The People's
New Testament

C O M M E N T A R Y

The People's New Testament

COMMENTARY

M. Eugene Boring

and Fred B. Craddock

Westminster John Knox Press
LOUISVILLE • LONDON

Book design by Drew Stevens
Cover design by designpointinc.com

First edition
Published by Westminster John Knox Press
Louisville, Kentucky

This book is printed on acid-free paper that meets the American National Standards Institute Z39.48 standard. ♾

PRINTED IN THE UNITED STATES OF AMERICA
04 05 06 07 08 09 10 11 12 13—10 9 8 7 6 5 4 3 2 1

Library of Congress Cataloging-in-Publication Data

Boring, M. Eugene.
The people's New Testament commentary / M. Eugene Boring, Fred B. Craddock.
p. cm.
Includes bibliographical references.
ISBN 0-664-22754-6
1. Bible. N.T.—Commentaries.   I. Craddock, Fred B.   II. Title.

BS2341.53.B67 2004
225.7—dc22   2004043029

To the congregations that have nourished us in the faith:
in some of which we have been members,
to some of which we have ministered

Central Avenue Christian Church, Humboldt, Tennessee
First Christian Church, Maryville, Tennessee
Glen Alice Christian Church, Rockwood, Tennessee
Post Oak Christian Church, Rockwood, Tennessee
First Christian Church, Custer City, Oklahoma
First Christian Church, Newport, Tennessee
Wildie Christian Church, Wildie, Kentucky
Burnside Christian Church, Burnside, Kentucky
Mount Pleasant Christian Church, Bedford, Indiana
Central Christian Church, Columbia, Tennessee
Kirklin Christian Church, Kirklin, Indiana
Central Christian Church, Enid, Oklahoma
First Christian Church, Dover, Tennessee
First Christian Church, Paris, Tennessee
First Christian Church, Decatur, Georgia
University Christian Church, Fort Worth, Texas
Cherry Log Christian Church, Cherry Log, Georgia

Contents

Preface

"This work has been prepared, not especially for the learned and critical class, but for the people." Thus begins the Preface to *The People's New Testament with Notes,* a two-volume work published in 1889 and 1891 and still available today (in a single volume, and on the Internet), 113 years later. The author was Barton Warren Johnson, a scholar, teacher, editor, and pastor in the American religious movement called the Disciples of Christ.

Mr. Johnson's work is the ancestor of this volume. Granted, *The People's New Testament with Notes* was just that: a New Testament with the King James Version (1611) and the Revised Version (1881) side by side, with notes on the text at the bottom of each page. This format is now familiar to Bible students who have used *The Interpreter's Bible* and *The New Interpreter's Bible.* The present volume is not a New Testament, in that the actual text of the New Testament is not reproduced here. This work is a commentary consisting of notes on the text, with such supporting articles as were deemed by the writers to aid the reader's understanding of the New Testament text. But the absence of the printed text of the New Testament is not to imply any distance from that text, or that this is a free-standing book. The proper use of this volume calls for a good translation of the New Testament, preferably the New Revised Standard Version or the New International Version, open beside this commentary for ready access.

This difference notwithstanding, *The People's New Testament Commentary* is a true descendant of *The People's New Testament with Notes.* The connection lies in the word *People's,* and the convictions carried in that word. First, let us be clear about what is not meant by the *People's* commentary. The term does not imply a marketing ploy, an attempt to broaden the target group to include laity as well as clergy. There is no "target" group. Nor are "the people" invited to overhear discussions of the biblical text among scholars, picking up pieces of information as they are able. Nor have the writers added water to the wine of scholarship so that the people can handle the sometimes troubling results of research.

On the contrary, this commentary is an expression of the fundamental conviction that the New Testament is the people's book. The book and the community of faith belong together, and out of the conversation between the text and the people come the preaching, teaching, believing, and behaving of the church. The people are not being "let in" on anything; the content of the New Testament belongs to them. The aim of this commentary is to clarify matters of history, culture, geography, literature, and translation so that the people can more readily listen to the text. And the people are not being protected from the findings of research. This commentary is in the tradition of trusting the people with the best of scholarship. The new, the surprising, the disturbing do not sever the relationship between the community of faith and its sacred texts. In fact, listening to the text carefully is the best antidote to superstition and unfounded claims *about* the Bible that the Bible itself will not support.

In this confidence, both in the New Testament and the people, this commentary is offered. If in its reading someone is prompted to explore further and more deeply, that happy condition will not mark a fault in this book, but will be taken by its writers as a high compliment. In fact, in anticipation of such a consequence, suggested additional reading can be found throughout at the appropriate places, and at the end.

M. Eugene Boring
Fred B. Craddock
Fort Worth, Texas, and Cherry Log, Georgia
July 21, 2003

Introduction: The New Testament as the Church's Book

We may thank God that we live in a time and place in which, if we choose to do so, we may own a copy of the Bible and read it without fear. It has not always been so. When we hold a Bible in our hands, we hold a book for which people have given their lives. Thus when we refer to the New Testament as "the church's book," we do not mean that only certain people may own and read it. The New Testament is certainly a cultural treasure; no other book has had more influence on the literature, art, and philosophy of Western civilization. It can profitably be studied from that point of view. One need not share the faith of the early Christian community that produced the New Testament in order to read its text with respect and appreciation. The Bible has become a cultural item that anyone may purchase at a bookstore or a department store, or may receive gratis from various agencies.

1. "TESTAMENT"

There is another sense, however, in which the New Testament belongs to the church, the Christian community. The word "testament" in biblical parlance is the same as the word "covenant." Thus English translations of the Bible use the terms "testament" and "covenant" interchangeably. "Old Testament" and "New Testament" mean the same as "Old Covenant" and "New Covenant" (see the title page of the New Testament in the RSV and NRSV). In the Bible, however, covenant terminology does not refer to a book, but to an act binding together two parties. It is somewhat like the English word "contract," with two important differences: (1) it is used of God's covenant-making act that binds people to God and to each other in a covenant community, and (2) it is unilateral, proceeding from God's side as gift, not negotiated between equal contracting parties. In the Bible, God made a covenant with one people, Israel, for the sake of all people (Gen. 12:1–3; see on 2 Cor. 3:5–6). In the Scriptures of Israel that became the Scriptures of the early church, covenant is an event, a saving act of God, God's own gracious unilateral act that creates a mission community and calls for

response, a life grounded in, oriented to, and expressing the reality of God's act.

2. "NEW"

Just as "testament" must not be defined in terms of contemporary English usage, so "new" must not be understood in terms of contemporary American culture, where "new" is a generally positive relative term and "old" tends to mean "outmoded, relatively inferior." The barrage of advertising hype for the "new and improved" version ("14 percent stronger") is not the context in which the Bible's language of newness can be understood. The Hebrew Scriptures use the language of newness in an absolute sense, as a term for God's eschatological fulfillment of the divine promises (see Isa. 43:19; 65:17; 66:22; Ezek. 11:19; 18:31). In such statements, "new" is not a relative term, but an eschatological one. The biblical concept of "newness" does not supersede the past relatively, but fulfills it absolutely. It is not the abolition of the old but its eschatological renewal. (Here and elsewhere, "eschatological" refers to the ultimate end of history, the final goal to which God is bringing the creation.)

3. "NEW TESTAMENT"

Jeremiah, sixth-century BCE prophet of Israel, specifically pictures the eschatological fulfillment of God's purposes as making a "new covenant," i.e. the eschatological renewal of God's covenant with Israel (Jer. 31:31–34). This vocabulary is not repeated elsewhere in the Old Testament as the expression of Israel's eschatological hope, but the idea is reflected several times (see Ezek. 34:25; 36:26; 37:26; Isa. 54:10; 55:3; 61:8, and 42:6; 49:8, where the Servant is representative of the covenant). The early Christian community interpreted the event of Jesus of Nazareth as God's definitive revelatory and saving event, saw this Christ event as the fulfillment of God's purposes for the world, God's eschatological renewal of the covenant. Thus the earliest document that reports Jesus' eucharistic words

1

presents him as speaking of his own body and blood as the expression of this "new covenant" (1 Cor. 11:23–26).

In the Bible, "New Covenant/Testament" never refers to a book. However, Christians now rightly use "New Testament" to refer to a book, a collection of documents. We understand, however, that this is only a shorthand way of saying "that collection of documents that bear authentic witness to the meaning of the Christ event, God's eschatological renewal of the covenant with Israel." The specific designation "New Testament" for Christian Scripture began to be used in the late second century, as the church began to select those documents that bore authentic witness to God's act in Christ.

From the beginning, the church had appropriated the Jewish Scriptures as its own Bible, and for two or three generations lived with these Scriptures as its only Bible (see 2 Pet. 3:15–16). When Christian writings were placed alongside them as the New Testament, these Christian writings did not become *the* canon for the church. The New Testament has always been a part of the Christian Bible only in combination with the Jewish Scriptures, which became the "Old Testament" counterpart to the "New Testament." In the church, these two collections of writings can never be separated from each other and interpreted independently of one another. In the church, the Old Testament has always been interpreted in the light of the Christ event; the New Testament has always been interpreted in the context of and in continuity with the Old Testament.

4. THE CHURCH'S BOOK

By "church" we of course do not refer to one particular denomination or adherents of one particular theology, but to the community of Christian faith through the ages and around the world. The New Testament is the church's book in the sense that it was written, selected, edited, transmitted, translated, and interpreted by the Christian community.

a. Written by the Church

The New Testament is the church's book in the sense that it was *written* by the church. The New Testament is not "Jesus' book," in the sense that he wrote it. The Christian Scriptures are thus very different from the Koran, which is "Mohammed's book," in the sense that he is responsible for its very words. While there are materials from Jesus in the New Testament, he personally wrote none of it.

The New Testament is not the "apostles' book." There is a real sense in which the New Testament as a whole is "apostolic," in that it is the authentic witness to the faith of the "one holy catholic apostolic church" of the Nicene Creed. But the documents of the New Testament do not come to us exclusively from the hands of the apostles. We cannot be sure who wrote several of the New Testament documents (see the introduction to each book). However, even if all the traditional ascriptions of authorship could be accepted as historically accurate, we still would have documents not only from the apostles Matthew, John, Peter, and Paul, but also anonymous documents (Hebrews), from Jesus' brothers who did not belong to the group of the twelve apostles (James and Jude), and from the nonapostles Mark the companion of Peter and Luke the companion of Paul. Traditionally, two Gospels have been ascribed to apostles (Matthew and John), while the other two are attributed to non-apostles.

Taken as a whole, the New Testament does not represent the product of a few brilliant individual writers, but the faith statements of the Christian community. Said theologically, the New Testament documents derive from the Spirit of God at work in the Christian community as a whole. The New Testament is the church's book because the church wrote it. "The church is the responsible author of Scripture."

b. Selected by the Church

The New Testament is the church's book in the sense that it has been *selected* by the church. Early Christianity produced much literature, much more than is included in our New Testament. We are aware of at least sixty-three documents that circulated as "Gospels" in the early church, as well as numerous "Acts," "Epistles," and "Apocalypses." This is not new or suppressed information, despite the sensationalizing claims sometimes made about the "lost books of the Bible." These documents are readily available (see bibliography).

The books in our New Testament were not selected by a few individuals, nor by a particular church council. In the life of the church as a whole, some books began to emerge as accepted and used in the mainstream churches. By the late second century, the Pauline letters and the four Gospels were generally accepted, but marginal documents such as 2 Peter were not generally included until the fourth century. The criteria were not authorship or date. In fact, no criteria were specified in advance. In an informal, unofficial process, the continuing Christian community heard in some documents authentic testimony to the meaning of the Christ event. These were preserved, read in the church's worship alongside the Jewish Scriptures, and finally were acknowledged to be authoritative Scripture, while other Christian writings were neglected or consciously rejected. The later bishops and councils only confirmed this; it was the church that selected the books that became our New Testament. This whole process was called canonization, and the result is the New Testament canon, the authoritative collection of documents the church acknowledges as normative for its faith and life.

c. Edited by the Church

The New Testament is the church's book in the sense that has been *edited and arranged* by the church. The books of the New Testament did not fall into their present arrangement and order by themselves. Nor is any particular individual or group responsible. Paul's letters were the first to be collected. Then collections of other letters and the Gospels were made. At first, there were different arrangements of the books, but finally the present arrangement was all but universally accepted. Though Luke and Acts are two volumes of one work (see Acts 1:1), Acts was early separated from the Gospel and placed before the Epistles, as a transition volume from the story of Jesus to the story of the church. Revelation, though not written last, was placed at the end as the fitting conclusion to the story of God's mighty acts in history. Matthew, though not written first, was placed at the beginning, so that the genealogy with which it begins served as a fitting transition from the story of Israel to the story of Jesus and the church.

The documents were originally without titles. In the process of collection and editing, the documents were given titles that may or may not represent original authorship, readership, and literary genre. Often the purpose was to designate the document as representing the apostolic faith, so apostolic titles were given. It may be that in this process different letters or letter fragments were edited together to form one document (see, e.g., introduction to 2 Corinthians). Occasionally glosses, annotations, or additions may have been added that then became part of the standard text (see, e.g., the endings of Mark; see on Mark 16:8).

The original authors did not write in chapters and verses. These markers were added later to facilitate reference. The chapter divisions made by Stephen Langdon, archbishop of Canterbury in the thirteenth century, gradually became adopted as standard. Verse divisions of the New Testament were not made until the sixteenth century, when the versification of Erasmus's Greek New Testament became generally accepted. Since the original manuscripts lacked punctuation marks, all punctuation in modern printed Bibles represents decisions made by a series of editors.

d. Transmitted by the Church

The New Testament is the church's book in the sense that the church has *transmitted* it to us. Until movable type was invented by Johannes Gutenberg ca. 1456, virtually all documents were copied by hand—which meant that no document of any length would be copied without deviations from the original, intentional or unintentional. No original document of any New Testament book has been preserved. This is true of all ancient writings; we have no "originals" of Plato, Aristotle, or any other ancient author. We have about 5500 manuscripts of New Testament books or fragments thereof. While most copies of the same text are very similar, no two are exactly alike. Careful scholarship, called "text criticism," is responsible for reconstructing the original text of each document. This can be done with great probability, but not with absolute certainty. There are thus numerous places in the New Testament where the interpreter must decide, on the basis of variations in the available manuscripts, what the author originally wrote (see footnotes in all modern translations of the New Testament, and comments below on, e.g., Matt. 5:25; 6:13; 21:44; Mark 7:4; Luke 22:19; John 7:53; Acts 27:37).

e. Translated by the Church

The New Testament is the church's book in the sense that the church has *translated* it for us. The New Testament was written in Koine ("common") Greek, the language understood by most of the literate population of the Hellenistic world. Koine Greek is not the native language of anyone in the contemporary world. (Modern Greek is the direct descendent of Koine Greek, but the Greek language has changed enough through the centuries that today Greek Christians need the ancient text to be translated into modern Greek in order to properly understand it.) Anyone in the twenty-first century, anyplace in the world, who wants to read the New Testament must either become an expert in Koine Greek or read a reliable translation.

Translation is not a simple task. Most words in both Greek and English have more than one meaning, and very few words in any two languages have precisely the same meaning or sets

3

of meanings. Translation can rarely be word for word, since no two languages are structured exactly alike. More than one legitimate English translation can be made from the same Greek words and sentences.

A variety of English translations, some made to support a particular viewpoint, had already been made by the sixteenth century. In the early seventeenth century, the Church of England appointed a group of scholars to make a reliable translation of the Bible into then-contemporary English, the Elizabethan English of the age of Shakespeare. Though James I, titular head of the Church of England, had sponsored the production of the new version, it was never officially "authorized" either by the king or any ecclesiastical body. Nevertheless, the work became known as the "Authorized Version" or "King James Version" and was gradually accepted by Protestant English-speaking Christianity as simply "the" Bible. This it remained for three centuries.

While a few private translations continued to be published, it was not until the twentieth century that a large number of modern-speech English translations began to appear, sometimes sponsored by individuals or groups who were dissatisfied with the "standard" translations and wanted a translation more in line with their political or theological agenda, sometimes sponsored by publishing companies—Bible publishing is a very profitable business. Currently, at least 140 English translations and versions of the New Testament are available (sixty English translations of the whole Bible, another eighty of only the New Testament).

"Which is the best translation?"

We are happily past the time when the church had one officially approved translation, and those who introduced new translations could be burned at the stake for corrupting the faith by their innovations. These times must never return, and will not. Yet the issue remains. Can just anyone select the books he or she thinks should be in the Bible, translate them in accord with his or her own knowledge, ignorance, theology, convictions, or prejudice, and have the result accepted as "the Bible"? In a free society and a free market, is the content and wording of Scripture to be decided on popularity and advertisers' ability to sway the mass of religious readers?

We suggest four criteria for a good translation:

1. The translation must be based on the oldest and best manuscripts of the Bible, most of which have been rediscovered only within the last 150 years, i.e., were not available to the translators of the King James Version.

2. The translation must be in contemporary language. Biblical texts originally spoke in the language and idiom of their own time. As the English language changes, biblical translations must also change to preserve the ancient meaning in contemporary language, so that modern readers of English may understand the original Greek texts as they were understood by their contemporaries.

3. The translation must be made by a committee commissioned for that purpose. No one person knows enough, or is unbiased enough, to translate the Bible adequately for the whole church. A large committee, qualified in the biblical languages and their interpretation, representing a variety of cultural settings and theological streams, will tend to cancel out individual and denominational biases and produce a translation representing the best insight into the meaning of Scripture for the whole church.

4. The translation must not be an individual or commercial enterprise, but must be sponsored by the church. While it is and must remain legal to translate and publish Bibles as any individual or group sees fit, the Bible belongs to the community of faith as its Scripture. The church as a whole must have a definitive say in what counts for "Bible" and what does not. Yet the worldwide church is not structured in such a way as to "authorize" Bibles for all Christians. No group or individual can presently speak for all English-speaking Christians. All translations and versions are someplace on the spectrum between purely individual translations and translations that are universally and officially approved by the church. There are purely individual translations, but no version of the Bible is officially approved by the whole church. Yet there are representative groups in various denominations and councils of churches that are ecumenically oriented and have the interests of the whole church at heart. Sponsorship by such groups is important in legitimizing any translation or version.

Among those that meet these criteria are the following:

NRSV—*The New Revised Standard Version* (1989). This is the revision of the *Revised Standard Version* (1946), which was a revision of the Authorized Version (1611). The NRSV is produced by American "mainstream" Protestantism with an ecumenical orientation. In our opinion, this is the best single translation available today. While we have used a large number of translations in this commentary, it is based principally on the NRSV, with frequent reference to the NIV.

NAB—*The New American Bible* (1986). This is an American Roman Catholic translation with an ecumenical orientation. (The NAB is to be distinguished from the *New American Standard Bible* (1960), a private commercial translation widely used in the evangelical community.)

REB—*The Revised English Bible* (1989), representing British Protestantism with an ecumenical orientation.

NJB—*The New Jerusalem Bible* (1985), a revision of the Jerusalem Bible, representing British Roman Catholicism with an ecumenical orientation.

Though representing commercial and institutional interests lacking in "official" church sponsorship, some other modern translations meet some of these criteria and can be commended:

NIV—*The New International Version* (1973), copyrighted and published by one publisher, translated by a representative committee of mostly North American evangelical scholars. We refer to it often in the comments of this volume.

TNIV—*Today's New International Version* (2002), an updated version of the NIV, differing from it principally by adopting gender-inclusive language.

CEV—*Contemporary English Version* (1995), a modern-speech translation published by the American Bible Society.

f. Interpreted by the Church

The New Testament is the church's book in the sense that the church *interprets* it for us and with us. Christians of all denominations are today encouraged to read the Bible for themselves, to encounter the Word of God that comes through these texts, to appropriate its meaning for their own lives on the basis of their personal engagement with the text of Scripture. Thus, when we affirm that the church interprets the Bible for and with us, we do not mean the acceptance of canned interpretations from church officials or the repetition of church dogmas and traditions as a substitute for one's personal reading, study, and reflection on the meaning of the biblical text. We have called our volume the "People's Commentary" because we believe the "common" people of the church—the laity, the people of God—are able and authorized to study the Bible on their own (see preface).

And yet, no reading occurs in a vacuum. Many biblical texts can have a variety of meanings, depending on their context. "Context" means not only literary context, but community setting. The twenty-seven documents of the New Testament were written from within the early Christian community, confessing, correcting, and nourishing its own faith. In this sense the New Testament is not the individual's book, not the book of society and culture at large, but the church's book. In this sense, the collection of documents is more like a family album than a rulebook or manual. As the church has moved through history, it has continued to cherish this book, to study it, to sort out valid and helpful interpretations from the perverse, misleading, and merely irrelevant. The church as the community of faith continues to embody this living tradition of dialogue with these sacred texts. We have attempted to distill some of that tradition and dialogue into this commentary, to facilitate the ongoing study of the New Testament within the life of the Christian community. We must study and interpret the Bible *for* ourselves; we must not do it *by* ourselves. The New Testament is the church's book.

For Further Reading

General and Reference Books
on the Whole Bible

Achtemeier, Paul J., ed. *HarperCollins Bible Dictionary*. San Francisco: Harper & Row, 1996.

Dunn, James D. G., and John W. Rogerson, eds. *Eerdmans Commentary on the Bible*. Grand Rapids: Eerdmans, 2003.

Metzger, Bruce G. *The Bible in Translation: Ancient and English Versions*. Grand Rapids: Baker, 2001.

Newsom, Carol A., and Sharon Ringe. *The Women's Bible Commentary*. Louisville, KY: Westminster/John Knox Press, 1992.

Extracanonical Texts

Charlesworth, James H., ed. *The Old Testament Pseudepigrapha*. 2 vols. Garden City, NY: Doubleday & Co., 1983, 1985.

Hennecke, Edgar, and Wilhelm Schneemelcher, eds. *New Testament Apocrypha*. 2 vols. Philadelphia: Westminster Press, 1964. Rev. ed., Louisville, KY: Westminster John Knox Press, 1992.

General Reference Books
on the New Testament

Brown, Raymond E. *An Introduction to the New Testament*. New York: Doubleday, 1997.

Harris, Stephen L. *The New Testament: A Student's Introduction*. 4th ed. Boston: McGraw-Hill, 2002.

Introduction to the Gospels

The most important issue for the interpreter of Gospel texts is that of their literary genre: what kind of writing is a Gospel? Texts will be understood differently, depending on whether the interpreter approaches them as biography, history, fiction, drama, or some other conventional literary type—or regards them as a distinctive genre created by early Christianity. Before deciding this question, however, two other important issues must be discussed: why the Gospels were written and how they were composed.

1. WHY WERE GOSPELS WRITTEN?

Two of the New Testament Gospels make statements about the author's purpose:

> John 20:30–31—Jesus did many other miraculous signs in the presence of his disciples, which are not recorded in this book. But *these are written that you may believe that Jesus is the Christ, the Son of God, and that by believing you may have life in his name.* (NIV, emphasis added)

John indicates that the purpose of his writing is not historical or biographical, but to generate and nourish Christian faith.

> Luke 1:1–4—Since many have undertaken to set down an orderly account of the events that have been fulfilled among us, just as they were handed on to us by those who from the beginning were eyewitnesses and servants of the word, I too decided, after investigating everything carefully from the very first, to write an orderly account for you, most excellent Theophilus, *so that you may know the truth concerning the things about which you have been instructed.* (NRSV, emphasis added)

Luke indicates that the readers may have heard or been taught various versions of the story of Jesus, and that he writes in order to guide the reader into the authentic understanding, rooted in the tradition that goes back to the eyewitnesses of Jesus' ministry.

Though there are historical, factual, and biographical elements in the Gospels, their writers' concern is *faith in Jesus as the Christ* and the *truth of the Christian message.*

2. HOW WERE GOSPELS WRITTEN?

Among the Gospel writers, only Luke, in the quotation cited above, shares any information on how the Gospels were composed. He delineates three stages by which the materials came to be written:

1. The first level of every Gospel text—though it is the one least directly available to us—is that of **the events that have been fulfilled among us.** The Christian faith is about events that happened in real history: the birth, life, death, and resurrection of Jesus of Nazareth. "Gospel" means "good news," not "good ideas" or "good advice." These events are not merely outstanding and wonderful occurrences in and of themselves; their significance is that they are the climax and **fulfillment** of a story, the mighty acts of God as portrayed in the Old Testament. By calling these events "fulfillment," Luke claims to be a theologian who interprets the significance of history, not merely a reporter who records it. It is not clear in the Greek text whether the **eyewitnesses and servants** [ministers] **of the word** represent one group or two. It is clear that there were those who saw and heard the original events—the gospel is not based on fiction—and that these events were interpreted and proclaimed by ministers of the word as the saving acts of God.

2. The second level of every Gospel text is the transmission process between the events of Jesus' life and the writing of the Gospel. Neither the author nor the readers personally experienced the original events; they are mediated to the author, to the original readers, and to us by the Christian community, the church. It is not a chain of individuals, but a community of faith, that mediates the gospel to later believers and inquirers. Notice the repeated plurals ("us," vv.

1, 2; see Deut. 5:1–5 and commentary on John 1:14, 16 and 1 John 1:1–4). The church handed on the tradition in its preaching, teaching, and worship, by composing hymns and rules for Christian conduct, by collecting, selecting, amplifying, and interpreting sayings of Jesus and stories about him. During this period, the church that handed on these materials interpreted and reinterpreted them from the perspective of faith in the risen Lord, so that all the materials in our present Gospels are seen in this light and reflect this faith (see an example of this in chart at Mark 14:3, p. 160).

Much of this tradition was oral, functioning in various settings in the life of the church, but after a while some of it was written down. Luke acknowledges that he is not the first, but the claim that "**many**" had written before him is part of the conventional style of such prefaces. We know of two such sources used by Luke (and by Matthew; perhaps also by John), namely, the Gospel of Mark and the collection of material (mostly sayings of Jesus) known as "Q" (the abbreviation for the German word *Quelle*, "source"). Since the Q document was also used by Matthew, it can be approximately reconstructed from the material common to Luke and Matthew but absent from Mark. Thus in the Synoptic Gospels (Matthew, Mark, and Luke), each paragraph ("pericope") can be designated as dependent on Mark, Q, or the sources peculiar to Matthew ("M") or ("Luke"), plus each evangelist's own interpretation and editing. While the first three Gospels are directly interrelated by their use of common sources, John has a different literary history and compositional technique. One helpful way of bringing Luke's (and Matthew's) own meaning into sharper focus is to compare his composition with his sources. We shall use this method often in the following commentary.

3. The third level of every Gospel text is the Gospel itself as it lies before us in the New Testament, as the author interprets his sources and traditions. This third level is actually the first and only level that is directly available to us, but its nature and meaning are often illuminated by working our way backward through the period of transmission in the church to the original event. This does not mean that authentic biblical interpretation means peeling away the "Gospel" and "church" layers in order to get back to "what really happened." It is rather the case that "level three," the composition of the evangelist, is what we actually have in the Bible. It represents the author's and the church's interpretation of the meaning of the original events. Biblical interpretation means attending to this final meaning, not reconstructing previous events and meanings, though awareness of these will often help us understand the final meaning of the text before us.

3. WHAT IS A GOSPEL?

A Gospel, like every other document of the New Testament, is at once a historical document, a literary composition, and a theological affirmation, and is thus properly interpreted by the methods appropriate to each of these perspectives. While advocates of historical, literary, and theological approaches to the Bible have sometimes argued as though these methods were mutually exclusive and attempted to approach the New Testament with only one method, an adequate interpretation requires that all these methods be used in order to bring the reader within hearing distance of the biblical text.

Historical

Each document of the New Testament is historical in a double sense:

1. It reflects the historical events on which the Christian faith is based. Jesus, Pilate, Herod, Peter, and Paul are not just characters in a story, but were real people who lived at a particular place and time in first-century Jewish and Roman history.

2. Each document reflects and addresses the historical situation in which it was originally written. Each Gospel, for instance, reflects not only the life of the historical Jesus but the historical setting of the church in and for which that Gospel was written (see introduction to each Gospel).

Literary

Every document in the New Testament is the literary composition of an author who had to decide how to begin, structure, and conclude it; what to include and what to omit; and what strategy of communication to use in order to communicate his message. In the Gospels and Acts, such literary concerns as plot, characterization, and narrator are important for understanding the text.

Theological

No New Testament author wrote only to report history or to compose interesting literature. All had a theological purpose; that is, all intended to interpret the meaning of God's act in Christ and to express it in ways it could be understood and appropriated in the writer's own time. The term for this category of theological thought is "Christology"; the Gospels are christological narrative.

Christology deals with the understanding of the person and work of Jesus Christ, Christ's relation to God and human beings, and the relation of the work of Jesus to the saving act of God. The church's confession is that the one true God is the One who is definitively present and revealed in the truly human being, Jesus of Nazareth. The New Testament thus speaks of Jesus as both truly human and truly divine. The Gospels handle this paradox in different ways. The Gospel of John is the most explicit in using God-language for Jesus (see on 1:1–2; 5:18; 20:28).

Within the Christian community, there has always been the temptation to confess faith in the deity of Christ in such a way that he is no longer regarded as really human. One group of Christians, later called Docetists and considered heretics, regarded Jesus as simply a divine being who had come to earth and only "seemed" to be human ("Docetism" is from the Greek word for "seem," "appear to be"). The Gospels and the New Testament as a whole oppose this view. While John, for instance, presents Jesus as the Preexistent One who was with God at the beginning and has come to earth to implement God's saving act (John 1:1, 14), he also presents him as the Truly Human One who suffered and died. Like the other Gospels, John deals with this paradox not by writing an essay that "explains" how a being could be both divine and human, but by telling a story in which both perspectives appear without compromise.

Since the full identity of Jesus did not become clear until after his death and resurrection—and on the basis of his death and resurrection—the post-Easter believer can perceive Jesus' real identity as Messiah and Son of God, but the people in the story cannot. For the Gospel writers, one can come to authentic faith in Christ only through the cross and resurrection—not on the basis of his miracles, his teaching, his ethical example. The story is told in such a way that the reader can understand and be addressed by the reality of Christ as the risen Lord, but the people in the story fail to grasp Jesus' identity and significance. Mark, who created the new literary form called a Gospel (see introduction to Mark) was the first to devise the "messianic secret," but all the Gospels in one way or another utilize the motif of secrecy and misunderstanding in order to communicate to the reader the significance of who Jesus was, though the people in the narrative continue to be unperceptive or misunderstanding. This technique has the double effect of placing the words and deeds of the human earthly Jesus in the perspective of the crucified and risen Lord, and of binding the declarations of the risen Lord to the actual life of the earthly Jesus. Again, John is the most explicit in this regard, insisting that both disciples and opponents could not understand Jesus during his earthly life, but only after the resurrection as an insight given by the Holy Spirit (John 2:22; 7:39; 12:16; 13:7; 16:4).

The literary form Gospel is most often compared to biography. Yet the Gospels are certainly not like modern biographies; they offer no physical description of the protagonist, do not narrate the development of his character during childhood and youth, and are unconcerned with the kind of chronological and historical data essential for modern biographical writing. The Gospels are more like ancient biographies, but even here there are crucial differences.

The Gospel paradoxically combines two perspectives on the Christ event: one that portrays Jesus as representing the saving power of God (strong like God) and one that identifies him as sharing the weakness and frailty of humanity (weak like us). This christological paradox, later affirmed in the church's creeds as "truly God and truly man," makes the Gospel form distinctively different from all other biographies ancient and modern.

The Gospel is not the story of a hero or "great *man*," but narrates the central segment of the story of *God's* dealing with humanity from creation to the eschaton, when God brings history to its final goal. The narrative is thus not only the "gospel of Jesus Christ" (Mark 1:1) but the "good news of God" (Mark 1:14) ("gospel" [NIV] and "good news" [NRSV] are equivalent translations; cf. NRSV footnote). The Jesus story is told not as an isolated story of a great individual but as the key to all God's acts in history. This is a distinctively biblical perspective. The biography of Socrates, for instance, was never regarded as the central scene in God's plan for all history.

The Jesus of the Gospels is not a fictional character but a real person who lived and died at a particular time and place in the past. The Gospels are thus basically oriented toward a *past* event, the life, death, and resurrection of Jesus of Nazareth. However, the Gospel is not merely the story of a past figure in history, who may now be admired and imitated; the central figure is not dead but alive, accompanying his disciples through history, and still calling people to discipleship as he speaks through the pages of the Gospel. The whole narrative is to be read at two levels—the there-and-then account of what Jesus said and did in his pre-Easter ministry, and simultaneously the here-and-now address of the risen Christ to the present (see on Mark 1:16–20).

From such a faith perspective, telling the "life of Jesus" is far different from recounting the biography of a hero of the past. The pre-Easter sayings and stories are presented in the light of the resurrection faith of who Jesus really was, so that the reality and significance of the living Lord is presented in the story of the pre-Easter Jesus. This is sometimes made explicit, so that the Jesus of the narrative story line in the Gospels speaks from the perspective of the post-Easter author and readers of the Gospels, seeming to look back on his own history from the standpoint of the later Christian community. For example, John 3:11–15 is set within a conversation between Jesus and Nicodemus, a Jewish leader, early in his ministry. Jesus refers to his coming death as still in the future (3:15) and in the same breath speaks of his ascension to heaven as something that has already occurred. Similarly, in Jesus' prayer in John 17, he both looks forward to his impending death and looks back on his life in this world as a past event (v. 11, "I am no longer in the world"). The Gospel of John is the most explicit in this regard, but this double perspective, this fusing of perspectives between past and present, is characteristic of the Gospel form and distinguishes the Gospels from all biographies. This is primarily due to the resurrection faith that permeates the telling of past history, but also reflects the contemporizing mode of biblical history as such, in which past events are understood as the living experience of the present (see, e.g., Deut. 5:1–6; 26:5–10).

4. THE ROLE OF THE GOSPEL'S PORTRAYAL OF THE "LIFE AND TEACHINGS OF JESUS" FOR CHRISTIAN FAITH

Readers will notice frequent reference to the fact that several New Testament authors, especially Paul, present their witness to the meaning of the Christian faith with minimal reference to the life and teachings of Jesus (see, e.g., on 1 Cor. 15:3–5 and Phil. 2:5–11). At those points the reader may wonder how it could be (or whether it is actually the case) that many early Christians confessed their faith in God's saving act in Christ without reference to the kinds of stories about Jesus and his teaching found in the Gospels, and what role the Gospels' narratives about Jesus have in Christian faith.

It is important to see that while all the New Testament documents point to God's act in Christ, they do not do it in the same way. There are basically two ways of confessing Jesus represented in the New Testament, related to the two basic types of Christology, the epistolary mode following Paul, and the Gospel mode following Mark.

a. In the **Epistles**, all attention is focused on the death and resurrection of Jesus, with Jesus' life and teachings playing a minimal role. In this approach to the faith, it is important that Jesus was born, lived a life of obedience to God, and died a truly human death, but Jesus' specific words and deeds are not crucial. The Apostles' Creed, which moves directly from "born of the Virgin Mary" to "suffered under Pontius Pilate," represents the epistolary Christology. This perspective on the Christian faith is theologically indispensable in that it allows Jesus to be portrayed as one who is born and who dies, presenting him as a truly human being, and focuses not on the personality of Jesus but on God's act in his life, death, and resurrection.

b. The **Gospels** point to the same saving act of God in the Christ event as the Epistles, but do this by portraying scenes from the earthly life of Jesus. We would be immeasurably the poorer without the specific pictures of Jesus' life and teaching presented in the Gospels. The Epistles speak of the humility of Christ, for example, by presenting a hymn praising the preexistent, cosmic Christ who humbled himself by coming to earth as a truly human being, living his life as an obedient servant, and willingly going to the cross (see on Phil. 2:5–11). The Gospels express the same gospel message by portraying an actual scene in which at the Last Supper the earthly Jesus assumed the role of a servant and washed the disciples' feet (see on John 13:1–20). Likewise, God is affirmed as the champion of the poor within the framework of the epistolary Christology by speaking of the heavenly Christ who for our sakes became "poor," so that we might become "rich" (2 Cor. 8:9), but here Christ's helping the poor is portrayed on a cosmic screen. The Gospels, on the other hand, portray the earthly Jesus in particular scenes as himself a poor person (e.g., Luke 2:22–24) who proclaims that the coming of God's kingdom means good news to the poor (e.g., Luke 4:18), pronounces blessing on the poor (e.g., Luke 6:20), and asks disciples to help the poor (e.g., Luke 18:18–30). In the Epistles, the fact that God has come to us in Christ as a truly human being is the essential message. In the Gospels, the kind of person in whom God's revelation comes to us is illustrated in numerous scenes, and he teaches us God's will in his own words and deeds. Gospel and Epistle are different, complementary ways of confessing faith in the one God who has come to us in Christ; the New Testament canon is essentially composed of these two kinds of writings.

For Further Reading

Boring, M. Eugene. *Truly Human/Truly Divine: Christological Language and the Gospel Form.* St. Louis: Christian Board of Publication, 1984.

Craddock, Fred B. *The Gospels.* Interpreting Biblical Texts. Nashville: Abingdon Press, 1981.

Keck, Leander E. *Who Is Jesus? History in the Perfect Tense.* Columbia: University of South Carolina Press, 2000.

Tatum, W. Barnes. *In Quest of Jesus.* Rev. and enlarged ed. Nashville: Abingdon Press, 1999.

The Gospel according to Matthew

INTRODUCTION

Matthew was the favorite Gospel of early Christianity, always appearing first in the various lists and manuscripts of New Testament books. It was the most quoted of the Gospels by the church fathers of the first five centuries. Favorite passages from the Jesus story are still most likely to be remembered in their Matthean form (e.g., the Sermon on the Mount, chaps. 5–7, containing the Beatitudes, 5:4–12, and the Lord's Prayer, 6:9–13).

Author

One reason for Matthew's popularity, then and now, is that it was believed to have been written by an eyewitness, the apostle Matthew (Mark and Luke were attributed to non-eyewitnesses, who could have received their material only indirectly). Like the other Gospels, however, the document itself is anonymous, and it is likely that it was attributed to Matthew as a way of affirming the authority of its apostolic message, not because it was written by an eyewitness (see Introduction to the Gospels). The Gospel does contain material that goes back to eyewitnesses, but, like Luke (see Luke 1:1–4), Matthew is based on sources and traditions from and about Jesus circulating in early Christianity, not on the author's own memory. The author seems to be a Christian teacher with a Jewish background, who offers a cameo portrait of himself in 13:52—a scribe "trained for the kingdom . . . who brings out of his treasure what is new and what is old."

Sources

Matthew adopts the Gospel of Mark as the major source of his narrative, reproduces almost all of its contents (with interpretative modifications), and follows its exact order from Matt. 12:22 (=Mark 3:22) to the end of the narrative. For the teaching material, Matthew draws mainly on an early collection of Jesus' sayings called "Q," also used by Luke (see Introduction to the Gospels), no longer extant, but which may be reconstructed with some probability by analyzing the portions of the gospels common to Matthew and Luke but not found in Mark (e.g., Matt. 3:7–10/Luke 3:7–9). In addition to these two major sources,

Matthew also had a collection of materials not found in any of the other Gospels. These passages peculiar to his own tradition and church, including Matthew's own editorial additions, are now designated "M" to facilitate convenient reference. Thus in terms of source analysis, every text in Matthew may be labeled Mark, Q, or M. Like each of his sources, Matthew also had his Jewish Scriptures, which he used in the Greek translation (primarily the Septuagint, LXX). Since Matthew understood the Jesus story to be the fulfillment of Scripture, his Bible also served as a source in composing his narrative (see "Matthew as Interpreter of Scripture" at 2:23).

Readership

Matthew has often traditionally been seen as "the Jewish Gospel," said to have been written "for the Jews." While there is a sense in which Matthew (like the other Gospels) is quite Jewish, Matthew writes not to convert or refute outsiders, but for members of his own Christian community, some of whom, like himself, had a Jewish background. The church for which Matthew writes, and perhaps the author himself, has gone through several stages from its Jewish origins to the time of the Gospel:

1. We may picture Matthew himself and numbers of his community as Jews who had grown up before the 66–70 war against the Romans that led to the destruction of Jerusalem and the desolation of the Jewish homeland. Like Jesus and the original disciples, Matthew and some of his church were originally Jews, with the synagogue as their spiritual home.

2. Prior to the destruction of the temple, they had encountered disciples of Jesus, probably related to or identical with the missionary-prophets of the Q community with their eschatological message of Jesus' return as Son of Man. They had been converted to faith in Jesus as the Son of Man, the fulfillment of their hopes for the coming Messiah, without ever dreaming that this would eventually alienate them from their religious and cultural home in Judaism.

3. Then tensions developed. Those who had become disciples of Jesus found themselves an

isolated group within the synagogue. In the generation following the 66–70 war and the destruction of the holy city and the temple, the surviving Jewish leadership, mainly Pharisees, restructured Judaism along the lines of Pharisaic tradition. Jewish Christians and other nonconformist Jewish groups found themselves under pressure to conform. Matthew's group found not only itself, but the synagogue, in the process of change, and tensions increased. (See "Conflicts with 'the Jews'" in the introduction to the Gospel of John, which reflects a similar situation.)

4. When Matthew writes, he and his community are separate and alienated from these developing Jewish structures, the restructuring of Judaism that occurred in the generation after 70 CE. Members of Matthew's community refer to their own gathering as the "church"— the word is found only in Matthew in the Gospels (16:16; 18:17)—and are carrying out and supporting a worldwide mission to Gentiles. They continue to affirm their Jewish past, of which they consider themselves the legitimate heirs, but in some ways now find themselves more oriented to the Gentile world than to the emerging shape of Judaism. Matthew and his church had lived through a period of rapid change; the Gospel of Matthew has much to say to a community experiencing social change to which it wants to adapt while being faithful to its Scripture and tradition.

Date and Place

The Gospel gives no direct indication of when or where it was written. The Gospel breathes an urban, cosmopolitan atmosphere reflecting the life of the church in a major city. Of the several suggestions for Matthew's location, to many scholars Antioch in Syria seems most likely for a number of reasons, including its connections with other literature and persons related to that area. Since it most probably uses Mark and Q as sources (see above) and seems to reflect knowledge of the destruction of Jerusalem (see 22:7) and developments in Judaism after 70, it was written sometime after 70 CE. It is reflected in the writings of Ignatius of Antioch ca. 110, so it was probably composed in the period 80–100, for which 90 may serve as a convenient symbolic figure.

Structure and Outline

From 1:2 through 12:21, Matthew arranges his materials from Mark, Q, and M according to his own principles, presenting Jesus as God's chosen king in the present and coming kingdom of God. The central panel of this first major section is the Sermon on the Mount (chaps. 5–7, "The Messiah in Word"), and the collection of ten miracle stories (chaps. 8–9, "The Messiah in Deed"). This central section is surrounded by sections on Jesus' disciples, John the Baptist, Jesus' opponents, and Jesus as messianic king.

From Matt. 12:22 (=Mark 3:22) to the end of the book, Matthew adopts the Markan outline and chronology, presenting the development and resolution of the conflict between God's kingdom and the dominion of Satan. Inserted into this structure are five major speeches that also form turning points in the outline. The structure of "Part One" is arranged chiastically, so that I corresponds to IX, II to VIII, and so on, with V, "The Authority of the Messiah in Word and Deed," at the pivotal point in the structure. See Figure 1.

For Further Reading

Boring, M. Eugene. "The Gospel of Matthew." In *The New Interpreter's Bible*, vol. 8. Nashville: Abingdon Press, 1995. Some of the material on Matthew in the following pages has been drawn from this more expansive treatment.

Meier, John P. *Matthew*. New Testament Message 3. Collegeville, MN: Liturgical Press, 1980.

Pregeant, Russell. *Matthew*. Chalice Commentaries for Today. St. Louis: Chalice Press, 2004.

COMMENTARY

1:1–12:21
PART ONE: THE CONFLICT OF KINGDOMS INITIATED AND DEFINED

In Part One of the Gospel, Matthew sets forth the conflict that results from the incursion of the eschatological kingdom of God into this world in the advent of the messianic king, Jesus of Nazareth. The omnipotent power of God's kingdom is represented by Jesus, whose kingship is characterized by nonretaliation and meekness (11:29; 21:5), and whose greatest command is love (22:34–40). The kingship of this world is the opposite of this, i.e., it is the "normal" human concepts of kingship that function by violence, intimidation, and selfishness. In Matthew's apocalyptic dualistic view, the "normal" administration of this world is portrayed as a kingship exercised by demonic power. When the Jewish leaders resist the kingship of God represented by Jesus, Matthew regards them as agents of Satan, who has usurped God's rulership of this world. Part One ends with the religious leadership's decision to kill Jesus, who does not retaliate but withdraws

(12:14, 15–21). In Part Two, 12:22–28:20, the conflict between the two kingdoms is developed and resolved.

1:1 A record: This verse is Matthew's own title to the whole document. The traditional title "The Gospel according to Matthew" is not from the author but from the early church. The word translated "record" (NRSV) or "account" (NIV) is thus better translated as "book," as elsewhere in the New Testament where the same word is used (e.g., Mark 12:26; Luke 3:4), often referring to a book of Scripture. **Genealogy:** This word too is translated differently elsewhere, often as "story" or "account" (see Gen. 2:4; 5:1, 6:9 NIV). Thus as Matthew's title for his whole work (not the genealogy), the phrase means "The Book of the Account of Jesus Christ." Since the Greek word translated "genealogy" is literally "genesis," the title for the first book of Matthew's (and our) Bible, the title also suggests the book of new beginnings, the new creation. **Son of David:** A messianic title, not merely a matter of ancestry (see on 22:41–45). **Son of Abraham:** The reference is to Jesus (not David) as "Son of Abraham."

While David was the paradigm of Jewish kingship, the model for the coming Messiah, Abraham at the time of his call was a Gentile, the one through whom all nations would be blessed (Gen. 12:1–3). Matthew begins his Gospel with a title proclaiming the Jewish Messiah as the one who represents God's saving act for all peoples (see the concluding words of the book at 28:18–20).

1:2–25
JESUS AS MESSIANIC KING: SON OF DAVID AND SON OF GOD

1:2–17
Genealogical Summary of the Story That Leads to Jesus
(See also at Luke 3:23–38)

Of the four Gospels, only Matthew and Luke give genealogies of Jesus; the two manifest considerable variations (see on Luke 3:23–38). Neither genealogy represents precisely accurate historical information based on research in family archives or interviews with family members; each is constructed from Old Testament lists and

---

Figure 1. Outline of Matthew

historical imagination to express the respective author's theological convictions. Matthew, for instance, compresses and changes the Old Testament lists of Davidic kings to fit into his schema of 3x14 generations leading from Abraham to Christ. In v. 8, three kings are omitted (Ahaziah, Joash, Amaziah; see 2 Kgs 12–14; 1 Chr. 3:11–12), and in v. 11 Jehoiachim should come between Josiah and Jehoiachin—the confusion of names was made by others in antiquity (see 2 Chr. 36).

In Matthew, the genealogy is not a list but a story that presents the unfolding redemptive plan of God from Abraham to Jesus. The genealogical story begins with the Gentile **Abraham** to whom the promise of blessing to all nations was made (Gen. 12:1–3), and proceeds to **David**, the chosen king through whom the promise seemed destined to be fulfilled, who stands at the apex of the Israelite story. But David, the anointed king, was not the one to bring in God's kingdom, for Israel and David broke the covenant and the story of Israel began a sharp decline, resulting in the destruction of the holy city and the temple and the **exile** of God's people to a Gentile land. It seemed that the Abrahamic promise and Davidic hope had been extinguished. But once again, things were not what they seemed. The story goes on, to arrive at the true "son of David," who will save his people.

The genealogy is unusual in that it includes the names of five women.

1:3 Tamar: The Canaanite wife of Judah's eldest son, Er, who died prematurely (Gen. 38:1–7). When the patriarch Judah refused her the normal considerations of remarriage, she tricked him into fathering her son, who then was incorporated into what was to become the messianic line (Gen. 38:8–30). Judah declares her "righteous" (Gen. 38:26), a key term in the Matthean story of Jesus' birth (see on 1:19).

1:5 Rahab: Matthew is the first, so far as we know, to insert Rahab into the Davidic line. The importance of Rahab is that she, like Tamar, was a Gentile. Again, the generations are compressed. In the Old Testament chronology, Rahab belongs to the time of the conquest (Josh. 2–6), while Boaz lived almost 200 years later (Ruth 2–4).

Ruth: A Gentile from Moab (Ruth 1–4). Moabites were specifically excluded from the Israelite community, even after ten generations (see Deut. 23:3; Neh. 13:1).

1:6 The wife of Uriah: Bathsheba, an Israelite, but here identified in relation to her marriage to a Hittite (2 Sam. 11–12), which would cause her to be considered Gentile by later rabbinic law.

1:16 Mary, of whom Jesus was born: The pattern of "X begat ['became the father of'] Y" is here broken. In the story about to be told, Jesus has no human biological father.

Since all the women mentioned are involved in some sort of sexual irregularity, it has often been suggested that this was Matthew's apologetic [defensive] response to nonbelievers' insulting versions of the Christian story of Jesus' birth from the virgin Mary. It could well be that, while not apologetic, Matthew is interested in affirming that the plan of God has often been fulfilled in history in unanticipated and "irregular" ways, as was the case in the birth of Jesus from Mary, and that Matthew is interested in showing that God worked through irregular, even scandalous ways, and through women who took initiative such as Tamar and Ruth. Yet the main reason for Matthew's inclusion of the women corresponds to one of the Gospel's primary themes: the inclusion of the Gentiles in the plan of God from the beginning. The genealogy shows that the Messiah comes from a Jewish line that already included Gentiles.

1:18–25
Joseph's Obedience Incorporates
Mary's Son into the Davidic Line
(See also at Luke 2:1–7)

This opening scene in is an overture to the whole Gospel. Like the narrative as a whole, it is presented from the narrator's post-Easter Christian perspective, so that the "infancy story" is an expression of the meaning of the whole Christ event. Within the thematic structure outlined above, chapter 1 presents Jesus as the royal son of David and Son of God, whose advent immediately initiates the conflict of kingdoms developed in chap. 2. Even as a baby, the new king does not retaliate but flees, finding safety among the Gentiles of Egypt (2:1–12). When he returns to the "land of Israel," he can no longer live in his own city, but becomes an exile in his own land, making a new home in "Galilee of the Gentiles" (2:13–23, see 4:15).

1:18 Mary had been engaged to Joseph: In first-century Judaism, this was a binding arrangement between people already considered legally husband and wife. **With child from the Holy Spirit:** Matthew and Luke (and only they in the New Testament) adopt the Hellenistic (Graeco-Roman) view that great leaders were often supernaturally conceived (Hercules, Augustus, and many others). Different from the Hellenistic stories, however, here God does not assume the male sexual role in procreation, but the Holy Spirit, the power of God, works in Mary to conceive a child without a human father. This is one of several ways the New Testament uses to express the faith that Jesus was Son of God (see on Luke 1:28–33; 2:7).

1:19 Joseph, being a righteous man: Joseph does not yet know what the reader knows, first learning it from the angel in v. 20. He can only assume that his bride is guilty of adultery. The biblical law specified capital punishment in such cases (Deut. 22:23–27). Though this had been mitigated by the rabbis of Matthew's time, the consequences were still severe and shameful. **Dismiss her quietly:** Matthew's main point is that Joseph the righteous man had already decided not to carry out the letter of the biblical and traditional law, but to act in mercy and preserve Mary's dignity with a quiet divorce. *How* it could be that a "righteous" person would not go by the written and traditional law of God is a theme of Matthew's whole gospel, for the church to which he writes respects and affirms God's law, but no longer lives by it literally (see on Matt. 5:17–48).

1:21 Jesus: This was a common name, borne by others in the New Testament (see Luke 3:29; Col. 4:11) and the Old (Joshua is the Old Testament form of the same name). The first-century Jewish historian Josephus mentions twenty different persons of this name, which means "God helps" or "God saves." **Will save his people from their sins:** The hoped-for Messiah was expected to save the Jewish people from their foreign oppressors; Matthew names the real enemy. The identity of "**his people**" will be a matter of dispute in the Gospel story.

1:22 To fulfill what had been spoken: On New Testament authors' Christian interpretation of the Jewish Scriptures, see excursus, "New Testament Interpretation of the Old Testament," at 1 Cor. 15:3, 1 Pet. 1:10, excursus, "Matthew as Interpreter of Scripture," at Matt. 2:23.

1:23 The virgin shall conceive: Formula Quote #1. The Hebrew text of Isa. 7:14 had promised a child to be born of a "young woman"; the Greek translation used by Matthew (the LXX) rendered the Hebrew word *almah* with *parthenos*, which can mean either "young woman" in general or "virgin" in particular. Matthew understands the Isaiah text in the light of his belief in the virginal conception. **They shall name him:** The Isaiah text has "she [the mother] shall name him"; the LXX has "you shall name him." Matthew's "they" does not refer to people in general, but is an indefinite way of referring to God. Since the verb "name" in biblical under-

standing does not mean merely "label," but has to do with the reality and being of the person, the meaning is: "People will call him 'Jesus,' the name Joseph will give him, but God will name [constitute] him Emmanuel, 'God with us.'"

1:25 Had no marital relations with her: Confirming the divine parentage of the child. **Until she had borne a son:** The implication is that afterwards Mary and Joseph had normal marital relations. Jesus' mother, brothers, and sisters are referred to later in the narrative (12:47–49; see Mark 3:31–35). While some later church traditions developed alternate explanations, Matthew seems to offer no basis for the doctrine of the "perpetual virginity" of Mary (see on 13:55–56).

He named him: Joseph obeys the command of God given by the angel. By naming the child, Joseph officially accepts him as his own and legally incorporates him into the line of David. The genealogy and birth story together serve to illuminate the Matthean meaning of Jesus as both "Son of David" and "Son of God." (See Rom. 1:3–4, where the tradition incorporated by Paul also combines "Son of God" and "Son of David" and relates Jesus' divine sonship to the power of the Holy Spirit, but locates it at the resurrection.)

2:1–23
CONFLICT WITH THE KINGDOM OF THIS AGE

Matthew tells the story of Jesus' birth as an advance summary of the meaning of Jesus' life, death, and resurrection. The birth story, told from the postresurrection perspective of Christian faith, is seen as a prefiguration of Jesus' rejection by the Jewish leadership and his acceptance by seeking Gentiles.

A king is born. But a king is already here; and there is room for only one king. The birth of Jesus, the messianic king, precipitates a conflict with the kingship already present in this world (see on 12:22–30). The conflict between the two kingdoms drives Jesus from his native Judean home to exile in Egypt and a resettlement in "Galilee of the Gentiles." The experience of Matthew's church, alienated from the synagogue where it once was at home but now finding a response among the Gentiles, is reflected in the way the story is composed.

2:1–12
Responses to the New Kingship:
Jewish Opposition and Gentile Worship

2:1 In the time of King Herod: Historically known as Herod the Great because of his vast building projects, this Herod was puppet "king" of

Judea at the pleasure of Rome. He ruled 37–4 BCE. **Bethlehem:** Five miles south of the temple city Jerusalem, this village was the hometown of David, where he was anointed king (1 Sam. 16). **Wise men:** Magi, i.e., astrologers. Later tradition made them into "kings" on the basis of Ps. 72:10–11 and Isa. 60:3. They were a priestly class of Persian or Babylonian experts in the occult arts such as astrology and the interpretation of dreams.

2:2 King of the Jews: The magi's question is both a reminder that Jesus is the royal heir of the Davidic promises and a prefiguration of his ministry proclaiming the kingdom of God and especially of the passion story, in which he will be crucified as "King of the Jews" (27:11, 29, 37). **His star:** There were pagan associations between the birth of a new ruler and unusual astral phenomena, as well as Jewish traditions connecting the hoped-for Messiah to the "star out of Jacob" (Num. 24:17). The military leader of the second Jewish revolt in 132–135 CE, Simeon bar Kosiba, was called "bar Kokhba," "son of the star," i.e., "star-man," the hoped-for deliverer God would send in the last days. Thus Jewish and Gentile hopes for salvation and world renewal were combined in the star imagery.

2:4 Chief priests and scribes: The established leadership of the Jerusalem temple, who cooperated with the Romans and their puppet king in administering the country, and the professional religious scholars and leaders. This is another anticipation of the later story, in which they will oppose Jesus and finally succeed in putting him to death.

2:5 They told him, "In Bethlehem": The Old Testament never speaks directly of a future Messiah, but in the first century Scripture texts such as Mic. 5:2 (here combined with 2 Sam. 5:2) were interpreted as predicting details about the life of the promised future king. By adding the Scripture text, Matthew has the quest of the Magi guided not only by pagan astrology, but by Jewish Scripture. In the present form of the story, Scripture reveals what pagan astrologers look for in the stars.

2:11 On entering the house: There is no stable in Matthew's story, just as there are no shepherds (contrast Luke 2). Matthew's and Luke's "Christmas stories" should not be homogenized, but each should be appreciated for its own witness to the meaning of God's act in the birth of the Messiah (on the distinctiveness of each story, see on Luke 1:5). **Gold, frankincense, and myrrh:** The three gifts are the basis

for the later tradition that there were *three* "wise men"; the story itself, of course, does not indicate how many there were.

2:13–23
The Messiah's Response: Exile in Egypt and Nazareth as Fulfillment

2:13 Angel of the Lord . . . in a dream: There are five communications of the divine will by dreams in the Matthean birth story (1:20; 2:12, 13, 19, 22). Matthew also has a dream play a key role in 27:19. There are no dreams at all in Luke's birth story—nor elsewhere in the Gospel of Luke. Thus dreams are Matthew's distinctive way of indicating that the story is providentially directed by God behind the scenes, but the account is not reporter-like history.

2:15 Out of Egypt I have called my son: Formula Quote #2 (see excursus, "Matthew as Interpreter of Scripture," at 2:23). Matthew sees all the Old Testament as pointing to its fulfillment in Christ. For early Christian interpretation of the Scripture, see excursus, "New Testament Interpretation of the Old Testament," at 1 Cor. 15:3. For Matthew's distinctive approach, see "Matthew as Interpreter of Scripture" at 2:23. Hosea 11:1 is cited here as referring to the flight of Mary, Joseph, and Jesus into Egypt to escape Herod's soldiers. In its original context, God's "son" was Israel, delivered from Egypt by God at the exodus. Matthew sees Jesus as God's greater Son, in whom the history of Israel is paralleled and fulfilled. See Figure 2.

The story is told in such a way as to parallel not only the history of Israel, but the story of Moses in particular. Moses and the Matthean Jesus both were born in a time in which God's people were oppressed by hostile forces (Moses/Egypt, Jesus/Rome), as babies had their lives threatened by the evil king (Moses/Pharoah, Jesus/Herod), went down to Egypt and came back, worked mighty wonders by

Figure 2. The Exodus/The Flight

Israel	Jesus
To Egypt and back	To Egypt and back
Red Sea	Baptism
Temptation in wilderness	Temptation in wilderness
Failure in the vocation to be God's servant to the nations	Faithful servant ministry

God's power, went through the waters (Moses/Red Sea, Jesus/baptism), were tested in the wilderness, and gave their authoritative teaching on the will of God from a mountain (Moses/the Law from Sinai, Jesus/Sermon on the Mount). In a traditional view current in Matthew's time (Philo, *De cherubim*, 12–15), the figure of Moses had been accommodated to that of the Hellenistic savior gods who had not been born of mortal parents, but were supernaturally conceived. Thus while not in the Old Testament, the image of Moses current in Matthew's time pictured him as having a miraculous birth. These parallels to Moses form an important element in Matthew's portrayal of Jesus throughout the narrative.

2:16 Herod . . . killed all the children: Other documents indicate that Herod was a cruel and unscrupulous man, but apart from Matthew there is no historical evidence of the "slaughter of the innocents." Taken as literal history, the story has problems not only of human ethics, but of divine: Would a merciful God warn only one family in Bethlehem of the impending slaughter, leaving the other babies of Bethlehem to be killed? Could not the angel have warned the others? Could not an omnipotent God have overruled or prevented Herod's decision in the first place? Such questions arise from taking the language of angelic communication and divine intervention at the objectifying, descriptive level. This is not the intention of Matthew, who tells the story as a confession of the church's faith that God was involved in the birth and preservation of the Messiah, that despite human evil God's purpose was fulfilled. Such language can be called "confessional language"—that kind of language in which believers confess their faith in what God has done, telling stories and making statements that point to the reality of God's act, without doing it in the mode of objectifying, literal language from which logical deductions can be made. Confessional language is true in what it confesses but does not provide material for further questions and inferences. The language of prayer and praise is such language. It is not purely subjective but points to something real, and yet is not merely neutral statement of facts that can be the basis for other statements. In this story, the reader is asked to believe that God's providential care protected the child Jesus from the forces of destruction, not necessarily that a heavenly messenger warned one family in Bethlehem while ignoring the others. On objectifying and

confessional language, see on Mark 2:10; John 5:9; Acts 1:9; 12:19; 13:19, "John's Use of Language" in introduction to Revelation, and the excursus at 9:35 below on "Interpreting the Miracle Stories."

2:18 Rachel weeping for her children: Formula Quote #3. See on 1:22 for the style of biblical interpretation. Jeremiah 31:15 pictures **Rachel**, matriarch of Israel, mother of the tribes of Benjamin and Ephraim (but not of Judah) weeping at Ramah for her "children," the Israelites, as they are led away captive to Babylon in Jeremiah's time, the sixth century BCE. Ramah, in Benjamin five miles north of Jerusalem, was chosen by Jeremiah because one tradition located Rachel's tomb there, at the site where Nebuchadnezzar's troops assembled captives for deportation (Jer. 40:1). Another tradition located Rachel's tomb at Bethlehem (the one shown to tourists today). Matthew combines these traditions to achieve the desired effect, and understands the text as pointing to the story of Jesus: the ancient matriarch weeps that the baby boys of Bethlehem have been destroyed.

2:23 Made his home in a town called Nazareth: Jewish scribal interpretation understood that according to biblical prophecy the Messiah must come from Bethlehem (vv. 4–6 above) and used Jesus' Nazareth origin (Mark 1:9; John 1:45–46) as an argument that he could not be the Messiah (see John 7:42). Both Matthew and Luke counter this objection by linking Jesus with both Nazareth and Bethlehem, but in different ways—in Luke the story begins in Nazareth, the home of Mary and Joseph, and moves to Bethlehem in order to enroll in the census, while in Matthew the story begins in Bethlehem, the home of Mary and Joseph, and moves to Nazareth after Mary and Joseph have been warned in a dream by an angel not to remain in the territory of Archelaus, and in order to fulfill the Scripture. **"He will be called a Nazorean":** Formula Quote #4. No such quotation is found in the present form of the Old Testament. There are similarities to the "branch" (Hebrew *netzer* of David's line) of Isa. 11:1 and/or to the class of Nazarites (those who had taken a special vow, see Num. 6; Judg. 13:5–7).

EXCURSUS: MATTHEW AS INTERPRETER OF SCRIPTURE

On biblical interpretation in early Christianity in general, see Excursus "New Testament Interpretation of the Old Testament" at 1 Cor. 15:3. There are some distinctive features of Matthew's interpretation:

—Matthew quotes the Scripture more than any of the other Gospels: forty direct quotations explicitly identified as such, with another twenty-one citations not so identified, plus scores of indirect references, allusions, and use of biblical phrases and imagery. Matthew's mind is steeped in the Scripture; he writes for a community intensely engaged with biblical study.

—Matthew takes over all thirty-three of the quotations already found in his sources Mark and Q, and adds an additional twenty-eight of his own.

—As is the case elsewhere in the New Testament, the Psalms is the most frequently cited book, with Isaiah a close second.

—As in Mark and Q, most of Matthew's quotations are from the Greek translation of the Old Testament (the LXX), which sometimes differs significantly from the Hebrew text on which our English translation is based. This is often the reason that the English reader does not find Matthew's quotations agreeing with the English version of the Old Testament (see, e.g., Isa. 7:14, cited in Matt. 1:23).

—A special category is formed by ten "formula quotations" (1:22–23; 2:15; 2:17–18; 2:23; 4:14b–16; 8:17; 12:18–21; 13:35; 21:4–5; 27:9–10). All are introduced by Matthew into their contexts. Except for the four formula quotations in the birth narrative, all are triggered by a Markan context. Except for Zech. 9:9, cited in Matt. 21:4–5, none is cited elsewhere in the New Testament. They thus seem not to belong to a standard repertoire of early Christian proof texts, but to belong exclusively to Matthew and/or his own tradition. They are distinguished from the other quotations, including the others peculiar to Matthew, in several ways. (1) Their introductory formula identifies an event in Jesus' life as the fulfillment of Scripture. The full introductory formula is found in the first quotation—"All this took place to fulfill what had been spoken by the Lord through the prophet" (1:22)—and is repeated with minor variations in all the others. (2) All the formula quotations are spoken not by a character in the story to other characters, but by the narrator to the reader. (3) The formula quotations have a different text type, i.e. their wording is different from both the Hebrew text and its LXX translation. It is debated whether this means they represent a lost text type, or are the products of a Matthean Christian scribal exegetical "school," or represent Matthew's own hermeneutical

work on the text. In any case, they seem to represent the result of a kind of Christian scribal activity (see 13:52). Such alterations in the biblical text are not as arbitrary as they may seem to us, but within the first-century Jewish context represent a sophisticated and subtle approach to Scripture. This form of interpretation that adapts the text to fit more closely presupposed fulfillment was practiced in other streams of first-century Judaism and bears some resemblance to the mode of interpretation practiced at Qumran.

—It has sometimes been thought that Matthew's use of Scripture is apologetic, i.e., that he is concerned to prove the messiahship of Jesus to the Jews by the use of their own Scripture. This is a mistaken notion for two reasons: (1) The Gospel of Matthew is not directed to outsiders in order to convert them, but to insiders to express, clarify, and strengthen their faith. (2) As "proof," Matthew's use of Scripture is not convincing. If he is thought to be assembling scriptural "evidence" for Jesus' messiahship, his Christian interpretation of the texts in opposition to their obvious original meaning, along with the changes he makes in the text itself, make him subject to the charge of manipulating the "evidence" in a way that could not be convincing to outsiders.

—Matthew's use of Scripture is not the language of apologetics directed to outsiders, but the language of confession directed to insiders. The conviction that Jesus is the Christ is the presupposition of his use of Scripture, not the result of it. From the earliest times, that the Christ is the fulfillment of Scripture was the universal conviction of early Christianity (see 1 Cor. 15:3). It is Matthew's conviction that as the Messiah Jesus is the fulfillment of the Scripture as a whole that comes to expression in his interpretation of individual texts.

—Given Matthew's presuppositions, he can then use the Scripture to add details to his story of Jesus. We can see this happening in Matthew, where we have Mark as a control, as in 27:42–43, where the words of the chief priests, scribes, and elders at the cross are taken from Mark 15:32 and then augmented with the words of Ps. 22:8. The question thus arises whether in those places where we have no direct control the Matthean scribal community, and Matthew himself, created narrative elements, or even whole narrative units, as an expression of their faith that the Scripture was fulfilled in Jesus. It may well be that the correspondence of "prediction" and "fulfillment," from Matthew's point of view, fits so well because elements of the narrative were generated by interpretation of the Scriptural text. This interpretive phenomenon went both ways. The fact that Jesus came from Nazareth generated a "prediction" in 2:23. This would also explain why the modern interpreter has difficulty in seeing the Old Testament as a "prediction" in the first place, since we no longer share Matthew's interpretive presuppositions and methods. The task for the contemporary interpreter of the Gospels is to share Matthew's faith that the Christ came as the fulfillment of Scripture, expressed in his theology illustrated and communicated by his own interpretative techniques, even though the modern reader must interpret the Bible with methods appropriate to our own time.

3:1–4:17
THE MINISTRY OF JESUS IN RELATION TO JOHN THE BAPTIST

3:1–12
John the Baptist and His Message
(See also at Mark 1:2–8; Luke 3:1–18; John 1:19–28)

This scene begins a new subsection, bracketed by John's appearance and preaching "repent, for the kingdom of heaven has come near" and concluding, after noting the arrest of John, with Jesus preaching the identical message (3:2=4:17). Here Matthew begins to follow and interpret his two major sources, Mark and Q, each of which began with the appearance of John the Baptist. Verses 3–6 are almost verbatim from Mark 1:2–6 (see there); vv. 7–12 are almost verbatim from Q, also preserved in Luke 3:7–9 (see there). Here, we will deal with the distinctive Matthean elements in his reinterpretation of the story.

3:1 In those days: These words have the archaic ring of biblical narrative (see 24:38, their only other occurrence to introduce a scene in Matthew). Mark had used them Mark 1:9 to introduce Jesus; Matthew transfers them to the beginning of the story of John's appearance. This subtle change is one of several instances of Matthew's paralleling of John and Jesus.

John the Baptist: John was a significant historical figure in his own right, a Jewish prophet with his own message and disciples, who ran afoul of Herod Antipas and was imprisoned and executed by him, as reported by the first-century Jewish historian Josephus (Ant. XVII 5.2; see further on 14:1–12). The group of dis-ciples founded by him continued not only after the baptism of Jesus (Matt. 9:14; 11:2–3), but after the resurrection and beginning of the Christian community (Acts 19:1–7). Early Christianity experienced the continuing Baptist group as a competitor, and in various ways reinterpreted the traditions about John from the Christian perspective to incorporate them into the developing Christian tradition. Our earliest source, Q, had proportionally the most to say about John, and cast him in the most independent role, like Jesus a prophetic spokesman for transcendent Wisdom (Matt. 3:7–10/Luke 3:7–9; Matt. 3:11–12/Luke 3:16–17; Matt. 11:2–19/Luke 7:18–35; 16:16). Mark had already interpreted John as "Elijah," who in Jewish tradition was expected to return as a harbinger of the eschatological advent of God (see Mal. 3:1; 4:5–6; Mark 1:6; 9:11–13). Corresponding to Mark's view of the messianic secret, the Markan John the Baptist never recognized or identified Jesus as the Messiah. Except for this literary device of the secret messiahship, Matthew takes over the Markan pattern with which he had long been familiar. In doing so, he both makes more explicit the Markan identification of John and Elijah (Matt. 11:14; 17:13, both Matthean additions) and makes John and Jesus parallel and complementary figures, though John is altogether subordinate to Jesus.

3:2 Repent, for the kingdom of heaven has come near: "Heaven" was a reverential Jewish way of avoiding pronouncing the sacred word "God"; thus this expression, used only by Matthew in the New Testament, means exactly the same as "kingdom of God." It does not refer to "heaven" as a place, but to God's royal power put into effect to make things right in this world (see at Luke 4:43). Both "kingdom of heaven" and "kingdom of God" mean primarily "God's reign," "the sovereign power of God functioning as ruler."

These words are taken from Mark 1:15, where they are a summary of the message of *Jesus*. Matthew makes the message of John and Jesus exactly parallel, introducing John as a preacher of the kingdom before the appearance of Jesus in the story. As in the preceding verse, here is another instance of John/Jesus parallels. Other such Matthean instances: John and Jesus have the same opponents, the unusual combination of "Pharisees and Sadducees"; in 3:7/12:34, 23:33, their opponents are described in the same way as "vipers"; in 3:10b/7:19, each announces that trees that do not bear good fruit will be cut down and thrown into the fire; in 14:1–12/chaps. 1–2, 26–27, opposition by the rulers brings about the death of each.

Matthew omits Mark's description of John's baptism as "for the forgiveness of sins" (Mark 1:4), and places the phrase at 26:28. It is Jesus (and the church, 9:8) who mediate God's forgiveness, not John. At the same time, this omission removes the problem of having Jesus baptized as a sinner.

3:3–6 See on Mark 1:2–6; Luke 3:1–6.

3:7–12 See on Luke 3:7–9.

3:7 Pharisees and Sadducees: Pharisees were lay leaders of the synagogue, advocates of Scripture and tradition and a strictly holy way of life (see at Luke 5:17). Sadducees were the priestly party associated with the temple. Historically, these two relatively small groups were opponents and competitors for the loyalty of the people as a whole. Matthew combines them to represent Jewish leadership as a solid, unified block opposed to John (and Jesus—see 22:15–46). In Luke 3:7, reflecting Q, these words of John are addressed to the multitudes of repentant sinners who came to be baptized by him. By changing the hearers from the crowds to the Jewish leaders, Matthew significantly changes the meaning of John's words, which are no longer addressed to those who came to be baptized, but to those who came to inspect and disapprove (see on 21:23–27). For John's message, see on Luke 3:7–9.

3:13–17
The Baptism of Jesus
(See also at Mark 1:9–11; Luke 3:21–22; John 1:29–34)

That Jesus was baptized by John is one of the most certain historical facts about Jesus. Yet here too Matthew is not merely reporting historical facts, but interpreting these events from his sources in a way that sets forth his understanding of the faith.

3:13 Jesus came . . . to be baptized: The grammatical construction, an infinitive of purpose, indicates that Jesus had already decided to be baptized before arriving at the Jordan, i.e., that the initiative and decision is his. At the very beginning, Matthew subtly indicates that Jesus is in charge (see v. 15).

3:14 John would have prevented him: Verses 14–15 are added by Matthew to his Markan source. Mark had portrayed John's baptism as "for the forgiveness of sins," and John had baptized Jesus without protest, since he did not

recognize him as the Messiah. The question of Jesus' sinlessness had not arisen for Mark (see Mark 10:18, and contrast Matthew's rewriting in 19:17). Matthew does not say how John recognized Jesus, since this is his first appearance in the Matthean narrative, but the reader should not insert the information in Luke 1, which Matthew and his readers do not have.

3:15 Fulfill all righteousness: Both "righteousness" and "fulfillment" are key Matthean theological themes. "Righteousness" here means, as often elsewhere, doing the revealed will of God. Here "fulfill" seems to mean simply "do, perform," and the meaning is that it is necessary for both John and Jesus to do God's will, which includes the baptism of Jesus. The plural "us" links John and Jesus together as partners in carrying out God's saving plan (11:2–19).

3:16 When Jesus had been baptized: There is no psychologizing of Jesus' "baptismal experience" in Matthew (or elsewhere in the Bible). Matthew does not speculate on what went on in the soul of Jesus. He does not encourage the reader to raise such questions as whether Jesus already knew he was Son of God or had some unique relation to God, or whether his baptism was the occasion when his mission first became clear to him. This is the stuff of novels, not of Gospels. The story of Jesus' baptism has a meaning for the church, but it is not presented by Matthew as a model for Christian baptism, as though the meaning is "since Jesus was baptized, we should be too." It is rather the case that Jesus' baptism is narrated in such a way that church theology and practice are reflected: as disciples are to be baptized into the name of the Trinity (28:19), so Father, Son, and Holy Spirit are all present in Jesus' baptism. As Christian baptism is a matter of obedience and receiving the Spirit, so was it with Jesus. As Christians are declared to be God's children in the act of baptism, so Jesus was declared Son of God when he was baptized.

3:17 A voice from heaven: The heavenly voice speaks in the words of Scripture, a combination of Ps. 2:7 and Isa. 42:1. The words, taken almost verbatim from Mark, represent a combination of christological themes that have become important to Matthew. Although Matthew has presented Jesus as Son of God in the birth story (1:18–25; 2:15), he has withheld the direct announcement until this scene, in which God himself confers the title. Matthew changes Mark's second person address "You are . . ." to third-person "This is . . ." In Mark the announcement is made only to Jesus, and, in keeping with Mark's perspective of the messianic secret, the other human characters in the story remain ignorant of Jesus' identity disclosed to the reader. In Matthew the announcement is addressed to a wider circle—at least John, more likely the bystander public in general, since in chapters 1–2 Jesus' identity is already a matter of family and public knowledge.

Although John hears the heavenly voice, he does not become a disciple, but continues his own work with his own disciples (9:14; 11:1). In Matthew, John remains a marginal figure, parallel to Jesus and subordinate to him, commended and respected, one that the reader must take seriously, yet one who does not join the group of Jesus' disciples. John is not quite "in," but neither is he "out." He represents an ally in the cause of the kingdom of God who yet does not belong to the Christian community and cannot be incorporated within it. This is but one example of Matthew's openness to accepting others as God's servants and messengers even if he can find no legitimate place for them within his theological understanding of the church. The picture of John, who never became a disciple (read "Christian" from Matthew's post-Easter perspective), might be kept in mind when interpreting Matthew's more negative pronouncements against other outsiders, including the Jewish people and their leaders.

In Matthew's perspective, the story is christological narrative. The heavenly voice declares Jesus to be both Son of God and Suffering Servant. Without minimizing the picture of Jesus as Son, it is the Servant picture, previously neglected in the tradition, which Matthew will emphasize, as he already does in this story.

3:17 My beloved, in whom I am well pleased: An echo of the first Servant Song of Isa. 42:1. Matthew will later (12:18–21) cite the entire song (Isa. 42:1–4), the longest scriptural quotation in his Gospel, as the concluding summary at the end of Part One of his Gospel, representing Jesus' response to the conflict his coming has initiated. The Servant picture fills in the content of the Son of God picture and affects the way Jesus fulfills his mission. Precisely as the "mightier one" who will baptize with the Spirit, precisely as the Son of David and Son of God, he submits to baptism at the hands of one who is "lesser." Though he is the Son, he is baptized in obedience to the will of God. Precisely as the Son he is the obedient one.

4:1–11
The Temptation
(See also at Mark 1:12–13; Luke 4:1–13)

See excursus, "Satan, the Devil, and Demons in Biblical Theology," at Mark 5:1. In the brief Markan account available to Matthew, the confrontation between Jesus and Satan is a test of strength, not a moral temptation, and no words are exchanged. The much more extensive Q story, followed by Matthew with only minor variations, is a verbal battle between Jesus and Satan, in which the tempter tries to divert the obedient Son of God from his path. The closest parallels are the debates between Jesus and the Jewish leaders (high priests, elders, Pharisees, Sadducees, scribes) in 21:23–27; 22:15–23:36. It appears that a Christian scribe in the Q community composed the story on this model to portray Jesus' victory in his confrontation with Satan at the beginning of his ministry. Matthew creates a literary bracket by having this dispute with Satan correspond to the disputes with the Jewish leaders at the end of the ministry, thereby suggesting the underlying cosmic conflict that surfaces in the confrontation between Jesus and the Jewish leaders (21:23–22:46).

The conflict throughout the Gospel, already anticipated in the conflict with Herod, the high priests, and scribes (and even the hesitation of John to baptize Jesus), is actually a conflict of kingdoms. Jesus is the representative of the kingdom of God; Satan also represents a kingdom (12:26). Thus, elsewhere in the Gospel the word for test/tempt is used only of the Jewish leaders (16:1; 19:3; 22:18, 35), and Jesus always resists them by quoting Scripture, as here. This conflict is not limited to the Jewish leaders but even emerges between Jesus and his own disciples (16:21–23). The conflict between Jesus and the Jewish leaders is a surface dimension of the underlying conflict between the kingdom of God and the kingdom of Satan. This is what Matthew is *about*. God is the hidden actor, and Satan is the hidden opponent, *throughout* the Gospel, though God is always offstage, and Satan appears only here as a character in the story. Satan is worked into the outline at strategic points, but the conflict between Jesus and Satan is not to be reduced to any one scene. In Matthew's theology, Satan, though defeated (12:28–29), continues his temptation during the ministry of Jesus (16:23!), at the crucifixion, and into the time of the church (13:19, 39), to be finally overcome at the eschaton (25:41).

4:1 Jesus was led up by the Spirit: All is part of the divine plan; Jesus' submission to temptation is not an accident or a matter of his being victimized by demonic power but is part of his obedience to God. **The wilderness:** Here, it means the barren desert near the Jordan, but the word also evokes the experience of Israel "in the wilderness" between Egypt and the promised land, Exod. 12–Deut. 34. In his debate with Satan, Jesus will quote exclusively from Deuteronomy.

4:2 Fasted forty days: The story has overtones of the experience of Israel, the "son of God" (Exod. 4:22–23; Deut. 8:2–5), who passed through the waters into the wilderness, was tested—and failed, by disobedience and worshiping other gods. Jesus, the true Son of God, who recapitulates Israel's experience in coming out of Egypt (Matt. 2:15), is tested in the wilderness and remains obedient to God, specifically refusing to worship another. In contrast to Israel in the wilderness, whose faith wavered until restored by the miraculous manna, Jesus is hungry but remains faithful without miracle. **Afterwards he was famished:** Matthew pictures Jesus as voluntarily fasting, using the technical term for the cultic practice current in Matthew's church (6:16–18; 9:14–15, changing Mark). In Matthew, the temptation begins only after the forty-day period of fasting that has strengthened and prepared Jesus for the encounter with Satan, but has also left him hungry. Jesus' humanness is documented before the conflict begins.

4:3 If: The Greek particle takes the statement at its face value, considering it a real case (as in 6:30, etc.) and could also be translated "since." Thus the devil is not attempting to raise doubts in Jesus' mind but is making an argument on a fact assumed to be true. The disputed issue is not whether or not Jesus is Son of God, but what it *means* for Jesus to be Son of God. It was a feature of some Jewish expectations of the Messiah that he would reproduce the miracle of the manna, as the messianic times were generally expected to provide a lavish supply of food (see John 6:25–58). Jesus is challenged to show that he qualifies as Messiah by these criteria. Matthew has changed the singular "stone" and "bread" (= "loaf") in Q to the plural "stones" and "loaves" (see Luke 4:3, which preserves the singular). Since one loaf would more than suffice for Jesus himself, the devil's argument is not only for Jesus to use his divine power for his own advantage, to alleviate his hunger, but to use his divine power to provide food, meeting an obvious human need. This would correspond to popular messianic expectations and carry enormous political power, but would also deny his humanity and the trust in God Jesus teaches in 6:24–34.

4:4 One [man] does not live by bread alone: "Man" of the NIV and the "one" of NRSV both translate the Greek word for "human being." The point is not maleness but humanity. Here Jesus places himself on the human side of the divine/human divide. He responds only in the words of Scripture, each time from Deuteronomy (see on 4:2 above). Jesus' words and deeds will later show the vital importance of providing food for hungry people (6:11; 14:13–21; 15:32–39; 25:31–46), but here Jesus insists that a truly human life must be nourished by the word of God.

4:5–7 To the holy city: On the different order of the last two temptations in Luke, see on Luke 4:9–12. The reference to the "holy city" is Matthew's addition. This somewhat rare phrase, like the manna expectation of the first temptation, has eschatological overtones (Isa. 48:2; 52:1; Dan. 9:24; Matt. 27:53, Rev. 11:2; 21:2, 10). The identity of the **pinnacle** of the temple is unclear, but it was not the roof or a spire. The temptation is to make some sensational demonstration that he is Son of God. The action is not obviously wrong or demonic (angels had protected Jesus in 2:1–23, and angels do come to serve him in 4:11), nor is the devil's quotation of Scripture for his purpose a case of obviously perverse exegesis. Matthew is illustrating that even the well-intentioned theologies and interpretations of Scripture in his own community can become the vehicle of a demonic alternative to the path of obedient suffering that Jesus has chosen as the path of messiahship. The alternative between angelic help and obedience to God's will that leads to the cross is pointedly expressed in 26:36–53, esp. v. 53. Again, Jesus rejects the temptation with words of Scripture (Deut. 6:16).

4:8–10 To a very high mountain: The "high mountain" is Matthew's addition, which he seems to have adopted from Mark 9:2 (see 5:1; 17:1=Mark 9:2; 28:16). It strengthens the allusion to Moses. The offer of "all the kingdoms of the world" strikes the note of the struggle between the kingdom of God and the kingdom of Satan (12:26) that reverberates throughout the Gospel, and reveals the real conflict inherent in the temptation scene. The temptation is to rule the kingdoms of the world, i.e., to assume the role presently played by the Roman Empire, and to do it by capitulation to the devil's kingship. At the end of this section, Jesus takes up his task of proclaiming the advent of God's rule (4:17) and teaches his disciples to pray for it to occur in this world (6:10). Jesus will not deviate from worship of the one true God, even for the noble-sounding purpose of taking over all the kingdoms of the world. At the conclusion of the story, on another mountain, Jesus announces that he has received all authority on earth, but it is from God, not Satan, and after the cross, not an alternative to the cross (28:18).

For the third time Jesus rejects the devil's proposal with the word of Scripture (Deut. 6:13). For the first time, he adds his own words, "**Away with you, Satan!**" only two words of Greek text, which express Jesus' authoritative command to which even Satan must now be subject. Jesus and his disciples will continue to struggle against the demonic throughout the Gospel, but it is a defeated enemy they face (see on 12:26–28).

4:11 Angels came: By placing the kingdom of God first, even though it means rejecting food and the help of angels, Jesus finally receives them both, thus becoming an anticipatory example of his own teaching (6:33!).

The story of the temptation of Jesus has been interpreted in basically three ways.

1. The *biographical/psychological* interpretation understands the story as a reflection of Jesus' own inner turmoil after his baptism, as he attempted to sort out the meaning of his baptismal experience and his dawning messianic consciousness. Jesus is pictured as toying with various ways to exercise his messiahship. Such an approach does violence to the Gospel genre, comprehending it as "report," and is uninterested in understanding the text in its concreteness.

2. The *ethical* interpretation seems more valid, since it makes contact with our own experience of being tempted. Jesus is presented as a model for resisting temptation (he quotes Scripture, refuses to use his power selfishly, prefers Word of God to "material things," etc.). There may be some indirect value in this approach, but the interpreter should not move too quickly from this text to "our own experience" in quest of cheap relevance. The text is not about the general activity of Satan in tempting people to do evil, for the temptations are not to lust and avarice, but

to do things that were always considered good, supported by tradition and Scripture.

3. The third approach is *christological*, understanding this scene as an expression of one dimension of Matthew's Christology. The issue is not the biographical/psychological one of how Jesus once thought of himself, but of how the Christians of Matthew's church (and ours) should think of Jesus as Son of God. Matthew presents Jesus as Son of God, who will work many miracles during his ministry about to begin. Yet this opening scene presents us with a picture that not only rejects violence and miracles but considers them a demonic temptation. Matthew's pictures of Jesus as powerful Son of God elsewhere in the narrative do not abolish or compromise the picture of Jesus as truly human. Messiahship is defined not only in traditional pictures of divine power, but in terms of Jesus' own suffering and death. Instead of the bread, circuses, and political power that "kingdom" had previously meant, represented in Jesus' and Matthew's day by the Roman Empire ("kingdom" and "empire" are the same word in Greek), in the Matthean Jesus we have an alternative vision of what the kingdom of God on earth might be. This is what was at stake in the temptation. To the extent that Jesus' temptation serves as a model for the Christian, it might teach that to be a "son/child of God" (a Matthean designation for Christians as well, 5:9; see 28:10) means to have a trusting relation to God that does not ask for miraculous exceptions to the limitations of an authentic human life.

4:12–17
To Galilee, Capernaum, and Beginning
of Preaching Ministry
(See also at Mark 1:14–15; Luke 4:14–15)

4:12 John had been arrested: Matthew follows Mark in having Jesus' ministry begin only after being signaled by John's arrest, in contrast to the Fourth Gospel, where Jesus and John the Baptist have overlapping ministries (see John 3:22–4:2). On "arrested," see commentary on Mark 1:14. **He withdrew:** The NRSV's "withdrew" catches the meaning of the Greek verb better than the NIV "returned." This word is found only twice in the other Gospels, but Matthew uses it ten times, almost exclusively for the response of Jesus to threat (see on 12:15; 14:13). It is not cowardice, self-preservation, or strategy, but represents Jesus' alternate vision of kingship,

23

which is nonviolent and nonretaliatory. Although he is the messianic king and Son of God, as the "Son of Man who has nowhere to lay his head" (8:20) Jesus is a displaced person in this world. This corresponds to the Matthean picture of Jesus who responds to aggression in a nonretaliatory withdrawal (2:14, 19–22; 4:12; 10:23; 12:14–21; 14:13; 15:2; 26:53–56) and reflects the post-Easter experience of his disciples (5:38–42).

4:13 Made his home in Capernaum: Nazareth was in the territory of the Old Testament tribe of Zebulun; Capernaum, in Naphtali, was a fishing village on the edge of the lake. Both were in Galilee, in the territory of Herod Antipas. Galilee had become Jesus' homeland in exile (2:19–21; 9:1; 13:54). Galilee, like much of Palestine, in Hellenistic times was a mixture of Jewish and Gentile culture. Jews were perhaps a minority, but Matthew considers Galilee "Gentile" on the basis of this text, not empirical demographics. It is because of Galilee's association with Gentiles that Matthew emphasizes it as the arena of Jesus' ministry.

4:14 Spoken through the prophet Isaiah: Formula Quote #5 (see excursus "Matthew as Interpreter of Scripture" at 2:23). Isaiah 9:1–2 speaks of the grand reversal that shall occur in the latter days, when the spiritual darkness of Galilee shall be dispelled by the dawn of the new age when the ideal king appears.

4:17 Repent: A reorientation of one's life based on the approaching kingdom of God, already manifest in Jesus' ministry (12:28). The word does not picture sorrow or remorse, but a change in direction of one's life. "Get yourself a new orientation for the way you live, then act on it" catches both the Greek and Hebrew connotations. **Kingdom of heaven:** See on 3:2.

"**Has come near**" (NRSV) is better than "**is near**" (NIV) or "**is at hand**" (RSV) in that it describes an event, not a static condition. The phrase makes a temporal statement, not a spatial one, referring to the eschatological kingdom that is already breaking in with the appearance of Jesus. Jesus announces that something has happened (the advent of the Messiah) and that this happening has brought near the final arrival of God's eschatological rule. This summary is already the anticipatory announcement of the Christian message about Jesus, entrusted to the disciples in these very words (3:2, 10:7). Matthew thus makes the proclamation of the kingdom of God the common denominator between Jesus' preaching

and that of the church, i.e., it is theocentric in both cases. As the church proclaims the act of *God* in Jesus, it also and thereby continues Jesus' own preaching of the kingdom of God. For Matthew the "kingdom of God" was not an ideal, principle, or abstraction, but was definitively revealed and embodied in the life and ministry of Jesus. This is why "kingship" language is so important throughout Matthew, from the opening scenes in which the newborn king is a threat to the kingdom already at home in this world (2:1–23) to the closing scenes in which the "king of Israel" is the crucified one who gives himself for others (note the kingship language of 27:11–54) and then vindicated and given "all authority" (28:16–20).

4:18–22
THE CALL OF THE DISCIPLES
(See also at Mark 1:16–20; Luke 5:1–11; John 1:35–51)

The call of the first disciples is the beginning of the messianic community, the church. Jesus' baptism and temptation were not merely individualistic religious experiences of a "great man," but the recapitulation of the birth of Israel in the Red Sea and the wilderness testing; so they lead to the formation of the new community, the Messiah's "people" (1:21). The story is not a straightforward report, but is transparent to the call of disciples in Matthew's church. The meaning of the text will be missed by a biographical/psychological approach that speculates about previous contacts between Jesus and the fishermen, attempting to combine Luke 5:1–11 and John 1:35–51 with this text or somehow to give a "rational" explanation for this miracle. The messianic community, the church, comes into being in response to Christ's own word.

4:18 Simon, who is called Peter: The first disciple-to-be is Simon "Peter." That Peter was called "**first**" is important to Matthew (10:2). (For discussion of his name and role, see on 16:16–18.)

4:19 Follow me: The call seems on the surface to be in the imperative, but the indicative of the divine initiative is fundamental (see on Mark 16:7; Rom. 6:6; 12:1; 13:14; 1 Cor. 5:6–8; 6:18–19; 2 Cor. 5:20; 1 Pet. 1:13). The fishermen are already at work, already have something useful and important to do, and are not looking for a new life. They do not seek him; he seeks and finds them (see John 4:23). The call of Jesus does not fill an obvious vacuum or meet an obvious need in their lives, but, like the call of prophets in the Old Testament, is intrusive and disruptive, calling them away from work and family. The divine sovereignty is clothed in the call for human response.

4:23–9:35
THE AUTHORITY OF THE MESSIAH IN WORD AND DEED

Matthew prepares to present the great central section on the words and deeds of the Messiah as the nuclear center of his creative Part One (see "Structure and Outline" in introduction to Matthew). Matthew has given a summary of Jesus' message (4:17) but has not yet presented Jesus as teaching, nor as performing any miracle. But, as he considers the "words and works of the Messiah" to be the paradigmatic picture of Jesus' life (see 11:2–6), he is preparing to give the first and major presentation of Jesus' teaching (the Sermon on the Mount, 5:3–7:29) and of Jesus' mighty works, including the calling and equipping of disciples (8:1–9:34). For Matthew, "words" precede "works," since he considers teaching to take precedence over working miracles. This major unit is bracketed by verbally identical summary statements, 4:23 and 9:35.

4:23–5:2
The Setting of the Sermon

4:23 Throughout Galilee, teaching: No content of Jesus' message is given yet. Matthew reserves this for his five great discourses, the first being the "keynote address" of the Sermon on the Mount. Prior to the resurrection the disciples do not teach; in Matthew, Jesus is the only legitimate teacher (see 23:8).

4:24 Syria: Matthew replaces the Markan "Tyre and Sidon" (Mark 3:8) with "Syria" (probably reflecting the home territory of the author and his church; see introduction) and the Decapolis, a league of independent Greek-speaking cities in Palestine with Gentile connections. **He cured them:** The acts of healing are narrated to place Jesus' instruction in the context of his own prior acts of announcing the kingdom and acting in mercy to illustrate its power and its nature. The people are healed without meeting any requirements or making any confession of faith. It is entirely the initiative and grace of the messianic representative of God's kingdom.

5:1 He went up the mountain: Luke locates the Great Sermon on the plain (Luke 6:7). The mountain setting in Matthew is not to be explained biographically or psychologically (as though Jesus attempted to get away from the crowds by going up the mountain). Rather, the mountain is part of Matthew's pattern of portraying Jesus in terms of Moses, the great lawgiver of Israel (see on 2:15). Matthew understands that the advent of Jesus brought something qualitatively new (see on 9:17), but it is important that Matthew does not specifically designate Jesus as a "new Moses" or his teaching as a "new Torah," just as he refrains from calling the church a "new Israel." Nonetheless, the image of Moses hovers in the background, and the sermon cannot be heard without reflecting on how Jesus' authoritative teaching from the mount relates to the Torah given on Sinai—a live issue in the Matthean community. Although more than one Galilean hill has been identified by Christian tradition (and tourism) as the "mount of the beatitudes," the location of the Sermon on the Mount is not geographical but theological, the mountain of revelation that corresponds both to Mt. Sinai and the mountain of 28:16 (see also 15:29; 17:1; 24:3 for mountain as place of revelation).

His disciples came to him: By "disciples" Matthew cannot mean the Twelve, since only four have been called (4:18–22; see 9:9; 10:1–4). This is an anachronism, but a theologically legitimate one, not a biographical mistake: disciples represent the church, not just the twelve, and the time barrier between pre- and post-Easter already vanishes. The real hearers of the sermon are the readers of Matthew's Gospel. The "report" of a sermon once delivered during Jesus' ministry becomes the present address of the Lord of the church who continues to be present (1:23; 18:18–20; 28:20). At the end of the sermon, it is clear that the "crowds" who originally occasioned the sermon (representing potential disciples at this point in the narrative) have also "overheard" it (see on 7:28–29).

5:3–7:29
Messianic Words: Sermon on the Mount
(See also at Luke 6:17–49; John 1:29–34)

The Sermon on the Mount is not a verbatim report of a speech once given by Jesus on a Galilean hillside. While it contains materials that go back to the historical Jesus, the present form of the speech is a Matthean construction, containing materials from Jesus, from the early church after Easter, and from Matthew's own composition. The sermon is the first, the longest (uninterrupted), and most carefully structured speech in Matthew's Gospel. Matthew and his church had long been thoroughly familiar with the Great Sermon in Q that began with beatitudes, continued with instruction on love, the

Golden Rule, attitudes toward others, and concluded with warnings about two kinds of ethical "fruit" and the story of the two builders (Luke 6:17–49). Matthew preserved the basic three-part outline of the Q sermon, and added traditional material from elsewhere in Q, from M, his own composition, and occasional touches from Mark. By utilizing his favorite means of composing in triads and the use of literary brackets, Matthew constructed a discourse with a new structure corresponding more closely to his own theological interests. See Figure 3.

At the very center of the sermon is the Lord's Prayer, itself the triadic center in a structure composed of triads. Matthew thus gave the sermon a new center and point of orientation, since the Q sermon had not contained this section on prayer.

5:3–12 The Beatitudes: Character and Destiny of the Disciples
(See also at Luke 6:20–26)

A "beatitude" (Latin) or "makarism" (Greek) is a statement in the indicative mood declaring certain people to be in a privileged, fortunate circumstance. The initial Greek adjective means "fortunate," "happy," "in a privileged situation," "well off." In a religious context, it means "blessed" (by God).

While the sermon has elements of wisdom tradition, Matthew's beatitudes are not practical advice for successful living, but prophetic declarations made on the conviction of the coming-and-already-present kingdom of God. This perspective results in the following principles of interpretation:

1. The beatitudes declare an *objective* reality as the result of a divine act, not subjective feelings, and thus should be translated with the objective "blessed" instead of the subjective "happy." The opposite of "blessed" is not "unhappy," but "cursed" (see the contrasts in Matt. 25:31–46; Luke 6:24–26).

2. The *indicative* mood should be taken seriously, and not transformed into an imperative or exhortation. For the prophets, the beatitudes were primarily a declaration of blessedness to those oriented toward the future reality of God's kingdom, with a powerful but indirect ethical imperative in the form of a call to decision.

3. There is, however, an *ethical* dimension to the beatitudes. The community that hears itself pronounced blessed by its Lord does not remain passive, but acts in accord with the coming kingdom. The life of those pronounced blessed is elaborated in Part II of the sermon, the instruction of 5:20–7:12.

4. The beatitudes are *unconditional performative* language. They do not merely describe something that already is, but bring into being the reality they declare. Like the patriarchal and priestly blessings, and like the prophetic word of the Scripture, the beatitude effects what it says, brings into being what it states.

5. Understood as prophetic pronouncements, the truth claim of the beatitude is not independently true, but *dependent on the speaker*. In the prophetic tradition, the truth of the prophet's word depended on his or her being an authentic spokesperson for God, the active authority behind the pronouncement. In the narrative context of the Sermon on the Mount, the speaker is more than a prophet, he is the Son of God and Lord of the church, already seen from the post-Easter perspective. The beatitudes are thus not observations about reality that others of lesser insight had simply overlooked, such as the truths of mathematics or logic. They are true on the basis of the authority of the one who speaks. Thus for Matthew, Jesus' beatitudes are related to the theme of the authority of Jesus (7:29; 8:9; 9:6; 21:23; 28:18).

6. The beatitudes are not historical but eschatological, not commonsense observations based on this-worldly logic, but pronouncements on the blessedness of those who orient their lives now to the coming kingdom of God.

7. The nine pronouncements are thus not statements about general human virtues—most appear exactly the opposite to common wisdom—but pronounce blessing on authentic disciples in the *Christian community*. All the beatitudes apply to one group of people, the real Christians of Matthew's community. They do not describe nine different kinds of good people who get to go to heaven, but are nine declarations about the blessedness, contrary to all appearances, of the eschatological community living in anticipation of God's reign. Like all else in Matthew, they are oriented to life together in the community of discipleship, not to individualistic ethics.

5:3 Poor in spirit: The "poor" of Jesus' original pronouncement of blessing, preserved by Q and Luke 6:20, refers not only to literal poverty, but also connotes the lack of arrogance and a sense of one's own need. Luke's beatitudes emphasize the literal, economic dimension. Matthew's addition of "in spirit" shifts the emphasis but does not exclude literal poverty. The Matthean Jesus is interested in the literally poor (see 11:5; 25:31–46). From the time of the Psalms, "the poor" had been

Figure 3. Outline of the Sermon on the Mount

Introduction: Setting of the Sermon	4:23–5:2	Mark 1:39; 3:7–13
		Luke 6:12, 17–20a

I. **Triadic Pronouncements That Constitute the Disciples as the Eschatological Community, 5:3–16**

A. The Beatitudes: Character and Destiny of the Disciples	5:3–12	Luke 6:20b–23
B. The Disciples as Salt	5:13	Luke 14:34–35
		Mark 9:49–50
C. The Disciples as Light	5:14–16	Luke 8:16; 11:33
		Mark 4:21

II. **Tripartite Instructions on the Way of Life in the Eschatological Community, 5:17–7:12**

A. Part One: "The Law," 5:17–48		
1. The Law and the "Greater Righteousness"	5:17–20	Luke 16:16–17
2. Three Antitheses Modeling the Greater Righteousness, 5:21–32		
a. Anger	5:21–26	Luke 12:57–59
		Mark 11:25
b. Lust	5:27–30	Mark 9:43
c. Divorce	5:31–32	Luke 16:18
		Mark 10:3–4; 11:12
3. Three Antitheses for the Disciples' Application, 5:33–48		
a. Oaths	5:33–37	M
b. Retaliation	5:38–42	Luke 6:29–30
c. Love	5:43–48	Luke 6:27–28, 32–36
B. Part Two: "The Temple Service": Three Acts of Righteousness before God, 6:1–18		
1. Giving to Charity	6:1–4	M
2. Prayer, 6:5–15		
a. Not Like the Hypocrites or the Gentiles	6:5–8	M
b. The Lord's Prayer	6:9–13	Luke 11:2–4
c. The Condition of Forgiveness	6:14–15	Mark 11:25(–26)
3. Fasting	6:16–18	M
C. Part Three: "Deeds of Loving Kindness": Additional Instruction in Authentic Righteousness, 6:19–7:12		
1. Serving God or Mammon	6:19–24	Luke 12:33–34
		11:34–36
		16:13
2. Anxiety	6:25–34	Luke 12:22–32
3. Judging	7:1–5	Luke 6:37–42
		Mark 4:24–25
4. Pearls before Swine	7:6	M
5. Asking and Receiving	7:7–11	Luke 11:9–13
6. Concluding Summary: The Golden Rule	7:12	Luke 6:31

III. **Three Eschatological Warnings, 7:13–27**

A. Two Ways	7:13–14	Luke 13:23–24
B. Two Harvests (False Prophets)	7:15–23	Luke 6:43–46
		13:25–27
C. Two Builders	7:24–27	Luke 6:47–49

Conclusion of the Sermon	7:28–29	Mark 1:22

understood as a characterization of the true people of God, those who know their lives are not in their own control and know their dependence on God. "Poor in spirit" makes this explicit. Those who are pronounced blessed are not those who claim a robust ego and strong sense of self-worth, but those whose only identity and security is in God.

Theirs is the kingdom of heaven: See on 3:2. Matthew presents Jesus as the ruler of the present and coming kingdom of God, the one through whom God's rule is and will be definitively manifested. As Jesus has reversed the idea of human kingship, so those to whom his kingdom belongs correspond to this eschatological reversal. As the king is meek and poor in spirit (see on 5:5), so are those to whom his kingdom belongs.

5:4 Those who mourn: Matthew here taps into the deep biblical tradition that one of the characteristics of the true people of God is that they lament the present condition of God's people and God's program in the world (Lamentations, the lament psalms such as Ps. 3–7, 10–12, 22, 44). This is the community that does not resign itself to the present condition of the world as final, but laments the fact that God's kingdom has not yet come and God's will is not yet done (6:10). The future passive "shall be comforted" is the divine passive of the eschatological future (as in vv. 6, 7, 9): "God will satisfy their yearnings by letting them see and participate in his eschatological celebration."

5:5 The meek: Psalm 37:9, 11 is here reformulated as a beatitude and presented as a saying of Jesus. Since "meek" is a key Matthean word that characterizes the reversal of this-worldly ideas of kingship (11:29; 12:18–21; 21:5), Matthew may have formulated this saying himself. "**Inherit the land,**" originally referring to the promised land of Palestine, has here become an eschatological metaphor for participation in the renewed earth (19:28).

5:6 Those who hunger and thirst for righteousness: Matthew interprets the literal hunger of the Q beatitude (see Luke 6:21) as a hunger for righteousness, which can also be translated "justice." All the occurrences of this key Matthean word have been added to the sermon by Matthew himself (5:6, 10, 20; 6:1, 33). "Righteousness/justice" means both the active doing of God's will to which Jesus' disciples are called (as 6:1–18; 25:31–46) and the eschatological activity of God that finally brings God's justice to this world (6:33; see Isa. 51:1, 5). Thus those who hunger and thirst for

righteousness are not those who merely long to be personally pious, but those who long for the coming of God's kingdom and the vindication of right that shall finally come with it. On the basis of this confidence that God will finally establish justice, they actively do God's will now. This longing is no empty hope, but **shall be satisfied** (another divine passive, i.e., God will satisfy it).

5:7 The merciful: The Greek word refers to concrete acts of mercy, not merely a merciful attitude. Throughout, the beatitudes refer to acts, not attitudes.

5:8 The pure in heart: Psalm 24:3–4 has been cast in the form of a beatitude and presented as a saying of Jesus (see on 5:5). Purity of heart is not merely the avoidance of impure thoughts (e.g., sexual fantasies), but refers to the single-minded devotion to God appropriate to a monotheistic faith. Faith in the *one* God requires that one be devoted to God with *all* one's heart, different from the functional polytheism that results in parceling oneself out to a number of loyalties (Deut. 6:4–5; see Matt. 22:37; see 6:22; 13:45–46; Phil. 3:13; Luke 10:42). The opposite of purity of heart is a divided heart (Jas. 4:8), attempting to serve two masters (6:24). "Purity of heart is to will one thing" (Søren Kierkegaard).

5:9 The peacemakers: The Roman emperors called themselves "peacemakers" and "sons of God." "Peacemakers" does not connote a passive attitude ("peace*keepers*"), but positive actions for reconciliation, bringing peace out of conflict and chaos.

5:10 For righteousness' sake: See on 5:6. The parallelism between "**for righteousness sake**" (v. 10) and "**for my sake**" (v. 11) shows that righteousness is not an abstract concept for Matthew, but has a christological foundation and is a matter of Christian discipleship.

5:12 Rejoice: The first imperative of the sermon is to "rejoice." The joy to which the disciples are called is not in spite of persecution, but because of it. This is not the expression of a martyr complex but the joyful acceptance of one's place in the eschatological community of faith, the people of God who are out of step with the value system of this age. Devotion to the right is devotion to the God revealed in Christ, and vice versa.

5:13–16 *The Disciples as Salt and Light*
(See also at Mark 4:21; 9:49–50; Luke 8:16; 14:34–35)
5:13 You are the salt of the earth: The saying is evocative and with multiple layers of mean-

ing. Salt had many connotations in Matthew's tradition and context, including sacrifice (Lev. 2:13; Ezek. 43:24); loyalty and covenant fidelity (Ezra 4:14; Num. 18:19; eating together was called "sharing salt," and expressed a binding relationship); purification (2 Kgs. 2:19–22); seasoning (Job 6:6; Col. 4:5); preservative. The "you" is plural—the life of Jesus' disciples is not individualistic, but is conceived throughout as life within the community of faith, a community charged with a mission to the world. The nonretaliatory essence of the new kingdom brought by Jesus is perfectly modeled: though out of step with the world and persecuted, like their master the disciples of Jesus live their lives for the sake of the world that persecutes them. Salt does not exist for itself, nor do the disciples; their life is turned outward to the world. The saying serves as a warning that if the disciples deny their mission, they (too) will be thrown out as useless. Salt loses its saltiness not by some impossible chemical miracle, but by becoming so impure, so mixed with other elements, that it loses its function (see on purity of heart, 5:8 above).

5:14 You are the light of the world: Like Jesus in 4:12–17, the community of disciples is light for the dark world. The metaphor pictures the church as having been lit, as recipients of light of which God is the source, and having been lit not for their own sakes, but for the world's. The primary function of light is not to be seen, but to let things be seen as they are. **A city built on a hill:** In a provocative contrast, the metaphor of the city on a hill presents the disciples as inevitably and unavoidably *being* seen, for it **cannot be hid.**

5:16 So that they may see your good works: Here, people are to see the good deeds done by Jesus' disciples, and they are to be done in such a way that they *can* be seen. On the tension with 6:1–18, esp. 6:3, see on 6:2.

5:17–48 "The Law"
5:17–20 *The Law and the "Greater Righteousness"*
(See also at Luke 16:16–17)

This section is a preface to the case studies that follow in 21–48. The general statements affirmed here are explicated and illustrated in the six antitheses of 5:21–48.

5:17 Do not think: The teaching of Jesus and his disciples about the Law was in fact misunderstood in Matthew's Jewish context (see Acts 7:13–14), but it is directed to outsiders only in a secondary sense. Matthew is addressed prima-

rily to insiders who find themselves belonging to a community that in fact has made fundamental changes in its practice of the Torah. This community must both answer the charges of outsiders and clarify its own understanding of the relationship of Christian discipleship and Torah observance (see on 1:18–25). **Not to abolish but to fulfill:** "Fulfill" does not here mean merely "do," as though Jesus claims that he performs everything required by the Law; or "interpret," as though what he offers is only a new interpretation of the meaning of the Law; or "sum up," as though Jesus claims his teaching is only a summary of the Law (as Gal. 5:14; Rom. 8:4; 13:8–10; Matthew must not be explained in Pauline terms, and vice versa). In line with Matthew's general theology of fulfillment, the best approach to this difficult, but key, passage seems to be as follows:

1. The *whole* Scripture ("Law and Prophets," every **letter** and **stroke**) testifies to God's will and work in history. Matthew does not retreat from this affirmation. He does not play off the (abiding) "moral law" against the (temporary) "ceremonial law."

2. God's work testified to in the Scripture was not yet complete; the Law and Prophets point beyond themselves to the definitive act of God in the eschatological, messianic future.

3. The advent of the messianic king proclaiming and representing the eschatological kingdom of God is the fulfillment of the Scripture, the Law and the Prophets, the goal to which they pointed. The Messiah has come. He embodies and teaches the definitive will of God. The Law and Prophets are to be obeyed, not for what they are in themselves, but because they mediate the will of God.

4. This messianic fulfillment does not nullify or make obsolete the Law and the Prophets but confirms them. The incorporation of the Law in the more comprehensive history of salvation centered in the Christ event is an affirmation of the Law, not its rejection.

5. But this affirmation by being fulfilled by Christ does not always mean a mere repetition or continuation of the original Law. Fulfillment may mean transcendence as well (see on 12:1–14). The Matthean Jesus elsewhere enunciates the critical principle that mercy, justice, love, and covenant loyalty are the weightier matters of the Law by which the rest must be judged (9:13 and 12:7, both of which quote Hos. 6:6; see 23:23). Jesus' declaration that his own life and teaching is the definitive revelation of God's will does indeed mean that

neither the written Torah nor its interpretation in the oral tradition (see on chap. 15) is the final authority.

Jesus' clear "I have come not to abolish the Law" is directed both to those who *fear* that the new freedom of Christian faith has rejected the Bible, and to those who (in their misunderstanding) *celebrate* that this is the case.

5:18 Truly I tell you: Literally, "Amen I say to you." "Amen" is not a Greek word, but a transliteration of a Hebrew word used as a responsive formula to something said previously. It is thus strange to *begin* a saying with this formula. This striking mode of speech is characteristic of the Jesus of the Gospels. Beginning some of his pronouncements with "amen" was a unique aspect of Jesus' own authoritative speech. **Until heaven and earth pass away:** This is not merely a folk expression for "always," but in apocalyptic fashion envisages a concrete event at the end of time, as does the identical expression in 24:35. The point is that, while the Law has continuing validity, it is not ultimate, in contrast to the word of Jesus, which is ultimately normative and will never pass away. For Jesus' disciples, the Law is affirmed but relativized by the advent and authority of Christ, who represents God's ultimate will.

5:21–32 *Three Antitheses Modeling the Greater Righteousness*

Matthew does not elaborate the meaning of this "greater righteousness" in an abstract essay, but explicates it by six concrete examples that take up older materials and place them in a new interpretative structure.

Each of the six units begins with a juxtaposition of what *was* said (divine passive, i.e., by God through Moses) "to those of ancient times" (i.e., the Israelites at Sinai) and what *is now being said* by Jesus to his disciples. "You have heard" refers to hearing the Scripture read in the synagogue. The antitheses contrast Jesus' word not merely with that of tradition or scribal interpretation, but with the Torah itself, which has been the subject since 5:17. Jesus does more than give a better interpretation of the old authority; he relocates authority from the written text of Scripture to himself, i.e., to God's presence in his life, teaching, death, and resurrection (see 1:23; 7:29; 18:18–20; 21:23–27; 28:18–20). No rabbi or scribe ever contrasted his own pronouncements with what God had said in the Torah. Still, the point is that Jesus' teaching is not transgression of the Law, but its transcendence.

The six antitheses are arranged in two triads; only the first set includes the "situational appli-

cation" element (see below). The scribal interpreter Matthew (13:52) follows a threefold structure devised by himself, which is seen most clearly in the first antithesis, 5:21–26. This format is carried through in the first set of three and then abandoned in the second triad—either because he had exhausted his materials for such elaboration or because the pattern had become clear and he leaves the hearer/readers to formulate their own applications. The dynamic of this repeated structure is that it does not answer all ethical issues in advance, but asks the disciple to discern God's will in the light of Torah and Jesus' teaching, and gives models for doing so.

The threefold structure is (a) *reaffirmation* of the Law, which is not abolished; (b) *radicalization* of the Law, which is not merely repeated but restated in a radical manner that expresses the ultimate will of God; (c) *situational application* of the radicalized Law, which provides counsel for imperfect people who want to live their daily lives in the light of God's absolute demand. Thus, without negating the call to perfection, Matthew selects other sayings of Jesus from his tradition that provide situational applications for disciples who *both* believe that the kingdom of God has come with the advent of Jesus, *and* pray for its final coming (6:10). The new age has come in Jesus, but the old age continues, and Christians live in the tension between the two.

In the first set of three antitheses (5:21–32), the reality of Christian existence "between-the-times" of the Messiah's appearance and the eschatological coming of the kingdom is addressed by giving examples for the creative application of Jesus' teaching by his disciples. These examples are not casuistic new laws but models for the disciples to adapt to their varied post-Easter situations. In the second set of antitheses (5:33–48), the concrete models are omitted, and the disciples are left to their own responsibility to discern the will of God in their own situation (see Rom. 12:1–2). All six are expressions of the love command (22:34–40) and keep it from being trivialized or sentimentalized.

5:21–26 *Love Shows No Hostility, but Prevents and Overcomes Alienation*

5:21 You shall not murder . . . liable to judgment (Exod. 20:13; 21:12; Lev. 24:17; Num. 35:12; Deut. 5:17; 17:8–13): For the form, see above. The Matthean Jesus begins with a verbatim quotation of the sixth of the Ten Commandments (Exod. 20:13).

5:22 But I say to you that if you are angry: The biblical command is not revoked, but reaffirmed and then radicalized. Jesus pronounces that anger makes one subject to judgment, without distinguishing between "justified" and "unjustified" anger. Many later manuscripts contain the later addition "without cause," which was printed in the King James Version. There is no doubt that the reading adopted by both NRSV and NIV represents Matthew's original (see "Introduction: The New Testament as the Church's Book," 4.d.). We do not have literal legalistic casuistry here. This is clear both from the fact that the demand is difficult or impossible to carry out—becoming angry is not usually under one's control—and from the absurdly disproportionate punishment, not to mention the fact that if it is taken literally, the Matthean Jesus violates his own injunction (23:17, 19). What we have is a declaration of the absolute will of God, who wills that persons not only not kill each other, but that there be no hostility between human beings.

5:23–26 So when you . . . remember that your brother or sister has something against you: What should happen when Jesus' disciples, who have resolved to live not only by the biblical command against murder, but by Jesus' radical demand not to be angry, nonetheless find themselves involved in anger and hostility? Matthew selects two illustrations from his tradition of Jesus sayings (see Q = Luke 12:57–59) that guide the disciples in applying Jesus' radical demand to their between-the-times situation of imperfect people living in an imperfect world. They are to consider reconciliation, overcoming alienation and hostility, to be even more important than worship at the altar (5:23–24), and to work for reconciliation in the light of the eschatological judgment toward which they are journeying (5:25–26). Neither picture is to be taken legalistically as a literal case. Corresponding to the antithesis of 5:22, this is not a realistic "case," but a nonliteral, noncasuistic, parabolic pointer to the kind of "greater righteousness" appropriate to those who belong to the kingdom of God. Likewise the picture in vv. 25–26, originally perhaps a fragment of this-worldly wisdom that it is sometimes prudent to settle out of court, has in this context become a testimony to the urgency of reconciliation before arriving at the eschatological judgment of God.

5:27–30 *Love Is Not Predatory in Deed or Look (See also at Mark 9:43–48)*
The formal structure devised by Matthew is also clearly seen in this pericope, which reaffirms the Law (5:27), radicalizes it (5:28), then provides two situational applications (5:29–30).

5:27: The absolute prohibition of adultery in the Ten Commandments (Exod. 20:14; Deut. 5:18) refers specifically to a married woman's having sexual relations with a man other than her husband, and is to be distinguished from "fornication," illicit sex in general. Adultery was considered a violation of the husband's exclusive right to his wife and the assurance that children born to her were his own. Both the woman and man involved were considered guilty of adultery, whether or not the man was married. The teaching of Jesus does not abolish the command of the Decalogue against adultery, but reaffirms it.

5:28 But I say . . . everyone who looks: Jesus radicalizes the intent of the Law with the pronouncement that every man who looks on the wife of another for the purpose of sexual desire is already an adulterer in his inmost being. Though both men and women can be guilty of adultery, Jesus presupposes the patriarchal setting of his own culture and of the original Decalogue by explicating his own command in terms of the man. This is remarkable, since the woman was often considered the offending party (see John 7:53–8:1). The androcentric perspective is also retained in that adultery is not seen as an offense against the unfaithful man's wife, but against the husband of the unfaithful wife. Strictly interpreted, this text does not deal with natural sexual desire and its associated fantasy, but with the intentional lustful look at the wife of another. This observation, however, should not be used to domesticate Jesus' radical demand. As in 5:21–27, not only the physical deed, but the intention of the heart, makes one guilty before the Law of God.

5:29–30 If your right hand causes you to sin: Once again the scribal Matthew does not leave the disciple who wants to live by the "greater righteousness" of the kingdom ethic standing helplessly before the radical, impossible-sounding demand. Without retreating from the command that expresses the absolute will of God, Matthew searches his tradition and finds sayings of Jesus that, when brought to this context, show both that from time to time the disciple will in fact not measure up to this absolute standard, and that such violations must be resisted by radical measures (see 18:8–9; Mark 9:43, 47). Matthew does not interpret the Jesus tradition by citing it and then writing explanatory comments, but by combining various sayings of

Jesus from the tradition into a tensive structure that suggests and helps generate the disciples' own creative interpretation.

While these instructions are not literal commandments applicable for all times and places, the teaching of Jesus does here impinge on the sexual ethics of his followers in later times, including ours. In this area above all others, in our culture we hear, "No one has any right to say anything to me about *this*. It is entirely my own personal business" (sometimes with the codicil "—so long as it is not hurting anyone else"). The Sermon on the Mount proceeds from other presuppositions: (a) Our sexuality, like all else, is a gift of God, not our private possession to dispose of as we will. (b) Right and wrong is not a matter of my individual decision, but of the revealed will of God. (c) My sex life does involve others and may hurt them even if I am unaware of it. (d) There are orders or structures of human life established by God into which my individual life should fit, including sexual and family structures. (This is what the later church has attempted to say in defining marriage as a sacrament.) (e) Even so, the radical demand must be applied and God's will discerned from case to case. Right and wrong in such matters cannot be handled prescriptively, legalistically, or casuistically, but go to the roots of human life in the "heart" and intention.

5:31–32 *Love in Marriage Is Not a Contractual Arrangement (See also at Mark 10:11–12; Luke 16:18)*
5:31 Whoever divorces his wife: The teaching of the Matthean Jesus in relation to the Law may be clarified by considering the following history of the hermeneutical tradition in which Matthew stands:

1. No teaching of the Torah commands divorce; neither is divorce prohibited. The Law of Moses assumes the legitimacy of divorce; the issue is remarriage. Divorce had to be official and regulated by the community, thus offering some protection to the divorced woman by granting her legal status and permitting her to marry someone else. The decision to divorce was strictly the prerogative of the husband, who did not have to go to court, but could simply make the decision himself, in the presence of certified witnesses.

2. Deuteronomy 24:1–4 was the locus of the scribal discussion in Jesus' day and Matthew's, the issue between the rabbinic schools being how strictly the grounds for divorce ("something objectionable," 24:1)

should be defined. The strict school of Shammai interpreted this to mean sexual sins or perhaps gross impropriety, while the liberal school of Hillel argued it could be anything that displeased the husband. In either tradition, divorce was relatively easy and frequent, encouraging a lax attitude toward marriage.

3. Against both Law and tradition, the historical Jesus proclaimed the will of God to be the absolute prohibition of divorce. Mark 10:2–9 and 1 Cor. 7:10–11 still reflect this oldest tradition, in which Jesus functioned as a prophet in the tradition of Mal. 2:14–16, who proclaimed the unqualified will of God, without making any adjustments for the demands of practical necessities.

4. Matthew's primary sources, Mark and Q, both preserved Jesus' saying about divorce, but reintroduced the issue of remarriage, a practical necessity in the case of the divorced woman (Mark 10:11–12 added to 2–9; Luke 16:18). In addition, Mark adjusted the saying to his Gentile context by adding the provision for a woman to divorce her husband (Mark 10:12). This provision was unknown in Jewish society except in exceptional cases such as royalty.

5. The original proclamation of Jesus, and the Markan and Q traditions that preserved it, indicated by their form that the man who divorced his wife was guilty of adultery. The pre-Matthean tradition had already reformulated this to fit the more traditional Jewish view that only the woman would be guilty of adultery (when she remarried), but preserved Jesus' charging the man with adultery by making him responsible for the woman's (subsequent) adultery (Matt. 5:32).

6. The whole stream of Christian interpretation has as its point of departure not the permission of divorce assumed by the Old Testament, but its absolute prohibition as initially proclaimed by Jesus. In this stream of tradition emanating from Jesus, marriage and the family is not a contractual arrangement regulated by law, but a part of the structure of creation itself, the good gift of God to humanity, and therefore not at human disposal.

7. Matthew himself functioned as a scribal interpreter of the whole tradition by including both the original demand of Jesus and both forms of its interpretation—the "Jewish" form here and the "Gentile" form in 19:3–12 (which see). He then added the "exception clause" to both forms, which allowed him to understand the logion against divorce as another instance

of his threefold pattern: Jesus (a) reaffirms the Law that had regulated the evil of divorce by (b) radicalizing it, outlawing divorce entirely, then (c) built in a situational application for Jesus' radical demand by including one exception. By including an "exception clause," Matthew has in principle indicated that if there is one exception, there can be others. He does not attempt to prescribe what these might be but illustrates that the teaching of Jesus must be interpreted from case to case, without establishing a rigid law that only one case is legally an exception.

5:33–48 *Three Antitheses for the Disciples' Application*

The second series of three examples has only the original law and Jesus' radicalization of it. The situational application is left for the disciples' own discernment. (See form above.)

5:33–37 *Love Is Unconditionally Truthful*

5:33 You shall not swear falsely: The Matthean Jesus formulates an antithesis that summarizes and paraphrases the Old Testament's teaching about oaths (Lev. 19:12; Ps. 50:14), then rules it out by his command that his followers take no oaths at all. Jesus abolished the distinction between words that have to be true and those that do not, between words one is compelled to stand behind and those one does not, and calls for all speech to be truthful. There may, indeed, be situations when utter candor violates the greatest command of love to God and neighbor, when a lie must be told in the service of love and truth, but Matthew refuses to give legalistic sanction or casuistic examples, casting the disciples on their own theological responsibility.

5:38–42 *Love Does Not Retaliate, but Foregoes Its Own Legal Rights (See also at Luke 6:29–30)*

5:38 An eye for an eye: The Old Testament does not command revenge but had sought to curb the tendency to unlimited private revenge (e.g., Gen. 4:23–24) by incorporating the law of retaliation into the institutionalized judicial system (Exod. 21:24; Lev. 24:20; Deut. 19:21). Jesus not only affirmed the thrust of the Law in opposing unlimited revenge; he called for his disciples absolutely to reject the principle of retaliatory violence. Retaliation and its associated violence represent the usurping counterkingdom of Satan, not the kingdom of God represented by Jesus. This antithesis, like the others, is not a matter of commonsense wisdom but is composed by Matthew in the perspective of the conflict of kingdoms that pervades his Gospel (see on 12:22–30). That means the "enemy" is seen not merely for what he or she empirically is, but in the light of the present-and-coming kingdom of God. This perspective takes evil seriously but does not consider it ultimate. The eschatological kingdom of God already breaking in with the advent of Jesus embraces even "the enemy." Thus Jesus' command not to resist evil goes beyond passive resistance as a strategy. It is positive action in the interest of the aggressor, as the examples immediately show.

5:39–42 Turn the other [cheek]: Superficially regarded, the five examples seem not to fit together. In the first three (being struck in the face, being sued in court, being requisitioned into short-term compulsory service for the occupying government), a person is victimized by powerful others, while in the last two the balance of power seems to have shifted, and one's help is sought by needy others (beggers, borrowers). From Matthew's perspective the common denominator for the five elements seems to be that they are all examples of aggression and pressure from other people that interfere with one's own selfish pursuits. What is called for is a response in terms of the good and the needs of the other, not one's own rights.

5:40 Give your cloak as well: This example portrays a court case in which a man is being sued and is literally losing his shirt (the Greek word refers was a long nightshirtlike main garment). The victim is commanded not only to give it willingly, but in addition to give the "cloak," the togalike outer garment that could not be legally taken away (Exod. 22:25–26; Deut. 24:12–13). Since the willing victim ends up nude in the courtroom, here too Jesus' teaching is hardly intended literally. It is a matter of being secure enough in one's acceptance by God to enable one not to insist on one's rights, legal and otherwise, but empowering one to renounce them in the interest of others, a perspective on the life of discipleship also affirmed by Paul (1 Cor. 6:1–11; 8:1–10:33; Rom. 14:1–15:7).

5:41 Go also the second mile: The third example reflects the Roman practice, taken over from the Persians, by which soldiers and government officials could compel citizens of the occupied country to give them directions or carry their equipment a prescribed distance (see 27:32, where Simon is compelled to carry

Jesus' cross on the way to execution). Rather than resisting the evil government or plotting how to get even, the disciple is commanded to do more than the law requires.

Though not given on an institutional level (Jesus does not legislate for worldly courts) but for the private lives of disciples, these commands still have implications for the involvement of these private lives in the public and political decisions for which Christians are responsible. These sayings indicate Jesus himself must have resisted the militaristic tendencies of those who opposed Rome and who finally plunged the nation into a catastrophic war (66–73 CE). In preserving these sayings and making them the climax of his antitheses, Matthew takes his stand with those who had resisted the disastrous attempt at a "military solution" he and his church had lived through.

5:43–48 *Love Extends Even to the Enemy (See also at Luke 6:27–28, 32–36)*

5:44 Love your enemies: Matthew has reserved the love commandment for this climactic spot, forming his sixth and final antithesis. Leviticus 19:18 had commanded the love of neighbor, but the context made clear that "neighbor" included only the fellow Israelite. There is no command in the Old Testament to hate the enemy, yet there are statements that God "hates all evildoers" (Ps. 5:5; see 31:6) and statements that imply that others do, and should do, the same (Deut. 23:3–7; 30:7; Ps. 26:5; 139:21–22). The group of insiders to be loved is constituted by the religious community; outsiders who are "hated" are those who do not belong. "Hate" in biblical parlance does not necessarily imply personal hostility, but may mean "not choose, not consider an outsider" (see Matt. 6:24; Luke 14:26; Rom. 9:13). This is made explicit in the Qumran community, who held it as a basic tenet of their faith that they were to "love all the children of light and hate all the children of darkness" (1QS 1:9–10; see 1:3–4). From a legalistic point of view, the question thus became how far the definition "neighbor" must be extended (see Luke 10:25–29, 30–37).

The Matthean Jesus makes love of God and neighbor the fundamental command on which all else depends (see 1 Cor. 13:4–7 on the meaning of *agape*) and makes the command to love enemies specific and concrete. In its absoluteness and concreteness, it is without parallel in paganism or Judaism. The command should not be understood abstractly:

"Love all people, including even enemies." In Jesus' situation it referred particularly to the occupying Roman forces, and thus to national enemies as well as competing religious groups and personal enemies.

Jesus bases the command not on a humanitarian ideal, a doctrine of human rights, or a strategy or utilitarian purpose (to win the enemy over) but (a) only on his authority to set his own command in juxtaposition to the Law (5:43), (b) on the nature of God, who loves all impartially (5:45), and (c) on the promise of eschatological reward (5:46). The idea of reward is not mere selfishness but a dimension of Jesus' fundamental proclamation of the present and coming kingdom as the basis for the radical lifestyle to which he calls his disciples. Thus "that you may be children of your Father in heaven" also represents Matthew's inaugurated eschatology: your conduct must be appropriate to your status as sons/children of God which you already are (6:4, 6, see 18) but which will be revealed and acknowledged by God at the last judgment (see 5:9).

5:46–47 Even the tax collectors . . . even the Gentiles: On "tax collectors" see on Luke 5:27. Though Jesus is presented as "friend of tax collectors and sinners" (9:11; 11:19) and Matthew's church includes Gentiles (28:18–20), he retains some of the vocabulary of the older Jewish-Christian tradition that disdained "tax collectors" and "Gentiles"—now understood not ethnically but as typical unbelievers.

5:48 Be perfect: What is the meaning of this troublesome, "unrealistic" demand? In the Gospels, the word is used only by Matthew, who has changed Q's "merciful," preserved in the Lukan version in 6:36, just as he has inserted it into the Marcan text at Matt. 19:21. It is thus not a problematic word he seeks to dilute, but a word he chose to sum up Jesus' demand in 5:2–48. Neither here nor in 19:21 does it express a two-level ethic, with "perfection" only for the elite; rather, it is the command of Jesus to every disciple. Matthew takes the word from his Bible (the LXX uses it often), particularly from texts such as Deut. 18:13: "You shall be perfect before the Lord your God." The biblical word is *tamim*, which means wholeness in the sense of not being partial (on God's impartiality, see v. 45). To "be perfect" is to serve God with the whole heart, to be single-minded in devotion to the one God, just as God is one—the ethical stance appropriate to a monotheistic faith (see 5:8 and Deut. 6:4–6). It is the kind of living called for in all the antitheses and is their appropriate summary, corresponding to the "pure in heart" of 5:8.

6:1–18 *"The Temple Service," Three Acts of Righteousness before God*

With this unit we move to the second major section of the Instruction (see p. 27 on structure of the Sermon on the Mount). The tradition in this section is derived from M, Matthew's collection of materials peculiar to his own tradition, with insertions of material also found in Q (6:9–13) and Mark (6:14–15). This section has no points of contact with the Q Great Sermon preserved in Luke 6:20–49, which Matthew has abandoned and will not resume until 7:1 (=Luke 6:37).

6:1–4 *Giving to Charity*

6:1 Beware of practicing your piety before others: This is the thematic heading that embraces the religious practices of almsgiving, prayer, and fasting taken over by the church from Judaism. There is no command to observe these religious practices; it is assumed that the disciples of Jesus will continue to make these fundamental elements of Jewish practice part of their own lives. The word here translated "piety" is the same word translated "righteousness" or "justice" in the preceding. This heading links this section thematically to the preceding, showing that the author makes no distinction between devotion to God expressed in acts of worship (6:1–18), and acts of personal integrity, justice, and love directed to other human beings (5:20–48), *all* of which are called righteousness/justice.

In all three examples, this heading makes clear that the point of contrast between "the hypocrites'" behavior and that required of the disciples is not the contrast between public worship and private (Matthew affirms both), nor the contrast between external and interior behavior (Matthew affirms both), but the contrast of motivations: the affirmation and applause of human beings with the "reward" of being accepted by God. (The NRSV, seeking to make the language gender-inclusive, translates "others" [contrast NIV's "men"], which is open to the misunderstanding that the contrast is "self"/"others." But the contrast is between conduct directed toward God and conduct directed toward human applause.)

6:2 Hypocrites: A neutral term in secular Greek, literally "stage actors," here applied metaphorically to those who perform their religious acts with an eye on the human grandstand. **Do not sound a trumpet:** The contrast is described in two striking metaphors, neither of which is literal. Contrary to a popular explanation, there is no evidence that in the synagogue worship trumpets were sounded to call attention to the presentation of large gifts. Nor is it literally possible for one hand to be unaware of what the other is doing. The emphasis is on doing one's religious duty to God—here, helping the poor—in such a manner that only God sees.

There is a tension between these instructions and 5:16 (see there). The tension is partly the result of Matthew's incorporating two different traditions, but is primarily due to the mode in which scribal wisdom functions. There are numerous such tensions in Matthew, e.g. 5:4 vs. 9:15; 5:9 vs. 10:34; 6:34 vs. 25:1–13; 8:12 vs. 13:38; 9:13 vs. 10:41; 16:6 vs. 23:3. Just as such tensions should not be pounced upon as examples of "contradictions in the Bible," neither should they too readily be "harmonized" into a bland "consistency," since they represent a potent dimension of scribal wisdom teaching (see, e.g., Prov. 26:4–5). This is the nature of proverbial wisdom in general: "look before you leap" but "he who hesitates is lost"; "fools rush in where angels fear to tread," but "damn the torpedoes—full speed ahead!" Matthew composes as a Christian scribe, one who transmits a tradition of proverbial Christian wisdom (see 13:52). Proverbial wisdom does not deal in bland platitudes, but is provocatively paradoxical. It is not intended as a set of rules but functions by stimulating the imagination and evoking personal responsibility. The jagged edges of Jesus' sayings should not be too quickly rounded off to make them "consistent" with other biblical teachings or even with each other. Talk of the kingdom of God generates a certain violation of conventional patterns of speech and logic that is lost if domesticated.

6:4 Openly: This word is not in Matthew's original but added in later manuscripts (see NRSV footnote). The promised reward is eschatological. This-worldly reward for discipleship is not in Matthew's perspective. God will reward with acceptance into the kingdom of God and the granting of eternal life.

6:5–15 *Prayer*

(See also at Mark 11:25–26; Luke 11:1–4)

Matthew rearranges the materials that come to him to make the section on prayer the structural and theological center of the Sermon on the

Mount, with the Lord's Prayer the core of this center (see "Structure" above).

6:6 Whenever you pray, go into your room: The "room" is the "closet" or "storeroom." With another provocative metaphorical picture the author rejects ostentatious praying aimed at applause from a human audience and commands that prayer be directed to God alone. This shows that for Matthew prayer was not understood psychologically, as though its value is its effect on the one praying and those who hear it, but like all worship is God-centered and understood as an objectively real event in which God hears the worshiper. Jesus does not here legislate against public community prayer, in which he expects the church to engage (18:19–20). The point is that prayer be addressed to God alone. Prayer does not require a holy place, but is sanctified when addressed to God in a storeroom. As elsewhere in this section, the direction is not intended literally—one can also ostentatiously call attention to going to the inner room to pray.

6:7 Do not heap up empty phrases: Authentic prayer is contrasted not only with hypocrites in the synagogue but with perverse Gentile practice. The "many words" of some pagan prayers refers not merely to their length. Matthew uses here an obscure Greek word that may refer to the invocation of many gods, to the ritual repetition of prayer formulas, to empty, insincere talk, or to glossolalia. All such speaking supposes one must impress or gain the attention of the deity, or use the correct formula in order to ensure the effectiveness of the prayer, and thus understands prayer to be a manipulative function for the self-interest of the one praying. In contrast, Matthew pictures Christians praying as an expression of trust in a God who knows our needs before we ask. "Asking," then, is not a matter of informing or manipulating the deity, but of aligning ourselves in trust and acknowledging our need.

Matthew 6:9–13 *The Lord's Prayer*

Over against such prayer, Matthew presents the Lord's Prayer as a pattern for the disciples. It has formal similarities with other Jewish prayers current in the first century, but the present form is due to Matthew and his community.

6:9 Our Father in heaven: Jesus' original invocation was "Father," as in Luke 11:2. "In heaven" represents the Matthean church's accommodation to the liturgical usage. In the first century both Jews and Greeks commonly addressed God as "Father." The common synagogue invocation was "our Father, our King." Jesus reflects this Jewish practice, with his own distinctive adaptation. "Abba" is originally a child's word (see "Dada," "Papa") but is not a childish expression, not baby talk; it was also used by adults within the intimate conversation of the family. It is thus family talk (see 12:46–50). Though God is spoken of as "Father" in the Old Testament and Jewish tradition (Exod. 4:22–23; Hos. 11:1–4; Isa. 63:16), no one prior to Jesus is known to have used this word in address to God. This made such an impression on the early Christians that Jesus' original word in his native Aramaic was preserved (see Rom. 8:15; Gal. 4:6). For Jesus and Matthew, "Father" was not a general term for the deity, but was first of all Jesus' word for his own relation to God. He then included his disciples, and then human beings as such in this relationship. As children of the one God, they are "brothers and sisters" not only to each other but to Jesus, sharing his personal relationship with God (12:46–50; Heb. 2:11). "Father" for Jesus means the one who loves, forgives, and knows how to give good gifts to his children (7:11; Luke 15:11–32). This word for God and its associated imagery were very important to Matthew, as it was for the other evangelists, especially the author of the Fourth Gospel. Father language not only dominates this section (6:1, 4, 6, 8, 9, 14, 15, 18); it is also found often elsewhere in the Sermon on the Mount (5:16, 45, 48; 6:26, 32; 7:11, 21) and in the remainder of the Gospel. Matthew and the Matthean Jesus can also use other images for God, including feminine images, but the centrality of this image in Matthew's theology and its basis in the teaching of Jesus should not be obscured.

6:9 Hallowed be your name: This is the first of three "thou" petitions. The first three petitions are not for three separate items, but for the eschatological event in which God's name will be hallowed, God's kingdom will come, and the will of God will be done. Thus all three are aspects of the central focus of Jesus' proclamation, the coming of the kingdom of God. Each petition is primarily eschatological, with an impact on the present that calls for corresponding action. "Name" in the biblical world was not a mere label but represented the reality and presence of the person. "Hallow" means to honor as holy. The initial petition is that God will be honored as God, the Holy One. It is not a pious wish but a prayer for a specific eschatological act of God (see Ezek. 36:22–23).

6:10 Your kingdom come: On "kingdom of God" see on 3:2; Luke 4:43. The eschatological nature of the whole prayer is focused in this one petition, which sums it up. Yet, as in each of the petitions, there is also a present dimension. The prayer acknowledges that God is God and is finally responsible for bringing in his rule, but one cannot pray this prayer without committing one's own will and action to fulfilling the will of God in the present and praying that other people will submit themselves to God's rule in the here and now (see 6:10b and 26:42).

Your will be done: Matthew adds this explanatory phrase (see Mark 14:36). As God's will is already done in heaven, so at the consummation all creation will be subject to the will of God. The kingdom image is (re)uniting, bringing the rebellious earth back under the rightful sovereignty of the Creator. Thus heaven/earth corresponds to the already/not-yet nature of the kingdom.

6:11 Our daily bread: Here begin the three "we" petitions, corresponding to the three "thou" petitions of vv. 9–10. The seemingly simple and natural prayer for daily bread has been interpreted in a wide variety of ways.

1. Since the prayer as a whole is eschatological, and since in a hungry world "bread" was a widespread symbol of the eschatological blessedness (see Luke 14:15; see 22:16), the prayer is for the eschatological bread of the final coming of the kingdom of God. So understood, the prayer is for the eschatological blessing of the messianic banquet, when all God's people will sit down together with food for all.

2. Bread has been understood for normal this-worldly needs, for survival. For the poor people among whom Jesus lived and worked, it would be difficult to exclude this natural meaning. The prayer represents Jesus' own solidarity with the poor and his concern that they have the minimal means of survival. Even an affluent, calorie-conscious church can pray this prayer in solidarity with the hungry and poor of the world. Such praying constitutes a readiness of those who have bread to share with those who have none.

3. Since this prayer early became an element in the church's eucharistic liturgy, "bread" was often understood to refer to the sacramental

bread. This could hardly have been part of Jesus' original meaning, and there is no indication that Matthew understands this petition eucharistically. "Daily" is the traditional translation of the unusual word *epiousios*, whose meaning is unknown since it occurs nowhere else in Greek literature not dependent on this text. It can mean "necessary," "continual," "for today," or "for tomorrow."

6:12 Debts: Jesus, like John the Baptist, Paul, and biblical theology in general, makes the assumption of universal sinfulness. Jesus assumes that every person who comes before the Holy One in prayer comes as a guilty one who needs God's forgiveness. Sin is here thought of as a debt owed to God, a debt one cannot repay. Without presumption, but in confidence, the disciple is taught to ask for God's forgiveness. God's forgiveness is unconditional, precedes human forgiveness of other human beings, and is its ground and cause. Yet prayer for God's forgiveness is unthinkable for one who is intentionally an unforgiving person. Matthew magnified this element in his Jesus tradition, the danger of presuming on God's grace and therefore being an unforgiving person oneself, emphasizing it at the conclusion of the prayer in 6:14–15 and especially in 18:21–35.

6:13 Do not bring us to the time of trial/Lead us not into temptation: In accord with the eschatological orientation of the prayer as a whole, it is best to interpret the petition as originally having primarily a reference to the ultimate future. In apocalyptic thought, just before the final victory of God and the coming of the kingdom, the power of evil is intensified, and the people of God endure tribulation and persecution. The disciple is instructed to pray that God, who always leads his people, will not bring them into this time of testing, when the pressure might be so great as to overcome faith itself (see 10:22, and see on 26:42, where the identical phrase occurs). Thus **"evil *one*"** is the proper translation of the final word of the prayer (as in NIV and NRSV), not "evil" in the abstract (KJV, RSV). Though originally primarily eschatological, the petition for deliverance from the final testing and the Evil One also has a present dimension. The "ordinary" testings and temptations are seen not as petty peccadilloes, but as manifestations of the ultimate power of evil. The disciple is instructed not to take them lightly but to see them as a threat to faith and to pray for God's deliverance from them.

The oldest and best manuscripts do not contain the final doxology. The mass of later MSS include some form of **"for yours is the kingdom and the power and the glory forever, amen"** derived from 1 Chron. 29:11–13. Earlier English translations such as the KJV were unaware of the oldest Greek texts, which had not yet been rediscovered, with the result that the common English form of the Lord's Prayer used in public worship quite appropriately includes the doxology. There can be no doubt, however, that it is a later addition long after Matthew's time (see "Introduction: The New Testament as the Church's Book," 4.d.).

6:16–18 *Fasting*

On fasting, see on Mark 2:18. As in the preceding instructions about almsgiving and prayer, the issue is whether such voluntary acts of piety are done with the goal of impressing a human audience, or as an act of devotion to God. Thus the disciples are commanded not to disfigure their faces (by wearing sackcloth, placing ashes on their heads, not washing or combing their hair), which makes it obvious they are fasting, but to perform their normal daily hygiene of washing and anointing—so that only God will be aware of their devotion.

6:19–7:12 *"Deeds of Loving Kindness," Additional Instruction in Authentic Righteousness*

This section corresponds to the third of the Three Pillars of Judaism, "Deeds of Loving Kindness." It begins with trusting and serving God with one's material possessions (6:19–34) and builds toward the Golden Rule (7:12).

6:19–24 *Serving God or Mammon*

(See also at Luke 11:34–36; 12:33–34; 16:13)

What seems to begin as prudent advice on long-term investments turns out to be a radical challenge calling for the reorientation of one's whole life. The identification and location of one's "treasure" turns out to be a matter of one's total self (this is the meaning of "heart," v. 21). How one handles property turns out to be not peripheral but a matter of saving or losing one's whole being.

6:19–21 Treasure in heaven: A common Jewish image for eschatological reward. Matthew does not spell out how the disciples are to store up treasures in heaven. Here, too, he leaves room for the disciple's creative response in his or her particular situation (see on 5:21–48).

6:22–23 The eye is the lamp of the body: In contrast to the modern understanding that regards the eye as a window that lets light into the body, the common understanding in the ancient world was that the eye was like a lamp (Prov. 15:30; Tob. 10:15; 2 Sam. 12:11; Dan. 10:6), i.e., an instrument that projected the inner light onto objects so they could be seen. In either case, however, if the eye is unsound, confusion and darkness reign within the person.

6:24 No one can serve two masters: The statement assumes the existence of slavery, which was made specific in Q (still preserved in Luke 16:13). By omitting the word "slave," Matthew makes it apply directly to the disciples. "Love" and "hate" are not emotional words, but represent the biblical idiom for "choose"/"not choose" (see on Luke 14:26). The point is that undivided service can be given to only one master; if there is more than one, every choice means a favoring of one and rejection of the other, and a split in the disciple's loyalty. Like the beatitudes (5:8, which see) and v. 24 below, this statement is a call for the unity of the person. Again, we see Matthew's radical "dualistic" understanding of discipleship that allows no middle ground (see 12:30).

It is a surprising turn to find Jesus placing worldly "goods" on a par with God as an object of "service," an idolatrous rival to the one God. The commonsense cultural understanding is that life is for "getting ahead," i.e., accumulating money and property. The Matthean Jesus understands authentic life to be oriented by a different compass. The concluding v. 24 only brings out the presupposition of the passage as a whole, that human life is not self-sufficient, that we find the meaning of our lives outside ourselves, that human life is inescapably "serving" something that gives it meaning. The choice is not whether we shall serve, but what or whom. It is this presupposition about who we are that confronts our self-understanding with a radical challenge.

6:25–34 *Anxiety*

(See also at Luke 12:22–32)

6:25 Do not worry: The prohibition "do not be anxious" (RSV; NRSV and NIV "do not worry") signals the beginning of the second unit in this section (see 6:19) and is repeated throughout as its dominating theme (25, 27, 28, 31, 34 [twice]). Yet there is a connection with v. 24, which shows that the section is not directed only to rich people inclined to the arrogance that comes with wealth. Poor and middle-class people can idolize that which they do not have.

6:26–29 Look at the birds of the air: The words are directed to people involved with sowing, reaping, barns, "toiling," and "spinning," but who are called to see that their life is not based on these things. The challenge to radical trust in God's providence does not exclude working and having property. Such people are not called to become birds or lilies but to consider God's providence for all creation, including birds, lilies, and human beings.

6:33 Strive first for the kingdom of God: See on Luke 3:2; 4:43. Matthew wants to relate his key word *dikaiosyne* ("righteousness/justice") both to the idea of the coming eschatological kingdom and to the idea of trust in the Father's providential care. The command to seek "first" the kingdom is not intended chronologically, as though the disciples were free to pursue material goods after seeking the kingdom, but means "above all else." The disciple can have only one priority, God's kingdom/will (see commentary on 5:8).

6:34 Today's trouble is enough: In the present context, this proverbial statement has no cynical overtone, nor is it intended to discourage planning for the future (25:1–13). The preacher on the mount is not an unrealistic exponent of nature romanticism, but one who knows that the sparrow will fall to the ground (10:29) and that trusting in God's providential care is not a strategy by which disciples can have it easy (5:10–12; 10:16–23). Jesus communicates the assurance that we do not live in a random universe but in the creation of the one God: address each day's problems as they come, confident that your lives are in the hands of a loving Father, who holds the whole world in his hands and will bring it to a worthy conclusion.

7:1–5 *Judging*

(See also at Mark 4:24–25; Luke 6:37–42)

The paragraph has two elements: (a) Jesus' absolute prohibition of judging in 7:1(–2) formulated in the plural, and (b) qualifications that presuppose judgments are actually made, formulated in the singular, that urge caution and a loving, "nonjudgmental" attitude (2–)3–5. The structure and function are thus reminiscent of the antitheses' radicalizing demand of Jesus supplemented by situational qualifications (see above on 5:21–48).

7:1 Do not judge: Although Jewish tradition contained exhortations toward moderation, toleration, and mercy, the absolute prohibition of judgment is without parallel. The verb here may mean either "be critical of" or "condemn." Jesus' original prohibition was absolute and may have embraced more than personal relations, forbidding all human judgments in the light of the dawning kingdom of God and the near advent of the Last Judgment. Here as elsewhere, Jesus' teaching is not a strategy for "success" in this-worldly relationships but a call to live in the light of the dawning kingdom of God.

7:2–5 The measure you give will be the measure you get: Here begins a series of qualifications that retain Jesus' original thrust but adapt it to conditions in a continuing world. Verse 2 presupposes that judgments will in fact be made (discrimination, not necessarily condemnation). The issue is how they are made, for at the Last Judgment God will measure us by the same standard we have used for others. Thus those who show mercy will receive mercy (5:7; see 18:21–35). **7:5 Then you will see clearly** shows Matthew does assume that occasions occur within the community when ethical discernment and community discipline are called for (see 7:15–20; 18:15–20), but they must be made by those aware of their own failures and of God's forgiveness. Community discipline, involving judgment and forgiveness, may be an expression of the deepest love, while "not judging" others by simply leaving them alone may be an easy way out that betrays authentic Christian love.

7:6 *Pearls before Swine*

"What is holy" is not an ethical term but is a biblical expression designating meat offered in sacrifice on the altar (Exod. 29:37; Lev. 2:3). For the Old Testament and Judaism, "swine" were the epitome of ritual impurity. "Dogs" are not pets, but semiwild, dangerous stray animals, like the wolves of 7:15. The general proverbial meaning is clear enough—the truism that holy things should not be profaned—but the particular meaning remains unclear.

7:7–11 *Asking and Receiving*

(See also at Luke 11:9–13)

7:7–8 Ask . . . seek . . . knock: Not three different actions—there no stages of spiritual experience here—but three Jewish expressions for prayer. These sayings may have originally been "beggars' wisdom" encouraging persistence—if you keep on asking, seeking, and knocking on doors, finally someone will help. Jesus or the early Palestinian church has transferred the picture to the relation between disciples and God and given it a transcendent meaning. The point is no longer human persistence, but divine goodness.

7:9 If your child asks for bread: Good human fathers are responsive and caring and would never respond to their child's request for bread by mockingly substituting a stone for the needed bread or a snake for the expected fish. This would be a cruel joke, since there is a striking resemblance between the flat cakes of bread and Palestinian stones (see 4:3), and between eel-like fish and snakes.

7:11 You then, who are evil: The statement presupposes universal sinfulness, including the fathers just mentioned and the disciples to whom the saying is directed (see commentary on 6:12). It is striking that Jesus seems not to include himself among sinners. There is no full-scale doctrine of the sinlessness of Christ here, though the elements are present in Matthew for its later development (see also 3:13–15 vs. Mark 1:4, 9; 19:16–17 vs. Mark 10:17–18). Nor is there an explicit doctrine of original sin here, but universal sinfulness is all the more striking as a presupposition for Jesus' thought in that it is assumed and mentioned only incidentally. It is a gross misunderstanding to juxtapose Jesus' "positive" view of humanity to Paul's "negative" view; Jesus, Paul, and Matthew have essentially the same view of the nature of human beings, as does the New Testament as a whole (see on Rom. 3:9–20).

7:12 The Golden Rule
(See also at Luke 6:31)

The Golden Rule (as it has been popularly known since the eighteenth century) was a part of the Great Sermon in Q (=Luke 6:31), where it was integrated into the command to love one's enemies. Matthew has relocated the saying to make it the climax and conclusion of the instruction and added "**everything**" as the opening word, making the Golden Rule an expression of the radical ethic of 5:21–47, especially of the Matthean perfectionism of 5:48.

There is nothing distinctively Christian about the Golden Rule in and of itself, nor is it a complete guide to Christian ethics. The distinctive Christian meaning is given by its identification with the Torah of Israel and the Great Commandment of love (see on 5:44), and by its editorial location as a summary of the teaching of Jesus who does not commend it as self-evident, but as the crucified and risen Lord who commands it on his own authority (28:18–20). So regarded in its canonical context, the Golden Rule is not an egocentric rule of thumb for getting what one wants. Neither is the Golden Rule a matter of self-evident natural law, common ground between Jesus and the advocates of a commonsense "ethic" of "enlightened self-interest." The focus is on doing for others, not on what one gets in return. It is not reciprocal, but initiatory (see 5:46–47!). "As you would have them do to you" is the anticipatory mental act of discerning the loving thing to do that does not wait for the action of the other and then respond.

In this final saying of the instruction, the disciples' action is related to human beings in general. Though spoken in the first place to disciples, and often focusing on inner community relations, this summarizing statement is cast in a universal horizon that springs all boundaries and relates the "greater righteousness" to which disciples are called not just to fellow members of the community, but to all human relationships as such (5:20; 5:21–7:11; see on 25:31–46).

7:13–14 Two Ways
(See also at Luke 6:23–24)

Matthew rewrites and amplifies the conclusion of the Great Sermon in Q to obtain another of his favorite triadic constructions. In Matthew's theology, the Christian life is thought of not in static terms, as a condition or once-for-all decision, but is the path or road of righteous living between the initial call of the disciple and the final goal of salvation. Thus he repeatedly emphasizes that many are called but few are chosen (9:13; 20:16; 22:14). The "many" here are then not the outsiders, unbelievers, or Jewish opponents, but are insiders, Christians who began to follow but "fell by the wayside."

The "many" and "few" are not informational, but hortatory. They function not to give a doctrinal statement on how many will be saved, but to exhort and admonish lagging disciples of the urgency of decision which must be made anew every day (12:30). Elsewhere, Matthew uses other imagery in which "many" are saved (8:11; 20:28). The initial warning sets the tone for the concluding section of the Sermon, presenting Matthew's characteristic dualism of decision. There are two and only two doors, ways, kinds of fruit, final destinies.

7:15–23 Two Harvests (False Prophets)
(See also at Luke 6:43–46; 13:25–27)

7:15 Beware of false prophets: The sermon here clearly reflects the post-Easter situation of Matthew's church, which has charismatic prophets among its leadership and membership (see on Acts 21:4; 1 Thess. 4:2, 15–17; introduction to Revelation, Rev. 1–3). They do not, of course, think of *themselves* as "false prophets." These are Christians who by the power of the Spirit speak the direct word of the exalted Lord (prophecy) and perform miracles (healings, exorcisms). Matthew sees them as dangerously misleading the church. They appear innocent ("**wolves in sheep's cloth-ing**," 7:15) and say "**Lord, Lord**" (7:22) to Jesus. Matthew affirms charismatic speech and miraculous deeds as the gifts of the exalted Lord to his church (10:41; 23:34). Matthew's objection is that they do not produce Christian "fruit," a common Matthean metaphor for true conversion resulting in the kind of righteous-ness called for in the Sermon on the Mount (see 3:8–10; 12:33; 13:8, 26; 21:34, 41, 43). They do not do "the will of my [= Jesus'] Father in heaven" (7:21), but practice *anomia* ("lawlessness" 7:23), Matthew's general word for unrighteousness (13:41; 23:28; 24:12). Matthew thus connects the "lawlessness" of false prophets and the relax-ing of Christian love (24:12). The point is that neither correct confession of Christian christo-logical titles ("Lord, Lord") nor the ability to perform spectacular miracles (which Matthew does not deny) will count in the final judgment, but whether one has done the will of God. This could be taken as works righteousness, except for the fact that the warning is directed to dis-ciples who confess their need of grace and for-giveness and pray for God's will to be done.

Matthew relates the sermon inseparably to the preacher, relates ethics inseparably to Christology. To be sure, there is no explicit Christology in the Sermon on the Mount. The subject matter of the sermon is not the person of Christ but the kind of life that Christ's dis-ciples are called to live. But the demands of the sermon are incomprehensible apart from the implicit Christology found there (see 5:1–12, 17–20, 21–48; 7:21–27). One cannot avoid Christology and appeal only to the "teaching" or "great principles" of Jesus, for these are inseparable from the claims of his person. But for Matthew the converse is also true: "cor-rect" christological understanding can never be a substitute for the kind of ethical living to which Jesus calls. Christology and ethics are inseparable for Matthew, just as Christology and discipleship are inseparable.

7:24–27 Two Builders
(See also at Luke 6:47–49)
Luke 6:47–49 has adapted the parable to the build-ing practices of a Hellenistic city, but Matthew's

version reflects the more original Palestinian situ-ation, where a house built during the dry season, when not a drop of rain falls in Palestine, seems secure until the fall storms come. Then the rain, wind, and floods that gush down the dry wadis overwhelm the house built on sand, while the house built on the rock stands secure. Though both builders seem to be getting along well in the pres-ent, only the one who has built with the coming storm in view is secure. The difference between the "wise" and the "foolish" builders is not a matter of intellect, but of insight into the eschatological situation, i.e., whether they are willing to hear in Jesus' words the revelation of God's will and to act on them. A provocative picture is called before the mind showing the crucial difference between doing the will of God and not doing it.

7:28–29 Conclusion of the Sermon
Here is the first of Matthew's five concluding/transitional formulae that mark out the five key discourses (11:1; 13:53; 19:1; 26:1; see introduc-tion, "Structure and Outline").

At the conclusion of the sermon the crowds reappear (see on 5:1–2). The crowds are not oppo-nents, but neither are they disciples. They repre-sent the uncommitted potential disciples to which Jesus appeals throughout the Gospel. Jesus' teach-ing is not esoteric instruction only for the initiated. Though directed to disciples, the Sermon on the Mount is "public" address that the uncommitted, potential disciples represented by "the crowd" can also overhear and act upon. Matthew here presents a model for the church's missionary address to the world: the community of disciple-ship speaks its own language, makes its own con-fession, addresses its ethical demands to those who are committed to Jesus as the Christ and the church's exalted Lord. Yet the church knows it is not an esoteric group but has responsibility to the world (28:18–20), so that even its "internal" talk is carried on with an awareness that the world is lis-tening in. For Matthew, the line between church and world is not so sharp. The text encourages the church to work out its own ethic based on the pre-suppositions of its own faith, but to do so with an eye on the "crowds" that share its ethical concerns even if they do not share its faith or consider it irrelevant. Such ethical concern and action is a mode of evangelism, a mode that can be taken seriously by the contemporary world.

8:1–9:35
Messianic Deeds: Miracles and Discipleship
Matthew has previously given a summary state-ment of Jesus' healing and exorcisms (4:23–24),

but here are the first miracle *stories* in the Gospel. There is no material peculiar to Matthew in this section. Here the author takes stories from his sources, Mark and Q (see introduction) and arranges them into a triadic outline of three sets of three stories. Since one story preserves the Markan intercalation of one story into another (see on Mark 2:1–10), there are ten miracles (in nine stories), again reflecting Matthew's Moses typology. As Moses worked ten acts of power in delivering the people of God, so does Jesus. But Jesus' mighty deeds are all acts of mercy and deliverance—even for the Romans—rather than judgment on the oppressor. As Matthew has transformed the violent, conquering "Son of David" into the healing king who does not retaliate but withdraws (see on 12:9–21), he has transformed the violent acts of deliverance into acts of compassion.

Since Jesus' own mighty works cannot be presented without calling for response, the section also includes statements about discipleship. So also the individual units have been carefully arranged to facilitate a certain movement to the story, leading to a particular climactic scene. Matthew wanted to conclude with the divided response to the exorcism of 9:32–34 in order to have the Pharisee's charge of collusion with Satan as the last item in this series. By 9:34, the reader is at a far different point in understanding the story of Jesus than at 8:1. For the first time in the Gospel, conflict emerges between Jesus and other human beings (at 9:2, from the scribes, on the issue of Jesus' pronouncement of forgiveness of sins). Previously, only the devil had opposed Jesus (4:1–11), the conflict between God's kingdom and Satan's having been prefigured in 1:18–2:23. Now, in response to Jesus' words and deeds of authority, a split occurs in Israel, and the community of Jesus' disciples is formed. The conflict is not because of Jesus' offense against the Torah, which he explicitly keeps (8:4), but because he acts in the place of God to forgive sins and accept sinners (see 1:21–23). The conflict escalates so that finally the Pharisees accuse him of acting by the power of Satan. The miracles are not denied; it is never at issue throughout all of 8:1–9:34 that they "really happened." But one may respond to the Christ who works miracles either in faith or unfaith, all the while accepting the miracles. See Figure 4 for a representation of Matthew's composition. For detailed comments on the individual stories, see on the Markan and Lukan parallel texts.

9:35 Then Jesus went about all the cities and villages, teaching . . . and curing every disease: This summary forms a literary bracket with 4:23, which it reproduces almost verbatim, making 4:23–9:35 into the central section, "The Words and Deeds of the Messiah" (see introduction, "Structure and Outline").

For comments on the individual stories, see on the corresponding sections of Mark and Luke. Here, we present a general discussion on interpreting New Testament miracle stories.

Figure 4. Matthew's Composition of 8:1–9:34

I. Christ Acts in Power for the Marginal and Excluded, 8:1–17

1. For a leprous person, 8:1–4 = Mark 1:40–45/Luke 5:12–16
2. For a Roman officer's paralyzed servant/slave, 8:5–13 = Luke 7:1–10
3. For a sick woman and many others, 8:14–17 = Mark 1:29–34/Luke 4:40–41

II. Christ's Mighty Acts Generate a Community of Disciples, 8:18–9:17

4. Christ calls into the storm,
   of which he is master, 8:18–27 = Mark 4:35–41/Luke 8:22–25; 9:57–62
5. Christ calls into new horizons,
   where he is master, 8:28–34 = Mark 5:1–20/Luke 8:26–39
6. Christ's call generates opposition,
   of which he is master, 9:1–17
   (*two* miracle stories combined) = Mark 2:1–22/Luke 5:17–39

III. Christ's Power Evokes Faith and Unbelief, 9:18–34

7. Faith in the Jesus who overcomes sickness, isolation,
   and death, 9:18–26 = Mark 5:21–43/Luke 8:40–56
8. Sight to the blind and the question of faith, 9:27–31 = Mark 10:46–52/Luke 18:35–43
9. Faith and unbelief: healing a speechless,
   demonized man, 9:32–34 = Mark 3:22/Luke 11:14–15

EXCURSUS:
INTERPRETING THE MIRACLE STORIES

1. Miracle stories are woven into the texture of the Gospel fabric in such a way that they cannot be set aside by dealing only with the "nonmiraculous" sections. Any interpretation of the Gospels requires dealing with their miraculous element. See Figure 5.

With the exception of the cursing of the fig tree (Matt. 21:18–19//Mark 11:12–14), all the miracles in the Gospels are performed for the benefit of human beings. Even the "nature miracles" are performed to help people in distress. In the Gospels, the genre of miracle stories already present in the Hellenistic world has been transformed by the character of Jesus himself, who embodies and makes present the love of God.

2. Miracle stories are included alongside nonmiraculous and antimiraculous traditions about Jesus.

Jesus is also pictured in nonmiraculous and antimiraculous ways in the New Testament and the Gospels. All New Testament epistles, following Paul, portray the act of God in Jesus in the incarnation, crucifixion, and resurrection without referring to any miracle story, and without giving any indication that the earthly life of Jesus was full of miraculous divine power. The Gospels themselves also contain traditions that portray the Christ event in nonmiraculous ways: Matt. 4:1–11/Luke 4:1–13; Matt. 12:38–42/Mark 8:11–12/Luke 11:29–32; Matt. 16:1–4/Luke 12:54–56; Matt. 26–27/Mark 14–15.

3. New Testament miracle stories need to be interpreted in relation to other miracle stories in the Hellenistic world.

In the Hellenistic world, miracle stories are told of others besides Jesus, in and outside the Gospels. The interpretation of New Testament miracles stories is illuminated by noticing both similarities and differences. According to the New Testament, miracles are performed (1) by God, directly (e.g., Acts 2:1–4; see 2:17); (2) by God, through an angel (e.g., Matt. 1:18–25; 2:1–12; Acts 12:6–11; 12:20–23; 16:25–28); (3) by Jesus (see figure below); (4) by apostles, including Judas (Matt. 10:1, 8, 20// Mark 6:7, 13; 13:11// Luke 9:2; 12:12 [exorcisms, healings, raising the dead]; Rom. 15:19; 2 Cor. 12:12; Acts 3:1–10; 5:1–11, 12–16; 9:32–25, 36–43); (5) by good disciples, missionaries, ordinary Christians (1 Cor. 12:10, 29; Gal. 3:5; Heb. 2:4; Acts 6:8; 8:6, 13; 14:3, 8–12; 15:12; 16:16–18; 19:11); (6) by bad, false, and unbelieving disciples (Matt. 7:22; Matt. 24:24// Mark 13:22 false Christs and false prophets); (7) by nondisciples: Jews and pagans (Matt. 12:27//Luke 11:19; Acts 19:13–16; 2 Thess. 2:9; Rev. 13:13–14; 16:14; 19:20). Conclusion: In the Hellenistic world, miracles belong to the realm of the possible and constitute an accepted part of the worldview of most people. Their *meaning* is what is disputed.

Miracles are likewise a given element in Old Testament–Jewish thought. The world is not a closed system of "nature" that God must interrupt in a "supernatural" way in order to act. The world functions as it ordinarily does because God wills it such; God can occasionally will it otherwise. This extraordinary activity of God, who is always active, is a "sign," "wonder," or "miracle," not a violation of "natural law."

Some streams of first-century Jewish thought supposed that these extraordinary acts of God or the Spirit were limited to the biblical period and would reappear at the eschaton. But there were also stories of miraculous deeds current among the rabbis and other Jews. A Jewish boy calms a storm at sea. Bread is miraculously provided for the wife of a famous rabbi. Stories exist about rabbis of Jesus' day who performed healings and exorcisms, and calmed storms.

Many miracle stories circulated in the first-century pagan world. Some examples: (1) There are many healing reports from tablets at Epidauros,

Figure 5. Miracle Stories in the Gospels

	Matthew	Mark	Luke	John	
Exorcisms	2	3	2	0	
Exorcisms/Healings	3	1	2	0	
Healings	8	8	10	3	
Raising the Dead	1	1	2	1	
Sea Miracles	2	2	1	1	
Provision Miracles	3	2	2	2	
Curse Miracles	1	1	0	0	
Totals	**20**	**18**	**19**	**7**	**Total 64 for Gospels**

the Lourdes of the Hellenistic world (mostly from the fourth century BCE) Asclepius was the healer god. (2) Pythagoras conversed with animals who did as he commanded, crossed the sea miraculously, calmed strong winds and stopped plagues, calmed raging rivers and seas. (3) The emperor Vespasian, a contemporary of Jesus, healed the blind with his saliva, healed a withered hand with pressure from his foot. (6) Philostratus' (third cent. CE) *Life of Apollonius* (first cent. CE) contains many miracles, exorcisms, and healings, but is written to "tone down" the earlier stories and present Apollonius as a more philosophical sage.
4. *New Testament miracle stories have been interpreted with a spectrum of approaches.*

They have been interpreted as *literal history* in which their factuality is the point. There are two variations of this view: (1) Miracles have always happened for faithful believers, in biblical times and later, including now. (2) Miracles happened in biblical times for the special purpose of confirming divine revelation, but no longer occur.

Rationalistic explanations have been given for biblical miracle stories. This view supposes that real events happened that were misunderstood as miracles, but they can now be rationally explained. Exorcisms and healings are examples of psychosomatic cures and the powerful, calming presence of Jesus and his word. Raisings of the dead were cases of (almost) premature burial. Feeding the five thousand was a lesson in sharing. Walking on water was a grammatical misunderstanding of an earlier story (the Greek preposition "on" also means "at edge of," so the story really only intended to picture Jesus wading in the surf), or an optical illusion, or mass hysteria, or planned deception (a raft!).

Mythological explanations do not claim that the stories are untrue, but that their truth lies on a plane other than the literal. In this view, the miracle stories may or may not have a historical core, but the stories themselves have been devised to express a transcendent, symbolic, "mythological" meaning. "Myth" in this sense does not mean "something untrue" but "deeper truth." In this view, miracle stories are akin to the parables told by Jesus. Interpreters of the New Testament should thus be wary of the expression "*just* stories" in evaluating Gospel narratives.
5. *In the Gospels, miracle stories are primarily kerygmatic and didactic narratives in which the miracle itself is often not the main point.*

This is a difference between Gospel stories about Jesus and similar stories about Hellenistic heroes such as Hercules, Asclepius, and Apollonius. In the New Testament, the stories point beyond themselves to express a Christology, God's act in the whole Christ event.

In the Gospels, miracle stories are not primarily evidential, for proving a point. Neither are they primarily manifestations of people's faith. They do not typically happen as the reward for someone's faith, so that the message is not "If you believe well enough, you will have miracles too; if you don't have miracles, it is because you do not have enough faith."

In the Gospels, the miraculous is an eschatological category. There was an expectation of a "prophet like Moses" (Deut. 18:15–18) who would renew the Mosaic miracles eschatologically. The coming of God's kingdom was portrayed in terms of wonderful miracles (e.g., Isa. 35:5–6). Thus the telling of miracle stories about Jesus is one way of claiming that in him God's kingdom has appeared, that the Christ event is the eschatological event. The miracle stories call the reader to decide whether Jesus Christ represents God's eschatological act for our salvation. They do not necessarily call for belief or unbelief in the literal facticity of the story.
6. *Here are some suggestions for the contemporary interpreter.*

a. Avoid framing the issue in such a way that believing the gospel is equated with accepting a particular worldview or cosmology. One's worldview is a given that cannot be changed at will. Just as we cannot decide to believe that heaven is "up" or that the earth is flat with four corners (Rev. 7:1) by an act of faith or an act of the will, so we cannot decide by faith for or against a Newtonian or post-Newtonian view of the way the universe works. Christian faith is not a matter of our worldview, but whether we believe that God has definitively acted in Christ to deliver us from the guilt and power of sin and to show us the way of life. The Christian message can be presented within the framework of more than one worldview.

b. Separate the meaning and validity of the story from its strict factuality. The meaning and validity of the story may be appropriated both by those who affirm factuality and by those who question it. On the one hand, if one accepts the miracle story as reporting a factual event, this does not necessarily mean one believes the gospel and has Christian faith, not even that one "believes the Bible." The approach we are suggesting does not necessarily ask one to give up the view that miracles happened but does not identify this view with Christian faith. (People in the stories sometimes believed in the facticity of the miracle but did not become disciples.) If one does not accept the facticity of the miracle or has questions about its facticity, this does not necessarily mean one disbelieves the biblical message and does not have a biblical Christian faith. The miracle story is not trying to get us to believe in miracles (=change our worldview), but to allow the miracle story to be to us a vehicle of the Christian gospel.

c. Evaluate the story mode of presentation as positively as the Bible does. Do not look pejoratively at "stories," as though the choice was "they really happened" or "are *just* stories." On any understanding, the texts are stories with nonfactual elements.

d. Attend to the linguistic category or categories (kind of language) to which miracle stories belong. Not all valid language belongs to the same linguistic category or functions in the same way. The language of miracle most often fits the category of confessional language, which is nonobjectifying and noninferential (see on Matt. 2:16; John 5:9; Acts 1:9–11; Rev. 6:15 excursus 3.b), akin to the language of prayer.

e. Respect the differences between modern categories of thought and those of the first century. The category of natural law is a modern understanding. Posing the issue as whether a particular event is either natural or from God is a modern way of looking at things.

f. Guard against any view that restricts God's presence, power, and activity to the *extra*ordinary. An apologetic "God of the gaps" that locates the act of God only in what is not otherwise explainable reduces the sphere of God's activity to that of our ignorance. Not only does this continually diminish the arena in which the presence of God is perceived; it discourages the expansion of one's knowledge by an appeal to faith.

g. Avoid confusing differences of approach and interpretation with degrees of faith or unbelief. Do not equate faith with believing in miracles and lack of belief in miracles as a lack of faith in general. Do not accuse others or yourself of a lack of faith as the reason for not believing in the factuality of miracle stories. The question must be posed of *what* the miracle story wants to communicate as the content of faith.

h. Respect the ethical issues inherent in affirmations of God's working by means of miracles. The issue is not only whether God *can* do such things, but whether God *should*. Healings and resurrections, if understood as objectifying reports, raise the ethical question of healing only a few when one has the power to heal and raise all. Sending an angel to warn one family of the impending danger to the babies of Bethlehem raises the question of why God warned only Joseph (Matt. 2:13–18). A Roman soldier who has done his duty well is executed because the prisoner he was assigned to guard was miraculously granted deliverance (Acts 12:6–19). Jesus miraculously feeds hungry people who were fortunate enough to be in his proximity, but children elsewhere in the world die of starvation (Matt. 14:13–21). Jesus heals one person at a distance, but others are left to suffer and die (Matt. 8:5–13). If attention is focused on the miracle itself, it then becomes a problem, not merely of physics, but of ethics, an obstacle to hearing what else the story wants to say. Miracle stories must not be interpreted in a way that casts God in a questionable ethical role.

9:36–10:42
THE DISCIPLES AUTHORIZED AND SENT

9:36 Sheep without a shepherd: This is a phrase from the Greek translation used by Matthew (the LXX; see Num. 27:17; 1 Kgs. 22:17; 2 Chr. 18:16; see Jer. 23:1–6; Ezek. 34:8; Zech. 10:12), taken from a different context in Mark 6:34. Matthew relocates the phrase here to describe the plight of "the crowds," the uncommitted masses of Israel who are potential disciples but are in danger of being misled by their leaders. Matthew considers Jesus to be their true shepherd (see 2:6; 26:31), who has compassion on the harassed and helpless flock. Jesus has compassion for Israel, not rejection, understanding his vocation to be sent to them (10:5; 15:24).

9:37 The harvest is plentiful: Harvest is a frequent symbol for eschatological judgment (Isa. 18:4; 27:12; Jer. 51:53; Hos. 6:11; Joel 3:13) used elsewhere by Matthew (3:12; 13:30, 39) and other writers in early Judaism and the New Testament (4 Ezra 4:26–37; 9:17; *2 Bar.* 70:1–2; Mark 4:26–29; 13:27; Rev. 14:14–20). The mission of the disciples that follows is seen as part of the eschatological events. As such, it is God's act, though involving human workers rather than the angels to whom this role is usually given. Thus the disciples are instructed to pray the Lord of the harvest (God) to send forth laborers into the harvest. The mission of the disciples is not voluntaristic do-goodism initiated by themselves; they are chosen, authorized, and sent by God through Christ (10:10).

10:1–5a
Disciples and Apostles
(See also at Mark 6:7; 3:13–19a; Luke 9:1; 6:12–16)

Matthew generally speaks of the "twelve disciples" (10:1; 11:1; 20:17) or simply "the Twelve" (10:5; 26:14, 20, 47). Only here does he call them "apostles," a term that seems not to have been important to him. Our earliest tradition speaks of "the Twelve" and "all the apostles" as two distinct, but overlapping groups (1 Cor. 15:5–7). It is the influence of Luke that has led the church to think of "the" Twelve Apostles. Historically, the apostles were a larger group of those to whom the risen Lord appeared and whom he commissioned as his authorized representatives, as indicated by lists of those called "apostles" in Figure 6.

The later need to identify the apostles with "the Twelve" and thus establish a list of only twelve apostles (as already in Luke–Acts) has led to the traditional attribution of two or more names to the same individual, e.g., identifying Mark's "Levi" with Matthew's "Matthew," and John's "Nathanael" with the Synoptics' "Bartholomew." There is no historical evidence for such identifications. The symbolism of the twelve was important for Matthew and for early Christianity, as it had apparently been to Jesus, for it pictured the eschatological reconstitution of Israel as the people of God (see on 19:28).

Matthew regards the mission of Jesus as continuing in the work of the disciples, who are given the authority to speak and act in Jesus' name (10:1; see 10:19–20, 40), i.e., to continue doing the same deeds of power Jesus himself has just done in 8:1–9:35 (though authority to teach was not given them until after the resurrection, 28:20). They preach the same message (4:17=10:7) and receive the same response (9:34=10:25). Thus the disciples are transparent to the post-Easter experience and mission of the church, and the mission discourse is to be heard as both the there-and-then address to his disciples in the pre-Easter setting of the story (for which 10:5b–6 may be representative), and as the address of the contemporary Christ who is still present with his church in its eschatological mission between the resurrection and the Parousia (see, e.g., 10:17–22, 32–33, which clearly depict a post-Easter situation).

10:5b–42
The Mission Discourse

Both Mark and Q contained versions of a missionary discourse by Jesus. Matthew typically combines them, while Luke includes them as separate discourses (see on Luke 9:1–6; 10:1–24).

10:5b–15 *Sharing the Authority of Christ and His Reception*
(See also at Mark 6:8–11; Luke 9:2–5; 10:3, 12)
As the disciples function with the authority of Christ (10:1), the discourse begins by charging

them to go to the same lost sheep of Israel as has Jesus (10:5b–6), to proclaim the same message (10:7=4:17), to do the same healings, exorcisms, and even raisings of the dead (10:8=8:1–9:35), to live the same wandering, dependent life of poverty (10:10=8:20), and to anticipate the same mixed reception (10:11–15=7:28–29; 8:16; 9:8 vs. 8:34; 9:34). The list reflects the "works of Christ" in chapters 8–9, as it prepares for 11:4–6.

10:5b–6 Go nowhere among the Gentiles: The disciples are sent to Israel, all Israel, and only to Israel. The Greek genitive expression **lost sheep of the house of Israel** does not designate only a part of Israel, but is an appositive genitive that identifies "lost sheep" with Israel as such. Historically, the mission of the earthly Jesus was limited to Israel (see Rom. 15:8). **Enter no town of the Samaritans:** See on Luke 9:52–54. This is the only reference to Samaritans or Samaria in Matthew; the inclusiveness of the Lukan perspective should not be read into Matthew. The picture of Jesus' mission as exclusively to the Jewish people is important in Matthew's theological story (15:24). Matthew thus omits or revises Markan stories that could portray a pre-Easter Gentile mission as already under way (e.g. Mark 5:19–20; see Matt. 8:34). After Easter, the Great Commission transcends this restriction by extending the mission to all nations (28:18–20).

10:9–10 No gold, or silver, or . . . bag: The original radicality of Jesus' own wandering life and of the missionaries of the Q community who probably founded Matthew's church (see introduction to Matthew) is retained. Mark had already modified the strictness of the command, permitting a staff and sandals (Mark 6:8–11). Luke considers the prohibition a temporary command belonging only to the special period of Jesus' earthly ministry (Luke 22:35–36). Matthew preserves the original strictness both as a witness to the radical call to discipleship once practiced by Jesus and the earliest disciples and perhaps still practiced by the wandering charismatic missionaries sent out by Matthew's church in his own day. Since any member of the community might be called upon to become such a missionary (see Acts 13:1–3), such commands are not dead relics of the past or an impossible ideal in Matthew's own situation. For both Jesus and his disciples, proceeding on a mission without even the basic equipment for sustenance and self-defense was a prophetic sign, an acting out of the presence of the kingdom similar to the symbolic actions performed by the

Figure 6. Apostles Listed in Scripture

Matthew 10	Mark 3	Luke 6/Acts 1	John	Paul
1. Simon Peter	1. Simon Peter	1. Simon Peter	1. Simon Peter	1. Simon Peter
2. Andrew	4. Andrew	2. Andrew	2. Andrew	
3. James	2. James	3. James	[3.–4. "the sons of Zebedee," 21:2]	
4. John	3. John	4. John		
5. Philip	5. Philip	5. Philip	5. Philip	
6. Bartholomew	6. Bartholomew	6. Bartholomew		
7. Thomas	7. Thomas	7. Thomas	7. Thomas	
8. Matthew	8. Matthew	8. Matthew		
9. James son of Alphaeus	9. James son of Alphaeus	9. James son of Alphaeus		
10. Thaddaeus	10. Thaddaeus			
11. Simon the Cananaean	11. Simon the Cananaean	11. Simon the Zealot		
12. Judas Iscariot	12. Judas Iscariot	12. Judas Iscariot	12. Judas Iscariot	
(13. *Lebbaeus* for Thaddaeus in some MSS)	(14. *Levi son of Alphaeus,* 2:14)	15. Judas son of James	17. Nathanael	19. James brother of Jesus (Gal. 1:19)
		[16. Matthias, Acts 1]	18. The Beloved Disciple	[20. Andronicus (Rom. 16:7)]
				[21. Junia(s)* (Rom. 16:7)]
				[22. Paul (1 Cor. 9:1, etc.)]

1 Cor. 15:6 indicates that Paul knew of more than twelve apostles.

*Depending on accentuation, this name can be read as either masculine (so RSV and NIV) or feminine (so KJV and NRSV).

biblical prophets (Isa. 20:2, 4; Jer. 13:1–11; 19:1–13; 27:1–28:14; Ezek. 4; 5; 12; Hos. 1; 3).

10:10 Laborers deserve their food: Here Matthew increases the strictness of the traditional predictions, changing Q's "the laborer deserves to be paid" to "laborers deserve their food" (see Luke 10:7). As Matthew opposes the developing rabbinic titles and status (see 23:5–12), so he also opposes missionaries who accept money for their work; they must be content with only the food necessary for survival. This may represent his polemic against an emerging tendency toward a paid class of "clergy" and corresponds to the initial prohibition of traveling with money (10:9; see 1 Cor. 9:3–12).

10:11–15 These instructions not only incorporate practical wisdom for the early traveling missionaries, who were dependent on the hospitality of fellow Christians; they are also an indirect prophetic warning to "settled" Christians to receive the "wandering" missionaries of the Matthean community. Hospitality, already a sacred obligation in the ancient Mediterranean world and emphasized in biblical stories (Gen. 18:1–8; 19:1–11; 24:14–61; see Judg. 19:10–25; Heb. 13:2), is here placed in an eschatological framework, concluding the section with a solemn prophetic *amen* pronouncement of eschatological judgment (see on 5:18).

10:13–14 Shake off the dust from your feet: It was customary for the Palestinian Jew returning to the sacred land to shake off the dust of pagan countries before entering the holy land. Here, as in 3:7–10 above and 10:16 below, Israel assumes the place traditionally occupied by pagan countries.

10:16–23 *Fate of the Disciples*
(See also at Mark 13:9–13; Luke 12:11–12; 21:12–19)

10:16 Sheep into the midst of wolves: Matthew presents a striking reversal of the Jewish tradition that compared the situation of Israel among the Gentiles to that of sheep among wolves (*1 En.* 89:55; 4 Ezra 5:18), an image that is reaffirmed as the prelude to this speech (9:36). As already in Q, the Christian missionaries are here seen as sheep—in solidarity with the "lost sheep" of Israel. But empirical Israel, the unbelieving Jews perceived as persecutors of the Christian community, are pictured as dangerous wolves. In 16b, Matthew refashions a proverbial saying (see Rom. 16:19). For him, the point is not the proverbial shrewdness of serpents, but the disciples' vulnerability and single-mindedness (NIV and NRSV: "innocent").

The mission instructions in Mark 6:7–13 give no hint that the missioners will be persecuted and rejected. To let this represent the post-Easter missionary experience of the church, Matthew imports a section of the apocalyptic discourse in Mark 13 (Matt. 10:17–25=Mark 13:9–13). It is profoundly important for Matthew's interpretation to note that the remainder of this section is taken from the eschatological discourse in Mark 13, where Jesus is pictured as looking beyond the resurrection to the time of the mission of the church and the eschatological events. By bringing these words predicting the post-Easter mission into the mission discourse that occurs in the pre-Easter story line and applying it to the mission of the disciples during the earthly life of Jesus, Matthew breaks down the temporal distinctions between the there-and-then story of the pre-Easter Jesus and the here-and-now mission of Matthew's post-Easter readership.

By the same token, he underscores that the mission of the church to the nations is not a mundane historical project initiated and carried on by human beings wanting to impose their religious views on others, but part of God's eschatological plan to bring all nations into the kingdom of God (Isa. 2:2–4). Thus the troubles and persecutions the church must endure are part of the eschatological woes that precede the final coming of God's kingdom, here pictured as the advent of the Son of Man (10:23).

10:17 Hand you over: See on Mark 1:14, 9:31. **Flog you in their synagogues:** The floggings referred to here are not random mob violence, but official punishments for those considered guilty of blasphemy or gross violation of the Torah (see Deut. 25:1–3, later elaborated in the Mishnah into punishments for heretics, blasphemers, and recalcitrant disturbers of the peace). Matthew's church is apparently still in some relation to the synagogue that requires its traveling missionaries to be subject to its discipline (as was Paul, see 2 Cor. 11:24–25). Yet the synagogue, the ancestral home of Matthew's own faith and community, is now "their" synagogue (vs. "my church" in 16:18).

10:18 Dragged before governors and kings: Prior to Easter, Jesus' disciples did not carry on a mission to Gentiles, did not suffer for the sake of Jesus' name, did not stand before governors and kings. The discourse here clearly modulates into the post-Easter address of Jesus to his Christian disciples in Matthew's present. The unsuccessful mission to Israel already lay in the past of Matthew's church, which now carries on a mission to all nations (28:18–20).

10:19–20 Do not worry about how you are to speak: See on Mark 13:11. The courtroom is not merely a threat, it is an opportunity for mission ("as a testimony to them," 18b). "Do not be anxious" (RSV) reminds the reader of 6:25, where the same words are used. There, the basis for encouragement was the Creator who cares for his creation. Here, eschatology forms the basis for encouragement. In Matthew's view, these are two aspects of the same God. This is the only reference in Matthew to disciples having the **Holy Spirit** (though see 3:11 and 28:19). Rather than conceiving the divine presence and help as the Holy Spirit given the disciples between Easter and the Parousia (as does Luke and John), Matthew thinks of the continuing presence of Jesus himself (see 1:23; 18:20; 28:16–20, and see the identification of the Holy Spirit and the presence of the risen Christ in Rom. 8:9–10; 2 Cor. 3:17–18).

10:22 You will be hated by all: In some streams of Jewish tradition, Mic. 7:6 had already been interpreted to refer to the eschatological terrors (*1 En.* 100:2). Apocalyptic thought understood that immediately prior to the end and as a sign of its nearness, the natural structures of the world break down, and even the most deeply rooted loyalties of the family are dissolved under the pressure of the approaching end. Matthew not only reflects the divisions that occurred in families as a result of Christian commitment; he follows Mark in interpreting these as eschatological ordeals inherent in the church's mission.

10:23 When they persecute you in one town, flee: Matthew underscores in yet another way the parallel between Jesus and the disciples to whom he entrusts his mission. As he has been persecuted, so will they be. As he did not retaliate, but withdrew (see on 12:14–21, and see 5:38–41), so the disciple is not to respond to hostility in kind or with prayers for vengeance, but is to withdraw and continue the mission elsewhere, in the glad confidence that the parousia of the Son of Man will bring the divine kingdom to full reality. **Before the Son of Man comes:** On Son of Man, see Mark 2:10. The affirmation of the nearness of the end turned out to be a chronological mistake; see on Rev. 1:3, "Interpreting the 'Near End'." The delay of the Parousia was for Matthew and his apocalyptic community not a concep-

tual problem to be solved or avoided, but a means of encouragement to mission. Since Matthew and his readers knew that the Son of Man did not come during the time of the historical Jesus, these instructions could be heard in his church as applicable to the continuing mission to Israel as part of the church's mission to all nations (28:18–20).

10:24–33 Call to Courageous Confession
(See also at Mark 4:22; Luke 6:40; 12:2–9)

10:24–25 Enough for the disciple to be like the teacher: Throughout, the discourse has emphasized that the disciples' life parallels that of Jesus' (see on 10:5b–15), including sharing the same fate of rejection and persecution (see on 10:16–23). This is summed up and dramatically focused in the charge of working by the power of Beelzebul, directed first to Jesus, then to his disciples (see on 9:34 and the key section 12:22–37; Mark 3:20–30).

10:26–33 Have no fear of them: The speech is directed to disciple missioners who experience such rejection and persecution and may be afraid to speak out boldly for their new faith. This section thus continues with a twice-repeated command not to be afraid (vv. 26, 31) and concludes with a promise and threat about publicly confessing Jesus (vv. 32–33). How can disciples of Jesus find the courage to live such a life? The Matthean Jesus gives three reasons, all adapted from Q (=Luke 12:2–7), why the disciple, contrary to all appearances and common sense, need not be afraid:

10:26–27 Nothing [is] secret that will not become known: The eschatological judgment soon to come will make everything public, so attempting to keep one's faith private is ultimately futile. What was originally conventional wisdom ("It's no use trying to keep things secret; everything becomes public sooner or later") had already been given an eschatological interpretation in Q (=Luke 12:2), to mean that the final judgment will reveal all secrets. Matthew reformulates this threat into an imperative (10:27). In the Matthean context, "what is heard in the darkness" refers to the nighttime meetings of the Matthean community where sayings of Jesus are passed on. The Christian message is to be publicly proclaimed and lived out by the disciples, not kept to themselves as "private religion."

10:28 Do not fear those who kill the body: Matthew expresses his warning in the Hellenistic language that distinguishes "body" and "soul" (see on Matt. 28:1; for a form of the saying expressed in the more Jewish understanding of the human self, see the parallel at Luke 12:4). Matthew's point is clear: there is a realm of human existence that the opponents cannot touch, but God can. Thus fear of God and the ultimate judgment overcomes fear of what human courts can do and sets the disciple free to be a courageous witness.

10:31 You are of more value than many sparrows: God is the faithful Creator who, however it may appear, cares for each creature (10:29–31). Sparrows were sold in the marketplace, sometimes in bundles of ten. Poor people bought them. Although sparrows are hunted and killed, this does not happen apart from the sovereign knowledge, power, and love of God the faithful Creator. No theoretical explanation is given, but as in 6:25–34, trust in the one Creator of all is called for. God as Creator and God as eschatological redeemer are united as the basis for these words of encouragement.

10:32–33 Everyone . . . who acknowledges me before others, I also will acknowledge: The section concludes with a promise to those who confess Jesus and a warning to those who do not. These texts are not concerned with the initial confession of faith in conversion; they address disciples who already profess Christian faith but are fearful of bearing public witness to it in the church's mission. The disciples' profession of faith is in continuity with Jesus' message, but not merely a repetition of it. The Matthean Jesus does not proclaim himself but the present and coming kingdom of God. The disciples not only preach what Jesus preached; they proclaim Jesus ("confess me"). Jesus is pictured here (as also in the Sermon on the Mount, 7:21–23) as claiming to be the eschatological judge, for whom the criterion of judgment will be the disciples' faithful confession of Jesus.

10:34–39 *The Cost of Discipleship*
(See also at Luke 12:51–53; 14:25–27; 17:33)

10:34 Not . . . peace but a sword: The "sword" here is not a political symbol but an eschatological one (see Rev. 6:4). Jesus' disciples are not to take up the sword to defend the cause of the prince of peace (26:52–54). The **"I have come"** form reflects the post-Easter perspective that looks back on the "coming" of Jesus as a whole and is present in all streams of the tradition (as 5:17=M; 9:13=Mark 2:17; 10:34–35=Q). The text reflects a real situation in Matthew's church, where people some-

times had to choose between their family and their faith (see on 10:22; Luke 14:26). Though no christological titles are used, the reader should not miss the claim that loyalty to Jesus has priority over even the closest human relationships and life itself, a claim that represents an implied Christology. Jesus here claims for himself the kind of absolute commitment that only deity can appropriately claim.

10:38 Take up the cross and follow me: See on Mark 8:34. The reader may be surprised at the abruptness of the reference to the cross, for which there is no explicit preparation in the preceding narrative. From reading the story of chaps. 1–9, the uninitiated reader would anticipate that the mission of the disciples would meet with spectacular success. But the discourse that begins with Jesus conferring his authority and power on the disciples concludes with the necessity of sharing Jesus' cross as well. In the narrative line, the suffering, death, and even crucifixion of disciples are elaborated before that of Jesus. The decision of the opponents to kill Jesus is not narrated until 12:14. The disciples *in the story* are not surprised, however—for they are transparent to the post-Easter readers of the Gospel. Matthew and his Christian readers look back not only on the cross of Jesus but on the martyrdoms of Christians that had already taken place. There is no evidence for the crucifixion of Christians in Palestine by Jews. By Matthew's time, however, it was well known that Christians, including Simon Peter, so important to Matthean Christianity, had been crucified in Rome under Nero. Like the reference to Judas in 10:4, this illustrates the retrospective post-Easter perspective of the whole narrative.

10:40–42 *Sharing the Presence of Christ and His Reception*
(See also at Mark 9:41; Luke 10:16)

The conclusion of the speech returns to the opening affirmations that authorize and empower the disciples as representatives of Christ. Here is added that Christ represents God—another implicit christological claim.

10:42 One of these little ones: Matthew's church includes Christian "**prophets**" as a distinct class, whose ministry Matthew affirms as legitimate spokespersons for the risen Lord (here and 23:34) but whom he also regards with some hesitation (7:21–23). "Little ones" does not refer literally to children but is Matthew's term for "ordinary" Christians, equivalent here to "disciples" (see 18:1–14). In Zech. 13:7 and *2 Bar.* 48:19, "little ones" is used as a synonym for the people of God. Matthew's egalitarian spirit may have chosen it in contrast to "rabbi," which means literally "my great one" (see 23:8). The **"righteous"** seems here to represent a distinct group (perhaps traveling missionaries who are non-prophets?), but elsewhere Matthew seems to have rewritten his tradition in order to get "prophets and righteous" as a pair representing the church as a whole (13:17; 23:29). "In the name of" is a Semitizing expression meaning "because one is" (see NIV). "Settled" disciples who receive and support "itinerant" disciples engaged in the church's mission share in their work and receive the same reward.

11:1–19
THE MINISTRY OF JESUS IN RELATION TO JOHN THE BAPTIST

The overarching concern of this passage is christological: the identity and role of Jesus in saving history. The christological question is here posed in terms of the relation of Jesus to the identity and role of John the Baptist.

11:1
Transitional Conclusion: Jesus Departs

Surprisingly, after picturing the disciples as hearing the mission discourse, Matthew does not narrate their departure and no mission is recounted as part of their past pre-Easter story. There is thus no "return of the disciples" in Matthew. By failing to anchor the speech in the past, Jesus' address to the reader is the more direct. The words are left hanging in the air, still addressing the post-Easter reader, and it is Jesus himself who continues his preaching mission (see the ending of Mark at 16:8). For the Matthean reader, this is another testimony that the risen Christ accompanies his church in its mission through history and is present and active in its preaching (see 1:23; 10:40; 13:37; 16:18; 18:20; 28:20).

11:2–6
"Who Is Jesus?"
(See also at Luke 7:18–23)

11:2 When John heard in prison: Matthew adapts the material from Q (= Luke 7:18–23), where these verses had a different context and meaning. Q began with John's preaching now found in Matt. 3:7–12//Luke 3:7–9; 16–17 but contained no reference to John's previous recognition of Jesus as the "coming one" or to

John's arrest and imprisonment. In its Q context, this story thus presented a positive view of John, who in the course of his continuing ministry is beginning to wonder if the "mighty one" whose near advent he had announced is in fact Jesus himself. In the Matthean story line, however, John has already recognized the messianic status of Jesus (3:14–15, a Matthean addition to his sources) and has been imprisoned (4:12, for which 14:1–12 is a flashback), so that the story in its present context represents the beginning of doubt rather than the dawn of faith.

11:3 Are you the one who is to come? Literally "the coming one," a generic term for the expected eschatological savior figure, widely used in early Christianity (see John's preaching in Matt. 3:11; Matt. 21:9=Mark 11:9; Matt. 23:39=Luke 13:35; John 6:35; Acts 19:4; Heb. 10:37; Rev. 1:8; 4:8). Since the "deeds of the Christ" of chaps. 8–10 are acts of compassion rather than the fiery judgment of the "coming one" announced in 3:11–12, John backs off from his previous confidence and asks whether Jesus is indeed the expected one, or whether we should wait for **another**.

To some extent John's question may already be ours. The John of Matthew's story may speak for those who were once sure of their faith but now are not so sure, or for those who are impressed by Jesus' accomplishments but wonder if there is some clue in them to the ultimate meaning of things, or for those who are beginning to doubt whether the way of gentleness and nonretaliation can ever really "work" in a world where the Herods still have most of the power. Matthew does not consider the asking of such questions to close the door to faith.

On the other hand, John's question may not be ours, so that if we ask ultimate questions at all, they may not take John's theological form, and Matthew's story of Jesus may want to teach us how to ask the question. His mode of asking, seeking, and knocking (7:7) excludes any individualistic "me and Jesus" approach, and reshapes the christological question to include Israel and history. To ask whether Jesus is "the one who is to come," i.e., the one in whom God has definitively revealed himself and acted for the world's salvation, is to ask what it is *all* about. Matthew's whole Gospel is his answer to John's question. The Gospel included a cross for Jesus and imprisonment and beheading for John. But those who affirm that in the events to which the

Gospel bears witness God is present with his people, know that they need not, and must not, look elsewhere for "another," even if from time to time they continue to ask the question.

11:4 What you hear and see: The words and deeds of Jesus and his disciples represent the works of the messianic age promised in Isa. 35:5–6; 42:18. "What you hear and see" corresponds to Matt. 5–7 and 8–10, the "words and works of the Messiah" framed by 4:23 and 9:35.

11:6 Takes no offense: The key theme of "taking offense," "falling away" (lit. "stumbling over") is here introduced. In the story line, it refers to Jesus' failure to conform to popular messianic explanations. The readers know it includes the scandal of a crucified Messiah and hear themselves included in the blessing.

Within the theological story world constructed by Matthew, John is a true prophet with a legitimate divine message who proclaims the same message Jesus will proclaim, recognizes Jesus as the Messiah when he comes for baptism, is imprisoned because his prophetic preaching offends the authorities, and dies a martyr's death. Nonetheless, this John wavers in his faith. For Matthew, this is the nature of discipleship and faith, which must be constantly renewed (see the similar presentation of Peter, 16:16–18; 26:57–75; 28:17). John becomes an object lesson to Christian believers, who cannot regard salvation as a static possession but must take heed lest they also fall away. Even "spiritual experiences" do not guarantee acceptance on the last day (7:21–23).

11:7–15
"Who Is John?"
(See also at Luke 7:24–28; 16:16)

11:7 A reed shaken by the wind? . . . Someone dressed in soft robes? The wilderness by the Jordan did contain reeds blowing in the wind and did contain palaces inhabited by people dressed in royal robes—Herod's fortress palaces of Herodium, Machaerus, and Masada. Some Herodian coins bore the symbol of a reed from the Jordan valley. Since John, like Jesus, represents an alternative kingdom, the Matthean motif of the conflict of kingdoms may shimmer in the background. So understood, Jesus' rhetorical question might mean "Reeds and royal robes are there, but that is not the reason you went into the wilderness. You went to see a *prophet*." Or the thrust of Jesus' rhetoric might be simply a contrast to John: he

was no weather vane who took his direction from changing political currents, but stood against the stream; he was dressed not in the finery of court lackeys but, like Elijah, wore the rough garb of the wilderness prophet. In either case, Jesus' point is to affirm the crowds' judgment that John was a prophet (14:5; 21:26).

11:10 See, I am sending my messenger ahead of you: See on Mark 1:2–3.

11:11 No one has arisen greater than John: John's borderline role in Matthew's theological scheme retains some ambiguity. On the one hand, John is paired with Jesus in having the same message of the kingdom (3:2=4:17); on the other hand, Matthew retains the traditional Q saying (see Luke 7:28) that distinguishes John from **the least in the kingdom**. This phrase probably refers to the disciples, i.e., from Matthew's perspective, Christian believers. John plays a decisive role in the history of salvation, forming a dividing line. He is the last and greatest of the prophets of the old eon. What matters, however, is not personal greatness but whether or not one belongs to the new eon of God's reign inaugurated by Jesus. For Matthew, John is a borderline figure who stands on the boundary between the old age and the new and between the disciples on the one hand and the opponents on the other (see on 3:17).

11:12 From the days of John the Baptist until now: This saying must be important for Matthew, since he has brought it from a different context in Q to this context (see Luke 16:16). The saying is difficult to understand and was already variously interpreted in early Christianity, as indicated by the different form and meaning in Luke 16:16. In its Matthean context, it probably expresses Matthew's conviction that the nonviolent eschatological kingdom represented by the advent of Jesus the meek king (21:1–9; see 12:22–30 and the Matthean addition in 21:5) has met violent opposition from representatives of the opposing kingdom.

11:16–19
The Call for Discernment and
Response of "This Generation"
(See also at Luke 7:31–35)

11:19 Wisdom is vindicated by her deeds: The Q community had originally understood both John and Jesus, as well as the members of their own prophetic community, as "children" of transcendent Wisdom, who vindicated the heavenly Wisdom by faithfully living out their prophetic mission and message (as in Luke 7:20). Matthew alters Q's "children" to "deeds," identifying Jesus with transcendent Wisdom herself and not merely as one of a series of Wisdom's messengers (see John 1:1–18).

11:20–12:14
CONFLICT WITH THE KINGDOM OF THIS AGE

From Jesus' initial pronouncement of "woe" to the concluding resolution of the Pharisees to kill Jesus, this section is one of growing conflict. It thus corresponds to 2:1–23, the initial conflict in Matthew's structure of Part One (see introduction to Matthew, "Structure and Outline").

11:20–24
Two Woes against Galilean Cities
(See also at Luke 10:12–15)

11:21 Woe to you: The woes are similar in form to the woes against foreign nations that are a common element of the prophetic books of the Old Testament (e.g., Amos 1:3–2:3; Isa. 13–23; Jer. 46–51; Ezek. 25–32; all of Obadiah). But the Matthean oracles announce a great reversal: the Gentile cities of Tyre, Sidon, and Sodom, which had become biblical symbols of utter evil, will fare better in the judgment than the Jewish cities of **Chorazin** and **Bethsaida**. Even Jesus' "own town" **Capernaum** (see 4:12–13; 9:1) is accused of exalting itself to heaven, as did ancient Babylon and its king (Isa. 14:13).

The problem is not that the inhabitants were skeptical of miracles as such. They indeed believed that the miracles happened, but Jesus' call for repentance (4:17), i.e., reorientation of life to accord with his announcement of the kingdom of God, had gone unheeded even by those who believed that Jesus and his disciples actually worked miracles. Like the Old Testament prophetic pronouncements of doom, these proleptic pronouncements of eschatological judgment function not as the announcement of an unalterable fate, but as a call to repentance. (See the Jonah story, shortly to be reflected in 12:38–41.)

11:25–30 Jesus' Prayer, Declaration, and Invitation
(See also at Luke 10:21–22)

The tripartite structure of this unit is a result of Matthean composition. The first two elements (vv. 25–27) are from a different context in Q (=Luke 10:21–22; Luke has made them a response to the jubilant return of the "seventy" from a successful preaching mission absent from

Matthew). Matthew has relocated them here and made them an integral part of this speech unit. The third element (vv. 28–30) is peculiar to Matthew, who extracted it from his own traditions or may have composed it himself.

The audience is still "the crowds" of 11:7 (the disciples disappear at 11:1 and do not reappear until 12:1). Even the prayer of vv. 25–26 is overheard by the crowds and the reader, and the concluding invitation (v. 28) is to "all." These striking sayings are thus firmly rooted in their context. By placing these sayings here, Matthew indicates that the negative woes and descriptions of the preceding verses are not the final and universal word. Jesus' message is rejected, but it finds acceptance among the "infants," the unpretentious little people (see 10:42; 18:6–14).

This passage is unique in the Synoptic tradition. It was once often considered to be similar to the declarations of "Hellenistic" savior figures, more akin to Johannine christological conceptions than to the Jesus of the Synoptics (see John 3:35; 5:19–20; 7:29; 10:14–15; 13:3; 17:2, 25). The immediate background, however, seems to be the wisdom tradition of the Old Testament and early Judaism. Beginning with a saying of the historical Jesus (11:25–26), the prophetic Q community expanded the saying by picturing Jesus as the messenger of transcendent Lady Wisdom (Sophia). Just as only God knows Wisdom (Job 28:12–27; Sir. 1:6–9; Bar. 3:32), so only the Father knows the Son. Just as only Wisdom knows God (Wis. 8:4; 9:1–18), so only the Son knows the Father. Just as Wisdom makes known the divine mysteries (Wis. 9:1–18; 10:10), so Jesus is the revealer of God's hidden truths. As the personified divine Wisdom calls people to take up her yoke and find rest (Sir. 51:23–30; see Prov. 1:20–23; 8:1–36; Sir. 24:19–22; Odes Sol. 33:6–13), so Jesus extends the same invitation. For Matthew, Jesus is not merely the messenger of Wisdom but is identified with the heavenly Wisdom of God; he speaks not only *for* Wisdom as other prophets did, but *as* the divine Wisdom (see on 11:20).

11:25 I thank you, Father: In the context given them by Matthew, these words are not a thanksgiving for a successful mission (contrast Luke 10:21), but are a prayerful reflection on the "failure" of the Galilean mission. These words thus function parabolically, and as in vv. 20–24 above, portray another reversal: those who accept are not the "wise and intelligent," but the "infants." Since Matthew elsewhere presents "wise" and "understanding" as positive attributes of the disciples themselves, these words are not a tirade glorifying ignorance (7:24–27; 13:51; 23:34; 25:1–13; see the concluding command "learn," v. 29, from the Jesus who has a "tradition"). As elsewhere (e.g., 16:17), Matthew affirms that those who recognize Jesus as the divine messenger do so, not on the basis of superior religious status or individual intelligence or shrewdness, but by revelation, as the gift of the God who chooses to give his revelation to babes, i.e., to those who are open and unpretentious. It is the little people without time, ability, or interest in religious learning, who have no religious basis for claiming the knowledge of God, to whom the divine revelation is given as sheer grace (see 18:1–14).

11:27 All things have been handed over to me: Jesus has a "tradition" delivered to him directly from the Father, in contrast to the scribes and rabbis, whose tradition is only on the human level (see 7:28–29; 15:1–20). Jesus is pictured not as a religious genius who has discovered the divine mystery, but as the beloved Son who is on intimate terms with the Father. It is the divine initiative of the Father, who, in a statement anticipating 28:18, has given "all things" to the Son.

11:28 Come to me: Speaking as the embodiment of the divine Wisdom, Jesus' invitation extends to all who are burdened. In his polemical situation, Matthew had in mind particularly the burden of religious obligation imposed by the scribes and Pharisees, which he understood as a barrier to communion with God (see 23:4). The saying has had a long life in the history of the church as a more general invitation to all who sense their need of God. To those who are put off by the pretensions of human religion, Jesus offers the direct invitation to communion with God.

In the Old Testament and Jewish tradition, **yoke** was a common metaphor for service. In contrast to the rabbinic custom of speaking of the "yoke of the Torah" or the "yoke of the kingdom," Jesus speaks of "my yoke," again placing himself in the divine role. Like **rest**, the **easy** yoke of Jesus is not an invitation to a selfish life of ease, but of deliverance from the artificial burdens of human religion, which Matthew saw as a barrier to the true fellowship of the kingdom of God (23:4). **Learn** is an important Matthean aspect of discipleship (see 9:13; 28:19), added by him here to the traditional saying.

I will give you rest: Like the divine Wisdom (Sir. 51:23–30), and like God in addressing Moses (Exod. 33:14), Jesus offers "rest," which

is not mere ease (see 10:17–39!) but is a synonym for salvation associated with the kingdom of God and eternal life (as in Rev. 14:13; Heb. 3:11, 18; 4:1, 3, 5, 10–11). The institution of the Sabbath also had these overtones. Jesus is here pictured as the true giver of Sabbath rest and all this implies (see Heb. 4), which binds this saying to the next pronouncements of Jesus, set in the context of Sabbath controversies.

12:1–14
Two Pronouncements from
the Lord of the Sabbath
(See also at Mark 2:23–3:6)

Matthew here refers to the Sabbath for the first time, gathering all his Sabbath material into this one story. Several layers of Jewish/Christian conflict are expressed in the present form of the story, from Jesus' original teaching and practice, through the use of this story in early Christian conflicts with Judaism expressed in the pre-Markan oral tradition, to the Gospel of Mark, and finally to Matthew. We are concerned here with the meaning of the Matthean text in its final form (see on Mark 2:23–3:6).

To understand this text, one must first gain some sense of the meaning of the Sabbath in first-century Jewish life (see on Luke 6:1). To observant Jews, the Sabbath was a joy, not a burden. Since the Sabbath was so central in Jewish life, it was important that it be observed properly. One of the Ten Commandments prohibits working on the Sabbath (Exod. 20:8–12). In view of the ambiguity of the Scripture itself as to what constituted "work," a body of tradition having the force of religious law had developed to guide the proper celebration of the Sabbath (see on 15:1–20). Humane considerations were paramount. Jewish tradition as preserved in the Talmud had already decided that "commandments that affect relations between human beings" take precedence over "commandments between God and human beings." God himself wills that human good take precedence over laws that concern God's honor. Thus, setting aside the strict observance of the Sabbath for human good was a way of honoring God. This point was already made in Judaism. Its exact application was disputed, however. Some rabbis taught that an animal that fell into a pit on the Sabbath could be helped out; others (including the Essenes of the Dead Sea Scrolls) specifically rejected this. Some Jews considered healing on the Sabbath to be permitted; others, only if life is in danger. The latter qualification was often understood very broadly, however; hunger could be considered life-threatening.

In the light of such considerations, the two scenes 12:1–14 as rewritten by Matthew should be seen as picturing Jesus' participation in this Jewish debate concerning the proper observance of the Sabbath, not a Christian rejection of "Jewish legalism." Matthew has taken care to rewrite the stories to emphasize that his position is not a rejection of the Law or the Sabbath as such.

It is not clear whether Matthew's community as a whole still continued to observe the Sabbath (see on 24:20). But the way Matthew handles Mark's and Q's Sabbath pericopes indicates that the way the Sabbath is observed is still an important issue in Matthew's community.

12:1 They began to pluck heads of grain and to eat: Matthew's specific notation that the disciples "were hungry" is to be taken seriously as a Matthean motif (see 4:2; 15:32; 21:18; 25:35–44; Jesus himself is hungry in 4:2 and 21:18). The picture is not of well-fed disciples enjoying a snack but of those who have "left all" (4:20, 22; 19:27) to follow Jesus and are genuinely poor and hungry. The Law provided that such people could pluck grain in fields that did not belong to them (Deut. 23:23–25); the issue was whether it could be done on the Sabbath.

12:2 Your disciples are doing what is not lawful: Matthew has omitted the question "why" from Mark, with the result that the Pharisees no longer ask a question, but make a charge, corresponding to the theme of *conflict* that dominates the section 11:20–12:14.

12:5–7 Or have you not read in the law?: In rabbinic debate, a point of law (halakah) could not be established on the basis of a story (haggadah), as Jesus had just done by referring to the account of David in 1 Sam. 21. A point of law required a clear statement of principle from the Torah. Matthew, conditioned by this rabbinic context, adds an example from Num. 28:9–10 (see the similar argument in John 7:22). Since the priests sacrifice according to the Law on the Sabbath, sacrifice is greater than the Sabbath. But mercy is greater than sacrifice, as the divine declaration makes clear (Hos. 6:6 again; see commentary on 9:13), so mercy is greater than the Sabbath.

12:6 Something greater than the temple: The declaration that "something" greater than the temple is here is Matthew's adoption of a Q formula (see 12:41–42) and does not refer only to the person of Jesus himself (the Greek word is neuter!). It seems to point provocatively to the *mercy* at the heart of God's Sabbath commandment (see 23:23, with reference to tithing), as explicated in the following. Note that Jesus does not claim something "greater than the Torah" is present. There is no polemic against the Torah as such in this pericope.

12:7 Mercy . . . not sacrifice: It would be a mistake to understand this section as an affirmation of commonsense humanitarianism against petty legalism. Matthew does not understand the Torah in general or Sabbath rules in particular to be a matter of pettiness (5:17–21). The "mercy and not sacrifice" text from Hos. 6:6 is not an abolition or negation of the sacrificial system or other ritualized practices of worship, but a Semitic way of expressing priority: mercy over sacrifice (5:23–24 specifically assumes the validity of the sacrificial system). Throughout this section, Sabbath rules are adjudicated not by common sense, but by the authority of the Son of Man (12:8), to whom the Father has given all authority (11:27; see 9:6; 28:18b). Precisely as in the Sermon on the Mount (5:17–20), the Torah is affirmed, but transcended by the authority of the one who speaks. Yet the crucial element for contemporary interpretation is the note sounded throughout Matthew: the one who speaks with transcendent authority is himself the representative of God's mercy for the hungering, which is even greater than the temple.

12:9 Entered their synagogue: Except for the summary statements of 4:23 and 9:35, this is the first occasion for Jesus to be in a synagogue in Matthew (elsewhere only in 13:54). In Matthew the synagogue is always an alien place of confrontation (contrast Luke 4:16; 6:6; 13:10). "Their" is added to Mark's "synagogue," and Jesus is deliberately provoked by a test question rather than being merely watched, as in Mark. The Pharisees' "question" is hostile—not for information or discussion of a disputed legal point but in order to accuse him. Sabbath violation does not, however, carry the death penalty and plays no role in the account of Jesus' trial in 26:57–75. Matthew is again at pains to recast the scene from Mark 3:1–6 into a dispute about proper observance of the Sabbath, not about the legitimacy of the Sabbath or the Torah as such. He omits the Markan note of anger and introduces here a saying reflected in other contexts in Q (see Luke 13:15; 14:5), in which Jesus is represented as the advocate of the more liberal Jewish interpretation, presumably the one in fact practiced by the peasant farmers of Galilee, which can be assumed as common practice, whatever the leading Pharisaic opinion.

Nonetheless, the Pharisees reveal their true nature by resolving to kill Jesus. Taken at the level of historical reporting, this might seem an overreaction to the modern reader. At the level of Matthew's story, it expresses the conflict of kingdoms that is its main theme (see on 12:22–30).

12:15–21
THE SERVANT KING
(See also at Mark 3:7–12; Luke 6:17–19)

12:15 When Jesus became aware of this, he departed: The conflict that first emerged in the ministry of Jesus in 9:1–8 came to its climax in 12:14 with the resolution of the Pharisees to put him to death. Jesus' response to this threat was to "withdraw." The withdrawal is not to passivity, but to the work of healing—still on the Sabbath. Instead of retaliating, Jesus heals. Matthew makes this pattern a programmatic christological paradigm in which "withdrawal" becomes a key theological term. Jesus' withdrawal in the face of threat is not a matter of cowardice or strategy but represents the divine response to human violence that will ultimately lead to the cross, in which human violence is met with divine self-giving. As Dietrich Bonhoeffer wrote, God allows himself to be edged out of the world and onto the cross. Here we have not the renunciation of divine sovereignty but its redefinition. It is the Christian redefinition of the Christ figure in terms of Jesus as the one who suffers at the hands of his enemies rather than making them suffer, the nonretaliatory mercy both taught (5:38–48) and practiced (26:50–54) by the sovereign Son of Man, who makes known his divine power in suffering love (16:21–23; 17:22–23; 20:17–19; 26:2).

12:16 Ordered them not to make him known: In Mark, the command to silence was addressed to the demons who had identified him, corresponding to Mark's theory of the secret messiahship. In Matthew, the command not to make him known is directed to those of the crowds he has healed, and is understood by Matthew as a dimension of his Servant Christology, for the Servant works quietly, avoiding publicity and acclaim, as expressed in the concluding formula quotation (see on 2:23).

12:18–21 What had been spoken through the prophet Isaiah: This Scripture quotation, the longest in Matthew, comes at a significant juncture in the structure of the Gospel, as the conclusion of Part One (see introduction to

Matthew, "Structure and Outline"). Though directly related to its context, the citation contains much more than the context calls for, and serves as a summary of the Matthean picture of the ministry of Jesus as a whole. Like the other formula quotations (see on 2:23, "Matthew as Interpreter of Scripture"), it has its own textual form, closer to the Hebrew Old Testament than the Greek LXX translation, and is particularly adapted to represent Matthean theology. The following points are significant:

1. The direct point of contact with the context is the retiring nature of the Servant, who does not **wrangle** or seek publicity but quietly utilizes those considered rejected by others. A **bruised reed** is good for nothing; it is trash. A **smoldering wick** must be thrown out or trimmed. But the Son/Servant rejects neither the one nor the other, just as Jesus calls as disciples those considered unacceptable by the religious authorities (11:25–30).

2. The quotation is from Isa. 42:1–4 [and 9], portraying the Servant of the Lord. In Matthew's time this text was already considered messianic. The Targum (the Aramaic paraphrase of Scripture used in the synagogue) reads "Behold my servant the Messiah." Since "my servant David" is a common biblical phrase, the term also has Davidic overtones. Matthew interprets Jesus in Davidic terms but understands the powerful Son of God/Son of David to be identical with the meek Servant of the Lord who heals and suffers on behalf of others (11:29; 21:5).

3. It is God who speaks in this quotation from Isaiah, describing the Servant. This is similar to the heavenly voice at Jesus' baptism, which also used Servant vocabulary in the context of the Spirit being given to Jesus (3:16/12:18), the divine declaration of Jesus' Son/Servant ministry filled with the Spirit, forming a literary bracket around the entire ministry of Jesus (3:16–17/12:18; see 17:5, adapted from Mark to make it fit the Isaiah vocabulary more closely).

4. As the quotation points back to the beginning of Jesus' ministry, it points forward to the conclusion, the last words of Part One striking exactly the same note as the conclusion of Part Two and the Gospel as a whole: the extension of the gospel to all nations (28:16–20).

5. The announcement of judgment/justice to the Gentiles/nations anticipates not only the end of the Gospel but the next section, the beginning of Part Two, in which the rejection of

Jesus and his message by [the leaders of] Israel becomes clear and "final." Until this point in the Gospel, Jesus and his disciples have preached exclusively to Israel. The offer has been refused by the Jewish leadership. A new community will be formed, comprising all nations. The double reference to nations/Gentiles (18, 21) anticipates and emphasizes this. The Servant will announce justice to the Gentiles as his disciples carry on the Christian mission after his death, a mission in which Jesus remains present and active in the work of his disciples (28:18–20; see 25:31–46).

6. The Servant, though meek and quiet, is ultimately victorious. The conflict that will result in Jesus' death is anticipated. The Matthean reader who will follow Jesus into the conflicts and passion story of Part Two must see all that transpires in the light of this declaration. Jesus is not victim, but victor. His cause cannot but triumph. But the way of universal victory is the way of the cross.

Jesus is thus the *meek king*, the king who redefines the meaning of rule, authority, and kingship. A major theme of the Gospel of Matthew emerges again in this section. On the one hand, Jesus is throughout 11:20–12:14 pictured as the authoritative sovereign who represents the kingdom of God. He has authority to pronounce judgment (11:20–24); he is exclusively the one who knows and is known by the Father, who has given "all things" into his hand (11:27); he is the one who gives the ultimate "rest," salvation in the kingdom of God (11:28–30). He exercises the authority of the eschatological Son of Man and represents something greater than the temple and is therefore Lord of the Sabbath (12:6, 8). Yet his self-description is that of the meek one (11:29), who declares that "mercy," not ritual, is what God wants from us (12:7), and whose whole life is represented by acts of loving response to human need (12:1–8, 12–13). Jesus as the meek one who as such represents the sovereign power of God is at the heart of Matthew's message and summarizes his view of the Christian faith (see on 2:23; 21:4–5, etc.). Such terms as "Christ" and "Son of David" are redefined in terms of who Jesus actually was. This section thus serves as the appropriate conclusion to Matthew's creative Part One, offering the final and climactic picture of the meek king, and serving as the transition to the key scene that has influenced the structure of 1:2–12:21 and for Matthew's theology as a whole.

12:22–28:20
PART TWO: THE CONFLICT OF KINGDOMS DEVELOPED AND RESOLVED

In Part One of his story (1:1–12:21), Matthew narrates the incursion of the kingdom of God into the world in the person of Jesus Christ, who redefined the meaning of kingship as suffering love and provoked the opposition of the kingdom of Satan represented by "this generation" and its leadership, the scribes and Pharisees, who finally resolve to kill him. In Part Two, which begins at this point, the conflict is developed and resolved. The conflict develops, and the disciples of Jesus become a separate community. The religious leaders succeed in their plot to kill Jesus, but precisely in Jesus' seeming defeat, the saving power of God is manifest both in the death of Jesus and in God's affirmation and reversal of this in the resurrection.

12:22–37
THE CONFLICT OF KINGDOMS AND THE NECESSITY OF DECISION
(See also at Mark 3:22–30; Luke 11:14–23; 12:10; 6:43–45)

This paragraph, usually designated the Beelzebul controversy, played a key role in Matthew's thought. Matthew chose this pivotal point in the Markan narrative as the goal of his extensive and creative Part One; after this, he never varies from the Markan order. As rewritten by Matthew, several important elements of Matthew's theology converge in this one paragraph: the kingdom of God (12:28) over against the kingdom of Satan (12:26); the power of the Spirit in Jesus' life (12:28, 31–32); Jesus as Son of David (12:23); forgiveness of sins (12:31–32). Further, the charge of collusion with Beelzebul is particularly significant to Matthew, who refers to it three different times as a charge leveled at both Jesus and his disciples (9:34; 10:25; 12:24).

Two kingdoms stand over against each other in this scene. Jesus represents the kingdom of God (12:28; see on Luke 4:43). But in Matthew, Satan also has a kingdom, the alternative to God's kingdom revealed in Jesus (12:26). In this pericope, the Pharisees who oppose Jesus are portrayed as representatives of Satan's kingdom. These two kingdoms vie for the loyalty of "the crowds," who are present at the beginning (12:23) and end (12:46) of Jesus' pronouncements.

12:23 All the crowds: Until the final scene in which they appear, the crowds in Matthew are potential disciples, neither aligned with the opposition nor committed to following Jesus (see 27:20–26). In the last appearance of the crowds in the story, they had responded to Jesus with wondering admiration (9:33). Here they go a step further in the direction of discipleship, entertaining the possibility that Jesus might indeed be the hoped-for Son of David, despite the fact that his merciful deeds do not correspond to the popular image.

12:24 When the Pharisees heard it: Matthew changes Mark's "scribes" to "Pharisees," i.e., those who have already decided to put Jesus to death (12:14). The Pharisees, rivals for the loyalty of the crowds, respond not to Jesus but to the crowds' growing appreciation of him. As before, they do not deny Jesus' miraculous healing and exorcism, but attempt to discredit him in the eyes of the crowds. In Matthew's perspective, their utter perversity is expressed by the fact that they attribute Jesus' mighty deeds of mercy to the power of Beelzebul, the prince of demons.

12:25 Every kingdom divided against itself: Comparison with the parallel passages in the other Gospels makes clear that Jesus' response in vv. 25–35 is a Matthean composition from materials in Mark and Q (see Mark 3:23–29; Luke 11:17–20, 23; 12:10; 6:43–45), with vv. 36–37 from M or his own composition.

12:30 Whoever does not gather with me scatters: Jesus' ministry is one of "gathering." This may connote imagery of the ingathering of the harvest and of the lost sheep of the house of Israel (9:36–38, also with the "crowds" in view) and/or the regathering of the scattered people of Israel. All are eschatological pictures. With the advent of the Messiah, the eschatological king, there can be no neutrality. One can only gather with Jesus or oppose his eschatological ministry by scattering.

In today's world, this means that those who take Matthew seriously cannot regard Jesus as merely a "personal savior" and the church as a religious support group for personal needs. Matthew's perspective lets us see our world as involved in a conflict of claims to sovereignty, a conflict in which we cannot be spectators but must take sides. In this conflict, the church is a missionary community standing against the idolization of cultural values, rather than putting a divine stamp of approval on them. As envisioned by Matthew, to be a disciple means to belong to the church, and be involved in its mission, and participate in its struggle.

12:31–32 Whoever speaks against the Holy Spirit will not be forgiven: These sayings are not a separate statement on "the unpardonable sin," but in their Matthean context are a constituent element in Jesus' response to the Pharisees' charge that he performs his exorcisms and healings by the power of Beelzebul (see on Mark 3:28–30). In Matthew's context, the sayings are not speculative statements about which sin or sins may be unpardonable, but a pronouncement of judgment against the Pharisees. In Matthew, the Pharisees are those who represent the kingdom of Satan, who have already decided to kill Jesus (12:14), who block others from entering the kingdom of God (23:13), who are not planted by God but represent Satan's work (15:13–14), and who are destined for condemnation at the final judgment. As elsewhere in Matthew, such pronouncements against the Pharisees at the narrative level function as warnings to church members and especially to church leaders. Their function is not to provide a doctrinal category of "unforgivable sins" about which Christians should be anxious.

12:33–35 The tree is known by its fruit:. Matthew has already used this Q material in the Sermon on the Mount (see on 7:16–20).

12:36–37 By your words you will be justified . . . condemned: These sharp pronouncements, peculiar to Matthew and from his own tradition or created by him, reflect not only the Semitic and biblical perspective on the importance of what one says (see on 5:33–37), but have a particular meaning in this context, which has to do with confession of Christ or denial of him. Matthew considers this act of verbal profession of one's faith to be very important (10:18–20, 26–27, 32–33). In the context of the synagogue, Matthean Christians had been tempted to keep quiet about their faith in Jesus as the Christ, or even to join in saying scandalous things about Jesus. Like other parts of the New Testament (e.g., John 12:42–43; Rom. 10:9–10), Matthew makes one's verbal professions a matter of ultimate concern, for which one will be accountable at the Last Judgment.

12:38–45
THE DECISIVE ISSUE: THE RESURRECTION OF JESUS AND ADVENT OF THE ESCHATOLOGICAL AGE
(See also at Mark 8:11–12; Luke 11:16, 29–32)

Three separate sayings (38–40, 41–42, 43–45) are taken by Matthew from their Mark and Q contexts, integrated into one unified speech, and placed by him in this context.

12:38 Teacher: In Matthew, the address "Teacher" is the badge of the unbeliever; no disciple so addresses Jesus ("Lord" is the disciples' address). The doublet in 16:1 adds "from heaven," apparently understood by Matthew to indicate some sort of cosmic sign making his divine authority absolutely clear, in distinction from his exorcisms and miracles, which were capable of other interpretations, as 12:22–37 had just illustrated.

12:39 An evil and adulterous generation: Matthew's addition of "adulterous" (as in 16:4) does not necessarily mean that his generation was characterized by unfaithfulness to marriage vows but is metaphorical for Israel's relation to God (as Hos. 3:1; see Jer. 3:9; 9:1; Ezek. 16:30–52, esp. 16:38).

In Mark 8:11–12, Jesus declares absolutely that no sign would be given. The Q tradition, preserved in Luke 11:29–30, makes the one exception: "the sign of Jonah" will be given to "this generation." It is unclear whether the Q form referred to Jonah's preaching or to Jonah's person, the sign that Jonah himself was. Matthew utilizes both the Mark and Q versions of this tradition (see Matt. 16:1–4; Mark 8:11–13; Luke 11:29–30) but makes the interpretation specific: the sign, and the only sign, is the resurrection of Jesus, who **will be in the heart of the earth** three days, just as Jonah was in the great fish three days. The death-resurrection event is a unity and the only sign given to "this generation."

12:41–42 See on Luke 11:29–32.

12:43–45 See on Luke 11:24–26. The original meaning of this saying is unclear. In a culture where sickness and demon possession were seen as related, it represented a bit of folk wisdom based on the observation that cures/exorcisms are often not permanent and that a relapse can be worse than the previous condition of sickness/possession. In their Matthean context, these words are an extension of Jesus' response to the Pharisees' demand for a sign, which was itself a continuation of the Beelzebul controversy. Despite Matthew's rewriting and insertion of additional material, he has preserved the connection present in Q, in which the saying about the return of the evil spirit was a response to the Pharisees' charge of collusion with Beelzebul. For the Matthean Jesus, the fragment of folk wisdom becomes an analogy of the experience of "this generation"—their last state is worse than the first.

Their encounter with Christ, filled with saving potential, has turned out for them to be for the worse (see John 9:35–41). The evil spirit who vainly seeks rest (12:43) contrasts with the rest offered by the Wisdom of God represented by Jesus (11:29).

12:46–50
THE NEW COMMUNITY OF DISCIPLES
(See also at Mark 3:31–35; Luke 8:19–21)

Despite the negative picture painted in the preceding denunciations of "this generation" that has rejected Jesus and his message, there are those who respond (see 11:25–27). Matthew reinterprets the scene in Mark 3:31–35 to portray the new community of disciples that emerges after the failure of the mission to Israel.

The crowds, as potential disciples, have been present throughout the disputation, overhearing Jesus' pronouncements against the Pharisees and "this generation." Matthew retained the Markan picture of Jesus' family standing "outside," which connotes religious distance, though he had eliminated the Markan setting in a house when he omitted the embarrassing statement that Jesus' family thought him to be deranged (Mark 3:20–21). Matthew's point is that those who have accepted Jesus' message and thereby have been called to place the kingdom of God even above family loyalties, as he himself had done (8:21–22; 10:21, 34-39; 19:29) have found a new family in the community of *disciples*—a term which Matthew specifically adds to his Markan source. The concluding pronouncement is doubly definitive: (1) Disciples are those who do the will of God. The essence of discipleship is not mere profession, right doctrine, or even charismatic phenomena, but doing the will of God (7:21–23, etc.). (2) Disciples are not only brothers and sisters to each other in the family of God; they are Jesus' "brothers and sisters," a term that is particularly important to Matthew as a designation of the members of the Christian community (see 23:8 [obscured there by the NRSV "students"]; 25:40; 28:10; see Heb. 2:11–12).

13:1–52
SPEAKING IN PARABLES

On the interpretation of parables, see at Mark 4:1.

Matthew has located the "parable discourse" in the midst of the conflict section, in which Jesus is being rejected by the leaders of Israel, the new community is being formed, and the inclination of the people as a whole hangs in the balance. The messianic words (chaps. 5–7), deeds (chaps. 8–9), and mission (chap. 10) had generated only conflict and rejection among the Jewish leaders (chap. 12). The section is preceded by the rejection by the Pharisees and by his own family, culminating in the announcement of a new community of those who do God's will and are thus Jesus' "family" (12:22–50). Immediately following the parables discourse, Jesus is rejected with hostility in his own home town (13:53–58). The separation of the community of Jesus' disciples from "the crowds" is the specifically Matthean context and purpose of the parable collection.

In 13:1–52, Matthew constructs one of his five major discourses around this theme (see introduction to Matthew, "Structure and Outline"). All the parables in Matt. 13 have an explicit reference to the kingdom of God/heaven. Matthew follows the pattern of the parable discourse already found in Mark 4:1–20, then expands it with material from Q, M, and his own composition, structuring the additional components into two sets of three parables each.

13:1–23
The Markan Parable Structure
Adapted and Interpreted

13:1–9 *The Parable of the Sower*
(See commentary at Mark 4:1–9; Luke 8:19–21)

13:10–17 *Why Speak in Parables?*
(See also at Mark 4:10–12; Luke 8:9–10)
13:10 Then the disciples asked him: Matthew is following Mark, who had pictured Jesus as using parables in order to prevent outsiders from understanding (Mark 4:10–12), a part of Mark's messianic secret (see there). Matthew does not share Mark's understanding of the secret messiahship and its corollary, the misunderstanding of the disciples. Matthew omits, modifies, or offers supplemental correction for every passage in Mark that pictures the disciples misunderstanding or failing to understand (see 13:14, 19, 23, 51; 14:31ff. [vs. Mark 6:52]; 16:9 [vs. Mark 8:17]; 16:12; 17:9 [vs. Mark 9:10]; 17:13, 23 [vs. Mark 9:32]). Here we see him struggling to reinterpret a Markan hard saying within the framework of his own understanding of Jesus' ministry. His considerable editorial expansion and modification of this passage begins with a clarification of the question. Whereas in Mark a larger circle had asked about the meaning of the parables, now it is those who do understand (the disciples alone) who ask specifically the reason for Jesus' speaking to "them" (the others) in parables. The question receives a fivefold response

representing Matthean theology and moderating the difficult statements in Mark 4:10–12.
13:11 To you has been given: Understanding is not a human accomplishment, but a gift of God. This is a Matthean theme elsewhere (11:25–30; 16:17). For Matthew, "understanding" is not merely conceptual but is understood biblically to include subjection to God's sovereignty. This is his understanding of Isa. 6:9–10 (and see Ps. 119:34). Matthew changes Mark's singular to the plural **mysteries**, more attuned to the Old Testament understanding of the hidden plans of God for history and the ultimate establishment of the kingdom of God (see the plural in Dan. 2:28–29, 47).
13:12 To those who have, more will be given: The reader of Mark 4:10–12 could well ask what kind of teacher generates only misunderstanding, and intends to do so. Matthew has corrected this in line with his view of Jesus as a good teacher, a dimension of his Christology. For Matthew, parabolic communication is a pedagogical strategy that rewards good students and penalizes bad ones. Jesus speaks in parables because he is a good communicator who wishes to challenge those who want to understand; those who fail to understand show that they are poor students, i.e., wrongheaded, not merely intellectually dull. This was standard scribal pedagogical strategy (see Sir. 3:29; 21:11–15; 38:31–39:3; on Matthew as scribe, see 13:52). To express this understanding, Matthew moves Mark 4:25 to Matt. 13:12, its new context providing an entirely new perspective.
13:13 The reason I speak to them in parables: Matthew changes Mark's conjunction meaning "in order that" to a different Greek word meaning "because," and omits the condemnatory "so that they might not turn again and be forgiven." The result is that the crowds are described as failing to understand because they are *already* imperceptive, rather than as in Mark, where their lack of understanding is the intentional *result* of Jesus' teaching in parables.
13:14–15 With them indeed is fulfilled the prophecy of Isaiah: The allusion to Isa. 6:9–10 already present in the preceding is now made specific, as Matthew adds the full quotation. Jesus speaks in parables, as he does much else, in order to fulfill the Scripture (see on 2:23).
13:16–17 Blessed are your eyes: Matthew brings this reassuring word from another context in Q (see Luke 10:23–24), which affirms not only that the disciples see and hear the deeper

meaning of what is happening before them, but that what they experience is what prophets and righteous persons have longed to see and hear, the eschatological events of the time of fulfillment!

13:18–23 *The Parable of the Sower Interpreted*
(See also at Mark 4:13–20; Luke 8:11–15)

Matthew essentially adopts the interpretation of the Sower as transmitted in Mark 4:13–20 (see there), with certain changes characteristic of Matthean theology. He designates the parable as "the sower," giving it a christological focus it had not had previously (see even more specifically 13:37). Matthew also slightly rewrites Mark 4:14 to avoid the direct clash between seed=word in v. 14 and seed=hearers in vv. 16, 18, 20—an attempt which does not quite succeed, since in 13:19b "what is sown in the heart" must be the word, but in vv. 20ff. "what was sown . . ." is "the one who hears."

The Matthean reading of Jesus' parable presents to the contemporary reader the following affirmations:

1. The victory of the kingdom of God is sure. The message of the parable is not an exhortation to work hard to bring in the harvest. Though as silent, mysterious, and unavailable to superficial observation as the germination of a seed in good soil, the kingdom for which the disciples pray (6:10) will certainly come. The seed has been sown by the Son of Man, who accompanies his church through history. The harvest is God's doing, and God is faithful.

2. But the line between sowing the word and reaping the eschatological harvest is not straight and unproblematical. The word encounters many difficulties between its original sowing and its eventual (but sure) results. Believers should not be surprised or discouraged that this is the case.

3. Though the responses and actions of believers do not effect the final coming of the kingdom, the choices they make are ultimately important, for they determine which side they are on at the final harvest. Believers may not blithely assume they are the good soil.

4. This picture of temporary and provisional pessimism but ultimate optimism also serves a theological purpose, similar to that of Rom. 9–11. The parable and its interpretation served to interpret to Matthew's readers their own history, in which the Messiah has been mostly rejected by his own people, yet the purpose of God (the "mysteries of the kingdom," 13:11 NRSV footnote) remains sure and will be fulfilled.

13:24–43 Three Additional Parables in the Markan Pattern
13:24–30 *The Parable of the Weeds*

This parable is M material, unique to Matthew. While there may be elements that go back to Jesus or the pre-Matthean church, it is the Matthean understanding of the story that is presented in the following comments.

13:25 An enemy came and sowed weeds: A wheatlike weed (darnel, cheat) is common throughout the Near East. The distinctive element in this parable is that it involves two sowings. In the Sower of 13:3–9, the seed per se was a symbol of the (good and potent) word of God that generates believers, and the issue was "what kind of soil are you?" (despite the garbled interpretation that confuses seed and soil). But in the parable of the Weeds, there are two sowings (corresponding to Matthew's apocalyptic dualism), and the question is "what kind of seed are you: the good seed sown by the exalted Son of Man or the evil seed sown by Satan?" Matthew's "two kingdoms" view comes again to expression here (see on 12:22–30; 13:36–43, 51–52).

13:31–32 *The Parable of the Mustard Seed*
(See at Mark 4:30–32; Luke 13:18–19)

The parable came to Matthew in both its Markan and Q forms; Matthew follows the Q form more closely.

13:33 *The Parable of the Yeast*
(See also at Luke 13:20–21)

13:34–35 *Why Speak in Parables?*
(See at Mark 4:33–34)

These words that were the conclusion to the Markan parable discourse (Mark 4:33–34) are made by Matthew into a transition to the next subsection with a different audience, corresponding to vv. 10–17 above. Similarly, Matthew introduces Ps. 78:2 as the eighth of his formula quotations (see excursus "Matthew as Interpreter of Scripture" at 2:23). Matthew is attracted to the saying not by its meaning but by the word "parable," and is concerned to show that not only the birth, itinerary, and death of the Messiah were matters of prophecy and fulfillment, but also that he taught in parables.

13:36–43 *The Parable of the Weeds Interpreted*

Matthew's interpretation understands the parable to be an allegorical portrayal of the eschatological judgment that urges a certain kind of conduct on the believer in the present.

13:36 Explain to us the parable of the weeds: For Matthew, the transition from the address to the "crowds" to the disciples represents the principle difference between "world" and "church"—the disciples are in the **house** (church) where Jesus explains everything to them. Inasmuch as the reader is given the opportunity to accompany them into the house and overhear Jesus' explanation, readers are implicitly understood to be within the in-group of disciples. In the Matthean perspective the believing community is privileged to be accompanied by the exalted Lord throughout their historical sojourn toward the coming of the kingdom at the last day.

13:37 The one who sows the good seed is the Son of Man: See on Mark 2:10. The Son of Man who is the sower is not only the historical Jesus, but the exalted one who accompanies his church through history as himself the sower of the word and the one who will judge both world and church at the end. The "seed" are sons/children/members of the kingdom, i.e., Christian believers.

13:39 The enemy who sowed them is the devil: The key to Matthew's understanding this parable is the *second* sowing, done by "the enemy," the devil. (On the language of Satan, the devil, and demons, see excursus at Mark 5:1.) Christians are the result of the "sowing" of the Son of Man. Unbelievers and opponents are the result of the activity of Satan. Matthew's dualistic perspective appears here once again, as in the conflict of kingdoms which pervades his presentation (13:38 **children of the kingdom/children of the evil one**; see 15:15 and discussion at 12:22–37). Thus it is important that **the field is the world**, not merely the church (v. 38). The traditional interpretation urging Christians not to pronounce judgment on fellow members of the community is not incorrect, but is too narrow. The admonition to forgo efforts to root out the "weeds" corresponds to 15:12–14 with regard to the Pharisees: they are not "planted" by the Father, who will deal with them in due time. Jesus' disciples are not to try to uproot them but to leave them be. Both the parable and the interpretation indicate that separation of authentic members of the covenant community from false is God's business and must await the eschatological judgment. The tension between these texts and 18:15–20 may reflect a debate within Matthew's church.

Matthew affirms both the church discipline of chapter 18 and the perspective of tolerance and patience represented by chapter 13, without clarifying how this is to be worked out in practice.

13:42 Weeping and gnashing of teeth: A Matthean stereotyped formula adopted from Q (see Matt. 8:12b=Luke 13:28) and added as a conclusion to five parables (13:42, 50; 22:13; 24:51: 25:30), highlighting Matthew's emphasis on the parables as pictures of eschatological judgment focusing especially on the fate of the condemned. This is not glee over the fate of outsiders, but warning to insiders.

13:44–52
Three More Parables in (a Variation of) the Markan Pattern

13:44–48 *The Parables of the Hidden Treasure, the Pearl, and the Net*

13:44 The kingdom of heaven is like treasure: Matthew apparently intends the parable of the Hidden Treasure to be interpreted together with the parable of the Pearl that immediately follows. They are similar in form, and their primary common feature is surely central to the meaning of each: the protagonist goes and sells everything for the sake of the one thing. Both the plowman and the merchant act with the single-minded response of the "pure in heart" (see on 5:8; see the *one* pearl).

The two parables are also different: (1) The plowman is doing his normal work, not looking for or expecting anything special, and comes upon the treasure quite by accident. It finds him rather than his actively seeking it. The merchant is actively seeking, knows what he is looking for, and still finds something beyond all his expectations. The kingdom can become real in either way (see 9:2, 22). (2) The great joy of the plowman is emphasized but is altogether absent from the merchant. This does not mean that his selling everything in order to obtain the pearl was joyless but that (subjective) joy is not the main point of either parable. (3) What the merchant did, though it may not have measured up to everyone's understanding of "common sense," was unquestionably legal. The same cannot be said of the plowman, whose action may have been questionable both legally and morally (we are not given enough details to know for sure). Some of Matthew's readers may have expected a law-abiding plowman to have reported his find to the owner of the field rather than cashing in on it himself. Sensitive contemporary readers may wonder about the ethics of, in effect, cheating the owner of the field out of his treasure, even if it was perfectly legal. The story does not legitimize the actions of the man. Jesus was certainly able to use questionable actions of characters in his parables in order to picture the urgency of acting to gain the kingdom while the opportunity is there (see Matt. 12:29's use of breaking-and-entering imagery and, more subtly, Luke 16:1–13!).

13:45–46 The kingdom of heaven is like a merchant in search of fine pearls: In the first-century Mediterranean world, the pearl was often a symbol of the highest good (as diamonds sometimes are in modern Western culture). The advent of the kingdom, sought for or not, brings about a reversal of values leading to the crucial action that obtains the new. It is this action, puzzling and out of step with those who live by the old values, that is central in each of these parables.

13:47–50 The kingdom of heaven is like a net: The net pictured here is a large dragnet, usually about six feet deep and up to several hundred feet wide, positioned in the lake by boats, requiring several men to operate (hence the plurals of v. 48). The picture is realistic, portraying an ordinary event with no surprising twists: the net brings in "every kind" of both good and bad fish, which are then sorted, the good being kept and the bad thrown out. Whatever the original meaning of the parable, Matthew's own ecclesiastical application already appears in the telling of the parable itself. The bad fish are called "rotten," a word inappropriate to fish that have just been caught but used four times previously in Matthew's description of bad "fruit" (=works) presented by Christians, where it is appropriate (7:17; 7:18; 12:33 twice; the word was taken over from Q [see Luke 6:43] and made into a Matthean theme).

13:49 So it will be at the end of the age: This interpretation is very like that of the Weeds, vv. 36–43 above (49a–50 is in verbatim agreement with 40b, 42; 49b is very like 41). Like the preceding interpretation, it concentrates entirely on the fate of the wicked, whose destiny is to be cast into the furnace of fire, with weeping and gnashing of teeth—all typical Matthean language for eschatological judgment, but not appropriate to fish, which are buried or thrown back into the water, not burned. The parable is not a picture of evangelism, "fishing for people," but a parable of

final sorting and separation. The eschatological sorting described in the parables is happening as Jesus speaks and as people respond or fail to do so. The church is to see itself reflected in the scene of this chapter as a whole: those disciples who respond to the word of Jesus and become the new community, the family of God (12:49).

13:51–52 *Understanding Parables*
13:51 Have you understood all this? The disciples answer with a clear "**Yes.**" These words added to Mark are to make clear that for Matthew, understanding is not an optional element of discipleship (see on 13:10–17 above).

13:52 Every scribe who has been trained for the kingdom of heaven: Vocabulary and style, as well as theology, indicate that Matthew himself has composed this concluding parable, with the (Jewish) scribe who has been trained (literally "discipled") for the kingdom of heaven being a cameo self-portrait (on Christian scribes, see 8:19–22; 23:34). Matthew affirms both the old and the new (see 9:17). Like a skilled scribe, he brings out of his storehouse the treasures of his Jewish past (Scripture, stock of traditional imagery, perspectives, and concerns), as well as older Christian tradition (Mark! Q!). But he does not merely repeat the past. Alongside the old he introduces the new, presenting the old in a new light, reclaiming it for the new situation in which he finds himself, seeing all things in the light of the Christ event and the coming of the kingdom.

13:53–17:27
THE FORMATION OF THE NEW COMMUNITY AMID CONTINUING CONFLICT

13:53–58
Jesus Is Rejected at Nazareth
(See also at Mark 6:1–6; Luke 4:16–30)

Jesus' hometown has the opportunity to receive him but joins the developing opposition.

13:55–56 Is not this the carpenter's son? Matthew probably changes Mark's "carpenter" to "carpenter's son" since it is important to picture Jesus as Son of David, incorporated into the Davidic line as the legal son of Joseph (see 1:2–25) and to avoid Mark's "carpenter" and "son of Mary," both of which could have been offensive (see John 8:41). There is no suggestion in the text of Matthew that Jesus' brothers and sisters are anything but the children of Mary and Joseph, a view still advocated by

Tertullian in the late second century with no suggestion that it was unorthodox. The later dogma of Mary's perpetual virginity generated other explanations. That they are stepbrothers and stepsisters, children of Joseph by a previous marriage, was already advocated in the late second or early third century by the *Protevangelium of James* and later became the dominant view in the Greek Orthodox Church, advocated also by some Roman Catholics such as the fourth-century Epiphanius. Jerome in the fifth century was the first to argue that they were cousins of Jesus, children of neither Mary nor Joseph, which became the dominant view in the later Roman Catholic Church. Matthew is untroubled by any of these later theological issues.

14:1–12
The Death of John the Baptist
(See also at Mark 6:14–29; Luke 9:7–9)

In Mark, the story was a "flashback" that had filled the narrative space between the sending of the Twelve in 6:13 and their return in 6:30. Since Matthew had moved that section of Mark forward to 10:1–42 and never narrates the departure or return of the Twelve on their mission, the story of John's death now falls directly after the rejection at Nazareth, with only a new vague transitional phrase "at that time" (see 3:1; 11:25; 12:1). This altering of the chronology has the effect of placing Matthew's specific identification of John as a prophet immediately after Jesus' implicit self-designation as a prophet in 13:57. Matthew has adopted the Deuteronomistic view of Israel's prophets already incorporated in Q, that Israel always rejected the true prophet, whose destiny it is to suffer (5:12; 23:37).

14:5 Herod wanted to put him to death: Over against John (and Jesus) as representatives of the kingdom of God, Matthew's understanding of Herod as representative of the anti-kingdom is seen in his rewriting of Mark to make Herod the direct opponent of John (see 12:22–30). Mark 6:18–28 had pictured Herod as admirer and defender of John, who is manipulated into executing him by the evil cunning of Herodias, responsible not only for his death but for his original arrest. Here, Herod himself arrests John and wants to kill him, his murderous intent restrained only by popular opinion of John as a prophet—precisely parallel to the conflict that will lead to Jesus' death (see 21:45–46).

14:9 The king: Matthew preserves Mark's title "king," which he knows is historically incor-

rect (see 14:1 and NRSV footnote, which gives the correct title **tetrarch**) in order to express his view of the conflict of kingdoms inherent in this story. Matthew wants to picture Herod not merely as an evil or weak individual but, along with other Jewish leaders, as a this-worldly representative of the kingdom of Satan opposing the kingdom of God.

Every perceptive reader knows that our lives are not lived in power vacuums or fire-free zones but within an arena of clashing force fields. Matthew's story throughout brings the reader within the conflict of kingdoms initiated by the advent of Jesus (see on 2:1–23 and 12:22–30). The story does not operate moralistically against oaths, divorce, partying, and dancing but, like the conflict between Herod and Jesus in 2:1–23, portrays the fundamental struggle initiated by the kingdom of God and the fate of those who are committed to it. Who wins in this conflict? John appears to be just another example of those who take their stand in behalf of the revealed will of God against the powers that be. His fate is more absurd than most, expending his one and only life as the result of a birthday party dance and a rash promise made while drunk. Matthew does not reassure the reader that John will somehow be vindicated or rewarded. The last picture we have of him is his headless corpse being interred by his disciples. Yet the story intentionally evokes the story of Jesus, for whom "he was buried" is followed by "on the third day God raised him from the dead." Like everything else in the Gospel of Matthew, the story of John cannot be proclaimed in isolation, but only as an element of the larger story of which it is a part. Each story calls the reader to faith in the crucified and risen one, and in the process redefines what it means to "win."

14:13–21
Healing and Feeding the Crowds
(See also at Mark 6:32–44; Luke 9:10–17; John 6:1–15)

On the issues involved in interpreting Gospel miracle stories in general, see excursus at 8:1, "Interpreting the Miracle Stories."

The contrast between the two kingdoms continues, as the banquet over which "king" Herod presides is implicitly contrasted with the meal provided by king Jesus. Matthew has altered the chronological connections so that Jesus' withdrawal comes as direct response to the announcement of John's death. Once again, the sovereign representative of the kingdom of God, when faced with the hostile power of the kingdom of this world, does not respond with violence, but demonstrates the nature of his kingship by withdrawing (see on 2:14, 19–22; 4:12; 10:23; 12:14–21; 14:13; 15:2; 26:53–56).

In its journey through the pre-Gospel tradition and in its Markan form, this potent story has been reinterpreted in many forms (there are six versions of it in the New Testament) to express many dimensions of christological faith, incorporating numerous features from the Bible, Jewish tradition, and Christian experience:

—the wilderness setting for the people of God, en route from captivity to the promised land (Exod. 13:18 etc.; "wilderness" occurs 92x Exod.–Deut.)

—recalcitrant Israelites/disciples, who doubt that food can be provided in the wilderness (Exod. 16:2–3=Matt. 14:15; Mark 6:35–38)

—God leading the people (who are like sheep without a shepherd, Num. 27:17=Mark 14:14; Mark 6:34)

—the people arranged in military companies (Exod. 13:18=Mark 6:40, omitted by Matthew)

—God as shepherd triggering Psalm 23 and its "green grass" (Ps. 23:2=Matt. 14:19; see Mark 6:39 [an allusion to Scripture, not a historical botanical note])

—the giving of the manna (Exod. 16; Num. 11; developed especially in the Johannine version of the story, John 6:1–58)

—Elisha's miraculous provision of food (2 Kgs. 4:42–44). The miracle followed the death of Elijah (= John, in the Gospel story); Elisha overcame protests and had a quantity left over. All of these are paralleled in the Gospel story.

—Jesus, accused of being a "glutton" (Matt. 11:19), providing table fellowship open to all, including "publicans and sinners."

—Jesus' eucharistic last meal with his disciples (Mark 14:17–25=Matt. 26:20–29), in which he assumes the role of head of the new family he is creating, providing food and pronouncing the table blessing (particularly appropriate in Matthew, where this story follows closely on 13:53–58)

—The messianic banquet as part of the eschatological imagery, which will include not only bread but fish or sea creatures (see 2 Bar. 29:3–8; 4 Ezra 6:52; see Ps. 74:14; Isa. 27:1).

Matthew does not develop all the overtones of this resonant story. He compresses the Markan version, making it one-third shorter, omitting and rewriting the elements that reflect badly on the disciples, omitting the features that picture

the community as the wandering people of God in the wilderness, and concentrating especially on the eucharistic features, which he emphasizes (compare 14:15–20 with 26:20–27).

14:16 You give them something to eat: Jesus' charge to the disciples is no longer met by the sarcastic response of Mark 6:37, but only by their volunteering the information of their inadequate resources. Not misunderstanding but lack of faith is the characteristic trait of Matthean disciples (see v. 31). This command of Jesus transcends the story framework and speaks directly to every reader who has food that could be shared with a hungry world.

14:21 Besides women and children: Matthew exploits the ambiguity of the Markan word *andres* ("men"), which can be understood in an inclusive sense, "people," or in the limited sense of "males." Mark obviously intended it in the broader sense, but Matthew takes it in the limited sense, in order to expand the numbers of people present and thus the greatness of the miracle (see on v. 35 below).

14:22–36
Walking on the Water and Healing the Sick
(See also at Mark 6:45–56; John 6:16–25)

Matthew's rewriting of Mark emphasizes the separation between Jesus and the disciples; Jesus was "alone by himself," and the disciples are "far from the land" (replacing Mark's "in the midst of the sea"). The boat/church symbolism of 8:23–27 is strengthened by representing the *boat* as "being tortured" by the waves (not the disciples laboring at rowing, as in Mark). This description is as strange as the earthquake in the sea of 8:24. In both cases Matthew allows his symbolism to shape his description, for in both cases he is thinking of the suffering the church will experience during its mission on which it is sent forth "alone" (i.e., "without" the Jesus who promised to be with them always, 28:20).

14:28–31 If it is you, command me to come to you on the water: These verses, probably composed by Matthew himself, are added to the Markan story (see Mark 6:50–51). The figure of Peter should not here (or elsewhere in Matthew) be psychologized as impetuous, but later failing. We do not have a psychological profile but a character in a story representing all the disciples, portraying the theological meaning of discipleship as such. Peter addresses Jesus as a believer: "Lord" (nonbelievers in Matthew use other titles). He has the "right" christological title and shows great personal faith, but he leaves the boat and

65

the community. Then he sees the power of the storm and begins to sink. For Matthew, his problem was not only that he took his eyes off Jesus, but that he wanted proof of the presence of Christ, and so left the boat in the first place. He cries out with the community prayer adopted from the Psalms and common in Christian worship, "Lord, save me" (see 8:25). Jesus stretches out his hand, and Peter is saved. The gentle rebuke identifies Peter as the typical disciple in Matthew; **little faith** is the dialectical mixture of courage and anxiety, of hearing the word of the Lord and looking at the terror of the storm, of trust and doubt that is always ingredient to Christian existence, even after the resurrection (see Mark 9:24; Matt. 6:30; 8:26; 16:8, 17:20). This last point is underscored by the peculiar word used here for **doubt**, which connotes vacillation, not skepticism. It is used elsewhere in the New Testament only in Matt. 28:17, of the disciples in the presence of the risen Lord (see James 1:6–8).

Peter is the first disciple and the typical one (see on 16:13–19). Matthew will shortly make it clear that even Peter can become the agent and voice of Satan (16:23). This potentially demonic aspect of discipleship is already present in this story. *Peter's* response to the reassuring "I am" of the divine presence is similar to *Satan's* first words to Jesus: **If . . .** (4:3). Peter hears the claim of Jesus, just as the contemporary reader of the Gospel hears the Matthean claim that Jesus is the one who makes God present to us (1:23; 28:20). In a chaotic world where such a claim often appears false, hollow, or meaningless, there is the temptation to want some experiential, spectacular reassurance that it is really so. Peter knows that Jesus had been left back on the beach, just as the modern reader knows that Jesus has been left back there in history. In both cases, it is clearly impossible that he could come to us. So when he appears, walking on the sea, it would be good news, if it could possibly be true. Peter's proposal to test the reality of Christ's presence doesn't sound like the voice of Satan, especially since Peter is willing to risk death himself to prove the presence of the divine reality (4:5–7!). As Jesus had responded to the demons' request with a one-word granting of permission (8:31–32), so he allows Peter to leave the boat. But the initiative was with Peter, and it was an initiative grounded in a lack of faith and a putting God to the test.

So the typical "lesson" derived from this text often borders on the demonic *mis*understanding of the nature of faith that Matthew wants to warn us against. The message is not "if he had had enough faith, he could have walked on the water"; just as the message to us is not "if we had enough faith, we could overcome all our problems in spectacular ways." This interpretation is wrong in that it identifies faith with spectacular exceptions to the warp and woof of the ordinary days of which our life is woven, days that are all subject to the laws of physics and biology. When our fantasies of overcoming this network of everyday life are shattered by the realities of accident, disease, aging, and circumstance and we begin to sink, this view encourages us to feel guilty because of our "lack of faith." Lack of faith is not just sinking but wanting to walk on the water in the first place. Faith is not being able to walk on the water—only God does that—but daring to believe, in the face of all the "evidence," that God is with us in the boat, made real in the community of faith as it makes its way through the storm, battered by the waves.

14:32–33: You are the Son of God: Matthew drastically rewrites the Markan ending of the story. Instead of utter astonishment, lack of understanding, and hardened hearts, we have falling down and worshiping Jesus, confessing that he is Son of God. The worshipful Christian confession with which the scene concludes illustrates the post-Easter perspective from which this and all the miracle stories are told. The story as a whole is reminiscent of the explicitly post-Easter John 21:1–14, especially the connection of feeding and the sea story, the initial lack of recognition preceding Jesus' self-identification, and Peter's getting out of the boat to come to Jesus.

15:1–20
Defilement—Traditional and Real
(See also at Mark 7:1–23; Luke 11:37–41; 6:39)

Verses 1–20 compose one unit pursuing a single theme. At the two extremes stand the Pharisees and scribes (opponents) and the disciples; the crowds stand in the middle and could go either way (wooed by the Pharisees but also addressed by Jesus as potential disciples).

15:2 Why do your disciples break the tradition of the elders? Two streams of Christian tradition have flowed into Matthew's own community: the earlier Q (and some M) traditions that represent a Christianity still loyal to the Torah, and the later Markan traditions representing law-free Gentile Christianity (see introduction to Matthew). Historically, it is not clear how these had been combined in Matthew's community. In any case, Matthew's perspective must be constructed from the Gospel as a whole, not merely from this passage.

15:3 He answered them: Their question, which seems on the surface to be a legitimate question, does not receive a response until v. 20b, and then not to the Pharisees who asked it but to the disciples in private. Instead of responding to the question, Jesus offers a counterattack, for at the level of the story the Pharisees are not asking a real question, since they have already decided to kill him.

15:4–6 God said . . . but you say: Matthew tightens the entire interchange he finds in Mark, making the parallels and antitheses more striking and more damning: over against the commandment of God, the Pharisees place their own tradition; over against what "God said" (Mark 7:10, "Moses said"), they place what they themselves say. **That person need not honor the father:** There is no documentation for such a practice outside the New Testament. What we have here is Christian polemics, seen from outside the Jewish tradition. In such situations, each side tends to look for data in its opponent's tradition and practice that can be interpreted adversely against the other side. Jews, for example, looking at Christian materials, could charge Christians with violating this same commandment of the Decalogue because they instructed their members to leave father and mother (10:34–37). Insiders on both sides of the conflict understand their own traditions quite differently from the ways polemical outsiders view them.

15:10–11 It is not what goes into the mouth that defiles a person: The theme now shifts explicitly to the issue of what defiles (=makes ritually unclean, separating one from the holy community and the holiness of God). In contrast to Mark 7:19c, which he omits, for Matthew Jesus' blanket declaration—that people are not made unclean by what enters their mouth but by what comes out of it—is not a comprehensive pronouncement nullifying the laws of the Torah regarding ritual defilement, such as the food laws. It is rather a thoroughly biblical and Jewish mode of declaring the relative importance of the inner commitments of the heart, as they come to expression in the way one speaks and acts, over against the ritual commandments, which

are still not abolished. This is the way Matthew understands Hos. 6:6, quoted twice by him (9:13; 12:7), which makes mercy more important than sacrifice, without abolishing the latter—and corresponds to the original meaning of Hosea.

15:12–14 Let them alone; they are blind guides of the blind: These verses are mostly composed by Matthew (with a Q point of contact, see Luke 6:39). He inserts them into the Markan story. In Matthew's dualistic theology, the Pharisees are pictured not as God's planting but the devil's, in terms reminiscent of 13:25, 39, and the same command is given here as there: leave them alone (13:30; 15:14) for the eschatological judgment of God (but see 17:24–27 and comments on 14:28–32). Since this is directed exclusively to the disciples, it functions as warning to insiders against overrating ritual correctness, not as polemic against outsiders.

15:15–18 Are you still without understanding? Matthew typically alters Mark's view that the disciples misunderstood, here by changing Mark's wording to signal that the disciples' misunderstanding is only temporary (see 13:10; 16:11–12). Matthew does not understand Jesus to be abrogating all the food laws of the Torah itself (unlike the Gentile Christian author of Mark), but only rejecting the oral tradition of the Pharisees. This is seen in his omitting Mark 7:19c ("Thus he declared all foods clean") and adding the summary conclusion of v. 20b.

15:20b To eat with unwashed hands does not defile: The concluding pronouncement, which sounds very much like a rabbinic legal decision on a disputed item of traditional religious law, returns to the initial question of 15:2, not only rounding off the unit with a neat literary bracket, but relating the whole discussion strictly to the Pharisaic oral tradition, without offering any challenge to the prescriptions of biblical Torah.

15:21–28
The Syrophoenician (Canaanite) Woman
(See also at Mark 7:24–30)

15:21 Jesus left that place: Again Jesus' response to the threatening Pharisees of the previous story is to withdraw (same verb as 4:12; see there), this time into Gentile territory, which is emphasized both by the biblical phrase "Tyre and Sidon" (Mark had only "Tyre") and by designating the woman a "Canaanite" (Mark had "Syrophoenician"). The scene draws from biblical imagery to portray a dramatic contrast between the Jewish Messiah sent only to Israel on the one hand and their archetypal enemies subject to demons on the other. Jesus does not enter a house (as he had in Mark 7:24).

15:22 Lord, Son of David: The woman addresses Jesus with the (later) Christian language of faith and worship: "Lord," "Son of David," "have mercy upon me" are all Christian confessions reflecting the liturgy of the church, adapted from the prayer language of the Psalter. Matthew had added these words; "Son of David" was a suspect title for Mark (see on Mark 10:47; 11:10; 12:35–37; on "Lord" in Mark, see on Mark 7:28).

15:29–39
Healing and Feeding the Crowds
(See also at Mark 8:1–10)

For interpretation of the details, see on the practically identical 14:13–21 and the Markan parallel.

16:1–12
The Pharisees and Sadducees Seek a Sign; Warning against Their Teaching
(See also at Mark 8:11–21; Luke 11:16, 29; 12:54–56)

16:1–4 is a doublet of 12:38–40 (see there). The Pharisees and Sadducees "test" Jesus. This is the first use of "test" since the temptation story of 4:1–11, used elsewhere only in 19:3 and 22:18, 35, each time of the Pharisees. Matthew thus draws a line of continuity between the devil's opposition to Jesus and that of the Jewish leadership. The conflict of kingdoms that is Matthew's major theme emerges again (see on 12:22–30). This theme extends into 16:5–12, and is one reason Matthew repeats 16:1–4 as its introduction. All of 16:1–12 thus leads into the key scenes of Peter's confession and Jesus' instruction to follow in 16:13–28, where the conflict between setting one's mind on "divine things" and setting it on "human things" comes to sharpest focus. On the demand for a "sign from heaven" itself and Jesus' response, see on 12:38.

16:4 Then he left: At the conclusion of this interchange, Jesus leaves the Pharisees and Sadducees. This represents Jesus' breaking off communication with the Jewish leadership (the verb used here sometimes means "abandon," "leave behind," elsewhere in Matthew only in 4:13; 19:5; 21:17). He will not see them again until the fateful and final confrontation that begins in Judea (19:3; 22:23).

16:5–12 See on Mark 8:14–21. Matthew has rewritten, streamlined, and relocated this Markan scene, which in Mark occurred in the boat during the crossing, so that it represents the interweaving of the two themes from the preceding two scenes: the feeding scene of 15:32–38, at which the disciples were last present, and the confrontation between Jesus and the Pharisees and Sadducees of 16:1–4, with the disciples absent. As Jesus has broken off communication with the Jewish leaders in the preceding scene, here he experiences a temporary breakdown of communication with his own disciples. The disciples are concerned with bread, v. 5. Jesus is concerned with warning the disciples against the teaching of the Pharisees and Sadducees, v. 6. The common denominator is "yeast," which the disciples understand in terms of their own interest in literal bread, v. 8. With divine insight (see 12:25; 26:9–10) Jesus is aware of their misunderstanding, which is not merely at the intellectual level but is a matter of "little faith." Jesus shifts from his own concern with the yeast/teaching of the Pharisees and Sadducees to deal with their concern. The next section toward which this scene is building will designate this as setting their minds on human things rather than divine things (16:23). By worrying about literal bread, they are threatening to abandon Jesus' teaching in the Sermon on the Mount (6:25–34) and join ranks with the Pharisees, who are on the side of the opposing kingdom and are united with Satan in "testing" Jesus—precisely as Peter is about to be accused of doing in the next section (16:23 again!). Jesus calls them to remember the extravagant divine provision manifest in the feedings of the five thousand and the four thousand. They get the point. Again in contrast to Mark (7:21), the disciples' misunderstanding was only a temporary aberration.

16:12 Then they understood: This verse is Matthew's editorial addition to his Markan source, where the disciples continue to misunderstand. In Matthew, the whole unit has been a teaching session, and a successful one, conducted by the master teacher and resulting in understanding disciples (see on 13:10).

16:13–28
The Disciples' Confession and the New Community

In this scene Peter declares the confession fundamental to the church's faith; Jesus pronounces Peter to be the foundation on which he will build his new community and sets forth the cost and meaning of adhering to this confession. Precisely in this section, 13:53–18:35, dealing with the formation of the church, Peter assumes a more prominent role, especially in the material added to the Markan narrative at 15:15; 16:17–19; 17:24–27; 18:21.

16:13–20 Jesus as Son of God: Peter as Rock
(See also at Mark 8:27–30; Luke 9:18–21)

This is the focal scene of the extended narrative unit 13:53–17:27. In the midst of what Matthew perceives as a blind and recalcitrant Israel, Jesus forms a new community of those who do perceive and confess his true identity.

16:13 Who do people say that the Son of Man is? On Son of Man, see on Mark 2:10. Matthew's addition to Mark 8:29 changes the nature of the question, incorporating Jesus' and the disciples own christological confession into the question itself. In the story line of Mark, no human being has as yet recognized and confessed Jesus' identity as the Messiah. In Matthew, Jesus' true identity is not new to the disciples, who have heard Jesus refer to himself in christological terms before, have understood him, and have already worshiped him as Son of God (14:33). All this means that the scene here pictured is not the same kind of christological breakthrough as it is in Mark, where no human being has correctly identified Jesus until Peter's confession of Mark 8:29. The Matthean emphasis is not on the identity of Jesus but on the formation of the church: it is the confession of faith in Jesus as messianic representative of God's kingdom that separates the new community Jesus is forming from those who oppose and reject it.

16:17–19 Jesus answered him: Matthew's most important editorial modification in this pericope is the addition of vv. 17–19 to Jesus' response to Peter. The origin of these words continues to be disputed, but the majority of scholars would attribute them to pre-Matthean tradition or to Matthew himself, rather than tracing them back to the historical Jesus.

16:17 Blessed are you, Simon son of Jonah: All the disciples have already received a similar pronouncement of blessing in 13:16–17, just as all have already confessed Jesus as Son of God in 14:33. Yet Jesus' singular blessing of Peter is significant, for in Matthew Peter not only represents all the disciples as their spokesperson and, with all his strengths and weaknesses, stands for the typical Christian; he also plays

a unique and unrepeatable role in the founding of the new community. **Flesh and blood has not revealed this to you:** Peter is not blessed because of a personal attainment or insight he has achieved. Knowledge of Jesus' saving role comes by divine revelation, as gift, not attainment. In this, Peter is representative of Christian faith generally (see on Matt. 11:25–27; 1 Cor. 12:3). The word for "revealed" connotes not some personal, individual spiritual experience but the divine disclosure of the eschatological secret.

16:18 You are Peter, and on this rock: Peter is the foundation rock on which Jesus builds the new community. On Peter's name, see introduction to 1 Peter. The wordplay of the passage means: "You are 'Rock,' and on this rock I will build my church." Peter is here pictured as the foundation of the church.

One of the achievements of contemporary ecumenical scholarship is that Protestant and Roman Catholic interpreters generally agree on the original meaning of the text: Jesus builds the church on Peter as the foundation (contrary to previous Protestant views), rather than on Peter's confession or Peter's faith, and the office of Peter was unique and unrepeatable (contrary to previous Roman Catholic views). The text pictures Peter as playing a unique and unrepeatable role in the foundation of the church. Later, Roman Catholic, Eastern Orthodox, and Protestant theologians all developed this meaning in their own ways, but there is now a consensus as to the original meaning. For contemporary Christian life, this means that the text need not have the polemical edge it has developed in the older Roman Catholic/Protestant/Greek Orthodox debates but can be heard again as the promise of Christ to build his church on the likes of Peter despite the forces of death arrayed against it. The church can take heart from this promise.

Although Peter is the foundation, Jesus is the builder of the church. Thus Peter does not compete with Jesus. Jesus himself is here portrayed as the one who constructs the new community, pictured as a building. This is part of Matthew's theology of the continuing active presence of Christ in the church (see on 1:23). The underlying image is that of the eschatological temple composed of the true people of God, common not only in early Christianity but also already at Qumran (see John 2:19–21; 1 Cor. 3:16–17; 2 Cor. 6:16; Eph. 2:21; 1 Pet. 2:4–5; Rev. 3:12; 4QpPs37 3:13–16) and sometimes related to a foundation stone and/or one who is a *pillar* or *foundation* (see Gal. 2:9 for "pillar" as a name for Peter, and Isa. 28:14–22). As the Son of David, Jesus builds the eschatological temple that the first David did not build. Matthew is able to picture the church built on Peter the rock without detriment to his later picture of the Christ being the chief cornerstone of the eschatological temple, the Christian community (21:33–43; see 1 Cor. 3:10–11, where the apostles are the builders and Christ is the only foundation).

16:18 My church: Over against "their synagogues" the Matthean Jesus speaks of "my church" (4:23; 9:35; 10:17; 12:9; 13:54). The word "church" is found only here and 18:17 in the Gospels. The word etymologically means "called out" and was used in Hellenistic Greek for the local political assembly (as in, e.g., Acts 19:32, 39, 40). Matthew means by "church" the renewed people of God constituted by the disciples of Jesus, the heir and continuation of empirical Israel that has forfeited its standing and role (21:43). This does not mean Matthew considered the church a replacement for Israel, but a special community of the new covenant within or alongside empirical Israel. **The gates of Hades** is a biblical expression (Isa. 38:10) that can mean the same as the "gates of death" (Job 38:17; Pss. 9:13; 107:18), i.e., the realm of the dead, not the place of punishment. The meaning is that the realm of the dead, which no human being can conquer, is nevertheless not stronger than the church founded on the Rock, and the church will always endure to the end of history, because accompanied by its Lord (28:20). Thus this text declares minimally that the church will never die. But "gates of Hades" may also refer to the portals of the underworld from which the powers of Satan emerge to attack the church, especially in the eschatological times (see the eschatological testing of Matt. 6:13 and 26:41 and the dramatic imagery of Rev. 9:1–11). Then the meaning would be that the church is undergoing attack by the powers of evil, but will never be vanquished, because founded on the Rock.

16:19 I will give you the keys of the kingdom of heaven: Matthew's synonym for "kingdom of God" (see on 3:2; Luke 4:43), "kingdom of heaven" is represented by authoritative teaching that lets heaven's power rule in earthly things (over against the power emanating from the gates of Hades). As Jesus has authority to teach (5:21–48; 7:29), so Peter as Jesus' representative continues to teach with Jesus' authority. The image of Peter with the keys is

not that of the doorkeeper to heaven of popular piety and cartoons. As the next image makes clear, Peter's function is not that of entrance monitor, deciding in the afterlife who is admitted and who is denied entrance to the heaven; Peter's role as holder of the keys is now, on earth, as chief teacher of the church. The language of **binding and loosing** is rabbinic terminology for authoritative teaching, for having the authority to interpret the Torah and apply it to particular cases, declaring what is permitted and what is not permitted. Jesus, who has taught with authority (7:29) and has given his authority to his disciples (10:1, 8), here gives the primary disciple the authority to teach in his name, i.e., to make authoritative decisions pertaining to Christian life as he applies the teaching of Jesus to concrete situations in the life of the church. In 18:18, similar authority is given to the church as a whole, and the way the last three antitheses are presented in 5:33–48 (see discussion there) shows such application of Jesus' teaching is the task of the whole community of disciples. Matthew portrays Peter as having a special responsibility as chief teacher as well as representative and model.

16:21–23 Jesus as Suffering Son of Man; Peter as Stumbling Stone
(See also at Mark 8:31–33; Luke 9:22)

On the passion predictions, see on Mark 8:31. Jesus' passion and the disciples' following are already presupposed and taught in Matthew (see 10:38), so this is not a dramatic new revelation (as in Mark) but now relates the confessional life of the disciples to the formation of the new community.

Matthew does not elaborate a reason for Jesus' death, only that it is necessarily a part of God's divine plan (see on 20:28). The suffering of the Son of Man is necessary ("must" NRSV; "destined" NIV). In Matthew this does not mean "fate" in the Greek sense but God's will as revealed in Scripture.

16:23 Get behind me, Satan: Jesus' counter-response (Mark's "rebuke" is omitted) is to call Peter to renewed and deeper discipleship and echoes the words of 4:19, the discipleship formula "behind me" being used in both cases. "Behind me" is not mere location but the posture of the disciple. Jesus is going to the cross; the disciple is to follow. But there is also an echo of the address to Satan in 4:10, the same Greek word for "go" being used in each place. The testing that Jesus had met and overcome in his initial encounter with Satan was not once for all; it reappears in the sincere and prayerful remonstrance of the disciple. Here Jesus' opponent is none other than the rock on which he will build the new community. Despite his revelation from God (16:17), Peter continues to think as good human beings are accustomed to think: reasonably, egocentrically, and in terms of human friendship and "success." This pericope does not contrast the commitment of Jesus with the failure of Peter, or even the blessed Peter of the preceding pericope with the Peter who becomes the spokesperson for Satan; rather, it contrasts the way of God in this world, which comes by a revelation of Jesus Christ, and the ordinary way of human beings thinking out of their own resources.

16:24–28 *The Cost and Promise of Discipleship*
(See also at Mark 8:34–9:1; Luke 9:23–27)

16:24 Jesus told his disciples: Matthew omits the crowds introduced by Mark at this point, making the teaching exclusively addressed to the disciples, in continuity with the preceding dialogue. Restricting the address to the disciples has the effect of focusing the instruction on the meaning of discipleship to those who are already within the community, those who have like Peter made the Christian confession but are still thinking according to human standards rather than the divine revelation (see v. 23b). These words are not an invitation to discipleship for outsiders but reflection on the meaning of discipleship for those who have already responded to the call of Christ. The NRSV **If any want to become my followers** is thus misleading. There is no word for "become" (see NIV, "if anyone would come after me," which is better at this point).

16:28 The Son of Man coming in his kingdom: On "Son of Man," see at Mark 2:10. In order to conclude this dialogue with Jesus' self-declaration as Son of Man, Matthew reformulates the saying of Mark 9:1 about the coming of the kingdom of God into a Son of Man saying. This brings Jesus' preaching of the coming kingdom of God and his identity as Son of Man into very close relationship. The nearness of the coming kingdom/Parousia of the Son of Man here functions as encouragement to follow the path of Jesus.

17:1–13
The Transfiguration
(See also at Mark 9:2–13; Luke 9:28–36)

By his editorial changes to his Markan source, Matthew has made all of vv. 1–13 an instructional

session for the disciples. Just as the preceding scene (16:13–28) juxtaposes the divine transcendence of Peter's confession of Jesus as Son of God based on a revelation from heaven (16:17) with Jesus' own teaching about the suffering Son of Man, so also in this scene the confession of the heavenly voice is juxtaposed with Jesus' self-confession as suffering Son of Man. It is therefore important to keep vv. 9–13 with 1–8, just as it is important not to separate 16:21–23 from 16:13–20.

17:2 His face shone: Matthew specifically adds this feature, another explicit allusion to Moses (see Moses in Exod. 34:29–35; Rev. 1:16; 2 Cor. 3:18).

17:3 Moses and Elijah, talking with him: By portraying Moses, Elijah, and Jesus as talking together in a scene of transcendent glory, Matthew confirms his view that Jesus is in continuity with and the fulfillment of God's work as represented by the Old Testament.

17:4 Lord, it is good for us to be here: As in the preceding scene, 16:13–20, Peter responds to the revelation, but his lack of understanding is somewhat alleviated (Mark 9:6 is omitted: "For he did not know what to say . . ."), and he speaks as a believer (Matthew's "Lord" for Mark's "rabbi"). Peter speaks more respectfully than in Mark ("if you wish" added to Mark) but still without complete insight, like the people in general still placing Jesus in the category of the prophets (17:4=16:14).

17:5 This is my Son . . . listen to him: Although three transcendent figures are present, the heavenly voice charges the disciples to hear *Jesus.* As in the Shema (Deut. 6:4), "hear" carries its Old Testament connotation of "obey" and is the same command given with regard to the "prophet like Moses" that God would send (Deut. 18:15; see on 13:57). The disciples fall on their faces in fearful response to the theophany, as in Exod. 34:30; Dan. 10:9; and Hab. 3:2 LXX.

The transfiguration story recalls the baptism of Jesus and the voice from heaven that designates him both (powerful) Son of God and (weak) Suffering Servant (see on 3:17). This commission is reconfirmed as Jesus begins to instruct his disciples on the meaning and cost of discipleship. It is thus important that the scene follows the first passion prediction, *confirming* from heaven what had been *questioned* by Peter, whose mind was "not on divine things but on human things" (16:23). The weak, crucified one (2 Cor. 13:4) is also the divine glorious one, and vice versa.

The transfiguration story recalls and confirms Peter's confession (16:16). Though Peter was still thinking in human categories despite the revelation he had received, he had understood the identity of Jesus, and this confession is confirmed by the heavenly voice.

17:14–20
Discipleship and Faith That Moves Mountains
(See also at Mark 9:14–29; Luke 9:37–43)

The story is closely attached to the preceding, to which it forms something of a counterpoint. This is rightly captured by Raphael's painting in the Vatican Museum, which contrasts the glory of the transfigured Christ on the mountain and the misery of the human condition below to which he returns to minister. His disciples, who have been commissioned with Jesus' power and authority, have been left in the mundane world below and are frustrated by their failure. But Jesus is with them nevertheless and has power to heal despite their failure (see on 14:22–33). The primary focus of this pericope is this relationship of the power of Christ and the disciples' ministry in the world below, on the mountain bottom experiences of service and failure rather than the mountaintop experiences of spiritual exhilaration.

17:17 You faithless and perverse generation: Matthew has added "perverse" to his characteristic "generation" (see Deut. 32:5), which has the effect of further distancing him from "this generation" (see 22:16; 12:41–42; 23:36; 24:34). As the Christ, the Son of God, and suffering, dying, rising, and coming Son of Man, he is now forming the new community over against the "perverse generation" of empirical Israel that rejects him. The struggle portrayed in this scene is whether the disciples, who have identified him and made the correct confession, will become the authentic community Jesus seeks to build or will regress into "this generation." Jesus has performed exorcisms and healings and has given them authority and power to continue his ministry. They cannot do it with their own power but only because Jesus is "with them," a Matthean theme called up by Jesus' sigh **How much longer must I put up with you**? Jesus' healing/exorcism is another instance of the kingdom represented by Jesus triumphing over the kingdom of Satan (see on 12:22–37). Jesus is the one who accompanies his church through history, who builds the church, and whose power continues in it. The disciples should have been able to heal and do this work

in the power of Jesus, as both they and Jesus recognize, but could not.

17:19 Why could we not cast it out? This is the point to which Matthew has (re)built the entire story. Matthew suppresses the Markan ending, imports a floating saying from a different context in Q (see Luke 17:6), and rewrites it as the concluding pronouncement of this story. **Because of your little faith:** The saying's importance to Matthew is seen in his using it again in 21:21 (see 6:30; 8:36; 14:31; 16:8).

17:20 You will say to this mountain: The proverbial saying about moving mountains is more than a rhetorical flourish on which to end. Matthew introduces it with a solemn *amen* saying (see on 5:18). Like the parables, the saying resists reduction to pedestrian logic. One cannot infer from it the guilt-inducing conclusion that when hoped-for miracles fail the problem must be our lack of faith, and that if we had "enough" faith we would be able to avert all tragedies and heal all afflictions. We cannot infer from it that faith is itself a power that accomplishes miracles, for God is the one who acts, not a commodity called "faith." Like the story in 8:5–13, this is not a saying about the power of faith but about the power of God, even if God language is not used in either place (see also on 21:18–22). This mind-blowing and disruptive picture pushes at us the gnawing reminder that as disciples we are agents of the church in which Christ himself is "with us," which means God with us (1:23; 28:20) and that with God nothing is impossible (see on 19:26), a guard against fitting God into our ideas of what is possible, and coming to terms too quickly with "the way things are."

17:22–23
The Second Passion Prediction
(See also at Mark 9:30–32; Luke 9:43–45)

On the passion predictions themselves, see on Mark 8:31. The disciples' response is not failure to understand as in Mark (9:32 is omitted) but sorrow—because they do understand. They have thus made progress since their initial protests in 16:21. The transfiguration and the period of instruction have had some effect. Their sorrow corresponds to their response at the Last Supper (26:22) when they learn of their own involvement in Jesus' being handed over, and to Jesus' own sorrow in Gethsemane *prior* to his prayer and resolution of his commitment to God (26:37–38). The disciples have a way to go, but they are becoming the church Christ has promised to build out of such as they (16:18–20).

17:24–27
Payment of the Temple Tax

This pericope comes at the conclusion of the extended section in which Jesus gathers the new community after his rejection by the leaders of Israel (13:53–17:27). In this section Peter has figured prominently, having become the spokesperson for the new community as well as the representative figure in developing new teachings for its life (see on 16:17–19). As a transition to the discourse on how community members are to live in relationship to each other (namely, in caring consideration for the well-being of one's brothers and sisters within the community), this pericope manifests the same concern with regard to outsiders: living in freedom as children of God, but concerned not to place a stumbling block in the way of others. As the Son of Man gives his life for others (17:22–23; see 20:28), so the community lives its life aware of its freedom but so concerned with the welfare of others that it is willing to sacrifice its freedom for their sake.

17:24 Does your teacher pay the temple tax?: As reported in Neh. 10:32–33, leading elements of the Jewish population took upon themselves a yearly obligation of one-third of a shekel for support of the temple cultus. The Pharisees later considered every male Jew throughout the world to be liable for a half-shekel and related it to Exod. 30:11–16. Strangely enough, Sadducees argued that the annual payment should be a voluntary gift rather than an imposed tax, from which priests were exempt. Diaspora Jews also (voluntarily) contributed their offering to the temple. The Qumran community understood the requirement in terms of Exod. 30:11–16 as a one-time-only contribution. Thus the question was a live issue in the spectrum of pre-70 Judaism concerning which Jesus might have been asked and to which he may have responded.

Outsiders approach Peter with a question about Jesus' (and the disciples') practice. A problem of Matthew's own time is dealt with by telling a story in which Jesus confirms the Matthean answer. The facts that Jesus is not asked directly and that Peter responds for Jesus suggest that the question presupposes a post-Easter setting where the practice of the disciples is the disputed point. As promised in 16:18–19, Peter speaks in Jesus' behalf, and Jesus confirms his answer as his own.

17:25–26 What do you think, Simon?: Jesus miraculously knows what has preceded (as 9:4; 12:25; 26:10, 25), and confirms Peter's response with a probing analogy. As earthly kings do not tax their own children, but others, so those who are children of God (literally "sons," as 5:9, 45—Matthew's term for Christian believers) are free from the temple tax. Thus Jewish Christians are in principle free from supporting the temple.

17:27 So that we do not give offense: In the post-Easter situation, the saying becomes the occasion for Christian teaching on the proper use of freedom. In Matthew's time, the temple no longer existed, but the Roman government had imposed a tax of two drachmas on all Jews for support of the temple to Jupiter in Rome, corresponding to the previous temple tax (Josephus, *War* 7.218–19). Though there was no legal choice for Jewish Christians in Matthew's church, the issue of whether to pay such a tax may have been a matter of conscience. In this situation Matthew could, to his own advantage, separate his community from any identification with Judaism. That he did not take this view indicates his community is not yet totally separated from Judaism and that, hostile as he is to the Jewish leadership, Matthew has a conciliatory attitude to the Jewish community as a whole. In this setting, Matthew offers this story as a Christian lesson on the proper use of freedom, analogous to Paul's instructions in 1 Cor. 8–9 and Luke's picture of Paul in Acts 21:17–26. Christians are to go the second mile (5:41!) in their efforts to avoid placing a stumbling block before outsiders (and insiders with "weak" consciences, as in Rom. 14).

Peter is once again representative speaker for both Jesus (to the opponents) and the disciples (to Jesus and the reader). Instead of being himself a stumbling block (16:13), he is now charged with the pastoral concern not to exercise his own freedom in a way that places stumbling blocks in the way of others (17:27).

Taken literally, the story has problems, not only of physics but of ethics, and conflicts with other pictures of Jesus who does not use his miraculous power for his own benefit (4:3–11, which considers such temptations demonic, and see 26:36–42, 51–54). See excursus at 8:1, "Interpreting the Miracle Stories."

18:1–35
LIFE TOGETHER IN THE NEW
FAITH COMMUNITY

This is the fourth of Matthew's major discourses that form part of the basic structure of his Gospel (see introduction to Matthew, "Structure and Outline"). This discourse focuses on how disciples relate to each other as they share their common life within the Christian community. The sayings have a different context in Mark and still another in Luke, illustrating again that each Gospel writer has arranged traditional materials to make his own theological point.

18:1–5
"Big People" and "Little People"
(See also at Mark 9:33–37; Luke 9:6–48)

There is no dispute about greatness, as in the Mark 9:33 source, only a question from the disciples about the kingdom. By inserting "kingdom" language into the opening question, Matthew sets the whole discourse into the framework of the conflict of kingdoms (see on 12:32–37). The concluding parable about a *king* brings out this contrast (see on 18:23).

18:2–3 Unless you change and become like children: Matthew rewrites Mark 9:35–36 by having Jesus make the child an object lesson of the saying Matthew has rewritten (or, more likely, has an older form of) from Mark 10:15. Introduced with the solemn prophetic *amen* (see on 5:18), Jesus first addresses their presupposition. They had supposed they were in the kingdom, and only asked about their relative rank. Jesus' radical prophetic reply challenges their assumption: to get in, one must be converted, which means become like the little child. This is the Synoptics' functional equivalent of John 3:3, 5, with the same gift and demand: following Jesus is not adding on one more worthy cause but starting all over (see 19:16–30).

18:4 Whoever becomes humble like this child: To become like a little child is to humble oneself, giving up all pretensions of self-importance, independence, and self-reliance and turning in trust to the heavenly Father (6:8, 32). The story is thus not a call to imitate the (presumed) character traits of children but to accept a radically different understanding of *status*. The first rule for life together in the new community formed by Jesus is to abandon the quest for status and accept one's place as already given in the family of God.

18:5 Whoever welcomes one such child: A concrete illustration of the meaning of humility called for in v. 4. To receive a child is to humble oneself genuinely, for the vulnerable, dependent child can do nothing to further one's selfish ambitions, and receiving him or her can have no ulterior motives, no hidden agendas. One who receives a child has been converted to the ethos of the kingdom represented by Jesus and is no longer concerned about being "greatest." In receiving a child one finds that, in the child, Christ himself is received (see on 1:23).

18:6–10
Against Disdaining "Little People"
(See also at Mark 9:42–50; Luke 17:1–2; 14:34–35)

The subject now shifts (but only slightly) from those who are immature in years, i.e., children, to members of the Christian community who are immature in faith. They are still "little people" without influence in the community, so that, like the children in the preceding pericope, they cannot advance one's religious career toward becoming greatest in the kingdom. What should the mature Christian's attitude be toward those "babes in Christ" (see 1 Cor. 3:1–3)?

18:6–7 A stumbling block before one of these little ones: Far from being dispensable, the "little people" in the Matthean community are to be shown the greatest consideration, and that without condescension. One must live one's own life of discipleship in such a way that no stumbling block is placed in the way of the weaker members of the community. **Great millstone:** literally, "donkey millstone," the upper millstone of a large mill where the upper stone is pulled by a donkey, rather than the small domestic mill. The expression is proverbial (see Rev. 18:21), but its application to the fate of one who places a stumbling block in the path of another's life of discipleship is unique with Jesus.

18:7 Occasions for stumbling are bound to come: Matthew elaborates the picture by inserting his modification of a Q saying (see Luke 17:1–2) on the necessity of such stumbling blocks. Though there is no avoiding living in a world where such things happen, the more mature members cannot use this as an excuse for their own lack of care for the little people of the community.

18:8–9 Your hand or your foot: In 5:29–30 the most stringent measures are called for in order to prevent one's sex drive from dominating one's life and making one into a predator against others. Here the will to power (wanting to be "great" in the community, me-first ambition at the expense of others) threatens to dominate one's existence, becoming a threat not only to oneself but to the faith of others and the life of the community.

18:10 In heaven their angels: NIV's **look down on** is better than NRSV's **despise**, which might be misunderstood as "dislike, hate." The "big people" in the community are not tempted to hate the "little people," but to disdain them, to regard them as insignificant (see Rom. 14:1–15:13). Though church leaders might be tempted to disdain them, the most exalted of the angels have been assigned to look after them. Matthew assumes that the Son of Man who accompanies his church through history has attendant angels who perform his ministry (13:39, 41; 16:27; 24:31; 25:31; 26:53). They not only attended the Messiah (4:6, 11) but attend the messianic people. Heaven has assigned only the most exalted angels, those that behold God's face, as helpers to the weaker members of the community. The point is clear: heaven does not give up on the marginal, lapsed, or strayed, and what heaven values so dearly cannot be disdained by the "big people" in the church on earth.

18:12–14
Concluding Parable: Concern for Straying Members
(See also at Luke 15:3–7)

Rather than disdaining the "little people," the alternative attitude which the "big people" in the community could take toward the others is to value them and seek them out when they go astray. As vv. 6–10 was directed to how the mature Christians are to live with the spiritual welfare of others in view, the parable that concludes this section is directed to actively seeking those members of the community who have gotten off the track despite the community's concern not to put obstructions in their way.

18:12 What do you think?: On interpreting parables, see on Mark 4:1. **If a shepherd has a hundred sheep:** During Israel's nomadic past, there had developed the image of Israel as the flock of God, the good shepherd (Pss. 23:1; 68:7; 100:3; Isa. 40:10; 49:9; Jer. 23:3; 31:10; 50:19; Ezek. 34:1–31; Mic. 4:6–8; 7:14). Jesus' original parable had portrayed a very dubious and risky decision, to leave the ninety-nine sheep in the desert (Luke) or on the mountains (Matthew) while going in search of the one lost sheep. Matthew focuses all Jesus' concern on the plight of the lost sheep, which has strayed and needs to be restored. This is the point Matthew intends for his readers, who are too inclined to disdain the "little people" of the community who cannot keep up.

In Matthew, the identity of the shepherd is not disclosed. The reader will think not only

of God (see references above), but also of Jesus who in Matthew represents the continuing presence of God with the church during its mission (see on 1:23; Jesus is the shepherd who seeks the lost in 9:36; 15:24; 26:31). Yet Jesus has conferred his authority and ministry on his disciples (see on 10:1–5a). The God who values the straying and lapsed and seeks them out is embodied in his Son, the Messiah, and the continuing ministry of the Son is embodied in his disciples, the church. In Matthew's view, the church's pastoral care ("pastor" = "shepherd") for its marginal and straying "little people" represents the continuing shepherding presence of God himself made real in Jesus, God-with-us.

18:15–20
Church Discipline and the Presence of Christ
(See also at Luke 17:3–4)

As vv. 6–14 above are concerned with marginal church members who are in danger of stumbling in their Christian life or have already wandered from the flock, so vv. 15–20 are concerned with members who are guilty of serious sin and remain unrepentantly and disruptively as participants in the congregational life. These are thus not general rules for personal relations but, like the preceding, are church rules for preserving and reconciling a straying member of the community, while preserving the community's integrity as the holy covenant people of God.

Matthew here offers a solution to something modern Western readers scarcely perceive as a problem, since we are inclined to see our sin as a matter between ourselves and God or, at most, between ourselves and the person who has wronged us. That it is a matter of the Christian congregation to which we belong, and may damage its life, comes as a surprise to both us and those who have wronged us, if they are as individualistic as we are. Whatever we think of the solution Matthew offers, we might first ponder the nature of the Christian life it presupposes. For Matthew, to be Christian is to be bound together in community; to pray is to say, "*Our* Father," even in the privacy of our own room (6:5–13).

18:15 Member of the church: Literally "brother," as in the NIV, in the inclusive sense of "member of the family of God" (see 12:46–50). **When the two of you are alone:** Although the sin is a matter of community concern, the private conversation between offended and offender is to avoid embarrassment, as with almsgiving in 6:3. Commitment to the priority of life together in community does not mean lack of sensitivity to the feelings of individuals but precisely the opposite: it is only by such sensitivity and care that people can live together in the new family of God gathered by Jesus.

18:16 Take one or two others: If the one-to-one encounter leaves the offending party unrepentant, the offended member attempts to resolve the problem by taking one or two fellow members of the congregation as "witnesses" (see Deut. 19:15), i.e., to protect from misrepresentation both the alleged offender and the one who claims to have been offended (see Lev. 19:17–18; Deut. 19:15; 1 Cor. 5:1–4, 11–13; Gal. 6:1; 2 Thess. 3:14–15).

18:17 Tell it to the church: "Church" here refers to the local congregation, unlike 16:17, where it is the universal body of believers. Cases of recalcitrant members who resist all private efforts to bring them to repentance are brought before the congregation and, if they do not heed the congregation's entreaty, are expelled (see 1 Cor. 5:1–4, 11–13; 2 Thess. 3:14–15).

Let such a one be to you as a Gentile and a tax collector: The language used seems strangely harsh, since Jesus (and his community) is accused of befriending tax collectors and sinners, as well as Gentiles (9:11; 11:19). The practice of excommunication also seems strange, from the perspective expressed in 7:1–5 and 13:37–43. These tensions may be due to the incorporation of conflicting traditions in the history of the community's development, and/or to applying them to different cases. It is clear, however, that if Matthew's church does not already have a procedure for disciplining dangerously errant members, one is here provided, spoken in the name of Jesus. While this procedure involves the judgment of the congregation, it is not clear whether this presupposes the presence of church leaders through whom the congregation acts, or whether the assembly functions as a committee of the whole (first-century congregations were not large). The goal is not only to maintain the holiness of the insiders but to bring straying members to an awareness of their sins, repentance, and eventual restoration.

18:18–20 Whatever you bind on earth will be bound in heaven: The authority given Peter to make legal decisions for the church as a whole is here given the congregation in matters of its own discipline. In v. 20 an originally independent saying assuring the church of the continuing presence of Christ during the time

of its mission—a major theme of Matthean theology, see on 1:23; 28:20—is here applied to the particular case of the church making its disciplinary decisions.

18:21–22
"Forgiveness" without Grace
(See also at Luke 17:4)

18:21 How often should I forgive?: Peter's proposal to forgive **seven times** sounds extravagantly generous, especially since there is no mention of repentance by the offending party (contrast Luke 17:4). It reverses the sevenfold pronouncement of vengeance in Gen. 4:15. Jesus' response is far beyond Peter's proposal, and not only in greatly extending the quantity. The Greek expression can be legitimately understood as "seventy-seven times" (as in Gen. 4:24, again a reversal of Lamech's pronouncement of vengeance) or "four hundred ninety times" (as in the ancient translations of the New Testament). The difference between Peter's proposal and Jesus' pronouncement, however, is not a matter of math or linguistics but of the nature of forgiveness. Whoever *counts* has not forgiven at all but is only biding his or her time (1 Cor. 13:5). The kind of forgiveness called for is beyond all calculation, as the following story communicates.

18:23–35
Concluding Parable: Grace beyond Imagining

As in interpreting all the parables (see on Mark 4:1), the reader must distinguish between the original potent stories told by Jesus as a means of proclaiming the kingdom of God, and Matthew's later interpretations applying them to life in the church. Here, Matthew's additions (vv. [34 and] 35) transform the parable into a vivid lesson on forgiveness. **The kingdom of heaven may be compared:** On "kingdom of heaven," see on 3:2; Luke 4:43. For Jesus, the story was about a Gentile king and his servant, only indirectly pointing to God. Matthew's allegorizing additions make the story from the beginning transparent to the relation between God and Christians. For Jesus, the king is a Gentile tyrant; for Matthew, the king already represents God, and "debt" represents sin (see 6:12–15).

18:23 Settle accounts with his slaves: The servant is not a household slave but a subordinate official (the NIV "servants" is here better than the NRSV). The debt was incurred through mismanagement of the king's resources and/or contracting to raise taxes from subject nations, not by personal expenditures.

18:24 Owed him ten thousand talents: A talent is the largest monetary unit, equal to the wages of a manual laborer for fifteen years. "Ten thousand" is the largest possible numerical unit. The combination is thus the largest figure that can be given. The annual tax income for all of Herod the Great's territories was nine hundred talents per year. Ten thousand talents would exceed the taxes for all of Syria, Phoenicia, Judea, and Samaria. The amount is intended to be fantastic, beyond all calculation.

18:25 He could not pay: The debt is unpayable. Casting the servant into prison will be punitive, i.e., will "pay him back" for his utter mismanagement, but it is utterly beyond the realm of possibility that the servant can repay his debt no matter how much time is given. The servant's situation is hopeless. He asks for mercy, and contrary to all expectation, the king responds with compassion.

18:28 Came upon one of his fellow slaves: The debt of the fellow servant is microscopic compared to what the first servant had been forgiven (1/600,000, if one attempted to be literal, but the figures are intended to represent an infinite contrast). Yet it is not an insignificant amount, representing a hundred days' wages for an ordinary laborer (see 20:2). When the first servant violently insists on repayment, it is not a trifling sum. The outrageous contrast between the way the first servant was treated by the king and the way he treats his fellow servant is not only a contrast of amount owed. In the first scene, there was no reasonable way to repay such a debt; one could only be condemned or receive mercy. The parallel and contrast between the two scenes is that one is "reasonable" (the second) and one is not (the first). To interpret the first in terms of the second is a mistake; the whole thrust of the parable is to bring the second scene into line with the first. This does not happen. The servant does not respond to his fellow servant as he has been treated by the king.

18:32 His lord summoned him: Again, the unthinkable happens. The king takes back his forgiveness, and the servant is condemned to eternal torment. Some scholars think Jesus' original parable ended with the question of 18:33 (see the ending of Jonah, 4:11), others that v. 34 was the original conclusion. In any case, Matthew has added v. 35 to make the point in the parable's present context unmistakably clear.

Matthew has clearly allegorized the parable, so that king=God, debt=sin, first servant=one who is forgiven an enormous debt of sin by God, second servant=one who has committed an "ordinary" sin against a fellow human being or fellow Christian. When the Christian does not forgive as he or she has been forgiven, God's own forgiveness is then invalidated. The parable thus becomes a vivid illustration of a point that Matthew states elsewhere (6:14–15). In the Matthean story, the problem remains that the king (= "God") went back on his forgiveness. It is better to let the story remain unallegorized, so that it is an earthly king who reneges on his original gracious forgiveness, and let it illustrate, in an analogous way, the awfulness of failing to forgive as God forgives.

19:1–22:46
CONFLICT AND ULTIMATE POLARIZATION

The first subsection continues the theme of the Christian community as the true family of God. By expansions and artful modifications of his source, Matthew has adjusted the Markan narrative so that the whole transitional section between Galilee and Jerusalem (19:1–20:34) becomes instruction to the disciples on the radically different kind of life called for by life together in the Christian community.

19:1–20:34
Instructing the Disciples En Route to the Passion

19:1–12 *Divorce, Remarriage, and Celibacy in the New Community*
(See also at Mark 10:1–12; Luke 16:18)

19:1 When Jesus had finished saying these things: This is Matthew's standard concluding formula to the five major speeches (introduction to Matthew, "Structure and Outline," and on 7:28), combined with the transitional statement in Mark 10:1.

19:3 For any cause?: Matthew alters Mark's question on the legality of divorce as such to the grounds for a legitimate divorce. At one level, this casts the debate as part of the continuing rabbinic argument between the conservative Shammaites and the more liberal Hillelites (see on 5:31–32).

19:4–9 Have you not read?: Matthew has rearranged Mark 10:3–12 so that Jesus' answer corresponds to the pattern of ethical reflection developed in the antitheses (see 5:21–48, esp. 5:31–32). Whereas in Mark Jesus speaks of divorce as a command and the Pharisees speak of it as a concession (Mark 10:3–4), in Matthew these terms are reversed (19:7–8).

And whereas in Mark Jesus begins with the concession and proceeds to the original will of God in creation, the Matthean Jesus begins with the absolute will of God and proceeds to the situational application (see on 5:21–48).

19:9 Whoever divorces his wife: Matthew omits Mark 10:12, reflecting the Gentile provision for a woman's initiating a divorce as not applicable from his Jewish perspective. As in 5:32 (which see for a full discussion), Matthew builds an exception clause into Jesus' absolute prohibition of divorce, thus in principle making the teaching of Jesus a situational application of the absolute ideal will of God rather than a legalistic code.

19:10–12 Not everyone can accept this teaching: This addition to Mark seems to be entirely Matthean composition, part of his effort to have Jesus speak to the new situation of the Matthean church, which not only still has strong Jewish roots and perspectives but also includes Gentiles with a completely different background and viewpoint. The disciples' response voices the objection of new Gentile members in the Christian community to the seemingly rigid marital ethic advocated by the Matthean Christians and serves to introduce the question of whether Christians should get married at all.

Most interpreters have understood **this teaching** to mean that while the pagan practice of literal castration as a religious practice is rejected (see Deut. 23:1; Lev. 22:24), those who **have made themselves eunuchs for the sake of the kingdom of heaven** refers to members of the community who choose to remain celibate in order to commit themselves fully to Christian work. While marriage and family life were valued by Jesus and the Matthean church as a gift from God and were the normal life of the disciple, exceptional people such as prophets and missionaries sometimes remained unmarried as a mark of their special calling. John the Baptist, Jesus, and Paul apparently belonged to this group. Matthew allows for it within the life of the church, but as with Paul (1 Cor. 7:7) it is for the minority who "can" (v. 12) do this because "it is given" to them by God (v. 11).

19:13–15 *Children in the New Community*
(See also at Mark 10:13–16; Luke 18:15–17)
Whereas previously Matthew had used children as symbols of the "little people" in the Christian community (see on 18:1–10), here he is concerned with the place of actual children in church life. In contrast to contemporary Jewish and pagan religious life, the Christian community encouraged participation by the whole family. Matthew thus changes Mark's ambiguous "touch" to **lay hands on and pray**, the typical acts of blessing by a revered teacher. It is likely that the practice of the Matthean church is reflected here, in which children are welcomed into the community in an act of blessing. Children are not merely tolerated but regarded as models of how the kingdom of God is received. The kingdom **belongs** not only to them, but to **such as these**—to all who receive it without presumption and self-justification.

**19:16–30 *Successful Young People
and the New Community***
(See also at Mark 10:23–31; Luke 18:24–30)
Matthew alone gives us the picture of a youth, twice calling him a "young man" (vv. 20, 22). In the present context, he represents wealthy, successful young people whom Matthew's church would like to attract to (or retain in) the way of Christian discipleship, but who often were uninterested in the different value system by which the Christian community lived.

19:17 Why do you ask me about what is good?: Matthew rewrites Mark 10:18 to avoid any misunderstanding that Jesus was not good (see Matt. 3:14–15). In Matthew, Jesus represents God's goodness in this world (1:23). In the following parable, understood by Matthew as an allegory in which the employer represents God and Jesus, the employer's climactic declaration is that he is "good" (20:15).

19:20 What do I still lack?: The young man has always been a law-keeping Jew who goes beyond the prohibitions of the Decalogue and attempts to live by the command of love for the neighbor. He still senses something is missing and asks, "What do I still lack?" (different from Mark, where Jesus takes the initiative in telling him of his deficiency).

19:21 If you wish to be perfect: This Matthean addition to Mark has traditionally been understood as the basis for the distinction between two degrees of discipleship, the ordinary Christians who keep the basic commandments and the "perfect," those who belong to religious orders and live according to the extra evangelical counsels of poverty, chastity, and obedience. But the passage does not distinguish two groups. The same goal is envisioned throughout, called "eternal life" (v. 16), "enter(ing) into life" (v. 17), "(being) perfect" (v. 21), "enter(ing) the kingdom of God" (v. 23) and "(being) saved" (v. 25). Verse

24 makes clear that selling all and giving to the poor is the requirement not only for the "second stage" for a Jew who is already saved to become a Christian, or for an ordinary Christian to become a perfect one but for entering the kingdom of God at all. Further, "perfect" does not have the sense of "sinless," but "whole, undivided," as in 5:48, where it is the divine requirement not for a special class, but for all who strive to be obedient to God. Jesus' final word to the young man is verbatim his call to Matthew, the wealthy publican who became a disciple (9:9; see 4:19, 21–22).

19:22 He went away grieving: Jesus let him go. His next words are not to the young man but to the disciples, for whom the whole scene has been played out. The disciples get the point, though many interpreters have attempted to moderate it. Their exclamation only serves to set up Jesus' pronouncement that everything is possible **for God** (not "with God," in the sense of collaboration).

19:25 Who then can be saved?: The young man is a fine specimen who "has it all": youth, money, morality, a sense that there is still something more, an interest in eternal things. Matthew resists the temptation to make the disciples (and his own church) look the better by painting the man in gloomy colors. He was a good, sincere young man, with money, and every church would be glad to "get" him. What *did* he lack? He anticipated being given one more commandment, one final achievement, and then his quest would be fulfilled. Not just the young man but also the reader is surprised when he is told that he lacks all, that his salvation is impossible. At one level, the story communicates that salvation is not any kind of achievement, that on human terms entering the kingdom is not merely hard but impossible. It is only when this no to all human claims is heard that the yes of God can be heard: **But for God all things are possible**. Binding this pronouncement to the call to discipleship keeps it from being cheap grace.

19:27–30 We have left everything and followed you. What then shall we have?: It is important to see this paragraph as a continuation of the preceding dialogue, for taken by itself Peter's question seems purely selfish, a quid pro quo understanding of discipleship. In the present structure devised by Matthew, Peter's question provides the occasion for Jesus to affirm the eschatological reward for those who have not depended on their own goodness but by following Jesus participate in the eschatological reversal of all things symbolized by the kingdom of God.

19:28 The renewal of all things: Matthew adds this saying to his Markan source. In some strands of Jewish apocalyptic thought, the regathering of the dispersed twelve tribes of Israel was one of the blessings of the last days (Ps. Sol. 17:28; the tenth petition of the Eighteen Benedictions). Even though the early Christian community's mission to the Jews had been mostly unsuccessful, this oracle announces that Israel will indeed be regathered at the eschaton—for judgment. As in other apocalyptic pictures, the saints participate with God or the Son of Man in this judgment scene, in which the tables are turned and those now rejected will act as judges (1 En. 45:3; 61:8; 62:2; 69:27; 108:12; 1 Cor. 6:2; see Rev. 20:4, 11; for "Son of Man," see at Mark 2:10). Matthew introduces the oracle here to portray the grounding of the life of discipleship in the vision of the present-and-coming kingdom of God and the reversal of values it expresses.

Matthew uses the phrase "the renewal of all things" to express the apocalyptic hope of the eschatological renewal of the earth. It is one way of picturing the meaning of the final coming of the kingdom of God, which will not negate the meaning of history but redeem and fulfill it (see "new heaven and new earth [= new creation] Isa. 65:17; 66:22; Rev. 21:1; 2 Cor. 5:17; Rom. 8:18–25). This text has sometimes been understood as giving the twelve apostles authority to rule the "new Israel," the church, through the centuries. This is a misinterpretation, since the picture is eschatological, not historical. The "renewal of all things" occurs at the Parousia, when the Son of Man comes and sits on the throne of judgment, as at 25:31–32, the only other instance of the Son of Man sitting on a throne. Thus Matthew omits Mark 10:30, "now in this time," to make the eschatological orientation clear.

19:29 Everyone who has left houses: The Markan form of the saying pictures the disciples' present experience as receiving many houses and families in the Christian community in exchange for leaving their literal family to become disciples. Matthew elsewhere affirms this view of the church as the family of God (12:46–50; 18:1–35) but here preserves the contrast between present appearances and eschatological reality. Eschatological reward is not only for the Twelve, but for everyone who, unlike the wealthy young man of 19:16–23, has left all to become a disciple.

20:1–16 *Parable of the Laborers in the Vineyard*

The original meaning(s) and function(s) in the context(s) of Jesus' own ministry must be distinguished from its meaning and function in the Matthean literary context (on interpreting Gospel parables, see on Mark 4:1). To hear it as Jesus originally told it, the reader must refrain from allegorically making the landowner into God and the payment the Last Judgment, for such a reading has the effect of letting the reader identify in advance with God, whose judgment is always right. Without this allegorical approach, the hearer tends to identify with those first hired, and the story can have its parabolic effect. The original parable ended at v. 13 or 14a; 14(b)–16 are Matthean additions to enhance his allegorical interpretation. Exegesis of Matthew is interested not only in hearing the original parable in Jesus' terms but in understanding the meaning of the text as we have it in Matthew, where it is closely related to the preceding context (see the issue of the "good" in 19:16; 20:15 [NRSV note] and the similar ending with the sayings in 19:30 and 20:16).

20:1 The kingdom of heaven is like a landowner: On kingdom of heaven/God, see on 3:2; Luke 4:43. The parable begins in the familiar world in which day laborers are hired at sunup and paid at the end of the day, in accordance with Torah regulation and Jewish practice (Deut. 24:14–15; Lev. 19:13). A denarius was a normal day's pay for manual laborers hired by the day but was barely enough to maintain a family at the subsistence level.

20:3 He saw others standing idle: The parable gradually fades into another dimension from that of the everyday world, as unusual features begin to accumulate for which no explanation is given. Instead of sending his manager, the wealthy landowner himself goes to the market to hire laborers (contrast v. 8). The landowner goes repeatedly, even at the "eleventh hour" (5:00 p.m.). No explanation is given as to why those "standing idle" had not been hired on earlier recruitment visits. The first group of workers is hired on the basis of an oral contract for the normal amount; the later groups are promised "whatever is right," thus raising, but not answering, the question of "right" (see on 1:19). Though the first group has a "contract" and the second can only trust in the master's sense of justice, in reality both groups are dependent on the trustworthiness of the landowner.

20:10 When the first came, they thought they would receive more: In the closing scene in which all are paid the same, the middle groups are ignored in order to focus on "first" and "last" (see 19:30 and 20:16, which bracket the parable!).

The closing scene in which payment is made contains the deeply disturbing element that makes the story a parable rather than an illustration of a logical point. At the landowner's (now called "Lord," 20:8) order, those last hired are paid first. They receive a full day's pay. Those hired first now expect that fairness demands that they will receive more (v. 10)—but they receive the agreed-upon amount. Matthean readers, too, assuming they are religious types committed to justice, equal pay for equal work, and the like, share the consternation of those who have worked all day, enduring its heat and fatigue.

The parable is upsetting because it functions to challenge and reverse conventional values, including the sense of justice and fairness conventional among Matthew's religious readership, and this is one reason Matthew chooses to preserve it and insert it here. Here as elsewhere, Matthew understands the parable allegorically, so that for him the landowner is the eschatological judge, God or Jesus, who is indeed "good," and the payment at the end of the day is the Last Judgment (as in the preceding context 19:27–29). The "first" and "last" in Matthew's view both refer to insiders, to Christians who have worked long and faithfully and latecomers who have not.

The parable deals with resentment toward others who have actually received the grace one affirms in theory. Strategically placed at the conclusion of the section 19:16–20:16, the parable invites reflection on the sovereignty of the good God, the One with whom there can be no bargaining because God is the Creator and the Sovereign (see Rom. 9–11). Likewise, the parable, while affirming the sovereign grace of God rejects *presuming* on grace. Grace is always amazing grace. Grace that can be calculated and "expected" (v. 10!) is no longer grace (see 22:11–14).

The story of the rich young man (19:16–30) is a picture of the rejection of grace by one who prefers to justify himself, to earn his own way. The parable of the Good Employer is a picture of the resentment of grace toward others by those who have worked long and hard themselves.

20:17–19 *The Third Passion Prediction*
(See commentary at Mark 10:32–34; Luke 18:31–34)

20:20–28 *The Disciples' Misunderstanding;
Model Reasserted*
(See also at Mark 10:35–45; Luke 22:24–27)
20:20 The mother of the sons of Zebedee: This
awkward phrase is the result of Matthew's
effort to spare the disciples, whom he usually
represents as understanding (see on 13:10).
Matthew replaces the disciples' own request
in Mark with one represented by their mother.
20:25–27 It will not be so among you: Jesus'
vision of the style of leadership as servanthood
corresponds to his alternative vision of kingship (see on 12:22–30). Over against the exalted
and powerful terms used for worldly rulership, Jesus substitutes **servant** (literally, "deacon," a table servant, waiter or waitress, also
used as a technical term for Christian ministry)
and **slave.** Rather than *replacing* the image of
kingship (potentially oppressive, and always
so in human kingdoms), Matthew *reinterprets*
it in terms of Jesus as the revelation of God.
20:28 Just as: Matthew changes Mark's simple
conjunction "and" to "just as," to make more
clear that Jesus as Son of Man is being
reasserted as a model for the disciples' own
lives and ministry. Again, one's understanding
of the nature of the church rests on Christology.

20:29–34 *Blindness Healed*
(See also at Mark 10:46–52; Luke 18:35–43)
This is a doublet of 9:27–31 but not merely a repetition. There, the focus was christological, on "the
works of the Messiah" (see on 8:1–9:35). Here, as
the conclusion of the section instructing and nur-
turing the disciples, the focus is on the disciples,
who like the blind men must have their blindness
cured by Jesus before they can see the new way of
life to which Christian discipleship calls them.

As in 9:27–31, Matthew doubles the number
of blind men. Though doubling is a stylistic trait
of Matthew, who throughout has added "two"
and/or doubled or reduced the number of individuals in Mark in order to get "two" (see 4:18,
21; 8:28, 9:27; 18:15–16, 19, 20; 20:21, 24, 30; and
even 21:2, 7, where Mark's one donkey becomes
two), here it may be theologically significant as
well. Just as the two sons of Zebedee represented
all the disciples in the preceding pericope, here
two blind men become transparent to all disciples who need to have their blindness healed (see
13:10–17). Doubling the number of blind men
makes them legitimate witnesses (Deut. 19:15;

see Matt. 18:16; 26:60) and a symbol of the community. Blindness is healed not individualistically but in the community.

Unlike its Markan source, the story as interpreted by Matthew is not a symbolic story of conversion. Three times the blind men call Jesus
Lord, the mark of believers. Twice they address
him as Son of David, a positive and correct christological title in Matthew, but not in Mark (see on
Mark 12:35–37). The Markan emphasis on their
faith is omitted, as are his "colorful details," so
that Matthew can concentrate all attention on
Jesus' compassion (added by Matthew) and his
word. It is not their faith that occasioned the healing but Jesus' powerful word. In yet another way
Matthew indicates that discipleship is a gracious
gift, not an achievement (see on 16:17). Precisely
as the conclusion and climax of this section
(19:1–20:34) in which Jesus has struggled to get
his disciples to see the nature of the life to which
he calls them, Matthew places a story showing
that when they finally "see it," it is a matter of
Christ's giving sight to the blind.

21:1–22:46
Jerusalem: The Final Confrontation

From Jesus' entry into Jerusalem through the Last
Supper, arrest, trial, crucifixion, and resurrection
Matthew follows the Markan order exactly,
except for slightly rearranging the fig tree incident (21:18–22=Mark 11:22–26; see below). In
Matthew the triumphal entry and cleansing of
the temple occur on the same day, Jesus' first day
in Jerusalem; in Mark these are divided into two
separate days. Matthew preserves all Mark's
materials except the story of "the widow's mite"
(Mark 12:41–44). This means that the differences
from Mark are additions of traditional material
from Q and M, plus Matthew's own editorial
additions and modifications. For more detailed
commentary, see on the Markan texts.

21:1–11 *The Spectacular Entry:
Conspicuously Meek*
*(See also at Mark 11:1–11; Luke 19:28–40;
John 12:12–19)*
In the Matthean story line, this is Monday, Jesus'
first appearance in Jerusalem, the city that joined
with wicked king Herod in being troubled at the
birth of Jesus (2:3), but which is nevertheless the
"holy city" (4:5; 27:53, even after the crucifixion)
and the "city of the great king" (5:35).
21:4–5 This took place to fulfill: Here Matthew
inserts his ninth "formula quotation," the first
since 13:35 (see excursus at 2:23: "Matthew as

Interpreter of Scripture"). The image of Zech. 9:9 had already impacted the (pre-)Markan form of the story, and perhaps influenced even Jesus' own symbolic act, but it is important to Matthew to make the reference to Scripture explicit. Zechariah's prophecy of the meek king who would ride not on a war horse but on a donkey was expressed in poetic parallelism, picturing the animal as "a donkey, that is, a donkey's colt." Although Matthew certainly understands the principle of parallelism in Hebrew poetry, he sees Scripture with rabbinic and scribal eyes in which every detail is important. To emphasize the fulfillment of Scripture, he has the disciples fetch two animals and has Jesus ride on both of them (v. 7). Matthew omits Zechariah's characterization of the king as "righteous and saving" (LXX; the Hebrew text reads "triumphant and victorious") in order to place all the emphasis on Jesus as the **humble** king who redefines the nature of kingship. Matthew also adds **Son of David**," a title of which Mark was suspicious (see Mark 12:37) but which Matthew has rehabilitated and reinterpreted to represent Jesus' authentic kingship (see on 1:2–25 and 22:41–46).

21:12–17 *Encounter/Disruption in the Temple*
(See also at Mark 11:15–17; Luke 19:45–46; John 2:13–17)

21:12 Jesus entered the temple and drove out all who were selling and buying: This encounter took place not in the sanctuary proper, but in the large court of the gentiles, where animals were sold for sacrifice and money was exchanged into the Tyrian coinage acceptable for gifts to the temple. Both practices were necessary and valuable, since sacrificial animals could not easily be brought from a distance and had to be certified as acceptable by the temple priesthood, and foreign currency often had idolatrous symbols inappropriate for temple use. Both practices were also subject to abuse, but there is no evidence of this in Matthew. (On "den of thieves" see on v. 14.)

The temple complex was large and secured by the Jewish temple police, augmented by Roman soldiers during festivals. It included among other things stalls for thousands of sacrificial animals and accommodation for the people who cared for them—an enormous barn and slaughterhouse. Apart from some tremendous manifestation of divine power (of which there is no suggestion in the narrative), Jesus, even with the aid of his small band of

disciples, could not have closed down, or even disrupted, the temple business, though he may have performed some dramatic symbolic act like those of the Israelite prophets. In any case, the temple was long since gone when Matthew writes, and he is not concerned with accurate reporting but with theological meaning. Both Matthew and his opponents acknowledged the destruction of the temple, which neither party expected to be rebuilt. The issue that divided them is, "What replaces the temple as the effective symbol of God's presence among his people, and what is the way forward for the people of God, given the destruction of the temple?"

Thus this scene should not be labeled "cleansing the temple," which implies that it had been ritually defiled and needed ceremonial cleansing (as in 2 Chr. 29:16; 1 Macc. 4:36–43; 2 Macc. 10:3–5), or, as in much traditional Christian exegesis, that "the Jews" had profaned the temple by making it into a price-gouging business enterprise. Neither interpretation has any basis in fact; the latter is particularly susceptible to anti-Jewish propagandistic use. "Cleanse" is never used by any New Testament writer with reference to Jesus' symbolic act in the temple.

21:13 "Den of robbers" does not refer to dishonest trade in the temple. The allusion is to Jer. 7:1–11, where the prophet charged the people of Judah with a false Zion theology that regarded the temple as a guarantee of divine protection, so that the temple became a robbers' hideout to which they could retreat in safety after their acts of injustice. Jeremiah's charge was thus against those who came to worship in the temple rather than those who sold animals and changed money there.

21:14 The blind and lame came to him in the temple, and he cured them: As Jesus *casts out* the insiders who see the temple as a safe place of refuge instead of prayer, he *welcomes* those who had been neglected and excluded—the blind, lame, and children (v. 14), thus extending the messianic works he had done in Galilee to Judea and Jerusalem (see Mic. 4:6–7; Zeph. 3:19; and on 11:5). Jesus does this as Son of David and is acclaimed as such by another marginalized group in Israel, the children (see on 18:1–14). Previously Matthew has specifically connected Jesus as Son of David with his ministry of healing (9:27–31; 12:22–24; 15:21–28; 20:29–34). As David was a violent person, the expected Son of David as a messianic figure was supposed to bring in God's reign with great violence against Israel's enemies. Matthew affirms Jesus as the fulfiller of the hopes associated with the Son of David (see on 1:1–17) but transforms the image in the light of who Jesus actually was (vs. Mark's hesitation about this title; see on Mark 12:37).

21:15 The children were crying out . . . Son of David: Jesus accepts the acclamation "Son of David," given him by the children. The first son of David, Solomon, built the first temple, which was destroyed by the Babylonians; Jeremiah and others interpreted the destruction as punishment for the sinful lives of the people who rejected God's covenant (Jer. 7:1–11). Jesus as Son of David builds a church—community, not building—in which the reality of God's presence is made known (1:23 etc.). This is recognized by the "little people," represented here by the children (see on 11:25–27; 18:1–14), but rejected by the "chief priests and scribes," who appear in the narrative for the first time since 2:4–6, where they "knew the Scriptures" but did not act on them.

21:16 Have you never read?: Again Jesus quotes the Scripture justifying the event (Ps. 8:2; the point is dependent on the LXX; see excursus at 2:23, "Matthew as Interpreter of Scripture"). There is no dialogue, only pronouncement.

21:18–22 *Withering the Fruitless Tree*
(See also at Mark 11:12–14, 20–26)

Matthew found the story in Mark, where the two acts of pronouncing judgment on it on one day and discovering it withered on the next day surrounded and interpreted the expulsion of merchants, buyers, and money changers from the temple (Mark 11:12–26). When Matthew extracts the middle element, the disruption of the temple business, and locates it on Jesus' first day in Jerusalem (see comments on chronology at Mark 11:1, 12), the Markan intercalation collapses, and the fig tree withers immediately, before the eyes of the disciples. Matthew also eliminates the troublesome Markan note "it was not the season for figs," but the difficulty of Jesus using his miraculous power for destructive purposes remains.

The primary meaning for Matthew seems to focus on two points important to Matthew elsewhere.

21:19 Found nothing at all on it but leaves: Matthew uses "fruit(s)" as a metaphor for good works seventeen times, more than any other writer in the New Testament. He never uses the word literally, but only in this ethical sense. The Lord comes seeking fruit from his tree; when he finds only leaves, he causes it to wither (see 3:10; 7:16–20). This represents the judgment of God on those who have the external appearance of productivity but no real fruits. The pronouncement is not a smug contrast between "fruitless Judaism" and "fruitful Christianity" but is directed as a warning to insiders in Matthew's own community.

21:21 If you have faith: These "fruits" are not self-justifying works; they are the products of faith, not its antithesis. Thus Matthew immediately makes the application to the prayer of faith, introduced by a solemn *amen* saying (see on 5:18). Those who have faith will not only be able to do what Jesus has done, i.e., pronounce the withering judgment of God on fruitless religion (in the *church*, not in another religious community), but will remove any obstacle, and will receive whatever they ask in prayer, if they believe. For discussion of "faith that moves mountains," see on 17:20.

21:23–27 *Jesus' Authority Questioned*
(See also at Mark 11:27–33; Luke 20:1–8; John 2:18–22)

21:23 When he entered the temple: When Jesus enters the temple in 21:23, he remains until 24:1, departing for the final time after pronouncing it desolate in 23:38. It is a dramatic, symbolic scene, as Jesus, the authorized teacher of God's will (7:28; 28:18–20), makes his final challenge to the Jewish leaders within the sacred setting of the temple court.

When the **chief priests and elders** question his authority, it is not a matter of personal petulance, nor a response to his action in the temple, which is never mentioned. From Matthew's post-Easter perspective, it concerns the dispute in Judaism concerning who are the authoritative teachers for the reconstitution of the people of God in the aftermath of the war and destruction of Jerusalem and the temple. Matthew has added to this scene the note that Jesus was teaching, which makes the discussion focus on Jesus' authority to *teach*. At the climax of the Gospel Matthew declares that God has given Jesus all authority, including specifically to teach (28:18–20).

This text puts John and Jesus in the same category. Those who reject John also reject Jesus. Their question about Jesus' authority is restated—not avoided—as the question of John's authority. Both are from God, yet they are very different. Their differences embraced not only their different religious "styles" (9:14–17; 11:16–19) but that John wavered and wondered (11:3), while Jesus spoke with unrelenting authority (7:29). For Matthew, God is also met in Christian missionaries, the "little ones" of the community, and in real children (10:40–42; 18:1–5). Yet this broad spectrum of figures whom one may encounter as authentic mediators of the divine presence does not mean that Matthew affirms a relativism in which all claims to divine authority are equally true and equally false. He calls for discernment (see on 11:16–19).

21:28–32 *The Two Sons*

This parable, unique to Matthew and saturated with Matthean vocabulary, style, and themes, seems to have been composed by Matthew himself as the preface for the traditional saying found in another form in Luke 7:29–30 and introduced by Matthew as a solemn *amen* saying in vv. 31b–32 (see on 5:18). In addition to illustrating the general Matthean theme that God requires deeds rather than empty words (7:21–23, etc.), the specific meaning in the context is that the Jewish leaders originally said yes to the prophetic message from God delivered by John. Matthew has not forgotten that he has pictured the Pharisees and Sadducees going to John to be baptized by him, 3:5–7a. But they did not accept his message and repent. Those who had been saying no to God's will revealed in the Torah, the tax collectors and prostitutes, changed their mind and accepted his message.

21:28 What do you think?: Jesus does not allow their previous strategic silence to stand. Since the question concerns characters in a story and thus is not directly about their own conduct, they cannot avoid answering it. When they give their answer, they who will sit in judgment on Jesus already condemn themselves. Their attempt to trap Jesus has resulted in self-condemnation.

21:33–46 *The Lord's Vineyard Given to Others*
(See also at Mark 12:1–12; Luke 20:9–19)

21:33 A landowner who planted a vineyard: Matthew identifies Mark's "man" as a "landowner" (as 13:52; 20:1), thus making him more transparent to the allegorical meaning Matthew intends: the Lord of the vineyard is God (v. 40).

21:34 The harvest time had come: Literally "the season of fruits"; both NIV and NRSV obscure Matthew's repeated reference to "fruits," twice here and added again in v. 41. For "fruits" as his key term for good works, see on 21:18–22 above. Unlike Mark, where the owner wants only his contracted share, here he unrealisti-

cally wants all the fruit, as allegorical meaning prevails over historical realism: God's claim can only be total.

21:37–39 Finally he sent his son: Matthew understands this sending of the son retrospectively as an allegory of the destiny of Jesus, who was sent by God as the climax of the series of rejected prophets. In Matthew's understanding the tenants represent the leaders of rebellious Israel, who conspire to kill Jesus. In the allegorical parable Matthew can be uninhibited by history and can make the Jewish leaders totally responsible—there is no second party to whom the son is turned over for execution. Matthew reverses the Markan chronology in which the son is first killed and then unceremoniously dumped outside the vineyard, having him first taken outside and then killed, corresponding to the actual passion story (27:32) and showing again that the parable is dominated by its allegorical interpretation.

21:42 Have you never read in the scriptures?: At this point Matthew restructures the Markan form to have Jesus pose a question (as in v. 28) that will allow the Jewish leaders to pronounce their own condemnation (see 2 Sam. 12:7; 14:12–13)—again as in the preceding pericope. They declare that God will destroy the wicked tenants and give the vineyard to other tenants. Matthew understands this as the destruction of Jerusalem and the growth of the church of Jews and Gentiles in Israel's place.

21:43 The kingdom of God will be taken from you: This verse is added by Matthew to Mark, apparently is composed by him, and represents the major theological issue in interpreting this passage. The issue is, who is the "you" from whom the kingdom is taken, and who is the "nation" to whom it is given? In the context, the addressees are clearly the **chief priests and the Pharisees** (the latter here added by Matthew), i.e., the Jewish leadership, not the people as a whole. Thus some interpreters have contended that Matthew here and elsewhere claims only that God will replace the present false leadership with faithful leaders. This requires understanding "nation," which is also the word for "Gentile," in an unusual sense, a new group of leaders for Israel. The more natural way is to understand "nation" as referring to **people**, so that (as in 1 Pet. 2:9) those to whom the kingdom is given are the renewed people of God, the church of Jews and Gentiles, who are called by God in place of unfaithful Israel. Many

Christians throughout history have been *too* willing to understand the text this way, which has fueled the fires of anti-Judaism and anti-Semitism. Many Christians today are hesitant to understand the text in any way that encourages a false understanding of supersessionism, that God has rejected Israel and replaced it with the church (Jewish and Gentile) as the people of God.

Neither past mistakes nor present Christian sensitivity to Jewish-Christian relations should inhibit our allowing Matthew to mean whatever he meant. If he believed God had now rejected the Jews as the elect people of God and replaced them with the church composed of people called from all nations, including Jews, historical honesty should accept this. It is possible that historical study of the Bible could document this as Matthew's view, even if his situational-conditioned perspective must not be allowed to dominate our own. Christians today who formulate their understanding of the role of the Jews in God's plan and the relation of Judaism and Christianity, must be informed not only by this text but by other canonical perspectives, such as that of Paul, another Jew who had become a Christian, who saw a larger plan of God that embraced both Israel and church (Rom. 9–11).

This text does not speak explicitly, however, of Israel's being rejected but of the "kingdom of God" being taken from "you"; i.e., in Matthew's view the saving activity of God continues in that community where taking up the "yoke of the kingdom" means adherence to the Torah as fulfilled in the teaching of Jesus (see 5:17–48; 28:20). Matthew, like the modern reader, here struggles with a difficult problem, one that he perhaps had as much difficulty in resolving with systematic clarity and consistency as does his modern reader. Even if the objective meaning remains not entirely clear, contemporary readers can still legitimately ask whether they themselves have set up other phony sovereignties in place of the one God and thus might be addressed in the "you" from whom the kingdom is taken.

21:44 The one who falls on this stone will be broken: This text, which does not occur in several important manuscripts, was once thought to be a scribal gloss imported from Luke 20:18 (RSV, NEB, still missing from REB; NAB brackets it as a later addition; see "Introduction: The New Testament as the Church's Book," 4.d). More recent evaluation tends to consider it a part of the original text of Matthew (NIV,

NRSV). If original, v. 44 functions to intensify the judgment expressed in the parable and in v. 43: the rock/kingdom/Son, who should be savior and Lord, becomes a terrible threat to the one on whom it falls or who falls against it.

22:1–14 *The Great Supper*
(See also at Luke 14:15–24)

Jesus told a striking and troubling story in which all the invited guests to a dinner party at the last minute refused to come, so the host rounded up a mélange of street people who found themselves guests at a party they had never dreamed of attending. The story circulated in a variety of forms in early Christianity (Q, Luke 14:15–24, and *Gospel of Thomas* 64, as well as here), in each case being interpreted contextually and modified in accordance with the theology of the author. Matthew has adapted the Q form, placing it in this context to serve as the final in his triad of judgment parables.

As in the preceding parables, Matthew builds his allegorical interpretation into the story itself, making the parable an allegory of salvation history from the initial sending of the prophets to Israel through the renewed invitation by Christian prophetic missionaries, concluding at the Last Judgment, when the good and bad in the church are sorted out. The original dinner party has become the messianic banquet given by the king (God) for his Son (Jesus), who invites guests who agreed to come (Israel) to the wedding celebration (salvation, the messianic banquet), but those who had agreed to attend refused the final invitations delivered by both the first group of slaves (the Hebrew prophets) and the second (the prophetic Christian missionaries).

22:2 A king who gave a wedding banquet: On the interpretation of parables, see on Mark 4:1. Matthew introduces the kingship motif; the "man" of Q who gave a dinner party now becomes a "king who gave a wedding feast for his son."

22:3 Call those who had been invited: In Matthew's allegorical understanding, the original invitation corresponds to the call of Israel, who accepted God's covenant. As in the preceding parable (but differently from the Lukan parallel closer to Q), slaves (plural) who are sent correspond to the prophets of Israel. In Matthew, no excuses are offered; those who had committed themselves to attend the banquet simply declare their unwillingness to come. Refusal of a king's invitation, especially in concert suggesting conspiracy, is equivalent to rebellion (2 Sam. 10:4).

22:4–6 Again he sent other slaves: The king is patient and does not retaliate but sends a second group of slaves. This element of the story is peculiar to Matthew, necessary to fit his allegorical understanding, for it corresponds to the prophetic Christian missionaries who by Matthew's time had already carried out a largely unsuccessful early mission to the Jewish community. Not only do those invited continue to refuse; they abuse and kill the messengers. This is one of numerous unrealistic elements in the story that points to its allegorical meaning: like the faithful prophets of Israel, some prophetic Christian missionaries had been killed (see on 23:34, 37; 1 Thess. 2:15–16).

22:7 He sent his troops . . . and burned their city: While dinner waits, the king wages war, kills those who had dishonored and rebelled against him, and burns their city, presumably also his own. On the historical level, this is not only an overreaction but hardly possible. Matthew is thinking in terms of his view of salvation history, not of an actual king who waged war while dinner waited. This is probably Matthew's retrospective view of the destruction of Jerusalem, understood as a judgment on rebellious Israel, who had rejected the Messiah, though it might be explained in terms of Matthew's reflection on Isa. 5:24–25.

22:8–9 Invite everyone: The rebellious old group has been judged, but the festival house is still empty. A third group of slaves is sent, representing the prophetic Christian missionaries, with a new invitation corresponding even in vocabulary to the Great Commission of 28:18–20. The invitation is no longer restricted to those who had accepted the previous invitation but is extended to all. Those who are **gathered** in are both bad and good, corresponding to Matthew's realistic picture of the empirical church in other parables peculiar to him (13:24–30, see the interpretation in 13:36–43; 13:47–50) and setting the stage for the appended conclusion of this scene.

22:11 A man there who was not wearing a wedding robe: This is not a separate parable, but functions only as an expansion of 22:1–10, into which it has been integrated to make one parable. The whole expansion seems to be Matthew's own composition, permeated with his vocabulary and theology. No trace of it is found in the forms of the story found in Luke and the *Gospel of Thomas.*

22:12 How did you get in here?: How could those unexpectedly herded into the wedding hall from the streets wear the expected clothing, which all but one of them seem to do? Again, "realism" is sacrificed to theological meaning—the theology is real, but not the history. In early Christianity, the new identity of conversion was often pictured as donning a new set of clothes; the language of changing clothes was utilized to express the giving up of the old way of life and putting on the new Christian identity (Rom. 13:12–14; Gal. 3:27; Col. 3:12; Eph. 6:11; see Luke 15:22; Rev. 3:4; 6:11; 19:8). At the allegorical level, the man was expected to have the deeds of an authentic Christian life, corresponding to the fruits in the imagery of the preceding parable. When confronted with his lack, the man has no response, for he is without excuse. The judgment seems harsh, but Matthew is thinking not of an actual wedding party, but of the Last Judgment; **weeping and gnashing of teeth** corresponds to 8:12; 25:30; 13:42, 50; 24:51, an apocalyptic Q expression (see Luke 13:28) that became a favorite of Matthew's to picture the terror of condemnation at the Last Judgment.

22:14 Many are called, but few are chosen: Matthew does not use "call" in the sense of "effective call," as does Paul (e.g., Rom. 1:1, 7; 8:28), but in the sense of initial invitation to become a disciple. Whether one is actually "chosen," belonging to the "elect" (i.e., accepted in the Last Judgment), depends on manifesting authentic Christian faith in deeds of love and justice. For the first time Matthew explicitly appropriates the term "elect," referring it not to a specific group (Jews, Christians), but to those who will finally be accepted in the Last Judgment (so also 24:22, 24, 31). The focus of an elect people of God has shifted from the Old Testament understanding of the people of Israel as a whole to that of the righteous remnant, a shift already made in some streams of Judaism (e.g., Wis. 3:9, 4:15; *1 En.; Apoc. Ab.* 29). The dispute between Matthew and the Pharisaic leaders of his own time concerned who constituted this elect remnant, the continuing people of God.

The theological point of 22:11–14 is that those who find themselves unexpectedly included may not presume on grace but are warned of the dire consequences of accepting the invitation and doing nothing except showing up. By concluding in this manner, Matthew makes it clear that such pictures, in which unfaithful Israel is condemned, are not an encouragement to smugness on the part of his Christian readers. The whole section is directed to the Matthean reader. It is instruction and warning to insiders, not a description of the fate of outsiders.

22:15–22 *On Paying Taxes to the Emperor*
(See also at Mark 12:13–17; Luke 20:20–40)

In the same breath in which he declares that paying taxes to support secular and pagan governments is not against the will of God, Jesus goes beyond their original question, declaring that what is God's must be given to God. This is not an in-principle division of the world into two realms with two sovereigns. Matthew's dualistic perspective is only penultimate; ultimately he is a monotheist who resists this kind of dualism. The kingdom of God represented by Jesus embraces all of life. In any case, by picturing Jesus and the Christian community as belonging to the series of Israel's prophets, Matthew could hardly advocate the separation of religion and politics.

While Matthew is clear that loyalty to God is a different and higher category than loyalty to Caesar, this text is not instruction on how people who live in a complex world of competing loyalties may determine what belongs to Caesar and what belongs to God. It simply declares that the distinction between what belongs to Caesar (as some things do) and what belongs to God (the ultimate loyalty) must be made, and it leaves it to readers in their own situations to be "Jesus theologians" who, in the light of Jesus' life and teachings, will make their own decisions in such situations (see on 5:21–48).

22:23–33 *Question about the Resurrection*
(See commentary at Luke 20:27–40)

22:34–40 *The Great Commandment*
(See also at Mark 12:28–34; Luke 10:25–28)

Matthew has already presented Jesus as teaching the centrality of love in the life of the disciples and has shown that love to the neighbor includes the enemy (5:21–48, esp. 23–48). Here the double commandment of love becomes part of the controversy series extending from 21:23 through 23:39. On the meaning of love (*agape*), see on 1 Cor. 13:4–7.

22:36: Which command in the law is the greatest?: In the corresponding section of Mark, a friendly scribe makes a sincere inquiry, Jesus replies, the scribe commends him for his answer, and Jesus responds positively, declaring that the scribe is not far from the kingdom of God (12:28–34). Matthew's rewriting changes the form and character of the peri-

cope from a scholastic dialogue to a controversy story. The lawyer's question is no longer sincere or collegial, as in Mark, but is to **test** Jesus (as in 4:1, 3; 16:1; 19:3; 22:18; only the devil and the Pharisees are the subject of this verb in Matthew). The address, "teacher," is insincere, and stands in contrast to the believers' address, "Lord." Jesus has just defended the Pharisees' point of view, as he does throughout this section (see 23:1–3!), yet their response is to "test" him as did Satan. In Matthew's understanding this is more than a religious debate; once again, the two kingdoms confront each other (see on 12:22–30).

The nature of the test is not clear. The clue may be given by Matthew's addition **in the law.** The rabbis had counted 613 commands (248 positive commands corresponding to the number of parts of the body; 365 negative commands corresponding to the days of the year). Though rabbinical teachers could indulge in giving "summaries of the Law," there was also the view that all commandments were equal, with any ranking of them being mere human presumption in evaluating the divine law, all of which was equally binding. The lawyer may be attempting to draw Jesus into this debate and get him to make some statement that could be interpreted as disparaging toward (some part of) the Law, such as declaring the moral law more important than the ceremonial law. This is a charge to which the Markan version of this story is very amenable, since not only Jesus but the scribes subscribe to it.

22:40 On these two commandments hang all the law and the prophets: Matthew's most dramatic change is to replace the Markan conclusion's positive interchange between Jesus and the scribe with this pronouncement by Jesus, who declares the command to love God and neighbor to be the key for interpreting all divine revelation—not only the law, but the prophets as well.

22:41–46 *The Question about David's Son*
(See also at Mark 12:35–37; Luke 20:41–44)

Mark had affirmed Jesus as Messiah but challenged the explication of this title in terms of Son of David (see on Mark 12:37). In contrast, Matthew is positive about Son of David as a christological title for Jesus (see esp. 1:2–25). He rewrites this scene as a bracket to 21:1–9, in which Jesus is properly hailed as Son of David. He transforms it from a monologue into a controversy dialogue in which Jesus exposes the

Pharisees as inadequate interpreters of Scripture. Matthew and his Pharisee opponents disagreed as to whether Jesus is the Messiah, but not on whether Son of David is a valid christological title. In this regard, the issue was the meaning of "Son of David."

22:43 What do you think?: See 17:25; 18:12; 21:28. The question Matthew wants to deal with is how David, presumed to be the divinely inspired author of Ps. 110, can call the Messiah "Lord" and yet have a **son** who is the Messiah, which Matthew emphatically affirms to be the case. The Pharisees, claiming to be the teachers of God's people, cannot explain this biblical question, but the teacher of Matthew's church can explain it: (1) As the Christ, Jesus is both Lord and Son of David—but one must have faith in Jesus as the Christ before this makes sense. (2) The Son of David idea is transformed in the process of Christian appropriation as a christological title. If the Son of David is *Jesus*, it has a new content.

23:1–25:46
THE JUDGMENT DISCOURSE

Chapter 23 is often seen as a separate speech, the "Woes against the Pharisees," with 24:1–25:46 constituting a distinct eschatological discourse. However, Matthew's overall structure calls for five major speeches (see introduction to Matthew, "Structure and Outline"). It is better to see Matthew as having added the speech against the Pharisees to the beginning and additional eschatological warnings to the end, thus constructing the apocalyptic discourse of Mark 13 into a grand concluding discourse that corresponds in length to the opening discourse (chaps. 5–7=chaps. 23–25). It also now corresponds in other ways as well: as the Sermon on the Mount begins with blessings, this speech begins with woes (5:1–12=23:13–33); both speeches involve a mountain on which Jesus sits to teach, with crowds and disciples as hearers (5:1; 7:29=23:1; 24:3); in the closing scene of each speech, false disciples say, "Lord, Lord," and are told, "I never knew you" (7:21–27=25:11).

Matthew's composition has the effect of incorporating Mark's "little apocalypse" (Mark 13) into a much larger discourse concerned with judgment, all addressed to insiders and potential followers. Rather than being seen as two speeches, one condemning outsiders and the other imparting eschatological instruction, the whole discourse functions as a warning to insiders to live an authentic life devoted to deeds of justice and mercy, in the light of the eschatological victory of God and coming judgment on present unfaithfulness.

23:1–12
Warnings
(See also at Mark 12:37–40; Luke 20:45–47)

23:1 Jesus said to the crowds and to his disciples: In Matthew's chronology it is still Tuesday, and Jesus is still in the temple precincts, where he has been since 21:23. The crowds represent potential disciples who are still positive toward Jesus (21:8, 9, 11, 26, 46; 22:33). Both groups are transparent to Christians and sympathizers in Matthew's own day. On **scribes**, see on Mark 1:22; on **Pharisees**, see on 3:7; Luke 5:17, 29–32. Together they represent the Jewish leadership of Matthew's time (but not necessarily that of Jesus). The conflicts between synagogue and church reflected in 23:1–39 reflect the growing Jewish-Christian conflict of the latter part of the first century.

23:2 Moses' seat: A metaphorical expression representing the teaching and administrative authority of the synagogue leadership, scribes and Pharisees. Surprisingly, and in contrast both to what precedes (16:6, 12) and what immediately follows (23:4, 16–22), it is only the practice of the scribes and Pharisees that is condemned, not their teaching. Matthew probably intends by the present passage that the Pharisees and scribes are right in founding their way of life on exposition of the Torah, which his Christian community also affirms (5:17–48), without here taking into account their differing interpretations (see on 15:1–20).

23:3 They do not practice what they teach: Here as elsewhere, Matthew juxtaposes mere talking with actual conduct (7:21–23; 6:1–18; 21:28–32). Of course there were Christians whose life was a contradiction of their teaching. It is to these that the word of the Matthean Jesus is actually directed.

23:4 They themselves are unwilling to lift a finger: After the destruction of the temple and the cessation of the functions of the actual priests, the Pharisees encouraged the people as a whole to live out their vocation as a priestly nation (Exod. 19:6). The Pharisees' multiplication of rules for the laity may be understood as their effort to apply the priestly purity laws to the people as a whole. Matthew understood their efforts as replacing God's law with human tradition, an intolerable and misdirected burden for ordinary people (15:1–20). The alternative to the **burden** placed on people's shoulders by the Pharisees is Jesus' own "yoke" (11:28–30), which is "easy" not because it is less stringent (5:17–48!) but because it is oriented in another direction.

23:5 They do all their deeds to be seen by others: After the destruction of Jerusalem in 70 CE, the emerging Pharisaic leadership emphasized external signs of piety, not because they were hypocrites interested in externals, but as distinctive markers of the holy people of God in a pluralistic society. They were concerned that Judaism not become homogenized into the surrounding world after the destruction of their national shrine. Matthew's church was tempted to conform to these practices and was under pressure from the Pharisaic leadership of the synagogues to do so. Thus Matthew's critique, though at the story level represented as Jesus' critique of the Pharisees of his own time, functions in Matthew's time as warnings to the leadership of his own church against these practices and the attitudes he understands them to represent. **Phylacteries** are the small leather boxes containing portions of the Torah (Exod. 13:1–16; Deut. 6:4–9; 11:13–32) strapped to the forehead and arm during the recitation of prayers, in literal obedience to Deut. 6:8. **Fringes** are those commanded as part of the dress of every Israelite, later understood as the tassels attached to the prayer shawl (Num. 15:38–39; Deut. 22:12).

23:6 Best seats: The places of honor at the front of the synagogue, facing the congregation, occupied by teachers and respected leaders.

23:8 You are not to be called rabbi: In Jesus' day "rabbi" had been a generic honorific title, but in the restructure of Judaism after 70 CE there was a tendency to restrict it to official teachers. **You are all students:** The word "disciple" means "student." Jesus' disciples have been indirectly the addressees throughout; Matthew now turns to them directly. The leadership of Matthew's church was tempted to imitate the clericalism he saw developing in his Jewish opponents; Matthew himself opposed it. Matthew may be emphasizing the literal meaning of rabbi (="my great one") in contrast to the Christian community as "little ones" (see 18:1–10). NIV's "**brothers** [and sisters]" is a better translation of the Greek text than NRSV's "students," the point being that members of the Christian community are members of the family of God (12:46–50) where distinctions emphasized by titles are inappropriate.

Matthew's church did have a class of leaders, to which the author himself probably belonged, but Matthew regarded them in a

more charismatic and egalitarian perspective. To be sure, one who claims to be just a "little one" can exercise more false pride than a sincere rabbi teaching the Torah. Here as elsewhere, externals such as titles are only pointers to the inner attitude, which is Matthew's real concern.

23:11–12 The greatest among you will be your servant: Leadership in the Christian community is to be servant leadership. "Minister" means "servant" (*diakonos*, "deacon"). An irony of Christian history is that there has often been little correlation between the use of titles and the attitude here called for: those in the Christian tradition who, despite the warning of this passage, adopted such titles as Father for leaders have often been truly humble servants; those who insisted on being only "ministers" have sometimes been arrogant and tyrannical. The conclusion of this section points to the eschatological judgment when authentic greatness and humility will be revealed and rewarded on a basis quite different from the adoption of titles.

23:13–36
Woes
(See also at Luke 11:39–51)

Like the prophets of Israel, Jesus undoubtedly had critical things to say against the religious leadership of his day. At the Matthean level of the discourse, however, the woes represent the conflict between the rabbinic group and Matthean Christians at the end of the first century, not an outburst of the historical Jesus against the 30 CE Pharisees, and it is Matthean readers who are actually addressed.

The woe form is from Old Testament prophets (Isa. 45:9–10; Jer. 13:27; 48:46; Ezek. 16:23). It was probably one form of Jesus' own prophetic speech. After Easter, the woe form was adopted by Christian prophets (Rev. 8:13; 9:12; 11:14; 12:12). Q contained a collection of seven woes spoken in Jesus' name, which already reflected conflicts between the followers of Jesus and the Jewish leaders (see Luke 11:39–52). Matthew adapts this Q speech to address his own opponents, represented by the scribes and Pharisees of his own time.

In the Deuteronomistic theology adopted by Matthew from Q, hypocrisy represents godlessness, not merely phoniness. The polemic is against one's placing too much value on the way one appears to others, which can be a form of idolatry. So understood, hypocrisy is not merely a transgression but represents a lack of trust in

God, a turning away from God toward what others think as the point of orientation for one's life.

23:13 You lock people out: Matthew transforms the Q woe into a saying about the kingdom (see Luke 11:52), corresponding to his view throughout that in the conflict between the Jewish leadership and the disciples of Jesus, two kingdoms confront each other (see on 12:22–30). The woes are not a petty outburst, but anticipatory pronouncements of the eschatological judge (see 25:31–46). Contrast Peter's role in 16:19.

23:15 You cross sea and land to make a single convert: Matthew, whose own church carries on a Gentile mission (28:18–20), understands the Pharisees to be carrying on a rival mission to the Gentiles, but of course requiring them to keep the Law as a condition of becoming Jewish proselytes. Missioners of Matthew's community may have encountered resistance not only from the Pharisees but from their Gentile converts who were now zealous for the Law and opposed what they perceived to be the Matthean Christians' lax attitude toward the Torah. These hostile encounters may help the modern reader understand (not to say excuse) the vitriolic description of both Pharisees and their converts as "children of hell" (literally "sons of," in the Semitic sense of "belonging to the category of"). We are aware of a few celebrated cases in which the Pharisees persuaded prominent Gentiles to convert to Judaism, but apart from this text, the existence of a large-scale Pharisaic mission to the Gentiles is unsupported by historical evidence.

23:16–22 Blind guides, who say, "whoever swears . . .": There may have been legitimate grounding for the Pharisees' rules interpreting the biblical legislation on oaths and vows (see on 5:33–37), the Pharisees' efforts to put the Law effectively into practice and prevent people from making casual oaths. Matthew understands the whole approach as casuistic hairsplitting, a devilish effort to find loopholes in the Law; his understanding of the teaching of Jesus has rejected the casuistic approach in principle (see on 5:17–48) and the making of oaths in particular.

23:23–24 You have neglected the weightier matters of the law: The Torah had commanded that a tenth of the increase of livestock, of fruit trees, and of grain, oil, and wine be presented to God for support of the priesthood and Levites (Lev. 27:30, 32; Deut. 12:17). While some passages seemed to limit the tithe on agricultural produce to grain, oil, and wine (Deut. 12:17; 14:23; see Neh. 13:5, 12), other texts seemed to extend the tithe to include all agricultural produce (Lev. 27:30; Deut. 14:22; see 2 Chr. 31:5). In order to be sure they complied with God's law, the Pharisees tithed even small garden vegetables used for seasoning. **Justice, mercy,** and **faithfulness** is another summary of the law dealing with responsibilities to one's fellow human beings. "Faith" here means "faithfulness," carrying out one's obligations under the covenant. Straining gnats out of liquids to be consumed in drinking or cooking represents their legitimate concern to comply with the law, since some insects were ritually unclean. Matthew, too, is concerned with the importance of the "least" commandments (5:18–20!). Matthew's critique is that in being concerned to filter out minor violations, they let major ones plop in unnoticed.

23:25–26 First clean the inside: Though the imagery is unclear, the point is not, continuing Matthew's polemic against concern with external appearance rather than internal integrity (6:1–18). As in 15:1–20, purity is first a matter of the heart, proceeding from within to affect external actions.

23:27–28 You are like whitewashed tombs: As a public service, tombs were whitewashed to make them obvious, since contact with the dead and with graves, even if unintentional, transmitted ritual impurity (Num. 19:11–22). This was especially important to pilgrims at Passover time, who would not be familiar with the local sites and who, if they inadvertently touched a grave, would be prohibited from participation in the festival for which they had come to Jerusalem. Matthew commandeers the image of such a tomb to express his picture of hypocrisy: ostentatious exterior, corrupt interior.

23:29–36 You are descendants of those who murdered the prophets: The final woe extends the tomb image and modulates into the concluding theme: Israel's rejection of the prophets God has sent, including John, Jesus, and the Christian prophets. Though only a few prophets suffered persecution in the Old Testament (e.g., Elijah, Jeremiah), tradition had long since developed that the true prophets of the past had been persecuted and killed. The Pharisees showed their repentance for the sins of their ancestors by building monuments to the biblical prophets and declared that if they had lived in the days of their **ances-**

tors or "fathers" who killed the prophets, they would not have participated in their murder. By exploiting the double Semitic meaning of the "father"/"son" terminology, Matthew turns both their word and their practice against them. Speaking of past generations as their "fathers" means they acknowledge that they are "sons" of those who killed the prophets. In the Semitic meaning of "son," this means not biological relationship but belonging to the same category (see Amos 7:14). Just as the Beatitudes climax by placing Jesus' disciples in the group of persecuted prophets (5:11–12), so the woes here climax by placing their opponents in the category of those who killed the prophets.

23:33 Being sentenced to hell: Literally, Gehenna, the Greek form of Ge-Hinnom, the Valley of Hinnom, a ravine immediately south of Jerusalem. Because it was the site of idolatrous worship during the time of the Judean kingship (2 Kgs. 23:10; 2 Chr. 23:8; Jer. 7:31), it became a garbage dump where perpetual fire burned. By the first century the word was already used metaphorically as a picture of the fiery eschatological judgment of God.

23:34–36 I send you prophets, sages, and scribes: The series of Q woes had concluded with an oracle in which the transcendent Wisdom of God speaks, picturing the series of Wisdom's messengers rejected through the generations and now climaxed by the present generation's rejection of John, Jesus, and the Christian prophets, who were pictured as messengers of transcendent Wisdom (see Luke 11:49–51). Matthew, however, identifies Jesus himself with divine Wisdom, so that the oracle is placed in his own mouth. The Jesus of the narrative is portrayed from the post-Easter community's faith in him as the exalted Lord, identified with transcendent Wisdom, who has sent prophets in the past and sends Christian prophets, sages, and scribes (leaders in the Matthean Christian community) to the present generation. Matthew understands his community to belong to the righteous who have always been persecuted, from Abel the first victim (Matthew adds "righteous" to Q; see Luke 11:50) to Zechariah, the last martyr in the Old Testament (Gen. 4:8–10; 2 Chr. 24:20–22). Since, in the order of the Hebrew Bible, Genesis is first and 2 Chronicles is last, this is equivalent to saying "all the prophets of the Bible."

23:36 All this will come upon this generation: "This generation" is a common expression in

Matthew, taken over from Q (see on 11:16; 12:41–42; 24:34). The pronouncement of judgment is made on the generation contemporary with John the Baptist and Jesus, not on the Jewish people as such. These words about all the blood (= guilt) coming "upon this generation" are the last words of Jesus heard by the crowd (see 23:1) before Jesus leaves with his disciples (24:1). It is thus a moment of decision for them as to whether they will choose to belong to the kingdom of God announced and lived out by Jesus or to the opposing kingdom represented by the prophet killers.

23:37–39
Lament
(See also at Luke 13:34–35)

Matthew has relocated these words (see Luke 13:34–35, spoken earlier in the narrative, long before Jesus had ever entered Jerusalem) to make them Jesus' last words in Jerusalem and its temple before he leaves it for the final time (24:1), to reenter the city only for his arrest, trial, and crucifixion. They continue the preceding theme of "killing the prophets," but the form is different: they are a lament. As the preceding woes are ostensibly addressed to "scribes and Pharisees" but actually function as a prophetic challenge to the crowds and disciples (23:1; also to the reader) not to belong to "this evil generation," so these concluding words are an invitation ostensibly addressed to Jerusalem, but function as an invitation to the crowds and disciples (and to the reader). They continue to picture Jesus as identified with transcendent Wisdom, grieved at the rejection of her messengers. Thus "how often" refers not to previous occasions on which Jesus has been in Jerusalem—in Matthew this is his first and only visit to Jerusalem—but to transcendent Wisdom's repeated appeals to Jerusalem/Israel through history.

23:38 Your house is left to you, desolate: For Matthew and his community, these words and the following explicit prediction of the temple's destruction functioned as an apologetic, explaining how the destruction of the temple fit into the divine program as a punishment for the people's sins in rejecting the prophets, including Jesus and the Christian prophets of the final generation (see Jeremiah, explicitly cited and mentioned by Matthew alone in the Gospels [2:17; 16:14; 27:9]).

23:39 Until you say, "Blessed is the one who comes in the name of the Lord": This acclamation from Ps. 118:26 has already been shouted by these same crowds during Jesus'

entry into Jerusalem (see on Matt. 21:9), so it cannot in Matthew refer to this occasion as it does in Luke, where it occurs much earlier (13:35). In Matthew it must refer to the Parousia, as the immediate context indicates. The crowds representing Jerusalem/Israel who presently will choose Barabbas over Jesus and shout, "Let him be crucified," will eventually shout, "Blessed is the one who comes in the name of the Lord!" While this could possibly mean that all people will finally be forced to acknowledge Jesus as Lord, Matthew's meaning is more likely that Israel's present rejection of the Messiah is not final. Before the Parousia they too will have been converted and will finally welcome him as God's representative (as Paul expects, Rom. 9–11).

24:1–36
The Coming of the Son of Man for Judgment
(See also at Mark 13:1–37; Luke 21:5–33)

Matthew incorporates the Little Apocalypse of Mark 13:1–32 almost exactly (see there), making slight but significant editorial modifications to adapt it to his later situation. Mark 13:3–8 had already been used in his missions discourse of 10:17–22. The Q materials also contained an apocalyptic discourse. Along with other materials, Matthew integrates these into one grand discourse.

24:20: On a sabbath: These words are added to Mark to the instructions for flight and may indicate that Matthew's church still observes the Sabbath, and that Jewish Christians are given a dispensation to flee even though it violates the Sabbath travel restrictions. More likely, the meaning is that in a Jewish context flight by a whole community on the Sabbath would be both difficult and conspicuous, and therefore both more dangerous than on other days, and scandalous and antagonistic to their opponents.

24:37–42
The Days of Noah
(See also at Mark 13:35; 17:26–36)

24:37–39 As the days of Noah were: The comparison with the days of Noah (Gen. 6–9) is not the wickedness of that generation but that life was going on as usual, with no striking or mysterious signs of the approaching judgment. Matthew's eschatological teaching is not that discerning disciples who know how to decode the prophetic Scriptures will be able to recognize when the end is near but that people did "not know," a theme he emphasizes

repeatedly (24:36, 39, 42, 43, 44, 48, 50; 25:13), thus downplaying the traditional saying taken over from Mark, "by this you will know" (24:33). What the disciples do know is not the time of the end but that it could come any time, and thus the urgency of active engagement in their assigned mission.

24:40–41 One will be taken and another left: Modern dispensationalism has understood those who are "taken" as those who are temporarily removed from the world at the "rapture" (see on 1 Thess. 4:13–5:11). However, like the rest of the New Testament, Matthew has no rapture in his eschatological understanding. Those who are "taken" refers to being gathered into the saved community at the eschaton, just as some were taken into the ark. To be a believer is faithfully to endure the tribulation that is part of the church's mission, not to escape from it. The point is that in the present the two men in the field and the two women grinding at the mill appear alike, but the Parousia will disclose that one is saved and one is lost. The eschatological judgment has a revelatory function. The crucified Jesus is already the Christ, and the persecuted church is already the elect people of God, but the reality is hidden except to eyes of faith. The eschaton will make the present hidden reality apparent to all, when the Crucified One is revealed to all as the Son of Man and his persecuted community is revealed as the elect people of God.

24:43–44
The Thief
(See also at Luke 12:39–40)

It was a bold metaphor to picture the return of Jesus as the breaking and entering of a thief, but one that became traditional in the prophetic stream of early Christianity (1 Thess. 5:2; Rev. 3:3; 16:15). That Matthew's metaphors are not to be interpreted as one consistent allegorical portrayal is seen from the fact that, previously, *not* knowing is the reason for vigilance, while in this parable it is the one who *does* know who is vigilant. The variety of pictures communicates the one point: the time of the Parousia cannot be calculated. Disciples are to be busy with the assigned mission, not with apocalyptic speculation.

24:45–51
The Good and Wicked Servants
(See also at Luke 12:41–46)

Since Matthew tended to interpret parables allegorically, he probably understood this parable to be directed especially to church leaders who, in the light of what they perceived as a delay of the Parousia, abused their authority for their own self-aggrandizement. Contrary to their calculations, the Lord will return unexpectedly and submit them to a horrible punishment, literally "cutting in two," the dismemberment traditionally practiced by Persian tyrants. Matthew adds to the Q saying that they will be counted as among the hypocrites, making contact with the woes of 23:13–36 and showing once again that, as here, they are directed as warnings to Christian leaders.

25:1–13
The Ten Bridesmaids
(See also at Luke 12:35–38)

The chapter division here is particularly disruptive, for this story continues the theme developed above. The story is not an independent unit that may be interpreted for itself, but, like all else in 23:1–25:46, is an integral part of the judgment discourse (see at 23:1).

The bridegroom is Jesus at his eschatological advent. This is clear not only from Matthew's previous use of this imagery (22:1–3; 9:15), but from the fact that he is addressed as Lord and speaks in solemn *amen* pronouncements (25:12; see 5:18).

The bridesmaids represent the church, the present mixture of faithful and unfaithful that will be sorted out at the Parousia (13:24–30, 36–43). They all have lamps and oil, and all sleep, but only some are really prepared for the eschaton whenever it comes. Although the image of Yahweh as bridegroom and Israel as bride was prevalent in the Old Testament and Jewish tradition and continued in the Christian community with Christ as the bridegroom and the church as the bride (2 Cor. 11:2; Eph. 5:25–32; John 3:29; Rev. 19:7; 21:2, 9, 17), that imagery does not fit Matthew's purposes here, and the bride does not appear at all. To represent the church, Matthew needs a *group* in which the members look the same to external appearances, but who will be separated at the Parousia. The "wise" and "foolish" terminology corresponds to 7:24–27, where two men built houses that superficially appear alike, but only one of which meets the eschatological test.

The delay of the bridegroom does not mean that Matthew himself expects a further long delay (see 24:48). In his situation there has already been a delay. His story points out that both those who thought the Parousia would never take place and those who counted on a long delay and thus still had time were tragically mistaken.

The arrival of the bridegroom is the Parousia, with the same phrase "to meet" used here as 1

Thess. 4:17. Since Matthew designates the story as "like the kingdom of heaven," this shows that the kingdom has a future aspect, that the final coming of the kingdom for which the church prays (6:10) is identical with the Parousia of the Son of Man. Both Son of Man and kingdom of God have present/future aspects (see on 3:2; Luke 4:43).

Oil, or rather *having oil*, represents what will count at the Parousia. Matthew will show in his final scene that having oil corresponds to the deeds of love and mercy in obedience to the Great Commandment (25:31–46). The problem was that some of those waiting lacked "oil," not that they went to sleep, since both "wise" and "foolish" slept. Here Matthew pictures preparation for the parousia as responsible deeds of discipleship, not constant watching for the end.

25:13 Keep awake: The conclusion is taken from Mark 13:35 but given a new content and meaning. In Mark, as the conclusion of a different parable, the identical words are properly translated "keep awake," i.e., "stay alert." But in the Matthean story, the maidens' problem was not that they went to sleep, which both good and bad did. To "keep awake" (or "keep watch," NIV) in the sense of constantly being on the alert for signs of the coming of the Son of Man is not Matthew's understanding of responsible discipleship. Matthew opposes the frantic quest for eschatological information and pictures faithful disciples as those who do their duty as disciples at appropriate times and are thus prepared for the Parousia whenever it comes. Such disciples can lie down to sleep in this confidence, rather than being kept awake by panicky last-minute anxiety.

25:14–30
The Talents
(See also at Luke 19:11–27)

A talent is a large sum of money, equal to the wages of a day laborer for fifteen years (see on 18:23). Precisely as a result of the wide circulation of this story, "talent" came into the English language in the Middle Ages as a term for God-given abilities, "gifts and graces." The talents of this story refer to money (25:18); the differing abilities of the recipients are referred to in other terms (25:15).

Matthew reads the Q parable as an allegory of the Parousia, rewrites it to serve that purpose, and inserts it into this context (contrast its different location in Luke 19, which is also closer to the original form). Matthew uses the story to fill in the content of the nature of the Christian life as waiting for the parousia. The meaning of being "good and faithful" is not mere theological correctness, passive waiting, or strict obedience to clear instructions, but active responsibility that takes initiative and risk (see on 5:21–48). In the story, the master had given no instructions as to what was to be done with the money, so faithfulness was not merely obedience to directions. Each servant had to decide how to use the time during the master's absence.

25:31–46
The Last Judgment

These are the last words of Jesus' last discourse, a climactic point to which Matthew has carefully built. Following the long series of parables and warnings about living responsibly so as to be ready for the coming of the Son of Man (24:32–25:30), Matthew reverts to the actual coming already pictured in 24:29–31. This scene is unique to Matthew. It is not a parable but an apocalyptic drama. Parables begin with familiar, this-worldly scenes that then modulate into a new dimension of meaning. This scene, in contrast, begins with an otherworldly depiction of the Parousia, the coming of the Son of Man with his angels and the gathering of all nations before his throne, and modulates into affirmations of the ultimate importance of ordinary, this-worldly deeds. While the evocative imagery cannot be reduced to a list of topics, Matthew has composed and located it so that several Matthean themes converge in this final scene.

1. *The two kingdoms*: The Son of Man who comes at the end is identified as the king (25:34, 40) who sits on his glorious throne (25:31) and admits the righteous to the final kingdom of God (25:34). This is the triumph of the kingdom represented throughout the Gospel by Jesus as the alternative to the this-worldly demonic kingdom represented by his opponents (see on 12:22–37). The two kingdoms that are confused and interwoven in the ambiguities of history now stand disclosed at the end of history. There are only these two kingdoms: the Son of Man with his angels, the blessed righteous, and the kingdom of God prepared from eternity stand on one side; the devil and his angels, the accursed, and the destiny prepared for the devil and his own stand on the other. The kingdom of God is disclosed as the only true kingdom; in this final scene, kingdom language not used of Satan's realm (contrast 12:26). The eschaton reveals that the dualism of the present struggle of the two kingdoms is only penultimate, and that ultimately only God is king.

2. *Christological basis*: A number of christological titles important throughout Matthew converge in this scene. Jesus is pictured as the *Son of Man* (25:31) who has God for his Father (25:34; thus an implicit *Son of God* Christology is present here also). He is called *"king,"* which connotes *Messiah* and *Son of David* in Matthew (1:1–2:2; 21:4–9), and *"Lord"* (25:37, 44). He is the messianic *shepherd* who cares for the sheep (2:6; 9:36; 18:12; 26:31), and the *judge* who makes the final separation between sheep and goats. Even as *"the one who comes"* (25:31) Jesus fills a christological role (11:3; 23:39), anticipated by various figures in the preceding parables who "come" for a judgment scene (24:30, 42, 43, 44, 46; 25:10, 19, 27).

3. *The primacy of ethics*: Like the New Testament writers in general, despite his apocalyptic orientation Matthew has been very restrained in picturing what actually transpires when the Son of Man comes. This is the only scene in the New Testament with any details picturing the Last Judgment. To the reader's surprise (ancient and modern), the criterion of judgment is not confession of faith in Christ. Nothing is said of grace, justification, or the forgiveness of sins. What counts is whether or not one has acted with loving care for needy people. Such deeds are not a matter of "extra credit" but constitute the decisive criterion of judgment presupposed in *all* of chaps. 23–25, the "weightier matters of the Law" of 23:23.

4. *The ultimacy of the love command*: Jesus has taught that self-giving care for others is the heart of the revealed will of God in the Torah and the key to its interpretation (5:17–48; 7:12; 22:34–40).

The fundamental thrust of this scene is that when people respond to human need or fail to respond, they are in fact responding to Christ or failing to do so. Yet this turns out to be a surprise to both groups (25:37, 44). Those who provided food, drink, clothing, and shelter and visited the sick and imprisoned respond entirely on the basis of the needs of "the least of these" and are surprised to learn at the judgment that there was a deeper dimension to their acts of human compassion—just as those who have lived their lives neglecting the needs of others are surprised to learn they had refused to serve the living Christ.

Matthew has also focused this general point on the reception of Christian missionaries, so that one concrete instance of the criterion of judgment would be whether or not the Gentiles to whom Matthew's church is carrying on a mission have supported or hindered the missionaries, and whether or not "settled" Christians have ministered to those missionaries who went out without money, food, or extra clothing and were subject to arrest and imprisonment (10:5–42). This indeed fits with Matthean statements elsewhere, where Christ is met in the "little ones" he sends out as missionaries, and those who give them even a drink of cold water are responding to Christ himself (10:40–42).

Here as elsewhere in the five discourses, Jesus speaks past the characters in the story, in whom the post-Easter reader can recognize the Christians of Matthew's church. As in the preceding paragraphs, the scene functions to encourage and warn the Christian reader that what will count in the judgment is deeds of love and mercy performed for the needy. Though the apocalyptic scene may picture "all the nations" and their treatment of Christian missionaries, the actual address is not to the nations but to the Christians themselves.

26:1–28:20
PASSION AND RESURRECTION

Matthew closely follows the Markan story, as elsewhere omitting some of Mark's more colorful details, but including every narrative element except 14:51–52, and adding within the Markan narrative only the stories of the fate of Judas (27:3–10), the guard at the tomb (27:62–66), and resurrection appearances after Mark's abrupt ending at Mark 16:8 (28:8–28). The distinctive Matthean meaning is expressed by subtle modifications to the Markan story and by enhancing its literary structure.

26:1–16
Jesus Plotted Against and Anointed
(See also at Mark 14:1–11; Luke 22:1–6)

26:1 When Jesus had finished saying all these things: Here is the final appearance of the formula that has concluded each of the five major discourses of Jesus in Matthew (see 7:28; 11:1; 13:53; 19:1). **All** is added here to signal that the teaching ministry of Jesus is now concluded (another reminiscence of Moses, see Deut. 31:30; 32:44). There will be no discourses of Jesus during the passion story, where Jesus is almost completely silent (Isa. 53:7; see Matt. 12:15–21).

26:2 You know: This is not a casual comment but includes the disciples as understanding the meaning of the coming events in advance, another indication of Matthew's abandonment of the Markan view that the disciples' did not understand until after the resurrection. **The Son of Man will be handed over to**

be crucified: On Son of Man, see Mark 2:10. Matthew launches the passion story with an additional passion prediction, a declaration showing it is Jesus himself who inaugurates the events to follow, which he will not only endure, but of which he is also in some sense master. The announcement is not mere information but a preemptive overruling of the plot of the chief priests and elders, who decide not to apprehend him during the Passover festival (vv. 4–5). When the course of events shows that Jesus is in fact put to death during the Passover festival, the reader will perceive from Jesus' announcement that the chief priests and elders, though supposedly in charge of events, are incorrect and without real authority.

26:6–13 A woman came to him: As elsewhere in the passion story, Matthew closely follows Mark. Two other versions of the story appear, in Luke 7:36–50 and John 12:1–8. Although there are variations in content, all forms of the story have the same form or structure (for details, see chart at Mark 14:3 and comments on Mark 14:3–9).

26:15 Thirty pieces of silver: Added by Matthew from Zech. 11:12–13, the obscure reference to the wage of the shepherd who puts the money back into the treasury (see excursus at 2:23, "Matthew as Interpreter of Scripture"). In both places, the sum is considered paltry, the price of an injured slave (Exod. 21:32). The contrast with the preceding story is intentional.

26:17–30a
Passover/Last Supper
(See also at Mark 14:12–26; Luke 22:7–30)

All the Gospels agree that the crucifixion was on the Friday of Passover week, and the Last Supper was on Thursday. Passover was always on the fourteenth day of Nisan, the first month in the ancient Jewish calendar, overlapping March–April in the modern calendar. The day of the month was fixed, so Passover could fall on any day of the week (like Christmas does, but unlike Easter). In the Gospel accounts, Nisan 14 was Preparation Day (Friday), the day before the Sabbath. The Passover lambs were killed in the afternoon of Nisan 14, and the meal was eaten in the evening, i.e., the beginning of Nisan 15 (the Jewish day begins and ends at sunset). In the Synoptic Gospels, following Mark, the Last Supper is the Passover meal. In John the Last Supper is eaten on the preceding day, and the crucifixion takes place at the time of the sacrifice of the Passover lambs. See Figure 7.

26:25 You have said so: Matthew adds this statement to make it clear that Jesus knows the identity of the betrayer in advance (nothing in Mark suggests this was the case) and to bring the hypocrisy of Judas into bold relief. Judas responds as do the other disciples, except for the address. They address Jesus as **Lord**, the typical insiders' term; Judas uses **rabbi**, the outsiders' term.

26:26–29 Jesus took a loaf of bread: The Markan text had expressed Mark's theology of the absence of Jesus between crucifixion and Parousia (see Mark 2:20; 14:7, 25; 16:7). Despite Matthew's own understanding of the presence of Jesus with his church during the time of mission between resurrection and Parousia (see on 1:23; 28:20), Matthew adopts the Markan form of the tradition, apparently the only form he knew. Matthew probably found his own understanding of the continuing presence of Christ in the words **This is my body**.

See the commentary on Mark 14:22–25 for further discussion of the Markan meaning adopted and adapted by Matthew, whose most distinctive changes are these: (1) The Markan narrator's words about the cup, "and they all drank of it," are made into a parallel command to the words over the bread, so that each action comprises a command of Jesus and obedient response of the disciples. (2) The command to **eat** is then added to the words over the bread, to enhance the parallelism to the newly formulated command to **drink**. (3) The whole action is related to **the forgiveness of sins**, the words dropped from Mark's description of John's baptism (Mark 1:4). Forgiveness is dissociated from John's baptism and related to Jesus'

covenant-renewing death. The forgiveness of sins is Jesus' primary mission (1:21; see 9:1–7). Forgiveness is accomplished by Jesus' death, understood here in terms of the sacrifice that seals the bond between God and the covenant people (see Exod. 24:8; Isa. 53:12; but see 9:2). (4) Matthew adds **with you** in v. 29, corresponding to his emphasis throughout on the presence of Jesus with his disciples—though here it is the future fellowship of the kingdom of God. (5) Mark's "kingdom of God" becomes **my Father's kingdom** (see Matt. 10:32–33//Luke 12:8–9; Matt. 12:50//Mark 3:35 for other instances of Matthew replacing "God" in his tradition with "my Father" in sayings of Jesus).

26:30b–56
Abandonment, Betrayal, Arrest
(See also at Mark 14:26–52; Luke 22:31–53; John 13:36–18:11)

Matthew follows the Markan narrative closely, but with subtle alterations that shift the focus of the presentation from the failure of the disciples to the sovereignty of Jesus, who continues to be the teacher who embodies his teaching in his own life.

26:39–46 He threw himself on the ground and prayed: Jesus falls prostrate before God in prayer (literally, "on his face," as in Gen. 17:3, 17; Num. 14:5; 2 Sam. 9:6; 1 Kgs. 18:39; and as the disciples themselves had done in 17:3). Matthew rewrites Mark, who has three occasions on which Jesus finds the disciples sleeping (Mark 14:37, 40, 41). Matthew explicitly delineates three periods of prayer, shifting the focus from the failure of the disciples to Jesus as himself a model of prayer. The contrast

Figure 7. Comparative Chronology of the Passion

	WEDNESDAY		THURSDAY		FRIDAY	
SYNOPTIC CHRONOLOGY					Arrest	
				Last Supper	Trials, Crucifixion, Burial	
JEWISH CALENDAR	NISAN 13		NISAN 14		NISAN 15	
			Slaughter of Passover Lambs		Passover Meal	
JOHANNINE CHRONOLOGY	THURSDAY		FRIDAY		SATURDAY	
			Arrest			
		Last Supper	Trials, Crucifixion, Burial			

between the willing spirit and the weakness of the flesh in v. 41 is not a dualistic anthropology but represents two aspects of the whole person that struggle with each other. Jesus himself is caught up in this struggle, and his prayer moves from praying for deliverance from death (as often in the Psalms; Ps. 118:17–18 had just been sung) to trust and commitment to God's will, using the identical words he had taught his disciples in 6:10. His three prayers form a dramatic contrast to the three denials of Peter, who had slept instead of praying. After the prayer, Jesus is resolute and sovereign and announces the arrival of the betrayer in words that also connote the advent of the kingdom.

26:51 One of those with Jesus: Mark represents one of those standing by (apparently one of the armed group that had come to arrest Jesus) as having drawn a sword and in the chaotic melee having accidentally cut off the ear of a servant of the high priest. Matthew takes this to be one of the disciples (the Fourth Gospel will make it specifically Peter, John 18:10) and makes it the occasion of Jesus' continuing to teach. Even in Gethsemane, Jesus remains the teacher, making three points:

26:52 Put your sword back into its place: *The way of nonviolence, nonretaliation, love of enemies is to be pursued to the end.* What Jesus has taught, he lives out, at the cost of his life (5:38–39, 43–48). As he himself practiced the prayer he taught his disciples, so he practices the nonretaliatory self-giving. Violence is self-destructive and futile, resulting only in a vicious spiral of violence. Jesus represents a redefinition of kingship; the way of God's kingdom, to absorb evil rather than inflict it, brings the spiral finally to an end.

26:53 He will at once send more than twelve legions of angels: *Jesus is not arrested against his will.* A legion is six thousand troops; "twelve" corresponds to Jesus and the remaining eleven disciples. He is confident in the Father's angelic protection but will not ask for it (see 4:6–7, 11). In this statement, added to Mark, Jesus is less the truly human victim than in Mark. Matthew here extends the picture of the powerful son of God further into the passion story than does Mark. Yet even here, the power is in God's hands, not in the hands of Jesus as a divine being, and his human trust in God is what is exhibited. (Again, see Matt. 4, where Jesus places himself on the human side of the equation.)

26:54 How then would the Scriptures be fulfilled? *The Scriptures must be fulfilled.* By this, the Matthean Jesus does not mean that the

prophecies are a prewritten script that Jesus must dutifully act out but that the Scriptures represent the plan and will of God, to which Jesus willingly and trustingly submits (see excursus at 2:23, "Matthew as Interpreter of Scripture").

26:57–27:1
Jewish Trial: Jesus' Confession and Peter's Denial
(See also at Mark 14:53–15:1; Luke 22:54–23:1; John 18:13–28)

26:59–63a Looking for false testimony against Jesus: In Mark the chief priests were looking for authentic testimony and found false witnesses; in Matthew they look for false witnesses and end up with true. Matthew rewrites Mark to show that the testimony of the final two witnesses is in fact true. For Matthew, Jesus is *able* to destroy the temple, "**I am able**" of v. 61 corresponding to that of v. 53. In each case, Jesus is able, by his divine power, to do something he does not in fact do. Like the Suffering Servant (Isa. 53:7), Jesus is silent in the face of his accusers.

27:2–31a
Roman Trial: Jesus Condemned and Mocked
(See also at Mark 15:2–20; Luke 23:2–25; John 18:29–19:3)

27:3–10 *Judas Fails to Make Restitution and Commits Suicide*

27:3 Judas . . . repented: Matthew is the only Gospel to continue the story of Judas after the scene of Jesus' arrest in Gethsemane, inserting a new scene into the Markan outline. Having realized that he has made a great mistake, Judas seems to do all the right things: he is sorry, he returns the money, he acknowledges Jesus' innocence and his own guilt. Yet Matthew seems to hold him up as a model of failed discipleship, one who had been better off if he had not been born (26:24). Why is his action unacceptable to Matthew, who pictures him as despairing and taking his own life? From Matthew's point of view, what Judas lacks, and what Peter has, is that fundamental reorientation away from the kingdom of this world represented by thinking "human things" to the kingdom represented by Jesus (thinking "divine things"; see on 16:21–23). The reader perceives this not from this pericope but from its context in Matthew as a whole, oriented to the new kingdom represented by the meek Son of David (see on 12:22–30). Thus Matthew has developed the story in terms of the biblical story of David, whose kingdom was threatened by an opposing kingdom and who had a friend who betrayed him and then hanged himself (2 Sam. 17:1–23). This story is not merely about the tragic situation of Judas, nor does it speculate on his eternal destiny. For Matthew, the story becomes another expression of the conflict of kingdoms, an illustration of how terrible it is to cast one's lot with the wrong side (12:25–30). Unlike Peter, Judas does not return to the community of disciples, where forgiveness abounds (18:21–35), but dies in individualistic despair.

27:4–8 What is that to us?: The high priests are represented as flat characters, uniformly evil. As they had decided in advance to kill Jesus and sought *false* witnesses, making a sham of the "trial" before the Sanhedrin, so they have only used Judas; now that his purpose is served, they literally have no more use for him. The priests consider the money paid to Judas, now retrieved from the temple, to be "unclean," thus acknowledging their own guilt. Yet their religious scrupulosity prohibits placing it in the temple treasury. They officially decide (the same phrase as 27:1) to use the money to purchase the **potter's field**, which then became known as the **Field of Blood**. In all this, there is a mixture of historical tradition and the confusion between "potter" and "treasury" in the manuscripts of Zech. 11:12–13 (the words are similar in Hebrew), along with the blending of Zech. 11 and Jer. 18–19, 32:7–9. Thus the fulfillment quotation, mostly from Zechariah, is labeled as from Jeremiah (on Matthew's use of Scripture, see excursus at 2:23, "Matthew as Interpreter of Scripture").

27:11–25 *Jesus Is Condemned; Jewish People Accept Responsibility for Jesus' Death*

In this scene Matthew follows Mark closely, making two additions (27:19, 24–25) and subtle modifications, all of which have the effect of making the decision of the Jewish crowds and the responsibility of the Jewish leaders all the more clear.

27:15 The governor was accustomed to release a prisoner: Matthew adopts the Markan picture of the annual custom of releasing one prisoner at the festival. The practice, not documented outside the New Testament, is omitted by Luke, who is more sophisticated in Roman matters.

27:16 A notorious prisoner, called Jesus Barabbas: The name can be translated "son of the

father." In the Gospels, this episode has the literary and theological effect of heightening the contrast between Jesus' true identity as the one who saves his people (1:21) and is the true Son of the Father (11:27). Matthew heightened this contrast if, as is probable, he added "Jesus" as Barabbas's given name (see NRSV footnote). The choice is thus between two men named Jesus, which means "God saves" (see on 1:21): Jesus the criminal, son of (whoever was) his father, and Jesus the Messiah, who saves his people from their sins, the true Son of the Father (3:17; 17:5; 11:25–27). Once again, two kingdoms stand over against each other.

27:19 I have suffered a great deal because of a dream about him: Verse 19 seems to have been composed by Matthew himself, reflecting his favorite themes of Jesus as the righteous one (see 3:15; 21:32) and divine revelation by dreams (in the New Testament only here and the Matthean birth story 1:20; 2:12, 13, 19, 22). These words could be taken as increasing Pilate's guilt—he now knows by divine revelation that Jesus is innocent and is commanded by God to have nothing to do with him. Matthew, however, probably understands the following episode of hand washing to represent Pilate's obedience to the divine message communicated by the dream, so that the words serve to release him from responsibility and heap guilt on the Jewish people.

27:24 I am innocent: Here Matthew makes his second addition to enhance the contrast between Jewish guilt and Gentile innocence. Writing from the post-Easter perspective of the (mostly) failed Christian mission to Jews and the success of the Gentile mission, he pictures Pilate as absolving himself of guilt and the Jewish people accepting the responsibility for Jesus' death (the "crowds" become "the people as a whole," in v. 25). The scene is only in Matthew and was probably composed by Matthew himself.

27:25 His blood be on us: The people respond with words accepting the guilt (for the biblical idiom, see Lev. 20:9–16; Josh. 2:19–20; 2 Sam. 1:16; 14:9; Jer. 26:15; 51:35). These words were destined to be tragically misinterpreted by Christians of later centuries who continued to blame the Jewish people as a whole for the death of Jesus. Matthew, however, looks back on the destruction of Jerusalem in 70 CE as divine punishment for rejection of the Messiah (see on 22:7; 23:34–36, 39). The people in Matthew's story do not invoke guilt on all future generations but on themselves and their children, i.e., the generation that experienced the devastation of Jerusalem and the destruction of the temple. Matthew is engaged in the anti-Jewish polemic of his time and offers his theological interpretation of a tragic event that had already happened as part of his polemic. He does not wish for eternal revenge or pronounce a sentence on all Jews forever.

27:26–31a *The True King Is Mocked*
(See commentary on Mark 15:16–20a)

27:31b–66
Jesus' Crucifixion and Burial
(See also at Mark 15:20–47; Luke 23:26–56; John 19:17–42)

27:34 They offered him wine to drink, mingled with gall: Mark had pictured Jesus being offered myrrhed wine, itself a delicacy but also used as a narcotic to ease the pain of the condemned (see Prov. 31:6). Matthew changes "myrrh" to "gall" corresponding to Ps. 69:21. Mark's helpful narcotic becomes in Matthew a cruel joke.

27:37 This is Jesus, the King of the Jews: The deep irony of the whole trial, mocking, and crucifixion scene is concentrated on the placard placed on the cross. Intended as a coarse joke, the reader knows it is profoundly true at a level the participants in the story cannot imagine. Matthew emphasizes this by adding "This is . . . ," transforming the insult into a Christian confession that even the executioners will acknowledge before the scene is over (v. 54).

27:38 Two bandits were crucified with him: The two crucified with Jesus are described, as in Mark, as "bandits," a word that can refer either to criminals, robbers (as in Luke 10:30; John 10:1; 2 Cor. 11:26; Matt. 21:13) or to revolutionaries, terrorists/freedom fighters (as Josephus, *War* 2.254). Matthew adopts Mark's word but has not described Barabbas as a revolutionary (see 27:16; omitting the description in Mark 15:7). In Matthew, Jesus is not classed with revolutionaries but with common criminals, thus increasing the humiliation (see Isa. 53:3, 9, 12).

27:39 Those who passed by: While Jesus is on the cross, he is derided by three groups. First, passersby **derided** him (the verb is literally "blasphemed," the same as 26:65) with the charge of claiming to destroy and rebuild the temple (see on 26:61). The "wagging of their heads" is an act of derision taken from Ps. 22:8

(see Ps. 109:25; Lam. 2:15). Their challenge for the one who saved others to save himself is not, as they think, the refutation of his claims, but ironically the very truth taught by Jesus (16:25). **If you are the Son of God** is added by Matthew, reflecting Wis. 2:13, 18–20, itself an interpretation of Ps. 22:9. Matthew adds "Son of God" because it is important to his Christology (see his similar addition in 16:16, and see 26:63) and to make the challenge of the passersby correspond to 4:3, 6, where the devil issued a similar challenge using the identical words. There too, Jesus placed himself in the category of humanity, as he does here by the most human act of all, dying a human death. The jeer of the passersby is thus more than a cruel taunt; it represents an opposing theology rejected by the canonical Gospels.

27:41 The chief priests . . . scribes, and elders: The second group is the whole Sanhedrin, as the chief priests, scribes, and elders join in the taunt, this time using the very words of Ps. 22:9 and Wis. 2:13, 18–20, with "Son of God" added again to the Markan text. They call him specifically the **King of Israel**, and **God's Son**, and challenge him to come down from the cross.

27:44 The bandits: The robbers join in the same derision; there is no repentant thief in Matthew (see Luke 23:39–43). Jesus suffers absolutely alone, with no friend, relative, disciple, or convert present.

27:51 The curtain of the temple was torn in two: Matthew sees this as the first of three eschatological signs that accompanied the death of Jesus. Matthew has in mind the veil that separates the most holy place from the rest of the temple (Exod. 26:31–35; 40:21). Ripping this curtain effectively demolishes the temple as the site of God's presence and is an anticipation of the temple's destruction. Matthew looks back on the destruction of Jerusalem and the temple, which he saw as divine judgment on Israel for rejecting the Messiah (see on 22:7).

27:52 The earth shook: The preceding sign was already in Mark, though understood differently by him. The remaining ones are added by Matthew. The eschatological signs continue with an earthquake that splits the rocks (see 24:8; 28:2).

27:53 After his resurrection they came out of the tombs: The tombs of Israelite saints surrounding the city and the Temple Mount are opened as Jesus dies. The rock tombs in which they are buried anticipates the rock tomb in which Jesus will be buried (27:60) and join

Christ and the saints in solidarity. These saints are Jewish people who are brought to life by Jesus' death—but not "this generation," which has rejected him. Since Matthew wants to connect the raising of the Israelite saints with the death of Jesus seen in eschatological terms, but also wants Jesus' own resurrection to be primary (as, e.g., 1 Cor. 15:20), this results in the peculiar picture of the saints being resurrected on Good Friday but remaining in their tombs (or in the open country) until after the Easter appearances of Jesus. That we have theology in narrative form, and not bare historical reporting, is clear. The eschatological events do not have to await the resurrection. Although no theory of the atonement is elaborated, it is clear that for Matthew the death of Jesus is not a mere minus that will be negated by the resurrection. Already in the death of Jesus the eon-changing, dead-raising power of God breaks in.

27:54 The centurion and those with him: Jesus' death and the eschatological events it triggers have a profound effect not only on Jewish saints but also on Gentiles. The Roman execution squad is converted by seeing these events (in Mark it was the centurion alone, on the basis of Jesus' death alone) and becomes a prefiguration of the Gentiles who were to be converted and form a large element of Matthew's own church. They signify this by reciting in unison the Christian affirmation rejected by "this generation": **Truly this man was God's Son!**

27:55–56 Many women were also there: In Mark, the surprising appearance of women at this point in the story and the surprising fact that they had been Jesus' disciples back in Galilee play a literary role. Matthew takes them over from Mark, but they no longer are Jesus' followers *in* Galilee; they follow him **from Galilee,** i.e., they made the pilgrimage trip south with him and his followers. Matthew minimizes the role of these women as earlier followers/disciples/ministers with Jesus, though they have a key role as witnesses to the crucifixion and resurrection and are still present after all the male disciples have fled (26:56).

27:57–61 A rich man from Arimathea: Joseph is a distinctive figure in the Matthean presentation: (1) In contrast to Joseph in Mark, he is not a member of the Sanhedrin; i.e., he is unrelated to the events that led to the condemnation of Jesus. (2) In Mark, Joseph is "waiting for the kingdom of God," but in Matthew Joseph is explicitly **a disciple.** Though Jesus is not

buried by any of the Twelve, who have abandoned him, neither is he buried by a benevolent member of the opposition, but, in another parallel to John the Baptist, he is buried by a disciple (see 14:12). (3) Only in Matthew is the tomb Joseph's **own new tomb,** and only in Matthew had Joseph hewn it **in the rock** himself. (4) Only in Matthew is Joseph wealthy (see Isa. 53:9), which coheres with his owning an expensive tomb but not with his doing the work to excavate it himself.

These distinctively Matthean touches add to the reflective, muted atmosphere that, in contrast to the previous scene, pervades the burial account. This is enhanced when, once again, the male disciple leaves, and the women sit down to keep vigil over the tomb. This provides continuity of witnesses, though the "many" has now dwindled to the two Marys. None of those who have heard Jesus' promises of resurrection are present; even Joseph, having performed his last service for his teacher, **went away** and is never heard from again. The Easter events will take place without him.

27:62–66 The next day: This story and its counterpart in 28:11–15 are both peculiar to Matthew, are written in Matthean style and vocabulary, and were probably composed by Matthew himself, perhaps with a traditional core.

27:63 The chief priests and the Pharisees: The Pharisees reappear for the first time since 23:29=22:41. Matthew has followed Mark in having them absent from the passion story proper but here reintroduces them in order to implicate them in the death of Jesus, and because they were present when Jesus indirectly predicted his resurrection (12:40).

27:64–65 Command the tomb to be made secure: As in the Roman trial scene of which this scene is reminiscent, Pilate has the authority but is persuaded by the evil Jewish leadership to fulfill their wishes. The Jews appear more and more hardened and guilty, Pilate more and more manipulated and innocent. The setting of the guard and sealing of the tomb are only in Matthew, to answer in advance the charge apparently current in Matthew's Jewish environs that the disciples stole the body (see on 28:11–15). As the story moves toward Easter morning, two affirmations about the future are juxtaposed: Jesus' own prediction of the resurrection and the Jewish leader's united front trying to guarantee that it could not happen. The two kingdoms that have stood over against each other throughout Matthew await the third and decisive day (see 12:22–30).

28:1–20
Jesus' Resurrection

EXCURSUS:
INTERPRETING THE RESURRECTION

1. The resurrection of Jesus, i.e., God's act in raising up Jesus, is central to Christian faith. While the virgin birth, miracles, and the teaching of Jesus appear in some New Testament books and are missing from others, faith in the resurrection is common to all.

2. Resurrection is not identical with belief in "life after death." Many people in the ancient world and today believe in the "immortality of the soul" but not in the resurrection. Immortality is a theory about *human nature*, that there is something within us that cannot die. Resurrection affirms something about *God*, that God acts for those who are dead. The resurrection refers to the act of God for a dead person, not the immortality of a being who cannot die (see on 20:27–40). Human beings are not immortal and do not have immortal souls; they die and are powerless unless God acts to grant life beyond death. Jesus shared this reality of human existence. He did not raise himself, or even "arise," but was raised by God. Christian hope is in the resurrection, not in immortality; it is hope in God, not in ourselves.

3. Resurrection is also to be distinguished from resuscitation, i.e., the restoration of a dead person to this-worldly life (see on Luke 7:14; Acts 26:23). In several biblical (and pagan) miracle stories, dead persons are raised (1 Kgs. 17:17–24; 2 Kgs. 4:18–37; Matt. 9:18–26; 10:8; Mark 5:21–43; Luke 7:11–17; 8:40–56; see Acts 9:36–43; 20:7–12), but this is a temporary reprieve from the threat of death, restoration to the life in this world, within which the restored person will still die. Jesus did not "come back to life." "Coming *back*" suggests a return to the previous mode of life; Jesus was raised to a new order of being beyond this life.

4. The concept of the resurrection developed late in Israel's history, as part of the apocalyptic hope. It developed as a way of affirming the faithfulness and trustworthiness of God, who will bring history to a worthy conclusion, raise the dead, and preside over the Last Judgment. The resurrection was part of the conceptuality developed to affirm the ultimate justice of God despite the injustice of the present. The concept of the resurrection, like the concept of the Christ, was thus an eschatological concept. When the end comes, there will be a resurrection of the dead; if there is a resurrection, then the end must have come.

5. For the earliest Christians, the resurrection of Christ was not an isolated event that only concerned something special that happened to Jesus, but the beginning of the end, the "first fruits" of the final eschatological harvest that would take place when Christ returned in the near future (see on 1 Cor. 15:20, 51–52; 1 Thess. 4:13–18).

6. The resurrection faith of the earliest Christians was expressed and communicated in several forms: songs (e.g., Phil. 2:6–11), creeds (e.g., Rom. 1:3–4; 1 Cor. 15:3–5), sermons (e.g., Acts 2:14–36) and stories (as in all four Gospels). The stories developed from two types of earliest traditions: the story of discovering the empty tomb and stories of Jesus' appearance to his disciples. These traditions were apparently originally separate but are combined in the Gospels (see on Luke 1:1–4 and "Introduction to the Gospels"). The Gospel stories point back to an event that really happened, God's act in raising Jesus from the dead, but they are not reporters' transcripts. Each Gospel reformulates the tradition into a story that expresses a particular set of meanings.

7. The Gospel stories of the resurrection are thus not to be harmonized. They differ on such items as who went to the tomb and when, the nature of the resurrection body of Jesus, and the location and chronology of Jesus' appearances. For example, in *Mark* three women go to the tomb, and there are no appearances (16:1–9a; 9b–20 is a later addition); in *Matthew* two women go to the tomb, Jesus appears to both, then later to all the apostles in Galilee; in *Luke* three named women go to the tomb (plus other unnamed women), there are no appearances to women, Jesus appears to two disciples (not apostles) on the road to Emmaus, who later learn that Jesus had already appeared "offstage" to Simon Peter, then Jesus appears to all the apostles. All this is on Easter Sunday, and there are no Galilean appearances. In *John*, Jesus appears to Mary Magdalene alone on Easter Sunday morning, then to ten disciples (without Thomas) that evening, then to the eleven disciples one week later, all in Jerusalem. In the Epilogue/Appendix of John 21, Jesus then appears to seven disciples in Galilee.

The proclamation of the resurrection in the canonical Gospels consists of the discovery of the empty tomb and appearances of the risen Jesus. Neither Matthew nor any of the other canonical Gospels narrate the resurrection event itself, which remains hidden in mystery. For the discovery of the empty tomb, Matthew has only his Markan source, which he follows to its end at Matthew 28:8a (= Mark 16:8a).

28:1–10 *The Two Marys Discover the Empty Tomb*

(See also at Mark 16:1–8; Luke 24:1–8; John 20:1–10)

Matthew brings his Gospel to an end by adopting the closing scene from the Gospel of Mark and composing three additional scenes climaxing in the Great Commission.

28:1 Mary Magdalene and the other Mary went to see the tomb: Matthew modifies Mark so that the women come only to "see the tomb," i.e., continue their vigil, rather than to "anoint the body," since the guard posted in Matthew makes anointing impossible, and since the body was already anointed for burial in 26:12. Likewise, they do not wonder who will roll away the stone, since they are not intending to reopen the tomb and anoint the body, which in any case is made impossible in Matthew by the guard.

28:2–4 A great earthquake . . . an angel: The eschatological drama of the crucifixion continues (see 27:51–53): the "young man" of Mark 16:5 is replaced by earthquake and angel. In this case, the apocalyptic signs do not convert (see 27:51–54). In contrast to the soldiers at the crucifixion, the guards at the tomb are shaken up and become **like dead men** themselves.

28:5–7 Go quickly and tell his disciples: In the Markan plot, the women were overcome with fear and kept silent, and the story ends by leaving the responsibility to proclaim the Easter message with the reader (Mark 16:8a). Matthew continues the story by adding joy to the note of fear, and the women become positive figures who obediently go to tell the disciples. Jesus had told the disciples he would meet them in Galilee (26:32), but the women had not heard this. Matthew thus adjusts the Markan "as he told you" to "I (the angel) have told you" (NRSV, **this is my message for you**). Galilee is for Matthew not mere geography but theology, "Galilee of the Gentiles" (see on 4:12–17), the appropriate setting for the Great Commission to all nations (28:16–20). As in Mark, so also in Matthew, there are no appearances to the disciples in Jerusalem or Judea and no room in the narrative for any such appearances (contrast Luke 24 and John 20). The stories of appearances of the risen Jesus cannot be harmonized into one narrative; each story is a testimony to the church's resurrection faith, not part of a single historical report.

28:8–10 Suddenly Jesus met them: In this scene, composed by Matthew, the women are not only the first witnesses of the empty tomb, but receive the first appearance of the risen Christ (contrast 1 Cor. 15:5). Jesus "meets" them, i.e., joins and accompanies them; they are already en route on their mission when they are joined by the risen Christ, a paradigm of Matthew's understanding of the reassuring presence of the risen Christ in the missionary activity of the church (see on 1:23; 10:40; 13:37; 14:22–33; 16:18; 17:17; 18:5; 20; 28:20). The disciples are now called **brothers** by Jesus himself. We have not seen the disciples since they all deserted him and fled (26:56), except for Peter, who denied him, and Judas, who betrayed him and then killed himself. The alienation has now been healed, from the divine side; the disciples may know that they again/still belong to the family of believers (12:46–50, Jesus' true family identified with his disciples). The women become not only missionaries of the resurrection message but agents of reconciliation.

28:11–15 *The Guards Are Bribed by the Chief Priests*

28:11 Some of the guards went into the city: This scene completes the story begun in 27:62–66. The scene with the guards forms a perverse parallel to that of the women, with corresponding sets of verbs (vv. 7–8/11, 13). The women have been commissioned to "go and tell" the good news of the resurrection and reconciliation; the guards, who have seen the same things as the women **went** and **told . . . everything that had happened**. Having hard empirical evidence or having observed the spectacular events themselves thus did not generate faith in the eschatological event of the resurrection, which is different from merely being convinced that Jesus' body came out of the tomb.

28:12–13 A plan to give a large sum of money: Again the chief **priests** and **elders** (Matt. 16:21; 21:23; 26:3, 47, 27:1, 3, 12, 20, 41; see 27:62 "chief priests and Pharisees") held an official consultation, as 12:14; 22:15; 27:1, 7. This is the height of irony, as they now become the perpetrators of the very story that setting the guard and sealing the tomb was designed to prevent, and the height of hypocrisy, which Matthew has opposed to discipleship throughout (Matt. 6:2, 5, 16; 7:5; 15:7; 22:18; 23:13, 15, 23, 25, 27, 28, 29; 24:51). As in the case with Judas, money oils the wheels of hypocrisy—though here the sum is greater. It costs more to suppress the resurrection message than to engineer the crucifixion. The Gospel concludes with the polar opposites of the two kingdoms represented throughout the Gospel (see 12:22–30, especially the "dualism of decision" represented by 12:30).

28:15 This story is still told among the Jews: The Christian story of the resurrection was opposed by a counterstory circulated by the synagogue. The phrase "the Jews" has been used previously in Matthew only in the phrase "King of the Jews" (Matt. 2:2; 27:11, 29, 37). The term is an outsider's term expressing some distance. Its use here indicates that after the eschatological event of the crucifixion/resurrection, in Matthew's view the "people of Israel" are now "the Jews," no longer as such the chosen people of God, but one of the nations of the world to whom the universal mission is directed.

28:16–20 *The Risen Lord Gives the Great Commission*
(See also at Luke 24:44–49)

28:16 The eleven disciples went to Galilee: This is the first scene in which the disciples have appeared since they fled during the arrest of Jesus (26:56). Presumably Matthew understands that they remained in Jerusalem until they received the announcement of the women (which is not narrated), on the basis of which they returned to the mountain Jesus had appointed for their postresurrection rendezvous (see on 26:32). The disciples thus have already come to faith in the risen Jesus and the reconciling message that they are again/still his brothers. The basis for this faith is not an appearance of Jesus to them but the testimony of the women, which they have accepted. The Jerusalem appearances of Jesus to his disciples recounted in Luke 24:13–43 and John 20:19–29 are not only not narrated in Matthew; they cannot be accommodated within the Matthean story line.

28:17 When they saw him, they worshiped him: Matthew provides no description of the risen Jesus. As in 28:9–10, the event is narrated as though it were an ordinary, this-worldly event. Their response, like that of the women in 28:9, is not amazement, fascination, or curiosity, but kneeling in worship. **But some doubted:** The concluding clause of v. 17 may legitimately be translated "but *some* doubted," referring to others besides the eleven (NIV and NRSV; so also KJV, ASV, NEB); "but some *of them* doubted," implying that while some of the eleven worshiped, others of them doubted (TEV, REB); or "but *they* doubted," referring to the same group that worshiped (NAB). The

last translation best represents Matthew's own theological understanding of the meaning of discipleship, which is always a matter of "little faith," faith that by its nature is not the same as cocksureness, but incorporates doubts within itself in the act of worship. The word is the same as in 14:31, in a scene composed by Matthew reminiscent of this one. Thus the same elements of worship, doubt, and little faith inhere in the church after Easter as before. Whatever the nature of the resurrection event, it did not generate perfect faith, even in those who experienced it firsthand. It is not to angels or perfect believers but to the worshiping/wavering community of disciples that the world mission is entrusted.

28:18–20 Jesus came to them and said to them: The risen Jesus comes to his wavering church, as in 14:25. Jesus' only action is to speak, and he is the only speaker. Acts 1–15 narrates the gradual process in which the community of Jesus' disciples after Easter came to realize under the guidance of the Spirit that it is the will of their risen Lord that the church be a universal, inclusive community of all nations. This process is here concentrated into one scene, composed by Matthew on the basis of traditions alive in his church. The scene represents Matthew's theological interpretation of the mission of the church in obedience to the command of the risen Christ. If the scene were a mere report of an occasion in which Jesus had literally commanded all the disciples to carry on a Gentile mission, it is difficult to understand their struggles in Acts 1–15.

All authority: See 11:27. The risen Jesus is pictured as Lord of heaven and earth, i.e., the cosmic ruler in God's stead (see Phil. 2:5–11; Heb. 1:1–3; Col. 1:15–18), the king in the present-and-coming kingdom of God, the one who represents God's cosmic rule. As God's representative, there is no competition between God as king and the authority of Jesus, just as there is no idolatry inherent in the worship of Jesus—who had declared that only God may be worshiped (4:9–10). Matthew has no explicit doctrine of the "deity of Christ" but presents the Jesus story in such a way that to encounter Jesus is to encounter the God who has defined himself in Jesus (see John 20:28).

All nations: The commission is to all the nations ("Gentiles" is the same Greek word). The Matthean Jesus had previously limited the missionary commission to Israel (10:5–6). But empirical Israel, now having lost its status as *the* people of God, is included among the nations to which the church's mission is directed.

Make disciples: The nations are to be "discipled" (Matthew has used "disciple" as a verb previously in 13:52 and 27:57; it occurs elsewhere in the New Testament only in Acts 14:21). Previously, Matthew has adopted the Markan usage in which disciples are exclusively the inner group of twelve men who have left all to follow Jesus, though Matthew has told the story in such a way that readers in the post-Easter church can see reflections of their own Christian experience. After the resurrection, the invitation to discipleship is open to all people, men and women, of all nations. That is, people are not called to become individual believers; they are to be enlisted as disciples within the Christian community, whose reception of the Christian message in faith must be actualized in their lives. The call to the fishermen (4:18–22), the tax collector (9:9), and the Twelve (10:1–4) is now extended to all, as an extension of the call to Abraham and in accord with the promise that all nations would finally be blessed through him (Gen. 12:1–3).

Baptizing them: Baptism is the transitional act from outside the Christian community to discipleship within it. Previously in Matthew, baptism has been associated only with John the Baptist; neither Jesus nor his disciples have carried on a baptismal ministry (contrast John 3:22; 4:1–2). **In the name of the Father and of the Son and of the Holy Spirit:** It is not clear whether "in the name of" with the Trinitarian formula refers to the authority by which baptism is carried out, to the liturgical formula pronounced over the baptized, or to fellowship with the divine reality into which the candidate is baptized (or elements of each of these meanings). Like the rest of the New Testament, Matthew has no developed doctrine of the Trinity (see on 1 Pet. 1:2). Yet Matthew, like other New Testament authors, has found that God talk in the light of the Christ event does modulate into a threefold pattern without denying the fundamental Jewish monotheistic affirmation (12:28; 22:43; see, e.g., Rom. 1:3–4; 8:3–4; 14:17–18; 15:30; 1 Cor. 12:3–6; 2 Cor. 13:13; Eph. 3:14–19; 4:4–6; 1 Thess. 1:2; Titus 3:4; Heb. 2:3; 6:4; Luke 1:35; 2:25–28; John 3:34; 1 Pet. 1:1–2; 1 John 4:2; 5:6–9 [NRSV and NIV, not KJV!]; Jude 20; Rev. 1:4–5; 14:13). The essential point is that the One encountered in Jesus as the Son of God and in the Spirit-led church as the people of God is not some subordinate deity, but the one true God.

28:18 I am with you: The Matthean Jesus does not ascend. His last words are a promise of his continuing presence during the church's mission (see 1:23; 10:40; 13:37; 16:18; 17:17; 18:5, 20; 26:29).

The Gospel according to Mark

INTRODUCTION

Author

As is the case with all the New Testament Gospels, the Gospel of Mark is anonymous (see "Introduction to the Gospels"). Second-century Christian tradition assigned this Gospel to "Mark," presumably the companion of Paul and Peter (Phlm. 24; see Col. 4:10; 2 Tim. 4:11; 1 Pet. 5:13), also identified with the John Mark of Acts 12:12, 25; 15:37–39. By ascribing the Gospel to a companion of the apostles, the church made the claim that it represents the apostolic faith, i.e., that it is an authentic witness to the meaning of the Christ event. We do not know the name of the actual author but can recognize from his work that he was an early Christian teacher who was a masterful interpreter of the story of Jesus.

Sources

The Gospel contains memories of the original eyewitnesses of Jesus' ministry, but the author was not personally present at the events he narrates, nor does he base his narrative directly on the personal reminiscences of Peter or other eyewitnesses. He draws from the oral and written traditions that circulated in the church the generation after Jesus' death. While some of these sayings and stories accurately preserve what the historical Jesus said and did in the pre-Easter settings of Galilee and Jerusalem, their value does not depend on their accuracy as history. The whole tradition had already been shaped and elaborated by the teaching and preaching of the early Christians. It was not biographical or historical interest that caused the stories and sayings of Jesus to be preserved, even though some represented accurate history. They were preserved as expressions of Christian faith in what God had done in the life, death, and resurrection of Jesus. The author drew from this stream of tradition, but he was the first to fashion the separate units into a comprehensive narrative.

Date, Place, and Readership

Since the book presupposes that the readers are unfamiliar with Jewish customs (see 7:2–4),

and since the author himself does not seem to have a personal knowledge of Palestinian geography, the Gospel was probably not written in Palestine but for Gentile Christians elsewhere. Early Christian tradition located the book in Rome just before or after Peter's martyrdom there ca. 64 CE, and some modern interpreters still consider that to be the best setting for understanding the Gospel. Many scholars, however, locate the author and his original readers in Syria, where both Peter and Paul had been active.

The discourse of 13:5–23 seems to reflect the persecution of Christians by Nero in 64 CE, and the Roman war in Palestine that destroyed Jerusalem and the temple in 66–70 CE. Since Mark seems to have been used by both Matthew and Luke (see Introductions to those books), it is probable that Mark was written for a Gentile Christian readership in Syria or north Galilee just before or just after 70 CE.

Genre

While there is some resemblance to the ancient biographical form, the Gospel form invented by Mark is different from the usual biography, ancient or modern (see "Introduction to the Gospels").

The Gospel was not written as a "book" to be circulated and sold in bookstores. It was written to be read aloud in the worship service of early Christian communities (see on 13:14) and was intended to be heard as one continuous reading. Just as a powerful movie cannot be experienced piecemeal, the impact of Mark's narrative is best experienced by hearing it read straight through from 1:1 through to 16:8, the original conclusion (see commentary there), which requires about an hour and twenty minutes.

Theological Themes

Mark is narrative Christology; it sets forth the saving act of God by telling the story of Jesus. The first half of the book portrays Jesus as the powerful Son of God who delivers humanity from all the threats that rob God's people of authentic life: meaninglessness; storms and the evils of nature; loneliness; alienation from themselves, others,

105

and God; sin and guilt; hunger; sickness; and the ultimate enemy—death. In this section of Mark, Jesus does what only God can do.

The second half of the book focuses on the human being Jesus as one in solidarity with the weakness and vulnerability of the human condition. Miracles cease, and he himself becomes the victim of human sin and death.

These two perspectives are held together by the secrecy motif: Jesus is presented as a manifestation of the power of God, but this is not recognized by the characters in the story until the cross and resurrection. To tell the story in such a way that Jesus' true identity could be recognized and that one could come to authentic Christian faith *prior* to the cross and resurrection would, from Mark's perspective, be inadequate: God's act in the crucifixion and resurrection is indispensable to true Christian faith. The "messianic secret" is thus not primarily an aspect of the 30 CE life of Jesus but is the Markan literary means of telling the Jesus story in such a way that the readers, from their post-Easter perspective, can see the power of God at work in Christ, which must be hidden from the people in the story until the end of the narrative (15:39!). Mark devised the distinctive literary genre Gospel to facilitate presenting Jesus as the one who represents the saving power of God and, at the same time, represents the weakness and vulnerability of the Suffering Servant. This Markan theology comes to expression in the way the author has structured the narrative.

Outline and Structure

Mark has composed his narrative in basically two parts, with an introduction and conclusion.

Figure 8. Structure of Mark's Narrative

1:16–8:21 Part One: Galilee	11:1–15:47 Part Two: Jerusalem
Miraculous ministry	Nonmiraculous ministry
Success	Rejection
Exorcisms	No exorcisms
Kingdom parables typical	Kingdom parables atypical
Calling disciples	No calling of disciples
Secrecy commands	No secrecy commands
Unhealed blindness	Blindness healed
No valid confession	Valid confession: Jesus, centurion

The carefully structured section 8:22–10:52 both separates and joins these two sections by representing the transition from blindness to sight. Thus the following outline:

1:1–15 Introduction
1:16–8:21 Part One—Galilee: The Secret Epiphany of the Son of God
    1:16–3:6 Positive Response and Beginning of Opposition
        1:16–45 Call of Disciples and Day in Capernaum
        2:1–3:6 Conflicts and Plot to Destroy Jesus
    3:7–6:6a Appointment of Twelve; Opposition Intensifies
    6:6b–8:21 Sending Apostles; Are They Too Blind and Hardened?
8:22–10:52 Transition—From Blindness to Discipleship, from Galilee to Judea
11:1–15:47 Part Two—Jerusalem: The Public Conflict and Suffering of the Son of Man
    11:1–13:37 Jesus' Ministry in Jerusalem
    14:1–15:47 Jesus' Passion
16:1–8 Conclusion—The Women at the Tomb

For Further Reading

Marcus, Joel. *Mark 1–8: A New Translation with Introduction and Commentary.* Anchor Bible 27. New York: Doubleday, 2000.

Hooker, Morna D. *The Gospel according to Saint Mark.* Black's New Testament Commentary. Peabody, MA: Hendrickson, 1991.

COMMENTARY

1:1
TITLE
(Matt. 1:1; Luke 1:1–4)

This verse is Mark's own title for his narrative. ("The Gospel according to Mark" is the church's title, added at the time when the four Gospels were selected and included in one authoritative collection.) "Gospel" means "**good news**," the Christian message (the same word is used in 1:14). The **beginning** refers not only to the following section about John the Baptist as the beginning of the Jesus story, but points to the narrative as a whole as the beginning of the story that continues to the readers' own day, in which they are involved, forming a bracket with 16:8 (see commentary there). On **Christ**, see on 8:29; on **Son of God**, see on 1:10–11; Luke 1:28–33.

1:2–15
INTRODUCTION

This compressed opening to the Markan narrative is a series of rapid-fire scenes in which the author portrays the events that were to happen at the end time, the time of the fulfillment of God's promises, *as already happening*: the fulfillment of Scripture (1:2–3, 14), the appearance of Elijah (John the Baptist; see Mal. 3:1; 4:5; Mark 9:11–13); the opening of the heavens, the return of the Holy Spirit, and the voice of God (1:10–11); the time of testing by Satan (1:12–13); the reappearance of the conditions of paradise (1:13); the advent of the kingdom of God (1:15); the coming of the Messiah (1:1); and the new creation (1:13).

1:2–8
JOHN THE BAPTIST
(See also at Matt. 3:1–12; Luke 3:1–18; John 1:19–28)

1:2–3 As it is written: The story that is about to unfold does not begin with Jesus, and not even with John. This story is the key segment of God's unfolding plan that began at creation, continued through the Old Testament prophets, comes to its definitive climax in Jesus, and continues after the resurrection in the lives of the readers, until the end of history at the coming of the Son of Man (13:24–27; see on 2:10). **In the prophet Isaiah:** The quotation is actually a combination of Exod. 23:20; Mal. 3:1; and Isa. 40:3. Such combinations were typical in first-century Judaism and elsewhere in the New Testament (e.g., Rom. 3:10–18; Heb. 1:5–13); the author has another combination in the heavenly voice of 1:11. The attribution to "Isaiah" is not merely a mistake; the visionary material of Isaiah plays a fundamental role in shaping the narrative to come. **I am sending:** The offstage voice heard by the reader is the voice of God speaking through the Scriptures. **My messenger:** In Exod. 23:20 this is the angel of the Lord. Since in both Hebrew and Greek the same word means "angel" and "messenger," Mark can here understand it to refer to John the Baptist. **Ahead of you:** The text is altered from Mal. 3:1 "before me." The "you" here is the offstage Christ, who has not yet appeared in the story. The reader (but not the characters in the story) know in advance that Jesus is the one already chosen by God, that Jesus has a **way**, and that John's role is to prepare the **way of the Lord**. This word, variously translated "road," "path," and "way," is a significant theological term for Mark (see 1:2, 3; 4:4, 15; 6:8, 8:27; 9:33–34; 10:17, 32, 46, 52; 11:18; 12:14). Here, God addresses Jesus with the divine title Lord, never used unambiguously of Jesus in the narrative itself (see 2:28; 5:19; 7:28; 11:3; 12:36–37). This is an aspect of the Markan "messianic secret" (see introduction to Mark).

1:4 John the baptizer: See on Matt. 3:1; Luke 1:5–25. **Baptism of repentance for the forgiveness of sins:** Repentance, reorienting one's life by turning back to God, was central in the Old Testament prophets and in first-century Judaism, where it was also related to the temple ritual as the means of appropriating God's forgiveness. Here John makes the temple sacrifices unnecessary for forgiveness and reconciliation with God, a foreshadowing of the Markan Jesus' own opposition to the temple (see on 11:11,15–16, 27; 12:35; 13:1, 3; 14:49, 58; 15:29, 38).

1:5 Whole Judean countryside and all the people of Jerusalem: From the beginning, Mark pictures the people as a whole (in contrast to the Jewish leaders) as responding positively to John and Jesus as messengers from God (but see 14:43; 15:8, 11, 15). **Were baptized:** On John's baptism, clothing, and dress, see on Luke 3:2–3.

1:7 The one who is more powerful: In 30 CE, John's original message pointed to the coming of God or to a heavenly savior figure such as the Son of Man (see on 2:10). Retrospectively, early Christianity, including Mark, understood the promise as referring to Jesus, and made John into the forerunner of Christ. In Mark, John has no independent message; his only function is to point to Christ. The first characterization of Jesus heard by the reader is that he is the **powerful** one (see 3:22–27; 9:28). The first half of Mark portrays Jesus as the mighty one representing the power of God (see introduction to Mark).

1:8 Water . . . Holy Spirit: Mark never reports the fulfillment of this promise, nor does he explain what he means by it. For Luke's understanding, see on Luke 3:16–17; Acts 1:4–5; 2:1–5. For Mark, the Spirit is given to Jesus' disciples after the resurrection and will be their guide, instructing them in what they should say in crisis situations. The Gospel of John elaborates extensively on this point (John 14–16).

1:9–11
THE BAPTISM OF JESUS
(See also at Matt. 3:13–17; Luke 3:21–22; John 1:29–34)

1:9 In those days: The chronology is not specific; the phrase sounds biblical and (like 1:2–3) is intended to set the narrative following into the context of biblical history. **From Nazareth of Galilee:** Mark says nothing of Bethlehem or of Jesus' birth there; throughout the Markan story Jesus is the "Nazarene" from Galilee (1:9, 24; 10:47; 14:67; 16:6). This is in contrast to the negative connotations of Judea, including the "Son of David" tradition associated with Bethlehem (see on 10:47–48; 11:10; 12:35). **Baptized by John:** In the Markan story, John is unaware of Jesus' identity (the reader knows), and there is no conversation (see on Matt. 3:13–17). John was baptizing for the forgiveness of sins (1:4). Mark's first picture of Jesus portrays him in solidarity with sinful human beings, being baptized along with them without a word of explanation. Mark does not feel compelled to explain that Jesus was not a sinner (see 10:18, "clarified" by Matt. 19:17). This does not mean that Mark rejected the idea of Jesus' sinlessness (2 Cor. 5:21; 1 Pet. 2:22; 1 John 3:5) but that the question in this form does not occur to him.

1:10–11 He saw: As an aspect of the messianic secret (see introduction to Mark), in Mark the heavenly vision is seen only by Jesus (and the reader). This corresponds to the heavenly voice, which speaks only to Jesus, **"You are my Son"** (contrast Matt. 3:17, "This is . . ."). The voice of God speaks in the words of Scripture (as in 1:2–3): the heavenly declaration is a combination of Ps. 2:7 and Isa. 42:1. (The wording is not as evident in the English Old Testament, based on the Hebrew text; Mark's wording reflects the LXX, the Greek translation used in early Christianity.) **My Son:** On Son of God as a title for Jesus, see on Luke 1:28–33. The phrase in Ps. 2:7 was addressed to the Israelite king, "adopted" by God at his accession to the throne. Unlike Matthew and Luke, Mark has no birth story in which Jesus is born as Son of God, and unlike Paul Mark has no doctrine of preexistence in which Christ was Son of God before coming to earth. This does not mean that Mark has an adoptionist Christology (that God "adopted" Jesus, an "ordinary man," at his baptism). Mark does not speculate on *when* Jesus became Son of God, but does have God address Christ as Lord offstage before the narrative begins. Thus 1:11 is a divine declaration of Jesus' identity as God's Son, not a statement that he is just now being adopted as Son. **Well pleased:** This echoes the language addressed to the Suffering Servant of Isa. 42:1–4; 49:1–6; 50:4–9; 52:13–53:12. The heavenly voice declares Jesus to be both the royal Son of God filled with divine power (the Spirit) and the Suffering Servant who carries out God's will in weakness and rejection.

1:12–13
THE TESTING BY SATAN
(See also at Matt. 4:1–11; Luke 4:1–13)

1:12 Satan: On the theological value (and dangers) of language about Satan and demons, see excursus at 5:1 and comments on Luke 4:1.

1:13 Tempted: The same Greek word means both "test" and "tempt." In Mark there is no debate between Jesus and the devil (as in Matt. 4:1–11; Luke 4:1–13), no "temptation" in the moral sense, but a testing of his divine power. In 12:15 the same word is translated "put to the test"; see 8:27 commentary. In the apocalyptic scenario, the devil appears at the end time to test God's people (see "lead us not into temptation" in the Lord's Prayer, and commentary on Matt. 6:13 and Luke 11:4). First-century Judaism had already understood the serpent of Genesis 3 to be Satan, so in Mark's context the scene has the overtones of Adam tested by Satan in the garden of Eden. The first Adam and all humanity have succumbed to Satan's power; will the second Adam (see Rom. 5:12–21) prevail? Mark does not describe the outcome of the battle (but see the following paragraph, and 3:23–27). **With the wild beasts:** Before the fall, Adam and all humanity had lived peaceably with all nature (Gen. 1–2). The promised messianic king will restore peace among all living things (see Isa. 11:1–9). Mark pictures this eschatological reality as already present in Jesus. The picture may also conjure up images in the minds of Mark's readers of the wild animals to whom Christians were thrown in Nero's persecution of the Roman church in 64 CE. **Angels waited on him:** This may also reflect a traditional view in first-century Judaism that in Eden the angels catered food to Adam and Eve; see also 1 Kgs. 19:4–9. In Mark, Jesus does not fast (see 2:18–20; vs. Matt. 4:2; Luke 4:2).

1:14–15
MINISTRY IN GALILEE: SUMMARY
(See also at Matt. 4:12–17;
Luke 4:14–15; 4:1–3; 43–46)

1:14 After John was arrested: A different chronology from John 1–4, where John and Jesus have parallel and overlapping ministries. **Arrested:** The word also means "delivered over" or "betrayed," the same word used for Jesus, who is "handed over" both by human hands (3:19; 14:10; 15:10) and, like the Suffering Servant, by God (Isa. 53:6; see on

9:31; 14:41). The destiny of John prefigures that of Jesus.

1:15 Kingdom of God: See on Luke 4:43. Jesus as the messianic king is the instrument of God's kingdom, not his own. God's rule is effected through the Christ event. **Has come near:** Unlike Matthew and Luke, Mark never explicitly says that the kingdom is already present. Its nearness already affects the present, but the full reality is still to come, even in the life of Jesus. **Repent:** The word literally means a "change of mind." The divine act calls for a response, a complete reorientation from the way humans normally think (see 8:33 in the context of 8:27–9:1). **Believe the good news:** The message of Jesus is summarized not as "good advice" or "great principles" but as good *news*: something has happened and is happening that makes all the difference—the saving act of God in Jesus Christ.

1:16–8:21
PART ONE—GALILEE: THE SECRET EPIPHANY OF THE SON OF GOD

In this major section constituted by the first half of Mark's narrative, Jesus is presented as the truly divine Son of God who functions by the power of God, delivering humanity from all the evils that prevent life from being what it was intended to be: an anticipation of eschatological salvation. The section is divided into three subsections, each of which uses the "call" vocabulary, and each of which portrays the call, commissioning, and sending of the disciples. In Mark, Christology and discipleship imply each other; the kind of discipleship one lives out is influenced by one's understanding of messiahship.

1:16–3:6
POSITIVE RESPONSE AND BEGINNING OF OPPOSITION

The first fifteen verses of Mark present the marvelous good news that the time of waiting is over, the time of God's salvation is dawning, Jesus is God's messianic king in the long-awaited kingdom of God. Elijah has come; the heavens have been opened; the Spirit has descended to empower Jesus with God's own power; the devil has been met and bested. All the pieces are in place; now begins the opening scene of the narrative proper. What mighty work will the Messiah accomplish to begin the work of transforming the sinful world into God's kingdom of justice and peace? The next paradigmatic

scene may be a disappointment to readers who have a different understanding of messiahship from Mark's: Jesus *calls disciples*.

1:16–45
Call of Disciples and Day in Capernaum
1:16–20 *The Call of the First Disciples*
(See also at Matt. 4:18–22; Luke 5:1–11; John 1:35–51)

1:16 Jesus passed by: See 6:48–50. God "passed by" in the theophany scene of Exod. 33:18–23. Jesus is the subject of all the verbs until the final clause of each scene; they are not seeking him, he finds and calls them. **Simon:** Later renamed Peter; see 3:16. **Fishermen:** They are not wealthy but people who work with their own hands; neither are they the poorest of the poor—they own boats and have houses (1:29) and employees (1:20), comparable to middle-class businesspeople of today.

1:17 Follow me: Mark has built to this moment with consummate artistry. These are the first actual words the reader hears Jesus say (1:14–15 are a generalizing summary, not, as here, specific address to particular people). **Fish for people:** The imagery and connotations are multilayered. In the Hellenistic world, fishing was a metaphor for teaching; in the Bible, fishing can be an image of judgment or of participation in God's eschatological work of restoring the people of Israel (see Jer. 16:16; Matt. 13:47). The image does not mean, in the sense of modern pop evangelism, that they will learn how to use the proper bait to win souls for Jesus.

1:19 He called them: This is what God does to make prophets (Isa. 6:1–8; 41:9; 42:6), not what rabbis did to gain disciples. In Judaism, would-be disciples sought out a teacher, not vice versa. Early Christianity used the language of "calling" to express how people became Christians (see Rom. 1:6, 8:28–30). Thus "those who are called" refers to the act of God in calling them, not to their own freedom and responsibility. The word for "church" in the New Testament (literally, the "called-out ones") is related to the word for "call." The followers of Jesus are not a voluntaristic society for promoting good, but those who have been drafted.

1:20 They left their father . . . and followed: See 1 Kgs. 19:19–21, on which this story is modeled; the call of Christ has higher priority than even the most sacred family obligations (see Matt. 10:37–38). Mark pictures this as the effect of the powerful, sovereign word of Christ. They do not reflect, weigh the advantages and disadvantages, and compare his teaching (which they have not yet heard) with other teachers, but without a word begin to follow. They do not even ask where they are going—they will learn this *along the way*. There are no psychological explanations to be offered here; Mark is not merely reporting what happened once upon a time back there in history but is presenting a scene in which the essence of becoming a disciple is powerfully portrayed. The post-Easter Christ speaks through the story from a pre-Easter setting (see Rev. 14:4, where "following" is used of disciples of the resurrected Lord). In reality, this is the first of Mark's miracle stories in which the power of God changes human lives.

The next three miracle stories introduce Jesus' public ministry with three scenes of deliverance, all of which point beyond themselves to the saving act of God in the Christ event as a whole.

1:21–28 Teaching and Exorcism
in the Synagogue at Capernaum
(See also at Luke 4:31–37)

On the language of demons, Satan, and exorcism, see excursus at 5:1. In 1:12–13 Jesus won a hidden victory in the offstage power struggle with Satan. Here and in the other exorcism stories the results of that victory are illustrated. Mark is the only evangelist to make an exorcism story an initial scene in Jesus' ministry, Mark's way of saying that a primary meaning of Jesus' advent is the defeat of Satan. In the Christ event, God has already defeated the cosmic power of evil; here, the this-worldly, "local" meaning of that victory is illustrated.

1:21 Capernaum: A fishing village on the northwest shore of the Sea (lake) of Galilee, the home of the four fishermen called in 1:16–20 (1:29). The city becomes the home base of Jesus during his ministry. **Entered the synagogue:** Archaeologists have excavated and restored a splendid synagogue from the fourth or fifth century CE, built on the foundations of a synagogue of the first century, probably the very one of this story. This is one of the few locations in modern Israel where visitors may stand today on a spot where Jesus himself likely stood.

1:22 As one having authority: This is not a matter of Jesus' tone of voice, confidence, or assertiveness; Jesus speaks as the eschatological king appointed by God and filled with the

Spirit, the representative of the dawning kingdom of God (1:10–11, 14). The issue between Jesus and **the scribes** is not the manner of their teaching but who represents the authority of God. The content of Jesus' teaching is not given; its power is due not to the great insights or principles it contains but to the person of Jesus. In Mark's theology, to have Jesus as one's teacher means to live in the light of God's revelation in the Christ event, not necessarily to cite the teaching of Jesus on this or that topic. **The scribes:** Not just secretaries but professional official scholars of the Bible and Jewish tradition, local Jewish leaders who will be Jesus' principal enemies throughout the story (e.g., 2:6; 3:22; 11:18, 27; 12:32–38) and who will finally participate in the plot to destroy him (14:1, 43, 53; 15:1, 31). In Mark's dualistic theology, one is either for Jesus or against him (9:38–40), on the side of God or on the side of Satan. This is the first hint that the scribes belong to the other side; there are no "Christian scribes" in Mark (see Matt. 13:52; but note Mark 12:28–34). Jewish scribes formed part of the opposition to the church in Mark's own setting; this post-Easter reality has influenced the way he composes the pre-Easter narrative. Here as elsewhere, Mark's readers see their own situation reflected in the Gospel story.

1:23 Unclean spirit: "Unclean" does not mean dirty or unsanitary, but ritually impure, in contrast to the Holy Spirit (see on Luke 2:22–24). Accordingly, Jesus is the **Holy One**, in contrast to the unholy spirit possessing the man.

1:24 Destroy us: Mark shares the apocalyptic view that at the eschaton God will destroy Satan (see Rev. 20:7–10; on apocalypticism, see introduction to Revelation). The demons acknowledge that they are already defeated. There is no struggle, no exorcistic technique—Jesus commands with a word, and the demons are gone. Thus Mark illustrates that the final victory of God over demonic evil is already present in the ministry of Jesus. **I know who you are:** The demons recognize Jesus, though humans do not, an aspect of Mark's messianic secret (see introduction to Mark).

1:27 A new teaching: Newness is an attribute of God's eschatological work (see on 2:21–22; Luke 5:36–38; 22:20; John 13:34; 1 Cor. 11:25). Mark's point is not that Jesus' teaching is original and innovative but that it represents the final, eschatological message of the time of fulfillment (1:14).

1:29–34 The Healing of Simon's Mother-in-Law and the Sick People of Capernaum
(See also at Matt. 8:14–17; Luke 4:38–41)

1:29 The house: Almost directly adjoining the excavated synagogue (see on 1:21), archaeologists have excavated a group of houses, one of which had an elaborate church building constructed over it in the fifth century CE, apparently because it was assumed to be the house of Simon Peter. This assumption is likely historical, in the light of the early Christian graffiti inscribed there. The earliest version of this cluster of stories may be the "founding story" of the church in Capernaum. In its Markan version, the transition from synagogue to house probably suggested to Mark's readers the pilgrimage of their church from its synagogue origins to the house churches of Mark's own time.

Of Simon and Andrew: When Jesus called them (1:16–20), they "left everything," including home and family (10:28–31), but here they still own a house. Such discrepancies indicate the disparate origin of the traditions combined in Mark's narrative.

1:30 Simon's mother-in-law: Simon Peter was married (1 Cor. 9:5), but the Bible preserves the name of neither wife nor mother-in-law. **Lifted her up:** The same word is used for God's raising Jesus from the dead; here and elsewhere, the healing stories point beyond themselves to the saving event of Christ's death and resurrection. **The fever left her:** Like the unclean spirit leaving the possessed man in 1:26. Jesus' healings also have the character of exorcisms, overcoming the power of Satan in order to restore people to the kind of life God wills for them. **She began to serve them:** The same word is used for the angels' service to Jesus in 1:13; see 15:41, where the same word is translated "provided for," and 10:45, where Jesus' own life is described with the same word, usually translated "ministry." The woman is set free from her affliction to minister to and with Jesus.

1:32 At sundown: The Sabbath was now over, and people could bring the sick to Jesus without violating the Sabbath restrictions. Mark suggests that pious respect for the Law is not contrary to invoking the help of Jesus (see 1:44).

1:34 Would not permit the demons to speak: Another messianic secret reference (see introduction to Mark, and see 1:24; 3:11–12). On the language of demons, Satan, and exorcism, see excursus at 5:1.

1:35–39 Preaching Tour in Galilee
(See also at Matt. 4:23; Luke 4:42–44)

1:35 Deserted place . . . prayed: At the very beginning of the narrative, Mark presents Jesus both as one filled with divine power who does what only God can do, and also as one distinct from God, a needy human being who seeks communion with God in prayer.

1:36 Hunted for him: Literally, "tracked him down," with a hostile overtone. The disciples expect Jesus to stay in Capernaum and enjoy his newfound success, but Jesus extends his ministry of preaching and exorcism to new areas. Here is the first hint of what will become the disciples' increasingly perverse misunderstanding of Jesus and his mission, and thus of what it means to be a disciple. **Let us:** Despite the disciples' misunderstanding, Jesus does not abandon them, but continues to include them in his ministry; this too is a Markan motif that will be repeated with increasing intensity.

1:40–45 The Cleansing of the Leper
(See also at Matt. 8:1–4; Luke 5:12–16)

Mark places the story here in anticipation of the next section, 2:1–3:6, where Jesus will repeatedly be charged with violating the divine Law. Here, while Jesus violates custom and expectations by touching the unclean man, he explicitly affirms the Mosaic Law by sending the man to the priest for certification that he had been cleansed and could reenter normal society.

1:41 Moved with pity: Some ancient manuscripts preserve the reading "becoming angry," which is more likely original. So also in v. 43 **sternly warning him** is a negative note, "growling" or "snorting" at him (or it). Such terminology may preserve traces of an earlier form of the story in which Jesus was presented as a magician-like figure who healed by esoteric techniques (which were thus eliminated in the Matthean and Lukan versions of the story). In both instances, Mark probably intends to present Jesus who is incensed not at the afflicted man, but at the demonic power that has robbed him of life; it is the eschatological anger of God who confronts and defeats the enemies of human life.

1:44 Say nothing to anyone: Historically implausible, but another expression of Mark's messianic secret (see introduction to Mark). **He went out and began to proclaim:** See on 5:19–20. Even when Jesus' commands to silence are disobeyed, the continuation of the narrative indicates that people still failed to recognize his true identity.

2:1–3:6
Conflicts and the Plot to Destroy Jesus

Here begins a new subsection, a collection of five conflict stories that extends to 3:6. The arrangement shows that it is the author who assembles similar materials and places them together to make his own point. It is hardly likely that in the life of Jesus some days of preaching and healing were met with tremendous positive response (1:14–45), only to be followed by a period of nothing but controversy (2:1–3:6). The author (or a pre-Markan teacher) has here collected a series of controversy stories dealing with sin and sinners, eating, and the sanctity of Sabbath laws. Each has a similar form, concluding with a decisive pronouncement by Jesus. At the conclusion, the religious leaders resolve to destroy Jesus.

2:1–12 The Healing of the Paralytic
(See also at Matt. 9:1–8; Luke 5:17–26; John 5:1–7, 8–9a)

The first story illustrates the Markan literary technique of combining two originally independent stories. This procedure of inserting one story into another as a means of interpreting both is called intercalation or "sandwiching" (see 3:22–30; 5:21–43; 6:7–30; 11:12–25; 13:5–27; 14:1–11; 14:18–25; 14:53–72). It is important to see the composition as the author's—Jesus did not consistently begin one event, do something else, and then return to complete the first event. Although the materials are from the life of Jesus and earlier church tradition, the arrangement is at the narrative level composed by the author, not the actual life of Jesus.

A controversy about authority to forgive sins, vv. 6–10a, has been inserted into a healing story. Note the repetition in vv. 5 and 10. Another indication of the insertion is the "all" of v. 12, which in the present combined form of the story incongruously has the hostile scribes glorifying God for the act they have just designated as blasphemy. With the stories together, each interprets the other.

2:1 At home: See on 1:29; 2:15.

2:2 Speaking the word: The content is not given, but see 1:14–15. The identical expression became almost a technical term for the later church's proclamation of the Christian message (see, e.g., 1:45; 4:14–15, 33; 8:32; Acts 8:4; 15:35). Jesus is pictured as proclaimer of the (post-Easter) Christian message; the horizons between Jesus' time and the later time of the church collapse, and Christ himself is both proclaimer and proclaimed.

2:4–5 Removed the roof: Literally, "dug through." The roofs of Palestinian houses were often made of wood crossbeams covered with thatch and held together with mud. To make an opening large enough to lower a man on a stretcher would effectively destroy the roof. No comment is made on this aspect of the story (see 5:13) or on the disturbance of Jesus' teaching caused by digging through the roof, with mud and thatch falling on the hearers. The reader is not to try to imagine the scene historically or biographically; all attention is focused on the word of Jesus.

2:6 Scribes: See on 1:22. **Questioning in their hearts:** The author composes his narrative with an omniscient narrator. Jesus and the reader, but not the other characters in the story, know what the scribes are thinking. Here as elsewhere, the account is not a matter of objective reporting but of telling the story in such a way that the meaning of the Christ event is communicated.

2:7 Blasphemy: Assuming the authority and prerogatives of God. **God alone:** An echo of the fundamental Jewish confession of faith in the one God (Deut. 6:4; see Mark 12:29).

2:9 Which is easier?: See on Luke 5:23.

2:10 The Son of Man: This is the first occurrence of this strange expression in Mark, where it occurs 14 times (30x Matthew; 25x Luke; 13x John; outside the Gospels only Acts 7:56; Heb. 2:6 [quoting Ps. 8]; Rev. 1:13; 14:14). The phrase occurs only in Jesus' own sayings and always with reference to himself. In each of the Gospels it is his most common self-designation. It is found in all the strata and sources of the Gospel tradition: Mark, Q, M, L, John (see "Introduction to the Gospels"). "Son of . . ." is a Semitic way of saying "belonging to the category of . . ." (see, e.g., 2:19 commentary). "Man" is the generic collective, "humanity." "Son of Man" thus means "belonging to the category 'human being,' member of the human race." The phrase was originally a Hebraic way of referring to a human being, usually in contrast to God, i.e., a "mortal" (as it is often translated in the NRSV; see, e.g., Num. 23:19; Job 25:6; 35:8; Pss. 8:4; 80:17; 144:3; 146:3; Isa. 51:12; 56:2; Jer. 50:40; 51:43; and 93x in Ezekiel). Daniel 7:13 is a key passage in the development of New Testament usage: a heavenly figure "like a son of man" is enthroned alongside God and given divine authority over all the earth. "Son of Man" thus does not refer only to Jesus as a human being, as though it were a contrast to "Son of God," but designates his role as the ultimate Savior figure sent by God, the heavenly figure of Daniel's vision who operates by God's authority and will come in the future to exercise divine judgment. The image of the future coming of the Son of Man sometimes is parallel to or identical with the future coming of the kingdom of God (8:38–9:1; Matt. 13:41; 16:28; Luke 17:20–22).

The Synoptic instances can be divided into three distinct groups (Johannine usage is different): the "present" Son of Man (e.g., 2:10), the "coming" Son of Man (e.g., 13:26–27), and the "suffering, dying, and rising" Son of Man (e.g., 8:31). The three categories are not mixed; there are no sayings, for instance, in which the Son of Man who presently acts with authority will be killed, nor any sayings in which the suffering, dying, and rising Son of Man will come again in glory. The three groups cohere as to their sources: the suffering, dying, and rising sayings are found only in Mark and in documents directly dependent on Mark. "Son of Man" is the only christological title applied to Jesus in the Q document, always referring either to the earthly Jesus or to the Christ who will come on the clouds at the Parousia. All this shows that "Son of Man" was used in various streams of early Christian tradition in a variety of ways to express the role of Jesus in God's saving plan.

2:10 Authority on earth to forgive sins: Jesus, Mark, and the opponents all agree that ultimate authority belongs to God. The issue is how this authority is mediated. If Jesus is Son of Man, he has been delegated to act with the eschatological authority of God. Here the ultimate authority of God is exercised not in judgment but in forgiveness. This story is not intended to tell the reader only about a 30 CE event in which Jesus claimed to forgive one person. Taken at that level, the story is very problematic—are the four who carried the paralyzed man still unforgiven (not to speak of the others in the house and at the door, and the four disciples Jesus has just called)? Like all the miracle stories, this story illustrates the meaning of God's saving act in the Christ event for humanity as a whole. It is expressed in the confessional language of faith, not the objectifying language of the spectator (see on Matt. 2:16).

2:11 Stand up: "Rise," the same word used at the resurrection. Here and elsewhere, the vocabulary of the healing stories points beyond the particular story to the cross-resurrection event.

2:12 Amazed and glorified God: In the present form of the story, this includes the hostile scribes, but Mark does not intend that the reader think that they have been converted (2:16; 3:22; 14:1). The crowds are astounded but, in contrast to the reader, do not perceive the identity of Jesus—another aspect of Mark's messianic secret (see introduction to Mark).

2:13–17 The Call of Levi
(See also at Matt. 9:9–13; Luke 5:27–32)

The author here combines two stories: 2:13–14, a call story parallel to 1:16–20 (see there), and 2:15–17, a controversy story about fellowship with "sinners."

2:13 Levi, the son of Alphaeus: Neither Mark nor any other Gospel tells us anything further about him. A "*James* son of Alphaeus" is listed as one of the twelve in 3:18. Matt. 9:9 changes the name to "Matthew." See chart and commentary at Matt. 10:2.

2:15 Levi's house: The Greek text does not make clear whether it is Levi's or Jesus' house (see NRSV footnote). Mark sometimes uses an ambiguous Greek expression that can mean simply a house or Jesus' own house (see 1:29; 3:19). Mark does not have the Matthean and Lukan picture, derived from Q, that Jesus was homeless (Matt. 8:28; Luke 9:58). Verse 14, "followed him," would suggest Jesus' house, and the recurrence of call imagery in the concluding v. 17 can be seen as portraying Jesus as the host. Mark's readers would think of the eucharistic setting in their house churches, where the risen Jesus as host "ate with sinners," i.e., the Markan church. However, Luke later understood the house as Levi's (Luke 5:29), perhaps in parallel to 1:16–18, 29–31, where Jesus calls Simon and then eats in his (= Simon's) house. **Tax collectors:** See on Luke 5:27. **There were many who followed him:** The call of Levi is presented as typical of discipleship in general. **Sinners:** Not in the general sense in which all human beings are sinners (see on Rom. 3:23) but in two overlapping particular senses: (1) Those who violated the biblical and traditional purity laws were considered sinners and ceremonially unclean. To eat with them was to be contaminated, disqualified from attending synagogue and temple, and contaminating others (see on Luke 2:22–24, 8:44; 1 Cor. 10:26–27; Rev. 14:4). (2) Those who violated the major divine laws such as the Ten Commandments. The tax collectors were widely regarded as thieves, liars, and traitors.

2:16 Scribes of the Pharisees: See on 1:22; Luke 5:17, 29–32. Not all Pharisees were scribes; not all scribes were Pharisees. **Why does he eat?:** Should the reader ask what the scribes themselves were doing at the dinner party they are criticizing? Or were they only looking in the windows, or waiting outside until the party was over in order to raise their objections? Such questions indicate that the reader should not seek a historical explanation; the scene is a matter of the author's stage management. Here and elsewhere Mark brings the opponents on the scene even in unlikely places (see 2:23–24) in order to voice the objections heard by Christian disciples in the author's and readers' own time: Why does the church violate the biblical and traditional standards of God's holiness by "eating with sinners" (see Acts 11:3)?

2:17 Need of a physician: Jesus adapts a proverb to express the Christian gospel: when physicians go among sick people, sickness does not contaminate them, but the healing power present in them overcomes sickness. Healing, not sickness, is contagious. Likewise, the holy power of God present in Jesus (1:7, 10; 3:28–30) is not contaminated by his association with sinners but overcomes sin. Holiness, not uncleanness, is contagious (see 2:10, and Paul's argument in 1 Cor. 7:14). God is the healer (Exod. 15:26); so as in 2:10, Jesus here casts himself in the role of God. **I have come:** Like the other miracle and conflict stories, this story points beyond itself to the meaning of the Christ event as a whole, in which the saving power of God has appeared to break down barriers and restore fellowship between separated groups of human beings, and between human beings and God.

    Regarding interpretation: A story such as this provides a good test case on how one interprets the Bible. If the modern reader understands the kingdom of God proclaimed and lived out by Jesus as "breaking down social barriers," "celebrating diversity," and "being inclusive," such readers will (or should) celebrate the act of Jesus in eating with those disdained by the rigidly orthodox and exclusive Pharisees. On the other hand, if the modern reader understands the kingdom of God proclaimed by Markan Jesus to be a matter of social reform, opposed to the "elite oppressors" such as the Roman overlords and their retainers and lackeys like the wealthy and deceitful tax collectors, such readers (like the scribes of the Pharisees) will (or should)

have objections that Jesus associates with such people without condemning their oppressive injustice. One cannot have it both ways. Perhaps one should not have it either way. The portrayal of Jesus eating with tax collectors poses problems for any co-opting of Jesus as an illustration of our own ideals of what discipleship is about, however worthy and just they may be by our own cultural standards. The Markan picture of Jesus and the meaning of discipleship cannot be merely a biblical warrant for our own social ideologies, whether to the right or the left, but is upsetting to all efforts to read our own commitments into the text. Such reflections may open the modern reader to pursue more closely the understanding of discipleship implicit in the biblical text, rather than using the text as reinforcement for our own worthy causes. See also comments on 7:24–30.

2:18–22 *The Question about Fasting*
(See also at Matt. 9:14–17; Luke 5:33–39)

This is a new scene, linked to the previous one by the theme of eating. Here, however, the issue is not with whom one eats, but whether or not one fasts. Only one day of fasting was prescribed in the Old Testament (Yom Kippur, the Day of Atonement [Lev. 16:29, 31; 23:27, 32; Num. 29:7]). Other liturgical fasts were apparently observed, though not prescribed (see Jer. 36:6); and a general fast could be called at special times of devotion or penance (1 Sam. 14:24; Ezra 8:21–23; Neh. 9:1). Other references to fasting involve smaller groups or individuals and are associated with the rites of mourning, personal penance, or special preparation for prayer (e.g., Ps. 35:13; 1 Kgs. 21:27; Num. 30:13).

2:18 The Pharisees (see on Luke 5:17, 29–32) went beyond the written law and fasted regularly as a sign of penitence, as a means of preparing Israel for the coming kingdom. **John's disciples:** For the first time the reader learns that John the Baptist not only proclaimed the mighty one to come (1:4–8) but had disciples of his own, parallel to the group of Jesus' disciples. While the Christian community interpreted John as only the forerunner of Christ, the historical reality was that a Baptist community existed alongside the Christian community and partly in competition with it (see Luke 7:18; 11:1; Acts 19:1–7). John and his disciples were ascetics who (unlike Jesus) rejected the comforts of civilization as a testimony to the coming judgment of God. Both John and the Pharisees considered the practice of purity rites and the discipline of fasting as ways of preparing for the coming of God's kingdom.

2:19 The wedding guests: Literally, "sons of the wedding chamber," those who belong to the wedding party (on meaning of "sons of," see on 2:10). While John and the Pharisees engage in religious disciplines to help implement the arrival of God's coming kingdom, in Mark Jesus is portrayed as announcing that the kingdom has already drawn near. The climactic happy ending of history is pictured as a wedding (see Matt. 22:1–11; Luke 7:32; John 2:1–11; 2 Cor. 11:2; Rev. 19:7, 9; 22:2, 9, 17). **The bridegroom . . . with them:** The time of preparation is over (1:14), and the dawning of the kingdom with the presence of Christ, the bridegroom, means that it is a time for celebration, not fasting.

2:20 The days will come: In Mark's own time, which looked back on the time of Jesus, the church did have times of fasting (see Acts 13:2–3; 14:23; *Did.* 8:1). **The bridegroom is taken away:** The first reference to the theme of the absence of Christ during the time of the church (see on 14:25; 16:6).

2:22 New wine into fresh wineskins: See on Matt. 9:16–17; Luke 5:36–38. Each evangelist adapts the saying to his own situation and theology. Matthew affirms the validity of both old and new (see Matt. 13:52); both Mark and Luke, in their different ways, emphasize the problem of mixing old and new. All of the Gospels represent the Christian faith not as a "fresh start" or replacement of the old but as in continuity with it. All emphasize, however, that the newness the gospel brings is not merely a remodeling or patching up the old but its eschatological renewal, which calls for new forms.

2:23–28 *Plucking Grain on the Sabbath*
(See also at Matt. 12:1–8; Luke 6:1–5)

2:23 Sabbath: For discussion of the Sabbath and comments on the story as a whole, see on Matt. 12:1; Luke 6:1. Gospel stories about Jesus in conflict with the Law of Moses and its traditional interpretation by the Jewish religious authorities reflect both the events of Jesus' ministry and the post-Easter situation of the readers of the Gospel, who were criticized for not living according to the biblical Law. Early Christians believed that the advent of Christ did not abolish the Law of Moses as a revelation of God's will but made a fundamental difference in how the Law was understood. **Made**

their way: This phrase, omitted by both Matthew and Luke, may have originally been important as an element in the Pharisees' objection, since "making a road" is a kind of work forbidden on the Sabbath ("road" and "way" are the same word in Greek). This may seem trifling to the modern reader, who might be easily misled into supposing that the point of the story is the contrast between the trivia of Jewish interpretation and the more substantial Christian view of religious obligation. This is not the point here (see on Matt. 23:23). For those who wished to obey God's law and refrain from working on the Sabbath, someone had to interpret the Sabbath tradition and decide what constituted work and what did not. Such decisions were serious business, as documented by the many rabbinic debates and traditions. While the story can be read at one level as an inner-Jewish debate about what constitutes proper Sabbath observance, the Markan point in this story and the next is that Jesus has the eschatological authority of God to decide such matters. The issue for Mark is thus not minor vs. major religious obligations but the status of Jesus in God's saving plan, i.e., whether or not he is the Messiah. In the Markan post-Easter situation, this is the overtone of all the conflict stories, an overtone that may also be significant for the modern reader who is no longer concerned with the fine points of Sabbath observance as such.

2:24 Pharisees: See on Luke 5:17, 29–32. We should not suppose that actual Pharisees made it a practice of hiding in the grainfields on the Sabbath in hopes of catching someone violating the Sabbath (see on 2:6). While Jesus and his disciples may well have heard such objections during Jesus' ministry, the story introduces them in order to have them voice the objection raised against Christians heard in the readers' post-Easter situation. In Mark's church, Sabbath observance had been relaxed on the basis of Christian faith that the Christ event had made a fundamental difference in how the Law is to be interpreted (see Gal. 3:1–5:12).

2:25 Have you never read what David did?: The point made in the commentary on 2:23 is here made more clear by Jesus' response, which at one level does not fit the question—when they object to his violation of the Sabbath, he responds with an example of David's practice in eating food prohibited by the law (1 Sam. 21). The point is again the authority of Jesus: as David in the Bible had transgressed the letter of the Law in response to human need—and David's authority to do so was apparently acknowledged by the biblical text and by the Pharisees—so Jesus and his disciples have the authority to interpret what constitutes proper Sabbath observance.

2:26 When Abiathar was high priest: In fact, Ahimelech was high priest at the time (1 Sam. 21:1–6), not his son Abiathar (1 Sam. 22:20). This is a mistake omitted by both Matthew and Luke, but Mark was not the first to confuse the two names (see 2 Sam. 8:17).

2:27–28 The sabbath was made for humankind: The rabbis also made declarations that Sabbath laws were to be interpreted in a humane way, such as "The Sabbath is handed over to you, not you to the Sabbath" (the rabbinic commentary on Exodus, the *Mekilta* on 31:14). Jesus' declaration can be read as in continuity with this liberal Jewish tradition of interpretation, but for Mark it is more than that. In Greek there is a linguistic connection between "humankind" of this verse and **Son of Man** of v. 28. In each text, the point is the authority of Jesus as the eschatological Son of Man (see on 2:10).

3:1–6 *The Man with the Withered Hand*
(See also at Matt. 12:9–14; Luke 6:6–11)

In the Markan narrative, this scene is the climax in the collection of Jesus' conflicts with the religious authorities in 2:1–3:6.

3:2 So that they might accuse him: The story, like the gaze of the Pharisees, is focused not on the healing of the afflicted man but on Jesus and his authority, which they judge according to whether he conforms to their understanding of the law.

3:5 With anger . . . grieved at their hardness of heart: These words are problematic for both Matthew and Luke, who omit them. They are important for Mark. The anger of Jesus manifests both his true humanity as one who shows human emotion, and Jesus as God's representative who reveals *God's* wrath (see, e.g., Rom. 1:18; 5:9; 12:19). Hardness of heart is also a Markan theme (see 6:52; 8:17; 10:5). Like God, Jesus grieves over the lack of perception of what God is doing in their midst. **Stretch out your hand:** Jesus neither touches the man, nor pronounces any words of healing, nor does anything else that could be considered work on the Sabbath. On one level, this could be considered mere human cleverness. Mark's point, however, is that even in the absence of specific evidence that would convict him, his opponents nonetheless decide to destroy him.

As at his final trial (14:1, 53–64), they had already made up their minds that he must be killed and were only looking for a pretext to carry out their decision. **His hand was restored:** The text does not say "Jesus healed him." The passive voice indicates divine action (as Luke 5:20; 12:8–9; 15:24; 24:16). God is the healer; in this scene, the figures of God and Jesus modulate into each other, and Jesus is the functional equivalent of God.

3:6 Pharisees: See on 2:16–18, 24; 7:1; 10:2; Luke 5:17, 29–32. **Herodians:** Historical study has not been able to make absolutely clear just who the Herodians were. The term is found only here and 12:13 (and the Matthean parallel 22:16; see Mark 6:14–22; 8:15). It apparently means "supporters of King Herod." During Jesus' ministry Herod Antipas, son of Herod the Great, was ruler of Galilee at Rome's pleasure. After Jesus' death much of Palestine was ruled by Herod's son Herod Agrippa I, who actively opposed the new church (Acts 12:1–23). In Mark's own time the grandson of Herod the Great, Agrippa II, was also unsympathetic to the Christian community (Acts 25–26). The rabbis of Mark's time, the successors of the Pharisees of Jesus' day, had a high regard for both Herodian kings. Thus the combination of Pharisees and Herodians, historically difficult to understand as referring to Jesus' time, fits well the situation of Mark's own time, when the successors of the Pharisees and the Herodian rulers of Palestine shared a common hostility to the new Christian community.

3:7–6:6a
APPOINTMENT OF TWELVE; OPPOSITION INTENSIFIES

Here begins the second subsection of Part One. As the first subsection begins with the call of the disciples that follows a summary of Jesus' preaching and teaching activity, so here a more elaborate summary is followed by the choosing of the Twelve (see Outline in introduction to Mark).

3:7–12
Jesus Heals Multitudes by the Sea
(See also at Matt. 12:15–21; Luke 6:17–19)

3:7–8 A great multitude came to him: The scene is painted in extravagant, post-Easter colors. As at Pentecost (see Acts 2), an international gathering from a large geographical area streams to Jesus, from the south (**Jerusalem, Judea, Idumea**), from the north (**Tyre and**

Sidon), from the east (**beyond the Jordan**), with the processions converging on **Galilee** at the center. (Since Galilee is bordered on the west by the sea, no crowds could be portrayed as coming from the west.) All this reminds the reader of the great crowds that made pilgrimages to the Jewish festivals at the temple in Jerusalem: the person of Jesus plays the role formerly occupied by the temple (see 11:11–17; 14:58; 15:28, 39). Though large crowds did sometimes gather around Jesus, this scene is not intended to report actual history; no questions are raised about the provisions for such crowds (contrast 6:32–36; 8:1–4), and such an international response to Jesus at the beginning of his ministry is difficult to imagine historically. The picture is theological rather than historical, portraying in advance the large international Christian community of Mark's own time.

3:11 You are the Son of God: See 1:1, 11; 9:7; 15:39. On the meanings of Son of God, see on Luke 1:28–33. For Mark, the title denotes more than human royalty. The demons recognize him as someone who belongs to the divine world and represents God's own power. Their confession already anticipates and refutes the charge to be made in 3:22 that Jesus is on the same side as the demons. On the language of demons, Satan, and exorcism, see excursus at 5:1.

3:12 Not to make him known: See 1:34. But it is too late! They have already made their announcement, which nevertheless seems to have no effect. Such puzzling scenes in Mark are not to be explained as a strategy of the historical Jesus, as though he commanded the demons to be silent in order to avoid having his ministry associated with demonic powers. Rather, we have here a classic expression of Mark's messianic secret (see introduction to Mark). In the Markan mode of telling the story, during his ministry Jesus' identity as Son of God is known only to himself, to God, to the demons—and to the reader.

3:13–19a
The Choosing of the Twelve
(See also at Matt. 10:1–4; Luke 6:12–16)

3:13 Called: As in 1:16–20, the initiative is with Jesus.

3:14 He appointed twelve: From among the larger group of disciples Jesus chooses twelve to be his special representatives. On the general meaning of apostleship and the significance of the number twelve, see on Luke 6:12–13. Mark often uses the phrase "the

Twelve," which plays a key role in Mark's story and theology; the term "apostle," on the other hand, is found only here and 6:30, where it has its generic meaning, "one sent," without the technical meaning "apostle." In 3:14 the word may be a latter scribal addition, harmonizing Mark with Matthew and Luke, since some important manuscripts lack the word here (see NRSV footnote). **To be sent out** is the verb form of "apostle." Their commission is first **to be with him**, then as authorized representatives to continue Jesus' own ministry of **proclaim(ing) the message** and **cast(ing) out demons** (see 1:39).

3:16 So he appointed the twelve: This repetition is omitted in some ancient manuscripts. The 3:14 reference to the Twelve is likely secondary, but here it is probably original, now understood in a somewhat "official" sense. While the number itself was theologically important, there was considerable variation in the names that constituted the list (see chart and discussion at Matt. 10:2).

Simon is the same as Simeon (see 2 Pet. 1:1), the name of one of the patriarchs of Israel (Gen. 29:33), and thus became a tribal name (Gen. 49:5–7; Num. 1:23; 26:14; Josh. 19:1–9). Simon was his Jewish birth name. **Peter** (Aramaic "Cephas"; both mean "rock") is not a proper name at all, nor is it merely a nickname. Jesus gave Simon this strange new name to represent symbolically his role in the church (see on Matt. 16:16–18; see Gen. 17:5, 15, Abram becomes Abraham; Sarai becomes Sarah; Gen. 32:28, Jacob becomes Israel). John pictures the renaming as occurring at Peter's initial call (John 1:42). Matthew 16:18 seems to locate it at the time of Peter's confession. **Peter** stands first in all the lists (and see 1 Cor. 15:5; Luke 24:34). Throughout the Markan story Peter plays the leading role in discipleship, failure, and ultimate renewal (see 16:7).

3:17 Boanerges: One would expect the next name to be Andrew, Simon's brother (see 1:15–20), but the names are arranged so that the group of Peter, James, and John is first. They form an inner circle, a primary group of three alongside the twelve, and play significant roles in the later story (see 9:2; 14:33). They (and only they) receive additional names from Jesus at the time of their call to be apostles. John and James were called Boanerges, which Mark translates as "sons of thunder." No explanation is given for any of the name changes. The name has sometimes been explained as reflecting the brothers' impetuosity (9:38–41; 10:35–45; see

Luke 9:49–50, 52–56), just as Peter, which means "rock," has sometimes been related to his personality. Such psychologizing interpretations are best avoided, however. Just as the patriarchs were renamed by God when they were constituted by God as the founders of the people that would become Israel, so the three pillars of the new Christian community receive a different name from Jesus, who acts in the place of God (see Gal. 2:9—though the James there is a different person).

3:18 Simon the Cananaean: The designation is not derived from Cana (see John 2:1–11) or Canaan (= Palestine) but is an Aramaic word meaning "enthusiast" or "zealot" (see Acts 1:13). Except for the primary three and Judas, nothing is said about any other of the Twelve throughout the Gospel. Later tradition developed legends about all the apostles, but Mark himself says nothing more about any of them except the primary three (and Judas).

3:19 Judas Iscariot, who betrayed him: Jesus did not give the name Iscariot to Judas; it was already a designation that distinguished him from other people of the same name (including a brother of Jesus, Matt. 13:35, and another of the Twelve, according to Luke 6:16). The meaning of **Iscariot** is disputed; it may refer to the Judean village from which he came ("man of Qerioth") or may be related to the Greek *sikarios*, "dagger man," "assassin," a term used of the later anti-Roman revolutionaries.

3:19b–35
Jesus, Beelzebul, and Jesus' True Family
(See also at Matt. 12:22–37 [9:32–34], 46–50;
Luke 11:14–15, 17–23; 12:10; 8:19–21)

This segment represents a very complex set of traditions, assembled by each Gospel writer in his own way (note the various locations of the parallel passages in Matthew and Luke). Neither Matthew nor Luke, for example, preserves Mark's opening scene, in which Jesus' relatives consider him to be out of his mind, and Luke locates the segments about Jesus' true family and the unpardonable sin in entirely different contexts. This disparity is due to at least three factors: (1) Some of the materials were handed on in different streams of tradition and thus preserved in different sources, so that Matthew and Luke found some of them in both Mark and Q. (2) Unlike Mark, Matthew and Luke have preserved stories of Jesus' miraculous birth, so that in their Gospels Mary certainly knew his divine origin and could not be portrayed as an unbelieving outsider who failed to understand the

identity of her son. (3) Neither Matthew nor Luke shares Mark's view of the messianic secret that is foundational for Mark's narrative and the origin of the Gospel genre (see "Introduction to the Gospels," introduction to Mark). It is thus necessary to read each Gospel from its own point of view; here as elsewhere, harmonization constructs a modern amalgamation of the New Testament texts that misses the point of each of the biblical Gospels.

Mark has constructed this scene from pre-Markan materials, using his typical "sandwich" technique (see on 2:1–12). Jesus' family consider him mentally disturbed and set out to apprehend him and get him out of the public view (3:20–21), but while they are on their way, Jesus responds to another charge from the Jerusalem scribes—that his power is derived from Satan. Then Jesus' family arrives but remain outsiders who do not understand or accept him. The scene thus pictures Jesus as rejected by two groups that should have recognized his divine mission: the religious leaders and his own family. This poses the choice for the reader: to stand with Jesus or to stand with those who reject him. In Mark's apocalyptic view, two kingdoms confront each other in this scene (see 1:15; 3:24); while the characters in the story can not yet understand what is going on, the reader, who stands this side of the cross and resurrection, sees the reality and must choose between the God represented by Jesus and the demonic power that rules this world, whose kingdom is already doomed.

3:19b He went home: The Greek expression can also mean simply "into a house" (see on 1:29; 2:15). **They could not even eat:** Not a matter of fasting (see 2:18–20). The press of the crowd and the concern of Jesus and his disciples to minister to them had a higher priority than eating.

3:21 His family: This is almost certainly the meaning, but the phrase is literally "those with him," i.e., "his people," which theoretically could mean his friends, his associates, or his family. The appearance of his mother, brothers, and sisters in v. 31 makes clear that "family" is the proper translation here. **People were saying:** Literally, "they were saying," which could mean that his family heard what others were saying and wanted to rescue him from this embarrassing situation. The context, and especially the grammar of the next clause, indicates that it was indeed his own mother, brothers, and sisters who considered him to be **out of his mind.** While the other Gospels sometimes paint a more positive picture of Jesus' mother, this is Mary's only appearance in Mark (though see on v. 35 and 15:40, 47; 16:1).

3:22 Scribes: See on 1:22. **From Jerusalem:** The point is not merely geography, but that Jesus' opposition is composed of representatives of the official center of the Jewish authority, the holy city and its temple (see on 3:7–12). **Beelzebul:** The word is of disputed etymology, but probably originally meant "Lord [Baal] of the House," referring either to a pagan household god, the god of a pagan temple, or the evil power that has usurped God's house, the created universe, and claims to be lord of this world. Already in the Old Testament it had been corrupted to the pejorative **Beelzebub**, "Lord of Flies," "Lord of the Manure Pile" (2 Kgs. 1:2). The NIV follows this tradition, already established by the King James Version, though "Beelzebub" occurs in no Greek manuscript of the New Testament. By Mark's time the etymology had long since been forgotten, and it had become a common designation for the devil, like Satan or Beliar (2 Cor. 6:15). Here Jesus' power to cast out demons is attributed to Satan the prince of demons. Note that Jesus' power to work miracles is not the disputed point—this was accepted by friend and foe alike; how one understands the *source* of this power, the *meaning* of his miraculous power, is the issue that separates disciples from opponents, insiders from outsiders, believers from unbelievers.

3:23 Parables: Jesus does not respond to the charge directly but with a series of proverbial analogical statements and rhetorical questions. "Parable," here used for the first time in Mark, in this text has its generic meaning "indirect speech," rather than the specific meaning illustrated in the next chapter (see on 4:2).

3:24 If a kingdom is divided against itself: For the first time since 1:15, the announced theme of Jesus' proclamation reappears, and it becomes clear that God's kingdom is proclaimed in a world that already has a kingdom—that of Satan, who has usurped God's rule. Jesus shows that Satan's kingdom is already doomed, even on the scribes' own premises, for even if Jesus does operate by Satan's power in casting out demons, this shows the divided demonic kingdom cannot endure.

3:25 A house ... divided against itself: Probably playing on the meaning of Beelzebul as "Lord of the House" (see above). If the "god of this world" (see 2 Cor. 4:4) is divided and one of his agents is casting out demons, then Satan's

kingdom is already doomed. This is Jesus' point, that the kingdom of God he proclaims and inaugurates has already destined the kingdom of evil to destruction (on "kingdom of God," see on Luke 4:43). Abraham Lincoln's 1858 speech made a different use of this proverb.

3:26 His end has come: On the language of demons, Satan, and exorcism, see excursus at 5:1. Demonic power continues in Jesus' world, in Mark's, and in ours, but in the life, death, and resurrection of Jesus God has asserted his royal power that announces and guarantees its ultimate end. Christians pray, "Thy kingdom come," in the assurance that the rule of God manifest in Jesus will finally prevail.

3:27 Tying up the strong man: The "strong man" is Satan, but overcome by the "stronger one" already announced (1:7). One image of the eschatological triumph of God is the binding of Satan and the **plunder(ing)** of his **house** (see on Rev. 20:1–3). Here, that longed-for victory of God is portrayed as already beginning to happen in Jesus' ministry; his triumphal march through Galilee vanquishing the demons (1:29–34, 39; 3:11) is the sign of the advent of God's own rule. While in Marcan theology (and in the New Testament generally) the means of God's action in overcoming satanic power is the love of God manifest in Jesus' weakness and vulnerability in going to the cross, the Markan Jesus does not hesitate to use violent imagery to communicate this victorious saving act. The binding of Satan sets his captives free, but not to be autonomous, self-centered individuals. In Mark's theology, as in Paul's (Rom. 6:15–23), one slavery is exchanged for another. It is an arrogant illusion for humans to suppose they can be self-sufficient masters of their own fate. In Mark's apocalyptic view, the only choice is whom to serve: the enslaving demonic power or the One "whose service is perfect freedom." This is also the message of Jesus (Matt. 6:24; 12:30).

3:28–30 People will be forgiven their sins: In the New Testament the saying has various forms and contexts (see Matt. 12:31–32; Luke 12:10). The Markan form juxtaposes two different statements: the first declares that all sins will be forgiven; the second specifies one sin that will not be forgiven. This is not the same as "All sins will be forgiven except one . . ." (found in none of the Gospels), nor is it the same form as the Matthean and Lukan saying, "This sin (speaking against the Son of Man) will be forgiven, but this other sin (speaking against the Holy Spirit) will not be forgiven." These forms are more readily amenable to ordinary human logic than the Markan form, which is the paradoxical juxtaposition of two different statements, each coherent and complete in itself, but logically problematical when placed together. The Markan form belongs to the same category as the pair of clashing statements in 9:24 (see commentary there).

For the modern reader, the meaning(s) of this sometimes troublesome text may be illuminated by considering its pre-Markan history and its interpretation in Mark. Three levels of history of the Markan form of this saying can be discerned: (1) This saying begins with an absolute, unconditioned announcement of divine amnesty: all sins will be forgiven. This radical declaration probably goes back to Jesus himself. (2) **But whoever blasphemes against the Holy Spirit:** In its Markan form, the announcement of universal forgiveness has been joined to another declaration that paradoxically conditions it: there is one sin that will not be forgiven. This dialectical, paradoxical manner of affirmation is not to be reduced to a less logically troublesome statement of clear propositional logic; in the form handed on by Mark it does not have a "meaning" that is simple and clear, like traffic laws or income-tax laws. The saying functions to communicate God's universal and absolute grace—"all sins will be forgiven"—and at the same time a most severe warning that this grace cannot be presumed upon—"not *every* sin will be forgiven." This is somewhat like Paul's adding Rom. 6 to his declaration of the amazing grace of God in Rom. 5. (3) **For they had said, "He has an unclean spirit":** This is Mark's own interpretation of the meaning of the saying in his context: those who have identified Jesus' work as the work of Satan are beyond the scope of God's forgiveness. (For Matthew's and Luke's particular interpretations of the form of the saying that came to them, see on Matt. 12:31–32 and Luke 12:10.) In the light of the saying's history, readers of the Bible thus should not worry that they might have "committed the unpardonable sin"—those who are worried about it have not done it and should hear the word of grace: "All sins will be forgiven." But those who presume on God's grace, assuming they can "continue to sin, that grace may abound," must hear the second half of the saying. Neither group can derive distress or comfort from Mark's particular interpretation of the saying

for his situation, by saying something like, "I have never attributed Jesus' works to Satan, so everything else I do is forgiven." Like Jesus' parables, this saying functions at a different level from specifying one act that is not forgivable, as though it then grants a license for everything else.

3:31 His mother and his brothers: The Greek word "brothers" is often used generically to mean "brothers and sisters" (e.g., Acts 16:40; Rom. 1:13; 7:1; 1 Cor. 1:10, 26; on Jesus' brothers and sisters, see on Matt. 13:55–56). **Outside:** See 4:10–12. Mark's dualistic theology divides all into "insiders" (believers who belong to the renewed people of God being created by Jesus) and "outsiders" (unbelievers who do not belong). This is not peculiar to Mark but is found elsewhere in the New Testament, based ultimately on apocalyptic dualism (1 Cor. 5:12–13; 1 Thess. 4:12; Col. 4:5; see John 8:23; 2 Cor. 11:13–15; chart at Gal. 3:18; introduction to Revelation). Jesus' natural family are outsiders (see John 7:5). Other New Testament texts indicate that after the resurrection Jesus' mother and some of his brothers became Christians (Acts 1:14; 1 Cor. 9:5) and that Mary came to be honored as a model for believers (Luke 1–2). In Mark, however, Jesus' family appears only in this one scene, where they are portrayed negatively. This has sometimes been explained as reflecting the rivalry among early Christian groups that honored the leadership of Jesus' family in the church (such as the Jerusalem church led by James) and other groups of Christians that did not, to which Mark and his readers supposedly belonged. It is probably better to see the portrayal here as the product of Mark's messianic secret: no one—not family, friends, or closest disciples—can properly identify Jesus and believe in him apart from the cross-resurrection event.

3:34 Those who sat around him: Not just the apostles or those who had been called personally by Jesus to be disciples, but all who are "insiders," who listen to Jesus' message as the rule for their lives, i.e., all followers of Christ, including the Markan readers. **Whoever does the will of God:** See 10:29–30. Some followers of Christ in Mark's situation, and in every generation since, have faced the agonizing choice between Christian faith and their own natural family. Jesus is here presented as the model for those who make doing the will of God a higher priority than even sacred natural family ties (see Luke 14:25–33). The inclusive "whoever" somewhat mitigates Mark's insider/outsider dualism (see 9:40). While the primary meaning here is that followers of Jesus are his true family, Mark does not limit doing the will of God to Jesus' disciples (see 9:40). This may be read as Mark's own version of Jesus' teaching in Matt. 25:31–46—those who do God's will are "insiders" who serve the God revealed in Christ, whether or not this is their own understanding of their religious identity. **Brother and sister and mother:** The absence of "father" from this list (also absent from 10:29–30) is to be explained neither biographically, as though Joseph had died prior to Jesus' ministry, nor as a pointer to the virginal conception of Jesus, a view which Mark does not share. Mark never mentions Jesus' earthly father for purely theological reasons, reserving the term "Father" for God, and thus theologically cannot cast believers in the role of Jesus' father.

4:1–25
The Parable of the Sower and
Parable Interpretation
(See also at Matt. 13:1–23; Luke 8:4–18)

Mark has often referred to the teaching activity of Jesus in the preceding narrative (1:21, 22, 27; 2:13) but without filling in the content of Jesus' teaching. **In parables:** For the first time in Mark, the reader gets a picture of the teaching of the earthly Jesus—it is primarily *parabolic.* In the Bible "parable" is used for a wide range of indirect communication, including figures of speech, aphorisms, proverbs, riddles, illustrations, lessons, allegories—almost any kind of metaphorical speech. How should the reader understand Jesus' parables in Mark? As elsewhere, the reader hears more than one voice from the layered Gospel text; here it is particularly important to keep in mind the three levels of Gospel texts discussed in "Introduction to the Gospels."

1. There is no doubt that Jesus himself taught in parables, and that, for example, the parable of the Sower in 4:3–8 is preserved essentially in the form and wording as spoken in Jesus' original teaching. In his teaching, however, parables were not allegories or illustrations of a point or points that could be stated in some nonparabolic manner, as though the parable were a disposable container for the message it contained. The definition of parable by the British scholar C. H. Dodd has found wide acceptance among contemporary interpreters: "At its simplest the parable is a metaphor or simile drawn from nature or common life, arresting the hearer by its vividness or strangeness, and leaving the mind in sufficient

doubt about its precise application to tease it into active thought." Jesus' parables did not deliver prepackaged meaning but challenged the hearer to respond. Parables are open-ended narrative metaphors that generate new meaning in new situations. While a parable cannot mean simply anything (it is not a Rorschach ink blot), it "teases the mind into active thought" in such a way that the hearer himself or herself must actively participate in deciding what the parable means, i.e., how the hearer should respond to it. Parables thus often function by beginning in the familiar world of the hearer but then presenting a different vision of the world that challenges the everyday expectations of the hearer.

2. In the New Testament we have not only Jesus' original parables, but the responses of faith by the believing community, i.e., interpretations of the parables given in Jesus' name by early Christian prophets and teachers. The church after Easter reinterpreted Jesus' stories in the light of their own situation. This was done in primarily two modes: (a) understanding parables as *example stories* (see, e.g., Luke 10:37b, appended to the parable of the Good Samaritan) and (b) understanding the parables as *allegories.* Mark offers two outstanding examples of the latter category: 4:13–20 appends an allegorical interpretation to the parable of the Sower, and 12:1–12 retells an earlier parable in which the allegorical interpretation has been built into the parable itself.

3. To the tradition, which includes Jesus' original parable and the later interpretation of the church, is added *Mark's own theological interpretation,* which presents his understanding of the reason Jesus taught in parables within his own theological framework (see on 4:10–12 below). The Markan perspective on the "parable chapter" as a whole is illuminated by its location immediately after the preceding scene, which deals with the triumph of the kingdom of God over the demonic kingdom of this world. Mark's readers might well have asked (as does the modern reader): "If God has already overcome the satanic kingdom in the Christ event, why does it appear that the world continues as usual, with demonic power still very much in control?" In Mark 4, the parables all deal with this "**mystery** (NRSV secret) **of the kingdom**" (4:11; see 26, 30) that has been imparted to Jesus' disciples, including especially the post-Easter readers. The reality of God's present-and-coming kingdom can be perceived, but it is not something on the surface of things that can be seen by anyone or demonstrated to others by those who perceive it

by faith. Its reality is apprehended only as a mystery, expressed in parables, and only by those who have "ears to hear" and "eyes to see."

4:3 Listen!: See the concluding admonition in v. 9, **Let anyone with ears to hear listen!** The first parable, presented as the key to understanding parables in general (see 4:13), is framed by the challenge to probe beneath the surface.

4:3–8 A sower went out to sow: The parable begins in the everyday world of the ancient hearer, realistically picturing the agricultural work as usually done. Contrary to modern Western practice, the seed is first broadcast and then plowed under. The farmer expects that some will be eaten by **birds**, some will fall on **rocky ground**, and some will fall **among thorns**—these are the normal risks of raising crops, compensated for by the expected harvest that will more than make up for the lost seed. So far, the story is within the framework of normal life, the world as we experience it. But if the farmer works hard and the weather is favorable, he can expect a crop of ten to twelve times what he has sown—the normal yield of an industrious and lucky planter. What is not expected is a yield from the **good soil** of **thirty and sixty and a hundredfold**. At this surprising turn of the story, the worldly wise hearer may walk away shaking his head, convinced that Jesus knows nothing about farming, about how the world "really is." Yet other hearers may recall having heard of the fabulous hundredfold harvest—from their reading of the Bible (Gen. 26:12). While such a harvest never happens in the everyday world, it is not unheard of, for the world of the Bible, the world in which God is active, tells the reader of such a wonderful event. The reader must decide whether the everyday world is the real world, or whether the world opened up by Jesus' provocative story, the world where God provides an extravagant life beyond all our experience, is in fact the real world. Jesus offers no explanation but leaves the reader to ponder and decide.

It is to be noted that the extravagant harvest is on the *borderline* between the everyday world and the unimaginable glory of God's kingdom. It is different, for example, from the apocalyptic picture found in several ancient Jewish documents of the coming glory of the new age: "The earth shall yield its fruit ten thousand fold. On each vine there shall be a thousand branches, and each branch shall produce a thousand clusters, and each cluster shall produce a thousand grapes, and each grape shall produce a cor [25–75 gallons] of wine." This picture is so obviously otherworldly that it must represent something altogether future. The picture in Jesus' parable, on the other hand, is close enough to the reality of the present world that it does not jolt or repulse the realistic hearer but "teases the mind into active thought" and calls for a decision.

4:4 On the path: The phrase can also be translated "at the side of the path," an ambiguity helpfully expressed in the NIV's **along the path**, which can mean either "on" or "alongside." While the original parable intended the former (see explanation of ancient Palestinian sowing above), Mark exploits the ambiguity by understanding it in the latter sense for his own situation (see on 4:15).

4:10–12 Since this section is oriented to Mark's own situation, we will deal with it below, with 4:21–25.

4:13–20 Understand this parable: This is the only parable in Mark with an explicit interpretation. The four results of sowing are understood as four different results of proclaiming the Christian gospel. In three cases, the word bears no fruit, and hearers are implicitly warned not to let this be the result of their own hearing of the gospel. In the fourth case, there is an amazing harvest; despite what appears to be devastatingly negative results, the word of God finally produces an astounding harvest. So understood, the interpretation, like the parable, has a positive message: however things may look to superficial observation, the harvest is sure. As indicated above, the interpretation is regarded by most interpreters as not from the pre-Easter historical Jesus but from an early Christian teacher who spoke in Jesus' name. Detailed reasons are given in the technical commentaries, but even the casual reader may note that the interpretation understands the *parable* as an *allegory*, and that the situations envisaged fit the life of the church as it proclaims the gospel, not the ministry of the earthly Jesus. Scholars also point out that the language and vocabulary fits later church usage, that the interpretation is not self-consistent (in v. 15, the seed is the word; in vv. 16, 18, 19, 20, the seed is "those sown," i.e., different kinds of people), and that the *Gospel of Thomas* has the parable but not the interpretation. The interpretation bears the marks of repeated reinterpretation in various settings of early Christianity.

Considering the interpretation to be secondary does not mean that it is second-rate, however, as though later accretions are to be peeled away to "get back to the real Jesus." For the church's faith and for Mark's, the "real Jesus" is not only the 30 CE man of Nazareth but the risen Lord who is active in the life of the church. This understanding of the presence of Christ himself with his preached word is found in the interpretation, as well as elsewhere in Mark. In the interpretation we hear an authentic response to Jesus' original parable. Since parables are open-ended, this is not the only possible response, not "the" meaning. Based on this model, which Mark presents as the key to understanding **all the parables** (v. 13), later readers may encounter and respond to the original parable in terms of their own setting—without setting aside the interpretation given in the text, which also comes to us as holy Scripture.

4:14 The sower sows the word: "The word" is often used to mean the gospel, the early Christian message of God's saving act in Christ (see 2:2; 4:33; 8:32; 16:20; Luke 1:2; Acts 4:4; 6:4; 8:4; 10:44; Gal. 6:6; Col. 4:3; 2 Tim. 4:2; 1 Pet. 2:8; 3:1). In the Old Testament the phrase was normally "the word of God" or "the word of the Lord." By using it in this unqualified way, Mark allows the word that generates faith to be understood as word of God, Christ, and the Christian preacher. As God speaks in Jesus' preaching, so Christ continues to speak in the message of Christian preachers; Christ identifies himself with the message about him and is present in and with it (see 8:35; 9:41; 10:29; 13:10–11; 14:9; Matt. 10:40; Luke 10:16; John 12:44–45; 12:45; 13:20; 2 Cor. 13:3). It is thus significant that in this interpretation, in which all other elements of the parable are given an allegorical identification, **the sower** remains unidentified (contrast Matt. 13:37). This allows the one who sows/preaches the word to be at one and the same time the Christian preacher, the living Christ, and God, whose word is heard in the message of Jesus and the church.

4:15 Satan immediately comes: If humans are casual about the potency of the divine word, the devil is not. The interpretation pictures those who hear the Christian message as caught in conflicting force fields in which not only human decisions are made, but Satan and God are active. To be sure, the interpretation challenges hearers to be responsive hearers of the word and to allow it to generate the fruits of the Christian life within them (see Rom. 8:23; Gal. 5:22). But the text does not deal only with human responsibility. The message is not

merely the moralizing "Take care what kind of soil you are." Soil in fact is passive, must receive what it is given, and cannot decide to become some other kind of soil. Likewise, in the very first instance, the birds that eat the seed before it can sprout represent **Satan**, who snatches away the word before the soil can produce fruit. Those who find themselves responding to the word and producing Christian fruit may not congratulate themselves, but can only give thanks that they have been preserved from the demonic raids that snatch away the life-giving word before it can do its work and that the Creator has allowed them to be "good soil." It is in this light that the third level of this text, the Markan editorial layer, may be heard.

4:10–12 Asked him about the parables: The disciples (the Twelve and others), the "insiders" of 3:31–35, also fail to understand the parables. Note the plural; the issue is not only the preceding parable of the Sower but Jesus' parabolic speech as such. Here as elsewhere, Mark tells the story at two levels. On the one hand, the characters in the pre-Easter narrative cannot "get it" prior to the decisive revelatory event of the cross-resurrection, and not fully until the eschaton—and this includes the disciples. On the other hand, the post-Easter Christian insight into the meaning of the Christ event is pictured as already revealed to the disciples. Here Jesus explains to his disciples what the crowds cannot perceive (see 4:34). Thus at this narrative level the crowds who do not receive the interpretation could not understand Jesus' parabolic teaching. Jesus is portrayed as a teacher who does not intend to be understood and is not. This represents the reality that the meaning of the Christ event was not understood prior to the resurrection and could not be. On the other level, Jesus is portrayed as preaching to the disciples, crowds, and general public with the expectation that his teaching, including his parables, will be understood (v. 33; see 7:14–15; 12:12; see 4:13a; 7:18a, which indicate the parables should be understandable without additional explanation). This double perspective permeates the Markan narrative and is fundamental to the literary genre "Gospel" (see "Introduction to the Gospels").

4:11 To you has been given: By God; the New Testament often uses the divine passive as a reverential way of referring to the action of God (as in, e.g., Luke 5:20; 12:8–9; 24:16; Acts 13:48; 1 Cor. 6:11; 2 Cor. 12:7). **The secret:**

"Mystery" is also a valid translation (as in KJV, NAB). The word refers not to a complicated idea that one may be able finally to figure out but to the divine plan that cannot be known at all by human discovery and reason, but only by revelation (see on Eph. 1:9–10; 3:5, 10). Some know what God is about in history; most do not. God's plan for history—centering in a crucified Messiah and a presently hidden kingdom that will be fully manifest only at the eschaton—is not obvious, something that can be read off the surface of the world and history. This insight comes only by revelation (see Matt. 16:17–18; 1 Cor. 12:3). The mystery is already revealed, already given to the disciples, though they do not yet grasp it (see Dan. 2:27–30). **Of the kingdom of God:** These words make explicit what is everywhere implied—Jesus' parables have to do with the nature of God's kingdom (see on Luke 4:43). **Those outside:** See on 3:31–34.

4:12 In order that: This difficult saying, which declares that the *intent* of Jesus' teaching in parables is to prevent his message from being understood, was so difficult for Matthew and Luke that they have rewritten it to make it less offensive (see on Matt. 13:10–17; Luke 8:9–10). In its Markan context, it must be understood within the framework of Mark's messianic secret as a whole (see above). **Listen but not understand:** The quotation is from Isa. 6:9–10, slightly revised but maintaining its essential point: the rejection of God's message is due to God's own hardening the hearts of those who do not hear. Other New Testament authors also found help from this passage in accounting for widespread rejection of the Christian gospel (Matt. 13:14–15; Luke 8:10; John 12:40; Acts 28:26; Rom. 11:8). Mark's community had been faithful in witnessing to the Christian message, but instead of joyous acceptance of the gospel, they had met with rejection and persecution, and their message went mostly unheeded. How could this be? Mark interprets the word of Jesus to this situation with several points: (1) This should be no surprise, for it is according to Scripture; as in Isa. 6, so in Mark's own time. (2) Acceptance or rejection of the divine message is not merely at human disposal but under God's sovereignty (as Paul elaborates in Rom. 9–11; see esp. 11:25–26, where "mystery" also appears). If one has eyes to see and ears to hear, one cannot congratulate oneself but only give thanks to God (see Deut. 29:2–4). (3) The rejection, though real in the present, is not the last word.

The sayings Mark has assembled in 4:21–25 illuminate this final hopeful point.

4:21–25 Nothing hidden, except to be disclosed: In this brief section, Mark has combined four separate sayings that circulated separately and are found in a variety of contexts in the other Gospels (see Luke 6:38; 11:33; 12:2; Matt. 5:15; 7:2; 10:26). Mark has placed them here not as a random sample of other aspects of Jesus' teaching, but as a counterpoint and interpretation of the previous section on Jesus' parabolic teaching. There, blindness and rejection, divinely intended as part of God's plan, were the dominant note. Here he assembles sayings that, in their present context, show that blindness and darkness, hiding and mystery, are only the next-to-last phase in God's plan for the ages, not the final result.

4:21 Nothing hidden, except to be disclosed: In other contexts, this saying is a bit of proverbial wisdom—"secrets finally come out, you can't fool people forever"—but here it is applied to the incongruity of Jesus' teaching in parables in order to conceal rather than reveal. This will not always be the case; in Mark's own post-Easter time, the original hiddenness has already been surpassed by the resurrection, and the present hiddenness of God's reign even in Mark's time and ours is to be finally overcome when God's light shines on all. The repeated "to be" in this section translates exactly the same Greek word as in 4:12 and might better be rendered "in order that" or "so that," as there. The same word is taken up and repeated four times in this brief passage, as if to emphasize that the divine judgmental "in order that" is not God's final word, but that the hiddenness and unbelief represent only a provisional and passing element in divine intent toward full eschatological disclosure to all.

4:24 Pay attention: Mark's theology, however, is not a simple progression, a period of secrecy that gives way to the final period of manifestation. Mark understands the sayings of vv. 21–25 as themselves parables that must be understood parabolically. As was the case with the time of Jesus, the present is both a time of concealment and a time of revelation—for those who have eyes to see. One cannot wait with passive resignation in the face of the divine hardening of people's hearts until the age of blindness is over and the final day of revelation has come. The revelation is already present, and overcoming the darkness is a matter not merely of waiting but of looking and listening with eyes and ears attuned to God's hidden act.

4:25 For to those who have: Originally a kind of folk wisdom like "the rich get richer and the poor get poorer," Mark sets it in this context to say that the divine gift of perceiving God's kingdom is not arbitrary but is given to those who have striven to understand and have developed their own insight. Paradoxically, those who have no such insight will have it taken away. Thus, while full of promise, vv. 21–25 is no simple "wait and God will take care of it" wisdom, but a mind-twisting challenge to look for the act of God in the present or face the consequences of not being able to see at all.

4:26–29
The Parable of the Seed Growing Secretly

This is the only parable found exclusively in Mark (though see echoes in Matt. 13:24–30). Mark's three seed parables are taken from a larger collection (see v. 33) and thus represent a Markan selection. Since all three parables deal with sowing, seeds, and harvest, and since Mark has made the sower the key to all the parables (v. 13), the identification of the seed with the word (v. 14) indicates that the preaching and teaching of the Christian message, identified as the word of God/Christ, is at the heart of his understanding of the kingdom.

4:26 Is as if: This expression corresponds to Jesus' Aramaic word that is best translated "it is the case with." The parables do not compare God's kingdom to some particular point or points in the story, but the parable as a whole in some unspecified way points to the nature and reality of the kingdom.

4:27 He does not know how: Jesus does not "explain" how the kingdom is present and/or is coming. God's kingdom can be spoken of only indirectly, obliquely.

4:28 Produces of itself: Literally, "automatically," but not in the impersonal sense of the English word. The term is found often in the LXX, the Greek translation of the Old Testament used by Mark, to represent God's act that is beyond human manipulation or control (e.g., Lev. 25:5; 2 Kgs. 19:29). The coming of the kingdom is not a matter of human cleverness, dedication, or preparation but belongs to God's sovereignty. Thus, while we and the original readers "know" that human activity is necessary for raising crops—not only planting, but fertilization, cultivating, and such—these human activities seem to be intentionally disregarded. The "point" is not that humans can do certain things to "prepare" for the coming of God's

kingdom, but precisely the opposite: God's word has been sown, and it will have its own effect, will bring its own harvest in God's good time (see Isa. 55:11). The farmer does not "raise" crops, but goes about his business and sleeps soundly, secure that God will bring his creative word to fruition.

4:29 When the grain is ripe: Literally, "permits," using the same word elsewhere used for the "handing over/betrayal" of John the Baptist, Jesus, and Christians (1:14; 3:19; 9:31; 13:12; 14:10, 41; see on 9:31). Note also the messianic connotations of "sprout," "shoot" (Zech. 3:8; 6:12; Jer. 23:5–6; 33:14–16). While the parable should not be allegorized, these allusions point to the relation between the "handing over" of John, Jesus, and Christians and the coming of God's kingdom. Such handing over appears to be defeat but is the instrument of God's present and coming rule. **Sickle . . . harvest:** Unmistakable eschatological imagery (Joel 4:13; Rev. 14:15). God's kingdom, already inaugurated in a hidden and paradoxical manner in the Christ event, will be brought to its full reality at the eschaton.

4:30–32
The Parable of the Mustard Seed
(See also at Matt. 13:31–32; Luke 13:18–19)

In the pre-Markan tradition this parable was handed on in tandem with the parable of the Leaven (see the Matthean and Lukan parallels); Mark has selected it as the third of his "seed" parables (see above).

4:30 We: This is the only time that the first person plural occurs as the voice behind Jesus' teaching. It should not be seen merely as an editorial we but represents the fusion of Jesus' word with that of his disciples (see above on vv. 13–20). This collapsing of the word of Jesus into that of the Christian community is extensively developed in the Gospel of John (see introduction to John and comments on John 1:14, 16; 3:11–12; 4:22; 9:4; 1 John 1:1; 4:1).

4:31 Smallest: Not technically, the orchid seed, for example, being actually smaller. But Mark's astounding small/great contrast remains.

4:32 Greatest of all shrubs: The mustard plant is not a tree but a large shrub, a distinction lost in the Q form of this saying preserved in Matthew and Luke. The imagery of Ezek. 17:23; 31:6; Dan. 4:10–12, 19–22 is in the background, where the kingdom of God is portrayed in terms of the common ancient Near East conception of the cosmic world tree representing world empire embracing a multitude of nations. In Jesus' parable and Mark's theology, it is the modest mustard plant, not the towering cedar, that communicates the manifestation of God's kingdom in the midst of the ordinary.

Birds of the air: A representation of Gentile nations in Ezek. 31:6. The Old Testament and Judaism expected the gathering of the Gentile nations into the people of God as God's act at the eschaton (see Isa. 2:1–4). Mark pictures this as already happening in the Christian community's response to the Christ event.

4:33–34
Summary: Jesus' Use of Parables
(See also at Matt. 13:34–35)

4:33 As they were able to hear: This concluding summary preserves the double perspective of the nature of Jesus' teaching discussed above, including the pre-Easter/post-Easter and insider/outsider tensions that are built into Mark's story throughout.

4:35–41
Stilling the Storm
(See also at Matt. 8:23–27; Luke 8:22–25)

The day of Jesus' parabolic teaching, in which God's power is represented as working in ordinary, hidden ways, is followed by a scene that combines pictures of Jesus as humanly weak and Jesus playing the role of God the Creator. See the excursus "Interpreting the Miracle Stories" at Matt. 9:35.

4:35 On that day: It is not clear when this day begins; the last temporal designation was 2:23, on a Sabbath, but this is a different day. Nor is it clear where the day's events end, but the day of parables apparently continues through 5:43, with a trip across the lake, calming the storm, an exorcism, the swineherds return to their town and the townspeople coming out to Jesus, a trip back across the lake, healing the woman with the flow of blood, and raising the daughter of Jairus, with the funeral still under way at this presumably late hour. It is not likely that Mark intends this as a literal chronology; such data only illustrate that his episodic narrative is not composed as biography. **The other side:** Up to this point, Jesus has conducted his ministry exclusively on the western, Jewish side of the lake. He now leads his disciples into a predominately Gentile area, prefiguring the later move from a purely Jewish-Christian group of Jesus' disciples to a predominately Gentile church such as Mark's own.

4:38 Asleep: An expression both of Jesus' human weakness—he is tired with a human weariness—and his trust in God's care (see v. 27). The story as a whole has several characteristics reminiscent of the Jonah story (departure by boat to a Gentile destination; violent storm at sea; the main character sleeping while experienced sailors are terrified; the storm is calmed in a way that involves the main character; the sailors responding positively to the amazing event). Although the Old Testament Jonah is something of an antihero who resists God's purpose, New Testament allusions to the Old Testament are sometimes based not on the Old Testament itself but on current interpretations that had been developed in Jewish tradition (see, e.g., comments on 1 Cor. 10:4). By the first century, Jonah had been reinterpreted as a hero who challenged and defeated the sea monster that caused the storm. Thus elsewhere in the New Testament Jesus is interpreted on the model of the Jonah story (Matt. 12:39–41; 16:4; Luke 11:29–32). Here, of course, there is also a great contrast with Jonah, the prophet who is reluctant to fulfill God's mission to the Gentiles, for Jesus leads his disciples into Gentile territory.

Teacher: This may seem to be a strange address in the situation, but Mark links teaching, authority, and power (see 1:22, 27) and also uses this address to bracket the section from 4:1 on as representative of Jesus as teacher.

Do you not care that we are perishing?: The threatened and persecuted Markan community (13:11–13) must have lifted such prayers to God in its time of trial. This is not an informational question, but an anguished prayerlike cry to Jesus, who now assumes the role of God. The disciples seem to assume that Jesus can do something about the storm but is sleeping rather than acting. But prayers are not made to rabbis. God is the one who commands the sea (Job 26:11–12; Pss. 104:7; 106:9, Isa. 51:9–10). God is also the one addressed in the psalms as sleeping on the job, not acting to save his people (Pss. 44:23–44; 35:23; 59:4). The figure of Jesus modulates into that of God, the human Jesus functions with divine power.

4:39 Rebuked: The same verb used for addressing demons, where **Peace!** is the same word translated "be silent" in 1:25 (see 1:27). Calming the storm is portrayed an the exorcism of the storm demon, another victory of Christ over satanic evil. On the language of demons, Satan, and exorcism, see excursus at 5:1.

4:40 Why are you afraid?: As "Don't you care that we're dying out here?" is suffering humanity's challenge to God, "Why are you afraid?" is God's challenge to humanity. The story functions not merely as a report of a once-upon-a-time amazing event at sea but, like the Gospel as a whole, as a christological narrative representing the divine-human encounter in the Christ event.

Have you still no faith?: If this is the original reading, it forms part of the preceding challenge of Jesus-who-represents-God to unbelieving humanity. Some manuscripts, however, read "Don't you yet have faith?" implying that they will indeed have faith later (4:21–25; 13:9–11). This corresponds to Mark's theology of the messianic secret, according to which Jesus' true identity as Son of God was not recognized until the cross-resurrection event made authentic faith possible.

4:41 Who then is this?: The disciples do not come to faith on the basis of the miracle but are still in uncomprehending blindness. The post-Easter reader knows the answer to their question, for which the characters in the story must wait on later revelation.

5:1–20
The Gerasene Demoniac
(See also at Matt. 8:28–34; Luke 8:26–39)

For detailed comment on this text, see the comments on the Lukan parallel; for particularly Marcan emphases, see below. Here we present a general discussion of the interpretation of the Bible's language for suprapersonal evil.

EXCURSUS:
SATAN, THE DEVIL, AND DEMONS IN BIBLICAL THEOLOGY

"Satan" has become in English a proper name for what was originally in the Hebrew Scriptures a generic word for "adversary." The word is often used in this generic sense in the Old Testament, especially in its specific use in the courtroom: "accuser," either as hostile witness or as prosecuting attorney (e.g., 1 Kgs. 11:14, 23, 25; Pss. 38:20; 71:13; 109:4, 30, 29). In three late (post-exilic) passages the accuser takes on a particular identity as one of the angels in the heavenly court, the divine prosecuting attorney who presses God's case or does God's work of probing the integrity of human beings (1 Chr. 21:1; Job 1:6–12; Zech. 3:1). In none of these instances, nor anyplace else in the Old Testament, is there a Satan as the personification of evil. In 1 Chr. 21:1 the "satan" does what God himself did in the earlier version of 2 Sam. 24:1.

During the intertestamental period, especially under the influence of Iranian dualistic religion and its evil god Ahriman, counterpart to the supreme god of light Ahura-mazda, the figure of Satan emerged in Jewish tradition as the personification of evil and the transcendent opponent of God. Jewish monotheism prohibited Satan from becoming a second god, but he became the leader of all evil spirits, with his own kingdom of darkness opposing the kingdom of God. Various versions of the origin of Satan as one of the fallen angels developed: (*1 En.* 6:1–16:4; *2 En.* 29). The full-blown myth of the origin of Satan and evil in the rebellion of the angels, popularized for English readers in Milton's classic *Paradise Lost*, did not develop until later, but its beginnings, though later than the Old Testament, are already found in the intertestamental apocalyptic literature. Satan, also called Satanail, Beliar or Belial (as in the Dead Sea Scrolls), and Mastema, now becomes what he is when the New Testament opens: the one who tempts humanity to discord, violence, and immorality (*T. Gad* 4:7; *T. Benj.* 7:1; *T. Reu.* 4:7; *T. Sim.* 5:3; *T. Ash.* 3:2; *Jub.* 11:5; *2 En.* 31:6). Although the idea of Satan had not developed when Gen. 1–3 was written, in the later retelling of the story in Jewish apocalyptic, the original sin of humanity was provoked by "the devil," "Satanail," now identified with the serpent (*2 En.* 31:1–8). As Satan was thought of as the cause of human sin and misery, in some contemporary Jewish documents such as the Dead Sea Scrolls the binding and destruction of Satan became a standard part of the hoped-for eschatological drama (1QH 3:35; 6:29; *T. Levi* 18:12; *T. Jud.* 25:3).

Early Christianity adopted this mythology as its way of expressing its conviction that evil, while not an eternal counterpart of God, was more than the accumulation of individual human sins. This supraindividual power of evil that has the world and humanity in its grasp is called by various names in the New Testament, including "the devil" (32x in the New Testament), "Satan" (33x), "Belial" or "Beliar" (2 Cor. 6:15), and "Beelzebul" (7x).

The Bible's talk of Satan and the devil is thus not peculiar, but belongs to the mainstream of Jewish and early Christian apocalyptic thought. The Gospels, Paul, Revelation, and the whole New Testament use language about Satan and the devil as a way of expressing their understanding of evil as a transcendent power. They do this in a variety of ways, however, which fall into two basic patterns:

1. Evil as Cosmic Power

Paul and his followers portray evil as a transcendent power pervading the universe and holding human beings under its control. Sometimes they can simply refer to this power as "sin" (see Rom. 6:1–23; comments on Rom. 3:19), but they can also use a variety of concepts and names for this cosmic power (see, e.g., Rom. 8:38–39; Gal. 4:8–11; Col. 2:15; Eph. 1:21; 2:1–2; 6:10–12). The Fourth Gospel likewise understands evil in cosmic terms (see on John 12:31) and has no exorcisms in which demons are cast out of individuals.

Revelation is perhaps the best-known example of the Bible's graphic Satan language. The author follows the Pauline model of portraying the cosmic evil power in personal terms, usually designating him "Satan" (Rev. 2:9, 13, 24; 3:9; 12:9; 20:2; 20:7) or "the devil" (Rev. 2:10; 12:9,12; 20:2,10). Echoing the sinister overtones of Satan's origin as the accuser in court, John refers to him as "the accuser" (12:10), a designation powerfully appropriate in the situation of the Asian Christians who found themselves accused before the Roman courts. John follows Jewish tradition—but not the Scripture—in identifying Satan with the serpent of the fall story in Gen. 3 (Rev. 12:9, 14, 15; 20:2). More importantly, in Rev. 12:1–13:18; 16:13; and 20:2 the author identifies both these figures with the primordial dragon, the chaos monster (Leviathan, Rahab, Tannin) subdued by Yahweh at the creation (see Job 7:12; 9:13; 26:12–13; Pss. 74:13–14; 89:9–10; Isa. 27:1; 30:7; 51:9–10). These superpersonal forces of evil are not speculative abstractions for John and his church but are met in their embodiments in the social structures of John's situation and in the institutionalized evil of the Roman Empire, as well as within the religious conflicts of his own community (Rev. 2:9, 13, 24; 12:1–13:18).

Although John shows no interest in taking over the mythical picture of the origin of Satan and evil (Rev. 12:7–12 does not refer to a precreation fall of the angels), he does adapt the traditional eschatological scenario for the destruction of the devil and all his influence. The decisive battle has already been fought and won in the Christ event (Rev. 3:21; 5:1–10; 12:7–10). Though defeated in the transcendent world of the heavenly court and only awaiting his execution, the devil still has power on earth and, knowing that his days are numbered, is still wreaking havoc, especially through his agents the beast and false prophet (Rev. 12:13–13:18). Yet his doom is sure. At the end of the final plagues, the devil will be bound for a thousand years while the earth enjoys an era of eschatological fulfillment (Rev. 20:1–6), then released for one last deceitful effort, after which he will be thrown into the lake of fire, the second death (Rev. 20:7–10).

2. Evil as Demon Possession of Individual People

The Synoptic Gospels and Acts (and, in the Bible, only they) often picture the evil power at work in this world as the possession of individuals by "evil spirits" or "unclean spirits." As the counterpart to the presence of the Holy Spirit, a number of *unholy* spirits are at work in the world, all under the control of the prince of evil, who may be called Satan, the devil, or Beelzebul. This way of thinking of the power of evil corresponds to the view of antiquity in general, which saw the world as inhabited by numerous spirits, good and evil, that could influence and dominate human life for good or evil. While it is true that phenomena now understood as epilepsy, paranoia, or other forms of physical or mental illness were attributed to evil spirits in a prescientific age, this is not sufficient to explain away such biblical stories as mere primitive superstition. Within the worldview of their times, they used evil spirits as a way of expressing the reality of evil powers to which human life is subject in every age. Modern readers may no longer believe in evil spirits in the same way as the people of the first century, but human beings in every age confront the powers of evil at work in their own world and within their own lives.

It is historically likely that within the cultural understanding of his times, Jesus in fact functioned as an exorcist, as did his disciples. However, the numerous stories of Jesus and his disciples casting out demons in the Synoptic Gospels and Acts not only represent historical reality; they also point to the meaning of the Christ event as a whole, understood as the act of God in which the demonic power of the world is overcome, a victory to be ultimately realized only at the final coming of the eschatological kingdom of God for which Christians pray (see on Matt. 6:9–13).

Summary

Such are the Bible's pictures of Satan as the power of evil. We do not have here a speculative metaphysical theory intended to satisfy intellectual curiosity about the origin of evil, but a variety of pictures of the evil powers to which human life is subject, and heartening good news that this power has been decisively broken in the Christ event, which points forward to the final victory of God over all the powers of evil.

Such language has both dangers and values. Among its chief dangers is a prosaic literalism, all the more dangerous because it supposes it is merely "taking the Bible for what it says," an encouragement to dwell in the story world of another culture and century and adopt its pictures as objectifying representations of the way things are. Comparative study of religious literature that brings to light the elaborate mythical stories of Satan, Beliar, and Mastema lets us see how restrained is the Bible's usage and also prohibits us from adopting it as an objectifying revelation from heaven of the way things are in the supernatural world. Such an approach can degenerate into a modern form of gnostic speculation, studying and constructing theories about Satan as curiosity-titillating bits of occult science masquerading as Bible study. It can result in a the-devil-made-me-do-it denial of responsibility for one's own actions. It can result in resignation in the face of concrete social and political manifestations of evil when we might take some effective measures against them. Including Satan in one's religious symbol system can even play into the hands of institutionalized evil, diverting attention from the real problem. In view of such real dangers, should not modern, intellectually honest Christians simply reject talk of Satan as an unfortunate vestige of a superstitious age?

Not necessarily. Satan language and imagery, like the language and imagery of apocalypticism generally, can be the vehicle of profound theological truths and may be the necessary vehicle for some essential Christian insights and affirmations. Not only fundamentalists, but responsible theologians of a variety of perspectives who have a social conscience, have found the New Testament's imagery for the demonic power of evil to be valuable when taken seriously but not literally. "Satan" as a symbolic way of thinking of the superpersonal power of evil is a valuable dimension of biblical theology. The power of evil is bigger than individual sins. The Bible often speaks in political and national terms when it talks of the power of Satan (e.g., Rev. 13:7; 18:3, 23; 20:3, 8). Satan is not merely the individualistic tempter to petty sins; he is the deceiver of the nations (Rev. 20:7–8). We might now label this as "systemic evil" or picture it as a vast, impersonal, computer-like network of evil in which our lives are enmeshed and that influences us quite apart from our wills.

A valuable dimension of this imagery is that it pictures the vastness of the reservoir of evil by which we are threatened and from which we cannot deliver ourselves. Another valuable aspect of such language is that it prohibits our treating human enemies as through *they* were the ultimate enemy. One of the major functions of the biblical revelation of the power of Satan behind the scenes is to disclose to adherents of the biblical faith that their real enemy is not those who in the name of other faiths or none oppose, harass, and even persecute Christian believers, but the power of evil of which they too are the victims.

5:1 To the other side: This story of Jesus' first public act in Gentile territory has several parallels to the exorcism and its response in 1:21–28, the inauguration of Jesus' ministry in Jewish territory.

5:3 Restrain him: See on 3:27.

5:4 No one had the strength: See on 1:7; 3:27.

5:7 Son of the Most High God: See on 3:11–12.

5:13 Two thousand: This incredibly high number is omitted by both Matthew and Luke, who want to make the story more in line with common sense. Mark's story does not function at the level of historical plausibility but witnesses to the defeat of satanic evil in God's ultimate triumphant act in the Christ event as a whole. Taken as literal history, the story portrays Jesus not only as destroying private property (two thousand swine represented a substantial investment), but as destroying needed food in a hungry world. Like all stories of miraculous divine intervention, the story raises ethical problems (see excursus on interpreting miracle stories at Matt. 9:35).

5:15 They were afraid: A double-edged word in Mark, that can mean either being frightened or experiencing the religious awe appropriate to being in the presence of God.

5:19 Go . . . and tell: A missionary commission similar to 16:7. The liberated man is a prototype of later Christian missionaries to Gentile lands. **The Lord:** Never used unambiguously of Jesus in Mark. **How much Jesus had done for him:** The alternation here of "Lord" and "Jesus" can be read to mean that the healed man misunderstood Jesus' instruction—Jesus intended God (as Luke 8:39 interprets), but the man understood Jesus as the (human exorcist) who had healed him. The reader understands the truly human Jesus as also the divine Lord, but this post-Easter Christology is still hidden from the characters in the story. The story as a whole is thus another illustration of Mark's messianic secret, which is preserved even in stories in which Jesus is openly proclaimed. It pictures the saving act of God in Jesus, liberating the world from satanic domination, but Jesus himself is misunderstood and rejected by some on the basis of common sense and understandable economic interests (the loss of two thousand swine!). Even those who hear and are **amazed** do not grasp his true identity.

5:21–43
Jairus' Daughter and the Woman with a Hemorrhage
(See also on Matt. 9:18–26; Luke 8:40–56)

The construction is a typical Markan "sandwich" that inserts one traditional story into another (see on 2:1–12). Mark's selection of these two stories is not arbitrary, for they have several points of contact: (1) The restored person in each instance is a nameless female, referred to with the respectful and affirmative "daughter"—one who belongs to Israel, the people of God. (2) Both stories use the language of healing/salvation that points beyond the immediate individual problem of sickness and death to its eschatological resolution in the Christ event; especially, the raising of the young woman points to the resurrection of Jesus. (3) The number twelve plays a role in each story: the woman has been sick for twelve years, the girl has been alive for twelve years. (4) Jesus' touch is healing, life-giving. (5) In both cases, the constantly menstruating woman and the dead girl, by biblical and traditional Jewish law, touching the person would render Jesus unclean, but his powerful touch communicates healing and life rather than receiving ritual uncleanness (see on 1 Cor. 7:14, and Gen. 18:22–33, where, contrary to the usual view that the sin of a few contaminates the whole community, the righteousness of a few is contagious and will save the whole community). (6) In each case, the traditional purity rules are boldly ignored, first by the woman, who courageously touches Jesus, and then by Jairus, who, aware that Jesus has now touched an "unclean" woman, persists in his invitation. (7) Both stories feature the language of *fear* (awe in the presence of the divine) and *faith* (trust in the power of God when it is already "too late").

5:22 Leaders of the synagogue: A lay not clerical office, analogous to the designated lay worship leader or the chairperson of the board of a modern Christian congregation. The story shows that not all the Jewish leaders opposed Jesus (see 12:28–34; 15:42–46).

5:23 Come: Though other stories present Jesus as being able to heal at a distance (7:24–30; Matt. 8:5–13; Luke 7:1–10; John 4:46–54), these two stories presuppose that the presence of Jesus is necessary for his healing touch to be operative. The perspective and presuppositions of the different stories should not be harmonized.

5:34 Your faith has made you well: The phrase also means "has saved you"; the healing story has the overtones of Christian conversion, of being delivered from the world of sickness and death into the eschatological community of salvation. Mark's readers (and modern ones) can see the experience of the woman as a prefiguration of their own experience, in which coming to Christian faith was the event that mediated new, eternal life. In these scenes, where Jesus represents God, to ask whether it is faith in Jesus or faith in God that saves is a false question (see on John 3:16). There is no magical or healing power in faith itself; it is the God who is present in Jesus who heals. No sick person who prays for healing and does not receive it should conclude on the basis of this story, "It's because I don't have enough faith."

5:41 Talitha cum: Mark preserves the language of Jesus' original Aramaic (see 3:17; 7:11, 34; 14:36; 15:22, 34). **Get up . . . the girl got up:** This is the same vocabulary used of Jesus' resurrection and of the future resurrection at the end of the age. The little girl was resuscitated, restored to life in this world, where she will die again, but the story, like the miracle stories in general, points forward to Jesus' resurrection and to the words God/Christ will speak at the last day (see John 5:25–29). Thus such stories are not promises to the believing reader that when our children die, as they do, Jesus will come now and restore them to life in this world, but that because of the Christ event, nothing, not even death, the last enemy, can separate us from the love of God (1 Cor. 15:26; Rom. 8:35–39), and that at the last day Christ will come and speak these life-giving words to all.

5:43 No one should know this: This is a striking example of Mark's narrative mode of telling the story in such a way that the post-Easter readers, but not the characters in the story, perceive Jesus' mighty works and their significance (see "messianic secret" in introduction to Mark). In this double story, Jesus, the woman, the girl's parents (and the reader) know what has happened, but the others fail to perceive or misunderstand. This is a particularly significant illustration of the way Mark's narrative mode is theologically significant but not (and not intended to be) historically realistic. How could the restoration of the little girl to life be kept secret, since her raising had happened during the funeral?

6:1–6a
Jesus Is Rejected at Nazareth
(See also at Matt. 13:53–58; Luke 4:16–30)

The problem of Jesus' having been misunderstood and rejected by his own people (though accepted by the Gentiles of Mark's time) troubled early Christianity (see the profound reflections of Rom. 9–11). This model scene reflects not only the events of Jesus' own day but the situation of the later church.

6:1 Came to his hometown: Nazareth in Galilee. Again, the chronology is vague, but the narrative is now in a different day from the events of chaps. 4–5 (see on 4:35).

6:2 Began to teach in the synagogue: In Mark, after this scene Jesus never again enters a synagogue, again reflecting the experience of the church, which began in the synagogue but had become primarily a Gentile Christian community in Mark's time and place.

6:2 Many who heard him were astounded: The initial response is positive. **This wisdom that has been given to him:** They acknowledge that his teaching and **deeds of power** are of more than human origin but do not specify that they are from God (see 3:20–35). Depending on how they are interpreted, the following references to his mother and brothers may continue the general positive acclamation ("See, one of our own young men has become somebody great!") or may already be a derogatory put-down ("We know this local kid; who does he think he is?"). **Son of Mary** could suggest that Jesus is illegitimate, a charge sometimes made in later anti-Christian Judaism, or it could be a normal designation for someone whose mother had become more prominent than his father (see, e.g., 1 Sam. 26:6 and often; Luke 7:12; Acts 16:1). There is no suggestion here of the doctrine of the virginal conception, which plays no role in Mark's theology (see Gal. 4:4). **Jesus and Joses and Judas and Simon . . . sisters:** See on Luke 2:7; 8:19–21; John 7:5; Acts 1:13. Mark shows no interest in the effort of some streams of later Christian tradition to understand these as Jesus' near kin, i.e., cousins or his half-brothers and sisters, the children of Joseph's previous marriage (see on Matt. 13:55–56). Joseph as Jesus' father is not mentioned in Mark and plays no role. **And they took offense at him:** Here the story makes a dramatic swerve. For no reason given in the text, the initial positive response now becomes negative, and the hometown folk become examples of those who see but do not perceive (see 4:10–12).

6:4 Prophets are not without honor: Jesus applies a traditional proverb to his own situation. While as one who speaks for God Jesus is indeed a prophet, he is more than a prophet, and "prophet" is not an adequate title designation for him (6:15; 8:28; see 14:65 commentary).

6:5 Could do no deed of power: Mark does not hesitate to portray this aspect of Jesus' human limitation, presenting Jesus as both humanly weak and full of the divine power (see introduction to Mark; Matt. 13:58 interprets the Markan text somewhat defensively, changing "could not do" to "did not do," and blaming the lack of miracles on the unbelief of the townsfolk; Luke simply omits the reference). **Except . . . a few:** Despite spiritual blindness and unbelief, the power of God continues to erupt through Jesus' human weakness, for those who have eyes to see.

6:6 He was amazed: Another human trait of the Markan Jesus, omitted by both Matthew and Luke. Mark's Christology paradoxically juxtaposes true divinity and true humanity, without qualifying or diluting either.

6:6b–8:21
SENDING APOSTLES; ARE THEY TOO BLIND AND HARDENED?

A new section begins here (see outline in introduction to Mark, and comments at 1:16–8:21).

A major narrative thread of this section is the theme of food and eating. Jesus twice feeds the multitudes (6:30–44; 8:1–9), offering life-giving bread as God did for the Israelites who had been liberated at the exodus (Exod. 16). Implicit in such stories is the later Johannine view that it is Jesus himself who has been offered to the world in the Christ event as "bread from heaven" (see on John 6:22–59). In contrast, John the Baptist is killed at a royal banquet, and his head is offered on a dinner plate to the startled guests (6:14–29). Food not only nourishes but separates people into exclusive and hostile groups; Jesus thus discusses food and the rules for eating, twice with his disciples (7:17–23; 8:14–21), and once with a Gentile woman (7:24–30).

In this section Jesus sends out the twelve disciples whom he has specially called and commissioned (see 1:16–20; 3:13–14). They share in his authority and message, but despite Jesus' continuing miracles and their own participation in his divine authority, they continue to misunderstand—an obtuseness that is focused in their inability to understand "about the loaves" (6:52).

6:6b–13
Commissioning the Twelve
(See also at Matt. 10:1–14; Luke 9:1–6; 10:1–12)

Another, more extensive version of Jesus' mission discourse circulated in early Christianity, preserved in Matthew and Luke (derived from Q), who combine it with the Markan instructions.

As elsewhere in his narrative, the story is narrated at two levels, the pre-Easter narrative level portraying Jesus sending out the Twelve and a post-Easter level addressing Mark's own church and later readers.

6:7 Called: See 1:16–20; 3:13. **Send them out:** This is the verb form of the noun translated "apostle" (see on 3:14; Luke 6:12–13). For the first time, the disciples are themselves active participants in Jesus' ministry, commissioned and empowered by him and doing the same things Jesus does: preaching, exorcising, and healing (see 1:14–15, 21–27; 2:1–11).

6:8–9 Take nothing for their journey: The word "journey" here translates the thematic Markan word elsewhere translated "way," "path," or "road," theologically significant in Mark as the "way" of Christ (see 1:2, 3; 4:4, 15; 6:8, 8:27; 9:33–34; 10:17, 32, 46, 52; 11:18; 12:14).

No bread ... bag ... money: As the Israelites liberated from Egypt were dependent on God, who provided them bread (the manna of Exod. 16) and clothing (see Deut. 8:4; 29:5), so the early Christian missionaries were to trust that God would provide for them through the hospitality of other Christians and those to whom they ministered. **Staff . . . sandals:** Also reflected in the exodus story (Exod. 12:11; Deut. 29:5). There is probably also a contrast here with the standard outfit of the itinerant Cynic preachers, who carried all their possessions in a bag but went barefoot. They made a point of being "self-sufficient"; the Christian preachers were dependent on God. The Markan Jesus does not want his missionaries to be mistaken for the common street preachers of the day.

6:11 Shake off the dust . . . on your feet: Although the Twelve had a successful mission in which there is no suggestion of opposition or rejection (see 6:30), the post-Easter missionaries were sometimes greeted with hostility and persecution. Here too the way the story is told reflects the later situation. When rejected, Jesus' disciples are to perform a symbolic, prophetic act, representing their separation from those who heard and rejected the Christian message, and leave them to the future judgment of God (see Acts 13:51; 18:6).

6:12 All should repent: Reorient their lives in view of the coming kingdom of God, the same message as Jesus (1:14–15). Their message is not about Jesus, but about God. During Jesus' earthly life, his followers could not yet proclaim the later Christian message of the saving act of God in the life, death, and resurrection of Jesus, but this later message was in continuity with Jesus' own message, though it did not merely repeat it. Mark's messianic secret is particularly concerned that the full Christian message could not be proclaimed during Jesus' lifetime, since it was not perceived or understood until the meaning of Jesus' life was completed by the cross and resurrection.

6:13 Many: In striking contrast to the **few** that Jesus had been able to heal in the preceding story (6:5). This does not mean that the people in Nazareth had no faith, so Jesus was ineffective, but that his disciples found many people with strong faith elsewhere in Galilee, so they could heal them. The contrast is between Jesus' earthly ministry, unspectacular in statistical terms, and the large numbers of people who were later transformed by the church's message (see the "greater works," John 14:12). **Anointed with oil:** Jesus is never represented as using this common means of healing (see Luke 10:34), which was adopted by the early church (Jas. 5:14), another indication that the discourse represents not only the life of Jesus but early missionary practice.

6:14–29
The Death of John the Baptist
(See also at Matt. 14:1–12; Luke 3:19–20; 9:7–9)

The disciples have been sent out and will return in 6:30. The intervening literary interlude in the form of a flashback is another Markan "sandwich" (see 2:1–12). The story of John's death fills the temporal interim during the disciples' mission but has a more important role: it serves both as a counterpoint to the next story of "king" Jesus' "banquet" in the wilderness (6:30–44) and as an anticipation of the fate of Jesus, who will also die at the hands of a ruler who is reluctant to execute him but succumbs to social pressure. There are thus several verbal parallels between John in this story and Jesus elsewhere: each is eagerly listened to (6:20/12:37); the ruler is curious about both (6:12/15:9–10, 14–15); Herod tries unsuccessfully to save John; Pilate does the same with Jesus (6:20/15:4, 9–14); each ruler does in fact arrest, bind, and shamefully execute his prisoner, who is buried by his followers (6:17, 27–29/14:46; 15:1, 16–47). Moreover, that some, including Herod, think of Jesus as "John raised from the dead" further identifies the two victims of state injustice.

6:14 King Herod: The first reference to the Galilean ruler in Mark. See on Luke 9:7. **Jesus' name had become known:** In the context, this means the works of Jesus' disciples were not done in their own name, but in the authority given them by Jesus (6:7). The story of *John's* death occurs in the context of a discussion of the identity of *Jesus*. **Elijah . . . a prophet:** An anticipation of 8:27–30 (see there).

6:16 John . . . has been raised: This was a popular view among the people and Herod's own view. Yet Mark does not consider it authentic resurrection faith, which is more than simply believing a dead man has been restored to life (see on Luke 7:14; excursus "Interpreting the Resurrection" at Matt. 28:1).

6:17 On account of Herodias: The first-century Jewish historian Josephus also recounts Herod's arrest and execution of John (*Antiquities* 18.116–19), but attributes the action to his fear that John might be fomenting revolution among his followers and locates the event in Herod's trans-Jordan fortress Machaerus. Josephus's account is more plausible historically and cannot be harmonized with Mark's account, which interprets the story theologically. Even so, it is not clear whether Mark's understanding is that Herod had John arrested to satisfy Herodias or placed him in protective custody to protect him from her assassins. Contrast the story in Matt. 14:1–12, where John's death is the result of Herod's own hostility.

His brother Philip's wife: This is apparently a mistake, but an understandable one, since the Herodian family tree is very complicated. Herod the Great, ruler at the time of Jesus' birth (Matt. 2:1; Luke 1:5), had ten wives and many sons and daughters, several of whom were called Herod or Herodias. There was much intermarriage within the Herodian family, so lines of relationship were difficult to keep straight. In Josephus's historically more reliable account, the first husband of Herodias was also called Herod. Mark or his tradition may have confused him with Herod Philip, Herodias's son-in-law, not her husband (Luke 3:19 omits "Philip," silently correcting Mark).

6:18 Not lawful: Lev. 18:16; 20:21. Like Elijah, John is portrayed as a righteous prophet unafraid to charge even the king with violating the law of God. (There is no suggestion that Jesus had criticized Herod on this count.) As in the case of Elijah, the king's evil wife attempts to destroy John (1 Kgs. 17–21; see Mark 1:2–8; 9:11–13 for other instances of Mark's casting John in the role of Elijah).

6:22 She pleased Herod: The expression often has sexual overtones in the LXX (Septuagint, the Greek translation of the Old Testament

used by Mark). See Esther 2:9; 5:3. The Esther story has provided a prototype and details for Mark's story.

6:29 His disciples . . . took his body: In contrast to Jesus, whose twelve disciples will abandon him (see 15:42–47).

6:30–44
Feeding the Five Thousand
*(See also at Matt. 14:13–21;
Luke 9:10–17; John 6:1–15)*

On interpreting New Testament miracle stories, see excursus at Matt. 8:1.

This is the only one of the miracle stories about Jesus to appear in all four Gospels; the image of Jesus who feeds the hungry was central to early Christian faith. Many levels of meaning reverberate through this symbolic story. The historical Jesus was one with compassion for the hungry, one who himself ate and drank with those who had been excluded by religious and social correctness. After Easter, stories of Jesus feeding the hungry were used to communicate God's answer in Christ to the hungers of humanity; in the story of feeding the five thousand, an image of the whole Christ event is given (see "Interpreting the Miracle Stories" at Matt. 9:35). Then each of the Gospels incorporates the story into their portrayal of Christ.

6:30 Apostles: See on 3:14. **All that they had done and taught:** See on 6:7–13. This is the only reference in Mark to the apostles' *teaching*. Elsewhere in Mark, no one teaches except Jesus. But since the disciples represent Jesus and function by his authority, they continue to represent his teaching ministry. Within Mark's narrative framework of the messianic secret and the disciples' misunderstanding, it is difficult to imagine the content of their teaching, but Mark's point is *that* they teach, not the *content* of their teaching. Mark intends this scene to represent the post-Easter reality of the church, where Jesus' disciples continue to teach in his name and by his authority.

6:31 No leisure even to eat: See 3:20–35. Being pursued by the crowds even when he wanted to be alone is reminiscent of 1:35–36—Jesus strikes a responsive chord in the people, who long for what he has to offer, even though they do not understand. The scene is historically problematic. Thousands of people in an area where the population of whole towns such as Capernaum was only two or three thousand is already astounding. That such a crowd is able to make its way around the lake on foot and get there ahead of Jesus and his small group, who take the more direct route by boat, suggests that here as elsewhere the focus of Mark's narrative is not historical reporting but theological meaning.

6:31 Deserted place: The same word often translated "desert" or "wilderness," the word used for the location of Israel's exodus journey between Egypt and the promised land. The word not only points backward to the memory of Israel, and their murmurings when they lacked bread and received the miraculous manna (Exod. 16), but also reflects the contemporary eschatological hopes of many Israelites, who expected Israel to be renewed and delivered in the wilderness. Thus Josephus tells of Jewish prophets in the first century who led groups of devotees into the wilderness in expectation of divine deliverance from the Romans (*Wars* 7.437–42; *Antiquities* 20.97–99, 167–72; see Acts 21:38).

6:34 Like sheep without a shepherd: A proverbial Old Testament expression for Israel without leadership or with bad leaders (Num. 27:17; 1 Kgs. 22:17; Ezek. 34:8; Zech. 10:2). God is himself the good shepherd (Ps. 23) who supplies authentic leadership to the people of God. Thus Moses and David, both of whom had been literally shepherds before being called to provide for God's people, provide models for New Testament images of Jesus and Christian leaders. In this scene Mark focuses on the Mosaic traits of Jesus—as Moses gave food in the wilderness, so will Jesus.

6:37 You give them something to eat: The Markan miracle stories in general are summary symbolic pictures of the character of God as revealed in the Christ event as a whole. In this story Jesus' action points to God who cares for the hungry, God who supplies food. In Mark's framework of the messianic secret, the people in the story saw the miracle but did not understand what was really happening—the saving work of God in Jesus—until after the resurrection. But sometimes the word Mark wants to deliver breaks through the framework of the story and addresses the reader directly (see 13:37; 16:8). Here perceptive readers overhear a word of God addressed to them in their own situation. Quite apart from how one understands the miracle story itself, the command of God to feed hungry people becomes a direct personal address: "You give them something to eat."

6:39–40 Groups . . . groups: Two different words are used. The first group is literally "sym-posia," eating groups, made famous by Plato's *Symposium,* the meal at which weighty matters were discussed. The second word is literally "garden plots," i.e., groups of people arranged in rows. **Hundreds and fifties:** The rowlike arrangement also connotes military order, reminiscent of Israel's army during the wilderness wanderings (see Exod. 18:21, 25; Deut. 1:15). One hundred rows of fifty totals five thousand; the group of Jesus' followers is pictured as the army of God in the wilderness. **Green grass:** Not just an incidental description or indication of the time of year; in the eschatological times, the desert will blossom (Isa. 35). This is another indication that the scene that unfolds reflects the eschatological reality, the time of plenty when all will have enough to eat.

6:41 Taking . . . blessed . . . broke . . . gave: These words echo the eucharistic liturgy of the early church (see Mark 14:22–25; Matt. 26:26–30; Luke 22:14–20; John 6:48–58; 1 Cor. 11:23–25). As the stories of Jesus' ministry were retold after Easter, they took on the features of church life, and Christian readers of the Gospels can see their own experiences reflected in them.

6:42–43 All ate and were filled . . . twelve baskets full: In the ancient world—and in large segments of the modern world—it was not taken for granted that whenever one ate, one ate one's fill, and that there would be food left over (see, e.g., the poignant comment in Ruth 2:14, "She ate until she was satisfied, and she had some left over"). But it is not God's will that any go away from the table hungry, and in the kingdom of God the hungry will be filled (6:21, 25; 14:15). Here we have eschatological abundance, a foretaste of the extravagance of the messianic banquet (see on 14:3–9; John 2:6–9).

6:44 Five thousand men: "Men" may be generic, "people," and represent a situation in which only adult males would leave home without provisions for an extended time in order to hear Jesus, or it may be a further pointer to the exodus typology in which only adult males were counted as part of God's army (see above). Matthew 14:31 ("besides women and children") understands it in the exclusive sense in order to enhance the miracle.

6:45–52
The Walking on the Water
(See also at Matt. 14:22–33; John 6:16–21)

On interpreting New Testament miracle stories, see excursus at Matt. 8:21.

6:45 To Bethsaida: On the northeast shore of the Sea of Galilee, in predominately Gentile territory, part of today's Golan Heights.

6:46 To pray: Jesus, who has just acted with the power of God to feed the hungry and who will come to the disciples on the water as only God can do, is also portrayed as a truly human being who seeks God in prayer (gods, angels, and divine beings do not pray). See on 1:35, and "Theological Themes" in introduction to Mark.

6:47–48 On the sea . . . alone on the land: Literally, "in the midst of the sea," emphasizing the separation between the disciples and Jesus (a distance of three or four miles, see John 6:19). **Early in the morning:** Literally, "the fourth watch." Roman military time divided the night into four watches corresponding to the changing of the guard. The fourth is 3:00–6:00 a.m. (see 13:35). **Straining at the oars:** Literally "being tortured in rowing"; Mark's readers would recognize the apocalyptic terrors they themselves are experiencing (cf. 13:9–13). They would wonder whether Jesus had left them and they were alone in this world with the responsibility to continue his ministry. The disciples had been called to "be with" Jesus, who had commissioned and empowered them (3:13–14), but now distance and darkness make it impossible for Jesus to see them, and the sea and the wind make it impossible for him to come to them. **He saw:** The penetrating gaze of Jesus (1:16, 19; 2:5, 14; 3:34; 8:33; 10:14, 23) represents the all-seeing eye of God; see 10:27; 14:35—all things are possible with God. **Walking on the sea:** Just as God walks on the sea (Job 9:8; Ps. 77:20; Isa. 43:16), so Jesus becomes present with them. On Mark's dialectic affirmation of Jesus' presence/absence, see on 14:22–25. **Pass them by:** Another use of God language to portray Jesus. In the Old Testament, God "passes by," i.e., passes in front of Israel or the prophet, exhibiting the divine glory (Gen. 18:3; Exod. 33:22; 34:6; 1 Kgs. 19:11; Hab. 3:15; Sir. 24:5–6).

6:49 Thought it was a ghost: See Luke 24:37–39. The disciples misunderstood, but Christ was with them anyway; his presence with them was and is not dependent on correct theology—though Mark writes to help reader disciples better understand and express their faith.

6:50 It is I: Literally, "I am," with echoes of God's self-designation in Exod. 3:13–15; Isa. 41:4; 43:10–11; see on John 6:35. This does not mean that the Markan Jesus claims to be God or that

Mark claims Jesus is God, but that the miracle stories in which *Jesus* is the central figure function to portray the act of *God*. When it is impossible for God to be present with his struggling, troubled people, God comes to them anyway. *The issue in this story is not whether Jesus could defy the law of gravity, but whether his disciples can ever come into a situation in which it is impossible for the God represented by Jesus to be with them.*

6:51 With them: This is one of several resurrection motifs in this story, which is told from the post-Easter point of view of the church's faith (see Matt. 28:20). Although Christ has been killed and raised to God's transcendent world, the risen Christ has not left his disciples in the world to do the best they can on their own; he can still be present with his church as it carries out its mission. There are other resurrection features of the story: it happens in the early hours of morning, as day dawns (Mark 16:1); the disciples have despaired of Jesus' presence and do not expect to see him; the appearance is altogether at Jesus' initiative; the disciples do not recognize Jesus and/or mistake him for a phantom (Luke 24:15–16); Jesus rebukes the disciples for their fear, unbelief, or hardness of heart (Matt. 28:17; Luke 24:11, 25; John 20:27; see Mark 16:11–14); the risen Jesus says, "I am" (Luke 24:39); there is a reference to eating bread and fish (Luke 24:30, 35, 41b; John 21:13); the disciples express awe and astonishment (Luke 24:41a).

6:52 Did not understand about the loaves: Verses 51b–52 are only in Mark, expressing his distinctive view of the messianic secret. The reader expects the disciples to be reprimanded for their lack of faith in his ability to come to them (see 4:40), and the reference to **bread** is at first surprising. Yet the larger unit has bread as a theme, with sixteen references to bread between 6:8 and 8:19 (see on 6:6b). Here and elsewhere, bread has eucharistic overtones, with its dialectic affirmation of the presence/absence of Christ (see on 14:22–25). **Hearts were hardened:** The disciples not only have hard hearts; their hearts have *been* hardened (passive voice). This is another allusion to the exodus account story, in which Pharoah both hardens his own heart—and so is responsible—and has his heart hardened by God, who remains sovereign. See on Mark 4:10–12, and comments on predestination at Rom. 8:28–29. Another Markan dialectic is at work here: on the one hand, the Lord of the storm who walks on the water does not have, or use, his divine power to change people's hearts. On the other hand, recognizing and understanding the presence of the sovereign God in Jesus is not an attainment but a divine gift, and its absence is not a personal defect but a divine judgment.

6:53–56
Healings at Gennesaret
(See also at Matt. 14:34–36; John 6:22–25)

6:53 Land at Gennesaret: See v. 45; they had set out, at Jesus' command, for Bethsaida on the east bank but land at Gennesaret on the west bank. It is not merely a matter of having the wind blow them off course; such historicizing biographical explanations mistake the nature of the narrative and its presuppositions—the Lord of the storm who walks on the water could bring the boat to the place he has designated. More likely, Mark's combination of traditional sources is at work here, and he has not thought it important to straighten out the geography. As elsewhere, theology, not historical or geographical accuracy, is Mark's concern.

6:56 Fringe: A progressive revelation of Jesus' power is found: from 3:7–12, where people touched Jesus to be healed, through 5:21–34, where the woman touches his clothes to be healed, to 6:56, where the **fringe** has healing power. These four tassels were the prescribed attire for all male Jews (Num. 15:39); that Jesus wore them presents him as an observant Jew and forms the transition to the controversy in the next section: when Jesus overrides the prescriptions of Jewish tradition and even of the Torah, is he simply an opponent of Jewish Scripture and tradition, or is something more profound and ultimate at work here?

7:1–23
Defilement—Traditional and Real
(See also at Matt. 15:1–20; Luke 11:37–41)

7:1 Pharisees: See on Luke 5:17. The feature of the Pharisees here emphasized is that they were champions of the oral law, the set of traditions that interpreted and supplemented the written Law. They believed both the written and oral Law had been revealed to Moses on Sinai, with the written Law handed on in the Scripture, the oral law handed on by a chain of authorized interpreters. In the Markan narrative, the Pharisees have already decided to destroy Jesus (3:6). **Scribes:** See on 1:22. **From Jerusalem:** See on 3:22; they believed he was inspired by Satan. The scene here is thus not

merely a report of an event in the life of Jesus but represents Markan dualism, with Jesus and his disciples on one side and his demonic opponents on the other.

7:2 Some of his disciples: That they criticize Jesus' disciples and not Jesus himself (who presumably had the same practice) points to the post-Easter context of the debate in Mark's own time. **Some:** Not all Jesus' disciples violated the Jewish tradition; the minority of Jewish-Christian members of Mark's church seems to have adhered to it. The story represents intrachurch conflicts between Jewish and Gentile Christians, not merely conflicts between Jews and Jesus or the church. The whole story is directed to insiders for their edification, rather than being an attack on or refutation of Jewish outsiders.

Defiled: Sometimes translated "unclean" (see on 1:23; Luke 2:22–24). The issue is not hygiene but ritual purity, an important matter in the Old Testament's and Judaism's understanding of being acceptable to God. **Without washing:** Hand washing before meals was not a part of the biblical regulations concerning ritual cleanliness. The only such regulations for laypersons in the Bible are found in Lev. 15:11, where ritual impurity contracted by a bodily discharge is not transmitted if the ritually unclean person's hands are rinsed in water. In Exod. 30:17–21, *priests* are instructed to wash their hands and feet as part of the ritual purification for ministering in the tabernacle (see Lev. 22:4–7). Apparently the Pharisees, a lay association alienated from the temple priestly establishment, adapted this priestly practice for themselves as an expression of their conviction that all Israel was a "kingdom of priests" (Exod. 19:6) and they attempted to implement it as a standard practice in the reconstitution of Judaism after the destruction of the temple in 70 CE. The practice in question here is therefore an item neither of the biblical purity code (such as the Sabbath and the kosher kitchen) nor of general practice in Judaism, but specifically a matter of Pharisaic tradition.

7:3 All the Jews: Mark attributes the Pharisees' rigid purity laws to all Jews, which is historically incorrect. That an explanation was called for indicates that the majority of Mark's readers were Gentile Christians. His inaccuracy suggests that he was not a Jew himself (see introduction to Mark, on authorship). **Thoroughly wash:** The word translated "thoroughly," literally "with the fist," is of disputed meaning. It may mean "up to the wrist," "with the hands cupped," or "with a handful of water." In all such ritual prescriptions, it is important to know what constitutes fulfilling them (see on 2:23).

7:4 Wash it: The manuscripts disagree as to whether the object of washing is the objects brought from the marketplace or the person who had visited the market. Different words are found in the manuscripts for "wash," one of which means "sprinkle" and one "immerse." Likewise, some manuscripts have beds as the last item in the list, and some do not. Since we do not have the original manuscript of Mark (or any other New Testament document), we are dependent on the work of skilled text critics to reconstruct the most accurate form of the original text (see "Introduction: The New Testament as the Church's Book," 4.d, and the footnotes throughout the NRSV).

7:5 Tradition of the elders: The elders are not (as in 8:31; 22:27; 14:43, 53; 15:1) the Jewish religious leaders contemporary with Jesus and Mark but the authorized chain of teachers who had handed on the tradition through the centuries from Moses' time to the first century. "Tradition" means literally "what is handed on." It is positively evaluated elsewhere in the New Testament as a valuable asset to the church (e.g., 1 Cor. 11:2; 2 Thess. 2:15; 3:6); in fact, no religious community can exist without tradition.

7:6 You hypocrites: Jesus does not respond with a reasonable theological rationale for the practice of his disciples, but attacks the Pharisees who made the charge as hypocrites, a word often found in disputes between different groups of Jews, each of which considered the other perverse. In the Markan narrative, this is not a sincere request for information or explanation; the interlocutors have already decided that Jesus is under the power of Satan and must be destroyed (3:6, 22).

As it is written: The Markan Jesus cites the Greek translation (LXX) of Isa. 29:13, which differs here from the original Hebrew text from which our English Bibles are translated (thus the difference between the version we find in Mark and our English translations of Isa. 29:13). The fact that the Markan point is found only in the LXX is another indication of the orientation of the story toward Mark's Gentile church situation, rather than the original setting in the pre-Easter life of Jesus.

7:7 Teaching human precepts as doctrines: This is probably the reversal of a charge made

against the Gentile Christians of Mark's day, who did not live by the Old Testament food laws (see on 7:19). Their opponents, Jewish and Jewish-Christian alike, understandably charged them with having abandoned the clear command of God contained in Scripture (e.g., Lev. 11:44) on the basis of a human teaching, i.e., that of Jesus. Here the charge is reversed: it is Jews and Jewish Christians who nullify God's biblical command with their tradition.

7:10 Moses said: Moses' command is here regarded as the word of God. This presupposition was shared by Jesus, the disciples of Jesus' and Mark's day, and the Pharisaic opponents before and after Easter. The issue was whether the command of God mediated by Moses was preserved only in Scripture or also in the oral tradition. This issue was debated within Judaism, with the Pharisees affirming and the Sadducees (for example) denying (see on 12:18–27). The issue should not be oversimplified into whether people will live by God's word or mere human teaching. Given this choice, all religious people will choose "God's word." But for all sides of the debate, God's word is not available directly, only through human mediation. The issue is actually dual: (1) *Which* words of Moses mediate God's word, only the written words of Scripture or the oral words handed on in tradition? (2) *How* are these words to be interpreted? All words, written and oral, must be interpreted before they can be understood and obeyed. All groups that claim to adhere to "the Bible alone" in fact have a tradition that gives it meaning. In this conflict of traditions and interpretations, members of each group tend to identify their own traditions and interpretations with the Bible as word of God and to denigrate those of their opponents as merely human tradition. Thus any community that honors Scripture as representing the word of God must also attend to its own understanding of tradition and interpretation. In the Markan community, Jesus' teaching about food laws (i.e., its own tradition) comes to take precedence over the laws actually found in Scripture.

Honor your father and your mother: One of the Ten Commandments (Exod. 20:12; 21:17; Deut. 5:16; see Lev. 20:9). **Speaks evil:** This prohibition must be interpreted, which inevitably happens within a tradition. Since those who violate this command receive the death penalty, it is important to have a clear and precise understanding of what "speaks evil" means from case to case—which statements about parents make one culpable and which do not. This point (not developed by Mark) illustrates that all who insist on "Scripture alone" must necessarily also have responsible rules of interpretation, which means a tradition not found in the Bible that validates its biblical interpretation as authentic.

7:11 But you say: According to this tradition, one could get out of supporting one's aged parents by a legal fiction: "giving" money or property to the temple, declaring it "consecrated" and thus unavailable for "secular" use, and thus becoming financially unable to help one's parents. No doubt Mark understood this to be possible within Judaism, but no such provision has been found anyplace in Jewish tradition. In Jewish writings dated later, rules are explicitly given that prohibit one from refusing to support one's parents on the basis of having made religious vows. The arrangement attributed to the Pharisees and scribes appears to be a product of inner-Jewish or Jewish-Christian polemic.

7:14 Called the crowd: Jesus' teaching is here modeled by Mark on the pattern of his teaching in parables (4:1–34), so that Jesus alternately addresses the crowd and his disciples. Here as there, the "parable" (see v. 17) is given to the crowd, but the "interpretation" only to the disciples.

7:15 Nothing outside a person: This aphorism, which could in itself mean several different things, including permission for sexual promiscuity, also requires to be interpreted. **The things that come out:** Likewise, these words require interpretation, particularly in a context discussing digestion, excretion, and the sewer. Jesus immediately interprets, but it is only those who have his teaching (tradition, interpretation) that understand (see on 4:10–24).

(7:16) This verse is in some manuscripts and not others; text critics judge it to have been added to Mark's original rather than omitted (see on 7:4 above and "Introduction: The New Testament as the Church's Book," 4.d).

7:19 The heart: "Heart" and "mind" are here interchangeable, since in the biblical perspective it is thoughts that come from the heart (Gen. 6:5 and often in biblical statements; see Mark 7:21). Taken with rigid literalism, Jesus' "parable" would advocate a mind/body dualism, so that what the body does would not affect the true person of the heart or mind. The gnostics did in fact later teach this: nothing that happens to the body is defiling, so absolute sexual freedom is appropriate to a "Christian" understanding of Jesus' teaching. Most Christians have considered this a drastic misunderstanding, i.e., that the gnostic tradition is wrong and the tradition represented by Mark represents the authentic meaning of Jesus' teaching.

Thus he declared all foods clean: The Markan Jesus here agrees with "later" Pauline understanding, which of course is actually earlier than the Gospel of Mark and one of its sources (see, e.g., Rom. 14:14, 20). In Mark the basis of this teaching is not argument, but Jesus' authority (see 1:21–22). Jesus is not here a wisdom teacher or philosopher who points out that these foods have always been clean, though mistakenly thought to have been defiling. The Markan Jesus and Mark himself accept the validity of the Scripture that upholds this distinction. The ritually forbidden foods of the Bible now become something they were not before; Jesus' declaration makes them clean; it does not merely disclose the status they have always had. The issue is thus whether one acknowledges the eschatological authority of God's representative, who announces a different time, the dawn of the kingdom of God in which previous distinctions, once authentic, no longer are valid. Here the gradual dawning of insight of the post-Easter church (see Acts 10–15) is summed up in one scene and made into a pronouncement of Jesus. Though Peter was present at this scene in Mark 7, the Peter of Acts 10 does not know that the issue had been decided. The result of the church's struggle narrated in Acts 10–15 is here made into a story set in the life of Jesus. This is what it means to be taught by Jesus in Mark. This chronology of where the community is located in God's plan, i.e., what *time* it is, will also be important in the next scene, for which Mark has here deftly prepared the reader.

7:21 From the human heart: Mark here gives a typical vice catalogue as an illustration of the evil that proceeds from the human heart (see on Rom. 1:28–32). It is striking that Mark, who is so strongly influenced by apocalyptic dualism with its understanding of Satan and demons, here explains human evil as erupting spontaneously from the heart. Here and elsewhere, he is influenced by Paul's understanding of the problematic nature of humanity and its divine solution (see on Rom. 1:18–3:20).

7:24–30
The Syrophoenician (Canaanite) Woman
(See also at Matt. 15:21–28)

It is important to note that Mark locates this story, which has to do with "bread" (see on 6:6b), as a transition between two feeding stories, *first* to Jews (6:30–44), *then* to the Gentiles (8:1–10).

7:24 Tyre: Outside Galilee, in Gentile territory, modern Lebanon. **Did not want anyone to know:** This is not a matter of the strategy or psychology of the historical Jesus but reflects the comprehensive pattern of the messianic secret that permeates Mark's narrative (see introduction to Mark). **He could not:** See on 6:5. **Escape notice:** See on 4:21–22. Although in Mark's theology the true light begins to shine only after Easter, even during the earthly life of Jesus the explosive power of the gospel breaks forth.

7:25 Unclean spirit: On "unclean," see at 1:23. Mark immediately identifies it as a "demon" (vv. 29–30) but, by referring to ritual impurity, links this story to the preceding discussion. The woman, as a Gentile, is from the Jewish perspective also ritually unclean, like the woman of 5:25–34. **Bowed down at his feet:** Worshipful respect, like the woman of 5:33.

7:26 Gentile: Literally "Greek," reflecting the Jewish categorization of all non-Jews as Greeks, as in Rom. 1:16—an important text in the background of this story. **Syrophoenician:** The Phoenicians had a prominent colony in Carthage, residents of which were called Libyphoenicians. This distinguishes the woman as belonging to Syria, north and east of Galilee, probably the location of the author and his readership (see introduction to Mark).

7:27 Let the children be fed: On Jews, God's covenant people, as God's children, see Deut. 14:1; Isa. 1:2. **Dogs:** In Jesus' Jewish setting, Gentiles were sometimes simply referred to as "dogs." The harshness of this insulting term should not be mitigated (see 1 Sam. 17:43; Isa. 56:10–11). One cannot escape from its reality by suggesting that Jesus' playful tone of voice or wink indicated he was only using conventional terminology nonseriously or that the diminutive form means only "puppy." In a Jewish setting, dogs were not household pets but semiwild scavengers, who *ate unclean food*. This latter aspect facilitated the use of "dog" as a crude metaphor for Gentiles. The natural tendency for Gentiles to be referred to in an insulting manner in the border state of Jewish Galilee was increased by the economic reality

that much of the product of the labor of Jewish peasant farmers in Galilee found its way to the tables of urban, wealthy Gentiles in Tyre, the closest large city. In Mark's own time near or during the Jewish war of 66–70, Galilean hostility to Tyrian Gentiles was intensified by murderous pogroms against Jews living in Tyre and by the fact that regiments of Tyrian soldiers served in the Roman army that devastated Palestine.

First: This is the key word of the story (see below), somewhat in tension with the second half of the verse. The first half of the verse makes feeding the dogs a matter of chronology: first the children, then the dogs. The Gentiles ("dogs") will be fed, but not before the Jews ("children"). The second half represents a situation in which the children's food is not given to dogs, period. That Mark preserves this tension, with emphasis on the first element, shows its importance for him. **Bread** is used throughout symbolically (see on 6:6b).

7:28 Sir: The Greek word is the normal word for "Lord," as in 1:3 (see 1:11); 5:18. Mark always uses the word ambiguously, with the characters in the story intending the respectful "sir," but the post-Easter believer knowing that Jesus is truly the Lord (see on 11:3; Luke 20:15; Acts 9:5; Rom. 10:9–10; 1 Cor. 8:6; Phil. 2:11). **The children's crumbs:** The woman does not respond to the insulting term but to the time frame implied: instead of waiting until the Jewish "children" have enjoyed the meal to the full (future fulfillment for Gentiles), cannot she as a Gentile "dog" already in the present receive some of the "bread" (present fulfillment)? In theological terms, purely linear futuristic eschatology is replaced with the already/not yet of an eschatology in the process of fulfillment (see below). The fragmentary crumbs are related to the leftover fragments from the extravagant distribution of bread in the feeding stories (6:42; 8:8), to the partial hearing, speaking (7:31–37), and seeing (8:22–26) in the present that will come to fullness in the future. But the eschatological future cannot wait; it already breaks into the present in a fragmentary but real way.

7:29 The demon has left your daughter: Already in Mark the Jew/Gentile issue had overshadowed the story's basic form as an exorcism (see on 5:1). The story in its present form communicates the victory of God manifest in Jesus over the demonic power of this world and how this victory is extended to the Gentiles, of which exorcising the woman's daughter is a symbolic example.

EXCURSUS:
JESUS AND THE
SYROPHOENICIAN WOMAN

This strange story bristles with problems for the modern reader: to begin with, the story is about an exorcism, strange to modern experience; Jesus journeys to a Gentile area but does not want to help the people there; though he is master of demons and nature, he is not able to secure the privacy he wants; in this text he is able to heal at a distance, but elsewhere his personal presence and contact are necessary; he is reluctant to heal, though he can do so without difficulty at a distance; Jesus uses abusive language that might seem both racist and sexist, then changes his mind on the basis of a sharp retort from the Gentile woman.

With no intent to domesticate or defuse this powerful and bothersome story, a number of observations may help the modern reader to come within its hearing and understanding distance:

1. The insulting manner in which Jesus responds to the woman should not be explained away. Yet hearing it in the context of Jewish-Gentile relations in first-century Palestine, especially in the context of the Jewish revolt against Rome, makes such terms understandable without excusing them.

2. The historical Jesus was a Jew and may well have used such language, but the story in its present form is no more a precise verbatim report of an event in the life of the 30 CE Jesus than are other stories in Mark's Gospel. While the story may well have a historical kernel, in its biblical form it is the vehicle of some aspect of the Christian faith (see "Introduction to the Gospels").

3. Though the word "faith" is not found in this story, Matthew is certainly right in designating it a story of persistent faith (see his addition at Matt. 15:28). Such faith is celebrated elsewhere in Mark (2:5; 5:35; 10:52) and in the Bible, faith that struggles with God in prayer, does not take the initial no as final, but perseveres (see Luke 18:1–8). Martin Luther interpreted this story as illustrating that God's ultimate yes is hidden in the preliminary no; true faith is persistent faithfulness, holding God to be true to his own character revealed in Jesus.

4. It is not incidental or unimportant that the key figure in the story, apart from Jesus, is female. Throughout Mark, while Jesus' male disciples are often imperceptive and bad disciples, women are sometimes insightful and representative of true discipleship (5:25–34; 7:24–30; 12:41–44; 14:3–9; esp. 15:40–41, 47; 16:1–8). The prominence of women in Mark likely reflects their sharing leadership roles in the Markan church.

5. It is inherently likely that the historical Jesus, as a growing and developing human being (see Luke 2:52), changed his perspective on various issues and that key encounters with significant women, from Mary his mother onwards, influenced his developing perspectives. Yet to interpret the present story as relating how Jesus was bested in an argument by a woman who cured his sexism and racism or as illustrating a strategy for how women can get their way in a predominantly male-oriented culture is to misconstrue the genre of the narrative and to read into it a modern agenda (see commentary on ideological interpretation at 2:17).

6. Yet Jesus does change his mind in this story, is persuaded to do something he initially was not going to do. However this is interpreted, it should not be understood in such a way that Jesus, who has power to heal suffering children at a distance, initially refuses to do so (like a doctor refusing to help a child because it is of another race), but then reluctantly decides to do so because he has been beaten in an argument. Jesus the Lord remains sovereign in this story; he is not unwillingly forced to deliver the girl from the enslaving demonic power. See on "Interpreting the Miracle Stories" at Matt. 9:35 and "confessional" and "objectifying" language at Matt. 2:16; John 5:9, Acts 1:9; Rev. 6:15, excursus 3.b.

7. In this story as elsewhere in Mark, Jesus represents God (see comments on "Lord" above). The story stands in a biblical tradition in which God has a plan for people and history but is persuaded to change the divine plan by dialogue with persistent human beings; the plan often has to do with the role of the non-Jewish world in God's plan (Gen. 18:16–33; Jonah). Mark too knows of a divine plan for history, but God revises it en route (see at 13:20). This story is not about an incident in the biography of Jesus but has to do with God's plan for history.

8. The biblical hope was that God had chosen the Jews not for their own sake but for the sake of all nations; its initial historical exclusivity was part of God's ultimate plan to bless all nations (Gen. 12:1–3). But in one major strand of biblical theology, the bringing in of the Gentiles was part of the eschatological fulfillment—Gentiles, now excluded, would be included in the final coming of God's kingdom at the end of history, a scene often portrayed as a great universal banquet in which there was food and fellowship for all (Isa. 2:2–4; 19:19–25; 25:6–10). It is not coincidental that the present story has to do with a table scene in which both Jewish "children" and Gentile "dogs" are present, and all are fed. The traditional schema was that at present God's people are called to

maintain their separation as a witness to God's plan for history, but in the eschatological fulfillment of God's plan the separation will be broken down and Jews and Gentiles will sit together at the one table of God.

9. Christian faith was that the Messiah had already come, the eschaton had already begun. Alongside the "not yet" of the still unfulfilled promise of God is the "already" that the Christ has come, and he is Jesus of Nazareth. What did this mean for bringing the Christian message to Gentiles? The inescapable reality was that Jesus was a Jew, the earliest Christians were Jewish, and the church only gradually became predominantly Gentile. Thus "first to the Jews, then to the Gentiles" was not only God's program for history but could be seen by observing the story of the first-century church. In Mark 7:27a, Jesus voices this theology, prominent in Mark and elsewhere in the New Testament, according to which God's plan unfolds in stages, and certain things must happen before its final fulfillment. This is the reason for the awkward insistence on "first" in v. 27: "first the children . . ." (see Mark 3:27; 4:28; 9:11–12; 13:10; Matt. 10:5–6 vs. 28:18–20; Acts 13:46; Rom. 1:16; 9:1–11:37).

10. Early Christianity knew, of course, that the Christian faith began in an exclusively Jewish context and then moved via a missionary enterprise to Gentiles to become a predominantly Gentile community. There was more than one way, however, of conceptualizing and narrating when and how this transition took place. When are the Gentiles accepted as full members of the people of God? In the Old Testament, this is the promise of the eschatological future (Isa. 2:2–4; 19:19–25; 25:6–10). In Ephesians, it is the post-Easter divinely given insight of apostles and Christian prophets (Eph. 2:20; 3:5). In Acts, it is the gradually dawning insight of the church led by the Holy Spirit (Acts 1–15, esp. chaps. 10–11, which has several contacts with Mark 7:24–30). In Matthew, the mission to Gentiles does not begin until after the resurrection (28:18–20), while the pre-Easter Jesus had explicitly restricted his mission to "the lost sheep of the house of Israel" (10:5–6). One can neatly picture the story of a Jewish Jesus sent only to Israel, then the post-Easter church under the guidance of the Spirit expanding the mission to Gentiles. But Mark is not so neat; the Messiah has already come, and though the time of fulfillment lies in the future—at Jesus' resurrection and the coming of the Son of Man at the end of history—Jesus is pictured as not waiting until the resurrection or the eschaton to open the door to Gentiles. While preserving the traditional frame-

work—"to the Jews first"—he tells the story in such a way that even during his ministry Gentiles were also recipients of God's special grace.

11. A shift of imagery takes place in the course of the story. "Dog" in its Jewish context is an outsider, scavenger, unclean eater of unclean food. "Dog" in its Gentile context is an insider, a "member of the family" who, though not "at the table," still plays under it and benefits from the excess of the children's food, and without waiting until the meal is over. As the gospel moved from its original Jewish setting to Gentile contexts, many such adjustments of imagery were made in adapting the message to new contexts. The missionary church is always called to do this, and always faced with the challenge of deciding when such adjustment is communicating the gospel and when it is an alternative to the gospel, the gospel's betrayal. Mark's story is told in the traditional framework, but in such a way that the explosive newness of God's act in Christ cannot wait. The gospel does not always wait for theology to catch up with it.

7:31–37
Jesus Heals a Deaf Mute and Many Others

This story is found only in Mark. Since it has several features that could be understood as casting Jesus in the role of a typical Hellenistic magician or "divine man," this is likely the reason both Matthew and Luke omit it.

7:31 By way of Sidon: This is a strange itinerary (trace it on a map). It is like saying that someone went from Toronto toward Lake Superior by way of Montreal, through the midst of the region of the Twin Cities. This may indicate that Mark was not familiar with Palestinian geography or that the theological point involved was more important than geography. The itinerary may also reflect the presence of Christian communities in the cities mentioned in Mark's own time (see Acts 9; 21:3–6; 27:3).

7:32 Deaf man . . . impediment in his speech: The inability to hear and the importance of speaking out in Jesus' name are both prominent Markan themes (4:9, 10–12, 33; 8:18; 13:9–10; 14:66–72). Although people, both insiders and outsiders, disciples and nondisciples are deaf and halting of speech during the ministry of Jesus, the day will come when the God at work through Christ will heal their ears and tongues, as Isaiah had prophesied for the time of fulfillment (Isa. 35:5–6). In Mark's healing stories, he shows that this final time is already breaking into the world in the ministry of Jesus (see the preceding story).

7:33 Fingers into his ears: This gesture, along with the use of saliva, sighing (the drawing in of breath/spirit prior to the healing act), and speaking exotic foreign words (such as **Ephphatha**) were part of the stock-in-trade of itinerant magicians and "divine men." Mark does not hesitate to use such pictures of Jesus, for his theology of the cross and his identification of Jesus with God make it clear that Jesus is no semidivine, semihuman "divine man."

7:35 His tongue was released: Literally, "unbound"—the one bound by Satan is set free; Jesus' healings are part of his liberating victory over the demonic world.

7:36 Tell no one . . . they proclaimed: See on 1:43–45; 5:19–20. Though they are disobedient to Jesus' command, the good news of God's act in Jesus breaks through the framework of the messianic secret. **Everything well:** An echo of the Greek translation (LXX) of Gen. 1:31, summarizing God's work of creation. Again, Jesus is indirectly cast in the role of God the Creator.

7:37 He even makes the deaf to hear: The miracle is for those who, during Jesus' ministry, are not only blind but blinded, not only deaf but deafened; their lack of hearing and seeing is the result of God's sovereign act. The healing story anticipates the future, post-Easter time, when their present deafness, blindness, and inability to speak will be taken away, not as their attainment, but as the gift of God, and the disciples will find the eschatological promise of Isa. 35:5–6 being fulfilled in their own experience.

8:1–10
Four Thousand Are Fed
(See also at Matt. 15:32–39)

This story has so many similarities to that of the feeding of the five thousand (6:35–44; see there) that most interpreters consider it to be a variation of the same story that circulated in the oral tradition. This may be the reason that both Luke and John have only the one story (note that John 6:5–13 has parallels to both stories, indicating either that he has merged the two traditions into one or that he combined the two Markan accounts).

We note the three distinctively Markan themes in this second story:

1. The biblical "in those days" suggests the time of eschatological fulfillment promised by the biblical prophets (see, e.g., Jer. 3:18; 33:15; Joel 2:29), and no early Christian reader could hear "three days" without thinking of the resurrection of Christ (see, e.g., Hos. 6:2; John 2:1; 1 Cor. 15:4). Such chronological indications are not merely reporter's incidental details but are laden with the overtones of biblical theology, illustrating again that Mark's miracle stories point beyond themselves to God's eschatological act in Christ.

2. As the five thousand represented Jesus' initial giving of the bread of life to the Jews, so the four thousand represent the (later; see on "first" in 7:27) inclusion of the Gentiles. There are several indications that the four thousand represent Gentiles: (a) The event is located by Mark in the Gentile Decapolis (see 7:31). (b) The note that some had "come from afar" uses phraseology associated with Gentiles. Jews thought of themselves as near to God and Gentiles as far from God (see, e.g., Eph. 2:11–13). (c) The story is located in the narrative outline after the transitional story of 7:24–30 involving a Gentile woman. (d) The differing numbers have Gentile connotations: in biblical typology, just as five and seven can suggest Israel and Judaism (five scrolls of the Law, twelve tribes), so four can suggest the whole world (four winds, four directions, four corners of the earth), and seven can suggest fullness, completion, the totality of the world (as in the creation story, Gen. 1, already alluded to in the preceding story); it can also be used specifically with Gentile overtones (seven nations in Canaan; seven Noahic commandments, seventy Gentile nations).

3. The disciples' lack of understanding continues to be a major theme expressing the messianic secret (see introduction to Mark). The disciples' incomprehension (8:4) is difficult to understand biographically or historically—how can they raise such a question after having experienced Jesus' miracle only two pages before? The post-Easter reader could never raise such a question. But Mark probably included the second story to illustrate their hardness of heart (see 6:52!) and to prepare the way for the dialogue in 8:14–21. Since Luke and John do not share Mark's form of the messianic secret, they consider the second story redundant and omit it.

8:10 Dalmanutha: The location is unknown; no site bears this name in ancient records. Matthew alters it to "Magadan" or "Magdala" (manuscripts of Matthew are inconsistent on this point). Here too, theological meaning and literary location in the Markan narrative are more important for the author than geography—Jesus is again on the western, Jewish side of the lake and immediately encounters hostile Jewish leaders, the Pharisees (see on Luke 5:17, 29–32; for Markan understanding, see 2:16; 3:6; 7:1).

8:11–13
The Pharisees Seek a Sign
(See also at Matt. 16:1–4; Luke 11:16)

Alongside the tradition that represented Jesus as a miracle worker full of the divine power, there was a stream of early Christian tradition that presented Jesus as a truly human being whose ministry was devoid of divine power (see "Introduction to the Gospels" and introduction to Mark; comments on Luke 4:9–11; Phil. 2:5–11). This scene represents the ministry of Jesus as without signs and miracles, and suggests even the desire for them to be illegitimate. This is an early tradition, as is clear from the underlying Aramaic grammar that still shines through Mark's Greek text, and from the circumlocutions to avoid using the divine name (**heaven** for God; "divine passive").

8:11 Testing him: During the whole section where bread is a dominant theme (see on 6:6b) Mark has adopted and adapted the Exodus account of God giving Israel bread in the wilderness through Moses as a model for narrating the story of Jesus. As the manna of Exod. 16 was followed immediately by testing God in Exod. 17, so here Jesus' feeding miracle is followed by the Pharisees' testing Jesus (see also overtones of Ps. 95:7–11). Their question is thus not honest seeking but demonic testing (see 1:12–13; Matt. 4:1–11; Luke 4:1–13).

8:12 Sighed deeply: As in the presence of demonic evil, see 7:34. **This generation:** The biblical term for unbelievers at the time of the flood and for Israel in the wilderness (Gen. 7:1; Deut. 1:35; 32:5, 20), here applied to the unbelievers of Jesus' and Mark's own generation.

No sign: In Mark, the refusal is absolute, attesting a stream of tradition that portrayed the Christ event without a miracle-working Jesus (see above). The other stream of tradition is represented by all the Markan miracle stories, including 2:1–11, where Jesus volunteers the kind of authenticating miracle he here refuses. Matthew and Luke each qualify this absolute rejection, but in ways that point to Jesus' preaching or resurrection and thus still indicate the life of Jesus itself was without signs (Matt. 12:39–40; Luke 11:29–30).

8:14–21
The Leaven of the Pharisees
(See also at Matt. 16:5–12)

If, as is generally believed, the combination of the two feeding stories above is editorial, then this section, which is based on the combination, must itself be editorial, i.e., it directly represents the views of Mark himself. This scene composed by Mark brings the first major section of Mark to an end. The disciples have seen God's power manifest in Jesus, but they are blinded to it and will not perceive the true power of God in Jesus until their eyes are opened by God's act in the cross and resurrection of Jesus.

8:14 Only one loaf: Since the section 6:6b–8:21 is dominated by the bread motif, which Mark elsewhere understands symbolically with reference to God's gift of Jesus, with eucharistic overtones (see 6:41, 52; 1 Cor. 10:17), and since "yeast" in the next verse is clearly symbolic, the reference to "one loaf" here also probably points to the presence of Christ himself represented in the Eucharist (see on 14:22–25). The imperceptive disciples worry about bread, when the Bread of Life is with them in the boat (see John 6:22–59).

8:15 Beware of the yeast: Yeast or leaven was not usually a separate element; bread was leavened by preserving a bit of the previous leavened dough and mixing it with the new batch. Thus "yeast" and "bread" were often used as synonyms, as here. **Pharisees . . . Herod:** See comments on Luke 5:17; Mark 2:16; 3:6.

8:16 Because we have no bread: The disciples miss the point by hearing Jesus' question only at the literal, surface level; the reader is implicitly warned *against* that.

8:18 Eyes . . . ears: An echo of 4:10–12, where unbelieving outsiders are so described, but there the disciples are given the secret of the kingdom of God about which Jesus is speaking. Here insiders appear to be subject to the same hardened hearts as outsiders. The several allusions to the Passover and exodus story (Exod. 12; see Deut. 25:2–4) point to God's people who receive divinely given bread in the wilderness. Here as there, they seem to be subject to the same divine judgment as Pharoah, who hardened his own heart but whose heart was also hardened by God (see Exod. 4:21; 8:15, 19, 32; 9:7, 12, 34, 35; 10:1; 11:10; 14:4, 17; 18:8).

8:20 Twelve . . . seven: One could see it as a lesson in simple math: if Jesus could feed five thousand from five loaves and four thousand from seven loaves, surely they need not worry that he can feed the thirteen of them with one loaf (see 8:14). Yet the meaning lies deeper. The point of the dialogue seems to be the abundant leftovers (see on 6:42). The act of Jesus means the promised eschatological age has dawned; the miraculous feedings were a foretaste of the eschatological messianic banquet, but they do not perceive it.

8:21 Not yet: Though the disciples do not understand (and in the perspective of Mark's messianic secret cannot understand prior to the cross and resurrection), their blindness is not permanent. This healing of their blindness will be pictured in the two stories of blind men that frame the next section.

8:22–10:52
TRANSITION—FROM BLINDNESS TO DISCIPLESHIP, FROM GALILEE TO JUDEA

This is a carefully structured Markan transitional section between Galilean epiphany and Jerusalem rejection (see introduction to Mark, "Structure and Outline"). The section is bracketed by two stories of healing blind men, the only two such stories in Mark (see 10:46–52). Although Matthew and Luke make healing blind people a general characteristic of Jesus' ministry (Matt. 11:15; 15:31; Luke 7:21), Mark has reserved this aspect of Jesus' ministry for these two stories. "Blindness" and "seeing" are heavily symbolic for Mark (see 4:10–12; 8:17–21). In the first story, the blind man is at first only partially healed, still does not see clearly. In the concluding "bookend" story of this section, the healing is complete, and the man whose sight has been restored follows Jesus in his way.

8:22–26
A BLIND MAN IS HEALED AT BETHSAIDA

This story is found only in Mark. Matthew and Luke probably omitted it because in it Jesus resembles too closely the typical Hellenistic magician (see on 7:31–37) and because they do not adopt Mark's structure, in which this story plays an important role.

8:22 Bethsaida: See on 6:45. Traditionally the home of Peter (see John 1:44), Andrew, and Philip. The following story has overtones of Peter's gradually having his blindness healed.

8:23 Saliva: See on 7:33.

8:24 I can see ... but: He is no longer totally blind; he sees but does not understand what he sees (see 8:27–9:1).

8:25 Saw everything clearly: Coming to clarity of faith and understanding does not happen all at once. Jesus' disciples did not understand who Jesus was or what they were getting into when they were originally called (1:16–20), and the process of developing theological clarity about the meaning of one's faith sometimes leaves things blurry for a while. The cross and

resurrection will effect a definitive revelation of the identity of Jesus and the nature of discipleship, but total clarity remains an eschatological hope never fully realized in this life (1 Cor. 13:12).

8:26 Do not enter the village: Another instance of Mark's messianic secret.

8:27–9:1
PETER'S CONFESSION
(See also at Matt. 16:13–28; Luke 9:18–27; John 6:66, 67–71; 12:25)

In contrast to the other Gospels, where Jesus' identity has been revealed and recognized by various people from the beginning (see Matt. 1–2; 14:33; Luke 1–2; 7:1–9; John 1:35–51), in Mark's narrative story line, no human being has yet perceived Jesus' identity. This scene represents a christological breakthrough, and yet they do not understand.

8:27 Caesarea Philippi: The setting is Markan (Luke 9:18; John 6:67 have different locations). Originally called Paneas, since it was the site of a pagan shrine where the god Pan was worshiped, it was rebuilt by Herod the Great and renamed after Caesar Augustus. Herod's son Philip enlarged it and renamed it after himself and Tiberius Caesar. In Mark's time, the war between Rome and the Jewish revolutionaries was raging or had just ended. Roman troops used this district as a staging area, and some Jewish POWs had been brought there, tortured, and killed. Caesar was honored in the civil religion as Lord, Savior, and Son of God. The issue of whom one confessed as Lord is already posed by the context in which Mark places this story—in a particularly powerful way if, as is likely, Mark and his readers live in this area. **On the way:** The same word elsewhere translated as "path" or "way," theologically significant for Mark (see 1:2, 3; 4:4, 15; 6:8, 8:27; 9:33–34; 10:17, 32, 46, 52; 11:18; 12:14). In this scene it becomes clear for the first time that Jesus' way leads to the cross, both for himself and for those who follow him (see vv. 31–34). **Who do people say that I am?:** Not an informational question, but posed to elicit inadequate answers as the backdrop for the authentic Christian confession. The christological question is not the identity of Jesus, but the identity of God: Is God the one who has definitively acted in the Christ event or not?

8:28 John ... Elijah ... one of the prophets: The Old Testament prophets were long since dead, and John had recently been killed (6:14–29), so this was a confession that Jesus was one who had been restored to life, i.e., resuscitated (see on Luke 7:14). Elijah had been taken to heaven without dying (1 Kgs. 17–2 Kgs. 2). Thus these are all high evaluations of Jesus (see 6:14), but they fall short of confessing Jesus to be the definitive revelation of God, the one in whom God acts decisively for human salvation.

8:29 Who do you say that I am? Emphasis is on the "you" (plural in Greek). Reciting and discussing the answers others have given is not the same as the personal response of faith. **You are the Messiah:** Peter speaks for all the disciples, and gives the answer that the later church knew to be correct. "Messiah" is the transliteration of the Hebrew word for "anointed," which became "Christ" in the Greek language of the New Testament. "Anointed" refers to the inauguration ceremony of the *prophet* (see 1 Kgs. 19:16; Isa. 61:1; and comments on Luke 4:18–21); *priest* (Exod. 40:13–14; Lev. 6:20–22); or *king* (1 Sam. 16), in which oil was poured on the head of the chosen one as a sign of consecration into the sacred office. Thus "Messiah" (Hebrew), "Christ" (Greek), and "anointed" (English) all mean the same thing: the one chosen by God and inaugurated into the office of prophet, priest, or king. There have been many prophets, priests, and kings, but to refer to Jesus as *the* Messiah means that one confesses Jesus to be *the* definitive spokesperson for God (prophet), *the* one who reconciles humanity to God and mediates the forgiveness of sins (priest), and *the* one designated by God to represent God's own rulership in the kingdom of God (king). The word is passive in form, pointing to God as the one who anoints the Messiah. To confess that Jesus is the Christ is a declaration not primarily about Jesus, but about God's act.

8:30 Sternly ordered them not to tell anyone: This is not a strategy of the historical Jesus but an aspect of Mark's literary-theological messianic secret. Although Peter has said the right words, it is not possible to understand them until Messiah is combined with cross and resurrection. The subsequent story shows that Peter has made the correct confession but still does not understand what he says.

8:31 Began to teach them: Once the Christian confession has been made, Jesus begins to fill the traditional words with new content. Three such passion predictions occur as structural elements in this section of Mark (8:31; 9:31; 10:33–34). **Son of Man:** See on 2:10. **Must undergo great suffering:** Jesus identifies Messiah and Son of Man and for the first time explains that being the Messiah means suffer-

ing, death, and resurrection. That the eschatological savior who will come at the last day and be the agent of God's judgment must suffer and die is a scandalous new idea. The suffering Son of Man appears only in Mark and in literature dependent on him and appears to be his own theological formulation. While it is likely that the historical Jesus reckoned with the likelihood that, like the biblical prophets, he too must suffer as part of his mission, the present form of the passion predictions reflects the post-Easter theological reflection of the church. That Mark places these predictions in Jesus' mouth is his way of affirming that the suffering and death of Jesus was not a tragic accident of history or a negation of God's plan but willed by God and accepted by Jesus. **The Elders, the chief priests, and the scribes:** The Jerusalem leadership; Pharisees are conspicuously absent and in Mark do not participate in the arrest, trial, and delivery of Jesus to the Romans for crucifixion. Likewise the Romans, who actually killed Jesus, are missing from this list. That Jesus suffers and dies means he is truly human; that he predicts his death and resurrection in advance and that he will **rise again** point to the truly divine dimension of Markan Christology. Here the active voice replaces the usual passive; see excursus "Interpreting the Resurrection" at Matt. 28:1.

8:32 Peter . . . began to rebuke him: This is not merely personal affection for Jesus, the response of a disciple who does not want him to suffer and be killed, but a theological response to Jesus' outrageous declaration that shatters all previous conceptions of what the Messiah would do and be.

8:33 Looking at his disciples: The issue is not between Jesus and Peter alone but is a matter of discipleship. One's understanding of Christ is always related to one's understanding of discipleship, and vice versa. **Get behind me, Satan:** In Mark's apocalyptic dualism, there are only two sides, and Peter is here on the wrong one (see on 1:22; 9:38–40). The rebuke thus places the event in a setting of cosmic conflict and is at the furthest pole from the-devil-made-me-do-it irresponsibility. To get behind someone means to follow them as their disciple; the identical Greek words are used in v. 34 for "follow me" (see 1:17; 5:23; Luke 23:26). Jesus' rebuke includes a renewed call to discipleship. **Divine things . . . human things:** See Rom. 8:2–8, esp. v. 4.

8:34 He called the crowd: This is not a historical reminiscence that Jesus had a crowd following him around in Gentile territory, which he could summon when he wanted to make a theological point. Rather, this is Mark's literary theological device that allows teaching to go "over the heads" of the disciples in the narrative and speak to the post-Easter reader. **If any want to become my followers:** Another indication that Jesus' word in the story now breaks through the narrative framework and addresses whoever will listen. **Take up their cross:** The scandalous disclosure of a crucified Messiah is joined to the shocking revelation that disciples must share Jesus' cross. While such persecution did not happen during the days of the earthly Jesus, by Mark's time Christians (including Peter) had been crucified in Nero's gardens in Rome, and the Roman armies had crucified many dissidents in their reconquest of Galilee and Judea. Mark's readers did not have to wonder what Jesus meant by this, which was a reality of their own experience (see Luke 9:23 comments for how later New Testament interpreters responded to this).

8:38 Me and my words: The Greek word translated "and" may identify Jesus with his words, i.e., to be ashamed of the Christian message is to be ashamed of Jesus himself (see on Rom. 1:16). **The Son of Man:** See on 2:10. Though the post-Easter church and Mark himself certainly understood that the Son of Man who would come on the clouds of heaven at the end of time would be the return of Jesus himself, the historical Jesus may have distinguished himself from the coming Son of Man and have meant by such words that his own ministry would be vindicated by the eschatological figure to come. **Will also be ashamed:** The Q form of this saying is both promise and threat (Matt. 10:32–33; Luke 12:8–9). Mark retains only the threat: the eschatological appearance of the Son of Man will condemn those who are not faithful to this confession. **In the glory of his Father:** As the Markan Jesus identifies Messiah and Son of Man, so he also identifies Son of Man and Son of God (see on Mark 14:61–62).

9:1 Some standing here: The advent of the Son of Man from heaven (13:26–27) is here identified with the coming of the **kingdom of God with power.** Both were expected to happen soon, within the lifetime of Jesus' disciples (see on 13:30; 1 Thess. 4:13–18; excursus "Interpreting the Near End" at Rev. 1:3; on "kingdom of God," see on Luke 4:43). That only "some" would still be alive probably indicates distress that the first generation was

almost gone, disciples had died, and the promised end had not come: Jesus said [only] "some" would still be alive (see on John 21:23). This indicates that Mark was written toward the end of the first Christian generation.

9:2–13
THE TRANSFIGURATION AND THE EXPECTATION OF THE COMING OF ELIJAH
(See also at Matt. 17:1–13; Luke 9:28–36)

These verses compose one Markan literary unit, juxtaposing images of the divine glory and the suffering and death of the Son of Man (see "Theological Themes" in introduction to Mark).

9:2 Six days: For the first time in Mark's narrative, the chronology becomes specific. Since the following story has several motifs derived from the manifestation of God to Moses on Mt. Sinai, the phrase may echo the six days of Exod. 24:15–16. **Peter and James and John:** See 5:37; 13:3; 14:33. **High mountain . . . by themselves:** The mountain is not identified. Speculation about which mountain (Hermon, near Caesarea Philippi, is often suggested) misses the point; Mark is teaching theology, not geography. **Transfigured:** As in 6:47–52, the divine, postresurrection glory of the Son of God breaks through the story of the earthly Jesus, as an anticipation and foretaste of the kingdom of God to come in power (9:1). The description may also relate Jesus to Moses (see Exod. 34:29; 2 Cor. 3:1–18).

9:4 Elijah with Moses: Both were prophetic figures who had worked miracles, had opposed the power structures of this world, had suffered for their faith and commitment, and had been vindicated by God. Elijah had been taken to heaven without dying, and in some traditions of first-century Judaism Moses too had not died but had been taken directly to heaven (Josephus, *Antiquities* 4.423–26). Both were expected to play a role in the eschatological events (Deut. 18:15–18; Mal. 4:5–6). There was speculation that Jesus was Elijah or one of the old prophets (6:14–15; 8:28). Mark presents Jesus as far superior to his prophetic predecessors; he too will be taken to heaven, but not without dying: the mission of the Son of Man and his vindication in the glorious presence of God leads through the cross, not around it.

9:5 Peter: Again spokesperson for the disciples, representing their misunderstanding. **Rabbi:** This Jewish title meaning "my great one," "my teacher," had been used generally of Jewish teachers in Jesus' day; in Mark's time, it was becoming an official, exclusive title for authorized Jewish teachers. There is thus a slight polemical tone in applying it to Jesus. But Mark also intends it as another Petrine misunderstanding—just as Jesus belongs to a different category from the revered heroes of Israel's past, so also to regard him as a merely human teacher of Israel's tradition is inadequate. **Three dwellings** (NRSV)/**shelters** (NIV): The imagery reflects both Israel's sojourn in the wilderness and the customs of the Feast of Tabernacles (also called Booths, see Lev. 23:33–43). Peter wants both to memorialize the dramatic occasion and to place Jesus in the same category as Moses and Elijah—showing he does not yet understand the significance of his own words in 8:29.

9:7–8 A cloud overshadowed them: See Exod. 14:15–16; 40:34–38; 1 Kgs. 8:8–10. In the Old Testament the arrival of the cloud signaled the divine presence and the validation of the tabernacle in the wilderness and the later temple in Jerusalem. Here the suggestion of building tabernacles is rejected, Moses and Elijah disappear, and the divine voice points out **only Jesus** as the ultimate revealer who mediates and symbolizes God's presence in the world. **This is my Son, the beloved:** The voice that spoke in 1:11 addressed Jesus alone in the second person; here the same affirmation is made in the third person. For Son of God, see 1:11; Luke 1:28–33; here the phrase means "belonging to the same world as God," a divine confession of what later came to be called the deity of Christ (see 14:61–62; 15:39). Like Jesus' statements that follow, the heavenly voice supplements and partially corrects Peter's confession in 8:29. **Listen to him:** As the Messiah and God's Son, Jesus speaks for God; his authority thus surpasses and supersedes that of Moses and the prophets (see 1:21–22; 7:19). Although the disciples' hearts are hardened and they are presently unable to hear (4:10–12; 8:17–18), the command that they are nevertheless to hear goes past them to the Markan readers. Mark intends especially such words of Jesus as the passion predictions (8:31; 9:31; 10:33–34) and his teaching about discipleship (8:34–9:1) to be understood by the post-Easter readers.

9:9 Tell no one: See 1:34; 3:11–12; 5:43; 7:36; 8:30. **Until after the Son of Man had risen:** For the first time, a clear terminus for the messianic secret is announced. After the cross and resurrection, the gospel can and must be proclaimed.

9:10 What this rising from the dead could mean: Like other Jews, they understood what the doctrine of the general resurrection at the end

of history meant (see 12:18–37). What they could not understand was that the savior, the Christ/Son of God/Son of Man, would be killed and raised.

9:11 Scribes: See on 1:21–22. Often in Mark, the scribes represent the opposing Jewish teachers of Mark's own time. One of their stock objections was that Jesus could not be the promised Messiah, because Scripture teaches that Elijah must return before the end (Mal. 3:1; 4:1–6). Since Elijah had not returned, Jesus could not be the Messiah. Mark here gives an answer, probably worked out by the Christian teachers of Mark's church. Elijah *has* in fact come; in fact his fate in being killed by the Jewish king anticipates the fate of the Messiah/Son of Man himself. Here too, the issue concerns what *time* it is, where the community stands on the timetable of God's plan for history (see on the analogous "first" 7:27).

9:14–29
JESUS HEALS A BOY POSSESSED BY A SPIRIT
(See also at Matt. 17:14–21; Luke 9:37–43a)

Except for the story of healing the blind Bartimaeus, which serves a special Markan purpose (10:46–52; see on 8:22–26), this is the last of Jesus' public miracles in Mark, forming a bracket with his first miracle, also an exorcism (1:23–27). Jesus' ministry is God's victorious conquest of a creation marred by demonic power, restoring it to the original goodness intended by the Creator (Gen. 1).

9:17 A spirit that makes him unable to speak: The exact opposite of the Holy Spirit, which gives the power to testify to the truth of the gospel (13:11). On the language of demons, Satan, and exorcism, see excursus at 5:1.

9:19 You faithless generation: The disciples, who were unable to perform the exorcism despite their commission and empowerment in 6:7, 13, also here belong to the unbelieving generation. For the terminology, see Deut. 32:5; Luke 24:25.

9:22 If you are able: See 1:7. Jesus' almost contemptuous response represents divine impatience with unbelief. As in v. 17, Jesus here looks at the human situation from a post-Easter and transcendent perspective. He is able, but Mark never forgets that the power of God at work in him is inseparably linked to his suffering and death (see 10:38–39). **All things can be done:** I.e., by God. This translation is better than the traditional "all things are possible" preserved in the NIV, for it points to God as the actor. That all things are possible is neither an abstract principle inherent in the scheme of things nor a matter of human faith or optimism, but a confession of faith in the Lord God Almighty (Rev. 19:6). Mark elsewhere links this universal divine possibility with human inability (10:27; 14:36, note "for you").

9:24 I believe; help by unbelief: This statement resonates with the experience of many believers, who realize that faith is not simply an alternative to unbelief. Paul Tillich expressed the nature of faith in declaring that "faith takes doubt into itself." It is important not to quantify or relativize these two statements. The man does not say something like, "I partly believe and partly doubt," or "I sort of believe and sort of don't." The man believes and *also* does not believe (see Matt. 28:17 comments). Mark's dialectic of faith is analogous to his christological dialectic, in which Jesus is truly human and truly divine, not partly or sort of each (see also 3:28). His affirmation captures the nature of faith as both human act and divine gift.

9:26–27 "He is dead." . . . Jesus . . . lifted him up: Just as the story reflects the victory of God in Christ over the demonic powers of this world, so, like the other miracle stories, it reflects the Christ event as a whole and points beyond itself to the act of God in raising Jesus from the dead and to the last day, when God through Christ will call all people forth from the power of death (see on 5:21–43).

9:29 Only through prayer: Mark connects faith, a central theme of this story, with prayer, the expression of one's dependence upon and need for God, and thus the authentic expression of faith. Again Mark is speaking over the heads of the disciples in the story, to the post-Easter reader. The depth of the meaning in the text is not perceived by explanations to the effect that if the disciples had only remembered to pray they would have been successful exorcists. Mark's theology cannot be reduced to such flat, neat (non)explanations.

9:30–32
THE SECOND PASSION PREDICTION
(See also at Matt. 17:22–23; Luke 9:43b–45)

9:31 Son of Man: See on 2:10. Though the details differ slightly, the suffering, dying, and rising Son of Man is the common element in all three passion predictions (see on 8:31). This one appears to be the oldest and the basis for the others. By using this christological title that affirms both the lowliness and suffering of the human Jesus and his transcendent divine authority, Mark expresses the paradox of the

Christian confession of the human Jesus as the divine act of God (see introduction to Mark, "Theological Themes").

Betrayed: Literally, "handed over" or "delivered up," which becomes a key word in the narrative from this point on. The word is used in Isa. 53:6, 12 (LXX, not in the Hebrew text from which our English Bibles are translated) for God's handing the servant of the Lord over to suffer for the sins of others. In Mark, it refers to the handing over to death of John the Baptist (1:14) and Jesus and to Christians' being handed over/delivered up because of their Christian confession (see 10:33; 13:9, 11, 12; 14:10, 11, 18, 21, 41, 42, 44; 15:1, 10, 15; see 1:14). In 9:32 the passive voice leaves it ambiguous as to who betrays/delivers up Jesus. The word does refer to Judas's betrayal of Jesus, but in Mark simultaneously points to God's act in delivering Jesus up (see 14:27). Judas's deed of betrayal is at the same time the fulfillment of the plan of God, who works in and through even the acts of unfaithful disciples. **Into human hands:** Not just Jews and Romans. Judas betrayed Jesus to the Jewish leaders, who handed him over to the Roman authorities, but the generic term here also points to God's delivering Jesus into the hands of sinful human beings and their defective religion and unjust courts. It is humanity as such, not some particularly evil first-century Jews and Romans, who are responsible for Jesus' death.

9:33–41
WHO IS AUTHORIZED TO REPRESENT GOD?
(See also at Matt. 18:1–5; 10:42; Luke 9:46–50)

The preceding section makes the scandalous claim that it is the crucified Christ who represents God. But who represents Christ? Mark affirms that Jesus' chosen apostles are his authorized delegates (3:13–19; 6:6b–13). Just who these apostles were and the nature of their authority were hotly debated issues in early Christianity (see Luke 6:12–13; 2 Cor. 10–13). Yet Mark does not have a rigidly hierarchical view of how Christ's authority is mediated in the church. In this section he shows both that official apostleship cannot be a matter of human greatness and prestige (just as messiahship is not) and that Christ's presence and authority come to the church in irregular, unofficial ways.

9:33 On the way: See on this significant Markan word at 1:2, 3; 4:4, 15; 6:8, 8:27; 9:33–34; 10:17, 32, 46, 52; 11:18; 12:14. It is ironic that their self-centered discussion about status happens precisely on the road of discipleship they are called to walk, a road that leads to the cross (8:34). **Who is greatest:** The scene reflects the post-Easter situation; even in the church, the struggle for leadership and status continues.

9:35 First . . . last: A "floating" saying of Jesus in early Christian tradition, inserted in various contexts by the Gospel writers (see 10:43–44; Matt. 23:11; Luke 22:26). **Servant of all:** The nature of Christian discipleship, corresponding to Christ's own mission (10:45), which calls for a renunciation of status and rights (see on 1 Cor. 8–10; Rom. 3:9–4:8, provides the theological basis for such unself-centered living).

9:36 Child: In the first-century Mediterranean world, the characteristic feature of children was not thought to be their innocence but their lack of status and legal rights. Here Christ is represented by the most vulnerable and insignificant, not only by the official apostles. There is a hierarchy here—God is represented by Christ, and Christ is represented by his own authorized delegates—but Jesus' teaching subverts the cultural expectations as to who these authorized representatives are and what the nature of their authority is. Alongside the "official" apostles stand the weak and vulnerable, who also mediate the presence of Christ (see Matt. 25:31–46).

9:38 Not following us: This is not a separate topic; the issue of the preceding continues: who represents the authority and presence of Christ? The reader expects "not following *you*"; the "us" points to Mark's post-Easter situation and its debates about who is to be considered the authentic "insiders," the true followers of Jesus. Since they act in Christ's name but do not follow "us," the reference is not to those with no Christian faith but, in contrast to the Matt. 25 text noted above, to other Christian groups.

9:40 Not against us: Although Mark still has the apocalyptic dualism of insider/outsider (see 4:10–12; 3:31), here he expresses it in a surprisingly inclusive manner. The neutral, uncommitted, are included unless they are specifically against Jesus. Contrast the Q version of the saying found in Matt. 12:30 and Luke 11:23, in which those not specifically for Jesus are deemed outsiders.

9:41 Whoever gives you: Mark's emphasis is on the "whoever"—even those who do not make the specific Christian confession are accepted by God when they do acts of compassion. **Because you bear the name of Christ:** A clear pointer beyond the pre-Easter narrative level to

the later situation of the church, when Jesus' followers were called "Christians" (see Acts 11:26).

9:42–50
Warnings concerning Temptations
(See also at Matt. 18:6–9; 5:13;
Luke 17:1–2; 14:34–35)

Here we have not a verbatim report of what Jesus once said on a particular occasion but individual sayings collected by Mark or the pre-Markan tradition. Sometimes the sayings, whose content is unrelated, are linked together on the catchword principle. See the variations on the word "stumble" in vv. 42, 43, 45, 47, and the domino linking in 48–50: stumble ⇒ fire ⇒ salt. The original and earlier meanings of these sayings is obscure; Mark includes them here as an expression of the rigorous demands of discipleship.

9:42 Little ones: See 9:36; 10:13–16. Here, not literal children, but immature disciples or believers with no social standing, the "little people" of the world who have found a home in the church family of God (see 3:31–35). **In me:** These words are not in all manuscripts, and may not be original (like vv. 44 and 46; see NRSV footnotes and "Introduction 4.d"). If original, this is the only text in Mark where faith is explicitly in Jesus rather than God—though Mark would not make this distinction so neatly (see on John 3:16).

9:44 Hell/Gehenna: See note on Luke 12:4–5.

10:1–12
TESTED BY PHARISEES ON DIVORCE QUESTION
(See also at Matt. 19:1–12; Luke 9:51; 16:18)

Jesus now leaves Galilee for Judea and Jerusalem. The Markan outline of Jesus' ministry is composed of two contrasting sections represented by Galilee and Judea (see "Outline and Structure" in introduction to Mark). All of chaps. 1–9 have transpired in Galilee or with Galilee as the base for brief trips elsewhere—but never to Judea. In Mark Jesus makes only one trip to Jerusalem, where he is killed. Matthew and Luke follow this Markan structure; John has Judea as the center of Jesus' ministry, with several trips back and forth from Judea to Galilee.

10:2 Pharisees: See on Luke 5:17, 29–32; Mark 1:22; 2:16, 18, 24; 3:6; 7:1–5; 8:11, 15. **Test him:** Jesus is teaching the crowds (v. 1), but the Pharisees do not here approach Jesus for teaching and information. They wish to pose a question that will expose him as unorthodox and publicly discredit him (see 12:13–17). They are not sincere but have already plotted his death (3:6). Like Satan and as his agents, they test Jesus (same word as 1:13; 12:15). In their Markan context, these verses should thus not be seen as the teaching of Jesus about divorce but as his winning another dispute with his demonic opponents. For Jesus as teacher on ethical issues, including specifically divorce, see on Matt. 5:21–48; 19:1–12. In Mark, Jesus functions as teacher not by giving new insights or items of content but by presenting himself as the authoritative revealer of God's will (see on 7:19).

10:4 Moses allowed: Deut. 24:1–4. Divorce is taken for granted in the Mosaic law and in Judaism; the debated issue was not whether divorce was permitted but what constituted appropriate grounds for divorce.

10:6 God made: Gen. 1:27; 2:24. What Moses permitted violated the original intention of God. As in 7:19, Jesus assumes sovereign authority to make distinctions in the Bible, to set aside clear biblical commands.

10:9 Let no one separate: The contrast is between the act of God in constituting a married couple an indivisible unity and the human act of separation. Like the Old Testament prophets, Jesus speaks in absolute terms of the ultimate will of God, not in terms of case law for various situations (see Matt. 5:31–32; 19:1–12).

10:11–12 Whoever: Mark reflects the Roman situation of the church after Jesus' time, in which women could initiate divorce. Matt. 19:9 omits and Luke 16:18 adjusts to their differing situations.

10:13–16
THE KINGDOM OF GOD
BELONGS TO CHILDREN
(See also at Matt. 19:13–15; Luke 18:15–17)

See comments on 9:33–37.

10:14 Kingdom of God: See on Luke 4:43; Mark 1:15; 4:1–34; 9:1. This scene is not primarily about children but about the kingdom. Children are an illustration of the kind of people who are included: those who have no claims but receive the kingdom of God as a gift.

10:17–31
THE COST AND REWARDS OF DISCIPLESHIP
(See also at Matt. 19:16–30; Luke 18:18–30)

For details, see on the parallel passages. Below are the distinctive Markan emphases.

10:17 On a journey: The same word elsewhere translated "road," "path," "way" (see on 1:3; 8:27). Mark locates the story after the crucial scene in 8:27–9:1. Even after Peter's confession

and the revelation that discipleship means walking the way of the cross (8:27–9:1), Jesus does not tell the young man what following means. Like the other disciples, he will have to learn along the way. But he refuses, rejecting the opportunity to grow and learn. **Good teacher:** Not flattery; the man sincerely wants to find the way to eternal life. **Inherit eternal life:** Equated with "enter the kingdom" in v. 24 and "be saved" in v. 26.

10:18 No one is good but God alone: Human beings, even the best, are only relatively good; God is the only one who can be called good in the absolute sense (Rom. 1:18–3:21). Here Jesus refuses to be placed in the same category as God and identifies with sinful humanity (see 1:4, 9). These texts do not mean that Mark considered Jesus a sinner but that the question of Jesus' sinfulness had not emerged for him (contrast Matthew, who adjusts both Markan texts in Matt. 3:13–15; 19:16).

10:22 He was shocked and went away grieving: See 10:13–16; the man had to learn how to be dependent like a child and receive as a gift what he supposed he could earn.

10:24 How hard it is: The illustration of the camel through the needle's eye shows it is utterly impossible. As the church has struggled with this difficult text through the centuries, traditional explanations have been developed attempting to make it easier to live with. Two examples: (1) Some scribes when copying the manuscript substituted "rope" (*kamilos*) for "camel" (*kamelos*). There is one Greek letter difference, and the two words were pronounced the same in Byzantine Greek. But the solution only seems to help; it is also impossible to get a rope through the eye of a needle. (2) According to a medieval legend there was a tiny gate in the Jerusalem wall called the Needle's Eye. It was too small for loaded camels to pass through, unless they were unloaded of their burdens, got down on their knees, and tried really hard. While it makes a good (but unbiblical) sermon, it misses the point of the story, which is not that it is hard for a rich person to get into the kingdom, but that it is impossible. Jesus clearly reached for the most extreme illustration of impossibility, and the disciples got the point (v. 26!). In any case, the gate never existed in the wall of Jerusalem—only in interpretations of this passage. This is an illustration of the Markan theme of the impossible possibility: what is impossible for human beings is possible with

God (v. 27). This is the Pauline doctrine of salvation: it is impossible for humans, even the best of us, but God, who creates out of nothing, justifies the ungodly, and raises the dead, can save the best of us as well as the worst (Rom. 3–5).

10:28 Left everything: See 1:15–20.

10:30 Receive a hundredfold now: See 3:35. Many Christians in Mark's church had had to make a choice between faith and family, but had received a larger family in the community of faith (see Rom. 8:12–17, which like this text combines the blessings of living as brothers and sisters in the family of God with the reality of persecution).

10:32–45
THE THIRD PASSION PREDICTION AND THE MEANING OF DISCIPLESHIP
(See also at Matt. 20:17–28; Luke 18:31–34; 22:24–30; John 13:4–5)

10:32: See on 8:27. The scene is transparent to the situation of the Markan church—Jesus had already gone ahead to suffering and death (see Acts 3:15; 5:31; Heb. 2:10; 12:2), as had some early Christian leaders, including Peter. **Those who followed:** Not just the Twelve (see 3:32, 34; 4:10).

10:33–34 The Son of Man will be handed over: The third passion prediction. See on 8:31, 9:31. **The Gentiles . . . will . . . kill him:** Although the complicity of the Jewish leaders is involved, Mark lays responsibility for the execution of Jesus squarely at the feet of the Roman government.

10:35–37 James and John: See 1:16–20. Along with Peter, James and John belong to the inner circle of the Twelve, who had witnessed not only Jesus' other miracles but the raising of Jairus's daughter (5:32–42) and the transfiguration (9:28) and who would be closest to him in the agony of Gethsemane (14:32–33). Like Peter (8:27–33), James and John continue to misunderstand the nature of Jesus' messiahship and, consequently, their own discipleship. **Right hand and . . . left:** The phrase next occurs at 15:27: those on Jesus' right and left are those who are crucified with him (see 8:34–38).

10:38 You do not know: And in Mark's narrative scheme they cannot know what they are asking until after the cross and resurrection. **Cup . . . baptism:** See 14:24, 36; Rom. 6:3–4. The post-Easter reader understands what the characters in the story do not (yet): Jesus' kingship is inseparably related to his self-giving love on the cross. "Cup" and "baptism" relate the two Christian sacraments to Jesus' death.

10:39 You will drink: One of the few Markan references that looks beyond the misunderstanding and failure of the disciples in the plotted narrative to the times of the church, when the disciples will, in the power of the Holy Spirit, have become faithful disciples (1:8; 13:9–13; 16:7).

10:43–44 It is not so among you: There is authorized leadership in the Markan church, but just as Jesus' messiahship is different from that of secular rulers, so leadership in the church is oriented to a different paradigm (see on 9:33–37; 10:13–16). **Servant:** The Greek word *diakonos* in v. 43 is also translated "minister," and is here equated with **slave** (*doulos* in v. 44).

10:45 Son of Man: See on 2:10. **Not to be served but to serve:** Verbal form of the word *diakonos* of v. 43. Ministry in the church is related to and derived from Jesus' own ministry. **Ransom:** In 4 Maccabees (a noncanonical Jewish book approximately contemporary with Mark), the death of a courageous Jewish woman and her seven sons who chose to die rather than renounce their faith is called "a ransom for the sin of our nation" (17:21). God accepts the faithfulness of the martyrs as a substitute for the nation as a whole, which had not been faithful. Mark does not portray the death of Jesus as a martyrdom, but such language of atoning death was available in the Judaism of his day. Mark's own understanding of Jesus' death is more closely related to that of Pauline theology, though he does not develop the imagery as Paul does (see on 14:24). Romans 3:24; 8:23; 1 Cor. 1:30; Eph. 1:7, 14; 4:30; Heb. 9:15; 11:35 all use related forms of the word "ransom" with reference to Jesus' death. **Many:** See Isa. 53:12, where the Suffering Servant gives his life for many, and Mark 14:24, which echoes this language. The Semitic idiom in the background contrasts "many" not with "all" but with "few." Mark's "many" is thus the equivalent of "all" in English and is so understood in 1 Tim. 2:6.

10:46–52
BLINDNESS HEALED, DISCIPLESHIP BEGINS
(See also at Matt. 20:29–34; Luke 18:35–43)

10:46 Jericho: On the west bank of the Jordan, ca. fifteen miles northeast of Jerusalem, the gateway to the holy city for pilgrims coming from the north and east, resonant with memories of Joshua and the Israelites' entrance into the promised land (Josh. 6). **A blind beggar:** The story is the complement to 8:22–26 (see there). **By the roadside:** The story presents the transformation from being *alongside* the road/path (like the seed of 4:4, 15 in Mark's understanding of the parable) to being *on* the way/road/path (see on 8:27).

10:47 Son of David: A popular title for the expected Messiah, who like David would bring in God's kingdom with military might. Though some New Testament authors reinterpreted this title and use it as appropriate for Jesus, Mark does not: those who regard Jesus as Son of David have not yet had their blindness healed (see on 11:10; 12:35–37).

10:48 Have mercy on me: In contrast to the rich man, he does not ask what he can do, but as a blind beggar knows he is totally dependent on God's mercy (see Luke 18:9–14).

10:49 Call him: See 1:15–20. The call of Jesus also comes through his disciples, even when they themselves do not yet understand.

10:50 Throwing off his cloak: Like the original disciples, he leaves everything to follow Jesus (1:16–20; 10:28–31; contrast 14:51–52). **My teacher:** The story illustrates the transformation of someone who blindly addresses Jesus as Son of David to a disciple who calls him "my Teacher."

10:51 What do you want me to do?: Contrast the scene of 10:36.

10:52 Your faith has made you well: On "faith," see 2:5; 4:40; 5:34, 36; 9:23–24. The word translated "made you well" also means "saved." Like all the miracle stories, this story has overtones of the totality of salvation offered by God in the Christ event (See excursus "Interpreting the Miracle Stories" at Matt. 9:35).

Followed him on the way: Called by Christ through his disciples, his blindness healed by Christ (which he could not do for himself), Bartimaeus is no longer alongside the way but follows the way of Jesus that leads to self-giving, even to the point of death (see 8:34–37). With this Markan summary portrayal of the meaning of authentic discipleship, the author now concludes the transition from Part One of his narrative and moves the story of Jesus to its climax in Jerusalem.

11:1–15:47
PART TWO—JERUSALEM:
THE PUBLIC CONFLICT AND
SUFFERING OF THE SON OF MAN

See introduction to Mark, "Outline and Structure."

11:1–13:37
JESUS' MINISTRY IN JERUSALEM

11:1–11
Jesus' Entry into Jerusalem
(See also at Matt. 21:1–9;
Luke 19:28–40; John 12:12–19)

11:1 Approaching Jerusalem: In Mark's narrative this is Jesus' first trip to Jerusalem. He has been followed by crowds from Jerusalem who were attracted to his ministry (3:8) and plagued by scribes from Jerusalem who charged him with being in the service of Satan (3:22). The Markan Jesus knows he will meet his death there at the hands of the Jerusalem religious leaders (8:31; 9:31; 10:33–34). His dramatic entrance into the city resembles the symbolic actions of Israel's prophets (Isa. 20:1–6; Jer. 13:1–11; 28:1–17; 32:1–15; Ezek. 2:1–3:3; Hos. 1:2–2:1). It is an acted parable of his kingship and of the coming kingdom of God (see 4:1–34).

In the Markan chronology the entrance occurs on a Sunday, with the temple "cleansing" the next day. Likewise in John the entrance is on Sunday, but the temple event had happened long before (John 12:12–19; 2:13–22). In Matthew and Luke the entrance is followed by the temple event the same day, which is on Monday in Matthew and unclear in Luke's chronology.

Mount of Olives: Directly east of Jerusalem, higher than the Temple Mount, affording a spectacular view of the city. It had apocalyptic overtones (Zech. 14:4). **Colt never been ridden:** This note suggests the consecrated animals of the Old Testament (Num. 19:2; Deut. 21:3; 1 Sam. 6:7). The colt as an indication of humility is probably suggested by Zech. 9:9, made explicit by Matthew and John.

11:2 Untie it and bring it: The reader should not look for rationalizing explanations, as though Jesus had made prior arrangements or had secret followers in Jerusalem. Though no miracles are involved, Jesus acts with sovereign authority.

11:3 The Lord needs it: The Greek word *kurios* can mean either "Lord" in the religious sense or "master" in the secular sense—our words "mister" and "sir" are related to it. The placing of the Greek modifier is such that the sentence can be read equally well as "Its master needs it" (as understood by the people in the story) or "The Lord needs it" (as the post-Easter Markan reader understands it). In contrast to the other Gospels, Jesus is never unambiguously called Lord in the narrative; the title is reserved for the post-Easter confession of faith (John 20:28; Rom. 10:9–10).

11:8 Leafy branches: Palm branches are only in John 12:13. The scene is reminiscent of Israel's royal festal processions (2 Kgs. 9:13; 1 Macc. 13:51; 2 Macc. 10:7).

11:9 Hosanna: In their acclamation of Jesus, the crowds use words from Ps. 118:25–26, the last of the Hallel psalms sung at Passover. "Hosanna" was originally a prayer, "save, I/we beseech thee," but by the first century had become a contentless festive shout, something like a religious "hurrah," with no more literal meaning than "Good-bye" (also originally a prayer, "God be with you"). Similarly the original meaning of Ps. 118:26 was a blessing pronounced on pilgrims coming to the temple, "Blessed in the name of the Lord is the one who comes" (to the temple to worship). But since "the one who comes" had developed eschatological and messianic overtones, the blessing is here applied to Jesus as a royal acclamation suggesting he is the Messiah to come (see Matt. 11:3; 23:39).

11:10 Our father (NRSV **ancestor**) **David:** The exuberant crowds misunderstand the nature of Jesus' kingship (see on 10:47; 12:35–37).

11:12–26
The Cursing of the Fig Tree
and Cleansing of the Temple
(See also at Matt. 21:18–22; 19:47–48; Luke [13:6–9; 14:13–14] 11:45–53; 19:45–46; John 2:13–17)

11:12 The following day: Monday in Mark's chronology. The references to the parallel sections of the other Gospels indicate how separate units of pre-Gospel tradition have been brought together by the different evangelists in different ways. See on 11:1 for differing Gospel chronologies for this section. Mark uses the story of cursing the fig tree as the framework for the story of "cleansing" the temple. On Mark's literary technique of intercalations, see on 2:1–12. Because of Mark's interweaving the two stories, each interprets the other. Luke and John omit entirely the troublesome story of Jesus cursing the fig tree, though Luke has an analogous edifying *parable* at 13:6–9, which may be the original source for this story. Matthew rearranges the story and omits the most bothersome v. 13b.

The Markan form of the story probably is intended to illustrate that the temple and its institutionalized worship have become like a tree without fruit and thus will be destroyed.

Mark's Gospel was written in conjunction with the destruction of the temple by the Romans, either just before, during, or just after (see introduction to Mark).

11:13 Nothing but leaves: The Israelite prophets had portrayed Israel as a tree without fruit that would suffer God's judgment (Jer. 8:13; Hos. 9:10, 16–17; Joel 1:7). In Mic. 7:1, God comes seeking fruit from his tree and finds none; Jesus is here cast in this role. **Not the season for figs:** Taken literally, this pictures Jesus as either ignorant of Palestinian horticulture or pronouncing a curse for an irrational reason—another good reason for understanding the story's meaning at a symbolic rather than literal level.

11:14 May no one: These words are called a curse in v. 21. Jesus' cursing the fig tree does not mean profanity but casts Jesus in the role of God who pronounces judgment. Nowhere else does Jesus use his divine power destructively (though see 5:1–20).

11:15–16 Would not allow: This comment, found only in Mark, depicts Jesus as closing down the whole temple complex. Historically, the temple event was more likely a prophetic symbolic action like the triumphal entry (see on 11:1). The point of Mark's comment is not to accentuate the sacredness of the temple, which is not to be used as a shortcut or place of business, but to emphasize Jesus' authority in bringing its business to a halt.

11:17 For all the nations: Isaiah 56:7; see Isa. 2:2–4. The temple was intended as Israel's worship place and the symbol of God's presence with Israel during historical times. Israel's prophets proclaimed the temple as the place where all nations would worship, but the promise was for the time of eschatological fulfillment. Mark and his community believed that with the coming of Christ the eschatological times had come. Thus the issue between Mark and his opponents was not narrow nationalism vs. inclusive multiculturalism, but "What time is it in God's plan for history?" (see on 7:24–30).

11:18 Kept looking: See 3:6, 22; 7:1; 8:31; 9:31; 10:33–34. The Pharisees disappear from the story when Jesus comes to Jerusalem, and the chief priests and scribes become the actual perpetrators of delivering him over to the Romans for death.

11:20 In the morning: This is Tuesday in Mark's chronology (see on 11:1, 12), a day that lasts until 13:37, representing one-seventh of

Mark's narrative. **The fig tree withered:** In Mark Jesus makes a pronouncement against the fig tree that is fulfilled a short time later, corresponding to his pronouncement against the temple that was to be fulfilled a short time later, in the time of the author himself (see 13:1–2; 14:57–58; 15:29; Acts 6:13–14).

11:22–26 Have faith in God: Mark here gathers independent sayings into a small catechism on faith. That faith can "move mountains" was a proverbial expression (see Matt. 17:20; Luke 17:6; 1 Cor. 13:2). For Mark the power is not in faith itself but in God; faith believes in a God who does what is humanly impossible (see 6:37–38; 8:4; 10:27; 14:36; Rom. 4; Heb. 11).

11:27–33
The Question about Authority
(See also at Matt. 21:23–27;
Luke 20:1–8; John 2:18–22)

Here begins the first of five controversy stories (11:27–12:37), corresponding to the five controversy stories of 2:1–3:6. In both cases, the series of stories reflects not only the situation of Jesus but the controversies between church and synagogue leaders of Mark's own time.

11:27 The chief priests, the scribes, and the elders: See on 8:31. Here Jesus enters the temple for the last time in Mark.

11:28 By what authority: From the beginning Mark has contrasted Jesus' authority with that of the scribes (see 1:21–22, 27; 2:10). In the Markan context, **these things** refers specifically to Jesus' action in the temple (11:15–19). Jesus shares his authority with his disciples (3:15; 6:7). Here, too, Christology and discipleship are inseparable themes.

11:30–32 The baptism of John: See on 1:2–11. **From heaven . . . of human origin:** "Heaven" is a reverent, indirect way of referring to God (see 8:11; 14:61–62). The contrast is God/human. Jesus and John are here placed in the same category, as representing God's authority (see 12:5); the chief priests and scribes acknowledge this at one level, but since in Mark's narrative they operate at the level of tactics rather than truth, they do not acknowledge Jesus'/God's authority. This is Mark's perspective, reflecting the conflicts of his own time (see 7:19; 10:1–12).

11:33 Neither will I tell you: Here, Jesus adopts the tactics of those testing him, challenging them to make their own position clear. In 14:61–62, Jesus answers clearly and boldly, as he calls his disciples to do (see 8:38; 13:11).

12:1–12
The Parable of the Wicked Husbandmen
(See also at Matt. 21:33–46; Luke 20:9–19)

12:1 To them: The parable is directed not to the people as a whole, but to the hostile chief priests, scribes, and elders of 11:27. It concerns the leadership of God's people. **In parables:** See on Mark 4:1–34. The original parable now functions in its Markan narrative context as an allegorical representation of the whole history of salvation. A version of this parable without the allegorizing additions is found in *Gos. Thom.* 65–66, which may be closer to Jesus' original parable. **Vineyard:** The people of Israel, God's people chosen from the nations of the world to be witnesses to God's love and care for all peoples (Gen. 12:1–3; Ps. 80:8–13; Isa. 5:1–7; 27:2–6; 42:1–7; Jer. 2:21; Hos. 10:1; Ezek. 19:10–14).

12:5 Some they beat, others they killed: Not a realistic story at the literal level, but reflecting the history of God's dealing with Israel by sending the prophets, many of whom were rejected and killed. In Mark's Christology Jesus' greatness is not that he is an outstanding individual, but that along with John the Baptist he is firmly rooted in the story of God's dealing with Israel as the climax and fulfillment of God's plan for history.

12:6 Beloved son: At the Markan level, a transparent reference to Jesus (see 1:11; 9:17).

12:8 Out of the vineyard: See 15:42–47; Heb. 13:12–13.

12:9 He will come: In the allegory, the son who has been killed is not raised and sent back in judgment, but the lord of the vineyard himself comes to settle accounts. For Mark, the return of Jesus is the coming of God himself in judgment (see 8:38–9:1; 13:26–27). **Give the vineyard to others:** The vineyard is not destroyed and replaced with another vineyard; Israel is not replaced by the church. There is no new vineyard but new tenant farmers. Leadership will be taken from the priests, scribes, and elders and will be given to Jesus and his disciples, all of whom are Jews.

12:10–11 Have you not read: Psalm 118:22–23 is understood as another picture of rejection being overcome. See excursus, "New Testament Interpretation of the Old Testament," at 1 Cor. 15:3. Here too the building is not replaced with another building, but the one rejected by those experts who should have known becomes the key figure.

12:12 They realized: In contrast to chap. 4 (see esp. 4:10–12), the "outsiders" do understand the parable, as does the post-Easter reader. Mark has no consistent "parable theory"; telling the story on two levels at once means that sometimes post-Easter understandings are communicated in a pre-Easter narrative framework. **Against them:** The leadership, not the people as a whole.

12:13–17
On Paying Tribute to Caesar and the Question about the Resurrection
(See also at Matt. 22:15–33; Luke 20:20–40)

12:13 They sent to him: In Mark the subject is still the chief priests, scribes, and elders of 11:27; 12:1, 12, whom Mark holds responsible for participation in Jesus' death (8:31), the masterminds behind the scenes who send various Jewish groups to challenge Jesus. **Pharisees and some Herodians:** See on 3:6.

12:15 Their hypocrisy: Though what they say about Jesus as teacher is true, *they* are not, for they only want to **trap him** (v. 13). **Putting me to the test:** Same word as in 1:13; 8:11; 10:2.

12:17 The things that are God's: (See on Rom. 13:1–10.) They had asked about whether a person loyal to God could pay taxes to a pagan government—a disputed issue among Jewish religious teachers of both Jesus' and Mark's day. Jesus' response affirms that his followers have obligations to participate in the political process of which they are a part; they are not to withdraw from the world and leave governmental responsibility to others, while keeping themselves "pure," even when the government is secular, atheistic, or oriented to some other religion. But Jesus introduces another element they had not asked about. All belongs to God, including Caesar and the denarius that bears his image.

12:18–27
The Question about the Resurrection
(See at Luke 20:27–40)

12:28–34
The Great Commandment
(See also at Matt. 22:34–40; Luke 10:25–28)

12:28 One of the scribes: Usually the scribes are presented as hostile in Mark (see on 1:22; 2:6; 8:31; 11:27; 12:38–40); this scribe is sincere. Not only do the Jewish people as a whole not oppose Jesus; their leadership, too, includes sincere people open to Jesus' message.

12:29 The Lord is one: This affirmation of the one God, taken from Deut. 6:4, became the central confession of Judaism, the Shema (the Hebrew word for "hear," the first word of Deut. 6:4).

While the monotheistic Jewish faith is basic to the whole New Testament, the Shema itself is explicitly quoted only here. Luke 10:25–28 relocates and rephrases the story so that the interrogator, understood to be hostile and insincere, is forced to answer his own question. Mark portrays Jesus as himself confessing the primary Jewish creed in the words of the Bible.

12:31 The second is: The scribe asked for one commandment and received two; love for God is inseparable from love for neighbor (see 1 John 4:19–20). **These:** The two commands are taken as a single command both here and in v. 33. On the meaning of "love" (*agape*), see on 1 Cor. 13:4–7.

12:32–34 You are right, Teacher: These verses are only in Mark. **More important:** The other commandments, including the ritual acts of sacrifice and the food laws, are not here abrogated but relativized (contrast 7:19; 10:1–12). That love, faithfulness, and obedience to God are more important than sacrifice is represented by a broad stream of Old Testament tradition (see 1 Sam. 15:22; Hos. 6:6; Pss. 50:12–15, 23; 51:17; Prov. 21:3). **Answered wisely:** The scribe does not just repeat Jesus' answer but draws inferences from it and reformulates it in his own words, a response that Jesus approves. **Not far from the kingdom:** See on 1:15; Luke 4:43. In Mark, the kingdom is a future reality that already affects the present; by responding in faith to Jesus and his message, one is prepared to enter the kingdom when it arrives.

12:35–37a
The Question about David's Son
(See also at Matt. 22:41–46; Luke 20:41–44)

After emerging victorious from the previous debates initiated by the Jewish leaders, Jesus poses a key question of his own.

12:35 Scribes: See on 1:22; 2:6; 8:31; 11:27; 12:28. **Messiah . . . Son of David:** Mark affirms Jesus to be the Messiah/Christ (1:1; 8:29; 14:61–62) but challenges the view that the content of "Christ" can be filled in from the "son of David" tradition. "Messiah" is the Hebrew word meaning "anointed," translated often "Christ" (see on 8:29). The Old Testament uses the term only for the prophets, priests, and kings of Israel, never to refer to the hoped-for messianic savior of the eschatological future. After the Old Testament was completed but before the birth of Jesus, many (but not all) Jews had come to express the hope for the final coming of the kingdom of God as God's sending of a David-like king (see Isa. 9, 11). The phrase denotes not merely one descended from David but one belonging to the Davidic category, one chosen by God to rule in God's kingdom. Son of David was one of the images found in first-century Judaism as an expression of its hope for the coming of a messiah as a great king like the Old Testament David (1 Sam. 16–2 Sam. 24) and was reinterpreted and adopted by some streams of early Christianity (Rom. 1:3–4; Matt. 1:6, 17, 20; 9:27; 12:3, 23; 15:22; 20:30–31; 21:9, 15, 42–45; John 7:42). The following quotation from a Jewish work from the first century BCE reflects the messianic expectation of some first-century Jews connected with the Davidic hope:

The lawless one laid waste our land so that none inhabited it, They destroyed young and old and their children together. . . . Behold, O Lord, and raise up unto them their king, the son of David, At the time in the which Thou seest, O God, that he may reign over Israel Thy servant And gird him with strength, that he may shatter unrighteous rulers, And that he may purge Jerusalem from nations that trample her down to destruction. Wisely, righteously he shall thrust out sinners from the inheritance, He shall destroy the pride of the sinner as a potter's vessel. With a rod of iron he shall break in pieces all their substance, He shall destroy the godless nations with the word of his mouth; At his rebuke nations shall flee before him, And he shall reprove sinners for the thoughts of their heart. And he shall gather together a holy people, whom he shall lead in righteousness, And he shall judge the tribes of the people that has been sanctified by the Lord his God. . . . So that nations shall come from the ends of the earth to see his glory, Bringing as gifts her sons who had fainted, And to see the glory of the Lord, wherewith God hath glorified her. And he shall be a righteous king, taught of God, over them, And there shall be no unrighteousness in his days in their midst, For all shall be holy and their king the anointed of the Lord. For he shall not put his trust in horse and rider and bow, Nor shall he multiply for himself gold and silver for war, Nor shall he gather confidence from a multitude for the day of battle. The Lord Himself is his king, the hope of him that is mighty through his hope in God. All nations shall be in fear before him, For he will smite

the earth with the word of his mouth for ever. He will bless the people of the Lord with wisdom and gladness, And he himself will be pure from sin, so that he may rule a great people. He will rebuke rulers, and remove sinners by the might of his word; And relying upon his God, throughout his days he will not stumble; For God will make him mighty by means of His holy spirit, And wise by means of the spirit of understanding, with strength and righteousness. (from Psalms of Solomon 17)

12:36 By the Holy Spirit: The same Spirit that inspired David and is at work in the Scripture came upon Jesus (1:10) and is given by him to his disciples (1:8; 13:20). The Markan Jesus claims that he and his disciples stand in the true succession of biblical interpretation. **The Lord . . . my lord:** Psalm 110:1, the most-cited psalm in the New Testament (Matt. 22:44; 26:64; Mark 12:36; 14:62; 16:19; Luke 20:42–43; 22:69; Acts 2:34–35; Rom. 8:34; 1 Cor. 15:25; Eph. 1:20; Col. 3:1; Heb. 1:3, 13; 8:1; 10:12). The argument assumes that David is the author of the psalm, who portrays God the Lord as speaking to another Lord, here assumed to be the Messiah (see 1:2–3). All these assumptions are troublesome to modern readers, but see excursus, "New Testament Interpretation of the Old Testament," at 1 Cor. 15:3. The logic of the argument is that the second Lord spoken of in the Psalm cannot be David, but refers to another Lord, whom the author understands to be Jesus. On "Lord" as a title for Jesus in Mark, see on 1:3; 2:28; 5:19; 7:28; 11:3; 12:36–37.

12:37b–40
Woe to the Scribes and Pharisees
(See also at Matt. 23:1–36; Luke 20:45–47)

On **scribes** in Mark, see on 1:22; 2:6; 8:31; 11:27; 12:28. For details of Jesus' critique, see parallels in Matthew and Luke.

12:41–44
The Widow's Offering
(See also at Luke 21:1–4)

12:44 Everything she had: Despite the Markan Jesus' opposition to the temple, he does not hesitate to commend people who show their devotion to God by contributing to the temple. In giving all, the woman represents a model of true discipleship, as in 1:16–20; 8:34, 35–38, but it is the God revealed in Jesus to whom sacrificial giving is to be devoted.

13:1–37
The Apocalyptic Discourse
(See also at Matt. 24:1–25:15;
Luke 21:5–33; 19:12–13; 12:38, 40)

This is Jesus' last and longest speech in Mark. It is often called the Little Apocalypse because of its resemblance to Revelation. While it contains some elements from the historical Jesus, some from the post-Easter church, and some from the author of the Gospel, the speech is indeed analogous to Revelation, i.e., the post-Easter address of the risen Lord to his troubled church (see on "Three Levels of Gospel Texts" in "Introduction to the Gospels"). Mark places the discourse within the pre-Easter framework of the life of Jesus, since he is distrustful of post-Easter "revelations" (see on 13:6, 21–22; 16:1–8; John 14:15–17; 16:12–14; Acts 21:4; 1 Thess. 4:2, 15–17; 1 John 4:1–4; introduction to Revelation; Rev. 2:1–3:22).

13:1 What large stones!: The Jerusalem temple was indeed a magnificent structure, an engineering feat that still calls forth wonder from architects.

13:2 Not one stone will be left here upon another: The prediction was not literally fulfilled, since tourists and pilgrims can still see the gigantic foundation stones of the temple in Jerusalem, the present Wailing Wall. Mark is written during or just after the Jewish war with the Romans that devastated the country and destroyed Jerusalem and its temple (see introduction to Mark). Jesus stands in the prophetic tradition that spoke against the temple (Jer. 26:6, 18; Mic. 3:12). This opposition to the temple played a role in his trial (14:58; see 11:15–16; 15:29). On Christian alternatives to temple piety, see Acts 7:48; 1 Cor. 3:16; 6:19; 1 Pet. 2:4–6. The destruction is final, with no mention here or elsewhere in the New Testament of rebuilding the temple.

13:3 Mount of Olives: See on 11:1; 14:26.

13:4 When will this be?: In Mark's time there was much apocalyptic excitement, as both Jewish and Christian prophets saw in the terrible war the signs of the end of the age. The apocalyptic discourse portrays the end as a drama in three acts: I. The beginning of the birth pangs, 13:5–13; II. The desolating sacrilege and great suffering, 13:14–23; III. Cosmic signs and the coming of the Son of Man, 13:24–37.

13:6 In my name: Those Mark warns against will not claim to *be* Christ, but to speak with his authority. The Markan Jesus warns the church of the author's time against those prophets who understand themselves to speak directly the word of the risen Lord.

13:7 The end is still to come: The catastrophic war of 66–70 was not the end.

13:8 As in Rev. 12:1–6 and Rom. 8:22–25, the troubles the world must go through to bring in the messianic age are the labor pains preceding the Messiah's arrival. Mark's point is that the wars, famines, earthquakes of his time are not the signs of the end (as the false prophets proclaimed) but only the **beginning** of the last period of history.

13:9 They will hand you over: The same word used for the arrest/delivering up of John the Baptist, Judas' betrayal of Jesus, the Jewish leaders delivery of Jesus to the Romans, and God's delivering up Jesus to death as the Suffering Servant (see on 1:14). The path of true discipleship follows that of Jesus (8:31–38; 10:32–45). Like John and Jesus, the disciples will suffer at the hands of all people, both Jews and Gentiles (see 2 Cor. 11:24–25; 1 Thess. 2:15–16). **As a testimony:** As in Revelation, the time of persecution is the opportunity for Jesus' disciples to bear witness to their faith. Though the disciples have been portrayed as misunderstanding and unfaithful during Jesus' earthly ministry, here they are shown to be faithful disciples in the post-Easter period (see on 16:8).

13:10 First be proclaimed to all nations: It is unlikely that the pre-Easter Jesus spoke of a mission to Gentiles (see Matt. 10:5–6; 28:16–20). This is another indication that it is the voice of the risen Christ who speaks within the pre-Easter narrative framework. Mark believes that the end will come in his generation (9:1; 13:30), but that the troubles of his own time, bad as they are, are not the immediate prelude to the end. There is still time within the plan of God for the church to carry out its universal mission. However long the world may endure, the disciples of Jesus in every period of history have only their own generation in which to proclaim the gospel.

13:11 Not you who speak, but the Holy Spirit: Jesus gives the Spirit of God to all Christians (1:8; see 1 Cor. 13:12). The Spirit does not protect them from persecution, but gives them the words to speak when they are accused. Not only the inspired prophets but every Christian can speak authentic, Spirit-given testimony in time of need (1 Cor. 12:1–3).

13:14 The desolating sacrilege: This phrase originally referred to a desecration of the temple in 167 BCE by the pagan king Antiochus IV Epiphanes, who sacrificed a sow on the sacred altar of the temple. This act defiled the temple, made it unclean, so that no Jew could worship there; i.e., it was a *sacrilegious* act that emptied the temple, made it deserted or *desolate*, hence "abomination of desolation" or "desolating sacrilege" (see Dan. 9:27; 11:31; 12:11; 1 Macc. 1:54). This act became an apocalyptic image reinterpreted many times in various contexts, projected into the future as some terrible blasphemy that would occur just before the end. **Let the reader understand:** Another clue that this is not the verbatim speech of Jesus to four disciples on the Mount of Olives but is the voice of Christ who speaks through the Markan text to the persecuted church. "The reader" is not the individual reading his or her own copy of the text privately but the lector who reads aloud the document to the assembled congregation (see Rev. 1:3). These cryptic words call for explanation; the lector is charged not to pass over them casually, but to interpret them. **Those in Judea:** An indication that the discourse (or its nucleus) originated in a pre-Markan, Judean setting, after Jesus but before Mark, who here takes up an earlier complex of tradition and reinterprets it for his own time. **Judea** was no longer *directly* relevant to Mark and his church, as it is not to the modern reader, but has an indirect message: Jerusalem is not the place of safety. Even the holy city and its temple will be destroyed and do not represent the final purpose of God.

13:17 Those who are pregnant . . . who are nursing: See on 1 Cor. 7:25–31.

13:20 He has cut short those days: In apocalyptic thought there is a divine plan, a schedule for the end. But in biblical theology, God is not bound to this plan but can alter it en route (see on 7:24–30). We too must have our theologies, our understandings of who God is and how God works. But Christian faith is not finally in its own theology but in the God who is not contained by any theology (see on Rom. 11:33–36). **The elect:** See on 1 Pet. 1:1.

13:22 False christs: Not people claiming to be Jesus, but some of the Jewish prophetic and military leaders of the 66–70 war (the author's own time), who saw themselves as God's anointed deliverers sent to deliver God's people in the last days. **False prophets:** Especially those Christian prophets who understood themselves to be spokespersons for the risen Lord (see on Acts 21:4; 1 Thess. 4:2, 15–17; introduction to Revelation; Rev. 1–3).

13:23 I have already told you everything: Mark's narrative of Jesus' ministry, suffering, death, and resurrection is God's final revelation. The author is suspicious of post-Easter revelations that claim to supplement or supersede this revelation.

13:24 After that suffering: The end will be a cosmic event marked by cosmic signs, distinct from the historical distress predicted in the preceding verses. Mark reassures his church that the war and persecutions of his own time are not the immediate prelude to the end.

13:26 The Son of Man coming: On Son of Man, see on 2:10. The end of history will be the return of Jesus as the Son of Man to establish God's kingdom in power (9:1). The point of such imagery is that at the end of history the One we meet is not a different God from the One we have already met in Jesus of Nazareth (see on Rev. 19:11–16).

13:27 Gather his elect: This is not a portrayal of a "rapture" in which Jesus returns to take his own out of the world for a period prior to the end (see on 1 Thess. 4:13–5:11).

13:29 You know that he is near: As anyone can tell that the summer is near by the budding of the fig tree, one can tell that the Son of Man is near by the cosmic signs observable by all and needing no interpretation. The readers are warned against the interpretations of the false prophets who see in the historical events of war, famine, and earthquake the signs of the end.

13:30 This generation: The time of Jesus' and the author's own contemporaries. Attempts to avoid the difficulty by translating "race" (of the Jews) are not convincing. **All these things:** The cosmic events, the coming of the Son of Man, and the end of history. Mark's expectation was not fulfilled. On the failure of the early Christian expectation of the Parousia to take place, see on Rev. 1:3, "Interpreting the 'Near End.'"

13:32–34 No one knows . . . you do not know: Mark warns against eschatological speculation. **Each with his work:** The master will return. The responsibility of his slaves is to carry out their responsibilities during the master's absence. On slave imagery for Christians, see on Luke 17:7–10; John 15:12–14; Rom. 6:15–23. Mark understands that the church has a mission to the world in the interim between Jesus' resurrection and the return of the Son of Man, and though the end will occur in his generation, there is time to fulfill the mission.

13:37 I say to all: Though in the narrative framework the speech is given privately to four disciples, here as elsewhere Jesus speaks "over the heads" of the characters in the story to the post-Easter readers. **Keep awake:** In some apocalyptic scenarios, there were signs by which one could determine that the end is near (as in 13:14–29). Other apocalyptic texts portray the end as erupting into history without warning (see Luke 17:20–37). Mark maintains the tension between these views. Readers can say *neither*, "Since we see the signs of war, earthquake, and famine, we know that the end is near," *nor*, "Since the sun has not been darkened and the moon turned to blood, we know that the end is *not* near."

14:1–15:47
Jesus' Passion

The concluding and climactic section of Mark's narrative is often called the passion story. The word "passion" in this context is related to the word "passive" in the grammatical sense—Jesus is not the actor but is acted upon; he does not die but is killed. While these are certainly historical events, the stories reflect not only what actually happened, but the church's reflection on the meaning of Jesus' death and resurrection, especially in the light of their reading of Scripture. This means that here, as elsewhere in Gospel study, the reader must not blend the different Gospels together but attend to the way the story is presented in each Gospel.

14:1–11
Betrayal and Anointing
(See also at Matt. 26:1–16; Luke 22:1–14; 7:36–50; John 12:1–8)

Mark has again inserted one story into another, so that they interpret each other (see on 2:1–12). The blindness and love of money of Judas and the religious leaders is contrasted with the generosity and perception of the unnamed woman. It is ironic that despite v. 9, Judas's deed of betrayal has been remembered more often than the woman's insight and service.

14:1 Two days before . . . : Wednesday, in Mark's chronology (see on 11:1, 20). **Passover . . . festival of Unleavened Bread:** In the Old Testament, these are two distinct festivals, but in the popular consciousness had been combined, as Advent and Christmas have been collapsed into the Christmas season among modern Christians. The Passover was celebrated on the evening of 14 Nisan (March–April) by sacrificing a lamb that was roasted and eaten at a family dinner or within a group formed for this purpose. It celebrated the exodus from Egypt, when the blood of a lamb placed on the doorposts of the Hebrews pro-

tected them from the scourge of death that caused Pharoah finally to release the Israelite slaves (Exod. 12:1–13). "Unleavened Bread" began on 14 Nisan and lasted seven days. The ancient Hebrews had left Egypt hurriedly, without the bread having had time to rise. The celebration involved removing all yeast from the house and eating no leavened bread for seven days (Exod. 12:14–20; 13:3–10; Lev. 23:5–6; Num. 28:16–17; Deut. 16:1–8). Both festivals were thus celebrations of the birth of the nation and created a patriotic atmosphere of expectation and hope of national liberation from the Romans. For the occasion, the governor of Judea, who usually resided on the coast at Caesarea, came to Jerusalem with extra troops to ensure order and keep the peace.

14:2 The chief priests and the scribes: See on 1:22; 3:6, 22; 7:1; 8:31. The Pharisees are absent from Mark's passion story; their last appearance was 12:13.

14:3–9 The Anointing: A form of this story occurs in all four Gospels; their similarities and differences are represented in Figure 9.

The same general form and numerous common details indicate that we have four versions of one story; the variations illustrate how the story was adapted and reinterpreted in the oral tradition prior to the Gospels; the different contexts and editorial modifications and additions show how the Gospel writers interpreted the story (see "three levels" in "Introduction to the Gospels"). Once again it is clear that not historical accuracy but theological meaning was primary. Responsible interpretation does not attempt to harmonize or reconstruct "what really happened" but attends to the meaning expressed in each Gospel.

14:3 Simon the leper: There is no indication that he had been healed. There are no miracles in the Markan passion story (see introduction to Mark). On leprosy, see on 1:40–45; Luke 5:12–16; 17:11–19. On Jesus eating with the outcast and marginalized, see on 2:16. **Poured the ointment on his head:** This is not a christological anointing, for which a different word is used (see on 8:29 and v. 8 below).

14:4 Some: Not identified in Mark, called "disciples" in Matt. 26:8, specifically "Judas" in John 12:4. See commentary on 14:47.

14:5 Three hundred denarii: An extravagant gift. Since a denarius was the standard day's wage for laborers, this is almost a year's pay (see 6:37; Matt. 20:1–16).

14:7–8 You always have the poor with you: In this context the issue is not helping the poor, which Jesus does and commands his disciples to do (6:37; 10:21; see Matt. 25:31–46; Luke 4:18; 14:13; 16:20–22; Acts 11:27–30; 2 Cor. 8–9; Gal. 2:10). The point is rather that the unnamed woman, in a daring act of great generosity and insight, recognizes the presence of Jesus as a special time in which celebration and extravagance are called for (see 2:18–20; 6:30–44; 8:1–10, 14–21; see John 2:1–11) and knows that Jesus' mission is to suffer and die. The disciples have been blind to this, and they will not be present at his death and burial. The woman accepted Jesus' own word about his mission (8:31; 9:31; 10:33–34), and **anointed his body beforehand.**

14:9 In remembrance of her: The phrase can also be translated "for her remembrance (before God)," as in Acts 10:4. On this reading, the telling of the woman's story will be a reminder to God, a call to God to remember and vindi-cate her deed. On either interpretation, the Christian message is always to be linked with the woman's generous and courageous act; here as elsewhere in Mark, Christology and discipleship are inseparable. There is no "in remembrance of me" in the Markan version of the eucharistic words in 14:22–25 (contrast Luke 22:19; 1 Cor. 11:25).

14:11 Promised to give him money: The amount is not specified (the "thirty pieces of silver" come from Matt. 26:15; Matthew derived them from Zech. 11:12–13). Mark contrasts Judas's receiving a relatively small amount of money for his betrayal of Jesus with the woman's giving the equivalent of a great sum of money to honor Jesus. **An opportunity to betray him:** The same Greek word is used for Judas's betrayal and God's "delivering up" Jesus as the Suffering Servant (see on 1:14). On Judas as an illustration of human responsibility and divine sovereignty, see on John 6:64–70; 13:2.

Figure 9. Form of the Anointing Story

FORM	MARK 14:3–9/MATT. 26:6–13	LUKE 7:36–50	JOHN 12:1–8
A. Setting	Bethany in Judea house of Simon the Leper reclining at table	(Not said:) Nain in Galilee house of Simon the Pharisee reclining at table	Bethany in Judea house of Mary, Martha reclining at table
B. Time	two days before Passover	weeks before Passover	six days before Passover
C. Identity of Woman	woman	woman of the city who was a sinner	Mary, sister of Martha and Lazarus
D. Material	alabaster jar, very expensive (Mark: pure nard)	alabaster jar	litra of pure nard (ca. 12 oz.)
E. Action	broke container poured on head		
		stood behind him cried wet feet with tears wiped feet with hair kissed feet	
	anointed head with ointment	anointed feet with ointment	anointed feet with ointment
F. Objector	Mark: some people Matthew: disciples	Simon the Pharisee	Judas Iscariot
G. Objection	Why this waste? Could have been sold and 300 denarii given to poor	If he were a prophet, he would have known what kind of woman this is.	Why not sell and give 300 denarii to poor?
H. Jesus' counter- objection	She did it for my burial. always have poor don't always have me	parable of two debtors 500 denarii mentioned Objection = Mark 2:7 "Your faith has saved you" (= Mark 5:34)	She did it for my burial. always have poor don't always have me
I. Concluding saying	*amen* I say to you gospel preached in whole world woman remembered	*therefore* I say to you loved much woman forgiven	[Note in John, too, the anointing story is surrounded by the plot against Lazarus's life, as in Mark/Matt. by plot against Jesus.]

14:12–25
Passover and Lord's Supper
(See also at Matt. 26:17–29; Luke 22:7–30; John 13:21–30)

Jesus was certainly killed on the Friday during the Passover festival, but the date is represented differently in the traditions behind Mark (followed by Matthew and Luke) and John, in order to bring out their differing theological points of view. Both traditions relate the death of Jesus to the liberating act of God memorialized in the Passover (see Exod. 12). The Synoptic Gospels do this by placing the Last Supper within the context of the Passover meal. In the Gospel of John, the Last Supper is not a Passover meal, but the evening before, and the crucifixion takes place prior to the Passover meal, at the time the Passover lambs are being sacrificed. Such differences on fundamental points show that the Gospel writers were throughout more concerned with theological meaning than with chronological accuracy. See chart at Matt. 26:17.

14:12 First day of Unleavened Bread: This is Thursday in Mark's chronology; see on 11:1, 20; 14:1. **Preparations for . . . the Passover:** This involved (1) locating an appropriate place within the city walls of Jerusalem, the only legitimate location for eating the Passover meal; (2) searching the room for leaven and removing any items that might contain yeast (bread crumbs, etc.); (3) obtaining a lamb and having it ritually slaughtered by the priests in the temple; (4) roasting the lamb and preparing it with the other necessary items for the meal in the place previously arranged. While it is important to Mark for theological reasons that the Last Supper was a Passover, he narrates none of the details associated with the Passover meal, concentrating on the new meaning given to the meal by Jesus, rather than on the items of the Passover ritual itself.

14:13 A man carrying a jar of water: This would have been unusual, since carrying water was usually done by women (see John 4:7). This is not, however, a covert, prearranged signal, as though Jesus had a secret network of disciples in Jerusalem. Novelistic reconstructions of Jesus' life have sometimes attempted to piece together such items into a conspiracy theory of "what really happened." Rather, this is Mark's way of indicating that, though Jesus will be killed (truly human), he is sovereign over the events of his death (truly divine). See the similar instructions in 11:1–6 and comments on 8:31.

14:15 Furnished and ready: Literally, "spread out, carpeted," i.e., a room prepared for a festive occasion in which the participants recline in Roman dining style, the posture of free people. The readers should not think of the modern Western table as portrayed in da Vinci's famous painting.

14:17 The twelve: Here equated with "his disciples" of v. 13 (see on 3:13–19).

14:18–19 One of you will betray me: Betray also means "hand over" (see on 1:14; 9:31). Again, Jesus' announcement shows that he is sovereign, not merely victim of circumstances. **Surely, not I?:** This translation captures the nuance of Mark's Greek better than the traditional "Is it I?" The grammar indicates the question is rhetorical, expecting a negative answer. The tone is not introspective soul-searching, but confidence, as in v. 31.

14:20 Bread . . . with me: An echo of Ps. 41:9, one of many such in the passion story. This is not a matter of details of Jesus' death being predicted in advance but reflects the conviction of the early Christians that Jesus' death was the fulfillment of God's purpose expressed in Scripture (see excursus, "New Testament Interpretation of the Old Testament," at 1 Cor. 15:3 and comments on 1 Pet. 1:10–11). Retrospectively, in the light of the resurrection, early Christians saw Jesus' death as part of the redemptive plan of God, not a random act of injustice carried out by religious and political leaders (see excursus "Why Was Jesus Killed?" at 14:53).

14:21 Son of Man goes as it is written of him: This is virtually another passion prediction, like 8:31; 9:31; 10:33–34 (see there). For Son of Man, see at 2:10. On human responsibility and divine purpose in the accounts of Judas' betrayal, see 1:14; 9:31; 14:41; John 6:64–70; 13:2, 27.

14:22–25 Institution of the Lord's Supper: On the several perspectives combined in the early Christian eucharistic celebration, see excursus, "The Lord's Supper in the New Testament," on 1 Cor. 11:23–26, and the parallel passages Matt. 26:26–30; Luke 22:15–20; John 6:51–59.

Blood of the covenant: Blood is a potent, many-faceted symbol. It represents life itself (see on Rom. 3:25; Heb. 9:14–22). Jesus gives himself, his life, to seal God's covenant. The covenant constitutes the people as God's own people, binding them together with God and each other. Mark relates blood to the covenant with Israel, which is here sealed (Exod. 24:6–8; Zech. 9:11). Jesus' disciples do not here have a different covenant but are incorporated into God's covenant with Israel. On Paul's and Luke's use of "new covenant" terminology, see on Luke 5:36–38; 22:19–20; 1 Cor. 11:25; 2 Cor. 3:1–18.

I will never [again] drink: Mark contains neither the command to repeat the eucharistic meal (as in 1 Cor. 11:24–25; Luke 22:19) nor the promise to be with his disciples in the interim between his resurrection and the Parousia. Since some manuscripts do not have the word "again," it is not clear in the Markan account whether Jesus himself drinks the cup with the disciples or abstains. In either case, there is here no promise of the presence of Christ at the church's eucharistic table. On Mark's dialectical understanding of the risen Jesus' presence/absence with his church, see on 2:20; 6:47–48, 52; 16:6. Until that day: Jesus does promise to renew his table fellowship with his disciples at the eschaton, when the Son of Man returns and the kingdom of God is fulfilled. This fulfillment is here pictured as the messianic banquet (see on 14:3–9; John 2:6–9; Isa. 25:6; Matt. 8:11–12; Luke 13:28–29; Rev. 2:7; 19:9). (On kingdom of God, see on Luke 4:43.) Jesus' final reference to the kingdom of God forms a bracket with his initial proclamation of 1:14–15.

14:26–31
Peter's Denial Predicted
(See also at Matt. 26:30–35;
Luke 22:31–34; John 13:36–38)

14:26 Had sung the hymn: Literally, "having hymned," the Greek construction not specifying a singular or plural object. Traditionally, the Passover was concluded by singing the Hallel psalms, 115–18. To the Mount of Olives: A brief walk across the Kidron valley to the adjacent hillside facing the city and the Temple Mount. It was rich in apocalyptic associations (see 11:1; 13:3). Although the narrative may well represent the course of events on the last night of Jesus' life, the details are also influenced by scriptural reflection (see on 14:20). In 2 Sam. 15, David is betrayed by a friend and goes to the Mount of Olives, where he prays.

14:27 For it is written: This is the only *formal* citation of Scripture in the Markan passion narrative, which is permeated with indirect allusions to the Scripture (see on 14:20). I will strike the shepherd: The section Zech. 9–14 contains numerous images and phrases whose original meaning was no longer clear

by the first century. This mysterious quality made them more amenable to being reinterpreted as referring to Jesus' passion and influencing the developing Gospel narratives (see excursus, "New Testament Interpretation of the Old Testament," at 1 Cor. 15:3). The Old Testament text of Zech. 13:7 quoted here has the plural imperative "strike," changed by Mark or his tradition to the first person singular future, "I will strike," making God the subject. Mark has adapted the biblical text to represent his conviction that Jesus' crucifixion was not only a human act, but an event in which God himself acted (see on "deliver up" at 9:31, and comments on John 3:16; 2 Cor. 5:19–21; Rev. 5:6).

14:28 After I am raised up: The passive voice points to God as the actor (see 8:31; 9:31; 10:33–34; 16:6). Both the crucifixion and the resurrection are seen as God's act. I will go before you: Jesus accepts the coming rejection and denial by his disciples and moves beyond it. God's act in raising up Jesus triumphs not only over death but over the failure of the disciples.

14:30 You will deny me three times: Like the predictions of his own faithfulness and sufferings (8:31; 9:31; 10:33–34), Jesus' predictions of his disciples' failures incorporate the whole scenario into the divine sovereignty without excusing the disciples of responsibility (see on 4:10–12; 6:52; 14:11; John 6:64–70; 13:2; Rom. 8:28–29).

14:31 All of them: As Peter was spokesperson for the Christian confession (8:29), so his denial of Jesus speaks for all the overconfident disciples, none of whom in the Markan account remains faithful to the end.

14:32–42
Gethsemane
(See also at Matt. 26:36–46; Luke 22:39–46;
John 18:1)

14:32 A place called Gethsemane: The name means "olive press." Mark mentions the name, and Matthew follows. Only John refers to a "garden," but without a name. Luke says simply the "Mount of Olives." Thus "Garden of Gethsemane" is a harmonizing construction of later tradition not found directly in the Bible (see "rich young ruler" of 10:17 and "three wise men" of Matt. 2:1).

14:33 Peter and James and John: See 1:16–20; 5:37; 9:2; 13:3. Distressed and agitated: The Greek expression is very strong, verging on breakdown. Jesus is overcome by horror and anguish as he faces death, expressed as he threw himself on the ground (v. 35). The Markan Jesus is not calm and self-possessed but humanly weak as he faces the cross (see "Theological Themes" in introduction to Mark).

14:34 Keep awake: As in 13:34, 35, 37, this is what Jesus asks of his disciples.

14:36 He said: Jesus prays elsewhere in Mark (1:35; 6:46), but only here is the content of the prayer given. It reflects the lamentations of Pss. 31:10–11; 42:5, 11; 43:5; 55:5. For the indirect influence of the Old Testament on the formation of the passion narrative, see on 14:20. One cannot understand Mark's Christology apart from reflection in the deep stream of lamentation in the Psalms. Abba: See on Matt. 6:9. As in 5:41; 7:34; 15:22, the original Aramaic of Jesus' native language is preserved in the Greek text of Mark and in our English translations. For you all things are possible: It is not the case that Jesus went to the cross because God could not deliver him. Human beings live lives of limited possibilities, but the Almighty, the Creator, is not bound by what is humanly possible (see 9:22–24; 10:27). This cup: The cup of suffering and death, which also has eucharistic overtones (see 10:38; 14:23–24).

14:36 Not what I want: Jesus' prayer is the model for all authentic human prayer, which does not try to bend God's will to ours, but ours to God's. To be truly human is to devote one's life to God's will, trusting that God finally wills our good.

In Mark's Christology, the death of *Jesus* is *God's* act for human salvation, though Mark does not elaborate an explicit theory of the atonement (see 10:45, and comments on 14:53; John 3:16; 2 Cor. 5:21). *That* Jesus' death represents God's saving act, not *how* this is so, is crucial for Mark.

As Jesus' Gethsemane prayer has earlier links with the lamentation tradition of Israel, so it has later links with the Lord's Prayer—the address to God as "Father," the prayer for God's will to be done, the reference to the "time of testing" (see on Matt. 6:9–13; Luke 11:2–4).

14:37 Simon: For the first time since receiving his new name in 3:16, Peter is addressed by his old name. In sleeping through Jesus' suffering and prayer, he has reverted to his old nature (see 8:29–33; Eph. 5:14). Time of trial: The same word can be translated "testing" or "temptation," see on 1:11–13; 8:11; 10:2.

14:38 The flesh is weak: The contrast between divine power and human weakness is common in the Old Testament (e.g., Job 34:14–15; Isa. 31:3). The reference is not only to Peter but to Jesus himself, who in Gethsemane and Golgotha participates fully in the weakness of humanity (see Rom. 8:1–17; 2 Cor. 10–13, esp. 13:4).

14:40 Did not know what to say: See 9:6. The disciples are dumbfounded both by Jesus' suffering and by his glory and must remain so until after the cross-resurrection (see "Theological Themes" in introduction to Mark).

14:41 Enough!: Both the NRSV and NIV so translate this obscure Greek expression, which may also be translated "it is all over," "the matter is settled," or "he [Judas] is taking possession of me." Such obscurities are rare in the Greek text, but there are words and sentences whose meaning remains in doubt. Let us be going: Despite their failure to understand, Jesus does not give up on his disciples but continues to call them to follow on the way to the cross (see 8:31–34; 10:32–34).

14:42 Is at hand: The same verb is used for the dawning of the kingdom of God in 1:14, correlating the coming of the kingdom with the crucifixion of Jesus as "King of the Jews" (see on 15:2).

14:43–52
Jesus Arrested
(See also at Matt. 26:47–56; Luke 22:47–53; John 18:2–12)

14:43 A crowd with swords and clubs: In Mark, no Roman soldiers or official temple police come to arrest Jesus but a "crowd" directed by the chief priests, the scribes, and the elders (see on 8:31). While historically this is probably not the same group that greeted Jesus in 11:9 and were on his side in 11:18, 32; 12:12, 37, Mark's use of the same terminology here indicates that the crowd is switching its loyalty (see 15:8, 11, 15).

14:44–45 The one I kiss: A usual greeting of students to their rabbi, like the greeting still common in the Middle East. There is nothing exceptional about Jesus' dress or physical appearance: he must be identified by Judas's deceitful act.

14:47 One of those who stood near: Nameless in Mark, who does not call him one of the disciples, who were presumably unarmed. Matthew and Luke identify him as a disciple; John specifies that it is Peter, and also gives the name of the slave of the high priest. The tradition becomes more specific as it is passed on (see 14:4 commentary).

14:48 Bandit: The same word as 11:17 and 15:27; used by the first-century Jewish historian Josephus for those involved in armed resistance against Rome, i.e., "freedom fighters" or "terrorists," depending on one's perspective.

14:49 Day after day: This comment seems to reflect an extended period, a different tradition from that of the overarching Markan chronology, according to which Jesus had taught in the temple only on Tuesday (see 11:20; Luke 21:37–38). Alternatively, the expression may mean only "by day" (in contrast to Jesus' arrest under cover of darkness). **Let the scriptures be fulfilled:** See on 14:20.

14:50 All of them deserted him: Except for Peter, who denies him in the next scene, this is the last appearance of the disciples in Mark. None are with Jesus at the crucifixion or burial, none come to the tomb. See on 16:7–8.

14:51 A certain young man: That the Scripture must be fulfilled is immediately illustrated (see Amos 2:16 and comments on 14:20). The young man has sometimes been identified as John Mark, traditionally presumed to be the author of the Gospel, whose home was in Jerusalem (Acts 12:12). However, this biographical, historicizing approach reflects more of the modern mentality of investigative reporting than the literary and theological orientation of Mark's narrative. The young man is a literary figure who epitomizes the flight of the disciples in v. 50, and stands in the series of desertions climaxed in 15:34. The scene forms a bracket with the *first* appearance of the disciples, who leave all to follow Jesus (1:16–20; 10:28). Here, the young man literally leaves everything *not* to be identified as a disciple. In the Bible, nakedness is often identified with shame (Gen. 2:25 vs. 3:10–11; Isa. 47:3; Rev. 3:18). Here nakedness represents the shame of those who deny rather than confess Christ (see 8:38).

14:53–72
Jesus before the Sanhedrin and Peter's Denial
(See also at Matt. 26:57–75; Luke 22:54–71; John 18:13–27)

EXCURSUS:
WHY WAS JESUS KILLED?

The question has two distinct but interrelated aspects: (1) historical, what actually happened, and (2) theological, how the event was understood in terms of God's saving act in Christ.

1. Historical: There is no more certain fact in history than the execution of Jesus by the Roman occupational forces in Jerusalem at a Passover festival ca. 30 CE. Jesus was executed as an actual or potential leader of political resistance against the Roman government. The placard on the cross sarcastically designated him "King of the Jews"—a rebel against Roman authority (Matt. 27:37; Mark 15:26; Luke 23:38; John 19:19).

Only slightly less certain is that Jesus was executed at the instigation of, and/or with the collaboration of, some of the priestly leadership in Jerusalem (not all the religious leaders, and not the people as a whole). The chief priests were responsible for working with the Roman officials to maintain law and order. They apparently recognized in Jesus a threat to religious and social stability and cooperated in making an example of him to other potential threats to peace (see John 11:47–53).

There is some connection between the life and ministry of Jesus and the manner of his death. It is difficult to know historically, however, just what this connection is, and how Jesus himself understood his death (see on 8:31). Although he centered his message on the present and coming kingdom of God, he did not engage in military resistance against Rome, nor teach his followers to do so. His talk of the rule of God and the large crowds he attracted may have been sufficient cause, from the Roman perspective, for his arrest and execution.

2. Theological: Early Christian understanding of Jesus' death began with the fact of it. Christian reflection did not begin with Jesus' birth and life and then ask from the pre-Easter perspective how and why he would die. For all his followers, Jesus' death was a terrible, unexpected surprise that shattered their hopes. However the disciples had understood or misunderstood Jesus and his mission prior to Easter, the resurrection experiences meant for them that God had validated Jesus as Christ and returning Son of Man, and that the whole event of Jesus' life, death, and resurrection must be reinterpreted as the eschatological act of God. Within this context, the meaning of Jesus' death was theologically understood in a variety of ways: as an expression of Jesus'/God's love (John 13:1; 15:13), as the means of God's forgiveness (1 Cor. 15:3), as an atoning sacrifice (Rom. 3:24–25; 2 Cor. 5:21), as an act of sealing or eschatologically renewing God's covenant with his people (Mark 14:24; Luke 22:20; 1 Cor. 11:25), as redemptive liberation from slavery (Rom. 3:24) or ransom from captivity (Mark 10:45), and in numerous other concepts and images that express the saving act of God in the death of Jesus.

When the stories of Jesus' arrest, trial, and crucifixion were elaborated within the early church's preaching and teaching, this theological dimension was primary. All Jesus' disciples had fled at his arrest (Mark 14:50); none were present at the trial or crucifixion, and there was little historical information available as to what actually transpired at his hearings and trials. This is reflected in the variations in the four Gospel accounts, which were to some extent filled in by interpretation of Scripture (see on 14:20). Each Gospel writer interprets his traditions and formulates his story of Jesus' trial and execution as a witness to the meaning of Christian faith, often influenced by the post-Easter experience of the Christian community, not as verbatim accounts of judicial proceedings.

In reading the whole story of Jesus' trial and execution, the modern reader should remember that Jesus did not die but was killed; that he was not killed by hoodlums in a back alley of Jerusalem but officially, by the government at the instigation of religious leaders; and that in the process his disciples had betrayed, denied, and abandoned him. The modern reader might well reflect that it was not the worst elements in the world that led to Jesus' death but the best, and ponder whether we can excuse ourselves with the thought that if we had been in charge, things would have been different. There was a sense in which all knew better, but there was another sense in which they did not and could not know with whom they were dealing (see Mark's messianic secret, and Luke 23:34; Acts 3:17; 7:60; 13:27; 17:30). Mark makes both points and leaves them logically unharmonized, as does the New Testament as a whole.

14:53 To the high priest: Not named in Mark; Caiaphas in Matt. 26:57. See John 18:13, 24. What follows is hardly a formal trial, but more of a hearing seeking grounds for an indictment before Pilate, presumably at the high priest's home. The Jewish council, called the Sanhedrin, is represented by the **chief priests, the elders, and the scribes** (see on 8:31).

14:54 Peter had followed him at a distance: Again Mark inserts one story into another, thereby interpreting each by the other (see on 2:1–12). By framing Jesus' "trial" with the account of Peter's denial, Mark contrasts Jesus' forthright confession (v. 62) with Peter's refusal to identify himself as a disciple of Jesus.

14:55 Looking for testimony against Jesus: His accusers had already decided Jesus must die (14:1; see 3:6); all pretense of a fair trial is abandoned as they look for a pretext to destroy

him. **Their testimony did not agree:** It did not meet the biblical requirement; see Deut. 19:15.

14:58 I will destroy this temple: Jesus had not said any such thing, but see 11:15–16; 13:1–2; 15:29; John 2:19–21; Acts 6:14. In Mark's time, the temple had in fact just been destroyed in the war or was about to be (see introduction to Mark). Mark's point is not what the historical Jesus may have said about the temple in 30 CE; his account reflects disputes between Jews and Christians and within the Christian community of his own time about the role of the temple in God's plan and what constitutes the proper continuation of temple worship for the people of God (see on 1 Pet. 1:22; 2:5).

14:60 The high priest . . . asked Jesus: When the false witnesses are not conclusive, the high priest attempts to wrest a self-incriminating statement from Jesus himself.

14:61 He was silent: Not reporter's notes, but another reflection of Scripture—the Suffering Servant is silent before his accusers (Isa. 53:7; see Ps. 38:12–14). **Are you the Christ?** See on 8:29–30. **The Son of the Blessed One:** The meaning is the same as "Son of God," on which see at Luke 1:28–33. The high priest reverently avoids using God's name.

14:62 I am: For the first and only time in Mark, Jesus declares his identity as Christ and Son of God. Since authentic Christian confession must acknowledge the Crucified One as God's Messiah, the Markan Jesus has withheld his own confession until this context in which he is condemned to die. **Son of Man:** See on 2:10. As in 8:29–31, Jesus interprets "Christ" in terms of the suffering, dying, and rising Son of Man, who will come with the clouds to establish God's kingdom. **Right hand of Power:** A reflection of Ps. 110:1, the most-cited Psalm in the New Testament, often interpreted christologically in early Christianity (see on Acts 2:34). Like the high priest's "Blessed One" of the preceding verse, "Power" is an indirect, reverential way of referring to God.

Six streams of Markan christological imagery converge in this crucial scene: Messiah (Christ), Son of God, Son of Man, Suffering Servant of Isa. 53, suffering righteous one of Wisdom of Solomon, and true prophet of God.

14:63 Tore his clothes: Not spontaneous anger or frustration, but a traditional ritual act communicating profound distress.

14:64 Blasphemy: It was not illegal or blasphemous, certainly not a capital offense, to claim to be the Messiah. In the Old Testament, blaspheming God's name is punishable by death (Lev. 24:16), but Jesus is not here accused of that. In any case, this would be a Jewish offense that would be useless when they bring their case to Pilate. The whole scene is written not to give an accurate report of what once happened at Jesus' hearing but to encourage Christians of Mark's day to stand fast in making their Christian confession (see 8:38; 13:9–13). We may surmise that the hearing before the high priest focused on getting evidence for a charge that could be brought to Pilate, i.e., associating Jesus with messianic claims that would be understood politically by the Roman governor.

14:65 Some began to spit on him: In Mark, this apparently refers to members of the Sanhedrin assembled at the high priest's house, but the detail probably comes from Isa. 50:6; 53:3–5. **Prophesy:** Here, the surface meaning is a taunt to the blindfolded prisoner to use his divine insight to identify the one who struck him, but Mark has a deep irony in mind: Jesus had in fact prophesied that he would be so abused, and his accusers unwittingly fulfill his prophecy (10:34). He is indeed a prophet (see 6:4).

14:66 Peter was below: The narrative camera swings back to Peter, for the second part of the sequence begun at 14:54. "Below" suggests the hearing was on the second floor, another "upper room" (see 14:15). The account of Peter's denial is one of the few Gospel incidents recounted in all four Gospels. It was particularly important for Mark's readers, who were facing a persecution in which some members of their community would deny that they were Christians. They could take both warning and consolation from the story of Peter, who had also failed—but who became a faithful disciple and leader in the church. So also those of Mark's church who had remained faithful are here reminded that they must be reconciled with those who had failed under pressure (see on 16:7–8).

14:67: With Jesus: The mark of a disciple; see 3:14.

14:68 He denied: See 8:38; Matthew 10:32–33.

14:70 You are a Galilean: It is not said how they know. Matthew supplies the missing explanation (26:73).

14:71 Began to curse: This does not mean that Peter reverted to his sailor's vocabulary, but that he invoked a curse upon himself to validate his word. See the Old Testament formula "may the Lord do so to me and more also,

if . . ." (see Ruth 1:17; 1 Sam. 14:44; 2 Sam. 3:35; 19:13; 1 Kgs. 2:23; 19:2; 20:10; 2 Kgs. 6:31). Since the word for "curse" usually takes an object, it may even mean that he pronounced a curse on Jesus to show he was not a disciple (see on 1 Cor. 12:3).

14:72 The second time: See the NRSV footnote at v. 68, which indicates that the "first" cock crowing is found in some manuscripts of Mark but not in others. There is much confusion on this point in the MSS of each of the Gospels, as scribes attempted to reconcile the various traditions (see "Introduction: The New Testament as the Church's Book," 4.d). In any case, the Markan point is clear: the crowing of the rooster reminds Peter of Jesus' word, and he **broke down and wept.** Peter is sorry, but remorse is not the same as repentance, and he must wait for the Easter message to be restored to true discipleship (16:7–8).

15:1–15
The Trial before Pilate
(See also at Matt. 27:1–26;
Luke 23:1–25; John 18:28–40)

15:1 As soon as it was morning: Friday, in the chronology of all the Gospels. In Mark, followed by Matthew and Luke, this is Passover day; in John, the day before Passover on which the lambs were sacrificed (see chart at Matt. 26:17). In either case, the meeting of the previous night would be illegal, and the council meets to confirm their decision. It is difficult to imagine historically that the Sanhedrin would have a special session early in the morning of a high holy day, but Mark is not thinking in terms of historical precision.

15:2 Handed him over to Pilate: On "handing over," see on 1:14. Pilate, prefect of Judea, has played no prior role in Mark's narrative (so also Matthew and John; contrast Luke, who mentions Pilate prior to the passion story in 3:1; 13:1; 20:20). Though traditionally known as governor, his actual title was prefect, as we now know from an inscription found at Caesarea. His headquarters were in Caesarea on the coast, but he came to Jerusalem with extra troops to maintain order during the patriotic festival. The historical situation is disputed with regard to the measure of local autonomy the Roman authorities permitted the Jewish leaders. They may have had some authority in cases involving religious matters, but Pilate as the Roman governor represented the real political power. On the basis of John 18:31, it has often been believed that during the

Roman governors' administration of Judea (6–40, 44–66 CE) the Jewish leaders did not have the power of capital punishment, but this has been disputed and opinions are divided. The evidence for the Jewish right of capital punishment all seems to point to exceptions, however, and John 18:31 seems to represent the historical situation. Whatever the historical reality may have been, in Mark's portrayal the Jewish leaders have authority to condemn Jesus, but it is Pilate who must carry out the execution.

15:2 Are you the King of the Jews? The Jewish leaders had presented the charges against Jesus in political terms, and represent themselves as pro-Roman in helping eliminate a threat to Roman rule. **You say so:** These are Jesus' last words in Mark, except for the cry from the cross in v. 34. The Greek phrase is sometimes understood as hesitant or ambiguous ("'King' is your word, not mine," "You could put it that way," or "So you say."). However, in Matt. 26:25 the same phrase is equivalent to the clear "I am," so the NIV translation is better here, **"Yes, it is as you say."** Mark intends the reader to understand the answer positively: Jesus is God's anointed king in the present and coming kingdom of God but not in the political sense assumed by Pilate. The phrase **"King of the Jews"** is repeated in vv. 9, 12, 18, 26; see v. 32, forming the ironic theme of the trial and crucifixion narrative.

15:3 Accused him of many things: The content of the other charges is not given. Mark's point is that despite the multitude of charges, Jesus does not defend himself but is silent like God's Suffering Servant of Isa. 53:7.

15:6 He used to release a prisoner . . . anyone . . . they asked: There is no extrabiblical evidence for this custom. It is historically difficult to imagine that the Romans would release a political rebel to the volatile crowds at a patriotic festival where mob action was feared (see 14:2).

15:10 Out of jealousy: This motive has not previously been mentioned. It could be that the leaders are jealous of Jesus' popularity with the crowds, but in this scene the crowds are on the side of the leaders. Since the Greek word and its Hebrew/Aramaic counterpart can also mean "zeal" (see Phil. 1:15; Jas. 4:5), the more likely meaning is that Pilate perceived that their interest in getting rid of Jesus was a matter of intensely religious/political zeal (see Rom. 10:2; 2 Cor. 7:11; Phil. 3:6).

15:11 Stirred up the crowd: See on 14:43. The crowd has a chance to save Jesus but is persuaded by the chief priests to choose Barabbas. They could have chosen Jesus, but then would have been responsible for the death of a popular revolutionary leader.

15:15 Wishing to satisfy the crowd: Pilate is pictured as weak and vacillating, knowing that Jesus is innocent but agreeing to his execution against his own conscience as a matter of expediency—like Herod's role in the death of John the Baptist (6:14–29).

15:16–20a
Jesus Mocked by the Soldiers
(See also at Matt. 27:27–31a; Luke 19:2–3)

Both the Jewish hearing and the Roman trial contain a scene in which Jesus is mocked (see 14:65).

15:16 The whole cohort: A cohort is one-tenth of a legion, which at full strength was six thousand men. Mark portrays a military unit of three hundred to six hundred soldiers.

15:17–18 Twisting some thorns into a crown: Humiliation and mockery, not merely increasing Jesus' suffering, is the point of the cruel charade. This scene is the height of Markan irony. Crown, robe, scepter, homage, and hailing him as "King of the Jews" represented a far deeper truth than the coarse humor of the mocking soldiers could be aware. **King of the Jews:** See on 15:2.

15:20b–41
The Crucifixion
(See also at Matt. 27:31b-56;
Luke 23:26–49; John 19:17–37)

Crucifixion was a sadistic form of capital punishment not found in the Old Testament, but devised by the Persians and later adopted by the Greeks and Romans. The condemned person carried the crossbar to the upright stake already erected in a public place, where he was stripped and beaten, then tied or nailed to both beams, and left to die of exposure, hunger, thirst, shock, and the gradual suffocation resulting from being bound in a cramped position. The Romans reserved crucifixion for the lowest classes of noncitizens (such as runaway slaves) and for rebellious provincials.

15:21 Compelled a passer-by: The Roman occupational forces could legally requisition the property of local inhabitants and impress them into limited service (see on Matt. 5:42, where the same word is used). **To carry his cross:** This is the same phrase as 8:34. Jesus was unable to carry the crossbeam himself, presumably too weak from the flogging of v.

15. Corresponding to its different Christology, the Gospel of John portrays Jesus as carrying the cross himself (John 19:17). **Simon of Cyrene:** Another Simon had been called to bear the cross (1:16–20; 8:34) but had so far refused (14:66–72). **Cyrene:** In north Africa, modern Libya. In Mark's story, the only person present with Jesus at Golgotha whose name we know is an outsider. Nothing else is known of this Simon, though he was apparently familiar to the first readers of Mark's Gospel. **Alexander and Rufus:** Otherwise unknown. The reference to a Rufus in Rom. 16:13 is sometimes used as evidence that Mark was composed in Rome, but there is no basis for identifying the two persons.

15:22 They brought Jesus: The verb can also be translated "carried," as in 2:13 and 6:27–28. Mark's presentation of the weak and exhausted Jesus may mean that he was physically carried to the place of crucifixion. **Golgotha . . . the place of a skull**: Perhaps so named from the shape of the hill—though it is never said in the New Testament that Jesus was crucified on a hill—or perhaps because, as the place of execution, human skulls were found there. The location is unknown, though it was outside the ancient city. The traditional pilgrimage sites in Jerusalem were first designated in the fourth century CE.

15:23 Wine mixed with myrrh: Here a sedative intended to reduce the pain (see Prov. 31:6). **Did not take it:** This is sometimes explained as Jesus' own desire to face death with a clear head. None of the evangelists wish to portray a drugged or unconscious Jesus on the cross, but one who can speak. In Mark, it may also reflect Jesus' continuing fast, his refusal of food and drink begun at the Last Supper (see on 14:25).

15:24 And they crucified him: Mark spares the reader the gory details. This is not because they were known to every ancient reader, for whom crucifixion was a common occurrence not needing to be described, and not because of squeamishness. Rather, the motive for following Jesus is not an emotional response to graphic descriptions of his suffering but faith in God's act in the Christ event as a whole, climaxed in the self-giving love manifest in his death. **Dividing his clothes . . . casting lots:** See Ps. 22:18, the lament of a sick person who, though he is not yet dead, sees relatives and friends already deciding who gets what. Such details may be derived not from historical memory of what actually happened at the

cross but from the earliest church's retrospective reflection on Scripture texts read in the light of the Christ event (see commentary on 14:20). Psalm 22, like Pss. 69 and 110, was especially important in this regard.

15:25 Nine o'clock: Literally, "the third hour," using the Roman system of timekeeping that begins at 6:00 a.m. The NRSV translates the temporal designations into modern terms, while the NIV preserves the biblical terminology. See John 19:14 for the different chronology of the Fourth Gospel. Such differences are not to be harmonized; each Gospel is to be read for its own distinctive message.

15:27 Two bandits: See on 14:48. From the Roman point of view, three dangerous rebels, threats to the peace and prosperity, law and order brought by Rome, had been executed. **Right . . . left:** See 10:37–40.

15:29 Shaking their heads: Another detail reflecting Ps. 22 (v. 7). In the ancient biblical world, this gesture represented not negation or lack of understanding but mockery. **Destroy this temple:** See on 11:11, 15–16, 27; 12:35; 13:1, 3; 14:49, 58; 15:38.

15:31 He saved others; he cannot save himself: An ironic expression of the truth of Jesus' teaching (8:35–38), by which he had himself lived and died.

15:32 Let the Messiah . . . come down from the cross now, so that we may see and believe: This is a crucial element in Mark's portrayal, indicated by its doubling (vv. 30, 32). The *logic of the chief priests* was clear: a Messiah who truly suffers and dies is inconceivable; the crucifixion is the ultimate proof that Jesus is not Messiah and Son of God. *Mark's theology* is that in Jesus God has fully identified himself with humanity, including weakness, suffering, and death (so also Paul, Hebrews, and other New Testament authors; see e.g. Phil. 2:5–11; Heb. 2:5–18). Contemporary readers might ponder whether their own way of understanding Jesus as the Christ corresponds more to the logic of the chief priests or to the theology of Mark. Some types of Christian theology have attempted to adopt the logic of the chief priests, arguing that the Jesus who walked on the water (6:45–52) *could* have come down from the cross. Since he *did* not, this must mean that he must have *chosen* to remain on the cross in order to purchase forgiveness or to show God's love. But such thinking separates Jesus not only from the two dying men on either side of him, but from all other human beings, none of whom have the choice of whether or not to die. Such thinking finally rejects the true humanity of Jesus. Some of the early Christian documents excluded from the Bible do not hesitate to follow this line of thinking to its ultimate conclusion, and explain that the Son of God could not suffer and die, but could and did come down from the cross. *The Acts of John*, for example, tells how during the three hours of darkness Jesus descended from the cross and spoke with the apostle John, explaining that he was not really suffering and dying, but only in appearance. Jesus then remounts the cross and acts out the charade to the end. Such an understanding was condemned by the early church as the heresy of Docetism (see on John 19:34; Acts 14:11; 1 Tim. 2:5–6). In Mark's theology, Jesus suffers and dies as a truly human victim subject to weakness and death. Though he was Messiah, he could not have come down from the cross; to suppose that he could is to share the false logic of the chief priests. Mark also shares and affirms the theology of the miracle stories he has preserved in the first half of his Gospel, in which Jesus is portrayed primarily as a divine being not subject to human limitations. No one theology can do justice to the act of God in the Christ event. Mark affirms two theological traditions, which he does not try to harmonize logically; the theological perspective operative in the crucifixion scene is not of the miracle-working Son of God but the human Suffering Servant (see introduction to Mark, "Theological Themes").

15:33 Darkness: See Amos 8:9, and notes on Mark 14:20.

15:34 Three in the afternoon: See on v. 25 above. **My God, why?:** The traditional seven last words are a combination of sayings from all four Gospels. In Mark, Jesus' only articulate word from the cross is the first line of Ps. 22, a lament of a suffering righteous person who calls out for divine vindication, which the psalm itself goes on to promise and celebrate, the Gentiles themselves finally joining in the celebration. The Markan reader, who knows the whole story, can rightfully think of Ps. 22 as an outline of the whole cross-resurrection salvation event that leads to the Gentile mission. But there are objections to this reading, in which the Markan Jesus has the whole psalm in mind, including its triumphant conclusion, encouraging the reader to imagine Jesus as triumphant in death. Luke did not understand it this way and substituted a different, more positive Psalm (Luke 23:45 = Ps.

31:6), and the bystanders in the Markan story did not understand it as an expression of confidence reflecting the psalm as a whole but as a desperate cry for help. The Markan Jesus should thus not be pictured as merely reciting the opening words of an outline of salvation history. The human Jesus is pictured as dying with a cry of anguish and abandonment on his lips, and yet not of despair. In the darkness and pain, he still addresses his lament to God, and as "*my* God."

In Mark this cry of derelicition represents the climax of a series of abandonments: first the religious experts and teachers, who might have been expected to recognize and acknowledge him (2:6; 3:6; 14:1); then his family (3:20–21, 31–35); then his hometown neighbors (6:1–6); then the crowds, receptive at first, ultimately rejecting him (11:8–10; 12:37; 15:13–15); finally his disciples. One disciple betrays for money (14:10, 43), their leader and spokesperson denies any association with him (14:29, 66–72), and all desert him and flee (14:50–52). Now Jesus is utterly alone—there is no repentant thief as in Luke 23:39–43—and his only word is a cry that God too has abandoned him. Is anyone left? (See on 16:1–8.)

15:35 Elijah: "Eloi" is mistaken for a call to the prophet Elijah. **Sour wine** is the typical soldier's drink. Some is offered to Jesus to keep him alive a bit longer to see whether Elijah will come to save him. But see on 1:2; 9:9–13—the Markan reader knows that "Elijah" has already come.

15:38 The curtain of the temple was torn in two: This curtain was apparently the veil that separated the most holy place of the inner sanctuary from the outer court (Exod. 26:31–35). Jesus had predicted that the temple would be destroyed (13:1–2), and the destruction already begins, to be completed in the disastrous war of 66–70 of Mark's own time.

15:39 The centurion . . . saw that in this way he breathed his last: Here at the cross the secret identity is revealed, in the most unexpected manner. The Roman officer in charge of the crucifixion turns out to the first and only human being in Mark to confess Jesus as Son of God. What prompts him to do this? Those who have looked for a basis for his confession have sometimes hit upon the rending of the temple veil in the preceding verse, but this is not Mark's meaning. (The tearing of the curtain is narrated to the reader but not visible to the participants in the story.) Others have pointed to Jesus' loud cry (v. 37) and argued that since most victims of crucifixion were unconscious by the time of their death, the centurion was impressed by Jesus' strength as he breathed his last. All such explanations miss the Markan understanding of faith, as though it were a matter of evidence (see on Luke 7:32, 39; 20:3–8, esp. comments on John 7:12).

Truly this man was the Son of God: To ask what a 30 CE Roman officer might have meant by these words is to miss Mark's point. For Mark, the centurion makes the Christian confession of faith (see 1:1), that this one who is truly human is also truly the Son of God. When the later church at Nicaea and Chalcedon developed the elaborate creeds testifying that it is the true God and not some lesser being who is manifest in Jesus, and that this Jesus is nonetheless truly human, it was only the elaboration of this basic biblical confession. The centurion's confession is only one step short of authentic Christian faith: he said "was," not "is," which must await the resurrection.

15:40 Women looking on from a distance: It is striking that until this point in the narrative Mark has withheld from the reader the fact that Jesus had women disciples, who **used to follow him** (v. 41) (the word for discipleship; see 1:15–20; 2:14; 10:21) when he was in Galilee and who were present with him in Jerusalem—including on the margin of the crucifixion scene from which the male disciples had fled. Women are prominent elsewhere in Mark (see 1:29–31; 12:41–44; 14:3–9), where in contrast to the male disciples they are portrayed in a uniformly positive light. This no doubt reflects the prominent role of women in the Markan church, as in the Pauline churches to which Mark has some connection. But, in contrast to Luke and John, who include women disciples in the earlier scenes of Jesus' ministry (Luke 8:1–3; 10:38–42; John 4:1–42; 11:1–43) Mark has withheld this picture from the reader until these closing scenes (see on 15:47; 16:1, 8).

Mary Magdalene ... Salome: There seems to be an intended ambiguity about the identity of these women. Though Christian tradition later developed legends about them, combining their stories with other similar figures, Mark gives no further information about either. **Mary the mother of James the younger and of Joses:** The only woman named Mary previously mentioned in Mark is the mother of Jesus (6:3), who had thought Jesus was deranged (3:20–21, 31–35), and who was also the mother of James, Joses, Judas, and Simon (6:3). Is this the same person who is here called

"mother of James the younger and of Joses," in v. 47 the "mother of Joses," and in 16:1 the "mother of James?" (See on 15:47.)

15:42–47
Jesus' Burial
(See also at Matt. 27:57–61;
Luke 23:50–56; John 19:38–42)

The Romans typically left the bodies of crucified prisoners on the cross to decompose and be consumed by birds and animals. In Judaism, the ultimate humiliation was to remain unburied (see Tob. 1:17–18; 2:4; 4:4; 6:15; 8:12; 12:12–13; 14:10). The recent discovery in Jerusalem of an ossuary containing the bones of a victim of crucifixion shows that there were exceptions.

15:42 The day of Preparation: Friday; in modern Greek, the word for Friday is still called Preparation.

15:43 Joseph of Arimathea: Mark had indicated that all the members of the Council had voted for his death. Both Matthew and Luke notice the discrepancy and alter this. While this could simply be generalizing exaggeration, more likely Mark intends to picture a transformed Joseph. As the crucifixion transformed the centurion, so also a previous opponent now acts as a disciple. **Boldly:** It was a risky and courageous act to identify oneself with an executed opponent of Rome, again in contrast to Jesus' disciples, who are not present to bury him (14:50–51) and who had denied any association with him (14:66–72). **Waiting expectantly for the kingdom of God:** In this last reference to the kingdom in Mark, it is still future (see on 1:15). Joseph here resembles the scribe of 12:34 who is praised by Jesus.

15:45 Learned from the centurion that [Jesus] was dead: That Jesus truly died is important to New Testament theology; witnesses to the cross and resurrection are careful to exclude theories that Jesus was only in a coma (see 1 Cor. 3:3–5; John 19:33–34, and comments on Docetism above). Here, the one who confesses that Jesus is Son of God also certifies that he died a truly human death.

15:47 Mary Magdalene and Mary the mother of Joses: See 15:40 and 16:1. Is the reader expected to recognize "Mary the mother of Joses" as the mother of Jesus? Or only to ask the question? If Jesus' mother, she, too, has been converted by the event of the cross, like the centurion and Joseph. In this case, Mark pictures the effect of the cross as transforming Jesus' enemies: the Romans who killed him, the religious leaders who rejected him, and his family who disbelieved in him. Perhaps by this allusive and indirect reference Mark leaves the reader to decide: can the message of the cross really effect such changes in people (see 1 Cor. 1:18–2:5)? Only one key group remains—will Jesus' disciples that have misunderstood and abandoned him also be redeemed by the message of the cross and resurrection?

16:1–8
CONCLUSION—THE WOMEN
AT THE TOMB
(See also at Matt. 28:1–8; Luke 24:1–12; John 20:1–13)

For general considerations on interpreting the resurrection, see excursus, "Interpreting the Resurrection," at Matt. 28:1.

Before one interprets the Markan narrative, one must decide whether or not Mark intended to end his narrative at v. 8, which seems to break off in midsentence, ending with the Greek conjunction *gar*. This would be analogous to ending an English sentence with "and, . . ." The oldest and best manuscripts end here. The fourth-century Christian historian Eusebius and the fifth-century theologian Jerome both reported that almost all the manuscripts of Mark in their day ended at v. 8. Yet later manuscripts have one or more of three different endings that seem to have been added, so that the vast majority of medieval manuscripts continue the narrative past v. 8. The King James Version of 1611 was translated before the most ancient manuscripts were rediscovered, so that most English Bibles prior to modern translations included vv. 9–20. Most modern translations now end at v. 8, or give notes indicating this is where the most ancient MSS ended (see NRSV and NIV). The comments below assume not only that all the longer endings are secondary but that the original ending has not been lost: strange as it may seem at first, Mark constructed his story to end in midsentence at v. 8.

This means that Mark's original conclusion contained the discovery of the empty tomb and the command to tell the disciples but not any scenes in which the risen Jesus appears. Mark's story concludes with the announcement of the resurrection but without any words of the risen Lord himself. Mark affirms the resurrection but is wary of post-Easter revelations from the risen Lord; he intends to bind the message of the risen Lord to the preceding narrative, the story of the Crucified One.

16:1 When the sabbath was over: The Sabbath ended at sundown on Saturday, but it is clear Mark sets the scene on Sunday morning. On the identity of the three women, see on 15:40, 47. **Bought spices to anoint him:** See 15:42, 46—because of the beginning of the Sabbath when no work could be done, the arrangements for Jesus' burial had not been completed. Despite Jesus' announcements in 8:31; 9:31; 10:33–34, the women came to the tomb to complete a funeral, not to celebrate the resurrection.

16:2 The first day of the week: This becomes the Christian holy day on which the church assembles for worship (Acts 20:7; 1 Cor. 16:2), the Lord's Day (Rev. 1:10), but for the world in general it remained a secular workday until becoming a legal holiday under emperor Constantine in the fourth century.

16:3 Who will roll away the stone? In Mark, the tomb is not sealed or guarded (see Matt. 27:62–66).

16:4 They looked up: The Greek word has a double meaning impossible to reproduce in English and thus can also be translated "they recovered their sight" (as the same word is translated in 8:24; 10:51–52). The light of the first Easter begins to remove the blindness that had prevailed during Jesus' ministry (see 4:10–12, 21–25; 8:22–26; 10:46–52). **Already rolled back:** In contrast to the apocryphal *Gospel of Peter*, the New Testament accounts never narrate the resurrection itself, which always occurs offstage, in the mystery of God.

16:5 A young man: In Matt. 28:2, the "angel of the Lord," in Luke 24:4, "two men in dazzling clothes," in John 20:12, "two angels" seen by Mary Magdalene alone. The resurrection accounts are not to be harmonized; each story is to be heard in its distinctive witness.

16:6 Jesus of Nazareth, who was crucified: The phrase is expressed by the Greek perfect participle, for which there is no accurate equivalent in modern English. The Greek perfect tense points to an event of the past that continues into the present. Old English had such a construction, as in "Joy to the world, the Lord *is* come," which is different from "has come" (past) and "is here" (present), and represents a combination of the two: "has come and continues to be present." Thus Jesus is here identified as the one who was crucified at a point in the past and whose continued existence is that of the Crucified One. In Mark's theology, crucifixion was not a temporary episode in the career of the Son of God, a passing phase to be nullified, transcended, or exchanged at the resurrection for heavenly glory. Even as the Risen One, he bears the mark of his self-giving on the cross as his permanent character and call to discipleship (8:31–34). **He is not here:** Mark has no appearances of the risen Lord and is suspicious of post-Easter prophetic revelations by Christian prophets who speak in his name. Thus the absence of Jesus during the time of the church between Easter and the Parousia of the Son of Man is a Markan theme (see on 2:20; 14:7, 25). Mark's understanding of Jesus' absence is dialectic: while the risen Lord is not present sacramentally or through directly inspired prophets who speak in his name, Christ does continue to be present and to speak through the story of the Crucified One. The Gospel itself mediates the presence and voice of the risen Lord. **He has been raised:** The NRSV is here more accurate than the NIV "he has risen," for the Greek verb is passive, pointing to God as the actor.

16:7 Go tell: The indicative of the resurrection message contains a built-in imperative; if it happened at all, it happened for all and must be shared (see on Rom. 6:6; 12:1; 13:14; 1 Cor. 5:6–8; 6:18–19; 2 Cor. 5:20; 1 Pet. 1:13). The angel commands the women to carry the message to the disciples, making them not only the initial witnesses of the empty tomb, but the first bearers of the glad message that "he has been raised [by God] from the dead." **And Peter:** "And" here can be translated "even." Peter is singled out as the apostolic leader; despite his failure, he is sought out, reconciled, and made into an authentic disciple by the resurrection message. **He is going ahead of you:** See 10:32, which already anticipates the post-Easter reality. The risen Christ is already "out there" in the world, ahead of the disciples. In their mission work they do not bring him to others; he is already there before them. **You will see him:** Though the text points to a particular event for the disciples in Galilee, a resurrection appearance that will happen offstage beyond the plotted narrative, the words also reflect the situation of the Markan readers and Christians generally— we live our lives between the testimony to the resurrection of the Crucified One and the return of the Son of Man when we shall "see him."

16:8 Fled and . . . said nothing to anyone: On this as the original ending of Mark, see above. To be sure, Mark knows that the resurrection message was communicated; the women and others shared it, or there would be no resurrection

faith, no apostolic testimony, no Gospel of Mark, no church that has continued through the centuries. But Mark has skillfully constructed his story to bring the reader to this point. *Now* we see why Mark has withheld reference to the women disciples until the story is almost over. It is for a literary and theological, not historical or biographical reason. Every group in the story had abandoned or rejected Jesus (see on 15:34). Then the women emerge. They are the only hope that the story will go on. But they, too, finally fail. Who is left? With great literary skill, throughout his narrative Mark has allowed the reader to be an invisible presence in every scene. The reader was present and heard the heavenly voice declaring Jesus to be God's Son, though the characters in the story did not (1:9–11). The reader remained "with Jesus" (see 3:14) when even his family misunderstood and remained outsiders (3:20–21, 31–35). The reader remained awake and heard Jesus' prayer, while the disciples slept (14:32–42). When all the disciples forsook him and fled (14:50–51), the readers were with Jesus through his trials, his mocking and beating. When Jesus cried out that God has forsaken him (15:34), the reader was still there. Then the women emerge within the story, and the reader is with them as Jesus is buried, and with them as they go to the tomb and hear the message to "go, tell" (16:7). The Gospel closes in midsentence with "they said nothing to anyone, for they were afraid, and . . ."

The beginning of 1:1 does not come to an end in the document itself. Mark leaves the story open-ended. Everyone in the narrative has failed, but the story is not over. He had not written "The End," but "To Be Continued." If the story is to continue, the reader has a decision to make.

16:9–20
THE SECONDARY ENDINGS OF MARK

Although Mark originally ended at 16:8 (see above), the three endings printed as text and footnotes of the NRSV are significant for two reasons:

1. They show that the church has always responded to Mark by realizing that the story it contains is incomplete. Not only these secondary manuscript endings added by Christian scribes, but the differing ways in which Matthew, Luke, and John extend the story beyond 16:8 witness to the church's perception that the Markan story must go on. In reading the various endings, we see early Christian responses to Mark's story, somewhat analogous to the ways in which early

Christian teachers wrote conclusions to Jesus' open-ended parables (see on 4:1–20).

2. While with most scholars we have interpreted Mark as ending at 16:8, we acknowledge that we cannot be absolutely certain and that Mark may have continued the story himself, with his ending either lost or embedded in one of the longer endings. We would not remove them from the Bible, even if we could. They represent sacred Christian tradition handed along with the biblical text, show how earlier Christians have interpreted Mark, and show that the line between Scripture and tradition is not always sharp.

The Gospel according to Luke

INTRODUCTION

The Gospel of Luke, volume one of a two-volume narrative, tells the Christian story from the birth of John the Baptist through the life, death, and resurrection of Jesus. The story is continued in volume two, the Book of Acts, which tells the story from the beginning of the church in Jerusalem to the preaching of the gospel in Rome by Paul.

Luke not only wrote more of the New Testament than any other person (27.5 percent), he contributed the framework of understanding the Christian story that has dominated Christian understanding and the liturgical calendar throughout the centuries until the present: Old Testament promises/birth of Jesus/ministry/death/resurrection/ascension/descent of the Spirit/mission of the church/parousia.

Author

Like the other Gospels, the Gospel of Luke does not contain the author's name but is anonymous. Like the other Gospels, the Gospel of Luke received a title in the second century, when the four canonical Gospels were selected from many others for inclusion in the canon, the normative collection of witnesses to the meaning of the Christian faith. From late in the second century, the author was understood to be Luke the companion of Paul mentioned in Phlm. 24 and 2 Tim. 4:11, called the "beloved Physician" in Col. 4:14, who speaks in the first person ("we") in Acts 16:10–17; 20:5–21:18; 27:1–28:16. Some scholars regard this identification as accurate history; others, perhaps the majority, believe that the "we passages" of Acts reflect the author's incorporation of the travel diary of one of Paul's companions, or consider them a literary device to add vividness to the story. On the author's medical language, see on Acts 3:7. In any case, the early church's attribution of the Gospel to Luke was not primarily a matter of historical correctness but a means of affirming that the narrative is an authentic representative of the apostolic faith. We will refer to the author with the traditional designation Luke, while considering the author's actual name to be unknown.

From the narrative itself we can learn that the author, though he may have been with Paul for a brief period, was not an eyewitness to the ministry of Jesus (see on 1:1–4). He was a sophisticated author who wrote excellent Greek, at a literary level superior to the other Gospels. If he was the Luke of Col. 4:14, he was certainly a Gentile (see Col. 4:11), and the narrative itself indicates the perspective of a Gentile Christian.

Genre and Readership

While Luke contains historical materials, it is clear that Luke is not concerned simply to write accurate biography or history but to bear witness to the truth of the Christian faith. "Theologically interpreted history" or "the story of God's mighty acts in history" perhaps best captures Luke's intent (see "Introduction to the Gospels").

The dedication to Theophilus does not mean that the narrative was written to one individual. Luke's readership is the wider public that has already been "informed" or "instructed" about the church and its message (1:4), but who need a deeper and more accurate understanding. This could be Christians who need a more informed faith, outsiders who are suspicious of Christianity, or both.

Sources

Luke refers to many prior authors who had compiled an account of Jesus' life and teachings prior to his own writing (1:1). While "many" is part of the conventional style of such introductions, we know of at least two documents that Luke used as sources: The Gospel of Mark and a (now lost) collection of Jesus' sayings called "Q." In addition, Luke had various oral and perhaps written sources not documented elsewhere. This material peculiar to Luke, including his own editorial modifications and expansions, is designated "L," so that all Luke's composition may be identified as Mark (about 50 percent), Q (about 25 percent) and L (about 25 percent):

1:1–2:52	L
3:1–6:19	Mark (+ Q for John the Baptist and Temptation sections)
6:20–8:3	Q + L
8:4–9:50	Mark
9:51–18:14	Q + L
18:15–24:11	Mark + L
24:12–53	L

It is clear from this (somewhat rough) outline that Luke composes in blocks, alternating sections of Mark and Q, interspersed with his special materials and own editorializing.

Date and Place

Luke–Acts was certainly written after the latest event it narrates, Paul's two-year imprisonment in Rome (Acts 28:30–31), i.e., after 63 CE. Since the Gospel of Mark is usually dated about 70 CE, Luke must have been written long enough after this to have considered Mark an authoritative source. Luke places himself in the second or third Christian generation (1:1–3) and seems to look back on the destruction of Jerusalem in 70 CE as having occurred sometime in the past (13:14; 19:43–44; 21:20). Thus most scholars place the composition ca. 80–90 CE, though there is no proof that the Gospel was written prior to the second century, when it first appears in quotations. There is no reliable evidence as to the place the document was composed, but this is not crucial for the Gospel's interpretation.

Theological Themes

Luke writes as a theologian to help the church clarify its faith. He weaves together several theological themes, including the following:

1. *Jesus as the "midst of time."* Jewish messianic hopes had looked forward to the coming of the Messiah and the establishment of God's kingdom of justice and righteousness at the end of history. When the earliest followers of Jesus were convinced by the resurrection that Jesus was the Christ, they understood that the end of history had come and expected Christ to return in the near future. Luke reinterpreted the historical schema so that the Christ was seen as the defining *center* of history, followed by the extended period of the church's mission before the coming of the end. He understood the "time of Jesus" to be a special one-year period in which the kingdom of God was realized on earth in the ministry of Jesus, preceded by the "time of Israel" and followed by the "time of the church." The time of Jesus was the ministry of Jesus, baptism to crucifixion, which in

Luke takes place within one year. During this unique one-year period, the kingdom of God was present and Satan was absent. Luke 3:1–2 identifies the year. At 4:13, after the temptation, Satan departs. In 4:19, Jesus announces the "year of the Lord's favor," with echoes of the Old Testament year of jubilee. In 9:22–23 Luke omits the reference to Satan at Caesarea Philippi (see Mark 8:33). In 11:20 Jesus' victory over the demons means the kingdom of God is present. In 17:20, the kingdom is declared to be "in **your** midst." At 22:3, on the last night of Jesus' earthly life, Satan returns. At the Last Supper Jesus explains to his disciples that the special time of the kingdom is over, that they will carry out the church's mission under the ordinary conditions of this world's continuing history (22:35–38). The church looks backward to the time when the kingdom was manifest in the life of Jesus and forward to the end of history, when it will be manifest to all.

2. *God as the champion of the poor and oppressed.* See 1:46–55; 2:8–14, 24; 3:10–14; 4:16–21; 6:20–23; 14:21–23; 16:19–31; Acts 2:44–47; 3:6; 4:32–35; 11:27–30.

3. *Repentance and forgiveness of sins as the content of the gospel.* See 3:3; 17:3; 24:47; Acts 2:38; 5:31; 8:22, and numerous other Lukan references to "repentance," which Luke uses twenty-five times, more than any other New Testament writer.

4. *The Holy Spirit.* As the power of God at work in Israel, Jesus, and the church, the Spirit binds their history together into the story of God's mighty acts in history (there are seventy-four references to the Spirit in Luke–Acts, e.g., 1:15, 35, 41, 67; 2:25–27; 3:16; 4:1, 14, 18; 10:21; 11:13; 12:10, 12; Acts 1:2, 5, 8, 16; 2:4, 17, 38; 4:31; 5:32; 6:3; 8:17; 9:31; 10:44–45; 11:28; 13:2; 15:28; 19:2–6; 28:25).

5. *The church as good citizens.* Neither Jesus nor his followers represent a political threat to the world order; though Christians are suspected of being politically subversive and the enemy of Rome, in Luke–Acts the church takes its place in history as good citizens alongside other institutions (1:1–4; 2:1ff.; 7:1ff.; 13:31ff.; 20:20–26; 23:13–16, 47; Acts 16:35–39; 18:12–17, and the other trial scenes in Acts when Paul appears before Roman governors).

6. *God as the Lord of the whole world and history.* God is not just the one who acts in the biblical and Christian history (Luke 2:1; 3:1; 24:47; Acts 14:17; 17:24–28; 26:26). The Christian story is set by God the Creator in the context of the whole world and its history, since the church has a mission to the whole world.

Outline

For Further Reading

Craddock, Fred B. *Luke*. Interpretation: A Bible Commentary for Teaching and Preaching. Louisville, KY: Westminster/John Knox Press, 1990. Some of the material on Luke in the pages that follow has been drawn from this more expansive treatment.

Culpepper, R. Alan. "The Gospel of Luke." In *The New Interpreter's Bible*, vol. 9. Nashville: Abingdon Press, 1995.

COMMENTARY

1:1–4
PROLOGUE

Among New Testament authors, only Luke prefaces his Gospel with a statement of his intention and method. In the Gospel, only here does the reader hear the narrator's voice in the first person, which reemerges briefly in the "we passages" of Acts (see on Acts 16:10–17). The preface functions as the vestibule that leads readers into the narrative world of the Gospel, where they can see and hear the story for themselves.

Luke 1:1–4 is one elegantly constructed sentence, at the literary level of historical works written for sophisticated readers of the first century. In Luke–Acts, Christian literature begins to address people of culture and education both within and outside the church, for one dimension of the author's purpose is to show that the Christian faith is not about something "done in a corner" (Acts 26:26) but belongs to the mainstream of world history. Theophilus is representative of such anticipated readers. Except for the fact that the author's name is not mentioned, the style and format are conventional, as in the prefaces to other historical works of the Hellenistic world (see, e.g., Josephus, *Against Apion* 1.1).

1:1 An orderly account: This does not mean that he is attempting to restore the correct chronological order of the life of Jesus, for we know from the way he handles his sources that this kind of historical accuracy was not his concern

(see on 4:14–30). His purpose seems rather to present an account that shows how the events fit into God's plan for the history of salvation, a theological order, rather than historical precision. The same word is translated "step by step" in Acts 11:4. So also, Luke's purpose that Theophilus **may know the truth** deals more with theological truth than with historical fact—though Luke is not unconcerned with the latter. We get Luke's understanding of truth by studying his narrative, not by importing our own ideas of accuracy and truth.

1:3 Most excellent Theophilus: The reference to Theophilus is not a direct address as in a personal letter—Luke addresses a much wider readership—but is more like a dedication. The Greek name Theophilus was also used by Jews and means literally "friend of God." Thus some interpreters have thought Luke was using the word symbolically to indicate his narrative is addressed to all friends of God whoever they were. More likely, Theophilus is an individual member of the Greco-Roman nobility, either actual or ideal. Since "most excellent" is found elsewhere in the New Testament only as a title for Roman governors (Acts 23:26; 24:3; 26:25), it may be that Luke has in mind Roman officials who must make decisions about Christianity. The word translated **instructed** (1:4) can also mean "informed, told" (as in Acts 21:21, 24), so Luke could have in mind Jewish Christians or Roman officials who had heard certain things about the Christian faith as represented by the Gentile Pauline churches, and writes his two volumes to give such people a more accurate understanding of what the church is about. Then Luke–Acts would have an *apologetic* purpose, i.e., it intends to defend the truth of the faith against misunderstandings and attacks. On the other hand, if Luke uses the word in the sense of "instructed" (as in 18:25), Theophilus represents Christian believers seeking a deeper understanding of their own faith. Thus whether or not Luke intended the "us" of 1:1 to include the original Theophilus, it includes all present readers of the Bible and invites us into the narrative that follows, to hear it as our own story.

1:5–2:52
THE BIRTH AND CHILDHOOD OF JOHN AND JESUS

This division is a narrative unit; 3:1 begins afresh. Infancy Narrative and Birth Story are traditional titles; the unit actually stretches from the annunciation of the birth of John the Baptist through the story of the boy Jesus in the temple at age twelve. Four features of the story as a whole require attention before study of its details.

1. *Length.* The story is a substantial narrative in itself, more than 10 percent of Luke's total narrative, more than three times the length of the only other New Testament narrative of Jesus' birth (Matt. 1:18–2:23), and longer than several of the books of the New Testament. Luke does not rush his readers into the heart of the story but prepares the way, just as John prepares the way for Jesus.

2. *Style.* Even the casual reader perceives the shift in style between verses 4 and 5. Those who are steeped in the Old Testament now find themselves at home, after the sophisticated introduction in the Greek style. The stories of Zechariah and Elizabeth, Mary ("Miriam" in Greek) and Joseph, Simeon, and Anna bring to mind the stories of Abraham, Sarah, and the birth of Isaac (Gen. 18–21); Elkanah, Hannah, and the birth of Samuel (1 Sam. 1–3); and Manoah, his wife, and the birth of Samson (Judg. 13). The story reads like the rest of the Old Testament and illustrates Luke's intention to join the story of John and Jesus to the story of the mighty acts of God in the Jewish Scriptures as their climax and fulfillment.

3. *Form.* It is artfully constructed of seven sections, the first five of which are arranged in the rhetorical pattern of a chiasm (shaped like the Greek letter Chi, which looks like an English X). The separate stories of John and Jesus are brought together at the visitation, then separated again for the birth of John and Jesus. To this chiastic arrangement two scenes in the temple are appended, giving the structure shown in Figure 10.

The diagram suggests that Luke disrupted his own neat scheme in order to add two scenes in the temple, thus beginning and ending the sec-

Figure 10. Chiastic Structure of Luke 1:5–2:52

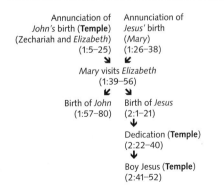

tion in the temple. The structure itself is the first indication that the Birth Story is not a prelude but an overture, not dispensable preliminaries but a Gospel in miniature that signals in advance major themes of the Gospel. One scholar has found twenty Lukan themes that are anticipated in chaps. 1–2: banquet, conversion, faith, fatherhood, grace, Jerusalem, joy, kingship, mercy, "must" (the divine necessity), poverty, prayer, prophet, salvation, Spirit, temptation, today, universalism, way, witness.

4. *Distinctiveness.* Luke tells the story in his own way, to bring out the theological meaning of the birth of Jesus. The genre is akin to Hebrew midrash, in which biblical stories were imaginatively amplified and interpreted to bring out their present meaning. It is a misdirected effort, then, to attempt to harmonize Luke's story with that of Matthew 1:18–2:23 (which is likewise midrashic storytelling, not factually accurate history). For instance, Luke's story of Jesus' birth begins in Nazareth and proceeds to Bethlehem, while Matthew's story begins in Bethlehem and moves to Nazareth. Each author has good theological reasons for telling the story this way, but their intended message is appropriated when the distinctive meaning of each is perceived, not from attempting to combine them. Not only are there no magi in Luke, and there is no room for them; there are no shepherds in Matthew, and to insert them is to disrupt Matthew's story. Where can the flight to Egypt (Matt. 2:13–21) be fitted into Luke's story? Where can the dedication in the temple (Luke 2:21–40) be inserted into Matthew's?

1:5–25
ANNUNCIATION OF JOHN'S BIRTH

John the Baptist was a Jewish apocalyptic prophet who announced the judgment soon to come (3:7–9). He had his own independent ministry of preaching and baptizing (3:1–6; John 3:22–24) and his own group of disciples (7:18) to whom he gave his own religious instructions (11:1). Luke knows that the group of John's disciples continued parallel to Jesus and his disciples, even expanding into the wider Mediterranean world after Easter (Acts 18:24–19:7). Historically, there was thus something of a competition between John's disciples and the Christian community.

Luke believes that while both John and Jesus were true prophets of God, only Jesus is the Christ, the Lord and Savior. He follows Mark by fitting John into the plan of God as the forerunner of the Messiah, the one sent by God to prepare the way. However, some of the hymns in this section may reflect the earlier view of John's own disciples that John was the forerunner of God himself (see Mal. 3:1; 4:5). Mark had already cast John in the role of Elijah, who was to prepare the way of the Messiah (Mark 9:9–13; see Mark 1:6/2 Kgs. 1:8). Luke affirms the role of forerunner for John but is hesitant to identify him with Elijah, since he also pictures Jesus in the prophetic colors of Elijah (see on 3:1–18; 7:11–17, 18–35).

1:5 King Herod: Herod the Great (37–4 BCE). Both the political and religious setting are given. The peculiarity that Jesus was born at least 4 BC is the result of an error in the centuries-later establishment of the calendar in common use today. Herod was the puppet king sponsored by the Roman Empire. This Herod ruled over all Palestine, but Luke sometimes uses **Judea** to refer to this whole territory, not only to Judea proper (see on 4:44).

1:9 Enter the sanctuary: The temple is the one central sanctuary in Jerusalem, in contrast to the local synagogues, of which there were many. The temple had been built by Solomon (tenth century BCE), destroyed by the Babylonians (586 BCE), and rebuilt after the exile (516 BCE). Thus the Judaism of Jesus' day is called Second Temple Judaism. This temple was extensively renovated by Herod and symbolized the unity of the Jewish people throughout the world and God's relationship to them and the world.

1:10–12 At the time of the incense offering: Zechariah and Elizabeth exude the atmosphere of Old Testament piety, just as they remind the reader of ancient saints who were childless but received the divine gift of children in their old age (see on 1:5–2:52 above). Zechariah is an authorized minister in the sacred temple in accord with biblical ordinances (1 Chr. 24:10). He has been chosen by lot (a way of determining the will of God, Acts 1:24–26) to offer incense within the holy place while the worshiping crowds wait outside. Most priests received this privilege only once in their lives. At this high moment, the angel **Gabriel** appears. (Angels in biblical stories are generally anonymous; the Old Testament names only Gabriel and Michael, both only in its latest book, Daniel. Jewish tradition later elaborated this into seven named archangels. The New Testament refers only to Gabriel and Michael—Luke 1:19, 26; Jude 1:9; Rev. 12:7). Angels are only one way of picturing God's communication with and care for human beings. While some biblical writers such as

Paul and John have a negative view of angelic beings and imagery (see on Rom. 8:38), Luke and Matthew use this imagery frequently to express God's presence and activity in the world.

1:13–17 The angel said to him: For the first time the reader learns that Zechariah and Elizabeth have been praying for a child. Zechariah now learns that their prayer has been heard. The child will be named **John,** and will be filled with the **Holy Spirit** even prior to his birth. Several streams of Judaism believed that God had once been active in the world by the power of the Spirit that inspired prophets and that in the eschatological times of God's victory at the end of the world the Spirit would return, but that in their own time the Spirit was absent. The announcement that John would be a Spirit-filled person was not a matter of personal spirituality, but of the eschatological gift of God, and meant that the time of fulfillment was dawning with the birth of John. Likewise, the instruction that John must **never drink wine or strong drink** is unrelated to the ethical question of the consumption of alcoholic beverages, but signifies that John will be a Nazirite (Num. 6:2–21) like Samson (Judg. 13:5–7) and Samuel (1 Sam. 1:11–22), prophetic Spirit-filled figures born of aged or barren parents, except that John shall be a Nazirite from his birth and for his whole life. No one would be able to say that John's unconventional activity and his strange words were a result of alcohol! (See Acts 2:13; Eph. 5:18.)

John will be **Elijah**-like (v. 1:17), but Luke comes just short of identifying John as Elijah (contrast Matt. 17:12–13, not found in Luke). John is to prepare a people for the coming of the Lord their God (1:17), of whom he is the forerunner. This promise sounds more like the original understanding of John's identity prevalent among his own disciples, rather than the later Christian view that John was the forerunner of the Messiah, and may reflect Luke's adoption of earlier materials. For Luke himself, John will be the forerunner of Jesus the Christ, as the following narrative makes clear (see "Three Levels of Gospel Texts," in "Introduction to the Gospels").

1:18–20 How will I know: Though Zechariah has been praying for a child, he cannot believe that it will happen without some additional evidence—though he is talking with an angel at the time! Luke has a nuanced view of how faith is generated, validated, and maintained. Here the message seems to be that even an angel telling us our prayers are heard does not necessarily result in faith (contrast the following story of Mary!). The punitive miracle for lack of faith that makes Zechariah unable to speak fits a Lukan pattern (see Acts 1:15–20; 5:1–11; 13:4–12; 19:13–16), though it is not found elsewhere in the Gospels.

1:22 He had seen a vision: Luke presents the experience as objectively real, but does not hesitate to use the word "vision" for these realities (see on 24:3, 23). He does not make the same kind of distinctions between subjective and objective reality customary among many modern thinkers.

1:26–38
ANNUNCIATION OF JESUS' BIRTH

God's initiative and surprising grace chooses a young unmarried woman from an obscure village to be the mother of the Son of God. Mary's response is that of a model believer. While in Matt. 1–2 Joseph is the primary figure, in Luke's presentation Mary and Elizabeth have the leading roles.

1:26–27 Nazareth was a small village of about fifteen hundred people in Jesus' time, mentioned nowhere in the Old Testament or other ancient writings. The village was located in the hill country of southern Galilee near the Valley of Jezreel, between the Sea of Galilee and the Mediterranean (about fifteen air miles from each), in the old tribal boundaries of Zebulun. As a young girl, Mary had been engaged to Joseph by her parents. Though she was still living with her parents, the arrangement was legal and binding; had Joseph died, Mary would be considered a widow (see also Deut. 22:23–24).

1:28–33 Greetings, favored one: Unlike Zechariah, Mary had not been praying for a child; the initiative is entirely God's. **Son of God** is used in the Bible in a variety of ways to express a special relation to God. It is used of angels and divine beings (Gen. 6; Job 1); Israel (Exod. 4:22); the Israelite king (Ps. 2:7); an especially wise or righteous person (Wis. 2:16–20); of Christian believers (Matt. 5:9; Luke 20:36; Rom. 8:14); and of Adam, who was "son of God" by creation (Luke 3:38). When Luke uses "Son of God" of Jesus, it denotes his unique nature and role as the Savior chosen and sent by God (3:22; 9:35). The story of the virginal conception is one of the ways the New Testament authors adopted to witness to their faith in Jesus as Son of God.

The New Testament has a variety of pictures that could be understood as portraying when Jesus "became" Son of God, e.g., at the resurrection (Rom. 1:3–4; Acts 13:33), the baptism (Mark 1:11 can be read this way, though see comments there), and prior to creation (Gal. 4:4; Heb. 1:1–4; see John 1:1–18). Luke does not picture the preexistence of Christ, but his birth story emphasizes that there never was a time when the earthly Jesus was not the Son of God.

The ancient world knew many stories of divine heroes begotten by the gods, but Jesus' conception is not pictured as the result of divine and human mating. Mary conceives not by sexual union with a divine being, but by the **power of the Most High** when the **Holy Spirit overshadows** her.

1:32 The throne of his ancestor David: Jesus will receive the throne of David forever. He is the fulfillment of God's promise to David (2 Sam. 7). God will deliver on the promise but in a most unexpected way: Jesus will not conquer and reign by Davidic violence but will inaugurate God's eschatological kingdom as the reign of love and justice, as the Gospel will make clear (see on Mark 10:47; 12:35–37).

1:34–38 How can this be?: See 1:18. Mary is pictured as the model disciple, the **servant of the Lord** who responds in faith (1:45) to the divine initiative. However, she too asked questions, in a way that paralleled Zechariah (who is said to disbelieve, see 1:18 and 34). Asking questions is not itself a mark of unbelief; to ask for signs is already an indication of lack of faith. Mary has a questioning faith; Zechariah wanted a sign on which to base his faith.

1:39–56
THE VISITATION

Luke brings the two story lines together (see on 1:5–2:52 above) in a poignant scene: the one woman is old, and her son will end an old era; the other is young and virgin, and her son will usher in the new. Even the unborn John knows the difference.

1:43 "The mother of my Lord": As one endowed with the prophetic Spirit, Elizabeth recognizes that Mary is pregnant and interprets the event as God's saving act. The same Holy Spirit interprets the movement of the unborn John (who likewise is already animated by the Spirit, see 1:15) as John's subordination to Jesus.

1:46–55 The Magnificat. See the Song of Hannah (1 Sam. 2:1–10). This is the first of the Lukan canticles that have become a traditional part of the church's liturgy (see Benedictus, 1:68–79; Nunc Dimittis 2:29–32). The names are derived from the first words of the Latin Vulgate version used for centuries as the standard text of the Bible in the Roman Catholic tradition. Luke's insertion of such songs does not mean that he has a verbatim report of what was spontaneously sung on these occasions, but that he has inserted traditional Jewish-Christian songs into the narrative. They have the effect not only of adding the note of joy and praise that permeates the Birth Story but also of interpreting the action somewhat in the manner of the chorus in a Greek play. The songs also slow down the action to allow the reader to ponder its meaning—just as do the characters in the story (1:65–66; 2:19, 51; see Gen. 37:11).

Mary's song emphasizes the eschatological reversal that is breaking in with the advent of John and Jesus. In a way that anticipates the blessings and woes of 6:20–26 (see there); the **proud** are brought down and the **lowly** are raised up, the **hungry** are filled and the **rich** are sent away empty. Another anticipation of an important Lukan theme is the generations-long perspective, as **all generations** will call Mary blessed, and God's mercy will endure **from generation to generation**. Luke is helping the church of the second and third generation to change its original perspective that had anticipated the soon return of Christ (see on 17:20–37; 19:11–27; 21:5–36; Acts 1:6–11).

1:57–80
BIRTH OF JOHN

The birth of John means the fulfillment of God's promise by the angel (1:13). Circumcision was practiced by several ancient societies; in Israel it was no longer a matter of hygiene or taboo but had come to signify the mark of God's covenant with Israel (Gen. 17:12; Lev. 12:3; Phil. 3:5). By circumcision and naming, John is incorporated into Israel, just as Jesus will be (2:21). Luke again emphasizes continuity. Zechariah, initially unbelieving (1:20), now obediently names John in accord with the divine plan.

1:68–79 The Benedictus. The second of Luke's inserted canticles (see on 1:46). The hymn celebrates the birth of a **mighty savior** in the **house of . . . David**, i.e., it is a song about the birth of Jesus inserted into the story of John's birth. As the **Holy Spirit** has been active in the life of Mary and Elizabeth, so also Zechariah speaks in the power of the prophetic Spirit. The same Spirit that inspired prophecy now is at work to interpret its fulfillment.

1:71 Be saved from our enemies: The song emphasizes the faithfulness of God, who had promised to save Israel from their enemies. Again, Luke emphasizes that the promises of divine deliverance are fulfilled in Jesus, without yet specifying the radically different way in which this salvation will come. The first part of the hymn, 1:68–75, pictures salvation in the traditional way, is like the Old Testament psalms, and could have been sung in Jewish and early Jewish Christian congregations. Several scholars consider 1:76–79 to be Luke's own addition, since it is thoroughly Lukan in style and content, giving two specifically Christian perspectives: (1) John will **go before the Lord** (Jesus) **to prepare his ways**, and (2) the deliverance will not be from political enemies, but from the guilt and power of sin. God is faithful in providing fulfilment for the Old Testament promises, but these promises must now be understood in the light of the fulfillment. Christ is the answer, but only to those who allow the answer to redefine the question.

1:80 The child grew: It is characteristic of Luke's schematic view of saving history that he concludes the story of John before turning to the story of Jesus (see on 3:1).

2:1–21
BIRTH OF JESUS
(See also at Matt. 1:18–25)

2:1 In those days: The story begins with a reference to the **Emperor Augustus** and **all the world**. Just as the first line of the story of John had set the narrative in the rule of Herod the Great, puppet king of Judea (1:5), so the first line of the story of Jesus' birth sets the narrative on the stage of world history (see 3:1–2). The Emperor (Caesar) Augustus was Octavian, the grand-nephew and adopted heir of Julius Caesar, born 63 BCE and confirmed by the Roman Senate as emperor in 27 BCE, when he was given the title Augustus ("august," "revered"). The title connoted not only political power but religious reverence. At the death of Herod in 4 BCE, Augustus had divided his territory and appointed his sons as rulers. Archelaus, appointed to rule Judea (see Matt. 2:19–22), was so unsatisfactory that ten years later (6 CE) Augustus made Judea into a Roman province administered directly by a Roman prefect or governor. This was the occasion for taking a census to facilitate Roman taxation.

2:2 Quirinius became governor of Syria, the Roman province to the northeast of Judea, in 6 CE, and carried out the census preliminary to the imposition of direct Roman rule of Judea. The idea that God's chosen people living in the holy land should pay tribute to a pagan government was outrageous to many Jews (see Luke 20:20–26). Militant protesters in Galilee began a violent resistance movement (see Acts 5:37) that was finally to eventuate in the armed rebellion against Rome in 66–73 and the destruction of Jerusalem and the temple in 70 CE.

Luke thus sets the story of Jesus in the context of political struggle, taxation, and the imperial and religious claims of Rome (Acts 26:26!). Luke's main point is clearly theological, but the details of his historical presentation are problematic. If Jesus was born in the days of Herod, the census or **registration** was at least ten years later, it was not of **all the world** but of Judea, and it was not Roman practice to have people return to their native towns to register. Luke, writing eighty or ninety years after the events he narrates, apparently did not have accurate historical information. The claim he makes is not dependent on the accuracy of historical detail; the issue is not the date and extent of the census, but the stand one takes in regard to whether it is the birth of Jesus or of Caesar that is *good news*, whether the title *Savior* is legitimately applied to Caesar or to Jesus (see below).

Though the story of Jesus is juxtaposed to that of Caesar, Jesus' parents do not resist the emperor's decree. One of Luke's later themes is that the Christian faith is not a political movement bent on the overthrow of Rome, that the church's talk of the kingdom of God is not a direct threat to Roman political order (see comments on 20:20–26; 23:47; Acts 18:12–16; 26:30–32; 28:30–31). Just as the unborn John had recognized Jesus' greatness (1:41–44), so the unborn Jesus is obedient to Caesar (see 20:20–26). Joseph is a descendant of David and returns to Bethlehem, David's town, to register. Unlike Matt. 2:1–6, Luke does not specify that the Christ must be born in Bethlehem in order to fulfill prophecy, but his emphasis on fulfillment of the Davidic promises suggests he is aware of that dimension of the story. In Luke the story begins in Nazareth, and the couple travel to Bethlehem in obedience to the emperor's decree. In Matt. 1–2, the story begins in Bethlehem, and the couple later move to Nazareth to fulfill the prophecy of Scripture (Matt. 2:19–23). Each way of telling the story expresses the author's faith that Jesus' birth was according to the plan of God

revealed in Scripture, but the accounts are theological confessions that are not to be harmonized historically.

2:7 Gave birth to her firstborn: Jesus is Mary's firstborn son, a term that is ambiguous in this context. Some later Christian teaching understood Mary as having remained a lifelong virgin and interpreted Luke's later references to Jesus' "brothers" (8:19–21) as meaning his near kin (e.g., cousins) or his half brothers, the sons of Joseph by a previous marriage (so the second-century *Protevangelium of James*). There is nothing unusual about the **bands of cloth** (KJV "swaddling clothes"), the normal clothing for new babies.

The later elaborations of Christian tradition are absent from Luke's story: there is neither innkeeper nor cave, nor is it clear that there was an **inn**. The word translated "inn" in KJV, NIV, NRSV, and others means basically "lodging," and may be translated "room," "guest room," or "house," as well as "inn." Its only other occurrence in the New Testament is 22:11, for the "upper room."

Three points of Lukan theology are clear:

1. In the birth story itself, Luke makes nothing of the "virgin birth," but presents the holy family as an engaged couple about to become parents. Although in Luke's perspective the birth of Jesus is the result of a miraculous conception (see on 1:26–38 above), the story of Jesus' birth itself does not reflect this view. In all of Luke or Acts, there is no reference or allusion to the virginal conception after 1:35. Except for Matthew 1:18–25, there is no other reference to the virgin birth in the rest of the New Testament. Like Matthew, Luke believed that Jesus was conceived in a unique manner, but he did not believe that this understanding was constitutive of faith in Jesus as the Son of God. To many modern readers, the unique aspect of Jesus' birth may seem to be its supernatural dimension. But in a world where there were many such stories, as well as many stories of divine beings who came directly from the heavenly world to earth, for Luke and Matthew the theologically important affirmation was that he was born at all—that he shared the vulnerability and weakness of human existence from its beginning. We may be inclined to emphasize the *virgin* birth, whether to affirm or deny it. Luke affirms the virgin *birth*. Luke affirms that the one true God is uniquely encountered in the truly human Jesus of Nazareth. For later readers, the story may witness to the "truly divine" character of

Jesus' life; for Luke, the emphasis was on the true humanity of the one who shared our life by being born, growing up, and finally dying.

2. There is "no place" for the newborn Messiah. From the very beginning, he is a displaced person for whom the world will not make a place. "No room" is not simply a matter of space—a place would have been found for Caesar or Quirinius—but a matter of the world's choice. The Jesus born in a stable will find "no vacancy" signs throughout his ministry (e.g., 4:24, 29; 9:37) and will finally be buried in a borrowed tomb (23:50–53).

3. The couple is poor (Matthew's gold, frankincense, and myrrh should not be inserted here). The child born in a stable and placed in a **manger** represents solidarity with the poor people of the earth, in dramatic contrast to the sleeping room of Caesar.

2:8 Shepherds: Both Matthew and Luke have visitors come to worship the newborn Messiah, but in Matthew the story is told as the birth of a king, the visitors are wealthy and learned visitors from the East, and the conversations take place in the palace with the scribes (Matt. 2:1–12). In Luke there is no star, there are no magi, and the announcement from heaven is made to lowly shepherds. The story of the shepherds and angels emphasizes God's affirmation of the poor and despised. In contrast to their positive image in the Old Testament, shepherds in first-century Hellenistic world were regarded as belonging to the lower class, irresponsible thieves who grazed their sheep on the land of other people, somewhat as gypsies are regarded in some countries today.

2:10–11 Good news of great joy: The angel brings good news, the gospel, the word that originally meant the victory message from the battlefield and was used in the Roman world almost as a technical term for the birth of the emperor. Once again, Jesus and Caesar are contrasted. The message is for **all people**, a Lukan theme in the story that began among the lowly of Galilee and Judea but will extend to Samaritans, Romans, and all the nations of the world (24:47; Acts 2:5–11). The **Savior** was also an honorific title often applied to the emperor; **Lord** was a designation for the emperor and for pagan gods, as well as for the God of the Old Testament. The **Christ** is the one anointed by God as the eschatological prophet, priest, and king, the fulfiller of God's promises in the Scriptures (see on 9:20; Mark 8:29). The angels thus announce the birth of

Jesus as the one who fulfills the aspirations and longings of all peoples, Jews and Gentiles, "the hopes and fears of all the years."

2:14 On earth peace: The traditional "peace on earth, good will among men" of the KJV is more correctly "peace on earth **among those whom he favors**," as found in the best ancient manuscripts of Luke, which were unavailable to the King James translators. This more correct reading testifies to Jesus' birth as the grace (unmerited favor) of God, rather than to a human quality. (The original text of no New Testament document has been preserved but must be painstakingly reconstructed from the hundreds of surviving manuscripts, no two of which are exactly alike. See " Introduction: The New Testament as the Church's Book," 4.d; commentary on Mark 16:9–20; 5:39; 8:26, 43; 10:1; 14:5; 22:19, 43–44; 23:34; John 7:53–8:1; Acts 8:37; 27:37; 1 Cor. 2:1; 14:34–35, and the footnotes throughout the NRSV and NIV.)

2:21 After eight days: This scene is parallel to that of the circumcision and naming of John the Baptist (see 1:57–79). Cf. comments at 1:57 on the significance of circumcision and naming in ancient Israel and in Luke's presentation of Jesus. This scene is not elaborated, but the next scene in the temple is given in great detail, once again showing Luke's great interest in connecting the story of Jesus to the temple.

2:22–40
PRESENTATION IN THE TEMPLE

2:22–24 The time came for their purification: Two ritual acts were required of Jewish parents: the redemption of the firstborn son and the purification of the mother. In the redemption ritual, the firstborn son was "bought back" from the Lord to whom he belonged (Exod. 13:2, 11–15; 22:29; 34:19–20; Num. 3:13). This had originally been a feature of the fertility religion of the ancient Near East. The deity who gave fertility has a claim on the firstfruits of the field, the flock, and the children. In earliest times, some cultures literally sacrificed the firstborn to the deity (see 2 Kgs. 3:27 and Gen. 22, which reflects the reinterpretation of this practice in early Israel). Luke does not elaborate on the redemption ritual in the case of Jesus but blends it into the act of purification for his mother. Luke's point is that Mary and Joseph were pious, observant Jews and that all was done **according to . . . the law of the Lord**.

The purification ceremony was for the mother, to make her ritually clean after the blood of childbirth (Luke's "their" may indicate an imprecise understanding of the ritual itself). The ritual was to take place in the temple, forty days after the birth of the son (Lev. 12:1–8). Modern readers must attempt to think themselves back into the cultic mindset of the Old Testament and early Judaism. Words such as "purification" and "cleansing" do not imply that the mother was considered dirty. Nor do such words as "defilement" have any moral connotation in such contexts ("sin offering" in Lev. 12:6 is an unfortunate translation, for the mother had not "sinned"; "purification offering" is better). There are no close modern analogies in our secularized culture, but we may think of the way "contamination" and "cleaning up" are now used with reference to radiation. In both cases it is a matter of power, of potency, and how such power is to be contained and regulated so that it does not "infect" society. After childbirth, as after menstruation, the woman was charged with the sacred, dangerous power of blood, the power of life itself. One had to undergo a purification in order to reenter ordinary society without unleashing this power in a dangerous way. Luke and his readers assumed all this, just as we assume that astronauts and workers in nuclear plants may sometimes have to be decontaminated before reentering society.

2:24 A pair of turtle doves: Luke's point is that Mary and Joseph lived according to the sacred law of Israel, with the added feature that their sacrifice was "a pair of turtledoves or two young pigeons." The law in Lev. 12:6 requires a lamb for the offering but has a "poverty clause" (12:8) that permits the offering of turtledoves or pigeons for those "who cannot afford a sheep." The one whose first sermon will announce "good news to the poor" (4:18) is here pictured as one of them, whose parents managed to get by with the religious equivalent of food stamps.

2:25 Simeon . . . Anna: In the temple they are encountered by Simeon and Anna, two aged prophets who, like the other characters in Luke's birth story, are **righteous** and **devout**. Luke characteristically presents pairs of men and women as witnesses to the saving event (Zechariah/Elizabeth [1:1–80]; Mary/Joseph [1:26–2:52]; demonized man/Simon's mother in law [4:31–39]; centurion's servant/widow's son [7:1–17]; good Samaritan/Mary and Martha [10:25–42]; the Good Shepherd who searches for the lost sheep/the woman who searches for the lost coin [15:3–10]; the persistent widow who prays/the humble publican

who prays [18:1–14]). The **Holy Spirit** brings them to Jesus and inspires them to speak. Simeon had been looking for the **consolation** of Israel, and Anna spoke to those looking for the **redemption of Jerusalem** (2:38). Both terms are from the prophecies of Isa. 40–53 that promise final salvation to God's people. This **salvation** (2:30) now appears in an unexpected way as the birth and dedication of a baby and has unexpected recipients—**all people**, both **Israel** and the **Gentiles** (2:30–32).

2:41–52
THE BOY JESUS IN THE TEMPLE

This concluding story of Luke's first section provides an opportunity to remind ourselves of the three levels to keep in mind when interpreting Gospel texts (see on 1:1–4 above).

1. The historical element is that Jesus was not a mythical or imaginary being but grew up as a boy in Nazareth within a religious Jewish family. Otherwise, the story provides a minimum of historical data. It bears the marks of composition in the post-Easter Christian community, rather than investigative reporting or the reminiscences of Mary or Jesus.

2. The story was apparently composed after Easter but prior to Luke. This story, like each of the other units of the birth story, was originally unconnected to the rest. It shows no awareness of the story of the virginal conception. **My Father's house** of v. 49 is not a "correction" of Mary's **"your father,"** as though Mary had forgotten about chap. 1. Rather, this story originally pictured the dawning of insight, in both Jesus and his parents, that Jesus is uniquely the Son of God. Already as a boy he knew that he must be **"in my Father's house"** (NIV, NRSV) or **"about my father's business"** (KJV) (the Greek phrase may be translated either way). It is one of the ways the early church projected its post-Easter faith back into its portrayal of the life of Jesus, and is thus to be understood as an expression of faith rather than a recording of historical detail.

3. In its Lukan setting, the story has three functions:

a. This story reconfirms the Jewishness of Jesus and the continuity between Judaism and Christianity. The lack of structural neatness (see diagram at 1:5–2:52 above) does not mean this story is an "afterthought," but that Luke is willing to violate his neat structural scheme in order to conclude the major section in the temple, as it began. All adult Israelite males were required to attend three pilgrimage festivals every year at the temple in Jerusalem (Passover, Pentecost, and Booths; see Exod. 23:14–17; Deut. 16:1–6). That Jesus' parents attended **every year,** including the year Jesus was **twelve years old** (just before bar mitzvah at age thirteen) shows once again that they and he were observant Jews.

b. In its Lukan setting, the story also responds to the readers' implicit question, "How should we imagine the boyhood of one who was born Son of God?" On the one hand, Luke pictures him as precociously religious, a Jewish lad who was very serious about matters of faith and his relation to God. Like other pious Jews, he prayed to God as "our Father," worshiped in the temple, and listened to those who taught there. His boyhood was *like* that of religious Jews.

On the other hand, Luke pictures his childhood as *unlike* that of "superboy" divine beings as pictured in the Hellenistic world. The later church—and perhaps already in Luke's time—was tempted to picture the boyhood of one born as Son of God as abnormal, not really human, but filled with divine power. *The Infancy Gospel of Thomas,* for instance, pictures the child Jesus as working miracles at a whim, terrorizing his playmates with his divine power, and confounding his first-grade teacher with his transcendent wisdom. In contrast, Luke pictures the boy Jesus without miracles, **increasing in wisdom, obedient** to his parents. When we compare this story with the twelve-year-olds we know, he seems very "divine." Luke's point is that if we compare him to other pictures attempting to portray him as the boy Son of God, such as those found in *The Infancy Gospel of Thomas,* he seems very human.

c. In its Lukan context, this story also has a literary function. Biographies of great figures of the Hellenistic world typically had a story of the boyhood of the hero in which his future greatness was anticipated. By including this story, Luke's narrative fits more readily into the world of the cultured readers Luke is addressing than did previous documents, such as the Gospel of Mark.

In Luke's own theological purpose, this story plays a transitional narrative role, anticipating the later life of Jesus. Just as the adult Jesus will make one trip to Jerusalem (in the Lukan narrative) to encounter the teachers in the temple and finally give his life in obedience to the Father's will, so the boy Jesus makes one trip to the temple (in Luke's account), encounters the teachers in the temple, and knows that doing the Father's will is supremely more important than family connections (14:25–33, esp. 14:26!).

Luke has also been preparing the reader, and this story serves as a literary bridge from the stories of Jesus' birth to the story of his ministry.

3:1–4:13
PREPARATION FOR JESUS' MINISTRY

At this point Luke begins to use and interpret his sources Mark and Q (see introduction to Luke). The Markan way of telling the story of Jesus' ministry was clear and direct: Jesus began his work in Galilee (Mark 1–9), made one journey to Jerusalem (Mark 10), where he disputed with the religious leaders and was executed by the Romans and was raised from the dead by God (Mark 11–16). This is different from John's way of telling the story, which is focused on Jesus' ministry in Judea, from where he makes at least three trips back and forth to Galilee. The Johannine outline involves three Passovers (hence the traditional three years of Jesus' ministry), while the Markan outline involves only one Passover and pictures Jesus' ministry as lasting one year or less.

Both Matthew and Luke adopt the Markan framework. Whatever the historical chronology may have been, for Luke it is theologically significant to portray the ministry of Jesus as one particular year (see on 4:19).

3:1–6
THE NEW BEGINNING: JOHN AS PROPHET
(See also at Matt. 3:1–6; Mark 1:2–6)

3:1–2a In the fifteenth year: As he begins this section devoted to Jesus' preparation, Luke locates this year in world and religious history with a sixfold synchronization.

Just as the story of Jesus' birth began with a reference to the Emperor Augustus (2:1), so the story that begins his ministry places it in the "fifteenth year" of the "Emperor Tiberius." Augustus died in 15 CE, so this was probably 29 CE, although there is some uncertainty about the calendar Luke used and whether he included parts of years in his calculations. Luke sets the Jesus story in the midst of world history.

When the puppet king Herod the Great died in 4 BCE, his territory was divided into four sections, and each of his sons was appointed by Rome to rule over one ("tetrarch" means "ruler of a fourth part"). **Herod** is Herod Antipas, who ruled Galilee and Perea 4 BC–39 CE, and was thus the ruler (by Rome's permission) of Jesus' home territory during Jesus' childhood and adult life. Herod's brother **Philip** ruled territories east of Galilee 4 BCE–34 CE. The identity of **Lysanias,** who ruled territories north of Galilee, is unclear. Archelaus, the son of Herod the Great appointed to rule

Judea, was so unsatisfactory that in 6 CE the Romans appointed governors to administer Judea as a Roman province. The fifth of these was **Pontius Pilate**, who governed 26–36 CE. These governors were often called procurators, since their chief responsibility was to gather Roman taxes. We now know from an inscription found at Caesarea that their official title was prefect. **The high priesthood of Annas and Caiaphas:** Only one high priest served at a time. Annas had been high priest 6–15 CE, until deposed by the Romans. He was wealthy and influential and managed to have five of his sons appointed to the office, as well as his son-in-law (according to John 18:13) **Caiaphas,** who served 18–36/37. This setting of the Gospel story is in real-world history, at the furthest pole from "once upon a time."

3:2b The word of God came to John son of Zechariah: Just as the preceding stories had breathed the atmosphere of Old Testament piety, so these words are reminiscent of the prophets of Israel (Jer. 1:1–5; Isa. 6:1; Hos. 1:1). Luke rarely refers to John as "the Baptist" (only 7:20, 33; 9:19; never in Acts). "Son of Zechariah" has an Old Testament ring. Luke wants to portray John as the last and greatest of the Old Testament prophets, a transitional figure who ushers out the old and announces the new. Thus in Luke his message of social justice (3:10–14) and his resistance to the oppressive establishment that imprisoned him for his prophetic stance (3:18–20) also cast him in the role of the prophets of Israel.

3:3 Proclaiming: John's announcement of **a baptism of repentance for the forgiveness of sins** may originally have had an antipriestly, anticultic emphasis, declaring that the expensive temple apparatus of animal sacrifice was not necessary, for God's forgiveness could be received directly by repentance and baptism. If so, John's original message of 29 CE would have fueled a populist movement against the temple hierarchy. This cannot be Luke's meaning, however (see the "three levels" of Gospel texts, commentary on 1:1–4), since Luke portrays John as from a priestly family devoted to the temple, and locates Jesus' life and ministry within the context of temple piety (see on 2:22–52). For Luke, the announcement of forgiveness of sins makes John a witness to the salvation announced in 1:76–77 that connects John to Jesus as the one who brings forgiveness.

Luke understands John's baptism from a Christian point of view, as having been commanded and authorized by God (see 7:29–30;

20:1–8), and does not ask about its historical meaning or antecedents. In later Judaism, a generation after John, we know that baptism was required of proselytes who converted to the Jewish faith. If this practice was already known in John's day, his call to repentance and baptism would have meant that even those who saw themselves as standing in the privileged community of Israel had to "start all over again" and repent if they would be members of God's people, just as was necessary for pagans. This fits John's message in 3:8.

While Luke regards John as preaching "with the spirit and power of Elijah" (1:17), he omits Mark's description of John as clothed with camel's hair and leather belt and eating locusts and wild honey (Mark 1:6; see the description of Elijah in 2 Kgs. 1:8), just as he will later omit Mark's identification of John as Elijah (Mark 9:11–13 is omitted at Luke 9:36; contrast Matt. 17:9–13, which makes the John = Elijah equation more explicit).

3:4–6 As it is written: Although Luke's extensive birth stories in 1:5–2:52 are permeated with the language and imagery of the Bible, there are no lengthy direct quotations (only the few words from Exodus and Leviticus in 2:23–24). As Luke here begins to follow the Markan story line, he adopts and adapts Mark's initial citation (see Mark 1:2–3). Luke eliminates the material from Exodus and Malachi that Mark had combined with Isaiah.

3:4 The prophet Isaiah: Isaiah (along with the Psalms) is central to Luke's theology of fulfillment. He here begins the narrative with a citation from Isaiah, has Jesus quote from Isaiah in his keynote sermon (see on 4:17–19), quotes from and alludes to Isaiah often in Luke–Acts (e.g., 7:22; 10:13–14, 18; 19:42; 20:9; 21:10, 24, 25, 35; 23:33, 34; 24:27, 46; Acts 2:39; 3:13; 4:27; 7:51; 8:23; 10:36, 38, 43; 17:29; 26:18, 23; 28:28), and brings the narrative to a conclusion by having Paul quote from Isaiah (Acts 28:26–27).

The passage from Isaiah 40:3, "In the wilderness prepare the way of the Lord," was originally an oracle celebrating God's leading the exiles back through the desert to the Jewish homeland after the Babylonian captivity, but was understood in first-century Judaism to be a promise of God's eschatological salvation. Thus the Qumran community (the people of the Dead Sea Scrolls) literally went to the wilderness, i.e., the Judean desert, to prepare the way for the Lord's final advent.

In the wilderness: Mark had already reinterpreted the oracle to apply to John's appearance in the wilderness as the forerunner of Jesus and now understood the wilderness as the location of the **voice** rather than the place where God's people were to prepare the way. Luke's further interpretation emphasizes **the way**, which will become a key image in his understanding of the Christian community (see, e.g., Acts 9:2; 18:25–26; 19:9, 23; 24:14, 22).

3:6 All flesh shall see the salvation of God: Luke extended the quotation from Isaiah beyond what he found in his Marcan source, to get to this thematic phrase central to his theology, making John an announcer of the universally inclusive dimension of Jesus' ministry from the very outset.

3:7–20
JOHN'S MESSAGE
AND THE PEOPLE'S RESPONSE
(See also at Matt. 3:7–12; Mark 1:7–8)

Luke's summary of John's message is significantly longer than that of the other Gospels. This is another indication that while Luke regards John as the forerunner of Jesus, he also wants to portray John as like the Old Testament prophets with his own independent message, the last and greatest of the prophets of Israel.

3:7–9 John said to the crowds: Of the sixty-four Greek words representing John's message, sixty-one are verbally identical in form and order with the parallel passage in Matt. 3:7b–10 (but absent from Mark), clear indication that Luke gets this material from the same written source used by Matthew (Q). John's theme is **repentance**, the fundamental aspect of one's relation to God as seen by the Old Testament prophets and first-century Judaism. The Hebrew word means basically "return" (to the covenant living to which God calls Israel), while the Greek word means "change of mind." Thus "repentance" does not signify mere grief, being sorry in a religious mood, but *a fundamental reorientation of the way one thinks about the world and life, a revolution in one's thinking that effects a change of direction in one's life.*

Even now: In John's message, like that of the biblical prophets of Israel, the motive for repentance is the coming judgment, the "day of the Lord" on which the **wrath to come** will be revealed against sinners (e.g., Isa. 2:11–22; Amos 5:18–20). Judgment is coming soon; the **ax** is already placed at the **root of the trees,** and only those who bring forth **fruits worthy of repentance** will be saved. Belonging to the "right" group, such as those who are de-

scended from **Abraham**, will not count in the final judgment, for the Creator God could make descendants of Abraham from **stones.** What counts is justice.

3:10–14 What then should we do?: (L, only in Luke.) In Luke John's message is directed to the **crowds**, i.e., the people as a whole, not only their leaders (see Matt. 3:7, "Pharisees and Sadducees"), and it is the people as a whole who respond. This brief text shows Luke's understanding of the kind of justice God calls for, the kind of justice expressed in a life of repentance (a reoriented life). All are called to share their **coats** and **food** with **anyone who has none.** Those who fit into the given social structure as **tax collectors** and **soldiers** (both employed by the Roman government) are not told to abandon their jobs or to attempt to overthrow a corrupt system, but to operate with justice and compassion within the social structure (see Luke's treatment of Cornelius, Acts 10–11). This corresponds to other efforts of second- and third-generation Christians to live out their faith in the midst of changed conditions, a faith that had originally been apocalyptic and socially radical or socially withdrawn (see on 1 Cor. 7:1–40 and 1 Pet. 2:11–3:12).

3:15 Whether he might be the Messiah: Once again Luke shows his awareness that some had regarded John himself as the final savior figure sent by God (see on 1:5–25) and that he regards John as a true prophet sent by God, but subordinate to Jesus the Messiah. This was not so clear to John's and Luke's contemporaries.

3:16–17 Holy Spirit and fire: John had originally proclaimed that the judgment of God soon to come would be carried out by an apocalyptic figure who would separate the world's present mixture of good and evil as **wheat** and **chaff.** Since in both Hebrew and Greek the same word means "wind," "breath," or "spirit," depending on the context, John's images of **wind** and **fire** probably originally reflected the scene at the threshing floor: the mixture was thrown into the air with the **winnowing fork**, the heavier grain fell back to earth, and the wind blew the chaff aside, where it was burned. When the **fire** is called **unquenchable,** the metaphor has already moved from the threshing floor to the final judgment. When the stories and message of John were reinterpreted in the Christian community (as in Mark), "wind" became "Spirit," and the distinction between wheat and chaff became the distinction between John's baptism and Jesus'. Luke has taken the reinterpretation one step further, so that for him the baptism with the Holy Spirit and fire is no longer the apocalyptic judgment, but is fulfilled in the phenomena of wind, fire, and Spirit on Pentecost (Acts 2:1–4).

3:18–20 He proclaimed the good news: John's original message of judgment has not been entirely replaced by Luke's Christian reinterpretation. Luke still lets it shine through the present narrative. It may seem strange to us that he considers this message of judgment to be **good news.** This is true not only because Luke interprets John in the light of the advent of Jesus, who brings good news, but because the future judgment of God is itself a constituent element in the gospel message. The present mixture of good and evil, the necessity to compromise with evil in order to do good, the constant choice between the lesser of two or more evils, is not the final word about the world. That God will finally sort all things out in a last judgment need not be heard as a threat but, as understood by Luke, can be liberating good news.

Shutting up John in prison: On John, Herod, and Herodias, see on Mark 6:17–18. Like his Old Testament counterparts, John's preaching of justice lands him in prison. A faithful, Spirit-filled ministry does not lead to success. This is the last time we see John in Luke's narrative. He sends a message from offstage in 7:18–21, but his death is not narrated (Luke omits Mark 6:17–29). Luke makes a crisp distinction between John, who belongs to the time of Israel, and the time of Jesus, and so removes John from the stage before beginning the story of Jesus' ministry.

3:21–22
THE BAPTISM OF JESUS
(See also at Matt. 3:13–17; Mark 1:9–11)

Luke has adopted the story of Jesus' baptism in Mark 1:9–11 (see there). For Son of God, see on 1:28–33. Luke's distinctive interpretation may be summarized in five points:

1. Luke completes the story of John before beginning the story of Jesus. Of course Luke understands, and expects the reader to understand, that Jesus was baptized by John. But Luke is concerned to tell the story of salvation as involving three distinct periods, the time of Israel, the time of Jesus, and the time of the church (see introduction to Luke). He is thus willing to complete the story of John, who belongs to the time of Israel, before beginning the story of Jesus' one-year ministry, the time of

Jesus, though this creates some awkwardness in the story line. (Contrast John 3:22–24; 4:1, where the ministries of John and Jesus overlap). We will see a similar concern at the beginning of Acts to distinguish the time of Jesus from the time of the church.

2. For some early Christians, that the Messiah had begun his ministry by being baptized by John was problematical in that it appeared to make Jesus a disciple of the Baptist (see the differing responses to this issue in Matt. 3:14–15 and John 1:32–34; 3:25–30). Some scholars have regarded Luke's separation of John and Jesus so that they never appear on the narrative stage at the same time, and thus his failure to narrate the actual baptism of Jesus, as another expression of this embarrassment. The above explanation of Luke's understanding of three distinct periods in the story of salvation is more likely, however. Moreover, from Luke's perspective, Jesus' baptism by John is not problematical but simply a part of Jesus' obedience to the will of God as revealed in the Law and the Prophets. As Jesus was circumcised and participated in the temple rituals in obedience to the Law (2:21–52), so he is baptized in obedience to the greatest of God's prophets (see 7:26–28; 16:16). In this way his baptism is an example to all believers.

3. As John's preaching had been to the people in general (3:7, 10, 15), so Jesus is only baptized after **all the people** had been baptized as an acknowledgment of the justice of God called for in John's preaching (see 7:29). While Luke cannot mean this in an absolutely literal sense, he does picture a large general response among the people to John's call to repentance and baptism, of which Jesus' own baptism is the climax. So also the baptism of Christian believers is not an individual matter between them and God but includes them in the renewed people of God (see Acts 2:41–42).

4. Only in Luke does Jesus receive the Spirit as he is **praying,** and not directly at his baptism. This points ahead to Jesus' ministry, which will be characterized by prayer at significant junctures (6:12; 9:18, 28; 22:40–46; 23:34, 46), and to the beginning of the church, when the Spirit will come upon the gathered disciples as they are praying (Acts 1:12–14; 2:1–4).

5. Only Luke emphasizes that the Spirit descends upon Jesus **in bodily form like a dove.** Luke is concerned that the Spirit be thought of not merely as subjective feelings, but in tangible ways—as on Pentecost it is accompanied by wind and fire (Acts 2:1–4). Yet, while Luke wants throughout his two volumes to help the reader

sort out the phenomena of the Spirit and claims about it in some kind of conceptual pattern, he has no rigid theological scheme into which all his stories of the work of God's Spirit must fit. He has no compulsion to explain, for instance, what it means that John the Baptist was filled with the Spirit from his prenatal period, but Jesus did not receive the Spirit until he was "about thirty" (v. 23), just as he feels no need to give a vignette from the boyhood of John to show what a Spirit-filled lad did and did not do (contrast his treatment of Jesus in 2:41–52). Luke knows that responsible talk of God and spiritual things must leave many loose ends, must neither be chaotic nonsense nor fit too neatly into a conceptual system.

3:23–38
JESUS' GENEALOGY
(See also at Matt. 1:2–17)

Only Luke refers to Jesus' age when he began his ministry, **about thirty** (see John 8:57, "not yet fifty"). While "about thirty" could suggest a young man between twenty-five and thirty-five, it was combined with the three Passovers mentioned during Jesus' ministry in John's Gospel to arrive at the tradition that Jesus was thirty-three when he was killed. Combining data from two Gospels in this way is very questionable, especially since Luke and John were not interested in biographical data about Jesus but in the theological meaning of his life and death. Luke's "about thirty" may be based on historical memory, or it may be another of Luke's ways of painting Jesus in biblical colors, since several Old Testament figures began their work at age thirty, e.g., Joseph (Gen. 41:46) and David (2 Sam. 5:4). Priests who served at the tabernacle began at age thirty (e.g., Num. 4:3), and genealogical documentation was especially important for priests. The combination of "thirty" and genealogy may indicate Luke sees Jesus as functioning in a priestly role analogous to his prophetic and kingly roles: the Messiah, the Anointed One, was God's true prophet, priest, and king (see on Mark 8:29).

Luke interrupts the narrative flow of the story to place the genealogy precisely here (contrast Matthew, who begins with it, 1:2–17). Luke's genealogy traces Jesus' lineage back to **Adam, the son of God.** "Son of God" imagery was important in the birth story (1:32, 35) and in the immediately preceding narrative of the baptism (3:22). In the next scene, the devil's first words to Jesus will refer to him as Son of God. Between these two scenes Luke places the genealogy that concludes with the term "son of God," as if to say that there is more than one way of understand-

ing the designation, but that it must *not* be understood in a way that separates Jesus from his Jewish ancestors and the Creator God.

Only Matthew and Luke portray Jesus as miraculously conceived without a human father; only Matthew and Luke include genealogies, in both cases of Joseph. It is probably too facile to say they each do it in order to show that Joseph was Jesus' legal father, and so he was legally entitled to the Davidic throne, or some such. While both Matthew and Luke are interested in presenting Jesus as the one who fulfills the biblical hopes for a Davidic ruler to establish God's final kingdom, neither thought that this was legitimized or proven genealogically. Jesus is confessed as Son of God in a sense that cannot be integrated into biology, ancient or modern. The paradoxical combination of virginal conception and genealogy of the earthly father is testimony to this mystery and a warning against explanations that reduce it to manageable proportions.

Luke's genealogy of Jesus, like that of Matt. 1:2–17, functions to fit Jesus into the broad sweep of the story of God's plan through the ages: Jesus is not a great man who appears on the stage of history as an outstanding individual, but is the climax and fulfillment of a story of which God is the director and producer. Many in the genealogy are otherwise unknown, but they played their role in the history that led to the coming of the Messiah.

Like their respective birth and infancy narratives, the genealogies of Matt. 1:2–17 and Luke 3:23–38 are not to be harmonized. Both have been constructed from traditional sources with some freedom and imagination. Matthew's is based on three cycles of fourteens (Matt. 1:17), but with only forty-one members. Luke's is constructed on a pattern of eleven cycles of seven totaling seventy-seven names between Jesus and Adam with Jesus beginning the twelfth cycle. Matthew specifies that there were forty-two generations from Abraham to Jesus, while Luke gives fifty-six generations for the same period. Both trace Jesus' lineage through David, but in Matthew it is Solomon the son of David who is Jesus' ancestor, while for Luke it is Nathan the son of David. The two genealogies diverge and reestablish contact at other points that cannot be reconciled biologically or historically. It is clear that theological confession and not biological accuracy is the concern in both cases. Significant features of Luke's genealogy are (1) the number of *priestly* names (see note above about "age thirty"), (2) the number of *tribal* names that seem to bind Jesus to "all Israel," (3) the genealogy's extension beyond

Abraham to Adam, connecting Jesus not only to Israel but to all humanity and ultimately to God.

4:1–13
THE TEMPTATION
(See also at Matt. 4:1–11; Mark 1:12–13)

Just as Israel was tested **forty** years in the **wilderness** after their deliverance at the Red Sea and before entering the promised land (Num. 10–26, esp. 14:33–34; Deut. 8:2), so the Son of God is tested for forty days after his baptism and before entering into his ministry. Israel failed the test of doing God's will, as has every other human being; Jesus overcomes the tempter as part of his messianic mission.

The **devil** appears only here as a character in Luke's story. On the language of demons, Satan, and exorcism, see excursus, "Satan, the Devil, and Demons in Biblical Theology," at Mark 5:1. The three temptations are all presented as invitations to do the greater good; there is no choosing between what is clearly good and what is clearly evil. In each case Jesus responds with biblical words from Deuteronomy—the book in which Israel's own career of testing and failure in the wilderness is documented.

4:2 For forty days he was tempted: The **wilderness** (NRSV) is better translated **desert** (NIV), the barren territory south and east of Jerusalem. The word translated **tempted** can also be translated **tested**, as in 4:13.

4:3–4 If you are the Son of God: "If" is better translated "since" or "assuming that." The devil is not challenging Jesus to question his identity proclaimed from heaven in 3:22 and established by his genealogy in 3:38, but to show by a miracle that he is Son of God. The issue is not *whether* Jesus is Son of God, but *how* he is to understand himself as God's Son, how he will exercise his ministry. After Jesus has fasted for forty days (like Moses, Deut. 9:18, and Elijah, 1 Kgs. 19:8), the devil's temptation is for him to satisfy his hunger by changing a **stone** to a **loaf of bread**. (Luke has the singular, Matt. 4:3 has the plural.) This is first and foremost a temptation to provide for his own needs by miraculous power, but in the context of the other temptations also proposes using his miraculous power to solve the social problems of the world. No one conscious of the hungry people of the world can take this temptation lightly. Like the other temptations, it presents itself as serving the greater good. Jesus' response is from Deut. 8:3. The one addressed by the devil as Son of God places himself in solidarity with human beings (the **man** of the NIV

and the **one** of NRSV in v. 4 both translate the Greek word for human being). Luke does not have the Matthean reference to living by the word of God (Matt. 4:4). The Lukan contrast is between divine and human, and Jesus here places himself among the latter.

4:5–8 Led him up: In the second temptation the devil lets Jesus **in an instant** see **all the kingdoms of the world.** Throughout the temptation story, it is the devil, not Jesus, who has miraculous power (see Matt. 7:21–23; Mark 13:22; 2 Cor. 11:13; 2 Thess. 2:9–10; Rev. 13:11–14). Only in Luke does the devil claim to have **authority** over all the nations and to be able to **give it to** one who will worship him. Luke does not dispute the reality of the claim; God is the ultimate ruler, but the present age is dominated by demonic power (see Job 1; 1 Cor. 2:6, 8; 2 Cor. 4:4). The devil claims one must acknowledge this if one wants to have power over the nations. The temptation is for Jesus to switch his allegiance from God to the realities of this-worldly power. It is not a one-time-only kneeling before the devil, but "serving him" (v. 8), i.e., adopting the values and methods of the devil-dominated world in order to gain control over it. This too is a Faustian temptation to the greater good— what good Jesus could do for the world if all its authority belonged to him! This is in fact the hope and promise of the Gospel of Luke: that the whole world will come back under the sway of its rightful sovereign, that the kingdom of God will come, and will come through Jesus (see Luke 1:32–33; 4:43; there are fifty-one references to the kingdom of God in Luke–Acts). Jesus perceives the ultimate choice involved in this temptation, and again responds with a word from Scripture, Deut. 6:13.

4:9–11 Took him to Jerusalem: Luke has rearranged the order of the temptations in his Q source from bread/temple/kingdoms (see Matt. 4:1–11) to bread/kingdoms/temple. This allows him to conclude the series in the temple, just as he had done with the birth stories (see pattern at 1:5), and corresponds to his ending the Gospel itself in Jerusalem (Luke 24). Matthew's arrangement that climactically ends on the mountain corresponds to Matthew's placing key scenes on a significant mountain (Matt. 5:1–2; 14:23; 15:29; 17:1; 18:12; 21:1; 24:3; 28:16). Each author has edited the materials to correspond to the themes he is developing. This rearrangement also fits Luke's use of Scripture in this text. In the first two temptations, Jesus responds by quoting the text of the Bible. In the final temptation, the devil himself cites Scripture in his effort to get Jesus to leap from the **pinnacle of the temple** and force God to fulfill the biblical promise of Ps. 91:11–12 that the **angels** would take care of those who trust and love God (Ps. 91:2, 14). This would also provide a public demonstration that Jesus is **Son of God**. For the third time Jesus replies from Deuteronomy (6:16), that God must not be **put . . . to the test**.

The temptations are primarily christological, i.e., at the story level they are directed to Jesus, challenging him about how he is to exercise his ministry as Son of God. At another level they are directed to the readers, challenging them as to how they think of Christ. While elsewhere Luke, like the other Gospels, expresses his faith in Jesus as the Christ by telling stories of Jesus' miraculous power, Luke also includes, as here, stories in which Jesus not only does no miracles but consider miraculous power, or the desire to have it, to be a demonic temptation (see, e.g., Luke 11:16, 29). Both images of Jesus, the powerful Son of God and the Son of God who takes his place with us humans who have no miraculous power, are vehicles of Christian faith.

This story also presents Jesus as the model for the Christian in testing and temptation. Those who, like Jesus, have been baptized and received the Holy Spirit are not immune from the assaults of Satan. Jesus' disciples too must be nourished on the text of Scripture, must affirm their identity as baptized children of God, must cultivate a trusting relationship to God that does not put him to the test and ask for miraculous exceptions to an authentic human life.

4:13 When the devil had finished every test: The devil is vanquished and departs, but only, Luke adds, **until an opportune time.** In Luke's way of telling the story, Satan will not return until the end of Jesus' ministry, 22:3 (see 22:28, 35–36, 40, 46, and often in Acts; Mark 8:33 at Luke 9:22). This is part of Luke's image of Jesus' one-year ministry as a special time when the kingdom of God was on earth, embodied in the life of Jesus, a time when Satan was absent (see the introduction to Luke and commentary on 4:20–21, 43).

4:14–9:50
JESUS' MINISTRY IN GALILEE

Luke divides Jesus' ministry into Galilee (4:14–9:50), Journey (9:51–19:27), and Jerusalem (19:28–24:53). See on 3:1–4:13.

4:14–15
INTRODUCTION TO GALILEAN MINISTRY
(See also at Matt. 4:12–17; Mark 1:14–15)

The beginning of Jesus' ministry is parallel to that of the church in Acts. Both are baptized (Acts 2:41), are filled with the Spirit (see Acts 2:1–13), teach (Acts 4:2; 5:21), and receive the acclaim of the people (Acts 2:47; 5:13). The same Spirit empowers Jesus and the church. The same God who acted in Jesus is at work in the life of the church. Just as the church is in continuity with Jesus, so Jesus is in continuity with Judaism, teaching in their **synagogues** (see on 4:16). For Luke, the ministry of Jesus is the bridge between Judaism and the universal church.

4:16–30
REJECTION IN NAZARETH
(See also at Matt. 13:53–58; Mark 6:1–6)

This scene also occurs in Mark 6:1–6 and Matt. 13:53–58, almost halfway through their narratives. Luke brings the story forward and greatly expands it to make it the keynote scene that begins Jesus' ministry, which is characterized by rejection (see on 2:7). Here we see Luke rearranging the chronology of Mark, his major source, in order to make a theological point.

4:16 Nazareth: The town (see on 1:26) had played a prominent role in the birth story as the home of Mary and Joseph (1:26; 2:4, 39, 51). Here the reader is reminded it is Jesus' hometown (see 4:23) **where he had been brought up. As was his custom.** Jesus was an observant Jew who attended the **synagogue** regularly. Synagogues were local places of Jewish worship that developed after Old Testament history was complete. The temple in Jerusalem was the one national center of Jewish worship authorized in the Bible. The **Sabbath** was Saturday, the Jewish day of worship. Christians later adopted Sunday as the sacred day of worship. Jesus has been teaching in other synagogues (4:15). Here he is invited to read the Scripture and address the congregation—another parallel to the early Christian preachers (see Acts 13:13–16).

4:18–19 The Spirit of the Lord is upon me: The text Luke pictures Jesus as reading is a combination of Isa. 61:1–2 and 58:6, omitting Isaiah's announcement of the coming day of vengeance. The reading is from the Septuagint version (the LXX), the Greek translation used in Luke's church, which differs from the Hebrew text of Isaiah translated in our English Bibles.

Anointed is the English word that means the same as "Christ" (Greek) and "Messiah"

(Hebrew). It refers to the inauguration ceremony of prophets (1 Kgs. 19:16), priests (Exod. 40:13–14; Lev. 6:20–22), and kings (1 Sam. 16:1–13) as part of their installation into office. The reference here points to Jesus as God's definitive spokesperson, the one anointed as God's eschatological prophet (see on Mark 8:29). Jesus is anointed not literally with oil, but with the Spirit, connecting this text to Jesus' baptism (3:22; see 9:20; Mark 8:29).

Luke understands this text to characterize the ministry of Jesus as a whole. It lasts one year, **the year of the Lord's favor**. The proclamation in Isa. 61 is already an interpretation of the law of the jubilee year, "you shall proclaim liberty throughout the land to all its inhabitants" (Lev. 25:10; this text is inscribed on the American Liberty Bell in Philadelphia). In Luke's theological understanding of history, the year of Jesus' ministry is a special year in God's plan. It is designated by a sixfold synchronism (3:1). This is the year that the kingdom of God was on earth, embodied in the ministry of Jesus (11:20; see the introduction to Luke on "Jesus as the 'Midst of Time'" and commentary on 4:43). It is characterized by the absence of Satan (4:13), who returns at the end of Jesus' ministry (22:3). To the question, "What do you mean by the kingdom of God," Luke points to the ministry of Jesus. The ministry of Jesus is **good news to the poor, the captives, the blind, and the oppressed**. See 1:46–55; 2:8–14, 24; 3:10–14; 4:16–21; 6:20–23; 14:21–23; 16:19–31. This ministry of Jesus is continued in the church by Jesus' disciples. See Acts 2:44–47; 3:6; 4:32–35; 11:27–30.

4:20–21 Today this Scripture has been fulfilled: "Today" refers to the time of Jesus' ministry, the time of salvation, not merely to the one day in the Nazareth synagogue. The biblical text comes from the later section of Isaiah called Third Isaiah by scholars (Isa. 56–66), written after the exile by a disciple of the original Isaiah. The text originally represented the proclamation of the Old Testament prophet, who was aware that God had called him, equipped him with the power of the Spirit to announce the advent of God's salvation (see Isa. 42:1; Mic. 3:8). In the Judaism of Jesus' day, these words were sometimes understood to refer to the eschatological prophet, God's final messenger (as in the Dead Sea Scrolls). Luke expresses the early Christian conviction that the ultimate meaning of the Old Testament is fulfilled in Jesus (see Luke 24:44–47; Acts 3:18;

see excursus, "New Testament Interpretation of the Old Testament," at 1 Cor. 15:3).

4:22 All spoke well of him: See above on 4:14–15. As is the case with Jesus' later disciples, rejection is preceded by an initially positive response (Acts 2:47; 5:13). The hometown folk are at first proud that one of their own can speak such **gracious words**. However, this Greek phrase may also be translated "words of (God's) grace." Their amazement may thus be understood as their objection that he spoke only of God's grace, omitting the words from the biblical text about God's vengeance (see Isa. 61:2). **Is not this Joseph's son?:** See 3:23.

4:23 You will quote to me this proverb: Luke's rearrangement of the Markan order has left some rough edges. The protest makes sense in the Markan context, for in Mark Jesus had already been to **Capernaum** (Mark 1:21; 2:1), but in Luke Jesus does not go to Capernaum until after his rejection in Nazareth, and as its result (4:31). **Physician, heal yourself!** (NIV): A common proverb among both Jews and Greeks; not an indication of Luke's medical interest (see 8:17–18; 9:58; 10:22; 11:9–10)

4:24 No prophet is accepted. Luke takes up the standard view of first-century Judaism that prophets are rejected in their own country (see 11:47–50; Acts 7:52). In his theology, the rejection of Jesus by Jews was the prelude to the Gentiles' acceptance, a pattern that is repeated in Acts (13:44–47; 18:6; 28:28; see Rom. 1:16; 9–11).

4:25–26 The time of Elijah (1 Kgs. 17:1–16). The Old Testament prophet was rejected in his home country but was sent by God to help a Gentile widow at **Zarephath in Sidon,** a Phoenician port city near Sidon, in modern Lebanon. **Three years and six months:** The "third year" of 1 Kgs. 18:1 has become the standard apocalyptic period of three and one-half years, as in James 5:17 (see Dan. 7:25; 12:7; Rev. 11:2, 9; 12:6, 14).

4:27 The time of the prophet Elisha (2 Kgs. 5:1–14). Even though Elisha was not rejected, God sent him to help a leprous **Syrian** soldier rather than healing those in Israel afflicted with leprosy. Both instances reflect the Lukan theme of God's acceptance of Gentiles (see Acts 10–11, also dealing with a Gentile soldier).

4:28–30 All in the synagogue were filled with rage: His "own people" are enraged (see Acts 7:58) by his references to God's mercy to Gentiles, a pattern that is repeated in Acts (see Acts 7:58; 22:17–22). Luke elaborates no miracle, nor does he comment on Jesus' courage or the power of his personal presence in walking through the midst of the hostile crowd. Luke's point is that despite hostile opposition, Jesus continues his mission in the power of the Spirit and under God's care. Again, this is a pattern repeated by Jesus' disciples in Acts (see Acts 4:1–22; 5:17–42; 12:1–17; 14:1–7, 19–20; 16:16–40; 23:1–11).

4:31–44
TEACHING AND HEALING IN CAPERNAUM
(See also at Mark 1:21–28)

Here Luke returns to his Markan source (Mark 1:21–39).

4:31 Went down to Capernaum: Jesus never returns to Nazareth after 4:30, but makes Capernaum the center of his Galilean ministry, though Capernaum also finally failed to respond (Luke 10:15). Capernaum, which means "village of Nahum," was a thriving fishing village on the northwest shore of the Sea of Galilee. The ruins of the synagogue that may still be seen there are from a building constructed much later, but recent excavations indicate that it was constructed on the foundation of a first-century synagogue, perhaps the same one in which Jesus preached.

4:32 Astounded at his teaching: Jesus teaches **with authority** (see v. 36), i.e., he does not establish the truth of his teaching by quoting the Bible, tradition, or other authorities such as the rabbis, but speaks directly as the anointed prophet of God who is also God's Son (see 3:22; 4:18–21).

4:33 Spirit of an unclean demon: Over against the Holy Spirit that empowers Jesus' ministry are the unholy spirits of the demonic world. Unclean does not refer to being dirty or unsanitary but to religious purity (see on 2:22–24). Luke pictures the power of evil that invades and dominates human life in personal terms but shows that Jesus has power to deliver from it. Exorcisms are a central feature in the Lukan picture of Jesus and his disciples, closely associated with the kingdom of God (see 4:41; 8:2, 27; 9:1, 42, 49; 10:17; 11:14–20; 13:32). On the language of demons, Satan, and exorcism, see excursus, "Satan, the Devil, and Demons in Biblical Theology," at Mark 5:1.

4:34 What have you to do with us?: This traditional formula (Judg. 11:12; 1 Kgs. 17:18; 2 Kgs. 3:13; 2 Chr. 35:21; 1 Esd. 1:24; Mark 5:24; Luke 8:28; John 2:4) indicates that the demons and Jesus belong to two different realms that were supposed to remain separate. **I know who you are:** The demons recognize Jesus' true identity, though the people in the story do not (yet).

Holy One is a title originally applied to God (see, e.g., 1 Sam. 2:2; 2 Kgs. 19:22; Job 6:10; Ps. 71:22; Isa. 1:4) that in the New Testament becomes a christological title (Mark 1:24; John 6:69; Acts 2:27; 13:35; 1 John 2:20; Rev. 3:7; 16:5).

4:35 Be silent. The demons are not to disclose Jesus' identity. This secrecy motif is adopted from Mark, where it plays a key role. In Luke's own way of presenting the story, Jesus' identity is known by his family, his disciples, and others. Yet Luke also preserves the dimension emphasized by Mark, that Jesus' identity as Christ, Lord, and Savior was not really recognized and understood until after the story was over, on the basis of the resurrection and the gift of the Spirit (see 24:13–49).

4:36 They were all amazed: Jesus' **authority** is not only a matter of teaching (v. 32) but includes power to deliver from the demonic powers that destroy lives. The crowds are impressed but do not understand (see 5:1, 15; 6:17–19; 7:11; 8:4; 9:11, 18, 37; 11:14; 14:25; 19:48; 20:19; 22:6, 47; 23:4, 13, 21, 48). Earlier in this chapter, Jesus' hometown folk did understand his claim and rejected it. Here they see his mighty words but do not understand his true identity or the nature of his claim. This is Luke's way of saying that coming to faith in Jesus and a true understanding of his identity is not merely a matter of evidence.

4:38 Simon's house: Simon will be called to become a disciple (5:1–11) and will be renamed "Peter" (6:8). In the Lukan chronology this has not yet occurred (contrast Mark 1:16–20; Matt. 4:18–22; John 1:35–42). The tourist to Capernaum may today view the excavated ruins of a house near the synagogue that was already revered in the second century as the house of Simon Peter and may indeed have been the exact location where this event occurred.

4:39 Rebuked: This is the same word as 4:35 with reference to the demon. The **fever** is in the same category as the demonic power; Jesus delivers from both. Though Jesus heals on the Sabbath, there is no protest here (contrast 6:1, 6–9; 13:10–16). The woman is not only healed but set free to serve. In Mark **them** referred to Jesus' disciples, not yet mentioned in Luke.

4:40–41 As the sun was setting: In the Jewish calendar, Sabbath begins and ends at sundown. The long list of Sabbath prohibitions included journeys, carrying, and healing (except in life-threatening emergencies). At sundown people were free to move about. **Diseases . . . demons:** Again Luke lumps these together as the powers that threaten life; God's power at work in Jesus is their master. **Son of God:** See on 1:28–33. **Messiah:** The same as "Christ" and "anointed." See on 4:20–21; 9:20; Mark 8:29. Although each of these titles, like "Holy One of God" in 4:34, has its own particular nuance, Luke uses them interchangeably to refer to the role of Jesus in God's saving plan (see 23:67–70). (See excursus, "Interpreting the Miracle Stories," at Matt. 9:35.)

4:42 At daybreak he departed: In Mark 1:35 Jesus seeks solitude to pray. Luke, who usually emphasizes the image of Jesus at prayer (3:21; 5:16; 9:18; 11:1; 22:32, 41; 23:34, 46), omits the reference here (but see 5:16). In Mark 1:36 it was Simon and the disciples who seek Jesus out. Here it is the crowds, who try to get the Jesus who heals and exorcises demons to stay with them (contrast 8:37).

4:43–44 For I was sent for this purpose: Jesus refuses to settle down and let people come to him. He represents the mission of God to the whole world (see 24:44–49; Acts 1:8) and is a model for the later church, which must not settle down and try to attract the world, but is always en route in carrying out its mission to the world (24:47–48). **Judea:** This seems out of place in a Galilean context and may indicate Luke's inaccurate knowledge of Palestinian geography. That some manuscripts have "Galilee" here shows already the ancient scribes perceived it as a problem. Luke seems to use Judea loosely to designate Jewish territory as a whole, i.e., Palestine (1:5; 6:17; 7:17; 23:5; Acts 10:37).

EXCURSUS:
THE KINGDOM OF GOD IN LUKE

For the first time Luke directly mentions the kingdom of God. Luke has waited until he has given some sample pictures of Jesus' message and ministry before introducing the term (contrast Mark 1:15; Matt. 4:17). The following notes are important for understanding this phrase in Luke–Acts:

1. The phrase is central in Luke's understanding of Jesus' life and message, with forty-seven references to the kingdom of God in Luke–Acts.

2. "Kingdom of God" means the same as Matthew's "kingdom of heaven" (cf., e.g., Matt. 5:3 and Luke 6:20). Matthew is the only biblical author to use "kingdom of heaven," in which "heaven" is a common Jewish reverential way of avoiding the word "God." "Heaven" in this phrase does not refer to a place but to a person. "Kingdom" in both phrases refers not to a place but to an action. The "kingdom of God" = "kingdom of heaven" refers to God's ruling, God's

assertion of kingly power over creation. In the Lord's Prayer, "Your kingdom come. Your will be done" (Matt. 6:10) is two ways of saying the same thing. Christians pray for something to happen, not for a place. "Strive first for the kingdom of God and his righteousness" (Matt. 6:33) means to strive for the righteous will of God to happen, not to strive for a certain place.

3. In first-century Judaism that forms the background and context for the New Testament, kingdom of God was understood in a threefold perspective:

a. *The eternal rule of God*, independent of all human action. God is always the Creator and ruler of the universe, and there is no other power that can ultimately resist God's rule. See Ps. 103:19 "The LORD has established his throne in the heavens, and his kingdom rules over all"; Ps. 145:13 "Your kingdom is an everlasting kingdom, and your dominion endures throughout all generations." God is already king de jure ("by rights," "in principle"), but not de facto, since rebellious humanity has rejected God's kingship.

b. *The present rule of God* in the individual lives of those who are obedient to God. Rabbis spoke of "taking upon oneself the yoke of the kingdom," i.e., submitting oneself to God's rule, especially as symbolized in the daily recitation of the Shema (Deut. 6:4). God's kingdom is present in the midst of a rebellious world as faithful members of God's covenant people obey God's will revealed in the Law.

c. *The future rule of God*. The present rebellious state of the world is not the last word. God will reestablish his kingdom over the whole creation, bringing the world and history as we know it to an end and restoring the creation to its unity under God's sovereignty. In Judaism this future dimension of the kingdom of God was thought of in a number of ways. One such apocalyptic vision of the coming kingdom is found in a Jewish document contemporary with Luke, the *Testament of Moses*:

> Then his kingdom will appear throughout
>   his whole creation.
> Then the devil will have an end.
> Yea, sorrow will be led away with him.
> Then will be filled the hands of the messenger,
>   who is in the highest place appointed.
> Yea, he will at once avenge them of their
>   enemies.
> For the Heavenly One will arise from his
>   kingly throne.
> Yea, he will go forth from his holy habitation
>   with indignation and wrath on behalf
>   of his sons.

And the earth will tremble, even to its ends
   shall it be shaken.
And the high mountains will be made low.
Yea, they will be shaken, as enclosed
   valleys will they fall.
The sun will not give light.
And in darkness the horns of the moon will
   flee.
Yea, they will be broken in pieces.
It will be turned wholly into blood.
Yea, even the circle of the stars will be
   thrown into disarray.
And the sea all the way to the abyss will retire,
   to the sources of waters which fail.
Yea, the rivers will vanish away.
For God the Most High will surge forth,
   the Eternal One alone.

Sometimes the future coming of the kingdom involved a Messiah that God would anoint from this world; sometimes it involved the coming of a heavenly figure such as the Son of Man (see on Mark 2:10); sometimes God is pictured as coming directly to establish his kingdom.

The future coming of the kingdom of God was an object of daily prayer. The Kaddish, which probably was already part of the synagogue liturgy in the first century, expresses this hope: "Magnified and sanctified be his great name in the world which he hath created according to his will. May he establish his kingdom during your life and during your days, and during the life of all the house of Israel, even speedily and at a near time."

4. In the Gospel of Mark, a source used by Luke, there are no clear references to the kingdom as already present in Jesus' ministry and the life of the church; hope is oriented toward the future coming of God's kingdom at the Parousia of Jesus (see Mark 1:15; 9:1; 14:25; 15:43). In Q, the other main source of Luke, the kingdom is primarily future (11:2; 19:12; 22:30), though it is also in some sense present (11:20). Luke clearly adopts both of these views. The Jesus who speaks in the Gospel of Luke presents the kingdom as an already/not yet reality. God's rule is present in Jesus' message and ministry, especially in his exorcisms, but it is to come in power in the future.

5. For Luke, the kingdom of God was present on earth in the ministry of Jesus, when God did indeed rule (see on 4:20–21; 11:20). But when Jesus ascended, the kingdom of God was no longer present in this world. The church lives in *hope* of the final coming of the kingdom and knows that it is not a utopian dream because God's kingdom *has appeared* in this world in the life of Jesus. The church *preaches* the kingdom, but in

Acts does not consider itself to *be* God's kingdom in this world. Although some later Christian theologians understood the church to be the earthly manifestation of the kingdom of God, Luke does not identify kingdom and church. Nor does he speak of the kingdom as being "in people's hearts" or talk of our "building the kingdom." In Luke's view, the good news of the kingdom is that it has appeared in the Christ event and will reappear when God brings history to a worthy conclusion. In the meantime, the church is to live by the revelation of the kingdom that has already appeared in Christ, to witness in word and deed to the reality of God's kingdom manifest in the life of Jesus, and to pray for and proclaim the coming triumph of God's rule at the end of history. In Luke's view the church is not the kingdom of God but preaches the kingdom of God, that is, the church proclaims in word and deed that the Christ, the anointed king in the kingdom of God, has come (see on 9:20; Mark 8:29). The church proclaims that Christ has ascended and will return (Acts 1:6–11), that is, that the kingdom of God will be fulfilled at the end of history. The church lives in the tension-filled period between the time of the kingdom on earth in the life and ministry of Jesus and the fulfillment of the kingdom at the end of history. The time of the church is not a parenthesis in God's purpose, but the time of witness, in word and deed, to God's act in Christ and the fulfillment of God's purpose at the end of history.

5:1–6:16
CALLING AND TRAINING DISCIPLES

For the structure of this section, see on 6:12.

5:1–11
Calling the Fishermen to Be Disciples
(See also at Matt. 4:18–22; Mark 1:16–20; see Matt. 13:1–3; Mark 4:1–2; John 21:1–25)

5:1–3 Lake of Gennesaret: Same as the Sea of Galilee in Mark 1:16 and elsewhere. Luke, a world traveler, avoids calling the small body of water in Galilee a "sea." Luke takes the setting from a different story in Mark 4:1–2 (see Luke 8:4, where the Markan setting is accordingly omitted). The chronological connection to the context is loose and vague (see also 5:12, 5:17). Luke has arranged the section 5:1–6:16 to begin with the call of disciples and to end with listing the Twelve.

5:3 Simon: This is the first reference to Simon, who will be renamed Peter ("Rock"; see Matt. 16:16–19). Unlike Mark and Matthew, he has delayed this scene until he has pictured Jesus as already preaching, healing, and manifesting the kingdom of God.

5:4–7 Let down your nets: See the similar story in John 21:1–14, in a post-Easter setting, and contrast the pre-Easter call stories in Matt. 4:18–22 and Mark 1:16–20. All versions of the story may go back to a common source, which the Synoptics have placed in the framework of the life of Jesus as the original call of the disciples, and John has placed in a post-Easter framework. That Luke is more like John than like the other Synoptics shows the fluidity in early Christianity between the earthly life of Jesus and stories of the risen Lord. All the earthly stories were retold from the post-Easter perspective of faith in the risen Christ; some post-Easter insights of the church were retrojected into the pre-Easter story of Jesus' life. (See excursus, "Interpreting the Miracle Stories," at Matt. 9:35).

5:6 So many fish: In John 21:11 there are 153. Here the extravagant catch almost sinks two large boats. That Peter and the other experienced fishermen have never seen such a large catch (5:9) shows that Luke pictures a miracle of eschatological extravagance (like John's picture of Jesus' changing water to 180 gallons of wine at the wedding feast, John 2:1–11). The picture modulates into the later image of Peter and the other apostles as evangelists who bring thousands to Christ (see Acts 2:37–41; 4:4; 21:20).

5:8 I am a sinful man: See Isa. 6:5. The story is similar to the call of Old Testament prophets. If originally a post-Easter story, Peter here remembers his denials of Jesus (see Luke 22:54–62).

5:10 You will be catching people: Calling disciples to be fishers for people is not a metaphor constructed on the spur of the moment. In Jer. 16:16 God calls for workers to participate in gathering people for judgment. In the first-century Hellenistic world, the gods and philosophers were pictured as fishers who catch people for divine service.

The call is directed to **Peter** alone (the "you" is singular), who is the first disciple called and who will regather the disciples after their failure at the crucifixion, reconstitute them as a community, and be the first leader of the church (Luke 22:31–32; Acts 1–12, 15). The focus on Peter, in the context of a miraculous event, makes the call of Peter more parallel to that of **Paul** in Acts (see list of parallels at Acts 28:31).

5:11 They left everything: The mark of a true disciple, referring to James and John, not just

Peter. Andrew is mentioned in Luke–Acts only in Luke 6:14 and Acts 1:13 (contrast Matt. 4:18; Mark 1:16, 29; 3:18; 13:3).

5:12–16
Cleansing a Leper
(See also at Matt. 8:1–4; Mark 1:40–45)

For the structure of this section, see on 6:12.

5:12 Leprosy: In the Bible, leprosy refers not mainly to Hansen's disease but to a variety of skin conditions. Details of the Israelite and Jewish understanding are given in Lev. 13–14. Even houses could be afflicted with leprosy. **In one of the cities:** According to Lev. 13:45–46, lepers are to live outside the community. Either this regulation was not in force, or Luke was unaware of it, or the leper had courageously violated the biblical rule. **Clean:** Ritually; see on 4:33. Social ostracization was the burdensome consequence of leprosy, somewhat like the manner in which AIDS today is regarded as having a social, religious, and moral stigma.

5:13 Jesus touched him: See 7:39; 8:44–47; 18:15; 22:51; 24:39. In Luke, only Jesus touches people, and his touch heals and cleanses. Luke may here intend the reader to understand that Jesus took the man's uncleanness on himself, sharing his ritual defilement and so having to withdraw to deserted places as lepers were supposed to do (5:16). Alternatively, Luke may understand that by touching the man Jesus communicated his own holiness to him (see 1 Cor. 7:14; Matt. 23:17). **Immediately:** Jesus' cures are portrayed as miraculous, not as psychosomatic suggestion. (See excursus, "Interpreting the Miracle Stories," at Matt. 9:35.)

5:14 Tell no one: Not reverse psychology, but an aspect of the messianic secret, adapted from Mark (see 4:35). **As Moses commanded:** Though Jesus had touched the man in violation of the Law, he also is pictured as affirming the Law. Luke's portrayal of Jesus' relation to the Old Testament regulations is complex but positive (see on 2:22–24).

5:16 Withdraw to . . . pray: See on 3:21–22. Though Jesus heals by the power of God, he is himself dependent on God.

5:17–26
Healing and Forgiving a Paralytic
(See also at Matt. 9:1–8; Mark 2:1–12)

For the structure of this section, see on 6:12. The unit 5:17–26 is itself a combination of two smaller stories, a healing story and a pronouncement story about forgiveness. The story-within-a-story combination had already been made in

Mark, a characteristic feature of Mark's literary style (see Mark 2:1–12; 3:22–30; 5:21–43; 6:14–29; 11:12–25; 14:1–11).

5:17 Pharisees: Their first appearance in Luke (27x Luke/9x Acts). Pharisees were lay (as opposed to priestly) leaders of the synagogue (as opposed to the temple). They were nonprofessional students of the Law, advocates of the oral tradition as the authorized interpretation and application of the Law, and considered it to have been revealed on Sinai along with the written Law. They accepted the "modern" ideas of demons, angels, and the resurrection (ideas not in the Pentateuch but only in the later strata of the Old Testament and in some streams of Judaism developing in the first century CE). They emphasized living an authentic, holy life, applying to all Israel the strict rules given only to priests in the Old Testament, on the basis that Israel as a whole was a priestly community, that all Israelites were priests (Exod. 19:6). Since the Pharisees were often the opponents of early Christianity, they mostly receive a bad press in early Christian documents, including the New Testament, but for the most part the historical Pharisees (as opposed to the literary figures of the New Testament) were sincere, serious advocates of the divine law, ethics, and the mission of Israel as a holy people among the nations. They were widely respected among the people and were themselves critical of hypocrisy in their ranks. They last appear in Luke in 19:39, i.e., they do not participate in the arrest, trial, and crucifixion of Jesus. Luke portrays them as sometimes friendly to Jesus (e.g., 7:36–39; 13:31; see Acts 5:33–39; 23:6–8) and sometimes hostile; Jesus can also denounce them as sometimes hostile to authentic religion (11:37–54). Here it is not clear whether they come to hear Jesus or only to investigate him.

5:18 Some men: Luke omits (or assumes) the Markan detail that the paralyzed man was carried by four. **Bed** (NRSV) or **mat** (NIV) refers to the stretcher on which the man was carried. Luke changes Mark's coarse military word, which might be translated "bunk" or "bedroll."

5:19 Roof . . . tiles: Luke adapts Mark's picture of a rough peasant house roofed with thatch and mud (Mark 2:4, literally "dug through the roof") to his more affluent Hellenistic environment and pictures a house with a tile roof. Tiles are removed and the man is let down through the opening.

5:20 Saw their faith: The courageous persistence of those who carried the invalid is here called

"faith" (see the presence of the leper in the preceding story, 5:12, who was in the city though he was supposed to "dwell alone" outside the gates; see persistence-as-faith in 8:48; 11:5–8; 18:1–8). Faith is not merely subjective but manifest in tangible behavior. No reference is made to the paralytic's faith or lack of it. **Friend** (literally "man," "human being," as in 12:14; 22:58). **Your sins are forgiven you:** The man had not been brought for forgiveness but for healing. There is no indication that the man was any more sinful than others. The story pictures the condition of human beings as such, all of whom stand in need of God's forgiveness but are powerless to effect it themselves (see on 11:4, 13). Thus this story, like the miracle stories generally, is a "gospel in miniature," presenting the meaning of the whole Christ event in the form of a single story from the life of Jesus. To be separated from God by sin is more fundamentally the human problem than any physical affliction, but the man recognizes his own real need only in retrospect in the light of the divine response to his need. The perfect passive grammatical form ("are forgiven") points to an act of God. Jesus is not claiming to be God but announces God's forgiveness. To speak for God is the role of a prophet such as John the Baptist, who also mediated God's forgiveness (1:77; 3:3).

5:21 Blasphemies: This is the first of a series of Jesus' conflicts with the religious authorities. The series of controversies extends through 6:11 and concerns Jesus' adherence to the Law of Moses as interpreted by the Pharisees. Blasphemy, understood as profaning the divine name or dishonoring God's glory, is punishable by death in Lev. 24:10–16. The scribes and Pharisees regard Jesus' pronouncement as a claim to assume the role of God. In Luke's time (though not in Jesus'), Jewish leaders understood Christian claims made for Jesus to compromise the monotheistic faith of the Bible and Judaism. In the Lukan narrative of Jesus' trial, in contrast to Matt. 26:65 and Mark 14:64, the charge of blasphemy does not play a role.

5:22 In your hearts: In the Markan source, the question had been silent; in Luke, it appears to be vocal (5:21 vs. Mark 2:6–8). Here, Luke retains the Markan picture; the question is in their hearts, whether silent or vocal. In Luke 6:8, Luke adds "he knew their thoughts" to the Markan account.

5:23 Which is easier?: Jesus' question contains an (intentional?) ambiguity. On the one hand, it is easier to *say*, "**Your sins are forgiven**," than to *say,* "**Stand up and walk,**" for the validity of the latter statement can be immediately determined but not that of the former. On the other hand, in terms of what really happens, it is easier to heal people—for other human healers do this—than to make God's forgiveness effective, for this is a divine act.

5:24–26 The Son of Man: See on Mark 2:10. **I say to you:** Here, the title Son of Man designates Jesus as the one who acts with God's authority to forgive sins. Jesus does not pray for God to heal the person but acts on his own divine authority (see 5:13 in the preceding story). The man was healed **immediately**—not a matter of psychosomatic suggestion but of God's power.

He went to his home, glorifying God . . . all of them . . . glorified God: Luke has doubled the single reference in Mark 2:12, emphasizing that the charge of defamation of God ("blasphemy") has been reversed: all see that Jesus' acts bring glory to God. Luke's christological focus does not compete with his theocentric emphasis (see 7:16; 8:24, 38; 9:20–22, 43; 13:13; 17:15; 19:37). The Pharisees misunderstand when they suppose that exalted claims for Jesus' status and function detract from the majesty of the one God. (See excursus, "Interpreting the Miracle Stories," at Matt. 9:35.)

5:27–39
Calling Levi, Party at His House, Question about Fasting
(See also at Matt. 9:9–17; Mark 2:13–22)

For the structure of this section, see on 6:12.

5:27 Tax collector: The same as "publicans" in earlier translations. Galilee had its own puppet king, but the Romans actually ruled. The taxes were exploitative and went to a foreign government. Those who collected them were often considered traitors. They purchased the right to collect taxes in advance and were thus widely suspected of overcharging to make the most of their investment. They were also resented because of their wealth, extracted from their poorer and more patriotic neighbors. They were not welcome at the synagogue, and were considered ritually unclean by the more pious because of their association with Gentiles. **Levi:** Thus an unlikely candidate for discipleship.

Follow me: Jesus takes the initiative. Jesus calls; Levi does not apply. Jesus does not present a teaching or set of principles, but himself as the one to be followed. He does not explain why Levi should respond or tell him where he

is going. Levi will learn along the way. The scene is another minigospel (see on 5:20 above) in which the gracious call of God extended by the Christian community to become disciples is compressed into this one symbolic scene from the life of Jesus. The call is sheer grace; Levi has no credentials or qualifications. The identity of this Levi is unclear, since no person by that name appears in the list of the Twelve in 6:14–16 or Acts 1:13. Since Matt. 9:9–17 tells an identical story about a tax collector named Matthew, it has often been thought that the one disciple had two names, but there is no basis for this in the text of Luke. Luke (and Mark, whom he is here following) may be drawing some analogy to the Old Testament, where the tribe of Levi was not considered to be among the twelve tribes but a special category (see, e.g., Num. 1:49; Deut. 10:8).

5:28 He got up: The same word used in 5:25 of the paralyzed man, related to the Greek word for "resurrection." **Left everything:** In Luke, Jesus' disciples abandon earthly possessions. Levi's response is taken as a model of responding to Christ's call. Though the Lukan Jesus' emphasis on renouncing one's possessions reverberates in this scene (e.g., 12:13–34; 18:28–30; Acts 2:44–45; 4:32–35), the following scene shows the call is to make a radical break with the old life and its values, not literally to walk away from all his assets and property.

5:29 A great banquet: Table scenes play an important role in Luke (5:29–39; 7:36–50; 11:37–54; 14:1–24; 22:14–38; 24:30–32; 24:36–49) and provide the context for understanding the mealtimes of the early church (Acts 2:42, 46; 6:1; 11:3; 16:34; 27:35).

5:30–32 The Pharisees and their scribes were complaining: On Pharisees, see on 5:17 (the NIV term "sect" is not in the Greek text). That the complaint is made to the **disciples** rather than Jesus himself suggests that the scene reflects the post-Easter life of the church, when Jesus' disciples were criticized for relaxing Jewish purity rules and having table fellowship with those previously thought to be unclean (see especially Acts 10–11; 15). The Pharisees believed that the way to be faithful to God's commission to be a light to the nations (Isa. 42:6) was to maintain the Law strictly, which involved not associating with those who might communicate impurity. In particular, it was important what one ate and with whom. This was not mere bigotry, but being faithful to the biblical dietary laws. Jesus spoke and acted with an authority that transcended even the biblical laws. There is an ambiguity in identifying who is **well** and who is **sick**, who are **sinners** and who are **righteous**. The Pharisees assumed they were the healthy and the righteous. Jesus challenges this assumption and declares that his mission is, like that of a good physician, to go to those who (know that they) need him.

5:33 John's disciples: John the Baptist is pictured in Luke–Acts as the forerunner of Jesus Christ, the last and greatest of the Jewish prophets (1:5–24, 57–80; 7:18–35). One would therefore expect that when Jesus appeared, John would have instructed his disciples to join the group of Jesus' disciples. But alongside his Christian interpretation of John, which fitted him into the Christian understanding of God's plan for history, Luke acknowledges the historical reality that John continued to have his own disciples who did not become followers of Jesus—though Luke believes they should do so (7:18; 11:1; Acts 19:1–7).

Fast and pray: Jesus responds only with regard to fasting, a practice found in many religions including Judaism and Christianity, in which the adherents abstain from food and/or drink for a definite time as a matter of religious devotion, in order to discipline their bodies and devote themselves to prayer. John and his disciples were ascetics who practiced fasting. John was a Nazarite who drank no wine and disdained the pleasures of civilization (1:15, 80; 7:33). He could thus pronounce judgment on the evils of society without being accused of participating in them and benefiting from them himself (3:7–17). This is another form of the purity mode of trying to do the will of God and prepare the way for God's kingdom. This is another form of what the **Pharisees** also attempted (5:30).

5:34 Wedding: Jesus did not stand aloof, but participated in society, rubbing elbows with its sinners. He declared that his own time was a special time, like a wedding, when celebration was appropriate (see on 4:13, 20–21). Prior to the special year of Jesus' ministry, godly people appropriately fasted (2:37). After the ministry of Jesus was over, the church would find it appropriate to fast at particular times (Acts 13:2–3; 14:23). Even during the special time of Jesus, those who did not recognize it as the time of the kingdom of God on earth (see on 4:13, 20–21, 43–44; 11:20; 17:21) will continue to fast. Not only the Pharisees, but the disciples of John did this. But the presence of Jesus signifies the presence of the kingdom of God, to which the appropriate response is celebration rather than fasting.

5:36–38 Parable: Here, a striking proverb (see Mark 3:22). The presence of the kingdom means the presence of that which is radically **new**. This newness is not relative, newer vs. older, but represents the absolute newness of God's reign, like the new covenant (Jer. 31:31–34; Luke 22:20 [1 Cor. 11:25]; Mark 14:24), the new creation (2 Cor. 5:17), or the new Jerusalem (Rev. 3:12; 21:2). That which Jesus brings is not a "new and improved version" of the old, a patching up of the old by tearing **a piece from a new garment** and sewing it on the old one, but an absolute renewal. Luke's version of the saying makes a slightly different point than his source, Mark 2:21. Luke emphasizes that trying to patch up the old with pieces from the new results in the destruction of the new. (In Mark, the result was a worse tear in the old.) In both versions of the saying, the point is that the newness of the kingdom of God calls for new forms; **new wine must be put into fresh wineskins**.

5:39 The old is better: It is striking to find this affirmation of the old embedded in a context that celebrates the new. Since it is not found in all manuscripts, it may be even be a post-Lukan addition (see NRSV footnote), as some scribe added a traditional proverb to the context (it is a truism that old wine is better than new). On the other hand, Luke may have added this saying to the Markan context he has been following (the saying is found only in Luke), and some scribes found it so problematical that it was omitted. If it is original, as is likely, it might be understood as Luke's ironic comment, the negative response of those who reject the newness brought by Christ. In Luke's view, one cannot measure the radical newness Jesus brings by the old standards; it must be measured by itself and allowed to create new forms for itself. Otherwise, one will always be locked into the old and never able to appreciate the newness Christ brings. This was the decision forced by the ministry of Jesus, then and now, and the struggle to come to terms with it is recorded by Luke in Acts 1–15. On the other hand, Luke may intend it in a positive sense as his own correction to what he saw as a superficial tendency to always prefer the new. He understands that the newness Christ brings is in fact a reaffirmation of the original will of God. It is the Pharisees who have introduced "new" departures from God's will; the newness

Jesus' brings is not innovation but reclaiming the ancient word and will of God. Throughout his two-volume work, Luke emphasizes that the new Christian faith is in reality the affirmation, continuation, and fulfillment of the old (see chaps. 1–2; Acts 17:21; 24:14; 26:6, 22). Luke's affirmation of old and new, the witness of Scripture and tradition to what God has done in the past and the experience of the new work of God in the present through the Holy Spirit, is not a simple "either/or."

6:1–11
Debating the Sabbath
(See also at Matt. 12:1–14; Mark 2:23–3:6)

For the structure of this section, see on 6:12.

6:1 Sabbath: See also 4:16, 39–41. The biblical and Jewish holy day was considered sacred, the violation of which was extremely serious (see Exod. 20:8; 31:14–15; Lev. 23:23; Num. 15:32–36; Deut. 5:12–14; Isa. 56:2, 6; 58:13). Jewish soldiers had died rather than violate the Sabbath (1 Macc. 2:29–41). The Sabbath was not considered a burdensome obligation but a joyous day of rest and worship, a memorial of God's rest at creation (Gen. 2:2–3) and of the liberation from Egyptian slavery (Deut. 5:15). The Sabbath day was a festive day of rest from labor, a day of eating and drinking on which it was forbidden to fast. From the beginning (Deut. 5:14–15) there had been an element of social justice expressed in the law, for servants and slaves received a much-needed rest of which they could not be deprived, and the poor and hungry joined in the eating and drinking.

One who wanted to honor God must obey the biblical law and refrain from work on the Sabbath. But what constituted "work"? In order to observe the commandment at all, one had to have an interpretation of the biblical command. The issue in this scene was not whether one would accept the text of the Bible (Jesus) or "human interpretations" (the Pharisees), but whose interpretation was legitimate. Interpretation is not the optional extra that one may add on (or not) to the text of Scripture; it is the vehicle that lets Scripture be operative as word of God. **Plucked . . . grain . . . rubbed . . . ate.** The violation was not that of private property, for in biblical law outsiders were permitted to eat from the fields of another (Deut. 23:24–25; see Ruth 2). The problem was that this was done on the Sabbath. By a strict definition of work, this activity could be seen as harvesting, threshing, and preparing food on the Sabbath.

6:2 Why are you doing?: His disciples were the ones charged (the "you" is plural), but Jesus responds, again suggesting post-Easter conflicts between the early church and its Jewish environment (see on 5:29).

6:4 David and the House of God: See 1 Sam. 21:1–6. The house of God was not the temple in Jerusalem, but the sanctuary in Nob. The bread of the Presence (Lev. 24:5–9) was the sacred bread placed in the sanctuary that only the priests were permitted to eat. In David's case, human need took priority over sacred tradition and even biblical rules. For Luke, Jesus is David's greater son (1:27, 32; 20:41–44). In the ministry of Jesus, something greater even than Solomon is present (see on 11:31).

6:5 The Son of Man is lord of the sabbath: On Son of Man, see on Mark 2:10. Luke omits Mark's explanation that legitimizes Jesus' Sabbath practice and makes it entirely a matter of Jesus' authority. The issue is not one of trifling legalism but the conflict of two eras: whether the biblical command will be interpreted by the tradition oriented to a past reality or in the light of the presence of the Christ who inaugurates the kingdom of God.

6:6–7 Whether he would cure on the sabbath: Jewish traditional interpretation of the Sabbath law was compassionate in that it allowed healing in emergency, life-threatening cases. Jesus affirms this interpretation of the Sabbath law that is concerned to save life. He extends the meaning of "life" to mean more than deliverance from literal death. In the presence of the kingdom, all that enhances authentic life is permitted on the Sabbath.

6:8 Come . . . stand: These two words are also words used for Jesus' resurrection (literally: "arise, stand up"). They may have an ordinary meaning, as here, but may also be understood to have a deeper connotation resonant with the overtones of the new life mediated by Jesus' resurrection. The scene pictures an enhancement of life, a transition from death to life (see 15:32).

6:9 To do good or to do harm: The choice is between giving life and destroying life; there is no holy do-nothing middle way. As in 5:23, Jesus' question is provocatively ambiguous: the Pharisees agree that life should not be destroyed on the Sabbath, but is it their interpretation of the Sabbath or Jesus' that enhances or destroys life? (See excursus, "Interpreting the Miracle Stories," at Matt. 9:35.)

6:11 Luke softens the Markan response, in which the Pharisees decide to destroy Jesus. In Luke the Pharisees are religious opponents who dispute with Jesus about interpretation of the biblical law but do not participate in the plot to kill him (see on 5:17).

6:12–16
Choosing the Twelve
(See also at Matt. 10:1–4; Mark 3:13–19)

The section begun at 5:1 with the calling of the first disciples is concluded by Jesus' "official" choice of the Twelve to be apostles. This section, which is framed with calling the disciples, also has a call scene in its midst (5:27–28). Within this framework, Luke has inserted stories of Jesus' mighty deeds of the kingdom of God, deeds that lead to conflicts with the traditions represented by the Pharisees. Luke thus interweaves the motifs of discipleship and conflict; to be a disciple is to be engaged in discernment and conflict on the issues of how the new era inaugurated by Jesus is related to the old. This is then narrated more explicitly in Acts 1–15.

6:12–13 Chose twelve . . . whom he also named apostles: In Luke Jesus prays at crucial points in his ministry (3:21; 6:12; 9:18, 28; 22:40–46; 23:34, 46), just as the later church will do. (Prayer is mentioned 32x in Acts; see especially 1:24, where Jesus' disciples pray as they choose a successor for Judas.) The **mountain** corresponds to Mark 3:13. See also Matt. 5:1.

In Luke's understanding, **disciples** represent a larger group than the twelve **apostles** (see 6:17). "Disciple" means "student," "learner," "follower" of a particular teacher. The word here translated "disciple" is not found in the Old Testament but was often used of the devotees of a Greek teacher. It represents one of the ways in which the Christian faith adapted its terminology and thinking to the modern world of its own day. It is found only in the Gospels and Acts (Gospels 233x; Acts 28x). "Apostle" means "one sent with a commission," such as a deputy or one's legal representative with power of attorney. Both words were ordinary secular words before being adopted by early Christianity and filled with particular religious meaning: for Luke, all followers of Jesus are disciples (e.g., Acts 6:1–2; 9:1, 10). From this larger group, Luke pictures Jesus as choosing twelve as apostles. We later learn that for Luke this means they must have accompanied Jesus from the time of John the Baptist until after the resurrection (Acts 1:21–22) and that they are to serve as authoritative leaders in the church (Luke 22:28–30; Acts 4:35; 8:14–25; 15:1–16:4). For Luke, there

are no "twelve disciples," but there are twelve, and only twelve, apostles. This is a different understanding from other New Testament writers, such as Paul, for whom there are more than twelve apostles (see 1 Cor. 15:3–8, where "the twelve" and "all the apostles" are different, but overlapping, groups, and where James and Paul himself, though not members of the Twelve, are nonetheless apostles). It is important to Luke that the church be apostolic, i.e., that it be guided by those commissioned and instructed by Jesus himself. "Apostle" means "authorized representative." After Jesus' death and resurrection, the issue of who continued to represent him and speak authoritatively in his name was of deep concern to early Christianity (see 2 Cor. 10–13; Gal. 1–2; Rev. 2:2).

Twelve is probably symbolic of the reconstitution of the twelve tribes of Israel, who had been dispersed during the deportation of the Israelites by the Assyrians (2 Kgs. 17) and the Judeans by the Babylonians (2 Kgs. 24–25). While the Judeans had returned after the exile, the tribes of the northern kingdom of Israel had been assimilated into the pagan world. In some streams of the Jewish eschatological hope, God would restore and reconstitute Israel at the end time. Jesus' choosing the Twelve is probably a symbolic action presenting his followers as the nucleus of renewed and restored Israel (see Num. 1:4–16; 13:1–16; Matt. 19:28). The Qumran community, the sectarian Jewish group that produced the Dead Sea Scrolls, also saw themselves as the renewed people of God of the end time and had a group of twelve leaders supervised by a smaller group of three, representing the twelve tribes and the three patriarchs (Abraham, Isaac, and Jacob), thus symbolizing all Israel. At Qumran too, "rock" imagery was important in portraying the group's leaders.

It was thus symbolically important for both early Christianity and Luke that there were twelve key apostolic leaders, but not so important precisely who they were. The lists in Matt. 10:2–4; Mark 3:16–18; Luke 6:14–16; Acts 1:13 do not exactly agree as to who constituted the twelve (see chart at Matt. 10:2). The discrepancy is often resolved by claiming that some apostles had two names, but there is no basis in the text for this. See chart at Matt. 10:1–5.

6:14 Simon . . . Peter: See on Mark 3:16. Luke has referred to Simon once previously as Peter (5:8) but seems to locate the change of name at his call to be an apostle. The interchange between post-Easter and pre-Easter traditions (see on 5:1–11) may indicate that Simon became Peter as a result of the resurrection appearances, when he was re-called and re-constituted the Twelve (see 22:28–32).

Andrew: Mentioned only here and Acts 1:13 by Luke, he plays no role in the narrative (contrast, e.g., John 1:40; 6:8; 12:22). **James and John:** Mentioned previously as Simon's partners in the fishing business (5:10). With Peter they form the inner circle of Jesus' apostolic band (8:51; 9:28). Later, Simon Peter and John form an important apostolic pair in Luke's narrative (22:8; Acts 3:1–11; 4:1–19; 8:14–25). Only Luke makes explicit that the other **Simon** was a **Zealot** (Greek for Mark and Matthew's "Cananaean," which means "zealous"). The nationalist military party just before the war with Rome in 66–73 called themselves Zealots. The name was not used in this sense in Jesus' day, but the term may have been used to indicate religious devotion, or that one of the Twelve later became a Zealot when that group emerged ca. 66. Note that (only) Luke's list mentions two men named Simon, two named James, and two named Judas.

6:17–49
THE SERMON ON THE PLAIN
(See also at Matt. 5–7)

6:17–20a Came down with them and stood on a level place: See Matt. 4:24–5:2. The Q source used by both Matthew and Luke had an inaugural sermon by Jesus. Matthew expanded it as the Sermon on the Mount (Matt. 5–7); Luke's version is closer to Q, but both Matthew and Luke offer an interpretation of Jesus' words appropriate to their setting.

Luke has Jesus choose the apostles on the mountain but come down to a level place for the sermon. This scene represents a transition from conflict with leaders of the old order (5:1–6:16) to instructing leaders of the new age. Luke constructs a scene with four concentric circles: Jesus in the center, surrounded by the twelve apostles (see on 6:12–16), then the wider circle of **a great crowd of his disciples**, and finally **a great multitude of people** including those from the neighboring country, a somewhat "international" gathering. All have come to **hear** and **be healed**, i.e., they are not hostile critics. But only the inner circles are committed disciples. The instruction is given to his disciples, but in the presence of the uncommitted but interested crowds (see 5:1, 15; 6:17–19; 7:11; 8:4; 9:11, 18, 37; 11:14; 14:25;

19:48; 20:19; 22:6, 47; 23:4,13, 21, 48). The Christian ethical teaching given by Jesus requires a prior commitment to Jesus as the Christ, the definitive representative of God, but this teaching is given "in public" to those who have not (yet) made such a commitment. This is a model for ethical instruction in the church.

6:19 Touch . . . power: In these words peculiar to Luke, Jesus is pictured as a Spirit-filled "divine man" who communicates the power of God by his very touch (see 8:44–46; Acts 5:14–15; 19:11–12). See excursus, "Interpreting the Miracle Stories," at Matt. 9:35.

6:20b–23 See Matt. 5:3–12. "Beatitude" means "blessing." A blessing is performative language, a pronouncement that causes the reality it names to happen (like "I forgive you," "I apologize," "I pronounce you husband and wife"). The blessings are thus not exhortations but announcements, in the indicative mood rather than in the imperative. They refer to an objective reality, not to a subjective state (thus "happy" is a poor translation). They declare a reality that exists by divine power, not what we should do.

It is thus startling to hear Jesus pronounce those blessed who are usually considered deprived and disadvantaged: the poor, hungry, and crying. Luke pictures the advent of Jesus as inaugurating the great eschatological reversal as in Isa. 65:13–16 (see 1:46–55; 2:8–14; 2:24; 3:10–14; 4:16–21; 14:21–23; 16:19–31; Acts 2:44–47; 3:6; 4:32–35; 11:27–30).

6:20 Poor: literally. Contrast Matt. 6:3, "poor in spirit." **Kingdom of God:** See on 4:13, 19–20, 4:41–44; 11:20; 17:21; see also 8:2, 27; 9:1, 42, 49; 10:17, 11:14–20; 13:32. Poverty is not romanticized, but neither is it the last word. Good news to the poor was the theme of Jesus' keynote address in this Gospel (4:18).

6:21 Hungry: literally. Contrast Matt. 6:6, "hunger and thirst for righteousness." **Weep . . . laugh:** At the eschatological coming of God's kingdom. Note contrast between the repeated "now" and the future kingdom. Though the promise of food for all is ultimately eschatological, this vision of what will be empowers Jesus and his disciples to feed the hungry now (see 6:1–5; 9:12–17; Acts 2:46; 6:1–4; 11:28–30).

6:22 Hate . . . revile . . . on account of the Son of Man: Reflects the marginalization of early Christians. **Son of Man:** an early christological title of Jesus, expressing his unique rule as God's representative (see on Mark 2:10).

6:23 The prophets: Though spokespersons for God and empowered by the Holy Spirit, the prophets were typically rejected. Luke sees Jesus' followers as such a prophetic community (see Acts 2:1–21).

6:24–26 Woes: Only in Luke. Each is the reversal of one of the Beatitudes. As the Beatitudes pronounce God's blessing, the woes pronounce God's judgment, in the tradition of the Hebrew prophets (e.g., Isa. 3:9–11; 5:8–11). Just as prophets were not essentially those who made predictions but those who faithfully spoke the word of God, so **false prophets** were not those whose predictions were not fulfilled, but those who falsely claimed to speak God's word. **Woe to you who are rich:** Riches were often thought to be a sign of God's blessing. The Lukan Jesus focuses on the dangers of wealth, as in Mary's Magnificat (1:53; see also 6:20–26; 12:13–21; 16:19–31; 18:22–25).

6:27–36 Love your enemies: Matt. 5:38–48. The imperatives that follow correspond to the preceding blessings in that they also represent a reversal of common wisdom. Things are to be used, and people loved—rather than the opposite orientation often found in the culture. Luke has doubled this command (vv. 27, 35), found only once in the Matthean parallel, and moved it to the primary position. **Love** represents the Greek word *agape* throughout, including 6:32, **even sinners love those who love them,** so neither here nor elsewhere in the New Testament does the word *agape* itself represent a special Christian or divine kind of love. In Greek as in English, one must explain what kind of love is meant (see 1 Cor. 13:4–7). Luke represents *agape* as the love of God manifest in Christ. As God loves even the enemy and is kind to the ungrateful and wicked, so also Christians are to love others without regard to whether the love is accepted and returned.

6:29–30 If anyone strikes you: Not only do the disciples of Jesus not seek revenge, they seek the positive good of those who abuse them. Jesus himself lived out this ethic that expresses the love of God for sinners (see on 23:34).

6:31 Do to others: The Golden Rule, found in both positive and negative forms in various pagan and Jewish moralists, is cited here as an expression of unselfish, uncalculating love for others.

6:33–35 Expecting nothing in return: Though difficult to practice literally, these commands express the utter unselfishness of the conduct called for by Jesus' disciples. **Credit** is the same Greek word elsewhere translated "grace." It does not refer to scoring points with

God, but points to those who live by God's grace rather than cultural expectations (retaliation, enlightened self-interest).

6:37–42 Judge not: Matt. 7:1–5. These instructions do not mean that followers of Jesus should blandly and indiscriminately accept all practices and lifestyles as equally valid, nor are they merely a strategy for getting along with others, nor yet are they a general plea to be more tolerant. Rather, Jesus here places all one's interpersonal relationships in the light of one's relation to God. One who knows God's acceptance despite human sin will see others in the same charitable light in which God has seen us. So also there is no selfish quid pro quo ethic advocated here, but the same unselfish orientation represented by love for the neighbor and the enemy. God's reward is precisely for those who live without the motivation of reward—and it will be extravagant beyond measure.

Can a blind person guide a blind person?: These instructions make clear that the preceding commands against judging do not mean the follower of Jesus is to be oblivious to the distinctions between good and evil in the name of tolerance. One can be discerning without a self-righteous, judgmental attitude. Jesus the **teacher** is the model. One's critical, discerning eye is to be turned first to one's own faults. Such a person can then help others see theirs.

6:43–45 Known by . . . fruit: Matt. 7:15–20; 12:33–35. Truly good words and deeds are the product of an inner transformation. Just doing or saying the right thing is like tying grapes on a bramble bush (see James 3:12). See Paul's contrast between the "works of the flesh" and the "fruit of the Spirit" (Gal. 5:19–25).

6:46–49 A man building a house: Matt. 7:21–27. The original story, preserved in the Q form represented more accurately by Matthew, portrayed a wise builder who built on the rock and a foolish builder who built on the sand of a wadi (dry riverbed). Luke has adapted the imagery to his non-Palestinian readership, so that a good builder constructs on a foundation and the bad builder builds without a foundation, but the point is the same: hearing and knowing the teaching of Jesus is not enough (see 8:21; 11:28; Jas. 1:22). Our culture encourages us to be concerned about an impressive superstructure; Jesus encourages us to think about the **foundation.** The foundation of a life that endures is not only knowing, but doing, the will of God manifest in Jesus.

7:1–10
HEALING THE CENTURION'S SLAVE
(See also at Matt. 8:5–13; see John 4:46–54)

A Lukan section begins here and extends to 9:51, where Jesus resolves to go to Jerusalem. Luke presents several scenes that reveal Jesus to be a prophetic figure filled with divine power, but greater than all the prophets including John the Baptist (7:18–35), because he is the Christ, the Son of God (9:18–36). The original point of the story as it circulated in the early church may have been that Jesus can still heal at a distance, i.e., from heaven. The Christian community that no longer lives in first-century Palestine still has the healing power of Christ available to it. The similar story found in Matthew and John has been elaborated by each evangelist to bring out his own theological point. In Luke, it is an anticipation of Acts 10:1–48.

7:1 Capernaum: See 4:31–40. This lakeside town, the residence of Simon Peter, became Jesus' headquarters during his Galilean ministry. Nonetheless, it did not respond in faith (10:15).

7:2 Centurion: A military officer responsible for one hundred troops (see "century," "centimeter"). They formed the mainstay of leadership in the army, much like sergeants in the American military. The contrast with "Israel" in 7:9 indicates he was a Gentile, though this is not specifically said.

Slave/servant: Later (7:7) the centurion uses the more general word that may be translated "servant," "slave," or "boy" (see John 4:46, which understands the boy as a son). Here, Luke uses the more specific Greek word that means "slave." Slavery was accepted as a given component in the social structure in the New Testament documents (and by Jesus). Jesus and the New Testament authors commend compassionate treatment of slaves by masters, as here, and loyal obedience by slaves to masters (e.g., Col. 3:22–4:1; see introduction to Philemon and 1 Pet. 2:13–3:12, esp. 2:18–25), but do not challenge the institution as such. It was only later, in the light of Christian faith, that Christians saw the need to transform unjust social institutions, including the abolition of slavery.

Luke draws a more subtly developed picture of the centurion than any of the other Gospels. He is a compassionate man who is concerned about his slave. He is a Gentile who loves and respects the religion of the Jewish community where he has military power and need not defer to them. He is a wealthy man who uses his money wisely, having built a synagogue for the Jewish community. He understands Jewish reservations about entering the homes of Gentiles, which might cause him to be ritually defiled. He gets along well with the leaders of the Jewish community, the **elders**, who praise him to Jesus as a man who is **worthy** (7:4), but he sincerely and modestly calls himself "not worthy" (7:6; see 18:9–14). He has come to have **faith** in Jesus not by direct contact with him but by the testimony of others. In all this, the centurion both serves as a model for the Gentile Christians of Luke's own church and prepares the reader for the similar centurion who becomes the first Gentile convert in the post-Easter Christian community (Acts 10–11).

7:6–7 Not worthy to have you come under my roof . . . But only speak the word: The centurion is also a model for later Christians, in that he believes Jesus can both hear and grant his request, that he can heal at a distance without direct contact. In this, the scene is like Christian prayer, a favorite subject of Luke's (see 6:12; 9:18, 28; 11:1–13; 18:1–8; 22:40–46; 23:34, 46). The power of Jesus' word, analogous to the word of God, is also a Lukan theme (cf 3:2; 5:1; 8:11, 21; 11:28; Acts 4:31; 6:2, 7; 8:14; 11:1; 12:24; 13:5, 7, 46; 17:13; 18:11).

7:8–9 Such faith: The faith that Jesus' praises is faith in the power of Jesus' word. Luke's own understanding of **authority** is articulated by the centurion, representing a kind of military chain of command. Just as the centurion is himself integrated into a chain of command, receiving orders from above and commanding those below him, so Jesus operates not by his own power but by the power of God (4:14; 5:17; see 19:12, 15, where the "son" represents Jesus). Luke is not troubled by later issues of whether the Son is subordinate to the Father, but understands the authority at work in the church somewhat hierarchically, as here. The apostles later become integral links in this chain that communicates God's power and authority, so that the "chain" is God $\Rightarrow$ Christ $\Rightarrow$ Apostles $\Rightarrow$ Church $\Rightarrow$ World. Luke understands God's authority and power to be delegated through channels (see 10:16; Acts 8; 15), and thus he has the centurion himself work by means of delegates he sends to Jesus, rather than coming himself (differently in Matt. 8:5–7). Luke understands hierarchy from the perspective of humility, not rank (see 9:46–48).

Not even in Israel: There is no contrast here between "unbelieving Jews" and "believing

Gentiles." Luke will later portray the church as one community of Jewish and Gentile believers (Acts 1–15). There have already been numerous Jewish believers in Luke's narrative (e.g., 5:12–26; 6:6–11; 6:17–19), and there will be others, such as the woman whose faith is praised in 7:50. The point is that one should expect to find faith in Israel, but here deep faith is found in an unexpected place. Again, the story of the later church is anticipated in this retelling a story from Jesus' ministry. (See excursus, "Interpreting the Miracle Stories," at Matt. 9:35.)

7:11–17
RAISING THE WIDOW'S SON

This story is only in Luke, but it has many points of contact with the story of Elijah's raising the widow of Zarephath's son (1 Kgs. 17:8–24), including such verbatim parallels as "he gave him to his mother" (Luke 7:15 = 1 Kgs. 17:23).

7:11 Disciples and a large crowd: See on 6:17–20; 11:14. **Nain:** A small village twenty-five miles southwest of Capernaum and six miles southeast of Nazareth, it is mentioned nowhere else in the Bible.

7:12 Only son . . . widow: The status of widows in the ancient world was often precarious. They were dependent upon their families or community charity (see Acts 6:1; 9:39; 1 Tim. 5:4, 9, 16; Jas. 1:27). Thus that the dead man was her only son only compounded the tragedy. The term "only son" was used in a christological sense by John (1:14, 18; 3:16, 18). Luke adds the designation to the story of the raising of Jairus's daughter (Luke 8:42; see Mark 5:23) and the healing of the epileptic boy (Luke 9:38; see Mark 9:17) but does not make anything specifically christological out of it. In every case, however, it allows the story of Jesus' healing or raising someone else to resonate with the larger story in which it is embedded—the story of God's raising Jesus, the only son in a unique sense.

7:14 Touched: Jesus touched the bier, not hesitating to come into contact with the dead (see on 5:13).

I say to you, rise: These words resonate with the word of the Son of God who will speak them to all the dead on the last day. The scene seems to modulate from an incident in the life of Jesus (the resuscitation of a dead man) to the future eschatological event of the resurrection. The reader should distinguish here between resuscitation (restoration of a dead person to the life of this world) and res-

urrection (the eschatological raising of the dead to eternal life, anticipated in the resurrection of Jesus). Luke explicitly declares Jesus to be "the first to rise from the dead" (see on Acts 26:23). One should thus not speak of the "resurrection" of the widow's son, except in the anticipatory and symbolic sense as pointing to Jesus' resurrection and the final resurrection at the last day. Again (in contrast to the scene in 1 Kgs. 17), the power of Jesus' word is manifest.

7:15 Jesus gave him to his mother: Verbatim echo of the Elijah story (see 1 Kgs. 17:23). Throughout, Jesus' compassion is directed not only to the dead man but to his mother.

7:16 Fear seized all of them: This does not mean that they were merely afraid but that they were overcome with the reverent awe that acknowledged they were in the presence of God. **A great prophet** is for Luke not a second-class christological title (see Acts 3:22; 7:37). The category "prophet" for Jesus allows Luke to affirm that Jesus' act was the act of God without making God and Jesus competitors. "God or Jesus" is a false question in such contexts. Here and elsewhere, Jesus' act is the act of God. Other New Testament authors and the post–New Testament church developed this affirmation in a variety of ways, resulting in such theological confessions as the Nicene Creed. All Luke's talk of the mighty works of Jesus is theocentric, as seen here when the people glorify God for what Jesus has done (5:25–26; 7:16; 8:24, 38; 9:20–22, 43; 13:13; 17:15; 19:37).

A great prophet has risen among us: "Has risen" is better translated "has been raised (by God)," another instance of how the stories of Jesus' mighty deeds are narrated in such a way as to reflect God's mighty act in raising up Jesus. The story as a whole, like all the Gospel miracle stories, points beyond itself to the central story of the Christ event itself, the story of what God has done for the world in Jesus (see excursus, "Interpreting the Miracle Stories," at Matt. 9:35).

God has looked favorably on his people: See 1:68, 78.

7:17 Judea: See on 4:44.

7:18–35
JOHN AND JESUS
(See also at Matt. 11:2–19)

7:18 Disciples of John: See on 1:5–25; 5:33–34; 11:1. John is in prison; this is the first reference to John since his imprisonment (3:18–20). See on 4:20–21, 43.

7:19 The one who is to come: John's question assumes that at the climax of God's plan at the end of history, God will send a mighty savior figure, or come himself, to establish justice and bring about God's ultimate purpose for the world. This Old Testament/Jewish hope was expressed in a number of different images: God himself will appear or will be represented by a prophetic figure such as the return of Elijah (see, e.g., Mal. 3:1–5; 4:1–5); God will raise up and empower a mighty kingly figure to establish divine justice (see, e.g., Isa. 9:1–7; 11:1–9); a heavenly figure such as the Son of Man will descend as judge for the unrighteous and savior for the righteous (Dan. 7:13; see on Mark 2:10).

Are you the one who is to come?: John does not doubt that the saving activity of God will finally be manifested by the appearance of the promised "one who is to come." His question is whether Jesus is that one. In the Gospel of Luke, this is a real question for John. In Matt. 3:13–17 and John 1:19–34, John had already recognized Jesus as the promised savior during his earthly ministry, but these scenes are not in Luke, who never has John and Jesus appear in the same scene. John's question thus does not represent a faltering faith that had previously been firm, but the dawn of faith that Jesus is the ultimate revealer and savior figure sent by God.

John had proclaimed one who would come in power to save the good and destroy the evil (3:15–17)—does this one who helps the helpless represent the power of God? The question is whether our initial expectation of who the savior must be will determine our evaluation of who Jesus is, or whether the kind of person Jesus turned out to be will reshape our expectations of what the ultimate power of God actually is.

7:20–21 Luke has added these verses to the traditional story (see Matt. 11:3), in order to have the messengers from John become actual eyewitnesses of the deeds of the Messiah. Luke is concerned with authentic witnesses to the revelatory event (see Luke 24:48; Acts 1:8, 22; 2:32; 3:15; 5:32; 10:39; 10:41; 13:31; 22:15, 20). This is probably why he adds the detail that there were two messengers from John (7:19; see Matt. 11:2), for two witnesses are required for valid testimony (Deut. 19:15; Matt. 18:16; 26:60; John 8:17; 2 Cor. 13:1; 1 Tim. 5:19; Heb. 10:28; Rev. 11:3).

7:22 What you have seen and heard: Jesus as the one who gives sight to the blind, makes the lame walk, cleanses the lepers, makes the deaf to hear, and gives life to the dead has been pictured in the preceding narrative and especially in the prophecies of Isa. 29:18; 35:5–6; 42:18.

7:23 No offense (NRSV), **fall away** (NIV): In Greek, literally "scandalize," "stumble" or "put a stumbling block in front of." Christ's blessing is pronounced upon those whose own expectations of what the Christ is supposed to be do not scandalize them, tripping them up and causing them to miss the revelation of God that is truly present in Jesus.

7:24–28 Jesus began to speak to the crowds about John: In the preceding section Jesus responds to John's question about his own identity; here Jesus asks the crowds about their understanding of John's identity. In the later first century, as people looked back on John's courageous life and death, he was highly respected in both Jewish and Christian circles, and some wondered if John himself was the ultimate savior figure (see 3:15; John 1:19–28; Acts 18:24–19:7; see on 1:5–25; 5:33).

Reed shaken by the wind: Points not only to something insubstantial, but also to the reeds of the Jordan valley that were a symbol of Herod's royal power, appearing on some of his coins. This connects to the reference to **soft robes** and **royal palaces.** John is contrasted with the political and economic power of Herod. Though John is in Herod's prison, he (and not Herod) is God's representative, God's **prophet.** Yet John is not only a member of the long line of God's prophets—he is their climactic final member before the advent of the **kingdom of God** that appears in Jesus (see on 4:5–8, 13, 20–21, 43–44; 11:20; 17:21). **Born of women** is simply a biblical way of saying "human being" (see Job 14:1; 15:14; 25:4). In Gal. 4:4 the expression is used of Jesus to affirm his true humanity. Here, the point is not only that John is the greatest of the prophets but that the **least in the kingdom** (including the tax collectors and sinners of 7:35) is even greater than John.

7:29–30 This is the author's retrospective comment, not presented as the words of Jesus. On **tax collectors,** see on 3:10–14; 5:27–29. They represented those who were considered socially and religiously unacceptable. On **Pharisees,** see on 5:17. **Lawyers** (also called scribes) are experts in religious teaching; the modern distinction between religious and secular law did not then exist. One would have expected Pharisees and lawyers to respond to God's revelation and tax collectors to reject it. But John's ministry itself had already shown the error of judging God's act by prior criteria of what God was supposed to do. By responding to John's call to be baptized, a call that included repentance (3:7–14), the tax collectors had **acknowledged that God's way was right** (NIV), i.e., they had ceased to depend on human standards of who is acceptable before God.

7:31–35 This generation: The motif of whether one judges God's act by human criteria of what is right permeates this entire section. John had been tempted to judge Jesus by his own understanding of how God will act (7:18–23) and to rank him too low on the scale. The people had been tempted to judge John by their own criteria of what a prophet is and to evaluate him too highly. Here, in evaluating both John and Jesus, the people are tempted to reject them both because they do not fit their previous criteria.

7:32 Played the flute . . . sang a dirge (NIV): John and Jesus were indeed very different. John did not participate in the niceties of civilized life but lived as an uncompromising ascetic. He could thus pronounce God's judgment on those who ate while others starved, who went to parties while others were tortured, without being involved in the ambiguities of civilized life himself. Jesus did eat and drink, celebrating life within the structures of human civilization, compromised with evil though they are. Forgiveness, rather than judgment, was the focus of his message. Yet those who measured John and Jesus by their own criteria found each of them wanting. Such critics are like children who refuse to participate when their friends try to get them to play funerals (like John's somber message), just as they had refused the invitation to play weddings (like Jesus' joyous message of God's acceptance). John is rejected as too fanatically strict, Jesus as not strict enough. John is too judgmental, Jesus is too accepting. Yet, different as they are, both are messengers from God, but one cannot evaluate this coolly from the sidelines as a spectator. One must join in the game.

7:34 Friend of . . . sinners: In the post-Easter development of Christian faith, many titles were rightfully applied to Jesus to express his role in God's saving plan (e.g., Son of God, Son of Man, Christ, Lord). These titles were probably not used by Jesus of himself, and their appearance in the Gospels represents the later retelling of the stories from the perspective of

faith. Once contemporary readers become aware of this, they may wonder if *any* of the titles go back to Jesus' own time. This one certainly does, and it contains the nucleus of many later developments. In representing God's mercy to us, Jesus was and is friend of sinners. That Jesus ate bread and drank wine with sinners scandalized the religious leaders of his day but became a central image of the later eucharistic life of the church.

7:35 Wisdom is vindicated by all her children: The application of this proverb is obscure. It may refer to John and Jesus, who, different as they are, are both "children of (divine) wisdom" who vindicate the divine revelation by their different ministries that have been rejected by human wisdom. More likely, in the light of 7:29–30, the proverb here refers to the followers of both John and Jesus, who recognized the activity of God in the lives of John and Jesus. The central question of this whole section is whether God's revelation confirms or upsets our previous understanding of how God acts.

7:36–50
A SINFUL WOMAN FORGIVEN
(See also at Mark 14:3–9; Matt. 26:6–13; John 12:1–8)

The Gospels contain three versions of this story, with Mark and Matthew having essentially the same and Luke and John each having different versions of recognizably the same event (see chart at Mark 14:1–9). The woman is not named in the Synoptic Gospels, but John 12 identifies her as Mary the sister of Martha and Lazarus. Post–New Testament traditions not only combined the stories into a single account but extended it by identifying the woman as Mary Magdalene, who is then described as a harlot, though the New Testament never makes either of these identifications. The interpreter's task (here and elsewhere) is not to attempt to reconstruct what really happened but to attempt to understand the meaning and message of each biblical text.

We concentrate on the Lukan meaning; Luke has placed it next to a story in which Jesus eats with sinners and is criticized by Pharisees.

The setting is another of Luke's numerous table scenes (see 5:29–39; 7:36–50; 11:37–54; 14:1–24; 22:14–38; 24:30–32; 24:36–49): Jesus eats and drinks at a dinner party, precisely what he had been rejected for doing in 7:34.

7:36 Pharisee: See on 5:17. Jesus eats not only with sinners but with Pharisees; there is no reverse discrimination but genuine inclusiveness in Jesus' ministry. Jesus' followers must guard against being proud as Pharisees that they are sinners (see on 18:9–14).

7:37 A woman in the city, who was a sinner: Jesus had been invited; the woman had not. Hellenistic houses had courtyards open to the street, so that those passing by could not only look in but enter. This made the entry of an uninvited guest less intrusive than it would be in a modern Western home, but it was still an extraordinary event for the woman to crash the party. That she is called a sinner does not mean that she was a prostitute, but that she did not observe the law of God, moral and ritual, as interpreted by the Pharisees (see 5:29–32, 34; 6:27–36; 7:34).

7:37–38 Bathed his feet . . . kissing . . . anointing: We later learn (7:44–46) that these are the normal acts of hospitality given a guest by the host. Simon had not done these, apparently assuming that a Pharisee's inviting a traveling preacher to dinner was consideration enough. The woman's acts go far beyond the normal niceties of conventional hospitality, however. In a daring display of devotion, she lets down her hair, wipes his feet, anoints them with perfume she has brought for the purpose, and kisses them. Jesus and the other guests are pictured as dining in aristocratic Hellenistic fashion, reclining on the floor around the low central table, with their bodies extending outward like the spokes of a wheel. This makes the anointing and caressing of Jesus feet during the meal more understandable and less disruptive than trying to picture it in terms of a modern Western dining table, but it hardly reduces the shock of how inappropriate the act was regarded by Simon.

7:39 Simon's response: See on "scandal" at 7:23 above. **If this man were a prophet:** Prophets were thought to have supernatural knowledge. Measured by Simon's criteria, Jesus is not a prophet. The irony of the scene is that Jesus not only knows the kind of person the woman is—much more than does Simon—but also knows Simon's thoughts.

7:41–43 A certain creditor: Jesus is also a prophet in that he tells a story that causes the hearer to pronounce judgment on himself, just as did the prophet Nathan (see 2 Sam. 11:1–12:14). In Jewish tradition, **debt** is often used as a metaphor for sin (see Matt. 6:12; 18:21–35; Luke 11:4). A **denarius** is approximately one day's pay for a hired laborer (Matt. 20:2); the debts are thus roughly two year's pay and two months' pay. Both are significant debts, but one is ten times the other. Both debts are forgiven, and the

debtors now owe exactly the same amount—nothing. The act of forgiveness has placed them on the same plane. This is what is difficult for Simon and those like him to accept.

7:44–47 You gave me no water . . . no kiss: Jesus' application of the parable to Simon corresponds to Nathan's prophetic "You are the man" to David (2 Sam. 12:7). The Greek conjunction (v. 47) translated **for** (NIV) or **hence** (NRSV) is an ambiguous element in an ambiguous statement, which does not make clear whether forgiveness generates love or love is the ground of forgiveness. The former is closer to Luke's overall meaning, but the point is not to establish whether love precedes or follows forgiveness but to show that they are inseparable.

7:48–50 Your sins are forgiven: See on 5:20–21, which also combines faith, persistence, Jesus' pronouncement of forgiveness, and shocked reaction. On this whole story, compare 18:9–14, which also features forgiveness, a Pharisee, and a person assumed to be a sinner (see 7:34!).

8:1–3
JESUS' FOLLOWERS: THE WOMEN

This paragraph is a Lukan summary found only in this Gospel. **Kingdom of God**: see on 4:13, 20–21, 43–44; 11:20; 17:21. **The Twelve:** See on 6:12–13. Luke emphasizes women in the story of Jesus more than the other evangelists, often pairing them with men (e.g., in the birth story Zechariah and Elizabeth, Mary and Joseph, Simeon and Anna [1:5–2:51], as well as the widow of Zarephath and Naaman the Syrian [4:25–27], the centurion and the widow of Nain [7:1–17], and the shepherd who finds the lost sheep and the woman who finds the lost coin [15:3–10]).

Mary, called Magdalene: Magdala, "Fish Tower," is usually identified as a town on the west bank of the Sea of Galilee, but the identification is uncertain. This Mary is mentioned among other Galilean women who followed Jesus in Mark 15:40–41, 47; 16:1, but only retrospectively at the end of the story. Matthew and John follow Mark in this, but Luke inserts this account into the story of the Galilean ministry itself. Later legends identified her with the woman who anointed Jesus (see 7:36–50 above) and described her as a former prostitute on the basis of the **seven demons** that Jesus had cast out of her. Demon possession, however, was not a matter of immorality of the person possessed (see on 4:33; see excursus, "Satan, the Devil, and Demons in Biblical Theology," at Mark 5:1). Nothing further is known of **Joanna** (see 24:10) and **Susanna**, who appear only in Luke. It is not clear whether Joanna is pictured as having left her husband in order to follow Jesus, but in any case, including women in his entourage would have been considered shocking (see on "scandal" in 7:23 above). The women are portrayed as people of some wealth who used their property in the service of Christ, a Lukan theme (see 12:15, 33; 14:33; 19:8; Acts 2:44; 4:32–37; 6:1–6; 11:27–29). Luke especially emphasizes that prominent women of means were won to the Christian faith (Acts 16:11–15; 17:4). This later situation in the church is here anticipated in the ministry of Jesus.

8:4–18
PARABLE OF THE SOWER
(See also at Matt. 13:1–23; Mark 4:1–25)

For general comments on interpreting parables, see on Mark 4:1.

Luke has already referred to Jesus' teaching in parables (4:23 [translated "proverb"]; 5:36; 6:39), but this is his first introduction of a parable in the strict sense, the narrative metaphors distinctive of Jesus' teaching. The parable here is not specifically called a kingdom parable but is framed with references to Jesus' teaching about the kingdom of God in 8:1, 10. For **kingdom of God,** see on 4:13, 20–21, 43–44; 11:20; 17:21.

8:4 A great crowd gathered: Luke has already used the Mark 4:1 seaside setting for the parable discourse at Luke 5:1. On the concentric circles around Jesus (apostles, disciples, crowds), see on 6:17–20.

8:5–8 For comments on the parable itself, see Mark 4:3–8.

8:9–10 Secrets of the kingdom of God: Luke here follows Mark, for whom the messianic secret was an integral part of his presentation of the story of Jesus' ministry. Luke does not subscribe to the messianic secret in the same way as Mark (see introduction to Mark and comments on Mark 4:10–12) but here reproduces with slight adjustments Mark's harsh view that Jesus taught in parables in order to conceal his meaning. Like Matthew (13:13–15), Luke eliminates Mark's troublesome "lest," dulling the impact of Mark's statement that the purpose of Jesus' teaching in parables was to prevent people from understanding, repenting, and being forgiven. The quotation from Isa. 6:9–10, originally directed to those who rejected the message of the eighth-century-BCE prophet, was often interpreted in early Christianity as a way of understanding the rejection of the Christian message by Jewish people to whom it was first proclaimed (Matt.

13:14–15; Mark 4:12; Acts 28:26–27; Rom. 11:8). Luke gives an abbreviated version of this quotation here but will use the full text in his climactic scene at the conclusion of Acts, 28:26–27.

The interpretation, vv. 11–15, reflects the later experience of the church and is often considered to be an addition to the original parable by an early Christian teacher. It represents one authentic reading of the parable within the context of the church but does not exhaust the meaning of the parable. The interpretation understands the parable as an allegory, in which each item of the story represents something else. Luke found the interpretation in Mark (see at Mark 4:13–20) and gave it some distinctive emphases:

8:11 The seed is the word of God: Luke specifies Mark's more open-ended "the word" as the word of God. Lukan theology often emphasizes this aspect of the growth of the church, sometimes simply equating the missionary expansion of the Christian community with the growth of the word of God (see Luke 3:2; 5:1; 8:11, 21; 11:28; Acts 4:31; 6:2, 7; 8:14; 11:1; 12:24; 13:5, 7, 46; 17:13; 18:11). As the stories in Acts will illustrate, conversion to Christ and growth to Christian maturity comes about not by mysterious spiritual causes, the church's marketing techniques, or psychological causes, but by encounter with the word of God mediated by the Bible and Christian preaching and teaching (see Acts 2:14–46; 3:11–26; 8:4–40; 9:1–22; 10:1–11:18; 13:13–52; 15:1–29; 16:11–35; 17:16–34).

8:13–15 In a time of testing fall away: Literally "become standoffish," keeping a low profile, distancing themselves from the Christian community in order to get along better in society. This is the opposite of the kind of witnessing to others Luke typically calls for (see, e.g., 11:48; 21:13; 24:48; Acts 1:8). By Luke's time the church had experienced persecution, and many of those who had been initially converted did not endure under pressure. Thus Luke emphasizes those who **bear fruit with patient endurance** (NRSV; "by persevering," NIV; "with patience" in older translations), using the word that became common in early Christianity for the undramatic, steady "hanging in there" under duress. The word is used 32x in the New Testament (e.g., Rom. 8:25; 15:4; Rev. 1:9; 2:3; 13:10), but among the evangelists only Luke uses it, here and 21:19.

8:16 That those who enter may see the light: Luke, concerned for the evangelistic mission of the church in bearing witness to outsiders, adds these words to Mark 4:21.

8:17 Nothing is hidden that will not be disclosed: As elsewhere (see 4:23; 8:18; 9:58; 10:22; 11:9–10; 12:3–4), this may have originally been a secular proverb pointing out the reality of village life: secrets always become public information sooner or later, one way or another. Jesus or the early church may have adopted and adapted this proverb to express the eschatological faith of the church: if you try to conceal your faith now, your failure will be revealed in the final judgment when all secrets are manifest. Luke takes it as encouragement to confess one's faith before the world now (see 12:2–9).

8:18 To those who have, more will be given: This too may have originally been a secular, somewhat cynical proverb—the rich get richer and the poor get poorer—adapted by Jesus and/or the church to express the realities of faith. Luke has attempted to moderate the provocative, contradictory form in Mark 4:25 by changing "what they have" to **what they seem to have**—without clarifying how what one only seems to have can be taken away.

8:19–21
JESUS' FOLLOWERS: HIS FAMILY
(See also at Matt. 12:46–50; Mark 3:31–35)

In the original Markan narrative framework for presenting the gospel, no human beings in the story could rightly understand Jesus' identity until after the crucifixion and resurrection—not the crowds, not the enemies, not the disciples, not even his family. Only God, the demons, and the (post-Easter!) reader could perceive Jesus as Christ and Son of God. Thus in Mark 3:21 Jesus' family, including Mary, seem to share the general opinion that Jesus is "out of his mind." Mark has no birth story and gives no indication that Mary or Jesus' brothers and sisters ever came to faith in him prior to Easter. Luke has a different perspective for telling the story, in which people of faith in the story line could discern the true identity of Jesus even prior to Easter. His birth story in 1:26–56; 2:1–40 presents Mary as one who responds in faith to the word of God, and his story of the church in Acts portrays Mary as among the Christian believers (Acts 1:14).

Luke adjusts the story to his own theological perspective by subtle changes to the Markan text: (1) he discreetly omits Mark 3:20–21 altogether; (2) he omits Mark's classification of "those around (Jesus)" and those "outside" that places the family of Jesus in the latter group; (3)

he explains that Mary and Jesus' brothers and sisters could not reach him "because of the crowd," though they were "wanting to see" him; (4) he places the whole incident later in the story than Mark, after the parable of the Sower rather than before, so that it now echoes the previous language of the "word of God" (8:11) and "hear the word of God and do it" (8:15), and Jesus' family becomes a positive example; (5) he replaces Mark's "brothers and sisters" (Mark 3:32) with "brothers" (v. 20), because "brothers/brethren" was a term used for the church in early Christianity (a point sometimes obscured by the NRSV but retained by the NIV). "Brother" was a generic term in first-century Greek, including male and female, and is thus often rightly translated elsewhere as "brothers and sisters" (e.g., Acts 16:40; Rom. 1:13; 7:1; 1 Cor. 1:10, 26).

In all this, Luke retains the Markan point that commitment to God through Jesus Christ is even more important than family commitments (see also 14:25–32, esp. 14:26).

8:22–25
STILLING THE STORM
(See also at Matt. 8:23–27; Mark 4:35–41)

Here Luke has three miracle stories that portray Jesus' power over natural catastrophes, demonic power, and sickness/death—that is, the power of God manifest in Jesus that overcomes these enemies of human life. All three stories point beyond themselves to the act of God in Christ. (See excursus, "Interpreting the Miracle Stories," at Matt. 9:35.)

8:22 One day: Luke has a different chronology, separating this story from its Markan context at the close of the day of teaching in parables from the boat (see on 8:4). **Lake/sea:** See on 5:1–3.

8:24 Master: This address to Jesus is found only in Luke (5:5; 8:24, 45; 9:33, 49; 17:13). It represents a change from Mark's "teacher," emphasizing the power of God manifest in Jesus.

Rebuked the wind and the raging waves: Jesus acts by his all-powerful word alone. By portraying him as commanding the wind and sea, Luke pictures Jesus as doing what only God can do (Ps. 107:23–25, 28–29; Job 9:8; Ps. 77:16, 19; Isa. 43:2). It is the power of God that is manifest in Jesus (on the theocentric character of Luke's Christology, see on 5:25–26; 7:16; 8:24, 38; 9:20–22, 43; 13:13; 17:15; 19:37).

8:25 Where is your faith?/Who then is this?: Luke concludes the story with two questions, each of which he has adjusted from his Markan source to his own perspective. The

"Have you no faith?" (literally, "How is it that you have no faith?") of Mark 4:40 has been softened to "Where is your faith?"—which assumes that the disciples do indeed have faith, but that it has receded or grown weak at the moment. Again, Luke modifies the harsh picture of the disciples Mark had drawn within the framework of the Markan messianic secret. This same motif was at work in Mark 4:4, in Mark expressing the disciples' lack of understanding. In its Lukan context, the question focuses the issue of the identity of Jesus, the theme of this extensive section that will climax in the confession of 9:20 (see 5:21; 7:20, 49; 9:9).

Like all the other Gospel miracle stories, this one points beyond itself to the act of God in the Christ event as a whole. The real question is not whether Jesus literally calmed a storm on a Galilean lake, but whether God has acted in Christ to deliver those who call on him. The story affirms that God is superior to any natural disaster, that even if our frail craft sinks and we must go down with the ship, God is the master yet, and delivers *through* and *beyond* (not necessarily *from*) the power of any natural disaster to destroy those who call on him in faith.

8:26–39
THE GERASENE DEMONIAC
(See also at Matt. 8:28–34; Mark 5:1–20)

On the language of demons, Satan, and exorcism, see excursus, "Satan, the Devil, and Demons in Biblical Theology," at Mark 5:1.

8:26 Gerasenes: Gerasa was a Gentile Greek town belonging to the Decapolis, thirty-seven miles to the southeast of the Sea of Galilee through rugged terrain. Thus some manuscripts read "Gadara," a town six miles from the lake, but still posing difficulties for the story, which pictures the pigs rushing down the bank directly into the sea (8:33). From the third-century CE it has been claimed that yet a third city, Gergasa, was located on the lakeshore, but there is no archaeological evidence for this. As the stories of Jesus were retold in early Christianity prior to their incorporation into the Gospels, such details became fluid among those who did not have an accurate knowledge of Palestinian geography.

8:27, 29 The man's deplorable condition—naked, homeless, ritually unclean by association with pigs (Lev. 11:7; Deut. 14:8), tombs (Num. 19:11; see Matt. 23:27), and demons (see 4:33 above), out of control, having lost his personal iden-

tity—fitly represents in a symbolic manner the human condition apart from God (Luke twice adds the word *anthropos*, "human being," to the Markan version of the story [8:33, 35]). As even a cursory reading of Homer's *Iliad* documents, many people in the ancient world understood life to be threatened by a multitude of spirits, demons, and angels that invaded and controlled their lives.

8:28 What do you have to do with me?: See on 4:34.

8:30 Legion: A Roman military unit comprised five thousand to six thousand men. The man experiences his life as a veritable mob of conflicting forces and has lost his personal identity represented by his own name. The original story probably had an anti-Roman slant; the wild boar was the logo of the Roman legion stationed in Palestine. The demonic Romans are reluctant to give up their occupied territory, but the natives are glad to see them driven into the sea. By the time it was incorporated into the Gospels, however, this connotation seems to have been lost. Mark has no anti-Roman polemic, and Luke is attempting to assure the Roman leaders that Jesus' followers are good citizens and loyal subjects. For Mark and Luke, the point of the name Legion is not explicitly political but the size of the demonic horde that has invaded the poor man, **for many demons had entered him**.

8:31 Abyss: Luke changes this from Mark's "out of the country" (Mark 5:10). The abyss is the depth of the sea, under the earth, the primeval world of gloom and darkness, the bottomless pit where demonic powers are confined by God (Jude 6; 2 Pet. 2:4; Rev. 9:1–2, 11; 20:1–3). This image places the scene in an eschatological context, lifting it from an individual story in Jesus' ministry to represent the final conflict between God and the demonic powers, in which they are vanquished forever. Christians believe this has already begun to happen in the Christ event. The story thus points beyond itself to the ultimate victory of God over all the powers that enslave human life.

8:32–33 The demons begged Jesus: At an earlier stage of the development of the story, it probably focused on the folk motif of "deceiving the demon." The demons get what they ask for, only to be destroyed anyway. Luke omits the fantastic and problematic number of two thousand pigs in the Markan account and does not raise the ethical question of Jesus' destruction of other people's property and the destruction of food in a hungry world.

8:36 Healed/saved: To Mark's account Luke adds this word that can mean either "healed" or "saved" (see Luke 6:9; 7:50; 8:12, 36, 48, 50; 9:24; 13:23; 17:19; 18:26, 42; 19:10; 23:35, 37, 39), thus facilitating the story's being understood as a symbolic representation of God's salvation. The meaning of salvation is pictured in that (1) the man is **clothed** and no longer dwells in the tombs, i.e., he is reintegrated into society; (2) he is **in his right mind**, i.e., he has "come to himself," like the prodigal son in the far country (15:17) and is no longer a slave to demonic powers; and (3) he is **sitting at the feet of Jesus**, the posture of a grateful disciple (7:38; 8:41; 10:39; 17:16). The story could thus be read by post-Easter readers as reflecting the conversion of Gentiles to Christ.

8:39 How much God has done: Luke changes Mark's ambiguous "Lord" (Mark 5:19) to "God," so that when the man, commanded to tell what God had done for him, relates what Jesus had done, it becomes the more clear that the story as a whole points beyond itself to God's act in Christ for all humanity. Again, the theocentric character of Luke's view of Christ is documented (5:25–26; 7:16; 8:24, 38; 9:20–22, 43; 13:13; 17:15; 19:37).

8:40–56
Jairus's Daughter and the Woman with the Hemorrhage
(See also at Matt. 9:18–26; Mark 5:21–43)

This story within a story was already combined in Mark, a characteristic feature of Markan style (see on 5:17–26). In this instance, it is not merely a matter of literary technique, but it expresses the close relationship between sickness (the woman) and death (Jairus's daughter). In biblical thought, sickness is already an anticipation of the last enemy, death. The prayers of sick people recorded in the Psalms speak of sickness as a kind of death (e.g., Pss. 9:13; 18:4; 22:15; 55:4; 78:50; 88:15; 107:18; 116:3).

8:41 Synagogue: See on 4:16.

8:43 A woman who had been suffering from hemorrhages: Her vaginal bleeding was not only a physical problem, but rendered her ritually unclean (see Lev. 15:25–31), and was thus a social problem as well. As in the case of the demoniac above, her salvation (see 8:48) not only restored her bodily health, but also restored her to the community life. **No one could cure her:** Some manuscripts of Luke refer to her having spent all her money on physicians, but only getting worse instead of better (as in Mark). Since we do not have the original manuscript of Luke (or any other biblical document), those who reconstruct the Greek text of the New Testament from which all our English translations are made must make a judgment call as to what Luke originally wrote (see "Introduction: The New Testament as the Church's Book," 4.d). In this instance, the NIV follows one reconstruction and the NRSV the other. Since it is doubtful that the author was "the beloved physician" of Col. 4:14, the interpreter should not see the omission as Luke's professional pride.

8:44 Touched: In the traditional view, her touch renders Jesus ritually unclean, just as does contact with the dead body of the little girl. Jesus' power and authority transcends the traditional understandings of ritual purity. On ritual purity, see 2:22–24. Now that Jesus is regarded as "contaminated," Jairus, as leader of the synagogue, also has a courageous decision to make: can he now ask Jesus to enter his house?

8:48 Your faith has made you well: Here as in 5:20; 11:5–8; 18:1–8, "faith" does not mean right belief but courageous persistence. The word translated "made well" can also mean "saved" (see on 8:36). The same pair of words occurs in Jesus' response to Jairus in v. 50.

8:49 Do not trouble the teacher any longer: Jairus and his family had believed that Jesus could heal the little girl. Now that she is dead, they give up hope (see 24:21). Human wisdom, even if it is believing wisdom, says, "While there's life, there's hope." This story, which is a prefiguration of the resurrection of Jesus, declares that even when it's too late, it's not too late.

8:52 She is not dead but sleeping: This does not mean, as the older rationalist interpreters thought, that Jesus sharply observed that the girl was only in a coma and intervened to prevent her premature burial. The girl was really dead (see John 11:11–13; 1 Thess. 4:13–14). "Sleep" is used as a metaphor for death, not because believers flee from the reality of death and disguise it by prettier names, but because it is not ultimate.

8:54 Get up: The word is the same one used for resurrection, "Arise!" (see on 7:14). Here too it is a resuscitation, not resurrection in the sense of Jesus' own resurrection to a new order of eschatological existence. The story of Jesus' raising the little girl points beyond itself to the story of God's raising up Jesus.

8:55 Her spirit returned: The Greek word *pneuma* means "breath," "wind," or "spirit." Here the meaning is that she started breathing again. Since living persons breathe, it is but a short step from literal breath to breath as an expression of one's life.

8:56 Tell no one: A reflection of Mark's messianic secret that Luke has adopted without casting the life of Jesus in the same secretive framework as in Mark (see on 4:35; 5:14; 8:9–10, 25).

9:1–6
SENDING OUT THE TWELVE
(See also at Matt. 10:1–14; Mark 6:6–13)

Luke found a story of Jesus' commissioning his disciples for missionary work in each of his two major sources, Mark and Q (see introduction to Luke). He uses the Mark 6 passage here as "Sending Out the Twelve," and the Q version, now also reflected in Matt. 10, as the "Sending Out the Seventy" (see 10:1–24 below).

These missionary instructions have at least four layers of meaning (see "Introduction to the Gospels" and comments on 1:1–4): (1) the historical Jesus probably sent out disciples to proclaim his message; (2) after Easter, the earliest Christians sent out missionaries and adapted Jesus' instructions to their later situation, just as their account of the earlier instructions is now influenced by their missionary context and its needs; (3) both Mark and Q included an account of this commission, interpreting it in the perspective of their literary and theological purposes; (4) Luke here reinterprets Mark 6:6–13 within the framework of his theology of the ministry of Jesus as the "midst of time." (See introduction to Luke and comments on the kingdom of God listed above.) For Luke, these instructions have validity in illuminating the missionary practice of his own time, but they primarily represent the special time of the one-year ministry of Jesus, when the kingdom of God was present; different instructions are given for the time of the church, in which Luke and his post-Easter readers live (see 22:35–38 and the comments there).

9:1–2 The Twelve: See on 6:12–13. Luke modifies his Markan source to emphasize the similarity of the apostles' deed to Jesus' own actions: casting out demons, healing, and preaching. They do not preach the later Christian message that Jesus is the Messiah but, like Jesus, preach the **kingdom of God** (see on 4:13, 20–21, 43–44; 11:20; 17:21). In the Synoptic Gospels (in contrast to the Gospel of John), Jesus does not proclaim himself but God's present and coming kingdom.

9:3–5 Take nothing for your journey: Early Christian missionaries were dependent on the hospitality of fellow Christians (Rom. 12:13; Titus 1:8; Heb. 13:2; 1 Pet. 4:9). Traveling without even the essentials of food, protection, and money would also be both an expression of solidarity with the poor—an emphasis of the Lukan Jesus (see at 1:46–55; 2:8–14; 4:18–19; 6:20–23)—and a dramatic symbolic act like that of the Old Testament prophets. That Jesus' followers stand in the succession of the prophets is also a Lukan emphasis (see 6:23; Acts 2:17–21). **No staff:** Luke (here following Q) is even more stringent that the Markan instructions, which permit a staff (Mark 6:8—"nothing . . . except a staff"). Luke also omits the Markan permission of wearing sandals. **Nor money:** Luke uses a different Greek word for "money" (literally "silver") from Mark's (literally "copper"). This is one of several indications that Luke writes for a church in a higher socioeconomic bracket than Mark's. His concern for the poor and for responsible use of money thus does not mean that he belongs to the poor class himself.

Stay there: Early Christian missionaries were sometimes tempted to shop around for the best accommodations. They could be confused with the indigent street preachers of other religions, who were sometimes interested only in living off the generosity or religious fears of others. Jesus' disciples are to make it clear in the conduct of their mission that their principal concern is their message and the welfare of their hearers. They are to arouse no suspicions that they are only out to make an easy living by being itinerant preachers.

Whenever they do not welcome you: Shaking off the dust of the feet was a vivid way of separating the messengers from those who had rejected them, a symbolic act of judgment indicating that the hearers had had an opportunity to respond to the good news of Jesus' message and had refused, so that the missionaries no longer were responsible for them.

9:7–9
Various Views of Jesus' Identity
(See also at Matt. 14:1–2; Mark 6:14–16)

9:7 Herod the tetrarch/ruler: On the division of the kingdom of Herod the Great (37–4 BCE), see on 3:1–2. This is Herod Antipas, who was ruler over Galilee and Perea during Jesus' ministry. Mark 6:14, Luke's source, calls him a king, but Luke gives the correct title of tetrarch (as NIV translates), a ruler (so NRSV) of a fourth part of the whole country. He was only a puppet ruler under the control of Rome.

This Herod appears twice more in Luke (13:31; 23:15), each time in passages peculiar to this Gospel. The activities of Jesus' missionaries had brought his followers to the attention of both the public and the ruler.

It was said by some that John had been raised from the dead: This note would be a surprise to the reader who did not already know Mark 6:17–29 (which Luke has omitted). The Lukan reader knows that John has been imprisoned by Herod (3:19–20) and that John has sent messengers to Jesus (7:18–23), but not that John has been killed. The idea of resurrection was widespread in Judaism in the first century, prior to and apart from Christianity, especially among Pharisees (20:27–40; Acts 23:6–9; John 11:17–24).

9:9 Who is this?: In Mark, Herod shares the view that Jesus is the risen John the Baptist, but by a very slight adjustment of the Greek text Luke transforms the statement into a question and lets Herod pose the central issue of this section of the Gospel, that of Jesus' identity. The popular identification of Jesus was that he was an outstanding prophet God had brought back from the dead. Luke does picture Jesus as in continuity with the ministry of John the Baptist, as an Elijah-like figure (see, e.g., on 7:11–17 above), and as the fulfillment of the Old Testament prophets (e.g., 4:21), as the prophet like Moses who was to come (Acts 3:22–26). Yet Luke is about to present scenes in which "prophet," though a true description of Jesus, does not adequately express his identity (9:18–36).

9:10–17
FEEDING THE FIVE THOUSAND
(See also at Matt. 14:13–21; Mark 6:32–44)

In the Lukan context, this story forms the link between Herod's question about Jesus' identity (9:9, "Who is this?") and the identification of Jesus as God's Messiah (Peter's confession, 9:20; Mark 8:29), the suffering, dying, and rising Son of Man (Jesus' self-testimony, 9:22), and the unique Son of God (God's testimony, 9:35). This transition that leads to the revelation of Jesus' true identity is made at a Eucharist-like meal over which Jesus himself presides, like the Lukan scene in 24:13–35. Here too, Jesus is "made known to them in the breaking of the bread."

9:10 Bethsaida: Only Luke introduces the scene as taking place in Bethsaida, a fishing town on the northeast shore of the Sea of Galilee. Mark, followed by Matthew, has the miracle occur in a "deserted place," and only afterwards do

Jesus and the disciples travel by boat across the lake to Bethsaida (Mark 6:32, 45). John has the feeding take place on a "mountain" (John 6:3; or in "the hills" RSV). Luke's reference to Bethsaida is especially puzzling since 9:12 presupposes the same deserted location as Mark. The reference may have something to do with Luke's omission of Mark 6:45–8:26 (Luke's Great Omission), which began and ended with references to Bethsaida (though Mark's geography is also confusing; the disciples leave for Bethsaida in 6:45 but arrive in Gennesaret in 6:53, only to arrive at Bethsaida much later in 8:22.)

9:11 The crowds . . . followed him: Not because they were expecting a free meal, but to be healed and to hear his message of the **kingdom of God** (see on 4:13, 20–21, 43–44; 11:20; 17:21.)

9:12–13 The twelve: They take the initiative (Mark 6:35, "his disciples"; John 6:5–6, Jesus himself). On the Lukan distinction between "disciples" and "the Twelve," see on 6:12–13. They have a humanitarian concern for hungry and homeless people and want to do what is humanly possible to assist them. **Send the crowd away:** Their well-intentioned response to the situation, their concern for others, causes them to notice. **You give them something to eat:** Jesus' paradoxical response. Christ does not act apart from their own actions. When the feeding happens, Jesus does not give the food to the multitudes directly, but through the apostles. This picture of God's concern for the hungry being implemented by the acts of Jesus' followers is followed up in Acts (2:42; 4:34; 6:1–6; 11:27–29). In Luke's version of the story, it is the Twelve themselves who have the bread and fish that are used by Christ to feed the hungry (9:13; see Mark 6:38; John 6:9).

9:14 About five thousand men: The number five thousand shows how great the miracle was. The story of feeding the four thousand (Mark 8:1–10; Matt. 15:32–39) is probably a variant of the same story (omitted by Luke and John). **Men:** May be generic, "people," or may represent a picture in which only adult males would leave home without provisions for an extended time in order to hear Jesus. Matthew 14:31, "besides women and children," understands it in the exclusive sense in order to enhance the miracle. **Groups of about fifty each:** This may reflect the organization of Israel during the exodus and wilderness period, the "wandering people of God" en route from Egypt to the promised land (Exod. 18:21–25). Luke portrays the life of both Jesus and the church as a journey and refers to the saving work of Jesus as an "exodus" (see on 9:31; 9:51).

9:16 Taking ... blessed ... broke ... gave: These words echo the eucharistic liturgy of the early church (see Mark 14:22–25; Matt. 26:26–30; Luke 22:14–20; John 6:48–58; 1 Cor. 11:23–25). As the stories of Jesus' ministry were retold after Easter, they took on the features of church life, and Christian readers could see their own experience reflected in the stories of Jesus in the Gospels.

9:17 All ate and were filled ... left over ... twelve baskets: Luke's picture of the one-year ministry of Jesus as the time when the kingdom of God was upon the earth represents it as a time when the eschatological extravagance of the final kingdom of God is already anticipated (see on 4:13, 20–21, 43–44; 11:20; 17:21 and introduction to Luke: "Jesus as the 'Midst of Time'"). There is plenty, and it is for all. In Luke's understanding, the church lives between the ministry of Jesus in feeding the hungry and the final messianic banquet in which there will be no hungry. The church's mission of feeding the hungry is a continuation of Jesus' ministry and an anticipation of the final kingdom of God for which it prays (11:2).

9:18–27
CONFESSION AND DISCIPLESHIP
(See also at Matt. 16:13–28; Mark 8:27–9:1)

From 8:4 through 9:17 Luke has been following the Markan story line quite closely. At this point, however, he omits an extensive section of the Markan narrative (Mark 6:45–8:26, the Great Omission). The reasons for this editorial decision are not evident, but the effect is clear: the next scene, in which Peter confesses Jesus to be the Christ, is brought into immediate conjunction with the question of Herod (9:9) and the feeding of the five thousand. This means the scene is no longer in the Markan context of Caesarea Philippi (Mark 8:27), but in the familiar Lukan setting of Jesus at prayer (see 6:12; 28; 22:40–46; 23:34, 46). The disciples in Luke are a larger circle than the Twelve (see on 6:12–13). Jesus takes the initiative and asks about the crowds, who in this context are those who have been following him, were present at the feeding of the five thousand, have seen him heal and heard his instruction about the kingdom of God, but are not (yet) committed disciples. They represent potential disciples.

9:19 John the Baptist ... Elijah ... one of the ancient prophets: See on 9:7–9. This repre-

sents a "high" Christology. The crowds believed that Jesus was a prophet of God, had been raised from the dead (i.e., resuscitated, not that he represented the eschatological act of God; see on 7:14), or was a being who had once lived on earth, had been taken to heaven, and had returned (Elijah, see 1 Kgs. 17–2 Kgs. 2). But these exalted views of Jesus as risen and returning from heaven did not make them disciples.

9:20 The Messiah of God: See on Mark 8:29. Luke's theocentric understanding of the Christ event is seen in his adding "of God" to "Messiah" of Mark 8:29 (5:25–26; 7:16; 8:24, 38; 9:20–22, 43; 13:13; 17:15; 19:37). The angels had announced the birth of the Messiah (2:11), the aged prophet Simeon had lived in hope of seeing the Lord's Messiah (2:26), people had wondered whether John the Baptist might be the Messiah (3:15), and the demons had recognized Jesus as the Messiah (4:41), but this is the first time any human being had confessed Jesus to be the Messiah. Luke understands the title to be the central Christian confession of faith (Acts 2:36) and to have played a crucial role in Jesus' trial and death (22:67; 23:2, 35, 39).

9:21–22 First Passion Prediction (Matt. 16:21–23; Mark 8:31–33). In Mark, Luke's source (see introduction to Luke), Jesus predicts his coming suffering three times in very similar words (Mark 8:31; 9:31; 10:32–33), and these three passion predictions form part of the integral structure of the Gospel. Luke adopts all three of the Markan predictions (see also 9:44; 18:31–34) and adds three others of a different form (12:50; 13:32–34; 17:25). They are all written from the post-Easter perspective of the church, which knew the details of Jesus' betrayal, trial, and crucifixion, and God's vindication of Jesus at the resurrection. The dual emphasis in both Mark and Luke is (1) that the role of the Messiah is fulfilled, not negated, by his suffering for others, and (2) that the suffering and death of Jesus were not a tragic accident of history or a negation of God's plan, but willed by God and accepted by Jesus.

As in Mark, the disciples identify Jesus with the correct title but still misunderstand his mission. For the first time, Jesus explains to them that being the Messiah means suffering, death, and resurrection (for Son of Man, see on Mark 2:10). Luke's theocentric understanding is again emphasized in that he changes Mark's "rise" (as though the Son of Man did it himself) to **be raised** (by God; 29; see 5:25–26; 7:16; 8:24, 38; 9:20–22, 43; 13:13; 17:15; 19:37). "Must," the word repeatedly used by Luke (2:49; 4:43; 9:22; 17:25; 21:9; 22:37; 24:7, 26, 44), is not a matter of personal compulsion but represents the divine plan to which Jesus submits himself. Luke here omits Mark's portrayal of the disciples' protest, Peter's rebuke of Jesus, and Jesus' calling Peter Satan (Mark 8:32–33), here as elsewhere enhancing the image of the disciples in comparison with the Markan picture.

9:23 To become my followers: Christology and discipleship are always related. How one understands Jesus' nature and role in God's plan directly affects how one understands what it means to be a follower of Jesus, and vice versa. A suffering Messiah (see 23:35, 39; 24:46) means that disciples are also called to suffering and self-sacrifice.

Daily: Luke adds this one word to the Markan saying (Mark 8:34), completely reinterpreting it to fit his own time. In Mark, written just after Nero's persecution of Christians in Rome, where Christians had been killed and Peter himself and others had been crucified, "taking up one's cross" was understood literally as the cost of discipleship. In Luke's situation about twenty years later, there is no direct persecution. By adding "daily" Luke does not water down the demand of Jesus; the cost of discipleship is still the same: one's whole life. But now it is not given all at once, in one dramatic act, but one day at a time, as Christ's disciples give their lives away in service to others. Thus the Lukan addition **to them all,** like the Lukan addition of "the crowds" in v. 18, has the effect of universalizing the call of Jesus to discipleship. It is no longer only to the martyr apostles of the original situation, but to all of Luke's readers.

9:24–25 To save their life: Just as Jesus as the crucified Messiah reverses everyone's expectations of what the Messiah would be, so these instructions about discipleship reverse everyone's commonsense standard of values of what a "successful" life is all about.

9:26 Those who are ashamed: If this saying is from the life of the historical Jesus, it may indicate that Jesus distinguished the coming **Son of Man** from himself and proclaimed that when the divine savior figure appears at the end of history, he will vindicate those who have been faithful to Jesus (on Son of Man, see at Mark 2:10). Luke and the early church certainly understood Jesus to be identifying him-

self as the Son of Man. Here the Son of Man has God for his Father, so "Son of God" should not be contrasted with "Son of Man." (On Son of God, see on 1:28–33.) All these sayings indicate that discipleship cannot be individualistic and private. Keeping one's faith to oneself, or just between the believer and God, is here understood as being ashamed of Jesus and his cross, and will be condemned in the Last Judgment. Discipleship is a matter of public confession of Jesus in one's words and deeds (see 12:4–12; Acts 1:8; 4:1–5:42).

9:27 Not taste death: This saying reflects the faith of first-generation Christians, who lived in the expectation of the soon return of Christ and the final establishment of the **kingdom of God**. It is not clear how Luke understands this saying in his later situation. Various interpreters' attempts to understand the saying as fulfilled in the transfiguration (9:28–36) or at Pentecost (Acts 2) are not convincing. Luke does not identify the kingdom with the church. For Luke, his disciples have indeed seen the kingdom in the life of Jesus and will see it in its fullness at the return of Christ (see on 4:13, 20–21, 43–44; 11:20; 17:21; Acts 1:6–11; 1 Thess. 4:13–18).

9:28–36
THE TRANSFIGURATION
(See also at Matt. 17:1–9; Mark 9:2–10)

9:28 Eight days: The reasons for Luke's changing from the "six days" of Mark 9:2 are unknown. **The mountain:** Its location is not identified in the Gospels. The point is not geography, but the parallel to Mt. Sinai (= Mt. Horeb), where both Moses and Elijah encountered God (Exod. 19; 1 Kgs. 19:1–18). **To pray:** Luke places crucial scenes in Jesus' life in the context of prayer (6:12; 9:18, 28; 22:40–46; 23:34, 46).

9:29 Face . . . clothes: Luke does not speak explicitly of a transfiguration, but portrays Jesus' appearance as already anticipating the glory into which he will enter at the resurrection and ascension (see 9:26, 31; 21:27; 24:26).

9:30 Moses and Elijah: Both were true prophets of God in the Old Testament. Elijah had been taken to heaven without dying (2 Kgs. 2). The biblical story of Moses' burial (by God) in a place unknown to humans (Deut. 34:5–5, 10) was understood in some later Jewish traditions to mean God had taken Moses to heaven.

9:31–33 These verses are a Lukan addition to Mark 9:4. Only Luke fills in the content of the conversation between the two visitors from the world of **glory**: they discuss the **departure** (literally "exodus") that Jesus will **accomplish at Jerusalem.** The heavenly world confirms in advance Jesus' decision to go to the cross, problematic as it was for Jesus' human disciples.

Make three shelters (NIV) **dwellings** (NRSV): The word may be related to the booths ("tabernacles") constructed annually by the Israelites in memory of the wilderness wanderings for the Feast of Booths (Lev. 23:42–43; Deut. 16:13, 16; 31:10). **Not knowing what he said:** Though Peter has given the correct answer to the question of Jesus' identity (9:20), he has not yet understood its meaning and here wants to memorialize the splendid experience on the mountaintop, rather than follow Jesus to the "exodus" (crucifixion) in Jerusalem.

9:34 Cloud: As on Mt. Sinai (Exod. 16:10; 19:9), but also as an anticipation of the clouds on which Jesus shall depart (Acts 1) and return (Luke 21:27; 1:9; see Dan. 7:13–14).

9:35–36 My Son . . . Jesus was found alone: Moses and Elijah disappear. Luke has understood Jesus to be the fulfillment of the promised prophet like Moses of Deut. 18:15–18 (24:19; Acts 3:17–26; 7:37) and has pictured Jesus with Elijah-like traits (see, e.g., Luke 4:25–26/1 Kgs. 17:1–16; Luke 7:11–17; 9:10–17/1 Kgs. 17:17–24). The hope for the promised prophet is indeed fulfilled in Jesus, but prophet is not an adequate category for Jesus' role in God's plan. As Peter rightly confesses Jesus to be God's Messiah (9:20; Mark 8:29), here God confesses Jesus to be his Son.

9:37–43a
JESUS HEALS A POSSESSED BOY
(See also at Matt. 17:14–21; Mark 9:14–29)

The scene at the bottom of the mountain is in stark contrast to the glory of the mountaintop experience the day before. This is more like the continuing experience of Jesus' disciples in the world where demonic power is still rampant, disciples who have not personally experienced the glories of the other world.

9:37–38 A great crowd: Not hostile, but potential disciples (6:17–20). **Only child:** See on 7:12.

9:40 Disciples: Not limited to the Twelve (see on 6:12–13).

9:42–43 Luke has radically compressed the Markan story in Mark 9:11–29, concentrating on **Jesus'** act that results in praise to **God**

(on the theocentric nature of Luke's Christology, see 5:25–26; 7:16; 8:24, 38; 9:20–22; 13:13; 17:15; 19:37).

9:43b–48
THE SECOND PASSION PREDICTION;
TRUE GREATNESS
(See also at Matt. 17:22–18:25; Mark 9:30–37)

Luke juxtaposes the crowd's awe at God's greatness to Jesus' second prediction of his coming suffering. What the crowd, and even the disciples, understand as either/or, Jesus affirms as both/and. It is precisely the greatness of God that is revealed in the redemptive suffering of the Son of Man.

9:44 Betrayed: the same word can also be translated "handed over." The word is used with intentional ambiguity for both human and divine actions. (See commentary on Mark 1:14.)

9:45 Concealed from them: Luke spares the disciples again. They do not understand, but they are not altogether responsible. It is not clear whether it is God or Satan (see 8:12) who keeps them from understanding, but in either case it was an aspect of the divine mystery by which God's act in Jesus was not recognized until after the resurrection and gift of the Spirit (see 18:34 and comments on 24:16).

9:46–48 The greatest: The disciples' lack of understanding is emphasized by juxtaposing it both to the greatness of God (9:43; only in Luke) and Jesus' announcement of his impending suffering that immediately precedes. **Aware of their inner thoughts:** See 2:35; 5:22; 7:39.

Whoever welcomes this child in my name welcomes me: Luke has a somewhat hierarchical understanding of how God's grace is mediated (see on 7:8–9; 10:16). Here the disciples misunderstand the matter in terms of rank and privilege, so the disciples are replaced in the divine order by children: God ⇒ Christ ⇒ little child. Unless they become as unpresumptuous little children who are not concerned with their own image and status, they cannot be Christ's representatives. Discipleship to Jesus is not a means of attaining our own goals, but represents a transformation of our values and commitments.

Whoever welcomes me welcomes the one who sent me: Luke's theocentric Christology (see 7:16; 8:24, 38; 9:20–22, 43; 13:13; 17:15; 19:37) has its own way of affirming Jesus as the functional equivalent of God.

The least among all of you is the greatest:
Not a strategy for becoming great by trying to
be least, but a renunciation of schemes of self-
advancement. Whoever receives a child does
so without regard for what the child can do in
return.

9:49–50
THE UNAUTHORIZED EXORCIST
(See also at Mark 9:38–41)

The issue here is deeper than personal pettiness
and involves the question of who is authorized to
speak and act for God. This is analogous to the
question of true and false prophets in the Old Testament (1 Kgs. 22; Jer. 23). Like the preceding scene,
this episode illustrates the disciples' misunderstanding of the commissioning in which the apostles and disciples represent Jesus, who represents
God (see 10:16). John, a member of the Twelve (see
6:12–14), objects that someone not a member of
their group (disciples or the Twelve?) is performing exorcisms. John's protest is the more regrettable
since the disciples had not been able to perform
exorcisms themselves (9:37–43). They are more
concerned with their own position than with overcoming demonic powers (contrast Phil. 1:15–18).

9:50 Whoever is not against you is for you: Luke
also preserves the more exclusive version of
this saying (11:23). Both present a dualistic
either/or. Decision for or against Christ
divides all humanity into two camps. One
must be either for or against; there is no category called undecided. John could not see that
God's work is sometimes done by those we
consider outsiders, those who "don't belong."
This scene is all the more powerful in that it is
in the New Testament narrative most concerned with order and structure.

9:51–19:27
THE JOURNEY TO JERUSALEM

The Gospel of Mark, Luke's major narrative
source, had basically a two-part outline: Jesus'
Galilean ministry (chaps. 1–9) and the passion
story in Jerusalem (chaps. 11–16), connected by
a brief transitional section in which Jesus journeys from Galilee to Jerusalem (chap. 10). Luke
preserves this overall outline but inserts a large
amount of his special material into the middle
section, so that it becomes a major section of his
Gospel, the Travel Narrative. Luke here abandons the Markan outline, to which he will return
in 18:14, and composes this section from Q and
L materials, formulating his own structure.

9:51–56
REJECTION IN SAMARIA

9:51 Set his face: Jesus resolves to carry out his
divinely given mission that will result in his
death in Jerusalem (see 9:22, 44).

9:52 Samaritans: The first reference in Luke (see
10:33; 17:11, 16; Acts 1:8; 8:1–25; 9:31; 15:3).
Samaria lay on the west bank of the Jordan
between Galilee and Jerusalem, but it is not
certain that Luke had a clear understanding of
Palestinian geography. In 17:11 Jesus is pictured as still on the border between Galilee and
Samaria, so Luke may think of Galilee as
immediately adjacent to Judea, with Samaria
parallel to both. The Samaritans were a people
ethnically and historically related to the Jews
but distinct from them in religious practices.
Jews thought of Samaritans as the semipagan
people of mixed blood who had been resettled
by the Assyrians after the conquest and deportation of the northern kingdom (see 2 Kgs.
17:24–41). Samaritans thought of themselves
as the true descendants of Israel, who had preserved the ancient ways and had their own
temple on Mt. Gerazim. They had been recon-
quered and forcibly "re-Judaized" in 128 BCE
by the Jewish Maccabean king John Hyrcanus,
who destroyed their rival temple. In Jesus' day,
lingering suspicions and hatreds existed on
both sides. Many Samaritans and Jews would
not associate with each other, not only for reasons of ritual purity, but because of racial and
national prejudice (see John 4:1–9, 19–20).

9:53 They did not receive him: Jesus was willing
to associate with them, but they not with him,
because he was going to Jerusalem, site of the
Jewish temple; the Samaritans had their own
temple on Mt. Gerazim (see John 4:19–20).

**9:54 Fire to come down from heaven and con-
sume them:** See 1 Kgs. 18:20–40; 2 Kgs. 1:1–18.
Elijah had brought down fire from heaven on
his enemies. Luke has modeled the portrayal
of Jesus' ministry on Elijah but abandons the
model of the prophet who punishes those who
reject him with fire from heaven—though his
disciples have not yet understood this. Once
again there is no room for Jesus, and he must
go elsewhere (see 2:7; 4:24, 29; 23:50–53).

9:57–62
DISCIPLE WANNABES
(See also at Matt. 8:18–22)

These three scenes emphasize the radical nature
of Christian discipleship. Following Jesus is not

something that can be added on to other good causes. Nor does Jesus formulate a marketing strategy to get as many followers as possible.

9:58 Foxes . . . birds: Since "son of man" can simply mean "human being" as well as be a title for Christ (see on Mark 2:10), this may have originally been a secular proverb: birds and animals have a home in the natural world, but humans are homeless in the world (see 4:23; 8:17–18; 10:22; 11:9–10; 12:3–4). Here, however, the phrase is used christologically to designate the wandering, rejected Christ (see 2:7; 4:24, 29; 9:53–56; 23:50–53). Those who become disciples cannot glibly say, "Where he leads me I will follow," but must count the cost (14:25–33).

9:59 First . . . bury my father: Respect for parents and burial of the dead were extremely sacred obligations in the Old Testament and Jewish tradition (Exod. 20:12; Tob. 1:16–20; 4:3; 6:15). Though Luke can use "dead" in a spiritual sense (15:32), interpreters should not too easily domesticate the saying to mean "let the spiritually dead bury the physically dead." The saying is intended to shock, to portray the radical nature of Christian discipleship in the most provocative way (see 14:26–27).

9:60 Kingdom of God: The call is to proclaim the **kingdom of God**: see on 4:13, 20–21, 43–44; 11:20; 17:21.

9:61 Farewell to those at my home: See 1 Kgs. 19:19–21. Again the story of Jesus evokes that of Elijah, but Jesus' call is more radical than Elijah's. **Fit for the kingdom of God:** Being "fit" is not a matter of worthiness—for none are worthy—but of being suitable, appropriate, and capable. One who plows and looks back will plow a crooked furrow. Following Jesus requires focus on the goal ahead.

10:1–24
Sending Out and Return of the Seventy
(See also at Matt. 9:37–10:24; 11:25–27; 13:16–17)

On Luke's two commissioning scenes, see on 9:1. There is some fluidity between the two scenes: Luke takes the element of sending out two by two from the Markan instructions to the Twelve (Mark 6:7), and in the instructions to the Twelve at the Last Supper in Luke 22:35, Jesus refers to these instructions to the seventy. The directions to both the Twelve and the seventy anticipate and reflect the later mission of the church in Acts, where early Christian missionaries must come to terms with the requirements of the Gentile mission, and often go out two by two (Acts 8:14; 11:30; 13:1; 15:39–40).

10:1 Seventy (-two): Some manuscripts have seventy-two, followed by NIV; other manuscripts have seventy, followed by NRSV. We do not know which Luke originally wrote ("Introduction: The New Testament as the Church's Book," 4.d). The symbolism is probably the same, reflecting the list of nations in Gen. 10, where the Hebrew text has seventy nations, the LXX (the Septuagint, the Greek translation of the Old Testament) has seventy-two nations. The title of the LXX itself manifests the same ambiguity. It is called "The Seventy," yet the legendary story about its translation tells of its miraculous translation by six scribes from each of the twelve tribes of Israel (*Letter of Aristeas*; Philo).

A historical setting in Jesus' ministry is difficult to imagine, for it calls for Jesus himself visiting towns and villages where his messengers have spent thirty-five or thirty-six times as much time preparing for his visit as he himself will spend. In any case, Luke tells of the return of the seventy and their report to Jesus (10:17–24) but never pictures Jesus' own visit to the towns and villages where they have announced his coming. The scene appears rather to symbolize the mission of the church between Jesus' first and second advents, proclaiming the kingdom of God that will be consummated by Jesus' final return (see on Acts 1:6–11).

10:2 Ask the Lord of the harvest to send out laborers: The harvest is a symbol of the eschatological ingathering (Joel 3:13; Mic. 4:11–13; see John 4:35–38) when the wheat will be separated from the chaff, an image Luke has already used (3:7–9). The seed has been and is being sown; the Christian missionaries reap the results (8:4–15). The whole body of Jesus' followers is charged with the mission, not just full-time Christian workers. Many (more than just the Twelve) are actively engaged in preaching, healing, and helping. All are involved in prayer and material support for the church's mission.

10:3–4 No sandals: For these and other instructions, see on 9:1–6. Luke follows the earlier, more severe instructions of Q rather than Mark 6:7–13, which allow rod and sandals. Luke pictures the missionaries as absolutely dependent, defenseless, and vulnerable (see the adjustment to the church's long-term mission in 22:35). Likewise, the command to **greet no one** would be a shocking symbolic sign of the urgency of the mission. Picture a group of travelers in the open country, who see two barefoot, unarmed persons approaching (perhaps two men, perhaps a man and a woman). They pass by without a word of greeting. Such conduct was as outrageous as Isaiah's walking naked and barefoot to symbolize his own message (Isa. 20:2–4).

10:6 Man of peace (NIV)/**Anyone ... who shares in peace** (NRSV): More literally, "son of peace." "Son" in Semitic idiom does not always refer to gender but in such expressions means "belonging to a particular category or group" or "having the character of." "Sons of peace" probably thus originally meant "members of the group devoted to peace." In Jesus' time and during the period of military buildup and political unrest prior to the disastrous war against the Romans in Palestine 66–70 CE, this would have referred to the followers of Jesus who rejected the militarist revolt against Rome, loved and prayed for their enemies (6:27–28), and refused to participate in the war. In Luke's context it had lost its direct political connotation, and referred to those who share the peace of God by participating in the Christian community, but still had the overtones of the antimilitarist life of Jesus.

10:7–11 Do not move about: These instructions give support from Jesus' teaching for the maintenance of Christian ministers (see 1 Cor. 9:14 and more specifically 1 Tim. 5:18). **Laborer:** Became a semitechnical term for Christian ministers (see 2 Cor. 11:13; Phil. 3:2; 2 Tim. 2:15). **Eating and drinking whatever they provide:** This directive is not only an admonition not to shop around for better room and board, but also dissolves the distinction between ritually clean and unclean foods, facilitating missionary work in Gentile areas (see Acts 10–11).

Whenever you enter a town: The three aspects of the mission were (1) establishing community, a matter of table fellowship, important both in the life of Jesus and the life of the early church; (2) healing, addressing the physical needs of the community; and (3) announcing the **kingdom of God** (see on 4:13, 20–21, 43–44; 11:20; 17:21). The eschatological expectation is already present in the life of Jesus.

10:12 Sodom: A city in the region of the Dead Sea, notorious for its lack of hospitality, a serious sin in the ancient Near East, as well as for its pride, its refusal to help the poor and needy, and its sexual immorality. It was destroyed by God for its great sin (Gen. 18:16–19:29; Isa. 3:9; Ezek. 16:48–49; Jude 1:7).

10:13–15 Woes to you!: That these verses are located in another context in Matthew (11:20–24) is one of several indications that the missionary discourse was originally a series of separate sayings, assembled in this context by Luke as instructions for Christian missionaries. **Chorazin:** a town two miles northwest of Capernaum. Apart from this text and its Matthean parallel (= Q), there is no other evidence that Jesus visited Chorazin or that any miracles were performed there. **Bethsaida:** A fishing town on the northeast shore of the Sea of Galilee. In Luke, Bethsaida was the site of feeding the five thousand; see commentary on 9:10. In other early Christian traditions, the home town of Philip, Peter, and Andrew (see Mark 6:45; 8:22; Luke 9:10; John 1:44; 12:21). **Capernaum:** The headquarters of Jesus' Galilean ministry, on the west bank of the Sea of Galilee, where Peter had a house with his mother-in-law (Matt. 4:13; 8:5; 11:23; 17:24; Mark 1:21; 2:1; 9:33; Luke 4:23, 31; 7:1; 10:15; John 2:12; 4:46; 6:17, 24, 59). **Tyre and Sidon** were important cities in Lebanon, often enemies of Israel in the Old Testament, condemned like Sodom by the prophets of Israel for their sins (Isa. 23:1–18; Ezek. 26:1–21; 27:1–28:24). Even the notorious pagan cities of Sodom, Tyre, and Sidon would have repented if they had had the opportunity that the Galilean towns had of encountering the kingdom of God as revealed in Jesus, so the unrepentant Galilean towns will receive the greater judgment. These pronouncements of doom probably reflect the rejection of early Christian missionaries.

Down to Hades: Words of judgment spoken against Babylon in Isa. 14:11, 13, 15 are here applied to Capernaum.

10:16 Whoever rejects you: To reject Jesus' missioners and their message is to reject the Jesus who sent them and the God who sent Jesus. This reflects the Jewish principle that the messenger is as the one who sent him, something like the modern concept of power of attorney. For Luke, the principle of delegated authority is important in the life of the church (see on 7:8–9; 9:46–48; Acts 8:4–25; 13:1–3; 15:1–35; 16:4).

10:17–20 The seventy returned: Their mission is characterized by joy and thanksgiving, the marks of the life of the Christian community. Christian mission is not an onerous task but is filled with joy (see Acts 2:46–47; 5:41–42). The missionaries had proclaimed and enacted the presence of the kingdom of God (see on 4:13, 20–21, 43–44; 11:20; 17:21). Their report emphasizes that the events expected to occur at the eschatological victory of God were already happening in the ministry of Jesus. The fact that **demons** are subject to them (contrast their earlier failure, 9:40) is interpreted by Jesus as the eschatological event of Satan's **fall from heaven**. This is not a reference to the myth of the rebellion of an angel who become Satan or the expulsion from heaven of Satan, who then tempted Adam and Eve (as in Milton's *Paradise Lost*). "Heaven" and "sky" are the same word in the biblical languages. Satan is sometimes pictured as dwelling in the sky, between our world and the divine world, as a barrier between humanity and God (see, e.g., Eph. 2:2; 6:12). The eschatological victory of God will mean the expulsion of Satan from the sky (Rev. 12:7–12). This was expected to happen at the end of history, as was the coming of Christ. In Luke's theology, the coming of Christ, the kingdom of God, and the fall of Satan are not only future events at the end of history, but already happen in the mission of Jesus and his disciples.

10:19 I have given you authority: See on 9:1 and 10:16 above. An anticipation of 24:45–49. **Snakes and scorpions:** Here not literally (as Mark 16:18; see Acts 28:1–6), but symbols for the power of evil (Gen. 3:1–14; Num. 21:6–9; Ps. 91:13; Rev. 9:3).

10:20 Your names are written in heaven: Another apocalyptic image transferred to the present (see Exod. 32:32–33; Ps. 69:28; Dan. 12:1; Mal. 3:16–17; Phil. 4:3; Rev. 3:5; 13:8).

10:21 I thank you, Father: These words are similar to the view of Jesus throughout the Gospel of John (e.g., John 3:35; 13:3; 17:2), and represent one of numerous points of contact between Lukan and Johannine traditions (e.g., Luke 5:1–11; John 21:1–14). **The wise and the intelligent . . . infants:** Not a discouragement of education and serious reflection, but a rejection of claims that humans can attain knowledge of God and his ways by their own achievement (see 1 Cor. 1:18–2:16; Rom. 11:33–36). We know God because God has graciously revealed himself to us in Israel, Christ, and the church, not on the basis of our own calculations or inference from evidence.

10:22 All things have been handed over to me by my Father: See Matt. 28:18–20. The statement affirms Jesus' status as representing God, while preserving the theocentric orientation of Luke's Christology (see 5:25–26; 7:16; 8:24, 38; 9:20–22, 43; 13:13; 17:15; 19:37). **No one knows . . . who the Father is except the Son:** This may

originally have been a secular proverb, in a setting in which trade secrets and family lore were passed on from father to son: "Only a son really knows his father" (see 4:23; 8:17–18; 9:58; 11:9–10; 12:3–4). It has been adopted and adapted to express the Christian faith that Jesus is the definitive revelation of God.

10:23–24 Blessed are the eyes: Jesus' followers live in the time of fulfillment; they experience what the people of God of previous ages only longed for (1:1; 4:21; 24:44; Acts 3:18; Eph. 3:4–6; Heb. 11:1–4; 11:39–40; 1 Pet. 1:10–12; Rev. 10:7).

10:25–37
THE GOOD SAMARITAN

This story that has become well known in the culture quite apart from the Bible has an obvious meaning that must not be lost: the way of God is the way of compassion and active help for those in need, even at personal risk, even against cultural expectations of what is proper. Yet the details of Luke's text are important for authentic biblical understanding. The section is composed of two elements: (1) the setting adapted from Mark and (2) the story of the Good Samaritan.

10:25 A lawyer stood up: The Good Samaritan is found only in Luke (L). He decided to place it in the setting of a conversation between Jesus and a lawyer (expert in religious teaching; see 7:29–30) found in a different context in Mark 12:28–34, where it is located in Jerusalem on Tuesday of the last week of Jesus' life. Luke places it much earlier, in the Travel Narrative (see on 9:51), omitting the Markan account when he comes to his own story of Holy Week, where in the Markan order it would appear between Luke 20:40 and 20:41.

To test Jesus: The lawyer is presented in an unfavorable light, not asking an honest question (in contrast to the scribe of Mark 12:28). His question is not about the greatest of God's commands but, "**What must I do to inherit eternal life?**" (see 18:18; Acts 16:30–31). Eternal life is not a matter of duration but of quality, the life of the age to come, the life of the kingdom of God. Inheriting eternal life, entering the kingdom of God, and being saved are all equated in 18:18–27.

10:26–28 What is written?: Jesus responds with a question, and the lawyer himself quotes the two greatest commandments of the Bible, love for God and love for neighbor (in contrast to Matt. 22:37–39/Mark 12:29–31, where it is Jesus who cites these commands). The first commandment is from Deut. 6:4–6, where the love of God is an integral part of the Shema, the primary confession of faith of Judaism, recited every day by pious Jews. The second command, to love the neighbor as oneself, is from Lev. 19:18. The combination is first found in Mark 12:30–31 as the Christian summary of the Law. The lawyer is here made to give the Christian answer to his own question. On the meaning of "love" (*agape*), see on 1 Cor. 13:4–7. **Heart, soul, strength, and mind** are not meant to divide up human anatomy or human life, but to represent human life as a whole that is offered back to God in grateful and loving response to God's saving acts. Love for God is not merely a "religious" matter that can reserve other "secular" areas of one's life and being; nothing can be withheld. **The neighbor** in the Old Testament is the one who lives nearby; in an Israelite or Jewish context, it means the fellow Israelite or fellow Jew.

Do this, and you will live: Jesus' answer likewise reflects Lev. (18:5 "You shall keep my statutes and my ordinances; by doing so one shall live"). Paul in Rom. 10:1–13 reinterprets these legal-sounding words that seem to advocate self-justification and works righteousness, understanding them in the Christian sense of justification by faith. It is not clear whether Luke has this in mind when in 10:29 he has the lawyer respond **wanting to justify himself**. In any case, the lawyer is still testing Jesus (10:25), seeking to establish himself.

10:29 Who is my neighbor?: The question could express a sincere moral issue, though the questioner in this context has questionable motives. If one assumes the validity of the command to love one's neighbor, it is legitimate to ask how far the boundaries of neighbor extend. All of us are in fact born selfish, absolutely self-centered, **loving ourselves**, and a major part of our socialization is to extend the boundaries of our self-love outward to include family, our local, regional, and national political groups, people who belong to our own race and religion, as representing "us" over against "them." The primal me becomes a social us, but the issue is how far do these boundaries extend? That is the lawyer's question, and it is not to be trivialized.

10:30 Jesus replied: Though it originally functioned as a parable, it is here called neither parable nor story, but is told straightforwardly as something that really happened. Until the last scene, it is utterly realistic. (On interpretation of parables, see on Mark 4:1.)

10:30 From Jerusalem to Jericho: A steep and dangerous descent, notorious for being infested by bandits. **A man:** The generic word for "human being" is used, and he is not otherwise identified by race, nationality, or religion. The original Jewish hearers would think of a Jew. Luke's Gentile hearers would think of a Gentile. The whole story is told from his point of view. He is left naked, wounded, dying, and alone. His only hope is that someone will happen to come by.

10:31–32 A priest . . . a Levite: A priest, **going down** from his service in the temple (there can be no excuse that he is going to the temple, and so must keep himself ritually pure), sees, but keeps his distance. Likewise a **Levite**, a subordinate temple worker (see, e.g., Num. 1:50–53), does the same.

10:33 But a Samaritan: On Samaritans, see above on 9:52. The original hearers probably expected the third traveler to turn out to be the hero, but anticipated that he would be a pious Israelite layperson, the "point" being that true religious duties are carried out not by the privileged clergy, but by sincere laypeople. When the Samaritan appears and responds with compassion and generosity, all expectations are shattered. (NB: This is what makes the parable difficult to hear today. The modern reader knows from the beginning that the Samaritan is good and the priest and Levite are bad. The story would have its original effect on us today if it were retold with two Samaritans passing by on the other side, followed by a compassionate Jewish priest who showed mercy. See on 15:11–32.)

The extravagance of the Samaritan's care is emphasized: he **came near** (the priest and Levite had seen but kept their distance). Luke has the Samaritan see only after he came near; the priest and Levite did not get close enough to really see. The Samaritan **saw, was moved** with pity, **went** to him, **bandaged** his wounds, **poured** on oil and wine, **put** the wounded man on his own donkey, **brought** him to the inn, and **took care** of him. He then **took** two denarii (two days wages, Matt. 20:2), **gave** them to the innkeeper, **said** for the innkeeper to take care of him at whatever cost, and promised to reimburse the innkeeper for the extra expenses. This series of twelve active verbs shows that the compassion of which Jesus speaks is not a matter of feeling, but of action.

10:36 Which of these three?: See 10:26. Throughout Jesus responds to the serious question not with information or advice but with questions and a story, which call the questioner to discern and decide for himself. It is not often noticed that Jesus' question reverses the original issue. The question is no longer "Who is my neighbor?" as though it could be answered in terms of how far my original selfishness should be stretched—to include family, friends, community, nation? It is thus a misunderstanding and misuse of the story to have it illustrate something like Jesus taught us to accept everyone, even if they are despised Samaritans. This is the liberal ideology that has co-opted the Jesus story for its own ideals (see on Mark 2:17). But in the story it is the Samaritan who **showed mercy**. It is a matter now of being a neighbor to whomever needs my help, not of defining boundaries, even if they are very inclusive ones.

10:37 Go and do likewise: Luke has understood the potent parable as an example story, which is one authentic reading of it, but not the only one (see on interpretation of parables at Mark 4:1).

10:38–42
Mary and Martha

10:38 Went on their way ... entered a certain village: Jesus is still on the journey from Galilee to Jerusalem (see on 9:51–52). The village is unidentified but cannot be the Bethany of Judea, where Mary and Martha are located in the Gospel of John (John 11:1). In John 11:1–12:1, Lazarus, the brother of Martha and Mary, is raised from the dead by Jesus, yet "the Jews" do not believe. In Luke, Martha and Mary are sisters but have no brother Lazarus, though there is a Lazarus in a story Jesus tells, a story that declares that even if Lazarus were to rise from the dead, the brothers of the Jewish rich man would not believe (16:19–31). Here we see another instance of how figures and motifs were interchanged and intertwined in the developing early Christian tradition (see on 1:1–4).

Martha welcomed him into her home: There is no male head of the household. Martha is portrayed as one of the propertied women who supported Jesus and his mission from their own resources (8:1–3).

10:39 Mary ... sat at the Lord's feet: This phrase means the person is the student or disciple of a respected teacher, like Paul at the feet of Gamaliel (Acts 22:3; see also the restored demoniac in 8:35. There may be a traditional connection here with the Mary of 8:2 from whom Jesus had cast out seven demons). In

the later tradition, all these features were woven together around the figure of Mary Magdalene (see on 7:36). Here, Mary violates conventional social codes by assuming a role usually reserved for men.

10:40 Lord, do you not care? ... Tell her then to help me: Martha has assumed the customary woman's role. Someone indeed must prepare the meal. Here it is not men who criticize a woman's not staying in her place, but the objection comes from another woman who is doing her needed work.

10:41–42 Many things ... one thing: Jesus does not make the work of one more important than the other. His contrast is between the distraction of many things (see 8:14) and concentration on one thing (not one *more* thing). Mary has found the organizing center for her existence, like Paul's "This one thing I do" (Phil. 3:13).

Luke has juxtaposed without comment the stories of the Good Samaritan (which instructs "Go and do likewise") and of Mary and Martha (which instructs that Mary's sitting and hearing the word is the **better part**). It is too facile to say something like "both are needed—sometimes we need to act, and sometimes we need to sit still and listen to the word of God." Luke's technique is more like that of the wisdom teachers of Israel, who placed opposing truths side by side without explanation, with the tension itself provoking the reader to deeper reflection (see, e.g., Prov. 26:4–5; Matt. 6:3 vs. 5:16).

11:1–13
Jesus' Teaching on Prayer
(See also at Matt. 6:9–13; 7:7–11)

Matthew has located these materials in the Sermon on the Mount, but Luke has taken the same items from the Q tradition, added a parable as the middle unit (11:5–8), and constructed a section illustrating Jesus' teaching on prayer.

11:1 He was praying: A typical setting for key points in the Lukan narrative (see 6:12; 9:18, 28; 22:40–46; 23:34, 46). **John taught his disciples:** Luke has pictured John as subordinate to Jesus and his forerunner but also is aware that John and his disciples constituted an independent group, by Luke's time somewhat in competition with Jesus' disciples, the later church (see on 1:5–25; 5:33–34; 7:18).

11:2–4 The Lord's Prayer was included in the Q document. Matthew 6:9–13 has expanded the wording. Matthew's version has seven petitions; Luke's has five.

Father: The historical Jesus addressed God in prayer in a distinctive, perhaps unique manner with the familiar, familial word "father" in his native language of Aramaic, "abba." This was so striking it was preserved in the later Greek-speaking church (see Mark 14:36; Gal. 4:6; Rom. 8:15). Luke preserves none of the original Aramaic of Jesus' words (contrast Mark 5:41; 15:34), but here the simple address, "Father," reflects Jesus' original practice. The believer comes to God in prayer without flattery, bribery, or manipulation but already has God's ear, just as a child has the attention of a good parent. Matthew's *Our Father* reflects a typical Jewish form of synagogue prayer. Luke's use of first person plural pronouns in the following verses ("us," "our," 11:3–4) shows that in Luke too the prayer is not individualistic but represents the prayer of the Christian community.

Hallowed be your name: The first petition prays for God's name to be sanctified, regarded as holy. The name represents the person (see on 6:14), so the prayer is that God himself will be regarded as holy, as the Creator who transcends all creation. Though the prayer begins with the familiar "Father," it is not cozily familiar but respects the transcendent holiness of God.

Your kingdom come: Here the kingdom is regarded as future (see on 4:5–8, 13, 20–21, 43). Luke himself looks back on the time when the kingdom was on earth in the ministry of Jesus, and forward to the time of its full manifestation at the return of Christ (Acts 1:6–11).

Daily: The rare word can also be translated "essential," "day by day," or "for tomorrow." **Each day** is typically Lukan (see his addition to Mark at Luke 9:23, and 16:19; 19:47; 22:53; Acts 2:46–47; 3:2; 16:5). The believer prays every day for daily sustenance. Literally poor believers (like Jesus' original hearers) ask God for daily food, which they do not take for granted. More well-to-do believers (like Luke himself) also confess in daily prayer their dependence on God for food.

Forgive us our sins: Luke has changed the Jewish metaphor for sin, "debts" (retained in Matthew), but retains it himself in the next line, **everyone indebted to us.** The Lukan Jesus assumes that all human beings are sinners in need of God's forgiveness (see the assumption expressed in 11:13). This view of human sinfulness is not only a Pauline idea (as, e.g., in Rom. 3:21). Forgiveness of sins was central in Luke's understanding of salvation (see, e.g., 5:20; 7:47–48; 24:47; Acts 2:38; 5:31; 10:43; 13:38; 26:18). Receiving God's forgiveness includes the readiness to forgive others.

Do not bring us to the time of trial (NRSV)/**lead us not into temptation** (NIV): The same Greek word may be translated "temptation" or "trial, testing." But it is not God who tempts people to sin; they are led away by their own desires (Jas. 1:13–14), or it is Satan who tempts (Luke 4:1–13). God does test his people (Gen. 22) and permits Satan to test them (Job 1–2). In the apocalyptic worldview, it was believed that just before the end, terrible trials would come upon the world, and the faith of believers would be tested. This prayer is that God would deliver believers from such testing, for they are not confident that they could endure it. Such a prayer is not confident in its own faith, but in God, and asks God not to permit faith to come to a testing it might fail.

11:5–8 Because of his persistence: Luke places this parable here to reassure believers that their prayers are heard and answered. If a grouchy neighbor awakened from sleep will respond to an urgent request for bread, how much more will God respond to our prayers! Verse 8 is difficult to translate and interpret. The Greek word translated "persistence" (NRSV) or "boldness" (NIV) understands it to refer to the petitioner, and understands the parable to encourage believers to be persistent in prayer (as 18:1–8). The word may instead refer to the shame and loss of face the sleepy neighbor will suffer if he does not respond, so that the story points to the hearer of the request rather than the petitioner. He responds to the request out of concern for his own honor rather than concern for the neighbor's need or his persistence (18:1–8 can also be so understood). Then the message would be that prayers are answered not because of something about the petitioner, but because of something about God. The believers' encouragement to pray rests on the character of God, not on our persistence.

11:9–13 Ask . . . search . . . knock: This collection of sayings is in another context in Matt. 7:7–11. Originally, vv. 9–10 may have been secular "beggar's wisdom": if you keep asking and knock on enough doors, somebody will finally respond (see 4:23; 8:17–18; 9:58; 11:9–10; 12:3–4). It may then have been adopted by Jesus or/and early Christian missionaries as encouragement to venture forth into the world on the Christian mission, depending only on friendly supporters along the way (see 9:1–6; 10:1–16). Luke here understands the sayings with reference to prayer: since God is eager to hear and respond to the believer's prayer, we may confidently ask, seek, knock—no longer on human doors, but on the gates of heaven.

If your child asks: If good human parents will not deceive their children but supply their needs, how much more will the heavenly Father respond to our prayers. The instruction on prayer in 11:1–13 turns out to be not techniques for effective praying but assurance about the nature of God. Prayer turns out to be worship and praise, rather than a shopping list.

Holy Spirit: The prayer in Q had "good things" (see Matt. 7:11). Luke's interest in the Spirit leads him to insert "Holy Spirit" here, also creating a parallel to Acts 1:14; 2:1–21, where the Holy Spirit comes on the church in response to prayer.

11:14–28
JESUS AND BEELZEBUL
(See also at Matt. 12:22–30, 43–45;
Mark 3:22–27; John 7:20; 8:48, 52; 10:20)

11:14–15 Casting out a demon: On the language of demons, Satan, and exorcism, see excursus, "Satan, the Devil, and Demons in Biblical Theology," at Mark 5:1. **Crowds . . . some of them:** In Mark 3:22 the objection is made by "scribes from Jerusalem," in Matt. 12:24 by "Pharisees." The crowds in the previous story in Luke have been neutral or potential disciples (see 5:1, 15; 6:17–20, 19; 7:11; 8:4; 9:11, 18, 37; 14:25; 19:48; 20:19; 22:6, 47; 23:4, 13, 21, 48). The crowds will appear in the passion story as hostile to Jesus (22:47, 23:4; but see 23:48). Here one begins to see a shift in the stance of the crowds. **Beelzebul:** See on Mark 3:22.

11:16 Sign from heaven: See on 11:29–32. Even though they had just witnessed a miracle, the appetite for miracles only is increased by what it feeds on.

11:17 Know what they were thinking: See on 2:35; 5:22; 7:39.

11:18 His (Satan's) kingdom: Although God is the sole Creator and ruler of the world, at the present, God's rule of the earth is usurped by demonic powers. Satan, too, has a kingdom (2 Cor. 4:4), but it is limited and temporary. The point here, however, is that it is united—all Satan's forces stand together; if they are divided, Satan's rule is in the process of coming apart. This is indeed what is happening with the appearance of the kingdom of God in Jesus' ministry.

11:19 Your exorcists: Here Jesus argues on the basis of the acknowledged presence of exorcists among the Jews (see, e.g., Acts 19:13–14). It is not only Jesus and his disciples who perform miracles (see excursus, "Interpreting the Miracle Stories," at Matt. 9:35).

11:20 The kingdom of God has come: In the ministry of Jesus. See on 4:13, 20–21, 43–44; 11:20; 17:21. **Finger of God:** See Exod. 8:19. This allusion to the exodus story pictures the ministry of Jesus as related to the saving power of God manifest in the deliverance of Israel from Egypt (see on 9:31).

11:21–22 A strong man . . . one stronger: Luke has elaborated the picture in Mark 3:27 of "tying up the strong man," which was already an allusion to the eschatological victory of God (on the image of binding Satan, see Rev. 20:1–3). Here, the ministry of Jesus is pictured as disarming and plundering Satan's kingdom (see Col. 2:15).

11:23 Not with me . . . against me: See on 9:50. There Luke presented the more inclusive Markan version, here the more severe Q version of the saying of Jesus. Both have the same point: after the appearance of Christ that represents God's defeat of the satanic kingdom there can be no middle ground, no holy neutrality. Everyone is either **gathering** or **scattering**, is either part of the solution or part of the problem.

11:24–26 Through waterless regions: The goal of the spiritual life is not emptiness, not merely a getting rid of evil practices. Following Jesus does not mean merely clearing out one's life of what is objectionable, getting rid of evil spirits, but being filled with the Spirit of God (11:13). The spiritual world, like the natural world, abhors a vacuum. Giving up things will not make one Christian, but only make one empty and more vulnerable to even greater evil. The powerful return of the evil spirits is a metaphorical way of presenting the truth of 2 Pet. 2:20. In the context in which Luke has placed this story, the reader might ask, What happened to the man from whom Jesus had cast out the demon? Did he become a disciple of Jesus, so that his life was filled with the Spirit of God? Or did even worse demons fill the empty space Jesus had created? And what of the one who reads this story?

11:27–28 Blessed is the womb that bore you: This conventional blessing (see Gen. 49:25) is not repudiated by the Lukan Jesus but becomes the occasion of pronouncing the true blessedness of those who hear and obey **the word of God** (see on 8:8, 15; 19–21).

11:29–32
THE SIGN OF JONAH
(See also at Matt. 12:38–42; Mark 8:11–12)

Again Luke omits the Pharisees of Mark 8:11, portraying them throughout in a more positive light than his sources (see on 5:17). **Crowds were increasing:** Indicates that their wavering in 11:14–16 has been overcome by Jesus' response. Here he responds to their demand for a sign in 11:16, declaring that asking **for a sign** is itself an indication of a lack of faith, can even be demonic (see 4:3–11).

11:30 Jonah became a sign: A progression in early Christian interpretation of this saying can be traced. (1) Mark 8:12: No sign at all shall be given to this generation, illustrating the view of some early Christians that Jesus' ministry was devoid of extraordinary divine power (see on 4:9–11; Phil. 2:5–11). (2) Q as represented in Luke 11:29b: No sign shall be given except the sign of Jonah. (3) Luke 11:30: This is interpreted by Luke as Jonah himself and his preaching, which brought the people of Nineveh to repentance. (4) Matthew 12:40: Matthew further interprets the "sign of Jonah" as Jonah's three days and nights in the belly of the big fish, corresponding to Jesus' three days and nights in the realm of death before his resurrection. All these interpretations understand the life of Jesus to be empty of divine manifestations of power, except for his message (3) or his resurrection (4).

Son of Man: See on Mark 2:10.

11:31–32 Queen of the South: The queen of Sheba, 1 Kgs. 10:1–13. Both she and the **people of Nineveh** were Gentiles who repented when Jews did not (see 4:25–27; 10:13–15). They did not repent on the basis of seeing miracles, but at the preaching of Jonah and the wisdom of Solomon, i.e., the word of God (see 3:2; 5:1; 8:11, 21; 11:28; Acts 4:31; 6:2, 7; 8:14; 11:1; 12:24; 13:5, 7, 46; 17:13; 18:11).

Something greater: The reference is not to "someone." Jesus recedes behind his message. It is the kingdom of God that is greater than Jonah and Solomon (see on 4:13, 20–21, 43–44; 11:20; 17:21).

11:33–36
CONCERNING LIGHT
(See also at Matt. 5:15; 6:22–23; Mark 4:21)

Luke here gathers a variety of sayings about light that appear in other contexts in Matthew and Mark. In this context, they are still concerned with the question of what will happen to the person from whom the evil spirit is cast out. His or her life can be filled with light or refilled with a darkness that is worse than the previous one, as though a person born blind, then healed, has now been reblinded.

The ancient understanding of the relation of the eye to light is important to understand these sayings. Modern people think of the eye as passive, responding to external light. These sayings reflect the ancient view, which understood the eye to be active, sending forth the inner light by which one can see. Just as modern people would speak of "the lens by which we see things," ancient people considered that which permits us to see to be built in, a part of ourselves. How we see things depends on our inner being, not just on external objects. The one whose inner being is changed sees a new world.

11:37–54
JESUS DENOUNCES PHARISEES AND LAWYERS
(See also at Matt. 15:1–9; 23:6–36;
Mark 7:1–9; 12:38–39)

11:37–38 Pharisee: See on 5:17. **Dine with him:** Luke often locates Jesus teaching in meal settings (see on 5:29). **Wash before dinner:** a matter of ritual purity, not of personal hygiene (see on Mark 7:1–23; Luke 2:22–24; 4:33; 5:13, 29–32; 8:44; 10:7–8).

11:39–41 Outside . . . inside: See 1 Sam. 16:7. **Fools:** Jesus' own use of the word here means the prohibition of Matt. 5:22 is not to be taken literally. In biblical understanding, being a fool is not a matter of intelligence but of arrogance (see Ps. 14:1 and often in Proverbs and Ecclesiastes; for New Testament usage, see Matt. 5:22; 23:17; Luke 11:40; 12:20; Rom. 1:22; 1 Cor. 15:36). **Give for alms those things that are within** (NRSV)/**Give what is inside the dish to the poor** (NIV): two possible translations of the ambiguous Greek original text of Luke. The NRSV understands the meaning to be a continuation of the earlier contrast between external ritual and true internal piety of the heart, though it is difficult to know what "giving those things that are within" would mean if one tries to express it in action. The NIV understanding is more in accord with Luke's general view elsewhere: give food to the poor and hungry, and this is the true "ritual purity" (see 1:53; 6:3, 21; 14:13; 16:9–31; 19:8). **Everything will be clean for you:** See Mark 7:19; Acts 10:15; Rom. 14:13–23, esp. vv. 14, 20.

11:42–54 Woe to you Pharisees . . . lawyers: Parallel to Matt. 23:6–36, i.e., Luke's adaptation of material from Q (see introduction to Luke). Luke has rearranged the material to give three woes each against Pharisees and lawyers; some of his woes against the lawyers are directed to Pharisees in Matthew. A woe is a pronouncement of judgment and/or lament, in the style of the Old Testament prophets (see Isa. 5:8–23 for a series of six woes that concludes with a "therefore" statement, the same arrangement Luke has constructed here).

Woe 1 (11:42): Against majoring in minors. Tithing of certain items was an Old Testament command (see Gen. 14:10; 28:22; Lev. 27:32; Num. 18:21, 24, 26; Deut. 12:17; 14:22, 28; 26:12; 2 Chr. 31:5; Neh. 8:38; 13:12; Mal. 3:10). The oral tradition of the Pharisees had greatly elaborated this command to include even garden herbs and seasoning, like tithing salt and pepper. Jesus does not here oppose the biblical rule of tithing as such, but the Pharisaic refinements that could trivialize the law at the expense of its main concerns: **justice** and **the love of God**. These two commands correspond to love of God and love of neighbor (see 10:25–28; Mic. 6:6–8). Love and justice are not alternatives. Love without justice degenerates into flabby sentimentalism; justice without love becomes legalistic, vindictive, and self-righteous.

Woe 2 (11:43): Against promoting one's public image. Followers of Christ are freed from concern with their image in order to serve others.

Woe 3 (11:44): Against contaminating others by one's internal rottenness. To touch a dead body or a grave brought ritual defilement (Lev. 21:1–4; Num. 19:11–22). Here, in contrast to 11:39–41, the defilement is considered to be real. Graves were normally marked in an obvious manner so people could avoid them and not become unintentionally or unknowingly defiled, but the Pharisees are like unmarked graves that defile others without their knowledge. A modern analogy might be an unmarked source of radioactive material, which we would consider dangerous, although the danger is not apparent on the surface. This image is developed differently in Matt. 23:27–28, where the Pharisees are like graves that *are* marked, but are full of rottenness within, continuing the contrast between correct exterior and phony interior.

Woe 4 (11:46): Against making religion burdensome to others. On **lawyers,** see 7:30; 10:29; 11:45, 52; 14:3. They are equated with scribes in 11:53. The lawyers represent religion as a list of burdensome rules, in contrast to following Christ, which is freedom and joy. Jesus takes away burdens, does not add religion as one more weight one must carry amid the other burdens of life (Matt. 11:28–30).

Woe 5 (11:47–51): Against honoring past prophets while killing present ones. Luke presents the church as the fulfillment and continuation of the prophetic line—Old Testament prophets, John the Baptist, and Jesus (see 6:22–23; Acts 2:17–21). Jesus charges the religious leaders of his time with honoring biblical prophets of the past but persecuting those of their own time who spoke in God's name. Jesus interprets their desire to **build the tombs of the prophets** in an ironic way: while claiming to honor the prophets, they are actually cooperating with their **ancestors. God in his wisdom said** (NIV)/**The Wisdom of God said** (NRSV): The words can picture as speaking either God or the personified Wisdom of God (see Prov. 1:20–33; 8:1–36) who was with God at creation and who sent forth the Old Testament prophets. This figure, sometimes identified with the preexistent and post-Easter, transcendent Christ (see John 1:1–18; 1 Cor. 1:24; Col. 1:15–20), also sends forth Christian prophets and apostles, thus binding the Old Testament and New Testament revelation into a unity. **Abel** (Gen. 4) was the first person to be murdered and is here considered a prophet, as is **Zechariah** (2 Chr. 24:22–24). Since 2 Chronicles was the last book in the arrangement of the Hebrew Bible, this is a way of saying "all the biblical prophets."

Woe 6 (11:52): Against dog-in-the-manger teachers. The lawyer-scribes were responsible to interpret and teach the law as a revelation of God's will, but their learning became a barrier both to themselves and to those they were supposed to teach.

In interpreting the woes, three items are to be kept in mind: (1) Luke does not present all Pharisees as guilty of these charges, but also knows of good Pharisees, including the converted Pharisee Paul (e.g., 7:36–39; 13:31; see Acts 5:33–39; 23:6–8). There is a danger in an approach to religion that wants a rule for every occasion, but the Pharisees are not here condemned as a body. (2) The Pharisees themselves had similar criticisms of hypocritical and superficial members of their own group. (3) Luke's writing is not directed to Pharisees but to Christians. It is followers of Christ who are here warned, not absent Pharisees.

12:1–12
To the Disciples: Against Hypocrisy; Exhortation to Fearless Confession
(See also at Matt. 10:26–33; 16:5–6; Mark 4:22; 8:14–15)

Here begins an extensive speech (12:1–13:9) in which Jesus alternates between addressing disciples (12:1–12; 23–53) and the crowds (12:13–21; 12:54–13:9). On the Lukan distinction between apostles, disciples, and crowds, see on 6:17–20. To understand these verses in context, one should hear them in the framework of this alternation, not as a series of individual sayings.

In 12:1–12 Luke combines Q sayings material with a Markan framework (see introduction to Luke), addressing a number of sayings originally in a variety of contexts to the one theme of courageous Christian confession. The concluding sayings in 12:11–12 indicate that the sayings presuppose the post-Easter time when Christians were persecuted (as in Acts 4–8; 12–28). These instructions appear in Matthew in the context of sending out the Twelve (Matt. 10:26–33; see Luke 9:1–6).

12:1 Crowds . . . disciples: While the crowds are present, Jesus speaks first to the disciples and the crowds overhear. Jesus' instructions here are not general teachings based on common sense, but require Christian commitment before they can be understood and appropriated.

Yeast of the Pharisees . . . hypocrisy: In 11:37–54 Jesus had pronounced judgment on those who pretended to be something they were not. Here the danger is that disciples will pretend *not* to be something they in fact *are*—disciples of Jesus (as Peter will do in 22:54–62). Keeping a low profile as a Christian to avoid embarrassment or trouble is the kind of hypocrisy warned against here (see Paul in Acts 24:10–21).

12:2–3 Nothing secret: See Matt. 10:27. Again, what could have originally been a bit of secular wisdom is here adapted to Christian proclamation (see 4:23; 8:17–18; 9:58; 11:9–10). Christian faith is not only a matter for the privacy of one's heart, home, or closest friends, but is to be visible in the workplace and public arena.

12:4–5 Friends: On Jesus' disciples as friends, see John 15:13–15; 3 John 15. **Fear** refers to the reverence and awe due to God as God (7:16). This reverence, akin to worship, must not be misdirected to human beings. God, not any human court, holds our ultimate destiny in his hands. **Hell:** here a translation of "Gehenna" (see

NRSV footnote), which originally meant Valley of Hinnom. This valley south of Jerusalem, once the site of pagan sacrifices, was later made the city garbage dump, where stench, maggots, and fire were always present—a powerful symbol of hell, the place of ultimate punishment for those who finally reject God.

12:6–7 Sparrows . . . hairs: Juxtaposed to the overwhelming picture of God's judgment is the equally stunning picture of God's love and care. Sparrows were trapped and sold in the market as the most inexpensive food for the poor, yet none of God's creatures dies apart from God's care. The argument is in the rabbinic form of *qal va-homer*, "light and heavy." Since God cares for sparrows, how much more for you! God's care is not "in general," but as particular as the hairs of our head.

12:8–9 Son of Man: See on Mark 2:10. The Greek text contrasts a court scene on the human level ("before men," NIV) and one on the divine level ("Son of Man"). Confession of Jesus in the court of human opinion will be vindicated in the heavenly court at the Last Judgment. Denial of one's faith by keeping a low profile in the present world of human life will result in being denied before the heavenly court. The heavenly world is represented in these sayings by the **Son of Man**, the **angels**, the **Holy Spirit**, and by **God** (God is implied by the passive verbs **will be denied . . . will be forgiven . . . will not be forgiven**).

Acknowledges me . . . denies me: This does not refer to the one-time event of making a public confession of Christian faith upon entering the Christian community or when standing before the court, but to one's witness in word and deed in the course of one's daily life.

12:10 Against the Holy Spirit: See also at Matt. 12:31–32; Mark 3:28–30. This originally independent saying appears in different forms and contexts in the Gospels. Its purpose is never to provide speculative information on the subject of which sins can be forgiven and which cannot; its meaning is conditioned by its context in each case. Luke has placed it within this context of encouragement to bold Christian confession. Here the **Son of Man** refers to the pre-Easter earthly Jesus (see further on Mark 2:10). The point in the context of Luke's theology seems to be that those who spoke against Jesus during his earthly life, such as Peter in 22:54–62, can be forgiven, but that those who harden themselves against God's offer of grace in the post-Easter era of the Holy Spirit will not be forgiven. Luke makes a clear distinction between the time of Jesus and the time of the church (see introduction to Luke: "Jesus as the 'Midst of Time'"). In its present context, the difficult saying does not intend to make legal distinctions between different kinds of sins, but to distinguish those who understandably did not recognize Jesus as the savior during his earthly life and those who reject the offer of God's grace made in the power of the Holy Spirit during the period of Christian proclamation (see on Acts 3:17; 17:30).

12:11–12 The Holy Spirit will teach you: See also at Matt. 10:19–20; Mark 13:11. This originally independent saying is connected to the previous one by the theme of the Holy Spirit. Here the point is not a threat to those who blaspheme the Holy Spirit but a promise of the help of the Holy Spirit to those who are accused before human courts. The meaning in the Lukan context is that when Christians resist the temptation to keep a low profile in this world and publicly acknowledge their faith, they will receive not only transcendent vindication in the heavenly world (12:8–10) but transcendent help in the present world. On whether Christians should prepare their defense beforehand, note the contrasting view in 1 Pet. 3:13–16.

12:13–21
TO THE CROWDS: WARNING AGAINST GREED; PARABLE OF THE RICH FOOL

Jesus responds to a question from the crowd (see on 12:1–12). In this context, his instruction about the danger of greed is not general human wisdom, but is evoked by his previous teaching to his disciples calling for a kind of commitment that now evokes this question from the crowd that has overheard his instruction to his disciples.

12:13–15 Tell my brother to divide the family inheritance: As a respected religious teacher, Jesus is asked to arbitrate a family dispute about the inheritance. Jesus' refusal does not mean that he is too spiritual to be involved in secular economic issues. A major thrust of Luke–Acts has to do with economic justice (see 1:46–55; 2:8–14; 2:24; 3:10–14; 4:16–21; 6:20–23; 14:21–23; 16:19–31; Acts 2:44–47; 3:6; 4:32–35; 11:27–30). Jesus rather addresses the underlying assumption of the noncommitted outsider, that "making a living" has to do with how much one has (see 9:25). The questioner is not an evil man; he simply shares the common assumption that life does in fact consist of one's possessions. This is what Jesus challenges.

12:16–21 Eat, drink, be merry: Likewise the man in the story is not inherently evil by cultural standards; he is in fact a model of cultural success. His harvest has greatly exceeded his expectations, so that his problem is what to do with his unanticipated wealth, much more than he has planned on having. The reader gets to hear his interior monologue, which reveals his true character (see 12:2–3). In public, the man might well have made proper statements about the welfare of the community, but in his inner thoughts no one comes on the scene except himself. His abundance could have been shared with hungry people, but the thought of others never enters his mind (see Sir. 11:24; Luke 16:19–31!).

Fool: See on 11:39–41. The man is smart and industrious, a model of success in the eyes of society, but God's judgment is that he is a fool. Note the contrast between his perspective ("many years") and God's ("this very night"). The man's affluence has brought with it great responsibility (see 12:48, with which this section closes), but he has thought only of himself.

12:22–53
TO THE DISCIPLES: ANXIETY, ALERTNESS, FAITHFULNESS
(See also at Matt. 6:19–21, 25–34; 10:34–36; 24:42–51; Mark 10:38; 13:33–37)

The discourse shifts back to the disciples (not just the Twelve), presented in the post-Easter perspective of the "little flock" (12:32) to which Peter belongs (12:41), those who are "waiting for their master" (12:35–37) and who can be contrasted with "the nations of the world" (12:30), the "unbelievers" (12:46 NIV). Luke's readers, however, overhear what is said to both disciples and the uncommitted crowds.

12:22–34
Trust in God instead of being anxious

Luke has placed these sayings in a different context from that of Matthew (see Matt. 6:25–34); in Luke they form a contrast to the preceding parable of the Rich Man (similar terminology: eating, sowing, reaping, barns, soul/life/self [the three words are the same in Greek]). The words are not addressed to hungry, naked, or homeless people, but are a warning to the disciples not to be like the rich man, who thought only of himself. Three reasons are given that the disciples are to trust in God for the basic necessities of life: (1) It is a matter of priorities. Life itself is more important than getting more and better food and clothing. Life here does not mean mere survival, but the quality of life that God intends, eternal life in the kingdom of God (see 6:6–8; 19:9–11, 25; 12:13–15). (2) The faith called for is not faith in general, but trust in God as the Creator. This God is not one among a number of competing powers, but the Creator of all. The idea is not that if our faith is strong enough, we will never be hungry or homeless—which would mean that the hungry and homeless of this world are to be blamed for not having enough faith. Rather, the believer is encouraged to trust that all things are finally in one hand, the hand of the loving Creator who cares for the whole creation. **Ravens . . . lilies:** They receive their food and clothing from the hand of the one Creator. They also die and are burned, but this does not remove them from the Creator's care. (3) Anxiety doesn't make anything happen, does not **add a single hour to . . . life.**

12:27 Solomon in all his glory: See 1 Kgs. 10:4–29.

12:31 Strive for his kingdom: Make the rule of God, for which the believer prays every day (11:2) the top priority in your life, rather than bigger barns and a life of ease (12:16–21). On kingdom of God in Luke, see 4:43–44).

12:32 Your Father's good pleasure to give you the kingdom: These words are added to Q by Luke (see Matt. 6:34). Here the kingdom is God's gift; in the preceding saying, the kingdom is a matter of human striving. The reality to which these two statements points should not be parceled out between them as though humans are partly responsible for the coming of the kingdom and God is partly responsible. Believers are totally responsible to orient their lives to the coming of God's kingdom, but whenever and however God's rule comes, it is totally God's gift. For similar dialectic on human responsibility and divine sovereignty, see Deut. 7:6–13; 30:6–10; Isa. 26:12; 1 Cor. 15:10; Gal. 2:20; Phil. 2:12–13; Col. 1:29; Rev. 20:11–14.

Little flock: The people of God in the Old Testament were sometimes thought of in the imagery of God as the shepherd and the people as his sheep (Pss. 23; 100:3; Isa. 40:11; Ezek. 34:11–16), an image that persists in the church regarded as the continuing people of God (Acts 20:28–29; 1 Pet. 5:2–3).

12:33 Sell your possessions: While this can hardly be understood as a literal, universal command to all disciples, Luke's readers should not rush to point out its symbolic nature. Luke portrays the earliest Christian community as actually practicing this (see on Acts 2:43–47; 4:32–37).

12:34 Where your treasure is: This is often cited as though it were an encouragement to get people to put their hearts into God's work, and their treasure will follow, or the opposite: get people to put their money into the church, and their hearts will follow. But chronology is hardly the point; this is not a command or exhortation but a statement of fact: people's hearts are in fact where their treasure is, whichever comes first. In the present context, the point is that those who have their finances and property invested in secular and selfish pursuits can hardly claim that their hearts belong to God.

12:35–48
Disciples as alert slaves

This section deals with the Christian life in the present, awaiting the final coming of the God's kingdom. Luke and his readers live in the second or third Christian generation, in which the first generation's hope for the speedy return of Christ was being abandoned or reinterpreted (see introduction to Luke: "Jesus as the 'Midst of Time,'" and excursus, "Interpreting the 'Near End,'" at Rev. 1:3). Luke is helping his church to rethink the meaning of the earlier proclamation that Jesus would return soon, and no longer believes that his own generation will see the return of Christ in the near future (see 19:11–27; Acts 1:6–11). Yet he does not want this revisionist theology of the delay of the Parousia to become an excuse for irresponsible Christian living. There will be a delay, but this is not a license to become careless or faithless. The general thrust of this collection of sayings is that Jesus' disciples do not know when the end will be but should live their lives as always ready to stand before God at the Last Judgment.

12:35–38 Slaves . . . alert: The image reflects ancient Palestinian wedding customs. The groom has gone to the wedding feast to be married at the home of the bride's parents. The slaves are to be ready to open the doors when the bridegroom appears, but they do not know when it will be, so they must be always ready. (Here as elsewhere, Jesus does not question the institution of slavery but accepts it as a given part of the social order. Later disciples saw that the institution of slavery as such was incompatible with Christian faith, but this insight had not been attained by Luke's time. See introduction to Philemon). The image of the wedding feast modulates into that of the eschatological banquet (see Isa. 25:6; Luke 13:29; 14:15–29; Rev. 19:7–9).

12:37 He will come and serve them: Reflects the eschatological reversal brought about by

Christ. Rather than being served, the returning bridegroom/Son of Man will serve his disciples at the messianic banquet (see 22:24–28). This image of the master who serves corresponds to the radicality of believing in a Messiah who is crucified. The Christian faith that the Christ is the crucified man of Nazareth reverses all our expectations and common-sense values, as illustrated by the whole preceding discourse on money and property.

12:39–40 The Son of Man is coming at an unexpected hour: The imagery shifts to the common New Testament metaphor of the unpredictable thief (see Matt. 24:42–43; 1 Thess. 5:1–3; Rev. 3:3; 16:15), but the point is the same: the time of the end cannot be predicted, so be always ready. In all this, the motivation for Christian living is not merely that the unsuspecting disciple will not be taken by surprise. Fear that Christ might return and catch the disciple engaged in unworthy behavior is not an adequate motive for Christian ethical conduct, so speculation about when the end might come is irrelevant for how one lives one's life.

12:41–48 For us [disciples] or for everyone?: Luke adds Peter's question to the Q materials (see Matt. 24:44–45). The question to whom these instructions are addressed raises the reader's consciousness of the distinction Luke makes within Jesus' speech (see on 12:1–12 above). Jesus answers the question with a parable. Instructions to **managers** probably are focused on leadership roles in the early church. During the (extended) interim period while the master is away, those in charge of his household must behave responsibly. The delay of the Parousia is no excuse for self-aggrandizement as church officials. Luke knows the value and necessity of church leadership and definite offices (Acts 2–6), but here acknowledges the tendencies toward selfishness, irresponsibility, and arrogance that sometimes are attached to them.

12:47–48 To whom much has been given: In the present context, these words (found only in Luke) seem to continue the focus on church leadership. At the final judgment, church leaders will be called to account and will be judged fairly (see 1 Cor. 3:5–22).

12:49–53
Division Caused by Decision

12:49 Bring fire to the earth: Luke reinterprets the Q saying (see Matt. 10:34) by adding the reference to Jesus as the bringer of fire. Many

of Luke's readers will have thought of the myth of Prometheus, who restored the gift of fire to humanity but was punished by Zeus. Since Luke connects this statement to Jesus' impending **baptism** of suffering (see Mark 10:38) in which he will be immersed in Jerusalem, Luke may have intended this association with Prometheus, who suffered for his gift to humanity. Luke clearly relates Jesus' statement to the prediction of John the Baptist that the coming powerful one would dispense baptismal fire (3:16), and to the fiery phenomena of Pentecost (Acts 2:3).

12:51 Peace? . . . rather division: Contrast 2:14; 10:5–6; 24:36; John 14:27; 16:33. The peace Jesus brings is not an alternative to decisions and new priorities that bring divisions even among families and close friends. The peace of God is not an anesthetic that makes one numb to the conflicts of the world; it may indeed sharpen them. As Christ contemplates the cross he will endure in God's service, he is not peaceful, but under **stress** (v. 50) and turmoil (23:39–47). The road to God's peace is not a detour around the cross but goes through it.

12:54–13:9
To the Crowds: Interpreting the Times, Be Reconciled before It Is Too Late; Repent or Perish
(See also at Matt. 5:25–26; 16:2–3)

12:54–56 How to interpret the present time: The preceding instructions have been directed to disciples (see on 12:1–12). Jesus now calls sympathetic outsiders who have not yet made the commitment of faith to interpret the present time. In Palestine, weather is determined either by the sea to the **west**, from which rain comes, or by the desert to the **south** and east. Weather can be reliably predicted by observing the **sky** and noting the direction of the **wind.** The crowds can discern the signs for changing weather, but not the sign of God's kingdom in their midst, which is Jesus himself (see on 4:43–44; 11:20; 17:20–21).

12:57–59 Another image from everyday life is the scene, common in first-century Palestine, of debtors being taken to court and prison, where they remained until their debt was paid. The debtor on the way to face the judge (see 11:4/Matt. 6:12) evokes the image of sinful people on the way to face God, the ultimate judge. No debtor would wait until he or she stands before the judge before trying to do something about the perilous situation. Jesus' hearers must first recognize their situation and then do something about it. The metaphor is not an allegory and does not mean that we can do something to achieve our reconciliation to God—this has already been done by God in Christ—but is a parabolic call to interpret the precarious time in which we live and respond in faith to God's act in Christ.

13:1–9 Unless you repent: The speech concludes by continuing the appeal to the sympathetic crowds that are still outsiders to the group of disciples. On repentance, see 3:7–9.

Blood Pilate had mingled with their sacrifices: The Roman governor's soldiers had killed some Galilean worshipers as they offered sacrifice at the temple. The cruel incident is otherwise undocumented, though Pilate is known to have done similar things. Although the one who reported the tragedy had raised no question, every such event has a question built into it: "Why?" People, especially religious people, want a satisfying explanation for tragedy. Those killed were sacrificing at the temple in obedience to the biblical command. Were they perhaps actually hypocrites, so that Pilate's outrageous slaughter was the just punishment for their sin? Jesus offers no explanation but eliminates the false idea that tragedy is God's punishment for sin. He then intensifies the issue with his own illustration: with no human cause, a tower fell on eighteen unsuspecting people—was this then an "act of God," punishing them for their sins that had escaped human notice, but not God's? Wrong again.

There are no explanations for such tragedies, but they still point us to the reality that we live in a world in which we are not in control, and constitute a call to repentance. Jesus' hearers are urged to avoid constructing an explanation for the evils of life and to see such calamities as reminders of the fragility of life; anyone, relatively good or evil, could find himself or herself standing before the final Judge without any advance warning. The address to the crowds that had begun with a story in which "relax" was the assumed goal of life (12:19) ends with the call of Jesus to repent as the crucial decision of life. Here too, repentance means the bearing of good fruit, as illustrated in the next paragraph, vv. 6–9.

13:6–9 A man had a fig tree: This conclusion of the discourse that began at 12:1 resembles the story of Jesus' cursing the fig tree in Mark 11:12–14, 20–24, a story Luke omits at that point. The tree exists to **bear fruit**. God is interested in lives that produce deeds of justice and compassion. If the tree remains fruitless, it is taking up precious ground, and must be **cut down**. The ax is already at the root of the tree (see 3:7–9). Yet there is a reprieve for **one more year**. In Luke, Jesus' ministry is a one-year special time in God's saving plan (see introduction to Luke: "Jesus as the 'Midst of Time,'" and comments on 4:20–21). Jesus' call for the crowds to repent (13:1–5) is not a summons for a general feeling of remorse about their bad lives but a call to discern the time in which they live, when they are confronted by the reality of the kingdom of God. The kind of radical reorientation of how one thinks and lives is not brought about by general resolves to do better, but by confronting the word and reality of God's kingdom as present in Jesus. The Lukan readers, though probably in the category of "insider" disciples, also hear the call to discern God's presence in the ministry of Jesus presented to them in the Gospel they are reading or hearing, and to reorient their lives to its truth.

13:10–17
JESUS HEALS A CRIPPLED WOMAN

The preceding discourse being finished, a new subsection begins here, 13:10–14:35, arranged in two corresponding patterns: a healing on the Sabbath brings controversy (13:10–17; 14:1–6) and leads to Jesus' teaching and warning the crowds (13:18–35; 14:7–35). The healing stories with which each section begins are only in Luke and are very similar (Sabbath setting, conflict with religious authority, analogy of freeing an ox). The two stories also represent Luke's characteristic pairing of female and male characters (see 2:25–38; 13:18–21; 15:3–10).

13:11 A spirit that had crippled her: Sickness was often associated with evil spirits (see on 4:33; 8:1–3; on the language of demons, Satan, and exorcism, see excursus, "Satan, the Devil, and Demons in Biblical Theology," at Mark 5:1). Verse 16 indicates the woman had been **bound** by **Satan**. Jesus' releasing her is part of his ministry of freeing the oppressed (4:18–19). **Eighteen years**: the detail connects with the reference in the previous story to eighteen people killed (13:4), illustrating the way stories were bound together with keywords during the period of oral tradition before the Gospels were written (see 1:1–4; for another example of keyword association, see Mark 9:42–50).

13:12 When Jesus saw her: Here Jesus takes the initiative and acts unilaterally; it is not a matter of the woman's quest and faith (contrast 8:43–48).

13:13 Laid his hands on her: An act of blessing and healing (see 4:40; Acts 6:6; 8:17–18; 9:12, 17; 13:3; 19:6; 28:8). **She stood up straight:** This is the obvious proof that the healing had taken place but may also have a symbolic meaning. In a social situation in which women were marginalized, Jesus restores not only health, but dignity that allows her to stand erect. **Began praising God:** The unity of God's act and the act of Jesus is implicit throughout Luke's theocentric narrative, which is not about Jesus, but about what God does in Jesus (see 5:25–26; 7:16; 8:24, 38; 9:20–22, 43; 13:13; 17:15; 19:37).

13:14–16 The sabbath: This is the third such conflict in Luke (see 6:1–6, 6–11) and will be rehearsed again in 14:1–6. Jesus is not pictured as simply rejecting the Sabbath (see 4:16), nor do his disciples (see 23:57). The issue was how to interpret the Sabbath law, i.e., whether responding to human need was "work" that violated the Sabbath. Jesus saw the Sabbath as a time of liberation, not of restriction (see the reference to the jubilee year in 4:18–19). Even the **ox** and **donkey** are **untied** on the Sabbath, so **ought not this woman . . . whom Satan bound . . . be set free** (same Greek word as "untie")? Again Jesus uses the rabbinic method of biblical interpretation that argues from the lesser to the greater ("light and heavy" see 12:6–7).

Daughter of Abraham: The woman, too, is a full member of the people of God (see Gen. 12:1–3; Luke 3:8; 19:9; Gal. 3:6–18, 28–29).

13:17 Put to shame: In first-century Mediterranean society, honor and shame were extremely important. Jesus and the woman are honored, the opponents are put to shame.

The entire crowd was rejoicing: The crowd, representing potential disciples of Jesus (see 5:1, 15; 6:17–20, 19; 7:11; 8:4; 9:11, 18, 37; 11:14; 14:25; 19:48; 20:19; 22:6, 47; 23:4, 13, 21, 48), had wavered in the preceding section (12:1–13:9) but now seems to be wholly on Jesus' side.

13:18–21
PARABLES OF GROWTH
(See also at Matt. 13:31–33; Mark 4:30–32)

On interpreting parables, see on Mark 4. These twin parables are together in Matthew but not in Mark or the *Gospel of Thomas*. Their combination reflects Luke's Q source, also used by Matthew, but it is Luke who has placed them in this context.

13:18 What is the kingdom of God like?: The question echoes Isa. 40:18, and does not prepare the way for an explanation, but calls the hearer to reflect on the incomprehensibility of God and the divine rule (see on 4:43). The twin parables do not explain the kingdom of God, but evoke provocative images that demolish conventional, inadequate ways of imagining God's rule in the world.

13:19 Mustard seed: Proverbial for its smallness (Matt. 13:32; Mark 4:31), yet Luke does not mention its size. That a tiny seed produces a large **tree** would be surprising, like the small beginnings of Jesus' ministry that eventuate in the coming of God's kingdom (see the surprising harvest at 8:8). Most surprising, however, is that the seed produces a tree at all. Although it could produce a large shrub (so Matt. 13:32; Mark 4:32), it no more produces a tree than a sunflower seed produces a sunflower tree. The tree reflects the imagery of Dan. 4:10–12; Ezek. 17:5–6, 23; 31:5–6, where the kingdom of God is represented by a mighty tree. In botanical terms, there is no way to get from a mustard seed to a tree. The imagery suggests that the coming of God's kingdom is not a matter of the potential in the seed—it's just not there—but of God's surprising sovereign act. So also one should not think of the potential present in Jesus and his "little flock," for the kingdom comes as God's surprising gift (12:32!). **Birds of the air:** Part of the imagery from Dan. 4:10–12, here they may suggest the inclusiveness of the kingdom, which embraces Gentiles and the unexpected, marginalized persons excluded by society (see 13:28–29).

13:20–21 Yeast that a woman took and hid: Again, the surprising elements in this imagery should not be domesticated to fit into conventional wisdom of how God's kingdom comes. To say that the kingdom works gradually, like leaven in dough, may be true, but that is not the thrust of the strange image of this parable, which only provokes questions: why is yeast used to communicate the meaning of the kingdom (it usually has only negative connotations, as in 12:1; 1 Cor. 5:6–8; Gal. 5:9); why did the woman want to **hide** the yeast? (See NRSV note; the translation "mixed" is an effort to fit the story into conventional thinking.) Why did she hide it in **flour**, of all places? And what is the meaning of the fabulous amount of flour? **Three measures:** About fifty pounds, enough to feed about 150 people. This corresponds to the extravagant, unrealistic harvest of 8:8, and the mustard seed that becomes a tree. Most people had never seen so much bread at one time—but had read about it in their Bible (Gen. 18:6; again, see the way 8:8 evokes Gen. 26:12). In reflecting on these strange stories, Jesus' hearers and Luke's readers may be challenged to reconsider whether their conventional explanations of how God works are adequate, and may be opened up to the mind-blowing advent of God's kingdom in our world.

13:22–30
THE NARROW DOOR
(See also at Matt. 7:13–14, 22–23; 8:11–12; 19:30; Mark 10:31)

13:22 One town and village after another: A reminder that this whole section is part of the Travel Narrative Luke has constructed from his sources and traditions (see on 9:51).

13:23 Only a few?: The question is not from a disciple and has the speculative quality of 13:1–5. But Jesus is not in the business of giving objective answers to abstract religious questions. As in 13:1–5 Jesus refused to give explanations for theoretical religious problems but called for repentance, so here he does not reply to the question but challenges the questioner's presuppositions. **Be saved:** See on 8:36. The reference is not to healing but to final acceptance into God's future kingdom and receiving the gift of eternal life.

13:24 The narrow door: Jesus' response puts all his hearers on the outside. None may presume they are already "in," as though the question were only who *else* will be included. As the preceding parables upset conventional understanding of the kingdom, so God's final salvation will be surprising to **many**, who will appear before the door assuming they will be admitted, but **will not be able**.

13:25–27 Shut the door: A time will come when it is too late for admission (see 12:57–59). Such images warn against presumption. Those who assume they are included find the door closed in their face (see 3:9–10). The mode of communication shifts to second person direct address, which now includes the readers.

I do not know where you come from: Means the same as "I do not know you" (see Matt. 7:23). Proximity to Jesus, hearing him teach, eating and drinking with him (all of which are important to Luke) do not in themselves guarantee that the person has come to know Christ and be known (= approved) by him. **Evildoers:** Reflects Ps. 6:9. Not where one

comes from or experiences with Jesus, but doing the will of God is what finally counts (see 3:9–10).

13:28–29 Abraham and Isaac and Jacob and all the prophets: The patriarchs of Israel, the past heroes and leaders of the people of God. **People will come from the east and west, from north and south**: What seems to be a narrow and judgmental view of who will be included in God's salvation turns out to be an inclusive picture of a multitude of people from many nations and cultures (see Luke's picture of the beginning of the church, Acts 2, and the spread of the gospel through many nations and cultures, Acts 2–28). Yet this broad picture of God's grace cannot be presumed upon; grace is always amazing.

13:31–35
JESUS' LAMENT OVER JERUSALEM
(See also at Matt. 23:37–39)

13:31 Some Pharisees: On Pharisees, see on 5:17. The reader has been conditioned by having repeatedly seen the Pharisees only in an aggressively hostile role, but here they appear as concerned friends of Jesus—a caution to the reader corresponding to the preceding parables (13:18–20) and warnings (13:21–30) not to deal in conventional stereotypes. **Herod:** Herod Antipas, ruler of Galilee (see on 3:1–2; 9:7–9). He finally does participate in Jesus' trial at which Jesus is condemned to death (23:7, 15; Acts 4:27).

13:32 Fox: Herod is sly, stealthy, and murderous. In this same context, Jesus will speak of himself as a mother **hen** (13:34) who tries to protect her chicks from danger. Who would suppose that the final victory belongs to the hen? Another surprising turning of the tables on conventional wisdom (see 13:18–30). Jesus leaves Herod's territory to continue his journey to Jerusalem, but not because his life and death are determined by fear of Herod. Jesus' future is determined by God's sovereign will and Jesus' willing submission to it (9:22, 30–32; 17:25; 18:32–33; 24:7, 26). Over against Herod's death plots, he places his own liberating and life-giving ministry. **The third day:** An allusion to the resurrection (9:22; 18:33; 24:7, 21, 46), one of many instances where the post-Easter perspective from which the Gospel story is told already shines through (see on 2:41–52; 5:4–8; 6:1–11; 7:34; 8:19–21, 36; 12:10–12).

13:33 A prophet to be killed: Luke affirms the designation of Jesus as prophet as a means of declaring his messianic role (see on 2:10–11;

3:23; 4:20–21, 24; 7:16, 39, 41–43; 9:20, 35–36; Acts 3:22–26; 7:37). Suffering and death had already become traditional in Judaism as the mark of the true prophet. **Jerusalem:** Though the holy city, it had played a key role in the persecution of God's messengers (11:49–51; Acts 7:52).

13:34–35 Jerusalem, Jerusalem!: Although in form a lament addressed to Jerusalem, Jesus is still on the way; the inhabitants of Jerusalem presumably addressed are actually absent (a different situation from the Jerusalem context of this saying in Matt. 23:37–39). In its Lukan context the saying actually functions as a warning and invitation to the hearers who accompany Jesus on his journey (and to the readers!) not to be among the ranks of those who reject and kill God's prophets, including Jesus.

How often!: The words do not refer to Jesus' previous visits to Jerusalem. (In Luke, the adult Jesus has not yet been in Jerusalem.) They are spoken as personified transcendent Wisdom, who represents God, who sends the prophets (11:49–51).

Blessed is the one who comes in the name of the Lord: These words from Ps. 118:26 were originally spoken to worshipers in the temple, meaning "Blessed in the name of the Lord are those who come to worship here." Early Christianity reinterpreted them to apply to Christ, the "coming one" (see on 7:19). At Jesus' triumphal entry into Jerusalem, Jesus' disciples raise this cry of acclamation, but the inhabitants of Jerusalem do not, and their leaders consider it scandalous (19:38–40). Jesus' prediction here points beyond the present period, when only his disciples confess him as Lord, to the time when, at the appearance of the Son of Man, even his enemies will acknowledge him as "the one who comes in the name of the Lord."

14:1–6
JESUS HEALS THE MAN WITH DROPSY

14:1 On the Sabbath: For the seriousness of the Sabbath issue, see on 4:16, 40–41; 6:1–11. This is the fourth such Sabbath conflict in Luke (see 6:1–6, 6–11; 13:10–17). For the structure of this section, see at 13:10; this story is parallel to 13:10–17 in the overall structure. **The Pharisees:** See on 5:17. **They were watching him:** See 6:7. They look for some infraction of biblical or traditional law, a hostile stance toward Jesus. The hostility is not returned. Jesus accepts an invitation to dine with the Pharisees, but not in order to condemn them. Just as he ate with the outcasts and sinners

(5:27–32), so he eats with the socially and religiously elite (7:36–50). In both cases he makes known and represents the loving presence of God. It is easier to fellowship with the one *or* the other as "my kind of people," but this is not real inclusiveness. The loving father has two sons, and loves and accepts them both (15:11–32). It is possible to be as proud and exclusive as Pharisees that we only eat with tax collectors and sinners, but that is not Jesus' style of inclusiveness (see on 18:9–14).

Jesus was going . . . to eat a meal: Table scenes play an important role in Luke–Acts (5:29–39; 7:36–50; 11:37–54; 14:1–24; 22:14–38; 24:30–32; 24:36–49) and provide the context for understanding the mealtimes of the early church (Acts 2:42, 46; 6:1; 11:3; 16:34; 27:35). The repeated scene of Jesus at table provides a bridge between the two worlds joined in the Gospel of Luke: (1) the Hellenistic culture, in which the picture of the philosopher or religious teacher carrying on serious conversation with colleagues and students at a meal was a common image (e.g., Plato's *Symposium*), and (2) the Jewish setting of the life of Jesus and early Christianity, where Jesus' table fellowship with all kinds of people and the eucharistic life of the church were central images.

14:2 A man who had dropsy: It is not clear whether the man is an invited guest or a passerby who stopped in to observe the banquet and the famous teacher. The latter would have been quite possible in the Hellenistic houses imagined by Luke, with their open courtyards, but unlikely in the Palestine of Jesus' own context. Dropsy is the archaic term for edema, a painful and debilitating disease causing excessive accumulation of fluids in tissue spaces or body cavities. Jesus takes the initiative. The man does not ask or expect to be healed and disappears from the story as soon as the healing takes place. (See excursus, "Interpreting the Miracle Stories," at Matt. 9:35.) All the attention is focused on Jesus and the Sabbath issue.

14:3 Is it lawful to cure people on the sabbath, or not?: The question is real. The Pharisees should not be caricatured as evil or stupid, as though the answer to the question were obvious. If modern readers too quickly side with Jesus, it may mean they have not grasped the seriousness of the question. To stand with Jesus on such issues does not mean merely to follow good common sense or common decency; this cheapens both Jesus' own radicality (which finally cost his life) and his call to follow him. It is no accident that the concluding paragraph of this section is on the cost of discipleship (14:25–33).

14:4 They were silent: Both before and after the miracle (see v. 6). The question calls for a decision, a risk. The safe way was not to answer, or to respond with an "on the one hand . . . on the other hand." But Jesus calls for a decision. Refusal to respond is already a negative decision. Jesus **healed him, and sent him away:** Jesus' answer to his own question was not a theoretical explanation but an act.

14:5 A child or an ox: Some manuscripts read "a donkey or an ox." We cannot be certain what Luke originally wrote (all original MSS of the Bible have been lost; the text must be reconstructed from later MSS, in which variations such as this occur. See "Introduction: The New Testament as the Church's Book," 4.d). If "child" (literally "son") is original, as is most likely, Jesus has escalated the traditional Jewish question, whether an animal in trouble could be helped on the Sabbath to the more crucial issue where the alternative is between helping a human being in distress or keeping the letter of God's Law. If Jesus' answer seems obvious to us, it is because we have not taken biblical teaching about the Sabbath as seriously as did first-century Jews—including Jesus (see Exod. 20:8; 31:14–15; Lev. 23:23; Num. 15:32–36; Deut. 5:12–14; Isa. 56:2, 6; 58:13).

14:7–14
JESUS AS DINNER GUEST

14:7–10 Not . . . at the place of honor: The preceding scene now continues as though nothing had happened. The following discussion presupposes the ancient Mediterranean culture in which honor and shame were extremely important. It was conventional wisdom that it was better to take a lower seat at a social occasion and be invited to come up higher, rather than suffer the shame of having placed oneself too highly and being asked to step down (see Prov. 25:6–7). For Jesus and Luke, however, the instructions are not merely about table manners, just as they are not a strategy for attaining the highest place after all.

14:11 All who exalt themselves: Rather, the Lukan punch line is understood in the ultimate sense: God is the one who exalts the lowly and brings down those who exalt themselves, as in Mary's song (1:47–55) and the eschatological reversal expressed in the Lukan beatitudes and woes (6:20–26).

14:13–14 Invite the poor: The preceding instructions (vv. 7–11) had been given to the *guests* (or

for occasions when the reader is guest). Here follows a parallel set of instructions for the *hosts* (or for occasions when the reader is host). Just as one should not plot where to sit at a banquet with a view to one's self-enhancement, so one should not make out the guest list for a party with a view to what those invited can do for the host. In both cases, those who would be Jesus' disciples are called to live as those who have been set free to live their lives before God without undue concern for one's image in the eyes of others—the making of such images is another form of idolatry. **The poor, the crippled, the lame, and the blind** are to be invited in the first place because of what the invitation does for the guests: they need food and fellowship generally denied them in the normal social pecking order. But they are also to be invited because of what such an invitation will do for the host: God will reward such conduct, because this corresponds to the invitation God extends to his own banquet (see 14:15–24).

Repaid in the resurrection of the righteous: In some eschatological views within Judaism, only the righteous will be resurrected at the last day. Luke reproduces this view here, which was already present in pre-Lukan tradition (see on 1:1–4), but his own view that there will be a resurrection of both righteous and unrighteous is presented in Acts 24:15. Doing the will of God for reward can be simply another form of selfishness, just as sitting at the lowest place in order to be invited to a higher one can be a self-serving manipulative strategy (14:10). There is a reward for God's faithful servants, but the reward goes to those who serve without thought of reward (see, e.g., Matt. 25:31–40). In all this, the Lukan Jesus takes the "ordinary" activities of giving or attending a dinner party and places them within the ultimate context of God's kingdom. An "ordinary" meal takes on the overtones of the eschatological banquet. In early Christianity, with whom one eats was a crucial issue of the nature of God and the Christian life (Acts 10–11; 15; Gal. 2:11–14). There are no purely secular areas of life that can be fenced off from God's demand; all of life is lived before God—on this point, Jesus and the Pharisees were at one.

14:15–24
PARABLE OF THE GREAT SUPPER
(See also at Matt. 22:1–14)

Jesus' table talk modulates into a story in which the kingdom of God is portrayed as a banquet.

14:15 Eat bread in the kingdom of God: In a world of scarcity—the world as most human beings throughout history have experienced it—the final coming of God's kingdom can be pictured as a great banquet. The messianic banquet was already anticipated in the Old Testament (Isa. 25:6–10). This hope had already become the subject of conventional piety, as expressed in this verse by one of the guests, but one cannot read his tone of voice from the text: Had he been won over to Jesus' view that "ordinary" talk of inviting people to dinner parties was a matter of God's kingdom? Or does he trivialize it by quoting a religious cliché?

14:16 Then Jesus said to him: The reader knows that the story is a parable like those of 13:18–21, but Luke does not identify what follows as a parable (contrast Matt. 22:1), so that the guests at the banquet (14:1, 7) hear it as a realistic story in continuity with the preceding discussion. On interpreting parables, see on Mark 4.

14:16 Someone gave a great dinner: Luke apparently has the more original and parabolic form of the story. The Matthean form (22:1–14) has added more allegorical traits, so that the "someone" becomes "a king," the "dinner" becomes a "wedding banquet for his son." The Lukan form is more in continuity with the everyday life of the preceding discussion, though it is clear the man is wealthy enough to have a servant and a large house appropriate for dinner parties, and that he is accustomed to invite those who can afford to buy property.

Invited many: The parable reflects ancient Mediterranean social customs involving an initial invitation that could be accepted or declined, then a second announcement, to those who had accepted, when all the arrangements were ready. The "many" obviously accepted this initial invitation, otherwise they would not have been contacted when the banquet was ready.

14:17 Come, for everything is ready now: The banquet is sheer grace; the host has provided it all. It is not a covered-dish or potluck dinner; the guests contribute nothing. The banquet does not just happen but takes place because the host has prepared it. Though the parable is not an allegory, the Christian reader can hardly avoid reflecting on the reality that those invited to the messianic banquet in the kingdom of God participate in what God has been doing through history since creation to reconcile humans to himself and to one other.

This is not what the parable "means," but it evokes such images and reflections among those with "ears to hear" (see 14:35 at the conclusion of this section).

14:18 They all alike began to make excuses: This is the first indication that the story, which began in the real world, is moving to a different plane, for in an actual situation it would be incredible that "all" of the "many" would send their regrets and that none of those who had accepted the original invitation would show up. A possibility that keeps the story within the realm of reality, however, is that, after accepting the initial invitation, all those invited asked around to see who else was coming and on this basis decided it was not to their social advantage to show up.

14:19 Bought a piece of land ... bought five yoke of oxen: The first two excuses are transparently false, since no one, then or now, would buy real estate or cattle sight unseen. The refusal of those invited to come to the party is thus doubly insulting to the host.

14:20 I have just been married: Though not as transparent, this excuse, too, is intentionally an offense to the host. Even if it is true, it shows that the original acceptance of the invitation was not intended seriously, since in ancient Hellenistic or Jewish society going through all the arrangements of preparing a wedding and getting married could not have been carried out between the time of the first and second invitations. In Luke, those invited only insult the host by their refusal; they do not abuse the messengers (as in Matt. 22:6). The excuses correspond to the bad soils of a previous parable who receive the seed, but the cares of the world and the distractions of seeking wealth choke it out so that it bears no fruit (8:14; see 12:13–21).

14:21 Bring in the poor, the crippled, the blind, and the lame: This corresponds to Jesus' instruction in 14:13 and is another illustration of the "good news to the poor" of Jesus' keynote address that began his ministry in Luke 4:18. The original invitation had been the *expected* invitation: the host invited those he was expected to invite, and those who were invited expected to be invited. The second invitation is the *unexpected* invitation. People found themselves at a party to which they had never in their wildest dreams supposed they would be invited. Grace, to be grace, must always be amazing grace (see 13:28–29).

14:22–23 There is still room: Another invitation is extended, out beyond the city to the **roads**

and lanes. Some interpreters see the two invitations as to the Jews and to the Gentiles (Luke develops this theme in Acts, in which the church begins as Jewish Christians and expands to become an integrated church of Jewish and Gentile Christians, Acts 10–11; 15).

Compel them to come in: Throughout, the initiative has been with the host. It is not the case in this story that the marginalized and disenfranchised have been standing at the gates, locked out, clamoring for their *right* to be admitted. The first group expected to be included and were finally rejected; the second group(s) did not expect to be included and had to be *brought* in (not "allowed" in). The sovereignty of the host is retained throughout. No one has a right to be at the party, but those who never expected to be there found themselves included, while those who wanted and expected to be asked (so they could turn down the invitation) found themselves excluded.

14:24 None of those who were invited will taste my dinner: The house has been filled, so now the first group could not come even if they changed their mind. The sovereign host confirms this. The original guests have been replaced or, rather, by their refusal have replaced themselves. The parable is not to be allegorized, as though it were a thinly disguised way of saying that the Jews who originally rejected Jesus have forfeited their opportunity and have been replaced by Christians (in contrast, e.g., to the teaching of Paul in Rom. 9–11). The story is rather a vivid warning against the presumption of those who come first or last—no one enters apart from God's invitation; no one is excluded except by his or her own choice.

14:25–35
THE COST OF DISCIPLESHIP
(See also at Matt. 5:13; 10:37–38; Mark 9:49–50)

14:25 Large crowds: On the difference between Jesus' speaking to committed disciples and to the crowds (potential disciples), see on 6:17–20; 11:14; 12:1. Jesus' last words to disciples were in 12:22–53. Since then, he has addressed interested inquirers and admirers. **Traveling with him:** The scene shifts from the table to the road. On the Lukan Travel Narrative, see on 9:51. The crowds travel with him but are not yet on the Way, as Christian discipleship will be described in Acts (9:2; 19:9; 22:4; 24:14, 22).

14:26 Hate father and mother: Two features of biblical language are helpful in understanding these shocking words: 1. Biblical speech is often extreme in order to make a point, a matter of "oriental hyperbole" that no one would think of taking literally (e.g., the camel through a needle's eye of 18:25, also in the context of discipleship), and yet such words lose their meaning if they are reduced to commonsense platitudes. The point of such expressions is that Christian discipleship is not just a matter of common sense but transcends all our expectations and categories.

2. In the Semitic idiom here reflected, "love" and "hate" are not emotion-laden words, but have to do with choice and priorities. "Hate" can mean "love less," as in Gen. 29:30–31: "So Jacob went in to Rachel also, and he loved Rachel more than Leah. He served Laban for another seven years. When the LORD saw that Leah was unloved . . ." "Hate" can also mean "not choose," as in Rom. 9:13, "As it is written, 'I have loved Jacob, but I have hated Esau,'" where God is pictured as hating Esau, that is, not choosing him but choosing his brother.

There can thus be no possibility that Jesus literally calls for his disciples to hate their parents. In Luke, Jesus himself is shown as loving and respecting his parents (2:41–51), but he is also shown as having a higher priority (8:19–21). This is what this saying is about. Christian discipleship cannot be merely added on to other obligations, but takes priority over all else.

14:27 Carry the cross: See on 9:23.

14:28–33 Build a tower . . . not able to finish: These sayings are found only in Luke. (The preceding sayings have been Luke's interpretation of material from Q; see Matt. 10:37–38.) Since the stories illustrate the point of the radical nature of the decision to become a disciple, their military imagery does not provide a biblical warrant for war and killing, just as the several illustrations that picture slaves and masters do not provide a biblical warrant for the institution of slavery. They show that in the secular world of building and military ventures, one cannot enter casually into such crucial actions as building a tower (defense) or going to war (offense). So also the decision to become a disciple of Jesus cannot be casual. Again, however, the metaphors are not to be taken literally or allegorized. The disciples called to follow Jesus in Luke's Gospel do not first make calculations and decide that they can handle it before deciding to follow Jesus (5:1–11, 27–28)—though in each case they "left everything" in order to become his disciples.

In the illustrations, the cost is seen in prospect; in the gospel itself, as in life, the cost of discipleship is learned along the way and seen in retrospect.

14:34–35 Salt that has lost its taste: These sayings, the Lukan interpretation of material also found in Mark 9:49–50 and Matt. 5:13 in other contexts with other meanings, here seem to speak to the issue of discipleship: those who decide to become Jesus' followers are called to live a distinctive life, just as salt is distinct from its surroundings. If food is not salty, it can be salted. But if salt itself is not salty, how can it be salted, and what good is it?

Let anyone with ears to hear listen!: This saying (repeated in various contexts in the Gospels: Matt. 10:27; 11:15; 13:9; Mark 4:9, 23; Luke 8:8) in its present context shows that the preceding speeches of Jesus have not been legalistic instructions to be literally followed but have been in the provocative mode of wisdom and parable. Such language calls for discernment and decision on the part of the hearer. One must lean into Jesus' teaching to hear and understand it; its meaning cannot be known until one is willing to respond.

15:1–32
THREE PARABLES

15:1–3
The Lukan Setting

On interpreting parables, see on Mark 4. Luke here clusters three similar parables, the first of which has a parallel in Matt. 18:12–14 and thus probably comes from Q. These parables are usually called The Lost Sheep, The Lost Coin, and The Prodigal Son ("prodigal" means not "immoral" but "wasteful"; this story could also be called "The Lost Son" [15:32]). The stories could also be called The Found Sheep, The Found Coin, and The Found Son, or simply The Joy of Finding, Parts I–III. We do not know how either Jesus or Luke would have entitled any of the parables. The titles here given (The Good Shepherd, The Persistent Woman, The Waiting Father) reflect the main actors in the stories and Lukan themes documented elsewhere. The reader should note that giving labels to parables, i.e., deciding what they are "about," already involves interpretation. So also, Luke's placing the parables in a particular context and adding editorial comments interprets the parables in a particular way.

It is important to distinguish the original meaning and function of the parables in the context of

Jesus' ministry from their later interpretation in the context of the Gospel, but this does not mean that later layers should be peeled away and discarded. (See "Introduction to the Gospels: How Were Gospels Written?") It is Luke who places these three stories together in the context of the Pharisees' and scribes' criticism of Jesus for eating with tax collectors and sinners, which gives them a particular meaning in the Lukan context.

15:1 Tax collectors and sinners: See on 3:10–14; 5:27–29; 7:29–30, 34–35.

15:2 Pharisees: See on 5:17. **Scribes:** Also called lawyers; see on 7:29–30. This combination is found often in Luke (5:21, 30; 6:7; 11:53). The scribes, but not the Pharisees, end up participating in the trial and execution of Jesus. **Welcomes sinners:** In Luke, Jesus not only does not reject sinners; he does more than merely tolerate or condescendingly accept them. They are guests at his table, where the note of joyous celebration permeates the whole (see vv. 5–7, 9–10, 23–24, 29, 32). **Eats with them:** See on 5:27–32; 7:36. On the importance of eating together in Luke–Acts, see Acts 10–11; 15; Gal. 2:11–14. That Jesus is "friend of sinners" (7:34) who "eats with them" has eucharistic overtones throughout Luke–Acts.

15:4–7
The Good Shepherd
(See also at Matt. 18:12–14)

15:4 Which one of you?: Jesus frequently teaches by means of probing questions that provoke reflection (see 6:9, 32–34, 39, 41; 7:24–26, 31, 42; 9:20, 25; 10:15, 26, 36; 11:11–13, 18–19, 40; 12:6, 14, 25–26, 42, 51, 56–57; 13:2, 4, 15–16, 18, 20; 14:3, 5, 28, 31, 34). He does not merely deliver authoritative instruction to be obeyed, but calls for the hearers' participation, discernment, and decision.

Having a hundred sheep: While the story is not an allegory in which the shepherd represents God or Jesus, in this context it still points to and evokes the image of the presence of God who in Jesus seeks out sinners and welcomes them. The image of the shepherd was a positive one in the Old Testament (e.g., Ps. 23:1) but had become a negative image in New Testament times (see on 2:8–20). Speaking of a good shepherd was a distortion of conventional imagery in somewhat the same way as speaking of a good Samaritan (see on 10:25–37), or using mustard seed and yeast as images for the kingdom of God (see on 13:8–21).

Leave the ninety-nine in the wilderness: The expression is unusual, for the ninety-nine are not "safely in the fold," as in the old gospel song. The imagery may reflect 1 Sam. 17:28, where David is charged with leaving the sheep "in the wilderness" while he defeats the enemies of Israel. In Luke, the phrase emphasizes the shepherd's concern for the one lost (not "strayed," as in Matt. 18:12) sheep.

15:7 Joy: The shepherd does not celebrate alone. Such joy must be shared. Heaven joins in, but not the Pharisees and scribes, who are offended by the extravagance of God's grace. **Righteous persons who need no repentance:** In this context refers to the Pharisees and scribes, the "righteous" in contrast to the "sinners." God rejoices at the repentance of sinners, not at the self-righteous who suppose they need no repentance. In Luke's theology, as in Paul's and Jesus', there are none who are absolutely righteous: all have sinned, all need to repent (see on 11:3; Acts 2:38; 17:30; Rom. 3:21–26).

15:8–10
The Persistent Woman

This story, only in Luke, is almost an exact parallel to the preceding one and has the same meaning. On Luke's pairing of male and female characters, see on 8:1–3. The **silver coin** was a drachma, in first-century Palestine considered the equivalent of a denarius, about a day's wage for a laborer. The lost coin is thus not a large amount but is still significant to the woman. Even though she still has 90 percent of her savings, she dwells on the lost coin, and seeks until she finds it. Her activity of **lighting a lamp** and **sweeping the** (dirt) **floor** indicates a typical poor home in Palestine with only one door and no windows. Here there is no mention of the presumably "righteous"—all attention is focused on the joy of finding the lost and the celebration that follows.

15:11–32
The Waiting Father

In the setting of Jesus' ministry the story is a this-worldly secular story of family life, but it is clear that Luke understands the father to represent God, the younger son to represent repentant sinners, and the elder son to represent the Pharisees and scribes who resented Jesus' acceptance of tax collectors and sinners (15:1–3).

15:11 There was a man who had two sons: On the basis of the preceding, the hearer/readers anticipate that here too an obvious truth will be used to challenge their present understanding. But in contrast to the two preceding

parables, this story does not begin with a rhetorical question that assumes the hearer/readers will agree that what is about to be recounted is self-evidently true. While the shepherd and the woman do what is expected, the pattern is here broken, and the father does not behave in the way everyone would have anticipated. He does not go in search of the lost son and seek until he finds him (but see comments on the concluding v. 32, and see John 4:22).

15:12 The younger (son): Often the favored one in biblical stories (see Cain and Abel [Gen. 4:1–16]; Ishmael and Isaac [Gen. 16; 21]; Jacob and Esau [Gen. 25–27]; Joseph and his older brothers [Gen. 37]). **Give me the share:** The younger son would inherit one-third of the estate at his father's death, the older son two-thirds (Deut. 21:17), but it was irregular and cold-bloodedly offensive to ask to be given the inheritance while the father was still living. It was as though the boy considered his father already dead (see v. 32!), and regarded himself as breaking family relationships forever.

15:13–16 Traveled to a distant country: The story unfolds with precipitous speed. The son converts all the property to cash, goes to a distant (Gentile!) country, wastes the money ("prodigal" means "recklessly wasteful") in **wild living** (NIV) (the elder brother, but not the narrator, relates this to hiring prostitutes [v. 30]). After the money is gone, a severe famine hits the country, and the young man is impoverished. How low he had sunk is illustrated by his accepting a job feeding **pigs,** abhorrent to any Jew, but even they have more to eat than he does. Everything is now gone: money, friends, religious scruples.

15:17 When he came to himself: This self-centered life is not his true self, and the young man realizes it. **My father's hired hands:** It never occurs to him to reassert his claim to be a son. He acknowledges he has forfeited all his privileges but realizes he will be better off as an employee of his father's than in his present situation.

15:18 I will say to him: The reader gets to hear the interior monologue of the young man, which shows that his later speech is sincere. **Father:** See on 11:2. He still addresses his father as "father" but has given up his rights of sonship. **I have sinned:** The young man places himself in the category of sinners (see 15:1–3; 18:9–14). Sin, not merely "inappropriate behavior," is the problem. Sin has a double dimension—it is against both God (here expressed with reverent Jewish reserve as "heaven") and human beings. This is the only reference to God in the story, which takes place on the horizontal plane of human relationships. But wronging other people is also sin against God (Ps. 51:4).

15:19 No longer worthy: He has given up all his claims to sonship, and will not ask to be readmitted on the basis of his status as a member of the family, which he assumes is a thing of the past, a situation of his own choice. **Make me like one of your hired men** (NIV): The transformation in process in the young man's life has taken him from "give me" (v. 12) to "make me."

15:20 So he set off and went to his father: In contrast to the two preceding stories, the father does not come to him. The sheep and coin are passive and are found by the shepherd and the woman, who persistently seek. The son is not a sheep or coin, must take responsibility for his own acts, and must not only have the nice internal conversation with himself but act upon it before he is finally received back into the father's house. Yet see the last word of the story in 15:32.

While he was still far off, his father saw him and was filled with compassion: Had the father been looking down the road? Yet the father does not go to meet the son until he sees the son coming to meet the father. **Ran:** This was considered extremely undignified; the father behaves in a somewhat embarrassing manner in the eyes of the community, somewhat akin to the scandalous manner in which Jesus ate with sinners (see 5:27–39; 7:34).

15:22–23 Robe . . . ring . . . sandals . . . fatted calf: The son does not get to complete his prepared speech, which is interrupted by the father's command to dress him in fine clothes and prepare a celebration. There is no apology, no penitence required, no preliminary making him feel guilty so he will appreciate forgiveness, but an extravagance of forgiveness granted without being asked for, restoration without being claimed or anticipated (see 14:23–24).

Joy permeates the whole (see vv. 5–7, 9–10, 23–24, 29, 32). God and the angels celebrate. Jesus and the sinners he receives celebrate. The scene of being received is not one of grim repentance but of celebration; in the Bible, repentance is not the alternative to joy but its ground and complement. Everyone celebrates except the Pharisees, scribes, and the elder brother, who had stayed home and been good. The story is reminiscent of the story of Jonah,

where everyone in the story, including God, repents—except for Jonah, who sulks at the mercy of God.

15:24 This son of mine: The father claims him as son, though the son had not claimed that status himself. **Was dead and is alive again:** Life in estrangement and alienation in the far country were not truly life. See on 10:25; 12:22–34; 18:18–27. **Was lost and is found:** Repeated as the last words of the story, 15:32. Although the son had taken the initiative in returning home, the final words still place him in the same category as the lost sheep and the lost coin, i.e., as passive being found rather than finding his own way back to the father's house. What seems like *our* act at the moment in retrospect is paradoxically seen as *God's* act. See on 12:32, especially Phil. 2:12–13.

15:25 The elder son was in the field: Traditionally, revivalistic piety has focused on the younger son, his sin and repentance, as though the story concluded at v. 24. But in the Gospel of Luke, Jesus told the story for the sake of those who are represented by the elder son (see 15:1–3). Now the reader remembers that the story begins with the declaration that "there was a man who had *two* sons." The elder son is hard at work (in contrast to the "wild living" of his younger brother). He hears the sounds of the party already going on in his absence: Had they not even invited him to the celebration? And what is being celebrated anyway? He asks a slave.

15:27 Your brother . . . your father: From the mouth of a slave, he is reminded of his own family relationships.

15:28 He became angry and refused to go in: Contemporary readers may have to remind themselves of the good reasons the elder brother could give himself for not joining the party. **His father came out:** While the father had not sought out the younger son, here he does seek out the elder son. The elder son fits into the category of the "lost" that is "sought" that has been established by the preceding two stories.

15:30 This son of yours: As he had not addressed his father with the respectful title of "father" (in contrast to the younger son), but brusquely began with "Listen!" so he identifies the young man not as "my brother" but "this son of yours." He is scandalized by the father's mercy (see Jonah 4!). The elder son is not lying when he speaks of having stayed at home, having been good, having worked hard (see 18:11–12, also a factual description). **Devoured your**

property with prostitutes: The elder brother's imagination has supplied this picture.

15:31 Always with me . . . all that is mine is yours: The status of the elder son too does not depend on his achievement. It is absolute: "always," "all." This is what the elder son could not (yet) accept. Those who have never messed up, who have considerable resources and achievements and wish to pay their own way, cannot rejoice when others who can't pay are still accepted, and do not realize that their own admission has already been paid by Someone Else. "No distinction" is a hard pill for the "righteous" to swallow, either at the level of being saved or of social and family relationships (Rom. 3:21; Acts 10:28, 34–35).

15:32 This brother of yours: Both the slave of v. 27 and the father identify the young man as brother to the moral, hardworking stay-at-home. It is not clear whether or not the elder brother ever accepted this reality and joined the party. The story concludes outside, with the father pleading, with the implicit question hanging in the air (again, like the conclusion of the story of Jonah, see Jonah 4:1–11). This story which does not begin with a question (see on 15:11) ends with one, for the reader.

16:1–31
RESPONSIBLE USE OF MONEY

Chapter 16 is a unit with a single theme, the responsible use of money and property. The section is framed by parables that begin with identical words, "There was a rich man." The first section is addressed to disciples (see on 6:12–13), the second to Pharisees (see on 5:17). While in the preceding chapter the Pharisees seem to represent self-righteous people who are offended by God's grace, in this present chapter they represent greedy people (see v. 14). In neither case is Luke presenting an accurate picture of historical Pharisees; he is using them as characters in his story to exemplify sinful opponents of Jesus and his message.

16:1–13
The Dishonest Manager

Jesus' original parable was not an allegory (see on parable interpretation at Mark 4), but in Luke's presentation it is clear that the rich man, who is called **master** in v. 3, represents God, and the manager/steward represents Christian leaders (see 1 Cor. 4:1–2; Titus 1:7; 1 Pet. 4:10).

16:1 Rich man: Responsible use of wealth is a Lukan theme; see 1:53; 6:24; 12:16, 21; 21:1. **Manager:** "Steward" in some translations;

one responsible for managing the property of another, in contrast to "owner." **Squandering:** Same word as 15:13, of the prodigal son. In both cases, though their actions are reprehensible, the persons themselves turn out to be accepted by grace. Their conduct is considered unrighteous, but they are "justified" (see on 18:14). Christians and their leaders are not owners, but stewards of God's creation; their irresponsible behavior squanders God's property entrusted to them.

16:2 Give me an accounting of your management: The coming judgment in which Christians and their leaders will stand before God and give account is a Lukan theme. "Judge"/ "judgment" occurs 36x in Luke–Acts (see, e.g., Luke 10:14, 11:31–32; Acts 17:31; 24:25).

16:3 Said to himself: An internal monologue, like that of the prodigal son in 15:17–19. In both cases, the sincerity of the person is represented, since the internal speech is not posturing before others, but is heard only by the reader. The quandary is that he is guilty of mismanagement, that judgment is inevitable, that he is going to lose his job, and that he considers it impossible to do manual labor or beg from others.

16:4 What to do: The manager allows his master's creditors, who do not know that he is soon to lose his job, to pay less than they had originally bargained for.

16:5–7 A hundred . . . fifty; a hundred . . . eighty: The substantial amounts indicate that his mismanagement was no trifle, was a matter not of individual households but of commercial transactions. The parable does not make clear the nature and meaning of the reduction. It has sometimes been thought that the manager was only sacrificing his own commission, in order to ingratiate himself with the creditors who would be obligated to help him in the future—especially in the first-century Mediterranean world in which patronage, honor, and shame played an important social role. In this view, the manager would be shrewd, but his actions would not be dishonest—his master would receive what was owed, but the manager would receive no commission. But since v. 8 calls the manager "dishonest," it is more likely that his actions actually caused the master to lose money. He is both shrewd and dishonest.

16:8a His master commended the dishonest manager: This is the most difficult and controversial verse in the story, which does not make clear whether the "master" is Jesus, who

241

is telling the story, or the rich man, who is a character in the story. Part of the difficulty is that there were no quotation marks in ancient texts, so modern translators and editors of English translations must decide where to insert them. If the direct quotation of Jesus' story ends at v. 7 (to resume at v. 9), then v. 8 is from the Lukan narrator commenting on the story, and "the master" is Jesus. More likely, however, is the understanding that Jesus remains the speaker throughout, so that the master is the rich man in the story. This parable then evokes the same type of shock as the parables of 13:18–21, in which the kingdom of God is presented in unexpectedly striking, even scandalous ways. In this understanding of Jesus' story, the master who had been wronged commended the dishonest manager because he had acted decisively in the face of the coming judgment—as Jesus' followers are called to do.

16:8b–12 Interpretations of the parable: The original parable thus probably ended at v. 8a, without comment. The early church, including Luke, was as bothered by this story as are modern readers, for it presents people acting in unconventional ways (see 15:11–31!). They thus derived meanings from it—"the moral of the story"—several of which are here appended to the original story. While these "applications" do not go directly back to Jesus, at least not in their present context, they allow us to hear the early church's interpretations of the meanings they found in *Jesus'* life and teachings, and are an indispensable element of the church's Scripture. The New Testament has preserved both Jesus' original teaching and the ways it was interpreted by the church and the authors of the New Testament (see on Luke 1:1–4 and Mark 4:1). However, the goal of adequate and responsible interpretation is not to peel away the later layers and get back to the original teaching of Jesus. This can sometimes be done, with more or less confidence from case to case, and is often illuminating for our New Testament texts. Responsible biblical interpretation, however, seeks to listen to the word of God that comes through the present form of the biblical text. In this instance, we can join with and overhear the early church struggling with a difficult text and profit from the additional meanings they found there. There are six of them:

1. **16:8b Shrewd . . . children of light:** The dishonest steward is commended not for his dishonesty but for his shrewdness (see 14:28–33;

Matt. 10:16). This saying assumes the apocalyptic dualistic perspective (see 9:49–50) in which Jesus' followers are "children of light" (see John 12:36; Eph. 5:8; 1 Thess. 5:5) and nonbelievers are **children of this age.** Jesus' followers already see the light that has come into the world in Jesus and orient their lives to the coming kingdom of God (see on 4:43), while others orient their lives to the present age and its values. The parable, however, is a "worldly" parable, not a directly religious one, and shows that Jesus' followers must not be naive, but need to learn the lesson of shrewd and decisive action as they prepare for the coming judgment (see 12:57–59).

2. **16:9 Make friends for yourselves by means of dishonest wealth:** In this interpretation, the parable points out that Christian believers should use the money entrusted to them wisely, i.e., in Christian service to others, so that in the age to come those they have helped will welcome them into the kingdom of God (see Matt. 25:31–46). There is a contrast between temporal money that belongs to this world, and the **eternal homes** of the world to come. Here, Luke recognizes the inherent ambiguity of wealth: on the one hand, money is "dishonest," i.e., tainted with sin. On the other hand, it is not to be rejected as such but to be used in a way oriented to the coming triumph of God's kingdom. Money is a means, not an end in itself. People are to be loved, and money is to be used, not vice versa.

3. **16:10 Little . . . much:** While the possession of wealth seems like a great thing in the present world, it is little in comparison with the true treasures of God's kingdom and provides a test of faithfulness.

4. **16:11 Dishonest wealth . . . true riches:** Being welcomed into God's kingdom by those we have helped by the responsible use of wealth is the "true riches" (see 19:11–27).

5. **16:12 What belongs to another . . . your own:** The present Christian life is a matter of stewardship, management of the world that belongs to God the Creator. The future inheritance is that of God's "sons," who are no longer managers and employees, but heirs (see 15:11–32; Rom. 8:12–17, 31–39; Gal. 4:8–5:1).

6. **16:13 Two masters:** Luke concludes the series of "lessons" from the parable with a saying from Q found in Matthew in another context (Matt. 6:24). The saying assumes that human existence as such is "serving" some "master," i.e., that we do not have it in ourselves to cre-

ate the meaning of our own lives, but must look outside ourselves for that which fulfills us and gives our lives meaning. As a human being, there is no choice but to serve some master—that "I am the master of my fate, the captain of my soul" (William Ernest Henley) is not only an illusion, but arrogance and rebellion against the Creator. The only choice is which master I will serve. Thus not merely greed, but idolatry, is the issue in the use of wealth. **Hate:** In biblical parlance, a matter of choice and priority (see on 14:26).

16:14–18
The Law and the Kingdom of God
(See also at Matt. 5:18; 11:12–13; 19:9; Mark 10:11–12)

The neat structure of this chapter that is framed by parables about the use of money seems to be disrupted by these verses that deal with the revelation of God's will in the Law and the Prophets. Each of the following sayings originally had its own meaning in a different context. Luke inserts them here, between the two parables about the use of money, addressed to "lovers of money." Luke seems to have placed them here as a reminder to the Pharisees—who regarded themselves as the interpreter of God's Law—that the revelation of God's will in the Scriptures is sufficient to reveal God's will as justice and compassion to the poor. In Luke's structure the second parable is thus itself framed by references to the Law of God revealed in Scripture (16:16, 31).

16:14–15 Pharisees, who were lovers of money: See on 5:17. As a group, the historical Pharisees were no more greedy than other groups. Luke here pictures the Pharisees as the foil for Jesus' advocacy of the poor and responsible stewardship of possessions. Pharisees **ridiculed** Jesus on the commonsense basis that everyone is interested in accumulating as much money as possible. The orientation of Jesus and his disciples to a different set of values seems ridiculous to those who simply adopt the values of this world. Since most people accept the worldly standard of judgment, the Pharisees **justify themselves in the sight of others**. (See 7:29–30.) Luke links concern for money and self-justification ("People respect and envy me because I am financially successful, so I must be OK"). Jesus has brought a reversal of conventional values, so that **what is prized by human beings is an abomination in the sight of God** (see 18:9–14).

16:16 Since then the good news of the kingdom of God is proclaimed: This difficult saying appears in a different form and different contexts in Matt. 5:18, 11:12–13. In Luke's understanding, John the Baptist stood at the transition period between the time of Israel and the time of Jesus (see introduction to Luke: "Jesus as the 'Midst of Time'"). Something radically new arrived in Jesus' proclamation of the kingdom, something that reversed conventional values. **Everyone tries to enter it by force:** The Greek verb can also be translated as a passive, "Everyone is pressed to enter it," more appropriate in this context. The Matthean form is different still, making the kingdom of God the subject of the verb: "the kingdom of heaven has suffered violence." In Luke's form and context, the saying corresponds to the pressure inherent in the other sayings that urge Jesus' disciples to make the radical decision in favor of the kingdom and its values.

16:17 Easier for heaven and earth to pass away: The dramatic new demand that Jesus' preaching of the kingdom brings does not nullify the revelation of God found in the Law and the Prophets of Israel's Scriptures. While Jesus introduces a radical new period in God's plan for history, there is continuity with the old.

16:18 Divorce . . . adultery: This is the most difficult of the four sayings to understand in this context. This, the only reference in Luke–Acts to divorce, is not to be understood as Luke's presentation of the teaching of Jesus about divorce. Many situations and cases are not dealt with (the saying deals only with the actions of the male partner and has no exception clauses, such as are found in Matthew and Paul, that relate this absolute teaching to particular situations; see Matt. 5:31–32; 19:3–12; Mark 10:2–12; 1 Cor. 7:10–13). Perhaps it is only an illustration of the preceding saying: the new era brought about by Jesus does not dissolve the older laws about marriage and divorce but intensifies and fulfills them. Since divorces are often brought about in order to obtain new sexual partners, the contextual meaning here may be a further contrast between the values of this age and the values of the kingdom of God. The quest for more money and more sexual partners is characteristic of this age, but the kingdom of God has reversed the values of the old age.

16:19–31
The Rich Man and Lazarus

For the general outline and major theme of the section into which this story fits, see 16:1–31.

16:19 There was a rich man: See 16:1; 13:16; 18:18–23. The Latin word for "rich" (*dives*) in the Vulgate translation was misunderstood as a proper name, Dives, but the man was anonymous, like all the characters in Jesus' parables (except Lazarus). **Clothed in purple:** Purple became the color of royalty, wealth, and position in the Roman Empire, due to the expensive process necessary in producing the dye (from a particular gland of mollusks found on the eastern Mediterranean coast). Wearing the color purple was regulated by law; how much purple one wore indicated one's status within the Roman system. The rich man **feasted sumptuously every day** in a world of scarcity. He lived in a gated house—to protect him from the have-nots.

16:20 A poor man named Lazarus: A form of the Jewish name Eleazar, which means "God helps." No one else in the story helps him. He is desperately poor, and sick. Lazarus is the only character named in any of Jesus' parables. The Gospel of John knows of a Lazarus who died and was raised, but the event still did not convince unbelievers to repent (John 11:1–57; 12:9–11).

16:21 Dogs: In Jewish society, dogs are not pets. These are the semiwild, dangerous animals that roam the streets. **Licking his sores:** Not a matter of gentle puppies helping soothe his pain, but a further illustration of the suffering and precarious situation of his daily life.

16:22–23 Died: Death is the great equalizer; here, death literally turns the tables. Just as the lives and earthly situations of the two men had been different, so their deaths were different. Lazarus is **carried away by the angels:** There is no speculative interest in whether this was his soul, spirit, or body. The story proceeds as though each person retained his or her former corporeal existence: Lazarus is at a feast where he presumably eats and drinks, while the rich man has a tongue, is thirsty, and experiences pain. **To Abraham's side** (NIV; see NRSV footnote): Abraham is the Old Testament patriarch, the "father" of all the family of the redeemed (see Gen. 12–22; Gal. 3:6–29). The picture is of people reclining at a banquet, in Greco-Roman style around a low central table, resting on one elbow with bodies extended outward like the spokes of a wheel (see 2 Macc. 7; see on John 13:23). At such a banquet, to lie "on someone's bosom" meant to recline next to them. As Abraham seems to be presiding, Lazarus is next to him in the place of honor.

The rich man also died and was buried: It must have been quite a funeral. Nothing is said of Lazarus's burial. To remain unburied was the ultimate dishonor. The rich man awakes in Hades, the place of the dead. The rendering "hell" found in some translations is inaccurate, though in some circles of Judaism by the first century the picture of Hades (Sheol) as the place of all the departed dead had sometimes been restricted to mean only the place of punishment for those who had done evil, with Paradise indicating a separate place for the departed righteous (see Luke 23:43; 2 Cor. 12:4; Rev. 2:7). Though he **was being tormented** in Hades, he could see Abraham, Lazarus, and the blessed dead.

16:24–25 Father Abraham: See 3:7–9; 13:16; 19:9. Abraham responds **"Child,"** graphic evidence of the truth of John the Baptist's preaching.

Remember that during your lifetime: The matter is not discussed in terms of "morality." The rich man is not pictured as being particularly evil, by the standards of this age, but as living as the well-to-do customarily do, admired and envied by all. Nor is Lazarus described as particularly virtuous. The only "point" of the story is the eschatological reversal: the ultimate verdict and situation brought about by the coming kingdom will be a reversal of the present world (see 1:52; 6:20–26). The reader must decide whether to live by the standards already in place in this world, or by the coming reversal manifest in Jesus.

16:26 A great chasm has been fixed: In this parable, deeds done in this life are the final determination of one's destiny, a destiny that cannot be modified after death (see 4 Ezra 7:36). During their earthly life, the rich man *would not* go to Lazarus; now, Lazarus *cannot* come to the rich man.

16:27–30 They have Moses and the prophets: See 16:14–18. Luke sees close continuity between the Old Testament Scriptures; the life, death, and resurrection of Jesus; and the word of God that continues to be mediated by Christian preaching. He thus emphasizes the adequacy of Scripture to mediate God's message. **Repent:** see on 3:7–9. Repentance was the fundamental theme of the preceding section, 15:11–32.

This story is a parable, not a documentary on what happens to people when they die. It does not purport to offer information on such questions as whether people will recognize one another in the next life, whether one can see hell from heaven, or whether there is an intermediate state between death and the final resurrection and judgment. The Christian hope (on "hope," see 24:21; Rom. 8:18–24) of life after death and the conviction of the final coming of the kingdom of God, resurrection, judgment, and eternal life are pictured in differing ways in the New Testament. In some, the faithful go directly to be with God in heaven at death; in others, this does not happen until the resurrection at the last day.

The general message of this parable is quite clear in its Lukan context: how one uses one's earthly resources is terribly important, for there are terrible consequences for neglecting the plight of the poor and hungry.

The parable provokes thought, as do all parables, without giving answers to the questions it raises for the thoughtful reader. It is clear that none of us would neglect a sick, starving beggar on our doorstep. But how far away must the person be before we are "no longer responsible" (see 10:29)? Down the street? In another part of town? In another town? Another state? Another country? If other people should be responsible in those more distant places, am I relieved of my responsibility, so that as long as no starving people are on my personal doorstep, I may continue my feasting in good conscience, secure in my gated community?

In this story, rich and poor are divided by table and gates, but Luke knows that in the early church such people are united around one table (Acts 2:43–47; 4:32–37; 10:1–11:18, esp. 11:3, 12), and Revelation knows of gates that do not exclude but are open to all (Rev. 21:12; 22:24–27).

17:1–10
FORGIVENESS AND FAITH

These four sayings were originally unrelated. Three of them are found in other contexts in Matthew and Mark (see Matt. 18:6–7, 15, 21–22; Mark 9:42). The final one, vv. 7–10, is peculiar to Luke, who has placed them all in this context.

17:1 Jesus said to his disciples: The change in addressees signals a break in the subject matter (see on 12:1; on crowds, disciples, apostles, see 6:17–20). **Occasions for stumbling** (NRSV)/**things that cause people to sin** (NIV) is translated from a Greek word that literally means "stumbling blocks" or "offenses, scandals." The word can be used in a positive sense, i.e., of Jesus' behavior that seems scandalous to the religious authorities (see on 7:23, 39). Here, it is used in a negative sense, of be-

havior that presents a problem for other disciples' faith and might "trip them up," causing them to compromise or abandon the faith. The striking thing to modern Western individualism that we have been conditioned to respect is that Jesus does not see faith and discipleship as merely an individual matter between the person and his or her conscience and God. Jesus presupposes that being a disciple also means being concerned for the spiritual wellbeing of one's fellow disciples and their relation to God. Two things are said about occasions when one disciple's behavior adversely affects another disciple's faith: (1) Such things are **bound to come.** To be a Christian means to belong to a community of faith, in which people's actions affect each other and the community as a whole. (2) **Woe to anyone** who causes them. This double affirmation means that in an imperfect church in an imperfect world, such things are bound to happen, but that no particular one "must" happen. The incredibly accurate prediction of how many accidents will happen on a holiday weekend may provide a modern analogy; accidents will happen, but no particular accident has to happen. No one who causes an accident can avoid responsibility by saying, "The insurance companies predicted that a certain number of people would die this weekend," just as no disciple can avoid responsibility by generalizations such as "these things happen." In the Christian community, people must care for each other's well-being. In particular, the "stronger" members of the community must take care not to cause the "weaker" members to stumble (see Rom. 14).

17:2 Millstone: The large, heavy circular stone fitted to the top of another stone, used for grinding grain. The top stone could weigh several hundred pounds, so much it was turned by a donkey. To be thrown into the sea with such a necklace is a vivid image of how serious it is to put an obstacle in the way of another person's faith, even if "I have a right to do what I think is right" and "I know I'm right" (see on 1 Cor. 8–10). **Little ones:** The expression is found only here in Luke–Acts, but in other contexts it seems not to mean "children," but "novice Christians," "those just beginning their Christian life." In Luke too, the warning is probably primarily against damaging the faith of fellow disciples, but it would still include a severe statement against obstructing the developing faith of children. **Thrown into the sea:** See on 17:6.

17:3 Brother (NIV)/**another disciple** (NRSV): The word literally means "brother (or sister)." The church was described in family metaphors. The saying deals with sins of fellow Christians against each other within the Christian family. Since Christian life means not individualism but living with other followers of Christ within the Christian community, one disciple will inevitably sin against another, intentionally or unintentionally. Here sin is not only against God but against a fellow Christian (see 15:18). Sin always has both a horizontal and a vertical dimension. The church developed and applied Jesus' sayings to address this situation. Such offenses are not to be ignored, even in a "forgiving spirit," but sometimes must be confronted before reconciliation can take place. This is not merely pandering to the feelings of the insiders, but a matter of Christian mission, for the mission of the church requires a community at peace within itself in order to carry on its work for others.

If he repents (NIV): In the Matthean form of the saying (Matt. 18:15, 21–22) forgiveness seems to be unconditional, and Matthew does not mention repentance, which is probably Luke's addition here—it is a special theme and interest of his (see on 3:7–9). In the Lukan view, repentance is the precondition of forgiveness and reconciliation (13:3, 5; 15:11–32; Acts 2:38; 17:30). This does not mean, however, that Luke instructs the offended party to withhold forgiveness until he or she receives an apology.

Seven times: The Matthean form has a different number, seventy-seven or seventy times seven, i.e., 490 times (see on Matt. 18:21). In neither case, however, is it a matter of calculation. Whoever counts the times has not yet forgiven the first time. Like the millstone in the preceding saying, the point is the incredible grace that is called for. Those who know they have been forgiven by God can "afford" to be forgiving to others, i.e., they are set free from concern with getting even, in order to share the grace they have received.

17:5 Apostles: See on 6:17–20. They are included in the instructions to disciples. **Increase our faith** is a surprising response to this teaching on forgiveness, which we might think would call for more toleration or love. But the ability to forgive others depends on the awareness that one has been forgiven by God, and this is a matter of faith. Faith is not merely vertical, between the believer and God, but is horizon-

tal, affecting relations within the community and thus its equipment for mission.

17:6 The size of a mustard seed: Proverbial for its smallness (see on 13:18). The Greek grammar of this saying is somewhat confused, with variations in the manuscripts. The meaning seems to be that the disciples had assumed they had a certain amount of faith, but that it needed to be increased. Jesus' response seems to indicate that what they need is not more faith, as though faith could be quantified, but simply that they need faith as such, the smallest amount of which can do amazing things. Casting the **mulberry tree** into the sea is a graphic hyperbole of the power of such faith that can allow one to forgive seven times in one day, because one has come to believe in God's grace toward one's own sin. The miracles spoken of here are not concerned with sensational flying trees, but with the miracle of a community of believers that lives by the ethic of the kingdom and its awareness of the grace of God.

In the sea: The occurrence of the phrase from v. 2 with different imagery is probably an indication of the catchword principle that caused individual sayings to be clustered together during the period of oral tradition prior to the writing of the Gospels (see on 1:1–4; 13:11).

17:7–10 Worthless slaves: Although the story itself seems to address people who owned slaves (**Who among you?**), in the Lukan context it is addressed to Jesus' disciples who did not own slaves. (Some of Luke's readers may have been wealthy enough to own slaves.) But the story forces the hearer into the point of view of the slave. In early Christianity, Christians were pictured as slaves and God or Christ as the master (e.g., Acts 2:18; 16:16; Rom. 6:16–19; 1 Cor. 7:21; but see also John 15:13–15; Rom. 8:15; Gal. 4:7, 31).

The imagery of this parable presupposes the institution of slavery as it existed in the first century (see on 7:32; 12:35–38; 14:28–33). The expectations of a slave were harsh; they rested only after taking care of the master (but see Jesus' surprising use of this imagery in 12:37, and see John 13:1–17). In Luke's understanding, the story seems to make two points: (1) No matter how much we do for God, we are not doing more than is asked or expected of us. The God who is our Creator and who is definitively revealed in Christ calls for our whole life (9:23), so that we can never do enough good deeds to build up credit so that

God would "owe" us. (2) The blessings of salvation we receive from God are a matter of grace, not of God's paying a debt to us. This is the meaning of justification by grace through faith, as expounded by Paul (Rom. 3:21–25), which Luke also profoundly understands (18:9–14).

17:11–19
CLEANSING AND GRATITUDE:
THE TEN LEPERS

17:11 On the way to Jerusalem: Not an incidental comment, but identifies this story as part of the Travel Narrative (see at 9:51). **Between Samaria and Galilee:** Luke seems not to have a clear picture of Palestinian geography (see on 4:44; 8:26; 9:10, 53). The note prepares the way for the introduction of the Samaritan at the conclusion of the story.

17:12 As he entered a village: See on 9:51–56. **Ten lepers:** See on 4:27; 5:12. **Keeping their distance:** See Num. 5:2–3; Lev. 13:45–46. Leprosy is an apt symbol of the sinful human condition before God, in that it is humanly incurable and separates the afflicted person from others, a kind of living death.

17:13 Master, have mercy on us: It is not clear whether they are only asking for alms, which would be the usual expectation, or if they have confidence in Jesus' power to heal and ask to be cleansed of their leprosy. In Luke's quasi-allegorical understanding, this is analogous to sinful human beings' calling out to God for mercy. The lepers ask for mercy, i.e., they have no "rights" to which they can appeal, and although they did nothing to fall into their appalling condition, healing is not "owed" to them.

17:14 Go and show yourselves to the priests: See Lev. 14:23; Luke 5:14. Jesus gives them a command, just as Elisha had done to Naaman the Syrian (see 2 Kgs. 5:1–14; Luke 4:27). There is no demand for faith, but a command to do something. **As they went, they were made clean:** They were to act as though they had already been healed, and when they did so, *then* saw that they had in fact been cleansed from their leprosy. This acting-as-if, on the basis of Jesus' word, is the nature of faith. They do not first simply "believe" and are healed, and then when they are healed proceed to have their healing certified by the priest.

17:15 One of them ... turned back: It was the others, in fact, who continued to do exactly what Jesus had told them to do. This is a completely spontaneous act, the expression of gratitude not commanded by Jesus. Gratitude cannot be commanded or exacted (see the previous parable in 17:7–10!). **Praising God:** Although *Jesus* had acted to make them whole, they gave praise to *God*. Luke's understanding of the relation of Jesus to God does not make them alternatives or competitors. It is God who acts in Jesus; Jesus is "the human face of God" (J. A. T. Robinson). On Luke's theocentric Christology, see 5:25–26; 7:16; 8:24, 38; 9:20–22, 43; 13:13; 17:15; 19:37. The leper responds with gratitude and praise. There is no presumption that "of course God heals/forgives/saves— that's God's business." Grace cannot be calculated; grace is always amazing grace. "Grace" and "gratitude" are related linguistically and theologically; just as the two words are derived from the same root, so there can be no awareness of grace without gratitude, no gratitude without an awareness of grace.

17:17 Were not ten made clean? All were cleansed. The healing was not reversed or cancelled. Ingratitude does not cancel grace. Human lack of faith does not cancel God's faithfulness (Rom. 3:3, 4). But there is hurt in the voice of Jesus that only one is grateful. The church is the community of the grateful, those who recognize that, while God's mercy extends to all, all are compelled to respond in gratitude. The others are just as cleansed by God but do not recognize that it calls forth the response of praise and thanksgiving.

17:18 This foreigner: See 10:25–37; Acts 10:28.

17:19 Your faith has made you well: See 7:50; 8:48; 18:42. Here faith does not mean the confidence that Jesus or God can work miracles— the others also had this—but the grateful response. To be saved is not only to be healed and forgiven but to be delivered from the self-centeredness that inhibits grateful praise.

17:20–37
THE COMING OF THE KINGDOM OF GOD
(See Matt. 24:17–41; Mark 13:5–23)

Apocalypticism deals with the future coming of the kingdom of God and the final triumph of God's purposes for the world. Two apocalyptic discourses attributed to Jesus circulated in early Christianity. One is incorporated in Mark 13:1–37 (adopted by Luke in 21:5–33); the other was in Q, incorporated here in Luke and by Matthew in Matt. 24:26–43 (on Luke's sources, see introduction to Luke, and comments on 1:1–4). A major difference in the two discourses is that according to the Markan version the end will be preceded by distinctive signs, but in the Q version the end will come in a completely unexpected manner. When Matthew found similar discourses in his two major sources, he characteristically combined them into one discourse; Luke, on the other hand, preserved them as two separate discourses. (See another example in the two evangelists' respective treatment of the mission discourses; see on Luke 9:1–6; 10:1–16.)

17:20 Jesus was asked by the Pharisees: A new section with a new audience begins here. Jesus has previously been addressing disciples and the healed leper. On the Pharisees, see at 5:17. Here as in 16:14 the Pharisees play the negative role in Luke's story, representing Jesus' opponents, who function as the foil for his own teaching. **When the kingdom of God was coming:** On kingdom of God, see 4:43; 11:20. In Luke's view, to ask when is to ask the wrong question (see 12:36; 19:11–27; 21:7; Acts 1:6–11). **Not coming with things that can be observed:** The presence of the kingdom of God is not a matter of objective verification, nor will its future appearance be preceded by "signs" that just anyone can observe (contrast Mark 13 and Luke 21:7–33; see discussion of Luke's sources above).

17:21 The kingdom of God is within (NIV)/ **among** (NRSV) **you:** The word translated "within" or "among" is ambiguous and rare (only here and Matt. 23:26 in the New Testament). This text has been understood and translated in two different ways. (1) "Within you" (KJV, ASV) suggests that the kingdom is an internal, spiritual reality "in the believer's heart," a personal, individualistic interpretation of the kingdom of God popular in American liberalism, but difficult to find in the Bible. There are no biblical texts that locate God's kingdom "in the heart" (see on 4:43). Jesus is here addressing the Pharisees; in this context it is unlikely that he would say to *them* that the kingdom is in their hearts. That the "you" is plural also argues against the individualistic interpretation. (2) Thus the second interpretation, "among you" (NRSV; REB) or "in the midst of you" (RSV) is better. It corresponds to Luke's own view that the kingdom was present in this world during the one-year ministry of Jesus (see introduction to Luke: "Jesus as the 'Midst of Time,'" and comments on 4:20–21; 11:20). The kingdom of God is present in Jesus' ministry, but the Pharisees do not see it. The kingdom was not the kind of thing that objective observers could validate but a matter of having the believers' "eyes of faith."

17:22 To the disciples: A change of audience takes place; the following instructions are directed to believers. On disciples, see 6:12–13; 12:1. **You will long to see one of the days of the Son of Man:** On Son of Man, see at 5:24; Mark 2:10. Here, the future coming of the Son of Man is equated with the future coming of the kingdom of God (see Dan. 7:13–14; Matt. 13:41; 16:28; 25:31–34). Luke belongs to the second or third Christian generation (see on 1:1–4) and knows that the kingdom of God/Son of Man did not come during the lifetimes of the original disciples: **you will not see it** (see Mark 9:1 and comments on Luke 9:27).

17:23 Do not go running after them (NIV): One of the early church's ways of coming to terms with the delay of the return of Christ was "realized eschatology," to shift the emphasis from the future hope to the present reality of what Christ had already brought (see on John 11). But Luke resists those who say the kingdom has already come in such a way that there is nothing to look forward to, as though the final victory of God were already completely present. Likewise, Luke resists those of his own time who regarded the second coming of Christ and his kingdom as still future, but very near (19:11–27; 21:8). In Luke's view there are three distinguishable periods in the coming of God's kingdom: (1) it was present in the ministry of Jesus; (2) when Jesus ascended to heaven, the kingdom was no longer present on the earth, just as the Son of Man was not (see Acts 7:55–56); (3) the kingdom will reappear in glorious power at the end of history with the return of the Son of Man. The church looks back on the reality of the kingdom as it appeared in Christ and forward to the end of history and the final coming of the kingdom of God, but in the meantime, the time of the church's mission, it proclaims the once-and-coming kingdom (see Acts 1:6–11).

17:24 As the lightning: When the Son of Man returns, there will be no more doubt about it than there is about the lightning that is visible to all, for it will not be an invisible, "spiritual" presence but the realization of God's kingdom in the visible social world. Luke's use of lightning as an illustration of something that is visible to all people is a reminder that he saw the world through first-century eyes, supposing that when the lightning flashed from one horizon to the other, all people could see it. We now know that even the brightest lightning flash is seen by only a tiny fraction of the world's population, and thus cannot serve us as an illustration of the final coming of the kingdom. Such reflections remind us of the difference between the essential elements of Christian faith—here, the final triumph of God's kingdom as already revealed in Christ—and the temporary, relative framework within which it must be expressed in every generation.

17:25 But first: Prior to the final victory of God lies both Jesus' own suffering and death that is part of God's plan and purpose for history (see on the "passion predictions" at 9:21–22, 43–44; 18:31–33) and the distress of the disciples who will long for the eschatological deliverance of the glorious future but will not see it in their own time.

17:26–30 Just as it was in the days of Noah: See Gen. 6–9. The signs that preceded the flood were not spectacular cosmic or political events, but business as usual. **As it was in the days of Lot** (Gen. 18:16–19:29): Though Noah's generation and the population of Sodom were considered notoriously wicked in the biblical accounts, Luke makes no point of this. Even spectacular evil is not a sign of the approaching end. Many generations have regarded the evil of their own times as so depraved that it must be the climax of evil just before the end, but Luke here rejects this view. There will be no signs; the end will come without warning (see 12:35–40; 1 Thess. 5:2; 2 Pet. 3:10; Rev. 3:3; 16:15).

17:31–32 Must not turn back: Such admonitions are typical of apocalyptic discourse; see Mark 13:14–16 for their meaning in another setting. Here, the Lukan emphasis is probably on concern for possessions (see 12:15!). **Remember Lot's wife:** Gen. 19:17, 26. Her error was that she "looked back," which the true disciple cannot do (Luke 9:61–62).

17:33 Those who try to make their life secure will lose it: At the eschaton it will be clear that our own efforts to make our lives secure have been futile. The final coming of the kingdom will reveal what has been worth doing and what not. Those who have been concerned only for themselves will be disappointed; those who trusted in God and lived their lives for others, rather than themselves, will be vindicated.

17:34–35 The great separation: The line that runs through humanity now, separating believer from unbeliever, is not visible. But at the eschaton, **one will be taken and the other left**, just as in the days of Noah and Lot. Neither here nor elsewhere does the Bible speak of a "rapture," in which believers are taken out of the world (see on 1 Thess. 4:13–5:11).

17:37 Where?: Just as the unbelieving Pharisees had begun this discourse with the inappropriate question "when?" so at its end the believing disciples still ask the inappropriate question "where?"—and that despite 17:23–24! Luke knows that faith does not give one immediate insight into God's purpose. Even after Easter, in the presence of the Risen One, the disciples will still be asking the wrong questions (Acts 1:6–11). But the coming of the Spirit will give the disciples of Jesus greater—but still not complete—understanding of God's purpose for the church and the world.

Where the corpse is: This is a proverbial saying, like "where there's smoke there's fire." Its exact application here is not clear, but it may refer to the visible character of the eschaton when it comes, as in 17:23–24.

18:1–8
THE PARABLE OF THE WIDOW
AND THE UNJUST JUDGE

This section continues with twin parables of similar form, each with two contrasting characters, each with Luke's editorial introduction giving the parable a particular interpretation. The first is to "them" (= the disciples of the previous discourse; see 6:12–13; 12:1); the second is to "those who trusted in themselves that they were righteous," illustrated in Luke's view by some of the Pharisees.

18:2 A judge: The judge who **neither feared God nor had respect for people** is, by biblical standards, a bad judge (Exod. 18:21; 23:1–3, 6–9; Lev. 19:15–16, 35–36; Deut. 1:16–17; 16:19–20; 17:8–13). Their responsibility was to settle disputes fairly and to restore justice. The weaker members of the community were dependent on them.

18:3 A widow who kept coming to him: Widows in Israelite tradition were extremely vulnerable—they could not inherit their husband's property, there was no organized social welfare program and for the most part no opportunity for independent employment for them. They were often dependent on the judge for protection and fairness, since they were easily victimized. In this story the judge is the woman's only hope for justice, and he is a bad judge.

18:4–5 Said to himself: The reader gets to hear his interior monologue, as in the case of the rich man of 12:17–19, the prodigal son (15:17–19) the dishonest manager (16:3–4), and also the Pharisee of the next story (18:11–12), and thus knows that the judge is speaking sincerely. **I will grant her justice:** As in the case of the dishonest manager (16:8), so also the unjust judge does the right thing for the wrong reason. **So**

that she may not wear me out: literally, "hit me in the eye," which may be intended literally (see NRSV footnote) or may be a metaphor, "give me a black eye" (before the public). In either case, here is the surprising element in the parable—even the bad judge does the unexpected thing in response to a powerless widow, and grants justice.

18:7 Will not God grant justice?: While the thrust of Jesus' original parable may have focused on the plight of the marginalized woman, Luke's interpretation emphasizes the importance of persistence in prayer (see 11:5–8): if an unjust judge responds, not on the basis of justice and compassion, but merely because of persistence, how much more will the just and loving God respond to those who appeal to him for vindication! In the context, **quickly** here is not a matter of chronology, but means God will not hesitate (as did the unjust judge) to vindicate those who call on him. **His chosen ones:** The elect, a title for Israel, the people of God, applied by Luke (only here) and other New Testament writers to Christian believers (e.g., Matt. 24:24; 31; Rom. 8:33; 1 Pet. 2:9).

18:8 When the Son of Man comes, will he find faith on earth?: Despite the affirmation in the preceding statement that vindication will come **quickly,** this reference to the Son of Man (see on 5:24; Mark 2:10) links the story to the preceding discourse that discourages speculation that the end will come soon. The question, expressed in the Greek grammatical construction that expects a negative answer, does not mean there will no longer be believers on the earth when the Son of Man returns, but is intended by Luke to discourage presumption and to prepare Jesus' followers for the endurance of the "long pull" that faith requires.

18:9–14
THE PARABLE OF THE PHARISEE
AND THE TAX COLLECTOR

On the pair of parables, see on 18:1. On interpreting parables in general, see on Mark 4. The careful reader will distinguish the original parable of Jesus, with its potential for multiple meanings leaving the hearer free to reflect and draw his or her own conclusion, and the particular interpretation Luke has given it by his editorial framework (see on 8:11–15).

18:9 To some who trusted in themselves that they were righteous and regarded others with contempt: Luke surrounds this parable with his editorial comments (see v. 14) that give the parable a particular interpretation.

Within this framework, the reader already has a negative impression of the Pharisee and a positive impression of the tax collector, before the story begins (see 5:32; 7:29–30, 34; 15:1–2; 16:14–15; 17:20).

18:10 Two men: See the "two sons" of 15:11. **One a Pharisee:** See on 5:17. **The other a tax collector:** See on 5:27. While the modern reader is prejudiced in favor of the tax collector, the ancient hearer of Jesus' original parable would have been prejudiced in favor of the Pharisee. The modern reader's problem is not only to derive the benefit of hearing the parable within the Lukan framework, but to hear it in its original context, which reversed the hearer's expectations.

18:11 Standing by himself, was praying (NRSV): This Greek phrase can also be translated "prayed about himself" (so NIV) or "to himself" (NIV footnote). The NRSV translation encourages the reader to understand the parable within the Lukan context, in which the Pharisee looks down on "sinners" with contempt and keeps his distance from them, while the NIV likewise understands the prayer to be self-centered and proud. But "to himself" may mean that the Pharisee's prayer was silent, and that the reader overhears the nonpretentious inner thoughts of the pious man (see the internal monologues at 12:17–19; 15:17–19; 16:3). His prayer contrasts himself with other people. Luke interprets this as "contempt." Apart from the Lukan framework, it could be understood in the sense of "There, but for the grace of God, go I," i.e., the Pharisee does not take the credit for his own piety but acknowledges with thanksgiving that it is by God's grace that he worships, prays, and tithes rather than steals, violates his marriage, and profits by working for a foreign government that exploits his own people.

18:12 I fast twice a week: On fasting, see 5:33. Although only one day of the year was designated a fast day in the Old Testament law (Lev. 26:23–32), by the first century some strict Jews had developed the practice of fasting on Tuesday and Thursday, while some strict Christians fasted on Wednesday and Friday (*Did.* 8:1). John the Baptist and his disciples fasted and prayed like the Pharisees, but Jesus' disciples did not (5:33). **I give a tenth of all my income:** The Old Testament required a tithe (tenth) of some items (see Num. 18:21–24; Deut. 14:22–26), but the Pharisee went beyond what was required and tithed all that he had. While Luke elsewhere pictures (some) Pharisees as "lovers of money" (16:14), this one is more generous than many Christians.

18:13 Standing far off: Luke interprets the Pharisee's distance as pride, but the tax collector's as humility. The hearer of the original parable had to decide how to interpret each, for the parable itself leaves the interpretation open. **Would not even look up to heaven:** Later Christian practice, partly on the basis of this passage, assumed the posture of bowing the head for prayer, but in the Bible the posture of prayer was to look up toward the sky/heaven (see 1 Kgs. 8:22–54; 1 Tim. 2:8, and depictions of Christians at prayer in early Christian art).

Beating his breast: An expression of grief and repentance (see 23:48). **God, be merciful to me, a sinner:** This is the prayer of the truly penitent who know that they are not righteous (see Ps. 51). It was also a standard element of the synagogue prayer, the sixth of the Eighteen Benedictions prayed regularly by Pharisees and all who worshiped at the synagogue:

> Forgive us, O our Father, for we have sinned; pardon us, O our King, for we have transgressed; for thou dost pardon and forgive.
> Blessed art thou, O Lord, who are gracious, and dost abundantly forgive.

18:14 This man went down to his home justified rather than the other: This was the unthinkable surprise to the original hearers. Luke's interpretation has taken away the surprising reversal for contemporary readers, and has added the generalizing conclusion that **all who exalt themselves will be humbled** (see Mary's song at 1:52–53). Luke's point too is a fundamental reversal of conventional expectations, which must not be ignored. But Christian readers of the Gospel have become accustomed to it, so that it is possible for us to be "as proud as Pharisees that we are publicans." Without losing Luke's valid interpretation, the modern reader needs to find a way to recover the original shock of the gospel of Jesus, which reverses *all* expectations, which never lets us *count on* "God's grace to the humble" in a manner that then becomes cheap grace. The grace of God is always *amazing* grace; when it can be *calculated*, even as "grace to the humble," it is no longer grace. For the modern reader who is already too familiar with this story, it would perhaps have its original function and effect by reversing the characters in the last line: the

Pharisee goes home justified, and the tax collector (who has come to "rely" on his "humility" that he knows God accepts) is rejected for his presumption.

18:15–17
JESUS BLESSES THE LITTLE CHILDREN
(See also at Matt. 19:13–15; Mark 10:13–16)

At this point Luke rejoins the Markan story line (see on 9:51). The saying of Jesus in vv. 16–17 agrees verbatim with Mark 10:14–16.

18:15–17 That he might touch them: The multitudes considered Jesus a holy man whose touch conferred divine power and blessing (see 8:43–48). **Even infants:** This is a Lukan modification of the "children" of Mark 10:13. Luke connects this incident with the preceding story, which emphasizes that salvation is not a matter of human achievement. Infants are absolutely dependent, can make no claims to be justified by their own attainments. They are thus the perfect illustration of those who **receive** and will **enter** the **kingdom of God** (see 4:43).

18:18–30
THE RICH RULER
(See also at Matt. 19:16–22; Mark 10:17–22)

18:18 A certain ruler: This figure is traditionally known as the rich young ruler, though "young" is found only in Matthew and "ruler" only in Luke. Since the man is a Palestinian Jew, "ruler" cannot mean "king," but refers to a local official. In 8:41 the same word is translated "leader" (of the synagogue), in 12:58 "magistrate," in 14:1 "leader" (of the Pharisees). Luke's addition of the word to his Markan source places the man among the "powerful" of this world (see on 1:52–53). **What must I do?:** See Acts 16:30. **Eternal life:** So also in Jesus' concluding words in 18:30; equated with entering the kingdom of God (18:24) and being saved (18:26).

18:19 No one is good: Human beings are only relatively good; only God is absolutely good. Here Jesus as "friend of sinners" (see 7:34) places himself on the side of humanity (see on 4:3–4).

18:20 The commandments: Jesus cites from the Ten Commandments (see Exod. 20:1–17; Deut. 5:16–21). The Lukan Jesus continues to affirm that God's will is revealed in the Hebrew Bible (the Christian Old Testament) and that what he proclaims and does is in continuity with God's revelation in the Scriptures (see 16:27–31; 24:26–27, 32, 45–47; Acts 15:19–21).

18:21 I have kept all these: The man does not claim to be perfect but is sincere in claiming that he has lived by God's Law (see the Christian Paul's view of his pre-Christian life as a law-abiding Jew, Phil. 3:2–16).

18:22 One thing lacking: Not "one *more* thing" (see on 10:41–42). The man lives in the world of relative demands and measures up well by human standards. But God is not relative, and the demand of the kingdom of God is absolute. There is one God (the "God alone" of 18:19 can also be translated "the one God," an echo of the Jewish confession of faith, the Shema of Deut. 6:4; see NRSV note there). This God asks for **all** (see on 9:23). The man supposed he was relatively near to pleasing God, and asks for what he needs to do beyond what he has already done. Jesus responds with three commands and a promise: (1) **Sell:** Luke adds "all" to Mark. (2) **Give:** Give to the poor. The problem is not merely that the man's property is a barrier between him and God and that he needs to divest himself of his wealth for the health of his soul, but that there are poor people in the world who desperately need what the rich man has. The issue is not between two parties, God and the rich man, but three parties: God, the rich, and the poor (see on 16:11–31). (3) **Follow me:** Helping the poor in Luke–Acts is not a matter of putting an ideal into practice, but of personal discipleship to Jesus. The ethics of the Gospels cannot be reduced to humanitarian principles but require faith in Jesus as the Christ and commitment to following him. (4) **You will have treasure in heaven:** Not "in order that . . ."; the statement is in the indicative, pointing to the eschatological reversal that occurs with the advent of the future kingdom of God. Giving to the poor is not a disguised form of personal selfishness, but means living one's life oriented to God's kingdom already manifest in the life of Jesus, God's rulership to be revealed in power in the future (see on 4:43).

18:23 He was very rich: Although this is the same meaning as in Luke's Markan source, Luke has adjusted the vocabulary ("rich" does not occur here in Mark) to conform to his polemic against the rich (see 1:53; 6:20–26; 12:13–21; 16:19–31).

18:25–26 Camel . . . through the eye of a needle: This is not merely an exaggerated way of saying "It's hard, but it can be done" (see on Mark 10:24). Jesus here reaches for an image of that which is absolutely unattainable. There is no rational explanation that can domesticate this

hard saying of Jesus, and **those who heard it** got the point: **Then who can be saved?:** The man was as good an example of human achievement as we can present; he was a genuinely religious man who had health, wealth, position, respect, morality, and a sense that something was still lacking. It is not just the worst examples of human beings of whom the pronouncement **impossible** to be saved is made, but the best.

18:27 Possible with God: The paradox of salvation is that in saving human beings, God does what is humanly impossible. God does not merely make up our lack, but justifies the ungodly (18:14; see Rom. 4:4–5; 5:6).

18:28 Left our homes and followed you: See 5:18; the disciples had done what the rich man would not do.

18:29 For the sake of the kingdom of God: See on 4:43.

18:30 Get back very much more: This is not a strategy for how to become wealthy after all but a picture of life in the Christian community pictured as the family of God, where Jesus' disciples are brothers and sisters and share their property, and no one is in need (see Acts 2:43–47; 4:32–37).

18:31–34
THE THIRD PASSION PREDICTION
(See also at Matt. 20:17–19; Luke 18:31–34)

On the three passion predictions Luke adapts from Mark and the three he adds to them, see on 9:21–22.

18:34 They understood nothing: Luke adopts aspects of the Markan messianic secret, according to which the true identity of Jesus could not be understood until after the crucifixion and resurrection (see on 24:16). **Was hidden from them** (by God): Luke is less severe than Mark in his picture of the disciples' lack of understanding, attributing their obtuseness to divine influence (see 9:45; 19:42; 24:16). This is Luke's way of saying that just as Jesus suffered and died according to the will of God, so in God's plan the disciples could not understand until after Easter, Pentecost, and the coming of the Holy Spirit (see Acts 1:6–7; 2:1–36).

18:35–43
A BLIND BEGGAR RECOGNIZES
JESUS AS SON OF DAVID
(See also at Matt. 9:27–31; 20:29–34; Mark 10:46–52)

18:35 Jericho: A fertile oasis city in the Judean Jordan valley, on the regular route of pilgrims from the north. The Travel Narrative is now coming to its conclusion (see on 9:51) and Jesus is in Judea, nearing Jerusalem. **Blind man:** He is called Bartimaeus in Mark, but Luke does not preserve the name. On Jesus as healer of the blind, see on 4:18; 7:21; see also 14:13, 21. **Begging** places him among the blessed poor in Luke's perspective (see on 6:20–26).

18:36 A crowd going by: It is the time of the Passover festival, with many pilgrims en route, but Jesus also has a sizable group of apostles, disciples, and the crowd of potential disciples and hangers-on in his train (see on 6:12–13, 17–20).

18:38 Son of David: More than merely "descendant of David," of whom there were many. The phrase is a messianic title (see on 20:41–44). The blind man sees what others do not, that Jesus is not only **of Nazareth,** but "of God" (see 9:20).

18:41 What do you want me to do for you? This is not a request for information. Jesus' evocative question elicits a decision and confession of faith from the man (see on John 1:38).

18:42 Your faith has saved you: See on 7:50.

18:43 Immediately he regained his sight: See excursus, "Interpreting the Miracle Stories," at Matt. 9:35. **Glorifying God . . . praised God:** As is typical in Luke, the saving act of Jesus calls forth praise to God. On the theocentric nature of Luke's Christology, see on 7:16; 8:24, 38; 9:20–22, 43; 13:13; 17:15; 19:37.

19:1–10
JESUS AND ZACCHAEUS

19:2 A chief tax collector: Tax collectors were assumed to be dishonest and unpatriotic (see on 5:27). A chief tax collector was considered even worse than the others, since he had to pay the Romans in advance for the tax assessed for his district, and then farmed out the actual work to employees, his profit consisting of all that he could extract from the population beyond his original purchase price. The system was open to abuse and was often abused. Luke specifically calls Zacchaeus **rich.** The reader thus receives mixed signals. On the one hand, in Luke the tax collectors are the prototypical models of those outcasts rejected by others but shockingly accepted by Jesus (see 5:29–32; 7:29, 34). On the other hand, in Luke the rich are the prototypical models of evil, accepted and fawned upon by others, but rejected by Jesus (6:20, 24; 12:13–21; 16:19–31). The reader remembers just having heard Jesus say that it is easier for

a camel to go through the eye of a needle than for a rich man to be saved (18:24–25). The initial description of Zacchaeus should warn the reader against stereotyping real people on the basis of Luke's previous literary descriptions, for Luke makes it clear that simple and clear categories of whom God accepts and rejects are inadequate (see Acts 10–11).

19:3 He was trying to see: The reader is reminded of the immediately preceding story of healing the blind man (18:35–42). Both the blind man and Zacchaeus cannot see at first but are granted real insight in their encounter with Jesus (see John 9:1–41, esp. vv. 39–41). **But on account of the crowd he could not:** As in the preceding story, the crowd is a preliminary obstacle overcome by the persistence of the man who is healed and by Jesus' gracious act. As the Gospel story nears its conclusion, the crowd of potential disciples (see 5:1, 15; 6:17–20, 19; 7:11; 8:4; 9:11, 18, 37; 11:14; 14:25; 19:48; 20:19; 22:6, 47; 23:4, 13, 21, 48) is becoming more distant from Jesus and some will finally join his enemies—though not without the possibility of repentance (see 22:47; 23:4, 48).

19:4 He ran ahead and climbed: It was considered more than merely embarrassing, but downright shameful, for an adult, especially a prominent and wealthy person, to run (see 15:20). By running and climbing a tree, Zacchaeus shows the same kind of decisive persistence and unconcern for public image as the women of 8:43–44 and 18:1–8.

19:5 Come down . . . I must stay at your house today: Jesus' response is surprising and unpredictable (the modern reader who has heard the story many times may have to work at perceiving the shock of the original story). The shocking element is not that Jesus invited himself to Zacchaeus's home—though this would never be done in modern North American culture, even by important public figures. The shock is that Jesus, who is a prominent religious teacher with such a large entourage that Zacchaeus had to climb a tree to see over the crowd, honors Zacchaeus by going to his (ritually unclean) home, rather than choosing some more conventional home such as that of a Pharisee or synagogue leader.

19:6–7 Welcomed him gladly (NIV) . . . **began to grumble:** This is the same contrast depicted in the parable of the Prodigal Son between those who celebrate the unexpected joy of salvation and those who grumble because it is happening to the "wrong people" (see 15:11–32; see also 5:30; 7:34).

19:8 Half my possessions . . . I will give to the poor: Zacchaeus is a picture of genuine repentance (see 3:13). The reader should not focus on the half of his wealth Zacchaeus keeps, nor on the contrast with 18:22. Such texts show that Luke is not thinking legalistically in either case, but is showing that it is possible for a rich man to be saved after all, and that salvation generates a concern to share one's wealth with others (18:26–27!). **I will pay back four times as much:** See Exod. 22:1; Lev. 6:5; Num. 5:7; 2 Sam. 12:6). The Old Testament required not only subjective feelings of "repentance," but actual restitution of what had been wrongly taken, plus additional compensation for the loss. These requirements had been somewhat relaxed in actual practice, but Zacchaeus declares he will voluntarily more than make right the wrong he has done.

19:9 Salvation: The word has many connotations in Luke–Acts, from physical healing to the gift of eternal life and reception into the eschatological kingdom of God. Here Zacchaeus's reincorporation into the community of God's people is called **salvation. Son of Abraham:** A true member of the people of Israel; see 3:8; 13:16. Zacchaeus belongs to the chosen people, despite the protests of those who have disqualified him.

19:10 Son of Man: See on 5:24, Mark 2:10. **To seek out and to save:** What began as a story of Zacchaeus's seeking Jesus is seen at the end to be God's seeking through Jesus to bring all the lost to salvation (see 15:3–7; John 15:16). **The lost:** The counterpart to the saved (see 15:32).

19:11–27
THE PARABLE OF THE POUNDS
(see Matt. 25:14–30; Mark 13:34)

19:11 He went on to tell a parable: On the interpretation of parables, see on Mark 4. A similar parable in Matt. 25:14–30 indicates that Matthew and Luke have adopted and adapted a parable found in their common source Q (see introduction to Luke), but the differences between the two versions show that each evangelist has interpreted it for his own situation by the context in which he has placed it and by making editorial modifications. The precise original form cannot be recovered, but distinctive items of the Lukan form reveal the editorial hand of Luke: (1) The principle character is a nobleman who becomes a king. This corresponds to Luke's interest in the kingdom of God as a comprehensive theme (see 4:43; there are fifty-one references to the kingdom of God

in Luke–Acts; see especially the image of Jesus as king that immediately follows this story in 19:38. (2) The beginning of the story involves ten slaves, but only three are dealt with in the concluding scene (as in the version of Matthew, who has only three slaves throughout). (3) Some influential people send a delegation to the emperor asking that the applicant not be made king. When he does in fact become king, he takes terrible vengeance on those who had opposed his kingship. This reflects the pattern that had become typical in the petty states of the Roman Empire, where local "kings" were made and unmade by Rome. This pattern had been repeatedly enacted in first-century Palestine, from the time of Herod the Great, who was appointed king in 40 BCE. (4) Luke surrounds the parable with editorial comment that indicates how he wants the reader to understand the provocative story as a lesson for post-Easter Christian disciples of Luke's own time (see on 10:25–29; 15:1–3). Luke does not turn the parable into an allegory, and yet it is clear that he wants the reader to reflect on the relation between the figure in the story who becomes king and Jesus, who will be hailed as king (19:38), the Jesus who is now absent in the time of the reader and who will return as God's anointed king in the coming kingdom of God (see on 4:20–21, 43; 11:20; 17:21).

They supposed that the kingdom of God was to appear immediately: This expectation is fueled as they approach the holy city Jerusalem. Luke belongs to the second or third Christian generation, which knows this expectation was a mistake, and wants to put the church's present in the proper perspective in the light of the delay of the return of Christ (see on 12:35–48; 17:22–23; 20:9; 21:8–9).

19:13 Until I come back: In Luke's understanding the kingdom of God is not now present, but this does not mean that the time between Jesus' ascension and his return is a passive time of waiting, as though the church were simply on hold until Christ returns. Rather, the present is also an integral part of God's plan for history, the time of Christian mission to all the world (Acts 1:6–11; see introduction to Luke: "Jesus as the 'Midst of Time'"). The time of the church between ascension and Parousia is a time of great responsibility for Christ's servants, which is suggested in the parable by the master's giving each of ten slaves a sum of money (about three months salary) and charging them to work with it until he returns.

19:14 We do not want this man to rule over us:
This is a Lukan insertion into the story (see above), emphasizing that some do not want the prospective king to be appointed. These are not the slaves, who belong to the future king, but others who have oriented their lives to the status quo. Their stance on the issue of who will be king in the future affects the way they live in the present. For Luke, Jesus' disciples are those who reorient their lives to the kingdom of God as revealed in the life and ministry of Jesus and believe that this kingdom will be manifest to all in the eschatological future.

19:15 When he returned: The story jumps immediately to the future return, the time between the master's departure and his return as king being told only from the perspective of the final judgment. **Having received royal power:** For Luke, there will come a time in which the present prayer of the church, "Your kingdom come," will be fulfilled; so the present should be lived in the light of this future fulfillment.

19:17 You have been trustworthy in a very small thing: See 16:10, with regard to another slave who had been entrusted with his master's money. **Take charge of ten cities:** The eschatological reward is extravagant and is pictured as sharing in the reign of God (see 22:28–30, which probably followed this parable in the Q source Luke is following; see the similar imagery in Rev. 2:25–27; 3:21).

19:21 I was afraid: The problem with the third slave was that he had played it safe, had had the wrong kind of fear with regard to his master, had supposed it was enough to hand back what had been given to him (on the proper fear of God, see 12:5). But the master has work to do in the world and wants the gifts he has given his servants to be used to carry on his work.

You are a harsh man: If the figure of the king in the story is intended to point to Christ as king in the kingdom of God, Jesus' call to discipleship and responsibility must not be taken lightly (see on 14:25–33). Of course the details of the imagery, which picture the king as selfish and vindictive, do not apply to Christ, just as details of other parables that point to God's kingdom are not literal or allegorical descriptions of the kingdom of God (see on 16:1–13). Some interpreters, however, understand the king in the story only as a contrast to the true kingship of Jesus (see below).

19:25: Lord, he has ten pounds: This is the seemingly righteous protest of those who operate by the usual standards of justice. Modern readers may well find themselves sympathetic to this protest (see Matt. 20:11–12). Some interpreters take this to be the point at which Jesus and Luke intend the reader to identify with the participants in the story, in which case the king is to be taken as an example of selfish, vindictive, and unjust conduct.

19:26 To all those who have, more will be given:
The interpretation that simply contrasts the king in the story with the kingship of Christ calls for taking the words of 18:26 to be a statement of the king in the story. The NIV makes this specific by adding the words "he replied," which are not in the Greek text. The NRSV likewise indicates the king in the story as the speaker by the way quotation marks are used—but there were no quotation marks in the Greek manuscripts. But since the saying begins with the formula characteristic of the Lukan Jesus, "I tell/say to you" (28x in Luke, elsewhere always introducing a saying of Jesus himself, including the "punch line" of the parable in 15:10; 18:8, 14), and since a similar saying is attributed to Jesus himself in Luke 8:18 (= Matt. 13:12; Mark 4:25), it is better to take this saying as modulating from the words of the characters in the story to the words of Jesus the storyteller. The protest of the bystanders seems just (see Matt. 20:11–12). Yet the coming kingdom of God operates by different standards.

19:27 Bring them here and slaughter them in my presence: These words of the parable evoke a terrible picture, one that has happened many times within the nationalistic and political struggles of history. That they somehow also point to the coming kingdom of God gives the reader pause, and provokes to reflection. This is what parables are intended to do. They are not merely colorful illustrations of conventional wisdom. To be sure, the coming kingdom of God represented by Jesus is not like that of the unsavory and vengeful king in the story, but the story still provokes the readers to ask whether they are those who look forward in hope to the coming kingdom of God but who must use their master's property responsibly in the meantime, or whether they are those who are committed to the present value system and want it to stay that way, those who will have to be listed among the enemies of God's kingdom when it finally comes. Like all such parables about the eschatological future, it casts its light on present decisions and priorities.

19:28–21:38
JESUS' MINISTRY IN JERUSALEM

Luke's story, which began in the Jerusalem temple (1:5), reaches its climax in Jerusalem, which had been for a thousand years the political, cultural, and, above all, religious center of Jewish life—in Jewish hearts if not in reality (see Pss. 125; 132; 137:4–6). Though Jesus was born in Bethlehem and reared in Galilee, he was dedicated in the Jerusalem temple, blessed by those who awaited the redemption of Jerusalem (2:21–38). At 9:51, Jesus steadfastly "set his face" to go to Jerusalem, and the Travel Narrative began as Jesus and his disciples made their way to the Holy City. In Luke, neither Jesus nor the disciples will return to Galilee, but the Holy Spirit will come on the disciples in Jerusalem, the church will be created, and the good news will proceed from Jerusalem to all the world (24:47; Acts 1:8).

19:28–40
JESUS' TRIUMPHAL ENTRY INTO JERUSALEM
(See also at Matt. 21:1–9; Mark 11:1–10; Luke 19:28–40; John 12:12–19)

19:29 The place called the Mount of Olives: The mountain directly to the east of Jerusalem, which affords a magnificent view of the city and especially of the temple. Only a few minutes walk down the western slope, through the Kidron valley, and up the eastern slope of Mount Zion brings the pilgrim to the gates of the city and the temple.

Bethany: Two miles east of Jerusalem on the eastern slope of the Mount of Olives. In the Gospel of John, Bethany is the home of Mary, Martha, and their brother Lazarus (John 11:1, 18), but in Luke, Mary and Martha live north of Jerusalem between Galilee and Judea (10:38). **Bethphage** is a nearby village, whose location has not been determined. In Mark and John, the triumphal entry takes place on a Sunday; in Matthew it is on Monday. Luke has Jesus in Jerusalem for an extended period before the passion story begins (see 19:47; 20:1) and does not make clear which day the procession into Jerusalem occurs.

19:30 A colt that has never been ridden: Triumphal processions of a conqueror or returning ruler were common in the first-century Roman world. Jesus is pictured as a triumphant king but fills the image with new content in that he does not ride a mighty warhorse but a young donkey. As the kingdom of God reverses the conventional values

of human culture, so Jesus redefines the meaning of kingship (see Zech. 9:9–10). As the prophets of Israel had sometimes communicated their message with dramatic signs (Isa. 20:2, 4; Jer. 13:1–11; 19:1–13; 27:1–28:14; Ezek. 4; 5; 12; Hos. 1; 3), so Jesus stages a provocative symbolic action that both points to the nature of his kingship and the division it brings about between those who celebrate it and those who are scandalized by it.

19:31 The Lord needs it: The Greek text could also be translated, "Its master needs it." This is intentionally stated in an ambiguous manner in Mark, Luke's source, but in Luke "the Lord" clearly refers to Jesus, who (unlike Mark) often uses the post-Easter Christian title in the story of Jesus' pre-Easter life.

19:36 Spreading their clothes on the road: This is both a sign of spontaneous jubilation and a symbolic gesture recognizing Jesus as king (see 2 Kgs. 9:13). There are no leafy branches as in Mark, and no palms as in John.

19:37 The whole multitude of the disciples: Luke has followed Mark carefully for most of this story, but this verse is Luke's own addition, making clear that it was the disciples (not the crowd or the Jerusalem population in general) that generated the spontaneous acclamation of Jesus as king. The disciples were a much larger group than the Twelve, but not the same as the "crowds" (see on see 5:1, 15; 6:12–13, 17–19; 7:11; 8:4; 9:11, 18, 37; 11:14; 14:25; 19:48; 20:19; 22:6, 47; 23:4, 13, 21, 48). *God* is praised for *Jesus'* mighty works (on the theocentric picture of the significance of Jesus, see 7:16; 8:24, 38; 9:20–22, 43; 13:13; 17:15; 19:37).

19:38 Blessed is the king who comes in the name of the Lord: This was originally a liturgical blessing on those who came to worship at the Jerusalem temple (see Ps. 118:26). **King:** Luke's key addition to Mark is the clear affirmation by Jesus' disciples that Jesus is king (in the coming kingdom of God). To call someone king was no small matter. Understood politically, it was the legal ground of Jesus' condemnation to death on the cross (23:3, 38). While it is profoundly true that Jesus was not the kind of king that the Jewish leaders, Pilate, or even his disciples understood him to claim to be, Christians should not rush to say that the claim has no political implications. While Jesus was indeed claiming a different kind of rulership from that exercised by worldly sovereigns (see 22:24–30), the reversal of conventional values manifest in the kingdom of God does indeed have political implications (4:16–21).

Peace in heaven, and glory in the highest heaven: Luke adds these words to his Markan source, so that this acclamation now corresponds to Luke 2:14 at the birth of Jesus, and the disciples join in the same song of praise as the angels. Just as there are no palms in Luke's account of Palm Sunday, so there are no hosannas.

19:39 Pharisees: See on 5:17. This is the last time Pharisees appear in the Gospel of Luke—they do not participate in the further Jerusalem conflicts and in the trial and execution of Jesus. Luke pictures two contrasting groups: the disciples, who celebrate Jesus as the humble king of the coming kingdom of God, and the Pharisees, who consider it scandalous and try to silence this confession. This is already a model of the post-Easter situation, when the Jewish leaders (not the Jewish people as a whole) oppose the Christian faith celebrated and lived out by Jesus' disciples (see Acts 3–7).

19:40 The stones will cry out (NIV): Jesus does not rebuke the disciples, who are celebrating that which they do not yet understand, but declares that their praise is appropriate. God's redemptive act that is about to take place in Jerusalem calls forth worship and praise as its appropriate response, not only from human beings, but from the creation itself, and if human beings do not respond in praise and thanksgiving, the rocks will (see Rom. 8:19–39).

19:41–44
JESUS WEEPS OVER JERUSALEM

The scene is not mere "objective reporting," but is written from Luke's own perspective at the end of the century, looking back on the terrible war between the Palestinian Jews and the Romans (66–70), in which Jerusalem was destroyed after its population had suffered the terrors of a long siege. Jesus does not celebrate the destruction of those who reject him, but weeps for them (and prays for them; see 23:34).

19:41 He wept: See John 11:35.

19:42 The things that make for peace: The Hebrew word for "peace," *shalom,* signifies more than the absence of war—though it includes that as well. It points to all that makes life worthwhile. The birth of Jesus was hailed by the angels as the good news of peace on earth (2:14), and Jesus' disciples had just echoed the angels' song (19:38). Jerusalem includes the Hebrew word for peace in its name (see Heb. 7:1–2), but Jerusalem does not recognize what brings authentic peace. In Luke's view, their rejection of Christ is a mat-

ter of ignorance, of not seeing and not knowing what is really happening before their eyes. From one point of view they are responsible; from another point of view, such ignorance and misunderstanding is an aspect of the divine mystery of life in the present fallen world, an ignorance and misunderstanding to which all, including the disciples, are subject. It is not an incurable ignorance, but the cure is not education but repentance (see 9:45; 18:34; Acts 3:17; 17:30).

This scene is filled with echoes and allusions to the Scripture; what is about to happen in and to Jerusalem is not random evil, but is taken up into the larger purpose of God as revealed in Scripture. Jesus cries over the fate of Jerusalem, as did the prophet Jeremiah (Jer. 9:1; 13:17; 14:17). Jesus' lament is reminiscent of the numerous laments in the Psalms, one of which also includes the terrible picture of the siege in which the city walls are finally torn down and children are dashed to the ground (Ps. 137:7–9).

19:45–48
JESUS CLEANSES THE TEMPLE
AND TEACHES THERE
(See also at Matt. 21:12–17;
Mark 11:11, 15–19 [John 2:13–17])

19:45 Then he entered the temple: On the temple, see 1:5–9. In Luke, Jesus goes directly to the temple on first entering the city, as did the king in the oriental triumphal precessions. **Began to drive out those who were selling things there:** In these few words Luke concentrates all the action of Jesus' demonstration in the temple, omitting many of the dramatic details in his Markan source. Luke does not elaborate on what was sold, but the modern reader should not think of a bazaar. Rather, as a service to worshipers, the temple priests made available animals already certified to be acceptable for sacrifice, as was customary in ancient temples. In Luke, nothing is said of money changers or of illicit profits. Likewise Luke does not call the demonstration in the temple a "cleansing." Jesus does not "cleanse" the temple, but displaces the merchants from the temple and takes it over to make it his own place of teaching. He makes no statements about the temple's "destruction" and does nothing that could be so interpreted. Luke does not speculate, nor encourage the reader to speculate, on how Jesus could perform this action in a large public institution that was guarded both by the temple police and the Roman soldiers (see Acts

21:27–36). Jesus' action in the temple, like the triumphal procession into Jerusalem, was like the symbolic actions of the prophets. *What Jesus' action symbolizes* is expressed in the combination of two prophetic texts, already combined by Mark.

19:46 My house shall be a house of prayer (Isa. 56:7)**:** Prayer is a major Lukan theme (see 6:12; 9:18, 28; 11:1–13; 18:1–8; 22:40–46; 23:34, 46). Luke inexplicably omits the Markan reference to "all nations," though Luke too sees the church as God's agent to all the nations (24:47; Acts 1:8). **You have made it a den of robbers** (Jer. 7:11)**:** The original image in Jeremiah was that of a robber's cave, where bandits hid out and stored their booty. The Lukan Jesus charges the religious leaders with making the temple into a safe hideout, protected by God, to which they could retreat in security, even though they practiced and permitted great injustice in the "secular" world. It is not clear whether Luke or his Markan source preserved this meaning of Jeremiah's text, but in Luke at least, there is no indication of actual robbery or cheating the people by the temple priesthood. The point of the "den of robbers" image is not that the priests were robbing the people, i.e., by overcharging for the animals they sold there, but that Jesus by his sovereign power now takes over the temple of God that had been misused, and conducts his own ministry in it.

19:47–48 Every day he was teaching in the temple: These words, and this image of Jesus' ministry in Jerusalem, are only in Luke and picture an extended period of teaching. In the Markan chronology that he has adopted and adapted, Jesus taught only one day prior to his arrest (see Mark 11–14). **The leaders** plot to kill him. **All the people were spellbound by what they heard:** Luke again distinguishes between the leaders and the people as a whole, and does not charge the whole Jewish people with complicity in the death of Jesus. **The chief priests** included the high priest, the leader of the Jewish Council, the Sanhedrin, that under the Roman government exercised leadership of the Jewish people in both religious and political matters. It was the responsibility of the high priest, not only to see that the temple worship was properly conducted, but to negotiate with the Roman authorities on whom the civil and economic well-being of the people depended. The chief priests therefore could not afford to allow disturbing elements among the population, for fear of cruel Roman reprisals against the population as a whole.

20:1–8
THE AUTHORITY OF JESUS QUESTIONED
(See also at Matt. 21:23–27; Mark 11:27–33)

20:1 One day: In Luke's narrative, Jesus spends an extended time in Jerusalem, teaching and preaching unmolested in the temple, which he has reclaimed as a true place of worship for his followers (19:45–48; Acts 2:46; 3:1–10; 4:1; 5:20–42; 21:26–30; 25:8). **Telling the good news:** Of the kingdom of God (see on 4:43). **Chief priests . . . scribes . . . elders:** The Jewish Sanhedrin was composed of members from these groups. The scribes were not secretaries, but experts in the traditional religious Law by which the nation was governed (NIV "teachers of the law"). In Luke the Pharisees are conspicuously absent from this list and form no part of the leadership that condemned Jesus to death (see on 5:17; 19:39).

20:2 By what authority?: The question is important, and the modern reader who identifies with Jesus as presented in this Gospel should not too quickly condemn those who raise the question. Jesus had staged a demonstration in which he was hailed as king and had taken charge of the national shrine (19:28–48). **These things:** Likely refers to Jesus' teaching in the temple. Modern "tolerant" individualistic readers are likely to take the authority to teach less seriously than did ancient readers. Modern individualism tends to suppose that there is no authority except the enlightened individual's ideals or common sense, and that whoever makes religious claims must justify them before this court. The New Testament does not assume that anyone can teach their own opinions as they choose, as though each individual could make up his or her own mind as to religious truth, but takes the question of authority very seriously.

20:3–6 The baptism of John: More than any other Gospel, Luke has emphasized the connection between John the Baptist and Jesus (chaps. 1–2; 7:18–35). Neither John nor Jesus cited his education, official religious status, the traditions he had learned from their teachers, or his own experience as the authority that legitimized his message. Both John and Jesus operated on the basis of the prophetic call (3:21–22; 4:16–21; 11:14–20). Jesus does not justify his call to discipleship to the modern reader with arguments from religious experience, conformity to commonly accepted ideals, or common sense, but confronts all with the prophetic word of God. In Luke's story, this authority is rejected by the religious leaders, who have their own respectable criteria by which religious claims may be measured and to which they must conform, but the common people accept him. The modern reader might well ask to which group he or she belongs, and whether those who measure Jesus' claim by their own criteria belong to the former group.

20:7 They did not know: Their answer was not a matter of information or truth but of expedient political calculation. They measured their response by the criterion of its practical consequences. Discipleship to Jesus, however, calls for decision on the basis of truth, not of "whatever works."

20:8 Neither will I tell you: Jesus' response was not a matter of clever strategy, not a matter of his outwitting his opponents at their own game. The Jesus of this story considers it pointless to provide information or arguments to those who make decisions on the basis of their own prejudice, or even on the basis of their own ideals or common sense. Those who claim to accept Jesus on this basis are merely confirming their own opinions, for which Jesus becomes a convenient illustration. The Gospel has repeatedly revealed, however, that Jesus' life and message are a challenge to conventional understanding and its values, not its confirmation (see 6:20–23; 10:25–37; 13:20, 24, 32; 14:7–10, 15; 15:11–31; 16:14–16; 18:13, 17; 19:30). The Jesus who reverses all our expectation of what the Christ, the definitive revelation of God, should be, refuses to validate his claim to authority before the bar of our own criteria. We have nothing beyond the divine revelation itself by which to validate Jesus as God's revelation—if we did have such criteria, these, and not the revelation of God in Jesus, would be our authority (see on Rev. 2:20). This scene thus gives no simple answer to the complex question of authority and discourages the reader from identifying *too* quickly with Jesus (14:25–35!).

20:9–19
THE PARABLE OF THE WICKED TENANTS
(See also at Matt. 21:33–46; Mark 12:1–12)

20:9 To tell the people: Luke adds this to Mark (where the parable is aimed at the chief priest, scribes, and elders), redirecting it to the people who are more responsive (see the contrast between leaders and people in 19:47–48). The leaders "overhear," however, and respond in 20:19. Luke uses the parable to widen the gap

between leaders and people. **Parable:** On interpreting New Testament parables, see on Mark 4. While the story may originally have functioned as a parable, Luke understands it as an allegory. The modern reader may grasp it at more than one level, seeing it as an allegory of God's dealing with the leaders of Israel who were entrusted with instruction and pastoral leadership of the people, but also at the more personal parabolic level, asking, "Where am I in this story? With which group(s) do I find myself identifying? What does it have to say to me personally in my post-Easter situation?"

At the level of Lukan allegorical understanding, the following symbolic meanings are transparent: **Vineyard:** The people of Israel, God's people chosen from the nations of the world to be witnesses to God's love and care for all peoples (Gen. 12:1–3; Ps. 80:8–13; Isa. 5:1–7; 27:2–6; 42:1–7; Jer. 2:21; Hos. 10:1; Ezek. 19:10–14). **The owner of the vineyard:** God, who is now absent but will come to judge at the end of history. **A long time:** These words added by Luke are part of his polemic against those early Christians who believed that the end was coming soon (see on 1:48; 17:20–37; 19:11–27; 21:5–36; Acts 1:6–11). **The tenants:** They do not own the vineyard, but only lease it, and are responsible to the owner. At the historical level, the tenants represent the leadership of Israel, who are to care for God's people and equip them for their mission. At the more personal level, modern readers can see themselves as stewards of God's world and God's mission in the world (see on 16:1–13). **The slaves:** The prophets whom God sends to warn Israel and its leaders, but who were consistently rejected (see 13:34). **The beloved son:** This figure clearly represents Jesus, who is the **heir** (see 3:22; 9:35). **The coming of the Lord to judge the tenants:** This refers to the Last Judgment, which plays a dominant role in Luke's theology (see 10:14; 11:31–32; 12:2–6; 22:30; Acts 10:42; 17:31; 24:45).

20:13 What shall I do: Luke adds these words, which picture God as deliberating how best to deal with the greedy and rebellious tenants (for other internal monologues in parables found only in Luke, see 12:17, 45; 15:17; 16:3–4; 18:4–5; 20:13). It is a remarkable scene. At the allegorical level, it pictures God as responding to the sinfulness of those he has entrusted with stewardship of the world and the divine mission in the world, not with vengeful retaliation, but by attempting to win them over by sending his beloved Son.

20:14 So that the inheritance may be ours: This may realistically reflect actual Palestinian situations in which, if an owner died without heirs, the tenants would have a legal claim to the property. Heir and inheritance are significant theological metaphors in the New Testament, especially in the Pauline tradition (see Rom. 8:14–17; Gal. 7:29–4:7; Eph. 1:11, 14; 3:6).

20:15 Threw him out of the vineyard and killed him: At the Lukan allegorical level, this points to the responsibility of the Jewish leaders for the death of Jesus (in distinction from the people as a whole). That the son was first taken outside the vineyard and then killed anticipates the actual course of events in the death of Jesus, who was killed outside the city (23:26–37; see Heb. 13:10–14). As in the passion predictions (see on 9:21–22), the story is told from the post-Easter perspective of the church, in which the details of Jesus' suffering and death were known.

What then will the owner of the vineyard do?: This is the punch line of the parable, which calls the readers to reflect. The owner's purpose has been frustrated, his slaves and even his son have been killed. Has he been defeated by the unfaithful tenants? At the allegorical level, the question is posed whether human rebellion against God's purpose, killing God's prophets and finally God's Son, means that God's purpose for the world has been defeated. But the owner is still in charge, and will hold a final judgment. The last word has not yet been spoken. He will come to his own property (see Mal. 3:1; 4:1–6), will destroy the false leaders, and will give their place to others. Luke does not understand the parable to mean that the people of Israel will be replaced in God's plan by the church of Jews and Gentiles, but that the unfaithful leadership of the Jewish people by the chief priests, scribes, and elders will be replaced by new leadership. This is in fact what happens in Acts, as the leadership of the church is assumed by Christian apostles, prophets, and elders. At the personal level, Christian leaders can then see themselves as tenants of God's vineyard who can in turn be replaced if they are not responsible. The word translated "owner" is mostly translated "Lord." Since Christians used "Lord" for both God and Christ, this terminology facilitated the modulation of the imagery in the story between God-the-Lord who as Creator is owner of the vineyard, and Christ-the-Lord who will return as judge at the end of history. The imagery flows back and forth between God and Christ.

20:17 What then does this text mean?: The question is rhetorical. The text cited is a combination of Ps. 118:22 and Isa. 8:13–14; 28:16 that circulated in early Christianity as an interpretation of what had happened to Jesus: human beings rejected him, but God made him the key figure in the renewed people of God (see, in addition to the Matthean and Markan parallels, Acts 4:11; 1 Pet. 2:7). The metaphor shifts from God's people as a vineyard to God's people as a building (see 1 Cor. 3:5–16, which in the context of a discussion of responsible leadership also refers to the people of God as both "God's field" and "God's building"). The image may refer either to the **cornerstone** (NRSV) of a wall or the **capstone** (NIV) of an arch, in either case the key stone that holds the building together.

20:20–26
THE QUESTION ABOUT PAYING TAXES
(See also at Matt. 22:15–22; Mark 12:13–17)

The New Testament deals with political realities, the stance that followers of Jesus should have to secular governments and political issues. Faith in Christ does not take believers out of the world or into some interior spiritual domain but intensifies their engagement with this world as God's world. "Messiah," "Christ," is a political term, referring to the one God has anointed as king in the present and coming kingdom of God (see on Mark 8:29). It was for this claim, misunderstood in the Roman sense that Jesus was a political revolutionary against the Roman government, that Jesus was executed (23:1–3). The New Testament is not an apolitical document. It speaks often of kings, governors, thrones, and the relationship of believers to the secular authorities, giving a limited variety of perspectives on the relation of the believer to the secular government (see the parallels to this passage in Matthew and Mark; Rom. 13:1–7; 1 Tim. 3:1–2; 1 Pet. 2:13–14; John 18:33–38).

This scene has already been presented in Mark 12:13–17 (see there). When Luke retells the same story about twenty years later in a different political situation, some of the emphases inherent in his interpretation are these: (1) Jesus appears on the stage of history as the representative of the kingdom of God (see on 4:43), an alternative to the kingdom of Caesar (see on 2:1–6). (2) But the birth of Jesus did not mean rebellion against Caesar's kingdom. Jesus was in fact born in Bethlehem in response to Caesar's decree calling for a census directly related to taxation. When, at Jesus' trial, he was charged with rebellion against the state and with refusing to pay taxes, the governor did not accept the charges, and the centurion in charge of the crucifixion pronounced him innocent of them (23:1–17, 47). (3) While the first generation of Christians expected Jesus to return soon and thus were not so concerned to come to terms with political leadership in this world, one of Luke's purposes in writing his Gospel is to help the church reinterpret the meaning of the Christian life in a continuing world (see on 1:48; 17:20–37; 19:11–27; 21:5–36; Acts 1:6–11). In his two-volume work, Luke is helping second- and third-generation Christians to settle into the world for the long pull, and this means, among other things, coming to terms with Christian responsibility within and to the secular state. (4) Thus Luke can picture Christians as serving the state, e.g., in the military or as wardens of a prison (Acts 10–11; 16:16–40), and as being protected by the state (e.g., Acts 21:27–26:32). (5) When choices between human authority and obedience to God must be made, Luke is clear that priority must be given to God (e.g., Acts 5:29).

20:20 So they watched him and sent spies: In his Markan source, it is the Pharisees who do this, but Luke has eliminated the Pharisees from the passion story (see on 19:39), replacing them here with the **scribes and chief priests** of 20:19. **Pretended to be honest:** The question about to be posed is not an honest question, seeking wisdom on how to settle the sometimes conflicting demands and responsibilities of allegiance to one's country and obedience to one's God. The spies present a disputed religious question, **"Is it lawful?"** i.e., is it in accord with the will of God as revealed in the law of Moses? If he answers that it is lawful and that believers should pay taxes to the pagan Roman state, this will condemn him in the eyes of the superpatriot religious zealots; if he answers that it is not lawful, this will make him guilty of rebellion against the Roman government. This latter answer is what the spies in fact hope for, and although they do not get it, they still make this charge at his trial (23:1–2).

20:21 You do not show partiality (NIV): This flattering statement is indeed true and is one of the great themes of Luke and Acts (see Acts 10:34), but the spies in fact do not believe it, just as they do not believe that Jesus teaches **the way of God in accordance with truth.**

20:23 He perceived their craftiness: By divine prophetic insight (see 2:35; 5:22; 7:39; 11:17).

20:24–25 Show me a denarius: The denarius was a Roman coin that bore the image of Caesar, with the inscription "Tiberius Caesar, Son of the Divine Augustus, Augustus." Jesus forces them to acknowledge that they are themselves carrying and using the Roman money, implying that they cannot require others to disavow its use in payment of Roman taxes. The portrait and inscription indicated it belonged to Caesar, i.e., to Caesar's realm of secular government. To pay taxes was only to give Caesar what they already acknowledged belonged to Caesar. Some interpreters see here an allusion to human beings as made in the image of God (Gen. 1:27), so that just as Caesar's image on the coin means it already belongs to Caesar, so God's image in humanity means that human beings already belong to their Creator, and cannot finally give ultimate allegiance to any other authority.

Jesus' aphorism, **"Give to Caesar what is Caesar's and to God what is God's"** (NIV), was not merely a clever way of extricating himself from a difficult situation by not answering directly (see on 20:3–8). Nor was it a simple solution to the problems of the relation of church and state. There are no simple answers here. There is certainly no intention to partition life into "Caesar's part" and "God's part." God does not ask for part, but the whole of life (9:23), and no part of life can be partitioned off as "secular" or "political" in which one's loyalty to God does not apply. Caesar and God both have legitimate claims on the believer, but this text does not tell the reader what belongs to Caesar and what belongs to God in any particular situation—this must be worked out by the followers of Jesus from case to case, together, under the guidance of the Holy Spirit, as Luke will illustrate in Acts. But the text does make two things clear: (1) Christian disciples do not violate their faith when they pay taxes to pagan secular governments; and (2) whenever there are conflicts between human loyalties, e.g., between one's country and one's God, there can be no question but that God must be served (Acts 5:29).

20:26 Amazed by his answer: See 2:47; 4:22; 8:25; 9:43; 11:14; but amazement and admiration are not the same thing as faith and commitment.

20:27–40
THE QUESTION ABOUT THE RESURRECTION
(See also at Matt. 22:23–33; Mark 12:18–27)

20:27 Some Sadducees: "Some" does not mean that only a part of the Sadducees rejected belief in the resurrection, but that some of this group here encounters Jesus. The Sadducees are mentioned only here in Luke, but 5x in Acts, always as hostile to the early Christians (unlike the Pharisees). They belonged to the wealthy, conservative, priestly stream of Judaism associated with the temple leadership. They probably acknowledged only the Pentateuch (Genesis–Deuteronomy) as Scripture, not the other books of the Hebrew Bible that were canonized later (see on 24:44). They did not accept the religious ideas that had developed relatively late, including the ideas of angels, demons, and the resurrection, that came into Jewish tradition as aspects of apocalyptic thought (see Acts 23:6–8). The idea of resurrection, for example, is not found in the Pentateuch, has only traces in the late prophetic books, and is first clearly stated in the latest book of the Old Testament, written ca. 165 BCE (Dan. 12:2–3). Neither did they accept the oral tradition, advocated by the Pharisees as a way of keeping the tradition up to date. Though religiously conservative, the Sadducees were politically liberal, cooperating with the Romans in administering Jewish political and religious affairs. **Resurrection** is the belief that God gives new life in the transcendent world to those who have died. It is to be distinguished from immortality, the view that there is something inherent in human beings that does not die. Immortality is a theory about the nature of human being; resurrection is a conviction about the act of God. Throughout the New Testament, faith in life after death is expressed in terms of resurrection, not of immortality—although there is a spectrum of views in how this is pictured or expressed.

20:28 Moses wrote: The Sadducees cite from the Pentateuch, which they regard as authoritative Scripture (Deut. 25:5–10; see Gen. 38:8; Lev. 18:6; Ruth 3:9, 12–13). **The man shall marry the widow:** The purpose of this law was to continue the name and memory of the deceased man, to protect the woman by providing her with a husband to support her in the present and children to provide for her in her old age, and to keep the property in the immediate family by prohibiting the widow from marrying someone from another clan or tribe.

20:29–33 Now there were seven brothers: This can hardly represent an actual case. It was rather an argument developed on the basis of the Bible to show that the late doctrine of the

resurrection was absurd, by presenting an instance in which following the biblical commands makes nonsense of the (to them) non-biblical doctrine of the resurrection.

20:34–36 This age ... that age: Jesus is pictured as responding in terms of the apocalyptic doctrine of the two ages, advocated by the Pharisees. The whole story could be seen as an intra-Jewish argument between Pharisees and Sadducees, argued on their respective grounds. While there is nothing distinctively Christian about the story, Luke has given it a Christian setting and interpretation, as had his Markan source before him. The point is that eternal life is not merely a quantitative extension of the categories of life in the present world, but life that is radically different in a qualitative sense from life as we now know it, life in a different mode of being. **Cannot die:** Eternal life is God's gift at the resurrection, not something inherent in human life as such (see above on resurrection and immortality). **Children of God:** Literally, "sons," a Semitic idiom for the members of a particular category (see on 1:28). Human beings in the heavenly world become **like angels**, who do not die and who are called "sons of God" (see Gen. 6:1–2; Job 1:6). The point is that life in God's new world to come will be another order of being, in which the earthly arrangements of marriage, birth, establishing families and inheritances will be transcended (1 Cor. 15:35–50). The text is not a devaluation of marriage and family, but a reminder that the nature of God's transcendent world is a mystery that cannot be captured within the categories of the present human world.

20:37–38 The fact that the dead are raised: Within the framework of midrashic argument from Scripture common in first-century Judaism, Jesus shows that not merely late tradition but the only biblical books considered canonical by the Sadducees also affirm the resurrection. The argument assumes the homogeneity of the Bible and will not be convincing to many modern readers. The logic is this: The Bible calls God the "God of Abraham." But God is the God of the living. Therefore Abraham must still in some sense be living, though he died centuries ago (see 16:19–31, a story told within the same framework of reference). The line of argument is actually more relevant for immortality than for resurrection, but the point remains the same: to believe in the resurrection is neither nonsense nor unbiblical. The Bible is actually a witness to the Christian faith in the resurrection rather than evidence that could be used to "prove" it (see excursus, "New Testament Interpretation of the Old Testament," at 1 Cor. 15:3). **To him all of them are alive:** See on Acts 17:24–28.

20:39–40 Some of the scribes: Luke here omits Mark 12:28–34, which he has already used at 10:25–28. This allows him to use the material at the beginning of that scene as the conclusion of this one. Jesus is commended by the scribes, but though they are silenced by having been bested in the argument, they are not converted.

20:41–44
THE QUESTION ABOUT DAVID'S SON
(See also at Matt. 22:41–46; Mark 12:35–37a)

The tables are now turned, and Jesus is the questioner rather than the questioned. This corresponds to the reality. The human situation is not that we pose questions to God and Christ, and if they can answer them to our satisfaction, we will become believers. Rather, we are always the ones placed in question by the revelation of God in Christ. We are not in the judge's seat with Christ on trial, but precisely the opposite.

20:41 The Messiah: See on 9:20; Mark 8:29. **David's son:** See 18:38. Mark, Luke's source, is cool toward the title (see Mark 10:47–48; 11:10; 12:35–37), but Luke, like Matthew, considers it a valid christological title (Luke 1:27, 32, 69; 2:4, 11; 3:31). For Luke, Jesus is the true Son of David, but he will represent God's kingship in a way radically different from the nationalistic and violent David.

20:45–47
JESUS DENOUNCES THE SCRIBES
(See also at Matt. 23:1–36; Mark 12:37b-40)

The Lukan Jesus has just defeated the scribes at their own game of biblical interpretation. He now addresses his disciples, and the people overhear (see on 6:12–13, 17).

20:46 Beware of the scribes: On the scribes, see on 7:29–30; 11:46, 53. Luke distinguishes the people and their leaders, does not condemn the Jewish people as a whole. Nor is there a blanket condemnation of the scribes. The Greek text is best translated as "Beware of the scribes who . . ." They are condemned for their grasping after public recognition. They do not have the security that comes from knowing they are accepted by God, and hence seek to establish their own sense of self-worth by being acknowledged by others. **Best seats in the synagogues:** Not as in a theater, the

seats from which one could best see, but the front seats facing the congregation, occupied by the elders and teachers, where they could *be* seen.

20:47 Devour widows' houses: Despite their show of piety, "business is business" when it comes to foreclosing on the mortgaged property of the poor or otherwise making a profit from their plight (as, e.g., in our time when media evangelists prey on widows of limited means by manipulating them into sending repeated offerings to support their broadcasts). On Luke's concern for the poor, see 1:46–55; 2:8–14; 2:24; 3:10–14; 4:16–21; 6:20–23; 14:21–23; 16:19–31; Acts 2:44–47; 3:6; 4:32–35; 11:27–30). **For the sake of appearance say long prayers:** Not the length of the prayer is condemned (see 6:12; 18:1–8), but prayer as a posturing before others, a concern with one's image as a religious person.

21:1–4
THE WIDOW'S OFFERING
(See also at Mark 12:41–44)

21:1 He looked up and saw: In Luke this is a continuation of the previous scene. There were no chapter divisions in Luke's manuscript, so that the story of the widow who placed her whole livelihood in the temple offering chest stood without a break immediately after Jesus' condemnation of the scribes who exploited poor widows. **Rich people putting their gifts:** Although Luke is severe in his treatment of the rich (see, e.g., 1:53; 6:24; 12:13–21; 16:19–31; 18:23–25), here there is no condemnation of their generous giving. However, the actions of the rich only serve as a contrast for the act of the poor widow. **Into the treasury:** These were thirteen large chests in the shapes of trumpets, located in the outer court of the temple open to all Jews (but not Gentiles). The offerings received there were voluntary and were used to support various charitable causes and the temple worship itself. Jesus offers no critique of this aspect of the temple system itself (see 19:45–48).

21:2 A poor widow: In ancient Israel widows had no inheritance rights and were dependent on family and charity, a situation that still prevailed in New Testament times (see, e.g., Acts 6:1–6). Widows play a special role in Luke, both as models of piety and as those in special need of support (2:37; 4:25–26; 7:12; 18:1–8; 20:28, 47). **Put in two small copper coins:** The lepton (pl. lepta), the same coin mentioned in 12:59. It was the smallest unit of money, equal to about two cents. She had only four pennies and put them all in the temple treasury.

21:3–4 Truly I tell you: Jesus speaks to his disciples and is overheard by the crowd (20:45), not to the woman herself, who does not know she is being observed. She would be surprised to know that Christ was watching her and that her act would be recounted in millions of Bibles in every language in the world. **Has put in more than all of them:** Just as Jesus' parables take a surprising turn, so also this story has a surprising conclusion. One could understand the scene cynically (If she only has a nickel anyway, why not put it in the church collection plate—what else can one do with it?) or even selfishly (If I give my last nickel to God, surely God will do something good for me). This last approach is in fact used by some media evangelists who exploit poor widows with such self-serving promises. Or one could, with some interpreters, understand Jesus' comment as a lament that the corrupt temple system, like the corrupt scribal establishment, takes the woman's last penny (see 20:47). But Jesus interprets the scene positively and makes only the one point, the contrast between those who **contributed out of their abundance** and the one who **out of her poverty** put in all she had. This story is another instance of God's asking for all (see on 9:23), which the woman gave, while the rich would not do so (see on 18:18–27). This is a difficult story and ought not to be reduced to manageable platitudes.

21:5–36
THE ESCHATOLOGICAL DISCOURSE
(See also at Matt. 24:1–36; Mark 13:1–32)

For general notes on Luke's eschatology, see introduction to Luke: "Jesus as the 'Midst of Time'" and comments at 4:43; 5:24; Mark 2:10; 17:23; Acts 1:6–11. Luke has already presented his interpretation of the eschatological discourse found in one of his sources, Q (see on 17:20–37). Here he takes up Jesus' discourse about the end of history found in Mark 13 (see there). The interpreter of Luke (or any of the Gospels) must be careful to distinguish (1) "what really happened" in the time of Jesus; (2) the reinterpretation of this in earliest Christianity after Jesus' death and resurrection; (3) the continuing reinterpretation in Luke's written sources Mark and Q; (4) Luke's own interpretation, set forth in the text before us (see commentary on Luke 1:1–4; and "Introduction to the Gospels: 2. How Were

Gospels Written?"). We will deal with the distinctive Lukan elements in Luke's adaptation of the Markan discourse for his own times, which may be summarized as follows:

1. The end of history will come. History is in God's hands and will not go on forever. God the Creator will bring history to a worthy conclusion.

2. The first Christian generation's understanding that they were living in the last times turned out to be mistaken. Terrible catastrophes and tragedies occurred in those days, including the persecution of Roman Christians by Nero in 64 CE, in which Christians were crucified and burned alive; the Jewish war against the Romans in 66–70 CE, which resulted in the destruction of Jerusalem and the temple, and the slaughter and enslavement of the city's population; the eruption of Vesuvius in 79 CE, which darkened the sky and changed the Mediterranean climate for a year. Many in the first Christian generation saw these events as signs of the end, but Luke looks back on them and can see that, terrible as they were, they were historical events, not signs of the end. (This is analogous to the way in which many Christians at the time of World War II saw the rise of Hitler, the Holocaust, the terrible events of the war, and the use of atomic weapons as signs that the second coming of Christ was near, but we may now look back on them as terrible events *in* history, not the end of history itself.)

3. The delay of the end and the reinterpretation of God's purpose in history is no reason for Christians to become complacent. The Jesus of Luke 21 calls for courageous testimony during the time of the Christian mission, not speculation about when the end will come or indifference because its date cannot be predicted.

21:5–19
The Destruction of the Temple Foretold
(See also at Matt. 24:1–14; Mark 13:1–13)

21:5 Some were speaking about the temple: In Mark, it is the disciples who do this, and Jesus takes four of them apart for private instruction about the eschatological events and the return of the Son of Man. In Luke, Jesus remains in the temple, where he has been teaching (see on 19:47), and the grandeur of the temple is pointed out by anonymous hearers. That Jesus is addressed as Teacher (21:7) indicates the inquirers were not disciples, who in Luke never address Jesus as Teacher but as Lord or Master. The eschaton, whenever it comes, will not be a secret matter, about which his followers will need instruction from teachers claiming special knowledge (see on 17:23–24), but will be unquestionably visible to all. So also instruction about the future course of history and its end is a matter of public teaching that all can hear and understand.

21:6 The days will come when not one stone will be left upon another: The temple was destroyed by the Romans in 70 CE at the conclusion of the siege, an unthinkable happening in both the time of Jesus (ca. 30 CE) and the time of Mark (ca. 70), but Luke and his readers can look back on it and know both that it happened and that it was not the end. Both Judaism and early Christianity had to rethink the understanding of their faith after the destruction of the temple.

21:7 When will this be?: In Luke's source the destruction of the temple was related to the end of history. Luke both discourages the question when (see Acts 1:6–11) and separates the destruction of the temple from speculation about the end of the world.

21:8 Beware that you are not led astray: The reference is to Christian prophets who spoke in Jesus' name, interpreting historical catastrophes as signs of the end. Luke adds **"the time is near!"** to what the false prophets will say; this is the specific error he wishes to oppose (see 19:11–12; 20:9).

21:9–19 The end will not follow immediately: These verses list the historical catastrophes that false prophets saw as signs that the end was near: wars, rebellions, **earthquakes**, **plagues** (epidemics), **signs** in the sky ("heaven" and "sky" are the same word in Greek), persecutions and trials. This last element is elaborated. These events will not be signs of the end, but a part of continuing history during which the church is called to bear witness to the world. Luke is careful to include all these events as part of the story of the Christian mission in Acts, showing that they are not eschatological signs but features of the church's mission. (**Do not**) **prepare your defense in advance:** See the different instruction in 1 Pet. 3:15. **I will give you words and a wisdom:** As in Acts 6:10; 18:9–10; 23:11. The risen Christ speaks from heaven, in dreams and visions, and by the Holy Spirit. **By standing firm you will gain life** (NIV): The Lukan Jesus calls for steadfast endurance, patient work in the Christian mission for the long haul, not apocalyptic sensationalism. Jesus' disciples save their lives by giving them away, just as Jesus

did (9:23–24; 17:33). In the instructions for courageous conduct during the Christian mission, Jesus does not ask his disciples to do anything he does not experience himself.

21:20–24
The Destruction of Jerusalem and the Times of the Gentiles
(See also at Matt. 24:15–22; Mark 13:14–20)

21:20 Jerusalem surrounded by armies . . . its desolation: Mark's eschatological discourse had spoken of the "desolating sacrilege" ("abomination of desolation" in older translations; see at Mark 13:14). Luke omits the phrase, preserving only the word "desolation," which he uses with a different meaning. What had been an apocalyptic event becomes in Luke a historical event—the destruction of Jerusalem by the Roman armies (see 19:43). The city is doomed; those inside must leave before the final battle, and those outside the city must not enter it. When the siege begins, Jesus' followers are to expect no miraculous deliverance of Jerusalem, as had happened in 2 Kgs. 18:13–19:35; Isa. 37:33–36; see 2 Kgs. 6:24–7:16.

21:22 Fulfillment of all that is written: In retrospect, Luke understands the destruction of Jerusalem to be a fulfillment of the biblical prophecies. This is his theological means of incorporating the tragedy into the overarching purpose of God, of affirming that God is nonetheless the Lord of all history (see Acts 17:24–30; see excursus, "New Testament Interpretation of the Old Testament," at 1 Cor. 15:3). It is important to understand this positively as Luke's theological interpretation of the event in retrospect, which is different from thinking of the destruction of Jerusalem as something predicted by the biblical prophets and by Jesus as something that was inevitable. Although Jesus, like the biblical prophets, may have made pronouncements against Jerusalem, in Luke we have an interpretation of the past, not a prediction of the future; it is history theologized, not the future prophesied.

21:23 Woe to those who are pregnant and those who are nursing infants: Originally a lament for those who live in the last days, when biological processes break down (see on 1 Cor. 7:25–31), Luke understands this as a lament for the noncombatants, the vulnerable civilian population that often must endure the ravages of a war for which they are not responsible. **Distress on the earth:** The Greek word translated "earth" also means "land." Mark understood the word in the planetary eschatological sense, but Luke understands it in the restricted historical sense, the land of Judea that will endure the terror of the Roman war. **Wrath against this people:** See on 1 Thess. 2:14–16. Like the reference to the **days of vengeance** in v. 22, this is not a matter of glee over the ruin of the city and the slaughter and enslavement of its population (see 13:34–35; 19:41–44).

21:24 Trampled on by the Gentiles, until the times of the Gentiles are fulfilled: The phrase, added by Luke to his Markan source, may refer to the extended period in history during which the followers of Jesus will be predominantly Gentiles. See Rom. 11:1–36, esp. v. 25, in which the Jewish rejection of the Christian gospel is not permanent, but the present is understood as the Gentile period of the church. Alternatively, Luke may not have any periodization of history in mind, but may mean only that Jerusalem will fall completely into the power of the Gentiles, i.e., the Roman empire. Since the next verses deal with the end of history, and since by Luke's time the church had in fact become primarily a Gentile institution, the former interpretation is preferable: the time of the Gentile church is a part of God's plan for history but is not the final goal in God's purpose.

21:25–28
The Coming of the Son of Man
(See also at Matt. 24:29–31; Mark 13:24–27)

After the time of the church's mission, which Luke understands to be an extended time (see introduction to Luke: "Jesus as the 'Midst of Time'"), there will be cosmic signs that signal the end. These are no longer historical events subject to various interpretations but will be visible to all (see 17:23–24). The church thus does not need teachers claiming special information or insights about the time of the end; when it comes, everyone will know it.

21:27 The Son of Man coming in a cloud: On the Son of Man, see on 5:24; Mark 2:10. The end of history, the consummation of God's purpose for the creation, is pictured as the return of Christ. At the end of history we do not meet a stranger, but the one who has already appeared among us as the definitive revelation of God. At the end of history we shall meet the same Jesus portrayed in this Gospel. Luke rejects the idea that the earthly appearance of Jesus in love and compassion was only a preliminary effort on God's part to win human-

ity back to himself, but that when Jesus returns it will be with violence and vengeance. The God represented by the Jesus of this Gospel will ultimately prevail.

The function of this eschatological discourse is not to satisfy curiosity about the time or manner of the end, but (1) to proclaim God the Creator as the lord of history, whose purpose for the world will finally be fulfilled, and (2) to call the readers to repentance and service.

21:29–36
The Parable of the Fig Tree
(See also at Matt. 24:32–36; Mark 13:28–32)

21:29–30 Look at the fig tree: The fig tree blossoms in late spring, so that when its leaves appear, summer must be very near. **You can see for yourselves:** You have no need for "interpreters of prophecy" who claim to have special insight about the nearness of the end.

21:31 The kingdom of God: See on 4:43. Luke changes Mark's "he" (the Son of Man) to "the kingdom of God," showing that he understands the final manifestation of the kingdom of God to be identical with the return of the Son of Man.

21:32 This generation will not pass away: This text, difficult for modern readers, was found by Luke in his Markan source and must have been difficult for him also. In Mark, it expressed the faith of the first generation of Christians that Jesus would return in their own time. Luke knows that this was a misunderstanding, yet he preserves the saying. Its meaning for Luke is no longer clear, but it may be a prospective reference to the last generation, which will see the unmistakable cosmic signs of Christ's return. *That* generation will not pass away, but the end will come immediately.

21:33 My words will not pass away: Throughout, Luke has cast Jesus as God's ultimate prophetic spokesperson, whose words communicate God's word. Just as the word of God spoken by the Old Testament prophets will stand forever (Isa. 40:8; Ps. 119:89; 160), so the word of God spoken by Jesus will abide (see 5:1; 8:11, 21; 11:28). Luke is the only Gospel to use the phrase "word of God" with reference to the message of Jesus, another instance of the theocentric character of his Christology (see 7:16; 8:24, 38; 9:20–22, 43; 13:13; 17:15; 19:37). *Whatever* the end may be like, and *whenever* the end may come, the word of God remains faithful.

21:34–35 Be on guard: Luke's reinterpretation of the expectation that Christ would return soon is no cause for complacency. Just as he opposed those who claimed to know that the end was coming soon (see above), so he opposes those whose message is "Relax, we know that the end is *not* coming soon" (see on 12:35–46). "Be always ready" is the watchword, without regard to eschatological timetables.

21:37–38
JESUS CONTINUES TO TEACH IN THE TEMPLE

See on 19:47. Luke pictures an extended time at the end of Jesus' ministry in which Jerusalem and the temple become the center of his operations. Jesus has reclaimed Jerusalem and the temple for the work of God's kingdom, and in Acts the Christian message will go forth from this new center until it is relocated in Rome, the center and capital of the world (Acts 1:8; see Acts 28:30–31).

22:1–24:53
JESUS' PASSION AND RESURRECTION

Here begins the account of Jesus' last meal with his disciples, his arrest, trial, crucifixion and resurrection. Luke continues to follow Mark's basic structure, with some omissions, additions, and modifications. In Luke, as in Mark and Matthew, this is Jesus' first and only trip to a Jerusalem Passover (except for the childhood trip of 2:41–52; contrast the Gospel of John, in which Jesus attends three Passovers during his adult ministry). Luke also follows the Markan chronology, in which the Last Supper was a Passover meal, rather than the chronology of the Gospel of John, in which the Last Supper was the evening before the Passover meal, and Jesus is killed at the time the Passover lambs are being slain (see John 1:29; 13:1; 18:28; 19:31, 36; see chart at Matt. 26:17).

22:1–6
THE PLOT AGAINST JESUS' LIFE
(See also at Matt. 26:1–5, 14–16;
Mark 14:1–2, 10–11; John 11:47–53; 13:2)

22:1 The festival of Unleavened Bread, which is called the Passover: On the religious meaning and patriotic overtones of the festival, see on Mark 14:1. Jesus, too, would accomplish an "exodus" at the time of the Passover, but the liberation he brings is not of the military or nationalistic kind (see on 9:14, 31, 51).

22:2 Chief priests: See on 19:47. **Scribes:** See on 20:1. Again Luke points out that it is the Jewish leadership, not the people as a whole, who are interested in his death. The issue is not whether he should be killed, which they have already decided. Luke does not mention when

or on what basis this decision had been made, but see 6:11, par. Mark 3:6. Their problem was that Jesus was supported by the masses, whom he taught daily in the temple (see 18:43; 19:48; 20:1, 6, 9; 21:38), so they could not arrest him there. **They were afraid of the people:** Though he did not live in a democratic society, Luke is aware of the power the "common people" have. Modern readers who live in a society where government is "of the people" might ponder the even greater power and responsibility they have, so that public policy and social evils cannot simply be blamed on "the politicians."

22:3–4 Then Satan entered into Judas called Iscariot: Luke here omits the story of the woman who anointed Jesus, found at this location in his Marcan source, in order to go directly to the story of Judas's betrayal (Luke has included a similar story in 7:36–50). The quandary of the chief priests is resolved by Judas's unexpected initiative. This is the first reference to the activity of Satan in the story since 4:13, when the devil left Jesus "until an opportune time." In Luke the one-year ministry of Jesus has been a time during which Satan was vanquished, the time when the kingdom of God was on the earth (see on 4:13, 19, 43; 10:18; 11:20; 13:16). Luke considers Judas responsible for the betrayal of Jesus, just as he considered Peter responsible for his denial of Jesus (22:54–62), but in and through Judas's decision the suprapersonal power of evil is at work, just as in and through Jesus' decisions the power of God is at work. **One of the twelve:** For the difference, in Luke's understanding, between the twelve apostles and the larger group of disciples, see on 6:12–13. **Officers of the temple police:** Jewish police charged with keeping order in the temple precincts. They are mentioned only in Luke and Acts, where they are involved in Jesus' arrest and in the later harassment of the apostles (22:4, 52; Acts 4:1; 5:24, 26).

22:5–6 Agreed to give him money: Judas had taken the initiative in the betrayal; in Luke the priests seem to have taken the initiative in offering him money. The amount is not specified (the "thirty pieces of silver" come from Matthew [26:15], who derived them from Zech. 11:12–13). **An opportunity to betray him:** The Greek word "betray" also means "hand over" or "deliver up" and is used for the action of God in delivering up the Suffering Servant (Isa. 53:6, 12; see on Mark 1:14). Luke can also use it with this overtone (9:44;

see Acts 7:42). Though Luke understands Jesus in terms of Isaiah's Suffering Servant (see Acts 8:26–35), he does not cite the passage in which the Servant is delivered up. It is nonetheless clear that Luke understands that Jesus' being delivered up to death is part of the divine plan (see on the passion predictions 9:22, 44; 12:50; 13:33–34; 17:25; 18:31–33). Judas betrays, but God delivers Jesus up. Judas betrays at his own initiative and responsibility, but Satan is also at work in his decision. Luke does not neatly parcel out responsibility among Judas, God, and Satan, but tells the story in such a way that the power of Satan, human responsibility, and God's overruling purpose are all at work.

22:7–13
Preparation for the Passover
(See also at Matt. 26:17–19; Mark 14:12–16)

22:7 The day of Unleavened Bread: Technically incorrect, since Unleavened Bread was a seven-day festival, but see the modern reference to Christmas as a "day," rather than the liturgical season of the "twelve days of Christmas." On the connection between Unleavened Bread and Passover, see on Mark 14:1. On the chronology, see chart at Matt. 26:17.

22:8 Peter and John: Luke specifies that the two anonymous disciples of Mark 14:13 are Peter and John (in Matthew all twelve seem to perform the chore). This anticipates the role of Peter and John in Acts 3–4; 8.

22:13 Found everything as he had told them: These arrangements are not part of a pre-arranged "plot," as though Jesus had secret accomplices in Jerusalem. Rather, as in 19:29–35, the fact that Jesus accurately predicts just what will happen shows that the tragic events about to unfold are not some fate that overtakes him against his will. Like the passion predictions (9:22, 44; 12:50; 13:33–34; 17:25; 18:31–33), they reveal Jesus' divine foreknowledge. This way of telling the story conveys to the reader that though Jesus will be killed by his enemies, his arrest, suffering, and death will not take him by surprise, but are part of God's plan. This represents the post-Easter perspective of the church, which saw in the events of Jesus' death and resurrection the saving act of God. **They prepared the Passover meal:** This involved procuring a lamb, having it ritually slaughtered by the temple priests, roasting it, and securing the

unleavened bread, wine, and bitter herbs that were part of the Passover meal.

22:14–38
The Last Supper
(See also at Matt. 26:20–35; Mark 14:17–31; John 13:1–17:26)

Luke expands and rearranges the account in his Markan source, placing here materials found in other contexts in Mark (22:24–27 = Mark 10:41–45) and Q (22:28–30; see Matt. 19:28), and from sources peculiar to him (22:14–16, 31–33, 35–38 are L, see introduction to Luke). Unlike Mark, Luke begins directly with the institution of the Eucharist.

22:14 The apostles with him: Only Jesus and the Twelve are present; see on 6:12–13. See excursus, "The Lord's Supper in the New Testament," at 1 Cor. 11:24. The comments below elaborate the distinctive Lukan perspective.

22:15 I have eagerly desired to eat this Passover with you: In these words peculiar to Luke, the connection of Jesus and his followers to the Passover and to Judaism is emphasized (see on 2:41–52; 4:14–15). The Last Supper is a Passover meal in Matthew, Mark, and Luke, but not in John (see on 22:1–24:53 above). On the Passover, see on 22:1. **Before I suffer:** In the Greek text, the words for "Passover" (*pascha*) and "suffer" (*pascho*) sound alike. Jesus relates his suffering and death to the significance of Passover, the Jewish festival of liberation from Egypt.

22:16 I will not eat it (again): The word "again" appears in some ancient MSS but not in others. The NIV includes it, the NRSV does not (but see note). It is thus not clear whether Jesus eats or abstains, but probably the meaning is that this is the last Passover in which Jesus will be present and eat with his disciples **until it is fulfilled in the kingdom of God.** In Luke's understanding, this fulfillment does not take place during the time of the church, but at the end of history with the return of the Son of Man (see on 5:24; Mark 2:10) and the final establishment of the kingdom of God (see on 4:43). One of the images of the final fulfillment of God's purpose for the world was the messianic banquet. Jesus will not eat the Passover again with his disciples until the final celebration of God's liberation of the world from the powers of sin and death.

22:17–18 Then he took a cup: One of the difficulties in interpreting Luke's account is that in the present form of the text Jesus gives his dis-

ciples two cups to drink. The Passover celebration involved drinking four specific cups
of wine, each with its particular blessing and
meaning. This first cup is not the eucharistic
cup of Christian significance but remains
within the framework of the Passover imagery. Like the Passover lamb itself, Jesus will
not drink it again **until the kingdom of God
comes.** In Luke, the Passover, but not the
Eucharist, is related to the kingdom of God.
For Luke, the earthly Jesus celebrated the
Passover (2:41–52; 22:15), but the Passover is
not to be celebrated by Christians until it is fulfilled at the return of Christ. The Passover is
related to the kingdom of God, which was
manifest in the life of Jesus and will come in
power at the end of history. It is a matter of
memory and hope but not of present experience. Thus Christians in Acts celebrate Pentecost (Acts 2:1; 20:16) but not Passover.

22:19 He took a loaf of bread: Here begin the
specifically Christian features of the Eucharist. **This is my body, which is given for you:**
While Jesus **broke** the bread, he does not refer
to his body as "broken" (see John 19:31–36).
Luke gives no explanation regarding the question later disputed by Christians as to how the
verb "is" should be understood (see below).
Note that the words from "which is given for
you" (v. 19) through "the new covenant in my
blood" (v. 20) are not found in some ancient
manuscripts and are more like 1 Cor. 11:23–25
than the Markan source Luke has been following. They may not represent the original
text of Luke but the addition of a later copyist.
Thus some modern editions of the Bible (e.g.,
1946 RSV) have not included them, but the
tendency of more recent scholarship is to
regard them as original (see "Introduction:
The New Testament as the Church's Book,"
4.d). **Do this in remembrance of me:** Unlike
the words about the Passover, Jesus commands the disciples to repeat the act, which
the church in Acts continued to do (Acts 2:42,
46; 20:7) and which millions of Christians have
continued to do until this day as the central act
of Christian worship.

22:20 He did the same with the cup after supper:
He gave thanks, gave the cup to the disciples,
and commanded them to continue to do it in
remembrance of him. **My blood:** God's covenant with Israel was sealed with sacrificial
blood (Exod. 24:3–8). This imagery is also used
in 1 Pet. 1:2. **The new covenant:** Jeremiah had
promised that God would renew the covenant

with Israel (Jer. 31:31). This would be the ultimate, eschatological renewal of God's covenant
with Israel, not its replacement. "New" in such
contexts refers to the ultimate fulfillment, not
a "new and improved version" that replaces
the old (see on 5:36–38). Luke omits the
Markan words "for many," which interpret the
death of Jesus as a sacrifice for sins. Although
other New Testament authors understand
Jesus' death as an atoning sacrifice (see on
Rom. 3:23–25), Luke is very reserved with
regard to this interpretation (see below on
22:24–27). The Passover lamb was not a sacrifice for sins, but a symbol of God's liberating
act at the exodus. For Luke, the Eucharist is
understood within the framework of the
Passover and is not related to the lamb sacrificed as a sin offering (see 1 Cor. 5:6–8).

22:21–23 The one who betrays me is with me:
Luke has rearranged and added to his Markan
source, resulting in a fairly extensive after-
dinner discussion, though not nearly so long
as the Farewell Discourse in the Gospel of
John (John 13–17). By reserving the announcement that one of his chosen apostles would
betray him until after the meal in which Jesus
has identified the bread and wine with his
body and blood, Luke has intensified the
pathos and shock: Jesus will be betrayed by
one who has participated in the first eucharistic celebration. The reader is thus called to self-
examination (1 Cor. 11:28), for participation in
the Eucharist does not automatically preserve
one from betrayal and denial of Jesus, just as
preaching and working miracles does not (for
Judas had been included in the apostolic band
that had done amazing works in Jesus' name
[9:1–6; see 10:17–20]).

The reader has known since 6:16 that Judas
would become a traitor, but the characters in
the story do not know. The whole Gospel story
is told from the post-Easter perspective, in
which the figures in the story only gradually
come to an awareness of Jesus' identity and
God's purpose, which the Christian believer
has known from the beginning.

**22:22 As it has been determined, but woe to that
one:** Luke provides no explanation but affirms
the paradoxical truth of divine sovereignty
and human responsibility. The modern reader
might well be wary of "explanations" that dispose of the mystery in which human beings
are fully responsible and accountable for their
actions, but God is the sovereign God, whose
purpose is worked out despite human sin.

Judas was not born to be a traitor, nor did Jesus choose him so that he could play a predetermined part in the Christian drama. Judas became a traitor (6:16!), and yet his betrayal did not overthrow the divine purpose but was incorporated within it. See excursus, "Predestination," at Rom. 8:28–29.

22:23 They began to ask one another: The apostles' response is represented differently in each of the Gospels. In Luke, their reaction is not soul-searching ("could I be the one?") but a group discussion—in which Judas participated—as to which of them could do such a thing.

22:24 A dispute also arose among them: Luke has rearranged the Markan chronology to bring this dispute into direct conjunction with the disciples' discussion of who will betray Jesus. Wanting to be great and denying Jesus are two sides of the same coin. Only Judas will literally betray Jesus, only Peter will literally deny him, but all engage in the self-seeking quest for status—which is also betrayal and denial. Lacking the sense of security that comes from knowing one is accepted by God, they attempt to establish their own status, becoming like the scribes who plot Jesus' death (see on 20:45–47).

22:25–26 Not so with you: Throughout Luke, Jesus represents the kingdom of God, which reverses the values of all earthly conceptions of rulership and authority. The difference between God's kingdom and worldly kingdoms is *not* a matter of "external" and "inner," as though Christ's kingship were only a matter of the individual heart. God's kingdom has to do with external relationships and power structures—but with a radically different understanding of what constitutes power. In the Greek text, the terminology of **those in authority, the youngest,** and **one who serves** reflects the vocabulary of church offices and positions of leadership (see Acts 2:17; 5:6, 10; 6:2; 7:10; 14:12; 23:18, 22; Rom. 16:1; 1 Cor. 3:5; 1 Tim. 3:8, 12; 5:1; Titus 2:6; 1 Pet. 4:10–11; 5:1–5; 1 John 2:13–14). Such passages show that the structure and terminology of the patriarchal family were adapted by the church to express its leadership roles. Here as elsewhere in the Gospel of Luke, the Christian readers of Luke's time can overhear in Jesus' instruction to his disciples an address to the squabbles and temptations of their own time.

22:27 I am among you as one who serves: This is the key to the reversal of worldly standards that has come into the world with the king-

dom of God as represented in the life of Jesus. Here Luke completely rewrites the saying in Mark 10:45, which expressed this reversal in different categories: the Son of Man who was to be the judge of all nations at the end time gives his own life as a ransom for many/all. Luke affirms the same kind of reversal, but without the language in which Jesus' death is an atoning sacrifice (see above on 22:20 and on Acts 2:36, 20:28).

22:28 You . . . have stood by me: Despite their failures, Luke gives a more positive view of the disciples than does his source Mark (omitting, for example, Mark 14:50–52 at Luke 22:53).

22:29–30 I confer on you, just as my Father has conferred on me, a kingdom: Just as Jesus participates in God's rule, so Jesus' followers will participate in Christ's rule. See the similar imagery in Rev. 2:25–27; 3:21. **So that you may eat and drink at my table in my kingdom:** This is not a reference to the church's celebration of the Eucharist, but to the final coming of the kingdom of God at the end of history, often pictured as the messianic banquet (see 9:17; 14:15–17; 22:16). **You will sit on thrones judging the twelve tribes of Israel:** What the disciples wanted on the earthly level is here transferred to the eschatological level. Another of the images used for the final coming of the kingdom of God in the eschatological future is the regathering of the scattered tribes of Israel and the reconstitution of the people of God (see Acts 1:6). The people of Israel in the Old Testament were composed of twelve tribes corresponding to the twelve sons of Jacob/Israel (Gen. 35:23–26). At the time of the destruction of the northern kingdom by the Assyrians in 721 CE, the northern tribes were deported and scattered, never to return (2 Kgs. 17). An aspect of the eschatological hope was that at the triumph of God at the end of history the "lost tribes" would be restored and Israel would be whole again. **Judging:** Here means ruling in the positive sense of a just ruler. There is no condemnation of Israel here, but rather the reverse: the fulfillment of God's kingdom is pictured as the restoration of Israel, but with the Christian apostles as its leaders.

22:31 Simon, Simon, listen! At this point in the Markan story, the group leaves the upper room for the Mount of Olives, where Jesus predicts that they all will fall away, and Peter objects that at least he will not. Luke has the conversation continue around the table. Simon was his birth name; Jesus renamed him Peter

(5:8; 6:14). Luke adds these verses that not only cushion Peter's fall to be narrated later, when he does actually deny Jesus (22:54–62), but also places the problem of unfaithful disciples in a larger theological context. The saying reflects the later perspective of the early Christian community, in which Peter did become a leader in the reconstitution of the group of disciples after the shattering experience of the crucifixion. The reference to **Satan** is more than the superficial "the devil made me do that"; it reflects the assault by the ultimate power of evil on the emerging kingdom of God (see 11:14–23). As Jesus began his ministry, Satan had tested Jesus, who emerged victorious (4:1–13); Satan had seduced Judas to betray Jesus (22:3) and now seeks (or has been granted permission; see NRSV footnote) to take over Peter's life.

22:32 But I have prayed for you: As Jesus prays for those who crucify him (23:34), so he prays for erring disciples. Here is a reflection of the mission of the Suffering Servant fulfilled by Jesus (Isa. 53:12) and a narrative representation of the Christology of Heb. 7:25. **When you have turned back:** Christ prays for Peter, but Peter must do the turning. Herein lies the difference between Judas and Peter. **Strengthen your brothers:** Salvation is not merely personal and individualistic, but for a role in the Christian community. God will add to the church those who are saved, Acts 2:47. Christ's prayer was answered, Peter did "turn back" (repent), and did become the leading figure in regathering the disciples after Easter to continue Jesus' mission.

22:33 Ready to go with you to prison and to death: In the immediate future, Peter will deny that he knows Jesus and belongs to the group of disciples. But Acts records that Peter was imprisoned for the faith, and later Christian history reliably indicates that Peter died a martyr's death in the Neronian persecution in Rome in 64 CE.

22:35 Did you lack anything?: Though Jesus here speaks to the twelve apostles, reference is actually to 10:4, where Jesus sent out the seventy missionaries (see on 9:1 for Luke's two commissioning scenes). The one year of Jesus' ministry had been a special time when the kingdom of God was present on earth in the person of Christ (see on 4:43; 11:20; 17:21; "Jesus as the 'Midst of Time'" in the introduction to Luke). The mission then had been conducted under the idyllic conditions of the kingdom of God.

22:36 But now: With the crucifixion and resurrection of Jesus, a new period in the saving plan of God begins. The mission of Jesus' disciples continues, but under radically changed conditions. Satan had been absent and defeated (4:13; 10:18; 11:20), but now has returned (22:3, 31). During its continuing mission the church looks not only forward to the victory of God at the end of history, but backward to the time of Jesus when the kingdom of God was present in one solitary life. The church's proclamation of the coming kingdom of God is thus no idle fantasy, no flight from the real world, because it looks back to a life in which God's rule actually happened.

The one who has no sword must sell his cloak and buy one: This is the most difficult element in the passage. The saying occurs only in Luke and perhaps was taken from some other context in which the meaning was clear. An occasional interpreter has argued that in reality Jesus wanted to establish an earthly kingdom by military violence, and that the picture of this revolutionary Jesus was mostly covered up by his later followers—as though here a fragment of the "original" picture still shines through. This goes against everything else in the Gospels and is certainly historically incorrect. The sole point seems to be that the sword was not a military or revolutionary weapon but a standard element in the traveler's equipment, for self-defense—like the staff of 9:3 they were forbidden to take earlier. The disciples never actually buy or use a sword in the story of the church's mission in Acts, and even the effort to use the sword in self-defense at Jesus' arrest is condemned by Jesus (22:49–51).

22:37 He was counted among the lawless: The allusion identifies Jesus with the Suffering Servant of Isa. 53:12, who does not use the sword even in self-defense, a figure whose suffering is for the healing of others (again, as in the scene at Jesus' arrest). Thus the whole point of this difficult passage seems to be that the special time of the kingdom is over, and the church must continue its mission under the ordinary conditions that dominate the world under the sway of Satan (4:6). No lessons can be drawn from it about the right and wrong use of weapons.

22:38 It is enough: Although here, too, the meaning is not clear, Luke's point seems to be that the disciples misunderstood Jesus' teaching, seeing only a prosaic, literal meaning, and that Jesus broke off the discussion. They would not understand until after the story is over and the Spirit has come (see Acts 1–2).

22:39–46
PRAYER ON THE MOUNT OF OLIVES
(See also at Matt. 26:36–46; Mark 14:32–42)

22:39 As was his custom: In Luke, Jesus is pictured as having spent an extended time in Jerusalem; see on 21:37. **Mount of Olives:** See 19:29. Matthew and Mark speak of Gethsemane, but not of a garden. John 18:1 speaks of a garden, but not of Gethsemane. Luke has neither. **Disciples:** Here refers to the Twelve, minus Judas, whose departure has not been mentioned by Luke.

22:40 Pray that you may not come into the time of trial: An echo of the model prayer (see on 1:4). "Time of trial" refers not to moral **temptation** (so NIV) but to the trials that come upon the faithful. Luke frames Jesus' own prayer with a command for the disciples to pray. He prays and is strengthened for the trial he is about to endure; they do not, and fail.

22:41–42 Knelt down: A more composed posture than the distraught Jesus of Mark 14:35. **Remove this cup from me:** "Cup" is an Old Testament symbol for God's wrath (Ps. 75:8; Isa. 51:17, 22; Jer. 25:12; 49:12; Lam. 4:21), but Luke does not picture Jesus as threatened with the wrath of God. In later Judaism, the cup came to symbolize the martyr's death, which is nearer to Luke's understanding of the meaning of Jesus' death. Jesus is no masochist, has no martyr complex, and shares fully the human desire for life. **Not my will but yours be done:** Jesus' death, seen in the retrospective view of the church, was part of God's plan, but Luke has no theory of the atoning death of Jesus that explains how this is so. Jesus illustrates that devotion to God's will is the highest priority, higher even than life itself, and that prayer strengthens one to do God's will.

22:43–44 An angel from heaven appeared: These verses are not in the oldest and best MSS, disrupt the formal neatness of the scene, and probably represent the addition of a later scribe. They present a different picture of Jesus than the composed worshiper of 22:41 (see 23:46 vs. Mark 15:34). **Drops of blood:** Jesus is not pictured as "sweating blood," but perspiring so profusely as he struggles in prayer that his perspiration flows like blood.

22:45 Found them sleeping: In Luke's source, Jesus had taken Peter, James, and John apart from the other disciples; it is to them he returns, and the scene transpires three times.

In Luke, Jesus prays only once and returns to all the disciples; his arrest follows immediately. **Exhausted from sorrow** (NIV): A Lukan addition that paints a more favorable picture of the disciples (see 22:28).

22:47–53
JESUS IS ARRESTED
(See also at Matt. 26:47–56; Mark 14:43–52; John 18:2–12)

22:47 A crowd came: The crowds had been potential disciples, and the authorities had been unable to arrest Jesus publicly because of the devotion of the crowd (see 5:1, 15; 6:17–19; 7:11; 8:4; 9:11, 18, 37; 11:14; 14:25; 19:48; 20:19; 22:47; 23:4, 13, 21, 48), but now the crowd seems to have switched its allegiance. **Judas, one of the twelve:** Luke has not mentioned either his departure from the group at the Last Supper or this prearranged signal. Kissing as a form of greeting was not unusual (2 Sam. 20:9; Luke 7:45; Rom. 16:16).

22:49 Should we strike with the sword: See on 22:36–38.

22:51 No more of this: In Luke, Jesus' last words before he is arrested are a renunciation of violence as the way of the kingdom of God he represents.

He touched his ear and healed him: Only in Luke. Jesus' ministry of healing continues until the very last. He does not wound others but heals those who have been wounded, even by the well-meaning mistakes of his followers.

22:52 As if I were a bandit (NRSV)/**Am I leading a rebellion?** (NIV): "Bandit" represents the perspective of the establishment, their term for the revolutionary "freedom fighters." Jesus is not suspected of being a thief, but of fomenting revolution against the Roman authorities and their Jewish supporters.

22:54–62
PETER DENIES JESUS
(See also at Matt. 26:57–58, 69–75; Mark 14:53–54, 66–72; John 18:15–18, 25–27)

Luke places this scene prior to the beginning of Jesus' hearing before the Jewish leaders, abandoning Mark's dramatic literary strategy of sandwiching Peter's denial into the scene of Jesus' confession. In Luke, both Jesus and Peter seem to be waiting in the courtyard during the night for the hearing to begin the next day (see 22:61).

22:54–55 Peter was following at a distance: He had been called to follow, and he was following, but he kept his distance and **sat among**

the enemy and the curious. Peter has set himself up for the failure to follow.

22:56 A servant-girl: In Mark, Peter's accusers are a servant-girl, who twice charges Peter with being a follower of Jesus, and the bystanders. Luke has modified this so that three different people, one woman and two men, identify Peter. The charge was serious: Jesus was accused of being a political rebel, and his followers could be arrested and condemned with him.

22:60 I do not know what you are talking about: He does not curse and swear, as in Mark 14:71, but feigns ignorance. It was a lie, of course. Peter the rock turns to sand. He is in danger of losing authentic life by trying to secure his own life (see 9:23; 17:33).

22:61 The Lord turned and looked at Peter: This dramatic note, only in Luke, informs the reader for the first time that Jesus had been present all along. Just as Judas's betrayal took place in the presence of Jesus, so also did Peter's denial. **Peter remembered the word of the Lord:** 22:31–34, which not only predicted that Peter would deny Jesus, but promised his repentance, restoration, and transformation into a strengthener of others.

22:62 Wept bitterly: Grief alone does not save. Peter not only was remorseful but repented (see 2 Cor. 7:9–10).

22:63–65
JESUS IS MOCKED AND BEATEN
(See also at Matt. 26:67–68; Mark 14:65)

In Matthew and Mark, this happens at the conclusion of Jesus' trial before the chief priests. Luke locates it in the courtyard during the night, waiting for the hearing to begin.

22:64 Prophesy: Prophets were supposed to be endowed with supernatural knowledge, not only of the future (see 7:39). The reader perceives the irony of the scene in which Jesus' prediction that Peter would deny him had just been fulfilled. Jesus suffers silently, without rebuke or condemnation of his tormentors.

22:66–71
HEARING BEFORE THE SANHEDRIN
(See also at Matt. 26:59–66;
Mark 14:55–64; John 18:13–24)

22:66 When day came: In Luke, there is no illegal hearing or trial at night. **Their council:** The Sanhedrin; see on 19:47.

22:67 If you are the Messiah, tell us: On the Messiah or Christ, see on 9:20; Mark 8:29. The title here has two levels of meaning. At the level of

the narrative, the Jewish leaders understand it in the political sense of the expected royal military leader who will defeat the Romans and restore Israel's sovereignty. There are no religious charges of blasphemy, which plays no role in the Lukan narrative of Jesus' hearing and trial. The post-Easter Christian reader hears the title in its religious sense as the Savior promised by God (2:11). **If I tell you:** Jesus' answer is not merely strategically evasive but reveals that the question is not an honest question (see 20:1–8). The chief priests and scribes have already decided to put Jesus to death (22:1–2).

22:68 The Son of Man will be seated at the right hand of the power of God: On Son of Man, see on 5:24; Mark 2:10. As in 9:20–22, when asked about the Messiah, Jesus responds in terms of the suffering, dying, and rising Son of Man. See Dan. 7:13; Ps. 110:1.

22:70 Are you, then, the Son of God?: On Son of God, see at 1:28–33. Luke here identifies the three christological titles Christ, Son of Man, and Son of God. **You say that I am:** This is not an evasive answer but the equivalent of the "I am" in Luke's source, Mark 14:61–62. The council understands it to be a clear affirmation.

In Luke, the hearing before the Sanhedrin should not be called a trial, since it does not result in acquittal or condemnation, no witnesses are called, and there is no reference to Jesus' having spoken or acted against the temple. With Jesus' admission that he claims to be the Messiah (understood politically), the Jewish leaders have enough evidence to bring him before the Roman court as a rebel.

23:1–5
JESUS' TRIAL BEFORE PILATE
(See also at Matt. 27:1–11;
Mark 15:1–5; John 18:29–38)

23:1 Pilate: See on 3:1–2. During Jesus' ministry Herod Antipas, a puppet king, ruled in Galilee at the pleasure of the Romans, but the troublesome territories of Judea and Samaria were ruled directly by a Roman governor. Whether at the time of Jesus the Romans permitted the Jews to carry out the death penalty is disputed among historians (see on John 18:31; Acts 7:58). In the Roman judicial system, for such cases there were no trials by jury, no prosecuting or defense attorneys, but the governor himself conducted the trial and made the decision. Pilate was legally authorized to dispose of the case as he chose.

23:2 Began to accuse him: Luke here completely rewrites his Markan source to specify that the charges against Jesus before the Roman court were political. The reader also knows that they are false (20:20–26). **The Messiah, a king:** See on 9:20; Mark 8:29; 19:38; 22:25–27, 67). Jesus is indeed the king in the coming kingdom of God (4:43), but the title here functions at two levels. The reader knows that Jesus' kingship is not an attempt to overthrow the Roman government by military violence.

23:3 Are you the king of the Jews?: Pilate is interested only in the political charge. **Yes, it is as you say** (NIV)/**You say so** (NRSV): Jesus' response is not absolutely clear in Greek. See the NIV and NRSV. The reader knows that Jesus is God's anointed king, but not in the sense that Pilate understands the question. Thus some interpreters have understood Jesus to answer ambiguously, "'King' is your word, not mine." However, the Lukan parallel to Mark 14:61–62 at Luke 22:67–70 makes it more likely that Luke intends Jesus' response to be a clear "Yes," as in the NIV.

23:4 The chief priests and the crowds: Here the crowds who have been Jesus' supporters stand with the chief priests, but their final decision is yet to be made. **I find no basis for an accusation against this man:** Pilate considers Jesus a harmless crank who has done nothing politically wrong and is no threat to Roman law and order. This is the first of three pronouncements of Jesus' innocence (23:15, 22).

23:5 From Galilee . . . to this place: The formulation expresses Luke's own theology that the gospel began in Galilee, moves to Jerusalem, and from there will spread to the whole world (Acts 1:8; 10:37). Pilate is pictured as a politician who is convinced of Jesus' innocence but is looking for a way out of a difficult situation without having to make the final decision himself. He is relieved to discover that Jesus comes from Galilee and that he can thus transfer his case to another jurisdiction.

Verses 4–5 are found only in Luke and represent the distinctive point of view he will develop in Acts, that the Roman government is not interested in religious disputes and does not find Jesus' followers to be politically dangerous (Acts 18:12–17; 24:14–15; 25:19; 26:2–3). Luke is writing for "Theophilus" (see on 1:1), to give guidelines as to how responsible Romans should regard the church of his own time and how Christians should understand their relation to the government: they are to stand fast for their religious convictions but are not a politically subversive movement in conflict with Roman order.

23:6–12
JESUS BEFORE HEROD

23:7 Sent him off to Herod: Herod Antipas, son of Herod the Great, at Rome's discretion ruler of Galilee and Perea (see at 3:1–2). Like the Roman governor, he is in Jerusalem for the festival. Pilate's sending Jesus to Herod (the scene is only in Luke) may represent political shrewdness of Pilate's part, by deferring to Herod's presumed authority in the case, but Luke more likely intends it as an illustration of Pilate's effort to avoid a difficult decision.

23:8 When Herod saw Jesus, he was very glad: Herod is interested in Jesus, but for the wrong reasons (see 9:7–9; 11:29; 13:31). Here his interest is not a matter of faith, but a kind of religious curiosity about miracles.

23:11 Put an elegant robe on him, and sent him back to Pilate: Like the crown of thorns (in Matt. 27:29; Mark 15:17; and John 19:2, 5, but absent from Luke), the robe is a cruel joke, mocking Jesus' claims to kingship. The claim of Jesus is handled in this section by attempts to dismiss it and let someone else decide, by an interest in Jesus at the level of curiosity about the miracles, and by dismissing Jesus as a crank or making a joke of the whole matter. All these efforts are still used to avoid taking seriously the claim of the kingdom of God that is present in Jesus. But the claim remains and must be dealt with sooner or later.

23:12 Herod and Pilate became friends: This seemingly casual historical note is to be seen in a larger theological context, the fulfillment of Ps. 2:1–2, in which the rulers of the world unite against the Lord's anointed (see Acts 4:25–26).

23:13–25
JESUS SENTENCED TO DEATH
(See also at Matt. 27:12–26; Mark 15:6–15; John 18:39–19:16)

23:13–16 I . . . have not found this man guilty of any of your charges: These verses are only in Luke, emphasizing the Lukan perspective that it is (some of) the Jewish leaders who accuse Jesus, but that Rome finds him innocent. The pattern is repeated in Acts, especially in the case of Paul, and was particularly relevant for the Christians of Luke's own time near the end of the first century. Although it was clear that Jesus had been executed by the Romans as a political threat, from the earliest times, as Christians told their story in the context of the Roman Empire, there was a tendency to blame the Jews and exonerate the Romans. This tendency, already present in Mark, is developed further in Luke. While later readers should sympathetically try to understand Luke's situation and his reasons for presenting the story with this emphasis, they should not continue to draw from his narrative the false conclusions about Jewish responsibility for Jesus' death that have plagued church history. Here as elsewhere in interpreting the Gospels, a distinction should be made between actual history and its theological interpretation in the Gospel (see Introduction to the Gospels, "3. What Is a Gospel?").

Neither has Herod: From Luke's point of view, the instance of Herod shows that not all the Jewish leaders thought Jesus should be condemned. The reader should also note that Luke carefully eliminates the Pharisees, the Jewish group that had assumed leadership in Luke's own day, from the passion story (see on 5:17). This means that Luke presents one group of Jewish leaders, the chief priests and their associates in the temple, as guilty of Jesus' death. By Luke's time the temple and its leadership had been destroyed in the war with Rome. Thus Luke emphasizes the guilt of a segment of Jewish leadership of a past generation, together with an unscrupulous Roman governor, all of whom knew Jesus was innocent.

23:16 I will have him flogged and release him: This was a severe penalty that could legally be administered only to those found guilty. Pilate is already violating justice by his offer to appease the priests and the crowds. But this ploy does not work, and he still must make a decision.

(23:17 Now he was obliged to release someone: This verse, present in the King James Version that was translated from late MSS, is not in the best and most ancient MSS, and is properly omitted by both the NIV and NRSV (see "Introduction: The New Testament as the Church's Book," 4.d). Without it, Luke does not indicate that the releasing of a dangerous prisoner at the festival was a Roman custom; rather, it was the spontaneous demand of the crowd to which Pilate capitulated. There is no evidence outside the New Testament for the custom of releasing a prisoner at the festival, and it is historically unlikely.)

23:19 Put in prison for an insurrection: There is supreme irony here—the priests and crowds call for the release of one who was actually guilty of the crime of which they had falsely accused Jesus.

23:22 A third time: See 23:4, 14. This emphasis on Jesus' innocence will be repeated by one of the criminals crucified with him (23:41) and by the centurion in charge of the crucifixion (23:47).

23:23 Their voices prevailed: Although Pilate's last words declare Jesus' innocence, he yields to the voices of the priests and the crowd. Luke emphasizes the Jewish insistence on Jesus' death, without eliminating the fact that the ultimate responsibility remained with Pilate.

23:26–49
THE CRUCIFIXION
(See also at Matt. 27:27–56;
Mark 15:16–41; John 19:17–37)

23:26 They led him away: The syntax, interpreted strictly, would mean that Pilate turned Jesus over to the Jews, and they led him away. But the subsequent story shows that the Romans were in charge of the crucifixion. **Cyrene:** In north Africa, modern Libya. Nothing else is known of Simon. As in Mark, Simon carries Jesus' cross, presumably because Jesus was too weak after the flogging. Luke records no beating (though see 23:16, 22). The scene becomes a vivid dramatization of the meaning of discipleship (see 9:23; 14:27). In the Gospel of John, Jesus carries his own cross (John 19:17).

23:27 A great number of people followed him: Verses 27–31 picturing the procession to the site of the crucifixion are only in Luke. The image of the lamenting crowds should not be historicized, as though Luke wants to say that some of the crowd had shouted for Jesus' death (23:23), but others retained their allegiance to Jesus. The crowds play a narrative role in Luke's story (see 5:1, 15; 6:17–20, 19; 7:11; 8:4; 9:11, 18, 37; 11:14; 14:25; 19:48; 20:19; 22:6, 47; 23:4, 13, 21, 48). Like Peter, they originally were potential disciples, became his strong supporters, wavered at the trial scene and joined the opposition, but here have returned to their allegiance to Jesus. **Women who were beating their breasts and wailing for him:** The traditional gesture of lamentation (see Zech. 12:10; Jer. 9:19, and the Wailing Wall in Jerusalem). Luke has also associated it with repentance (18:13!). Here and in v. 49, the crowds lament the death of Jesus and repent of their involvement in it.

23:28 Weep for yourselves and for your children: In Luke, the tragedy of Jesus' death is part of a larger tragedy, the destruction of the holy city that had rejected and killed God's prophets and even now does not recognize the time of its visitation by God (see 19:41–44; 21:20–24).

23:29–30 Blessed are the barren: Normally, to be childless was considered a great misfortune. In the eschatological times, however, it is better not to have a family (see 1 Cor. 7:25–31). Luke here takes eschatological imagery and applies it to the tragic historical event of the destruction of Jerusalem in the war of 66–70, which was already in the past as he writes (see on 21:7–33). **Then they will begin to say to the mountains, "Fall on us":** This too is eschatological imagery (see Rev. 6:16) that Luke applies to the destruction of Jerusalem. Jesus here looks forward not to the Last Judgment, but to the coming historical judgment of the terrors of the destruction of Jerusalem. Just as the impending crucifixion means the suffering of an innocent person at the hands of Rome because of the city's rejection of its Messiah, so in the coming war it will be especially the innocent who will suffer, and it will be better not to have children.

23:32 Two others also, who were criminals: Luke does not specify their offense. Their traditional designation as "thieves" is taken from the older translations of Matt. 27:44.

23:34 Father, forgive them: Though absent from some of the oldest and best manuscripts, Jesus' first saying from the cross is typically Lukan: Jesus prays (6:12; 9:18, 28; 22:40–46; 23:46); Jesus forgives his persecutors, practicing in the most extreme circumstance what he has taught his disciples (6:27); those who perpetrate the evil deed do so in ignorance (see 9:45; 18:34; Acts 3:17; 7:60; 13:27; 17:30). The first Christian martyr will pray a similar prayer, rather than asking for God's vengeance on his murderers (Acts 7:60). **Cast lots to divide his clothing:** See Ps. 22:18, and commentary at John 19:24.

23:35 The people . . . the leaders: In Luke, the crowds and bystanders do not join in the mocking (see on 23:27), and it is only the leaders who are guilty. **Let him save himself:** This challenge is repeated by the leaders, the soldiers (v. 37), and one of the criminals (v. 39), emphasizing their misunderstanding of Jesus' teaching in 17:33. Jesus was hailed by the

angels at his birth as the Savior (2:10), and now the scandalous truth is revealed that the saving plan of God includes the death of Jesus. In Luke's understanding, Jesus' death is part of the saving plan of God, but he has no theory of the atoning death of Jesus (see on 22:20).

23:36 Sour wine: Wine was sometimes given to the condemned man as a sedative, but here it seems to be a part of the mockery.

23:38 This is the King of the Jews: Since crucifixion was intended as a deterrent, the offense for which the condemned was being executed was posted on the cross. This inscription shows that Jesus was killed by the Romans on a political charge, not by the Jews on a religious charge. That Jesus was indeed the anointed king in the coming kingdom of God is the ironic truth of the placard (see 4:43). (See excursus, "Why Was Jesus Killed?" at Mark 14:53.)

23:39–43 One of the criminals: This scene is only in Luke. Mark has both criminals revile Jesus, but Jesus does not respond (Mark 15:32). It symbolically represents that the cross of Jesus erected in our world divides people into those who respond in faith and repentance and those who continue to rebel and reject him. **This man has done nothing wrong:** The leading motif throughout has been that Jesus is innocent (see 23:4, 14–15, 22, 47). **Remember me when you come into your kingdom:** The meaning is not precisely clear, just as whether Luke wrote "in" or "into" is not certain (see NRSV footnote). It is clear that the dying criminal recognizes that the placard "King of the Jews" is somehow true, and that the rule of God represented in Jesus will somehow be vindicated. How he came to know this, the story is not concerned to tell us, but the reader who has followed the narrative throughout, and knows that the kingdom of God stands at the center of Jesus' life and ministry, understands (see summary and references in comments at 4:43). **Today you will be with me in Paradise:** The abode of the blessed dead is sometimes called paradise (e.g. 2 Cor. 12:4; Rev. 2:7). Here Jesus and the dying criminal are pictured as going directly to the realm of the blessed (see 16:19–23). Elsewhere Luke portrays the blessed life after death in terms of a future resurrection (14:14; 20:36; Acts 24:15). In neither case is Luke concerned to give a chronology or geography of what happens after death, but to affirm that death is not the end for those who trust in God. This faith is pictured in more than one way by New Testament authors, ways that cannot be integrated into one systematic picture.

23:44 Noon . . . until three in the afternoon: Luke does not designate the time when the execution began, omitting Mark's note that it was 9:00 a.m. (see Mark 15:25). **Darkness came over the whole land:** The same word may be translated "earth" or "land" (see NRSV footnote). In Mark, the darkness was probably to be understood as a cosmic sign of eschatological proportions, so the translation "earth" is appropriate. For Luke, the crucifixion is a tragic historical event marked by portents in the natural world, which he pictures as an eclipse that covered the whole land (of Judea). In terms of astronomy, an eclipse could not occur at Passover, the time of the full moon, but Luke is concerned with theological meaning, not astronomy.

23:45 The curtain of the temple was torn in two: Jesus had predicted that the temple would be destroyed (21:6), and the destruction already begins, to be completed in the disastrous war of 66–70, which Luke also links to the death of Jesus in 23:27–31. The tearing of the temple veil was interpreted theologically in Heb. 9:6–28 as the abolition of the separation between God and humanity by the sacrificial death of Jesus. Luke understands it as one of the portents (like the darkness) that revealed the transcendent significance of the death of Jesus.

23:46 Father, into your hands I commit my spirit (NIV): "Spirit" means simply "breath," "life." Luke has replaced the despairing cry of Ps. 22:1, "My God, my God, why have you abandoned me?" found in Mark 15:34 with a quotation from Ps. 31:5, a psalm of quiet confidence and trust. As Jesus' prayer of forgiveness was a model followed by his disciples, so his dying prayer of trust in God is echoed by Stephen (Acts 7:59).

23:47 Praised God: The way *Jesus* died brought glory to *God*, just as throughout his ministry the mighty acts of Jesus were seen as the work of God (see theocentric emphasis of Luke's Christology throughout, e.g., 7:16; 8:24, 38; 9:20–22, 43; 13:13; 17:15; 19:37). **Certainly this man was innocent:** Luke replaces Mark's christological affirmation (Mark 15:39) with a political judgment. Rome recognizes that Jesus' death was a great miscarriage of justice, that in executing Jesus they had killed an innocent man. This political dimension of the Christian faith, the status of Christians in the Roman empire in Luke's own time, is a major theme throughout Luke–Acts (see introduction to Luke: "Theological Themes").

23:48 All the crowds . . . returned home, beating their breasts: See on v. 27. The crucifixion scene closes on a dismal, shattering note. Luke's readers know already that the resurrection is to follow, but Luke does not rush to the joy of Easter morning. Easter can be grasped only by those who have stood at the cross and pondered their own involvement in the sins of humanity that have led to the rejection of God's definitive revelation in Jesus. The tax collector who lamented and beat his breast in repentance (18:13) did not presume that he would go home justified, and the mourners at the crucifixion did not already anticipate the resurrection. In both cases, grace can only be amazing grace.

23:49 The women who had followed him from Galilee: See on 8:1–3. They are not named until 24:10. Here and in v. 55 they serve as the guarantors of continuity between the pre-Easter ministry of Jesus and the resurrected Christ.

23:50–56
THE BURIAL
(See also at Matt. 27:57–61; Mark 15:42–47; John 19:38–42)

23:50–51 A member of the council: Luke has frequently distinguished between the people as a whole and their leaders, charging only the latter with responsibility for Jesus' death. He now indicates that even this cannot be a blanket charge, that there were **good and righteous** people among the Jewish leaders. **Waiting expectantly for the kingdom of God:** See on 4:43.

23:53 A rock-hewn tomb where no one had ever been laid: As Jesus had entered into Jerusalem on a colt on which no one had ever ridden before (19:30), so he is buried in a tomb in which no one has ever been placed. As he was laid in a borrowed manger when he was born, so he is laid in a borrowed tomb at his death. "No Vacancy" has been the response of the world from beginning to end.

23:54 The day of Preparation: The Jewish word for Friday, because one prepared for the Sabbath on Friday (see Mark 15:42).

23:56 Prepared spices and ointments: What does one do after such a shaking, catastrophic event? Nothing seems appropriate. At such times the importance of rituals becomes apparent. They prepared to complete the funeral arrangements, the anointing of the body that could not be done on Friday. Then they observed the Sabbath as usual. As the story of Jesus had begun in the temple among observant Jews, so his life comes to an end among pious women who observe the Jewish Sabbath, as Jesus himself had done (4:16). That they prepared to anoint the body on Sunday morning shows that, despite Jesus' announcements, his disciples did not anticipate the resurrection. They supposed the story was over (see 24:21).

24:1–12

THE WOMEN DISCOVER THE EMPTY TOMB
(See also at Matt. 28:1–8; Mark 16:1–8; John 20:1–13)

For general considerations in interpreting the resurrection faith, see excursus, "Interpreting the Resurrection," at Matt. 28:1. Luke retells the Markan story of the discovery of the empty tomb (Mark 16:1–8 = Luke 24:1–12) with modifications and additions to express his own theological perspective. He then adds three additional stories found in none of the other Gospels: the appearance to the two disciples on the road to Emmaus (24:13–35), the appearance to the apostles in Jerusalem (24:36–49), and the ascension (24:50–53), all of which happen in the environs of Jerusalem on the first Easter Sunday.

24:1 The first day of the week: Sunday, not a holy day in the Jewish or Roman calendar, and not previously mentioned in Luke. As the day of Jesus' resurrection, Sunday became the Lord's Day (Rev. 1:10), replacing the Jewish Sabbath as the Christian holy day. Henceforth, Christians would gather on this day for worship, including the reading of Scripture, preaching, presenting of offerings for God's work, and celebration of the Eucharist (Matt. 28:1; Mark 16:2; John 20:1, 19; Acts 20:7; 1 Cor. 16:2; Rev. 1:10). **They came:** The women of 23:49, 55, including (but in Luke not limited to) Mary Magdalene, Joanna, Mary the mother of James (see v. 10). There were, of course, no chapter divisions in the ancient manuscripts, so "they" binds this story most closely with the preceding. The story of Jesus' death is incomplete without the resurrection; the Easter story cannot begin here but must presuppose the story of the cross. **Taking the spices:** The women had not come expecting a resurrection, but expecting to complete the burial procedures interrupted by the Sabbath.

24:2 They found the stone rolled away: The stone has not been previously mentioned in Luke, who presupposes his Markan source. The tomb was cut out of solid rock, sealed with a large wheel-like stone that rolled in a track before the entrance. Luke does not mention any guard at the tomb or any concern by the

women about how they would move the stone. In none of the New Testament Gospels is the resurrection itself described; it had already happened when the empty tomb was discovered or when Jesus appeared to his disciples. The reality of the resurrection is witnessed to by the stories of the empty tomb and the appearances, but "what really happened" at the resurrection event itself is something that the New Testament veils as a divine mystery.

24:4 They were perplexed about this: Seeing the empty tomb itself did not generate faith but perplexity. The bare fact needs interpretation. **Two men:** Called "angels" in 24:23. As angels had heralded Jesus' birth (2:8–14), so they announce his resurrection. Luke's high evaluation of angels as a way of talking about the activity of God is not shared by all New Testament authors (see on Rom. 8:38). What is described here as objectively real is called a "vision" in 24:23. Luke was unconcerned with the modern distinction between objective and subjective reality and often uses the word "vision" to express the manifestation of transcendent realities (1:22; Acts 2:17; 9:10, 12; 10:3, 17, 19; 11:5; 12:9; 16:10; 18:9; 26:19). The dazzling clothes of the two "men" indicate that they belong to the transcendent world (see 9:29).

24:5–6 Bowed their faces to the ground: In worship, which is not here rebuked (see Acts 10:25–26; 14:15; Colossians 2:18; Rev. 19:10; 22:8–9). Colossians 2:18 opposes both worship of angels and interest in visions. **The men said to them:** Verses 6–7, a summary of the Christian message of Jesus' death and resurrection, are added by Luke to the Markan story. Luke alters the Markan command to go to Galilee to a command to **remember** what Jesus had said in **Galilee**. Having reached Jerusalem, the disciples must not return to Galilee (see on 24:49). **He . . . has risen:** Better translated "He has been raised (by God)." The resurrection was not something Jesus did, but something God did for the dead and powerless Jesus. Just as Jesus did not die but was killed, so Jesus did not rise but was raised (see Acts 2:36; 3:15; 4:10). **Remember:** Emphasized again in v. 8. The word of Jesus now lies in the past, and must be remembered and heard in the post-Easter perspective (see 22:61; Acts 11:16; 20:35).

24:7 The Son of Man must be handed over: The angels rehearse the passion predictions Jesus had repeatedly made (9:21–22, 44; 12:50; 13:32–34; 17:25; 18:31–34). Only Luke has "Son of Man" as part of the resurrection story (see on 5:24; Mark 2:10).

24:9 The eleven: The apostles, minus Judas. **The rest:** See on 6:12–13. In contrast to Mark, where the women are commanded to tell the apostles but say nothing to anyone, here the women receive no command from the angels, but act on their own initiative in telling the apostles. Luke follows Mark in that the risen Christ does not appear to the women (contrast Matt. 28:9–10; John 20:1–18).

24:10 Mary Magdalene: The women are finally named. On Mary Magdalene and Joanna, see at 8:2. **Mary the mother of James:** Taken by Luke from Mark 15:40; 16:1, otherwise unidentified. The mother of Jesus is strangely absent, but she reappears in Acts 1:14. As in 8:1–3, Luke mentions that there were other women whose names he does not report.

24:11 These words seemed to them an idle tale: The apostles hear of the empty tomb first from the women, but it does not produce faith in them, just as it had not in the women themselves. The empty tomb can be explained otherwise than by Christian faith in the resurrection, as Matthew also knows (Matt. 28:11–15).

24:12 Peter . . . ran to the tomb: This verse is not in some ancient manuscripts and may represent cross-fertilization in the copying process between John 20:3–10 and the Lukan story (it was thus omitted by the RSV), but most scholars now consider it a part of the original text of Luke. According to v. 24, Peter was accompanied by other apostles. Seeing the empty tomb for themselves created amazement, not faith. On the **linen cloths** see John 20:6–7.

To this point, the female and male disciples of Jesus have seen the empty tomb, been reminded of Jesus' teaching, and seen a vision of angels, but as yet there are no Christian believers. The Markan story ended at this point, but Luke's additions will provide profound reflections on how Christian faith in the resurrection actually arises, and on what basis.

24:13–35
JESUS APPEARS TO TWO ON THE ROAD TO EMMAUS

This resurrection story, more elaborate than any other in the Synoptic Gospels, is found only in Luke and reveals most clearly his own understanding of the meaning of the resurrection faith (see excursus, "Interpreting the Resurrection," on Matt. 28:1).

24:13 Two of them: Members of the wider community of Jesus' followers composed of apostles and disciples (see on 6:12–13). **That same day:** Sunday, to become the Christian Easter. **Village called Emmaus:** Its location is still unidentified. Most manuscripts say it was sixty stadia (seven miles) from Jerusalem, though some say 160 stadia (nineteen miles).

24:14 Talking with each other: The setting for the revelatory encounter with the risen Christ was a discussion among his disciples about the meaning of the events **that had happened** among them.

24:16 Their eyes were kept from recognizing him: See 9:45; 18:34; John 21:4. The passive voice points to God as the actor. That Jesus' disciples did not perceive the meaning of the Christ event until after their encounter with the risen Christ and reception of the Spirit is seen in retrospect as part of the divine plan. This is a theological way of saying that merely being with the earthly Jesus, hearing his teaching, and seeing his miracles and the example of his life are inadequate apart from the revelation of the risen Christ and the gift of the Holy Spirit. Recognizing God's act in Jesus is not a matter of human insight but is itself a divine gift. This means that those who have this faith know that they cannot congratulate themselves but must give thanks to God for it (1 Cor. 2:6–16; Eph. 2:8–10).

24:18 Cleopas: Otherwise unknown.

24:19 What things?: Luke's story reflects the pattern of stories of pagan gods in which the incognito deity feigns ignorance in order to investigate what mortals really think and do (see also v. 28). Luke's Bible also contained stories of the unrecognized divine visitor (Gen. 18; Judg. 6:11–24; Tobit). **Jesus of Nazareth . . . a prophet mighty in deed and word:** Their summary was not wrong but did not perceive that Jesus was the promised Messiah and Savior, despite—or because of—his death on the cross. They recite the correct events but still do not perceive what has happened, as in 9:20 Peter had recited the correct words without perceiving Jesus' true identity.

God's saving work in Jesus was a matter of both word and deed. He spoke the word of God, just as did his later followers in the church (5:1; 8:11, 21; 11:28; Acts 4:31; 6:2, 7; 8:14; 11:1; 12:24; 13:5, 7, 46; 17:13; 18:11), and his deeds reflected the divine justice and mercy that represent the kingdom of God, just as his later disciples not only spoke the gospel but embodied it in their lives (e.g., Luke 4:18–19; 5:17–26, 29–31; 9:1–6, 10–17; 10:1–12; Acts 2:43–47; 3:1–10; 4:32–37; 11:27–30). Word and deed were an integrated whole in both Jesus' life and the life of the early church. In Acts 6:1–7, for example, the church's provision for the poor is called the spread of the word of God. All recognize that words without deeds are hypocritical and hollow; it is also true that deeds without the word of the gospel do not point to God's act in Christ as the source and norm of loving conduct. While the church in the past has been guilty of speaking without acting, the modern church may sometimes be guilty of acting without speaking the word of God.

24:20 Our chief priests and leaders: Again Luke distinguishes leaders from the people as a whole and makes (some of) them responsible for Jesus' death.

24:21 We had hoped: The birth of Jesus had been the birth of hope (2:10–14, 25–32). Jesus' followers were not cool cynics who thought it foolish to believe that the present unjust world is the final state of things, which one must simply accept and make the best of, but neither were they "optimists" who always looked on the bright side. They believed that God was present in Jesus' word and works and that God's kingdom of justice was about to dawn. Then came the crucifixion and the shattering of their hopes. Human wisdom says, "While there's life, there's hope." The death of Jesus had been the death of hope. They had Jesus' message, his example, and his mighty deeds, but the crucifixion meant that Jesus was only another failed idealist, and they had no reason to believe that Jesus' way was right despite, or even because of, his death on the cross. Human wisdom had written, "The End," but by the resurrection God wrote, "To Be Continued."

The **one to redeem Israel:** The hope that God would send the Messiah was sometimes expressed in the Jewish imagery of the restoration of the nation and its freedom from oppression. These disciples still perceive God's redeeming work in these nationalistic terms, but such imagery can point to the larger horizon of God's redeeming work for all. Luke has utilized this imagery (1:68–79; 22:30) but interprets it as God's act in Christ for all peoples, as the continuing story that unfolds in Acts will show.

24:23 A vision of angels: The men in dazzling garments seen by the women at the tomb are here called angels, and the experience is called a vision (see 1:22; 24:4).

24:25–26 Slow of heart to believe all that the prophets have declared: Jesus rebukes his dis-

ciples, not for having the wrong information, but for not interpreting it in the light of the Scripture and the resurrection. **Necessary that the Messiah should suffer and then enter into glory:** The resurrection of Jesus did not merely restore Jesus to the ordinary life of this world (which would be a resuscitation; see 7:11–17; 8:40–56) but raised him to the eternal world of God, never to die again (see Rom. 6:9; Heb. 7:16, 25). Luke repeatedly sees the revelation of God in the Christ event in continuity with the revelation of God in Scripture (16:27–31). Who Jesus is cannot be grasped apart from the revelation of God's purpose in the Scripture, just as from the Christian perspective the meaning of the Old Testament is incomplete until it is seen as pointing to the definitive act of God in Christ. Jesus was not a "great personality" whose identity is resident in himself; he is who he is as the climactic fulfillment of God's purposes as revealed in Scripture. Luke understands that the Old Testament as a whole points to God's ultimate act in Christ; the way he expresses this conviction is that all the Old Testament prophets predicted the coming of Christ (see excursus, "New Testament Interpretation of the Old Testament," at 1 Cor. 15:3). This understanding of the Scriptures of Israel, the Christian Old Testament, is itself an expression of the Christian faith, not a charge that if Jews believed their own Scripture, they would see that it points them to Christ. Christians read their Old Testament Scripture in the light of their faith in Jesus as the Christ, the Risen One. Luke knows that the Christian meaning of the Old Testament is not transparent, but requires interpretation (see on Acts 8:26–35; 2 Cor. 3:12–18).

24:27 He interpreted to them the things about himself in all the scriptures: After Easter, Jesus' disciples eagerly reread their Bible in the light of their Christian faith, and discovered there many passages that illustrated their new faith. They did not give credit for these new insights to their own wisdom or cleverness, but believed that the risen Christ, through the Spirit, was guiding them into the true meaning of the Scriptures (see John 2:22; 12:16; 16:12–13; 20:9; 1 Pet. 1:10). In this beautifully composed symbolic scene, Luke compresses the gradual process of reinterpreting the Scripture under the guidance of the risen Christ into a single scene (see the similar technique in Acts 2:1–47; see there).

24:29 They urged him strongly: They do not recognize him as the Christ, but only as a weary fellow traveler, and they extend the invitation to food and fellowship. As they do that, Christ is revealed to them (see Matt. 25:31–46).

24:30 He took bread, blessed and broke it: Christ had not forced himself on them, but when invited, the guest becomes the host. The words are the familiar words of the eucharistic celebration (see 9:16; 22:19), but the meal is an "ordinary" meal, not a communion service. As in Acts, the boundary between "ordinary" meals and the Eucharist grows thin. Every meal can point to the risen Christ.

24:31 Then their eyes were opened, and they recognized him: As their eyes had been closed by God (see on v. 16), so now they are opened by God. The revelation is a gift that cannot be manipulated. **He vanished from their sight:** That Christ *had been present* among them is made known in the breaking of bread. This corresponds to Luke's understanding that Christ was once present among us, is now absent, and will return to bring the kingdom of God to fulfillment (see introduction to Luke: "Jesus as the 'Midst of Time'"). While some New Testament authors and some strands of later Christian theology emphasized the real presence of Christ at the Eucharist, Luke (and Mark) look backward in history, forward to the Parousia, and upward to the transcendent world for the presence of Christ (see excursus, "The Lord's Supper in the New Testament," at 1 Cor. 11:24). They do not picture Christ as present at the church's celebration of Holy Communion. In Acts, Luke portrays the church as breaking bread together, but does not picture Christ as present at the eucharistic celebrations. In Luke's schema, Christ is in heaven, from whence he will return at the Parousia (Acts 1:6–11), and from heaven he sometimes reveals himself or speaks to special messengers (Acts 9:1–17). From heaven, Christ has sent the Holy Spirit to empower and accompany the church in its earthly mission (Acts 2:1–36). This is Luke's christological schema, but perhaps it should not be pressed too rigidly in this scene that pictures the church, under the guidance of the risen Christ, gathering about the Table, reading its Scripture with new eyes, and receiving the assurance that Christ is risen indeed. The Lukan church eats and drinks together, breaks bread in Jesus' name, and does so in the power and presence of the Holy Spirit that represents Christ (Acts 20:7). Thus, while Luke does not have the explicit doctrine of the eucharistic presence of Christ found elsewhere in the

New Testament, he may well share Mark's dialectical view of the presence/absence of Christ (see on Mark 14:25).

24:33 That same hour: Luke has all these events happen on one symbolic day. Since it was already evening when they began the meal, this is difficult to imagine historically, and would call for the ascension of 24:51 to have happened at night. The narrative is symbolic throughout, but points to the reality of what happened in the church's experience after Easter. **Jerusalem:** This was the goal of the pilgrimage of the earthly Jesus (9:51) and becomes the center for the mission of the early church. **The eleven and their companions:** The twelve apostles (minus Judas) and the larger circle of Jesus' disciples (see on 6:12–13).

24:34 The Lord has risen indeed, and has appeared to Simon: The reader hears the overtones of early Christian liturgy and creedal statements (see 1 Cor. 15:3–5). As in Mark 16:7 and 1 Cor. 15:5, the risen Christ appears first to Peter (see Luke 22:31–32; contrast John 20:1–18). This scene is never narrated but in each instance happens offstage.

24:35 What had happened to them on the road: After Easter, under the guidance of the Spirit, the community of Jesus' disciples reread their Bible with new eyes, and found that it testified to them of Christ. The report of Jesus' life and teachings, his martyr death, even the report of the empty tomb had not made the reality of the Christ event present to them. But as they worshiped together around the Lord's Table, the meaning of Christian faith and the reality of the risen Lord became real. Scripture and Eucharist were the setting and means for reinterpreting the story of Jesus, now seen in a new light.

24:36–43
JESUS APPEARS TO HIS DISCIPLES
(See also at John 20:19–23)

24:36 While they were talking: The disciples are gathered at the table (see vv. 41–42). As in 24:15, Jesus becomes present as they talk with each other about the Easter events. **Peace be with you:** This is the customary Jewish greeting, "Shalom," here filled with new meaning (see Rom. 5:1; Phil. 4:7).

24:37 They were startled and terrified: In the New Testament stories of the resurrection, the appearance of the Risen One is often met at first with doubt and consternation (see, e.g., Matt. 28:18). The resurrection was not an unambiguous event that could have been captured by a video camera, but was a mysterious phenomenon that could be interpreted more than one way and could evoke doubt and fear as well as faith and joy. **Thought they were seeing a ghost:** See Mark 6:49–50, omitted by Luke. The New Testament is concerned to guard against *misunderstandings* of the resurrection. While it is presumptuous to suppose that the mystery of the resurrection can be reduced to the categories of human understanding (see 1 Cor. 15:35–49), misunderstandings can be avoided. Just as the resurrection is not a resuscitation (see on 7:11–17; 8:40–56), so the risen Lord is not a ghost. Luke portrays the body of the risen Christ as having **flesh and bones** (v. 39) and eating **a piece of broiled fish** (v. 42) to dispel the idea that he is only an apparition. Paul, on the other hand, denies that the resurrection is a matter of flesh and blood, to dispel the idea that the resurrection life is merely a continuation of the conditions of this-worldly existence (1 Cor. 15:50; see on Luke 20:27–40). The New Testament thus pictures the reality of the resurrection in different ways that are not to be harmonized. Each image brings out some theological meaning of the resurrection or closes the door to some misunderstanding; the variety of imagery points to the divine mystery that cannot be captured in one representation.

24:41 In their joy they were still disbelieving: Again Luke spares the disciples (see 22:45).

24:44–53
JESUS' LAST WORDS AND ASCENSION

At the close of his Gospel, very late on the first Easter Sunday, Luke pictures Jesus as blessing the disciples and ascending to heaven (though a few ancient manuscripts, apparently to avoid a conflict with Acts, omit the ascension in 24:51). In Acts 1:9–11, after a forty-day period of instructing the disciples, Luke pictures Jesus as promising his disciples that the Holy Spirit would come upon them, and then ascending to heaven. Thus Luke has two "reports" of the ascension, on different days. That Luke consciously does this, and in Acts 1:2 even refers back to the ascension in the Gospel before narrating the "second" ascension in Acts, shows that theology, not chronology, is his point, and that he is perfectly aware of this. "God raised up Jesus and made him Lord of all" is central to the Christian faith (see Phil. 2:5–11), but it can be pictured in a variety of ways, even by the same biblical author. On objectifying language, see on Acts 1:9.

Only Luke narrates the ascension as an event separate from the resurrection (though see John 20:17). Paul's view is more typical of other New Testament authors, for whom Christ was exalted to heaven at the resurrection, so that all the appearances of the Risen One were from heaven (1 Cor. 15:3–11).

24:44–45 These are my words: This does not refer to a particular previous teaching but is a summary of Jesus' message, now seen in post-Easter perspective. **The law of Moses, the prophets, and the psalms:** This represents the Hebrew Scriptures as a whole, the three divisions of which are the Torah (Genesis–Deuteronomy), the Prophets (Joshua–2 Kings; Isaiah–Malachi), and the Writings (the rest of the Old Testament books, represented here by Psalms). The Law and Prophets had long been standard elements in the Hebrew canon of Scriptures, but in Luke's time at the end of the first century, the final decisions as to what books were to be included in the Writings were still in the process of being made. Luke's point is that the Scripture as a whole points to Christ as the fulfillment of God's purpose. **Opened their minds:** See on 24:27, 35; 2 Cor. 3:12–18. The insights given to the two disciples on the road are now given to all the apostles and disciples. Acts 2:22–32 gives an example of how Luke understands the Old Testament to testify to Christ's resurrection.

24:46–47 To be proclaimed . . . to all nations: The Gospel closes with the risen Christ commissioning his disciples to bear the good news of what God has done in the Christ event to all nations. The community of Jesus' disciples is not merely a support group of individuals that celebrate their own spiritual quest and private salvation, but is the continuing people of God with a mission to the world. **That the Messiah is to suffer and rise from the dead:** The content of the message centers on the death and resurrection of Jesus (1 Cor. 15:3–5), and this is what the church proclaims in Acts. The gospel of the kingdom of God that Jesus has preached (see on 4:43) now becomes the gospel of what God has done in Jesus. The proclaimer becomes the proclaimed, but the kingdom of God is the common denominator that binds together the message of Jesus and the message of the church.

Repentance and forgiveness of sins: The content of the gospel; see on 3:2–3, 7–9, and introduction to Luke: "Theological Themes: Repentance and Forgiveness of Sins." Acts will record the struggle of early Christianity to fulfill this mandate that the gospel is "to all nations," for all. What Acts presents as a gradual dawning of insight, Luke here pictures as the command of the risen Lord (see on Acts 10:14–15).

24:48 You are witnesses of these things: See on Acts 1:8.

24:49 I am sending upon you what my Father promised: The Holy Spirit, who will empower the disciples for the mission ahead of them (Acts 1:5). **Stay here in the city:** In Luke the disciples obey these words spoken on the first Easter evening and do not return to Galilee (contrast Mark 16:7; Matt. 28:16–20; John 21). For Luke, to return to Galilee would be a rever-

sal of the course of the Gospel, which began in Galilee, moved to Jerusalem, and from the temple city and capital of Judaism goes into all the world (Acts 1:8).

24:52 They worshiped . . . with great joy: The Gospel ends in the temple, as it had begun, on the note of worship and joy. Luke here achieves closure to the Gospel story, which can be read meaningfully by itself. But it also points ahead to the continuing story of the church in Acts.

The Gospel according to John

INTRODUCTION

For the nature of New Testament Gospel writings, see "Introduction to the Gospels." While John contains some historical materials, the author has interpreted, modified, and expanded them to interpret the meaning of God's presence in Jesus for his own time. He claims—and the church accepted this claim—to have done this reinterpretation under the guidance of the Holy Spirit (see 14:15–17, 25–26; 15:26–27; 16:26–27). As in the other Gospels, the pre-Easter life of Jesus is retold from the perspective of the post-Easter faith, but in John this is made more explicit; not only *did* not the eyewitnesses understand what was really happening in the life of Jesus, they *could* not do so until after the resurrection and the gift of the Spirit (see 7:39; chaps. 14–16). This is John's way of saying that the meaning of Jesus' life is not apparent on the basis of historical, "objective" research but is the gift of God. Whoever understands the life and message of Jesus as the presence of God's grace cannot take credit for this insight on the basis of his or her intelligence or achievement, but can only give thanks for the insight that comes by the Spirit. This is the perspective from which the Gospel is written.

Author

Like the other Gospels, the Gospel of John is anonymous. The titles given to the canonical Gospels late in the second century express the traditions that were current at that time. More importantly, the titles represent the church's claim that the contents of the Gospels represent the apostolic faith, i.e., that they present the Christ event as understood by its authorized interpreters. From the time of Irenaeus (ca. 180), but not earlier, the Fourth Gospel was known as the Gospel of John, and understood to be the composition of John the son of Zebedee, one of Jesus' original twelve disciples (Mark 1:19–20; 3:16–19; Matt. 4:21; 10:2; Luke 5:10). This claim is not supported by the Gospel itself. The Gospel itself never refers to the disciple John (though see 21:2). One of Jesus' followers present at the Last Supper and in the story of Jesus' trial, crucifixion,

and resurrection is called "the disciple whom Jesus loved" (see on 13:23–24). He represents the authoritative witness that stands behind the Gospel, and the concluding comment in the epilogue may attribute the composition of the Gospel to this anonymous Beloved Disciple, though this is not clear (see on 21:24). The name John was apparently attributed to the author because tradition had identified him with the author of Revelation, whose name was indeed John (Rev. 1:4, 9). This John, however, was not one of the Twelve (see introduction to Revelation).

We will continue the tradition of referring to the book and the author as "John," though we do not know his (or her) real name. Though it would satisfy our curiosity, knowing the author's name is theologically unimportant and does not affect the authority of the Gospel as holy Scripture, for the Gospel is offered to the church and the world not as the composition of an individual author, but as representing the "we" of the early Christian community that transmitted the apostolic faith (see the "we" of 1:14, 16; 3:11–12; 4:22; 9:4; 1 John 1:1; 4:1 and the comments there). Here and elsewhere, the New Testament is not an individualistic document, but the church's book—written, preserved, translated, and interpreted within the community of faith (see "Introduction: The New Testament as the Church's Book").

Sources

John had predecessors. In the view of most scholars, the Gospel of Mark was the earliest Gospel (see introduction to Mark). Mark created a distinctive new narrative form as the vehicle of Christian faith. Matthew and Luke then adapted, expanded, and reinterpreted Mark for their later situations. Did John do the same? The ancient church was of the general opinion that John knew the other Gospels and wrote last as a "supplement" and "theological interpretation" of them. The Synoptics were supposed to tell the history, for which John composed a theological interpretation—hence the traditional title "St. John the Divine (= theologian)."

It is now clear that all the Gospels, and not just John, are combinations of historical facts and theological interpretations of the Christ event, and that when John and the Synoptics differ, it is sometimes John who has the more "historical" account. Today the majority opinion among scholars is that John is independent of the Synoptics. It is certainly true that John does not incorporate material from Matthew, Mark, and Luke as sources the way Matthew and Luke use Mark and Q as sources. John is quite different in outline and content from the Synoptics (see below), but this need not mean that he did not know them at all. It seems more likely that he knew they existed and was sometimes influenced by their form and even their wording. For the majority of the Gospel, the author had his own traditions and sources not used in the Synoptics. These may have included some written sources such as a collection of Jesus' "signs," and John may have had a written source for the passion story. In any case, he used his traditions and sources in an independent manner as he interpreted his materials and composed his Gospel.

Process of Composition

The internal evidence of the Gospel itself suggests that the Gospel was not composed all at once but grew by a series of expansions and revisions. Some of the more obvious indications of this process are:

1. The end of the Last Supper narrative, 14:31, connects seamlessly to 18:1. Thus 15:1–17:26 may represent an insertion into an expanded edition.
2. The present order of chaps. 4–6 is difficult to imagine as original. At the end of chap. 5, Jesus is in Jerusalem. But 6:1, with no transition, presupposes that Jesus is in Galilee. If chaps. 5 and 6 are reversed, this difficulty disappears, for 4:54 connects well with 6:1, and 7:1 follows smoothly after 5:47; see on 4:54.
3. The book seems to come to an end with the concluding words of 20:30–31, yet chap. 21 continues as an epilogue, and another conclusion follows at 21:25.

With some probability the following four stages can be distinguished in the formation of the Gospel of John:

1. The original events as remembered and repeated after Easter by eyewitnesses. For the Johannine community, chief among these was the Beloved Disciple, the original leader and teacher of their community, who was the guarantor of the community's tradition.
2. The original stories and sayings were transmitted in the worship and teaching of the church, expanded and adapted to the needs of the developing community. In this phase, the preaching and teaching of the community reshaped the tradition in its own idiom. Thus the long speeches of Jesus in the Farewell Discourses (chaps. 13–17) are not verbatim reports of Jesus' last words. They are unlike the teaching of Jesus in the Synoptic Gospels but closely resemble the teaching of the community itself as found in 1 John. The community felt free to reshape traditional sayings of Jesus and compose new sayings in his name because it believed the Spirit of Christ was present in the community, and the community was authorized to speak for Jesus.
3. These reformulated traditions formed the basis for the "first edition" of the Gospel, which set forth the work and words of Jesus in a dramatic new way.
4. Some time later, a "second edition" of the Gospel was composed, adding the epilogue of chap. 21 and making other additions and changes. This final edition took into account new insights of the community, especially in its dialogue with the larger church. This is the edition we have, the version of the Gospel that was accepted into the Bible.

Johannine School and Johannine Community

The author represents the Johannine school, a group of theological teachers and interpreters within the Johannine community, a particular stream of early Christianity whose center was apparently Ephesus, on the west coast of Asia Minor, modern Turkey. This Johannine school produced the Gospel and three Letters of John. Though not written by the same author as the Gospel, Revelation also comes from this area and has some points of contact with the Johannine school. For example, both the Gospel and Revelation refer to Christ as the Word (John 1:1, 14; Rev. 19:13); both use Lamb as a central image for Christ (John 1:29, 36; see on 13:1; 18:28; Rev. 5:6 and often); both regard witness/testimony and conquering as important themes (e.g., John 3:11; 16:33; 1 John 1:2; 2:13, and often; Rev. 1:2; 2:7, and often); both understand the Christian community to be guided by Christian prophets who speak the word of the risen Lord by the Spirit (John 14:15–17; 16:12–14; 1 John 4:1–4; Rev. 2:1–3:22); both represent the church as opposed by Jews (John 5:1–18 and often; Rev. 2:9; 3:9). From within the Johannine school, the Gospel of John presents a distinctive interpretation of Christ and the church that was at first suspect in developing "mainstream" Christianity but liked by the stream of Christians later considered to be gnostics and heretics. On gnosticism, see on John 1:1, 14; 18:20; 19:34; 1 Cor. 12:3; 1 Tim. 4:1–5; 6:20–21; 1 John 2:20, 27; Rev. 1:3). The first commentary on John (or any other New Testament document) was written by Heracleon, a gnostic teacher in the mid-second century. The "mainstream" church, developing catholic Christianity, finally overcame its reservations, partly because the Gospel seems to have been slightly revised by the addition of an epilogue (chap. 21) and other additions to bring its theology into line with developing orthodoxy. Thus the Gospel of John, originally written for a distinctive, somewhat sectarian Christian group, was accepted by the mainstream of the church, which thereby received one of its most profound statements of the meaning of Christian faith.

Intended Readership

Some of its earliest readers had apparently been members of the Jewish synagogue, and then excluded after they became Christian believers (see below). This makes the hostility to "the Jews" more understandable—not to say excusable—and also helps the modern reader understand the Jewish focus of the Gospel. John's Gospel is in polemical dialogue with the synagogue, while at the same time affirming its Jewish heritage (4:22).

But not all the original Christian readers were Jewish Christians. The Johannine community also included many Gentiles—probably the majority by the time the Gospel was written. The Gospel reflects the evangelistic effort of the early church to interpret what was originally a gospel message conceived in biblical (Old Testament) and Jewish terms to a public that did not have this background (see on 1:35–51), and is thus particularly valuable for the modern church to study. We too attempt to interpret a faith conceived in biblical and Jewish terms to a secularized world. The Fourth Gospel provides a biblical model for the mission of the church in every generation to interpret its faith afresh to itself and the world.

Conflict with "the Jews"

Jesus, his disciples, and almost all members of the earliest Christian community were Jews. The church began as a faction within Judaism among those Jews who had come to faith in Jesus as the Messiah. The earliest church would have appeared to the external observer as a Jewish sect, like the followers of John the Baptist or the Essene community at Qumran, both of whom were alienated from mainstream Judaism. During the time of Jesus, Judaism contained a variety of groups—Pharisees, Sadducees, Essenes, priests, Levites, sectarian reform movements and baptizing groups such as John the Baptist's, and others. In the Jewish war against Rome (66–70 CE) that devastated Palestine, only one group survived as leaders in the Jewish community—the Pharisees. Under their leadership, a group of rabbis and scholars met intermittently at Jamnia (also spelled Jabneh or Yabneh) for a generation or more. Their purpose was to restructure and regulate the shattered Jewish community. This included discussing and clarifying the canon (i.e., which books belonged in the Jewish Scriptures, determining their official text among the variety of versions in circulation), setting standards and rules for rabbinic ordination, and purging the Jewish community of fringe groups and heretical movements deemed to be dangerous to community life. This setting of boundaries is a normal part of any institution's life. Every religious group must sometime define who is "in" and who is "out," which writings and traditions are authoritative and which are not, who is an authorized religious teacher and who is not. Jewish Christians, gnosticizing Jews, and other sectarian Jewish groups were caught in this squeeze and forced to conform or leave (see "Readership" in introduction to Matthew for an analogous situation).

In Jesus' own day he and his disciples had disputes with other Jews, but there is no indication in the Synoptic Gospels that Jesus or his disciples were threatened with expulsion from Judaism or the synagogue; their conflicts were internal to Judaism. Luke 21:12 indicates this would happen *after* Jesus' death, and the early chapters of Acts present the early church as a group within Judaism, only gradually assuming a separate identity. The Gospel of John reflects the situation of a Christian community sometime later, at the time when the parting of the ways between Jews and Christians had become clear and painful. This community believes it has been rejected, excluded, and persecuted by the leaders of the Jewish community (see 9:22; 12:42; 16:2). For the most part, the opponents are called simply "the Jews," often identified with the "Pharisees." The earlier distinctions are gone; the only Judaism known to John is Pharisaic Judaism. In John's time and place, the term "Jews" is thus not merely an ethnic or religious category. It does not refer to the Jewish people as a whole or all members of the Jewish religious community. Jesus and the earliest disciples were Jews in this sense; the author of the Gospel may also have been an ethnic Jew who had grown up in the synagogue. In the Fourth Gospel, "Jew" sometimes means "Jewish leader," with whom the Jewish population as a whole could be contrasted. Sometimes it means "Judean," i.e., an inhabitant of Judea. Sometimes it means a member of the synagogue who is sympathetic to Jesus (i.e., in the Gospel's time, sympathetic to the Christian faith) but has not made a public declaration. Often "Jew" is used in a representative symbolic sense, to mean those who reject and oppose faith in Jesus as the Messiah (see on 7:11).

It is this last sense that pervades John's narrative. This has had terrible consequences, as the Fourth Gospel has sometimes been used to give a "biblical" basis for anti-Semitic racism. This is a tragic misunderstanding. It remains a problem as to how to translate "the Jews." No one translation ("Judean," "Jewish leader") conveys the complexity of John's meaning (see commentary on 7:11). Thus most modern translations of the Bible, while aware of the difficulty, have found no better solution than to continue to translate the term as "the Jews," but historical explanations must be given to avoid misunderstanding John as delivering wholesale condemnation of the Jewish people. Since most modern readers of the New Testament will tend to think of Christianity and Judaism as two separate religions and to read the negative statements about "the Jews" in the light of modern racism and anti-Semitism, it must be emphasized here that this was not yet the case in the time of the Gospel of John. The conflict in the New Testament had nothing to do with race or racism. *The conflict between the Jews and Jesus and his disciples was an intramural Jewish conflict,* as Catholic/Protestant conflict at the time of the Reformation was not the persecution of one religion by another but an intramural Christian conflict. Also in contrast to the later situation, in which Jews were a religious minority persecuted by the majority representing a different religion, in New Testament times the church was a persecuted religious minority within Judaism, itself a religious minority struggling for its identity in the Roman Gentile world.

Place and Date

The earliest tradition (late second century) locates the Gospel and Letters of John, as well as Revelation, at Ephesus, on the west coast of Asia Minor, modern Turkey. Revelation was certainly written in this area, most probably ca. 95 CE (see introduction to Revelation). The connections between Revelation and the other Johannine literature suggest Ephesus as their location as well.

First John is cited by Polycarp in his letter *To the Philippians,* ca. 115–20, so it was circulating in Asia Minor by then. The Gospel is not directly cited in other extant literature until the middle of the second century, but we know that Heracleon wrote a commentary on it by 150 CE, and we have a papyrus fragment of John 18 from Egypt that must be dated 125–50. The latest date for the Gospel would then be about 125. If the Gospel reflects the Jewish decisions about 80 CE in Jamnia, and the Synoptic Gospels (70–90), then the earliest date would be about 90. The range of possible dates is thus 90–125 CE, with most scholars opting for a date about the turn of the century or a little earlier. Most scholars date the Letters after the Gospel, but some see the Letters as the earliest representatives of the Johannine writings, with the Gospel as their crowning and summarizing definitive statement. Since the Gospel seems to have been revised at least once before attaining its present form, it may be that the Letters were written after some early form of the Gospel, but prior to its present form, which is the latest representative of Johannine theology and its definitive statement.

Outline

In the Synoptic Gospels (Matthew, Mark, and Luke) Jesus' ministry is located in Galilee in the north, climaxed by the one dramatic trip south to Jerusalem, where he is killed. In the Synoptics, Jesus' ministry lasts less than a year. John locates the center of gravity of Jesus' ministry in the south, in Judea, from where he makes a few brief trips to Galilee. In John, Jesus is in Galilee only in 2:1–12; 4:43–54; and 6:1–7:9. After 7:9, Jesus is always in Jerusalem or Judea. Whereas in the Synoptics Jesus attends only one festival, the Passover at which he is killed, in John three Passovers are mentioned (2:13; 6:4; 11:55), indicating a ministry of between two and three years. Other Jewish feasts are mentioned (5:1 [also a Passover?]; 7:2 [Booths, Tabernacles]; 10:22 [Dedication, Hanukkah]), all of which are attended by Jesus. Whereas in the Synoptics Jesus teaches his disciples throughout the Galilean ministry, speaking in brief parabolic and aphoristic sayings, in John all his teaching to his disciples is compressed into one evening, in the extended monologues of the Farewell Discourses at the Last Supper (John 13–17). In the Synoptics the Eucharist is instituted in Jerusalem at the Last Supper, which is a Passover meal. In John the Last Supper is on the night before the Passover meal, and there is no institution of the Eucharist; John's eucharistic teaching is placed earlier, in Galilee, in connection with the feeding of the five thousand (6:51b–58). The narrative thus has a shape very different from the Synoptic story. The theological structure of John's story is represented in the following outline:

For Further Reading

Smith, D. Moody. *John*. Abingdon New Testament Commentaries. Nashville: Abingdon, 1999.

O'Day, Gail R. "The Gospel of John." In *The New Interpreter's Bible*, vol. 9. Nashville: Abingdon Press, 1995.

COMMENTARY

1:1–18
PROLOGUE

There is nothing like this in any of the other Gospels. Before beginning his narrative, John presents a hymnic prelude that places the whole narrative in a cosmic framework. The Prologue lets the reader know in advance what is really happening in the story to follow, although the people in the narrative will not be able to understand until the story is over and the Spirit is given (7:39). Like an overture to an opera or oratorio, it strikes the major themes that will occupy the following narrative:

God as Creator;
the whole universe as God's creation;
the universal revelatory Word of God that
    is present and gives life to the whole
    creation;
the role of the preexistent Christ in creation;
light and darkness;
life and death;
the role of John the Baptist;
the real incarnation of the Word in Jesus;
the world's rejection of Jesus and his
    acceptance by his "own," who are
    children of God born "from above";
the relation of Christian faith to Moses and
    the revelation that came through him;
Jesus' relation to the Father, the one God.

These verses are poetic (with prose insertions in vv. 6–8, 15) and thus probably represent a hymn that was sung in the Johannine community. The early church used hymns with solid theological content as teaching instruments (see on Col. 1:15–20; 3:16, and Phil. 2:6–11). Apart from the prose insertions, the Prologue falls into three parts: The Word at creation (1:1–5), the Word in history (1:9–13), and the Word incarnate and named in Jesus (1:14–18).

1:1 In the beginning: An echo of Gen. 1:1. John's story of Jesus begins not with Bethlehem but with creation. Neither here nor elsewhere in the Bible do we find any interest in mythological stories of what happened *before* creation—in contrast to Gnosticism, which "explained" the evil of the present world with precreation myths that accounted for how one good God could allow a world with evil to come into being. The biblical story begins with creation and unfolds in *this* world, without attempting to offer explanations, defenses, or excuses for the present world. (On Gnosticism, see on John 1:1, 14; 18:20; 19:34; 1 Cor. 12:3; 1 Tim. 4:1–5; 6:20–21; 1 John 2:20, 27; Rev. 1:3.)

The Word: The Greek word is *logos*, which has a wide range of meanings, including word, speech, discourse, language, thought, reason, message, account, document, book. Since *logos* had been used in a wide variety of religious, cultural, and philosophical streams, people from a variety of backgrounds could relate to it. Stoics spoke of the *logos* as the immanent rational principle present in the whole uni-

verse, and conceived of no higher God than this. Platonists thought of the *logos* as a divine rational principle, but posited a God beyond this. John's readers who had no biblical or Jewish background would still find his opening words understandable—there is a divine Reason that permeates the world and makes it a meaningful universe rather than a chaos.

Those from a biblical and Jewish background would think of the creative word of God as in Gen. 1:1, and the prophetic, revelatory word of God that spoke through the Old Testament prophets. In biblical and Jewish tradition, this Word was closely associated with, and sometimes identified with, the creative Wisdom of God (e.g. Prov. 8:22; Wis. 7:22–26; 9:1–2). As in Prov. 8, this Word/Wisdom was sometimes personified or regarded as a heavenly being present with God at creation. In Philo, a first-century Jewish philosopher, this transcendent Word was also called the Son of God, and spoken of as divine, as belonging to the category God. John's theology is certainly indebted to this biblical-Jewish context. A full-blown Wisdom myth may be reconstructed from the numerous references in the Old Testament and Jewish Wisdom literature, but the whole cosmic "career" of Wisdom is never explicitly stated. The following may be the presupposed story of Wisdom:

Wisdom, a preexistent being (Job 28:27;
    Sirach 24:9; Wis. 7:22; Prov. 3:19; 8:30;
    2 En. 30:8), was God's partner or
    helper at the creation (Prov. 8:22–30;
    Sir. 1:1–9; 24:3, 9; Wis. 8:3; 9:4, 9. See
    also Philo).
She sought, and still seeks, a dwelling
    place among human beings, but her
    seeking was in vain (*1 En.* 4:1–3; Prov.
    1:20–32; 9:5–6).
Her preaching was, and is, rejected (Prov.
    1:23; Sir. 6:23; Bar. 3:12).
She came to what was her own (for she had
    created it), but her own did not accept
    her (Sir. 24:6; *1 En.* 42:1–3; 84:3).
So she returned to the heavenly world,
    where she lives in hiding (Job 28:12–17;
    Bar. 3:15).
Though people seek her now, they can no
    longer find her. God alone knows the
    way to her (*1 En.* 5:8; 91:10; Wis. 7:14,
    27; Job 28:20–33; Bar. 3:19–31).
Nevertheless there are rare exceptions,
    people to whom Wisdom reveals her-
    self, who accept her, and whom she

thereby makes friends of God and prophets (Wis. 7:12).

She will reappear at the last times, when her spirit will dwell in the Son of Man; he will act in the power of Wisdom and execute judgment (*1 En.* 49:1–4).

The word *logos* had also developed Christian connotations by John's time. The Christian message, the good news of God's saving act in Christ, was sometimes called simply "the word" (e.g., 1 Thess. 1:6, 8; Rom. 9:6; Acts 4:4). From this perspective, John would be claiming that the life-giving word of the Christian message is the same creative word of God of Gen. 1 (see 2 Cor. 4:1–6). The Word of God that addresses us in Christian preaching is the same Word encountered in creation, in the prophetic word of the Old Testament, and definitively in Jesus Christ. **With God . . . was God:** John believes in only one God (17:3), and that as Son of God Christ is subordinate to the Father (14:28). Thus he can speak of the preexistent Christ as a separate being who was "with" God. Yet John can use God language of Christ (20:30) and have the earthly Jesus declare, "The Father and I are one" (10:30). The preexistent Christ, the One incarnate in Jesus, is no less than God, though there is only one God. John's language oscillates dialectically between these two poles; he does not reduce them to manageable logic, but is unwilling to let go of either pole. John is not yet a Trinitarian theologian, but later Trinitarian theology will attempt to give an appropriate conceptual expression to the divine reality manifest in Jesus.

1:3 All things . . . through him: Since the subject is the Word, one could also translate "through it," but the author may already be thinking of the personal Word incarnate in Christ. For Christ as the agent of creation, see also 1 Cor. 8:6; Col. 1:15–20; Heb. 1:1–4; Rev. 3:14.

1:4 In him was life . . . the light of all people: Here the author claims that the particular revelation made known to Christian faith in Jesus Christ is the same revelation of God universally revealed in the creation to all people (see Acts 14:17 commentary; see the similar dialectic of particular and universal revelation in Ps. 19). When John claims that no one comes to God except through Christ (14:6), this does not mean that those who do not know or believe in Jesus have no knowledge of God. The light of the one God the Creator shines on every human being in the world (v. 9, see NRSV footnote). John does claim that the God known in

creation by people of other religions and none is the God definitively revealed in Jesus. John's theology is that whoever knows God, whether or not they are Christian, knows *this* God (however *they* may describe God).

1:6–8 A man sent from God: John the Baptist (though the Fourth Gospel never uses "the Baptist") is presented without introduction, assuming the readers know who is meant. This is one of several indications that the Gospel is written for initiated readers, insiders to the Christian community, who already know the Christian tradition. The Gospel is written not to inform nonbelievers, but to clarify, strengthen, and even correct the faith of insiders in the Christian community. John does not wait until he has finished the poetic Prologue to insert this prose comment, which anticipates the narrative proper that begins in 1:19. **He himself was not the light:** Ephesus, where the Gospel was probably written (see introduction to John) still had a community of disciples of John the Baptist more than a generation after his death (see on Luke 3:3; Acts 18:25; 19:4). The author emphasizes that John the Baptist was truly a prophet sent from God, but that he was a witness to Jesus the Messiah, not himself the Messiah (see 1:19–34).

1:11 He came to what was his own: The world, for he had made it. **His own people did not accept him:** The Jewish people. While there were many Jewish Christians, most Jews did not come to faith in Christ. By John's time, Christianity had become predominately a Gentile religion. Like Paul (see Rom. 9–11), John struggles with the problem that most of the Messiah's own people did not believe in him as the Messiah and deals with this fundamental problem in the narrative that follows.

1:12 To all who received him: Whether Jews or Gentiles. **Power to become children of God:** John reserves the title Son for Christ. This is in contrast to, e.g., Jesus in the Sermon on the Mount (Matt. 5:9) and Paul (Rom. 8:14, 19 [the Greek text has "sons" in the generic sense]). For the Fourth Gospel, Christian believers become God's children through faith; they have a "supernatural" birth, having God as their father rather than deriving their relation to God from any human source. John has no doctrine of Jesus' virgin birth (see 1:45) but believes that all Christians are "born from above" in a way that involves no human father (see 3:1–16; 1 John 2:29; 3:9; 4:7; 5:1, 18).

1:14 The Word became flesh: Until this point, the sophisticated ancient reader could understand what had been said in his or her own terms. Now comes the scandalous element in the Christian proclamation: not an idea, but an event, something that happened. The Word is the transcendent, the Eternal One, the Creative Word there at the beginning, the Reason that permeates the universe and gives it meaning. The Word is identified with God. "Flesh" is the biblical term for true humanity, humanity in contrast to God (see Gen. 6:12; 9:16; Deut. 5:26; Ps. 56:4; Isa. 31:3; 2 Chr. 32:8; Luke 3:6; Rom. 7:25). In this affirmation, the later church's confession of Christ as truly human and truly God is already implicit. The one true God is manifest in the truly human Jesus of Nazareth. **We have seen his glory:** The form shifts from the narrative third person to the first person plural of the confessing church. The "we" does not refer just to the apostles and literal eyewitnesses but to the whole Christian community (see Deut. 1:30; 5:2–5; John 3:11–15; 21:24; 2 Pet. 1:16–18; 1 John 1:1–3). **Lived among us:** The RSV ("dwelt") and NIV ("made his dwelling") are more precise translations than "lived." John's Greek word means literally "tented," and is related to the Old Testament word for "tabernacle," "tent," and "temple," in which God lived among his people. John will be concerned to show that what the tabernacle and temple stood for is now fully represented by Christ and his community, the new temple (see 2:18–22).

1:17 Law . . . grace: Like Paul, John here contrasts law and grace. Also like Paul, this does not mean that he claims the Law of Moses is superseded by Christ. The following narrative will show in what sense Christians too continue to honor the Law as given by God through Moses.

1:18 No one has ever seen God: But see 14:9 and 2 Cor. 4:6. When Christians are asked what God is like, they point to Jesus, the "human face of God" (J. A. T. Robinson). This knowledge of God is not a matter of human attainment or the achievement of human reasoning. We know God because God has definitively revealed himself in his unique Son, who is himself identified with God. **God the only Son:** See NRSV footnotes. Later manuscripts read simply "Son," but the oldest texts read literally "the only (begotten) God." On "only/only begotten," see on 3:16. Though the phrase is difficult, it is almost certain that the original reading was "God," not "Son." As John began his Prologue with a reference to the Word as

God, so he ends it, and so he will end his Gospel (20:28).

1:19–51
INTRODUCTORY TESTIMONY

Following the poetic Prologue comes a prose introduction that sets the stage for the first of the revelatory signs that will begin Jesus' ministry. It is composed of two parts, the first identifying John the Baptist and the second identifying Jesus.

1:19–34
JOHN AND JESUS
(See also at Matt. 3:1–17; Mark 1:2–8; Luke 3:1–18)

On John the Baptist, see at Luke 1:5–25. That the story of Jesus began with John impressed itself deeply on the memory of the early church (e.g., Acts 10:37), and all the Gospels refer early in the narrative to Jesus' baptism by John. This also constituted a problem for early Christianity, which was concerned to show that in God's plan John was subordinate to Jesus. Each of the Gospels does this in a different way. John is the most extensive and pointed, the most concerned to reduce John's status in comparison with Jesus.

1:19–21 The testimony of John: When the narrative curtain opens, John is on the stage. His only function is to bear testimony to Jesus. His first statement is, **"I am not the Christ"** (see the narrator's urgent interruption at 1:8, "He himself was not the light"). Some of John's followers had persisted into the time and place of the Gospel, apparently claiming messianic status for John (see Acts 18:24–19:7). In the Fourth Gospel, John also denies he is **Elijah** (contrast the Synoptics, who present John as Elijah in dress and demeanor, and see specifically Matt. 11:17; 17:12–13; Luke 1:17). **The prophet:** Based on Deut. 18:15–18, some streams of Judaism expected a prophet like Moses, the eschatological prophet who would appear just before the end. John also rejects this identification.

1:23 I am the voice: The author divests John of all eschatological titles and functions, and makes him only a voice that testifies to Jesus. In the Fourth Gospel, John is not even "the Baptist." Here too, he must yield to Jesus, who baptizes more than John (see 3:22; 4:1). John has no independent message but has an extensive understanding of who Jesus is: the one who will baptize with the Holy Spirit (v. 33), the preexistent one (v. 30), the Lamb of God (vv. 29, 35), the Son of God (v. 34). This is not the testimony of the historical John, but the retrospective faith of the Christian community, for which John is portrayed as a witness (see "Introduction to the Gospels"). John speaks retrospectively; the baptism of Jesus is not narrated but reported by John as something that has already happened "offstage" in the narrative past.

One crying in the wilderness: Isaiah 40:3, applied to John the Baptist in all four Gospels. Here it is quoted according to the text found in the Synoptics, not in the form found in the Hebrew Bible, i.e., it reflects the Christian reinterpretation of the Old Testament (see excursus, "New Testament Interpretation of the Old Testament," at 1 Cor. 15:3).

1:29 The Lamb of God: John the Baptist here becomes a witness to the Christian doctrine of the atonement, the sacrificial death of Jesus for the sins of others. The Christ event here replaces the temple ritual as the means of God's forgiveness. The image is related to the Suffering Servant of Isaiah, who dies as an innocent lamb for the sins of others (Isa. 53:6). "Lamb" imagery is important for the Fourth Gospel. The passion story is told in such a way that Jesus dies at the same time the Passover lambs are being sacrificed in the temple (19:16–30; see 13:1 commentary; 18:28). Lamb is also the central christological image in Revelation (see on Rev. 5:6). It had already been used by Paul in a letter written from Ephesus, the area with which both the Gospel of John and Revelation are associated. On Jesus' death understood as atoning sacrifice, see on Rom. 3:25; 1 Cor. 15:3; Heb. 1:3; 2:17; 5:1–10. The Passover lamb was not a sacrifice for sins, as was the regular sacrifice of lambs in the temple (Lev. 1:3–4; 5:6), but there is some overlapping of imagery here. Already Paul, who understands Jesus' death as a sacrifice for sins (Rom. 3:25; 1 Cor. 15:3), can also consider Christ as the Passover lamb sacrificed for us (1 Cor. 5:8; see 1 Pet. 1:19).

1:33 The one who sent me: "The one who sent me" is used twenty-six times in John, elsewhere always of Jesus. Although John is emphatically subordinated to Jesus in the Fourth Gospel, he is nonetheless regarded as a true prophet sent by God. **Baptize with water . . . baptizes with the Holy Spirit:** This contrast is traditional, being found in all the other Gospels. It functions differently in John, however, since Jesus too baptizes with water—even outbaptizing John (3:22; 4:1). The promise of Spirit baptism is interpreted

differently in each of the Gospels. In John, Jesus confers the Spirit on his disciples from the cross and on Easter Sunday (see on 19:30; 20:22), and has no separate Pentecost scene (vs. Acts 1–2).

1:35–51
JESUS' FIRST DISCIPLES
(See also at Matt. 4:18–22; Mark 1:16–20; Luke 5:1–11)

The reader familiar with the Synoptic Gospels will miss the stories of Jesus' baptism and temptation, none of which is narrated in the Fourth Gospel. Of the material in Matt. 3:1–4:11; Mark 1:1–13; Luke 3:1–4:13, John contains only the contrast between the Baptist's own water baptism and Jesus' baptism by the Spirit, and the Baptist's testimony that he saw the Spirit descend on Jesus—but this is not directly related to Jesus' baptism. There is no place in John for a temptation story, for the Johannine Jesus is always in communion with God and not subject to human temptation (8:29; 10:30; 11:42).

The Synoptic scene in which Jesus calls four fishermen by the sea of Galilee is replaced by a scene in which some of John's disciples become disciples of Jesus. This probably reflects the original historical reality—Jesus was baptized by John, and when he left the group of John's disciples to begin his own ministry, some of John's disciples followed him. More importantly, this is what the author believes should happen in his own time: disciples of John the Baptist should become Christians.

1:38 What are you looking for?: These are the first, programmatic words of Jesus in the Fourth Gospel. They are not a verbatim report of what Jesus once said but express the theology of the evangelist. Jewish people had a variety of messianic hopes and images of the coming consummation of God's purpose. If one is looking for the Messiah, the coming king in God's kingdom, then Jesus will identify himself as the Messiah (e.g., 1:41; 4:26). But if one is not a Jew—as was the case for most of John's readers—he did not insist that one must first learn from the Bible and Jewish tradition to look for God's Messiah. The Johannine Jesus asks, "What *are* you looking for?" Every human being, Jewish or not, has deep hopes for the fulfillment of life, for salvation; every human being is "looking for something" as the fulfillment of life. In the Fourth Gospel, this quest is expressed in universal human symbols: bread, water, light, life, truth, the way. To each of these human longings, the Johannine Jesus says, "I'm it" (literally "I am"; see commentary on the "I am" sayings at 6:35). The following series of dialogues applies the spectrum of Jewish messianic hopes to Jesus, but his initial question expresses the Johannine faith that in Christ God fulfills all human hopes, Jewish and non-Jewish.

Where are you staying?: These seemingly almost trivial words, the first words of Jesus' disciples in the Gospel, also bear more meaning than appears on the surface. The word translated "staying" also is translated as "abide," "stay," "live," "dwell," and is found in the Johannine literature more than in all the rest of the New Testament together. A central question of the church at the end of the first century was, "Where is Jesus?" The first generation had expected his soon return from heaven. It had not happened. Where is he? This question, which troubles the Johannine church, will be dealt with in the course of the Gospel and is placed in the mouth of the earliest disciples as their first words.

1:39 Come and see: Jesus does not explain, but invites his hearers (including the readers of the Gospel) to learn from their own experience and from the narrative of the Gospel where Jesus dwells today.

1:40 Andrew, Simon Peter's brother: In the Synoptics, Peter is the first disciple called by Jesus and retains his primacy throughout. This reflects his leadership in the early Christian community. Here Andrew and the "other disciple" are first, and they become the means by which Peter becomes a disciple. The Johannine Christians regard the Beloved Disciple as their leader (see commentary at 13:23). He may have been intended by the unidentified disciple of vv. 37, 40. The story is told throughout the Gospel in a way that demotes Peter from first place in favor of the Beloved Disciple.

1:41 We have found the Messiah: John translates the Hebrew "Messiah" into the Greek "Christ" (English "anointed"). See extended commentary on Mark 8:29. As John had to explain "Messiah" and "Christ" to his non-Jewish readers, so the Christian community today must explain the meaning of "Christ" to our secularized culture (and to ourselves) before the *Chris*tian confession can be intelligently accepted *or* rejected. "We have found" sounds like a human achievement, but see 4:23—God is the ultimate seeker. Augustine's prayer is Johannine: "We could not seek you, O Lord, if you had not already found us."

1:42 Simon/Cephas/Peter: Simon was Peter's birth name. "Cephas" is the Aramaic word for "rock." In Greek, the word for "rock" is "Peter" (see on Matt. 16:16–18). Although as a result of Christian tradition, Peter is now a common name, when Jesus renamed Simon as Peter, it was a striking and mysterious symbolic event. Prior to this, no one had ever been called Peter. It would be like renaming someone Tree or Dirt in our own time and was intended to be provocative. Jesus' designation of Simon as Rock was not merely a nickname but corresponds to the biblical tradition in which a new name signals a new reality: Jacob becomes Israel (Gen. 32:22–32), Abram becomes Abraham (Gen. 17:1–8), Sarai becomes Sarah (Gen. 17:15–16). Simon is not yet a rock; Jesus renames him for what he will become.

1:43–44 Follow me: In contrast to the preceding, in this scene Jesus takes the initiative and uses the same commanding words as in the Synoptic call stories (see Mark 1:17; 2:14). **Bethsaida:** On the northeast side of the sea of Galilee. In the Synoptics, Peter's home is in Capernaum, on the western shore (Mark 1:21–29).

1:45 Nathanael: Not mentioned in the Synoptics. There is no reason to identify him with Bartholomew, though this is often done in order to harmonize John's list of disciples with those of the other Gospels. **The one about whom Moses . . . and the prophets wrote:** John does not repudiate the Jewish Scriptures, the Christian Old Testament, but reinterprets them as a witness to Christ (see 5:39 and excursus, "New Testament Interpretation of the Old Testament," at 1 Cor. 15:3). **Jesus son of Joseph:** This declaration is never qualified or replaced in the Fourth Gospel. John does not know, or does not accept, the story of the virginal conception of Jesus (see on Matt. 1–2; Luke 1:28–33; 2:7; 2:41–52). He has a profound faith in Jesus as Son of God but understands this in a way that does not conflict with his normal human birth. In John's understanding, the Word became flesh (1:14) in a truly human way. A part of the scandal of the incarnation is that the Son of God is a truly human being who comes from the nothing-town of Nazareth. John knows the tradition that the Messiah is to come from Bethlehem (see on 7:42), but the reality of who Jesus was upsets all expectations of who the Messiah was supposed to be. This is supremely expressed in the fact that he was crucified, but the scandal of the cross is inherent in the incarnation itself.

1:46–49 Come and see: Jesus' own invitation to learn who he is in one's own experience is echoed in the disciples' invitation to others (see v. 39). The original word of Jesus that invites to faith and generates it is mediated in the word of his disciples. **An Israelite . . . no deceit:** The story of Gen. 27:30–38 is reflected, in which wily Jacob obtains his brother's blessing by deceit. "Jacob" means "supplanter," the one who takes over the property of others (by deceit). His name is later changed to "Israel," which means "prince of God," and he becomes the ancestor of the people of Israel (Gen. 32:22–28). In the meantime, Jacob/Israel had had the dream of "Jacob's ladder," in which he saw heaven and earth connected, at Bethel, which means "house of God" (Gen. 28:10–17). In becoming a disciple of Jesus, Nathanael does not abandon his Bible or his ancestral faith, but is a true *Israelite*, not like the untransformed *Jacob*. While John often uses "Jew" in a pejorative symbolic sense to represent "unbeliever" (in Christ), he uses "Israel" in a positive sense to represent those Jews who see in Jesus the fulfillment of their own Jewish hopes. Thus Nathanael declares Jesus to be Son of God and King of *Israel*, titles equivalent to Messiah, but Jesus' enemies will later ridicule him as "King of the *Jews*" (John 3:19, 21). **King of Israel:** "King" is one of the meanings of "Messiah/Christ," as is "Son of God" (see on Mark 8:29). On the Johannine understanding of kingship, see on 6:14–15; 18:33–38.

1:50 I saw you under the fig tree: Like God, the Johannine Jesus has supernatural knowledge of people's hearts and lives (2:23–25; 4:16–19; 6:70–71; 13:21–26). **Greater things than these:** One of the themes of the Gospel is that faith in Jesus based on his miraculous signs is only preliminary. The signs are to point to a greater reality, the presence of God in Christ. He is himself the "Jacob's ladder," the bridge between heaven and earth, Bethel the house of God, the place where God is revealed and dwells on this earth (see Gen. 28:10–17). In the Bible, Jacob *saw* this ladder; Jesus *is* this bridge between God and humanity. On Son of Man, see commentary on Mark 2:10.

In the Synoptic Gospels, faith only gradually dawns on his disciples, and they come to a realization of his true identity only at the climax of the story (see Matt. 16:13–28; Mark 8:27–9:1; 15:39 commentary; Luke 9:18–27). John retells the story in such a way that at the very beginning, before Jesus' ministry begins, his disciples confess faith in him with the whole range of christological titles: Lamb of God, Rabbi/Teacher, Messiah/Christ, Son of

God, King of Israel, Son of Man. This is an aspect of the collapsing of horizons inherent in the Gospel genre (see "Introduction to the Gospels").

Having heard these declarations about the identity of Jesus Christ, the reader is now prepared to hear the story of Jesus' revelatory ministry.

2:1–12:50
PART ONE—THE BOOK OF SIGNS: JESUS REVEALS HIS GLORY TO THE WORLD

In Part One of John's narrative Jesus manifests his glory to the world in a series of signs that reaches its climactic point in the raising of Lazarus. Jesus is met with increasing misunderstanding and hostility that finally results in the determination to kill him. The signs point to the one great sign of Jesus' death and resurrection, but the figures in the narrative do not, and cannot, understand what is really happening until the story is over. Part One begins and ends with symbolic scenes not found in the Synoptic Gospels, chosen and composed by John himself to portray the meaning of the Christ event (2:1–11, the wedding at Cana; 11:1–57, the raising of Lazarus).

2:1–4:54
THE NEW BEGINNING

This first subsection of Part One begins and ends at Cana (4:46), a town mentioned only in John. The first two episodes of this subsection portray Jesus' manifestation of his (= God's) glory. The first scene is at a family festival in Galilee in which he transforms the traditional water of purification into the wine of celebration; the second pictures Jesus as the fulfillment of the temple as the place of God's presence.

2:1–11
The Wedding Festival at Cana

2:1 On the third day: This date does not fit the preceding chronology (see 1:29, 35, 43). Early Christian readers could hardly hear the phrase "the third day" without thinking of the resurrection (see v. 19 and Matt. 16:21; Luke 14:7, 21, 46; 1 Cor. 15:3). The story is set in the pre-Easter framework of the life of Jesus but is a "resurrection story." **Wedding:** The joyous celebration of a wedding festival is often used in the New Testament as a picture of the meaning of eschatological salvation: Christ is the bridegroom, the bride is the redeemed people of God, the time of engagement is over, and the intimate new life together begins (see Matt. 9:15; 22:1–11; John

3:29; 2 Cor. 11:2; Rev. 19:7, 9; 22:2, 9, 17). While this story is not an allegory, it evokes these images of the time of salvation. **Cana of Galilee:** Exact location unknown; the site shown to tourists today is one of several possibilities. **The mother of Jesus:** Never called Mary in John.

2:4 Woman: The address sounds rude in our culture, but in the Bible is the normal address, connoting no disrespect (like "Frau" in German or "Lady" in old English). **What concern is that to you and me?:** Literally "What is there that is both to you and me?" i.e., "What do we have in common?" These are the same words used by the demon addressing Jesus in Mark 1:24, indicating that they belong to two different orders of reality. That is the point here; Jesus' mother speaks from the world of earthly concerns; Jesus "comes from above" (3:7, 31; 8:23) and represents a different order of existence. **My hour:** Not a sixty-minute hour, but the long hour of Jesus' glorification, which is the hour of his crucifixion and exaltation (see 7:30; 8:20; 12:23–27; 13:1; 17:1). The signs that Jesus does all point to *the* sign, his death and resurrection. This hour cannot be rushed, cannot come at human initiative.

2:5 Do whatever he tells you: Although there is no story of Jesus' miraculous conception in John, Mary seems to know of his authority and power. Jesus does not respond immediately to her request, but as the representative of God acts on his own initiative (see 7:1–10; 11:1–7).

2:6 Jewish rites of purification: This water was used for ceremonial purposes to remove the ritual impurity that kept people from being acceptable to God (see Lev. 15; 17:15; 22:6; Mark 7:1–4). Jesus will transform the water of the old purification ceremonies into the new wine of salvation (see Matt. 9:17). **Twenty or thirty gallons:** This quantity in each of the jars results in 120–180 gallons of wine. This is a fabulous, extravagant amount of wine, unheard of in a village family celebration and reminiscent of the extravagance expected in the messianic days of salvation. See this hope as expressed in a first-century Jewish document: "The earth shall yield its fruit ten thousandfold. On each vine there shall be a thousand branches, and each branch shall produce a thousand clusters, and each cluster shall produce a thousand grapes, and each grape shall produce a cor [25–75 gallons] of wine" (2 *Bar.* 29:5). On extravagance as a mark of eschatological salvation, see John 6:12–13; 12:3; 19:39; Mark 4:3–8; Luke 5:6; 6:37–38; 9:17; 8:5–8; 13:20; 15:22; 19:17; Rom. 5:15.

2:9 The water that had become wine: There were also pagan stories of changing water to wine, especially associated with the wine god Dionysus (Greek) or Bacchus (Roman). See excursus, "Interpreting the Miracle Stories," at Matt. 9:35. The sign points the reader to the meaning of the Christ event as a whole, not merely to an incident in Galilee. As a symbolic story of the meaning of God's act in Christ, it portrays the joy and extravagance of God's saving act. Taken literally, it raises questions not only of metaphysics but of ethics: in a world where children starve, is this a responsible use of miraculous power?

2:10 Become drunk: The wine was not unfermented grape juice. **The good wine until now:** Saving the best till last is a mark of eschatological salvation. John pictures Jesus as the climax of God's saving work. The eschatological joy is already present. Without knowing it, the master of ceremonies at the wedding festival confirms the miracle—a Johannine pattern (see 4:46–53, also related to Cana, and 9:15).

2:11 The first of his signs: Not only chronologically, but the premier sign of the meaning of the advent of Christ. The other seven miracle stories in John have parallels or analogies in the other Gospels, but this story is unique in the New Testament, the prototype of the Christ event as a whole. Since a "second" sign is enumerated in 4:54, with other signs that nevertheless come in between (2:23; 3:2), some scholars have taken this as evidence for a pre-Johannine "signs source" he has adopted. By declaring this to be Jesus' *first* sign, John may also intend to reject stories about the boy Jesus who worked miracles (see on Luke 2:41–52). **His disciples believed in him:** This is the purpose of signs, to generate faith (20:30–31). Yet John knows that faith based on signs can be superficial unless the believer transcends miracles and apprehends that to which the miracle stories point: God's saving act in the Christ event as a whole, focused in the death and resurrection of Christ (see 2:23–25; 3:2–5; 4:48; 6:2, 26).

2:12–25
"Cleansing" the Jerusalem Temple
(See also at Matt. 21:12–13; Mark 11:15–17; Luke 19:45–46)

This scene occurs at the end of Jesus' ministry in the Synoptics, where he makes only one journey to Jerusalem, which results in his death. John transfers this symbolic scene to the beginning of Jesus' ministry, on his first of several visits to Jerusalem. As Jesus replaces the water of Jewish purification ceremonies with the wine of the presence of salvation (2:1–11), so he appears at the temple, disrupts its business, and presents himself as the new locus of the revelatory presence of God, the new Beth-El, the new "house of God" (see 1:51; 4:19–23). When John writes this, the Jerusalem temple had already been destroyed by the Romans in the war of 66–70, and both Jews and Christians were reinterpreting the significance of the temple. Jews located the presence of God in the synagogue and study of the Torah; Christians saw the Christian community itself, the "body of Christ," as a new house of God (see 1 Cor. 3:16; 12:27–39; Eph. 2:22; Rev. 3:12; 21:3). The Johannine community seems to have been influenced by these Pauline ideas circulating in Ephesus. In this scene Jesus is portrayed as expressing this Johannine theology.

2:13 Passover: See "Outline" in introduction to John and commentary on Luke 22:1.

2:15 Drove out . . . the sheep and the cattle: Different from the Synoptics, where animals are not mentioned, and Jesus drives out only the money changers. In John's time the temple had been put out of business by the Roman destruction, but in John's understanding it was Jesus himself who closed down the temple as a place of animal sacrifice; he himself is the Lamb of God (see 1:29, 36).

2:17 His disciples remembered: Not immediately, but after Easter, in the light of the resurrection (v. 22). **Zeal for your house:** The quotation is from Ps. 69:9, a different text giving the scene a different "point" than that found in the Synoptic parallels (see on Luke 19:46). Jesus' radical act is not because he (and his followers in the time of the Gospel) was antitemple, but because they were protemple in its essential meaning—the presence of God in this world. **Consume me:** Holy zeal for God's presence not only provokes Jesus to react vigorously but will finally lead to his death.

2:18–19 Destroy this temple: Here is the Johannine version of a saying found in different form in other contexts (see Matt. 26:59–61; Mark 14:55–59; Acts 6:14). Elsewhere, Jesus is charged with threatening to destroy the temple. Here, Jesus' opponents will destroy the temple, but Jesus will raise it. As often in John, the saying functions at two levels, pointing both to the Jerusalem temple and to Jesus himself. The Jews, not Jesus or the Christians, are responsible for the destruction of the temple, by the disastrous war they had caused. (This had not yet happened in Jesus' day but was

already an event of the past in John's.) Yet Jesus will raise up a new temple, his body, the body of Christian believers, that represents the presence of God in the world.

2:20 The Jews then said: Of course Jesus' hearers in the story could not understand the symbolic, Christian meaning of his words and deeds, and misunderstand his statement at the mundane level. This Johannine technique of the "inept question" occurs often (see 3:3–4; 4:10–11, 33–34; 6:51–52; 8:19, 22, 33, 57; 11:11–12, 23–27; 14:5, 8, 22). Neither opponents nor disciples can understand the meaning of the Christ event until it is completed in the death and resurrection (see on 10:6 and "Introduction to the Gospels"). **Under construction for forty-six years:** This would locate the present scene in 27–28 CE. The original temple built by Solomon had been destroyed by the Babylonians in 586 BCE. The second temple, rebuilt after the return from exile, a modest building (Ezra 1; 3; Hag. 1–2; Zech. 6:9–15), was enlarged and remodeled in an extravagant building program by Herod the Great. The project was begun about 20 BCE, was still under way in Jesus' day, and was completed only in 63 CE, shortly before it was destroyed by the Romans in 70 (Josephus *Ant.* 15.380; 20.219). This period 520 BCE–70 CE is thus called Second Temple Judaism.

2:23–25 Many believed in his name: See commentary on 2:11. **He himself knew what was in everyone:** Jesus is pictured by John as having divine omniscience (see 1:48; 4:16–19; 6:64, 70–71; 13:21–2). Here as elsewhere, he represents God (see on 5:18).

3:1–21
The Discourse with Nicodemus

There were of course no chapter breaks in the original text; the Nicodemus story is joined directly to 2:23–25. Nicodemus is one of those who "believe" on the basis of signs, but who has not come to an authentic faith (see 12:42). He reappears in a more positive light in 7:50–52, as the defender of Jesus, and in 19:39, as the one who courageously gives Jesus a royal burial.

3:2 By night: Darkness has a symbolic meaning in Johannine dualism (see 9:4; 8:23; 11:10; 13:30; 19:39; 21:3). **We know:** Nicodemus is a good man, a respected religious leader who declares his positive evaluation of Jesus based on his own this-worldly standards (see the discussion of "criteria" at 7:12). His "we" signals that he speaks not just for himself as an individual.

3:3 Jesus answered him: Jesus seems to give an abrupt or even rude response to Nicodemus's respectful approach, but John's point is that Jesus is "from above," that he and Nicodemus belong to two different worlds (see 2:4), and that Nicodemus (and everyone else) must be born from above before they can grasp Jesus' true identity. **Very truly:** Literally "amen amen." Jesus had used "amen" in a distinctive manner (see on Matt. 5:18). The church continued to use it in editing and interpreting the tradition of Jesus sayings. Only John has it in doubled form, which became the traditional "verily, verily I say unto you" of the King James Version. **The kingdom of God:** Only here and v. 5 in the Fourth Gospel. The Synoptic Jesus spoke often of the kingdom of God, but John has almost entirely reinterpreted this phrase from Jewish tradition into the more universal "eternal life." **Born from above:** John's Greek word has a dual meaning, either "from above" (as in 3:31) or "again" (as in Gal. 4:9). This ambiguity cannot be represented in English, for we have no one word that conveys both meanings. Jesus means "from above," but Nicodemus takes it to mean "again." The issue is not how many times one has been born (Nicodemus's misunderstanding) but the origin of one's life (Jesus' meaning). This kind of misunderstanding is a frequent Johannine literary and theological technique, with Jesus intending his statement at one level, but being heard only at a different, mundane level (see 4:10–15; 6:30–58; 7:33–36; 9:39–41; 11:11–13, 23–27; 13:6–10). The metaphor of new birth was widespread in the pagan religions of the Hellenistic world but had also been taken over by Judaism. Other New Testament authors use the metaphor of new birth for conversion and beginning a new life (see 1 John 3:9; 5:8; Titus 3:5, Jas. 1:1; 1 Pet. 1:3, 23; 2:2), but John develops it with particular theological sharpness.

3:4 How . . . ?: John makes repeated use of the inept question, in which characters in the story respond at the wrong level in order to set the stage for the contrasting truth of Jesus' answer (see the list at 2:20).

3:5 Water and Spirit: Here the new birth is related to Christian baptism, in which the Holy Spirit is given to new converts (see Acts 2:38; Titus 3:5).

3:6 Flesh . . . Spirit: Johannine theology is sharply dualistic (see list at 8:23). On "flesh," see 1:13–14; "Spirit" refers to the transcendent world of God (see 4:24). "Flesh" is not evil, for it is God's good creation, but as human reality

of itself it is incapable of attaining to the divine presence. This life must come from God's side.

3:7 You: Here Jesus' address switches to the plural "you" (not apparent in English). The conversation is gradually modulating from the there-and-then dialogue between Jesus and Nicodemus to the here-and-now of the Johannine reader, in which Jesus speaks for the Johannine church and Nicodemus represents the unbelieving outsiders.

3:8 The wind blows where it chooses: In Greek the same word (*pneuma*) means "wind," "breath," or "spirit" (see English pneumonia, pneumatic tires). Again the Johannine vocabulary has a double meaning: the wind is an invisible force beyond human control, but its effects can be observed—the Spirit of God is not at human disposal, but its effects can be seen. **Everyone who is born of the Spirit:** Every Christian believer is meant, not a special class of "born again" Christians (see 1 John 5:1). Each believer is to understand his or her faith as a gift from God, not a human achievement. At birth, we receive the gift of life entirely as grace, without our decision, without getting to vote on it. We can only be grateful for it. John understands the mystery of conversion and salvation as this kind of divine grace. For the paradox of human decision that is involved in the gift of faith, see on 3:16 below.

3:9 How . . . ?: With this question, Nicodemus fades from the scene, and the dialogue becomes the Johannine church speaking in Jesus' name to the unbelieving world. There is no explanation that corresponds to this human question, "how?" which may be an honest question and/or an expression of human pride and arrogance (see on 1 Cor. 15:35–41).

3:11 We: As the "you" has become plural, now the "I" of Jesus becomes the "we" of the witnessing church (see on 1:13–14). The Christian community speaks, as in 1 John 1:1–4.

3:13–15 Ascended . . . descended: Here pre- and post-Easter perspective are collapsed into one, and the speaker (Jesus/the church) looks "back" on the resurrection and ascension. The pre-Easter Nicodemus could not be expected to understand these realities, which can be perceived only by the post-Easter church in the light of the resurrection and the gift of the Spirit (see also 7:39!), but the text is in fact addressing its post-Easter readers in the form of a story from Jesus' ministry (see "Introduction to the Gospels"). Since the following verse refers to Moses, **No one has ascended:**

May refer to claims made for Moses, who in some streams of first-century Judaism was supposed not to have died, but to have been taken to heaven. **Serpent in the wilderness:** See Num. 21:4–9. The story about Moses is understood to find its deeper fulfillment in the Christ event (see excursus, "New Testament Interpretation of the Old Testament," at 1 Cor. 15:3). **Lifted up:** Another Johannine double meaning, referring both to Jesus' being lifted up on the cross and to his exaltation to heaven (see 8:28; 12:32, 34). His crucifixion is his glorification; his return to the Father, which is the saving event for humanity, occurs by his self-giving love that leads to the cross. **Son of Man:** See on Mark 2:10. **Eternal life:** The discourse that begins with a statement about the kingdom of God has now modulated into the Johannine equivalent. Eternal life does not mean just an endless extension of this-worldly life, but a new order of being, the life of the age to come, in John's theology already present in the life of Christian faith.

Since the original one-on-one conversation has faded seamlessly into the address of the Johannine community to the world, it is not clear where quotation marks should be placed, i.e., where Jesus stops speaking directly to Nicodemus and the narrator addresses the reader in the name of Jesus and the Johannine community. Some translations place the quotation marks here; others extend the quotation through v. 21. The original author and the ancient manuscripts, of course, did not use quotation marks, so all such decisions are modern editorial judgments. In any case, "Jesus or Johannine church" is not a necessary choice from the point of view of the author's theology. When the church speaks in Jesus' name, it is (the risen) Jesus who speaks (see on chaps. 14–16).

3:16 For God so loved the world: Although John 3:16 can be trivialized, this text is rightly regarded as a summary of Johannine theology and of the Christian faith. Even so, it cannot be interpreted apart from its context, but must be understood in the context of the whole narrative of John's Gospel. Almost every word is important; we will comment on only a few key words. **So:** The Greek word can mean "so much," but its primary meaning is "in this way," "in this manner," and that is its meaning in all its other thirteen occurrences in the Gospel of John (see, e.g., 3:8, 14; 21:1). While God's love is indescribably infinite, the point here is not how much but how—God gave his

Son. **World:** While the world is often pictured in the Fourth Gospel as hostile to God, it is also God's creation. God loves his enemies, those who have rebelled against him, and is thus the model for Christian love. **Gave his . . . Son:** This should not be pictured as though God sacrificed or punished someone else for the sins of humanity (see on 2 Cor. 5:19–21; Rev. 5:6). Here it is important to see the Johannine theology that identifies God and Christ (1:1, 5:18; 10:30; 14:9; 20:28), as later explicated in Trinitarian theology. God does not punish someone else, but takes human sin into himself; Christ's giving himself is God's self-giving love. **Only:** Translates the Greek word *monogenes*, which means "unique," "the only one of its kind," as in all its other New Testament occurrences (Luke 7:12; 8:42; John 1:14, 18; 3:18; Heb. 11:17, 1 John 4:9). It was misunderstood in the Latin Vulgate and translated "only begotten," as though it had to do with the birth of Jesus. John is not interested in the birth of Jesus and has no doctrine of the virginal conception (see on 1:12–13, 45; 3:3–5). In the Fourth Gospel, *Christians* are begotten/born children of God, but *Jesus* is the unique Son of God in a different, paradoxical way. "Begotten" was used in yet a different sense in the later Trinitarian creeds ("begotten not made") to refer not to Jesus' birth but to the "eternal generation" of the Son, i.e., to refer to the eternal relationship of the preexistent Christ to God, as opposed to understanding the Son as an angelic creature who was not truly identified with God. Although John is not yet thinking in Trinitarian terms, this understanding expressed in the Nicene Creed is in fact closer to John's meaning than mistakenly understanding it as referring to his miraculous birth.

Whoever believes: Here belief or unbelief is obviously a human possibility and responsibility. This is combined with the statements about conversion as being born "from above" in 1:12–13; 3:3–5. Pictured as birth, conversion is the gift of God, the result of God's choice and initiative, for which the believer can only give thanks. Pictured as faith, conversion is the result of human decision and responsibility. These two views are juxtaposed but not combined or harmonized in the New Testament. On the value of the language of predestination and election, see excursus, "Predestination," at Rom. 8:28. **In him:** To ask whether "him" refers to faith in God or Christ is to ask an un-Johannine question. John identifies God and Christ. The sometimes laudable effort to avoid gender-specific language in reference to God (God is indeed not a male or female being) is misleading in texts such as John 3:16. The ambiguous Greek pronoun here points to both God and Christ; to substitute "God" or "Christ" as a means of avoiding the masculine pronoun is to miss an important point of Johannine and New Testament theology (see the many similar instances elsewhere, e.g., Matt. 3:3; Mark 1:3; Luke 1:15–17; 3:4, and many passages that refer ambiguously to "the Lord"; John 1:1–13; 3:34–35; 1 Cor. 1:8; 15:25–28; Gal. 1:3–5; 2 Tim. 1:9; 4:1, 8; 1 John 1:6–19; 2:1–6, 26–29; 3:7, 23–24; 4:17; Rev. 1:1; 6:17 (?); 11:4, 15; 22:4). **Perish:** Not physical death, but the opposite of eternal life (see 3:15).

3:17–21 Not condemned . . . condemned already: While John still pictures a great judgment on the future last day, he has shifted the emphasis to the present (see on 5:25–30). **Light has come into the world:** See 1:4–9; 8:12; 9:5; 12:35–36, 46; 1 John 1:5, 7; 2:8, 10). God did not send the Son, the Light, to condemn the world, but the coming of the light inevitably casts shadows, and people must choose whether to remain in darkness or to live in the light. **Those who do what is true:** Truth is a theme of the Fourth Gospel; see on 18:38. For John, truth is not an abstraction that may be possessed, but a relation to God that is a matter of one's doing.

3:22–36
John's Testimony to Christ

The structure of this section is like that of the preceding: a dialogue between a Jew (instead of Nicodemus) and the rabbi (in this case John instead of Jesus) that fades into a monologue in which finally the voice of there-and-then teaching of the rabbi modulates into the address of the Johannine church to the reader.

3:22–24 And baptized: This statement is interpreted or corrected in 4:1, another indication that the Gospel has gone through more than one edition. That Jesus conducted a baptismal ministry during his earthly life is unique to the Gospel of John. Since Jesus had begun as a disciple of John and had been baptized by him, this is not historically unlikely. The point here, however, is not history but theology—the Johannine community here anchors its own baptismal practice in the life of Jesus. **Aenon near Salim:** The site has more than one identification in ancient literature and maps but probably refers to a location on the west side

of the Jordan south of Roman Scythopolis (Beth-shean). **Not yet thrown into prison:** In contrast to the Synoptics (see Mark 1:14; Matt. 11:2–19; 14:1–12). Only in John do the ministries of John and Jesus overlap. Again, the Gospel writers are more interested in theology than chronology; in the Synoptics John *precedes* Jesus as his *forerunner*; in John he is *contemporary* with Jesus as a *witness*. Each can make a valid theological point; they cannot both be historically correct.

3:25–30 Purification: John's baptism is linked to forgiveness of sins in Mark 1:4 and Luke 3:3—though not in John, who considers the only reason for John's baptizing ministry to be the identification of Jesus as the Christ (1:31–33). John's baptism was nonetheless understood to effect forgiveness and purification, and thus to compete with or replace the temple rituals. This provoked the discussion with "a Jew" (though John was of course himself a Jew; see introduction to John: "Conflict with 'the Jews'"). **Rabbi:** See Nicodemus's address to Jesus, 3:2. Though John, like Jesus, would not have qualified as a rabbi in the post-70 Judaism, of the author's own time, in pre-70 Judaism before strict "ministerial" standards of ordination had been enforced, whoever gained a following was considered a rabbi. Among other things, this represents the author's protest against the restructuring of Judaism, which had excluded the Christian community. **All are going to him:** Jesus' preaching and baptizing exceeds that of John (see 4:1–2). In baptizing, as in all else, Jesus is superior to John, and John happily acknowledges his own subordinate role—he is the best man, not the bridegroom (for the imagery, see on 2:1). **I am not the Christ:** See 1:19–23.

3:31–36 The one who comes from above: It is not clear whether this section that expresses the Christology of the Johannine church is intended to be a continuation of the quotation from John or is the author's own affirmation (see on 3:13–15 above). Some scholars think the section has been displaced or relocated in the editing of different editions of the Gospel and that it originally followed 3:12 or 3:21, though the parallel structure of 3:1–21 and 3:22–36 argues for its present location as original. In any case, the final editor(s) of the Gospel placed it here. **Has certified . . . that God is true:** Whoever believes the message from and about *Jesus* responds to the word of *God*. Here as elsewhere in John's theology, God and Christ are distinguished and identified at the same time.

Placed all things in his hands: The post-Easter perspective, as in Matt. 28:18; see Matt. 11:27; Luke 10:22. **Believes . . . disobeys:** The opposite of faith is not only unbelief but disobedience. For John, as for Paul, faith is not merely the intellectual acceptance of a claim as true, but the response with one's whole life, which includes obedience (see on Acts 16:31; Rom. 1:4, 17).

4:1–42
The Discourse with the Woman of Samaria

In this lengthy episode Jesus encounters a woman, a foreigner, of questionable reputation, who becomes a hesitant but effective witness, resulting in the conversion of many Samaritans. There is an obvious contrast with the preceding narrative featuring the male rabbinic teacher of Israel who never understands.

4:1–3 Jesus . . . baptizing . . . disciples: See on 3:22, 26. The correction or clarification of the earlier statement points to the editorial history of the document, which has been revised perhaps more than once (see introduction to John).

4:4 Samaria: On Samaritans, see commentary on Luke 9:52. According to Josephus, it was not unusual for Jews to go through Samaria en route to Galilee, though sometimes they went through Perea, on the east side of the Jordan.

4:5–6 Jacob's well: The **plot of ground** is mentioned in the Old Testament (see Gen. 48:22), but not the well. That Jacob = Israel is to be kept in mind throughout (Gen. 32:22–28). The literary motif of the man of God meeting a woman at a well and asking for a drink is biblical (Gen. 24; 1 Sam. 9:11; 1 Kgs. 17:10) and has the effect of setting the present story in continuity with biblical history. **Tired out:** One of the indications of Jesus' humanity, in this Gospel so concerned to emphasize his divinity.

4:7 A Samaritan woman: The Fourth Gospel emphasizes the role of women in the life of Jesus (2:1–11; 4:27; 11:17–44; 12:1–8; 19:25–27; 20:1–18), a reflection of the prominent role of women in the life of the Johannine church. At the end of the first century some streams of Christianity were modifying the earlier freedom with regard to cultural standards (see Gal. 3:27–28) and conforming their practice to the current social expectations, which limited the active role of women in Christian congregations (see on Col. 3:18–4:1; 1 Pet. 2:11–3:12; 1 Tim. 3:1–13). The Johannine church, however, was a charismatic community in which the Spirit held sway and generated leadership.

Although emerging church order in other streams of Christianity was inclining toward male leadership and ordination, the Spirit was no respecter of persons. Since leadership in the Johannine churches depended on endowment by the Spirit rather than official ordination, women played an active role (as in the modern Pentecostal movement, which has always had women ministers). This is reflected in the Johannine stories that feature women.

4:9 You, a Jew: Despite the tensions between Jews and Christians evident in John (see introduction to John), Jesus is portrayed as a Jew and recognizably so. This is not a matter of racial characteristics, for Samaritans are not ethnically distinguishable from Jews. **Jews do not share things in common with Samaritans:** The modern reader should not read this in terms of "White Only" signs in previously segregated America or South Africa. It was a matter of religious cultic purity laws. Jews had to obey certain ritual prescriptions that Samaritans did not observe, so they could not share the same eating and drinking vessels (see on Mark 7; Acts 10).

4:10–15 The gift of God: See 3:16. **Living water:** Literally "running," "flowing" water, as opposed to stagnant water. Here the deeper meaning is "water that gives life, true, eternal life." In the Old Testament and Judaism the symbol of living water had repeatedly been used of God himself and the salvation God gives, sometimes understood as mediated by the Torah (e.g., Jer. 2:13; 17:13; Ezek. 47:1–8; Zech. 14:8; Sir. 24:21; Prov. 13:14; 18:4; see Rev. 22:1–2). In John this living water is Jesus himself, mediated by the Spirit (7:37–39). **Where do you get?:** Another example of the Johannine inept question (see on 2:20).

4:18 You have had five husbands: Another example of Jesus' divine knowledge. He is like God, who does not look on the outward appearance, but knows our hearts (1:48–50; 2:24–25; 4:29; 6:64, 70–71; see 1 Sam. 16:7). Jesus knows the woman's life, but does not condemn her (see 8:11). The woman has an abnormal and unrespectable past, but need not be thought of as a notorious sinner. In a society where women were subject to men's decisions, she may have been handed around without any decision on her part. In any case, this person who was disdained as a woman and as a Samaritan by Jews, and as a disreputable character among her own people, is accepted by Jesus and becomes an evangelist of his message.

4:19 You are a prophet: Not merely an adroit change of subject. She recognizes that Jesus is a prophet, on the basis of his supernatural knowledge (see Luke 7:39; 1 Cor. 14:24–25; the repeated prophetic "I know" of Rev. 2:2, 9, 13, 19; 3:1, 8, 15).

4:20–21 You say: The "you" is plural, "you Jews" (in contrast to "we Samaritans"). **This mountain:** Gerazim, where the Samaritan temple had been built, and which was still the holy place of Samaritans. **Jerusalem:** The site of the Jewish temple. In Jesus' day, the Samaritan temple was gone, but the temple in Jerusalem was active (see on 2:20). In the author's and readers' day, both temple sites were in ruins. The hoped-for prophet of the end time was expected to settle disputed religious issues and restore the true and final will of God. **Neither on this mountain nor in Jerusalem:** In John's view the Christ event had inaugurated an era in which true worship was no longer bound to a particular location.

4:22 You worship what you do not know: Again, the "you" is plural, meaning "you Samaritans." The Jewish Jesus declares that authentic worship is a matter of Jewish faith and practice, that **salvation is from the Jews.** John believes, however, that the saving plan of God that came through Judaism is now fulfilled in the Christian faith. The Johannine Jesus takes his stand with the God of Moses, Isaiah, and the Psalms, all cited in John, and with the Jerusalem temple as the (now fulfilled) sign of God's presence. In Samaria, Jesus identifies himself as Jew over against the Samaritans— but then declares that what he represents transcends both.

4:23 The hour is coming, and is now here: See 5:25; 12:23; 16:32; 1 John 2:18. For John, Jesus' "hour" is the climactic event of his death-resurrection-glorification, the saving event of God's act in Christ taken as a whole (see on 2:4). From the point of view within the narrative, this hour is still to come, for Jesus is not yet glorified. But here as elsewhere, the Jesus in the narrative line of the Gospel story speaks past the characters in the story to the post-Easter readers. For author and readers, this Johannine "hour," this time of salvation, is both present and to come. This corresponds to the message of the kingdom of God preached by the Jesus of the Synoptic Gospels (see on Luke 4:43–44). This corresponds to Christ himself, who has already come but is also still to come at the end of history (4:25–26; see on Luke 17:23; 21:5–36; see excursus, "Interpret-

ing the 'Near End,'" at Rev. 1:3). The Johannine Jesus does not say that the (supposedly) coming hour is already here, i.e., he does not reduce supposedly mistaken futuristic hope to present reality. Nor does he say that the hour of salvation is "partly" now and "partly" to come. This already–not yet paradox is inherent in the Christian faith. **The Father seeks:** See on 1:41.

4:24 God is spirit: This is not a "definition" of God; the point here is that God is to be worshiped in a way that corresponds to his own being, i.e., in the Spirit that God sends through Jesus (14:16), not by animal sacrifice at a specific location (see on 1:14, 29; 2:15–25).

4:25 Messiah . . . Christ: See on Mark 8:29. The Samaritans had their own version of the messianic hope, in which they did not expect a Jewish Messiah descended from David, but an analogous figure they called the *Ta'ev*, "Restorer," i.e., a saving figure God would send at the end of history to restore God's own rule over the creation. The Samaritan woman's speech is here adapted to the Jewish tradition and that of the readers.

4:26 I am he: This is the first of the Johannine Jesus' "I am" statements (see on 6:35). In contrast to the Synoptic Gospels, in John Jesus clearly reveals his identity from the beginning of the story and throughout, but the people in the story still cannot come to an authentic understanding of his identity until the story is over (see on 10:6 and "Introduction to the Gospels").

4:27 Disciples . . . were astonished: Jesus, and the Johannine church, crossed the cultural barriers of race and gender. The woman had already expressed amazement that a Jew talked with a Samaritan.

4:29 He cannot be the Messiah, can he?: The Greek grammatical construction expects a negative answer. The woman's faith and testimony are hesitant but real. In the story, God uses even this wavering affirmation as the vehicle of the conversion of the Samaritans. Even today, God does not wait for us to have perfect faith or correct theology to use our efforts at Christian evangelism and mission.

4:33–34 Surely no one has brought him something to eat?: In the Greek text, a question expecting a negative answer. On the misunderstanding expressed in the inept question, see 2:20. **My food:** See Deut. 8:3; Matt. 4:4; Luke 4:4.

4:35–36 Four months more: The harvest was an eschatological symbol, the time of the final salvation of Israel and the bringing in of the Gentiles in the triumph of God's kingdom. In some streams of Jewish theology, this was supposed to happen at the eschaton. It was not human responsibility to bring in the Gentiles, which would be God's business at the end of history. In the meantime, it was the responsibility of God's people to maintain the boundaries that distinguished them as witnesses to the one God and God's plan for history. Typical of Johannine theology, Jesus here declares that the events expected at the end time are already happening. **Sower and reaper . . . rejoice together:** See Amos 9:13. The eschatological times would be so fruitful that the reaper would overtake the sower, the times of sowing and reaping would be collapsed into one joyous occasion. Jesus announces that this time is now.

4:37–38 Others have labored, and you have entered into their labor: This text reflects the combination of pre- and post-Easter perspectives characteristic of the Gospel genre. During the ministry of the historical Jesus, there was no mission to Samaritans and other Gentiles (see Matt. 10:5 and the struggle the church had in Acts 2–15 regarding inclusion of the Gentiles). Under the guidance of the Holy Spirit sent by the risen Christ, the church did launch a mission to Samaritans and then other Gentiles (see Acts 8–11). The Johannine church already looks back on this history and enters into the labors of others. This is true of every Christian generation, including ours. None of us starts at square one of the Christian pilgrimage through history, but enters into the previous life and mission of the church that brought the faith to us, and it becomes our own story and mission.

4:39 Many . . . believed in him because of the woman's testimony: Although it was incomplete and faltering (see above), it was still effective.

4:42 No longer because of what you said: They progressed beyond secondhand faith based on the miracle reported by someone else. **We have heard for ourselves:** This is not an alternative to hearing and believing on the basis of the testimony of others, for the Gospel of John praises those who believe on the basis of the word received from others (17:20; 20:29). The Gospel's readers of a later generation, who could not have firsthand personal experience as described in this chapter, are still not secondhand or second-rate believers. In the author's theology, all believers belong to the Christian community that has "heard," "seen," and even "touched" Christ personally (see on 20:26–30; 1 John 1:1–4, and the series of conversion stories in 1:35–51, in which the distinction between secondhand and personal experience disappears). **Truly the Savior of the world:** Not "my personal savior," though there is an irreducible personal element in the decision of faith. God is at work saving the world, not saving individual souls out of the world; believers are saved with the world, not out of it. This chapter sees a progress in recognition of Jesus from the respectful "sir" (4:12–15) through "prophet" (4:19) and the Samaritan and Jewish "Messiah"-"Christ" (4:25–29) to the climactic "savior of the world" (4:42).

4:43–54
The Royal Official of Capernaum
(See also at Matt. 8:5–13; Luke 7:1–10)

This story is very similar to its Matthean and Lukan counterparts, and illustrates the way stories of Jesus' miraculous deeds were reinterpreted as they circulated in early Christianity and incorporated in the Gospels. In its Johannine context, it is the second sign to be narrated, and has been rewritten to correspond very closely to the first sign in 2:1–11. There are at least eleven points of comparison: (1) the event is called a "sign" (2:3/4:47); (2) the sign is numbered (2:11/4:54); (3) the sign is located at Cana (2:11/4:54); (4) a request is made to Jesus (2:3/4:47); (5) the request is initially repulsed by Jesus (2:4/4:48); (6) the petitioner persists 2:5/4:49; (7) Jesus commands 2:7–8/4:50; (8) Jesus' command is obeyed 2:8–9/4:50; (9) The miracle happens offstage (2:9/4:51); (10) the miracle is (unwittingly) verified (2:10/4:51–53); (11) there is a response of faith (2:11/4:53). This correspondence is not accidental, but represents John's deliberate literary structuring so that this story forms an inclusio (literary bracket, "bookend") with the first Cana story, thereby constituting 2:1–4:54 a literary unit and signaling that a new section begins at 5:1.

4:44 No honor in the prophet's own country: This saying is found in other contexts in the Synoptic Gospels (Matt. 13:57; Mark 6:4; Luke 4:24), where his home town in Galilee is the place where he is not received. In John, Jesus is welcomed in Galilee (4:45), but his ministry is centered in Judea, where he is not at home. Jesus is recognized as an outsider in Samaria (4:9), but in Judea he is called a Samaritan (8:48). For John, Jesus is the Son of God from heaven, who is a stranger everywhere in this world.

4:46 Cana in Galilee: See on 2:1. **A royal official:** In the parallel story in Matthew and Luke, he is an officer in the Roman army, a Gentile. This is not so clear in John, though Josephus, the first-century Jewish historian, uses the same word for the Gentile soldiers in the army of Herod Antipas (who was himself considered hardly Jewish by many strict Jews). If John intends the reader to understand the official as a Gentile, which is likely, the progression in the literary unit 2:1–4:54 reflects the expansion of early Christianity: Jerusalem, Judea, Samaria, Gentiles (see Acts 1:8 and the narrative Acts 1–15). **Whose son lay ill:** In Matthew the lad is a servant, in Luke a slave. In the original story he was probably called *pais*, a Greek word comparable to English "boy," which may be understood as servant, slave, or son. The variations indicate something about the nature of early Christian transmission of the tradition from and about Jesus.

4:47 Heal his son: See excursus, "Interpreting the Miracle Stories," at Matt. 9:35. The original "point" of this story as it circulated in early Christianity may have been that Jesus can still heal from a distance, i.e., that the risen Christ can still heal from heaven. Like Matthew and Luke, John has adapted it to express the theological message he wants to communicate in his own situation.

4:48 Unless you see signs and wonders: Jesus' response sounds disparaging and off-putting (see 3:1–3) and is odd in that one of the themes of the Gospel is that signs are given to generate faith (12:37; 20:29–30). Such texts may indicate that John has incorporated prior traditions and sources that had differing valuations of signs, or that there is more than one level of belief—faith can be focused on the sign itself, which is not authentic faith, or can look beyond the sign to the one to whom it points. For John, authentic faith is not finally in signs, but in the sign-giver, the God who is present and active in Christ.

4:50 Go, your son will live: Only in the Johannine version of the story does the reader get to hear the healing word of Jesus. **The man believed the word:** For John, faith comes by the word of Christ, who is the incarnate Word of God (1:14). The man believes on the basis of the Word before he has seen any sign.

4:54 The second sign: See 2:11. Though there have been intervening signs that happened offstage (2:23; 3:2), this is the second sign that has been narrated, and the second sign in Cana. Some scholars have taken this enumer-

ation, which does not exactly fit the present narrative, to be evidence of a pre-Johannine "signs source" John has incorporated and interpreted.

(It has often been noted that 6:1 connects well here, as 7:1 follows well after 5:47, so that the chapter order 4–6–5–7 makes better chronological and geographical sense, and that some aspects of the narrative read better if chap. 7 follows chap. 5. Yet the references to signs in 6:2 presupposes the signs of 4:46–54 and 5:1–8, and thus the present order of the chapters. Likewise the reference to thirty-eight years in 5:5 and to the approaching Passover in 6:4 fit better in the present order. Such difficulties show that the Gospel of John was not the product of one day, but that it grew through more than one revision over a considerable period of time. However, we can no longer see how many such stages and authors or the length of time involved in its composition. We must interpret the text in its final canonical form, but it is sometimes helpful to see the process by which this text came to be. [See "Process of Composition" in introduction to John.])

5:1–11:57
THE LIFE THAT LEADS TO CONFLICT, DEATH, AND RESURRECTION

5:1–30
THE LIFE-GIVING WORD GENERATES CONFLICT

At this point the narrative takes a deadly turn. Previously, Jesus has been met with suspicion, skepticism, and challenge, but not overt hostility. In this episode begins the real conflict, which quickly escalates into a decision by his opponents that Jesus must die. This section has similarities with Mark 2:1–3:6, in which Jesus' miracles generate conflicts that result in his enemies' resolve to kill him. There is in fact verbatim agreement between Jesus' words in 5:8 and Mark 2:9, but this does not necessarily mean John is using Mark directly as a source. Here as elsewhere, John takes the Synoptic tradition, melts it down, and recasts it in his own idiom. There are also similarities to John 9:1–41, where a miracle story results in a hostile dialogue that modulates into a monologue by Jesus.

Chapter 5 is clearly a literary unit that begins with a miracle story (5:1–9a), resulting in a controversy dialogue, which escalates into a decision to kill Jesus for his christological claims (5:9b–18), followed by a monologue on the authority of Jesus as Son of Man (5:19–30) and the (five?) witnesses that testify to Jesus (5:31–47).

5:1 After this: See on end of chap. 4. **A festival of the Jews:** If this was a Passover, there are four Passovers mentioned in John, and Jesus' ministry is portrayed as lasting more than three years. See on "Outline" in introduction to John.

5:2 In Jerusalem: In the Synoptic portrayal of Jesus' life, there are no healing stories recounted in Judea or Jerusalem. **A pool:** This pool has now been excavated, on the north side of the temple court, near St. Anne's Church. It does indeed have five porticoes, showing the author or his source had accurate knowledge of Jerusalem. **Beth-zatha:** Alternate names are given in various manuscripts. See NRSV note. We cannot be sure of the actual ancient name.

5:3b–4 An angel ... stirred up the water: Though found in the King James Version, these verses are missing from the oldest and best manuscripts (which were unavailable to the 1611 translators) and apparently were added by a later scribe to explain the statement in v. 7, which does seem to presuppose something like this.

5:5 Thirty-eight years: The only other biblical reference to "thirty-eight" is to Deut. 2:14, the period Israel spent in the wilderness between Egypt and the promised land, a time of rebellion and grumbling. This motif of the crowds grumbling in the wilderness reappears in 6:25–59, and seems to be prepared for here.

5:6 Do you want to get well? (NIV): Jesus takes the initiative and speaks first; the sovereign Jesus who represents God acts unilaterally (see v. 14; 2:3–4; 7:1–10; 11:1–7). This is not an informational question, which the Johannine Jesus practically never asks, since he operates with divine knowledge (see 1:48–49; 2:24–25; 4:17–18, 29; 6:64, 70–71, and, e.g., 6:6). Nor is it a foolish question, as though of course the man wanted to be healed, since that is what he had been waiting by the pool for all these years. Johannine theology is involved—those who are healed/saved by Jesus must want the gift he has to offer (see 4:10; 7:17). While such stories are not to be psychologized, it is also true in the Johannine sense that the man must decide whether he wanted the radically new gift of freedom and the responsibility it brings. For thirty-eight years his identity had been that of the sick, apparently paralyzed man who could do nothing but lie by the pool and complain that he was not able to get into the

healing waters in time. On the day he is healed, he must assume a new understanding of himself and his responsibilities. The healing gift of God brings a new identity, new freedom, and new responsibilities. We have grown accustomed to our old identities in which no one blames us, and we do not blame ourselves, for doing or being anything different. Whether anyone wants to accept this joyful/frightening offer is indeed a real question.

5:9a At once the man was made well: See excursus, "Interpreting the Miracle Stories," at Matt. 9:35. What he had sought in the water he found in Jesus himself (see on 9:7). The reader should note that Jesus heals only *one* of the multitude; both Jesus and the narrator ignore the others. This is not because Jesus plays favorites or due to the man's faith or character (as though he "deserved it" and the others did not). Nothing is said of the man's faith, he doesn't know who Jesus is, and in fact he turns against him (5:12–16). Such miracle stories are told in the mode of confessional language that communicates the theological meaning of the Christ event, not in the mode of objectifying that allows such (otherwise reasonable) questions (on confessional language, see commentary on Matt. 2:16; excursus, "Interpreting Revelation's Violent Imagery," 3.b, at Rev. 6:15). On the "aloofness" of the Johannine Jesus, see commentary on 11:6.

5:9b Now that day was a Sabbath: We now learn this for the first time, almost as an afterthought. On the importance of the Sabbath in Jewish life, see on Luke 4:16, 39–41; 6:1–11, esp. on 6:5; 13:14; 14:1–5 (and Jesus is a Jew, 4:9, 22). This is the first reference to the Sabbath in John; it sets up the conflict to follow.

5:10 The Jews: See introduction to John: "Conflicts with 'the Jews.'"

5:14 Do not sin any more: See Mark 2:5; John 8:11; 9:1–3 (where Jesus opposes the view that physical suffering and handicaps are a punishment for sin).

5:17 My Father is still working: Father as a name for God was already found in the Old Testament and in Jewish tradition, but it is not this "ordinary" use to which his opponents object. On Jesus' distinctive address to God as father, see on Luke 11:2. Nor is it the Christian understanding that all believers or all people are children of God that is here rejected. Here and elsewhere the Johannine Jesus claims a unique relation to God.

Jesus' debates with his opponents reflect early Christian debates within Judaism and (after Christianity became primarily a Gentile religion) with Judaism. The historical Jesus had been an observant Jew and had not in fact violated the Sabbath in spectacular, profane ways, but also had not observed all the strict refinements developed by the Pharisees. After Easter, the church continued and extended Jesus' nonrigid adherence to the Sabbath law and then, as the church became more and more Gentile, replaced the Sabbath with Sunday, the day of resurrection. In conflicts with Jews on whether they had abandoned the law of God by their relaxation of the Sabbath, Christians searched the Scripture, the Bible they had in common with Judaism, to find justification for their relaxation of the Sabbath. Such debates are projected back into the life of Jesus, who is claimed as their authority for the new practice. (On early Christian interpretation of the Bible, see "New Testament Interpretation of the Old Testament," excursus at 1 Cor. 15:3.) Here the Bible is found to support their practice, in that God continued to work after the six days of creation (see Gen. 1:1–2:3). The argument is that since God does not strictly keep the Sabbath, neither does Jesus or his followers.

5:18 Making himself equal to God: There is a double escalation in 5:1–18: (1) an escalation from a Sabbath controversy such as occurred within Judaism, to a christological controversy typical of debates between Jews and Christians in the author's own day; and (2) an escalation from inquiry and opposition to a resolve to put Jesus to death. It is not entirely clear whether "equal with God" is a way of describing Jesus' relation to God that the author himself affirms, or he only places it in the mouth of Jesus' Jewish opponents as their misunderstanding of Christian claims for Jesus. It is clear that Jews were concerned to protect their monotheistic faith and understood Christian claims about Jesus as violating this fundamental tenet of faith. (Such claims were not made during Jesus' lifetime; the author is here expressing the post-Easter issues of his own time within the pre-Easter framework of the story of Jesus. See "Introduction to the Gospels.") It is also clear that Christians were concerned to claim that in the truly human Jesus of Nazareth the one true God is encountered, and to do this in a way that does not compromise Jewish and Christian monotheism. That there is only one God is as fundamental to the author, who is probably himself a Jewish Christian, as it is to his Jew-

ish context (see 5:44; 17:3). He never himself says, or has Jesus say, that Jesus is "equal to God," but quite the contrary (see 14:28). Yet he wishes to be clear that it is not some subordinate being less than God who is incarnate and present in Jesus (see on 1:1–2, 14; 10:30; 14:9; 20:28). For John, there is thus a sense in which Christ is "equal with God," but to think of him as a separate god alongside the one God is a misunderstanding of Christian faith. Later Trinitarian theology was concerned to find a way to express the Christian claim that it is not someone less than God who is present and active in Christ, and to do this in a way that does not compromise faith in the one God. Such christological discussions in the mouth of Jesus are unique to the Gospel of John; nothing like them is found in the Synoptic Gospels. They reflect the christological reflection and debates of the Johannine community.

5:19 The Son can do nothing on his own: Jesus does not directly deny the charge of claiming "equality with God," but neither does he give a theoretical, metaphysical "explanation" of his divine nature. He responds in terms of his unity with God's mission and work; he is the functional equivalent of God (see on Luke 9:46–48). The roots of the Johannine theology are already present in the Synoptic Gospels and in the life and teaching of Jesus himself. **Whatever the Father does, the Son does:** In a culture in which the father's vocation was taught to the son, this may well have been a common proverb. It is here taken up in a theological sense and applied to the relation of Jesus' work to God's.

5:20 Greater works: Jesus will (as God's agent) raise the dead, preside at the eschatological judgment, and grant eternal life. See 14:12, where the disciples too will do "greater works" than the pre-Easter Jesus, i.e., they will be Christ's agents in proclaiming the gospel and in creating the church as the community of ministry and reconciliation.

5:21–22 Raises the dead . . . judges: In traditional Old Testament and Jewish theology, this is the work of *God* in the eschatological *future*. In Johannine theology, these divine acts *already* begin in the life and ministry of *Christ*, before and after the resurrection. Judgment is not only the great separation at the end of history (see Matt. 25:31–46) but happens already in response to the presence and message of Christ.

5:22–23 Father . . . Son: This saying has the same form and content as the Synoptic (Q) saying in Matt. 10:40/Luke 16:16, but different wording.

It illustrates the Johannine style of taking traditional sayings and recasting them in his own vocabulary. In all the Gospels, to deal with Jesus is to deal with God, which corresponds to the Jewish principle that a man's messenger is the same as the man himself. God's act in *Jesus* is God's *own* act. This Christian conviction common to the New Testament is here expressed in the distinctively Johannine idiom.

5:25 Is coming, and · . . . is now here: See on 4:23. Here as elsewhere, John thinks bitemporally. **The dead:** Those who are physically alive, but since they "live" apart from God, have no real life (see Luke 15:24). **Those who hear will live:** Here the eschatological resurrection happens already, in the encounter with the life-giving Word (see 11:24–27; Col. 2:12; 3:1–4; Eph. 2:6; contrast 2 Tim. 2:18).

5:26 Just as . . . so: Here the christological paradox is stated in another way. Christ is like God in that he has *life in himself* (= underived, independent); yet *God has granted this* to the Son (= derived, dependent; see v. 30).

5:27 Son of Man: See on Mark 2:10. Only here in John does Jesus assume the traditional role of Son of Man as eschatological judge.

5:28–29 The hour is coming: Since the eschatological judgment is here portrayed as entirely future, some have seen this as the work of a later editor who has reinserted the traditional futuristic eschatology. While it is true that the Gospel has gone through at least one revision in the process of coming to its present canonical form (see introduction to John; commentary at 5:54), it is probably not the case that there was ever a form of the Gospel of John that was totally devoid of the future hope. The tension between present and future was there all along and is inherent in the Christian affirmation that the Christ has come but the Christ is still to come; the decisive event has occurred, but the final purpose of God for the creation is not yet fulfilled.

5:30 I can do nothing on my own: See 14:10 note. **I seek to do not my own will:** See Matt. 26:39. Jesus' final prayer in Matthew here becomes the trademark of his whole life. Human beings were created to do the will of God, but since Gen. 3 human beings have never escaped the temptation to replace God's will with their own, to place themselves in God's place (see on Rom. 5:12–21). The uniqueness of the human being Jesus consisted in his total transparency to God, the unity of his will and God's. In this sense he is the one truly human being; the rest of us fall short not only of God,

but of our own true humanity. In this sense John can picture Jesus as truly God without violating his true humanity, but indeed as an expression of it.

5:31–47
TESTIMONY TO JESUS

John presents this concluding section of the discourse in the light of two principles that were important in biblical and Jewish tradition for ·evaluating witnesses and testimony: the truth cannot be established on the basis of only one witness (Num. 35:30; Deut. 17:6), and the truth cannot be established about a person solely on the basis of that person's testimony. John thus presents five witnesses to Jesus: John (31–35), Jesus' "works" (36), the Father (37), the Scripture (39), and Moses (46). This is not a matter of gathering "evidence" on the basis of which Jesus is "proved" to be God's Son (see on 7:12). Faith in Christ is not a matter of rational inferences drawn from reliable evidence; Christian faith is generated by the Word of God that is heard in the testimony from and about Jesus.

5:32 Another who testifies on my behalf: On the surface level, this is John the Baptist, whose only role in this Gospel is to offer testimony to Jesus (1:19–34; 3:22–26). But at a deeper level, the one who testifies is God, for it is God's word that is heard in John's testimony (v. 37). This is true of all the other witnesses as well.

5:34–35 Not that I accept such human testimony: Jesus makes it clear that the series of witnesses here introduced is not for *Jesus'* benefit, to establish his identity on the basis of (good) human criteria (see on 7:12). Rather, Jesus speaks for *their* benefit, i.e., their salvation. **A burning and shining lamp:** Literally, a lit lamp. It is Jesus, the incarnate Word, the embodiment of the light that enlightens everyone, who is the light of the world (1:4–14; 8:12). John's light is secondary and derivative; he has *been lit*, while Christ inherently *is the light* of God. John was the lamp directing people to the wedding celebration, but people stopped at the sign (for John was a popular and interesting character) rather than going ahead to the wedding festival and the bridegroom himself (see 3:25–30).

5:36 The works . . . testify: For those who have eyes to see, Jesus' deeds testify to the presence of God. This does not mean that we can look over Jesus' works, compare them with others, and decide on the basis of our own criteria and value system that Jesus is God's Son. We do not authenticate him as from God on the basis of our own judgment, which would be a way of keeping control in our own hands (see on 3:1–3; 7:12). We have nothing with which to measure and authenticate the Word of God, which asserts itself and creates faith. But Jesus' works become the vehicle of this word of testimony.

5:37 The Father . . . has himself testified: This does not refer to the voice from heaven at Jesus' baptism or transfiguration (Mark 1:11; 9:7), neither of which is reported in John. God's testimony is not one of a series that includes John, Jesus' works, and the Bible, but transcends and speaks through them all. **Have never heard his voice:** See 1:18.

5:39 You search the scriptures: The same Greek verb form can be translated as imperative (as in KJV, "Search the scriptures") or indicative (as in NRSV and practically all modern translations). Jesus does not here command to study the Bible, but is critical of those who study the Bible supposing that eternal life is to be found in a book, when the book itself testifies to the living Word of God, Christ himself, who represents God. Christian faith is not finally in the Bible, but in the God of the Bible. Believing the Bible can be an idolatrous barrier to faith in God. Just as admirers of John the Baptist stopped short of faith in Christ to whom John pointed, so believing the Bible can become faith in a book rather than in the living God to whom the Bible points.

5:42 The love of God: Love for God, the reflection of God's love for us (1 John 4:19). Paradoxically, those who hear God's word in Scripture are those who already love God, a matter of one's will rather than intellect (7:17).

5:43 In my Father's name: The Johannine Jesus claims to represent not himself but God. The Christian confession that Jesus is the Christ, the Son of God, is not in answer to the question, who is Jesus? as though he were some great man for whom we need to find an adequate title. Rather, the Christian confession responds to the question, who is God? (see on Acts 9:22). God has defined himself as the one present and active in the life, death, and resurrection of Jesus. The Scripture points to God; Christ is identified with God, so that from the perspective of Christian faith the (Old Testament) Scripture points to Christ, i.e., it points through him to God. Christians have not rejected the Old Testament but, without denying that it spoke and speaks the word of God to Jews as their Scripture, hear it speaking to them as the same God definitively revealed in Jesus Christ (see on 2 Cor. 3:1–18).

5:46 Moses . . . wrote about me: From the perspective of Christian faith, Christ is the one to whom Moses and all the prophets ultimately point. Thus Christians do not reject Moses (as John's Jewish opponents claimed) but accept the real testimony of Moses to Christ. In early Christianity, this was often understood to mean that Moses (and the Old Testament generally) were not speaking to their own times but predicting Jesus and the church. More critical modern Christians no longer affirm this in the way the ancient church did; the Old Testament did indeed have a message for its own times, but in the Christian view the will and purpose of God to which the Old Testament testifies point to the ultimate fulfillment of God's will as represented by Christ. On Christian appropriation of the Old Testament, see on Luke 21:22; 24:27; Acts 1:16–17; 2:16; 3:18; excursus at 1 Cor. 15:3, "New Testament Interpretation of the Old Testament"; and 1 Pet. 1:10.

6:1–71
THE BREAD OF LIFE

This chapter represents the only section of Jesus' ministry in John that has the same events in the same order as the Synoptics: feeding the multitudes, walking on the water, Peter's confession. Here and elsewhere, it is still not clear whether John knows the present form of the Synoptics or whether the events he narrates were already clustered together in the tradition common to all the Gospels. While following the Markan order, John has nonetheless given the section his distinctive structure: a sign followed by interpretative dialogue that tends to become a monologue. In the Synoptics, the christological message of each miracle story was implicit (see on Luke 9:10–17); John makes this meaning explicit by having Jesus give a long speech interpreting its significance.

6:1–15
Five Thousand Are Fed
(See also at Matt. 14:13–21; 15:32–39;
Mark 6:32–44; 8:1–10; Luke 9:10b–17)

This is the only miracle story that occurs in all four Gospels, with Matthew and Mark each having two versions of the story (five thousand, four thousand). John's version reflects elements from all the other versions. On sequence and editing, see on 4:54.

6:1 The other side of the Sea of Galilee: In contrast to Matthew and Mark, John locates the feeding on the east side of the lake (see also vv. 16–20). Luke places it in Bethsaida. This illustrates the freedom each evangelist exercised in retelling the story of Jesus, in which the goal was theological meaning, not reporter-like accuracy. **Sea of Tiberias:** This designation, which occurs only in John (6:1; 23; 21:1), has political overtones. Tiberias had been founded by Herod Antipas about 20 CE as his new capital, replacing Sepphoris. Tiberias, located on the southwest shore of the lake, was named for the reigning emperor (see Luke 3:1). It was built over an ancient Jewish cemetery, making it ritually unclean for all observant Jews. This meant that whoever lived there, including all Herod's court and administrative officials, had to consider Hellenistic culture, Rome, and Herod more important than Jewish tradition. Jesus is never reported as being there or as having mentioning the city in his teaching.

6:4 Passover: See "Outline" in introduction to John and commentary on Luke 22:1.

6:6 To test him: The Johannine Jesus, representing God, hardly ever asks informational questions (see 1:48; 4:16–19; 6:64, 70–71; 13:21–2; but see 11:34). Typical of the Johannine presentation, Jesus takes the initiative.

6:9 A boy . . . barley loaves: These details, only in John, seem to reflect the similar story of Elisha in 2 Kgs. 4:42–43. Since Jesus was considered the fulfillment of the Old Testament, details from the traditional biblical story enriched the retelling of the Jesus story.

6:11–13 When he had given thanks: Matthew and Mark have "blessed" in the feeding of the five thousand, "given thanks" in the feeding of the four thousand. The Greek word for "give thanks" is *eucharizo,* from which "Eucharist" is derived. As the story was repeatedly retold in the early church, it took on features of the Christian celebration of the Eucharist. The early Christians could not tell stories set in the pre-Easter life of Jesus without hearing in them the overtones of their own post-Easter experience. John's version of the Last Supper (13:1–17:26) has no institution of the Eucharist; he places all his eucharistic material in this section. **He distributed:** In contrast to the Synoptics, there is no "breaking" of the bread (see on 19:31–37), and Jesus himself distributes the bread. In the Christian Eucharist, the living Christ is present; he is the one who offers the believer the bread of life. **As much as they wanted . . . they were satisfied:** All the Gospels point out that the people ate their fill and that there was much food left over. In the modern affluent West, we must remind ourselves that "eating all you want" has been an extraordinary event in the lives of most of the human race for most of its history (see, e.g., Ruth 2:14), and thus served as a symbol of ultimate salvation. In John's picture, the satisfaction of this universal human hunger is already present in Christ. **So that nothing may be lost:** John emphasizes that Christ loses nothing of what has been entrusted to him (6:39; 18:9). The **twelve baskets** of fragments testify to the extravagance of the messianic banquet (see on 2:6). The bread supplied by Jesus enables more than survival. The leftovers are gathered and preserved. The manna of Exod. 16 and Num. 11 could not be preserved. The next day it "bred worms and stank."

6:14–15 The prophet: See Deut. 18:15–18. This identification is true, though partial and not finally adequate (see 4:19). **Make him king:** The crowd realizes that one who can multiply bread can end the world's hunger problem and rule the world (see Luke 4:3–4). It seems so right, and modern readers should not too easily dismiss Jesus' first Jewish hearers as expecting only an "earthly king." They too were interested in feeding the hungry and ending the unjust inequality of the way the goods of this earth are divided. In John's view, Jesus is indeed the promised king of the end time who will bring the world back under God's rule (1:49; 3:3–5; 12:15; 18:33, 36–39; 19:3, 12–21). But the kingship of God represented by Jesus transcends even our best vision of how to establish justice. Humans cannot make Jesus king; we do not elect him to be the Christ. He comes from God and transcends even our best vision of what rulership and justice should be.

6:16–21
The Walking on the Water
(See at Matt. 14:22–33; Mark 6:45–52)

6:22–59
The Bread of Life

6:23 The Lord had given thanks: See 6:11–12. The whole preceding scene is here summarized with eucharistic overtones; the phrase could almost be translated "after the Lord had celebrated the Eucharist."

6:25 When did you come here?: Since John has the feeding occur on the eastern side of the lake, he utilizes the account of getting Jesus and the crowds back on the western side to raise this question of Jesus' origin. From the very first, the questions, where is Jesus? and how did he come here? understood in their ultimate sense, are important for Johannine theology (see the disciples' first question, 1:38). On "where are you from?" see 19:9.

6:26 Signs . . . ate your fill: On John's ambivalent perspective on signs, see 1:48–49; 2:1, 4, 11; 3:1–2; 4:48. The *signs* are intended to *point to* the saving act of God in the Christ event. Believing in a particular miracle, i.e., that it "really happened," means that one has not really seen the sign, even if one's stomach is full of miraculous bread.

6:27 Food that endures: Even the Old Testament manna did not provide lasting satisfaction (Exod. 16; Num. 11). Neither did the miraculous food Jesus had just provided. See 4:13–15, 32. **Work . . . Son of Man will give:** Here in one statement the paradox of human responsibility and divine gift is expressed. Human beings cannot simply be passive and wait for God to act, but are to work for that which really satisfies their ultimate longings, just as they are to seek God's kingdom first (Matt. 6:33). But what they work for they do not achieve by their own efforts, for it is finally the *gift* of the Son of Man (see on 3:16). **God . . . has set his seal:** See 3:33. God is the one who certifies Jesus. Human beings do not make him the Christ (vs. 6:15; see Luke 20:17; Acts 2:36).

6:28–29 What must we do?: God is the author of salvation; it is God's act that finally saves. Yet the question of human responsibility, human *response* to God's grace, is a crucial question (see Mic. 6:8; Luke 10:25; 18:18; Acts 16:30). **Work . . . believe:** As in Acts 16:31, faith is the human response to God's grace. Faith is obedience in personal-trust (see on 3:31–36).

6:30–31 What sign? . . . bread from heaven: As in Mark 8:1–12, the feeding miracle is followed by a demand for a sign. They had seen the miracle, which they believed, but had not seen it as a sign pointing to the true identity of Jesus himself as God's saving act. The sign must be given by God's initiative; it cannot be God's response to human criteria (see on 7:12). They refer to the story of Moses and the manna in the wilderness (Exod. 16; Num. 11) and cite Ps. 78:23–25. Much in the remaining discourse seems to be an interpretation of this psalm and reflects the preaching of the Johannine church in dialogue with Jewish objections to the church's faith.

6:32–33 Not Moses gave . . . God gives: The contrast is between what Moses did in the past (i.e. what God did through him) and what God does in the present (i.e., in the Christ-event, which through the resurrection and the gift of the Spirit did not remain an isolated event of the past). **The true bread:** In such Johannine expressions, "true" means "real, ultimately real"; its opposite is not "untrue," but "unreal" (see 1:9; 4:23; 15:1; 17:3). **That which (he who):** The Greek can be translated either way. John intends the ambiguity. The audience in the story hears "that which"; John speaks to the post-Easter readers who know it refers to Jesus himself. **Gives life to the world:** The true bread that sustains real life is neither the manna of the Old Testament nor the miraculous bread Jesus has just supplied, but Christ himself, the gift of God from heaven who gives eternal life.

6:35 I am the bread of life: Only in the Gospel of John does Jesus speak of himself in this distinctive "I am" form (6:35, 41, 48, 57, "bread" or "manna"; 8:12, "light"; 10:7, 9, "door"; 10:11, 14, "shepherd"; 11:25, "resurrection and life"; 14:6, "way, truth, life"; 15:1, 5, "vine"; 4:26; 8:28, 58; 13:19; 18:5, 6, absolute "I am," but see Mark 6:50; Matt. 14:27). The formula has antecedents both in the Bible and in pagan culture and is used four ways: (1) the *presentation* form, responding to the implicit question, who are you? as in Gen. 28:13; Rev. 1:17; (2) the *qualification* form, responding to the implicit question, what are you? as in Ezek. 28:2, 9; (3) the *identification* form, in which the speaker identifies himself, "I am the one who . . ."; see the colloquial "it's me"; (4) the *recognition* form, in which the "I" is not the subject, but the predicate, as in 1 Sam. 9:19; see John 9:9. The implicit question was not, who are you? but, who is the X? where the meaning of X was already known, but *who* is to be identified as X was at issue. We might think of the day after a disputed election for the presidency, when it is known that *someone* is the president, but *who* this is remains disputed. Then a figure steps forth and settles the question by saying "I am"— more colloquially, "I'm it," or "It's me." This is precisely the case in 9:9, where the healed man says, "I am the man," in Greek simply "I am." The French translation thus appropriately renders it "c'est moi." See Louis XIV's famous expression of political absolutism, "L'ètat c'est moi"—"I am the state," or "the state, that's me." Some forms of pagan religion used a combination of these forms. The "Hymn to Isis" had a long list of self-affirmations by the goddess: "I am the eldest daughter of Time. . . . I am wife and sister of King Osiris. . . . I am she that riseth in the dog star. . . .

I am the Queen of War. . . . I am the Queen of the Thunderbolt. . . . I am the Lord of rainstorms." People are aware that there is a mysterious power in the storm and everywhere in nature; Isis says, "I am," "That's me."

Ancient Israel was aware that there were various claims to be God. The God of Israel had revealed his divine name as "I am," in the Johannine understanding, "I'm the One," "That's me" (see Exod. 3:13–15). When the Johannine Jesus uses this formula, it is not a direct claim to be God (see 9:9, where the blind man uses the "I am" formula). Yet the use of this expression evokes the story of the revelation of God's name and reminds the reader that Jesus is the representative of God, who is united with and identified with God (1:1–2, 14, 18; 5:18; 10:30; 14:9; 20:28). It is important to see that the Johannine usage represents the *recognition* form described above. If one is a Jew, one looks for the Messiah sent by God as savior of the world. To such a person, Jesus says, "I am" (see 4:26). If one comes from a background in Gentile culture, one is still looking for something as the fulfillment of life. In John, these universal human aspirations are pictured as bread, water, life, light, truth. In our own time, one might think of money, security, love, acceptance. All these are symbols of what we are really looking for, often at a level deeper than our own awareness or ability to articulate. To all such human longings, Jewish and Gentile, religious and secular, the Johannine Jesus says, "It's me," "I'm it," "I am" (see on 1:38).

6:36–37 Have seen . . . do not believe: On the Johannine dialectic of seeing and believing, see on 20:24–29. **Everything (NIV All) that the Father gives me will come to me:** On the dialectic of divine sovereignty (predestination) and human responsibility, see on 3:16. The Greek neuter emphasizes the collective idea involved (as in 3:6; 10:29; 17:2, 24) and might better be translated "all" (people). They are both given to the Son by the Father (divine initiative and responsibility) and come to Jesus (on their own decision and responsibility).

6:38–40 Not to do my own will: See on 5:30. **Raise . . . on the last day:** Repeated four times in this context, showing that while the eschatological center of gravity has shifted in the Gospel of John, the hope of future resurrection remains (see on 5:29).

6:42 Jesus, the son of Joseph: See 1:45. **Whose father and mother we know:** See discussion of human criteria in evaluating Jesus at 7:12.

How?: As in v. 52, this is not an informational question, but the "how" of human pride that presumes to reject trust in God until God has answered our reasonable questions and we can see on our own terms how God's truth can be true (see 1 Cor. 15:36–41). **I have come down from heaven:** The paradox is that the one who is the son of Joseph *is* the one who has come down from heaven. No space trip is pictured here, but Jesus' origin and the source of his mission (see "nonobjectifying language" at Acts 1:9).

6:44 No one can come to me unless drawn by the Father: We find God because God first finds us (see 1:38–51; 4:23, and excursus, "Predestination," at Rom. 8:28–29).

6:45 All be taught by God: John may be responding to the claim in his own church situation that there are special teachers with esoteric knowledge to initiate believers into deeper mysteries of the faith. John believes that in the Spirit-led community of faith, all instruction comes from God, and one needs no elite "gnostic" teachers (see on John 1:1, 14, 18:20; 19:34; 1 Cor. 12:3; 1 Tim. 4:1–5; 6:20–21; 1 John 2:20, 27; Rev. 1:3).

6:51–59 The bread . . . is my flesh: Salvation, the saving gift of eternal life, is often pictured in the Bible as eating and drinking together with God's people. See Isa. 55:1. The life-giving divine Wisdom offers herself as food and drink (Prov. 9:5). In John, Jesus is the incarnate Wisdom of God (see on 1:1–14). Jesus gives himself as living bread and living water, 4:10; 6:35. We well-fed modern Westerners tend to forget that eating and drinking is a matter of life and death, but John's readers did not need this reminder. **Drinks my blood:** This is an extremely shocking phrase to Jewish ears (see Lev. 17:10–14; Acts 15:20). On Jesus' blood in Christian symbolism, see on Luke 22:19–23; John 19:34–35; Acts 20:28; Rom. 3:25; 1 Cor. 5:6–8; Heb. 9:1–10:18, and often; 1 Pet. 1:2, 13, 19; 1 John 1:7; 5:6; Rev. 1:5, 5:9; 6:9–11; 7:14; 19:13.

The whole discourse has eucharistic overtones (see on 6:11), but John does not mean to reduce the meaning to participation in the Eucharist (see on 13:30—in the Johannine narrative of the Last Supper, only Judas receives bread). It is Christ—who is present in the eucharistic service and to whom the bread and wine point—who gives life, not a magical effect of the eucharistic elements themselves. Yet John's insistence on the importance of participating probably has a particular point in his own situation, where Jewish (and Gentile) believers were tempted to have their own private, individualistic faith that did not expose them to religious, social, and political difficulties. See 12:42–43. Participation in the eucharistic service was an act of Christian confession, a testimony to others of the truth of the Christian faith (like baptism, which John also emphasizes, 3:3–5, 22, 26; 4:1–2; see 19:34).

6:60–71
Many Disciples Take Offense at Jesus;
Peter's Confession
(See also at Matt. 16:13–20;
Mark 8:27–30; Luke 9:18–21)

As in the Synoptic Gospels, the feeding miracle is followed by Peter's confession of Jesus as the Christ, speaking in behalf of all the disciples. The story here has both different details and a different function. In Mark, this is the dramatic turning point in the story, the first time a human being has perceived Jesus' true identity. In John, Jesus has been acknowledged by his disciples as the Christ from the first page (see 1:41).

6:60 This teaching is difficult: Not difficult to understand, but a "hard saying" in the sense that it is offensive and off-putting. The disciples are not puzzled by it, but offended (v. 61). In this it corresponds to the nature of the Christian gospel itself, centered in a crucified Christ, which is always a shock to our conventional ways of thinking, an offense that must not be adjusted to make it more palatable; the message that the one true God has definitively acted in the life and death of a crucified Jew is inherently offensive and resists being domesticated (Gal. 5:11).

6:61–62 Complaining: The word is the same used for Israel's grumbling during the wilderness wanderings between Egypt and the promised land. Here it is applied not to the Jews but to Jesus' disciples. **Offend:** Literally "cause you to stumble" or "scandalize." As in 16:1, the danger is that they will fall away from their faith, yield to the external pressure, and abandon their calling as disciples. This reflects the danger present in the church of John's own time. **The Son of Man ascending:** On Son of Man, see on Mark 2:10. "Ascending" is by way of the cross; Jesus is "lifted up" in crucifixion, which is his exaltation to heaven (3:14; 8:28; 12:32–34).

6:63 The flesh is useless: John can use "flesh" (and "world") in more than one sense (see 1:14; 3:6). On the one hand, the Johannine Jesus uses "flesh" to insist on the reality of the incarnation (1:14). On the other hand, these words coming so quickly after 6:52–58 show

that "flesh" there is not crudely literal, that the Eucharist does not function mechanistically. **The words that I have spoken to you are spirit:** The Greek word means both "spirit" and "breath" (see 3:8). Human words are literally our "breath," our "life." The word of Christ is his breath or spirit that gives life.

6:64 Jesus knew from the first: See 1:48–49; 2:23–25; 4:16–19; 6:70–71; 13:21–26. The text is not about Judas and is not directed to the question of whether he was responsible, but is about Jesus: as the representative of God, he is all-knowing.

6:65 No one can come to me unless it is granted: See v. 44. This is not an "explanation" for the mystery of why some respond to God's grace and some do not, but a confession of gratitude. Every believer must look at Judas, not with a sense of superiority, but with the confession, "There but for the grace of God go I."

6:66–69 Many of his disciples turned back: This reflects the situation in the Johannine church, when many were abandoning the faith due to persecution or internal schism of the Johannine community (see on 1–3 John). **To whom shall we go:** A question that transcends John's own situation. **The Holy One of God:** A synonym for "the Christ," "the Messiah," "the Savior" (see Mark 1:24; Luke 4:34; 1 John 2:20; Rev. 3:7). Unlike Paul and the New Testament generally, the Gospel and Letters of John reserve the term "holy" for God and Christ, never using the plural, translated "saints," as a term for Christians (but see fourteen times in Revelation).

6:70 One of you is a devil: This may refer to the fact that Judas was inspired by the devil to betray Jesus (13:2). But both the Greek and Hebrew words for "devil" also mean "slanderer"; the Satan is the one who slanders or accuses God's people before the heavenly court (Job 1–2). The same word is translated "slanderer" in 1 Tim. 3:11; 2 Tim. 2:26; 3:3; Titus 2:3. In John's situation, Christians were sometimes brought before synagogue courts because they had been "turned in," i.e., betrayed, by fellow Christians. Judas is here portrayed as the prototype of such Christians who accused their brothers and sisters before the synagogue court. This is one reason the Fourth Gospel makes so much of judicial imagery. As the Holy Spirit is the Counselor, i.e., the attorney who is the advocate of the Christian's cause before such courts, so people who accuse Christians are like Judas. The question had arisen in John's situation, how could one who has been called by Christ into the church turn against his or her fellow Christians? Was he not really called in the first place? The Johannine answer: Judas was called by Christ, but he became a slanderer and accuser (= "devil"). See 6:64–65.

6:71 The twelve: "The twelve" occurs only here and 20:24 in John. They are not called "apostles," a word which occurs only in 13:16 (translated in the nontechnical sense as "messengers"). Nor does the expression "twelve disciples" occur in John.

7:1–11:57
LIGHT AND LIFE, MANIFESTATION
AND REJECTION

7:1–52
Conflict at the Feast of Booths

7:1 After this: See on chronology and editing at 4:54. **The Jews were looking for an opportunity to kill him:** On "the Jews" see introduction to John. This threat connects well to chap. 5 (see 5:18); in the present order, some time (and several pages of text) intervene between the threat and the continuation of the theme.

7:2 The festival of Booths: Also called "Tabernacles" or the "festival of ingathering" (see Exod. 23:16; Lev. 23:34; Deut. 16:13; Num. 29:12), this fall harvest festival had come to commemorate the period when Israel dwelt in booths or tents before they settled down in the promised land. It also involved water rites looking forward to the beginning of the fall rains, necessary for the agricultural year. Both water symbolism and tent-tabernacle symbolism is involved in the action and dispute that follows. In the Synoptics, Jesus attends only one festival, the final Passover (see introduction to John: "Outline"). John mentions three Passovers, an unnamed feast (5:1), Dedication (Hanukkah, 10:22), and Booths.

7:3 Brothers: The term, generic in Greek, can include sisters. **Disciples:** The Synoptic Jesus has no Judean disciples, but in John, Jesus' disciples, like his ministry in general, are concentrated in Judea.

7:5 Not even his brothers believed: Jesus' brothers and sisters did not believe in him during his earthly life; some came to believe after the resurrection (1 Cor. 15:7; 9:5).

7:6 My time: See his response to his mother concerning his "hour," 2:4, and see 7:30; 13:1.

7:7 The world ... hates: See 15:18. The world cannot hate those who belong to it, but Jesus and his disciples do not belong to this world. On "hate" see commentary on Luke 14:26.

7:8 Not (yet): Some manuscripts reflect scribal efforts to keep Jesus from contradicting himself or changing his mind, by inserting "yet" (see v. 10 and NRSV note) but the original text read simply "not." As in 2:4–7 and 11:5–11, the point is not duplicity or pettiness, but the divine initiative so important to Johannine theology. Jesus never does anything at the behest of others but, as the one who represents God, acts only unilaterally.

7:11 The Jews: See introduction to John. This chapter illustrates the complexity of John's use of "the Jews." Here they are distinguished from "the crowds," as though Jewish leaders, not the people as a whole, are meant. In 6:41, however, the crowds (in Galilee!) are identified as "Jews," so the word cannot consistently mean "Judeans." In 7:19 it is the crowd, not just the leaders, who try to kill Jesus. In 7:25 "some of the people in Jerusalem" are distinguished from those who are trying to kill Jesus, namely, "the rulers." In 7:49, the high priests, rulers, and Pharisees are distinguished from the crowd. In this whole section, there is a range of responses, from positive to murderous, by the various figures in the story, all of whom are "Judeans," but not all are "Jews" in John's symbolic sense. Only the Pharisees, the enemies of the church in John's own time, are consistently negative. In all this, it is clear that there is no neat way to isolate John's meaning of the term "the Jews": neither "Judeans" nor "Jewish leaders" consistently expresses John's meaning, which is nuanced and symbolic. It is clear, however, that by "Jews" he does not mean the Jewish people indiscriminately and taken as a whole.

7:12 A good man . . . deceiving the crowd: Throughout the Gospel, the appearance of Jesus evokes contrasting responses. Here and elsewhere, people respond on the basis of their own criteria of whether he acts and speaks as the expected prophet or Messiah should. Even those who respond positively do so on the basis of their own judgment about how God acts (see 3:1–3). In the conflict scene portrayed in chap. 7, the author concentrates several examples of this mistaken attempt to evaluate Jesus by human criteria:

1. *Positive*: Jesus is a "good man," apparently based on their judgment of what is good (v. 12; see Nicodemus's similar evaluation, 3:1–3).

2. *Negative*: Jesus does not meet their image of how the people should be led, so he is a deceiver (v. 12).

3. *Negative*: Since Jesus (mistakenly, they think) believes people are trying to kill him, they charge him with being demon-possessed, i.e., paranoid, mentally ill (v. 20). But even if they had known what the reader knows, that the leaders had in fact decided to kill him (5:18), this would not deliver them from their false assumption that they can judge Jesus by their own criteria.

4. *Negative*: They know where Jesus comes from, but the Messiah is supposed to be of mysterious, unknown origin (v. 27).

5. *Positive*: Jesus must be the Messiah, on the basis of the number of signs he does (v. 31).

6. *Negative*: Jesus comes from Galilee and the Messiah is to come from Bethlehem, so Jesus cannot be the Messiah (v. 42). The point is not that Jesus in fact was born in Bethlehem (of which there is nothing in John—see on 1:45), so they are right in their criteria but wrong in their data. It is thus irrelevant whether the author is unaware of the story of Jesus' birth in Bethlehem, or knows the story but does not accept it, or knows it and believes it to be reliable history. Their problem, from John's point of view, is their effort to accredit *or* disqualify Jesus on the basis of their criteria, even if they had in fact been better informed.

7. *Positive*: No one ever spoke like Jesus (v. 46).

8. *Negative*: None of the religious authorities believed in him (v. 48).

9. *Negative:* No prophet is to arise from Galilee (v. 52). See #6 on v. 42.

This pattern is found elsewhere in John (e.g., 3:1–3; 12:34; classically in 9:16). People attempt to judge Jesus, but they cannot, for Jesus himself is the standard of judgment, the self-authenticating incarnate Word of God, beyond which there is no appeal. This is classically portrayed in the passion story, which on the surface appears to be Jesus on trial before the high priests and Pilate, but the reality is that Jesus himself is the judge (see 19:13, in which this is summed up). The people involved need not be judged by the reader to be bad or dishonest people, as though we more honest types would see that Jesus does meet biblical, traditional, and commonsense criteria for messiahship, and so we accept him. The people in the story attempt to certify or disqualify him by their *this-worldly* criteria (the only ones we

humans have or can have). The Johannine point (which still eludes many modern readers who wish to justify themselves and their faith as their own accomplishment) is that Jesus' origin and accreditation (certification, 3:33; 6:27) come from God and transcend our ability to validate or invalidate. For one to come to authentic faith in Christ, God must act, and—without eliminating or minimizing the ultimate seriousness of human decision—faith must be a gift (see 3:8, 16; 4:10–15; 6:27). The point is made for the final time in the encounter between the risen Jesus and Thomas, 20:24–29. See excursus, "Testing Prophecy," at Rev. 2:20.

7:14 Began to teach: The content of Jesus' teaching is not given, here or elsewhere. For John, the important point is not that Jesus teaches certain items of good content, but that he is the teacher authorized by God (see v. 46). On this, John is the authentic successor of Mark (see on Mark 1:22; 4:38; 10:2; 50.

7:15 Never been taught: Jesus (and his later disciples) did not have formal rabbinic training (see Acts 4:13). Here is reflected the charge against the church that they are reinterpreting the Scriptures in the light of the Christ event without having any official standing as religious teachers (see 7:48).

7:17 Anyone who resolves to do the will of God will know: John claims that those who want to do the will of God will recognize it when they see it embodied in Jesus. Willing and doing take precedence over theoretical knowing; authentic religious discernment is a matter of one's heart, not just of verifiable criteria. This does not mean that there is no place for rational, traditional, or biblical criteria, but that these cannot have the last word. See 6:45. **Speaking on my own:** See 5:30; 7:28; 8:15; 10:18 commentary.

7:20 You have a demon: See Matt. 12:22–32; Mark 3:20–30; Luke 11:14–23; 12:10, where Jesus is charged with casting out demons by the power of Beelzebul, the chief demon. In contrast to the Synoptic Gospels, in John Jesus performs no exorcisms. Jesus does not liberate individual people possessed of demons, but the Christ event as a whole is the overcoming of the power of Satan on a cosmic scale (12:31).

7:22 You circumcise a man on the sabbath: A reminder that the conflict of 5:10–18 over Sabbath observance continues here. There Jesus' conduct was authorized by his own authority as Son of God. Here an argument from the Bible and Jewish tradition is introduced. The Scripture commanded circumcision on the eighth day after the child's birth (Gen. 17:12; Lev. 12:3; see Luke 2:21). What happens when the eighth day falls on a Sabbath? Jewish tradition had already decided that the circumcision law takes precedence over the Sabbath commandment. The Johannine Jesus argues that the healing of a whole person all the more overrules the Sabbath—and that consequently he (and his later disciples) are not violating the Sabbath. In these arguments we hear the echoes of disputes between the later (largely Gentile) church and the synagogue.

7:24 Judge with right judgment: Like God, who looks on the heart and not the outward appearance, and like the messianic king promised in Isa. 11:3.

7:30 His hour had not yet come: The repeated attempts to arrest Jesus all fail, not because he is too clever for his opponents (7:32, 45; 10:29; 11:45–53), but because the hour when God acts for human salvation is decided by God alone. In the Fourth Gospel, Jesus is not the victim of the power of others but is the victorious one who goes to the cross on his own initiative and at a time he alone (representing God) decides.

7:33–36 The Dispersion . . . and teach the Greeks: "Diaspora" means "scattered" (see NIV). The Dispersion or Diaspora was that large number of Jews living outside Palestine. Another Johannine example of the people misunderstanding (see on 3:3). As in 11:50–51; 19:5, 14, they utter a profound truth without knowing it, for by John's time the Christian faith had already become primarily a Gentile religion—the risen Christ was indeed teaching the Greeks in the Diaspora (see 11:52).

7:37 Let anyone who is thirsty come: Alongside John's emphasis on divine sovereignty and salvation as God's gift, he maintains his insistence on human decision and responsibility.

7:38 Out of the believer's heart: "Believer's" is not in the Greek text, which has "his," and represents the NRSV's effort to use non-gender-specific language. Here the Johannine point may be lost, for "his" more likely refers to Jesus, the ultimate source of the water of life. The water imagery is appropriate to the water rites at the festival of Booths (see above). **The scripture** intended is uncertain, for there is no such text in the Old Testament (but see Isa. 44:2–3; Zech. 14:8, a text read at Booths).

7:39 As yet there was no Spirit: In the Fourth Gospel's understanding, the Spirit given in the cross-resurrection event (19:30; 20:22–23; see

Acts 2) was not yet present in Jesus' ministry. The Spirit is given to all **believers**, not just to apostles or a spiritual elite, and provides the only basis for understanding who Jesus is. Thus the people in the story are incapable of understanding what is going on in their presence, but the post-Easter believer reading the story is addressed by its true meaning.

7:40–48 A division in the crowd because of him: On the division Jesus causes, and the inadequacy of human criteria, see on 7:12 above.

7:52 Search and you will see: The Jews are factually correct; no prophet or Messiah is predicted to come from Galilee. For John, the tragic mistake is supposing that Jesus' status as God's Messiah can be validated or invalidated by study of the Scripture. See on 5:39. Christians should learn from such texts not to fault those who do not see the Christian Messiah "prophesied" in the Old Testament (see on Luke 21:22; 24:25; Acts 3:24; excursus, "New Testament Interpretation of the Old Testament," at 1 Cor. 15:3).

The Johannine narrative continues at 8:12; 7:53–8:11 is a later insertion.

7:53–8:11
The Woman Caught in Adultery

Although this text is a precious story from early Christian tradition and communicates an unforgettable picture of the meaning of Jesus' life and ministry, it is historically certain that it was not a part of the original Gospel of John. It is not found at all in the earliest and best MSS of the Gospel. In later MSS, it appears at other places in the Gospel of John (after 7:36; 7:44; or 21:25) or the Gospel of Luke (after 21:38; after 24:53; a total of six different places in various New Testament manuscripts), often marked with obelisks to indicate it was a secondary addition. In most of the medieval manuscripts on which the King James Version was based, it appears here, after John 7:52, and thus entered the standard English Bible tradition. Here we have a story that circulated in early Christian tradition, where it may be attested as early as 125 CE, but it is first found in New Testament manuscripts dating from the third century. The text thus teaches us not only something about the character of God and the nature of sin and forgiveness, but also something about the nature of the Bible itself. The line between Scripture and tradition is not as sharp as many Protestants have believed. We have this text because it was handed on in the church and later inserted into the Bible at various points, not because any biblical author included it in the text of the Bible. See "Introduction: The New Testament as the Church's Book" 4.c, 4.d.

The story is lacking in Johannine features but resembles the pronouncement stories of the Synoptic Gospels that narrate the attempts of Jesus' opponents to entrap him, which Jesus frustrates by a memorable and wise concluding pronouncement (see, e.g., Mark 12:13–17).

8:1 Mount of Olives: Across the valley from the Temple Mount, on the east side of Jerusalem. Jesus teaching daily in the temple and spending the night on the Mount of Olives is typically Lukan (see Luke 21:37). This, along with other characteristic Lukan features, accounts for this story having been inserted at Luke 21:38 or 24:53, rather than here.

8:5 Moses commanded us to stone: This was the penalty for adultery in the Old Testament law, but both the man and the woman were to be killed (Lev. 20:10; Deut. 22:22–24). Since according to John 18:31 the Romans had reserved the death penalty for themselves, the present story may resemble Mark 12:13–17, not only in form but have the same function: Moses commands the death penalty, the Romans forbid it—shall we obey the Bible or the Romans?

8:6 Wrote with his finger on the ground: This may represent a historical memory that Jesus was among the minority that could read and write (see 7:15; Luke 4:16ff.), or may be derived from Jer. 17:13 (see commentary on 6:9).

8:7 Let any one . . . who is without sin: If the story has the same pattern as the Markan one, Jesus escapes their trap by a profound saying that has its own force. It is to be noted that Jesus here assumes the universal sinfulness of humanity, which is not only a Pauline doctrine, but the general perspective of biblical theology (see also Luke 5:20; 7:47–48; 11:4; 24:47; Rom. 3:21).

8:11 Neither do I condemn you: The Synoptic Jesus claims the divine role of forgiving sins (Mark 2:1–12), but this portrayal of Jesus is not found in John. **Sin no more:** Jesus does not condemn the woman, but his forgiveness does not mean he is "nonjudgmental" in the sense that he has no judgment about her behavior, as though that were "her own business." Jesus is clear that he condemns what the woman (and the man) did as sinful, but he forgives the woman herself. She is set free from the guilt of sin, but is not free to continue her sinful life.

8:12–59
The Conflict Continues

The scene that follows continues the conflict theme of chap. 7 but is not directly connected. The hostility between Jesus and the Jews leads to name-calling and contemptuous statements on both sides of the debate. On the one hand, Jesus' declarations against the Jews cannot be taken as verbatim statements of the historical Jesus or as a license for his followers today to adopt similar language and perspectives—though this has tragically happened in Christian history. On the other hand, Christians of today may not self-righteously justify themselves by condemning the presumed "anti-Judaism" of the Fourth Gospel. In this text we overhear the heated language of the debate between the church of the late first century CE (that spoke in Jesus' name), expressed in the framework of their own theology. As in the study of every New Testament text, the first task is to understand the text within its own setting.

8:12 I am the light of the world: See Matt. 5:14, on Jesus' followers. On the "I am" sayings, see on 6:35. If the setting is still thought of as at the feast of Booths (7:2), the reference to light is especially appropriate. The festival was begun by lighting four enormous candelabra, symbolizing the light of God (see, e.g., Pss. 27:1; 36:9; 119:105; 130). Light was not only a Jewish symbol but a universal human symbol of divine truth. In the Fourth Gospel, Jesus himself is the embodiment of the light of God (1:4–5, 9).

8:13 Testimony: See on 5:31–47; 8:18.

8:15 You judge by human standards: See on 7:12. **I judge no one:** This seems to be a contradiction of 5:22, 27, but here the author presupposes the distinctive Johannine "on my own" (see 5:30–31; 7:17, 28; 8:28, 42, 54 [same Greek expression]; 12:49). Jesus does in fact judge, but his judgment is not "on his own," but represents the judgment of God, who sent him.

8:19 Where is your father?: As often in John, the dialogue proceeds on two levels, facilitating the "Johannine misunderstanding" (see 3:3–4; 4:10–11, 33–34; 6:51–52; 8:22, 33, 57; 11:11–12, 23–27; 14:5, 8, 22). Jesus is speaking of heavenly realities, but they hear him at the level of biological paternity.

8:20 His hour: See on 2:4. As the passion story indicates, Jesus will be arrested at his own decision and on his own initiative, and his death will be voluntary, not forced. Since he represents God, he is throughout victor, not victim (see 18:1–12).

8:23 Below . . . above: Equated with "this world . . . not of this world," this is another example of the dualism that forms the framework of John's thought. The following pairs recur constantly in the Johannine writings:

God	devil
light	darkness
above	below
spirit	flesh
heavenly	earthly
life	death
saved	condemned
love	hate
deeds done in God	evil deeds
truth	lie
believers	unbelievers
children of light	those who love darkness

We may think of ourselves as more tolerant, sophisticated types who know that life is not black and white but shades of gray. Much biblical thought also has this nuanced view, but there is also a necessary role for either/or thinking, and not only both/and. Dualistic thought is prominent in Jesus, Paul, and elsewhere in the New Testament, not only in John (see, e.g., comments on Matt. 12:30; 25:31–46; Luke 9:49–50; 16:8; 26:18; 1 Cor. 6:1; 2 Cor. 11:13–15; Gal. 3:18; introduction to Revelation, and Revelation throughout).

8:26 I declare . . . what I have heard: See 3:11–12. Jesus never divulges the content. His revelation is himself, not particular items of "heavenly information," but that he is the one who has come from God. The Christian revelation is that God has acted in Christ, not that Jesus has brought us data from the other world (see 8:24 "believe that I am he").

8:28 Lifted up: On the double meaning, see 3:13; 12:32–34.

8:30 Many believed: These have seen no signs but come to faith based on Jesus' word. See on 2:11. Yet they turn out not to be very good believers, as the following verses show. John can use "believe" and "believers" in a variety of senses. Here he may have in mind those who "believed" but were unwilling to pay the price connected with public confession of Christ (see 12:42 and on 6:51–58). He also may be reflecting tensions and the split among believers that already had occurred or was occurring in the Johannine church (see 1 John 2:19).

8:32–33 The truth will make you free: This is a general truth, i.e., that the truth about bacteriology

and medicine sets people free from a superstitious understanding of disease and makes possible cures, the truth about meteorology sets people free from the fear of storm demons that must be placated to obtain good weather, and the like. Thus this text is emblazoned on the entrance to many universities. Yet Jesus is not speaking of the march of scientific progress. In the Fourth Gospel, truth is personal, embodied in Jesus himself (14:6). It is this truth, learned not from books and laboratories but in encounter with the Word of God present in Christ, that sets free. **We . . . have never been slaves:** This freedom is not merely social or educational; the slave driver is not human social systems, not ignorance and superstition, but sin, thought of as an enslaving power. Here and elsewhere in this chapter, Pauline thought seems to be reflected (see, e.g., Rom. 6; Gal. 4:21–31).

8:37 You look for an opportunity to kill me: See v. 40. Strangely enough, these words are addressed to those who "believed" in Jesus (8:30–31).

8:38 The Father . . . your father (or the Father): The same Greek word can be translated either as imperative, as in the NRSV, in which case **the Father** is God, or as an indicative, as in the NRSV footnote, which would mean that Jesus already contrasts *his* Father, God, and *their* father, the devil (see v. 44). In either case, this is another expression of the Johannine theology that origin determines character and destiny (see on 3:3–5).

8:39 Abraham is our father: The original promise made to Abraham and Sarah in Gen. 12:1–3 is very important in biblical theology. To be **Abraham's children** means to be heirs of God's promise, participants in the salvation God has promised. Thus debates between first-century Jews and (Jewish and non-Jewish) Christians sometimes focused on who were the true children of Abraham (see Matt. 3:7–12; Rom. 4; Gal. 3).

8:41 We are not illegitimate children: I.e., we are authentic children of Abraham. There may also be an insulting reference to Jesus' own paternity, if stories of Jesus' miraculous birth were circulating in the Johannine context. John himself makes to reference to Jesus' supernatural birth (see on 1:45; 3:16; 7:42). In later Jewish tradition, the Christian story of Jesus' birth was sometimes explained by Jews as a case of illegitimacy, but we do not know if this was already the case in John's time.

8:43 You cannot accept: A better translation would be "you are unable to hear" (so NIV). In

Johannine theology, one must be given the gift of faith; one cannot simply attain it on one's own (see on 3:16; 5:42; 6:27). The mystery of why so many rejected Jesus' message is dealt with in a similar way elsewhere in the New Testament, drawing on Israel's reflections in the Old Testament as to why so many rejected the word of God that came through the prophets (see Isa. 6; Matt. 13:10–23; Mark 4:10–20; Luke 8:9–10; Acts 28:17–31; Rom. 9–11).

8:44 Your father the devil: Another expression of Johannine dualism; one is either from God or from the devil, and origin determines character and destiny (see above). This dualistic contrast that distinguishes children of God and children of the devil has a Jewish origin and background (see *Jub.* 15:26–32; *T. Dan.* 4:7; *Apoc. Ab.* 13–14). As illustrated by the writings of the Jewish group that produced the Dead Sea Scrolls, Jewish groups used harsh words in their religious debates. The debate between Jews who did not believe in Jesus as the Messiah and those who did was such an acrimonious debate; we hear it reflected in the debates between Jesus and his opponents in the Fourth Gospel. Within the schism that occurred in the Johannine church, Christians used such language of each other; some Christians called others they considered heretical and false believers "children of the devil"; in dualistic thought in which everyone belonged to God or the devil, all evildoers were "children of the devil" (1 John 3:8, 10, 15). Though such texts have tragically been used to justify both anti-Semitism and anti-Judaism, and though many Christians now see that such attitudes and language cannot be reconciled with Christian faith, such historical considerations as presented here may help contemporary readers to see that the texts were neither anti-Semitic nor anti-Jewish, and to interpret them in their historical context.

8:46 Which of you convicts me of sin?: The Johannine Jesus here speaks as representing God; all human beings are sinful, but here Jesus is placed in the divine category.

8:48 Samaritan . . . demon: In Samaria, Jesus is considered a Jew; in Judea, he is charged with being a Samaritan. He who came to break down such barriers and gather into one the dispersed children of God was himself everywhere rejected as "not our kind of person." On the charge of demon possession, see 7:20.

8:51 Never see death: See on 5:24; 11:25–26.

8:53 Who do you claim to be?: Better, as in *Today's English Version*, "Who do you think you are?"

This is not an informational question, but the way the sinful creature addresses the Creator and Savior. We hear the arrogant pride of sinful humanity, which is not willing to be God's creature and does not see any need for a Savior. This is prideful religious humanity unwilling to let God be God and resentful of God's identification of us as sinful creatures (see Gen. 2:15–3:24, the story of humankind's refusal to be a creature, wanting to play the role of God).

8:56 Abraham rejoiced . . . saw my day: This does not mean that Abraham literally had a vision of the future coming of Christ, or that Jesus and Abraham were somehow contemporaries. The Jews understand Jesus' statement at this prosaic level, and reject it—another example of the "Johannine misunderstanding" and "inept question" (see on 2:20). Jesus claims Moses (5:39, 45–46) for his cause, as he will claim Isaiah (12:41). The Johannine Jesus expresses the early Christian understanding of Jesus, that those ancient Israelite worthies who were granted prophetic insight into the meaning of God's purpose for history in fact "saw Christ" or "wrote of him" (5:46), for Christ is the key and fulfillment of God's purpose.

8:57 Not yet fifty: The Jews again characteristically misunderstand Jesus' statement literally in terms of this-worldly reality. "Fifty" may be part of a proverbial expression, meaning simply that Jesus is too young to have known Abraham. Plato repeatedly mentions "fifty" as the commonly accepted age of maturity and respect (e.g., *Laws* 12.951). It may also reflect an alternative tradition from that of Luke 3:23, that Jesus was "about thirty" when he began his ministry. Except for the birth stories in Matthew and Luke that place his birth shortly before Herod's death in 4 BCE, this is our only indication in the New Testament of Jesus' age. John may reflect another view that circulated in early Christianity, according to which Jesus was older when he was killed, and thus was able to experience all the seasons of human life, from infancy to old age.

8:58 Before Abraham was, I am: Not "I was." In this "I am" saying (see on 6:35), Jesus refers to his preexistence, which mystifies and scandalizes his hearers but is by now well understood by the Johannine reader (1:1–14, 15, 30; 3:13; 8:23; 17:5, 24).

8:59 Hid himself: Not from fear. As representing God, Jesus is in charge of his own destiny and will not be arrested or killed before "his hour" (see on 2:4; 8:20). The Old Testament figure of

Wisdom hid herself when she was repeatedly rejected by sinful humanity; this myth is part of the background of the incarnate Logos (see on 1:1).

9:1–41
Jesus Heals the Man Born Blind

This section continues the series of episodes that began at 7:1. The setting is still Jerusalem, at the feast of Booths. The Johannine pattern continues: a miracle story somewhat like one in the Synoptic Gospels, followed by a controversy dialogue, which fades into a monologue by Jesus (see 5:1–47; 6:1–71). Although God did not send the Son to judge the world but to save it, this episode illustrates the inevitable judging effect of the Light of the World (see 3:17–21; 8:12; 12:35–46). One cannot turn on the light without creating shadows. In an absolutely dark room, all are equally blind. But when the light is switched on, the coming of the light separates those who are truly blind from those who can see. The light does not create blindness but separates those who are (willingly, in John's theology) blind from those who see (those who choose to see by the new gift of light,).

Throughout the Gospel the story is a two-level drama in which the post-Easter situation of the Johannine church is superimposed on the story of Jesus' pre-Easter mission, but this is especially clear in this chapter (see introduction to John). The image of Jesus who heals blindness becomes a defining image of his mission as a whole (10:21; 11:37).

9:2 Who sinned?: The assumption that misfortune is the result of sin is widespread, even among those not overtly religious—"What did I do to deserve this?" Human beings intuitively resist the idea that we live in an immoral or morally neutral universe. This innate human desire sometimes finds expression in a particular theology that "explains" physical evil as the result of sin. A person *born* blind poses problems for such a theology.

9:3 Neither this man nor his parents: See Luke 13:1–5 and the entire book of Job. The man's misfortune is the result of neither his own nor inherited sin. Nor is Jesus' response to be understood as a mechanical "explanation" of this particular instance, as though God blinded this man at birth so that God or Jesus could later be glorified by healing him. The words "he was born blind" are not in the Greek text, but are supplied to give a particular English sense. The addition makes the sentence too simple, too clearly an explanation.

The sense is that the presence of the blind man provides the occasion to do something about it, something that will glorify God. Here and elsewhere, the Bible simply begins with the reality of evil, without providing explanations. The attractiveness of Gnosticism, in both its ancient and its modern forms, is that it claims to provide profound explanations for the problem of evil, which the Bible leaves as a mystery. (See introduction to John: "Johannine School"; comments on John 1:1, 14; 18:20; 19:34; 1 Cor. 12:3; 1 Tim. 4:1–5; 6:20–21; 1 John 2:20, 27; Rev. 1:3.)

9:4 We must work: The "we" includes the Johannine church with which Jesus identifies (see 1:14; 3:11–13). **Night is coming:** At one level, this refers to the end of Jesus' earthly life and ministry, and the urgency of his completing his work. It then broadens out to include the community (**no one,** not just the pre-Easter Jesus), which also has only a limited time in which to fulfill its mission.

9:7 Siloam (which means Sent): This note is a clue to the perceptive reader that the story works at a symbolical level (not allegorical; on the difference, see on Mark 4:1–20; Luke 8:11–15; 12:57–59; 14:16–24, 28–33; 15:4–7; Gal. 4:21–5:1). In the Fourth Gospel Jesus is repeatedly the "sent one," and Jesus' distinctive title for God is "the one who sent me" (found twenty-five times in John, e.g., 5:37; 6:44; 7:28; 8:16, 18, 26; 12:49). There is a sense in which Siloam represents Jesus himself, his mission from God. The man was blind *from birth*, i.e., his blindness was not the result of disease or accident, but was "the way he had always been," representing the given human condition. The man longs to be able to see but does not ask to be healed; he is not consciously "seeking" anything. Jesus takes the initiative and gives him a command. Washing is a reflection of Christian baptism. He does not have to obey it, but he does. He is given something to do, and he does it, but his healing is still a gift, an act of grace, not his achievement. His blindness is healed. By water from the Sent One, i.e., by the water represented by Christ himself (see 3:5; 4:10–15; 5:7–8; 7:2, 38; 13:1–20; 19:34). Again the miracle happens offstage (see 2:9; 4:46–53). See excursus, "Interpreting the Miracle Stories," at Matt. 9:35.

9:9 I am the man: The words "the man" are added to clarify the English meaning; the Greek phrase is simply "I am," the recognition formula (see on 6:35). Its use here shows that "I am" by itself can be simply a "secular" phrase, not an echo of God's name or claim to divinity.

9:10 How?: This repeated question (vv. 15, 16, 19, 21, 26) is not an informational question, but represents the desire to incorporate God's act into human understanding and thereby validate it on our own terms. See on 1 Cor. 15:35, on 9:16 below, and the comments at 7:12.

9:13 Pharisees: See introduction to John. They were the sole leaders of Judaism in John's day; he uses the term as interchangeable with "the Jewish leaders" and "the Jews."

9:14 Sabbath: See on 5:9. The miracle story–discourse pattern is the same as in chap. 5, where the reader also learns only late in the narrative that the event occurred on the Sabbath.

9:16 This man is not from God: On the biblical and religious basis that he does not keep the Sabbath, they reject his claim that he is from God. Others, on the basis of the signs they have seen him do, declare he cannot be a sinner. In John's view, *both* sides of this discussion are wrong because they presume to judge Jesus on the basis of their criteria—even if their criteria are correct (see full discussion of this important Johannine point at 7:12). This is related to their repeated **we know** (see vv. 24, 29; and discussion at 3:1–3).

9:17 Prophet: This is a correct, but inadequate, identification of Jesus' role and status (see 4:19; 6:14–15; 7:12, 52).

9:18–23 Two-level drama: In this paragraph the nature of the Gospel as combining pre-Easter and post-Easter perspectives is most clearly seen. The parents apparently believe that Jesus has performed the saving act but are hesitant to confess their "faith" because they did not wish to be expelled from the synagogue. This reflects the situation in the author's own time and place. It is understandable that Jews who had come to faith in Jesus as the Messiah wanted to remain Jews in good standing within the synagogue. They did not understand their Christian faith as an alternative to Judaism, as having chosen a different religion. In John's day (but not in Jesus'), Judaism and Christianity had come or were coming to a parting of the ways. John considers this to be a result of pressure from the Jewish side. Nonetheless, he insists that authentic faith must be confessed, that one cannot have a purely personal, private Christian faith (12:31; see on 6:51–58; 12:11). The parents are unwilling to take this public stand; the once-I-was-blind-but-now-I-see son courageously confesses his faith and is expelled. John clearly holds him up as an example of the authentic believer.

9:24 Give glory to God: This seems to be something of an oath formula, akin to swearing in a witness (see Josh. 7:19). The Pharisees are conducting a judicial procedure. The Johannine community was familiar with appearing before Jewish courts (see Luke 21:12; Acts 9:1–2; 2 Cor. 11:24; 1 Thess. 2:14–17).

9:25 Though I was blind: The man does not make a theological argument but speaks from his own undeniable experience. It is only later that he becomes clear about the identity of the One who has given him sight. This is the reflection of Christian experience; Christ does not wait on us to have the right christological understanding before calling us to discipleship (see on Mark 1:16–20).

9:28–29 Moses . . . this man: Again the debate reflects John's own situation. From the perspective of the synagogue, discipleship to Moses and discipleship to Jesus were simply alternatives—one had to choose between Moses and Jesus, or even between the God who had spoken through Moses and the God who, as the Christians claim, had spoken and still speaks definitively through Jesus. The Johannine church did not so understand the situation, and considered it a false choice: in choosing to follow Jesus, they did not understand themselves to have rejected Moses and the Jewish Scriptures, which, in their understanding, in fact testified to Jesus (see on 5:39, 45–47). The issue, of course, was who was authorized to interpret the Scriptures, for the Jewish community resisted the Christian understanding of Scriptures illuminated by faith in the Christ event. Christians also affirmed the Jewish claim that **God has spoken to Moses**; they added that this same God had now spoken definitively through Jesus Christ (see 1:18; Heb. 1:1–4). **We do not know where he comes from:** Another illustration of their making their own criteria the supreme court of religious faith (see on 7:12 and 9:16 above).

9:34 They drove him out: Literally "cast out," as in 9:22, not just from the courtroom but from membership in the synagogue. This is what Jesus had promised he would not do to those who come to him, 6:37.

9:35 Son of Man: See on Mark 2:10. Only now does the man learn of Jesus' true messianic status. His healing did not depend on having the correct Christology, but the story shows it is important to learn who it is who has given us light and life.

9:38 Lord, I believe: The content of his faith is that Jesus is the Son of Man, equated by John with Christ, Son of God, Lord. He now confesses Jesus as "Lord" (see NRSV footnote), and worships Jesus. Since the whole Bible, including the Johannine tradition, rejects worship of anything or anyone but the one true God, this is a way of identifying Jesus with God (see 1:1–2; 20:28; Matt. 4:10; Rev. 19:10; 22:8–9).

9:39–41 I came into this world for judgment: Not the purpose, but the effect, of Jesus coming (see introduction to this chapter). **That . . . those who do see may become blind:** These concluding words make more obvious what has been clear all along, that the story is not merely a literal description of the healing of one blind person in Judea ca. 30 CE, but a representation of the meaning of the Christ event as a whole. Jesus never literally blinded anyone, but the effect of his advent and the Christian message was to show that those who claim to see by their own standards have become blind, and those who acknowledge their blindness are given sight by the one who is himself the Light of the World. Sight is a gift of God for which no one may take credit. That those with Christian faith see "how things really are" in this world is not their own achievement, of which they can boast, but the gift of faith for which they can only give thanks.

10:1–21
Jesus as Gate and Shepherd

Jesus has been in Jerusalem since the festival of Booths in chap. 7. Indeed, if in a previous edition of the Gospel chap. 6 once preceded chap. 5 (see note at 4:54), Jesus has been in Jerusalem since 5:1. The scene thus continues from chap. 9, but the chapter division does signal a change in theme. The reader is reminded of the overall structure of John's narrative (see introduction to John: "Outline"): in chaps. 2–12 Jesus confronts the hostile world; only from 13:1 on does he address "his own." Thus throughout chap. 10 Jesus *addresses* his opponents, and talks *about* his disciples in the third person, as though they were not present. Jesus' disciples were with him in 9:1 but, typical of Johannine style, have since evaporated from the narrative (see in the episode of 3:1–36 the disappearance of Nicodemus after 3:10).

The chapter is a united whole but has clear subdivisions: 10:1–18, Jesus' discourse on himself as gate and shepherd; 10:19–21, division among the Jews; 10:22–39, Jesus' final encounter with his opponents at the festival of Dedication; 10:40–42, Jesus' departure across the Jordan.

The word "parable," found forty-eight times in the Synoptics, never occurs in John. Instead of the Synoptic parables of the kingdom as the substance of Jesus' message, in John Jesus delivers extended metaphorical discourses focused on himself and his mission. The Synoptic Jesus preaches the *kingdom of God*; the Johannine Jesus proclaims *himself*. This is not the egotism of Jesus but the theology of the Johannine community.

The **figure of speech** (v. 6) deals with God's people, represented as God's flock, sheep who need a shepherd but sometimes have false leadership—a common biblical metaphorical configuration (e.g., Num. 27:16–17; Pss. 23; 77:20; 100:3; Isa. 40:11; Ezek. 34; Zech. 11:4–10; Mark 6:34; Matt. 9:36; 10:6; 15:24; John 21:16–17). The imagery is not a simple allegory in which each element neatly stands for something else. The imagery would be simpler (and more manageable, more readily adapted to our preconceived ideas of what it is "supposed to mean") if it were two separate sets of images, one in which Jesus is gate and one in which he is shepherd. But "gate" and "shepherd" are already intertwined in vv. 1–5. The reader anticipates that Jesus will be the shepherd who enters by the gate, and he indeed is prefigured as such in vv. 3–5, yet the first explicit christological identification is Jesus as gate (not shepherd) in v. 7. Like the parables of the Synoptic Jesus, this metaphorical style keeps the reader off balance, frustrates too quick and too easy efforts to reduce the imagery to simple "points" (see on Mark 4:1).

10:1 A thief and a bandit: The identity of the false, would-be leaders of God's people is not clear. Is Jesus referring to the Pharisees themselves, whom he is addressing, thought of as false teachers by the Johannine community? In John's time, as they reconstituted Judaism after the catastrophic war (see introduction to John), they were claiming to be the authorized leaders of the people of God. Or is the reference to false messiahs, especially those who had appeared during the war and had contributed to the calamity by the false hopes they had generated (see on Matt. 24:5)?

10:3 The sheep hear his voice. . . . He calls his own sheep by name: In John's understanding, the mark of the true people of God is that they recognize God's voice in the message of Jesus. It is a personal voice, addressed to each one by name (see 20:11–18, esp. v. 16).

10:6 They did not understand: In the nature of the case, no one can understand Jesus' message or identity until the story of his life is concluded in the cross and resurrection. This is the christological nature of the Gospel narrative (see "Introduction to the Gospels"). All the Gospels have some form of the messianic secret, but John's is very different from the Synoptics. The Johannine perspective can be summarized in four points: (1) The illumination of the Holy Spirit is necessary in order to understand Jesus and the Christian message, and this Spirit was not given until after Easter (7:39; 14:19–20; 15:26–27; 16:7, 12–13; 20:22). (2) During his ministry, Jesus speaks in "figures of speech" that are not clear until later (10:6; 25; 29). (3) The Scriptures that point to Jesus are not understood until after the resurrection (2:22; 12:16; 20:9). (4) Even Jesus' disciples fail to understand him during his ministry (10:6; 11:11–12; 13:7, 29; 14:7 in some MSS and translations; 16:17–18; see 21:1–3).

10:7 I am the gate: On "I am" sayings, see 6:35. The imagery seems to be suggested by the practice of Palestinian shepherds, who slept at night lying across the entrance to their sheepfolds, providing security for the sheep within by blocking the entrance of intruders and by keeping the sheep themselves from straying. The idea of the temple as the "gate of heaven" also hovers in the background. In Johannine theology Jesus himself is the access to God previously symbolized by the temple (see Gen. 28:17; John 1:14, 29, 51; 2:19–22; 4:20–21; 14:6; Rom. 5:1–2).

10:9 Be saved . . . Come in and go out and find pasture: These are all aspects of one event, the salvation brought by Christ, not a chronological series of separate stages of conversion and discipleship.

10:10 May have life . . . abundantly: The life that Jesus brings and is provides more than survival. On the extravagance of the messianic salvation, see on John 2:6; 6:12–13; 12:3; 19:39; Luke 5:6; 6:37–38; 8:5–8; 9:17; 13:20; 15:22; 19:17; Rom. 5:15.

10:11 The good shepherd: On "I am" sayings, see 6:35. Like the other such sayings, this is a *recognition formula*. It is not directed to the question, who is Jesus? but who is the Good Shepherd? While shepherd was also a universal, Gentile image, in the Bible and Judaism it was especially significant as a metaphor for God (e.g., Ps. 23) and the good leadership God provides for his people (e.g., Ezek. 34) It is not a soft, warm-fuzzies image; shepherd was used for the kings of Israel (e.g., Jer. 2:8; 3:15; 10:21; 25:34–38; Mic. 5:2; see Ezek. 34) and connotes both power that commands obedience and personal devotion to the sheep. **Lays down his life for the sheep:** Jesus as one with God is not a third party who dies for human sin,

but is God's own act for human salvation. On Jesus' death understood as atoning sacrifice, see on 3:16; Rom. 3:25, 1 Cor. 15:3, Heb. 1:3; 2:17; 5:1–10.

10:12 The hired hand: The good shepherd also provides the image for the good minister, the leader of the congregation ("pastor" means "shepherd"), and is contrasted with bad church leaders, who are only employees. **Wolf . . . scatters:** The good pastor protects the sheep from division and false teachers.

10:16 Other sheep: Christ is not *a* shepherd but *the* shepherd and is responsible for all God's people. Most interpreters have thought of the "other sheep" as the Gentiles, who will be brought into the community of Christian faith by the post-Easter church under the guidance of the risen Lord. Jesus' mission is indeed to *all* (4:42; 12:20–21; 17:20; 20:29). This text may also reflect the divisions within the church that were already occurring in John's time. The Johannine community was caught in divisive currents (see 2–3 John; 1 John 2:19), but the author has an ecumenical heart and sees Christ as guiding the church to be **one flock, one shepherd**. See 21:1–23, which has as one of its goals the portrayal of a (re)united church that respects variety but still finds its unity under one shepherd.

10:18 No one takes it from me: Jesus gives his life voluntarily for the salvation of his people. He is presented throughout the Fourth Gospel as victor, not as victim (see 7:30, and the passion story throughout, 18:1–20:31). **Of my own accord:** This phrase, found eight times in the Fourth Gospel, is everywhere else something that Jesus denies about himself—he does not come on his own authority, does not speak on his own (5:19, 30; 7:17:28; 8:28, 42; 14:10). The only thing he does on his own is to give his life willingly for others. **I have power to take it up again:** Usually the resurrection is represented in the New Testament as the act of *God* (see on Luke 24:1–12); Jesus does not rise but is raised. God is the actor in the resurrection event. When Jesus is here pictured as having power to raise himself, from the point of view of Johannine theology this is no contradiction of the usual view, for in John Jesus paradoxically represents both humanity and deity: **I have authority . . . from my Father** (see on 5:18).

10:20 He has a demon: See on 7:20; 8:48, 52; 10:33; Mark 3:21. At the end of his discourse, there is a split reaction. While some are nearer the truth than others, in John's perspective all are wrong in supposing they can judge Jesus by their own criteria (see on 7:12).

10:22–42
Jesus at the Feast of Dedication in Jerusalem

10:22 Festival of the Dedication: Hanukkah, the festival celebrating the rededication of the temple in 164 BCE by Judas Maccabeus, after it had been defiled by Antiochus IV Epiphanes (1 Macc. 4:52–59). The festival lasted eight days, beginning on the twenty-fifth of Kislev (Nov–Dec).

10:24–25 If you are the Christ, tell us: This demand is difficult to understand, since in the Fourth Gospel (in contrast to the Synoptics) Jesus has not been secretive but has repeatedly affirmed his identity as Messiah and its equivalents, Son of Man and Son of God (see 1:49–51; 3:13–14; 4:26; 5:25–27; 7:26, 27, 31, 41, 42; 8:28; 9:37; on the public, open character of Jesus' teaching in John, see 18:19–20). This scene may thus represent the Johannine development of the crucial trial before the high priests found in Mark 14:55–64, which has the same sequence: questioning whether Jesus admits to claiming to be the Messiah–Son of God, his response with "I am," the charge of blasphemy, and condemnation by the Jewish court. This scene does not appear in the Johannine account of Jesus' trial, for his whole ministry has the form of a trial before a hostile court, in which he openly confesses his claim to be the Messiah. Since another element in the Markan account, the saying about destroying the temple, is found in another context in John (Mark 14:58; John 2:19–21), it may well be that John has constructed his account based on this Markan scene, or on the same tradition used by Mark. Such observations may grant us an insight into the manner in which our Gospel traditions developed and were composed. **The works that I do:** See 5:36; 10:38; 14:11–12. Even in John, where he much more overtly declares his divine mission and identity, he points more to his works than his claims as the basis for faith in him (see Matt. 11:2–6; Luke 7:18–23).

10:26 Because you do not belong to my sheep: This connects to 10:1–6, still in the reader's mind from the previous page, but in the Johannine story line it had happened at the previous festival some months before. Such phenomena show that the story is constructed to address the reader, not for the benefit of the hearers in the framework of the story itself. As elsewhere, faith is both human decision and divine choice in a paradoxical unity (see on 3:16; 6:27, 37).

10:29 Greater than all: These words are transmitted in a bewildering number of variations in the Greek manuscripts, so that it is very difficult to know what John originally wrote (see "Introduction: The New Testament as the Church's Book" 4.d). The NRSV understands the subject to be **What my Father has given me,** which is probably closest to the original Greek, but is difficult to make sense of in this context. Most other translations render **My Father is greater than all,** which is probably the original sense despite the confusion in extant manuscripts. **No one can snatch them:** That Christ will preserve those whom God has given him is a dominant theme in John (see 6:39; 17:12; 18:9).

10:30 The Father and I are one: The fundamental confession of Judaism, then and now, is the Shema of Deut. 6:4, "God is one." Judaism stood practically alone against pagan polytheism; Jews had suffered and died rather than disavow their faith in the one God. John uses God language of Jesus without ceasing to be a monotheist, incorporating Christ's unity with the Father into the confession of the one God (see "Introduction to the Gospels" and comments on 1:1, 18; 5:18; 14:8–11; 20:28).

10:33 Blasphemy: Any claim to be on a par with God was considered blasphemy. **You, though only a human being, are making yourself God:** This is the way John's Jewish opponents heard Christian claims for Jesus, but John's point is that this is not the way Christians themselves express it (see on 5:18). John's is not a Christology from below, in which a human being claims to be divine. Jesus does not make himself anything (see on "of my own accord" at 10:18). John's is Christology from above, the story of God's becoming human, not the divinization of a human being—incarnation, not apotheosis. The Roman world was very familiar with the divinization of human beings, in the Caesar cult and elsewhere (see introduction to Revelation, comments on Rev. 13). John wants to distinguish Christian belief about Jesus from such views.

10:34 You are gods: John's Jewish opponents objected to the Christian use of God language for Jesus (the debate hardly reflects a situation in the life of Jesus, where this was not an issue). As in the case of controversies about the Sabbath (see on 5:17), Christians scoured the Bible they shared with Judaism in quest of texts that illustrated the legitimacy of their theology. Psalm 82:6, quoted here, became a useful Christian text in this battle. It may seem to deny the very point John wishes to make, i.e., denying Jesus' unique relation to God by reducing him to one of a number of people to whom the word of God came. Jesus seems blandly to say, "You should not be bothered that I use God language of myself, since our Bible uses such language of us all." Yet John's logic—also common among the rabbis—may be an example of *"qal va-homer,"* "light and heavy," i.e., "from the lesser to the greater": what is true of a minor element is all the more true of a major (see 7:22). Thus the argument would be this: since our Bible teaches us that it is legitimate to refer to human beings who proclaim the word of God as gods (or sons of God, the next verse in Ps. 82), how much more legitimate it is to use God language of the one who is uniquely *the* Word of God.

10:35 Scripture cannot be annulled: Not a statement about the Bible's infallibility, in the sense of modern fundamentalism, but the claim of the Johannine community that, rather than denying the Jewish Scriptures, they joined with Jews in affirming the Scriptures—when understood in the light of Christ, the definitive revelation of God.

10:39 Tried to arrest him again: See on 2:4; 7:30; 8:20, 59; Jesus will decide when his hour comes, when it is time for him to be arrested and willingly lay down his life (see 18:1–11).

10:40 Across the Jordan: See 1:28. The reference to John the Baptist and his testimony brings the story of Jesus' ministry full circle and forms a fitting close to his public ministry. At one stage in the development of the Gospel, the narrative may have gone directly from here to the passion story. In the Gospel's present canonical form, Jesus makes another public appearance, a new plot is devised for his arrest, and he retires again (chap. 11). This double conclusion to his ministry corresponds to the double conclusion of the Gospel as a whole (chaps. 20–21). The Gospel is best read and understood not as though it were written by a single author all at one time but as the product of the church's continuing development of multilayered insights into the meaning of the Christ event.

11:1–57
The Raising of Lazarus

In the Fourth Gospel this is the final sign in Jesus' ministry, which leads to his death. The story is not found in the Synoptics, though there, too,

Jesus and his disciples restore life to the dead (Matt. 9:18–26; 10:8; Mark 5:21–43; Luke 7:11–17; 8:40–56; see Acts 9:36–43; 20:7–12). Though interpreters sometimes refer to it as the resurrection of Lazarus, the New Testament never uses the word "resurrection" of those Jesus or his disciples restored (see on Luke 7:14; Acts 26:23; Matt. 28:1). Rather, this climactic episode resembles the other miracle stories, in which people are healed but will get sick again (chaps. 5, 9), are fed (chap. 6) but will get hungry again. Lazarus will die again (see 12:10!). Like the other miracle stories, the wonderful deed is only a temporary reprieve, not the final defeat of the ultimate enemies of life. But it *points* to the ultimate saving event. The healing stories point to the final salvation accomplished by the Christ event, feeding stories to the ultimate satisfaction of that for which we hunger. The story of the raising of Lazarus points to the death and resurrection of Jesus, the final defeat of death and the means of eternal life.

All the miracle stories point beyond themselves to the saving event of Jesus Christ as a whole (see at Matt. 9:35); John has taken particular care to narrate the Lazarus story as a parallel to and prefiguration of Jesus' own death and resurrection. There are at least ten parallels and points of contact:

1. The previous narrative has been structured on the principle of sign/discourse, as in 6:1–58. John 11 reverses the order by placing the discourse first (11:17–42), followed by the miracle itself (11:43–44). This corresponds to, and prepares the reader for, the final discourse (chaps. 13–17), followed by the final sign (chaps. 18–20).
2. John 11:2—John makes anachronistic connection with Mary, not previously introduced, who will anoint Jesus' body for burial. This has the effect of placing the death and burial of *Lazarus* within the framework of the story of *Jesus'* death and burial.
3. John 11:4—Lazarus's death was for the glory of God, and so was Jesus'.
4. John 11:6, 21, 32—Jesus' delay in letting Lazarus die is inexplicable on the human plane, but reflects God's delay in letting Jesus die.
5. John 11:34—The question concerning Lazarus is also asked about Jesus (20:13, 15): "Where have you buried him?"
6. John 11:38—The tomb of Lazarus is like that of Jesus: a cave with stone door.
7. There are common descriptions of Lazarus's and Jesus' burial and tomb: binding; crying,

"Where have you laid him?"; Martha and Mary's misunderstanding at the tomb.

8. John 11:41–42—Jesus prays at Lazarus's tomb and prior to his own death and resurrection (17:1–26), and nowhere else in the Fourth Gospel (though see 12:28–30, also with motifs from Jesus' death and resurrection).

9. John 11:45–53—Lazarus's life is linked to Jesus' death.

10. John 11:43—The motif of calling by name occurs in both stories (20:16).

There are also, of course, contrasts: Lazarus is restored temporarily to this life, Jesus is raised to eschatological life; Lazarus comes forth bound, Jesus leaves the grave clothes behind; Lazarus is called forth by Jesus' word, but Jesus comes from the tomb directly by God's power. Even these contrasting motifs show that the two stories are thought of in relation to each other.

11:1–2 Lazarus, Mary, and Martha: This chapter introduces new characters into the story; not only Lazarus and his sisters Mary and Martha, but also Thomas and Caiaphas emerge for the first time in the narrative. A character in Jesus' parable is called Lazarus (Luke 16:19–31), but as a character in the Gospel story itself, Lazarus is unique to the Fourth Gospel. **Mary and Martha** are sisters, as in Luke, where they live in an unnamed village in the north (not Bethany, as in John), though there they have no brother. John also identifies Mary with the nameless, sinful woman of Luke 7:37 (see 12:1–8), which later gave rise to identifying her with Mary Magdalene, who was still later identified as a prostitute on the basis of Luke 8:3. See chart at Mark 14:1–9 for the complex interweaving of traditions in early Christianity. **The one who anointed the Lord:** This flash-forward to chap. 12 indicates that the reader is expected to recognize this story that has not yet been narrated. Such phenomena suggest (1) that the Gospel was designed for repeated reading (and indeed its message cannot be appropriated at a single reading) or (2) that the intended readership is already acquainted with the story from one or more of the Synoptic Gospels or oral tradition, or (3) that the order of the Gospel of John itself has been revised, with 12:1–8 prior to chap. 11 in some preceding edition (see note on 4:54), or (4) some combination of the above. In any case, the Gospel was written for initiated readers, not for beginners.

11:3 The one you love (NIV): On this basis some have identified the anonymous Beloved Disciple (see 13:23 commentary) as Lazarus. But

Jesus loved all three (v. 5), i.e., they were not only his disciples but his personal friends. That Jesus, who in the Fourth Gospel represents God and has few purely human traits, should have personal friends may sound a bit *too* human for the Johannine Jesus. But the author is also concerned to show that the one true God incarnate in Jesus has truly entered our human life, and that means having friends as well as disciples (on Jesus' humanity in the Fourth Gospel, see on 1:14; 4:4; 10:18; 11:34–36; 19:34). **Is sick** (NIV): The sisters' report is not mere information, but an implicit request for healing. If Jesus can get there in time, he can heal Lazarus (11:21, 32). The reader, but apparently not the sisters, knows that Jesus can heal at a distance (4:46–54).

11:4 Does not lead to death: Lazarus will die, but death will not have the ultimate victory. Even after being restored to life, Lazarus will die again (see above), but the story points beyond itself to God's ultimate victory over death in the Christ event. Thus Lazarus's sickness and death are for the glory of God (see 9:3). Here, death and the glory of God are two contrary realms of being, and Lazarus's sickness and death belong to the second.

11:6 Stayed two days: On the level of human understanding and compassion, this seems brutally cruel. From the human perspective and that of objectifying language (see on Matt. 2:16; Acts 1:9; Rev. 6:15, excursus, "Interpreting Revelation's Violent Imagery," 3.b), Jesus let Lazarus die and let the sisters despair in order to make his own point. It does not help to say that he waited "only" two days, and Lazarus had been dead four days when Jesus arrived (11:17), so Jesus couldn't have gotten there in time anyway. Jesus can heal at a distance (4:46–54), and in any case to make excuses for Jesus who represents God is to force the Jesus story into the human framework of understanding (see on 7:12). That Jesus' behavior is inhumane (= transcends the merely human) is precisely the point. As representing God in the Johannine story, Jesus acts on his own initiative, not at human directives (see on 1:43–44; 2:4; 7:1–10; 18:1–11). On the "aloofness" of the Johannine Jesus, see on 12:6.

11:8–10 Are you going there again?: Bethany was a suburb of Jerusalem (11:18), where Jesus' life had repeatedly been threatened, but his enemies could not prevail, because his hour had not yet come (2:4; 8:20, 59; 10:39). But now, at his own initiative, he moves to initiate the final scenes of the divine drama.

11:11–14 Fallen asleep . . . speaking about his death: See on 1 Cor. 15:6; 1 Thess. 4:13–14; 5:10, where some English translations preserve the Greek "asleep" and others translate "dead" or "have died." Even the disciples are subject to the "Johannine misunderstanding" (see on 3:3–5; 4:10–15; 6:30–58; 7:33–36; 9:39–41; 10:6; 11:23–27).

11:16 Thomas: In the Synoptics, Thomas is mentioned only once in each Gospel, in the list of the Twelve (Matt. 10:3; Mark 3:18; Luke 6:15), but plays no narrative role. John has no list of the Twelve, a group he mentions only in 6:66–71, but repeatedly refers to Thomas, who is a significant character in the Fourth Gospel (11:16; 14:5; 20:24–28; 21:2). **Called the Twin:** Didymus is the Greek word for "twin." His twin brother or sister plays no role in the New Testament. Here he is represented positively. His comment is not cynicism, but the awareness that Jesus' mission is to give his life for others, and that his disciples are called to the same mission (see on 13:37; Mark 8:34; 14:31).

11:17 Four days: In the hot climate of the ancient eastern Mediterranean, it was customary to bury the unembalmed corpse on the day of death. On the chronology, see commentary on 11:6. According to a rabbinic tradition often cited in this connection, the spirit of the deceased person hovered in the neighborhood for three days, so "four days" meant "thoroughly dead," "beyond hope"—but this reflection is seldom applied to Jesus' own resurrection and should not be pressed. John is not thinking of whether Lazarus's spirit is still hovering nearby; his point is expressed in 11:40.

11:19 Many of the Jews had come: John frequently has a negative picture of "the Jews," but here they are portrayed as genuinely sympathetic—more so than Jesus, who had lingered two days before coming to Bethany.

11:21–22 If you had been here: See v. 32. Both Martha and Mary seem unaware that Jesus can heal at a distance (4:43–54) and suppose that the only hope Jesus (as God's agent and representative) could offer ended at the death of Lazarus. While there's life there's hope, but hope ended when Lazarus died with no answer from Jesus. Thus uncountable millions of those who have prayed for healing of a loved one must have felt when death finally came without the prayer being answered. In this story, Jesus' conduct models that of God, and the other characters in the story reflect people's response to the God who did not answer their prayer. **But even now:** Without being able to articulate it, Martha dares to believe and hope beyond the conceivable—"Even when it's too late, it's not too late" (see on Mark 5:21–43, another story in which God grants life through Christ, though it is already "too late").

11:23 Your brother will rise again: On the resurrection hope in the Old Testament and Judaism, see on Mark 6:16; 12:18–27; Luke 20:27–40; 24:1–12. As often elsewhere in John, Jesus' words can be appropriated at two levels (see on 3:4–10). Martha understands him to affirm the traditional hope shared by Pharisees and some other Jewish groups (but not by the Sadducees) of the future resurrection of the dead at the end of history. Without denying or rejecting the future hope, Jesus explains what he means:

11:25–26 I am the resurrection and the life: On Jesus' "I am" sayings, see 6:35 comments. The Johannine Jesus declares that the eschatological hopes for the end of history are already present for those who believe in Christ. What believers hoped for in the final victory of God's kingdom—the return of Christ, the defeat of Satan, the resurrection of the dead, the judgment, eternal life—are already present in Christ. In the Fourth Gospel, the emphasis has shifted from future hope to present experience: realized eschatology. **Even though they die . . . will never die:** Such language indicates that "die" is being used in more than one sense, but it is too neat simply to speak of physical death and spiritual death, as though John/Jesus is saying, "Christian believers will die physically, but not spiritually." "Never die" is in Greek literally "not die in(to) the age (to come)," suggesting that death in this world does not mean for believers that death prevails over them in the world to come. Thus some have helpfully proposed that the meaning could be paraphrased, "Those who believe in Jesus, even though they die in this world, will not die with respect to the next." This is more in accord with John's thought than the physical/spiritual explanation above, which has more of the pagan connotation of immortality than the biblical doctrine of resurrection (see excursus, "Interpreting the Resurrection," at Matt. 28:1). Still and all, these mysterious, paradoxical words should not be reduced too neatly to clear, conceptual ideas; as the next verse indicates, what is at stake is personal faith in God through Christ, not a schematic idea of what happens when we die.

11:27 Yes, Lord, I believe: The Greek verb is in the perfect: "I have come to believe and still believe (despite Lazarus's death and our unanswered prayer to you)." **You are the Messiah, the Son of God:** She responds to Jesus' declaration about resurrection not by agreeing to a particular doctrinal understanding of life after death, and/or the presence of eternal life now, but by confessing her faith in Christ as Lord. The content of the faith is Christ, the act of God in Christ. It is personal, not doctrinal. This is the fundamental Christian confession, the author's goal for the readers in writing the book (20:30–31; see Mark 8:29).

11:33–35 Greatly disturbed . . . deeply moved . . . Jesus began to weep: See v. 38. These words are sometimes taken as revealing Jesus' divine indignation at human misunderstanding and unbelief, but John also presents Jesus as truly human. These expressions of deep human emotion reveal the humanity of the Word become flesh (see on 1:14) and provide a counterbalance to John's lack of the Gethsemane scene (see on 12:27–28). There is a sense in which this, too, is the Johannine Gethsemane. **Where have you laid him?:** Jesus typically does not ask informational questions (see on 5:6; 6:4), but in this paradoxical scene, where Jesus operates with the power of God who raises the dead, he also illustrates his true humanity.

11:36 See how he loved him: This need not be considered a misunderstanding. Like other human beings, Jesus weeps at the grave of a loved one.

11:37 Could not he . . . have kept this man from dying?: There are various types of religious, supernatural, and faith healers, but death is the end of all human possibilities. It never occurs to them that in this situation Jesus too is not helpless.

11:39 Already there is a stench: King James English is more pungent, "He stinketh." For John, over against the gnostics, who disdained this world, it is precisely in this stinking world of death and decay that the power of the resurrection has been let loose (see Phil. 3:10).

11:40–41 If you believe: It is not the power of their faith that accomplishes the miracle, but God's gracious unilateral power. Yet seeing it as a sign pointing to the glory of God is a matter of faith. Jesus' opponents also believed the miracle happened, but it only hardened their determination to get rid of him (11:47–53). **Glory of God:** See 11:4. **Father, I thank you:** The Johannine theology of Jesus' identity with God makes it difficult for John to portray Jesus praying as other human beings do (see 12:27–30;

17:1–25). Here his prayer is not a request but a thanksgiving that he is in constant communion with God, and is not for Jesus' own benefit but a testimony to the spectators.

11:42 That you sent me: For John, faith in Jesus *is* faith in God, not an alternative to it or an addition to it.

11:43 He cried with a loud voice: The eschatological shout that calls forth the dead from their graves (see 1 Thess. 4:16) rings out already in the call of Jesus who gives life. See 5:25–29.

11:44 Bound . . . unbind: The prototypical image of the freedom Christ gives. See 8:32.

11:45–47 Many of the Jews believed: See 8:31; 9:18; 12:11. John's picture of the Jews is nuanced, not altogether negative (see introduction to John). **Chief priests and the Pharisees:** Historically, it was very probably the Jerusalem temple leadership, the chief priests, that were instrumental in delivering Jesus to the Romans, who put him to death. The major reason was his disruption of the temple business for which they were responsible and the threat that he might provoke a popular uprising. The Pharisees were the opponents of the Johannine church in the author's own time (see introduction to John) and probably played a negligible role in the actual historical events of Jesus' death—they do not appear in Mark's or Luke's passion story at all. In one phrase John blends the 30 CE events of Jesus' actual life and the situation of the Johannine church at the end of the first century, typical of his "two-level drama." **Council:** The Sanhedrin, composed of high priests, scribes, and elders; the latter two groups never appear in John. This is the first official decision to put Jesus to death (see 5:18). This scene corresponds to Mark 14:53–65, Jesus' "Jewish trial" after his arrest, which does not appear in John—who has the decision made by the official council before Jesus was arrested.

11:48–50 The Romans will come and destroy: This argument needs to be read without cynicism and with some sympathy, especially by modern Americans, who have always been the dominating power that other, smaller countries have had to come to terms with and have never experienced the kind of political decisions necessary in a small nation occupied by a foreign empire. The decision of the council does not reflect personal malice against God and Jesus but the realities of the political situation. If the only choice is the death of one person, though innocent, or the destruction of a whole country, in which thousands of innocent people will die, who would not vote for the death of one person? John here pictures the realities of this-worldly politics, and that is his point—it is this world that calculatingly put to death the Son of God. With consummate Johannine irony, Caiaphas says more than he knows—**one man die for the people** is in fact the summary of John's Gospel (3:16). Ironically, when John writes, he knows that, though the decision was made in order to avoid Roman intervention that would destroy the nation, the Romans destroyed it anyway.

11:52 Gather into one: See 10:16; 17:20–22. **Children of God:** Believers, 1:12–13; 3:3–5, who in John's time were not only scattered but divided into hostile groups. The Fourth Gospel has an ecumenical perspective on the church that was already suffering division (see 10:16; 21:1–23).

11:53 From that day . . . put him to death: See 5:18. In the Synoptic Gospels, the temple cleansing, which occurred on Jesus' one and only visit to Jerusalem, precipitated the decision that he must die. While this is probably closer to the historical reality, John has placed the temple cleansing early in Jesus' ministry (2:13–22), with several visits to Jerusalem having occurred since, and thus finds another event that triggers the final opposition against Jesus.

11:54 Went . . . to a town called Ephraim: A village several miles northeast of Jerusalem. There is a parallel withdrawal at the end of the preceding section (see commentary at 10:40). The stage is now set (again!) for the final events of Jesus' ministry.

12:1–50

Transition and Summary

Chapter 12 comprises three units: (1) Jesus' anointing (12:1–11) and (2) his triumphal entry into Jerusalem (12:12–19), each of which has counterparts in the other Gospels, and (3) Jesus' final proclamation summarizing his message and its results at the end of his public ministry (12:20–50), unique to John. This chapter forms a transitional section between Jesus' public ministry confronting the unbelieving world and his private instruction to "his own" (see introduction to John: "Outline").

12:1–11

The Anointing at Bethany

(See also at Matt. 26:6–13; Mark 14:3–9; Luke 7:36–50)

12:1 Six days before the Passover: A very similar story appears in all four Gospels, but the four versions are located in three different times and places (see chart at Mark 14:1–9). John places the story in Bethany near Jerusalem in the house of Mary, Martha, and Lazarus, on the Saturday evening before Palm Sunday. Since in Jewish reckoning the day begins at 6:00 p.m., this meal is after the Sabbath, on Sunday (see on Acts 20:7). Matthew and Mark place this event after the triumphal entry, "two days before the Passover" (Matt. 26:2; Mark 14:1), in the house of Simon the leper. Luke locates it earlier, during the Galilean ministry, in the house of a different Simon, a Pharisee.

On the Passover, see on Luke 22:1. This is the third (or fourth) Passover in the Johannine chronology (see introduction to John: "Outline"). **Lazarus . . . raised:** See on 11:1.

12:2 Martha served: On Martha, Mary, and Lazarus, see on 11:1–2. John here reflects the same perspective on the roles of Martha and Mary as Luke 10:38–42. John and Luke share many distinctive elements, but it is not clear whether John knows Luke or whether they share elements of the same tradition.

12:3–5 Pound: A Roman pound of 12 ounces, a very large amount, and very expensive. **Three hundred denarii:** Three hundred days' wages for a day laborer (see Matt. 20:2). On the Johannine understanding of messianic extravagance, see John 2:6; 6:12–13; 12:3; 19:39; Luke 5:6; 6:37–38; 9:17; 8:5–8; 13:20; 15:22; 19:17; Rom. 5:15). **Feet . . . hair:** As in Luke 7; in Matthew and Mark the woman anoints Jesus' head.

12:6 The poor: There is no reference to helping the poor, here or elsewhere in the Gospel of John. The motif is a relic of the Synoptic tradition that John does not develop. The reader may have allowed images of the Synoptic Jesus to infiltrate the Johannine picture and may not have noted the distinctive profile of Jesus in the Fourth Gospel; in John there are no poor, no wicked rich, no publicans and sinners, no widows, no children, no women fellow travelers, no unclean demoniacs, no lepers, no shepherds, no fishermen (except in the appended chap. 21), no prostitutes, no reference to Jesus' compassion or pity.

John is oriented to Christology on a cosmic scale, not to developing a characterization of the individual deeds of Jesus and his disciples. The center of John's attention is focused on the Christ event as a whole as the expression of God's saving grace for the world (see 3:16), rather than particular acts of grace for specific individuals or groups. Thus the Johannine

Jesus can be perceived as "aloof" (see, e.g., 5:9, 8:23; 11:6). The New Testament elsewhere provides pictures of the compassionate acts of the man Jesus as models for the believer (esp. in the Gospel of Luke); John is focused on another approach to Christology, which also has its necessary role in Christian belief. Thus we see the importance of a plurality of distinct Gospels and the danger of simply choosing among them or harmonizing them.

He was a thief: The mystery of why one of Jesus' closest disciples betrayed him puzzled early Christianity. Only the Fourth Gospel pictures Judas as the treasurer for the group, who stole from the common fund. John does not have the Synoptic story that Judas took money from the high priests as payment for betraying Jesus, but like the Synoptics presents greed as a cause in his betrayal. Despite the Johannine perspective discussed in the previous verse, the fact that Judas the bad disciple did not care for the poor implies that true disciples do care for them. Although John expresses it differently from the way it is articulated in the Synoptics, in the Fourth Gospel, too, the love of God is not restrictive, but for all (see on 3:16). Here the reader again hears the narrator's voice, like a commentator at the side of the stage who speaks to the audience, though the characters on the stage do not hear his voice. There are numerous such inserted footnotes or narrative asides in John; depending on one's criteria, from fifty-nine to more than one hundred have been counted (e.g., see 1:8; 3:16–21; 4:2, 9, 25; 6:6, 23, 59; 12:6; 33).

12:7 So that she might keep it: The Markan version of the saying is clear: "she has anointed my body beforehand for burial" (Mark 14:8). The Johannine meaning is not clear; the NRSV and other translations have added words in an attempt to clarify the meaning (see NRSV note), but the puzzle remains as to how Mary can keep the ointment for Jesus' burial after she has already used it for the anointing.

12:10–11 Many of the Jews were believing: See commentary on 11:44. Here, the high priests are contrasted with "the Jews," illustrating again that John uses the term in a nuanced way (see introduction to John). **Put Lazarus to death:** Here Lazarus becomes a prototype of the post-Easter Christian witness to Jesus. He has received new life, he eats and drinks with Jesus and his disciples, the testimony of his life leads others to faith. Like some Christians in the Johannine church, he is now under the

threat of persecution and death because of his testimony. Such statements do not reflect the time of Jesus' own ministry but imply a time when the disciples of Jesus had already separated and/or been expelled from the synagogue, some Jews were leaving the synagogue to join the groups of Christians, and they were suffering duress from Jewish leaders for their "apostasy" (see 9:22; 16:2; 1 Thess. 2:14–16; Acts 9:1–2).

12:12–19
The Triumphal Entry
(See also at Matt. 21:1–9; Mark 1:1–10;
Luke 19:28–40)

12:12 The next day: Sunday, in the chronology of John and Mark; Monday in Matthew's chronology; Luke is unclear as to the day of the week. See chronological note at 12:1. In the Synoptics this is Jesus' first entrance into Jerusalem; in John, he has been there often before. Thus in John the crowd from the city is expecting him and goes out to meet him, while in the Synoptics they approach the city with Jesus. There is also "a crowd that was with him" (12:17), a combination of the Synoptic view and John's own perspective.

12:13 Branches of palm trees: Palms are mentioned only in the Fourth Gospel, giving the name to Palm Sunday. **King of Israel:** See 1:49; 6:15; 18:33, 37, 39; 19:3, 19. John always uses "Israel" positively, "Jews" in subtle and nuanced ways. Like other characters in John, the crowds say more than they know, do not understand the deeper sense of what they are saying—but the post-Easter reader does (see vv. 11:50–52; 19:5, 19–22).

12:14 Jesus found: In the Synoptics, the disciples find the colt and bring it to Jesus. The Johannine Jesus, representing God, acts directly and unilaterally (see 6:11; 19:17).

12:16 His disciples did not understand: See on 10:6. **Then they remembered:** See on 2:22, 20:9. It is not just their later commonsense retrospective insight, but the gift of the Spirit, that makes post-Easter understanding possible (7:39).

12:19 The world has gone after him: What the Pharisees say within the framework of the pre-Easter ministry of Jesus reflects the frustration of the Jewish leadership as perceived by John in his own day, when many Jews were becoming disciples of Jesus and leaving the synagogue (see 11:42; 12:10–11). On characters within the story saying more than they know, see 11:50–52; 12:13; 19:5; 19:22.

12:20–36
Greeks Seek Jesus; Discourse on His Death

12:20–22 Some Greeks: See 7:35. The word in itself usually refers to non-Jews, but in the context—they have come to Jerusalem to worship—they are to be understood as Hellenistic Jews, such as Paul, who lived in the Diaspora and had adopted the Greek language and customs. During Jesus' ministry, Gentiles did not become his followers. By John's time, Christianity had become primarily a Gentile, i.e., Greek, religion. The author wants to show that this was already anticipated in Jesus' own time. Like Luke in Acts 2, who knows that the church began as a group within Judaism, he paints its beginnings in a way that foreshadows its later development (see on Acts 2:5–11). **Philip . . . Andrew:** The "Greeks" do not approach Jesus directly (also appropriate to the historical reality) but through two disciples, both of whom have Greek names.

12:23 The hour has come: See 2:4; 4:23, 5:25; 13:1. For the first time, Jesus "hour" is announced as present, as having come. The arrival of the Greeks signals that Jesus' earthly ministry is over and the time for his death/resurrection has arrived. **Son of Man:** See commentary on Mark 2:10.

12:24 Falls into the earth and dies: Paul uses the image in the same way, with reference to the resurrection, but does not apply it directly to Jesus (1 Cor. 15:36–37). Jesus' story of the seed in Mark 4:1–9 is there interpreted so that the seed is the word (Mark 4:14; even more explicitly in Luke 8:11). For John, Jesus is the Word made flesh (1:14), who brings life by himself dying and being placed in the earth.

12:25 Those who love their life lose it: A saying similar in form and meaning, but with different vocabulary, is found in Mark 8:35 (reproduced in Matt. 16:24 and Luke 9:24) as well as Matt. 10:39/Luke 17:33, a Q saying. John has reformulated the saying in his own idiom and placed it in a different narrative setting, namely at the summary and capstone of Jesus' public ministry. Following Jesus means not merely admiring his teaching and life, but adopting the model of unselfish love for others as the orientation of one's own life. For John too, Christology is not real until it is translated into discipleship. **Those who hate their life:** "Hate" in biblical idiom does not mean "detest," but "not choose," i.e., make something else the top priority (see on Luke 14:26; Rom. 9:13). Discipleship is here presented as a matter of choice, not of self-hatred. "Feeling good about myself" is still focused on "myself"—the Johannine Christ frees his followers from this compulsive service to one's own image, which is also a form of idolatry.

12:27–28 What should I say?: Here the Johannine Christ explicitly rejects a portrayal of Jesus who trembles before death and asks to be delivered from it (see the Gethsemane scene of Mark 14:34–42; Matt. 26:36–46; Luke 22:39–46; see Heb. 5:7–10). John ponders this scene from the other Gospels or their tradition, rejects it in advance, makes the extensive prayer of John 17 into his substitute for the Gethsemane prayer (see 5:30; 11:40–41), and presents a different image of Jesus in the garden where he is arrested (see 18:1–11, but also on 11:33–35). **A voice came from heaven:** The heavenly voice at Jesus' baptism and transfiguration does not appear in John's story. Here, the only words explicitly attributed to God in the Fourth Gospel, the heavenly voice speaks with the accents of Johannine theology. **I have glorified it:** *God's* name has been glorified in *Jesus'* ministry. **And I will glorify it again:** *God's* name will be glorified in *Jesus'* coming death and resurrection.

12:29 It was thunder: Though God does speak directly from heaven, the divine voice must be interpreted. One can always explain God's act as natural phenomena. **An angel:** From John's perspective, this is not much better than the previous interpretation. Although God truly acts in history, God's act is not obvious to the uncommitted observer; God does not force his way into our lives. God acts, but we must decide whether it is God or we will explain the action some other way. The Egyptians and the Israelites both saw the waters recede at the Red Sea, but only the Israelites said, "God has acted for our salvation." The Egyptians presumably said something like, "Lucky for them the wind came up," and pursued the Israelites to their own destruction (Exod. 14; see on Acts 2:12–13).

12:31 Now is the judgment: Courtroom imagery plays a large role in the Gospel of John, partly because the Johannine community itself appeared before synagogue courts in which Christians were accused (see 2 Cor. 11:24), partly because the life of Jesus had ended in a double trial scene before Jewish and Roman courts, and partly because the Last Judgment to be conducted by the Son of Man as God's agent was a recurrent theme in early Christian theology (e.g., Matt. 25:31–46). The constant issue revolves around who is really the judge, who is being judged (see 18:33–19:16, esp. 19:13), and when the judgment takes place. Without denying the future judgment, here the point is that the Last Judgment already takes place as people respond to Jesus and his message. **Now the ruler of this world:** John believes, as do all biblical authors, that the ultimate ruler of this world is the one God, the Creator, who has not abdicated his sovereignty (1:1–3; 17:3). But in the apocalyptic view John shares with other New Testament writers, God's rulership has been usurped by the rebellious creation, headed by the Satanic power of evil (see on Luke 4:41; 2 Cor. 4:4). **Will be driven out:** Although casting out demons is a characteristic feature of Jesus' ministry in the Synoptic Gospels, there are no exorcisms in John. As in Paul's theology, the Christ event itself accomplishes a cosmic exorcism. In Jesus' death and resurrection, God casts out the demonic power that presently rules the world and reasserts his own divine sovereignty over the universe (see Eph. 2:2; 6:12; Col. 2:15).

12:32 When I am lifted up: The Greek verb has a double meaning in John—lifted up on the cross, and exalted to be with God. Those who "lift up" Jesus are both those who crucify him and God, who exalts him to heaven; the human act of crucifixion is paradoxically the divine act of exaltation. The conjunction is "when," not "if"—there is no condition attached. Thus "lifting up Jesus" is not something contemporary preachers and Christians are charged to do, but something that has been done by God's act at the cross and resurrection. **Draw all people:** This does not refer merely to the psychological effect the cross may have on some people in attracting them to follow Jesus, who gave his life for them, but represents God's act, the divine initiative without which no one can come to God (6:37, 44, 65). But God finally draws **all**. This does not here mean that God attracts all, but not all respond; God's act is effective. This is one of the universalistic passages (all are finally saved) that paradoxically lie side by side with particularistic passages (only believers are finally saved). On "universal salvation," see excursus, "Universal Salvation and Paradoxical Language," at Rev. 22:21.

12:33 The kind of death: On the narrator's voice, see 12:6. The kind of death is crucifixion, one of the most horrible deaths human ingenuity has devised as a "deterrent" to crime. In the New Testament generally, it is important not just that Jesus died, but that he died officially as a condemned criminal at the hands of humanity's highest religion and the world's best government. The Johannine paradox is that this depth of injustice, humiliation, and human suffering is at the same time Jesus' glorification as God's representative. As in the Synoptics (Mark 8:31; 9:31; 10:33–34), Jesus knows his suffering in advance.

12:34 The Messiah remains forever: There is no specific text that declares this, but it is nonetheless true that the hoped-for messianic deliverer of Old Testament and Jewish expectation was not thought of as one who would accomplish God's deliverance by suffering and death, but as one who would establish God's ultimate and eternal rule as the last act of the historical drama. This topic was not actually debated in the pre-Easter ministry of the historical Jesus; the dialogue represents the retrospective view of what actually happened to Jesus, in view of Christian claims that he was nonetheless (or rather, all the more) the Messiah sent by God. **Who is this Son of Man?:** See on Mark 2:10. This is the only occurrence of "Son of Man" in the Gospels not on the lips of Jesus. The dialogue here assumes information previously given to the *readers* by the narrator, another indication that the Gospels are not verbatim reports, but interpret the significance of Jesus to the post-Easter reader.

12:36 Children of light: Another expression of Johannine dualism (see on 8:23). The phrase is literally "son of . . . ," a Semitic idiom (see on Mark 2:10; Luke 16:8; 1 Thess. 5:5; Eph. 5:8). **Departed and hid:** See 8:59.

12:37–43
The Unbelief of the People

Jesus' public ministry ends at 12:36. John 12:37–43 presents the narrator's concluding comment and summary of Jesus' public encounter with "the world." In 12:44–50 Jesus himself then presents an epilogue, not spoken within the narrative framework, but "over their heads" to the reader.

12:37 So many signs . . . did not believe: "They" here seems to represent the crowds (see 12:34), i.e., the Jewish people as a whole, not just the leaders. Though there is no blanket condemnation of the Jews in the Fourth Gospel, by the author's time it was clear that most Jews were not going to be converted by Christian preaching, and that the church was mainly Gentile.

12:38 To fulfill the word spoken by the prophet Isaiah: The citation is from Isa. 53:1, which introduces the Suffering Servant passage that many early Christians saw as pointing to Jesus (see on Luke 9:43–48; 22:5, 32, 36; Acts 8:27–33; 1 Cor. 11:23–26; 15:3; 1 Pet. 2:21–25; Rev. 5:6). Paul also cites the same text in the same connection (Rom. 10:16).

12:39 They could not believe: Early Christians found the rejection of Jesus by most Jews already prefigured in Israel's rejection of the prophets. In this regard Isa. 6:9–10 was a key explanatory text also in Matt. 13:10–17; Mark 4:11–12; Luke 8:9–10, and as the concluding reflection (as here) at Acts 28:26–27. On the paradox of divine sovereignty and human responsibility, see 3:16; 5:42; 6:27, 44; 10:26 and especially excursus, "Predestination," at Rom. 8:28–29.

12:41 Isaiah . . . saw his glory: The early Christians saw the Old Testament as a whole as pointing to the climax of God's plan of salvation in the Christ event (see excursus, "New Testament Interpretation of the Old Testament," at 1 Cor. 15:3; 1 Pet. 1:10). John claims Abraham, Moses, Isaiah, and the psalmists as witnesses to Jesus (see 1:17, 45–51; 5:39, 46; 8:56; 9:28–29; 10:34).

12:42 Many, even of the authorities, believed: On John's multileveled use of "believe," see 2:23–25. Here, their "faith" does not lead them to the public profession that is the mark of authentic discipleship (see on 6:51–58; Matt. 10:32). **Because of the Pharisees:** See above on 11:45–47. **Put out of the synagogue:** See 9:18–23. In 16:2 this is only "predicted" from the narrative standpoint within the story. Here it is represented as already present during Jesus' ministry. On the two-level drama in John's dual perspective, see "Introduction to the Gospels" and comments on 9:1–2.

12:43 Human glory . . . glory that comes from God: John plays on the double meaning of the Greek word, which means not only "glory" but also "opinion, what people think." He is critical of those who value what others think of them, or their own self-image, more than how they appear in God's eyes. To be freed from the tyranny of protecting one's image, even to oneself, is part of the freedom Christ brings (8:32).

12:44–50
Jesus' Summary of His Ministry

In this epilogue to his public ministry the Johannine Jesus looks back over his ministry and summarizes his message and its results. Most of his hearers had not understood him or believed in him. In John, it is only the small group of disciples at the Last Supper, who receive the revelation of the cross and resurrection and the gift of the Holy Spirit, that comes to authentic faith and understanding. Jesus here summarizes the message of the book so far for the reader, who already shares the postresurrection perspective the disciples are to receive in chaps. 13–20.

12:44–45 Whoever believes in me believes . . . in him who sent me: The paradox that faith in Christ is faith in God, that faith in God means faith in Christ. Faith in Christ is not something Christians have added on to faith in God, as a second, optional step. Nor is it the case that Christians believe in two deities, while Jews (and Muslims) believe in only one. This is the very heresy John opposes. Rather, Christians believe in the "one true God" (17:3), but they cannot think and speak about this God apart from his definitive revelation in Christ. The God who sent Jesus is the one true God; Jesus is the functional equivalent of God. This is expressed in John's reformulation of a saying also found in Matt. 10:40 and Luke 10:16. John only makes explicit what is already implicit in the Synoptic Gospels; one cannot avoid the high Christology of John by fleeing to the Synoptics.

12:46 I have come as light into the world: The light of God has always been in the world, for the creation reflects the light of the Creator and is available to every human being (1:1–4, 9; Acts 14:17). Yet this primal light that illuminates every person has come into the world as a person (1:14; 8:12). Here we have the Johannine paradox of the universal and the particular. Each side of the paradox has become a stumbling block to some; John (the Johannine Jesus) affirms them both in tandem.

12:47–48 I came not to judge the world: God's intention is to save, not judge (3:17–18). **The one who rejects me . . . has a judge:** The only options are "believe in me" and "reject me." In the Johannine dualism there is no place for "sort of," "sometimes," or "maybe," but here too John only expresses in his distinctive way the message of Jesus also found in the Synoptic Gospels (Matt. 12:30; Luke 11:23). The coming of the light of God forces an either/or decision between living by the light and remaining in darkness. God wants all people to come to the light but will not force his will on those who choose to remain in darkness. **On the last day:** In one sense the separation that is presently taking place as people respond to the light by either accepting or rejecting it, is already the judgment (12:31), but not in such a way that it replaces the future Last Judgment. **The word that I have spoken will serve as judge**: The Johannine version of Matt. 7:24–27; in John the norm of judgment is the word that Jesus is, the Christ event as a whole, not only Jesus' teaching communicated in his sayings. This word spoken once for all in the event of Jesus Christ, the word Jesus spoke and was (1:14), is the ultimate criterion of God's judgment.

13:1–20:31
PART TWO—THE BOOK OF GLORY: JESUS REVEALS THE GLORY OF HIS DEATH AND RESURRECTION TO THE DISCIPLES

13:1–17:26
THE FAREWELL DISCOURSES

The second major part of John's narrative is composed of two parts: the Farewell Discourses at the Last Supper (chaps. 13–17) and the account of Jesus' glorification, i.e., his death and resurrection (see introduction to John: "Outline"). All the Gospels recount Jesus' last meal with his disciples on the evening before he was killed. This is done quite briefly in Matt. 26:17–29 and Mark 14:19–25, somewhat more expansively in Luke 22:7–38 (one of numerous points at which John is more like Luke than Matthew and Mark). Yet John's account of the Last Supper is several times longer than Luke's. John's account overlaps the Synoptic story only slightly. He agrees with them in having Jesus foretell his betrayal and in predicting Peter's denial but has no institution of the Lord's Supper. This is not because John is unaware of or rejects Jesus' eucharistic teaching; John's church celebrates the Eucharist (see on John 6:11–12, 23, 51–59; the references to wine in 2:1–11, to the vine in 15:1–8, and to blood in 19:34 also have eucharistic overtones). John has inserted the story of Jesus' washing the disciples' feet in the place occupied in the Synoptics by the institution of the Eucharist (see on 13:14–15).

While the Synoptic Jesus has a few words to say at the Last Supper, there is nothing there comparable to John's lengthy Farewell Discourse, which resembles the style and content of 1 John much more than that of the Synoptic Jesus. Here we have a good example of the post-Easter church developing Jesus' own teaching under the guidance of the Holy Spirit and speaking in

Jesus' name (see "Introduction to the Gospels," and comments on John 14:25–26; 16:7–15).

13:1–20
Washing the Disciples' Feet

The scene is not in the Synoptics (see above).

13:1 Before the festival of the Passover: Here we have John's first chronological note since 12:12, on Palm Sunday (see 12:1). The Passover lambs were killed on the afternoon of the 14th of Nisan and eaten that evening, which according to the Jewish reckoning of time was already the 15th. While all the Gospels agree in placing Jesus' Last Supper on Thursday evening, the Synoptics regard it as a Passover meal on the 15th of Nisan (Matt. 26:17–19; Mark 14:12–16; Luke 22:11–15), but John represents it as occurring on the 14th, with the crucifixion itself occurring the next day, still the 14th, at the time of the slaughter of the Passover lambs (see John 13:29; 18:28; 19:14; see chart at Matt. 26:17). In each case the point is theological: Matthew and Luke, following Mark, portray the Last Supper itself as a Passover meal, the fulfillment of the Jewish Passover; John has the meal take place on the night before, so that Jesus' death will coincide with the death of the Passover lambs (see on 1:29; 18:28; 19:16–30, and chart at Matt. 26:17).

Jesus knew: As God's representative, the Johannine Jesus has divine omniscience. The impending arrest, trial, and crucifixion do not take him unawares (see 18:1–11, esp. 18:4). **His hour had come:** See 2:4; 4:23, 7:30, 13:31; 16:32; 17:1. **His own:** See 1:11. In contrast to the world that had rejected him (chaps. 1–12; see on 12:37–48), those who believe in God through Jesus are "his own." In the Fourth Gospel's narrative, there is no reason to think that only the Twelve are present (see 6:66–70). **Who were in the world:** Jesus is departing; his disciples remain in the world. "World" occurs forty times in chaps. 13–17, more than in all the rest of the Gospel. This shows that the Farewell Discourses do not represent a retreat from the world, as though after being rejected in chaps. 1–11 Jesus abandons the world and withdraws with his disciples into some kind of private domain. As Jesus in chaps. 1–12 represents God's love for the *world* (3:16), so Jesus' disciples will be sent into the *world* (17:15, 18, 21, 23). It is for the sake of God's mission to the world, represented by Jesus and continued in the church, that Jesus now speaks to "his own." His instruction is not a private blessing to be enjoyed by his disciples, but is equipment for mission.

Loved them to the end: The Greek phrase can be translated "completely," or "utterly," but John's point is better preserved by the literal translation represented here. The Johannine Jesus thinks of his death on the cross, when he will say, "It is finished" (19:30). Love is not an emotion but an event, the act of God's self-giving love on the cross (see on 3:16; 1 Cor. 13:4–7).

13:2 Devil had already put it into the heart: See 13:27. Judas is both personally responsible and also the victim of Satan; see 6:66–70. On the dangers and validity of the Bible's Satan language, see excursus, "Satan, the Devil, and Demons in Biblical Theology," at Mark 5:1; Luke 4:1–13; 22:3–5; Acts 5:3; 2 Cor. 11:13–15; Rev. 12. **During supper:** Not a Passover meal, as in the Synoptics. Some older translations follow the mass of later MSS that read "after supper," which harmonizes better with the Synoptics—one can imagine that the Eucharist has already been instituted. Such harmonizing interpretation should be resisted. The best and oldest manuscripts read "during supper." On such text-critical decisions every translation must make, see "Introduction: The New Testament as the Church's Book," 4.d.

13:3 Jesus, knowing: See on 13:1. The Jesus of the Fourth Gospel, unlike the Synoptic Jesus, is always aware of his preexistence. **Placed all things in his hands:** See on 3:35.

13:4–5 Began to wash the disciples' feet: In the dusty first-century Mediterranean world, where walking was the usual mode of transportation and sandals the customary footgear, this was a normal act of hospitality but was considered beneath the dignity of the average person and thus almost always performed by a slave (see Luke 7:36–50). Here the preexistent Christ lays aside his celestial dignity and performs the service of a slave. There are several parallels to the hymn of Phil. 2:5–11. What Paul pictures as a cosmic drama of preexistence-incarnation-exaltation, John portrays as a solemn incident in the life of the earthly Jesus. But John also understands it as a pointer to the whole Christ event (see v. 8): just as Jesus at the Last Supper laid aside his garments, assumed the role of a slave, then arose, was called Lord, and resumed his previous mode of existence and rejoined his disciples at the table, so the preexistent Christ laid aside his celestial glory, became an example to the Christians as a truly human servant

of all, was raised and declared to be Lord of all, and meets them at the Lord's Table. John has replaced the institution of the Lord's Supper with the footwashing scene.

13:6 Lord, are you going to wash my feet? It is a natural response, yet in typical Johannine fashion, Peter (mis)understands at the everyday level an event that points beyond itself to the transcendent act of God. On the typical "Johannine misunderstanding," see on 3:3–5; 4:10–15; 6:30–58; 7:33–36; 9:39–41; 11:11–13; 23–27.

13:7 You do not know . . . later you will understand: Again the nature of the Gospel genre is illustrated—the church's post-Easter insight into the meaning of Jesus' life, death, and resurrection became available only from the perspective of the resurrection and by the gift of the Holy Spirit (see 2:22; 7:39; 12:16; 14:26; 16:13).

13:8 Unless I wash you, you have no share with me: The conversation has moved to another level that only the post-Easter reader can grasp. It becomes clear that "washing" is not merely the literal removal of dirt from the body, but refers to the cleansing, saving act of God in the Christ event as a whole, an event that the believer experiences as personally real by being baptized and participating in the Eucharist. This washing puts one into a new relation with Jesus. (See Acts 22:16; Rom. 6:3–4, where, as here, baptism is related to Jesus' death; and see 3:5, 19:34, where water evokes the image of Christian baptism.) After his humble service on this earth, the risen Lord, reclothed in his divine glory, meets believers at the Lord's Table, eats and drinks with them.

13:9 Not my feet only: Peter continues to (mis)understand at the literal level, as did Nicodemus (3:3–5) and the Samaritan woman at the well (4:14–15)—each dealing with life-giving "water" that grants life, not literal water. (For the "Johannine misunderstanding" see also 2:19–22; 6:30–58; 7:33–36; 9:39–41; 11:11–13, 23–27.)

13:10 Except for the feet: This difficult text is more understandable if this phrase is omitted, as in some manuscripts (see NRSV note). Then we would read Jesus' response as "One who has bathed [been baptized into the new life] does not need to wash, but is entirely clean." The cleansing Jesus' gives makes secondary washing irrelevant, just as the water Jesus gives means one will never thirst again (4:14–15). Peter's question and Jesus' response shows that Peter continues to understand spiritual truth at the literal, everyday level.

13:10–11 You are clean: "You" is plural. As in the dialogue with Nicodemus (3:7–11), the one-on-one conversation modulates into an address to all the disciples, including the readers. **He knew who was to betray him:** See 6:64–70.

13:15 I have set you an example: As in Phil. 2:5–11, the humility of the Christ who stoops to serve is a model for the disciples' own conduct. In early Christianity, still in a culture where washing the feet was a normal expression of service and hospitality, footwashing became a symbol of the Christian life as such (see 1 Tim. 5:10). While the church has sometimes appropriately adopted footwashing as a liturgical, symbolic act of mutual humility, it would be a misunderstanding on the same level as Peter's in the story to take **wash one another's feet** as a literal command for all times and places. The humility of the Christ event itself, in which the eternal Word became flesh and dwelt among us (1:1–2, 14) for the service of all humanity, is the model of the Christian life. This example is not necessarily followed by repeating the literal act, but by allowing oneself to be incorporated into the Christ event, permitting the same self-giving love of God present in Christ to be present and active in Christ's disciples. Thus the Johannine writer here gives one vivid symbol of the dictum presented elsewhere in the straightforward language of the Johannine school: "We love, because he first loved us" (1 John 4:9–19, esp. 4:19). The story of the footwashing at the Last Supper thus serves as a kind of Johannine replacement of the story of instituting the Eucharist. While it is possible to think of the Eucharist as an act in which the believer only passively receives, here the Christ event is symbolized in a way that calls for active participation and emulation of the example of Christ (see 2 Cor. 8:1–9 comments).

13:16 Messengers: This is the NRSV translation of *apostolos*, usually translated "apostle," but here understood in its usual, nontechnical sense. The word is not found elsewhere in the Gospel of John or the Letters of John, but see Rev. 2:2; 18:20; 21:14. See 6:66–70.

13:18 To fulfill the Scriptures: Ps. 41:9. See excursus, "New Testament Interpretation of the Old Testament," at 1 Cor. 15:3. John explains elements in his tradition that could be interpreted as illustrating Jesus' human weakness as having happened in order to fulfill the Scripture (see 19:28). Here, that one of Jesus' own disciples betrayed him is explained not as Jesus' lack of knowledge (see on 6:64), but as according to God's plan as revealed in the Scripture. On John's paradoxical view of Christ as truly human–truly divine, see introduction to John, and on 1:14; 5:18, 30; 11:33–34. On Judas as an illustration of human responsibility and divine sovereignty, see 6:64–70; 13:2.

13:20 Whoever receives one whom I send . . . receives me . . . (and) him who sent me: Although John does not use the terminology of "apostolic Christianity" (see 13:16 commentary), he has an apostolic understanding of the church analogous to that found in other New Testament writers: as Christ is the representative of God to the world, so Christians are representatives of Christ to the world (see Luke 6:12–13; Acts 19:6; 1 Cor. 4:1–13; introduction to 2 Corinthians; 2 Cor. 4:7–5:10; 5:18–20; Gal. 1:1–5; 1 Pet. 5:1–5).

13:21–30
Jesus Foretells His Betrayal
(See also at Matt. 26:21–25;
Mark 14:18–21; Luke 22:21–23)

13:21 Troubled in spirit: Despite divine foreknowledge, the human Jesus is grieved (see on 11:33–35).

13:23–24 The one whom Jesus loved: This figure, traditionally called the Beloved Disciple, is not a matter of Jesus playing favorites. Rather, this anonymous disciple represents the ideal follower of Jesus, the ideal human response to the love of God manifest in Jesus. He is not found in the Synoptics, is not to be identified with any of the Twelve, and appears here for the first time (see 18:15–16; 19:26, 35; 20:2, 3, 4, 8; 21:7, 20, 24; also 1:40?). He may represent an ideal figure not to be identified with any historical person, but more likely represents the idealized memory of the founder of the Johannine school, the "patron saint" of the Johannine church, the one through whom the community originally attained access to Jesus and whose testimony is still the basis of that continuing relationship. **Next to him:** Traditionally translated in the quaint King James English "on his bosom." Jesus and his disciples are pictured as reclining, Roman style, around the central table like the spokes of a wheel. Diners reclined on the left hand and used the right hand for eating, so the Beloved Disciple was on Jesus' right, the place of honor (see Gen. 48:13–20; Ps. 110:1; Col. 3:1; Heb. 8:1; 12:2). The place "next to him," or "on his bosom" reflects the closest communion; the same Greek word is used in 1:18 of Christ's relation to God—as Jesus is the representative and interpreter of God, so the Beloved Disciple (as the ideal follower of Jesus) is the representative and interpreter of Jesus (see 13:20). In some other streams of early Christianity, Simon Peter is given this role (see, e.g., Matt. 16:16–18; introduction to 1 Peter). Throughout the Fourth Gospel—until the epilogue of chapter 21—there is a not too subtle contrast between the Beloved Disciple and Peter, in which the Beloved Disciple always appears in the superior role. Here, the Beloved Disciple is closest to Jesus, and Peter must ask him what Jesus means. The incident does not merely recount an event around the table at the Last Supper, but reflects competing understandings of church leadership in early Christianity.

13:27 Satan entered into him: See on 13:2. **Do quickly what you are going to do:** The announcement of the betrayer is in all the Gospels, but only John gives this elaboration. This is not a report of the historical Jesus' giving permission or issuing a command for Judas to betray him, but is John's way of showing that Jesus is not an unwilling victim of his betrayal, arrest, and crucifixion; rather, representing God, Jesus is in control even during his passion (see on 18:1–11). On Judas as treasurer for the group, see on 12:6. John does not contain the Synoptic explanation that Judas betrayed Jesus for money.

13:29 Buy . . . for the festival: In the Fourth Gospel, the last supper is not a Passover meal, which has not occurred yet (see chronological note on 13:1). The disciples typically misunderstand (see on 10:6).

13:30 After receiving the piece of bread: In the Fourth Gospel, only Judas is portrayed as receiving bread at the Last Supper. While the Johannine church celebrates the Eucharist, receiving the communion elements is not understood in a mechanical or magical manner (see on 6:51–59). **It was night:** Not chronology but theology. On John's light/darkness dualism, see 3:2, 19; 8:12, 23, 9:1–41; 11:10; 12:36, 46; 19:39; 21:3.

13:31–35
The New Commandment of Love

13:31 Now the Son of Man has been glorified: On Son of Man, see Mark 2:10. Here as elsewhere, the Johannine Jesus "looks back on" his earthly career from the post-Easter perspective of the church (see "Introduction to the Gospels"). **Glorified** means "crucified"; the "lifting up" on the cross is also Jesus' return to the glory of God the preexistent

Christ shared with the Father (see 3:13–15; 12:23–24, 32; 17:24).

13:33 Little children: This is not a condescending comment by the historical Jesus on the childishness of the disciples. This word occurs only here in the Gospels, but seven times in 1 John as a designation of Christian believers, and nowhere else in the New Testament. In the Fourth Gospel, Jesus speaks in the idiom of the Johannine community, in which believers address each other as children of God (see 1:11–12; 3:3–5; 1 John 2:1, 12, 28; 3:7, 18; 4:4; 5:21). **Where I am going, you cannot come:** See 7:34.

13:34 A new commandment: In the Synoptic Gospels, Jesus cites as the greatest commandment the Old Testament the command to love God and neighbor (Deut. 6:4–5; Lev. 19:18; Matt. 22:34–40; Mark 12:28–34; Luke 10:25–28), and commands love even to one's enemies (Matt. 5:43–48; Luke 6:27–36). In John, Jesus does not cite the Bible in this regard, but gives the command on his own authority, as "new," i.e., eschatologically renewed, analogous to the "new covenant" (see on 1 Cor. 11:25; Luke 5:36–38; 22:20). There was some discussion in the Johannine community as to whether and how the command of Jesus was "new": 2 John 5, not . . . a new commandment; 1 John 2:7–8, "no new commandment, but a new commandment"; John 13:34, "new commandment."

13:35 Love for one another: On the meaning of love in the New Testament, see on 1 Cor. 13:4–7. Though the command seems to apply only to the community, love in the Fourth Gospel is not exclusive but reflects the love of God, directed to all people (3:16; 1 John 4:19). Yet it was important to remind the persecuted disciples in John's church of the solidarity that each member enjoyed with a loving community that supported them in their trials, that God's universal love is made concrete within a particular community of faith. **Everyone will know that you are my disciples:** The disciple's experience of the love of God is not an individualistic personal blessing, but a testimony to the world that Christians are not merely "nice people," but agents of God's love for the world revealed in Christ.

13:36–38
Peter's Denial Predicted
(See also at Matt. 26:30–35; Mark 14:26–31; Luke 22:31–34)

See comments on Synoptic parallels. Only John reflects that the narrative is written after Peter had already become a martyr (see on 21:18–19; introduction to 1 Peter). Since there were no punctuation marks in ancient manuscripts, v. 38 could also be punctuated as a declaration, rather than a question: "You will lay down your life for me."

14:1–31
Jesus' Departure and the Arrival of the Paraclete

Although the chapter divisions were placed in the text long after it was written and are not always felicitous, here the division is appropriate, for chap. 14 does in fact comprise a distinct literary unit. The preceding section has been somewhat parallel to the Last Supper in the Synoptic Gospels, but there is nothing comparable to the material that begins at 14:1. The unit comes to a clear end at 14:31. The reader could proceed to 18:1 with no break in the thought. Thus chap. 14 may have been an original core of the Farewell Discourses, amplified in the extended editorial process that produced the Fourth Gospel (see introduction to John and 4:54 commentary).

14:1 Do not let your hearts be troubled: These words, often read at funerals and during the grief over a departed loved one, have brought comfort and courage to countless millions. This is not a misuse of this text, but it originally had nothing to do with the death of Christians. In its context, it addresses the perplexity of disciples who are troubled at the departure of Jesus. More concretely, in the situation of the Johannine church at the end of the first century, these words address the situation of those who wonder what it means to be a disciple of Jesus, who is no longer present. How can one follow an absent Lord? Where *is* Jesus now? This question of where Jesus "abides" was expressed in the first words of the disciples (1:38) and has been on the edge of the author's mind throughout. The Farewell Discourses respond to this question in a number of different, overlapping ways.

Believe in God . . . in me: Since in John's Greek the second person plural uses the same form for indicative and imperative, and since the word translated "also" can also mean "even," "that is," "namely," there are theoretically several equally legitimate translation possibilities, including "You believe in God and you believe in me," "Believe in God and believe in me," "You believe in God, believe also in me," "Believe in God, and you believe in me." On the basis of Johannine theology, it is probably best to take both verbs as imperative and understand the "also" as meaning

"that is": "Believe in God, that is, believe in me." In any case, Jesus' statement must *not* be understood as though one can first believe in God and then, as an optional extra, add on faith in Christ. In John's theology, faith in God is nothing else than faith in the one who reveals God, and vice versa.

14:2 In my Father's house: The word also means, and is here better translated, "household"—family, not building. Whether Gentile Christians can be members of the family of God had been a live issue in early Christianity (see Acts 2–15, especially the Jerusalem council in Acts 15, and Paul's heated argument in Galatians). Ephesians 2, probably written from the same area as John and a few years before, celebrates that Jews and Gentiles are now fellow members of the one household of faith. **Many dwelling places:** In 1611, when the KJV was translated, the English word "mansion" meant simply "residence," with no suggestion of palatial luxury. The point is that there is a lot of room in God's household, that God has a big family (see Rev. 21:16).

14:3 I will come again: Each of the Synoptic Gospels has a lengthy eschatological discourse near the end of the narrative in which Jesus teaches about the ultimate future (Matt. 24–25; Mark 13; Luke 21). John's Farewell Discourses fit into the outline at the same traditional point, and have some of the same language and concerns (see 16:21). By John's time it was clear that the hope of earliest Christianity for the soon return of Jesus had to be rethought (see, e.g., Mark 9:1; 13:30; 1 Thess. 4:13–17; and excursus at Rev. 1:3, "Interpreting the 'Near End'"). John shifts the emphasis from the future hope to present experience but does not abandon the future hope. This promise can be understood to refer to the resurrection, the coming of the Holy Spirit, or to the return of Christ at the end of time. **Where I am:** The assurance and joy of the believer is to be with Christ (see Phil. 1:23), not to have a luxurious "mansion."

14:4–5 You know the way . . . we do not know: In chaps. 1–12, the world that has no or inadequate faith has typically claimed to know, and Jesus reveals that it does not know (see 3:3–15). Here, among "his own," they appropriately claim not to know, and are told that they *do* know—because they know Jesus himself.

14:6 I am the way, and the truth, and the life: On Jesus' "I am" sayings in the Fourth Gospel, see on 6:35. Jesus does not claim to teach the way, or to give instruction about the truth, or to present *a* way, but to *be* the way, the truth, and the life. As a human claim, this can only be heard as exclusive, narrow-minded arrogance. It is understandable only in the perspective of Johannine Christology, in which Jesus represents God (see introduction to John: "Christology," and 1:1–2, 14 comments). **No one comes to the Father except through me:** The claim is exclusive and should not be diluted to mean that Jesus is one of a number of ways, one of a number of perspectives on truth, and such. Modern readers accustomed to relativistic pluralism may be offended by this claim, just as modern exclusivistic Christian fundamentalists may celebrate it and condemn adherents of all other religions. Neither approach grasps the Johannine point. In this text Jesus does not start with the presumption of a number of ways to God and narrow them down to one, namely himself. Neither here nor elsewhere does the Bible assume that a large number of ways to God exists, ways that people can discover for themselves. Rather, the biblical assumption is that sinful humanity has closed off its own access to God and that there is no way back to God from the human side. When *all* access is closed, to announce that there is *one* way open to God is good news. The reader is to celebrate what the text affirms—the way to God is now open through (what God has done in) Jesus Christ, not by our own achievement (see Rom. 5:1–2; Heb. 10:20). The text does not claim that adherents of all other religions are doomed if they do not make a personal confession of faith in Jesus before they die. The text affirms that all who come to God come to the God who has revealed himself in Christ. John shares the monotheism of Judaism—there is one God (Deut. 6:4; Mark 12:27–33; John 17:3; Rom. 3:30; Gal. 3:20; James 2:19). This God is the Creator, universally present and active, the light that illuminates every human being, the reason and meaning inherent in the world itself (1:1–9). For John, whoever comes to God comes to *this* God, the only God there is, whether or not this is the way they would understand it, whether or not they have conscious awareness of the God revealed in Jesus. For John, faith in God is nothing else than faith in the God revealed in Jesus, for it is *this* God who is the Creator, Sustainer, and Light-giver to all people. This is analogous to the Jewish claim that there is only one God, and that whoever worships God worships the God revealed as the Creator and Redeemer in Jew-

ish history, Scripture, and tradition. Such claims are inherent in a monotheistic faith. And John is a monotheist (17:3).

14:7 You do know him and have seen him: There is a long and varied biblical tradition that relates faith to "seeing God." The mainstream contrasted faith and sight, and asserted that no one has ever seen God, whose majesty and holiness is unendurable by human eyes (see Exod. 33:20), that not God himself but only the hem of God's heavenly robes could be seen (Isa. 6:1, 5), or that only God's backside and not God's face was seen (Exod. 33:33). The Johannine school knows and affirms this tradition that "no one has ever seen God" (1:18; 6:46; 1 John 4:12, 20). Yet Judaism and the Jewish Scriptures also speak of people "seeing God" (e.g., Gen. 32:30; Deut. 5:24; Judges 13:22) and hold out the hope of the eschatological vision, when God will be seen face to face (Job 19:26; see Matt. 5:8). The Johannine community can also use this mode of theological language, in which "believing" is not contrasted with "seeing" but is equated with it—to believe is virtually equivalent to "seeing God" (3 John 11). The Johannine Jesus here speaks of "seeing God" in this sense. The complexity of this variety of statements should not be reduced to a simplistic conceptual consistency or assigned to different sources, layers of tradition, or different writers. The dialectic of the hidden and revealed God is interwoven into this complex of statements, all of which come from the same community of faith.

14:8 Show us the Father: Even Jesus' disciples still understand his words at the "earthly" level; they will not be able to truly "see" until they receive the post-Easter illumination of the Holy Spirit.

14:9 Whoever has seen me has seen the Father: Throughout, Jesus has insisted on his functional unity with God (see 10:30 and comments on 1:1–2; 20:28).

14:10 Not . . . on my own: See 5:19, 30; 7:16–17, 28; 8:28, 42; 14:10. Jesus is the definitive revealer of God precisely because he is not selfishly egoistic but is truly obedient to God. In him alone, being truly human and truly divine are not alternatives (5:30; 19:5). **The Father . . . does his works:** The *Christ* event is the act of *God* (see 2 Cor. 5:19, and the meaning of Christ as the one whom God has anointed; Mark 8:29; Luke 9:20; Acts 2:36).

14:11 Believe me: The verb shifts to the plural. As in the Nicodemus story (3:7–15) and elsewhere, a conversation between Jesus and one other person fades into an address to all the disciples, including the readers.

14:12 Greater works: While it is true that after Easter the community of Christian faith has in Jesus' name multiplied the healing, feeding, and reconciling work of Jesus millions of times, this is not John's primary meaning. The Johannine Jesus already speaks from the eschatological perspective of the transcendent world in which God rules. The disciples still belong to this world, and cannot yet grasp the extravagance of living in the realm of eternal life. It is this unexplainable "greater" to which Jesus points, a greatness that cannot be quantified.

14:14 If in my name you ask me for anything: See 15:7, 16; Matt. 7:7; Luke 11:9–13. Here too, there is no "explaining" this profound text, but some comments may bring us closer to hearing it aright. First, praying "in Jesus' name" is not merely a particular formula, a magic word that makes the wish come true. There are numerous Christian prayers recorded in the New Testament, none of which concludes with "in Jesus' name we pray" or the like. Throughout the Bible, "name" is more than a label; it represents the self. To pray in Jesus' name means to acknowledge that our access to God is not on our own but has been opened up by God through Christ (see on 14:6). Second, all those unanswered prayers in Christian history made in Jesus' name are not to be explained as a lack of faith or not knowing the right formula. They are not to be explained at all. Petitionary prayer—asking God in Jesus' name for needed forgiveness, healing, food, world peace, reconciliation among estranged families, friends, neighbors, and nations—is a matter of confessional language, the natural, uncalculated response of faith to the loving goodness of God (on confessional language, see Matt. 2:16; Acts 1:9; excursus, "Interpreting Revelation's Violent Imagery," 3.b, at Rev. 6:15). As in the reference to "greater works" above, this mind-blowing promise is to be explained neither literally nor "spiritually," for here we are confronted by a reality beyond ourselves, beyond our capacity to explain. It is thus an encouragement to pray, to bring our petitions before a God greater than all our theology. Whoever must have an explanation before praying will either cease praying or reduce their prayers to the confines of their own explanation, unworthy of address to the transcendent God.

14:15–17 Another Advocate: This is the first of five Paraclete sayings (14:15–17; 14:25–26;

15:26–27; 16:7–11; 16:12–15) in which Jesus promises that after his death and resurrection the Holy Spirit will come to the aid of his disciples. In the New Testament the Greek noun *parakletos* is found only in the Gospel of John and 1 John 2:1, but is related to the verb *parakaleo*, often translated as "beseech," "encourage," "comfort," and to the noun *paraklesis*, "comfort," "encouragement," exhortation." *Parakletos* means literally "one called alongside" and thus was used for a helper, encourager, and, in the courtroom, "advocate," "counselor" in the legal sense. The King James translation "comforter" was appropriate in 1611 English, but today its connotation is too soft." Since John often uses the forensic language of the court and regards the ministry of Jesus as a judicial confrontation with the world, "counselor" in the legal sense is perhaps the best translation. That the Paraclete is called "another Advocate" means that Jesus himself is considered the first counselor, whose place in this world will be taken by the Holy Spirit (see 1 John 2:1). The figure of Jesus modulates into that of the Holy Spirit; the presence of the Holy Spirit in the life of the church is the continuing presence of Christ (see on Rom. 8:9–10). In this text, the Paraclete–Holy Spirit will come to believers; in 14:18, 28, Jesus himself will come to believers; in 14:23, the Father and the Son will come to believers. John does not intend distinct experiences; these all refer to the one reality of the continuing presence of God with the community of faith. **The Father . . . will give:** Here, God sends the Spirit at the Son's behest. In later Christian theology, whether the Spirit proceeded from the Father alone, or from the Father and the Son (*filioque*) became an important issue that played a role in the separation of the Eastern churches from the Western (see the phrase in the Nicene Creed representing the Western church, "We believe in the Holy Spirit, the Lord, the giver of life, who proceeds from the Father [and the Son]"). John was of course not yet thinking of these later important theological subtleties and uses a variety of expressions for the one reality. Here, the Father sends the Spirit; in 15:26, the risen Jesus sends the Spirit from the Father; in 16:7, the risen Jesus sends the Spirit.

Love me . . . keep my commandments: The Holy Spirit is the promise and gift of God. Yet from the human side, love for God expressed in keeping Jesus' commandments is the prerequisite for reception of the Spirit. The Johannine Jesus does not give a list of specific commands, but the one command of love, i.e., caring for others, which includes all that God requires. **With you . . . in you:** As in Acts 2 and 1 Cor. 12, the expression refers primarily to the presence of God's Spirit in the community; individuals participate in the life of the Spirit not on an individualistic basis, but by belonging to the community of faith animated and guided by God's Spirit. The pronouns and verb forms are in the plural throughout (see NRSV note, "among you"). **With you forever:** In contrast to the historical Jesus, who was departing, the risen Christ/Holy Spirit will remain with the church until the end of history (see Matt. 28:20).

14:18 Orphaned: The new community of faith is a family of brothers and sisters, born of water and the Spirit, with God as their Father. The departure of Jesus does not change this new reality that has come into being.

14:19 You will see me: The "world" will see the same empirical data as Jesus' followers, but only believers will see Christ in them (see 12:29). The reality of the Risen One and the Spirit he gives is not something that can be demonstrated to the uncommitted observer, however honest and impartial. This "seeing" is not contrary to reason, but is not *based* on it and is not a matter of the accumulation and presentation of "evidence" (7:12).

14:20 You in me: While the Johannine Jesus speaks with a certain "mystical" tone, it is not mystical spirituality that is offered, but concrete reality in the world of the Christian community that finds its new life "in Christ" (see commentary on 2 Cor. 5:17).

14:22–23 Judas (not Iscariot): Mentioned only here, Luke 6:16, and Acts 1:13; one of numerous points of contact between Luke and John. Until Judas Iscariot made the name unpopular in Christian Western culture, Judas was a common name. **Jesus answered him:** In typical Johannine style, the dialogue fades into a monologue (see on John 3:9). Jesus now speaks without interruption through 16:16.

14:25–26 The Advocate . . . will teach you everything: The second Paraclete saying. See on vv. 15–17 above. When the Holy Spirit comes, he will not only guide the disciples into new truth, giving new revelations in the name of the risen Lord (see on 16:13), but will remind them of the message of the pre-Easter Jesus. The Holy Spirit represents Jesus in the church after the crucifixion and resurrection, and binds together the earthly and risen Lord. The

new insights brought by the Spirit after Easter develop the meaning of the Christ event, but there is no *independent* revelation through "spiritual experiences." The continuing revelation brought by the Spirit is in continuity with the definitive life and message of the earthly Jesus. The new understanding brought by the post-Easter perspective is not merely the advantage of hindsight but the gift of the Spirit that transcends empirical, this-worldly knowledge. **Remind you:** This does not mean that the disciples will miraculously and accurately remember every word that Jesus said, as shown by the variations in Gospels, but that they are not merely left to their own resources to preserve the memory of Jesus. The Spirit of God is active in the preservation, interpretation, modification, and expansion of the Jesus tradition to adapt and adopt the message of Christ to new situations.

14:27 Peace I leave with you: Peace is not mere peace of mind, but resonates with the Hebrew greeting, "Shalom," representing wholeness and well-being, the all-inclusive gift of God (see on Luke 12:51; 19:42; 24:36; Rom. 5:1; 1 Thess. 1:1). In 20:19, it is the first word of the risen Lord to his disciples. **Not . . . as the world gives:** "Peace be with you" was already a secular, commonplace greeting, but the Christ event and Christian faith filled it with new content by Jesus who *is* "our peace" (Eph. 2:14).

14:28 Rejoice that I am going to the Father: The disciples are to rejoice not for Jesus' sake, as though they were commanded to be happy that "he is going back to heaven," but for their own sakes—it is better for *them* that the earthly Jesus be absent and that they live in the Spirit-empowered Christian community rather than in direct contact with the earthly Jesus (see 16:7). The Johannine Jesus affirms that it is not a second best to be a disciple in the church of those reading the Gospel at the end of the first century (or in the twenty-first century), a church guided and empowered by the Holy Spirit to do greater things than the earthly Jesus (14:12). It is better to be such a post-Easter Christian of later generations or centuries than to have been an eyewitness and companion of the earthly Jesus; such eyewitnesses did not and could not grasp what was happening before their eyes. In John's view, the church is not a memorial society looking back in admiration to the earthly Jesus who *once* lived, regretting that he is no longer with us. In John's view, it is better for the earthly Jesus to have departed, so that the Spirit of

Christ would be released through his church to minister to the world in his name. Thus the risen Jesus commands Mary not to hold on to him (see on 20:17).

If you loved me: The Greek grammar of this conditional sentence indicates an unreal condition: "If you loved me, but you don't." This is not a criticism or complaint against Jesus' pre-Easter disciples, but another indication that true love for Christ is not possible prior to the event of the cross-resurrection and the gift of the Spirit. After that decisive event (the time in which the readers already live), true love for God in Christ is poured into the believer's heart by the Spirit (see Rom. 5:5; 15:30), and believers are glad that Christ has ascended to the Father.

The Father is greater than I: On the Johannine christological paradox, see "Introduction to the Gospels," and 1:1–2, 14; 5:18, 26; 10:18; 12:44–45.

14:30 The ruler of this world: See on 12:31.

14:31 Rise, let us be on our way: The discourse seems to conclude here; the reader could skip directly to 18:1. Chapters 15–17 may represent a later editorial stage in the process of forming the Gospel. See introduction to John and on 4:54. While the consideration of such possibilities helps the reader to understand the nature of the Gospel composition, the reader's task today is to interpret the final canonical form of the Gospel, not to analyze possible sources and preliminary forms of the text.

15:1–8
Jesus the True Vine

While Jesus continues his speech without interruption (see on 14:23), a new topic begins.

15:1 I am the true vine: On Johannine figurative language, see on 10:1–6, and see 16:25. On the "I am" sayings, see 6:35 commentary. In this final "I am" saying, Jesus includes his disciples. "True" in such Johannine sayings (1:9; 17:3; 1 John 2:8; 5:20) means "ultimately real." Its opposite is not "false" but "unreal." As shepherd and sheep are often in the Bible metaphors for God and God's people (see on 10:1–6), so vine, vineyard, and vinedresser also are used as images for Israel and its leaders, including God their ultimate leader (see Ps. 80:8–16; Isa. 5:1–7; Jer. 2:21; Ezek. 17:6–8; 19:10–14; Hos. 10:1). The Jesus of the Synoptic Gospels also had used the vineyard metaphor (Matt. 21:23–43; Mark 12:1–12; Luke 20:9–19); John seems to have developed the Synoptic story in his own style. Like Paul's image of the

church as the body of Christ (1 Cor. 12, Rom. 12), the metaphor of vine and branches is organic. Membership in the people of God is not names on a list, but living branches of a living vine. As Christ is the whole body in Paul's image, so Christ is the whole vine in John's. Christ is not the stem or trunk, to which branches are attached, but Christ is the vine as a whole, into which believers are incorporated. Here the whole point of the Farewell Discourses comes to vivid expression: Jesus has not "established the church" and left it behind in the world to "carry on his work," but God/Christ/Holy Spirit continues in, with, and *as* the church on its missionary journey through history.

15:2 He removes every branch: God acts in and on every branch of the vine. Those that are unproductive are removed; those that are productive are not congratulated or left alone, but "pruned" or "cleansed" so that they will bear more fruit. On "bearing fruit" as metaphor for the Christian life, see Matt. 3:8–11; 7:17–19; 12:33; 13:23; 21:19, 34; Mark 4:20; 11:14; 12:2; Luke 3:9; 6:43–44; 8:14–15; 13:6–7, 9; 20:10; Gal. 5:22–25.

15:3 Already . . . cleansed by the word: The Greek verb for "prune" also means "cleanse." The cleansing of which Jesus speaks takes place in encountering the Word of God that he speaks and is (1:14).

15:4 Abide in me: See 14:20; 2 Cor. 5:17 commentary. This statement is the death of all purely individualistic Christianity. The Johannine Jesus understands discipleship to him as necessarily incorporating the believer into the Christian community. The individual branch has its life-giving connection, not only in the personal relation with God through Christ, but in relation to all the other branches that comprise the vine with which Christ identifies himself. To be connected with Christ is to be organically related to his church (see 1 Cor. 12:12–31).

15:7 Ask for whatever you wish: See on 14:14.

15:9–17
Abide in My Love

15:11 So that my joy may be in you: The preceding may sound stern and demanding, but the life of discipleship is not merely solemn obligation and obedience—though it is no less than that—but "rejoicing in God" (see 17:13; 1 John 1:4; Luke 1:47; Rom. 5:11; 1 Pet. 1:8; James 1:2).

15:12–14 This is my commandment . . . love one another: These verses are a summary of

Johannine ethics. The Jesus of the Fourth Gospel does not give a list of commands but summarizes all in the one command of love (see on 14:31–35).

15:15 I do not call you servants: The Greek word is better translated "slave," as often in the New Testament (e.g., Matt. 8:9; 10:24; John 4:51; 8:33–35; 18:10, 18, 26; and often in Paul as an image of Christians' relation to their Lord). Jesus has also just used this common New Testament image for his disciples (13:16), but now qualifies it. His disciples are not those who offer him a blind, mechanical obedience, but are friends (not a casual word in the Hellenistic world) of Jesus and of one another, those who are in the know and obey with informed commitment.

I have made known to you everything: The Johannine Jesus never spells out the content of this knowledge he has received from God and shares with his disciples. Here and elsewhere, the point is not a body of information that Jesus reveals, but that he is the revealer. He does not bring the revelation but is himself the revelation. John emphasizes that there is no secret, mysterious body of knowledge known only to elite super-Christians (the gnostics of his day), but that the Christ event itself is the full revelation of God. (See on John 1:1, 14; 18:20; 19:34; 1 Cor. 12:3; 1 Tim. 4:1–5; 6:20–21; 1 John 2:20, 27; Rev. 1:3.)

15:16 You did not choose . . . I chose: This is news to the disciples, as it is news to most Christians and to the reader. In the stories of their becoming disciples in 1:35–51, it seemed to them and to the reader that they were making their own decisions to follow Jesus. Now they learn, in a way that does not eliminate or minimize their own responsibility, that the initiative has been with Christ. On the paradox of divine sovereignty and human responsibility, see 3:16; 5:42; 6:27, 44; 10:26; and especially excursus at Rom. 8:28, "Predestination."

15:18–25
The World's Hatred

15:18 The world hates you . . . hated me: The discourse shifts from love (13:1, 23, 34–35; 14:15, 21, 23–24, 28, 31; 15:9–10, 12–13) to hate (15:18, 19, 23, 24, 25; 17:14). There is no middle ground in Johannine dualism (see on 8:23). "The world" hates Jesus' disciples, but they do not reciprocate. Though in the Fourth Gospel there is no explicit command to love one's enemies, the followers of Jesus are to reflect God's own love for the world (3:16). The role previously

occupied by "the Jews" as the opponents of Jesus and his disciples is now filled by "the world." Each term is complex and ambivalent. As there are Jews who become Christian believers (see on 2:11; 7:11; 8:31; 9:18–23; 11:19, 45–47; 12:10–11, 20, 42), so God loves the world (3:16), and some in "the world" will hear, believe, and become disciples (17:20–23). The dualistic boundaries between light and darkness, love and hate, the "world" and Jesus "own" are there, but they are not absolute, and they can be crossed in both directions. Unfruitful branches that belong to the vine that Christ is can be removed (15:1–2), and unbelievers that belong to the "world" can become believers.

Jesus is not only the model for the believers' life; they are incorporated into him and share his fate. As he loves God and knows he is loved by the Father, so do they; as he is hated by the world, so those who belong to him receive the world's hatred. **The world would love you as its own:** The followers of Jesus are not the only people in the world who love; the world too knows love, but on its own terms, and hates the followers of Jesus because they do not fit into its this-worldly categories.

15:19 I have chosen you out of the world: See v. 16. Christians still live in the world; they do not disengage from the life of this world and withdraw into their own "spiritual" domain. But they are no longer *determined* by the world. The world cannot understand the different criteria by which Jesus' followers live, are scandalized by them, and hate them as "not belonging, not our kind" (see 3:6).

15:20 Servants . . . master: See 15:12–14.

15:22 If I had not come: See 3:17–21; 9:41. The meaning is not that by coming into the world Jesus introduced into their lives the sin of rejecting God, as though they would have remained sinless if he had not come. As the light of the world, Jesus does not introduce sin but forces the decision that reveals what people already are.

15:24 Seen and hated both me and my Father: To reject Jesus' followers is to reject Jesus, which is to reject God (see 12:44; 13:20). On "seeing God," see 14:7–9. Here even unbelievers "see God," without realizing it.

15:25 In their law: The inexact quotation is from Ps. 35:19 or 69:4. The whole Scripture, to which the Psalms belong, is called "law" as the revelation of God's will. See 10:34 (Ps. 81:6); 12:34 (Ps. 109:4; Isa. 9:6; Dan. 7:14). This usage is also found in Paul, e.g., 1 Cor. 14:21 (Isa. 28:11f), and in first-century Jewish authors. "Their" does not mean that Jesus or the Johannine Christians did not acknowledge the Jewish Scripture (the Old Testament) as their own (see 5:39, 46), but that *even* the Scripture acknowledged by Jews points to Christ (as read from the Christian perspective, of course—see excursus, "New Testament Interpretation of the Old Testament," at 1 Cor. 15:3).

15:26–27
The Witness of the Paraclete

15:26 When the Advocate comes: The third Paraclete saying (see on 14:15–17). Here the risen Jesus sends the Spirit, who "proceeds" from the Father (see on 14:26). **He will testify:** In this text, the Greek masculine pronoun "he" could refer either to "the Spirit of truth" or to "the Father." In 16:13–14, however, it clearly refers to the Spirit. Since the word for "Spirit" is neuter in Greek, this means that the author here thinks of the Holy Spirit in personal terms, "he" rather than "it." (Of course, the issue is not male-or-female, but personal-or-impersonal.) The Paraclete-Spirit, the believer's Counselor in the legal setting, will also be a witness and will testify on Jesus' behalf (see the series of witnesses in 5:31–47).

15:27 From the beginning: Unlike 1:1, but like 1 John 1:1, "beginning" here refers not to the creation but to the beginning of Jesus' ministry. In the latter part of the first century when the Fourth Gospel was written, a variety of Christian groups were competing (sometimes cooperating) with each other, each claiming to be a or the legitimate representative of the faith. In this situation it was important for each group to be able to claim that its version of the faith was in continuity with the original life and teaching of Jesus (see 19:35; 21:24; Luke 1:2, 22; 1 John 1:1–4; 2:7, 13).

16:1–6
On Persecutions

16:1 To keep you from stumbling: The verb is the same as in 6:61, where it is translated "offend." Here it can better be translated as in the REB, "to guard you against the breakdown of your faith," or the NJB, "that you may not fall away." The Farewell Discourses are not general meditations on the religious life but are intended to strengthen a persecuted Christian community (see introduction to John: "Conflict with 'the Jews'").

16:2 Put you out of the synagogues: Here the situation represented in 9:22 as already present during Jesus' ministry (see 12:42) is only pre-

dicted for the later time of the church. See "Introduction to the Gospels." **Kill you . . . think . . . they are offering worship to God:** Unlike the Synoptic Gospels, where Jesus' adversaries are often charged with hypocrisy (see, e.g., Matt. 23), John always regards the hostility of those who persecute Jesus and his disciples as sincere. They are like modern people who believe capital punishment is the just punishment for treason, and that it must be implemented for the good of the nation, though they have no personal hostility against traitors and insist on the death penalty "for the good of the country." Paul was such a persecutor of Jewish Christians before his conversion (see Acts 9:1–9; 22:4–11; 26:10–18; 1 Cor. 15:9; Gal. 1:13). After his conversion he was probably the victim of such an attempt on his life (see 2 Cor. 11:25).

16:4 I told you about them: Here and elsewhere the Fourth Gospel represents Jesus as having divine omniscience (see on 2:23).

16:5 None of you asks me: But see 13:36, where in the present arrangement Peter had asked precisely this question only a few minutes before. Since much of chaps. 15–16 seems to be a variant parallel version to chaps. 13–14, this may be another indication of the editorial stages in the development of the present form of the Gospel (see on 4:54; 14:31).

16:7–15
The Work of the Paraclete

These verses all deal with the coming of the Holy Spirit. They are usually divided into two different "sayings," the fourth and fifth Paraclete sayings (see on 14:15–17), with vv. 8–11 portraying the relation of the Holy Spirit to the world and vv. 12–15 his relation to the church.

16:7 It is to your advantage that I go away: The presence of the Holy Spirit who "replaces" the "absent" Jesus is not a second best; the Counselor is no consolation prize for those who could not live in first-century Palestine and experience the presence of the "real" Jesus (see on 14:28). **I will send him:** See on 14:15–17.

16:8–10 When he comes: In the Fourth Gospel's understanding of the Holy Spirit, the world as such does not receive the Spirit, but is affected by the Spirit's work in the life of the Christian community, particularly as it inspires Christian preaching that allows the prophetic preachers of the Johannine community to speak in Jesus' name and by his authority and power. The work of the Holy Spirit in relation to the world is described as a threefold forensic function as God's advocate/prosecuting attorney in the cosmic courtroom drama played out in the Johannine narrative (see 5:20–30; 12:31, 47–48). The earliest Christians supposed that they needed a defense attorney to stand by them and speak for them against the accusations and threats of Jewish and Roman courts (see Mark 13:9–11). The Johannine church found its whole existence to be a trial, had learned in its own experience that the Spirit of God not only was with them in the courtroom but was a constant guide and help, and that the Holy Spirit was God's prosecuting attorney, pressing God's case against the unbelieving world. The church discovered its mission was not merely to defend itself, but in its life and message to press God's case against the world. As in the great trial scene of 18:28–19:16, where a scene in which Jesus is tried and condemned is actually the portrayal of Jesus as the ultimate judge (see esp. 19:13 NJB), so also in the work of the Holy Spirit in the world: when Christians are charged before the courts, it is the world that is on trial, with the Holy Spirit as prosecutor.

He will prove the world wrong about: Or "convict" (so NIV), in the legal sense. The forensic setting is the framework for the whole context. "Convince," found in some translations, is misleading. A guilty felon in court may or may not be convinced of his guilt, but is convicted nevertheless. So also with the world—whether or not the Holy Spirit convinces it of the truth of God's claim in Jesus, it is convicted of its sin of rejecting God's offer. "Convict" is not a subjective feeling of guilt, but an objective reality, whether or not the person feels guilty.

About sin: The primal sin is not breaking a commandment, but failure to trust in God. Faith is the authentic response of human beings to their Creator; lack of faith is the underlying sin from which all individual sins originate. On faith as obedience in personal trust see on 3:31–36; 6:28–29. On sin as rebellion against God, see summary comments at Rom. 3:19 and Rom. 5:12 (John shares the Pauline understanding of sin, which is the general biblical perspective).

About righteousness: Also translated "justice" (REB) or "what is right" (NJB). The point is God's vindication of Jesus, God's assertion of divine justice in raising Jesus from the dead, overruling the injustice of Jesus' condemnation and death sentence by a human court. For the persecuted Johannine community, this

meant that just as God had vindicated Jesus, so God would vindicate his oppressed disciples. This realization and reality is not obvious on the surface of things but is the work of the Holy Spirit.

16:11 About judgment . . . the ruler of this world has been condemned: It appeared that accused Christians were being condemned in this-worldly courts. As the divine prosecutor, the Holy Spirit will prove that it is not the Christians who are condemned, but their accuser. This accuser is not merely the Jews in the earthly courts, but Satan, the Grand Accuser, who stands behind them (see Job 1–2; John 8:44; 13:2; Rev. 12:7). It is important to note that the world itself is not judged-condemned; Jesus came to save it, not to condemn it (3:17–18). But the world's (mis)judgment of Jesus is itself judged and condemned, shown to be wrong, and Satan, who stands behind the world's rejection of God, is condemned.

16:13 He will guide you into all the truth: The fifth and final Paraclete saying (see on 14:15–17). During Jesus' earthly life, what was really happening—the definitive revelatory act of God for human salvation—was not adequately perceived and understood, even by his disciples. The truth of who Jesus was and the meaning of his life and teaching were understood only after his death and resurrection, by his disciples who grasped this only as they were empowered by God's gift of the Spirit (see on 10:6; 14:25–26). On the necessity of the Spirit to understand God's gifts, see on 1 Cor. 2:6–16.

After Easter, the Holy Spirit led the church into new truth not perceived during Jesus' lifetime. One clear example of this is the reception of Gentiles into the people of God (see on Matt. 10:5 vs. 28:15–18; Luke 24:47; Acts 10:14–15).

He will not speak on his own: See 14:10 note. As Jesus does nothing "on his own" but only as he represents God, so the Holy Spirit is not an independent generic spirituality, but represents Jesus and speaks for him in the post-Easter situation. Here John reflects the presence of Christian prophets in his community (see on Acts 21:4; 1 Thess. 4:2, 15–17; introduction to Revelation). Christian prophecy represented the continuing voice of Jesus in the post-Easter Christian community. As in Rev. 1:1–3, John here conceives of this continuing revelation as a prophetic chain of command from God through Christ, the Spirit, and Christian prophets to the church and the world.

16:16–28
Sorrow Turned to Joy

16:16 A little while: The importance is emphasized by the threefold repetition (16, 17, 19). In earlier Christian tradition, the focus had been on the "little while" before the return of Christ. John's reinterpretation shifts the emphasis to Christ's return at the resurrection and the coming of the Holy Spirit that represents him.

16:17 Some of the disciples said: This is the first response from the disciples since 14:22, and signals that Jesus' long monologue is at an end. The remaining vv. 17–33 basically summarize themes already treated and may represent alternate forms of the tradition (on the multistage editorial process behind the present form of the Fourth Gospel, see on 4:54; 14:31).

16:18 We do not know: See on 10:6; 14:4.

16:21 A woman is in labor . . . anguish: This imagery and vocabulary reflects the original apocalyptic discourse that is here extensively reinterpreted (see on 14:3). The earlier connotation of such imagery pointed to the return of Christ at the end of history, expected by many early Christians to occur in their lifetime (see, e.g., Mark 9:1; 13:8; 30; Rev. 12:1–17). John here characteristically reinterprets it to apply to the present, ongoing faith of the church in Christ's resurrection.

16:23–24 If you ask anything: See on 14:14.

16:25 Figures of speech: See on 10:1–6.

16:28 I . . . have come into the world: Here is a clear summary of the Johannine Christology. God's salvation is not represented by the particular things Jesus says or does in the narrative, but by the Christ event as a whole.

16:29–33
Prediction of the Disciples' Flight

16:30 We believe that you came from God: Though the disciples will not grasp its significance until after the resurrection, they are presented as already understanding the basics of the saving message of Jesus' advent (see "Introduction to the Gospels: Genre" and comments at 10:6). Even so, the disciples make no reference to Jesus *going* to God, i.e., the crucifixion-exaltation, and so are still to some extent in the dark.

16:31–32 Do you now believe? Jesus' response indicates that, though they claim to already understand, authentic faith must await his resurrection. The immediate future will show their lack of faith as they abandon him and are scattered. But this is not the final word. Jesus looks beyond their present lack of faith and understanding, will pray for them (see Luke 22:32), and knows they will finally be his faithful witnesses to the world. His magnificent prayer for them then follows.

16:33 I have conquered the world: Like 16:11, which declares Satan has already been judged, and much of the prayer to follow, this statement looks back at the life of Jesus from the post-Easter reader's perspective. In the eyes of the world, Jesus was a loser who was conquered by the world. But Jesus' death was also his victory; giving one's life in the service of God is not defeat but victory. "Conquering" in this paradoxical sense also plays a key role in the thought of 1 John (2:13, 14; 4:4; 5:4, 5) and Revelation, where forms of "conquer" occur seventeen times (2:7, 11; 5:5; 12:11, etc.), always referring to the victory won by Jesus or Christian martyrs whose death seemed to mean they were defeated.

17:1–26
The Intercessory Prayer

In the Synoptic Gospels, on the night before his crucifixion Jesus struggles with his impending death, wavers, and finally resolves to go through with it (Matt. 26:30–46; Mark 14:26–42; Luke 22:39–46). His prayer is a prayer of distress and anguish. The Jesus of the Fourth Gospel has already considered and rejected this posture before God (see 12:27; but also on 11:33–35); he has already overcome the world (16:33). This is John's "replacement" for Jesus' prayer in Gethsemane. He will have Jesus go to the garden, but there will be no further prayer. It will be a serene, already victorious Jesus who goes to meet his captors (18:1–11).

Thus these final words that the disciples will hear from Jesus represent the double perspective apparent throughout the Gospel. In the narrative story line, Jesus and his disciples are still gathered at the Last Supper. But the Jesus who speaks already looks back on his mission as a whole, and already presupposes that his disciples too are in the postresurrection time when they are no longer the misunderstanding, confused group they have been during his ministry. Jesus prays for and about the disciples; they hear his prayer for them. He does not pray for their courage and understanding, which they are now presumed to have, but for their unity. The readers of the Gospel recognize their own situation, in which the exalted Christ in heaven intercedes for his church on earth, as in Rom. 8:9–27 and Heb. 4:14–5:10. John does not use the term "high priest" of Jesus, but this prayer has rightly been known as Jesus' great high-priestly prayer, because it portrays him as the intermediary between the heavenly world and the church (see on 19:24).

No new theological insights emerge. In these last words his disciples will hear from him, Jesus summarizes his mission and message he has been reiterating throughout the Gospel.

17:1 Looked up to heaven: The characteristic biblical posture in prayer (see Pss. 121:1; 123:1). **Father:** As in 11:41; 12:28; 17:11, 21, 24, 25, the typical address of Jesus in prayer. It probably represents the striking, original address to God as *abba*, which Jesus taught his disciples to use (see on Matt. 6:9; 11:25; Luke 10:2; 11:2; Mark 14:36; Rom. 8:15; Gal. 4:6). **The hour has come:** See 12:23; 13:1, 31; 16:32 (vs. 2:4; see 5:25). Jesus' "hour" is not a matter of sixty minutes, but the decisive time of his death-resurrection as the saving event. Since 12:23 time has been "frozen" as this hour is accomplished.

17:2 You have given him authority over all people: Here, as elsewhere in the Gospel but particularly in this prayer, the pre-Easter and post-Easter perspectives coalesce. As in 3:31–36 and elsewhere, Christ speaks as the risen Lord to whom all authority has been given (Matt. 28:15–20). As the representative of the one God, the Creator, his lordship extends not only to his own followers in the church, but over all people and the whole creation—whether known and acknowledged by them or not.

17:3 This is eternal life: In the Johannine perspective of realized eschatology, eternal life is the believer's present experience, not only the future glorious existence in heaven (see 3:3, 13–15; 4:10–15; 11:25–27; 1 John 5:12). **The only true God:** Alongside his use of God language for Jesus, John has throughout insisted on monotheism (see 5:18; 10:30; 14:6, 1 John 5:20–21). **And Jesus Christ:** This "and" could be translated "that is," or "namely" (see on 14:6). Christ is not a second deity alongside the one God. For Johannine theology, the one true God has definitively revealed himself in the Christ event.

17:5 Before the world existed: See 1:1–2. The Johannine Jesus is aware of his own preexistence. While 1:1 affirms the Logos was (already) there when the world was created, here (and in 17:24) the preexistent Christ was present *before* the creation. Yet there is no

mythological content given, here or elsewhere in the Bible, elaborating on what happened before the creation. The biblical narrative begins at creation and ends at the eschaton, and does not attempt to speculate on before or after the history of the world. Though understanding the life of this world in a transcendent context, the Bible is a very this-worldly book.

17:6–7 I have made your name known: In biblical theology, the name is more than a label; it represents the person, the self. Jesus reveals who God is, the being and person of God, not a particular designation by which God is called. Yet the story of Exod. 3:13–15 also shimmers in the background. Though the Johannine church affirms Moses (see on 5:39, 45–47), it is Jesus, not Moses, who has brought the definitive revelation of God (see 1:17). In first-century Judaism, the name of God ("Yahweh") was considered ineffable, too holy to pronounce. Jesus does not pronounce God's traditional sacred name or reveal a new divine designation. It is the person of Christ himself, the Christ event as a whole, not what Jesus teaches, that represents the person and being of God, God's "name." **Those whom you gave me:** See on 6:36–37. **Have kept your word:** In 14:23 the perspective is still future; here, the disciples are regarded as already faithful in the post-Easter time of the church. So also in v. 7, **now they know** is in contrast to 14:4, which represents the pre-Easter narrative time.

17:9 I am asking on their behalf: This is not at all, or not only, a once-upon-a-time prayer for particular disciples, those gathered about the table at the Last Supper in the narrative context of the Fourth Gospel. The Johannine merging of temporal perspectives means that this prayer also represents the intercession of the exalted Christ for his church on earth. On the content of his petition for them, see below.

17:11 I am no longer in the world: Another indication that the prayer already looks back at the time of the historical Jesus from the later time of the church. **They are in the world:** Though Jesus has "gone on ahead" (see 14:1–2), his disciples of the readers' time have been "left behind" to carry out Christ's mission in and for the world. **So that they may be one:** See vv. 21–23 below; 10:30.

17:12 The one destined to be lost: Literally "the son of destruction," the one who belongs to the realm of lostness. The same expression in 2 Thess. 2:3 is used of the eschatological agent of Satan, the anti-Christ. Judas is here described as agent of Satan (see 13:27). The

Johannine community interpreted the eschatological expectations as already present. See on 1 John 2:18. **So that the scripture might be fulfilled:** Judas's defection is explained, not as Jesus' inability to choose trustworthy disciples, but as foreseen in Scripture (see on 19:28).

17:14 They do not belong to the world: But they remain in the world. Jesus' prayer for them is not for them to be withdrawn from the world, but that they not be overwhelmed by its evil power (see Matt. 6:13; Luke 11:4). Jesus' final prayer in John has several points of contact with the Lord's Prayer of Matthew and Luke.

17:17 Sanctify: The word is related to "saint" and "holy." Jesus' disciples are never called saints in John, though this is a common word for the church elsewhere in the New Testament (see on Acts 9:13). The same idea is present here: Jesus' disciples are to be a holy community, not physically withdrawing from the world, but separate from it and not sharing its values. **Your word is truth:** The word of God is the means of the disciples' sanctification. Christ himself is the incarnate Word (1:1, 14). The Bible is the witness to this word but is not identical with it (5:39).

17:20 Those who will believe in me through their word: The apostolic testimony is the basis of all later faith in Christ.

17:21 That they may all be one: In John's setting at the end of the first century, the unity of Jesus' followers was threatened by competing streams of Christianity, especially rivalry between "apostolic" Christians who honored Peter, and John's own group that who saw the Beloved Disciple as the guarantor of the church's message and tradition (see on chap. 21). John's church was also threatened by internal dissension caused by false teaching (see on 1–3 John). Like Paul, the Fourth Gospel has an ecumenical perspective that affirms unity without rigid uniformity (see on 1 Cor. 1:10–17; 3:21–22; 2 Cor. 10–13). **So that the world may believe:** For both Paul and John the unity of the church was not an end in itself but a means to the evangelistic mission of the church in the world. Each segment of a divided church is oriented to enhancing its own fragment of the Christian community; a united church is oriented to its mission in the world.

18:1–19:42
THE PASSION NARRATIVE

The account of Jesus' suffering and death is traditionally called the passion story because Jesus is passive, i.e., he is acted upon; he does not just die, but is killed (see on Luke 22:1). The term is more appropriate to the Synoptic Gospels, in which the human victimization of Jesus is portrayed, than to the Fourth Gospel, which represents Jesus as in control throughout, exercising his sovereign will that corresponds to the will of God. In John, though Jesus dies a truly human death, he is presented as victor rather than victim (see 7:30; 8:20; 10:18).

Here John begins to agree more closely with the Synoptic accounts, but nevertheless there are many differences of detail and theological perspective. The author has omitted or modified most of the elements that could be interpreted as portraying the human weakness of Jesus, and added comments that illustrate his sovereign divine power. There can be no doubt that Jesus was actually arrested, tried, convicted, and died on the cross. But here as elsewhere, the Gospel writers are theological interpreters of the meaning of the event, not mere reporters of historical data. It is certainly historically true that the Romans were responsible for Jesus' arrest and execution, with some collaboration with the Jewish leadership in Jerusalem and one of his own disciples, while his other disciples denied and abandoned him. John schematizes this drama by presenting it in four distinct scenes: (a) 18:1–12, Jesus is arrested under the leadership of Judas; (b) 18:13–28, Jesus is brought before the high priests Annas and Caiaphas, while Peter denies him; (c) 18:29–19:16, Jesus is tried and condemned by Pilate, the Roman governor; (d) 19:17–42, Jesus is crucified and buried.

18:1–12
Jesus Arrested
(See also at Matt. 26:47–56; Mark 14:43–52; Luke 22:47–53)

18:1 A garden: The Synoptics refer to the place of Jesus' arrest as Gethsemane, but do not call it a garden; John has garden but no Gethsemane. Traditional harmonizing has combined the two accounts into the Garden of Gethsemane, which is not in the Bible. All accounts agree that the location of Jesus' arrest was somewhere on the eastern outskirts of the city, but the precise location is unknown. The traditional site shown to tourists must be near the actual location.

John omits the vivid account of Jesus' intense suffering and wavering before the prospect of death, which does not fit his theological perspective on Jesus' sovereign self-control (see on 12:27 and 18:11). Jesus does not go to the garden to pray. He has just prayed the long, serene high-priestly prayer of 17:1–26, which is John's replacement of the agony of Gethsemane narrated in the Synoptics. In John, Jesus' only motive for going to the garden is to "be in the right place" for Judas to find him (v. 2; see 13:1–2, 27).

18:2 Jesus often met there: The reader should not think of Mark's and Matthew's chronology, in which Jesus is in Jerusalem for the first time during his ministry and has only been there for three (Mark) or four (Matthew) days. In the Fourth Gospel, Jesus has often been in Jerusalem, and this garden had become his customary meeting place with his disciples. In the Fourth Gospel there is no Holy Week chronology (see on 12:1, 12).

18:3 Soldiers . . . police: In the Synoptics, it is an armed "crowd" that arrests Jesus. John depicts the arrest as carried out by Roman soldiers and the Jewish temple police. A **detachment** (sometimes translated "battalion" or "cohort") of soldiers normally represented six hundred men. In v. 12 the word translated "officer" is *chiliarch,* literally "commander of a thousand." **Lanterns and torches:** Mentioned only in John, an illustration of Johannine symbolism and irony—they represent the powers of darkness and need artificial light in the presence of the light of the world (see 1:4–5; 3:19–20; 8:12; 12:35–36).

18:4 Knowing all that was to happen: John emphasizes Jesus' divine foreknowledge throughout (see 1:48–49; 2:24–25; 4:17–18, 29; 6:6, 64, 70–71). Jesus is not arrested as a victim of surprise, but knowingly and willingly goes to meet his death (see 10:18). **Came forward and asked:** Jesus takes the initiative and is in control throughout the scene.

18:5 I am he: Judas does not kiss Jesus to identify him; Jesus identifies himself. On the "I am" formula, see 6:35 commentary; it is found three times in this brief scene. Here it is the simple recognition formula, as in 9:9. At the narrative level, "I am" is not here a claim to be God or a use of the divine name (see Exod. 3:13–15), but the knowledgeable reader recognizes it as resonant with divine authority (see on 8:58–59). **With them:** Judas does not approach Jesus but has taken his stand with the powers of darkness (see 13:30).

18:6 Fell to the ground: This is not because they were stunned that Jesus had spoken the sacred name of God (which he had not done, see above). Roman soldiers would not have understood or been scandalized by Jesus' use of the Hebrew name for God. The point is rather that Jesus' powerful word overcomes them, so that when Jesus is arrested, bound, and taken away, it is a voluntary act of his own.

18:8 Let these men go: Jesus commands the troops that arrest him, and they obey. It is a historical fact that only Jesus was arrested. John apparently knows the story of the disciples' flight found in the Synoptic Gospels (Matt. 26:56; Mark 14:50), but reinterprets it as Jesus' sovereign will rather than their cowardice.

18:9 The word that he had spoken: See 6:39; 17:12. Here Jesus' word is on a par with Scripture, which is fulfilled in his suffering and death (see 18:32; 19:24, 28, 36).

18:10 Malchus: Though this incident is found in the Synoptics, the slave's name is not mentioned. The story here prepares for 18:15b, 26, also found only in John.

18:11 Am I not to drink the cup?: This is an echo of the language of the Gethsemane scene in Matt. 26:39, 42/Mark 14:36/Luke 22:42 but is given a different twist. John here omits the scene in which Jesus has doubts, trembling before the prospect of death. In John's story, it is only the disciples, not the sovereign Son of God, who wavers. The reader should resist harmonizing the Synoptic portrayal of Jesus' agony in Gethsemane with the cool sovereignty of the Johannine Jesus, for these cannot be biographically combined without blurring the sharpness of each account. Neither should the reader ask how it "really was," as though one must choose between the two accounts. Each has its own essential theological point to make. The Synoptics portray the truly human Jesus who shuddered before death and asked to be delivered from it; the Fourth Gospel presents Jesus as the representative of God, who is sovereign over all, in control even of his own death. See "What Is a Gospel? in "Introduction to the Gospels." John too affirms the true humanity of Jesus, but in this story it is the divine self-giving of Jesus, not his human weakness, that is emphasized.

18:13–28
The Interrogation before the High Priests; Peter's Denial
(See also at Matt. 26:57–27:2a;
Mark 14:53–15:1a; Luke 22:54–23:1)

See excursus, "Why Was Jesus Killed?" at Mark 14:53.

The large contingent of Roman soldiers and temple police—an unlikely combination historically—takes Jesus not to the Roman governor but to Annas, who had previously been high priest and was father-in-law of the current high priest. The section has several such historical improbabilities, but John is primarily concerned with theology, not precise history. This section has been called the Jewish trial (in contrast to the Roman trial of 18:29–19:16), but the distinction is not neat: Romans are present in Jesus' arrest and first hearing, and Jews continue to be present and active in the trial before Pilate. Nor is trial an accurate description. In the Synoptics, there is a formal trial before the official Jewish council, the Sanhedrin, composed of the high priest, the other chief priests, the scribes, and the elders. Charges are brought, witnesses are heard, Jesus is cross-examined, a verdict is pronounced. None of this is in John, which only has a preliminary hearing carried out in two phases. Perhaps there is no Jewish trial in the Fourth Gospel because the whole first part of the Gospel, chaps. 2–12, is a "trial" in which charges are made, witnesses are brought, and a verdict is rendered. John has dramatically reversed the characters in the drama, so that it is the Jews who are on trial, with Jesus himself the eschatological judge.

As in the Synoptics, the story of Peter's denial is interwoven with the account of Jesus' appearance before the high priest(s). The narrative camera shifts back and forth from Jesus to Peter.

18:13 First . . . to Annas: In the Bible and Jewish tradition, the high priest was to serve until his death. But the Roman occupying power had assumed the right to install and remove high priests at their pleasure. Annas had held the office 6–15 CE and had been succeeded by five of his sons for brief periods. Caiaphas, who was in office ca. 18–36 CE, was his son-in-law (according to John; the relationship is not otherwise documented). Thus at the time of Jesus' arrest Caiaphas was the actual high priest, though several previous holders of the office were still alive. By the time the Gospels were written, there was some confusion as to the high priests contemporary with Jesus (see, e.g., Luke 3:2; Acts 4:6). In v. 19 Annas is called high priest, though Caiaphas was actually in office. **That year:** An unusual way to designate the term of the high priest, which was not annual. While technically not incorrect, this is not the way an insider to the Jewish tradition would state the matter (somewhat like referring to Pope John Paul II as "pope that year"— an expression no informed Roman Catholic would use in a circumstance analogous to the present one). There may also be a touch of irony or sarcasm in John's comment: the high priest was supposed to be in office for life

according to the law, but John and the readers knew that the Romans replaced them from time to time according to their own needs, and the high priest actually continued in office only at the pleasure of the Romans.

18:14 One person die for the people: See 11:49–50.

18:15 Another disciple: Presumably the Beloved Disciple, as in 20:2–4 (see on 13:23). As Peter had had to rely on him at the Last Supper (13:21–30), so here too the other disciple must come to Peter's aid (see on chap. 21).

18:17 I am not: Jesus had identified himself with a threefold "I am" in the immediately preceding scene (18:5–7). Now Peter will make a threefold denial using the same "I am" language, but negating it.

18:18 Charcoal fire: Only in the Fourth Gospel. This literary motif will recur powerfully in 21:9.

18:19 Disciples . . . teaching: Surprisingly, the focus of the interrogation is not Jesus' claims to messiahship, which had been the bone of contention throughout the Gospel (e.g., 5:18; 7:19; 8:40; 10:31–39). This is in contrast to Mark, where Jesus is asked point-blank if he is the Messiah, and for the first time in that Gospel replies with a clear yes (Mark 14:55–65). The reader will remember that, in contrast to the Synoptics, the Jesus of the Fourth Gospel has openly proclaimed his messiahship throughout.

18:20 I have said nothing in secret: Again in contrast to the Synoptics, where, following Mark, Jesus does not speak openly of his messiahship to the world but instructs his disciples privately. This motif of the messianic secret plays a different role in John (see on 10:6). John is not merely "correcting" Mark on this point—though his narrative is very different from Mark's—but may be addressing a different issue from Mark. In John's time and place, a gnostic version of the Christian faith was becoming very attractive. One aspect of such Gnosticism was the view that the earthly Jesus had communicated secret teaching to his disciples, which had been handed on in esoteric circles and was not known to ordinary Christians, but only the gnostic elite. John seems concerned to oppose this view: Jesus is a public figure, and discipleship to him is not a matter of being initiated into a secret order. (See on John 1:1, 14; 19:34; 1 Cor. 12:3; 1 Tim. 4:1–5; 6:20–21; 1 John 2:20, 27; Rev. 1:3.)

18:23 Testify to the wrong: Though bound and beaten, Jesus maintains his sovereign authority. His reasonable challenge is unanswered, and he is sent to Pilate without any charges having been made or proved.

18:25–27 You are not, . . . are you? On Peter's denial, see on the parallel texts in the other Gospels. As in v. 17, the Greek grammar expects a negative answer, properly represented in the NRSV translation. **The cock crowed:** Just as Jesus had predicted, 13:38; see 16:32. This is the distinctive Johannine emphasis in this traditional passage: the events that befall him in the arrest, trial, and crucifixion are the fulfillment of his own prediction, just as they fulfill the Scripture (see 18:9).

18:28 The praetorium (NRSV **Pilate's headquarters**/NIV **palace of the Roman governor**): The Roman "courthouse" in Jerusalem. Its location is disputed, but near the temple area. **Did not enter . . . so as to avoid ritual defilement:** On Jewish understanding of purity laws, see on Luke 2:22–24; 4:33; Acts 10:28. In John's chronology it is the morning of the day on which the Passover lambs will be killed; the Passover meal has not yet occurred (see on 13:1). To enter a Gentile residence would render Jews ritually unclean and disqualify them from participation in the Passover meal. Here is another example of Johannine irony—the religious leaders are scrupulous in their preparations for the Passover, while oblivious to the Lamb of God who stands before them (see on 1:29).

18:29–19:16
The Trial before Pilate
(See also at Matt. 27:2b–26; Mark 15:1b–20a; Luke 23:2–25)

Here begins the Johannine version of the Roman trial (see on 18:13–28). It is much more extensive than the Synoptic parallels, representing the climax of John's narrative of Jesus' confrontation with "the world" (represented by Pilate and the Jews). Throughout the narrative, the world supposes it has placed Jesus on trial and condemned him by its own criteria (see on 7:12). In this ironic scene, John reveals to the reader that it is "the world" that is on trial, and that in condemning Jesus, it condemns itself.

18:29 What accusation do you bring?: Pilate responds as though this is the Romans' first involvement with Jesus, though in the Fourth Gospel Jesus has been arrested by Roman soldiers under Pilate's command (18:3) and has been interrogated by the Jewish high priests, but without charges being brought. These are among the points that illustrate John is more

focused on theology than on accurate history. The author is interested in showing the guilt of the Jews and the relative innocence of the Romans in relation to Jesus' death (see introduction to John "Conflict with 'the Jews,'" and comments on Luke 23:13–16).

18:31 Judge him according to your law: Pilate assumes the dispute is only an internal debate among Jews, not a matter of Roman law for which he is responsible (see Acts 18:12–17). **We are not permitted to put anyone to death:** Judicial murder, not a fair trial, is their intent; they have long since decided that he must die as a threat to true religion and social order (5:18; 7:1, 19, 25; 8:37, 40; 11:53). In their sincere religious understanding, Jesus was a dangerous threat to religion and society, who by biblical and Jewish law merited the death penalty. They are no more evil than other advocates of the death penalty as a means of preserving the values of their religion and society; the pre-Christian Paul is an example (see Acts 9:1). The Jewish leaders did not have the authority under Roman occupation to carry out the death penalty, and must persuade Pilate to execute Jesus, though the Romans in fact have nothing against him. This is the author's understanding of the scene he here portrays. **The Jews:** 19:15 makes it clear that it is not the Jewish people as a whole, but the high priests, who are Jesus' opponents and instrumental in putting him to death.

18:32 To fulfill what Jesus had said: See on 18:9, 25–27. **The kind of death:** For John, it was important not only that Jesus died but that his death was by crucifixion, practiced by Romans but not by Jews, for whom death by stoning was the mode of capital punishment (Lev. 20:2, 27; 24:14, 16, 23; see Acts 7:58–60). The shedding of Jesus' blood was involved in crucifixion, but not in stoning. For the importance of blood in Johannine theology, see on 6:53 and 19:34. Furthermore, the Johannine double meaning of "lifting up" (see 3:14–15; 12:32) is fulfilled in crucifixion but not stoning. This, of course, represents John's after the fact reflection on the meaning of Jesus' death, which had occurred in an obscenely bloody manner.

18:33 Pilate . . . summoned Jesus, and asked him: Now begins the extensive verbal exchange between Pilate and Jesus. This is not found in the Synoptics, where Jesus is practically silent in his trial before Pilate. The dialogue is replete with Johannine theology. **Are you the King of the Jews?** The charge that Jesus was claiming to be a king, i.e., was a rebel against the Roman rule, was probably the historical charge at his trial and the reason for his condemnation and death. At another level, the issue is who is king over God's people, who is God's authorized "anointed one" (Messiah). This theological motif dominates not only the passion story but the Gospel as a whole. At the narrative level, Pilate's specific question has not been prepared for by the Johannine story line. The scene presupposes the readers' knowledge of the Synoptic Gospels or the traditions that lie behind them (see Luke 23:2, which would lead appropriately to Pilate's question). John generally uses "Israel" for the people of God, and "Jews" to designate worldly unbelief in the role of religious leadership; "Israel" is generally a good word for him, and "Jews" a bad word (though there are exceptions; see 4:22). Though Jesus' disciples and the crowds had confessed him to be "king of Israel" (1:49; 6:14–15; 12:15), this was a different kind of kingship from the political threat to Roman rule Pilate had in mind.

18:36 My kingdom is not from this world: Though some translations render the Greek preposition "of" or "belongs to," the NRSV's "from" is important to the Johannine meaning. For John, one's origin determines one's being and character. Thus Jesus is "from above" and his opponents are "from below"; he is not "from this world," but his opponents are "from this world" (8:23; see 9:29–30). The point is that Jesus is indeed God's appointed king in the present-and-coming kingdom of God, but that the source of his authority and power are not from this world, are not based on this world's assumptions, and does not use this world's methods. **My followers would be fighting:** All this-worldly governance rests on violence or the threat of violence. This is true, not only of dictatorships and militant nationalism, but of every human state and all forms of democracy. Jesus' alternate vision of the ultimate reality of God's rule rests on self-giving love, but every human state must regard this as "unrealistic" (see on Matt. 5–7). The followers of Jesus live in the tension between the realities of this world—which is also God's world and to which Christians belong—and the ultimate reality of God's present-and-coming kingdom already manifest in Jesus Christ (see on Luke 4:43–44). Jesus' statement does not mean that his followers are to retire into a "spiritual kingdom" and turn the political realities of this world over to those for whom this-worldly politics constitute the only reality.

18:37 You say that I am a king: The Greek phrase can be translated more than one way, e.g., "King is your word" (REB); "You are right" (NIV); "It is you who say that I am a king" (NJB). See on Luke 23:3. In the Johannine context, Jesus' answer is best understood as an affirmation, not a denial or clever avoidance of the issue. He is a king, but not in Pilate's understanding of the word. **For this I was born:** This is the only explicit reference to the birth of Jesus in the Fourth Gospel. Some early Christians were so persuaded of Jesus' divinity that they pictured him as coming directly from heaven and considered his involvement in the pain and messiness of a human birth to be beneath his divine dignity (e.g., Marcion, ca. 150). Such views were finally considered heretical and rejected by mainstream Christianity. The New Testament maintains the paradox that Jesus' origin is from heaven and from Nazareth, he is Son of God but born of human parents (see 1:45; 2:1; Gal. 4:4).

18:38 What is truth?: Truth is a major theme of the Fourth Gospel. The word occurs twenty-five times (only seven times in the other Gospels combined). Pilate's question, though apparently sincere, is wrongly put. One cannot get a good answer to a bad question. Like many moderns, Pilate assumes truth is a "what," that truth has a definite objective content that can be clearly stated. This is not the understanding of truth in the Fourth Gospel, where Jesus is never said to *teach* the truth. He does not deliver the truth to his disciples, who are never said to "have" the truth. Truth is not an object, a body of material that can be possessed. Jesus is not a great teacher who gives disciples "great truths" to live by. He gives himself; he himself is God's truth (14:6). Truth is a "who," not a "what," a matter of personal encounter and relationship, a matter of worship and commitment that is experienced in the power of the Holy Spirit, the Spirit of truth who guides Jesus' disciples into all truth (see 4:23–25; 16:12–15). Truth is a matter of doing (John 3:21), of ethics, of wanting to do the will of God, not a matter of abstract principles one may weigh objectively and then decide whether what Jesus teaches is true (7:12, 17). There is great Johannine irony in this scene where Pilate with apparent sincerity asks what is truth? when the one who is the incarnate truth of God stands before him (see 1:14, 17; 8:32–36; 14:6).

18:38b I find no case against him: See 19:4, 6.

18:39 You have a custom: This custom is not documented outside the Gospels. It is historically unlikely that a governor would release an accused terrorist in the midst of a patriotic festival. **Barabbas was a bandit:** The same word as Matt. 27:38; Luke 22:52 (see there). It can also be translated "robber" or "revolutionary." In Roman eyes he was a bandit; in Jewish eyes a freedom fighter.

19:1–3 Pilate . . . had him flogged: The mockery of dressing Jesus up like a king and beating him is also found in Matthew and Mark, but at the end of the proceedings. In Luke 23:6–12, Jesus is dressed in royal robes during an interlude in which he is sent to the Jewish king (at Rome's permission) Herod Antipas of Galilee, who was in Jerusalem for the festival. Since in the Fourth Gospel the trial before Pilate continues for some paragraphs, John's rearrangement has the effect of placing the mocking and beating in the middle of the proceedings. Jesus, dressed in a crown of thorns and royal robes yet beaten and mocked is the height of Johannine irony.

19:4 Pilate went out again: Since the Jews would not enter the Praetorium (see 18:28), Pilate is pictured as shuttling back and forth between the Jews outside, who call for Jesus' death, and Jesus himself, whom he knows to be innocent. Pilate's dilemma is real. He would like not to make a decision about Jesus but is being forced into it. John uses Pilate to illustrate that, in view of the incarnation, there can be no neutral ground. Either God has come to the world in the Christ event, or God has not done so. Though expressed in terms of Johannine dualism (see 8:23), the either-for-me-or-against-me nature of the Christ event is common New Testament theology (see Matt. 12:30; Luke 11:23). To attempt to be neutral or to avoid a decision is already to be on the wrong side.

19:5 Here is the man: The traditional translation, "Behold the man!" (Latin *ecce homo*), captures the ironic acclamation better. Pilate may be making a play for the sympathy of Jesus' accusers, or attempting to appease them, by presenting them with the beaten and humiliated Jesus dressed in the crown of thorns and mock royal attire. At another level, he declares a profound truth—here is a truly human being, man as he was created to be, the one made in God's image and truly obedient to God, the only one of whom this can be said without qualification. Like Caiaphas (see 11:49–52), he proclaims Christian truth at its deepest level without realizing it: "If you want to see what a real human being is like, look at Jesus" (see Rom. 5:12–21).

19:7 We have a law: There is no specific law in the Old Testament or Jewish tradition that forbids one from claiming to be a Son of God. Understood in a nonmetaphysical sense, the title was actually used by Jewish kings (see Ps. 2:7; 2 Sam. 7:14). The law of Lev. 24:16 against blaspheming the name of God could apparently be understood in this sense (see the equation of Jesus' claim to be the Messiah, the Son of God, with "blasphemy" in Mark 14:61–64, a scene not in the Fourth Gospel). **Claimed to be the Son of God:** Finally the real objection of the Jews comes out (no charge had surfaced in the hearing before the high priests of 18:13–27). "Claimed to be" is literally "made himself to be." Their objection is thus a misunderstanding of Jesus, who has repeatedly asserted that he does not "make himself" to be anything (5:18–19; 10:18, 33).

19:8 More afraid than ever: For the first time, the reader learns that Pilate is already afraid. We should not ask about the inner turmoil of the historical Pilate, with which John is not concerned and about which he has no way of knowing. In the narrative story line, John's point is that Pilate's apprehension is increased as he sees he is being forced into making a decision about Jesus, whether he wants to do so or not.

19:9 Where are you from? Another example of the two-level, double meaning involved in John's literary technique. At one level, it is the normal administrative question to an accused suspect. At the deeper Johannine level, origin determines nature and character; Pilate suspects he may be dealing with someone "not from this world" (see 18:36).

19:10 I have power to release you: Jesus agrees that Pilate has power, but rather than intimidating Jesus, this fact serves to point out Pilate's own responsibility when he decides not to release Jesus. In John's eyes, Pilate is also guilty, despite his placing the principal blame on the Jews.

19:13 Sat on the judge's bench: The Greek text can be translated either as indicating that Pilate took his place in the judge's seat, or that he continued the mockery by seating Jesus, still wearing the crown of thorns and dressed in his royal robes, on the judge's bench (see the NRSV, note "seeated him"; the NAB and NJB adopt this translation in their text). Either way, the scene is profoundly ironical. If Pilate is seated on the judge's seat, it portrays his real judge standing before him in the prisoner's role, though Pilate is unaware of the real situation. If Jesus is on the judge's seat, Pilate supposes he is continuing the mockery, though he has in fact staged the real situation: Jesus is the one who exercises the final judgment of God (see 5:22, 27; 7:12; 8:15; 12:31; 16:8–10; 18:13–28).

19:13 The Stone Pavement . . . Gabbatha: Some stone slabs with the markings of soldiers' dice games scratched on them, probably dating from the Roman era, have been found in excavations in the temple area. These are sometimes identified as the pavement mentioned here, but the location and identification are far from certain.

19:14–15 Preparation for the Passover . . . about noon: John's point is that the Passover lambs have not yet been slaughtered and the Passover meal has not yet been eaten (see on 13:1; 18:28). **Noon:** literally "the sixth hour"; since John uses Roman time, which began counting at 6:00 a.m., Jesus is still in Pilate's judgment hall at noon. This is a different chronology than the Synoptics, in which Jesus has already been crucified by 9:00 a.m. (see Mark 15:25; Luke 23:44). **Here is your King:** An ironic acclamation similar to 19:5. **The Jews . . . the chief priests:** Another indication that by "the Jews" John rarely means the Jewish people as a whole. In Mark 15:13 it is the crowds who cry out for Jesus' crucifixion; here it is only the priestly leaders, which is certainly nearer to the historical reality.

We have no king but the emperor: Who is Israel's true king? (See 18:33.) This question was focused in the particular issue of whether faithful Jews could acknowledge the Roman emperor as king, a concern with a long history that had deeply troubled and divided first-century Judaism. The Zealots claimed that only God was Israel's king and advocated open resistance to Rome (see on Mark 12:13–17; Luke 20:20–26). At the Passover festival, a religious-patriotic hymn was sung:

> From everlasting to everlasting thou art God—
> Beside thee we have no king, redeemer, or savior.

It is thus the climactic irony, when John portrays the Jewish leaders as proclaiming that Caesar is their only king, that they are more Roman than the pagan governor Pilate.

19:16 Then he handed him over: The same word is used of Judas's betrayal (18:2), of the Jewish leaders' handing Jesus over to Pilate (18:30,

35), and of Pilate's handing Jesus over to be crucified. The word is also used of God's handing over the Suffering Servant to die for the sins of others (Isa. 53:12). Though John does not explicitly cite this text, he indicates that in and through the sinful actions of human beings, including Jesus' own followers, it is God who is at work "handing over" Jesus to atone for human sinfulness, i.e., that God himself takes the penalty for human sinfulness (see on 3:16; 10:11; Rom. 3:25; 1 Cor. 15:3; Heb. 1:3; 2:17; 5:1–10). In John's view, Jesus was handed over to death not only by Judas, the chief priests, and Pilate, but by all who reject him (see Heb. 6:6)—and ultimately by God, who in Jesus delivered himself over as the atonement for human sin. **To them:** Strictly interpreted, this means Pilate handed Jesus over to the Jews for crucifixion. Yet John obviously knows that Jesus was actually crucified by Roman soldiers (v. 23) and that Pilate himself was in charge of supervising the crucifixion (vv. 20–22, 31, 38). John's point here is thus that Pilate knuckles under the veiled threat of the Jewish leaders (see 19:12) and hands him over to their demand.

19:17–42
The Crucifixion and Burial
(See also at Matt. 27:27–66; Mark 15:20b-47; Luke 23:26–56)

All the Gospels present Jesus as the truly human being who suffers and dies a real death. At the same time, in their various ways they present Jesus as representing the eternal God. They thus are all faced with the theological and literary problem of how to narrate the death of one who is both truly human and truly divine. Mark, who has emphasized Jesus' divinity in the miracle stories, emphasizes his human weakness in the passion story; Matthew and Luke follow Mark, but allow more of Jesus' divine nature to be seen. For John too, Jesus has truly human characteristics and dies a real human death. That Jesus' death was not a sham, staged by a divine being who in fact could not suffer and die, is an important part of his own testimony. Accepting this as a given, John is more interested than any of the other Evangelists in narrating the story of his death in a way that emphasizes his deity. The comments below point out several examples.

John's story of the death of Jesus is in many respects closely parallel to that of the other Gospels. He omits only a few major items found in them, including the derision and insults from the chief priests and the brigands crucified with him, the rending of the temple veil and the darkness at midday, and the centurion's confession (see the Synoptic parallels listed above). On the other hand, he elaborates, modifies, or adds extensive material in order to bring out his own theological perspective. Among the major Johannine additions are that Jesus carries his own cross; that the placard on the cross was in three languages; that Pilate refused to change the inscription; that Jesus' robe was seamless; that his mother, three other women, and the Beloved Disciple were present at the cross; that his side was pierced so that blood and water came out; and that Nicodemus was involved in providing him an extravagant, royal burial. John also adds references to Scripture not found in the Synoptics. The following comments focus on these distinctive Johannine elements; see on the other Gospels for their interpretative accounts of Jesus' death. Here as elsewhere, the differing accounts should not be combined and harmonized, but each writer's presentation should be appreciated for itself.

19:17 Carrying the cross by himself: This contrasts with Matt. 27:31–32/Mark 15:20–21/ Luke 23:26. John avoids presenting the weak, victimized, crucified Jesus (see 2 Cor. 13:4), and replaces him with the strong, triumphant Jesus, who goes resolutely to death as his own act (see 10:17–18).

19:18 There they crucified him: Crucifixion was an obscenely horrible death, a public spectacle intended by the Romans as warning and deterrent. In contrast to the kind of martyr stories found, for example, in 4 Macc. 6–12, but like the other Gospels, John does not dwell on the grim details. This is not due to squeamishness, but because the motive for following Jesus is not an emotional response to graphic descriptions of his suffering, but faith in God's act in the Christ event as a whole, climaxed in the self-giving love manifest in his death.

19:20 Near the city: This description fits the traditional location of the crucifixion now enshrined within the Church of the Holy Sepulcher, which was just outside the walls of the ancient city (inside the present city walls). It does not fit the Garden Tomb site near the Jerusalem bus station, a modern identification of the site shown to tourists. **Hebrew, Latin, Greek:** Only the Fourth Gospel presents the placard on Jesus' cross in such an international manner (see 4:42, "savior of the *world*"). The trilingual inscription points to the universal meaning of the Christ event, which was not

"done in a corner" (Acts 26:26). Jesus' kingship is placarded in Hebrew, the language of the Bible and the only monotheistic religion; in Latin, the language of law and empire; and in Greek, the language of philosophy and human wisdom. It was not the hoodlums of Jerusalem's back alleys who killed Jesus—he died at the hands of the representatives of humanity's highest religion, government, and education. This is John's way of saying that God's salvation came not by religion, law, or education, but by God's own act in Christ, culminating in the self-giving love that placed him on the cross. John thus agrees with Paul that the cross is the abolition of all claims to human achievement as the way of salvation (1 Cor. 1:17–2:5).

19:22 What I have written I have written: The Jewish leaders attempt to make Jesus' kingship a matter of his own claim, but Pilate again becomes an unwitting witness that Jesus' lordship is not merely his "making himself" something (5:18–19; 10:18, 33).

19:23–24 To fulfill what the scripture says: Ps. 22:18, originally a lament of a sick person near death who sees his friends and relatives already dividing up his clothing as though he were already dead. The early Christians understood this text (and much else in Ps. 22) as pointing to Jesus, and used the psalm to fill in details of the crucifixion scene, thus making it appear that they were predicted in the Old Testament. See excursus, "New Testament Interpretation of the Old Testament," at 1 Cor. 15:3; 1 Pet. 1:10. **Seamless, woven in one piece:** Similar language is used of the high priest's robe in Exod. 36:35; 39:27, especially in the Greek translation used by John. The first-century Jewish historian Josephus refers to the high priest's robe as "woven from a single thread" (*Antiquities* 3.161). Though he does not make it explicit, this may be John's way of pointing to the role of Jesus as the true high priest (see Heb. 7–9, which repeatedly makes this specific). As the Fourth Gospel presents Jesus as the true judge when he stands before Pilate, who claims to be his judge, so John may here be presenting Jesus as the true high priest in the presence of the high priests who condemned him (see 17:1–25).

19:25–27 Standing near the cross of Jesus: In the Synoptics, all the disciples flee when Jesus is arrested, and none are present at the cross. His mother is not mentioned. Some other women observe from afar. In the Fourth Gospel, Jesus' mother, whose name is never given in John, and three other women (two of whom are named Mary) are present at the cross, as is the Beloved Disciple (see on 13:23). **He said to his mother:** In the Fourth Gospel, these are Jesus' first words from the cross. John omits the "My God, why" cry of dereliction of Mark and Matthew. No Gospel has all of Jesus' "seven last words from the cross," which is a traditional combination from all four Gospels. Such combinations, if taken as representing what Jesus actually said, do violence to the Gospels, each of which has its own theological point to communicate. The cry of despair in Mark and Matthew cannot be combined historically or psychologically with the calm assurance of the Johannine Jesus. **Here is your son . . . here is your mother:** Jesus is self-possessed, presiding over the situation, making arrangements for his mother. The scene is unique to John and has sometimes been seen as Johannine symbolism, in which the anonymous mother of Jesus (the people of God or Jewish Christianity) is committed by him to the ideal disciple, representing Gentile Christianity. See on Rev. 12:1 for an analogous case in the Johannine writings in which an anonymous woman represents the people of God as the mother of the Messiah. The case is not so clear in John.

19:28 I am thirsty: Though the human being Jesus can get thirsty (just as he can get tired (4:6–7), here Jesus asks for a drink not from thirst but to fulfill the Scripture. See Pss. 22:15; 69:21; and commentary at 19:24.

19:29 Hyssop: All the Gospels have the presentation of vinegar or sour wine to Jesus on the cross. Only John mentions hyssop, a small fragile plant that could hardly be used for the purpose here described (Mark 15:36 refers to a "stick"). Hyssop was part of the Passover ritual (see Exod. 12:22; Lev. 14:6; Num. 19:6; 1 Kgs. 4:33). The small, flowerlike plants were tied into bunches and used as a brush to sprinkle blood on the doorposts in Egypt. John has apparently inserted the reference to correspond to his understanding that Jesus is the Lamb of God, who dies at the time the Passover lambs are being slain (see on 1:29; 13:1).

19:30 It is finished: Better, "It is accomplished"; see 17:4. Jesus remains sovereign over his own destiny until the end and then himself announces that his work is finished. **Gave up his spirit:** Another Johannine double-meaning; the same Greek words can be translated "handed over the Spirit" (to his followers; see 7:39; 14:16–17). John tends to compress the whole saving event into the cross scene.

Although he narrates the traditional resurrection story as something that happened on Easter Sunday, he also sees the crucifixion itself as Jesus' exaltation, his being "lifting up" (3:14–15; 12:32–33). Just as he compresses resurrection, ascension, and the pentecostal giving of the Spirit to Easter Sunday (see on 20:21–22), so here he hints that everything, including the giving of the Spirit, is already accomplished on the cross.

19:31 That sabbath: In John's chronology (see on 13:1), the Passover begins on the Friday evening of the crucifixion. The next day was thus not only the usual Sabbath, but a particularly holy day that was the Passover as well. **Have the legs of the crucified men broken:** This is not an additional cruelty to the tortured victims, but a merciful shortening of their suffering. The bodies could not remain on the cross during the Sabbath and the Passover (see Deut. 21:23). With broken legs, the victims could no longer support their body weight, were unable to breathe, and thus died quickly of asphyxiation.

19:34 Blood and water came out: This is not a medical explanation of the physiological cause of Jesus' death, but a double theological point:

1. The lance thrust and pouring out of bodily fluids shows that Jesus was not a ghostly divine being, but had truly died a human death. Some versions of early Christianity thought of Jesus as so divine that his suffering and death were only an appearance. John opposes that view, held by some gnostic Christians and later called the heresy of Docetism ("seemism").

2. Blood and water point to the two Christian sacraments of Eucharist (blood; see 6:51–58) and baptism (water; 3:3–5, 22–24), both of which are here grounded in the reality of Jesus' death.

19:35 He who saw this has testified: The Beloved Disciple, the patron saint of the Johannine community, the guarantor of its tradition and testimony (see 21:24). **He knows/There is one who knows:** See the variant translation suggested in the NRSV note. The one who knows that the Beloved Disciple's testimony is true may be the disciple himself, the author who is reporting it, or (most likely) the risen Christ who validates the testimony of the Beloved Disciple on which the Gospel is based.

19:36–37 So that the scripture might be fulfilled: See 19:24 commentary. **Broken:** The Passover lamb was to be roasted whole; its bones were not to be broken (Exod. 12:10, 46). Since Jesus is depicted as the Passover lamb, dying at the same time the lambs are being slaughtered in the temple (see 1:29; 13:1), his bones were not broken (see NRSV note on "broken" in some manuscripts of the eucharistic words of institution, 1 Cor. 11:24). **They will look . . . :** This quotation from Zech. 12:10 is also applied to Jesus in Rev. 1:7. Since there is no other New Testament reference to it, this suggests it was a current interpretation in the Johannine community to which both the author of the Gospel and the author of Revelation belonged.

19:38–39 Joseph of Arimathea: Involved in Jesus' burial in all four Gospels. John interprets his appearance here in the perspective of 9:22 and 12:42–43, i.e., as an example of those Jewish believers in Jesus who need to step forth publicly and declare their faith. So also **Nicodemus** (see 3:1–13; 7:50), who appears only in the Fourth Gospel, becomes increasingly public in his confession of Jesus. **Hundred pounds:** This extravagant (and very expensive) amount portrays Jesus as having been given a royal burial commensurate with his role as "king of Israel." On Johannine pictures of extravagance, see on 2:6; 6:12–13; 12:3; 19:39; see also Luke 5:6; 6:37–38; 9:17; 8:5–8; 13:20; 15:22; 19:17; Rom. 5:15, for pictures of salvation as extravagance. As in the reference to hyssop above, this is a theological image of the meaning of Jesus' death, not accurate history.

20:1–31
THE RESURRECTION OF JESUS AND COMMISSIONING OF THE DISCIPLES

This chapter constitutes the "original" conclusion of the book (see 20:30–31!), i.e., its conclusion at the next to last stage of its development toward its present canonical form (see on 21:1–25; see introduction to John and commentary at 4:54).

For general considerations, see excursus, "Interpreting the Resurrection," at Matt. 28:1. The comments below concentrate on the distinctive Johannine perspectives.

20:1–10
The Empty Tomb
(See also at Matt. 28:1–8; Mark 16:1–8; Luke 24:1–12)

20:1 The first day of the week: Sunday, which as the Lord's Day, i.e., the day of the resurrection, later became the Christian holy day in place of the Old Testament–Jewish Sabbath (Saturday). **Mary Magdalene:** All the Gospels report a woman or women as being first at the tomb.

Only John reports a visit of Mary Magdalene to the tomb alone; only in John does she receive the first appearance (vs. 1 Cor. 15:6; Luke 24:34). It is not said why she comes. In Mark 16:1 and Luke 24:1 the women come to anoint the body, but in John 19:39–40 this has already happened in a royal style. **While it was still dark:** Contrast Mark 16:2. In several places John seems to be intentionally "correcting" the version of the story found in the Synoptics (see also other parts of the Gospel, e.g., 3:24 vs. Mark 1:14). Darkness may also be symbolic, as in 13:30—apart from the resurrection, the world lies in darkness. **The stone:** Not previously mentioned in John—one of several indications that the story presupposes the Synoptic Gospels or their tradition. See the "we" of vs. 2, which corresponds to the Synoptics but not to John and may be a holdover from a prior form of the story now found in the Synoptics. **Had been removed:** In all the canonical Gospels, the resurrection itself is not narrated, but happens "offstage"—when the narrative curtain opens, the tomb is already empty. (Contrast the later apocryphal *Gospel of Peter*, which pictures Jesus coming out of the tomb.) For the New Testament writers, the event itself remains an indescribable mystery.

20:2 Simon Peter and the other disciple: See on 13:23. There is nothing parallel to this scene in the Synoptics, where the women report to all the disciples (though see Luke 24:24, only present in some MSS). **They have taken the Lord:** The open tomb itself does not generate resurrection faith. Mary apparently assumes that the body had been stolen by grave robbers (it had been a royal funeral, 19:39–40) or removed by the authorities (see her plaintive request in v. 15).

20:4 The other disciple outran Peter: The footrace to the tomb, in which the Beloved Disciple finishes in first place, is not a matter of athletic ability, but reflects the first-century struggles for church leadership. Tensions between early Christian leaders were not merely a matter of petty politics, but expressed the community's concern for the authentic tradition and its legitimate bearers. In the Fourth Gospel, Peter consistently comes in second. Peter was the traditional leader of what in John's day was becoming mainstream apostolic Christianity. The Beloved Disciple was the traditional and revered leader of another, somewhat competitive stream of Christianity. Although the tradition of the "apostolic" church revered Peter as the Easter hero who received the first appearance (1 Cor. 15:5; Luke 24:34), the Johannine community's version of the story favors the Beloved Disciple throughout (without dismissing Peter—see on chap. 21).

20:5 Saw the linen wrappings: In the Fourth Gospel Jesus was not buried in a single linen wrapping, a shroud, but was wrapped in mummylike strips, with a separate wrapper around his head (see 19:40 and the analogous description of Lazarus, 11:44). The famous shroud of Turin is based on the Synoptics and ignores the Johannine account. While Peter was the first to enter, the Beloved Disciple was the first to "see," and due respect is paid to both the Petrine and Johannine traditions.

20:7 Rolled up in a place by itself: There is something significant about the arrangement of the left-behind grave clothes. Their neat arrangement, and the fact that they were left behind, at least shows that the empty tomb was not the work of grave robbers and contrasts with the raising of Lazarus, who needed to be "unbound" (see 11:44), but there may be a deeper significance not apparent to the modern reader.

20:8 Saw and believed: Both Peter and the Beloved Disciples "saw," but only the Beloved Disciple believed. Faith is not merely a matter of evidence—each saw the same facts, each had the same data, but only one believed. On the paradox of faith as human decision and divine gift, see 3:16; 5:42; 6:27–29, 44; 10:26, and especially excursus, "Predestination," at Rom. 8:28. On the Johannine dialectic of seeing and believing, see on 2:23; 6:36–40; 11:45; 14:7, 19; 20:24–29. The Beloved Disciple is again represented as the faithful witness; what he has seen is important for the foundation of the community's faith (see 19:35; 21:24). But there is a sense in which all Christians have "seen" (see on 1 John 1:1–4; 3 John 11).

20:9 Did not yet understand the Scripture: The Christian community reinterpreted the Old Testament on the basis of the Easter event (see excursus, "New Testament Interpretation of the Old Testament," at 1 Cor. 15:3; 1 Pet. 1:10). When read with post-Easter eyes, the Hebrew Scriptures were seen as witnesses to Christian faith (see, e.g., Acts 2:24–27). In the Fourth Gospel, Jesus himself has not specifically predicted his own resurrection (as, e.g., in Mark 8:31; 9:31; 10:33–34), though he has spoken of it in symbolic, allusive language (e.g., 3:14–15; 10:18; 12:32–34; 16:16). Thus the disciples in John are not in the situation of having heard such predictions from Jesus himself that they did not understand or believe. For the Fourth Gospel's theology, resurrection faith is supported by rereading the Old Testament as illumined by the insight provided by the post-Easter gift of the Holy Spirit (see 2:17, 22; 7:39; 12:16; 14:15–17, 25–26; 15:26–27; 16:7–15).

20:10 To their homes: The reference here is not to Galilee, the home of all the disciples except the Beloved Disciple, but to wherever they have been staying while in Jerusalem. John is not here concerned with such details; his comment serves to get the disciples offstage so the significant encounter between the risen Jesus and Mary Magdalene can have the readers' full attention.

20:11–18
Jesus Appears to Mary Magdalene
(See also at Matt. 28:9–10 [Mark 16:9–11]; Luke 24:10–11)

This scene is John's equivalent of the Synoptic stories in which women discover the empty tomb and (in Matthew) encounter the risen Jesus. Mary Magdalene is included in every case, the only name common to the various groups. We have here not an accurate historical report, but an exquisite summary, in story form, of the Johannine understanding of how resurrection faith comes to be.

20:11 Mary stood weeping: The story is only loosely integrated into the narrative context; it may originally have been a continuation of v. 1, with vv. 2–10 the insertion of an independent story. In the present form of the narrative, this is Mary's second appearance at the empty tomb. John does not narrate her arrival. Presumably she was not present with Peter and the Beloved Disciple in the preceding scene, for she seems unaware of their experience and that the Beloved Disciple has come to faith in the risen Christ.

20:12 Two angels in white: In Mark the women see a young man in white, in Matthew the angel of the Lord, in Luke two men in dazzling clothes, later identified as angels (24:23). John seems to combine all these elements of earlier stories into his account. Nothing is said of the grave clothes that convinced the Beloved Disciple in the previous scene. Mary responds to the angels with the same words as 20:2b.

20:14 Saw Jesus . . . but did . . . not know: Readers should avoid novelistic and psychological explanations for Mary's lack of perception (overwhelmed by grief; blinded by tears, etc.). John is not writing a biographical account or data for psychological explanations, but narrative theology: there is a kind of "seeing" that still does not result in faith (see on vv. 24–29 below).

20:15 Whom are you looking for?: The initial question of 1:38 (see commentary there) recurs at the end of the Gospel, now transformed into its more authentic form by the intervening Gospel narrative itself. It turns out that, after all, the goal of the human quest is not a "what" but a "who," not things or something, but the personal One who is the source and goal of our existence. The personal God manifest in Christ is the unrecognized goal of all human longing and striving, though often disguised as various forms of "what" that promise a happiness they cannot deliver.

20:16 Mary . . . Rabbouni: When Mary thinks Jesus is the gardener, she addresses him with the respectful "sir"; when she recognizes his true identity, her address becomes the familiar but still respectful "rabbouni," "my teacher." The pronoun "my" built into the word is important (see Thomas in 20:28, "*my* Lord and *my* God"). The Christian confession is not in an abstract truth, but in the personal God, who knows our name and numbers the hairs of our head (Matt. 10:30). Mary had previously seen the stone rolled away, the empty tomb, two angels, and the risen Jesus himself, but they did not produce the response of personal faith. The personal address of the risen Lord himself, the One who calls his sheep by name (10:3), generates authentic faith that overwhelming "evidence," including visions of angels, could not. For John, people come to Christian faith not by weighing the evidence judged by their own criteria (see on 7:12), but as a response to the voice of the living Christ that continues to be heard in Christian preaching and the testimony of Christian words, deeds, and lives.

20:17 Do not hold on to me: The REB and NJB translate "do not cling to me." For John, Christian faith is not a continuation of the warm familiarity with the earthly Jesus that had been enjoyed by a few Palestinians in the first century (see on 14:28; 2 Cor. 5:16). Fascination with the earthly "historical Jesus" is not the same as Christian faith in God's act in Christ. Believers of the second and later generations (including us), for whom John writes, are not only at no disadvantage—it is *better* not to hold on to the earthly Jesus, so that authentic faith in the risen Christ, generated in the power of the Holy Spirit, can lead believers into the "greater works" they have to do in the world in the

name of the living Christ (see 14:12; 16:7). Christian faith is not holding on to a past that recedes ever farther into the distance, but experiencing a living present in which everything is different because of what once really happened and continues to happen.

I have not yet ascended . . . I am ascending: The risen Christ is not a resuscitated Jesus. The resurrection places Jesus in a different mode of reality, does not merely restore him to live in this world (contrast Lazarus, 11:1–57). Unlike Luke, John has no separate ascension scene, but thinks of the resurrection event as including the ascension to heaven and transformation into the transcendent mode of reality. Mary is forbidden to "hold on to" a Jesus who still belongs in our realm of existence; he is "in the process" of becoming the ascended Christ. Jesus will later invite Thomas to touch him, for the resurrection-ascension event is then "complete." Of course John is not inviting the reader to think of various trips to heaven and back, but is affirming the unity of resurrection and ascension. So also in John's theology, the pentecostal giving of the Spirit is not a separate event from the resurrection-ascension, but occurs on the same day (20:22). In fact, resurrection–ascension–bestowal of the Spirit are all aspects of the cross event itself (see on 19:30). Though narrating the story requires stretching its various elements out on a chronological line, for John the saving event is the cross-resurrection event, which includes ascension and Pentecost.

My brothers: As in Matt. 28:10, the exalted Christ does not hesitate to refer to his disciples as his brothers (see Heb. 2:11), whom he also calls not slaves but friends (15:14). **My Father and your Father . . . my God and your God:** Neither here nor elsewhere in the New Testament does Jesus speak of "our Father" in a way that includes both himself and his disciples. The Lord's Prayer instructs the disciples, "When *you* pray, say 'Our Father . . .'" Despite the intimacy of "brother" and "friend," Jesus' unique relation to God is not the same as that of his followers, but the basis for it.

20:19–23
Jesus Appears to His Disciples
(Thomas Being Absent)
(See also at Luke 24:36–43)

20:19 Evening on that day: In John as in Luke, the risen Jesus appears to his disciples while they are still in Jerusalem; in Mark there are no appearances at all, though the young man in the tomb promises that Jesus will meet his disciples in Galilee (Mark 16:7). In Matthew Jesus appears to the women in Jerusalem, to the male disciples in Galilee. **The doors . . . locked:** John does not speculate on the nature of the resurrected body of Jesus but presents it as a tangible body still bearing the marks of crucifixion, a body can be touched (v. 27) and yet that can mysteriously appear inside a locked room. **For fear of the Jews:** There is no evidence that the Jewish leaders sought Jesus' disciples immediately after the crucifixion, but by the author's time, church communities sometimes lived in fear of Jewish persecution (16:1–4; see Acts 9:1–2; 10–14). **Peace be with you:** Though a conventional Jewish greeting in antiquity, "peace" ("shalom") is here filled with eschatological meaning as the fulfillment of Jesus' promise (14:27; 16:33).

20:20 He showed them his hands and his side: The risen Christ is the continuing presence of the Crucified One. John has been more graphic than any of the other Gospels in portraying the flesh-and-blood reality of the crucifixion. Only John has nails. Only John has blood. Only John has the spear-thrust in the side (19:34–35). While John has the most exalted Christology of the Gospels, in which Jesus is truly divine, he also is most insistent that Jesus is truly human, that Jesus' death was not a sham but the supreme instance of the Word (true God) who became flesh (true human). John's presentation of the Easter-Pentecost story does not consider the crucifixion as an episode of past history that is now superseded by the resurrection and the Spirit, but the continual making present of the significance of that event. The exalted Christ does not put the nail prints behind him, but reigns only as the Crucified (= self-giving, even to death) One.

20:21 So I send you: The resurrection was not merely an individual and private religious experience, but a corporate reality that involved a mission to the world. This mission is not at the church's own initiative, but the by-product and continuation of God's mission in sending Jesus (17:18; Matt. 10:40). Our sending is an extension of God's own sending. Jesus incorporates his disciples into his mission, but Jesus was not a great man who concocted his own mission. He too was sent. God is the primal missionary; the church's work is not the *church's* work but is an extension of God's own mission. As the next verse indicates, this mission is not carried out in the disciples' own power and insight, but is enabled by the Holy Spirit that guides and energizes Jesus' followers.

20:22 Breathed on them: The single Greek word *pneuma* means "breath," "wind," and "spirit" (see on 3:3–8). Jesus breathed on them, and they received the divine, life-giving breath, God's breath-Spirit (see Gen. 2:7; Ps. 104:29–30). **Receive the Holy Spirit:** The bestowal of the Spirit that occurs fifty days later on the day of Pentecost in Luke's chronology (see on Acts 2:1) occurs on Good Friday–Easter Sunday in John's compressed theological chronology (see on 19:30; 20:17).

20:23 If you forgive . . . if you retain: Somewhat surprisingly to the reader of the Synoptic Gospels, this is the only reference to forgiveness in the Gospel of John. In the Johannine community, forgiveness of sins was thought of primarily in intracommunity terms (1 John 1:9; 2:12). As the sending into the world and the reception of the Spirit applies to all the disciples in this scene, so the power of forgiveness is also given to the believers as a group, primarily as a matter of the internal life of the church that requires forgiveness (see Matt. 9:8; 16:16–18; 18:18). Just as it is God who sends Christ, who sends the church, so it is God who forgives through Jesus, "the Lamb of God who takes away the sins of the world" (1:29). But though this happened before us and apart from us in a once-for-all event on Golgotha, it remains only theology, doctrine, until it is made real in the life of the Christian community. As Christians share in the *missio Dei* that sent Christ as the primal missionary, so Christians share in God's act in Christ that announces, mediates, and models forgiveness. While the church in its mission to the world does announce and mediate both God's grace and God's judgment, it is not pictured here or elsewhere in the New Testament as an institution that stands between God and the sinful world as the only access to God's forgiveness.

20:24–29
Jesus and Thomas

In the most common traditional understanding, Thomas has been blamed (as "doubting Thomas") because he insisted on seeing for himself rather than believing the apostolic testimony. A minority view has praised Thomas as a model of individualistic tough-minded skepticism. Both approaches tend to flatten out the subtlety of the Johannine interplay between seeing and believing.

For John there is a kind of seeing that produces, or can produce believing (see 2:23; 6:40;

11:45; 20:8). Even in this text, Jesus' invitation to Thomas to "see and believe" seems authentic. The initial disciples are invited to "come and see" without reproach, and they become believers (1:39, 46). Even the Beloved Disciple sees before he believes (20:8), and his faith-based-on-sight becomes the basis of the faith of others who have not had the opportunity to see for themselves (19:35; see 17:20; 20:29). Even so, the Johannine church is urged to understand itself to be a community in which every member of every generation has seen, heard, and touched the Word of Life (1 John 1:1–4).

Yet sometimes the relation between seeing and believing is judged negatively (4:48; 6:30; 20:25), and there is a kind of seeing that does not produce faith (6:35). John thus has a dialectic of seeing and believing. There are those who see and do not believe, who see and believe, who do not see and do not believe, who do not see and yet believe. Thomas's problem is not that he is a tough-minded skeptic who will not believe until he has seen with his own eyes, but that he insists on submitting the revelation that has come in Christ to his own criteria. He is thus the final example of an issue that permeates the Gospel (see on 7:12). With dramatic subtlety, the author leaves it to the reader to decide whether Thomas reached out and touched; presumably he did not.

20:25 The mark of the nails: Jesus has already displayed these marks to the other disciples, without reproach. It is important to John, and to the New Testament generally, that the resurrected Christ be seen in continuity with the Crucified One. The crucifixion was not an unfortunate episode in Jesus' career en route to resurrection glory, that could now recede into the past; the Resurrected One maintains his identity as the Crucified One (see Mark 16:6; 1 Cor. 1:17–2:5).

Crucifixion did not always involve nailing; its intent was that the victim die slowly, not by loss of blood. Often the condemned was tied to the cross in an awkward position and hung there for days before dying. In the New Testament, only John specifically mentions nails; the shedding of Jesus' blood was an essential part of John's Christology (see on 6:53; 19:34–35).

20:28 My Lord and my God: The original Gospel narrative ended on this climactic note. The narrator has indicated to the reader that it is God who has become incarnate in Jesus (1:1–2, 14, 18; see 5:18–24; 10:30; 14:8–11), but God language has not been used directly of Jesus by the characters in the pre-Easter narrative, including Jesus himself. Now the resurrected Lord

can be addressed using language appropriate only to the one God. Although the later church fathers spoke of Jesus as God, the New Testament is very restrained in this regard (see clearly Titus 2:13; Heb. 1:8–9; other possible instances not as clear: Rom. 9:5; 2 Thess. 1:12; 2 Pet. 1:1; 1 John 5:20).

20:30–31
Conclusion and Purpose of the Gospel

20:30 Many other signs: The author is aware that he has not written a biography, but illustrative scenes that point to the meaning of the Christ event as a whole. By speaking of "other" signs in this context, he indicates that the immediately preceding Thomas episode was a sign, i.e., that the encounter calling for faith in the Risen One who continues to bear the marks of crucifixion is the climactic sign, summing up the meaning of the narrative as a whole. **In the presence of his disciples:** Like the "you" of the next verse, these words indicate that the signs were done for the benefit of disciples, to deepen and clarify their faith, not to convince the unbelieving world. For John, faith is not merely a logical deduction based on observing Jesus' miraculous signs (see on 3:16; 6:27; 7:12).

20:31 These are written: The author's written composition mediates the living voice of Christ that appeared in history and generates and strengthens faith. **That you:** As in 19:35, the narrative shifts into direct address to the readers. Such a "you" is unheard of in the Hellenistic literature of the time and shows that the book is not a biography designed for private reading, but addresses the congregation in the language of the preacher. **Come to believe/continue to believe:** Two forms of the Greek verb appear in the manuscripts; it is not clear which is original (see NRSV and notes). While non-Christians can indeed be addressed through the Fourth Gospel by the life-giving word that generates faith, as has repeatedly happened, it seems clear that the Gospel was written primarily for those already interior to the Christian community and familiar with the stories contained in the Gospel, in order to deepen and clarify the faith they already had. **That Jesus is the Christ, the Son of God:** This is the author's summary of the content of the Christian faith, the content of the Christian creed (see on Luke 9:18–27; Acts 17:3; 18:5, 28). **Have life in his name:** The final goal is not believing something about Jesus, but the eternal life that comes through him, i.e., through God's act in him.

21:1–25
EPILOGUE

The Gospel seems to come to a proper conclusion at 20:31. Most scholars regard chap. 21 as added after the composition of the main body of the narrative, indeed representing its final edition. The more technical commentaries and monographs offer detailed reasons of vocabulary, content, and style that seem to justify this conclusion. On the process of growth of the Gospel, see introduction to John and commentary at 4:54.

Chapter 21, while representing the latest stratum of composition, is not an appendix in the sense of an unrelated postscript to the main part of the Gospel. It is better thought of as an epilogue, i.e., the final phase of the Gospel's composition that integrates some of its competing elements in an ecumenical perspective that now permeates the whole Gospel, all of which is now to be read in the light of these concluding scenes. There are at least three of these elements: (1) the rivalry between Simon Peter and the Beloved Disciple is resolved; (2) the Gospel's emphasis on the realization of eschatological hopes in the present is now balanced by highlighting the hope of Jesus' future return; (3) the resurrection accounts of exclusively Galilean appearances to the apostles (Mark, Matthew) or exclusively Judean appearances (Luke; John 20) are now balanced, so that John is the only Gospel that combines Judean and Galilean appearances (Mark 16:9b–20 is not original; see commentary there).

21:1 Sea of Tiberias: Another name for the Sea of Galilee (see 6:1).

21:2 Sons of Zebedee: James and John (Mark 1:19–20). This is the only reference in the Fourth Gospel to the John to whom the authorship of the Gospel was later attributed. Even here, he is not mentioned by name—it is assumed that the reader is familiar with the Synoptic Gospels or their traditions. **Nathanael:** Mentioned in the New Testament only in John 1:45–49 and here. Though **Cana** (also mentioned only in John) appears in 2:1, 11, 46, only here does John connect Nathanael and Cana. **Two others:** A total of seven; the anonymous Beloved Disciple must be one of these (v. 7, 20–23; see on 13:23). The Twelve do not figure in John's resurrection stories.

21:3 I am going fishing: It is difficult to conceive that the Simon Peter who has received the Holy Spirit directly from Jesus and has been commissioned for the Christian world mission in 20:19–23 now decides to return to his old life as if nothing had happened. We have

here an indication that this story is an independent element in Johannine tradition that does not presuppose the appearances of the risen Jesus in chap. 20, but represents (one version of) the initial appearance of Jesus to his disciples after the resurrection. Again John seems to presuppose the Synoptic stories in which four of the original disciples were fishermen, since this description of them has not appeared earlier in the Gospel itself. **That night they caught nothing:** The story in its present Johannine location illustrates Jesus' saying at the Last Supper, "Apart from me you can do nothing" (15:5). There are several similarities and identical details to the story of the initial call of the disciples in Luke 5:1–11. In the early, pre-Gospel tradition of the sayings and stories about Jesus, no firm line was drawn between the life of pre-Easter earthly Jesus and the post-Easter risen Lord, so that the same story might be located either before or after the resurrection by different teachers, preachers, and evangelists. Luke has apparently told the story within the pre-Easter narrative framework; the Johannine tradition takes it as an Easter story. Even the stories of Jesus' earthly ministry were seen in the light of the resurrection faith (see on Luke 5:1–11).

21:4 Did not know that it was Jesus: Recognizing the presence of the Risen One was not merely a matter of objective "seeing" (see on Luke 24:15–16; John 20:15).

21:5 Children: As in the Farewell Discourses, Jesus addresses his disciples in the vocabulary that had become typical of the later Johannine community (see 13:33; 1 John 2:1, 12, 14, 18, etc.).

21:7–8 It is the Lord: Peter is again first on the scene (see 20:3–8), but again the Beloved Disciple is the first to have insight into what really happened.

21:9 A charcoal fire: With this deft literary touch, the reader is immediately reminded of the scene in which Peter denied Jesus three times (18:18), and the stage is set for the following exchange between Jesus and Peter. **Fish . . . bread:** Likewise, the present story evokes the scene in which Jesus fed the multitudes and then declared that he himself is the bread of life (6:9).

21:11 A hundred fifty-three: A special "triangular" number, the total of all the numbers in the series 1–17. Such numbers had a quasi-mystical symbolism in some ancient philosophies such as Pythagorianism, but if the number was symbolic to John, its significance has been lost. In any case, the underlying symbolism is clear: the disciples, who have been called to be "fishers for people" (Mark 1:16–20; Luke 5:1–11), now draw in a large number of all kinds of "fish" in a net that is still unbroken. Here is an expression of the inclusiveness of the Johannine church that includes Jew and Gentile, slave and free, male and female, and a plurality of Christian traditions. John is about to emphasize that the one church has room for both the Petrine and the Johannine understandings of church leadership. **Hauled** (NIV **dragged**) is the same word used in 6:44 and 12:32 of God and Christ's drawing people to faith and salvation; that mission is here implemented by the disciples, led by Peter.

21:14 The third time: See 20:19, 26. The enumeration does not count 20:11–18; evidently Mary Magdalene is not here counted as a disciple, here used as the equivalent of apostle, differently from the way it is used in the body of the Gospel. In the trend toward the early catholic church's understanding of apostolic leadership represented by this stratum of the Gospel, the church appears to be losing some of the charismatic emphasis on egalitarian leadership by both men and women that had prevailed in the earlier Johannine community. This is analogous to the development between first-generation Pauline Christianity and the Pauline Christianity represented by the Pastoral Letters (see on 1 Tim. 2:11–14; 3:1–13).

21:15 Do you love me? . . . You know that I love you: As Peter had denied Jesus three times (18:15–27), here around another charcoal fire he reaffirms his love for Jesus three times. There is no particular significance in the fact that different Greek words for "love" are used by Jesus and Peter in the first two exchanges (see on 1 Cor. 13:4–7). The words are synonyms, used interchangeably by John, as are the words for feed/tend and sheep/lambs in the same context. **More than these:** The Greek can mean "more than you love these things" (boat, fishing business, your former life), but more likely in this context it means "more than these other disciples love me" (as Peter had claimed in Mark 14:29; Matt. 26:33; but not specifically in John; see 13:37).

21:16 Tend my sheep: Love for Jesus is expressed in care for his flock. Peter is here three times commissioned to shepherd the flock of God. Petrine leadership of the whole church as a symbol for its apostolicity and unity was becoming dominant in some streams of Christianity in John's time (see Matt. 16:16–18; introduction to 1 Peter). John's own commu-

nity, which had revered the Beloved Disciple as its leader and guarantor of its tradition, is here incorporated into the developing universal church that respects Petrine leadership.

21:18 You will stretch out your hands: An apparent reference to death by crucifixion. By the time the Fourth Gospel was written, Peter had died a martyr's death in Rome, according to reliable tradition crucified upside down in Nero's arena, at the site where the basilica named for him was later built.

21:19 Follow me: This terse command echoes the language of Jesus' initial call to discipleship found in all four Gospels (Matt. 8:22; 9:9; 16:24; 19:21, 28; Mark 2:14; 8:34; 10:21; Luke 5:27; 9:23, 59; 18:22; John 1:43; 10:27). The good news for every reader who has responded to this call but has betrayed or denied Jesus is that the risen Christ repeatedly restores his disciples and renews their commission to serve him.

21:20 The disciple whom Jesus loved following: The author again subtly contrasts Peter with the Beloved Disciple. Though Peter must be restored and called to follow, the Beloved Disciple has never denied but has always been following. He was present when Peter denied Jesus but remained faithful (18:15–27). He was the only male disciple present at the cross, when the others had fled (19:25–27).

21:22 Until I come: Unlike the body of the Gospel, the epilogue reemphasizes the traditional future eschatology (see on 5:28–29; 11:25–26; 14:22–24; 17:3).

21:23 The rumors . . . that this disciple would not die: The first generation of Christians expected the return of Jesus in their lifetime (see, e.g., 1 Thess. 4:13–18; 1 Cor. 15:51; Mark 9:1; 13:30). Some in his community had thought that at least the Beloved Disciple would remain until the end, but he had apparently died. The author, who belongs to the second or third generation, explains that the expectation of the first generation had misunderstood the chronology. The early church had to reinterpret its eschatological hopes without abandoning them. John 21 represents *one* of the theological possibilities of dealing with the delayed Parousia (see excursus at Rev. 1:3, "Interpreting the 'Near End'").

21:24 This is the disciple who is testifying these things: In Greek, "testify" comes from the same root as "martyr." Peter had become a literal martyr by giving his life in the Neronian persecution. The Beloved Disciple had lived to a ripe old age, but nonetheless had been a martyr-witness in a different sense—not by dying a martyr's death but by living his life as a witness of the authentic tradition of the meaning of Jesus' life, death, and resurrection (see 19:35). This the readers of the Gospel, then and now, can also do (see on Luke 9:23). **And has written them:** This may refer to direct authorship or, as in 19:1, 19, to causing something to be written and standing behind it as the legitimizing authority. In this latest layer of the Gospel, the reader hears the testimony of the Johannine school that the Beloved Disciple is the legitimate authority that stands behind the Gospel, or was himself its author. In still later church tradition, the claim to authorship was understood literally, and the Beloved Disciple was identified both with the

John of Rev. 1:9 and John the son of Zebedee (Mark 1:19, etc.; see John 21:2). The Beloved Disciple did not die a martyr's death, but in his long life he became the mediator of the word of the living Christ that continues to call the church into being and send it forth on its mission.

21:25 The world itself could not contain the books: While this is a conventional exaggeration found at the end of other heroic tales in antiquity (e.g., 1 Macc. 9:22), it here indicates in this latest layer of Johannine tradition that the community is aware of a number of books (only later called Gospels) containing Jesus' life and teaching. See comments on Luke 1:1–4, and "Introduction: The New Testament as the Church's Book," 4.d.

The Acts of the Apostles

INTRODUCTION

The Book of Acts, volume two of a two-part narrative, tells the Christian story from the ascension of Jesus through the beginning of the church and its expansion from Jerusalem, the center of the Jewish faith, to Rome, the capital of the Gentile world. The story is a continuation of volume one, the Gospel of Luke, which tells the story from the birth of John the Baptist and Jesus to the death, resurrection, and ascension of Jesus. In the narrative as a whole, the reader follows the progress of the story from the angel's announcements to a priest in Jerusalem and to a peasant girl in Galilee (Luke 1–2) to the final scene in which the Christian missionary Paul preaches the gospel in the capital city of the world, "with all boldness and without hindrance" (Acts 28:31). For introductory issues to Luke–Acts as a whole, see the introduction to Luke.

In the process of the formation of the New Testament canon, the Gospels were placed together, with the result that Luke and Acts were separated, but a proper understanding of them requires that they be read together. The present location of Acts, however, reflects the church's sense that in the New Testament story as a whole, Acts is the connecting link between the story of Jesus in the Gospels and the letters written by early Christian leaders to church members as instruction for the Christian life. Acts is thus the only New Testament book that portrays the beginning and expansion of the church. Only here does the reader get to see the church at work in evangelism and mission. It continues the work of Jesus and continually rethinks its own self-understanding as it reinterprets what it means to be disciples of Jesus in new times and places. Only here are there narratives of people being converted to the Christian faith, providing models of what people do in order to become Christians.

Title

We do not know what title the author gave his work. The title "The Acts of the Apostles," with several variations such as "Acts of Apostles" or "Acts of the Holy Apostles," was added in the second century when the book was separated from the Gospel and included in the developing New Testament canon. The title is not altogether accurate, since the book focuses on Peter, who was an apostle, and Paul, whom Luke admires but does not consider an apostle (see on 1:12–26; 14:4, 14). A title appropriate to Luke's own understanding might be "The Story of God's Act in Jesus Continues in the Life of the Church."

Genre and Readership

On the importance of genre for understanding a New Testament text, see "Introduction to the Gospels." Luke–Acts is not a private communication written only for "Theophilus," to whom it is dedicated (see on 1:1), but is written for a wider readership. Luke certainly writes for Christian believers to confirm them in their faith and expand their horizons, but also may have a wider, non-Christian public in mind. Acts can be read both as an evangelistic document to witness to the truth of the gospel and as an apologetic document, i.e., a defense of the faith to interested outsiders who might misunderstand the new religious group as a subversive or superstitious and dangerous religious cult.

There is nothing else like Acts in the New Testament. But in Luke's Bible (the Christian Old Testament) there were a number of books that recounted the story of Israel, the people chosen by God to witness to his mighty acts. Luke intentionally continues the biblical tradition of confessing the faith by retelling the story of God's guidance of the chosen people through history. Thus the fact that Acts exists at all is testimony to Luke's conviction that the extended time of the church's mission after Easter, a time that he saw extending for generations (Luke 1:48), is not a parenthesis in God's plan but is the continuing story of the people of God.

Sources

It may be that the author incorporates earlier written narratives about early Christianity, but if so, he has so reworked them according to his own style and perspective that their extent and character can no longer be determined. The author will have had oral traditions from the particular Christian communities that play central roles in his story, such as Jerusalem, Antioch, and Ephesus. Many of these traditions may contain accurate historical memories of what actually happened, but the primary purpose for which they were preserved was not to chronicle history, but to interpret the meaning of the faith. Both Luke's sources and his own narrative belong to the category of theologically interpreted history.

If the "we passages" (see on 16:10) are understood as reflecting the author's own recollections (rather than as incorporating the travel diary of another, or as a literary device to add vividness), then the author's own memory of the part of Paul's missionary work in which he participated would be one of his sources. The author, however, seems to look back on the first generation of Christian history with admiration, not as one who participated in these events himself (see on Luke 1:1–4).

Speeches

About one-third of Acts is composed of speeches. While some of them may contain elements of older traditions, they are not verbatim reports of what was actually said on any given situation, but Lukan compositions that interpret the meaning of the story. This was the common practice of first-century historians, who made no use of footnotes, parentheses, or quotation marks, all of which are modern paraphernalia of a later age interested in investigative reporting. Especially the evangelistic sermons of the early preachers are intended as summaries of the Christian message and models of preaching for Luke's own and later times.

Historical Accuracy

In regard to the question of the historical accuracy of Acts, we are in a situation different from that of the Gospels. The Gospels provide us with four secondary sources narrating some of the same events in the life, death, and resurrection of Jesus a generation or two after the events themselves (see "Introduction to the Gospels" and comments on Luke 1:1–4). Their differences allow us to see that the Gospels are a combination of fact and interpretation, communicating the meaning of the Christ event. In Acts, we have only one account of the beginning and growth of the early church, i.e., we have no parallel account with which to compare it. But, unlike the situation in the Gospels, we have letters from one of the main characters in the story (Paul) that deal with some of the same events, with which we may compare the way the story of Acts itself is told. It is as though we had letters from Jesus or Peter, written during the life of Jesus, with which to compare the Gospel accounts.

Sometimes Paul's letters confirm the historical accuracy of Acts, even in minor details (e.g., Acts 9:23–25 // 2 Cor. 11:33). Such incidental confirmation of the accuracy of events narrated in Acts makes it clear that the narrative is not fiction. At other times, discrepancies between Paul's letters and the Acts account allows us to see that the author of Acts is composing in order to present a theological truth in narrative form, rather than presenting straightforward accurate history (compare the number of Paul's visits to Jerusalem in Gal. 1–2 and Acts 9–15, and the discussion in the comments below at 15:35 on Luke's account of the Jerusalem Council in Acts 15 and Paul's account in Gal. 2).

Sometimes secular historical information confirms the accuracy of Luke's knowledge of first-century Roman history (see, e.g., on 18:12–17), while at other places he seems to be misinformed, confused, or altering history to make a theological point (see on 5:33–39).

The comparison of the Acts narrative both with Paul's letters and with secular historical sources shows that Luke sometimes transmits accurate historical data and sometimes adapts historical reports or composes his own scenes to communicate theological truth in a narrative form. Such scenes as the beginning of the church on Pentecost (Acts 2) are composed, not reported. Even in those places where accurate historical data may be gleaned from Luke's story, this is incidental to Luke's main point, which is the truth of the Christian faith (see on Luke 1:1–4). The factual historical data transmitted in Luke's account shows that the Christian gospel is not a myth but is anchored in the historical act of God; Luke's deviations from factual history show that his point is the meaning of the origin of the church and its continuing mission, not accurate "reporting" of "what actually happened."

Theological Themes

On the themes of Luke–Acts as a whole, see the introduction to Luke. Some distinctive themes of Acts are these:

—*The Holy Spirit in the Life of the Church:* In Acts, the Holy Spirit leads the church into new truth the followers of Jesus had not apprehended during the earthly life of Jesus. Luke attempts to coordinate and somewhat "standardize" the variety of expressions and understandings of the Spirit in early Christianity.

—*The Church in a Non-Christian Culture:* The church to which Luke belonged was a tiny minority in a non-Christian society that already had numerous sophisticated and persuasive religions and philosophies that shaped the lives of most people. When Paul or the other early Christian missionaries came to a new town, they were the first and only Christians there. It was necessary for them to proclaim and explain what the Christian faith was and when people were attracted to it, to explain to them what they should do in order to become Christians. The modern church is different in that it has a long tradition of Christian history behind it, but is also like Luke's situation in that it now lives in an increasingly secular culture where Christian assumptions do not prevail, where the Christian message must be explained and defended, a situation in which if people are to be Christian they must stand against the cultural stream. In all of this, the contemporary church can learn and be encouraged by the story of the church in Acts.

—*How to Become a Christian:* In past generations of a "Christian" culture, many people were baptized as babies or children in a situation in which there were commonly shared assumptions that people should become Christians and how this came about. This is no longer the case for the church in any country in the world. Only Acts provides narratives in which the reader can see people converted to the Christian faith. The numerous conversion stories in Acts (2:1–47; 8:4–25; 8:26–40; 9:1–19 [22:1–16; 26:2–18]; 10:1–48; 16:11–15; 16:25–40; 17:16–33) allow the modern reader to hear what was proclaimed as the Christian message and to observe what people did in response to it when they decided to become Christians. Since many contemporary Christians are embarrassed or at a loss for words when it comes to talking about conversion, Acts can help the modern reader to discern the question, "What must I do to be saved?" (16:30) as an important question in a secular society, and to see the pattern of the biblical responses.

—*The Church as the Continuation of the Plan and Purpose of God:* The earliest Christians expected Jesus to return soon. Luke writes for a church that recognizes this did not happen and is struggling to understand and live out the Christian faith for the long term in a continuing world.

—*The Relation of Christians to the Secular World:* A part of rethinking the meaning of faith is developing a Christian understanding of the relation of Christians to other religious groups and to the secular government.

—*The Unity of the One Church:* The tensions between various understandings in the first-generation group of Jesus' disciples could have resulted in Jesus' followers of the second and third generations settling for a divided church. Luke shows how the church's developing insight incorporated different groups and understandings within the one church of God. The "harmonizing" of Peter and Paul manifest in Acts is part of this program.

Outline

For Further Reading

Dunn, J. D. G. *The Acts of the Apostles.* Valley Forge, PA: Trinity, 1996.

Johnson, Luke Timothy. *The Acts of the Apostles.* Sacra Pagina 5. Collegeville, MN: The Liturgical Press, 1992.

COMMENTARY

1:1–26
THE EARLIEST DISCIPLES
CHARGED TO BE WITNESSES

1:1–11
THE ASCENSION OF JESUS

1:1 The first book: The Gospel of Luke. Here Luke takes up the story of the Gospel and briefly recapitulates its ending. **Theophilus:** Common Greek name, "lover of God." The two volumes are dedicated to him. He may have been the author's patron or sponsor. See on Luke 1:1.

1:2 Until the day when he was taken up to heaven: Unlike Paul and other New Testament writers, Luke thinks of the ascension as an event distinct from the resurrection. Luke recounted the ascension at the end of the Gospel, where it is pictured as taking place on Easter Sunday evening. See comments at Luke 24:44. These two reports of the ascension can be understood in two ways: (1) In Luke's view Jesus was translated to "glory" at the resurrection, and he makes all his appearances, including the Easter appearances, from heaven, "ascending" after each earthly appearance (see Luke 24:26). In this view, Jesus does not stay on earth after the resurrection until the ascension, but appears a number of times to his disciples during the forty-day period, at the close of which the account in 1:9–11 is the last and definitive such appearance. (2) Alternatively, Luke understood Jesus' exaltation to heaven as a two-stage process, resurrection to live forty days on this earth, followed by ascension to heaven, where he remains until the Parousia. The latter view is the more likely, since it fits Luke's theology elsewhere. However, the two reports that locate the ascension on two different days show that Luke did not think of the ascension as an event that can be objectively dated, but as a way of expressing God's act for Jesus after his death. God not only restored him to life and overcame death, but exalted him to be Lord of all (Phil. 2:5–11). For Luke, Jesus is not only an example in the past to believers look back—though he is that—but is the enthroned Son of Man who will come again as judge.

1:2 The apostles whom he had chosen: See on Luke 6:12–13. **Through the Holy Spirit:** The disciples have not yet received the Spirit (1:5; 2:1–21), but the presence of the risen Jesus is the presence of the Holy Spirit. The Spirit is very important in Luke's understanding of the life and mission of the church (57x in Acts), but he is also aware of the danger of unbridled spiritual enthusiasm or fanaticism, so that in his first sentence he links the Holy Spirit to the life and work of Jesus (see on 1 Cor. 12:1–3).

1:3 Presented himself alive: See Luke 24:1–49. The disciples were convinced of the reality of the resurrection by their encounters with the risen Christ. **By many convincing proofs:** See on 9:22.

Speaking about the kingdom of God: The central theme of Jesus' message and Luke's theology. See on Luke 4:43. In the early years of the church, as the disciples of Jesus grew in their understanding of the faith under the guidance of the Holy Spirit, they came to a deeper understanding of the meaning of God's kingdom that had been revealed in Christ. Luke pictures this as happening in one paradigmatic scene, a forty-day seminar on the kingdom taught by the risen Christ (see his picture of the risen Christ reinterpreting the Scripture to his disciples, Luke 24:27, 45).

1:4 While he was eating with them (NIV): The Greek expression can mean either "staying with" (so NRSV) or "eating with" (literally, "sharing the salt"). The NIV is better here; mealtime scenes played a prominent role in the Gospel of Luke (5:29–39; 7:36–50; 11:37–54; 14:1–24; 22:14–38; 24:30–32; 24:36–49), and the risen Jesus made himself known to his disciples during their common meals (Luke 24:35). The translation "staying with" forces such wrong questions as whether the risen Jesus slept and, if so, where. Despite Luke's objectifying of the spiritual reality of the resurrection, he does not entertain such questions and does not wish to evoke them in his readers. **He ordered them not to leave Jerusalem:** See Luke 24:6, 49. In Luke, there are no appearances of the risen Jesus in Galilee, and no room for them in the narrative. The gospel has progressed from Galilee to Jerusalem and will proceed from Jerusalem to Rome. This progression is important to Luke theologically as symbolic of the universal growth of the church that begins in the Jewish capital (2:1–42) and is finally proclaimed in the Roman capital (28:30–31).

1:5 You will be baptized with [or in] the Holy Spirit: See on Luke 3:16–17; 1 Cor. 12:13. For Luke, the promise is fulfilled in the Pentecostal events he narrates in 2:1–21; see also 10:44–48; 11:15–18; 19:1–7.

1:6 Is this the time when you will restore the kingdom to Israel?: Despite their forty days of instruction, they still misunderstand both the nature of the kingdom and its chronology. They still suppose it means the restoration of Israel's sovereignty, i.e., driving out or destroying the Romans. Luke repeatedly points out the futility of asking when the kingdom or the end will come (see Luke 12:35–48; 17:22–23; 19:11; 20:9; 21:8–9). Jesus replies that only God knows the time of the coming of the kingdom. Instead of answers for their futile eschatological speculation, the disciples are given a job to do.

1:8 You will receive power when the Holy Spirit has come upon you: The church's mission is history is not carried out in its own strength. The church is not merely a group of good people trying hard to make the world a better place. The church functions by the presence and power of God. **You will be my witnesses:** Sums up one of the major themes of Acts. "Witness," like "disciple" and "Christian," is an important word to Luke for designating a follower of Jesus (Acts 1:8, 22; 2:32; 3:15; 5:32; 10:39, 41; 22:15; 23:11). Though eyewitnesses of Jesus' ministry are important in Luke's understanding (see Luke 1:1–4), **witnesses** here refers to the whole group of Jesus' followers, including those who later became disciples without having been eyewitnesses of Jesus' ministry (e.g., Paul, Acts 22:15). They are called to bear witness not to their internal spiritual experiences or to anecdotes in their own biography, but to the mighty acts of God in history, culminating in the Christ event (see Acts 1:11). Christians are not only to follow Jesus in the way they live their lives, by adopting his priorities and continuing to serve others as he did; they are also called to declare verbally why it is that they live that way (see Luke 12:8–9). For Luke, there can be no merely private, individualistic followers of Christ.

Jerusalem . . . Judea . . . Samaria . . . the ends of the earth: This is the outline of the story to be told in Acts. It represents not only a numerical and geographical expansion of the church, but a widening of its theological perspectives as it grows into its true being and mission. The church inherits the charge to Israel in Isa. 49:6, where the Servant of God is charged to be God's witness to the nations to the ends of the earth. These words commissioning Jesus' followers reorient their perspective, from looking *up* expecting the Parousia to looking *out* into the world and their mission in it.

1:9 He was lifted up: By God. Just as Jesus did not "rise" but "was raised" (see on Matt. 28:1), so he did not "ascend," but was exalted by God. Here Luke portrays a spiritual reality in objective terms. Like his objectifying the resurrection, this description is a testimony to the reality of the event of God's having exalted Jesus to be Lord, not a report in photographic terms. Here and elsewhere (e.g., in narrating the transfiguration and the resurrection), Luke portrays the events in objective language. This is analogous to modern portrayals of atoms as a nucleus of small, colored balls orbited by electrons pictured as other balls of various colors. Likewise, the phenomenon of light is sometimes pictured as tiny particles that bounce off objects and into our eyes, or as waves in the ether. Electricity is portrayed as a current of electrons flowing through a wire. Such models are necessary for us to think and talk about these phenomena at all, but no one believes that the reality they represent is actually composed of waves, particles, or colored balls. So also the biblical authors' portrayals of transcendent events in objectifying language is neither to be taken as a literal description nor to be dismissed as mere subjective fantasy. Luke's objectifying language cannot be understood literally, but it points to something real, just as do the models of atoms. Such objectifying language is sometimes called myth by theologians, by which they do not mean that it is untrue, but that a transcendent reality is represented in this-worldly pictures and language. Such language says what it has to say in a mode that does not allow us to make inferences from it; it makes its own "point," but we cannot deduce other "points" from it (see on "confessional language" at Matt. 2:16). **A cloud received him:** Not meteorology, but the biblical symbolism of the cloud as the presence and power of God (see, e.g., Exod. 13:21; 19:16; 40:34; Ps. 68:4; Ezek. 1:4; Dan. 7:13).

1:10 Two men in white robes: See on Luke 24:4, 23. The heavenly messengers declare that Christ will return. Luke has made it clear that the church's job is not to be concerned with how soon the Parousia might be, but to be engaged in the mission that continues Jesus' life and work. First, they must receive the power of the Spirit.

1:12–26
MATTHIAS CHOSEN TO REPLACE JUDAS

1:12 The Mount of Olives: See Luke 19:29; 22:39; 24:50. **Sabbath day's journey:** A little over half a mile, so called because this is the maximum distance observant Jews could travel on the Sabbath without it being considered work. The rule is not found in the Old Testament, but later rabbis derived it from Exod. 16:29 and 20:8–11; deriving the two thousand cubits from Num. 35:5.

1:13–14 The room upstairs: See Luke 22:12. In Luke 24:53 the disciples return to the temple. **Peter . . . Judas son of James:** The names of the twelve apostles (minus Judas) are given again (see Luke 6:12–16), establishing continuity between the post-Easter church and the group of Jesus' pre-Easter disciples. **Together with certain women:** See Luke 8:2–3; 23:49, 55–56; 24:1–9. **Mary the mother of Jesus:** Luke deals more extensively with Mary than does any other New Testament author (Luke 1:27–56; 2:1–52), but Mary disappears from the story in Acts after this reference. **His brothers:** They are not named here or in Luke 4:22 or 8:19–21 (see Mark 6:3). James will emerge in 12:17 as a leader of the church in Jerusalem (see 15:13; 21:18), but Luke never designates him the brother of Jesus.

1:15 Peter stood up among the believers: Peter fulfills the role Jesus had promised (Luke 22:31–32), that he would be the one to reconstitute the apostolic group after the death and resurrection of Jesus. **About one hundred twenty persons:** The original Christian community in Jerusalem, led by the apostles (see on Luke 6:12–13). Nothing is said in Acts as to what happened to the other followers of Jesus in Galilee (though see 9:31). The Twelve are Galileans (2:7); it is not clear whether the 120 are from Galilee and, if so, whether they have moved to Jerusalem or are there only temporarily. Luke is writing schematically about the progress of the church from Galilee to Jerusalem and ultimately to Rome.

1:16–17 The scripture had to be fulfilled: This was an early Christian theological way of affirming that the difficult events they had experienced nevertheless somehow belonged within the will of God. The crucifixion itself was the most severe such problem. Since the Scriptures revealed the will of God, they were searched to find texts that could be seen as illustrating the events of the passion story. Once this had been done, texts were also found that illuminated Judas's role in the suffering and death of Jesus (see on Luke 21:22; 24:25; and excursus, "New Testament Interpretation of the Old Testament," at 1 Cor. 15:3).

1:18 Acquired a field: Luke has repeatedly pictured Jesus as warning against the dangers of acquiring property (Luke 1:52–53; 6:20–26; 12:13–21; 16:19–31; 18:22–25, 28) and will picture his true disciples as selling property to help the poor (4:32–37). In all of Luke–Acts, the only disciple who *buys* property is Judas. **All his bowels gushed out:** This account of Judas's horrible death is not to be combined with the different story in Matt. 27:3–10. Other early Christian legends give even more gruesome accounts. The point of all of them is the same: how terrible it is to resist God's will (see 12:23 on the death of Herod).

1:19 Their language: Here Luke has Peter speak as though Aramaic was not his own language and that of his hearers in the story, i.e., Peter speaks directly to Luke's Greek-speaking readers. This is one of several indications that the speeches in Acts are not verbatim reports but Lukan compositions to communicate the meaning of the events to the reader (see introduction to Acts). **The Field of Blood:** So called because it was defiled by Judas's own blood (see the different explanation in Matt. 27:8). The location is unknown. The site shown to tourists today was first identified in the fourth century.

1:20 Let another take his position: The necessity to replace Judas is found in a Christian interpretation of Scripture. The two citations are modified versions of Ps. 69:25 and Ps. 109:8. Ps. 69 (like Pss. 22 and 110) was cited frequently by New Testament authors as pointing to Christ and the church (Matt. 27:34, 48; Mark 3:21; 15:23, 36; Luke 13:35; 23:36; John 2:17; 15:25; 19:28; Rom. 11:9–10; 15:3; Phil. 4:3; Heb. 11:26; Rev. 3:5; 16:1). **Overseer:** The same word was used later for the office of bishop.

1:21–22 Beginning from the baptism of John: See Luke 3:1–21; 16:16; Acts 10:37. In Luke's time at the end of the first century, several versions of Christianity contended with each other as representatives of the authentic faith. In Luke's understanding, the validity of the faith is guaranteed by connecting it with those who were eyewitnesses of Jesus' ministry from the very beginning. Luke's stream of tradition will eventually become the mainstream, but this was not apparent in his own time. It is to be noted that by the criteria given here, Paul does not qualify as an apostle. Though Luke admires Paul as a great missionary of the founding generation of the church, he does not consider him an apostle (see on 14:4, 14). On apostles, see on Luke 6:12–13.

1:23 Joseph called Barsabbas . . . and Matthias: Nothing more is known of either; they do not reappear in the story. It is important for Luke that the Twelve be reconstituted, since in his understanding of the church the apostles, though originally from Galilee, continue to reside in Jerusalem, where they formed a kind of governing board for the church as a whole as it expanded and adapted to new situations (see 6:1–7; 8:1, 14–17; 9:26–29; 11:1, 19–24; 15:1–2). As the church expanded numerically and geographically, crossing national and cultural boundaries, it was not necessary that the church remain the same, but it was important that authorized representatives of the original faith guide and approve the new developments. This is the meaning of the "apostolic faith" for Luke, and why it is important to have authentic apostles as the church's leaders.

1:24–26 They cast lots: See Exod. 28:30; Lev. 27:21; 1 Sam 14:41; Prov. 16:33. This was understood as the way God chose Judas's successor. Though the church participated by praying, it was not a democratic process. Just as the original Twelve had not volunteered or been elected, but had been called by Jesus (Luke 5:1–11; see John 15:16), so the risen Lord chose Judas's successor. The church, its mission, and its leadership are not matters of human efforts to do good, but of divine initiative.

2:1–8:3
THE CHURCH WITNESSES IN JERUSALEM

2:1–13
The Coming of the Holy Spirit

The New Testament writers in general affirm that after the death of Jesus his followers were united, guided, and empowered by the experience of the risen Christ, who empowered them by the Holy Spirit to carry on his work. All agree that the church began not by human initiative, but in the conviction that the presence and power of God (= the risen Christ, the Holy Spirit) generated the renewed Christian community. The New Testament authors have different ways of conceptualizing and expressing this. The Gospel of John, for instance, does not have a separate Pentecost scene but pictures Jesus as giving the Spirit to his followers on the first Easter day by breathing on them (see on John 20:22; the Greek words for "breathe" and "spirit" are related). Luke portrays the coming of the Spirit in a separate scene, just as he had pictured the ascension as an event distinct from the resurrection (see on 1:2 and Luke 24:44–53). In the story of Pentecost, Luke sums up a gradual process in one paradigmatic scene (see on Luke 24:27).

2:1 The day of Pentecost: The Jewish festival called the Feast of Weeks in the Old Testament (Exod. 23:14–17; 34:18–24; Deut. 16:16). Originally an agricultural festival celebrated seven weeks after the beginning of the grain harvest (Deut. 16:9), in later Judaism it was celebrated fifty days after Passover ("Pentecost" means "fiftieth"). The agricultural associations faded away, and the festival was increasingly related to Israel's sacred history. As Passover was the celebration of the exodus from Egypt, Pentecost became the celebration of the giving of the Law on Mount Sinai, and its annual observance pointed to the renewal of the covenant. While Luke does not make these connections explicit, his language seems to reflect that the church began with the coming of the Holy Spirit on the day associated with God's giving the Law and making the covenant with Israel (Exod. 19–23).

They were all together: Whether Luke intends the Twelve or the 120 is not clear, but the later story focuses on the twelve apostles (2:14).

2:2–3 A sound like the rush of a violent wind . . . tongues, as of fire: Although the coming of the Spirit on Jesus' disciples was and is an experience that defies objective description, and can be interpreted by observers in more than one way (see on 2:12–13), Luke pictures it in objective, observable terms (see on 1:9 above). Wind and fire represent the presence and power of God (see Exod. 3:2; 14:20, 24; 19:16–25; 1 Kgs. 19:11–12; Ps. 104:4).

2:4 Filled with the Holy Spirit: A common biblical expression for being empowered by God, used of Old Testament artisans, prophets, Jesus, and Christians (Exod. 31:3; 35:31; Ezek. 43:5; Mic. 3:8; Luke 1:15, 41, 67; 4:14; Acts 2:4; 4:8, 31; 7:55; 9:17; 13:9, 52; Rom. 15:13; Eph. 5:18). Luke also calls this the baptism of (in/with) the Holy Spirit (1:5) and the gift(s) of the Spirit (2:38; 8:15–17; 10:45–47; 11:16–17). The Spirit sometimes empowers Christians to minister in extraordinary ways, as in this scene, but is not limited to the spectacular (see on 1 Cor. 12). Luke pictures a variety of manifestations of the Spirit in the life and work of the church but does not have a systematic doctrine of the Spirit (see on 8:15–17).

Began to speak in other languages: Speaking in tongues was a common and valued experience in some streams of early Christianity, especially in the Pauline churches. It was the expression of a deep religious experience that could not be expressed in ordinary human language and was thus considered by some to be the "language of angels" (see 1 Cor. 12:10, 28, 30; 13:1; 14:2, 4–6, 9; Acts 10:45–46; 19:6). It occurs in other religions besides Christianity and seems to be a universal phenomenon of religious experience that, wherever there is deep religious feeling, some members of the community give expression to this feeling in ecstatic speech.

Only here in the New Testament is the phenomenon understood as the ability to speak (and hear) in actual human languages that one has not learned. (Elsewhere in Acts, Luke pictures "speaking in tongues" in the Pauline sense, as ecstatic speech, inspired but unintelligible; see 10:45–46; 19:6.) Luke constructs this model scene in Acts 2 to represent the church as a community that, though it began as a Jewish sect, will become a universal, inclusive community transcending languages and cultures. His reinterpretation of the gift of tongues as the ability to speak foreign languages serves his view of the nature of the church. At the tower of Babel, God's judgment on human sin was to confuse people's language so that they could no longer understand each other (Gen. 11:1–9). Just as the primal human sin of arrogance had not only separated humans from God but alienated them from each other, so the reconciling act of God in Christ and the beginning of the Christian community was the reversal of this judgment, the founding of a community that transcended race, language, and culture. Luke pictures the church as the undoing of Babel. The story in the rest of Acts will show that this did not happen all at once, that the church had to grow into its true identity. But Luke's opening scene of the church's life presents a picture of what the church ideally is and is to be.

2:5 Jews from every nation under heaven: The church began as a distinct group within Judaism, "the sect everywhere spoken against" (28:22). Jesus, the apostles, and all the earliest Christians were Jews. What separated Christians from other Jews was their faith that Jesus was the Messiah. Yet Luke knows that the church is destined to become a universal community and in his model opening scene pictures the church in as international a manner as possible within the historical constraints of its actual beginnings within Judaism. Thus "every nation under heaven" is not literally true, but neither is it mere hyperbole—it is Luke's symbolic way of picturing the church

at its beginnings as already containing the seeds of what it was to become.

2:9–11 Parthians . . . Arabs: The list of fifteen nations is symbolic of the whole world. It reflects ancient lists of nations such as Gen. 10:1–32 (which immediately precedes the tower of Babel story!) and thus omits many actual nations known to Luke, such as Greece and Macedonia. The list transcends the Roman Empire, including Parthians on the eastern border, its constant enemy and threat. Jews and Arabs are both embraced in the vision of the universal church. **Jews and proselytes:** Those born into Jewish families, and those who had converted to Judaism from a Gentile religion. Thus, though all are Jews, an ethnic and racial diversity is represented in the church at the very beginning. **Visitors from Rome:** Luke's story will conclude with the arrival of Paul in Rome and his preaching there (27:1–28:31), but Romans were present at the beginning of the church.

2:11 God's deeds of power: A biblical expression for the mighty acts of God (Deut. 3:24; 11:2; Pss. 71:18–20; 105:1–2; 145:4; Sir. 36:7; 42:21), referring to God's acts in creating the world, delivering Israel from Egypt and making a covenant with them, guiding and delivering them through history. For Luke, this series of God's mighty acts reaches its climax in the coming of Christ, his life, death, and resurrection, as well as the coming of the Holy Spirit to create the church. The first Christian preachers did not merely discuss general principles of ethics, personal piety, and social justice, but announced the good news of God's acts in history. The church is founded not on good advice, but on the good news of God's act, that something has happened that makes all the difference.

2:12–13 Amazed and perplexed. . . . They are filled with new wine: The miraculous phenomena themselves do not generate faith but confusion (see on Luke 24:4, 37). The events themselves are ambiguous and subject to more than one interpretation. One can be in the presence of the Spirit's activity and regard the participants as merely drunk (see Eph. 5:18), just as one could stand at the Red Sea and see only a fortunate wind rather than an act of God (Exod. 14–15). God's acts are never so obvious that they cannot be understood as natural or even demonic events (see Luke 11:14–23). They require the interpreting word that first calls for a decision. This follows immediately in Luke's presentation of the first Christian sermon.

2:14–36
PETER ADDRESSES THE CROWD

On the speeches in Acts, see the introduction to Acts. Peter becomes the spokesperson for the apostolic faith (see Luke 22:31–32) and delivers the first Christian sermon. It is missionary and evangelistic, i.e., it proclaims the central elements of the Christian faith to people who are not Christians, calling them to repentance and faith. In the modern world, most sermons preached in churches are not evangelistic but address those who already profess faith. In an increasingly secular world, the church can learn from the sermons in Acts the nature of evangelistic preaching, which does not presuppose faith but generates it. In this first instance, we see that such preaching is not a discussion of general moral principles or "inspirational" encouragement to live a better life, but a proclamation of what God has done in Jesus (see above on 2:11).

2:14–15 Men of Judea: There is no indication in the text that only men were present (see 2:17). **These are not drunk:** Peter's sermon begins where the hearers are, with their objection. **Nine o'clock in the morning:** While it is not impossible to be drunk so early in the day, drunkenness cannot be the real explanation for the pentecostal phenomena.

2:16 This is what was spoken through the prophet Joel: See Joel 2:28–32. Joel had predicted the coming of the Holy Spirit in the last days, i.e., as part of the eschatological events of the "day of the Lord." In first-century Judaism, many Jews believed that the Spirit of God had been active in previous generations, "biblical times," but was no longer present and would return only at the eschaton. Thus the Christian claim that the Holy Spirit was again present, like the claim that Jesus was the Messiah, was heard as a blasphemous claim that the fulfillment of history had come (see on Luke 11:14–23). The earliest Christian view was that they were living in the final generation of history and that the presence of the Spirit was testimony that they were living in the last days (see introduction to Luke: "Jesus as the 'Midst of Time'"; comments on Luke 1:13–17; 21:5–36). On the New Testament's understanding of the Old Testament as pointing to Christ and Christians, see excursus, "New Testament Interpretation of the Old Testament," at 1 Cor. 15:3. Peter is pictured as here quoting a modified

version of the Greek translation of the Old Testament (the LXX, the Septuagint), which would not have been the Bible used by the Aramaic-speaking Peter in Jerusalem but was the Bible of the Gentile church in Luke's own day.

2:17 In the last days: Some manuscripts read "after this," which may be the original reading. Luke does not understand the coming of the Holy Spirit to signal the near eschaton but the beginning of the new age, the final period of history that will extend for some time, the time of the church's mission to all nations. See 3:24, where Luke understands "all the prophets" to "predict these days," i.e., not only the time of Jesus but the days of the church. **All flesh:** This is a biblical expression for "everyone." In the Old Testament, the Spirit had been reserved for prophets and special religious leaders; now it is given to the whole community of God's people, including men and women, old and young, slave and free (see Gal. 3:27–28). **Shall prophesy:** Not predict the future but speak by the power of the Holy Spirit.

2:19–21 Portents . . . and signs: The cosmic signs Joel had predicted for the end of history are not literally a part of the Pentecostal events that Luke sees as the fulfillment of Joel's prophecy. It is not clear whether Luke historicizes the imagery, as he has done with other eschatological prophecies (see on Luke 21:20), or whether he includes this reference to cosmic signs only because he wanted to extend the quotation to v. 21, which affirms that **everyone who calls on the name of the Lord shall be saved**. The affirmation that God's grace is for everyone is central to Luke's theology. See Luke 3:4–6, where Luke also extended the traditional quotation to the point where "all flesh shall see the salvation of God." On Jesus as Lord, see 2:36. On being saved, see on 16:30.

2:22 Jesus of Nazareth, a man: Luke's understanding of Jesus does not include the incarnation of the preexistent Son, as in Paul (Phil. 2:5–11) and John (1:1–18), but begins with the man Jesus. See "this man" of v. 23, and 1 Tim. 2:5–6, which expresses a similar Christology. **Attested to you by God:** This is Peter's summary of the ministry of Jesus that the reader knows from the Gospel of Luke—but of which Peter's hearers in the story would be unaware. The deeds of Jesus point to God; on the theocentric character of Luke's Christology, see on Luke 7:16; 8:24, 38; 9:20–22, 43; 13:13; 17:15;

19:37. While the reader knows the life and teachings of Jesus from the Gospel, the early Christian preachers in Acts are not portrayed as telling of Jesus' life, but of God's act in his death and resurrection.

2:23 You crucified: By turning Jesus over to the Romans, **those outside the** (Jewish) **law**. While Luke has previously distinguished between (some of) the Jewish leaders as responsible for Jesus' death and the people as a whole (see Luke 19:39, 47; 23:23, 35, 51; 24:20), here he charges the people assembled from all nations with crucifying Jesus. Even though historically only a few people were responsible for the crucifixion, Luke understands it theologically as the guilt of humanity as a whole that led to Jesus' death (see reflections on Luke 23:23; Acts 3:13). **According to the definite plan and foreknowledge of God**: Without explanation, Luke again affirms both that humans have responsibility for Jesus' death and that it was a part of God's plan. Luke has no specific doctrine of the atonement—neither here nor elsewhere does he picture the early Christian preachers proclaiming that Christ died "for our sins" (see excursus at 1 Cor. 15:3)—but he does not regard Jesus' death as merely a human tragedy. God is sovereign over human history and included Jesus' death within the divine plan.

2:24 God raised him up: This is the central message of the first Christian sermon, the first main subject and verb in its proclamation, and remains at the heart of the Christian faith (see 2:32, 36). The resurrection as God's act vindicates the life of Jesus as the way of life that had been rejected by humanity. God's act in raising Jesus overcomes the human evil of crucifying Jesus, so that humanity's sin is not the last word.

2:25–28 For David says concerning him: Ps. 16:8–11. Though by a variety of composers, the Psalms had been traditionally ascribed to David. Again Luke has Peter cite the LXX and understands the biblical text to point to Christ as its fulfillment (see on 2:16 above). **You will not abandon my soul to Hades**: The first person speech of the author of the psalm is understood as though Jesus himself were speaking (see 1 Pet. 1:11; Heb. 2:12–13). In this undeveloped sense Luke does have a view of the preexistence of Christ (see on 2:22 above). David is pictured as speaking for the (future) Messiah. The original psalm was a thanksgiving for healing. But deliverance from sickness is rightly understood as deliverance from (the

threat of) death. In Luke's day Jewish rabbis had already reinterpreted this text as evidence of the resurrection, but had not applied it to the Messiah. Hades is not hell, but the abode of the dead. **You have made known to me the ways of life**: In the original psalm, the author gives thanks for being restored to life after being deathly sick. Luke understands that in the resurrection of Jesus, God vindicated the kind of life Jesus had lived as the way of life, the way God wants people to live (see 3:15; 5:20; 9:2; 11:18). Luke uses "life" as identical with "salvation" and "entering the kingdom of God" in Luke 18:18–26. The term has an ethical dimension, a particular "way of life." It is by no means obvious to all that the "right way to live" is represented by Jesus' unselfish life, his care for others, his inclusion of everyone as loved by God, his lack of interest in wealth and prestige. Most people then and now consider it a delusion or an unrealistic ideal. In Luke's theology, it is because God raised up Jesus that we know his way is the way of life. In the crucifixion, humanity had said no to that life, but in the resurrection, God had said yes to it.

2:30 Since he was a prophet: The Old Testament never calls David a prophet or portrays him as such, but as we now know from the Dead Sea Scrolls, first-century Judaism considered David to be a prophet and the Psalms to be predictions of the messianic age. See 3:24: David is among "all the prophets" who speak of the Christian age.

2:32 This Jesus: The resurrection vindicated the particular life of Jesus of Nazareth. See 2:28 commentary.

2:33 Having received from the Father the promise of the Holy Spirit: Luke understands that God gave the Holy Spirit to the exalted Jesus, who gave it to the church. Though there is no developed doctrine of the Trinity here or elsewhere in the New Testament, the elements of the church's later expression of the faith in Trinitarian terms are found here (see on Matt. 28:19; 1 Pet. 1:2). Without ceasing to be monotheists, the church found that it could not give full expression to God's definitive revelation without also speaking of Christ and the Holy Spirit.

2:34 Sit at my right hand: Ps. 110:1. The right hand was the place of honor. Luke understands the psalm to point to the exaltation of Jesus to the transcendent realm, where he reigns with God (see Phil. 2:5–11). The early church often referred to Ps. 110:1 to express its

Christology (Matt. 22:44; 26:64; Mark 12:36; 14:62; Luke 20:42–43; 22:69; Acts 2:34–35; 5:30; Rom. 8:34; 1 Cor. 15:25; Eph. 1:20; Col. 3:1; Heb. 1:3, 13; 8:1; 10:12).

2:36 God has made him both Lord and Messiah: The summary and climax of the sermon. **Lord:** The title used for God in the Old Testament, the title for various Hellenistic gods (see 1 Cor. 8:5), and the title used for the divinized Caesars in the Roman world. It thus represented the highest authority in every realm of Luke's world (see Phil. 2:9–11, "the name that is above every name"). **Messiah:** Christ, the anointed one, the one chosen and commissioned by God to establish justice and represent God's rule in the coming kingdom of God. See on Mark 8:29.

2:37–47
THE FIRST CONVERTS

2:37 Were cut to the heart: They were not previously burdened with guilt, but had a clear conscience (see 23:1). Their awareness of guilt was an effect of hearing the gospel proclaimed. Even though they were not personally involved in the death of Jesus, they acknowledged their guilt (see on 2:23). Luke here presents it as a unanimous response, though see v. 41; 17:32–34. The proclamation of the word calls for a decision that separates those who respond from those who do not. **What shall we do?:** God's saving act calls for human response. The followers of Jesus are called to declare clearly what this response should be. See 16:30; 22:10. Luke will contrast the response given here to Luke 3:10–14, where John the Baptist gives the pre-Christian answer.

2:38 Repent: The evangelistic message concludes with a call to conversion. On repentance, see on Luke 3:2–3, 7–9. Christians in common with Judaism affirm the necessity of repentance. **Be baptized:** Symbolic immersion in water as a means of God's grace and incorporation into the Christian community. For these first converts, baptism was not a traditional formality but a radical break with the values and presuppositions of their culture. Throughout Acts, those who come to faith in Christ are baptized as part of their conversion (2:41; 8:12–13, 36–38; 9:18; 10:37, 48; 11:16; 13:24; 16:15, 33; 18:8, 25; 19:3, 5; 22:16). Elsewhere, the New Testament writers assume that all Christians have been baptized (Rom. 6:1–4; Eph. 4:5). John the Baptist had already introduced baptism as the symbol of a new beginning required of all (Luke 3:1–3), but

Christian baptism now goes beyond John's (Luke 3:16; Acts 1:4–5; 18:24–19:7). **In the name of Jesus:** See 2:21, 38; 3:6; 4:7, 10, 12, 17, 18, 30; 5:28, 40, 41; 8:12, 16; 9:14, 16, 21, 28; 10:43, 48; 15:14, 17, 26; 16:18; 19:5, 13, 17; 21:13; 22:16; 26:9). In biblical theology, "name" is more than a label and represents the authority and reality of the person himself or herself. This is not merely a reference to the formula pronounced at the time of baptism, but means that the rite is administered by the authority of the risen Lord. For the Trinitarian formula, see Matt. 28:19. **So that your sins may be forgiven:** The human problem is pictured as rebellion against and alienation from God. Salvation is to have this alienation removed and to have one's sins forgiven. **The gift of the Holy Spirit:** See on 1 Cor. 12:1–31. Empowerment by the Holy Spirit is no longer only for special religious leaders such as prophets, as in the Old Testament, but is granted to everyone who turns to God (2:17–18). The Spirit is not an individualistic gift, but is given to the whole community of faith. The church throughout Acts will carry out its mission in the power of the Spirit.

2:39 The promise is for . . . everyone: Although in the story line of Acts only Jews were included in the beginning of the church, the message already anticipates the universal church that spans the generations and the nations.

2:40 Save yourselves: Luke, like Paul (Rom. 3:24; 4:16; see Eph. 2:8), presents salvation as the gift of God's grace (Acts 15:11), but human response is necessary. Paul can also combine the challenge to work out one's own salvation with the declaration that God is the one who accomplishes it (Phil. 2:12–13).

2:41 Those who welcomed his message were baptized: The proclamation of the gospel calls for a decision and creates a division. Everyone responds, but not everyone responds positively (see 17:32–34 for the spectrum of responses). The church is composed of those who come to faith as a response to hearing the Christian message. Faith is not an innate disposition or self-generated quality, but a response to the preached word (Rom. 10:14–17). This is a challenge to the church to continue the kind of evangelistic preaching, in word and deed, formally and informally, that calls forth the response of faith. **About three thousand persons were added:** By God (v. 47). Salvation is not individualistic, but means being incorporated into the people of God.

2:42 The apostles' teaching: Those who become Christians are further instructed in the meaning of the faith by its authorized representatives. On apostles, see Luke 6:12–13; Acts 1:23. On the key role of teaching in the Christian community, see Luke 4:15, 31–32; 19:47; 20:1, 37; Acts 2:42; 4:2, 18; 5:21, 25, 28; 13:1, 12; 18:11; 20:20; 28:31. **Fellowship:** *Koinonia* is not merely a congenial feeling of being together (though this is included), but refers to the shared life of believers, including sharing of property (see 2:44, where "common" is a form of the same word). **Breaking of bread:** Though this could refer to "ordinary" meals, by Luke's time the phrase had come to designate the church's eucharistic celebrations (see Luke 22:14–20; 24:35; Acts 2:46; 20:7, 11; 27:35; 1 Cor. 10:16; 11:23–34). The line between ordinary meals and the Eucharist was not yet so firmly drawn. **Prayers:** As prayer had characterized the life of Jesus (Luke 6:12; 9:18, 28; 22:40–46; 23:34, 46), so Jesus' followers in the post-Easter church continue to be a community devoted to prayer (e.g., Acts 1:14, 24; 3:1; 4:31; 6:4, 6; 7:59; 8:15, 22, 24; 9:11, 40; 10:9; 12:5; 13:3; 14:23; 16:25; 20:36; 21:5).

2:43 Wonders and signs . . . done by the apostles: The mighty deeds of Jesus' own ministry continued within the church (see Luke 9:1–6; 10:1–12; 17–20; Acts 1:1–2).

2:44–45 All who believed were together and had all things in common: Luke presents the life of the earliest church as an idealized picture of true Christian community. The later story of Acts shows that the practice was not universal and did not last (see 5:4), but it should not be regarded merely as a failed experiment. It is Luke's way of holding before the reader a picture of discipleship in which Jesus' own lack of selfishness and his concern for others was actually realized. His true followers did what the rich young ruler refused to do (Luke 18:18–30). While Luke does not call for a restoration of the way of life of the earliest Jerusalem church (see on Luke 22:35–38), he holds this picture before later generations as a challenge. Jesus' followers need not simply assume that the call to discipleship is an unrealizable ideal. See on 4:32 below.

2:46 Spent much time together in the temple: In the Gospel of Luke, Jesus had taken over the temple and made it the base of his own teaching ministry (Luke 19:45–47; 20:1; 21:37; 22:39). Jesus' followers continue as faithful Jews; their baptism did not make them members of a new religion. Although Luke knows that later the church would separate from the synagogue, here and elsewhere he stresses the continuity between Judaism and Christianity (see Luke 1:5–23; 2:21–52; 4:14–15; 24:57; Acts 3:1–10; 18:18; 21:17–26; 22:3; 24:1–21; 26:6; 28:20).

2:47 Those who were being saved: This is one of Luke's designations for Christians. **The Lord added to their number:** "Joining the church" is not a secondary, optional human decision made after one is saved, but is an aspect of salvation itself. Salvation is personal but not individualistic. The same Lord who saves adds those who are saved to the community of faith. On the Lukan meaning of salvation, see at 16:30.

3:1–11
PETER HEALS A CRIPPLED BEGGAR

An instance of the general statement of 2:43. See excursus, "Interpreting the Miracle Stories," at Matt. 9:35.

3:1 Peter and John: John is the son of Zebedee, brother of James (Luke 5:1–11). Only Luke has Peter paired with John (Luke 22:8; Acts 3:1; 4:13, 19; 8:14). Here and elsewhere, Peter is the spokesperson, John is the silent partner. On Peter as the leading apostle, see on Luke 22:31–32. On Christians continuing to worship in the temple, see on 2:46. **The hour of prayer:** The time of the evening sacrifice (see Exod. 29:39; Num. 28:3–4, 8; 1 Kgs. 18:36) when devout Jews came into the temple courts to pray (see Luke 1:8–10).

3:2 Lame from birth: A "hopeless case" (see John 9:1, 32). **The Beautiful Gate:** Not mentioned in ancient descriptions of the temple; location unknown. **Ask for alms:** Apparently without family, in a society without public welfare, the man was dependent on the goodwill of worshipers who visited the temple.

3:6 I have no silver or gold: Not necessarily because Peter, like the other disciples, has contributed his property to the common fund (see 2:44–45). Luke has consistently pictured those who responded to Jesus' call to discipleship as without property (Luke 5:11, 28; 9:57–62; 14:33; 18:22–23). **In the name of Jesus Christ:** On the "name," see on 2:38. Jesus had performed miracles in his own authority; his disciples do signs and wonders in his name. While Jesus himself is not present in the church, the power of his name continues to be effective.

3:7 His feet and ankles: These are unusual anatomical terms, occurring only here in the New Testament, and thus were once thought to represent the "medical language" of Luke the "beloved physician" (see Col. 4:14). Further research has shown that they are the typical vocabulary of the more educated Hellenistic authors, also found, for instance, in Philo and Josephus. Luke also uses sophisticated words of the legal profession and navigational and nautical terms from the world of sea travel, but such vocabulary shows only that he was a well-educated world traveler, not that he was a lawyer or ship captain (see on 25:17). The medical language of Luke–Acts thus shows that Luke had an advanced education, not that he was a physician. On the authorship of Luke–Acts, see introduction to Luke.

3:8 Jumping up . . . leaping: This vivid detail not only expresses the exuberance and joy of the man who has been healed but recalls Isa. 35:6, "the lame shall leap like the deer," part of the imagery of the messianic age that Luke sees as now fulfilled in the time of the church (3:24).

3:9 Praising God: Neither the apostles nor Jesus is praised. As Luke had consistently presented the acts of *Jesus* as resulting in praise to *God* (Luke 7:16; 8:24, 38; 9:20–22, 43; 13:13; 17:15; 19:37), so the signs and wonders that transpire in the church are seen in a theocentric perspective.

3:10 They were filled with wonder and amazement: The crowds are convinced that the miracle has happened, but this does not make them Christian believers. Faith is generated by hearing the gospel message (see on 2:41). Thus the miracle becomes the occasion for Peter's second sermon.

3:11 Solomon's Portico: A colonnade in the public courts of the temple, the exact location of which remains unknown (see 5:12; John 10:23).

3:12–26
PETER SPEAKS IN SOLOMON'S PORTICO

3:12 Why do you stare at us?: Peter and John resist being applauded as "celebrity Christians" or as "divine men" (see on Acts 8:10; 14:15).

3:13–14 The God of our ancestors: The miracle points to God. This God is not a new deity of a new religion but points to the same God that Peter, John, and their fellow Jews have always worshiped. **Glorified his servant Jesus:** A prophet in the Isaiah tradition whose oracles are contained in Isa. 40–55 had pointed to the "Servant of the Lord" as the agent of God's final salvation (Isa. 42:1–9; 49:1–6; 50:4–11; 52:13–53:12). While the Servant is identified in the Old Testament as the people of Israel (Isa.

41:8–9; 44:1–3, 21–22), Luke and other early Christians saw the ultimate fulfillment of the Servant's mission in Jesus (see 8:26–35).

You handed over and rejected: Peter is addressing "all the people" (3:11). While Luke elsewhere charges (some of) the Jewish leaders with responsibility for Jesus' death, rather than the people as a whole, here they are all judged to be guilty. This historical tension is the result of the dual theological point Luke intends: (1) On the one hand, the responsibility for Jesus ' death is laid at the feet of some of the Jewish leadership, so Christians and others should not continue to blame "the Jews" as such for the death of the Messiah. (2) On the other hand, Luke also wants to show that Jesus' death was the result of general human failure, not just Jewish sin, so that none may blame others (see on 2:23).

The charge is made in a series of contrasts that ring like hammer blows: **You handed over and rejected/Pilate . . . had decided to release** (see 23:4–22); **You rejected the Holy and Righteous One/asked to have a murderer; You killed the Author of Life/God raised from the dead.**

3:15 To this we are witnesses: The apostles bear witness not to their own religious experiences, but to God's act in Christ. See on 1:8.

3:16 Faith in his name: Nothing is said of the man's faith, who had asked for only money, not healing. The faith is the apostolic faith at work in the church. The "name" stands for the person of Christ himself; see on 2:38.

3:17 In ignorance: Again a theological tension (see 3:13). The proclamation of the Christian message combines two theological points: (1) On the one hand, those who reject God's revelation should know better, for God has revealed it (2:22; see on Rom. 1:18–2:29). Human beings are responsible, and cannot offer excuses. (2) On the other hand, they did not know, and could not have known, what they were doing when they rejected the Messiah. God's deeds are always ambiguous, can always be explained in other ways. No one is compelled to faith. Especially with regard to the Christ event, it was not clear who Jesus was until the story was over. His true identity was discerned only in the light of the resurrection and the gift of the Holy Spirit (see on the messianic secret in Mark). Luke in particular emphasizes the latter aspect (see on Luke 9:45; 18:34; 19:42; Acts 17:30).

3:18 All the prophets: Luke repeatedly emphasizes that the Christ event and the foundation of the church did not produce a strange new religion but represent the fulfillment of God's purpose declared in the Old Testament. **That his Messiah would suffer:** Not found in any text in the Hebrew Scriptures. The logic of Luke's statement, which he shares with the early church in general, is this: (1) God's will, purpose, and plan are revealed in the Hebrew Scriptures, the Christian Old Testament; (2) Christ is the fulfillment of God's purpose, therefore the fulfillment of the Old Testament; (3) contrary to all expectations, rather than punishing the enemy and providing political liberation, Christ suffered and died as the fulfillment of God's purpose; (4) therefore the Old Testament as a whole must point to the suffering Messiah.

This was seen only in retrospect, as a matter of Christian conviction in the light of faith. No one saw it in advance. Christians may not blame non-Christians, especially Jews, for not finding the suffering Messiah in the Old Testament apart from prior Christian faith. See excursus, "New Testament Interpretation of the Old Testament," at 1 Cor. 15:3; and comments on 2 Cor. 3:12–18.

3:19 Repent . . . and turn to God: See on 2:38.

3:20 Times of refreshing: Another expression for "the time of universal restoration"; see on 3:21.

3:21 The Messiah appointed for you: The Messiah is not elected by his followers but appointed by God. See on Mark 8:29. The phrase reflects a very early Christology, in which Jesus was not seen to be Messiah during his earthly life or at the resurrection, but is the Messiah-designate who will become the Messiah when the kingdom of God comes at the Parousia. The way in which the early followers of Jesus understood Jesus to be the Christ (= Christology) developed by stages, several of which are reflected in the New Testament.

In the earliest Christology, reflected here, Jesus was seen as the one chosen by God who would return as Christ at the last day. (This is not Luke's own Christology; he is here using an earlier tradition. Such data show that, though Luke has composed the speeches in Acts, he has sometimes used earlier traditions.) Other texts present Jesus as having been made the Christ at the resurrection (e.g., Acts 2:36), at baptism (Mark 1:9–11, but see the comments there), or already at birth (Matt. 1–2; Luke 2). The New Testament has more than one way of picturing the Christ event, but not just any way was acceptable. No one theology can do justice to the act of God in Christ. The limited variety

found in the New Testament, even in the same author, prevents Christian readers from absolutizing any one way of presenting the Christian faith (see on 1 Cor. 3:21–23).

Likewise, a variety of christological titles are used in the New Testament, seven of which are found in this one passage: servant (3:13, 26); Holy One (3:14); Righteous One (3:14); Author of life (3:15); Messiah (3:18 = Christ, 3:6; see on Mark 8:29); Prophet like Moses (3:22–23; see Deut. 18:15–18); offspring of Abraham (3:25 NIV; see Gal. 3:8–16). Though "Son of God" is important to Luke's own Christology, it is strikingly absent from Acts (only 9:20; see 20:28).

3:21 The time of universal restoration: Some streams of early Christian theology pictured the ultimate outcome of God's act in Christ as the salvation of the whole creation, the summing up of all things in Christ (see Rom. 11:36; Phil. 2:8–11; Eph. 1:7–10, 20–23; Col. 1:15–20; Rev. 5:13–14). While Luke resonates with this inclusive view (see 3:25), he preserves other views as well. See excursus, "Universal Salvation and Paradoxical Language," at Rev. 22:21.

3:22–23 Prophet like Moses: For Luke, "prophet" is a legitimate christological title (see Luke 7:11–17; 9:8, 19; 24:19). The office of Messiah includes the role of being God's definitive spokesperson (see on Mark 8:29). Deuteronomy 18:15–18 had promised that after Moses' departure, God would continue to deal with Israel through a prophet like Moses. This was originally intended to point to the succession of later Israelite prophets, but Luke understands it to be fulfilled in Jesus (see on "Servant of the Lord" at 3:13).

3:24 All the prophets . . . predicted these days: The days of the church as the continuation of God's plan for history disclosed in Christ. On "all the prophets," see above on 3:18.

3:25 In your descendants (NRSV)/**Through your offspring:** The word is singular and can be understood of one individual (as in NIV; see Gal. 3:8, 16) or collectively of the people of Israel (NRSV). **All the families of the earth shall be blessed:** This was the promise to Abraham and Sarah, Gen. 12:1–3. Luke joins other early Christians in seeing it fulfilled in Christ (Gal. 3:8; Heb. 11:8; Rev. 1:7).

3:26 Sent him first to you: Peter's speech betrays Luke's later perspective (see 13:46; 18:6ff.; Rom. 1:16; 2:9–10). In the Acts story line, Peter only gradually became aware that God's plan includes all peoples (Acts 10–11).

4:1–22
PETER AND JOHN BEFORE THE COUNCIL

4:1 The priests, the captain of the temple, and the Sadducees: See 4:5, 15. The same official religious leadership that had been instrumental in the arrest of Jesus now for the first time opposes the group of Christian disciples that continues Jesus' mission. Putting Jesus to death had not resolved their problem (see Luke 22:1–6, 47, 54, 66; 23:1). To be a disciple of Jesus means to accept the same opposition he received (see Luke 12:4–12). On Sadducees, see on Luke 20:27.

4:2 Teaching . . . and proclaiming in Jesus . . . the resurrection of the dead: While the Sadducees denied the doctrine of the resurrection affirmed by the Pharisees (see Luke 20:27–40; Acts 23:6–11), it is not this general issue that leads to the arrest of the apostles. "The resurrection," like "the name" and the "word of God," became a designation of the specifically Christian message. While there were conflicts between Jewish leaders and Jesus' followers from the earliest days of the Christian community (see 1 Thess. 2:14–16), the scene here portrayed by Luke also reflects Luke's own time, when Jewish leaders opposed the Christian faction as such.

4:4 Five thousand: See 1:15; 2:41. The embryonic Christian community is growing very quickly. This, too, alarmed the Jewish leaders (see 13:45). Modern readers might ponder their own reaction if uneducated traveling preachers of a new religious movement came into established churches and lured thousands of them away as followers of an executed criminal that they claimed to be God's final revelation.

4:5 Annas was actually an ex–high priest, still given the honorary title. **Caiaphas** was the current high priest, who served 18–36 CE (see on Luke 3:2). The burial cave of the high-priestly family of Caiaphas has recently been found in Jerusalem, including ossuaries inscribed with their names.

4:7 By what power or by what name?: The charges are vague. This is part of the Lukan pattern of showing that the hostility against the Christian group has no legitimate grounds. This is illustrated extensively in the case of Paul in the latter half of Acts (see 25:26–27). The "name" plays a crucial role in this scene (3:6; 4:7, 10, 12, 17, 18, 30; see on 2:38). The issue of the resurrection is dropped, and "the name" becomes the summary designation of the Christian faith.

4:8 Peter, filled with the Holy Spirit, said: Peter is the chief spokesperson for the apostles throughout the Acts story until 12:17.

4:9 If we are questioned today: The charges are vague, but the response is clear. This is a reversal of Peter's previous behavior, in which the charge was clear but his response was evasive (Luke 22:54–62). Luke presents Peter as a model example of bold Christian testimony under pressure. **This man has been healed:** The word here translated "healed" is rendered "saved" in v. 12.

4:10 Jesus . . . whom you crucified . . . God raised from the dead: The Jewish leaders had played a role in Jesus' arrest and conviction, but the Romans had crucified Jesus. Luke charges them with the general human guilt involved in the death of Jesus (see on 2:23).

4:11 This Jesus is the stone that was rejected: The quotation is from Ps. 118:22, slightly modified ("by you" is added). This text had also been cited by Jesus (see on Luke 20:17). The citation shows that the issue of the resurrection was not a theoretical doctrinal issue of life beyond the grave, but the specific act of God in raising up Jesus and reversing the human evaluation of his life. What was rejected by human beings has been made the cornerstone of God's work. In such contexts, "cornerstone" is not merely the decorative inscribed stone placed in a building at its completion, but is the keystone or capstone that holds the structure of the building together.

4:12 There is salvation in no one else: This verse has often been used as a proof text to affirm that only baptized Christians are finally saved. The following considerations should be kept in mind for a more adequate interpretation:

1. In the context, the declaration refers to the healing of the lame man ("save" and "heal" are the same word in Greek).

2. Luke, like other New Testament authors, often uses the word "save" to mean deliverance from sickness, demon possession, or other dangers that threaten human life (Luke 6:9; 7:50; 8:36, 48, 50; 17:19; 18:42; 23:35, 37, 39; Acts 14:9, 27:20, 31).

3. However, biblical authors generally, including Luke, recognize the connection between the granting of physical life by salvation from physical dangers and the gift of eschatological salvation, and the one is often used as a symbol of the other. Thus a story of healing or cleansing from leprosy, when told in the context of the Christian faith, has overtones of the eschatological salvation accomplished

by God in the Christ event. It has not been wrong, then, to raise the question of eternal salvation in relation to this text, though that is not its primary meaning.

4. When the larger issue is raised, modern readers should still keep the context of this saying in mind. In the story, Peter is addressing an actual situation of the people of Jerusalem, who have heard the message of the saving act of God in Jesus. Luke is not here addressing the theoretical issue of the eternal destiny of people in distant centuries and countries who have not heard the Christian message.

5. From Luke's theology, as well as the New Testament as a whole, the modern reader may be clear with regard to two points: (a) Christians are not encouraged to believe that the Christian way is only one of "many roads to God"—see at John 14:6; (b) but neither are Christians encouraged to believe that only confessing Christians are finally accepted by God. For Luke and the New Testament generally, as there is only one God, there is only one way of salvation provided by God: the grace of God manifest in Jesus Christ. Whoever is saved is saved by this God, the only God there is. But this text has nothing to say on the issue of whether one must consciously confess faith in Christ before the grace of God manifest in Christ is effective for that person. On the basis of this text, Christians ought to say neither that only Christians shall ultimately be saved nor that people can be saved through a variety of saviors. Christians should confess their faith that the God revealed in Christ is the only Savior, without claiming that only those who respond in faith will be saved (see excursus at Rev. 22:21, "Universal Salvation and Paradoxical Language").

6. On the understanding of salvation in Luke–Acts, see further on Acts 16:30.

7. On the issue of universal salvation, see excursus at Rev. 22:5.

4:13 The boldness of Peter and John: Not just their personal brashness, but that they spoke the truth without regard to prevailing social, political, and religious opinion. What they said was not a matter of tactics, but truth (contrast the council itself in vv. 14–16). **Uneducated and ordinary men:** Without rabbinic theological credentials, and without rhetorical training. They are "amateurs." Paul uses the same word of himself in 2 Cor. 11:6, there translated "untrained."

4:15–16 Ordered them to leave the council: The religious leaders deliberate privately. The

modern reader should not ask how Luke gets this "information." In terms of literary criticism, the story throughout Luke–Acts is told by an omniscient narrator who knows what transpires in secret meetings and when people are alone, as well as the private thoughts of the characters in the story (see Luke 12:17; 15:17; 18:4, 11–12; 20:13). The truth of Luke–Acts is not the truth of investigative reporting. The religious leaders do not ask about truth, but strategy (see on Luke 20:1–8).

4:18 Ordered them not to speak or teach at all in the name of Jesus: On the name, see 2:38. Both the council and the author of Luke–Acts take speaking and teaching more seriously than do many modern Christians. That Jesus and his disciples were teachers, and that their teaching had a certain content, were not considered harmless items by the authorities or by Luke. The faith is spread and nourished by apostolic teaching (see Luke 4:15, 31–32; 19:47; 20:1, 37; Acts 2:42; 4:2, 18; 5:21, 25, 28; 13:1, 12; 18:11; 20:20; 28:31), which Luke considers vital to the growth and health of the church.

4:19 Listen to you rather than to God: See 5:29.

4:20 What we have seen and heard: The Christian faith is not a cluster of ideas, but the mighty acts of God in history culminating in the Christ event. See on 1:8; 2:11; 1 John 1:1–4.

4:21 Praised God: As in the ministry of Jesus, so the deeds of his disciples bring glory to God. The story challenges the church of later generations to conduct its mission in a way that points to God, so that observers do not respond merely by congratulating them as nice people, but by glorifying God. While living and acting out the faith are indispensable, speaking and teaching the faith are important in order to point to God as the source and ground of the church's service to other people (see Matt. 5:14–16).

4:22 This sign of healing: "Sign" points beyond itself. Luke has related the story not just as an incident of healing one person, but as a means of pointing to the salvation that has come into the world through Christ.

4:23–31
THE BELIEVERS PRAY FOR BOLDNESS

4:23 They went to their friends: No longer the whole church, which now numbers more than eight thousand.

4:24 Raised their voices together: Following the example of Jesus (Luke 6:12; 9:18, 28; 22:40–46; 23:34, 46) the church in Acts is portrayed as praying often (e.g., 1:14, 24; 2:42; 3:1; 6:4–6;

8:15; 12:5; 13:3; 16:25), but only here and the brief 1:24–25 is the content of the prayer given. It does not follow the model Jesus had given in Luke 11:2–4, but consists of two elements: affirmations of praise to God and a petition to God for boldness. The prayer is not a verbatim report of a unison prayer, but Luke's summary of how Christians should and did pray in difficult situations. The prayer is in biblical language (see 2 Kgs. 19:15–18/Isa. 37:16–20; Pss. 2:1–2; 146:6).

4:24 Sovereign Lord, who made . . . everything: God is praised as the one who made all things and is sovereign over them. This is not mere theological speculation. Under duress, the disciples confess before God their faith that all things are finally in one hand. Such monotheistic faith in the one God, the Creator, understands life and its troubles to rest securely in the hands of God. This God is not one competing power among others, but is the Almighty, sovereign over all (contrast the understanding of life expressed in the polytheistic prayers in Homer's *Iliad* and *Odyssey*).

4:25 It is you who said by the Holy Spirit: As in the preceding affirmation, this is not said as information, but as praise. God is praised as the one who has spoken. These two affirmations are fundamental to the Christian faith that undergirds prayer in difficult situations: God is the Creator of all, and God is the one who has not remained hidden, but who has spoken, i.e., the one who has revealed his character and purpose in the word of God spoken by prophets and apostles. **David your servant:** Psalm 2:1–2 is cited as from David, although the Old Testament does not attribute it to him. Luke reflects the traditional view that all the psalms were composed by David. On David as prophet, see 2:30. On interpretation of Old Testament passages as predictions of Jesus, see on 1:16–17; 2:16; 3:18 and excursus, "New Testament Interpretation of the Old Testament," at 1 Cor. 15:3. "Servant" is the same word used for Jesus in v. 27 as a christological title (see 3:13, 26).

4:27 You anointed: See Luke 4:18; 9:20; Mark 8:29 comments; Acts 10:38. The title, "Christ, Messiah, Anointed One," points to God as the actor. As in Paul's theology, the act of God in sending the Messiah is summed up with reference to Jesus' suffering and death, without reference to his ministry (see 1 Cor. 15:3–5). **Herod and Pontius Pilate:** See Luke 23:6–12, 15. Only Luke includes an appearance before Herod in the story of Jesus' trial. The disciples

now share the destiny of Jesus by being opposed and persecuted by the rulers.

4:28 To do whatever your hand and your plan had predestined to take place: See excursus, "Predestination," at Rom. 8:28. On the combination of human responsibility and divine sovereignty, see on Mark 4:10–12; 6:52; Luke 22:3, 22; John 6:64–70; Acts 2:23; Phil. 2:12–13.

4:29 Grant to your servants: When the prayer turns from praise to petition, it is not for deliverance, but for boldness under pressure. Persecution is seen as an opportunity to witness. This cannot be done by silent suffering; the disciples must speak up in order to show why they are willing to suffer and what they are suffering for (see 1 Pet. 3:13–16, which addresses a similar situation). All this is the polar opposite of private, uninvolved religion.

4:30 While you stretch out your hand . . . and signs and wonders are performed: The prayer is prayed in the confidence that God will continue to act as in 3:1–4:22 and that the church will continue to witness.

4:31 The place . . . was shaken: For earthquake as sign of God's presence, see Exod. 19:18; Isa. 6:4; Acts 16:26. **All:** The experience of Peter and John becomes a model for the whole church—all are filled with the Spirit, all speak out boldly despite the cultural pressure to keep a low profile (see Luke 12:1–12).

4:32–35
THE BELIEVERS SHARE THEIR POSSESSIONS

4:32 Of one heart and soul: Luke presents the earliest church as a model of Christian unity (see Eph. 4:1–6). When tensions do arise later, the community works through them without dividing (6:1–7; 10:1–11:26; 15:1–35; 21:17–26). The church as presented in Acts is not a cluster of competing groups, but one community of believers sharing a common faith and mission. **Everything they owned was held in common:** See on 2:44. Their unity was not only religious, but economic. Luke has throughout emphasized that discipleship to Jesus involves one's possessions (Luke 6:20–26; 12:13–21; 16:9, 19–31; 18:22–25; 19:1–27; 21:1; Acts 11:27–29). Luke's presentation reflects the ideal of sharing property that was widely admired in the Hellenistic world and occasionally put into practice by philosophic associations or exclusive religious groups such as the Essenes, the people of the Dead Sea Scrolls. Luke wants to show that the teaching of Jesus was not merely an ideal but was concretely practiced. Not a word is said about eschatological motivation; i.e., it was not the case that the early church believed the end of the world was coming soon, so they could "afford" to abandon their earthly property. While Luke has a wholesome eschatology (see on Acts 1:6–11), he provides instruction not for the "last generation" but for a church that has settled down in real history for the long pull (see on Luke 17:20–37; 21:5–36). The picture of authentic discipleship presented here is the antithesis of the view that Christian faith brings wealth and success. Faith results in giving, not in getting. While the general message of this picture is clear—Jesus' disciples unselfishly provide for the needs of others—the details remain ambiguous. Does Luke want the reader to understand the sharing of goods as obligatory or voluntary? Did all practice it, or only some? Was it only in Jerusalem, or in Christian groups elsewhere as well? Was the obligation to share one's goods made a part of the entrance requirements of the church, or were new Christians only later informed that they must share their property? When such questions are posed, it becomes clear that Luke is not presenting, reporter-like, the details of an actual situation, but has composed a model scene to show that unselfish sharing was not an ideal to which Jesus' disciples paid lip service, but actually happened.

4:33 With great power the apostles gave their testimony to the resurrection: Again, the Christian faith is summarized in the message of the death and resurrection (see on 4:27). Although the readers have before them the images of Jesus' life and teaching in the Gospel of Luke, the church in Acts is portrayed as basing its radical new life not on Jesus' example, but on the message of Jesus' death and resurrection—not on what Jesus had done, but on what God had done in the whole Christ event. (For the role of the Gospel stories of Jesus' life in the formation of Christian faith, see on "Introduction to the Gospels," 4.)

4:34 There was not a needy person among them: The benevolence seems to be directed to insiders of the Christian community. (See on "love one another" in John 13:34–35; 15:17; 1 John 3:11, 14, 23; 4:7, 11–12; 2 John 5.) The church begins with limited horizons, but in the power and insight provided the Spirit, it will increase its vision. The readers know that God's will revealed in Jesus is not only love for fellow believers, but compassion for the neighbor, whoever he or she is (Luke 10:25–37).

4:35 Laid it at the apostles' feet: Placed it at the disposal of the church, to be administered by

the apostles. Charity was not private and individual, but was administered through the church leadership. This is another of Luke's ways of showing that Christian acts of compassion are not merely the result of the goodness of the hearts of individual people, but are included in God's act of sending the Christ and founding the church. The church will shortly see the wisdom of dividing up this administrative responsibility (6:1–7).

4:36–5:11
POSITIVE AND NEGATIVE EXAMPLES

The chapter divisions were first added in the thirteenth century and often do not fit the author's structure of the narrative. The verses 4:36–37 belong to what follows, not the preceding section. After portraying the earliest church's sharing of goods, Luke gives positive (Barnabas, 4:36–37) and negative (Ananias and Sapphira, 5:1–11) examples of how it actually worked out.

4:36 Joseph . . . Barnabas: To his original Jewish name Joseph the apostles added a surname by which he will be known in the Gentile world (not an informal nickname). The translation and etymology of **Barnabas** is unclear, but in no known language does it mean "son of encouragement." Luke may reflect a folk etymology connecting "bar" to Aramaic "son" (see Matt. 16:17, Bar-Jonah = son of Jonah), and may relate "nabas" to the Hebrew word for "prophet," i.e., one who offers divine encouragement (see 1 Cor. 14:3). Barnabas is the first nonapostle to be named among the church's leaders (see on 14:4, 11). He is presented as a model disciple who will play a prominent role in the missionary expansion of the church (9:27; 11:22–30; 12:25; 13:1–15:22). **A Levite:** Not necessarily a tribal designation (Judg. 7:17 refers to a Levite who belonged to the tribe of Judah), but a subordinate order of priests (Exod. 32:25–29) who were later charged not only with performing the sacrifice ritual but with responsibility for teaching the divine law (Deut. 17:18; 33:10), with carrying the sacred ark (1 Chr. 15:11–15) and providing music for the worship services (1 Chr. 16:4–37). Like Paul whom he will later accompany as a Christian missionary, Barnabas embodies the continuity between Israel and the church. He is also a transitional figure in that he comes from **Cyprus**, a large island in the eastern Mediterranean, later to be evangelized by Paul and himself.

4:37 Sold a field that belonged to him: In sharp contrast to Judas (see on 1:18). According to

Num. 18:20 and Deut. 10:9, Levites were not to own property in Israel. It is not clear how this restriction applied to Levites of the Diaspora.

5:1–11 Ananias and Sapphira: This is a difficult story. Its problems should neither be minimized nor exaggerated. The reader should be wary of resolving its difficulties too quickly and easily, either by refusing to take it seriously by rejecting it out of hand, or by accepting it too quickly as a straightforward illustration of how God works. The following observations may help the modern reader apprehend the message Luke intends:

1. It is problematic to take the story simply as an objective report of an event from which moralizing lessons may be drawn. Its problems include at least the following:

a. The sin of which Ananias and Sapphira are guilty is common enough—wanting credit for what we have not done, wanting more credit than we deserve. They are not the only people in the church, then or now, guilty of this sin.

b. The judgmental attitude of God and Peter, who strike the pair dead without opportunity to repent, must be pondered carefully. The reader must wonder what has happened to the teaching of Jesus given to Peter in Luke 17:3–4 and the example of Jesus on the cross (Luke 23:34; see Acts 3:17; 13:27–28; 17:30), imitated by Stephen, who forgives murderers, but not by Peter, who rather cold-bloodedly participates in the death of Christians guilty of what seems to be a relatively minor infraction. Peter will later give an opportunity for repentance to the baptized magician who has violated the Holy Spirit for economic reasons (8:14–25)—but not here.

c. The church now numbers many thousands (2:41; 4:4), so they could not all be gathered at the same place, and yet the story is told as though the church as a whole were present.

d. Ananias is buried immediately and unceremoniously without his wife's knowledge. The church apparently sits still for three hours, is silent when Sapphira enters, and thus participates in this "entrapment" drama. The lack of compassion—not to speak of cruelty—inherent in this scene taken as objective reporting of literal history seems to violate all that the disciples have been called to be.

2. These problems cannot be resolved by ignoring them, or by ignoring or rejecting the biblical text in which they stand. To do so would be to enter on the slippery slope that results in eliminating all the biblical texts that

objectify the actions of God as judge of human sin, including much of the message of Jesus (see, e.g., Matt. 25:31–46, much used as an affirmation of divine compassion). The reader's own principle of selectivity then becomes the criterion for what can be "accepted" in the Bible and what cannot, and the Bible becomes a cafeteria. This story simply brings into inescapably sharp focus all the Bible's teaching about God's judgment on human sin, from Gen. 3 through the Old Testament prophets and John the Baptist to Jesus himself. The problem remains and must be faced.

3. The story should be seen as an aspect of Luke's telling the story of the church in continuity with the story of Israel, painting Christian events with colors taken from his Bible. As John the Baptist functions "in the spirit and power of Elijah" (Luke 1:17), as the beginning of the church is the undoing of the tower of Babel (Gen. 11/Acts 2), so this story at the beginning of the church's life is analogous to the story of Achan's sin in Joshua 7. In the Old Testament story, the selfish individual sin of Achan led to defeat of the whole people of God, and he was summarily exposed and punished. The Old Testament story is replete with punitive miracle stories that illustrate the judgment of a righteous God on sinful humanity. The liberating exodus and creation of the Old Testament people of God is told in terms of punitive miracles (the plagues against Egypt and Pharoah, including the death of all the firstborn sons in Egypt). These stories too have ethical problems if taken as objective reporting of God's acts; the point here, however, is that Luke's story stands in that tradition and must be interpreted in the same way as other such biblical stories of God's judgment.

4. It is helpful in attempting to understand such biblical passages to distinguish between the message of the biblical text and the objectifying language in which it is told (see on 1:9 above and comments on confessional language at Matt. 2:16). All stories in which God acts in the human scene pose problems when the stories are taken as reports of objective events from which readers may make their own independent inferences. Rather, the reader should seek the theological message embedded in the text without making further inferences on the basis of objectifying the story. Some of these are pointed out in the commentary following.

5:1–2 Sold a piece of property: The similar vocabulary to the preceding story of Barnabas shows that the story is the negative counterpart of the positive example of Barnabas: **sold . . . brought . . . laid at the apostles' feet**. The only difference is expressed in the word **kept back** (emphasized in both v. 2 and v. 3), which is the same word used in Josh. 7:1 for the sin of Achan—see (3) above. The modern reader should read Josh. 7 in its larger context of God's formation of the people of Israel and gift of the land.

5:3 Why has Satan filled your heart?: That Ananias is himself responsible is also clearly affirmed in 5:4. See on 4:23 above, Luke 22:3, and John 13:2, on the paradox of human responsibility and the instrumentality of Satan. Responsibility is not parceled out between Ananias and Satan, but Ananias is portrayed as making his decision in the force field between the power of the Holy Spirit operative in the church and the power of Satan at work in the world. Like all Christians, Ananias lives in both church and world and must decide what will determine his life. This agrees with the general biblical perspective, in which human life is not autonomous, but will be ruled by good or evil, by Satan or God (see on Rom. 6:15–23; Phil. 2:7; Matt. 6:24). It is part of the illusion of human sin that we ourselves are our masters of our own fates, captains of our own souls.

5:4 Did it not remain your own?: Here the picture of the church's community of goods (2:44; 4:32, 34) is seen as voluntary and not universal. Luke's portrayal here seems to reflect the Old Testament rule that one did not have to make vows to God, but that, once made, such vows are taken with absolute seriousness. The story of Achan in Josh. 7 is also told in terms of the violation of a solemn vow. **Not to us** (NIV **men**) **but to God:** The sin of Ananias and Sapphira turns out to be more serious than it appeared at first. They had supposed that the church was a human institution, had not recognized that to deal with the church was to deal with God. This is analogous to responses to Jesus—Pilate, Herod, and the high priests supposed that in dealing with him they were dealing only with a human being. Without any exalted theoretical Christology, Luke has made it clear that Christian faith affirms that to deal with Jesus is to deal with God. Here, in an analogous way, he affirms that to deal with the church is to deal with God (see 9:4—to persecute the church is to persecute Christ).

5:5 Fell down and died: Rationalizing explanations (heart attack, fright, shame) miss the point of Luke's story, which he intends as a miracle. See "Interpreting Miracle Stories," excursus at Matt. 9:35. Luke also portrays Paul as having effected a punitive miracle (13:4–12; on Peter/Paul parallels, see list at 28:31). Paul also takes seriously the view that God's judgment on sin that violates the holiness of the church can be punished with death; see on 1 Cor. 3:16–17; 5:1–5; 11:30.

Great fear seized all who heard of it: Not fright at the prospect of sudden death, but the fear of God, reverent awe that comes with the awareness one is in God's presence. This is what Ananias and Sapphira had lacked; they supposed they were dealing only with human beings, as when people, inside and outside the church, suppose that the church is only a human institution, another worthy cause or support group.

5:6 Young men: Probably not merely an indication of their age, but a reflection of the structure of the church in Luke's own time, when "the younger" may have designated a certain status in church leadership, the counterpart to "elder" (see 1 Pet. 5:1–5). In Luke's time the church had not developed firm orders of clergy, but it was moving in that direction, as Luke's reference to "elders" indicates, and as illustrated in 6:1–6.

5:7–10 His wife came in: Sapphira is throughout treated by Luke as an equal, not merely an appendage to her husband. Here her identity is "his wife," just as Ananias's identity in v. 8 is "her husband." She is equally responsible with him and receives the same punishment. He had not decided for her, even in economic matters, but she had decided for herself. **Not knowing what had happened:** See above on the evident lack of compassion. The story is told from the point of view of responsibility before God, the by-product of which is to present the church as uncaring and judgmental— but the story is focused on another point. See on Matt. 2:16 and Acts 1:9 on objectifying language.

5:11 Great fear seized the whole church: Another parallel between Ananias and Sapphira. On "fear," see 5:5. This is the first use of the word "church" in Acts, though it is clear that Luke has considered the community formed in 2:37ff. as the church throughout the whole narrative. He will use the word frequently after this (never in Luke; 23x in Acts), mostly for individual congregations of Christians at particular places (e.g., 8:1; 13:1), but also for all the Christians in a given area (9:31).

While the word can be used in its secular sense of "assembly" (19:32–40), Luke understands it primarily as the community of faith, the people of God, and can use it, as does his Bible, of Israel, the Old Testament people of God (7:38).

5:12–16
MANY SIGNS AND WONDERS

5:12 They were all together: The twelve apostles (see on Luke 6:12–13). The location is not large enough for the whole church (see 2:41; 4:4; the numbers continue to grow, see 5:14; 21:20). **Solomon's Portico:** See on 3:11. The apostles' ministry, like that of Jesus, is conducted in continuity with the Jewish temple.

5:13 None of the rest dared to join them: The apostles are a special authorized group called and commissioned by Christ (Luke 6:12–16; 24:44–49; Acts 1:12–26; 2:1–14; 8:14–25; 15:1–29).

5:14 More and more . . . believed in the Lord and were added (NIV)/**Believers were added to the Lord** (NRSV): The Greek phrase can be translated either way. In both translations, when people respond in faith and obedience to Christ, God adds them to the church (see 2:41, 47). Just as one cannot voluntarily "join" the apostles (v. 13), so in Luke's understanding one cannot "join" the church as one joins other human institutions and organizations. The point of the preceding story is the danger of regarding the church only from a human point of view. The NRSV translation "added to the Lord" identifies the church with Christ, analogous to 9:4. To be added to the church is to be joined to Christ (see Paul's understanding, Rom. 6:3; Gal. 3:27). "The Lord" is used in Acts of both God (e.g., 3:22) and Christ (e.g., 2:36).

5:15 Peter's shadow: Like the hem of Jesus' garment in Luke 8:44 and the handkerchiefs and aprons that had touched Paul's body (Acts 19:12), healing power resides in the presence of Peter. While such views border on magic, Luke (who distinguishes Christian faith from superstition and magic, see 8:9–25; 19:19–20) understands these to be expressions of the power and presence of God in the church.

5:16 The towns around Jerusalem: The first indication that the faith is spreading beyond Jerusalem; see 1:8. **Those tormented by unclean spirits . . . were all cured:** The power of the Holy Spirit active in Jesus (Luke 4:36; 8:2, 29; 9:42). See excursus, "Satan, the Devil, and Demons in Biblical Theology," at Mark 5:1.

5:17–42
THE APOSTLES ARE ARRESTED AND THREATENED

5:17 Sadducees: See on Luke 20:27. **Sect:** Not here used as a pejorative term, the word means simply a group within Judaism. The first-century Jewish historian Josephus uses the same term to designate Pharisees (the group to which he belonged), Sadducees, Essenes, and Zealots. Luke uses the word of other Jewish groups (15:5; 26:5), including Christians as a group that originated within Judaism (24:5, 14; 28:22). **Filled with jealousy:** The word can refer to the leaders' jealousy at the numerical success of the church, as possibly in 13:45 (Luke's only other use of the word), but can also mean religious zeal, even if misdirected (see John 2:17; Rom. 10:2; Phil. 3:6).

5:18 Put them in . . . prison: As Paul, representing the same Jewish authorities, is to do later in the story (9:1–2; 22:4–5; 26:9–10). Luke and his readers already look back on this.

5:19 Angel: Angels play a prominent role in Luke–Acts (see on Luke 1:10–12). For Luke, the appearance of angels is a way of expressing the presence and act of God. In this story, to obey the angel's instruction is to obey God (see vv. 21, 32). Some New Testament authors affirm this way of talking about God (e.g., Matthew and Luke), while others are suspicious or hostile to it (John and Paul). On the ethical problems inherent in such language, see on 12:6–19.

5:20 The whole message about this life: The Christian message is not merely speculative doctrine about God and Jesus, but has to do with life: the purpose and meaning of life, and how to live. A message claiming to be Christian but unrelated to ethics is no Christian gospel (see on 2:28).

5:21 Teaching: As elsewhere in Luke–Acts, teaching plays a decisive role (Luke 4:15, 31–32; 19:47; 20:1, 37; Acts 2:42; 4:2, 18; 5:21, 25, 28; 13:1, 12; 18:11; 20:20; 28:31). Neither the apostles nor their opponents consider teaching to be a harmless matter of mere words. As the message about Jesus is summed up in "what he did and taught" (Acts 1:1), so in the church both actions and words are necessary. Words without actions are empty; but actions without words fail to communicate the meaning of God's act in Christ.

5:24–26: Wondering what might be going on: Like the discovery of the empty tomb (see on Matt. 28:1; Luke 24:1–12), the bare miracle itself does not generate faith. **Afraid of . . . the people:** Again Luke distinguishes between the Jewish people as a whole and their leaders (Luke 19:39, 47; 23:23, 35, 51; 24:20; but see also comments on Acts 2:23). **Standing in the temple and teaching the people:** The apostles did not take the opportunity provided by their miraculous deliverance to flee to safety, but returned to their mission as instructed by the angel. See the later conduct of Paul and Silas (16:16–34).

5:27 Had them stand before the council: The Sanhedrin, the Senate of the Jewish people that mediated between the Roman authorities and the people, the same official group before which Jesus had appeared (Luke 22:66–23:1). There is no further reference to the miraculous deliverance from prison, which seems to be forgotten both by the narrator and the participants in the story, and—typical for Acts—attention is now focused exclusively on the speeches of Peter and Gamaliel.

5:29 Peter and the apostles answered: Peter is spokesperson for all the apostles, as in Acts 1–12 generally (see on Luke 22:31–32). **We must obey God rather than any human authority:** See 5:4. The Sanhedrin and all readers will agree. The difficult issue, however, is to discern what is divine and what is merely human. The priests sincerely supposed that by preserving the temple cult, by maintaining law and order and public peace in cooperation with the Roman authorities, and by suppressing civil revolution and religious heresy, they were in fact obeying God, while the apostles were advocates of a dangerous sect that rested only on mistaken human foundations. The remainder of this scene is Luke's narrative presentation of this issue. All concerned wish to obey God and recognize the Savior God sends—but how is this done? The speeches of Peter and Gamaliel respectively spell this out.

5:30 God raised up Jesus, whom you had killed: The remainder of the scene is bracketed by the apostles' proclamation of the Christian message, with the alternatives presented by Gamaliel sandwiched between. Peter responds with a summary of the Christian message of the death and resurrection of Jesus (as in 2:14–36; 3:17–26; 4:8–12). He does not present rational arguments or persuasive general ideals and principles to show what obeying God means, but witnesses to God's act in Christ. **The God of our ancestors:** The Christian faith is not a new religion, but the decisive act of the same God Jews have always wor-

shiped. **God exalted him at his right hand:** See on 2:33–34 (Ps. 110:1). **Savior:** First use of this title in Acts; see on Luke 2:11. **Repentance and forgiveness of sins:** See on 2:38; Luke 3:3; 24:47. Repentance is both a human act and the gift of God (see on Luke 15:24; 22:22).

5:32 The Holy Spirit as witness: In Luke's view, the Holy Spirit witnesses to the truth of the Christian message not only by the "signs and wonders" that occur in the life of the church, but also in and through the obedience of those who respond to the Christian message (see 2:38).

5:33 Wanted to kill them: Not primarily personal hostility but religious conviction, the judgment that what the apostles were doing was sufficiently dangerous as to warrant capital punishment (see Paul's similar view as portrayed in 26:9–10). The judgment against Jesus is now extended to his followers (see Luke 22:1–2; Acts 6:8–15; 7:54–8:1).

5:34 Gamaliel: An illustrious Jewish teacher, the grandson of the great Hillel, and grandfather of Gamaliel II, who played a leading role in Judaism in Luke's own time at the end of the first century. According to 22:3, Paul himself had studied with him in Jerusalem. **Pharisee:** See on Luke 5:17.

5:35 Consider carefully what you propose to do: Gamaliel's general counsel is that the religious authorities should adopt a laissez-faire policy toward the new Christian group. This is Luke's own view of how both the religious and secular leaders should respond to the Christian community (see his last word of the book, 28:31, to which his whole story is building). The issue before the group is how to respond to claims that a particular leader is the savior sent by God. Gamaliel points to two illustrations in the past that bear out his proposed policy.

5:36 Some time ago Theudas rose up, claiming to be somebody: The first-century Jewish historian Josephus describes Theudas as claiming to be the eschatological prophet who would deliver Israel from Roman oppression by the miraculous power of God, as Joshua had originally conquered the land by God's power. He led his followers to the Jordan, which he promised would part before them (see Josh. 3, where the story is modeled on the deliverance of Israel at the Red Sea, Exod. 14). The Romans executed him, his followers were scattered, and his movement came to nothing.

5:37 Judas the Galilean: Judas likewise led a revolt against the Romans and was likewise destroyed by them. Gamaliel's point is that God will empower the true deliverer and his followers so that they cannot be destroyed, but false claims will perish in the ordinary course of history. As a political tactic, Gamaliel's advice is not helpful to those who cannot "wait and see"—we all have 20/20 hindsight—but must decide in the moment, before later historical results are in. But Gamaliel's advice does embody Luke's own view of the church: it is not just a human movement, but is empowered by God, and those who oppose it oppose God (see 5:1–11). This understanding of the church later was dogmatized and used to support the imperialistic claims of the church. It is a dangerous ecclesiology when it leads to unquestioning obedience to the church as represented by its officials. It is, however, a biblical point of view that needs to be taken more seriously in times when the church is seen only as a human institution.

5:38 This plan: Gamaliel uses precisely the word Luke has used twice before to signify the plan of God for history, of which Christ is the determinative midpoint (2:23; 4:28; see introduction to Luke: "Jesus as the 'Midst of Time'"). **What might be going on** (5:24) in the events that are happening in Jerusalem is precisely the plan of God, and to oppose it is to oppose God.

History and theology: The speech contains two historical problems: (1) Theudas was executed by the Romans ca. 44 CE, several years after Gamaliel is purportedly making the speech. Luke and his readers could know about it in retrospect, but it had not yet happened when Gamaliel is purportedly speaking. (2) The episode involving Judas the Galilean happened in connection with the census under Quirinius, i.e., in 6 CE, many years before Theudas, though Luke locates Judas after Theudas (v. 37). Efforts to get Gamaliel (and Luke) to be historically correct on these points have thus far failed. Luke's point, however, is theological and is not dependent on accurate historical data. The issue is, who is the deliverer sent by God, and how can this be known? Luke presents the Christian claim that God has validated Jesus by the resurrection and continues to work in the church by the Spirit, so the church cannot finally be successfully opposed.

5:40 Had them flogged: The beating was a form of punishment for religious violations to which Paul himself was later subject (see 2 Cor. 11:4). They do not wonder where the angel is now (5:19). The God who sent the angel lets them be severely beaten.

5:41 Rejoiced that they were considered worthy to suffer dishonor for the sake of the name: See Matt. 5:12; 1 Pet. 4:13.

5:42 They did not cease to teach and proclaim Jesus as the Messiah: The unit is framed with references to apostolic preaching of the Christian message. On Jesus as the Messiah, see on Mark 8:29. A more accurate translation would be "that the Messiah is Jesus." The question throughout is not who is Jesus? but who is the Messiah, the Savior sent from God? (see 3:20; 17:3; 18:5, 28).

6:1–7
SEVEN CHOSEN TO SERVE

Except for the episode of Ananias and Sapphira (5:1–11), the young church now faces its first internal difficulties. Previously, the church has been portrayed as under duress from outsiders, but internally "of one heart and soul" (4:32). Luke consistently minimizes the actual internal struggles of the church, as we know from a comparison with Paul's letters; when problems within the church do arise, Luke pictures the church as working them out harmoniously under the leadership of the Holy Spirit, as instructed by the apostles.

6:1 The disciples were increasing in number: See the 120 of 1:15, the 3000 of 2:41, the 5000 of 4:4, and the additional multitudes of 5:14. This story shows that the church is growing not only in numbers but theologically, as it adapts to its mission in the world. The church was not born full grown, but under the guidance of the Spirit it creates new structures to fulfill its mission. **Disciples:** See on Luke 6:12–13. This is the first occurrence of the word since Luke 22:45, but henceforth it is used often to designate members of the Christian community. **Hellenists . . . Hebrews:** This denotes a linguistic distinction within the Jerusalem church. Hellenists were Jews whose native language was Greek, who read their Bible and prayed in Greek, and who knew little or no Aramaic, the native language of Palestinian Jews. There was a significant population of Greek-speaking Jews resident in Jerusalem, as evident from recovered ossuaries. Hebrews were Jews who, even if they also knew Greek, spoke Aramaic, and who worshiped and prayed using Aramaic or Hebrew. Paul would be an example of the latter group (21:40; 22:2; 26:14; 2 Cor. 11:22; Phil. 3:5). The situation would be analogous to Hispanic Christians in New York or Houston, some of whom speak only Spanish, attend Spanish-speaking worship services, and read their Bible in Spanish, while others, though they can speak Spanish, know English well, attend English-speaking congregations, worship and read their Bible in English. In Acts 6, the Hellenists were monolingual and had attended Greek-speaking synagogues in Jerusalem prior to becoming Christians, while the Hebrews were bilingual, and attended synagogues where Aramaic and Hebrew were the languages of liturgy and prayer. The new Christian community now includes Jews from both backgrounds. The first test of its unity is whether to become a segregated community with Hellenistic and Hebrew branches, or whether it will be one church. Luke has presented the story of the founding of the one church of Jesus Christ that transcends linguistic and cultural diversity (see on 2:1–13), but now the church faces tensions and a decision. Like Israel in the wilderness, people **complained** (same word as in Num. 11:1). Luke clearly has the Num. 11 scene in mind as he presents this story of the church facing its first structural problem. **Daily distribution:** See 4:35. "Distribution" is literally "ministry"; the same Greek word (*diakonia*) is translated "wait on" (tables) in 6:2, "serving" (the word) in 6:4, and "ministry" in 1:25; 20:24; 21:15. **Widows:** See on Luke 7:12.

6:2 The twelve: The apostles, distinguished from the disciples (see on Luke 6:12–13). **Called together the whole community:** Though now numbering many thousands, Luke pictures the church as able to come together in one place and transact its business in a plenary session. The picture is difficult to imagine historically: where would such a place be available to the new religious group, and how could they do it without incurring the resistance of the Roman authorities, who reacted violently to anything that appeared to be a mob? **Wait on tables:** The Greek phrase is also used in the world of banking to mean "keep accounts" (Luke uses the same term in Luke 19:23). It hardly pictures the apostles as personally delivering food each day; it is a matter of administering a welfare program that had become large and complex.

6:3 Select from among yourselves seven men: Although in the Gospel Luke has told the story of Jesus in such a way as to emphasize women among Jesus' disciples (Luke 1–2; 8:1–3; 10:39–41; 21:1–4; 23:50–24:12), he has yet to portray any women in leadership roles in the early church, but see 16:14–15, 40; 17:12, 34; 18:2, 24–28; 21:8–9. The apostles have authority to

summon the church, to decide that a new structure be instituted, to specify the criteria for the new administrators, to approve the seven candidates selected, and to ordain them to the new work, but not without the church as a whole, which selects the men and presents them for ordination. Here and elsewhere Luke presents a harmonious church working together under apostolic leadership and authority.

6:4 To prayer and to serving the word: "Prayer" is not only personal devotions, but leading the community's worship. "Serving the word" is the preaching and teaching of the new faith to insiders and outsiders, the ministry of evangelism and nurture. Nothing may distract the church from the ministry of the word, which is central to its mission. See on Luke 24:46–49; Acts 2:41; 5:21; and Luke's frequent summing up the life and mission of Jesus and the church as "the word of God" (Luke 3:2; 5:1; 8:11, 21; 11:28; Acts 4:31; 6:2, 7; 8:14; 11:1; 12:24; 13:5, 7, 46; 17:13; 18:11). Two "orders" of ministry emerge, one devoted to worship and the ministry of the word, the other to administering the benevolence program of the church. This passage later became the model and scriptural point of contact for the ministry of bishops, elders, and priests as ministers of the word and sacraments, and deacons as ministers of the church's administrative and benevolence programs. However, none of this terminology is found here. The language of deacons is used for both the apostles and the seven. Language later applied to bishops is used of the seven ("select" [6:3] is related to the word later used for bishops). Elders first appear in Acts 11:30 as church leaders, and then often. Later ideas of church leadership should not be read back into this account, which is not presented as a warrant for a particular kind of church government, but as a model of how the church preserves its unity while adapting to new situations.

6:5 Full of faith and the Holy Spirit: The work of administration also calls for spiritual people nourished in the faith. All seven have Greek names, which may indicate that all belonged to the group of Hellenists (though Hebrews such as Paul could also have Greek names). Since the seven are later shown only as engaged in the ministry of the word (Stephen, 6:8–8:1; Philip, 8:4–40), the division of labor pictured by Luke may represent his own theological picture of the emerging church structure rather than the historical reality. Lying behind Luke's portrayal may be two independent or competing groups of early Christians, one led by the Twelve and one led by the Seven. Such reconstructions are speculative, however, and even if established with some confidence, the church's guide is not a reconstruction of "what really happened" but the present text of Scripture.

6:6 The apostles . . . prayed and laid their hands on them: See Num. 8:10, where the Levites, a secondary order of priests, are commissioned by the laying on of hands, and 27:18–23, where Joshua as Moses' successor is so commissioned. For the laying on of hands as an act that sets certain Christians apart for a particular ministry, see 13:3; 1 Tim. 4:14; 5:22; 2 Tim. 1:6.

6:7 The word of God continued to spread: See on 6:4. **Many of the priests:** Luke does not say they ceased to be Jews or priests when they became members of the new Christian community. **Obedient to the faith:** They obeyed the Christian message. See 5:32. "The faith" is here not subjective belief, but the content that is believed. The early church does not proclaim merely that people should believe, but in its preaching and teaching delivers the substance of the faith to be believed (see Luke 4:15, 31–32; 19:47; 20:1, 37; Acts 2:42; 4:2, 18; 5:21, 25, 28; 13:1, 12; 18:11; 20:20; 28:31).

6:8–7:1
THE ARREST OF STEPHEN

6:8 Wonders and signs: See 2:19–20; 4:30, the signs that the church was begun and continues by the power of God. Such signs were ambiguous and had to be interpreted; they obviously do not convince Stephen's opponents. Stephen (and Philip, 8:4–40) continue to do what the apostles did, despite their selection to "wait on tables" (see on 6:2, 5).

6:9 Synagogue of the Freedmen: These are descendants of Jews taken as slaves to Rome by Pompey in the preceding century, who have returned to Jerusalem and have their own synagogue. They would have been Hellenist Jews like Stephen himself (see on 6:1). Though Luke has presented Jesus as champion of the poor and oppressed (e.g., Luke 4:18–20), he does not romanticize freed slaves, but knows that once liberated they too can become oppressors, as here. **Cyrene and Alexandria** (NIV) were in north Africa; **Cilicia and Asia** were part of what is now Turkey. It is Diaspora Jews, either resident or temporarily present in Jerusalem, who foment the charges (see the similar case of Paul in 21:7, with similar charges).

6:10 The wisdom and the Spirit with which he spoke: Stephen continues as a "minister of the word," despite the division of labor and his ordination to administrative work in 6:6.

6:11 Blasphemous words against Moses and God: On blasphemy, see Luke 5:21. Luke is aware that in his sources the charge of blasphemy was leveled against Jesus and played a crucial role in his trial (Mark 14:64; 15:29) and that Jesus was charged with planning to destroy the temple (Mark 14:58; 15:29), but neither of these plays a role in his account of Jesus' trial (Luke 22:54–23:12). What he has omitted with reference to Jesus he now includes in the portrayal of Stephen's trial.

6:12 The people: As in the Gospel of Luke the people who were at first supportive of Jesus turned against him at his trial (Luke 23:4–5), so in Acts the people as whole who have not been included in the official opposition to the church now join in the charges against Stephen.

6:13–14 False witnesses: The reader knows they are false, but the people in the story do not. Like Jesus, Stephen is finally killed not on the basis of false witnesses, but because of his own true testimony (7:2–8:1). **This holy place:** The temple. In Luke, though Jesus had predicted the destruction of the temple (21:5–6), he had not claimed to destroy it. That Jesus will **change the customs that Moses handed on to us** is also a new charge, and a false one. The church in Acts continues to worship in the temple, and Jewish Christians such as Paul continue to observe the Jewish law and traditions (see 16:3; 18:18; 20:16; 21:17–26).

6:15 His face like the face of an angel: Stephen, like Jesus, is transfigured before them, yet the transformation does not result in their conversion or his deliverance.

7:1 Are these things so?: The high priest has not been a party to arranging for the false witnesses and gives Stephen a chance to defend himself.

7:2–53
STEPHEN'S SPEECH TO THE COUNCIL

The speech is composed by Luke, partly on the basis of traditional source material he has received (see introduction to Acts: "Sources" and "Speeches"). Stephen's speech, the longest in Acts, stands at a transitional point in the story line that will introduce Saul (Paul; 8:1–3), the hero of the second half of Acts. Both its length and its location point to its importance for Luke. The speech will rehearse the history of Israel from Abraham to Stephen's own time, concentrating on the times of Joseph, Moses, and David-Solomon, but its function is not to inform either Stephen's original hearers or the reader about the Old Testament story, for the speech presupposes familiarity with the Bible. Rather, the speech illustrates a particular reading of the Old Testament and Israelite history. This was what was at stake in the church of Luke's time. The church shared the Scriptures of Israel with the Jews, but read them differently (see on Luke 24:25–27, 32, 45–48; Acts 3:17–18, 24). The fact that the speech differs at some points from Luke's own understanding and emphases indicates he has composed it on the basis of earlier tradition, which has its roots ultimately in Diaspora Judaism. For the first time in Acts it becomes visible that some streams within the Christian community itself saw themselves as separating from contemporary Judaism. This was a development of tensions already present between Hellenistic and Palestinian Jews.

7:2 Brothers and fathers: Throughout Acts, the followers of Jesus address non-Christian Jews as members of the same religious community, sharing the same history and Scriptures, not as adherents of another religion (3:17; 13:16–17, 26; 22:3; 23:1; 26:2–8; 28:17–20). "Fathers" is his respectful address to the Sanhedrin, the leaders of the Jewish nation. **The God of glory:** See Ps. 29:1. "God" is the first word of Stephen's speech and the active subject throughout. **Before he lived in Haran:** A town in northern Syria. In Gen. 11:31 Abraham is already in Haran when God speaks to him. Thus Gen. 15:7 was later interpreted to mean that God spoke to Abraham in Ur (in Babylon, contemporary Iraq). Stephen pointedly adopts this Jewish interpretation, though it is in tension with the text of the Bible itself. This is the first of at least ten such discrepancies between Stephen (Luke) and the Old Testament (see below at 7:43).

7:3 Left the country: See Gen. 12:1–3, the foundational promise of the Old Testament. After the human rebellion against God in Eden (Gen. 3), at the time of the flood (Gen. 6–9) and at the tower of Babel (Gen. 11), God ceases to let humankind go their own way to destruction and initiates a saving plan that is both particular and universal. God calls the particular family of Abraham and Sarah and promises to make of them a particular people through whom all the nations of the world will be blessed.

7:4 After his father died: The chronology of the Genesis text (itself composite) makes it appear that Abraham left his aged father in Haran, a violation of later Jewish sensibilities. Hel-

lenistic Judaism had already reinterpreted the chronology to avoid this problem, though it created a tension with the text of the Bible itself (discrepancy #2; see below on 7:43). **The country of the Chaldeans:** Babylon, where Abraham had originally lived. **This country:** Israel, the promised land.

7:5 Even though he had no child: Though Abraham himself never inherited any of the promised land, God's amazing promise was that the covenant people God would create through Abraham and Sarah would inherit the land—a promise made when they were very old and Sarah was sterile (see Gen. 12:1–3; 15:1–6; 17:1–18:15).

7:6 His descendants would be resident aliens: People living in a foreign country without citizenship rights. The image was used in the early church for the situation of Christians (Eph. 2:11; 1. Pet. 1:1; 2:11). **Four hundred years:** Exodus 12:40–41 and Gal. 3:17 give the time as 430 years (discrepancy #3; see below on 7:43).

7:8 Covenant of circumcision: See Gen. 17:1–14; Lev. 12:3; Rom. 2:25–29; 4:9–12; Gal. 5:2–12; Phil. 3:3. The covenant was God's gracious choice of the people Israel to be in a special relationship with him, and to have special responsibilities as God's witness among the nations of the world. The mark of this covenant was circumcision, which came to mean the sign of acceptance by God and the assurance of salvation (see on Acts 15:1–29). **Abraham . . . the twelve patriarchs:** A summary of the story line of Gen. 21–36.

7:9–10 The patriarchs, jealous of Joseph: Stephen takes the Joseph story of Gen. 37–50 as a prototype of the Christ event: in each case the innocent one is rejected by the patriarchs (see the "fathers" Stephen is addressing, 7:2!) but is vindicated by God and becomes the bearer of the promise. The pattern of Acts 2:36 is anticipated. **Favor . . . wisdom:** Another point of contact with Jesus (see Luke 2:52).

7:13 Joseph made himself known to his brothers and . . . to Pharoah: The one who had at first not been recognized becomes known both to Hebrews and Gentiles. This is analogous to the case of Jesus, whose true identity was not recognized until after the resurrection, but who then was seen by both Jews and Gentiles to be God's Messiah.

7:14 Seventy-five in all: Gen. 46:27 gives the number as seventy (discrepancy #4; see on 7:43 below). The problem had already been noted by Hellenistic Jews such as Philo and resolved by allegorical interpretation.

7:16 Shechem: In Gen. 50:13 the bodies are brought to Hebron and buried. **Abraham had bought:** In Gen. 33:19 it is Jacob who buys the property (discrepancies #5 and #6; see on 7:43 below).

7:17 The fulfillment of the promise: In Luke's view the leading motif of the Hebrew Scriptures is that of promise. God promised a land to resident aliens, a nation to a childless couple, and deliverance from Pharoah to powerless slaves. Luke sees the ultimate fulfillment of God's promises in the Christ event and the continuing history of the church, of which the Old Testament stories are prototypes (see on Luke 1:1–4; Acts 3:18).

7:20 At this time Moses was born: The central and longest section of Stephen's speech is devoted to Moses (vv. 20–44), whom he specifically designates as the prototype of Christ (7:37). This is Luke's own theology, also placed in Peter's speech (3:22–23). Just as Luke sees the history of God's saving work as divided into three periods (Israel/Christ/Church; see introduction to Luke: "Jesus as the 'Midst of Time'"), so he explicitly divides the life of Moses into three corresponding periods, each forty years in length:

1. *The People of Promise.* The time of the patriarchs, when God was creating the nation destined to be the covenant people. This corresponds to the time of Israel in Luke's scheme.

2. *The Rejected Deliverer.* The time of Moses himself, who like Jesus to come was "mighty in word and deed" and who was not recognized or understood by the people he tried to deliver.

3. *The Church on the Way.* The "congregation in the wilderness" (7:38) is the true people of God, delivered from bondage and finding itself en route to the fulfillment of God's purpose for them, restructuring itself along the way in order to fulfill its mission.

Luke points out the continuity of all three periods by the occurrence of "signs and wonders," and by the presence of the Holy Spirit, the work of the one God that binds them into one whole. This understanding of the Moses story is the retrojected image of Luke's theological reflection on the place of Jesus and the church in God's plan for the ages. It illustrates how the Old Testament was read in the church as a testimony to the Christian faith, and how the proper way of reading the Bible was a key issue between Jews and Christians.

7:25–26 They did not understand: Just as Moses' own people did not understand that he was the one sent by God to deliver them until after the exodus had already happened, and therefore rejected him at first, so the Jewish people, including Jesus' own disciples, did not understand until after God had raised Jesus from the dead and sent the Holy Spirit (see on Luke 24; Acts 1–2). **God through him was rescuing them:** Literally "providing salvation for them," using the same word elsewhere used of Christian salvation (13:26, 47; 16:17). **Tried to reconcile them:** Literally "bring them together in peace," using the same word used when the angels proclaimed the birth of Jesus as Savior (Luke 2:11–14).

7:29 When he heard this, Moses fled: In Exod. 2:14–15 Moses flees because of his fear of Pharaoh; here, it is because he is rejected by his fellow Hebrews, providing a better prototype of the Jesus story (discrepancy #7).

7:30 When forty years had passed: See Exod. 3:1. The Old Testament does not specify the length of the period, but Luke inserts the data into the story here to make the periodization clear (see above at 7:20; discrepancy #8). **An angel appeared:** See vv. 35, 38, 53. Here and elsewhere in Luke–Acts, angels are regarded positively as agents of God's own activity (see on Luke 1:10–12).

7:32 I am the God of your ancestors, the God of Abraham, Isaac, and Jacob: Just as Luke regards the Christian faith not as a new religion but as the continuation and fulfillment of the old, so Moses did not bring a new God to the Israelites, but represented the one God of their ancestral faith.

7:33 The place: In the exodus story, the reference is to Mount Sinai where the Law was given, but "this place" later was used by the Jews of the holy place in Jerusalem where the temple was built (John 4:20; 11:48; Acts 6:13; 21:28). Stephen's point is that God appeared to Abraham and Moses, but not at the temple, and without sacrifice. God appeared to them in a foreign land, to people born and educated in the ways of the Gentiles. This reflects the ideology of some streams of Hellenistic Judaism, in which an antitemple polemic had developed. When such Jews became Christians, they brought this view of the temple with them. This is not Luke's own perspective; he has a positive view of the temple (see on Luke 1:5–2:52; 1:5–12; 2:22–52; Acts 2:46; 3:1). Such data indicate that the speeches in Acts are not entirely Luke's own composition, but reflect traditional materials.

7:35–36 Who made you a ruler and a judge?: God had sent Moses as their deliverer, but they rejected him as acting on his own authority. But God reversed the human decision and sent Moses back as ruler and judge. The parallel with Jesus is clear, further confirmed by the reference to **wonders and signs** in v. 36.

7:37 God will raise up a prophet for you from your own people: Deut. 18:15–18. See on Luke 9:35–36; Acts 3:22–23.

7:38 The congregation in the wilderness: Here Luke uses the same word he uses for the Christian community, elsewhere translated "church" (e.g., 5:11; 8:1). As Luke sees the life of Moses as parallel to that of Jesus, so he regards experience of Israel in the wilderness between the Red Sea and the promised land as parallel to the time of the church between Easter and the Parousia (see "Jesus as the 'Midst of Time'" in the introduction to Luke).

7:40 This Moses: See "This Jesus" of 2:23, 32, 36.

7:41–42 Reveled in the work of their hands: Without knowing it, those who rejected Moses had rejected God and thus became idolaters. **God . . . handed them over:** God's punishment for idolatry is to let them be idolaters (see Deut. 4:16; Hos. 13:2–4; Rom. 1:24, 26, 28).

7:42–43 As it is written: Amos 5:25–27. During the wilderness period between Egypt and the promised land, Israel did not offer sacrifice, and yet God was with them. **Moloch . . . Rephan:** The names of pagan gods. Luke portrays Stephen as citing the LXX (Septuagint, the Greek translation of the Hebrew Scriptures), which has names for these gods different from the Hebrew text of Amos translated in the English Bible (see on 2:16; discrepancy #9). **I will remove you beyond Babylon:** Exile is God's punishment for idolatry. The text of Amos, both Hebrew and LXX, reads "beyond Damascus," referring to the deportation of the Israelites by the Assyrians in 2 Kgs. 17. Stephen understands the text to refer to the later deportation of Judeans by the Babylonians, and changes the text accordingly (2 Kgs. 24). This is discrepancy #10 between Stephen's speech and the present text of the Old Testament.

EXCURSUS:
INTERPRETING DISCREPANCIES
IN THE BIBLE

Attention to such details as pointed out above should not be considered pickiness or lack of respect for the Bible, but the opposite: precisely because the Bible is the church's normative Scripture that mediates the Word of God, it should be studied with great care. Such study brings to light the kind of discrepancies pointed out above. How should they be understood? Four approaches have been suggested:

1. The discrepancies are only apparent, and further study will reveal that in every point both the Old Testament and Stephen's speech are entirely accurate. Such apparent discrepancies must be harmonized, or the Bible is not "true." Since Christian faith believes the Bible to be true, a way must and can be found to harmonize each of the apparent discrepancies. This view rests on a prior judgment about what the Bible must be like if it is true, a view not derived from the Bible itself.

2. The discrepancies are real and cannot be resolved by further study. Such mistakes show that the Bible is false and cannot be trusted. Christian faith must be abandoned or must be based on foundations other than the Bible. This view has the same (unbiblical) understanding of the nature of God's revelation in the Bible as the first view stated above, but draws the opposite conclusion from the biblical data itself.

3. The discrepancies are real, but in this instance they are not a problem, since it is Stephen, not the Bible, that is in error. Luke accurately reports what Stephen said, but he made at least ten errors in his references to the Old Testament text. Both Acts and the Old Testament are preserved as totally accurate at Stephen's expense. This approach runs into difficulties, however, when Jesus, Paul, or other inspired apostles are "accurately" quoted as having made mistakes.

4. The discrepancies are real and cannot be harmonized. The truth of the biblical message is not dependent on infallibility in detail. This need not be a grudging concession, but can be celebrated as part of the biblical witness that God has chosen to work through fallible human beings, that the treasure of the gospel is placed in clay jars (2 Cor. 4:7). This is the view represented by this commentary.

7:44 The tent of testimony: The tabernacle, the sacred tent that Israel constructed during the wilderness period as the symbol of God's presence among them (Exod. 25–27). "Testimony" refers both to the witness to God's presence symbolized by the tabernacle, and to the tablets of the Law, called the "testimony," that it contained. **According to the pattern he had seen:** Exod. 25:9, 40; see Heb. 8:5. Stephen's point is that the tabernacle was built by divine command according to a heavenly pattern, but that this was not true of the later temple.

7:45–50 Until the time of David: The story moves very quickly from the time of Moses to the time of David. Luke regards both Moses and David as prototypes of Christ. Stephen's point is that neither constructed a temple. Stephen does not mention that when **Solomon** (David's son) built the temple, this, too, was by God's command, but cites a prophetic critique of (misuse of) the temple (Isa. 66:1–2). Neither does he mention that at the dedication of the temple, Solomon's prayer emphasized that God dwells in heaven, and that no house made by human hands can contain him (1 Kgs. 8:27–30).

7:51–53 You stiff-necked people: Stubborn, self-willed (Exod. 33:3, 5); Stephen shifts abruptly from recitation of Israel's history to a direct charge against his own accusers, but maintains the biblical idiom. **Uncircumcised in heart and ears:** Not really belonging to the covenant people, though you bear the external mark of the covenant (Lev. 26:41; Deut. 10:16; Jer. 4:4; 6:10; 9:26). **Forever opposing the Holy Spirit:** Not previously mentioned, but Stephen expresses the Jewish view that the **prophets** were inspired by the Holy Spirit, so to oppose the prophets was to resist the Holy Spirit. **The law as ordained by angels:** See 7:38; Gal. 3:19. Stephen expresses the later Jewish view that God did not give the Law directly, but through angelic mediators. Here the phrase is understood positively: the Law is good and comes from God (through angels); the temple, in contrast, is a human imposition. On the variety of New Testament perspective on angels, see on 5:19; Luke 1:10–12. **Have not kept it:** By building the temple, for which the Law made no provision.

7:54–8:1a
THE STONING OF STEPHEN

7:54 When they heard these things, they became enraged: The same reaction as in 5:33, expressed with the same phrase. This time, the religious leaders carry out their murderous intent, and Stephen becomes the first Christian martyr ("martyr" is derived from the same root as "witness"; see on 1:8).

7:55 Jesus standing at the right hand of God: See on 2:33–34; 5:30. The Jewish leaders realize that the claim Jesus is now enthroned in heaven is not a speculative christological point. If Stephen really sees the risen Christ at God's right hand, then the Jewish council has become God's enemy, as Gamaliel had warned (5:39).

7:56 The Son of Man: See on Mark 2:10. The title is found only here outside the Gospels, and

almost always on the lips of Jesus himself (though see Rev. 1:13; 14:14).

7:58 Outside the city: One of numerous parallels between the death of Jesus and the death of Stephen (Luke 4:28–29; 23:26–33; see Heb. 13:13). **Began to stone him:** Stoning was the prescribed method of capital punishment for several offenses in the Old Testament law, including the crime of blasphemy, of which Stephen is accused (Lev. 24:10–23). While the trial takes place before the official council, and there are witnesses, Luke's description resembles a riot and lynching more than an official verdict and execution (see 21:27–36). Whether the Jewish leaders had authority for capital punishment is a disputed historical point (see Luke 23:1).

7:59 Receive my spirit: Psalm 31:5. Like Jesus, Stephen dies with a psalm of trust on his lips (see Luke 23:46). **Spirit** here means "breath" (the same word in Greek); see Luke 2:46; 8:55.

7:60 Lord: In the previous verse "Lord" specifically refers to (the exalted) Jesus; here, the word addresses a prayer to God, like that of Jesus. In Luke's Christology the images of God and Jesus flow into each other. See on 5:4. On the theocentric nature of Luke's Christology, see Luke 7:16; 8:24, 38; 9:20–22, 43; 13:13; 17:15; 19:37. **Do not hold this sin against them:** Another parallel to the death of Jesus (see Luke 23:34; Rom. 12:19; contrast Ps. 69:27; 2 Chr. 24:22, and the deaths of the Maccabean martyrs, e.g., 2 Macc. 7:17).

8:1 Saul: The Jewish name of Paul (his Roman name; see on 13:9), who will be the missionary hero of the second half of Acts (9:1–30; 13:1–28:31). Saul first appears in the story as a persecutor of the church. He will later be subject to the same kind of persecution from zealous and sincere Jewish authorities, including stoning (22:4, 20; 26:10; John 16:2; 2 Cor. 11:23–28).

8:1b–3
SAUL PERSECUTES THE CHURCH

8:1 A severe persecution began against the church in Jerusalem: The earliest church experienced persecution at the hands of Jewish leaders (1 Thess. 2:14–16). This historical reality should be distinguished from the later Christian perspective in which it is presented by Luke. Historically, it was a matter of internal Jewish conflicts that sometimes became violent. In the troubles of the Maccabean period, some Jewish groups opposed others with violence, even killing those considered to be renegades (1 Macc. 1–2). The Jewish group at Qumran experienced violence at the hands of the Jerusalem leadership. The earliest Christians were Jews and were opposed by the defenders of Jewish orthodoxy, not because they confessed faith in Jesus as the Messiah, but because their practice was considered a violation of Jewish identity. In 6:8–7:60, Stephen is killed, not because he is a Christian, but because of his violation of Jewish practice.

Luke does not here give the reasons for the persecution, but in 5:17–52 he has already indicated that it is "for the sake of the name," i.e., people are persecuted by Jews because they are Christians. This represents the perspective from within the Christian community of Luke's own day, when the Christian disciples had become a separate religious community distinct from Judaism. In Jewish eyes, Jews guilty of conduct dangerous to Judaism were being controlled and disciplined; from the later Christian perspective, believers were being persecuted because of their confession of Jesus as Son of God (9:1, 22).

8:2 Scattered throughout the countryside of Judea and Samaria: If the story is taken literally, this means that thousands of Jerusalem Christians left their homes and property and became refugees (see 2:41, 4:4). Luke's interest is in the fulfillment of Jesus' command and prediction in 1:8, that the church that began in Jerusalem will spread to Judea, Samaria, and beyond. Eventually this dispersion of the church resulting from the persecution that followed Stephen's death will lead to new churches in Phoenicia, Cyprus, and Antioch (11:19), but Luke does not inform the reader of that yet, since he wishes to unfold the story of the church's expansion gradually and systematically, by definite stages.

Except the apostles: Historically, this may reflect that the first persecution was directed against Hellenistic Christians like Stephen, who opposed the temple and relaxed the Law, without affecting Palestinian Jewish Christians such as the apostles. Luke's point, however, is that the apostles are Christ's authorized representatives and that Jerusalem is something like an "official headquarters" of the developing church, as indicated in vv. 14–25 (see 9:26–30; 15:1–35).

8:3 Saul was ravaging the church: See Gal. 1:13; Phil. 3:6 for Paul's own confirmation of his pre-Christian life as a persecutor, and 2 Cor. 11:24; 1 Thess. 2:14–16 for confirmation of Jew-

ish persecution of early Christians, seen from Paul's perspective after he himself had become a Christian. **Men and women:** Luke often pairs men and women as sharing both the triumphs and troubles of the life of the church (5:1, 14, 8:3, 12; 9:2; 17:12, 34; 22:4).

8:4–40
THE CHURCH WITNESSES IN JUDEA AND SAMARIA

8:4–25
PHILIP PREACHES IN SAMARIA

8:4 From place to place, proclaiming the word: Though pictured as refugees driven from their homes, the church under stress does not turn inward, concerned only with personal or institutional survival, but continues its mission even under the worst of circumstances. So also Paul, though taken to Rome as prisoner, will incorporate his arrest and imprisonment into his call to be a missionary, and continue his mission even as prisoner (21:27–28:31; see 16:19–40).

8:5 Philip: One of the seven chosen to administer the welfare program of the Jerusalem church (6:1–6). Like Stephen, also one of the seven, his further activity is pictured as evangelistic and missionary, as a preacher and worker of miracles. **Went down:** Philip went north; just as one customarily spoke of "going up" to the mountain city of Jerusalem, so also one "went down" from Jerusalem in whatever direction. **Samaria:** The name of both the district and its leading town (cf. New York, NY). In accord with 1:8, the church now enters a new phase of its mission. On Samaritans, see on Luke 9:52. Of the Synoptic Gospels, only Luke is concerned with Samaritans (see Matt. 10:5!), but he shares this concern with the Gospel of John (John 4:1–42). **Proclaimed the Messiah:** See 17:3; 18:5, 28 (8:37). That Jesus is the Christ is the central affirmation of the Christian faith (see on Mark 8:29). Philip did not proclaim new ideas, theories, or principles, but that God had acted decisively for human salvation by sending the Messiah. The same Christian message is summarized in v. 12 as the "kingdom of God," and "the name of Jesus Christ," and in v. 14 as the "word of God." The Samaritans did not share the Jewish expectation of a coming Messiah, but had their own expectation of a final deliverer that God would send, the eschatological prophet called the "Restorer." Luke does not picture the missionaries as first getting the Samaritans to share the Jewish expectation, but has Philip proclaim the message of the Christ as the fulfillment of the Samaritan hopes. This is the first step of the church beyond its Jewish origins, its first adaptation to preaching the gospel in the wider pluralistic world. The Samaritans do not have to become Jews before they can become Christians, but move directly from their Samaritan faith to Christian faith. Christian missionaries do not preach a different message among Samaritans than they have preached among Jews, but present the Christian faith as the fulfillment of the Samaritan hope, just as it is for the Jewish hope.

8:7 Unclean spirits: On the language of demons, Satan, and exorcism, see excursus at Mark 5:1. The Holy Spirit at work in the church encounters the other spirits at work in the world and overcomes them.

8:9–10 Simon . . . previously practiced magic: Often called Simon Magus (Simon the magician) in later tradition, he appears only here in the New Testament. The Bible consistently distinguishes magic from Jewish and Christian faith, often putting magicians over against advocates of authentic faith (e.g., Gen. 41:8–24; Exod. 7:11, 22; 8:7, 18–19; 9:11; Ezek. 13:8; Dan. 1:20; 2:2, 10, 27; 5:11; Acts 13:8; 19:19). Magic is the belief in supernatural forces and the attempt to manipulate them for human benefit. Unfortunately, this is the way "religion" is sometimes defined. Biblical faith makes it clear that faith is a personal relation to a personal God, not merely a belief in mysterious supernatural forces. **This man is the power of God that is called Great:** Behind this description may be Simon's own claim to represent a divine being. "Great" may be the Greek form of a Semitic word for "revealer." Thus more may be at stake here than merely a local trickster. A rival religious claim may be represented by Simon, who already had a following among the Samaritans.

8:12 Kingdom of God: See on Luke 4:43. **Name of Jesus Christ:** See on 2:38. On these terms as summaries of the Christian message, see 8:5 above.

8:13 Simon believed . . . (was) baptized: It is not said that his faith is insincere. He does the same things that others do to become Christians, and becomes a member of the church (see on 2:38).

8:14 The apostles at Jerusalem: See on Luke 6:12–16; 24:44–49; Acts 1:12–26; 2:1–14; 8:14–25; 9:26–30; 15:1–29. Luke understands

the apostles as a group specially chosen and authorized by Jesus to supervise the developing church. Jerusalem serves as the church's headquarters during this period of geographical and theological development. New developments are welcomed, but cannot happen haphazardly; they must be approved by the apostles. This is Luke's way of affirming the church's unity that embraces variety. **Accepted the word of God:** See Luke 3:2; 5:1; 8:11, 21; 11:28; Acts 4:31; 6:2, 7; 11:1; 12:24; 13:5, 7, 46; 17:13; 18:11). This is another way of summarizing the Christian message (see 8:5).

8:16 As yet the Spirit had not come upon any of them: This statement is in stark contrast to 2:38 and 5:32, which indicate that God gives the Holy Spirit at baptism to all who are obedient. This and other tensions have sometimes been explained by an elaborate systematizing of Luke's doctrine of the Spirit. The explanation goes back to Reformation times (John Calvin) and has been popular in some traditional streams of Protestantism. It attempts to harmonize Luke's statements about the Spirit by sorting them out into three categories:

1. The *baptism of the Holy Spirit*, assumed to have occurred only twice: Acts 2:1–13, at the inauguration of the church among Jews, and Acts 10:44–47, at the inauguration of the church among Gentiles. The special mark of the baptism of the Holy Spirit is speaking in tongues, and it is given directly by God. After the establishment of the church among Jews and Gentiles, the baptism of the Holy Spirit was no longer needed and has not occurred since. Christians in general are not baptized in the Spirit.

2. The *special gifts* of the Holy Spirit, which convey the power to work miracles such as healings and exorcisms. This ability was given to the young church to confirm its faith and aid its missionary enterprise. It was not given to Christians generally, but was received only by imposition of the hands of the apostles. It disappeared after the death of the apostles and those to whom they had conferred this special gift.

3. The *general gift* of the Holy Spirit, conveyed at baptism to every believer. This gift of the Spirit incorporates believers into the church and empowers them for the Christian life. It is not miraculous or spectacular, but results in the "fruits of the Spirit" (Gal. 5:22), the greatest of which is love (1 Cor. 13). The baptism of the Spirit and the special gifts of the Spirit passed away with the first Christian

generation, but the general gift of the Spirit abides with the church throughout the ages.

This neat arrangement has been popular in some traditions because it seems to make coherent sense of the variety of descriptions of the work of the Spirit found in the New Testament, but is too systematic to do justice to the biblical data, including Luke's view presented in Acts. Here are some of the difficulties: (a) The biblical terminology is not as consistent as called for by this scheme. Paul uses "baptism in the Spirit" as a designation for what happens to Christians generally (1 Cor. 12:13), and does not distinguish between "special gifts" given to some Christians and a "general gift" given to all—all Christians have gifts of the Spirit, some spectacular, some not (1 Cor. 12–14). Luke uses the same Greek word, *dorea* ("gift") to designate all the manifestations of the Spirit: baptism, special gifts, general gifts (Acts 2:38; 8:20; 10:45; 11:17). Speaking in tongues is not limited to the baptism of the Holy Spirit as called for by the presumed systematic scheme, either by Luke or Paul (see Acts 19:6; 1 Cor. 14). Luke pictures believers as repeatedly filled with the Spirit to empower them for special occasions, in ways that do not fit into the neat scheme outlined above (Luke 1:15, 41, 67; 2:4; 4:8, 31; 5:3; 9:17; 13:9, 52; see Rom. 15:13; Eph. 5:18).

Rather than presenting a systematic doctrine of the Holy Spirit, Luke's concern seems to be to include a variety of ways that the Spirit was experienced and understood in early Christianity within the one church, and yet to "regulate" the work of the Spirit by the apostolic norm. Luke is concerned to hold together three elements of the life of the church: baptism, the Holy Spirit, and apostolic approval. In his understanding, all Christians are baptized, all Christians receive the gift of the Holy Spirit, and all Christians live together in the one church guided by the apostles. When in his story he comes across deviations from this pattern, he shows that it was remedied by responsible church leadership. Thus, as here, when people are baptized but do not receive the Holy Spirit, he shows that they did in fact receive it by apostolic approval (see 18:24–19:7). When people receive the Spirit without being baptized, he shows that they can and must then be baptized (10:44–48). In his understanding of the church, there can be no baptized believers without the Holy Spirit, and none can have the Holy Spirit without becoming baptized believers. There can be no

individualistic bearers of the Spirit for whom church membership is optional, just as there can be no Christians who have "just been baptized" but who do not participate in the life of the Spirit given to the church. But Luke does not have a uniform pattern or systematic doctrine of the Spirit that accounts for all this.

8:17 Laid their hands on them, and they received the Holy Spirit: As in 10:44–48; 11:15–18, the coming of the Holy Spirit signals the divine approval of incorporating the Samaritans into the one church of God.

8:18 Simon . . . offered them money: Luke's concern in this story is not to present a systematic doctrine of the Spirit, but to warn against its commercialization. It was not unusual in pagan religions for offices to be bought. Priesthood in some pagan cults was available for purchase. Simon reflects a pagan understanding of the church that Luke rejects. Luke is concerned with the danger of greed and its relation to the faith (see 16:16–22; 19:24–25). The later church referred to the sale of ecclesiastical offices as "simony."

8:20 May your silver perish with you: More colloquially, "To hell with you and your money" (as translated by J. B. Phillips).

8:22 Repent . . . and pray: Luke is aware that baptized believers are not instantly made perfect. The remedy is repentance (reorientation of life and priorities; see on Luke 3:7–9). Simon realizes that he not only needs to pray himself, but belongs to a community that prays for him. Simon plays a large role in later legendary accounts as an archheretic, but Luke gives no indication of this and ends the story on a positive note.

8:25 Proclaiming the good news: The whole story is framed by references to the missionary preaching of the church (see 8:4). Wherever the church of God finds itself, in word and deed it bears witness to the saving act of God in Christ. **They** (NIV): Includes Philip, who is back in Jerusalem in the next scene. **Peter and John** are not in the Greek text; see NRSV note.

8:26–40
PHILIP AND THE ETHIOPIAN EUNUCH

Luke continues to display the step-by-step progress of the church in becoming a universal, inclusive community representing God's love and acceptance of all (see chart at 15:1).

8:26 The angel of the Lord: On angels in Luke–Acts, see on Luke 1:10–12; Acts 5:19. The angel modulates into the Spirit at 8:29; see 8:39.

The point is that transitions to new horizons in the church's mission are made at the divine initiative. **Go toward the south:** (May also be translated "at noon"; see 10:9; 26:13) In the previous story, the gospel is taken north to Samaria. In the remainder of Acts, this progress will be traced further north to the key city of Antioch, from which it will proceed westward to Europe and finally to Rome. But first Luke gives a brief vignette presenting the conversion of an African. Acts is entirely silent on the progress of the gospel eastward. **To Gaza:** In the Old Testament, one of the five cities of the Philistines; southwest of Jerusalem, on the road to Egypt and the African interior. The story will conclude at Azotus (= Ashdod; 8:40), another of the Philistine cities. Luke may already be conjuring up in the reader's mind the image of "uncircumcised Philistines," i.e., outsiders to the people of God, but people who will be evangelized and brought within the Christian community. **A wilderness road:** Perhaps more than a mere geographical note. "Wilderness" was the location of the wandering people of God led by Moses, the "church in the wilderness" (see 7:30, 36, 38, 42, 44; 13:18), the prototype of the Christian community.

8:27 Ethiopian: Not identical with the modern state, ancient Ethiopia (Old Testament "Cush") was the kingdom in the Nile valley of southern Egypt and northern Sudan. **Eunuch:** Castrated males were employed as guards and chamberlains in the palaces and harems of Eastern monarchs. The term then came to be used of chamberlains and court officials generally, not only of those who had been surgically changed. **Court official:** Literally, "powerful one," since he was secretary of the treasury. **The Candace:** Not a proper name, but a title, Queen Mother. **He had come to Jerusalem to worship:** Nothing is said of the religious status of the eunuch. That he worships in Jerusalem and reads the Jewish Scriptures suggests that he is a Jew, but this would violate the development of Luke's story line (see on 15:1). According to Deut. 23:1, physical eunuchs were excluded from the people of God, but Isa. 56:1–8 points to a time when eunuchs and foreigners will be included, and God's house will be "a house of prayer for all peoples." Luke sees the Ethiopian as a transitional figure who worships the Jewish God, reads the Jewish Scriptures, but is still an outsider to the people of God. He will now be evangelized and baptized by Philip and incorporated into the Christian community.

8:28 Reading the prophet Isaiah: Isaiah 53:7–8, a passage about the Servant of the Lord (see on 3:13). Isaiah is Luke's favorite book, appearing at key passages in the narrative, including its programmatic opening and closing scenes (e.g., Luke 3:4–6 [Isa. 3:4–6]; 4:18–19 [= Isa. 61:1–2]; Acts 28:26–27 [Isa. 6:9–10]).

8:29 The Spirit: (= the angel of 8:26; see Heb. 1:7 = Ps. 104:4). Whether conceptualized as angel or Spirit, God is directing the expansion of the church. The spiritual phenomena do not directly convert the Ethiopian, but serve to bring him and the evangelist together. Despite all the supernatural phenomena in the conversion stories in Acts, it is the message of the gospel that generates faith. See on 9:10; 10:9.

8:30 Heard him reading: Even private reading was done aloud in the ancient world. Centuries later, Augustine was surprised that Ambrose of Milan read silently. All the Bible was written to be read aloud and perceived by the ear. The modern reader can often come to good insights about the meaning of the text by hearing it read aloud.

8:31 How can I, unless someone guides me? Luke does not understand the meaning of Scripture to be transparent. Scripture is not in fact self-interpreting, but requires a community of faith in order to be faithfully interpreted. The Bible is not the individual's book, but belongs to the church (2 Pet. 1:19–21; 3:14–18; see "Introduction: The New Testament as the Church's Book," 4.f). This is of course no discouragement of private Bible reading and study, but means that Christian readers of the Bible should avail themselves of the insights into the meaning of the Bible provided by the whole community of faith as represented in its preaching, teaching, study groups, and commentaries and aids to biblical interpretation. Books such at *The People's New Testament Commentary* mediate not merely individual insights, but the treasure of the whole church's wisdom gathered through the centuries and around the world.

8:32–33 So he does not open his mouth: Luke understands the text to point to Jesus (see excursus, "New Testament Interpretation of the Old Testament," at 1 Cor. 15:3, and comments on Luke 21:22; 24:25). In the Synoptic Gospels, Jesus is virtually silent at his trial (in contrast to John 18:19–19:12). **Justice was denied him:** In his account of Jesus' trial, Luke emphasizes that Jesus was innocent of the charges against him (see Luke 23:4, 15, 22, 47). **Who can describe his generation?** (NRSV):

This translation understands the Greek text as a reproach against Jesus' contemporaries who denied him justice. **Who can speak of his descendants?** (NIV): Another possible translation, referring to the Old Testament figure who was put to death before he fathered a family, and so left behind no descendants, a great tragedy in the Jewish perspective. This translation is to be preferred, since it also allows the eunuch to identify with the Servant. **His life is taken away from the earth:** Luke understands the death of Jesus to be part of God's saving plan, but avoids citing the specific elements of this passage that point to the death of the Servant as an atonement for sin (see Isa. 53:5–6, 10–11, which are interpreted elsewhere in the New Testament in terms of the atoning death of Jesus [1 Pet. 2:24–25]). See on Luke 22:20; Acts 2:23.

8:34 About whom . . . does the prophet say this?: The question was already disputed in ancient Judaism. The Servant was sometimes interpreted as referring to Israel (the view of most modern interpreters), but was sometimes seen as an individual such as Jeremiah who suffered in behalf of the people. Whether the passage was already understood to point to a future Messiah in early Judaism remains a disputed point.

8:35 Proclaimed to him the good news of Jesus: Philip (and Luke) are clear that the Scripture points to Jesus. The content of his message is not given, but it must have included not only the story of Jesus' life, death, and resurrection, but his call to discipleship and command to be baptized.

8:36 What as to prevent me?: Perhaps reflecting part of the early Christian baptismal liturgy, in which, after the candidate for baptism had confessed his or her faith, the question was raised (as in the traditional English marriage ceremony). The Bible itself had hindered the eunuch from participating in the covenant people of God (Deut. 23:1), but now the same book of Isaiah that had promised full participation to those excluded (Isa. 56:3–4), interpreted in the light of Christ, removes all hindrances.

8:37 I believe that Jesus Christ is the Son of God: These words are not in the best and most ancient manuscripts of Acts and probably represent an early marginal gloss that later was incorporated into the text. While probably not from Luke, they do indeed represent an accurate Lukan summary of the faith that is to be confessed when one is baptized. Such phenomena as the uncertainty of what is the orig-

inal biblical text and what is later church tradition illustrates that the boundary between Scripture and tradition is not sharp. (The original text of no New Testament document has been preserved, but must be painstakingly reconstructed from the hundreds of surviving manuscripts, no two of which are exactly alike. See discussion in "Introduction: The New Testament as the Church's Book" 4.d, and comments on Mark 16:9–20; Luke 5:39; 8:26, 43; 10:1; 14:5; 22:19, 43–44; 23:34; John 7:53–8:1; Acts 8:37; 1 Cor. 2:1; 14:34–35, and the footnotes throughout NRSV and NIV.)

8:38–39 Went down into the water . . . came up out of the water: Immersion as the mode of baptism is here presupposed. See on Rom. 6:1–11.

8:39 The Spirit of the Lord snatched Philip away: Like the Old Testament prophets Elijah (2 Kgs. 2:16) and Ezekiel (Ezek. 11:24). The Spirit is not thought of as a subtle internal "spiritual" suggestion, but as a dynamic power. The dramatic ending of the story corresponds to its beginning, showing the power of God at work in the growing and changing church.

8:40 Azotus: On the correspondence of Azotus and Gaza, see on 8:26. **Proclaimed the good news to all the towns:** See on 8:25. The two stories end on a similar note. **Caesarea:** By bringing the story line to Caesarea, the stage is now set for the next great step in the church's geographical and theological expansion (10:1–11:26). But first, the second leading actor in the unfolding drama must be reintroduced and converted.

9:1–14:28
THE CHURCH WITNESSES TO GENTILES

9:1–19a
CONVERSION OF SAUL/PAUL

Paul never refers to his encounter with the risen Lord as a conversion, either in Acts or his own letters, but speaks of his call (e.g., Rom. 1:1; Gal. 1:15). He never thought of himself as being converted from one religion to another, as conversion was understood in the later history of the church. Paul does undergo a fundamental transformation and reorientation of his life in his encounter with the risen Christ, and in this sense we may properly continue to speak of his conversion.

Paul was not converted from one religion to another. He never ceased to be a Jew, and in his day Christianity had not become a separate religion, but was a group within Judaism that believed that Jesus of Nazareth was the Messiah sent by God. Paul was not converted from being irreligious to being religious—he was already a very religious person, and persecuted Christians on the basis of deep religious convictions. Paul was not converted from unbelief to belief—he was already a person of deep faith. He was not converted from insincerity to sincerity—his pre-Christian life was entirely sincere. He was not converted from atheism to theism—he had always believed in the one God of biblical and Jewish faith. He was not converted from not believing in a Messiah to believing in a Messiah. As a Jewish Pharisee, he already believed that God would send the Messiah to fulfill the divine plan and bring in the kingdom of God. In what, then, did Paul's conversion consist? *The one life-transforming change was that he came to believe that God had sent the Messiah, and his name was Jesus of Nazareth.* The one who had previously believed that the Christian claims for Jesus were delusion or deceit came to believe that they were true: God had acted decisively for the salvation of the world; the crucified and risen one is God's Messiah.

Luke considers Paul's conversion to be so important that he relates it three times: once in the words of the narrator (9:1–19) and twice in speeches given by Paul (22:1–21; 26:2–23). The event was also important to Paul, who refers to it in 1 Cor. 9:1; 15:8–10; Phil. 3:6–8; and especially in Gal. 1:11–16. Just as Luke's accounts are not biographical, so Paul's are not autobiographical; both are concerned with the theological meaning of the event. Nor is there any psychological interest. When he encounters the risen Christ, Paul is not searching, consciously or unconsciously, for God, but is pursuing what he confidently assumes to be God's will.

9:1 Threats and murder: Paul's ardor is not personal hostility, but is like that of a prosecuting attorney determined to eliminate organized crime (see on 5:29; 8:1). He persecutes Christians, not because they are members of another religion, but because they represent a dangerous element in his own religion. Thus he goes to the Jewish **synagogues** in Damascus, not to the population in general. In Luke's story line these would presumably be Jerusalem Jewish Christians who had fled to Damascus (8:1–3), not indigenous Jews who had become Christians. **Damascus:** A large city in Syria, northeast of Jerusalem, it is strategically located and has been an important city from the most ancient times (Gen. 14:15; 15:2) until today. At the time this story takes place, it was loosely a part of the Roman Empire, but controlled by the Nabatean king Aretas IV. **The Way:** Only in Acts as a description of the church (18:25, 26; 19:9, 23; 22:4; 22:14, 22; see Isa. 40:3; Luke 3:4). The people of Qumran (Essenes) also saw their community as the fulfillment of Isa. 40:3, and in the Dead Sea Scrolls referred often to their group as the Way. The term designates the Christians as a particular group within Judaism.

9:3 A light from heaven: In Luke's view, the appearance to Paul was different from the preascension appearances to the Twelve (Luke 24:36–53; Acts 1:1–11), and does not qualify Paul to be an apostle (see the Lukan qualifications for apostleship in Acts 1:21–22, and the comments on 14:4, 14). Contrast 1 Cor. 9:1; 15:3–11; Gal. 1:1, 11–16, where it is important to Paul to emphasize that he encountered the risen Lord in the same way as the other apostles.

9:4 Why do you persecute me?: The heavenly Lord identifies himself with his disciples on earth. Luke does not have the Pauline concept of the church as the body of Christ (1 Cor. 12:12–27; Rom. 12:3–8), but affirms the same reality in his own way.

9:5 Who are you, Lord?: Since Saul does not yet know the identity of the speaker, "Lord" is here used in the conventional sense of "sir," as in Luke 13:25; 19:16, 18, 20, 25.

9:6 Enter the city, and you will be told what you are to do: It is not directly from heaven that Paul receives the content of the gospel or what he should do in order to become a Christian. This will be communicated to him in the way that Luke considers "standard," by the church's own messengers. As in the other conversion stories in Acts (2:1–42; 3:11–4:4; 8:26–40; 10:1–48; 16:11–15, 25–40; 17:16–34), God is at work in the conversion process, but those who are converted do not receive instructions directly from heaven or from their inner experiences. God uses human agents to communicate the gospel and to guide people into the Christian way.

9:7 They heard the voice but saw no one: See Dan. 10:7. Luke models the call of Paul on the call of the visionary experiences of the Old Testament prophets. See 22:9, where Paul's companions saw the light but did not hear the voice. Though the other members of Paul's party participate in the transcendent experience, they do not become Christians. All attention is focused on Paul. Luke will later have Paul refer to this experience as a vision (26:19), but this does not mean for him that it was any less objectively real.

9:9 For three days he was without sight: Paul's blindness is not punitive (contrast 13:4–12), but is symbolic of his unbelief (see Isa. 6:9–10; Acts 28:26–27). The scales that fall from his eyes in v. 19 represent an authentic conversion.

9:10–11 Ananias: A disciple in Damascus, but Luke provides no details as to whether he is a resident or one of the refugees from the Jerusalem church (8:1–3). So also **Judas,** who has a **house** in Damascus. Luke focuses all attention on the conversion of Saul, so that to ask for historically realistic details is to miss the point. Unlike Saul, Ananias registers no surprise or fear at the vision. In the story line, it represents the work of God behind the scenes to bring together Saul and Ananias (see 8:26–29; 10:1–16). **A man of Tarsus named Saul:** Tarsus is named for the first time. In previous references to Saul, the reader would suppose he is from Jerusalem (7:58; 8:1; 9:1–2). Tarsus was a large city in the southeast of what is now Turkey, at that time the capital of the Roman province of Cilicia, a cultural and intellectual center (see 21:39, "no mean city" [KJV, RSV]). **He is praying:** Although Saul has seen the heavenly light, heard the heavenly voice, and is praying, this does not make him a Christian. Luke is not an advocate of religious experience in general, but of faith in Christ and incorporation into the church by baptism. This happens to Saul by the "ordinary" means of responding to the Christian message in faith and by being baptized; Ananias is the agent of the church's evangelistic mission that brings Saul into the Christian community. See on 8:29; 10:9.

9:13–14 Your saints: Another name for members of the Christian community, here used for the first time in Acts (see also 9:32, 41; 26:10). "Saints" is not found in the Gospels as a term for Jesus' disciples, but is common in Paul and the literature dependent on him (58x, e.g., Rom. 1:7; 1 Cor. 1:2; 2 Cor. 1:1; Heb. 13:24; Rev. 13:10; 22:21). "Saint" does not indicate a person of exceptional piety, but means "Christian," a member of the holy people of God, a synonym for **all who invoke your name.**

9:15 An instrument whom I have chosen: Saul is called to be a special missionary to both Gentiles and Jews; the term "apostle" is strikingly absent. God chose Saul, not vice versa (see John 15:16). The story is about God, not about Saul. The whole story is not about Saul's successful quest for God, but about the grace

of God that transforms a persecutor into a missionary. Readers are called not to admire Saul, but to rejoice that they belong to a church whose mission is empowered and directed by such a God.

9:16 Suffer for the sake of my name: See 5:41. The terminology reflects the later period of Luke's own time, when wearing the name "Christian" itself could be a cause of persecution (see on 1 Pet. 4:16). The divine intervention in Saul's life does not stop the persecution itself. Others will continue it, but henceforth Paul will be on the receiving end.

9:17 Laid his hands on Saul: For healing his blindness (9:12), not for commissioning (see 13:1–3) or for receiving the Holy Spirit (see 8:18). **Be filled with the Holy Spirit:** by being baptized (see 2:38). **Brother Saul:** Fellow Israelite, as 2:29, 37; 7:2, 26.

9:19b–25
SAUL PREACHES IN DAMASCUS

9:19 Several days: In Acts, Paul remains in Damascus; there is no trip to Arabia (see Gal. 1:17). He immediately begins the mission to which he has been called. There is no period of meditation or reorientation.

9:20 Began to proclaim Jesus in the synagogues: The one who had come to Damascus to arrest those in the synagogues who confessed Jesus to be the Christ is now their advocate. Paul does not immediately go to the Gentiles, but continues the church's mission of proclaiming Christ within the context of the Jewish faith. In Luke's portrayal, the events of chaps. 10–11, in which Peter plays the leading role must happen before Saul's Gentile mission can begin. **He is the Son of God:** Though "Son of God" is an important christological title for Luke himself (Luke 1:32, 35; 3:22; 4:3, 9, 41; 8:28; 20:13; 22:70), it occurs only here in Acts (though see 13:33). The reader knows that "Son of God" is one of several ways designating Jesus as the saving act of God, but that the title itself is not necessary for the authentic proclamation of the gospel. That "the Messiah is Jesus" (v. 22) is the indispensable Christian confession, though it can be expressed in other ways.

9:21 Made havoc in Jerusalem: Saul's initial preaching is understandably met with distrust (as in 9:26). As in the Gospel, the reader is privy to information of which the people in the story are unaware. Though the reader knows that God has truly acted in Saul's life and his conversion is real, not everyone in the story is immediately convinced.

9:22 Proving that Jesus was the Messiah: Better, "that the Messiah is Jesus" (see on 17:3; 18:5, 28). The Christian confession "Jesus is the Christ" answers the question, who is the Messiah? not who is Jesus? Ultimately, it responds to the question, who is God? for Christian faith is theocentric (see Luke 7:16; 8:24, 38; 9:20–22, 43; 13:13; 17:15; 19:37; Acts 2:22, 36). In Christian faith, God is identified as the one who has definitively revealed himself by sending his Son, Jesus the Christ. The issue for Christian faith is not whether there is a god in general, but whether God is the one who has acted decisively in the Christ event to disclose the nature of divine reality and to restore humanity to himself. "Proving" is literally "bringing together," making a coherent case from the Scripture. It is not "proof" in the logical or laboratory sense; otherwise those who are not convinced would be either stupid (in that they could not follow the argument) or evil (in that they see the truth of the argument but are unwilling to accept what they know to be true).

9:23 Some time: See Gal. 1:18, "three years." The chronology of Acts gives the impression of a briefer period. **Plotted to kill him:** As in 9:29; 23:12–30. See on 5:29, 8:1. In 2 Cor. 11:31–33, it is the agents of King Aretas, not "the Jews," who attempt to destroy Saul.

9:25 His disciples: The terminology reflects the later generation of Luke's own time, when there were disciples of Paul (contrast Paul's own perspective, 1 Cor. 1:10–17). **Through an opening in the wall:** Critical scholars might be tempted to regard this colorful detail as a legendary accretion if it were not confirmed by Paul's own incidental reference to the incident in another connection (2 Cor. 11:31–33). Such phenomena show that Acts is not fiction and should provide a brake on scholarly skepticism (see introduction to Acts: "Historical Accuracy").

9:26–31
SAUL IN JERUSALEM

This summary follows the same outline as Saul in Damascus: initial hesitation of the church to receive him, his acceptance as an authentic Christian leader, his preaching that evokes opposition, a plot against his life from which he escapes.

For a comparison of the Acts chronology of this period of Paul's life and the picture Paul himself gives, see chart at Gal. 2:14.

9:26 Attempted to join the disciples: Saul's conversion experience was not for himself alone,

but made him part of the Christian community. The Jerusalem church is understandably hesitant to welcome him with open arms.

9:27 But Barnabas: The "son of encouragement" (4:36) does not just make cheerful comments from the sidelines, but takes the risk of recommending the potentially dangerous Saul (see also 11:19–26). **Brought him to the apostles:** Not "to the *other* apostles." In Luke's view Paul is disciple and missionary, but not apostle (see on 1:15–26; 14:4, 14). Contrast Paul's view of himself, 1 Cor. 9:1; Gal. 1:1, 11–2:10. In Gal. 1:18–24 Paul insists that on this visit to Jerusalem he saw only Peter and James.

9:29 The Hellenists: Not Hellenistic Christians, like Stephen (6:1), but Greek-speaking Jews, perhaps from the Diaspora (as 21:27–29). **Attempting to kill him:** In all religious sincerity, as Saul had previously done (9:2; 22:4; 26:10).

9:30 The brothers (NIV)/**the believers** (NRSV): The NRSV attempts to avoid gender-specific language; the NIV, literally more correct, attempts to preserve the designation of members of the family of God. All translations must make such choices; there is a gain and loss in each case. Elsewhere, the NRSV rightly renders the Greek "brothers" as "brothers and sisters" (e.g., Acts 16:40; Rom. 1:13, and often).

The hesitation of v. 26 is overcome, and the Jerusalem church accepts Paul as a true Christian brother and saves the life of the one who had previously participated in the death of Christians. **Caesarea:** The center of Roman government in Judea on the Mediterranean coast (not the same as the city of Matt. 16:13; Mark 8:27). It plays an important role in the story line of Acts (8:40; 9:30; 10:1, 24; 11:11; 12:19; 18:22; 21:8, 16; 23:23, 33; 25:1, 4, 6, 13). **Sent him off to Tarsus:** In 22:17–21, Paul's departure is attributed to a direct command of the risen Lord received while praying in the temple. On Tarsus, see on 9:11.

9:31 The church throughout Judea, Galilee, and Samaria: Here "church" refers not to a congregation, but to the whole body of Christians in a broad area. Local congregations are not independent entities separate from other congregations, but all are part of the one church of God (see Eph. 4:4–6). Only here does Luke mention that there were Christians in Galilee, the original scene of Jesus' preaching and the call of his earliest disciples, but he does not tell us how or when the church there originated— an instance of the fragmentary nature of the Acts account (see 20:5; 21:1; 27:3; 27:14). Luke is not concerned with a complete "history of early Christianity," but wants to show the movement of the church from Galilee to Jerusalem, and from there to all the world (see on Luke 24:6, 49; Acts 1:8).

9:32–11:18
PETER BEGINS MISSION TO GENTILES

9:32–43
Peter in Lydda and Joppa

See excursus on "Interpreting the Miracle Stories" at Matt. 9:35. The two miracle stories serve to reintroduce Peter and prepare for his role in bringing Gentiles into the church in 10:1–11:18. Peter's last appearance in the story was in 8:14–25, where he was instrumental in granting apostolic approval of incorporating Samaritans into the one church of God.

9:32 As Peter went here and there: Peter is now pictured as traveling, rather than remaining in Jerusalem as part of the apostolic college (see on 8:1), though it is not clear whether Luke intends to portray an evangelistic trip or an "inspection" tour by the principal leader of the Jerusalem church. **Saints:** See on 9:13. **Lydda:** An ancient town located at an important crossroads, Old Testament Lod (1 Chr. 8:12; Ezra 2:23; Neh. 7:37; 11:35), modern Lud, site of the main Israeli airport near the modern Tel Aviv.

9:33 Aeneas: Appears nowhere else in the New Testament. **Make your bed:** As evidence of the reality of the miraculous cure.

9:35 Lord: Jesus, as in v. 42. The converts were Jews who already worshiped the one God. In Luke's delineation of early Christian history, Gentiles do not become Christians until chap. 10. **Sharon:** The fertile coastal plain in which Lydda was located (1 Chr. 5:16; 27:29; Song 2:1; Isa. 33:9; 35:2; 65:10).

In contrast to 8:26–40, an angel appears not to the evangelist but to the one to be converted. In both cases conversion is brought about not by the "religious experience" of having visions or being visited by angels, but in response to the word proclaimed by a Christian evangelist.

9:36 Joppa: Modern Jaffa, on the coast near Tel Aviv. **Tabitha:** Her Aramaic name, with **Dorcas** the Greek translation. Her English name would have been Gazelle. **Good works and acts of charity:** She was concerned for the poor, a Lukan theme (see at Luke 1:46–55; 2:8–14; 4:18–19; 6:20–23; 16:19–31; 18:18–30; Acts 2:44; 4:32–33; 11:27–29).

9:37 Became ill and died: Her death evokes lamentation (see 8:2), but not consternation or doubt (see on 1 Thess. 4:13–18).

9:38 Lydda was near Joppa: About ten miles. **Sent two men to him:** They make no specific request, except for Peter to come. They do not anticipate the resuscitation of Tabitha.

9:39 Widows: In Luke's time (but not Peter's), widows were already being organized into something like an order of Christian women who did charitable work in behalf of the church and took a vow not to remarry (see on 1 Tim. 5:3–16). That Luke distinguishes widows and saints in v. 41 indicates that he tells the story influenced by the structure of the church in his own day.

9:40–41 Peter put all of them outside: The masculine pronoun in Greek indicates others beside widows were there. The miracle story is modeled on that of Jesus, which in turn was modeled on the stories of Elijah and Elisha (1 Kgs. 17:17–24; 2 Kgs. 4:18–37; Mark 5:40–41; Luke 7:11–17; 8:41–42, 49–56). The people are put outside, the hand is extended to the dead person, who is commanded to rise. **Tabitha, get up:** Reflects the Aramaic command of Mark 5:41 (in Luke's source, but rewritten by him at Luke 8:54). Luke does not confuse such stories of resuscitations with the resurrection of Jesus (see on 26:23). **He showed her to be alive:** No words of Tabitha herself are given, no report of "what it was like." Luke's story focuses on the miracle as a testimony to the truth of the gospel and has no interest in satisfying curiosity about what happens when we die.

9:43 With a certain Simon, a tanner: Tanning hides for the making of leather was an unsavory trade avoided by strict Pharisees, but was not considered religiously defiling. The stage is thus set for the following story, in which Peter is hesitant to enter the house of a Gentile.

10:1–33
Peter and Cornelius

This story is traditionally labeled the conversion of Cornelius, but might also be called the continuing conversion of Peter. In 10:1–11:18 Peter is instrumental in bringing Gentiles into the church and defends the new development before the other apostles and the Jerusalem church. After Easter, under the guidance of the Holy Spirit, the followers of Jesus gradually realized that the Christian community as the new people of God should include all people (see on 15:1). This story is the climactic scene of that development, compressing the gradual dawning of insight into one dramatic scene in which Peter plays the leading role (see Luke 24:25–27, 45–48; Acts 2:1–42, for other such Lukan model scenes).

10:1 Caesarea: See 9:30. As Jerusalem was the setting in which Jews received the Holy Spirit and the church was begun, so Caesarea, seat of the Roman government in Judea and named after the Roman emperor, is the setting for the "Gentile Pentecost." **Centurion:** Commander of a hundred soldiers. **Italian Cohort:** A cohort was one tenth of a Roman legion, i.e., six hundred soldiers. The Italian Cohort is not otherwise documented as present in Judea before 69 CE. It was prior to Luke's time, but may have been later than Peter's time, and thus may represent another Lukan anachronism (see on 5:36–37).

10:2 A devout man who feared God: See 10:22 and Luke 7:5. "Godfearers" was a semitechnical term for those interested and supportive Gentiles who formed a penumbra around the synagogue community without becoming Jewish proselytes. "Fear" here means "worship," as often in the Bible. They were impressed with Jewish monotheism and ethics and sometimes attended the synagogue, but remained Gentiles, were not circumcised, and did not keep the Jewish food laws.

10:3 Three o'clock: See 3:1; 10:30.

10:4 Your prayers . . . a memorial before God: God hears the prayers of non-Christians (10:31). Cornelius is a good man who prays and gives to the poor and has had a vision of angels, yet these good deeds and spiritual experiences do not make him a Christian (see the Ethiopian of 8:26–40).

10:5 Simon . . . called Peter: There are two Jews named Simon in the house. On Peter, see Luke 5:3; 6:14.

10:7 Two of his slaves: No objection is made to the institution of slavery, here or elsewhere in the New Testament. See introduction to Philemon; comments on Luke 7:2; 1 Pet. 2:18–25. As in Luke 7:5 (contrast Matt. 8:5–13), Luke uses the literary device of having a centurion send a delegation.

10:9 About noon: See 26:13, where Paul's vision comes at noon, and perhaps 8:26 (see commentary there). **To pray:** Both Peter and Cornelius pray, the prayers of both are heard, and both have visions in which they receive revelations from heaven. The answer to their prayers is to bring together the Christian messenger and those who needed to hear the

gospel (see 10:22, and comments on 9:10; 8:29). For Luke, people become Christians, and the church grows as the word of God is proclaimed, heard, and believed (Luke 3:2; 5:1; 8:11, 21; 11:28; Acts 4:31; 6:2, 7; 8:14; 11:1; 12:24; 13:5, 7, 46; 17:13; 18:11). **Fell into a trance:** As in the experience of Jesus (Luke 3:21–22) the heavens are opened, and Peter hears a heavenly voice. The spiritual phenomena in themselves are only to facilitate the spread of the Christian message that generates faith and discipleship.

10:12 All kinds of . . . creatures: The biblical laws made a sharp division between "clean" animals that could be eaten and "unclean" animals that could not be eaten by Jews (Gen. 1:24; 6:20; Lev. 11:1–47). Gentile readers of the Bible should not trivialize these laws. Like circumcision and keeping the Sabbath, observance of the food laws was an essential mark of the people of God, a part of their witness to the nations (see Ezek. 22:26; 44:23; Dan. 1). Jewish martyrs had died rather than dissolve Jewish identity by eating prohibited food (2 Macc. 7:1–42).

10:13 Kill and eat: The heavenly voice commands him to violate the biblical and traditional purity laws that constituted Jewish identity.

10:14 By no means, Lord: On Lord, see on 9:5. Cornelius addresses the heavenly messenger with the same word (10:4), which might be translated "sir." Peter is not rejecting a direct command of God. He is following the biblical command that the revealed Law of God is to be obeyed and that visions and dreams that instruct one to do otherwise are to be resisted (Deut. 13:1–5; see Gal. 1:6–9). Thus Peter's refusal here should not be understood simply as his pettiness or prejudice, as though it is "obvious" that God intends to include all people in the holy community, but Peter is simply too narrow-minded to accept what is clearly God's will. The modern reader must here remember that such visionary experiences are ambiguous, must be interpreted, and call for discernment by the community of faith as a whole (see 10:17, 19, 28, 34). The great insight here achieved by the early Christian community should not be trivialized, as though the modern ideology of "tolerance" were "obvious," and it is only Peter's prejudice that keeps him from seeing it (on ideological use of the Bible, see on Mark 2:17). The modern ideology is based on the view that such things as religious rituals, laws, and traditions simply do not matter anyway; Luke and early Christianity presuppose that they matter supremely, so that discerning the will of God for people who have different traditions to accept each other and live together in one community was a great breakthrough in the development of the church. **I have never eaten anything that is profane or unclean:** Peter has never eaten nonkosher food. In Luke–Acts, Jesus and his disciples and the earliest Jerusalem church are portrayed as continuing to keep the food laws. In Mark 7:19 Jesus is pictured as having already nullified them during his earthly ministry, but Luke has omitted this scene (but see Luke 11:41).

10:15 What God has made clean, you must not call profane: On the one hand, here is a fundamental declaration of the Christian faith. God is the Creator of all people, the one who loves and accepts all people, the one who wants to create a community within the divided world that will be God's witnesses to the inclusiveness of God's love. Peter himself finally sees this, not merely as the result of the vision, but on the basis of further experience within the Christian community (10:28, 34). The church in every generation and nation stands under the judgment of this text whenever it has tried to limit the Christian community by nation, race, gender, sexual orientation, or social or economic status.

On the other hand, the scene must not be trivialized by simplistically juxtaposing God's will to Peter's prejudice. Of course, *if* God has made something clean, no human being should consider it profane. But whether in fact God has dissolved the distinction between clean and unclean is precisely the issue. The Old Testament, Peter's Bible, made it clear that the distinction was God's own command. The Scripture had not called these laws on which this distinction rests a temporary measure that would pass away when the Messiah came, but had declared their validity was forever (see Lev. 10:9, 15; 16:25, 31; 17:7; 23:14, 21, 31, 41; 24:3, 8; 25:32). See the similar issue with regard to circumcision, and comments at Acts 15:1–2. In Luke–Acts up to this point, both Jesus and his disciples have followed the biblical purity laws. If God has now reversed the precedent of both Bible and Jesus, then Peter will obey God (5:29). But despite the vision, he has not yet seen that this is God's will. The will of God will become clear only in subsequent events and their interpretation in the life of the community.

In these scenes we see the post-Easter church under the guidance of the risen Christ and the Holy Spirit coming to insights about the will of God that were not clear during the ministry of the historical Jesus. No one says anything like "Don't you remember that Jesus taught us to ignore the food laws and accept everyone into the group of disciples?" The situation is the same when, much later, the church faces such issues as the institution of slavery and the leadership role of women in the church. The church becomes more inclusive than its Bible had been, more inclusive than Jesus had been. The study of Acts can warn the modern reader against a too superficial reading of the New Testament, as though the historical Jesus were the source of all liberation, while the later church domesticated or suppressed his revolutionary way of life. It is God's act in Christ that is the liberating, saving power, the meaning of which is only gradually discerned. Luke presents the church as developing true insights into the meaning of the Christ event that were not apparent to anyone during the earthly life of Jesus.

10:17 Greatly puzzled: Peter neither dismissed the message of the heavenly voice nor perceived it to communicate a clear divine directive. The ambiguity of such revelatory phenomena becomes clear only in the light of further events and dialogue within the Christian community.

10:22 What you have to say: See on 8:29; 9:10; 10:9. Miraculous phenomena, dreams, and visions do not effect Christian conversion apart from the apostolic message.

10:23 Invited them in: Though the meaning of the vision is not yet clear, Peter is already changing, in that he does not hesitate to invite two Gentile slaves and a Roman soldier into the house to spend the night. **Some of the believers from Joppa accompanied him:** The vision is not a matter of private interpretation (see 2 Pet. 1:20–21).

10:26 I am only a mortal: Though a worshiper of the one God (10:2), the Roman is too willing to accord divine honors to others. For a similar scene in which Paul rejects divine honors, see 14:8–18. Contrast Dan. 2:46. For a list of such Peter-Paul parallels, see list at 28:31.

10:28 God has shown me: What was not clear in the vision itself has now become clear in the light of subsequent events, dialogue, and reflection. In 11:12 this insight is attributed to the Holy Spirit. This is the way God's revelation works in the community as it continues to face new situations and discover the will of God (see on 15:28). **Not call anyone profane**

or unclean: The distinction between ritually clean and unclean peoples is dissolved. The words are religious terms, not a matter of personal hygiene but of ritual purity (see on Luke 2:22–24; 4:33). No one is to be considered outside God's grace, unacceptable to God.

10:33 To listen to all that the Lord has commanded you to say: The stage is set for Peter's sermon as Cornelius rehearses the events that have led to this occasion.

10:34–43
Gentiles Hear the Good News

As the gospel is now addressed for the first time to Gentiles, Luke provides the most complete statement of the Christian message about Jesus to be found in the Acts speeches.

10:34 God shows no partiality: A radical statement, difficult for all to hear who have been socialized to always think in terms of an "us/them" mentality. That God loves and accepts "them" as well as "us" (whoever "them" is thought to be) is part of the scandalous good news of the Christian gospel. See Rom. 2:10–11; 3:22 ("no distinction"); 3:29; Gal. 2:6; 3:27–28.

10:35 Anyone who fears him and does what is right is acceptable to him: Taken by itself, this statement could be an expression of works righteousness that reintroduces a partial God. This is not Luke's understanding (Luke 15:11–32; 18:9–14; Acts 15:11). The issue here is not how to be saved (works or grace), but who is acceptable to God, and the answer in this context is not only Jews, but Gentiles who turn to him. The whole point of this scene is that acceptance by God is not a matter of race, nation, culture. Nonetheless, the statement succinctly shows what God expects: worship (this is the meaning of "fear him"; see on 5:5; 10:2) and ethics ("doing what is right").

10:36 You know: In the story line, those addressed (the Gentile Cornelius, his family, and Gentile friends) do not know the story of Jesus that is about to be rehearsed, but the readers do. This is another indication that the speeches of Acts are primarily Lukan compositions directed to the reader (see 1:19; introduction to Acts: "Speeches"). He (God) sent: God is the active subject in the following story about Jesus. The Christian gospel is a matter of God's initiative and act, not of human seeking and religiosity. Preaching peace by Jesus Christ: God continues as the actor. On the theocentric perspective of the story of Jesus and the church, see on Luke 7:16; 8:24, 38;

9:20–22, 43; 13:13; 17:15; 19:37. It is God who speaks in the message of Jesus (see God was with him, v. 38), just as it is God who continues to speak in the message of the apostles and the continuing message of the church through the centuries. While Luke insists on the full and true humanity of Jesus (and the church), he also presents God as the one who acts and speaks in the ministry of Jesus and the church, so that the work and growth of the church can be summarized as "the word of God" (Luke 3:2; 5:1; 8:11, 21; 11:28; Acts 4:31; 6:2, 7; 8:14; 11:1; 12:24; 13:5, 7, 46; 17:13; 18:11).

10:38 God anointed: See Luke 4:18–21; 9:20; Acts 2:36. Doing good and healing all who were oppressed by the devil: Thus Luke summarizes Jesus' ministry, the details of which are known to the reader from the Gospel of Luke. Usually in Acts, Luke follows the Pauline pattern of concentrating on the death and resurrection of Jesus as the essence of the gospel (see 1 Cor. 15:3–5; Phil. 2:5–11). Only here does he include a summary of Jesus' ministry.

10:39 We are witnesses: See on 1:8. The witnesses are not volunteers, but created by God, a part of the saving event itself (v. 42).

10:39–40 They put him to death . . . but God raised him: See on 2:23–24. The resurrection is God's gracious act that reverses the human act of the rejection of Jesus. "God raised him" and "he rose" are equivalents for Luke (see the next verse below, and 1:3).

10:41 Ate and drank with him after he rose from the dead: Not with everyone, but also not with the apostles alone. See Luke 24:13–35, 36–43. This is both a testimony to the reality of the resurrection and to the importance of the common meals Jesus shared with his disciples.

10:42 He is the one ordained by God as judge: See 17:31. The future judgment in which all will give account to God is an important element of Luke's theology, as it is for the New Testament as a whole (see Matt. 25:31–46; Rom. 14:9–10; 2 Cor. 5:10; 2 Tim. 4:1; 1 Pet. 4:5; Rev. 20:11–15). One way of pointing to the ultimate significance of Jesus is to represent Christ as the one who exercises God's final judgment.

10:43 All the prophets testify about him: See on 3:18, 24. The Christian message is not a clean break with the past, but the continuation and fulfillment of God's plan revealed in the ancient Scriptures. This was also important to emphasize in presenting the gospel to Gentiles who did not know the Old Testament (then and now), who are too inclined to misunderstand Jesus in celebrity terms as a significant personality, a great teacher, a visitor from another world, or an individualistic wonder worker. Throughout Acts, it is important to integrate the Christian message into the continuing plan of God for all history. **Everyone:** Jews and Gentiles alike—the point of the whole story. **Who believes:** Acceptance before God is a matter of faith, not of works (see v. 35 above). **Forgiveness of sins:** A summary of the meaning of salvation, having one's alienation from God overcome (see 2:38). **Through his name:** See 2:38; 4:12.

10:44–48
Gentiles Receive the Holy Spirit

10:44 The Holy Spirit fell upon all who heard the word: The initiative comes from God. **Circumcised believers:** Jewish Christians. An anachronism showing the story is told from Luke's later perspective—in his chronology there were as yet no non-Jewish Christians. **Were astounded:** That God includes the Gentiles in the community of faith without their becoming Jews first.

10:45 Gift of the Holy Spirit: See on 8:16. Here the "gift" of the Spirit and the "baptism of the Holy Spirit" are identified (cf. 11:15–16).

10:46 Speaking in tongues: Not in "other" tongues. See on 2:5.

10:47 Can anyone withhold the water for baptizing these people?: A similar expression to that in 8:36, which may reflect part of the early baptismal liturgy. In Luke's theology, baptism in water, as the act of entrance into the church, and receiving the Holy Spirit belong together. The human act of water baptism and the divine act of bestowing the Holy Spirit are complementary, two aspects of the one event. This story shows that wherever the Spirit has been received, people must be incorporated into the church. Elsewhere, Luke narrates stories that illustrate that where people have been baptized, the Spirit must be received (8:14–17; 18:24–19:7). Such stories are part of his "standardization" of the variety of views of baptism and the Spirit circulating in early Christianity. **Received the Holy Spirit just as we have:** A sign that God shows no partiality.

10:48 So he ordered them to be baptized: Peter speaks with apostolic authority. No one objected that since they had the Spirit already, they did not need baptism. This is the same Peter who had objected to associating with Gentiles (10:14), but who now **stays** with them **for several days**. The whole story shows not

only the conversion of Cornelius, but the conversion of Peter.

11:1–18
Peter's Report to the Church at Jerusalem

11:1 The apostles and the believers who were in Jerusalem: The radical new step must be approved by the apostles and the church as a whole. Though Peter is the leading apostle, he does not settle such issues on his own authority (see on 15:1–29). On "believers" (NRSV) or "brothers" (NIV), see on 9:30. Luke does not explain how the disciples scattered in 8:1 are again in Jerusalem. **Had also accepted the word of God:** Luke's summary term for Christian faith. See on 6:2, and Luke 3:2; 5:1; 8:11, 21; 11:28; Acts 4:31; 7; 8:14; 11:1; 12:24; 13:5, 7, 46; 17:13; 18:11.

11:2 The circumcised believers: Jewish Christians. See on 10:45.

11:3 Why did you . . . eat with them?: In ancient Judaism, "eating with" implied intimate fellowship and complete acceptance and was regulated by strict taboos and religious laws (somewhat like "sleeping with" in contemporary American culture; see on Luke 5:29–30). "Eating with" is the summary term for accepting into fellowship, standing for all aspects of associating with others as equal members of the community of faith. The objection is not that Gentiles could be baptized so long as separate table fellowship is maintained, but to accepting Gentiles into the Christian community.

11:4 Peter began to explain to them: In vv. 5–17 Luke gives as a speech of Peter what has already been recounted in the narrator's voice in 10:1–48. (See on Paul's conversion, 9:1–19a, repeated as speeches of Paul in 22:1–21 and 26:2–23.) Such repetitions impress on the reader the importance of the event. **Step by step:** The same word as in Luke 1:3, there translated "in order." Luke is concerned throughout Acts to show the gradual and orderly progression of the church's development from a group of disciples of a Galilean prophet to a world religion (see on 1:8); the inclusion of the Gentiles under Peter's leadership is a major step in this development.

11:14 Be saved: The language of salvation had not been used in the previous account in chap. 10. One of the meanings of salvation is inclusion in the people of God (see on 4:12; 16:30).

11:16–17 Baptized with the Holy Spirit: See on 1:5; 2:4; 8:15–17. Here the "baptism of the Holy Spirit" is equated with the "gift of the Holy

Spirit." **When we came to believe:** Luke has portrayed Peter as a disciple since Luke 5:1–11, but he did not receive the Spirit until the Pentecost event of Acts 2. Does this mean that Peter first came to "believe" then? Luke may simply be presenting Peter as speaking for the Judean Christians present, who became believers in response to the post-Easter preaching of the apostles. More likely, he here indicates that Peter did not truly become a believer until after the Easter and Pentecost events. Christian faith does not come about merely by following the earthly, historical Jesus, but is the response to the act of God in Christ seen only in the light of the resurrection and by the power of the Holy Spirit. Peter is here made the spokesperson for the general Christian experience.

11:18 Praised God: They did not brag on Peter for overcoming his prejudices, but gave glory to God who includes all peoples in his saving work. The Jewish Christians of Jerusalem do not reluctantly accept the inclusion of the Gentiles as God's will, but celebrate it. **God has given . . . repentance:** Repentance is the human act of reorienting one's life in response to the word of God. Yet it is also the gift of God. On human responsibility and divine sovereignty, see on 4:28. **To life:** Salvation, entrance into the kingdom of God (see on Luke 18:18, 24, 26).

11:19–12:25
THE CHURCH CONTINUES
THE GENTILE MISSION

11:19–29
The Church at Antioch

11:19 Those who were scattered: A flashback to 8:1, recounting events that apparently happened prior to 10:1–11:18. After tracing the "step by step" progression of the gospel from Jews to Gentiles (see 11:4; 15:1–35), Luke now informs the reader for the first time that this quantum leap had already been accomplished elsewhere. **Phoenicia:** Modern Lebanon. Among its important cities were Tyre and Sidon, where Christians are later found (21:7; 27:3). **Cyprus:** The large island south of modern Turkey; a Roman province with many Jewish inhabitants, the original home of Barnabas (4:36). **Antioch:** Large seaport, seat of the Roman governor of Syria, a Gentile city with a large Jewish population. Antioch will become the pivotal center in the spread of the gospel from Jerusalem to Rome. In Luke's account

Antioch is (1) associated with the first mission to Gentiles, a congregation that becomes a missionary church sending out Paul and Barnabas (13:1–3), to which Paul returned as his "headquarters"; (2) the church where disciples of Jesus first received the distinctive name "Christian" (11:26); (3) the first church to provide benevolent support for needy fellow Christians in other parts of the world (11:27–29); but also (4) the location of the first dispute about how Jewish and Gentile Christians could live together as one church (15:1–29; see Gal. 1:11–2:10). **Spoke the word to no one except Jews:** The disciples of Jesus are still a community within Judaism, and the events of 10:1–11:18 have not yet happened.

11:20 Men of Cyprus and Cyrene: Hellenistic Jewish Christians originally from the Diaspora. Cyrene was in north Africa. **Began to speak to Greeks also** (NIV): The NIV translation "Greeks" is better than the NRSV **Hellenists** (see on 6:1). The whole point of this story is that those addressed were not Jews at all, not that they were another type of Jew. The scattered church crosses traditional religious and cultural boundaries and begins to include people in the church who have never been Jews at all. Here is an "unauthorized" new development in the actual historical chronology, but the reader learns of it only after it has received divine and apostolic approval in 11:1–18. **The hand of the Lord was with them:** The narrator's comment makes it clear to the reader that the new step is guided and empowered by God, and is not merely the daring step of renegade liberal disciples—but the participants in the story, the members and leaders of the Jerusalem church, do not know this yet.

11:22 They sent Barnabas to Antioch: As they had sent Peter and John to check out and authorize the new developments in Samaria (8:14–17). On Barnabas, see 4:36; 9:27. He has already demonstrated his open and generous spirit and his willingness to take risks.

11:23 He . . . saw the grace of God . . . rejoiced: The grace of God is tangible and visible, but only to eyes illumined by the Holy Spirit. Others looked at the new development and saw only abandonment of the Bible and tradition (15:1). On the basis of the accomplished fact that God's grace had been extended to Gentiles, Barnabas encourages them to continue. As in 10:44–48, the new, creative act of God does not wait on Christian theological reflection to make it possible. The movement goes the other way: Christian theology interprets the acts of God in history, what God has already accomplished.

11:24 Full of the Holy Spirit: Not merely a matter of personal piety, but a way of saying that Barnabas's approval of the new development was guided by the Holy Spirit (see 15:28!). **Many people:** The integrated church of Jews and Gentiles flourishes.

11:25–26 Went to Tarsus to look for Saul: See 9:30. Saul is now reintroduced after the story line had switched to the account of Peter's introduction of the Gentiles into the church. **They met with the church and taught a great many people:** The new converts were not abandoned, but were instructed. What it means to have become a Christian is not immediately obvious, but requires teaching and learning. Luke summarizes the ministry of Barnabas and Saul, as he had summarized Jesus' ministry, as "teaching" (e.g., Luke 4:15, 31–32; 19:47; 20:1, 37; Acts 2:42; 4:2, 18; 5:21, 25, 28; 13:1, 12; 18:11; 20:20; 28:31). The picture is of an ecumenical, worldwide community, Jewish and Gentile Christians in the one church of God as manifest in Antioch, being instructed by Christian teachers from Jerusalem and Tarsus, one of whom is a Hellenistic Jewish Christian from Cyprus (Barnabas), the other a Pharisaic Jew of the Diaspora who had studied with famous teachers in Jerusalem before becoming a Christian (Saul/Paul).

11:26 The disciples were first called "Christians": The term "Christian" is a relatively late development in early Christianity, occurring in the New Testament only here, 26:28 (mockingly), and 1 Pet. 4:16. The word understands "Christ" as a proper name, and formulates the new designation on the linguistic analogy of "Herodians" (Mark 3:6; 12:13). After 10:1–11:21 there are large numbers of people in the church who are not Jews, and the disciples of Jesus can no longer be seen as only a particular faction within Judaism. It is not clear whether "Christians" is a self-designation by disciples themselves, or a derogatory epithet given them by outsiders to distinguish them from Jews and other religious groups (the Greek grammar can be understood either way). Probably outsiders first applied the designation to the group of disciples, perhaps in a derogatory sense ("Christ-lackeys"), but it was adopted by them as a badge of honor (see "Methodist," "Baptist," "Dunker"). Prior designations in Acts have been "believers," "dis-

ciples," "saints," "brothers and sisters," in the next scene "those who belong to the church" (12:1). Luke waits until there is an integrated church of Jews and Gentiles carrying on a world mission of evangelism and compassion before he applies to it the name "Christian."

11:27 Prophets: Those Christians who speak by the power of the Holy Spirit in the name of God or the risen Lord (see Matt. 23:34; Luke 11:49; Acts 13:1; 15:32; 1 Cor. 12:28–29; 13:1; 14:1–40; Rev. 1:1–3; 19:9–10; 22:8–9.) **Agabus:** See 21:10. He is the first prophet specifically named in Acts, though see 2:17–18. Luke understands Christian prophets in the same way he understands the prophets of Israel, primarily as predictors of the future.

11:28 A severe famine over all the world: Early Christian prophets frequently spoke of cosmic and worldwide catastrophes that were to be part of the eschatological events, including famines (see Rev. 6:8; 18:8). **This took place during the reign of Claudius:** The years 41–54 CE. Luke historicizes the prediction, as in Luke 21:20 (see there), providing another reminder that the church's story is set in the midst of world history (see on Luke 2:1; 3:1–2). The famine is otherwise unattested in history.

11:29 Each would send relief to the believers living in Judea: (= Jerusalem, 12:25). The new Christians have been well enough instructed in the meaning of their new faith (11:26) that they realize it calls on them to share with those in need (2:44; 4:32–34). Their compassion extends beyond their own community to people in another country with a different culture and ethnic background. In addition to Christian compassion, their act also manifests their solidarity and unity with the Jerusalem church. They are not merely a new group of enthusiastic individual believers, but belong to the wider church, to which they send offerings and from which they receive teaching and leadership (vv. 25–26).

11:30 Elders: The benevolent work of the church is not done individually and privately, but is administered by elders—Luke does not comment on what had happened to the seven (6:1–6). This is the first reference in Acts to Christian leaders called "elders," though Jewish elders have been often mentioned (e.g., 4:5, 8, 23). Luke will later picture every church as led by elders (14:23; 15:2, 4, 6, 22; 20:17). The office of elder was a relatively late development in early Christianity, still unknown in the undisputed letters of Paul (though see 1 Tim. 4:14; 5:17, 19; Titus 1:5; Jas. 5:14; 1 Pet. 5:1,

5; 2 John 1; 3 John 1). "Elder" at first was a mark of the wisdom and leadership that comes with age, but then became the designation of an office not directly related to age. **By Barnabas and Saul:** This visit is not mentioned by Paul, unless it is identical with that of Gal. 2:1–10. On the chronological tensions between Acts and Paul's letters, see chart at Gal. 2:14.

12:1–19
Peter Delivered from Prison

12:1 About that time: The time of the famine and sending of money that had connected the Antioch church with Jerusalem. The scene switches back to Jerusalem and its leading apostle, Peter. **King Herod:** Herod Agrippa I, grandson of Herod the Great of Luke 1:5, and second cousin of Herod Antipas, who had ruled Galilee during Jesus' ministry. At first (37–41 CE) ruler of only the northeast section of Transjordan, he briefly (41–44) ruled Samaria and Judea as well (at the pleasure of the Romans). **Laid violent hands upon some who belonged to the church:** For the first time it is not the priests and temple leadership that oppose the new Christian community, and it is "ordinary" Christians, not only apostles or leaders, who are harassed. Luke gives no reason for Herod's opposition, but it was apparently suspicion of the potential political power and perception of the disciples of Jesus as a religiopolitical movement that spoke of the "kingdom of God" and Jesus as Messiah (= king).

12:2 He had James, the brother of John, killed: One of the Twelve, the son of Zebedee (see Luke 5:1–11; 6:12–16; Acts 1:13). He becomes the first martyr among the apostles. It is not clear whether he was arrested or simply assassinated by royal order. Though the Herods ruled only by permission of the Romans, they could administer the death penalty at their own discretion in their own territories (as in the case of John the Baptist, Mark 6:14–29). The early church lived in a situation of arbitrary power, in which believers could be abused, arrested, and killed without hearing or trial.

12:3 Proceeded to arrest Peter also: As the leader and chief spokesperson for the Jerusalem church. **The festival of Unleavened Bread:** A part of the Passover festival; see on Luke 22:1. Peter's arrest at this time is parallel to that of Jesus.

12:4 Four squads of soldiers: One for each three-hour watch. Each squad was composed of four men. **Bring him out to the people:** No reason is given, but apparently to exploit public approval of his suppression of the new community.

12:5 The church prayed fervently: See 4:23–31.

12:6 That very night: The verses following tell of Peter's miraculous deliverance from prison, his acknowledging the leadership of James the brother of Jesus, and his departure from Jerusalem. The miracle happens the night before he would have been condemned and killed. See excursus on "Interpreting the Miracle Stories," at Matt. 9:35. On the ethical issue connected with this particular miracle story, see on vv. 18–19 below. **Peter, bound with two chains:** The miraculous nature of the deliverance is heightened by emphasizing how securely Peter is imprisoned: chained between two guards, with two sentinels at different posts outside the cell (see 12:10).

12:7 An angel of the Lord: On angels in Luke–Acts, see on Luke 1:10–12; 24:4, 23. **Chains fell off his wrists:** As the door opens by itself in 12:10. Both features are repeatedly found in Hellenistic stories of miraculous deliverance.

12:9 He thought he was seeing a vision: As elsewhere in Luke–Acts (Luke 1:22; 24:23, 43; 26:19; Acts 2:17; 7:31; 9:10, 12; 10:3, 17, 19; 11:5; 16:9, 10; 18:9), "real" means for Luke "in the space-time world, objective reality observable by anyone," in contrast to a "vision," which is also real, but belongs to another (and higher) order or reality. See 2 Cor. 12:2–3.

12:12 The house of Mary: Nothing more is known of her. She is apparently a person of some means (see Luke 8:1–3; Acts 16:11–15; 17:4), with a house large enough to accommodate a congregation of the Jerusalem church. She is the head of a household that includes slaves (v. 13). If she is a widow—there is no such indication—she does not belong to the group mentioned in 6:1; 9:39–41, nor has she sold her property (see 4:32–34). **John whose other name is Mark:** His first introduction in the Acts story; he will reappear in 12:25; 13:5, 13; 15:37–39. Traditionally identified with the Mark of Phlm. 24 and Col. 4:10 and with the author of the Gospel of Mark (the latter is especially dubious).

12:13 A maid named Rhoda: The same word is translated "slave" in Luke 12:45 and Acts 16:16. On slavery in the New Testament world, see introduction to Philemon and comments on Luke 7:2; 1 Pet. 2:18–25. The slave girl believes it is Peter, but in her joy forgets to let him in.

12:15 You are out of your mind: Although they had been praying for Peter's release, they are astounded and cannot believe that their prayers have really been answered. **His angel:** Convinced that someone is actually at the door, they still do not believe it is Peter himself. Folk religion had come to believe in guardian angels that were the double of the person to whom they were assigned (see Ps. 91:11; Matt. 18:10; Heb. 1:14)

12:16 They saw him and were amazed: The whole story provides opportunity to reflect on the meaning of answered prayer. Its main point is to show God's care for the developing church: despite the opposition of the king, the church continues to worship and to grow. Caution must be exercised in drawing other lessons from the story, as though it were simply reporter language from which we may draw our own inferences (see on "confessional language" at Matt. 2:16). In dealing with the mystery of God's ways and the reality of prayer, one should be wary of simplistic formulae that reduce it all to objectifying, reporter-type language, such as "if we have enough faith, our prayers will be answered." In this story, prayer is answered and God's deliverance comes even though those who were praying did not expect it to happen. Presumably prayer had also been made for James, but he was killed. One can say neither, "If we had had enough faith, James would have been spared," nor "Since we had enough faith, Peter was spared." Prayer is the confession of our dependence on God and praise for God's grace, but there is no mechanical connection between the power of prayer and God's acts, as though God waits on our knowing how to pray correctly or our having enough faith before acting in response to our prayers. The church continues to pray, with more or less faith, and God continues to act, whether God's actions fit our mental models or not.

12:17 Tell this to James: The brother of Jesus, who became the leader of the Jerusalem church (see on Gal. 1:19; 2:9, 12; Acts 15:3; 21:18) and was later considered its first bishop. We do not know how or when leadership shifted from Peter to James, or whether it involved some internal power struggle within the developing church. Luke pictures the transition very deftly and has Peter acknowledge James's leadership.

Went to another place: At this point Peter drops out of the story of Acts and gives place to Paul (to reappear only briefly in Acts 15:7–11 at the Jerusalem Council). Peter served as a traveling missionary (1 Cor. 9:5; Gal. 2:11) and eventually went to Rome, where he suffered a martyr's death under Nero (never mentioned by Luke, who gives this honor only to Paul [19:21; 23:11; 28:14, 16]; see introduction to 1 Peter).

12:18 No small commotion: Luke frequently uses litotes, a figure of speech in which an affirmative is expressed by the negation of its opposite (see 15:2; 19:23, 24; 20:12 NRSV; 21:39 NIV; 12:35–48; 17:22–23; 20:9; 21:8–9; see English "not bad"). This stylistic feature appears in Acts, but not in the Gospel, where Luke is more dependent on his sources. **Among the soldiers:** They had done their job rightly and could not have been aware of or prevented the miracle that was happening. They are simply innocent bystanders to the miraculous deliverance.

12:19 Herod . . . examined the guards: Of course they had no explanation for the disappearance of their prisoner. Herod could only assume that the escape was due to their neglect. **Ordered them to be put to death:** Guards were responsible for their prisoners and had to pay with their own lives if the prisoners escaped (see 16:28; 27:42–43). The reader should note that if all this is taken as objectifying language, then one must regard the God and the angel who had effected the miracle as standing idly by while innocent people are put to death for an event they had no way of comprehending. One must think of the wives and families of the soldiers. One must ask whether the same God who miraculously acted to deliver Peter could not have miraculously acted to deliver the soldiers (or James). One must ask why neither Peter nor the author expresses any concern or compassion regarding the fate of the guards. All this is the result of understanding the miracle stories as objectifying language (see excursus, "Interpreting Miracle Stories," at Matt. 9:35; comments on Matt. 2:16; Acts 1:9; 5:1–11; excursus, "Interpreting Revelation's Violent Imagery," 3.b, at Rev. 6:15). The problem inherent in all talk of God's acting in miraculous ways is focused in a story such as this, but it is present in every miracle story. The solution is not to reject, ignore, or allegorize miracle stories, but to understand them as a representing a particular kind of confessional language appropriate to speaking of God's act, a language that does not tolerate the kind of inferences and conclusions discussed above.

12:20–25
The Death of Herod

12:20 Tyre and Sidon: The two leading cities of Phoenicia, the neighboring state on the Mediterranean coast, modern Lebanon. **Blastus, the king's chamberlain:** Otherwise unknown; like the eunuch of 8:26–40, an important official who had influence with the king.

12:22 The voice of a god, and not of a mortal: See 10:24–26; 14:15. Peter and Paul both refuse such idolatrous accolades.

12:23 Because he had not given the glory to God: His crimes of murdering James, attempting to murder Peter, and killing innocent guards seem to be ignored (recall the discussion of confessional and objectifying language above). The story here has one point, God brings down the arrogant ruler (see Mary's song, Luke 1:52), and does not permit other inferences, such as that it is even worse to take credit for a good speech than to commit murder. **He was eaten by worms and died:** The motif of the horrible death of those who arrogantly oppose God (or the gods) was widespread in antiquity (see 2 Macc. 9:5–28, and the death of Judas in Acts 1:18–19; Matt. 27:3–10). The first-century Jewish historian Josephus has a story similar in many details: Herod wears a splendid garment woven with silver that gleams in the rising sun and evokes the impression of deity. When the crowds applaud him as a god, he accepts the acclamation, but immediately sees an owl, an omen of his death. He then dies five days later of severe abdominal pain. Such parallels illustrate that Luke is dealing with real events in history and that he is treating them from his own theological perspective.

12:24–25 The word of God continued to advance: Luke's summary for the continued growth of the church and the Christian mission (see Luke 3:2; 5:1; 8:11, 21; 11:28; Acts 4:31; 6:2, 7; 8:14; 11:1; 12:24; 13:5, 7, 46; 17:13; 18:11). **After completing their mission:** See 11:30. **From Jerusalem** (NIV) **to Jerusalem** (NRSV): The NIV translation is better. The text cannot mean "to Jerusalem" because of the context, which requires them to return to Antioch from Jerusalem, and because John **Mark** is a native of Jerusalem who now comes to Antioch (not vice versa) to join Barnabas and Saul in the mission that is about to be launched there (13:1–3). The Greek can also be translated "after completing their mission in Jerusalem." On the tensions concerning this visit, reported

in Acts but missing in Galatians, see chart and discussion at Gal. 2:14.

13:1–14:28
PAUL'S FIRST MISSIONARY JOURNEY

Here begins a new stage in the story of the church's expansion (see 1:8). From this point on, the figure of Paul dominates the story, as had Peter in the first half of Acts (for Peter/Paul parallels, see list at 28:31). Luke will structure the remainder of Acts around three missionary journeys of Paul and Paul's trial in Jerusalem that eventuates in his journey to Rome as a prisoner (see Outline in the introduction to Acts). Between the first and second journeys comes the Jerusalem Council, so his first journey serves as preparation for the council. Though broadly historical, all this is Luke's structure. There are both overlaps with data from Paul's own letters that confirm the accuracy of much of Luke's account, and tensions between Luke's structure and Paul's letters. (There is no place in Luke's structure, for example, for Paul's mission to Illyricum referred to in Rom. 15:19.)

13:1–3
Barnabas and Saul Commissioned

13:1 Prophets and teachers: The leadership of the Antioch church. It differs from the Jerusalem church in that no apostles or elders are mentioned. No sharp distinction is made between prophets and teachers, but prophets are those who speak the word of the risen Lord directly, which they receive in visions and revelations, while teachers are those who hand on and clarify the meaning of the church's tradition, including materials from and about the historical Jesus (see on 11:27; 1 Cor. 12:28–29; Eph. 4:11). Not only the prophets, but also the teachers are guided by the Spirit. **Simeon who was called Niger:** "The Black." **Manaen:** A boyhood comrade friend of King **Herod** (Antipas, ruler of Galilee during Jesus' ministry), he is now a leader of the Christian community. Nothing further is known of any of these except Barnabas and Saul.

13:2 The Holy Spirit said: Through one of the Christian prophets. **The work to which I have called them:** Paul's call by the risen Lord (9:1–9) is here seen as the work of the Holy Spirit. Barnabas and Saul are commissioned to a special ministry of proclaiming the gospel to Gentiles. The Holy Spirit is active in the "ordination" process (see 1 Tim. 1:18; 2 Tim. 1:14). The Holy Spirit guides the expanding mission of the church, but through an orderly procedure.

Luke affirms both the charismatic presence of the Spirit in the life of the church, and the orderly process of selection and ordination by the church to particular ministries. Charisma and structure are not incompatible alternatives.

13:3 After fasting and praying, they laid their hands on them: See 6:6. Though Paul had been directly called by God through a special revelatory experience, his mission is not his own project. He is set apart, authorized, sponsored, and supported by the church, to which he will return and report (14:24–28). Barnabas also is the delegate of the Spirit and the church, though the way in which he initially became a Christian and missionary is not narrated (4:36; 9:27; 11:22–30; 12:25).

13:4–12
A Confrontation in Cyprus

13:4 Seleucia: Seaport of Antioch. **Cyprus:** large island in the northeast Mediterranean, home to many Diaspora Jews. Barnabas was originally from there (4:36). Jerusalem Hellenistic Christians had already done evangelistic work on the island, but only among the Jewish population (11:19). Christian converts from Cyprus had been the first missionaries to preach to Gentiles and had brought this gospel to Antioch (11:20).

13:5 Salamis: Seaport on the eastern coast of Cyprus, formerly the capital city. **In the synagogues:** According to the pattern of "first to the Jews" that Paul will follow throughout Acts (9:20; 13:14; 14:1; 16:13; 17:1–2, 10, 17; 18:4–6, 19; 19:8; see Rom. 1:16). **John to assist them:** John Mark of Jerusalem, who had returned with Barnabas and Saul to Antioch (12:12, 25). He plays only a minor role, is not part of the commissioning event in 13:1–3, and soon returns to Antioch (v. 13). There is no report of any response to their first preaching, either positive or negative.

13:6–7 Paphos: About one hundred miles from Salamis, on the west coast of the island; the current capital. **Bar-Jesus:** A Jewish name, "son of Jesus-Joshua." He is a renegade Jew who had become a magician and poses as a prophet who works as a sorcerer in the court of the governor. As the Jerusalem mission led by Peter first encountered a magician who was defeated by the power of the Holy Spirit, so the mission (to be) led by Paul initially encounters and defeats a magician in the power of the Spirit. (For list of Peter/Paul parallels, see 28:31.) **The proconsul, Sergius Paulus:** Luke here as always uses the correct title for the Roman leader, no

minor accomplishment in the complicated system of designations for Roman ranks. This is one of several indications that Luke's story is in close touch with historical reality. As Peter's first Gentile convert was a prominent Roman official, so also with Paul—another parallel. Sergius Paulus was proconsul 46–48 CE. The first missionary journey of Acts 13–14 is in the period 46–49 CE, with the Jerusalem Council of chap. 15 in 49. For **word of God** as a way of summarizing the Christian message, see Luke 3:2; 5:1; 8:11, 21; 11:28; Acts 4:31; 6:2, 7; 8:14; 11:1; 12:24; 13:5, 7, 46; 17:13; 18:11.

13:8 Elymas: The meaning of the name is unknown, but it is not a translation of Bar-Jesus in any known language. Luke is fond of folk etymologies (see 4:36).

13:9 Saul, also known as Paul: Rather than the usual understanding ("he was called 'Paul' as well as 'Saul'"), the meaning is probably "Saul, like the governor, has as his Roman name 'Paul.'" Saul was his Jewish name, Paul his Roman name. Since he was born a Roman citizen (22:28), he received this name at birth. It was not a new, "Christian" name given him at conversion, baptism, or ordination. As the Gentile mission now begins, Luke drops the Jewish name (except for the flashbacks in 22:7, 13; 26:14) and will refer to the hero of the rest of the story exclusively as Paul. Paul himself uses only his Roman name in his letters; were it not for Acts, we would not know his Jewish name.

13:10 Son of the devil: See John 8:44. This was an epithet used by Jews in inter-Jewish controversies. **Making crooked the straight paths of the Lord:** The false prophet is contrasted with the true prophet John the Baptist, who did the opposite (Luke 3:4).

13:11 Immediately mist and darkness came over him: A punitive miracle like that of Peter against Ananias and Sapphira (see on 5:1–11, and excursus, "Interpreting the Miracle Stories," at Matt. 9:35).

13:12 The proconsul . . . believed: He is converted both by witnessing the miracle and by the **teaching about the Lord**. The miracle itself is ambiguous and does not generate faith in either Elymas or in the others present (contrast the response of Simon Magus [8:14–25], and of Paul, who was likewise temporarily struck blind [9:8–19]). Teaching is necessary to clarify the faith (see Luke 4:15, 31–32; 19:47; 20:1, 37; Acts 2:42; 4:2, 18; 5:21, 25, 28; 13:1, 12; 18:11; 20:20; 28:31).

This scene is a vignette that aptly summarizes Luke's theological reflection on what happened in early Christianity in general as the disciples of Jesus made the transition from a Jewish sect to a universal religion: Jews generally rejected the Christian message, leading Romans accepted, and God confirmed the transition with amazing signs, all happening as a result of human freedom and divine sovereignty. This will be confirmed in the model scene that follows (13:13–52), which portrays Paul's first missionary sermon and the responses to it, and in the closing scene in Acts (28:17–31), and repeatedly throughout the rest of the narrative.

13:13–52
Paul and Barnabas in Antioch of Pisidia

In this section Luke presents Paul's first missionary sermon in Acts, which is also Paul's longest speech (with 26:2–23 it forms a literary bracket framing the ministry of Paul). The speech is an evangelistic, missionary sermon addressed to a mixed audience of Hellenistic Jews and Gentile "Godfearers" (see on 10:2). Modern readers who mostly hear sermons addressed to insiders might well ponder the message of these speeches addressed to non-Christians. The speech resembles Peter's speech on Pentecost (2:14–36), as the speeches of all the characters in Acts are very similar (see "Speeches" in introduction to Acts). The speech is mainly the standard Lukan composition, but preserves some traces of Paul's distinctive theology, showing that Luke did not compose it without data from and interest in the Pauline tradition.

13:13 Set sail: A semitechnical term in Greek, like "embark" in English, indicating the author is something of a world traveler. There is more such semitechnical language of transportation in Acts than medical language (see on 3:7; 25:17; and 27:1). **Perga in Pamphylia:** A river town some miles inland. Paul and his party landed at Attalia (see 14:25) and changed ships or went overland. **John . . . returned:** John Mark; not to Antioch, but to Jerusalem, his home (12:12, 25). Luke gives no reason, so we can only speculate. Perhaps he saw the arduous and dangerous journey that lay before them (v. 14). His departure was later to become a problem (16:36–41).

13:14 Antioch in Pisidia: More accurately "Pisidian Antioch," "Antioch facing Pisidia," since the town was actually located in Phrygia on the Pisidian border (cf. Kansas City, MO). The town bears the same name as Antioch in Syria, from which Paul and his party had set out. Both were named for the line of Syrian

kings named Antiochus, successors of Alexander the Great (just as there were several cities named Caesarea after the Roman ruler). The city was ca. one hundred miles inland, over dangerous roads (see 2 Cor. 11:23–28). **Sabbath . . . synagogue:** Luke again emphasizes the continuity between Judaism and the new faith. See the similarity of this scene to Jesus' appearance in the synagogue at Nazareth (Luke 4:16–30).

13:15 Officials of the synagogue: Lay leaders responsible for organization and order of worship in the synagogue.

13:16 You Israelites: Better translated "fellow Israelites," as Luke continues to emphasize that Paul speaks as a Jew to Jews and worshipers of the Jewish God. This is also communicated by the reference to **the law and the prophets** (v. 15) and by Paul's reference to **our ancestors** (v. 17; see **my brothers, to us,** v. 26).

The sermon is divided into three parts by the repeated direct address to Paul's fellow Jews. God is the subject and principal actor in all three parts. The sermon is not advice about what human beings must do or general principles for them to consider, but an announcement of the mighty acts of God (see 2:11) that calls for a response: (1) "Fellow Israelites" (13:16–25)—a rehearsal of the story of God's saving acts for Israel; (2) "My brothers, you descendants of Abraham's family" (13:26–37)—showing how Israel's history leads to its climax in God's act in Christ; (3) "My brothers" (13:38–41)—an exhortation to receive God's offer of salvation in Christ.

13:17 God . . . chose: The people of Israel came into being by God's sovereign choice. Throughout the history of salvation, the initiative is with God. Paul will conclude on the same note regarding those who respond in faith to the Christian message (13:46, 48). **He led them out:** When the Israelites became slaves in Egypt, God delivered them (Exod. 1–15).

13:18 In the wilderness: The story of Exodus–Deuteronomy is summarized in a line.

13:19 Destroyed seven nations in the land of Canaan: The book of Joshua is summarized as God's gift of the land to Israel. The seven "nations" are listed in Deut. 7:1. The language is confessional language, not objectifying language (see on 5:1–11; 12:16–23; comments on Matt. 2:16; Acts 1:9; Rev. 6:15 excursus, "Interpreting Revelation's Violent Imagery," 3.b). The confession of thanksgiving to God is made from the grateful believer's perspective, not from an objectifying perspective in which

God destroyed the Canaanites and gave their property to others.

13:20 Four hundred fifty years: The phrase occurs at different places in the manuscripts and can thus refer either to the time of Egyptian slavery and wandering in the wilderness or to the period of the judges between the exodus and the beginning of the Israelite monarchy.

13:21 God gave them Saul: The establishment of the Israelite kingship is here presented as the gift of God, without reference to the difficulties of 1 Sam. 8–10. King Saul of the tribe of Benjamin was Paul's namesake and from the same tribe. Paul was proud of this ancestry (Rom. 11:1; Phil. 3:5).

13:22–23 He made David their king: The Old Testament story is seen as finding its climax in David's kingship. **Of this man's posterity God has brought to Israel a Savior:** The story now jumps to the Christ event. David is seen as a prototype of God's saving act in Christ (see 2 Sam. 7:12–16; Rom. 1:3–4; 2 Tim. 2:8). In the story of Jesus' birth, Luke has already elaborated his view that Jesus is the descendant of David in whom the promises to David are fulfilled (Luke 1:27, 32, 69; 2:4, 11; 3:31; 6:3; 18:38–39; 20:42–44; Acts 1:16; 2:25, 29, 31, 34; 4:25). Here as elsewhere in Luke–Acts, Jesus' messiahship is grounded not in the virginal conception but in his Davidic ancestry (see on Luke 2:7).

13:24–25 John had . . . proclaimed a baptism: John the Baptist was not important in the theology of Paul himself and is never mentioned in his letters. But John had an important role in Luke's understanding of the Christian faith as the last of the prophets of Israel who pointed to the coming of Christ (see on Luke 1:5–25; 5:33). Here as elsewhere, Luke presents Paul as representing the theology important in Luke's own setting. **I am not he:** John makes no such statement in the Gospel of Luke, but see John 1:20; 3:28, and the Lukan narrator's comment at Luke 3:15).

13:26 My brothers: The second major section of the speech begins, as Paul summarizes the message about God's act in Jesus. The story moves from John to the crucifixion and resurrection. The reader knows the story of Jesus' ministry in the Gospel of Luke, but the people in the story of Acts are presented with the cross and resurrection as the central events of the gospel. The good news of the Christian faith is not the life and teachings of Jesus, but the act of God manifested in raising him from the dead. Here Luke is true to Paul's own understanding of the

gospel as focusing on Jesus' death and resurrection (see 1 Cor. 2:1–2; 15:3–5), but he does not present Paul's view of Jesus' death as an act of atonement for human sins (see on Luke 22:20; Acts 2:23). Instead, he tells the story of Jesus' death as an evil act of human ignorance, rectified by God who vindicated Jesus by the resurrection (see on 3:17; 17:30).

13:31 They are now his witnesses: On the importance of "witness" in Luke's understanding of the Christian life, see on 1:8. God's placing in the world authentic witnesses to the reality and meaning of the Christ event is God's gift, part of the Christ event itself. The Lukan Paul does not claim to be an apostolic witness of the resurrection himself, but points to the testimony of those God chose (10:41; 14:4, 14; contrast Paul's own view in 1 Cor. 9:1; Gal. 1:1, 11–17).

13:33 As also it is written in the second psalm: Psalm 2:7; see Heb. 1:5; 5:5. On Luke's understanding of the whole Old Testament as pointing to Jesus, see on 3:18, 24; see also excursus, "New Testament Interpretation of the Old Testament," at 1 Cor. 15:3; and comments on 2 Cor. 3:12–18. **You are my Son:** On the meanings of "Son of God" in the New Testament, see on Luke 1:28–33. **Today I have begotten you:** The words were originally addressed to the Israelite king, as part of the inauguration ceremony. In contrast to the claims of pagan rulers, the Israelite king was not considered divine by birth, but was "adopted" as "Son of God" at his coronation. These words are here reinterpreted as referring to Christ. The "begetting" is understood to occur at the resurrection (rather than the conception) of Jesus, when God made him "Lord and Christ" (see 2:36).

13:34–35 No more to return to corruption: Isaiah 55:3 and Ps. 16:10 are also reinterpreted to refer to the Christ event. Peter had already so interpreted Ps. 16:10 (2:27, 31) with reference to the same point, that David's body decayed in the tomb, but Jesus' did not—another of the many Peter/Paul parallels in Acts (see list at 28:31).

13:38 Therefore, my brothers: The final section of the speech begins (see outline at 13:16). It comprises the offer of forgiveness through Christ and a warning against disbelieving the Christian message. **Forgiveness of sins is proclaimed to you:** Also central in Peter's first proclamation of the gospel (2:38).

13:39 Could not be freed by the law of Moses: Like the reference to the grace of God in v. 43, here we have a distinctive Pauline emphasis (Rom. 3:28; 8:3; Gal. 3:23–25), found only here in Acts. This shows both that Luke knows the Pauline theological perspective and that he expresses it in terms of his own later theological emphasis.

13:41 In your days I am doing a work: Habakkuk 1:5, originally addressed to the Babylonian conquerors of Jerusalem ca. 600 BCE, here reinterpreted to address Luke's contemporaries. That God is "doing a work," acting in the Christ event and the Christian mission, is Luke's primary point.

13:42–43 As Paul and Barnabas were going out: Luke reports no specific invitation to accept the Christian faith and be baptized, though the later references urging them to **continue in the grace of God**, to those who **followed Paul**, and to **disciples** (v. 52) suggest that some of his initial hearers responded to the message and became Christians.

13:44 Almost the whole city: Luke dramatizes the effect of the Christian mission, which "was not done in a corner" (26:26). One can ask historicizing questions such as how so many people could get in the synagogue and whether the service was moved to the theater, but the reader who approaches the text from this direction will probably miss Luke's point.

13:45 Filled with jealousy: See on 5:17. "Jealous" and "zealous" are alternative translations of the same Greek word. The Jewish leaders may not have been merely *jealous* of the church's numerical success, but rather sincerely *zealous* for their faith, which they saw being corrupted by the traveling preachers—as Paul himself had believed in his pre-Christian days.

13:46 Necessary that the word of God should be spoken first to you: "To the Jews first" was part of the divine plan; see Mark 7:24–30; Acts 3:26; 13:5; Rom. 1:16. **We are now turning to the Gentiles:** The missionaries continue to go first to the Jews and to turn to the Gentiles only after Jews have rejected the Christian message (e.g., 18:4–6, 19; 19:8; 28:17–31; see on 13:12). **Judge yourselves to be unworthy of eternal life:** No one is "worthy" in the sense of "deserving," but salvation is a matter of God's forgiveness and grace (vv. 38–39, 43). The meaning is that they made their own decision to reject the offer of salvation in Christ (see v. 48).

13:47 I have set you to be a light for the Gentiles . . . to the ends of the earth: The "you" is singular, in the quotation from Isa. 49:6 referring to the "Servant of the Lord," the personification of Israel (see on 1:8; 3:13; 8:27). Luke reinterprets this text in terms of the Christ event and the Christian mission.

13:48 As many as were destined for eternal life became believers: The Greek phrase can technically be either passive ("were destined") or middle ("destined themselves"). While the latter harmonizes more neatly with v. 46, Luke probably means that God is the one who destines people for belief. Thus the passage affirms both human responsibility and divine sovereignty. On the paradox of human action as God's action, see excursus at Luke 22:3, 22; Acts 2:23; 5:3; Phil. 2:12–13. On predestination, see excursus at Rom. 8:28.

13:49 The word of the Lord spread: Lukan shorthand for the founding of churches (see Luke 3:2; 5:1; 8:11, 21; 11:28; Acts 4:31; 6:2, 7; 8:14; 11:1; 12:24; 13:5, 7, 46; 17:13; 18:11).

13:51 Shook the dust off their feet: See on Luke 9:5, 10:11; Acts 18:6.

13:52 The disciples: Although this could refer to Paul and Barnabas, it is more likely the Lukan summary of the results of the conversion of those who had "followed Paul and Barnabas" (13:43). When Paul and Barnabas arrived in Antioch, they were the only Christians in town. When they left, as a result of their testimony, there was a church. Modern readers of the New Testament who are rarely in a situation where Christian communities do not already exist might ponder what Christian witness is in a world that is nonetheless increasingly secular.

14:1–7
Paul and Barnabas in Iconium

14:1 At Iconium: About ninety miles southeast of Pisidian Antioch. **As usual** (NIV): Despite the declaration of 13:46. The evangelistic preaching of Paul and Barnabas receives a believing response, and a united, integrated church of Jews and Gentiles is formed.

14:2 The unbelieving Jews: In this scene Luke thus pictures the situation of the church in every time and place. Some Jews believe, and some Gentiles believe. Some Jews oppose, and some Gentiles oppose (v. 5). All Jews were believers in the one God, in the will of God as revealed in the Hebrew Scriptures (the Christian Old Testament), and in the Jewish faith as interpreted by their teachers. "Unbelieving" in this context means they did not accept the Christian message. Here and elsewhere in Acts, it is not Judaism or Jews as such that constitute the problem, but unbelief. The dividing line is not ethnic, national, or cultural, but runs between belief and unbelief in the Christian message that God has sent the Messiah, Jesus.

Poisoned their minds: Luke has in mind active opposition to the Christian message, but in every situation one's own response affects the response of others. Every hearer of the gospel is responsible not only for himself or herself, but for the influence his or her response makes on others.

14:3 The Lord . . . testified to the word of his grace: The risen Lord acts through the signs and wonders of his messengers to confirm the word. Yet the signs are ambiguous and do not persuade all (see on 2:12–13; 3:17; 6:8; 10:14; 13:12).

14:4 The residents of the city were divided: The proclamation of the gospel unites peoples of various national, cultural, ethnic, and social backgrounds in the one community of faith (see Gal. 3:27–28). But wherever the gospel is faithfully proclaimed, it brings a division, because not all respond in faith (see Luke 12:51–53). **Some sided with the Jews, some with the apostles:** The missionaries were themselves ethnic Jews, as were Jesus and all the earliest Christians. "Jews" here refers to the unbelieving Jews in the sense of v. 2. Luke uses "apostles" for Paul and Barnabas only here (and v. 14; the NRSV reference in v. 6 is added to the Greek text). On "apostle," see on Luke 6:12–14; Acts 1:12–26; 9:3, 15, 27). Like all the religious vocabulary of the New Testament, "apostle" was an ordinary secular word before it was used in a special religious sense. Its ordinary meaning is "authorized messenger," "delegate," "representative." In early Christianity it was used in both an official and an unofficial sense, as we use the word "minister" or "secretary." Elsewhere Luke uses "apostle" only in an official sense, for the Twelve chosen and authorized by the earthly Jesus. Their qualifications are listed in 1:21–22. Paul (and Barnabas) do not qualify in this official sense. Luke regards Paul as apostle in the sense of "missionary," indeed the great missionary hero of the first generation, but does not consider him an apostle in the same sense that Peter was, for there were only twelve apostles. This is different from the understanding of Paul, who also can use the word in the informal sense of "a missionary authorized by the church" (2 Cor. 8:23; see 1 Thess. 2:7), but who insisted that he was an apostle in the official sense, in the same category as Peter and the earliest apostles (1 Cor. 9:1–2; Gal. 1:1–17). For Paul, but not for Luke, the group of official apostles was wider than the Twelve (1 Cor. 15:3–11) and included Paul himself.

14:6 Fled: Sometimes, as in this same episode, Christian responsibility called for the early missionaries to resist persecution and stand fast, even to the point of death (see 4:1–31; 5:17–42; 7:1–60; Rev. 2:10). At other times, it was the better part of wisdom to flee persecution in order to continue the Christian mission (Matt. 10:23). Early Christian missionaries received both instructions in the name of the risen Lord, but had to decide from situation to situation whether to resist or flee.

14:7 Lystra: About twenty-five miles southwest of Iconium. The town was a Roman colony and thus included many Roman citizens like Paul himself. **Derbe:** About sixty miles to the southeast of Lystra. Antioch, Iconium, Lystra, and Derbe were all in the Roman province of Galatia (though not in ethnic Galatia; see the introduction to Galatians).

14:8–20
Paul and Barnabas in Lystra and Derbe

14:8 Crippled from birth: See the parallel to the man healed by Peter, 3:2.

14:9 Seeing that he had faith to be healed: "Healed" is the same Greek word as "saved"; see on 4:9, 12. In New Testament healing stories, faith is sometimes a prerequisite and sometimes not. See on Luke 5:20, Acts 3:16; 4:9–12; and excursus on "Interpreting the Miracle Stories," at Matt. 9:35. Neither here nor elsewhere does the New Testament encourage the view that if prayers for healing are not answered, the problem must lie in the lack of faith of those who pray.

14:10 Sprang up: See 3:8. The healed man literally jumps for joy, dramatic proof of the reality of the miracle. Modern readers who walk and jump without reflecting on the miracle involved in this "normal" activity might reflect on the ability to walk as itself a gift of God.

14:11–12 In the Lycaonian language: Greek had become the common language of the Hellenistic world, but it was the native language of only a relatively few. Most learned it as a second language to facilitate communication. Paul and Barnabas preached in Greek, which was almost universally understood. All the New Testament documents were written in Greek. Here the inhabitants revert to their native language. **The gods have come down to us in human form:** The idea that gods would disguise themselves as humans and roam the earth incognito was a common pagan idea. A famous example is the legend of

Philemon and Baukis, an elderly couple in Ovid's *Metamorphoses* (Book VIII). They entertain Jupiter (**Zeus**) and Mercury (**Hermes**), supposing them to be needy humans, and are richly rewarded for their kindness. Some heretical branches of early Christianity understood Jesus to be a divine being who disguised himself as human (Docetism), but orthodox Christianity insisted on the true humanity of Christ, the divine One who had become human (John 1:1, 14; Phil. 2:5–11). This incarnational view of God is distinctive of early Christianity. Luke here contrasts the pagan view with the Christian and maintains the sharp distinction Jews and Christians have always made between God and human beings. **Paul . . . the chief speaker:** The description seems to presuppose that Barnabas is still the leading person, but that Paul is the more fluent speaker (contrast 2 Cor. 10:10).

14:14 Tore their clothes: As in Gen. 37:29; Esth. 4:1; and Mark 14:63, a sign of consternation. The misunderstanding gives Paul the occasion for his first speech to pagans.

14:15 Turn from these worthless things to the living God: Previously he has addressed mixed congregations of Jews and Gentiles in the synagogues, all people who share the Jewish faith in one God. In speaking to Jews and Godfearers, Paul and the early Christian missionaries begin with the Hebrew prophets and the story of God's acts in the history of Israel (2:14–36; 7:2–53; 13:16–41). Here, in speaking to pagans who do not already have this faith, Paul begins with the proclamation that there is one God, the Creator of all. The Christian faith, like the Jewish faith, is theocentric (see Luke 7:16; 8:24, 38; 9:20–22, 43; 13:13; 17:15; 19:37; Acts 2:22, 36). For Christian faith, this God has revealed himself in nature and human experience, but is definitively revealed in Jesus Christ. In Lystra, Paul is interrupted before he comes to the christological climax, but see the speech to a similar situation in 17:22–31. "**Living God**" is in contrast to idols. This reflects the authentic preaching of Paul (see 1 Thess. 1:9). Pagans considered their gods to be living, of which the statues were only symbols, but Jews and Christians supposed pagans worshiped the statues themselves as gods, and therefore ridiculed the dead idols in contrast to the living God (see Isa. 44:9–20).

14:17 He has not left himself without a witness: The Paul of Acts proclaims that the one God of Jewish and Christian faith is also testified to by nature and human experience, so that pagans who have no special revelation are addressed by God. Rain from heaven, the provision of food, and the joy of life all point to the reality of the one God (see 17:23–29; Rom. 1:20). Unlike the Paul of the letters, the Paul of Acts does not blame the Gentiles for rejecting and perverting this revelation.

The sermon is entirely God-centered, with no reference to Christ. But since Paul left Christian disciples in the town, including Timothy, who will later play a major role in the story, Luke must have presupposed that he preached the Christian gospel, baptized those who responded in faith, and established a church there (see vv. 21–23; 15:37; 16:1–2).

14:19 Jews came there from Antioch and Iconium: Just as Paul himself had previously pursued Christians into other cities (9:1–2; 22:3–5; 26:9–11). **They stoned Paul:** See 2 Cor. 11:25. How "official" this attempt on Paul's life was is unclear (see on 7:58), just as it is not clear whether Paul actually died and revived (see 20:7–10).

14:21–28
The Return to Antioch in Syria

14:21 Made many disciples: See Matt. 28:19. Their faith was not merely personal and individualistic; the disciples are added to the church by God (as 2:41). **Returned to Lystra, then on to Iconium and Antioch:** Pisidian Antioch is meant (see 13:14). **Strengthened the souls of the disciples:** Here Paul exercises the same function Jesus had promised to Peter (Luke 22:32; for list of Peter/Paul parallels, see at 28:31).

14:22 Through many persecutions: Paul and Barnabas themselves were examples of what the new Christians could expect. The motive for becoming a Christian was not in order to have one's life go smoothly, to obtain supernatural help in becoming healthy and wealthy, but to **enter the kingdom of God** (see on Luke 4:43–44). Jesus' devotion to God's kingdom led to the cross, not to a life of luxury; his disciples can expect persecution as the badge of their identification with him (see Luke 9:23).

14:23 Appointed elders: Literally "stretched out the hand," originally as a way of voting; the word later was generalized to mean simply "choose." Since Paul and Barnabas are the subjects, it is not a matter of election but of appointment. The authorization extended to Paul and Barnabas by the church is now extended to the elders of the church. Luke does not yet have the rigid hierarchical understanding of church structure that developed later, but he does portray a structured church: Christ conferred authority on the apostles (Luke 6:12–16; 9:1–6; 24:44–49; Acts 1:12–26; 2:1–42), who approved the work of the Antioch church (11:19–30), which commissioned Paul and Barnabas (13:1–3), who now authorize local church leadership. Elders were a relatively late development in church structure, unknown in the undisputed letters of Paul, and thus here anachronistically reflect the church structure of Luke's own time at the end of the first century. See 20:17–38; 1 Tim. 5:1–2, 17, 19; Jas. 5:14; 1 Pet. 5:1, 5; 2 John 1; 3 John 1.

14:24–26 Pisidia . . . Pamphylia . . . Perga . . . Attalia . . . Antioch: Paul and Barnabas retrace their steps, except that they do not return to Cyprus and go directly back to Antioch (see 15:39—Cyprus later gets a return visit from Barnabas).

14:27 Related all that God had done through them: Paul and Barnabas had not been independent missionaries operating on their own initiative. The missionaries report to the church that sent them out. They were called by the Holy Spirit at work in the life of the church, and were commissioned by the church for their mission (13:1–3). Presumably the Antioch church also supported the (relatively expensive) mission financially, though this is not directly stated. They do not report to the "mother church" in Jerusalem, but will shortly appear there on other business, with the result that the Jerusalem church will approve and authorize the mission of Paul to the Gentiles. The stage is now set for what was perhaps the most important event in the life of the early church.

15:1–35
THE JERUSALEM COUNCIL

This scene, carefully prepared for and composed by Luke, marks a turning point in his portrayal of the growth and development of the church. Paul too looked back on it as a crucial debate (Gal. 2:1–10). The Jerusalem Council comes almost exactly in the center of Acts. The previous chapters represent the "primitive" church to which Luke looks back with respect and appreciation, as it has grown to maturity under the leadership of Peter and the original apostles. After this scene, Peter and the Jerusalem apostles disappear from the story. After chap. 15 the

Christian community is portrayed as like the church in Luke's own time, looking back to the time of the church's origins as part of its own history, but not attempting to reproduce it.

During the first fifteen chapters the church becomes a universal, inclusive community representing God's love for and acceptance of all:

—*Jesus and the Twelve:* The story begins in Galilee with the Jew Jesus and Galilean Jews.

—*The Seventy:* Jesus' disciples are still Galilean Jews, but "seventy" has the connotation of "all the nations."

—*The three thousand* (Acts 2:1–42): The church that began in Jerusalem is composed entirely of Jews, but they are "from every nation" and specifically include proselytes, i.e., converts to Judaism who are not ethnic Jews.

—*Hellenists and Hebrews* (Acts 6:1–6): The church is still entirely Jewish converts, but embraces the whole spectrum of Judaism, including Hellenists, Hebrews, priests (6:7), and Pharisees (15:5).

—*Samaritans* (Acts 8:1–26): A major step is taken when the gospel is extended to the Samaritans, who had Jewish roots but were regarded by orthodox Jews as outsiders. Samaritans had their own temple and considered themselves to be a different religious community distinct from Judaism. In Acts 8:1–26 Jews and Samaritans are embraced in the one people of God.

—*The Ethiopian eunuch* (Acts 8:26–40): A transitional figure who had previously been excluded is baptized into the one church.

(In Acts 9:1–31 Paul is converted, the one designated to be the principal missionary to the Gentiles [22:21].)

—*Gentile Godfearers* (Acts 10–11): The role of including the first Gentiles in the church is given to Peter. (Only after this crucial story is told in detail does Luke incidentally mention that Gentiles had already been included; see on 11:19–21.)

—*Full, unqualified Gentiles* (Acts 13–14): Paul and Barnabas then conduct a mission that brings full Gentiles, who had no previous contact with Judaism, into the church. With this climactic development, the question is raised from within the church as to whether Gentiles can simply become Christians, without becoming Jews first. This sets the stage for what has been considered the most important event in the history of earliest Christianity, the Jerusalem Council.

15:1 Certain individuals: Luke makes it clear that they are operating on their own initiative and do not represent the Jerusalem church (see v. 24). However, their insistence that all Christians keep the Law of God as revealed to Moses does pose an inescapable problem for the church. This issue had not been recognized and faced squarely before. Complete plans for the future church and instructions for all future occasions were not given in advance by Jesus or the early apostles. Led by the Spirit, the church grows and develops as it responds to new situations.

Unless you are circumcised: On the importance of circumcision in Judaism, see on 7:8. Here and elsewhere, the issue of circumcision does not concern merely the ritual itself; circumcision represents the mark of the covenant, the commitment to keep the Law of God as revealed to Moses and recorded in the Bible. **According to the custom of Moses:** See 6:14. Luke somewhat dulls the point of the opposition by expressing their argument in terms of a "custom." Although a few late Hellenistic Jewish documents such as 1 Maccabees occasionally spoke of the obligations of the Law as "customs," this word never occurs in the Hebrew Bible itself for God's law. The Judean Christians did not represent the issue as whether or not they would continue a particular custom, but whether or not they would live by God's law as revealed in the Bible.

You cannot be saved: On the Lukan understanding of salvation, see on 4:12; 16:30. These Judean Christians insist on maintaining the clear teaching of the Bible that membership in the people of God, the community of faith and salvation, requires the mark of the covenant.

15:2 No small dissension and debate: On the figure of speech, see 12:18; 19:23, 24; 20:12 NRSV; 21:39 NIV. The problem was serious, with sincere and devout Christians on both sides. It should not be trivialized by the modern reader as though the answer is obvious. Advocates of circumcision could quote the Bible that circumcision and the other rituals of the Mosaic Law were given by God forever, and were not to be superseded by some later revelation (see Exod. 31:17; Lev. 10:9, 15; 16:29, 31; 17:7; 23:14, 21, 31, 41; 24:3, 8; 25:32; Deut. 12:28; 29:29). Jesus himself had been circumcised (Luke 2:21). Genesis 17:13 specifically declares that circumcision is "an everlasting covenant." Advocates of law-free Gentile Christianity could respond that these laws were only given for Jews, that Gentiles were never expected to obey them. The response of the Judean Christians was that the laws were given to the covenant community, and whoever joins it must keep the Law, including even aliens who are sojourning among Israel (see Exod. 12:48).

The apostles and the elders: Not to the "other" apostles; in Luke's view Paul and Barnabas are not official apostles (see on 1:15–16; 9:27; 14:4, 14). The phrase "apostles and elders" is important to Luke, who repeats it five times in this scene (vv. 2, 4, 6, 22, 23). On apostles, see Luke 6:12–15. On elders see on 11:30; 14:23. Previously in Acts the apostles have functioned as a kind of central authority for the expanding and developing church (see 6:1–7; 8:1, 14–15; 9:26–30; 11:1–18, 19–26). Now the apostles, in conjunction with the elders, are seen as a central council that can decide issues for the church at large. It is different from the later ecumenical councils of the church, which included delegates from the church as a whole, though the later church councils looked back on Acts 15 as model and authorization.

Paul and Barnabas: They are authorized teachers and missionaries in the Antioch church (13:1–3), which itself has been approved by Jerusalem (11:19–30). It was their mission to Gentiles of Acts 13–14 that had precipitated the issue. Luke's story line makes it clear both that they did not wait on apostolic approval when launching the Gentile mission, and that they regarded apostolic approval as essential for the unity of the church and its mission. As delegates of the Antioch church, Paul and Barnabas had followed the guidance of the Spirit in leading the church in new directions that created problems. *Then* the issue must be resolved by the church meeting in a structured council.

15:3 Brought great joy to all the believers: Along the way to Jerusalem, Paul and Barnabas announce what God had done through them among the Gentiles (see v. 4). Christians in Phoenicia and Samaria do not wait for Jerusalem's approval before celebrating what God has done.

15:4 When they came to Jerusalem: According to Acts, this would be Paul's third trip to Jerusalem after his conversion (see 9:26–30; 11:27–30; see 12:25). It was in the year 49 CE, fourteen (or seventeen) years after Paul's call to be a Christian (Gal. 2:1).

15:5 Believers . . . Pharisees: On Pharisees, see on Luke 5:17. Becoming Christians did not dissolve their status as strict Jews, just as it did not for Paul himself (23:6–9; 26:5; Phil. 3:5; see 2 Cor. 11:22).

15:6 Consider this matter: The will of God is not immediately clear even to the apostles. They do not regard it as a matter of "whether or not we are going to go by the Bible," "whether or not we are going to follow the guidance of the Spirit," or a matter of "let each individual decide for himself or herself." It is a matter of churchly importance, but its resolution must await further insight. Speeches are made by Peter, Paul and Barnabas, and James, but Paul plays no role in the decision-making process itself.

15:7 Peter stood up and said to them: This will be Peter's last appearance in Acts, as the focus of the story shifts to Paul. **In the early days:** In the Lukan chronology the events of chaps. 10–11 to which Peter appeals had happened after Paul's conversion and prior to Herod's death (9:1–30/12:1–5, 20–23), i.e., in the mid-30s, which in general agrees with Paul's own sketch of early Christian history (see 13:6; 15:4; Gal. 2:1). The church had thus been receiving Gentiles into membership for ca. fifteen years, but in Luke's story line it is the objections of some strict Jewish Christians to Paul's Gentile mission of Acts 13–14 that provokes the present debate and decision. In this section Luke is not concerned to establish a precise chronology, but to make three theological points: (1) God has already included Gentiles in the church; what is being discussed is a fait accompli; (2) this happened through Peter, i.e., Peter and Paul agree on this crucial issue; (3) the work of the Spirit in the wider church needs to be discerned and approved by the responsible church authorities. **The gospel** (NIV)/**The good news** (NRSV): This noun is found only twice in Luke–Acts, here in the mouth of Peter and 20:24 in the mouth of Paul (see list of Peter/Paul parallels at 28:31).

15:8 Giving them the Holy Spirit: The presence of the Holy Spirit in the lives of Gentile Christians is the sign that God has already included them (see Gal. 3:2). *Discerning* the presence of the Spirit, however, is an ambiguous human judgment. What appears to be the work of the Holy Spirit to one person may appear to be blasphemy to another (see Mark 3:22–28; Luke 11:14–23). Consistently in the New Testament, the ability to discern the work of the Holy Spirit is itself a gift of the Spirit (1 Cor. 12:11; 1 Thess. 5:19–22; 1 John 4:1–3). Peter's argument is not airtight objective logic that would be convincing from the disinterested spectator's point of view, but presupposes sharing the life and faith of the Christian community filled with God's Spirit.

15:9 Cleansing their hearts by faith: The issue of ritual purity was the problem that divided Jews from Gentiles, an issue that modern secularized readers should not trivialize (see on Luke 2:22–24; 5:27–32; 11:37–41).

15:10 Putting God to the test: By imposing circumcision and the requirements of the Mosaic Law on Gentile Christians. "Testing God" is what rebellious Israel did during the wilderness wanderings (e.g., Exod. 15:22–27; 17:2; Num. 14:22; Deut. 6:6), but what Jesus refused to do (Luke 4:12). **Yoke:** The harness by which animals were linked together to pull a common load. It was used as a positive metaphor for the Law in Judaism, which spoke of obeying the Law of God as "taking on oneself the yoke of the kingdom"—as a gift received with joy rather than as a burden to be borne. Jesus also used the metaphor in a positive sense of discipleship to himself (Matt. 11:29–30). Paul used the image in a negative sense, describing the Law as the "yoke of slavery" (Gal. 5:1; see 3:19). Peter here uses the word in the Pauline sense.

15:11 We will be saved through the grace of the Lord Jesus: Paul could not have said it better (see Rom. 3:19–26; Gal. 3–5; Eph. 2:1–10). Salvation, acceptance by God, is not a matter of belonging to the right group or doing the right thing, not a matter of human achievement at all, but is the gift of God's grace. Just as in Acts Peter (rather than Paul) is credited with being the first to admit Gentiles to the church, so here he expresses the Christian doctrine of grace in a distinctively Pauline manner. In the second or third generation of Christianity Luke is concerned to show that the two major leaders of the first generation agreed on the fundamentals of the faith. **Be saved:** The original issue, 15:1. On the Lukan understanding of salvation, see on 4:12; 15:30. **Just as they:** Grace is the great equalizer. If salvation is based on merit, then there must be different classes of Christians, for there are different levels of achievement. But if salvation is indeed God's gracious gift rather than human achievement, then the community of salvation is a community in which all are equal (see Rom. 3:21–26, esp. 3:22, "no distinction," to which Rom. 10:12 corresponds; see also Gal. 3:27–28).

15:12 Kept silence: More than mere politeness while someone else is speaking, it reflects the openness of the different groups to listen to those with whom they disagreed. The objections are in fact silenced, and Peter's argument is found to be persuasive.

15:13 James replied: There were two of the original twelve apostles named James (Luke 6:14–15), but this is a different person, the brother of Jesus. Like the rest of Jesus' family, he had not been a believer during Jesus' lifetime (Mark 3:19–21, 31–35; Luke 8:19–21; John 7:1–9). The risen Jesus had appeared to him (1 Cor. 15:7; see further on introduction to James). Here he emerges as the leader of the Jerusalem church (see 12:17, 21:18).

15:14 Simeon: Reflects the Hebrew form of "Simon." See 2 Pet. 1:1. Luke certainly understands it to refer to Simon Peter, though in his source it may have referred to Simeon Niger, a teacher in the Antioch church (13:1), who had been sent to Jerusalem to consult James and the leaders about conflicts in Antioch about Jewish dietary regulations for Gentile Christians. The unusual use of "Simeon" may be an indication that Luke has combined two separate incidents in his narrative of 15:1–29 (see on historicity at 15:35 below) **A people for his name:** "People" is the "people of God," a designation reserved for Israel (see Jer. 13:11; Luke 2:10, 32; 3:9, 11; 4:10; 5:34; 7:29; 10:41), but now expanded to include Gentiles. On the importance of "the name," see on 2:38.

15:15 This agrees with the words of the prophets: The Scripture is reread in the light of the Christ event and is seen to confirm the experience of the church in admitting Gentiles (see on Luke 21:22; 24:25; Acts 3:18; 8:32–33; 2 Cor. 3:12–18; and excursus at 1 Cor. 15:3, "New Testament Interpretation of the Old Testament"). The meaning of the Scripture in Christian perspective was not clear in advance of the church's experience; otherwise the council and deliberation would not have been necessary.

15:16–17 I will rebuild the dwelling of David: As elsewhere, Luke emphasizes that the promises made to David find their fulfillment in Jesus and the church (see 4:25; 7:45–50; 13:22–23). The point of the text quoted depends on the Greek translation used by Luke (the LXX; the original Hebrew is different); i.e., it is the Bible of the Greek-speaking Gentile church of Luke's time and place, not the Hebrew Bible of the Jerusalem church (see on 2:16).

15:19 I have reached the decision: On the basis of the discussion. For the criteria on which the decision was based, see on v. 28 below. There is no vote, but a consensus is discerned. While James has considered the discussion and the criteria, he is portrayed as making the decision himself, by which the church abides, somewhat in the style of later bishops. In James's and Luke's setting, the office of bishop had not yet evolved. Since in Luke's theology it is the "apostolic college" of the Twelve in Jerusalem, led by Peter, by which the church is supervised, the scene here probably reflects both the source Luke is using and the historical reality behind it, in which James early emerged as the primary leader of the mother church in Jerusalem—though by Luke's criteria he is not an apostle.

15:20 Write to them to abstain: The directions here given are traditionally called the Apostolic Decree, though it is formulated by James and approved by apostles, elders, and the Jerusalem church as a whole (see vv. 22–23). The decree does not address the original issue. It contains four prohibitions, all ritual. Gentile Christians are to abstain from the following:

1. *Things polluted by idols:* This refers to meat ritually slaughtered and dedicated to an idol (v. 29; see on 1 Cor. 8–10).

2. *Fornication:* The Greek word can refer to sexual immorality in general. That is most likely not the meaning here, since then it would be the only moral command in the list (the others being ritual commands), and the absence of other moral commands, such as prohibition of lying and stealing, would be difficult to explain. One would then have to ask why only Gentile Christians are given this command. As we now know from the Dead Sea Scrolls, in first-century Judaism the word was also used to refer to marriage within proscribed kinship limits (incest).

3. *Whatever has been strangled:* This refers to meat not properly slaughtered so that the blood has been drained from it, nonkosher meat.

4. *Blood:* The eating of food made from blood was proscribed by the Old Testament (e.g., Gen. 9:4) and by Jewish law.

The four prohibitions thus represent a minimal observance of the Jewish ritual law that would make it possible for Jewish and Gentile Christians to live and work together in one church. They are modeled on the regulations for resident aliens living among Israelites in the holiness code of Lev. 17–18. A later edition of Acts, long after Luke's own time, attempted to transform the rules into ethical admonitions by understanding the first as a prohibition of idolatry, the second as a prohibition of sexual immorality, omitting the third, and understanding the fourth as a prohibition of murder, and by appending a form of the

Golden Rule ("whatever you wish not to be done to you, do not do to others"). This form of the text is found in a group of manuscripts called the Western Text. It is not original, but represents an effort of later scribes to make a ritual law for a particular time into universal ethical instruction.

15:21 In every city ... Moses has had those who proclaim him: The decree is directed to Gentile Christians and is not intended to abolish the Law of Moses for Jews and Jewish Christians, who are here assumed to continue to worship at the synagogue (see 21:17–26).

15:22 Apostles and elders, with the consent of the whole church: James formulated the compromise, but it is issued in the name of the Jerusalem church and its apostolic and presbyterial leadership. Though literally the council involved only the Christians of Jerusalem, Luke intends it to represent the wider church. **Judas called Barsabbas and Silas:** Authorized representatives of the Jerusalem church accompany the delegates of the Antioch church. Luke portrays the whole development as a matter "officially" handled between churches, not as the result of enterprising individuals. Nothing further is known of **Judas**. **Silas** is the same person as the "Silvanus" of 2 Cor. 1:19; 1 Thess. 1:1; 2 Thess. 1:1; 1 Pet. 5:12. He will play an important role as Paul's missionary companion later in Acts.

15:23 The brothers ... to the believers ... in Antioch ... greetings: The Jerusalem church is pictured as adopting the standard Hellenistic letter form, "A to B, greetings" (see 23:26; James 1:1). The Pauline letters significantly modify this stereotyped form (see on 1 Thess. 1:1).

15:24 No instructions from us: The letter plainly indicates that the original disturbers of 15:1 had not represented James and the Jerusalem church. The letter does not refer to the contents of the original dispute directly, but in its present context makes it clear that circumcision and keeping the Mosaic law are not necessary for acceptance by God and inclusion in the church (see v. 28).

15:25 We have decided unanimously: The Christian Pharisees in the Jerusalem church who had originally objected to the admission of Gentiles who do not keep the Mosaic Law had been convinced that the new developments were the will of God. **Our beloved Barnabas and Saul:** The phrase does not suggest a grudging acceptance of Gentile Christians. Luke pictures the Jerusalem church as fully endorsing the new Gentile mission. The order

"Barnabas and Saul" is not Luke's own after 13:9 and suggests he is accurately citing an older source that contained the letter.

15:28 Seemed good to the Holy Spirit and to us: The Holy Spirit is not mentioned in vv. 1–27. In Luke's understanding of God's guidance of the church, the Holy Spirit works through human reflection, struggle, discussion, and decision. The church was not complete at the beginning, was not born full grown. The reader knows God has been guiding the expansion of the church by the Holy Spirit, not only numerically, but theologically. This is Luke's version of "discerning the spirits" (see 1 Cor. 12:1–31; 14:29; 1 John 4:1–3). The people in the story must decide whether it is the Spirit of God or a seductive evil spirit leading them away from God's truth revealed in the past. How does this process of discernment take place? Barnabas and Paul rehearse their experience, Peter does likewise, and others give their objections based on the Bible, tradition, and experience. The teaching and example of Jesus is strikingly absent. Although the readers of Acts know the sayings and stories of Jesus in the Gospel, the characters in the story do not here make these the basis of the church's decision. The Bible is studied again. And in the process of group discussion under responsible leadership, a decision is made. The Holy Spirit is not mentioned in the process, there are no miraculous signs, and it appears to be a matter of human judgment. Then, in retrospect, the whole process is called "the Holy Spirit and us." This is not done in such a way that some things can be assigned to "the Spirit" and some to "us," but the Spirit works within the church. It is a matter of risk and trust, with no absolute certainty possible (see excursus at Rev. 2:20 on "Testing Prophecy"). It is also a matter of theology, of faith seeking understanding, of reflecting on the nature of the church and God's continuing act.

These essentials: Keeping the minimal ritual requirements is necessary not for salvation, but for the unity of a church that has both Jewish Christian and Gentile Christian members. Neither here nor elsewhere in Acts is there an expectation that Jewish Christians will abandon their Jewish practices, though they must not attempt to compel Gentiles to practice them. For the church to be one fellowship and work together in one mission, Gentile Christians must make some accommodations. For an analogous issue from another perspective, see Paul's discussion in 1 Cor. 8–10.

15:31 Rejoiced at the exhortation: The Antioch Christians did not consider themselves independent of approval by the Jerusalem church. This is an aspect of belief in the unity of the one church of God, a view that Paul too affirms from another perspective (see on Gal. 2:2).

15:32 Judas and Silas . . . prophets: They were directly inspired spokespersons for the risen Lord (see on 11:28–29; 13:1–3). Luke portrays harmony between those who speak the word of God by direct inspiration and those who make decisions through "official" church structures. The institutional church does not exclude the guidance of the Holy Spirit; those spoken to by the Spirit do not disdain church structures and discussion on the basis of Christian experience and human insight (see on v. 28 above).

15:33 Those who had sent them: The second "sent," referring to the delegates from Jerusalem to Antioch, is the verb form of the word "apostle," and suggests the communication of apostolic authority from Jerusalem to Antioch.

15:34 Silas . . . remain there: This verse is not in the oldest and best manuscripts and was added later by Christian scribes in order to harmonize with 15:40. Such phenomena show that Luke is using sources that he has incorporated without making them totally consistent with his own narrative (see Luke 1:1–4).

Paul also describes the Jerusalem Council in Gal. 2:1–10 (see there). Since Luke's account of the Jerusalem Council is the only instance where we have an extensive primary source written by a participant in the scene Luke describes, it affords us a good opportunity to assess the combination of historical fact and theological interpretation manifest in Luke's writing. See Figure 11 (see also chart at Gal. 2:10).

The comparison thus reveals numerous agreements, but also significant disagreements. Some differences may be only a matter of emphasis and perspective, while others resist harmonization (especially #3, #7, and #10). The most likely solution to the central focus on the Apostolic Decree in Acts 15 and its absence in Gal. 2 is that Luke has combined the accounts of two separate events in his sources into one grand scene (see his composition of the Gospel, comments on Luke 1:1–4). The Jerusalem Council on which Paul reports dealt with circumcision and keeping the law. A *later* meeting in Jerusalem, at which Paul was not present, dealt with the question of dietary rules in the Antioch church, probably as a result of the dispute Paul reports in Gal. 2:11–14. This would explain both Paul's lack of reference to the Apostolic Decree in Gal. 2:1–10 and why even in Acts he seems to be informed of it for the first time in 21:25.

Luke seems to have taken the accounts of two separate meetings and reformulated them into a ideal portrayal of how differing groups in the church work through their difficulties with mutual respect and a concern to maintain the unity of the one church of God: Jewish Christians do not insist on circumcision and keeping the Mosaic Law for Gentile Christians, and Gentile Christians agree to keep a minimum of the ritual law for the sake of church unity and mission. Luke's narrative in Acts 15 provides a model of decision making for maintaining the unity of the church under the guidance of the Holy Spirit, a model also valuable for later generations of Christians. While it contains historical materials, precise historical accuracy is not its main point.

15:36–20:38
PAUL CONTINUES THE UNIVERSAL MISSION OF THE CHURCH

15:36–18:22
PAUL'S SECOND MISSIONARY JOURNEY

15:36–41
Paul and Barnabas Separate

15:36 Paul said to Barnabas: After 13:1, Paul is the leader of the missionary team. Paul's proposal to revisit the churches seems to be a matter of human initiative (contrast the initial missionary impulse, 13:1–3), but Luke does not distinguish human initiative and guidance of the Spirit, understanding the whole mission of the church to be under the supervision of the Spirit (see on 15:28). **Visit:** The Greek word is related to the word for "supervisor," "bishop," and was later used for episcopal oversight. See commentary on 15:33. The church as portrayed by Luke does not yet have the later official structures, but the language he repeatedly uses indicates it is on the way to developing them. **Every city where we proclaimed the word:** The churches established on the first missionary journey of Acts 13–14.

15:37 John called Mark: See on 12:12, 25; 13:13. Does Luke consider his having deserted them (13:13) an illustration of Luke 9:62?

15:39 The disagreement became so sharp that they parted: The presence of the Holy Spirit in the lives of both Barnabas and Paul did not exclude such disagreement. Luke does not mention that theological tensions had also developed between Paul and Barnabas (see Gal. 2:11–14, "even Barnabas"). Barnabas and John Mark disappear from the story in Acts at this point as they return to **Cyprus** (Barnabas's original home, 4:36) to continue the mission work there (see 13:4–12). Paul's letters and the later Pauline tradition refer to a Mark who worked with Paul (Phlm. 24; Col. 4:10 [which indicate Barnabas and Mark were cousins]; 2 Tim. 4:11; see also 1 Pet. 5:13). If this is the same person and all these traditions are accurate history, then Paul and Mark were later reconciled.
15:40 Paul chose Silas: See on vv. 22, 32. **He went through Syria and Cilicia:** Here begins the "second missionary journey," which will continue until 18:22, beginning and ending in Antioch (see Outline in the introduction to Acts). Now that the kind of Gentile mission Paul has initiated has been approved by the Jerusalem church, the remainder of Acts will be devoted to Paul's further mission work, which will finally bring him to Rome. **Believers commending him to the grace of the Lord:** The Antioch church also blesses Paul's work and sends him forth. The mission is not his personal enterprise.

16:1–5
Timothy Joins Paul and Silas

16:1 Derbe and Lystra: Towns in which churches had been established on the first missionary journey (14:8–21). **Timothy:** Luke does not indicate whether he and his mother had been

---

Figure 11. A Comparison of the Jerusalem Council as Represented in Acts and Galatians (cf. also chart at Gal. 2:10)

1. In both Galatians and Acts, the issue is whether Gentile Christians must be circumcised and keep the law of Moses (Gal. 2:3; Acts 15:1).
2. Both Galatians (2:2) and Acts (15:2, 31, and implied throughout) consider the approval of the Jerusalem church and its apostolic leadership as vitally important.
3. In Galatians, the Council visit is Paul's second visit to Jerusalem after his conversion (Gal. 1:18; 2:1). In Acts, it is his third visit (9:26–30; 11:30; 15:2).
4. In Galatians, the Council visit is fourteen (or seventeen) years after his conversion (Gal. 2:1). This is compatible with Acts' chronology, though Luke does not locate it precisely (see on Acts 15:7).
5. In Galatians, Paul is accompanied by Barnabas and Titus, an uncircumcised Gentile Christian who becomes a test case of the issue that occasioned the Council (Gal. 2:1, 3). Acts nowhere mentions Titus, and Paul is accompanied only by Barnabas (Acts 15:2).
6. In Galatians, Paul goes to the meeting "by revelation," i.e., at the direct command of the risen Christ received in a vision or prophetic oracle (Gal. 2:2). In Acts, he is sent as a delegate of the Antioch church (Acts 15:2).
7. In Galatians, Paul as an apostle has a private meeting with the pillars of the Jerusalem church: James, Cephas (Peter), and John (Gal. 2:2, 9). In Acts, Paul meets with the apostles, elders, and the whole church (Acts 15:4), and Paul is pointedly not an apostle (see on Acts 14:4, 14).
8. In Galatians, Paul speaks of those Jerusalem leaders who advocate circumcision and keeping the law as "false brothers" (Gal. 2:4). Acts speaks of them as "believers who belonged to the sect of the Pharisees" (Acts 15:5).
9. In Galatians, Paul set before the group the gospel that he preached among the Gentiles (2:2). In Acts, he and Barnabas rehearse the signs and wonders that God had worked during their mission (15:12).
10. In Galatians, Paul insists that his own view carried the day, and that the Jerusalem leaders added nothing to him (Gal. 2:6, 10). In Acts, the Apostolic Decree is formulated, and Paul willingly delivers it to the Antioch church and his own mission churches (15:30; 16:4).
11. In Galatians, the only request made by the Jerusalem leaders is that Paul "remember the poor" (Gal. 2:10), i.e., that he take up an offering from the Gentile churches for the poor Christians of Judea. There is no reference to this in Acts 15, but cf. 24:17.
12. Galatians speaks of a division of labor in which Paul will go to the Gentiles and the Jerusalem leaders to the Jews (Gal. 2:9). Acts reports no such arrangement.

converted on Paul's previous mission or by the evangelistic work of the church in the meantime. According to 1 Cor. 4:17 he had been converted by Paul personally. Timothy will join the missionary team and in Acts will play a somewhat subordinate role, always in conjunction with others (see 17:14–15; 18:5; 19:22; 20:4). In Paul's letters, Timothy is a partner with Paul, entrusted with important assignments on his own (Rom. 16:21; 1 Cor. 4:17; 16:10; 2 Cor. 1:1, 19; Phil. 1:1, 2:19; 1 Thess. 1:1; 3:2, 6; Phlm. 1). He also plays an important role in the deutero-Pauline literature (Col. 1:1; 2 Thess. 1:1; 1–2 Tim; see Heb. 13:23).

16:3 Had him circumcised because of the Jews: This is the same Paul who has just successfully resisted those who advocated the circumcision of *Gentile* converts. Timothy is a borderline case, with a Jewish Christian mother and a Gentile father. The status of such offspring was disputed in ancient times. He had not previously been a Jew (otherwise he would already have been circumcised), and is known only by his common Greek name. Or perhaps Luke wants us to understand that he had been a "Jewish" Christian whose Greek father had prohibited circumcision. In any case, Paul could be seen as compromising the very principle for which he had fought (see 1 Cor. 7:18–19; Gal. 2:3). Yet Luke presents Paul as wanting to avoid placing any unnecessary stumbling blocks in the way of those who might come to faith, and willing to be misunderstood for the sake of the gospel (see 21:17–26). This accords with the stance Paul himself expresses in his letters (1 Cor. 8–10; see esp. 9:19–23). Just as circumcision in itself is not ultimately important, neither is *un*circumcision (Gal. 5:6; 6:15). Paul is not concerned with his image as liberal or conservative, but that the gospel be heard and accepted without false stumbling blocks.

16:4 They delivered to them for observance the decisions: See 15:23–29. Though originally in a letter addressed to the churches in Syria and Cilicia, the decisions are for Luke now relevant for the whole church. Here is a model for the later church's appropriation of all the New Testament documents, which were originally addressed to Christians in another time and place.

16:5 Increased in numbers daily: Just as Paul himself was a missionary evangelist, so the churches he founded were evangelistic, proclaiming in word and deed the good news of God's act in Christ, and winning converts to the Christian faith. Evangelism was the prin-

cipal mission of the church in Acts (Luke 24:45–49; Acts 1:8; see Matt. 28:16–20). God had acted in Christ for the salvation of the world, and the good news had to be shared. The new faith had implications for life together in the new community and eventually for the transformation of society. But the church's mission began with proclamation of the gospel and the invitation to Christian faith and membership in the Christian community. Paul and the other missionaries in Acts did not enter the towns of the ancient Mediterranean world as social reformers. They mainly accepted the social structures of their day, as had Jesus. But the new community would finally have transforming effects on society as well.

16:6–10
Paul's Vision of the Man of Macedonia

16:6 The region of Phrygia and Galatia: The towns of Iconium, Lystra, and Derbe were in the Roman province of Galatia, which did not correspond to the ancient territory of ethnic Galatia, settled originally by Gauls from central Europe. Paul and his party now turn northward into ethnic Galatia, in the central part of what is now Turkey. They had intended to go to the south and west to the Roman province of Asia, the capital of which was Ephesus, but were forbidden by the Holy Spirit. Luke does not say how the Spirit guided the mission. Elsewhere he portrays the Spirit working both through extraordinary means (visions, revelations through prophets) and within ordinary occurrences such as human insight and discussion (see on 15:28).

16:7–8 Attempted to go into Bithynia: To the populous areas in the north, in the direction of the Black Sea. **Troas:** An important city on the west coast, the nearest seaport to Europe. Its proper name was Alexandria, but it was popularly called Troas, after the nearby site of ancient Troy, to distinguish it from Alexandria in Egypt. The origins of Christianity and its earliest communities were all in Asia; the mission of the new community will only now cross the Aegean to Europe.

16:9 A vision: The guidance of the Spirit in restricting their previous movements now becomes clear. Luke frequently portrays communication from the heavenly world as a vision (2:17; 9:10–12; 10:3, 17–19; 11:5; 12:9; 18:9; 26:19). In his understanding such visions are objectively real.

16:10 We immediately tried to cross over: For the first time the narrative shifts from the third person to the first person. The "we passages" in Acts comprise 16:10–17; 20:5–15; 21:1–18; 27:1–28:16 (a few ancient manuscripts begin the "we" sections at 11:28, but the reading is hardly original). The "we" in these passages may indicate the personal presence of the author during the scenes in which "we" occurs or the incorporation of sections of a diary of one of Paul's companions, or this may be a literary device (see "Sources" in introduction to Acts). **Macedonia:** A Roman province to the north of Greece, which will be the first setting for the proclamation of the gospel in Europe. **Being convinced that God had called us:** The work of the "Holy Spirit" and of the "Spirit of Jesus" are here identified as the work of "God." While there is no developed doctrine of the Trinity in the New Testament, the elements for the later doctrine are present (see 2:33, comments at Matt. 28:19; 1 Pet. 1:2).

16:11–15
The Conversion of Lydia

The first Christian convert in Europe is a woman. For other Christian women in Acts, see 1:14; 5:1–14; 8:3, 12; 9:2; 16:1; 17:4, 12, 34; 18:2; 22:4.

16:11–12 Samothrace: An island port in the Aegean, en route to **Neapolis**, the seaport of **Philippi:** Paul's missionary strategy was to establish churches in large cities, from which the gospel would spread. A strong church was established in Philippi, to which Paul developed close and tender ties, a church that provided financial support for Paul's mission trips (Phil. 1:1; 4:15–16). **A Roman colony:** The Philippians enjoyed the same rights as Roman citizens of towns in Italy. Their patriotism will play a role in the later story (16:20–21) and will provide the setting for the first introduction of Paul's status as a Roman citizen (16:37–38).

16:13 On the sabbath: Paul and his companions continue to worship as observant Jews and continue to go to the Jews first (see on 3:26; 13:46). There are as yet no specific references in Acts to Sunday, the first day of the week, which was to become the Christian holy day (see on 20:7). **Place of prayer:** A synagogue could be so called, but this appears to be an informal gathering of Jews and Godfearers, since no formal worship service is described (contrast 13:13–16).

16:14 Worshiper of God: A technical term, "Godfearer" (see on 10:2). **Thyatira:** Later a church is found there, one of the seven to which Revelation is directed (Rev. 2:18). **Purple cloth:** The point is not just its color, but that Lydia dealt in cloth colored with the distinctive dye associated with royalty (see Mark 15:17, 20; Luke 16:19; John 19:2, 5; Rev. 17:4, 12, 16). Lydia is portrayed as a prosperous businesswoman dealing in expensive goods. **The Lord opened her heart:** See on 13:46, 48. To ask why the Lord did not open the hearts of the other women is to mistake the kind of language being used. On "confessional" and "objectifying" language, see on 1:9; 5:1–11; Matt. 2:16; excursus, "Interpreting Revelation's Violent Imagery," 3.b, at Rev. 6:15; Rom. 8:28–38.

16:15 Her household: If she is a widow, the household would include her children. If, as is more likely, the phrase indicates she is unmarried, her household would consist of her slaves (on slavery in the New Testament world, see the introduction to Philemon). **Were baptized:** As elsewhere in Acts, it is assumed that acceptance of the Christian message includes being baptized and added to the church. **Stay at my home:** Lydia becomes a model of that minority of early Christians who were wealthy and whose homes functioned as meeting places for the church and provided hospitality for traveling missionaries (see v. 40 and Luke 8:1–3; 9:1–6; 10:1–12; Acts 12:12; 18:1–3; 21:4, 8, 16). This network contributed greatly to the expansion of early Christianity.

16:16–40
Paul and Silas in Prison

16:16 We met a slave-girl: Neither here nor elsewhere does anyone in the New Testament challenge the institution of slavery as such. On New Testament perspectives on slavery, see the introduction to Philemon. **A spirit of divination:** Literally a "python spirit," so called from the legend of the great snake that guarded the oracle at Delphi. The phrase then came to mean any spirit that enabled one to predict the future. **Great deal of money:** Luke–Acts is concerned throughout with the danger of greed and with the relation of money to matters of faith (see on Luke 1:53; 6:24; 12:16, 21; 21:1). The theme here emerges for the first time since 8:18–24.

16:17 The Most High God: The girl's statement functions at two levels. From her pagan perspective, the "most high god" is Zeus, and the missionaries' message proclaims "a way of salvation," i.e., one of many ways in the Hellenistic world that people could attain a happy life ("salvation" was a synonym in the Roman world for the peace and prosperity brought by the emperor; on the Lukan understanding of **salvation,** see below on v. 30). Luke and his Christian readers will understand the "Most High God" to be the one God, the Creator, the Father of Jesus Christ, and "the way of salvation" to be the one way revealed in Christ. Note that the NIV translates "the way," while the NRSV translates "a way." Either is a technically correct rendering of the Greek text. The NIV represents Luke's own understanding, the NRSV that of the girl in the story. Understood in Luke's sense, what the girl said is true, but Paul is angered by its association with an evil spirit. The Christian faith is not a matter of magic and belief in spiritual phenomena (see on 8:9–24; 13:6–12; 19:13–20), of which the Hellenistic (and modern) world was full, but of the good news of God's act in Christ.

16:18 Come out of her: The power of Jesus' name (see on 2:38) that heals (3:6) also delivers from the power of evil spirits. The same Holy Spirit at work in Jesus continues to be effective in his disciples; see excursus, "Satan, the Devil, and Demons in Biblical Theology," at Mark 5:1.

16:19–20 Their hope of making money was gone: Monetary greed was their real motive, which they cloaked in religious and patriotic reasons. See 19:24–25. **Disturbing our city:** See 17:6. The opponents of Christianity understand themselves to be advocates of public order, defending it against new Eastern superstitious movements.

16:20–21 They are Jews: The Christian community is not yet recognized as separate from Judaism. Paul and Barnabas were Jews (Jewish Christians). The "we" of the author (see 16:10) fades away at this point, so it is not clear whether he is included as Jewish. The author is not arrested and beaten. **Advocating customs not lawful for us Romans:** Both anti-Jewish and patriotic sentiments are exploited in order to discredit the missionaries. Philippi as a Roman colony (16:12) shared the belief that Rome had brought order, peace, prosperity, and security to a chaotic world, and were suspicious of any group that seemed to threaten the Roman way of life. Their charge was untrue. Throughout Luke–Acts, the author is concerned to show that Jesus and the church are not a political threat, and in fact have the approval of insightful Roman leaders (see e.g., Luke 23:15, 22, 47; 18:12–17; 26:30–32).

16:22–23 Ordered them to be beaten with rods: Paul explicitly refers to this abuse in 1 Thess. 2:2, written shortly afterwards from Corinth (see also Phil. 1:30; 2 Cor. 11:25).

16:24 Innermost cell, fastened their feet: See the imprisonment of Peter, 12:4–6, and list of Peter/Paul parallels at 28:31.

16:25 Praying and singing hymns: Not because they felt cheerful or religious, but as an expression of praise to God who continues with them in their mission and allows them to suffer for his name (see 5:41). It is not said that they were praying to be set free. The deliverance comes at God's initiative, now because they knew how to pray properly. **The prisoners were listening:** Not as entertainment. Paul and Silas do not directly preach to their captive audience, but the way they respond to their troubles becomes a testimony to the Christian faith to the other prisoners.

16:26 Earthquake: To ask how the quake affected the other people in the area is to take the story in an objectifying sense and miss its confessional point (on objectifying and confessional language, see on Matt. 2:16; Acts 1:9; 5:1–11; excursus, "Interpreting Revelation's Violent Imagery," 3.b, at Rev. 6:15). **All the doors were opened and everyone's chains were unfastened:** Not only Paul's and Silas's. **About to kill himself:** The penalty for allowing prisoners to escape was death (see on 12:18–19; 27:42–43).

16:28 We are all here: Not just Paul and Silas. The other prisoners likewise do not avail themselves of the opportunity to escape (though they are lost sight of as the story continues).

16:30 What must I do to be saved?: Many modern readers of the Bible, especially in the mainline churches, are uncomfortable with the language of salvation. Yet such language pervades the New Testament, where the Greek words for "savior," "save," and "salvation" occur 176 times, of which 44 are in Luke–Acts. Since there is some variety in the ways the various New Testament authors use these words and what they understand by them, we will here confine ourselves to Luke–Acts as representative of broad streams of early Christian understanding.

EXCURSUS:
WHAT MUST I DO TO BE SAVED?

The question, What must I do to be saved? itself is alien to our modern secular world, which when confronted by the language and thought world of the Bible is more likely to ask, "What does it mean to 'be saved'?" Answers should not be read into the Bible from the theology of American revivalism, which has preserved the language of "being saved" in a way that does not always correspond to biblical usage. The following observations are offered to aid the modern reader toward a more biblical understanding:

1. *Jesus and the church did not invent the language of salvation, which was already present both in the Old Testament and in the Hellenistic world, in both secular and religious senses.* The Caesars were regularly called saviors, and the good life they took credit for bringing to the world was called salvation. In the Greek translation of the Old Testament, the term "Savior" was applied to God (e.g., Deut. 32:5; 1 Sam. 10:19; Ps. 24:5) and to the deliverers God sent, the judges (e.g., Judg. 3:9, 15), and "salvation" was used for God's deliverance of his people from various threats to their life and well-being (e.g., Pss. 18:2; 38:22; 74:12; Isa. 12:2; 25:9; 49:6). Jesus and the early church found the language of salvation used frequently both in their secular world and in their Bible.

2. *The biblical language of "being saved" presupposes that life as we know it is incomplete, that it lacks something to be what life should be, and that God has graciously acted in Jesus Christ to supply that lack.* This threat to true life may take many forms. In the following list, the Greek words for "be saved" and "salvation" are translated in several ways, but all represent the New Testament idea of salvation. In Luke–Acts, God's people are said to be saved from enemies (Luke 1:71); from the guilt of sins (Luke 1:77; 5:31); from sickness and disease (Luke 6:9; 7:50; 8:48; 17:19; 18:42; Acts 4:9, 12; 14:9); from demonic powers (Luke 8:36); from isolation and exclusion from the people of God (19:9–10); from troubles, distress, and the threat of death (Luke 23:37–39; Acts 7:25; 27:20, 31, 34); and from death (Luke 8:5). Salvation is also used in a comprehensive sense that includes deliverance from the guilt and power of sin, inclusion in God's people, acceptance before God at the Last Judgment, eternal life in God's heavenly kingdom (Luke 8:12; 9:24; 13:23; 18:26; Acts 2:21, 40, 47; 11:14; 13:26, 47; 15:1, 11; 16:27, 30–31). In Luke 18:18–26, "be saved," "inherit eternal life," and "enter the kingdom of God" all mean the same thing. In Luke–Acts, the language of salvation is never used with reference to "hell" (but see Luke 12:5). In Luke–Acts there are no pictures of what salvation beyond death is like—no pictures of heaven and the like, and being saved does not mean primarily going to heaven when you die. Being saved is having one's life put in right relation with God and other human beings, being given one's life as it was intended to be by God in this world, and being given the sure and certain hope of eternal life beyond this world. As such, being saved is sometimes the opposite of "being lost" (Luke 15:4, 6, 9, 24, 32; 19:10).

3. *The question, "What must I do?" presupposes the act of* God. The question asks what human beings should do, but the New Testament never indicates that human beings are capable of remedying their own lack, of doing certain things that in themselves result in salvation. Salvation is predicated on the grace of God given in Christ (Acts 15:11). The jailer at Philippi has heard Paul's preaching of salvation that comes from God and asks what he as a human being should do in response. This question should not be avoided by modern secularized Christians. The church needs to be able to recognize this question, even when it is no longer asked in these terms (e.g., "How can I be really happy?" "Is there any such thing as right and wrong?" "When confronted with a variety of attractive and persuasive options, how should I live my one and only life?" "Is there a God, or are we the highest and best there is in the universe?" "What's worth doing?"). The church needs to be able to give a clear and biblical response to this question, even when the questioners are not clear what they are asking (in Luke's story, it is not likely that the jailer understood the Christian doctrine of salvation when he raised his poignant question).

16:31 Believe on the Lord Jesus: This is Luke's comprehensive summary of what is required of human beings in response to God's act in Christ. It is not a first step in a "plan of salvation," but contains in itself the whole answer to the jailer's question. It includes faith in Jesus as Lord and Christ, turning away from sin, commitment to doing God's will, baptism and incorporation into the Christian community, and living one's life in the service of the God revealed in Christ. Elsewhere in Acts it can be called "repentance" (11:18); "turning to the Lord" (9:35; 11:21; 15:19; see 26:18, 27); "becoming obedient to the faith" (6:7); "being persuaded" (17:4); "believing in God" (16:34); or, as here, simply "believing" (e.g., 2:44; 4:4; 8:12–13; 17:12, 34; 18:8, 18, 27; 19:2, 4; 21:25; 22:19; 28:24). In such contexts, believing does not mean merely holding the opinion that such and such is true (as in "I believe it will rain tomorrow"), but is a matter of personal trust and commitment. One theologian has aptly described the New Testament meaning of faith as "obedience in personal trust." With this conversion story, compare the other accounts in Acts of what people do in order to be saved–become Christians (2:29–42;

3:17–4:4; 8:4–17; 8:26–39; 9:1–9 [22:3–16; 26:2–18]; 10:34–48).

And your household: His family and/or slaves in his household (NRSV "his entire family" of v. 33 is an interpretation of the Greek phrase, literally "all his"). While Jesus had warned that discipleship to him would split families (Luke 12:51–53), in Acts households are consistently united in Christian families (see 16:15; 18:8).

16:32 They spoke the word of the Lord to him: Instruction in the basics of Christian faith and life preceded baptism, but it was not a lengthy process, since he and his household were baptized the same night.

16:33–34 Washed their wounds . . . set food before them: The genuineness of his conversion is not a matter of internal spirituality, but is manifest in deeds of compassion for prisoners who have espoused an unpatriotic cause (see Ps. 146:7; Isa. 42:7; 49:9; Jer. 37:17–21; 38:7–13; Matt. 25:36–44).

16:35–36 Let these men go: The remainder of the story proceeds without reference to the earthquake and dramatic events of the preceding night; v. 35 could join seamlessly to v. 24. The civic authorities have decided that the missionaries have been adequately punished and will leave town without causing any more problems. **Roman citizens:** Silas is apparently included. Here is the first reference in Acts to a feature of Paul's identity that will play an important role in the subsequent narrative (21:39; 22:25–29; 23:27; 25:11–12).

16:40 Went to Lydia's home: See 16:15. **Encouraged the brothers and sisters there:** Lydia's home is now the meeting place of the new Christian community. In Philippi (as elsewhere), when Paul and Silas arrived they were the only Christians in town. When they left, there was a church in Philippi. Wherever early Christians went, they did not passively place their new faith on hold until they came to some town where there was already a church, but became the nucleus of a new Christian community. The modern church in a secularized society has much to learn from the early church in this regard.

17:1–15
The Uproar in Thessalonica and Beroea

17:1 They: The Greek "they" is retained by the NIV but interpreted as "Paul and Silas" by the NRSV (though Timothy was also apparently with them; see v. 15). **Thessalonica:** The capital, modern Thessaloniki (or Thessalonike or Saloniki), already an ancient city in Paul's time (founded 315 BCE). Paul had apparently passed through **Amphipolis** and **Apollonia** because there were no Jewish synagogues there. For Paul's own account of his mission in Thessalonica, see 1 Thess. 1:5–2:16.

17:2 Paul went in, as was his custom: See on 13:46. Paul continues to go "first to the Jews." First Thessalonians gives no indication that the church in Thessalonica had a Jewish Christian nucleus (see 1 Thess. 1:9!). **From the scriptures:** The Hebrew Scriptures, the Christian Old Testament, accepted as a common authority by Judaism and Christianity. The issue is not authority but interpretation. Christians understand the Old Testament to point beyond itself to Christ and the church; Jews understand it to point to the continuation and further development of God's purpose in the synagogue and Jewish tradition. On Christian interpretation of the Old Testament, and whether it specifically predicts the death and resurrection of Jesus, see on 3:18, 24, and the excursus at 1 Cor. 15:3. **Three sabbaths:** Philemon 4:9 and 1 Thess. suggest that Paul's sojourn in Thessalonica was for a longer period.

17:3 This is the Messiah: On the meaning of "Messiah/Christ," see on Mark 8:29. The hope for the Messiah was common to Judaism and Christianity. The issue was whether the hope for the Messiah was fulfilled in Jesus of Nazareth, or whether we should "wait for another" (see Luke 7:19–20). In the Christian confession "Jesus is the Christ," "Christ" is the subject and "Jesus" is the predicate noun, so it might more accurately be rendered "The Christ is Jesus." The question is not, who is Jesus? but who is the Christ? (see 18:5, 28).

17:4 Some of them were persuaded: Both Jews and Gentiles respond to the message; both Jews and Gentiles reject it. Those who were persuaded (see on 16:31) believed the Christian message, were baptized, and constituted the nucleus of a church in Thessalonica, a congregation composed of Jewish Christians and Gentile Christians who had been Godfearers (see on 10:2). **Not a few of the leading women:** From the beginning the church included influential women in its membership (see on 16:11–15), who played a more active role in church leadership than had been possible in the synagogue.

17:5 The Jews became jealous: Or "zealous" (see on 13:45). **Ruffians in the marketplaces . . . set the city in an uproar:** Luke acknowledges that response to the Christian mission did sometimes produce conflict and disturbance of the peace, but attributes this to the misguided zeal/jealousy of some of the Jews and to the ignorance and gullibility of "lower class" people. He is eager to show that the Christian message appealed not just to the lower economic and social strata, but to the wealthy, respected, and influential people as well (see 4:34–5:2; 8:27; 10:1–2; 11:29; 12:12; 13:7; 16:14–15; 17:4, 7, 11, 18, 34; 18:1–3, 24; 19:19–20). Though in the Gospel Luke had portrayed Jesus as champion of the poor and oppressed (1:46–55; 2:8–14; 2:24; 3:10–14; 4:16–21; 6:20–23; 14:21–23; 16:19–31), in Acts Luke never specifically mentions that slaves, the poor, and the socially marginalized were included in the church (though see 2:44–47; 3:6; 4:32–35; 11:27–30). This is different from Paul's perspective in 1 Cor. 1:26–31. Luke wants to show his readers that the new Christian community is not what the suspicious Roman public is inclined to believe about it (see on vv. 6, 12 below). **Attacked Jason's house:** This Jason is otherwise unknown, but was apparently a wealthy Jew sympathetic to the missionaries' cause (see 18:17). There is no reason to identify him with the Jason of Rom. 16:21.

17:6 Turning the world upside down: See 16:20; 24:5, 12. This is not merely an emotional outburst, but a serious charge. The Romans were understandably proud of the order they had brought to the world and were suspicious of those who might disrupt it. It is true that the Christian faith effected a revolution in the lives of those who accepted it, and that eventually it would achieve dramatic social transformations. Luke's concern is to show that the new faith is not socially disruptive in the sense feared by the Romans. The modern reader might ponder whether the Christian faith is indeed more socially revolutionary than its advocates are often inclined to think.

17:7 Acting contrary to the decrees of the emperor: This charge is actually false (see on Luke 2:1–7; 20:20–26; 23:47; Acts 18:12–16; 26:30–32; 28:30–31). **Another king named Jesus:** See the placard on the cross, Luke 23:38, and the discussion of the political charges against Jesus in the comments on Luke 23:1–47. Jesus' and the early church's preaching of the kingdom of God was easily misunderstood as the program of an anti-Roman political movement, as though Christians advocated disloyalty to Caesar and support of a rival emperor. But the New Testament proclamation of God's rule may have more and deeper political implications than many

modern Christians suppose. On "kingdom of God," see on Luke 4:43. For a different perspective on Jesus' kingdom, see John 19:12.

17:10–11 Sent Paul and Silas off to Beroea: On the missionaries' flight to avoid persecution, see on 14:6. **Beroea** is modern Verria, about fifty miles from Thessalonica, a city where the evangelists were no longer subject to the political authorities of Thessalonica. **Went to the Jewish synagogue:** See commentary on 17:2. **Of more noble character** (NIV)/**More receptive:** literally, "better born," i.e., belonging to "a better class of people." Modern democratic and egalitarian readers rightly resist such an understanding, but Luke's point continues to be that it was not only irresponsible riffraff who were attracted to the Christian faith (see on vv. 4, 5, 12). Luke himself makes the egalitarian, inclusive nature of discipleship to Jesus clear in, e.g., Luke 5:27–32; 7:36–50; 14:1. Here, his point is apologetic.

17:12 Greek women and men of high standing: See on vv. 4–5, 10. Luke is concerned to present the church's story in an apologetic light, i.e., to defend it against charges circulating in his environment ("a bunch of unpatriotic, superstitious riffraff") in order to open the way to people's understanding and accepting the truth of the Christian faith (see his statement of his purpose in Luke 1:1–4).

17:13 Jews of Thessalonica . . . came there too: See on 14:19, and Paul's own account in 1 Thess. 2:14. On **word of God** as a summary of the Christian faith, see Luke 3:2; 5:1; 8:11, 21; 11:28; Acts 4:31; 6:2, 7; 8:14; 11:1; 12:24; 13:5, 7, 46; 17:13; 18:11. This is of course the Christian perspective. The Jews of Thessalonica did not regard the Christian message as "word of God," but as a perversion of the authentic faith.

17:14 Silas and Timothy remained behind: To strengthen the new church. Apparently Luke thinks they are not as threatened as Paul, the leader of the group. In 1 Thess. 3:1–2 much of this account is confirmed, but Paul there indicates Timothy accompanied him to Athens. Luke either compressed the account or did not have accurate information. Even if the author is identical with the "we" of 16:10ff, he had remained at Philippi and was not personally acquainted with the events in Thessalonica, Beroea, and Athens.

17:16–34
Paul in Athens

17:16 Athens: Though Athens was still renowned as the glorious city of classical times (fifth–fourth centuries BCE) where Plato and Aristotle had taught, its actual importance had greatly declined in the first century. In the time of Paul and Luke, Corinth had already outstripped Athens commercially and politically. The setting is symbolically important to Luke, who portrays Paul as confronting the assembled representatives of pagan culture with the Christian message. **Deeply distressed to see that the city was full of idols:** The historical Paul had been in idolatrous cities his whole life. Tarsus, his home town, was much like Athens. The scene is set up by Luke as the occasion for Paul's speech. Jews had two fundamental objections to the statues of pagan gods that adorned every Gentile city: (a) Gentiles worshiped many when there is only one God (Deut. 6:4–6), and (b) Gentiles worshiped lifeless images they themselves had made, rather than the true God who is invisible to human eyes (Exod. 20:4–5; Isa. 44:9–17). Both charges were valid against much of the folk religion of antiquity, but many thoughtful pagans had come to believe in one God who was represented in the variety of gods and goddesses, praying to "Zeus of many names," and most would have said they did not worship the statue itself, but the god it symbolizes.

17:17 In the synagogue with the Jews and the devout persons: As elsewhere (e.g., 17:2, 10) Paul begins with Jews and Godfearers who attended the synagogue, but in this scene they are quickly forgotten, for Luke wants to concentrate on the encounter between Paul and the intellectual leadership of the Gentile world. The Christian faith is to be proclaimed not only in houses of worship, but **in the marketplace every day.**

17:18 Epicurean and Stoic philosophers: Two of the three leading philosophical perspectives in the Hellenistic world (Cynics are missing here and elsewhere in the New Testament, though Cynicism represented a popular philosophy). Philosophy here does not refer to the abstract doctrine of an academic seminar, but to philosophy of life (like capitalism, communism, competition, the American way of life). Such philosophies were advocated vigorously by street preachers, discussed in everyday conversations, and taken seriously as of practical importance. Epicurus had taught in Athens in the fourth century BCE. His followers were materialists who believed in the gods, but taught that human life was free from interference from them, and was ruled only by the chance combination of atoms. In the ancient context, this was a liberating doctrine that called for a sober life of human responsibility. The Epicureans considered individual, personal happiness the supreme value and did not participate in public and political life. Since human life was an accident of nature, it had no future beyond death. Stoicism was founded by Zeno, who taught in the Stoa ("porch") in Athens in the fourth century BCE. His followers did not believe in a personal god or gods, but in a universal reason (the "logos," related to "logic") that permeated nature, including human beings. "All things are unfolding as they should," according to universal cosmic reason. The good life accepts the reasonableness of the world and lives calmly in accord with it, taking what life gives without celebration or complaint. Morality is to live by the dictates of reason. Of course these few sentences do not do justice to these two approaches to life that were advocated in the Roman world with sophistication and passion.

Babbler: Literally "seed picker," picturing a bird hopping around the market place pecking at various seeds, but without a coherent systemic view of life. **Want to say:** The Greek grammatical construction indicates an unreal condition, as when in English we say, "If I were you." The meaning is thus "What would he say, if only he could manage it?" Their response expresses the disdain of the cultivated Greek world to what they considered the simple-mindedness of Jewish and Christian primitive superstition. **A proclaimer of foreign divinities:** Not just a conversational comment, but a serious charge. Athenians were forbidden by law to introduce novel religions, especially those from the "Orient." Socrates had been executed on this charge. **Jesus and the resurrection:** This has sometimes been understood as though Paul's hearers perceived him to be advocating two new gods, Jesus and Anastasis (resurrection). While the reader of Luke's account might so understand the expression, Paul's actual hearers in the story could hardly have misunderstood him in this way. The summary of the Christian message is not focused on Jesus' teaching or example, but on God's act in Jesus, culminating in the resurrection (see 2:36).

17:19 Brought him to the Areopagus: The Hill of Ares, the Greek god of war, identified by the Romans as Mars, so the place is also called Mars Hill. The name was applied both to the hill and the judicial assembly that met there (see v. 22).

17:20 We would like to know what it means: Luke portrays a dramatic scene: the leading Christian missionary is taken seriously and invited to address the representatives of pagan culture (contrast Paul's view in 1 Cor. 1:18–25). With regard to the church's message, what does it mean? is a good question when asked by outsiders (see on 16:30), a question the church should be prepared to answer (see on 1 Pet. 3:15). Paul gives a model for this in the following speech.

17:21 Nothing but telling or hearing something new: On the one hand, there is a sense in which Luke himself affirms the newness of the Christian faith (see on Luke 1:39; 3:2; 5:36–38). On the other hand, Luke regards the Athenian interest in novelty as superficial and misguided, for he presents Christ and the church as the continuation and fulfillment of the old, not its abolition. In speeches to Jews, the Christian preachers connect what they are doing with the story of Israel in the Hebrew Bible (e.g., 7:1–53; 13:16–41). Here in the Gentile setting, Paul will present the Christian message as in continuity with the act of God from creation through world history (vv. 24–31). Paul does not announce a new God, but the act of the one God whose purpose for the world and history (Israel's and that of all nations) is fulfilled in Christ.

17:22 Extremely religious: The word so translated is found only here in the New Testament, but see the related word understood pejoratively in 25:19. The Greek term can be taken in a positive or negative ("superstitious") sense, but the Lukan Paul here takes it positively as a point of contact for his own message.

17:23 To an unknown god: Many ancient altars have been discovered in Athens, but none with this inscription. The original meaning in its Athenian context may have been to a god not known locally, i.e., a foreign god. Alternatively, the altar may have been erected in gratitude to some gift or act of the gods (e.g., healing, deliverance from shipwreck) by someone or a group that did not know which particular god had helped them. Paul understands the inscription in his own positive sense: the pagan worship of the Athenians, and of Gentiles in general, is directed to the one true God, though they have previously been ignorant of his identity. **You worship as unknown:** Here Luke acknowledges that pagan worship is unknowingly directed to the one true God. On the "igno-

rance motif" in Luke's theology, see 3:17; 13:26; 17:30. **This I proclaim to you:** In Luke's theology, Christians do not bring God, or the worship of God, to people of other religions, for the one true God is universally present. Christians must still bear witness to their faith that the God already present and worshiped in paganism is in fact the God who has definitively revealed himself and acted in Jesus Christ. This is Luke's theology of mission. It is opposed to two other views: (a) the claim from the right that only Christians are in touch with the one true God, and must bring this saving message to those who as yet have no experience of God, and (b) the claim from the left that since God is universally present and people of all cultures and religions already worship God, Christians have no mission to them. Luke understands the Christian gospel to concern the mighty acts of God, and Christian mission to be testimony to these acts (see on 2:11). For the ancient Christians, the mission of the church involved "going" to other lands and cultures with the Christian message. In the modern world, in which there are congregations of Christians in every nation, mission strategy is not primarily "going" (though it does not exclude that), but witnessing to its faith that the one God already present and (unknowingly) worshiped is the God of Jesus Christ.

17:24 The God who made the world and everything in it: The one God, the Creator, is universal. Note the number of universal words in this passage: "everything" (v. 24), "all mortals" (v. 25), "all things" (v. 25), "all nations" (v. 26), "whole earth" (v. 26), "all people everywhere" (v. 30). **Does not live in shrines made by human hands:** See also on Stephen's speech to Jews, 7:48, and 1 Kgs. 8:27; Isa. 57:15. Just as good Jews built a temple while acknowledging that God did not actually inhabit a house in this world, the more thoughtful pagans regarded their temples and statues in the same perspective.

17:25 Gives to all life and breath and all things: Whether they worship or not, whether they know whom they worship or not. The creation of the world and the sustaining of it, the gift of life itself, are already witnesses to the grace of God (see 14:16–17).

17:26 From one ancestor he made all nations: A major implication of faith in one God the Creator is the unity of the human race. Polytheism can affirm that people of other nations and races do not really belong to "us," because they have their own god. But if the one God is also their Creator and sustainer, all peoples belong together as children of the one God. **Allotted the times . . . and the boundaries:** The one God is the Lord of history, not only of nature. Luke represents the Jewish and Christian view of God who is active in history, not an absentee landlord, not an immanent impersonal force or process oblivious to or unconcerned about the rise and fall of nations and the course of human history. This statement does not mean that God has predestined which nation shall control which territory and for how long; human beings must bear responsibility for this. Luke claims that God is sovereign over the whole course of human history. On human responsibility and divine sovereignty, see on Luke 22:3, 22; Acts 2:23; Phil. 2:12–13.

17:27 So that they would search for God: Luke understands the idolatry of pagan religion, i.e., human religion as such, as a human quest and affirmation that human life is not self-sufficient and does not contain its meaning within itself, that there is a God to be found. But Luke's own theology is not that God is lost or hidden and needs to be found by human searching. Rather, the one God is omnipresent, is always already there (vv. 27–30), and this God has definitively acted in Jesus Christ (v. 31). Humans do not finally find God, but are found by the God who has come to us (see John 4:23).

17:28 We too are his offspring: Luke uses the language of being "children of God" in a way different from some other New Testament authors, who use it as a synonym for Christian believers (see John 1:12; Rom. 8:14; 9:8; Gal. 3:26; 1 John 3:1, 10; 5:2). For Luke, all people are children of God by creation (see Luke 3:38; Adam is "son of God" by creation). No individual, people, race, or nation is an accident of nature or creature of some other god; all are children of the one God.

17:30 God has overlooked the times of human ignorance: See 3:17; 13:27; 14:16. For Luke, the principal problem of humanity is not human perversity but human ignorance. God's act in Christ has now remedied that problem, so that ignorance is no excuse. **Commands all people everywhere to repent:** This was also the Jewish message, though the content of "repentance" was different. For Luke, it includes confession of faith in Jesus as the Christ. **All people everywhere** includes Jews and Gentiles. Though God is already present in Jewish and Gentile religion (and modern secularism),

God's definitive saving act in Christ calls for faith and repentance as its response.

17:31 He has fixed a day: To this point everything in the sermon could have been proclaimed by a Hellenistic Jew. Only here does the Lukan Paul introduce the specifically eschatological and christological proclamation inherent in the Christian faith. **He will have the world judged in righteousness:** As in Peter's speech in 10:11–42, the conclusion points to God's eschatological judgment to be accomplished by Christ. "In righteousness" means "in justice." God will bring world history to a worthy conclusion, in which the present injustice is seen not to be the last word about the world and human life, and the justice of the kingdom of God will prevail. **A man whom he has appointed:** This is the only statement made about Jesus in the entire sermon: Jesus is God's designated agent for eschatological judgment and salvation. **By raising him from the dead:** Here as elsewhere in the Acts sermons, the resurrection of Jesus is the act of God. It is not a dispensable postscript to the sermon, but its climax. The function of the resurrection here is to validate Jesus as God's chosen agent (see 2:36). Here as elsewhere in Acts, there is no message of the cross itself as an act of atonement or reconciliation (see on Luke 22:20; Acts 2:23; 13:26).

17:32–34 Some scoffed: The proclamation of the resurrection proved to be the stumbling block. Had Paul preached the immortality of Jesus' soul, there would have been no problem, for the issue was not whether there is some sort of life after death, but whether God has acted to restore the crucified Jesus to life and make him Lord of all (see on Luke 20:27), whether the consummation of history, including the final resurrection, has already begun in Jesus Christ. **We will hear you again:** While this could simply be a polite dismissal of Paul's claims, Luke more likely intends it as a second kind of response: some scoffed and overtly rejected the gospel, others postponed the issue and refused to decide (see 24:25). **Some . . . became believers:** This is the third and authentic response. Luke has pictured a model scene of the proclamation of the gospel in a secular culture: some make fun of the Christian message and openly reject it, others politely postpone a decision and go on to other things, some respond in faith. Nothing further is known of **Dionysius the Areopagite** (i.e., a member of the assembly that met on the Areopagus) or **Damaris,** but the reader notes that, as in

Thessalonica and Beroea, both women and men of high social standing became members of the Christian community (see on 17:4, 12).

18:1–17
Paul in Corinth

18:1 Corinth: The capital of the Roman province of Achaia (Greece). See the introduction to 1 Corinthians.

18:2 A Jew named Aquila . . . with his wife Priscilla: Jewish Christians, here identified as Jews because it was as Jews that they had been forced to leave Rome. Luke is interested in showing that the Romans consider Christianity to be a branch of Judaism (18:12–17). Priscilla is the same as Prisca of Paul's letters, where she is always named first (Rom. 16:3; 1 Cor. 16:19; see 2 Tim. 4:19). **Native of Pontus:** On the Black Sea (see 2:9; 1 Pet. 1:1). **Claudius:** Roman emperor 41–54 CE. According to the Roman historian Suetonius (*Life of Claudius* 25), Jews were expelled from Rome in the ninth year of Claudius (49 CE) because they "constantly made disturbances at the instigation of Chrestus." Since Chrestus, a common Roman name, was pronounced the same as Christos, the Greek word for "Christ," which would not be familiar to the Romans, Suetonius apparently misunderstood disturbances in the Roman synagogues caused by the Christian proclamation of Jesus as the Christ as caused by someone named Chrestus. All Jews, including Jewish Christians (again: the Romans made no distinction) were forced to leave Rome.

18:3 Tentmakers: The exact meaning of the Greek word is still disputed; it may mean "leatherworkers." Paul often supported himself during his mission by working at his own craft, but he also accepted financial support from some churches he had founded (see 20:24; Rom. 15:24; 1 Cor. 9:3–14; Phil. 4:15–17).

18:4 Would try to convince: The Greek verb may also mean "he kept convincing," i.e., he was successful in his attempts to persuade some of his hearers of the truth of the Christian faith.

18:5 Silas and Timothy: In the Acts account, they had been left in Beroea (see 17:14–15; for a slightly different chronology, see 1 Thess. 3:1–6). Paul's letter to the Thessalonians was written at this time (ca. 51 CE; see the introduction to 1 Thessalonians). **Testifying to the Jews that the Messiah was Jesus:** For the meaning of "Messiah," see on Mark 8:29. In the Greek text the grammatical subject is "Messiah" and the predicate is "Jesus," i.e.,

not "Jesus is the Messiah" but "the Messiah is Jesus." See on 17:3; 18:28.

18:6 Shook the dust from his clothes: See on 13:51. **Your blood be on your own heads:** A biblical expression meaning, "I have fulfilled my responsibility; now you are responsible" (see Ezek. 3:17–21; 33:1–6; Matt. 27:25). **From now on . . . to the Gentiles:** Paul repeatedly makes this pronouncement, but nonetheless continues to go "to the Jews first" (see 13:46; 28:28; see 18:19).

18:7 Titius Justus: Otherwise unknown. **A worshiper of God:** A Gentile Godfearer (see on 10:2).

18:8 Crispus, the official of the synagogue: A lay leader responsible for organization and worship (see 13:15), perhaps the same person mentioned in 1 Cor. 1:14. **Many . . . became believers and were baptized:** See on 2:38, 16:31.

18:9 The Lord said to Paul in a vision: Instead of responding to rejection by going to another town (see 13:51; 14:6; 16:35–40; Matt. 10:23), the missionaries obey the vision and stay in Corinth. This is Luke's way of indicating that the progress of the mission is under the direction of the risen Lord (see on 16:6–10).

18:11 A year and six months: Ca. 51–52 CE Paul and his associates spend an extended period in Corinth, and develop a strong and lively church with which Paul will later have an intense and stormy relationship (see 1–2 Corinthians). His ministry is summed up as **teaching,** which includes both evangelizing non-Christians by proclaiming the Christian message and nourishing the faith of new converts by instructing them in the meaning of the Christian faith and life (see 2:42; 4:2; 5:25, 28, 42; 13:12; 15:35; 17:19; 20:20; 28:31). **The word of God:** A summary for the Christian message (see Luke 3:2; 5:1; 8:11, 21; 11:28; Acts 4:31; 6:2, 7; 8:14; 11:1; 12:24; 13:5, 7, 46; 17:13; 18:11).

18:12 When Gallio was proconsul: Gallio was a friend of the emperor Claudius and brother of the philosopher Seneca, who was tutor to Nero, who was to be the next emperor. Governors were sent from Rome to the provinces to rule for one year. Fragments of an inscription discovered in Delphi in 1905 and 1910 refer to Gallio as the governor. The Gallio Inscription almost certainly identifies Gallio's administration as 51–52 CE. Presumably Paul was brought before him soon after his arrival, i.e., in 51. This is one of the few references in Acts to secular history that allow the Acts chronology to be established with a high degree of probability.

432

Brought him before the tribunal: Literally the "platform" or "rostrum" on which the judge's bench was located. This platform can be seen today in the excavations of ancient Corinth, near the modern city of Corinth.

18:13 Contrary to the law: Some Corinthian Jews attempt to charge Paul with having violated Roman law by advocating the "new" religion. The incident is historical (though never mentioned in Paul's own letters). Gallio's speech, however, is Luke's own creation (see "Speeches" in the introduction to Acts), giving the reader the ideal Roman response to the church's missionary work (see on Luke 1:1–4; Acts 28:31).

18:15 Your own law: The governor pronounces the case to be an internal religious dispute among Jews, not a matter of Roman law. Judaism was an authorized religion (*religio licita*). If Christianity were to be regarded as a separate, new religion, it would not be legal for Romans to practice it, nor could missionaries legally try to win converts to it. Luke portrays the Roman governor as advocating what in his eyes is the proper Roman attitude toward the Christian community: they are guilty of no infraction of Roman law and receive the legal protection afforded Jews. The first time the issue comes up in Acts, a Roman governor declares that Christianity is not a crime. **Words and names:** Whether or not the Christ is Jesus was the disputed point (see on v. 5).

18:16 Dismissed them from the tribunal: Using the same word as in v. 12, forming a neat bracket: the Jews bring Paul to the judge's platform, the Roman sends him away from it. "Unbelieving" Jews suppose Christianity is something to be dealt with before the courts, but "good" Roman governors dismiss the case.

18:17 Sosthenes: The successor of Crispus as leader of the synagogue. If this is the same person who is mentioned in 1 Cor. 1:1, he later became a Christian convert. **Beat him:** The reason is not given, but apparently he was seen as supporting the Christian cause. Jews subject to synagogue discipline could be beaten for violations of religious law. Paul himself continued to be subject to this discipline (see 2 Cor. 11:24). Why Paul was not also beaten is not clear. **Gallio paid no attention:** Not merely a personal observation about Gallio. See the last word of Acts, to which Luke is already building (see on Acts 28:31). Luke wants to impress upon the reader that the mission of the church is a matter that Rome need not be concerned with, and should *not hinder*.

18:18–23
Paul's Travels

18:18 After staying there for a considerable time: Paul was not deterred by being hailed before Gallio's court, but continued his work in Corinth for a total of a year and a half (v. 11). **Sailed for Syria:** His destination is Antioch in Syria, the church that had sent him forth. Jerusalem of Judea is also in the Roman province of Syria, but in Luke's story line he will visit there only in passing, v. 22. Note how quickly the story moves in 18:22–23 from Ephesus to Jerusalem, to Antioch, and back to Ephesus in 18:24. This journey to "report to the home church" that divides the "second" and "third" missionary journeys may be Luke's construction, and Paul may actually have remained in Ephesus. The center of gravity for world evangelism had shifted from Jerusalem to Antioch—and will move westward to Ephesus (19:1–41) and finally to Rome (28:14–31). **Priscilla and Aquila:** See on 18:2. That Priscilla is mentioned first (and v. 26) suggests that she was the more prominent figure of the two and had a leadership role in the church. **Cenchreae:** The harbor of Corinth on the east. **Had his hair cut, for he was under a vow:** The details are unclear, but the vow is probably that of a nazirite (a word that means "one who has taken a vow"). See Num. 6:2–21; Judg. 13:5–7. Luke's point is that Paul the Christian continues to be an observant Jew (see 16:3, 13; 20:16; 21:17–26).

18:19 Ephesus: Capital of the Roman province of Asia, on the west coast of what is now Turkey. Ephesus was then a major seaport, but the harbor has since silted up, so that the ruins of the ancient city now lie six miles inland. See further on the introduction to Ephesians and comments at Rev. 2:1. Ephesus will become the base of Paul's mission during his "third missionary journey." **He himself went into the synagogue:** See on 13:46; 18:4–6, 19; 19:8; 28:17–31. Luke reports no results of Paul's discussion with the Ephesian Jews, except that they want him to stay and he promises to return, a foreshadowing of the important Ephesian mission of 19:1–41. **Left them there:** As was the case in Corinth (18:1–4), Priscilla and Aquila actually preceded Paul and had been doing evangelistic work and establishing a church prior to Paul. But Luke has told the story in such a way as to indicate Paul's priority (see the manner in which Peter's admission of the "first" Gentiles is told in 10:1–11:18, followed by the Lukan anachronistic comment in 11:19–21).

18:22 Landed at Caesarea: The major seaport on the west coast of Israel, residence of the Roman governor of Judea. Here Cornelius and his household were converted (10:1–11:18), and here Paul will spend two years as a prisoner (23:33–26:32) before being sent to Rome for trial. **Went up to Jerusalem and greeted the church:** Luke is concerned to show that the missionary to the Gentiles maintained respect for, and good relations with, the Jewish Christians in Jerusalem under the leadership of James the brother of Jesus. Though differing traditions and theologies prevailed in various sections of the early church, Luke portrays it as one united church. **Went down to Antioch:** The Syrian church that had originally commissioned Paul's mission and continued to authorize and support it (13:1–4; 16:40).

18:23 After spending some time: In the Lukan chronology, about one and a half years, but Luke does not dwell on Paul's time spent at the "home church"; he moves immediately to narrate the next phase of the mission. **Through the region of Galatia and Phrygia:** See on 16:6. Here begins the "third missionary journey" (on the structure of Luke's narrative, see on 13:1 and Outline in the introduction to Acts). Luke speaks only of Paul, without companions.

18:23–20:38
PAUL'S THIRD MISSIONARY JOURNEY

18:24–28
Ministry of Apollos

18:24 To Ephesus: The scene unfolds in Ephesus prior to Paul's return, one of the few scenes in the latter half of Acts in which Paul himself is not present. Since Luke's narrative is very selective, he must have regarded it as conveying an important message to have included it at all. **A Jew named Apollos:** He is a Jewish Christian (see the similar description of Aquila and Priscilla in 18:2), for he **has been instructed in the Way of the Lord**. On "Way" as a designation for the Christian community, see on 9:2. **Alexandria:** One of the four principal cities of the empire (along with Rome, Antioch, and Corinth), the political capital of Egypt, and a center of culture with a famous library. Alexandria was also an important center of the cultural life of the Diaspora, the home of Philo, a Jewish teacher who adapted Judaism to the Greek language and culture. It was a center of rhetorical and biblical study.

18:25 Knew only the baptism of John: See on Luke 3:3; Acts 19:4. The details of this description are problematic, since Apollos had been **taught accurately the things concerning Jesus**. Luke's point is clear, however. Both this scene and the next (19:1–10) illustrate Luke's concern to "regularize" the variety of understandings and practices of Christian baptism and how it is related to the Holy Spirit (see on 2:38; 8:15–17; 10:44–48). Luke's narrative shows how Christians of differing understandings and traditions were incorporated into the developing mainstream, the one church of God.

18:26 He began to speak boldly in the synagogue: Apollos, Aquila, and Priscilla are all portrayed as Jewish Christians who continue to attend the synagogue. Whether they also attended separate Christian worship services (which would be on Sunday, not on the Jewish Sabbath) is not made clear. There is no indication that Ephesian Jews opposed the Christian disciples (see 18:19–20). **Explained the way of God more accurately:** The content of this explanation is not given, but presumably it corresponded to the understanding of baptism and the Holy Spirit given elsewhere in Acts (see on 2:38; 8:15–17; 10:44–48). There is no indication that Apollos is (re)baptized (see 19:5). In his case, it was a matter of receiving a better understanding of the meaning of Christian baptism, i.e., a more adequate theology of baptism. Luke considers this something that was needed—all theologies are not created equal. How one understands and articulates the faith is important. But since he is not (re)baptized, it is also clear that the efficacy of baptism does not depend on having the proper baptismal theology.

18:27 The believers encouraged him: The phrase indicates there was already a church in Ephesus under the leadership of Priscilla and Aquila before Paul's arrival (see on 18:19–21). **Wanted to cross over to Achaia:** To Greece, of which Corinth had become a leading center of the Christian mission. In Acts, Apollos leaves Ephesus before Paul arrives, and their paths never cross (contrast 1 Cor. 3:4–9; 16:12). Apollos will be very influential in the Corinthian church (1 Cor. 1:12; 3:4–6; 4:6). **Wrote to the disciples to welcome him:** Congregations of Christians in each city realized they belonged to the one church of God. On Christian letters of recommendation, see Rom. 16:1–23; 2 Cor. 3:11–13.

18:28 Showing by the scriptures: See on 3:18, 24; 2 Cor. 3:12–18; and excursus, "New Testament

Interpretation of the Old Testament," at 1 Cor. 15:3. **The Messiah is Jesus:** See on 17:3; 18:5.

19:1–22
Paul in Ephesus

19:1 Paul . . . came to Ephesus: See 18:19–21; introduction to Ephesians. "**Found some disciples:** Luke uses the word "disciples" 28x in Acts, always of Christians. That they had "become believers" (v. 2) also indicates he considers them Christians in some sense (see 16:31). Yet it is difficult to fit this group into a coherent picture of how early Christianity developed. Luke is apparently using the discovery of a group of disciples of John the Baptist to illustrate his view of how the original spectrum of groups that clustered around John the Baptist and Jesus became (or should become) the one church of God.

19:2 Did you receive the Holy Spirit when you became believers?: In Luke's view, Christian baptism and receiving the Holy Spirit are inseparably connected. Where either is already present, the other should also be (see on 2:38; 8:15–17). The Lukan Paul asks the question (in itself historically implausible) to introduce the scene in which "irregular" Christians are incorporated into the mainstream. **Not even heard that there is a Holy Spirit:** This is difficult to imagine historically, since in Luke's narrative John the Baptist was "filled with the Holy Spirit . . . even before his birth" (Luke 1:15) and had proclaimed the coming of the Holy Spirit as a central element of his message (Luke 3:16).

19:3 Into what then were you baptized?: Again presupposing that all baptized Christians have received the Holy Spirit. **Into John's baptism:** On the historical relation between the followers of John and those of Jesus, see on Luke 1:5–25. Historically, John's disciples formed a parallel, competing group to those of Jesus. Luke understands that in the plan of God John was only a forerunner of Jesus, so there should be no parallel group of competing disciples. Just as he has pictured Apollos and Paul in such a way that there is no rivalry between them, so he pictures John and Jesus, and their disciples, as uniting in one harmonious group. In Acts Luke pictures a variety of ways in which the developing church incorporated the variety of early Baptist and Christian groups into the developing mainstream. Sometimes it was done by instruction (see 18:24–28), sometimes by baptism and the laying on of hands (19:1–7; see 8:15–17).

19:4 John baptized with the baptism of repentance: Luke 3:3, 15–18; Acts 13:24. **Believe in the one who was to come after him:** See on Luke 7:18–19. In Luke's understanding, John the Baptist's message had actually pointed to Jesus as the Christ, but he and his disciples did not yet realize this. In this verse, the "disciples" and "believers" in Ephesus seem to learn of Jesus as the Messiah for the first time (contrast vv. 1, 2). Luke understands them already to be Christians of a sort who are now properly incorporated into the one church, though his source apparently understood them to be disciples of John the Baptist who now become Christians.

19:5 Baptized in the name of the Lord Jesus: See 2:38. Luke probably does not understand this as *re*baptism, since they had never received Christian baptism at all, but he is not dealing with the details of this later issue.

19:6 Laid his hands on them: The Spirit was originally conferred by the apostles (8:18). In Acts the apostles disappear from the narrative after the Jerusalem Council of Acts 15, but the church continues to act by apostolic authority (see 13:1–3; 15:33). Luke has no rigid doctrine of "apostolic succession"—for him the apostles have no successors. In Luke's understanding, Paul is not one of the apostles (see on 1:15–26; 9:27; 14:4, 14), but the authority given to the apostles by the risen Christ continues to be effective in the church. **Spoke in tongues and prophesied:** As in Acts 2:1–13; 10:44–48, these signs of the Spirit's presence certify that the Baptist's disciples are included in the one church to which God has given the Holy Spirit. As in 10:44–48 and 1 Cor. 12–14, "tongues" here does not refer to foreign languages, but to ecstatic speaking under the power of the Spirit. "Prophecy" does not mean prediction, but speaking by the inspiration of the Spirit.

19:8 Entered the synagogue: See on 13:46; 18:4–6, 19; 19:8; 28:17–31. **For three months:** The Ephesian Jews are more open to the Christian message than elsewhere, and are initially receptive (see 18:20–21; contrast 13:50–14:7; 14:19; 17:1–13; 18:6, 12–17). **The kingdom of God:** Another way of summarizing the Christian message, for Luke equivalent to "the Messiah is Jesus" (see 2:36; 17:3; 18:5, 28). On kingdom of God, see on Luke 4:43.

19:9 The Way: a designation of the Christian community; see on 9:2. **Taking the disciples with him:** The new Christian group in Ephesus was for three months composed entirely

435

of Jewish Christians within the synagogue, and leaves only reluctantly and under duress. This is in contrast to the picture of Paul as going strictly or primarily to Gentiles. **Argued daily in the lecture hall of Tyrannus:** Paul is portrayed as an itinerant teacher who rents a lecture hall as the setting for his instruction, a common picture in the Hellenistic world. Tyrannus is otherwise unknown. The Christian community spreads and preserves its authentic identity by teaching (see on Luke 4:15, 31–32; 19:47; 20:1, 37; Acts 2:42; 4:2, 18; 5:21, 25, 28; 13:1, 12; 18:11; 20:20; 28:31).

19:10 This continued for two years: Ca. 54–56 CE. In 20:31 Paul's residence in Ephesus is given as three years. His most extensive ministry was located in Ephesus, which later became a center of Pauline Christianity. Luke pictures **all the residents of Asia** hearing the Christian message that emanated from the Ephesian church. During this time Paul writes 1 Corinthians, probably Philippians and Philemon, and perhaps parts of 2 Corinthians and Galatians (see introductions to those books, where alternate possibilities are also given). **Both Jews and Greeks:** What began as a distinctive Jewish community within the synagogue now becomes one church of Jews and Gentiles. **The word of the Lord:** As a summary of the Christian message; see Luke 3:2; 5:1; 8:11, 21; 11:28; Acts 4:31; 6:2, 7; 8:14; 11:1; 12:24; 13:5, 7, 46; 17:13; 18:11.

19:11 Extraordinary miracles: All miracles are extraordinary, of course, but Luke wants to picture Paul as he had portrayed Peter, as especially endowed with miraculous power (see 5:12–16; for list of Peter/Paul parallels, see excursus at 28:31). On interpreting New Testament miracle stories in general, see excursus at Matt. 8:1. **God did:** Luke is careful to point out that Paul does not do such deeds by his own power, again as in the case of Peter (see 3:6; 5:15–16).

19:12 Handkerchiefs or aprons: Healing by contact with such articles could easily be considered a form of magic, but in this same chapter Luke is careful to distinguish the Christian faith from belief in magic (as in 8:9–24).

19:13 Itinerant Jewish exorcists: See Mark 9:38; Luke 9:49–50; 11:19. On the language of demons, Satan, and exorcism, see excursus at Mark 5:1. Most people in the ancient world believed in possession by evil spirits. There were many pagan exorcists, but Jews were sometimes thought to have special powers in this regard. They were thus sometimes sought

by pagan rulers and wealthy people to aid them against evil spirits, and some (renegade) Jews took advantage of this situation.

19:14 A Jewish high priest named Sceva: Otherwise unknown. While the Greek text can be understood to mean he belonged to one of the high-priestly families of Jerusalem (so both the NIV and NRSV), it can also mean "a Jew, a high priest," i.e., exercising priestly functions in a pagan cult in Ephesus. We know that the title "high priest" was used in Ephesus for such functionaries, so it is better to understand Luke as intending to portray a renegade Jew who with his sons has hired himself out as an exorcist and cult official in Ephesus. Impressed by the power of Jesus' name as used among the Christians, they add it to their repertoire of exorcistic spells. The situation is thus analogous to the stories of Bar-Jesus, the Jewish magician who was employed in a pagan court in 13:4–12, and Simon the magician of 8:9–24.

19:15 Jesus I know and Paul I know: As in the Gospel, the demonic powers are pictured as recognizing the superior power of Christ and his agents, even when this is concealed from human beings (see Luke 4:33–37). But they do not recognize the Jewish exorcists as legitimately exercising this same power.

19:16 Fled out of the house naked and wounded: Another punitive miracle (see on 5:1–11; 13:4–12). The whole incident is related without interest in the plight of the suffering possessed man; it is an example of confessional language to make one theological point, not objectifying language from which other conclusions may be drawn (on confessional and objectifying language, see on Matt. 2:16; Acts 1:9; 5:1–11; Rev. 6:15, excursus, 3.b). This is Luke's way of showing the danger inherent in attempting to use the power resident in the Christian community to one's own advantage. The power of the Holy Spirit at work in the life of the church is not an impersonal force that may be manipulated to one's own advantage, but requires commitment in faith and repentance to Christ and his way of life.

19:18–19 Those who had become believers ... disclosed their practices: The incident causes the new Christians to realize the difference between magic and Christian faith. Here Luke affords us a glimpse into the mixture of magic and superstition that was sometimes combined with Christian faith in the early churches. Further experience revealed their incompatibility. Former pagans did not instantly become mature Christians, but required nurture and growth in the community of faith. **Those who practiced magic:** Presumably the new converts from paganism. **Fifty thousand silver coins:** About thirty-five thousand dollars. The new faith required considerable financial sacrifice in turning from the old life to the new, an expenditure they did not realize at first. Apparently all the implications of the Christian life were not explained in advance, but after instruction in the basics of the faith they were baptized and then learned the cost of discipleship in the course of their Christian life.

19:21 Paul resolved in the Spirit: Unless otherwise specified, the Greek word for "spirit" can mean either the human spirit (one's internal consciousness) or the Spirit of God. Here the NIV understands it in the former sense and the NRSV in the latter. In either case, Luke understands the expanding mission of the church to be under the guidance of God's Spirit. **To go through Macedonia and Achaia:** To make a western circuit across the Aegean, visiting the churches before heading back east **to Jerusalem.** Paul's letters indicate that the main purpose of this visit was to receive the offering the Gentile churches were collecting for the Jerusalem church (see on Rom. 15:25–32; 2 Cor. 8–9), but Luke does not mention that here and makes only minimal and indirect allusion to it elsewhere (see on 24:17). **I must also see Rome:** Paul's ultimate plan is to extend his mission to the capital city of the empire (see Rom. 1:11–15; 15:22–29). The form of expression is literally "it is necessary for me . . . ," the same form used repeatedly by Luke to signal the divine plan into which Paul's life fits, just as did that of Jesus (see on Luke 9:22).

19:22 Timothy: Last mentioned in 18:5, we now learn he has been with Paul in Ephesus. See 1 Cor. 4:17; 16:10. The **Erastus** mentioned in Rom. 16:23 may refer to the same person; see 2 Tim. 4:20. **Stayed for some time longer in Asia:** During this period Philippians and Philemon were probably written (see "Introduction to the Pauline Letters").

19:23–41
The Riot in Ephesus

19:23 No little disturbance: On litotes, see 12:18. It was in fact a riot. **Concerning the Way:** See on 9:2.

19:24 Artemis: A Greek goddess, identified with the Roman Diana, daughter of Zeus (the Roman Jupiter). In the course of the centuries Artemis had absorbed the features of the great mother goddess, known variously as Cybele, Atargatis, Ashtarte, Ashtoreth, Asherah, and Ishtar, the female consort of the Canaanite high god El. She was variously depicted as the huntress with bow and arrow and the many-breasted Great Mother. **Brought no little business to the artisans:** Luke again pictures the opposition to Christianity as based on economic reasons (see 16:19).

19:26 Gods made with hands are not gods: See on 14:15; 17:16–17. Jews in Ephesus had been affirming this with impunity for some generations (see v. 34), but it was the numerical success of Paul that threatened the idol business. An economic interest is disguised as a religious issue. **Almost the whole of Asia:** Luke's description reflects the situation of his own time at the end of the century. This is reflected in a letter written a few years later by the governor Pliny of Pontus, who describes the results of his repression of Christianity: "The temples, almost deserted previously, are gradually gaining more and more visitors, the long neglected sacred festivals are again regularly observed, and the sacrificial meat, for which buyers have been hard to find, is again being purchased."

19:27 The temple of the great goddess: The temple of Artemis in Ephesus was one of the Seven Wonders of the World, brought thousands of pilgrims from all over the world, like Jerusalem in Paul's time and Rome and Mecca in later centuries, and was the center of economic life of the capital city. It was an ancient temple, begun in the eighth century BCE, and remodeled and rebuilt over the centuries. **All Asia and the world:** Artemis was not a local goddess but the symbol of a world religion. The reader of Acts will remember the commission of Jesus in 1:8 to be his witnesses to the ends of the earth. The old world religion is here confronted with what is to become the new worldwide faith.

19:29 To the theater: An impressive amphitheater that seated twenty-four thousand spectators. It is now excavated and on the tourist circuit, and one may stand with some confidence on the same pavement that Paul once walked. **Gaius and Aristarchus:** See 20:4; Rom. 16:23; 1 Cor. 1:14.

19:31 Officials of the province of Asia: Paul has friends among the responsible officials of Asia. It is only the business interests that oppose him. Paul appears in this scene only indirectly and then disappears.

19:32 The assembly: The Greek word *ekklesia* is used three times in this passage (see vv. 39, 40). The word means literally "the called out" ones and was regularly used in secular Greek for the legal assembly meeting to conduct official business. It was used in the Greek translation of the Old Testament for the "assembly" of Israel, the congregation of the holy people of God, and thus came to be the common word for the body of Christians, translated "church" elsewhere in the New Testament. Only here in Acts does it preserve its secular meaning. Luke here uses it informally for the mob that had gathered, and contrasts it with a real, legally constituted assembly.

19:33 Alexander, whom the Jews had pushed forward: We do not know what their instructions were, for he never gets to carry them out. Luke's portrayal of the Jews elsewhere in Acts (e.g., 18:12–17) would suggest that the Jews wanted to distinguish the Christian missionaries from themselves and make it clear that the commotion was not provoked by Jews.

19:34 When they recognized that he was a Jew: The Ephesian worshipers of Artemis rightly classify Christianity as related to Judaism. This is Luke's point, made in another way in 18:12–17. Jews were recognized as opponents of idolatry and advocates of monotheism, but had not been considered a problem until the numerical success of Paul and his fellow missionaries created an economic threat.

19:35 The town clerk: The word is elsewhere translated "scribe." He is in an official position, one who understands the legal and political ramifications of the day's activities. He does not want to draw the attention and disfavor of Rome; the Roman leaders did not take riotous public assemblies lightly. It is his interest in the continued peace and prosperity of the city, more than justice per se, that motivates his appeal. Thus Luke shows that enlightened self-interest among pagan officials calls for a halt to public protests and demonstrations against the Christian missionary enterprise. **The statue that fell from heaven:** This feature of the Artemis cult is not otherwise documented in ancient literature, although the idea is associated with other gods and goddesses. The feature may be entirely mythological, or may be related to the making of cult statues from meteorites.

19:37 Neither temple robbers nor blasphemers of our goddess: See on Rom. 2:22. Paul and the Christian missionaries are cleared in advance of this potential charge that was sometimes made against Jews. Monotheism and the denial of the reality of the pagan gods was not considered a legally culpable offense.

19:38–39 The courts are open, and there are pro-consuls: Luke places the appeal for orderly, regular procedure in the mouth of an enlightened and responsible pagan official. This is the position that Luke wants to prevail among the Roman leadership (see on Luke 1:1–4; Acts 28:31). In Luke's time and place, he regards the threat to the Christians to be not legal, public prosecution—where they will prevail if given the opportunity—but unofficial harassment as a suspect and disdained group (see the introduction to 1 Peter). **In the regular assembly:** The present one is irregular, i.e., not an official assembly.

19:40 We are in danger: The official even argues that the tables might be turned, should the matter be pursued legally. The moral to Luke's story is that the new Christian faith has a legal right to exist and propagate its faith in the Roman world, that level-headed pagan officials recognize that Christianity is not a violation of city or Roman law, and that they should discourage popular reactions against the growth of the Christian community, for such responses are themselves illegal. The law and the state stand on the side of Christianity, when it is rightly understood. Luke is attempting to help both church and state to find their way forward in a time when the issues had not yet been clarified. The church was to suffer much before such clarification was achieved.

20:1–16
Paul Begins His Final Journey to Jerusalem

20:1 Left for Macedonia: As on the "second missionary journey" (see 18:18), Paul intends to return and report to the mother church in Jerusalem and to the Antioch church that sent him forth, but first he will visit the churches in Macedonia and Greece he had founded on the previous mission tour (see on 19:21). We know from his letters that his purpose included gathering the offering for the Jerusalem church, but Luke is silent about this (see on Rom. 15:25–32; 2 Cor. 8–9; Acts 24:17).

20:2–3 When he had gone through those regions: This is actually a very stormy time in Paul's life. Paul's letters reveal severe internal strife within his churches and conflicts between Paul and elements within his churches (see Galatians, 2 Corinthians, probably Philippians). Luke tells only of external problems.

He came to Greece, where he stayed three months: The winter of 55–56. This period was spent mostly at Corinth, where the internal problems of the church had been resolved.

The letter to the Romans, written at this time, reveals the profundity of Paul's thinking. **A plot was made against him by the Jews:** Not mere personal hostility, but the zeal of religious leaders to protect what they saw as the authentic faith, as Paul himself had once done (see 8:1; 13:45; 17:5).

20:4 He was accompanied by: Luke lists seven men from various churches as Paul's traveling companions—a rather large entourage for a trip that lasted many weeks, thus involving considerable expense. Historically, Paul was collecting a large sum of money to be delivered in Jerusalem, and the men were something like delegates from the churches who would accompany him. For another seven chosen by the churches to administer funds, see 6:1–6. Luke is not concerned with the logistics of the enterprise, but with Paul's encouraging the young churches (20:1–2) by his preaching and teaching. Except for **Timothy** (see on 16:1), little is known about the seven except what is given here. For **Aristarchus** and **Gaius**, see 19:29. For **Tychicus**, see Col. 4:7; Eph. 6:21; Titus 3:12; 2 Tim. 4:12. For **Trophimus**, see 21:29; 2 Tim. 4:20.

20:5 For us: The author of the "we source" joins the group at Philippi, where the first unit of the "we source" ended (16:17; see on 16:10). **Troas:** Previously mentioned only in 16:8–11, but now site of a congregation of Christians. Here is another of many indications of how fragmentary the story of Acts is, and of how little we know of the beginnings and growth of early Christianity (see 9:31; 21:1; 27:3).

20:6 We sailed from Philippi: I.e., from its port city of Neapolis (see 16:11–12). **After the days of Unleavened Bread:** Not mere chronological data, but indicating that Paul and his party celebrated the Jewish Passover festival with the Philippian Christians. Luke rarely misses an opportunity to point out the continuity between Judaism and Christianity, and the fact that Paul the Christian continued to be an observant Jew (e.g., 16:3, 13; 20:16; 21:17–26).

20:7 The first day of the week: Sunday, the day of Christ's resurrection, gradually replaced the Jewish Sabbath as the Christian day of worship (Matt. 28:1; Mark 16:2; Luke 24:1; 1 Cor. 16:2; Rev. 1:10). If the Jewish reckoning of time is followed, Sunday would begin on Saturday evening. It is not clear here whether the church meets on Saturday evening or Sunday evening. The church met in the evening not only because the first Eucharist was an evening meal (Luke 22:14–23), but also because Sunday was an ordinary working day and Christian meetings had to be held after work. Sunday did not become a public holiday until the empire was "Christianized" in the fourth century under Constantine.

We met to break bread: This is not an ordinary meal, but the celebration of the Christian Eucharist—which did, however, take place in the context of a regular meal (see 1 Cor. 11:17–34). The primary purpose of the Christian gathering was to celebrate the Lord's Supper. Luke is strikingly reserved in his references to this central act of Christian worship, which the early church celebrated every Lord's day. This is the first reference to "breaking bread" since 2:42, but this minimal reference is no indication of marginal importance. The situation is analogous to the letters of Paul, which explicitly mention the Eucharist only in 1 Cor. 10:14–17 and 11:23–29, though it was central in Paul's own understanding of Christian worship.

Paul . . . continued speaking until midnight: Not only or primarily conversation, but Christian preaching and teaching.

20:9–10 Eutychus . . . began to sink off into a deep sleep: This text has since encouraged many a sleepy churchgoer, but Luke is setting the stage for the miracle to follow. "Eutychus" means "lucky." **Was picked up dead . . . his life is in him:** Luke intends to recount a miracle, not merely an astute diagnosis by Paul. The story not only reflects the story of Elijah (1 Kgs. 17:21–24) and Elisha (2 Kgs. 4:18–37), but is parallel to that of Peter (9:36–41; see list of Peter/Paul parallels at 28:31). See excursus, "Interpreting Miracle Stories," at Matt. 8:1. Luke does not confuse such stories of resuscitations with the resurrection of Jesus (see on 26:23).

20:11 Broke bread . . . talking until daylight (NIV): These words can refer either to ordinary conversation and eating, or to the continuation of the worship service that consisted of Eucharist, preaching, and teaching. The dramatic event did not keep the worship service from continuing, and Paul continues to speak. Here and elsewhere, Luke pictures the church as called into being and maintained by the word of God that comes through the human words of preaching, teaching, and conversation (see Luke 3:2; 5:1; 8:11, 21; 11:28; Acts 4:31; 6:2, 7; 8:14; 11:1; 12:24; 13:5, 7, 46; 17:13; 18:11).

20:12 Were not a little comforted: On this feature of Lukan style, see on 12:18.

20:13–15 We went ahead: The "we source" resumes after vv. 7–12 were narrated in the third person (see on 16:10).

Set sail for Assos . . . Mitylene . . . Chios . . . Samos . . . Miletus: These travel details reveal a precise knowledge of geography and sailing patterns of the time, showing that what Luke writes is not fiction but anchored in real history. The details come either from the author's personal experience or that of the author of his source. The five-day trip covers thirty air miles. Miletus was excavated in the nineteenth century (when national treasures of weaker countries were gathered into the museums of the more powerful countries). The city gate and adjacent wall (constructed in the second century CE) were taken to Berlin and reconstructed in the Pergamon Museum, where today one can look upon the gates of the city through which Paul passed two millennia ago.

20:16 Eager to be in Jerusalem . . . on . . . Pentecost: See on 20:6. Seven weeks separate Unleavened Bread and Pentecost. The trip today can be made in less than two hours by airplane.

20:17–38
Paul Speaks to the Ephesian Elders

20:17 Asking the elders of the church to meet him: On elders = presbyters, see on 11:30; 14:23. Luke expends no words on items about which we are curious, such as the authority of Paul in summoning the elders, how many there were, and how the Ephesian church was structured (one elder per house church, or a plurality; was there a presiding officer or did they function by consensus), the logistics involved (it was a three-day round trip; how could the elders drop everything and come for a conference with Paul?). Luke focuses all his attention on the speech itself, the only speech by Paul in Acts directed to Christians. It is cast in the form of a farewell speech, a last will and testament, such as several biblical figures gave as their death approached (e.g., Gen. 49:1–27; Josh. 23–24; John 14–17). Though reflecting some of the distinctive aspects of Paul's own life and theology, the speech is a Lukan composition (see on "Speeches" in the introduction to Acts), presenting what Luke wants the elders of his own time to hear from the great missionary hero and martyr of the past. All that is said serves to present Paul to the elders as an example of ministerial leadership (v. 35).

20:19 Humility . . . enduring the trials: The first characteristic mentioned is humility, suggesting that authoritarianism and arrogance were a particular danger to which church leaders were subject (see the similar stance of 1 Pet. 5:1–5, which presents Peter as a model for the elders of the author's time). In the first century, church leaders were particularly subject to trials and harassment, and so are called to endurance.

20:20 I did not shrink from doing anything helpful: The Greek can also be translated "I did not hesitate to tell you what was for your own good." This is a standard of authentic ministry. From the first century until the present, church leaders have been tempted to say what will make them liked and successful in their congregations and denominations, especially, but not only, in congregationally governed churches. Paul's integrity in putting the good of the church above his personal popularity still resulted in being respected and loved by those to whom he ministered (see 20:37). **Proclaiming the message . . . and teaching:** Paul had modeled this central aspect of ministry that is to be followed by the elders (see 1 Tim. 3:2; 2 Tim. 2:24, which also list teaching as a fundamental responsibility of the elder-minister). In Luke's view the church is nourished by the word of God that comes through the human words in preaching and teaching (see Luke 4:15, 31–32; 19:47; 20:1, 37; Acts 2:42; 4:2, 18; 5:21, 25, 28; 13:1, 12; 18:11; 20:20; 28:31). **Publicly and from house to house:** The church of Luke's time did not yet meet in public buildings, but in private homes (e.g., 20:8). Christian ministers not only instruct insiders by teaching in the house churches, but also proclaimed the Christian message to outsiders, in public places (see Paul's practice in 19:9).

20:21 To both Jews and Greeks: Luke has shown in chaps. 1–15 how the church was guided by the Holy Spirit finally to see that the gospel was for everyone. In Paul's time, the burning issue had been whether Gentiles could be included (see chaps. 10–11). In more recent times, an important issue is whether Jews should be included, whether Christians should preach the gospel to Jews. In Luke's view, Christians do not represent another religion, and the task of Christian evangelists and missionaries is not to try to convince Jews of the superiority of Christianity. Their task is to witness to their faith that the Messiah is Jesus, and this testimony is to be shared with everyone, Jews and Gentiles.

Turn to God in repentance and have faith in our Lord Jesus (NIV): The first of four brief summaries of the Christian message found in Paul's speech. Repentance is standard Jewish teaching (see on Luke 3:7–9; Acts 2:38). The distinctive Christian element is faith in the Lord Jesus, i.e., that he is the promised Messiah (see on Luke 9:22; Acts 17:3; 18:5, 28).

20:22–23 I am on my way to Jerusalem: As in the Gospel Luke has presented Jesus as "setting his face to go to Jerusalem" (Luke 9:51), where he knows he will be rejected and killed, so Luke presents Paul as making his final resolute journey to Jerusalem. Here the "Pauline passion story" of Acts is anticipated, parallel to that of Jesus in the Gospel (see on 21:1). **Not knowing what will happen:** Poignantly Rom. 15:30–31 records Paul's own anxieties about what might happen to him in Jerusalem, including his fear that the offering he had been gathering might not be accepted by the Jewish Christians in Jerusalem (Luke is silent about the latter issue; see on 24:17). **The Holy Spirit testifies to me in every city:** Inspired Christian prophets spoke of Paul's future destiny (see 11:27–28; 21:4, 9–11). Luke here indicates that such prophets were widespread in early Christianity, without conflicting with the structured leadership of the presbyters, which he also assumes is a universal feature of the church.

20:24 I do not count my life as of any value to myself: As a model for the elders, Paul considers his ministry the absolute top priority, more important than life itself. Luke's readers know that these words are not empty rhetoric, and that Paul had been misunderstood and arrested and had sealed his ministry in his own life's blood (see 1 Cor. 9:24–27; 2 Cor. 4:7–12; 6:4–10; 1 Thess. 2:8; Phil. 1:20–23; 2:16; 2 Tim. 4:17). **The good news of God's grace:** The second summary of the Christian message (see 20:21). "Gospel" means "good news," an announcement of what God has done (see on 2:11). God's grace is not an idea, but an event that has happened in history. Here Luke accurately represents Paul's own understanding of the gospel, though Paul's letters do not contain the exact phrase "the good news of God's grace" (see e.g., Rom. 3:21–26). "Gospel" occurs only here and 15:7 in Luke–Acts, once each in the mouth of Peter and Paul, in each case summarized as grace (for list of Peter/Paul parallels, see on 28:31).

20:25 Proclaiming the kingdom: The third summary of the Christian message in this passage (see 20:21, 24). On "kingdom of God," see on Luke 4:43. The concept and terminology of the kingdom actually played a minor role in Paul's own theology, but in Luke–Acts it is a major way of expressing the meaning of the Christian faith and binds together the message of Jesus in the Gospel and the church's message about him in Acts. **None of you . . . will ever see my face again:** Luke writes after Paul's death, and his readers know that Paul will be arrested and killed, never to return to Ephesus (see on 28:31).

20:26 I am not responsible for the blood of any of you: Not a reference to his pre-Christian acts as a persecutor, in which he had been involved in bloodshed (see 7:58; 9:1; 22:4; 26:10), but a biblical expression meaning he had played the role of the watchman with honesty and forthrightness (see 18:6; Ezek. 3:17–21; 33:1–6; the imagery of Ezek. 34:1–10 on the responsibility of shepherds of God's flock also hovers in the background).

20:27 The whole purpose of God: The fourth summary of Paul's message (see 20:21, 24, 25).

20:28 Keep watch over yourselves: Christian leadership is not merely a matter of individual charisma or ambition, but means belonging to a group of elders that exercises collective and mutual oversight within the group. It cannot be assumed that Christian leaders are always properly shepherding the church, but they are exhorted to call each other to accountability. **The Holy Spirit has made you overseers:** We do not know how they were chosen to be elders. In 14:23 they were appointed by Paul and Barnabas. Later they were elected or designated by charismatic prophets (see 1 Tim. 1:18; 4:14). But the Holy Spirit is at work in whatever human process the church uses to choose its leaders (see on 15:28). It is important that both the church and its leadership be aware of this. Just as the word for elder (*presbyter)* later became "priest" or "minister," so the word here translated "overseer" later came to mean "bishop." In the second century the church developed a clear structure of bishops, priests, and deacons, but this development is still incomplete when Luke–Acts was written (see Phil. 1:1; 1 Tim. 3:1–7; Titus 1:5–7 [which also equates presbyters and overseers/bishops, as here]; 1 Pet. 2:25; 5:1–5). Here it is important to see that the local elders represent the church's guidance by the Holy Spirit, that they are the ones who supervise the work of the church and exercise pastoral leadership with apostolic authority (see on 14:23). **Obtained with the blood of his own Son:** This is the distinctively Pauline view of the redemptive significance of

Jesus' death, not found elsewhere in Luke–Acts (see on Luke 22:20; Acts 2:23). Here the point has to do with the nature of the church: it belongs to God, who has paid a magnificent price for it, and its leaders dare not comport themselves within it as though it belonged to them (again, see Ezek. 34:1–10).

20:29 After I have gone: Luke presents the church of the first generation as practically free from internal doctrinal disputes, a kind of "golden age" when the church was united in one faith, as it should be. When disputes did occasionally occur, the church resolved them without heretical groups splitting off (see 15:1–35). Luke considers the factions that had developed and were present in his own time to have developed after Paul's death. **Savage wolves:** Luke does not consider false doctrine as a harmless matter of opinion (see Matt. 7:15). Like Paul his hero, Luke limited pluralism within the Christian community and pictures the earliest church as being united without being uniform (see on 1 Cor. 3:21–23), but like Paul he also sets limits to this variety, so that not just anything can be considered Christian (see on 2 Cor. 10–13). The consistent New Testament canonical pattern: more than one thing is acceptable, but not just anything is acceptable.

Some even from your own group: Luke knows that after the death of Paul, Paul's own followers disputed over the right way to interpret the Pauline message to a later generation, and that Ephesus was the center of the Pauline tradition in the second and third generations, when this issue was hotly debated and competing groups of Christians arose within the Pauline tradition (see Col. 2:8; Eph. 5:6–14; 1 Tim. 1:19–20; 4:1–3; 2 Tim. 1:15).

20:31 Warn everyone with tears: Twice in this brief speech (see v. 19) Paul refers to his ministry as laced with his own tears, and the elders will shed tears at Paul's farewell (v. 37). Like Jesus, who wept over Jerusalem (Luke 19:41), Paul is a model for other Christian leaders, whose teaching the Christian faith is not to be a matter of cool objectivity or a part-time avocation, but something that passionately involves their whole being.

20:32 I commit you to God and to the word of his grace (NIV): The pattern of the "farewell speech" that Luke has been following (see on v. 17) concludes with a blessing on the hearers. Paul's concluding blessing to the elders emphasizes that they who are agents of the divine word are themselves to be nurtured by it.

20:33 Silver or gold or clothing: Those in positions of religious leadership are tempted to personal financial gain (see 1 Pet. 5:2). Luke again reflects Paul's own affirmations as we know them from his letters (1 Cor. 9:4–12; 2 Cor. 7:2; 11:8–9; Phil. 4:10–11). There were enough unprincipled preachers who used their identification as Christian ministers for personal gain that Paul had to take care that his financial dealings were unselfish and scrupulously honest, and were seen to be so (2 Cor. 8:16–24).

20:34 I worked with my own hands to support myself: See on 18:3. Paul could not be accused of having profited from the Ephesians, and he presents himself as a model for the Ephesian elders.

20:35 In all this I have given you an example: Not only his instruction about unselfishness, but the whole speech presents Paul as an example of Christian ministry. **Remembering the words of the Lord Jesus:** This saying is not found in the Gospels, but is one of the sayings attributed to Jesus that circulated in the oral tradition of the church (see on Luke 1:1–4). **It is more blessed to give than to receive:** These words are often cited as a general truth of the Christian perspective on life, and so they are: the Christian life means loving care for others rather than selfishness (including "enlightened self-interest"). It is not simply an idea, but an act, the active response to God's love for us (1 John 4:19). Though frequently cited in the church *by* ministers (often as an "offertory sentence"), it was originally directed *to* ministers, affirming that Christian ministry is a matter of the blessedness of giving (Luke 9:23).

20:37 Embraced Paul and kissed him: Paul is authentically portrayed as exercising his ministry in such a way that his authoritative teaching and uncompromising integrity were not represented by a distant, authoritarian Paul. He embodies Christian leadership that generates personal friendship and love. This too is presented as a model.

21:1–28:31
PAUL'S PASSION STORY AS WITNESS TO THE GOSPEL

Here begins the final section of the story of Paul, parallel to the story of Jesus in the Gospels. As there, the narrator slows down the "narrative clock," taking more space to cover a smaller amount of actual time. Paul's two years in Ephesus, for example, take one chapter (Acts 19), while two weeks in Jerusalem takes three and a half chapters (Acts 21:17–24:23). This illustrates how selective the story of Acts is, how the emphasis of the story lies in the hands of the storyteller, who can extend or compress the narrative at will, and thus how important the "Pauline passion story" is in Luke's composition.

21:1–23:22
Arrested in Jerusalem

21:1–16
Paul Continues His Journey to Jerusalem

21:1–2 When we had parted: The "we passage " resumes; it had been interrupted at 20:16 by Paul's speech to the Ephesian elders (see on 16:10). **Cos . . . Rhodes . . . Patara . . . Cyprus:** Again Luke's geographical data are consistent and accurate. He knows Mediterranean geography and travel better than Palestinian (see on Luke 9:51; 17:11). **Tyre:** A major port on the coast of Phoenicia, modern Lebanon. Luke has previously referred to the city in Luke 6:17; 10:13–14; and Acts 12:20, but there has been no previous indication of a church there. This is another indication of the fragmentary nature of the Acts account (see 9:31; 20:5; 27:3).

21:4 We looked up the disciples and stayed there for several days: They apparently had no advance notice that they would be entertaining a sizable entourage (see 20:4—Paul and seven associates). Luke's interest in supplying such details is not only human interest in the story of Paul, but to point out the crucial role that hospitality for visiting missionaries played in the expansion of the church (see on 16:15), and the family feeling that Christians had for each other. They are brothers and sisters in the same family, not merely members of the same organization or institution (see on Luke 8:19–21; 18:30; Acts 9:30). **Through the Spirit:** Christian prophets speak in the name of the risen Lord by inspiration of the Spirit (see 2:18; 11:27–28; 13:1–3; 16:6–7; 19:21; 20:22–23; 21:7–14; for Paul's own discussion of charismatic speech by Christian prophets, see 1 Cor. 12–14). The church's mission is guided by the Holy Spirit. **They told Paul not to go on to Jerusalem:** He went anyway. Luke believes in divine revelation through prophecy, in both the prophets of Israel as recorded in the Bible and the revelations of Christian prophets. Yet he also knows that such oracles must be evaluated and interpreted (see 1 Cor. 14:29; 1 Thess. 5:19–20), that sometimes (as here) prophecy stands against prophecy, which also happened

in biblical prophecy (1 Kgs. 18:17–40; 22:1–40; Jer. 23:9–22; 28:1–17). For list of biblical criteria for evaluating prophecy, see excursus, "Testing Prophecy," at Rev. 2:20.

21:7 Ptolemais: Paul and his group are now back in the land of Israel, at a port city near the modern Haifa. As in Tyre, they find a church not previously mentioned in Acts (see on 21:4).

21:8 Philip the evangelist: "Evangelist" is related to the Greek word for "gospel," the good news of God's redeeming act in Christ. It is found elsewhere in the New Testament only in Eph. 4:11 and 2 Tim. 4:5, i.e., in the later Pauline tradition, indicating a particular type of Christian minister. The structure of church leadership is still developing, and there is as yet no consistent terminology for Christian ministers. **One of the seven:** To be distinguished from the Philip who was one of the Twelve (Luke 6:13–16; see on 6:1–6; 8:4–40). **Stayed with him:** Again a Christian leader is pictured as having a large home able to accommodate several unexpected guests.

21:9 Four unmarried daughters who had the gift of prophecy: Prophetic leadership in the early church included women prophets (see 2:18). Celibacy was often associated with the prophetic gift. John the Baptist, Jesus, and Paul were all unmarried, very unusual among first-century Jews; all were prophetic figures (see 1 Cor. 7:7).

21:10 Agabus: Yet another Christian prophet (see 11:27–28). In this section Luke mentions only charismatic leaders and is silent about elder-presbyters (until Paul arrives in Jerusalem). The church began with charismatic leadership and developed structured leadership only gradually. Luke portrays the transitional period, but, as usual, without any hint of conflict between the original Spirit-led leadership and the later more institutional leaders. **Bound his own hands and feet:** Agabus is portrayed as one of the biblical prophets who acted out their message with symbolic acts (see Isa. 20:2; Ezek. 4:1; Jer. 13:1–13; 16:1–4; Hos. 1–3).

21:11 Thus says the Holy Spirit: A formula of Christian prophecy analogous to the biblical "Thus says the Lord" (see 15:17, plus 418x in the Old Testament). Agabus's prediction is not literally fulfilled (see 21:27–36), but Paul will be arrested by the Romans as a result of Jewish misunderstanding and provocation, parallel to the case of Jesus in the Gospels.

21:13 I am ready . . . to die in Jerusalem: Again parallel to Jesus' resolute decision to go to Jerusalem (Luke 9:51) and to his premonitions of his own death there (Luke 9:21–22, 44; 12:50; 13:32–34; 17:25; 18:31–34). **For the name of the Lord Jesus:** On the significance of "the name," see on 2:38. In Paul's day, Jesus' disciples were not yet persecuted "for the name," i.e., simply because they were Christians, but this was happening in Luke's time at the end of the first century (see on 1 Pet. 4:14).

21:14 The Lord's will be done: A counterpart to Jesus' Gethsemane prayer (Luke 22:42), another parallel to the Gospel's passion story.

21:16 The house of Mnason of Cyprus: Otherwise unknown. Luke points out another example of Christian hospitality in the service of mission (see on 16:15 and v. 4 above).

21:17–26
Paul Visits the Church in Jerusalem

21:17 We arrived in Jerusalem: Here ends the "third missionary journey" (see on 13:1 and Outline in the introduction to Acts). **The brothers** [and sisters] **welcomed us warmly:** Strangely, the NRSV retains "brothers" here (see on 9:30). The whole church of Jerusalem is meant.

21:18–20 James . . . all the elders: James the brother of Jesus is now the leader of the Jerusalem church (see on 12:17; 15:13, the last reference to James), but elders also play a role in its leadership (see on 11:30; 14:23; 20:17–38). Paul rehearses all **that God had done among the Gentiles through his ministry**, and the Jerusalem leadership **praised God**. This is the image that Luke wishes to impress upon the mind of his readers: rather than there being any tension or opposition to Paul from James and the Jerusalem leadership, the mother church in Jerusalem welcomes Paul back from his Gentile mission and praises God for it. At this point the "we source" is interrupted, not to be resumed until 27:1—two years later in Luke's chronology (see on 16:10).

   Many thousands of believers . . . among the Jews: As Paul has reported the success of the Gentile mission, James reports the success of the Jewish mission (see Gal. 2:9). Luke emphasizes parity and mutuality between the two wings of the one church. (Yet in 21:30ff. most of the city seems to belong not to the "believers among the Jews" but to the non-Christian Jewish opponents of Paul.)

21:21 They have been told about you: See on Luke 1:4. One of Luke's purposes is to clear up misunderstandings of what Christian faith involves. **You teach all the Jews living among the Gentiles to forsake Moses:** Literally

"apostasy from Moses." This is clearly a misunderstanding not only of Paul as presented in Acts, but of Paul's practice as documented in his letters; see 16:13; 1 Cor. 9:22.

21:23 Do what we tell you: As in 15:19–20, James proposes (somewhat authoritatively!) a solution that builds bridges between the two wings of the one church and will help maintain its unity. **Four men who are under a vow:** Similar to Paul's own vow; see on 18:18. **Pay their expenses** (NIV): Both as a gesture of goodwill and because the participants themselves were poor. We do not know the amount involved, but it was substantial, for Josephus reports the king Herod Agrippa I had performed a similar service for poor Jews (*Ant* 19.6.1, 293–94). Luke makes no reference to the large offering that Paul has brought to the Jerusalem church (except the indirect allusion in 24:17; see there). It is not clear whether Paul himself here participates in the nazirite ritual or only sponsors those who are doing so. Neither would involve a compromise for Paul, who had never insisted that Jewish Christians abandon the temple ritual or the Law of Moses. His objection, both in Acts and in his own letters, was to the attempt to impose the Law on Gentile Christians.

21:25 As for the Gentiles . . . we have sent a letter: See on 15:20, 29. Paul seems to be told of this for the first time, an indication that this letter was not part of the Jerusalem Council, in which Paul had played a key role, but was the result of a later decision made in his absence. Luke seems to have combined the two occasions, intentionally or without being aware of the actual history.

21:27–36
Paul Arrested in the Temple

21:27 Jews from Asia: The Roman province of Asia Minor on the west coast of modern Turkey, where Paul had recently been evangelizing. They are sincere, religious people who, like Paul, have made the pilgrimage from Asia to be in Jerusalem at the festival of Pentecost (see 20:16). Like Paul himself prior to his call, Diaspora Jews had regularly opposed Paul's work (13:50; 14:2, 5, 19; 17:5–9; 18:12–17). Luke makes it clear that it was not Jerusalem Jewish Christians who instigated the riot that resulted in Paul's arrest.

21:28 Against our people, our law, and this place: They understood Paul to be profaning the holy people, the Torah, and the temple that are at the heart of Jewish faith and life. This was the prevalent misunderstanding that James and Paul wanted to avoid (21:20–21). **Has actually brought Greeks into the temple:** The temple area was divided by walls into several courts. Gentiles could come into the outermost court, which was separated by a wall on which was the following inscription: "No one of another nation may enter within the wall and enclosure around the temple. Whoever violates this shall have himself to blame for his death that follows." Like all observant Jews, Paul in fact scrupulously observed this law.

21:29 They had . . . seen . . . and they supposed: Since they had in fact seen Paul in the city with one of his missionary companions, **Trophimus the Ephesian**, and since they knew that Paul brought such Gentiles into the Christian community, they jumped to a false conclusion based on their stereotypes of the new group and its practices. They were sincere, but sincerely wrong. As in the case of Jesus, Luke tells the story with great irony: in the very process of going the second mile to avoid misunderstanding, Paul (like Jesus) is misunderstood, arrested and finally killed because of a deep and deadly misunderstanding generated by prejudice and a lack of information. Modern Christian readers might learn from this not too hastily to accept stereotypes of other denominations and other religions, including the Jews who oppose Christianity.

21:30 The doors were shut: A security measure, but Luke sees it as a symbolic act. The Christians, who have previously worshiped in the temple (see 2:46; 3:1; 5:42; 22:17 [a flashback]), now have its doors shut against them. Though historically Jewish Christians continued to worship at the temple until it was destroyed in 70 CE, Luke will make no further reference to Christians in the temple.

21:31 All Jerusalem was in an uproar: Characteristic Lukan hyperbole, which does not include the thousands of Jewish Christians mentioned in 21:20. In Luke's story it is only Jews, not Jewish Christians, who are responsible for Paul's troubles. **Tribune of the cohort:** A cohort was a thousand soldiers, commanded by the tribune. They were stationed in the Tower of Antonia in the northwest corner of the temple area overlooking the courts, for the purpose of maintaining order especially during the festivals in which Jewish nationalist feeling ran high.

21:33 Arrested him: Paul is arrested by the Romans, not the Jewish temple police. From this point on, Paul will be a prisoner of Rome. About half of Acts is devoted to Paul, and half of this portrays Paul in Roman custody. In Luke's presentation, Rome becomes his protector from the Jewish threat and mob violence. **Bound with two chains:** Another parallel to Peter (12:6; see list at 28:31). **Inquired who he was and what he had done:** The Jews from Asia had not done this. Again Luke portrays "bad" Jews and "good" Romans (13:12; 18:16), but neither here nor elsewhere does he intend the picture as a stereotype, for he also knows that there are good Jews and bad Romans. He draws a symbolic scene of what he argues should happen in Christianity's confrontation with the Roman world. Christianity can well survive examination, but suffers from prejudice and hasty conclusions based on misinformation, even if made by sincere people. His own two-volume work is directed to correcting this situation by communicating **the facts** (v. 34; the same word is translated "the truth" in Luke's preface of Luke 1:4; see Acts 19:32; 22:24, 30).

21:36 Away with him: Another parallel to the passion story of Jesus; see Luke 23:18 (see on 21:1).

21:37–22:21
Paul Defends Himself

21:37 Do you know Greek?: Romans spoke Latin, their native language, among themselves, but Greek was the international language that Romans used in administering their multicultural empire. They did not bother to learn the native Aramaic of Judea, but many Judeans would know Greek.

21:38 The Egyptian: The tribune supposes that Paul was an Egyptian prophetic agitator who had previously assembled a large group of followers whom he had convinced that God would miraculously destroy the Romans and liberate Judea (see 5:36–37; the incident is also reported in the first-century Jewish historian Josephus, *Ant.* 20.8.6, 169–72 and *War* 2.13.5, 261–63). Roman troops had dispersed and killed many of his followers, but "the Egyptian" had escaped. The tribune supposed he had finally apprehended him.

21:39 I am a Jew: Not "I am a Christian." Here as elsewhere, Paul places himself within Judaism, as he does in his letters (Rom. 11:1; 2 Cor. 11:22; Phil. 3:5). Luke's point is that the Christian community should be regarded by Rome as a group within Judaism and should receive the toleration and protection Rome granted to Jews (see on 18:12–17; 28:31). This perspective became increasingly difficult to sustain as Christianity became more and more a Gentile religion. Luke writes in a transition period. **A citizen:** As he emphasizes his Jewish identity, so also his identity as a citizen of a prominent city (see 22:25–29). Luke is concerned to show that Christianity is not a backwoods superstition (see 26:26). In the next scene an even more important citizenship will be disclosed (22:27). **No ordinary city:** On the figure of speech, see 12:18.

21:40 In the Hebrew language: The native Palestinian Aramaic was called "Hebrew." See on 6:1. Paul is a Diaspora Jew who is nonetheless a "Hebrew of the Hebrews" (Phil. 3:5). The tribune is surprised that he can speak Greek, the language of the Gentile world, while the Jerusalem crowds are surprised that he can speak Aramaic, the native language of Palestinian Judaism, the language that Jesus and the earliest disciples had spoken. Luke portrays Paul as a bridge figure between two worlds, the key figure in the Jerusalem-to-Rome story of early Christianity. It well illustrates the task of the church and its preachers and teachers in every age, who must be "bilingual" in the sense that the church must know both the original vocabulary of its faith, articulated in the Bible and tradition, and the language of its own time and place, and be faithful to both. The church is always in the missionary situation represented by the Paul of Acts, always mediating between the world of the Bible and the world in which it finds itself.

22:1 Brothers and fathers: Paul addresses his Jewish brothers and their leaders, in exactly the same terms as had Stephen (see on 7:2). "Fathers" was more appropriate there, in that Stephen spoke to the Sanhedrin. Paul addresses the mob assembled in the temple court, but Luke has him speak to Judaism and its leadership. **Listen to the defense that I now make:** The final seven chapters of Acts are essentially speeches made by Paul connected by appropriate narrative settings. All are Lukan compositions (see "Speeches" in the introduction to Acts). This is the first of six such speeches:

—22:1–21, to the Jerusalem Jews on the barrack steps in the temple court
—23:1–6, to the Sanhedrin in Jerusalem
—24:10–21 to the Roman governor Felix in Caesarea

—25:8–11 to the Roman governor Festus in Caesarea
—26:4–23, 25–27, 29, to Festus and the Jewish king Herod Agrippa II in Caesarea
—28:17–20, 25–28, to the Jewish leaders in Rome

The first five speeches are all made in **defense** of Paul's ministry, i.e., in defense of Christianity as such. They are different from the evangelistic missionary speeches in which the gospel is proclaimed to outsiders. "Defense" is here a semitechnical term, *apologia*. The apologists of the second century (such as Justin Martyr) were Christian leaders who explained the Christian faith to the Roman world in order to guard it from misunderstandings and to defend its right to exist as a legitimate religion. Luke is already moving in that direction, is something of a precursor of the apologists. Of the eighteen instances of *apologia* and the related verb form in the New Testament, ten are in Luke–Acts. The speeches do not respond to the particular situation, but are general defenses of the validity of the Christian faith. Thus Paul here does not even mention the particular charge against him that had infuriated the crowd: that he had defiled the temple by bringing a Gentile into it. The main line of defense is that Christianity is not a new and dangerous religion, but a legitimate outgrowth of Judaism (see on 18:12–17). Thus the first words of the first *apologia* are:

22:3 I am a Jew: See on 21:39. **Born in Tarsus:** See on 9:10. In 9:1–19 Luke has already narrated the conversion and call of Paul. Now he has Paul recount it again in his own words, and will do so yet again in 26:2–23. The story is mainly the same in each case, but each version has significant variations. For comments on most of the details, see on 9:1–19. **Brought up in this city:** Jerusalem. Though born in the Diaspora, the Paul of Acts was sent to the holy city as a child. Paul's sister and her son were currently living in Jerusalem (23:16). **At the feet of Gamaliel:** Paul is pictured as a rabbinical student taught by the great scholar Rabbi Gamaliel I (see 5:34). Paul's letters never refer to this phase of his biography. **Being zealous for God, just as all of you are today:** Luke wants the reader to understand that the Jewish opposition to the Christians was a matter of sincere religious conviction, of which the pre-Christian Paul himself is the best model. Here, the Christian Paul remains proud of his past achievements as a Jew (see Phil. 3:7–10).

22:4 This Way: See on 9:2.

22:9 Saw the light but did not hear the voice: In 9:7 the companions hear the voice but do not see anyone. Luke is apparently not concerned with the conflicting details. His point is that those with Paul can confirm that something strange really happened and that it was not Paul's subjective imagination. On Luke's concern for objective reality of the transcendent events he narrates, see on Luke 1:22; 3:21–22; 6:20–23; 24:4; Acts 1:9.

22:12 A devout man according to the law: Both Paul and Ananias are here portrayed as devoutly observant Jews. This detail is absent from the chap. 9 narrative, but is included here as part of the Lukan apologetic.

22:14 The God of our ancestors: This biblical title for God (e.g., Exod. 3:15–16 at the prophetic call of Moses) emphasizes the continuity between the Christian faith and Judaism. **To see the Righteous One:** As in 3:14 and 7:52, a christological title for Jesus, but here particularly relevant. Luke is emphasizing that Paul and Ananias are Law-keeping Jews. Jesus himself is designated by a title that emphasizes his Jewishness. The same title (in a nonchristological sense) was given to James the brother of Jesus, who was called James the Just (i.e., Righteous) because of his devotion to the Jewish Law.

22:15 To all the world: To all people, including Gentiles (see 9:14). Luke makes this a little less explicit here in order to allow the later commission to the Gentiles (v. 21) to become the decisive point at which the crowds object.

22:16 Be baptized, and have your sins washed away: See 2:38, where baptism is related to the forgiveness of sins and the name of Jesus.

22:17 Returned to Jerusalem: On the differing chronology of Gal. 1:13–2:10, see on 15:35. **I was praying in the temple:** This is a new detail, different from the accounts in 9:15 and 26:17, 20, which indicate that Paul was commissioned to go to the Gentiles at the time of his conversion. In this scene, Luke has this revelation come while Paul is praying in the temple, in order to further bind the Christian faith to its Jewish roots: even the mission to the Gentiles was authorized within the temple. **Fell into a trance:** Peter too learned that he was to go to the Gentiles as the result of a trance (see 10:10ff; for list of Peter/Paul parallels, see 28:31).

22:20 I myself was standing by: See Acts 7:58; 8:1. In his letters Paul himself never mentions the Stephen incident.

22:21 I will send you . . . to the Gentiles: Luke has amended the earlier account in 9:1–19 so that Paul first learns of his commission to the Gentiles not at his call but at a later stage of his ministry, while worshiping in the Jerusalem temple.

22:22–29
Paul and the Roman Tribune

22:22 Up to this point: See the analogous response to Jesus' inaugural sermon in Luke 4:28—the crowds listen to the speaker until God's grace to the Gentiles is introduced, at which point there is a violent reaction.

22:23 Shouting . . . throwing dust into the air: These are not merely emotional outbursts, but signs of revulsion and consternation, symbolic acts like that of tearing the garment (Matt. 26:65; Mark 14:63) or shaking the dust from one's feet (Luke 9:5; 10:11; 13:51; 18:6).

22:24 Examined by flogging: The Roman administration of "law and order" in the provinces was ruthless.

22:27 Are you a Roman citizen? . . . Yes: Citizenship gave one rights that noncitizens did not have, including freedom from arbitrary examination by torture. Paul's claim seems to be accepted at face value, without verification. Having been a citizen since his birth, he is more of a Roman than his captor—just as, having studied with the great Gamaliel, he is "more Jewish" than his accusers. In his letters, Paul refers neither to himself as a Roman citizen nor to having studied in Jerusalem. Like the Lukan Paul's period of rabbinic study in Jerusalem, Paul's Roman citizenship may be a dimension of the Lukan picture of Paul, or either or both may be historical reality. Luke's point is to show that there is no incompatibility between being Christian leader and a Roman citizen, and to portray Rome as responsible protector of Christians.

22:29 Afraid, for he realized: The tribune later distorts the chronology to make himself look better to his superiors (23:27). The commander now finds himself in a strange situation, holding a Roman citizen in custody with no charges against him. He has no authority to settle the matter himself, but does not act arbitrarily. He calls together the Sanhedrin to clarify the issue. It is doubtful historically that a local army officer could call a meeting of the Sanhedrin (only one of several historical problems in the narrative), but Luke is concerned to give the reader an impression of Roman order that operates judiciously and is protective of the rights of Christians.

22:30–23:11
Paul before the Council

22:30 He wanted to find out what Paul was being accused of: More literally "determine the truth." See on Luke 1:4; 21:33–34, where the same word is used. Thus Luke constructs the intervening narrative to set up Paul's second apologetic speech (see on 22:1). **The next day:** Another parallel to the trial of Jesus (see Luke 22:26).

23:1 Clear conscience: Luke presents Paul as a sincere Jew loyal to his Jewish faith, before and after his conversion. He had a clear conscience while opposing the Christians and their presumed violation of the Jewish law, just as he continued to have a clear conscience after his conversion, which placed him on the side of those who were being persecuted, his present situation. This is also Paul's view expressed in his own letters (Phil. 3:5–6). The contemporary reader might learn that, while conscience is not to be violated, neither is it a reliable guide to what is right and wrong. People of good conscience can be on opposite sides of the same issue; the same person can switch positions while preserving a good conscience. One's own conscience must be critically evaluated (1 Cor. 4:4).

23:2 The high priest Ananias: He was in office 47–59 CE, and thus fits the scene narrated by Luke, one of several points in this scene where Luke is historically accurate.

23:3 God will strike you: The Lukan Paul does not respond as the Jesus of the Gospel had instructed (Luke 6:29), but this is not Luke's point, which is rather to present Paul as pro-Law. Luke does not allow the reader to place "the Jews" and "their Law" on the one side, with Paul and the Christians on the other. He tells the story in such a way that Paul the Christian is more Torah-observant than the high priest himself (see on 22:27). **White-washed wall:** See Ezek. 13:10–15; Matt. 23:27.

23:5 I did not realize: Ananias had not been high priest many years before, when Paul was a delegate of the Jerusalem authorities (9:1), but this is not Luke's point. The incident gives the Lukan Paul the opportunity to continue his affirmation and support of the Jewish Law (he cites Exod. 22:27) and his respect for the office of the high priest. Historically, it is difficult to imagine how in this setting Paul (or anyone else who is present) would not know that Ananias was the high priest, but Luke overrides

historical probability in order to make his theological point: Paul and the Christians are not anti-Law, anti-priest, anti-temple.

23:6 Sadducees . . . Pharisees: On Pharisees, see on Luke 5:17. On Sadducees, see on Luke 20:27. **I am a Pharisee, a son of Pharisees:** For the first time in Acts, Paul is identified as a Pharisee. The historical Paul also emphasizes that he had been a Pharisee (Phil. 3:5). As he had been born a Roman citizen (22:28), so he had not become a Pharisee only casually and late in life, but is the heir of a long Pharisaic tradition. **I am on trial concerning the hope of the resurrection of the dead:** The original accusation of defiling the temple has long since been forgotten on both sides, and the scene has modulated into a general legal confrontation between the leadership of Judaism and the leading Christian missionary. By stating the issue in this way, the Lukan Paul presents himself as the advocate of one group within Judaism. This is the way Luke wants the issue to be seen in his own time. Paul had recounted how the risen Jesus had appeared to him. The Pharisees categorize this within their understanding of believing in the general resurrection and the appearance of angels and spirits to human beings, thus making it possible to incorporate the basic Christian message of the resurrection of Jesus within the theology of Pharisaism and allowing the dispute about the Christian faith to be seen as an intra-Jewish dispute. On the specific reference to the resurrection of Jesus, see on 25:15. On Pharisees siding with Christians, see 5:17–39.

23:9 We find nothing wrong with this man: This is not an incidental comment, but the key declaration Luke wishes to emphasize: one party of the Jewish Sanhedrin in an official meeting declares that Paul's message and mission are perfectly acceptable. In Luke's time (but not in Paul's), the Pharisees were the sole surviving group, representing Judaism as such. This Jewish declaration of innocence will correspond to the repeated Roman declaration (23:29; 25:26; in 26:31 the Jewish king and the Roman governor will agree that Paul has done nothing illegal). It is thus only *some* Jews who oppose Paul and Christianity, and the dispute about the Christian message is internal to Judaism and protected by Roman law.

23:10 Bring him into the barracks: Again Roman power emerges as the protector of Christians from the violence of internal Jewish disputes.

23:11 The Lord stood near him: Paul's testimony before the Sanhedrin has been apologetic, and only indirectly evangelistic. It is here given the divine stamp of approval. Luke thus commends this approach to the threatened church of his own day as the right way to represent the faith before the Roman authorities. Like the visions in 16:6–10; 22:17–21; 18:9–10; and 27:23–26, the vision here documents Luke's view that the expansion of the church from Jerusalem to Rome is under divine direction. Paul in his letters also speaks—however reluctantly—of having received visions and revelations from the risen Lord (2 Cor. 12:1; see Gal. 1:11–12; 2:2). **You must bear witness also in Rome:** See 19:21, on Jerusalem and Rome as Paul's goals. He has faithfully carried out his witness in Jerusalem, and is assured that he will do the same in Rome. The reader thus knows that despite the troubles and conflicts of the remaining chapters, Paul and the Christian message he proclaims will reach its goal in Rome. Luke's story began in the Jerusalem temple (Luke 1:5) and will conclude in Rome, spanning the distance between the capital of the Jewish faith and the capital of the Gentile world.

23:12–22
The Plot to Kill Paul

23:12 The Jews joined in a conspiracy: The reader now knows that "the Jews" means only "some Jews." A conspiracy had also been involved in the arrest of Jesus, another parallel between the passion story of Paul and that of Jesus (see on 20:22; 21:1).

23:16 The son of Paul's sister: The Lukan Paul had not only grown up in Jerusalem himself (22:3), but has a sister and nephew who still reside in the city. Again, this is not merely incidental biographical information, but portrays Paul as integrally related to Jerusalem. Although he is a Diaspora Jew, he is no outsider in Jerusalem.

23:17 Called one of the centurions: Paul is not presented as a cringing and humiliated prisoner, but as a rather commanding figure (see 27:10, 21–26, 31, 33–38; 28:1–10).

23:23–26:32
Testifies in Caesarea as Prisoner

23:23–35
Paul Taken to Caesarea

23:24 Take him safely to Felix the governor: Felix is mentioned by the Roman historian Tacitus and the Jewish historian Josephus as governor ca. 52–60, which fits the Lukan

chronology. The number of military personnel assigned to protect Paul (470, almost half the Jerusalem contingent) seems improbably large and is likely part of the Lukan portrayal of Rome as respecting the rights of Christians, as is his picture of Paul the "prisoner" riding, while most of the soldiers walk.

23:25 He wrote a letter to this effect: One should not ask how Luke came into possession of official Roman correspondence, since this is part of Luke's dramatization of the scene. By saying **"to this effect"** Luke acknowledges that the wording of the letter is his own creation, though it presents the substance of what he supposes such a Roman would or should write on such an occasion. See the speeches as Lukan compositions based on historical data (see "Speeches" in the introduction to Acts). **Claudius . . . to . . . Felix, greetings:** This is the standard Hellenistic letter form, also followed in 15:23. It will be theologically modified by Paul in his letters (see on 1 Thess. 1:1). **His Excellency:** The same word used in Luke 1:3 and Acts 24:3, placing Theophilus in the same social category as the Roman governors. The sending of such a letter and its content documents Luke's view that Christian cases that come to the attention of the Roman authorities should be handled by the orderly process of law at the level of provincial government by its official representatives, not by the whim of local authorities. Thus this section contains references to Jerusalem, Antipatris, Caesarea, and Cilicia (see 26:26).

23:29 I found that he was accused concerning questions of their law: The pattern of 18:12–17 is followed again. This is the model Luke wants to impose on the consciousness of his readers and their public: the dispute about Christianity is interior to Judaism, a legal religion. Neither here nor elsewhere in Acts does Luke bring up the issue that Rome considered threatening: that Christians spoke of the kingdom of God and of Jesus as king (see on Luke 23:1–25, 47, where Jesus had been pronounced innocent of these charges by the responsible Romans). **Charged with nothing deserving death or imprisonment:** As the Pharisees had pronounced Paul innocent, so also the Roman officer in charge. Paul will thus arrive in Caesarea in Roman protective custody against the plots of some fanatical Jews, having been declared innocent in Jerusalem by both Jews and Romans.

23:31 Antipatris: Ca. thirty-six miles from Jerusalem, twenty-eight miles from Caesarea.

23:33 Caesarea: See on 9:30. Paul will be here more than two years (24:27).

23:35 Your accusers: In the story line, these should be the Diaspora Jews from Asia who on a misunderstanding had charged Paul with defiling the temple by bringing Gentiles into its inner courts reserved for Jews (21:27–30). This particular charge has long since been forgotten by all involved, and Luke has modulated the issue into a matter between the leaders of Judaism, represented by the Jerusalem Sanhedrin, and the leading missionary to the Gentiles. Luke retells the particular incident of the 50s in a way that generalizes it and makes it a paradigm for his church in the 90s. Just as he has retold the Markan narrative of ca. 70 so that it speaks to the 90s, Luke has recast the stories he has about Paul's earlier conflicts so that they address his own situation. The modern church might hereby learn a biblical model of retelling the ancient story in a way that communicates to the contemporary world.

24:1–27
Paul before Felix in Caesarea

Paul's experience in the following chapters is an example of what was foreseen for Christians in Luke 21:12, and a model of how they should conduct themselves under such duress.

24:1 The high priest . . . with some elders . . . to the governor: This is the same configuration that combined to put Jesus to death (Luke 22:54–23:1). Luke knows it will eventually lead to Paul's death as well (20:25, 38), though he will end his narrative with Paul still in prison (see on 28:31). Unlike the situation in Jesus' trial, the priests also have employed **an attorney, Tertullus.** While his accusers have a professional prosecutor, Paul acts as his own defense (see Luke 12:11–12).

24:3 Your Excellency: See on Luke 1:3; 23:25. Verses 2–3 represent the customary formalities in such a courtroom speech, though somewhat exaggerated (see Paul in v. 10). From the point of view of those Palestinian Jews who saw the Romans as protectors from the revolutionary bandits that were beginning to roam the country, assassinating Jews who cooperated with the Romans (the Sicarii, "dagger men"), Felix had brought a measure of peace to the country. From the point of view of Jewish patriots who were to become the Zealot party, Felix had killed Jewish freedom fighters. Tertullus represents the priestly point of view that generally advocated cooperation with the Romans as best for the country.

24:5–8 We . . . found this man: He comes to the charges and names four:

1. He is a **pestilent fellow:** Not merely a personal insult, but a quasi-legal term for people who are threats to the public welfare, who therefore should be apprehended by the Romans responsible for law and order.

2. **He is an agitator among all the Jews throughout the world:** There is a measure of truth in this description, for wherever Christianity went, it did provoke controversy (see, e.g., 16:10; 17:6; 19:23–41; see on 18:2 on events in Rome under Claudius). Tertullus portrays this as political sedition, while Luke is concerned to represent it throughout as a religious conflict within Judaism that is not illegal and is no threat to the Roman peace.

3. **He is a ringleader of the sect of the Nazarenes:** "Sect" represents a Greek word that may mean simply "organized group," like the English word "party." Josephus, the first-century Jewish historian, uses it to describe the groups within Judaism: Pharisees, Sadducees, Essenes, and Zealots. It may be used in a positive or neutral sense, as when one speaks descriptively of the Democratic or Republican party as a group on the political scene in the United States. It may also be used in a negative sense, as when we speak of a "party spirit," or "the party line." Tertullus uses the word in a negative sense, but the Lukan Paul accepts it in his sense as an accurate description of the Christian disciples as one group within Judaism (see 5:17; 26:5; 28:22). **The Nazarenes:** This became the standard Jewish term for Christians, i.e., the followers of Jesus of Nazareth.

4. **He tried to profane the temple:** For the first time since his arrest, the charge that originally provoked the attack on Paul is brought up (see 21:27–36). The charge was the result of a prejudiced misunderstanding that had not been investigated.

24:10 I cheerfully make my defense: See on *apologia* at 22:1. Paul makes his defense "cheerfully" as a model for Luke's Christian readers, who welcome the opportunity to speak out in behalf of their faith, confident that they will be vindicated (see on Luke 12:1–12). **For many years:** Felix's term as governor was ca. 52–60 CE, the longest term in turbulent Judea since Pontius Pilate in the time of Jesus (26–36 CE).

24:11 You can easily verify (NIV): Luke places in Paul's mouth the view that he himself advocates throughout Acts: the suspicions of and charges against Christians will not stand up under impartial investigation, from which Christians have nothing to fear (see 25:24–27 for the same verdict from the point of view of the prosecution). **I went up to worship at Jerusalem:** Paul's journey as represented as a Jewish pilgrimage. "Going up" is the customary term for going to worship at the temple, situated on a mountain. The psalms sung on the pilgrimages were called psalms of ascent (Ps. 120–134).

24:13 Neither can they prove: Paul speaks with the confidence of one who knows that the misunderstanding that got him arrested had become an unexamined assertion that would not stand up under examination.

24:14 This I admit: The word can also be translated "confess," which is better here. Christians do not reluctantly admit their faith, but confess it (see on Luke 8:17; 12:1–12). **According to the Way, which they call a sect:** Paul accepts Tertullus's description but understands it positively: the Christian faith is a group within Judaism. On "Way" as a designation of the Christian community, see on 9:2. **I worship the God of our ancestors:** No new god, but the same God worshiped in Judaism. **Believing everything ... law ... prophets:** The "Law and the Prophets" designated the Hebrew Scriptures as a whole (Luke 16:16; see 24:44). No new Scriptures, but the same Scriptures read in Judaism. When Paul speaks and when Luke writes, there is as yet no New Testament. A selection of Christian writings was not to become part of the Christian Bible until the next century. Paul does not appeal to a different Bible, but understands the same Bible in the light of the Christ event (see "New Testament Interpretation of the Old Testament," excursus at 1 Cor. 15:3).

24:15 A hope that they themselves also accept: The same God, the same Scriptures, the same hope. Here Paul regards Judaism as pointing beyond its own present to the eschatological future, the resurrection of the dead. He knows that not all Jews affirm this (see on Luke 20:27), but takes the Pharisees' belief in the resurrection as representative of Judaism as a whole. Luke's point is that this Pharisaic faith in the resurrection is legitimate Judaism, though not all Jews accept it, and he wants Christianity to be understood in this same light. What Paul believes is what Jews believe; his faith does not violate Judaism. **A resurrection of both**

the righteous and the unrighteous: In the undisputed letters of Paul, there is no reference to a resurrection of the unrighteous (see on 1 Cor. 15). Here, the Lukan Paul makes the generic belief in the resurrection (not specifically the resurrection of Jesus) central to his message. The reader knows that Christians believe in the resurrection not only as a future hope, but as an eschatological event already begun in the resurrection of Jesus; in the story line of Acts the emphasis is the general principle that faith in the resurrection is authentic Jewish faith (though see 25:15).

24:16 A clear conscience: See 23:1.

24:17 I came to bring alms ... and to offer sacrifices: These are the activities of a pious Jew on pilgrimage to Jerusalem. "Alms to my nation" portrays Paul the Jew bringing his personal offering of charitable gifts to be used to care for poor Jewish people, as did many other Jewish pilgrims. The reader of Paul's letters, however, knows that the major reason for Paul's final visit to Jerusalem was to bring an offering from the Gentile Christian churches, of which the Jerusalem Christians were suspicious, not only or even primarily for charitable reasons, but as a symbolic expression of the unity of Jews and Gentiles in the one church of God (Rom. 15:25–32; 1 Cor. 16:1–4; 2 Cor. 8–9; Gal. 2:10). Paul was fearful that the conservative Jewish Christians of Jerusalem would not accept the offering, considering it "tainted money" and symbolizing something they could not affirm (Rom. 15:30–31). Luke is almost entirely silent about this offering, never mentioning it as part of Paul's mission work in chaps. 16–20 or during his two weeks in Jerusalem (21:17–23:30), and giving only an oblique and ambiguous reference to it here, after Paul has already left Jerusalem. Some interpreters have supposed that Luke did not know about the offering, but this is difficult to imagine, since he gives detailed information about Paul's final missionary journey on which the money was collected, including the list of delegates chosen to accompany the offering to Jerusalem (see on 20:1–6). If the author was actually included in the "we" of 20:6–21:17 and 27:1–28:16 (see on 16:10 and "Sources" in the introduction to Acts), it is incredible that he remained unaware of something so important to Paul. Why then the minimal reference to it in Acts? Apparently Paul's fears were realized, and the Jerusalem Christians led by James decided they could not in good conscience accept the offering. It is indeed striking that Luke has nothing to report about the Jerusalem church's support of Paul after his arrest and imprisonment. It is Paul's relative living in Jerusalem who comes to his aid, not the influential James. There is no indication that anyone in the Jerusalem church supported Paul during his more than two years incarceration in Judea. The deep differences that divided Christians who supported the Gentile mission and those who opposed it (see on Acts 15; Gal. 2) were apparently not healed in Paul's day. Luke writes a generation later, retelling this part of the story in the best possible light, with the purpose of allowing later generations of Christians to see that they are heirs of "both sides" of an issue that had divided earliest Christianity. It is good for the modern reader to be aware of the actual history, some of which must be read between the lines, on the basis of other sources such as Paul's letters. In interpreting the text of Acts, however, the modern reader should attempt to understand and appreciate the message and purpose of Luke, who writes not as an objective historian, but as an ecumenical theologian who wants his readers to appropriate the story of Acts as the story of the one church of God.

24:18–19 Some Jews from Asia . . . ought to be here: As in 4:5–22, the accused is more specific about the charges than the accusers, Luke's way of showing that Christians have nothing to fear from clear, impartial investigation. His point is that those who misinterpreted his action in the temple and initiated the riot that led to his arrest are not present as witnesses, a tacit admission that the original charge could not be sustained. **Completing the rite of purification:** Precisely the opposite of their original charge. Rather than "defiling the temple," Paul was carrying out a ritual of purification indicating his respect for the temple.

24:21 This one sentence: This is not Paul's "admission" that he had distorted the facts by his strategic move that divided his accusers in the previous hearing. Paul stands by his statement, insisting that the one thing he declared before the Sanhedrin that had caused such a tumult is actually an intra-Jewish dispute about the resurrection faith.

24:22 Felix, who was well acquainted with the Way: Luke's description may be historically accurate, since Felix was married to Drusilla, a Jewish princess, daughter of Herod Agrippa I (v. 24). Luke's point, however, is that Roman governors who must make judicial decisions about accused Christians can do so only if they are well informed (Luke 1:1–4). **I will decide your case:** The governor postpones making any decision, a stance he will reaffirm in v. 25. Luke has indicated this as one of three possible responses to the Christian message, two of which are wrong (see on 17:32–33).

24:23 Keep him in custody but let him have some liberty: As in 28:30, Paul is pictured as a respected gentleman prisoner, in protective custody but not abused. Luke is putting the best possible face on the historical facts, needing to explain why it was that Paul was arrested, imprisoned, and finally killed by the Romans, if in fact he was innocent of any crime. **Permit his friends to take care of his needs** (NIV): Ancient prisons were places where accused people were held for trial, at which time they were released, executed, punished by fine, confiscation of property, or corporeal punishment. Imprisonment was not itself a means of punishment for condemned criminals. Thus there were no provisions for feeding and caring for prisoners on a long-term basis, and it was important for friends of those accused to have access to them. This access could be granted or denied. Paul is pictured as being treated as favorably by Rome as the facts will allow.

24:24 Concerning faith in Christ Jesus: This is not in addition to what Paul has already declared, but more explicit. Luke does not picture Paul as concealing his basic Christian faith in order to fit into Judaism. He here makes it clear that being "on trial concerning the hope of the resurrection" (see 23:6; 24:21) means specifically faith that God has raised Jesus and made him to be Lord and Christ (2:36). Though Luke does not give the content of the conversation, it is clear that it is evangelistic as well as apologetic.

24:25 Justice, self-control, and the coming judgment: Further dialogue with the governor reveals that the substance of the Christian faith has implications for social and personal ethics. For the eschatological judgment as a fundamental element in the message of the missionaries in Acts, see 10:42; 17:31. **Felix became frightened:** He had sent for Paul out of curiosity and an interest in learning about the new religious movement, as some modern people enjoy studying various religions. The encounter with Paul reveals that the Christian message cannot be treated merely as fascinating data to be discussed, but calls for a decision. Again Felix backs away from actually deciding on the truth of the message Paul presents. **When I have an opportunity, I will send for you:** He never did.

24:26 He hoped that money would be given him by Paul: This information is part of Luke's own apologia for Paul, since he must explain why an innocent man would be kept in jail by the Romans. Since there is no reason to suppose that the tentmaker Paul would have enough personal funds to impress a Roman governor, this note is another indirect indication that Luke knows Paul is in charge of a considerable sum of money (see on 20:4; 24:17).

24:27 Two years had passed: While a few scholars have argued that some of Paul's "prison letters" (Philippians, Colossians, Philemon, Ephesians, 2 Timothy) were written during this period, we in fact have no information from this period in Paul's life, either from Acts or his letters. **Porcius Festus:** His term lasted ca. 60–62 CE. **Felix left Paul in prison:** His procrastination and lack of decision turns out to be a decision. **Wanted to grant the Jews a favor:** The influence of his Jewish wife may have been a factor. This is also a part of the Lukan apologia (see v. 26).

25:1–12
Paul Appeals to the Emperor

25:1 From Caesarea to Jerusalem: From the seat of the Roman government in Judea to the center of Jewish religious leadership. Though not necessary, it was politically expedient for the new governor to confer with the high priest and the Sanhedrin, and vice versa.

25:2 Chief priests and leaders of the Jews: The "leaders" are called elders in 25:15. They are thus the same official group that has constituted the opposition to Jesus and his followers (Luke 9:22; 20:1; 22:52; Acts 4:23; 23:14; 25:15). They continue to be the villains in the story, and Rome continues to be the protector of Christians. This is the Lukan perspective throughout.

25:3 Planning an ambush: See 23:12–25. Paul is in fact in protective custody in Caesarea because of a similar plot more than two years previously.

25:5 If there is anything wrong about the man, let them accuse him: See the similar attitude of the town clerk at Ephesus, 19:38–41. Luke has confidence in the orderly procedures of Roman courts, a confidence he wants to commend to his readers. For Luke, the way forward for the church in his own situation at the

end of the first century is to fit into the Roman world as loyal citizens, trusting in the validity of Roman justice. See the differing perspectives in 1 Peter and Revelation, written slightly later and in a different situation, which also deal with the proper conduct of Christians under Roman rule.

25:6 Took his seat on the tribunal: Literally the "bench," or "judgment seat," as in 18:12, 16, 17.

25:7 Many serious charges . . . which they could not prove: A repeat of the scene under Felix (24:1–13).

25:8 Paul said in his defense: The fourth apologetic speech; see on 22:1. Details are not given, but the main lines of the Christian defense are summarized. Paul's case is presented as a model for the Christian situation in Luke's own time, and the defense is that the Christian faith is not against the Jewish **law**, the Jewish **temple**, or the Roman **emperor**, i.e., that it is perfectly legal from the perspective of both Jewish and Roman law.

25:9 But Festus, wishing to do the Jews a favor: Luke knows, however, that law is not always administered fairly, that local politics and corrupt officials hinder the just administration of the law. Nonetheless, Luke's story advocates the view that when Jews and Romans judge Christians fairly by their own laws, Christians are vindicated. The story of Paul illustrates, both to Luke's Christian readers and the Roman authorities to whom he hopes to appeal (see on Luke 1:3), that Christians are only harassed and persecuted when Roman justice is perverted by plots (23:12–22; 25:3), bribes (24:26), and misunderstandings (21:27–34). These factors, and not Jewish or Roman law, are the causes of Paul's continuing imprisonment. **Asked Paul:** Though the governor has authority to make such decisions, Paul throughout his trials is presented by Luke as an imposing figure respected and consulted by the Roman authorities (see on 23:17; 24:23).

25:10 This is where I should be tried: In the Lukan story, Paul the Roman citizen can insist on this, but most Christians of Paul's and Luke's day could not. They were at the mercy of the local Roman and Jewish officials (see the situation presupposed in Pliny's letter to the emperor, cited in the introduction to Revelation).

25:11 I appeal to the emperor: The emperor was Nero, who ruled 54–68 CE. This is not a personal appeal, but a legal action analogous to appealing to the Supreme Court in the legal system of the United States. In the story line of Acts, however, the legal basis for Paul's appeal is unclear. Normally the appeal was made after a verdict had been reached in a local court, but Paul's ambiguous legal situation has not yet resulted in a verdict. Some scholars of Roman law argue that Roman citizens had the right to appeal to the emperor when a change of venue for their case was proposed, as here. Luke is not interested in the precision of legal details, but in the general picture he wishes to project: Rome is the protector of Christians from the arbitrary intrigues of local Jewish and Roman officials.

25:12 To the emperor you will go: With this decision, the plot of the remaining story of Acts is set, and the concluding chapters will portray Paul's journey to Rome. In the concluding scene of Acts Paul in the capital of the empire is "proclaiming the kingdom of God and teaching about the Lord Jesus with all boldness and without hindrance" (28:31). This is the goal to which the whole story is directed.

25:13–27
Paul Brought before King Agrippa

In this section Luke sets up Paul's fifth and last apologetic speech (see on 22:1), the climactic address before King Agrippa in 26:2–29. Paul has stood as a Christian witness before synagogues and governors, and now he will stand before a king, fulfilling the predictions of Luke 12:12 and Acts 9:15–16. The Roman governor will have the accused Paul appear before Herod, just as had happened in the Lukan account of Jesus' trial (23:6–12), another Jesus/Paul parallel in the "Pauline passion story" (see 20:22; 21:1).

25:13 King Agrippa and Bernice: The king is Herod Agrippa II, son of the Herod who appeared in 12:1–2, 20–23 and thus brother of the Drusilla of 24:24. At his father's death he had been only seventeen, but was made "king" of a small territory northeast of Galilee. He served the Romans well and territories were gradually added to his kingdom until they included not only parts of Lebanon and the area northeast of the Sea of Galilee, but most of Palestine except for Judea and Samaria, still under direct Roman control. Though actually subject to the Romans, he was something of a peer of the new Roman governor to the south and pays him a royal courtesy call. He was the last Judean king, ruling until the war of 66–70 brought an end to any kind of Jewish rule in Palestine. Bernice was his sister, who had been married to her uncle, after whose death she came to live with her brother. There was much gossip about the

apparently incestuous relationship. Luke is silent about all this (contrast his treatment of another Herod, which recounts John the Baptist's condemnation of his illegal marriage [Luke 3:19–20]).

25:14 Festus laid Paul's case before the king, saying: Here is a good example of an extensive speech composed by Luke himself, but narrated as though a verbatim account. (Otherwise the interpreter must imagine that verbatim records were made of the conversations between Festus and Agrippa, and that Luke somehow gained access to these.) The speech expresses what Luke considers to be appropriate on the occasion that would be edifying for his readers. See on "Speeches" in the introduction to Acts.

25:17 Lost no time: Literally a legal technical term, "postponement." Luke's report of Paul's trials uses other forensic technical terminology (such as "send up" in v. 21, a technical term for the transfer of a prisoner to a higher jurisdiction, and "cast my vote against them" in 26:10). Luke will also use a sophisticated nautical vocabulary in his recounting of Paul's sea voyage in 27:1–28:14, but neither the one nor the other is evidence that the author was a lawyer or a sea captain. Similarly, his somewhat sophisticated "medical language" is not evidence that he was a physician. The sophisticated vocabulary in all such cases shows that the author is well educated, but indicates nothing about his vocation or profession (see on 3:7).

25:19 Certain points of disagreement ... about their own religion: Festus here uses a form of the same word Paul had used in describing Athenian religion (17:22). **A certain Jesus ... whom Paul asserted to be alive:** Luke here lets the reader see how Christian faith in the resurrection of Jesus appears to a cultivated Roman. The comment also shows that the "generic" assertions of the resurrection in the preceding defenses included the specific affirmation of the resurrection of Jesus (23:6; 24:21).

25:20 At a loss how to investigate these questions: Luke pictures the Roman governor in an awkward situation, holding as a Roman prisoner one who is guilty of no infraction of Roman law, but is involved only in Jewish religious disputes. Luke thus sends a message to prospective Roman readers: don't arrest Christians, or you will find yourself in an embarrassing legal situation.

25:22 I would like to hear the man myself: The Greek can also be translated "I have been wanting to hear . . . ," which would make the parallel to Herod Antipas's role in Jesus' trial more explicit (Luke 23:8; thus another parallel between the passion stories of Jesus and Paul; see on 20:22; 21:1). This would also suggest that in each case the motive was a matter of curiosity rather than a quest for truth (see on 24:25).

25:23 With great pomp: Luke sets up the dramatic scene in which the itinerant missionary tentmaker is the center of gubernatorial and royal attention, surrounded by the locally prominent.

25:24 The whole Jewish community: Luke has allowed the story to modulate from a dispute between "some Jews of Asia" and Paul over their misunderstanding of his presence in the temple (21:27–33) to an issue between Jews as such and Christians as such.

25:25 He has done nothing deserving death: Though this is what "the whole Jewish community" clamors for. Once again the responsible Roman official declares the Christian missionary to be innocent of breaking any Roman law (see 17:35–39; 18:12–16; 23:29; 26:32; see the multiple declarations of Jesus' innocence by the Roman governor and centurion, Luke 23:1–22, 47).

25:26 Nothing definite: Luke again uses a form of the word for "the truth" or "the facts" that is the goal of his own writing (see on 1:4; 21:34; 22:30). Roman rulers such as Festus who wish to be informed as to what the Christian community is really about can learn this by reading Luke's two volumes. **Our sovereign:** The same word, *kyrios* ("Lord"), that Christians use of God and Christ is here applied by the Roman ruler to the emperor (Nero). This is apparently the earliest documented instance of applying the term absolutely to the Roman emperor and reflects the time of Domitian at the end of the first century. Luke, however, is unconcerned with the christological issue and never shows any uneasiness with Roman worship of the emperor (contrast Revelation). Differing New Testament authors choose different battlefields on which to contend for the faith.

26:1–32
Paul Defends Himself before King Agrippa

This is the climactic finale of Paul's five apologetic speeches (see on 22:1). As in the others, Paul does not merely report a past event in Paul's life, but presents Paul's experience as a model for Christians of his own day as they respond to the suspicion and harassment of a non-Christian world.

26:1 Began to defend himself: Once again, "defend" designates the speech as an apologetic. At the conclusion of this final speech, however, the Lukan Paul modulates back into the evangelistic and missionary mode, addressing the king personally and calling for a decision. It is never far from Luke's mind that the church is not in the world to defend itself, but to persuade others.

26:2 The Jews: Though Paul has explicitly identified himself as a Jew (21:39; 22:3), he can refer to others as Jews (as did Paul in his letters; see 2 Cor. 11:24; 1 Thess. 2:14). **I consider myself fortunate:** Not flattery, but the conventional formality, as in 24:2, 10.

26:3 You are especially familiar: See 24:22. **Jewish customs and controversies:** Luke again emphasizes that Christianity is to be judged not as a new religion but as a particular community within Judaism (see on 9:1–19; 18:13; 21:39; 23:6; 24:5, 14).

26:4 My way of life from my youth: Here begins the third narration of Paul's conversion (see on 9:1–19 and 22:1–21).

26:5 The strictest sect of our religion . . . a Pharisee: On Pharisees, see on Luke 5:17. For Paul's identification of himself as a Pharisee, see 23:6. On "sect" as a neutral term, see 24:5.

26:6 My hope in the promise made by God to our ancestors: Again Luke emphasizes the continuity between Judaism and Christianity (see Luke 1:5–23; 2:21–52; 4:14–15; 24:57; Acts 3:1–10; 18:18; 21:17–26; 22:3; 24:1–21; 26:6; 28:20). Though not all Jews saw it that way, Paul the Pharisee considers the eschatological triumph of God at the future resurrection as the hope for which Israel longs, a hope that for some Pharisaic Jews would include the coming of the Messiah. Within this framework, Paul the Christian believes that this eschatological event has already begun in the resurrection of Jesus (v. 23). Luke has frequently portrayed the Christian perspective that the coming of the Messiah is the hope of Israel (e.g., Luke 1:47–55, 68–79; 2:39–32; 24:21).

26:7–8 Our twelve tribes: See on Luke 6:12–13; 22:29–30. The reference to the twelve tribes also evokes the hope of Israel that included the restoration of the "lost tribes." **Because of this hope . . . that God raises the dead** (NIV): This, of course, is not his accusers' formulation of the charges against Paul, but the Lukan understanding of what actually was at stake. Here the Christian understanding of the Jewish hope is expressed generically as the hope that God raises the dead (pl.). The Lukan Paul incorporates within this Jewish framework the Christian affirmation that the Messiah has come, has been rejected by human beings, but has been vindicated by God who raised him from the dead (see 2:36). Luke's point is that the Christian message of God's act in raising Christ corresponds to the traditional Jewish hope of the resurrection and is in fact its fulfillment. **Why is it thought incredible by any of you?:** Here the Pharisee Paul addresses his fellow Jews, making the resurrection of the dead (pl.) an intra-Jewish debate. **Your Excellency:** Here Paul addresses the king directly. Better translated as in the NIV, "O king," or "Your Highness," since "Excellency" is a title Luke reserves for the Roman governor (see on Luke 1:3; Acts 23:25; 24:3).

26:10 Many of the saints: Another term for Christians, those who belong to the church, the holy people of God. Holiness in such contexts refers to being set apart for a special purpose, not to personal piety. The church as a whole is set apart for the purpose of carrying on God's mission in the world. See on 9:13, 32, 41. **Cast my vote against them:** Another legal technical term in Greek (see on 15:17). It is not clear whether Paul uses it literally, meaning that he had played an official role in condemning Christians to death, or metaphorically, meaning only that he had stood on the side of those who did so (see 7:58; 8:1). On Jewish execution of Christian Jews in the first century, see on 22:4; 1 Thess. 2:14–16; Matt. 10:21; John 16:2. In such contexts it must not be forgotten that this is not the persecution of one religion by another, as in the later Christian anti-Semitic persecutions, but the Jewish community's internal regulation and discipline of those they considered dangerous and on whom they imposed the supreme penalty.

26:11 By punishing them . . . I tried to force them to blaspheme: New information not found in the previous accounts of Paul's prior life. **Punishing them** refers to the disciplinary floggings administered by the synagogue authorities, which the Christian Paul later himself endured. Here he portrays his pre-Christian period, in which he administered such punishment himself. Blaspheme means to revile God or his representative. The event is here interpreted in his later Christian perspective. At the time Paul did not understand himself to be forcing the Christians to blaspheme, but to abandon their faith in Christ, perhaps with some such formula as "A curse on Christ" (see on 1 Cor. 12:3; Gal. 3:13).

26:14 When we had all fallen to the ground: In 9:4; 22:7, only Paul falls to the ground. For Luke's lack of interest in consistency in his three reports of this event, see on 9:7; 22:9. **In the Hebrew language:** In Aramaic, the native language of Palestine (see on 6:1). The detail is added to increase the solemnity of the revelation and to emphasize again that Paul (who is speaking Greek to Festus, Agrippa, and the assembled nobles) is a "Hebrew of the Hebrews" (Phil. 3:5). Though the risen Christ speaks in Aramaic, he quotes a Greek proverb. **It hurts you to kick against the goads:** The Greek saying is a common proverb, documented in at least three authors, that illustrated how futile it was to struggle against the Greek gods who control human destiny. The image is taken from goading oxen with sharp sticks to make them move faster; when the oxen respond by kicking, it only hurt them more severely. There is no allusion to Paul's psychology, as though he were unconsciously aware that he should not be persecuting the Christians and were intensifying the persecution in order to try to overcome his inner doubts. Such psychological subtleties are foreign to Luke and alien to the actual experience of the pre-Christian Paul. The saying has a better explanation within its ancient context: it is useless for Paul to resist the divine purpose, for God has called Paul to become a Christian missionary, and God's purpose cannot be resisted.

26:15 I am Jesus whom you are persecuting: In Luke's theology, this means that though the risen Lord is absent, he still maintains solidarity with his people on earth, and to persecute them is to persecute him.

26:16 I have appeared to you for this purpose: Paul is made a servant and a witness by the vision (see v. 19), but pointedly not an apostle (see on 14:4, 14).

26:17 The Gentiles—to whom I am sending you: In this version of Paul's call, he receives the commission to go to the Gentiles immediately and directly from the risen Lord (contrast 22:17–21), Ananias plays no role (contrast 9:10–19; 22:12–16), and there is no reference to Paul's blindness, baptism, and receiving the Holy Spirit.

26:18 To open their eyes: This reflects Isa. 42:7, where opening the eyes of the blind is part of the commission of the Servant of the Lord. The call of Paul is here shaped according to that passage, for Paul is called as a servant (26:16; see Isa. 42:1) who will bring God's justice to the nations (i.e., Gentiles; 26:17; see Isa. 42:1,

6) and who will bring light to the Gentiles who live in darkness (26:18; see Isa. 42:6). Like Paul, the Servant in Isaiah is chosen and called by God, who places his Spirit upon him (Isa. 42:1, 6), and foreign countries wait for his teaching (Isa. 42:4; see Acts 16:6–9). While Luke elsewhere uses the imagery of the Servant in Isaiah to interpret Jesus (e.g., 8:28–35), here he applies the imagery to Paul—another parallel between the passion stories of Jesus and Paul (see 20:22; 22:1).

In this verse Luke gives a succinct summary of his understanding of salvation, expressed as the transfer from the realm of the world, where one set of realities is operative, to the Christian community, where another reality prevails:

Eyes closed	Eyes opened
Darkness	Light
Power of Satan	Power of God
Unforgiven	Forgiven
No inheritance	Inheritance ("a place")
Unholy	Holy ("sanctified")
Unbelief	Faith

For additional comments on the Lukan understanding of "being saved," see on 16:30. Here as elsewhere, salvation for Luke is not an individualistic experience, but a corporate experience, becoming part of the saved people of God (see 2:47).

26:19 I was not disobedient to the heavenly vision: The experience was real, but visionary (see on 12:9). Such visionary experiences are not for personal enjoyment or the titillation of one's religious sensibilities, but call for obedience. Paul complied.

26:20 Jerusalem . . . countryside of Judea: Contrast Gal. 1:22. The Lukan account emphasizes Paul's incorporation into the Jerusalem church and its mission, to which he was subordinate (see on 9:26–30; 13:1–3; 15:1–35; 18:22; 19:21; 21:17–26). In his letters, Paul himself emphasizes his independence from the original apostles and the Jerusalem church (Gal. 1:1; 1:11–2:14). **Do deeds consistent with repentance:** Though this note is not often sounded in Acts, Luke's portrayal of the Christian message in Acts has not lost sight of the ethical message of volume one, the Gospel of Luke: repentance is not only a shifting of one's beliefs and attitudes, but must have concrete effects in one's ethical life (see, e.g., Luke 3:7–9, especially the Lukan addition, 3:10–14, that makes "repentance" concrete; see also Acts 24).

26:21 For this reason the Jews . . . tried to kill me: Here the original charge reemerges, seen in the Lukan perspective. "Gentile" (v. 23) is the operative word. Paul was originally apprehended because some Asian Jews mistakenly thought he had illegally brought Gentiles into the inner court of the temple and defiled it (21:27–32). Though Paul was innocent of the specific charge, the real issue between Paul (and the Christians he represents) was whether Gentiles could be brought into the church as the continuing people of God without first becoming Jews (see on 15:1). The Jewish objection to Christians was not their faith that Jesus is the Messiah, but that the holy people of God could include people who were uncircumcised and did not keep the Law of Moses. Christians understood Jewish objections as though they were against their faith in Jesus; Jews understood themselves to be defending the integrity and reality of Israel, the covenant people of God.

26:22 Testifying to both small and great: In the Gospel of Luke, the author had been intent on presenting Jesus as God's agent, who breaks down the economic and social barriers that separate people, and especially on sounding the note that Jesus' ministry meant "good news to the poor" (Luke 4:18). In his efforts in Acts to show that Christianity is not a foreign superstition that appeals only to the "lower classes," Luke has emphasized its appeal to, and reception by, especially the "upper classes" (see, e.g., 4:34–37; 10:1–2; 13:4–12; 16:11–15; 17:4, 12; 17:34; 18:8). But Luke has written the Gospel and Acts as two parts of one message and here reminds the reader that the Christian message includes both "little" people and "big" people—though at the moment Paul is pictured as addressing only a governor, a king, and assembled nobility (25:23). **Saying nothing but what the prophets and Moses said:** Again Luke stresses the continuity between Judaism and the church (see Luke 1:5–23; 2:21–52; 4:14–15; 24:57; Acts 3:1–10; 18:18; 21:17–26; 22:3; 24:1–21; 26:6; 28:20), arguing that the Christian faith does not go beyond the Jewish Scriptures. The difference, of course, was in how these Scriptures were interpreted. See on 3:18, 24, and excursus, "New Testament Interpretation of the Old Testament," at 1 Cor. 15:3. The Hebrew Bible (the Christian Old Testament) nowhere speaks of a Messiah who must suffer, die, and rise from the dead. The modern reader of Acts might reflect on the fact that the pre-Christian Paul had studied the Scriptures thoroughly, and had never come to this conclusion. It was only after his meeting the risen Christ and in the light of this event that he began to see that the Scriptures pointed to Christ. In conversations with Jews, Christians should keep in mind that it is this interpretation, derived from a prior conviction about the Christ event, that distinguishes a Christian reading of the Bible from a Jewish one. **By being the first to rise from the dead:** Though the phraseology of Jesus' "rising" is conventionally used, here as elsewhere God is understood as the active subject in the resurrection (2:36; 10:40; 17:31). A new note in Paul's apologetic speeches emerges here, though it has been presupposed all along. The Lukan Paul claims that the "generic" doctrine of the resurrection of the dead (pl.) is the common faith of Jews and Christians. For Christians, this faith is a matter of the eschatological event having already begun with the resurrection of Christ; i.e., it is another way of claiming that "the Messiah is Jesus" (17:3; 18:5, 28). That the resurrection of Jesus is the first installment on the general resurrection is also the understanding advocated by Paul in his letters (e.g., 1 Cor. 15:20), as well as other New Testament writers (e.g., Rev. 1:5). That Jesus was the **first** shows that Luke does not understand the resuscitations he has reported in Luke 7:11–17 and Acts 9:36–43; 20:7–12 to be in the same category as Jesus' resurrection.

26:24 You are out of your mind: The Gentile governor takes Paul's talk of the resurrection and his interpretations of the Jewish Scriptures to be **insane**, the product of too much study (see the response of the Gentile Athenians, 17:32). **Too much learning:** In contrast to the Jerusalem apostles, 4:13.

26:25–26 The sober truth: As Peter had responded to the charge of drunkenness by giving a direct response in terms of Scripture (2:13, 15), so Paul responds to the charge of madness by an appeal to both Bible and history. Luke emphasizes that the Christian faith is not a mania, not a matter of hyperemotional "religious experiences," but a matter of events that can be investigated, for they happened in the public arena. The story of Luke–Acts, the story of Jesus and the church, is not esoteric, not something for "religious fanatics" in the backrooms with candles and incense or in the privacy of individual hearts. **This was not done in a corner:** It happened in the world of Caesar, Pilate, and Herod (Luke 3:1). The mighty acts of God (2:11) are in the real world of history.

26:27 Do you believe the prophets?: Paul understands Christian faith to be a matter of believing the Hebrew Scriptures, not of rejecting them. But the equation may not be reversed— to believe the Hebrew Scriptures does not make one a Christian. One must first come to Christian faith before the Hebrew Scriptures testify to Christ (see above, and, e.g., 8:26–35).

26:28 Are you so quickly persuading me to become a Christian?: On "Christian," see 11:26. The Greek text here is ambiguous, the chief difficulty being whether the Greek phrase "in/by a little" applies to persuasion ("with a little more persuasion") or time ("in a little more time"). Paul's response indicates the latter interpretation is more probable. In either case, Agrippa's question is not serious, but ironic and sarcastic. He turns away Paul's "speaking the sober truth" (v. 25) with a condescending joke: "You think you're going to make a Christian out of me in such a short time?" As Felix, when he felt himself in danger of actually being converted by Paul's message, postponed the discussion until another time (which never took place [24:25]), so Agrippa, as a defense against taking Paul's message seriously, responds with royal cuteness. He was not the last to attempt to avoid the claims of the Christian faith by joking about conversion.

26:29 Paul replied: Paul is not repulsed by Agrippa's response, but concludes his speech with a succinct comment that might be taken as a summary of major elements of Lukan theology: (1) eschatology, (2) mission, (3) political apologetic.

1. **Quickly or not:** Paul's comment transcends its reference to how long it might take Agrippa to become a Christian. A major issue in Luke's church had been whether or not the end is coming soon (as the first generation of Christians had believed), and thus whether the church had time for its mission to the world. Luke had retained several of the traditional affirmations that the end is coming soon, though his own view is that the church must settle down in history for the long pull (see "Jesus as the 'Midst of Time,'" in the introduction to Luke, and comments on Luke 12:35–48; 17:22–23; 20:9; 21:8–9). In reality, whether it is "quickly or not" does not effect the church's missionary mandate.

2. **All . . . might become such as I am:** The mission of the church is to all peoples, Jew and Gentile. Paul the Jewish Christian prays that all might become believers in Jesus as the Christ.

3. **Except for these chains:** In five speeches (see on 22:1) he has explained, and the narra-

tive has indicated, that his arrest and imprisonment are unjust, that Christians can fit legally into the Roman world and in fact should enjoy protection from harassment and false arrest by the government. Luke has explained how it came to be than Paul is nonetheless in chains, but does not conclude without a reminder that it ought not to be so.

26:31 Said to one another: On Luke's "source" for such information, see on 25:14–22. The departing officials, including a Roman governor and a Jewish king, have not been converted. Luke's point is that they do not need to be converted in order to see the injustice of Paul's situation, that **This man is doing nothing to deserve death or imprisonment.**

26:32 This man could have been set free: The final verdict after Paul's five defense speeches is "not guilty" (see 23:25; 25:29). It was Paul's appeal to the emperor, the reasons for which the narrative has made clear to the reader, that prevents his immediate release. Thus Luke explains to the reader Paul's imprisonment and death despite his innocence (see on 25:25). Just as outsiders to the faith could ask in all sincerity, "If Jesus was not a criminal and enemy of Rome, why was he crucified under official Roman authority?" so they could sincerely ask, "If Christianity is not an illegal religion, how do you explain the fact that Paul, a leading Christian missionary, was arrested, kept in prison for some years, and then sent to Rome where he was finally executed?" Luke considers these to be legitimate questions, which his narrative sets out to answer with a forthright account, the "sober truth" (26:25). So understood, the narrative now proceeds to the final account of Paul's journey to Rome.

27:1–28:31
JOURNEY TO ROME, TESTIMONY AS PRISONER IN THE CAPITAL

In this last section of his narrative, Luke switches from the apologetic style of the preceding chaps. 22–26 (see on 22:1). Now we have an almost novelistic style that combines adventure, travel, danger, shipwreck, and a "happy ending," but which still expresses elements of Luke's theological message. The trip to Rome has been foreshadowed as part of the divine plan that God would see through to its completion (see 19:21; 23:11; 27:24). Paul's letters also refer to his travels, including three shipwrecks, during one of which he spent a night and a day adrift at sea, but these are all some years prior to the time covered by Luke's story (see 2 Cor. 11:25). This is

another indication of the fragmentary account of the Acts narrative (see 9:31; 20:5; 21:1; 27:3).

The author is unconcerned with questions that arise for the modern reader, e.g.: How long would the trip from Caesarea to Rome normally take? If it is necessary to spend the winter en route (see 27:9–12), why not remain in Caesarea and then sail directly to Rome? Who is paying the expenses of Paul's companions? The story has another focus: God's providential care for the hero Paul, who brings the whole group safely through the storm and shipwreck, and who will finally enable Paul to preach and teach the faith in Rome, openly and unhindered (28:31).

27:1–12
Paul Sails for Rome

27:1 We were to sail for Italy: The final "we passage" begins, extending through 28:16, though it contains several insertions in the third person (see on 16:10 and "Sources" in the introduction to Acts). **A centurion of the Augustan Cohort, named Julius:** Nothing is known of him outside this story, where he is the respectful protector of Paul, representing Luke's view of the ideal attitude of Rome to the Christian community. On centurions, see 10:1. The Augustan Cohort is known from Greek inscriptions.

27:2 Adramyttium: The modern reader requires a map in order to locate the numerous geographical references referred to in this section. The geography throughout is accurately described. The story also manifests a thorough awareness of travel routes and sailing strategies (see v. 4). Such details document that the biblical story is grounded in real history. **Aristarchus, a Macedonian from Thessalonica:** See 19:29; 20:4; Col. 4:10; Phlm. 24. It is not clear whether he is also a prisoner or is accompanying Paul as a helper. He is sometimes thought to be the author of the "we source" that Acts incorporates. If this is an actual travel dairy, one should reflect on how the fragile papyrus survived the shipwreck.

27:3 Sidon: Presumably Paul's **friends** there are Christians, though we have not previously heard that there is a church in Sidon—yet another testimony to the selective nature of the Acts narrative (see 9:31; 20:5; 21:1).

27:4 We sailed under the lee of Cyprus: See on 4:36; 11:19; 13:4–5; 21:1. At this season of the year, the ship takes a route different from that of 21:1–3, where they sailed across the open sea, because the winter storms are coming on and the large island afforded protection from the strong west winds.

27:6 Found an Alexandrian ship bound for Italy: We later learn that it was a large cargo vessel carrying wheat from Egypt to Rome with 276 passengers and crew (27:37–38).

27:8 Fair Havens, Lasea: Small towns now famous because of their connection with Paul described here, but hardly known by anyone in the first century except those who had had occasion to visit there—another indication that the voyage here described is rooted in real history.

27:9 The Fast had already gone by: The reference is to the Day of Atonement, the only fast specified in the Old Testament, which was observed in the last week of September. Such incidental references would be lost on the ordinary Hellenistic reader of the first century, as they are to the modern reader, unless the reader is thoroughly aware of biblical and Jewish traditions. That Luke assumes his readers understand such allusions without further explanation is evidence that he writes for well-informed insiders as well as inquiring outsiders (see on Luke 1:1–4). **Paul advised them:** In actual history, it is likely that Paul was in chains in the hold of the ship, but Luke presents him throughout as a commanding figure who repeatedly intervenes in the direction of the journey (see also 23:17; 27:21–26, 31, 33–38; 28:1–10).

27:10 Loss of our lives: Luke is not bothered by the fact that this "prophecy" of Paul turns out to be wrong, and that it is "corrected " by a later prediction (27:22).

27:11 Spending the winter: The Mediterranean was unnavigable during the winter months, ca. November–March. They do not hope to reach Rome before winter (see 2 Tim. 4:21), but only to find a more adequate harbor town in which to wait for navigable seas in the spring.

27:13–38
The Storm at Sea

27:13 They weighed anchor: One of six interpolations into the "we source" in the third person. This indicates either that the "we passages" are a literary device temporarily dropped or, if it is an actual source, that the author does not use it "as is," but edits it with his own insertions.

27:14 A violent wind, called the northeaster: This was a wind of hurricane force, that in a day prior to global communication of weather information could not have been predicted even by seasoned sailors.

27:16 The ship's boat: The dinghy used for ferrying passengers to and from shore and for

other purposes, normally left in the water and drawn behind the larger boat, but here hoisted aboard to prevent it from being smashed against the side of the ship.

27:17 They took measures to undergird the ship: In some manner the sailors reinforced the ship against the violence of the waves, but while several explanations have been given, the procedure remains unknown. **The Syrtis:** A reef or sandbank on the African coast.

27:20 All hope of our being saved was … abandoned: The characters in the story do not know what the readers know, that God's purpose will be fulfilled and Paul and his company will arrive safely in Rome. Their despairing words are analogous to those in the last chapter of the Gospel of Luke (24:21). **No small tempest:** On this figure of speech, a feature of Lukan style, see on 12:18. **Neither sun nor stars:** Their only means of navigation were hidden, so that they had no idea where they were (see 27:39).

27:21 You should have listened to me: Throughout, Paul comports himself as an authoritative figure (see 23:17; 27:10, 21–26, 31, 33–38; 28:1–10).

27:22 There will be no loss of life: See on 27:10.

27:23 An angel of the God to whom I belong and whom I worship: On angels in Luke–Acts and other New Testament authors, see Luke 1:10–12; 20:27; 24:4; Acts 5:19; Rom. 8:38; Gal. 1:8–9.

27:24 You must stand before the emperor: The fulfillment of this angelic promise is certain, but it is not narrated in Acts. In Luke's view, Paul's testimony in Rome is part of the divine plan. The same sovereign divine purpose according to which Jesus had to suffer in Jerusalem has decreed that Paul shall bear witness in Rome (see on Luke 9:21–22).

27:31 Paul said to the centurion: See on 27:9.

27:34 None of you will lose a hair from your heads: See 1 Sam 14:45; Luke 12:7.

27:35 Took bread … giving thanks … broke it: While the context indicates that this is an "ordinary" meal for nourishment, the initiated reader cannot miss the eucharistic overtones (see Luke 9:16; 22:14–20; Acts 2:42; 20:7).

27:37 Two hundred and seventy six: Some manuscripts give the number as "seventy-six," others as "about seventy six." The variations in the number given in various manuscripts is a reminder that we do not have the original document written by Luke (nor of any other biblical manuscript). In the present instance, the larger number is almost certainly original.

Luke wants the reader to see a large ship (see "Introduction: The New Testament as the Church's Book," 4.d).

27:39–44
The Shipwreck

27:39 Did not recognize the land: See v. 20. They had providentially struck Malta. The modern reader who examines a map might reflect on the statistical chances of this happening to a boat driven westward through the Mediterranean by a storm, and what would have happened if the boat had been a few miles further north or south.

27:40 Anchors . . . steering-oars . . . foresail: Three of the numerous technical nautical terms found in this account (see 3:7; 25:17).

27:42 The soldiers' plan was to kill the prisoners: This was not a matter of personal hostility or cruelty, but reflects the Roman practice of holding the guards responsible for prisoners entrusted to them, and the severe consequences of allowing them to escape (see on 12:18–19; 16:27–28).

27:43 The centurion, wishing to save Paul: Once again a Roman official becomes the agent of God's providence, a view Luke wishes to reinforce in the reader's mind and to encourage in Roman officials among his potential readership (see 18:12–16; 19:35–41; 21:31–36; 22:29; 23:12–35; 24:22–23; 25:12; 26:30–32).

27:44 They all were brought safely to land: Paul's predictions are fulfilled, and he is vindicated (27:22, 24, 26, 34), as is the benevolent behavior of the centurion to him.

28:1–10
Paul on the Island of Malta

28:1–2 Malta: A large island south of Sicily. It had been controlled by the Romans since the third century BCE and was an important commercial and shipping center. **The natives:** Greek "barbarians," which originally meant all those who did not speak Greek, i.e., "foreigners." As the narrative illustrates, the word does not imply "uncivilized" people.

Unusual kindness: Literally "not the normal," another example of the Lukan use of litotes (see on 12:18). The term is literally "philanthropy," ordinary human kindness and decency, as shown by the centurion in 27:3. The inhabitants are all pagan polytheists and idolaters. Throughout Acts, Luke portrays pagans as generally kind and decent people when not influenced by the misunderstanding of Jewish agitators (contrast Paul's picture

of pagan society in Rom. 1:18–32). **Kindled a fire and welcomed all of us around it:** The scene here (as in v. 7) seems to presuppose a small group. Luke appears to have forgotten the 276 people of 27:37.

28:3 A viper . . . fastened itself on his hand: "Viper" is used generically for poisonous snakes, as in Luke 3:7 (metaphorically).

28:4 This man must be a murderer: A common Hellenistic literary genre typically relates how a criminal, who flees human justice by ship, is overtaken by the goddess Justice and destroyed through a storm at sea (see Jonah 1, which is also a variation on this theme). In Acts 27, Luke has incorporated the Pauline story within this literary framework, altering it to illustrate Paul's vindication by being saved from the storm. The **natives** have this model in mind, and suppose that though Paul is a criminal who has escaped the storm, he has not escaped Justice, who now operates through the poisonous snake.

28:6 Nothing unusual happened to him: See Mark 16:18; Luke 10:19 for other early Christian views that faithful Christian missionaries are protected from the dangers of poisonous snakes. **Began to say he was a god:** See 14:11, and the parallel to Peter in 10:25–26. Here, however, Paul offers no protest, just as there is no Pauline indignation at the polytheism of the islanders (contrast 17:16), and there is no preaching of the gospel by Paul. The whole story is here told within the framework of a general humanitarianism, without reference to the Christian evangelistic mission. The reader may already have noticed that there have been no converts since the "third missionary journey" concluded at 21:16. The historical reality was otherwise, but Luke the skilled storyteller focuses the readers' attention on only one aspect at a time. The missionary journeys of chaps. 13–21 were for evangelism, and many converts were won. The five apologetic speeches of chaps. 22–26 are to explain and defend the Christian community to those who were suspicious of it, and no converts are won. The narrative of the trip to Rome is to enhance the image of Paul (though a prisoner in Roman custody) as he journeys to the "ends of the earth" in accord with the divine plan (1:8). In Rome he will offer his final testimony.

28:7 The leading man of the island, named Publius: Otherwise unknown. **Entertained us hospitably:** All 276 people (see 27:37)? Luke's selective focus has also allowed the large number of passengers to skip into the background of the readers' awareness.

28:8 Cured him by praying and putting his hands on him: Jesus had healed by laying his hands on sick people (Luke 4:40), but without prayer (by his own authority). **The rest of the people . . . were cured:** Though Paul does not engage in missionary preaching during the three months on Malta, he heals all the sick there. See excursus, "Interpreting the Miracle Stories," at Matt. 9:35.

28:11–16
Paul Arrives at Rome

28:11 Three months later: The group was on Malta ca. December–February, 60–61 CE. **The Twin Brothers:** Castor and Pollux, sons of Zeus who were honored as protectors of those on the high seas. Cf. the later Christian adoption of St. Christopher as patron saint of travelers. The association has continued until modern times, when a space capsule was named Gemini, "The Twins."

28:12 Syracuse: Then as now, an important seaport on the east coast of Sicily. The large island off the southern coast of Italy had been under Roman control for centuries, and in Paul's and Luke's time was a Roman province.

28:13 Rhegium: Port city at the southwestern tip of the Italian boot. **Puteoli:** A major seaport and port of entry to Rome, though ca. 120 miles from the capital. From here the party will make its way overland to Rome.

28:14 There we found believers: Literally "brothers," i.e., brothers and sisters of the Christian community (see on 9:30). A church already exists in an Italian town not mentioned previously in Luke's narrative, another example of the fragmentary nature of his narrative (see 9:31; 20:5; 21:1; 27:3). **Stay with them seven days:** The selective focus of the storyteller now concentrates on Paul and his party, the others of the 276 having long since been forgotten. In this scene Luke even seems to forget that Paul is a prisoner under the control of the centurion, and to portray the group simply as though they were traveling Christian missionaries who availed themselves of the hospitality of other Christians (see 16:15, 40 and Luke 8:1–3; 9:1–6; 10:1–12; Acts 12:12; 18:1–3; 21:4, 8, 16). **And so we came to Rome:** The fulfillment of the divine program of 1:8, for which Paul thanks God (v. 15). That the party seems to arrive in Rome a second time in 28:16 may reflect Luke's combination of more than one source (see on Luke 1:1–4). **The**

Forum of Appius: About forty miles from Rome; **Three Taverns:** About thirty miles from Rome. There is already a church in Rome, but we do not know how it was begun (see the introduction to Romans). These Christian believers go to extravagant lengths to show their welcome to the great missionary, but they are not mentioned again after Paul arrives in Rome itself.

28:16 Paul was allowed to live by himself: In a sizable house or apartment (v. 28). Paul is a prisoner under house arrest, chained to **the soldier who was guarding him** (v. 20), but still portrayed by Luke as a "gentleman prisoner" respected and protected by Rome.

Here the final "we passage" ends (see on 16:10). Luke concludes his two-volume narrative with a paradigmatic scene that sums up many of the themes of his narrative:

28:17–31
Paul Preaches at Rome

The final scene to which Luke has been building is actually two subscenes, one in which Paul invites the Roman Jewish leaders to his residence, at which time they express not hostility, but an openness to hear what Paul has to say (28:17–22), and the final one, in which Paul presents his message to them (28:23). There is a mixed response (28:24–25a), Paul makes a final pronouncement including a key citation from Scripture (28:25b–29), and the narrator has the last word (28:30–31). In this concluding scene Luke draws together ten themes, all of which have been presented throughout his narrative:

1. *Paul the Jew.* In this context where all are Jews, Paul does not specifically identify himself as a Jew (as he does in 21:39; 22:3), but makes his identity as an observant Jew clear by addressing his guests as **brothers** and by references to **our people** (v. 17; see 13:15, 26, 38; 22:1; 23:5). He presents himself as one who honors **the customs of our ancestors** (v. 17; see 16:1–3; 18:18; 21:17–26) and who is imprisoned on account of the **hope of Israel** (v. 20; see 23:6; 24:15; 26:6–7). Paul's Christian identity is not an alternative to his Jewish identity, but is incorporated within it. Luke wants his readers, Christian and non-Christian, to understand Christianity not as a new cult, but as a community within and an outgrowth of the ancient religion of Judaism, which enjoys Roman protection.

2. *Paul, though innocent, arrested and handed over to the Romans.* Paul (and Christians generally) had violated neither Jewish nor Roman law

(25:8). This theme is elaborately developed in Paul's five defense speeches in chaps. 22–26 (see on 22:1). Being arrested in the first place was a mistake, but when he was delivered over to the Romans, they acted with respect and care and repeatedly found him to be innocent.

3. *Christians as a "sect" within Judaism.* When the Roman Jews call Christianity a "sect" (v. 22), this is not in itself a negative evaluation (see on 5:17; 15:5; 24:5). This particular sect has been widely discussed and objected to within Judaism, but that it *is* a group within Judaism is important to Luke.

4. *The Christian message as fulfillment of the Scriptures.* Paul argues his case on the basis of the (Christian understanding of) Scriptures, as he and the other Christian missionaries have done throughout (e.g., Luke 3:4–6; 4:17–21; 24:27, 32, 45–47; Acts 2:16–21; 3:18, 24; 8:30–35; 13:26–41; 17:1–3, 10–11; 26:22–23, 27; see on these passages, and excursus, "New Testament Interpretation of the Old Testament," at 1 Cor. 15:3).

5. *Proclaiming the kingdom of God and teaching about the Lord Jesus.* In this closing scene Luke twice uses this formula to sum up the Christian message (vv. 23, 31). (See on Luke 4:43; 6:20; 7:28; 8:1, 10; 9:2, 11, 27, 60, 62; 10:9, 11; 11:20; 13:18, 20, 28–29; 14:15; 16:16; 17:20–21; 18:16–17, 24–25, 29; 19:11; 21:31; 22:16, 18; 23:51; Acts 1:3; 8:12; 14:22; 19:8; 28:23, 31.) The Christian message can also be called **this salvation of God** (v. 28), for "being saved" and "entering the kingdom of God" mean the same thing for Luke (see Luke 18:24–26; for other summary terms for the Christian message of salvation, see on 16:30–31). In Luke's understanding, the kingdom of God is a primary element in the continuity between the message of Jesus and the message of the church. The church preaches the same message as did Jesus, except that now Jesus himself is incorporated into the message as the divinely appointed king in the coming kingdom of God.

6. *Divided response.* Some of the Jews were convinced, and some were not (v. 24). This is typical throughout Acts for both Jews (17:4–5; 18:5–10) and Gentiles (17:32–34).

7. *First to the Jews, then to the Gentiles.* Despite repeated announcements to the contrary (13:46; 18:6), Paul again takes the initiative in bringing the gospel message first to the Jews. Some of them in fact accept his message (v. 24), but when others reject, he announces that he is going to the Gentiles, who will listen. This is a paradigm of the actual course of early Christianity, which was becoming predominantly a Gentile religion in Luke's time. This scene, however, like the earlier ones in 13:46 or 18:6, is not to be regarded as a "final rejection" by or of the Jews, but a dramatic illustration of the principle of Rom. 1:16 and the actual course of history.

8. *At his own expense.* This comment in v. 30 is not biographical, but illustrates the principle Luke has illustrated throughout: the mission of the Christian community is not attempting to make money from the secular society. Its missionary efforts are not economically motivated, and Christian missionaries pay their own way (18:3; 20:33–34). It is the opposition to Christianity, in fact, that is economically motivated (16:16–24; 19:23–27).

9. *The representative of a church that welcomes all.* Luke has deftly sketched how the group of Jesus' followers that began as a sect within Judaism followed the step-by-step leading of the Holy Spirit to become a universally inclusive community of faith (see the outline at 15:1). In the final scene Luke pictures the Jewish missionary to the Gentiles in the capital city of the world, welcoming all.

10. *Without hindrance.* Luke has skillfully composed his narrative in order to conclude with this key phrase. He has throughout shown that as the ideal response of informed Roman officials (e.g., 18:12–16; 19:35–41, and the whole series of events involving Paul's final defense speeches in chaps. 22–26). Luke's closing words contain an implicit assignment to both the church and the secular world. Like Paul, Christians are to teach about the Lord Jesus Christ **with all boldness** (v. 31), and the secular world need not be convinced of the truth of the message to grant Christians to do this **without hindrance**.

Luke has done his work so skillfully that the reader almost forgets that Paul is in fact a prisoner. "But the word of God is not chained" (2 Tim. 2:9).

Why does Acts end as it does? To some readers, the ending of Acts seems abrupt. Thus speculation has developed that Luke wrote a third volume, which has been lost, or that he planned to write a third volume, which never appeared. Since the story ends with Paul in prison in Rome about the year 62 CE, a few scholars have thought that Luke–Acts was written in Rome at the end of Paul's two years there, prior to his trial, so that in effect Luke brought the story up to his own time and told the reader all he knew. Most scholars are convinced, however, that the author writes near the end of the century and looks back on the story he has recounted as that of an earlier generation (see the introduction to Acts).

The ending of Acts is illuminated by reflecting on what actually happened. This can be reconstructed with some confidence from other early Christian literature. (On the final period of Paul's life, see further on "The Death of Paul and the Continuation of the Pauline Tradition" in the introduction to 1 Timothy.) Paul did appear before the imperial court in Rome and was condemned. Nero was the emperor. In 64 CE there was a persecution of Christians in Rome, since they were made the scapegoats for a fire that destroyed much of the central part of the city—a fire for which Nero himself was widely regarded as responsible, in order to make way for his grandiose "urban renewal project." Christians were rounded up and executed in the most cruel ways. Simon Peter had also recently come to Rome (see the introduction to 1 Peter). Both Peter and Paul became victims of this barbarous act against the Roman Christian community. Luke looks back on this and wants to put Nero's cruelty in its proper perspective—not an expression of what sober and responsible Roman policy should be, but the cruel act of a deranged emperor. It was still the case, however, that Paul was condemned and executed by the Romans. Luke and his readers knew that Paul had never left Rome alive (20:25, 38). It would have been terribly anticlimactic for his story, however, to have narrated the death of Paul, which Luke considered untypical of Rome. Luke wished to correct the image of how Rome had treated Christians with a final scene portraying how Rome at its best should respond to the Christian community and its mission. It is thus only a superficial reading of Acts that finds the conclusion abrupt. The Christian message is being proclaimed to all, Jew and Gentile, in the capital city of the world, openly and unhindered—and this is as it should be.

Parallels between Peter and Paul in Luke–Acts

1. The risen Jesus appears to both (to Peter, chap. 1 (see Luke 24:34); to Paul, chaps. 9, 22, 26

2. Peter and Paul both begin their ministry by healing a lame man: Peter, chap. 3; Paul, chap. 14

3. Both not only work miracles—many people in early Christianity do that—but do so in outstanding ways: Peter, with his shadow, chap. 5; Paul, with cloths that have touched him, chap. 19

4. Demons flee before both: Peter, chap. 5; Paul, chap. 19

5. Each meets and vanquishes a magician: Simon Magus by Peter, chap. 8; Elymas bar-Jesus, by Paul, chap. 13

6. Each raises the dead: Peter Dorcas, chap. 9; Paul Eutychus, chap. 20

7. Both at first oppose preaching the gospel to Gentiles, but are "converted," and the conversion is narrated three times in each case; each conversion involves a vision, a voice, and a call to the Gentiles: Peter, chaps. 10, 11, 15; Paul, chaps. 9, 22, 26

8. Each falls into a trance while praying and receives a vision sending him to the Gentiles: Peter, 10:10–15; Paul, 22:17–21

9. Both have a noontime vision: Peter, 10:9; Paul, 26:13

10. Each has a "conversion" by a heavenly vision, but the vision does not tell him specifically what to do; each must go to another town where he learns what the vision requires of him: Peter, chaps. 10–11; Paul, chaps. 9, 22, 26

11. Both are presented as initiators of major new evangelistic developments in the life of the church, although they in fact had predecessors: Peter, 10:1–11:18; 11:19–21; Paul, 18:1–4, 18–19:10

12. The first Gentile convert of each is a prominent Roman: Peter, Cornelius, 10:1–48; Paul, Sergius Paulus, 13:6–12

13. Both are worshiped as divine, but reject the divine honors: Peter by Cornelius, chap. 10; Paul by people at Lystra, chap. 14

14. Both accept the hospitality of a Gentile God-fearer who has become a Christian: Peter, 10:48; Paul 16:15

15. Both are supported by Pharisees in the Sanhedrin against Sadducees: Peter (by Gamaliel, Paul's teacher), chap. 5; Paul, chap. 23

16. Both are imprisoned, and miraculously delivered: Peter, chap. 12; Paul, chap. 16

17. The Spirit initiates a mission after previous unfaithfulness. Peter, 2:1–4; Paul, 13:1–4

18. Both champion the Gentiles against more narrow Jewish Christians: Paul throughout, esp. chaps. 11–15; Peter as the one who initiates and struggles for the Gentile mission, chaps. 10–11

19. Both Peter and Paul remain loyal to Jewish traditions even though their Gentile converts

are not required to "Judaize": Peter, 3:1, chaps. 10–11; 15:1–29; Paul, 21:17–26; 15:1–29

20. Each goes to a spiritually deficient Christian group and gives the Spirit by the laying on of hands: Peter, 8:14–17; Paul, 19:1–6

21. Each appoints leaders in the churches by prayer and laying on of hands: Peter, 6:1–6; Paul, 14:23

22. Each is bound with two chains: Peter, 12:6; Paul, 21:11

23. Each experiences an earthquake in response to prayer: Peter, 4:31; Paul, 16:25–26

24. Both strengthen their fellow disciples: Peter, Luke 22:32; Paul, Acts 14:22

25. Their speeches are parallel:

The word "gospel" only twice in Luke–Acts, in each case identified with "grace": Peter, Acts 15:17; Paul, Acts 20:24

Each quotes Ps. 16 in first speech, interpreting Ps. 16:10 by making the point that David's body suffered corruption, so the words of Scripture must refer to Christ and not to David: Peter, 2:27; Paul 13:35

Each refers to Galilean witnesses of the resurrection: Peter, Luke 23:35; Acts 1:11, 22; Paul, Acts 13:31 (This excludes Paul from being such a witness [see on Acts 1:21–22].)

Each goes from Israel to John the Baptist to cross and resurrection, without reference to Jesus' ministry: Peter, 1:22; Paul, 13:24–27

Each refers to the death of Jesus as human evil corrected by God, not as saving event: Peter, 10:39–40; Paul, 13:28–30

Each announces forgiveness of sins as the content of salvation: Peter, 2:28; Paul, 13:38 (absent from Paul's undisputed letters)

Introduction to the Pauline Letters

We know very little about the life of Paul before his call/conversion to become a Christian. Even for Paul's Christian period, we do not have the materials to write anything like a biography.

The New Testament attributes thirteen letters to Paul. Modern historical study has shown that it is probable that Paul did not directly write some letters ascribed to him (see the introduction to 1 Timothy) and that some extant letters may be editorial combinations of authentic Pauline letters (see the introduction to 2 Corinthians). Acts was written by an admirer of Paul who may have accompanied him on some of his missionary journeys and who had some reliable traditions concerning Paul's life and message, but it is also written from a perspective after Paul's death. The following sketch combines primary material from Paul's undisputed letters and secondary material from Acts, where it seems to be confirmed by the letters or to be inherently probable. While some points are disputed, the following outline represents the conclusions of a broad spectrum of scholarly study.

OUTLINE OF THE LIFE OF PAUL

Birth, Childhood, Education, Advocate of Judaism

Paul was born of Jewish parents in Tarsus and was a Roman citizen from his birth (Acts 21:39; 22:3). We do not know the date of his birth, but he was presumably about the same age as Jesus, therefore probably born between 5 BCE and 5 CE. Like many Diaspora Jews, he received a Hebrew name, Saul, and a Roman name Paul (see on Acts 8:1; 13:9).

He received a Greek education, speaking and writing Greek as his native language, though as a "Hebrew born of Hebrews," he belonged to a family that spoke Aramaic at home and attended the synagogue, where the liturgical language was Hebrew. He was educated as a strict Pharisee (see on Phil. 3:3–5). According to Acts 22:3, he studied in Jerusalem with the important rabbi Gamaliel I, though Paul's own letters make no

reference to this. Even if he had spent some time in Jerusalem, there is no reason to suppose that he had seen Jesus. Like all Pharisees, he learned a trade; he became a tentmaker or leather worker (Acts 18:3; 1 Thess. 2:9; 1 Cor. 9:6), by which he supported himself even after he became a Christian missionary.

As a zealous advocate of strict observance of the Jewish law, Paul became a persecutor of the Jewish followers of Jesus (Gal. 1:13–14, 23; 1 Cor. 15:9; Phil. 3:6).

33 Conversion/Call

In the neighborhood of Damascus, Paul encountered the risen Christ and became a zealous advocate of the faith he had been persecuting (Gal. 1:11–17; Acts 9:1–19; 22:3–21; 26:4–18). After becoming a Christian, Paul never ceased to be a Jew; he did not regard his call to be a Christian and apostle as a conversion from one religion to another. Though he speaks of his "call" (e.g., Rom. 1:1; Gal. 1:15) and describes the experience in language reminiscent of the call of Old Testament prophets (see Jer. 1:4–10; Gal. 1:15), in a real sense his encounter with the risen Christ resulted in a radical transformation of his life and can properly be called a "conversion"—a fundamental change.

36 First Visit to Jerusalem for Fifteen Days

Paul received Christian traditions from the Damascus church, became a missionary in the Damascus area and in "Arabia," and after three years made his first visit to Jerusalem (see on Gal. 1:16–24).

36–50 Missionary Activity in Syria and Cilicia (and Beyond)

During this period on which both Paul's own letters and Acts are silent, Paul apparently continued his missionary work and matured as a Christian leader. At the end of this period he and Barnabas engaged in their "first missionary journey" (according to the Acts chronology; see Acts 13–14) under the sponsorship of the Antioch church.

50 Second Visit to Jerusalem (Jerusalem Council)

The success of Paul's Gentile mission created tensions with the Jerusalem Jewish Christians, resulting in a conference of apostolic leaders in Jerusalem (Gal. 2:1–10; Acts 15:1–29).

Upon his return to Antioch, Paul had a confrontation with Peter, resulting in a break with the Antioch church.

50–56 Mission in Galatia, Asia, Macedonia, and Achaia

Paul launched his own mission and never returned to Antioch. From this relatively late period in Paul's career, some of his letters are preserved and allow the modern reader an interior view of Paul's life and thought. In the Acts chronology, 1 Thessalonians was written during the "second missionary journey" (and possibly 2 Thessalonians and Galatians); the others come from the "third missionary journey."

50	**1 Thessalonians** (and **2 Thessalonians**, if written by Paul) [Galatians?]
54	**1 Corinthians**
54–55	**Philemon, Philippians** (if from Ephesus; see the introduction to Philippians and the introduction to Philemon)
55–56	**2 Corinthians**, probably as more than one letter
	Galatians
	Romans

56–57 Collection Tour

During what Paul saw as the final phase of his mission work in the east, he collected a substantial sum of money as an offering from the Gentile churches to aid the Jewish Christian churches in Jerusalem and Judea (2 Cor. 8–9).

57–64 Arrest and Imprisonment

Paul was arrested by the Romans during his final visit to Jerusalem to deliver the offering (Acts 21). After a series of defenses in Jerusalem and Caesarea, resulting in two years imprisonment in Caesarea, he was sent to Rome, where his imprisonment continued two more years (Acts 22–28). In some chronologies, **Philippians** and **Philemon** were written from this Roman prison (as well as **Colossians** and **Ephesians**, if by Paul). He was probably condemned and executed ca. 64.

[64–68 Release and Second Roman Imprisonment]

According to some traditions, Paul was released and continued his missionary activity and writing (see the introduction to 1 Timothy), then was arrested again. His second Roman imprisonment ended in his death. In this view, **1 Timothy** and **Titus** were written during his release, and **2 Timothy** from his final imprisonment.

For Further Reading

Barrett, C. K. *Paul: An Introduction to His Thought.* Louisville, KY: Westminster John Knox, 1994.

Cousar, Charles B. *The Letters of Paul.* Interpreting Biblical Texts. Nashville: Abingdon, 1996.

Keck, Leander, and Victor Paul Furnish. *The Pauline Letters.* Interpreting Biblical Texts. Nashville: Abingdon, 1984.

The Letter of Paul to the Romans

INTRODUCTION

The early church arranged the collected letters of Paul on the basis of length; as the longest letter, Romans was placed first—though actually it was among the last of Paul's extant letters, probably the very last (see Outline of the Life of Paul in "Introduction to the Pauline Letters"). In a real sense, however, Romans is indeed the premiere Pauline letter, for in the history of the church it has had the most influence, contains the longest sustained argument of any Pauline letter, and comes closest to being a summary of Paul's faith. Its overarching outline is clear: the universal sinfulness of humanity (1:1–3:20) has been met by the gracious act of God in Christ (3:21–8:39) as worked out in God's plan for history that includes Jews and Gentiles (9:1–11:36), which forms the basis for Christian living (12:1–16:27). Nonetheless, Romans is not an essay, but a genuine letter reflecting the particular situation of both Paul and the Roman church.

Paul has established churches in several major cities in the eastern Mediterranean, and regards his work there as complete (15:18–23). He has recently struggled with the problems in the churches in Corinth and Galatia and now looks back on a successful resolution of the difficulties in Corinth (2 Cor. 10–13; 1:1–2:13; 7:5–15). He is happily settled for a few weeks in Corinth, where he writes this letter about 56 CE (16:23; see 1 Cor. 1:14; in Luke's chronology, Romans comes at Acts 20:4). He intends to visit the Roman church, which he had not founded and with which he is so far personally unacquainted (1:13), and wants them to support his projected mission to Spain (15:22–24). Before sailing westward, however, Paul must once again go to Jerusalem to deliver the collection he has organized among the Gentile churches (15:25–29). The collection, if received by the Jewish-Christian Jerusalem church, will concretely symbolize the unity of the one church of Jews and Gentiles (see on Gal. 2:1–10; 2 Cor. 8–9). But Paul is not sure the offering will be received (15:30–31). As Paul writes Romans, therefore, the situations of four different churches are on his mind and influence his composition:

1. The Roman church to which Paul writes. He wants support from it and is concerned to allay their possible suspicions of him by setting forth the gospel he preaches. The church itself is composed of both Jewish and Gentile Christians (see 1:13; 2:17; 3:9; 11:13), and needs instruction on the role of Jews and Gentiles in God's plan. In 49 CE, seven years prior to Paul's writing, Jews and Jewish Christians were forced to leave Rome (see on Acts 18:2). This left the Roman church, originally composed predominantly of Jewish Christians, a Gentile Christian church. In the meantime, the Jewish Christians have returned to Rome, making the relation of Jewish and Gentile Christians within the church not only a theological issue, but a practical one.

2. The Corinthian church from which Paul writes. This church has just been through stormy debates on the legitimacy of Paul's apostleship, the importance of charismatic gifts in the life of the congregation, and such issues as the eating of meat sacrificed to idols and Christian participation in pagan social life.

3. The Galatian churches with which Paul has recently been in debate. Jewish Christian teachers have intruded into the Gentile churches in Galatia, teaching that the new converts there must be circumcised and keep the Jewish Law in order to be authentic "children of Abraham" and belong to the people of God. These arguments still echo in Paul's mind as he writes Romans.

4. The Jerusalem church to which Paul is en route. The "mother church" is suspicious of Paul's law-free Gentile mission. He wants to explain and clarify his gospel that embraces Jewish and Gentile believers in the one church of God. These issues are especially on his mind as he writes to Rome and contribute to shaping the letter.

Outline

1:1–17 Introduction of the Letter
   1:1–7 Salutation
   1:8–15 Thanksgiving
   1:16–17 Thesis Statement: The Power of the Gospel
1:18–11:36 Part One—God's Righteousness in History

For Further Reading

Achtemeier, Paul J. *Romans*. Interpretation: A Bible Commentary for Teaching and Preaching. Louisville, KY: Westminster/John Knox, 1985.

Barrett, C. K. *The Epistle to the Romans*. Black's New Testament Commentaries. London: Adam & Charles Black, 1957.

COMMENTARY

1:1–17
INTRODUCTION OF THE LETTER

1:1–7 Salutation

On the special form and meaning of the Pauline letter salutation, see on 1 Thess. 1:1.

1:1 Paul: Only here in the undisputed letters of Paul does he address the church exclusively in his own name. Timothy and others are with him as he writes (16:21–23), but Paul accepts sole responsibility for the following letter. **Called to be an apostle:** Better translated "a called apostle" (see on 1 Cor. 1:1; Gal. 1:1–5). Paul has a special call (Gal. 1:11–16; Acts 9:1–19), but all Christians are called (1:6, 7), i.e., have become Christians not as a result of their own initiative but in response to God's call through the gospel (see 8:28–30; 2 Thess. 2:14).

1:2–4 Promised beforehand: The gospel is an expression of God's unilateral promise (see on Gal. 3:15). **Four Descended from David . . . declared to be Son of God:** See Matt. 1:2–25; 2 Tim. 2:8. Paul expands the stereotyped salutation formula especially by this insertion of traditional material representing an early Jewish-Christian creed that would be recognized by the Roman congregation and thus establish common ground. On Davidic imagery in Christian confession of Jesus, see on Luke 1:28–33, 68–79; 6:4; 18:35–43; 20:41–44; Acts 13:22–23. The creed affirms both the authentic humanity of Jesus ("descended from David") and his authentic divinity ("Son of God," "Lord"). Here the matter is thought of chronologically, from humanity to divinity, with the resurrection being the transition point. In this way of thinking about Jesus, he became Son of God at the resurrection. Although Paul includes and affirms this "two-stage" creedal statement adopted from earlier tradition, his own way of conceptualizing the person of Christ is as a "three-stage" drama: (1) the preexistent Son of God, who (2) descends to earth, fully shares human existence, and dies a truly human death, then (3) is raised by God to transcendent power (Phil. 2:5–11). Both the traditional creed he cites and his own understanding differ from the Gospels, which portray Jesus as the powerful Son of God during his earthly life (see on "Introduction to the Gospels," 4). The New Testament includes a limited variety of ways of conceptualizing God's saving act in the Christ event—not just any way is valid, but more than one way is affirmed.

1:5 Obedience of faith: Authentic obedience derives from and is grounded in faith (rather than fear or promise of reward); authentic faith leads to obedience (rather than passive inaction). Paul insists on a gospel that generates and requires both faith and obedience, in such a way that the Christian response is not two things that could be separated, "faith plus obedience," but one inseparable act, obedience in personal trust as the meaning of faith (see on Acts 16:31). **Among all the Gentiles:** The gospel calls for the response of obedient faith from people of all nations. As apostle to the Gentiles Paul is authorized to write to the Christians in Rome, capital of the Gentile world, even though he did not found the church there and has had no personal contact with or claim upon it. Paul has authority only as one under authority, himself servant (slave) of Christ the Lord.

1:7 Saints: See on 1 Cor. 1:2; 1 Thess. 3:13.

1:8–15

THANKSGIVING

On the thanksgiving as a standard component of Paul's letters, see on 1 Thess. 1:2.

1:8 Your faith is proclaimed throughout the world: The churches of the first century were small and mostly unnoticed by society at large, but Christians throughout the world were aware that they belonged to something bigger than their local congregation, and took courage from the news that there was a faithful congregation in the capital city.

1:9 I remember you always in my prayers: Not an empty formality. Paul prays for people he has never seen in a church he has never visited, because all Christians are members of the one body of Christ (12:4–8; 1 Cor. 12:12–13; Eph. 4:4–6).

1:11–12 Share with you some spiritual gift: The Holy Spirit had given Paul special apostolic gifts ("charisms") to strengthen the church,

gifts he wants to share with the Roman Christians, but he immediately adds that sharing the gifts of the Spirit is not a one-way street: the Spirit is at work in the life of every Christian and every congregation, and each has something to give the other (12:6–8; 1 Cor. 12:13–13:13).

1:14 I am a debtor: When Paul received the gospel, he received something that belonged not to him but to everyone. The treasure of the gospel and the gifts of the Spirit are not just for the enjoyment and edification of the individual Christian. The gospel is from the one God, Creator of all, who sent his son to die for all; so the good news of God's saving act in Christ already belongs to all people. Evangelism is not imposing "our" religion on "them," but announcing the good news of the treasure that already belongs to them as God's beloved creatures. **To Greeks and to barbarians:** Romans considered themselves the heirs of Greek culture, spoke Greek even in Rome (Paul writes to them in Greek), and numbered themselves among the "Greeks." Thus from the first-century Roman perspective, "Greeks and barbarians" (like "Jews and Gentiles" or "Jews and Greeks") is a way of saying "everyone," something like "civilized and uncivilized," "cultured and uncultured." Paul's point: the Christian gospel transcends all cultural differences; it is for everyone alike.

1:15 To proclaim the gospel to you who are in Rome: The church there had already heard the Christian message—otherwise, there would not be a church there. But the gospel is to be preached not only to "outsiders." Those already baptized need their faith constantly renewed by hearing the gospel proclaimed.

1:16–17

THESIS STATEMENT:

THE POWER OF THE GOSPEL

This is Paul's carefully composed thesis statement for the whole letter, which will elaborate his own meaning of each of its major terms.

1:16 Not ashamed: In the biblical vocabulary on which Paul is dependent, "being ashamed" is not a matter of personal embarrassment, but of being disappointed by something in which one had placed one's hope and trust (see 5:5; Ps. 119:6; Isa. 54:4). Thus the meaning is "I have complete confidence in the gospel" (so TEV) as God's way of dealing with sinful people and the sinful world (see Mark 8:38). **The gospel:** The good news of God's saving act in Christ, for Paul centering in the cross and res-

470

urrection (see 1 Cor. 15:3–5). **Power of God:** The gospel is not merely *about* God's power, but *is* God's power, it makes God's power effective. **Salvation:** This-worldly restoration to fellowship with God, reconciliation with oneself and others leading to transformation of the world, and confident hope of eternal life in the coming kingdom of God (see on Acts 16:31). **To everyone who has faith:** Salvation is dependent on faith generated by the gospel, but not in a legalistic sense—as though instead of our works we offer our faith as the basis for acceptance with God. Faith points us away from ourselves, even from our own act of believing, to the grace of God as the only ground of our salvation. Faith is not something we do so that God will accept us, but the trust that God has accepted us in Christ. **To the Jew first and also to the Greek:** The meaning is not that in a particular location Jews are given preferential treatment, as though the gospel goes first to them and only secondarily to Gentiles, but that Israel had priority in God's saving plan for history, in which Gentiles were only later included (chaps. 9–11). That the impartial God is no respecter of persons is a fundamental element in the gospel. Paul will go on to show that Jews and Gentiles are equally needy sinners and equally recipients of God's love and grace.

1:17 Righteousness of (NRSV)/**from** (NIV) **God:** No one English translation can bring out the meaning of the multifaceted Greek phrase (see the difference in NRSV and NIV, each of which apprehends one aspect of its meaning). Included in the Greek phrase are (1) righteousness as a quality of God the Righteous One; (2) God's act of setting things right; (3) God as the source of righteousness, the One who declares us to be righteous even though we are sinful, conferring his own righteousness on us (see Paul's elaboration in 3:21–5:21; Phil. 3:7–10). **Is revealed:** Not only "made known" but "put into effect." God's revelation is more than a matter of information. **By faith from first to last** (NIV): This difficult phrase can have several meanings (see also NRSV "through faith for faith"), but most likely is best translated as in the NIV. Salvation does not come by "faith plus" something else (see on Gal. 2:21), but is a matter of faith from beginning to end. The phrase may also mean that the message—that salvation is not our achievement but comes by trust in God—itself generates such trust (while the idea that salvation is by doing good works generates either false pride that we do them or

despair that we cannot be good enough). The word "faith" itself here has different levels of meaning, pointing both to God's faithfulness shown in the faith of Jesus (see on Gal. 2:16) and the believer's responsive obedience in personal trust (see 1:5). **As it is written:** Paul finds a key text in Hab. 2:4 that he understands as a summary of his doctrine of "justification by faith" (see also Gal. 3:11; Heb. 10:38). On Paul's use of the Old Testament, see excursus, "New Testament Interpretation of the Old Testament," at 1 Cor. 15:3. **The one who is righteous will live by faith:** Alternate translation: "Those who are justified by faith will live" (= receive salvation). The issue is how sinful people can be accepted as righteous or justified-acquitted. The answer is not by their own achievement, but by their trust in God's faithfulness manifest in Christ. Throughout Romans (and the New Testament as a whole) the reader should keep in mind that in both Hebrew (the language of the Old Testament) and Greek (the language of the New Testament) the adjective, noun, and verb forms for "justice" and "righteousness" are from the same stem. Hebrew and Greek can speak of God as just, doing justice, and justifying someone, or of God as being righteous, doing righteousness, and "righteousing" or "rightwising" someone, but of course proper English cannot do this. Though different words must be used in English, the fundamental idea throughout is that the righteous God makes unrighteous people righteous, or the just God justifies unjust people.

1:18–11:36
PART ONE—GOD'S RIGHTEOUSNESS IN HISTORY

1:18–8:39
The Meaning of God's Righteousness

1:18–3:20
The Human Condition: The Sinfulness of All Humanity

Here the argument of the letter itself begins, the first point being that all human beings, religious and irreligious, Jews and Gentiles, are sinful and in need of God's grace. Paul first shows the sinfulness of Gentiles, who do not have the law of God (1:18–32), then the sinfulness of Jews, who do have God's law (2:1–3:7), then concludes with a medley of Scripture passages that show that all human beings without distinction are sinners in need of God's grace (3:8–20).

1:18–32 The Guilt of the Gentiles

Before presenting God's saving act, Paul will show the reader the human condition to which the Savior is sent. The view is retrospective, seen only in the light of Christ. Paul has already presented God's grace manifest in the gospel as fundamental, and his thought moves from solution to problem, not the other way around. Paul does not present a sinful humanity longing for a savior, but a darkness that was not realized until the light appeared.

1:18 The wrath of God: Not emotional rage, but the impartial and just response of God's holiness to human sin. **Revealed from heaven:** Paralleled to the righteousness of God (1:17). "Revealed" means "put into effect" in both instances. It is not as though God showed his righteous side to some and his wrathful side to others, or first his wrath and then his righteousness. The two are revealed simultaneously and to all people. This revelation is both present and future. God's justifying act ("righteousness") and his judging act ("wrath") both participate in the already/not yet reality of God's definitive act in Christ. **All ungodliness:** Not merely sensational sins; the word means "without religious devotion," i.e., without worship. The human condition is marked not only by ignorance, weakness, and wrongdoing, but by being "without worship." In failing to respond to God in worship, human beings deny their own created existence and make themselves the center of their own universe. Martin Luther thus defined sin as "the curvature of the self in on itself."

1:20–21 Without excuse: God's creative power is shown in the natural world. People should see this revelation of God in the created world, but they willfully do not **honor him as God or give thanks**. Worship, grateful praise to God, is not a religious "extra" added on to "normal" human life, but the appropriate response of every human being for the gift of God and the created world. The revelation of God in the created world could be compared to radio waves, which are always present, whether people are "tuned in" or not. But the situation Paul describes is not that "waves" are present but we have no "receiver." Rather, our situation is that the radio waves of God's revelation are always present; we do have a receiver, we have heard, we didn't like what we heard and not only switched off the set but unplugged it, with no possibility of switching it back on ourselves. God's revelation is universally present, but we cannot hear because we will not.

1:23 Exchanged the glory of the immortal God for images: In Old Testament and Jewish thought, idolatry is the primal sin from which all other sins spring (see Exod. 20:1–6). Modern sophisticates may presume to have outgrown primitive idol making, but Paul identifies idolatry as serving **the creature rather than the Creator** (v. 25). Orienting one's life to *things* in the created world (including status and self-image) is idolatry (see Col. 3:5).

1:24 God gave them up: Repeated three times (also 1:26, 28), this phrase does not mean "God gave up on them," but "God handed them over" to their own choices. Instead of worshiping and serving the Creator as grateful creatures, they worshiped the material world. God's judgment was not to rain fire and brimstone from heaven, but to turn them over to their own desires.

1:26–27 Degrading passions: Sexuality is a gift from God, a part of God's good created order, to be gratefully used in God's service (Gen. 1:27–28; 2:18–25). The distortion of sexuality is illustrative of human sin as such. Interpretation of New Testament texts dealing with homosexual acts should keep in mind the following:

1. The Christian ethical perspective on homosexuality is a complex subject involving legal, social, psychological, and medical points of view as well as theological and biblical statements. Although biblical teaching on sexuality and sin is an indispensable factor in Christian ethical decision making, this issue cannot be settled by quoting a few biblical texts.

2. There are very few biblical references. There are no references to homosexuality in the Gospels. So far as we know, Jesus never mentioned the topic, apparently assuming traditional Jewish teaching on the subject. In the New Testament, only the Pauline tradition refers explicitly to homosexual acts, and that only three times (Rom. 1:26–27; 1 Cor. 6:9; 1 Tim. 1:10).

3. Each of the three New Testament references appears not as a topic in itself (which the New Testament never addresses as such), but as an item in a list illustrating a larger, more fundamental point: human sinfulness seen from the point of view of the Old Testament and Jewish tradition. The Romans text occurs in the theological section illustrating a doctrinal point on the basis of the standard Jewish understanding of Paul's day (chaps. 1–11), not in the parenetic section instructing Christians how to live (chaps. 12–16). That other sins such as greed and party spirit (cliquishness) appear

in these lists should give all readers pause in singling out one act as especially sinful.

4. Paul regards homosexual acts, like the other sinful acts he mentions, as the willful choice of a heterosexual person who has intentionally perverted the way God created him or her. The concept of homosexuality as a sexual orientation not chosen by the person, but received as part of God's creation, was unknown to Paul.

5. In much of his argument in Rom. 1:18–32 Paul reflects the line of thought of Hellenistic Judaism, according to which Gentile idolatry inevitably led to immorality and "the exchange of natural sexual roles," an argument explicitly developed in Wisdom of Solomon (see 11:15–16; 12:24–27; 14:12, 26).

1:28–32 Every kind of wickedness: Such vice catalogues were a common technique of ancient moralists (see also 1 Cor. 5:10–11; 6:9–10; Gal. 5:19–21; Eph. 4:31; 5:3–5; Col. 3:5, 8; 1 Tim. 1:9–10; 6:4–5; 2 Tim. 3:2–4; Titus 3:3). They are illustrative of the nature of sin, not definitive.

1:31 Foolish, faithless, heartless, ruthless: The list is not a random accumulation, but derives its rhetorical power from its cumulative impact climaxing in these four well-chosen words. **Applaud others:** This comment portrays sin not as human weakness that fails to live up to its ideals, but as active rebellion, arrogantly replacing God the Creator with its own assertive ideas of right and wrong, celebrating its own lifestyle.

2:1–16 The Righteous Judgment of God

2:1–3 Judge others . . . condemn yourself: Paul now turns to those respectable and moral types (Jews or Gentiles) who join in condemning the more flagrant sins of the Gentile world, but who assume they are immune from God's righteous judgment (see the same rhetorical strategy in Amos 1–2). While they are free from the vices condemned by the culture, they commit the root sin of refusing to honor God as God, living in their own self-centered world. Thus Paul addresses not merely a negative "judgmental attitude," the opposite of which would be "tolerance"—worldly society joins in condemning the former and praising the latter. What Paul opposes is the more fundamental sin of supposing that condemning social wrongs exempts one from accountability before God.

2:4 God's kindness meant to lead you to repentance: God's forbearance, delay in punishing sin, is not to be misunderstood as approval (see

2 Pet. 3:9, 15). Again, Paul is following the standard teaching of Hellenistic Judaism, which had already declared this (Wis. 11:23; see on Rom. 1:26–27 above). Repentance is not mere sorrow for individual sins (which the self-righteous person does not acknowledge anyway), but reorientation of life (see on Luke 3:7–9).

2:6–8 Repay according to each one's deeds: The principle of God's judgment is at stake here: God functions as judge only by rewarding good and punishing evil. This is God's standard of judgment. Paul is not here discussing whether people actually live in such a way as to be acceptable before the righteous judgment of God on their own merits. He will later make clear that if God carried through the divine judgment on this basis, no one would be saved (3:9–4:8). Yet Paul's affirmation of grace cannot be heard prematurely; God's yes cannot be heard until the no to human sin is sounded. God's gracious yes must be heard in such a way that God's ultimate standard of righteous judgment is not compromised but affirmed. All this shows how seriously Paul takes the image of the Last Judgment. That God is the righteous judge is axiomatic for Paul (see 5:9; 12:19; 13:4–5; 14:10; 1 Cor. 4:4–5; 11:31–32; 2 Cor. 5:10; 1 Thess. 1:9–10).

2:8 Self-seeking . . . who obey not: The ultimate sin is not a matter of the peccadilloes and compromises of daily life ("nobody's perfect"), or even the violations of the Ten Commandments. These are only the expression of the deeper self-orientation, the making of myself the center of my universe, making myself into my own God, and thus refusing to obey God as God. Such self-orientation is often affirmed in our culture as having a healthy ego and sense of self-esteem.

2:9–11 There will be: The righteous judgment of God is not manifest in everyday life, in which the wicked are often healthy, prosperous, and socially applauded. God's ultimate judgment is still future and final (2:16).

2:11 No partiality: God's ultimate judgment is universal and plays no favorites. **Jew first and also the Greek:** See on 1:16–17.

2:12–16 Apart from the law . . . under the law: If all human beings are ultimately judged by the same divine standard, what is the role of the law in God's plan, and what is the meaning of God's choice of Israel to be a special people called by God and given the law? This profound problem troubled Paul and his readers, and Paul often pondered it deeply (Rom. 7;

9–11; Gal. 3–4). Here Paul only makes a twofold point: (1) All human beings live under the law of God, whether it be the law of the Creator revealed in nature (1:18–32) or the law of Moses revealed on Mount Sinai (2:17–29). (2) What counts, however, is not merely having the law, but living by it, for this is the basis of God's judgment.

2:17–29 The Jews and the Law

2:17 You call yourself a Jew: Paul, of course, is not addressing Jews in general, but the Jewish-Christian readers in the Roman church (see the introduction to Romans). He addresses Jewish people not as though they were inherently self-righteous or hypocritical, but because they represent the very best moral and religious life the world had to offer (see 9:4–5; Phil. 3:3–11 on Paul's reflection on his own experience as a good Jew; see on Luke 18:18–30).

2:19–24 A light to those in darkness: Paul does not compose ad hoc charges against the Jews, but alludes to the role of Israel as portrayed in the biblical prophets: Israel's mission is to teach the world God's law, to bear witness to God among the Gentiles as a "light to the nations" (Isa. 42:6), but Israel's own failure to keep God's covenant law caused **the name of God** to be **blasphemed among the Gentiles** (Isa. 52:5; Ezek. 36:20).

2:25 Circumcision: The sign of God's covenant with the Jews (Gen. 17:1–14; Lev. 12:3; 4:9–12; Gal. 5:2–12; Phil. 3:3). In some Jewish thought of Paul's day, God will honor those marked with the covenant sign and deliver them from judgment because they belong to the chosen people (see Luke 3:7–9). Paul follows some streams of Old Testament thought and Hellenistic Judaism in reinterpreting the sign of circumcision in an interior, spiritual manner (see Deut. 10:16; Jer. 4:4; 9:26; Ezek. 44:7).

2:29 It is spiritual and not literal: See 7:6; 2 Cor. 3:6; 1 Sam 16:7.

3:1–8 Paul Counters Jewish Objections

3:1 What advantage has the Jew? The reader following the line of Paul's argument (see the introduction to Romans, comments on 1:18) expects the answer "None! All persons stand on equal footing before the God who judges impartially." Paul does in fact come to this conclusion in 3:9–20. But the paradoxical logic of God's saving plan makes room both for God's impartiality in judging the whole world and for God's faithfulness to his promises made to the covenant people Israel.

3:2 The oracles of God: Israel received not only God's revelation in nature, but God's revelation of his will in the Law and his covenant promises contained in Scripture.

3:4 By no means!: This very strong Greek expression, used 14x by Paul and elsewhere in the New Testament only in Luke 20:16, can also be translated "God forbid" (KJV), "May it never be" (NASB), "Certainly not" (TEV), "Of course not" (NAB), "Out of the question!" (NJB). **Let God be true** (NIV): Paul cites Ps. 51:4 and alludes to Ps. 116:11.

3:5 Should we say . . . God is unjust?: Paul wants to avoid misunderstanding by posing the argument of an imaginary objector (a common ancient rhetorical technique called "diatribe"). "If our unrighteousness only serves to show by contrast how righteous God is, is it not wrong for God to condemn us for it? And if our sin only gives God more opportunity to show how gracious he is in forgiving it, should we not continue to sin to further illustrate how good God is?" The argument was not meant literally, but was intended to reduce Paul's gospel of unconditional grace to absurdity and show that it was a danger to moral decency. Then as now, objections to the grace of God are made in the name of preserving moral standards. Paul's full answer to this objection is found in 6:1–23. Here he simply rejects the charge by appealing to God's judgment of the world, axiomatic for him (see on 2:6–8).

3:9–20 None Is Righteous

3:9 All . . . under the power of sin: The noun "sin" occurs here for the first time in Romans (see on 3:20 below). Human sinfulness is here thought of not as an accumulation of mistakes, but as being subject to a power that sweeps all human beings before it like an irresistible flood (Paul elaborates in 6:15–7:25). The Jew/Gentile distinction, like the righteous/unrighteous distinction, disappears into the common situation of all humanity in bondage to the power of sin.

3:10–18 Paul recites a collection of biblical passages he has assembled to show that the understanding of universal human sinfulness he advocates is not a new Christian doctrine, but is repeatedly documented in the Jewish Scriptures. Nor is his view of human sinfulness a matter of observing the human scene (which always appears to us as a mixture of good and evil). This perspective on the human situation is a matter of revelation, derived from Scripture and the Christ event. While the revelation was given in Israel's

Scripture, it reveals the situation of humanity as a whole.

3:10–12 No one who is righteous: See Eccles. 7:20. **Not even one:** Ps. 14:2–3.

3:13–14 Throats . . . tongues . . . lips . . . mouths: Ps. 5:9; 140:3; 10:7. One might expect the bodily location of sin to be in the "heart," stomach, or genitalia, but Paul selects images of human sinfulness that focus on speech, a theme of biblical theology that locates language at the center of our being (see Isa. 6:5; Matt. 12:36–37).

3:15–17 Feet . . . paths . . . way: Isa. 59:7–9. The other image on which Paul focuses is the path one walks, one's "way of life." In this collection of images, sin is not a matter of attitude, but of concrete words and deeds, what one says and what one does.

3:18 No fear of God: Ps. 36:1. See on 1 Pet. 1:17. The root sin is failure to worship God as God (1:20–21; 2:1–3).

3:19 Speaks to those who are under the law: Paul has cited texts from the Psalms and Isaiah, but uses "law" as the generic term for God's revelation, as is common in Judaism (see also 1 Cor. 14:21). In this context, the point is that the Jewish Scripture not only condemns flagrant Gentile sins, but addresses Jews, to whom the law was entrusted, and specifically includes them in its declarations of universal human sinfulness. **Every mouth may be silenced:** The result of Paul's argument and citation of Scriptures is that no human being, Jew or Gentile, may raise a claim against God. All stand justly condemned in the divine courtroom.

3:20 No human being will be justified: Paul concludes with a paraphrase of Ps. 143:2 (see Ps. 130:3), but adds his characteristic **"by deeds prescribed by the law"** (see Gal. 2:16), summing up his argument that no one can be accepted before God on the basis of claiming to have kept God's law. **Through law comes the knowledge of sin:** Although the law cannot justify, it is from God and serves God's purposes, one of which is to reveal human sinfulness. The law can reveal the difference between right and wrong, but as law it is powerless to produce the right it calls for (Paul elaborates in 7:7–12).

The first part of Paul's argument concludes by having silenced all human claims before God. All—Jew and Gentile, "good" and "bad"—stand condemned before the holy God. There is nothing that can be done from the human side to bring about reconciliation and salvation.

EXCURSUS: THE PAULINE UNDERSTANDING OF SIN

1. Paul's understanding of universal human sinfulness is sometimes seen as too "pessimistic," in contrast to the "positive" view of human potential in the teaching of Jesus. But while the Jesus of the Gospels does not develop a "doctrine" of human sinfulness, like Paul he simply assumed that all human beings are sinful and in need of God's forgiveness (see, e.g., Matt. 6:12; 7:11; Luke 11:4). On this issue, one cannot flee from Paul to Jesus.

2. Sin not a matter of "one's own business," but is directed against God and affects others. Paul rejects the popular cultural understanding that "I can do what I please as long as I'm not hurting anyone else." For Paul (and Jesus), every act has "horizontal" social consequences, for every human life is enmeshed in the whole human network, and "vertical" consequences in regard to one's relation to God. Actions "only" against oneself or other humans are also—or primarily—against God (Paul cites Ps. 51:4; see Luke 15:18).

3. In the biblical perspective sin is not a "mistake," a "missing the mark" (though the Greek word itself can mean this), but rebellion against God. Sin is thus aggressive, not passive, an assault against the truth of God, the "way things are" (1:18).

4. Paul almost always uses the term in the singular, as a quasi-cosmic power to which human beings are subject, not in the plural, as the accumulation of individual wrong actions.

5. Perhaps the most difficult aspect of Paul's biblical understanding of human sinfulness is that there is **no difference** (3:23 [NIV], the climax of his argument). We naturally relativize our sins, and can always point to people who are worse than we are. Is there really no difference between Hitler and Mother Teresa? Of course Paul and the Bible generally affirm the important relative differences between human good and evil. This is never questioned. But Paul's point is that in terms of one's standing and acceptance before God, all such distinctions are blotted out, and all are equally unable to justify themselves before God.

Paul's portrayal of the desperate human situation prepares the way for the good news to come.

3:21–4:25
The Divine Response: God's Act in Christ for the Salvation of All Humanity

Paul now turns to the good news of God's act in Christ and its meaning for Christian faith and life.

475

3:21–31 God's Justifying Righteousness
This paragraph is one of the most concentrated, tightly woven statements in all Paul's letters, partly adapted from previous Jewish-Christian creedal and liturgical material (3:25–26). It is not easy reading, but rewarding to the patient student who works carefully through it (in more than one English translation) pondering each phrase.

3:21 But now: The contrast is not between two religious theories, law and grace, but between the human situation seen apart from Christ and the human situation regarded in the light of God's saving act in the cross of Christ. Paul does not regard the crucial turn in saving history to be the "life and teaching of Jesus," but God's act in the cross and resurrection. Though expressed in temporal-sounding then/now language, the contrast is not chronological, as though God changed his relationship to humanity at Bethlehem or Golgotha. Paul will emphasize in the next section (4:1–25) that God has always been gracious and that believers have always been justified by trust in God's faithfulness. **Apart from law:** Acceptance by God is (and has always been) on another basis than keeping the Law. **The righteousness of God:** See on 1:17 for the meaning of this crucial phrase. **Is attested by the law and the prophets:** Justification by grace through faith is not a change of plans on God's part. As Paul is about to illustrate (4:1–25), the Jewish Scriptures document that this has always been God's way of accepting those who trust in him.

3:22–25 The faith(fulness) in Jesus Christ: This ambiguous Greek phrase can mean either human faith or God's faithfulness manifest in Christ—or both meanings simultaneously (see on Gal. 2:16). **No distinction . . . all have sinned:** See on 3:20. **His grace as a gift:** Salvation is not earned by human merit, but granted freely by God's grace. Salvation is not based on who we are and what we have done, but on who God is as revealed in Christ, and what God has done in the event of Christ's life, death, and resurrection. **Redemption:** The image is that of liberating someone from slavery (see Paul's elaboration in 6:15–23). **Whom God put forward:** Jesus did not put himself forward in our place to appease an angry God. God himself provides the sacrifice, taking human sin and alienation into himself and thus nullifying it. The event involves two parties, God and humanity, not three parties, God, Jesus, and humanity (see on 2 Cor. 5:19). **As a sacrifice of atonement:** The language and imagery is taken from the Old Testament sacrificial ritual of the Day of Atonement (Lev. 16:13–15), in which sacrificial blood was poured on the lid of the ark of the covenant in the innermost sanctuary of the tabernacle. This mercy seat was the place where God *dwells* (1 Sam. 4:4; 2 Sam. 6:2; Ps. 80:1), where God *speaks* (Exod. 25:22; Num. 7:89), and where God *atones and reconciles* by the shedding of blood (Lev. 16:13–15). This "mercy seat" provided by God is Christ, who represents God in all three roles. **By his blood:** I.e., by giving his life. In biblical terminology "blood" and "life" are often used synonymously (Gen. 9:4; Lev. 17:11, 14; Deut. 12:23; Ps. 72:14; Ezek. 3:18; Jonah 1:14; Mark 14:24; John 6:53–54; 1 Pet. 1:19).

3:26 He himself is righteous: God's saving act does not compromise God's own righteousness, but manifests and confirms it. God's righteousness is not a passive quality, but an active putting-things-right, an act of God that creates a new situation. God's act in Christ does not change God, but creates a new situation, a new relationship between God and humanity. Paul here affirms the early Christian faith that the world really is different because of God's act in Christ.

3:27 What then becomes of boasting?: The terminology reflects Paul's recent dispute with Jewish Christian opponents in Corinth (see 2 Cor. 1:12; 5:12–13; 7:4; 11:1, 22; 12:5). The REB catches Paul's meaning here: "What room then is left for human pride? It is excluded. And on what principle? The keeping of the law would not exclude it, but faith does." Salvation by grace excludes the possibility that one group could flaunt its own privilege or accomplishment against another group, whether it be law keepers versus lawbreakers or believers versus unbelievers. The affirmation of God's grace means that even faith cannot be seen as a human attainment that allows believing insiders to "boast" that they are believing insiders. As the Old Testament as a whole is now seen in the light of God's act in Christ, the Law has become for Christians the **law of faith** (see 8:2; 1 Cor. 9:21; Gal. 6:2).

3:28 Justified by faith: Luther's translation added "alone" to this verse; though the word is not explicitly in the Greek text, "faith alone, without works of the law" is Paul's meaning (see on 1:5, 16–17). James 2:14–26 rightly warns against a misunderstanding of Paul, but nonetheless Paul's own view will not allow salvation to be seen as a combination of faith and works or a cooperative enterprise between God and humans—salvation is entirely the gift of God's grace appropriated by faith. This faith must not be seen as a human achievement for which the believer can take credit, but is itself the gift of God (see on 8:28–30; Eph. 2:8; 1 Pet. 1:1–3, 21).

3:30–31 God is one: An echo of the Shema, the basic Jewish confession of faith (see Deut. 6:4; Mark 12:29; 1 Cor. 8:4; Jas. 2:19). Since God is one, the Creator of all that is and of all people, God does not have one program for saving Jews and a different program for saving Gentiles. **Do we then overthrow the law?:** As in 3:19 and 1 Cor. 14:21, "law" includes the whole Old Testament. In Paul's situation "overthrowing the law" was not a hypothetical issue. His Jewish-Christian opponents suspected that his law-free gospel both rejected God's revelation in the Scripture and undermined morality (see on Gal. 3:1–5:1). **We uphold the law:** Salvation by faith does not mean that God's revelation in the Law and Prophets can be simply set aside. Though in the heat of argument Paul sometimes seems to have only a negative view of the role of law, he insists that the Law is from God, plays its proper role in God's saving plan, and must be understood positively in the light of God's act in Christ (he elaborates in 7:1–25).

4:1–12 The Examples of Abraham and David

In 1:2 and 3:21 Paul had declared that the gospel of justification by faith was not a Christian innovation but was witnessed to by "the law and the prophets" of Jewish Scripture, the Christian Old Testament. He now illustrates this by the examples of Abraham and David.

4:1 Abraham is introduced not as a random example, but as the hero of Jewish faith who had already been used as the key example by Paul's Jewish-Christian opponents in the Galatian dispute (see on Gal. 1:7; 3:6–18). The Abraham story is found in Gen. 12–23, presenting God's new beginning after the judgment of the world in the flood (Gen. 6–9) and the tower of Babel (Gen. 10–11). God, the Creator of the world and all peoples, calls Abraham and Sarah to found a new family that will become a new covenant people as God's agent and mission in the world, a mission that is ultimately for the sake of blessing all peoples (Gen. 12:1–3). **Our ancestor according to the flesh:** Not just biologically, but "from a human point of view" (see Gal. 4:23; 2 Cor. 5:16).

4:2 Something to boast about: Boasting is not necessarily bragging, crowing, and strutting, but may mean "taking credit for, accepting responsibility for" (see 3:27).

4:3 Believed God: During the dispute with the Galatian false teachers, Paul had reread the Abraham story through his Christian eyes and discovered this text (Gen. 15:6) that presents Abraham as already declared "righteous" by God on the basis of his faith, not on the basis of his own achievement. (On Paul's use of Scripture, see excursus, "New Testament Interpretation of the Old Testament," at 1 Cor. 15:3, and 1 Pet. 1:10.) Even Abraham's faith was not something he could "boast" about (see 3:27; 4:2), since it was a response to God's initiative, call, and promise. Genesis 15:6 had already been interpreted in some streams of first-century Jewish tradition in a way that combined Abraham, faith, and righteousness in a manner similar to Paul (see 1 Macc. 2:52; Jub. 14:7; 30:17; and from the Dead Sea Scrolls, 1 QS 11:2–22; 4QMMT, last line). It is this stream of Jewish interpretation that Paul develops in the light of God's saving act in the cross of Jesus. Thus Judaism should not be stereotyped as uniformly advocating "works righteousness." So also Jas. 2:21–24 cites this same verse, understood in the light of Abraham's willingness to sacrifice his son Isaac (Gen. 22), and thus understands Gen. 15:6 in a way different from Paul. These examples illustrate that the interpretation of Scripture is never absolute but is always conditioned by its location within a particular tradition at a particular time, place, and social location.

4:5 Him who justifies the ungodly: The shocking nature of Paul's statement is intensified when one remembers that the Old Testament had forbidden "justifying the ungodly" (Exod. 23:7; Prov. 17:15; Isa. 5:23). Abraham is not, of course, called "ungodly" in the Bible; Paul extends the example of Abraham to include everyone (as he will next illustrate by appealing to David, 4:6–8). Paul's radical point is that God does not merely supply the lack that good (but not quite perfect) people have, but graciously justifies those who are totally lacking. The gospel is not that if you try hard and do your part, God will make up the rest, but that God's grace extends even to the ungodly, those Paul has described from Scripture in 3:9–20.

4:6–8 So also David: The Psalms, too, are found already to teach justification by faith. (Martin Luther came to his great insight while lecturing on the Psalms.) Abraham had been the model of the "good" person who does not trust in his own goodness, but in God's grace. David (assumed to be the author of Ps. 32:1–2 that Paul here quotes) was the model of the "bad" person (= repentant sinner). Paul's radical point: "no difference" (3:23)—they are *equally* in need of God's grace, and *equally* recipients of it. The word "reckon" (also translated "credited" [NIV], "counted as" [REB]) that binds together the two passages has legal connotations, but is not a matter of a "legal fiction," as though the judge treats the accused "as if" they were not guilty. The judge's pronouncement of "guilty" or "acquitted" is not a legal fiction, but is performative language that creates the reality it pronounces. Those who trust in God are declared righteous, accepted, by the divine judge, and so they *are*.

4:9 Only on the circumcised?: On the importance of circumcision as the sign of God's covenant, signifying that one belongs to God's people, see on Gal. 1:7, 10; 2:3; 3:6; 5:2–6; Acts 7:8; 15:1. His opponents' insistence on it is not mere "legalism," but their understanding of being faithful to God's commands written in the Bible. Paul's proclamation of the law-free gospel to Gentiles, including them in the continuing people of God without circumcision and obedience to the food laws, is a serious problem to some of his Jewish-Christian colleagues, including leaders in the Jerusalem church to which he is en route as he writes Romans (see the introduction to Romans, 15:22–32). It is thus important for him to clarify that his gospel is not a rejection of God's Law written in Scripture.

4:10–11 Before or after: Just as Jesus in similar situations had appealed "over the head" of Moses and the Mosaic Law to Scripture's statement of God's original intention (see, e.g., Mark 10:2–12), so Paul appeals to God's original promise to Abraham, who antedated Moses (see Gal. 3:6–29, still fresh in Paul's mind, but here expressed in a more moderate tone to a readership that—in contrast to the Galatians—includes Jewish Christians). Paul's point is that God had already accepted Abraham on the basis of his faith, prior to the command to be circumcised. Circumcision was thus the sign and seal of faith, not the condition of his acceptance by God. Abraham who became the "father" of Jews was an uncircumcised "Gentile" when called and accepted by God (see Matt. 1:1). **Ancestor of all who believe:** The "according to the flesh" of 4:1 is now extended, as is the "our." The Genesis

story of Abraham, like the whole Old Testament story of God's dialogue with Israel through history, is now regarded as the story of all people of faith, Jew and Gentile. All who believe like Abraham are his "children," i.e., belong to the chosen people of God, and Abraham becomes a symbolic figure uniting believing Jews and Christians.

4:13–25 God's Promise Realized through Faith

4:13 The promise ... not ... through the law: These phrases summarize two fundamentally different and mutually exclusive ways of relating to God. The one way relies on God's promise; the other way relies on human achievement. The promise is not exacted but is God's free choice; it does not exclude human response and responsible action, but it does exclude making a legal claim on God by human action, whether this be the human action of keeping the law or the human action of "believing in Christ." Even "faith" can be presented to God as a "work," a human achievement substituted for "keeping the law." Paul's gospel of salvation is oriented to God's promise, not to human acts, whether these be "works" or "faith." **Inherit the world:** The original promise to Abraham was the land of Canaan, later known as Israel and Palestine (see Gen. 15:18–20; 17:8). By Paul's time the promise had already been reinterpreted to refer to ultimate salvation on a renewed earth (see Matt. 5:5), a symbolic picture of eternal life, ultimate salvation.

4:17 Father of many nations: See Gen. 17:5. Originally, the incredible promise that the aged and impotent Abraham would become the ancestor not only of Israel, but of the other nations physically descended from him (Moabites, Ammonites, Edomites, the Arab clans). Paul now understands this in the light of Gen. 12:3 and the Christ event to mean that Abraham is the spiritual father of all believers, the whole people of God, Jews and Gentiles. **Gives life to the dead:** Paul, whose own faith is centered on the God who raised Jesus from the dead (4:25; 1 Cor. 15:3–5), sees Abraham as already having a kind of resurrection faith. The God who gives life from the dead, who generates hope when there is no hope, is the God who acted in the "dead" bodies of Abraham and Sarah to give new life (4:19). (For another perspective on Abraham's resurrection faith, see Heb. 11:17–19.) For Paul, God's act in raising Jesus is the paradigmatic event that defines the meaning of faith, but those such as Abraham who trust in God's impossible promises have resurrection faith without ever having heard of Jesus. Abraham, who never heard of Jesus, can be for Paul the model of Christian faith because Abraham's God is the same God active in Jesus, and Abraham's faith is the same faith active in Christians. Paul provides a way of affirming the particularity of God's act in Christ as definitive for who God is and what faith is, without disqualifying as believers those who have not come to this explicit faith in Christ's resurrection. Here is a chapter written by a Jewish Christian that can be pondered by both Jews and Christians engaged in Jewish-Christian dialogue. **Calls into existence:** The God of resurrection is the God of creation—and vice versa. God is the one who creates out of nothing, the Creator who is not hampered by having nothing to work with. This is the same God who "justifies the ungodly" (4:4).

4:18–19 Hoping against hope: The God who raises the *dead*, creates out of *nothing*, and justifies the *ungodly* is the God who gives hope when there is no hope, when humanly speaking there is no reason to hope, when the only commonsense "realistic" thing to do is to give up hope and accept things as they are. Abraham and Sarah are the models of believers who, with full awareness of "the facts," trust in God's promise. Some scribes in copying this text inserted the word "not" before "**considered his own body**," supposing that Paul's meaning must have been that in order to believe, Abraham looked away from the reality of his impotent old body. This is the opposite of the radicality of Paul's understanding of faith, which trusts in the promise of God while looking the reality of the situation squarely in the eye.

4:21–22 God was able to do what he had promised: Faith was in God, not in abstract ideas. God had promised, and Abraham believed God's word, even though he did not see *how* the promise could be fulfilled. Paul does not mention that Abraham even tried to help God out of the "impossible" difficulty, getting God off the hook by trying to have the promise fulfilled in Abraham's and Sarah's own "commonsense" way (see Gen. 16–17). Even this lack of faith did not eliminate Abraham from the roll of those who truly believe; authentic faith is never "pure," can never say "of course," but is always mixed with doubt, which it incorporates into itself and presents honestly and trustingly to God.

4:23 Written not for his sake alone: See 15:4; 1 Cor. 9:10. In Paul's view the stories found in Scripture are not mere ancient history, but are addressed to later generations of Christian believers, who find their own faith reflected and nourished there. Just as later generations of Israelites were urged to read the earlier stories as events that happened to them (Deut. 5:1–10; 26:1–11, noting the change from "them" to "us"), so biblical faith is never merely the acceptance of ideas found in the Bible, but telling and retelling the story as *our* story.

4:24–25 Believe in him who raised Jesus our Lord: The twofold formula of v. 25 ("was handed over . . . was raised") probably represents pre-Pauline Christian tradition, a creedal summary of the faith analogous to 1:3–4; 3:25–26; 10:9–10; and 1 Cor. 15:3–5. The creed is about God (not about Jesus). God is the subject of clauses. The Christian God is not God-in-general, but the God who has defined himself by his saving act in Christ's death and resurrection.

5:1–8:39
The Christian Life as Freedom

A new section begins at 5:1 and extends through 8:39. As the previous sections have shown the saving act of God in response to universal human sinfulness, this section presents what it means to live in the world as those who trust in the God who has accepted them in Christ without any merits of their own. Paul presents what it means to be Christian, not as following the teachings and example of Jesus (the Gospels approach discipleship more from that perspective), but as life in the community of faith in God's saving act. The basic thesis of this section: Christian life is a life of *freedom*, a life in community liberated from the threats that destroy life. The contents of this section might be captured in this rough outline:

Chapter 5: Freedom from alienation, judgment, and the wrath of God
Chapter 6: Freedom from sin
Chapter 7: Freedom from the Law
Chapter 8: Freedom from death and the cosmic powers that separate from God

5:1–11 The Results of Justification

5:1 We have peace with God: Not subjective "peace of mind," but the objective state of peace that is the cessation of hostilities, living one's life in the situation of no longer being at war with God, no longer alienated and hostile, no longer under the threat of God's righteous judgment. "Peace" also connotes the objective state of well-being, the good life God intends expressed in the Hebrew *shalom.*

5:2 We have obtained . . . we stand . . . in our hope: On the language of salvation, see on Acts 16:31. Paul repeatedly emphasizes the three dimensions of God's saving act. (1) Salvation is based on something that really happened in the *past,* namely, Christ's death and resurrection, and the believer's conversion and coming to faith—"we have obtained." (2) Salvation is a *present* process, a matter of present experience—"we stand." (3) The process is not yet complete, but awaits a *future* consummation—"our hope." See also the threefold pattern in vv. 8–9:

past: **while we were still sinners Christ died for us**

present: **now that we have been justified**

future: **will be saved through him from the wrath of God**

So also in v. 10:

past: **while we were enemies, we were reconciled to God**

present: **having been reconciled**

future: **we will be saved by his life**

    (i.e., by the reality that he still lives)

This three-dimensional, already-but-not-yet understanding of salvation is characteristic of biblical theology, so that the biblical answer to the question, "Are you saved?" (a legitimate question that ought not be abandoned to fundamentalists) is, "Yes, I was saved by God's act in Christ; yes, I am in the process of being saved; and no, I am not yet saved, but confidently await salvation at the victory of God's kingdom." **We also boast:** Christians "boast" in God's saving act (as in 5:11), not in their own achievements (contrast 3:27; 4:2). **The glory of God:** What was lost by human sin (3:23) is restored in the future triumph of God's kingdom.

5:3–4 Suffering . . . endurance . . . character . . . hope: The Christian life does not spare believers from present troubles, but places them in the framework of God's ultimate purpose for the world ("produces hope") and molds believers into the image of the suffering Christ ("produces character"). The point is not that suffering develops character in the cultural sense of making one tough or improving one's personality, but that one's life is seen to be incorporated into God's larger purpose for the world and history, a purpose that will finally prevail. Paul's theology makes no sense apart from this eschatological hope—the sure confidence in the final coming of God's kingdom. In this Paul and Jesus are one.

5:5 God's love: The context indicates the primary meaning is God's love for us, but our love for God and others is also included. **Poured into our hearts through the Holy Spirit:** Love is the result of God's work in us, not the product of our own efforts. We love because God first loved us (see 1 John 4:19).

5:6–9 We were still weak: I.e., unable to extract ourselves from the vicious circle of human sinfulness described in 3:9–20. **Christ died for the ungodly:** I.e., for all, see on 1:18; 4:5. The fundamental sin common to all humanity is "ungodliness," refusal to worship God as God. **God proves his love . . . Christ died:** It was God who acted in Christ; God's love was made known in Christ's willingness to go to the cross (see on 3:25; 2 Cor. 5:19). **Justified by his blood:** See on 3:25. **Saved . . . from the wrath:** From the righteous judgment of God (see on 1:18; 1 Thess. 1:9–10).

5:10 We were reconciled to God: Not "God was reconciled to us." The cross did not overcome God's hostility to us—it was never there—but human alienation from God. Most people have never thought of themselves as hostile to God, and do not discover this by self-examination. This aspect of the human situation is a matter of God's revelation (see 1:18–3:20). Paul understands the human instinctive drive for self-defense and self-justification, the effort always to be sure that one is "OK" in the eyes of others and oneself—Paul understands this drive as making us actual *enemies* of the God who loves, accepts, and justifies us freely by his own grace. This asserting of ourselves, concern with our image and our self-image, is the placing of a "graven image"—an idol—in the place God reserves for himself, an effort to be our own God (Gen. 3:1–5; Exod. 20:1–6). The acceptance of God's grace is the end of all efforts at self-justification, ends the hostility, and opens up one's life to God, others, and oneself.

5:12–21 Adam and Christ

5:12 Through one man: The story of the "fall" (= rebellion) of humanity is found in Gen. 1–3. God created the world and human beings "good," but humans were not content to be God's grateful creatures. Adam and Eve wanted to be "like God" (Gen. 3:6). Paul understands this story of the primal human sin as the story both of the human race as such and of the individual person Adam (which means "human" in Hebrew). **Death came through sin:** Death is here understood not as the "natural" end of human life, but, like "sin," a transcendent power (see 3:9) that overcomes and enslaves human life. **Because all have sinned:** Some older translations, based on the Latin Vulgate and not on the original Greek text, translated "in whom," thus supporting the view of "original sin" as the genetically transmitted sin and guilt of Adam's transgression. The better translation is "because" or "with the result that." The meaning is not that God punishes all later human beings for the sin of Adam, but that Adam's story is the representative story of everyone.

5:14 Death exercised dominion from Adam to Moses: God's Law was not given until Moses' time (Exod. 20), so sin was not "reckoned" (counted, registered, attributed to each person's "account") between Adam and Moses. But the presence and power of sin was nonetheless clear in that all people died. Sin and death are inseparably connected in biblical thought, but the correlation is not individualistically one to one, as though only those who sin die. The thought is corporate, involving the human race as such: all humans die, because the universal power of sin has all humanity in its grasp.

The type of the one who was to come: Adam was a prototype and model of Christ in that the act of each had universal effects. Adam released sin and death into the world for all people; Christ released justification and life into the world for all people (see also Paul's use of this image in 1 Cor. 15:20–28).

5:15 The free gift is not like the trespass: Adam and Christ are not merely compared, but contrasted. God's act in Christ does not merely balance what Adam had done, but extravagantly overbalances it. **Many . . . many:** In biblical terminology "many" is often used in the inclusive sense, being contrasted not with "all" but with "few" (see, e.g., Isa. 53:6, 12; and compare the "many" of Mark 10:45, rightly understood as "all" in 1 Tim. 2:6). The point is not "many-but-not-all" (for Adam's sin affected all in that all die, not just "many"), but "many, not few"—in other words, "all." Thus Paul himself replaces "many" with "all" in 5:18. Paul's whole point is that God's act in Christ is as universal as Adam's act, affecting all human beings. What Adam undid for all, God in Christ has more than restored for all. This is one of several "universal salvation" passages in Paul, but it is not to be understood undialectically, without regard for human responsibility and decision, as Paul himself immediately makes clear in 6:1–23. For reflec-

tions on "Universal Salvation and Paradoxical Language," see the excursus at Rev. 22:21.

5:19 One man's obedience: The fundamental relation of human beings to God is that of creature to Creator, servant to Lord. This is what Adam (and the "Adam" in every human being) resists and rejects. All humans since Adam are "disobedient," i.e., refuse to have God as their God. Some know they should be obedient to God, but cannot or will not. Most reject even the idea that the meaning of human life is grateful acknowledgment of one's status as creatures who owe God gratitude, obedience, and praise. Over against this universal picture of human disobedience, Paul presents Jesus as the one person in human history who realized in his own existence what it means to be a truly human being. He was truly obedient to God. Here—rare in Paul's theology—it is not only Jesus' death but also how he lived his life that is the saving event (cf. Phil. 2:8, where Jesus' whole life is characterized as "obedience"). Jesus' obedience was God's saving act that reversed previous human history and created a new humanity. Christians are incorporated into this new reality by baptism (6:1–11; 1 Cor. 12:13), so that their lives are no longer determined by the old Adamic reality.

5:20 But Law came in: Paul continues to respond to the Jewish-Christian concern for the role of the Law in God's plan (see 2:12–16; 7:7–25; Gal. 3–4). The Law is from God, but it cannot control sin.

5:21 Sin reigned . . . so also grace might reign (NIV): In Jesus Christ the rule of sin is broken, and a new sovereignty takes over. **Through Jesus Christ our Lord:** Paul concludes each section (later to be numbered as chapters—see structure above) with this solemn formula. Throughout he is not expounding a theory of religious truth, but explicating the meaning of God's act in Jesus Christ our Lord.

6:1–14 Dying and Rising with Christ

6:1 Should we continue in sin?: This is the classical objection to salvation by grace, always sincerely made by those who fear that without the requirement of the Law and the threat of punishment, morality is undermined and there is no reason to try to live an ethically responsible life. "Law restricts sin; grace encourages sin" is the banner not merely of "legalists," but of some whose concern is for right living, for living according to God's will. Paul's previous reference in 3:5–8 shows the objection was not merely theoretical, but an actual personal charge made against Paul. How may one respond to the charge, if God graciously forgives and saves all anyway, why even try to "be good"? The section 6:1–7:6 gives a three-part response. You cannot continue in sin because (1) (6:1–14) something has happened that makes it impossible: Christ has died to sin and you have been joined to Christ in baptism; (2) (6:15–23) you are no longer a slave to sin but belong to a new master; (3) (7:1–6) a new situation has been brought about by the death of someone else that makes continuing in the old situation impossible.

6:2 By no means!: "Absolutely unthinkable!" With this very strong expression (see on 3:4) Paul could not say more forcefully that the proclamation of God's grace takes the reality of sin seriously and in fact delivers from sin's power in a way that the religion of law and threat could never do. The doctrine of grace never backs away from the declarations Paul has made (e.g., 2:1–16) about human accountability to God for moral conduct. **We who died to sin:** Paul responds to the charge not with an abstract argument but by appealing to something that has happened, a twofold event: Christ died to sin, and you have been baptized. These two events are integrally related. In 5:12–21 Paul has already explained that the death of Jesus was not the isolated event of a single individual, but that Christ was a representative figure, the founder of a new humanity. The meaning of Jesus' death has been explicated in 3:21–26 as effecting not only forgiveness and reconciliation with God, but also "redemption," i.e., liberation, freedom. Jesus' death was a dying-out-from-under the power of sin, not only for himself, but for all those united with him. It effected not only forgiveness, but deliverance from the power of sin (see also 2 Cor. 5:14–21).

6:3 All of us who have been baptized: Paul assumes that all Christians have been baptized. He never argues *for* baptism, but *from* baptism, as the common history of all Christians to which he may appeal. **Baptized into Christ:** Baptism is not only a personal experience, but places a person "in Christ," i.e., in the body of Christ, the church (see 1 Cor. 12:13; Gal. 3:27). Baptism is not individualistic but a matter of incorporation (literally "embodiment") within the Christian community. The Christian's life is lived in a new sphere of existence, a new force field that determines all his or her relationships (see on 2 Cor. 5:17 for the Pauline phrase "in Christ"). For Paul, baptism

is not a mere initiatory ritual, entrance requirement, or subjective experience, but an event in which something really happens, an event in which God is active. The Christian is **united with him** (6:5) in baptism, literally "fused" together with Christ, so that the story of Christ becomes the Christian's story. The meaning of baptism is not determined by the believer's feelings about or understanding of baptism, but by God's act. As in a marriage ceremony, something objective happens that changes the person's status. It may take a lifetime of experience and reflection to probe the meaning of the event, but its reality is not determined by the candidate's feelings or doctrine at the time.

6:4 Buried with him: The imagery reflects baptism by immersion, the universal practice of the church in Paul's day. By passively being lowered into the life-threatening and life-giving water, the believer enters the world of death and is raised to a new life. This is not only an imitation of Christ's example—though it is this, since Jesus, too, was obedient to God by being baptized (Matt. 3:13–17; Mark 1:9–11; Luke 3:21–22; John 1:29–34)—but a reenacting of the saving event of Jesus' death and resurrection in which Christ's story becomes the believer's own biography.

6:5 If we have been united with him: "If" here has the meaning of "since," as one might say to a U.S. citizen who was shirking his or her duty, "If you are an American, you will. . . ." The argument is "since X has happened, Y will follow." **We will be united in a resurrection like his:** The Christian life is lived between two poles, the "already" and the "not yet." We *have already been* united with Christ's death in baptism, and we *will be* united with him in the future resurrection. In the meantime, our present life is determined by these two real events, one past and one future (on the past/present/future dimensions of salvation, see above on 5:2). Paul here comes short of saying that Christians are already "risen with Christ." The resurrection is a firm future hope, but in the present the Christian's life is marked by solidarity with Jesus' self-giving love for others on the cross, not by the triumph of the resurrection (see also Phil. 3:10–11). Later writings in the Pauline tradition relaxed this tension and saw the Christian life as already participating in the power of the resurrection, as did some writers in the Johannine school (see Col. 2:12; 3:1; John 11:1–44). Paul himself considered this a dangerous view, and other members of the later Pauline tradition rejected it as heretical (see 2 Tim. 2:18). Paul's point here is not abstract theology, but concretely practical: you cannot go on willfully sinning by appealing to God's grace, because you have been united to Christ's death in baptism, and your life, which will someday share the triumph of the resurrection, now bears the mark of the cross.

6:6 Our old self: As elsewhere in the New Testament, words for "body," "soul," and "spirit" are used interchangeably to refer to the whole person, the "self" (see on Luke 10:26–28; 1 Cor. 3:3–5; 6:14; 1 Thess. 5:23). The "old self" is the self determined by belonging to Adam, my "natural, this-worldly self," understood in its own terms apart from God. This self has died, has been put to death when Christ was put to death. This radical statement of Christian self-understanding is not an "ought," as though Paul were saying "we really must try harder to kill the old, pre-Christian desires that still plague us and try to live by new Christian ideals." He has imperative statements (see 6:12–23), but every imperative is based on the reality of a preceding indicative. Here the statement of Paul in Gal. 2:27, "I have been crucified with Christ," is not the rigorous ideal of super-Christians like Paul, to which we ordinary folk might aspire but mostly can only admire from a distance. Rather, "our old self was crucified with him" is the simple statement of fact, the reality of what has happened to every baptized Christian. It is not an ideal to be admired, but a reality to be lived out.

6:7 Whoever had died is freed from sin: This standard dictum of rabbinic theology affirmed that only death frees from sin. Paul adopts and adapts this saying to his Christian perspective: the death that frees from sin has already happened in Christ, and the Christian already participates in this victory over sin's power.

6:8–10 Death . . . sin: These two powers are linked in Paul's thought (see 5:12–21; 1 Cor. 15:56). The defeat of sin was the defeat of death; death loses its power over those who know they are forgiven and accepted by God's grace.

6:11–12 Consider yourselves dead: This is not a matter of fantasy or mental gymnastics, but a call to awareness: Think about what it means that you have been joined to Christ in baptism. The first imperatives directed to the reader are found here (see 6:6 above on indicative and imperative). **Do not let sin reign:** Sin is a defeated power that need not dominate our lives. Based on this indicative, the imperative

is no longer simply a noble human struggle against evil, but means that every willing sin is a needless concession to a defeated enemy, an orienting of one's life to a lame-duck administration on the way out.

6:14 Sin will have no dominion over you: Unless you let it, yielding to a defeated enemy. **You are not under law but under grace:** Human beings are not autonomous, not finally in control, have no voice in whether they are born and die; all human life is "under" some external power. Human beings cannot choose whether their lives will be subject to external powers; believers can choose which power they will live under. The good news is that the dominion of the triumvirate Sin, Death, and Law has been defeated, and that believers' actual life is in the sphere of God's triumphant grace.

6:15–23 Slaves of Righteousness

6:15 What then?: Paul begins afresh with the challenge of 6:1, setting forth his second response (see on 6:1), this time with a different image: slavery. The metaphor is objectionable to us, but was an unchallenged element in the social structure of the first century. Both Paul and Jesus (e.g., Matt. 6:24) used this imagery to portray the meaning of authentic life before God. Paul's second response: "You cannot go on willfully sinning, because you were a slave subject to sin's domination, but you have been set free in order to serve a new master!"

6:16 You are the slaves of the one whom you obey: Paul and other biblical writers consider human life itself to be inherently a kind of slavery; human beings are by nature not autonomous subjects free from all constraints, but creatures. Our life is not self-contained, but always finds its meaning and point of orientation in some allegiance beyond itself. We are born into a human race already enslaved to sin and death (see on 5:12–21), and live in a world alienated from God and subject to hostile external forces that prevent it from being the good life for which human beings were created (see on 8:19–22). Thus for Paul, Christ's willingness to enter this world meant assuming human nature and the role of a slave (Phil. 2:7; cf. also on Gal. 1:10). By Christ's death and resurrection, believers are delivered from slavery to the power of sin, but are not thereby transferred into some autonomous realm of self-centered "freedom"—this illusion is itself a kind of slavery. The situation is analogous to a prisoner's release from jail: the new freedom is freedom indeed, but is now subject to another set of constraints, those of society. The effort to live in absolute "freedom," ignoring the rules of society, simply lands one back in prison. Christians are set free to serve God, to be slaves of God, "in whose service is perfect freedom" (*Book of Common Prayer*).

6:17 The form of teaching: Though Paul has never visited Rome (1:13), he can presuppose that the Roman Christians have received a collection of Christian teaching that sets forth the meaning of the Christian faith. We do not know the particular contents of this body of tradition, but it presumably included such creedal and instructional material alluded to by Paul in 1:3–4; 3:25–26; and 4:25. When his Roman readers became Christians, they were entrusted to this body of Christian teaching (not vice versa), i.e., they were committed by God to a new pattern of living set forth in the living tradition of the church. This tradition assumed an authoritative role in the shaping of their Christian lives. They did not simply get together and discuss their opinions on religious issues, but were instructed in a form of teaching that helped them be servants of God rather than servants of sin. **6:23 Wages . . . free gift:** The contrasting words are carefully chosen. The point is not that if one works for sin, the payment is death, but if one works for God, the payment is eternal life. Sin pays its debts, but eternal life is the free gift of the gracious God, not the payment for services rendered. **In Christ Jesus our Lord:** See on 5:21.

7:1–6 An Analogy from Marriage

The general theme of chapter 7 is freedom from the law (see structure at 5:1). Paul's "teaching" about the law is complex and many-sided. He never writes a systematic treatise, an essay that neatly pulls together his variety of statements about the role of the law in God's plan, but responds ad hoc to the various needs of his churches (see especially Gal. 3–4; 2 Cor. 3).

7:1–3 Do you not know, brothers and sisters?: This paragraph is a continuation of his response to the objection, "If God is gracious, why not keep on sinning?" (see structure outlined at 6:1). Here Paul's point is a legal one: the death of one partner in a marriage places the other partner in a completely different situation. **If her husband dies, she is discharged from the law:** The analogy would seem to call for the death of the law, but Paul continues.

7:4–5 You have died to the law: He is dealing with the objection, "How can the death of someone else affect my situation?" The mar-

riage analogy does illustrate that. But it is not the law that died. The "someone else" who died is Christ. His death is the central event that makes everything different (see 3:23–26; 5:1–11; 6:2–8). Paul's point is that the death of Christ with which believers are united in baptism sets them free, not only from sin and death, but from the law. **So that you may belong to another:** In the back of Paul's mind is the image of Israel the people of God as God's marriage partner, i.e., bound in covenant to God so that worship of other gods was spiritual "adultery" (see, e.g., Hos. 1–3; Ezek. 16; 23; Isa. 50:1; 54:1–6; Ps. 45; and the Song of Solomon were also interpreted this way in early Judaism). The Jewish Christians Paul addresses were trying to be faithful to this biblical image. They were tempted to think that acknowledging Gentile Christians who did not keep the law as full members of the people of God meant abandoning the covenant. This would be a kind of spiritual "adultery," i.e., a rejection of their true "husband" ("Lord" and "husband" were the same word in the Hebrew Bible). Paul explains that a death has occurred that makes the "legal" situation different. The analogy is not neatly exact, since Christ both died and was raised, is both the one whose death sets us free from the old law and himself the new "marriage partner" who allows us to begin a new life (see Mark 2:18–20; John 3:29–30; Eph. 5:22–33; Rev. 19:1–10; 21:1–9; 22:17). The new union is blessed by God and is to bring forth the fruits of the Christian life in the Spirit (see Gal. 6:22–25). **While we were living in the flesh:** See on 7:14.

7:6 Old written code . . . new life of the Spirit: See 2:29; 2 Cor. 3:6. The "letter" that kills is not the law itself, but the law as controlled by sin, as Paul hastens to clarify.

7:7–13 The Law and Sin

7:7 The law is sin? Paul's negative statements about the law, as well as Paul's proclamation of salvation by grace apart from the works of the law, could well lead the unwary reader to think that Paul considers the law itself as sinful (see 3:20; 4:15; 5:13, 20; 6:14–15; 7:1–6; see esp. Gal. 3–4). The equation of "dying to sin" (6:10) and "dying to the law" (7:6) seems to confirm this. **By no means!** See on 3:4. Paul utterly rejects the charge that his gospel equates the law with sin. **I would not have known sin:** See 3:20. Through the centuries the chief problem of interpretation for Rom. 7

has been the identification of the "I." There are three main positions:

1. The "I" is autobiographical, as Paul describes his pre-Christian experience. In this view, Paul recounts how he tried to keep the law as a Jew, ended in despair, and thus welcomed the gospel of grace he found at his conversion to Christianity. But elsewhere Paul never indicates that in his pre-Christian life keeping the law was a burden or problem, and Phil. 3:1–6 indicates precisely the opposite.

2. The "I" is autobiographical, describing the internal conflict that Paul first experienced as a Christian. When Paul received the Holy Spirit at his conversion, this initiated an internal conflict common to all Christians who struggle to live by the Spirit rather than the old life of the "flesh." This view has been held by Augustine, Luther, and many Protestant interpreters, and seems to be confirmed, not only by the struggles that all Christians experience, but by Paul's own statement in Gal. 5:16–18 which does refer to the Christian life. In this context, however, it is difficult to see Paul describing a Christian struggle, since he has just written 6:6–7, 17–18, which portrays the Christian as delivered from the power of sin, and will continue with 8:1–39, which celebrates the Christian's life in the Spirit that overcomes the struggle with sin and death.

3. The best solution, preferred by most interpreters today, does not regard the "I" as primarily autobiographical, but as representative of human experience as such. Paul recounts the human story and the story of Israel in the personal "I" form with which every reader can identify, recounting human experience prior to and apart from Christ, but as seen only from the Christian perspective. This corporate, generalizing use of the first person is found often in the Psalms (e.g., Ps. 23:1) and is frequently used elsewhere by Paul (3:7; 1 Cor. 6:15; 10:29–30; 13:1–3, 11; 14:11, 14, 15; Gal. 2:18–21; 6:14). Paul now sees, from his Christian perspective, the reality of his situation under the law, though he did not see it then. His point has to do with the objective situation under the law, not the subjective experience of the person. The real subject throughout 7:7–25 is sin, the power that commandeered God's good law and perverted it into an instrument of condemnation. **You shall not covet:** Exod. 20:17, the last of the Ten Commandments. Paul knows that a respectable person of good morals can check off most of the commandments (You shall not murder, you shall not steal, you shall not commit adultery, etc.) with the authentic response, "I may not be perfect, but I haven't done *that*." Such a person is tripped up by the last commandment, which forbids not only external acts, but internal desires. Such people usually do not notice that the same is true of the first and primal commandment to worship God and no other (Exod. 20:1–6; see on Rom. 1:18–25).

7:8 Apart from the law sin lies dead: Paul is recounting in universally personal terms the experience of the human race he has described in 5:12–14. Sin was there prior to the giving of the law, but not recognized for what it was. When the law appeared on the scene, the good law given by God was commandeered by the power of sin, so that it actually provoked sin. The negative command is not only powerless to prevent sin, but actually provokes it (like the dentist saying, "Now don't swallow"). Paul knows that this is true not only for those who are obvious lawbreakers, but insidiously true of those who like himself had kept the law. His very zeal to do God's will as revealed in the law had actually led to his persecution of the church (see Gal. 2:13–14; 1 Cor. 15:9). The law is not sin, but the deceptively evil power of sin is seen in that it works through the law that is **holy and just and good (7:12)**, and through the sincere intention of those who try to live by the law.

7:11 Deceived: The Law misled its devotees into believing that it was more powerful than sin, that all one needed to defeat sin was a good law and the will to follow it.

7:14–25 The Inner Conflict

7:14 The law is spiritual . . . I am of the flesh: The conflict is between the will of God revealed in the Law, which is "holy and just and good" and "spiritual," i.e., comes from God, and my earthly, human existence apart from God. The conflict here described is thus not an internal one between "components" of human existence, the "lower" fleshly part and the "higher" spiritual part. In Paul's terminology, "flesh" refers to the whole of our human existence, including our highest ideals and aspirations, as belonging to this world (see 8:5–13; 1 Cor. 3:1; 2 Cor. 5:16; 10:2; Gal. 3:18; 4:23, 29). Thus the NEB's translation of "flesh" by "our lower nature" is misleading and unfortunate. The solution to the human dilemma is not resolutely to follow our "higher nature," but to rely on God's grace revealed in Jesus Christ and to live in the power of the Holy Spirit given by God to all Christians (see 8:1–17). Thus what is described here is not the internal struggle of the Christian (see on 7:7), but universal human experience prior to and apart from Christ, as seen from the Christian perspective.

7:15 I do not understand my own actions: The word translated "understand" can also mean "approve," "recognize and accept as my own." It is not a matter of cognition but of *recognition*, not of knowledge but of *acknowledging* one's actions as representing oneself (see Amos 3:2, where God is aware of all nations, but "knows" [= acknowledges, approves] only Israel; Ps. 1:6 RSV; Matt. 7:23; 1 Cor. 8:3).

7:16 The law is good: This is the point of the whole discussion: justification by grace through faith apart from the works of the law does not mean the law itself is sin.

7:17 No longer I . . . but sin: This is not a superficial claim to avoid responsibility for one's own actions ("Don't blame me—the devil made me do it"). Paul describes the objective situation of humanity apart from Christ, under the domination of sin (6:15–23). The Christian counterpart is found in Gal. 2:20: "No longer I, but Christ."

7:24–25 Wretched man that I am: While there is a sense of incompleteness in the Christian life that longs for the deliverance and justice of God's eschatological future (see 8:18–27; Matt. 5:6), in this context Paul can hardly intend this despairing cry of wretchedness to be the self-understanding of the Christian. It represents the objective situation of the person apart from Christ, who can never extricate himself or herself from the world's evil and from personal sin by his or her own efforts. **This body of death:** There is here no contrast between the "good" soul or spirit and the "evil" body. "Body" refers to the whole person as belonging to the world of sin, law, and death (see on 7:14). **Through Jesus Christ our Lord:** See on 5:21. **With my mind . . . with my flesh:** This statement seems to be in such conflict with its context that it may belong earlier in the paragraph as a summary of the human situation apart from Christ, or, as many interpreters believe, may be a later marginal gloss by a scribe mistakenly copied into the text here. In any case, it cannot represent Paul's summary description of Christian existence as presented in the following paragraphs.

8:1–17 Life in the Spirit
Chapter 8 continues the section 5:1–8:39, which describes the life of those justified by God's grace

through faith (see structure at 5:1). Just as believers are accepted by God through no merit of their own, so their present Christian life is not merely the result of their own efforts (though not without them), but is empowered by God's Spirit at work in the Christian community.

8:1–2 No condemnation: The law has lost its power to condemn, and Christians no longer live under the threat of God's punishment. **In Christ Jesus:** On the meaning of "in Christ," see on 2 Cor. 5:17. **The law of the Spirit:** The law, the revelation of God's will, was originally and inherently "spiritual" (7:14) before being commandeered by sin. The Christian is set free from the law as dominated by the powers of sin and death to live by the revelation of God's will, the law as it was intended to be, namely, "life in Christ." When the law is linked with the life-giving Spirit instead of sin, it recovers its life-giving original function (see Deut. 30!) and no longer enslaves and condemns (see 13:8–10, and Matthew's way of presenting the same issue, Matt. 5:17–20). Paul here summarizes the law in the light of God's Spirit as "life in Christ." God's revelation of the way of life is not finally a set of rules for every occasion (not even the "teachings of Jesus"), but living in a manner appropriate to those who belong to Christ. What this means in particular is not always easy to discern (see on 12:2). The law so understood is not enslaving but liberating (1 Cor. 9:21; Gal. 6:2; see Jas. 1:25; 2:12). For other "summaries of the law" see 13:8–10; Matt. 22:34–40. **Set you (NRSV)/me (NIV) free:** Some manuscripts read "you" (sing.) and some read "me." We do not have the original text of any New Testament document, which must be painstakingly reconstructed from the hundreds of manuscripts, no two of which are exactly alike (see "Introduction: The New Testament as the Church's Book," 4.d, and comments on Mark 16:9–20; Luke 2:14; 5:39; 8:26, 43; 10:1; 14:5; 22:19, 43–44; 23:34; John 7:53–8:1; Acts 8:37; 1 Cor. 2:1; 14:34–35, and the footnotes throughout the NRSV and NIV).

8:3 The law, weakened by the flesh: On "flesh," see on 7:14. Though such terminology is awkward to modern ears, Paul's meaning is better retained throughout this section by the NRSV than the NIV's translation of "flesh" as "sinful nature," which suggests that Paul is talking about one component of human nature, in contrast to our "higher nature." Here "flesh" in Pauline terminology refers to human life as a whole and as such, not one aspect or part of it in contrast to our "better nature." Paul's point is that the law was not able to overcome the power of sin in the world, but—like humanity and God's good creation as a whole (see 8:18–23)—was itself overcome and victimized by the domination of sin. God sent the law and it was not sufficient to deal with the problem. God sent his Son, i.e., God himself came in the person of his Son and overcame the domination of sin. **In the likeness of sinful flesh:** This does not mean that Jesus came in a human disguise, only appearing to be human. Christ assumed a fully human existence, was like all other humans with one exception: he was truly obedient to God. Paul is not concerned with the "sinlessness" of Jesus in the sense of personal transgressions of the law. Paul thinks of sin as a dominating power, not merely as violation of commands. His point is that Jesus entered fully into sin's domain, the world of human beings, and defeated sin on its own turf.

8:4 Requirement of the law might be fulfilled in us: The law aimed at realizing the will of God in people's lives, but was itself overcome by sin and failed. The sending of Christ to do what the law could not do does not mean that God abandoned the original purpose of the law. God did not simply set the law aside, but met its requirement in a new way: the will of God is not realized by obeying a list of rules, but by living one's life "in Christ" in the power of the Spirit.

8:5–8 Minds on . . . the flesh . . . the Spirit: The "mind-set" oriented to this world and its possibilities is contrasted with the mind-set oriented to the world as transformed by God's act in Christ. See the similar contrast between two ways of orienting one's life in Jesus' teaching in the Gospels (Matt. 16:23; Mark 8:33). **Those . . . in the flesh:** Here "in the flesh" means the same as "according to the flesh" of 8:12, referring to those who live their lives in the realm dominated by the flesh (7:14; see Gal. 4:23). Paul can also use the phrase in a neutral sense referring to the bodily existence "in the flesh" of all human beings including Christians (see Gal. 2:20; Phil. 1:22).

8:9–10 Spirit . . . Spirit of God . . . , Spirit of Christ . . . Christ in you: These phrases are all identical and are different ways of referring to the presence and power of God at work in the life of the Christian community and the believer (see on 1 Cor. 12:12–31, esp. 12:13). Rather than being the property of some "spiritual" elite within the church, the Holy Spirit is the life-giving breath that animates the body of Christ

to which all Christians belong. **If anyone does not have the Spirit of Christ** (NIV): The reference is not to the "attitude" of the earthly Jesus that Christians should imitate, but to the objective reality of the Spirit given to every Christian at baptism (Acts 2:38; 1 Cor. 12:12–31).

8:13 You will die: The word "death" throughout this section points beyond mere physical death—which is the lot of all, believer and non-believer alike—to the life-destroying power of death that, in partnership with sin and the law, keeps life from being what God created it to be. Paul's contrast between "death" and "life" is analogous to the contrast between "perishing" and "eternal life" in John 3:16 (see Deut. 30 for the ultimate context).

8:14 Children (NRSV)/**sons** (NIV) **of God:** The Greek text reads "sons," as in 8:15, 19, 23, 29, 32, a designation for all Christians, male and female, and interchangeable with "children" in 8:17, 21. It is important to realize that Paul's word "son" is the same word he uses for Jesus as "Son of God" (Paul never uses "child" in this christological sense). In Paul's culture and in biblical tradition generally, "son" had a different set of connotations than "child." "Son" implied heir, agent, and image of the father. All these connotations are present in designating Christians as "sons" of God, coheirs with Christ the Son, our "elder brother" (see 8:29).

8:15–17 When we cry "Abba": See on Mark 14:36; Gal. 4:5. **Joint heirs with Christ:** The image of "heir" captures the already/not yet reality of Christian existence: Christians already have full confidence in belonging to God's family as those whose full inheritance lies in the eschatological future (see 1 Pet. 1:3–5). **Suffer with him . . . glorified with him:** Life in Christ is marked in the present by the sign of the cross, self-giving love in the service of others, and in the future by sharing in the resurrection life of the glory of God at the fulfillment of God's plan for history (on "glory," see 1:23; 2:7, 10; 3:23; 5:2; 6:4; 8:21; 9:4, 23).

8:18–30 Future Glory

8:19 The creation waits with eager longing: Like all biblical apocalyptic thinkers (including Jesus), Paul believes that God is not concerned merely with saving individual souls out of the world, but is determined to save the creation itself (see on Rev. 20–22). The created world is portrayed in personal terms, standing on tiptoe awaiting the future transformation that Paul and other first-generation Christians believed was soon to come.

8:20 For the creation was subjected to futility: Sin not only overwhelmed and perverted human life, but enslaved the whole creation, preventing it from being the good world God originally made (repeatedly in Gen. 1:1–2:4; esp. 1:31). When humanity sinned,

> Earth felt the wound, and Nature from her seat
> Sighing through all her Works gave signs of woe,
> That all was lost. (John Milton, *Paradise Lost* 9:30)

Paul and other apocalyptists did not see the violence and evil of the "natural" world—in which, for example, every living thing lives by devouring other living things—as simply "natural," the "way things are." Neither is the world "fallen," as though there is something inherently wrong with the matter of the physical universe (as the gnostics argued), but it was subjected to futility by God, as part of God's judgment on human sin (see Gen. 3:14–19).

8:21–22 The creation itself will be set free: The present state of the world with its evil is accepted as real, but it is not the Creator's last word. This is not merely Paul's speculation, but is a firm element in biblical hope (see Isa. 11:6–9; 65:17, 25; 66:22, and the daily prayer of Christians, "Thy kingdom come, thy will be done *on earth*"). Along with humanity, the creation itself has been **groaning in labor pains**. On "labor pains" as an image for the present suffering of the world that will eventuate in new life in the birth of the "messianic age," see Mark 13:8; 1 Thess. 5:3; Rev. 12:1, and the introduction to Revelation: "Apocalyptic Language and Symbolism."

8:23 The first fruits of the Spirit: As creatures in God's world, Christians sigh along with the whole creation, longing for God's eschatological triumph. As the firstfruits of the coming age, the Spirit within and among them is already a promise, foretaste, and guarantee of God's new world that has dawned in Christ (see on 1 Cor. 15:20).

8:24 In hope we were saved: On the three-dimensional nature of salvation, see on 5:2. This is the only place in Paul's undisputed letters where "saved" is used in the past tense, and here it is inseparably attached to future hope. Hope does not mean pious wishing ("we hope we win the game," "we hope we will get a raise next year," "we hope she gets well"), but sure confidence in the future reality, though it is not yet seen.

8:26 We do not know how to pray: This confession is part of the anguish of an unredeemed creation. Paul prays, in community worship and in private, but despite his theological education, his encounter with the risen Lord, and the depth of his religious experience including miracles and visions, he does not claim that he knows how to pray. This is not false modesty, but the acknowledgment that speaking to God is not a casual matter that can be learned. Yet in our stammering efforts to pray, despite all our confusion and doubts about what prayer really is, the Holy Spirit within and among us knows our deepest longings that we cannot articulate even to ourselves, and brings them before God. The community of the Spirit need not turn its praying over to spiritual experts, or wait until it has "learned how to pray" before it really prays. Prayer too is a gift of God, not a human achievement.

8:28 In all things God works for the good (NIV): The NIV is here more accurate than the NRSV. Some ancient manuscripts of Romans have a Greek text that can be translated "**all things work together for good**" (see NRSV, and comments on 8:2). Paul is not claiming, however, either that God directly causes everything that happens, or that in some impersonal, Pollyanna way everything works out for the best. Rather, Paul's faith, based on God's act in raising the crucified Jesus and vindicating him as Lord, is that no matter what happens, the sovereign God is not helpless, but works in all things for the good. This is not demonstrable to the uninvolved spectator, but is a matter of faith **for those who love God** and **are called according to his purpose**. On Christians as called by God, see on 1:1.

8:29–30 Foreknew . . . predestined . . . called . . . justified . . . glorified: Here Paul uses the language of foreknowledge and predestination as assurance to believers that they participate in God's saving plan that stretches from eternity to eternity, not as explanation for why some are not believers. Paul is not writing an essay on God's foreknowledge, predestination, and election, but a pastoral letter to a particular situation. He is not speculating on such deep questions as whether God knows all the details of the future, or whether God can know what will happen without causing it to happen. In chaps. 9–11, he elaborates on his meaning in this particular context.

EXCURSUS: PREDESTINATION

Since language about foreknowledge, election, and predestination is particularly bothersome to many modern readers of the Bible, the following general considerations for interpreting such language are presented to help place biblical statements in their broader biblical and theological context:

1. Foreknowledge, election, and predestination are not minor or marginal themes in the Bible, but come to expression in many biblical texts emphasizing God's sovereignty, including Prov. 16:4; Isa. 6:9–10; 42:9; 46:10; Dan. 2:28; Matt. 13:10–17; 24:22, 31, 36; Mark 4:10–12; Luke 8:9–10; 10:20; 18:7; John 6:64, 70; 13:1, 11; 15:16; 18:4; 19:28; Acts 3:18; 4:28; 15:18; Rom. 8:28–33; 9:11; 11:2; Eph. 1:4; 3:11; 2 Tim. 2:10; 1 Pet. 1:2, 20; Rev. 13:8; 17:8; 20:12.

2. It is easier to say what predestination does not mean that what it means. Predestination does not mean that God is to be blamed for the decision of those who do not believe, or that everything that happens "had to" happen, as though our lives and all history were simply the playing of a tape made in advance.

3. Biblical language of predestination often applies to groups and categories, not to each individual within those categories. The language about "Jacob" and "Esau" has to do not just with the individuals, but with the nations designated by these names (i.e., Israel and Edom). God is pictured as the one who controls the destinies of nations and groups, not the one who predetermines who will belong to those nations and groups. Thus in Rom. 8:28–30, God predestines that those "in Christ" will finally be conformed to the image of his Son, and is not portrayed as deciding in advance which individuals will be "in Christ." As in Rom. 9–11, what is at stake is God the Creator as Lord of history, not the God who makes separate lists in advance of "those accepted" and "those rejected."

4. What God knows and does in the eternal world is expressed in chronological before-and-after terms in our world, but God's act can never be adequately described in this-worldly chronological categories. In Rom. 8:29–30, the past/present/future dimensions of salvation (see 5:2) are all collapsed into past tense statements, so that even the believers' future glory is already spoken of as though it were in the past. Using the past tense for the "not yet" is a way of affirming strong

faith—it is "as good as done" (see the Magnificat, Luke 1:47–55).

5. The language of predestination thus expresses the difference between the human temporal perspective and the divine eternal world. At the moment of decision and action, I know that I am free and responsible to decide and act; in retrospect, I thank God for calling me to the decision and allowing me to make it. At the moment of enlistment, I make my own decision and consider myself a volunteer; in retrospect, I know I am a draftee. Thus in the Gospel of John people come to Jesus in a variety of ways, making their own decision to believe and become Jesus' disciples (John 1:35–51). Yet already in 1:45 the "we have found" is preceded by the "Jesus found" of 1:43, and Jesus later declares to his disciples at the Last Supper that *they* did not choose *him*, but *he* chose *them* (15:16; see 6:70). Augustine prayed, "We could not seek thee, if thou hadst not already found us."

6. In the Bible the language of predestination is not an alternative to "free will." Alongside predestination statements affirming God's sovereignty are "free will" statements affirming human responsibility. Thus in the same context of the Gospel of John salvation is attributed both to (new) "birth" (over which we have no control and do not get to choose) and "belief" (our own free decision) (John 3:3–5, 16, 36). This is biblical language. For example, in 2 Sam. 7:1–17, God promises to David and his descendants that they will always rule over God's people. The promise is unconditional, entirely a matter of God's own sovereign grace and faithfulness; David's descendants are "predestined" by God to rule. It is explicitly said that if the Davidic king sins, he will be chastened and disciplined, but the throne will not be taken away from him; Davidic rule will last forever, for the promise is unconditional (vv. 14–16). This unconditional promise is repeatedly reaffirmed: 1 Kgs. 11:36; 15:4; 2 Kgs. 8:16–19; 2 Chr. 21:7. But the editors of the historical books of the Old Testament have included a series of narratives in which the same promise is made to David's house, with one exception: it is entirely dependent upon the obedience of the Davidic kings to God's covenant demands. This conditional version of the promise to David is found in 1 Kgs. 2:14; 6:12; 8:25; 9:4; 11:38. Here too divine sovereignty and human responsibility are both absolutely affirmed, without any effort to harmonize them. Analogous to the truly human/truly divine christological statements, the juxtaposition of divine sovereignty/human responsibility is not 50/50 or 60/40, but

100/100. God is absolutely sovereign, and we are absolutely responsible. In the Bible, statements of God's predestination are affirmed only in conjunction with statements of human responsibility, without any effort to superficially harmonize them.

7. Predestination statements express the sovereignty and initiative of God, and function as the believers' grateful expression of praise to God for salvation, as the alternative to either taking credit for one's own salvation or making salvation a cooperative enterprise between God and humans.

8. The language of predestination is confessional language, not objectifying analytical language (see on Matt. 2:16; Acts 1:9; Rev. 6:15, excursus 3.b). Though such language points to something real in the transcendent world, the reality it attempts to describe cannot be reduced to objectifying language. It is the language of confession and praise, not discursive language that fits into a logical system from which further inferences can be drawn.

9. The language of predestination is thus never in the Bible a denial of or excuse for human inaction or irresponsibility. It is at the furthest pole from resignation, cynicism, or fatalism. Such language is a joyful call to action, assured that finally all things are in the hands of a loving and faithful Creator.

10. The Bible's language of predestination is the language of worship, the language of grateful praise given by insiders in response to God's gracious choice, not the analytical language of outsiders explaining why God did not choose others.

8:31–39 God's Love in Christ Jesus

8:31–34 If God is for us: "If" does not express doubt, but has the meaning of "since" (see 6:5). **He . . . gave him up for all of us:** The love of God that is the ultimate basis for Paul's hope (5:5–8) is not a theory, but an act (as in John 3:16; see on 2 Cor. 5:19). **It is God who justifies:** The believer need not fear the divine courtroom, since it is the judge himself who has already made the pronouncement, "Acquitted!" **Christ Jesus . . . intercedes for us:** In a related image, it is the risen Christ who pleads the Christians' cause in the heavenly judgment chamber (see Heb. 7:25; 9:24; 1 John 2:1).

8:35–39 Who will separate us?: The enemies are real and must be resisted and endured. But neither this-worldly enemies (Paul's sevenfold list, **hardship . . . sword** [v. 35]) nor transcendent, cosmic powers (Paul's tenfold list, **death . . . anything in creation** [vv. 38–39])

can separate the believer from God's love manifest in Christ. **For your** (God's) **sake we are being killed:** Ps. 44:22, originally a lament and complaint to God, is reinterpreted by Paul as an expression of confidence, but still acknowledging that the people of God are out of step with this world and will be resisted by it. **More than conquerors:** Not by a heroic mustering of our own resources, drawing on our "inner strength" and the like, but **through him who loved us. Death nor life:** Not only is "death" a threat that can potentially separate from God, but so is "life." Some faith is stronger in the face of threatening death than when confronted with a "successful" life that appears to get along quite well without God. But even this insidious threat cannot finally separate us from God's love. **Angels . . . rulers . . . powers:** Paul lists "angels" among the hostile transcendent powers that stand between humanity and God and attempt to separate us from God. Other biblical authors refer to angels as God's good messengers and agents, but Paul's undisputed letters speak of them only in this negative sense (see on Luke 1:10–12; Acts 5:19; Gal. 1:8). **Nor anything else in all creation:** Because the universe is not a neutral mass of matter but the creation of the one God, the believer's life and destiny is secure in the hands of the Creator. This was the faith of Jesus (Matt. 6:25–34; 10:26–31).

9:1–11:36
THE IRREPLACEABLE ROLE OF ISRAEL IN GOD'S PLAN FOR HISTORY

This difficult section has often been either ignored as a parenthesis in Paul's argument, falsely assumed to be about individual salvation, or taken as providing proof texts for the doctrine of double predestination. Recent study of Paul's theology has shown, however, that Paul's argument actually reaches its climax here (see the introduction to Romans). The main theme of Romans is not about the individual's standing before God, but God's plan for history that includes both Jews and Gentiles. The three chapters can be roughly outlined as follows:

9:1–29: *The Freedom of God,* who has not broken his word by justifying Jews and Gentiles by faith

9:30–10:21: *The guilt of Israel,* who is presently responsible for her own rejection

11:1–36: *The hope of the world,* which includes Israel's final redemption, for the present rejection is not God's last word

9:1–18
God's Election of Israel

9:1–3 I have . . . unceasing anguish: The Christian faith began among Jews—Jesus and all his earliest followers were Jews—but by the time Paul writes Romans (ca. 56 CE), though there are numerous Jewish Christians like himself, the church's evangelistic mission to the world had found minimal response among Jews and the church is becoming predominantly Gentile. Paul had always understood that the gospel was directed "to the Jew first" (1:16; 2:9–10). Paul did not intend to preach the Christian message that God accepted Gentiles without the works of the law in such a way that that most Jews would reject it; when they did so, it was a source of great pain to him. If it were possible (8:35, 39), he is willing to be rejected by God (**accursed**) if it would mean the salvation of Israel (see Moses' offer to God, Exod. 32:31–32).

9:4–5 To them belong: Paul lists the blessings that belong to God's chosen people. **The Messiah:** The Hebrew word translated "Christ" or "anointed one," referring to the savior figure who comes from Israel and brings God's salvation to the world (see on Luke 4:20–21; 9:20).

Who is over all, God: The grammar is ambiguous, so that "God" may refer to Christ, or the blessing may be pronounced to God (see John 1:1; 20:29; Titus 2:13, where God-language is used of Christ). Paul's theology suggests that the reference is to God, the actor throughout chaps. 9–11. The acclamation of praise to God here thus forms a bracket with the concluding paean, 11:33–36.

9:6 Not as though the word of God had failed: The major theme of the whole section is the faithfulness of God to his word. God has made promises that Israel would be the chosen people of God, playing a special role in God's plan for the blessing of all peoples (Gen. 12:1–3; Isa. 42:1, 6–7), and this word of God is still valid.

9:7–8 Not the children of the flesh . . . but the children of the promise: On "flesh," see 7:14. As in Gal. 3–4, Paul refers to the Old Testament story in Gen. 18–21 to show that God's promise, not physical descent, is the key factor in belonging to the chosen people (see Gen. 18:10, 14; 21:12; Matt. 3:7–10).

9:10–13 God's purpose of election . . . not by works but by his call: The story of the birth of the twins Jacob and Esau (Gen. 25:19–33) illustrates Paul's point. Both were equally descendants of Abraham; neither had yet done anything right or wrong, but God's promise was extended through the family of Jacob (the Israelites) rather than through Esau (the Edomites). See Gen. 36:8, "Esau is Edom"; and excursus at 8:29–30, "Predestination," 3). The point has to do with God's choice of nations through which the divine purpose in history is accomplished, not the selection of individuals for salvation or damnation. **I loved Jacob but hated Esau:** Malachi 1:2–3. "Love" and "hate" in this biblical idiom have nothing to do with affection and hostility, but mean simply "choose" and "not choose" (see on Luke 14:26, and Deut. 5:9, where "hate" means "not choose," i.e., "reject").

9:14–16 Is there injustice on God's part? See 3:5. God's plan for history reveals God both as finally and absolutely just and as finally and absolutely merciful. **By no means!:** See on 3:4. **I will have mercy:** From the Moses story in Exod. 33:19. **It depends . . . on God who shows mercy:** On Paul's language of predestination in general, see excursus at 8:29–30. On the use of Pharaoh as example, see in particular #8 there. The Pharaoh example is chosen carefully to show that God's election is not random or whimsical, but a matter of God's asserting his power into the human scene to fulfill his purpose for history—a purpose resisted by Pharaoh.

9:19–29
God's Wrath and Mercy

9:19–20 You will say to me: See on Paul's diatribe style at 3:5. Raising such objections himself shows Paul is not composing spontaneously, but is presenting a carefully thought-through argument that takes account of legitimate objections that he takes seriously. **Who indeed are you, a human being, to argue with God?:** If God is God, there is no higher court to which the objector can appeal. Paul first wants to establish God's "right" as the one God, the Creator of all, the One who cannot be called to account by any of his creatures (see Job 4:33; 38:1–42:6).

9:21 Has the potter no right?: Paul utilizes the biblical image of the potter, which had been used not to illustrate the election of individuals, but God's power in forming history and nations (Isa. 29:16; 45:9; Jer. 18:1–11; Wis. 15:7; Sir. 33:13). As Creator, God has the "right" to do as he wills; if God "must" or "should" do something else, then God is something less than God. If the objector believes he or she has something "higher" than God to which to appeal, something to which even God must conform, then the objector has placed something else in place of God, i.e., has made an idol, even if this something is the objector's own ideas of "love" or "justice." This is what Paul will not allow, in the name of the first commandment (Exod. 20:1–6). God must remain God, the One beyond whom there is no higher court to which one may appeal. *This* point must first be established, but it is the presupposition, not the conclusion, of the good news Paul wishes to share. Grace cannot be exacted or compelled, or it is no longer grace.

9:22–24 What if God: God *could* rightfully create some to be accepted and some to be rejected. The point, once made and accepted, turns out to be hypothetical. In *fact*, the God revealed in Jesus Christ has not arbitrarily chosen some and rejected others, but has **endured with much patience . . . in order to make known the riches of his glory for the objects of mercy. Including us:** This phrase reveals that throughout Paul has not been describing the work of God from some assumed spectator stance, but is confessing his own faith that God has in fact chosen and called "us"—apostle and Roman readers, Jews and Gentiles alike—to be his people.

9:25–29 As indeed he says in Hosea: Hos. 1:10; 2:23. In Hosea God is portrayed as the husband who takes back his undeserving wife Israel after her repeated unfaithfulness—the love that will not let us go. Originally directed to sinful Israel, Paul understands this text to point to the inclusion of Jews and Gentiles in the one people of God. **Only a remnant:** The point is not that only a few Israelites are included in the authentic people of God, but—returning to the point of 9:6–8—that those included are the result of God's gracious choice, i.e., that God's *word* has not failed ("sentence" in v. 28 is the same Greek word as "word" in 9:6). Except for God's mercy, Israel is in no better position than the cities of **Sodom** and **Gomorrah,** which received God's judgment. Paul points out this is not his own innovative view, but was already proclaimed in Israel's Scripture (Isa. 10:22–23; 1:9).

9:30–10:4
Israel's Present Stumbling

9:30–33 Gentiles . . . have attained . . . but Israel . . . did not succeed: The topic is not Israel's unbelief but differing perceptions of the role of the law in God's plan. Relying on a combination of texts from Isa. 28:16 and 8:14, Paul

presents a summary statement of why the church of his day was increasingly Gentile, an utterly unexpected development of God's original choice of Israel. He sees the role of the law in God's plan for history as the crucial factor. Gentiles who do not keep the letter of the law but who live by the "law of the Spirit" (see on 8:2) are being added to the people of God by faith, while Israel is increasingly missing out on the new development in God's plan by continuing to insist on a wrong view of the law. The foundation stone laid by God, the gospel, had become a stumbling block to those who did not accept it, precisely like the law. Paul elaborates this in the next section.

10:1 My . . . prayer to God for them: See 9:1–2.

10:2–3 Zealous for God . . . not based on knowledge (NIV): In Paul's view, this zeal misunderstands the nature of God's law, regarding keeping the law as the basis for acceptance before God. **The righteousness that comes from God . . . their own:** See on 1:16–17. God's righteousness is here understood as a power at work in the world, which one may submit to or resist (see 6:12–23).

10:4 Christ is the end of the law: The meaning of the word translated "end" is not clear, for it can mean "end" in the sense of either "termination" or "goal." Paul has already made it clear that the law as such is not abolished by Christ (3:31; see Matt. 5:17–19), but the misunderstanding of the law as the means of works-righteousness comes to an end in Christ, and is replaced by its proper understanding as the "law of faith" (3:27). Paul also understands Christ to be the goal in God's plan for history to which the law was leading (Gal. 3:23–26).

10:5–21
Salvation Is for All

10:5 Moses writes: Paul illustrates both the false and the true understanding of the law from the law itself. As in Gal. 3:12 (which see), he cites Lev. 18:5, "the person who does these things will live." The point is not that no one is able to keep the law perfectly, but that the law is unable to deliver the life it promises.

10:6–8 The righteousness that comes from faith says: It is important for the Christian reader of the Bible to see that Paul does not turn from the Old Testament law to cite the New Testament gospel, but cites another passage from the law itself (Deut. 30:12–13) as testimony to the righteousness from God that comes through faith. At one level, this may seem to be a twisting of the clear meaning of Deuteronomy to force it to give a Christian meaning. But Paul, like the early church in general, understood the Old Testament Scriptures to be the word of the one God, who has definitively revealed himself in the Christ event, and thus found the Christian message already contained in his Bible (see excursus at 1 Cor. 15:3, "New Testament Interpretation of the Old Testament," and 1 Pet. 1:10). The law read in the light of Christ thus becomes the "law of faith" (3:27) and the "law of the Spirit" (8:2).

To bring Christ down . . . to bring Christ up: The original point of this passage in its own context is that Israel need not wonder where God's will is revealed—it is neither in heaven nor in the abyss of the grave, but is clearly revealed in the law. Paul understands these declarations in terms of the revelation of the ultimate will of God in Christ. The law itself forbids trying to do for oneself what God has already done in Christ. The incarnation has already happened—Christ is no longer in heaven, but has come to earth to reveal and fulfill God's will. And the resurrection has already happened—Christ was not left in the defeat of death, but God vindicated him at the resurrection—so God's will is made known in Christ, and God's saving act has already become present reality in Christ. The believers' task is not to reach for God's will and attempt to establish their own righteousness, but to live out their faith in what God has already done. **The word of faith that we proclaim:** Paul identifies both the word of God mediated by the Old Testament law itself and the word about which it speaks as the Christian message.

10:9–10 Confess with your lips that Jesus is Lord: Paul cites two traditional creedal texts from the liturgy or instruction of the pre-Pauline church. Though the Bible rejects ostentatious displays of faith, Christian faith cannot remain a purely personal internal matter between the believer and God, but must be expressed in words and deeds. Paul has in mind not only the "good confession" made by the new convert before the congregation prior to baptism, but the expression of faith in everyday life that acknowledges Christ as Lord (Matt. 10:32; Luke 9:26; 12:1–12). **God raised him from the dead:** Here the whole of Christian faith that God acted in Christ for our salvation is summed up in the confession that God raised Jesus from the dead (see on Matt. 28:1; 1 Cor. 15:3–5). **Heart . . . mouth:** Chris-

tian faith is a matter of the heart, but cannot be confined there. "Internal" faith without "external" confession is as defective as external pretense without faith in the heart, a different kind of hypocrisy, but nonetheless a lack of integrity and faithfulness to God (Luke 11:42–52; John 12:42).

10:11 Put to shame: See 1:16. Paul's citation of Isa. 28:16 (again; see 9:33) means those who confess faith in Christ will not be disappointed, for God will fulfill the promises made in the gospel. He adds the word "**all**" to the Old Testament quotation on the basis of Joel 2:32 immediately cited.

10:12–13 No distinction: The saving counterpart to 3:22. **Everyone:** The citation of Joel 2:32 (see Acts 2:21) emphasizes that the distinction between Jew and Gentile is not obliterated, but no longer matters in Christ (Gal. 3:27–28). **Calls on the name of the Lord:** More than saying, "Lord, Lord" (Matt. 7:21–22; 25:11; Luke 6:46). The invocation of Christ's name in baptism is the initial response of faith to God's act in Christ, which places the whole of one's life under the lordship of Christ (6:1–23).

10:14–15 How are they to call?: The sequence presupposed is (1) *sending* of preachers; (2) the *proclamation* of the Christian message; (3) *hearing* the message; (4) *believing* the message; (5) *calling* Christ's name on the believer in baptism. Paul does not introduce this list in order to explain the process of conversion, but as part of his argument that Israel has had every chance to accept the Christian message. Preachers have been sent, the word has been proclaimed, and they have heard it. The responsibility lies with them—they have not responded to the gospel and invoked Christ's name on themselves. This text has often been used in the discussion of the church's missionary responsibility to carry the gospel to all nations. While the church is indeed under a missionary mandate (Matt. 28:18–20), this passage is not oriented to urging the church to send missionaries. As in Matt. 9:37–38, here the point is that God is ultimately the one who sends forth preachers, and that Christian faith arises from a chain of events initiated by God.

10:16 Not all have obeyed: Paul makes no distinction between "believing" and "obeying" (see on 1:5). Two quotations from Isaiah (52:7; 53:1) point to the joy of those who see messengers of good news approaching (they have "beautiful feet") and the sadness that many do not accept the good news and continue to live as though Christ had never lived. Paul presupposes throughout that the *good news* of which Scripture speaks is the Christian message of God's saving act in Christ, good news rather than good advice, the *announcement* that something has happened that makes all the difference, *not more advice* about "how to live a good life."

10:17 Faith comes from what is heard: It is not the act of hearing (NIV) that generates faith, but the content of what is heard (NRSV), the message of the gospel. The **word of Christ** is not Jesus' teaching, but the word **about Christ** (see NRSV note), the content of the Christian message.

10:18–19 Their voice: Paul understands Ps. 19:4, originally referring to the testimony of the creation to the Creator, as the preaching of Christian missionaries, who in Paul's day had already extended the Christian preaching to large areas of the Mediterranean basin, here rhetorically called "the ends of the world." **Have they** (Israel) **not heard?:** The issue Paul is dealing with is Israel's rejection of the Christian message (see on 9:1–3). The explanation cannot be that they have not heard, for the message has gone throughout the world. **Did Israel not understand?** Paul does not here answer this rhetorical question, but in 10:1–4 has already indicated that Israel's lack of understanding is precisely the problem: they continue to (mis)understand God's revelation in the law in the old, pre-Christian way. Paul cites Deut. 32:21, interpreting **those who are not a nation** as Gentiles. He later elaborates the point that Israel's misunderstanding is in fact providential, for it opened the door to the Gentiles, which will itself provoke Israel to "jealousy" and lead to God's ultimate inclusion of Israel (11:11–36). Thus as Paul agonizes to make some kind of sense of Israel's present rejection of the gospel (9:1–5), he sees God's present inclusion of the Gentiles as itself an expression of God's love for Israel—God's means of provoking them to come to a right understanding that will mean their inclusion with believing Gentiles in the one people of God—and understands this schema to have been already foreseen in Scripture.

10:20–21 Isaiah is so bold as to say: Paul understands Isa. 65:1–2 to apply to the Gentiles who are presently included in God's people (**those who did not seek me**) and those Jews who are presently excluded (**a disobedient and contrary people**). But this is not the last word in God's plan for history.

11:1–10
Israel's Rejection Is Not Final

11:1–4 Has God rejected his people? The Greek grammar indicates this is not a real question, but a rhetorical question anticipating a negative response: "God has not rejected his people, has he?" Throughout this section, Paul is not concerned with the difference between Jewish and Christian faith, but the faithfulness of God to his promises to Israel despite their present lack of faith in Christ. **By no means!:** See on 3:4. Paul supports this conviction three ways: (1) **I myself am an Israelite:** He presents himself as a parade example of a Jew zealous for the law who has come to faith in Christ as the fulfillment of the law and has been included in the renewed people of God. (2) **God has not rejected his people** reflects the promise of Ps. 94:14, where the verb is in the future tense. (3) The example of Elijah (1 Kgs. 18:20–19:18) shows that in a time of widespread rejection, thousands remained loyal to God.

11:5 So too: In Paul's time, though most Jews have not been persuaded by the Christian message, **there is a remnant, chosen by grace**. The Old Testament already saw the purpose of God continued through history not by the people of Israel as a whole, but by a nucleus, the "remnant" (see, e.g., 2 Kgs. 19:4, 31; Ezra 9:8; Neh. 1:3; Isa. 1:9; 10:20–22; 11:11; 37:31–32; Jer. 23:3; 31:7; Ezek. 6:8; 14:22; Amos 5:15; Mic. 2:12; 5:3; Zeph. 3:13; Zech. 8:12). Sometimes, "the remnant" identifies those who have remained faithful while the majority were unfaithful. Other passages refer to those graciously spared by God from a catastrophe that has engulfed the people as a whole. In the present context it is to be particularly noted that Paul understands "remnant" in the second sense—the remnant is constituted not on the basis of Israel's faith or lack of it, but is a matter of the grace and faithfulness of God. Paul sees in the faithful Jews of his own time (in his view, the Jews who like himself had become Christians) the continuity between pre-Christian Israel and the completion of God's plan that will include all peoples, Jew and Gentile, and thus as the proof that God has not abandoned his people.

11:6 Grace . . . works: Paul's argument throughout has been that God has always accepted people on the basis of grace, an absolute alternative to works (see, e.g., 3:21–4:12).

11:7 The rest were hardened: See on 8:29–30; 9:14–18.

11:8–10 As it is written: Paul supports his view of the temporary "hardening" of Israel in God's plan by appeal to Israel's own Scripture, "the law, the prophets, and the psalms" (see on Luke 24:44), by citing Deut. 29:4; Isa. 29:10; and Ps. 69:22–23. Here as elsewhere, the quotations do not agree exactly with our English Bible, which has been translated from the original Hebrew texts, because Paul customarily used the Septuagint (LXX), the Greek translation regularly used by Hellenistic Jews and the early Christians.

11:11–24
The Salvation of the Gentiles

11:11–12 Stumbled so as to fall? By no means!: The same grammar and function as 11:1. **Salvation has come to the Gentiles:** The sovereign God who does not directly *cause* everything that happens but who works *in* everything for good (8:28!) is able even to bring good out of the present situation, when most Jews, the covenant people of Israel chosen by God, have rejected Christian faith. The present unbelief of traditional "insiders" has become the occasion for previous "outsiders," the Gentiles, to be included in the people of God. **Full inclusion:** The argument is that if Israel's present rejection of the gospel has meant blessing to the Gentiles, **how much more** will their future acceptance mean (anticipating 11:26).

11:13–14 Now I am speaking to you Gentiles: Paul has not been writing an abstract essay on Jewish-Christian relations, but is writing a letter to a particular church in a particular situation, the Roman church of 56 CE, composed of Jewish and Gentile Christians who have together experienced a particular history (see introduction to Romans). Developments in Rome had allowed Gentile Christians to become the majority and to neglect the Jewish roots of their own faith. **Make my own people jealous:** Paul sees the church's present Gentile mission as a step in God's plan finally to include Jews and Gentiles in the one redeemed people of God.

11:15 Rejection . . . acceptance: Israel's temporary "stumbling" will not mean their ultimate "fall" (11:11), but their reconciliation and acceptance, described in the eschatological language of **life from the dead**. Paul anticipates that the Jewish people will become "jealous" (the word also means "zealous," i.e., for the law in its true sense as witnessing to Christ), and thus will be ultimately accepted by God within the one renewed people of God. He does not see this as an ordinary event on the plane of ongoing human history, but as a component of the eschatological events by which God will bring history to a worthy conclusion. Paul believed this would happen in the near future, and that his mission to the Gentiles was part of God's preparation for the triumphal end of history. Paul, like other first-century Christians, was mistaken in this view, but it does not invalidate either his faith or the theological insights that this perspective allowed to emerge (see excursus at Rev. 1:3, "Interpreting the 'Near End'").

11:16 First fruits: See 8:23; 1 Cor. 15:20. The present nucleus of Jewish Christians is the pledge that all will finally be included; the holiness of the **root** (faithful Israel) points to the holiness of the whole vine (the whole people of God composed of Jewish and Gentile believers). The metaphor modulates from believing Israel as pledge for the whole people of God to the believing community of Jews and Gentiles as pledge for the whole of humanity. As the "remnant" (9:27–29; 11:5) is the pledge of the future consecration of "all Israel" (11:26), so the church of Jews and Gentiles is the pledge of the future acceptance of all people by God's mercy (11:32).

11:17–19 The olive tree: The image of God's people as a tree planted and tended by God is biblical and traditional (Ps. 1:3; 92:12–14; Isa. 61:3; Jer. 11:16–17). In Paul's analogy, **some of the branches were broken off,** i.e., Jews who did not accept the Christian message were excluded from the ongoing people of God that had been eschatologically renewed by God's sending the Jewish Messiah (see 9:4–5). **You . . . were grafted in:** Gentile Christians were incorporated into Israel and became "honorary Jews." Paul emphatically does not represent God as rejecting Israel and "starting all over" with the church in Israel's place (supersessionism, the doctrine that the church has now taken the place of Israel in God's plan). It is rather the case that Israel the people of God continues through history, and that Gentiles who have come to faith in Jesus as the Jewish Messiah have been incorporated by God into Israel, while those Jews who rejected the Messiah have been temporarily excluded.

11:18 Do not boast: As though God had changed his mind and now favors Gentiles over Jews.

The impartial God has no favorites (1:16; 2:9–11; 3:1–2, 9–20). **The root . . . supports you:** Christians can never be anti-Jewish without rejecting their own roots, their own foundation, their own parents. Salvation comes to them only in continuity with God's choice of Israel as the covenant people in which they are now graciously included.

11:20 Do not become proud: The faith by which Gentile Christians stand is not a human achievement of which they may boast, but a gift of God for which they can only give thanks (3:24–28; 4:2–3, 13; 5:15; 6:23; 9:10–25).

11:23 For God has the power: God is the active subject throughout chaps. 9–11. Human faith and unbelief are finally subordinate to God's purpose and power; even human unfaithfulness cannot nullify God's faithfulness (3:3–4). Without minimizing human responsibility, Paul makes salvation finally a matter of God's sovereignty and faithfulness (see on 8:29–30).

11:24 How much more: See on 5:15. God's eschatological resolution will not merely balance the historical claims of Jews and Gentiles. God's amazing grace will overbalance all claims.

11:25–36
All Israel Will Be Saved

11:25 I want you to understand this mystery: As in Dan. 2:18–19, 27–30, "mystery" does not refer to something necessarily difficult to understand, but to something that has been concealed and can only be known by revelation; the same word is translated "secret" in Mark 4:11 and 1 Cor. 2:7 (see Rom. 16:25; 1 Cor. 4:1; 15:51; Eph. 1:9; 3:3–4, 9; Rev. 10:7). Paul does not claim that he has unraveled the secret of the divine plan on the basis of his own study and reflection, but that it has been revealed to him or some other Christian prophet (see on 1 Thess. 4:2). The "mystery" is God's plan for history that finally unifies Jews and Gentiles in the one people of God. The divine secret is a three-step plan: (1) the present "hardening" of part of Israel, leading to (2) the full number of the Gentiles being admitted to the people of God, which eventuates in (3) the salvation of all Israel, the resurrection of the dead, and the final coming of God's kingdom.

11:26–27 Out of Zion will come the Deliverer: "Zion" is a traditional name for Jerusalem. Paul does not speak of a mass conversion of Israel but of an act of God. He finds his hope expressed in Scripture, combining Isa. 27:9; 59:20; Jer. 31:33. **Ungodliness:** See on 1:18, with which this word forms a bracket. The long and complex argument that began at 1:18 with the revelation of universal sin ("ungodliness" is the primal sin of failure to worship God) now concludes with God taking the responsibility for removing ungodliness (see Hos. 11:8–9).

11:28–30 Enemies: The NRSV adds the interpretative phrase "of God," but Paul may be thinking of Jews who now reject the crucified Messiah as enemies of the gospel (see Phil. 3:18). **Received mercy because of their disobedience:** I.e., it was the Jewish rejection of the gospel that encouraged the Christian missionaries to turn to the Gentiles (see repeatedly in Acts, e.g., 13:42–52).

11:31–32 God . . . merciful to all: Both Jews and Gentiles will finally be accepted by God on the basis of God's mercy, i.e., because of who God is, not because of who they are or what they have or have not done.

11:33–36 The riches and wisdom and knowledge of God: Paul has presented his understanding of how Jewish rejection of the Christian message and Gentile acceptance of it fit into God's plan for history, in Paul's view soon to reach its climax. But history continued, and Paul's projections turned out to be wrong: the world did not end soon, and Gentile acceptance of the gospel did not provoke Jews to jealousy and cause them to accept it. At one level, modern readers of Romans should simply acknowledge this and not try to read contemporary history as though Paul had made predictions about Jews and Christians in the twenty-first century. But does Paul's error invalidate the deeper significance of his theology? He envisioned a history in the hands of God, in which a gracious God will finally bring all peoples, Jew and Gentile, into one redeemed people. A thoughtful rereading of Romans as a letter addressed to a particular situation, a letter full of anguish and hope, still reveals a profound vision of God and God's purposes for humanity that cannot be invalidated by what now appear to be the inadequacies of his first-century apocalyptic worldview (see on Rev. 1:3).

Paul closes his argument with a worshipful confession from Scripture that God's ways are finally beyond our grasp (Isa. 40:13 and Job 41:11, perhaps already combined into a Christian hymn). This has not caused Paul to fold his theological hands in his lap and refuse to engage in hard theological thinking. He has presented his best thinking, based on revelation, Scripture, the experience of the church, and his own personal struggle, but he still does not claim to have understood the mind of God (see 1 Cor. 13:11–12). He has given his best understanding, but at the end of the day, he does not claim that God must finally act in accord with his own theology. Adapting a formula from the Stoic philosophy of impersonal "nature" and applying it to the personal God revealed in Jesus Christ (**from him . . . through him . . . to him**; see 1 Cor. 8:6; Col. 1:16; Heb. 2:10), he commits himself to the Creator and Redeemer of **all things**, confident that even when our best theology is inadequate to fathoming the depths of God's wisdom, we and all creation are in the hands of a faithful and merciful Creator, outside whose care nothing exists.

12:1–15:13
PART TWO—THE CHRISTIAN LIFE AS RESPONSE TO GOD'S GRACE

At 12:1 the content and tone of the letter shift dramatically: from struggling with profound theological issues to practical instruction on life together in the Christian community. Yet one cannot make a neat distinction between Paul's theology and his ethics, as though the one were mere theory but the other is commonsense practice. In Christian ethics, nothing is so practical as a good theory, and on occasion one may offer the serious objection, "That may be OK in practice, but will it work in theory?" We are thinking beings, and action without thought, even if it is right, cannot finally satisfy.

12:1–8
The New Life in Christ

12:1 Therefore: The following instructions on living a life "in Christ" are at the farthest pole from general moralistic advice. They presuppose that one shares the faith presented in the preceding eleven chapters (esp. chaps. 5–8). The imperative of the Christian life cannot stand alone, but is based on the indicative of God's act in Christ and the incorporation of the believer into the Christian community (see on 6:6). **By the mercies of God:** As made real in God's concrete act in Christ (3:21–26; 11:30–32). **To present your bodies:** "Body" is the self, the total person (see on 6:6, 13, 16; 8:23). **A living sacrifice:** The old law required animals to be killed and offered to God on the altar (e.g., Exod. 20:24 and Lev. 3–9 specify the regulations for such sacrifices). Paul here joins that stream of Old Testament and Jewish tradition that emphasized repentance and devotion to God as the real meaning of sacrifice (e.g., Ps.

50:14, 23; 51:15–17). **Your spiritual worship:** The phrase can also be translated "reasonable, rational worship." Authentic worship is devotion to God with the whole self, including the mind (see Matt. 22:37), but it is a "**renewed mind**" (12:12) that no longer claims God must conform to human logic (11:32–36).

12:2 Do not be conformed to this world: "This world" is literally "this age," in contrast to "the age to come" that has already dawned in Christ, the coming age to which the Christian's life is already oriented. The "renewal of the mind" that takes place in Christian faith in the community of the Holy Spirit no longer measures life and its meaning by the standard of secular values. Christians will not only join with other people in opposing the obvious evils of society also rejected by the culture, but often will find themselves swimming against the stream of what is considered self-evidently right by the values commonly accepted. **So that you may discern what is the will of God:** The Christian life is free from the law in the sense that it no longer has in advance a rule for every occasion, but must from case to case discern the will of God for that situation. It is not always the case that **what is good** is clear, the only issue being whether we will do it or not. People of goodwill may differ on what in fact is the will of God for the particular situation. Paul uses the plural "you" throughout, like our colloquial "you all," "y'all" (unlike English, Greek distinguishes singular and plural in the second person). This usage, taken with his discussion of the Christian life in the body of Christ in the same context (12:3–8) shows that Paul does not understand Christian freedom in individualistic terms, with each person free to do what he or she considers right, without regard to the convictions of others (see further on 14:1–15:6). The variety of individual opinions are pooled in the corporate body of Christ, so that in interaction with each other under the guidance of the Spirit, Christians are called on to discern the will of God together. We must decide for ourselves, but not by ourselves.

12:5 We, who are many, are one body in Christ: See Paul's discussion in 1 Cor. 12:12–30. That Paul's list of gifts here overlaps, but does not exactly conform to the list in 1 Cor. 12 shows that Paul does not have a firm inventory of specific "gifts of the Spirit," but celebrates the variety of talents and abilities, "special" and "ordinary," that make real the power of God's Spirit in the life of the church. Though clearly

Paul understands the abilities to live the Christian life and strengthen the life of the church for its mission to be manifestations of God's Spirit, he discusses them as human skills and abilities, and mentions the Spirit specifically only in 12:11. His emphatic "spiritual" terminology in the previous discussion of the same theme in 1 Cor. 12 was occasioned by the Corinthian congregation's own infatuation with spiritual phenomena. Likewise, here there is no ranking of the gifts, unlike the Corinthian situation (see 1 Cor. 12:8), for Paul is not disputing a false evaluation of the more "spectacular" gifts such as tongues, which he does not even mention here. Paul emphasizes the egalitarian activity of the Spirit, who distributes to each and all the variety of gifts needed for a congregation to function as one body of Christ and to carry on its mission in the world.

12:9–21
MARKS OF THE TRUE CHRISTIAN

12:9–13 Let love be genuine: As in 1 Cor. 13:1–3, Paul here considers love to be the supreme gift of the Spirit. As in 1 Cor. 13:4–7, love is not an emotion, but is expressed in concrete caring deeds for the benefit of others. **Contribute to the needs of the saints . . . extend hospitality to strangers:** The Christian community is by definition multicultural, a community where inherited prejudices are overcome and care is extended to those of another language, culture, and race. The particular focus is on traveling Christians and missionaries (see 1 Tim. 3:2; Titus 1:8; Heb. 13:2; 1 Pet. 4:9).

12:14 Bless those who persecute you: See Luke 6:28. The following instructions reflect the way Jesus himself lived as portrayed in the Gospels. Yet, in setting forth the ethics of the Christian life, Paul rarely appeals directly to the sayings of Jesus (explicitly only 1 Cor. 7:10–11; 9:14; 11:23–25). For Paul and much of early Christianity (as represented in all the New Testament letters and in much early Christian tradition), the Christian life is not guided by trying to live according to specific teachings of Jesus and the example of his earthly life, but by living in the faith and light of the Christ event as a whole as the manifestation of God's saving love. The community that shares this faith and is enlivened by God's Spirit is the context and source of power for making Christian ethical decisions and living them out in daily practice. (On the role of the Gospel stories of the "life and teaching of

Jesus" in Christian faith, see "Introduction to the Gospels," 4.)

12:18 Live peaceably with all: Peace is more than the absence of hostility; it refers to the wholeness of the good life God intends (see 5:1). The Christian life is not oriented only to "insiders," fellow members of the Christian community, but to "outsiders," i.e., to all, as Christians exercise their social responsibility in the conviction that all finally belong to God (5:18–21; 11:32–36).

12:19 Never avenge yourselves: See Deut. 32:35; Proverbs 20:22; 24:29. **I will repay:** This is not so much a threat to the offending party as a warning to the Christian, that to take revenge into one's own hands is to encroach on God's territory. Here is an instance where the Christian ethic clashes with the values of a secular culture that admires the wronged person who strikes back ("I don't get mad; I get even").

12:20 If your enemies are hungry, feed them: Proverbs 25:21–22. It is striking that Paul cites the Old Testament, not the teaching of Jesus (see commentary on 12:14 above, and see Matt. 5:44; 25:35; Luke 6:27). This kind of nonretaliatory life can be lived by those who have nothing to prove, who are secure in their own acceptance by God, and who do not have to justify themselves in their own eyes or in the eyes of others. **You will heap burning coals on their heads:** Two explanations have been offered for this difficult image: (1) The coals represent the burning shame and remorse the offending party feels, which lead to repentance. Thus the repentance and acceptance by God of the other is the goal of Christian behavior. (2) If one responds to the enemy's hostility with genuine love and he or she remains hostile, the enemy is then consigned to an even more severe judgment by God. This "kill them with kindness" approach can be a subtle form of revenge in the guise of love and humility.

13:1–7
BEING SUBJECT TO AUTHORITIES

13:1 Be subject to the governing authorities: Paul is not writing an essay on church and state or general instructions for all times and places, but a letter to a specific situation (for general principles of interpretation, see on 1 Pet. 2:11). The disturbances in Rome of 49 CE were a matter of recent history (see the introduction to Romans; comments on Acts 18:2). Christians in Rome were already suspect by the government, a suspicion that would break out again a few years later (64 CE), when the emperor Nero would blame the great fire that destroyed much of the city on the Christians as "enemies of the human race." In such a situation Paul wants to make it clear that the Christian life itself does not call for resistance against government authority or withdrawal from public life. This line of thought is developed in later situations by subsequent New Testament authors, as they attempt to teach Christians responsible citizenship and reassure the empire that Christians are not its subversive political enemies (see the introduction to Luke; comments on Luke 2:1–21; 20:20–26; 1 Pet. 2:13–14; 1 Tim. 2:1–2).

Those authorities that exist have been instituted by God: Paul here draws on the legal, prophetic, wisdom, and apocalyptic traditions of the Old Testament and Judaism, all of which present the social order itself as established as part of the divinely given structures of the world (see, e.g., Deut. 32:8–9; Isa. 41:1–4; 45:1–6; Dan. 2:21, 37–38; 4:17, 25, 32; Prov. 8:15–16; Wis. 6:1–3; *Let. Aris.* 196, 219, 224; *1 En.* 46:5; *2 Bar.* 82:9; Acts 17:26; John 19:11; 1 Pet. 2:13–17). God is not the God of disorder but of peace (1 Cor. 14:33). But no particular political or economic system (e.g., monarchy, democracy, communism, capitalism) may claim to be instituted by God, just as no particular ruler may claim to rule by divine right. This text has often been used by those in power to maintain their position, and has even been misinterpreted by those under repressive regimes to mean that they should do nothing to change the government.

13:4 It is God's servant for your good: The Greek text can also be translated "he is God's servant" (so NIV). Nero was Roman emperor as Paul wrote. Even though he had not yet shown his demonic character as ruler, Paul is more likely thinking not of Nero personally ("he") but of governmental authority as such ("it") as a divinely given restraint on evil. Paul assumes commitment to "the good," wherever it is found, and assumes that government power promotes the common good. He is not discussing civic and Christian responsibility when government ceases to do this (as, e.g., in Nazi Germany).

The authority does not bear the sword in vain: The reference is to the executioner's sword. Capital punishment was commonly practiced in the Roman Empire, but this text no more authorizes capital punishment as God's law than it establishes the Roman Empire itself as God's kingdom.

13:5 One must be subject . . . because of conscience: The Christian fits into and participates in the governmental structures not only from fear of punishment, but as a willing participant in regulating the social structure for the common good. The readers' situation has dramatically changed since Paul wrote—we no longer live under the Roman Empire, when "being subject" or "rebellion" were the only political options. The modern reader can hear Paul's instruction as a call for responsible participation in government, both by informed voting and by serving in office. Paul takes care that his instructions in 12:2 not be misunderstood as a call for withdrawal from the world; in our situation this would mean turning its governing structures over to unbelievers with a different set of values. Paul's call is to active involvement in society, precisely because its structures have a divine warrant.

13:7 Pay to all what is due them: Paul insists that the payment of taxes, customs fees, and respect, even for a pagan government, is a Christian responsibility. Again, it is striking that Paul does not refer to the saying of Jesus on this issue, a saying that would support his point (Mark 12:13–17; see on Rom. 12:14, 20).

13:8–10
LOVE FOR ONE ANOTHER

13:8 Love one another: Paul's instruction that Christians pay their legitimate debts (taxes and other government fees) reminds him of the general orientation of the Christian life: care for the well-being of others (see on 12:9; 1 Cor. 13:1–13; Luke 6:27–36; 10:26–37). It may seem strange to the modern reader to connect Christian love to the payment of taxes, but this would be a misunderstanding of the nature of love as a private feeling. Taxes (and other arrangements in which people pool their funds for the common good, like insurance, plans such as Social Security and Medicare, and retirement plans) can be thought of not merely as personal investments for one's own benefit, but as using one's surplus wealth for the benefit of others. From the perspective of Christian love, the appropriate question would then not be am I getting what I paid into it? but, is the money being used properly for the benefit of all? From this point of view, Paul's affirmation that love is the one obligation that can never be "paid off" can be understood by every Christian.

13:10 Love is the fulfilling of the law: As Paul has argued throughout, the coming of Christ does not abrogate the law, but illuminates and makes effective its original intention (3:31; 7:14; 8:2–4; 10:5–8; Gal. 5:14). The negative mode of stating the love command, **Love does no wrong to a neighbor:** Does not mean mere passivity or selfishness, as though it authorized one to "do as I please and mind my own business, as long as I do not hurt anyone else." Paul's own call for active love in this very context, and such texts as Luke 6:25–31; 10:26–37 show that inactivity and passivity also do wrong to a neighbor and violate the command to love.

13:11–14
An Urgent Appeal

13:11 You know what time it is: Christians live in the already/not yet tension between the advent of Christ that inaugurates the kingdom of God and the final consummation of God's kingdom at the end of history (see on the three tenses of salvation at 5:2 above; see also comments on 1 Cor. 4:7; 15:45–49; and Luke 4:43). As in 1 Cor. 13:8–13, Paul connects the love command with the eschatological hope. **Salvation is nearer:** The end of history is pictured as the return of Christ, which Paul believed to be near (1 Cor. 15:20–24; 1 Thess. 4:15–18; see excursus, "Interpreting the 'Near End,'" at Rev. 1:3). "Near" is the same word for the dawning of the kingdom of God used in Mark 1:15.

13:12 The night is far gone, the day is near: Christian existence is like living in the time of early dawn. It is still night, the old age is still with us, the sun has not yet come up, but in the east the sky is already becoming bright as the signal that the new day is dawning. Christians are those who know what time it is, that "the darkness is passing away and the true light is already shining" (1 John 2:8), and who thus orient their lives to the dawning new age, rather than the lame-duck administration of darkness that is already passing away.

13:13 Orgies . . . drunkenness . . . sexual immorality . . . debauchery . . . dissension . . . jealousy (NIV): It is striking that along with the traditional sins of the "night life" of sensual pleasure, Paul lists the more respectable sins of dissension and jealousy (which may also be translated "selfish ambition"). Though quite a respectable virtue in most societies, Paul places egocentric drive for "success" in the same category as the more sensational "sins of the flesh" that belong to the value system of the old age that Christ brings to an end.

13:14 Put on the Lord Jesus Christ: Christian existence as "in Christ" (6:2–3; 8:1–4; 2 Cor. 5:17) is thought of as putting on a new garment that surrounds one's whole life. That which in Gal. 3:27 is stated in the indicative as an objective reality is here given as a command (see comments there). The reality that has happened to the believer in baptism must be constantly realized anew in daily conduct. The Christian life always stands under the imperative: "Be what you are."

14:1–12
Do Not Judge One Another

The section 14:1–15:6 deals with a particular problem, how "weak" and "strong" Christians may live and serve God together in one congregation. The identity of each group becomes clear only as the discussion proceeds.

14:1 Welcome those: The church's welcome embraces both "weak" and "strong," prior to any discussion of the convictions of each (this section at 15:7 concludes with the same command to receive one another as Christ has received all). The potentially divisive issues include both **faith** and **opinions,** which may not be neatly distinguished: one person's "opinion" is another person's "faith." The group Paul calls "weak" (he identifies himself with the "strong" in 15:1) did not so designate themselves; each group considered itself "strong." The initial address to the whole church to welcome the "weak" members indicates that the "strong" were in the majority.

14:2 Eating anything . . . only vegetables: The "weak" are represented as vegetarians; the "strong" have no religious restrictions on what they may eat. The prohibitions of the "weak" also include drinking wine (14:21) and the observance of certain days as particularly holy. "Weak" and "strong" cannot be neatly identified with "Jewish" and "Gentile" respectively, for Jews were not vegetarians and had no restrictions against drinking wine. The descriptions also fit pagan ascetic practices, as does the observance of certain days considered particularly favorable or unfavorable on the basis of astrology and pagan religious traditions. The Roman church included previous adherents of various pagan cults, as well as Jewish Christians. All brought their previous ideas and practices into the church; some "baptized" them and continued to observe them as a matter of Christian piety. In particular, in the Roman situation Jewish Christians who still observed Jewish holy days and maintained a kosher kitchen regarded the continuing obser-vance of these rules as a matter of God's law. In the urban environment of pagan Rome, where most meat and wine sold in the marketplace had been devoted to some pagan god, some strictly observant Jews (and Jewish Christians) may have given up meat and wine entirely as a matter of faithfulness to God (see Dan. 1:8–17; see on 1 Cor. 8–10). Thus Paul deals with the issue at length, as part of the larger concern that dominates his argument throughout Romans —the relation of Jews and Gentiles in the one people of God. In Paul's view, those Jews and Gentiles who as Christians continued to observe their former religious scruples were not yet strong enough in their faith to see that Christ had liberated them from their previous laws, and unless or until they came to this con-viction themselves, their views and practices should be respected.

Modern Christians face something of the same problem in deciding how "conserva-tive" and "liberal" Christians may live and serve God together in the same denomination or congregation. Recognizing that the corre-spondence is not exact, in reading this chap-ter, one can substitute "conservative" for those whom Paul calls "weak" (though, as in Paul's day, they consider themselves "strong") and "liberal" for "strong" Chris-tians who believe they are liberated from the scruples of their more conservative brothers and sisters. Paul identifies himself as among the "strong," but argues that God affirms and accepts both (see on 15:7). How can such dif-fering groups live and serve together in the one church of God? One "solution" never occurs to Paul: let those of similar liberal or conservative opinions cluster together in the same congregation or denomination, forming different congregations or denominations, each claiming to be the "strong."

14:3 Despise . . . pass judgment: With keen dis-cernment, Paul places his finger on the prob-lem of each group. "Despise" does not mean "hate"—this is not the liberals' temptation—but "disdain," the belittling attitude of the "enlightened" toward their less progressive brothers and sisters. "Pass judgment" refers to the temptation of the conservative to con-demn the liberal. This does not necessarily mean a personally censorious negative atti-tude, as though the person needed simply to become more "tolerant," but refers to the seri-ous theological problem of one who has strong convictions about what constitutes cor-

rect religious faith and practice, and simply does not see how God can accept one who vio-lates what appears to be clearly God's law. "How can one claim to be Christian when he or she disregards the clear word of the Bible?"

14:4 Who are you?: Paul's response: *You* do not have to understand how the person could be Christian by your standards. Those with whom you disagree are **servants of another**, namely, the God revealed in Jesus Christ. Paul's words in 14:6–9 show he presupposes that all concerned confess Christ as Lord and attempt to serve him in the church; the divi-sive issue is how this is to be done. **The Lord is able to make them stand:** Whether or not the conservatives see how this can be, accord-ing to their theology.

14:5–6 Let all be fully convinced in their own minds: All do not have to agree or have the same practice, but none may violate their own conscience (14:22–23). **They give thanks to God:** Whatever their practice in eating and drinking or abstaining, each group does what it believes to be God's will. The dispute is thus much more than mere personal preference, for which "tolerance" would be the recom-mended solution, but a matter of devotion to God. That each group **gives thanks** shows they are no longer enslaved to the primal sin that separates human beings from God and each other (1:21).

14:7 We do not live to ourselves: Paul does not make the issue merely a matter of individual opinion, as though the solution would be sim-ply to show a human respect for the opinions of others. That Christians are bound together in the Christian community, that they live their lives together before God, is what makes mutual acceptance both necessary and possible.

14:9 Lord of both the dead and the living: The "communion of saints" to which the believer belongs embraces not only Christians of dif-ferent races, cultures, languages, and cus-toms; it includes those who have already died, but have not thereby been marked off the list of God's people (see Heb. 11:1–40, leading to the climactic "cloud of [heavenly] witnesses" of 12:1–2). If Christ is Lord of all and has accepted all, Christians of differing traditions must find a way to accept each other.

14:10–12 We will all stand before the judgment seat of God: See on 2 Cor. 5:10. This reference to the Last Judgment is not introduced here to produce anxiety. In Paul's view, salvation by grace does not negate the role of God (or Christ; see NRSV note) as the ultimate judge

(2:28–29). Paul here uses the picture of the Last Judgment as a prohibition against Christians judging each other (1 Cor. 4:1–5). **For it is written:** The quotation is primarily from Isa. 45:23, but see also Isa. 49:18; Jer. 22:24; Ezek. 5:11. **Every tongue shall give praise to God:** See Phil. 2:10–11. Paul's point here is that, though all, conservative and liberal, must stand before God at the Last Judgment, **each of us will be accountable to God** for ourselves, not for others. And each will then see that God vindicates and accepts both, for in this picture none is condemned, but all confess and give praise to God.

14:13–23
DO NOT MAKE ONE ANOTHER STUMBLE

14:13 No longer pass judgment on one another: From here to the end of this section at 15:6, Paul primarily addresses the "strong." His warning against judging others in the church shows it is not only the "weak" who are prone to judge the other group. **Never to put a stumbling block in the way of another:** Throughout Paul stresses that as a Christian one must consider not only what one personally believes to be right, but how the practice of one's faith affects the faith of others. The issue is not whether the "weak" Christian approves of the way the "strong" practice their own understanding of the faith, but whether this becomes a problem that trips up the weak person's own effort to live a Christian life.

14:14 I know and am persuaded in the Lord Jesus: Paul's own convictions align him with the "strong" (15:1). **Nothing is unclean in itself:** "Unclean" is not a matter of sanitation, but refers to the ritual impurity of eating prohibited foods. On the importance of laws concerning ritual purity, see on Mark 7:1–23; Luke 2:22–24; Acts 10:1–11:18. The food laws of the Old Testament and Jewish tradition are not mandatory for Gentile Christians. **It is unclean for anyone who thinks it unclean:** The food is not unclean in itself, but in the "weak" (= unliberated) conscience of the conservative believer. For a person with such convictions then to proceed to do something he or she believes to be wrong would actually be a violation of conscience and a sin before God (14:23).

14:15 Injured by what you eat: I.e., encouraged by your example to violate his or her own conscience. **Do not . . . cause the ruin of one for whom Christ died:** This instruction shows the seriousness with which Paul regards the whole matter. Paul balances the freedom of the liberated (including himself) to eat and drink according to their own conscience against the destruction of a "weak" brother or sister's Christian life. In such a situation, "strong" Christians actually show their own weakness by continuing to insist on their own liberated views. True freedom is the freedom to renounce one's "rights" for the sake of others.

14:17 The kingdom of God is . . . righteousness and peace and joy in the Holy Spirit: This is Paul's own summary of his portrayal of Christian existence in chaps. 5–8. On "kingdom of God," see on Luke 4:43. Such a vision of what it means to live one's life "in Christ" (see 2 Cor. 5:17) far transcends one's "right" to eat and drink what one pleases.

14:19 Peace and mutual upbuilding: The criteria for Christian conduct are not simply personal convictions, but the well-being and strengthening of the church for its mission.

14:20 Everything is indeed clean: Paul repeats his conviction of 14:14 that he is not compromising his liberated view that there is nothing inherently wrong with drinking wine and ignoring the food laws and prescribed festivals of the Old Testament and Jewish tradition. But there is something very wrong with placing obstacles in the path of another, "less enlightened" Christian. What one actually eats and drinks, which days one observes as holy, and the like, must then be decided by the "strong" from case to case—unlike the situation of the "weak," for the "strong" there are no binding rules that tell one in advance what must always be done (see 1 Cor. 9:19–23).

14:22 Blessed are those who have no reason to condemn themselves: Paul's only use of the beatitude form (see Matt. 5:3–12). The meaning is not that "those who approve wrong things are condemned." In this context Paul makes a practical application of his doctrine of justification by faith, and pronounces a blessing on those who know their acceptance before God is not a matter of food and drink, and who thus are free to eat and drink or not to do so, depending on what is helpful for the Christian lives of their brothers and sisters in the church.

14:23 Whatever does not proceed from faith is sin: This is not a general definition of sin (Paul is writing a letter, not an essay), but in this context means that those who eat and drink in violation of their own conscience are sinning against God—and thus that the "strong" should not force the "weak" into situations where this can happen. Just as it is wrong for one (the strong) to eat when one's actions corrupt the faith of others, so it is wrong for one (the weak) to eat when one believes it is wrong.

15:1–6
PLEASE OTHERS, NOT YOURSELVES

15:1 We . . . ought . . . not to please ourselves: This is not general moralizing advice that, taken out of context, would seem to commend an unhealthy rejection of one's own happiness. The command to love the neighbor as oneself (13:9) presupposes love for oneself. In this context, the point still has to do with the preceding issue of "weak" and "strong" (14:1–23), and the command is that the strong not insist on their own freedom to the detriment of their fellow brothers and sisters. They are not merely passively to put up with the failings of the weak, but actively to support them in their Christian life together.

15:3 Christ did not please himself: Christ's sacrifice of his life expressed his love for sinful human beings (8:32–35). Jesus is the example, but the words quoted are from the Old Testament, not the sayings of Jesus (Ps. 69:9; see commentary on 12:14). The psalmist originally expressed the lament of an Israelite worshiper who had been insulted because of his zeal for God's house. Paul understands it to mean Jesus bore the insults aimed at God, i.e., he did not please himself.

15:4 Written in former days . . . for our instruction: Paul reads the Jewish Scriptures in the light of the Christ event, and finds them filled with Christian meaning (see on 1 Cor. 15:3; 1 Pet. 1:10). Psalm 69 cited here was often seen in early Christianity as pointing to Christ (see Matt. 27:34, 48; Mark 3:21; Luke 13:35; 23:36; John 2:17; 15:25; 19:28; Acts 1:20; Rom. 11:9–10; Phil. 4:3; Heb. 11:26; Rev. 3:5; 16:1).

15:5–6 May the God of steadfastness and encouragement: Paul knows that the letter will be read aloud in the worship service of the Roman Christians. He concludes the section that began at 14:1 with a prayer that, despite their differences in theology and practice, the different groups in the Roman church will continue as the one church of God and **live in harmony with one another**, joining together **with one voice** in united praise to God. What began with mutual suspicion and disdain over differences of opinion about what Christians can eat and drink concludes with prayer and praise (see 11:33–36 as the conclusion to 9:1–11:36).

15:7–13
THE GOSPEL FOR JEWS AND GENTILES ALIKE

15:7 Welcome one another: "Weak" and "strong" are not merely to "put up with" each other (15:1), but to welcome one another, for no one perspective has a monopoly on the truth. Liberals and conservatives need each other; each has something to contribute to the body of Christ in which not all members are alike (12:4–8; 1 Cor. 12:12–30). **Christ has welcomed you:** Weak and strong, conservative and liberal, Jew and Gentile.

15:8–12 Truth of God: God's faithfulness to his promises to Israel (see 9:6). **His mercy:** God's grace to Gentiles who had no claim on the covenant with Israel, but who are now mercifully included in the one people of God.

As it is written: Paul cites four texts from the Jewish Scriptures that show God intended to include the Gentiles (Ps. 18:48; Deut. 32:43; Ps. 117:1; Isa. 11:10). Paul's point is clear only in the LXX (the Septuagint, the Greek translation of the Old Testament used by Hellenistic Jews and early Christians; see 11:7). **Gentiles, with his people:** The LXX version of Deut. 32:43 is crucial to Paul's point, for (unlike the original Hebrew text translated in English Bibles) only it pictures Gentiles celebrating *with* Israel, the covenant people of God (see NRSV note at Deut. 32:43).

15:13 The God of hope: The God who gives hope (secure confidence) in seemingly hopeless situations (see on 4:16–21; 8:18–25).

15:14–16:27
CONCLUSION OF THE LETTER

15:14–21
PAUL'S REASON FOR WRITING SO BOLDLY

15:14–15 You yourselves are . . . able . . . nevertheless: Paul tactfully wishes to avoid the presumption of having written authoritative instruction to the Roman church he had neither founded nor previously visited (see 1:8–15). More than tact and personal diplomacy are involved. It is not as though they were incapable of instructing themselves, for they have able teachers and leaders (12:3–8), the Scripture, and the church's traditions, to which Paul himself has alluded (e.g., 1:3–4; 3:25–26; 4:25; see 6:17). **Boldly by way of reminder:** Paul does not consider his teaching an innovation, but an affirmation of the common core of Christian teaching already available to the Roman church. This view was shared by other early Christian teachers (see 2 Pet. 1:12; 3:1; 1 John 2:21).

15:16–19 A minister of Christ . . . in the priestly service: Paul was not literally a priest, but portrays his ministry as bringing the Gentiles as a holy offering to God (see Isa. 66:20). **I have reason to boast:** On "boasting," see on 3:27; 4:2; 5:2; 11:18–20. Paul boasts not of his own achievements (Phil. 3:2–10), but of what Christ has accomplished through him. **The power of signs and wonders:** Paul never refers to any miracles Jesus performed during his earthly ministry (see on 2 Cor. 12:12; 13:4; Phil. 2:5–11), but locates the power of Christ in the work of the Holy Spirit in the life of the church. **Fully proclaimed the good news:** I.e., established churches in the major cities of Asia Minor, Macedonia, and Greece. **Illyricum:** A Roman province on the eastern shore of the Adriatic, comprising parts of modern Bosnia, Serbia, Croatia, and Albania. Neither Acts nor Paul's other letters mention a Pauline mission to Illyricum. The point is that Paul's work in the eastern Mediterranean is complete, and he now intends to extend his mission to Spain, visiting the Roman church en route (15:22–23).

15:21 Those who have never been told: Paul finds in the promise of Isa. 52:15 an expression of his own commission to preach the Christian message in areas where other Christian missionaries have not founded churches. He is especially reluctant to work in areas where Jewish-Christian missionaries have already evangelized (see Gal. 2:7–8). His aversion **to build on someone else's foundation** must also mean that the Roman church had not been founded by other apostles (e.g., Peter); otherwise Paul would not have been willing to preach in Rome (see 1:15). The Roman church had apparently been established by Christians who had been converted elsewhere and had moved to Rome. Paul believed they needed an apostolic visit.

15:22–32
PAUL'S PLAN TO VISIT ROME

15:24 To be sent on by you: This included, but was not limited to, financial support for his projected Spanish mission. Paul's arrest in Jerusalem and imprisonment in Caesarea and Rome apparently prevented this mission from becoming reality.

15:25–27 I am going to Jerusalem in a ministry to the saints: Paul had collected a large offering from the Gentile churches in **Macedonia** and **Achaia** (Greece) to help ease the poverty of the Judean Christians and as a symbol of the unity of Jewish and Gentile churches (see on Gal. 2:10; 2 Cor. 8:1–9:15).

15:30–31 Join me in earnest prayer: Paul's anxiety about what might befall him in Jerusalem is twofold: (1) He is concerned that **unbelievers**, i.e., zealous non-Christian Jews such as he had once been himself, will try to arrest or kill him, as indeed turned out to be the case (see Acts 21:27–36). (2) He is worried that **the saints,** i.e. the Jerusalem Christians, who were suspicious of his Gentile mission, might be unwilling to accept the offering he is bringing, considering it "tainted money" from churches that had abandoned God's law. The minimal and oblique references in Acts to the offering suggest that Paul's hopes for his final meeting with the Jerusalem leaders were not fulfilled and that the offering was in fact refused (see on Acts 19:51; 20:1, 22–23; 21:23; esp. 24:17).

16:1–16
RECOMMENDATION OF PHOEBE
AND PERSONAL GREETINGS

The concluding chapter of Romans has sometimes been considered a separate note written by Paul to Ephesus, later added to Romans during the editing process in the formation of the New Testament (see the introduction to 2 Corinthians). Among the reasons given are these: (1) It is unlikely that Paul knew so many people (and their circumstances) in a church in a city he had never visited. (2) Some of the people mentioned are located in Ephesus by other New Testament texts. (3) The concluding doxology of 16:25–27 is found after 15:33 in one of our oldest MSS of Romans. Against these arguments, this may be said: (1) Given the mobility of Christians, especially Christian leaders such as Paul himself and his associates, it would not be unlikely that many of them would gravitate to the capital city of the empire. Since Paul wanted to establish good relations with the congregation with which he was personally still a stranger (1:8–15; 15:14–29), he names as many contacts as possible. (2) A "letter" consisting almost entirely of a list of names is conceivable in the day of the vacation postcard, but hardly in Paul's day. (3) There are no MSS of Romans without chap. 16. The variations of the location of the concluding benediction (and other peculiarities in the MS tradition) are accounted for by the fact that Marcion, a second-century Christian leader who became a heretic, circulated truncated versions of Paul's letters that influenced the way MSS were copied in subsequent generations. Though it was once the dominant scholarly opinion that Romans was originally written without chap. 16, the majority of recent students of the New Testament consider the chapter an integral component of Romans.

The chapter is mostly composed of greetings to Paul's friends and coworkers now in Rome. Twenty-six individuals are named, plus their associates, with greetings from eight individuals with Paul in Corinth as he writes (see the introduction to Romans). Including Paul and Phoebe, this total of thirty-six named individuals indicates something of the intensely personal character of the Christian faith as documented in the New Testament (which names a total of 423 different individuals).

16:1–2 Our sister Phoebe: "Sister" means a fellow member of the church, the family of God. **A deacon:** See NRSV note. It is not clear how "official" ministerial "offices" were in Paul's time, but Phoebe is obviously a leader and valued colleague of Paul in **the church at Cenchreae**, the port city of Corinth. The incidental reference to the church there, not otherwise attested in Acts or Paul's letters, is an indication of how fragmentary our picture of his missionary career is (see 15:19 on Illyricum). Phoebe was apparently en route from Corinth, where Paul writes Romans, to Rome, and was likely the bearer of the letter. **A benefactor of many:** This is a quasi-technical term (lit. "patron") for that type of wealthy and influential person who played an important role in Hellenistic society structured on the patron-client pattern. She may have owned a large house in which the congregation in Cenchreae met for worship and instruction. It was assumed that Christians were members not only of a particular congregation, but of the one church of God scattered throughout the world, and that when they moved from one place to another they belonged to the congregation in that place. Letters of recommendation such as Paul here writes facilitated leaders of one congregation assuming an active role in the congregation to which they were moving (see Acts 18:27; 1 Cor. 16:15–17).

16:3–5 Prisca and Aquila: Prisca is always called Priscilla in Acts (18:2, 18, 26), but Prisca by Paul (1 Cor. 16:19; see 2 Tim. 4:19). Prisca and Aquila are among those listed whose last known location prior to the writing of Rom. 16 was Ephesus, not Rome (see 1 Cor. 16:19; Acts 18:11, 18–26), and thus evidence that Rom. 16 was originally addressed to Ephesus (see above). **Who risked their necks for my life:** Probably during the tumultuous days described in Acts

19:23–41; see 18:26. **The church in their house:** As in other large cities, the church was composed of small house churches that met in the houses of the wealthier members (see Col. 4:15; Phlm. 2). On moving back to Rome, Prisca and Aquila had resumed their role of active leaders.

16:7 Junia (NRSV) is a woman's name; **Junias** (NIV) is a man's name, though not otherwise attested in antiquity (see NRSV note). The church fathers uniformly understood the word as feminine. Some medieval copyists who assumed that a woman could not be an "apostle" apparently changed the original Junia to Junias in some manuscripts. The expression may mean that the couple were highly regarded by the apostles, or that they themselves were apostles—a word used for a wider circle than the Twelve (see on 1 Cor. 15:4; Luke 6:12–13; Acts 14:4, 14).

16:13 Rufus . . . his mother . . . a mother to me: During Paul's mission work he had apparently been included as a "member of the family" in Rufus's household (see Mark 3:32; 10:29–30). If this is the same **Rufus** mentioned in Mark 15:21 as the son of the person who carried Jesus' cross (a differing tradition from that of John 19:17), it is strange that Paul does not mention the "famous" father, Simon of Cyrene. It is thus unlikely that Paul's reference to a **Rufus** in Rome connects the Gospel of Mark with Rome.

16:16 Greet one another with a holy kiss: See on 1 Cor. 16:20; 1 Thess. 5:26.

16:17–23
FINAL INSTRUCTIONS AND GREETINGS

16:17 Keep an eye on those who cause dissensions: The uncertainty about how Paul himself ended the letter (see above) suggests the possibility that this concluding warning is not from Paul himself. It does not fit the tone of the letter as a whole (see, e.g., 15:14–32), which has no indication that the Roman church is plagued with the kind of disruptive false teachers Paul had just opposed in Galatia and Corinth. Yet here too Paul's own recent history may have caused him to make a preemptive strike against the possibility that his opponents in Galatia, Macedonia, and Greece would attempt to win over the Roman church to their position.

16:20 The God of peace will shortly crush Satan under your feet: This is the only direct reference to Satan in Romans, but the eschatological hope of God's final victory over demonic powers is never far from the surface throughout (see, e.g., 8:18–25, 37–39; 13:11–14).

16:21–23 Timothy . . . Lucius . . . Jason . . . Sosipater . . . Tertius . . . Gaius . . . Erastus . . . Quartus: Several of Paul's coworkers are with him as he writes, but do not join in the composition of the letter, which is Paul's alone (see 1:1). Timothy is one of Paul's trusted colleagues and fellow missionaries (see on Acts 16:1). Tertius was the scribe to whom Paul dictated the letter. Gaius was wealthy enough to have a house in which the **whole church** in Corinth could meet (see 1 Cor. 1:14). On Erastus, see Acts 19:22. He was another of the few wealthy and influential members of the Corinthian church. His becoming a Christian did not mean he had to abandon his position as **city treasurer** (see 1 Cor. 8:1–11:1 on the difficulties of maintaining one's faith in a pagan culture without withdrawing from society—which the New Testament nowhere recommends).

16:25–27
FINAL DOXOLOGY

These verses resemble the liturgical doxologies in the later letters written by Paul's disciples (Eph. 3:20–21; 1 Tim. 1:17; see Jude 24–25). Since Romans circulated with a number of different endings (see above and NRSV note y), this liturgical conclusion may have been added later. Paul's own closing benediction may be contained in 16:20b. Whether directly from Paul or from the later church, these verses are authentic testimony to the Christian faith, and illustrate that the boundary between "Scripture" and "church tradition" is fluid (see, e.g., comments on Matt. 6:13; Mark 16:9–20) and that here as elsewhere we receive our Bible from the hands of the church.

The First Letter of Paul to the Corinthians

INTRODUCTION

In Paul's letters to the Corinthian Christians we have the most extensive correspondence in the New Testament from the apostle's hand. The letters let us see the person of Paul as he is intensively engaged with a church he had founded and loved, the clarifying of his message in the process of this engagement, and many aspects of the life of an early Christian church.

Corinth

The ancient Greek city had been destroyed by the Romans in 146 BCE, had lain in ruins for a century, and then had been rebuilt in 44 BCE by Julius Caesar, who repopulated it with Roman military veterans and freed slaves and made it the capital of the Roman province of Achaia (Greece). By Paul's day it had again become a thriving commercial center with two ports: Cenchreae, the Aegean port on the east, and Lechaeum, on the western gulf leading to the Adriatic and Rome. Corinth's strategic location on the narrow isthmus separating the two seas contributed to its wealth and cultural variety. The reputation of the older city as a center of prostitution and other forms of sexual immorality had been exaggerated by Corinth's commercial rivals. The Roman city of Paul's day was probably no better or worse than other large Mediterranean seaports. Corinth was a typical Hellenistic city in which "gods many and lords many" were worshiped (8:5); this has been documented by the excavation of temples and shrines to Apollo, Asclepius, Aphrodite, Demeter, Poseidon, Isis and Serapis, the Great Mother, Artemis, Helios, and others.

Setting in Paul's Mission

See "Introduction to the Pauline Letters."

According to the Acts account (18:1–17) the church was founded by Paul, Silas, and Timothy during the "second missionary journey." Paul found there two other Christians, Priscilla and Aquila, who had recently arrived from Rome. They became his coworkers, and for a year and a half they conducted a vigorous mission. In Acts

Paul began his work in the synagogue but when his message was mostly rejected, quickly turned to the Gentiles. That the church to which 1 Corinthians is addressed appears to be mainly Gentile (12:2) is important for understanding the letter. Its recipients had for the most part been adherents of pagan religions who did not entirely leave their previous understandings of religion and ethics behind when they were baptized.

Paul left a vital Christian congregation in Corinth and continued his mission in Ephesus. When he wrote 1 Corinthians, he had not visited the church again, though he had written them a letter (see 5:9; now lost, unless it is partially preserved in 2 Corinthians). In the meantime, the church had been visited by Apollos, whose emphasis on "wisdom" was quite different from Paul's presentation of the gospel, but whom nonetheless Paul regarded as brother and colleague (see Acts 18:24; 19:1; 1 Cor. 1:12; 3:4–5, 22; 4:6; 16:22). The Corinthians had been unduly impressed by Apollos's "wisdom," as well as by followers of Simon Peter who had joined the congregation and by the spiritual phenomena manifested by some of their members, especially speaking in tongues.

Paul writes 1 Corinthians from Ephesus (16:8) in the late fall of 53 or early spring of 54 CE, about three years after the founding of the church. He writes in response both to their letter inquiring about various problems (see on 7:1) and to what he had heard from the bearers of the letter (16:15–17), as well as to reports he had received from "Chloe's people" (1:11). Some internal tensions within the letter (e.g. 8:1–13 vs. 10:14–30) have caused a few scholars to regard 1 Corinthians as a combination of two or more letters, but most scholars today consider the tensions to be better resolved by careful interpretation and regard the letter as a unity—in contrast to 2 Corinthians.

Since the letter is in response to particular practical problems of Corinthian church life, the letter is our best window into the life of a first-century Christian congregation. As is the case in reading all New Testament letters, however, the situation of the addressees must be reconstructed by "mirror reading" what Paul says to them, often already interpreted in terms of his own perspective. While the Corinthians have asked Paul about "practical" issues, Paul's response is invariably theological, illustrating his conviction that all of life is to be understood in the light of the gospel.

Outline

For Further Reading

Fee, Gordon D. *The First Epistle to the Corinthians.* The New International Commentary on the New Testament. Grand Rapids: Eerdmans, 1987.

Hays, Richard B. *First Corinthians.* Interpretation: A Bible Commentary for Teaching and Preaching. Louisville, KY: Westminster John Knox, 1997.

COMMENTARY

1:1–3
SALUTATION

On the greeting form of Pauline letters, see on 1 Thess. 1:1.

1:1 Called to be an apostle: There is no "to be" in the Greek text. Paul identifies himself as a called apostle, an apostle who has been called, i.e., not a volunteer but a draftee (Gal. 1:1; Acts 9:1–19; 22:1–21; 26:2–23). On "apostle," see at Luke 6:12–13. **Sosthenes:** If the same person as in Acts 18:17, he had been a leader in the synagogue before becoming a Christian (see also Crispus [Acts 18:8]).

1:2 Called to be saints: "Saints" does not mean persons of outstanding piety or exceptional religious discipline, but is the designation adopted from the Old Testament for God's people Israel (see Ps. 31:23; the same word is often translated "holy"; see, e.g., Lev. 20:26). The word thus means simply "Christians," members of the church, the holy people of God. See on 1 Thess. 3:13; 1 Pet. 1:1. Again, there is no "to be" in the Greek text. They are saints by virtue of God's call through the gospel, not by their own initiative (see 1:9; Rom. 8:28–30; 2 Thess. 2:14). **Sanctified:** In Greek as in English, a related form of the word for "saints," thus means "made holy." Despite the serious shortcomings and problems of the Corinthian Christians, they are nonetheless sanctified by being included in God's holy people (see 7:12–14; Exod. 19:5–6). **Together with all those . . . in every place:** Their calling to be Christian is not only not *individual*; it is not only *congregational*. The call of God adds them to the one *universal* church. This has practical consequences: they cannot simply decide to go their own way in the Christian life (see 11:16; 14:36).

1:3 Grace . . . and peace: See on 1 Thess. 1:1. **The Lord Jesus Christ:** That "Christ" occurs four times in this brief greeting is not mere religious decoration, but shows Paul's own Christ-centeredness, that he can hardly say hello apart from the reality of the world made new by God's act in Christ.

1:4–9
THANKSGIVING

On the thanksgiving section of Pauline letters in general, see on 1 Thess. 1:2. As elsewhere, in the opening thanksgiving Paul signals major concerns of the letter to follow.

1:5 Speech and knowledge: "Speech" refers especially to the charismatic utterances of tongues and prophecy, while "knowledge" points to the insights given by the Spirit (chaps. 12–14). While Paul will later be critical of the exaggerated importance attributed to these gifts by (some of) the Corinthians and can speak negatively and sarcastically of them when they become the objects of human pride (see 1:17–18; 8:1–13), here he is genuinely grateful that God's Spirit is at work among them.

1:7 Not lacking in any spiritual gift: See the "catalogues" of 12:9–11, 27–31; 14:26. The word "spiritual" is not in the Greek text, but has been added by both NRSV and NIV to make clear that Paul is referring to the gifts given by the Spirit discussed in chaps. 12–14. Paul's own word is *charismata*, not found prior to his letters and perhaps invented by him. It is related to the word for "grace" (*charis*), and points to the spiritual phenomena occurring in the Corinthian church as God's gift, not something in which they could take a kind of spiritual pride (see 4:7). **As you wait for . . . our Lord Jesus Christ:** See 1 Thess. 1:9–10. This reflects Paul's own perspective on how they should understand the Christian life more than how they actually did understand their present experience. Paul understood Christian existence as a tension between "already" and "not yet," living "between the times" of Christ's first coming, which inaugurated the eschatological age, and Christ's return to bring the triumph of God to fulfillment. The Corinthians had interpreted the spiritual phenomena occurring among them as evidence that the final time of fulfillment was already present, and they underestimated the "not yet" character of the Christian life (see on 4:8; Phil. 3:10–21; 2 Thess. 2:2). Paul here places the Corinthians' exuberance about their present spiritual experience in the larger framework of the whole church throughout the world (1:2),

a church still looking forward to the triumph of God as the fulfillment of history.

1:8 The day of our Lord Jesus Christ: Paul Christianizes an Old Testament concept (see on 1 Thess. 5:4–6).

1:9 The fellowship of his Son: "Fellowship" is elsewhere translated "sharing," "participation," "communion." It may have either the "vertical" reference of communion with God and Christ (as, e.g., 10:16) or the "horizontal" dimension of communion with fellow Christians, including those with whom one does not agree (as in Gal. 2:9). First John 1:3 has both dimensions, which may also be intended here. Participation in the Christian fellowship is not an optional second step after conversion, but is included within God's initial call. **God is faithful:** God is the actor in the Christian drama throughout. Humans have their own response-ability, but it is God who calls the Christian community into being, and God who sustains it until the end (see also Phil. 2:12–13).

1:10–6:20
PART ONE—PAUL'S RESPONSE TO WHAT HE HAD HEARD

Paul had received a letter from the Corinthians inquiring about various problems (see 7:1). The first extensive part of his letter, however, is directed to issues that they had not considered problematic, but about which he had heard from Chloe's people (1:11) or from the bearers of their letter.

1:10–17
DIVISIONS IN THE CHURCH

1:10 No divisions: The Corinthian church had formed competing groups, but *they* saw it as no problem and had not inquired about it. Paul saw it as the number-one problem to be addressed. **Be united:** The word is used elsewhere of mending nets (Matt. 4:21), i.e., of restoring an original unity. The "quest for Christian unity" is not an attempt to impose the human construction of a new united church, but the *re*construction of an original unity given to the church by God. The letter makes clear that Paul does not have in mind uniformity (3:21–23; 12:4–6, 12–31), but a deeper unity that transcends the diversity of differing gifts in the one body of Christ.

1:11 Chloe's people (NRSV)/**household** (NIV): Chloe was apparently a businesswoman in Corinth or Ephesus (where Paul is writing, 16:8) who has relatives, slaves, or employees who travel across the Aegean on business. If she herself was a Christian (not clear from the context), her large house may have been the meeting place of one of the Corinthian house churches. **Quarrels among you:** The quarrels were not a matter of personality conflicts or personal differences—though social and economic distinctions probably played a role (see 11:19–22), nor were the competing groups structured organizations like denominations. The factions were religious cliques promoting their favorite religious leader within the one church at Corinth.

1:12 I belong to Paul . . . Apollos . . . Cephas . . . Christ: In the pagan model of religious associations and mystery cults that had formed the background of many of the Corinthian converts, a significant bond was formed between the one who initiated new members into the group and the new initiates. On **Apollos,** see the introduction to 1 Corinthians; Acts 18:24; 19:1; 1 Cor. 3:4–5, 22; 4:6; 16:22. **Cephas** is the Aramaic name for Peter, both of which mean "Rock" (see Matt. 16:16–19; 1 Cor. 15:5; Gal. 2:8–9; introduction to 1 Peter). "**I belong to Christ**" is the most difficult slogan to interpret. Apparently some Corinthian Christians had made "Christ" into the name of a particular group, probably claiming direct relationship to Christ without any human mediation (see Paul himself in Gal. 1:1, 11–12).

1:13 Has Christ been divided? Paul takes it as axiomatic that there is one Christ, just as there is one God, one Spirit, one church, one faith, one hope, one baptism (8:6; see Eph. 4:4). **Crucified . . . baptized:** Paul does not respond to the competing groups with an appeal for openness and tolerance, but with an affirmation of the redemptive event of Jesus' death and by a reminder that their baptism united them with Christ and with each other (12:13; Rom. 6:3–4). The bond of unity is not good-natured tolerance (sometimes hardly indistinguishable from indifference), but the common gospel and common baptism already shared by all Christians.

1:14 I baptized none: Paul does not minimize the importance of baptism, which he everywhere assumes, but does minimize the importance of the particular person who performs the baptism. **Except Crispus:** In Acts 18:8 the ruler of the synagogue. **And Gaius:** In Romans 16:23 the "host" to the whole church in Corinth. He had a house large enough to serve as meeting place for all the scattered house churches in Corinth, a man of some wealth, one of the few in the Corinthian congregation (1:26).

1:16 Also the household of Stephanas: See 16:16–17. This "afterthought" shows not only Paul's own minimizing of the importance of the baptizer, but also the oral style retained in the unrevised letter, which functions to bring the apostle's living voice into the congregation.

1:17 Not . . . to baptize: Paul's mission was not to form a group of his own "followers," but to proclaim the good news of God's saving act in Christ. This reference to the gospel introduces the second major item on Paul's agenda, which actually was the context and cause of the quarreling groups—the contrast between human "wisdom" and the message of the cross.

1:18–31
CHRIST THE POWER AND
THE WISDOM OF GOD

1:18 The message of the cross (NIV): Two thousand years of usage as a positive religious symbol, as decoration, and as jewelry have dulled the impact of the words "cross" and "crucify." The Romans used crucifixion to make an example of those who disturbed the good life of the Roman peace, the *pax Romana*, as a public display of how important they considered "law and order." Roman citizens who committed crimes were not crucified. The punishment was reserved for revolutionaries, terrorists, the worst criminals, and slaves. "Cross" had the connotations of ugliness, contempt, weakness, loser, criminal, slave, unpatriotic lowlife.

Who are perishing . . . who are being saved: In Paul's perspective the Christ event divided all humanity into two categories: nonbelievers, who rely on their own potential or achievement, and believers, who respond in faith to God's grace. Both groups represent an action in process. Nonbelievers are not necessarily eternally doomed, and believers are on the way, not in the "already" state of "having arrived" (contrast the attitude of some of the Corinthians, 4:8).

1:19 It is written: Isa. 29:14. Such citations (see 1:31 = Jer. 9:23–24) show that the Christ event does not represent a change of plans on God's part, but that the God definitively revealed in Christ is the same God manifest to Israel and the prophets.

1:20 This age: Paul's apocalyptic thought contrasts the present **age** or **world** with the age/world to come (on apocalypticism, see the introduction to Revelation). The Corinthians suppose they already live in the age of fulfillment (4:8), but their evaluation of things in terms of human wisdom reveals that their thinking still belongs to the present age.

1:21 The world did not know God through wisdom: See Paul's elaboration in Rom. 1:18–31. **The foolishness of what was preached.** (NIV): Not the act of preaching but its content is foolishness by human standards. Paul's word is related to the English word "moron." A "crucified savior" was a contradiction of terms, an oxymoron. The Christian faith is thus not the confirmation of our best efforts and insights, but their replacement. The gospel overturns not only our worst, but our best. The God revealed in the cross of Jesus does not and cannot fit into our ideas of how the world works. The cross is a reversal of all our expectations, not just those that are evil or stupid.

1:22 Jews . . . Greeks: These are not empirical ethnic or national terms, but represent Paul's way of describing all humanity (see 10:32; 12:13; Rom. 1:16; 2:9; 3:9; 10:12; Acts 14:1; 18:4; 19:10, 17; 20:21), corresponding to the Jewish way of speaking of "Jews and Gentiles" and the Greek way of designating the whole of humanity as "Greeks and barbarians." "Jews" here represent the people who suppose that God's act is made obvious and clear by miraculous events, while "Greeks" represent those who assume that God's way of working is a confirmation of their own intellectual system or ordinary "common sense." Both types presume that God works according to their presuppositions. The cross stands both sets of expectations on their heads. To claim to believe the Christian faith because it has measured up to our expectations—whether of miracle or intellect—is still to operate with the wisdom of this world, which has been shattered by the unanticipated, unpredicted, incalculable event of the cross. Grace that is not amazing is not grace.

1:23 Stumbling block: Literally "scandal." There is a necessary scandal of the cross (Gal. 5:11). When it is watered down or eliminated, the gospel has been domesticated to our expectations, and the Christian faith only a projection of our "best" insights and ideologies (see on Mark 2:17).

1:24 Those who are the called: Paul's term for Christians (see on 1:2). **Christ the power of God and the wisdom of God:** What we could not attain or verify by miracles or intellectual systems or common sense, God has freely provided in the surprising event of the crucified Messiah.

1:26 Not many of you: Paul appeals to the composition of the Corinthian church as testimony to his point. The community of faith God has called together to be his witnesses in this world is not composed of mainly Caesars and senators, outstanding celebrities, or the wealthy and influential. But there are some—e.g., Crispus, Gaius, and Stephanas, mentioned above. The exceptional thing about the church, then and now, was that it included both rich and poor, slave and free, male and female, Jew and Gentile (see Gal. 3:28). This too was part of the message of the cross, the overturning of all human priorities and expectations.

1:28 Things that are not . . . things that are: The Corinthian church was not a matter of God or Paul's developing the human potential, but the work of the Creator God, who is not dependent on good raw material but creates out of nothing (see Rom. 4:5, 17; 2 Cor. 4:6).

1:29 No one may boast (NIV): The Corinthians wanted to be proud of their church, their preachers and apostles, and were upset with Paul in that he did not fit the mold. The only appropriate stance before God is not pride, but grateful praise.

1:30 It is because of him (NIV): Believers may not even be proud of their own "accomplishment" in accepting Christ as Lord, and can never say or think something like, "Sure, salvation comes from God, and is offered freely to all, but most have rejected it and *we*—unlike others—have accepted it." In retrospect, the believer does not take credit for his or her own faith, but gives thanks to God (see on Rom. 8:28–30).

1:30 Christ . . . became for us wisdom from God . . . righteousness . . . sanctification . . . redemption: The meaning is not that Christ became four things, but one thing: the wisdom of God. But the true wisdom is not intellectual systems or common sense into which the gospel is retrofitted. Christ as the wisdom of God is God's act in the cross, which is explicated in three metaphors: righteousness means living in right relation to God; sanctification means the holiness appropriate to the people of God (see on 1:2); redemption is the buying of people out of slavery and setting them free. All this was accomplished by God in the cross of Jesus. This is true wisdom, "what it's all about."

1:31 It is written: Jer. 9:23–24.

2:1–5
PROCLAIMING CHRIST CRUCIFIED

2:1 When I came to you: At the time of the founding of the church (Acts 18:1–17). **The mystery of God** (NRSV)/**The testimony about God**

(NIV): The NRSV follows one set of manuscripts, the NIV a different set. (Here as elsewhere, the original document has been lost, and the available manuscripts contain such variations.) The Greek words for "mystery" and "testimony" are very similar. Here the NIV has probably chosen the original reading. See "Introduction: The New Testament as the Church's Book," 4.d. **Lofty words or wisdom:** Paul was himself an educated person who wrote letters of considerable rhetorical power, including the present passage. He is not glorifying ignorance or crudeness, but reminding his readers that his own missionary preaching was not an "explanation" of how God's plan fits into rational human intellectual systems, but was the shattering of all such systems, including "common sense."

2:2 Jesus Christ and him crucified: The grammatical form (perfect passive participle) points to the continuing identity of Christ as the Crucified One. The cross is not an incident in the cosmic career of Christ that was left behind at the resurrection, but has indelibly stamped itself on the divine identity. At the cross God revealed himself as the One who gives himself and suffers on behalf of others, the One whose power is revealed in weakness (see 1:23; 2 Cor. 4:10; 5:19; Gal. 2:20; 3:1; Mark 16:6).

2:3–4 Weakness . . . fear . . . trembling: Paul's own presence among them was not impressive by human standards, but corresponded to the message of the cross. Paul was afflicted with some physical ailment (see on 2 Cor. 12:7) and retained the effects of several severe beatings (see 2 Cor. 11:23–29). The **demonstration of the Spirit and of power** refers to the spiritual phenomena that accompanied the conversion of the Corinthians (see on chaps. 12–14). Such "spiritual experiences" are not a violation of or alternative to the message of the cross.

2:5 That your faith might not rest on human wisdom: They had not become believers because Paul had presented persuasive evidence that Jesus was the Christ, but by the **power of God** that was at work in his testimony to the crucified Jesus whom God raised from the dead. Even though they may have thought that they had come to faith on the basis of preaching that appealed to their common sense or scientific or philosophical wisdom, faith had actually been generated by the word of God that came through the message of the cross.

2:6–16
THE TRUE WISDOM OF GOD

In this section Paul appears at first to reverse or even contradict his previous argument, but he is actually taking up the language of the Corinthian advocates of (worldly) "wisdom" and using it against them—with a heavy dose of irony. Paul is clearly *not* proposing an elitism in which there are "spiritual" Christians and "ordinary" Christians. He understands the Holy Spirit to have been given to all Christians when they were baptized (12:13). The Corinthians have the Holy Spirit by virtue of their being incorporated into the church, the body of Christ, but they are still living by the "wisdom" of the old age.

2:6 The mature: In contrast to the "infants" of 3:1. Both words probably reflect the Corinthians' own vocabulary. They considered themselves "mature" in contrast to "baby Christians" and objected that Paul had not given them the sophisticated "wisdom" provided by their later teachers—and wondered whether Paul perhaps belonged to the "baby" class himself.

2:7–8 Not a wisdom of this age: Paul has already declared that the true wisdom of God is the crucified Christ (1:30). Paul and the Corinthians agree on the importance of the Holy Spirit and the gift of divine wisdom. But for Paul it is important that the gift of the Spirit be seen in corporate terms, not the individualistic terms of the present age (see on chap. 12), but in terms of the Christ event that inaugurated the new age to which the Spirit belongs.

The rulers of this age: Paul may be thinking of the actual political and religious power structures of the present world, or the demonic forces that are manifest in them (see Rom. 8:38; 1 Cor. 15:24–26; 2 Cor. 4:4; Gal. 4:3, 8–9; Eph. 2:2; Col. 2:15), or both.

God's wisdom, secret and hidden: This is not a matter of esoteric revelations communicated in trances, mystical "spiritual" experience, or a mysterious code known only to the initiates. God's wisdom was "secret" and "hidden" because it was manifest in the crucified Christ, a revelation that no one could recognize apart from the work of the Holy Spirit. **Before the ages:** Salvation through Christ was not a late change of plans on God's part. The self-giving of the weak, crucified one revealed who God has always been, is now, and ever will be.

None of the rulers of this age understood this: The value system of this world, manifest in its power structures and representing the demonic forces that stand behind it, could not perceive that God was acting in the life and death of Jesus. Luke–Acts expresses this in a different mode, that of human ignorance (see on Acts 3:17).

2:9 As it is written: Paul clinches his point by citing Scripture. Since this text is not found in the Old Testament, Paul may be paraphrasing a loose combination of Isaiah 64:4 and 65:16. More likely, he is citing a lost document that he considered Scripture—the canon of the Old Testament was not yet firmly fixed in Paul's day. Origen, a third-century Christian leader, stated that the quotation is from the (now lost) *Apocalypse of Elijah.* The words are found in the *Testament of Jacob* and (as words of Jesus!) in *Gospel of Thomas* 17, both of which are later than Paul but may have been citing the same source he here quotes.

2:10 Revealed to us: To the Christian community, not just to Paul and his associates or a special "spiritual" group. **Through the Spirit:** The church's insight into Christ as the saving act of God is a matter of revelation from God's side, not of human attainment.

2:11 What is truly human (NRSV)/**thoughts of a man** (NIV): Here the NRSV's effort to use gender-inclusive language transforms Paul's meaning into a generalization that misses what he wants to say. Though not using inclusive language, the NIV is here more accurate. Paul's point has nothing to do with "what is truly human" in the general sense. He intends to say that a person's inner thoughts are truly known only to that individual and those to whom he or she chooses to reveal them. But when this self-disclosure actually happens, others *do* know the real thought of the person, which they could never have figured out on their own. Since "spirit" also means "mind," "inner consciousness," "purpose," "intent," Paul can use this reality of human experience as an analogy of God's revelation: what we could never know on our own, no matter how profound our "wisdom," God has revealed.

2:12 So that we may understand: The perception that the good things we have are neither our achievement nor "good luck," but the gifts of God, is itself a gift of God. This is true of the supreme gift of salvation through God's Son. Being able to see that God acted in the cross of Christ is not a matter of human cleverness or sophisticated wisdom. No one can *explain* how or why God "had to" send Christ and why Jesus "had to" die for human salvation. The response to this saving act by those who

have come to faith is not, "I'm smart," but "Thanks be to God" (15:57; 2 Cor. 8:16).

2:13 Those who are spiritual: All Christians, not a special "spiritual" group. The Greek text is ambiguous and can be translated more than one way (see NRSV, NIV, and their respective notes). The context deals with both "**spiritual people**" (3:1) and "**words . . . taught by the Spirit.**" The reference to "words" does not mean that the words of Paul's letters are dictated by the Holy Spirit, but that his message of the cross (composed and communicated in his own words and ideas) is not merely a matter of human insight but is the work of the Holy Spirit.

2:14 Those who are unspiritual: In this whole section, whether or not one is "spiritual" does not depend on one's attitude or personal piety, but is a matter of living in accord with the Holy Spirit active in the life of the church. **Foolishness:** See 1:18–2:5. The contrast is between conventional common sense and the truth of the Christian faith manifest in the Crucified One.

2:15 Subject to no one else's scrutiny (NRSV)/**judgment** (NIV): See 4:3–4. This does not describe a spiritual elite who can claim to be above the judgment of the community itself—as the rest of 1 Corinthians indicates—but means that those who operate by the divine wisdom of the crucified Messiah (those who live their lives in the light of the Christ event) are not subject to judgment by the criteria of those who operate on the basis of purely worldly wisdom. The Spirit is to be measured by the cross, not by human standards, even "spiritual" ones.

2:16 Who has known the mind of the Lord?: From Isa. 40:13. The rhetorical question implies, "No one—as a matter of their own achievement by human wisdom." **The mind of Christ:** Not a personal attitude but the corporate wisdom of the community of faith. See Phil. 2:1–11.

3:1–22
ON DIVISIONS IN
THE CORINTHIAN CHURCH

In this section Paul returns directly to the problem of divisions in the church as a result of their fascination with human wisdom.

3:1 Spiritual people: This was their own term for themselves; they had complained that Paul had not treated them as "spiritual" enough. Paul replies that they are still **people of the flesh.** This does not mean that they were necessarily guilty of "spectacular" sins of sexual

513

lust, gluttony, and the like. Rather, the Christ event, the coming of the Holy Spirit, and their baptism into the community of faith where the Spirit is active are presupposed. However, they continue to live and think as though none of this had happened, living their lives as though they still belonged to the world. Paul is not here advocating a spiritual elitism that contrasts those who are "spiritual" with those who are only "babes"—this is the Corinthian view he is against—but declaring that their present behavior reflects the worldly values from which they have been set free, rather than the life of the Spirit into which they have been baptized (12:13). Paul redefines spirituality in the light of the cross.

3:2 Milk, not solid food: Not Paul's own vocabulary, but standard philosophical parlance, as was the contrast between "mature" and "babes." The Corinthians (or some of them) had adopted this language, considered themselves "mature" and "spiritual," and complained that Paul had not fed them with solid food of impressive philosophical explanations of the faith, but only with "milk," the simple gospel of Christ crucified and risen.

3:3 Jealousy and quarreling: The mark of "spiritual" people, i.e., of the work of the Holy Spirit in their lives, is not infatuation with "wisdom," but the absence of jealousy and self-centered competitive rivalry. The Spirit creates concern for the whole body of Christ (see chaps. 12–14). The word for "jealousy" may also be translated "zeal" (as in John 2:12; Rom. 10:2; 2 Cor. 7:7; 9:2; Phil. 3:6). What Paul opposes is not mere pettiness, but zealous concern for religious issues about which people have deep convictions. These include issues discussed in 1:10–3:22 (e.g., the meaning of baptism and the cross of Jesus, the nature of commitment to particular theologies and religious leaders, the relation of faith to human wisdom). Nor is Paul commending a shallow tolerance that says such things don't really matter. The unspiritual behavior is the kind of narrow religious zeal that promotes rivalry and division.

3:5–7 What is Apollos? . . . Paul? Paul refuses to enter into the competitive Corinthian game that makes "belonging to Apollos" and "belonging to Paul" alternatives ("Peter" is here curiously absent; see 1:12). Though he and Apollos are different, they are partners, not rivals. The one God works through both.

3:9 God's fellow workers (NIV): Not, as in older translations, "Fellow workers with God," but

fellow workers with each other, both working on God's farm. God as owner and Lord of the farm sends laborers with different tasks into his fields. One plants, another waters. It is God who makes the church grow.

3:10 I laid a foundation: Paul's switch of metaphors illustrates that in Corinth he did have the priority in founding the church (see Rom. 15:20), and that later both he and Apollos, as well as others, built on this foundation. For a different image, see Eph. 2:20, where the apostles and prophets are the church's foundation, and Matt. 16:18, where Peter is the rock on which the church is built. Here, the original preaching of the crucified and risen Christ (not human wisdom, not human leaders) is the one foundation of the church.

3:13 The Day will disclose it: Paul's apocalyptic perspective looks forward to the final judgment (as 1:7–8; see 1 Thess. 5:2; Rom. 2:5, 16; 14:10; 2 Cor. 5:10) that will be a fiery trial of the work of Christian leaders. Paul is speaking neither of purgatory after death nor of the fate of individual souls, but of how well church leaders have built on the one foundation of Jesus Christ. This is not apparent to human eyes at present. What may appear to be a "successful" or "growing" church may be growing in numbers and enthusiasm by promoting current ideologies and cultural ideals in response to the religious market.

3:15 The builder will be saved: Here one's salvation is a matter of God's grace, not a matter of being a "good minister" (see 9:24–27, where Paul seems to present a different perspective). But each minister will give account for his or her ministry. Those who have built by faulty standards will suffer loss, and those who have built well will be rewarded. Here Paul remains with his metaphor. When a well-built building withstands storm, earthquake, or fire, the builder is praised. When structures that seem splendid now collapse under stress, the builder may be fined.

3:16 You are God's temple: The temple in Jerusalem was still standing as Paul writes this. For every faithful Jew, it was the visible center of God's presence in this world. The sectarian Jewish community at Qumran (where the Dead Sea Scrolls were found) had become convinced that the temple in Jerusalem was defiled by the priests who, in their understanding, were unauthorized to be there. They therefore withdrew to the desert, where they came to understand that the real temple of God was in their own holy community that offered spiritual sacrifices (see Rom. 12:1). Here Paul makes an analogous reinterpretation: God dwells not in a particular building but in a consecrated community. The pronoun "you" and the corresponding verbs are plural. Paul is not talking about the Holy Spirit in each individual Christian's life (cf. 6:19–20) but the community of faith as filled with God's Spirit and therefore a dwelling place of God (see Eph. 2:22). Here the point is that the temple is holy and God will not tolerate its being defiled or destroyed by remodeling it along the lines of human wisdom.

3:18 You should become fools: This is not a general statement praising lack of sense, but returns to the theme of 1:18–2:16, the Corinthians' infatuation with impressive "wisdom," "deep" understanding of the Christian faith that "explains" the divine mysteries and leads to elitism and factionalism. Paul nails down his point with citations from Job 5:12–13 and Ps. 94:11.

3:21–23 All things are yours: If the Corinthians could get past their regarding various leaders in a competitive, exclusive way, they might see that they do not belong to any particular religious leader, but that all belong to them. Each Christian belongs to the one church of God, not to a party, denomination, sect, or movement. Thus all authentic Christian leaders belong to the whole church—not only Paul, Apollos, and Peter, but Augustine, Aquinas, Luther, Calvin, Wesley, Campbell, Teresa, King, and a great cloud of witnesses too vast to be named (see Heb. 11). This is so not because Paul is promoting a liberal and tolerant attitude, but because **you belong to Christ and Christ belongs to God.**

4:1–13
THE MINISTRY OF THE APOSTLES

The chapter break (added much later) is not the beginning of a new topic. In 4:1–21 Paul sums up and concludes his understanding of apostolic Christian ministry. The Corinthians had exalted ministers who impressed them with "wisdom." Paul himself did not measure up well by those standards.

4:1–2 Servants . . . and stewards: Here the metaphor shifts again—apostles are God's household servants, working in their master's house and responsible only to him, a metaphor also used by Jesus (see Luke 12:42–43). In Paul's social world a slave could be given weighty responsibilities and represent the master, something like a manager or foreman

in our social system. **Mysteries:** The Corinthians may have heard this in terms of the pagan mystery cults, but Paul is using biblical language for the revealed plan of God, what God is about in history (Amos 3:7; Dan. 1:18, 27–30; 4:9; see at Eph. 1:9). The word does not refer to puzzling riddles or complex abstractions, but to that which has previously been concealed from ordinary human understanding but now has been made known (e.g., Rom. 16:25; 1 Cor. 2:1; 13:2; 14:2; 15:51; Eph. 1:9; 3:3–5, 9; Col. 1:26–27; 2:2).

Trustworthy: This is the qualification for ministers. It not only refers to personal integrity, but includes an awareness that they have been **entrusted** (NIV) with something they did not create, the gospel handed to them through the church.

4:3 Judged by you: Paul does not judge his ministry by whether or not he measures up to human criteria of what a "good minister" should be. Accountability is the issue here. Although Paul and all authentic ministers "belong" to the church (3:21–23), they are finally accountable only to the God who called and authorized them. The Corinthians cannot judge someone else's servant (Rom. 14:4).

4:4 My conscience is clear (NIV): On the one hand, Paul never advises going against conscience (see Rom. 14:1–9). On the other hand, just because one's conscience is clear does not mean one is acceptable to God. Paul is not here asserting a self-centered individualism ("I did it my way," "I don't care what people think," etc.). On the contrary, he places himself with the Corinthians rather than over against them. His point is that how either they or he himself judge his ministry does not matter; only God's evaluation at the Last Judgment is what counts.

4:5 Do not pronounce judgment before the time: This is not a general statement about having a judgmental attitude, but a particular statement about evaluating Christian ministers: only the eschaton will reveal who has been a good minister and who not (3:10–15). In 5:12, Paul calls on them to judge (= critically discern and make a decision), and he himself is judging the Corinthians in this sense throughout the first four chapters.

4:6 All this: Paul now pulls together his whole argument. **Do not go beyond what is written** (NIV): This statement continues to puzzle scholars, so much so that some consider it a non-Pauline gloss and omit it entirely. NRSV and NIV are probably correct in considering it a quotation familiar to the Corinthians, a popular proverb of some sort. It could be a generalization like "Play by the rules!" (as in the NEB "Keep within the rules"). Then the meaning would be that they have been treating both Paul and Apollos unfairly, i.e., not "going by the rules." More likely is that "what is written" refers to the Scripture, as elsewhere in Paul, and that he is referring to the scriptural texts he has quoted in the preceding that reject pride in human wisdom. **Puffed up:** As in our expression "full of hot air." See 5:2; 8:1; 13:4, where this is the opposite of Christian love. **One against another:** Probably not a generalization, but referring specifically to Apollos and Paul, whom the Corinthians consider to be rivals and alternatives. Paul and Apollos are indeed different, but Paul regards Apollos as a partner who complements his own ministry, rather than a competitor.

4:7 What do you have that you did not receive? Though there is a general truth here—God is the Creator of all—the point has to do with Christian faith and ministry. The Corinthians did not *discover* Christian faith in a "quest for spirituality" but received it from the preaching and teaching of Paul and his fellow missionaries. Modern Christians do not discover or invent the faith afresh, but receive it from the community of faith of past generations. Since this is so, the only appropriate response is gratitude.

4:8 Already: Paul's theology, like that of the New Testament in general, maintains the tension between the "already" and the "not yet" inherent in the Christian faith. The Christ has already come and the kingdom is in a certain sense already present, but the Christ is still to come, Christians still rightfully pray, "Thy kingdom come," and God's plan for history and the world is not yet fulfilled. The Corinthians have practically abandoned the eschatological perspective they received from Paul and relaxed this tension in favor of the "already." This may be due to a perversion of Christian theology that abandoned the future hope, or a reinterpretation of Christian faith in terms of contemporary wisdom speculation. In the latter view, the "wise" knew that whatever their external circumstances, in their inner individual selves they "reigned as kings." This was the language of popular Stoic philosophy of Paul's day. **Without us . . . with you** (NIV): Their understanding not only abandoned the forward-looking eschatological horizon of Christian faith, but had become individualistic. Paul reasserts the communal

view of the Christian life as belonging to the body of Christ.

4:9 Apostles . . . last of all: The metaphor is that of the parade of a victorious Roman general, who led his captives in a triumphal procession. Those condemned to die as gladiators or be thrown to wild animals brought up the rear. This is the spot that God has assigned the true apostles. Paul's image of ministry is not prestige and honor, but a public spectacle corresponding to Christ as the crucified one. **To angels:** Here as elsewhere in the authentic Pauline letters, angels are seen in a negative light. Like the unbelieving world, they view the apostolic ministry with consternation.

4:10–13 Fools for the sake of Christ: By worldly standards, including its "wisdom," it is foolish to regard the crucified man of Nazareth as God's definitive revelation and saving act (1:18–2:16). Authentic ministry participates in this "foolishness," as does authentic Christian life. Being a disciple of Jesus is not a means to enhancing self-esteem and gaining the respect of others. Here Paul uses sarcasm and irony, contrasting his view of ministry with theirs. As the opposition to Paul in Corinth intensifies, so does Paul's sarcastic style (see 2 Cor. 10–13). **When reviled, we bless:** Beneath the sarcasm is the authentic embodiment of Jesus' own loving response to those who rejected him (Matt. 5:44; Luke 6:28; 23:34). **The work of our own hands:** Manual labor was looked down upon by many in Paul's world, especially by the traveling philosopher teachers honored by the Corinthians. They resented Paul's refusal to accept money from them so he would not "have to work." Paul earned his own living as a way of distinguishing himself from the itinerant philosophers (see 1 Thess. 2:9; 2 Cor. 11:7–11). **Rubbish . . . dregs:** In Paul's situation authentic apostles could not be honored by the worldly standards the Corinthians were using, but are considered the **scum** (NIV) of the earth and the world's trash.

4:14–21
FATHERLY ADMONITIONS

4:14–15 As my beloved children: His words take a warmer tone. The sharpness of Paul's rebukes is within the context of family relationships, concerned with the well-being of the Corinthians, not simply defensiveness or scoring points on his own behalf. Likewise, "father" is not merely a reflection of the patriarchy of the times (shared by Jesus, Paul, and the New Testament authors in general with their culture), but (1) common terminology for the teacher-student relationship; (2) an expression of Paul's conviction that they were "begotten" by the word of God preached by him that had generated new life (see Phlm. 10; 1 Pet. 1:3, 23; Jas. 1:18). Thus Timothy is his "son," and they are his "children." Paul, like Jesus, adopts the language and thought world of patriarchy but fills it with new content—his only power is the power of the gospel of the weak, crucified Jesus (2 Cor. 13:4). Paul is their only father, their other teachers are only **guardians**—the trustworthy slaves who conduct children to school (see on Gal. 3:24).

4:16 Be imitators of me: This is not egotism, but an extension of the father metaphor. Children learn by having good parents as role models. The church in Corinth was new and had no tradition. They did not need laws for the Christian way of life, but they did need role models of what it meant to have one's life shaped by the gospel of the crucified and risen Lord. Paul claims that the apostles are authentic representatives and models of the kind of life to which Jesus calls his disciples.

4:17 My ways in Christ: On the key Pauline phrase "in Christ," see on 2 Cor. 5:17. Paul does not deliver a new set of Christian rules, but teaches Christians to live in ways appropriate to their new situation "in Christ."

4:19–20 Not the talk . . . but their power: This is not the conventional contrast between words and deeds, saying and doing (as, e.g., in Matt. 7:22–23; 23:1–3). "Talk" here translates *logos*, as in 1:5 (= "speech"), 1:17 (= "eloquent wisdom"), 1:18 (= "message"), 2:1 (= "lofty words of wisdom"). The contrast is thus between rhetorical wisdom and the power inherent in the message of the cross. The same contrast between "word" (*logos*) and "power" is found in 2:4. Throughout, the contrast has been between the supposed powerful speech of those enamored of "wisdom" and the apostolic gospel of the crucified Jesus, whose power is made perfect in weakness (2 Cor. 12:9; see Rom. 1:16). **Kingdom of God:** Occurs often in the Synoptic Gospels, but is rare in Paul and John. On the meaning, see Luke 4:43–44.

4:21 Stick (NRSV); **whip** (NIV): This word would be better translated "rod," as in Prov. 13:24; 22:15; 23:13–14, since it is not Pauline bravado but a continuation of the "father/children" metaphor. Paul's question is, when he next visits the Corinthian congregation as their spiritual father, shall he come in fatherly tenderness or fatherly discipline?

5:1–8
SEXUAL IMMORALITY DEFILES THE CHURCH

The subject shifts for the first time since 1:10 (see the introduction to 1 Corinthians, Outline). Again the issue Paul deals with is not something they had asked about and did not consider to be a problem.

5:1 Pagans: Literally "nations," "Gentiles," the term used by the Old Testament, Israel, and Judaism of non-Jews, since Israel as the holy people of God did not count itself among the "nations." The Corinthian Christians themselves were mostly Gentiles, but Paul here addresses them as those who have been incorporated into the people of God (see Gal. 6:16; 1 Pet. 2:12; 4:3). **Living with his father's wife:** As in contemporary English, "living with" indicates a long-term sexual relationship. The woman was not his own mother, but another of his father's wives, as is made clear by Lev. 18:7–8, to which Paul is here alluding. The relationship was not "incest" in the sense of cohabiting with a blood relative. Apparently the father had died and the son and stepmother were living together as man and wife. Both the Old Testament and Gentile law forbade such unions as a violation of community standards. That the woman involved is not condemned probably means she was not a Christian.

5:2 You are arrogant: The Greek pronoun is plural. It is striking that Paul never addresses the guilty individual, but the church as a whole. He is concerned not merely with the individual's sin but with the nature and mission of the church. Clearly Paul does not consider the modern view that one's sex life is "nobody else's business" as applicable to Christians who have been added to the church and who must take its corporate witness and mission into consideration in all their relationships (see chaps. 8, 10, 12). "Arrogant" is literally "puffed up," the same word as in 4:6, 18; 8:1; 13:4, the same stance called "boasting" in v. 6. They were proud of their newfound Christian freedom, which liberated them from cultural conventions and "what other people think," but had misunderstood Paul's own doctrine of freedom that included responsibility for the church's mission. Their pride was not that they were tolerant of a sinful situation, but that they were "enlightened" and did not consider the relationship wrong, though their less enlightened neighbors were scandalized by it.

See on their motto, "All things are lawful for me," at 6:12 and 10:23.

5:3 Absent in body . . . present in spirit (or **Spirit**): The first step in understanding this difficult passage is to acknowledge that it is expressed in terms of the ancient worldview, in which Paul and his readers were "at home," but which is no longer presupposed by modern readers. Two things are clearly not meant: (1) The modern expression "I'm with you in spirit," in the sense of "I'll be thinking about you, I can't be there, but you'll be in my thoughts." Paul means he will really be there, not that they should proceed "as if" he were there. (2) The ancient Greek dualistic way of thinking that divided human being into a physical body and an internal soul or spirit, so that the spirit could be one place and while the body is another. Paul understood human being in the unified sense of the Old Testament, so that "flesh," "body," "mind," "heart," "soul," and "spirit" were not separable components, but different ways of speaking about the whole person (see on Mark 12:30; Matt. 22:37; 1 Thess. 5:23). Paul believed that when his letters were read out in the assembled congregation, his voice was really there, and there was a sense in which he was personally present. Yet this is not the whole explanation. In some way strange to modern thought patterns, Paul believed that he would be present to participate in the congregational decision (see Ezek. 11:1–11; Matt. 18:18–20; Acts 8:39; 2 Cor. 12:1–5).

5:4 When you are assembled: Though Paul has already passed judgment, his judgment is not effective on its own, but requires the consent and cooperation of the church as a whole. Paul's point is that the whole matter is not just between the person and God or a difference of opinion between the offender and Paul, but is a concern of the whole congregation. **In the name of the Lord Jesus:** "Name" connotes presence, power, and authority. It is not clear how the phrase is grammatically connected to the rest of the sentence. If related to "pronounce judgment," then the meaning is that Paul makes his pronouncement with the authority of the risen Christ himself (so RSV, NRSV, TEV). If connected to "assembled," the meaning is that the congregation comes together in the power and presence of Christ, a common view of early Christian worship (so KJV, NIV, NEB, JB, REB). The most natural way to read the phrase is connected with "done," which would mean that the offender

had entered into his relationship with the woman claiming that it was authorized by his freedom in Christ, that he was violating community standards precisely on the basis of his Christian conviction (so NRSV note and several recent scholars).

5:5 Hand this man over to Satan: Expel him from the community; no longer regard him as a Christian brother. This means not to impose some new punishment upon him, but to place him *back* where he was before he became a Christian, namely, in the world dominated by Satan (see 2 Cor. 4:4). **So that the sinful nature** (NRSV **flesh**) **may be destroyed** (NIV): Exactly what Paul has in mind here is not apparent to modern readers, but again it seems clear that he is not thinking in terms of ancient Greek dualism that regarded a person as composed of mortal flesh and immortal spirit. It is evident that the disciplinary action is intended to lead to the ultimate salvation of the man, so the NIV translation is probably best: the man is to be placed outside the church in the realm of Satan, there to experience troubles and shame that will lead him to repentance and readmission to the church. Clearly the punishment is provisional and remedial, with the ultimate salvation of the man the goal of the whole proceeding.

5:7 Clean out the old yeast: It is just as clear that the overarching concern of the whole section is preserving the church as the people of God, guarding it from becoming indistinguishable from the world around it. These verses transfer the whole issue into the framework of the exodus story, in which Israel was delivered from Egypt and constituted as the holy people of God (Exod. 12–13; see also comments at 10:1–13; 1 Pet. 1:13–17). The Corinthians could only have understood this paragraph if they were familiar with the story of Exod. 12–24 (esp. 12–13) and understood themselves as addressed by this text as the continuing people of God. The "old yeast" had to be cleaned out of the houses in order to celebrate the festival of Unleavened Bread associated with the Passover. It was a negative symbol of the old evil way of life, the slavery from which they had been delivered.

You really are unleavened: The church is pictured as the new unleavened bread used at the Passover. The imperative to purify the community is based on the indicative that the community is pure, another example of the Pauline ethic of indicative/imperative: be holy because you are holy. God's gracious act and human responsibility are here set alongside each other. **Our paschal lamb, Christ:** The Passover lamb was not a sacrifice for sins, but the symbol of the Hebrews' deliverance from slavery and their constitution by God as a distinctive people. The blood of the lamb on the doorpost of the house separated and protected those inside from the destroyer that raged outside. Paul applies this picture to the church. The offender is to be removed from the exodus community of faith and placed back in the secular community where the destroyer is at work.

5:8 Celebrate the festival: Here the life of the Christian community as a whole is pictured as a continual festival of thanksgiving and communion.

5:9–13
Sexual Immorality Must Be Judged

5:9 I wrote to you: Paul's previous letter to the Corinthians has been lost, or perhaps part of it may be found in 2 Cor. 6:14–7:1.

5:10 You would then need to go out of the world: Paul's lost letter had addressed the problem of Christians continuing to live according to the pagan standards of sexual morality, in which premarital and extramarital sex was usually considered normal, violating neither community nor religious standards. They had misunderstood his command not to associate with such immoral people as though it applied to people in general, which would mean the church would have to withdraw into a holy conclave like the sectarian Jewish group of Qumran near the Dead Sea. But Paul understands God to have placed the church in the midst of the world, where it is to continue to live and carry on its mission, rubbing elbows and associating with all types of people.

5:11 Anyone who bears the name of brother or sister: Paul's directions apply to internal church discipline, not to contacts with outsiders.

5:13 Drive out the wicked person from among you: This is quoted from Deuteronomy (17:7), the book directed to the exodus people of the Old Testament. It is thus probable that the list of six specific sins of v. 11 reflects the six categories of sinners in Deuteronomy that so defile the community that they must be removed (see Deut. 13:1–5; 17:2–7; 19:16–19; 21:18–21; 22:21–22, 30; 24:7). The parallel is close, but not exact. In any case, it suggests that Paul is addressing the church as God's new Israel (see Gal. 6:16), a community that must remain distinctive if it is to fulfill its mission in the world.

For at least three reasons this passage is difficult for many modern Christians, especially mainline Protestants, to hear as an effective word of God for their own time:

1. The whole concept of the church as a community that disciplines and even expels its members is strange to many such modern readers. They may be acquainted with, and affirm, the disciplinary procedures for ordained ministers who have committed flagrant sins, but not with similar measures for "ordinary" church members. The argument is that the ministry of such a member of the clergy has been damaged or destroyed, so discipline or expulsion is not a personal condemnation but is necessary for the mission of the church, which cannot function with ministers whose lives contradict the message of the church. Paul did not make this clergy/laity distinction, and applied this kind of thinking to the church as a whole.

2. Modern Protestants are not accustomed to taking seriously the biblical understanding of the church as a holy community ("saints"), in which the Holy Spirit and the risen Christ are actually present. The biblical concept and language of "holiness" are alien to most secularized Protestants. Even those who would object to crude violations of the holiness of the sanctuary (having a cocktail party around the communion table, using the chalice for mixing drinks; using the baptistry as a bathtub) would tend to express their intuitive discomfort in terms of taste and aesthetics, though what they would be struggling to express is their rightful sense of the church as a holy community. On holiness, see on 7:12–16; Acts 5:1–11; 1 Pet. 1:15–22. Paul regards the church not as a voluntaristic association of seekers or do-gooders, but as the holy community God has called into being for God's mission in the world.

3. Modern Protestants are accustomed to having a variety of "churches" in the community with different standards of tolerance, so that if one is "too conservative" or "too liberal," those who are expelled—usually informally—from one may find another where they are more comfortable. In such a "marketing" atmosphere, each type of congregation or denomination is inclined to have the same pride as the Corinthians concerning those who fit into "their" church but are unwelcome elsewhere. The disciplined and excluded member at Corinth knew he was excluded from the church, and could not

find another congregation more to his taste. The divided church of our own time is a hindrance to our understanding biblical texts such as this.

6:1–11
LAWSUITS AMONG BELIEVERS

Some Christians in Corinth were taking each other to court before pagan judges. In addressing this issue (which, again, they did not see as a problem, and concerning which they did not ask Paul's counsel) Paul does not turn to a different topic, for his continuing theme is that as Christians they have not become simply "spiritual" individuals, but that they now belong to the community of faith. Paul continues to respond in terms of the true nature of the church thought of in eschatological and apocalyptic terms. His impatient, heavy-handed, sarcastic tone reflects his frustration that they have little understanding of who they are as baptized members of the body of Christ who participate in the life of the Spirit.

The social situation also plays a role. The disputes in court were about property, which reflects an upper-class activity. The wealthier members of the congregation were using the court system as an instrument of injustice against the poorer members (see 1:26).

6:1 The unrighteous . . . the saints: Paul's dualistic manner of referring to non-Christians and Christians. See "those who have no standing in the church" (v. 4) and "unbelievers" (v. 6). Such dualism is characteristic of the apocalyptic worldview (see 5:5 and the introduction to Revelation). Paul's consternation that Christians do not settle disputes among themselves but go to pagan courts also reflects Paul's background in the Jewish community, which had its own courts that settled disputes among Jews.

6:2–3 Saints will judge the world: In some streams of apocalyptic understanding, God's people will assist the divine judge at the Last Judgment (see Dan. 7:22; Wis. 3:7–8; Matt. 19:28; Luke 22:30; Rev. 3:21; 20:4). **We are to judge angels:** See 2 Pet. 2:4; Jude 6. Apocalypticism often attributed evil in the world to rebellious angels, who will be judged at the eschaton. Paul pictures Christians as participating in this judgment.

Ordinary matters: A better translation than the NIV's **things of this life,** which implies that Christians are not concerned with this world but only the next. Paul's point is rather that Christian faith gives one the eyes to reevaluate the matters prized by this world—chiefly money, property, and prestige—as no longer of central importance.

6:4 Those who have no standing: The Greek text is ambiguous. The verb may be either indicative or imperative. The NRSV understands it as indicative, so that Paul charges the Corinthians with pleading their case before pagan courts that (should) have no standing among Christians, who will themselves participate in the final judgment. The NIV takes it as an ironic imperative, to the effect that it is better to place the disputes before even the least-capable church members than to go to court before pagans. The NRSV is here the more probable meaning.

6:5 No one . . . wise enough: Extremely sarcastic, in view of the Corinthian glorification of "wisdom" and their claim to be "wise" (1:17–30, 2:13; 3:10, 18–20). **A believer . . . against a believer** (NRSV)/**Brother . . . against brother** (NIV). The Greek text is literally "brother," understood in the inclusive sense "brother or sister." Paul's point is that disputes among Christians are family matters to be settled within the family, since members of the church have been born anew into the family of God and made brothers and sisters to each other (see 4:14–15; 5:11).

6:7 To have lawsuits at all . . . is already a defeat: Regardless of who "wins" in court, all in fact lose—plaintiff, defendant, and the church as a whole. The statement is partially colored by Paul's expectation that the divine judge would come soon to establish the final justice of God. Paul's instruction here cannot be reduced to this, however, as though it has nothing to say to later generations who do not share Paul's eschatology. Christian faith provides a radical transformation of what "winning" and "losing" are (see on Rev. 5), just as it calls Christians to "sit loose" to what are considered the primary values of the world (see 7:29–31). Christians who no longer expect the second coming to happen soon are nonetheless called to eschatological existence within the community of faith. This instruction is part of Paul's larger teaching that the unity and mission of the church are more important than individual interests, more important than any private property, and is related to Jesus' teaching that it is better to suffer wrong than to wrong another person (see Matt. 5:39–40; Luke 6:28–30).

6:9 Wrongdoers will not inherit the kingdom of God: On "kingdom of God," see on 4:20, Luke

4:43–44. Paul here expands his vice list of 5:10 from six to ten items, but in neither place is his purpose to draw up a list of those who will enter the kingdom and those who will not (e.g., liars, murderers, child molesters, and those guilty of many other serious crimes are not mentioned). Paul's point is to illustrate the new reality to which the Corinthians now belong. This list illustrates the way some of them *were*, but Paul's point is they no longer belong to the world where these kinds of sins prevail. The problem is that they are living as though they were still resident members of the old world, taking each other to court over property matters. It is ironic that much recent discussion of this text focuses on items in Paul's illustrative list (especially the reference to homosexual acts) and ignores his main point. **Male prostitutes:** The word literally means "soft," and was often applied to the more passive member in homosexual activity. **Homosexual offenders** (NIV): A rare word apparently referring to the more active partner in homosexual acts (NRSV "sodomites"). For a brief discussion of interpreting New Testament passages dealing with homosexuality, see on Rom. 1:27.

6:11 Washed ... sanctified ... justified: The verbs are all passive, pointing to God's act, the basis for Paul's call to the moral life: "Be what you are." "God has placed you among his holy people. Live like it." The three words are not a chronological series of the "steps of salvation," but three metaphors of what happens at conversion. Former pagans are washed (baptismal language; see Acts 22:16), sanctified, (made holy as members of God's holy covenant community), and justified (an image from the law court in which the accused person is acquitted and pronounced righteous).

6:12–20
GLORIFY GOD IN BODY AND SPIRIT

Except for the Jewish community, the world into which Christianity was born made little connection between religious faith and sexual ethics. Sex prior to and outside marriage was generally accepted as normal (for males) and was not considered a religious or moral issue. The Corinthian Christians, most of whom had been Gentiles before their conversion, brought these attitudes with them into the church.

Paul's response is not in terms of a general sex ethic for the secular world. No one in the Bible (including Jesus) attempted to make general moral pronouncements apart from the framework of faith.

6:12 Everything is permissible for me (NIV): **All things are lawful** (NRSV): NIV better, since the issue is not a matter of law but of the autonomy and freedom of the individual. See the NEB "I am free to do anything." Paul is apparently quoting and responding to a series of Corinthian slogans that expressed their reduction of complex issues of faith and life to a kind of bumper-sticker theology. There were no quotation marks in ancient documents, so modern editors and translators must insert them according to their understanding of the context. This Corinthian slogan was probably a perversion of Paul's own emphasis on the freedom of the Christian life (see 9:1, 19; Gal. 5:1) and his call for Christians not to live merely by cultural values and expectations (Rom. 12:1).

Paul does not deny that Christians are free, but insists they use their freedom (1) for the benefit of others and (2) in a way that does not bring them back into the slavery from which they have been delivered. Paul recognizes that Christian freedom is not only "freedom from" but "freedom for," that Christians are set free in order to serve, not to become slaves of their own self-centered autonomy.

6:13–14 Food is meant for the stomach and the stomach for food: Apparently another Corinthian slogan, which argued that sex is simply a natural appetite like hunger and can be satisfied innocently. **God will destroy both one and the other.** Both NRSV and NIV take this as Paul's response, but it makes more sense to see it as a continuation of the Corinthian slogan. They argued that since the body will be destroyed (but not their "immortal spirit"), deeds done in the body do not finally matter.

Body ... for the Lord: Paul, along with the Bible generally, rejects this dualism of body and spirit (see further on Matt. 28:1; 1 Cor. 15:1–58). The body is not a temporary "shell" or "husk" for the "real" person inside, so it is not the case that the body can do what it wills without affecting the "spirit" or "soul." The body is God's good creation, and is destined for resurrection, not destruction. **Raised the Lord ... will ... raise us:** Christian faith looks back on the resurrection of Jesus and forward to the resurrection of Christians. This is another example of Paul's "eschatological reservation." In Pauline theology, Christians are not yet raised, do not yet live the resurrection life, are not yet free from the responsibilities of living appropriately in this world (4:8; Rom. 6:1–4; 8:17; 2 Cor. 4:10; Phil. 3:10–11; 2 Tim. 2:18).

6:15–16 Never!: See on Rom. 3:4. **One body . . . one flesh:** The sex act involves more than physical union. Paul's point is that sexual intimacy, unlike satisfying hunger for food, involves the whole person. Whether they so understand it or not, the participants are involved at the deepest level of their selves, so sexual activity cannot be treated casually. Paul cites Gen. 2:24 to show that from the very beginning sex was declared by God to be a personal union.

6:17 One spirit: Here Paul uses "flesh," "body," and "spirit" interchangeably, not as "components" of the human being, but as virtual synonyms, each of which refers to the whole person from a particular point of view. The point is that just as being a Christian is more than casually having one's name on a church roll, but is personal union with Christ, so sexual activity is also deeply personal. Casual sex violates Christ as well as the Christian.

6:18–19 Outside the body: Though not in quotation marks in the NRSV or NIV, "Every sin that a person commits is outside the body" was also apparently a Corinthian slogan, expressing their view that whatever the *body* does has nothing to do with sin. Paul responds that sexual immorality is against the body, i.e., the person. His argument has nothing do with the possible physical harmful effects resulting from casual sex (venereal disease, etc.) but moves at a deeper theological level. **Your body is a temple:** The image of 3:16 in which the Christian community is a temple is here applied to the individual believer. The Spirit of God dwells in the Christian because he or she has been added to the body of Christ in which Christ's Spirit is present and active (see on 12:1–31). Note again the Pauline understanding of indicative and imperative: *Since* God's Spirit dwells in your body, keep your body holy. This is the polar opposite of the moralizing "*If* you keep your body holy, God's Spirit will dwell in it."

6:20 You were bought with a price: The metaphor is the purchasing or ransoming of a slave or captive. The result is that the Christian has been freed, but is free to serve a new master (Rom. 6:15–23). **Glorify God:** Paul's inference from Christian freedom is the exact antithesis of their "I am free to do anything." Life is to be God-centered, rather than self-centered.

7:1–16:22
PART TWO—PAUL'S RESPONSE TO THEIR LETTER

7:1–40
QUESTIONS ABOUT MARRIAGE

7:1 Matters about which you wrote: For the first time Paul addresses the Corinthians' questions. The formula "now concerning" occurs as he takes up each question in turn (see 7:25; 8:1; 12:1, 16:1, 16:12). Their letter to him was not merely writing the apostle for friendly advice that they were sure to accept. He had already written them (5:9), and their letter back to him (now lost, as is his first letter to them) probably had an adversarial tone, challenging his views and reasserting their own. The entire chapter deals with issues of marriage and divorce—indeed such issues are discussed more fully here than any place else in the Bible. This does not mean, however, that here we have a compendium of the Christian teaching on marriage. What Paul writes is not an essay on marriage but part of a letter conditioned by one particular situation. The chapter has three parts: (1) counsel for the married (those presently married or who have been married, i.e., widows and widowers)—7:1–16; (2) the general principle: remain in the social situation in which God called you—7:17–24; (3) counsel for the unmarried (engaged couples)—7:25–40.

7:1–16
Counsel for Those Who Are or Have Been Married

7:1 It is well for a man not to touch a woman: A motto expressing the view of some of the Corinthians. "Touch" means sexual contact, a euphemistic expression like contemporary English "sleep with." The interpretation "marry" is not in the Greek text (vs. NIV). Some Corinthian Christians were arguing that married couples should abstain from sex as an expression of their "spirituality." The NRSV is correct in understanding it as a quotation of the motto of some Corinthian Christians (see on 6:12). This is certainly not Paul's own view (vs. NIV). Why would anyone suppose sex between married partners is sub-Christian? We must remember that this is a new church with no Christian tradition to guide it, in a thoroughly pagan world. Five reasons can be given: (1) The pagan dualistic separation of body and spirit (see on 6:12–20). While some interpreted this dualism to mean "since I am spiritual, the body in which my 'I' is contained can do as it wills," others made the opposite inference: "since I am spiritual, I should not participate in the pleasures of the body in which my true 'I' is contained." Paul's understanding of Christian bodily existence rejects both extremes. (2) Some Stoic and Cynic philosophers argued that true seekers after wisdom should renounce marriage in order to devote themselves completely to wisdom, and those already married should live together as though unmarried. (3) A hyper-realized eschatology, i.e., a belief that the realities promised for the end time were already ("spiritually") present. If Jesus had taught that at the resurrection there would be no sexuality or marriage, but the redeemed would be like the angels in heaven (Matt. 22:30), and the end time has already arrived, then Christians are already like the angels and should abandon sex, which belongs to the old world. Some Corinthians probably believed they already spoke the "language of angels" (13:1) and thus should live like the angels (see also 11:2–16). (4) Sayings of Jesus that called for abandoning family life in order to be his disciples (e.g., Mark 10:29–31; Luke 14:26) may have circulated at Corinth and may have been understood in this literalistic ascetic sense. (5) John the Baptist, Jesus, and Paul himself were unmarried.

7:2–4 Each man should have his own wife and each woman her own husband: "Have" is meant in the sexual sense, as in 5:1 (see NIV, which there translates literally; NRSV translates the sense, "living with"). This is therefore not Paul's grudging advice for couples to get married as a second-best status, but precisely the opposite. (Paul's address to those who have never been married begins in v. 25.) He counsels—against the practice of Corinthian "spiritualists"—that married couples have a normal sex life. Otherwise, one or both of them may be tempted to fornication. Paul here presupposes the Jewish and Christian view that sex is the good creation of God, that marriage is established by God, and that sexual activity is permitted only within marriage. The equality and mutuality of Paul's counsel should be noted (also 11–14). Rather than considering sex to be the husband's privilege and the wife's duty, Paul considers it the obligation of each partner to fulfill the other's sexual needs.

7:5–6 By agreement for a set time: Withdrawing from sex for a brief time is not Paul's idea, but his concession to the Corinthians' understanding that a deep prayer life and sexual activity are incompatible. **Concession, not . . . command:** Christian faith does not give rigid rules for such matters but leaves them to the couples' informed good judgment.

7:7 As I myself: Paul (like Jesus) was unmarried and without sexual relationships. **A particular gift from God:** Paul considers the ability to live happily as an unmarried person without sex a spiritual gift from God (same word as 1:7; 12:4, 9, 28, 30), but everyone does not have the same gift. Both marriage and celibacy are gifts from God; neither state is more "spiritual" than the other. This is a remarkable statement from one with Paul's Jewish background, where marriage was considered the norm and a religious obligation. It affirms the dignity and value of the single life before God, and needs to be reaffirmed in modern contexts wherein the name of "family values" marriage is assumed as the normative state.

7:8–9 Unmarried and widows: In this context, "unmarried" probably means "widowers" (see distinction in 7:34), so that this is another of the male/female pairs Paul consistently uses throughout this section. The issue is whether they should remarry or not. The Corinthians and Paul agree that it is better to remain unmarried, but for different reasons —they because the unmarried state is more "spiritual," Paul because of the times (see on vv. 26–31). Although the passing of time has shown that Paul's expectation of the near Parousia was wrong, the difficult point for the modern reader is not his incorrect chronology, but his insistence that decisions about sex and marriage are to be made not as individual personal decisions, but in the light of one's belonging to Christ. For Paul, marriage is neither a sacrament nor merely a legal arrangement of a secular culture, but is an aspect of Christian discipleship. **Aflame with passion:** None of Paul's discussion is to be understood as though in his eyes marriage is a second best, only a means of avoiding sexual promiscuity. In context, his point is that widowers and widows who want to get remarried should do so. It is not Paul but the hyperspiritualists at Corinth who regard celibacy as more Christian. For Paul, if one does not have the gift of celibacy, the Christian thing to do is to get married.

7:10 Not I but the Lord: Paul distinguishes his own apostolic instruction—which he also considers authoritative—from direct commands of the Lord. Only four times in all his writings does Paul quote "sayings of the Lord" (here, 9:14; 11:23–25; 1 Thess. 4:15–17). One should note not only the paucity of such references in his letters, but that he makes no clear distinction between sayings of the historical Jesus and sayings of the Lord spoken in the church by Christian prophets (see on 1 Thess. 4:2, 15–17). The saying here does not agree in wording with the Gospel forms in Matt. 5:32; Mark 10:11; Luke 16:18. All this illustrates that early Christianity made no rigid distinction between the Jesus "back there" in history and the risen Christ "up there" in heaven and present in the life and worship of the church.

7:12 I . . . not the Lord: Paul also considers his own teaching the command of the Lord (7:25, 40; 14:37). He means here that he does not have a saying of Jesus or of the exalted Lord that bears directly on the issue at hand.

7:14 The unbelieving husband is made holy through his wife: Holiness is thought of in tangible terms, like electricity. Note that the issue has to do with ritual purity, so that **unclean** here is a ritual term, not a moral one (see Luke 2:22–23; 4:33; 5:27; Acts 10–11; 15). The Corinthians were worried that Christians would be ritually defiled by having sexual relations with unbelieving spouses. Paul reassures them that in this case it is holiness that is transmitted, not unholiness (see Gen. 18:22–23; Matt. 23:17; Rom. 11:16). The believer is not made ritually impure by sleeping with an unbelieving spouse, but the unbeliever is sanctified by the relation to the believer, as are the children.

7:15 Not bound: In some cases Paul considers divorce the best solution (here, when an unbelieving spouse no longer wishes to live with a Christian partner).

7:17–24
General Principle:
Remain As God Called You

When God called them to be Christians, their social situation was irrelevant. The call of God does not depend on whether one is married, separated, divorced, widowed, or single. This is Paul's point. He illustrates it with two examples, the Jew/Gentile distinction and the slave/free distinction. God's call to be Christian transcends and relativizes all such social distinctions (see Gal. 3:28). This is Paul's point, but when taken out of context it seems to make him much more of a social conservative than he was. Otherwise, it would be utterly cruel and unrealistic to say to a slave, **"Do not be concerned about it."** His

meaning is that God's call comes to slave and free alike, not a Christian endorsement to the institution of slavery. The institution itself was simply assumed (also by Jesus). Both slave and master have their real being "in Christ" (see on 2 Cor. 5:17), so that the master is Christ's slave and the slave is one who has been freed by Christ. Both master and slave are both free and slave. That is Paul's mind-blowing point.

7:21 If you can gain your freedom: The words that follow are ambiguous in Greek, and can mean either remain a slave as a Christian witness (NRSV) or take the opportunity to be free (NIV). Here the NIV's understanding better fits the context.

7:24 In whatever condition you were called . . . there remain: The present point is that marriages should not be dissolved on the basis of "spirituality." Those who are married should remain married. The point is strengthened by Paul's eschatological considerations in the next section.

7:25–40
Counsel for the Unmarried

7:25 Now concerning: Again introducing a new topic, those who have never been married (see v. 1 on structure of the chapter). Although Paul's general point in this section is clear, since we do not know exactly the Corinthian situation to which he is responding, there is much uncertainty as to his precise meaning. **Virgins:** Probably refers to young women engaged to be married.

7:26 Present crisis (NIV)/**Impending crisis** (NRSV): The NIV translation is here more accurate than the NRSV. The Greek word always elsewhere refers to that which is already present (see, e.g., 3:22, where the same word is used in contrast with what is to come). We do not know precisely what crisis Paul refers to, but it is conditioned by his apocalyptic perspective. He sees present troubles as the prelude to the near end (see vv. 28–31). Since the word for "crisis" is translated "necessity" in v. 37 and "obligation" in 9:16, in reference to Paul's obligation to preach the gospel, he may be referring here to the urgency of the Christian mission. In view of the urgency to evangelize the world before the end comes, marriage is not the best option for faithful believers. He also has in view the tribulations that precede the end, which Paul sees as already beginning in the present distress the church is suffering. In apocalyptic thought, as the end approaches, the normal processes of nature will break down, as reflected in this quotation from the Jewish historian Josephus (*War* 6:289–92):

Thus there was a star resembling a sword, which stood over the city, and a comet, that continued a whole year. . . . also, a heifer, as she was led by the high priest to be sacrificed, brought forth a lamb in the midst of the temple.

So also the apocalyptic book of 2 Esdras/4 Ezra 5:8; 6:20–21:

There shall be chaos also in many places, fire shall often break out, the wild animals shall roam beyond their haunts, and menstruous women shall bring forth monsters. . . . When the seal is placed upon the age that is about to pass away, then I will show these signs: the books shall be opened before the face of the firmament, and all shall see my judgment together. Children a year old shall speak with their voices, and pregnant women shall give birth to premature children at three and four months, and these shall live and leap about.

Within this thought world, if one believes the apocalyptic times have dawned, it is not a good time to get married and start a family— though it is not "sinful," as the Corinthian hyperspiritualists claim.

7:29–31 As though . . . : For Paul, Christian life is not a flight from this world into interior spirituality or a withdrawing into a community separated from worldly concerns (5:9–10). Christian life is firmly rooted in the everyday concerns of this world, but in a way that is not dominated and ultimately controlled by worldly circumstances. Christians mourn and rejoice, buy and sell, marry and stay single, but none of these is the ultimate determiner of one's existence. This is neither the Stoic's internal aloofness and indifference nor the apocalyptist's escape from or abandonment of this world, but the confident awareness that God is leading the world to a worthy conclusion.

7:34 His interests are divided: Here Paul seems specifically to address the young man who is engaged and is deciding whether or not to go through with the marriage. In the light of the short time before the end, Paul advises him to stay single. The advice is certainly influenced by Paul's personal opinion and preference for celibacy (v. 7), but is not to be reduced to that. The point is not that married life is second-rate existence for those who are truly "spiritual," but that for those who have the gift, to live in the unmarried state allows them to give undivided devotion to God (see on Luke 10:41–42). Single-minded service to God is the focus of Paul's concern, not the making of rules about marriage. Many Christians have found married life less distracting, allowing wholehearted devotion to God.

7:36–38 Behaving properly toward his fiancée: The Greek text of this paragraph is ambiguous and can refer to (1) an engaged couple, as in the preceding paragraph; the NRSV and NIV both so understand it; (2) a father who is deciding whether to give his daughter in marriage, as understood by the AV, ASV, and JB; (3) a "spiritual marriage" as presumably advocated by some Corinthians, in which husband and wife lived together without sexual relations as an expression of their spirituality; the NEB and JB notes so understand it. Probably the first option is what Paul intended. He recommends that the couple stay single in view of the near Parousia, but that it is no sin if they proceed with their wedding plans. As throughout, the decision is not legislated or manipulated, but left to the persons involved to decide in the context of their understanding of life in Christ (not their individualistic autonomy). This chapter as a whole should be pondered by those who tend to regard Paul as an authoritarian dogmatist. His pastoral advice is a model of pastoral concern, urging theological discernment and reflection in the context of Christian freedom.

7:39–40 She is free . . . she is more blessed: The concluding summary has nothing really new, must be understood in the context of the whole chapter, and forms a bracket with the opening words of 7:1–7.

8:1–11:1
Food Offered to Idols

The new section that begins here extends to 11:1, all dealing with the issue of how the new Christians in Corinth are to come to terms with one feature of their pagan environment: the eating of meat sacrificed to idols. It was a complex issue. Practically all meat sold in the marketplace had been ritually slaughtered in connection with some temple. Could Christians continue to purchase and eat such meat at home? (Almost the only alternative was to become vegetarians.) Could they continue to attend dinner parties at the homes of their non-Christian friends, where such food would be served? Could they continue to "eat out"? The nearest things to "restaurants" in the ancient Mediterranean world were the dining rooms attached to temples, where civic and social as well as religious occasions were held. People regularly had birthday parties and wedding receptions at such places as part of normal social life. These were disputed points in several streams of early Christianity. The issue was not merely what is "right" for a Christian to eat, but how Christians were to fit into the pagan culture around them, how decisions on such issues affected the Christian mission, and how Christians of differing convictions on such issues were to live and work together in one church. Sometimes clear, if one-sided or compromising, answers were given (see on Acts 15:22–29; Rev. 2:14, 20). Paul considers it an issue that must be thought through as a whole, in contrast to the Corinthians' sloganistic "bumper sticker" approach. There are three main thrusts to his argument: (1) The basis of Christian ethical decisions is not "knowledge" but love (8:1–13). (2) His own understanding of the rights of an apostle, and how he has exercised them, illustrates his approach (9:1–27). (3) Explicit participation in pagan temple meals is forbidden, and all other conduct is to be governed by care that it does not lead to the weakening or destruction of the faith of a Christian brother or sister (10:1–11:1). Paul discusses a similar issue in Rom. 14:1–23.

8:1–13
"Knowledge" vs. Love

8:1 Now concerning: This phrase again signals a change of topic in response to their question (see on 7:1). The context indicates that the question was not an inquiry for friendly advice, but a challenge to Paul's own understanding and practice. **All of us possess knowledge:** The NRSV is probably correct in taking this as another of the Corinthian slogans (hence the quotation marks; see on 6:12). The NIV understands it as Paul's own statement. **Knowledge puffs up:** This is not a general anti-intellectual declaration as though Paul were glorifying ignorance. "Knowledge" here refers to the religious attitude of the "liberated" Christians in Corinth who parade their "enlightened" Christian freedom (see on 6:12). **Love builds up:** Paul contrasts "knowledge" not with ignorance, but with love.

8:2 Does not yet have the necessary knowledge: What they lack is not content; the problem is not what they know but how they practice it.

8:3 Anyone who loves God: The reader might anticipate "has true knowledge" to follow, but Paul reverses the expected logic to emphasize that the initiative is with God (cf. 13:12; Gal. 4:9). Being known by God, not knowledge, is what constitutes the Christian life.

8:4 No God but one: This is also a Corinthian motto, but one with which Paul agrees. It reflects the basic creedal statement of Judaism, the Shema (Deut. 6:4; Mark 12:29; Rom. 3:30; Jas. 2:19). Several of the Corinthians' slogans are in fact distortions or exaggerations of Paul's own theology. The Corinthians have been converted to Jewish and Christian monotheism and know that idols have no real existence and that the one God does not accept or reject people on the basis of diet.

8:5 Many gods and many lords: Many of the "so-called" gods and lords had ancient and impressive temples and shrines in Corinth (see the introduction to 1 Corinthians). Although they had no real existence as gods, in Paul's view they somehow represented evil spirits (10:14–22; Gal. 4:8–9).

8:6 Paul agrees with this "knowledge" and elaborates it by citing an early Christian creed. Though this is not clear in the English translation, the rhythmical form and parallel structure of this verse indicate Paul is not here composing ad hoc, but citing a creedal statement probably already known by the Corinthians. The Jewish Shema (Deut. 6:4) used both "God" and "Lord" in affirming the oneness of God. With early Christianity in general, Paul affirms the lordship of the one God in terms of both Father and Son, without compromising Jewish monotheism (see John 1:1–3, 14, 18; Phil. 2:5–11; 1 Pet. 1:2; Rev. 1:4–5). Neither here nor elsewhere does he attempt to "explain" this, but knows that Christians cannot talk about the one God without at the same time talking about the one Lord Jesus Christ. Later Trinitarian theology attempted to articulate this more systematically. Paul is not discussing abstract theology, but making a practical point, which here as elsewhere cannot stand without a theological foundation.

8:7 Their conscience, being weak, is defiled: Conscience is here understood not in the popular modern sense of the inner voice that tells us right from wrong (an understanding alien to the Bible), but means something like their "moral and religious awareness." For Paul, conscience is not an infallible guide to right and wrong (4:4), but he still considers it wrong for believers to go against their own conscience (Rom. 14:13–23). Paul is concerned that some of the new Christians at Corinth, if they see their fellow "enlightened" Christians continuing to attend the meals in pagan temples, will be encouraged to attend such occasions themselves, though they misunderstand it as a kind of reversion to idol worship, or a placing Christ among the pagan deities as another of the "many lords" worshiped in the Hellenistic world. Although those who claim to "possess knowledge" do not understand it this way, intentionally or not they are contributing to the demolition of the faith of a fellow Christian.

8:10 If others see you: The Christian life is not limited to one's individual convictions before God, but takes into consideration how others are affected by one's actions. It is thus quite possible that a "strong" Christian with "knowledge," by doing something that in itself is perfectly right or innocent, still damages the faith of a "weak" Christian who does not understand. An aspect of the lack of understanding of the "weak" is that they consider their rigid version of the faith actually the "strong" Christian response, and their liberal brothers and sisters to be the "weak." The burden is on the "strong" in such cases.

8:12 Sin against members of your family: Literally "brothers," as the NIV. Paul is referring to one's brothers and sisters in the Christian community. **Sin against Christ:** Christ is encountered in the Christian brother or sister, even (or especially) in the "weak" ones. To serve them is to serve Christ; to harm their faith is to sin against Christ (Matt. 10:40–42; 18:6–7; 25:40, 45; Acts 9:4; Heb. 6:6).

8:13 A cause of their falling: The issue revolves around causing a fellow Christian to fall away from the faith, not whether the more conservative are "offended" (in the sense of "bothered") by the conduct of the more liberal. Paul is not discussing a matter of personal sensibilities—though it is also true that Christians should not unduly scandalize their fellow Christians who have differing convictions on matters of personal lifestyle, such as the use of alcohol and tobacco. Paul is dealing with conduct that, when misunderstood by others, damages their Christian faith. To be sure, "eating meat sacrificed to idols" is no issue for modern Christians. However, the way we conduct our "personal" lives (eating, drinking, sex, money) is an issue for contemporary Christians to ponder in the light of 1 Cor. 8–10, if it encourages other Christians to think of

Christian faith as only a liberated view of personal "rights." **I will never eat meat:** Paul declares his own stance. He agrees that neither eating nor not eating matters before God (v. 8). But he will renounce any conduct that damages the spiritual life of others. This leads to a fuller presentation of his own apostolic "rights" and how he has used them.

9:1–26
The Rights of an Apostle

9:1 Am I not an apostle? On Paul as apostle, see on Luke 6:12–13; Acts 1:21–22; Gal. 1:1. This is not a new topic or an abstract discussion of apostleship, but an illustration of the meaning of Christian freedom (which includes the freedom to give up one's rights). The issue has been raised in the Corinthians' letter to Paul. The question concerns not only Paul, but the Corinthians. Since he (and his coworkers) founded the church at Corinth, they may have feared that if Paul is not a legitimate apostle, they are not really a church. Paul claims to be an apostle because he has seen the risen Jesus and has been personally commissioned by him (Acts 9:1–22; 22:3–21; 26:9–20; Gal. 1:10–17). The Corinthians are an authentic church, and its existence testifies to the authenticity of Paul's apostleship.

9:3–5 My defense to those who would examine me: This statement, along with the general tone of this section, shows that the question about idol meat to which Paul is responding (see 8:1) is not a friendly request for information, but a challenge to his apostolic authority. **Food and drink . . . accompanied by a believing wife:** Questions of whether marriage and certain foods were appropriate to "spiritual" people had troubled some Corinthians (7:1–8:13). **Brothers of the Lord:** See Mark 6:3. Paul elsewhere mentions only James, who assumed a leading position in the Jerusalem church (15:7; Gal. 1:19; see Acts 12:17; 15:13; 21:18; Jude 1). **Cephas:** Simon Peter (see 1:12) was married (Mark 1:30).

9:6 Refrain from working for a living: Not an appeal for idleness or sloth, but a claim that Christian missionaries are authorized to devote their time and energy to evangelism and church leadership, rather than supporting themselves by secular work.

9:7 On human authority?: After giving analogies from military service, agriculture, and shepherding, Paul turns to his Bible for support. Among the Old Testament's humane regulations for the treatment of animals is that a working ox must be allowed to eat from the grain it is "threshing" by treading it out on the threshing floor (Deut. 25:4). Paul here interprets the Bible allegorically, denying its literal meaning and replacing it with Christian interpretation. Jesus or Matthew might have argued the point differently: "If God is concerned for oxen, as the Scripture shows he is, how much more is God concerned for the support of faithful Christian missionaries" (see Matt. 6:25–34).

9:12b Nevertheless, we have not made use of this right: Paul's first point is to establish that he *has* the right to their financial support, his second that he has the freedom not to insist on this right (see 9:1, 15, 23; 10:31–11:1). This is a surprising turn in the argument. After all the reasons that he has the right to their monetary support—with more to come in vv. 13–14—the reader expects the conclusion to be Paul's insistence that they provide it. They were in fact more than willing to do so. Other missionaries and apostles accepted money from them, which was more in line with the expectation of traveling philosophers and teachers, and the Corinthians felt somewhat demeaned by Paul's refusal, as well as suggesting that this meant Paul was not very confident about his own apostolic office (see 2 Cor. 11:7–11; 12:13–14). For his own reasons, he has resolutely decided to support himself (see Acts 18:1–4), and declines to accept that to which he has every right. This is the model of the Christian life Paul presents to the Corinthians, agreeing that they have the right and freedom to eat and drink, but their conduct should be governed by a higher calling than asserting their individual rights. **An obstacle in the way of the gospel:** When others misunderstand Paul's rightful actions based on Christian freedom, and their misunderstanding becomes an obstacle to the church's mission, Paul will change his behavior for the sake of the gospel. This is the governing principle of his life. For the sake of the gospel he is willing to be misunderstood as more liberal or conservative than he really is, for he has the inner security of having been freed from concern with his own status and image. Each issue is decided on the basis of whether it furthers the mission of the church or whether it hinders it.

9:13 Those who serve at the altar: An additional argument or analogy for the right of Christian ministers to be supported by their congregations.

9:14 The Lord commanded: Paul's final authority is not his argument from nature, farming, shepherding, the temple, or the Bible, but the command of Christ (Matt. 10:10; Mark 6:10; Luke 10:7).

9:16 Woe is me if I do not proclaim the gospel: The issue here is not the content of the message Paul preaches, i.e., whether it is really the gospel or not, but whether and why he is a Christian missionary. His point is that he preaches not for financial reward but because he has been charged with a commission to which he must be faithful. Thus the cry, "Woe is me," is not an expression of Paul's psychology or an inner compulsion, but precisely the opposite. He has been given a job to do by the risen Lord. Paul's own contribution to the mission is to serve at his own expense.

9:19 Free . . . slave: Paul's own life represents the paradoxical unity of freedom and servitude inherent in the Christian life as such (7:22).

9:20–23 All things to all people: Paul serves as an agent of reconciliation, bringing fragmented humanity, people of diverse races and backgrounds, into the one church of God (2 Cor. 5:11–21). To the extent that he could do so without compromising the truth of the gospel, he accommodated his life to Jews and Gentiles, to "weak" Christians and "strong" Christians. This meant that, depending on the situation, Paul was convinced he was free to eat or not eat, obey certain religious laws and customs or ignore them, if it served to communicate the faith. In this context, the particular meaning is that when Paul was with Gentiles he ate idol meat from the marketplace, but that when he was with Jews he did not eat. (This did not solve the problem of mixed groups and could lead toward having segregated, homogenized churches.) Such a strategy also left him open to the charge that he really had no convictions, that he simply tried to please everybody.

Under Christ's law: The stance of Gentile Christians to the Old Testament law was not a problem at Corinth, though it was to become a hot issue later in the Galatian churches (see Galatians). Here Paul can portray his own stance without the pressure of polemics on the subject of the law. To Jews, he becomes as one **under the** Jewish **law,** and to Gentiles as one **outside the law,** but in each case he makes it clear that neither position is really where he stands. His is not determined by the law—neither in keeping it nor in not keeping it—but by the new reality in Christ, which transcends this apparent either/or. The new reality does not leave him in an autonomous, "lawless" state. Nor does being under Christ's law mean Paul has now traded the Law of Moses for a new law such as the Sermon on the Mount. Paul's understanding of the Christian life is not to adopt the "teaching of Jesus" as a list of "rules for Christian living," but to have one's whole life determined by the Christ event.

9:26 I do not run aimlessly: Paul's flexible strategy of evangelism is not that of following the path of least resistance. Paul uses familiar metaphors from the Corinthian games (held every two years, second in importance only to the Olympics). Serving in the Christian mission calls for the discipline of an athlete who has his eyes firmly fixed on the goal line and who exerts himself completely to attain the goal. The options are to win, lose, or be disqualified, and the outcome is not clear until the race is complete. (Unfortunately, Paul had no awareness of team sports—all the Greek games were only individual competition—though Paul's own point would be better served by the team analogy.) Confidence in God's grace is not incompatible with disciplined training and struggle to complete the race (Rom. 6:1–23). There is no false security for the Corinthians or for himself.

10:1–22
Warnings from Israel's History

The subject continues to be the same: to what extent Christians can participate in pagan culture, especially attendance at festive meals in pagan temples. Paul's previous argument (chaps. 8–9) is that even "enlightened" Christians should avoid such participation because it endangers the "weak" brother or sister. His argument now takes a new and more direct turn: such conduct endangers those who participate.

10:1 Our ancestors: Some of the Corinthians apparently believed that baptism and the Lord's Supper had a quasi-magical effect by which they were insulated from the pagan influence from which they had been delivered (see 15:29). Paul interprets the biblical story of Israel in order to provide a warning against this. Old Testament Israel represents the spiritual ancestry not only of Jews, but also of Christians, who have been incorporated into the ongoing people of God (Rom. 11; Gal. 6:16). Paul reminds the Gentile Christians of Corinth that the Old Testament stories are also, by God's grace, our story as well.

10:2 All were baptized into Moses: See Exod. 13:17–14:31. Paul must stretch a bit to find something like Christian baptism in the Old Testament (the Egyptians, in fact, were more thoroughly "baptized" in the Red Sea than the Israelites). Paul reads the Old Testament through Christian lenses (see excursus, "New Testament Interpretation of the Old Testament," at 15:3).

10:3–4 Spiritual food: The manna, the miraculous "bread from heaven" (see Exod. 16:1–36). **Spiritual drink:** The water miraculously supplied from the rock during Israel's wilderness wanderings (Exod. 17:1–7; Num. 20:1–13). Paul does not rehearse the biblical stories, assuming his readers are familiar with them, even though they are new converts from paganism. Many modern readers will have to refresh their memory before Paul's words receive their evocative power. **Rock that followed them:** This is not in the biblical story, but later rabbinic tradition elaborated it so that it was the same stone that produced water wherever the Israelites camped. Paul's application reflects both the Old Testament and this tradition, and interprets it in terms of Christ. In applying the rock imagery to Christ, Paul presupposes his view of the preexistence of Christ. This is not mere speculation, but a way of saying that the God who is met in Jesus Christ is the same God met in the story of the deliverance of Israel (see on Phil. 2:5–11). There may also be an indirect polemic against the view of Peter's followers that he was the foundation rock on which the church was built (see 1:12; 3:11; Matt. 16:18).

10:5–6 They were struck down in the wilderness: The story was written as an **example** (literally "type," "model," see v. 11) for Christians, but was not a "prophecy" or "prediction" of them. What happened to Israel need not happen to the church—though it *could*. Paul's warning is that mere enjoyment of the spiritual privileges of God's call and election, and participating in the sacraments, do not guarantee one will not fall back into idolatry and incur God's wrath.

10:7–8 Do not become idolaters: Paul regards attending the festive meals in pagan temples as participation in idol worship (vv. 14–22). The story of Israel in the wilderness provides specific warning examples: see Exod. 32:1–6; Num. 11:4–6, 34; 21:5–6; 25:1–11. **Sexual immorality:** In the Num. 25 example, eating and drinking in the setting where idols are worshiped leads to sexual immorality. Paul shared the Jewish view that false worship and false ethics were inseparably connected, and supposed that those "strong" Christians who continued to attend festive meals in pagan temples would inevitably indulge in sexual sins as well (see on 6:12–20, where the connection between sex ethics and temple also appears).

10:9–11 Put Christ to the test: See v. 4; Christ was already present in the Old Testament story (see also 1 Pet. 1:11). **Written down to instruct us:** Rom. 15:4. **On whom the ends of the ages have come:** Paul believed that he lived at the end of the present age, and that God would soon bring the glory of the coming age. The plural of both "ends" and "ages" may well mean that he saw Christians as living in the extremities of both ages—the "overlapping" of the old age and the new, in the tension between "already" and "not yet."

10:15 Judge for yourselves: This is neither a general "everyone should follow his or her own opinion" nor Paul's settling the issue by decree. He is confident that the Spirit of God present in the congregation helps the community of faith to discern the will of God. He is equally confident that when they do so, they will arrive at his own understanding of the matter (see 11:16; 14:37–38).

10:16 Participation in the blood . . . body (NIV): "Participation" was translated as "communion," in the King James Version, the source of this term for the Eucharist. For a fuller discussion of Paul's understanding, see excursus, "The Lord's Supper in the New Testament," at 11:17–34. Paul is not discussing the nature of the elements or what happens to them in the eucharistic ritual, but what is involved in eating and drinking in the temple of a pagan god. He introduces both biblical and pagan analogies to support his claim that participation in festive meals in pagan temples is not just a harmless social occasion, but a religious one that violates God's exclusive claim on them. In the Old Testament, eating sacrificial meat in the presence of God's altar was a covenant ceremony with both "vertical" and "horizontal" implications, binding the participants to both God and one another.

10:20 They sacrifice to demons: This is the only reference to demons in Paul, though he often refers to cosmic powers of evil that permeate the present world, something akin to what moderns call "systemic evil" (e.g. 15:24; 2 Cor. 4:4; Rom. 8:38; Gal. 4:3, 9; see Col. 2:20; Eph. 2:2; see excursus, "Satan, the Devil, and Demons in Biblical Theology," at Mark 5:1). Idolatrous worship is an expression of these powers. Christians cannot participate in it as

though it were innocent. Throughout, Paul still has in mind the analogy of Israel's experience in the wilderness (Deut. 32:17–21).

10:21 You cannot partake of the table . . . of demons: Christian freedom does not allow actual participation in pagan ceremonies. Such an exclusive attitude represents Jewish and Christian monotheism, but was unusual in the tolerant world of pagan religion, where sacrificing at the shrine of one god did not preclude similar sacrificial worship at the shrines of other gods.

10:22 Jealousy: The one God of the Bible is jealous, will not be accepted as one of several, but demands exclusive loyalty (see, e.g., Exod. 20:5; 34:14; Deut. 4:24). **Stronger than he?** The "strong" in Corinth, whose "superior knowledge" allowed them to visit idol temples with impunity, are challenging God (see Deut. 32:21).

10:23–11:1
Do All to the Glory of God

Here Paul makes clear that all along he has been dealing with the issue introduced at 8:1. While participation in idol worship is prohibited, there is nothing wrong with the meat as such, even though it has been ritually slaughtered in a pagan temple.

10:26 The earth . . . is the Lord's: Ps. 24:1 was traditionally used as a table blessing in Jewish families. Since God is the Creator of everything, there are no inherently "unclean" foods, and Christians need not withdraw into some "holy" sphere where they are "uncontaminated" by the "evil" world (see on 5:9). Christians can in good conscience attend dinner parties in the home of their non-Christian friends and neighbors, and eat whatever is served.

10:28 If someone says to you: Apparently the helpful comment of a fellow Christian guest, who has scruples about eating meat sacrificed to idols (or supposes the one to whom he or she offers this friendly advice does).

10:30 Why should I be denounced? The two rhetorical questions of vv. 29b–30 may be Paul's quotation of the objection of the "strong" who resist having their freedom restricted by the scruples of the less liberated, and thus should be included in quotation marks (as in the NEB; see on 6:12–13 above). It is less likely that they are Paul's own protest (as in NRSV and NIV), since this self-imposed restriction on one's liberty is actually what Paul is advocating.

10:31 Do everything for the glory of God: Over against the slogan of Corinthian freedom, "All things are lawful for me" (10:23; see 6:12), Paul places "All things for the glory of God." Their slogan focused on their own rights; Paul's is oriented to God. Before other human beings one may claim rights, but before God one can only respond in worship and obedience. In all this Paul refuses to give a Christian rule that tells them whether to eat or not. As 10:24, 29 point to consideration for the "other" as the norm of Christian conduct, so here Paul points to God. Christian conduct is not to be governed by the compulsive desire to exercise one's freedom, but by devotion to God and others. This is Paul's practical application to a concrete case of the double commandment of love to God and neighbor (see Matt. 22:34–40).

10:32–33 Give no offense: This is not a matter of manners (though exercising common courtesy and sensitivity to others' feelings is a matter of loving the neighbor). "Offense" here means "stumbling block," an obstacle placed in the path of another person's approach to God. Paul urges that Christians not place false stumbling blocks in the way (such as matters of diet, entertainment, and dress), so that those addressed by the gospel may face the real stumbling block of God's revelation and saving act in the cross and resurrection of Jesus (1:23; Gal. 5:11). **Not seeking my own advantage:** Such a concern for others is a reversal of both the values and the strategy of the world.

11:1 Be imitators of me: The conclusion of the discussion begun at 8:1 (the chapter divisions, made centuries later, here obscures this). Paul's offering himself as an example is not egotism (see 4:16), but because his own life is an example of giving up rights in order to reach out to others—just as did Jesus (Rom. 15:3).

11:2–14:40
QUESTIONS ABOUT WORSHIP

The section that begins here deals with disruptive behavior in the Corinthian worship services. Their letter had asked him about charismatic phenomena, and his response extends from 12:1 through 14:40 (see 12:1). Prior to responding to their question, Paul deals with two items they had not asked about, but about which he had heard (see 11:18): head coverings (11:2–16) and abuses at the Lord's Supper (11:17–34).

11:2–16
Head Coverings

The section is not about appropriate headgear in general, but has to do with conduct in Christian worship, particularly by those who play prominent roles of leading in prayer or inspired preaching (vv. 4–5). The passage is difficult and leaves the modern reader with many unanswered questions. It has sometimes been understood as Paul "keeping women in their place," and therefore either welcomed or rejected. This text has seemed to a few scholars to be so different from Paul's teaching elsewhere that they consider it a post-Pauline interpolation. This is not impossible, since Paul's letters were edited in the process of including them in the canon, in order to bring them into line with his teaching as later understood (see on 14:33b–34 and "Introduction: The New Testament as the Church's Book," 4.c, d). If the passage is not from Paul, like the post-Pauline letters composed in Paul's name, it is still Scripture and must be taken seriously in the life of the church (see the introductions to Colossians, Ephesians, 1 Timothy, 1 Peter). Assuming that it was written by Paul, interpreting the text as though it taught the subordination or inferiority of women is clearly a misreading, since it clashes with Paul's teaching and practice elsewhere (Gal. 3:27–28), including in this letter (7:1–7) and in this section itself (v. 12).

Modern readers should once again remember that they are not reading timeless essays or rules, but a letter. The modern reader does not know the social customs that are presupposed, the meanings intended by some of the vocabulary, or the Corinthian letter to Paul to which 1 Corinthians is a response. Even the original readers who knew all of this still sometimes misunderstood (see on 5:9–13).

11:2 You . . . maintain the traditions: The powerful gift of the Holy Spirit had broken (or was threatening to break) through the cultural conventions, some of which were oppressive. Paul celebrated this new freedom, but knew that the young church needed the guidance of tradition. They belong to a community bigger than their local congregation (see 1:2). The church as a whole provides guidance on how to steer the congregation's life in a pagan culture. Paul has provided such guidance by teaching them church tradition (see, e.g., 11:23–26; 15:3–5). Here he commends them for adhering to (some of) these traditions, before giving them further instruction on points where they are violating Christian tradition.

The Corinthians and Paul knew what the issue in Corinth was, but we can only infer it from Paul's response. They seem to be convinced that since the "new age" has already arrived, they are already "as the angels" and the sexual distinctions of "this age" no longer apply (see on 4:8; 7:1). Their powerful experience of the Spirit seems to them to mean that they are free from the social conventions of human culture.

11:3 The head of every man is Christ, and the head of the woman is man (NIV): Here the NIV is better (see NRSV note). Paul is not dealing with husbands and wives, but with the role of men and women in worship. **God is the head:** Some have interpreted this as a strict hierarchy: God⇒ Christ⇒ man⇒ woman. Yet if hierarchy is his point, he presents the series in a peculiar order (Christ, man; man, woman; God, Christ), and at the end of this paragraph Paul asserts his standard view of the equality and mutuality of man and woman before God (v. 12). "Head" throughout may be translated "source." Since Paul uses the creation story that tells of the source of both man and woman, and since he refers to birth from the woman as the source of the man, "head" probably does not express his meaning in regard to human relationships. He apparently chose this ambiguous word because he wanted it to have a double meaning in terms of human relation to God, who is both "head" in the sense of authority and "source" in the sense of Creator.

11:4 Disgraces his head: Paul reflects some social or religious convention of his time, but we no longer know what it was. The double meaning of "head" here means that the man who wears a head covering (we no longer know whether Paul refers to a hat or to long hair) not only violates this social convention, but brings dishonor on Christ, his "head." Such ambiguities show that Paul is responding to a specific situation, not attempting to provide rules for Christians of all times and places.

11:5 Prays or prophesies: On prophecy, see 14:1–40. Here as elsewhere, Paul assumes that women have leadership roles in the church, that they lead in prayer during congregational worship and preach as inspired by the Spirit (contrast 14:33b–34). **Head unveiled:** The same expression could be translated "let her hair down," so it is not clear whether the issue is hairstyle or wearing of veils. We no longer know what was signaled by either veils or hairstyles in the Corinth of Paul's day, though in some sections of the first-century Mediterranean world certain hairstyles indicated promiscuity, homosexuality, or participation in the frenzied worship of some pagan cults. Also, since women wore their hair and headdress differently in the privacy of the home

than they did in public, we do not know whether they considered Christian worship in the small house churches where Christians were all "brothers and sisters" as being "in public" or "at home."

11:9 Woman for the sake of man: Paul supports his point by an unclear argument that combines the two creation stories of Gen. 1–2 (see Gen. 1:26–27; 2:21–23).

11:10 Authority on her head: Some have interpreted this as a **symbol** (NRSV) or **sign** (NIV) of a married woman's subjection to her husband, but the Greek says simply that the woman has authority on (or over, about) her head, which probably means she has the authority to decide whether or not to wear the conventional head covering or hairdo in worship (see NRSV note). Yet some elements of the context indicate Paul recommends that women go along with convention, even though they are free to do otherwise, as in the issue of eating idol meat (see 8:1–11:2). **Because of the angels:** Many interpretations have been given to this obscure reference, such as: (1) since the Greek word for "angel" can also be used of a human messenger (e.g., Luke 7:27 [though Paul never uses "angel" in this sense]), Paul is referring to visiting messengers from other congregations who will be scandalized by the unconventional dress or hairstyle of the Corinthian women; (2) Christian worship is observed by angels who keep account of irresponsible behavior; (3) since Christians will judge angels (see on 6:3), the Corinthian women can certainly exercise authority over such a small matter as headgear. The Corinthians were infatuated with angels and authority (see 4:9; 13:1), and these words were probably introduced into the discussion by them. Their reference is no longer clear to us.

11:14 Nature itself: Paul identifies social convention with "nature," i.e., what seems natural to him in his cultural setting.

11:16 If anyone is disposed to be contentious: Paul has introduced arguments from his interpretation of Scripture and from his understanding of "nature," but his final appeal is to the fact that the Corinthians belong to the church at large. He does not finally command what they should do. Throughout, he is true to his theology that, while we must decide for ourselves, we do not decide by ourselves. The Corinthians are urged to abide by the custom of the church as a whole.

Because of the obscurity of the passage and because it is conditioned by the customs and conventions operative in first-century Corinth, there is little in this text that can be *directly* transferred to other situations, including our own. Yet this is true to some extent of everything in the Bible, so that the passage provides a model exercise in interpreting its word to us in a different setting. What is clear, and what may challenge our own understanding of the Christian life, is that the church's evangelistic mission to the world is of primary importance. Thus Christians should make decisions about dress and hairstyle in such a way that people are not struck by our peculiarity, judged by cultural norms, and sidetracked into responding to superficial phenomena rather than to the gospel itself. Paul wants outsiders to ask about the gospel, not about whether Christians wear unconventional hats or hairstyles—even if in principle they are free to do so. These instructions are then informed by the same theology that undergirds the discussion about eating food sacrificed to idols (8:1–11:2).

11:17–34
The Lord's Supper

11:17–22 Abuses at the Lord's Supper

11:17 More harm than good (NIV): This is a terrible charge to make, that the regular gathering of the congregation about the Lord's Table is not an expression of the gospel but a barrier to it. What was going on at Corinth that provoked this charge? The central act of worship was the Eucharist, which was celebrated in the context of a real meal. The congregation met in private homes of those wealthy enough to provide for such meetings. The church service somewhat resembled a dinner party. The dining room held eight or ten persons, the adjoining atrium forty or fifty more. It was absolutely "normal" in such settings that those of higher status received privileged places and better food in the dining room, while slaves and those of lower status ate in the atrium—just as we regard it as normal that those in the first-class cabin have better food and drink than those in economy, and that dignitaries have reserved parking places and special seats in the worship service. In such a context, the central symbol of Christian worship was radically egalitarian—slaves and masters, rich and poor, men and women all ate together as an expression that they were one body in Christ (10:17). Their problem was that they were transferring the understanding of social relationships normal in their culture into the life of the church, without realizing

that the very event they were celebrating—the death and resurrection of Jesus—had made everything new (2 Cor. 5:17).

11:18 To some extent I believe it: Paul believes it, as the following clearly indicates. This is his way of communicating his shock: "I can hardly believe it!" (see Gal. 1:6). He finds it "incredible" that they would take the experienced symbol of the church's unity and make it into a display of their social distinctions (see Jas. 2:6).

11:19 There have to be factions among you: A different view from 1:10–12. Here Paul reflects the apocalyptic perspective that just before the end, heresies and divisions emerge in the people of God, forcing believers to show their true colors.

11:23–26 The Institution of the Lord's Supper

11:23 I received from the Lord: Paul was converted after Easter and thus was not present at the Last Supper (see Matt. 26:26–28; Mark 14:22–24; Luke 22:19–20). Yet this is not a claim to have received these instructions directly from the risen Christ (see on Gal. 1:1, 11–12). The words "received from" and "handed on" are the technical terms for the transmission of tradition. Paul identifies the church as the continuing living body of Christ (12:12–31). Christ continues to be present and active in the life of the church. To have received the tradition from the church is to have received it from Christ. **The night when he was betrayed:** The same word means "handed over," "delivered up," and here refers to God's delivering up Jesus for our sins rather than—or as well as—Judas' act of betrayal (see Isa. 53:6, 12, where the same word is used repeatedly for God's act of delivering up the Suffering Servant for the sins of others; see the same word in Rom. 4:25; 8:32; and notes on Mark 1:14, 9:31).

11:24 Broken: This word, not found here in modern translations of the Bible but often heard in eucharistic liturgies and prayers, was not in the original texts but is found in the later MSS of the Bible used by the King James translators. The bread is broken, but not the body of Jesus (see John 19:31–37 and the Passover symbolism; Exod. 12:46; 1 Cor. 5:7).

EXCURSUS:
THE LORD'S SUPPER IN
THE NEW TESTAMENT

There is no systematic discussion of the meaning of the Lord's Supper in the New Testament. The following represents the variety of perspectives found in the spectrum of New Testament authors. For further discussion, see the comments on the particular texts mentioned below. The Eucharist is a symbolic act instituted by Jesus that cannot be reduced to one or several "meanings," but points the participant in several directions:

1. The Eucharist points *backward* to something that really happened:

—It points back to the Passover, the festival that celebrated God's liberation of Israel from Egypt (Luke 22:15).

—It points back to the covenant made with Israel that is now eschatologically renewed (1 Cor. 11:25; for "new covenant," see on Luke 5:36–38; 22:20).

—It points back to the inclusive meals Jesus celebrated with his disciples and with the outcasts (Luke 5:29–32; 7:29, 34).

—It points back to the Last Supper of Jesus with his disciples (Matt. 26:26–29; Mark 14:22–25; Luke 22:15–20; John 13–17).

2. The Eucharist points *forward* to the future:

—Since there is one loaf and one cup (1 Cor. 10:17), it points forward to the time when the one church will be manifest in reality, when all Christians can celebrate together the breaking of bread in the name of Christ.

—The Eucharist points forward to the end of history (Mark 14:25; 1 Cor. 11:26), the final consummation of the kingdom of God, pictured as the messianic banquet where all are included and where there is food, drink, and fellowship for all.

3. The Eucharist points *outward*:

—The Eucharist points out to the whole church, a reminder that discipleship is not individual and Christian life is not just congregational. As there is one body, one church, one faith, one hope, one baptism (Eph. 4:4–5), so there is one loaf and one table for all (1 Cor. 10:17).

—The Eucharist points out beyond the church to the world, as a testimony to God's act in Christ. It is itself a proclamation of the death of Jesus and its meaning (1 Cor. 11:26).

4. The Eucharist points *inward*. While it is not an individualistic sacrament that concerns only the believer and God, there is always a personal element of self-examination involved in Holy Communion. In 11:27–28 believers are urged to examine themselves (not their neighbors!), but the "examination" is not in order to see if they are "worthy," for none is worthy, least of all those who suppose that they are. The Lord's Supper is the supreme testimony to the grace of Christ, who eats and drinks with sinners (Luke 5:29–32). The self-

examination is to see that the Eucharist is celebrated in a proper manner and does not degenerate into a casual and empty ritual, a secular dinner party, or a meal that emphasizes the distance between rich and poor and thus violates the unity of the church. Still and all, the worshiper reflecting on the meaning of Jesus' body and blood cannot but become more aware of personal sin and forgiveness.

5. The Eucharist points *upward* to the reality of the divine world and to the experience of the presence of God in Christ. Through the centuries the church has developed more than one way of attempting to express the presence of Christ in the eucharistic celebration ("transubstantiation," "consubstantiation," "real presence"). Such theological discussion is important, for Christ's followers should think their faith through as clearly as possible. Yet the fact of the presence of Christ in the Eucharist does not depend on how it is explained. It is important for believers to understand that the Eucharist is more than "just" a symbol, that something really happens in the breaking of bread (Luke 24:28–35; 1 Cor. 10:14–22).

11:27–34 Partaking of the Supper Unworthily

11:29 Without discerning the body: The problem was not that they had forgotten that the bread symbolized the body of Jesus—they apparently had a "high" view of the sacraments (see on 10:1–22). What they failed to discern was the body of Christ, the church, in which their "normal" distinctions of social status no longer existed. To fail to discern this is to eat and drink in such a way as to bring God's judgment on the community.

11:30 Weak and ill, and some have died: Paul understands the celebration of the Lord's Supper to be more than "just" a symbol, to be like the Old Testament festivals of eating and drinking in God's presence, a festive meal in which the powerful presence of Christ is manifest. To disregard this is as serious as the biblical scenes in which people profaned the festivals, as though God were absent, and suffered God's judgment (Exod. 32; see 1 Cor. 10:1–22). The meaning is not that those who "partake unworthily" are likely to get sick and die. The judgment is against the community as a whole, not just the guilty. Paul interprets sickness and death in the community as God's judgment on the community as a whole for its abuse of the Lord's Supper.

11:33 Wait for one another: If the word means "wait," the situation is that some—the wealthier—were coming early and enjoying a good meal before others—slaves and the working poor—arrived and found little to eat. This would be a violation of the meaning of the Lord's Supper. However, the word translated "wait" also means "receive, welcome," so that the meaning is more likely that the Eucharist should be a setting in which fellow Christians accept one another rather than segregate themselves from each other. In either case, the punch line of the whole discussion has to do with the reality of the egalitarian Christian community, not abstract eucharistic doctrine.

12:1–11
Spiritual Gifts

12:1 Concerning spiritual gifts: The phrase indicates Paul here begins to make a specific response to their letter (see on 7:1; 11:2).

12:2 When you were pagans: Literally "nations," "Gentiles," the way Jews thought of non-Jews. Paul here applies the Old Testament–Jewish understanding of the people of God to the self-understanding of the church (see on Rom. 11:17–36; 1 Pet. 1:1; 1:13–2:20). Prior to their conversion they had already experienced various spiritual phenomena, including inspired speech. The Corinthian Christians are concerned with two basic types of inspired speech: (1) prophecy, i.e., intelligible speech directly inspired by a god or spirit; and (2) tongues, glossolalia, i.e., unintelligible directly inspired speech. Prophecy and tongues occur wherever people are intensely religious. Paul did not introduce religion to Corinth, but proclaimed the gospel of God's saving act in Jesus. The human response to the gospel is always necessarily expressed in the religious forms already present—e.g., prayer, prophecy, tongues—but fills them with new content and gives them a new orientation. Paul begins by reminding them that "inspired speech" as such is not necessarily an indication that the Spirit of God is present.

12:3 Jesus is Lord: This is one form of the fundamental Christian confession (see Rom. 10:9–10). The issue is the question of what can be said as an expression of the presence and power of God's Spirit. Is the church at the mercy of anyone who claims to speak directly for God? Or are there criteria that can be applied to the claims to prophetic speech to sort out true prophets from false (see excursus, "Testing Prophecy," at Rev. 2:20). Paul takes up two polar opposite examples as test cases. His main point is clear: *No one* who says,

"**Jesus be cursed,**" is inspired by the Holy Spirit, but *everyone* who says, "**Jesus is Lord,**" is inspired by the Spirit (see Matt. 16:17). The Holy Spirit is active in the life of the church as a whole, not just in a few specially inspired speakers in tongues or prophecy. The real test of the Spirit's presence is not flashy "spiritual experiences," but confession, in word and deed, that the crucified man of Nazareth is Lord of one's life and Lord of the church and world. There is no agreement among scholars regarding the problematic "Jesus be cursed." Interpretations can be classified as follows:

1. It is a statement actually made by non-Christian outsiders.
   a. Pagans who said such things against Christians in their "inspired" utterances.
   b. Jews who consider the claim that Jesus is the Messiah to be blasphemy.
   c. An autobiographical example of what Paul himself might once have said when he was still a persecutor of the church (see Acts 26:11).
2. It is a statement actually made by Christian insiders:
   a. Some Christians who, carried away during worship by spiritual exuberance, had said something like this, not quite knowing what they were doing.
   b. Some Christians who, when charged before the courts, had denied their Christian faith using such language, and then claimed that they were led by the Holy Spirit to do so (see Mark 13:11; see the reference to "cursing Christ" in Pliny's *Letter to Trajan* in the introduction to Revelation). This is probably anachronistic, since as far as we know, such incidents did not happen until a generation or two later.
   c. Some "spiritual" Christians who magnified the exalted Christ but disdained the earthly Jesus and displayed their "spirituality" by pronouncing a curse on the earthly Jesus. Later gnostic Christians did this, but so far as we know this distorted theology had not developed this early. It could, however, represent a misunderstanding of Paul's own theology that minimized the earthly Jesus, except for the crucifixion, since Paul too knew of situations in which the crucified one could be spoken of as a "curse" (see Gal. 3:13).
3. It is a hypothetical example invented by Paul as a shocking contrast to authentic

Christian confession, to illustrate that not just anything could be attributed to the Holy Spirit.

The best understanding is either 2.c or 3.

12:4–5 Different . . . same (NIV): Paul's theme throughout this section emphasizes the variety of gifts given to the church by the one God. **Gifts:** Paul switches from their favorite term, "spiritual phenomena," to his own. The Greek word, *charisma*, found only in Paul and in literature dependent on him, was probably invented by Paul. It is related to the word for grace (*charis*), and emphasizes the sovereign gift of God, not the "abilities" of the believer (see v. 11). **Spirit . . . Lord . . . God:** Paul does not have a systematic doctrine of the Trinity, but experiences and expresses the reality of God in a proto-Trinitarian way that was later more systematically formulated (see 8:6; Matt. 28:19; 1 Pet. 1:2).

12:6 All of them in everyone: The Greek expression is even more comprehensive (as in 8:6; Rom. 11:36; Acts 17:25); the God at work in the variety of ministries and services of the church is the same Creator who energizes the universe.

12:7 For the common good: The gifts of the Spirit are not for individualistic enjoyment or display, but for strengthening and equipping the church for its mission. Paul's emphasis is not on "each one" (NIV), but "the common good." See on v. 13. Concentration on "discovering which is *my* gift" is more individualistic than the biblical understanding.

12:8–11 To one . . . to another: Paul here illustrates the rich variety of the work of the Spirit by mentioning several gifts, but the list is not a precise or complete catalogue. See the variations in Paul's other lists in 12:28–13:3, where love—not mentioned here at all—is the supreme gift of the Spirit. See also Rom. 12:6–8; Eph. 4:11; 1 Pet. 4:10–11. Paul begins with **wisdom** and **knowledge**, especially valued by the Corinthians (see 1:5–6; 1:18–2:16). **Faith,** like love (see 13:1–13) may be the general gift of Christian faith and life, or the special faith that enables **healing** and **miracles**. **Prophecy** is preaching directly inspired by the Spirit, not necessarily prediction (see 14:1–40; introduction to Revelation). The **discernment of spirits** is the Spirit-given ability to sort out claims to speak by the Spirit (see 1 Cor. 14:12, 14, 29, 32; 1 John 4:1–4). **Kinds of tongues . . . interpretation of tongues:** As Paul's list begins with gifts especially prized by the Corinthians, so he concludes with the gifts they had magnified. On tongues, see on Acts

2:5. There is no indication in 1 Corinthians that Paul or the Corinthians regarded "tongues" as actual human languages. They apparently thought of themselves as speaking the "language of angels" (13:1). The tongues thus had to be "interpreted," either by the tongues-speaker or by another member of the church who by the power of the Spirit translated the unintelligible words of the tongues-speaker into coherent speech.

12:12–31
One Body with Many Members

12:12 One body . . . many members: Paul adapts a common political metaphor as a way of understanding the nature of the church, with two important modifications: (1) In Roman society, the "body politic" metaphor was often used to urge members of the lower social classes to "stay in your place," since this is needed and healthy for society as a whole. Paul emphasizes the equality of members of the body. (2) The body is the body of Christ, not the body of Christians. Without speculating on the "mystical" connection between Christians and Christ, Paul insists that being a member of the church is actually participating in the body of the living Christ. "Member" thus means a functioning organ in a living body, not "membership" in the sense of having one's name on a list and paying one's dues. The church is organism not organization, corpus not corporation.

12:13 In the one Spirit we were all baptized: The Greek word for "spirit" also means "breath" (see on John 3:1–5). Paul thinks of the Spirit of God as the divine breath that enlivens the body of Christ, the church. The Spirit is given to the church, and individual members participate in the life of the Spirit as members of the body of Christ (12:13). The NRSV translation "in" is consistent with Paul's usage elsewhere, and better than the NIV's "by." Being baptized in the Holy Spirit is not a second-level experience that happens to a special "Spirit-filled" group within the church, but something that happens to all Christians by virtue of being incorporated into the body of Christ. It is not identical with water baptism, but is inseparably connected with it (see Acts 2:38; Gal. 3:2–3; Rom. 8:14–17; see esp. comments on Acts 8:15–17). **Made to drink:** The imagery probably alludes to the Eucharist. While there is nothing magical or mechanical about baptism and the Lord's Supper, when Paul thinks of participating in the life of the Spirit, he thinks of the symbols that express the corporate life of the church: baptism as the initiatory rite, the Eucharist as the continuing expression of this participation (see 10:1–4).

12:14 Not . . . one member but . . . many: Paul assumes the unity of the one church, but his emphasis here is on variety. The one body is not homogenized. Unity is not uniformity. In a living body, variety is *necessary*, not merely tolerated (v. 19). The Christian life is a matter of interdependence, not independence. The "superior" members (in either social status or "spirituality") cannot say to the "inferior" members, "We can get along without you." But the converse is also true: the "common folk" who "have the Spirit" cannot disdain the "high and mighty."

12:26 One . . . all: Paul draws the practical consequences: members of the congregation and of the one worldwide church, though they have a variety of gifts, have the same care for one another. When one's foot hurts, one does not say, "My foot hurts," but "*I* hurt." Or when one's stomach stops hurting, one says, "*I* feel good." It may be more difficult for some Christians to "rejoice with those that rejoice" than to "weep with those who weep" (Rom. 12:15). In stressing mutual dependence, Paul departs from the religious ideal of much ancient religion, which magnified cool self-sufficiency.

12:27 You are the body of Christ: Paul states a fact; he does not urge an ideal. The indicative of God's action precedes and is the basis for Christian ethic. *Since* God has constituted the one body of Christ as a variety of many members, Christian conduct must be based on this reality.

12:28–31 The greater gifts: This paragraph seems to be in tension with his previous emphasis on equality. Yet neither here nor elsewhere is Paul interested in giving a precise and complete list of spiritual gifts and then ranking them from best to worst. The various lists are only illustrative (see on 12:8–11). Nonetheless, from the perspective of building up the church, some gifts are to be preferred and cultivated. In Paul's understanding, leadership in the church occurs not by the church's electing or appointing people to specific offices, but as the work of the Spirit active in the congregation. **Apostles:** See on Luke 6:12–13. **Prophets:** See 14:1–40 and the introduction to Revelation. **Teachers:** See 4:17; Acts 13:1; Rom. 12:7. **Deeds of power:** Working of miracles, as in 12:10. **Assistance:** Not a particular "office," but the capacity to do concrete deeds of helpfulness to others in need—which Paul lists as a gift of the

Spirit. **Leadership:** Not only administrative and organizational competence, but the ability to offer wise counsel and guidance. **Tongues:** Along with the interpretation of tongues, named last in all Paul's lists. Although Paul is not offering a precise ranking of gifts in which apostleship is first and tongues are last, chap. 14 makes it clear that with regard to building up the congregation, Paul gives tongues a low priority.

13:1–13
The Way of Love

This famous passage is not an independent poem idealizing love. It is not a poem at all, but lyrical prose. And it does not understand love as a general ideal, but as the concrete expression of the Christian life in the midst of the conflicts of a first-century church that was fascinated with "spirituality" and "spiritual gifts." It is an integral part of the context discussing spiritual gifts (12:1–14:40) and apart from its context is too easily misunderstood as sentimentality. Love is not itself a "spiritual gift" superior to others, but is the "way" of the Christian life as such that guides the use and application of all gifts of the Spirit.

The three units of the section make three related affirmations: (vv. 1–3) without love, any other "spiritual gift" amounts to nothing; (vv. 4–7) love acts in distinctive ways; (vv. 8–13) unlike the other gifts, which are temporary and provisional, love lasts into the new age that is already dawning.

13:1 Tongues of mortals and of angels: Some of the Corinthian Christians were enthralled by their gift of glossolalia (see 12:1–3, 10, 27–30; Acts 2:5). The "tongues" they spoke were not earthly languages. Some apparently believed that their unintelligible speech was the heavenly language of angels, and that they already participated in the worship of the heavenly world (see 7:1; 11:2–6, 10). The *Testament of Job*, a Jewish document written sometime in the period 100 BCE–100 CE, refers to ecstatic speaking as "the language of angels." Even if this were true, says Paul, if done without love it is mere sound, a cymbal solo. **Clanging cymbals** were used in the ecstatic worship of some pagan rituals.

13:2 Prophetic powers: Not predicting the future, but inspired speech that directly reveals the will of God (see 14:1–25; 1 Thess. 5:19–20; Matt. 7:21–23). **Faith so as to remove mountains:** See 12:9; Matt. 17:20; Luke 17:6.

13:3 Give away all my possessions: The giving of money and property to the poor or to support the mission of the church can indeed be an expression of Christian love. It can also be thinly disguised selfishness, done in order to win applause (see Matt. 6:2) or as a false and unnecessary effort to win God's approval. Since love is action that expresses care for the needs of others, the question throughout is whether such acts are oriented to the well-being of others or are only a refined form of self-interest. **Hand over my body:** As in the case of Jesus, giving one's own body can be the ultimate expression of love, but can also be done without love. **So that I may boast** (NRSV)/**To the flames** (NIV): There is only one letter difference between the Greek words translated these two different ways. The majority of MSS have "flames," but the oldest and most reliable have "boast," which is probably what Paul wrote.

13:4–7 Love is patient: "Love" can mean many things in both Paul's Greek and contemporary English. The Greek word Paul uses is *agape*, but there is no magic in the word itself, which could also be used in a bad sense for selfish love (as in Luke 6:32; 2 Tim. 4:10; 2 Pet. 2:15). Thus Paul must describe the content of what he means by love, just as we must in our own time. These four verses contain fifteen verbs, seven positive and eight negative, that describe what love does and does not do. As with God's love, of which it is a reflection (Rom. 5:5; 1 John 4:19), Christian love is not an abstract quality, attitude, or feeling, but a distinctive action. All fifteen verbs are action words, not "qualities" or "attitudes," and would better be translated "Love acts with patience, love does deeds of kindness," and the like. Several of the verbs fit precisely the situation in Corinth and reveal their unloving actions. **Not envious:** See 3:3, which uses the same word. **Boastful:** See 1:29–31; 3:21; 4:7; 5:6. **Arrogant:** Literally "puffed up" (see 4:6, 18–19; 5:2; 8:1). **Rude:** In Greek a stronger word, which refers to living outside the expected standards of propriety (see 11:2–16). **Bears all things:** See 9:12 for Paul's own example.

13:8 Love never ends: The traditional KJV translation, "never fails" (preserved in the NIV), can be misunderstood to mean that love "always works." But love does sometimes fail in this sense. Love is not commended by Paul as a surefire strategy that "works." His point is that the spiritual gifts with which they are infatuated are provisional and temporary; they belong to this age and will pass away

with it at the return of Christ and the establishment of God's kingdom. They are incomplete, but love will last into the new eschatological age that will commence with the advent of Christ.

13:10 The complete . . . the partial: The present manifestations of the Spirit (except for love) are partial and incomplete; the final kingdom will be complete and will never be superseded (15:20–28). Some interpreters have claimed that the spiritual gifts were given only for the first period of the church's history and were destined to pass away and be superseded by the New Testament, as though once the church had the Bible, it no longer needed the Spirit. Paul never expected the gifts of the Spirit to disappear in this age, nor did he foresee the collection of his writings and others into a Christian "New Testament," but he did expect the age to come to appear very shortly in his own time (see 15:51–52; 1 Thess. 4:15; Mark 9:1; John 21:22–23; see excursus at Rev. 1:3, "Interpreting the 'Near End'"). Paul's point is that Christian love is not a provisional and temporary arrangement given to the church only for its earthly pilgrimage, but that it represents the nature of God himself and will last into the new age.

13:11 Child . . . adult: The Corinthians considered the spiritual phenomena occurring among them to be proof that they were "mature" and "advanced" in their faith. Paul takes their fascination with such things to be a mark of immaturity rather than Christian maturity.

13:12 In a mirror . . . face to face: Many commentaries incorrectly speak of the indistinct image given by ancient mirrors, but the metal mirrors of antiquity reflected clear images. The point is that a mirror image, however clear, is still not direct and is always incomplete. Paul has in mind the biblical contrast of Num. 12:6–8. All present knowledge is indirect, a part of the "not yet" aspect of Christian existence. Direct knowledge (such as the Corinthians claimed for "now") is yet to be experienced at the eschaton. **Now . . . then:** Present knowledge, even revealed, inspired knowledge, is fragmentary and indirect. Even prophecy, which Paul values highly, is not a complete revelation. **As I have been fully known:** God's knowledge of us is the foundation for our knowledge of God—now fragmentary, then to be complete (Gal. 4:9). It is personal knowledge, not informational knowledge.

14:1–40
Gifts of Prophecy and Tongues

14:1 Love . . . spiritual gifts . . . prophesy: Paul now returns to the specific issue (see 12:1). Love is the essential activity that must permeate all the Christian life (13:1–13). Of the charismatic speech gifts, prophecy is the most valuable for edifying the community because, in contrast to tongues, it may be understood by all. This is the main point of the remaining discussion (14:1–40) on the topic begun at 12:1. **Pursue . . . strive for:** Although God the giver decides "who gets which gift" (see 12:11), this is not done in a way that eliminates seeking and cultivating the more helpful gifts.

14:2–3 Tongues . . . not to other people but to God: Paul understands tongues to be a personal, private devotional experience between the believer and God. But congregational worship is not just a collection of such individual experiences. "What do I get out of it?" is the commercial question of the marketplace, but is not the attitude of Christian worship, in which the congregation as a whole directs its prayer and praise to God. Prophecy is intelligible inspired preaching that is for the benefit of the community as a whole. It is neither the prepared sermon nor prediction of the future, but spontaneous inspired speech directed to the congregation's **upbuilding, encouragement, and consolation** (in 14:31, also **learning**). Prophetic speech strengthens the faith of those who hear. The Greek word for "encouragement" is related to the word for the Paraclete of the Fourth Gospel, the post-Easter gift of the Spirit that enables speaking in the name of the risen Christ (John 14:15–16, 25; 15:26; 16:7–11, 12–15).

14:6 Revelation or knowledge or prophecy or teaching: Samples, not a precise or exhaustive list, of forms of speech inspired by the Spirit. Since they are intelligible, they can strengthen the church.

14:11 The speaker a foreigner to me: Paul considers this anti-Christian. The purpose of the church is to break down the walls that separate people, not to increase distance and alienation among its members. Paul gives illustrations from the concert hall (v. 7) and the battlefield (v. 8) to emphasize the necessity of clarity and intelligibility in Christian worship.

14:13–17 Pray . . . sing praise . . . say a blessing: Rather than in unintelligible gibberish, the language of worship is to be **with the mind.**

Anyone in the position of an outsider: The word used here can be translated "non-expert," "uninitiated," and in later church history was used of a special class of "inquirers" who attended worship and catechetical instruction before being baptized. Here the reference is probably to interested outsiders. Christian worship is to be directed to God, but with an eye on the seeking unbelievers, and must not repel them with unintelligible speech. **Say the "Amen":** As an informal part of worship, congregational members sometimes responded with this Hebrew word, which meant something like "I heartily agree."

14:18 I speak in tongues more than all: Paul sometimes tends to speak in rhetorical, exaggerated style (see 15:9–10; 2 Cor. 11:5–33; Phil. 3:2–11; see the post-Pauline 1 Tim. 1:15 in this same tradition). The Corinthians may well have criticized Paul for not being "spiritual" enough, and for lacking what they considered the supreme manifestation of the Spirit. Here Paul (surprisingly, to many modern readers) indicates that he too speaks in tongues, just as he has other personal ecstatic experiences; yet he considers them to be part of his private devotional life and not to be introduced in public worship as a matter of spiritual pride (see 2 Cor. 12:1–10).

14:20 In thinking be adults: The Corinthians were enthralled by spectacular and entertaining displays of spirituality that made them feel good, but were unwilling to engage in the discipline necessary to think through the meaning of the Christian faith. But this, not spiritual display, is the mark of Christian maturity. Even their attachment to "wisdom" was immature (see on 3:1–23).

14:21 Strange tongues: Paul cites Isa. 28:11–12 to show their speaking in unintelligible tongues was a mark of God's *judgment*. See 14:11 "foreigner." That Paul uses actual foreign languages as an analogy of what their speaking in tongues is *like* shows that for neither him nor them was glossolalia actual speaking of foreign languages (see on Acts 2:5). They thought of "tongues" as the "language of angels" (13:1), not actual human languages.

14:22–25 Tongues . . . are a sign . . . for unbelievers: Here Paul takes the negative meaning of "sign," i.e., a sign of God's judgment, while prophecy is a positive sign of God's acceptance. The following illustration seems to reverse this evaluation, since prophecy is "for unbelievers" in the sense that they respond to it and are converted by it. While the analogy may be confused by Paul's rhetoric, the point is clear: tongues confirm unbelievers in their unbelief, but prophecy may lead to their conversion. **Out of your mind:** The idea is not that outsiders might think tongues-speakers were crazy, for before they became aware of Christianity the Corinthians were well acquainted with the phenomenon as it occurred in pagan cults. The danger was rather that they would confuse the church with such pagan cultic worship, in which ecstatic speaking was the mark of possession by the god or the spirits. Christian worship has a responsibility to outsiders to make clear the distinction between the Christian faith and pagan religion. **God is really among you:** A citation of Isa. 45:14 (in contrast with the quote from Isa. 28:11–12 above). This is a goal of Christian worship. While it is directed to God, it must be intelligible to outsiders and beginners and lead to their own confession of the presence and power of God. Thus worship has an indirect evangelistic aspect.

14:26 When you come together: The early Christian worship services had no "order of service" or authorized "worship leaders." Unless Phil. 1:1 refers to bishops and deacons (the words there may also be translated unofficially as "superintendents and servers"; see Rom. 16:1), in the Pauline churches there were as yet no bishops, priests, elders, or deacons. No "church officers" are mentioned in the Corinthian letters. The congregation of house churches at Corinth gathered, and those who felt led by the Spirit made their contribution. Into this lively but chaotic situation Paul attempts to introduce some order (see vv. 33, 40). The later Pauline churches established a more orderly ministry and order of worship (see, e.g., 1 Tim. 2:1–3:13).

14:27 Let one interpret: Paul minimizes, but does not absolutely forbid, tongues in worship— but only if they are interpreted in intelligible language.

14:29 Let the others weigh what is said: The "others" are the congregation as a whole to whom the Spirit is given (12:1–13), not merely the other prophets. The claim to speak by direct inspiration of the Spirit is to be respected, but not accepted uncritically (1 Thess. 5:19–21). In the presence of such claims, the congregation has a responsibility to discern the word and will of God (see on Rom. 12:1–2; Rev. 2:20).

14:33 As in all the churches: This phrase properly ends the preceding paragraph (contrary to both NRSV and NIV). Verses 34–35 are then a separate section. Paul reminds the Corinthians that their worship must be regulated in the context of the church as a whole to which they belong (see v. 36; 1:1; 11:16). Each congregation is not "free" to conduct its worship without regard to the larger community of faith.

14:34–35 Women should be silent in the churches: There is good evidence that these two verses were not written by Paul himself, but were added to the letter a generation or two later. For a full statement of the evidence, see the more detailed commentaries. Persuasive to many scholars are the following data: (1) A large number of manuscripts contain the verses at a different location, at the end of chapter. This suggests that they were originally a marginal gloss, incorporated into the body of the text at two different locations. (The original text of no New Testament document has been preserved, but must be painstakingly reconstructed from the hundreds of surviving manuscripts, no two of which are exactly alike.) See on Mark 16:9–20; 5:39; 8:26, 43; 10:1; 14:5; 22:19, 43–44; 23:34; John 7:53–8:1; Acts 8:37; 1 Cor. 2:1; the notes throughout the NRSV and NIV, and see "Introduction: The New Testament as the Church's Book," 4.c, d. (2) The text conflicts with 11:2–12, which assumes that women speak in church. (3) The text conflicts with other Pauline statements in which women play leadership roles, including speaking in the congregational worship (e.g., Rom. 16:1–2, 3–4, 7; Gal. 3:27–28; Phil. 4:2–3; Acts 5:1–11; 18:8–28). (4) The text reflects developments in the post-Pauline church in which restrictions were placed on women's activity as an effort to conform to cultural expectations and not unduly hinder the mission of the church—a practice Paul himself had commended on other issues (see 1 Tim. 2:11–12; 1 Cor. 8:1–11:1). (5) Efforts to harmonize this text with Paul's teaching elsewhere have failed. For instance, it is false to claim that this text forbids only women "babbling" in church, on the purported basis that the Greek word used here (*laleo*) means "babble." This explanation is not only demeaning to women, but incorrect Greek. *Laleo* does not mean "babble," but is often used by Paul and others as the normal word for "speak" (296x New Testament; see, e.g., 1 Cor. 2:6, 7, 13; 14:3, 16, 19, 29; Matt. 10:20; 12:46; Rev. 10:3).

While apparently not from Paul, these words are nonetheless part of holy Scripture. Like other parts of Scripture influenced by their times (e.g., the passages accepting slavery), they must be interpreted to address the modern situation. On this point, other voices, such as that of the authentic Paul, must prevail.

14:37 Acknowledge that what I am writing to you is the Lord's command (NIV): Paul affirms the claim that by the Spirit the risen Christ continued to address his church. Yet he knew that such claims must be evaluated. Apostolic writings are one criterion to which claims to inspired speech must measure up. By making his own letters a norm by which the church may judge where the word of God may be heard and where not, Paul takes a decisive step in the direction of the formation of the canon, the Christian Bible.

15:1–58
THE RESURRECTION OF CHRIST
AND CHRISTIANS

On interpreting the New Testament witness to the resurrection in general, see at Luke 20:27–40 and excursus at Matt. 28:1.

Here begins a new topic, which Paul has saved for the conclusion and climax of the letter. It is not in response to their letter (see on 7:1). For Paul, the resurrection is not one topic among others, but is integral to several of the ethical problems the Corinthians had asked about or on which they had challenged him. Some of them had minimized or eliminated the future dimension of Christian faith, supposing that they already lived the full life of the Spirit and were like the angels (see on 4:8; 7:1; 11:2; 13:1).

The chapter has three sections (1) 15:1–11 The Foundation and Core of Christian Faith—the Death and Resurrection of Christ; (2) 15:12–34 The Future Resurrection of All; (3) 15:35–58 The Resurrection of the Body.

15:1–11
The Foundation and Core
of Christian Faith—the Death
and Resurrection of Christ

15:1–2 Remind you of the good news: The gospel, the basic Christian message. Paul begins by stating the common ground. **Proclaimed . . . received . . . stand . . . saved . . . hold firmly . . . believe:** This series of six verbs all have to do with the gospel. What Paul is about to declare stands at the center of Christian faith and life, not at the margin.

15:3–5 Handed on . . . received: As in 11:23, these are the technical words for transmission of sacred tradition. Paul is about to quote verbatim the creed, i.e., the summary statement of the Christian faith he had been taught at his conversion and which he in turn had taught to the new converts at Corinth at the founding of the church. (For other such creeds or creedal fragments, see Acts 8:37; Rom. 1:3–4; 3:25; 4:25; 10:9; 1 Thess. 1:9–10.) Thus 15:3–5 is very ancient Christian tradition, formulated within a very few years of Jesus' death and resurrection. It is crucial to see that this earliest summary of Christian faith does not portray the "life and teachings of Jesus" as a great hero to be emulated, but refers to his death (his truly human life) and his resurrection (God's act, not an "accomplishment" of Jesus). The death and resurrection stand for the Christ event as a whole, the act of God for human salvation. This is the gospel, the good news, of God's act in Christ. (For the role of the Gospel stories of Jesus' life in the formation of Christian faith, see on "Introduction to the Gospels," 4.)

The formula has two parallel parts with four elements each:

I.
  A. That Christ died
    B. for our sins
    C. in accordance with the scriptures
  D. And that he was buried

II.
  A. And that he was raised
    B. on the third day
    C. in accordance with the scriptures
  D. And that he appeared to Cephas, then to
    the twelve

A = *event.* Christ's death and resurrection were events that happened, not ideas. The gospel is good news, not good advice.

B = *interpretation.* The bare event must be interpreted. Jesus' death was "for our sins," using the sacrificial language of Isa. 53:4–12. Jesus' resurrection was "on the third day," which in this pattern is not a chronological note, but probably refers to Hos. 6:2 and other Old Testament pictures of the triumph of God after apparent defeat for his people.

C = *theological validation.* Both death and resurrection were "in accordance with the scriptures," i.e., in continuity with the will and plan of God as revealed in the Bible.

D = *historical validation.* Both death and resurrection really happened in the real world. Neither was an illusion or mere subjective experience. This is the meaning of "was buried"—he really died, we are talking about a corpse placed in a real grave. "Appeared to Peter" is the validation that the resurrection was not a subjective projection, but something that really happened. Nothing is yet said about *how* the resurrection happened, or what it means to talk of God raising the dead (see below).

In accordance with the scriptures: The creed cited by Paul does not list specific Scriptures, and Paul probably has none in mind himself. The point here is not that the Bible had made specific predictions that were fulfilled by Christ, but that the good news of the Christ event is in accord with the nature and plan of God revealed in the Scriptures as a whole.

EXCURSUS:
NEW TESTAMENT INTERPRETATION
OF THE OLD TESTAMENT

In scores of passages the New Testament quotes or alludes to its Bible—the Jewish Scriptures, the Christian Old Testament—as having been fulfilled in the Christ event, including the life of the Christian community. But not all New Testament authors interpret the Old Testament in the same way, and a variety of interpretative approaches may be found in the same author. Here are some guidelines to keep in mind when studying the New Testament's interpretation of the Old:

1. The early church regarded the Scripture as a whole ("Law and Prophets") as testifying to God's will and work in history.

2. God's work testified to in the Scripture was not yet complete; the Law and Prophets point beyond themselves to the definitive act of God in the eschatological, messianic future.

3. The advent of the Messiah proclaiming and representing the eschatological kingdom of God is the fulfillment of the Scripture, the Law and the Prophets. The Messiah has come. He embodies and teaches the definitive will of God. He is the fulfillment of the Scripture viewed as a whole. All God's promises find their yes in him (2 Cor. 1:20).

4. This messianic fulfillment does not nullify or make obsolete the Law and the Prophets, but confirms them. The incorporation of the Law in the more comprehensive history of salvation centered in the Christ event is an affirmation of the Law, not its rejection (Matt. 5:17–19; Rom. 3:31).

5. But this affirmation by being fulfilled by Christ does not always mean a mere repetition or continuation of the original Law. Jesus' declaration that his own life and teaching is the definitive revelation of the will of God does indeed mean that neither the written Torah nor its interpretation in the oral tradition (see on Matt. 15) is the final authority.

6. No one in the New Testament plays off the (abiding) "moral law" against the (temporary) "ceremonial law."

7. The ways early Christians interpreted the Scripture are different from our modern, more historically oriented ways. We rightly ask for the "original meaning," but they used other methods. Paul and other early Christians used the exegetical methods standard in their days in both the Jewish and Greek worlds, ways that did not seem strained or "proof-texting" to their contemporaries.

8. Early Christians understood the Old Testament not only to point to its fulfillment in Jesus, but to predict specific events in the life, death, and resurrection of Jesus and the beginning of the Christian community. To modern readers, their interpretations often seem far removed from the original meaning (see, e.g., 9:8–10 above).

9. Neither Paul nor other early Christians began with the Old Testament and found predictions that then led them to Christ. Paul had studied the Old Testament his whole life without seeing prophecies of Christ there. But when he was converted by his encounter with the risen Christ, he felt that scales fell from his eyes (Acts 9:18) or a veil was lifted from his reading of the Bible (2 Cor. 3:12–18). He saw the same texts with new eyes, and understood them from a new perspective.

10. If modern Christians ask, "What is the Old Testament *about*?" New Testament writers might well answer, "God, the one God, the God definitively revealed in the life, death, and resurrection of Jesus." In *this* sense the whole Old Testament can be heard as pointing to Christ, but not in the sense of specific predictions, without doing violence to the text of the Bible. (For further reflections on early Christian interpretation of the Old Testament, see excursus, "Matthew as Interpreter of Scripture" at Matt. 2:23 and comments on 1 Pet. 1:10–11.)

15:5 He appeared to Cephas: Paul appears not yet to know the later Gospel stories of the discovery of the empty tomb in which Jesus' first appearance was to women (Mark 16:1–8; Matt. 28:1–10; Luke 24:1–12; John 20:1–17). While Paul did not believe the resurrection was a matter of flesh and blood (15:50) but of a transformed body (15:35–55), he would have found it difficult to formulate his understanding of the resurrection if he had believed that the body of Jesus had decomposed in the tomb. His manner of affirming the resurrection was not to tell stories of the discovery of the empty tomb, but to list the witnesses to whom the risen Jesus had appeared. The list of appearances is not intended as evidence to convert unbelievers—neither here nor elsewhere does Paul attempt to "prove the resurrection"—but to reconfirm the proper understanding of the resurrection for believers.

Cephas: Peter. Both words mean "rock," the nickname given to Simon (1:12; 3:22; 9:5; see John 1:42; Matt. 16:18; introduction to 1 Peter). **The twelve:** A smaller group included in "all the apostles" (see on Luke 6:12–13).

15:6 Five hundred: This event is otherwise unknown, but may refer to something like the Pentecost event of Acts 2:1–42. Paul's point is that the resurrection is not some twilight zone, never-never-land event in the mythical past, but an event in recent history to which many of his own generation could testify.

15:7 James: The brother of Jesus, who remained an unbeliever during the life of Jesus (John 7:5), but was converted and became leader of the Jerusalem church (Gal. 1:19; 2:9, 12; Acts 15:13–21; 21:18).

15:8 Last of all: The series of resurrection appearances did not continue indefinitely, but belonged only to the initial period that founded the church. Paul understands himself to have been the last apostle called. **As one untimely born:** Literally "the abortion," "the miscarriage," perhaps a derogatory nickname given Paul by his opponents, with overtones of "the freak." It may refer to something repulsive about Paul's physical condition or appearance (see on 2 Cor. 12:5–10).

15:9 Least: "Paul" means "little," "small." Again, this may take up a taunt of his opponents that Paul turns into a testimony to the gospel: "Little as I am, God's grace made me into an apostle."

15:10 Worked harder than any: See on 14:18–19 for Paul's exaggerated style. Here Paul is not merely bragging, but pointing to the effect of the overwhelming grace of God in his life. This grace was not his personal possession, but impelled and empowered him to mission.

15:11 Whether I or they: Though the various apostles had different ways of expressing the faith, and different emphases, they all proclaimed essentially the same message (see on 3:21–23).

15:12–34
The Future Resurrection of All

15:12 Christ is proclaimed as raised from the dead: Paul appeals to the fact of the matter. This is what the church proclaims, this is what Paul preached to the Corinthians, this is

what they and he believe. Note that *Jesus* did not *"rise,"* but *God raised* him (see on Luke 20:27–40; Matt. 28:1). The Corinthians did not reject the general idea of "life after death"; what they objected to was the raising of dead bodies, which sounded crude within their framework of sophisticated pagan philosophy.

15:14–19 If Christ has not been raised: The resurrection is not optional or marginal, but essential and central to Christian faith. Paul lists the theological consequences of rejecting it:

1. The **proclamation** of the church **is in vain,** useless (15:14).

2. **Faith** is **in vain,** useless (15:14). Christian faith is not believing in general, but believing *something,* i.e., that God acted to vindicate the crucified Jesus as Lord of all.

3. The church is **misrepresenting God** (15:15), since the church does not proclaim a god-in-general, but the good news of God's act in Christ.

4. **You are still in your sins** (15:17). The forgiveness of sins is not a general truth to be discussed, but results from God's act in Christ, and is included in the basic affirmation of 15:3 that "Christ died for our sins."

5. **Those who have died in Christ have perished** (15:18; see 15:29). Here "perished" is as in John 3:16, where it is opposite "eternal life." If there is no resurrection, then the dead are gone forever, their life counts for nothing; it is the same as if they had never lived.

6. We are **most to be pitied** (15:19). Those who have lived an unselfish life in the service of others have built on an illusion. They should have been living for themselves, and have wasted the chance (see 15:32).

15:20 First fruits: The image is from the harvest ritual, in which the first sheaf of grain was dedicated to God as pledge and guarantee of the harvest of the remainder of the crop (see Lev. 23:9–14). In early Christianity the resurrection of Jesus was not regarded as something special that happened to Jesus, but as the beginning of the eschatological event in which all the dead would be raised.

15:22 Adam . . . Christ: See 15:45; Rom. 5:12–21. Here "all" seems to be identified with "those who belong to Christ" (see 15:23). All those in Adam (= the whole human race) corresponds to all those in Christ. But having begun this line of thought, the "all" reaches out from its earliest reference to all Christians to embrace all humans. The Christ event, the new creation in Christ (see 2 Cor. 5:17), becomes as universal as the original creation, so that the meaning progresses from "all in Christ" (exclusive sense) to "in Christ all" (inclusive sense), as in Rom. 5:12–21.

15:23 Each in his own order: Paul is not here concerned to give a detailed chronology of the end-time events, but to make three points important in the context: (1) the resurrection of Christ was not an isolated event, but the prelude to the final end and the resurrection of all; (2) Christ has already been raised, but the resurrection of Christians is still in the future (see Phil. 3:4–10; contrast 2 Tim. 2:18); (3) God will finally be "all in all" (see 12:6). Paul had no interest in the later question of whether Jesus would return to earth and have a "millennial reign" before the final end (see Rev. 20:1–6). Likewise, Paul is untroubled by the later questions of Trinitarian theology, whether the Son is subordinate to or "co-equal" with the Father. Paul's point is that Christ is the agent of God in bringing about the ultimate divine victory, and that finally the one God will be supreme over all. In making his case, Paul understands two psalms as expressions of Christian theology, Ps. 110:1 (see also Matt. 22:44; 26:64; Mark 12:36; 14:62; 16:19; Luke 20:42–43; 22:69; Acts 2:34–35; Rom. 8:34; Eph. 1:20; Col. 3:1; Heb. 1:3, 13; 8:1; 10:12) and Ps. 8:7 (see Eph. 1:22; Heb. 2:8).

15:29 Baptism on behalf of the dead: This text continues to be a puzzle. A 1950 study catalogued more than forty explanations, and others have been offered since. Paul and the Corinthians knew what he was referring to, but we later readers do not (see 11:2–16). This is further testimony to the letter character of 1 Corinthians (and of much of the New Testament), which was written not as a general essay but for a particular situation. It may be among the things Paul intended to straighten out when he got to Corinth (11:34!). Whatever it meant, Paul takes it as an argument for the resurrection.

15:32 Wild animals at Ephesus: This is not literal, but a common metaphor for intense struggles. See 16:8–9. If literal, Paul would not have survived. **Eat and drink, for tomorrow we die:** A quote from Isa. 22:13, originally a secular drinking song. Paul cites it as appropriate to the Corinthian mood, which misunderstood the resurrection and emphasized their "advanced" knowledge, which allowed them to eat and drink what they pleased (see 8:1–11:1).

15:33 Bad company ruins good morals: This quotation from the Greek poet Menander had become a common proverb by Paul's time. Paul cites it not as a bland generalization, but in reference to the Corinthian situation: their conversation with seemingly sophisticated teachers of "advanced wisdom" had corrupted not only their theology but their ethics.

15:34 Right mind . . . sin no more: Paul considers right thinking about the Christian faith (= good theology) and right living (= ethics) to be inseparable. What he says here does not have as its goal mere speculation about "what happens when we die," but is aimed at a Christian life based on a proper understanding of the Christian faith. There is an inseparable moral dimension to faith in the resurrection (6:13–14). **No knowledge of God:** The opposite of their profession to have advanced knowledge (see 8:1–13).

15:35–58
The Resurrection Body

The point of this whole section is that future existence of resurrected believers in the transcendent world of God will be neither the continuation of the flesh-and-blood existence of this world nor the ghostly "spiritual" existence of disembodied spirits, but will involve an unimaginable transformation. Christian hope involves the "redemption of our bodies" along with the whole creation (Rom. 8:23), not redemption *from* them. The life of the world to come will manifest both continuity and discontinuity with the present world.

15:35 How are the dead raised?: This is not a request for an explanation, but a rhetorical question. It expresses the challenge of the Corinthian "spiritualists," who believed they had already entered fully into the new life of the age to come (4:8), that they already lived the life of angels and spoke their language (7:1–16; 11:2–16; 13:1), and that all that stood between them and the heavenly world was sloughing off their fleshly bodies and entering totally into the world of the Spirit. In their view, the "body" was the enemy of true spirituality and would be disposed of at death, so they resisted the idea of the resurrection of the body, either of Jesus' or their own.

15:36 Fool!: In biblical parlance, being a "fool" has nothing to do with intelligence or education. It cannot be measured by an IQ, SAT, or GRE test. The fool is the one who fails to take God into account, who lives as though God does not exist and all issues must be settled in terms of his or her own intelligence—which may be quite high (Ps. 14:1; 53:1; 92:6;

12:16–21). Paul contends that anyone who must have a rational "how" before believing the divine "that" is a "fool" in this biblical sense. They thought they knew what "resurrection" meant—the resuscitation of corpses, the same body that was buried coming out of the tomb—and so they rejected the whole concept. Paul challenges the presupposition of their argument. He agrees that resurrection existence is not the restoration of present physical existence. Thus such questions as, will we know each other in heaven? will babies that died in infancy still be babies in heaven? and how can there be a resurrection when bodies have been eaten by worms, which were in turn eaten by other living creatures? are all irrelevant. See on Mark 12:18–27; Luke 20:27–38.

Unless it dies: See John 12:24. Resurrection is for dead people who are without hope unless God acts in their behalf, not for beings who have an immortal soul that cannot die.

15:38 God gives it a body: Paul's analogy of the seed that becomes a flower is an apt analogy, but only an analogy. He has already indicated that the transformation involved in being taken into God's eternal world is more than human minds can grasp, and must be a matter of trust in God, rather than "understanding" what is involved. Yet it is *like* planting a seed. For the ancient mind, that one planted seeds and reaped a harvest was not "natural," but a miracle. People did not "raise" crops; the divine miracle created new life from the seed planted in the earth. Just as there is continuity between seed and flower, so there is continuity between this life and the next. All that is valuable here is redeemed and preserved there. Yet we are no more capable of imagining what life in God's new world is like than of projecting the image of a flower by looking at a seed.

15:42 So it is with the resurrection of the dead: Paul proceeds with a series of contrasts. The left column represents present earthly life, which we can grasp; the right column represents future eternal life, which defies our imagination:

Perishable	Imperishable (v. 42)
Dishonor	Glory (v. 43)
Weakness	Power (v. 43)
Physical body	Spiritual body (v. 44)
Of dust	From heaven (v. 47)
First Adam	Last Adam (v. 45)
Mortal	Immortality (v. 54)
Death	Victory (v. 54)

15:45–49 The first man, Adam ... the last Adam: Human existence is corporate existence, as part of the human race created by God and heir to its weaknesses; Christian existence is incorporation in the new humanity created by God in Christ, and participating in its coming glory. Paul is concerned to emphasize the already/not yet dimension of Christian existence: we *already* participate in Adamic humanity, but *not yet* in the resurrection life of the new humanity (Phil. 3:4–11, 20–21). Paul illustrates his point with a paraphrase/interpretation of Gen. 2:7. In the creation story Adam was first made of dust; then God breathed the divine spirit/breath into him (in both Greek and Hebrew, the same word means "breath" and "spirit"). His point is that we now share in the earthly reality of the first Adam, and at the resurrection we shall share in the spiritual reality of the second Adam. The Corinthians are mistaken in supposing that they already share the full resurrection life; this is part of the "not yet" aspect of Christian existence.

15:50 Flesh and blood: Especially to be noted in the above list is that "physical body" appears only in the left column. The Bible nowhere teaches the "physical resurrection" of either Jesus or ourselves, but the "bodily resurrection" conceived in terms of the right-hand column. The resurrection is a matter of the "body," the essential self, not a matter of "**flesh and blood.**" "Spiritual body" does not mean a body made of "spirit," as though it were composed of ethereal vapor. Paul is not talking about the "components" of such a body— he has already argued that such ideas are beyond human comprehension—but that the resurrected body shares the power of God's transcendent world, just as the earthly body shares the weakness of this world.

15:51 Mystery: Not merely a puzzle, but the truth of God that cannot be discovered by human wisdom. Once hidden, it is now revealed in Christ and by prophets (2:7; Rom. 11:25). **We will not all die:** Paul himself expected to be alive at the second coming (1 Thess. 4:15–17; see Phil. 1:23). **We will be changed:** Both those who have died and those who remain alive at the parousia. This physical body does not enter into the final coming of God's kingdom, but neither is it simply abolished (see Phil. 3:20–21; Luke 20:34–36).

15:54–55 Victory: Isa. 25:8; Hos. 13:14. These Old Testament texts are now read through Christian eyes (see excursus at 15:3 above). In biblical theology, death is not "natural," a "part of life," but the *enemy* of life caused by human rebellion against God (Gen. 1–4). But the enemy has been defeated, and God's original purpose for the creation has been restored.

15:56 Sin . . . law . . . death: These are pictured as suprapersonal powers that conspire to hold present human life in bondage, but from which we will be freed at the resurrection and final coming of God's kingdom (see Rom. 5:12–14; 7:7–13).

15:57 Thanks be to God: The conclusion is not a neat "explanation" that satisfies the understanding, but thanksgiving and worship. Readers are asked not to believe a concept of "what happens when we die," but to trust in God in grateful praise—the God who raised Jesus from the dead (see Rom. 11:33–36).

16:1–4
THE COLLECTION FOR THE SAINTS

Paul has concluded the theological and ethical part of the letter and turns to practical matters—which he also considers an expression of the theological and ethical concerns of the Christian life.

16:1 Now concerning: Introduces a new topic about which they had inquired (see on 7:1). **The collection for the saints:** On "saints," see 1:2. Paul was engaged in taking a substantial offering for the poor among the Jerusalem Christians, both to relieve their poverty and as a symbol of unity between Gentile and Jewish Christians (Rom. 15:25–32; 2 Cor. 8–9; Gal. 2:10; see Acts 11:17–30; 24:17).

16:2 First day of the week: Sunday, the new Christian holy day that eventually replaced Saturday, the Jewish Sabbath (see Acts 20:7; Rev. 1:10). Though Sunday did not become a government-supported holiday until the fourth century, it was already the regular day for Christian worship and assembly. Christians thus met on a "workday," before or after work.

16:5–12
PLANS FOR TRAVEL

16:5 I will visit you: See the introduction to 2 Corinthians for Paul's travels that involved the Corinthians. Paul changed the plans projected here, making him all the more suspicious to some Corinthians (2 Cor. 1:15–2:4).

16:6 Spend the winter: Paul is writing prior to Pentecost in the spring of 54 CE (v. 8). Since ships did not sail during the winter, he is writing in the fall of 53 or the early spring of 54. He plans to arrive in Corinth late the next fall,

spending some months in Macedonia. He will then spend the winter in Corinth. Such a schedule does not suggest casual visits, but extended periods of teaching and supervising the new churches. As he writes, Paul has a great opportunity for mission despite the opposition, about which we know no details.

16:10 Timothy: See 4:17–21. There is no further reference in the New Testament to this visit. Paul is worried that Timothy, as Paul's representative, will not be well received. Paul's own next visit to Corinth was a disaster (2 Cor. 2:1–11; 7:12).

16:12 Now concerning: The final reference to their letter (see 7:1). On Apollos, see 1:12; 3:5–6, 22; 4:6; Acts 18:24; 19:1. Although some of the Corinthians considered Apollos to be the leader of a rival faction, Paul considers him a Christian brother and colleague.

16:13–22
FINAL MESSAGES AND GREETINGS

16:14 All . . . in love: Not a merely a platitude on which to end. Paul mentions love three times in his closing comments, because its central role in the Christian community had been neglected by the Corinthians (see vv. 22, 24; 8:1–3; 13:1–13).

16:17 Stephanas and Fortunatus and Achaicus: See 1:16. These, along with the "household of Chloe" (1:11), had reported to Paul on the conditions in the Corinthian congregation. They represent the church and had probably brought the Corinthian letter to which Paul has been responding since 7:1, and probably carried 1 Corinthians back to Corinth. **Made up for your absence:** Despite Paul's severe criticism of the theology and practice of the Corinthian congregation, he genuinely loves them and wants to be with them (v. 24!).

16:19 The churches of Asia: In these closing comments, Paul incidentally mentions churches in Jerusalem, Galatia, Macedonia, Asia, and Ephesus. This is another reminder that the Corinthians are not an independent congregation, but like all congregations are part of the one church of God scattered throughout the Mediterranean (see on 1:2). **Aquila and Prisca:** Prisca is also called Priscilla. They first met Paul in Corinth, are now with him in Ephesus, will later appear in Rome, always as Christian leaders whose home accommodates a house church (see Acts 18:2, 18, 26; Rom. 16:3).

16:21 My own hand: The rest of the letter had been dictated to a secretary. Here Paul takes the pen himself to complete the letter (see Rom. 16:22; Gal. 6:11; Col. 4:18; Phlm. 19; 2 Thess. 3:17).

16:20–24 Greet one another: The letter concludes with five elements that later became standard items in the liturgy, probably indicating that Paul anticipated his letter being read in worship just prior to the celebration of the Eucharist.

1. **Holy kiss:** A kiss was a conventional greeting in the first century among friends and especially in the family; "holy" means it has been incorporated in Christian worship as a sign that Christians are brothers and sisters in the one family of God (see Rom. 16:16; 2 Cor. 13:12; 1 Thess. 5:26; 1 Pet. 5:14).

2. **Let anyone be accursed:** Not a flash of anger, but a solemn ritual pronouncement against those who pervert the life and message of the church (see Gal. 1:8–9). The apostolic faith tolerates considerable variety, but has limits to what is acceptable (see on 3:21–23).

3. **Our Lord, come:** Paul's churches preserved the Aramaic prayer from the earliest days of the Jerusalem church, *Marana tha,* "Come, Lord." It is an eschatological prayer for the return of Christ, who will bring the final coming of the kingdom (see Matt. 6:10), and shows that the very earliest post-Easter followers of Jesus both confessed him to be Lord and expected the near Parousia. That the Aramaic prayer was repeated in Gentile churches (like "Amen" and "Abba" [Mark 14:36; Rom. 8:15; Gal. 4:6]) shows the continuity of Jewish and Gentile Christianity. The prayer also served as an invocation for the risen Lord to "come" and be present at the Eucharist.

4. **Grace . . . be with you:** The closing benediction of the letter that also begins with grace (1:3).

5. **Amen** (NIV): Not in all manuscripts (see NRSV note), but likely written by Paul, who intended his letter to be read as part of the Corinthian worship.

My love be with all of you: See v. 14. Even after the formal close of the letter, Paul adds one more reference to the most important element of all.

The Second Letter of Paul to the Corinthians

INTRODUCTION

While 1 Corinthians often deals with issues of how the Christian relates to the world and culture outside the church, 2 Corinthians deals almost entirely with an internal issue—the meaning of apostleship and whether Paul is a genuine apostle. Some in the Corinthian church had challenged Paul's standing as an authentic apostle. Paul's response is not mere pride or ego, but deals with a fundamental issue of Christian theology: who is authorized to interpret the meaning of the Christ event? What is authentic ministry in Christ's name? Classical Christianity has maintained from the first century to the present that authentic Christian faith cannot be whatever one wants it to be, a matter of personal taste and individual opinion, but must be apostolic, i.e., must be true to the original authorized interpreters. In his struggles against the "false apostles," Paul also shows us his most personal side and innermost feelings.

Chronology

We know that Paul wrote at least four letters to the Corinthians. From the letters and the information in Acts, the following chronology may be pieced together:

1. The church is founded by Paul (and Timothy and Silvanus?) (1 Cor. 1:14, 2:1; see Acts 18:1–17).
2. Apollos (and Peter?) visits Corinth (Acts 18:24–9:1; 1 Cor. 1:12; 3:4–6, 22; 4:6), but is no longer there (1 Cor. 16:12).
3. Paul writes Letter A (1 Cor. 5:9), now lost, unless a fragment has been edited into 2 Corinthians.
4. The Corinthians send a letter to Paul (1 Cor. 7:1), and Paul hears oral reports from Corinth about matters they had not reported in their letter (1 Cor. 1:11; 16:17).
5. Paul writes Letter B, our 1 Corinthians (ca. 54, from Ephesus, 16:8).
6. Timothy visits Corinth and returns to Paul (1 Cor. 4:17; 16:10; 2 Cor. 1:1; see Acts 19:22).
7. Paul sends Titus back to Corinth instead of coming himself. For some reason(s) Paul changed his original plans to come to Corinth

from Ephesus shortly after Pentecost (1 Cor. 16:5–7) and sent Titus instead, with instructions about the collection (2 Cor. 1:13–17). (This visit of Titus is different from and earlier than the one mentioned in 2 Cor. 7:6ff.).

8. Fresh difficulties arise at Corinth: "false apostles" arrive, who "make slaves" of them (2 Cor. 10:7, 10; 11:12–13, 20–23; 12:16–17).
9. The "painful visit"—not in Acts—during which Paul is grossly insulted and humiliated by someone (local? missionary?) and leaves Corinth in defeat (2 Cor. 2:1, 5–8; 7:12; 12:14; 13:1).
10. Letter C—the "severe letter," "painful letter" (2 Cor. 2:3–9; 7:8–12)— is written. This letter, either lost or (partially) preserved in 2 Cor. 10–13, is sent with Titus or perhaps ahead of him.
11. Titus visits the church at Paul's behest (2 Cor. 7:7).
12. The church repents, reaffirms its loyalty to the *Pauline* Gospel, and punishes the offender (2 Cor. 2:6; 7:9–11). It is not clear whether it was Paul's harsh letter, Titus's pastoral visit, or both, that brought about their repentance.
13. Paul is endangered in Ephesus and leaves (Acts 19 uproar; 2 Cor. 2:8–9). Paul goes to Troas and has a great missionary opportunity, but pushes on to rendezvous with Titus "somewhere in Macedonia" (2 Cor. 2:12–13; 7:6–16).
14. Letter D is sent by Titus and the "two brothers." This is our 2 Corinthians, or part of it.
15. Paul comes to Corinth, has a positive relationship to the church, receives the collection, prepares to take it to Jerusalem, writes Romans from there ca. 55 or 56 (Rom. 15:25ff.; see Acts 20:2f.).

Integrity

The primary historical issue in understanding 2 Corinthians is its "integrity," a technical term used by scholars to refer to the literary unity of the letter. The issue is whether 2 Corinthians as we now have it was written all at once by Paul, or whether it was edited into one document from two or more of the letters Paul wrote to Corinth (see above). This possibility cannot be ruled out in advance, since we know that the Pauline letters were edited in the process of combining them into one corpus, circulating them, and finally placing them in the canon. Here and elsewhere, we receive the New Testament not directly from the apostles, but from the hands of the church (see "Introduction: The New Testament as the Church's Book," 4.c). The question must be decided on the evidence from case to case (see, e.g., comments on 1 Cor. 14:34–35 above). Some of the evidence will be mentioned in the comments below, but the reader must consult a more detailed technical commentary to get a more complete picture. If one reads the letter as a whole at one sitting, the disjointed nature of the document becomes apparent. For example, 6:14–7:1 seems to interrupt the train of thought, resumed at 7:2. Paul's intense discussion of his travel plans is broken off at 2:13 and taken up again at 7:5. The first part of the letter, especially chaps. 1 and 7, is full of joy and reconciliation, looking *back* on the troubles between Paul and the Corinthians that are now over, while chaps. 10–13 are bitter, sarcastic, and appear to be written in the midst of a conflict still in full swing. Some scholars nevertheless find 2 Corinthians to be a unity, explaining the differences as mood swings or a "sleepless night" during the composition of the letter. Most find at least two letters, with the major division between chaps. 1–9 and 10–13. A few scholars find 2 Corinthians to be a combination of as many as six letters. The following comments are written from the perspective that chaps. 1–9 and 10–13 belong to different letters, and that chaps. 1–9 may itself be a combination of more than one letter.

Outline

For Further Reading

Best, Ernest. *Second Corinthians*. Interpretation: A Bible Commentary for Teaching and Preaching. Atlanta: John Knox Press, 1987.
Furnish, Victor Paul. *II Corinthians*. The Anchor Bible. Garden City, NY: Doubleday & Co., 1984.

COMMENTARY

1:1–2
SALUTATION

1:1 Apostle: See on Luke 6:12:13; Gal. 1:1. **Including all the saints throughout Achaia:** This is not a circular letter; it is addressed to only one congregation and its problems. But again (see 1 Cor. 1:1) Paul reminds them that as members of the one church of God they belong to something bigger than their local congregation. The letter is not a private letter. *He* is an apostle authorized by God, and his letter carries divine authority; *they* are part of God's worldwide church, also called by God.

1:2 Grace to you and peace: On this innovative greeting formula, see on 1 Thess. 1:1.

1:3–11
BLESSING

1:3 Blessed be God: In the formal structure of a Greek letter, the salutation was followed by the thanksgiving (see on 1 Thess. 1:2). Here the thanksgiving vocabulary of the letter is replaced by the blessing terminology taken from synagogue worship (as in Eph. 1:3; 1 Pet. 1:3; see Luke 1:68).

1:4 Who comforts (NIV)/**consoles** (NRSV): The word refers to the act of God in giving strength and encouragement to endure trouble, not merely to soothing one's feelings. Paul praises

God for deliverance from the threat to his life he has just experienced (1:8) and for the good news he has received about the Corinthian church from Titus (7:5–7).

1:5 The sufferings of Christ flow over into our lives (NIV): Paul does not focus on his individual troubles, but includes them in the sufferings of the church at large, in which the Corinthians also participate. Paul understands that the suffering of the Christian life as such is included in the sufferings of Christ. The Christian life participates in the suffering and resurrection of Christ; it is christomorphic, i.e., the disciple's life has the same shape as the Christ event itself. Paul interprets individual Christian sufferings, i.e., sufferings endured for the sake of the Christian message, in the larger context of the suffering of the whole church and the Christ event itself. In the death and resurrection of Christ, the nature of God and the ultimate meaning of all things are disclosed, and individual sufferings are seen in this ultimate context (see Rom. 6:1–11; Gal. 2:19–20).

1:8 The affliction we experienced in Asia: Paul may have been imprisoned in Ephesus, and feared that he might be condemned to death; Philippians may have been written from this Ephesian imprisonment (see "Introduction to the Pauline Letters"). In any case, Paul is not reflecting on human sufferings in general (sickness, bereavement, accident, loss of job, divorce, and family troubles), but suffering that comes to one because of commitment to Christ and the Christian mission (see 11:23–29).

1:9 Rely on . . . God who raises the dead: When he thought that his life and ministry were going to end in Ephesus, where he would die as a misunderstood condemned prisoner, Paul realized the personal meaning of God's act in raising Jesus (who had been killed in Jerusalem as a misunderstood condemned prisoner). For Paul the resurrection was not only something that happened to Jesus and something that will happen to Christians in the future, but something that determines the whole of Christian life. It means that in every hopeless situation God still gives hope (see on Luke 24:21).

1:11 Many will give thanks on our behalf: Paul's troubles on the mission field are not just his personal concerns, but involve the church that prays for him. The "thanksgiving" form is here reversed (see 1:3 above); instead of beginning with his thanks for them, he speaks of their thanks for him. None of this is egocen-

tric; all is theocentric. Paul is focused on God's act in Christ that is now expressed in God's act in delivering Paul—for which all give thanks to God, both he and the Corinthians.

1:12–9:15
PART ONE—PAUL ASSURES THE CORINTHIANS OF HIS CONCERN FOR THEM

1:12–2:4
INTEGRITY OF PAUL'S CONDUCT AND HIS CHANGE OF TRAVEL PLANS

The body of the letter begins with Paul's defense of himself, occasioned by their misunderstanding. The Corinthians (or some of them) were suspicious because Paul had promised to visit them and had abruptly changed his plans (see 1 Cor. 16:5–9; 2 Cor. 1:15, 23). Just as his proposed visit was not merely personal but part of the apostolic supervision and strengthening of the churches, their suspicion was not mere personal pique, but reflected their growing doubt that he was a trustworthy apostle. In addition, Paul's missionary strategy of being "all things to all people" (see on 1 Cor. 9:19–23) had been perversely misunderstood by some as evidence that Paul vacillated under pressure, saying only what was convenient and self-serving (see 1:17). Paul protests that this is a misunderstanding and attempts to set the record straight.

1:12 This is our boast: The terminology of "boasting" seems strange to the modern reader. Paul's meaning, however, is not "bragging," but refers to the eschatological confidence of standing before God and giving account of one's ministry. The word expresses Paul's and the Corinthians' interrelatedness—they are all linked together in God's saving purpose. He wants to stand with them among the redeemed on the coming day of the Lord, rejoicing in their acceptance by God as they rejoice in his. He wants to be proud of them and wants them to be proud of him. This is what "boasting" means to him (see 1 Thess. 2:19). If chaps. 10–13 are part of the earlier "tearful letter" (see the introduction to 2 Corinthians), Paul had already used "boasting" with bitter sarcasm, and is now taking up the word in a different sense and removing its sting. Paul lives his whole life, including making his travel plans, as one who lives in God's presence and will finally give account to God—not just to them (see 1 Cor. 4:1–5). He wants them to understand his conduct and change of plans in this light (this is why he presents the elaborate theological excursus in 1:18–23).

1:16 To Judea: Since writing 1 Cor. 16:1–4, Paul has decided that he will go to Jerusalem himself to take the offering (see chaps. 8–9).

1:18 Our word to you has not been "Yes and No": See above. Some of the Corinthians were suspicious that Paul said what his various publics wanted to hear, saying yes and no on the same disputed issues, and that he sometimes said yes when he had no intention of fulfilling his promise, i.e., that his yes was really a no. It is characteristic of Paul that he takes seemingly small incidents and places them in the grand context of God's gracious act in Christ (see, e.g., 8:9; 1 Cor. 8:1–11:1). The point is that Paul's own yes is not duplicitous, but is embraced in the ultimate yes spoken by God.

1:20 In him every one of God's promises is a "Yes": In the Bible God had made many promises of coming salvation, expressed in a variety of ways. Some of these seemed never to have been fulfilled. Does this mean God is unfaithful? No, Paul replies—all God's promises, however expressed, are fulfilled in Jesus Christ, God's grand Yes to all humanity. This is what we mean when we sing at Advent and Christmas, "The hopes and fears of all the years are met in thee tonight."

We say the "Amen": "Amen" is a Hebrew word adopted by early Christianity from synagogue worship, where it is the liturgical response to prayer (see on 1 Cor. 14:16). The word is related to "yes" as the affirmative response, and alludes as well to the ideas of God's faithfulness (v. 18) and God's confirming his promises (v. 21), to which it is linguistically related. "Amen" comes from the same Hebrew root that means "be faithful."

1:21 God . . . has anointed us: "Christ" means "anointed" (see on Mark 8:29). Paul here understands "Christians" to be anointed by God just as Christ was (see 1 John 2:20, 27). The further references to the **seal** and the **Spirit** suggest the language of baptism. Although in the later church, beginning in the second century, the baptism ritual involved anointing with oil and sealing with the sign of the cross, Paul is not explicitly referring to elements of the baptism ceremony. He uses the language metaphorically, recalling to the Corinthians their transition into the community of faith in which they were baptized into the body of Christ and received the Holy Spirit (1 Cor. 12:13).

1:23 To spare you: Paul here returns to explaining his actions, his change of plans in not coming to Corinth as promised. Since a visit then would have been detrimental, it was for their sakes that he had not come (see 1 Cor. 4:21; 2 Cor. 13:2). His conduct has not been self-serving, but was arranged—and changed when necessary—in order to benefit the church and its mission.

2:1 Another painful visit: See chronology in the introduction to 2 Corinthians. Paul's brief unexpected visit to them had resulted in conflict with some of the Corinthians and their new leaders (see on 2 Cor. 10–13; esp. 11:13). Paul himself was terribly humiliated by someone during this visit and left in defeat and consternation.

2:3 I wrote as I did: Letter C, the "severe letter," "painful letter"; see 2 Cor. 2:3–9; 7:8–12. See chronology in the introduction to 2 Corinthians. This letter is either lost or (partially) preserved in chaps. 10–13.

2:4 The abundant love I have for you: Paul is at pains to explain and put the best construction on the harsh letter he had sent, a letter he once wished he had never written (7:8). In retrospect, he sees that it had a good effect, that it was written not out of personal pique or in his own interest, but in the interest of the Corinthians—an expression of his love for them.

2:5–11
FORGIVENESS OF THE OFFENDER

2:5–7 Forgive and console him: Though both the Corinthians and Paul were vividly aware of the incident, exactly what had happened is unclear to us. This is another example of the letter character of New Testament documents: written to specific situations, not written for later generations, documents that can be brief and allusive and need not report information already known to the readers. Understanding such documents poses a challenge to later readers. It is clear that during Paul's hasty, unscheduled second visit to Corinth (see Chronology in the introduction to 2 Corinthians) Paul had been grossly offended by one of their members or leaders, and the church had not defended Paul. The person responsible is clearly not the man of 1 Cor. 5:1–11, but someone who attacked the legitimacy of Paul's apostleship. Paul left Corinth in defeat and humiliation. In the meantime, as a result of Paul's letter and Titus's visit, the church repented, returned to the support of Paul's mission, and punished the offender. Paul is not vindictive and urges forgiveness and restoration of the offender. As always, he insists that church discipline be redemptive and constructive, not merely punitive (see 7:9–11).

Not to me . . . to all: Paul was terribly hurt by the incident, but does not nurse his personal wounds. The damage to the church is what concerns him. He will not reduce the incident to the level of a mere personality conflict. The solution is not conflict management or damage control, but a theological understanding of how this involved and damaged the whole church and its mission.

This punishment by the majority: "Majority" does not necessarily imply a split decision, but that the disciplinary action was by the church as a whole. We do not know what this was. It could have been a variety of actions taken by the church, ranging from excommunication to congregational rebuke. On disciplinary measures in the early church, see 1 Cor. 5:1–12; 2 Cor. 10:1–6; 13:1–10; 2 Thess. 3:14–15; Matt. 18:15–20.

2:9 To test you: See 2:4. Another retrospective effort to explain his previous severe letter. **Obedient in everything:** Not personal domination, but acceptance of apostolic authority, is Paul's goal.

2:11 Outwitted by Satan: Paul regards the church to be in a struggle with hostile demonic powers that resist its mission. Discord within the congregation is more than a problem of interpersonal relationships. Internal conflicts hinder the mission of the church and are thus a strategy of Satan.

2:12–13
PAUL'S ANXIETY IN TROAS

2:12–13 Troas . . . Macedonia: See map. Troas (Acts 16:8, 11; 20:5, 6; 2 Tim. 4:13) was a major Roman port on the west coast of Asia Minor (modern Turkey), ten miles south of ancient Troy of the Homeric legends. Paul had arranged to meet Titus there and receive his report on the status of the Corinthian church. Titus was delayed. Even though Paul had a good opportunity for mission work in Troas, he did not wait for Titus, supposing he had missed the last boat of the fall sailing season and was making his way overland through Macedonia. Paul brings this up not merely to report his travels, but to document his concern for the Corinthians. The modern reader may wonder how Paul could be sure that he and Titus would meet, and the answer must be that he knew Titus would check in with the churches along the way in Macedonia, as would Paul himself. This networking of early Christian congregations and missionaries was very important in the expansion of early Christianity.

Since this discussion is abruptly broken off and not continued until 7:5, some scholars see 2:14–7:4 as part of an earlier letter to the Corinthians, inserted here in the later process of editing the letter (see the introduction to 2 Corinthians).

2:14–17
GOD'S TRIUMPHAL PROCESSION

2:14 God . . . leads us in triumphal procession: The metaphor compares the Christian mission to a Roman victory parade in which prisoners of war were forced to march. However, Paul and the missionaries are cast in the role not of conquering soldiers, but of the prisoners (see 1 Cor. 4:9; 2 Cor. 4:7–12; 6:4–10). Paul was often a prisoner (Rom. 16:7; Phlm. 9, 23; 2 Cor. 11:23) and may have just been released from an imprisonment in Ephesus (see 1:8 and "Introduction to the Pauline Letters").

2:15–16 Those who are being saved . . . those who are perishing: See 1 Cor. 1:18. The response to the proclamation of the gospel divides humanity into two groups. In each case the use of the present tense indicates a process, not a completed result. The image portrays everyone as on the way to salvation or being eschatologically lost, but those in either group may decide to switch to the other.

Aroma . . . fragrance: This metaphor had been used in Jewish religious texts of the presence and knowledge of God mediated by the Law and by divine Wisdom (e.g., Sir. 24:15), which to some had the fresh pleasant aroma of life, and to others the stench of death. Paul applies this metaphor to the Christian message.

Who is sufficient?: The word might be translated "adequate" or "competent" and recurs in 3:5, thus bracketing this literary unit that introduces a new major topic. The issue at Corinth was the legitimacy of Paul's apostleship, which is here introduced and developed in this section, which extends to 6:10. It is not an abstract question, for Paul's standing as an authentic apostle had been challenged by the new missionaries who had recently come to Corinth (see Chronology in the introduction to 2 Corinthians, item 8).

2:17 Like so many: This indirect reference is the first reference in the present form of the letter to the rival missionaries at Corinth. If chaps. 10–13 are part of the earlier "painful letter," Paul is here looking back to the conflict with the false apostles, a conflict that has now been resolved. Professional traveling teachers and preachers were common figures in the first-century Mediterranean world (see 1 Thess. 2:3), and they expected to be paid. They often tailored their teaching to the desires of their clients. Paul places his opponents in this group of hucksters who profit from the Christian message, in contrast to his own stance as commissioned by God and presenting his message without the profit motive (see also 1 Cor. 9:1–12).

3:1–18
MINISTERS OF A NEW COVENANT

3:1 Beginning to commend ourselves again?: In the present order of the Corinthian correspondence, Paul has not "commended himself." If chaps. 10–13 were written earlier, this would refer to the practice of the new missionaries at Corinth who commended themselves, and to which Paul had already responded with his own "foolish" self-commendation (see 10:12; 10:18–12:11).

Letters of recommendation: Early Christians, including Paul, often wrote letters commending Christians from one congregation to another (see Rom. 16:1–2; 1 Cor. 16:15–18; Phil. 4:2–3; 1 Thess. 5:12–13). Paul's opponents had arrived with letters from other Christian congregations that claimed to validate their own apostolic ministry.

3:3 You are a letter of Christ: The existence of the Corinthian congregation itself is all the "letter" Paul needs to validate his apostleship to them (see 1 Cor. 9:1–2). He did not go to churches founded by others, where he might present his "credentials." He founded churches where none existed before. They themselves are his letter, written on human hearts, not written by Paul or any human authority, but from Christ. God's message to the world is the Christian community, the church, not merely the apostle or the ministry, not even apostolic letters. Paul did not "found" the church (1 Cor. 3:5–7) and did not "write" the "letter" that the Corinthians are. **Tablets of stone:** Paul is already thinking of the contrast between the old covenant represented by the Ten Commandments, written on stone tablets, and the new covenant inaugurated by God's act in Christ (Exod. 31:18; Deut. 9:10; see Jer. 31:33; Ezek. 11:19; 36:26).

3:5–6 Our competence is from God: Paul returns to the question of competence introduced in 2:16. In contrast to his opponents, he claims no competence of his own.

Ministers of a new covenant: See Jer. 31:31–34; Luke 22:20; 1 Cor. 11:25; Heb. 8:8, 13;

9:15. God's covenant with Israel has not been abrogated or replaced, nor merely revised like an outdated constitution, but eschatologically renewed. "New" refers to God's eschatological new creation that is already begun and anticipated in the Christ event, but is not yet fulfilled. This same usage of "new" is found in the Old Testament's promise of "new heavens and new earth" (Isa. 65:17; 66:22; see 2 Cor. 5:17; Gal. 6:15; 2 Pet. 3:13; Rev. 21:1, 5); the image of the "new Jerusalem" (Rev. 3:12; 21:2); Jesus' image of the "new wine" for his message and ministry (Matt. 9:17); Paul's image of the "new person" that the Christian becomes at conversion (Col. 3:10; Eph. 4:24); and the "new humanity" that God is creating by the Christ event (Eph. 2:15). In all these cases, "new" does not mean "new and improved" in the sense of commercial products, i.e., relatively better, but "eschatologically renewed"; the old is taken up, affirmed, and transformed as the climactic act in the coming of God's kingdom.

Paul's understanding of the covenant may be outlined in these five steps:

1. God made a covenant with Israel to be a special elect people among all the peoples of the world (who are also God's people by creation). Israel's election and covenant were not to privilege but to mission.

2. Israel did not live up to the responsibilities of the covenant, and in this sense broke the covenant, but God did not revoke it. Israel's unfaithfulness did not nullify God's faithfulness (Rom. 3:2).

3. The old covenant was associated with external, written laws that spelled out Israel's responsibility.

4. The Law itself was holy and good, but was commandeered by the evil power of sin, which perverted it from its original good purpose and function (Rom. 3:31; 7:7–25).

5. By the Christ event God overthrows the power of sin and renews the covenant in such a way that God's law is no longer an external constraint that rules and condemns, but an internal power that accomplishes God's will in the believer by the power of the Spirit. It is not just an internal attitude (as in the phrase "the spirit of the law, not the letter of the law"), but the eschatological gift of the Holy Spirit at work in the life of the church. The new covenant is distinguished by a series of contrasts based on Jer. 31:31–33 and Ezek. 16:59–62; 34:25–26. These are letter vs. Spirit; death vs. life; glory vs. more glorious; condemnation vs. justification; temporary vs. permanent.

3:8 How much more: Despite the language, this is not a *comparison* of the relative merits of the old and new covenants, but a *contrast* between that which is historically relative and that which is eschatological and eternal (as in 1 Cor. 13:8–11). It is like comparing the old Adam and the new Adam (Rom. 5:12–21) or the historical kingdom of Israel led by David and the eschatological kingdom for which Christians pray (Matt. 6:9), but which is also already in some sense present. Speaking of the new covenant or new testament thus does not mean that Christians claim to have a relatively better covenant than the Jews within history, but is a contrast between historical reality—in which of course Christians also continue to participate—and the eschatological renewal of all things inaugurated by the Christ event.

3:12 Since . . . we have such a hope: The new covenant, the new relationship with God in which Christians already participate, is not yet completely fulfilled, just as the kingdom is not yet completely here (1 Cor. 4:5), and Christians themselves are not yet completely transformed into the new persons God wills them to be (3:18). Here, too, Christians live in the tension between the "already" and the "not yet."

3:13 Moses . . . put a veil: See Exod. 31:1–35. In the Old Testament story the veil was to protect Israel from the radiance associated with the presence of God (see modern fear of radiation). As in 1 Cor. 10:1–5, Paul may be depending on a later traditional expansion and interpretation of the story than the one found in the Bible, or he may himself present a Christian allegorical interpretation with two different aspects, neither of which is in Exod. 34:

1. Paul understands the veil as a device to keep Israel from noticing that the glory of the old covenant was temporary. Paul concedes that the old covenant manifested the glory of God, but like the temple, the sacrificial system, and the Law itself, was not intended by God to continue into the eschatological age.

2. Paul interprets the veil as the barrier that keeps Israel from seeing the true meaning of their Scriptures, which from his perspective point to the fulfillment of God's plan in Christ (see excursus at 1 Cor. 15:3, "New Testament Interpretation of the Old Testament"). This is a Christian confession of faith, not a description of objective reality (for objectifying and confessional language, see on Matt. 2:16; Acts 1:9; excursus at Rev. 6:15, "Interpreting Revelation's Violent Imagery," 3.b).

3:14 Their minds were hardened: See Deut. 29:4; Isa. 6:9–10; 29:10; Mark 4:10–12; Luke 8:9–10; Rom. 11:7–8. Early Christians struggled with the mystery of why some who heard the Christian message responded in faith while others remained unbelievers. By subordinating the whole process to God's sovereignty, they did not minimize human responsibility. As in the case of Pharoah, who hardened his own heart but whose heart was also hardened by God (see, e.g., Exod. 4:21; 8:15), humans are considered absolutely responsible for their own decisions, but those who decide for God give praise to God for being included, rather than taking credit for their decision themselves. This issue comes to expression in the New Testament's language of predestination and election (see excursus, "Predestination," at Rom. 8:29–30. On the combination of human responsibility and divine sovereignty, see on Luke 22:3, 22; Acts 2:23; Phil. 2:12–13).

Reading of the old covenant: This refers to the reading of the Scripture in the synagogue. The language is from the Christian perspective, that the new covenant had been inaugurated in Christ, because of course the Jews did not consider their covenant to be "old." There was as yet no Christian Bible divided into the "Old Testament" and the "New Testament." This terminology first appears in the late second century in Melito, bishop of Sardis.

Only in Christ is it set aside: The veil, not the old covenant, is set aside. The documents of the Jewish Scriptures, the Christian Old Testament, remain the same as before, but those who have come to faith in Christ read them with new eyes. Christians regard the Christ event as the definitive revelation of God and read the Old Testament from this perspective (see 1:20; excursus at 1 Cor. 15:3). This should not be interpreted to mean that people of Jewish faith do not hear an authentic word from God as they read the same Scriptures from their perspective, for such a reading has sustained their faith through many terrible trials in the course of history.

3:16 When one turns to the Lord, the veil is removed: This is Paul's paraphrase of Exod. 34:34, which referred to Moses. When Moses spoke to the people, he retained the veil, but in God's presence, he removed it. Paul understands this to picture the experience of a Christian, who encounters God in the reading of Scripture.

3:17 The Lord is the Spirit: To ask whether "the Lord" is God or Christ is a misplaced question, since Paul is not dealing in the later subtleties of Trinitarian theology. "Turning to the Lord" was a standard phrase for conversion to the God revealed in Christ (1 Thess. 1:9–10). The "Spirit of the Lord" was a standard Old Testament phrase for God's Spirit (23x Old Testament, e.g., Judg. 3:10; 6:34; 1 Sam. 10:6; Isa. 11:2; 40:13; 61:1, See Luke 4:18; Acts 5:9). Paul's point is not to discuss abstract explanations of the nature of God, but to say that when people are converted to Christ, they enter the realm where God's powerful Spirit, the Spirit of freedom, is at work.

3:18 We . . . all reflect the Lord's glory (NIV) / **All of us . . . seeing the glory of the Lord as though reflected in a mirror** (NRSV): Equally valid ways of translating Paul's Greek. The former pictures Christians themselves as a reflection of God's glory, as was Moses; the latter regards Christians as seeing God's glory, but not directly. Christians see the reflection of God's glory in something or someone else. Since Paul continues to speak of Christ as the "image of God," he may have in mind that Christ is the "mirror" in which Christians see the glory of God. In the latter case, in contrast to 1 Cor. 13:12, the point is not that Christ is only a partial or imperfect reflection, but as in 1 Cor. 13:12 there may still be a "not yet" aspect to the Christian's seeing. As long as Christians are in this world, their reading too is still somewhat veiled, for perfect seeing comes only in the future consummation of God's kingdom.

We are being transformed: The terminology is the same as in the story of Christ's transfiguration (Matt. 17:2; Mark 9:2). Though not yet complete, eschatological transformation into Christ's image has already begun in the Christian who still lives in the old world but already reflects the radiance of the coming age (NIV reading) or who sees the reflection of God's glory in Christ, but not yet perfectly (NRSV reading). See Rom. 12:2; 8:29; 1 Cor. 15:49–51; Phil. 3:21.

4:1–6
THE GLORY OF GOD AND THE GOSPEL

4:1 We are engaged in this ministry: Though he uses much profound theological imagery often foreign to the modern mind, Paul's point is not to explain theological ideas but to place his ministry in the context of God's gracious act in Christ. Theology is important not in itself but as illuminating and undergirding ministry.

4:2 We refuse to practice cunning or to falsify God's word: Paul has been accused of operating in underhanded ways and distorting God's word found both in the Bible and in the Christian message. In chaps. 10–13 he will reverse these charges and accuse his opponents.

4:3 If our gospel is veiled: The good news of God's act in Christ proclaimed by Paul was in fact not accepted by most who heard it. In Paul's understanding, people do not "get it" not only because of their own decision, but because Satan has veiled their minds. Previously Paul had assigned this to God's hardening of people's hearts (see on 3:14). Paul here reflects the apocalyptic understanding (as in Revelation) according to which the one sovereign God temporarily allows lesser powers to carry out their rebellious purposes, though these powers have already been defeated and will ultimately be destroyed or redeemed (see John 12:31; 1 Cor. 2:6, 8; Eph. 1:15–2:3).

4:4 Christ . . . the image of God: When Paul says "God" he does not have in mind an abstract force or principle, or even a supreme being, but the One who has personified himself and is met personally in Christ. It is God who was and is at work in Christ (5:19); Christ is the human face of God (4:6).

4:5 Not . . . ourselves . . . Jesus Christ as Lord: "Jesus is Lord" was an early Christian creedal affirmation (Rom. 10:9; 1 Cor. 12:3; Phil. 2:10–11).

4:6 Let light shine: See Gen. 1:3; Isa. 9:2. The one Creator God, who originally called light into being, has also acted to create light in the believers' hearts. God the Creator continues to create. Just as resurrection is not an abstract idea of what happened in the past, but a reality in the believer's life (see on 1:9), so creation is not only an event in the past, but an experienced reality in the believer's present (see also 5:17; Rom. 4:17). In biblical theology, the heart is the center of planning, willing, and acting, nor merely of feelings.

4:7–5:10
TREASURE IN CLAY JARS

This is all one section that must be understood as a unit. It is especially important to see that 5:1–10 is part of the whole argument in this section. The theme is the apostolic ministry. It is not an abstract discussion of the nature of ministry, but responds to the concrete criticisms Paul has received from the Corinthians and their new would-be leaders: that Paul's ministry looks undignified and is not appropriate to the glory of the gospel. Paul has been in prison; he does not accept pay for his ministry among them, but works at manual labor to support himself while he preaches; he does not do the "signs of an apostle," sensational miracles that show he belongs to the new age of the power of the gospel. Paul's response is not personal defensiveness, but showing that authentic apostolic ministry is oriented to God's act in the cross of Jesus. This section is a reaffirmation of his message in 1 Cor. 1:18–2:5 (see there) in the light of the new charges against him made by the new missionaries that have recently come to Corinth (see Chronology in the introduction to 2 Corinthians).

4:7 Treasure . . . clay jars: Paul uses some of the dualistic language and imagery of the Hellenistic understanding of human being, but not in the typical Hellenistic sense of an immortal soul trapped in a mortal body (see on Luke 20:27; Matt. 28:1; 1 Cor. 15:42–44). The glory of which Paul has been speaking belongs to God, who is made real in the gospel. This good news is the treasure (4:3–4), the "unsearchable riches" (Eph. 3:8), but the ministers themselves are earthly vessels by which the gospel is shared with others. The glory belongs to God, not the ministers (4:16).

4:9 Struck down, but not destroyed: Paul contrasts the indignity and weakness of his own ministry (when measured by the standards of human culture) with the high-and-mighty ways of his opponents in Corinth, who claim to be superior apostles. His powerful and carefully composed rhetorical contrasts are impossible to preserve in English translation. Some of the imagery is taken from the athletic arena and could be expressed in the English phrase "down but not out." His apostolic ministry was not attained by his own efforts, but is the result of God's initiative and grace (4:1). It bears the authentic marks of the cross, and is sustained by the power of God who raises the dead (see 1:9). Thus the troubles he recounts and his endurance through them is not a matter of Stoic inner tranquility and aloofness, a retreating within oneself, where the world cannot touch one's true inner being, nor is it merely a psychological matter of "how you look at it." The troubles are real, and Paul does not flee from them to an inner sanctuary, but is deeply troubled and distressed by the problems of the churches. It is God who sustains him, not some inner resources or internal "spirituality."

4:10 Always carrying in the body the death of Jesus: Paul's opponents claimed to live already the life of the resurrection. He identifies his ministry with Jesus' cross (Gal. 2:20). **So that the life of Jesus may also be made visible:** It may be that Paul's opponents had made the "life of Jesus" a slogan of their own leadership, emphasizing Jesus' miraculous deeds that they reproduced in their own ministries. Paul claims the life of Jesus is also evidenced in his ministry, but Paul identifies with Jesus' cross, not with his miracles (which he never mentions in any of his letters—see on 11:4; 13:4).

4:11 Always being given up to death: Paul is not referring to literal martyrdom, though he occasionally faced this threat (1:9), but to the daily giving away of one's life in the service of others. The life of Christian ministry he points to is not the dramatic beheading or being burned at the stake, but the undramatic acts of ministry, when one gives oneself an hour at a time or five minutes at a time. For Paul the normal Christian life may mean being thrown to the lions or being nibbled to death by goldfish, but in either case it is a continual life of unselfish acts that receive no public applause. **For Jesus' sake:** Better translated "on account of Jesus." The troubles he recites are not the ordinary human troubles to which all are subject—sickness, bereavement, career disappointments—but the abuses suffered in the service of Christ.

4:12 Death is at work in us, but life in you: This is Pauline irony (see 1 Cor. 4:8–10). Probably "death" and "life" should be enclosed in quotation marks, as referring to the death and life of Jesus as sloganized by Paul's opponents. *They* claim to manifest the powerful *life* of Jesus; *Paul* is identified with his *death*. *They* already celebrate the *resurrection* power at work among them and the presence of the kingdom; *Paul's* ministry manifests Jesus' self-giving on the *cross* validated by God's raising him from the dead—but not yet us (see the reference to the resurrection as future in 4:14, Paul's characteristic "eschatological reservation").

4:13 I believed, and so I spoke: Here Paul quotes verbatim the Greek translation of Ps. 116:10. The original Hebrew translated in our English Bibles is quite different. He claims to speak manifesting the same faith found in his Bible, for it is the same **spirit of faith** that inspired both the psalmist and Paul's own preaching.

4:14 Will raise us: Paul believes that the Christian life is stamped with the reality of Jesus' death and resurrection. Romans 6:1–11, written a few months later after the dispute with

Corinth was over, presents this more reflectively and less argumentatively. The Christian life in the present is identified with the cross (Mark 8:34; Gal. 2:19–20; 1 Cor. 15:31), lived in faith in God's act of raising Jesus in the past and in the confident hope of God's act for believers in the future (Phil. 3:21–4:1).

4:16 We do not lose heart: Paul's confidence is expressed in a series of contrasts that extend through 5:10. The two columns in Figure 12 could be labeled "death—life" or "cross—resurrection."

The unit concludes in **5:9–10**, which brings present and future reality together before the judgment seat of Christ, where the life one has lived in this world is judged by Christ in the transcendent world. The two columns thus do not represent a timeless contrast between "here below" and "up there" or a psychological contrast between the world "out there" and one's "inner spiritual life," but a contrast between the historical present and the ultimate future. Paul characterizes Christian life as "between the times." Though Paul thinks in terms of kingship rather than democratic government, a modern analogy would be the period after the election but before the inauguration. The old administration, though still in power (4:4!), is a lame duck. By faith the Christian already experiences the reality of the not-yet kingdom that is sure to come. While living and fully participating in the present reality, believers must decide whether to orient their lives toward the present that is on the way out (the left column) or the future that already impinging on the present (the right column).

5:1 For we know: The "for" is important, for it signals that this paragraph is not a separate discussion of "what happens when we die" or the like, but is an integral part of the discussion of authentic ministry in 4:7–5:10 (see above at 4:7; Paul has already given his basic teaching on the resurrection in 1 Cor. 15). A key dimension of true ministry is that it is not oriented to what can be seen, i.e., to empirical "results" or the "image" one has when measured by worldly standards ("from a human point of view," 5:16), but is measured in terms of God's eternal world. This does not mean it is otherworldly, but that what is done in this world is measured from God's perspective, not the standards of worldly success.

5:2–4 Tent . . . clothed: Paul now thinks most believers will die before the Parousia (contrast 1 Thess. 4:13–17). He uses and mixes two metaphors for life after death: (1) moving from a tent into a building, and (2) taking off old clothes and putting on new ones. In neither case is there an adoption of the Hellenistic idea of an immortal soul in a perishable body (see on 4:7). Present life is tent existence, eternal life is in a building. The difference is between the transient existence of our present life and settling down in a permanent home. The clothing metaphor reflects the imagery that already at baptism the believer takes off the clothing of the old life and begins a new life in new clothing (Gal. 3:27). Thus the future "being clothed" is the fulfillment of what has already begun in the believer's life at baptism. In all this, two different ways of picturing God's gift of eternal life are given. In the one picture, eternal life comes at the Parousia, the future resurrection (e.g., 1 Cor. 15; Phil. 3:7–21; 1 Thess. 4:13–17). In the other picture, the believer goes directly to the heavenly world to be with Christ (Phil. 1:21–23; 2 Cor. 5:1–9;

Figure 12. Paul's Confidence

Outer	Inner (4:16; see on 4:7)
Wasting away	Renewed (see 3:18)
Slight	Beyond all measure (4:17; cf. Rom. 8:18)
What can be seen	What cannot be seen (4:18)
Temporary	Eternal (4:15)
Tent	Building (5:11)
Destroyed	Eternal
Groaning, longing	Heavenly dwelling (5:2; cf. Rom. 8:23)
Naked	Clothed (5:2–3)
Mortality	Life (5:4)
Spirit as down payment	Full inheritance
At home in the body	At home with the Lord (5:6)
Faith, confidence	Sight (5:7; cf. 1 Cor. 13:12)

1 Thess. 3:13). These pictures are metaphors; they do not tell us how it "really is" but point to the meaning of an inexpressible reality (see on Luke 20:27–40; 1 Cor. 15:35–36). This is the value of having more than one picture; no one picture is adequate. They are not to be harmonized by attempting to picture what happens to the "soul" in an "intermediate state" between death and the final resurrection. All such speculation is beyond us, and Paul never attempts it. Neither are the two pictures to be reconciled in terms of Paul's "development," as though he began with the idea of a future resurrection, but then shifted to the idea of going directly to heaven at death as his theology "matured" or as he became convinced that he would not live long enough to experience the Parousia personally. Paul uses both metaphors side by side, as in Phil. 1:21–23/3:7–21; 1 Thess. 3:13/4:13–17; and 1 Cor. 15/2 Cor. 5). All such language is true and referential in that it points to something real, but it is nonobjectifying language (see on Matt. 2:16; Acts 1:9; excursus at Rev. 6:15, "Interpreting Revelation's Violent Imagery," 3.b).

5:8 Away from the body . . . at home with the Lord: As throughout, the point is not where the believer lives, but the orientation of one's life, where one's ultimate loyalty lies. Without disparaging this world, which is God's creation, the Christian has shifted orientation to the world of God's eternal realities and evaluates ministry from that perspective. As in Phil. 3:20, the "home address," the "true citizenship" of believers is in the coming kingdom of God, whether they are in this world or the next, whether they are alive or dead (Rom. 14:7–12).

5:10 Judgment seat of Christ: See on Matt. 25:31–46; Rom. 14:10; 1 Cor. 3:10–15; Rev. 20:11–15. Sometimes God is pictured as judge at the Last Judgment, and sometimes Christ acts as God's agent in this role, but there is only one Last Judgment. The Last Judgment itself is one of several pictures in which God's final victory is portrayed (see on comments on Rev. 19:11–22:5). Again, two pictures point to the ultimate reality. Elsewhere, Paul emphasizes that when believers stand before God at the Last Judgment, they are saved entirely by God's grace, not by any deeds of their own (e.g., Rom. 3:21–25; 5:1–21). In the picture presented here, at the Last Judgment all Christians (Paul is thinking especially of ministers, missionaries, those claiming to be apostles) are called to account for their deeds. Again,

these pictures are not to be harmonized. The one picture points to the absolute sovereignty and grace of God—we are saved because of who God is and what God has done—but this cannot be expressed in some way that minimizes or excuses human responsibility. Romans 6 must always be read with Rom. 5. Paul's point here is not to explain a doctrine of salvation or what will happen at the Last Judgment, but to insist that ministry in Christ's name—both his and his Corinthian opponents'—is not to be measured by human standards of success. What finally counts is how it is evaluated by Christ.

5:11–6:10
THE MINISTRY OF RECONCILIATION

5:11 Fear of the Lord: Reverent awareness of the holiness of God and that ministers are accountable to God, not to what human beings think of them. **We . . . persuade people:** The same theme is dealt with in Gal. 1:10, where the verb is translated "please." Paul has been accused by his Corinthian opponents of "persuading" or "pleasing" people, i.e., adapting his message to what people find persuasive, catering to the wants of the religious marketplace (see on 1 Cor. 9:20–23). Paul does persuade people, but does it in the fear of the Lord.

5:12 Boast about us: See on 1:12–14.

5:13 Beside ourselves: The same word was used of Jesus in Mark 3:21. It may refer to Paul's unconventional behavior in general, which was considered outrageous by some who measured ministry by worldly standards. More likely, the allusion is to Paul's (purported lack of) charismatic gifts of the Spirit, of which his opponents boasted (see 1 Cor. 12–14; 2 Cor. 10–12). The charge could be made because Paul did not parade his "ecstatic" spiritual experiences, but considered them a matter of private devotion, between himself and God (1 Cor. 14:1–5, 18–19, 28; 2 Cor. 12:1–10). But when Paul speaks in his **right mind,** with sober, reasoned speech, it is for the upbuilding of the Corinthians.

5:14 The love of Christ: Theoretically the Greek expression, like the English, could mean either Christ's love for us or our love for Christ. The context and Paul's usage elsewhere makes it clear that the former is meant. **Urges us on** (NRSV)/**Compels us** (NIV):** Better translated "lays claim to." The love of Christ had claimed Paul, so that he was "bought with a price" (1 Cor. 6:20; 7:23). His point is that he was not free to conduct his ministry however he pleased; the compelling love of Christ has laid hold of him. **One died for all:** See Rom. 5:6–8; 1 Cor. 15:3; Gal. 2:20; 1 Thess. 5:10. This was a basic affirmation of one of the earliest Christian creeds (see on 1 Cor. 15:3–5). This is a given, a fundamental aspect of human existence. Something has been done for us—for us all, all humanity—prior to our decision about it. We cannot choose whether or not to be born, and we cannot choose to be born into some other world than the one for which Christ died. **Therefore all have died:** We might have expected "Therefore all do not have to die," as though Paul's meaning were that since Christ died in our place, we don't have to die. But Paul is thinking globally, not individually. Christ's death brought the end of one world and the beginning of another, the death of one world and the advent of the new world where life prevails. In Paul's view the death and resurrection of the Messiah brought the death of the old world and the birth of the new. As part of the old world, we all died with it.

5:15 That those who live might no longer live for themselves: We have no choice but to belong to the old world that has died, and we have no choice but to live in the world made new by Christ's resurrection. But we can choose whether or not to orient our lives to the new world that has dawned in Christ, or to continue to live as though the old world were the only one. Here Paul shows he is not talking theological abstractions: to orient one's life to the new world is to live unselfishly. The self was the center of the old world. Concrete deeds of care for other people manifest the reality of the new world (see Matt. 25:31–46).

5:16 From a human point of view: Literally "according to the flesh," a distinctive Pauline phrase that means "by worldly standards." Judged by these standards, the ministry of Jesus was a failure. **We once knew Christ:** This does not mean that Paul had been personally acquainted with Jesus, but that he once evaluated the message about Jesus preached by the church by the normal standards of the world. **We know him no longer in that way:** Often our prejudices against other people, especially people of other ethnic, racial, or social groups, can be changed simply by getting to know them better. This, however, is not what Paul is talking about. His view of Christ was changed by the encounter with the risen Christ (Acts 9, 22, 26; Gal. 1). It was not changed by "getting to know him better" by

historical study or by interviewing those who had known him personally. The Gospels make clear that even those who had had a direct and close personal knowledge of Jesus were often not changed by this kind of knowledge (see Mark 3:20–22; John 7:1–7).

5:17 If anyone is in Christ: The phrase "in Christ" or some variation thereof ("in the Lord," "in Jesus," "in the beloved," "in him," "in whom") is found in the New Testament 171 times, only in Paul and in the literature influenced by him. Paul himself apparently originated this peculiar phrase. Jews do not speak of being "in Moses" or "in Abraham," adherents of Islam do not speak of being "in Mohammed," Buddhists do not refer to themselves as "in Buddha." While it is not correct to speak of Paul's "Christ mysticism," Paul thinks of Christ as more than a mortal who once lived on earth and is now in heaven. Christ is a corporate, cosmic reality, a sphere of existence, a force field that determines one's life. When one is baptized, one is united with Christ (Rom. 6:5), puts on Christ (Gal. 3:27), is joined to the body of Christ as an integral member of Christ himself (1 Cor. 12:12–27).

There is a new creation: See Gal. 6:15. There is no subject or verb in the Greek, so they must be supplied. Thus NIV translates "he is a new creation," similar to the King James's "he is a new creature." From the context and from Paul's theology as a whole, the NRSV is to be preferred. So also the New English Bible ("When anyone is united to Christ, there is a new world. The old order has gone, and a new order has already begun") and the Jerusalem Bible ("For anyone who is in Christ, there is a new creation; the old creation has gone, and the new one is here"). The meaning is not that the individual becomes a new person while the world remains unchanged. Nor is the meaning psychological, as though the world remains the same but for those who have come to faith, "everything looks different." Paul means the statement objectively. In the Christ event something happened to the world, not just to individual souls. The background is the biblical hope (Isa. 11:1–9; 65:17; 66:22), developed in Jewish and Christian apocalyptic (e.g., *1 En.* 72:1; *2 Bar.* 32:6; *Jub.* 4:26; 2 Pet. 3:13; Rev. 21:1, 5), that at the eschaton God would not merely save souls out of the world, but would renew the world itself. The "new creation" became one of the ways Christians thought and spoke of the final saving act of God. There is an already/not yet dimension to all these realities. Christians do not merely look forward to the coming of Christ—the Christ has come. And God has already begun to renew the world by the Christ event. The new world is there because the Christ has come; the new world is still to come because Christ is still to come. This is not mere subjectivity but the act and promise of God.

5:19 In Christ God was reconciling the world to himself: The older translation, "God was in Christ," was incorrect in that it represented Paul as here speaking about the incarnation. Paul is not here making some metaphysical statement about God being "in" Christ. The phrase here means "through Christ." Here, "in Christ" in reference to God's act is different from "in Christ" as the sphere of the believer's life (5:17). God is the actor, Christ is the agent.

Reconciliation is here the metaphor for God's saving act. It is not God who is reconciled, but the world. Paul pictures estranged, alienated parties brought together again in a restoration of personal relationships. The reconciliation was accomplished by God in the Christ event. Paul's point is that what was accomplished in the life, death, and resurrection of *Christ* was the act of *God*. God is the actor. The saving act was a two-party action involving God and the world, not a three-party transaction in which Christ reconciled an angry God with a sinful world.

5:20 We are ambassadors for Christ: Though in context the "we" refers primarily to the missionaries and apostles in Paul's circle, he nonetheless pictures the role of the church in the world as Christ's representatives with the message of reconciliation. This message spoken by the church as God's representative is from God himself (see Matt. 10:40; John 13:20). The indicative that God has reconciled the world generates the imperative "Be reconciled," "Be what you are," "Don't continue to live as if God's reconciling act had not happened." The reconciling act between God and humanity is to be expressed in the reconciliation of alienated groups and individuals. On the basis of the cross that broke down the barrier between God and humanity, all the barriers between humans are to be broken down (see Eph. 2:11–22, where the Jew/Gentile separation is the model).

5:21 Made him to be sin: This sentence may reflect a creedal formula like 2 Cor. 8:9 and Phil. 2:5–11. That Jesus was "made to be sin" may refer to the incarnation, by which the Son of God

became a participant in the sinful life of humanity (see Rom. 8:3), or to the crucifixion, a terrible form of execution reserved for the worst offenders and thought to indicate that the person was under God's curse (see Gal. 3:13). The same word is sometimes used in the Old Testament for "sin" and "sin offering" (e.g., Lev. 4:3; 7:37; see Num. 8:7), so the imagery here most likely expresses the meaning of Jesus' death as a sacrifice for sins (see Rom. 3:21–26). Again, this is not a three-party transaction, as though Jesus was sacrificed to appease an angry God (see on 5:19), but a two-party transaction: God identifies himself with the suffering Jesus, God takes the guilt and penalty for sin into himself. Since the Old Testament imagery of sacrifice is alien to most modern readers, it may be difficult for this interpretation of the significance of Jesus' death to be meaningful to us. Nonetheless, it is a powerful image of God himself absorbing the suffering involved in human sin. This is why it is important to have some understanding of the "deity of Christ"—at the cross we meet not a third party, but the one God of love and grace.

Who knew no sin: Jesus died not for his own sins but for the sins of others (see John 8:46; Heb. 4:15; 1 Pet. 2:22).

6:1 As God's fellow workers: Here the NIV translation is better. There is no "with him" in the Greek text, though it may be supplied from the connection with 5:21. The sentence should not be understood in such a way that human beings do their part and God does his part in the work of salvation. The doctrine that God and humans cooperate in the work of salvation, called *synergism*, was later condemned as a heresy. For Paul salvation is entirely a matter of the **grace of God**. "All is from God" (5:18). The meaning is that the church and Christian missionaries work together in a program instituted by God (see 1 Cor. 3:9).

6:2 Now: Salvation was accomplished once for all in God's act in Christ, a reality of past history. Salvation will be consummated by God's victorious act in the eschatological future. But God's act must be appropriated every day. This "now" is every day of the Christian life. It lasts until death. It lasts until the end of time.

6:9–10 Having nothing . . . possessing everything: This paragraph (vv. 3–10) dramatically presents a series of paradoxical contrasts that portray authentic ministry as clashing with worldly understandings of power, authority, and "success," yet sustained by God under the sign of the cross (see 11:23–29). Paul was confident not because he could point to objective "results" or because his own life was untroubled, but because it bore the mark of God's act in the cross of Jesus and was sustained by God's continuing presence.

Unknown . . . yet well known: This may refer to the obscurity of the Christian community, which did not attract much public attention until the second century, two generations after Paul's time. Unnoticed by the public and led by missionaries who are unknown (not "celebrity Christians"), they are yet known by God and within the minority Christian community. The words may also be translated "unacknowledged," "unrecognized," i.e., without proper credentials that legitimate their authority, yet acknowledged and recognized by God.

6:11–13
AN APPEAL TO THE HEART

6:11–13 We have spoken frankly: Literally "our mouths are open," a biblical idiom for candid speech. Paul emphasizes his deep friendship with the Corinthians, which has permitted him to speak frankly. **Open wide your hearts:** Not only his mouth, but his heart is open to them; he longs for the same kind of loving response from them that he has shown to them. Paul's previous protests that acceptability by human standards means nothing in God's eyes do not mean that he does not care what the Corinthians think about him. He loves them deeply and longs for them to return his love.

This paragraph is continued at 7:2.

6:14–7:1
THE TEMPLE OF THE LIVING GOD

Even a casual reading of this section in context reveals that it sits uncomfortably in its present location, that it is disruptive, some sort of insertion or digression. If 6:14–7:1 is skipped, 7:2 follows 6:13 smoothly. This section has several features of vocabulary, style, usage, and theology that are in tension with what Paul writes elsewhere. But in all ancient manuscripts of 2 Corinthians the passage occurs precisely at this point. Scholars recognize some kind of problem here, but have come to differing conclusions: (1) Paul composed the passage himself as he wrote the letter, as a kind of digression; when he recognized this, he returned to his previous train of thought at 7:2. This is still probably the majority

opinion of recent scholarship. (2) Paul himself inserted and slightly edited a paragraph of pre-Pauline tradition, as he had elsewhere (e.g., 1 Cor. 15:3–5; Phil. 2:6–11). (3) The passage is part of Letter A, referred to in 1 Cor. 5:9 and inserted at this point by the editors of the Pauline corpus (see the introduction to 2 Corinthians). (4) The section is a fragment of non-Pauline (or even anti-Pauline) writing, inserted by the editors at this point, either intentionally or in the mistaken belief that Paul had written it. In any case, the passage is part of the Christian Bible. Such considerations do not affect the value and authority of the passage, but do influence how it is understood.

6:14 Mismatched (NRSV)/**Yoked together** (NIV): The issue here is the relation of believers and unbelievers, not the relation of differing Christian groups or individuals—though it has been cited to justify congregational and denominational splits. The passage does fit into the situation of first-generation Christianity, where practical questions of the relation of believers to other people in a society permeated with idolatry were live and important issues. Can a Christian work for a pagan boss or client who engages in idolatrous practices? What is the Christian member of a business partnership to do when the pagan partner proposes that a pagan priest bless the business in the name of a pagan god to ensure success? Can the Christian partner participate in business meetings held in an idol temple (see 1 Cor. 8–10)? Can Christians participate in pagan athletic, patriotic, and social events, i.e., can they participate in the life of their own community, or must they withdraw? Whether from Paul or not, here is one ringing and clear answer to such questions. How it applies in modern situations is a matter of critical discernment. It is clear that Paul himself did not understand marriages between believers and nonbelievers in these terms, and does not call for the dissolution of "mixed marriages" (1 Cor. 7:12–14). On the issue as a whole, 1 Cor. 5:9–10 should be kept in mind.

6:15 Beliar: A variation of "Belial," one of the Jewish names for Satan.

6:16 Temple: Here a genuine Pauline note is struck—Christians are the temple of God, and should keep this temple holy (1 Cor. 3:16; 6:19).

6:16b–18 God said: In his other letters, Paul does not use this introductory formula to cite the Scripture, nor does he ever refer to any of the texts here quoted. The passage is a patchwork of several biblical texts, none of which is cited exactly (see Lev. 26:11–12; 2 Sam. 7:8; Isa. 43:6; 52:4, 11; Ezek. 20:34, 41; 37:27).

7:2–4
THE APPEAL RESUMED

7:2 Corrupted . . . taken advantage: Could also be translated "defraud." This sentence connects to 6:13, whether Paul himself now returns to his argument or the preceding section is an insertion by another hand. Paul would not make this protest unless he had been charged with taking advantage of his Corinthian readers. Apparently his opponents had charged (or insinuated) that even though he would not accept their offer of support, he was taking an offering for "others" that he would somehow turn to his own profit (Rom. 15:25–32; 2 Cor. 8–9; Gal. 2:10; Acts 11:17–30; 24:17; see esp. 2 Cor. 12:14–18).

7:3 To die together and to live together: This was a common proverb for close friendship, but Paul may be using it in the deeper meaning of Christians who are bound together by having been united in the death and resurrection of Jesus (see 1:4–7; 4:10–12).

7:4 I often boast about you: See also 7:16. It is difficult to see such expressions of joy and confidence as part of the same letter as chaps. 10–13. See especially 12:19–21 (see the introduction to 2 Corinthians).

7:5–16
PAUL'S JOY AT THE CHURCH'S REPENTANCE

This section appears to be the resumption and completion of 1:3–2:13, whether as a result of Paul's own digressions or the consequence of later editing (see the introduction to 2 Corinthians). Paul had left Ephesus without having met Titus and without knowing how things stood between him and the Corinthian congregation. He met Titus in Macedonia, where he received an encouraging report of the church's repentance (see Chronology in the introduction to 2 Corinthians, and comments on 2:5–13).

7:5 Disputes without and fears within: Even in the Macedonian churches that had remained loyal to him (e.g., Philippi, Thessalonica, Beroea), there were disturbing problems both outside and inside the churches (see the introduction to Philippians).

7:8 I did regret it: Paul had had second thoughts about the angry letter he had sent to them (see Chronology in the introduction to 2 Corinthians), but in retrospect he is glad he sent the letter, because of the positive results it (and Titus) produced.

7:9 Your grief led to repentance: Repentance means a change in one's life based on a reorientation of one's thinking (see on Luke 3:7–9). Being sorry one has done wrong is not itself repentance—it can be only another form of self-interest—but may be a step in the right direction. Repentance is part of the process of conversion, and stands at the beginning of the Christian life, but it is not a once-for-all initial act that can be "done" and then put behind one. Being Christian involves a constant reorienting one's life to the will of God as expressed in the Christian gospel. The change that transpired in the life of the Corinthian congregation was not only a restoration of personal relations with Paul—though the element of personal friendship was very important to him—but meant acknowledging Paul to be an authentic apostle, God's representative who presented the truth of the Christian gospel in word and deed. It is a testimony to the depth of the Corinthians' faith that they were able to hear and accept Paul's rebuke and to place themselves again under his apostolic leadership. Their former suspicion and antagonism had changed to zealous support of his mission, so that they had even punished the offending member who had insulted Paul (see on 2:5–11).

7:12 In order that your zeal for us might be made known to you: In retrospect, Paul is no longer accusatory. He lets them (and himself) off the hook of the previous conflict, which had involved the "painful letter," by offering yet another explanation of its severity—it allowed them to see the matter, and themselves, in the proper light, and to realize that after all they were devoted to the truth of the gospel as represented by Paul.

7:13 The joy of Titus: Paul is encouraged not only by Titus's report, but by Titus's own obvious delight at what had transpired at Corinth as a result of Paul's letter and Titus's visit. Paul had sent Titus into a hostile situation with the delicate task of presenting and interpreting the harsh letter from Paul, participating in the soul-searching discussions it caused, leading the church back to the Pauline gospel, and reintroducing the touchy matter of the collection (see on 1 Cor. 16:1–4; 2 Cor. 1:15; 7:2; chaps. 8–9). The collection was an especially sensitive issue, since the Corinthians had been suspicious of Paul's handling of money and his promotion of the offering for Jerusalem (see 1 Cor. 9:3–18; 2 Cor. 8:20; 11:7–11; 12:14–18). The (re)conversion of the Corinthians may owe as much to Titus's pastoral skills as to Paul's theology and harsh letter.

8:1–9:15
THE OFFERING

Most scholars regard chaps. 8 and 9 as a continuation and conclusion of the previous discussion, but some have concluded that these two chapters were not written at the same time as the rest of the letter, but are parts of an earlier letter or letters inserted into this document at the time of its final editing (see the introduction to 2 Corinthians). They deal entirely with the offering that Paul and his colleagues were gathering to take to poor people among the Jerusalem Christians (see on Acts 24:17; Rom. 15:25–27, 31; 1 Cor. 16:1–4; Gal. 2:10). The Corinthian congregation had previously committed itself to participating in the offering. Then came the break with Paul. Now that harmonious relations have been restored, Paul sets about organizing the arrangements for completing the collection, which was a substantial sum. Gathering the collection involved three provinces (Galatia, Macedonia, and Achaia) and the work of several people over a year's time; several people made an overseas trip of some weeks in order to deliver the offering to Jerusalem (see 1 Cor. 16:3–4; 2 Cor. 8:16, 18, 22–23; Acts 20:4).

Paul never explicitly spells out the reasons for the offering, but the following considerations were probably involved (certainly the first two):

1. *The actual poverty of some of the Jerusalem Christians.* Jesus and his original followers had come from the lower economic classes, and many early Christians had suffered economic reprisals for their faith. Christians in Judea needed economic help. It is not the case, however, that the sharing of goods in the earliest church had resulted in a "failed communism" from which the "capitalist" Christians of the west had to rescue them (see on Acts 2:44–45; 4:32–37). Nor does Paul base his appeal on sympathy for the plight of Judean Christians. He presents no "poster children." Motivation for the offering had theological grounds (see below). Yet the poverty in Judea was real, and Gentile Christians were called upon to do something real about it.

2. *A symbol of the unity of Jewish and Gentile Christians in the one church of God.* See Gal. 2:10. This was one of Paul's major reasons for gathering the collection. As Gentile Christians, who did not observe the law, sent by their own chosen representatives a significant amount of money to aid the original church in Jerusalem, a church that continued to observe the Jewish law and

was suspicious of law-free Gentile Christianity, the collection, giving, and reception of the offering became a symbolic healing of the breach that had threatened the unity of the church.

3. *An annual gift of the Jewish Diaspora throughout the world for the support of the temple in Jerusalem.* This "temple tax" (see Matt. 17:24–27) was not only a financial support, but a symbol of the unity of the one people of God, scattered throughout the earth but loyal to its one temple in Jerusalem. Paul and other Jewish Christians may have seen the offering as a Christian equivalent or analogy: by supporting financially the poor among the Jerusalem Christians, they honored the original church that was the source of their own faith. A few months later Paul would write that as they had received from Jerusalem spiritual things, they now responded with material things (Rom. 15:27).

4. *One picture of the "last days," in which God brings history to a glorious conclusion and the Gentile nations bring gifts to Jerusalem* (see Isa. 2:2–4; Mic. 4:1–2; Isa. 60:5–6). Paul understands the Gentile mission to be the next to the last step in the plan of God for the ages (11:11–36), and so may have understood the event of Gentiles bringing a thanksgiving offering to Jerusalem in eschatological terms.

All Christians today are concerned about supporting the mission of the church financially. As church budgets are made and financial campaigns are designed and implemented, congregations today could deepen their faith and understanding of the Christian life by lingering in prayerful reflection over these two chapters.

8:1–15
Encouragement to Be Generous

8:1 The grace of God: For Paul the offering itself is a matter of grace, i.e., it is a gift of God to be able to participate in it and to be willing to do so. "Grace" and "gratitude" are related theologically and linguistically. Giving is a matter of gratitude; it presupposes the grace of God. Christian giving is a human action, but it is a reaction to the primary gift of God. This is symbolized in many congregations by the action of placing the offering on the communion table. Our gifts to others are in response to God's gift to all. Paul's "fundraising letter" does not begin with gimmicks, but with a declaration of God's grace.

8:2 Poverty: While Paul does not dwell on the poverty of the needy people in Jerusalem for whom the gift is made, he does point out the poverty of the Gentile Macedonian

Christians, who insisted on participating in the offering. Paul had apparently not asked them to give, but they had heard of the offering and wanted to participate. While this could be seen as a means of shaming the Corinthians to whom he is writing into increasing their pledge, for Paul it is not merely strategy, but inherent in the nature of the Christian faith. Giving is based on who God is, what God does, what it means to be a believer; so no one should be excluded from the opportunity to share just because he or she is poor. Likewise the reference to the generosity of the Macedonians should not be reduced to a mere tactic on Paul's part. His basis for giving is not comparison with others or competition with them, but the nature of God and the nature of the Christian faith itself.

8:4 Sharing in this ministry: Both words are loaded with theological freight. "Sharing" is *koinonia,* often translated "fellowship" or "partnership," and used in theological contexts having to do with sharing the life, faith, and material resources of the church with other people. "Ministry" is *diakonia,* from which the word "deacon" obviously is derived, the same word used for the self-giving ministry of Jesus himself (Mark 10:45). Paul refers to the offering as a "collection" only once (1 Cor. 16:1–2). Otherwise, as here, he uses theological designations: the offering is designated or related to "grace" (8:1; 9:14), "generous act" (8:9), "generous undertaking" (8:6, 7, 19), "generous gift" (8:20), "blessing" (9:8), "thanks" (8:16, 9:15), "ministry" (8:4, 9:1, the same word translated "relief" in 8:13), "rendering of this ministry" (9:12, 13), "obedience to the confession of the gospel" (9:13), and "administering" (8:20), "glory" (8:19, 23; 9:13), and "sharing" in the sense of "participation" (8:4; 9:13).

8:5 Gave themselves: This is what Christianity is *about.* It is not self-interest, not even enlightened self-interest. The life, ministry, and death of Jesus stands our commonsense ideas of what's what on their heads, demolishing the assumption that everyone always finally acts in his or her own interest. Here Paul points to ordinary people, quite poor people, who gave a substantial part of their limited resources to help people they had never seen, because of their faith in Christ. They did this only because they first gave themselves. They gave themselves because they had come to believe in the God revealed in Christ, that at the heart of the universe is not the struggle for survival, nature "red in tooth and claw," but self-giving love. "Oh

heart I made, a heart beats here." **To the Lord and . . . to us:** The reference is not to two things, but to one. To give oneself to God is to give oneself to other people. To give oneself to other people is to give oneself to God (Matt. 25:31–46).

8:7 Excel also in this: When Paul mentions **faith, speech,** and **knowledge** as "spiritual gifts" in which the Corinthians already excelled (see 1 Cor. 1:5), he is not referring to these as ordinary capacities that all Christians have, but to the special gifts of the Spirit prized by the Corinthians (see 1 Cor. 12–14, esp. the lists in 12:8–11, 28–31; 13:1–3). Just as Paul had instructed them that love is the supreme gift of the Spirit (1 Cor. 13), so here he regards giving as a spiritual gift. Their zeal for spiritual gifts should be manifest in their desire to excel in this gift also. When Paul writes Romans a few months later, he will specifically add "giving" to the list of spiritual gifts (Rom. 12:7–8).

8:8 Not . . . as a command: As an apostle, Paul has the authority to command, but knows that authentic giving, like love, cannot be done in obedience to a command.

8:9 For your sakes he became poor: Here is the supreme theological model that is the basis for all Paul's talk about Christian giving. The picture is not of the poverty of the earthly Jesus, as though Jesus had been a rich man who left his riches to share the life of poor people (as did Buddha). So far as we know, the earthly Jesus was always literally poor, but that is not Paul's point. Rather, as in Phil. 2:6–8, the picture is of the preexistent Son of God, who left the riches of the eternal world to share the life of human beings. Here Christology is not a speculative abstraction, but is expressed in the concrete realities of the situation, wealth and poverty. **So that by his poverty you might become rich:** To interpret this in economic terms, as though Paul is promising that those who contribute to the offering he is gathering will be rewarded by becoming wealthy themselves, is to reduce Christian faith to a clever form of selfishness, and thus to reverse and pervert the meaning of the whole passage and of the Christian faith. As in 6:10 and often elsewhere in the New Testament, "wealth" is a metaphor for the spiritual reality that comes to the believer by participating in the kingdom of God (see Luke 16:11; Rom. 2:4; 9:23; 11:12; Phil. 4:19; Col. 1:27; 2:2; Eph. 1:18; 2:7; Jas. 2:5; Rev. 3:17–18). That which people usually seek in wealth, believers find in the reality of salvation.

8:10 Not only to give but also to have the desire to do so (NIV): We might have said it the other way, "not only want to, but actually to do it." Long before Shakespeare, however, for Paul and Jesus "the gift without the giver is bare," and doing the "right thing" without actually wanting to do so (e.g., under the pressure of guilt, manipulation, or coercion) is not adequate.

8:13 A fair balance: Literally "equality." Paul is here interested in equality in two senses: (1) those who have money in the west sharing their resources with those who need it in the east, and (2) those who share, those who are contributing to the offering, doing so in a way that expresses their equality. Those who have more are responsible to give more, those who have less are responsible to give less, but all are equally responsible to give.

8:15 As it is written: Exod. 16:18. Paul appeals to a biblical story to illustrate his point. When the hungry Israelites grumbled during their wilderness wanderings, God sent an amazing gift of "manna," breadlike material that fell from heaven. The Israelites could gather only enough for one day's needs at a time. If they tried to gather a supply for several days, the excess became rotten and stank. Those who were able to gather only a little still discovered that it met their needs. The miracle of divinely provided bread was also a miracle of equality.

8:16–24
Commendation of Titus and
the Two Brothers

8:18 The brother who is famous: Paul is sending Titus back to Corinth (see Chronology in the introduction to 2 Corinthians, and 2:13; 7:6, 13, 14; 8:6, 16), along with two other Christian leaders ("brother" means "fellow Christian," "fellow member of the family of God") to organize the collection of the offering before he arrives with the other delegates from Macedonia. Their names are not given, and their identity remains unknown. It cannot be deduced from other texts, but see Acts 20:4, which must include these two. They had been **appointed by the churches** (8:19), i.e., were independent of Paul. In v. 23 they are called **messengers of the churches,** where the word is literally "apostles." The offering was not merely Paul's pet project, but the responsibility of the churches, who had selected people to collect and deliver it. Here as in Phil. 2:25 Paul uses "apostle" in the nontechnical sense (see Luke 6:12–13) of those who have been chosen, authorized, and sent on church business. They are not apostles in the sense of Paul

himself, chosen by the risen Christ to be an authorized representative and interpreter of the Christian faith.

8:21 In the sight of others: See 1 Thess. 2:5; 2 Cor. 2:5, 17; 12:14–18. Paul and his colleagues had been suspected of collecting money to line their own pockets, as did many of the pagan traveling teachers and preachers. His handling of funds had been particularly suspect by his opponents in Corinth, so he was particularly careful to keep church finances a matter that was open and aboveboard. Even in later and different situations where there is no personal suspicion, it is right that church budgets and expenditures should be open to inspection by all members of the church.

8:24 Boasting: See on 1:12; 5:12–13; 7:4, 16.

9:1–15
The Collection for the Christians
in Jerusalem

9:2 Macedonia . . . Achaia: Paul's instructions illustrate that the churches were in this together, that the offering was not a personal or congregational project, but involved Macedonia and Achaia. These were Roman provinces on the Greek peninsula. Corinth was the capital of Achaia, Thessalonica of Macedonia. Paul and his colleagues had established churches in the capitals and other major cities in each province, and the Christians there had spontaneously spread the faith to smaller towns. The churches in Galatia, across the Aegean, were also participating in the offering. In good faith Paul had "boasted" to the Macedonian churches that the churches of Achaia had already completed the offering, and then the troubles with Corinth came, and he learned that the collection had stalled. Here he urges the Corinthians not to disappoint and embarrass both himself and themselves. Again, this is not to be reduced to a tactic—though it is also that. Christians may learn and have their own faith deepened by being informed of the way others give. Christians have the obligation to let others learn from the way they give. Though followers of Jesus are not to make their giving a matter of prideful publicity (Matt. 6:2–4), making Christian giving an absolutely private matter robs it of part of its meaning. Followers of Jesus are also to let others see their good works in a manner that brings glory to God (Matt. 5:14–16). There are no rules for deciding how and when to do each. Here Paul decides that informing the Corinthians of the

Macedonian gifts will deepen their faith and Christian action.

9:5 As a voluntary gift and not as an extortion: Paul is interested in more than the bottom line. He is not interested in himself as a successful fund-raiser, but in helping the Corinthians be the kind of Christians who give of their own free will.

9:7 God loves a cheerful giver: Paul clinches his point with a quotation from the Bible (Prov. 22:8 in the Greek translation, not present in the Hebrew original from which our English Bibles are translated).

9:9 As it is written: Paul cites the description of the righteous person of Ps. 112:9. In the Old Testament the NRSV pluralizes the Hebrew text's generic masculine singular to retain inclusivity, but retains the singular in Paul's quotation, for here it is not clear whether the subject is "Christ" or the "righteous person." While the Psalms were often understood in early Christianity to refer to Christ or to represent Christ as speaking (see, e.g., Acts 2:25–36), here Paul most likely understands the reference to be to the good person who shares with others. The point is that God will supply the resources for such a person to help others.

9:11 Enriched in every way: Such statements can be perverted to mean that giving to Christian causes is a good investment, that it will reward the giver, that by giving our material means we receive spiritual riches, or that we give in order to receive the heavenly reward later. All this is a refined kind of selfishness. Throughout, the image of 8:9 should be kept in mind, for it dominates Paul's whole discussion. Paul consistently contrasts the free gift of God with payment due for good works (e.g., 8:1; Rom. 4:4; 6:23). The point is not the self-serving "generosity pays off," but that God provides the means to be generous.

9:13 The testing of this ministry: The phrase means "the test which this ministry is." The offering is here called "ministry" (see 8:4). How one responds to the opportunity to give is a test that reveals whether or not one takes the confession of faith seriously. **Obedience to the confession:** See Rom. 10:9–10 for the basic Christian confession, "Jesus is Lord." To call Jesus Lord not only is a statement about his status, but places those who make this confession under his lordship. The confession calls for obedience.

9:15 Thanks be to God: Throughout, Paul's appeal is God-centered. Giving glorifies God (v. 13) and produces thanksgiving to God (v.

11). The goal is not merely that the recipients of charity in Judea will regard the Corinthians as nice people, but that they will give thanks to God for such people.

We do not know for sure how the offering turned out. When Paul writes from Corinth to the Romans a few months later (see the introduction to Romans), he seems to be satisfied with the results in gathering the collection from the Gentile churches in the west (Rom. 15:26), but is anxious that after all it may not be received by the leaders of the Jerusalem church (Rom. 15:30–31). It may be that his fears were realized, that his ecumenical vision was not shared by the Jerusalem leaders and the gift was declined (see on Acts 24:17).

10:1–13:13
PART TWO—TRUE AND FALSE APOSTLES

With 10:1 the reader encounters such an abrupt change of both subject and mood that it is difficult to understand chaps. 10–13 as originally part of the same letter as chaps. 1–9 (see the introduction to 2 Corinthians). The minority of scholars that regards 2 Corinthians as an original unity must explain what happened between chaps. 9 and 10. The explanations are speculative: after composing chaps. 1–9, Paul received further bad news from Corinth and added chaps. 10–13 without revising the first part of the letter; or he had a sleepless night; or chapters 1–9 represent Paul and Timothy's views together (see 1:1), while from 10:1 to the end Paul takes the pen himself and expresses his own anger and frustration, which were not shared by Timothy. Most scholars regard chaps. 10–13 as (the major) part of a different letter Paul wrote to Corinth, later combined with chaps. 1–9 in the editing and canonizing process that led to the New Testament.

The subject is the legitimacy of Paul's apostleship, which is rejected by new traveling missionaries who have come to Corinth claiming that they are the authentic apostles whom the church should heed. Paul's response is bitter and sarcastic. He is engaged in a battle (10:3) with those he considers "false apostles," "deceitful workers" (11:13), and ministers of Satan. Paul does not use this strong language of all those who disagree with him. His ministry tolerates a broad spectrum of theological points of view and ways of understanding Christian life and ethics (Rom. 14:1–23; 1 Cor. 3:5–9, 21–23). Paul is not a narrow-minded dogmatist who believes that everyone who disagrees with him is wrong and condemned. There is more than one way of bearing witness to the truth of the gospel. But not just anything goes. In Paul's view the boundaries of authentic Christian faith are wide, but there are boundaries. The rival apostles at Corinth, like the Judaizers in the Galatian churches (Gal. 1:6–9), present not merely another form of the gospel, but a different message that in Paul's view denies the truth of the gospel itself. Thus Paul addresses his letter not to the opponents, but to the Corinthian congregation, who must decide for themselves who authentically represents the Christian faith (see extended comments at Rev. 2:20). They did not have a New Testament or a long Christian tradition on which to draw. The rival apostles were more impressive. But it is clear that the Corinthians decided for the Pauline gospel, because we have his letters in the New Testament, rather than the writings of his opponents, whose identity has even been lost to us.

Who were these opponents? Both Paul and the Corinthians were aware of their identity and character, so Paul has no need to describe them. We can reconstruct their claims only by "mirror reading" what Paul says about them, i.e., by supposing that Paul's assertions about himself are mostly responding to some assertion they had made about him. This indirect, allusive means of historical reconstruction does not yield absolutely clear results. Keeping in mind that we have only Paul's hostile report (what if we had only their picture of Paul?), we may glean the following data from Paul's letter:

What they said about Paul (the converse of their view of themselves)

10:1 Paul is timid when present, but bold when absent.

10:2 Paul lives his life and conducts his ministry "according to human standards" (*kata sarka*).

10:8 Paul boasts about his authority.

10:9–10 Paul writes impressive letters, but in person he is weak, and his speech is contemptible.

10:13–16 Paul has overstepped his bounds in claiming authority over them.

11:6 Paul is "untrained in speech."

11:7 Paul preached at no charge (which he would not do if he were a "real" apostle).

11:11 Paul does not love them (but is interested in himself).

12:11 Paul is a "nobody."

12:16 Paul is crafty and took them by deceit.

What they said about themselves

10:7 "I am of Christ."

10:9–10 We are personally impressive, and our speech is impressive (as you Corinthians can see by observing our style of ministry).

[11:12 We are Paul's equals.]

11:13 We are apostles of Christ (not just of the churches).

11:13 We are ministers of Christ.

11:14 We have seen visions of angels. (See 1 Cor. 13:2, the claim to speak the language of angels.)

11:15 We are ministers of righteousness.

13:3 Christ speaks in us (but not in Paul), a phenomenon that is "provable."

13:4 Christ is powerful and was not crucified in weakness. (The opponents seem to have emphasized the "life of Jesus," in which he was the powerful Son of God, and/or the power of the exalted Christ, but not his death—see 4:10–12.)

What Paul said about them

10:5 They raise up obstacles against the knowledge of God.

10:12 They commend themselves.

10:12 They do not show good sense.

10:15 They boast in the labors and field of others.

11:4 They come from outside. (The "someone" may be generic, or may refer to one particular individual, their leader, perhaps the one who had wronged Paul.)

11:4 They proclaim another Jesus.

11:4 The manifest a different spirit, or offer a different Spirit.

11:4 They proclaim a different gospel.

11:5 They are "super-apostles" (probably reflecting their own vocabulary in which the word "super" played a prominent role [Greek *hyper*, see English "hyper"]).

11:12 They want an opportunity to be equal with Paul and they claim to be equal with Paul.

11:13 They are false apostles (perhaps on the analogy of "false prophets").

11:13 They are deceitful workers ("workers" was a quasi-technical term for "missionaries").

11:13 They disguised themselves as apostles of Christ.

11:15 They are Satan's ministers.

11:15 Their end will match their deeds.

11:20 They make slaves of you, prey on you, take advantage of you, put on airs, slap you in the face.

11:22 They are Hebrews, Israelites, descendants of Abraham.

12:1 They claimed visions and revelations.

12:12 They "proved" the legitimacy of their apostleship by miracles.

10:1–18
PAUL DEFENDS HIS MINISTRY

10:1 The meekness and gentleness of Christ: Paul is not here referring to the personality and ministry of the earthly Jesus, as though he had in mind such scenes from the Gospels as Jesus' riding into Jerusalem on a donkey instead of a warhorse (Matt. 21:1–11) or washing the disciples' feet (John 13:1–20). If Paul knew such stories, he never referred to them. When Paul thinks of the character of Christ, he thinks in terms of the incarnation, the preexistent one who chose to come to the earth and share the lowliness of human life as such (8:9; Phil. 2:5–11). The description "meek" and "gentle" comes not from the life of Jesus but from Paul's Bible, the Christian Old Testament, which he understood to speak of Christ (see, e.g., Ps. 45:4 in the Greek translation used by Paul; Zech. 9:9).

Humble . . . bold: Paul begins on the sarcastic note that pervades the whole section. This is not Paul's own view of himself; he is quoting what his opponents had said about him in Corinth (note quotation marks in NIV).

10:2 According to human standards: His opponents in Corinth charged him with not being "spiritual" enough, with living his life by worldly standards (*kata sarka*, "according to the flesh," a characteristic Pauline phrase). By this they probably meant that he did not manifest the spectacular gifts of the Spirit, such as speaking in tongues and working miracles, that he did not perform the "signs of an apostle" (see 12:12), that he acknowledged his own inferiority by not accepting financial support from the church, and that he mishandled the finances he claimed were for relief of the poor in Jerusalem (see 1 Cor. 9:1–23; 12–14; 2 Cor. 8–9; 11:7–11; 12:16–18).

10:3 We live as human beings: *En sarki,* "in the flesh"; like all Christians, Paul lives in the world, but not by worldly standards.

Wage war: Paul is not only on the defensive but on the offensive. The war metaphor is common in the Old Testament (e.g., Ps. 24:8), the stories of Jesus (Luke 14:31–33), and the New Testament letters (e.g., Eph. 6:11, 13; 1

Tim. 6:12; 2 Tim. 4:7). His is a war to destroy false words, ideas, and theologies, not to destroy persons (see Rev. 19:13–21).

10:6 Punish every disobedience: After those in Corinth who heed the apostle's warning repent, he will punish the others when he arrives. This sounds strange to modern ears, for we rarely think of the Holy Spirit in terms of judicial and punitive power. Paul will not invoke the aid of civil authorities to punish heretics, as the church later did; neither will he administer corporal punishment as the synagogue did, but by the power of the Spirit he will invoke God's wrath on the offenders in some way foreign to modern understanding (see on Acts 5:1–11; 13:4–11; 1 Cor. 5:1–5; 11:27–32; Gal. 1:8–9; 1 Tim. 1:20). **When your obedience is complete:** Paul is referring to their obedience to Christ and their own confession (9:13), not merely to Paul himself—though he sometimes blurred the line between these.

10:7 Belong to Christ: This had earlier been the motto of one group within the Corinthian church (see 1 Cor. 1:12). It is unlikely that Paul refers to them here, since he is dealing with intruders from outside who have arrived in Corinth since then. They may have had the same self-understanding, however, claiming to belong to Christ in some special way, whether by their spiritual experiences that directly connected them to the risen Christ, or by their missionary practice that authorized them to be supported by the churches rather than doing manual labor themselves (see Mark 9:41, where the same expression is translated "because you bear the name of Christ"). The rival apostles may have claimed they belonged to Christ because they observed his command, and that Paul did not because he supported himself. Paul insists he belongs to Christ just as much as they do.

10:8 For building you up and not for tearing you down: Paul often pictures the task of the ministry as "building up" the church, i.e., strengthening it for its life and mission (Rom. 15:20; 1 Cor. 3:10–17; 8:1, 10; 10:23; 14:4, 17; Gal. 2:18; 1 Thess. 5:11). Here he alludes to the words of Jeremiah (1:10; 24:6), a prophet who had to contend with false prophets, who himself was abused and unimpressive over against the claims of his rivals, but whose message was finally accepted by the community of faith as representing the will of God (see Jer. 23:9–40; 28:1–17).

10:10 His letters are weighty and strong: Not only modern readers find Paul's letters ponderous and sometimes difficult to understand (see 2 Pet. 3:16); his ancient readers, including his opponents, were also impressed with their depth. Here, however, the remark is not intended as a compliment, but as a contrast between how Paul writes when absent and how he speaks when present. **His bodily presence is weak:** We do not know what Paul looked like, but apparently he was not a commanding figure. He had often been beaten and in prison, and may have been chronically ill (see on 11:23–29; 12:7; Gal. 4:15). **His speech contemptible:** Judged by cultural standards, he was not an effective speaker. He did not express himself in the refined rhetorical manner that was the mark of an educated person, nor did he manifest the spontaneous power of one filled with the Spirit.

10:12 Commend themselves: Paul's response is not what we might expect. He does not recite his successes, how many churches he has established, how many converts he has made, how many people he has baptized. Judged by human standards, these are legitimate accomplishments, and it is not likely that his opponents could have matched them. They commended themselves, i.e., measured themselves by the criteria and values that were operative in their own group, and thus received high grades. Paul refuses to enter into such comparisons—though he would have come out well, even by their standards—since the only evaluation that mattered to him was how he appeared in God's sight.

10:13 The field that God has assigned: This could refer to the agreement Paul had made with leaders of Jewish Christianity (Gal. 2:7–10), in which he had accepted responsibility for the Gentile mission and they for the Jewish mission. Corinth was clearly in Gentile territory, and the Corinthian church was composed of Gentile Christians. Thus Paul had remained within the agreed-upon territorial assignments. His Jewish Christian opponents had not abided by the agreement, but had invaded "his" Gentile territory, interfering with churches they had not planted. Paul could regard the decision reached at the Jerusalem Council as the command of God (see Gal. 2; Acts 15:22–29, esp. 22:28). However, Paul is here more likely referring to his own apostolic commission to go to the Gentiles, which included the Corinthians.

10:15 The labors of others: Since practically all readers of the words on this page will live in communities in which churches have existed for generations and centuries, it is difficult for us to imagine either the pioneering work of a missionary apostle such as Paul, who founded new churches in pagan territory, or his indignation at others who invade his territory and attempt to "correct" his converts. In most things we join projects already under way; we inherit and build on the work of others. Paul, however, considered himself the spiritual father of his congregations (see on 1 Cor. 4:14–16). Perhaps we can understand his response if we think how we as parents react when someone else attempts to take over the parental responsibility of instructing our children, leading them in a different direction from that which we have taught them, giving them a different set of values and lifestyle from our own parental instruction. Paul understood himself to be called to found churches and refused to build on foundations laid by others (Rom. 15:20–21). He deeply resented it when others attempted to build on the foundation he had laid, but it was more than personal resentment. He saw it as a matter of the truth of the gospel.

10:17 Boast in the Lord: On "boasting," see on 1:12; 5:12–13; 7:4, 16. Paul had already cited this text from Jeremiah in 1 Cor. 1:31. In the present context it takes on a new meaning as it becomes clearer that to "boast in the Lord" means to "boast in weakness" (v. 13; 12:5), to make the cross of Jesus the criterion of what one can "boast" about and what one must be ashamed of.

11:1–15
PAUL AND THE FALSE APOSTLES

11:1 A little foolishness: Although Paul deplores "boasting" about one's own credentials, since he feels forced into it by the claims of the rival apostles who have come to Corinth, he will do it only in the literary form of the "fool's speech," a stance which he preserves throughout chaps. 10–13.

11:2 I am jealous for you (NIV): The meaning is that Paul cares deeply for them with the same kind of jealousy that God manifests toward his people Israel (see, e.g., Exod. 20:5; 34:14; Deut. 4:24; 5:9). His protests are not self-serving defenses of his own status but an expression of his concern for them. **I promised you in marriage:** God as the husband and Israel as the bride or wife was a common metaphor in biblical portrayals of God's covenant with Israel, an image adopted by Jesus and the early church for the relation between God and the church (see, e.g., Hos. 1–3; Ezek. 16; 23; Isa. 50:1; 54:1–6; Ps. 45; and the Song of Solomon were also interpreted this way in early Judaism; Mark 2:18–20; John 3:29–30; Rom. 7:4; Eph. 5:22–33; Rev. 19:1–10; 21:1–9; 22:17). The present was seen as the time of engagement, and the wedding feast would be celebrated at the Parousia (see Matt. 22:1–14; 25:1–13; Luke 12:35–40; Rev. 19:1–10). Christians live "between the times" of engagement and wedding, a time of "already" and "not yet." Paul has portrayed himself as the father of the believers that were converted by his preaching (see 1 Cor. 3:6; 4:14–15; 1 Thess. 2:11–12, where maternal imagery is also used). The imagery reflects first-century Jewish marriage customs in which the young woman was promised by her father to the bridegroom, and was then responsible for her sexual purity in the time between the engagement and the wedding. Paul is fearful that the Corinthians' purity will be violated by their new "suitors," who will lure them away from their commitment to Christ. The first-century marriage customs no longer fit our culture and our sensitivities, but we can still imagine the happy and proud moment to which Paul as father of the bride looks forward when he will present the bride to the bridegroom.

11:3 As the serpent deceived Eve: See Gen. 13:3. In Rom. 5:12–21 it is Adam who is guilty for introducing sin into the world. Here Paul focuses on Eve in order to retain the feminine imagery of the bride. **Someone comes:** The opponents are not local members of the Corinthian church, as in 1 Corinthians, but itinerant missionaries who have come from elsewhere.

11:4 Another Jesus . . . spirit . . . gospel: These may be only general descriptions of the false message and ministry of the rival apostles, or in Paul's mind they may have had specific content. "Another Jesus" has been understood in several different ways:

1. The opponents may have emphasized the life and teachings of the earthly Jesus, whom Paul had not known. The details of Jesus' earthly life did not play a role in Paul's own gospel, which focused on the act of God in the whole Christ event, not on stories about and sayings of the earthly Jesus.

2. The opponents may have contrasted the exalted heavenly Christ and the purely human Jesus, one who could be disdained and even cursed (see on 1 Cor. 12:3). If so, it means that before their arrival in Corinth some

Corinthians already leaned toward this view, which the new missionaries elaborated and exploited.

3. Since Paul places their Christology in contrast to his own, which emphasizes the vulnerability and weakness of the crucified Christ (see 1 Cor. 1:18–2:5; 2 Cor. 13:4; Phil. 2:5–11), they may have emphasized the power of the miracle-working "divine man" Jesus, a view that had no place in Paul's own understanding. It may be that they saw the power at work in Jesus' life as continued in their own powerful ministry, just as Paul saw the self-giving of the victimized and crucified Jesus as continued in his ministry. Neither group saw a way of combining the pictures of Jesus the divinelike miracle worker and the Jesus who died a human death on the cross. Paul chose the weakness of the crucified Jesus as the power of God; they chose the power of the miracle-working Jesus as representing the power of God. The Gospels, which were not written yet, were the first to combine these two ways of picturing the saving act of God in Christ (see "Introduction to the Gospels").

"Another Spirit": The lower case *s* of both the NRSV and NIV is an editorial decision to signal their understanding that Paul is talking about the human spirit, i.e., "attitude," of the rival apostles. The Greek text makes no such distinction, so Paul may be referring here not to their attitude, but their understanding of the Holy Spirit, which is so different from his own that he does not consider it the same Spirit.

"Another gospel": Like the false teachers in Galatia (see Gal. 1:6–9), the rival apostles in Corinth preach a different gospel from Paul's own message. Paul spells out the difference in his letter to the Galatians, but we should not assume that the "different gospel" of his rivals in Corinth is the same problem as in Galatia. There it was clearly Judaizers (Jewish Christians zealous for the Law) attempting to impose on Gentile Christians Jewish laws, including circumcision and the food laws. Although Paul's opponents in Corinth are from a Jewish background (11:22)—as he himself is—there is no indication that they emphasized circumcision and the Jewish law.

11:5 These super-apostles: On apostles, see at Luke 6:12–13. Those who came to Corinth did not claim to be among the original Twelve, but probably claimed to be more than apostles of the churches (see on 8:19, 23). Like Paul, they probably claimed to be directly authorized by the risen Christ. Some interpreters have understood these to be the original Jerusalem apostles and leaders of the Jerusalem church, a different group from the "false apostles" of v. 13. It is more likely, however, that only one group is meant, and that "super-apostle" is Paul's sarcastic adoption of some of their own language. The Greek preposition *hyper* is very flexible and is often used in the New Testament, including in combination with other words to heighten their meaning, like "super-" and "hyper-" in English. Its density in this section of 2 Corinthians is many times the normal usage, and probably echoes the opponents own *super*ior claims.

11:6 Untrained in speech: See on 10:10. The opponents were themselves skilled orators and considered Paul an amateur. **Not in knowledge:** It is the substance of the faith, not the rhetorical form in which it is presented, that is important to Paul. The knowledge that is important is not speculative and theoretical explanations, but the knowledge of God, expressed in love for others. Paul opposes the kind of knowledge that makes one feel superior to others (1 Cor. 8:1–13; 13:2).

11:7 Humbling myself . . . free of charge: See on 1 Cor. 4:12; 9:3–18; 1 Thess. 2:9; Acts 18:3. In a day when there was no public education, traveling teachers commanded a substantial fee for their services. So Paul's opponents considered his doing manual labor and refusing fees for his teaching to be an admission that he really did not belong to the educated class and lacked the credentials to instruct the Corinthian church. The relation between patron and client in first-century Mediterranean culture was a tricky one for modern readers to understand. Paul's refusal to accept their money meant a refusal to be their patron, a refusal to be obligated. Though he accepted no money for himself, his raising money for the poor in Jerusalem (see on chaps. 8–9) could have been understood as a tactic to get their money without becoming obligated to them himself. In the social structure and conventions of first-century Corinth, his opponents could claim that he really cared nothing for the Corinthians, but had devised a way to get their money and remain independent of them. Paul was willing to risk that his decision and procedure could be misunderstood as a social insult that could be used against him. This is the meaning of his protestation that he does indeed love them (v. 11).

11:12 Those who want . . . to be recognized as our equals: We do not know all Paul's motivation for his procedure, but here he gives us one reason: those who accepted money for their ministry in Paul's churches could not claim that their ministry was equal to his.

11:13–15 False apostles: See the general discussion above at 10:1–13:13. Though Paul considers them false, they were probably sincere Christian leaders whose differences with the Pauline mission were so great that they considered him a false apostle, a danger to the churches, whose converts had to be "corrected." **His (Satan's) ministers:** The language is severe. Later Christians should be extremely hesitant to imitate it. Paul's thought reflects the apocalyptic dualism found in much of the New Testament, in which all matters are seen as either/or, God-or-Satan, black-or-white, with no shades of gray in between. Not only Revelation, but the Gospels and Jesus, thought in these terms (see, e.g., Matt. 12:30; 25:31–46). While Paul's apocalyptic worldview, including its Satan-language, should not be adopted literally by modern readers, it points to something real. One theological asset of Satan-language is that it allows us to see that our theological and secular opponents are not themselves the ultimate enemy, but are themselves the victims of the transcendent power of evil, as we all are to some extent.

Angel of light: Paul reflects the variety of Jewish legends current in the first century according to which Satan disguised himself as a good angel in order to deceive Adam and Eve. Thus the *Apocalypse of Moses* 17:1–2: "Satan appeared in the form of an angel and sang hymns like the angels." Paul's world was fascinated with angels, and his opponents may have appealed to visions of angels to validate their claims, just as they supposed that they spoke in the language of angels (see on 1 Cor. 13:1; Gal. 1:8; Col. 2:18; Heb. 1:5–14). Paul himself never has a good word to say about angels (see on Luke 1:10–12; Acts 5:19; Rom. 8:38).

11:15 Their end will match their deeds: While all Christians will give account to God and Christ at the Last Judgment (5:10; Rom. 14:10), those who have misled the church may expect a severe judgment (see Phil. 3:19).

11:16–33
PAUL'S SUFFERINGS AS AN APOSTLE

11:16 Accept me as a fool: The "fool's speech" continues, with its heavy sarcasm.

11:17 Not with the Lord's authority: Paul shifts out of his apostolic role in order to engage in the "boasting" called for by his opponents' behavior. Paul cannot imagine Jesus rehearsing his "qualifications" nor instructing his followers to do so.

11:20 Preys upon you: This list of the rival apostles' behavior gives Paul's evaluation of the high and mighty ways of their style of ministry.

11:22 Hebrews . . . Israelites . . . descendants of Abraham: The rival apostles boasted of belonging to the chosen people. Hebrews probably refers to their ethnic background, they or their parents having come from Palestine, with Aramaic being spoken at home (see Acts 6:1; Phil. 3:5). They probably did not contest Paul's actual Jewishness, but considered him a renegade Jew.

11:23–29 I am a better one: Paul sarcastically takes up their claim to be "better" ("super-," "hyper-"; see on v. 5), but his own claim to "superiority" has to do with sharing the suffering and rejection of Christ. Paul presents his credentials, his résumé, which shows he is an authentic apostle. His list of achievements is an overwhelming crescendo of the suffering and indignities Paul had endured as a Christian missionary. While some are mentioned in Acts, most are unknown otherwise. The list is a reminder of how much we do not know about the life of Paul and earliest Christianity. **Forty lashes minus one:** See Deut. 25:1–3. Synagogues administered corporal punishment to those they considered offenders against Jewish Law. Paul was punished not for preaching that Jews should abandon the Law, but for preaching to Gentiles, i.e., for attempting to bring Gentiles into the holy people of God without requiring them to keep the Law (1 Thess. 2:16). Being publicly whipped was a painful and humiliating experience. None of these beatings is mentioned in Acts. **Beaten with rods:** This was a Roman punishment, probably administered to Paul as a disturber of the peace. If he was a Roman citizen (see Acts 16:37–38; 21:39; 22:25–29; 23:27; 25:11–12), his citizenship did not protect him from such punishment. Only one beating is mentioned in Acts (16:37–38). **Stoned:** See Acts 14:19, where it is the result of a riot, not the Jewish capital punishment administered by stoning (see Lev. 20:2, 27; 24:14, 16, 23; Deut. 13:11; 17:5; 21:21, 24; 1 Sam. 21:10; Num. 15:35–36; Josh. 7:25; Deut. 22:21). The context here may indicate an unsuccessful judicial execution at the hands of a Jewish court. The litany of dangers, including not only physical suffering and deprivation, but **many a sleepless night** and **the daily pressure because of**

my anxiety for all the churches, shows that faith and prayer are not sedatives that numb one to worldly and church troubles.

11:33 I was let down in a basket: Over against the exalted image of themselves as "ministers of Christ" promoted by the rival apostles in Corinth, Paul pictures for them his undignified escape from Damascus (see Acts 9:23–25).

12:1–10
PAUL'S VISIONS AND REVELATIONS

12:1 Visions and revelations: The rival apostles claimed to have visionary experiences in which the risen Lord spoke to them and revealed the secrets of the heavenly world (see Revelation), and made these experiences the basis of their authority. Paul does not deny their claims. Such spiritual phenomena occur in and out of the church (see on 1 Cor. 12:1–3). The Corinthians were very interested in such phenomena and found the new leaders appealing. Paul too had such experiences (see 1 Cor. 14:1–19), but he did not parade them. His criterion asks what builds up the church, not what impresses, fascinates, and entertains people. Nonetheless, he is forced by his opponents' tactics to describe one of his own experiences, which he does reluctantly and still under the category of "foolishness."

12:2 A man in Christ (NIV): See 5:17. Paul is clearly referring to himself. Fourteen years ago: Since 2 Corinthians was written ca. 56 CE, this would be about 42 CE, several years before Paul's founding visit to Corinth. He had apparently not mentioned this experience in his preaching then. Paul had such "ecstatic" visionary experiences (see 1 Cor. 9:1; 15:8; Gal. 1:12; 2:1–2; Acts 16:9; 18:9; 22:17–21; 27:23), but apparently not very often, and considered them personal and private, not the substance of the gospel to be shared with others. **Was caught up:** By God. Paul is passive. He does not manipulate the experience by prayer, fasting, or spiritual disciplines, but experiences it at God's initiative. It is not repeatable at will. **The third heaven:** The apocalyptic worldview conceived the transcendent world to be a number of levels or stages, with God dwelling in the highest. Some apocalyptic documents such as 2 Enoch and the Apocalypse of Moses pictured seven heavens, with others portraying ten or as many as seventy-two. One other document speaks of three heavens (Testament of Levi), the view Paul seems to share here. He identified the third heaven with "paradise" (v. 4; see Luke 23:43; Rev. 2:7).

There is no consistent biblical map of the transcendent world, which was thought of in a variety of ways in the ancient world.

12:3 In the body or out of the body: In the predominant Greek way of thinking, the "soul" leaves the body for such otherworldly experiences. In the predominant biblical and Jewish way of thinking, the person is a unity, and heavenly journeys involve the whole person (see, e.g., Gen. 5:22–24; Sir. 44:16; 49:14; Heb. 11:5). Paul has no theory of how to understand the experience, but is certain of its reality.

12:4 No mortal is permitted to repeat: He had made the heavenly journey and seen and heard wonderful things, but this is not the content of his gospel. He is to preach the act of God in Christ, the gospel shared by all Christians, not his interesting personal spiritual experiences. (For another perspective, see Rev. 1–3, but see also Rev. 10:4; 14:2–3.)

12:5 Not boast, except of my weakness: See on 10:17; 11:21–30.

12:7 Exceptional character of the revelations: Some translations render the phrase "abundance of revelations" (so RSV). The variation depends in part on how modern editors punctuate the ancient manuscripts, which lacked punctuation. Paul emphasized the nature of the revelation, not their quantity. **Thorn was given me in the flesh:** That this was both given by God (this is the meaning of the passive voice) and a **messenger of Satan** is no contradiction. In biblical theology the one God is ultimately in control, but permits or makes use of Satan to accomplish his purposes (see Job 2:6–7). No one today knows the nature of Paul's "thorn," though his readers obviously did. Interpreters through the centuries have made various suggestions: the persecutions and opponents that opposed Paul's mission, moral temptations to which he was subject, or physical afflictions such as migraine headaches, leprosy, malaria, a speech impediment, a chronic disease, or a repulsive eye disease. Some physical problem is most likely, but we cannot further identify it (see Gal. 4:13–14).

12:8 Three times I appealed: Even Paul's prayers were not answered in the way he supposed was best for him and his mission (see Mark 14:32–42). It was only in retrospect that he understood the "thorn" as an aspect of God's will for him, but he did not at the time (or he would not have repeatedly prayed for its removal).

12:9 My grace is sufficient: This was God's answer to Paul's prayer. He received no "explanation"

along the lines that suffering was somehow good for him in that it strengthened character, developed patience, and the like. His only "answer" was the grace of God—which was enough. **My power is made perfect in weakness** (NIV): Paul's own life and ministry became an embodiment of the Christian message that the power of God is effective in the weakness of the crucified Jesus (13:4). On weakness as the dominant theme of this section, see 10:10; 11:21, 29–30; 12:5, 9–10; 13:3–4, 9.

12:11–13
THE SIGNS OF A TRUE APOSTLE

12:12 Signs and wonders: Just as Paul does not validate his own ministry by appealing to "visions and revelations," so he did not attempt to prove his apostleship by appealing to miracles. The rival apostles in Corinth did appeal to their miracle-working ability, just as they probably appealed to the miracle stories of Jesus, seeing their own ministry as a continuation of his miraculous deeds (see on 4:7–5:10; 10:2; 11:4). Paul does not dispute that his opponents work miracles. If one wants to appeal to such credentials, he also can point to miracles in his own ministry (see Rom. 15:19; 1 Cor. 2:4; Gal. 3:5; 1 Thess. 1:5; for Acts' portrayal of Paul as miracle worker, see on Acts 19:11). Paul has the double task of showing that by their criteria ("signs and wonders") he is as much an apostle as his opponents, but also showing that this is an inadequate criterion. **With great perseverance** (NIV)/**with utmost patience** (NRSV): The NIV is the better translation here. The point is not "patience" (NRSV), but that the miracles that occurred in Paul's ministry were in the context of suffering and service, in which they play a subordinate role.

12:14–21
PAUL'S CONCERN FOR
THE CORINTHIAN CHURCH

12:14 Third time: See Chronology in the introduction to 2 Corinthians.

12:16 Crafty . . . took you in by deceit: His opponents (willfully?) misinterpreted Paul's refusal to accept financial support for himself, claiming that his promotion of the offering for others (see chaps. 8–9) was in fact Paul's clever way of taking money from them without being obligated to them. See on 11:7.

12:19 Defending ourselves before you: See 1 Cor. 4:2–4. Paul loves the Corinthians dearly, but wants to be clear that what he is doing in these chapters is not an attempt to vindicate himself before a human court. He wants the Corinthians to return his love for them, but he knows he finally must give account to God and not to them (see on 1:12).

12:20–21 Quarreling ... sexual immorality: Paul gives two vice catalogues composed of traditional materials (see on Rom. 1:29). The first (v. 20) illustrates the effects of false leadership, the breakdown of trust and relationships, and theological squabbles. The second (v. 21) emphasizes moral, especially sexual sins, not previously a concern of this letter (but see 1 Cor. 5:1; 6:12–18; 10:8). If these sins are still present when he arrives, he will deal with them severely, but he hopes to have a happy reunion with the Corinthian congregation.

13:1–10
FURTHER WARNING

13:1 Third time: See Chronology in the introduction to 2 Corinthians. Paul regards his impending visit as a trial scene with himself as a judge, and speaks of his three visits as the "witnesses" required in biblical and Jewish tradition (see Deut. 19:15; Matt. 18:16). In Palestinian Jewish law of the time, the Deuteronomy text was sometimes understood to call for warning the offender two or three times before punishment.

13:4 Crucified in weakness: In Paul's view the earthly Jesus shared the weakness inherent in the human situation and was not filled with miraculous power that could have enabled him to escape death. His power was manifest in the post-Easter work of the Holy Spirit effective in the church (see Rom. 1:3–4; 15:19; Phil. 2:5–11).

13:5–8 Jesus Christ is in you: "You" is plural; modern individualistic readers tend to think of this as though Christ were in each believer, but Paul thinks more corporately of the congregation as a whole. See the imagery of the body of Christ (1 Cor. 12:12–27), in which Christ or the Spirit of Christ dwells (see Rom. 8:9–10 for the interchangeability of these terms). **Nothing against the truth:** Paul refers not to general or abstract truth, but to the truth of the gospel (as 4:2; 6:7).

13:11–13
FINAL GREETINGS AND BENEDICTION

13:12 Holy kiss: See on 1 Cor. 16:20.

13:13 The grace of the Lord Jesus Christ: This Trinitarian-sounding text is not a theoretical statement about the nature of God, though Paul, like other New Testament writers, speaks of God in ways that were later properly explicated in Trinitarian theology (see on 3:17; Matt. 28:19; 1 Cor. 8:6; 1 Pet. 1:2).

The Letter of Paul to the Galatians

INTRODUCTION

This letter contains some of the most sublime statements of the meaning of Christian faith and life found in the New Testament (e.g., 2:19–20; 3:26–28; 5:1, 22; 6:14–15), as well as some of its most angry and bitter denunciations (e.g., 5:12). Galatians, a key text in Martin Luther's sixteenth-century struggle to reform the church, has thus played an important role in Protestant understanding of the faith and has been called "the charter of Christian liberty." Yet like all the other New Testament letters, it is not a timeless tract or essay, but a real letter addressed to a particular situation, to a church threatened by issues such as the role that circumcision and food laws play in making one acceptable to God—issues that may at first seem remote from modern concerns. A more careful reading reveals that the letter addresses basic issues of Christian faith and life and holds great rewards for those who think themselves into hearing distance of its distinctive message.

Authorship and Integrity

Galatians is solidly among the undisputed letters attributed to Paul. We can be sure that we have the letter practically verbatim as it came from his hand.

The Burning Issue

Paul (perhaps with his coworkers) had founded the Galatian churches (4:13–14) and launched them on their new Christian life. It is not clear whether Paul had also visited them a second time (see 4:13). After Paul left for other mission work, Jewish Christian missionaries arrived who taught the new converts that Paul's version of the Christian faith was incomplete, that in order to be authentic members of the people of God they must be circumcised, as the mark of being included in the covenant people (5:2–6, 11; 6:12–13; see Gen. 17:9–14), and observe other Jewish religious laws (4:10). These itinerant teachers are not the same group of Jewish Christian missionaries that had troubled the Corinthian church, for circumcision was no issue at Corinth (see the introduction to 2 Corinthians,

and comments on 2 Cor. 10–13). Both groups, however, considered Paul an inadequate apostle, misleading his converts by relaxing the requirements for belonging to the people of God. Paul considers the message of the Jewish Christian evangelists in Galatia to be not merely a variation of the one gospel, which he would have celebrated and affirmed (see on 1 Cor. 3:21–23), but a substitute gospel, a false gospel, a perversion of the true gospel (1:6–7).

Galatia and the Galatians

The Gauls of France and the Galatians of the New Testament have a common ethnic ancestry. In the third century BCE Celtic tribes from central Europe migrated both westward into France and Britain and southward into central Asia Minor (modern Turkey). In the area around Ankara they established their own kingdom, which lasted until 25 BCE, when it was annexed by Rome and became part of a Roman province. The Romans called the province Galatia, and extended its boundaries southward to include regions not inhabited by ethnic Galatians. Thus in Paul's day Galatia could refer either to the multicultural Roman province or only to the old Galatian region in the north. In which of these areas were the churches to which the New Testament letter is addressed?

In the Acts account of Paul's missionary journeys prior to the Jerusalem Council of Acts 15, Paul and Barnabas established churches in the southern part of the province of Galatia (Iconium, Lystra, and Derbe, Acts 13–14), but did not at that time venture into ethnic Galatia in the north. They then later twice passed through the northern region of Galatia (Acts 16:6; 18:25). Acts never mentions churches in the north, regional Galatia, while Paul never refers to any churches in the southern part of the province of Galatia. Paul seems to address his readers as ethnic Galatians, belonging to the old region of Galatia in the north (3:1). Thus while some students of the life of Paul have argued that the letter was addressed to the "south Galatian churches," the letter itself is better understood on the presupposition that its readers were in churches in north Galatia. Now the majority opinion of scholars who have studied the issue, this is the perspective from which the following comments are written.

The question is more important than it might seem at first. It bears on the reconstruction of the outline and chronology of Paul's life, and the date of the letter (which could have been written early, even before the Jerusalem Council, only if addressed to churches in south Galatia). It is important for efforts to harmonize the account of Paul's life in Acts with data from his own letters. Especially, whether the letter is addressed to regional ("north") or provincial ("south") Galatia is important for understanding the letter's harshly polemical statements about "Judaism," the "law," the "two covenants," and the relation of the church to Judaism. There is no evidence of Jews in north Galatia in Paul's time, while south Galatia had a Jewish population and south Galatian churches would have Jewish Christians in their membership. However, there is no indication that there were any Jewish Christians among the Galatian churches to which this letter is addressed; their members had all previously been Gentiles (4:9). This would have been true only in north (ethnic) Galatia. What Galatians has to say is addressed to Gentile Christians who are now being told by Paul's opponents that they need to add various Jewish practices to their Christian faith. The questions of whether Jewish Christians should continue their traditional practices and how Jewish Christians and Gentile Christians may live and work together in one church are not addressed in Galatians.

The Setting of Galatians in Paul's Mission

Galatians cannot be absolutely dated, and even its relative dating with regard to Paul's other letters is disputed. Some advocates of the south Galatian theory (see above) regard Galatians as the earliest of Paul's letters, written before the Jerusalem Council. Most interpreters today are convinced that the letter was written later, at about the time of the Corinthian correspondence, either just before 1 Corinthians or just after the latest section of 2 Corinthians. The many similarities to 2 Corinthians and especially Romans makes it more likely that it was written between 2 Corinthians and Romans (see on 2:1, 14; Acts 11:29–30; 15:1–35; Outline of the Life of Paul in "Introduction to the Pauline Letters").

Outline

For Further Reading

Cousar, Charles B. *Galatians*. Interpretation: A Bible Commentary for Teaching and Preaching. Atlanta: John Knox Press, 1982.
Martyn, J. Louis. *Galatians*. Anchor Bible. New York: Doubleday, 1997.

COMMENTARY

1:1–5

SALUTATION

1:1–5 To the churches in Galatia: These verses form one long sentence, Paul's expansion of the typical brief Hellenistic letter form (see on 1 Thess. 1:1). Within Paul's own pattern, there are three distinctive features here:

1. The reference to the addressees is not expanded. Paul elsewhere says something warmly affirmative about the recipients (see Rom. 1:6–7; 1 Cor. 1:2; 2 Cor. 1:1; Phil. 1:1; here it is only the terse and distancing "To the churches of Galatia." This is the only Pauline letter written to a group of churches in an extensive area. Paul expects each congregation to gather and hear the letter read as part of the worship service (see below).

2. Paul elaborates his own identity only in a polemically negative way, **sent neither by human commission nor from human authorities**. His opponents are teaching the Galatians that Paul has no direct authority from God or

Christ, but is only a secondary apostle authorized by the church in Antioch or Jerusalem (see Acts 13:1–2; 14:4, 6; 2 Cor. 8:23), and that he had compromised the teaching he had received from them. Paul's insistence on his own apostleship is not a matter of ego, status, or authoritarian personality, but of the truth of the gospel. The fundamental problem at Galatia was not their rejection of Paul, but their perversion of the gospel. The truth of the faith Paul proclaimed was related to the issue of whether he had been called as an authentic apostle, or his message was only his own secondhand alteration of the Christian message he had received from the "real" apostles in Jerusalem. The classical Christian creeds rightly spoke of the Christian community as "one holy catholic *apostolic* church." On the importance of the apostles for Christian faith, see on Luke 6:12–13; Acts 1:21–22; 1 Cor. 9:27; 2 Cor. 10–13.

3. Paul's typical pronouncement of **grace and peace** is expanded into a liturgical doxology concluding with the **Amen** in which the congregation is expected to join. This indicates that Paul wrote his letters not for private or individual reading, but to be read aloud in the church's worship. They are the substitute for his personal presence (Gal. 4:20), the sermon he would preach if he were there. Galatians (like all Paul's other letters) is not merely personal correspondence, but a launching of the apostolic message into the worship of congregations gathered in the presence of God, the church called to hear the Word of God that comes through the proclamation of the apostolic gospel.

1:4 Who gave himself for our sins: The first clause seems to reflect traditional Christian material and is probably extracted from the church's liturgy, with which the Galatians were already acquainted. Thinking of Christ as the divine response to the human predicament of "sins" (plural) is pre-Pauline tradition (see 1 Cor. 15:3). Paul affirms this traditional view that the saving event is God's act in Christ for the forgiveness of sins. Paul's own formulation of the human problem is that of being enslaved by Sin (singular) thought of as a power; the divine saving event is the liberation from this oppressive power as expressed in the following clause, which presents Christ as the one who gave himself **to set us free from the present evil age**. This saving event is **through Jesus Christ and God the Father** (v. 1). Three times in this brief passage Paul writes of God as "Father." This emphasis is not a matter of patri-

archy or the masculinity of God, but is in response to the agitators at Galatia who insisted the new Gentile Christians must become "children of Abraham" by being circumcised and keeping the Jewish law. Over against "Father Abraham" Paul puts "God our Father" as the only One who gives life. The juxtaposition of Jesus Christ and God does not mean that two different figures cooperate in the saving act, but that God and Christ are functionally identified—it is the one God who is at work in the Christ event (see on 2 Cor. 5:19–21). Thus the Christ who gave himself for our sins was not offering a sacrifice to a third party, appeasing an angry God, but represented God himself acting for human salvation.

1:6–2:21
PART ONE—THE VALIDITY OF PAUL'S APOSTLESHIP

1:6–10
THERE IS NO OTHER GOSPEL

The body of the letter begins abruptly, without the expected thanksgiving section (see on 1 Thess. 1:2).

1:6 So quickly: There seems to have been an extended period during which the church remained faithful to the gospel as preached by Paul (5:7), but then with surprising suddenness they had abandoned, or were in the process of abandoning, their original faith and replaced it with the new teaching. **The one who called you in the grace of Christ:** God, not Paul. Again, God and Christ are spoken of together in a way that almost identifies them (see above). The same God who called Paul to be an apostle called the Galatians to be Christians (see on 1 Cor. 1:2; Rom. 1:1; 6:7).

1:7 A different gospel—which is really no gospel at all (NIV): Paul launches immediately into the main problem. There is only one gospel of the saving act of God in Jesus Christ. The attempt of the new missionaries in Galatia to supplement the gospel Paul preached had actually resulted in changing it into a nongospel or antigospel. From Paul's response to their message in the rest of Galatians ("mirror reading") and from parallel texts from Jewish Christianity, we may formulate the message of the new teachers in Galatia somewhat as follows:

God originally called Abraham, gave him the covenant of circumcision, and promised that all nations would be blessed in him (Gen. 12:1–3; 17:1–14). This covenant with Abraham was confirmed by the giving of the law to Israel, Abraham's descendants, by Moses on Mount Sinai (Exod. 19–24), in which God's people were given the moral way of life and special holy days and festivals to observe to show that they were God's people. Now God has confirmed the law by sending the Messiah, Jesus, who opened the way of inclusion of the Gentiles in the covenant with Abraham and the people of Israel. The law was originally given by God with the assistance of angels (Deut. 33:2; see Acts 7:38), just as angels were present when the promise was made to Abraham (Gen. 18:1–2; see 19:1). At the climax of history, the final good news that God is sending forth his law to all the world will be proclaimed by an angel (see Rev. 14:6). We are the messengers of this final announcement of salvation, but Paul has given you only a compromised version of it, having omitted the requirements of the law that make you members of the people of God. You already believe in Christ, but if you want to be saved and belong to the true people of God, you must keep the primary commandments that identify God's covenant people in this world: circumcision, the food laws, and the holy days and festivals. Furthermore, unless new Christians are taught to live by the law of God, they will be overcome by evil influences and immorality will abound.

The new evangelists were sincere missionaries who supported their message with biblical interpretation and their claim that they represented the mother church in Jerusalem. Their message was attractive to the new converts of Galatia. It was not merely a matter of confusing the new converts, but of threatening them with loss of salvation. The expression **some who are confusing you** is hardly strong enough; the phrase is translated more literally as "the troublers," or "the agitators" (see 5:12, "those who unsettle you"). These derogatory terms, of course, are from Paul's own perspective. They saw themselves as sincere missionary evangelists representing the traditional faith of the Jerusalem church from which Paul had deviated.

1:8–9 An angel from heaven: This may be only exaggerated rhetoric emphasizing the point

that the gospel itself is the authority, not Paul or anyone else, not even a heavenly being. More likely, it reflects the claim of Paul's opponents that their message is validated by angels, just as the law originally was (see above and on 3:19). The account of the expansion of Christianity in Acts portrays the early Christian mission emanating from the Jerusalem apostles as guided by angels (Acts 5:19; 8:26; 10:3, 7, 22, 11:13; 12:7–11). Paul himself never had anything positive to say about angels (see on Luke 1:10–12; Acts 5:19; Rom. 8:38). **Let that one be accursed:** This is not merely an emotional outburst or personal vindictiveness. It assumes the congregation assembled in the presence of God (see on 1:3), who alone can place those who pervert the gospel under a curse (see 4:30; 1 Cor. 5:3–5; 14:38). **What we proclaimed . . . what you received:** The formulae used are similar to those of 1 Cor. 15:3. The gospel Paul preaches is not his personal formulation, but the authentic gospel handed on in the church's tradition.

1:10 Seeking human approval: Paul makes a general point—the church is not in the business of doing market research, determining what people want, and then delivering it to them in order to grow numerically. But the point is also specific to the situation in Galatia. Paul's opponents understood the gospel of grace as proclaimed by him to be a watering down of the strict requirements of the law in order to gain human approval. They understood themselves as adhering to the strict requirements of circumcision, keeping the food laws, and holy days and festivals necessary to belong to Israel, the people of God. This strictness was in fact more appealing to many people, then and now, than the radical gospel of grace proclaimed by Paul, which seemed not "religious" or "spiritual" enough. **Pleasing people . . . slave of Christ:** As the NRSV note indicates, "servant" here is "slave." While in Galatians Paul usually presents slavery in a derogatory light, as the opposite of Christian freedom, like Jesus (Matt. 6:24) he does not hesitate to present the Christian life as slavery to Christ. As in the first of the Ten Commandments (Exod. 20:3), *exclusive* service to God is the point. Moses had addressed Pharaoh in the name of God, "Let my people go, so that they may worship me" (Exod. 9:1). They were delivered from bondage in Egypt in order to be servants of God. Human existence as such is finite, "enslaved" existence. We are not the masters of our own fate, the captains of our own souls; to want to be otherwise is to reject being a creature and to want to be "like God" (Gen. 3:1–7). Our only choice is which master we will serve. Service to money (Matt. 6:24) and self gives the illusion of freedom; it is nonetheless demeaning slavery. Faith in Christ delivers one from that slavery, to be a "slave" of Christ, not to selfish, individualistic "freedom" (see Rom. 6:15–23).

1:11–24
THE DIVINE ORIGIN OF PAUL'S GOSPEL

This section (through 2:14) is the most extensive "biographical" account Paul gives and is of supreme importance in reconstructing the outline of his life and ministry. Yet Paul does not write it for biographical purposes, as though he were composing his memoirs. His twofold purpose is to document (1) how *little* contact he had had with the Jerusalem apostles (1:11–24) and (2) that his message is in harmony with theirs and recognized by them, and is not an alternative to the gospel as proclaimed by them (2:1–10).

1:11 Not of human origin: Paul's point is that the ultimate source and authority of his message is from God and manifest in his encounter with the risen Christ. He is not merely a secondhand apostle, dependent on the other apostles, but was called to be an apostle directly by Christ himself (see 1 Cor. 9:1; 15:8–10; 2 Cor. 4:6). Though Paul here emphasizes his direct call by God, this does not eliminate mediation of the contents of the Christian faith to him by church tradition and others who were Christians before him. Both he and the Galatians are called by God; both he and they also receive the faith as mediated by church tradition (1:1, 6, 8–9; 5:8, 13; 1 Cor. 11:23–26; 15:3–5; 1 Thess. 1:5; 2:12–13; 4:1–2). See Acts' combination of these two dimension of Paul's call, 9:1–19, though the author of Acts emphasizes human mediation of the gospel to Paul more than Paul himself does.

1:13 My earlier life in Judaism: Paul's present stance toward the law is not the result of ignorance. He was a Pharisee thoroughly educated in both the law and in the authoritative traditions that constituted its interpretation (see 2 Cor. 11:22–25; Phil. 3:4–7). **Persecuting the church of God:** Paul did not persecute Christians as such, but only Jewish Christians. His persecution was not because they were Christians, but because they were unfaithful Jews. He attempted to root out from the synagogue

those Jews who had come to Christian faith. Such Christians were relaxing the law, blurring the boundaries that separated the Jewish people from Gentiles, and thus were seen by him as a threat to the very existence of the people God had chosen to be witnesses to the one God, a "light to the nations" (Isa. 42:6; 49:6). Christians were also proclaiming that one accursed by the law was actually God's Messiah (see 3:13 below). For the pre-Christian Paul, the Christian group posed the issue of whether God's final revelation was to be found in the law or in the crucified and risen Jesus of Nazareth. After his conversion, Paul the Jewish Christian experienced from zealous Jews the same kind of discipline and persecution in which he had previously participated (see 1 Thess. 2:14–16; 2 Cor. 11:24–26; Matt. 23:29–36; John 16:1–2; Acts 7:54–8:1; 9:29; 12:1–3; 14:19–20; 21:27–32; 23:12).

1:15–16 God, who had set me apart: God is the subject of this long sentence. Paul does not discuss his call in terms of his feelings or external circumstances. His call to be an apostle was at the initiative of God, not the fulfillment of his own spiritual quest. He uses the language of the call of the prophets (Jer. 1:5; Isa. 49:1–6) to portray his own call. But Paul's call to be a Christian and apostle was a conversion in the sense of personal transformation. Paul's "conversion" was not the conversion from one religion to another, not from Judaism to Christianity. Paul remained a Jew and did not see his confession of Christian faith to be an abandonment or rejection of Judaism, though it was a reorientation and reevaluation of priorities he had once held (see 2 Cor. 11:22–25; Phil. 3:4–7).

Reveal his Son to me: The phrase can also be translated "in me." Paul came to an insight on the true identity of Jesus and his role in God's plan, not on the basis of common sense or historical research, but as a matter of God's revelation; this is true for every Christian (see 1 Cor. 12:3; Matt. 16:17), even though Paul's direct encounter with the risen Lord is not a model for others. **Set apart . . . called . . . reveal** may be a sequence or an emphatic way of speaking of the same experience three different ways. **Proclaim him among the Gentiles:** This expresses the purpose of Paul's call. Paul does not speak of the results of his conversion as "peace and joy for me" or the like, but of mission.

Did not confer with any human being: The main subject and verb of this long sentence is found here. Paul's main point is that his gospel is not derived from and dependent on others. See the somewhat different picture in Acts 9:10–19. In Acts, Luke is concerned to show the continuity between Paul's mission and the church prior to him; Paul himself is here concerned to show its discontinuity.

1:17 Into Arabia . . . and returned: Not found in the Acts account. See Figure 13. Paul does not tell us what his activities there were. Arabia is not the desert, but the populated area south and east of Damascus, ruled by King Aretas. Since Aretas tried to arrest Paul, he was probably engaged in missionary activity there (see 2 Cor. 11:32). We should not think romantically of a quiet retreat in which Paul prepared for his future ministry by withdrawal and mediation. He began immediately to proclaim the faith he had once persecuted, both in Arabia and Damascus. This period lasted for three years.

1:18 Then after three years I did go up to Jerusalem: There were no "three years in Arabia." This is Paul's first visit to Jerusalem after his call. In the Acts picture of Paul's life, he had both studied there as a young man (Acts 22:3) and persecuted the church in Jerusalem (Acts 8:1–3; 9:1–2; 26:9–11). Paul's letters give no indication that he had ever been in Jerusalem prior to this visit (see 1:22). From his letters alone, one gets the impression that Paul had been living in Damascus at the time of his conversion and that his persecution of Jewish Christians began with the Damascus synagogue of which he was a part (see on Acts 9:1–2). **To visit Cephas:** "Cephas" is the Aramaic word for "rock," as "Peter" is the Greek word. Paul almost always uses the Aramaic word, though the Gospel and Acts use the Greek word (see on Matt. 16:18; John 1:42). We should not romantically picture Paul, who had not known the earthly Jesus, as zealously inquiring of Peter what Jesus was "really" like. This is the very point of view advocated by his opponents, against which he is defending himself. Paul's understanding of the Christian faith was not greatly concerned with the life and teachings of the earthly Jesus. Though Paul could have learned much from Peter during this two-week conversation, picking up interesting stories and sayings from the earthly Jesus was not central to his theology, which focused on God's act in the death and resurrection of Jesus (1 Cor. 2:2; 2 Cor. 8:9; 10:1; 11:4; Phil. 2:5–11). During the meeting, Paul probably did at least as much talking as listening.

1:19 Except James the Lord's brother: James, who did not believe in Jesus during his min-

istry (John 7:5) became an apostle on the basis of an appearance of the risen Lord to him (1 Cor. 15:7) and later a leader of the Jerusalem church (Gal. 1:19; 2:9) and then its sole leader (Acts 12:17; 15:13; 21:18).

1:21 Into the regions of Syria and Cilicia: After leaving Damascus, Paul became a missionary apostle of the Antioch church, along with Barnabas, carrying on his mission to Gentiles in the area around Antioch and Tarsus, his home town. This is difficult to identify with the "first missionary journey" of Acts 13–14, which entered the southern part of the province of Galatia (see the introduction to Galatians).

2:1–10
PAUL'S MEETING WITH
THE JERUSALEM LEADERS

Paul here describes the conference in Jerusalem discussing the relation of Paul's Gentile mission to the Jewish mission conducted under the leadership of the Jerusalem apostles. See Acts 15:1–35 for Luke's later account of this same meeting, more oriented to the central role of Jerusalem in the expanding mission of the church.

2:1 After fourteen years: It is not clear whether the period is counted from the last visit or from Paul's call. Since parts of years were reckoned as years, the total period from Paul's call to this meeting could be from twelve to seventeen years. Paul's point: so far from being dependent on the Jerusalem leadership, Paul was in Jerusalem only twice during this extended period, and each time his independent mission was acknowledged by the Jerusalem leaders. **Barnabas** was a respected missionary in both the Jerusalem and Antioch churches (see Acts 4:36; 9:27; 11:22–30) and, along with Paul, conducted a mission tour sponsored by the Antioch church just prior to the conference (Acts 13:1–14:28). **Titus** was a Gentile Christian apparently converted in the process of the preceding mission. Though prominent in Paul's mission to Asia Minor, Macedonia, and Greece (2 Cor. 2:13; 7:6, 13–14; 8:6, 16, 23, 18), he is not mentioned in Acts.

2:2 In response to a revelation: Paul emphasizes that he was not summoned or called on the carpet by the Jerusalem authorities, as though he had to give account to them, but went at the initiative of God. **Though [only] in a private meeting:** There is no word "only" in the Greek text. Though ambiguous, the Greek is probably better translated to mean that after a meeting with the whole church, Paul also had a private meeting with the leaders. It is the leaders who decide. **To make sure that I was not running . . . in vain:** Though Paul considers himself in no way subordinate to the Jerusalem apostles, the unity of the one church of God is crucial to him. There can be two parallel missions, but only one church. Just as there cannot be two Israels, there cannot be two churches, each with its own gospel and mission. Thus Paul acknowledges that his mission would be in vain—in the sense that it would result in splitting the one church—if it were not recognized by the Jerusalem leadership as initiated and empowered by God.

2:3 Titus . . . not compelled to be circumcised: Whether Gentile Christians must be circumcised, i.e., become Jews, in order to belong to the one people of God was the issue between Paul and his Galatian opponents (see the introduction to Galatians; comments on 1:7).

2:4 False brothers (NIV): Not Peter or James, but other influential leaders of the Jerusalem church who argued, like the new Galatian teachers, for the necessity of circumcision. **To spy on the freedom:** The "false brothers" had apparently investigated the law-free mission of the Antioch church in which Barnabas and Paul were engaged, and now bring their objections to the Jerusalem leaders, attempting to discredit the new "open membership" practice on the mission field.

2:6 Supposed to be acknowledged leaders: Paul uses the same Greek expression three times (2:2, 6, 9), apparently reflecting a title of honor used in Jerusalem. While Paul is ambivalent about the title, the Greek phrase does not have the same sarcastic ring as the English translation. **God shows no partiality:** This key principle of Pauline theology (see Gal. 3:27–28) is reflected in his view of church leadership. Paul does not exalt himself, nor does he acknowledge the exalted status of others. Authority resides in the gospel message itself as the vehicle of the word of God, not in particular persons. **Those leaders contributed nothing to me:** That is, they made no additions to the Pauline gospel, such as the requirement of circumcision or adherence to the food laws, as the new Galatian teachers were attempting to do.

2:7–9 Peter: Except for this passage, Paul always elsewhere uses the Aramaic name Cephas. This is one of several indications that these two verses echo traditional material already formulated, reflecting an older agreement that acknowledged the legitimacy of Paul's mission to the Gentiles—perhaps formulated at the time of the

visit with Peter in 1:18 and here affirmed by all the Jerusalem leaders. **Acknowledged pillars:** "Pillar" was a traditional honorary title in Judaism, where for example Abraham, Isaac, and Jacob were considered the pillars on which Israel was built. The metaphor in which Peter was the rock on which the church was constructed is here expanded to include other Jerusalem apostles; Paul considers Christ the only foundation and is leery of both titles applied to human beings (see Matt. 16:18; 1 Cor. 3:5–11).

Recognized the grace that had been given to me: They acknowledged the legitimacy of Paul's mission to Gentiles, which did not require them to *begin* keeping the law in order to become Christians, as parallel to the Jewish mission, which did not require Jews to *stop* keeping the law in order to become Christians. The point was not that they authorized Paul's mission, but that they recognized God had authorized both missions as the mission of the one church. **Right hand of fellowship:** The outward symbol of the unity of the one church. They did not reject him as competitor, compromiser, or destroyer, but gave him their blessing as a partner.

2:10 Remember the poor: The meaning is concrete: Paul is encouraged to collect an offering from the Gentile churches to help the poverty stricken members of the church in Judea. Paul was glad to do this; it constituted no compromise to his law-free gospel, helped needy people in the name of Christ, and provided a concrete expression of the unity of Jews and Gentiles in the one church of God (see 1 Cor. 16:1–4; 2 Cor. 8–9; Rom. 15:25–29).

2:11–14
PAUL REBUKES PETER AT ANTIOCH

2:11 When Cephas came: We do not know whether the visit was incidental, part of a mission trip, or to receive offerings from the Antioch church as promised in 2:9. **Antioch:** An integrated church with Jewish Christian and Gentile Christian members (see on Acts 11:20–24). It was not unlawful for Jews to eat with Gentiles, but Jews could not eat nonkosher food and had to avoid contact that would result in ritual impurity (see on Mark 7:1–23). Their eating together (which would have included the eucharistic meals) involved the Jewish Christians' relaxing of biblical and Jewish food laws. Peter participated in these common meals.

2:12–13 Certain people came from James: They carried a message from James, the brother of

Figure 13. A Comparison of Paul's Missionary Career as Represented in Galatians and Acts
(See also chart at Acts 15:35)

	Galatians	Acts
1. Early life in Judaism		
a. zealous, "advanced"	1:14	7:58; 8:1
b. persecutor	1:13	8:3; 9:1–2
2. Call	1:15	9:3–19
a. set apart before born	1:15	
b. not human origin, not taught	1:11	call not of human origin; *Ananias instructs him*
c. revelation of Jesus Christ	1:12	
d. reveal Son to me	1:15	
d. to proclaim among Gentiles	1:16	
3. After call		*9:19 Damascus "several days"*
a. not human beings	1:16	*powerful preaching*
b. not to Jerusalem	1:17	
c. to Arabia	1:17	
d. back to Damascus	1:17	*9:23 Damascus "some time"; plot to kill him* *2 Cor. 11:33 through wall in basket*
4. Jerusalem #1	1:18	
a. after three years	1:18	*9:26 Return to Jerusalem seems to be soon*
b. saw only Peter, James	1:18	
c. fifteen days	1:18	
d. did not know Judean churches	1:21	*9:28–30 "went in and out"; plot to kill him; sent to Tarsus* *11:25–26 integrated Antioch church; Barnabas brings Saul to Antioch* *11:27–30 famine visit with Barnabas (not Titus)*
e. into regions of Syria and Galatia		"first missionary journey" of Acts 13–14 here?
5. Jerusalem #2		(chap. 15)
a. after fourteen years	2:1	
b. with Barnabas and Titus	2:1	15:2 "Paul, Barnabas, and others"
c. by revelation	2:2	
d. private meeting with "pillars"	2:2	15:4 "apostles and elders" (*Paul not "apostle"*)
e. Titus accepted without circumcision	2:3	
f. false (brothers) believers	2:4	
g. pillars added nothing but "remember the poor"	2:6, 10	*15:20 added "apostolic decree"*
h. division of labor/right hand of fellowship	2:9	
6. Confrontation in Antioch	2:12–14	No Peter/Paul confrontation; in Acts they look alike

The above chart makes the differences in the two chronologies apparent. A harmonization that would remove the apparent contradictions would require:

1. Identifying the Jerusalem visit of Gal. 2 with Acts 11:27–30 rather than the Acts 15 visit.
2. Identifying the recipients of the letter as residents of south Galatia (provincial Galatia), so that the letter could have been written after the "first missionary journey" but prior to the Jerusalem Council of Acts 15, making it the earliest of Paul's extant letters (see introduction to Galatians).
3. Imposing the Acts picture of Paul on Paul's letters (see introduction to the Pauline Letters and introduction to Acts).

Most scholars regard all three as historically improbable and/or theologically illegitimate, and thus prefer to let the tensions stand unharmonzied.

Jesus, now the primary leader of the Jerusalem church. Their message apparently indicated that Peter's joining in the common meals was a hindrance to the mission to observant Jews, of which Peter was supposed to be the leader and model (2:9). This incident should be evaluated in terms of Gal. 2:1–10, without reference to Acts 10–11, written from a later perspective harmonizing the earlier views of Peter and Paul (see there). **Kept himself separate:** He reverted to the lifestyle of an observant Jewish Christian, appropriate to the leader of the Jewish mission. **The circumcision faction:** The group within the Jerusalem church that advocated circumcision of Gentile Christians (elsewhere called the "false brothers" by Paul, 2:4).

2:13 This hypocrisy: Peter saw himself as acting sincerely; Paul saw this as a conscious compromise of the agreement worked out in 2:10. Apparently, that agreement had envisioned two parallel missions, equally valid, but did not foresee the problem of a mixed congregation of Jewish and Gentile Christians and thus did not address the issue of how an integrated congregation would conduct its common life. Paul understood that the unity of the one church of God required Jewish Christians in an integrated church to relax the food laws, and that their effort to maintain them would compel Gentile Christians either to form a separate church or to conform to the Jewish food laws. Either option was impossible in Paul's view: although there could be two distinct missions, there could not be two separate churches. Jewish Christians could continue the observance of the food laws, but could not impose them on Gentile Christians as the price of a united church. In all this Paul saw a reintroduction of the law as a condition of acceptance by God. Since Peter did not believe *this*, Paul considered his withdrawal a matter of hypocrisy.

2:14 I said to Cephas before them all: Paul reports his rebuke of Peter "before them all," aware that his letter will be read to the Galatian churches in the presence of their new teachers. Paul cites his speech to Peter, which really addresses the Galatian teachers, in the presence of the whole church. **Compel the Gentiles to live like Jews:** This was the issue for Paul, imposing the law on Gentiles as a condition of acceptance by God and belonging to the church. These two aspects are inseparable. The issue is corporate fellowship, not individual salvation. Paul is not against the

law or Judaism as such, but opposes the imposition of the law on Gentile Christians.

2:15–21
JEWS AND GENTILES ARE JUSTIFIED THROUGH CHRIST'S DEATH

Since ancient manuscripts had no quotation marks, it is not clear where Paul's citation of his speech to Peter ends (see the different punctuation in NRSV and NIV). It is clear that what began as a description of a there-and-then encounter between Paul and Peter modulates into a here-and-now address to the Galatians (cf. John 3:1–21).

2:15–16 We ourselves are Jews by birth: Initially, Paul and Peter as Jewish Christians, but now including the new teachers in Galatia (not the Galatians themselves, who are Gentiles). **Justified not by the works of the law:** Already as Jews and Jewish Christians, they did not consider the law the means of being accepted by God, which has always been a matter of God's grace. **But through faith in Jesus Christ:** The Greek phrase used here (and in 2:20; 3:22; Phil. 3:9; Rom. 3:22, 26) is ambiguous, and can mean either faith *in* Christ (= a human act) or the faith *of* Christ (= Jesus' faithfulness even to the point of death, representing God's act for us). There is no doubt that Paul considers the human act of faith to be essential, as in the latter part of this verse. But here the phrase may refer to Jesus' own faithfulness. Paul does not contrast the human act of keeping the law, which does not save, with the human act of believing, which does save; he contrasts the human act of keeping the law with God's act in giving over Christ to die for human sins and Christ's faithfulness in doing this. **No one will be justified:** An echo of Ps. 143:2. Paul argues that the view that one is justified not by the law but by the free grace of God is not a Christian innovation, but was already a matter of Hebrew Scripture and Jewish faith.

2:17–21 Is Christ then a servant of sin?: The logic may seem strange to us. Paul is apparently reflecting the charges made by the new Galatian teachers to the effect that Paul's encouraging Gentile Christians to live without the law removes the guards against sin, and that his law-free gospel of grace thus makes Christ an agent of sin (see Rom. 6:1–11). **By no means!:** See on Rom. 3:4. **I have been crucified with Christ:** Paul's representative "I" is not an expression of his own subjective piety, but speaks for every Christian (see Rom 7:7–25). In the crucifixion of Christ, God acted to end the power of sin, law, and death, and included all people in this cosmic victory. The death of Christ meant the death of the old world, to which Paul and all belong, and the dawn of the new creation. **21 I do not nullify the grace of God:** This is what the new teachers in Galatia are doing by "supplementing" faith in Christ with observance of the law. But there can be no such thing as "grace plus a requirement." If something has to be added, grace is no longer grace, but acceptance with God has become a matter of human achievement. Paul's radical understanding of grace is still upsetting to many Christians, who wish to do something themselves to be sure of their acceptance by God.

For this whole section of Galatians, see Romans 1:18–8:39, where the polemical formulation of justification here argued in Galatians is set forth in a more reflective manner. Romans was written shortly after Galatians and represents Paul's own elaboration and commentary on the views he argues here.

3:1–5:12
PART TWO—LAW AND FAITH

The previous section, 1:6–2:21, argues that Paul's own history validates his gospel. This section shifts from narrative to theological arguments from Scripture.

3:1–5
THE EXPERIENCE OF THE SPIRIT

This unit is transitional: as Paul's experience validates the truth of his gospel, so does the experience of the Galatians.

3:1 Foolish Galatians: Lack of understanding, not deficient IQ, is the problem. The address "Galatians" indicates the addressees live in regional, ethnic Galatia (see the introduction to Galatians). **Who has bewitched you?:** Their lack of understanding is pictured as the result of someone having cast a spell on them; the modern equivalent is brainwashing. The question is rhetorical; both Paul and the Galatians know well it is their new teachers who had changed their understanding of the nature of Christian faith and life. **Jesus Christ publicly exhibited as crucified:** Paul's message centered on God's act in the death and resurrection of Jesus (see 1 Cor. 1:21–25; 15:3–5). This phrase does not mean that Paul elaborated the gruesome details of crucifixion—they already knew what crucifixion meant—but that his preaching kept before their mind's eye the faithfulness of Jesus in giving himself up to death (see on 2:16) as the central element of the gospel.

3:2 Works of the law . . . believing what you heard: Paul appeals to their own remembered experience. They had already encountered the reality of the Holy Spirit in the life of the church prior to the arrival of the new teachers. This was not a matter of their own attainment, but of God's gift and act. The emphasis is on what they heard, God's act in Christ, not on their own act of believing. As above, Paul does not contrast two human acts (working and believing), but all human acts and God's own act (see further on Rom. 4:1–25).

3:4–5 Experience so much: The NRSV is more accurate than the NIV ("suffered"). It may be that in fact the Galatians had already suffered for their faith (see 1 Thess. 1:14), but Paul's point is that they had already experienced the life of the Spirit prior to the arrival of the new teachers. We do not know the particulars of the earliest days of the Galatian churches, but they and Paul did. Whatever their experiences were (miracles, tongues, personal transformation), it was convincing evidence that they had entered fully into the Christian life through Paul's preaching, and did not need religious "supplements."

3:6–18
THE PROMISE TO ABRAHAM

Here Paul begins an involved argument from Scripture. Some of the texts introduced and Paul's interpretations may seem strained to us, but he is using the methods of interpretation common in his day (see excursus, "New Testament Interpretation of the Old Testament," at 1 Cor. 15:3). He presumes a knowledge of the texts among his recent Gentile converts, probably indicating that he is giving his own counter-interpretation of texts already used by his opponents in Galatia and familiar to his readers. He repeatedly cites from the law (Gen. 12:3; 15:6; Deut. 21:23; 27:26), showing that his own gospel does not reject the law but regards it as the authoritative revelation of God. While the Scripture as a whole could be called "the Law," the phrase refers specifically to the first five books of the Bible, the Torah attributed to Moses.

3:6 Abraham believed God: Paul cites Gen. 15:6, quoting a passage from the Law (the Pentateuch, the first five books of the Bible). The covenant with Abraham, of which circumcision was the sign and seal, had apparently been introduced by the new teachers. Paul's point is that salvation, acceptance with God, has always been by faith. The law itself had always indicated only one way of salvation, and it was not by keeping the law. God has not changed the plan of salvation, as though the law once granted justification, but now faith is the way of salvation. Abraham's faith was not a "work," an achievement that he offered God, but was itself the result of God's act and initiative that called forth Abraham's response. Again, the contrast is not between human working and human believing, but between human achievement and [trust in] God's act.

3:7 Children of Abraham (NIV): Paul's opponents apparently quoted Gen. 12:3, arguing that the Gentile Galatians could become Abraham's children only by becoming Jews, by being circumcised and keeping the law. Paul argues that it was always those who shared the faith of Abraham who were his "children," not those who were his physical descendants (see Rom. 9:6–13).

3:10 Under a curse: His opponents had probably already brought up the threat of God's curse found in the Bible (e.g., Deut. 27–28). Paul argues that law religion as such places one under curse rather than blessing. This text has often been understood to mean that the law requires perfect obedience in order to grant life and salvation, but since "nobody's perfect," the law actually condemns everyone, placing them under a curse. Paul does not say this. He does not understand the law to be a way of salvation, even if one could keep it perfectly (see Phil. 3:4b–6). His point is rather that law as such does not grant life, but pronounces a curse on all, whether they "keep" it or not (3:21). Blessing comes from God, but curse comes from the law. The opponents will reply "But the law comes from God." Paul deals with this objection in 3:19–4:7.

3:11–12 Live by faith: Paul cites Hab. 2:4. See on Rom. 1:17. **The law does not rest on faith:** The problem with the law is not simply that no one can keep it perfectly, but that it operates on another basis than grace and trust; it is a matter of doing, not trusting. Doing the law establishes a claim, an entirely different kind of relationship from personal trust. Law, even when it is kept, does not give life, 3:21. **On the contrary:** Paul cites Lev. 18:5, in which the law itself says that life comes by doing its commandments. Paul sees this as a false way of salvation, the negative voice of the law promising what it cannot deliver.

3:13 Christ redeemed us: Set us free from slavery (see 1:4, 10). Salvation is not only forgiveness,

but deliverance. **Becoming a curse for us:** See on 2 Cor. 5:21. The text Paul cites from Deut. 21:23 forbade Israelites from exposing the corpse of an executed criminal by hanging it up for public display for more than one day, since such an exhibition would be punished by God's cursing the whole land. Paul's selective interpretation understands **one who hangs on a tree** to refer to crucifixion, and makes the curse come from the law, not from God.

3:15 Brothers and sisters: Despite his harsh language (3:1), Paul still addresses them as beloved fellow members of the family of God (4:6; see on 1 Thess. 2:7; 4:9). **A person's will:** In Greek the same word is used for "covenant" in the religious sense and for "last will and testament" in the secular sense. Paul explains the biblical meaning by an illustration from its secular use. His point throughout is that God's covenant is not a contract negotiated by two or more parties, but, like a will, the unilateral act of one party. Like a will that bestows property on the heirs, God's covenant is a matter of promise and grace, not a matter of a compulsory law that forces the testator against his or her will, just as it is not a matter of achievement that entitles the heirs to claim it on the basis of their accomplishment. **No one:** A different party from the testator. **Adds to it or annuls it:** A will can be changed only by the testator. Another person cannot later annul or add stipulations to the will. God originally made the covenant ("testament," "will") with Abraham as a matter of grace and promise. The law that came later cannot annul or add provisions to God's promise.

3:16 To your offspring, that is, to one person: Literally "seed," meaning descendants in the collective sense in the passages to which Paul is referring (Gen. 13:15; 17:7–10; 24:7). Paul was of course aware of this collective meaning, and elsewhere in this same passage he interpreted these verses in that sense himself (3:29; see Rom. 4:13–17). Here, however, he understands the passage as pointing to Christ (see excursus, "New Testament Interpretation of the Old Testament," at 1 Cor. 15:3). His point throughout is that God's promise to Abraham points to Christ, and that those "in Christ" are heirs of the promise. The "one person" corresponds to the one Christ (3:28) into whom Christians are baptized, and ultimately to the one God (3:20).

3:17 Four hundred thirty years later: The promise was made to Abraham (Gen. 12:3), but the law did not appear until the time of Moses and the exodus (Exod. 19–23). In Jewish tradition, Abraham already kept the law; indeed, the law had existed forever, and God himself studied it. Paul relativizes the law by having it come on the stage only relatively late in God's plan and, in contrast to the standard phraseology in the Old Testament and Judaism, never says it was "given" by God.

3:18 If the inheritance comes from the law: The Old Testament and Judaism had traditionally understood law and covenant together. Paul contrasts them, placing law on the negative side of his dualistic understanding, in opposition to the **promise**. Throughout this section Paul expresses himself in the either/or categories of dualism (see on Luke 9:49; 16:8; the introduction to Revelation). Note the following contrasts in Figure 14.

This dualism is not ultimate, two equal forces balanced against each other, between which the individual must choose. God's act in Christ, represented by the right-hand column, has already prevailed, and its final victory is sure. But the Christian still lives in the force field between these two powers. The left-hand column is constitutive of the old world, from which Christians are delivered, but in which we still live—but without being ruled by it (see 1:4; 3:28; 5:16–17; 6:14).

3:19–29
THE PURPOSE OF THE LAW

Again, the reader must remember that Galatians is a letter to a specific situation, namely to a Gentile church now being urged to adopt the law in order to be acceptable to God. In opposing this false teaching, Paul has presented the law in purely negative terms. He has not written an abstract essay on the role of the law in God's plan, but has shown only its negative side. In the more reflective letter to the Romans, written to a church with a strong Jewish Christian element, Paul will give a more balanced discussion (see on Rom. 3:31; 7:7–13). Here his point is that the law had a negative and temporary function.

3:19–20 Because of transgressions: This may mean "to increase transgressions," i.e., to make a wrongdoing an actual legal offense (see Rom. 5:20), or "to restrain transgressions," i.e., as a curb on the evil in the world. **Ordained through angels:** That angels had a role in delivering the law is a widespread tradition, developed from Deut. 33:2 and Ps. 68:17. In Jewish tradition this connection with angels enhanced the glory of the law; the new teachers had likely presented the law to the Galatians in this glowing perspective. Paul has a negative view of angels and stands this tradition on its head: the

law is somewhat second-rate, not having been given by God himself, but only indirectly through angels and a mediator. On the negative Pauline view of angels, see on 1:8; Rom. 8:38; Luke 1:10–12; Acts 5:19. **By a mediator:** Moses (see Exod. 19–20). **A mediator involves more than one party:** This difficult verse has been interpreted in more than three hundred different ways! Whatever the exact meaning, Paul's point seems to be twofold: (1) the law did not come directly from God (Christ did!); (2) a transaction that involves a mediator is necessarily bilateral, something like a contract involving negotiation, but God's promise is unilateral and nonnegotiable, a covenant not a contract.

3:21 Is the law then opposed to the promises of God?: The context suggests, "Yes, it certainly is" (see figure above). But Paul draws back from this inference. The traditional interpretation of this statement is that, though the law has a temporary negative function, in the overall plan of God it plays a positive role. In this context, however, the meaning is more likely that the law that came later than God's promise cannot effectively oppose it, so that God's promise stands despite the law.

3:22 The scripture has imprisoned all things: Sin is pictured as an enslaving power, aided and abetted by the law (the Scripture). In Paul's overall view, both the world and the law are God's good creation, but both the world and the law have been commandeered by Sin, so that in their present fallen state they function as powers opposed to God (see Rom. 7:7–13).

3:23 We were imprisoned: Salvation is not only a matter of *forgiveness* of sins, a judicial metaphor in which debts are cancelled and guilty people are acquitted, but a matter of *deliverance*, a royal, military metaphor in which enslaved people are set free (see 1:4). The Christ event does not merely change the books on guilt and forgiveness, but reestablishes God's rule over his rebellious creation, setting the captives free.

3:24 The law was our disciplinarian: The traditional translation "schoolmaster" is too positive. The point is not that the law educates us to the point where we can see the value of accepting Christ, but that the law was the stern supervisor, usually a slave, who protected children on their way to and from school, a necessary but negative guardian required by those who are not mature and free (see 4:1–2).

3:27–28 Baptized into Christ: These two verses are almost certainly pre-Pauline traditional

Figure 14. Law and Promise in Galatians

Verse	Negative, "the present evil age" (1:4)	Positive, "age to come" that has already dawned in Christ
3:2	works of the law	believing what you heard
3:3	flesh	the Spirit / spirit
3:5	works of the law	believing what you heard
3:6		Abraham believed God
3:7		those who believe are the descendants of Abraham
3:8		By faith
3:9		those who believe
3:10	works of the law / under a curse, cursed	
3:11	no one is justified before God by the law	The one who is righteous will live by faith
3:12	whoever does the works of the law will live by them (This quotation of Lev. 18:5 is, in Paul's view, an impossible requirement, so that the law never gives life. The life it promises is actually found only in the right column.)	faith
3:13	curse of the law	Christ / blessing / Abraham
3:14		Christ Jesus / the promise / the Spirit / faith
3:16	offsprings . . . many	Abraham / the promises / the offspring / one
3:17	law / later	covenant ("Law" and "covenant" are in different columns. Law is here not identified with covenant, but contrasted with it.) / Christ
3:18	the law / from the law	previously / the promise / from the promise / the inheritance / Abraham
3:18, continued		Granted (as a gift) / God (Here God, Christ, Abraham, covenant, faith, promise, one, spirit, seed, inheritance, making righteous, prior all stand together against law, many, curse, doing, works, later.) / owners
4:1–2	minors, slaves / under guardians and trustees	date set by the father
4:5	under the law	adoption as children (lit. "sons")
4:6		Spirit of his Son; "Abba, Father"
4:7	slave	child, heir through God
4:8–9	Formerly, when you did not know God enslaved to beings that by nature are not gods / weak and beggarly elemental spirits	Now . . . know God . . . be known by God
4:19		Christ is formed in you
4:21	subject to the law	
4:22	by a slave woman	by a free woman
4:23	according to the flesh	through the promise (equated with "according to the Spirit" [v. 29])
4:24–26	One woman, in fact, is Hagar, from Mount Sinai, bearing children for slavery. Now Hagar is Mount Sinai in Arabia and corresponds to the present Jerusalem, for she is in slavery with her children.	But the other woman corresponds to the Jerusalem above; she is free, and she is our mother.
4:27	the children of the one who is married	"Rejoice, you childless one, you who bear no children, burst into song and shout, you who endure no birthpangs; for the children of the desolate woman are more numerous . . ." / Children of the promise, like Isaac
4:28		the child who was born according to the Spirit, now also ("Spirit" corresponds to "promise" of v. 23)
4:29	at that time . . . child who was born according to the flesh persecuted	
4:30	Drive out the slave and her child; for the child of the slave will not share the inheritance	with the child of the free woman
4:31		So then, friends, we are children, not of the slave but of the free woman
5:1	a yoke of slavery	For freedom Christ has set us free

material used in the baptism ceremony. The Galatians had heard these words before. Paul reminds them of the words directly addressed to them at their baptism. **You . . . have clothed yourselves with Christ:** Baptism is not an empty ritual; God acts in baptism to incorporate the believer into the body of Christ (see 1 Cor. 12:13; on "in Christ," see on 2 Cor. 5:17). Thus "have clothed yourselves" is an unfortunate translation; the text does not point to the believers' own act, but to what happens to them in baptism. In the early Christian baptismal ceremony practiced a bit later than Paul, candidates disrobed on one side of the baptistery, symbolizing leaving the old life, were immersed, and emerged on the other side of the baptistery to put on new clothes symbolizing the new life. In this new life the old social distinctions no longer count before God. Although the external social conditions did not immediately change, the new reality did effect relationships in the Christian community, where Paul, the free Jewish male, worked with Gentiles, slaves, and women as equal partners in the Christian mission (see on Philemon; Rom. 16:1, 7; 1 Cor 7:1–24). **All . . . one:** The law divides and separates; Christ unites.

3:29 You are Abraham's offspring: See on 1:4, 7; 3:7, 16.

4:1–7
HEIRS AND CHILDREN OF GOD

Paul communicates his point with a twofold metaphor: (1) a minor child who will one day be heir, but who is not free to exercise the status he actually has until the legal age of majority; (2) a slave who is adopted as a son with the full rights of freedom.

4:1 No better than slaves: Paul's metaphor makes only one point. From another perspective, the son is certainly better than a slave; he knows it and his guardians know it—for he is in fact the son and will one day be the heir. The already/not yet tension of Christian existence is implicit in the metaphor.

4:3 Enslaved to the elemental spirits of the world: The NRSV translation is here more appropriate. Though the same expression can elsewhere refer to the "basic principles of the world" (NIV), as in Heb. 5:12, here Paul refers to those transcendent cosmic powers that oppress humanity, the enslaving conditions of human existence as such (see v. 9; Rom. 8:38–39; 1 Cor. 15:20, 24; Eph. 2:2, 3:10; 6:12; Phil. 2:7; Col. 1:13, 16; 2:10, 15, 20; 1 Pet. 3:22).

By saying **"we,"** Paul includes himself and all Jews as well as all Gentiles. The evil powers had commandeered God's good Law, just as they had taken over God's good creation, so that apart from Christ all were under the same oppressive slavery, whether Jews or Gentiles (see 3:19; 4:9).

4:4 The fullness of time: See Mark 1:15; Eph. 1:10. The time was set by God himself (see v. 2, **the date set by the father**), was not the result of developments in human history. **God sent his Son:** The liberating event was God's act in Christ. It was not a matter of human beings adopting a new attitude or resolving to follow the "great principles taught by Jesus." **Born of a woman:** There is no reference to the miraculous birth of Jesus as portrayed in Matt. 1:18–25 and Luke 1:26–2:6. As in Matt. 11:11, the phrase means that Jesus belonged completely to the human race. **Born under the law:** This also identifies Jesus not only with Jews but with all people, for human existence as such is servitude to law. Jesus was indeed a Jew (Rom. 1:3), but Paul's point here is not the Jewishness of Jesus, but his accepting the conditions of human life as such, sharing its restrictions with all other human beings.

4:5 That we might receive adoption: For Paul, human beings are not "naturally" children of God, but become God's children by the free grace of God's act in adopting former slaves into his family. The liberating act does not abandon in front of the prison doors those who have been set free, now "on their own" with no place to go. In the community of faith they receive God's Spirit, enabling them to call out, "Abba," as their address to God ("Father," Jesus' distinctive word for God in his native Aramaic, taken from the intimate language of the family; see on Matt. 6:9; Mark 14:36; Rom. 8:16–17). Once again (see 3:2, 5, 14) Paul appeals to their corporate experience of the Spirit as proof that they already belong fully to God's people without additional conformity to the prescriptions of the biblical law.

4:8–11
NO TURNING BACK

The Galatians are compared to convicts released from prison who, frightened by freedom and responsibility, welcome the opportunity to return to the security of their cells, where everything was organized and decided for them. The new teachers were persuading the Gentile Christians of Galatia that by adopting the practices of the Jewish law they were progressing toward full membership in God's people. In Paul's view, for them as Gentiles to adopt the Jewish law would be turning back to their previous religion, in which the **elemental spirits** of the world were manifest as idols. For pagans, these cosmic powers had been manifest as idolatry; for Jews, servitude to the cosmic powers was expressed in religious devotion to the law. All, Jews and Gentiles, had been subject to the powers of this world. God's redeeming act in Christ was for all. The Galatians had been set free, but were about to return to the same religious servitude in another form.

4:10 You are observing special days, and months, and seasons, and years: Paul does not object, of course, to Christians observing special holy days as such; he assumes Christians regard Sunday as a special day for worship (1 Cor. 16:2) and regulates his own life around the major festivals (1 Cor. 16:8). What he resists is the Gentile adoption of Jewish laws as though that makes them more religious and acceptable to God (see also Col. 2:16).

4:12–20
AN APPEAL TO FRIENDSHIP

In trying to bring the Galatians back to an authentic understanding of Christian faith and life, Paul has previously appealed to his authority as an apostle and the authority of the one gospel (1:1–2:21), to the Galatians' own experience of the Spirit (3:1–5), to [his interpretation of] the Scripture (3:6–22), to the traditional baptismal confession they had made (3:23–29), and to God's plan for the ages of which Christ (not the law) is the center and climax (4:1–7). Now he appeals to the heart—to the personal relation they have with him as pastor and friend.

4:12–14 Brothers and sisters: See on 1 Cor. 6:5; 1 Thess. 2:7, 4:9. **I have become as you are:** The Jewish Christian Paul lives in freedom from the law among the Gentile churches (see 2:14; 1 Cor. 9:19–23). On Paul seeming to make an example of himself, see on 1 Thess. 1:6; 1 Cor. 4:16; 11:1. **Because of a physical infirmity:** Paul's first missionary visit to Galatia was apparently an unplanned stop because of his health problem. We do not know the details (see on 2 Cor. 12:7). **Welcomed me as an angel of God:** The Galatians, encouraged by their new teachers, were impressed by angels. For Paul's negative view of angels, see on 1:8 and Rom. 8:38; for other perspectives, see on Luke 1:10–12; Acts 5:19.

4:15 Torn out your eyes: The expression may be simply proverbial (like "give you the shirt off his back," "cut off his right arm for you"), or

it may suggest Paul had a repulsive eye disease (see 6:11).

4:17 They want to exclude you: By their teaching that Christian faith and baptism are not enough to be included in the people of God, but that the Gentile Christians must be circumcised and keep the law. **Make much of them:** The new teachers want to impress the Galatians with their credentials and "professional distance," while Paul numbered himself among his converts as a brother and fellow disciple.

4:19 I am again in the pain of childbirth. Here Paul's pastoral heart is revealed. He is not the self-centered, authoritarian figure he is sometimes made out to be. His dispute with the Galatians is not for personal status or leadership, but for the truth of the gospel. Paul uses fatherly, motherly, and brotherly imagery of his relation to his fellow church members (see on 1 Thess. 2:7). Despite his sharp critique of them, he loves them with a mother's heart. He once labored to give them a new birth. Since they have drifted away from the gospel, he must now "reconvert" them, with all the pain and labor involved.

4:21–5:1
THE ALLEGORY OF HAGAR AND SARAH

In this section Paul compares two covenants (or two understandings of God's covenant that are presently being practiced in the church, see below) with Hagar and Sarah and the children they bore to Abraham (Gen. 16–21). Paul is not discussing the Old Testament and New Testament as parts of the Christian Bible, nor is he speaking about Judaism and Christianity. Both the covenants of which he speaks are Old Testament in that sense, i.e., from the time of Abraham. His passionate discussion and interpretation of the Scripture addresses the situation of his own time, in which Jewish Christian missionaries, claiming support of the Jerusalem church, invade the Gentile churches Paul has established in Galatia, teaching a new understanding of the covenant different from what Paul had taught (see the introduction to Galatians, comments on 1:6–8; 3:6–18). For Paul's discussion addressed to a church of both Jewish and Gentile Christians, see Romans, esp. chaps. 9–11.

4:23–24 According to the flesh . . . through the promise: Paul speaks of two realms of existence. "**Flesh**" refers not to a person's "lower," physical nature, in contrast to a "higher," spiritual nature, but to the world as determined by human abilities, resources, and values (see

1 Cor. 3:1; 2 Cor. 5:16; 10:2; Rom. 8:5–13). "Promise" (identified with "Spirit" in v. 29) refers to the world as determined by God. See Paul's apocalyptic dualism as presented in the chart at 3:18 above.

4:24 Allegory: Paul understands the Old Testament story to point beyond itself to spiritual realities. This kind of interpretation was common among rabbinic scholars of Paul's day. The new teachers at Galatia also no doubt interpreted the Scripture with this method, but had given a different interpretation, to which Paul here responds. **These women are two covenants:** Paul's symbolic interpretation can be outlined as shown in Figure 15.

This was not, of course, the original meaning of the Old Testament story, but represents Paul's theological reading from his Christian perspective (see excursus, "New Testament Interpretation of the Old Testament," at 1 Cor. 15:3). There is only one covenant in the Old Testament story. Paul sees this covenant as now understood in two very different ways. The two covenants are thus not the "old" and the "new"—they are both interpretations of the "old." Paul understands it as a covenant of promise and grace in Christ; his opponents associate the covenant with Sinai and the Law. Neither was in the Old Testament story, which Paul understands one way in order to illuminate his point, and his opponents understand in a different way.

4:26 The Jerusalem above: As the earthly Jerusalem to which his opponents appeal is the Jerusalem church, the heavenly Jerusalem to which Paul appeals is the heavenly counterpart of the people of God. His opponents appeal to the earthly Jerusalem church for their authorization; Paul is an apostle authorized from heaven, representing the heavenly community of God's people, the true locus of their citizenship (see Phil. 3:20).

4:27 It is written: Paul appeals to Isa. 54:1, which he also understands symbolically, representing the originally barren Sarah who by God's promise became the mother of many nations.

4:29 Persecuted: There is no reference in the Old Testament story to Ishmael persecuting Isaac (see Gen. 21:9). Paul bases his interpretation on current Jewish traditions in which Isaac was persecuted by Ishmael (see on 1 Cor. 10:3–4). This is not a reference to Jewish persecution of Christians (see on 1 Thess. 2:14–16), but to the opposition Paul had experienced from the Jewish Christian leaders of the Jerusalem church.

4:30 What does the scripture say?: Paul cites Sarah's command to cast out Hagar and Ishmael from the family as the word of "Scripture." Paul understands it as authorizing the Galatians to throw their new teachers out of the church (see 1 Cor. 5:1–13, especially the concluding command). Paul had considerable tolerance for a broad range of understandings of the Christian faith, but also recognized a line at which it was not only a different perspective, but a different gospel that was being proclaimed (see on 1 Cor. 3:21–23; 2 Cor. 10–13).

5:1 Christ has set us free: The good news of God's liberating act in Christ is the core of the gospel. Freedom is from the power of sin, law, and death. **Do not submit again to a yoke of slavery:** By subjecting themselves as Gentiles to the Old Testament and Jewish laws of circumcision, food laws, and special holy days, as though they were required of Gentiles for salvation. Like all of Galatians, this is addressed to Gentile Christians tempted to submit to the law; it is not a polemic against Judaism.

5:2–12
WARNING AGAINST CIRCUMCISION

5:2–4 Christ will be of no benefit: Observance of the law cannot be added to faith in Christ as an extra religious accomplishment. Salvation cannot be both by grace and, even partially, by human religious achievement. **Obey the entire law:** Paul sees the matter entirely in either/or terms. To accept circumcision, the food laws, and the Jewish calendar of holy days is to obligate oneself to keep all the law's commandments. The new teachers in Galatia had not been clear about this. **You have fallen away from grace:** This does not mean that if

Figure 15. Hagar and Sarah as Two Covenants

Galatians 4:24–30	
Hagar	Sarah
Slave child born from slave mother	Free child born of free mother
"According to the flesh"	"According to the promise/spirit"
Mount Sinai in Arabia	
Present Jerusalem church our "mother"	Heavenly Jerusalem our "mother"
Children of the flesh like Ishmael	Children of the promise like Isaac
Persecutes other group	Is persecuted by other group
Cast out and does not inherit	Receives the inheritance

believers sin after becoming Christians, they have "fallen from grace," but that those who submit to the law thereby reject the way of God's grace.

5:5 Hope of righteousness: "Hope" here means not "maybe" but "confident assurance of a reality that is still future" (see Rom. 8:18–25). "Righteousness" refers both to justification of the individual and the establishment of God's justice throughout creation. Here too the tensive already/not yet of salvation is affirmed.

5:6 Neither circumcision nor uncircumcision: See 6:15; 1 Cor. 7:19. Neither doing the law nor not doing the law can be matters of human achievement. The distinction itself is obliterated in the new creation God is accomplishing through Christ (see 6:15; 2 Cor. 5:17). **Faith working through love:** Literally "faith energized by love." This, and not religious law-keeping, is the essence of the Christian life.

5:11 If I am still preaching circumcision: This may point to Paul's pre-Christian work as a Jewish missionary, who made proselytes to Judaism by "preaching circumcision" (see Matt. 23:15), as the false teachers in Galatia did presently doing. Or, after his conversion, did Paul continue to "preach circumcision" for a time as part of the Christian message, rather than preaching "freedom from the law" from the very first? Possibly, but more likely, the reference is to a false report or misunderstanding of Paul's Christian missionary practice, as though Paul, too, occasionally preached that Gentile Christians should be circumcised and keep the law (see Acts 16:1–3; 1 Cor. 9:19–23). **The offense of the cross:** That God acts to save through the cross is a scandal to all "common sense" ideas of human religion as a meritorious achievement (see 1 Cor. 1:18–2:5). This offense is a mark of authentic faith and must not be surrendered or domesticated.

5:12 Those who unsettle you: See on 1:7. **Castrate themselves:** This is at least a crude and angry outburst against those who are promoting circumcision. It may, however, be more than that. Since Paul has called for expulsion of the false teachers from the church (4:30), he may be making an ironic allusion to the fact that the law itself requires expulsion of those who have been sexually mutilated (Deut. 23:1). Also, in some pagan cults the devotees of the goddess castrated themselves as a mark of their devotion, so Paul may be saying in effect, "If you are going to insist on circumcision that puts you back under the this-worldly enslaving religious powers from

which you have been delivered by Christ, why not practice self-castration like some of the pagan cults?"

5:13–6:18
PART THREE—THE RIGHT USE OF FREEDOM

As is typical of the Pauline letter, the foundational theological section is followed by a section on Christian ethics; a right understanding of the Christian message leads to the Christian life and is its basis. The ethical section of Galatians (1) emphasizes that the gospel of grace itself calls for ethical living, (2) refutes the false teachers' charge that the gospel of grace does not provide guidance for daily living, and (3) provides practical instruction on how Christians should live.

5:13–15
FREEDOM AND LOVE

5:13 You: The pronoun is plural in Greek, here and elsewhere. Paul deals with the individual only in the corporate life of the Christian community. **Opportunity for self-indulgence:** Literally "as a supply base for the flesh." The picture is military. God's act in Christ has initiated a cosmic battle in which God's Spirit invades and reclaims the realm of the "flesh," God's creation that has been captured by the power of sin. Christians have been delivered from the realm of law, sin, and death, but are not to allow their freedom to become the empty staging area where the hostile army can reassert itself as in charge of the "real" world (see on 1:10). As God's slaves they express their new freedom by serving one another (see on 1:10).

5:14 Whole law is summed up: In the sense of the revealed will of God, the law itself contains a statement that fulfills the meaning of the whole (Lev. 19:18; see Mark 12:28–32; Matt. 22:34–40; Luke 10:25–28; Rom. 13:8–10). Paul's gospel is not against the law as such. Here Paul is entirely positive about the law, which not only has the negative voice that condemns and curses (Deut. 27:26; Lev. 18:5; see 3:10–13 above), but also has the positive voice that reveals the will of God as manifest in Christ. The law itself can be cited in both tones of voice (see the similar view of Jesus in Mark 10:2–9).

5:16–21
THE WORKS OF THE FLESH

5:16–18 Spirit . . . flesh: See on 4:23 and chart at 3:18. When referring to "Spirit" and "flesh," Paul is not talking about two components of the human self, but about the Christian life lived in the conflicting force field between two powers. On Paul's later reflections on a similar point, see Rom. 7:7–25.

5:19 The works of the flesh: Not the products of our "lower nature," but the results of the power of sin at work in the Christian community. The "flesh" destroys relationships and community not only by flagrant immorality, but by generating the socially acceptable (even admired!) sins of envy, excessive ambition, and divisions into cliques.

5:22–26
THE FRUIT OF THE SPIRIT

5:22 Fruit: While the "flesh" results in a plurality of works, **the Spirit** (God's Holy Spirit, not the internal conscience of the believer) generates a singular fruit. **Love** is not one "virtue" or "ideal" among others, but the care for others expressed in concrete acts of unselfishness, the mainspring of all the other activities (see 1 Cor. 13:4–7).

5:23 There is no law against such things: Pauline irony. Acts of Christian love will not violate the law they are so tempted to idolize.

5:24 Those who belong to Christ have crucified the flesh: Again, this does not mean that Christians mistreat part of their own selves, e.g., self-flagellation of their bodies, in an effort to be more "spiritual." The enemy is "the flesh," the hostile power of the sinful world. A real death stands between Christians and the old world, a death by crucifixion. Christ's crucifixion was the price of deliverance from the old world; Christians are united with Christ in that death. The statement is to be interpreted in the light of 2:19–20; 6:14; Rom. 6:6; 7:1–6; 8:13.

6:1–10
BEAR ONE ANOTHER'S BURDENS

6:1 You who have received the Spirit: Not a special group within the church, but the Christian congregation as such is charged with the restoration of straying members. Such efforts at restoration are a risky business, involving the possibility of further misunderstanding and conflict, self-righteousness, and offending the straying member even further. As his own letter shows, for Paul the business of being a caring congregation *is* risky, and it accepts the risks.

6:2 Bear one another's burdens: The effort to live a Christian life is not a solo performance but is playing in a symphony, being members of a family in which there is mutual care (v. 10). **The law of Christ:** See Rom. 3:27; 8:2; 1 Cor. 9:21. Though free from the law as a way of salvation, acts of Christian love fulfill the law as illuminated by Christ (see 5:13–14).

6:5 All must carry their own loads: The tension with v. 2 is not to be resolved. The caring congregation affirms both individual responsibility before God and its members' responsibility for each other.

6:6 Those who are taught the word: Paul had appointed teachers in the churches of Galatia as part of his original mission, who were supported by gifts from the congregations. Either the new teachers had dismissed them, or their teaching had caused their support to dwindle. Paul insists that faithful teachers of the gospel be financially supported (see on 1 Cor. 9:14).

6:8–10 Flesh . . . Spirit: See on 3:18; 4:23; Rom. 8:1–17. **Sow . . . reap:** Metaphors for present actions and the Last Judgment. **Work for the good of all:** The doctrine of salvation by grace without meritorious works does not cut the nerve of social action. While Paul urges mutual care for **those of the family of faith**, i.e., fellow members of the Christian community, Christian concern is not limited to taking care of the needs of church members, but is directed to all. The church is in the world to represent God's care for the whole world, whether or not the world responds.

6:11–18
FINAL ADMONITIONS AND BENEDICTION

6:11 I am writing in my own hand: Paul dictated his letters, but customarily wrote a personal note at the end in his own hand (see 1 Cor. 16:21; Phlm. 19; Rom. 16:22; 2 Thess. 3:17; Col. 4:18). His concluding words here, however, are not warm and personal. As he begins without thanksgiving (see 1:6), so he concludes without personal warmth or mentioning any names. Instead, he provides a harsh summary of the message of the whole letter.

6:14 I: Paul's "I" is not merely his individualistic personal experience, but representative of Christian existence as such (see 2:19; 5:24; Rom. 7:7–25).

6:15 Neither circumcision nor uncircumcision: The old world was marked by distinctions and separation. One received one's identity by being this or not this, Jew or Gentile, law-keeper or law-ignorer, male or female, slave or free. The new world that came into being in Jesus Christ has overcome not only the law and circumcision, but nonlaw and noncircumcision, religion and nonreligion. The Galatians are reminded again of the pronouncement they heard at their baptism (see on 3:27–28).

6:16 And upon the Israel of God: The meaning of the little word "and" is not clear. It could be an addition to the previous phrase describing the church, so that the blessing is pronounced on both church and Israel, i.e., Jews. Paul does later develop a view like this in Rom. 9–11. Here, however, the "and" probably means "that is," "that is to say" (a common meaning of the Greek conjunction *kai* [= "and," "also," "even," "that is," "namely"]). Paul's point is then that the Galatian Gentile Christians are in fact already included in Israel, the people of God, without adding on circumcision and becoming law-observant Jews. In neither understanding does Paul intend to say that the church has now replaced empirical Israel as God's people.

6:17 The marks of Jesus: The scars from his missionary experience (see 2 Cor. 4:7–10; 6:4–5; 11:23–27). Paul not only proclaims the message of the cross; it is imprinted on his body. Few modern Christians in North America can point to anything similar, but one's commitment to the crucified Christ might be visible in checkbook and (lack of concern with) self-image.

The Letter of Paul to the Ephesians

INTRODUCTION

The Traditional View

Ephesians has traditionally been regarded as written by Paul from his Roman prison (3:1; 6:20) to the church in Ephesus (1:1), as one of the last of his letters, sent at the same time as Philemon and Colossians (see introductions to those books). This is the view reflected in the title, which of course was provided by later church tradition, not by the author himself. As is the case with other New Testament documents, the titles represent the conviction of early Christianity that the document represents the apostolic faith, i.e., that it is a trustworthy guide to the meaning of God's act in Christ, rather than necessarily providing accurate historical information. If written by Paul, the letter was most likely written from Rome in the early 60s.

The Critical Approach

"Critical" of course, does not mean "negative," but "with careful, analytical study." The opposite of "critical" is not "believing" but "uncritical," i.e., "naive." In the judgment of some critical scholars, Paul is still to be considered the author of the work, but it is almost universally accepted that the letter was not addressed to the church at Ephesus. The author is unknown to the readers (1:15; 3:2–4), and the letter contains no personal details about either writer or readers. There are no personal greetings (contrast, e.g., 1 Cor. 16:5–18 and Eph. 6:21–24). Moreover, at 1:1 the words "in Ephesus" are missing from key ancient MSS, suggesting the letter was originally a general letter.

Most critical scholars have been convinced that the internal evidence of the letter indicates it was not written by Paul personally, but by one of his associates some years after his death, to reinterpret the Pauline gospel in a new situation. (See "The Death of Paul and the Continuation of the Pauline Tradition" in the introduction to 1 Timothy.) Some of the types of evidence on which this conclusion is based are these:

1. *Vocabulary and style.* The vocabulary and style of Ephesians differ markedly from that of the undisputed letters of Paul. Details cannot be given here, but lengthy (and somewhat tedious) lists of examples are found in the technical critical commentaries. While anyone can change his or her style as circumstances require, the differences on these points between Ephesians and the undisputed letters are not of the type that can be so explained. Moreover, Ephesians is very different from Philippians (as can be perceived in a close reading even of the English text), which according to the traditional view was written about the same time as Ephesians.

2. *Theological differences.* There are numerous differences in theology from the unquestioned Pauline letters, especially the abandonment of the expectation of the soon coming of the Lord and the shift toward an emphasis on the present experience of Christian faith. While Paul affirmed the already/not yet tension in the experience of salvation, his emphasis was on the believer's identification with the crucified Jesus and the future fulfillment of God's saving act at the resurrection. In Ephesians the center of gravity is on the present status of believers as already risen and seated with Christ in the heavenly places. These are not minor differences; numerous others will be pointed out in the comments. The point is not that Paul's theology is valid and that of Ephesians is not, but that they are different, that Ephesians represents a reinterpretation of Paul's message for a later time.

3. *The relation to Colossians.* The two letters have the same outline, with Ephesians being an expanded version of Colossians. Similarity extends to many details, giving Ephesians the appearance of a revised version of Colossians, with details from the other Pauline letters worked in. Yet in the overlapping texts, Ephesians represents a more developed theology than Colossians, not a repetition of it. Compare, for example, Col. 3:18–4:1 with Eph. 5:21–6:9. Both are different from Paul, but Ephesians is different from Colossians.

To many scholars, such evidence is better explained by regarding Ephesians as having been written by a member of the Pauline school in Ephesus that carried on his ministry after his death, writing in his name as a way of continuing to promote his message, reinterpreting it for a new situation.

Pseudonymous Letters
in Early Christianity

If we begin with our world and its cultural pre-suppositions, words beginning with "pseudo" raise immediate problems, especially when associated with the Bible. On the other hand, we are acquainted with several kinds of documents not written by the purported author: forged checks, plagiarized term papers, literary forgeries such as the alleged Hitler diaries published in 1983, the Book of Mormon (from a non-Mormon perspective), the ghost writing of books and speeches for politicians and celebrities, research books written mostly by assistants but published under the professor's name, authors' pen names (Samuel Clemens = Mark Twain, Mary Ann Evans = George Eliot), business executive's letters written by a secretary "over my signature," letters to the editor as a transparent literary device ("A Letter from Martin Luther King Jr. to the People of Memphis," dated 2003). Some of these involve legal rights, copyright laws, ethical issues ("intent to deceive"), and others do not. On this spectrum of possibilities, the issue would be whether New Testament authors who wrote in the name of an apostle were using a "transparent literary device" with no "intent to deceive," or whether such documents should be considered "forgeries." If one must consider such pseudonymous writings forgeries, then many readers of the Bible will object to the whole notion of "pseudonymous" writings in the Bible, and rightly so. But should we begin with our culture and its presuppositions?

Within the biblical tradition of the ancient world, it had for centuries been common and accepted practice to write in the name of a revered figure of the past and to attribute collections of such material to an ancient author. Thus, since Moses was the representative lawgiver, the first five books of the Bible (including the account of his own death in Deut. 34) were attributed to Moses; the Psalms as a whole were attributed to David, though he clearly did not write many of them (see, e.g., Pss. 132; 137; and the title to Ps. 90), and all the Wisdom materials were attributed to Solomon, the principle "wise man" of Israelite history. New documents were composed in the name of each of these figures as a way of continuing their tradition.

So also in the first-century Hellenistic world into which Christianity was born; it was common and accepted practice to write in the name of famous philosophers of the past. Almost all the great figures of Greek and Roman intellectual history had a comprehensive correspondence attrib-uted to them. We know that the early church continued this practice. Bishop Ignatius of Antioch, for instance, wrote seven letters to churches in Asia Minor. Soon after his martyr death, not only were his letters collected and published, but new ones were composed in his name to continue his teaching and influence. Modern scholarship can easily distinguish "authentic" from "inauthentic" letters of Plato and Ignatius.

If we approach this issue from within the context of early Christianity, the issue was not, is it a forgery or authentic? but how may we continue to express the apostolic faith? Of the twenty-two letters in the New Testament (considering Revelation as a letter), only eight are undisputed as to their authorship (Romans, 1 and 2 Corinthians, Galatians, Philippians, 1 Thessalonians, Philemon, Revelation). Some of the others may also be by their purported authors (see the introductions to each book for details). But in no case should the modern reader perceive the issue as whether or not the Bible contains forgeries. The issue in each case is whether the document concerned represents the apostolic faith. The fact that the books are in the canon indicates that the early church, under the guidance of the Holy Spirit, heard in these documents the word of God, the authentic witness to the apostolic faith, as it tried to find its own way forward after the death of the apostles but before any authoritative tradition, canon, or organizational structure had been accepted. In such later New Testament writings, the voice and teaching of the apostles continued to be heard. Thus the production of pseudepi-graphical documents was not the work of individuals who wanted to foist their own opinions on the church by attributing them to some famous leader of the past, but the extension of the apostolic witness into a later time.

Structure and Outline

Ephesians follows the standard pattern of the Pauline letter, in which the first part is theological-doctrinal, primarily in the indicative mode, and lays the foundation for the second part, which is primarily in the imperative mode, giving instruction for the Christian life. The distinctive aspect of Ephesians is that the Introduction and whole of part one is presented in the mode of worship. The liturgical introduction flows seamlessly into theological reflection in part one of the body of the letter. After the opening greeting come a liturgical blessing (1:3–14), a thanksgiving (1:15–23), and a recitation of God's mighty acts as in the Psalms (2:1–3:13), concluded by a prayer report and doxology (3:14–21). Ephesians, especially chaps. 1–3, is better understood within the context of the grateful praise of the community than the logical analysis of the solitary reader.

As is typical of letters in the Pauline tradition, part two of the body of the letter consists of ethical exhortations, drawing out the implications for Christian life of the theology expressed in the first part.

The letter then concludes with greetings and a benediction, ending as it began on the note of worship. The letter is permeated with worship materials, and, like other letters in the Pauline tradition, is intended not for private reading and analysis, but for reading aloud in the worship of the assembled congregation. This structure may be represented by the following outline:

1:1–23 Introduction
  1:1–2 Salutation
  1:3–14 Blessing
  1:15–23 Thanksgiving
2:1–6:20 Body of the Letter
  2:1–3:21 Part One—Theological Reflection
    2:1–10 God's Act in Christ Brought Us from Death to Life
    2:11–22 God's Acts Created Unity in Christ
    3:1–13 The Role of the Apostle in God's Plan for the Ages
    3:14–21 The Apostle's Prayer and Doxology
  4:1–6:20 Part Two—Ethical Exhortations on Living as Christians
    4:1–16 Building Up the Body of Christ
    4:17–32 The Old Life and the New
    5:1–14 Living as Children of Light
    5:15–20 Life as Thanksgiving and Praise
    5:21–6:9 Life in the Orderly Christian Household
    6:10–20 Armed with God's Armor
6:21–24 Conclusion

This structure is clearly an expansion of the identical outline of Colossians, one of numerous indications that Colossians formed the basis for the composition.

For Further Reading

Perkins, Pheme. "The Letter to the Ephesians." In *The New Interpreter's Bible*, vol. 11. Nashville: Abingdon Press, 2000.

Martin, Ralph P. *Ephesians, Colossians, and Philemon*. Interpretation: A Bible Commentary for Teaching and Preaching. Atlanta: John Knox Press, 1991.

COMMENTARY

1:1–23
INTRODUCTION

1:1–2
SALUTATION

On the form and meaning of the Pauline letter introduction, see on 1 Thess. 1:1.

1:1 Paul: In contrast to all the undisputed letters except Romans, no cosenders are mentioned; all emphasis is on the apostle himself. **Apostle . . . by the will of God:** See on Gal. 1:1–5; Luke 6:12–13. **Saints:** See on Acts 9:13. **In Ephesus:** This phrase is missing from the oldest and best MSS, which read "to the saints who are also faithful" (see footnotes in NRSV and NIV). This is another reason to regard Ephesians as a circular letter written to the churches of a large region (see introduction; 1:15; 3:2). **In Christ:** See on 2 Cor. 5:17.

1:3–14
BLESSING

This section is one continuous sentence in Greek, giving the impression of solemn and joyful liturgy. In the conventional Greek letter, the salutation was followed by a thanksgiving (see on 1 Thess. 1:2). Paul had developed this convention in such a way that the thanksgiving provided a substantial theological preamble to the letter, signaling its main themes. On one occasion, the thanksgiving assumed the form of the Jewish liturgical "blessing" familiar from the synagogue (2 Cor. 1:3; see 1 Pet. 1:3). The author of Ephesians adopts both forms, combining blessing (vv. 3–14) and thanksgiving (vv. 15–23) into a long liturgical introduction praising God and giving thanks for his mighty acts climaxing in the Christ event.

1:3 In the heavenly places: As Christ is already exalted to heaven, so believers, who are "in Christ," already share his heavenly reign. In the undisputed letters, Paul identifies Christian life with the crucifixion and death of Jesus (Rom. 6; Gal. 2:19–20), and resurrection glory is still in the believer's future (see Phil. 3:12–21). Colossians goes beyond this to "raised with him" (Col. 2:12–3:1). Ephesians goes even further to "seated with him in the heavenly places" (see 2:6). Ephesians lacks the "eschatological reservation" typical of the undisputed letters (see on Rom. 6:14). The tension of the Pauline already/not yet is maintained, but the center of gravity has shifted decisively to the "already."

1:4 Chose us in Christ before the foundation of the world: God's saving act in Christ was not a response or reaction to mythical or historical events or powers, but proceeds from his own gracious will, entirely a matter of the divine initiative. As Christ existed before creation (John 1:1–2; Col. 1:15–20; 1 Cor. 10:3–4; Phil. 2:5–11; Heb. 1:1–4; 1 Pet. 1:11, 20; Rev. 13:8), and believers are "in Christ," so the church participates in the program of God that began before time. On the New Testament's language of foreknowledge and predestination, see excursus at Rom. 8:29–30.

1:7 Through his blood: Though stretching from eternity to eternity and established in the transcendent world "in the heavenly places," the saving event is not a metaphysical theory—it is grounded in the this-worldly historical event of Jesus' death.

1:9–10 Made known to us the mystery of his will: Insight into the saving plan of God is not a matter of human discovery or speculation, but has been revealed through God's act in apostles and prophets (3:5) and definitively in the Christ event. **A plan for the fullness of time:** History does not wander aimlessly through the centuries and eons, but has a beginning, a revelatory center in the decisive event of Jesus Christ, and an end. Ephesians here has its own way of expressing standard New Testament theology (see on Luke 4:43–44; Rom. 5:1–5; 1 Pet. 2:9). **To gather up all things in him:** God's plan for history is to unite and reconcile the fragmented, alienated, and hostile universe. The Christ event is God's decisive act in this divine plan for the ages. Since this event has already happened, for the author of Ephesians this unification and reconciliation have in principle already been accomplished. The decisive victory is already won, though the battle still continues (6:10–17; see Rev. 12). **In heaven and . . . on earth:** This biblical expression includes the whole creation (as in Gen. 1:1, etc.). The author's cosmology has no "under the earth," but the earth itself is the lowest point (see note on 4:9 and contrast, e.g., Phil. 2:10).

EXCURSUS:
THE BIBLICAL STORY AS A
DRAMA IN FIVE ACTS

The author's phrase in Ephesians 1:10, "a plan for the fullness of time," at the center of which stands the Christ event, represents a summary of biblical theology. Although the biblical authors have a variety of ways of expressing it, and do not all have the same perspective and emphasis, there is a view of God's purpose for the world that is common to the Bible as a whole. The biblical story can be summarized as a drama in five acts, a drama of which God is the author, producer, and director:

Act 1. *Creation: God created all things and all persons.* (Gen. 1–11)

The first article of Christian faith and the first page of the Bible affirm that, however it is understood scientifically, God is the Creator. In Christian faith, there is no ultimate dualism; there is nothing and no one who is not a beloved creature of God.

Something has gone wrong with God's good creation. When we human beings first become aware of ourselves, we live in a world that, while it continues to be God's good creation, is already in rebellion against its Creator. The story of Adam and Eve in Gen. 3 is the story of humanity writ small (Rom. 5:12–21). The stories of Gen. 1–11 picture the creative act of God and the human rebellion that gives us our present world.

Act 2. *Covenant: God made a covenant with one people for the sake of all people.* (Gen. 12–Mal. 4)

God did not let that be the end of the matter. When human beings were incapable of restoring the intimate relationship with God and the sense of themselves as God's creatures, God acted. God chose Abraham and Sarah and made a covenant with them that through their descendants all the world would be blessed (Gen. 12:1–3). Among the peoples of the world, all of whom are created and loved by God, in response to God's initiative and call there emerged a particular people, Israel, called to be the witnesses and vehicle of God's blessing for all the earth.

The story of God's covenant with Israel, its ups and downs through faithfulness and unfaithfulness, its interpretation by sages and prophets, is the story of most of the Hebrew Bible, Gen. 12 through the final chapter of the Old Testament, Mal. 4.

Act 3. *Christ: God sent his Son as Revealer, Redeemer, and Lord.* (Matthew–John)

At the center of the drama of God's mighty acts in history stands not a proposition or principle, but a person, Jesus of Nazareth, as the definitive truth about God. In his life and teaching, he taught and lived out the sovereign love of God the Creator. In his death and resurrection, God acted definitively for the salvation of the world. The significance of his life and person is summed up in the affirmation "Jesus is the Christ," classically unfolded as the threefold office of prophet, priest, and king (see on Mark 8:29).

This act of the drama is not merely one incident among others, but is the defining center for the whole drama of God's mighty acts in history and serves as the interpretative key by which they are all to be understood and appropriated. This means that the God truly known in the history of Israel and mediated to us in the Old Testament is no other God than the God definitively revealed in Jesus Christ. The story of Jesus and his significance can be pictured more than one way, but not just any way. The four Gospels present the normative pictures of the Christ event for Christian faith.

Act 4. *Church: God continues to act in calling and sending the community of the eschatologically renewed covenant, the church.* (Acts–Jude)

The Christ was supposed to be the savior king God would send at the eschaton to establish justice and bring in the kingdom of God. But instead of destroying injustice, Jesus was himself killed as the victim of injustice. Jesus was believed in as Christ, not because he fit the traditional expectation, but because God raised him from the dead, reversing all expectations. The result of his ministry was not a renewed world purged of evil, but a community of believers who now understood that God's ultimate purpose for the world is represented in the life and ministry of Jesus. The church is the community of those who have responded in faith and obedience to the act of God in Jesus Christ.

In this biblical understanding of the drama of God's mighty acts in history, the church does not live in some sort of parenthesis in God's plan or pause in God's activity. The same God who created the world, called Israel into being, acted definitively in Jesus, continues to act in the deeds of witness, mercy, and justice as the church carries out its mission. The church is a mutual ministry to its own members, providing fulfillment of life's meaning, celebration of life's good-

ness, and consolation and support for life's problems. Yet the church does not exist for itself, but as the expression of God's mission to the world, the continuation of Jesus' own ministry of love and justice. This story of the church is told in Acts and reflected in the Letters.

Act 5. *Consummation: God will bring history to a worthy conclusion.* (Revelation)

The drama is not over. Christians live in Act 5, looking back on God's decisive revelatory act in Christ, but also looking forward to the consummation of God's purpose. History will not go on forever. Only God is eternal. As the physical world and human history had a beginning, so they will have an end. As Genesis gives us canonical pictures of God the Creator with which to think of the ultimate beginnings, so Revelation gives us canonical pictures with which to think of the ultimate end of this world and human history. This "grand far-off divine event to which the whole creation moves" is celebrated in the Bible not as the destruction or frustration of God's purpose, but as the glorious consummation of God's will for the creation, the final answer to Jesus' prayer and ours, "Your kingdom come." The book of Revelation pictures the Christian hope, this final act in the cosmic and historical drama.

1:11 Accomplishes all things: Literally "the one energizing all things." The universe is not an independent entity, but is energized and held in being by the Creator (see Col. 1:17). This does not mean God directly causes everything that happens; the one God who works in all things for good (see on Rom. 8:28) is not an impersonal force, but the God and Father of our Lord Jesus Christ (1:3).

1:13 Marked with the seal of the promised Holy Spirit: An allusion to Christian baptism (see 4:5; 1 Cor. 12:13; 2 Cor. 1:22; Col. 2:12).

1:14 The pledge of our inheritance: As in Rom. 8:23 and 2 Cor. 1:22, the gift of the Holy Spirit given to the believer in the present (Acts 2:38) is the "down payment" on the future fulfillment of eschatological salvation. While Ephesians focuses on the present reality of salvation, the future hope is not missing (1:21; 2:7; 4:30; 5:5; 6:8, 13). **To the praise of his glory:** The blessing concludes by pointing the reader/hearer/worshiper to God (see vv. 6, 12).

1:15–23
THANKSGIVING

For structure, see on 1:3.

1:15 I have heard of your faith: The author writes in the persona of Paul, but presents him as not knowing the addressees personally. The letter contains no greetings or personal references. Since Paul was well known to the church in Ephesus (Acts 18–20; 1 Cor. 15:32; 16:8), this means the letter is either not by Paul or not to Ephesus, or both (see introduction). The familiar Pauline triad of faith/hope/love (1 Thess. 1:3; 5:8; Rom. 5:1–5; 1 Cor. 13:13; Col. 1:4–5) is completed by the reference to **hope** in v. 18 (see 4:2–5).

1:17–19 I pray . . . a spirit of wisdom and revelation: Though centered in the ministry of apostles and prophets (2:20; 3:5), the revelatory ministry of the Holy Spirit is not rigidly confined to particular church leaders, but rests in the church as a whole (see Acts 2:14–21). Insight into God's purpose does not come merely by human reason—though reason is not excluded—but is the gift of God's Spirit at work in the whole community of faith. The apostle is pictured as praying that the church will receive insight regarding three aspects of the meaning of God's act in Christ:

1. **The hope to which God has called you:** On the meaning of Christian hope, see the comments on Luke 24:21; Rom. 8:18–24; Matt. 28:1–8; 1 Cor. 15:35–58; 1 Thess. 4:11–5:11; Rev. 6:9–11. Ephesians emphasizes how this hope transforms the *present* life of believers.

2. **What are the riches of his glorious inheritance:** The phrase refers to God's inheritance, not the believers'. In Old Testament theology, Israel as God's chosen people is often called God's inheritance (Deut. 4:20; 9:26, 29; 2 Sam. 21:3; 1 Kgs. 8:51, 53; Pss. 28:9; 33:12; 68:9; 78:62, 71; 94:14; 106:5, 40; Isa. 19:25; 47:6; 63:17; Jer. 10:16; 51:19). For the author of Ephesians, to be in the church is to be incorporated into the continuing people of God, Israel (2:11–12).

3. **The immeasurable greatness of his power:** The church does not function merely by the good intentions and exertions of its own members, but by the surprising power of God at work within it. This is not obvious—the human weaknesses and foibles of the church are apparent even to the casual observer—so the apostle prays for the revelatory work of the Holy Spirit to enlighten **the eyes of (their) heart** to see what is really happening in the church as the people of God, energized by God's own power.

1:20 When he raised him from the dead: While Paul emphasized the *cross* as the manifestation of God's power in weakness (Phil. 2:8, 3:10–11), the author of Ephesians focuses on the resurrection and ascension. He is thus sometimes thought of as intending to replace Paul's "theology of the cross" (1 Cor. 1:18–2:2; 2 Cor. 12:9; 13:4; Phil. 2:5–11) with a triumphalistic "theology of glory." While there is a danger here, the author has mainly shifted the emphasis, without denying the role of Jesus' suffering and death (1:7; 2:13, 16).

Right hand: A reflection of the Christian interpretation of Ps. 110:1. See on Acts 2:34, Col. 3:22.

1:21 This age . . . age to come: See commentary on 1:14.

1:22–23 Has put all things under his feet: An interpretation of Ps. 8:6 as referring to Christ (for christological interpretation of the Old Testament, see excursus at 1 Cor. 15:3). This psalm is also interpreted in Christian terms in 1 Cor. 15:28 and Heb. 2:18, where the "not yet" dimension is emphasized. The author of Ephesians characteristically emphasizes the "already" of the "already/not yet" tension inherent in Christian faith (see on Luke 4:43–44; John 4:23; Rom. 1:18; 8:17; 13:11; 1 Cor. 15:45–48; 2 Cor. 5:17; 2 Tim. 2:18).

Head over all things: Christ is already exalted to share God's role as ruler of the universe (Phil. 2:5–11; Rev. 3:21; 22:1, 3). **For the church, which is his body:** There are two images here that must be kept separate. Christ is "head," i.e., Lord, of the cosmos, not of the body. Head and body metaphors are here distinct. In this world the church (not the cosmos) is the body of Christ, i.e., the agent of his will. As head, Christ's reign is over all, but it is for the benefit of his people, the church.

The fullness of him who fills all in all: Better translated "who is filling," i.e., is in the process of filling. The destiny of the universe is here pictured as finally being filled with the "fullness" of God—then God will be "all in all" (see 1 Cor. 15:28, also in view here in relation to the interpretation of Ps. 8). Since in the author's theology the church is already this "fullness," the church is pictured as already that reconciled, believing, worshiping community that the whole universe will become—the destiny of the universe is to become "church." While this can be understood as prideful Christian triumphalism, it need not be; it is a Christian confession that the love of God *already* manifested in the Christ event and confessed in the Christian community will finally prevail (see excursus, "Universal Salvation and Paradoxical Language," at Rev. 22:21, and comments on the texts listed there).

2:1–6:20
BODY OF THE LETTER

Here the body proper of the letter begins, but it is also a continuation of the preceding worship format. The introductory blessing and thanksgiving fade seamlessly into the main body of the letter, which is composed of two parts: the theological basis (2:1–3:21) for Christian living (4:1–6:9); see "Structure and Outline" in the Introduction above.

2:1–3:21
PART ONE—THEOLOGICAL REFLECTION

Worship in Israel and Judaism often included recitation of God's mighty acts of salvation (see, e.g., Ps. 105; 106, which have several points of contact with Ephesians). This function is fulfilled in Ephesians by affirmations of what God has done in Christ that brought salvation to lost individuals and unity to divided humanity and the fragmented cosmos.

2:1–10
God's Act in Christ Brought Us from Death to Life

In the preceding section the author had reported his prayer for the readers' increased insight into the power of God at work in calling the church into being, so that they would have a deeper understanding of what it means to say, "I belong to the church." This section comprises a compact summary of Pauline teaching found in Romans: the sinful human situation (Rom. 1:18–3:20) is met by the grace of God (Rom. 3:21–11:36), to which the believers' response is good works (Rom. 12:1–16:27). In the Greek text, 2:1–7 is one sentence; the main subject and verb constituting the core of the sentence are found in vv. 4–5: God made us alive.

2:1 You were dead: Seen from the perspective of the new life in Christ, the previous world in which we lived was dominated by death and sin. Death is not just the event that brings physical life to an end, but the power that permeates and determines human life as a whole. **Trespasses and sins** are not merely our own individual evil actions, but the effect of living in the realm where this-worldly values and assumptions prevailed.

2:2 Ruler of the power of the air: The devil, as 4:27; 6:11. The author understands the demonic

forces to be located in the air, i.e., not the atmosphere, but the realm between earth and heaven, separating us from God (see on 1 Thess. 4:17).

2:3 All of us: The author describes the situation of all people, Jew and Gentile, including himself. **Following its desires and thoughts (NIV):** The translation of the NIV is here better than the NRSV, for it correctly indicates that in the natural human situation apart from the grace of God, both "flesh" and "thoughts" are corrupt. There is here no mind/body dualism, as though the mind had noble ideas but the weakness of the flesh prevented their being carried out. As in Rom. 1–3, the whole person is seen as **disobedient** (v. 3), oriented to self rather than to the Creator.

2:4 But God: When sinful human beings could do nothing to attain the life for which they were striving, and when they did not understand their own situation and were not seeking God, the initiative came from God's side, entirely as a matter of divine **mercy** and **love.**

2:5 Made us alive . . . with Christ: God's act in raising Christ is primary, but since Christians are united with Christ, they too are "risen with him" (see 1:3, 20). The Paul of the undisputed letters emphasizes the Christian's identity with Christ at the point of death and burial (Rom. 6:1–6; Gal. 2:20), which are here omitted.

2:7 In the ages to come: The future dimension of salvation is not lacking in Ephesians (see on 1:14), but is subordinated to the present reality. Christians are already chosen and incorporated into the body of Christ, sharing in advance his resurrection life of the age to come, but this is not merely for their own sake—the existence of the church is a testimony to God's grace through ages to come. The author of Ephesians looks ahead to this role of the church in history. The modern reader can look back on more than nineteen centuries of church history as enduring Christian testimony to God's grace, and can gain insight into the continuing nature and mission of the church.

2:8 By grace . . . through faith: Faith is not a meritorious work, but the response to God's grace. **You have been saved:** In the undisputed letters, Paul is reluctant to speak of salvation as something already accomplished, but speaks of it as a present process based on the past event of God's act in Christ and as a future hope (see Rom. 5:1–11; 8:24; Cor 1:18). **This is not your own doing:** The Greek grammar makes it clear that "this" refers not specifically to faith, but to the whole event of salvation, including the believer's faith. Human responsibility is not excluded, but in retrospect the believer sees that faith is not his or her own achievement, but **the gift of God.**

2:9 Not the result of works: The author writes in a later situation than the debate between Paul and the Judaizers of Galatians, and thus does not contrast grace with "works of the law." The point is not that salvation does not come by adhering to the Jewish law, but that salvation, acceptance before God, is granted purely as God's gift rather than by any human achievement. Faith in Christ and a Christian life are not a "work" that makes us acceptable before God, but the grateful response to God's grace.

2:10 We are what he has made us: Literally "we are God's poem." God is here the poet-author who writes our lives as a poem, as God's own creative composition. See on Paul's "new creation" language in Gal. 6:15; 2 Cor. 5:17. Thus even our good works are not something for which we can take credit, any more than we can take credit for the creation of the world. **Created in Christ Jesus for good works:** Still, the author is not "antiworks," as though the Christian life were just trusting in God's grace and continuing to live our previous self-centered little lives. He understands and affirms the Pauline teaching that those accepted by God's grace cannot "continue in sin in order that grace may abound" (see on Rom. 6). In chaps. 4–6 he spells out the content of Christian good works. Here he is intent on instructing the reader that God desires good works from us, but that they are the result of God's gracious, saving act in Christ, not the source and ground of salvation. Throughout, the author preserves the Pauline paradox that Christians are called to do good works, but it is God who works within us (Phil. 2:12–13).

This contrast between "salvation by works" and "salvation by grace through faith" is not a contrast between Old Testament and Jewish works-righteousness and Christian grace and faith. The Old Testament, the Jewish writings from Qumran, and the rabbinic writings all testify to acceptance by God on the basis of God's grace, not human works.

2:11–22
God's Act Created Unity in Christ

The section is divided into three subunits: (a) vv. 11–13 look again at the believers' past, "the way we were," this time from the perspective of God's historical act in choosing Israel, and how the church is related to the chosen people; (b) vv.

14–18 apparently adapt an early Christian hymn celebrating Christ as God's act that created unity; (c) vv. 19–22 summarize the present significance of the church, the imagery modulating from the holy community and family of God to the temple in which God dwells.

2:11 Gentiles by birth: By the author's time, the conflicts of Paul's time, reflected in Galatians, now belong to the past, and the church is primarily a Gentile community. **The uncircumcision . . . the circumcision:** Since circumcision was the mark of God's covenant with Israel (Gen. 17:10–14; Lev. 12:3), these were terms for "non-Jewish" (= Gentile) and "Jewish." Already in the Old Testament, circumcision was understood in more than a physical sense (Deut. 10:16; 30:6; see Rom. 2:25–29).

2:12 Remember: The history of God's mighty acts in the past, in the time of Israel, also now belong to their history (see Deut. 5:1–5). **At that time:** They were not aware of it at the time, but in retrospect they can see that as Gentiles they have only recently been incorporated into God's plan for history (see on 1:10). They were then "outsiders," but did not then realize it; it is only now that they are "insiders" that they can see their former status and give thanks that they are now included. As 2:1–3 had presented their previous situation as caught in the human condition generally in its alienation from God, here their prior condition is described as not (yet) included in God's redemptive plan that began with the election of a particular people. This is the author's reinterpretation of Rom. 9–11 (see 9:4). Israel had the hope for the **Christ,** participated in the **covenants,** had **hope,** believed in the one true **God.**

2:13 But now: The grand turning point. Their deprived past is seen only from the perspective of the blessed present. **In Christ Jesus:** The change in their situation was not brought about by their own quest, but by God's act in Christ. **Far off . . . brought near:** This is the language of Isa. 57:19 combined with Isa. 52:9, which had already been adapted in Judaism to apply to proselytes, Gentiles who had adopted the Jewish faith and been incorporated into Judaism. The author himself appropriates this language to express his conviction that Gentiles (and Jews who accepted the Christian faith) have been incorporated into the new (= renewed) people of God, the one church of Jews and Gentiles. Here there is no struggle for this basic Pauline understanding of the nature of the church; unlike the earlier period represented by Galatians (and portrayed in Acts

9–15), the unity of Jews and Gentiles in the one church of God is presented as an accomplished fact. The author is not trying to persuade his readers, but to appreciate their present situation that already exists.

2:14–15 He is our peace: Careful analysis of vv. 14–18 have convinced several scholars that these verses are the author's reworking of an early Christian hymn (see on Phil. 2:6–11; Col. 1:15–20). The hymn originally celebrated Christ as the cosmic victor who had restored unity to a fragmented universe. The author refocuses this cosmic meaning on the historical act of creating the new community, the church, that unites fragmented humanity. Here as elsewhere in the Bible (e.g. Rom. 5:1), **"peace"** is resonant with the overtones of the Hebrew *shalom,* i.e., it implies not merely the cessation of hostilities but the positive sense of wholeness, what life was created to be. Christ did not teach peace merely as an ideal we should strive to emulate; he himself, in his own person, is the peace of God, who unites divided humanity in his body, the church. The Pauline concept of corporate humanity, Christ as the second Adam (1 Cor. 15:22, 45; Rom. 5:12–21), is in the background of the author's thought. **Made both groups into one:** The primal division between Jews and Gentiles is here taken as the paradigm of divided humanity. **Broken down the dividing wall:** In the original hymn, this probably referred to the wall that separates the heavenly world from earth, an idea common in some religious thought of the ancient world. The hymn praised Christ as the one who removed the wall that separated heaven and earth and opened up access to God, thus restoring cosmic unity. The author understands the wall to refer to a historical reality that had separated Jews and Gentiles, not a cosmic wall separating heaven and earth. Some interpreters have seen a reference to the literal wall in the temple that separated the court of Israel from the court of the Gentiles, a wall that had literally been broken down in the 70 CE destruction of Jerusalem, but it is unlikely the Gentile readers in Asia Minor would have understood this without further explanation. But Judaism spoke of the Law as a "fence" that separated Jews from Gentiles, and the author here specifically interprets the dividing wall that has been broken down as meaning the **law with its commandments and ordinances**. In the author's understanding, this law has been **abolished** by Christ.

A generation earlier, in the thick of debate about the validity of the Old Testament-Jewish law, Paul had presented a more complex view, but one clear element of his understanding that remained constant was that Christian faith did not mean that the law was abolished (Rom. 3:31; see Matt. 5:17–20). In the Ephesian author's situation, that debate is over, and from his perspective in the present context he can simply declare that the law that separated Jew from Gentile has been abolished in the Christ event. This does not mean, however, that the Old Testament is no longer Christian Scripture—the author repeatedly cites from it and understands it in a Christian perspective (see, e.g., 4:8, 25; 5:30). In 6:2–3 he will explicitly cite the law as giving positive instruction to Christians.

One new person: The author does not have an individual "person" in mind, but, like Paul in Rom. 5:12–21, is thinking in corporate terms of the human race as a whole. As Adam represented all humanity, so Christ represents the new, renewed humanity. The church that finds its reality "in Christ" is thus the prototype of reunited humanity, in which all us/them thinking is broken down. In the author's theology, the Jew/Gentile division so important for Old Testament and Jewish thought is taken as the model for all the divisions that fragment humanity. Christ (= God-in-Christ) is here the Creator of the church, which is not a voluntaristic society for improvement of the world, but the agent of God, who called it into being as witness and agent for the reconciliation of all humanity to God and to each other.

2:16 Reconcile both groups in one body through the cross: With the dissolution of the dividing wall that separated Jew and Gentile, all human insider/outsider mentality, all us/them divisions are removed. As *all* humanity, Jewish and Gentile, is seen as previously under God's wrath, so *all* are now reconciled by God's act in Christ. (Otherwise, the author would be advocating the strange view that the Jewish Messiah in fact benefits only Gentiles.)

2:17 He came and proclaimed peace: The peace proclaimed is not primarily that Jews and Gentiles are now reconciled to each other, but that God's act has reconciled *both* to God, i.e., it is primarily "vertical" and *then* "horizontal" (Rom. 5:1). The division between Jews and Gentiles (and all other human divisions) can in fact be healed because God has already acted to reconcile all of humanity to himself (2 Cor. 5:19). This gospel of peace refers to the

Christ Event as a whole, not to the preaching of the earthly Jesus. Paul and the Pauline tradition never refer to the content of Jesus' preaching. In any case, Jesus' proclamation as represented in the Gospels does deal with the unity of Jews and Gentiles (Matt. 10:5–6!). It is rather the risen Christ, as he works through his apostles and prophets, who brings his disciples to the insight that God is now uniting all peoples in one community (Matt. 28:16–20; Acts 1–15; see on Eph. 2:20; 3:5, 4:11 below).

2:19 No longer strangers and aliens: Those who formerly were outsiders have been made insiders, **members of the household** and fellow **citizens. With the saints:** The word actually means "holy ones" and could refer to angels, but more likely refers to the whole church of Jews and Gentiles, as elsewhere in Ephesians.

2:20 Foundation of the apostles and prophets: The reference is to the apostles of the founding generation of the church and the early Christian prophets (not Old Testament prophets; see the word order and 3:5). In contrast to 1 Cor. 3:9–11, where Christ is the sole foundation, here the foundation is provided by the first-generation Christian leaders who, inspired by the Holy Spirit, forged the constitution of the new community. Christ is then the cornerstone (of the foundation) by which all else is aligned, or perhaps the keystone that holds the whole structure together (see NRSV note and NAB "capstone").

2:21 Grows into a holy temple: The imagery shifts from body to building, but retains the growth metaphor. **Built together spiritually into a dwelling place for God:** The destruction of the Jerusalem temple in 70 CE caused both Jewish and Christian communities to rethink the meaning of the temple as God's earthly residence. The sectarian Jewish community at Qumran, convinced that the Jerusalem temple was illegitimate and staffed with unauthorized priests, had already developed the imagery of the community itself as the temple of God (see 1 Cor. 3:9–11; 1 Pet. 2:6; Rev. 21:14).

3:1–13
The Role of the Apostle in God's Plan
for the Ages

3:1 This is the reason: The author begins a prayer, which he interrupts with a digression on Paul's own apostolic ministry, then returns to the prayer mode in 3:14, repeating the same introductory phrase. The effect is to insert affirmations about the place of Paul's own ministry in God's saving plan as that for which the community hears Paul give thanks. **This** refers to Paul's ministry proclaiming and implementing the unity of Jews and Gentiles in Christ, as explicated in 1:3–2:23. The author looks back on the life of Paul as a whole as the reason for his suffering and imprisonment, not merely on one particular incident that provoked a particular arrest.

3:2 The commission of God's grace: Commission is the same Greek word translated "plan" in 1:10 and 3:9. Paul's *mission* is part of God's gracious *plan*. **Given me for you:** Paul's apostleship was not merely something special about Paul, but was for the sake of the church, especially the Gentile believers for whom Paul had struggled.

3:3 The mystery was made known to me by revelation: The revelation of the unity of all peoples in the one church of God was not a part of the teaching of Jesus, but the post-Easter insight given through Christian apostles and prophets on the basis of the Christ event understood as a whole (2:20; 3:5). In the Pauline school of the author's time, Paul is considered the leading member of the group through whom the revelatory insights came. Though considered innovative and controversial in Paul's own time (see Gal. 2; Acts 15), in Ephesians the unity of the one church of Jews and Gentiles is considered as established truth given by God's revelation.

As I wrote above: "Above" can also be translated "before," "previously," or "already." The NRSV takes it to refer to the previous paragraphs of this same letter, but it may better be understood as referring to Paul's previous letters, already being collected and circulating in the author's time and forming the basis for Christian instruction in the Pauline churches of Asia Minor.

3:4 A reading of which will enable you to perceive: Though revealed to apostles and prophets (v. 5), the new revelation is confirmed as having come from God by being recognized and validated by the Christian community as a whole (see at Rev. 2:20). The Spirit of God is at work not only in particular charismatically endowed individuals, but in the church as a whole. The revelatory gestalt, the configuration by which prophetic revelation is received, is event + prophetic interpretation + community reception. Prophets do not simply speak the word of God "out of the blue," but as interpreters of God's acts in history. The action of

God is always ambiguous and can be interpreted in more than one way. At the Red Sea, *something happened,* an event that allowed Israel to escape from the pursuing Egyptians. One could say either, as the Egyptians presumably did, "Lucky for the Israelites the wind came up and dried out an escape route for them," or, "Praise God, who has delivered his people." The prophet Moses declared the event an act of God, and the community of Israel was enabled to perceive it as such. In the case to which Ephesians is pointing, the event was the revolutionary acts of some churches in accepting Gentiles into the holy people of God previously confined to Israel (see Acts 10–11). The event is ambiguous—it could be a new and definitive phase of God's plan for history, or it could be another failure of God's people in not maintaining the divinely given standards, watering down the revelation they had been given to preserve by keeping the distinction between the holy and the profane. Prophets (or some of them) declare the event to be God's will. Yet the apostolic or prophetic say-so does not in itself settle the issue—particularly in a situation where there are competing prophetic voices. The Spirit-endowed community itself and as a whole discerns among the rival claims which is the authentic word of God. In this case, the church, led by the Holy Spirit, discerned that the prophetic interpretation of Paul and his associates was authentic: it is God's plan for history to unite all things and all persons, Jew and Gentile, in the one church of God.

3:5 Not made known . . . in other generations . . . now been revealed (NIV): The author does not operate according to the prophecy/fulfillment schema in interpreting the Old Testament. Though the Old Testament is Scripture for him (see 4:8, 25; 5:31; 6:2), he does not understand Old Testament prophets as having predicted the saving events of Christ and the church (contrast Paul; see "New Testament Interpretation of the Old Testament," excursus at 1 Cor. 15:3). For Ephesians (as Col. 1:26), God's eschatological plan of salvation—the Christ event that generated the one church of Jews and Gentiles—was not known until revealed through Christian apostles and prophets. **Revealed to his holy apostles and prophets:** In Col. 1:26, the author's model for this paragraph, the revelation was to the church in general. Ephesians manifests a later narrowing to more "official" bearers of revelation.

3:8 The very least of all the saints: Paul's statement about himself in 1 Cor. 15:9–10 is here both intensified and generalized. "Very least" is literally an ungrammatical Greek expression, the comparative of a superlative, "less than the least," "leaster." Paul in 1 Corinthians compared himself to other apostles, here to all Christians. This unprovoked insistence on his own humility would be strange for the historical Paul, but was common in the church fathers of the second century, who illustrated the grace of God by pointing to the unworthiness of the apostles. Thus *Barn.* 5:9, "When he chose his own apostles who were destined to preach his gospel (who were sinful beyond all measure in order that he might demonstrate that 'he did not come to call the righteous but sinners' . . .")."

3:9 God who created all things: The scheme of redemption centered in God's act in Christ is not a contingent plan worked out by God in response to human failure, but the sovereign, unconditioned will of the Creator.

3:10 Through the church . . . made known: The principalities and powers **in the heavenly places** (see Rom. 8:38; 1 Cor. 2:7–8; Col. 1:16, 26; 2:15, 20; Eph. 2:2; 6:12) are not to be feared, as though these supernatural powers were the source of deeper wisdom. The church does not learn "mysteries" from them; they first learn of the "mystery," God's saving plan for history, by observing God's acts in Christ and the church (see 1 Pet. 3:18–19). The transcendent powers in the heavens are amazed at the act of God in forming a new human community in which all barriers are broken down.

3:13 I pray: The reader is reminded that all of 1:3–21, though full of heavy theological content, is presented in the mode of prayer rather than cool theological analysis. **Not lose heart over my sufferings for you:** As in the case of Jesus' suffering and humiliating death, the readers are reminded that Paul's suffering is not a reason for despair but for hope: **they are your glory.** The God who works in all things for good (see Rom. 8:28) has incorporated Paul's suffering (and death, of which the readers were aware—see the introduction to Ephesians) into his eternal purpose (see Col. 1:24; 2 Tim. 2:10).

3:14–21
The Apostle's Prayer and Doxology

The section consists of two sentences in Greek, the apostolic prayer-report in vv. 14–19 and the doxology of vv. 20–21 that concludes the first major part of the two-part letter (see "Structure and Outline" in the introduction to Ephesians).

3:14–15 For this reason: Identical phrase to 3:1, picking up the thought broken off by the digression on Paul's apostolic role of vv. 2–13. **From whom every family . . . takes its name:** "Family" is Greek *patria,* similar to *patera,* "Father," of the preceding clause. The word-play cannot be reproduced in English. The point has to do with the greatness of God, not human or heavenly families: God is the Creator and sustainer of all the structures in which earthly and heavenly beings are organized (see 3:9; 4:6).

3:17 Christ may dwell in your hearts: See 2:20 and Paul's immediate qualification. In the believer's experience, the reality of the risen Christ and the presence of the Holy Spirit are one and the same; see their interchangeability in Rom. 8:9–11; 2 Cor. 3:17; Rev. 2–3 (*Christ* speaks; hear what the *Spirit* says to the churches). That believers are "in Christ" is an objective reality (see on 2 Cor. 5:17). The author prays that they may experience in their own lives their actual situation. **Rooted and grounded in love:** See on 1 Cor. 13. Love is not a moral character trait, but the sphere of the believer's existence.

3:18 Power to comprehend, with all the saints: The insight and spiritual strengthening the apostle prays that the readers might experience is neither a personal attainment (it comes **with power through his Spirit** [v. 16]) nor an individual matter (it is **with all the saints**). The Holy Spirit is the divine breath that breathes through the body of Christ and enlivens the Christian community for its mission. The individual Christian finds his or her strength and insight not via a lonely spiritual quest, but through participation in the body. **The breadth and length and height and depth:** All four nouns are governed by one article in Greek, indicating (differently from English grammar) that the four nouns all refer to one thing. While divine Wisdom is sometimes described in terms of these four dimensions (Job 11:5–9; Sir. 1:3), and while Ephesians is interested in the readers' attaining deeper wisdom (1:8, 17; 3:8, 10), the one referent here is more likely **the love of Christ.** Christ's love is not distinct from God's love (see, e.g., Rom. 8:35–39); the figures of God and Christ fade into each other; it is God's love that is made known in Christ.

3:19 To know . . . that surpasses knowledge: The author knows he is straining human language past the breaking point, that the mystery of the mighty acts of God cannot really be grasped in human thoughts and language. Rather than being paralyzed, reduced to silence by this awareness, it frees him to use human language to point to the inexpressible reality of God. This accords with the meaning of the incarnation, in which the absolute and infinite is revealed in the relative and finite (see on John 1:1–14).

Filled with all the fullness of God: This is the same language used of Christ in Col. 1:19, the author's model. Christians are "in Christ," the Christ reality is their reality. The author prays that they will *realize* it, let it be active in the way they live their lives (see v. 17).

3:20 More than all we can ask or imagine: All of 3:14–21 is a prayer. Yet the answer to prayer is not merely the fulfillment of our expectations and requests. We do not know how to pray as we ought (Rom. 8:26–27). Yet when the author prays, his prayer is big, for it glorifies a great God. There is nothing petty or trivial about the author's understanding of worship, prayer, or the church, all of which is shaped by his vision of the greatness of God.

3:21 Glory in the church and in Christ Jesus: The conclusion and summary once again unite Christ and church, but place the church first. This in no way suggests that the church is superior to Christ, who calls it into being and empowers it for its mission. But the church, the Christian community, is the visible sign of God's once-for-all act and continuing presence. The church is not here to glorify itself but to praise God. Worship is part of the church's *mission* in the world; by its own worship and being it calls the world to glorify its Creator. **Forever and ever:** Not a mere concluding liturgical flourish. The Christ event and resulting Christian community are God's ultimate (eschatological) plan for the world, not to be superseded. There is no Plan B.

4:1–6:20
Part Two—Ethical Exhortations on Living as Christians

In typical Pauline style, the author turns from the grand theological vision of the nature of the church to the nature of the Christian life—sometimes expressed as from indicative to imperative, from theology to ethics, from theory to practice. Such descriptions are helpful, but not entirely accurate or sufficient. The "ethical" section continues to be heavily "theological," just as the preceding "theoretical" section is not mere speculation but already has "practical" life in view.

4:1–16
Building Up the Body of Christ

The first paragraph of parenesis, "practical instructions," is still oriented not to individualistic ethics but toward Christian responsibility as life in the church.

4:1 I therefore . . . beg you: These are the same Greek words as in Rom. 12:1 and have the same function at the same structural location in the letter. The "therefore" is not unimportant; as in Rom. 12, ethics do not stand alone, but require a theological foundation. What one believes and how one understands it (theology) affect the way one lives (ethics). **The calling to which you have been called:** See on 1:17–18; 2:15.

4:2 Humility and gentleness: In the Hellenistic world of the first century, humility was regarded not as a virtue but a sign of weakness and servility. In the Old Testament and Jewish tradition reflected here, humility before God is not a matter of weakness of character or low self-image, but the appropriate stance before the faithful Creator. Insecure people need constant reassurance and reinforcement of their self-image in order to "feel good about themselves." The personal security found in authentic faith has been delivered from self-centeredness. **Bearing with one another in love:** Love is not here an idealistic virtue one should strive for, but the considerate, unselfish concern for others essential in the life of a family—the household of faith (2:19), where all are brothers and sisters in Christ.

4:3 The unity of the Spirit: Not a subjective attitude, but the objective reality of the unity of the one body of Christ given by the Holy Spirit.

4:4–6 One body . . . one God: Christians are called to maintain and exhibit this unity given by God, not to create it. The point here is that there is one church, one faith, one baptism, just as there is one Lord, one God. This is an inclusive view of the church. The author does not view his particular group as "the" one church, but urges his readers to see themselves as already belonging to the one body of Christ composed of various groups.

4:7 Each of us was given grace: The word for "grace" also means "gift"; the point here is that within the one body there is still a variety of "gifts and graces" (see Rom. 12:3–9; 1 Cor. 12:4–31). This sedtion (vv. 4–7) has many verbal similarities to 1 Cor. 12 and Rom. 12, on which it is based, but there Paul's emphasis was on the diversity necessary in a local con-

gregation for it to function as a living body; here the emphasis is on the one body of the universal church.

4:8 It is said: In Ps. 68:18, which the author understands christologically. The New Testament authors have a variety of ways of appropriating the Old Testament Scripture as a Christian book (see excursus at 1 Cor. 15:3). The ancient psalm was about God's leading Israel out of Egypt to the promised land, where God was enthroned in the temple and received gifts. It had already been reinterpreted in some streams of Jewish tradition in terms of Moses and his "ascension" and associated with the festival of Pentecost. The Jewish Targum (a paraphrasing interpretation read in the synagogue) had already changed the second person passive "you received" to third person active "he gave." Thus, while the author of Ephesians understands the psalm in a manner different from the way it was originally intended, his interpretation is not an arbitrary Christian imposition on the text, but is in line with the developing Jewish tradition and the accepted methods of his own day.

4:9 The lower parts of the earth: The "of" here is appositional, as in "the city of Fort Worth"; so the meaning is "the lower parts, namely, the earth." The author's cosmology has only two realms, heaven and earth, as in Gen. 1:1, not three, as in, e.g., Phil. 2:10, Rev. 5:13. **He ascended . . . he had also descended:** The author's reinterpretation of the psalm has been understood in three ways in the history of the church: (1) Christ descended into the realm of the dead between crucifixion and resurrection, liberated the redeemed held captive there, and took them with him to heaven at his own ascension (see 1 Pet. 3:18–21 and the variety of interpretations proposed for it). This interpretation is unlikely; it fits neither the author's cosmology nor his theology. (2) The reference is to Christ's descent at the incarnation and ascent at the resurrection. (3) The reference is to Christ's ascent at the resurrection and "descent" in the person of the Holy Spirit to give gifts to the church. In this interpretation, Christ is identified with Spirit (as in 1:13; 4:30; 3:16–17; see 1 Cor. 15:45; Rom. 8:9–11; 2 Cor. 3:17). Although (2) is quite possible, (3) is to be preferred, since the psalm had already been interpreted with reference to Pentecost, and since in the context the risen Christ gives the gifts of ministry to the church, which happened not at the incarnation but after the cross/resurrection/ascension event.

4:11 The gifts he gave: The meaning here is different from v. 7, in which gifts are given *to* each member of the body of Christ, the church. Here ministers *are* gifts of the risen Christ to the whole church. For **apostles,** see on Luke 6:12–16. **Prophets:** Not predictors of the future, but directly inspired spokespersons for the risen Lord (see on Acts 2:17; 11:27; 21:4; 1 Cor. 14; 1 Thess. 4:2, 15–17; Rev. 1). **Evangelists:** Missionaries beyond the local congregation who found new churches. **Pastors and teachers:** A distinct group charged with teaching and pastoral care of congregations. In Paul's time, apostles, prophets, and teachers were all contemporaries. For the author of Ephesians, apostles and prophets belong to the past founding generation (2:20; 3:5), while contemporary church leadership is represented by evangelists and pastor-teachers. In contrast to the later Pastorals (see on 1 Tim. 3), church leadership is not yet a matter of ordination, but there is already an identifiable group of ministers. The ministries of evangelism, pastoral care, and teaching are distinct, but overlapping.

4:12 To equip the saints for the work of ministry: The Greek text can be punctuated two ways; the first edition of the RSV had "for the equipment of the saints, for the work of ministry," the comma signaling that equipping the saints and the work of ministry were the responsibilities of pastor-teachers. In the NRSV, the NIV, later editions of the RSV, and other modern translations, the absence of the comma identifies "the work of ministry" as the responsibility of the laity, for which they are equipped by pastor-teachers. The ministry of the laity, the service of the whole community of faith to each other and the world, is an important element in New Testament theology as a whole, but here the meaning if more likely that pastor-teachers are charged with "the work of ministry." In the author's time and place, the church is finding it necessary to have a more structured and "official" ministry than previously, though there is as nothing yet in Ephesians about ordination or a clear line between clergy and laity. Teaching the faith is a major responsibility for the church in a non-Christian society in which the culture itself does not pass along Christian values and perspectives.

4:13 Until all of us come to the unity of the faith: The unity of the one faith is both a divinely given gift (4:5) and a goal to be attained. In the Pauline dialectic of indicative/imperative, already/not-yet, the church is called to become what it truly already is. **To maturity, to . . . the full stature of Christ:** The church is already "in Christ," but must grow into its true identity.

4:14 We must no longer be children: It is a mark of immaturity when members of the church are drawn away by every fascinating new religious idea. The risen Christ gives pastor-teachers to help the church mature and resist such childish interests.

4:15 Speaking the truth in love: The author's perspective is ecumenical, not merely congregational ("church" appears nine times in Ephesians, always of the universal church, never of the local congregation). The truth of which the writer speaks is the authentic Christian tradition mediated by apostles and prophets, the "apostolic faith" (2:20; 3:5). Thus this instruction is not only about how church members should get along with each other in the local congregation, but how Christians of different groups relate to each other in the one church of God. Neither truth nor love can be one-sidedly appropriated. Ecumenicity requires commitment to both. The truth of the faith can be claimed in an unloving way that violates the very claim to Christian truth; love can be affirmed in a shallow manner indifferent to truth.

4:17–32
The Old Life and the New

4:17 No longer live as the Gentiles live: Though themselves ethnically Gentiles (2:11–12; 3:1), the readers now belong to the new Christian community that transcends the Jew/Gentile division (see on 2:14–19). Though not ethnically Jews, they can look on the unbelieving world and their own unbelieving past as a "Gentile" way of life that cannot continue (see 1 Pet. 1:13; 2:11–12).

4:20–21 The way you learned Christ . . . you were taught in him: The Christian faith is transmitted by teaching. The readers have become Christian and have entered into a new life by "learning." The author lived in a pre-Constantinian world in which the church could not expect the culture to transmit the faith; people did not learn what it meant to be "Christian" by absorbing the ethos of the dominant culture. The "Christian culture" of the West has dissolved. As the world of the twenty-first century becomes more and more secularized, the church finds itself in the same situation as the readers of Ephesians and must develop its teaching/learning strategies to pass on the authentic Christian faith.

4:22–24 Put away ... your old self ... clothe yourselves with the new self: See on Gal. 3:27–28. Conversion to the new life is compared to taking off old clothes and putting on new, clean garments. The later church symbolized this by having baptismal candidates disrobe on one side of the baptistery and put on new clothes as they emerged from the other side. We do not know if this practice was as early as Ephesians. The message is addressed to insiders; conversion is not a once-for-all event that can be checked off the "to do" list and left behind.

4:25 Speak the truth to our neighbors: An allusion to Zech. 8:16. The Christian life is a matter not only of theological truth (4:14–15), but of truth in everyday personal relations. The universal human assumption is that people say what is to their own advantage, that projecting a desirable self-image is primary in what people say. Christians are freed from this concern with the self (see 2:3, 10; 4:2, 22–24). The "neighbors" (not just fellow Christians) will note the way Christian talk is dedicated to truth rather than self, and this becomes a powerful evangelistic witness.

4:26 Be angry but do not sin: A quotation from Ps. 4:5 in the Greek translation used by the author (LXX). Here and in the previous verse the author weaves biblical texts into his exhortation without calling attention to their source. **Do not let the sun go down:** Anger itself is not necessarily sinful, but nursing grudges disrupts and poisons the life of the community.

4:28 Have something to share with the needy: The warning against stealing is not only a matter of individual morality or honest labor. It is assumed that those who have this world's goods will share with others.

4:30 Marked with a seal for the day of redemption: The basis for Eph. 4:29–5:2 is provided by Col. 3:8–14; see further comments there. Thus 4:30 corresponds to Col. 1:14.

4:32 Forgiving ... as God in Christ has forgiven you: See the variations on this theme in Matt. 6:14–15; 18:21–35.

5:1–14
Living as Children of Light

See further comments on Col. 3:5–9, which formed the basis for this section elaborated by the author of Ephesians.

5:1 Be imitators of God: The specific point to be imitated is God's forgiveness (see the preceding point), but the instruction presupposes a wider perspective. Christian life involves patterning our behavior toward others after God's. There is no specific call to imitate Christ, but to imitate God's behavior, as Jesus did. As was also the case with Paul, the author's ethic does not involve a call to imitate Jesus' conduct; the details of the earthly life of Jesus are not the author's model for Christian life. Rather, it is the life of Christ as a whole, summed up in his going to the cross, that represents his unselfish sacrifice for others. This is not something different or distinct from the love of God. Particularly in this section, 4:32–5:5, the figures of God and Christ modulate into each other. Christ's love for others *is* God's love.

5:3 Fornication: Any kind of sexual immorality, including adultery. The author understands all extramarital sex to be immoral. Sex ethics is not a matter of accommodating oneself to changing cultural mores, but of living out the implications of one's life "in Christ," with one's body incorporated into the body of Christ. **Not even be mentioned:** The repeated references in this section to one's conversation as an element in sexual ethics (see v. 4) reveal the connection between talk and behavior. Coarse sexual humor as entertainment does not take sex seriously enough as God's gift, but degrades something that is holy, trivializes a divine gift as a common element of this world.

5:5–6 One who is greedy (that is, an idolater): The author can lump greed, idolatry, and sexual immorality together in one category of sinful behavior, for all are self-centered, locating the center of life in this world, which should rather be seen as the good creation that points to the Creator, the appropriate center of life (see Rom. 1:21–25, in the back of the author's mind as he writes this section). Thus instead of coarse entertaining talk of sex, Christian talk is **thanksgiving** (v. 4), oriented to the Creator in grateful response for the good gifts of life rather than idolizing the creation, including our own psyches and self-images—which also violate the command against making idolatrous images (Exod. 20:4–5).

No ... inheritance ... wrath of God: See Paul's warnings in 1 Cor. 6:9–10; 15:50; Gal. 5:15–21. Understanding God as the God of infinite love and ultimate inclusiveness does not exclude pictures of God's wrath against sin, of how terrible it is to reject God's grace (see discussion at Rev. 6:15; 14:16; 16:1–21). **Kingdom of Christ and of God:** See Rev. 11:15.

5:8 Once ... darkness ... now ... light: On the dualism of New Testament thought, see on

John 8:23; 12:47–48; 13:30; Luke 9:49; 16:8; introduction to Revelation. Believers once belonged to the darkness; they are now not only in the light, but are light (see Matt. 5:14), i.e., they participate in and mediate the light of Christ to the world.

5:11 Take no part . . . but instead expose them: Light does not exist only for itself. Here the function of light is to expose and reprove sinful deeds of others. Other places in the New Testament point out the dangers of a self-righteous judgmental attitude (Matt. 7:1–5), but hesitancy to judge others does not mean an individualistic withdrawal into oneself, as though what others do is "none of my business." Light, simply by being what it is, reveals the dark side of human life.

5:15–20
Life as Thanksgiving and Praise

5:14 Everything . . . is light: The Christian light that shines in the world's darkness is not only to expose and reprove, but to allow the darkness itself to become light, i.e., to allow unbelievers to see their situation in the light of Christ and to become believers themselves. The shining of the light is part of the work of the gospel that will finally transform the whole creation into the kingdom of God (see on 1:10, 23). Christians may let their light shine (see Matt. 5:16) in the glad hope that the light of God will finally prevail, for it has already happened to them—they themselves were once darkness but are now light (5:8). **Sleeper, awake!:** The latter part of v. 14 is probably an extract from a familiar baptismal hymn. The newly baptized are greeted by the congregation as those who have awakened from sleep, have risen from the dead (see Col. 3:1–4), and have been transformed from darkness to light. This has already happened to the readers (indicative), but they are now reminded of their baptism and called to be what they are (imperative).

5:15 Be careful then how you live: This section is closely related to Col. 3:16–17; 4:5. There, however, the believers' behavior is related to its impression on outsiders; here, internal relationships, especially the worship of the community, are the focus.

5:18 Wine . . . Spirit: The author emphasizes the vitalizing role of the Spirit in the Christian congregation (see 1:3, 13, 14, 17; 2:18, 22; 3:16; 4:30; 6:17, 18), reintroducing a perspective that had been present in Paul but minimized in Colossians (see on Col. 1:9). The author is aware of the use of alcohol in some religions

to "get the spirit," just as he is aware of the danger of charismatic excesses, being carried away with exuberant feelings mistaken as the work of the Spirit. see Prov. 23:31; Acts 2:1–21, esp. vv. 13–15. **Be filled:** Reminiscent of 1:23; 3:19; 4:13, where the church is described as the fullness of God and Christ. To be filled with the Spirit is the functional equivalent of being in Christ or having Christ in us. This fullness of God and Christ is mediated to the church by the Spirit—another of the implicit Trinitarian aspects of the theology of Ephesians. Since the instruction proceeds to speak of community worship, the exhortation is not to the cultivation of individual private "spiritual experiences," but to participation in the life of the community, especially its worship, where the Spirit enlivens the church as the breath gives life to the body ("spirit" and "breath" are the same word in Greek; see 3:18).

5:19 Psalms . . . spiritual songs: See Col. 3:17.

5:21–6:9
Life in the Orderly Christian Household

The author expands and interprets the household code found in Col. 3:18–4:1. See comments there. On interpreting the household codes in the New Testament, see especially the "principles of interpretation" at 1 Pet. 2:11–3:12. Here we consider only the elements distinctive of Ephesians.

5:21 Be subject to one another: This general command addressed to all Christians is the context in which the following directions are to be understood. In the social structures of the day, wives were subject to husbands, children to parents, slaves to masters; in the Christian community there is a mutual serving of one another that takes precedence over all social structures. The imperative in the English translation renders a participle in the Greek text that, instead of beginning a new section, continues the preceding instructions for wise and Spirit-filled living (5:15, 18). The household code is not a law, but an expression of living according to Christian wisdom and in the realm of the Spirit. **Reverence for Christ:** Literally "in the fear of Christ," in the same sense in which the traditional biblical phrase "fear of God" is used—not fright or terror, but worshipful awareness that one is dealing with the Creator (see 2 Cor. 5:11). God-language is again used with reference to Christ; Christian life in the home is not a matter of social convention, but of one's worshipful obedience to God.

5:22 Wives, be subject: See on Col. 3:18–4:1; 1 Pet. 2:11–3:12. The subordination called for means to fit in with the given orders of social structure, to the extent that one can do so without compromising the fundamentals of Christian faith. The submission called for is not blind obedience, but adapting one's family life to the expectations of society in a way that does not hinder the mission of the church.

5:23 As Christ is the head of the church: The author adopts the image of the church as bride of Christ, itself adapted from the imagery of the Old Testament in which Israel was the bride of God (see Hos. 1–3; Ezek. 16:8–14; Mark 2:18–22; Matt. 22:1–14; 25:1–13; Luke 12:35–38; John 3:29; 2 Cor. 11:2; Rev. 19:7, 9; 22:2, 9, 17). Weaving back and forth between this christological image and earthly family life has the effect of lifting the marriage relationship to a sacred level (in the Hellenistic world it was a secular contract without religious associations). While in Paul and the other New Testament references listed above, the present is the time of engagement with the marriage to be celebrated in the eschatological future, the author of Ephesians characteristically shifts the emphasis to the present: the church is already the bride of Christ, and Christian marriage should reflect this. To be sure, the imagery throughout is androcentric, reflecting the male-dominated culture of the times. Modern readers may well ask why it is that only the husband is thought of as representing Christ, only the wife as the subordinate church, but this perspective had not yet emerged in the author's time.

5:25 Husbands, love your wives: The instructions to husbands are greatly expanded from the Colossians model—one line has become a paragraph (see Col. 3:19).

5:26 Washing of water: A reference to baptism by which people were incorporated into the body of Christ, becoming Christ's "bride." **By the word:** The act of baptism was accompanied by the interpreting word, which may be either the confession of faith spoken at baptism (see Acts 8:37; Rom. 10:9–10), the words of the minister administering baptism (including the name of Christ or the Father, Son, and Holy Spirit; see Acts 2:38; James 2:7; Matt. 28:19), or the purifying word of the Christian message as such (see John 15:3; 17:17).

5:28–29 He who loves his wife loves himself: Husbands are to love their wives with the same kind of self-giving, self-sacrificing love that Christ shows to the church. Since the church is Christ's body (1:23; 4:4; 5:23), and since the husband **tenderly cares** for his own

body, even this "self-centered" love becomes a model for the love of husband for wife.

5:31–32 The two will become one flesh . . . I am applying it to Christ and the church: The author sees in the unity of man and wife in Gen. 2:24 a prototype of the unity of Christ and the church. Better said from the author's perspective: the author sees the love of Christ for the church as the prototype of human marriage, in which two separate persons are merged into one.

6:1 Children, obey your parents: See Col. 3:20. Children are directly addressed, as responsible members of the congregation who will hear the letter read and can make their own decision to respond. Thus the directive does not include infants or small children.

6:2–3 Honor your father and mother: One of the Ten Commandments (see Exod. 20:12; Deut. 5:16). **So that . . . you may live long:** The perspective no longer expects the soon coming of the Lord, as in Paul's day. Thus the church adjusts to the new situation and orders its family life for its extended journey through history and its mission to the world.

6:4 Bring them up in the . . . instruction of the Lord: The responsibility for Christian education is placed on the shoulders of the head of the family. This is added to the earlier instruction in Col. 3:21, as the church becomes more concerned about passing on the faith to future generations (see on 4:12).

6:5–9 Slaves, obey your . . . masters: See on Col. 3:22–4:1 and the introduction to Philemon. **There is no partiality:** This concluding line is added to the Colossian household code; the author of Ephesians ends as he began, with a reminder that even the conventional patriarchal structures of first-century Asia Minor are here adopted only in the perspective of the universal Lord who shows no partiality and calls all members of the church not to domination and subordination, but to mutual unselfish service (see 5:21).

6:10–20
Armed with God's Armor

6:10 The strength of his power: God's power revealed in Christ is that of suffering love for the sake of others, the power of God made perfect in weakness (see 1 Cor. 2:2; 2 Cor. 12:9; 13:4). The image of "the Christ" was originally the powerful military figure who would bring about God's righteous reign by violence (see Isa. 11:1–9); this image was transformed and filled with new content by God's act revealed in the suffering and death of Jesus. Both Jesus (Matt. 10:34; Luke 14:31) and Paul (1 Thess. 5:8; 2 Cor. 6:7; 10:3, 4; Rom. 6:13, 23; 13:12) used military imagery, as did the nonviolent Martin Luther King Jr., as the vehicle for the nonviolent gospel. Thus the military imagery here is not a call for Christians to support militaristic politics. See 2:15—the paradox is that the gospel of peace makes one ready for "war," i.e., struggle against entrenched evil.

6:11 The whole armor of God: The armor God supplies. Both God and the coming Messiah are portrayed in the Old Testament as armed for battle (Isa. 11:4–5; 49:2; 59:17). It is God's own armor that is provided for Christians, who need not rely on their own resources in the struggle against evil.

6:12 Not against enemies of blood and flesh: While there are dangers in the use of "Satan language," there are also theological values, one of which is that it keeps us from identifying our fellow human beings as the ultimate enemy (see excursus, "Satan, the Devil, and Demons in Biblical Theology," at Mark 5:1; Rev. 20:3). **Against the cosmic powers . . . the spiritual forces of evil in the heavenly places:** See on 2:2; 3:10; Rom. 8:38; 1 Cor. 2:7–8; Col. 1:16, 26; 2:15, 20). Individual sins and crimes and entrenched systemic social evil are the expressions of an even deeper evil; earthly evil is here seen in the perspective of its transcendent source, located in the author's understanding of the universe as "in the heavens," i.e., as the barrier between heaven and earth (see on 2:2). The combatants are God and the devil, but the battle is already decided. The readers are not urged to help God win, for the victory is already won (see 1:17–23; Rev. 12:7). The result of the battle is not in doubt, for believers live in the "already" of God's victory. But the power of evil still exerts its force, so believers cannot be complacent or passive, but must be armed to resist.

6:14 The belt of truth: See Isa. 11:5. Truth here is not an abstract principle, but the trustworthy faithfulness of God. **Breastplate of righteousness:** See Isa. 59:17; 1 Thess. 5:8; 2 Cor. 6:7. "Righteousness" here is God's justifying act that results in the believers' own good deeds (see 2:8–10; Rom. 1:17; 3:21–22).

6:15 As shoes . . . the gospel of peace: See Isa. 52:7; Rom. 10:15. Having received the gospel of peace themselves (2:14–17; Rom. 5:1), believers may stand firmly against the forces of evil.

6:16 The shield of faith: See Gen. 15:1, Pss. 5:2, 18:2 and many other Old Testament texts in which God himself is the believer's shield.

6:17 The helmet of salvation: See Isa. 59:17. In 1 Thess. 5:8 Paul had used the same image, but there the helmet was the "hope of salvation." The author has characteristically taken the future imagery of Paul's theology and shifted it toward the present. **The sword of the Spirit . . . the word of God:** Again the Messiah's weapon becomes the Christian's (see Isa. 11:4). The word of God is not identified as the Bible, but as in 1:13 and 6:15, the Christian gospel in and through which God speaks.

6:18 Pray in the Spirit: See Rom. 8:15–15. **For all the saints:** See 1:15; 3:18; 1 Cor. 1:2. Prayer is not only a private act for personal needs, but a churchly act for the whole church. The "our" of "Our Father who art in heaven" is a universal "our," joining the believer with all Christians who pray to God through Jesus Christ.

6:19 Pray also for me: The author continues to speak in the persona of Paul. The prayer is not for "Paul's" personal needs, which were no longer present in the reader's time, but for Paul's ministry and the apostolic gospel, which did and does continue. **To make known with boldness the mystery of the gospel:** Even apostles are not assumed to have mastered the evangelistic mission, which must be refashioned in every situation without losing the fundamental truths of the gospel. Even apostles need to be supported by the prayers of the church in the effort to communicate the gospel—thus indirectly the author urges the whole church to pray for the progress of its evangelistic mission.

6:21–24
CONCLUSION

6:21 Tychicus will tell you everything: See Col. 4:7–9, most of which is here reproduced verbatim. Tychicus was a coworker of Paul who continued to play a leading role in the post-Pauline school (Acts 20:4; Eph. 6:21; 2 Tim. 4:12; Titus 3:12). Some have suggested he was the actual author of the letter. While this is too speculative, Tychicus does symbolize both the continuity and discontinuity between Paul's generation and the later Pauline mission in Asia Minor, as does Ephesians itself. The task of reinterpreting Paul's gospel to later generations continues in our own time. Ephesians has been placed in our Bible as a reliable guide and model.

The Letter of Paul to the Philippians

INTRODUCTION

That Philippians was written by Paul is beyond dispute; that it is a letter is apparent from the literary features common to all of Paul's correspondence: salutation, thanksgiving, body of the letter, greetings, benediction or doxology. The congregation at Philippi probably received the letter by hearing it read aloud in their assembly (Col. 4:16; 1 Thess. 5:27). A letter assumes a relationship on which it draws and to which it contributes.

The letter is addressed to the church at Philippi, founded about 50 CE, the first church established by Paul in Europe (Acts 16:12–40). The city of Philippi, nine miles from the port of Neapolis, was founded by Philip of Macedon, father of Alexander the Great, in 356 BCE. Commercially important because of nearby gold mines and its location on the main east-west artery (Egnatian Way), Philippi had achieved political status as a Roman colony.

Dating the letter depends on determining the place of origin. Paul was in prison (1:7, 13, 17), but where? Mention of the Praetorian Guard (1:13) and Caesar's household (4:22) makes Caesarea and Rome (Acts 24:26–27; 28:30) the most likely choices. Ephesus is a possibility but a lengthy imprisonment there is not known (1 Cor. 15:32; 2 Cor. 1:8). Rome poses the problem of distance but modes of travel made possible the four trips implied in the letter: the church learns of Paul's imprisonment; the church sends Epaphroditus; the church learns of the illness of Epaphroditus; Paul returns Epaphroditus. If from Ephesus, the date of the letter would be 54–55; if from Caesarea, 57–59; if from Rome, 60–61. See "Introduction to the Pauline Letters."

The purposes of the letter are several, mostly personal. Paul is sending Epaphroditus back to Philippi with expressions of gratitude for the gift sent by the church (2:25; 4:14, 18) and to allay concerns about Epaphroditus's health (2:26–30). Paul responds to their concern for him, saying he hopes for a positive outcome to his trial (1:25). He hopes to come soon, but in the interim is sending Timothy (2:19–23). The letter is warm and filled with expressions of mutual affection. There are no Old Testament citations. Paul does refer to his former life in Judaism, and in a way unlike self-references in other letters (3:4–11). Autobiographical notes enable the readers not only to understand life in Christ Jesus (1:29–30; 2:12–13; 3:12–17), but also to refute intruders who are disturbing the church (3:2–4, 17–19). Central to all Paul's reminders about Christian conduct and relationships is his portrait of the self-emptied, God-exalted Christ Jesus (2:5–11).

Outline of the Letter

1:1–2	Salutation
1:3–11	Thanksgiving
1:12–26	Autobiographical Notes
1:27–2:16	Exhortations
2:17–3:1a	Autobiographical Notes
3:1b–4:9	Exhortations
4:10–20	Thanksgiving
4:21–23	Closing

For Further Reading

Craddock, Fred B. *Philippians*. Interpretation: A Bible Commentary for Teaching and Preaching. Atlanta: John Knox Press, 1985. Some of the material on Philippians in the pages that follow has been drawn from this more expansive treatment.

Osiek, Carolyn. *Philippians, Philemon*. Abingdon New Testament Commentaries. Nashville: Abingdon, 2000.

COMMENTARY

1:1–2
SALUTATION

1:1 Paul and Timothy, servants: On the special form and meaning of the Pauline letter salutation, see on 1 Thess. 1:1. The signature reveals a great deal about the mood, purpose, and content of a letter as well as the relationship between writer and reader. Here the absence of Paul's usual credentials says that his relationship with the readers makes that unnecessary. **Servant** (slave) flavors the entire letter. He will call upon the readers to be servants of one another, just as Christ himself took the form of a servant (2:7). Timothy was not coauthor of the letter—Paul writes in the first person singular (1:3). Timothy's name here signals that Paul worked as part of a team. Timothy was well known to the church at Philippi, since he had been with Paul at its founding and had later visited there (Acts 16; 19:22). He was soon to be sent to Philippi as Paul's emissary (2:19–23). On **saints,** see commentary on Acts 9:13; 26:10; 1 Cor. 1:2.

Paul gives the saints two addresses: "in Christ Jesus" and "in Philippi." He will elaborate upon this double designation later, when he calls upon them to let their life in Christ Jesus be evident in their life in Philippi (2:5; on "in Christ," see at 2 Cor. 5:17). Being God's people in Philippi was strategic for the whole Christian mission. Philippi was a Roman colony, an administrative center of the empire, whose proud inhabitants were Roman citizens and whose official language was Latin.

Bishops and deacons: Mentioned only here in the undisputed letters of Paul. No definite articles are used. The reference is not to the ecclesiastical positions later so designated. The terms, now used of clergy, were in that culture rather common secular words, referring to overseers or superintendents and servants or attendants. "Deacon" was a common term for servant. An overseer ("bishop") could be a state or local official, or a leader of a religious guild; these persons were responsible for collecting, managing, and distributing taxes or other funds. Some persons in the church at Philippi may have functioned in such a capacity, since the church had committed a large amount of money in underwriting Paul's mission and in helping the famine victims among the Christians in Judea (4:10–20; 2 Cor. 8–9). **Grace and peace:** See on 1 Thess. 1:1.

1:3–11
THANKSGIVING

On the thanksgiving section of Pauline letters, see on 1 Thess. 1:2. The threefold structure of the section may be viewed in either of two ways: In *content*, there is the expression of gratitude (vv. 3–6), the expression of Paul's affection for them (vv. 7–8), and a prayer for the church (vv. 9–11). In terms of *movement*, however, the passage can be viewed in terms of Paul's relation to the Philippians' past (vv. 3–6), present (vv. 7–8), and future (v. 9–11). The notes below follow this latter perspective, because it maintains the centrality of the writer-reader relationship.

1:3–6
THE PAST

1:3 I thank my God: Having expressed the blessing of God's grace in the greeting (v. 2), the clear responding word was "thanks." One can see the word "grace" (*charis*) in the word "I give thanks" (*eucharisto*). Paul can sometimes use exactly the same word for grace and gratitude (2 Cor. 9:14–15), binding together giving and receiving. **Every time I remember you:** Can also be translated "all your remembrance of me." In the latter rendering, Paul would have clearly in mind their gifts to him. The orientation of 1:3–11 as a whole makes the former more appropriate here.

1:4 Constantly praying: Paul may be emphasizing that he prays for **all** of them, not a favored few. Paul certainly uses *all* noticeably (vv. 4, 7, 7b, 8), and later comments reflect some tension and disunity (2:1–11; 4:2–3). Or the key word may be *joy*. Paul may be trying to assure close friends who are heavy with the news of his imprisonment that being in prison and facing death have not robbed him of joy. Or it may be that the Philippians, themselves suffering hostility and conflict (1:28–30), have lost their joy; and Paul knows that if they can see that he remains joyful, they might recover their own joy.

1:5–6 Your sharing in the gospel: Paul remembers with gratitude that from the time of his arrival in Philippi, he had experienced the faithful as participants, partners, partakers, sharers. The word *koinonia*, from the root "to have in common," is variously translated according to what is being shared: money, suffering, work, or grace. Its frequency in the letter (1:5, 7; 2:1; 3:10; 4:14) testifies to the full identification of the Philippians with Paul's message and mission. Paul's confidence is expressed with his characteristic symmetry: The one who started the work of grace in Philippi will not abandon it in a state of incompleteness. God will perfect, complete, finish, bring to fulfillment that work **by the day of Christ Jesus**.

1:7–8
THE PRESENT

1:7 I have you in my heart (NIV): The NIV translation here fits Paul's thought better (see NRSV note). **My imprisonment:** Paul surprisingly relates grace to prison bonds and courtroom scenes. In 1:29–30 he says that it has been granted (graced) to them to suffer for Christ and to engage in the same conflict which was his. Such grace participates in the very suffering of Christ (3:10). The present form of that grace for Paul is prison (see 1:29; comments at 1 Pet. 2:19–20; 5:12). We do not know what charges were brought against him. References to the praetorian guard (1:13, NRSV "**imperial guard**," NIV "**palace guard**") and those of Caesar's household (4:22, NRSV "**the emperor's household**") tell us Paul is in the powerful hands of Roman authority. Paul is apparently being held in a barracks or guardhouse where Roman officials and supporting military are quartered. Imprisonment was for persons awaiting trial, and not punishment following conviction. While it is Paul who is in prison, he understands it is the gospel that is on trial. Thought of distancing himself from the gospel for his own security apparently never entered his mind.

1:8 I long for all of you: Paul's yearning for them is "**with the** affection (*viscera*) **of Christ Jesus**." The signals are too clear to miss: vv. 7–8 and the parenthetical verse 4 reflect a problem in Paul's relationship with the church at Philippi. The exact nature of the matter is not clear, but it does seem to be an issue of intimacy, not distance. Has Paul been very close to some members while others felt slighted? The thanksgiving (1:3–11) has alerted us that the letter will deal with at least two subjects: Paul's own personal situation and his relationship with the church at Philippi.

1:9–11
THE FUTURE

1:9–10 This is my prayer: Paul concludes the thanksgiving with an eschatological reference (see 1 Cor. 1:7; 2 Cor. 1:10; 1 Thess. 1:10). **The day of Christ:** A Christianized version of the day of the Lord in the Old Testament (Amos 5:20; Zeph. 1:14), it refers to the Parousia, the coming of Christ. The controlling image is the day of Christ, but the form of the reference is prayer. Just as Paul opened with a twofold thanksgiving, he concludes with a twofold petition. First, he prays that the Philippians will grow and mature in love, a love that is joined to knowing and understanding, to probing and discerning, to putting itself to the test in real-life situations and making moral choices in matters that count (see Rom. 12:2). Second, Paul prays that at the day of Christ they will be pure and blameless (having neither stumbled nor caused to stumble).

1:12–26
AUTOBIOGRAPHICAL NOTES

Here begins the first major unit in the body of the letter. There is but one subject: Paul's imprisonment and its effects on the gospel, the church, and Paul. Within 1:12–26 there are two subunits: in vv. 12–18 Paul reports on the welfare of the gospel and in vv. 19–26 he reports on his personal welfare and its effect upon his relationship with the Philippians. Paul is in bonds but the gospel is not, and at every opportunity he concerns himself with the defense and vindication of the gospel, not of himself.

1:12–18
THE EFFECT OF PAUL'S IMPRISONMENT
ON THE GOSPEL

1:12 I want you to know: What the Philippians need from Paul is not simply a news report on how he is faring. When a Christian minister, a missionary, a preacher of the gospel is arrested, imprisoned, waiting for Roman authorities to decide his fate—that is a condition that demands interpretation. Very likely there were some Christians in Philippi who were beginning to wonder if their church was really of God. If preaching the gospel gets you arrested, what will happen to us? Is Paul's fate to be ours as well? Paul needs to interpret his chains. Paul writes his concerned friends in Philippi to assure them in joyful tones that his imprisonment has served to **advance the gospel** (NIV).

1:13 Known throughout the whole imperial guard: It has become clear that Paul's bonds are for Christ. This does not mean necessarily that some guards were converted. Paul's witness, supported by a spirit and behavior consistent with that witness, made Paul's imprisonment into a testimony to Christ.

1:14 The brothers and sisters ... made confident: Paul's imprisonment has generated new courage among (most of) the Christians in the area of his confinement, and they are speaking the word of God most fearlessly. It was Christ—or as Paul sometimes said with no difference in meaning, the Holy Spirit—who gave heart to the believers so that the arrest of a leader actually strengthened the church. Only by the Holy Spirit can the church experience the miraculous shift of attitude from assuming that wherever the Lord is, there is no suffering, to believing that wherever there is suffering, there the Lord is.

1:15 Some proclaim Christ from envy and rivalry: Paul reports that his imprisonment has advanced the gospel in a most unexpected way: Those who preach with a spirit of rivalry and competition, envious of another's success, see in Paul's confinement a chance to get ahead and so have accelerated their activity. This is not true of all, of course; some out of love and goodwill increase their labors to help compensate for the loss of Paul's ministry. In that fact Paul rejoices. What is most unusual is that Paul also rejoices that the competitive preachers, operating out of partisanship (a term common in that day to describe persons hired to do electioneering), hoping both to advance themselves and afflict the confined Paul, were at least preaching the gospel.

1:18 What does it matter?: What we do not expect is for Paul to say, **Christ is proclaimed, . . . whether out of false motives or true; and in that I rejoice.** Are we to sense in this statement a shrug of the shoulders? Is the old soldier too weary to rise anymore to reveille? These divisive preachers are not the famed Judaizers of Corinth, Galatia, and perhaps chap. 3 of Philippians, who preached another gospel and for it received Paul's anathema (Gal. 1:6–9). Here the issue is not message but motive. Paul did not approve such motives; he had renounced the shameful things (2 Cor. 4:2). The power of the gospel is not contingent upon the motives or feelings of the one preaching. For all the dangers of opening the doors of ministry to charlatans, it must be affirmed that the gospel has its own life and efficacy.

1:19–26

THE EFFECT OF PAUL'S IMPRISONMENT
ON THE CHURCH AND HIMSELF

In this passage it is amply evident that Paul is experiencing intense mental conflict: "**I am hard pressed between the two**" ("I am pulled two ways" [REB]; "I am caught from both sides" [TEV]) (1:23). He quotes Job, the very personification of struggle, in v. 19; and the awkward grammar, the disjointed sentences, testify to the apostle's frame of mind. We have here a soliloquy, a thinking out loud, in the presence and confidentiality of close friends, about dying and living. Apparently Paul needs to speak about it, and the church needs to think about it. That he chose to share these resolved/unresolved thoughts and feelings with the Philippians is high compliment.

1:19–20 For I know: Paul begins by saying he *knows*, he is certain of, the outcome of the events which now are beyond his control: He will be delivered (Job 13:16–18). He surely means deliverance or salvation in a sense larger than release from prison; otherwise the description of his struggle is emptied of meaning. The deliverance he has in mind is not contingent upon his being released or executed. Paul is not filled with dread. On the contrary, his mood is one of eager expectation ("looking out the window in anticipation"; see Rom. 8:19) and hope. These words were not for Paul mere synonyms for wishing. What Paul firmly anticipates is that whether Rome says yes or no over his life, his witness by word and conduct will honor and magnify Christ. Paul states this hope most dramatically by counterposing two vivid terms: **shame** and **boldness.** Rather than being ashamed (shrinking back, failing, Pss. 25:3, 20; 31:1, 17; 119:6) in that hour, Paul expects to be, as always, courageous, or perhaps more precisely, "out in the open" with his witness (see this sense of the word in John 7:4, 13; 11:54; 16:29).

1:21 Living . . . dying: Living or dying (Rom. 14:8), waking or sleeping (I Thess. 5:10), Paul belongs to Christ; but there is a sense in which living will differ from dying. Living is **Christ** (Gal. 2:20; 2 Cor. 4:10, 16; 5:15), but dying would be **gain.** If living is Christ, what was there to gain by dying? The gain would be the avoidance of what he most feared (lest I myself be disqualified, 1 Cor. 9:27), the attainment of what he most desired (to know Christ fully, Phil. 3:10–14). What if Paul does not die, but is released? That, too, is an attractive alternative, for life in the flesh ("flesh" here has no negative moral implications) would give opportunity for further ministry for Christ.

1:22 I do not know: Which shall I choose? What an extraordinary thing to say! Since Paul is neither judge nor jury but the one on trial, what possible meaning could there be in his struggle with his choice? In one sense, of course, Paul has absolutely no decision; he awaits the decision of others. In another sense, though, Paul can take the initiative, walk into his own future, embrace rather than resist necessity. He talks as one who had done it and now is free. What can the world do to him? Even death, the last enemy, is subdued, domesticated, and could, if called upon, render Paul a most desirable service.

Two notes are appropriate here. First, Paul is not discussing eschatology in general, but is

615

talking with friends about his death. Second, that this account of Paul's own pilgrimage in Christ and to Christ has been canonized as Scripture does not mean it is normative for all of us. Paul does not speak to the Philippians in the imperative; in fact, he never made his conversion, his call, his charismatic gifts, his elevation to the third heaven, nor any other such experience the rule in his churches.

1:24 To remain . . . is more necessary for you: To speak in terms of what is necessary is not new ground for Paul; his preaching of the gospel was a matter of "obligation," "am compelled" (NIV) (a secular term referring to fate or destiny, 1 Cor 9:16), not choice. Paul realizes that he is first of all an apostle, a pastor, a preacher. Martyrdom is a luxury and will have to wait.

1:27–2:16
EXHORTATIONS

It is clear that 1:27 begins a new direction in Paul's thought that concludes at 2:16. The entire passage before us (1:27–2:16) is rich with images of the Christian life, but as we shall see, it is the image of servant, of which Christ is the supreme model (2:5–11), which effectively focuses Paul's discussion of living the gospel.

Within 1:27–2:16 there are three sub-units: (a) Christian conduct in relation to a hostile, unbelieving community (1:27–30); (b) Christian conduct within the believing community (2:1–11); (c) Christian conduct in relation to Paul, the church's founding apostle (2:12–16).

1:27–30
CHRISTIAN CONDUCT IN RELATION TO A HOSTILE COMMUNITY

1:27 Whether I come and see you or am absent: The cooling effect, the sense of distance in this phrase is difficult to miss. He is being professional rather than personal in the sense that he must not allow those to whom he ministers to become dependent upon him. Paul's presence or absence is not the determining factor in their living out the gospel of Jesus Christ. **Live your life in a manner worthy:** Suspicious of any persons or movements not aligned and loyal to Caesar, probably quite anti-Semitic (Acts 16:20–21), this city could and did make it difficult for the disciples of Jesus. Paul knows this firsthand and uses the local term for living out one's citizenship. He means by it one's manner of life as it faces upon and intersects with life in the city. It is incumbent upon them to live among the people and insti-

tutions of Philippi in a way that is informed and disciplined by the gospel of Christ.

1:28 In no way intimidated: Nothing the opponents say or do must be allowed to frighten ("stampede," as with horses) them. If they cease to act and simply react, then it is no longer the gospel but the culture that gives the church its identity. What Paul knows, however, is that united, firm, consistent living out the gospel of Christ will be an omen, a sign, a manifestation, a preliminary demonstration of the future; and the omen will be to the **opponents**. To them Christian conduct will be a sign of what will occur at the end: the **destruction** of the opponents and the **salvation** of the believers.

1:29 Not only of believing . . . but of suffering for him: The Philippian Christians have more than a sign, however; they have clear evidence of God's grace, for it has been granted (graced) to them not only to believe in Christ but to suffer for Christ (see 1:7). Verse 30 certainly gives the impression that the Philippian church is in a situation with the threat, if not the reality, of arrest and possibly of death. Paul is inviting the believers at Philippi, beleaguered as they are, to understand their suffering through his, which means finally as sharing the suffering of Christ.

2:1–11
CHRISTIAN CONDUCT WITHIN THE BELIEVING COMMUNITY

This section, 2:1–11, is tied inseparably to 1:27–30. The conjunction "then" or "so" (2:1) looks back to what has been said and builds upon it. The "one spirit, one mind" (1:27) quality essential for standing and struggling together in the face of hostility is now to be given increased attention as Paul characterizes a believing community that is in Christ Jesus (2:1–5).

2:1 If: In our usage, "if" most commonly expresses uncertainty or a condition contrary to fact. The Greek language also has a way of saying such things as, "If I were the king (but I am not)." Greek had another way of saying "if" that stated what was actually the case; for example, "If I am your friend (and I am)." Such is the case in 2:1: "If there is any encouragement in Christ" (and there is). One could just as well begin the four clauses in 2:1 with "since."

2:2 Make my joy complete: The imperative governs vv. 2–4: "complete (fill, make completely full) my joy." Paul so completely identified both with Christ (1:8) and with the church (1:7) that his joy was not his alone, and neither was it simply an emotion or feeling. The joy of Paul and of the church was, as he put it, "in Christ Jesus," nourished by their relationship with each other and by the Spirit.

For emphasis as well as clarity he says what he has in mind in four expressions: being of **the same mind** (the phrase does not refer to agreeing on everything, but to having a common attitude or orientation); having **the same love**; being **in full accord** (joined souls); and **of one mind** (he repeats the call for a common attitude or mindset). The word twice used in 2:2 and translated "mind" is extremely important in this letter (also 1:7; 3:15, 19; 4:2). By his double use of the word in 2:2, Paul is preparing his readers for his elaboration upon what the Christian mindset, attitude, or orientation is, beginning in 2:5: "**Let the same mind**" (NRSV); "**your attitude should be the same**" (NIV).

We do not know what lay at the root of the discord in the Philippian church. There may have been polarization around the two women who had worked faithfully with Paul in the past but were at odds with each other (4:2–3). The dissension could have been generated by the preaching of those who sought to bring elements of Judaism into the faith and practice of the church, against whom Paul lashes out in 3:1b–6. Or it could have been the case that the disunity in Philippi was related to Paul himself. If Paul's unusually strong insistence that he loves and prays for all of them (1:4–8) implies that some members felt they were not in the circle of Paul's favor and affection, then that could be the condition further addressed in 2:1–11.

2:3–4 Do nothing from selfish ambition: After being totally positive about their past experiences (v. 1) and about the unity to be sought (v. 2), Paul presents the forms of conduct and relationships to be avoided. He does so by the use of three negatives: nothing from selfishness (the word was used in 1:17 to describe the "partisan for hire" mentality of some preachers); nothing from **conceit** (literally "empty glory"; obviously Paul is looking ahead to his portrayal of Christ as one who emptied himself of claims to glory); and looking **not to (one's) own interests**.

2:5 Let the same mind be in you: Paul regards as inappropriate to the body of Christ the selfish eye, the pompous mind, the ear hungry for compliments, and the mouth that spoke none, the heart that had little room for others, and the hand that served only the self. Paul is not opposed to individualism in the sense that one

is to be responsible for oneself and bear one's own burden (Gal. 6:4–5). If minding one's own business means an unwillingness to bear another's burden, then such individualism is destructive of the community and a contradiction of the gospel. There is, he says, a way of "minding," an approach to life, to others, to self, to God that characterizes those who are in Christ Jesus; and he calls upon the Philippians to "let the same mind" qualify all their relationships with each other (v. 5). Since the latter part of v. 5 lacks a verb, the NRSV simply inserts "was": "that **was** in Christ Jesus." Paul proceeds to clarify in vv. 6–11 what the "in Christ Jesus" mind is.

The form of Paul's elaboration is that of a hymn. There is no general agreement on the literary analysis of the hymn. Some view the hymn as structured upon the pattern of the descent and ascent of the Redeemer and therefore framed as two major strophes (vv. 6–8, 9–11), each consisting of three stanzas. Others see in the passage three strophes, each describing a phase of the Christ story: preexistence, earthly career, glorification. Neither is there agreement as to whether Paul composed the hymn or quoted one already available to him and the church. The majority opinion is that Paul is quoting a hymn that arose in another context to address another problem, perhaps a christological question. Christological hymns and confessions are not uncommon in Paul's writings (e.g., 1 Cor. 8:6; 2 Cor. 8:9; Col. 1:15–20).

The hymn is so rich in statement and inference that one can easily forget what Paul sought to say to the Philippians by means of the quotation. Only two questions need to be pursued here: What does the hymn say? (and more importantly here) What does Paul say by quoting the hymn?

Philippians 2:6–11 is a rehearsal of the Christ story in three movements: preexistence, existence, postexistence. To say that Christ preexisted, was with God prior to life on earth, is not uncommon in the New Testament (John 1:1–2; Heb. 1:1–4; Col. 1:15; 2 Cor. 8:9); but the passages are difficult for us because the category of preexistence is for many of us a foreign notion. In some quarters the category of preexistence was used as a way of affirming the transcendence of Christ. Because in Jesus of Nazareth they experienced God, the Christians used preexistence as one way of saying that in the very human, crucified Nazarene they had encountered reality beyond all contingencies of time, place, and history. The church has always proclaimed this paradox about Jesus Christ, but always with difficulty. Appropriate words and images are scarce.

The hymn says that Christ did not hold on to his preexistent state. Though **in the form of God** (the words translated "form" and "likeness" in vv. 6–8 are imprecise in meaning and much debated), **equality with God** was not regarded as **something to be grasped** (NIV). The expression "to be grasped" does not in itself tell us if equality with God was already possessed or was a quality to be seized, as in the case of Adam (Gen. 3:5) or Lucifer (Isa. 14:13–14). The point is that all such claims are abandoned in the choice of the Christ to empty himself. The description is of Christ coming under all the conditions of the human lot, becoming a servant, obedient even to death. In this picture of the saving event, as in the letters of Paul and other New Testament letters, the earthly life of Jesus is portrayed as empty of the divine power, nonmiraculous, like that of other human beings except for his total obedience to God. (For the role of the Gospel stories of Jesus' life in the formation of Christian faith, see on "Introduction to the Gospels," 4.)

2:9 Therefore God also highly exalted him: Here the subject of the hymn changes. Up to this point it is Christ who decides and who acts, relinquishing claims, emptying himself, becoming human, serving, obeying, dying. Now it is God who acts in the exaltation of Christ. The name bestowed upon Jesus is *Lord*, acknowledged in what may be the earliest form of the confession of faith among Gentile Christians: Jesus is Lord (Rom. 10:9; Acts 2:36). Submission to the lordship of Christ, however, is not confined to the human realm; Christ is Lord over every power in the created order. There is no place in the universe beyond the reach of the redeeming act of the servant Christ.

If that is what the hymn says, what is Paul saying by quoting it? Clearly the passage is to be taken as a whole, not fragmented into lessons to be learned, examples to be followed. Paul's point is that Christ acted in our behalf without view of gain. That is precisely what God has exalted and vindicated: self-denying service for others to the point of death with no claim of return, no eye upon a reward. In Paul's judgment, what the church needs is not a scolding but a reminder of the event that created and defined their life together.

It may be objected that such a conclusion as to the function of the quotation fails to make full

use of this christological hymn; that is, Paul's answer would seem immeasurably larger than the problem that evoked it. But Paul's response even to pettiness was a big answer: a hymn, a creed, a confession of faith, a reminder of the central event that begets, nourishes, and matures the community of faith.

2:12–16
CHRISTIAN CONDUCT IN
RELATION TO PAUL

2:12 Now in my absence: In 1:27 he opened by urging a kind of behavior "whether I come or . . . am absent." Now he concludes by calling for obedience "not only in my presence, but much more now in my absence." There is no question but that Paul's presence *personally* made a difference in the life of the church. There is no question but that Paul's presence *apostolically* made a difference in the life of the church. But Paul wishes to set them, in his absence, in *God's* presence with fear and trembling. Therefore, his statement in 2:12 is stronger than in 1:27: The "whether or not" of 1:27 becomes "more in my absence than in my presence" in 2:12. Paul's mind is now tilted toward not seeing them again.

Nothing is more vital for understanding Philippians than sensing the inseparable bond between Paul and the church, dramatically expressed in the presence/absence motif. Paul expects even greater fidelity and obedience in his absence. It is quite obvious that Paul used for a model here the farewell speech of Moses (Deut. 31:24–32:3), but he has not adopted the negativity of that speech. Moses: "I know that after my death you will surely act corruptly" (Deut. 31:29); Paul: "as you have always obeyed, . . . much more now in my absence" (2:12). Moses: "his degenerate children have dealt falsely with him, a perverse and crooked generation" (Deut. 32:5); Paul: "that you may be blameless and innocent, children of God without blemish in the midst of a crooked and perverse generation" (2:15).

2:12 Work out your own salvation: This passage is loaded with words for "work." The Philippians are to work out their salvation; God is at work, both to will and to work; and Paul labors and by his labors will be measured in the day of Christ. From work, no doctrine of grace protects us; and there is no reason to protect Paul from himself in these sentences. The work of the Christian life and mission is not parceled out, with God doing "God's part" and believers doing "their part." Salvation is totally the work of God, who began the work within them and will see it through to the end (1:6); it is the total responsibility of believers, who cannot rely on cheap grace but whose response of faith requires their whole being. Just as authentic Christology does not think of Christ as "partly human and partly divine," so the Christian life is wholly our work and wholly God's work (see Deut. 7:6–13; 30:6–10; Isa. 26:12; 1 Cor. 15:10; Gal. 2:20; Col. 1:29; Rev. 20:11–14). The church is to actualize in concrete ways, in energy-burning, time-consuming endeavors, the mind of Christ.

2:17–3:1a
AUTOBIOGRAPHICAL NOTES

The situation reflected in 2:17–3:1a is not difficult to reconstruct. Paul, in prison, facing trial and possibly execution, cannot come to resume his ministry in Philippi. As was often his practice, between the sending of a letter and his own arrival, Paul plans to send a trusted associate as his emissary; in this case Timothy. However, if Timothy went immediately, he could not give a report about Paul's fate before the Roman tribunal. As soon as the gavel falls in declaration of freedom or death, Timothy will come and after a stay of uncertain length return to Paul (provided, of course, he is still alive) with news of the church. In the meantime, Epaphroditus is being sent immediately to Philippi. He was sent by the church to minister to Paul, became gravely ill, has recovered, and by his return will relieve not only his anxieties but Paul's and the church's as well.

As in 1:12–26, he regards it his first duty to interpret for the church what is taking place. The major event to be interpreted is his own situation in the hands of Roman power. Again, as in 1:19–26, he sends a double message: I may even now be at the point of death; I trust in the Lord that I will come soon (vv. 17, 24). As stated in 1:19–26, here again is testimony to an unusual relationship. Paul can share with them honestly, without careful attention to consistency and logic. Yes, he hopes to die and be with Christ; yes, he hopes to come to them soon; yes, this is very likely his farewell to them; yes, he trusts in the Lord to be with them shortly. He and they have been partners in the gospel from the beginning (1:5), are now partners in prison and trials (1:7), will again share in fruitful labor if he is released (1:22–26), but if not, his death will intimately involve them as well (2:17).

2:17 I am being poured out as a libation: Paul wants them to see his death as an act of wor-

ship. The imagery is strangely beautiful. The Philippians are portrayed as priests at an altar offering up the sacrificial gift of their faith. Paul's lifeblood is being poured out as a libation (a practice in pagan cults and in Israelite worship), the completion or crowning touch to their offering of faith.

2:19–22 I hope . . . to send Timothy: Like a son with a father was Timothy to Paul. In Paul's opinion Timothy was one of a kind, and so it was not a difficult choice for Paul. In fact, one gets the impression that Paul really had no choice, since his other associates in ministry **are seeking their own interests, not those of Jesus Christ.** There certainly is no evidence that Paul regarded Timothy any less a minister than himself. Timothy's signature is on the letter (1:1), and Paul's reference to him as a son is a term of affection, not subordination. If Paul is executed, the work falls upon Timothy, a prospect that seems not to worry the apostle at all.

2:25 Necessary to send . . . Epaphroditus: Known only here in the New Testament, Epaphroditus was probably a convert from paganism, judging from the fact that he was named for the goddess Aphrodite. He was from the church at Philippi, sent to Paul with gifts (4:18), and commissioned to remain indefinitely with Paul to serve him in all the ways they themselves could not. He became deathly ill. Through God's grace and Paul's prayers he has now recovered. Paul wants to return him now to Philippi, an act that will relieve Paul (he is in no position to wait upon the sick), the church (which has heard of Epaphroditus's illness), and Epaphroditus himself (who has been distressed that the church was distressed). Paul wants to relieve all anxieties and to pave the way for a joyful return. In relation to Paul, Epaphroditus is brother, fellow worker, and fellow soldier; in relation to the church, he is their messenger (*apostolos*, used here as in 2 Cor. 8:23) and minister (in vv. 25 and 30 ministry is imaged as an act of worship, as liturgy).

3:1b–4:9
EXHORTATIONS

Readers of Philippians have been struck by the conclusion-like nature of 2:17–3:1a and the radically different material beginning at 3:1b. The fact that there is a rough seam in the fabric of the letter is clear to all. Some account for the break by an interruption in Paul's writing at 3:1. He begins to conclude, remembers a problem with

Judaizers in Philippi, addresses it, and then resumes his farewell at 4:8. Others theorize that upon the occasion of collecting Paul's letters, all the notes and letters from Paul found at Philippi were put together as his Philippian correspondence. The issue remains unresolved. See "Introduction: The New Testament as the Church's Book," 4.c, and the introduction to 2 Corinthians.

The parallels to the previous section are unmistakable: As the "mind in Christ Jesus" governed instructions as to conduct and relationships, so here Paul is the one to be imitated (3:17); what they have learned, received, heard, and seen in Paul they are to do (4:9). Even as Christ gave up all claims, so has Paul, relinquishing everything so that he might be identified with Christ totally: in suffering, in death, in resurrection.

3:1b–16
Look to Paul, Not the Judaizers

3:2 Beware: The threefold "Beware of" warning posted before the eyes and ears of the Philippian Christians carries two messages. First, the danger to the church is such as to arouse in Paul the most intense passion. Whether Christians had to obey the law of Moses in order to be saved was a question fully and finally clear in Paul's mind (Gal. 1:8–9; 2:16). But Judaism was not for Paul simply a backdrop of black velvet against which to cast the diamond of his new creation. For Paul the covenant with Abraham, who believed God and whose faith was accounted as righteousness, was still in effect (Rom. 4:1–12). The law of Moses was not intended to be and is not the means by which one stands acceptable before God. Justification by law would annul the grace of God and put the spotlight on human achievement (Gal. 2:16–21). Salvation does not rest with us but with God. Just as one should not boast of circumcision, neither should one boast of uncircumcision; just as one should not boast of keeping the Sabbath, neither should one boast of not keeping it. For Paul it was not the law but the law moved to the center as the ground of human righteousness, that caused him to yell, "Beware!"

The second message carried by Paul's threefold warning is that those preaching the necessity of obeying the law of Moses are a very real threat to the church. Gentile Christians may be especially enticed by the laws and rituals of a tradition which not only lay behind Christianity but which offered identity, certainty, and promise through its sacred texts.

The dogs: Who are these who are a threat to the Philippian congregation? Paul's names for them do not help us: dogs (a Jewish term for Gentiles; unclean animals; prowlers and scavengers—Paul could have had all or none of this in mind), **evil workers, those who mutilate the flesh.** This last phrase translates *katatome*, a parody of *peritome*, which means circumcision. We who accept God's grace in Christ, says Paul, are the true circumcision, truly members of God's covenant people (Rom. 2:28). Most likely they are not Jewish Christians, but Jews seeking to win Christians over to the synagogue. Some synagogues were quite evangelistic (Matt. 23:15). The intruders in Philippi are preaching a distortion, not just of Christianity, but of Judaism as well. The issue was the adequacy of the grace of God to make righteous those who trust in that grace.

3:3–6 No confidence in the flesh: This is the phrase that Paul will now develop. By "flesh" he is referring to the rite of circumcision in particular, but in the broader sense "flesh" is a synonym for human effort or achievement (see Gal. 4:23; 2 Cor. 5:16; Rom. 7:14, 25; 10:3). Paul's claim that he has more reason for confidence in the flesh implies "more than they do." This could mean that while he was born and bred a Jew, the opponents were proselytes, Gentile converts to Judaism. Paul's credentials as a Jew make more sense if laid beside those of one not born a Jew. For example: **circumcised the eighth day** (not as an adult); **of the people of Israel** (not just a Jew religiously); **of the tribe of Benjamin** (a family genealogy, not just a certificate of circumcision); **a Hebrew born of Hebrews** (probably a reference to his family preserving the native tongue in the home); **as to the law, a Pharisee** (the Jewish party committed to full obedience to the whole law written and oral and not to selected rules such as circumcision; see on Matt. 3:7; Luke 5:17); **as to zeal a persecutor of the church** (the logical conclusion for one tied to the tradition and not as those whose zeal is satisfied with circumcision of Christians); **as to righteousness under the law, blameless**.

3:7–9 Whatever gains I had: Paul does not extol the virtues of his new life in Christ by a deprecating description of his life in Judaism. He does not say of his former life that it was in the loss column of the ledger, but rather that in his new way of reckoning he counted gain as **loss.** This difference is most important. Paul does not say Judaism is worthless, that it is **rubbish** (garbage, excrement), that intrinsically that way of life is of no value. What he is describing is his consuming desire to know Jesus Christ, to be in Jesus Christ, to have the **righteousness** that is God's gift to the one who believes; and for the surpassing worth of that, he *counts* gain as loss. It is not the law that is dead; Paul is dead to the law. Paul does not toss away junk to gain Christ; he tosses away that which was of tremendous value to him. What Paul is saying is that Christ surpasses everything of worth to me. Paul's model in 2:6–11 is the Christ who did not relinquish the low and base for something better, but who gave up all claim to equality with God in exchange for obedient service. Paul tells his own story here for the same reason. Giving ourselves up to God is total trust, having no claims, seeking no advantage, but in service to one another leaving our status before God entirely in God's hands.

3:10–11 The power of his resurrection: Paul ends with resurrection as his final hope. He has referred to it in Philippians as the day of Christ (1:6, 10; 2:16). **If possible:** Paul's reminder to himself and to his readers that those who think they stand should take heed lest they fall (1 Cor. 10:12).

Paul also begins with resurrection. Present participation in Christ's resurrection is a matter of power. Although he provides here no particulars as to how that power expressed itself in his life, Paul probably is referring to the enabling of his ministry. Between these references to future and present benefits of Christ's resurrection, however, Paul speaks of **sharing** Christ's **sufferings** and **becoming like him** (being conformed with) **in his death.**

3:12 Not that I have already attained: In vv. 12–14 Paul is again the runner (2:16). Faith for him involved running, wrestling, striving, and fighting, none of which would end until the day of Christ. For Paul all effort was not for merit, but was rather the activity of one who had abandoned all claim to merit. Trust in God's grace did not make Paul less active than the Judaizers, but rather set him free now to run without counting his steps, without competing with other servants of Christ. His goal is clear: to be with Christ in the resurrection. To that end he can seek, because he has been found; he can know because he has been known; he can apprehend because he has been apprehended. In a word, Paul sought to lay hold of him who had already laid hold of Paul. His language is vivid, tense, repetitious: pressing, stretching, pushing, straining. In those words the lungs

burn, the temples pound, the muscles ache, the heart pumps, the perspiration rolls.

3:13 Forgetting what lies behind: In pursuit of that prize Paul not only strains forward but he forgets what lies behind. Whether he is speaking of his former life in Judaism is uncertain. The use of the word "perfect" in the sense of maturing in faith and love is not uncommon for Paul (1 Cor. 2:6–3:3; 13:11). It is regrettable that popular usage of the word "perfect" ("Nobody's perfect") almost always means "flawless in morals," a definition that hardly fits any of the many New Testament uses of the word. Paul is calling the Christians to continued growth and maturity.

3:15 Be of the same mind: Here Paul modifies slightly his earlier usage. When he offered the Christ model in 2:5–11, he said without qualification, "Let the same mind be in you," but now, when offering himself as model, he says, "Be of the same mind, and if you think differently about anything," God sheds upon the path light that is not mediated through Paul. God may lead the church around, beside, beyond, or even in spite of its leaders, and a mark of a great leader is to be able to say just that.

3:17–4:1
LOOK TO PAUL, NOT TO THE LIBERTINES

3:18 Enemies of the cross: Who are these? Paul's description does not fit either the opponents of 1:27–30 or the competitive preachers of 1:15–18, whose motives were unworthy but who nevertheless were preaching Christ. Are they the dogs and evil workers of 3:2? Perhaps 3:17 is the resumption of the intense emotion with which Paul began his attack. How one identifies the group determines one's understanding of the phrases in vv. 18–19.

However, it is most likely that 3:17–4:1 addresses a problem different from that represented in 3:1b–16. The issue with Judaizers had to do with one's status before God; the issue in 3:17–4:1 has to do with conduct and specifically with attitude toward and use of the physical body. Paul's description of the troublemakers in vv. 18–20 is clearly that of persons who represent indulgence of the body as an expression of the new life in Christ. Food and sex are to them god and glory (vv. 19–20). Since the body is the center of this lifestyle, the end of the body is their destruction.

It is not difficult to understand how some could arrive at such a view. The missionary preachers had proclaimed freedom in

Christ. Paul himself was a foremost preacher of freedom. What more natural way to demonstrate one's freedom than indulgence in the areas of former restriction? Wherever Paul's gospel of freedom from law was heard, it was also misheard. Some, perhaps, were too immature to see that liberty become license is really a new kind of bondage.

The characteristic of the opponents of 3:17–4:1 most offensive to Paul was their conduct, and it is at that point he counters them. Against their lifestyle he offers his own and that of others whose example is to be emulated. This, and not egotism, is the meaning of the phrase "join in imitating me" (v. 17).

3:20 Our citizenship is in heaven: Only here does Paul call Christ Savior, and only in this place does he say our citizenship is in heaven. "Citizenship" would have been especially meaningful in Philippi, with its high patriotism as a Roman colony. We are, says Paul, a colony of heaven (see earlier remarks on the same word at 1:27).

3:21 He will transform the body of our humiliation: As Paul countered lifestyle with lifestyle, so he countered teaching about the body with teaching about the body. As a Jew and as a Christian, Paul accepted the body as created of God and as an integral part of one's identity. It is not a substance foreign to our true nature. Naturally enough, then, Paul's doctrine of resurrection was just that, resurrection from the dead and not the survival of an immortal soul free at last (see on Luke 20:27; Matt. 28:1). As far as the body was concerned, resurrection meant the transformation of this lowly body to conform to Christ's glorious body.

4:2–3
LET FELLOW WORKERS BE RECONCILED

4:2 Euodia ... Syntyche: Paul returns to the problem of dissension that had occupied him earlier (2:1–16), using the very same admonition directed to the congregation (2:2) to address two women who are leaders in the church. Paul is not just trying to embarrass two members by having their names read aloud in a worship service; he is reminding them that they are leaders and therefore are able by words or deeds to polarize the congregation, destroying the one soul, one mind, one body. Paul expects the church to help with the healing. This is precisely the nature and function of the congregation as a partnership.

For all the dispute about Paul's attitude toward women, they are very visibly and significantly present in his references to associates in ministry. Women preached and prayed in Paul's churches (1 Cor. 11:5) and their names are many in Paul's remembrances of a lifetime of shared service (Rom. 16:1–16). In fact, Luke says the church at Philippi was begun when Paul went to a place of prayer and "spoke to the women who had come together" (Acts 16:13).

4:4–7
ONCE MORE, REJOICE

4:4 Again I will say: Paul urges the church not to be victimized by its problems within and without. The joy and forbearance (gentleness, 2 Cor. 10:1) that constitute part of the church's witness to the world (vv. 4–5a) are grounded in the church's faith. Two of the tenets of that faith form a parenthesis around them not only making joy and **gentleness** possible but liberating them from anxiety.

4:5 The Lord is near: Most likely Paul meant this eschatologically, an expectation he never lost (Rom. 13:11; 1 Cor. 16:22).

4:7 Peace of God ... will guard: In a striking paradox, Paul describes this peace with a military term: The peace of God "will stand sentry watch" over your hearts and minds. Because the day of Christ is near and because the peace of God stands guard, the church can rejoice.

4:8–9
PRACTICE WHAT PAUL SAID AND DID

4:8–9 Finally, beloved: For the second time Paul says, "Finally" (3:1; 4:8). This may be a return to 3:1 after a digression or the conclusion of what once was a separate letter. He commends to the Philippians a list of admirable traits drawn from Greek moralists: the **true,** the **honorable,** the **just,** the **pure,** the **lovely,** things of **excellence,** and **worthy of praise.** Use of such lists not only of virtues but also of vices (Rom. 1:20–32; 1 Cor. 6:9, 10; Gal. 5:19–21) was a common practice for Paul, just as it had been in the Jewish community for generations (see Wisdom of Solomon).

Think about these things: This virtue list is not given to the Philippians for thoughtless embrace. They are to consider, give thought to, reason out. Paul offers his own life for their consideration. **Learned and received:** Refers to passing along a tradition. There is a body of teaching giving identity and continuity to the Christian community.

4:10–20
THANKSGIVING

As literature, 4:10–20 is a gem; as a note of thanks to close friends who have sent a gift, the passage is full of surprises. Paul and the Philippians do not represent what one would regard as a standard apostle-church relationship. They were his partners: In the gospel (1:5), in prison and court defense (1:7), in conflict and suffering (1:30), and unlike all the other churches, they shared repeatedly in financial support of his ministry (4:15–16).

4:10 Now at last: He chides them a bit ("after so long," REB), and his immediate modifier, "you . . . had no opportunity," does not fully dull the edge of the reproach. Paul gives a brief testimony to the effect that he has contentment in either abundance or want, and being in Christ is adequate for all situations (vv. 11–13). Paul makes sure they understand that his desire was not for the gift but for the fruit or profit from it (apparently referring to his ministry [1:22]) which would be credited to their account.

4:12 In any and all circumstances: The intimacy of giving and receiving must be balanced with distance, discourteous as it may sound. So Paul reminds his friends that he is free. He is able to live with abundance, but it is not necessary that he have it. He is able to live in hunger and want, but it is not necessary that he be poor. He is defined neither by wealth nor by poverty but by a contentment that transcends both and by a power in Christ that enables him to live in any circumstance. It is important for his friends to see their gift in this context.

4:21–23
CLOSING

4:21 Greet every saint: Having spoken throughout the letter to "all of you," Paul now wants each member personally to hear a word from him. The word "greet" is in the imperative. Paul does not say, "I greet," but calls on someone to greet each person. Whether he is here calling on the reader of the letter or the bishops and deacons (1:1) or each member to take responsibility to greet the others, we do not know.

4:22 All the saints greet: The second word of greeting is extended in behalf of Paul's associates. Paul had many partners in ministry who were especially helpful during times of the apostle's imprisonment. Through them he was able to continue his work. Of that group, the name of only one who was with Paul at this time is given: Timothy. **Caesar's household** (NIV)/**The emperor's household** (NRSV): A term applied to those in Roman civil service, consisting primarily of slaves and freedmen. Why greetings especially from these? Perhaps some of them were originally from Philippi; or since Philippi was a Roman colony, perhaps some had formerly served in Philippi and wanted to be remembered.

4:23 The grace of the Lord: Paul's last word is his first word (1:2): grace.

The Letter of Paul to the Colossians

INTRODUCTION

Author

This letter presents itself as written by Paul (1:1) in his own hand (4:18). He joins to his signature the name of an associate, in this case, Timothy (1:1), and even though the writer will often say "we," including Timothy and other companions (4:7–14), it is clear that the readers are receiving a message from Paul. There are, however, within the letter clues sufficient to persuade some students of Paul that while the message is essentially Paul's, the letter as we have it was written in Paul's name by someone in the Pauline tradition. (See "The Death of Paul and the Continuation of the Pauline Tradition" in the introduction to 1 Timothy, and "Pseudonymous Letters in Early Christianity" in the introduction to Ephesians.) Those who hold this view do not at all wish to diminish the value or dilute the message of this letter as part of the New Testament. Rather they notice quite a bit of vocabulary not found elsewhere in Paul and the absence of some of his characteristic terms, such as "law," "righteousness," "promise," and "sin" in the singular. In Colossians, believers have died, not to sin, but to the elemental powers of the universe (2:20). In fact, the church, while occasionally referred to as a local community (4:15–16), is primarily presented as a cosmic body including all creation in heaven and on earth, visible and invisible, embracing all principalities and powers conquered and reconciled. Of this body, Christ is the head (1:15–20). While a future coming of Christ is not an absent theme (3:4), this familiar Pauline teaching has receded in favor of a more realized or already experienced eschatology (2:9–15; 3:1–4). The reader of Colossians has the sense that the faith of Paul, usually hammered out as he writes, has become a transmitted tradition, the faith in which the church has been instructed and to which it must hold fast (1:23; 2:7; 3:16). Has the vibrant language of Paul's faith in process now become minted phrases to be preserved in the churches?

Perhaps, and perhaps not. In the undisputed letters, Paul used liturgical materials already formally structured (Phil. 2:6–11; 2 Cor. 8:9; 1 Cor. 15:3–5). In those letters he also dealt with the cosmic dimensions of Christ's lordship (Rom. 8:18–39; Phil. 2:5–11; 1 Cor. 15:20–28), especially as it dealt with hostile principalities and powers. Likewise, Paul elsewhere underscores fulfilled as well as futuristic eschatology (Rom. 6:1–11). And the absence of references to Torah is not peculiar to Colossians; such references are also lacking in Philippians and Philemon. In short, supporters of Pauline authorship find no phenomena in Colossians that cannot be accounted for by the fact of Paul's never having been to the church addressed and by his practice of shaping his message to the contours of the problems of his readers. The reader of this commentary may or may not wish to enter into the debate over authorship in the process of studying the letter. Hereafter the author will be referred to as Paul or the apostle.

Addressees

The letter is to the church in Colossae (1:2), a town in southern Phrygia in Asia Minor, a few miles east of the larger and more influential city of Laodicea, on the route between Ephesus and Tarsus. Colossae was destroyed by an earthquake in 60–61 CE, and it is uncertain whether or not it was rebuilt. Paul was not known personally to the church (2:1), the congregation having been started by Epaphras, whom Paul commends highly (1:7; 4:12). The membership seems to be Gentile (1:27; 2:13), but a number of Jewish practices are a part of the church's life (2:11, 16). In fact, in an unusual statement, Paul points out that three of his coworkers are "of the circumcision" (4:10–11).

Occasion for the Letter

On a personal level, the return of Onesimus to Colossae (and presumably to Philemon; see the Letter to Philemon), accompanied by Tychicus, provides an opportunity for the church to be updated on Paul's situation (2:1; 4:7–9). Paul is in prison (1:24; 4:3, 18), and the church will be encouraged by news of him. The letter is also a means of sending greetings from himself and his associates to friends not only in Colossae but also in Laodicea. The two churches are to exchange letters from Paul (4:10–16).

On a pastoral level, the letter addresses a serious theological and ethical problem that has gained a foothold among some of the members. Paul calls it a philosophy and a deception with empty promises (2:8). Apparently this "heresy" offers perfection and spiritual fulfillment through a mixture of visions, worship of angelic beings, festivals and rituals based on the calendar, dietary restrictions, and asceticism (2:9–23). For the adherents, Christ was only the beginning in their movement toward full maturity. The burden of the writer is to alert those not yet seduced and to remind everyone that in Christ they have all they need, for in him is the "whole fullness of deity" (2:9).

Date and Place of Writing

Here we face uncertainties, whether or not the letter was penned by Paul himself. If he was the writer, it probably could be dated in the mid-fifties, sent from a prison, perhaps in Asia Minor. Onesimus, the slave, had found his way from Colossae to Paul, so more distant imprisonments such as at Caesarea and Rome are less likely. Ephesus is a possibility; not all of Paul's frequent imprisonments (2 Cor. 11:23) are known to us. If Colossians consists of Paul's thoughts written by a student of his or someone in his tradition, then a reasonable date would be a generation later, but still from somewhere in Asia Minor.

Outline

1:1–14 Introduction
  1:1–2 Salutation
  1:3–14 Thanksgiving
1:15–4:6 Body of the Letter
  1:15–2:23 Theological Reflections
    1:15–20 The Christ Hymn
    1:21–23 The Hymn Applied
    1:24–2:5 The Role of the Apostle
    2:6–23 Disputing False Teachers
  3:1–4:6 Ethical Exhortations on Living as Christians
    3:1–4 Summary
    3:5–17 The Old Life and the New
    3:18–4:1 Life in the Orderly Christian Household
    4:2–6 Concluding Admonitions and Prayer Request
4:7–18 Conclusion
  4:7–9 Concerning the Apostle
  4:10–17 Greetings
  4:18 Farewell

For Further Reading

Lincoln, Andrew T. "The Letter to the Colossians." In *The New Interpreter's Bible*, vol. 11. Nashville: Abingdon Press, 2000.
Lohse, Eduard. *Colossians and Philemon. A Commentary on the Epistles to the Colossians and to Philemon.* Hermeneia. Philadelphia: Fortress Press, 1971.

COMMENTARY

1:1–14
INTRODUCTION

1:1–2
SALUTATION

1:1 Paul ... and Timothy: These names are joined elsewhere in salutations (2 Cor. 1:1; Phil. 1:1), but not equally. Paul is the apostle, Timothy the **brother,** joining Timothy both to Paul and to the recipients (1:2). However, Timothy probably bore no special relationship with the Colossian church since his name appears no more, not even in the greetings. Paul as **apostle** seems undisputed; no further reference is made to it. Verse 1 is exactly the same as 2 Cor. 1:1.

1:2 Saints: The recipients are "saints" (a noun; hence NRSV is preferred to NIV "holy"); that is, set apart as God's own (Exod. 19:6; Rom. 1:7; Phil. 1:1). The faithful brothers (and sisters) are located geographically (**in Colossae**) and theologically (**in Christ**; on the phrase, see on 2 Cor. 5:17). **Grace ... and peace:** This familiar greeting is not as brief as in 1 Thess. 1:1, but not as elaborate as the more frequent "from God our Father and the Lord Jesus Christ," found in MSS.

1:3–14
THANKSGIVING

The thanksgiving, a staple in Paul's correspondence, except for Galatians, functions, as elsewhere, not only to thank God for the recipients and for God's work among them, but also to introduce themes to be developed later in the letter. Good reports about the faith and life of the community (Rom. 1:8; 1 Thess. 1:7) prompt the thanksgiving which is marked by a flourish, an expansiveness expressed by repeated uses of the words "all" and "every": "all the saints" (v. 4); "all the world" (v. 6); "all spiritual wisdom and understanding" (v. 9); "pleasing him in every way" (v. 10); "in every good work" (v. 10); "with all the strength" (v. 11); "endure everything" (v. 11). As Paul will say later, Christ's sufficiency needs no supplements.

1:3 We always thank God: Verses 3–8 are one sentence, difficult to follow, even when broken into several sentences, as in English translations. The prayer joins to God the Father **"our Lord Jesus Christ,"** the phrase expected in the greeting.

1:4–6 Faith . . . hope . . . love . . . : Paul's familiar triad of faith, hope, and love appears here. Faith is in Christ, love is toward the saints (Phlm. 5), and hope is in the expected consummation of the end. Hope here is not only an orientation but also a content **laid up . . . in heaven** (Heb. 6:19). One thinks of Christ now in God's presence whom the apostle will soon describe as "the hope of glory" (v. 27). Hope thus understood is integral to the content of the gospel that was preached to them.

The word of the truth, the gospel: This message they heard has taken root and become fruitful not only in Colossae but **in the whole world** (Rom. 1:8; 1 Thess. 1:8; 2 Thess. 1:3–4). The combination of truth, the message they received, their full understanding of it, and the grace of God truly anticipate an adversary to be addressed later.

1:7 Epaphras: Evidently his preaching gathered the church in Colossae. He is now with Paul, a **fellow servant** and according to Phlm. 23, a fellow prisoner. He is the source of Paul's information about the church in Colossae. Paul commends him highly as a **faithful minister of Christ** who continues to struggle in prayer for the believers (4:12–13). His absence from Colossae likely made the church more vulnerable to false teachers.

1:9 Not ceased praying: Here the thanksgiving moves into intercession, but there is no break in the tone and flow of thought. Verse 9 continues v. 3 and the vocabulary of vv. 9–14 is very much that of vv. 3–8. News about the church from Epaphras prompted the ceaseless prayers of Paul and his associates (v. 9), and as will be seen, especially in chap. 2, shaped the content of the prayers. Paul and his coworkers pray **in order that** (NIV) the church may be filled, not with speculative wisdom about the invisible world of spirit powers, but with **knowledge of God's will,** having the **wisdom and understanding** "in the Spirit/spirit" (v. 5). Here, "spirit" may refer to Paul's spirit (see on 2:5), his internal life, rather than the Holy Spirit, for Colossians is very reserved in speaking of the Holy Spirit—probably as a

reaction to the spiritual excesses of those following the "philosophy" of 2:8–23. In contrast to the undisputed letters of Paul, Colossians has no clear references to the Holy Spirit.

1:10–12 So that you may lead lives worthy of the Lord: To what end are they to be filled with God's wisdom? Not to feel superior, able to judge and disqualify others (2:16–18), but (1) to **lead lives worthy of the Lord;** (2) to **please God** in every way; (3) to **bear fruit** in every good work; (4) to **grow in the knowledge** of God; (5) to **be made strong** by God to endure all things patiently in a spirit of joy; (6) to **give thanks** to God the Father, who has made possible our sharing **the inheritance** reserved for **the saints in the light.** All these extraordinary expressions—working, walking, growing, knowing, enduring, waiting, praising, and thanking—are in no way related to transcendental speculation, but to conduct. The prayers of intercession have a single focus: that the believers, among themselves and in Colossae, live out their faith daily.

1:12–14 Giving thanks to the Father: The phrase returns the reader to v. 3, "We always thank God the Father." One could, therefore, conclude the thanksgiving at v. 12, joining vv. 13–14 to the hymn in vv. 15–20. However, the hymn is to the Son, not the Father, and the "he" (who) in v. 13 refers to the Father. Verse 13 concludes with a statement of what God has done through **his beloved Son** (literally "the Son of his love," a Hebrew idiom). At this point the subject becomes the Son, **in whom we have redemption.** Verse 14 is then transitional, moving primary attention from Father to Son, who, at v. 15, becomes the subject of an extraordinary hymn. **Enabled you:** The apostle says that God has **enabled you** (plural) to share in the light; at v. 13, God **has rescued** (see Matt. 6:13) **us** from the authority (or **power) of darkness.** The shift from second to first person may be due to v. 13 being a creed of the community used in worship and quoted here. In any case, the believers have experienced a change of dominion from the power of darkness to the **kingdom** of God's beloved Son (Acts 26:18). Redemption, usually related to freedom from prison or bondage, is here defined as forgiveness of sins (Eph. 1:7). Sins is far less frequent in Paul than "sin," the power in human life which results in sins. That forgiveness of sins was commonly associated with baptism (Mark 1:4; Acts 2:38; 22:16, etc.) supports the view that the Christ hymn in vv. 15–20 was from a baptismal liturgy.

1:15–4:6
BODY OF THE LETTER

1:15–2:23
THEOLOGICAL REFLECTIONS

1:15–20
The Christ hymn

I

He is the image of the invisible God
    the firstborn before all creation
For in him all things were created
    in the heavens and
    on the earth
    the visible and
    the invisible
        whether thrones
        or dominions
        or principalities
        or powers
All things were created through him
    and for him
And he is before all things
    And all things cohere in him
And he is the head of the body,
    the church

II

He is the beginning
The first born from the dead
    In order that he might be first in
    all things
For in him all the fullness was pleased
    to dwell
And through him to reconcile all things
    to him
        Making peace through the blood
        of his cross through him
    Whether on earth
    or in the heavens

The hymn in 1:15–20 may seem misplaced in an instructional section. However, the hymn provides both language and themes for the church's instruction (see 3:16), for Paul to express the nature of his ministry, and for the apostle to address christologically the false teachings disturbing the church.

Even though v. 12 begins liturgically ("giving thanks"), and even though v. 13 begins in a way common to ancient formulas in praise of famous persons (relative pronoun "who" is translated as "he" plus a verb; see Phil. 2:6; 1 Tim. 3:16; Heb. 12:2), clearly the hymn proper begins at v. 15. Verses 12–14 attend very much to "us" and "we" while vv. 15–20 focus entirely on Christ. There are two stanzas, one beginning at v. 15, the other

at v. 18b. The stanzas have parallel beginnings; both speak of Christ as **firstborn**; both refer to **all things in, through,** and **for** him; a form of "all" appears in eight lines of the hymn; and both stanzas present Christ's influence cosmically, in **heaven** and **on earth**. Students of Colossians believe the hymn is quoted by Paul but that he inserted "**making peace through the blood of his cross**" (v. 20), just as he inserted the line about the cross in the Christ hymn in Phil. 2:6–11. The hymn may have been part of a baptismal liturgy, the introductory contrasts of light-darkness, power-kingdom, sin-redemption (vv. 12–14) serving well to mark the transition in baptism from one realm to another. As will be seen, the hymn addresses issues in the congregation.

1:15–17 Firstborn of all creation: The first stanza relates Christ to all creation as the image of God prior to creation; the Son is the pretemporal, precreation expression of God's creative activity and the one through whom God creates. The early church took from the Wisdom tradition of Judaism (Prov. 8; Wis. 7; Sir. 24) the Word-Wisdom figure and applied it to Christ as image of God and means of creation (John 1:1–5; Heb. 1:2–3; 1 Cor. 8:6). Relating Christ to creation has at least two functions: (a) it affirms that creation is not by its nature evil; (b) it affirms Christ is total and not partial Redeemer. After all, if there are forces and arenas beyond his saving work, then for complete redemption one would need Christ *plus* something else. The heretics in Colossae were apparently advocating something else, and this hymn is already pointed at them. Through the Son **all things** (a formula for "the totality of all that is") were created (past tense) and remain in the state of being created (perfect tense; v. 14). That is, nothing else is divine or eternal; nothing is equal to or superior to the Son; no creature is to be worshiped. Because **all things** are **in, through,** and **for** the Son, all creation will have its purpose, its fulfillment, in him. Within the expression "all things" Paul identifies only **thrones, dominions, rulers,** or **powers.** These powers in the spirit world were integral to Paul's understanding of the work of Christ, since these hostile forces had to be either destroyed or reconciled (1 Cor. 8:5; 15:24–26; Rom. 8:38–39; Phil. 2:11; Eph. 1:21; 6:12). These spirit powers were also important in the theology of the heretics (2:15–19), but in a far different way. For Paul, their fate is in the hands of the Son, who created them. After all, he is before them (preeminent) and in him they **hold together**; that is, cohere, have their unity, constitute a cosmos not a chaos.

1:18a The head of the body, the church: The beginning of v. 18 may have been inserted in the hymn by Paul. It introduces the church as cosmic body of which Christ is the head. If the heretics thought of redemption as Christ plus, they probably thought of the realm of redemption as the church plus. Not so, says Paul; the church is all-embracing, including the totality. Hence, the church as "body" is a cosmic reality, not as in 1 Cor. 12, where the apostle is thinking of the local congregation.

1:18b–20 The firstborn from the dead: The second stanza turns to the redemptive work of the Son. As he was firstborn of all creation, he is firstborn in redemption, here summarized as death and resurrection. As in creation he was preeminent, so in redemption he holds first place. As he was the image of God in stanza 1, so here all the plenitude **(fullness)** of God dwells in him. As all things were created in, through, and for him, so his act of reconciliation embraces the totality. The realm of redemption is coextensive with the realm of creation. There is nothing in creation beyond his act of reconciliation, which is, in typical Pauline thought, effected by means of the **cross.**

1:21–23
The Hymn Applied

1:21–23 Once . . . now: The darkness-light contrast in vv. 12–13 is now brought to bear directly on the readers. Being **estranged and hostile** means they were Gentiles, not Jews. It is rather common in Pauline letters to have the ugly past recalled as a background against which to display the present state of grace (Rom. 6:17–22; 1 Cor. 6:9–11; Gal. 4:8–9). Being **reconciled** through Christ's **fleshly body** is a restatement of v. 20, again accenting the physical reality of his death, lest someone spiritualize it. Their reconciliation is for the purpose of presenting them before God **holy, blameless, and irreproachable** (Phil. 2:15; Eph. 5:27). This description of the believer is drawn from liturgical language, but refers to daily conduct. The reconciliation is Christ's act, but the condition is that they remain firm on the foundation of faith, **without shifting.** And since redemption is for all creation (v. 20), then naturally the gospel with its word of hope is a message **proclaimed to every creature.** As transition to the next section, Paul now introduces himself ("I" not "we") by name and vocation: **I, Paul . . . a minister (servant) of this gospel.** Elsewhere he is minister of God (1 Cor. 6:4) and of Christ (2 Cor. 11:23) but only here

minister of the gospel, the message to the whole world.

1:24–2:5
The Role of the Apostle

1:24–26 Rejoicing in my sufferings: Paul, although not known personally in Colossae (2:1) is bound to them by his sufferings (2 Cor. 1:4–7; Phil. 3:10) on their behalf and on behalf of the whole church. For Paul, the sharing of Christ's suffering binds together Christ, Paul, and the church, which also suffers with Christ (Phil. 1:29; 3:10; Gal. 6:17). Paul's suffering is here interpreted as making up, **completing what is lacking in Christ's afflictions.** This is not to say that Christ's suffering was insufficient, needing to be supplemented. Rather, the context is the Jewish and early Christian belief in the "woes of the Messiah," the sufferings and misery expected to precede the return of Christ (Mark 13:5–27). By his suffering, Paul is foreshortening the final afflictions and hastening the dawn of the coming glory. His suffering is therefore in behalf of the church. Paul now identifies himself as a minister of the church entrusted with a **commission** (office, stewardship; 1 Cor. 9:17) **given** to him from God **for you** (the church).

To make the word of God fully known: His assignment is to complete; that is, to make fully known the gospel to all creation. Recall his word to this effect in Rom. 15:19. The word of God is characterized as a **mystery.** Since the message is a revelation, what has previously been **hidden** is **now revealed** (1 Cor. 2:7–8; 1 Tim. 3:16; Rom. 16:25–26). The concealing of the mystery could be "from the eons and the generations," referring to the hostile principalities and powers (1 Cor. 2:7–8), but it should more likely be taken as a temporal expression (as NRSV and NIV do); that is, concealed for ages past but now revealed. The revelation is not to a select few spiritually elite but is made known **among the nations (Gentiles).**

1:27 Christ in you: The content of the mystery is now stated: "Christ among you, **the hope of glory.**" The same word translated "among" in reference to the nations should be "among" here. "In," while possible (as in NRSV and NIV), can be read as too subjective, too private. Preaching is properly "among you" (2 Cor. 1:19). This, says Paul, is what "we" (again including his associates) announce, following up the proclamation with **warning** (admonition) and **teaching.** The instruction **in all wis-**

dom is not in esoteric speculation but in matters related to Christian living (1:9–10; 4:5) in order that all become **mature (perfect) in Christ.** Such maturity was vital, given the presence of false teaching in the church. This ministry, says Paul (shifting again to "I"), is a continuous struggle, possible only with the energizing power of Christ.

2:1–3 For I want you to know: This is a familiar introduction to an important message from Paul to a church (Rom. 1:13; 1 Cor. 11:3). Since he had never been to Colossae, as he had never been to Rome, it is important in both letters to establish personal relations as a basis for being heard in subsequent remarks. Paul uses the word describing his worldwide ministry (**struggling,** 1:29) to characterize his work in behalf of the church in Colossae and in nearby Laodicea. **Hearts . . . encouraged:** Paul's struggle has as its goal the encouragement (the word can also mean "exhortation," but not here) of the believers, their being brought together **in love,** their possession of the full confidence that comes with **understanding,** and their **knowledge of God's mystery,** which is **Christ. Hidden . . . treasures:** It is in Christ that **the treasures of wisdom and knowledge are hidden.** The image of hidden treasure is a dramatic one, but the apostle has not only said that they are revealed to the writer (1:24), but here he also discloses their hiding place in Christ. By saying "all the treasures," Paul is again affirming the complete and total adequacy of Christ for the redemption of Colossae and of the world.

2:4–5 No one may deceive: The apostle speaks more directly to the situation: I am warning you about those with beguiling speech and persuasive arguments. Aware of the disadvantage of the distance between his prison and Colossae, Paul assures them that **in spirit** (his spirit and the Holy Spirit may blend here) he is with them and is delighted to see the **morale** and **firmness** (terms drawn from military life: soldiers in rank at a bulwark) of their **faith in Christ.** Apparently they will not be surprised by opposition.

2:6–23
Disputing False Teachers

2:6–7 Continue: The readers are urged to hold true to what they have been taught and to conduct themselves (to walk) in the life which flows from that teaching. Reminding his readers to hold fast to the received tradition is a commonplace in Paul (Gal. 1:9; 1 Thess. 4:1; 1

Cor. 11:2; Phil. 4:9). So also is the joining of images from farming and building (**rooted and built up;** see 1 Cor. 3:9; Eph. 3:17), thereby urging both growth and stability. And, of course, Paul urges **thanksgiving,** which includes the whole act of praise to God.

2:8 See to it: This phrase (NRSV, NIV) is hardly strong enough to convey the urgency and importance of the warning now stated. "Watch out! Be alert! Beware!" would be better (see 1 Cor. 3:9; 10:12; Gal. 5:15; Phil. 3:2). Those who threaten faith are not named; perhaps "lest anyone" more forcefully express the hidden danger. **Takes you captive:** To capture or to snare or to carry away as booty is a word used only here in the New Testament. The means of capture is **philosophy,** immediately branded as **empty,** deceptive, and **human tradition;** that is, not the apostolic tradition. Philosophy, love of wisdom, had a wide range of meanings, often quite distant from the careful, critical thinking of Greek intellectuals. Religious groups using magic and rites of initiation into the mysteries of the universe often called their teachings "philosophy." If such exercises had a long history, they carried the authority of tradition. The **elemental spirits (basic principles,** NIV) **of the universe** on one level simply refers to the basics, the ABCs, which, in an analysis of the universe, would be earth, air, fire, and water. However, in many religious circles of the time, these elements were the fundamental spirit beings controlling the universe and human life. For Paul they were principalities and powers, angelic beings hostile toward humanity, demanding worship and service (see Gal. 4:3, 8–9; also Rom. 8:38–39; Eph. 6:12).

2:9–15 For in him the whole fullness of deity dwells: But for those in Christ any fear of, worship of, or desire to please these spirit powers is not only superfluous, but is in fact contrary to Christian faith. Beginning in v. 9 the truth of this conviction is spelled out. First, in Christ dwells the whole fullness of deity, a reassertion of 1:19. It is all here; no supplement needed. **Bodily** recalls both the incarnation and the church (1:22, 25). Second, Christ is, both by creation and by redemption, **the head** of all these spirit powers (1:15–20). Third, in Christ the believers have in baptism put off the life **of the flesh** and have put on new life in that they have died and risen with Christ (see on Gal. 3:27–28). This unique comparison of **baptism** and **circumcision** implies the practice of circumcision among the heretics, but with an interpretation quite non-Jewish. Apparently circumcision was for them a ritual of discarding the physical body, viewed as evil, in order to enter into the world of the spirit powers. What the believers have experienced through baptism is death to sin and trespasses, forgiveness, and resurrection to new life in Christ (Rom. 6:4, 8). Resurrection is both a present and a future experience. Finally, in Christ the believers are set free from legalism and from the spirit powers back of all legal demands. If the heresy at Colossae included the Jewish element of circumcision, perhaps it also embraced legalistically some of the demands of the Mosaic Law. Hence the reference to the consultation of the written code.

Nailed to the cross: Rather than referring to Christ himself, a dramatic expression saying that with the crucifixion all the charges against God's people were cancelled, rendered null and void. To say this is to say that all the spirit powers with their hold over human lives have been **disarmed,** stripped of their authority, and paraded publicly as defeated enemies. Paul speaks elsewhere and in different imagery of this writing of God through the reconciling death of Jesus (Phil. 2:11; 1 Cor. 2:6–8; 15:24–28; Gal. 4:3–9). Interestingly, in Gal. 4 Paul joins legalism (a perversion of the nature and intent of Torah) to the activity of the principalities and powers, as he does here at 2:14–15.

2:16–19 Food or drink: Among the legal demands were observances of the calendar of the movement of celestial bodies, as well as regulations concerning permitted and forbidden foods and drinks (Gal. 4:9–10). While these practices were obviously drawn from Judaism, it is clear that they have been put to new ends. It is not Moses being honored and obeyed, but the spirit powers set forth by the heretics as the forces to be worshiped and obeyed. Those so persuaded graded themselves as spiritually superior and sat in condescending judgment of those members who did not enter into these observances. These practices are in the category of appearance (**shadow**) while the reality (body, **substance**) is Christ. This distinction between the shadow and the true reality, drawn from Plato, was used among some early Christians to distinguish between the earthly (shadow) and the heavenly (true form or substance; see Heb. 8:5; 10:1). Again a warning: do not let these who practice **false humility** (NIV), **worship** the spirit powers (**angels**), claim **visions** (a strange expression, perhaps a quotation from the heretics, perhaps referring

to out-of-body experiences) or a fleshly mind disqualify you or condemn you or rob you of the prize rightly yours. Whatever role the false teachers accorded Christ in their "philosophy," it certainly was not acceptable. He is not one of the angels; he is not a step along the way to perfection. Christ is the **head** of the body, the church, from whom all the body is **nourished,** enjoys **growth,** and has its center, absolutely necessary for functioning.

2:20–23 Why do you live . . . to the world?: The warning to the church takes the form of a rhetorical question. If in baptism you died with Christ, then you died to the world with all its dominating powers. Why, then, continue as though you did not? The line of thought parallels Paul's words to the Romans: you died to sin (6:2); you died to the law (7:4). Why continue to submit to rules such as the heretics lay on you: **Do not handle, Do not taste, Do not touch?** These taboos are part of a humanly conceived legalism which forgets or denies that God through Christ has created all things. Why treat created things as evil? To be sure, such abstinence, such asceticism, might impress others as deeply spiritual and prompted by divine wisdom. The truth is, such exercises in **self-imposed piety** and **humility** are self-centered, fixed on the very world of values they appear to deny. There is no lasting value in such "spiritual" practices; in fact, they perish in the very process. And they have absolutely no value in the real battle we face: **checking self-indulgence**—even though some are seduced into thinking that what they are doing is restraining such indulgences.

3:1–4:6
ETHICAL EXHORTATIONS ON LIVING AS CHRISTIANS

3:1–4
Summary

3:1 Therefore (So NRSV/**Then** NIV): In typical Pauline fashion (Rom. 12:1; Eph. 4:1), the hortatory section begins. The basis for exhortation is what has already been said. Having been **raised with Christ,** the believer is to keep his or her mind on Christ and that means **above,** because Christ is now at God's **right hand** (Ps. 110:1), where he remains till all his enemies are absolved. The spatial categories (above, below) are often used in the New Testament to indicate contrasting realms of value and meaning (1:5; Gal. 4:26; Phil. 3:14). Paul repeats the thought expressed in "you have been raised" by the corollary phrase **you have died.** As with any death, the deceased is no longer visible, no longer accountable, no longer bound; the hold of the world is broken. The believer's life is in Christ and Christ is with God. This is no otherworldliness in its popular sense, but rather an understanding of the source, means, and end of one's life. However, dying and rising with Christ, a present experience, also has its future reference. **When Christ is revealed** at the end of the age, what is now **hidden with Christ** will be **revealed with him in glory** (1 John 3:2). "Glory" describes the unhindered and unending presence of God in which believers finally live.

3:5–17
The Old Life and the New

3:5–9 Whatever . . . is earthly: This unit urges the believers to live out their faith in specific conduct and relationships. Since you have died with Christ and have been raised with him, then to certain behavior from your past (v. 7) you are to be dead; to behavior that befits Christ you are to be alive. The lists of vices and virtues are rather traditional and should not be read as a profile of this particular church. However, at points the lists seem to be contoured to fit what has been said in chaps. 1–2. The language of dying and rising fits the occasion of baptism as the setting for such exhortations. This possibility is further supported by the expression **stripped off** (v. 9) and **clothed yourselves with** (v. 10), perhaps a reference to the ritual of changing garments as a symbol of one's change of conduct and status before God. One does not put off the body, as would be the view of antiworldly spiritual groups (perhaps the Colossian false teachers?), but one puts off, one dies to, behavior centered on the created rather than on the Creator. Foremost among the evils to be discarded are sexual sins and covetousness (**greed,** v. 5). Covetousness, setting the heart on material wealth, is **idolatry** because it is to have a god other than the one true God (also Eph. 5:5). **Fornication,** with its attendant **impurity, passion**, and **evil desire**, makes the vice lists among many churches (1 Cor. 5:10–11; 6:9–10: 2 Cor. 12:21; Gal. 5:19–21; 1 Thess. 4:3; 1 Tim. 1:9–10). On such evils the **wrath of God**'s judgment is visited (Rom. 1:18–3:20; 1 Thess. 1:10; 2:16). The list of five vices in v. 5 is followed by five more in v. 8. These center on speech and attitudes destructive to relationships in the believing community. To these is added a sixth, lying (v. 9). All these vices belong to the one who is dead (v. 3), and hence, like a soiled garment, are to be "striped off."

3:10–17 Clothe yourselves: See on Gal 3:27–28. The apostle begins to consider what the one raised to new life in Christ is to put on as the clean garment of the baptized. Using the language of Gen. 1:26–27, the new person in Christ is a new creation in the image of God (1:18); all the baptized are in Christ; and he, as the head of the body, the church (1:18–20), is **all in all,** the totality. Since he is all in all, the usual ethnic, racial, economic, and social distinctions are excluded (Gal. 3:28). Addressing the readers now as **God's chosen ones, holy and beloved** (Rom. 8:33; 1 Pet. 2:9), the writer offers another list of five qualities, five virtues to be **put on (clothe yourselves).** All five characterize how Christians should relate to other people. To the list the apostle adds **bearing with one another** and **forgiving each other.** Complaints and tensions occur in the believing community as in any other, but those who have been **forgiven forgive.**

3:14–17 Above all . . . love: Surpassing all other virtues is love (Rom. 13:8, 10; 1 Cor. 13) which is the bond which ties all together in completeness (perfection). The one body of Christ is complete. Verse 15 has the quality of a prayer for the rule of Christ's **peace** within and among them (John 14:27; Phil. 4:7); to such life together they have been **called.**

Be thankful is literally "Be the grateful ones." Thanksgiving recalls the liturgical character of much of the letter (1:3; 1:12; 2:7) and at this point both introduces and concludes a brief description of the worship of the community. The first element in the service is the **word of Christ** (the gospel), which is at work in the community through teaching and admonition **in all wisdom** (1:9–10; 2:3, 23; 4:5). The second element is **singing with gratitude in your hearts** (not with lips only). It is neither necessary nor possible to distinguish among **psalms, hymns, and spiritual songs.** All are offered in praise and gratitude to God for what God has done in Christ. Verse 17 is the summary: **everything** said or done is to acknowledge the lordship of Jesus, thanking God in Christ's name.

3:18–4:1
Life in the Orderly Christian Household

This unit, Rules for the Household, is self-contained without connections with what precedes or follows. While the undisputed letters of

Paul have no such instructions, similar household codes are found in Eph. 5:22–6:9; 1 Tim. 2:8–15; 5:1–6:2; Titus 2:1–10; 1 Pet. 2:13–3:7. See on those passages, especially the principles of interpretation at 1 Pet. 2:11–3:12. Such codes of conduct, found among Jewish and Greek moral teachers, had apparently been embraced by the church, with some modifications. Early Christians found helpful teachings in the culture that were congenial with their own standards. There is little evidence of attempts to react or revolutionize at first, even though it was inevitable that the teachings of Christ would at times and places run counter to culture with radical effects. Some women and slaves, on the basis of such Pauline mottoes as Gal. 3:27 (only partially repeated in Col. 3:11) may have taken their new-found freedom to extremes, abolishing all authority and social distinctions in the name of Christ and the Spirit; the household codes may in part have represented a response to what were considered dangerous and easily misunderstood extremes. Such lists of household duties are given not only for the internal purpose of regulating the Christian household, but were an aspect of the church's mission—witnessing to outsiders that the new Christian community was not subversive or disruptive, but fit into the conventional cultural norms to the extent that it could do so without compromising its fundamental faith (see on 1 Pet. 2:11–3:12). The sequence of instruction is in three pairs, beginning with the subordinate in each pair: wives and husbands, children and parents, slaves and masters.

3:18–19 Wives . . . husbands: The wife is to accept her role as subordinate to her husband as proper. To say such a role is **in the Lord** is to say the church affirms it as appropriate for the Christian. Neither the writer nor the reader dreamed of any other understanding. The gospel's gradual social revolution had not even begun. As for husbands, they are instructed to love their wives, never being bitter, harsh, or cruel toward them. The wife of such a husband could have a good life but not a free one, and even a good life under the authority of another, however benevolent, in time ceased to be a good life.

3:20–21 Children . . . parents: As for children, obedience to parents was time-honored in Jewish and Greek circles, and the church affirmed it as God's will. On the other hand, fathers were not to initiate, provoke, or embitter their children. Under such oppression and provocation children in their powerlessness become disheartened.

3:22–4:1 Slaves . . . masters: On slavery in the first century, see the introduction to Philemon. The relationship between slave and master is here treated more elaborately, perhaps because the incongruity between freedom in Christ and human slavery was being felt in the church. If "there is no longer . . . slave and free, but Christ is all" and in all (3:11), how does Christian love work itself out in a world in which slavery is accepted as normal? And since the readers knew the case of the slave Onesimus, referred to as "the faithful and beloved brother, who is one of you" (4:9; see Philemon), what instruction could be given? (This passage will be understood differently if Colossians is not contemporary with Philemon but represents a later interpretation of Paul. See the introduction to Colossians.) Quite obviously there is no thought of changing society at large, but personal relationships are to be before God, service is to be **as for the Lord**, and the behavior of even a slave is to be genuine and not simply pleasing the master. Not even a slave is to be one person when seen by the master and another when unseen. Let service be to the Lord, and the promised **reward** will be theirs. However, the Lord who rewards also punishes, with **no partiality.** This is to say, the circumstances of slavery do not provide an excuse for wrongdoing. As for masters, the admonition is quite brief, perhaps because a letter read to the church would be heard by many slaves but few masters. The **master** is to treat slaves **justly** and **fairly,** mindful that the master had a **Master.** In sum, both slaves and masters were in the service of the same Lord.

4:2–6
Concluding Admonitions
and Prayer Request

4:2–4 Devote yourselves: Following the rules for household duties (3:18–4:1), the subject matter returns to that of 3:17, but now in a series of loosely joined exhortations. Verses 2–4 have to do with prayer with its elements of thanksgiving, watchfulness, petition, and intercession. The call to continuous **prayer** was made to the church everywhere (Luke 18:1–8; Acts 1:14; 2:42, 46; 6:4; Rom. 12:12; 1 Thess. 5:6; etc.). The apostle requests intercession for himself and associates that they may have an opportunity to continue preaching beyond their present imprisonment. God opens **doors for the word** (1 Cor. 16:9; 2 Cor. 2:12). **The mystery of Christ** (1:26; 2:2) that Paul preaches landed him in prison, but he wants to resume the open proclamation of that message.

4:5–6 Toward outsiders: Nonbelievers; 1 Thess. 4:12; 1 Cor. 5:12–13. Believers are to walk **wisely**, further evidence that, unlike the false teachers, the apostle views wisdom as practical, related to behavior (1:9–10, 20; 2:3; 3:16). Being Christian is not secret activity confined to the group; it is before the world and is constantly being evaluated by the world. **Making the most of** (redeeming [KJV]) **the time:** Taking advantage of the opportunity. "Time" here does not refer to chronological time but "opportune time," time that God gives (Gal. 6:9–10; 1 Pet. 1:5; 5:6; recall Jesus' references to his time in the Gospel of John; e.g., 7:6). In every situation one's **speech** should **be gracious** ("in grace"; 3:16), **seasoned with salt** of wisdom and appropriateness so as to represent properly the Christian faith.

4:7–18
CONCLUSION

4:7–9
CONCERNING THE APOSTLE

4:7–9 Tychicus . . . One claims: No details about Paul's condition are stated in the letter; the church will hear those from Tychicus (Acts 20:4; Eph. 6:21; 2 Tim. 4:12; Titus 3:12) and Onesimus (see Philemon), **who is one of you,** that is, from Colossae. That no reference is made to his being a slave but rather a **faithful and beloved brother** does not mean he is not the Onesimus of the Letter to Philemon. The two messengers are more than news bearers; they are to **encourage** (comfort; also exhort) the church in Colossae.

4:10–17
GREETINGS

4:10–17 My co-workers: Verses 10–14 contain greetings from companions of Paul. First mentioned are three Jewish Christian coworkers who are special to Paul, being of his own background, being the **only ones of the circumcision** sharing his mission, and very likely providing entry for ministry among populations not necessarily hospitable to the gospel. They are **Aristarchus** (Phlm. 24; Acts 19:29; 20:4; 27:2); **Mark**, cousin of Barnabas, likely

the John Mark of Jerusalem (Acts 12:12, 25), who had a long history of service with Paul (Acts 13:13; 15:37, 39; Phlm. 24; 2 Tim. 4:11) and Peter (1 Pet. 5:13), about whom the church in Colossae had already received instructions (from whom?); and **Jesus**, about whom we know nothing more except he called himself **Justus**, perhaps as an accommodation to a Gentile world or perhaps out of an unwillingness to use the same name as his Lord.

4:12–13 Greets you: Epaphras, who has been with the church since its inception (1:7–8), sends greetings. Why he is presently absent from Colossae is not clear. He has worked hard in Laodicea and Hierapolis as well as Colossae, and even now wrestles in constant prayer for the church, that it be mature and fully confident of God's will for them. **Luke** sends greetings (Phlm. 24; 2 Tim. 4:11). Only here is he called **the beloved physician**, and there is no word as to whether he attends Paul as a physician or as a fellow missionary who happens to be a physician. **Demas** (Phlm. 24) is last to be mentioned. According to 2 Tim. 4:10, Demas later abandoned the Pauline mission.

4:15–17 Give my greetings: Paul adds his own greetings to be sent along to the church **in Laodicea** and especially **to Nympha(s)** and **the church** which meets **in his/her house** (on house churches, see also Phlm. 2; Rom. 16:5; 1 Cor. 16:15). Manuscript evidence is divided but somewhat favorable toward "her" house, making the homeowner a woman, Nympha. The letter to Colossae and one that had been written to Laodicea were to be read publicly and then exchanged for a second reading. A special directive is given to **Archippus** but the **task** he is to complete (v. 17) is unknown to us. Archippus is mentioned in Phlm. 2 as "our fellow soldier," but that his ministry was related to the disposition of the case of the runaway slave Onesimus is only speculation. That the names in Phlm. 23–24 are the same as those in Col. 4:10–14 seems to join the two letters to Paul and to Colossae. For those who hold Colossians was written in Paul's name by one of his associates, the names in Colossians were copied from Philemon to give this letter authenticity and authority, and descriptions were added not found in Philemon.

4:18
FAREWELL

4:18 Grace be with you: The farewell is brief, containing three themes. First, Paul's greeting is in his **own hand**. This was rather customary, even if a letter were dictated (Rom. 16:22; Gal. 6:11; 1 Cor. 16:21; 2 Thess. 3:19). Second, Paul asks that they **remember** his imprisonment, implying that they remember why he is in bonds, his ministry in their behalf, and his desire to resume his mission (4:2–4). And finally, Paul commends them to God's **grace**. So he concludes as he began (1:2), with a reminder that he and they live by and within God's gracious favor.

The First Letter of Paul to the Thessalonians

INTRODUCTION

Authorship

In the earlier days of critical biblical scholarship when everything was challenged, a few scholars doubted that Paul wrote 1 Thessalonians. Critical study is long past that phase, and today no scholar doubts that the letter was written by Paul.

Date and Setting in Paul's Ministry

Prior to the Jersualem Council ca. 50 CE (Acts 15; Gal. 2:1–10) Paul had served with Barnabas as a missionary of the Antioch church (the "first missionary journey" of Acts 13–14; on Luke's structuring Paul's ministry into three "missionary journeys," see on Acts 13:1). After the Jerusalem Council and the confrontation with Peter in Antioch, in which Barnabas, too, was alienated from the Pauline view of what "freedom from the Law" meant (Gal. 2:11–21), Paul chose Silas as his partner and began a new mission that established churches in Europe: Philippi, Thessalonica, Athens, and Corinth (the "second missionary journey" of Acts 15:40–18:21; see 1 Thess. 1:5, 9–10; 2:2; 3:1). Along the way, Timothy was recruited as a fellow missionary (see Acts 16:1–5). The letter was written a few weeks or months after the founding of the church by Paul, Silas, and Timothy. Since according to Acts Paul went from Athens to Corinth, where he was rejoined by Timothy (Acts 18:1, 5; see 1 Thess. 3:1), 1 Thessalonians was apparently written from Corinth. Correlation with the mission in Corinth allows us to date the letter about 50 CE (see "Introduction to the Pauline Letters"). It is the earliest of Paul's extant letters, and thus the earliest extant Christian document of any kind.

Addressees

Thessalonica (modern Thessaloniki, Thessalonike, or Salonika) was a large seaport on the northwest coast of the Aegean Sea, on the Via Egnatia, the main highway to Rome. It was a cosmopolitan, multicultural city, the capital of Macedonia and the seat of the Roman government of the area. Many religions had temples and adherents in the city, which also had at least one Jewish synagogue. Though Acts pictures Paul's mission as centered in the Jewish synagogue (Acts 17:1–9), the letter represents the new Christians as converts from sophisticated pagan religions (1:9). They had not been irreligious people converted by Paul to become religious, but religious people who had responded to the good news of the Christian gospel.

Situation

Paul was anxious about the new congregation. He knew it was experiencing harassment and persecution (1:6; 2:14). He was worried that they might misunderstand his intentions as those of a traveling preacher interested in his own bank account. More than once Paul had attempted to return to Thessalonica himself, but "Satan blocked our way" (2:18). During his mission at Athens Paul sent Timothy back to Thessalonica to encourage the church and report on their condition (see the contrasting chronology in Acts 17:10–18:5). Timothy brought an encouraging report, but also news of distress that some members had died, since the new church had apparently understood that Christians would all live to experience the return of Christ (see 4:13–18). First Thessalonians is Paul's letter in response to Timothy's report.

Outline

For Further Reading

Gaventa, Beverly Roberts. *First and Second Thessalonians*. Interpretation: A Bible Commentary for Teaching and Preaching. Louisville, KY: Westminster John Knox, 1998.

Smith, Abraham. "The First Letter to the Thessalonians." In *The New Interpreter's Bible*, vol. 11. Nashville: Abingdon Press, 2000.

COMMENTARY

1:1
SALUTATION

In contrast to the modern letter form that has the addressee at the beginning and the writer's signature at the end, letters in the first-century Graeco-Roman world began with a standard form "A to B, greeting." James 1:1 and Acts 15:23; 23:26 follow this form exactly. It can be seen from figure 16 that Paul adopts this form but changes it in distinctive ways so that it is no longer a mere formality, but an elaborate theological affirmation.

First Thessalonians, the earliest letter, is the simplest, and Romans (probably) the latest letter, is the most elaborate.

Paul, Silvanus, and Timothy: Paul writes as one conscious of his apostolic authority (see 2:7; on the meaning of "apostle," see on Luke 6:12; Gal. 1:1). Yet he begins his letter without any official claim (contrast Galatians, 1–2 Corinthians, Romans, in the chart above). His inclusion of his fellow missionaries shows he does not write as an authoritative individual, but as a representative of the church and its mission. Though "we" occurs often in 1 Thessalonians, it is clear that Paul himself is the writer (e.g., 2:18; 3:1, 5). Silvanus is the Silas who first appears in Acts 15:22 and then accompanies Paul on his mission trips. On Timothy, see on Acts 16:1–5. Both became seasoned missionaries.

The church of the Thessalonians: The one church of God as it is represented in the congregation in Thessalonica. "Church" means "assembly," those "called out" (see on Acts 19:32). Paul can use it for the one Christian community in the whole world (1 Cor. 10:32; 12:28); for all the Christians in a particular town, as here (Rom. 16:1; 1 Cor. 1:2); or for a congregation that meets in a particular house (Rom. 16:5; 1 Cor. 16:19). **In God the Father and the Lord Jesus Christ:** On Paul's distinctive "in Christ" expression, see on 2 Cor. 5:17.

Grace to you and peace: This is Paul's most distinctive change in the traditional letter formula,

and became his trademark. Though now a familiar church expression, Paul was the first to use it in a letter greeting formula. It occurs in all his undisputed letters, but nowhere else in ancient literature except in dependence on Paul's own usage. The customary form was *chairein*, translated "greetings," but this was a purely formal word without content, functioning like the English "Hi." Paul changes it to the similar-sounding *charis*, the Christian theological term "grace." Grace is the free, unmerited favor of God, granted as a gift without conditions or achievements (see Rom. 3:24; 4:4, 16; 5:2, 15–21; 11:6; 1 Cor. 5:10; Gal. 2:21; Eph. 2:8; John 1:17; Luke 15:11–32; 18:9–14). The traditional Jewish greeting was (and still is) "shalom," translated "peace." For Paul, peace is the result of grace, the state of salvation and restored relationship with God that comes through God's act in Christ (Rom. 5:1). By adapting and combining the traditional Graeco-Roman and Jewish forms of greeting, Paul gives expression to the inclusive nature of the Christian faith (Gal. 3:27–28; Rom. 1:16) and to his own sense of mission as a Jewish Christian who is apostle to the Gentiles.

1:2–3:13
PART ONE—EXTENDED THANKSGIVING

Following the salutation, the traditional letter form often had a brief section called the thanksgiving, which typically said something like "I thank the gods that you are in good health and pray that you will continue to prosper." It too was a formality, a matter of polite communication (like "Dear Sir or Madam" and "Thanks for your letter of the nineteenth"). Here too Paul transforms a traditional form by filling it with Christian content. He typically begins his letters with an extensive thanksgiving to God for the addressees (absent only in Galatians in the undisputed letters).

In the Hellenistic world people did not thank each other. This does not mean they were less polite than modern Americans, but represents a cultural difference. In that culture, to say "thank you" to another was a way of settling the matter, paying the debt, ending the relationship. Thus neither here nor elsewhere does Paul say "thanks" *to* human beings, but thanks God *for* them. The Pauline thanksgiving is a real prayer expressing Paul's interest in and concern for the readers, filled with theological content and signaling the contents of the letter to follow. In 1 Thessalonians, the thanksgiving that begins in 1:2 does not really conclude until 3:13, embracing much of the substance of the letter within the

Figure 16. Form of Greetings in Letters

Typical Hellinistic Letter Form

Jas. 1:1

James, a servant of God and of the Lord Jesus Christ, To the twelve tribes in the Dispersion: Greetings.

Acts 15:23

The brothers, both the apostles and the elders, to the believers of Gentile origin in Antioch and Syria and Cilicia, greetings.

Acts 23:26

Claudius Lysias to his Excellency the governor Felix, greetings.

Pauline Letter Form

1 Thess. 1:1

Paul, Silvanus, and Timothy,

To the church of the Thessalonians in God the Father and the Lord Jesus Christ:

Grace to you and peace.

1 Cor. 1:1–3

Paul, called to be an apostle of Christ Jesus by the will of God, and our brother Sosthenes,

2 To the church of God that is in Corinth, to those who are sanctified in Christ Jesus, called to be saints, together with all those who in every place call on the name of our Lord Jesus Christ, both their Lord and ours:

3 Grace to you and peace from God our Father and the Lord Jesus Christ.

2 Cor. 1:1–2

Paul, an apostle of Christ Jesus by the will of God, and Timothy our brother,

To the church of God that is in Corinth, including all the saints throughout Achaia:

2 Grace to you and peace from God our Father and the Lord Jesus Christ.

Gal. 1:1–5

Paul an apostle—sent neither by human commission nor from human authorities, but through Jesus Christ and God the Father, who raised him from the dead—2and all the members of God's family who are with me,

To the churches of Galatia:

3 Grace to you and peace from God our Father and the Lord Jesus Christ, 4who gave himself for our sins to set us free from the present evil age, according to the will of our God and Father, 5to whom be the glory forever and ever.

Phil. 1:1–2

Paul and Timothy, servants of Christ Jesus,

To all the saints in Christ Jesus who are in Philippi, with the bishops and deacons:

2 Grace to you and peace from God our Father and the Lord Jesus Christ.

Phlm. 1–3

Paul, a prisoner of Christ Jesus, and Timothy our brother,

To Philemon our dear friend and co-worker, 2to Apphia our sister, to Archippus our fellow soldier, and to the church in your house:

3 Grace to you and peace from God our Father and the Lord Jesus Christ.

Romans 1:1–7

Paul, a servant of Jesus Christ, called to be an apostle, set apart for the gospel of God, 2which he promised beforehand through his prophets in the holy scriptures, 3the gospel concerning his Son, who was descended from David according to the flesh 4and was declared to be Son of God with power according to the spirit of holiness by resurrection from the dead, Jesus Christ our Lord, 5through whom we have received grace and apostleship to bring about the obedience of faith among all the Gentiles for the sake of his name, 6including yourselves who are called to belong to Jesus Christ,

7 To all God's beloved in Rome, who are called to be saints:

Grace to you and peace from God our Father and the Lord Jesus Christ.

framework of prayer. Paul did not write doctrinal essays to be analyzed in seminars, but, letters to be read aloud in the worship service (5:27), expressing his message within the context of thankful praise.

1:2–10
THE THESSALONIANS' RECEPTION
OF PAUL'S GOSPEL

1:2 We always give thanks to God for all of you: Paul, Silas, and Timothy had preached in Thessalonica (2:2, 13); some—we have no idea how many—had responded (1:9–10) and were now enduring harassment and persecution for their faith (1:6; 2:14). Yet Paul does not thank them for their response (as a modern evangelist might), but gives thanks to God. This is partially a difference in ancient Mediterranean and modern North American culture (see above). Primarily, however, the difference between Paul's and our presuppositions is theological, not cultural: Paul did not consider coming to faith a matter of human initiative or achievement, but of God's initiative and call. They had not been religious seekers who finally found what they were looking for in Paul's new religion, just as Paul had not been seeking a deeper religious experience when he was confronted on the Damascus road by the risen Christ (Acts 9:1–19; Gal. 1:13–17). In each case, it was a matter of God's choice and call, not of human seeking (see on v. 4).

1:3 Work of faith . . . labor of love . . . steadfastness of hope: Although the triad appears repeatedly in Paul's letters (5:8; Rom. 5:1–5; 1 Cor. 13:13; Gal. 5:5–6) and later Pauline tradition (Col. 1:4–5), it is not a list of "Christian virtues" or "Christian attitudes." Faith is here not an attitude but the God-given power to do Christian work; love is not an emotion but the mainspring of labor (see 1 Cor. 13); hope is not optimism but the confident expectation of the triumph of God that will occur when Christ returns (1:10; 2:19; 3:13; 4:13–5:11).

1:4 He has chosen you: This is a key theme of the letter (2:12; 4:7; 5:24). They had not been seeking a deeper religious experience. God's choice or election means inclusion in the chosen people of God, the people chosen to serve God and witness to his mighty acts (see on Rom. 8:28–30; 1 Pet. 1:2). It is not a matter of God arbitrarily choosing some individuals for salvation and others for damnation, nor is it a denial of human responsibility, but an affirmation of God's initiative in forming the chosen people. In the Old Testament, Judaism, and earliest Christian-

ity, this people was understood to be Israel. A few years after Easter, the church at Antioch came to understand God's will as opening the doors to membership in the chosen people to all nations (Acts 11:19–26). After his conversion Paul had worked within this church and represented its inclusive point of view in his mission work (Acts 13–14), which he had successfully defended at the Jerusalem Council (Acts 15; Gal. 2). In Thessalonica, Paul and his coworkers had preached to Gentiles who accepted the faith and were incorporated into the chosen people.

1:5 Not in word only: The Thessalonians became Christians in response to the preaching and teaching of Paul and his colleagues. The Thessalonians respond to God's word, i.e., to the thoroughly human word of the preaching and teaching of Paul, Silas, and Timothy, the **message of the gospel**. This is how they are called (2 Thess. 2:14). Yet in and through this human word the **power** of the **Holy Spirit** was at work (2:13), so that the church was called into being by God's powerful word. On the human level, Paul preached and some of them responded. In retrospect, God was at work both in Paul's preaching and in their response. They do not take credit for it but give thanks to God. It is our freedom and responsibility to decide for or against the gospel. If we respond in faith, we are inclined to think we are volunteers. In retrospect and thanksgiving, we see that we are draftees (John 15:16, 19).

1:6 You became imitators of us: This is not egotism. When Paul presents himself as an example (as also, e.g., 1 Cor. 4:16; 11:1), he is reflecting the standard Hellenistic pattern in which teachers set forth their own life before their students as an example of their philosophy. Not to have done so would have made Paul appear hypocritical. Paul does not have in mind detailed ethical prescriptions but his basic orientation; his life is now determined by his faith in God's act in Christ. **And of the Lord:** So also when Paul holds up Christ as example, he is not thinking of the details of daily life. He speaks of the exalted Lord, not of Jesus. For Paul, the pattern of Christian life is determined not by the example of the Jesus in Galilee and Jerusalem, but by the incarnation, the divine Son who condescended to become a servant (Phil. 2:5–11; 2 Cor. 8:9).

1:7–8 You became an example . . . the word of the Lord has sounded forth from you: The new Christians of Thessalonica were not mere consumers and imitators. The evangelized became evangelists themselves. Those who adopted the pattern of life manifest in the Lord Jesus and the apostle Paul became themselves examples to other new Christians.

1:9–10 How you turned to God from idols: These two verses reflect a pre-Pauline Christian creed, a summary statement of the faith probably developed in the Antioch church and adopted and elaborated by Paul. The statement of faith can easily be set out in two stanzas of three lines each, in which the first line refers to the past, the second to the present, and the third to the future:

You turned to God from idols	a. past
to serve a living and true God	b. present
(and) to wait for his Son	c. future
from heaven	
Whom he raised from the dead	a. past
Jesus who rescues us	b. present
From the wrath that is coming	c. future

The three verbs of the first stanza summarize Christian experience: **turn**, **serve**, **wait**, that correspond to the "faith, love, hope" of 1:3. Just as first two are active—the past step of conversion and the present life of service—the orientation toward the future is not a passive waiting, but an active awaiting of the final triumph of God. Yet this summary of the faith is not a list of human duties, a new law, but is centered on God.

The first and last lines represents the traditional Jewish missionary message of the one God over against pagan idols, the God whose ethical seriousness is manifest in that he will bring all human beings to a final judgment. **The wrath that is coming** is not the emotional anger of God, but the standard image for God's eschatological judgment, in which sinners will be punished (of dozens of biblical examples, see Isa. 63:3–6; Jer. 7:20; 21:12; Amos 1:11; Mic. 5:15; Zeph. 1:15; Matt. 3:7; John 3:36; Rom. 1:18; 2:5, 8; 3:5; 4:15; 5:9; 12:19; Col. 3:6; Rev. 6:16). These two features made Judaism very attractive to many people in the Hellenistic world: monotheism instead of polytheism, and ethical responsibility validated by the final judgment. For Christians, the living God is the one definitively manifest in Jesus, the God who raised Jesus from the dead, the one through whom God saves at the final judgment. The pattern is the traditional Jewish one, now transformed by faith in Christ, so that the final judgment is a matter of faith in the God who saves through Christ, rather than an evaluating of whether good works outweigh bad ones.

For other places where Paul adopts and amplifies previous Christian traditions that already had a fixed form, see 4:14; Phil. 2:5–11; 1 Cor. 11:23–26; 15:3–5; Rom. 1:3–4; 3:23–26.

That the new Thessalonian Christians had turned to God from idols shows that they had previously been Gentiles (an impression different from the synagogue-oriented mission described in Acts 17:1–9).

2:1–16
PAUL'S WAY OF LIFE IN THESSALONICA

2:1 You yourselves know: This repeated reminder (see 1:5; 2:1, 2, 11; 3:3, 4; 4:2, 4; 5:2) recalls the story of the founding of the church in Thessalonica, their response, Paul's conduct among them, and his previous instructions. To be a Christian is not an individual vertical relationship to God, but means belonging to a community of faith with a particular history.

2:2 Shamefully mistreated at Philippi: See Acts 16:20–24. **The gospel of God:** "Gospel" means "good news" (not "good advice," "good ideas," "good principles," etc.). It announces the act of God in Christ for human salvation. God is both content and source of the gospel (see Mark 1:14; Rom. 1:1; 15:16; 2 Cor. 11:7; 1 Thess. 2:8–9; 1 Pet. 4:17).

2:3–5 Deceit or impure motives or trickery . . . flattery . . . greed: Paul seems on the defensive, and it may be that some of the Thessalonians were tempted to classify Paul with the traveling teachers and philosophers who operated for their own profit, exploiting their new students and then moving on. However, the phrases are stereotyped and part of the conventional declarations of teachers in Paul's world. The letter nowhere else indicates personal distrust between the church and Paul; rather, the relationship seems to be one of mutual love and trust.

2:7 Demands as apostles of Christ: For meaning of "apostle," see on Luke 6:12–13. The word appears here for the first time in Christian literature. In later letters Paul will include it in his opening salutation and distinguish his own apostolic ministry from that of his coworkers (see on 1:1), but here he uses it incidentally in a way that includes Silas and Timothy. Paul can use the word not only in its "official" sense of commissioned representatives to whom the risen Lord has appeared, but in its general sense as "missionaries" (see 2 Cor. 8:23, where "messengers" of the churches translates the Greek word "apostles" [see NRSV note], and see on Acts 14:4, 14). The issue of Paul's status as an "official" apostle has not yet arisen (see on Gal. 1:1). Here, the point is that church missionaries have the right to be supported by the congregations they have founded, but rather than exercising this right, Paul had worked to support himself during the mission in Thessalonica (see v. 9 and 1 Cor. 9:1–18).

Gentle among you: For "gentle" some MSS read "infants" (see NRSV note), which is more likely the original reading. There is only one Greek letter difference (*epioi / nepioi*). Some scribes changed "babies" to "gentle" because it seemed to fit the context better. In such cases, the more difficult reading is often more original, since scribes attempted to "correct" the text by making it clearer, not more difficult. But Paul often changes metaphors suddenly. "Babies" is one element of a constellation of family imagery Paul here uses for the church: "brothers and sisters" (2:1, 9), "nurse" (2:7), mother caring for "her own children" who (in nursing) "shares her own self" (2:8) with them; "father with his children" (2:11); "orphans" (2:17). For Paul, joining the church was not adding on another worthy cause to our list of obligations, but incorporation into the family of God. The variety of imagery tempers Paul's parental and patriarchal imagery. He is not only the father as head of the household, but mother and nurse, baby, brother, and orphan—with the Thessalonians in the "parental" role. Though conscious of his authority and responsibility as apostle and founder of the church, Paul's understanding of church leadership is mutuality rather than hierarchy.

2:8 Share with you not only the gospel . . . but also our own selves: Ministry is not merely the delivery of a commodity or providing a service. It is a giving of not only what one has but what one is. Sharing one's own self pictures Paul as the nursing mother.

2:12 God, who calls you: The call is effective. Paul refers to an accomplished fact—they are in the church, and they are there because God has called them. **Into his own kingdom and glory:** On "kingdom of God," see at Luke 4:43–44. Paul uses the phrase occasionally to refer to the present reality of Christian existence (as Rom. 14:17; 1 Cor. 4:20), but more often of the future coming of God's kingdom (1 Cor. 6:9–10; Gal. 5:21). Here he seems to combine the meanings.

2:13 The word of God that you heard from us: Paul and the other missionaries preached in human language, using human words and concepts, just as the Thessalonian Christians them-

selves did (1:7–8). Yet Paul is grateful to God that in and through his preaching the divine word was spoken, that they had **accepted it not as a human word but as what it really is, God's word.** This does not mean that every word Paul spoke was directly given by God, but that God spoke in the truly human word of preaching. It is this word that calls the church into being and sustains it, for it continues **at work in you believers.** The key term here is "believers." It is only to eyes of faith that God can be seen in the ministry of Paul, who to all outward appearances was a renegade Jew in trouble with his own synagogue, a traveling tentmaker preacher who was not very impressive as a speaker, one who embodied the "foolishness" of declaring that the crucified carpenter is really the power and wisdom of God (see 1 Cor. 1:18–25; 2 Cor. 10:10).

2:14–16 You . . . became imitators of the churches of God in Christ Jesus that are in Judea: Paul's main point is clear: the sufferings endured by the new Christians in Thessalonica are part and parcel of the sufferings that Christians in other parts of the world suffer. When they joined the church, God added them to the one worldwide church, which has a common mission and destiny (see 1 Pet. 5:9). To confess faith in Christ is to find oneself at odds with mainstream human culture. Their sufferings are not unique or exceptional, but inherent in the Christian life.

While Paul's point is clear, his illustration is so problematical that some scholars have considered all or parts of vv. 14–16 to be a post-Pauline addition to the text. These words do seem in fact to be an interruption of the context; the connection between v. 13 and v. 17 seems to be improved by omitting them. Some have seen 2:16b, **God's wrath has overtaken them at the last,** as the comment of a later scribe looking back on the destruction of Jerusalem (70 CE), understood as punishment of Jewish sins. Further, Paul nowhere else charges "the Jews" with "killing the Lord Jesus," and elsewhere Paul, who is himself a Jew, declares his love for the Jewish people and his confident hope for their final salvation (Rom. 9:1–5; 11:25–36). It is indeed *possible* that these verses are a later addition made when the Pauline letters were edited into one corpus, various letters were combined (see "Introduction: The New Testament as the Church's Book," 4.b.c.d; and the introduction to 2 Corinthians), and some passages, such as 1 Cor. 14:34–35, were added (see there).

In this case, however, it seems Paul actually wrote the passage. There is no manuscript evidence for an interpolation, and closer study reveals it is more integrally related to its context than first appears. The question is therefore how to understand it. Since 1 Thessalonians is Paul's first extant letter and Romans is probably his last, it could be that Paul's earlier "anti-Judaism" later moderated. Yet Paul had been a Christian missionary for seventeen years when he wrote 1 Thessalonians, and Romans is only five or six years later. While no completely satisfactory solution is available—this is the nature of ancient letters in which the meaning was clear to the ancient writer and readers but obscured by time—the most adequate interpretation regards the passage as a piece of early Christian tradition adapted by Paul to the present context. Since Jews did not participate in pagan society, they were often called "haters of humanity" and the like. This Gentile charge against Jews has been taken up by this tradition. While it was actually the Romans who "killed the Lord Jesus," there was some sort of Jewish complicity, and early Christian tradition tended to make the Jews more and more responsible (see, e.g., Acts 2:23; 3:14–15; 13:27–28; Matt. 27:25). There was in fact Jewish hostility against the early Christian community resulting in persecution and even death (see, e.g., 2 Cor. 11:24–26; Matt. 23:29–36; John 16:1–2; Acts 7:54–8:1; 9:29; 12:1–3; 14:19–20; 21:27–32 23:12). All of this cannot be Christian propaganda; some of it represents the historical reality. The final phrase, translated "God's wrath has overtaken them at last," is ambiguous Greek, and may mean "God's wrath [the final judgment, see above] is about to come upon them" or "God's wrath has come upon them until the end." The latter translation would mean that God's wrath already rests on disobedient Israel in the present, and will last until the final eschatological salvation, as elaborated in Rom. 11. The text as a whole, however, remains obscure.

Paul's illustration here is unfortunate. He himself later acknowledges having written things that he afterwards regretted (see 2 Cor. 7:8). What is clear is that it is a gross misunderstanding to read it in a racial, anti-Semitic sense, or even in a wholesale anti-Jewish sense. Paul himself is a Jew both ethnically and religiously and knows of many other Jewish Christians. (See further comments at John 8:44; Rev. 2:9.)

2:17–3:5
PAUL'S CONCERN FOR THE THESSALONIANS WHILE ABSENT

2:17 Orphans: See on 2:7 above.

2:18 Satan blocked our way: We have no information on the empirical causes that prevented Paul from returning to Thessalonica, but sometimes physical sickness interfered with and determined the course of Paul's missionary moves (see 2 Cor. 12:5–10; Gal. 4:12–14). Paul sees himself and his mission engaged in the final eschatological struggle, in which the power of Satan was very real. Every obstruction of his mission was seen in retrospect as the effort of Satan to hinder the Christian cause (see 2 Cor. 12:7); every departure from the faith was not mere human lack of interest, but succumbing to "the tempter" (3:5). Paul lives life with theological eyes of faith, not "commonsense" secular eyes. As it was God who spoke in authentic Christian preaching (2:13), so it is Satan who hinders the Christian message (see Mark 4:15).

2:19 Boasting: Paul sees "boasting" as utterly wrong if it is a matter of one's own status or achievement; he will "boast" only of his fellow Christians in the churches, which represented God's activity and faithfulness, not human achievement (Rom. 3:27; 4:2–3, 11; 5:2; 15:17; 1 Cor. 1:29–31; 15:31; 2 Cor. 1:12; 7:4; 8:24; 9:2; Phil. 3:3; Gal. 6:11). **Our . . . joy . . . before our Lord Jesus at his coming:** Paul looked forward to presenting his churches to the returning Lord Jesus in the near future. This would be the mark of his faithfulness as an apostle (see 2 Cor. 1:14). Thus Paul's concern for the church in Thessalonica was more than just hoping that things were going well in "their" church. He sees the Christian mission as the task of the one church in which he, the Thessalonian Christians, and all other churches are involved. Their lives are intricately woven together. What happens to them, that they continue to exist and thrive as a church, is extremely important to him in this sense—and difficult to understand for many modern readers who have substituted a later "service institution" model of the church for Paul's biblical model.

3:1 Left alone in Athens . . . sent Timothy: See the different chronology of Acts 17:14–15; 18:5, where Silas and Timothy remain in Beroea and Paul goes alone to Athens, then to Corinth, where he is joined by Silas and Timothy.

3:2 Sent: This implies some authority on Paul's part (contrast, e.g., 1 Cor. 16:12). Paul has a group of coworkers of which he is the director. His brotherly and collegial attitude does not exclude apostolic authority.

3:3–4 Destined . . . to suffer persecution: Paul sees the troubles he and his new converts are enduring (see 1:6; 2:14) as part of the intensified activity of Satan just before the end. This is the typical apocalyptic pattern, manifest not only in the Pauline tradition (see, e.g., 1 Cor. 7:25–31; 2 Thess. 1:4–5; 2:3–12) and Revelation (1:9; 2:10; 6:9–11; 12:7–17), but in Jesus and the Gospels (see Matt. 6:13; Mark 13:3–27). Paul sees the church as the eschatological community of faith chosen and gathered by God to be his witnesses in the (to him brief) time between Jesus' resurrection and his return in glory. This is a time of suffering and endurance for the church, and is thus its normal state.

3:6–13
TIMOTHY'S ENCOURAGING REPORT

3:6 Brought us the good news: This is a form of the same word used elsewhere for preaching the gospel of Christ. Here it concerns the state of the church and the relation of Christians to each other. Paul does not separate these. His response to the report of their continued endurance in the faith is exuberant joy.

3:7 Encouraged . . . through your faith: As in 1:7 the Thessalonians are an encouragement to all Christians in Macedonia, so here they are an encouragement to the missionaries. Here is another instance where it is clear that the dimensions of Christian faith are not only private and personal, are not even confined to the members of one's local congregation thought of as a "support group," but involve one in the wider circles of the Christian community in state, nation, and world.

3:10 Restore whatever is lacking in your faith: Paul wants to see them not only as a matter of personal relationships, but to instruct them on matters in which their faith is deficient. His close relation to them does not prohibit this frank statement (see his more diplomatic statement to a church he does not know personally, Rom. 1:11–12). While Paul does not insist on uniformity in how one understands and expresses the faith (see 1 Cor. 3:21b-23; 15:1–11, esp. v. 11), he also does not consider faith a matter of "one's own business," as if no Christian should attempt to nourish, inform, supplement, and correct the faith of another. This is at the furthest pole from the view that "no one has the right to tell another person what they should believe." Christians decide about the faith for themselves, but not by themselves.

3:12 Abound in love for one another and for all: Christian love as the summary of the Christian life (see Matt. 22:34–40; 1 Cor. 13) is not only for those in one's own congregation but for "all." God has added each Christian to the whole church; each Christian loves and is loved by the whole community of faith, even those of other nations and cultures they have never seen. Here Paul is thinking of love within the whole community of faith, though "all" implicitly includes all God's creatures, as does God's own love (see 5:15).

3:13 Strengthen your hearts in holiness: See on 1 Pet. 1:15. As Paul makes the transition to the next section on the particularities of the Christian life, he summarizes it as love and holiness. These are not attitudes or particular virtues, but the summary description of the Christian life as a whole, the new life oriented to God's act in Christ.

The coming of our Lord Jesus with all his saints: Since "saints" is literally "holy ones," some interpreters have thought Paul is here referring to the angels that early Christian tradition sometimes pictured as accompanying Christ at his triumphal return (see, e.g., Matt. 25:31). In Zech. 14:5, which seems to be reflected here, the "holy ones" are angels, as also in Jude 14. A text Paul has adopted from earlier Christian tradition portrays the "archangel" as accompanying Jesus at the Parousia (see below on 4:16). However, elsewhere Paul always uses "holy ones" (= "saints") to mean Christians, members of the holy people of God (23x in the undisputed Pauline letters, e.g., Rom. 1:1; 8:27; 15:25; 16:2; 1 Cor. 1:2; 6:11; 16:11; Phil. 1:1; 4:22). It is also the case that Paul has a negative view of "angels" (Rom. 8:38; 2 Cor. 11:14; Gal. 1:8; 3:19; see on Luke 1:10–12). In 1 Cor. 6:2–3 "holy ones" (= "saints") are in contrast to "angels." In this text Paul thus portrays Christians who have died as presently "with Christ" (see Phil. 1:23). The Lord Jesus will bring them "with him" (4:14) at his return. Paul has more than one way of picturing the destiny of Christians after death (see on 4:13–18).

4:1–5:22
PART TWO—THE LIFE TO WHICH CHRISTIANS ARE CALLED

The preceding has been one long paean of praise and thanksgiving that rehearses the story of the church's founding and its present situation. In part two of the letter, Paul turns to specific instructions about the Christian life.

4:1–12
A Life Pleasing to God:
Practice Good Public Morality

4:1 How you ought to live and to please God: Biblical ethics are not a matter of what is "right" on its own merits or the application of principles and ideals judged (by whom?) to be inherently "right," but a matter of doing God's will. Biblical ethics are not self-fulfillment or conformity to community expectations, but depend on the faith that God is the Creator and human beings are not autonomous but are creatures of God. Thus Paul gives no motivation for ethics such as "going to heaven" or "health and prosperity." "Be good, for it pays off" is finally a form of selfishness. Paul's ethic is oriented to God.

4:2 Instructions we gave you: Paul's initial preaching not only proclaimed God's act in Christ (see on 1:9–10), but also included ethical directions on living the Christian life (see 1 Cor. 4:17). The first-century Hellenistic world had moral standards, some of them advocating high ethical norms, but they were mostly based on philosophical or humanitarian theories or community expectations and were unrelated to religious commitment. The Thessalonians, previously Gentile adherents of pagan religions (1:9), had been accustomed to thinking of religion as one thing and ethics as another, unrelated area of life. For Paul, profession of Christian faith included ethical commitment. He thus did not hesitate to give instructions on **how you ought to live** (see above on 3:10; 4:1). **Through the Lord Jesus:** This is related to "in the Lord Jesus" of v. 1. Paul's ethic was not a matter of rehearsing and applying the teachings of Jesus, which are reflected only minimally in Paul's letters. Nor should we picture Paul as drilling his new converts on the "sayings of Jesus" (see on 1 Cor. 7:10). Rather, for Paul Christian conduct is that which is oriented to the revelation of God's will in the Christ event as a whole. What this means in particular cases must often be determined in the situation by the guidance of the Holy Spirit within the context of the Christian community (see on Rom. 12:1–2). The community had its store of traditions from and about Jesus that served as guidelines, but not as laws, in making its ethical decisions. These would also include new insights, reve-

lations of the "word of the Lord" by Christian prophets that proclaimed the will of God for new situations (see 4:15 below; the introduction to Revelation; and Rev. 2:20; see Matt. 23:34; Luke 11:49; Acts 11:27; 13:1; 15:32; 1 Cor. 12:28–29; 13:1; 14:1–40).

4:3 Sanctification: The same as "holiness" of 4:7; see on 3:13 above. **Abstain from fornication:** The word is a general term for sexual immorality. In contrast to the typical understanding of the Hellenistic world, Paul follows the biblical and Jewish ethic that directly relates religious commitment and responsible sexual behavior. See on Rom. 1:26–27 and 1 Cor. 6:12–7:40 for Paul's more detailed response to particular issues.

4:4 Control your own body: The Greek word for "control" can also be translated "acquire or possess"; the Greek word for body is literally "vessel." Thus the KJV translates literally, "That every one of you should know how to possess his vessel in sanctification and honor." The second word can also be used metaphorically either for one's own body or self (as in 2 Cor. 4:7) or for one's spouse (as in 1 Pet. 3:7). Thus the RSV translated "that each one of you know how to take a wife for himself in holiness and honor." All translations make it clear that Christian faith is incompatible with adultery and sexual promiscuity.

4:5 Like the Gentiles who do not know God: The readers were Gentile Christians (1:9; see 1 Cor. 6:9–11). Paul here follows the stereotypical image Jews tended to have of Gentiles, regarding them as dominated by lust and sexual immorality and perversions. There were of course immoral Gentiles, just as there were immoral Jews, but there were also many Gentiles who had a high standard of sexual morality. The distinctive element in Paul's Christian ethic is not so much its content as its orientation. For Paul as for Jesus, ethical behavior is not a matter of personal fulfillment and autonomy, but of pleasing God and respecting the neighbor; it is oriented not to self but to God and to others. This, and not its particular requirements, is what contrasts biblical ethics with the modern American view of the autonomous individual or relative community standards as the final authority in such matters.

4:9 Love of the brothers and sisters: Prior to the New Testament, the Greek word *philadelphia* had been used almost exclusively for relations within the family. The early church regarded itself as truly a family (see above on 2:7). **Taught by God:** By the revelation of God in the Christ event; by the continuing presence of the Holy Spirit in the life of the church (4:8; 5:19–21; see John 6:45; 1 John 2:27); and by the word of God that comes through human teachers (2:12–13; 4:1–2).

4:10 Indeed you do love all the brothers and sisters throughout Macedonia: Love here is not a nice feeling of sentimental attraction or personal affection for people they have never seen, but a matter of concrete Christian acts: prayer and financial support of the wider church to which they belong, hospitality and support for visiting missionaries and traveling Christians.

4:11 Live quietly . . . mind your own affairs . . . work with your own hands: This is not merely a rehearsal of conventional middle-class individualism. Such a stance is excluded by the letter as a whole, which calls for involvement in the Christian community and its world mission. It appears that the eschatological expectation of the soon coming of the Lord had been understood by some to mean that they could abandon their everyday occupations and become irresponsible busybodies preoccupied with religion. Paul's understanding of the Christian hope includes both fervent expectation and continuing responsibility for one's daily duties. One is reminded of Martin Luther's dictum in the same spirit: "If I knew that the world would end tomorrow, I would still plant an apple tree today." Many in the ancient world disdained manual labor as the work of slaves and the ignorant, but Paul stands in the Jewish tradition that affirmed the dignity of working with one's own hands, expressed in the lives of Jesus the carpenter and Paul the tentmaker.

4:13–5:11
THE COMING OF THE LORD

The chapter division at 5:1 is unfortunate, for the section 4:13–5:4 has a unified topic. The discussion of the Parousia is in the "practical" Part Two of the letter (see Outline in the introduction to 1 Thessalonians, and contrast the setting of 2 Thess. 2:1–12). They are not doctrinal speculations or instructions about "what happens when we die," but pastoral care for a grieving community.

4:13 Have died (NRSV)/**Fall asleep** (NIV): The NIV translates the Greek more literally; the NRSV gives the plain meaning. The New Testament does not avoid calling death by its real name (see John 11:11–14). The phrase was common among both Jews and Gentiles of Paul's world, without any connotation of what lies beyond death.

Some members of the new congregation in Thessalonica had died. The church had apparently understood that Jesus would return while all believers were still alive. Paul expected to be alive at the Parousia (4:15; 1 Cor. 15:51–52), and his new converts were shocked that some of their members had died before the return of Jesus. Did this mean they were not true believers, or that they would miss out on the salvation bestowed by Christ's triumphal return? The problem was not isolated in early Christianity (see Mark 9:1; John 21:22–23).

You may not grieve as others do: Of course they grieved, and Paul does not offer the false "comfort" of lecturing them that death is "natural" (see on 1 Cor. 15:26) or "inevitable" or that their loved ones "no longer suffer." They grieve, as Paul grieves (and see Jesus, John 11:35), but in a way different from others **who have no hope**. This phrase is not an objective statement about the eternal prospects of the "others" (as though it meant "there is no hope for them"), but is a statement about how people grieve. Members of the Christian community grieve as those who share the Christian hope; others grieve without this hope. There were in fact many in Paul's day who believed in a life after death as the immortality of the soul, but the Christian hope is in God who raises the dead (see on Luke 20:27; 24:1–12).

4:14 Jesus died and rose again: This is the basis of the Christian hope—not a theory of life after death but God's act in Christ. For Paul and earliest Christianity, Jesus' resurrection was not an isolated act that concerned Jesus alone, but the beginning of the final triumph of God (see 1 Cor. 15:20–23). These words are from an early Christian creed adopted by Paul, whose own language is to speak of God as raising Jesus, not of Jesus rising. **Bring with him:** See on 3:13 (see also Phil. 2:23; 2 Cor. 5:1–9).

4:15–16 By the word of the Lord: No such saying is found in the Gospel tradition, though it could be a saying of Jesus that was not recorded in the Gospels (like Acts 20:35). Much more likely, it is a saying of the risen Jesus from a Christian prophet, probably preserved by Paul from his Antioch period that immediately preceded the mission to Thessalonica (see Outline of the Life of Paul in "Introduction to the Pauline Letters"). On Christian prophets, see the introduction to Revelation. The Antioch church had such prophets in its leadership, to which both Silas and Paul had once belonged (Acts 11:27–29; 13:1–3).

Will by no means precede: This, and not apocalyptic information, is Paul's point in quoting the "word of the Lord." Those Christians in Thessalonica who have died will not be left out or disadvantaged when Christ returns. **The dead in Christ will rise first:** It is not selected individuals, but the church, the community of faith, that will meet Christ at the Parousia. Here the church is pictured as being reassembled: dead Christians will be raised first and be reunited with the believers still alive at the Parousia, and they will meet Christ together as his church. This is a different picture from 3:13 and 4:14, which picture the dead as already "with" Christ. Paul's intention is not to give *information* on "where are the dead," but to give *assurance* that the Christian dead are included in God's final triumph. This assurance can be pictured in more than one way. Like the pictures of the end in Revelation, such differing portrayals should not be "harmonized" into "how it really is" (see on Rev. 3:12; 6:9–11; 7:16; 19:11–16; 20:12).

4:17 We who are alive: Paul expected the return of Christ to occur during his own lifetime. On interpreting the "near end" in early Christianity, see the excursus at Rev. 1:3. **Caught up in the clouds:** Taken into God's presence. The clouds were originally related to the storm god, imagery adopted by Israel from the nature religion of Canaan to speak of the presence and power of God (e.g., Exod. 19:16–25; Pss. 29; 97:2) and then applied to the return of Jesus as the Son of Man (Mark 13:26; Matt. 26:64). Theology, not meteorology, is the content (as though Paul thought Jesus would not return on a clear day). **To meet the Lord in the air:** So also "the air" is not the atmosphere, but as in Eph. 2:2 the realm between the heavenly world of God and the earthly human world, the dwelling place of supernatural powers that separate this world and the transcendent world. Like the word "parousia," **to meet the Lord** is part of the semitechnical language used for the arrival of a monarch. A delegation of his or her subjects went out to meet the king or queen and ushered them back into the city. The picture is thus not of a "rapture" in the sense of modern dispensational interpretation, in which believers meet Jesus in the sky and are then taken to heaven. Rather, Jesus is pictured as returning to earth as its rightful sovereign, and Christian believers—those already dead and those still alive—going together to lead him in a triumphal parade back to earth. These words and pictures utilize common apocalyptic imagery (see the introduction to Revelation) that seems strange to modern eyes and ears—as they did to most of the Thessalonians, who had no previous exposure to such Jewish ways of thinking. Modern readers need not take them literally, but must take them seriously.

We will be with the Lord forever: Salvation is finally not a matter of a place, but of a relationship (on the language of salvation, see on Acts 16:31). Being with the Lord is the final fulfillment of the relationship to God already begun in this life.

4:18 Encourage one another: Pastoral encouragement, not theological speculation, was the purpose of **these words.** Engagement with such words and communicating their encouragement to others was the responsibility of not only "religious experts" such as pastors and teachers; the community of faith studies them together as a matter of mutual encouragement.

5:1–3 Concerning the times and the seasons: In view of the unexpected death of some of their members, the Thessalonians wondered whether they had misunderstood Paul's preaching about the nearness of the Parousia. He reassures them that the Lord will certainly come, but the time cannot be calculated, for it will be **like a thief in the night,** an expression that became proverbial in early Christianity (Matt. 24:43; 2 Pet. 3:10; Rev. 3:3). Although other texts point to observable signs signaling that the end is near (Mark 13:5–8, 14–23; 2 Thess. 2:3–12), Paul here pictures the end as coming unexpectedly, when the world is conducting business as usual in **peace and security** (as in Luke 17:20–37; see there).

5:4–6 You . . . are not in darkness: The final day of God's triumph was called in the Old Testament the Day of the Lord (Isa. 13:6, 9; Jer. 46:10; Ezek. 13:5; 30:3; Joel 1:15; 2:1, 11, 31; Amos 5:18, 20; Zeph. 1:7, 14; Mal. 4:5). Early Christians understood this in terms of the Lord Jesus, and referred to the return of Christ as the Day of the Lord or simply the Day (1 Cor. 1:8; 3:13; 5:5; 2 Cor. 1:14; Phil. 1:6, 10; 2:16; 2 Thess. 2:2; 2 Pet. 3:10). This imagery then leads to thinking of the present as the darkness before the dawn (as in Rom. 13:12–13; see Eph. 6:12).

5:8 We belong to the day: Although the final Day had not yet come, Christians have already oriented their lives to the fulfillment of God's kingdom at the end of history. The time in which Christians live is pictured as analogous to the time between the election of a new administration and its inauguration. During

645

this in-between time, one can orient one's life to the "lame duck" administration still in power, or to the new administration to which the future belongs. Christians do not belong to the present darkness but already to the coming Day. **Faith . . . love . . . hope:** See on 1:3. Paul concludes the letter with the same formula with which he began. The image of the "Christian's armor" was originally "God's armor" (see Isa. 59:17; elaborated in Eph. 6:14–17). The imperative of the NRSV ("put on") and the participle of NIV ("putting on") are poor translations of the Greek, which does not give the believers something else to do, but declares they are in fact already clothed with God's own armor of faith, love, and the confident hope of salvation (see on Gal. 3:27–28).

5:9 Wrath: See on 1:9. **Destined:** See on Rom. 8:28–30.

5:10 Who died for us: See on Rom. 3:25–26; 5:6–11; 1 Cor. 15:3. This is finally the motivation for Paul's Christian ethic. He never makes the soon coming of Christ the basis of Christian conduct in the sense that "you wouldn't want to get caught doing something wrong when Jesus comes back." It is not fear that motivates the Christian life, but gratitude for what God has done for us through Christ.

5:12–22
LIFE IN CHRISTIAN COMMUNITY

5:12 Respect those who have charge of you: The church of Paul's day does not yet have a firm structure and knows no distinction between clergy and laity (for later developments, see on Acts 14:23 and 1 Tim. 3:1–13). Yet there are already acknowledged leaders in the congregations (see on Phil. 1:1). The mission of the church requires some form of leadership, and that this role be acknowledged and respected. The word translated "have charge of" also means "be a leader, have authority over, manage; care for, give help; engage in, practice."

5:14 Admonish the idlers: See on 4:11. "Idlers" can also be translated "disorderly" or "disruptive." The church has a mission to carry out, which requires some structure and order. Those on the margin of the congregation's life (the "idlers," the **weak**, the **faint-hearted**) are not to be written off, but admonished, encouraged, and helped. Paul lays the responsibility for such pastoral care on the congregation as a whole. **To one another and to all:** See on 3:12.

5:16–22 Rejoice always: The catalogue of instructions that begins in v. 16 is not a random list but a roster of staccato commands with (in the

Greek text) rhyme and rhythm. **Always . . . without ceasing . . . in all circumstances:** Christian faith embraces the whole of life and is not a matter of moods or "giving God his part." Even in the harassed situation of the new congregation at Thessalonica (see 1:6; 2:14), all of life can be a joyous celebration of the presence of God and salvation. This is a matter not of how one feels but of what God has done.

5:19 Do not quench the Spirit . . . test everything: The church lives not by its own determination, but by the life-giving presence of the Holy Spirit in its midst, the energy that sometimes erupts in speaking in tongues, miracles, and prophecies (see on 1 Cor. 12–14). This sometimes leads to excesses and cultivation of the more spectacular phenomena, which then causes an overreaction by some against all manifestations of the Spirit. As in 1 Cor. 12–14, Paul steers a middle course: neither extinguish the flame of the Spirit, nor accept everything uncritically. The congregation as a whole is the bearer of the Spirit, not merely gifted individuals, so spiritual claims are to be evaluated by the whole congregation. On testing the utterances of Christian prophets, see the excursus at Rev. 2:20.

5:23–28
GREETINGS AND BENEDICTION

The letter concludes with what was to become the typical pattern in Paul's letters: a concluding prayer for the church, a request that they pray for him, greetings to members of the congregation, instruction to share the holy kiss, and the benediction of grace and peace.

5:23 Spirit and soul and body: Not an analysis of the "parts" of the human being, but a way of saying "your whole self" (see Mark 12:30; Matt. 22:37).

5:24 He will do this: It is God who called them (1:4; 2:12; 4:7), and it is God who will bring his work to completion in them. Paul does not eliminate human responsibility, but reminds them that the initiative throughout is with God, who will complete the work he has begun (Phil. 2:12–13).

5:25 Pray for us: Not an empty formality. The apostle recognizes that he is not adequate in himself, but that his work is part of the church's mission, and that he is dependent on their prayers (see Rom. 15:30–31; Col. 4:3; Eph. 6:18–20).

5:26 Holy kiss: Kissing was a conventional greeting in biblical tradition and in Paul's world (see, e.g., Exod. 18:7; Ruth 1:14; 1 Sam. 10:1; 20:41; 2 Sam. 19:39; 20:9; Matt. 26:48; Luke 7:38, 45; Acts 20:37). In the Pauline churches it became a standard part of the liturgy (1 Cor. 16:20; 2 Cor. 13:12; Rom. 16:16; 1 Pet. 5:14). Though the liturgical kiss was not erotic, "holy" does not mean "chaste, nonsexual," but "signifying belonging to the holy community, the people of God" (see on 3:13; 1 Pet. 1:15).

5:27 This letter be read: The letter is a personal communication to friends, but it is more than that: an apostolic letter to be read aloud as part of worship. The church obeyed this command, repeatedly read and preserved this letter, not only for itself but for the church at large. This command at the close of the earliest Christian document already initiates the way that led to the later collection, selection, preservation, and editing of other letters and Gospels that formed the New Testament canon.

The Second Letter of Paul to the Thessalonians

INTRODUCTION

If 2 Thessalonians was written by Paul, it was written as a response to recent developments at Thessalonica, a few weeks or months after 1 Thessalonians, and reflects the same general situation (see the introduction to 1 Thessalonians). An increasing number of scholars, however, have become convinced that 2 Thessalonians was written by an associate or disciple of Paul after Paul's death to represent Paul's message in a later situation. A sample of the evidence:

1. The structure is modeled precisely on that of 1 Thessalonians, which differs from all the other Pauline letters. This includes such incidental features as the second thanksgiving of 2 Thess. 2:13 (= 1 Thess. 2:13), difficult to explain except on the basis that the author of 2 Thessalonians had 1 Thessalonians before him. Only 1:5–10 and 2:1–12 are new elements; otherwise, 2 Thessalonians rehearses the same topics as 1 Thessalonians, and in the same order.

2. Many details and verbatim agreements, such as the following:

1 Thess. 1:1 2 Thess. 1:1–2
  greetings almost verbatim identical
1 Thess. 1:3 2 Thess. 1:11
  work of faith
1 Thess. 1:3 2 Thess. 1:3–4
  combination of **faith, love,** and **steadfastness**
1 Thess. 1:4 2 Thess. 2:13
  brothers and sisters beloved by God/the Lord
1 Thess. 2:9 2 Thess. 3:8
  labor and toil, . . . we worked night and day, so that we might not burden any of you.
1 Thess. 4:1 2 Thess. 3:1
  Finally at the same structural point, considerably before the end.

There are a large number of such instances. These can best be seen by making a careful comparison oneself, underlining common words and phrases. This phenomenon is difficult to explain on the basis of Paul's remembering and recycling his earlier letter. Romans was written shortly after 2 Corinthians, for instance, but does not manifest this phenomenon. Second Thessalonians appears to represent literary dependence on 1 Thessalonians.

3. Second Thessalonians also has several differences from 1 Thessalonians that are difficult to explain if written by the same author separated by only a brief interval. The most obvious is the view of the nearness of the return of Christ. First Thessalonians represents the Parousia as near and to occur without signs (e.g., 1 Thess. 4:15; 5:2–3, 10) while 2 Thessalonians warns against those who teach that the day of the Lord has already come or is near (see on 2:2), for there must be a delay and obvious signs will announce its coming (see on 2:1–12). Further, 2 Thessalonians lacks the warm personal tone of 1 Thessalonians, lacks its concern for ethics (which it reduces to the one item of the "idlers" [2 Thess. 3:6–13]), seems already to be aware of a collection of Paul's letters and that people are writing letters in Paul's name (2:2, 15; 3:17), and reflects a time of more severe persecution in which the persecutors are more harshly condemned (2 Thess. 1:4, 6; 3:2–3 vs. 1 Thess. 1:6, 2:14; 3:3).

Such evidence, only a sample of which is given here, has convinced many scholars that 2 Thessalonians was written by a member of the Pauline school to interpret his message in a later situation. It is not written to a particular congregation, but is written to the church at large in the form of a letter of Paul to Thessalonica. The questions of authorship and date make a difference for understanding the theology of Paul himself and for interpreting 2 Thessalonians, but do not diminish the authority and significance of the letter as sacred Scripture, for the church heard in it an authentic witness to the meaning of the Christian faith and included it in the New Testament canon. (See "The Death of Paul and the Continuation of the Pauline Tradition," in the introduction to 1 Timothy, and "Pseudonymous Letters in Early Christianity" in the introduction to Ephesians.)

Outline

1:1–2 Salutation
1:3–4 Thanksgiving
  (1:5–10 First Insertion: The Judgment at Christ's Coming)

1:11–12 Thanksgiving Continued
  (2:1–12 Second Insertion: The Day of the
    Lord)
2:13–17 Thanksgiving Concluded
3:1–15 The Life to Which Christians Are Called
  3:1–5 Prayer for the Missionaries
  3:6–13 Warning the "Idle"
  3:14–15 Warning the Disobedient
3:16–18 Greetings and Benediction

For Further Reading

Gaventa, Beverly Roberts. *First and Second Thessalonians*. Interpretation: A Bible Commentary for Teaching and Preaching. Louisville, KY: Westminster John Knox, 1998.

COMMENTARY

1:1–2
SALUTATION

Almost verbatim copy of 1 Thess. 1:1; see there. The greeting of "grace and peace" is no mere formality but recurs in the conclusion (3:16, 18), including the letter's threats of judgment and damnation within the framework of the peace of God.

1:3–4
THANKSGIVING

On the "thanksgiving" section of a Pauline letter, see 1 Thess. 1:2. The unusually long thanksgiving of 1 Thessalonians is here adopted, extending through 2:17 with two insertions (see Outline). **Faith . . . love . . . steadfastness** is retained from 1 Thessalonians, but "hope" is missing (4x in 1 Thessalonians, but in 2 Thessalonians only in 2:16, where it does not refer to the Parousia).
1:4 We . . . boast of you: Reflecting 1 Thess. 1:7–9; 2:19. If 2 Thessalonians is not by Paul, this no longer reflects a concrete situation, but reminds the readers of a later time that their faith is celebrated by their fellow believers throughout the whole church—and thus more readily includes the modern reader.

(1:5–10
FIRST INSERTION: THE JUDGMENT AT CHRIST'S COMING)

The joyful note of 1 Thessalonians is replaced by the somber announcement of judgment.
1:5 The kingdom of God: See on Luke 4:43–44.

1:7 His mighty angels: In contrast to Paul, the author pictures the returning Lord in the traditional apocalyptic scenario as accompanied by angels (see 1 Thess. 3:13; on Paul's view of angels, see on Rom. 8:38).
1:8 Vengeance: This note, which resounds through this passage, is rightly troublesome to modern readers. Like Revelation, 2 Thessalonians reflects the intensified situation of persecution near the end of the century. Vengeance is not vindictiveness, but justice, **the righteous judgment of God** (v. 5; see on Rev. 6:9–11; 16:1–21). Such statements are not to be harmonized with Jesus' teaching about love for one's enemies and prayer for one's persecutors (Matt. 5:43–48). The description is not objectifying language about what God will do to unbelieving persecutors, but functions as encouragement and warning to the believers addressed by the letter: vengeance is a matter for God in the age to come, not something we may take into our own hands now (see Rom. 12:17–18). **Flaming fire:** The presence of God is accompanied by fire, as at the burning bush (Exod. 3:1–5) and the giving of the Law on Sinai (Exod. 19:16–19). The image portrays the return of Christ as Sinai-like, not hell-like. **Those who do not know God:** Not mere conceptual knowledge, but personal relationship involving faith and turning toward God (as Prov. 2:5; Hos. 4:1; 6:6; Mark 14:71; 1 Cor. 15:34; 2 Cor. 5:17; 10:5; Col. 1:10; 2 Pet. 1:2); here applied to the persecutors, not non-Christians in general.
1:9 Eternal destruction: The Paul of the undisputed letters does not dwell on the fate of unbelievers. Second Thessalonians is more explicit about the future judgment of persecutors than the future reward of believers. There is no speculation here on either "eternal" (whether it means "forever" or "belonging to the future age") or "destruction" (whether it means annihilation or torment). The point is that the punishment of persecutors is God's business in the age to come, not the Christian's business in the present age. **From the presence of the Lord:** As salvation is being "with Christ" (1 Thess. 4:17), so damnation is to be separated from God.

1:11–12
THANKSGIVING CONTINUED

Here 2 Thessalonians resumes the pattern of 1 Thessalonians.
1:11 Our God will make you worthy of his call: On Christians as called, see 1 Thess. 1:2, 5; 2:12; 2 Thess. 2:13–14. Christians are not worthy in

and of themselves; God confers worthiness on them. **His power . . . (our) good resolve and work of faith:** Second Thessalonians preserves the Pauline paradox that God is sovereign and Christians are responsible (as, e.g., Phil. 2:12–13), without making salvation into a "cooperation" between human beings and God.

1:12 Our God and (the) **Lord:** There is no second article in the Greek text, which might better be translated "Our God and Lord Jesus Christ" (see NIV note). Paul was careful to distinguish "God" and "Christ," but in the later first century God-language was applied to Christ (e.g., John 1:1; 20:28). Even later, the classical creeds of Nicaea and Chalcedon struggled to express in philosophical terminology the Christian conviction that it is not some lesser being, but the one true God, who is definitively made known in Jesus. The occasional use of God-language for Christ in the New Testament is already moving in this direction. Here the author speaks of Christ as the true manifestation of God in contrast to the "lawless one" to come, who will use God-language of himself (2:3–4).

(2:1–12
SECOND INSERTION: THE DAY
OF THE LORD)

2:1 The coming of our Lord Jesus Christ and our being gathered together to him: See 1 Thess. 4:13–18. This is the most important section of 2 Thessalonians and the primary reason it was written—to correct mistaken eschatological views that had developed in the Pauline churches. The instruction on the "day of the Lord" is here part of the doctrinal section, in contrast to its location and function in 1 Thessalonians.

2:2–3 By spirit (NRSV)/**By some prophecy** (NIV): The writer is concerned that the readers are upset and confused by a mistaken view they may have received by purported revelations of Christian prophets who (supposed that they) spoke in the power of the Spirit (see 1 Thess. 5:19–21). **By word:** By rational deduction or by an insight supposed to be inspired by the Spirit (see 1 Cor. 12:8, where "utterance" [NRSV] or "message" [NIV] is the same term here translated "word"). **By letter as through us:** In the generation after Paul, his followers struggled to interpret his teaching in a new situation and presented their interpretations as letters written in Paul's name. Second Thessalonians itself is probably such a letter (see the introduction to 2 Thessalonians). Here the author warns against other Paulinists who advocate a different understanding of eschatology.

To the effect that the day of the Lord is already here: On "day of the Lord," see on 1 Thess. 5:4–6. The misunderstanding that the day is already here may mean that in the events presently experienced (e.g., persecution) the final day of the Lord has already begun, so that Christ must certainly return immediately. More likely, the false understanding interpreted the "day of the Lord" as the present experience of believers in such a way that no future Parousia is to be expected. Paul, like the first generation of Christians in general, had expected Christ to return in their own time. When this did not happen, believers could either abandon the faith as mistaken or reinterpret its meaning in the light of the delay of the Parousia. For the spectrum of responses, see excursus on "Interpreting the 'Near End,'" at Rev. 1:3.

Here the author of 2 Thessalonians reinterprets the first generation's expectation of "soon" in terms of an apocalyptic pattern supposed to have four acts: (1) the present distress, i.e., the persecution of Christians near the end of the first century (1:4–5); (2) the apostasy (translated "rebellion" in NRSV and NIV), a rejection of God and intensification of evil as a prelude to the last days of history; (3) the appearance of God's final adversary, here called "the lawless one, the one destined for destruction"; (4) the return of Christ on the "day of the Lord," who will defeat the final adversary, judge sinners, and establish God's final kingdom in which believers will rejoice. Such imagery seems bizarre to many modern readers; for suggestions on understanding it, see the introduction to Revelation. The author is not interested in speculative information about the future, but interpreting the meaning of his readers' present—more specifically, in warding off the deceptive false interpretation advocated by some in their church. His point is that the end has neither already come in some "spiritual" way, nor is it about to come any minute, for the reader's present distress is not the "day of the Lord." The readers' present is neither the time of the final fulfillment nor the time just before the end, but the time of the church's mission in spreading the word of God (3:1), the time of the church's service that still looks forward to the triumph of God at the end of history, whenever it may come.

The rebellion comes first: The readers cannot be living in the time of fulfillment or the last days, since in God's plan there are events that must happen before the end, and these have not even begun to occur (see Mark 13:5–8, responding to an analogous situation, and also insisting that before the end the gospel must be preached to all nations, and that there is time for that to happen). **The lawless one . . . destined for destruction:** The author's term for the anti-God figure to appear at the end of history, summing up its evil and making one last gasp to overthrow the sovereignty of God. In Christian history this figure has often been called the anti-Christ, though the word itself occurs in the Bible only in 1 John 2:18, 22; 4:3; 2 John 7, applied to the false teachers of the author's own day.

2:4 Takes his seat in the temple of God, declaring himself to be God: As throughout this section, the author draws upon traditional apocalyptic imagery. There was an extensive tradition that the final opponent of God would claim divine honors and enter and profane God's temple. This imagery had already been applied to the king of Tyre (Ezek. 28:2) and the Babylonian king (Isa. 14:13); to Antiochus Epiphanes, the Greek Syrian king who entered and profaned the Jerusalem temple at the time of the Maccabees (1 Macc. 1:29–40; Dan. 11:36); to the Roman general Pompey, who in 63 BCE entered the temple and was surprised to find no idol in the Holy of Holies; to the Roman emperor Caligula, who in 41 CE attempted to install a statue of himself in the Jerusalem temple. The author thus finds the image in his Bible and his tradition; the temple is a firm part of this tradition, so it is irrelevant that the Jerusalem temple (which he never mentions) had probably already been destroyed when he writes.

2:5 I told you these things: By portraying his present instruction as only a reminder of what Paul had taught when he was among them, the author insists that his teaching is not an innovation, but is in continuity with Paul's teaching in the first generation (in contrast to the errors he warns against), and is thus the authentic understanding of Paul's message for the present.

2:6 You know what is now restraining him: If the original readers were familiar with apocalyptic ideas, perhaps they knew what (or who—both neuter and masculine forms are used) is restraining the appearance of the "lawless one." We no longer know. Interpreters have argued for the Roman Empire (the traditional interpretation already in the second century), for an angelic power (see Rev. 7:1–3), and for Paul himself as the restraining influence. Ultimately it is God himself who is in control of the way history comes to an end; who (through whatever agent[s]) extends history as the opportunity for repentance and mission (Mark 13:7–8; 10; 2 Pet. 3:8–9).

2:7 The mystery of lawlessness: The power of rebellion, evil, and lawlessness that will intensify climactically at the end of history is already present. Although the "day of the Lord" is not already present, the church constantly confronts the power of sin that is already present.

2:8 The Lord Jesus will destroy with the breath of his mouth: This reflects the promise of the messianic king of Isa. 11:1–9, who will redeem and transform the world into the reign of God's justice and will finally destroy evil without a struggle, by the word that comes from his mouth (Isa. 11:4). This is pictured in more vivid apocalyptic form in Rev. 19:11–21 (see there).

2:9 The coming of the lawless one: The final manifestation is a parody of the true God and his Christ (see on Rev. 13:2–3, 11; 17:8). "Coming" here is *parousia*, parallel to "the coming of our Lord Jesus Christ" (2:1). Both have a "revelation" (1:7/2:8); God-language is used of both (1:12/2:4). His agents do signs and miracles (2:9), as did the Christian missionaries.

2:10 To love the truth: In biblical understanding, truth is not abstract, but is a matter of action (John 3:21; 1 John 1:6); its opposite is not merely error, but unrighteousness (Rom. 1:18; 2:8; 1 Cor. 13:6), so that truth is not only a matter of how one thinks, but how one lives.

2:11 God sends them a powerful delusion: This should not be understood superficially as though God deceives people. It is a theological way of avoiding dualism and affirming that finally all things are in one hand. It does not diminish human responsibility. Pharaoh hardens his own heart (e.g., Exod. 8:15), but God hardens Pharaoh's heart (e.g., Exod. 4:21). People choose sin, and God responds by turning them over to the sin they have chosen (Rom. 1:24–25, 28). Throughout this section, the reality and depth of evil is emphasized. Evil is pictured not as mere ignorance that can be overcome with education, or personality defects that can be overcome by psychological means, but as rebellion of creatures against their Creator (Rom. 1:18–23). The church presently struggles against this power of evil already in the world and in the church itself, but does so in the confident hope that evil does not have the last word, that love also exists in the world, and that when evil is finally summed up, it will be destroyed "at the coming of our Lord Jesus Christ and our being gathered to him" (2:1).

2:13–17
THANKSGIVING CONCLUDED

The writer resumes his procedure of following the structure of 1 Thessalonians.

2:13 God chose you: See on 1 Thess. 1:4. Believers give thanks to God, for they have escaped the strong delusion (v. 11) not by their own efforts, but by God's grace. **Sanctification by the Spirit:** See on 1 Thess. 4:3.

2:15 Hold fast to the traditions: The tradition handed on by the community of faith is its guide in living an authentic Christian life (see 1 Cor. 11:2). At the end of the century, when the author is probably writing, this tradition is represented orally **by word of mouth** and **by our letter,** i.e., the letters of Paul and the Pauline school, including 2 Thessalonians (see the introduction to 1 Timothy). Here are the rudiments of what later became Scripture and tradition as the guidelines of the church's life.

3:1–15
THE LIFE TO WHICH CHRISTIANS ARE CALLED

3:1–5
PRAYER FOR THE MISSIONARIES

3:1 Pray for us: See on 1 Thess. 5:25. **That the word of the Lord may spread:** The Christian mission to the whole world (Matt. 28:18–20) is not thought of in terms of statistical "church growth," but as the spread of the Christian message identified as God's word (see 1 Thess. 1:8; 2:13; Acts 6:7; 12:24; 13:49; 19:20). The church is the work of God, who calls people into it through the gospel (2:14).

3:2 That we may be rescued: Nothing like this in 1 Thessalonians, but see Rom. 15:31. The author apparently looks back on this later plea of Paul. In his (and our) situation it becomes a plea for the church to pray for all its representatives in the worldwide mission.

3:3 He will guard you from the evil one: See Matt. 6:13.

3:6–13
WARNING THE "IDLE"

Here the author addresses a problem in his own time by extensively elaborating the passing remarks of Paul in 1 Thess. 4:11 and 5:14 (see there). This is the only part of Paul's instruction on ethics and Christian life in the church on which he elaborates.

The traditional explanation is that some church members had become so excited about the return of the Lord in the near future that they had quit their jobs and had become a nuisance and burden to the church that supported them. We have seen above, however, that the error the author opposes is probably not an overheated expectation of the immediate Parousia, but the view that the time of fulfilment is already present and there will be no future Parousia at all. Second Thessalonians does not relate the "idleness" to false eschatological expectations. "Disorderly" or "disruptive" is a better translation than "idle" or "loafer." It seems more likely that the problem was those traveling Christian missionaries of the late first century who went from church to church designating themselves as "apostles" (= missionaries) and "prophets" (= spokespersons for the risen Christ), teaching and preaching and expecting the churches to support them. The situation is portrayed in another document of the late first or early second century responding to this situation (*Did.* 11:3–12:5):

Concerning the apostles and prophets, conduct yourselves according to the ordinance of the Gospel. 4 Let every apostle who comes to you be received as the Lord; 5 but he shall not abide more than a single day, or if necessary, a second day; but if he stays three days, he is a false prophet. 6 And when he departs, he is to receive nothing except bread to supply him until his next station; but if he asks for money, he is a false prophet. 7 And do not make any judgments about any prophet speaking in the Spirit; for "every sin shall be forgiven, but this sin shall not be forgiven." 8 Yet not every one speaking in the Spirit is a prophet, but only if he manifests the "ways of the Lord." The false prophet can be distinguished from the true prophet on this basis. 9 No prophet ordering a table in the Spirit shall eat of it; otherwise he is a false prophet. 10 And every prophet teaching the truth, but not living according to his own teaching, is a false prophet. . . . **12** And do not listen to anyone who says in the Spirit, "Give me silver" (or anything else); but if he tells you to give on behalf of others that are in want, then he is not to be judged. . . . **12:2** If the new arrival is a traveling missionary, assist him, so far as you are able; but he shall not stay with you more than two or three days, and then only if it be necessary. **3** But if he has his own trade and wishes to settle with you, let him work for and eat his bread. **4** But if he has no craft, according to your wisdom provide how he shall live as a Christian among you, but not in idleness. **5** If he is not willing to do this, he is making Christ into a cheap way of making a living. Beware of such people. (Trans. MEB)

The two generations after Paul also saw the development of a resident "clergy," ordained bishops, elders, and deacons, some of whom were apparently salaried and devoted their full time to the work of the church. The Pastoral Letters (1 Timothy, 2 Timothy, Titus) represent this development within the Pauline school. Second Thessalonians opposes this later development of a separate "class" of ministers supported by the churches by appealing to the example of Paul himself. He considers such ministers as "disorderly" and "disruptive," though they probably thought of themselves as advocates of the new structures and orders of Christian ministry. The author represents the point of view that ministry in the church cannot be relegated to a particular group but is always "lay" ministry. Another member of the Pauline school presents a mediating view in which God gives specialized ministries to the church, but the special vocation of pastor-teacher is to equip the whole church for its mission in the world (Eph. 4:7–13). In 2 Thessalonians, the Pastorals, and Ephesians the modern reader can overhear a debate among the followers of Paul on the development of new forms of ministry.

3:6 Keep away from: See v. 15.

3:9 This was not because we do not have that right: Paul himself had had to contend with the objection that his refusal to take money for his services was an acknowledgment that he was not a "real" apostle (1 Cor. 9:1–23; 2 Cor. 11:7–11; 12:13–14). Here the author reasserts Paul's claim that apostolic authority is not related to being salaried by the church.

3:10 Anyone unwilling to work should not eat: A bit of proverbial wisdom (see, e.g., Prov. 6:6–11; 10:4), here applied to a specific situa-

tion within the church, not a general social or political principle that may be uncritically applied to later issues.

3:11 Mere busybodies not doing any work: In the perspective argued here, these are "full time ministers and missionaries" who do not do any (secular) work but are supported by the churches. What they saw as being free to devote their full time to the ministry of the word (see Acts 6:1–4), the author sees as simply idleness, living off the work of others, and meddling in the life of the church.

3:14–15
WARNING THE DISOBEDIENT

3:14 Those who do not obey: "Paul" expects to be obeyed. This is not the purported authoritarian personality of Paul himself, but the second-generation affirmation that to be a Christian is not merely an individual matter, but means belonging to the church ordered by apostolic authority. The issue continues to be not merely loafers who have become busybodies, but disruptive ministers who resist apostolic example and authority. **What we say in this letter:** The continuing authority of the apostle is mediated by the written text. Though the "official" canon of the New Testament was a later development, the consciousness that the church is guided by normative documents that bear witness to the authentic faith is already present here (see 1 Thess. 5:27).

3:15 Not . . . as enemies . . . but as believers (= brothers and sisters in the family of God; see NIV and NRSV note): Disruptive leaders and members deviating from the apostle's example should neither be ignored nor excommunicated, but they are to be warned and avoided (see v. 6; Matt. 18:15–18; 1 Cor. 5:3–5, 11; 2 Cor. 2:5–11). Modern readers may be shocked to find that the New Testament contains instructions to avoid, admonish, discipline, or even in some cases exclude members from the church. This shock is found wherever the church is thought of as a voluntaristic association for doing good or a support group for developing one's personal faith, whose existence depends on maintaining the goodwill of its customers or clients, who will go to another congregation or denomination if their own offends or upsets them. In the New Testament, the church is understood to be the people of God called into being by God's word and given a mission to witness to the world of God's gracious act in Christ, a community of faith in which discipline is necessary.

The New Testament shows only the beginnings of the variety of ways the church has attempted to exercise this discipline. Crucial for 2 Thessalonians is that deviant members and ministers are still regarded as insiders (Greek: "brothers" = "brothers and sisters"), still members of the family of God. Contrast 1 Cor. 5:9–13 and 2 John 7–11.

3:16–18
GREETINGS AND BENEDICTION
(See on 1 Thess. 5:23–28)

3:17 The mark in every letter of mine: See 1 Cor. 16:21; Gal. 6:11; Col. 4:18; Phlm. 19. Paul is pic-

tured as dictating his letters to a scribe (see Rom. 16:22), but taking the pen in hand himself for the final words. "Every letter of mine," taken literally, would disqualify 1 Thessalonians, which lacks this mark. The phrase is better understood as indicating a time when one or more collections of Paul's letters were circulating, a time when the church must critically distinguish between those that represent the apostolic faith and those that do not. The author here establishes the claim of 2 Thessalonians to represent the real teaching of the apostle (see 1 Tim. 1:1–2).

The First Letter of Paul to Timothy

INTRODUCTION TO THE PASTORAL LETTERS

The two letters to Timothy and the letter to Titus are similar in content and style, and will be treated together as the Pastoral Letters.

The Death of Paul and the Continuation of the Pauline Tradition

When Paul wrote Romans from Corinth about 56 CE, he was planning to come to Rome after he had delivered the collection from the Gentile churches to the mother church in Jerusalem. He then hoped to be sent by the Roman Christians on to Spain for further mission work (Rom. 15:22–32). This is the last clear picture we have of the life of Paul.

The traditional reconstruction of the latter period of Paul's life is that he went to Jerusalem, where he was taken into custody by the Roman authorities, and sent to Rome as a prisoner in the early 60s (Acts 20–28). From his Roman prison he wrote Philippians, Philemon, Colossians, and Ephesians. In this reconstruction, Paul was then released and continued his mission work, during which time he wrote 1 Timothy and Titus. He was then arrested again (the "second Roman imprisonment") and wrote 2 Timothy from prison shortly before he was condemned to death.

Although the New Testament itself nowhere provides this chronology, this traditional view is reconstructed from Acts 20–28, which is harmonized with data from the letters, some of which were probably not written by Paul or from Rome (see Pseudonymous Letters in Early Christianity, in the introduction to Ephesians). The more likely historical scenario is that Paul was taken as a prisoner from Jerusalem to Rome, where he was condemned and executed (see on Acts 28:31, "Why does Acts end as it does?").

The martyrdom of Paul about 64 CE meant that one of the most important leaders of early Christianity was gone, but the Pauline tradition was continued by his disciples and associates. According to Acts, Ephesus had been a center of Paul's missionary efforts, from which he and his coworkers established churches in the surrounding regions of Asia Minor. There is considerable evidence that after Paul's death a group of Christian leaders who looked back to Paul as the primary apostolic leader of the church continued to interpret and adapt his message to later contexts. Paul himself had been no individualist, but the principal leader of a missionary and theological group. He did not work alone, but had numerous coworkers (about forty can be listed). In his letters to churches, Paul characteristically joined his name with others, which was extremely unusual. The content of Paul's letters reflects the work of a school that developed and passed on traditions, including liturgical and hymnic pieces and interpretations of particular texts of Scripture. Thus something like a "Pauline school" already existed during his lifetime, as pictured in Acts 19:9–10. It was not Paul's death that first generated such a school; when Paul was killed, the group of which he had been leader continued his work, passing on the Pauline tradition and composing documents in his name (see Pseudonymous Letters in Early Christianity, in the introduction to Ephesians).

Author and Readers, Time and Place

On the traditional view, Paul wrote to his trusted coworkers Timothy and Titus, giving them instructions for the work of Christian ministry. Timothy is mentioned often in Acts from chap. 16 on and in Paul's letters; Titus plays a role in 2 Corinthians and Galatians, but is absent from Acts. The following lines of evidence have convinced most scholars that the letters were not written directly by Paul, but by later advocates of the Pauline tradition (see above):

1. They are clearly documented only in later sources. They are missing from $\mathfrak{P}^{46}$, the oldest papyrus MS of the Pauline letters, and from B, the fourth-century Vaticanus MS. The Muratorian Canon, a list of authoritative Christian books compiled perhaps as late as the fourth century, has the Pastorals listed separately from the other letters of Paul. Marcion, the mid-second-century heretical church leader, compiled an authoritative list of Paul's writings from which the Pastorals are missing, but it is not clear whether this is because he did not know them or simply that

he rejected them. In any case, the first certain reference to the Pastorals is found in the writings of Irenaeus, ca. 180 CE.

2. The vocabulary and style are very different from the undisputed letters of Paul, but resemble that of the church fathers from the second century. More than a third of the vocabulary is not found in the unquestioned Pauline letters. Several distinctive Pauline words and phrases are found not at all or only sparingly, such as language of justification by faith, the church as the body of Christ, the "in Christ" vocabulary, emphasis on the Holy Spirit, and "Son of God" as a title for Christ.

3. The church situation depicted seems to be later than that of Paul. Church organization has become more institutionalized, with bishops, elders, and deacons, ordination ceremonies, and lists of qualifications. The false teaching described fits the later author's time, but not that of Paul.

4. It is difficult to fit the events presupposed into the life of Paul as we otherwise know it; thus a hypothetical reconstruction of Paul's release from the "first" Roman imprisonment, a period of mission work otherwise unattested, and a "second" imprisonment must be made in order to fit the Pastorals into Paul's life.

5. It is difficult to understand the letters as appropriate communications from an actual Paul to a historical Timothy and Titus. They were seasoned missionaries (see on Phil. 2:19), but are addressed as young and inexperienced. It is also difficult to understand such elementary instruction given in letter form from a Paul who is only temporarily absent, but who had already spent an extensive amount of time with them. The letters assert Paul's authority in a way understandable in letters addressed to churches of a later time by one of his disciples, but not by Paul himself in a personal letter to close associates (e.g., 1 Tim. 2:7).

6. There are significant theological differences between the Pastorals and the unquestioned letters of Paul, e.g., the expectation of the near Parousia has waned, the gifts conferred by the Holy Spirit function only through ordination, and marriage and a conventional household are considered the standard Christian life.

7. The letters are rhetorical compositions that seem intended for public reading in the church, i.e., they are not personal letters, but are really addressed to the Christian congregations. The concluding greetings in each letter are *plural*.

As will be pointed out in the comments on particular texts below, all these difficulties are cleared up if the letters are seen as written in Paul's name for the instruction and edification of churches a generation or two after Paul's death.

Though various authors have been proposed (Luke, Polycarp), the real author—hereafter called the Pastor—remains unknown; he wants only the voice and message of Paul to be heard.

The letters were all probably composed at the same time and circulated together, corresponding to the corpus of Pauline letters that was already beginning to circulate by the end of the first century CE. There is no indication of a specific time and place in the letters themselves. If not by Paul, they could have been written any time from ca. 90 to ca. 150 CE. They probably derive from the Pauline tradition centered in Ephesus.

Outline

For Further Reading

Bassler, Jouette. *1 Timothy, 2 Timothy, Titus*. Nashville: Abingdon, 1996.

Collins, Raymond F. *I and II Timothy and Titus: A Commentary*. New Testament Library. Louisville, KY: Westminster John Knox, 2002.

COMMENTARY

1:1–2
SALUTATION

Paul had adapted the conventional Hellenistic letter form to express his own message (see on

1 Thess. 1:1). Here the Pastor adapts Paul's formula to represent the continuation of apostolic authority into his own time.

1:1 Paul: The author writes in Paul's name (see introduction), and Paul alone is represented as the sender (contrast 1 Cor. 1:1; 2 Cor. 1:1; Phil. 1:1; 1 Thess. 1:1; Phlm. 1). **An apostle:** See on Luke 6:12–16; 7:8–9; Acts 1:23; Rom. 1:1–7; 1 Cor. 1:1; Gal. 1:1–16. The Pastor is concerned that the church in the generations after Paul continue to be apostolic, i.e., that they represent legitimate interpretations of the meaning of the Christ event. Paul recognized that there were "false apostles" (2 Cor. 11:13), but did not consider himself the only apostle or believe that all other apostles had to agree with him on every issue (1 Cor. 3:21–23; 15:3–11). The Pastor represents Paul as the model of the apostolic office and mentions no other apostles. **God our savior:** The phrase reflects the Old Testament (e.g., Isa. 12:2; 43:3; Hos. 13:4) rather than Paul, who never uses it; the Pastor uses it 6x. Though here God as savior is distinguished from Christ, in 2 Tim. 2:10 Christ is called savior; God and Christ merge into one savior figure (see on Titus 2:13). **Christ Jesus our hope:** The Pastor focuses on hope as the key christological feature—an initial implicit response to the author's opponents, who minimized the future hope by reducing it to present Christian experience (see 2 Tim. 2:18).

1:2 Timothy, my loyal child (NRSV)/**true son** (NIV): The word translated "loyal" or "true" can also mean "legitimate." In the second and third generation of the Pauline tradition, the issue was who continued to be the legitimate heirs of Paul's teaching and authority. These words establish the claim that what follows in the Pastoral letters, rather than the message of the teachers the author opposes (see Titus 1:4), represents the true succession.

1:3–20
INTRODUCTION

In standard personal letter form, the salutation is followed by the thanksgiving (see on 1 Thess. 1:2). Here the author jumps directly into the subject matter of the letter (see Gal. 1:6). Though the form is abrupt for a personal letter, it is found in letters from officials to subordinates. This signals to the reader that we do not have a conventional letter from the historical Paul to the historical Timothy, but official instruction from the apostle presented to the churches in the form of an apostolic letter. This was the claim of the Pauline school (see introduction).

1:3–7
FALSE TEACHERS

1:3 Remain in Ephesus: There is no known situation in the career of Paul when he left Timothy in charge in Ephesus while he was in Macedonia. The scene corresponds to the time after Paul's death, when his followers, here represented by Timothy, had been "left behind." Paul has departed, but still instructs the church through the writings of his followers. In the two generations after Paul's death, Ephesus was the center of the Pauline school (see introduction). **Not to teach any different doctrine:** The Pauline understanding of the Christian faith was considered normative by the author and his associates. He understands his own reinterpretation of Paul to be legitimate, to stand in the authentic Pauline tradition, and that of his opponents (who also appealed to Paul as their authority) to be deviant. The later church acknowledged this claim by placing the Pastoral letters in the canon—but not the writings of the teachers he opposes.

1:4 Myths and endless genealogies: "Myth" had been a positive term in earlier Greek philosophy, used for the symbolic communication of that transcendent reality accessible only to faith. But by the author's time, "myth" had become among Hellenistic philosophers a standard derogatory description of the opponent's teaching, and this is the way it is used in each of its five appearances in the New Testament. Genealogies refers here not to the family trees often found in the Old Testament, but to the fanciful (but impressive) interpretations of the Bible as later illustrated by those gnostics who found their mythological system in the Bible (see v. 7). These often dealt with elaborate lists of divine "emanations" between the heavenly world and our world, i.e., a kind of "genealogy" of the divine world.

Divine training (NRSV)/**God's work** (NIV): The expression is the same as in Col. 1:25; Eph. 3:2, 9, a key phrase summarizing the Pauline school's understanding of the faith. It is thus better to translate it as "divine plan," as in Eph. 3:5 (see NRSV note). The author opposes the imposing, profound-sounding biblical interpretation of the false teachers with the affirmation of God's saving plan worked out in history, a divine drama in five acts: Creation/Covenant/Christ/Church/Consummation. See excursus at Eph. 1:9.

1:5 The aim of such instruction: The Christian life is oriented to **love, a pure heart,** and sincere faith, not the mastery of a complex system of biblical interpretation.

1:7 Desiring to be teachers of the law: The false teachers propagated their teaching by means of their interpretations of the Bible (the Jewish Scriptures, the Christian Old Testament). The author does not enter into debate with them, offering reasons why the interpretations of his own group are superior, but simply rejects them as having departed from the authentic tradition. From other references in the Pastorals, we learn that the teachers were ascetics who disdained marriage and a normal family life and who demanded abstinence from certain foods (see on 4:3) and from wine (see on 5:23). This ascetic understanding of the Christian life seems to have been based on their understanding that the material world was not the good creation of a good Creator (see on Titus 1:15). They rejected future eschatology (see on 2 Tim. 2:18) and emphasized "knowledge" ("gnosticism," i.e., speculative, philosophical science; see on John 1:1, 14, 18:20; 19:34; 1 Cor. 12:3; 1 Tim. 4:1–5; 6:20–21; Titus 1:16; 1 John 2:20, 27; Rev. 1:3).

1:8–11
Right and Wrong Interpretation
of the Law

For Paul, the issue of the law involved one's acceptance before God; it was a matter of salvation—see the heated debate in Gal. 3–4 and the profound reflections in Rom. 2–7. By the author's time this debate was a matter of past history. The Pastorals nowhere suggest that the false teachers advocated that one must keep the law to be saved. Rather, the false teachers are using the Law (Torah, Jewish Scriptures) as the biblical basis for their false (presumably gnostic) doctrine. The Pastor will not relinquish the law to them, nor does he argue that the law is second rate.

1:8–9 The law is good: Reflecting Paul (Rom. 7:12, 16), he argues that the law is good (it comes from God, is inspired; 2 Tim. 3:16). But God's purpose in giving it was to place a restraint on evil. It was given **for the lawless and disobedient**, not as a basis for imaginative interpretations that support false doctrine. (But see the Pastor's own interpretation at 5:18, and the comments there.) **The godless and sinful, for the unholy and profane:** Vice lists were common in the Hellenistic world as a means of moral instruction; about twenty are found in the New Testament (e.g., Mark 7:21–22, Rom. 1:29–31). The point is not the specific vices listed, which often overlap, but

the general impression of overwhelming evil that is to be avoided. This list is not random, but is structured as a reflection on the Ten Commandments.

1:10 Sodomites: On interpreting New Testament references to homosexuality, see on Rom. 1:26–27.

1:12–17
The (Delayed) Thanksgiving

A conventional formal element of first-century letter writing appears here in altered form (see on 1:3 above). Instead of giving thanks for the health of the recipient, the thanksgiving paragraph focuses on Paul himself, who has become a model of Christian conversion.

1:12 Judged me faithful: The passage suggests that Paul was not made an apostle immediately at the time of his call/conversion, as he himself understood it and as reflected in Acts (Gal. 1:13–17; Acts 9). Rather, since Paul is the model for Christian ministry, he too must first be tested and considered trustworthy before entering his office, just as is the case with ministers in the Pastor's time (3:6).

1:13 Formerly a blasphemer, a persecutor: See Acts 8–9; Gal. 1:13. If such a person could be converted, it can happen to others. Present blasphemers might become faithful ministers; the church should not give up hope on anyone (see 1:20; 2 Tim. 2:25–26; see Titus 3:10).

1:14 The grace of our Lord overflowed: The wording affirms extravagant grace, as in Rom. 5:20: more than more than enough. Despite his emphasis on conventional morality and values, the Pastor understands and affirms Paul's radical doctrine of grace (see Titus 3:3–8).

1:15 The saying is sure: The first of five "faithful sayings," representing key elements of traditions developed in the Pauline school that have a somewhat creedal function to summarize the faith and keep the church on course (see 3:1; 4:9; 2 Tim. 2:11; Titus 3:8). The sayings may have been recited in worship, with "the saying is sure" as a congregational response, analogous to "Amen." ("Sure"/"faithful" is linguistically related to "Amen.") Here the pithy traditional element affirms Christ's coming to save sinners and presents Paul as a model example. The Pastor would not welcome the later trivialization of "Jesus saves."

1:18–20
Charge to Timothy

1:18 The prophecies made earlier about you: On Christian prophecy, see on 1 Cor. 14; 1 Thess.

4:15; introduction to Revelation. The spiritual spontaneity of the earlier generation has now given way (or the Pastor thinks it should) to more orderly structure. Prophecy still occurs, but it designates particular people for ordained ministry (see 2 Tim. 1:6, 14; Acts 13:1–3).

1:20 Hymenaeus and Alexander: There is no way of knowing whether these were actual opponents of Paul whose names have been handed on in the tradition (they are not mentioned in the undisputed Pauline letters), actual opponents of the Pastor's own time, or literary figures in the fictive world projected by the letters. **Turned over to Satan:** See on 1 Cor. 5:3–5.

2:1–6:19
BODY OF THE LETTER

The body of the typical Pauline letter is composed of two parts, the first of which provides the theological foundations for the second part dealing with practical instructions for the Christian life (see the outlines of Romans and Galatians, and the comments at Rom. 12:1; Gal. 5:13; the introductions to Ephesians and Colossians; and comments at Eph. 2:1; 4:1; Col. 3:1). In contrast, the Pastor's letters are composed throughout of practical, ethical instructions, with theological materials and rationale woven in from time to time (see especially Titus 2:11–15; 3:4–7).

2:1–15
INSTRUCTIONS CONCERNING
PROPER WORSHIP

2:1–2 Prayers . . . for kings and all who are in high positions: The government was pagan and often made divine claims for itself (on emperor worship, see the introduction to Revelation). Nonetheless, it is God's world they administer. **A quiet and peaceable life:** The early Christians were often thought to be a disruptive influence, a threat to community decency and order (see, e.g., Acts 19). The Pastor wants his readers to see themselves, and to be seen by others, as good constructive citizens (even in a pagan state; see Rom. 13:1–7). This was a continuation of the Jewish practice; prayers were offered daily in the synagogue *for* the emperor, though Jews had resisted to the death the practice of praying *to* the emperor as a deity. Though they cannot participate in the state-sponsored worship of the emperor and the pagan gods, the readers are instructed to pray for rulers so that the church may live peaceably and fulfill its mission (see on Acts 28:30–31).

2:3–4 God our Savior, who desires everyone to be saved: "Savior" was often used of the emperor. The Pastor restricts this title to the one God. In contrast to the developing Gnosticism, which restricted salvation to a "spiritual" elite, the Pastor emphasizes that God's saving intention includes all people. See 4:10, and excursus on "Universal Salvation and Paradoxical Language," at Rev. 22:21.

2:5–6 There is one God: Vv. 5–6 are not an ad hoc composition, but cite an early Christian creed (among the other traditional materials cited by the Pastor, see 3:16; 5:7–8, 11–12, 15–16; Titus 3:4–7; and the list of "faithful sayings" beginning at 1 Tim. 1:15). That "God is one" is the central creedal affirmation of Judaism (the Shema; see Deut. 6:4–9), reaffirmed in the Christian community in contrast to pagan polytheism. Christian declarations of the deity of Christ must be made, as in the New Testament, in a way that does not compromise this fundamental monotheistic faith. **One mediator:** This is in contrast to the developing Gnosticism in the author's context, a kind of Christian theology that affirmed a complex system of many levels and emanations between the divine and human world. In this view, later condemned as heretical, Christ was represented as more than human but less than divine, neither truly human nor truly divine, but one of a series of quasi-divine mediators between God and humanity. **Christ Jesus, himself human:** See 3:16. Though the author can also confess the deity of Christ (see Titus 3:4), here he emphasizes Christ's true humanity (see on Luke 2:7; "Introduction to the Gospels"; introduction to John; comments at John 1:14; 5:18, 30; 11:33–34; 14:10). The Christians' understanding of Christ contrasts with the demi-god status attributed to the divinized emperors and the series of divine beings advocated by developing Gnosticism. The latter led to a docetic view of Christ in which he only "seemed" to be human.

2:6 A ransom for all: The saving act of God is pictured in terms of redemption—liberating slaves by buying their freedom. The ransom metaphor represents God as redeeming human beings from the bondage of sin and death (as in Rom. 6). As God is the savior of all, Christ's death is for all (see on Mark 10:45). The metaphor should not be pressed literally, as though God had to pay someone (the devil) a purchase price (the death of Jesus) to obtain humanity's release (see on 2 Cor. 5:19). Nonetheless, the redemptive act was costly (1 Pet. 1:18–19).

2:8 Men should pray: The section 2:8–3:1a deals with the community at worship. In contrast to synagogue practice, men and women worshiped together in a common assembly in the house of one of the members. Instructions are given to both men and women. Men pray, preach, and teach, but, in contrast to the practice of earlier Pauline churches, women do not participate verbally. **Lifting up holy hands:** The normal posture for prayer in the ancient world was standing, with open palms upraised, an attitude of respect and openness.

2:9–15 Also . . . the women: The Pastor is concerned with women's place in church life (in addition to this section, see 3:11; 5:3–16; Titus 2:3–5). All such directions must be understood as specific directions in a particular historical context, not as universal rules for all time. On interpreting the household codes in the New Testament, see especially the "principles of interpretation" at 1 Pet. 2:11–3:12. The earlier freedom and equal standing of women in the Pauline churches (Gal. 3:28; 1 Cor. 7) is here seen as dangerous, being misunderstood by outsiders as representing the destruction of what was then regarded as traditional family values. If modern readers ask how Christian women should conduct themselves in a church situated within an Islamic culture, we may gain some insight into the Pastor's reasons for writing these restrictive instructions (see on 1 Pet. 2:13–17; 3:1–6).

2:9 Modestly and decently in suitable clothing: Many parallels can be found in the moral instructions of the first-century world. Here the church is instructed to accommodate itself to the culture for the sake of the Christian mission. Paul had earlier warned against accommodation to the ethos of "the world" (Rom. 12:1). In every situation, the church must decide when to accommodate to and when to resist the dominant cultural ethos. Whichever decision is made must be on the basis of the church's mission, not lethargy or a desire to fit in, but also not on the basis of individual personal feelings and "rights."

2:11 Let a woman learn in silence: Contrast Paul's instructions in 1 Cor. 11:2–16, where women pray and preach (see there).

2:12 No woman to teach or to have authority: In early Judaism, women were not permitted to study the Torah, and thus could not teach. The Pastor here adopts that perspective, in contrast to the earlier Pauline churches, where

women held leadership roles and taught others, including men (Acts 18:24–28; Rom. 16:1, 7; 1 Cor. 11:5). The Pastor now attempts to curb this earlier freedom, which is in danger of being misunderstood in a gnostic or heretical sense and was thus endangering the mission of the church.

Though such instructions were valuable in their own context, and still have something to say to modern Christians when interpreted historically, they are misused when cited as "biblical authority" against the full participation of women in the leadership of the church of all later times and places.

2:13–14 Adam . . . Eve: This exposition of Gen. 3 is a traditional interpretation that had been developed in the Pauline school—a "faithful saying" (3:1 probably refers to the preceding verses). Contrast Paul's interpretation of Gen. 3 in 1 Cor. 11:3, 8–9, which emphasizes mutual responsibility, and in Rom. 5:12–21, in which "Adam"—humanity as such—is guilty, not merely Eve (but see 2 Cor. 11:3, which is developed here). The Pastor emphasizes that only Eve was deceived (in contrast to Gen. 3 and Rom. 5), because it was particularly the women in his church who were being deceived by the false teachers (2 Tim. 3:5–7).

2:15 Saved through childbearing: The text is difficult, addressing a situation to which we are no longer privy. Of course the Pastor does not mean that childless women cannot be saved. It is a false way out of the difficulty, however, to interpret the text as referring to the "birth of *the* child" (Jesus) as the means of salvation. The author is opposing the ascetic false teachers (4:3) who reject marriage and family in the name of true spirituality, teachers who were probably appealing to the earlier words of Paul in 1 Cor. 7:1–16, 25–40 (see there). Such teachers later taught "that marrying and generating come from Satan" (cited in Irenaeus, *Against Heresies* 1:24.2; 1.28.1). Paul gave the earlier instructions when the return of Christ was expected soon. The Pastor properly saw that in his own later time it was a misuse of Paul's earlier instruction to cite it as opposing marriage in general. He sets forth the normal family life of his day as the model of a saved, redeemed life. **Continue in faith, love, and holiness:** "They" here refers to the mothers, not the children. The point is that having children itself is not a matter of one's salvation, but is an aspect of the Christian life of faith, love, and holiness as a whole.

3:1–13
INSTRUCTIONS CONCERNING
CHURCH LEADERSHIP

3:1 The saying is sure: The second of the "faithful sayings"; see on 1:15. Both NRSV and NIV take it as referring to the following. Other translations relate it to the preceding paragraph, a traditional unit of Scripture interpretation in the Pauline school.

In Paul's time, congregational leadership was relatively unstructured, dependent on the spontaneous guidance of the Spirit (see on 1 Cor. 12:28–31; yet see Phil. 1:1; 1 Thess. 5:12; Gal. 6:6). Here, we see stages of development toward ministerial offices, as charismatic leadership becomes more structured. There is still some variety; such development did not proceed uniformly along a common front (see Titus 1:5–9). The Pastor is not introducing innovations, but giving instructions regarding offices already established—though he may be contending against competing views of church polity. The role and function of these ministerial offices, already known to the original readers, are not always clear to the modern interpreter.

The office of bishop: Literally "overseer," "supervisor," one who "looks after" others to be sure all is going well. In some New Testament references, the term "bishop" seems to overlap or be identical with "elder" (see Acts 20:17, 28; 1 Pet. 5:1–2; Titus 1:5, 7). Here, "bishop," always used in the singular, seems to be distinguished from the "elders," who are treated in a different section (4:14; 5:17–22), always in the plural.

3:2 The bishop must be: All the following sixteen virtues are found in typical lists of the qualifications expected of civic and military leaders in the Hellenistic world. Thus the first-century philosopher Onosander lists the qualities of a good general: "temperate, self-restrained, vigilant, frugal, hardened to labor, alert, free from avarice, neither too young nor too old, indeed a father of children if possible, a ready speaker, and a man of good reputation." Church leaders are to have the same qualities that would be admired in other leaders in the author's context. **Married only once:** Literally a "one-woman man." Marriage is not commanded but assumed; the context indicates that it is presupposed the bishop is a family man. This addresses both the suspicion of outsiders that devotees of the new Christian cult are under-

mining traditional family values, and the false teaching of some insiders who rejected marriage and exalted a celibate, ascetic lifestyle (4:3). The discussion in 5:9–16 suggests that "one-woman man" not only prohibits polygamy (or adultery, forbidden to all Christians). As a development of Paul's instructions in 1 Cor. 7:8, 39–40, the Pastor's intent is that bishops, if divorced or widowed, not be remarried. **Hospitable:** Not merely a congenial host, but one willing to provide lodging for traveling missionaries (see Phlm. 22; 3 John 5–8). **An apt teacher:** The bishop is not only administrator, but a knowledgeable and skilled teacher of the Christian faith.

3:3 Not a drunkard: Excess drinking is prohibited; temperate use of wine is commended (5:23), in opposition to the ascetic doctrine of the false teachers.

3:5 Manage his own household: In 5:14 the wives also manage the household. Since the early churches met in private homes—there were no church buildings until generations after the Pastor's time—the (patriarchal) structure of the household influenced the developing offices in the church, the "household of God" (3:15).

3:6 Condemnation of the devil: Since the same word in Greek means "slanderer" (as 3:11) and "devil" (as 2 Tim. 2:26), it is not clear whether the meaning here is "be condemned by outsiders who slander the church" or "be trapped and condemned by the devil." The next verse suggests the former interpretation, the general context the latter.

3:7 Well thought of by outsiders: The goal is not necessarily respectability as such, but that the church's leaders not cause non-Christians undue concern over the way they conduct their personal and family lives. This missionary/evangelistic concern is basic to the Pastor's instruction about household and family (see on Col. 3:18–4:1; Eph. 5:21–6:9; 1 Pet. 2:13–3:12).

3:8 Deacons: The word itself means "server," "minister" (in the nonclerical sense). It was used by Paul in a variety of senses for those who serve in the church. As in the case of "bishop," the word is on the way to describing a definite church office, but has not yet attained its distinct clerical status of later centuries. The qualifications are quite similar to those for the bishop, but do not include oversight or teaching.

3:9 Mystery of the faith: "Mystery" here refers to the content of the faith, what is believed (see

3:16). The distinction that became popular later, according to which bishops and elders are responsible for the "spiritual" life of the church and the deacons take care of "practical" matters, should not be pressed. Deacons, too, must be people who accept, understand, and can articulate the church's faith.

3:11 Women likewise: Greek uses the same word for "wife" and "woman" (like contemporary German "Frau"). It is thus not clear whether the reference is to wives of the deacons (and bishops/elders) or to female deacons. Since the Pastor excludes women from some leadership roles (see on 2:11–15), and since the instruction continues in v. 12 with regard to (male) deacons, one could argue that v. 11 refers to the deacon's wife. On this view, it would then be surprising that no corresponding instruction is found with regard to the bishop. So also, the absence of the possessive pronoun ("their wives") and the word "likewise" corresponding to v. 8 seems to make the women parallel to the male deacons, not a description of the qualifications of their wives. The author does have specific roles for women in the church, including their belonging to an "order" (5:3–16). The present text was clear to the original readers, but remains ambiguous to contemporary interpreters.

3:14–16
THE CHURCH'S GREAT CONFESSION

3:15 If I am delayed: These words would be unnatural in the lifetime of Paul himself (see the introduction to 1 Timothy), but in the later context of the Pastor indicate that after Paul's death his letters (including the Pastorals) will serve as guidelines for the church's life until the eschaton. In contrast to the hopes of the first generation, the return of Christ may be delayed. The ministers in the Pauline communities will give account not only to God and Christ, but to Paul (see 1:2; 4:13).

The **church . . . the pillar and bulwark of the truth:** The Pastor believes that God has provided the community of faith with Scripture, tradition, and ministerial leadership to keep it on course in its journey through history. However, the foundation of God's truth in this world is not the Bible, tradition, or clergy, but the believing community itself as the extension of God's incursion into the world in the Christ event (see 1 Cor. 3:10–12; Eph. 2:20). The author proceeds immediately to cite an early Christian creed, i.e., an accepted element of the tradition summarizing the church's faith.

3:16 Without any doubt: This phrase translates one Greek word, which in secular parlance means "obviously" or "by general agreement"; here it means "according to the common Christian confession" (see RSV "We confess," NASB "By common confession"). The author presents the following six-line formula as an element of Christian tradition that was confessed by all. The English "con" + "fess" corresponds to the Greek word *homologeo*, and means to "say with," or to "agree," i.e., to join with the whole Christian community in expressing the faith by the same words.

The formula consists of a relative pronoun "who" that refers to God/Christ, followed by six lines, each of which begins with a passive verb in the past tense. The formula is constructed on the pattern a-b-b-a-a-b. Each of the "a" lines refers to this historical, temporal, material world ("flesh," "nations," "world"); each of the "b" lines refers to the divine, transcendent world ("spirit," "angels," "glory"). In the incarnation and resurrection, the act of God in Christ bridges this chasm. The entire creed/hymn affirms that it is in this world that the transcendent God has acted in the Christ event, and that this is the message proclaimed and believed throughout the world.

4:1–5
THE "LATER TIMES" PREDICTED

4:1 The Spirit expressly says: This section describes the false teachers of the author's time, a theme to which he returns in 6:3–10. These two sections form a framework around the section of instructions for ministers, 4:6–6:2 (see Outline). Paul is portrayed as reporting the prediction of a Christian prophet about the last days, the time of trouble just before the end. See the introduction to Revelation and comments on Luke 21:8; Acts 11:27–28; 21:4; 1 Thess. 4:2, 15–17. **In later times:** As in Acts 20:28–30, Paul's own time is portrayed as maintaining the purity of the faith, with destructive heresies emerging only after Paul's death. The "prophecy" actually reflects the deviant teaching of the Pastor's own time (see introduction; 2 Tim. 3:1; 4:3; 2 Pet. 3:3; Jude 18). **Deceitful spirits . . . demons:** The author's opponents also appeal to guidance by the Spirit, but the Pastor regards their teaching as inspired by Satan (see 2 Cor. 11:13–15). As in Mark 3:22–30 and Col. 2:8–23, the reality of "spiritual" phenomena is not questioned; the issue is whether the Holy Spirit or other spiritual powers are at work.

4:3 They forbid marriage and demand abstinence from foods: As in the case of the Colossian false teaching (see Col. 2:8–23), the author's opponents advocate an otherworldly asceticism as the mark of an authentic Christian life. Their views on renouncing marriage and family as the mark of an authentic Christian life had profoundly affected the second- or third-generation Pauline churches for which the Pastor writes. His views on women, marriage, and the family may be seen as an (over-?)reaction to the teaching of his opponents, which was attractive to many, especially the women of his churches (see 2:9–15; 3:11; 5:2–16; 2 Tim. 3:6; Titus 2:3–4).

4:4 Everything created by God is good: This is not a platitude, but another response to the false teaching. Some later strands of gnostic Christianity taught that the present world is evil because it is the botched creation of an inferior divine being, a god different from the true God represented by Christ. The author insists that the Creator and Redeemer are the same God, the only God (2:5). Food and sex are not secular, profane realities, but the good gifts of God's creation, sanctified by God's word that created them (Gen. 1:3, 6, 9, 11, 14, 20, 24, 26), and declares them to be good (Gen. 1:4, 10, 12, 18, 21, 25, 31), and by the human response of grateful prayer (see 1 Cor. 10:30; Titus 1:15).

4:6–6:2
INSTRUCTIONS FOR MINISTERS

This extensive section is sandwiched between the author's descriptions of the false teachers (4:1–5; 6:3–10; see Outline). Faithful ministers are part of the antidote to false teaching. The author's selection of topics and emphases is influenced by the false alternatives threatening his own situation. As elsewhere, "Timothy" here sometimes represents church members in general (who hear the letter read in congregational worship), sometimes the ordained ministers, sometimes their superior who ordains and disciplines them.

4:6–16
Characteristics and Character of the Good Minister

4:6 A good servant: Literally "deacon," here used in its generic sense, "minister." Verses 5–16 address the duties of ministers in the form of instruction from "Paul" to "Timothy" (see introduction). The whole section emphasizes *teaching* as central to the minister's role (vv. 6,

11 13, 16), and the minister's responsibility to guard the church against false teaching.

4:7 Profane myths and old wives' tales: See 1:4. This is the Pastor's derogatory description of his opponents' teaching, which seemed impressive and profound to those not firmly established in the tradition (see 2 Tim. 3:6). The opposing teachers considered their doctrine to be deeply theological interpretations of the Bible and philosophy; the Pastor puts it in the same category as gossip exchanged by elderly housewives over the back fence.

4:8–9 The saying is sure: The third of the "faithful sayings" (see on 1:15) is the preceding verse, not v. 10. **The life to come** refers to the renewed world brought into being at the return of Christ, the era of eschatological salvation. All the "faithful sayings" refer to salvation.

4:10 Savior of all people: See on 2:4. This saying seems to declare both that God saves all people and (in some special sense) saves only believers. This tensive pair of statements has been understood as meaning (a) God is potentially the savior of all, but actually saves only those who believe; (b) the second clause simply "corrects" the first; (c) the issue of who is saved at the eschaton can only be expressed dialectically: God saves all (God is sovereign and his saving will for all cannot finally be thwarted even by human unbelief) *and* God saves only believers (every human being is responsible, and God will not overrule human unbelief). In view (c) the Pastor properly leaves the tension unresolved, as had Paul (see Phil. 2:5–13). See excursus on "Universal Salvation and Paradoxical Language," at Rev. 22:21.

4:12 Let no one despise your youth: Timothy is portrayed as youthful and inexperienced, in need of elementary instruction. This corresponds to the need for pastoral instruction in the church of the author's time, but not to that of the historical Paul and Timothy. The actual Timothy to whom Paul would have addressed a letter after his "first" Roman imprisonment (see introduction) would have been a seasoned missionary of mature years, having already proven himself by weathering many crises with Paul. See Acts 18:15; 19:22; 20:4; Rom. 16:21; 1 Cor. 4:17; 16:10; 2 Cor. 1:1, 19; Phil. 1:1; 2:19; 1 Thess. 3:2, 6. The young ministers of the Pastor's church, however, who were sometimes called on to teach and even reprove church members older than they, needed to be instructed to conduct their ministry in such a way that it could not be disdained or dismissed because of their relative youth.

4:13 Until I arrive: See note on 3:14. **Public reading of scripture:** A knowledge of the Bible was one of the church's defenses against false teaching. Church members, however, did not generally have personal copies of the Bible until centuries later. Scripture (i.e., the Old Testament) was appropriated by hearing it read aloud in the worship assembly. Long passages, including whole books, were read repeatedly as part of Christian worship. It was the minister's responsibility to facilitate this. The minister is not to offer his own summary of biblical teaching, but to allow the congregation to appropriate the text of the Scripture for themselves. **Exhorting:** Preaching and admonition based on Scripture and Christian tradition (in this case Pauline). **Teaching:** In the Pastor's view, the Pastor is primarily a minister of the word, engaged in proclaiming and teaching the faith (see Eph. 4:12).

4:14 Gift . . . prophecy . . . laying on of hands: Although the initial charismatic phenomena of the first generation of the Pauline churches (see 1 Cor. 12–14) had waned or had come to be considered theologically dangerous, the experience and conviction remained that Christian ministry was not merely voluntaristic do-goodism, but was the gift of the Spirit to the church (see Eph. 4:1–16). This spiritual gift is now "regularized" by associating it with ordination (see on 1:18; 3:1–13). Unlike Paul, the Pastoral Epistles provide no suggestion that the Holy Spirit provides a variety of gifts to the whole body of Christians. There is one gift, and it comes through proper ordination. For Paul, there is a variety of spiritual gifts, and each Christian receives a gift by virtue of being baptized (1 Cor. 12:13–31); for the Pastor, there is one gift, given to ministers by virtue of being ordained. The development of this understanding was one way the church protected itself from false teachers and self-proclaimed ministers. **The council of elders:** Literally "the presbytery" (see NRSV note). In 2 Tim. 1:6 the gift of ministry is conferred by Paul's hands. The point is that Paul's apostolic authorization continues in the regular ordination process conducted by the elders. This is not yet "apostolic succession" in the sense of an unbroken chain of ordained clergy that extends back to the apostles, but it does claim that the regular ordination by elders represents an apostolic ministry. In the laying on of the presbytery's hands, Paul's hands are laid on the ordinand, i.e., he is affirmed as a legitimate representative of the apostolic faith.

5:1–2
The Minister in the Household of God

The section 5:1–6:2 follows to some extent the pattern of a household code (see on Col. 3:18–4:1), but the author has adapted the pattern to his purpose, which is more concerned with church order in the household of God (3:15) than private family life. The real thrust of this passage has to do with groups among whom problems had arisen: "widows" (5:3–16), "elders" in the official sense (5:17–25), and slaves and masters within the church; but all is to be done with the love and sense of fairness appropriate to life in a good family.

5:1 An older man: The same word as 5:17, 19, and Titus 1:5, where it is used in an "official" sense (see NRSV note). The minister's relation to other church members is not "professional," but that of one member of the family to another.

5:2 Younger women: The young minister is to be particularly careful that his relation to the younger women be above suspicion.

5:3–16
Widows

5:3 Honor: Has to do not only with respect, but with financial considerations. Thus the Decalogue's command to "honor father and mother" (Exod. 20:12) includes providing for them in their old age. **Widows** were often among the vulnerable members of ancient society, which had no social welfare programs and provided limited opportunities for single women to be self-supporting. Thus the Old Testament and Jewish tradition were very concerned to protect and provide justice for widows (see Exod. 22:22–24; Deut. 24:19–22). The church early on incorporated this biblical tradition into its own life by providing organized assistance to widows (Acts 6:1; 9:36–41). This arrangement could be taken advantage of by those who were not really needy, just as it could be exploited by households that did not want to take care of aged widows.

Real widows: Some interpreters see the issue discussed here entirely within the context of the church's social welfare program, the problem being certainty that only qualified needy widows with no other means of support receive church benevolent funds. While this concern is certainly included in the Pastor's instructions, most interpreters now understand "real" widows to be those who belong to an emerging official "order" of single women, whether previously married or not, who take a vow to remain unmarried and to serve the church full-time, a precursor of the later orders of nuns. This was certainly the case in some streams of church life by the early second century. By ca. 112 CE, Ignatius, bishop of Antioch, could refer to "the virgins who are called widows" as an established element in the church's structure (*Smyrnaeans* 13.3). There is some evidence that a preliminary form of such orders is addressed here: women are **put on the list** (5:9) and take a **pledge** or vow that they violate if they marry (not "remarry," 5:11–12). The qualifications are strict, resembling those for the bishop (3:1–7). Such an understanding could well be a development of Paul's earlier instructions in 1 Cor. 7:10–11, 25–38. Thus, just as not all elderly men in the congregation were elders in the official sense, so also not all women whose husbands had died were widows in the official sense. Such a life of devotion to the church that freed women from the patriarchal household, with financial security provided by the church, seems to have been attractive to a number of women. This attractiveness seemed a dangerous development to the Pastor, who apparently regarded it as a threat to the normal family life of the culture he affirmed (2:9–15), and who feared it would open the door to exploitation by his opponents (who certainly discouraged marriage and appealed to the women of the congregation [4:3, 2 Tim. 3:6]). The Pastor affirms the office and role of "widows," but places them under strict regulation—somewhat as Paul had responded to glossolalia in 1 Cor. 12–14.

5:17–25
Elders

5:17 Elders who rule well: On elders as a church office, see Acts 11:29–30; 14:23; 20:17–38; Titus 1:5–9; Jas. 5:13; 1 Pet. 5:1–5; 2 John 1; 3 John 1. The functions of the office are here described as "ruling," **preaching,** and **teaching** (5:17, i.e., they are ministers, not laypersons). They are paid for their work, and those who do it well are to be both respected and compensated. This is probably the meaning of "**double honor,**" not that they are to be paid twice as much as the others. In dependence on 1 Cor. 9:9, where Paul had interpreted Deut. 25:4 as meaning that the church should support its missionary preachers, the author calls on the same text to argue the congregation should support its resident elder-ministers.
5:18 The laborer: This proverb is also cited in Matt. 10:10 and Luke 10:7. Its presence here in associ-

ation with the Scripture text from Deuteronomy does not mean that the author considered Matthew or Luke Scripture. "Laborer" had become almost a technical term for ministers and missionaries (see Matt. 9:37–38; 10:10; 20:1–2, 8; Luke 10:2, 7; Acts 19:25; 2 Cor. 11:13; Phil. 3:2; 2 Tim. 2:15).
5:19 Accusation against an elder: Here "Timothy" represents the role of those who **ordain** (v. 22) and hear complaints against elders; the office he represents is superior to theirs, corresponding to that of the later bishop. Such leaders are instructed to be fair. **Two or three witnesses:** See Deut. 19:15; Matt. 18:16. The Old Testament–Jewish injunction designed to guarantee a fair hearing is followed.
5:23 Take a little wine: The advice seems to interrupt the context, but it is appropriate from the Pastor's perspective. In this context on the proper character and function of ministry, he instructs ministers to drink wine rather than embrace the ascetic rigidity of the false teachers (see 4:3).

6:1–2
Slaves

This section is included here as part of the household code pattern at the basis of 5:1–6:2. On slavery in the early Christian world, see introduction to Philemon and comments on Col. 3:22. Unlike other household codes in the New Testament, these verses address only slaves, with no corresponding instruction to masters. The author is here concerned neither with the institution of slavery nor with personal relations between slaves and masters as such, but with the influence church life has on outsiders (see 1 Thess. 4:11–12; 1 Cor. 14:23–24; Eph. 5:21–6:9; 1 Pet. 2:11–3:12).

6:3–10
THE OPPONENTS

The author returns to the theme that brackets his instructions to ministers (see commentary on 4:1–5, and Outline). These opponents are often described as "gnostics," a particular stream of early Christianity later regarded as heretical (see on John 1:1, 14; 18:20; 19:34; 1 Cor. 12:3; 1 John 2:20, 27; Rev. 1:3). The Pastor struggles against an early form of this dangerous false teaching.
6:3 The sound words of our Lord Jesus Christ: The Greek phrase can also be translated "about our Lord Jesus Christ," and this is its probable meaning here. The author is not referring to the Gospels or to a collection of Jesus' sayings available in his church. The

author's theology, like Paul's, does not function by citing stories and sayings from the life of Jesus, but by drawing out the meaning of the Christ event as a whole.

6:5–6 Imagining that godliness is a means of gain: "Godliness," used 10x by the Pastor but never by Paul, means for him true religious devotion and the corresponding Christian life. Then as now, the "gospel of prosperity" was preached by the false teachers, who supposed that religious faith was the means to material success. **Contentment:** The word means "self-sufficiency," not being dependent on external things for internal peace and happiness. It was a favorite virtue of first-century Stoics and other pagan philosophies, here understood in a Christian sense (in which the Christian is not self-centered, but dependent on God for peace and happiness).

6:8–10 Food and clothing: The author in fact knows and affirms faithful Christians, including church leaders, who have substantial financial resources and large homes in which the church meets, and slaves to serve such households (2:9; 3:1–7; 5:8, 16; 6:2). It is greed, the **love of money** that is **a root of all kinds of evil,** not wealth as such. Like the pagan philosophers from Plato and Aristotle on, he teaches that money is a means that becomes evil when it is regarded as an end in itself, a good servant but a poor master.

6:11–19
FINAL EXHORTATION TO TIMOTHY

6:11 Shun all this: Timothy, as representative of Christians and especially of ministers, is commanded to flee the love of money and religion-as-success doctrine he understood to be advocated by the false teachers.

6:12 The good confession: On "confession," see 3:16 commentary. The content is not given; the author understands the confession to be the Christian faith as handed on in the church, especially in the form expressed in the Pauline tradition. The confession is not a matter of private, personal faith, or of secret doctrines handed on in esoteric circles, but something declared publicly, in the presence of **many witnesses.** At the ordination of ministers, after testing the candidates the council of elders were witnesses who vouched for the validity of the candidates' confession (1:18–19; 4:14; 2 Tim. 1:14).

6:13 Christ Jesus . . . made the good confession: "Timothy" (and all ministers and Christians) conduct their ministry in the time of the church, the period between Jesus' own public testimony, given in a hostile environment, and his return at the end of time, when the church and its ministry must give an account of its confession. **I charge you:** Another indication that 6:11–21 reflects the ordination liturgy, or at least the kinds of responsibility with which ministers were charged at their ordination.

6:14 Keep the commandment: "Keep" here means "preserve intact." The "commandment" is the charge received by ministers to preserve the deposit of faith entrusted to them by faithfully teaching it to their contemporaries and handing it on to future generations until Christ returns (see on 6:20; 2 Tim. 1:14).

6:16 He alone . . . has immortality: Gnostics taught that the souls of elite Christians were immortal, had existed before their birth in the divine realm to which they will return at the death of the body, in which they are presently trapped. The Pastor affirms the biblical theology that humans are mortal, only God is immortal, and humans' only hope is in the immortal God, who raises the dead. See the distinction between "immortality" and "resurrection" at Luke 20:27; 24:1–12.

6:17 Everything for our enjoyment: The Pastor is not antienjoyment, but antiascetic. In contrast to his gnosticizing opponents, the Pastor celebrates the goodness of the created world (see on 4:3). A rabbinic dictum states that "we shall give account to the Almighty for every good thing in creation we have not enjoyed."

6:20–21
EPISTOLARY CONCLUSION

The conclusion sums up and reaffirms the main theme of the letter.

6:20 Guard what has been entrusted to you: See on 2 Tim. 1:12, 14.

Contradictions of what is falsely called knowledge: "Knowledge" translates the Greek "gnosis," the basis for the English words "gnostic" and "Gnosticism." On "gnostics," see on John 1:1, 14; 18:20; 19:34; 1 Cor. 12:3; 1 Tim. 4:1–5; Titus 1:16; 1 John 2:20, 27; Rev. 1:3. "Contradictions" can also be translated "Antitheses," the title of a book by Marcion, a gnostic teacher of the early- and mid-second century. Marcion's *Antitheses* listed 140 contradictions between the (in his view) second-rate Creator god of the Old Testament and the true God of the New Testament revealed in Jesus. The Pastor's final admonition can thus be read as meaning,

"Avoid Marcion's book called *Antitheses*, a product of that movement falsely called 'knowledge,' 'science,' or 'Gnosticism.'" Since Marcion's book may have been published too late for the Pastor to have known and objected to it, most scholars now reject this identification. The options are (1) a remarkable coincidence, the Pastor's objection to Gnosticism having accidentally used a word that a leading gnostic later adopted as the title for his book; (2) the Pastorals were written later than generally believed, late enough to object specifically to Marcion; (3) Marcion's book was earlier than previously believed, early enough for 1 Tim. 6:20 to specifically target it. In any case, the readers are urged to hold fast to the traditional faith and reject the speculative theology of the "knowers."

6:21 Grace be with you: The "you" is plural. In this last word, the author drops the literary form of a letter addressed to Timothy and addresses the churches for which it was intended.

The Second Letter of Paul to Timothy

INTRODUCTION

For a general introduction to the Pastoral Epistles (1–2 Timothy, Titus), see Introduction to 1 Timothy. Here 2 Timothy is understood to have been written in Paul's name by a later disciple, reinterpreting Paul's message to the Pauline churches of Asia Minor in the second or (more likely) third Christian generation (see on 1:5; 2:2). The document represents Paul writing from prison (1:8, 2:9), presumably in Rome (1:16–17, see Acts 28:16), shortly before his death (4:6–8). The letter thus belongs to the category of testamentary literature, in which a religious hero of the past blesses and exhorts his followers, preparing them to continue his work without him (see Gen. 49 [Jacob]; Deut. 31 [Moses]; Josh. 24 [Joshua]; John 14–16 [Jesus]; Acts 20:18–38 [Paul]). There are numerous examples of testaments in the Jewish literature of the period, e.g., *The Testaments of the Twelve Patriarchs, The Testament of Job, The Testament of Moses, The Testament of Solomon, The Testament of Adam.* All these are literary compositions of the author who composed the document, not verbatim reports of the hero's last words. The Pastor has been influenced by this literary model.

Outline

1:1–2 Salutation
1:3–4:18 Body
    1:3–2:26 Thanksgiving, Encouragement,
    Instructions
    3:1–9 False Teachers and the
    Last Days
    3:10–4:8 Paul's Charge to Timothy
    4:9–18 Personal Instructions
4:19–22 Final Greetings and
    Benediction

For Further Reading

Bassler, Jouette. *1 Timothy, 2 Timothy, Titus.* Nashville: Abingdon, 1996.

Collins, Raymond F. *I and II Timothy and Titus: A Commentary.* New Testament Library. Louisville, KY: Westminster John Knox, 2002.

COMMENTARY

1:1–2
SALUTATION

1:2 Beloved child: This does not mean that "Timothy" is young (see on 1 Tim. 4:12), but that he is *chosen* as an authoritative representative of the Pauline faith (see on 1 Tim. 1:2).

1:3–4:18
BODY

1:3–2:26
THANKSGIVING, ENCOURAGEMENT, INSTRUCTIONS

1:3 I am grateful: A brief thanksgiving, a standard formal element in Hellenistic letters (see on 1 Thess. 1:2; 1 Tim. 1:3). **As my ancestors did:** The Paul of the Pastorals emphasizes his continuity with past religion, not his discontinuity. In the Pastor's time, new cults were suspect. For the Pastor, it is the false teachers, not Paul, who were innovators (3:1; 4:3). **I remember you constantly in my prayers:** During his lifetime, Paul prayed for his churches and associates (see, e.g., Rom. 1:9; Phlm. 4; 1 Thess. 1:2). Here, the "absent Paul" (whose martyr's death is reverently remembered) prays for "Timothy," i.e., the Christians and ministers of the later Pauline churches. The communion of saints joins Christians of present and past generations, who pray for each other (see 1:18).

1:5 Lois . . . Eunice . . . you: "Timothy" is portrayed as belonging to third-generation Christianity, the situation of the actual readers. Timothy comes from a family in which the Christian tradition had been faithfully transmitted (see 2:2; 3:15; and contrast Acts 16:1–3). Although the Pastor resists the teaching role of women in the public assembly of the church (1 Tim. 2:9–15), he affirms their role as transmitters of the faith within the family. Nothing else is known of Lois and Eunice, who are among the twenty-three names (+ Paul and Timothy) mentioned in 2 Timothy, most of whom are not mentioned elsewhere. The tradition tends to gather names as it is passed along.

1:6 The gift of God: The charismatic gift of ministry. The Holy Spirit is given to every believer at baptism (Titus 3:5; Acts 2:38; 1 Cor. 12:13). See on 1 Tim. 4:14, where the gift is imparted through ordination by the elders. The gift is received at ordination, but must be constantly rekindled by the minister's own responsibility: it is both gift and assignment.

1:8 Do not be ashamed: See v. 12; see Rom. 1:16. Christianity was not yet "respectable." Jesus had died a shameful death by being executed at the hands of the government. **Suffering for the gospel:** The author, along with the whole New Testament, assumes that Christian faith always brings one into conflict with the dominant values of the culture. Suffering here is not with *Christ* (as in the undisputed letters of Paul), but suffering with *Paul,* who in the theology of the Pauline school was himself an integral part of the Christ event (see on Col. 1:24).

1:9 Who saved us and called us: Verses 9–10 represent a liturgical fragment, part of a traditional creed or hymn (see 1 Tim. 1:15; 2:5–6; 3:16; 6:7–8, 11–12, 15–16; Titus 3:4–7). **Not according to our works . . . but . . . his grace:** See Titus 3:5, which also reflects the Pauline doctrine of grace developed in Rom. 3:21–5:21.

1:10 Immortality: See on 1 Tim. 6:16.

1:12 What I have entrusted to him: This phrase is the translation of one Greek word, *paratheke,* translated "treasure" in 1:14 (see commentary below) and "what has been entrusted to you" in 1 Tim. 6:20. The better translation here is represented in the NRSV note, "what has been entrusted to me" (see commentary on 1:14). As an apostle, Paul had been *entrusted* with an authentic understanding of the gospel, which he transmits to Timothy, who is to transmit it to others (2:2). **He is able:** Though ministers are themselves responsible for faithful preservation and proclamation of the Christian faith, they are not alone, but conduct their ministry by faith in the power of God who works in and with them. See Phil. 2:12–13, and **with the help of the Holy Spirit** (v. 14).

1:13 The standard of sound teaching: In contrast to the false teachers (3:1–9; 1 Tim. 4:1–5; 6:3–10), Paul is the model for both the content of the gospel message and for faithful adherence to it despite opposition.

1:14 Guard the good treasure: The word translated "treasure" is *paratheke,* used three times in the Pastorals, each time with the command "guard/keep" (1 Tim. 1:18; 2 Tim. 2:12, 14), and nowhere else in the New Testament. The corresponding verb is found in 1 Tim. 1:18 and 2 Tim. 2:2. The word is a synonym for "tradition," often translated "deposit" (of tradition). The picture is of a deposit of sacred tradition given to someone for safekeeping; it refers to the content of the Christian faith, as expressed especially in the Pauline tradition. The minister's responsibility is to *preserve* it, but not merely for his own spiritual welfare. He is to be a faithful teacher of what he has received and pass it on to future generations (see 2:2). This means he (in the Pastor's context, ministers were exclusively male) must also adapt it to changing times, as the Pastor himself has done with the Pauline tradition he received. But the pastor/teacher is to adapt *it,* the given body of tradition, not begin afresh with his own resources in every generation and situation. The task and challenge of the church's ministry in every generation is to adapt and reinterpret the traditional faith so that it is relevant to changing needs and times, without losing it or letting it simply become an echo or reflection of current values and ideologies (see on Mark 2:17). The Pastor proposes to offer a model for such ministry in his own writings, which are faithful to the Pauline tradition without merely repeating it—which, in a situation different from Paul's, would mean being *un*faithful to it.

1:15 All who are in Asia have turned away: This reflects the author's own time, when the traditional Pauline gospel was being rejected in Asia Minor, in favor of the new, "progressive" gnosticizing understanding of the faith. **Phygelus and Hermogenes:** Nothing more is known about these two men except that they represent the group that had abandoned Paul's teaching (see 2:17; 4:10–15).

1:16 Not ashamed of my chain: Analogous to not being ashamed of Jesus' cross (1 Cor. 1:17–18; Gal. 5:11; 6:12, 14). Respectable, religion-as-success Christianity was embarrassed by Paul's imprisonment, as it was of Jesus' cross, but authentic faith overcomes this scandal (1 Cor. 1:18–2:5).

1:18 Service he rendered in Ephesus: Onesiphorus (only here and 4:19 in the New Testament) is an example of those who were faithful to the Pauline gospel, a person well known in Ephesus, the center of the Pauline school (see introduction to 1 Timothy). He had apparently died, since only his family is mentioned in 4:19. This text has been cited as the earliest Christian example of prayers for the dead (see 2 Macc. 12:43–46 for Jewish precedent).

2:2 What you have heard from me: The authentic Christian faith rests on a tradition that goes back to the original apostles, in the Pastor's view concentrated in the person of Paul himself. "Paul" represents the apostolic faith; "Timothy" represents the teachers of the Pauline school who continued to transmit and reformulate Paul's message; **faithful people who will be able to teach others** represent the bishops/elders/pastors/teachers of the congregations contemporary with the Pastor. The chain of tradition is thus "Paul" ⇒ "Timothy" ⇒ teachers ⇒ church of the present and future. The concern is not merely for individualistic personal faith, but for transmitting the faith to future generations.

Through many witnesses (NRSV)/**In the presence of many witnesses** (NIV): The NRSV understands the Greek expression to refer to the chain of reliable witnesses through whom the tradition was transmitted. To receive it through the faithful Christian community *is* to receive it from Paul (see 1:6 in relation to 1 Tim. 4:14, and comments on Paul's understanding of tradition at 1 Cor. 11:23). The NIV is a possible translation of the same Greek phrase. In either case, the point is that the Christian faith is not esoteric and private information from one individual to another, but is openly and reliably transmitted by the church.

2:7 Think over . . . the Lord will give you understanding: Another example of the Pauline dialectic of human responsibility and divine gift: ministers are responsible to do rigorous thinking about the faith, and are encouraged to do so. But when insight comes, it is not the result of the minister's own diligence and mental capabilities, but the gift of God (see Phil. 2:12–13).

2:8 Risen from the dead . . . descendant of David: See Rom. 1:3. Verses 8–9a are another fragment of creedal, hymnic, or catechetical material (see on 1 Tim. 2:5–6).

2:10 I endure everything for the sake of the elect: In retrospect, the Pauline school regarded Paul's suffering and martyrdom as an integral part of the Christ event itself (Col. 1:24; Eph. 3:13).

2:11–13 The saying is sure: The fourth of the "faithful sayings" (see on 1 Tim. 1:15). **Died with him:** See Rom. 6:1–11. **Will also live with him:** The Pastor here reasserts the future eschatology; see on 2:18 below. **Reign with:** See Rom. 5:17; Rev. 3:21.

Deny him . . . deny us: This pair of statements preserves the classic Pauline dialectic of divine sovereignty and human responsibility. Believers are called on to confess their faith before the world, in deed and words. To fail to do so is to disavow God, who will disavow those who deny him (Mark 8:38; Matt. 10:32–33; Rev. 2:10; 3:5). This statement makes humans absolutely responsible and is to be taken with utmost seriousness: it is our responsibility to be faithful witnesses, *entirely* our responsibility. But alongside it is another statement, absolutely surprising in this context. One expects: "If we are unfaithful to God, God will be unfaithful to us." But what we read is astoundingly unexpected: God's faithfulness is not dependent on ours; God's acceptance of us is based on who God is, not on who we are or what we have done. This paradox permeates the whole New Testament (see, e.g., Phil. 2:12–13; Rev. 20:11–15).

2:15 Worker: Often used as a technical term for Christian ministers (e.g., Matt. 9:37; Rom. 16:3, 6, 9; 2 Cor. 11:13; Phil. 3:2). **The word of truth:** A phrase used by Paul for the Christian message (see 2 Cor. 6:7). A primary task of the minister is to be a student and teacher of the Bible for the church, interpreting it in the context of the authentic Christian tradition (see 2 Pet. 1:20–21; 3:16). **Rightly explaining:** Found elsewhere in the Bible only in Prov. 3:6; 11:5, where it is translated "cut a straight path."

2:16–17 More and more impiety: On the claims of the false teachers to be "progressive," see on 3:9. The minister is here warned against getting sidetracked into the kind of dispute exemplified by **Hymenaeus and Philetus** (v. 17), who deviated from the path of authentic understanding advocated by the Pastor.

2:18 Already: Like Jesus (see on Luke 4:43–44) and John (4:23), Paul had taught the already/ not yet dialectic of the reality of salvation (Rom. 8:15; 13:11; 1 Cor. 15:45–49; Gal. 4:1; 5:5). At baptism Christians are united with Christ in his *crucifixion*, i.e., the Christian life is marked by the sign of the cross, characterized by Jesus' own self-giving for others (Rom. 6:1–5; 1 Cor. 6:14; 15:23–28; Gal. 2:19–20; 5:24; 6:14). Being united with Christ in his *resurrection* life, however, is still a matter for the eschatological future, so that the Christian life is lived in the tension between cross and resurrection (Phil. 3:7–14).

The apocalyptic view of the future resurrection (see on Luke 24:1–12) was sometimes reinterpreted as "realized eschatology," as a matter of the present Christian experience: the resurrection happens to believers when they die and rise with Christ in baptism (Col. 2:12; 3:1–5; John 5:25; 11:25–26). In the New Testament, this reinterpretation is primarily a shift of emphasis and is not affirmed in such a way as to deny the future resurrection.

In the gnosticizing Christianity opposed by the Pastor, the false teachers had reduced the resurrection hope entirely to present experience, and resurrection language became simply a metaphor for what happened at conversion. The dialectical already/not yet of Jesus and Paul became the simple "**the resurrection has already taken place**." We see examples of this in later gnostic documents:

The disciples ask Jesus, "When will the resurrection of the dead occur, and when will the new world come?" He said to them, "What you expect has already come, but you do not recognize it." (*Gospel of Thomas* 51)

If one does not receive the resurrection while still alive, one will receive nothing at death. (*Gospel of Philip* 73.1–5)

You already have the resurrection. (*De Resurrectione*, as cited in Hippolytus, Fragment 1)

The Pastor rejects this hyperrealized eschatology and reasserts the future Christian hope of the triumph of God in the ultimate future, including the resurrection of the dead (see 2 Thess. 2:2; Rev. 20:5).

2:19 God's firm foundation: See on 1 Tim. 3:15. The citations reflect, but do not quote exactly, Num. 16:5; Job 36:10; Isa. 26:13.

2:21 Become special utensils: This is the Pastor's ethical application of Paul's theology of election in Rom. 9:19–26.

2:22 Shun youthful passions: On "Timothy's" youth, see 1 Tim. 4:12. The phrase can also mean (more appropriately here) "avoid innovations"—of the "progressive" false teachers—and stay with the traditional Pauline faith.

2:24–25 Kindly to everyone . . . correcting opponents with gentleness: The Pastor's own words to "Timothy" about the false teachers

are hardly kind and gentle (see 3:1–9; 1 Tim. 4:2; 6:3–10). What we have here, however, is indirect communication, descriptions of the kind of outsiders to be avoided in a message addressed to insiders (see the analogous situation in Matt. 23). When actually addressing those whose teaching deviates from the apostolic norm, the Pastor wants those who teach in the church to correct with gentleness those teaching false doctrine. The false teachers are considered insiders, fellow Christians with a dangerous misunderstanding of the faith, but they too may be brought back to God's way by a renewed understanding and delivered from Satan's trap.

3:1–9
FALSE TEACHERS AND THE LAST DAYS

3:1 The last days: In the typical apocalyptic scheme, the final victory of God at the end of history is preceded by a period in which evil is intensified (see Mark 13:3–23; introduction to Revelation; and Rev. 6–11). The Pastor shares this worldview, according to which there will be a moral decline and appearance of false teachers just before the end. The opponents "predicted" are in fact already present in the author's own time (see 1 John 2:18–21) and have been opposed throughout his writings from 1 Tim. 1:3 on (see 1 Tim. 4:1–3).

3:2–4 People will be: On such vice catalogues, see on Rom. 1:28–32, a Pauline text that probably serves as the basis of the Pastor's own list. Such lists were a general polemical tool often found in Hellenistic moralists, not specific descriptions of particular people. The list is composed with rhetorical power and artistry, beginning with **lovers of themselves** and concluding with the counterpart **rather than lovers of God**.

3:6 Make their way into households: While most of the list is conventional, vv. 6–9 are specific to the author's situation. "Households" are churches (see 1 Tim. 3:15; 2:20–21). The opponents are not kidnappers who break into private homes, but false teachers who disrupt the house churches with their seductive doctrine.

Silly women: Literally "little women," in the derogatory sense, somewhat like "little old ladies" in the stereotypes of American culture. The author shares the cultural stereotypes of women that permeated his culture, in which women were mostly uneducated and confined to the home. His point, however, is not to further denigrate women, but to disqualify the false teachers by showing that they appeal only to the ignorant and easily swayed. They prey on the (presumed) weaker members of the community. Some women in the Pastor's congregations were in fact attracted to the opponents' teaching, not because they lacked intelligence, but because the opponents continued Paul's original emphasis on women's equality (Gal. 3:28) and freedom to serve in positions of leadership. In the Pastor's time, however, these teachers had perverted Paul's teaching in a gnosticizing ascetic direction that encouraged women to abandon home and family, and thus brought the church and its mission into disrepute. This is documented in a second-century Christian writing, *The Acts of Paul and Thecla*, which portrays Paul as encouraging women to abandon their families. This was seen by the Pastor as such a violation of the accepted social structure that his own perspective on women's role in the church seems retrogressive and reactionary in comparison with Paul. Both Paul and the Pastor, of course, must be interpreted in their historical context, not seen as providing universal prescriptions.

3:7 Always being instructed: The Pastor portrays those who follow the false teachers as following current religious fads, but not grounded in **the truth** of the traditional Pauline faith.

3:8 Jannes and Jambres: Though not named in the Old Testament, these are the names traditionally given to the magicians of Pharaoh's court who opposed Moses (Exod. 7:11, 22). The names are found in the Targums (later Aramaic paraphrases of the Hebrew text) and in the Dead Sea Scrolls.

3:9 Not make much progress: The false teachers presented themselves as "progressive," in contrast to the "simple, traditional" faith advocated by the author (see 2 John 9). The Pastor ironically turns their own buzzword against them: in 2:16 they "progress" all right—to more and more ungodliness. Here the "progressives" are said not to progress much.

3:10–4:8
PAUL'S CHARGE TO TIMOTHY

3:10 You have observed: Paul is presented as a model for ministers and Christians for the following generations. This is not egotism of the historical Paul, but the theology of the Pauline school that has adopted Paul's life as the ideal for later ministers and Christians. In contrast to Jannes and Jambres, "Timothy" has followed the apostle's teaching and example

(see on 1 Tim. 1:2). **Teaching:** In the Pastorals, "teaching" is always singular when it means the traditional authoritative apostolic teaching, and plural ("teachings") when it refers to the doctrines of the false teachers.

3:11 My persecutions and my suffering: See 2 Cor. 10–13 and comments there. In the Pauline tradition, it was not particular sayings and events in the life of Jesus that served as models of the Christian life, but the character of God revealed in the Christ event as a whole. Paul is here seen as the model for the unselfish suffering on behalf of others (see 1 Tim. 2:10) represented by the love of God manifest in the incarnation (John 1:1, 14; 3:16). As in 2 Cor. 10–13, this is in deliberate contrast to the attitude and conduct of the false teachers. **Antioch, Iconium, and Lystra:** Not mentioned in the undisputed letters of Paul, but see Acts 13–14.

3:12 All: In regard to suffering for the faith, Paul's suffering is the model not only for ministers, but for all believers. This is not a matter of encouraging Christians to develop a martyr complex, but a declaration that the Christian faith inevitably brings believers into conflict with the dominant value system of the culture.

3:13 From bad to worse: See note on "progress" at 3:9.

3:14 Continue in what you have learned: In the midst of the confusion caused by the new teachings attractive to many, "Timothy" is instructed to hold fast to the traditional faith as taught in the Pauline tradition. **From whom:** Paul is the ultimate source of this tradition, but the plural form of "whom" indicates it comes to the ministers in the Pastor's churches through the teachers of the Pauline school, not directly from Paul.

3:15 From childhood: The Pastorals present "Timothy" as a third-generation Christian; see on 1:5. **The sacred writings:** See on 1 Tim. 3:15. In the author's view, God has provided the church with three resources to guide it in its pilgrimage through history: the Scripture (the Old Testament, read from the point of view of Christian faith), the tradition (as distilled in firm instructional elements and creedal affirmations—see on 1 Tim. 2:5–6), and Christian ministers (properly prepared and ordained to serve as authorized teachers of the faith).

3:16 All scripture: The reference is to the Old Testament; Christian writings were not yet considered Scripture (see on 2 Pet. 3:16). Though in the Pastor's time some writings, such as Paul's letters, were beginning to be highly revered, in the fictive setting represented here the Scriptures that "Timothy" would have known in his youth could only be the Jewish Scriptures. **Inspired:** The Greek phrase could also be translated "Every Scripture inspired by God is also . . . ," as in the NRSV note. The author assumes the Old Testament is inspired; this is not the disputed point. The issue in his context is whether these documents are valuable for Christian instruction. Some later gnostics such as Marcion did not regard the Old Testament as Christian Scripture, but as the inferior product of the Jewish god who had created this evil world, a different god from the Father of Jesus Christ, who saves souls out of this world. The author here resists all such tendencies and reclaims the Old Testament as Christian Scripture. The author does not define what he means by "**inspired.**" The word literally means "God-breathed," and reflects both the current understanding of how Greek oracles came into being through the "spirit/breath" of the gods (see John 3:3–5) and the Genesis story of the creation of Adam (Gen. 2:7). As in the biblical picture Adam is created from both the earth's soil and the divine breath, so the Scripture is the product of both human and divine action.

3:17 The man of God (NIV): The NRSV's effort to use gender-inclusive language, usually laudable, here misses the Pastor's point by translating "**everyone who belongs to God.**" As in 1 Tim. 6:11, where the same Greek phrase is found, the reference is to the authorized church leadership—exclusively male in the Pastor's setting. Ministers are to be capable interpreters of the Bible as part of the divinely given protection against false teaching.

4:1 God and . . . Christ: The Pastor continues the charge to Christian ministers in the most solemn language, reminding them that their responsibilities are assigned and accepted in the presence of God. Here as often elsewhere in the New Testament, the figures of God and the exalted Christ modulate into each other. One should not ask whether it is God or Christ who judges and whose kingdom will come (see John 3:16 commentary). This is what later Trinitarian theology attempted to articulate, as in the Nicene Creed.

4:2 Proclaim . . . teaching: For the Pastor as for Paul, ministry is basically ministry of the word; ministers are essentially preachers and teachers. The good news of God's saving act in Christ is to be proclaimed in preaching and explored and clarified in teaching.

4:3 The time is coming: As in 3:1 and 1 Tim. 4:1, the "prediction" actually portrays the situation of the Pastor's own time.

4:6 Already being poured out: See Phil. 2:17. What is there considered future is here already happening.

4:7 I have kept the faith: Again Paul is presented as the model for faithful ministers. "The faith" is not the subjective act of believing, but the objective content of the deposit of faith handed on in the Pauline tradition (see on 1:12, 14).

4:9–18
PERSONAL INSTRUCTIONS

The realistic personal details of this section are sometimes taken as evidence that at least 2 Timothy was written directly by Paul himself. Such details were a common feature, however, of pseudepigraphical letters of the time. Here they give a realistic, personal tone to the letter as a whole: the readers are to understand it as really Paul's voice they hear in the compositions of the Pauline school that continues to represent the apostle's teaching after his martyrdom (see the introduction to 1 Timothy). The details are not mere stage setting or window dressing, nor are they an attempt to deceive the original readers, who recognized the literary form. They present a particular picture of the suffering apostle that is to serve as a model of authentic ministry. The fifteen individuals mentioned in this section (apart from Paul, Timothy, and the opponents) illustrate that the Pauline gospel is not dependent on Paul himself. After his death, the large group of coworkers continues his message and mission. So also the listing of places (Thessalonica, Galatia, Dalmatia, Ephesus, Troas, Corinth, Miletus) highlights the continuing influence of the Pauline gospel in the area he and his associates had evangelized.

4:10 Demas: See Phlm. 24; Col. 4:14. **Crescens:** Mentioned only here in the New Testament. **Titus:** See the introduction to Titus.

4:11 Only Luke is with me: Phlm. 24; Col. 4:14. Once-faithful followers are now (in the Pastor's time) abandoning Paul (see on 1:15). **Mark:** Phlm. 24; Col. 4:10; Acts 12:12, 25; 15:27, 39. The names of Mark and Luke were attached to the anonymous Gospels that bear their name (see introduction to Mark, introduction to Luke). This may have already happened in the time of the Pastor. If so, the Gospels and their authors (neither of whom was an apostle) are portrayed as finding their leader and guide in Paul, i.e., the Gospel form is legitimated by its association with the earlier Pauline kerygma.

4:12 Tychicus: Not mentioned in the undisputed letters of Paul, but five post-Pauline documents picture him as a faithful coworker of Paul: Col. 4:7; Eph. 6:21; Acts 20:4; 2 Tim. 4:12; Titus 3:12.

4:13 Cloak: On the one hand, we have here a personal note, full of pathos—winter is coming and Paul needs his cloak (see v. 21). There is also an embedded theological meaning: the cloak was the symbol of authority (see 1 Kgs. 19:19–21; 2 Kgs. 2:6–15). As we still speak of the "mantle of leadership" being passed from a departing senior official to the leader of the next generation, so the apostolic cloak "Timothy" is charged to bring symbolized the apostolic authority that would be transmitted to Paul's successors in the Pauline school responsible for the authorship of the Pastoral epistles. **Books . . . parchments:** We do not know the nature or contents of these documents. The former may point to the Pauline letters that had been collected and were beginning to be considered sacred, the latter to the Scripture. The three together suggest the symbols of authority being passed from the founding generation to the leadership of succeeding generations: the cloak of apostolic authority (later symbolized by vestments received at ordination), the Scriptures (the Old Testament; see on 3:15–16), and the apostolic writings themselves that would become the core of the developing New Testament.

4:14 Alexander the coppersmith: See 1 Tim. 1:20; Acts 19:33. Here and in vv. 10–12, the Pastorals share with Acts several details not found in the undisputed letters of Paul. Luke–Acts stands in the same post-Pauline tradition as the Pastorals. By the Pastor's time Luke–Acts may have already been associated with Luke the companion of Paul. Both the Pastorals and Luke–Acts contend for a similar "orthodox" interpretation of Paul against that of the false teachers.

4:17 The Lord stood by me: Others abandon Paul; the Lord stands by him. Paul is pictured as being given a brief reprieve before his impending death, so that the Christian message could continue to be proclaimed to all the world—again, Paul is the model for faithful ministry.

4:19–22
FINAL GREETINGS AND BENEDICTION

4:19 Prisca and Aquila: See Acts 18:2, 18, 26; Rom. 16:3; 1 Cor. 16:19. **Onesiphorus:** See 1:16. **Erastus:** Acts 19:22; Rom. 16:23. **Trophimus:** Acts 20:4; 21:29.

4:21 Come before winter: These are represented as Paul's last words. He wants to see his friend and coworker Timothy; he needs the cloak in the cold, damp prison (v. 13). The words are not triumphalistic, but resonate with the pathos of a truly human servant of Christ who suffers for the faith, whose weakness and vulnerability is itself a testimony to the meaning of the cross of Jesus (see on 2 Cor. 10–13). **Eubulus, Pudens, Linus, Claudia:** Though later legends developed about all of these, this bare reference is all that is known about them from the New Testament.

4:22 The Lord be with your spirit: The letter is unique in having two concluding benedictions. In this first, the "your" is singular, the personal address to "Timothy." In the second, **Grace be with you,** the "you" is plural, the fictive mask of a letter to "Timothy" is dropped, and it becomes clear that the letter is addressed through "Timothy" to the church and its ministry. **Amen:** This concluding word is found in most, but not all MSS. The letter concludes with a liturgical response, showing it was written for reading aloud in public worship, like the undisputed Pauline letters written for churches.

The Letter of Paul to Titus

INTRODUCTION

Titus was a Gentile Christian coworker of Paul's who accompanied him to the Jerusalem Council as a "test case" (see Gal. 2:1–10), helped him resolve the problems in the Corinthian church (2 Cor. 2:13; 7:5–16), and assisted with the collection from the Gentile churches to be presented in Jerusalem (2 Cor. 8:6, 16–24). This document represents Paul writing to Titus, whom he has left on Crete to organize new churches in the Pauline mission. This situation fits neither the chronology inferred from the undisputed Pauline letters nor that of Acts (which never mentions Titus or a mission to Crete). In order to fit this situation into the life of Paul as we otherwise know it, one must postulate that Paul was released from his "first" Roman imprisonment after Acts 28:31 and established churches on Crete. It is more likely that Titus, like 1–2 Timothy, was written in Paul's name by a disciple of the second or third Christian generation, and that the situation projected by the letter belongs to the literary world projected by the letter rather than to the actual life of Paul. For a general introduction to the Pastoral Epistles (1–2 Timothy, Titus), see the introduction to 1 Timothy.

Outline

1:1–4 Salutation
1:5–3:11 Body
  1:5–9 Elders
  1:10–16 Warnings
  2:1–10 Instructions for the Christian Household
  2:11–15 Theological Basis: The Appearance of Christ
  3:1–2 Instructions to the Whole Church
  3:3–8 Theological Basis: Conversion and Baptism
  3:10–11 Final Warning
3:12–15 Travel Plans, Greetings, Benediction

For Further Reading

Bassler, Jouette. *1 Timothy, 2 Timothy, Titus*. Nashville: Abingdon, 1996.

Collins, Raymond F. *I and II Timothy and Titus: A Commentary*. New Testament Library. Louisville, KY: Westminster John Knox, 2002.

COMMENTARY

1:1–4
SALUTATION

1:1 Paul ... an apostle: The letter to Titus, like the other Pastorals, sets forth the apostolic faith in opposition to the seductive false teachings that threatened the church in the postapostolic period. In the understanding of the Pauline school, Paul played the key apostolic role in the saving plan of God that extended from before creation to the end of time, of which the Christ event was the center. While such a long explanation of the meaning of apostleship (the longest in the New Testament) would be inappropriate in a personal letter to a trusted coworker of many years, this officious-sounding greeting is appropriate in establishing the apostolic claim of the letter for the later generations to which it is in fact addressed. This passage, along with 2:11–15 and 3:4–7, constitutes the Pastor's summary of Pauline theology (see there).

1:2 Hope: The Pastorals oppose the hyperrealized eschatology of the false teachers that reduces everything to present experience (see 2:13 and see on 2 Tim. 2:18), and thus all emphasize the reality of the future hope in their opening words (see 1 Tim. 1:1; 2 Tim. 1:1).

1:3 I have been entrusted: Paul is regarded as the guarantor of the authentic gospel handed on from the first generation (see 2 Tim. 2:2).

1:4 My loyal child: Better, "legitimate," as in 1 Tim. 1:2. In the two generations after Paul's martyrdom, the disputed issue in Pauline Christianity was who were the authentic heirs and interpreters of the Pauline tradition. **The faith we share:** See Jude 3. Paul had used the term "faith" primarily to express the believer's relation to God and Christ, "obedience in personal trust." In the Pastor's theology, "faith" usually refers to the content of the authentic Christian tradition, the faith that is to be believed, rather than the faith with which one believes.

1:5–3:11
BODY

The thanksgiving section, which occurs at this point in the conventional letter form, is omitted here (see on 1 Tim. 1:3).

1:5–9
ELDERS

1:5 I left you behind in Crete: This situation is not otherwise documented in the undisputed Pauline letters or in Acts, but represents the situation in the Pastor's time. Paul has been martyred and has left his disciples and coworkers behind to continue the church's mission (see on 1 Tim. 1:3; 3:14; 4:13). **Elders in every town:** The letters that unquestionably come from Paul never refer to elders (see on 1 Tim. 3:1–13). Church offices developed in the following two generations to lead the church in its mission and to protect it from false teaching. The Pastor attributes the establishment of such offices to the authority of Paul. The house churches in each city were governed by a representative council of elders (presbytery; see 1 Tim. 4:14). **As I directed you:** The line of authority is from Paul to "Titus" (representing the Pauline school) to local elders to churches (see on 1 Tim. 4:14; 2 Tim. 2:2).
1:6 Blameless, married only once: On the qualifications for church leaders, see on 1 Tim. 3:1–13. As elsewhere, the Pastor requires church leaders to be respectable citizens who have married and raised orderly families, in opposition to the ascetic views of the false teachers (1 Tim. 4:3). While 1 Tim. 3 distinguishes "elders" from "the bishop," here the two terms seem to be used interchangeably (see Acts 20:17, 28), or at least to overlap. The difference between 1 Timothy and Titus on this point probably indicates that the development of church structure did not proceed evenly in all the Pauline churches. Titus seems to reflect a transitional phase in which one elder is assuming the rule of overseer (bishop), a development that had already occurred in the churches reflected in 1 Timothy. By the time of Ignatius (ca. 112), the churches in Asia Minor seem to have developed the threefold ministry of deacons and elders in local churches,

presided over by a bishop who was responsible for all the congregations in a particular city or region. This later became the standard pattern of church structure.

1:9 Must have a firm grasp on the word: Ministers are essentially ministers of the word (see 1 Tim. 4:13). **Trustworthy in accordance with the teaching:** See the RSV, "must hold firm to the sure word as taught." Among the competing new interpretations of Paul in the Pastor's time, the elder/bishop has the responsibility to keep the churches on course (see 2 Tim. 2:2). He does this not by authoritarian decrees, but by being a good teacher of the traditional faith.

1:10–16
WARNINGS

1:10 Especially those of the circumcision: See v. 14. The Pastor is particularly distrustful of Christian teachers who have some connection to or fascination with Judaism, who claim to be experts in the Old Testament law (see on 1 Tim. 1:4–11). Crete had a sizable Jewish population, and converts from Judaism who continued to interpret the new Christian faith in Jewish categories may have been part of the problem. Some Gentile gnostic Christians were also fascinated by the Old Testament, which they interpreted allegorically as a basis for their heretical teachings.
1:11 Upsetting whole families: See 3:6; 1 Tim. 3:5, 15. Since the early churches were house churches, meeting in the homes of believers whose houses could accommodate them, there was often no firm line between "household" and "congregation."
1:12 Cretans are always liars: This pejorative caricature was expressed in a well-known proverb from the sixth-century BCE poet Epimenides, a native of Crete. **Prophet:** Used here in its generic sense, "spokesperson." The point is that one of their own called them liars. Such polemics, common in ancient rhetoric, do not authorize the modern Christian to engage in racial, national, or sex stereotyping.
1:15–16 To the pure all things are pure: The opponents advocate an ascetic lifestyle that attends to the purity laws of the Old Testament and later Jewish tradition. The Pastor understands adherence to such laws as a denial of the goodness of creation and locates impurity not in things, but in the heart (see 1 Tim. 4:1–5; Mark 7:1–23).
  Their minds and consciences are corrupt: For the Pastor's descriptions of the false teachers, see on 1 Tim. 4:1–5; 2 Tim. 3:1–9; and the notes there.

2:1–10
INSTRUCTIONS FOR THE
CHRISTIAN HOUSEHOLD

In this section the Pastor adapts the traditional form of the household code in order to present instructions to various groups in the Christian household, the church (see on 1 Tim. 3:15; Col. 3:18–4:1; 1 Pet. 2:11–3:12). Though written to "Titus," the literary form of the pseudepigraphical letter serves as the vehicle for instructions to the church as a whole (see introduction to 1 Timothy). While in the Pastor's context he believed it was appropriate that only authorized men serve in teaching roles (1 Tim. 2:11–15), every Christian of whatever status in any social situation can serve as a teacher of the faith by the way he or she reflects the faith in daily life.

2:1 What is consistent with sound doctrine: Christian life is based on Christian theology, how the faith is understood. Doctrine is not merely abstract and theoretical, but the basis for life (see on Rom. 12:1).

2:2 Older men: A different Greek word than that for "elders," a church office, in 1:5. **Endurance:** Replaces "hope" in the familiar Pauline triad of "faith, hope, and love" (1 Thess. 1:3; 5:8; 1 Cor. 13:13). Here "endurance" is not merely putting up with various troubles, but the steadfast active waiting for the fulfillment of God's promise of eternal life at the Parousia of Christ (1:2; 2:13; 3:7; see Rom. 5:1–5).

2:3 Older women: Their teaching responsibilities are here confined to the home (see on 1 Tim. 2:11–15), where they are to inculcate the "feminine virtues" of good household management.

2:4 Love their husbands . . . children: Corresponding to the cultural assumptions of the time, it is assumed that younger women will be married and raise families (see on 2 Tim. 3:6).

2:5 So that the word of God may not be discredited: The ancient author of course had no awareness of the social and legal equality of women and men in the modern sense. His concern throughout is with the mission of the church; he does not want outsiders to think that the new religious community and its mission, of which they were already suspicious, undermines traditional "family values." Christians of whatever social status are to conduct their lives and express their faith in ways that do not violate community standards and bring disrepute to the faith. Potential converts, beloved of the God who wills the salvation of all (1 Tim. 2:4), are not to be put off by breach of cultural norms and prevent them from getting within hearing distance of the gospel. There is a scandalous element in the Christian faith, but it is the crucified Christ (Gal. 5:11). False stumbling blocks should not be erected that might serve as pretexts for unbelievers to continue rejecting the faith.

2:8 Having nothing evil to say of us: Likewise the conduct of young men must not be merely according to their own standards of what is good and right; they must live their lives in view of how the Christian community to which they belong and which they represent will be regarded by unbelieving neighbors.

2:9 Tell slaves to be submissive: For slavery in the ancient world, see the introduction to Philemon. Regarding New Testament instruction to slaves, see on Col. 3:22; Eph. 6:5–9; 1 Pet. 2:11–3:12. Some slaves had become Christian when whole households were converted, and thus had the same religion as their masters. Others became Christians independently of their masters and had thus already shown some courage. Here they are addressed as persons in their own right, who can make their own decisions, not as mere property or chattels of their masters.

2:10 Complete and perfect fidelity so that . . . : As in the case of free women and men (vv. 5, 8), so even slaves are to do their work responsibly, in a manner that will bring honor to the faith they profess.

2:11–15
THEOLOGICAL BASIS:
THE APPEARANCE OF CHRIST

The discourse now moves to another level. This passage, along with the theological summary of 3:4–7 and the summary of the meaning of apostleship in 1:1–4, constitutes a brief synthesis of the traditional Pauline faith. In all three passages, the Pastor is not composing freehand, but incorporating traditional creedal and liturgical material. Three main points are made:

1. *The universality of God's grace.* That grace has **appeared** (v. 11) illustrates that grace is an act, not merely a personal quality. The same is true of God's love (see on John 3:16). The NRSV's **bringing salvation to all** (v. 11) can also be translated **has appeared to all**. In either case, the point is that God's grace is not exclusive, not limited either to a chosen people in the Jewish sense or to spiritually elite in the gnostic sense; the Pastor is opposing both tendencies. God's grace is for the salvation of everyone; the last word of the Bible is the word "all" (see 1 Tim. 2:4–6; 4:10; and

the excursus, "Universal Salvation and Paradoxical Theology," at Rev. 22:21).

2. *The saving act of God in Christ as the key to the meaning of life and history.* The paragraph speaks of two appearances of Christ, one in the past (v. 11) and one in the eschatological future (v. 13). The first advent/appearance is centered on the saving death of Christ, which is not a different reality from the self-giving act of *God* (see commentary on 2:13 below, and discussion of the saving event as a two-party transaction at 2 Cor. 5:19–21). The **for us** of v. 14 is correlated with the "for all" of 1 Tim. 2:6, and maintains the tension between universal and limited salvation, between divine sovereignty and human responsibility.

3. *The transforming power of God's grace:* A transformed life is the result (not the cause or condition) of God's gracious act in Christ. The Christian people addressed in 2:1–10 not only must, but can fulfill their responsibilities because they live between the two advents of Christ, the first of which redeemed them (= set them free) from the powers that enslaved them, so that they could in fact be **a people of his own who are zealous for good deeds** (v. 14). Here, without any suggestion that the church has superseded Israel as the people of God, the language of the Old Testament chosen people is applied to those of Christian faith (see Paul's full discussion in Rom. 9–11). The Pastor emphasizes the "not yet" dimension of Christian faith (see 2 Tim. 2:18). There is a second appearance of Christ, still to come. Christian life looks back to the appearance of God's grace in Christ, and forward to the triumph of that grace, bringing salvation to all.

2:13 Our great God and Savior: This phrase was used on an inscription in Ephesus devoted to Caesar. In the Pastor's Christology, not Caesar but Christ is the manifestation of God; the figures of God and Christ fade into each other. This is one of the few places in the New Testament where God-language is used of the exalted Christ (not the human being Jesus of Nazareth; see John 1:1; 20:30). In a way that compromises neither the humanity of Jesus nor monotheistic faith in the one God, Christ and God can be spoken of together as one reality (see on 2 Cor. 5:19–21; John 3:16). Later Trinitarian theology, as in the Nicene Creed, attempted to safeguard this mystery in appropriate language.

3:1–2
INSTRUCTIONS TO THE WHOLE CHURCH

3:1 Remind them: These instructions were already current in the Pauline tradition circulating in the Pastor's churches; see Rom.

13:1–7; 1 Tim. 2:1–2; 1 Pet. 2:13–17. Even in a pagan society, Christians are not to withdraw from the world but to conduct themselves as good citizens. In the Pastor's view, obedience to authorized authority—to the order God has established in the political world, the family, and the church as the household of God—is integral to the life of faith.

3:2 Courtesy to everyone: Christians relate to all people as God's beloved creatures whom he wills to save, whether they realize it or not (2:11). Christian faith and insight into God's saving act causes one to treat all people with loving respect.

3:3–8
THEOLOGICAL BASIS:
CONVERSION AND BAPTISM

As in 2:1–10, 11–15, so also here the ethical instructions are grounded in a substantial theological affirmation derived from the church's liturgical and creedal tradition (see 1:1–4; 2:11–15). Verses 4–7 are identified in v. 8 as a "faithful saying" (see on 1 Tim. 1:15). The unit reflects the threefold schema derived from Paul's own theology and elaborated in Romans:

1. The human condition apart from God's grace (see Rom. 1–3)
2. God's saving act (see Rom. 4–11)
3. The Christian life (see Rom. 12–16)

The Pastor, however, begins with the Christian life (vv. 1–2), then sets forth its theological basis (vv. 3–7).

3:3 We ourselves were once . . . disobedient: The Christian life is contrasted with the human situation prior to receiving God's grace. When writing to Gentile Christians, Paul had portrayed their former life in lurid terms (Rom. 1:19–31; 6:17–19; 1 Cor. 6:9–11); contrast Paul's estimate of his own pre-Christian life in Phil. 3:4b–6. The Pauline school made Paul himself into a model of conversion from sinful depravity to Christian "good works" (Eph. 2:1–10; 1 Tim. 1:12–16).

3:4 The loving kindness of God our Savior appeared: The first coming of *Christ*, the appearance of Jesus in history, is seen as the epiphany of *God*. On this identification of Christ with God, see on 2:13. The advent of Christ is both *revelatory* in that it discloses the character of God, and *effective* in that God acts through the Christ event for human salvation.

3:5 Not because of any works of righteousness that we had done: As in Paul, salvation is entirely the gift of God, not the reward for human good works (see Rom. 3:21–26; 4:1–

5:11). **Good works** are the response to God's grace, not its cause (v. 8). **Water of rebirth:** Baptism is here related to conversion, pictured as rebirth (see John 3:3–5). As in Paul, baptism unites the believer with the Christ event, incorporating the believer's own life into that of Christ at the point of crucifixion and forgiveness, not at the point of resurrection and glorification, which remains future (Rom. 6:1–11; see Col. 3:1–4; Eph. 2:1–6; 2 Tim. 2:18).

3:7 Heirs according to the hope of eternal life: Like Paul (Rom. 5:1–11; 8:24), the Pastor can speak of salvation as both a past event (v. 5) and a future hope. The Christian life is located between the first and second advents of Christ, both of which are called "epiphanies" (translated "manifestation" or "appearance" in 1 Tim. 6:14; 2 Tim. 1:10; 4:1, 8; Titus 2:13). On the "between-the-times" character of Christian existence, see on 2:11–15.

3:8 The saying is sure: The fifth and final of the "faithful sayings"; see on 1 Tim. 1:15. The Pastor here identifies 3:4–7 as reliable, authoritative traditional material.

3:9 Controversies, genealogies: See on 1 Tim. 1:4; 2 Tim. 2:23.

3:10–11
FINAL WARNING

3:10–11 Anyone who causes divisions: Those who advocate the new "progressive" doc-

trines the Pastor rejects (see 1 Tim. 4:1–5; 2 Tim. 3:1–9). **First and second admonition:** See Matt. 18:15–17. **Have nothing more to do with:** See 1 Cor. 5:11; Rom. 16:17; 2 Thess. 3:6, 14–15. **Perverted:** By departing from the traditional Pauline theology.

3:12–15
TRAVEL PLANS, GREETINGS, BENEDICTION

On personal details, see on 2 Tim. 4:9–18. The passage expresses a concern for continuity in ministry: the absent Paul authorizes Titus to act in his stead (as 1:5), who in turn is to send forth other ministers, Zenas and Apollos. Titus himself is to be replaced by Artemas or Tychicus. Some of these are known from other New Testament references: **Tychicus** (see on 2 Tim. 4:12); **Apollos** (Acts 18:24–19:1; 1 Cor. 3:5–15; 16:12). Others are mentioned only here in the New Testament, and nothing more is known of them: **Zenas, Artemas**. The letter thus concludes with an allusive, indirect portrayal of the church in the Pastor's time (and ours): named and anonymous Christians and ministers continuing the work of the absent Paul, in continuity with the tradition he has left behind, as instructed in this letter. The closing blessing on **all of you** (v. 15) is again plural (see on 2 Tim. 4:22), embracing all readers of the letter who continue in the apostolic faith, then and now.

The Letter of Paul to Philemon

INTRODUCTION

No one has presented a convincing argument against Philemon as an authentic letter of Paul. The letter is not private, since Apphia, Archippus, and the church meeting in Philemon's house are included in the address (v. 2). The greeting of grace and peace is to all of them (plural "you," v. 3). However, the message of the letter is a personal one from Paul to Philemon; the "you" is singular from v. 4 until v. 22b. Since Paul's letters were read aloud in the assembly of the congregation, a direct message to one in the presence of all presents an interesting dynamic. Although some attempts have been made to identify Philemon with a letter to the Laodiceans mentioned by Paul in Col. 4:16, that theory has not been established. Given the correspondence of names of persons with Paul and persons to whom he sends greeting (Col. 1:1, 7; 4:7–17; Phlm. 1, 2, 10, 23–24), Philemon and Colossians appear to be companion letters to the same city and from the same place of Paul's imprisonment (Col. 4:3, 10, 18; Phlm. 1, 9, 13).

The destination is Colossae (compare especially Col. 4:9 and Phlm. 10–11), but the place of origin is less clear. Some scholars opt for Rome, a known place of imprisonment, which would date the letter in the early 60s and satisfy Paul's self-description as an old man (v. 9). However, the distance between Rome and Colossae argues against this theory. Would a runaway slave go all the way to Rome? Would Paul from Rome request the preparation of a guest room in anticipation of a visit soon? Some scholars are more satisfied with Ephesus as the place of origin and the mid-50s as a date. But the apostle of many imprisonments (2 Cor. 11:23) could have written from a number of places unknown to us.

The letter is occasioned by Onesimus, a fugitive slave from the household of Philemon, who has come to Paul and become a Christian and a helper to Paul in prison. Now he is being returned to Philemon with Paul's request that he be received as a brother and fellow worker. In making the request, Paul presents himself to the reader and listeners as a man of wit, humor, understated authority, gentle persuasion, and not at all hesitant to call in IOUs.

Slavery in the Hellenistic World

Slavery was a social institution almost universally accepted in the first-century Mediterranean world. While a few philosophers taught the essential equality of all human beings, slave or free, even they did not advocate abolition of slavery as an institution, and practically everyone accepted slavery as a given and necessary part of the social and economic order. The question was not raised, just as the question of the legitimacy of the injustice brought about by private property is not raised in a capitalist culture. In the first-century world, only the Jewish sect of the Essenes rejected slavery (Josephus, *Antiquities* 18.1.5 §21; Philo, *De vita contemplativa* 9 §70–71; see Quod omnis probus liber 12 § 79), just as they rejected other social institutions such as marriage. They rejected neither slavery nor marriage as a social institution for the public at large, but as the practice of their own sect. There were no protests against the institution of slavery as such in the Hellenistic world. The Gladiatorial War against Rome, led by the escaped gladiator slave Spartacus in 73–71 BCE, was not an attempt at social revolution, just as the war of independence fought by the American colonists was for their own freedom, not an attempt to abolish monarchy as an institution.

Slavery meant that one person was owned by another; it was a matter of property and property rights. Slaves could thus be bought and sold, rented, and given to others as gifts. One could become a slave by being born of slave parents, by being exposed as a baby, by being kidnapped by pirates, as a prisoner of war, or by selling oneself into slavery to pay one's debts. Most slaves in the first century had been born as slaves and had a well-defined place in the household and social structure. Many slaves were well-educated, and they constituted a significant element of the managerial class (as, for example, in the stories of Jesus in Matt. 18:23–35; 24:45–51; and Luke 16:1–13—some translations soften the picture by rendering the word as "servant" rather than the more accurate "slave"). It was to the owner's advantage to provide education for his or her slaves, since this enhanced both their usefulness and their value. Slaves could be bought out of slavery by others or could accumulate enough money to purchase their own freedom. Slaves had some limited legal rights, e.g., if their master treated them too harshly, they could demand to be sold to another master. Some slaves were paid wages, with which they purchased their freedom; some even owned their own slaves.

Slavery was not a matter of race; slaves could not be recognized as slaves on the street. While the slave's life was usually not easy in the ancient world, North American readers should not read into the New Testament the terrible pictures of the enslavement of Africans by Europeans and Americans. There was not always a wide gap between slaves and free, most slaves were humanely treated by their owners, and the modern reader should not assume that every slave wanted to be free. Like Jesus, Paul and other early Christians never questioned the institution of slavery as such, but the Christian community declared that "in Christ" the distinction between slave and free had been abolished (see Gal. 3:27–28) and attempted to live as Christians within the existing social structures (see on Col. 3:18–4:1, Eph. 5:21–6:9; 1 Pet. 2:13–3:7).

Outline

For Further Reading

Fitzmyer, Joseph A. *The Letter to Philemon: A New Translation with Introduction and Commentary.* Anchor Bible 32C. New York: Doubleday, 2000.

Lohse, Eduard. *Colossians and Philemon.* Hermeneia. Philadelphia: Fortress, 1971.

Osiek, Carolyn. *Philippians, Philemon.* Abingdon New Testament Commentaries. Nashville: Abingdon, 2000.

COMMENTARY

1–3
SALUTATION

1 Paul, a prisoner: Paul does not add his usual "apostle" or "servant of Jesus Christ" to his name. However, "prisoner of Christ Jesus" is not without authority. To be in prison for the gospel (v. 13), to share in the sufferings of Christ, gave Paul credentials worthy of the church's ear. And as will be seen, Paul will continue throughout the letter with the emo-

tional appeal of understated authority. **Timothy our brother:** As elsewhere, Timothy is Paul's associate (2 Cor. 1:1; Col. 1:1), but apart from Timothy's participation in the "our" of vv. 1–3, the letter is from Paul alone.

To Philemon our dear friend: Literally "beloved," "loved" (by God and by Paul). Philemon is called "**beloved**" just as Onesimus will be later (v. 16). The ground is laid for owner and slave to be brothers in God's love.

2 Apphia, our sister: May be Philemon's wife who has a share in decisions to be made. At least as a member of the Christian community, she is a leader, as the location of her name in the address implies. **Archippus our fellow soldier:** See Phil. 2:25; an image of one who shared in ministry "under fire," under adversarial circumstances (see 1 Cor. 9:7; 2 Cor. 10:3–4). In Col. 4:17 Paul had a specific directive for Archippus. The entire church meeting in Philemon's house is included in the address, meaning they were to hear what Paul said to Philemon (for other house churches, see Rom. 16:3–5, 23; 1 Cor. 16:15, 19; Col. 4:15; Acts 12:12; 16:40).

3 Grace and peace from God the Father and the Lord Jesus Christ: Of course, all are included in Paul's customary greeting.

4–7
THANKSGIVING

4–5 When I remember you: Paul now speaks directly to Philemon as the singular "you" makes clear. The Pauline thanksgiving, elsewhere addressed to a church (Phil. 1:3–11; Col. 1:3–8; 1 Thess. 1:2–5), here focuses on Philemon. He is constantly in Paul's prayers, and with gratitude (v. 4), because of the good report he has received about Philemon. The report contains two elements: **love** for all the saints and **faith** in the Lord Jesus. In the Greek text, love for all the saints is a split expression opening and closing v. 5, an arrangement that highlights this element of the good report. Obviously, Paul is anticipating the appeal soon to follow.

6 I pray: Here Paul turns to the second element of the report: Philemon's **faith**. It is Paul's prayer that **the sharing** (fellowship) of Philemon's faith will be **effective** (operative) in the knowledge of all the good in us for Christ. The "good" may refer both to all that God has granted us and to the good work God performs through us (Rom. 8:28; 1 Thess. 5:15; Gal. 6:12). If God's good is in us, then the good deed Paul expects from Philemon (v. 14) is neither unreasonable nor unexpected.

7 I have indeed received: Paul returns again to the theme of Philemon's **love**, which has been a source of **joy and encouragement** for Paul and for the faith community a source of refreshment for the heart. Precisely what Philemon has done for the saints is not stated, but it has **refreshed** (renewed) their **hearts**. At v. 20 Paul will ask Philemon to refresh his heart by receiving Onesimus as a brother.

8–22
MESSAGE

8 For this reason: Paul feels he has laid the foundation for his "therefore," the actual request to be made. Even so, he still moves to it slowly. He has not yet mentioned Onesimus; rather Paul begins with the basis of his appeal. His restraint is persuasive. He is bold enough to proceed from apostolic authority and command Philemon to do **"what you ought"** (NIV; literally what is fitting). That which would be fitting is soon spelled out.

9 I would rather appeal to you: The course Paul prefers, however, is marked by two words: "appeal" (beseech, encourage) and "love," of which Paul has repeatedly spoken (vv. 5–7). And who makes this appeal of love? Paul the old man, Paul the prisoner who shares Christ's suffering (v. 9). He has Philemon's attention and respect. In fact, Paul's approach, heard in the presence of the church, is stronger than a command.

10 My child, Onesimus: Again Paul says "I appeal to you," and in the Greek text does not name Onesimus until he has called him **my child, whose father I have become during my imprisonment** (the Greek word is literally "generate" and can mean either "beget" or "give birth to"). Paul often spoke of believers as his children (1 Cor. 4:15–17; Gal. 4:19; 1 Thess. 1:11). This is not paternalism, but reflects the Jewish teaching preserved in the Talmud that if a man teaches Torah to another's child, it is as if he had begotten that child (*b. Sanh.* 19b). Since Paul also converted Philemon (v. 19), Philemon and Onesimus are now brothers. It was not uncommon in that culture for persons of power and influence to intercede for slaves or prisoners.

11 Formerly . . . but now: Onesimus, whose name means "useful" or "helpful," was, of course, useless to Philemon as a runaway, but now he is useful to both Philemon and Paul. The words "useless" (*achrestos*) and "useful" (*euchrestos*) constitute not only a play on

words but the root word *chrestos*, which was pronounced similarly to the word "Christ." A rough paraphrase would be, "he was un-Christ to you, but now is good-Christ to you." Paul's choice of words keeps Philemon in a Christian context.

12–14 Him . . . my own heart: For Paul, to return Onesimus is to send his own heart. The treatment accorded Onesimus upon his return is thus treatment accorded Paul. Paul could well have retained Onesimus as Philemon's representative attending to the prisoner's needs, but Paul wants Philemon's willingness from the heart, **not** his **forced** obedience.

15 Perhaps this is the reason: At this point Paul muses on God's will, wondering if the temporary separation between Philemon and Onesimus might have been to bring about a larger good, that they be joined forever **in the Lord**, not as master-slave but as **brothers**.

17 Welcome him as you would welcome me: Paul's appeal becomes direct; what was implied in v. 12 (I am sending back my own heart) is now stated clearly. If we are partners, welcome him as you would me. If reparations or compensations are in order, Paul asks that such charges be put on his **account**. There is no clear implication that such was or was not the case, but Paul speaks in the appropriate legal and economic terms.

19 I will repay it: In fact, above his own signature he gives his promissory note, with the subtle but forceful reminder: "Speaking of debts, I will not mention the fact that you owe me your very life." By this nonstatement statement, Paul moves the topic out of the courtroom and accounting office into the gospel and the freedom of God's grace that all three now enjoy.

20–22 Let me have this benefit: To this Paul adds three statements, each one seeming to be his last, thus finishing with a persuasive rhetorical flourish. First, **refresh my heart** (recall v. 7); grant me this **benefit** ("benefit" is a form of the word Onesimus). Second, I am persuaded that you will go beyond my request and **do even more**. Third, prepare a lodging for me because I hope **through your** (plural, the whole community) **prayers to be restored** (returned) **to you** and all the church there. If any hesitation remained in Philemon, certainly it was now dispelled.

23–24
GREETINGS

23 Sends greetings: Just as the presence of the church surrounding Philemon gave weight to the letter at the point of reception, so the company of fellow workers with Paul strengthened the letter at its sending. Philemon would know that not only Timothy (v. 1) but also five other Christian leaders would be aware of the letter. The names of these coworkers correspond with the list in Col. 4:7–17. For someone who was not commanded in what to do but who was left to act freely from his heart, Philemon has been pointed to a path well lighted with no attractive alternative.

25
FAREWELL

25 Grace: The grace that Paul desired for Philemon and the church in his house at the letter's beginning (v. 3) is here repeated. **With your spirit:** Used elsewhere by Paul (Gal. 6:18; Phil. 4:23). The farewell reminds all the recipients that the community has all its life and relationships in the grace of our Lord Jesus Christ.

The Letter to the Hebrews

INTRODUCTION

Hebrews, traditionally identified as a letter, is designated by the author himself as a "word of exhortation" (13:22). This same expression occurs at Acts 13:15 to refer to Paul's speech in vv. 16–41, a speech noticeably similar to Hebrews. In other words, Hebrews is a sermon. In the sermon, expositions of Scripture are followed by exhortations based on the texts cited, altogether serving as fuel to keep alive a fire that seems to be flickering out. A host of literary devices and communication strategies are used in this letter-sermon. Metaphors abound, drawn from athletics, agriculture, education, architecture, seafaring, courts of law, and more. Verbs are noticeably in the present tense, and the language of speaking prevails over that of writing (2:5; 5:11; 6:9). However, Hebrews is not simply a sermon, but a sermon containing sermons (1:5–2:4; 2:5–3:1; 8:1–10:25). In this respect, Hebrews resembles Deuteronomy, which is Moses' final sermon to Israel but also a collection of sermons within the sermon. In the commentary to follow, Hebrews will sometimes be called a letter and sometimes a sermon.

Authorship and Date

As to authorship, the identification with the apostle Paul has a long history. In a third-century manuscript, Hebrews follows Romans among the letters of Paul. Both Clement and Origen, leaders in the great Christian intellectual center of Alexandria, judged the content of Hebrews to be from Paul. However, the style of the letter was so different from the remainder of the Pauline corpus that they concluded the actual writing had been done by another, perhaps Luke or Clement of Rome. In the Western church, early writers did not include Hebrews among the letters of Paul. Tertullian, for example, suggested Barnabas as the author. However, by the fifth century, the Western church accepted Pauline authorship, a position dominant until the Reformation. But the debate would not die. Students of both Paul and Hebrews found difficulty in attributing to Paul the language and literary style as well as in the admitted second-generation position of the letter (2:3). Other candidates have included Silas, Priscilla, and Apollos. Fortunately, neither canonical authority nor theological merit depends on having the name of the author. However, the unnamed writer does have some visibility as a Christian who lives and thinks within the apostolic tradition (2:3). Timothy has been a companion in ministry and may be again (13:23). The writer is temporarily distanced from the readers, but expects to return to them soon (13:19, 23). Their situation is known in great detail, either through their leaders (13:7, 17, 24) or by direct association. The writer joins strong pastoral concern with the authority of either person or office. Both the instructions and the exhortations of the letter reveal a person well educated in Greek rhetoric as well as in Judaism, especially Hellenistic Judaism formed, in part, by a Greek translation of the Old Testament called the Septuagint (LXX).

Dating Hebrews is likewise a problem. Clement of Rome quoted from it in a letter usually dated 95–96 CE, but how much earlier was it written? According to 2:3, the author belongs to a generation following the apostles. In addition, we are told that Timothy is still active in ministry (13:23). If this is the same Timothy who was a young companion to Paul, a date between 60 and 90 would be appropriate.

Addressees

Who and where were the readers? The writing appears with the title "To Hebrews" in the earliest MSS, but the heading raises more questions than it answers. Certainly the intended readers are Christians (3:6, 14; 4:14; 10:23) and not Jews. The readers and the writer are second-generation believers (2:3–4), having been baptized (6:4–5; 10:22) and fully instructed (6:1–2). In fact, they have been believers long enough to have become teachers (5:12), but they have stalled in their growth. On the one hand the writer chastises them for their infantile spiritual state (5:11–14), and on the other hand he assumes that they are capable of following a lengthy and complex christological argument (6:9–10:39). But now the readers are a faith community in crisis. Some members have grown lax in their attendance at their assemblies (10:25), and commitment is waning. If the writer's urgings are problem-specific, then the letter presents a painfully clear image of their condition. The writer does not think the addressees have hopelessly fallen away (6:4–8). In fact, better things are expected of these believers in view of their past record of love and good works, a record that has not totally come to an end (6:9–10).

Situation

What is the root cause of this crisis in the church? The readers have been under extreme external pressure. Some have been imprisoned, and others have suffered the confiscation of their property (10:34). They have not yet shed blood for their faith (12:4), but the writer does speak of persecution (10:33), hostility (12:3), and torture (13:3 NRSV). By no means the least painful form of pressure was public abuse and ridicule (10:33). The best guess is that the readers are Hellenistic Jewish Christians located in Rome. When the writer says "those from Italy send you greetings" (13:24), it is not clear whether the expression locates the writer or the readers in Italy. However, early knowledge of Hebrews by Clement of Rome makes that city a likely candidate as the location of the addressees. As the letter will make abundantly clear, the author addresses the readers in their critical condition with instruction, warning, exhortation, and encouragement lest their condition become fatal.

Outline

For Further Reading

Craddock, Fred B. "Hebrews." In *The New Interpreter's Bible*, vol. 12. Nashville: Abingdon Press, 1998. Some of the material on Hebrews in the following pages has been drawn from this more expansive treatment.

Williams, R. M. *Hebrews.* New Century Biblical Commentary. Grand Rapids: Eerdmans, 1987.

COMMENTARY

1:1–4
INTRODUCTORY STATEMENT OF FAITH

The first four verses are one carefully composed sentence in the Greek text expressing the faith held in common with the readers. The writer may be quoting from the liturgy of the church addressed or from the "confession" often mentioned (3:1; 4:14; 10:23), creating an atmosphere of trust by beginning on common ground. In addition, the writer introduces the major themes to be developed in the sermon, even using the language of two Old Testament texts very central to all that follows, Pss. 2 and 110.

1:1–2 Long ago God spoke: The sermon that we call Hebrews is predicated on the affirmation that God speaks (1:5–13; 3:7; 4:3; 5:5–6; 7:21; 8:8–13) and on the injunction "See that you do not refuse the one who is speaking" (12:25). This foundational conviction is broadly framed in a balanced statement:

> God spoke   God has spoken
> in the past   in these last days
> to our ancestors   to us
> by the prophets   by a Son

God's past revelation is described in three ways. First, it was in segments or episodes, not continuous. Second, God's speaking took many forms (e.g., voices, events, visions, dreams, stories, and theophanies). Third, revelation came through the prophets, understood in the broad sense as those who spoke for God. Continuous with and distinctly different from past revelation is that which is **to us**. God's speaking is here presented with two qualifying phrases. **In these last days:** The expression is not so much chronological as eschatological. For early Christians, the eschaton was inaugurated by the advent of Jesus Christ. **By a Son:** The absence of the definite article "*the* Son" seems quite purposeful. As a general rule in Greek, the presence of the definite article serves to identify; its absence serves to qualify. In other words, what is the quality or nature of God's speaking? It is through the person of a Son.

Although God continues to be the subject of the verbs in v. 2 ("appointed," "created"), the reader's attention is now being drawn to the Son. **Heir of all things:** This affirmation of the Son is based on Ps. 2:7–8, which will be one of the major sources for developing the Christology of Hebrews. The expression refers to the Son's preexistent life with God; nothing that belongs to God is withheld from the Son. **Through whom he also created the worlds:** The Son was God's agent of creation. That God worked through an intermediary in creating is an idea that developed in Jewish theology (Prov. 8:22–31; Wis. 7:22), the intermediary being called Sophia (Wisdom) or Logos (Word). The church appropriated these terms in developing its understanding of the relation of Christ to God and the praise of Christ as agent of creation entered early into hymn and creed (1 Cor. 8:6; Rom. 11:36; Col. 1:16; John 1:3, 10).

1:3 He is the reflection ... and the exact imprint: Verse 2 spoke of God's relation to the Son; v. 3 speaks of the Son's relation to God. This verse may be all or part of an early christological hymn that has been skillfully incorporated by the writer (see Phil. 2:6–11; Col. 1:15–20; 1 Tim. 3:16). Jewish Wisdom theology contributes the first two of the four statements concerning the Son. Wisdom was God's agent in relating to the world in creation, providence, revelation and reconciliation. According to Wis. 7:24–27, Sophia is the mirrored reflection (radiance) and exact imprint (representation) of God's being. God's being is here called essence or substance, the word (*hypostasis*) used at 11:1 to describe faith as the essence or substance of things hoped for. In other words, what God is, the Son is (John 1:1). The author also appropriates for the Son Wisdom's sustaining relation to the created order. The Son's word not only speaks life into being, but sustains it continually. **He had made purification for sins:** The verse ends with the humiliation and exaltation of the Son. The whole of the Son's earthly career is gathered up in one image: a priest at the altar making purification for sin (see 2 Pet. 1:9). **He sat down at the right hand of the majesty:** Both the completion of the Son's work on earth and his elevation to the highest station are summed up as the Son-Priest is enthroned. Psalm 110 joins king and priest in the presentation of Jesus Christ. Son-Priest-King: already the writer has set out the themes of his sermon and the burden of his argumentation. **1:4 Superior to angels:** This final affirmation about the Son serves as a transition to the first major unit of the text, 1:5–2:18, in which the subject is the Son's relationship to the angels. To say the Son is greater than the angels implies that some persons of a contrary view are in the audience or known to the audience.

1:5–2:18
THE SON AND THE ANGELS

Notice the ways this unit contributes to an understanding of the method and the content of the epistle as a whole.

First, the reader is immediately immersed in citations from the Old Testament. Beginning at 1:5, direct quotations begin and continue with great frequency until the end of the letter, which cites more than thirty Old Testament passages, most of them from the Psalms. On early Christian interpretation of the Old Testament, see the excursus at 1 Cor. 15:3.

Second, in this early unit the reader meets the writer's habit of introducing biblical quotations with verbs of speaking (God says) rather than of writing (it is written). In Hebrews the introductory formula "it is written" occurs only once in a direct citation (10:7) and the noun form (writings or Scripture) not at all. Hearing the Old Testament being "said" to them has significance at two levels for the reader. On one level is the rhetorical impact. After all, Hebrews is a sermon (13:22), and therefore we should expect the author to employ rhetorical strategies. On the theological level, the implications of the author's rhetorical style are unmistakable: the Old Testament is the very speech of God, addressing the hearer in the present.

Third, the structure of 1:5–2:18 is quite clear: exposition (1:5–14); exhortation (2:1–4); exposition (2:5–18); this pattern of alternating exposition and exhortation is sustained throughout.

1:5–14
THE SON SUPERIOR TO ANGELS

Why all this attention to angels? We have to assume that asserting Christ's superiority over angels is important for both writer and readers. It is not a matter of debating the existence or nonexistence of angels; these beings were common to the assumed worlds of early Judaism, Christianity, and other religions of the Near East. Angels (the word means "messengers") were commonly portrayed as God's intermediaries in all the ways God relates to creation and to humanity in particular. In some quarters angelologies were very complex, even including angels who revolted against God and devoted themselves to thwarting God's purposes (Matt. 25:41; Rom. 8:38; Gal. 4:3). Four reasons have been proposed for the author's beginning with this discussion of the relation of Christ to angels: (1) The writer felt the need to elaborate on the reference to angels in the creedal formula in 1:1–4. (2) The nature and role of angels was not a live issue for the readers and therefore provided a perfect foil for a recital of the greatness of Christ. (3) Angels are taken seriously since it was believed that the law was given through angels (2:2), and any adequate defense of the superiority of Christianity to an audience steeped in or attracted to Judaism must establish that Christ is superior to angels. (4) The writer may be confronting the problem of angel worship in the church of his readers (see Col. 2:18; Rev. 19:10; 22:8–9). The interpretive task is to make a judgment as to which answer the text best supports.

Except for the writer's connecting comments and closing remark in v. 14, this unit consists of seven quotations from the Old Testament: five from the Psalms, one from Deuteronomy, and one from 2 Samuel. One can find parallel arrangements of texts in the rabbis and in writings from Qumran. The scarcity of commentary by the author and the absence of polemic elaboration may indicate that the readers were already familiar with this combination of texts.

1:5 You are my Son: That Ps. 2:7 would be used by Christians as appropriate at Jesus' baptism (Mark 1:11) and at his resurrection (Acts 13:33) raised for some the question, when did Jesus become Son of God, at birth, at baptism, or at resurrection? John and Paul would join the Hebrews writer in adding, or in preexistence? Of the several ways to express Christ's sonship, the one most recurring in Hebrews is preexistence, the essential first phase of the formula: pre-existence, humiliation, exaltation (2:8–13; 7:3; 10:5; 11:26).

1:6 Firstborn: Implying authority, privilege, and inheritance; used of David (Ps. 89:27), Israel (Num. 11:12; Hos. 2:1), and elsewhere of Christ (Rom. 8:29; Col. 1:15, 18). But to what event or christological moment does the writer refer with the expression "when he (God) brings the firstborn into the world"? Technically the adverb "again" may modify the verb, and hence "bring again" could refer to the Parousia, the second coming, but it is more likely that "again" is simply a connective, as at 1:5; 2:13a,b; 4:5; 10:30. Thus understood, the bringing of the firstborn into the world is without chronological clues, and therefore may refer to the incarnation, the Parousia, the world to come (2:5), or the exaltation into the "world" of the angels who are commanded to worship him. Originally Deut. 32:43 called for all the sons of God to worship

God. A version of the LXX changed "sons" to "angels," obviously a version preferred by the writer. The other alteration, directing angelic praise to the Son rather than to God, is the writer's own modification.

1:7 He makes his angels winds: The Hebrew of Ps. 104:4 reads, "who makes winds to be his messengers and fire and flame his servants," while the LXX reverses the expressions: "who makes his messengers (angels) to be winds and his servants to be fire and flame." The point here is that angels are as transient and temporary as wind and fire (LXX text). This will be abundantly clear momentarily. The contrast between Christ and the angels is that of permanent/transient.

1:8–9 Of the Son he says: The writer introduces Ps. 45:6–7 by saying that what follows applies to the Son. Psalm 45 is a marriage song praising the king as bridegroom and calling on the bride, a princess from Tyre, to abandon all former loyalties in recognition of the superior status of the groom. The Hebrews writer does not develop the marriage theme; rather, Ps. 45 yields other themes appropriate to the Christ-angels discussion. First, the angels are changing and transient; the throne of the Son is forever and ever (13:8). Second, because the Son is a king whose reign is marked by righteousness, the writer anticipates the discussion of Melchizedek, king of righteousness, beginning at 7:1. Third, that God **has set you above your companions** (NIV) has clear implications for the issue of Christ's relation to the angels. No special attention is given to the most shocking feature of the quotation: the king, and hence the Son, is called God. References to the Son as God can be found in early liturgical texts (Rom. 9:5; John 1:1; 20:28; Titus 2:13; 2 Pet. 1:1).

1:11–12 They will perish, but you remain: Ps. 102 is a lament of a person ill and dying. The psalmist contrasts his own condition with the abiding nature of a never-changing God. This description of God is here used concerning the Son. There is no doubt that the one addressed as Lord is the Son. Psalm 102:25–27 contributes several themes to the discussion. The role of the Son as Creator and sustainer of the universe (1:2–3) is here elaborated to highlight the contrast between Christ as Creator and angels as creatures. This leads to a second contrast between the Son who never changes and creation that perishes. One also observes here the writer's practice of anticipating future ideas by dropping words and phrases that will receive fuller attention later. For example, as creation grows old and wears out like clothing, so the old covenant grows old, soon to disappear (8:13). Again, as the Son remains the same forever, so will this unchanging quality characterize Christ's priesthood (5:6; 6:20; 7:3; 7:17). Or again, as creation perishes, so will there be a shaking and an end to all things in the eschaton, leaving only the kingdom that cannot be shaken (12:26–28). Telegraphing ahead themes yet to be developed is sound rhetoric and effective pedagogy.

1:13 To which of the angels has God ever said?: The chain of citations in 1:5–13 ends as it began, forming an inclusion (a passage that ends as it begins) with the same rhetorical question. The writer now quotes the text to which he alluded in 1:3, Ps. 110:1, which provides the scriptural authorization for the unique Christology of Hebrews. This psalm is also frequently employed elsewhere in the New Testament in christological debate (Mark 12:35–37; 14:62; Acts 2:34; 1 Cor. 15:25, et al.). Psalm 110, God's address to the king, contains two oracles: the offer of a place of power at God's right hand (v. 1) and the declaration of the king's priestly office after the order of Melchizedek (v. 4). Only Hebrews in the New Testament develops v. 4 as a christological text. In the present context only v. 1 is quoted, and it is presented as the words of God to the Son. In addition to the affirmation of the supremacy of the Son, the psalm predicts the final subordination of all enemies of the Son. Later in the epistle the writer will discuss the Son's victory over the two great enemies, sin and death (2:14–15; 10:27).

1:14 Angels . . . sent to serve: Unlike the Son, who sits at God's right hand, angels are sent out on mission, and the beneficiaries of their service are those soon to inherit salvation (Ps. 104:4). This verse serves as a transition, speaking positively of the work of angels, providing an opening for a statement about one of the significant tasks of angels, the giving of the Law (2:2). In addition, it announces salvation, a subject soon to be developed (2:3–4). And finally, v. 14 introduces those who will inherit salvation, the group to be strongly admonished in 2:1–4.

2:1–4
THEREFORE LISTEN CAREFULLY

The hortatory portion begins and will reappear from time to time (3:12–4:13; 5:11–6:12; 10:19–39; 12:14–29). The author does not separate himself from the readers in an accusing tone, but uses the inclusive "we" throughout.

2:1 Therefore: This exhortation is clearly linked to what precedes it; not to 1:14 specifically, but to the entire presentation of the Son's superiority to angels. **Pay greater attention:.** Matthew uses the same word repeatedly (6:1; 7:15; 10:17; 16:6, et al.) as a term of strong warning: Beware, watch out! The danger is not that of willful engagement in ethical or doctrinal error but rather the potential to **drift away from** one's mooring. The condition addressed is a serious one. Toward the message they have heard the readers are displaying a laxity, a carelessness, a loss of attention.

2:2–3 If the message declared through angels: The "if" clause of this conditional sentence most likely states a certainty: "since the message declared" (cf. Phil. 2:1). The argument is from the lesser to the greater, from the angels to the Lord. This form of argumentation (a fortiori) is a favorite of the writer (7:20–22; 9:13–15; 10:28–29). The sentence continues the language begun at 1:1, and since both angels and the Lord are referred to as agents, the assumed speaker is God.

Even though Exod. 20:1 gives no indication of mediating angels at Sinai, the belief came later on to be held among both Jews and Christians. (*Jub.* 1:27, 29; Acts 7:38, 53; Gal. 3:19). Since the Son is greater than angels, so the word of the Son is greater than the message delivered through angels. At this point, exactly what will not be escaped is not spelled out, but it will soon be clear that the writer has in mind eschatological punishment (6:8; 10:27, 31; also Luke 21; 36; Rom. 2:3; 1 Thess. 5:3). The danger among the readers is neglect (2:1) or indifference. At stake is a **great salvation** (1:14), which, interestingly enough, is portrayed as something spoken. Its reality and certainty are secured in God's having said so; that is enough. This salvation means exemption from eschatological punishment (9:28; 10:25), but the epistle will also detail present benefits (4:16; 6:5; 8:7–12; 9:13–14, 26–28; 10:2, 15–18, 22).

2:4 God added: God now becomes the actor, the one who through signs, wonders, powerful deeds, and distributions of the Holy Spirit offers supporting testimony to the word spoken (see also 6:5). Signs and wonders had long been joined (Exod. 7:3; Deut. 4:34; 6:22; Ps. 135:9; Jer. 32:20–21; Neh. 9:10), and early Christians often added "deeds of power" (Acts 2:22; Rom. 15:19; 2 Cor. 12:12; see Gal. 3:5; 1 Cor. 12:12).

2:5–18
The Son Lower Than Angels

The writer returns to the exposition of biblical texts. Instead of continuing the comparison of the Son and angels, the author now argues that just as angels were not the means of redemption, neither are they the beneficiaries of it. With this new orientation toward humanity, toward those "who are to inherit salvation" (1:14), the primary consideration of the epistle will have been established. After 2:16, angels will no longer be a factor in either exposition or exhortation.

This unit falls easily into two parts: 2:5–9, which consists primarily of a christological exegesis of Ps. 8:4–6 (8:5–7 LXX), and 2:10–18, which elaborates on that exegesis and anticipates the fuller development of the high priesthood of Christ. Portions of Ps. 22 and Isa. 8 support the argumentation.

2:5 Someone has testified somewhere: Ps. 8:4–6, the centerpiece of 2:5–9, is introduced as speech of indefinite citation (see also 4:4; 7:17; 12:5, 6). This may have been a common homiletic practice; undivided attention on content can often best be served by indefinite referencing. However, most quotations are introduced as the speech of God or Christ or the Holy Spirit.

2:7 A little lower than angels (NIV): The author uses the Greek text (LXX) of the psalm, which differs from the Hebrew "a little lower than gods (*elohim*)." This may have a temporal meaning, "a little while." This seems to be the writer's sense in the exegesis (v. 9), and so the NRSV translates it (vv. 7, 9). The NIV keeps the qualitative meaning in its rendering, "a little lower." The NRSV has honored its commitment to more inclusive language by translating "man" and "son of man" (synonymous parallels) "human beings" and "mortals." This obscures the shift from plural to singular in the application of the psalm to Christ. Similarly, the phrase "son of man" is lost, and it is possible that it was this phrase that first attracted christological interpretations of the psalm by the early church.

2:8b–9 We do not yet see everything: Having spoken of what we do not see, the writer now announces what "we do see" (1:9). The Greek construction is especially impressive. Between two expressions from the psalm, the one made "for a little while lower than the angels" and the one "crowned with honor and glory," the author places the principal clause, **we see Jesus.** The two expressions that had been joined as a description of humanity now are separated as

two phases of the temporal journey of the Son: lower than angels for a little while, crowned with glory and honor forever. There is no shrinking back from or minimizing what happened to Jesus during that "little while." **Taste death for everyone:** It was because Jesus suffered death that he was crowned with glory and honor (Matt. 16:28; John 8:52).

During the "little while" the drama of redemption was played out. The essential vocabulary of that drama has already been introduced: suffering, death, grace of God, for everyone (v. 9), and now, consistent with a literary pattern already employed, the writer will elaborate on that vocabulary.

2:10 It was fitting that God: What occurred during the "little while" of Christ's incarnation was at the initiative of God. **For whom and through whom:** This omnipotence formula removes even a hint of accident, coincidence, or historical contingency. This activity of God is totally appropriate to the character of God and to God's relationship to humankind. Speaking of what is proper behavior for God is unique to Hebrews in the New Testament. God's purpose is to lead **many children to glory** (the word is "sons" [see NIV], but is unquestionably inclusive). Honor and glory belong to Jesus (v. 9), but now many others will share in that glory (see John 12:28–32). **Perfect:** Perfection is not a term for moral flawlessness; that quality of blamelessness is otherwise stated in 4:15; 7:26; and 9:14. Rather, it refers to the completeness of Jesus' preparation for his priestly ministry. Any life short of suffering and death would have been less than identification with humankind.

2:12–13: In these verses, the author portrays Jesus as speaking in the words of Ps. 22:22; Isa. 8:17–18.

2:14 Since, therefore: The transition announces the gathering up of what has been said thus far and the projection of lines of thought stated here but to be developed later. Since all human beings share (perfect tense, indicating an abiding condition) blood and flesh, Jesus in every way participated (aorist tense, indicating a completed act in the past) in the same things. **Flesh and blood:** A common way (here "blood and flesh") to summarize the human condition (Matt. 16:17; 1 Cor. 15:50; Gal. 1:16). To say Jesus **destroys** the devil very likely means "to break the power of" (see 1 Cor. 5:5; 10:10; 15:24; John 8:44).

2:16 Not . . . angels: While angels are in divine service for the benefit of those who inherit salvation (1:14), they are neither the agents nor the beneficiaries of that salvation. With this sentence angels leave the stage of Hebrews, but they leave honorably.

2:17–18 High priest: Here the first application to Jesus of the title "high priest" occurs, and to speak of Jesus as high priest is unique to Hebrews in the New Testament. In this introduction of the title, the author distills into four statements the matters for exposition in chaps. 3–10. (1) It was necessary that Jesus be in every respect **like his brothers and sister**s. (2) Christ's being totally like us was for the purpose of being **a merciful and faithful high priest in the service of God**. That he is faithful will be presented in 3:1–4:14; that he is merciful, in 4:15–5:10. (3) Jesus became a priest in order to make atonement (NIV), **make a sacrifice of atonement** (NRSV), make expiation (REB) for the sins of the people. Neither in the LXX nor in the New Testament does the word mean "propitiate," in the sense of placating or appeasing God, since it is not human but divine initiative that effects mercy and atonement. (4) The priestly ministry of Jesus has to do with his capacity and willingness **to help those who are being tested**. A priest not only offers sacrifice for sins but also makes intercession for those in need. Those addressed have endured suffering, public abuse, persecution, imprisonment, and the confiscation of property (10:32–34). To them Jesus ministers not only as the pioneer and model who "endured the cross, disregarding its shame" (12:2), but also as the high priest making intercession for them from his place at the right hand of God (4:15–16; 7:25).

3:1–5:10
CHRIST THE FAITHFUL AND MERCIFUL HIGH PRIEST

In the literary pattern of Hebrews, the essential content of the next section is announced in the preceding one by means of a phrase or concise statement. So at 2:17, "so that he might be a merciful and faithful high priest in the service of God" introduces the primary subject matter of 3:1–5:10. The modifiers "merciful" and "faithful" will now be developed but in reverse order, the second one mentioned being the first for consideration. Both Gen. 2:2 and Ps. 95:7–11, supply proof for the writer's argument in 3:1–4:13, but especially Ps. 95:7–11 which is not only quoted (3:7–11) but which reappears in part at 3:15; 4:3, 5, 7. In 4:14–5:10, Ps. 2:7 and Ps. 110:4 are quoted

for use in an argument delayed until 7:1. As in the preceding section, the text will alternate between exhortation and exposition.

3:1–4:13
CHRIST THE FAITHFUL

The writer turns to examine two qualities of the high priest, faithfulness and mercy. In 3:1–4:13, note the pervasive use of vocabulary developed from the stem word "faith": faithful, faithfulness, obedience, unfaithful, faithlessness, disobedience.

3:1–6
Brothers and Sisters

The readers have already been called brothers and sisters (2:11, 12, 17), as well as those who are sanctified (2:11) and partners with Christ in the human condition (2:14). **Partners in a heavenly calling:** That the calling is "heavenly" points not only to its source, but also to its goal (2:10). The readers are addressed directly in order to urge them to "give attention to" (Luke 12:24, 27; Acts 7:31–32) Jesus in his unique role in their salvation. The role of Jesus is captured in two terms: **apostle** and **high priest**. The noun "apostle" is applied to Jesus only here in the New Testament, but that he was "sent" of God is the testimony of many (Mark 9:37; Matt. 10:40; Luke 10:16; Gal. 4:4; John 3:17, 34; 5:36; et al.). **Confession:** may refer both to the act of confessing and to the content of the community's faith (see also 4:14; 10:23).

The quality of Jesus as apostle and high priest underscored here is fidelity to God (v. 2), and it is this fidelity which joins Jesus and Moses. Even though **Moses** and **Jesus** were both **faithful**, they differ in station: Moses is **a servant**, while Jesus is **a son** (1:2, and frequently thereafter). They differ also in function: Moses serves **in God's house** while Jesus as son is **over God's house** (vv. 5–6). That Moses is a servant in God's house does not diminish him (Num. 12:7–8).

3:7–11
The Faithless People

This unit consists entirely of a quotation of Ps. 95:7b–11 in the LXX. The writer will provide commentary in 3:12–4:11.

3:7 Therefore: The conjunction joins the quotation to the conditional clause in v. 6b, **if we hold firm**. The writer thus telegraphs ahead that the quotation from Ps. 95 will be in the service of urging fidelity. **The Holy Spirit says:** Earlier scriptural citations have been presented as speeches of God (1:5–9, 13) or of Christ (2:12–13). The effect of such attribution is to allow no discontinuity between past and present people of God. The application of Ps. 95 to the present readers assumes the correspondence between the situations of Israel and the church as the pilgrim people of God. On early Christian interpretation of the Old Testament, see the excursus at 1 Cor. 15:3.

3:10 For forty years: In the LXX of Ps. 95:9–10, the forty years refers to God's anger: "For forty years I was angry with that generation." The writer of Hebrews has inserted a "therefore" before the expression "**I was angry with that generation**," leaving the forty years to be attached to the preceding statement, "**though they had seen my works for forty years.**" Contrast this with v. 17, "**With whom was he angry.**" Here the author reads the LXX correctly: God is angry for forty years. Apparently both statements stand: the ancestors observed God's providential activity forty years; God was angry forty years, doubtless the same forty years. Instead of quoting the historical books (Exod. 17:1–17; Num. 20:2–13; 14:20–23, 28–35) to recall Israel's rebellion and testing God, and God's oath that they would never see the land of promise, the author uses the memory of those events as preserved in Ps. 95:7–11. If Hebrews was read in a worship assembly of the church, the words heard and the words remembered would have compounded effect.

3:12–19
Failure to Enter God's Rest

At 3:12 the author begins the commentary on Ps. 95:7–11 in the form of a homiletical midrash; that is, an interpretation of a passage of Scripture for a particular audience in a situation sufficiently similar to that of the text so as to make the application reasonable. Key words and phrases of the text (**today, turn away, rebel, unbelief, listen, harden, disobey, rest**) are brought directly to bear on the readers' spiritual condition. Behind Ps. 95 stands Num. 14, the account of Israel's unbelief and disobedience at Kadesh. The commentary on the quoted psalm assumes the readers of Hebrews are now at their own spiritual Kadesh and must learn from Israel's failure. There are three units in the commentary, 3:12–19; 4:1–5; 4:6–11, each unit being built around a quoted portion of the psalm.

3:12 Take care: This repeats 3:1 in addressing the **brothers and sisters**, but strengthens the verb from "consider" so that it is a warning (see Matt. 24:4; Acts 13:40; 1 Cor. 10:18). The community of believers is to see that not a single one of their number turns away from God. **Evil,**

unbelieving heart: Such a label is characterized by faithlessness and turning away from God; that is, disobedience. The words are taken from Jer. 16:12; 18:12, Ps. 95:7, and Num. 14:22, 29, 32 and do not refer to agnosticism or atheism, but to rebellion against God. What is involved in turning away (apostasy) the writer spells out in 6:4–8; 10:26–31; 12:15–17, 25.

This condition can be avoided by daily exhorting (encouraging) each other, an activity that may imply preaching (Luke 3:18; Acts 14:22; 2 Cor. 1:4) as well as admonitions on specific matters (Rom. 12:1; 16:17; 1 Cor. 16:15; Phil. 4:2). The **today** of Ps. 95:7 and Heb. 3:13 remains open, and the invitation to hear God's word still stands, but the implication is that the door of salvation could close. God's offer is available, but so is the deceptive sin that hardens the heart toward God.

3:14 First confidence: The word may be translated "resolution," "standing firm," or the "very essence" of a matter. Apparently the author is saying that the fundamental core of their faith commitment must be as securely held at the end as at the beginning.

3:15–18 The writer is speaking *about* Israel but in so doing is speaking *to* the readers. The quotation is inescapably appropriate to the readers; but the writer drives it home with three rhetorical questions and answers (vv. 16–18). The questions draw upon the language of Ps. 95, the answers from what happened to Israel at Kadesh according to Num. 14.

3:19 So we see that they were unable to enter: In Num. 14, when Israel realized their sin, they sought to prove their repentance by attempting to enter the land in spite of warnings that God was not with them. The result was tragic defeat at the hands of occupants of the land (Num. 14:39–45). Perhaps the preacher of Hebrews is preparing the readers for the strong language concerning second chances in 6:4–8; 10:26–31; 12:16–17.

4:1–11
God's Rest Still Available

At 4:1 the text shifts from exhorting by means of talking *about* Israel (3:15–19) to exhorting by means of direct address *to* the hearers. This unit begins and ends with strong imperatives ("let us take care"; "let us make every effort") and strong warnings ("that none of you should seem to have failed to reach it"; "that no one may fall").

4:1–2 Let us take care: Since the promised rest of God is still available, we must take care that no one fail to enter. Our situation and Israel's are parallel in that all of us heard **the good news** (literally "were evangelized," v. 2), but we differ from Israel in that we received the good news in faith and are entering that rest.

4:3–4 We . . . enter that rest: The use of the present tense emphasizes that the rest is not only an eschatological future but also a present favorable state, as the sermon will unfold later. But what is this rest? By interpreting the noun "rest" in Ps. 95:11 by citing the verb form of the same word in Gen. 2:2 (LXX), "**God rested**," the author moves beyond the idea of a land to that of a condition in which we participate with God. "Rest" now becomes a synonym for salvation, the presence of God now and in the future. But what is the rest of God, the Sabbath rest? In the New Testament apart from Hebrews, rest is spoken of quite apart from notions of the land or the seventh day (Matt. 11:28–30). Thus the view that while "rest" transcends place and history, it is also experienced here and now (4:3, 10) is not the creation of the author of Hebrews. "Rest" is an eschatological reality in the sense of being grounded in the ultimate purpose of God for God's people. It neither began nor ended at Kadesh (Num. 14). Rest is a reality existing from **the foundation of the world**. God "rested on the seventh day from all his works" (Gen. 2:2), just as those who enter God's rest will do (4:10). While the Sabbath was later justified on humanitarian grounds (rest for all creation), for historical reasons (remember the Exodus), and for liturgical purposes (the praise of God), Gen. 2:2 is its birthplace. The Sabbath reminds of a central truth: God rested and invites others into that rest with all the blessings attendant to the presence of God.

4:6–7 Today: How can an ancient offer to Israel be understood as an offer to believers in the present? The writer's reasoning is as follows: God's offer of rest was not accepted **because of disobedience**, and **therefore, it remains open** to those of faithful obedience "today." This "today," says the author, was spoken by God through David in Ps. 95, and **David** lived **much later** than the wilderness generation led by Joshua. This clearly means that the offer in Joshua's day, having been rejected, was at a later day still open.

4:12–13
God's Word Still Active

In the writer's theology, words of Scripture are words of God to us today. Hence, the word is living and active (see Isa. 55:11), sharper than any

two-edged sword (see Isa. 49:2; Eph. 6:17; Rev. 19:15). The word that creates is also able to discern and judge (Amos 1:2; Ps. 51:6). **Soul from spirit, bone from marrow:** These terms are drawn from the anthropology of the day, as a forceful way of saying that no part of the human life is beyond the knowing gaze of God. The word of God serves as the eyes of God, seeing everything the heart devises and feels. These two verses could be read as a digest of Ps. 139. **Account:** The passage ends as it began, with *logos* ("word"), but here it is not God's word but ours; hence the translation "account" (as in 13:17; also Luke 16:2; 1 Pet. 4:5). It is as though the writer expects the readers to respond, not with "Amen," but with their lives.

4:14–5:10
CHRIST THE MERCIFUL

The description of Christ as a merciful and faithful high priest at 2:17 provided the structure for 3:1–5:10. Just as 3:1–4:12 developed Christ's (and our) faithfulness; 4:14–5:10 will focus on his mercy. Of key interest in this unit are two moves by the writer: the joining of Ps. 2:7 and Ps. 110:4, and the introduction of the scriptural ground for presenting Jesus as a priest when genealogically and liturgically he was not.

4:14 Passed through the heavens: This evokes the image of the Jewish high priest on the Day of Atonement passing through the veil of the temple and entering the Holy of Holies, the place of God's presence. That Jesus has entered God's presence was implied at 1:3, 13, but is now stated with the obvious intention of recalling the imagery of the wilderness tent of meeting, as well as of anticipating more detailed discussion of Jesus passing beyond the veil (6:19–20; 8:1–2; 9:11; 10:20). By joining **Jesus** and **Son of God** the writer may be drawing on the language of the confession. The two terms join the two qualifications of a priest: to be made like his brothers and sisters (Jesus), and to be appointed of God (Son of God). This presentation of Jesus as one who shares our lot and who also bears a special relation to God is made especially important for two reasons. First, it is essential as a basis for assurance that our approach to God will be met with sympathy and understanding. That Jesus experienced completely the human condition gives confidence to a prayer life that fully expects both mercy and help. And since Jesus, having been as we are in every respect, entered into God's presence, access to God has been opened for us, with Jesus already there interceding in our behalf (7:25; 9:24). Second, this presentation of Jesus as being both of the people and of God is a clear anticipation of 5:1–10, where the writer begins the difficult task of establishing that Jesus was and is a priest.

4:15 Weaknesses: The reference is to the human condition as such, not to physical weakness or illness (see 5:2; 7:28; Luke 2:7; John 19:17–42; Rom. 6:19; 1 Cor. 1:18–2:5; 15:43, 50; 2 Cor. 13:4; Phil. 2:5–11). **Yet without sin:** That Jesus was without sin was variously expressed by early Christian writers (John 7:18; 8:46; 1 Pet. 1:19; 2:22; 1 John 3:5), in each case with a particular understanding of sin. Here, being without sin refers to Jesus' unwavering firmness in his faithfulness to God. As the ancients expressed it, he was as we are, and therefore *will* help; he was not as we are, and therefore *can* help.

5:1 High priest: Though Hebrews is the only New Testament document to develop the concept of Christ as high priest, fragments of related ideas are found in the New Testament outside Hebrews: the tearing of the temple veil at the death of Jesus (Mark 15:38); Jesus' words, "Destroy this temple, and in three days I will raise it up" (John 2:19); Jesus' giving his life as a sacrifice and, therefore, functioning as a priest; Jesus as the place of atonement (mercy seat) for our sins (Rom. 3:25). The concept could have developed out of the church's wide use of Ps. 110. Although it is Ps. 110:1 that is so much employed, Ps. 110:4, which declares, "You are a priest forever," lies close at hand. Other possible influences have been found in the Logos-priest of Philo of Alexandria, the Messiah-priest of Qumran, or the priest of late Jewish apocalyptic visions. Of course, a church that reread and reappropriated its own sacred texts and heritage in Judaism quite possibly created a liturgy out of a Christian interpretation of the Day of Atonement (Lev. 16). **Offer gifts and sacrifices for sins:** The writer begins presenting the essential qualities of any high priest before moving to the consideration of Christ as high priest in vv. 5–10. Sacrifices for sin were efficacious under circumstances of unwilling or unintentional errors and breaches of God's law due to ignorance (Lev. 4:13; Ezek. 45:20; Luke 23:34; Acts 3:17; 1 Tim. 1:13). Such sins, according to the Hebrews author, are quite different from those committed willfully (6:4–8; 10:26–31; 12:17). The high priest's own sins made it necessary for him to offer first a sacrifice for himself and then a sacrifice in behalf of the people (v. 3; Lev. 16:11–17). This difference between

the Aaronic high priest and Christ will be noted later.

5:2 Deal gently: This was not in the list of credentials for Aaronic priests; very likely the author is reading backward from qualities of Christ to qualities of the Aaronic high priest. The high priest is to behave with restraint toward the ignorant and wayward, a restraint born of the priest's awareness of his own weakness.

5:4 Just as Aaron was: Aaron serves to demonstrate that priests must be called by God. Just as the Aaronic priesthood was not by human initiative but by the call of God, so Christ did not glorify himself; on the contrary, glory and honor were bestowed on him by God (2:9).

5:5 Son . . . begotten: The title "Son," introduced at 1:2, is the constant term for referring to Jesus Christ in chaps. 1–4. The word "begotten" does not refer to Jesus' birth; here the term is from the language of appointment not parentage, just as it is in the psalm's original sense: God appointed or designated Israel's king as God's son (see Acts 13:33). Being "God's son" has roots in royal ideology. The writer is guided by the psalm's own meaning: God grants to the king a place above all other monarchs and princes. The text thus join two christological motifs: kingship and priesthood (see 7:1–3).

5:7 In the days of his flesh: The "for a little while lower than the angels" (2:9) is elongated into a vivid description of life "in the days of his flesh." **Prayers and supplications:** The image of Jesus in fervent prayer, with loud cries and tears appealing **to the one able to save him from death,** brings to mind Jesus in Gethsemane (Mark 14:32–42; Matt. 26:36–46; Luke 22:40–46). The language of v. 7 carries echoes of Pss. 22; 39; 116; Isa. 65; and Job 40, but clearly fits the context. For example, Jesus **offered up** prayers, a term used to describe the sacrificial activity of a priest (5:1, 3). That Jesus' prayers were heard and yet he still suffered locates Jesus more firmly among his brothers and sisters whose experiences are precisely the same. Though "from" death can be translated "out of" death, making his prayer a petition for resurrection, there is no reason not to take it in its plainest sense; like the rest of us, he cries out to God in the face of the immediate prospect of death. **Reverent submission:** What is being said about Christ? That he was worshipful, filled with awe, reverent, devout, in fear of God? At 12:28, the author's only other use of the word, it is in a context of priestly service before God and therefore describes the attitude or behavior appropriate to that service: bowing in reverence.

5:8 Although he was a Son: Being God's Son did not exempt Jesus from learning, from **obedience**, from suffering, so complete was his identification with all who share flesh and blood. By learning obedience through suffering, Jesus is qualified as both intercessor and model.

5:9 Made perfect: In summarizing Christ's preparation for and fulfillment of his ministry as our high priest, the perfection of Christ is not a reference to moral achievement but to the "completion" of his preparation as high priest through testing, suffering, and death. No doubt the author is using the word "perfect" in its cultic sense, borrowing the term from its use in the LXX to describe the priest of Israel's tabernacle. There the word is translated "consecrated" or "ordained" (Lev. 4:5; 8:33; 16:32; 21:10; Num. 3:3).

5:11–6:20
PREPARATION FOR THE DIFFICULT QUESTION

The phrase, "a high priest according to the order of Melchizedek," that frames this unit at 5:10 and 6:20 alerts the reader to the distinct nature of the material between those markers. The passage before us now will introduce a question that disturbed the early church for generations: the question of postbaptismal sins and the possibility of a second repentance.

5:11–6:3
A CALL FOR MATURITY

Further discussion of the high priesthood of Christ will not only contribute to the maturity of the readers (6:1), but also requires a degree of maturity for its progress (5:14).

5:11 We have much to say that is hard to explain: The expression is literally "the word has much to say to us difficult to interpret." It is with "the word" that both writer and reader must struggle. The accent on God's speaking, from 1:1 onward, is recalled, as is the lyrical prose in praise of the living, active word of God in 4:12–13. Literally, the readers are accused of being "dull or sluggish of hearing." It is toward the word already preached and the word now to be further explored that the readers have become **dull** or sluggish.

5:12–14 Basic elements: The vocabulary and analogies are drawn from educational circles of the Hellenistic world. Anyone moving normally through the stages of education available would be expected to progress from the **basic elements** (the NEB renders the expres-

sion "the ABC of God's oracles") to discourses of some complexity. The congregation is encouraged to go back to school. This may be an allusion to formal catechetical instruction, which later was institutionalized as lengthy (one to three years) preparation for baptism. We do not know how structured such education was at this time and place, nor whether it preceded or followed baptism. The content of such instruction is **the oracles of God**, a familiar designation for the Jewish Scriptures (Num. 24:16; Ps. 107:11; Acts 7:38; Rom. 3:2). **Milk:** An image for "the basic elements of the oracles of God" while **solid food** is **the word of righteousness**, which is the capacity in the believer **to distinguish good from evil**. The writer focuses only on moral and ethical discernment. Having one's faculties (senses) trained by practice is athletic imagery, common in the New Testament (1 Tim. 4:7; Heb. 12:11; 2 Pet. 2:14).

6:1 Go on toward perfection: Earlier the term "perfect" described Christ as one who was made so through full identification with humankind, including suffering and death (2:10; 5:9). His incarnation, humiliation, and exaltation perfected or completed his redemptive work, and hence he is "perfect forever" (7:28). However, in the text immediately before us, at 5:14 and again at 6:1, the term is used to describe the moral, ethical, intellectual, and spiritual goal of the believer's life, a goal achieved by learning, practice, and teaching others, a goal expected of all who submit themselves to the resources for Christian growth. In the discussion of 5:11–6:20, it is, therefore, appropriate to translate the word "mature" or, in its noun form at 6:1, "maturity." **Leaving behind:** In this pilgrimage language, the eschatological flavor of the word "perfection" should be kept in mind. Believers not only practice the disciplines of Christian living that lead to maturity, but also receive a completeness or perfection granted by the perfection of Christ. The exercises of the Christian life are always performed under the benediction of grace. This may be implied in the writer's choice of the passive "let us be carried" (translated "let us go on"). We not only move on toward maturity; we are carried along toward perfection.

The basic teaching about Christ: The expression can also mean Christ's own teaching (subjective rather than objective). The phrase following, **repentance from dead works and faith toward God**, seems to support this interpretation since, according to the Gospels, Jesus came preaching, "Repent and believe the good news" (Mark 1:15). In addition, the author assumes some knowledge about the historical Jesus (5:7–8), further supporting the view that the basic instruction of Christians involved teaching what Christ himself taught. If, however, "Christ" is read as objective, then the instruction here referred to was about Christ and may well have included material such as we find in 1:1–14. In the absence of certainty, there is no reason not to accept both interpretations: "the basic teaching of/about Christ." When the canon of the New Testament was determined, teachings both by Christ and about Christ were included. **The foundation:** This foundation is described as one of repentance and faith, further defined as teaching in four subject areas. The writer has only to mention them without comment, because they were already familiar to the readers. **Repentance from dead works and faith toward God:** This expression summarizes the entire movement from the former life to the present life. The writer uses the phrase here and at 9:14 as a general characterization of the activities and rituals of the readers' former life, whether in Judaism or some Hellenistic religion.

6:2 Baptisms: The word is better rendered "washings"; another form of the word is used in the New Testament to speak of Christian baptism. Just as Paul had to distinguish between the eucharistic meal and pagan ritual meals (1 Cor. 10; 11), so perhaps new Christians needed to understand differences between ritual washings of other groups (Traditional Judaism? Qumran? The disciples of John the Baptist? Pagan ablutions?) and the baptism of the church.

6:4–12
STERN WARNING, WITH HOPE

The pattern occurs again of a stern warning (vv. 4–8) followed by words of encouragement and hope (vv. 9–12; see 2:1–9; 4:1–16). The writer wants the reader to hear the words about the impossibility of restoring certain persons to a second repentance as part of the larger message of pastoral encouragement.

6:4 It is impossible to restore again to repentance: This statement must be understood in its context in Hebrews, rather than combining it with other texts about an "unpardonable sin" (Mark 3:28–29; Matt. 12:32; Luke 12:10; 1 John 5:16). Matching texts that are similar in rigor can lead one away from the issue of sub-

stance: what is the condition of those who are, in the mind of the writer of Hebrews, beyond the possibility of being restored to repentance? What is meant by "falling away" (v. 6)? The writer does not specify with whom the impossibility lies: God cannot? The preacher cannot? The listener cannot? Such precision is unnecessary. The impossibility lies in the writer's understanding of the once-for-all act of God in Jesus Christ. The author repeatedly finds the expression "impossible" useful in clearing away from the Christology of the letter any modifiers, any alternatives, any exceptions (6:18; 10:4; 9:9; 10:1, 11; 11:6). For Hebrews, impossibilities are implied in the writer's affirmation: "once for all" (10:10). **Have once been enlightened:** Being "enlightened," moving out of darkness into light, was a widely used metaphor for the trustful reception of the message about Christ (John 1:9; 2 Cor. 4:4–6; Eph. 1:18; 2 Tim. 1:10; 1 Pet. 2:9). The author uses the expression again at 10:32 in recalling the readers' firm stand in their confession. **Have tasted the heavenly gift:** The vivid metaphor refers to direct personal experience (2:9; Ps. 34:8; 1 Pet. 2:3). The heavenly gift is most likely a reference to God's grace. **Have shared in the Holy Spirit:** The language of partnership has already been used in relation to the heavenly calling (3:1) and to Christ himself (3:14). God's distribution of the Holy Spirit in the community was assumed by the author as being the experience of the readers (2:4).

6:5–6 Have tasted the goodness of the word of God and the powers of the age to come: No provision necessary for the believers to enter God's rest is lacking. In confirmation of this promise, the qualities of that age to come break in upon the present. **Have fallen away:** The author has here chosen a verb which appears nowhere else in the New Testament. In the LXX the word occurs, being variously translated: "acting faithlessly" (Ezek. 14:13, NRSV; "breaking faith," REB); "dealing treacherously" (Ezek. 20:27, NRSV). The sense is that of rejection, violation of a relationship, breach of faith, abandonment. The act of falling away is against the Son of God. This is not a charge of one side of a debate against the other; rather, it is the sin of abandoning God, Christ, and the fellowship of believers (see 10:25).

6:7–8 Crop . . . thorns and thistles: The image carries echoes of Old Testament texts doubtless familiar to the readers: thorns and thistles of Gen. 3:17–18, blessing and curse of Deut.

11:26–28, and perhaps the fruitless vineyard of Isa. 5:1–7. Ground that produces a crop is blessed by God; ground that produces thorns and thistles is under a curse and destined for burning.

6:9 Beloved: The readers are addressed affectionately as "beloved" (v. 9), the only time they are so greeted in the sermon. **We are confident:** The preacher speaks softly here, offering the strongest signal that salvation and not damnation lies before the congregation. **Better things:** That the author is confident of "better things" is in no way to be taken as an apology for the harsh warning. The warning was appropriate; there were clear signs that some were slipping away (drift; neglect; inattention; dullness of understanding; 2:1–3; 5:11–12). Nor is the writer simply trying to put a happy face on a sad situation.

6:10 Better things: Two factors have persuaded the preacher of better things from the congregation. One is the justice or faithfulness of God (2:4; 6:4–5). The second factor is that God's investment in them has borne fruit in their love and service in God's name toward the saints (fellow believers).

6:11 Show the same diligence: The words not only recall 3:14 and anticipate 9:28, but also join in the New Testament's admonition to all who cling to faith under great duress (Mark 13:13; Rev. 2:10). Such faithfulness enables them to throw off the sluggishness (dullness) which had overtaken them (5:11).

6:12 So that you may not become sluggish: The readers are not infants; 1:1–5:10 is not addressed to the immature. And it is clear the writer intends to proceed in serving solid food, demanding more and more of them in digesting the profound message of Christ's high-priestly work.

6:13–20
THE GROUND FOR HOPE

6:13–14 Abraham: Presented as a prototype of those who trust in God's promises (Rom. 4:3; Gal. 3:6; Heb. 11:8–19). The brevity of the treatment suggests that the readers were already familiar with the story (see 12:17, "afterward, as you know" [NIV]); Abraham will reappear in chap. 11 as the model faith pilgrim. God's promise to Abraham was twofold: the multiplying of his offspring (Gen. 12:2; 15:5; 22:17) and the possession of the land (Gen. 13:14–17; 12:7). **I will surely bless you and multiply you:** The statement is not really a quotation but rather a sharpened summary of Gen. 22:17

that follows the most severe trial of Abraham's faith, the offering of his son Isaac (Gen. 22:1–14). God had promised earlier, but now, in view of Abraham's trust beyond comprehension, God undergirds the promise with an oath, which further strengthens the reader's confidence in the dependability of God.

6:17 By an oath: Drawing on this analogy from human discourse, the author now explains the meaning of God's oath. God's words do not, of course, require confirmation, but God wanted to show even more clearly (demonstrate more abundantly) the unchanging nature of God's purpose. **Guaranteed:** Rendered as "confirmed" in the NIV, the word is literally "interposed" or "mediated," but in the legal language of the passage, refers to the act of an intermediary in offering security or a guarantee.

6:18 Encouraged: In this context, "encouraged" is the translation preferred over "exhorted," even though both are possible (12:5, 13:22). Those who are thus encouraged are identified as **we who have fled** (NIV; taken refuge, NRSV). The flight from Egypt comes to mind, since the exodus theme was developed earlier in chaps. 3–4. Alternatively, the reference could bring to mind persons fleeing for their lives who run to the place of worship and lay hold of the altar where they would be safe from pursuers (see 1 Kgs. 1:50–51; 2:28–30). Or the writer may be recalling the LXX, where the Greek word used here for "those who flee" is used to describe persons fleeing from avengers to designated cities of refuge for asylum (Deut. 4:42; 19:5; Josh. 20:9). **Hope set before us:** This hope is present as assurance (6:11) but it is also eschatological. The participle "set before us" permits both present and future reference.

6:19–20 We have this hope: The description of hope continues, but also turns the reader's attention to the work of Jesus as high priest, the major subject next to be developed. In v. 18, hope was the goal set before fleeing refugees; in v. 19, hope is an anchor of the soul. This nautical metaphor for stability was rather common in Greek literature, but is absent elsewhere in biblical writings. **Inner shrine behind the curtain:** By introducing the imagery of the tabernacle and the scene of the mediating work of the high priest, the author returns us to the subject briefly delayed at 5:10: Jesus as our high priest. The curtain or veil mentioned here refers to the partition between the holy place and the most Holy of Holies in the desert tabernacle (Lev. 16:2, 12, 15; Exod. 26:31–35). That Jesus went inside this curtain specifically recalls the entry into the inner shrine by the high priest on the Day of Atonement (Lev. 16:2). In the cultus of the tabernacle or temple, the high priest was not a forerunner; no others, not even priests, followed him into the Holy of Holies; he went alone. By contrast, Christ, even though his salvific work of offering himself was peculiar to him, was a forerunner; that is, he prepared for others to follow.

7:1–10:39
THE DIFFICULT DISCUSSION

The writer of Hebrews comes now to an earlier delayed subject: the high-priestly ministry of Christ. Nothing in the Gospel traditions of the preacher, teacher, exorcist Jesus provided a basis adequate to support a high-priestly Christology. After all, Jesus was not a Levite, and never in his visit or visits to the temple in Jerusalem is he in the role of a priest. The writer looks, then, not to those accounts but to Ps. 110:4 for an exegetical foundation. The author goes back to the priesthood of Melchizedek to ground a priestly Christology in Jewish Scriptures and, most importantly, in the plan of God before there ever was a tabernacle or a Levitical priest.

7:1–28
CHRIST AND MELCHIZEDEK

Obscure figures of the Old Testament whose portraits are very briefly sketched or whose stories contain elements of mystery attracted great interest in subsequent generations. Enoch vanished from the earth because God took him (Gen. 5:24); Moses' grave was never found (Deut. 34:6); Elijah ascended in a whirlwind (2 Kgs. 2:11). It was not simply curiosity that drew poets and scholars to these characters; the gaps and ambiguities provided room for traditions to develop around these figures in support of various theologies and institutions. The shadowy and mysterious Melchizedek belongs in this company.

7:1–3 King Melchizedek: The meeting of Melchizedek and Abraham in Gen. 14:17–20 is here summarized. Hebrews picks up the story of Gen. 14 after King Melchizedek appears, offering bread and wine. That Melchizedek was a king is also important for Hebrews, because Ps. 110, the central text for the Christology of the letter, joins kingship (Ps. 110:1) and priesthood (Ps. 110:4). The primary importance here is his priesthood: he **blessed** Abra-

ham and from Abraham received a tithe of all Abraham had (Gen. 14:19–20).

7:5–8 A tenth of the spoils: Melchizedek received a tithe of the very best, placing him above the Levitical priests. Since the tithe comes from Abraham, it is the greatness of Abraham which argues for an even greater Melchizedek. **Collected tithes from Abraham and blessed him:** Abraham was the progenitor of all Israel, the one who received the promises from God (v. 6; 6:13–15), superior to the law of Moses by which the Levites operate (v. 5). Melchizedek blessed Abraham, and the one who blesses is always greater than the one who is blessed. **Testified that he lives:** Melchizedek received a tithe as one who was totally apart from a genealogical record since he was a priest "in perpetuity" while Levitical priests were mortal (lit. "dying men") and hence had to be replaced.

7:11 Perfection: The ineffectiveness of the Levitical priesthood lay in its inability to "perfect" the people. We have noted earlier the writer's fondness for the word "perfection" (see comments at 2:10; 5:9; 6:1) and the range of meanings in its usage: the Son is perfected through sufferings, and the believers are to grow into perfection (maturity). But here the writer introduces yet another use of the term: the perfecting of the people through priestly activity, a theme to be elaborated later. **On the basis of** (NIV)/**Under this priesthood** (NRSV): The NIV captures the meaning better; the law was based on the cultus, not merely contemporary with it.

7:12 When there is a change: The Levitical (Aaronic) priests were called and appointed by God (5:1–4), but they functioned, says the author, in a system that was incomplete, unable to fulfill its adherents.

7:13 Belonged to another tribe: The author finally addresses the objection that has hovered over every reference to Christ as a priest: he was not of the tribe of Levi, but of the tribe of Judah (Matt. 1:1; Acts 13:22–23; Rom. 1:3); so how could he be a priest? The writer turns this objection into an affirmation, embracing the priest of a different (translated "another") tribe; he was of a different order, the order of Melchizedek.

7:15–16 Resembling: The writer substitutes "resembling" (v. 15; also v. 3) for "in the order of," making it clear that Christ's being a Melchizedek priest is not a matter of lineage or tradition or succession but of likeness or similarity to Melchizedek. **Indestructible life:**

The resurrection of Jesus is likely in the author's mind here. The power or authority of his work comes from his eternal nature and the life he has, exalted at God's right hand (Ps. 110:1). **Legal requirement:** The authorization typical of Levitical priests is a sharp contrast. **Concerning physical descent:** Literally "fleshy commandment," this refers to the genealogical ground of the Levitical priesthood.

7:17 Forever: More appropriately, "unending." Of the ten allusions to or quotations of Ps. 110:4 in Hebrews, seven occur in this chapter. The psalm is offered as proof of the preceding assertion that Christ's life, unlike that of a Levitical priest, was "indestructible." The resurrection-exaltation of Christ is surely in the writer's mind here.

7:18–19 Abrogation: For the writer, the law and priesthood are inseparably joined (7:5, 11, 12, 16); the replacement of one means the replacement for the other. **Weak and ineffectual:** In the language of Hebrews, the ineffectiveness of the law lay in its inability to make "**perfect.**" The writer thus looks to Christ, a priest like Melchizedek, to fulfill this eschatological expectation of being in God's presence, since he is, on our behalf, at the right hand of God (Ps. 110:1). **A better hope:** This access to God is present through our prayer and Christ's intercession (4:14–16), but is also a hope (7:19). That this hope is "better" is no surprise to the reader, given the writer's demonstrated fondness for this word (1:4; 6:9; 7:7; 7:22; 8:6; 9:23; 10:34; 11:16, 35, 40; 12:24).

7:20 Confirmed with an oath: In this first argument for the superiority of Christ's priesthood over that of Aaron's line, priesthood confirmed by an oath (Christ's) is superior to priesthood **without an oath** (Levitical, Exod. 28:1).

7:22 A better covenant: The hope of which the writer speaks (v. 19) will have its implementation within a covenant relationship between God and the believing community. Of this better covenant Jesus is the **guarantee** or surety, guaranteeing the work or commitments of another, even at the risk of property and even life itself. The God who promises and makes oaths also guarantees the covenant with Christ's priestly offering of himself for us. See chap. 8 for a more complete discussion on "covenant."

7:23–25 Many in number: The familiar transient/permanent contrast between the Levitical priesthood and that of Christ is reframed in terms of "many" and "one." The Levites are many; that is, generation after generation, because they are subject to death. Christ, however, is one, because he **continues forever**. He has no successor, but rather remains. **For all times:** The temporal sense is to be preferred, but with no loss of meaning if translated "completely" (as in the NIV). This quality of salvation rests on two affirmations about Christ. First, he continues alive forever, and therefore his priestly endeavors for his followers never cease. Second, his priestly ministry involves making **intercession**. His sympathy for us because he was one of us (4:15; 5:1; 5:7–9) and his access to God as one appointed of God (5:5–6) join as the twin credentials qualifying him to intercede in our behalf (4:14–16). Since his salvation is "complete," intercession is not episodic or reserved for only certain conditions.

7:26: Christ as high priest is presented in terms of character, achievement, and status. **For it was fitting:** This expression was used at 2:10 to speak of God's making the pioneer of our salvation perfect through suffering. Whether from the perspective of God's activity or of our need, the fittingness lies in God's purpose. **Separated from sinners, and exalted above the heavens:** These two phrases refer essentially to the same event, the elevation of Christ to the presence of God. It is in this sense that he is apart from sinners and not in any way that would diminish his capacity for human sympathy, a point the writer has taken great pains to make repeatedly (2:10–18; 4:14–16; 5:1–2, 7–8).

7:27 Unlike the other high priests: Christ is unlike other high priests, who offer sacrifices repeatedly, and first for their own sins (5:1–3). Had the writer said "year after year" rather than "day after day," the statement would have been historically correct, but perhaps "day after day" was chosen to sharpen the contrast between the repetition of the Levitical system and the "once for all" sacrifice of Christ. **He offered himself:** Up to this point the writer has spoken of Christ's high-priestly work as primarily that of intercessor (2:18; 4:14–16; 7:24–25); his sacrifice of himself for sin is a theme yet to be developed.

8:1–10:18
THE HIGH-PRIESTLY MINISTRY OF CHRIST

The writer has now employed the titles on which all further argument will depend. He is Son (Ps. 2:7; Heb. 5:5), king (Ps. 110:1; Heb. 1:3, 13), and high priest (Ps. 110:4; Heb. 2:17; 3:1; 4:14; 5:5, 10;

6:20; 7:26, 28). High priest will be the title most prominent in what follows, but it must be established that this high priest had the essentials of a priestly ministry: a sanctuary; a covenant between God and humanity within which a priestly ministry has its efficacy; and something to offer, that is, a sacrifice. The centerpiece for the section is Jer. 31, drawn upon to authorize an exegetical homily on covenant and atoning sacrifice.

8:1–6
A Better High Priest

8:1 At the right hand of the throne: This paraphrase of Ps. 110:1 recalls 1:3. The image of a heavenly throne was deeply imbedded in Judaism (Pss. 11:4; 47:8; Isa. 6:1; 66:1; Ezek. 1:26) and abundantly used in apocalyptic literature, including the Apocalypse of John (Rev. 4–5; 7:15–17). The affirmation that Christ is seated at God's right hand does not serve at this point to declare Christ's lordship but rather to establish the location of his ministry as high priest.

8:2 Sanctuary and the true tent: This distinction between the sanctuary and the tent as a whole not only reflects the structure of the desert tent of meeting (Lev. 16:16, 20, 33), but also anticipates Christ's ministry in the inner sanctuary, where only the high priest enters. The tabernacle that the Lord has pitched is the "true" one; that is, the real, genuine, lasting one (also 9:24; 10:22).

8:5 Worship in a sanctuary: The earthly tent that served Israel in its desert journey was of God, not simply in a general sense but with specific instructions to Moses. The earthly tabernacle was not of human origin, and therefore not deserving of general indictments. Its limitations and inabilities lay in its transient nature and defined purposes; it was unable to do what it was not intended to do. **Sketch and shadow:** This is the author's interpretation of Exod. 25:40; the real tabernacle is the one in heaven. That there is a heavenly sanctuary and that there are correspondences between it and earthly ones is an idea widespread in both Jewish and Hellenistic sources.

8:6 More excellent: His ministry is "more excellent" in that he mediates a better covenant, enacted on better promises. **Better:** Notice the writer's continued fondness for this comparative (1:4; 6:9; 7:7, 19, 22), which carries the weight of a superlative. The new covenant is not newer, but the one eschatologically renewed covenant; it is not better in the relative sense, but in the ultimate sense (see "eter-

nal covenant," 13:20). In the nature of the case it cannot be superseded by a still better covenant (see on Luke 5:36–38; 22:10; John 13:34; 2 Cor. 3:5–6; Rev. 21:1–22:7). The better covenant, introduced at 7:22, will be the subject matter of the quotation of Jer. 31:31–34 and the discussion that follows. Christ serves this better covenant as mediator (8:6; 9:15; 12:24).

8:7–13
First Covenant

The function of the introduction is not to draw out the benefits of the new covenant, but rather to underscore the need for it. Had the first been without fault "no place (room, opportunity, Acts 25:16; Rom. 12:19) would have been sought for another" (the NIV is preferred here).

8:8 With them: The fault lies not only in the covenant but also in the people. **He says:** The oracle in Jer. 31:31–34 is introduced with "God says," recalling the pattern in Hebrews of using verbs of speaking rather than "it is written," and in the present tense, as though directly addressing the readers (1:5, 6, 7, 8; 2:12; 3:7 et al.). This is the lengthiest quotation in the entire New Testament. **A new covenant:** See on v. 6; here it is enough to observe that this very phrase makes the first covenant old (obsolete).

The core of Jer. 31:31–34 subtly remains the textual centerpiece by centering on the location of the new covenant in the heart and the promise of forgiveness of sin.

9:1–6
Earthly Sanctuary

The "sanctuary" refers to the entire tabernacle and not to a particular part of it. The adjective "earthly" (worldly) anticipates its opposite, the heavenly sanctuary. The descriptions in Hebrews, while generally in accord with Exod. 25–31, do not always exactly agree with the details of the Old Testament depiction, and may reflect a different liturgical tradition and a knowledge of other texts pertaining to tabernacle and temple services.

9:2 The first one: The writer's references to two tents are to be understood as two compartments or distinct areas of the one tabernacle. **Golden altar of incense:** The strongest traditions locate the altar of incense at the rear of the Holy Place near the curtain. However, biblical references to the location of this altar are not exactly clear (Exod. 30:1–10; 37:25–28; 40:5, 26; Lev. 16:18; 1 Kgs. 6:20, 22). **Ark of the covenant:** According to Exod. 16:32–34 and

Num. 17:10–11, a pot of manna and Aaron's rod that budded were placed "before the covenant." Hebrews places them inside the ark with the stone tablets.

9:7–14
Entering the Holy Place

9:7 Once a year: On the Day of Atonement (Yom Kippur). The writer selects appropriate details from what was an elaborate day of rituals (Lev. 16:29–31). The high priest first sacrificed a bull and sprinkled its blood on the ark of the covenant for his sins and those of his family (Lev. 16:6, 11, 14), quite unlike Christ, who had no need to offer a sacrifice for himself (5:3; 7:27). Then the high priest sacrificed a goat and offered its blood for the sins of the people (Lev. 16:15, 30). Hebrews qualifies this sacrifice as being effective for inadvertent sins, a distinctive quite important to the writer (10:26; Num. 15:22, 30).

9:8 The Holy Spirit indicates . . . the way: For Hebrews the role of the Holy Spirit is not solely inspiring Scripture (3:7), but also making God's word present "today," and disclosing (make clear, reveal, 1 Cor. 3:13; 2 Pet. 1:14) what had not been understood. The Holy Spirit makes clear that the way into the Holy of Holies will be made open by the priestly act of Christ (2:10; 4:16; 10:19–20).

9:9–10 Sacrifices are offered: The author understands that the sacrificial system of the first tent serves a purpose: the ritual cleansing of persons who had been in violation of regulations concerning foods, drinks, the body, and the essential utensils for daily living. Laws of purity were many, and breaches of those laws called for rituals of restoration. But none of this priestly activity could **perfect** the worshiper (see comments at 5:9; 7:11–19). **Until the time comes to set things right:** Along with "the present time" of verse 9, "the time of correction" is to be viewed not simply chronologically, as though one time ended and another began. The references are similar in meaning to "this age" and "the age to come." Both "this age" and "the age to come" are here now but they are qualitatively different realms of being (see commentary on 1 Cor. 10:11).

9:11–12 Good things: These things are not here specified, but two have been mentioned earlier: access to God and the perfecting of the conscience (vv. 8–9). **Through the greater and perfect tent:** In its straightforward sense the phrase means Christ went through the tent, entering the Most Holy Place (Holy of Holies), that is,

the presence of God. **Entered once for all into the Holy Place:** This obviously refers to the Most Holy Place, the Holy of Holies. Christ entered the heavenly sanctuary, into the presence of God, and entered once and for all. This affirmation stands in sharp contrast to the repetition of the activities of the Levitical priests. Christ secures redemption that is eternal; that is, not repeated (v. 9) but possessing eschatological finality (5:9). While the word "redemption" is rather rare in the New Testament (9:12, 15; Luke 1:68; 2:38), this metaphor for salvation is common in both Judaism and Christianity, sometimes referring to freedom from slavery, sometimes from prison, sometimes from death, sometimes from sin. The sacrifice of Christ is, therefore, consummated in heaven. **His own blood:** In contrast to the Levitical sacrifice, Christ's sacrifice is the offering of his own blood, not the blood of another. Christ's offer of himself purifies the inner self, the conscience (see comments at v. 9), from dead works.

9:13 Ashes of a heifer: Why the reference to this ritual of the red heifer (for its details and purpose, see Num. 19) is not clear. That the heifer was slaughtered and burned "outside the camp" may anticipate 13:12, 13. Certain elements in the ritual of the heifer do serve to set up the contrasting sacrifice of Christ: the blood is sprinkled on the outside of the tabernacle, reminding the reader of the external efficacy of the Levitical system; the heifer is referred to as a sin offering; and the ashes of the heifer in the water of purification cleanse the bodies (flesh) of those sprinkled.

To worship: The purpose of Christ's sacrifice for us is in order that we may worship (serve, NIV) the living God. The expression "to serve" comes from the cultus and has the immediate sense of worship, but throughout the New Testament includes service to God much more broadly (12:28; Rom. 1:9; Phil. 3:3; Luke 1:74; Acts 27:23).

9:15–22
Sacrifice and the New Covenant

The writer now returns to the theme of covenant and to the explicit language of Jer. 31. Two benefits of Christ's death are stated. First, his death provided an inheritance for those who are called. Here salvation is cast in terms of the promised inheritance developed earlier (4:1–11; 6:12–20). Second, Christ's death sets free from transgressions under the first covenant.

9:16–17 Where a will is involved: The same Greek word means both "covenant" and "will." The writer argues the necessity of Christ's death by playing on the ambiguity of the word. A will does not go into effect until the death of the one making the will. Yet even if the key term is understood as "covenant," the writer is arguing on the basis of ancient rites of covenant making in which the slaughter of an animal symbolically represented the parties who pledged with their lives the keeping of the covenant. The person or persons ratifying the covenant have thus in a symbolic manner given their lives.

9:18–21 Not . . . without blood: The shedding of blood is essential in the inauguration of a covenant. The writer draws on the tradition of the covenant at Sinai to make the point (Exod. 24). There are noticeable differences. Apparently the writer of Hebrews is either following a tradition other than Exod. 24 or is taking the "first covenant" in a general sense and hence feels free to amalgamate various rituals performed "under the law" (v. 22). However, the writer draws the reader's attention to one element only: **This is the blood of the covenant that God has ordained for you** (v. 20; Exod. 24:8).

9:22 Almost everything: An acknowledgment that in the Levitical system there were some rituals of cleansing using substances other than blood. **Without the shedding of blood there is no forgiveness:** Read here no "putting away" or "removal" ([9:22b] The NRSV adds "of sins," which is not in the Greek text). The statement is a fitting summary of the claims made about blood thus far in this chapter: blood provides entrance before God (v. 7), purification of the conscience (v. 14), inauguration of a covenant (v. 18), cleansing of those entering a covenant (v. 19), and purifying almost everything (v. 22). Understanding Hebrews requires placing oneself within a cultus in which the above-mentioned vocabulary and actions were integral to rituals of cleansing, renewal, approaching God, and community forming. The writer presents the benefits of Christ for believers in these same images, obviously with hope for the same effects: cleansing, renewal, approaching God, and community formation.

9:23–10:18
Better Sacrifices

Interpreters are divided as to how far to press the analogy in v. 23. Animal sacrifices purify the earthly sanctuary (Lev. 16:16; 20:3, 21:23; Num. 19:20); does this mean that the better sacrifice of Christ purifies the heavenly sanctuary? If thus pressed, then there is sin or impurity in the heavenly realm in need of cleansing. It seems wiser to take the analogy in a broad and general sense, to understand that Christ has entered the heavenly sanctuary with a better sacrifice, that is, himself, but to draw no more detailed comparisons than the writer does in the resummarizing that follows (vv. 24–26).

9:24–26 On our behalf: The intercessory function of Christ's ministry (2:18; 4:15; 7:25) is not to be separated from the cross that preceded it. **At the end of the age:** Christ's sacrifice of himself is portrayed as an eschatological event. The phrase "the end of the age" is found elsewhere in the New Testament in Matthew (13:39, 40, 49; 24:3; 28:20), but the view of Christ as the central eschatological event is more widely expressed (1 Cor. 10:11; Gal. 4:4; 1 Pet. 1:20).

9:27–28: The descriptions quite possibly contain lines drawn from the catechesis the readers had received at baptism (6:1–2). **Die once, and after that the judgment:** The comparison between the common human experience and Christ's salvific work is formally balanced, perhaps an excerpt from a larger confessional statement. But whether from a catechism or original, the central point is not our death and judgment; these serve as analogies to underscore the emphasis on the once-for-all nature of Christ's high-priestly ministry. Christ's second appearance will not be to deal with sin, since that work was done once for all. Rather, the second coming will be for the consummation of salvation for those eagerly awaiting his coming.

10:1 The law . . . only a shadow: Previous chapters used spatial categories; but here the "shadow" and the "true form" are temporal categories, reminiscent of Plato's philosophy, which refer to what the law "foreshadows" and the "good things to come" in Christ. **Things to come:** That the benefits in Christ are "to come" does not mean that they are totally futuristic from the believer's perspective, but that from the perspective of the law they were "to come." By returning to the temporal categories (past, present, future) the writer can again discuss the historical dimension of Christ's high-priestly ministry, namely, his death on the cross.

10:2 Consciousness of sin: "Conscience" is a key term in the discussions of the subjective side of Christ's sacrifice for sin. The word, used in Hebrews five times—variously used in Hellenistic, Jewish, and Christian writers to refer to the human capacity for self-knowing, self-accusing, and when liberated, self-affirming—is the writer's term of choice for locating the place where the "objective" act of Christ's sacrifice meets the "subjective" self of the believer.

10:5–6 Sacrifices and offerings you have not desired: Ps. 40:6–8 is introduced as words of Christ at the time of his incarnation, his coming into the world. Attributing Old Testament citations to Christ is fully in accord with Hebrews Christology (1:1–4) and has been done previously at 2:12–13. In its own context Ps. 40:6–8 is a familiar prophetic warning against excessive dependence on ritual and a testimony to God's preference for obedience and observance of the law within the heart (1 Sam. 15:22; Ps. 50:8–10; Isa. 1:10–13; Jer. 7:21–24; Hos. 6:6; Amos 5:21–26). **Body you have prepared for me:** In the Hebrew text Ps. 40:6 reads, "Ears you have dug for me." The image is of one prepared to listen and to obey (Isa. 50:5). However, the writer of Heb. 10:5 uses a variant reading of the LXX text of Ps. 40:6 that replaces "ear" with "body." This alternate reading fits perfectly the argument now being brought to a close; that is, not through the repeated rituals of the law's system but through Christ we have been sanctified (2:11; 9:13; 10:10, 14, 29; 13:12).

10:7 In the scroll of the book it is written of me: The parenthetical reference could refer to the common notion of God making entries in a book about each of us, what we are to do and what we do (Pss. 56:8; 139:16). Or the psalmist may have in mind the book of the laws governing the conduct of the king (Deut. 17:18).

10:9 He abolishes the first in order to establish the second: The Old Testament tradition is presented as attempting to correct itself (Ps. 40:6–8), rather than a Christian critique of the Old Testament.

10:11–13 Every priest . . . but when Christ: The priests stand, because their work never ends but is rather a day after day after day tedium of ineffectiveness; in contrast, Christ sits, because his single offering once for all has been completed, and he has only to wait until all its effects are brought to fruition. **Footstool for his feet:** Citing Ps. 110:1, with which this section began (8:1), the writer pictures the eschatological consummation of Christ's sacrifice, which will see this end to all his enemies.

10:17 Remember their sins . . . no more: This theme from Jer. 31 describes the new covenant, now in place, and its benefits are ours. This is the last word. And the very last words are "no more" and "no longer"; no more remembrance of sin, no longer any need for the continuation of cultic acts that by their very repetition testified to their ineffectiveness.

10:19–39
LIFE IN RESPONSE TO THIS MINISTRY OF CHRIST

The hortatory material in 10:19–39 parallels in form that which preceded the exposition of Christ's priestly ministry in 7:1–10:18. As in 5:11–6:20, the exhortation consists of admonition (10:19–25), stern warning (10:26–31), and encouragement based on the church's prior performances (10:32–39).

10:19–25
A Threefold Admonition

A statement of christological grounds is followed by a threefold admonition, each portion beginning with the hortatory formula, "let us": let us approach God, let us hold fast, and let us help one another. The first admonition centers on faith, the second on hope, and the third on love, giving the paragraph the balanced and rounded-off quality of a homily.

10:19 We have confidence: The boldness of which the writer has previously spoken in a strongly subjective sense (3:6; 4:16) now carries more objective weight in that the believers' boldness has been given firm footing, "authorization," by the entrance of our pioneer, our forerunner (2:10; 6:20) Jesus. **By the blood of Jesus:** Our entrance is into the sanctuary, the Most Holy Place, where God dwells and where Christ now is (2:10; 4:3, 10; 6:19). As unique as his act was, our entry by the new and living (4:12; 7:25; 10:31) way will be after the manner of his, and that is by obedience to God's will (10:5–10).

10:20 He opened for us: This echoes the entire new covenant discussion (see 9:18) and sets the reader in that theological context. **Through the curtain (that is, through his flesh):** The debated issue regarding this phrase is whether the reader is to take "flesh" as appositional to "curtain," thereby identifying his flesh as the curtain or veil. But nowhere else in Hebrews, with all its discussion of the veil of the tabernacle, is the veil identified as Christ's body. Rather, the way through the veil has been provided by the offering of himself (9:12–14, 10:10).

10:22 Let us approach: Our approach to God, of which the writer has already spoken (4:16; 7:19), does not have here a stated purpose, but undoubtedly it is "to worship the living God" (9:14). Our approach should be with sincerity and integrity ("true heart," Isa. 38:3) and with abundant faith (6:11). **Sprinkled clean:** This obvious reference to baptism testifies to the early church's joining of baptism to inward changes in the one being baptized. The language here may be liturgical. The similarity to 1 Pet. 3:21 is striking.

10:23 Let us hold fast: Confidence and firmness to the end must characterize hope because the final results of Christ's work are not yet in, and there are many enemies (10:13). This confidence is grounded finally not in the strength of our grasp, but in the trustworthiness of the one who keeps promises (6:13–18).

10:24 Let us consider: This is now the second time the writer has called on his readers to "consider" (3:1). **How to provoke:** The word can also be translated "pester." Provocation can, of course, have a negative sense (Num. 14:11; Deut. 1:34; Acts 15:39; 1 Cor. 13:5), but the word also had a positive use in the sense of disturbing the apathetic or fearful into activity.

10:25 Neglecting: Some members of the community are neglecting (abandoning; see 2 Tim. 4:10, 16; Matt. 27:46) the assembly, the gathering for worship, and acts of mutual support. Reminders that the Day was near (Rev. 1:3) were integral to sustaining the eschatological expectation of the community.

10:26–31
Warning about the Future

Similar to 6:4–8, the warning includes four statements: the prior experience of the believers; the apostasy, the impossibility of renewal, the final fate.

10:26 Persist in sin: The use of the present tense of continuing action ("keep on sinning" [NIV]) makes it clear that the violation and its penalty concern sin that is intentional and continuous. The author is recalling the language of Num. 15:22–31, where it is stipulated repeatedly that atonement ceremonies under the first covenant dealt with "unintentional" sins. **After having received the knowledge of the truth:.** Having "knowledge of the truth" was used by early Christians to refer to their faith experience (John 8:32; 17:3; 1 Tim. 2:4; 4:3).

10:27 Prospect of judgment: Now that sacrifices are not repeated, there awaits only a certain judgment of fire. A general conflagration was widely associated with God's final judgment (Zeph. 1:18; Isa. 26:11; Matt. 25:41; 2 Pet. 3:7, 12).

10:28 The law of Moses: Under the law of Moses the death penalty was stipulated for murder (Lev. 24:17), blasphemy (Lev. 24:14–16), and idolatry (Deut. 17:2–7). This last violation is the one in the writer's mind, since it constituted a breach of covenant. In an argument from "lesser to greater" (a fortiori), those who reject life under the new covenant can expect even more severity. Greater blessings imply greater judgment.

10:29 Profaned the blood: Having treated the blood of the covenant as common, vulgar, and profane, the violators have **outraged** ("insulted" [NIV]) **the Spirit of grace.** The participle is a form of the word transliterated "hubris," used in the Hellenistic culture to refer to a haughty arrogance that belittles others. Two texts are cited that remind everyone that judgment belongs to God alone (Deut. 32:35a, with a slight variation from the LXX, and Deut. 32:36; also Rom. 12:19).

10:31 A fearful thing: This proclamation has the ring of prophetic pronouncement. The living God is held before apostates as "a consuming fire" (12:24). The behavior described here and at 6:4–8 can be understood through the language of covenant. In the patron-client relationships prevalent in the first-century Mediterranean world, persons in position to bestow favors (freedom, money, political advantage, etc.) entered into relationships, directly or through a mediator (broker), with persons needing and seeking those favors. In return, the clients gave to their patrons gratitude and honor. If a client were ever to violate that relationship, either by public denial or gradually drifting away, the affront to the person and honor of the patron would be of such gravity that the patron and client would become adversaries. The position and public esteem of the patron would require severe punishment of the former client.

10:32–39
Recall Those Earlier Days

The activation of the community's memory was basic to preaching in both synagogue and church (Lev. 19:33–34; the entirety of Deuteronomy; 1 Cor. 15:1; 2 Tim. 1:6; 2 Pet. 3:2). The recollection is of times when the readers were subject to verbal and physical abuse, but times, nevertheless, when they were firm, bold, and sympathetic.

10:32 Struggle with sufferings: This contest with sufferings came only **after you had been enlightened** (v. 26; 6:4). Becoming followers of Christ did not end hardship, but began it in new and intense ways.

10:33–34b Endured a hard struggle: Four expressions, framed as a chiasmus, a literary pattern (ABBA), reiterate two aspects of the congregation's sufferings: those endured directly and those endured in sympathy with others. This description is in sharp contrast to the tendency of some to absent themselves from the church assemblies (v. 25). **Compassion for those who were in prison:** Demonstrating sympathy for those imprisoned involved more than a feeling of sadness or regret; rather it meant visits, providing food, running errands, and perhaps interceding (Phil. 2:25; Matt. 25:36). All these activities meant risk of further abuse. **Cheerfully accepted the plundering:** The plundering of the property of Christians may refer to official seizure, mob violence, or perhaps the burglarizing of the homes of believers who were taken to prison. Citizens of the Roman Empire often made life miserable for minority groups, ethnic or religious. The Christians were sustained by the certainty that they had another kind of possession, "better" (1:4; 7:19; 8:6) and "permanent" (7:3; 11:14–16; 13:14); they cheerfully anticipated it, embracing a perspective traced back to Jesus himself (Matt. 5:12; Luke 6:22; Rom. 5:3; Acts 5:41).

10:35–36 Great reward: What is at stake is the final reward, the lasting possession, that God will give in the day of judgment. **Endurance:** To the "very end" (6:11) can be a long time, but for them "endurance" was the very definition of God's will. At the end of endurance lies the promise, a term already familiar as a reference to the salvation provided by Christ (4:1, 8; 6:12, 17; 8:6).

10:37–38 Live by faith: This final quality urged on the readers is introduced by a composite quotation of Scripture, Isa. 26:20 and Hab. 2:3–4, adapted to bring out the messianic references in the text.

10:39 Not among those who shrink back: The writer here anticipates a roll call of those among whom we live, men and women who did not shrink back but who held firmly to their faith in God. Such will be the content of chap. 11.

11:1–12:17
A CALL TO FIDELITY AND MUTUALITY

The movement of this section is from the earlier experiences of faithful endurance by the readers (10:32–39), to examples from redemptive history (11:1–40), to Jesus and the Christian community

(12:1–17). Hebrews 11:1–40 is a single literary piece, in form, function, and theme. Verses 2 and 39 form an inclusion by the use of the unusual passive form of the verb "to witness." When so used, it is variously translated "received approval," "was attested," "were commended" (vv. 2, 4, 5, 39). Some variant of the noun "faith" appears twenty-four times as exemplary figures from history are presented, despite the frequent lack of any reference to faith as the moving force in their lives in the Old Testament texts (even though it may be strongly implied). The phrase "by faith" names the perspective of the writer's rereading of the Old Testament. The eighteen repetitions of the phrase "by faith" (a rhetorical device called anaphora) impact memory when teaching, impress listeners when used in an oration, and have cumulative effect when employed in argumentation. Brief lists with sermonic functions can be found elsewhere in Jewish tradition, at Josh. 24:2–13 and 1 Sam 12:6–15. In Wis. 10:1–11:1, Wisdom functions in the recital very much as Faith does in Heb. 11. The hymn to the ancestors ("Let us now praise famous men") in Sir. 44:1–49:16 has much in common with Heb. 11, but the closest parallel to our text is in the Christian epistle *1 Clement* (17:1–19:3). However, for Clement the virtue being extolled is not Faith but Humility.

11:1–2
FAITH REFOCUSED

11:1 Faith is: We find not a "definition" of faith; after all, the word "faith" will sometimes indicate trust or belief and sometimes refer to the quality of loyalty or faithfulness. Rather than offering a definition, the author provides thematic unity to the discussion. The orientation remains eschatological, and that perspective will prevail through v. 40. As used here, faith cannot be severed from hope. **Assurance of things hoped for:** The word is used at 3:14 with the obvious sense of "confidence" on our part, but at 1:3 the meaning is more philosophical, referring to the very essence of substance or being of God. The association with faith, then, joins the subjective and the objective: "faith is the substance of that for which we hope." **Conviction of things not seen:** This key word "conviction" is more at home in a court of law and can properly be translated "proof" or "demonstration": "faith is proof of the unseen." That which is not seen may be a reference to the future, given the orientation of the entire chapter toward what lay in promise for all the faithful.

11:2 Our ancestors: The persons referred to are called "elders," but not in any technical sense (as at Mark 7:3, 5); they are the characters in the recital soon to begin (v. 4). The approval they received is literally "received testimony"; this is to say, their lives are in the biblical record as lives of faith. That the Scripture bears witness to them (7:8, 17; 10:15) is the equivalent of saying that God testifies to their faithfulness. The brief sketches in the roll call that follows are thus to be read as God's testimony about their lives.

11:3–7
FAITH: FROM CREATION TO NOAH

11:3 We understand: By beginning uncharacteristically with "we" as the subject, rather than one of the ancestors, the writer begins the narrative as it ends, in the first person (vv. 39–40). This is to say, the roll call of the faithful springs from the earlier word, "we are among those who have faith" (10:39) and moves toward the conviction that "apart from us, they would not be made perfect" (11:40). **Made from things that are not visible:** The assertion here is that the visible came from the invisible, and the invisible is the word of God. That the word of God (Gen. 1: "And God said") brought into being the universe is a tenet of faith that is proof of the unseen.

11:4 Abel: The interest in Abel is as focused as the very sparse record in Gen. 4:4: his life is distilled into a single act, the offering of a sacrifice to God which, in comparison with his brother's was "better" or "greater." The NRSV says "more acceptable," but on what grounds? The writer does not speculate; it is enough that it was offered by faith and God testified (approved, attested) that through that faith Abel was righteous (Hab. 2:4 at Heb. 10:38; also Matt. 23:35; 1 John 3:12).

11:5–6 Enoch: The slightly elaborated translation of Gen. 5:24 that "Enoch pleased God" provided the author an exegetical base for a general principle regarding faith. The argument unfolds in this way: if Enoch pleased God, then he was a person of faith because **without faith it is impossible to please God. Rewards those who seek him:** That God rewards faith is a clear conviction of Hebrews (10:35) and an important feature of the recital in chap. 11 (e.g., 11:26).

11:7 Noah: Noah's faith is that he trusted God's warning (8:5; 12:25) about what was not yet apparent, the flood (Gen. 6:8–9:17). **By this he condemned the world:** The antecedent of "this" can be either "faith" or "ark." Most likely it was his faith that served to judge the world, a judgment that could have been indirect in the way that a person of faith is a judgment on unbelieving contemporaries.

11:8–22
FAITH: FROM SARAH AND ABRAHAM
TO JOSEPH

This unit is the heart of the narrative, and Abraham, with Sarah, is its central figure (Gen. 12–22). It becomes apparent during the three narratives concerning Abraham that in this narrative faith and hope are one, and life is pilgrimage. God makes promises and keeps them (recall 6:18–20), regardless of the time that passes and the circumstances that seem hopeless.

11:8–9 Abraham: Abraham's faith is expressed in obedience, implied in Gen. 12 but explicitly stated here, a quality Abraham shares not only with Christians (5:9) but with Christ himself (5:7). **Set out for a place:** The substitution of "place" for "land" (Gen. 12:1) seems also deliberate, opening the door to a new interpretation of Abraham's destination (vv. 10, 13–16), an interpretation already suggested at 4:8 and 8:15. That the place Abraham was to receive was an inheritance is clearly implied in the Genesis story (15:7; 22:17; 28:4), but the word is used here to attract the positive associations of that term already presented to the reader (1:2, 4, 14; 6:12, 17; 9:15; 11:7). **Living in tents:** In this place he lived temporarily as in the home of another. The terminology recalls not only the experience in Canaan (Gen. 17:8; 23:4; 37:1), but also the time in Egypt (Gen. 12:10; 15:13; Acts 7:6). Some Christians found this language also appropriate to characterize their life in the world (Eph. 2:19; 1 Pet. 1:17; 2:11).

11:10 He looked forward: This Christian interpretation makes Abraham's hope eschatological, not to be fulfilled by possession of a piece of real estate. For a sense of the intensity of his "looking forward," see the same word at Acts 17:16; 1 Cor. 16:11; Heb. 10:13; and Jas. 5:7. In contrast to the tent home, the image of life that is temporary and vulnerable, Abraham anticipated a city, permanent and with sure foundation; that is, the heavenly Jerusalem (v. 16; 12:22, 28; 13:14).

11:11 Received the power of procreation: This brief summary gathers up all that the Genesis accounts say about both Abraham and Sarah with reference to advanced age, sexual inactivity, and barrenness (Gen. 15:1–6; 17:15–22; 18:9–15; cf also Rom. 4:19).

11:13–16 The recital of ancient models of faith is temporarily halted in order to reflect on its meaning. **All of these:** Likely a reference to Abraham, Isaac, and Jacob (v. 9), the pilgrim patriarchs; the context makes it clear that the promise not received was **a homeland** (v. 14). This was true in the literal sense as a reference to Canaan, but in the present discussion the homeland is the **better country, that is, a heavenly one** (v. 16). The homeland they see from a distance is one seen with eyes of faith. The "better country" that the resident aliens "desired" is "better" by reason of being heavenly rather than earthly. This vision empowered them not only to live as **strangers and foreigners on the earth** but to confess publicly that such was their life. They could have abandoned the pilgrimage and settled into the values, goals, and relationships of the land in which they now lived as strangers. Instead, they lived as strangers and aliens, and in that culture had to endure the verbal abuse, the disgrace, and often the economic mistreatment heaped on persons of lower social status (see comments at 10:32–34).

11:17 Abraham . . . offered up Isaac: The next example of Abraham comes from Gen. 22:1–8, the offering or, as expressed in Jewish tradition, the binding (Akedah) of Isaac. A prominent feature of the Gen. 22 account and of the tradition around it is the introductory statement, "God tested Abraham" (Gen. 22:1). None of the other exemplars of faith presented in Heb. 11 is so portrayed. His offering of his son is a testimony to his faith. In other words, by faith Abraham offered his son to God.

11:18 Of whom he had been told: The unusual nature of Abraham's faith is accented by contrasting the promise and the test. The promise of progeny was tied to the birth of Isaac; the test calls for the end of Isaac's life. The testing of Abraham thus seems to contradict his faith, the promise, and the character of the God in whom he trusted. The offering of Isaac is, in Kierkegaard's famous expression, "the suspension of the ethical" in the service of one's faith.

11:19 He considered the fact that God is able even to raise someone from the dead: Faith that God is able to raise someone from the dead is not a part of the Gen. 22 story. However, it is in the tradition. Of the Eighteen Benedictions of the synagogue service, the second concludes, "Blessed are you, O God, who raises the dead." **Figuratively speaking, he did receive him back:** It is unusual that the author would say "figuratively" (literally "in

a parable" or "parabolically speaking") since Abraham did in fact receive back Isaac. In the writer's earlier use of the word "parable" at 9:9, the first tabernacle was called a parable of the true tabernacle yet to be. This is to say, "parable" was used eschatologically to point to a future reality, and its function at 11:19 is very likely the same. That which is foreshadowed in this parable is not only the resurrection of Christ, although that is included (13:20), but the vindication, the deliverance, of all God's faithful.

11:20–22 Isaac . . . Jacob . . . Joseph: The briefer sketches of these heroes have in common the future orientation of faith; that is, faith is in large measure hope. In the cases of Isaac and Jacob, this hope-filled faith is expressed in the blessing of descendants; with Joseph it is evident in prophetic words about the future of his people, a future in which he wanted to share even as a corpse. **Bowing in worship over the top of his staff:** The reference quotes the LXX of Gen. 47:31. The Hebrew text has "head of his bed." The image is of a man of faith worshiping the God of promises and reaffirming faith in those promises by blessing his grandsons. By faith, both Jacob and Joseph joined the exodus and even in death claimed the promise. Thus Joseph's story moves the narrative forward to the exodus itself.

11:23–31
FAITH: MOSES AND ISRAEL

Abraham and Moses are clearly the principal figures in the recital of heroic faith, each being treated at much greater length than the others. The movements of Moses' own life of faith are four: his being hidden as a child (v. 23); his identification with his own people rather than with the Egyptians (vv. 24–26); his flight from Egypt (v. 27); and his institution of the Passover (v. 28). This structure parallels the telling of the Abraham story.

11:23 Moses was hidden: This is in fact a witness to Moses' parents' faith. They (Exod. 2:2 in the LXX; the Heb. text mentions only the mother) hid him three months because he was "beautiful." The child's comeliness was taken as a sign of God's favor. In Stephen's speech rehearsing Israel's history, Moses is said to have been "beautiful before God" (Acts 7:20). The parents' faith is expressed in their boldness or courage in the face of the Egyptian king's edict. In the biblical text it is the midwives who fear God (Gen. 1:17, 21), but perhaps the writer here felt that such a characterization of the parents was a justifiable inference.

11:24–26 Refused to be called a son of Pharaoh's daughter: That Moses had become "a son of Pharaoh's daughter" is based on the statement of Exod. 2:10, "He became her son." This clearly implies that Moses would be an heir of the monarch's house. Moses' act of refusal was likely the killing of the Egyptian who was beating a Hebrew (Exod. 2:11–15). Moses' choice was clear: he turned his back on the palace life with its fleeting pleasures of sin and joined his own oppressed people (vv. 24–25). Moses' choice, like Abraham's before him, was to act out of faith in God, knowing the hardships that would follow such a choice. Given the readers' social and economic situation (10:32–34), the lesson from Moses' faith could hardly be missed.

11:26 Greater wealth: The greater wealth is the "abuse" ("disgrace" [1 Tim. 3:7]; "insults" [Rom. 15:3]; "abuse" [Heb. 10:33; 13:13]) of Christ. But what of the enigmatic expression, "the reproach of Christ"? Who or what is the Christ, the Anointed One? The language of Heb. 11:26 seems to be that of Ps. 88:52 LXX (89:52 Heb. text): "They have reproached your anointed one (Christ) by way of recompense." This psalm gives to the writer of Hebrews the key terms: reproach, anointed one (Christ), and reward (recompense). Hence, the writer of Hebrews seems to say that Moses envisioned the day of Jesus Christ and participated in his shame and reproach.

11:27 He left Egypt: This move parallels the first movement of Abraham's faith: "he set out for a place that he was to receive as an inheritance" (v. 8). **Unafraid of the king's anger:** This contradicts Exod. 2:14, where Moses was afraid of the king. The best solution is to regard Moses' fearlessness as an overall trait of his life, even though his impulse after killing the Egyptian was to run. Faith overcame fear, for Moses as for his parents (v. 23), the two examples underscoring an important lesson for the readers. Likewise vital to faith is perseverance (endurance), obviously another quality drawn from Moses' life because it addressed a need of the readers (6:11). **Him who is invisible:** This term for God, not found in the LXX, apparently arose in Hellenistic Judaism and was adopted by early Christians (Rom. 1:20; Col. 1:15; 1 Tim. 1:17).

11:28 He kept the Passover: The vocabulary and phrasing of Exod. 12 are preserved. The statement is straightforward, with no suggestion that the Passover or the pouring of blood was to be taken figuratively or symbolically, as was the case in the offering of Isaac (v. 19).

11:29–31: Three events, not characters, among the community are now utilized as examples "by faith." In each of these three episodes the contrast is made between the faith of Israel and the unbelief of Israel's opponents, with predictable consequences in each case. Believing Israel walked through the sea as on dry ground; the Egyptians drowned. Believing Israel captured Jericho; the inhabitants perished. Believing Rahab along with her family was rescued; the disobedient (unbelieving) inhabitants of Jericho were destroyed. By her act of hospitality Rahab cast her lot with Israel, and therefore Israel's faith was hers as well. The only woman besides Sarah mentioned in the list of exemplars of faith, Rahab was immortalized as a symbol of hospitality (Jas. 2:25), as was Abraham (Heb. 13:2). In the present context her faith is important in that she believed that the future belonged to Israel's God.

11:32–40
FAITH: PROPHETS AND MARTYRS

11:32 Time would fail me: The reader's familiarity with the stories is assumed, and the stories appear out of chronological order. This highlights the fact that the preceding narrative is not being sustained but is now replaced by dipping here and there into the story of salvation history.

11:33 Who through faith: The "who" would lead one to assume the nine activities refer back to the persons listed in v. 32, but as the list unfolds, it becomes evident that other persons from Israel's history are in the writer's mind.

11:35 Women received their dead by resurrection: This is surely an allusion to the widow of Zarephath (1 Kgs. 17:17–24) and to the Shunammite woman (2 Kgs. 4:32–37). **Others were tortured:** For these assorted descriptions, faith is faithfulness, a tenacity of hope of something better. The "torture" some endured is not a general reference to physical abuse; the word derives from the term for "drum," hence, beat as one would a drum.

11:37 Stoned . . . sawn . . . killed by the sword: These descriptive terms seem to come from a martyrology, and both ancient Jewish history and the more recent Maccabean revolt provide cases of such suffering. According to tradition Isaiah was sawn in two (*Ascen. Isa.* 5:1–14). **They went about . . . destitute:** Every period of revolt in Israel's history produced guerrilla warriors who hid out in the deserts and in mountain caves, surviving almost like animals, in order to strike another blow against the enemy. Living by values beyond the understanding of their contemporaries, these homeless and pursued faithful were not only a enigma to the world, they were beyond its deserving.

11:38–39 All these: In the conclusion, the inclusive phrase puts into one category all the exemplars of faith, from Abel to all those nameless ones since Eden **of whom the world was not worthy. Did not receive what was promised**: That they did not receive the promise is not due to any flaw in their faith; rather it was due to the unfolding purpose of God.

12:1–17
A CALL TO CONTINUE IN FAITH

With the endurance evident in the lives of exemplars of the past, the present aim of the writer is to encourage the readers to endure in their sufferings (10:32–34). Although some of the persons described were martyrs, the call is not for death but for endurance. In fact, the cross will be spoken of as something Jesus endured (12:2).

12:1 Cloud of witnesses: The ancient exemplars are gathered about the Christian community as a "cloud," here gathered as spectators at the athletic event in which we are runners. They now gather around us for whom the race is not finished. They are spectators whose presence exercises a strong positive influence on the runners. **Lay aside every weight:** The race easily lent itself as a metaphor for moral and ethical struggle, involving as it did rigorous training, self-discipline, intense effort, and laying aside anything that encumbered the contestant.

12:2 Looking to Jesus: Literally, the participle says, "looking away to," which implies looking away from everyone and everything else and concentrating on a single object. The writer has in mind the historical Jesus, who was one of us, tested as we are, subject to suffering and death (2:9–18; 4:15; 5:7–9). Apart from him, the forward-looking faith of the ancient exemplars could not be made perfect (complete, fulfilled [11:39–40]). **Who for the sake of the joy:** The preposition is variously translated "for," "for the sake of," "instead of." Until the Protestant Reformation, the most common translation was "instead of." This rendering presents *Jesus as* self-consciously choosing to suffer (10:5–7) instead of maintaining the joy of his preincar-

nate life (1:2). The alternate view—that is, that the joy was not already his but lay in prospect and "for the sake of" which he suffered—continues the forward-looking nature of faith presented earlier.

12:3 Endured such hostility: The word translated "hostility" indicates verbal opposition and abuse, referring back to the shame and disgrace of v. 2 and recalling a major element of the reader's own suffering (10:33). This text does something surprisingly rare in the New Testament: it argues for Christian conduct by a presentation of Jesus as example. There have been earlier occasions (esp. chaps. 2, 5), and there will be a subsequent one (13:13) for noting the importance of the historical Jesus in the message of Hebrews.

12:4–5 Not yet resisted: The author now turns from the example of Jesus to the second ground for exhortation: suffering as divine discipline. **The exhortation that addresses you:** By applying this text from Prov. 3 directly to the readers, the writer is, in effect, calling them children (lit. "sons") of God. It is very important that the congregation understand their experiences in the context of the parent-child relationship.

12:6 For the Lord disciplines: There is no doubt but that in Prov. 3 the discipline described involves punishment and correction. There were, however, ample uses of the word translated "discipline" in a nonpunitive sense of education and character formation available to the writer, especially in the Hellenistic culture and in Jewish writings strongly influenced by that culture (e.g., 4 Macc. 1:17; 5:24; 10:10; 13:22). While the writer is by no means offering a broad theology of suffering, there certainly is an attempt to provide a way of interpreting the present hardships of the readers. When their suffering is understood as discipline from God, then it can be seen, not as evidence of God's rejection, but as a sign of God's embrace.

12:9–10 Subject to the Father of spirits: The discipline of human parents and of God is compared, from lesser to greater. God's discipline is not given a time frame, because we do not outgrow the need. **As seemed best:** While human parents are guided by what seems best to them, implying both good intention and fallibility, God disciplines for the explicit purpose of sharing in God's holiness.

12:12 Lift your drooping hands: See Isa. 35:3, Prov. 4:26. The word is clear: recover your strength, stay on course, avoid careless worsening of your condition, and accept the healing that will enable you to finish the race.

12:14 Pursue peace: The congregation is reminded to be involved in aggressive initiatives toward peace and holiness. To "pursue peace" is a biblical expression (Ps. 34:14; 1 Pet. 3:11) that echoes v. 11b, and the effort to attain holiness continues a thought from v. 10b. Holiness has moral overtones, to be sure, but it has already been made clear that to be holy is to be sanctified by the self-giving of Christ (2:11; 9:13–14; 10:14). **With everyone:** The writer reminds the readers of the communal nature of the Christian life. The pursuit of peace "with everyone" is a congregational reference and not an injunction regarding their relationship with the larger society (contra NIV). Some members of the congregation are lagging behind and beginning to absent themselves from the assembly (10:25). Toward these the others are to assume some responsibility (3:12–14; 10:24).

12:15 That no root of bitterness springs up: Watchfulness is called for, lest one or more of their number "fall short" (same verb as at 4:1) of God's grace. The one who does so is not a single fatality; such a person is a "root" (a metaphor for a dangerous element in a society, 1 Macc. 1:10), a source of community disruption. If unchecked, the bitterness can spread to the entire church, with the result that **many become defiled.** The term "defiled" is cultic, the opposite of "sanctified" (see John 18:28; Titus 1:15).

12:16 See to it that no one becomes like Esau: The NIV is correct in translating the first adjective "sexually immoral" rather than simply "immoral" (NRSV), and sexual issues may have been a cause for concern among the readers (13:4). However, fornication was a metaphor for all kinds of unfaithfulness, especially idolatry (Deut. 31:16; Judg. 2:17; Jer. 2:20). The story of Esau in Genesis does not include accounts of fornication. However, the primary thrust of the warning is inescapable: some of those who are in line to inherit salvation and all the promises of God (1:14; 6:12, 17; 9:15; 11:7–8) are in danger of relinquishing it all for something worthless by comparison.

12:17 He was rejected: The blessing of his father Isaac was lost (Gen. 27:30–40), despite Esau's attempt to persuade his father to reverse the prior act of giving the blessing to Jacob. He **found no chance to repent.**

12:18–13:19
FINAL EXHORTATIONS

The final section of Hebrews consists of two units, a rhetorical flourish of metaphors on Mount Sinai and Mount Zion in 12:18–29 and pastoral words to conclude the letter in 13:1–19. The readers are as pilgrims who have come to Zion, the heavenly Jerusalem, in festive assembly with God, with Jesus, with all the saints, and with angels in joyful song. But again the church is warned: Christians have not arrived at a soft and permissive place; the proper posture is worship in reverence and awe. God remains "a consuming fire" (v. 29).

12:18–29
Not Something That Can Be Touched

Chapter 12 concludes with two sharp contrasts: what is palpable (can be touched) with what is heavenly (vv. 18–24), and what is shaken with what cannot be shaken (vv. 25–29). The first is between Mount Sinai and Mount Zion. Details of the description of the theophany at Sinai are taken primarily from Exod. 19:16–22; 20:18–21; Deut. 4:11–12; 5:22–27; 9:19, although "gloom" is probably the writer's contribution to the scene.

12:18–21 Fire, and darkness, and gloom, and a tempest: These traditional symbols of God's presence create a net effect that the people cannot bear it. **So terrifying was the sight:** The writer makes clear that the conditions under which the old covenant was given were dread, fear, distance, and exclusion (Exod. 19:23).

12:22 You have come: The verb "come" is cultic, referring to one's approach in worship. **Mount Zion, the city of the living God**, and **the heavenly Jerusalem** are in reality a single eschatological reference. Since the time of David, Zion and Jerusalem were regarded as the location of God's presence, sometimes both being named, sometimes one or the other (Ps. 2:6; Isa. 8:18; Mic. 4:1; Joel 2:32; 3:16–17). **Innumerable angels in festal gathering:** Within the heavenly city are thousands upon thousands of angels in joyous celebration who fill God's court and attend God's self-disclosure (Deut. 33:2; Ps. 68:17–18; Dan. 7:10; Rev. 5:11).

12:23 The assembly of the firstborn: The firstborn receive the inheritance (12:16), and they share in the benefits of him who is the Firstborn of God (1:6; see Col. 1:15, 18). That "you have come" to **God, the judge of all** is in this context a positive and welcome experience.

The judge is the God of all and therefore, the believers can anticipate fairness, impartiality, and vindication. **Spirits of the righteous:** This presence before God is a traditional figure (Wis. 3:1; Rev. 6:9–10), but to it the writer joins a familiar theme: perfection. This means the righteous dead have completed their pilgrimage, to be joined by the faithful readers.

12:24 To the sprinkled blood: That the blood of Jesus speaks **a better word than** that **of Abel** is not a contrast but a comparison; reference to Abel recalls 11:4, which refers to his acceptable sacrifice of an animal (Gen. 4:4).

12:25–26 See that you do not refuse: This warning uses previous language to establish a contrast, a contrast between Sinai and Zion, between earth and heaven, between what will be shaken and that which cannot be shaken, between Israel and the readers. The unbelieving and disobedient people did not escape God's punishment (2:3; 3:16–18; 4:11; 10:27–28). How unreasonable, then, to think that we will escape if we refuse the voice from heaven. **At that time:** The earth-heaven contrast becomes a then-now contrast, introducing the quotation of Hag. 2:6. This was Haggai's word of assurance concerning the future splendor of the temple in a time of great confusion and disappointment. The writer of Hebrews quotes only one-half the verse to point to an eschatological shaking of the old universe.

12:27–28 Removal of what is shaken: In the eschatological convulsion, all created things will be removed. Creation is here portrayed, not as evil or corrupt, but as temporal and transient. That which is unshakable has been there all along, but will be fully evident after the removal of all that is temporary. This contrast again echoes Ps. 102:25–27, cited at 1:10–12. **Since we are receiving a kingdom that cannot be shaken:** This phrase from Dan. 7:10 is stated in present time. Again the future is balanced with the present because the event that determines the eschaton has already occurred and the community of faith is already participating in its benefits (4:14–16; 9:14; 10:19–22). **Worship with reverence and awe:** The access to God already available is lived out in their worship, and worship that pleases God (13:16, 21; recall Enoch, 11:5) is marked by gratitude, reverence, and awe—for it is God whom we approach in worship.

12:29 God is a consuming fire: In biblical texts, such as this quote from Deut. 4:24a, fire is often associated with the presence of God (1:7; 12:18; Acts 2:3; Joel 2:3; Sir. 45:19), and especially with scenes of judgment (6:8; Matt. 25:41; 1 Cor. 3:13; 2 Thess. 1:78; 2 Pet. 3:7). The writer concludes this exhortation with the same stern voice with which 10:26–31 ended, not simply because of the nature of worship, which reveres the awesomeness of God, but because of pastoral concern for a church plagued by neglect, apathy, absenteeism, retreat, and near the point of apostasy. But stern warnings are followed by instruction and encouragement.

13:1–19
LIFE IN THE FAITH COMMUNITY

The author, unable to be present to deliver the sermon, changes style and concludes the sermon as a letter to be read to the congregation.

13:1 Mutual love: Four couplets, each stating a pair of related exhortations with comments interspersed that provide support and motive for the action enjoined, begin the ending of the letter.

13:2 Do not neglect to show hospitality to strangers: Among those things that cannot be shaken is the mutual love within the covenant community. But this mutuality is not a closed circle; the community is not to "**forget**" ([NIV]; **neglect** [NRSV]) love of strangers. The strangers in mind here are most likely the itinerant Christians who depended on local Christian communities for hospitality (Matt. 25:35; Rom. 12:13; 1 Tim. 3:2; 1 Pet. 4:9). It is understandable, however, why some house churches, either living in an atmosphere of suspicion due to opposition and persecution from society, or facing the upheavals created by traveling heretics, would become reticent about extending hospitality. Some even used certain criteria for "testing" strangers before welcoming them (3 John 9–10; *Did.* 11). **Entertained angels without knowing it:** The implication is that such a pleasant and blessed possibility existed for the readers. The allusion is most likely to Abraham and Sarah welcoming three visitors who brought the good news of a promised son (Gen. 18:1–21), but there are other stories of hospitality to mysterious strangers (Gen. 19:1–14; Judg. 6:11–18; 13:3–22; Tob. 12:1–20; Matt. 25:35–36).

13:3 Remember: Remembering involves solidarity. The author earlier had spoken with appreciation of the readers' partnership with those suffering public abuse (10:33) and compassion for the imprisoned (10:34). Here the language of solidarity is even stronger: behave as though you yourselves were in prison with them, as though you yourselves were being mistreated. **As though you yourselves were being tortured:** This negates the ability to distance oneself from those suffering out of fear of becoming the target of mistreatment; the writer urges providing for the needs of prisoners, even though this meant exposing oneself as a fellow Christian, and being present with the sufferers in every way that might encourage and give relief. Even intercession with local authorities would not be out of the question.

13:4 Let the marriage bed be kept undefiled: The Christian community continued Judaism's high regard for marriage and its strong prohibition against adultery, the violation of the marriage vow (Exod. 20:14). The Roman governor Pliny, investigating the Christian community in Bithynia early in the second century, reported to Emperor Trajan that Christians bound themselves with an oath that included abstaining from adultery. The author brings marriage into the circle of sanctification essential to worship that is acceptable to God (12:28).

13:5 Love of money: This fourth and final couplet uses the negative form of the word used in 1 Tim. 6:10. **Be content:** Contentment with what one had was a commonplace in Greek morality and was embraced by early Christians (Luke 3:14; Phil. 4:11; 1 Tim. 6:8). The writer's addressing the problems of sexual misconduct and greed together is probably due not to the frequent link between these two vices in society, but rather to the prohibitions against them in the seventh and eighth of the Ten Commandments (Exod. 20:14–15). **For he has said:** Deut. 31:6, Ps. 118:6. The Scripture citations combine to say that the believer's trust in God makes trust in money not only misplaced but a contradiction of faith (recall Matt. 6:24–34).

13:7 Remember your leaders: Benefit for life and fidelity is to be derived from remembering former leaders. Good examples are good teachers, as chap. 11 argued abundantly. There is no indication that these leaders held particular offices; the term used here for "leaders" is a general one, used not only in religion but also in politics and the military (Luke 22:26; Acts 15:22; Sir. 17:17; 1 Macc. 9:30). They are identified only by their function: they spoke the word of God, that is, they preached the gospel (Acts 4:29, 31; Phil. 1:14; 1 Pet. 4:11). These leaders may have been the founders of the congregation. **Consider the outcome of their**

way of life: There is some uncertainty here as to precise meaning. The outcome (result, end) could be the result of their preaching, or it could be a reference to their deaths. Martyrdom may be implied, but more likely the sense is that they were faithful to the end (6:11–12; 10:39). It is their fidelity that is to be imitated.

13:8–9 The same yesterday and today and forever: This acclamation about Jesus Christ may be a traditional formula drawn from elsewhere, perhaps from a confession of faith. The sameness of Christ can anchor the fidelity of the church. While the faithful leaders whose fidelity was exemplary have passed on, Jesus Christ whom they preached has not; he remains eternally the same. Therefore, the eternal sameness of Jesus Christ is the place to stand when the congregation is called on to deal with **all kinds of strange teachings**.

Do not be carried away: The warning about teachings (Jude 12) became a rather standard warning in battles with heresy (Eph. 4:14–16; Col. 2:8; 1 Tim. 1:3–7). **Regulations about food:** That problems arose in some congregations over meals—that is, what to eat, who is to eat, and the manner of eating—is evident from other writings (Acts 11:3; 15:20; Rom. 14; 1 Cor. 8, 10–11). There were ritual meals in Hellenistic religions that held some attraction, as well as confusion, for some Christians (1 Cor. 10). All Jewish meals have a ritual and numinous meaning, and it could have been that some members of the congregation with a background in Judaism continued certain ritual meals. Another possibility is that the issue over foods was due to an interpretation of the Lord's Supper. If some were making the Lord's Supper a sacrificial meal with meanings drawn from either Jewish or Hellenistic influences, then perhaps the author regarded such an interpretation a contradiction of the once-and-for-all nature of Christ's sacrifice. At any rate, the statement in v. 9 is not polemical as though there were a heretical intrusion threatening the congregation, but is rather pastoral exhortation, instructing and correcting.

13:10 We have an altar: Given the lengthy argument distinguishing old covenant and new, old priesthood and new, earthly tent and heavenly in 7:1–10:18, it seems *wisest to* understand our "altar" in a metaphorical sense; that is, as the place of our having received and continuing to receive the grace of God through the high priesthood of Christ.

13:11–12: The readers are asked again to recall the Day of Atonement (9:1–14; Lev. 16). The focus is on the point that the bodies of the sacrificial animals were not eaten by the high priest, but were burned outside the camp (Lev. 16:27). Not even the sacrifices under the old system were eaten; so, by implication, why would Christians interpret their participation in the sacrifice of Christ as a ritual meal in which Christ is regarded as a food? If some are attempting to bring into the congregation an interpretation borrowed from the Levitical system, they need to read again Lev. 16; there was no meal of the sacrifices. **Jesus also suffered:** That Jesus sanctified (2:11; 9:13–14; 10:10, 14, 29) **by his own blood** is here a reminder of a previous argument and not a new one. Jesus suffered **outside the city gate,** the equivalent of "outside the camp" (v. 13). The writer again reveals some knowledge of the tradition about the historical Jesus (John 19:20 and at least implied at John 19:17; Mark 15:20; Matt. 27:32).

13:13 Let us then go to him outside the camp: It was outside that animal carcasses were destroyed and criminals were executed (Lev. 24:14, 23; Num. 15:35–36; Deut. 22:24). Just as the writer had earlier spoken of the manner of Jesus' death as one of shame and disgrace (12:2), so here the place of his death is one of **abuse** (reproach; disgrace; used of Moses at 11:26). And just as the readers were called on to "look to" the Jesus on the cross of shame (12:2), so here they are called on to "go to him" and bear his abuse "outside the camp." To go to Jesus outside the camp is to join Abraham and all the company of faith pilgrims who left a homeland in search of the homeland, who left a city in search of the city (11:8–16). By declaring themselves strangers and aliens on the earth (11:13), they took on the abuse that goes with the life of a pilgrim, which is to be without identity, without status, without place in the world.

13:15 Continually offer a sacrifice: The reader cannot allow the abuse and shame heaped on them to define who they are and to sever their relation to God. On the contrary, a continual sacrifice of praise is to be offered. **Fruit of lips:** Along with "sacrifice" this expression was used in Judaism to characterize genuine worship of God, which did not always rely on material offerings (Hos. 14:3; Ps. 50:14, 23; 107:22). Here such unending praise is characterized as being **through him** (Christ) and **confess(ing) his name** (3:1; 4:14; 10:23).

13:16 Do not neglect to do good: The final admonition of this unit enlarges on the cultic image

of sacrifice to include noncultic activities in the congregation: doing good (the only use of this word in the Scriptures) and fellowship or sharing.

13:17 Obey your leaders: Instructions to congregations to be subordinate and obedient became commonplace in the generations after the apostles (e.g., *1 Clem.* 42:2; Ignatius, *To the Trallians* 2:1). Clement (ca. 100 CE) even uses a military analogy and refers to leaders as "generals" (*1 Clem.* 37:1–5). The leaders **are keeping watch** ("staying alert" [Mark 13:33; Luke 21:36; Eph. 6:18]), perhaps for the threat of "strange teachings" (v. 9) and **will give an account** of your conduct. The leaders can, with your help, do their work **with joy** (10:34; 12:2, 11) rather than with groaning ("sighing" [NRSV] is not quite strong enough; see this word at Rom. 8:23; Mark 7:34). To behave in such a way as to bring groans and grief to the leaders would be "unprofitable," or more strongly, **harmful** to the membership.

13:18 Pray for us: The writer is included among the leaders in the request for prayer. The use of "I" in the next verse seems to indicate a literal use of "us" here. This does not necessarily mean that the writer is one of a formal body of leaders. All that can safely be said is that the writer is among those who have responsibility for the congregation and therefore will have to give account. To pray for leaders was a standing petition among the churches (2 Thess. 3:1; Rom. 15:30; Col. 4:3; 1 Thess. 5:25) and need not imply a crisis. **We have a clear conscience:** The claim has to do with the will or the motive of the leaders. It is their desire to act honorably in everything.

13:19 I urge you all the more: The shift is from the plural "we" to a personal petition by the writer. The general request for prayer for the leaders is now personalized and made a more urgent appeal. **That I may be restored to you very soon:** While less a clue into the nature of the former relationship between writer and readers, the petition reveals a relationship that is personal and draws the writer toward the church again with great urgency. This reference to travel plans, although brief (vv. 19, 23), was a commonplace in early Christian correspondence.

13:20–25
BENEDICTION AND GREETINGS

Paul is usually credited with modifying letter writing in the Greco-Roman world in order to make it an extension of his ministry, and Hebrews is but one example of a modification of Paul's modification. The epistle form permitted the writer to do many things other than pass along information. By concluding this sermon as an epistle, the author was able to achieve many purposes integral to the leader-congregation relationship: nourishing, guiding, renewing, adding anticipation, and providing self-disclosure, sketchy as it is.

13:20–21 Now may the God of peace: This opening title recalls the call to pursue peace (12:14) and the instructions on how to achieve it (13:1, 2, 7, 17–18). That God raised Jesus from the dead is foundational and almost universally stated in early Christian literature. In Hebrews, this affirmation is implied and assumed, but here is directly said for the first time. The metaphor **Jesus, the great shepherd of the sheep** is at 13:20 new to Hebrews. The phrase **blood of an eternal covenant** is more at home in Hebrews than in other New Testament writing, here reviving in the reader's mind the heart of the sermon. May God provide, equip (translated "prepare" at 10:5 and 11:3) you with everything necessary to do God's will. God not only equips for obedience, but works in (among) us to accomplish what is pleasing to God. That which pleases God is faith (11:5), worship in reverence and awe (12:28), doing good, and sharing what one has (13:16). The ascription of praise (**glory**) seems to be to Jesus Christ, since his name is the closest antecedent. But if one looks at the benediction as a whole, the ending may have returned to its beginning: God. The God announced at 1:1 as the subject of this sermon-letter is the governing thought in the framing of the final benediction.

13:22 I have written: The letter-sermon was a second choice to being present with the congregation, but it is the writer's clear expectation to remedy that very soon. **My word of exhortation:** The phrase may be a semitechnical term for sermon (see Acts 13:15). The ground for the writer's appeal that they bear with the letter-sermon is that it is brief. This may be a conventional phrase. Perhaps there is rhetorical irony in the understated appeal, just as there may be in saying that he has written **briefly** ("a short letter" [NIV]). Of New Testament letters, only Romans and 1 Corinthians are longer (and Revelation, if considered a letter).

13:23 Timothy has been set free: That this is the Timothy who was Paul's companion and co-worker there is no reason to doubt, but the meaning of his being set free is unclear. The verb was commonly used in referring to release from prison (Matt. 27:15; John 18:39; Acts 3:13; 16:35–36). To try to answer our questions from Acts and Paul would not satisfy inquiries addressed to Hebrews. The writer plans to come to the congregation very soon (v. 19). Those plans include Timothy with whom, if he comes very soon, the writer will see them.

13:24 Greet all your leaders: The sending of greetings was a standard feature of a letter (Phil. 4:21–22; 2 Cor. 13:12; 2 Tim. 4:19, 21). **Those from Italy:** The identity of this group is difficult if not impossible to determine (see introduction).

13:25 Grace be with all of you: The farewell blessing puts Hebrews in the company of most of the letters of the New Testament. The expression may have already become a part of the church's liturgy, although the forms of the blessing vary slightly. The form here is exactly the same as in Titus 3:15. The word "grace" appears but eight times in Hebrews, but the readers are never given reason to doubt that all God's actions toward them have been and are gracious.

The Letter of James

INTRODUCTION

This letter bears the name of its writer, but further identification has been difficult to ascertain. The New Testament knows five persons by the name "James" (Mark 1:19; 3:18; 6:3; 15:40; Luke 6:16), but only two achieved enough prominence to be candidates for authorship. One, the son of Zebedee, and brother of John, was executed by Agrippa I in 44 CE. The other, a brother of Jesus, was killed by stoning in 62 CE according to the Jewish historian Josephus. Both Luke (Acts) and Paul (Galatians) testify to the prominence of James, brother of Jesus, in the Jerusalem church and to James's influence beyond Jerusalem in behalf of Jewish Christianity. Those who hold this James to be the writer have to account for the author's apparent education in Greek grammar and rhetoric, the scant references to Jesus (1:1; 2:1), the absence of Jesus from the biblical examples of good conduct, the allusions to words of Jesus without a single "Jesus said," the absence of issues central to early Jewish Christianity (circumcision, Sabbath, food laws, Jew-Gentile relations), and the church's rather late embrace of the letter in the canon (no evidence before 200 CE). Others find these obstacles insurmountable and attribute the letter to another James or to someone who in the name of James, brother of Jesus, represents Jewish Christianity of Palestine or perhaps Syria at the close of the first century. (See "Pseudonymous Letters in Early Christianity" in the introduction to Ephesians.)

The letter is addressed to "the twelve tribes in the Dispersion" (1:1; see 1 Pet. 1:1). If the writer assumes the church is the new Israel, then this could mean "to all Christians everywhere." The addressees could also be all Jewish Christians outside Palestine. The contents of the letter, while dealing with issues as specific as economic discrimination and landowner-worker tensions, do not yield geographical certainty. While "the poor" are addressed sympathetically, it is unclear where they are or who they are, since "the poor" could be a synonym for "the saints" (see comments).

Beyond 1:1, James bears little resemblance to letters such as we have from Paul. However, there were in antiquity so many different forms and purposes of letters, public and private, that one should not be too hesitant to call James a letter.

Following the salutation, James has been variously described as moral discourse with the conventional uses of aphorisms, repetition, catchwords, and rhetorical questions; as an ethics handbook; as a baptismal catechism; as a synagogue manual slightly modified for the Christian community; and as Christian wisdom, drawing instruction from plants, animals, and persons, a feature common to Wisdom literature. Affinities with Proverbs and with the moral instructions of Jesus as recorded in Matthew are quite evident, but hardly more than one would expect from a treatise on Christian conduct. The mode of the letter is heavily imperative.

If there is a pattern or structure to James, it is difficult to discover. Expressions of direct address ("listen," "brothers and sisters," "you double-minded person," etc.) seem to mark transitions to new subjects, but not always. There are several discernible self-contained units within the letter: Christian morals and the Law (2:1–13); faith and works (2:14–26); responsible speech (3:1–12); Christians and conflict (3:13–4:12); concerning wealth (4:13–5:6); life within the faith community (5:7–20). Chapter 1 is not unyielding to attempts to find a literary pattern. One does find in chap. 1 subjects discussed later in the text, and therefore, this introductory material may function as the thanksgiving sections found early in Paul's letters, that is, as a summary sketch of issues later to be treated.

James has suffered among Christian readers, especially Protestant, since Luther's unfortunate reference to it as "a right strawy epistle." More recent students of James have found the tension between Paul and James overdrawn and unfair to both, failing to credit Paul with attention to works and James with attention to faith.

Outline

4:13–5:6   Concerning Wealth
5:7–20   Life within the Faith Community

For Further Reading

Johnson, Luke T. "The Letter of James." In *The New Interpreter's Bible,* vol. 12. Nashville: Abingdon, 1998.

Sleeper, C. Freeman. *James.* Abingdon New Testament Commentary. Nashville: Abingdon, 1998.

COMMENTARY

1:1
SALUTATION

This salutation, while lacking the elaboration familiar from Paul's letters, is typical for the time: identification of the writer and the person or persons addressed, and a word of greeting. The writer feels no need to claim any more right or authority to gain the readers' attention than **servant** (slave) of God and of Christ. Within the letter the writer claims to be no more than a teacher among teachers (3:1). Apparently, the readers knew and respected the writer (see the introduction to James on efforts to identify this James). The readers are addressed as **the twelve tribes of the Dispersion**. Since James in Greek is *Iakobos* (Jacob), the letter is from Jacob to the twelve tribes scattered after the exile. The symbolism for Jewish Christians, wherever they lived, is clear and strong (see 1 Pet. 1:1). The greeting is simple and conventional. It is found elsewhere in the New Testament in the letter to the churches from the apostles and elders following the Jerusalem Council (Acts 15:23).

1:2–27
PERSPECTIVES ON CHRISTIAN CHARACTER

As indicated in the introduction, a number of subjects treated briefly here will reappear later in the text.

1:2–8
ON BEING MATURE

1:2–4 Consider it nothing but joy: When tests or trials are viewed as purposive, they can not only be endured but actually received with joy. The **trials** are not specified; perhaps they are related to the socioeconomic condition of the readers (1:9–11; 2:5–7; 4:13–5:6). Trials can be productive of **endurance** (patience), endurance can produce maturity and fullness of life (see Rom. 5:3–4).

1:5–8 If any of you is lacking in wisdom: However, some on this growth journey may still lack the elusive and desirable quality, wisdom (*sophia*; Prov. 8; Wis. 7:7–8:21; Sir. 51:13–26). True wisdom is a gift from God and must be sought in prayer (Wis. 8:21; 9:6; Sir. 51:13). The prayer must be full of faith and free of doubt (vv. 6–7; Mark 11:24). Finding analogies and lessons in nature (waves **tossed by the wind**) is characteristic of wisdom literature. Being **double-minded**, a term peculiar to James in the New Testament (also at 4:8), is similar to Matthew's anxious mind (6:25–34) that looks in two directions rather than being focused on God alone (see on Matt. 5:8). Such uncertain and **unstable** faith expects nothing really, and hence receives nothing.

1:9–11
ON POOR AND RICH

The subject matter in this brief unit will receive further treatment at 2:1–7, 14–16; 4:13–5:6. The word "poor" is not used; instead, we find a word ordinarily translated "humble" but surely referring to the poor in contrast to the **rich** (v. 10). The reversal of the fortunes of the poor and the rich, the humble and the proud, is a theme in the Gospels (Matt. 23:12; Luke 1:51–53). Using another analogy from nature, this time echoing Isa. 40:6, the writer envisions the rich disappearing in the middle of being very **busy**. This gloomy prospect for the rich anticipates more such words, doubtless encouraging to the poor.

1:12–16
ON BEING TESTED

1:12–16 Anyone who endures temptation: The writer returns to the theme of vv. 2–8: being tested and enduring. In contrast to vv. 2–8, in which testing produced endurance and endurance produced maturity, here failure to endure produces blaming God, sin, and death. **Test** or **trial** and **temptation** translate the same word; context determines translation. The introduction of **desire, sin, evil,** and deception in vv. 13–16 has led both NIV and NRSV to shift to **temptation,** even though the test or temptation remains unspecified. The one who endures receives a blessing (Matt. 5:11–12) that is the **crown of life** (Rev. 2:10; 3:11, also referring to those who endure).

Those who love him: Whereas in 1:2–8 God gave to the one with strong faith, here it is to the one "who loves him." James rejects the excuse that God is the source of temptation. God is neither the source nor the object of temptation (v. 13). The source is in human desire. The word "desire" may carry sexual overtones but not necessarily; it can also be translated "covet" or "desire to possess." The writer, however, does find sexual desire an appropriate image to characterize the downward slide of the one who does not endure. First, God is blamed; then desire, the real culprit, conceives and **gives birth to sin**; finally, sin, when it has fully matured, **gives birth to death** (vv. 13–15). Death, then, is the result of being deceived about true cause and inevitable effect. Against this deception the writer warns **the beloved brothers** (v. 16), a favorite way of addressing the readers (see NRSV note).

1:17–18
ON GOD THE GIVER

1:17 Every perfect gift: Having said that God gives wisdom (v. 5) and the crown of life (v. 12), the writer now speaks of God as the source of all gifts. Because two different words are used for gift, the NRSV translates one "giving" and the other "gift," making v. 17 a bit awkward. However, it can properly be said that both giving and the gift are **from above**; that is, from God. To think of life and its resources as gifts of God is important for both rich and poor. This God is uniquely portrayed as **Father of lights** (Gen. 1:3–5; Ps. 136:7), a creation image, but as different from the lights (sun, moon, stars) in that God is not subject to **change**. In a description peculiar to James in the New Testament, God neither revolves (our word "parallax") nor rotates; that is, with God there are neither seasons nor night and day. God is not fickle in giving and can be trusted.

1:18 He gave us birth: This dependable God has a purpose, a new creation, a new humanity. In pursuit of that purpose, God has given us birth (same word as in v. 15 to speak of sin giving birth to death), in order that we may be the **first fruits**, the beginning of harvest with the promise of more to come (Rom. 8:23; 1 Cor. 15:20, 23). That our birth is by the word of truth echoes the creative activity of God's word in creation (Gen. 1:1–26) and in Jesus Christ (John 1:1–18).

1:19–20
ON SELF-CONTROL

The use of an imperative (**understand**) and direct address (**my beloved brothers;** see NRSV note) marks a transition at v. 19. The subject of hearing

and speaking, to which the writer will return at 3:1–12, is introduced with a bit of proverbial wisdom that has almost an exact parallel in Sir. 5:11. According to Matthew, Jesus spoke repeatedly about responsible speech (5:22, 37; 12:32–37). In fact, Jesus related speech and anger (Matt. 5:22), which the writer here apparently does (v. 19). More listening and deliberate speech help keep anger in check (Sir. 1:22–24). **Anger** is nonproductive, interfering with one's relation to God and the quality of life God expects (v. 20).

In a loosely related general exhortation, in v. 21 the readers are to remove and to receive. That to be removed is summarily categorized as filth and evil. That to be received is the heard and believed **word** of truth (v. 18) which must continually be embraced. A similar form of moral instruction is found in the "put off" and "put on" passage in Col. 3:5–17.

1:22–25
ON HEARING AND DOING

The writer returns to the matter of listening, only briefly mentioned in v. 19. The joining of hearing and doing echoes teaching of Jesus (Matt. 7:24–27; Luke 11:28). In Greek, "hearing" and "obeying" are from the same root. Hearing the word can deceive one into a false estimate of one's character. Listening to sermons without response in action has no lasting value. It is like glancing in the **mirror** and then quickly **forgetting** what was seen (vv. 23–24). By contrast, one who stares, who looks long and hard at God's requirements, which are complete and liberating, will be impressed sufficiently to act on what is said and heard. To that person comes the blessing of God (v. 25; Luke 11:28).

1:26–27
ON SPEAKING AND DOING

The writer now returns to v. 19 to pick up the theme of speaking. Just as listening without acting is empty and deceptive, so is talking **religion** without a life which confirms one's words. Religion (a rare word in the New Testament; Acts 26:5 and Col. 2:18) that is meaningful rather than empty must have the integrity of word and work. If one wonders what is to be done, the answer is very practical: **care for** those who cannot fully care for themselves. Socially, these persons were to be given the community's attention. To do so is to live acceptably before **God, the Father,** if such attention to others is joined to an effort to resist the values and pursuits of an unbelieving culture.

2:1–13
CHRISTIAN MORALS AND THE LAW

The entirety of 2:1–26 can reasonably be treated as one unit. However, both the NRSV and NIV honor the fact that both v. 1 and v. 14 begin with "my brothers and sisters" and a rhetorical question by regarding these markers as transition points.

2:1–7
ON A PARTICULAR VIOLATION

2:1 Your acts of favoritism: The issue of showing partiality is raised with a rhetorical question expecting a negative answer: "By showing partiality you do not **really believe in our glorious Lord Jesus Christ,** do you?" That is, such behavior contradicts faith in Jesus Christ (the name appears only here and at 1:1). Partiality violates Lev. 19:15, which Jesus embraced not only in his behavior but also in his citation of Lev. 19:18. For the church, then, this text is "law," an understanding not uncomfortable for Jewish Christians.

2:2 If a person: The form of "if" beginning v. 2 implies a hypothetical case. If so, the writer had presented a dramatic illustration to address a very real problem, as vv. 6–7 indicate. The word translated **assembly** (NRSV) or **meeting** (NIV) is actually "synagogue," but this is hardly proof that James was originally a synagogue manual of conduct. The word means "assembly" and very likely lingered as such among Jewish Christians. If the congregation was made up of the poor, as vv. 5–7 imply, then they very likely would have welcomed rather profusely visitors from among the rich landowners. Such fawning favoritism was evil, as all discriminating is.

2:4–7 Have you not made distinctions: The readers knew it, as the question in v. 4 with its anticipated yes answer makes clear. Verses 5–7 drive home the point made in vv. 1–4 with four strong rhetorical questions, each portraying an actual situation and each expecting a yes answer. Imbedded in the passage in the biblical theme that **God has chosen** the weak, the neglected, the poor to receive special favor which confounding the rich and powerful (1 Cor. 1:26–31). Echoed here are the Beatitudes of Jesus (Matt. 5:3; Luke 6:20 along with the woe on the rich, Luke 6:24), as well as the reversal of fortunes (Luke 1:48–53 and elsewhere). The oppression and legal suits against the believing poor by the rich are not specifically identified. It may have been actions of landlords against laborers. Such actions, along with verbal abuse, **blasphemed** the **name** of Christ which was the identifying mark of the believers (v. 7).

2:8–13
ON THE LAW BEING VIOLATED

By means of a series of "if" clauses, the writer now argues in principle the point made in the particular instance of favoritism.

2:8–11 The royal law: The "royal" (of God; of the kingdom) law is clear, not only in Lev. 19:15 but especially in Lev. 19:18, the law of love toward the neighbor. Jesus quoted this text as one of the two greatest commands (Matt. 22:37–39; also Rom. 13:9; Gal. 5:14). James is not involved in Paul's law and gospel debate; his concern is morality grounded in Hebrew Scriptures, interpreted by Jesus, especially as presented in the Sermon on the Mount. Note especially the references to **adultery** and **murder** and Matt. 5:21–30. One does not, says the writer, pick and choose among the moral commands and give them different degrees of seriousness. To violate the law is to violate the law, and discriminating between rich and poor violates the law (v. 9). The writer is heading off any excuse such as "at least I did not murder or commit adultery."

2:12 The law of liberty: In v. 12, the writer returns to the themes of speaking and doing and the law of liberty in 1:22–27. However stern and demanding the moral law of God may seem, its purpose is not to bind but to set free. The themes of judgment on the judgmental and mercy on the merciful are familiar from the teaching of Jesus (Matt. 5:7; 9:13; 12:7; 18:23–35; Luke 6:36).

2:14–26
FAITH AND WORKS

The unit falls naturally into two parts: the first (vv. 14–17) consists of a series of questions and a concluding piece of proverbial wisdom; the second (vv. 18–26) consists of a series of arguments concluding with a repetition of the proverb in verse 17.

2:14–17
ON FAITH'S INSEPARABILITY FROM WORKS

2:14 If you say you have faith: The Greek word for the "if" in the questions with which the writer peppers the readers indicates hypothetical cases presented to underscore a point. Keep in mind James is not dealing with Paul's Jews-Gentile, works-faith debate; James is focused on Christian moral conduct. Has someone among the readers misunderstood Paul and used him to justify inactivity as a way of honoring faith (see Rom. 6:1)? Perhaps. But regardless of the situation that prompted this discussion, the writer reduces to the absurd any view of Christian faith that addresses basic human needs with pious words alone (vv. 15–16). The answer is too obvious to be stated; a proverb will suffice: **Faith by itself, if it has no works, is dead** (v. 17).

2:18–26
On Faith's Proper Expression in Works

2:18 But someone will say: This subunit is in a form similar to a diatribe in which one debates an imaginary opponent. Here, however, the opponent seems to state the writer's position, not the opposite. It seems wiser, therefore, to picture a hypothetical dispute over the issue in vv. 14–17: Can faith and works be separated? Verse 18 denies that faith can be shown apart from works. Verse 19 insists that even confessing faith as expressed in the Shema (Deut. 6:4), "**God is one**," is empty if unaccompanied by deeds.

2:19 Even the demons believe, and they are demons! Then assuming the opponent wants further proof (how senseless can you be!), the writer offers two examples from Scripture.

2:21 Abraham justified by works: The first example is that of Abraham, a presentation punctuated with **you see** (vv. 22, 24). Abraham's willingness to offer Isaac (Gen. 22:1–18) expressed his faith (v. 21), which was brought to fulfillment in action (v. 22). Since Scripture affirms that **Abraham believed God** (v. 23) and was justified (Gen. 15:6), it is clear (to the writer) that the story of Abraham demonstrates that his faith was expressed in action and did not stand alone (v. 24). Again, it would be unfair to James and his stress on Christian conduct to evaluate him by Paul and the issues he faces in Rom. 4 and Gal. 3–4.

2:25 Rahab the prostitute: The second example of faith completed in works is Rahab (Josh. 2:1–21). Her hospitality and aid to Israelite spies show her faith in Israel's God, a faith that later saved her and her family (Josh. 6:22–23). Interestingly, Abraham and Rahab appear in the recital in Heb. 11 of those who lived by faith. The writer concludes the argument as at v. 17, but with an additional analogy: just as

the body without its vital life force is dead, so **faith without works is also dead** (v. 26).

3:1–12
RESPONSIBLE SPEECH

The subject matter of this unit, marked by "my brothers and sisters" at vv. 1 and 12, has already been introduced at 1:19, 26; 2:12. However, here multiple analogies are provided, mostly from the realm of nature. Learning from animals, reptiles, birds, water, fire, wind, and plants is characteristic of Wisdom literature, looking as it does more to creation than to historical events. The vocabulary of much of this unit is unique in the New Testament.

3:1 Not many . . . become teachers: The discussion of disciplined speech begins with those for whom speaking is a vocation: teachers. The writer numbers himself among them ("we," v. 1), feels the heavy responsibility, and anticipates **greater judgment** (translated literally, stronger than either NRSV or NIV). This is more than teacher evaluation; it is standing before God.

3:2 Anyone: Now the audience is enlarged to **all of us**. All stumble at times, and this includes speech. In fact, anyone who does not stumble in speech is perfect, because control of speech is control of the **whole body** (person, self). The extraordinary importance of speech here recalls Jesus' words in Matt. 12:36–37. The reintroduction of the word **bridle** (1:26) as an image of control, not only of the tongue but of the whole body, moves the discussion easily to bridles that control **horses** (v. 3) and to **rudders** that control **ships** (v. 4). The tongue, the bridle, the rudder: all are small but all have great power (v. 5).

3:5 How great a forest: Thus far, everything said is positive and possible because there is control. Without control, just as a small fire can destroy an entire forest, so the tongue can destroy one's whole life. It creates a **world of iniquity** (injustice), it **stains** (recall "unstained" at 1:27) everything it touches, it destroys the **cycle of nature** (wheel of birth), probably meaning "the whole course of life" (NIV), and it is itself continually replenished by the fires of **hell** (v. 6). Hell is Gehenna, referring to the Valley of Hinnom south of Jerusalem where trash burned. It came to be an image of fiery punishment (Matt. 5:22; 18:9; Mark 9:42–48). The four classes of animals—**beast**, **bird**, **reptile**, and **sea creature** (v. 7; see Deut. 4:17–18)—can be tamed, but not the tongue, which is evil and full of poison. The view of the tongue has become so totally negative that the instruction to "bridle the tongue" seems now to be lost.

3:9 With it we bless . . . curse: In vv. 9–12 the writer modifies the totally negative view of the tongue and addresses the problem of contradictory uses of speech. With the same tongue we bless God as **Lord and Father** (perhaps referring to the church's liturgy) and **curse** fellow human beings created **in God's likeness** (NIV). Nowhere else in all creation is there such contradictory and inconsistent behavior. A spring does not produce both sweet and bitter water (v. 11); a **fig tree** does not **yield olives nor a grapevine figs** (v. 12); salt water does not produce fresh water. The point is inescapable: of all God's creatures, only humans violate the integrity and consistency of creation. **This ought not to be so** (v. 10).

3:13–4:12
CHRISTIANS AND CONFLICT

Even though 3:13–18 is dominated by discussion of wisdom, it is evident, even in the opening question (v. 13), that there is a problem being addressed, and that it has to do with behavior. Among the readers is a climate of envy and disorder, the discussion of which leads naturally to chap. 4 and the subject of conflict. Hence 3:13–18 is joined to what follows rather than to what precedes.

3:13–18
WISDOM AND CONDUCT

3:13 Who is wise: The opening question and the imperative "Show it" imply claimants to wisdom among the readers, persons who lack the **humility** (NIV) appropriate to a quality which is, after all, a gift from God (1:5). That one has wisdom should be shown in lifestyle, in works, and in attitude (v. 13). Four qualities show that one does not have the wisdom from God: **envy, ambition**, boasting, and being **false to the truth** (v. 14). The truth is very likely the word of truth by which God gave us birth (1:18). Such a life, if it be called wise, is produced by a cleverness that is of the earth, merely human (in contrast to spiritual, 1 Cor. 2:1–16), and demonic (in contrast to being of God, v. 15). The result in the faith community is **disorder** and **wickedness of every kind** (v. 16).

3:17 Wisdom from above: By contrast, wisdom from God produces persons who are **pure, peace-loving** (NIV), kind, yielding, merciful, **full of good fruits, without partiality** (recall 2:1–13) or **hypocrisy** (v. 17). Verse 18, appar-

ently given as a summarizing statement reiterating the priority on peace, is difficult to translate. Along with the NRSV and NIV, consider **And the fruit of justice is sown in peace among those who make peace**.

4:1–6
CONFLICTS AMONG BELIEVERS

4:1 Conflicts . . . where do they come from?: The language describing the situation among the readers becomes even stronger: **war, murder**. Perhaps the writer is drawing on a conventional discussion of the self-destruction of a community full of selfish desire, pleasure seeking, and jealousy, or the words may present the hypothetical rather than the actual situation. In any case, strife and conflict are traced to desires for pleasure that are battling (a military term) within you (v. 1). The **within you** may be too subjective; the expression literally is "in (or among) your members." The conflicts seem more communal than private.

4:2 You want something: Verse 2 is difficult not only to translate but to punctuate. The NIV is more exact, but the NRSV captures the sense better. The progression is from desire to failure to obtain to **murder** (recall 5:21–22); from **jealousy** (trans. **covet** in NIV and NRSV) to inability to acquire to fighting and war (the two words in noun form in v. 1). The frustration and failure described are due to misguided means, object, and motive. The proper means of gaining what is desired is to ask it of God (v. 2c; 1:5–8). The proper object of one's petition is that which is wise, good, and mature (v. 3; 1:5–8, 17). The proper motive for asking is for the good of the brothers and sisters (vv. 11–12), not one's own **pleasures** (v. 3).

4:4 Adulterers!: The use of the feminine **adulteresses** (trans. with the generic masculine in NRSV; **adulterous people** in NIV) probably recalls Israel's unfaithfulness to God. The uncompromising choice between God and the world echoes Jesus in Matt. 6:24 and even earlier, the two ways of Joshua (Josh. 24:14–15) and of Moses (Deut. 30:19).

4:5 Scripture says: Verse 5 presents three problems. First, if Scripture is being quoted or paraphrased, we have no record of such a text, in or out of the Bible. Second, how then is the verse to be translated? Perhaps as two sentences: "Or do you think the Scripture speaks vainly (emptily)?" and "The spirit which he (God) causes to dwell in us yearns jealously." Third, what does this mean? The first part can refer to the authority of Scripture used earlier and in the future: it addresses the situation of the readers and is to be heeded. The second part can be answering an unspoken objection that since the spirit of life in us is from God, surely it has no objectionable craving and jealousy, so the writer has been saying. Yes, it does, says the writer. Of course, the NRSV and NIV offer reasonable alternatives to this reading of v. 5. But in v. 6, the writer returns to the God who gives. Even greater than all the wrongs described in vv. 1–5 is the grace God gives. But by quoting Prov. 3:34, the writer is able, even in a presentation of grace, to return to a familiar theme: humility, not arrogance, is the appropriate posture of the believer.

4:7–12
EXHORTATIONS FOR THOSE IN CONFLICT

Verses 7–10 contain ten imperatives, all of them concise, crisp, and like maxims in general, portable to a range of contexts. Whether the writer is drawing on a collection of moral instructions is not clear, but one wonders, when one sees that the three items in 4:6–7 are found in 1 Pet. 5:5–9, and in the same order. Antecedents to all ten imperatives are found in early Judaism among those who presented Israel's faith as moral instruction rather than as ritual and historical memories. All ten imperatives in vv. 7–10 deal with one's relation to God, while vv. 11–12 concern one's relation to the neighbor.

4:7 Submit yourselves . . . to God: The list begins and ends with the theme of humility, already frequent in the letter. Clean **hands** and pure **hearts** (v. 8), while originating in the rituals of the priesthood (Exod. 30:17–21), came to be used widely in a moral sense (Pss. 24:4; 73:13; Sir. 38:10). Verse 9 uses the dramatic and emotional imagery of biblical Judaism to call for repentance and sorrow for sin. The exaltation of those who humble themselves echoes a teaching of Jesus (Matt. 23:12; Luke 18:14).

4:11 Do not speak evil: Verses 11–12 set the reader, not before God, but in the presence of the brother (and sister) and neighbor. Speaking (1:19–20, 26; 3:1–12), judging (2:13), and law (1:22–25; 2:8–12) have been treated previously, but now are tightly drawn in one brief passage that concludes the discussion of conflict in the Christian community. Addressing the readers as brothers and sisters sets in sharp relief the issue of criticism and slander against one's brothers and sisters. The law against slander was clear (Lev. 19:16), just as it was on love of neighbor (Lev. 19:18). In the writer's movement of thought, to speak against a

brother or sister is to **speak against the law** that forbids it. Just as speaking against another is judging another, speaking against the law is judging the law. Judging the law is putting oneself above the law, and to put oneself above the law is to sit in God's seat. However, we know there is only one God, one giver of law, one judge. Conclusion: do not even begin this dangerous and futile journey by slandering or speaking against a neighbor. "Who do you think you are?" is a sharp way to end such a discussion (v. 12).

4:13–5:6
CONCERNING WEALTH

This unit resumes the discussion of rich and poor in 1:9–11 and 2:5–7. There are two sub-units, each beginning **Come now** (4:13; 5:1), the first a denunciation of the pursuit of wealth (4:13–17) and the second a denunciation of the behavior of those possessing wealth (5:1–6).

4:13–17
ON THE PURSUIT OF WEALTH

4:13 Come now: It is not clear whether those addressed here are businesspeople seeking to improve their lot or some of the poor, perhaps farmers (5:4), trying to climb out of poverty. In any case, according to the writer the error is not the quest for material gain, although that may be implied, but rather the presumption that life can be planned apart from God. The evil is not the plan, but the fact that it is a godless plan. Not only is tomorrow an unknown (v. 14), but life itself is brief and uncertain, like a mist that quickly rises and quickly disappears. Rather one should say, "If the Lord wishes"; then we will live and within God's will be able to pursue a goal (v. 15).

4:16 You boast in your arrogance: Again the writer centers on boasting and arrogance (2:13; 3:14) as the root of the problem. Verse 17 is a maxim that could be applied to any situation and be appropriate. In the present context, the message is, "You have now been informed; ignorance is no excuse. To act otherwise is sin without excuse."

5:1–6
ON THE POSSESSION OF WEALTH

5:1 Come now, you rich people: An address to persons (or things) absent is called an apostrophe. Here is a rhetorical flourish that indicts persons absent, to the delight of those present. "Come now, you who say" at 4:13 may have been an apostrophe; 5:1 is surely one. It is not likely that "rich" is in effect a word of encouragement to the poor, oppressed field workers. The weeping and wailing of the rich is not a show of repentance; it is an expression of misery. The eschatological judgment ("Woe to you rich" [Luke 6:24]) has already begun. All their possessions are worthless: all that has been stored up is destroyed by **moth** and **rust** (Matt. 6:19–20), now reduced to piles of ruin giving silent witness against their owners in the day of fiery judgment (vv. 2–3).

5:4 Wages of the laborers: But even stronger witness against the rich is the wages withheld from poor field workers. That such fraud was a violation of the law of God is amply stated in Scripture (Lev. 19:13; Deut. 24:14–15; Jer. 22:13). In fact, the prophetic word against such oppression in Mal. 3:5 includes the same expression for God as here: **the Lord of hosts,** an image of a militant God opposing evil. And for what use did the rich fraudulently accumulate wealth? Their own **pleasure** and **luxury** (v. 5), not realizing that they were as penned animals being **fattened** for **slaughter** (Jer. 12:3). The final charge against the rich (v. 6) is the most serious: you have **murdered the righteous one.** There is no reason to take this as a reference to the death of Jesus. More likely it is a vivid statement of their crime against the passive and powerless poor: "To take away a neighbor's living is to commit murder; to deprive an employee of wages is to shed blood" (Sir. 34:26).

5:7–20
LIFE WITHIN THE FAITH COMMUNITY

In this closing unit the writer treats three subjects: patience and endurance (vv. 7–11), swearing (v. 12), and relationships (vv. 13–20).

5:7–11
ON PATIENCE AND ENDURANCE

5:7 Be patient . . . until the coming of the Lord: The three key words in this subunit are long suffering, translated **patience** in both NRSV and NIV (v. 10), and **endurance** (NRSV) or **perseverance** (NIV) (v. 11). Of patience the writer offers three examples: **the farmer** waiting for heaven's blessing to bring a harvest (v. 7); **the prophets,** who in the midst of suffering were patient and endured (vv. 10–11a); and **Job** whose endurance **you have heard** and the end of whose story (the purpose of the Lord) **you have seen** (v. 11b). The appeal for patience and

endurance is grounded in the twice-stated coming of the Lord (v. 8; again in a different expression in v. 9b). The approach of the Parousia (**coming**) of the Lord is not intended simply to strike fear in the heart of the believer; after all, the one who judges **is compassionate and merciful** (v. 11). The reminder about the Lord's coming is intended, however, to put an end to grumbling and murmuring in the congregation, a condition not uncommon in circumstances in which patience wears thin (v. 9).

5:12
ON SWEARING

5:12 Above all: The introductory "Above all" can signify the primary importance of what follows, but it can also alert the reader to the approaching end of the letter, much as one would use the expression "And finally." The writer has spoken frequently about responsible speech (1:19, 26; 3:2, 9–10, 14:3, 11–12); now the subject is addressed with new seriousness. The taking of an **oath,** the calling in as witness something or someone greater than oneself as a way of establishing the truth of one's words, was permitted in Judaism. What was forbidden was swearing falsely (Lev. 19:12; Exod. 20:7). Contrary to popular understanding, swearing did not involve profanity. One might say, "As God is my witness," or "I swear on a stack of Bibles," or "On my mother's grave." An oath supports one's word. James says that one's word should need no support; rather, if one has integrity, yes is yes and no is no. Without integrity, no amount of swearing will make a false word true. Speech that assumes one is a liar comes under the judgment of God. At no point in the letter does the writer more clearly echo a teaching of Jesus (Matt. 5:33–37). The working of the tradition in James differs somewhat from that in Matthew, but beyond question it is the same teaching. That the saying is not attributed to Jesus is thought-provoking. Perhaps, in a circle familiar with Jesus' words, the absence of his name would effectively prompt recognition and involvement in their own remembrance of him.

5:13–20
ON RELATIONSHIPS

5:13 Any among you: Verses 13–18 deal with prayer, introduced with a series of three questions: Is anyone **suffering?** Is anyone **cheerful?** Is anyone **sick** (vv. 13–14)? The answers are brief and clear: **pray; sing; call for the elders of the church.** Only here are "elders" and "church" mentioned in James. They have a pastoral function, praying and **anointing with oil** (v. 14), a ritual associated with healing the sick (Mark 6:13).

5:15 Will save the sick: The act of anointing was not to be construed as healing in and of itself; it was done **in the name of the Lord** (v. 14) and accompanied by a **prayer of faith** (v. 15). It is the Lord, not the elders, who heals (the meaning of **save** in this context), and it is a prayer of faith which appropriates God's healing power. The addition of forgiving sins implies a connection between sickness and sin, but the connection is not as clearly drawn as in Mark 2:5–11 where the pronouncement of forgiveness precedes the pronouncement of healing. Here in 5:15, healing occurs, followed by the less certain "**And if he has sinned**" (the NIV is more exact here). At this point, the writer enlarges on the themes of forgiveness and healing by calling on the entire community, not only the elders and the one sick, to engage in mutual confession and prayer (v. 16). Again, the writer enlarges on the theme of prayer by stating a general maxim that could fit many contexts: **The prayer of the righteous is powerful and effective**. An illustration of this truth is drawn, not from nature as is common in James and all wisdom literature, but from Scripture, a more rare source for him (Abraham, Rahab, Job [2:21–25; 5:11]).

5:17 Elijah: Not to be considered a rare example of effective praying, says the writer; he was a person **like us** (having "like feelings"). In other words, our prayers can be no less effective. The story of Elijah is in 1 Kgs. 17:1–2 Kings 2:12, but tradition (oral or written?) had added material and interpreted the original story. Thus James uses elements not in the Old Testament. For example, the "three years" of 1 Kgs. 17:1 has become the standard apocalyptic period of three and a half years (see Luke 4:25; Rev. 11:3, 6; reflecting Dan. 7:25; 8:14; 9:27). Elijah's prayer brought drought; his prayer brought rain (v. 18). As the writer says, "**The prayer of the righteous is powerful and effective**" (v. 16).

5:19–20 If any one wanders: The letter closes with a pastoral appeal to restore the erring to the community and its fellowship (recall a similar appeal in Gal. 6:1–5). The image is of someone in the group wandering off, going astray. The wandering is not specified except as being **from the truth** (v. 19). The use of "the truth" in 3:14 implies moral rather than doctrinal content, and that may be the sense here. When effectively pursued, this effort at restoration **will save his soul from death**. Whose soul, the wanderer or the restorer? Both the NRSV and the NIV translate the phrase so as to identify the soul saved as that of the wanderer. Most likely that is the proper interpretation, but the text itself is unclear. Covering a multitude of sins is an expression echoing Prov. 10:12, "Love covers all offenses." In a slightly different context, 1 Pet. 4:8 draws on the same source: "Love covers a multitude of sins." On this positive and healing note the letter of James to the twelve tribes in the Dispersion (1:1) comes to a close.

The First Letter of Peter

INTRODUCTION

The Man: The Historical Simon Peter

Simon's father's name was Jonah (Matt. 16:17) or John (John 1:42; 21:15)—two different names are represented in Aramaic and Greek, as in English. His mother's name is unknown. As a contemporary of Jesus, Simon was presumably born sometime in the period 10 BCE–10 CE, perhaps in the bilingual and multicultural Bethsaida (see John 1:44; 12:21). Simeon (Hebrew)/Simon (Greek) apparently received this double name at birth. It is likely that, like many people in Galilee, he could handle Greek as well as his native Aramaic, but the extent to which he may have been competent in Greek is not known.

Simon was married (Mark 1:30–31) and accompanied by his wife on later mission trips (1 Cor. 9:5). He, along with his brother Andrew, was in the fishing business. This means that Simon belonged neither to the upper class of tax collectors, who farmed out fishing rights from the government (the social class to which Matthew/Levi belonged, Mark 2:14; Matt. 9:9), nor to the lower class of day laborers who did most of the actual work—and who were largely illiterate—but to the "middle" class of small businesspeople and craftspeople such as Paul the tentmaker.

Sometime during his ministry, Jesus of Nazareth called Simon to be his disciple, and Simon responded. We know nothing of Simon's religious orientation before he became a disciple of Jesus. Similarly, we know little if anything about Simon's personality. Though often pictured in sermons and popular legend as volatile and impulsive, this romanticized image of popular piety is based on the ways the literary character of Simon is portrayed in New Testament narratives, which were written for theological purposes.

In becoming a disciple of Jesus, Simon's life was completely reoriented. He left home, family, and business and became an itinerant follower of Jesus and participant in his mission. Not only so, it is clear that he became a or the leading member of the group of disciples. He is pictured as belonging to the inner circle (e.g., Mark 9:2; 13:3; 14:33), as being the spokesperson for the other disciples (e.g., Mark 8:29; 9:5—it is such texts that give rise to the picture of Peter as "impulsive"), as being the disciples' representative to whom Jesus speaks and with whom he deals (e.g., Mark 8:33), and as the representative member of the group whom others approach (e.g., Matt. 17:24).

During Jesus' ministry Peter is reported to have made some sort of confession of Jesus as uniquely sent from God ("Messiah" Mark 8:29; "God's Messiah" Luke 9:20; "Messiah, Son of the Living God" Matt. 16:16; "Holy One of God" John 6:69). Simon's understanding of Jesus during his earthly life was incomplete; he misunderstood and finally denied him (e.g., Mark 8:29–33; 14:66–72).

The risen Jesus appeared to Simon and (re)constituted him to be the Rock on which the new Christian community is established (1 Cor. 15:5; Mark 16:7; Luke 24:34). Despite his misunderstanding and failure during Jesus' earthly ministry, the encounter with the risen Lord enabled Peter to become the principal leader in regathering the disciples and in the formation of what was to become the church. Jesus gave Simon a new name that embodied this role in the establishment of the church: Rock (Aramaic, Cephas; Greek, Peter; Matt. 16:16–19; John 1:42). Since Peter has since become a common name in Western culture influenced by Christianity, it is important to remember that Cephas/Peter was not a name at all in first-century Judaism, but was a metaphorical title, Rock. Jesus' designation of Simon as Rock was not merely a nickname, but reflects to the biblical tradition in which a new name signals a new reality: Jacob becomes Israel (Gen. 32:22–32), Abram becomes Abraham (Gen. 17:1–8), Sarai becomes Sarah (Gen. 17:15–16).

Peter was clearly the principal leader of the earliest Christian community in Jerusalem, which was composed of both Hebrews and Hellenists, i.e., Christians of Aramaic-speaking Palestinian culture and Christians of Greek-speaking Hellenistic culture. Acts 2–6 pictures Peter as a bridge between the two groups, not just as leader of one.

In Paul's letters, Peter appears at first as the leading figure in the Jerusalem church (Gal.

1:18), then several years later as one of the three "pillars" (Gal. 2:9), then as an influential leader in the Antioch church (Gal. 2:11–14). We lose sight of Peter after the Antioch incident (ca. 51 CE), though he apparently continued various missionary journeys (1 Cor. 9:5). These mission trips, however, did not include the provinces to which 1 Peter is addressed (1 Pet. 1:12). In Acts, Peter disappears abruptly from the narrative at 12:17 (mid-40s CE) and departs Jerusalem for "another place," to reappear later in the narrative only once, at the Jerusalem Council (ca. 50 CE).

Peter later came to Rome, where he continued his apostolic ministry, which he finally sealed with a martyr's death (1 Clem. 5–6; Ignatius, To the Romans 4:3; see John 21:18–19).

The Tradition

The ministry of the apostle Peter continued among disciples influenced by him and in a stream of tradition emanating from him, somewhat analogously to the Pauline school that continued to reinterpret Paul's message after his death (see introductions to Colossians, Ephesians, 1 Timothy). In the second and third Christian generations, the issue of who could legitimately present themselves as representatives of the Christian faith meant that several streams of Christian tradition vied with each other for recognition.

While the traditions represented by Paul and Peter were different, they were not mutually exclusive alternatives and were not seen as such by the Roman church, which in the latter part of the first century began to see itself as supporter of and teacher to other struggling churches outside Rome. By the end of the first century, there had been an amalgamation of Pauline and Petrine traditions in Rome, which is acknowledged in the next generation by 2 Peter's claiming Paul as a brother apostle, whose teaching, however, must be understood within the perspective of the Petrine tradition (2 Pet. 3:14–16).

Authorship and Date

First Peter represents this Roman combination of Petrine and Pauline tradition focused in a particular letter to churches in Asia Minor to encourage and instruct them to live as Christians in their hostile social situation. Although written in the name of the beloved apostle, it was most likely written not by Peter himself (who was killed in 64 CE), but by one of his disciples in Rome, about 90 CE. This conclusion is based on (1) the sophisticated Greek, some of the best in the New Testament, not likely to have been written by a Galilean fisherman; (2) the reflection of much of the language and thought of the Pauline letters; (3) the association of Paul's companions with Peter (Silvanus = Silas; Mark, 5:12–13); (4) indications of a late date, such as using "Babylon" as a designation for Rome, which became current only after 70 CE; (5) the similarities to 1 Clement, written from Rome about 95 CE; (6) the letter's lack of the kind of material one would anticipate from an eyewitness, such as sayings of Jesus that would be relevant to the author's purpose; (7) the explicit indication that the letter was written by an elder (5:1). (See "Pseudonymous Letters in Early Christianity" in the introduction to Ephesians.)

A Real Letter

While it contains and interprets a considerable amount of earlier Christian tradition, including materials used in teaching and liturgy, it is not, as once was often thought, a baptismal sermon modified into the letter form. Not a letter to individual churches, 1 Peter is a circular letter to all the Christians in a wide area. Like the Pauline letters, it was intended for reading in the worship services of the congregations, not for private study.

First Peter is addressed to Christians in a broad geographical area, the five Roman provinces comprising most of present-day Turkey. While there were likely some Jewish Christians among the addressees, the letter indicates that the readers were primarily Gentiles who had formerly not known the true God and who had lived the sinful, idolatrous life of pagans (1:14, 18, 21; 2:1, 9–11, 25; 4:3). Indeed, the principal reason for their social marginalization and distress was due to their having withdrawn from participation in aspects of their former life they now considered to be sinful (4:4).

The letter was written to distressed churches in Asia Minor facing a difficult social situation. While Christians are called to suffer "for the name" (4:15–16), the abuse is mostly verbal (2:22–23; 3:9–12, 16). There is as yet no government persecution, except for occasional arbitrary acts by subordinate officials; 1 Peter's positive attitude toward the state (2:13–17) makes it clear that there was no government policy of persecution of Christians as such. First Peter attempts to offer realistic encouragement and instruction to Christians attempting to live faithfully in such a situation (see Pliny's Letter to Trajan in the introduction to Revelation).

Outline

1:1–2 Salutation
1:3–12 Thanksgiving
1:13–5:11 Body of the Letter
    1:13–2:10 The New Identity as the Elect and
      Holy People of God
    2:11–3:12 Christian Existence and Conduct in
      the Given Structures of Society
    3:13–5:11 Responsible Suffering in the Face
      of Hostility
5:12–14 Conclusion

For Further Reading

Craddock, Fred B. *First and Second Peter and Jude.* Westminster Bible Companion. Louisville, KY: Westminster John Knox, 1995.

Boring, M. Eugene. *1 Peter.* Abingdon New Testament Commentary. Nashville: Abingdon, 1999. Some of the material on 1 Peter in the pages that follow has been drawn from these more expansive treatments.

COMMENTARY

1:1–2
SALUTATION

Regarding the form of salutations, see on 1 Thess. 1:1. The author here adapts the Pauline letter opening. These two verses comprise one carefully constructed sentence:

  A. Peter, apostle of Jesus Christ
  B. To the elect resident aliens of the Dispersion in Pontus, Galatia, Cappadocia, Asia, and Bithynia,
    [elect] 1. according to the foreknowledge of God the Father,
      2. through the sanctification of the Spirit,
      3. for obedience and sprinkling of the blood of Jesus Christ,
  C. May grace and peace be multiplied to you.

1:1 Apostle: Authorized representative (see on Luke 6:12); attribution to **Peter** expresses the claim that the letter represents the apostolic faith.

Pontus, Galatia, Cappadocia, Asia, and Bithynia: Five Roman provinces comprising most of modern Turkey. The Christians are addressed as belonging to something much larger than a local church. The **Dispersion** (Diaspora) is the technical term for the **scattered** (NIV) people of Israel who live as Jews throughout the world, united not by having a

homeland but by belonging to the chosen people of God. The author addresses his Christian readers as the inheritors of this status (see John 7:35; Jas. 1:1).

Chosen/elect: Election is the characteristic biblical designation of Israel as the chosen people of God (e.g., Deut. 7:6; 10:15; 14:2; 1 Chr. 16:13; Ps. 105:6; Isa. 43:20–21; 45:4; 65:9). Like other New Testament documents (e.g., Gal. 6:16; Phil. 3:13; Jas. 1:1), 1 Peter considers the Christian community, as members of the renewed Israel, to be the continuing people of God, though the author never uses the terms "Israel," "Jew," or "Judaism." The author does not speculate on when this election took place, nor does he make it an alternative to human responsibility. Though people are responsible to respond to God's saving act, the initiative belongs to God (see Rom. 8:28–30; 11:5; 1 Thess. 1:4; John 13:18; 15:16, 19).

Exiles (NRSV)/**strangers** (NIV): The author's key designation of the status of Christians in society. The term is relatively rare (only here, 2:11, and Heb. 11:13 in the New Testament; only Gen. 23:4; Ps. 39:12 in the Old Testament), but it is paralleled with "sojourner" in 2:11 and in each of the Old Testament references. The term designates "sojourners" or "resident aliens," people living in a land where they are more than tourists but do not have the rights of citizens (see Gen. 23:4; Ps. 39:12; Heb. 11:13). "Transients" or "migrant workers without documents," as these words are used in North America captures something of their social status. **In the world** (NIV) does not refer to Christians' exile from their heavenly homeland, but to their marginal social status in this world.

1:2 Father . . . Spirit . . . Christ: They are **chosen** because God the Father has **destined** them, through the Spirit that has **sanctified** them (made them holy, set them apart for a special purpose), **to be obedient** to Jesus Christ. This proto-Trinitarian formula is centered on the activity of the one God. Among other examples of proto-Trinitarian texts: Matt. 3:16–17; 12:28; 28:19; Luke 1:35; 2:25–28; 4:18–19; 10:21; 12:8–12; John 3:3–5, 34; Acts 2:32–38; 4:8–10; Rom. 1:3–4; 8:3–4; 14:17–18; 15:30; 1 Cor. 6:11; 12:3–6; 2 Cor. 13:13; Gal. 4:6; Eph. 4:4–6; Col. 1:3–8; 1 John 5:6–9; Rev. 1:4–5. For both Israel and the church, election is not for privilege but for obedience. Both obedience and **sprinkled with his blood** reflect the language of the Old Testament covenant (see Exod. 24:3–8). The readers are addressed as members of this (renewed) covenant, now sealed with the blood of Christ (Mark 14:24; 1 Cor. 11:25; Heb. 9:20; 10:29; 13:20).

1:2 Grace and peace: As in Paul, grace (the word occurs 10x in 1 Peter) is the absolutely unmerited favor of God made concrete in the Christ event, the sole ground of the believer's acceptance before God. Peace, as in the closing benediction of 5:14, is neither merely the lack of hostilities nor a subjective state of tranquility, but refers to all the blessings, material and spiritual, personal and social, that comprise the good life willed and given by God, practically representing the Jewish *shalom* and a synonym for salvation.

1:3–12
THANKSGIVING

Verses 3–12 are a single complex sentence in the Greek text, broken into several sentences by English translations in the interest of readability. This section corresponds to the typical unit that followed the salutation of Hellenistic letters. See on 1 Thess. 1:2. The author again adapts Pauline usage. The skillful construction is tripartite, corresponding both to the proto-Trinitarian structure included in the salutation (Father, 3–5; Christ, 6–9; and Spirit, 10–12) and to the body of the letter to follow.

1:3 Blessed be . . . God: The thanksgiving section typically began with "I thank God" (as, e.g., Rom. 1:8; 1 Cor. 1:4), but once Paul adopted the familiar synagogue form of prayer, "Blessed be God" (2 Cor. 1:3; see Eph. 1:3). The author of 1 Peter here follows this tradition. Adopting this form places the whole letter in the mode of worship. Instruction for the Christian life is given in the framework of praise, corresponding to the fact that the letter itself was not written for private reading, but like Paul's letters was read aloud in the worship service of the churches.

New Birth: See 1:23. Another way of emphasizing the divine initiative. No one chooses to be born; we find that we have been given life. In the New Testament this metaphor for becoming a Christian is found only in John 1:12–13; 3:3–5; 1 John 3:9; 5:8; Titus 3:5; and Jas. 1:18. This imagery is not found in the Old Testament, the Synoptic Gospels, Acts, or Paul's letters, but was frequent in pagan Hellenistic religions. Here the author adapts an idea current in his religious world to express the Chris-

tian faith. As elsewhere, the author does not merely take over Hellenistic ideas wholesale, but gives them a Christian interpretation. The Christian does not receive a new immortal nature on the basis of an initiation ritual, but a new life of hope **through the resurrection of Jesus Christ from the dead** when encountered by the word of God in Christian preaching (1:12, 23). In the perspective of 1 Peter, the believer is given a new life by being incorporated into God's plan for history and into the people of God, who bear witness to God's mighty acts (2:9). The perspective is communal not individualistic, horizontal not vertical, historical not natural.

Living hope: The Christian life for 1 Peter has an essential *future* dimension. Hope plays an even more decisive role than faith for this author, and can serve as the one word that sums up the meaning of the Christian life as such (e.g., 1:3; 3:5, 15). Hope in biblical perspective refers to that which is *real*, but *not yet*. Hope is not psychological, a matter of one's attitude, but lives in the light of the certain future victory of God. It has to do with the **inheritance** God has already **kept in heaven** (v. 4) for believers, but the picture here is not of going up to heaven to receive it, but going forward in history (horizontally *through* the present trials, not vertically *out of* them) to receive it **in the last time** (1:5), **when Christ is revealed** (1:7). God is active in the present troubled experience of Christians, who **are being protected by the power of God through faith** (1:6).

1:5 Salvation: Already/not yet, with both a present and future aspect.

1:6 Various trials: Not the ordinary difficulties of everyday life, not even bad health, accidents, or personal tragedies, but the harassment and discrimination they suffer on account of their faith (see the introduction to 1 Peter). **You rejoice:** Not a command, but a statement. The joy here described is not a superficial "feel good," but a deep, inexpressible joy permeated by the presence and glory of God, i.e., it is "in him [God]" or "on the basis of God's mighty acts" (2:9). This joy is unforced, is not a matter of cranking it up within ourselves by convincing ourselves to have the right attitude, but a response to God's acts of the past, present, and future.

1:8 You have not seen him is not in contrast to the author, who also has not personally seen Jesus, but is a statement about the Christian life as such. Christians love, trust, and obey Christ on the basis of the faith that has come to them by Christian preaching and the power of the Holy Spirit (1:12).

1:9 Salvation of your souls: In the biblical understanding, soul is not a part of the person, immortal or otherwise, but is a way of talking about the whole person (see 1:22; 2:25; 3:20; 4:19 in which the same Greek word is used).

1:10 The prophets who prophesied of the grace that was to be yours: The author, like many early Christians, understood the Old Testament as predicting the times of Jesus and the early church, rather than speaking to the prophets' own times (see, e.g., 1 Pet. 2:6–8, 10; Matt. 1:23; 2:6; 2:15, 18, 23; Mark 1:2–3; 14:49; Luke 4:18–19, 21; 24:25–26, 44–49; John 5:39; Acts 3:24; 8:29–35; Rom. 1:2; 10:5–13; 1 Cor. 15:3, 4). When modern readers study these Old Testament texts, they often do not appear to be predictions of Christ or the church. The following theses may help to put the affirmations of 1 Peter and other such New Testament claims in a biblical perspective:

—The prophets of Israel addressed primarily their own contemporaries, promising God's blessings on those who were faithful and obedient (see Ezek. 12:26–28).

—In later situations when faithfulness to God resulted not in blessing but in persecution, some apocalyptic thinkers reinterpreted earlier prophecies, understanding them to be predictions of the long-range future, sealed up for a future day (e.g., Dan. 12:5–13). Thus already the Old Testament tradition reinterpreted earlier prophecies as speaking to the situation of later readers.

—However, most of the Old Testament prophets had in fact spoken from within an eschatological perspective. That is, while they addressed their own contemporaries, they did so in the light of the ultimate purpose and victory of God.

—The early Christian community rightly saw that the biblical prophecies had a future orientation, pointing to a later time of fulfillment of the ultimate plan of God. Since they believed that the Christ had come and that the eschatological age had begun, they reread their Bible in the light of this conviction and found many texts they believed were predictions of Christ and the church.

—Modern Christians can and should affirm the conviction of 1 Peter and early Christianity that the event of Jesus Christ is rightly interpreted as the fulfillment of the

hopes of the Old Testament prophets. We need *not* do this in the same *way(s)* that early Christians did. For modern Christian readers, the original meaning of the Old Testament texts in their own historical contexts must be considered.

—We must be especially careful not to understand the Old Testament prophets in such a way that claims that only Christians can understand what the biblical prophets were saying in their own times, as though Jewish readers cannot understand their own Bible without Christian faith.

—For further reflections on early Christian interpretation of the Old Testament, see the excursus, "New Testament Interpretation of the Old Testament," at 1 Cor. 15:3.

1:11 The Spirit of Christ: First Peter claims that the Spirit that inspired the prophets was the Spirit of Christ speaking of the future Christian age. This conviction is an expression of Christian faith, seeing the Old Testament through Christian eyes. Like the Pauline tradition (Gal. 4:4; Phil. 2:5–11; Col. 1:15–20), the Gospel of John (1:1–18), and Hebrews (1:1–4), 1 Peter pictures Christ as standing not only with God at the end of history as its goal, but with God at the beginning of history as its Creator. This means that the acts of God in the Old Testament could be seen as the acts of the pre-existent Christ as God's agent. This is not a matter of speculative theory, but a way of saying that the one God who is the Creator and Lord of history is the one who has defined himself in Christ, so that God's acts can be spoken of as Christ's acts. In believing in the God revealed in Christ, Christians do not believe in a new God, but in the God who has always been.

1:12 Those who have preached the gospel to you by the Holy Spirit sent from heaven (NIV): The readers came to faith as a response to Christian preaching. In such preaching the Spirit of God is active and effective. On the surface it appears to be human words and human activities; here the theological depth is revealed—in and through the human words and acts, God's Spirit has been at work.

Angels long to look: The author of 1 Peter concludes the thanksgiving by portraying the eschatological existence of Christian believers, who live in the climactic time of God's plan for history, as the envy of both the biblical prophets and the angels (1:10–12). Again, this is not a matter of speculative fantasy, but plays a practical role. First Peter addresses those who are at the margins of society, reviled and accused. They know how they appear in society's eyes. They need a larger perspective, which the author provides not in psychological or sociological terms of self-esteem, but by helping them see their privileged place in the context of God's plan for history, a privilege they had not achieved but had been granted by God's grace.

1:13–5:11
BODY OF THE LETTER

1:13–2:10
THE NEW IDENTITY AS THE ELECT
AND HOLY PEOPLE OF GOD

1:13 Therefore: First Peter is concerned to instruct Christians on how to live faithfully in the midst of a hostile society. It thus contains many commands: in the Greek text there are thirty-five direct imperatives, seventeen participles that function as imperatives, as well as other ways of communicating what God requires Christians to do, but none of these is in the first twelve verses. A series of imperatives begins at 1:13. As in the Ten Commandments, before the imperatives of human responsibility are set forth, there is the indicative of God's action (see Exod. 20:2–17; Deut. 5:6–21). The "therefore" of 1:13 presupposes the indicatives of 1:3–12.

Prepare your minds for action: Literally "gird up the loins of your mind" (KJV). The flowing garments worn in the ancient Near East were tightened about the waist and hips in preparing for work. "Roll up your mental sleeves and get ready for hard thinking" is the modern equivalent. The ancient Israelites ate the first Passover with their "loins girded" (Exod. 12:11; see Luke 12:35). The author of 1 Peter throughout applies to Gentile converts the whole exodus experience of Israel: former slaves are freed by the mighty act of God, are redeemed by the blood of the lamb, have been made participants in the divine covenant within which they have pledged their obedience, and are presently under way through a series of testings and harassments toward their promised inheritance, en route to becoming a holy people and royal priesthood. As Israel in the wilderness longed for the fleshpots of Egypt, Christians are now tempted to long for their former social life.

Hope: The first command in 1 Peter. Hope is his summary of the Christian life (see on

1:3). Is hope something that one can do in response to a command? Here as elsewhere in 1 Peter, the imperative is related dialectically to the indicative. Authentic hope can only be a response to God's act. Verse 13 presupposes verse 3; since God *has* acted, definitively and eschatologically, Christians can live a life of hope that is not illusory self-confidence or merely striving for a positive attitude.

1:14 Obedient children: The reference is not to maturity or "finding one's inner child," but to being reborn into the family of God (1:3, 23). Obedience is not servile or mindless, but the conduct of those who engage in disciplined thinking (1:13).

1:15 Be holy: Holiness is the quality of being separate from the ordinary. It belongs first of all to God, the Holy One, the Wholly Other, the Creator who is different from everything created (see 1 Sam. 2:2; 2 Kgs. 19:22; Job 6:10; Ps. 71:22; Isa. 1:4; 5:19–24; 6:1–5; 40:25; 60:9, 14; Jer. 35:7; 51:5; Hos. 11:9). God's people are holy because God has **called** them to live a distinctive life within the world as witnesses to God's mighty acts (2:9). The command to be holy is not something they can achieve on their own (see the command to hope in the preceding verse). Again the imperative rests on the indicative: "be what you are," or better, "show yourselves in your daily, public conduct to be what you in fact have been made by God's act."

1:16 For it is written: Lev. 19:2, see Lev. 11:44–45; 20:7, 26. Leviticus was the priests' manual. The citation is from a subdivision of Leviticus known as the Holiness Code (Lev. 17–26), which, in contrast to the rest of Leviticus, understands all Israel, and not only the ordained Levitical priests, to be priests to God for the sake of the world (see on 2:9).

1:17 Live your lives . . . in reverent fear (NIV): Fear is not cowardice or lack of trust, but honoring God as God, not becoming too casual or cozy with the Creator (4:19). Paul too had pictured pre-Christian life as those who "have no fear of God" (Rom. 3:18, citing Ps. 36:1) and connected holiness and the fear of God (2 Cor. 5:10–11; 7:1). Such reverent fear is not only compatible with calling upon God as Father, but in the ancient world was inherent in this invocation. Christians are to live lives of reverent fear as those who in their prayers invoke God as Father (the lack of article with "Father" indicates it is used adverbially, "fatherwise"), remembering that God is the One **who judges all people impartially**, not by their theology but by their lives.

1:19 The precious blood of Christ: Christ as the Passover lamb (see Exod. 12:1–28). This lamb was not a sacrifice for sins, but the means of deliverance from death and slavery. First Peter clearly affirms the atonement theology of the early church, according to which Jesus died to mediate God's forgiveness and reconcile sinful human beings to God (see 2:24; 3:18), but that is not in view here. The ransom of Jesus' blood does not here deliver us from the guilt of sin, but from the old way of life, as another expression of the exodus imagery that forms much of the metaphorical framework for this section.

Blood terminology, though alien to many modern readers, permeates biblical language and must be understood within its own framework of biblical theology. "Blood" is a shorthand way of saying "life." It was a maxim of the biblical world that "the life is in the blood," so that "blood" and "life" are virtual synonyms (Gen. 9:4; Lev. 17:11; Jonah 1:14; etc.). To say Jesus gave his blood for us is to say he gave his life, himself, for us.

1:22 Love: Jesus made the love command supreme (Mark 12:28–34; Matt. 22:34–40; Luke 10:25–28; John 13:34; 15:12, 17). The special quality of Christian love is defined christologically: the caring, self-giving, unconditional love revealed in the life and death of Jesus. Love so understood is not a feeling but an action.

Having purified your souls: "Souls" is a synonym for "persons" or "selves," as in 3:20 and consistently in 1 Peter. "Purified" echoes the biblical word found 34x in the LXX, used of the consecration or sanctification of priests, Levites, Nazirites, and the people of Israel as a whole. The word is used in the LXX almost exclusively for ritual purity, the kind of cultic holiness necessary for priests and the temple. First Peter uses it in a spiritual but real sense of the Christian community that, as a whole, has been sanctified as a priesthood to God, a spiritual house, where spiritual sacrifices are offered (see on 2:5).

This love should not be sentimentalized or romanticized. "See how they love one another" was said by outsiders of ancient Christians not as a compliment, but with resentment and suspicion of those who had been charged with "hatred for the human race" (see Tacitus, *Annals* 15.44; Tertullian, *Apology* 39). A Christian community such as the readers of 1 Peter could be tempted to turn their love exclusively to each other, as did the Qumran community, whose "Manual of Discipline" urged members to "love all the children of light and hate all the children of darkness" (1QS 1.10). First Peter specifically resists yielding to this pressure.

1:23–25 All flesh is like grass: Isa. 40:6–7, 8–9. The new life is not a matter of developing innate qualities, but of being **born anew** by the **living and enduring word of God** heard in Christian preaching in the power of the Holy Spirit (1:12). In 1:3 the new birth was by the resurrection of Jesus Christ; here it is through the word that is inseparably bound to this event and mediates it to the believer. Rebirth is not a matter of experienced feelings, but of the divine word.

Word of the Lord: The Old Testament has "our God." The author changes this to "Lord," which can refer to Christ as well as God, to express his conviction that it is the word of Christ that is heard in the Old Testament prophets (1:11).

2:1–3 Therefore: The chapter division here is unfortunate, since 2:1–10 goes with the preceding as the concluding literary unit of the first major section of the letter, 1:13–2:10.

Malice, deceit, hypocrisy, envy, slander (NIV): The author focuses on the attitudes and behavior that destroy community. It is aimed specifically at the internal life of the church as those who have been born anew into a new household, and whose ethic cannot be individualistic and privatistic.

Newborn infants: Continues the imagery of new birth (1:3, 23) and the church as the family of God. This is a baptismal image, as is **rid yourselves** (literally "lay aside"), since the Christian's entrance into a new life was sometimes symbolized in early Christianity by taking off one's old clothes, entering naked into the baptistery, and emerging on the other side to don new garments (see, e.g., Rom. 13:12; Col. 2:12; 3:8–10). First Peter is not addressed to a group of new converts within the church, but to the churches of the five provinces of Asia Minor as a whole, most of whom were not newly baptized. As Paul in Romans 6:1ff. appeals to the fact that the readers have been baptized (long after their actual baptism) as a foundational element in their ethical decisions, so 1 Peter continues to refer to the status of believers as those who have been born/begotten anew as basic to their understanding of themselves as Christians in a hostile society. Baptism, conversion, entrance into the household of faith was not a passing event that could be left behind in the past; it continued to be crucial in the believer's Christian life. **Long for the pure,**

spiritual milk: In 1 Cor. 3:1–2, "infants" and "milk" are negative images for immature Christians. Here the image is positive: as new babies instinctively long for milk that will nourish them, so Christians must seek the spiritual nourishment that makes them strong: the word of God that comes in Scripture, preaching, teaching, and Christian testimony in word and deed to the mighty acts of God (2:9). Christians never outgrow this. The picture of Christians as babies longing for their mothers' milk means they can never be satisfied, must always be hungry for the word of God by which they live (Deut. 8:3; Matt 4:4).

Verse 3 cites Ps. 34:8, where "Lord" refers to God; here the author understands it as referring to Christ. The author returns to this psalm in 3:10–12.

2:5 Living stones . . . spiritual house: Not each individual Christian, but the church itself, the community of believers, is the temple in which God dwells (see 1 Cor. 3:16, where the pronouns are plural).

2:6–8 Making use of a collection of three "stone" texts that had already become traditional, the author understands the rejected-but-vindicated stone to be both Christ and the Christians. This same combination of Old Testament texts had been used by Paul in Rom. 9:25–33 (Isa. 28:16; Isa. 8:14; Hos. 1:6–9). Christian lives are placed in parallel to the life of Christ. He was and is rejected by the world in general (not just by the Jewish leaders); the Christian readers of 1 Peter recognize their own experience of being rejected by pagan society. Christ was vindicated, and the rejected stone turned out to be the chief cornerstone; Christian readers will be vindicated at the eschaton.

The elect status of Christians is now explicated in seven images. Each of the seven images is taken from the Bible, was originally applied to Israel, and designates the church as the continuing people of God:

1. As heirs of Israel, the readers are addressed as "living stones" who are being built into a spiritual house (2:5).

2. As heirs of Israel, the readers are addressed as a "holy priesthood" or "royal priesthood" (2:5, 9). The later issue of whether there is a special order of priests within the church, or whether every individual is a priest, is not here in view. The point is that the Christian community as a whole plays the role of the continuing people of God in history, which includes being a priestly community on behalf of the world.

3. As heirs of Israel, the readers are addressed as a "chosen race" (2:9).

4. As heirs of Israel, the readers are addressed as a "holy nation" (2:9).

5. As heirs of Israel, the readers are addressed as "God's own people" (2:9). "People" (*laos*, from which our term "laity" is derived) is the common word for Israel in the LXX. The phrase translated "God's own" (NRSV) or "belonging to God" (NIV) literally means "for (a) possession." Translations have added the word "God" for clarity, but the phrase could also mean "a people destined for vindication."

6. As heirs of Israel, the readers are addressed as the "people of God" and

7. as those who have "received mercy" (2:10). These last two designations are taken from Hosea 1:6, 9–10; 2:23 (also used in a similar context by Paul in Rom. 9:25). In Hosea, the contrast was between unfaithful Israel rejected by God and the renewed eschatological Israel accepted by God. First Peter applies this to the Gentile past of the readers, who have now by the divine mercy been incorporated into the continuing people of God. The final word is one of divine initiative and mercy. The readers' identity is established not by their own deed, but by God's choice and effective call.

2:9 That you may proclaim: Like the Israel of the Bible and history, the church as the people of God is called into being not for its own sake, but as an expression of the divine mission to the world, and is itself charged with a mission. The gift becomes a responsibility.

The worship life of the Christian community, in both its liturgical and everyday forms, though directed to God, is already a testimony to the world. But the church also has a mission more directly oriented to the world: in word and deed to proclaim God's **mighty acts**. The church does not witness to itself and its own experiences, but to what God has done, is doing, and will do. The "mighty acts of God" can be outlined as Creation, Covenant, Christ, Church, Consummation. See on Eph. 1:9

2:11–3:12
CHRISTIAN EXISTENCE AND CONDUCT IN THE GIVEN STRUCTURES OF SOCIETY

For many modern Christians, this section is the most difficult part of the letter to take seriously. It gives instructions for Christians to live their lives in the given social structures in such a way that the church bears witness to the Christian faith, with a view to winning others to Christ. The section is structured as follows:

2:11–12   General introduction (to all)
2:13–17   General instruction: subordination to the given social structures, illustrated by respect for governmental authority
2:18–25   Specific instruction to slaves, modulating into christological affirmations that provide a model for all
3:1–7   Specific instruction to wives and husbands
3:8–12   General instruction to all, concluded with extensive Scripture citation

EXCURSUS: "INTERPRETING LANGUAGE ABOUT SUBMISSION"

Let it be clearly said: this section of the biblical text does instruct Christian readers to be subject to the imperial governing authorities, slaves to be subject even to harsh masters, and wives to be subject to husbands. These instructions are problematic to modern readers. Some contemporary Christians, wishing to respect the authority of the Bible, attempt to follow the instructions literally—as did the advocates of slavery in early nineteenth-century America. Other modern readers (perhaps the majority) are puzzled, embarrassed, or resentful that 1 Peter instructs citizens, slaves, and wives to be subordinate to those who are above them in the social structure, raising no questions about the validity of the structures and institutions themselves. The following comments suggest ways to understand the text in its own setting (rather than defending, apologizing for, or subverting its intention).

1. *The text is to be interpreted historically as a letter (not an essay).* The text before us is not a programmatic essay on the state, slavery, or the role of women. The question addressed in 1 Peter is not whether the Roman Empire, the institution of slavery, or the patriarchal family should exist, but how Christians in Asia Minor at the end of the first Christian century should live out their faith within these given social structures. The letter allows the modern reader to see a *specific application* of the kerygma mediated by the Pauline/Petrine tradition in a particular situation, a social situation different from that of the modern reader.

2. *The text includes a household code.* Hellenistic Jews and Christians in the Pauline tradition had already adapted the traditional table of household duties as a means of teaching Jewish and Christian ethics (see Col. 3:18–4:1; Eph. 5:22–6:9; Titus

2:1–10; 1 Tim. 2–3; 5:1–6:3; *1 Clem.* 1.3; 21.6–9; Poly. *Phil.* 4.1–6.1; *Did.* 4.9–11; *Barn.* 19.5–7). The author of 1 Peter is not formulating new rules, but joining a discussion and adapting a tradition.

3. *The text in its entirety is directed to "all."* Just as the whole letter was addressed to all the churches in an extensive area (1:1), so this section, 2:11–3:12, including the instructions to slaves and wives, is addressed to the whole church. Since 2:13–3:7 does not cover all cases and classes, instructions to slaves and wives are to be taken as *illustrative.* It is not as though there is nothing here for bachelors, widows, divorcees, children, employees. The whole community is to learn from what is said to slaves and wives.

4. *The text of the whole letter is oriented to the weak and vulnerable; it sees the world from the underside.* The situation of the church as a whole and the Christian life as such can be addressed in instructions to those who most clearly represent social weakness and vulnerability. The slaves and women here addressed have already made a courageous decision to join a despised foreign cult that is not the religion of their non-Christian masters and husbands. That is, they have already shown that they are *not submissive.* Their profession of the Christian faith can itself be seen as a form of social protest—though it must not be reduced to that. It can also be that they simply believed the gospel to be true and were prepared to take the consequences. This makes them a model for the church as a whole.

5. *The text does not merely command docility, submission, and obedience, but subordination.* God is the Creator of order—though no particular social structure can claim divine authorization. The author instructs the whole church to fit in to the recognized social order as a part of Christian responsibility in that situation. This is illustrated by instructions to slaves and women. The author does not justify the institution of imperial government, slavery, or the patriarchal family. Mission, not submission, is the goal.

6. *The text is to be understood in its wider theological context.* The author stands in the Pauline tradition of justification by faith as the basis for declaring that all Christians are free, all are slaves (2:16). As those who are already freed and accepted before God, their identity does not depend on the social status others attribute to them. They are freed from obsession with their self-image to place their lives in the service of the Christian mission (see Rom. 6; 1 Cor. 8–10).

7. *Mission, not submission, is the focus of this text.* The challenge is to remove a false stumbling block, so that people may decide for or against the

truth of the Christian message without being put off by [their perception of] the cultural forms associated with it. To be good citizens subordinate to the civil authorities is to silence the objections of outsiders, i.e., it is in the service of the Christian mission (2:15). By voluntarily living in accord with the patriarchal family structure, wives may win over husbands who have not been won by preaching to them (3:1). Members of the people of God on pilgrimage through history must take responsibility for the community's witness to the mighty acts of God (2:9).

2:11–12
General Introduction (To All)

Religious rituals were interwoven into every aspect of pagan life. All social, community, political, and educational occasions involved rites that Christians could only regard as "lawless idolatry" (4:6). When Christians did not participate in the life of society around them, they were suspect and maligned **as evildoers**, considered to be "atheists," "haters of the human race," and unpatriotic traitors.

Gentiles: Though ethnically they were mostly Gentiles themselves, the readers now understand themselves to be incorporated into the holy people of God (see on 2:1–10). Their conduct is to consist of **honorable deeds** that outsiders can see, with a view to their being converted, so that they will **glorify God when he comes to judge.** The general principle of this whole section is that Christian conduct within the given structures of society is to be seen as part of the church's evangelistic mission.

Desires of the flesh that wage war against the soul: See on 1:9. "Soul" is not the "true inner self" in contrast to "evil flesh." See 4:2, where "human desires" are contrasted with the "will of God."

2:13–17
General Instruction

The **emperor** and **governors** are to be honored along with all other human beings, but only God is to be feared (see on 1:17).

2:18–25
Instructions to Slaves (And to All)

On slavery in the first century, see the introduction to Philemon.

No pre-Christian household codes address slaves directly. *All* New Testament household codes directly address slaves as responsible members of the inclusive Christian community. The section is paradigmatic for the whole Chris-

tian community, which has been addressed as "slaves" who are nonetheless "free" (2:16).

The reality of unjust suffering is not explained, excused, or justified. The author of 1 Peter chooses this point, precisely in the midst of instruction purportedly directed to the most beleaguered and vulnerable group in society, to introduce his most profound discussion of the motivation for such a Christian life. He stands in the Pauline tradition, in which unjust suffering for the sake of Christ is understood as a gift from God.

2:19–20 Suffering unjustly: These verses start and end with a phrase that is literally translated "this [unjust suffering] is grace from God" (see 5:12, and Phil. 1:29, which uses a form of the same word for grace, and comments on Phil. 1:7). Unjust suffering is not just a strategy in 1 Peter. It is inherently right, as revealed in Christ. The nature of God and the universe embraces unjust suffering. This is the polar opposite of saying that Christians may cause, contribute to, or excuse unjust suffering. But when they are called upon to endure it, they can do so as grace from God, as was the cross itself (2:19–20; 5:12).

2:21–25 Christ also suffered: Often taken to be a fragment of an early Christian hymn (see Phil. 2:5–11; Col. 1:15–20). The Suffering Servant of Isaiah 53 is the model (2:22/Isa. 53:9; 2:24/Isa. 53:5, 11; 2:25/Isa. 53:6, 10).

Example: The Greek word pictures a sketch, tracing pad, or outline used to teach children to write the alphabet. It is thus a guideline to be used in one's own composition, not a mechanical pattern to be duplicated. **In his steps:** These words often used to picture Christ as the model for all Christians were originally addressed to slaves (and through them to all Christians).

2:25 You have returned: The author does not take credit for being able to live such a life of self-sacrifice for the sake of others. Those who do so are called by the divine initiative (1:21) and, though once straying sheep, have been *brought* back (so TEV; Greek text has passive voice in 2:25) by/to their divine shepherd who has given his life for the sheep.

3:1–7
Instructions to Wives, Husbands, (And to All)

For general principles of interpretation, see above.

3:1 In the same way: Like all other Christians, including husbands and young people (the same word is used in 3:7 and 5:5) wives are to fit into the existing social order as part of the Christian mission (see on 2:13). **Accept the authority:** Better translated "be subordinate," reflecting the Christian's relation to the orders of society (see above).

3:3 Braiding . . . hair . . . gold . . . fine clothing: Romans were suspicious of foreign cults such as the Isis cult from Egypt, which encouraged women to engage in public processions, wear loud clothing, and call attention to themselves. Christians are to remove suspicion that they belong to such a cult. Their dress is not to call attention to themselves. For women in another culture to adopt these instructions as normative rules would make them stand out—the precise opposite of their intention.

3:4 Gentle and quiet spirit: Inner integrity rather than outward show is the model for all Christians, not just for women (3:16; see 1 Sam. 15:7; Matt. 5:5; 11:29; 1 Cor. 4:21; Gal. 6:1).

3:6 Sarah: See Gen. 18:12. "Lord" = "Sir," a show of respect. The case is not exactly analogous, since Sarah was not the believing wife of an unbelieving husband, and since in the Genesis story she is quite independent.

3:7 Christian **husbands:** They are not simply to accept the dominant role assigned to them by first-century society, but are to **show consideration** and **honor** to their wives as coheirs of the **gift of** (Christian) **life** received from God. Husbands are to relate to their wives not merely in terms of cultural expectations, but **according to knowledge** (KJV), i.e., as those who understand the Christian faith as articulated in 1:3–2:25 (see 2:15).

3:8–12
Concluding Instructions to All

The unit explicitly returns to address all Christians. Jesus had taught nonretaliation (Matt. 5:44/Luke 6:28). Typically, to support his point the author does not quote Jesus, but the Old Testament (Ps. 34:13–17).

3:13–5:11
RESPONSIBLE SUFFERING IN THE FACE OF HOSTILITY

3:13–17
Suffering for Doing Good
(= Doing Right)

3:13 Do what is good: Readers are instructed to do what is right despite the temptation to drop out or retaliate against a society that misunderstands and excludes them.

3:14–16 Even if you do suffer: Christian conduct is not a strategy for success. **Make your defense:** Not only before the courts if need be. Be able to give a coherent explanation of the meaning of the Christian faith to outsiders who misunderstand. **Hope:** Summary for the whole of Christian faith and life (see on 1:3). **In Christ:** See on 5:10.

3:17 Suffer for doing good: Christ is the model (2:18–25).

3:18–22
Lesson from an Early Christian Hymn

3:18–19 Christ . . . suffered: The ethical conduct to which Christians are called is grounded not on the basis of logic, general principles, or common sense, but christologically. This obscure passage is probably part of an ancient Christian hymn familiar to the readers but now lost. Such hymns celebrated the cosmic victory of Christ (see Phil. 2:5–11; Col. 1:15–20; 1 Tim. 3:16). **Flesh . . . spirit:** Not two "parts" of Christ, but the earthly world in which he was killed and the transcendent world in which he was vindicated. **Spirits in prison:** Probably the rebellious transcendent beings (also called "angels," "demons," and "sons of God") who corrupted the human race and were imprisoned in the nether world awaiting eschatological judgment (see Gen. 6:1–4; *1 En.* 10:4–6; 1 Cor. 6:3; Jude 6; 2 Pet. 2:4). It is not clear whether the **proclamation** Christ made to them after his death communicated doom or salvation.

3:20–21 Baptism: As the waters of the flood separated **Noah** and his family from the old world, so baptism separates Christians from their old life. As only **a few** in Noah's time were delivered, so the minority status of Christians in society does not mean they are rejected by God. Baptism **saves** not by some magical power in itself, but **through the resurrection of Jesus Christ.** The imagery may also point to baptism as a reenactment of Christ's sojourn into the nether world, as the believer enters into the world of death and reemerges sharing Christ's victory over the hostile powers.

3:22 Angels, authorities, and powers made subject to him: May point to their final redemption (see Phil. 2:9–11; Eph. 1:9–10, 19–22; Col. 1:19–20). **Right hand of God:** The imagery is based on Ps. 110, the most quoted psalm in the New Testament (e.g., Matt. 22:44; 26:64; Mark 12:36; 14:62; Luke 20:42; 22:69; Acts 2:34–35; Rom. 8:34; 1 Cor. 15:25; Eph. 1:20; Col. 3:1; Heb. 1:3, 13; 8:1; 10:12).

4:1–6
Application to the Christian Life

4:1–2 Finished with sin: May refer to Christ, Christians, or both. The sinless Christ (2:22) suffered to bring the reign of sin to an end. Christians, who participate in Christ's suffering and death because they are baptized, and whose own sufferings are part and parcel of the Christ event that is now their own story, have finished with sin, in the sense that they can never return to their old way of life.

4:3 Gentiles: The term is not meant ethnically, but as in 2:12; the Christian community is identified as the holy people of God, to which outsiders are Gentiles. The list of vices is stereotypical and does not reflect the particular evils of the readers' setting (see on Rom. 1:29).

4:4 No longer: The readers once belonged to the society that now rejects them.

4:6 The gospel was proclaimed even to the dead: Obscure, but probably unrelated to the "spirits in prison" above (3:19). More likely refers to Christians who have died. From the perspective of this world, their death was a judgment, but they are vindicated in the transcendent spiritual world (see on Rev. 14:1–20).

4:7–11
Eschatological Encouragement

4:8 Above all . . . love: See Mark 12:28–34; Matt. 22:34–40; Luke 10:25–28; 1 Cor. 13; Rom. 12:9; 13:9–10. Best translated as "caring." In the biblical understanding, the opposite of love is not hate, but not caring, indifference. **Covers . . . sins:** Prov. 10:12; Jas. 5:20; see 1 Cor. 13:5.

4:9 Offer hospitality . . . without grumbling (NIV): Literally, "be friendly to strangers." The church was already a multicultural community, uniting in Christ people from various economic, linguistic, racial, and national backgrounds. The church needed to provide for traveling missionaries and other Christians who needed support and shelter. Old prejudices die hard, and the church is reminded that love is a matter of concrete acts for the benefit of others who may be different; cultural xenophobia is overcome in the Christian community (see Rom. 12:13; 1 Tim. 3:2; Titus 1:8; Heb. 13:2).

4:10 Gift: This Pauline word (*charisma*) is found only here outside the Pauline tradition (see 1 Cor. 12:1–31; Rom. 12:3–9). Every Christian has received a gift, there is a variety of gifts, and the gifts are not for individual self-aggrandizement but for strengthening the Christian community as a whole.

4:12–19
Suffering in Joy and Hope

4:16 Christian: In the New Testament only here, Acts 11:26; 26:28. Originally probably a demeaning term, the name "Christian" later became a badge of honor.

4:18 Proverbs 11:31, an Old Testament wisdom text now understood in the perspective of eschatological judgment.

4:19 In accordance with God's will: It is not the case that God wills the readers' particular sufferings, but that God's plan is the framework for understanding their meaning. **Faithful Creator:** The eschatological hope that reverberates throughout 1 Peter (see on 1:3) is the other side of the faith that all things are finally in one hand, the hand of the one God who is the Creator of all and who will bring the world and history to a worthy conclusion. **Continuing to do good:** See on 3:13, 17. The Christian response to unjust suffering is not sullen resignation but actively doing good.

5:1–11
Church as Support Group
Structured for Mission

5:1–5 An elder myself: The author is a presbyter (elder) in the Roman church, who writes with apostolic authority (1:1; see introduction to 1 Peter; on elders, see Acts 11:30; 14:23; 20:17–38; 1 Tim. 5:17–25; Titus 1:5–9; Jas. 5:13). **Witness of the sufferings of Christ:** Does not mean the author claims to have been present at the crucifixion, but that he bears witness to the meaning of the cross, as all Christians are called to do, and as he has done in this letter.

The churches addressed are led by **elders** (v. 1) who, like the author, participate in the apostolic authority, but all are subordinate to Christ the **chief shepherd** (v. 4). Their temptation to exercise their ministry for **sordid gain** (v. 1) may refer to their responsibility for church funds, or that by the time of 1 Peter elder was already a salaried office (see 1 Cor. 9:7–14; 1 Tim. 3:8; 5:17–18).

Good church leaders exercise their authority by being **examples** (v. 3), in a spirit of **humility** (v. 5).

The **younger** (v. 5) probably refers not to youthful members, but to the rest of the congregation, which is divided into "elders" and "younger," i.e., leaders and followers. While there is a structure of authority in which some are subordinate, all are to be subject to one another (see 2:13–3:12).

5:7 He cares for you: Literally "it matters to him [God] what happens to you."

5:9 Your brothers and sisters in all the world: The little house churches in Asia are members of the one church, a worldwide community of faith. **Suffering:** Does not refer to official persecution, but to the harassment and discrimination all Christians suffer wherever they are.

5:12–14
CONCLUSION

5:12 Silvanus: Also called Silas (see 1 Thess. 1:1; 2 Cor. 1:19; Acts 15:22; and often in Acts). "Through Silvanus" does not mean he is coauthor or secretary in the composition of the letter, but that he was active in delivering it (see Acts 15:22–23). "Written . . . with the help of Silvanus" (NIV) is an incorrect translation. **This** [unjust suffering for the sake of Christ] **is the true grace of God:** See on 2:19–20; see Phil. 1:7, 29 comments.

5:13 Babylon: Rome (see Rev. 17:5, 18), for Babylon had destroyed Jerusalem in 586 BCE (2 Kgs. 25; Jer. 52), just as the Romans did in 70 CE (an indication that 1 Peter was written some time after 70 CE).

My son Mark: Not literal, but refers to Mark as Peter's convert and younger coworker, as Paul had referred to himself as "father" of Onesimus and Timothy (Phlm. 10; 1 Cor. 4:17; see 1 Tim. 1:18; 2 Tim. 1:2). Both Silvanus/Silas and Mark had been associated with Paul (1 Thess. 1:1; Phlm. 24). Their association with Peter is here a signal of the later combination of Petrine and Pauline traditions in Rome (see the introduction to 1 Peter), as is the use of the Pauline expression **in Christ** (see on 2 Cor. 5:17).

Kiss of love: A modification of the Pauline "holy kiss" (see on Rom. 16:16), reflecting the author's understanding of the church as the family of God, the household of faith (see on 2:1–10).

The Second Letter of Peter

INTRODUCTION

Second Peter is a letter, as are most of the writings in the New Testament. This literary form had, by the time of this letter, become so popular that the form alone may have helped to gain acceptance, or at least a hearing, in the church. In fact, letters of Paul had already been collected into a body of writing and were being circulated in the churches as Scripture (2 Pet. 3:15–16). Not all the features of a Pauline letter are present in 2 Peter (signature, address, greeting, thanksgiving or praise, message, closing greeting, farewell), but not all are essential to qualify a writing as an epistle. Nor does being a letter mean that all the content is conversational or informal. Epistles often contain formal elements such as hymns, creeds, liturgies, lists of virtues or vices, and lists of domestic duties. For example, 2 Pet. 1:5–7 bears the marks of an oratorical form with its rhythm of repetition and addition providing ease of listening and memory. However, the most noticeable literary feature of this epistle is that it is structured as a valedictory or farewell address, sometimes called a testament. This form appears with some frequency in the Bible (Gen. 47:29–49:32; Deut. 1–3; 28–31; Josh. 23–24; 1 Sam. 12; John 14–16; Acts 7; Acts 20:18–35). In a farewell address the one approaching death recalls experience in common with the readers, warns of dangers on the horizon, and charges the faithful to remain steadfast. The pattern will be apparent in the comments on the text.

Audience

Second Peter is a general letter. This is to say, it does not address particular persons or congregations. Of course, the original readers may have felt they were being addressed personally, but information about place and names is unavailable today. It may have been the writer's intention to leave the address open so that the letter could circulate among several churches. The readers, wherever they were (Asia Minor, if the audience is the same as addressed in 1 Pet. 1:1), are plagued by controversies over the interpretation of Scripture (1:20–21) and destabilizing teachings about moral conduct (1:5, 10; 2:2; 3:14) that in the writer's opinion, were the fruit of rejecting the doctrine of the return of Christ and final day of God (1:16; 3:3–5, 9). The letter is a defense of the prophetic and apostolic tradition on the subject. In that defense a portion of chaps. 2–3 is remarkably similar to the Letter of Jude. Whether 2 Peter incorporated Jude, as most scholars believe, or Jude borrowed from 2 Peter, or the two used a common source, the problem of locating the readers in time and place remains unsolved.

Authorship

As to authorship, the letter bears the name of Simeon Peter. However, several features in the epistle itself argue against the authorship of Peter. Paul's letters have been collected and are read as Scripture (3:15–16). Paul is obviously dead, and since he and Peter both died in the mid-sixties, Peter must be also. Likewise, the message "spoken through your apostles" (3:2) implies the writer and readers live in a time subsequent to the apostles. Furthermore, the mount of revelation has now become "the holy mountain" (1:18); reverence has replaced reporting. Probably someone from the circle of Peter's disciples honored the apostle by writing what Peter would say to the church in a new time and place. Writing in the name of Peter was a way of claiming the message of the document represented the apostolic faith. See "Pseudonymous Letters in the New Testament" in the introduction to Ephesians.

Outline

1:1–2 Salutation
1:3–11 Summary of God's Blessings and the Believer's Response
1:12–3:16 The Writer's Farewell Address
  1:12–15 A Personal Word
  1:16–21 The Message Remembered and Confirmed
  2:1–22 Attack upon False Teachers
  3:1–16 Certainty of the Lord's Coming
3:17–18a Closing Admonition
3:18b Doxology

For Further Reading

Craddock, Fred B. *First and Second Peter and Jude.* Westminster Bible Companion. Louisville, KY: Westminster John Knox, 1995. Some of the material on 2 Peter in the pages that follow has been drawn from this more expansive treatment.

Watson, Duane F. "The Second Letter of Peter." In *The New Interpreter's Bible*, vol. 12. Nashville: Abingdon Press, 1998.

COMMENTARY

1:1–2
SALUTATION

The three-part salutation, common to correspondence of that day, is familiar to us through Paul's letters.

1. Sender: **Simeon:** This is a rare form of the name Simon (Acts 15:14), joined to the name Jesus gave him (Matt. 16:18; John 1:42; see the introduction to 1 Peter). Simon was called to be an apostle (Mark 3:13–19). Identifying him as **servant** (slave) **and apostle** may have been patterned after Paul (Rom. 1:1), whose letters the writer knew (3:15–16).

2. Addresses: Broad and inclusive. If a specific church was in the writer's mind, we are not so informed. The readers are Christians who **have received a faith** (Rom. 12:3; 1 Cor. 12:9) **as precious as ours**; that is, distance of time or place from the apostles makes no one a secondhand believer. How so? All receive equally from a righteous (just) God. **Our God and Savior Jesus Christ:** Whether God and Jesus Christ are to be understood separately or as one is unclear. To refer to Jesus Christ as God is unusual in the New Testament but not unique (John 1:18; 20:28; Rom. 9:5; Heb. 1:8; see on John 3:16). Governor Pliny reported that Christians in Asia Minor sang hymns to Christ "as to a god."

3. Greeting: Here in the form of the apostolic blessing, probably originating with Paul. **In abundance:** This is an added flourish to the usual blessing. **The knowledge of God and of Jesus our Lord:** Unlike v. 1, God and Jesus are clearly separated. This knowledge is important in this letter (1:2, 3, 5, 6, 8; 2:20; 3:18), a claim of the promise of the new covenant (Jer. 31:34), of the purpose of Christ's coming (John 1:18; 17:3), and the work of the Spirit (1 Cor. 2:9–10). The attack on false teachers is anticipated.

1:3–11
SUMMARY: GOD'S BLESSINGS AND THE BELIEVER'S RESPONSE

This unit parallels the thanksgiving with which Paul usually followed the greeting. The function is basically the same: to provide a summary of the message of the letter, setting up the reader's expectation of matters to be discussed.

1:3–4 His divine power: Notice the divine initiative. God has **given**, has **called**, has **given**. All resources needed for life appropriate to God's nature are provided. Knowledge (v. 2) of God, though not defined, will be joined to the tradition in which the readers have been instructed (1:12–15). **Very great promises:** Moving from this corrupt world into the realm where God is. **Corruption:** Not the nature of creation, but **because of lust**; that is, problems are moral and ethical. **Participants of the divine nature:** He became as we are so that we may be as he is (1 John 3:2; 1 Cor. 15:42–44a).

1:5–11 You must make every effort: Believers respond to God's initiative with "every effort" (v. 5) to grow in Christian virtues (v. 8). Virtue lists were common among moral philosophers of the day and often embraced by Christians (Gal. 5:22–23; Col. 3:5–9; 2 Tim. 3:2–5). **Support** (NRSV)/**Add** (NIV): The same word translated "provided" or "will receive" in v. 11. We supply Christian virtues, God supplies **entry into the eternal kingdom** (v. 11). The list (vv. 5–7) begins with **faith**, ends with **love**. The rhythm of repetition and addition aids the reader's (listener's) memory. **Goodness:** Right conduct based on self-discipline. **Mutual affection:** Reciprocal love. **Love:** As God loves, including strangers and enemies. These virtues make the believer effective and fruitful (v. 8), confirm God's initiative of grace toward us (v. 10), protect against **stumbling** (falling, v. 10), and prepare for entry into the **kingdom** God will provide (v. 11). To be without these virtues is to be **nearsighted**, **blind**, and **forgetful** (v. 9), three common words to describe the lost.

1:12–3:16
THE WRITER'S FAREWELL ADDRESS

The main body of this letter is structured as a valedictory or farewell address. Approaching death is stated, common tradition and experiences are recalled, warnings of dangers are given. See the introduction to 2 Peter.

1:12–15
A PERSONAL WORD

1:12 Reminding: The message that follows is a reminder of the truth with which both writer and readers are familiar and in which they are firmly grounded.

1:13 Refresh your memory: The writer makes it his primary mission to rehearse the Christian tradition. With the passing of time, preserving the word passed from Christ through the apostles to the church becomes critically important.

1:14 Death will come soon: Obviously a reference to John 21:18–19, in which Jesus predicts the martyr's death that awaits Peter. According to tradition, that death occurred in Rome in the mid-sixties.

1:15 Recall: The tradition must not die with Peter. The life of the church depends on its memory.

1:16–21
THE MESSAGE REMEMBERED AND CONFIRMED

1:16a: The power and coming of our Lord Jesus Christ. The message here is clearly the second coming, the return of Christ. **We made known to you:** No need for lengthy review; they already know the teaching. **Cleverly devised myths.** The writer is already debating opponents who claim the doctrine of Christ's return is speculation, a created story passed off on the church. Later the writer will accuse them of creating deceptive views (2:1–3). Truth vs. myth was a common framing of debate in the early church (1 Tim. 1:4; 4:7; 6:20; 2 Tim. 2:16; Titus 1:14).

1:16b–21 Message more fully confirmed: A threefold confirmation is presented.

1. **We had been eyewitnesses of his majesty** (v. 16b). This is further elaborated in v. 18: **We ourselves heard this voice come from heaven** and **we were with him on the holy mountain.** The event is usually understood as the transfiguration (Matt. 17:1–5), but may refer to a post-Easter revelation (see Matt. 28:18–20). The "we" may not be the personal "we" of the original apostles, but a past event now claimed as the experience of the whole church (see John 1:14; 1 John 1:1–4). The transfiguration or post-Easter revelation argues for the second coming in that the majesty, power, and glory that will mark Christ's return have already been demonstrated in advance of his return. What will be seen is what has been seen.

2. **We have the prophetic message** (v. 19). No specific citations from the Old Testament are given (as also in Luke 24:25, 27, 44–47). Perhaps the writer assumes the well-instructed readers will know. Prophecy serves believers as **a lamp shining in a dark place** until Christ comes. **Morning star:** the term appears nowhere else in the Bible, but see Num. 24:17; Rev. 22:16).

3. **Men and women moved by the Holy Spirit spoke from God** (v. 21). Since the church did not write the Scriptures on its own initiative, so interpretation of Scripture is not a private matter (v. 20) but the task of the believing community. The Bible is the church's book. Not false teachers who come in, but the writer and the church grounded in the apostolic tradition can interpret aright. The doctrine of the Lord's return is both given and received by the Holy Spirit (Acts 28:25–27; 2 Tim. 3:16).

2:1–22
ATTACK UPON FALSE TEACHERS

In a farewell address, a leader may warn followers of their own moral failure (Deut. 31:29), of opposition from without (John 16:2, 4–5), or of false teachers within their ranks (2 Tim. 4:3–4). This last source of difficulty is now addressed. In all such addresses the problems are not future, but present.

2:1 False prophets: In contrast to true prophets (1:19–21). **Among the people:** Israel (Jer. 5:12; 6:14; Ezek. 13:10). **There will be:** In a farewell address, future means present: "there are." **False teachers:** See Acts 20:30; Jude. **Secretly:** Insinuating and deceptive. **Destructive opinions:** Views that divide the church. **Deny the Master who bought them:** By word and life turning from the one who rescued them from sin and death. **Swift destruction:** If those who turn from Christ seem to be faring well (1 Kgs. 18:27; Pss. 10:11, 13; 73:11), that condition is soon to end.

2:2 Licentious ways: They sell their ministry to the highest bidder and use their followers as a source of gain.

2:3 Pronounced against them long ago: Discussed in the verses that follow (vv. 4–10).

2:4–10a Judgment: One long conditional sentence: If (v. 4), then (v. 9). Three cases of God's judgment are recalled:

1. **2:4 Spare the angels:** Reference to Gen. 6:1–4: sons of God married earthly women and their offspring brought war, violence, and idolatry into the world. The Genesis account is elaborated in a Jewish writing, *1 Enoch*

(dated between third cent. BCE and first cent. CE), in which these sinning angels are cast into hell (Tartarus), confined in dark pits until judgment day. The writer of 1 Peter assumes the readers know *1 Enoch* and regard it as an authoritative report of God's activity.

2. **2:5 Noah:** Gen. 6–8 recalled. **The ungodly:** The image is appropriate for the false teachers, since their erroneous teaching is joined to immoral living. God's judgment involves both punishment and rescue.

3. **2:6–8 Sodom and Gomorrah:** Gen. 19 is recalled. The more elaborate treatment of this segment includes not only the destruction of the cities and the rescue of Lot but also Lot's vexation and grief due to living among the ungodly. No doubt the writer and the readers of 2 Peter saw themselves in Lot's predicament.

2:9 Then the Lord knows how: The three examples serve to prove that God can handle the situation of the beleaguered church: rescue the godly and hold under punishment the ungodly until the final judgment.

2:10a Those who indulge their flesh . . . and despise authority: Again the writer joins moral and doctrinal error. Here the statement is stronger, charging depraved lust and arrogant mocking of the apostolic tradition and the position of authority held by the Lord's apostles. The behavior of the false teachers is described in 2:10b–19. The heretics continue to be referred to as "they," even though they are present in the church (v. 13). This is the style of a farewell address. In addition, treating them as not present adds edge to the indictment. The rhetorical rampage in this unit was familiar to audiences of the time. It belonged to a form of oratory called "in praise or blame." Exaggerated flourishes were used to praise or to blame a person or a group of persons.

2:10b Not afraid to slander the glorious ones: Verbal abuse of angelic beings (vv. 10b–11) constitutes a brief allusion to a story found in the Jewish writing *The Assumption of Moses*, in which the archangel Michael refuses to condemn the devil, leaving that judgment to God. See the more extended treatment at Jude 8. The false teachers are more bold and arrogant, blaspheming angels, the spirit beings who carry out God's will in creation, and proclaiming their own freedom and secularity.

2:12 Like irrational animals: Beasts of the field, with no life of understanding, are killed for human use. So the false teachers, blaspheming without understanding, move toward

their own destruction, a just end for their own wrongdoing.

2:13 Revel . . . blots and blemishes . . . dissipation while they feast with you: That they carouse in the daytime is evidence of how morally degenerate the heretics are (Eccl. 10:16; Dan. 5:11–12). They are "blots and blemishes"; that is, morally bankrupt, the very opposite of what they are expected to be at the Lord's coming (3:14). They even make drinking parties out of the church's fellowship meals and eucharistic services.

2:14 Eyes full of adultery . . . entice unsteady souls . . . trained in greed. Accursed children! The false teachers are on the lookout for partners in adultery while seducing the unstable, immature (new Christians) to join in their vices. The immature are unsuspecting, while the seducers are experts through long exercises in evil. The writer screams at them: they are under God's curse.

2:15–16 Following the road of Balaam: See Num. 22. The **straight road** is the image of obedience (Prov. 2:16), but they, like Balaam, have turned aside, selling their ministries for money. A speechless donkey knew more and behaved better. "Son of Beor" in Num. 22 is here **son of Bosor.** Bosor, similar to the Hebrew word for "flesh" may have been the writer's creation to describe his opponents. In v. 12 they were like animals; in v. 16 they are even lower.

2:17 Waterless springs . . . mists driven . . . deepest darkness: The promises of the false teachers are empty of the water that nourishes life; they are transient and not dependable, subject as they are to the outside forces that determine their direction. As for their punishment in caves of darkness, see 2:4, 9; Jude 13.

2:18 Bombastic nonsense . . . desires of the flesh . . . people who have just escaped: Empty, boastful words (NIV) is a better reading. Unsteady novices, only yesterday pagan, and now still wet from baptism, are easy prey to flourishes of oratory and lifestyles of greed and indulgence.

2:19 Freedom . . . slaves: The promise of freedom from authority and the moral demands of the Christian tradition actually bring a new kind of bondage to passions of the flesh, a bondage in which the false teachers are also trapped.

2:20 Again entangled: This description of the heretics should warn and deter those in danger of coming under their spell. The knowledge of Christ (1:3–5) had provided for the false teachers an escape from the **defilements** (corruption) **of the world,** but they chose to return, becoming enslaved and overcome by the very life they mistook for freedom. As a result, their condition is worse than their pre-Christian state. This statement recalls a story Jesus told about a man with an unclean spirit whose last state was worse than the first (Matt. 12:43–45).

2:21 It would have been better: Verse 20 is here restated in a form, borrowed by the church from Judaism, that underscores the magnitude of certain erroneous conduct (Matt. 5:29, 30; 12:45; 1 Pet. 3:17).

2:22 The dog . . . the sow: The writer returns to the analogy of animals to describe the false teachers (2:12), in this case drawing on proverbs about the filthy habits of dogs (Prov. 26:11) and hogs. The two animals, despised in that culture, were joined in a negative portrait in a teaching of Jesus (Matt. 7:6). The gravity of the sin of turning back from faith once embraced is here presented in a way reminiscent of Heb. 6:4–6. The church struggled long and hard with the possibility of a second repentance for such persons (*The Shepherd of Hermas*, a second-century Christian writing, focuses on this issue). For the writer here, the core of the heretics' unspeakable wrong was **turning back from the holy commandment that was passed on to them** (v. 21). The "passing on" translates a term for handing on a tradition. No doubt the author has in mind the apostolic tradition that conveys the saving knowledge of Jesus Christ.

3:1–16
THE CERTAINTY OF THE LORD'S COMING

The rhetorical rampage in which the writer attacked and exposed the opponents is now completed and the text returns to the issue stated in 1:16: "the power and coming of our Lord Jesus Christ." For the false teachers to scoff at the doctrine of Christ's return, to disparage and deny it, is for the writer an error with catastrophic results for the Christian and for the church. For 2 Peter, the doctrine of the second coming is fundamental for motivating and sustaining the Christian life. About this the writer is passionate, as 2:1–22 makes abundantly clear. He is now ready to return to the subject matter of 1:16–21 and to debate it with the false teachers and those influenced by them.

3:1–2
The Message Stated

3:1 The second letter: Perhaps a reference to 1 Peter, although what the writer says he is try-

ing to do in the two letters does not fit 1 Peter. The two letters are quite different in style, vocabulary, and content. The "second letter" may imply a prior letter unknown to us. On the relation of 2 Peter to Simon Peter himself, see the introduction to 2 Peter. **Reminding you:** A return to the stated purpose in 1:12–15, to bring to remembrance, a central feature of farewell addresses.

3:2 Prophets . . . the Lord and Savior . . . your apostles: Again the appeal is to the unbroken tradition of prophets, Christ, and the apostles. "Your apostles" sounds like the words of a later generation appealing to the apostles, not the words of one of the apostles. It is important to the writer that the prophets agree with each other, that the apostles agree with each other, that the prophets and apostles agree, and that what they present is the commandment of the Lord. Whatever moral and ethical content may be couched in **commandment**, it is clear from what follows that all of it concerns the behavior of those waiting for the return of Christ (vv. 3–15). Therefore the case for the second coming must be made.

3:3–10
The Message Argued

As stated at 1:12–15, a major component of a farewell address is a prophecy of trouble following the leader's death. For the church of 2 Peter, this trouble is the appearance of persons who scoff at the doctrine of Christ's return.

3:3 The last days: In the Old Testament, prophets spoke of those who mocked the delay of the day of judgment (Amos 9:10; Mal. 2:17), and in the New Testament, there are many prophecies of false teachers in the last days (Matt. 7:15; Mark 13:22; Acts 20:29–30; 1 Tim. 4:1–3; 1 John 4:1–3). The viewpoint of the scoffers is not the result of a different interpretation of Scripture, but is born of fleshly lust; that is, their theology follows and supports a lifestyle of greed and lust.

3:4 Where is the promise?: A rhetorical question referring to the promise of Christ's return within the lifetime of the first generation of Christians (Mark 9:1; 13:30 et al.). **Since our ancestors died:** The first generation of believers are now dead, the Lord has not returned, and there is no evidence it is about to happen. The world moves on without change since creation. The scoffers argue that there is no proof of God's beginning anything new or ending anything old.

3:5–9 They deliberately ignore: The false teachers, says the author, close their eyes to three facts:

1. **The word of God** (vv. 5–7). God's word is active and powerful. By the word, God created the heavens and the earth. By that same word, **water** stored up for judgment was released at the flood that destroyed the world. Now the present world awaits destruction by **fire**, according to that same word. The writer may here be referring to Jewish writings of an apocalyptic nature or to certain Old Testament texts (Deut. 32:22; Isa. 66:15–16; Zeph. 1:18). Verses 5–7 recall the flood, the fire, and being shut up **until the day of judgment** in 2:3–9.

2. God's time and human time (v. 8). The scoffers ignore the fact that judgment is God's business and will be done in God's time. What humans experience as a long delay can be viewed another way. Using Ps. 90:4, the writer reminds the readers that in God's sight **a day** may be **like a thousand years** and **a thousand years like one day**, so calculating the fulfillment of the prophetic promises on the basis of the human calendar should be abandoned. For other New Testament perspectives in delaying with the delay of Christ's coming, see excursus, Rev. 1:3, "Interpreting the 'Near End.'"

3. The character of God (v. 9). Throughout the Bible God is portrayed as **patient** and long-suffering. God's behavior toward Nineveh in the book of Jonah is a classic example. Rather than doubting or scoffing, the church should be grateful that what has seemed a delay in the return of Christ and its attendant judgment is in reality an expression of God's patience and grace. With this line of argument the writer concludes his attempt to silence the false teachers and to rehabilitate the teaching about the second coming of Christ.

3:11–15a
The Application of the Message
of the Lord's Return

3:11 All these things: The fundamental elements of creation, both heaven and earth (v. 10). Those who denied the doctrine of the Lord's return openly flaunted a libertine way of life. Doctrine is joined to behavior. By contrast, believers who hold to the doctrine should manifest their faith in **holiness and godliness**. Such quality of life is prompted not only by expectation of judgment but also by the realization that all created things are transient and pass away. The anticipation of new heavens and new earth (Isa. 65:17; Rev. 21:1) has a sanctifying influence (v. 13).

3:12–13 Hastening the coming of the day of God: If the day of God has been delayed to allow for repentance (v. 9), then godly lives (morally alert) should shorten the time. If the readers match God's patience with their own, then they will experience the time and place **where righteousness (justice) is at home** (v. 13).

3:14–15 Therefore, beloved: The writer closes the exhortation with direct address and underscoring what has been said. **While waiting for** the attendant blessings of the day of God, believers are to **strive** (be diligent), unlike the false teachers who wallow in false freedom. They are to be **at peace**, unlike the heretics who agitate and disturb the body of Christ. They are to be **without spot or blemish** (Eph. 1:4; Col. 1:22; 1 Thess. 3:13), unlike the opponents who are "blots and blemishes, reveling in their dissipation" (2:13). They are to welcome God's **patience** as further opportunity for the working of God's grace, unlike the false teachers who interpret the delay of the day of God as evidence that such a day will never come. If these qualities are theirs, then they will welcome being **found** (a very positive New Testament word for the redeemed of God) by the one who will come with the suddenness of a thief (v. 10; Matt. 23:43–44; 1 Thess. 5:12; Rev. 3:3).

3:15b–16
The Message of the Lord's Return
Supported by Paul

The message is concluded, but it is important that the readers understand that Paul is in agreement. Why Paul? Peter has already identified himself with the apostles as a group who with one voice, along with the prophets, pass along the normative tradition from Jesus (1:1, 16–19). In this apostolic circle is **our beloved brother Paul**, who was also inspired (**according to the wisdom given him**) and whose **letters**, now collected and being read in churches to which they were not originally addressed, are regarded as **scripture**. Given the status of those letters of Paul, that Paul agrees with Peter about the coming day of the Lord (1 Cor. 1:7–8; Phil. 1:10; 1 Thess. 3:13; 5:23) is strong support for the writer's position against his opponents. But, in addition, Paul is singled out because apparently his writings have been used by the false teachers in support of their position. Admittedly some of Paul's writings contain **difficult** passages, but the **ignorant and unstable** (the opponents and the novices in the faith whom they recruit) pervert Paul's meaning. In fact, says the writer, they misuse all the Scriptures in the same way. For example, the heretics might support their promise of freedom (2:19) with Paul's arguments for freedom from law in Gal. 5:1 and Rom. 5–8. They would omit, of course, Paul's caution, "only do not use your freedom as an opportunity for self indulgence" (Gal. 5:13). Or they might understand Paul's experiential eschatology (Rom. 6:1–11) to mean that we have already died and have been raised with Christ, arguing against a doctrine of an end to this age and the beginning of a new. The occasional nature of Paul's letters, the range of issues treated, and the styles of his argumentation make such misuses possible. In the first century, the church's Bible was the Old Testament, read from a Christian perspective. The collection and selection of particular Christian writings that came to be regarded as Scripture did not occur until the second century. This reference to Paul's letters having been collected and read as Scripture argues for a date for 2 Peter later than the lifetime of Simon Peter, though the letter could certainly have come from a disciple of Peter.

3:17–18a
CLOSING ADMONITION

3:17 Beloved: A common literary term, much like our "Dear," and not a clear indicator of the relationship between writer and reader (3:1, 8, 14). Being **forewarned** of dangers to come is one of the ingredients of a farewell address (See comments at 1:12; 2:1–3; 3:3–4). The read-

ers are stable and confirmed in the truth of the prophetic and apostolic tradition (1:22), but they can be destabilized by "the ignorant and unstable" false teachers and their followers (2:14; 3:16; 2:15).

3:18 But grow: Being firmly grounded and stable does not mean the readers are not to avail themselves of all resources and relationships that enable growth. **Grace and knowledge:** This salutation returns the message to 1:3 and the repeated accent on knowledge of Jesus Christ, which, as we have seen, is fixed in prophecy and in the inspired apostolic tradition (1:12–21). A key element in this "knowledge" is the teaching concerning the return of Christ. Otherwise, the readers will remain in danger of being influenced by "the lawless."

3:18b
DOXOLOGY

To him: To Christ. This doxology reminds the reader of the Christ portrayed in the entire letter. He is not here presented as the historical Jesus providing an ethical model, nor is he the crucified one, bearing our sins. Rather, he is the ascended, exalted, and glorious Christ, who will, on the day of God (3:12), return to terminate the reign of evil and to bring the dawning of a new day (1:19) in which "righteousness is at home" (3:13).

The First Letter of John

INTRODUCTION

Five of the twenty-seven writings of the New Testament are associated with the name John: the fourth Gospel, the Apocalypse, and the three epistles. However, of these only the Apocalypse bears the name (1:1). That the Fourth Gospel is associated with John is due to a statement by Irenaeus (Bishop of Lyon in France ca. 180 CE) to the effect that the apostle John "published a gospel while residing in Ephesus" (*Against Heresies* 3.1.2). Irenaeus cites as witnesses Polycarp and Papias, said to have been disciples of John. As will be mentioned often in the comments, 1 John was familiar with some version of the Gospel of John or the tradition out of which it came. Therefore, the attribution of this letter to John is quite understandable. Since Polycarp knew 1 John (Pol. *Phil.* 7:1), and since Polycarp wrote about 120 CE, many students of 1 John join the lines of testimony and conclude that 1 John was written by John about 100 CE in Ephesus. Others question this evidence and find the conditions addressed in the letter more appropriate to Syria than Asia Minor. Because of differences as well as similarities not only between the Gospel and 1 John, but among the five writings associated with John, many find it more acceptable to speak of a Johannine circle of Christianity, out of which the writings came without having to argue single authorship (see the introduction to John).

It is impossible to locate the intended readers, if indeed 1 John was written for a single congregation. If it was a document for broader circulation, that fact would account for the lack of personal features. Referring to 1 John as a letter creates the expectation of such personal marks as name, salutation, address, and greetings. Indeed 2 John and 3 John are letters; 1 John seems to be something else, but what? Because the writer is announcing or proclaiming (1:2, 3, 5), perhaps it is more like a homily or sermon. Like Hebrews, which has both epistolary and sermonic traits, 1 John may be called an epistolary sermon. The distinctions are not critical to the reader's understanding.

The author writes to remind the readers of their common tradition (1:1–3; 2:7; 3:11) and to underscore certain themes within that tradition

(as presented in the Fourth Gospel?) that seem to have been both understood and misunderstood. Some have left the ranks (2:19), and false prophets are about (4:1–3). There seem to be disputes about Christology (2:22; 4:2, 15) but the more frequent accents in the letter have to do with practical matters of Christian living such as loving one another and avoiding sin, themes visited over and over again. The author does so without recourse to Scripture (Old Testament) except for one allusion to Cain (3:12).

The writing moves forward in a series of alternating affirmations and exhortations with both being repeated, often with slight variations, so as to give the reader a sense of circularity.

Outline

For Further Reading

Rensberger, David. *1 John, 2 John, 3 John*. Abingdon New Testament Commentary. Nashville: Abingdon, 1997.

Smith, D. Moody. *First, Second, and Third John*: Interpretation: A Bible Commentary for Teaching and Preaching. Louisville, KY: Westminster/John Knox, 1990.

COMMENTARY

1:1–4 Prologue

1:1–2 We declare to you: The writer seems to assume a knowledge of the Prologue of John's Gospel and wishes to evoke that knowledge by using some of the same vocabulary: beginning, have seen, word, life, with the Father (God). This resemblance is especially striking in the Greek text, which begins with **That which was from the beginning** reserving the main verb "we declare (proclaim)" till the close of the sentence. However, while the Gospel Prologue begins before time and creation and arrives at the incarnation in v. 14, "the Word became flesh," here the incarnation itself is "the beginning." The beginning is not their Christian experience (as in Phil. 1:5), but the Christ whom we have **seen**, **heard**, **looked at**, **touched**. He is **the word of life**, mediated to the readers through the word proclaimed, the word that brings the revelation and the reality of life eternal from God. This is the core of the writer's message. The "we" of these declarations refers not merely to the original apostles, but to the whole community of Christian faith (see on John 1:14). About 180 CE Irenaeus, bishop of Lyon in France, could still write, "We would not be able to know, unless we had seen our Master and heard his voice with our own ears." Of course this was no claim to be a literal eyewitness, but this "ecclesial we" was the insistence that membership in the church means belonging a community that has personal, visual, tangible experience of the presence of Christ.

1:3–4 We are writing these things: The author writes with a twofold purpose: **so that you also may have fellowship with us**, and **so that our joy may be complete** (clearer in the NIV). The fellowship mentioned here (and at vv. 6–7) is probably what Paul meant by partnership in the gospel (Phil. 1:5), but the writer asserts rather than assumes that this fellowship is initiated and sustained by God's gift of the Son, Jesus Christ. No doubt this fellowship provides the note of joy on which the first series of exhortations will be made.

1:5–2:17
EXHORTATIONS

1:5–10
THE MORAL MEANING OF FELLOWSHIP

1:5 We have heard . . . and declare to you (NIV): Since the writer is saying in a concise way what is repeatedly stated in John's Gospel (John 1:4–5; 3:19–21; 8:12), some form of that Gospel or its tradition is probably intended. **From him:** This very likely refers to Jesus as the revealer of God.

1:6 If we say: Verses 6–10 are framed on a series of five "if" clauses on the pattern of negative, positive, negative, positive, with the fifth clause breaking the rhythm, as if to say some things are true without condition, with no "if"

(see the similar pattern at 2 Tim. 2:11–13). All these clauses spell out the moral seriousness of fellowship with God and with one another. **We have fellowship with him:** The theme of fellowship, introduced in the prologue (v. 3), is further developed. Fellowship that is in God must be appropriate to God's own nature, which is light (v. 5). Evil loves darkness, thinking thereby to be hid from God (Ps. 139:11–12; John 3:19–21).

1:6 While walking in darkness: The first "if" clause warns against the talk without the walk (Gal. 5:25), an inner contradiction which constitutes a lie.

1:7 The blood of Jesus his Son: The second "if" clause, by contrast, portrays two positive effects of living in God's light: genuine **fellowship** with other believers and the removal of our **sin** by the sacrifice of Christ. Since according to the ritual language of Judaism the life is in the blood, biblical writers would speak meaningfully of the blood without fear of charges of superstition or cannibalism.

1:8–10 Deceive ourselves: The third conditional clause reminds the readers that any claim of sinlessness is no more than self-deception. In contrast, v. 10 returns to the denial of sin in v. 8, stating that denial more forcefully ("**have not committed a sin**"), and then draws the conclusion that such a denial is an attack on the character of God who is light. But God still offers reconciliation when one confesses to a breach in the relation to God. A denial of sin is not only a lie, but by its rebuff of God's offer, also treats God as **a liar**, and effectively negates any positive working of God's word in us.

2:1–6
THE CHRISTIAN WALK AND JESUS

2:1–6 That you may not sin: Lest statements made in 1:5–9 be taken as opening the door of mercy so widely as to weaken ethical demands (see on Rom. 6:1), the writer restores the demand for Christian conduct in four ways. First, he insists that the purpose of writing was that they not sin (v. 1). Second, by referring to Jesus Christ as **the Righteous One** (NIV), the author reminds the readers of the quality of life of the one they follow (v. 1). Third, knowledge of and love of Christ are joined to obedience (vv. 3–5; see John 7:17; 14:15). And finally, Jesus' followers are to **walk just as he walked** (v. 6). This appeal to the life of Jesus as an ethical model is not detailed, but knowledge of that life has been clearly stated as a presupposition (1:1–2). That the life of a disciple is a continuing demand is captured both in the word "walk" and in the expression **abide in him** (v. 6). Abiding in Christ is familiar from John's Gospel (40x; esp. chap. 15) and will occur 24x in 1 John. The expression is similar to Paul's "in Christ Jesus" (e.g., Phil. 2:5 and often; see commentary at 2 Cor. 5:17).

But if anyone does sin: This is not to say that grace toward the sinner is forgotten in the exhortation to Christian conduct. One expects it in the opening term of endearment, "**My little children**" (v. 1; also 2:12, 28; 3:7, 18; 4:4; 5:21; see on John 13:33; 21:5), and the gracious word is immediate: "But if anyone does sin" (v. 1). In such case, Christ functions in two ways: he is our **advocate** (*paraclete*, a Johannine term for Christ and the Holy Spirit; see on John 14:15–17), the one who intercedes for us and speaks in our defense; and he is **the atoning sacrifice for our sins** (v. 2). Here the idea in 1:7 is repeated with a new accent: Christ is the reconciling meeting place between humans and God, recalling the mercy seat in the temple Holy of Holies, where the sacrificial blood was sprinkled on the Day of Atonement (Rom. 3:25; Heb. 9:14–15). It bears repeating, however, that this subunit begins and ends with reminders of ethical demands.

2:7–11
Something Old, Something New

The writer's use of metaphor (light, darkness) to convey the message continues in this subunit, as does the frequency of contrasts (old/new, light/darkness, love/hate; on Johannine dualism, see commentary at John 8:23). The concern continues to be conduct and relationships.

2:7–8 No new commandment: The not new, but **old**, yet **new** command (vv. 7–8) is to love one another, recalling the one governing command in the Gospel of John (13:31–35; 15:10, 12, 17). It is old in that it goes back to Jesus, and yet it is new in that it is the signal characteristic of the new age. The same love that was evident in Jesus and now fills the church (v. 8) moves the writer to sense an end to **darkness** and the dawning of **light** (v. 8).

2:9–10 Whoever says: But religious claim and personal behavior must agree (vv. 9–11). While the author is aware of God's love for the whole world (2:2; see John on 3:16; 13:35), the focus here is on love within the Christian fellowship, among brothers and sisters. Regardless of what one may claim, hating a fellow Christian

is walking in the dark and being a stumbling block to relationships in the church (v. 10). By contrast, the one who loves the brother and sister lives (abides, a favorite Johannine word for continuing, staying, remaining) in the light and can see the way clearly.

2:11 Whoever hates: The one who hates is lost, confused, and blind.

2:12–14
The Church Family Addressed

2:12 I am writing to you: The writer has addressed the readers as little children (2:1) and beloved (2:7) and has spoken of them as brothers and sisters (2:10–11), giving the image of the church as family (see John 1:11–13; 3:3–5). Now he breaks down the constituency in three groups: children, fathers (parents), and young people. Elsewhere in the New Testament, household lists of duties are used (Col. 3:18–4:1; Eph. 5:21–6:9; and elsewhere), but here no duties are assigned. On the contrary, these three groups are addressed **because** (or **that**; the Greek conjunction can be translated either way) they have behaved in a commendable way. Even though both NRSV and NIV use the present tense "I am writing" or "I write" throughout vv. 12–14, the Greek verb shifts from present to aorist at v. 14, marked by the shift from "am writing" to "write" in the NRSV, not marked at all in the NIV. The aorists of v. 14 could also be translated as an English past tense, "I wrote." The shift could thus be a reminder of what has already been said in the letter, lest negative statements in preceding comments tend to discourage.

Verses 12–14 consist of two parallel units, each addressing children, fathers, young people. Since **children** elsewhere refers not to youngsters within the family, but to all members of the Christian family as "children of God," **fathers** and **young people** may designate particular semiofficial ecclesial groups corresponding to the "elders" and "young people" of 1 Pet. 5:1–5 (see also Acts 5:6, and commentary at 2 John 1). The vocabulary and ideas are drawn from chaps. 1–2, with the exception of what is said to the young people. They are **strong** (v. 14), not with the vigor of youth but because **the word of God abides** in them. This source of strength enables them **to overcome the evil one** (vv. 13–14). In sum, what the writer has exhorted and urged thus far is, in these verses, an affirmation of approved behavior.

2:15–17
A WARNING ABOUT THE WORLD

This unit of exhortations (1:5–2:17) concludes with a clear command (v. 15), reasoning in support of the command (v. 16), and a statement of the folly of doing otherwise (v. 17).

2:15–16 Do not love the world: The writer does not equivocate: love of the world and love of God are mutually exclusive. To understand this, one has to have in mind the Johannine view of "world"; otherwise one might have a directive against responsibility to family, community, or environment. Through the Word God created the world (John 1:10), but the world, loving darkness rather than light, did not know God (John 1:10, 17, 25). Yet God loves the world, and for its salvation sent his Son into the world (John 3:16–17) just as the church has been sent into the world (John 17:18). But being *in* the world is not being *of* the world (John 17:14); that is, the world as created does not replace the Creator as the source of identity, meaning, and purpose. The world as God's creation is, therefore, not evil. Evil (idolatry) arises in the inordinate **desire** (v. 16; lust, but not confined to sex) for what one can acquire and possess, things visible not spiritual. From such acquisitions comes the proud illusion that life has been attained. Nothing could be farther from the truth. In fact, everything created is transitory, as is the appetite for it. It is entirely foolish, therefore, to make such an investment of one's life. Only the Creator and those who put the Creator's will foremost will continue to live after all else has passed away.

2:18–27
AFFIRMATIONS

No unit in 1 John is totally exhortation or totally affirmation, but noticing the major accent of a passage aids in moving through material often circular and repetitious.

2:18–19
CONCERNING THE ANTICHRISTS

2:18 We know: While "we know" in the Gospel of John is often a negative signal of human presumption and lack of understanding (see on John 3:1–3; 9:16; and the discussion at 7:12), in 1 John the phrase is always a positive sign of Christian assurance, equivalent to "we believe" (2:3, 18; 3:2, 14, 16, 24; 4:6, 13, 16; 5:2, 15, 18, 19, 20). For both the Gospel and the Epistle, faith is not betting on the probabilities when

one cannot have objective "factual" knowledge, but is the assurance that comes from personal trust in God through Jesus Christ. In this sense, believing is not to be contrasted with knowledge, but is its own kind of knowledge.

It is the last hour: The writer's declaration is not a jarring surprise; it is duplicated elsewhere in the New Testament (Mark 9:1; Phil. 4:4; 1 Thess. 4:15–17; Rev. 1:3; and others). What is striking here is that the antichrist (counterchrist) has already come, and there are many antichrists (v. 18). "Antichrist" is a term peculiar to 1 John in the New Testament, although some identify the figure with "man of sin" and "the lawless one" of 2 Thess. 2:3–9. The appearance of the antichrist is a sign of the end, since it was a common tenet of apocalyptic thought that evil would intensify just before the end (Mark 13:6, 21–22). The readers have heard that such a figure would appear, but the writer announces that not one but many are already here. Who are they?

2:19 They went out from us: Whether "they" identifies the antichrists or describes the result of the antichrists' influence is not clear. What is clear is that the division in the community and the departure of some members is the evidence of the antichrist at work. This congregational crisis is the result; the theological reason will be stated in the next verses.

2:20–23
THE TRUTH AND THE LIE

2:20 You have been anointed (NRSV)/**You have an anointing** (NIV): "Anointing" represents the Greek word *chrisma.* Either translation reflects the relationship to the word for Christ, *the* anointed one. The writer is confident in the belief that the readers know the truth, unlike those who have departed the community and obviously have embraced a lie (vv. 20–21). How is it the readers know the truth? Because they have been anointed **by the Holy One** (God? Christ?). The nature of the anointing and the time of its reception are not specified. Very likely it is a reference to the giving of the Holy Spirit to the followers of Jesus. According to John's Gospel, the Spirit is the Spirit of truth that will teach the truth and remind the disciples of the truth (John 14:17, 26; 15:26; 16:7, 14–15; 20:12).

2:21–22 The truth: That Jesus is the Christ (i.e., that the Christ is *Jesus*; see on Mark 8:29; Acts 17:3; 18:5, 23; 1 Cor. 12:3). **Lie:** The denial that **Jesus is the Christ**, which is, in effect, also a denial of the Father who sent him (4:15; 5:1; see John 5:23;

12:44–45). But what specifically is being denied is not clear at this point. At 4:2 and 2 John 7, that which is being denied is the incarnation, that the heavenly Christ actually came in the flesh. At 2:22; 4:2; and 2 John 7, the heretical view is attributed to the antichrist, and it is reasonable to conclude that the denial is the same in all three references. In any case, response to the Son is a response to the Father (4:15; John 14:6–9; 15:23).

2:24–25
Therefore Remain in the Truth

2:24 What you heard from the beginning: The writer urges no more than a steadfast continuation in the tradition they received. The verb is again the familiar Johannine "remain" (NIV) or "abide" (NRSV), the word often used to characterize the relation among Father, Son, and believer (1:3; 2:5–6; John 6:56–58; 15:1–10; 17:21–23). In this abiding is life eternal (1:3; 3:15; 5:11, 13, 20; John 3:36; 17:3).

2:26–27
This Anointing Is Adequate
to Sustain Them

2:27 The anointing that you received: The best understanding of the anointing that abides in the readers is the giving of the Spirit of truth to the disciples by Jesus (see on v. 20).

2:28–3:24
EXHORTATIONS

Again, exhortations are so mingled with affirmations that divisions and headings are rather arbitrary, but may aid in laying hold of material that appears to be circular and repetitious.

2:28–3:3
Being Confident When Christ Appears

2:28 When he is revealed: When the writer spoke of this being "the last hour" (2:18), there followed warnings about the appearance of the antichrist and urgings to hold fast to the tradition in which they had been instructed. Now the writer turns to the future and the coming, not of the antichrist, but of Christ himself. Those who abide in Christ now will welcome Christ's coming with **confidence** (boldness) and without shame.

2:29 Everyone who does right has been born of him: Throughout the New Testament, "born again" language refers not to an elite spiritual group, but to all Christians (see on John 1:11–13; 3:3–5). In the controversy and split within the Johannine church (see 2:18–22), the author

here regards all who are true Christians (i.e., those who have remained with the traditional faith and have not followed the new heretical teachers) as born of God. Here the formula we might have anticipated ("all who are born of God do what is right") is reversed, and all who do right are considered children of God (see also 4:7, "everyone who loves is born of God"). While these statements that identify all who practice love and justice as born of God may originally have had only the narrower intention of identifying authentic Christians within the church controversy of the author's time, in view of the universal sweep of the Johannine logos theology, the ultimate meaning may be that all who do what is right in God's eyes are accepted by God as his children (see Matt. 25:31–46). This abiding in him carries an obligation to justice ("what is right," 2:29 [NIV]) and to purity of life (3:3), which may be understood as moral uprightness (see 1 Pet. 1:22; 3:2). The writer further describes abiding in Christ in terms of family: "born of him" (2:29; John 1:13; 3:3–8; 1 John 3:9; 4:7; 5:1, 4, 18) and **children of God** (3:1–2). As God's children, we bear resemblance to the Father in conduct and relationships (4:17; Matt. 5:43–48), but at the appearance of Christ that resemblance will become similarity (like him, 3:2). How that transformation will occur is not yet clear, of course (3:2), but anticipation of it has a purifying effect even now (3:3). Confirmation of the truth of these affirmations lies in the fact that the world does not know Christians, just as it did not know Christ (3:1; John 15:18–21; 17:14).

3:4–10
Of God or of the Devil

The writer returns to the sharp contrasts which characterized chaps. 1–2: light/darkness, love/hate, truth/lie, God/world (see John 8:23).

3:8 A child of the devil: Here the contrast is vivid and strong: children of God or children of the devil, with attendant behaviors (see on John 8:44). The flavor of the wording is eschatological, introduced at 2:18 and explicit again at 2:28; 3:2. The end time is characterized by accelerated activity by the devil to frustrate the just reign of God, activity described as lawlessness (v. 4) and deception (leading astray; v. 7). The lines are clearly drawn (3:4, 7–10). The repetition of earlier comments about sinning and not sinning give the impression of urgently addressing a real problem.

3:9 Those who have been born of God do not sin: See on John 1:11–13; 3:3–5; 1 John 2:29. What is not clear is how members of the church could possibly associate the Christian life with sin and lawlessness, the very conditions the Son of God came to destroy (3:8). Apparently the deceivers (3:7) have succeeded in creating a climate of moral confusion. What is clear, however, are the practical criteria by which children of God and the children of the devil are distinguished (revealed, 3:10): doing what is just (right) and loving the brothers and sisters (3:10).

3:11–18
WE SHOULD LOVE ONE ANOTHER

See on John 13:34–35. These verses are an elaboration of v. 10, an elaboration that picks up on earlier themes: the message from the beginning (1:1, 5); enmity between the church and the world (2:15–17; 3:1); demand for just behavior (2:29; 3:7); love of brothers and sisters (2:10); and Christ as the example of justice and love (2:1, 6).

3:12 We must not be like Cain: Cain, who killed his brother Abel (Gen. 4:1–16), provides an antecedent for the dynamics in the text and apparently in the church: brother vs. brother, love vs. hatred, evil vs. righteousness (vv. 11–15). Cain, belonging to **the evil one** (not in Gen. 4), hated his brother because Abel was righteous. Likewise, **the world hates** the believers (John 7:7; 15:18). But within the church there is hatred (v. 15) and hatred of a brother by a brother is for the writer the equivalent of murder (v. 15; see Matt. 5:21–22). And the one who hates is himself dead, but the one who loves has **passed from death to life** (v. 14; 1:2; 2:25; John 5:24). Eternal life is not only future but present as well.

3:16 We know love by this: This life-giving love has its model in Jesus, who **laid down his life for us** (v. 16; 1:7; 2:6; John 10:11–18; 15:12–13). Thus, while hatred takes the life of another, love gives its life for another.

3:17 Anyone who has the world's goods: If laying down one's life for a brother or sister in the literal sense of martyrdom is a rare event, then more available, repeatable, and practical expressions of love lie in the many opportunities to share one's goods with those in need (v. 17). Such actions exceed in merit any talk of sacrificing life (v. 17), but all expressions of love must be recognized for what they are: the fruit of the love of God within us (v. 17).

3:19–24
CONFIDENCE BEFORE GOD

3:19 We will know: See 2:18 note. In 3:18 the author urged love that was "in truth"; that is,

in a life in which words and deeds are joined. Now in vv. 19–24 the reader is given the assurance that they can know they are of God and of the truth. In case one has a self-condemning heart (v. 20)—if one lives with inadequate self-understanding or with a lingering sense of guilt—then God, who knows us better than we know ourselves, overrules our opinion and sets our hearts at ease (v. 19). In case **our hearts do not condemn us** (v. 21), then we stand boldly **before God** confident that God will answer our prayers (vv. 21–22; 5:14). Such confidence waits on the condition of obeying and pleasing God (v. 22; John 8:28–29).

3:23 And this is his commandment: Again this requirement boils down to faith in Jesus Christ as God's Son and love toward one another. This obedience confirms, in turn, that we are of the truth and **abide in him** (v. 24; 2:6; 4:13).

3:24 We know . . . by the Spirit: This mutual "abiding," the believer in Christ and Christ in the believer, has further if not final confirmation by the gift of the Holy Spirit. Although the Spirit is clearly implied as the "anointing" in 2:26–27, this is the first explicit reference to the gift of the Spirit, echoing the five Holy Spirit (Paraclete) promises of Jesus in John 14–16.

4:1–6
AFFIRMATIONS

4:1 Do not believe every spirit: The introduction of the Spirit in 3:24 raises the question needing an answer: How does one know the Holy Spirit from other spirits? This discussion does not take the writer away from his train of thought, but is rather integral to themes already introduced: false prophets and the antichrist, life in God rather than from the world, and truth and falsehood. **Test the spirits:** Again the readers are reminded to be discerning and to test the spirits, since many false prophets (antichrists, 2:18) have left the fellowship (v. 1; see on 2:18–25 and Rev. 2:20).

4:2 Confesses that Jesus Christ has come in the flesh: At 2:25 the problem with these false prophets and their followers was the denial that Jesus was the Christ. Such a statement could be variously interpreted, but here at 4:2–3 the christological problem is more specifically stated: those who acknowledge Jesus Christ has come in the flesh are of God; those who deny it are of the antichrist (also 2 John 7). That the Word became flesh and dwelt among us (John 1:14) is a nonnegotiable teaching. It is not clear from this brief statement whether the opponents had problems with Jesus' humanity in connection with his earthly ministry or with the cross or with the resurrection. Apparently a Christ totally divine, totally spiritual in nature was more acceptable to them.

4:4 Little children: See on 2:1; John 13:33; 21:5. The author responds to the community's need for instruction on life in the Spirit in a world of error. He first says "Good riddance" over those who have left the fellowship. The rift has been clarifying. Whatever the arguments of the opponents, they failed, because the Spirit in the believers is stronger that the spirits in those who are in error about Jesus Christ.

4:5–6 They are from the world . . . we are from God: In Johannine theology, one's origin, "where one is coming from," determines behavior (John 3:6; 1 John 3:8–9). However much it may seem a rationalization, the writer's position is clear: whoever has God's Spirit listens to those with God's Spirit; whoever is of the world and all its falsehoods listens to those who are of the world and who speak falsehoods (see on John 7:17). The two audiences have formed and it is now clear to the writer who has the Spirit of God.

4:7–5:5
EXHORTATIONS

In this unit the christological and theological themes of the prior unit are spelled out in terms of Christian conduct.

4:7 Love is from God: Again, the mode of address is "Beloved," and here most appropriately so, since the subject is love from God and for each other, making the readers doubly beloved. God's love is prior to ours and, in fact, makes ours possible. The writer expresses even more forcefully that our capacity for love is from God by saying that the one who loves not only **knows God** but is **born of God** (John 1:13).

4:8 Whoever does not love: In his characteristic manner of using contrasts to accent a truth, the writer states that the one who does not love **does not know God. God is love.** "Love" is here a noun, not an adjective, "loving." Though it is true to say that God is "loving," it is not enough for the author. Love is not just a characteristic of God, but his very being. It is enough to say that God is love, and not let God's essential being be lost in a string of modifiers. God's love has been chiefly expressed in the giving of **his only Son** (v. 9). All who love are children of God, begotten of God (v. 7; John 1:13) but Jesus Christ is the "only begotten" in

the sense of unique or one of a kind (v. 9; John 1:14, 18; 3:16).

4:10 This is love: The message of vv. 7–9 is repeated: God's love precedes ours and makes ours possible, and the love of God is revealed in the sending of his Son to remove our sins and reconcile us to God (see comments at 2:2). In view of God's extraordinary love, our love for one another should follow (v. 11). Of course, **no one has ever seen God** (v. 12; John 1:18; 3:13; 6:46; on "seeing God" in Johannine theology, see on John 14:7). Nonetheless, God is evident among us through our love for one another. Through such love God abides among us and **his love is perfected**, made complete, matured among us. This description of love is not subjective, as though it were found in the individual heart, but among us, in the community of believers.

4:13 We abide in him: On **we know**, see on 2:18. In the subunit 4:13–21, the writer uses two key terms found in v. 12 to gather up and to extend what has been said since v. 7. The two terms are the oft-used and now familiar "abide" or "remain" (sometimes "live" in NIV; prominent in the Gospel of John as well) and "perfected love." Verse 13 restates 3:24b: the gift of God's Spirit assures the church of its continuing relation to God (John 14:26; 16:13–14; Rom. 8:9–17).

4:14 We have seen: See on 1:1–2. Verses 14–16a gather up earlier themes in new constellations. Although no one has ever seen God (v. 12), in the Son we have seen and heard the Word of God (1:1–2; John 14:7–9). To confess faith in Jesus as God's Son is to **abide in God** and God's love (vv. 15–16).

4:16 God is love: See on 4:8. To abide in this love is a continuing process resulting in **perfected** (mature) love (v. 17). Mature love gives one **confidence** (NIV) or **boldness** (NRSV) **on the day of judgment** (v. 17), but not only in the judgment; in this world we are, as Christ is, clear and constant witnesses to God's love (v. 17b). And mature love does not live in fear of punishment but in the assurance of God's abiding love, which always precedes and motivates our own (vv. 18–19). As we have come to expect from the writer, love of God and love of brother and sister are inseparable: to claim one without demonstrating the other is to live in duplicity (vv. 20–21).

5:1 Everyone who believes: To believe in **Jesus is the Christ** is to be **born of God** (John 1:12–13; 3:3–5; see 1 John 2:29; 4:7) and to be born of God is to have God as parent and other believers as brothers and sisters. This means one loves both the parent and the children, and love is expressed in obedience to God's commands (vv. 2–3; John 14:15). This obedience is not oppressive nor **burdensome** (Matt. 11:30); on the contrary, it is triumphant, overcoming a confused and deluded world (vv. 3–4; 2:13–14; 4:4). Love's obedience to God thus confirms the truth of 2:8. Strikingly, the author returns in vv. 4–5 to the affirmations of vv. 1–2. The one who believes is born of God; whoever is born of God loves; whoever loves obeys; whoever obeys overcomes the world; whoever overcomes the world believes (see John 16:33). Thus faith, love, and obedience are tightly joined.

5:6–12
AFFIRMATIONS

5:6 The one that testifies: The writer has used the verb "to witness" or "to testify" at 1:2 and 4:14, but in this brief section it occurs 4x (vv. 6, 7, 9, 10). The noun "testimony" is not used elsewhere in the letter, but here it occurs 6x (vv. 9–11). Witnessing is therefore central to this passage, just as it is in the Gospel of John. In the Gospel, witness is given to Jesus by the Baptist (1:7–8, 15, 19, 32–34), by God (5:31–40), by Jesus himself (8:13–18), by the Spirit (15:26–27), and by the disciple Jesus loved (19:35; 21:24). If the writer is assuming the reader's knowledge of the Gospel or the tradition on which it is based, v. 6 may be clearer than otherwise. Although **water and blood** may refer to baptism (Jesus' baptism is implied but not narrated in John's Gospel) and Eucharist (John 6:53–56), it is more likely that this is a reference to the cross. According to John 19:34, blood and water came from Jesus' side following his death. The author has already stressed the importance of Jesus' atoning death (1:7; 2:2). Likewise, that the Spirit bears witness to Jesus has also been repeatedly stated (3:24; 4:6, 13; John 15:26). The Spirit has already testified that Jesus Christ came in the flesh (4:2). Here the Spirit joins witness with the water and blood that a central feature of Christ's coming in the flesh is his death on the cross (vv. 6–7). This threefold witness is not human in its source but divine. (A few very late MSS insert the Trinitarian formula here as found in the King James Version [v. 7], but it was certainly not in the original text; see notes in the NRSV and NIV, and "Introduction: The New Testament as the Church's Book," 4.d.)

5:9 If we receive human testimony: If, then, a human under oath is believed, how much more should we believe God who is never guilty of perjury? Those who believe embrace this testimony; those who do not, in effect, regard God as a liar (v. 10). Literally, those who believe have this testimony "in him," not in his or their hearts (NIV, NRSV). The translations' addition of "heart" may make the statement more subjective than the writer intended. The accent is on God's action. God not only gives testimony but God also gives the Son who is the means of eternal life. Hence, to have **the Son** is to have (present tense) **life**; otherwise one does not have life but remains in death (vv. 11–12; John 3:36).

5:13–21
EPILOGUE

5:13 I write . . . that you may know: The writer concludes his message by returning to the familiar refrain (see 1:4; 2:1, 3, 7–8, 12–14, 21, 26; 3:2, 5, 14, 16, 19, 24; 4:2, 6, 13, 16). The epilogue has two foci: praying (vv. 13–17) and knowing (vv. 18–21).

5:14 If we ask anything according to his will: It cannot be coincidental that just as 1 John 1:1–4 is similar to the Prologue to the Gospel, so 1 John 5:13 is like John 20:31: what is written is joined to faith that issues in life eternal. Verses 14–15 elaborate on 3:21–22: confidence in prayer. This confidence is born of asking according to God's will (John 4:34; 5:30), certain that God hears such prayers, and that if God hears, God answers. In fact, the prayer is already answered.

5:16 Your brother or sister: Verses 16–17 deal with intercessory prayer: when is it appropriate, and when is it not appropriate? In a rather enigmatic way, the writer distinguishes between sin that leads to death and sin that does not lead to death (NIV translates the Greek better than the NRSV). Intercession for a member of the community who sins but not leading to death is effective, and life is given to that person. The writer is not urging prayer for anyone who commits a sin leading to death. But there is no certainty as to what sin the writer has in mind. Within the context of the letter, there are two candidates. According to 2:18–25, to deny Jesus is apostasy from the fellowship and, in effect, returns one to the world of death. Or the writer may have in mind the hatred of a brother or sister, which is to live in a state of death (3:14–15). In the writer's mind, both are sins leading to death.

5:18 We know: See on 2:18. Not surprisingly, the author returns in closing to the language of family and affection: born of God, children of God, little children. And not surprisingly, the subject of sin returns. The writer has recognized that sin exists in the fellowship of believers; to deny that is to lie. But such sin is dealt with through confession and intercession. But according to 5:18, **those who are born of God do not sin**. Perhaps the NIV has properly located the difference in translating the Greek present tense as **does not continue to sin**. That is, sin is not a continuing way of life. The moral seriousness of the writer is evident, but so also is the encouragement offered the reader. The one born of God is guarded from the malicious intent of the **evil one** (v. 18). The guard is **the one who was born of God**. Very likely this is a reference to Christ (John 1:14, 18; 3:16, 18). Three times the readers are assured **we know** (vv. 18–20), and that certainty is dramatically reinforced by stating by contrast the condition of the unbelieving world: the evil one seeks to harm; the evil one controls; the world lives in idolatry (v. 21). The certainty of believers is not blind: **understanding** of God has come

through the revelation in God's Son (v. 20; John 1:17). In him are truth and **life** (v. 20; John 14:6). **He is the true God:** The reference is to Jesus Christ (see on John 1:1–2; 20:28. The one true God is the one made known in Jesus Christ (John 14:7–9; 17:3).

5:21 Keep yourselves from idols: Verse 21 is abrupt and seems to introduce a new topic, idolatry; but putting anything or anyone in the place of the one God made known in Jesus Christ is idolatry (see Col. 3:5). One can assume idolatry was a very present option for all Christians in the ancient world, those addressed here being no exception. But the writer has prepared the way for such a warning in vv. 18–20. Having returned to a favorite format, a series of contrasts, the final positive assertion about the "true God" (v. 20) invited an expression of its opposite: false gods, or idols. The lure of idols, especially when accorded cultural, economic, and political support, was strong enough to elicit from the writer a final warning: be on guard.

The Second Letter of John

INTRODUCTION

The three letters to which church tradition has attached the name John are arranged in the canon by size: the largest is thus 1 John, next in size (245 words in the Greek text) is 2 John, barely edging out 3 John (219 words). Unlike 1 John, both 2 John and 3 John are, in both form and content, genuine letters. Each would fill one page of papyrus of standard size.

The author identifies himself as "the elder" (see v. 1 commentary). Kinship between this letter and the other two in both vocabulary and themes suggests common authorship. In fact, similarities to the Gospel of John (truth, love, abiding in truth and love, Jesus Christ in the flesh) convince many that the Gospel and the three epistles, if not from the same pen, come from a common tradition. The writer has a good relationship with the readers, hoping to visit them soon (v. 12).

The readers are addressed as "the elect lady and her children" (v. 1). This way of referring to a congregation is expressed again in v. 13, "the children of your elect sister send you their greetings." Very likely the image derived from the metaphor of the church as the bride of Christ (2 Cor. 11:2; Rev. 12:17; 19:7; 21:2, 9). It has been surmised that the readers may have been in Asia Minor, since the earliest reference to 2 John is from Polycarp, bishop of Smyrna, in his letter to the Philippians (if indeed Pol. *Phil.* 7:1 refers to 2 John 7 rather than 1 John 4:2). The date would probably be the last decade of the first Christian century.

The concern of the writer is that the readers continue in obedience to Christ's command to love one another (vv. 5–6) and that they abide in the truth that Jesus Christ has come in the flesh (v. 9). The concern is an urgent one because false teachers are moving among the churches, deceiving the believers with doctrine to the contrary (vv. 7–8). To such persons the hospitality of the church is not to be extended (v. 10); to associate with false teachers is to be accessory to heresy (v. 11).

Outline

For Further Reading

Rensberger, David. *1 John, 2 John, 3 John.* Abingdon New Testament Commentary. Nashville: Abingdon, 1997.

Smith, D. Moody. *First, Second, and Third John*: Interpretation: A Bible Commentary for Teaching and Preaching. Louisville, KY: Westminster/John Knox, 1990.

COMMENTARY

1–3
SALUTATION

1 The Elder: The author identifies himself in warmly personal terms, but "elder" does not here mean simply "older person." In the New Testament, "elder" refers primarily to a position of church leadership (see Acts 5:6; 6:4; 14:23; 15:2, 20:7–34; 2 Thess. 3:6–13; 1 Pet. 5:1–5). The author has authority beyond his own congregation and writes to another sister congregation—but his authority is also disputed. The letter reflects a time of transition in church polity, on the way to a more structured institution. **The elect lady and her children:** The sister congregation, probably in the same area, another congregation in the Johannine tradition near Ephesus. Church members are not individualistic Christians, but "children" of "mother church." **All who know the truth:** The author writes to a particular congregation, but also has his eyes on the church as a whole. On truth as a theme in the Johannine churches, see on John 14:6; 8:32; 18:38. The word occurs 27x in the three letters of John, 5x in this brief letter. Here, "knowing the truth" is not an abstract, general reference, but reflects the struggle against false teachers who deny the incarnation of God in Jesus Christ, who is the truth (John 14:6). Such teachers are threatening to mislead the churches.

3 Grace, mercy, and peace: An adaptation of the letter greeting formula that had been developed by Paul (see on 1 Thess. 1:1), who had made the church letter form a standard form of Christian communication and instruction by the time of the elder. **Truth and love:** The integrity and unity of the church must be based on both (see Eph. 4:15, written from about the same time and place). Truth without love can lead to arrogant (though "orthodox") harshness; love without truth can lead to shallow (though "tolerant") subjectivity. The author takes the more difficult path of holding on to both.

4–11
AFFIRMATIONS AND WARNINGS

4 I was overjoyed to find some of your children walking in the truth: Verse 4 expresses the writer's cautious joy. The source of the joy is in learning of those members who keep God's command to walk in the truth (comments on vv. 1–2). "Walking in the truth" (3 John 3–4) is a way of saying what is more frequently expressed by "abiding in the truth." The caution is heard in the qualifier "some of your children," implying "but not all." A warning can be anticipated. Before classifying what it means to obey God's command by walking in truth, the writer reminds the reader that what is being said is the received tradition and is not new (v. 5; 1 John 2:7). The command is to **love one another** (vv. 5–6; John 13:34–35; 1 John 3:11, 23).

7 Many deceivers: Verses 7–8 reveal the central problem for the readers: the intrusion of those who deceive (lead astray) by denying Jesus Christ has come in the flesh. The language is that of 1 John 1:8; 2:26; 3:7; 4:6 (see John 1:1, 14), even to identifying the deceivers as the antichrist (2:18; 2:28; 4:3). In the face of this approaching if not present danger, the writer calls on the readers to be alert, to be **on guard** (v. 8). Although they have been well taught and abide in truth and love, the deception can insinuate itself and rob them of their progress and their future reward. The centerpiece of vv.

9–11 is **the teaching of Christ,** mentioned here three times and most likely meaning the teaching *about* Christ; that is, his true humanity, his coming in the flesh (v. 7). In contrast to those who "abide" in this teaching (v. 9) are the deceivers who **run ahead** (NIV) or **go beyond** the teaching (NRSV). The writer may be using a characterization that the false teachers used of themselves: progressives, more mature, cutting edge (see 2 Tim. 3:9). So crucial is the issue that to deny the incarnation is to be without both Father and Son. Therefore, neither greeting nor hospitality was to be accorded those who did not confess that Jesus Christ has come in the flesh (v. 10). To do so would be to become accessory to their wickedness and, by implication, share in their judgment (v. 11). Hospitality was not merely a matter of personal friendliness. Early missionaries and teachers were dependent on the hospitality of local congregations and Christian families in order to spread their message (see Matt. 10:1–42; Mark 6:6–13; Luke 9:6–9; 10:1–20; Phlm. 22; 2 John 5–8).

12–13
PERSONAL COMMENTS AND SHARED GREETINGS

12 I hope to come to you soon: To close a letter expressing preference for a face-to-face (literally mouth-to-mouth) visit over words on paper (papyrus) was rather common, but being customary did not mean it was insincere. In fact, such a visit would make complete **our joy.** The "our" could refer to writer and readers or to those believers who join in sending greetings (v. 13). **Children of your elect sister:** A family image returning the reader to v. 1. In view of the exhortation to withhold greetings from false teachers, the closing greeting is especially positive and important for the church.

The Third Letter of John

INTRODUCTION

This is the briefest of the three Johannine letters and is therefore placed last among them. In fact, 3 John is the briefest document in the New Testament. Like 2 John, it is a letter, but more private in nature, being addressed to an individual rather than directly to a congregation. The congregation, however, is included in the greetings (v. 15), and the message is not a personal note but a matter of church concern. In form and content, 3 John is similar to a letter of reference or recommendation. As in 2 John, the writer is "the elder," and there is no reason to doubt that 2 John and 3 John are from the same pen. Whether 3 John 9 is a reference to 2 John is a matter of dispute. As to time and place of writing, we again can only speculate (see the introduction to 2 John).

The addressee is one Gaius, apparently a person close to the writer (vv. 2, 5, 11), perhaps even a convert or pupil of the writer, if being one of the writer's "children" (v. 4) can be so interpreted. The letter concerns leadership and authority in the church. Gaius and others who welcome itinerant preachers are commended, but one Diotrephes, having promoted himself into leadership, shuts the door of such hospitality. A prior letter to the church by the elder has been ineffective. The elder, with support of Gaius and a certain Demetrius, who is highly commended, hope to counter the influence of Diotrephes on an upcoming visit.

Outline

1   Salutation
2–4   Reason for Joy
5–8   Support Itinerant Preachers
9–10   Charge against Diotrephes
11–12   Commendation of Demetrius
13–15   Personal Word and Greetings

For Further Reading

Rensberger, David. *1 John, 2 John, 3 John*. Abingdon New Testament Commentary. Nashville: Abingdon, 1997.

Smith, D. Moody. *First, Second, and Third John*: Interpretation: A Bible Commentary for Teaching and Preaching. Louisville, KY: Westminster/John Knox, 1990.

COMMENTARY

1
SALUTATION

The elder to the beloved Gaius: The elder (see the introduction to 2 John and commentary on 2 John 1) opens and closes the letter in the first person singular, but in the body of the letter seems to be representing the views of others, referred to as **we, brothers, friends,** and **children**. The recipient Gaius is **beloved,** one who is loved **in truth.** Love and truth are familiar Johannine themes (John 17:17–19; 1 John 3:18–19; 2 John 2–6) which will appear again in this letter (vv. 2, 3–4, 5–6, 11, 12). Gaius cannot be identified further. Perhaps he was a leader in a church known to the elder and located in the same general area.

2–4
REASON FOR JOY

I pray that all may go well with you: The wish that one's correspondent be in good health, body and soul, was rather conventional for the time. For this writer it is a prayer, not a wish. Noticeably absent is some form of the greeting as in 2 John, "grace, mercy, and peace." The elder is overjoyed by reports from itinerant brothers that Gaius is faithful and walking **in the truth** (v. 3; 2 John 4); that is, living out the Christian faith with integrity and in accord with the tradition they had received (1 John 1:6–7; 2:6, 11). The truth may be shorthand for the word of Christ and about Christ, who is not mentioned by name in the letter. Such conduct by **my children** (v. 4; converts? members of a church founded by the writer?) is a source of joy and satisfaction to the elder. Hence the elder and Gaius are mutually encouraged.

5–8
SUPPORT ITINERANT PREACHERS

Whatever you do for the friends: See NRSV note, indicating the translators have rendered the Greek "brothers" as "friends" in the interests of inclusive language. However, in the Johannine church "friends" is a designation for Christians as such (see on John 15:12–14; 3 John 15). "Brother" (and "sister") in 3 John may have a more specific usage, pointing to traveling missionary teachers (as in vv. 5, 10). Gaius is commended for the faithful work of extending hospitality to traveling Christian missionaries. There was a great deal of movement among Christians, and these itinerant preachers could be both blessing and bane for the church (2 John 9–11). But hospitality was a mark of the church going back to Jesus (Matt. 10:40–42), even if those arriving at the door were **strangers** (Heb. 13:2; Rom. 12:13). Hospitality involved not only receiving but sending them on their way (v. 6); that is, offering financial assistance for the journey (v. 8; Acts 15:3; Rom. 15:24; 1 Cor. 16:6, 11). In this way, host and guest become **coworkers** (v. 8). It was expected that the church thus provide for its own. No support was accepted from "Gentiles" (v. 7; here meaning unbelievers; see on 1 Pet. 2:12; 4:3) as a matter of conviction about their community and their identity as people of "the name" (v. 7; the NRSV [see note] inserts "Christ").

9–10
CHARGE AGAINST DIOTREPHES

I have written something to the church: It is difficult to identify the church to which the elder has written; perhaps it is not the one to which Gaius belongs but one very nearby. Nor can we know what was written. There is no evidence that the message was 2 John 9–11. Were that the case, Diotrephes is only guilty of doing what the elder himself was doing. The charges against Diotrephes—he loved being in charge, he did not accept the elder and his friends, he spread false charges against the elder and his friends, he does not give hospitality to delegates of the elder, and he ousts those who do—seem not to be doctrinal.

Perhaps the text reflects a power struggle in the church. The elder hopes to improve his position by a visit to the church (v. 10).

11–12
COMMENDATION OF DEMETRIUS

Whoever does good is from God: See on 1 John 2:29; 4:7. Origin determines conduct (see on 1 John 4:5–6). In contrasting Diotrephes and Demetrius, the writer uses familiar Johannine language about not seeing God and being of God (v. 11; on the Johannine understandings of "seeing God," see on John 14:7–9). Demetrius, the elder's advocate to the church of Gaius, is probably the bearer of the letter. He is commended by the elder, the associates of the elder, and by **the truth itself** (v. 12), probably an expression to indicate his consistent embrace of the Johannine tradition. That tradition is echoed in the statement that **our testimony is true** (v. 12; John 19:35; 21:24; 1 John 1:1–4).

13–15
PERSONAL WORD AND GREETINGS

I have much to write to you: The ending of the letter is very similar to 2 John 12–13. The conventional preference for direct communication over writing and the anticipation of a visit soon are both expressed. The blessing of peace is especially appropriate, given the tensions over hospitality. The elder expects to be well received, but even so, he aids his own reception by extending greetings from the elder's circle and by requesting that Gaius's circle of friends be greeted **each by name** (v. 15); that is, greet each one individually. There is no question: the elder's visit is extremely important for the church.

The Letter of Jude

INTRODUCTION

Jude is a letter, its opening and closing being clearly in the epistolary tradition of Paul. The author intended to write another, different letter, but a crisis in the church (v. 4) prompted the writer to set aside the planned letter and to send this one instead (v. 3). Our clarification of the document as a general letter is simply that, our clarification. That the readers are not identified by name or location does not necessarily mean that the author did not have a specific church in mind. The style of the letter is dignified, at times poetic, and embodies several rhetorical strategies of persuasion. Verses 6–19 are so strikingly similar to 2 Peter 2 that the question of borrowing is inevitable. Which borrowed from the other, or did they use a common source? The majority opinion is that 2 Peter found Jude 6–19 appropriate to its message and included it.

The Letter of Jude intends to be received as written by a brother of Jesus, even though the claim is made indirectly: "servant of Jesus Christ and brother of James" (v. 1). Two of Jesus' four brothers were Jude and James (Mark 6:3), a fact that weakens the nomination of other Christian leaders named Jude (an apostle other than Iscariot [Luke 6:16], and a prophet of the church [Acts 15:22, 27, 32]). However, it was not uncommon for unknown authors to write under the name of a person known to and respected by the readers. The author is steeped in the texts and traditions of Judaism, making the brother of Jesus a possibility. On the other hand, "the faith that was once for all entrusted to the saints" (v. 3) and "remember the predictions of the apostles" (v. 17) are expressions that hint of a later generation. (See "Pseudonymous Letters in Early Christianity" in the introduction to Ephesians.)

It is futile to attempt to locate the readers geographically. The condition of the church addressed could characterize a congregation in Palestine, Asia Minor, or elsewhere. The theological location of readers is a bit more discernible. They have been fully instructed (v. 5) in the teaching of the apostles (v. 17), in the Old Testament (vv. 5–11), and in early Judaism (vv. 9, 14–15). However, the readers now face the dangers brought by certain intruders (v. 4) whose destructive influence is not so much doctrinal as it is behavioral. By denying the second coming and the judgment, they effectively remove the moral constraints that kept many from immorality. According to the author, the license promoted in the name of Christian freedom amounted to a denial of Christ. The letter, therefore, is designed to warn against danger, to urge firm faithfulness, to call for growth in grace, and to encourage mercy to those who are faltering.

Outline

1–2	Salutation
3–4	Occasion of the Letter
5–7	Lessons from History
8–13	Indictment of the Intruders
14–19	Lessons from Prophecy
20–23	Final Appeal
24–25	Concluding Doxology

For Further Reading

Craddock, Fred B. *First and Second Peter and Jude.* Westminster Bible Companion. Louisville, KY: Westminster John Knox, 1995. Some of the material on Jude in the pages that follow has been drawn from this more expansive treatment.

Watson, Duane F. "The Letter of Jude." In *The New Interpreter's Bible,* vol. 12. Nashville: Abingdon Press, 1998.

COMMENTARY

1–2

SALUTATION

The three parts typical of early Christian letters are all present: the sender, the recipients, and a greeting (here a blessing). **Brother of James:** See the introduction for a consideration of the names Jude and James. Interestingly, for Paul (Rom. 1:1) and Peter (1 Pet. 1:1), stating one's relation to Jesus Christ was sufficient introduction; here the author adds "and brother of James." Is this an attempt by a leader in the postapostolic church to establish a connection with the authoritative tradition from Jesus to the apostles to the church? Is the reference to James providing that connection?

Perhaps. The readers are identified in relation to God's activity toward them. The identification is threefold: God has called them; God is holding them in constant love; God is keeping them safe for Jesus Christ. **Kept safe:** Being "kept safe" (also v. 24) until the coming of Christ was a widely held affirmation (John 17:11–12, 15; 1 Thess. 5:23; 1 Pet. 1:5). This image of security is the opposite of promises made by intruders who are "clouds carried along by the winds" and "wandering stars" (vv. 12, 13). The threefold blessing, while somewhat standard, seems especially appropriate for these readers: the blessing of mercy reappears three times in the final appeal (vv. 5, 16, 19); and the blessing of God's love offers a place for believers to dwell (vv. 1, 21). This blessing therefore, anticipates the affirmation, the argument, and the exhortation of the entire letter.

3–4
OCCASION OF THE LETTER

The author was in the process of writing a letter to recipients, a letter affirming and celebrating their common salvation, when news of the crisis came. The writer feels such responsibility for the church that addressing the crisis is **necessary.** The urgent appeal is for the readers to **contend for the faith** (v. 3). The word "contend" is literally "agonize," a term borrowed from Greek athletic games and used to describe the struggles of moral living (1 Cor. 9:24–27; 1 Tim. 6:12) and of missionary activity (Rom. 15:30; Col. 1:29–2:1; Phil. 4:3). At stake is "the faith," the core teaching of the apostles concerning God's act in Christ. Faith is not a vague feeling; it has content. Formulations of this content circulated early (1 Cor. 15:1–8; 1 Tim. 3:16). **Once for all entrusted to the saints:** Literally "the faith . . . traditioned." Because God's act in Christ is once for all (Rom. 6:10; Heb. 9:12; 1 Pet. 3:18), the identity of the Christian community is determined by this tradition. Any siege against the tradition is a call to action.

Certain intruders: The crisis is precipitated from without by intruders who have **stolen in** (**secretly slipped in**, NIV). Very likely these are itinerant teachers and preachers, who were often a source of doctrinal and moral confusion for congregations. The writer describes them: they sneak in from the outside; they deny the sovereignty and lordship of Christ, probably not in a doctrinal attack but in their libertine conduct; they cheapen God's grace by twisting liberty into license, using freedom as an opportunity to indulge the flesh (Gal. 5:13). However, the writer calms the reader with a reminder: these intrud-

ers **long ago were designated for this condemnation** (v. 4). In other words, God is neither surprised nor threatened; these disturbers appeared in prophecy long before they appeared in church. The author will enlarge on this statement beginning with a prophetic use of Old Testament stories.

5–7
LESSONS FROM HISTORY

The lessons drawn here are but reminders of that which the readers already know. They have not only been **fully informed** in Old Testament content but apparently are also familiar with a moral use of the Old Testament in Christian preaching. The intruders are indicted by three Old Testament stories of judgment: the exodus (v. 5), the rebellious angels of Gen. 6:1–4 (v. 6), and the fall of Sodom and Gomorrah (v. 7). Second Peter 2:4–8 likewise cites three Old Testament lessons, but with two noticeable differences: Peter recalls the flood, while Jude remembers the exodus; and Peter intersperses stories of divine rescue, while Jude speaks only of judgment.

Out of the land of Egypt: The exodus is, of course, a story of deliverance, but the account here is on the punishment of those who did not live by faith. Between Israel's departure from Egypt and their arrival at the promised land was a wilderness in which moral and spiritual tragedies occurred. Jude joins Paul (1 Cor. 10:1–13) and the writer of Hebrews (3:7–4:2) in drawing on Israel's failure to warn their readers.

Angels: The lesson from the obscure story of angels in Gen. 6:1–4, expanded and interpreted in the noncanonical book *1 Enoch* (chaps. 6–8), does not focus on unbelief as in story one, but on rebellion against God. (See the comments on 2 Pet. 2:4, where this story is used in the same way.) As with 2 Peter, Jude understands rebellion against authority in the church as a threat against the defining apostolic tradition.

Sodom and Gomorrah: The third and final lesson from the Old Testament warns against sexual immorality by recalling the fate of Sodom and Gomorrah (v. 7). The **unnatural lust (perversion,** NIV) is apparently not a reference to homosexuality. The men of Sodom and Gomorrah **"pursued different flesh"** in their desire to have sex with the two supernatural beings who visited Lot (Gen. 19:1–29). This is similar to the relation between mortals and angels in Gen. 6:1–4. There may have been some perverse fascination with angelic beings among the intruders. Union with the divine through sex was a claim in many ancient fertility rites and continues in the promises of some cults today.

8–13
INDICTMENT OF THE INTRUDERS

The broad warnings from Old Testament history in vv. 5–7 now give way to direct words of judgment on the intruders. With stabbing repetition the author uses an expression that says literally, "These are the ones who" (vv. 8, 10, 12, 16, 19). They are characterized as **dreamers**, substituting their own wishful imagining for the apostolic tradition. They grant sexual license to themselves and to any who will join them. They prove their freedom by **rejecting authority**, shake the fist at heaven, and insult angels as God's messengers and executors of God's judgment. Such arrogance is not even found among beings of a higher order. For a discussion of vv. 8–9 and the story about Michael, found in *The Assumption of Moses*, a writing of early Judaism, see comments on 2 Pet. 2:10–11. Such behavior, says the author, shows kinship with brute creatures, ignorant and unaware of any higher quality of life (v. 10; see comments on 2 Pet. 2:12).

Woe to them: The writer pronounces over the intruders the classic form of God's judgment (Matt. 11:21–24; Rev. 8:13). Their behavior is in the tradition of the infamous trio: **Cain** (Gen. 4), **Balaam** (Num. 22–24), and **Korah** (Num. 16). Jewish rabbis had linked these three as examples of those who have no share in the life to come. Cain was a heretic in that he denied God's justice; Balaam was willing to bless or curse as long as the money was right (see comments at 2 Pet. 2:15–16); Korah rebelled against authority and created division in the faith community. Now follow in v. 12 vivid images of the conduct of the intruders, who, as members of a Christian community, share at the church's fellowship meals. At the table they are **blemishes**, an unusual word that may also be translated "spots" or "ugly blots" (NEB at 2 Pet. 2:13), or "rocks," such as pose a danger to ships. **Feeding themselves:** Literally "shepherding themselves." The intruders may have posed as pastors, but the sheep existed only to be exploited. The indictment concludes with four analogies from nature: **clouds, trees, waves, stars.** However, these four represent creation gone awry, as will be the case in the cosmic convulsions of the last days. Recall from elsewhere in the New Testament darkness at noon, sun and moon refusing to shine, rocks splitting, mountains falling (e.g., Mark 13:24–15; Rev. 6:12–16. See also *1 En.* 80:2–6). The intrud-

ers are not only being described by these images, but their behavior is indirectly offered as a sign that the last days are near.

14–19
LESSONS FROM PROPHECY

This unit consists of two parallel statements of prophecy and fulfillment (vv. 14–16, 17–19). The two prophecies, while coming from sources outside our Bible, were from traditions regarded as true and authoritative. In each case, the prophecies are fulfilled by the intruders in the church addressed.

Enoch . . . prophesied: The first prophecy (vv. 14–16) is from *1 En.* 1:9 (with some phrases from elsewhere in that book), a Jewish writing from the second and first centuries BCE that can be found in the collection of Old Testament Pseudepigrapha. Enoch was a holy man who never tasted death (Gen. 5:24; Heb. 11:5) and therefore was regarded as especially qualified to speak of God. God's coming became for Christians Christ's coming (Matt. 25:31; Mark 8:38) with the holy angels. The crisis in the church prompts Jude to speak only of the judging work of Christ upon **the ungodly** (stated three times). They are without reverence for God and they complain as did Israel in the wilderness (Exod. 15:24). Their behavior is licentious; they talk loud to attract attention and then ingratiate themselves to pull weaklings into their circle.

Predictions of the apostles: The second prophecy (vv. 17–19) is from the apostles of Christ. The exact source is unknown; perhaps 2 Pet. 3:3 or Acts 20:29–30. Neither do we know at what the intruders are scoffing. In 2 Pet. 3:3–4 it is the second coming of Christ; perhaps here it is the apostolic tradition and the moral demands of Christ. These divisive persons are obviously engaged in a vulgar flaunting of a lifestyle contrary to all held sacred by the church. That the apostles predicted such mockers is a comforting word, because a larger plan is being worked out, and the final word is God's.

20–23
FINAL APPEAL

Here is instruction in Christian living equal to any in the New Testament. Given the crisis created by the intruders, one might expect a final word of judgment or at least of damage control. Instead, the author offers words of restraint and mercy. The comments are not about others (as in 5b–16), but to the faithful. There are in these four verses seven phrases of pastoral exhortation. The first four (vv. 20–21) address the reader's own spiritual welfare and focus on faith, prayer, love, and hope, staples in any Christian discipline. **Pray in the Holy Spirit:** Only the word about prayer contains ambiguity. Paul speaks of praying "with the Spirit" as well as with the mind (1 Cor. 14:15), and since we in our weakness do not know how best to pray, he is confident that the Spirit, who knows the mind of God, "intercedes with sighs too deep for words" (Rom. 8:26). Perhaps Jude has in mind what Paul does. At least, Jude is urging prayer that is within God's purpose and will.

Some who are wavering: The final three instructions (vv. 22–23) deal with appropriate behavior toward those who have wavered or are wavering. The Christian faith is morally serious, but wavering and stumbling will occur, especially in a church influenced by persuasive intruders who offer freedom from restraint. Therefore efforts at forgiveness and restoration were widely urged (Matt. 18:15–22; Gal. 6:1–5; James 5:19–20; 1 John 5:16–17). Those to whom mercy is to be shown are mentioned in the order of increasing seriousness. First are the wavering, those on the edge who are in danger of being drawn away. Second are those in **the fire**, trusting in the mercy of God, which does not give up. The final group, though unclearly described, seem to be most deeply engaged in profligate and corrupt behavior. Ministry to them must be done **with fear**, perhaps of becoming contaminated or of slipping

into the same lifestyle that had been made to appear attractive to those now trapped.

24–25
CONCLUDING DOXOLOGY

This is perhaps the most familiar portion of Jude, being frequently used as a benediction in worship services. The charges against troublemakers and the exhortations to the faithful are complete; the writer now concludes in a burst of praise. Although broad enough to be appropriate for any church, this doxology is especially appropriate to this letter. **Able to keep you from falling:** Notice this phrase in light of frequent references to God's power to keep, to guard, to secure (vv. 1, 6, 13). **To make you stand without blemish in the presence of his glory:** This recalls the references to the end time (vv. 1, 6, 13, 14, 15, 18, 21). **Before all time and now and forever:** Here the doxology affirms God's noncontingent stability to a church off course, disturbed by winds and waves and stars (vv. 12–13). **Glory, majesty, power, and authority:** The ascription of glory, majesty, power, and authority—similar to the doxology added to the Lord's Prayer in Matt. 6:9–13—may have become by the time of Jude a common liturgical practice. The source for such ascriptions of praise may have been 1 Chr. 29:10–13. Certainly reading this letter in the worship assembly of the church it addressed did not interrupt that worship, but rather was itself an act of worship.

The Revelation to John

INTRODUCTION

A Unit to Be Read as a Whole

There is no book of *Revelations* in the New Testament. The Revelation is singular, one document designed to be read aloud and heard all at once (1:3). The writing cannot be understood by extracting a sentence or paragraph from its context, but must be experienced as a whole. No one should venture comments on the "meaning" of a text in Revelation without having heard the letter as it was intended to be heard. The best way to begin to grasp what Revelation has to say to the contemporary church is to gather in a worship setting, join briefly in praise and prayer, then have a good reader (or several) read aloud the whole text without interruption or comment. This takes about an hour and a quarter. A second, less satisfactory option is to read Revelation to oneself straight through, without pausing to ask about the "meaning." Discussions and books about Revelation (including this one) will be of little help without an encounter with the content of the book as a whole, which presents the reader with a vision of the risen Christ that leads through a series of disasters to pictures of the final triumph of God's kingdom.

A Letter Not Written to Us

Revelation is a letter, like 1 Corinthians or 1 Peter. (The prophetic messages of chaps. 2–3 are sometimes called the letters to the seven churches, but all of Revelation is one letter addressed to all the churches.) The realization that Revelation is a letter removes much of the mystery about how to approach it. It is immediately clear, for instance, that just as 1 Corinthians was not written to us or about us, yet communicates the meaning of the Christian faith to us when we first understand it in its own terms, so also Revelation is to be read as a message to other people, in the first century, a letter that they understood, but that requires some explanation before the modern reader can understand it. To understand a letter, one needs to know who wrote it, when it was written, to whom it was written, and the situation addressed. Only then can the modern reader ask about its contemporary meaning.

Authorship

The author designates himself simply as "John," a brother and fellow servant of the readers (1:4, 9). In the second century CE, when it became important to associate all the writings judged to communicate the authentic Christian faith with the original apostles, the tradition developed that the apostle John, son of Zebedee (Mark 1:19; 3:17), was the author of the Gospel and Letters of John, as well as Revelation. The designation was theologically valid, for Revelation does communicate the apostolic faith, but it is historically incorrect. Here are the major reasons modern scholars regard Revelation as written by someone other than the author of the Gospel and Letters of John: (1) The difference in language (which does not show up so well in English translations, which necessarily smooth out the differences). The Gospel is written in good Greek with a distinctive vocabulary. Revelation has an entirely different Greek style, with many grammatical mistakes, the kind of Greek written by one who thinks in his native language—Hebrew or Aramaic—but writes in a second language he learned late in life and imperfectly. Even in an instance where Revelation and the Gospel of John share a similar theological concept, Christ as the "Lamb of God" (e.g., John 1:29; Rev. 5:6 and often), they use different Greek words for "Lamb." (2) Revelation and John share the same faith, but have different ways of conceptualizing and expressing it, i.e., they have different theologies. The Gospel communicates its faith in the transcendent Son of God by telling stories about the earthly Jesus; Revelation has practically no information about the pre-Easter life of Jesus and gives no indication that the author was a witness to that life. The Gospel of John has shifted the emphasis away from the hope of the future return of Christ to the affirmation of the presence of Christ now; in Revelation, these emphases are reversed.

Revelation does not claim to be by an apostle, but speaks of the twelve apostles as others who belonged to the founding generation of the church (21:14; see Eph. 2:20). The author speaks of his composition as "prophecy" (1:3), belongs to a group of prophets (22:9), and describes his ministry as "prophesying" (10:11). The author was thus one of the Christian prophets, a leading member of that group of Christians who spoke by the power of the Holy Spirit directly in the name of God or the risen Lord (see Matt. 23:34; Luke 11:49; Acts 11:27; 13:1; 15:32; 1 Cor. 12:28–29; 13:1; 14:1–40). John was a pastoral leader in the churches of Asia Minor who knew their situation well, an inspired "traveling preacher" who normally would have delivered his messages in their worship services. He has been arrested and deported to the island of Patmos because of his preaching activities (1:9) and, like Paul, composes a letter to be read aloud in worship (1:4; 2:1–3:22) as a substitute for his personal presence.

Date

The original readers, of course, knew when the letter was written and received, but modern readers need to know the date in order properly to understand it. The oldest church tradition locates the writing near the close of the reign of the emperor Domitian, i.e., about 95 CE. This is confirmed by the document itself, which reflects the political and social situation of the late first century in Asia Minor. Among the items that seem to confirm this date is the use of "Babylon" as a symbolic name for Rome. This occurred only some time after 70 CE, when Roman armies destroyed Jerusalem, just as Babylon had done in 586 BCE (see on 1 Pet. 5:13).

Addressees

The letter is addressed to "the" seven churches of Asia (1:11; 2:1–3:22). The seven represent all the churches, for there were more than seven churches in Asia (e.g., Colossae, near Laodicea; see Col. 4:15–16). Asia is the Roman province on the west coast of what is now Turkey. The churches were in the area in which the Pauline mission had founded new churches a generation earlier, and where a strong tradition of Pauline Christianity, centered in Ephesus, continued after his death.

Situation

John addresses his hearer-readers as Christians who are submerged in a severe crisis. The extent to which they themselves were aware of it is unclear, and part of the dynamic of the letter itself. The status of Christians in Asia Minor is illuminated by Pliny's *Letter to Trajan*. When Pliny arrived from Rome as the new governor of Pontus about 111 CE, he found some charges against Christians already on the court docket over which he had to preside and render judgments. A few citations from Pliny's letter to the emperor Trajan, written about twenty years after Revelation and from the same geographical area to which Revelation is directed, illuminate the way Christians were perceived by the government and their neighbors, and illustrates the precarious situation of a religious minority at the mercy of suspicious neighbors and arbitrary state power:

I have handled those who have been denounced to me as Christians as follows: I asked them whether they were Christians. Those who responded affirmatively I have asked a second and third time, under threat of the death penalty. If they persisted in their confession, I had them executed. For whatever it is that they are actually advocating, it seems to me that obstinacy and stubbornness must be punished in any case. Others who labor under the same delusion, but who were Roman citizens, I have designated to be sent to Rome. . . .

An unsigned placard was posted, accusing a large number of people by name. Those who denied being Christians now or in the past, I thought necessary to release, since they invoked our gods according to the formula I gave them and since they offered sacrifices of wine and incense before your image which I had brought in for this purpose along with the statues of our gods. I also had them curse Christ. It is said that real Christians cannot be forced to do any of these things.

Others charged by this accusation at first admitted that they had once been Christians, but had already renounced it; they had in fact been Christians, but had given it up, some of them three years ago, some even earlier, some as long as twenty-five years ago [this would be near the time of Revelation]. (Pliny the Younger, *Letters*, X:96–97)

A Document of Christian Prophecy

As a prophet, John understands himself to write what has been revealed to him in a vision from the risen Lord. This is what the church of his time needed, as they faced the crisis of deciding how to respond to the social pressure to acknowledge the Roman emperor as divine. Scribes and teachers could hand on the tradition from and about Jesus, but the historical Jesus had said nothing that specifically applied to their critical situation. Christian prophets gave new "words of the Lord" for new situations faced by the church.

The biblical prophets functioned as interpreters of history. The events of history, when seen from the human perspective, are ambiguous and can be interpreted entirely in terms of this-worldly causes (physical, sociological, psychological). The wind that drove back the marshy waters of the Red Sea could be seen as a lucky break for the Israelites (the Egyptians regarded it as such; Exod. 14). It was the prophet Moses (Deut. 18:15–18; 34:10; Acts 3:22; 7:37) who interpreted the event as the mighty act of God that delivered Israel from Egypt and made them into God's people (Exod. 15), but this was not obvious apart from the prophetic word. The escalating military power of Assyria that became a threat to Israel and Judah could be interpreted empirically in terms of world politics, imperial ambitions, and military strategy, but the prophets of Israel interpreted it as the judgment of God against Israel's sins (Amos, Hosea, Micah, Isaiah). So also the cultural pressure of John's day, the growing insistence that the church adapt to Roman religion and culture, could be seen as a more or less harmless historical phenomenon to which the church should adapt. But the prophet John interprets what is really going on. He is allowed to see behind the scenes of world history and perceives the events through which he and his churches are living as a great struggle between God and Satan, a struggle that has already been decided by God's act in Christ, a struggle that calls for decision and faithfulness on the part of the church.

The claim to speak the word of the risen Lord does not mean that John simply records, reporter-like, what he saw in his visions. Though John, like Paul, had real visionary experiences (see, e.g., 2 Cor. 12:1–10), he stood in a tradition that developed a conventional set of imagery to express the reality of the heavenly world and the acts of God. Like the prophets of Israel, as he gives literary expression to his revelatory experience, he utilizes this store of traditional imagery, much of which was already familiar to his readers. Again like Paul and the Old Testament prophets, in composing his prophetic and pastoral letter John makes use of older sources, probably including prophetic oracles from his own past experience or from his fellow prophets (e.g., see below on 11:1–2). Just as Paul quoted hymns (e.g., Phil. 2:5–11) and sections of his own previous compositions (e.g., 1 Cor. 13) in composing his letters, so also John utilizes older materials to communicate the meaning of his revelation. In particular, John's Scriptures (the Christian Old Testament) provided source material for his prophecy. Although he does not explicitly quote the Bible a single time, his forty-nine pages of Greek text contain around five hundred allusions and echoes of the biblical text, with Ezekiel and Daniel

playing major roles. His mind is absolutely saturated with biblical language, so that both the original reception of the visions and his communication of them to his readers is overwhelmingly influenced by biblical imagery. (For one example, see the comments on 1:13–16.)

In designating his book as prophecy, John does not claim to predict the long-range future. Although some prophecies contain predictive elements, the essential element of prophecy is the claim to speak directly the word of the Lord, not the prediction of the future. When prophets do make predictions, it concerns the future that directly affects their hearers, including the ultimate future of the eschatological victory of God's kingdom, but not the long-range historical future. As prophecy, Revelation announces both the word of the risen Lord Jesus to his church for the crisis they are facing in the first century and the final coming of God's kingdom at the end of history, which John believed would happen soon (see at 1:1). John does not predict historical events generations and centuries later than his own time, though he has often been misunderstood in this way (see on 1:3, "The time is near").

Apocalyptic Language and Symbolism

The language and imagery of Revelation, with its angels, beasts, heavenly streets, and fiery pits, is strange—even bizarre—to many modern readers. This may have been the case with some of the original readers as well, if they were Gentile converts who had not been previously acquainted with this traditional genre of language and imagery. However, John himself and most of his original readers recognized this type of language as a powerful vehicle for communicating the divine message already found in the Bible and in several streams of Judaism. Apocalyptic writings were already present in John's Bible (e.g., Isa. 24–27; Dan. 7–12). By John's time, this style of writing had become very popular in some streams of Judaism, represented by numerous documents such as *Jubilees* (ca. 150 BCE), *Sibylline Oracles*, Book III (from ca. 150 BCE onward), *Testaments of the Twelve Patriarchs* (latter part of second century BCE), *Psalms of Solomon* (48 BCE), *Assumption of Moses* (6–30 CE), *1 Enoch* (second cent. BCE to first cent. CE), *2 Enoch* or the *Book of the Secrets of Enoch* (first century CE), and some of the Dead Sea Scrolls such as the *Habakkuk Commentary* and the *Description of the New Jerusalem* (second century BCE to first part of first century CE). Many of these are available in the Jewish Pseudepigrapha.

One that is readily available is 2 Esdras (also called 4 Ezra), included in the Apocrypha or deutero-canonical books printed as part of many English Bibles. Second Esdras is a Jewish document with Christian additions, written at about the same time as Revelation, using much the same kind of imagery. It is immensely valuable for modern readers interested in understanding Revelation to read through 2 Esdras, for it becomes immediately clear that Revelation belongs to a literary type familiar in the ancient world, but not to us. Such a reading gives the modern reader a category within which to fit Revelation, a category already familiar to John's original readers. To take a modern analogy: A picture of a man wearing a red, white, and blue suit struggling with a bear holding a banner on which a hammer and sickle are found would be an absolute mystery to a person unacquainted with the category of "newspaper political cartoon" and the history of the struggle between the United States and the Soviet Union of the decades after World War II. Most modern readers instantly recognize the cartoon, but to some it already belongs to past history with which they are not familiar, and must be explained. To place such a cartoon in a category of several similar cartoons with their traditional stereotyped images is a necessary step in understanding. The reading of just one ancient apocalyptic document in addition to Revelation places it in a category that opens up understanding.

Some features of first-century apocalyptic language and imagery also found in Revelation:

The use of (often bizarre) symbolic language to represent the transcendent world. Evil powers are often represented by beasts and monsters. Particular numbers such as four, seven, and twelve have special meanings. This-worldly realities and events are placed in a broader context of meaning by clothing them in symbolic form. This is not the same as a "code," in which there is a one-to-one correlation between symbol and meaning. Once a code is understood, it is no longer needed, for its message is clear in ordinary language. This is not the case with the symbolic language of Revelation (or of the Bible in general). Biblical symbols are not disposable containers for an ordinary meaning that can be stated in ordinary language, but serve to evoke, provoke, even irritate and disorient the mind accustomed to thinking only in ordinary categories, pointing to the transcendent reality that cannot be expressed otherwise than in irreducible pictorial imagery. It is thus false, for example, to suppose that Revelation was written in a code language to communicate to Christians but to conceal its meaning from the Roman authorities. The anti-Roman message of Revelation is clear enough (see

17:9, 19). The symbolic language functions at a more profound level than code language.

The perception of all reality in dualistic terms, in which good and evil, light and darkness, truth and falsehood, God and Satan, are all sharply contrasted. For apocalyptic thought, there are only two categories. All issues are black and white, with no shades of gray. The only response to God's word can be yes or no. The Jesus of the Gospels also reflects this apocalyptic way of thinking (see, e.g., Matt. 12:30; 25:31–46). Apocalyptic thought permeates not only Revelation, but much of the rest of the New Testament. To learn to interpret Revelation better is thus to open the door to much else in the New Testament. On the language of demons, Satan, and exorcism, see the excursus at Mark 5:1.

The expectation of the near end of history, in which the kingdom of God will triumph. Revelation shares the apocalyptic expectation that the end is coming soon (see on 1:3), an expectation also found elsewhere in the New Testament (see, e.g., 1 Thess. 4:13–17; 1 Cor. 7:25–31; Rom. 13:11–12; 1 Pet. 4:7; Mark 9:1; 13:30–31). This is not the result of speculative curiosity, but is an aspect of apocalyptic theology's understanding of the faithfulness of God. That is, apocalypticism's affirmation of the near end of the world is not a response to the speculative question "When is the end coming?" but to the theological questions "How can God be faithful?" and "What is the meaning of our present suffering?" Biblical and Jewish faith affirmed that God was the almighty Creator who was just and loving. When this faith was confronted with the radical evil of the world in which God's people suffered precisely because they were faithful (as in Daniel and Revelation), apocalyptic theologians affirmed the faithfulness of God by interpreting present evil as the prelude to the final victory of God. In extreme situations represented by persecution, the present suffering was understood as the "labor pains" that precede the birth of God's new world (see Mark 13:8). The fact that the labor pains had begun must mean that the coming end in which God's love and faithfulness will be clear to all is not far away. The translation of "Jesus is coming soon" is "No matter how it looks from the human perspective, the God revealed in Jesus Christ is faithful and will deliver on his promises." Present troubles are placed in the context of God's plan for history, which is perceived to be hastening to its conclusion. With the aid of 20/20 hindsight, the modern reader can perceive that in terms of chronology, the apocalyptists were wrong. Within the framework of their apocalyptic theology, their affirmation of the goodness and faithfulness of God is not thereby invalidated. Each modern reader must respond in faith or unbelief to their claim that—no matter how it looks to the human eye—God is faithful and will bring the creation to a worthy conclusion, and that this is not a matter of speculation but of revelation.

A Book That Must be Interpreted

It is quite possible to be addressed by the message of Revelation simply by reading it or (better) by hearing the message read aloud, just as it is possible to be impressed, even overwhelmed, by a great symphony or work of art without any "explanation" as to its "meaning." But as soon as one asks, "What does this *mean*?" it becomes clear that Revelation requires interpretation, for *any* response to this question is an *interpretation*. One can be *addressed* by Revelation merely by reading it, but *understanding* requires interpretation.

Revelation must be interpreted because it is a letter written to other people in another time and place. This is true not only of Revelation, but of all New Testament letters. It is inherent in the letter form as such, which is not an essay of general timeless truths, but a particular address to particular people in a particular time and place with a particular set of problems. It thus corresponds to the nature of the Christian faith, which deals not with a set of general ideas or principles, but with the particular act of God in the person of Jesus of Nazareth.

Four main types of interpretation have been developed in the history of the church. The great number of differing interpretations are all variations and combinations of these four basic types:

1. The *idealist* interpretation understands Revelation to portray timeless images of the victory of good over evil. For example, the Beast represents evil, whenever and wherever it appears, and its destruction represents the ultimate victory of God, but without relating it to any particular historical situation. Prophecy is understood to be the announcement of general principles.

2. The *continuous-historical* or *church-historical* interpretation understands John to predict the history of the church from his own time to the end of the world, usually understood as to happen in the interpreter's own time centuries later. Thus some visions refer to the development of the papacy, the Reformation, the Napoleonic wars, the rise of Hitler and the Soviet Union, and the like. The great variety of these interpretations has given Revelation the reputation of having many different interpretations, but these are all variations of one approach to the meaning of the book.

3. The *futurist* (also called *dispensationalist* or *premillennialist*) interpretation understands John to predict the last few years of world history, centuries after his own time, still in the interpreter's own future. This interpretation, developed in the nineteenth century and popularized by some televangelists, attempts to understand the imagery literally, and regards the Beast as an anti-God power soon to come that will signal the approach of the end of the world.

4. The *preterist* or *past-historical* interpretation regards the message of Revelation as directed to the churches of his own time and understood by them. Its predictions are for the future of its original readers, not the long-range future. This is the interpretation adopted by practically all modern scholars of all denominations, and the only interpretation appropriate to the understanding of Revelation as a letter. This is the interpretation represented in the following comments. Revelation has a message for the church of our own day in the same way that, e.g., 1 Corinthians has a message for later Christian readers: though not written to us—we are neither Corinthians nor members of one of the "seven churches" of Revelation—the ancient document still mediates the word of God to us, and we understand its message to us only by first understanding its message to its original readers.

Outline

For Further Reading

Boring, M. Eugene. *Revelation.* Interpretation: A Bible Commentary for Teaching and Preaching. Louisville, KY: Westminster/John Knox, 1988. Some of the material on Revelation in the following pages has been drawn from this more expansive treatment.

González, Catherine Gunsalus, and Justo L. González. *Revelation.* Westminster Bible Companion. Louisville, KY: Westminster John Knox, 1997.

Hill, Craig C. *In God's Time: The Bible and the Future.* Grand Rapids: Wm. B. Eerdmans Publishing Co., 2002.

COMMENTARY

1:1–3:22
GOD SPEAKS TO THE CHURCH IN THE CITY

1:1–8
INTRODUCTION AND SALUTATION

1:1–2 The title "The Revelation to John" was added by the church in the process of the formation of the New Testament. John's own title to the document, which summarizes its content, is **the Revelation of** (from) **Jesus Christ.** The revelatory chain of command proceeds from **God**, the ultimate source, through **Jesus Christ**, the defining center, to the **angel**, who mediates the revelation to **John**, who delivers it to the other **servants** of God, the churches—whose mission it is to bear witness to the world. The individual members of the "revelatory chain" modulate into each other, so that the whole document that presents "all that he saw" can be called not only John's word, but **"the word of God and the testimony of Jesus Christ." John** identifies himself with no special titles, but only as one of the **servants of God** (see 1:9; introduction to Revelation on "Authorship").

1:1 What must soon take place: The phrase is from Dan. 2:28, and connects John's revelation with previous prophecy as its fulfillment. "What must take place" is not a matter of fate or impersonal destiny, but the plan of God (see 4:1–5:14).

1:3 Blessed: Though they are not numbered, Revelation contains seven such beatitudes (1:3; 14:23; 16:15; 19:9; 20:6; 22:7, 14). **The one who reads aloud:** The letter was designed to be read aloud in the worship service at one hearing. **The words of this prophecy:** See the introduction to Revelation for the biblical meaning of prophecy. **Keep what is written in it:** "Keep" means not merely preserve, but obey. Revelation calls for obedience to the command of the risen Christ to resist the cultural pressures that erode the church's witness to the truth of the Christian message.

EXCURSUS:
INTERPRETING THE "NEAR END"

Revelation begins and ends with the declaration that the return of Christ and the end of history are near (1:1, "What must soon take place"; 1:3, "For the time is near"; 22:20, "Surely I am coming soon"). This motif is not incidental, but is woven into the fabric of the message throughout:

2:16—The risen Jesus warns those in Pergamum to repent, because he is coming soon. This word functions as a warning, and loses its power if there is a lot of time left in which to get ready to meet the Judge.

2:25—The risen Jesus encourages the faithful at Thyatira to hold fast what they have "until I come." This word functions as encouragement to steadfast endurance. If in fact a centuries-long period is intended, it no longer encourages the reader to hold on. Similarly 3:11.

3:20—"Behold I stand at the door and knock" is not only a spatial image for the church at Laodicea, but a temporal image, often found in apocalyptic, that reflects the shortness of time before the coming of Christ: he is already at the door (see Mark 13:29; Luke 12:36; Jas. 5:9).

6:11—The souls of the martyrs already in heaven cry out for God's eschatological judgment of the world and ask, "How long?" They receive the response that they must wait only "a little longer."

10:6—The "mighty angel" in the vision swears by the Creator that there is to be "no more delay," but that the "mystery of God, as he announced to his servants the prophets," i.e., the divine plan for the establishment of God's just rule at the end of history, is about to be fulfilled.

11:2–3; 12:6—The longest period mentioned in Revelation is this span of time described variously as forty-two months, or twelve hundred and sixty days, derived from the period of three and a half years prophesied in Daniel 7:25; 8:14; 9:27; 12:7, 11, 12. This period became a traditional apocalyptic time frame (see Luke 4:26 and Jas. 5:17 vs. 1 Kgs. 17:1; 18:1). The period is not meant literally, but still represents only a short time.

12:12—The devil intensifies his persecution of faithful believers precisely because he "knows that his time is short."

17:10—There are to be seven "kings" altogether, and John and his hearer-readers live in the time of the sixth. Again, while the precise numbers may not be literal, it is clear that John sees himself and his readers as living near the end.

22:6, 7, 10, 12, 20—Revelation ends with a cluster of assurances that Christ will return soon.

That the end of history is near in the writer's own time is a constituent part of apocalyptic thought (see the introduction to Revelation).

How should the modern reader come to terms with this apparently erroneous expectation? The New Testament itself offers help on this problem,

for it was already faced in New Testament times. During the first Christian generation, there were several crises that convinced some early Christians that they were indeed experiencing the final events of history and the end was now upon them. There was widespread apocalyptic excitement among both Jews and Christians when the emperor Caligula attempted to place a statue of himself in the Jerusalem temple in 39, as there was during the terrible Neronian persecution of Christians in Rome in 64, during the catastrophic war in Palestine 66–70, and in the wake of the famines, earthquakes, and eruption of Vesuvius in the following decades. Yet these crises came and went, and the end did not come. How could Christians respond to this apparent disappointment of their eschatological hopes?

1. *Rejection.* It is striking that no New Testament author simply rejected the apocalyptic hope as such, despite its failure to materialize as expected. Some other early Christians, however, whose writings were not included in the New Testament, decided that apocalyptic expectation as such was an error, and simply rejected it. Gnostic streams of Christianity abandoned the hope that God would redeem the horizontal line of history in a mighty eschatological act, and retreated to a verticalism in which individual souls are saved into the transcendent world and/or already enjoy the eschatological realities in their present religious experience. Such views may have been shared by John's opponents among the Nicolaitans (Rev. 2:6, 15) and the followers of "Jezebel" (2:20) who advocated the teaching of "Balaam" (2:14). Some contemporary interpreters have responded in this way to Revelation's apocalyptic expectation of the near end of history, i.e., by simply rejecting apocalyptic in general and Revelation in particular. This is often done without an awareness of how deeply rooted apocalyptic ideas are in the New Testament as a whole and in Christian faith as such.

2. *Reinterpretation.* Other Christians held on to the apocalyptic language of the first generation, but reinterpreted it in the light of the failure of the end to appear. There were basically two varieties of such interpretation:

a. *Reinterpretation of "soon."* The author of 2 Peter represents this point of view. He discovered Psalms 90:4, which declared that a thousand years in God's sight is only a day, which helped him to understand "soon" in a different way than had the first generation of Christians (2 Pet. 3:3–13). Likewise the author of Luke–Acts reinterpreted the near-expectation of the previous generation in such a way that the earlier expectation was postponed to the indefinite future (see the introduction to

Luke: "Jesus as the 'Midst of Time,'" and comments at Luke 4:43; 5:24; Mark 2:10; 17:23; 21:5–36; Acts 1:6–11). So also the author of 2 Thessalonians postponed the end (see 2 Thess. 2:1–12).

b. *Reinterpretation of "end."* In this view, the promised "end" did in fact come soon, but it was not the end of history. The outpouring of the Spirit and the beginning of the church was considered the fulfillment of the promised return of Christ. The eschatological realities were no longer understood in a literal manner, but spiritualized and understood to be a part of the present experience of the Christian life. This kind of "realized eschatology," elements of which had also been a dimension of the faith of the first generation, was developed especially by the authors of the Gospel and Epistles of John. These authors reinterpret all the realities expected to come at the eschaton as already present realities: the antichrist is reinterpreted as the presence of false teachers in the church (1 John 2:18; 4:3); the second coming of Christ is reinterpreted as Christ's coming again as the Spirit, the Paraclete (John 14–16); the defeat of Satan happened in Jesus' ministry (John 12:31). Furthermore the resurrection happens in the new life of the Christian (John 11:21–26; see 8:51); the judgment happens in the present encounter with Christ the judge (John 3:18–19; 12:31, 48), and eternal life is already the present possession of the believer (John 3:36; 6:47; 17:3). The Johannine authors did not absolutely reject the future hope, however (see, e.g., John 5:28–29; 12:48; 21:22–23), but did strongly subordinate it to present Christian experience.

3. *Reaffirmation.* In times of threat and persecution, Christians of the second and third generations revived the older apocalyptic expectations with the conviction that even though earlier predictions were wrong, *now* the end has indeed come near. In their situation, apocalyptic language once again made sense and supplied an urgently needed means of holding on to the faith despite all the empirical evidence to the contrary (see the introduction to Revelation, pp. 762–64). Thus in 1 Peter, written in a situation similar to John's, the author revives the expectation of the nearness of the end as a motive for Christian steadfastness in the face of persecution and trial (4:7; see 4:16; 5:9).

Revelation is best understood as fitting into this category. When John said "the time is near" (1:3, etc.), he meant the time for the happening of all the events his letter envisions, including the return of Christ, the destruction of evil, and the everlasting glory of the new world. He meant both "soon" and "end." John was simply wrong about this. Christians who reverence the Bible as Scripture, the vehicle of God's word, ought not to hesitate to acknowledge that its authors made errors. It is an aspect of the humanity of the Bible, a part of the meaning of the incarnation, that God uses human thought (with its errors) and human beings (with their errors) to communicate his message. Apocalyptic thought was one of the human ways of thinking about God and the world prevalent in the first century. That the end was near was one of the ingredients of apocalyptic thought. When John adopted apocalyptic as the vehicle of his message, he adopted its errors as well, just as would have been the case with any other form of thought available to him (or us). Just as John accepted a flat earth with corners as the spatial framework within which he expressed his message (see Rev. 7:1), so he accepted a world shortly to come to an end as the temporal framework within which he expressed his message. As he was wrong in the one case, so was he wrong in the other case. But in neither case does the error of his worldview nullify the validity of the message expressed in it. One must distinguish between gift and wrapper, baby and bathwater, the truth of the message and the form in which it is expressed.

1:4–8 is the letter opening. **1:4–5a** is John's adaptation of the Pauline letter formula (see on 1 Thess. 1:1). **1:5b–6** is an ascription of praise that corresponds to the thanksgiving section of a Pauline letter (see on Rom. 1:8–15). **1:7–8** are two prophetic pronouncements that form the transition to the body of the letter proper.

1:4–5 The seven churches that are in Asia: Asia is the Roman province on the west coast of what is now Turkey. There were more than seven churches in Asia (e.g., Colossae, near Laodicea, see Col. 4:15). The seven are representative of the whole church. Seven not only represents completeness but signifies the divine order (seven days in the week, seven "planets" known to the ancient world). Portraying the church as represented by seven churches symbolizes its role in God's plan (see at Eph. 1:9). **Seven** is used 55x by John and is a primary structural principle of his book. Not only are there seven churches, seven seals, seven trumpets, seven bowls (see Outline), but, e.g., seven spirits (e.g., 1:4), seven angels (e.g., 1:20), seven emperors (17:9–10), and several series of seven that are not specifically numbered (e.g., the beatitudes listed above). All this testifies to the careful literary composition of the book.

From him who is: God is the Creator who is present with and rules the creation and will come at the end to bring history to a worthy conclusion. **From the seven spirits:** This reflects the view of first-century Judaism that there were seven principal angelic spirits that carried out God's will in the world (Tob. 12:15; *1 En.* 90:21). John does not here refer to the Holy Spirit or Spirit of God (phrases that do not occur in Revelation), but the function of the "seven spirits" is that of the Holy Spirit. **And from Jesus Christ:** This threefold way of designating the divine reality is not yet a developed Trinitarian understanding, but the elements of this later development are found in the New Testament (see on 1 Pet. 1:1). "Jesus" is the proper name; "Christ" is the office (see on Mark 8:29).

For John, "Christ" has not become a name, but still connotes the office of God's anointed messiah as prophet, priest, and king. Christians share in this ministry. As we shall see below, John understands the church to be a prophetic community (see on 11:1–13), and he here declares it to be a royal and priestly community. As a prophetic community the church mediates the word of God made known in Jesus to the world. As a priestly community the church mediates to the world God's reconciliation of the world in Jesus, the sacrificed priest, and instead of sacrificing to the emperor on the Roman altar, sacrifices itself on the true altar of God (see 6:9–11). As a royal community the church represents and signifies the rule of God as already present in the world.

The role of Jesus as the Christ is elaborated with three additional titles appropriate to John's situation: (1) **The faithful witness:** The same phrase is used in 2:13 of Antipas, a Christian who had already suffered martyrdom. The Greek word for "witness" is literally "martyr." See on 11:3. In Revelation the word already connotes one who bears witness by being truthful under duress even to the point of death, but the word did not come to explicitly signify martyrdom until two generations later. Testimony-by-giving-one's-life was what Jesus did when he stood before the Roman governor; this is what John's readers are called to do (see 2:10; 11:3). (2) **The firstborn of the dead:** Though he died, God raised him. "Firstborn" connotes status, not merely chronology (see on Acts 26:23; Col. 1:18). (3) **The ruler of the kings of the earth:** See 19:16. This was the claim of the Roman emperors. The kingship represented by Jesus' suffering love for others presents an alternative to Roman kingship, a reinterpretation of what it means to "conquer" (see on 5:6–14).

1:5–6 Freed us from our sins by his blood: See on 19:13; Rom. 3:25. **A kingdom, priests:** See Exod. 19:6; 1 Pet. 2:5, 9. The Christian community is portrayed with the attributes of Israel. Just as a specific group of priests mediated between God and Israel, so the people of Israel as a whole plays a priestly role with regard to the world. Just as priests exist for the sake of the people as a whole, so Israel and the church as the continuing people of God exist for the sake of the world. All Christians are priests, mediating between God and the rest of humanity. In Revelation, the church shares in the priestly and kingly work of Christ (3:21; 20:4).

1:7 Every eye will see him: For John, the return of Christ is not an inward spiritual experience of what happens to the individual at death, but will be visible to all at the end of history. See commentary on John 19:37.

1:8 The Alpha and the Omega: The first and last letters of the Greek alphabet. See 21:6, where God is again the speaker, and 22:13, where the risen Christ is the speaker—one of several places in Revelation where the same language is used of or by both God and Christ. In Revelation, the figures of God and Christ are not kept distinct but modulate into each other, a way of portraying the one God as represented by Christ.

1:9–20
THE PRESENCE OF THE RISEN CHRIST

1:9 I . . . your brother who share with you: John does not claim to be an apostle or eyewitness of the life of the earthly Jesus, but a fellow member of the church who shares the common Christian experience, which is identified in three ways: (1) **Persecution:** There was as yet no official empirewide persecution of the church, which did not occur until the third century. Nonetheless, in John's situation at the end of the first century, to be a Christian is to be subject to harassment that could sometimes result in arrest and even death (see Pliny's *Letter to Trajan* in the introduction to Revelation). (2) **Kingdom:** To be a Christian is to participate in God's rule of the world inaugurated by Christ, at present visible only to eyes of faith, to be consummated at the end of history. (3) **Patient endurance:** The key Christian virtue in Revelation, a word that occurs seven (!) times. It connotes not mere passivity, but the tough-minded resistance to cultural pressures to conform that can be exercised by those who know that "the Lord our God the Almighty reigns" (19:6). **In Jesus:** Like "in the Lord"

(14:13), a reflection of the Pauline "in Christ" (see on 2 Cor. 5:17). **The island called Patmos:** A small island about ten miles long and six miles wide at its widest point, located about forty miles from the mainland of Asia Minor. There is no evidence for the tradition that it was used as a penal colony by the Romans. **Because of the word of God and the testimony of Jesus:** This pregnant phrase used often by John (see 1:2, 9; 6:9; 20:4; see 12:17; 14:12) identifies or closely associates the word of God and the word of/about Jesus. The "testimony of Jesus" can mean either the testimony Jesus gave or the testimony of others (the church) about him, or can combine both meanings. Roman governors sometimes punished criminals and troublemakers by deporting them to an island. John had been banished because of his preaching.

1:10 I was in the Spirit: This does not refer to John's subjective feelings, but indicates that he was inspired by the divine Spirit, that he fell into a prophetic trance (see Num. 11:25–29; Luke 1:67; Acts 2:18; 19:6; 2 Cor. 12:1–10; Eph. 3:5; 2 Pet. 1:21; 1 John 4:1; Rev. 19:10). The phrase occurs four times, 1:10; 4:2; 17:3; 21:10. **On the Lord's day:** Not the Jewish Sabbath (Saturday), but Sunday, the first day of the week, the Christian day of worship celebrating Jesus' resurrection (Mark 16:2, 9; Luke 24:1; John 20:1, 19; Acts 20:7; 1 Cor. 16:2). John has his vision at the same time the churches on the mainland are having their worship services. If he were present among them, he would deliver his prophetic message personally, as the "sermon" during worship (see 1 Cor. 14:26–33). Since he is separated from them, he writes his revelation to be read aloud during worship (1:3).

1:11 Write what you see: The vision itself and its narrative description is the word of God and testimony of Jesus Christ that is to be delivered to the churches (1:2). **The seven churches:** see on 1:4.

1:12–16 describes the vision of the risen Christ. Three things are important to note about the vision as a whole:

1. *Cosmic proportions:* The vision does not portray the pre-Easter historical Jesus, but the risen and exalted Christ. He is not a mythical heavenly being, but the same Jesus who was killed in Jerusalem (1:7, 18; 11:8). Yet he is now the representative of God as the exalted Lord of the universe, who spans the cosmos and hold the stars in his hand (1:16). All this is not mere speculative fantasy, but expresses the faith of the church that the Jesus for whose tes-

timony they are now called upon to suffer is not merely an admirable hero of the past, but the cosmic Lord. John wants his hearers to bear their own witness in the confidence that the Jesus they serve "has the whole world in his hands."

2. *Biblical language as medium of communication:* The "data" John utilizes to describe this figure are not merely his "observation" of what the risen Jesus is like. The overwhelming experience is expressed in new combinations of imagery taken from Scripture.

1:13 Seven golden lampstands: Exod. 25:31–35. The lampstand was part of the furniture of the Old Testament tabernacle and temple. Its light represented the divine presence, the light of God's own word. John will explain it as the symbol for the church (1:20). The scene combines the fullness of the divine presence in the heavenly worship scene and the presence of the Son of Man on earth "in the midst of the lampstands/ churches. John's imagery, like the Old Testament's imagery for God, combines the transcendence of Christ who is in heaven and will come again with the image of Christ's presence among his churches. **One like the Son of Man:** Dan. 7:13; see commentary on Mark 2:10. "Son of Man" is a Hebrew expression for "human being." On this peculiar phrase, see on Luke 5:24, Mark 2:10. Like the figure in Daniel, the risen Jesus has a human form, is "like" a human being, but now transcends historical human existence. **Clothed with a long robe . . . with a golden sash:** Imagery is combined from the heavenly beings of Ezek. 9:2, 11 and Dan. 7:9.

1:14 Hair . . . white as snow: Here the description of the Ancient One (God) in Dan. 7:9 is applied to Jesus. **1:14–15 His eyes . . . like blazing fire . . . his feet . . . like bronze glowing in a furnace, and his voice . . . like the sound of rushing waters** (NIV) are all taken from the description of the angelic heavenly beings of Dan. 10:6 and Ezek. 1:24. **1:16 The sharp double-edged sword** (NIV) coming from his mouth reflects Isa. 49:2, and his face **like the sun shining with full force** reflects the language of Judg. 5:31.

3. *Evocative nonliteral language:* This language is not literal, but evocative. It cannot be represented graphically, but only in words that disorient the mind in its effort to picture them. The same cosmic hand that holds the stars (1:16) is in the next sentence the personal hand placed upon John (1:17). The sword coming from Christ's mouth says something powerful about the nature of Christ's word, but

any effort to picture it is grotesque. Does the sword recede into Jesus' mouth when closed, or remain hanging outside? Such questions reveal that these words have been misunderstood as objectifying language. (On objectifying language, see on Matt. 2:16; Acts 1:9; Rev. 6:15, excursus 3.b.) Such language is not merely subjective fantasy. It points to something real that it cannot literally express.

1:17 Fell at his feet as though dead: See Isa. 6:5; Acts 9:3–4. The encounter with the risen Christ is not a pleasant, chummy experience, but the overwhelming sense of being in the presence of the divine. **Do not be afraid:** The first word to John and his churches. Though the conventional response of a heavenly messenger to the fear generated by his appearance (see Gen. 15:1; Judg. 6:13; Dan. 10:12; Luke 1:13, 30; Acts 18:9; 27:24), it is also significant that the first word from the risen Christ addresses the situation of John's churches who face a fearful ordeal. **I am the first and the last:** The risen Christ uses the same language as God in 1:8 and 21:6. Literally there can be only one who is first and last. John's Christology does not compromise his monotheism. This is what the later Trinitarian theology attempted to express.

1:18 I am . . . the living one. I was dead . . . I am alive forever: Christ died a real death. He was not immortal, who did not "really" die. His word of hope to his disciples is not that they are immortal, but that even if they have to die in his service the One who raised him will also raise them. On the difference between the pagan doctrine of immortality and the Christian affirmation of resurrection, see on Matt. 28:1; Luke 20:27. **I have the keys of Death and of Hades:** Hades is not hell, the place of punishment, but another word for the realm of the dead. **The keys** reflects the pagan image of Hekate, a goddess popular in Asia, portrayed as having the keys of death. This image has been transferred to the risen Christ, who is in charge of death and life. See Matt. 16:19.

1:19 Write what you see: The report of his vision mediates the word of God and testimony of Jesus (1:2). The vision comprises two elements, **what is** (the true state of the world and church in John's time) and **what is to take place after this** (the ultimate fulfillment of God's purpose for the world, the final coming of God's kingdom, which John sees as happening in the near future). It is a popular misunderstanding to see this verse as the "outline of the book," as though "what you have seen" = the vision of chap. 1, "what is" = the seven

churches of chaps. 2–3, and "what is to take place after this" as chaps. 4–22. Rather "what you see" comprises the whole vision, which includes present and future of God's world and God's people.

1:20 As for the mystery: This is one of very few places in Revelation where the symbolic language is translated into ordinary discourse, and even here it is not done as though Revelation were written in "code" (see on symbolic language in the introduction to Revelation). The "explanation" still leaves the sense of mystery and disorientation.

The seven stars are the angels of the seven churches: Since "angel" means "messenger" and can be used for human beings (such as John the Baptist [Matt. 11:10] or the messengers sent by Jesus [Luke 9:52]), it has sometimes been thought that the "angels" are the bishops or prophetic leaders of each church. On this interpretation, since in chaps. 2–3 each message is addressed not directly to the church but to its "angel," the meaning would be that John writes to the leader of each congregation, who is to read the letter to the group. This somewhat pedestrian interpretation does not sufficiently take into account either the nature of Revelation's symbolism in general or the particular fact that of the sixty-seven references to angels in Revelation, all the others clearly refer to transcendent beings. John operates out of the apocalyptic tradition within which earthly realities have their counterparts in the heavenly world. Just as each nation has its representative angel in the heavenly world (see, e.g., Dan. 10:2–14, 20–21), so each congregation has its representative "guardian" angel in the heavenly world. The church is not merely a human worthy cause, but participates in the reality of the eternal world. John writes to the churches, but not merely as one concerned Christian to others; the communication of the divine message takes place on another level. It is thus better to understand the angels as heavenly counterparts of the churches, their alter egos. To address the angel is clearly to address the church as a whole, but in a transcendent context. This is not without precedent: In Isaiah 40:1 the prophet's message is addressed to the beings of the heavenly court, and is only "overheard" by the earthly reader.

John's thought world includes such heavenly beings, but he is concerned not to give them too exalted a status. There was considerable angel speculation in the churches of

Asia in the generation after Paul (see Col. 2:18). People were fascinated with stories of angelic beings. John shares this world of ideas, but is concerned to reduce the status of angelic beings to that of the church members themselves: angels too are servants of God, who can be obedient or disobedient. They can be admonished, as in the messages to the seven churches, but they are not to be worshiped (see on 19:9–10; 22:8–9).

The seven lampstands are the seven churches: This, too, should not be reduced to the level of code language. The church is the bearer of God's light to the world (Matt. 5:14). The lampstands are part of the heavenly temple, the scene of the heavenly worship. The churches are not merely human institutions for promoting good causes, but somehow participate in the heavenly world. Medieval art and architecture attempted to represent this by, for example, painting the inside of church domes and ceilings in a way that connected heaven and earth, with the legs of little angels dangling over the parapet of heaven and into the sanctuary. As the church participates in the heavenly world, so the living Christ is present on earth and walks in the midst of the lampstands/churches (1:13).

2:1–3:22
The Messages to the Seven Churches

The seven churches were real congregations of real people with real problem in real cities at the end of the first century. They do not symbolize "seven ages of church history." John did not foresee a long period of church history after his own time, but expected the end to come soon (see on 1:3).

Although the individual letters reflect the particular situation of the church in each city, all the messages are addressed to all the churches. Each congregation is to hear not only the message addressed to it, but "what the Spirit is saying to the churches," as declared at the end of each letter. The messages do not have the form of the Hellenistic letter—Revelation as a whole has that (see 1:4–5; 22:21)—but they do resemble imperial edicts of Hellenistic kings and the Roman emperors, thus placing what the risen Christ as "king of kings" says to the churches over against the emperor who falsely claims this role of world rulership (see 17:14; 19:16).

The messages all have the same form:

1. *Address to the "Angel"* (see on 1:20).
2. *The City.* Each of the cities named had a Roman law court, i.e., was a location where

Christians had been or could be charged with membership in the Christian sect suspected of being subversive, and at least the first three (Ephesus, Smyrna, Pergamum) addressed were sites of temples dedicated to Caesar.

The letters are addressed to churches in sizable cities. By the end of the first century, Christianity was an urban phenomenon. The Christians in John's churches were not simple peasant people of the back country, but residents in the principal cities of their time, struggling with the issues of how the Christian witness could be made real and viable within the political and cultural life of a sophisticated urban population. The contrast between two cities, Babylon and the new Jerusalem, forms the burden of John's visions in the body of the book to follow, chaps. 4–22. Whether Christians who lived in the mundane cities of Asia would orient their lives to the "Great City" of Babylon or the "Holy City," the new Jerusalem, is a major theme of Revelation.

3. *Prophetic Messenger Formula.* The standard prophetic messenger formula in the Old Testament was "Thus says the Lord," with the message following in the first person. The prophet did not speak as a reporter of what he had been instructed to say, using indirect address in the third person, but directly in the person of the Lord who had commissioned him or her. John adopts that style and its accompanying formula, the repeated "The words of him who . . ." (NRSV) being exactly identical to the LXX translation of "Thus says the (Lord)." For Christian prophets, the Lord who speaks is the risen Lord Jesus.

4. *Christological Ascription.* At the beginning of each letter is a christological affirmation, mostly taken from the attributes of the vision of Christ in 1:9–22. These christological statements at the beginning of each letter are neither casually chosen nor mere decorations, but serve a theological purpose. The letters contain ethical instructions and warnings, the commands of the risen Christ for living a faithful Christian life in a trying situation. Such commands cannot stand alone; they are not general or obvious moral truths. Their truth is bound up with the truth of the vision of 1:9–20, that the crucified one is the exalted Lord vindicated by God and made Lord of all. Here, as elsewhere, the ethical imperative is founded on the christological indicative; the Christian life is founded on the fact and reality of Christ.

5. *The Divine Knowledge.* The exalted Lord says, "I know," to each congregation, whether in threat or reassurance.

6. *The "Body."* The body of each letter is composed of praise and/or blame, promise and/or

threat. Only two churches (Smyrna and Philadelphia) receive unqualified praise.

7. *The Call to Attention and Obedience.* A characteristic element in Old Testament prophetic forms was the call to attention, "Hear!" (Isa. 1:10; 7:13; 28:14, 23; 48:1, 14; Jer. 2:4; 5:21; 6:18; 7:2; 10:1; 13:15; Hos. 4:1; 5:1; Amos 3:1, 13; 4:1; 5:1; 7:16; 8:4). The word carries its full meaning of not only listening, but acting on what is heard (as in "I tried to tell you, but you wouldn't *listen* to me"). John incorporates this call to hear/obey in the closing words of each message: "Let anyone who has an ear listen to what the Spirit is saying to the churches." The formula is one of the few places where John's prophetic idiom echoes the words of the historical Jesus—or where the words of Jesus in the Synoptic Gospels have been adapted to the familiar forms of Christian prophets who spoke in his name (see Mark 4:9, 23; Matt. 11:15; 13:9, 43; Luke 18:8; 14:35). John does not distinguish the risen Christ and the work of the Spirit; what the risen Jesus says is what the Spirit says to the churches.

8. *Eschatological Promise to Those Who "Conquer."* Each letter concludes with a promise of blessing, expressed in apocalyptic terms, to the Christians who "conquer." "Conquer" was translated as "overcome" in the King James Version and stands behind the song of hope, "We Shall Overcome." Christians are "winners," those who "conquer" or "overcome," but the Christian meaning of "winning" has been redefined by the Christ event (see on 5:5–6).

2:1–7
The Message to the Church in Ephesus

2:1 Ephesus: After Rome, Alexandria, and Antioch, the largest city in the Roman Empire (ca. 150,000) and the most important city in Asia; the political, economic, and cultural capital of the province. Ephesus was then a harbor city, but the harbor has silted up over the centuries, and the city is now six miles inland. Tourists can still visit its impressive ruins, including its magnificent theater and library. It contained numerous temples, including no less than six dedicated to Roman emperors. A large temple with a colossus to Domitian was excavated in 1960. A generation before John's time, the city had been a center of the Pauline mission (see Acts 18–21; 1 Cor. 15:32; 16:8), and it was still a flourishing center of Pauline Christianity as well as for Christians of other traditions. **Seven stars . . . seven golden lampstands:** see 1:12, 16, 20.

2:2 Tested those who claim to be apostles: Not the original Twelve, but traveling missionaries (see 2 Cor. 10–13). Not all claims to represent the Christian faith are to be accepted. As indicated by the later inclusion of four different Gospels and a variety of letters in the New Testament, more than one way of expressing the faith is to be affirmed, but not just any way. On criteria for such discernment, see excursus at 2:20.

2:3 Bearing up for the sake of my name: See 2:13; 1 Pet. 4:15–16.

2:4 Abandoned the love you had at first: Revelation, sometimes wrongly thought to be mainly a book of revenge and wrath, also magnifies love as the supreme Christian virtue (see Mark 12:28–34; 1 Cor. 13). The Ephesian church had begun as a church empowered by love for God and others, but in John's time their original Christian conviction had waned (see Matt. 24:12; and the church at Laodicea, Rev. 3:15–16). They rejected false apostles and the doctrine of the Nicolaitans, but were unloving. It is possible to be orthodox and still miss the "more excellent way" (1 Cor. 12:31; 13:1–3).

2:5 Repent: All the churches except Smyrna and Philadelphia are challenged to repent. On repentance, see on Luke 3:7–9. Repentance is not a once-for-all act as a part of initial conversion, but is also a continuing aspect of the Christian life, which must be continually reoriented to the call of Christ. **If not, I will come to you:** This does not refer to the return of Christ at the end of history (which John believed was to take place soon in any case), but is the conditional threat of coming in judgment to this particular congregation (so also 2:16). Even to John, the "coming" of Christ can be interpreted in more than one way.

2:6 The Nicolaitans (and followers of "Balaam" and "Jezebel"): These are all groups of Christians within the churches of Asia. The identity of the Nicolaitans is unclear; neither is it known whether they are identical with those who accept the teaching of "Balaam" (2:14) and "Jezebel" (2:20). "Balaam" and "Jezebel" are not the actual names of John's opponents, but are derogatory labels taken from the Old Testament. Balaam was a pagan false prophet who misled Israel during the wilderness period after the exodus from Egypt (Num. 22–24; Deut. 23:5; Josh. 13:22; 24:5). Jezebel was the pagan wife of King Ahaz, who persecuted the true prophets (1 Kgs. 16–21; 2 Kgs. 9). The Nicolaitans were probably named after an actual leader. Some Church Fathers of the second century supposed the Nicolaus of Acts 6:5 later developed teachings that were considered heretical by John, but there is no evidence for this. Even if they represented different groups, their common denominator was that in the name of "progress" they advocated accommodation to pagan culture, represented by participation in festivals and social occasions that included eating meat ritually sacrificed to idols. John considered such actions an unacceptable compromise with paganism. That the groups existed at all shows that even though John was a Christian prophet who claimed to speak the word of the Lord, his leadership was not uncontested.

2:7 The tree of life: See Gen. 2:9; 3:22–24. In the symbolic story, sin had caused humanity to lose its access to the source of life in the garden of Eden, and so death prevails over all humanity. The triumph of God's kingdom at the end of history will restore this original blessedness of creation. Revelation does not picture a return to the garden, but the bringing forward of the garden into the eschatological new Jerusalem. This means a forward-looking, hopeful affirmation of human history in this world rather than its ultimate negation (see on 21:1–22:5).

2:8–11
The Message to the Church at Smyrna

2:8 Smyrna: Modern Izmir, it was a large city (ca. 100,000) located on the coast forty miles north of Ephesus, its commercial rival. It is not otherwise mentioned in the New Testament; we know nothing of the origins and previous history of the church there. Smyrna had been the first city in Asia to build a temple to the goddess Roma (193 BCE) and by John's day had become a center of emperor worship. **Who was dead and came to life:** From 1:17–18. The risen Christ characterizes himself in this way especially to a church facing life-and-death decisions.

2:9 Your poverty: Though riches and poverty could be used in a spiritual sense in the New Testament, as already the case in Judaism (see Matt. 5:3; 1 Cor. 4:8; Eph. 3:8; Rev. 3:17), here literal poverty is meant. This is not because Christianity attracted only poor people in the first century (see Luke 8:1–4; Acts 4:36–37; 8:26–39; 10:1–48). More likely, church members in Smyrna had suffered economic reversals because of their faith (losing jobs, confiscation of property, vandalization and boycott of their businesses). The church has borne up well under this distress. It is one of only two churches of whom nothing negative is said (the other is Philadelphia, 3:7–13).

Those who say they are Jews and are not, but are a synagogue of Satan: To understand such harsh words from a Christian (see also John 8:44, also written by a Jewish Christian), spoken in the name of the risen Christ, one must remember several factors:

1. "Jew" in this sentence is a positive characterization. The problem with those he speaks against is not that they are Jews, but that they do not live up to their name (see Rom. 2:28–29).

2. Race is not involved. The statement is not anti-Semitic in the racial sense, but expresses a religious conflict.

3. Such epithets were routinely used in inter-Jewish religious conflicts, in which each party called the other "children of the devil," a practice adopted by Christians: in 1 John 3:4–10 "children of the devil" is applied by Christians to other Christians. On the language of demons, Satan, and exorcism, see the excursus at Mark 5:1.

4. Such language represents the dualistic framework of thought inherent in apocalypticism (including the language of Jesus; see the introduction to Revelation above).

5. In John's situation Jews were a substantial minority in the Roman population (a total of about three million Jews in the Roman Empire of about sixty million, about 5 percent of the total population = fifty Jews per thousand). Though an old and often respected community, they also had to deal with suspicion and prejudice, and sometimes had a precarious existence. But the Jewish community was thirty times the size of the Christian community. Estimates of the number of Christians in the Roman Empire at the end of the first century range from 50,000 to 320,000. Taking 100,000 as a rough median figure, there would have been 1.6 Christians per thousand population—a much smaller, more recent, and more suspect minority than the Jewish community. Non-Christian Jews were understandably resentful that some Jewish Christians attempted to maintain their identity with the synagogue, thus making trouble between the Jews and the Roman authorities. It is understandable that in such a situation Jews sometimes denounced Christians to the Roman authorities. Something like this had apparently happened in Smyrna (and Philadelphia, see below). John responds by charging them with being a synagogue of Satan.

6. While historical study can make such New Testament texts more understandable, it does not authorize later generations to make use of such language. No one today may refer to Jews in such terms. Modern Christians, precisely on the basis of the New Testament, can only lament that such texts have been used in Christian history to support anti-Semitism.

2:10 The devil is about to throw some of you into prison: On the language of demons, Satan, and exorcism, see the excursus at Mark 5:1. The Romans did not use incarceration as a punishment. People were put in prison in order to force them to comply with certain demands (here, probably emperor worship), or as a place of detainment awaiting trial or execution. **Ten days:** Not literal, but another reference to the shortness of the time before the final deliverance (see on 1:3). **Be faithful unto death:** This responds to the question "To what extent should I be faithful?" not "How long?" Christians in Asia Minor were asking, "At what point can I deny the faith? When they make fun of me at school? When I lose my job? When my property is confiscated? When I am fined or beaten?" The answer: Christ asks for your life, whatever it may cost. The original meaning was not, "Be faithful your whole life long," but as translated in the *Jerusalem Bible*, "Even if you have to die, keep faithful." This is spoken in the name of the One who gave his own life, and who now lives (2:8).

2:11 The second death: This is one of John's apocalyptic images for the ultimate judgment of God (20:6, 14; 21:8). Those executed for their faith by human courts will be vindicated by God's own verdict at the Last Judgment. See the similar teaching of the Matthean Jesus (Matt. 10:26–33, esp. 10:28). The Jesus of Revelation is no more severe on such issues that the Jesus of the Gospels.

2:12–17
The Message to the Church in Pergamum

2:12 Pergamum: Another large city (ca. 100,000), ca. seventy miles northwest of Smyrna. It was known for several impressive temples, including the great altar to Zeus, an artistic masterpiece that has been removed to the Pergamon Museum in Berlin, where it is a tourist attraction now as it was in the first century. **The sharp two-edged sword:** see 1:16.

2:13 Satan's throne: May refer to a specific location in Pergamum, such as the Zeus temple (altar and throne were associated in the ancient world), one of the temples to Rome

and the Caesars, to the Roman court where Christians were tried, or to the Roman opposition to Christianity in general that permeated Pergamum. **You are holding fast to my name:** See 2:3; 1 Pet. 4:15–16. Christians have always been tempted to be "anonymous" (literally, "without the name"), i.e., to make their faith a nonpublic individual matter between themselves and God. But the New Testament regards faith as a matter of corporate and public testimony—it has a horizontal, not merely a vertical dimension. **Antipas:** Nothing more is known of him, except that he was executed for his confession of Christ. **My witness:** Literally "my martyr" (see on 1:4; 11:3).

2:14 Balaam: See on 2:6. **Eat food sacrificed to idols:** Most people in the ancient world did not regularly eat meat—only on religious or festive occasions, which were in the framework of pagan worship. Most meat purchased in the public meat market was the by-product of pagan sacrifice. Whether Christians could or should eat such meat was a disputed point in early Christianity, to which more than one solution was presented (see further on 1 Cor. 8, 10; Acts 15:20, 29; 21:25). In John's situation, he regarded eating such meat to be an unacceptable compromise of the Christian faith. His opponents in the church, the "Balaamites," "Nicolaitans," and followers of "Jezebel," all considered eating such meat to be a legitimate expression of the faith. **And practice fornication:** It is not clear whether this was meant literally or not. Jews considered idolatry inevitably to lead to sexual immorality. Pagan religion was sexually permissive by Jewish and Christian standards. But participation in pagan worship itself was considered "fornication," i.e., unfaithfulness to one's true Lord (see Hos. 1–3).

2:16 Repent then. If not, I will come to you soon: See on 2:5.

2:17 The white stone: May originally reflect a magical use of amulets, and/or the entrance ticket to social/business occasions from which Christians who hesitated to participate in pagan society were excluded. **Hidden manna:** Reflects the Jewish despair over the destruction of the temple by the Babylonians in 586 BCE. At that time, the sacred ark that contained some of the manna (Exod. 16:1–36; see Heb. 9:4) was hidden and never recovered, but it was believed that it would be revealed at the eschaton. All the lamentation, hopes, and overtones of feeling associated with the Wailing Wall and the people of God's longing for the restoration of the true worship of God in the true temple are compressed into the image of the "hidden manna." This is combined in Christian tradition with the eucharistic imagery of eating the true bread with the Messiah at the ultimate messianic banquet, already anticipated in the eucharistic celebrations (see John 6:1–65, esp. 49–51; Rev. 3:20–21; 11:19).

2:18–29
The Message to the Church in Thyatira

2:18 Thyatira: A center of industry and commerce forty-five miles southeast of Pergamum, mentioned elsewhere in the New Testament only as the home city of the Christian businesswoman Lydia (Acts 16:14). **Son of God:** Used only here in Revelation (see "my Father" 2:28; 3:5, 21; "his Father" 1:6; 14:1). The title contrasts the risen Christ with the Caesars, who also often claimed to be "sons of God," i.e., natural or adopted sons of their deified predecessors.

2:19 Love as the primary Christian "work" (see 2:4).

2:20 Jezebel: See on 2:6. John was not the only leader in the churches of Asia who claimed to speak directly in the name of the risen Lord. Jezebel and her group also made such claims, but their message was the opposite of John's.

EXCURSUS:
TESTING PROPHECY

What does the community of faith do when confronted with rival prophet claims to speak for God? Throughout the centuries Israel and the church developed various criteria for testing revelatory claims:

1. *Miracles.* The true prophet is validated by his or her ability to work miracles and signs (1 Kgs. 17–19). But false prophets also work miracles (Deut. 13:1–3; Matt. 7:21–23; Rev. 13:11–18 [see 16:13]; 19:10; 20:10).

2. *Accurate predictions.* The true prophet is validated by the accuracy of his or her predictions (Deut. 18:18–22; 1 Kgs. 22:28; Isa. 30:8). But, apart from the fact that the bulk of prophecy is not predictive anyway, the hearers must typically decide before this criterion could be helpful. Strictly applied, this criterion would exclude some canonical prophets (e.g., Amos 7:11 vs. 2 Kgs. 14:29; 2 Kgs. 22:30 vs. 23:29; Ezek. 26:7–14 vs. 29:17–20; Jonah 3:4 vs. 3:10; Jer. 22:30 vs. Matt. 1:12).

3. *Vision vs. dream.* The true prophet receives his or her message in a vision, while the message of false prophets comes through dreams (Jer.

23:16–18, 25–28). Yet dreams are also evaluated positively by those who affirm prophetic revelation (Num. 12:6–8; Dan. 2; 4; 7:1; Matt. 1–2).

4. *Doom.* The true prophet proclaims doom, the false prophet salvation (Jer. 23:17; 28:8; 1 Kgs. 22; Ezek. 13:10). This criterion too would exclude some canonical prophets such as 2 Isaiah (Isa. 40–55). In any case, most prophecies contain a combination of the two.

5. *Covenant loyalty.* Fidelity to the covenant God and righteous conduct (not merely miracles) are the sign of the true prophet, while false prophets are immoral (Deut. 13:1–3; Matt. 7:15–20; *Did.* 11:8, 10). But what constitutes such fidelity and immorality is often a matter of interpretation.

6. *Creedal loyalty.* True prophecy is in accord with the fundamental faith of the community as expressed in traditional creeds (Deut. 13:1–3; 1 Cor. 12:3; Rom. 12:6; 1 John 4:1–3; 2 John 7–9). Yet such creeds are not universal, and they too must be interpreted.

7. *Personal unselfishness.* True prophets will not order meals for themselves in the Spirit, or ask for money for themselves, or want to stay more than three days (*Did.* 11:9; 12:2). Here the criteria are clear enough, but of limited usefulness.

8. *Hearing the [orthodox] message.* In 1 John 4:6, whether the opposing claims to speak by the Spirit are authentic is determined by whether they hear "us." Those that do are from God; those that do not are from the world.

Three observations:

1. *One criterion is noticeably absent: sincerity.* It is assumed that all prophets believe their own revelation. The point of the peculiar story in 1 Kgs. 13 is apparently that each prophet must be true to the message he or she has received, even when it conflicts with other revelatory claims. Prophets may be deceived by the deity (1 Kgs. 22) or themselves, but the term "false" in the phrase "false prophets" means that their message is false, not that they think of themselves as false prophets. All the biblical prophets were thought of as false prophets by their opponents, and vice versa. Jeremiah himself had no criteria by which to measure true and false and agonized over the validity of his own message, while his prophetic opponents were self-assured (Jer. 20:7–18; 27). The prophets' sincerity does not help the community to adjudicate conflicting claims. "Jezebel" and her followers were just as sincere as John.

2. *Biblical revelation, including prophetic revelation, is always ambiguous.* Consider the alternative: if revelation is unambiguous, then those who do not accept it are dumb or evil or both, and those who do accept it can pride themselves on

being smart or good or both. (See the danger inherent in 1 John 4:6 taken alone.)

3. *Criteria of some sort are indispensable.* Yet criteria that claim to validate the word of God can be demonic, as among Jesus' opponents in the Gospel of John. The community that receives revelation must use its best judgment in applying its best criteria. Yet it is the Spirit at work in the community of faith that recognizes, receives, and validates the prophetic message as the word of God in a way beyond objectivization or demonstration. There is no escape from the risk of faith in affirming the prophetic word, but it is not individualistic faith. Prophecy is a church phenomenon, and the church as a whole is charged with the responsibility to "test everything; hold fast what is good" (1 Thess. 4:21; 1 Cor. 14:29; Eph. 3:1–7). In the present instance, the community of faith preserved John's prophecy and finally rejected that of the "Jezebel" group, but this was not so clear in John's day.

2:22 Those who commit adultery with her . . . her children: Figurative expressions for those who accept "Jezebel's" teaching and practice.

2:24 Deep things of Satan: This may have been the claim of Jezebel's followers, i.e., that they could explain deep truths about Satan, how evil originated, why an almighty God permits evil, and such. Alternatively, they in fact may have claimed to explain the "deep things of *God*" (see 1 Cor. 2:10), which John parodies (see 2:9; 3:9, "synagogue of Satan" as John's term for what his opponents considered God's synagogue).

2:26–27 Authority over the nations . . . rule them with an iron rod: These phrases are taken from Ps. 2:8–9, understood to portray the reign of the Messiah (as in 12:5; 19:15). The second psalm was often understood in this sense in the New Testament (Matt. 3:17; Acts 4:25–26; 13:33; Heb. 1:5; 5:5). Revelation understands Jesus' followers to participate in his messianic reign. Christians will not literally lord it over others and break them like clay pots, nor do they want to do so. Christ reigns through suffering love, and his followers share his role by participating in this ultimate power of the universe (see on 5:5–7).

2:28 The morning star: The planet Venus, thought to be a star in antiquity, the brightest light in the sky after the sun and moon. Since there is only one "morning star," it cannot be given to every believer individually; here as elsewhere, the eschatological reward is corporate (see on 21:10).

3:1–6
The Message to the Church in Sardis

3:1 Sardis: A large (ca. 75,000) city forty miles southeast of Thyatira, the capital of Lydia and location of the legendary King Croesus. Sardis is not mentioned elsewhere in the New Testament. **The seven spirits of God and the seven stars:** See 1:4, 16. **A name of being alive, but you are dead:** The reputation of being "a lively church" is seen differently through the eyes of the risen Christ.

3:3 Remember then what you received and heard: The prophet points to the original Christian message and tradition as the source of renewed life. Charismatic prophets who speak the present word of the Lord and affirmation of the church's tradition are not alternatives. **I will come like a thief:** Despite Revelation's elaborate presentation of "signs of the end," the author affirms that the return of Christ will be unexpected. This saying of the risen Lord also appears as a saying of the earthly Jesus (Matt. 24:42–44; Luke 12:39–40; see 1 Thess. 5:2; 2 Pet. 3:10; Rev. 16:15). Traditional sayings of Jesus were taken up by Christian prophets and elaborated as the present address of the risen Lord. Sayings of the risen Jesus from Christian prophets were included in the Gospels as sayings of the historical Jesus. Earliest Christianity did not distinguish between what Jesus had "really" said during his earthly life and "sayings of the Lord" first spoken by post-Easter Christian prophets. This one was probably originally a prophetic oracle that in the Gospels became a saying of the historical Jesus.

3:4 Not soiled their clothes . . . dressed in white: Probably an indication of the priestly function of the church (see Exod. 19:5–6; Rev. 1:6).

3:5 If you conquer: See 5:5–7. **The book of life:** The registry of those who belong to God's people, and thus a metaphor for salvation (Exod. 32:32; Dan. 12:1; Luke 10:12; Phil. 4:3; Rev. 13:8; 17:8; 20:12, 15; 21:27). The saved are enrolled in it from the foundation of the world (13:8), i.e., by God's grace, but they are erased from it by their actions, for which they are responsible. The picture thus paradoxically combines salvation by grace and human responsibility (see on 20:11–15). **I will confess your name before my Father and before his angels:** Those who do not try to be anonymous Christians but confess Jesus' name before the world will be acknowledged by Jesus at the Last Judgment, where he will confess their names before God. See Matt. 10:32 and Luke 12:8; here is another instance of an oracle of the risen Jesus being included in the Gospels as a saying of the historical Jesus. (See on 3:3.)

3:7–13
The Message to the Church in Philadelphia

3:7 Philadelphia: Modern Alashehir, twenty-eight miles southeast of Sardis, not mentioned elsewhere in the New Testament. The city honored the emperors by adding "New Caesarea" and "Flavia" to its name in gratitude for Roman help in rebuilding after the devastating earthquake of 17 CE. **The holy one:** Not only a frequent designation of God in the Old Testament (e.g., 2 Kgs. 19:22; Job 6:10; Ps. 78:41; Prov. 9:10; Isa. 5:19; Jer. 51:5; Ezek. 39:7; Hos. 11:9; Hab. 3:3), but also used of the Caesar in the emperor cult. On the meaning of "holy," see on 4:8. **The key of David:** The authority of the Davidic kingdom (Isa. 22:22). For the early church's picturing the coming kingdom of God as the renewal of David's kingship, see on Luke 1:28–33; 3:23; 20:41–44; Acts 13:22–23.

3:8 I know your works: Only the churches in Philadelphia and Smyrna (2:8–11) receive unqualified praise. **I have set before you an open door:** This may refer to the opportunity to evangelize ("witness," in Revelation's vocabulary), as in 1 Cor. 16:9; 2 Cor. 2:12; Col. 4:3. If it is related to possessing the key of David, it more likely refers to Christ's power to grant access to the new Jerusalem, i.e., eschatological salvation. Since it is Christ who has opened that door and no one can close it, entrance does not depend on the disciples' own power—of which the Philadelphians had little.

3:9 Synagogue of Satan: See on 2:9. **I will make them come and bow down before your feet:** The imagery is from Isa. 49:23; 60:14, in which the eschatological victory of God is pictured as the pagan nations bowing at the feet of Israel. Here the imagery is reversed: at the final coming of God's kingdom the Jewish people who regard the Christians as heretics and outsiders to the people of God will see that God has chosen them: Jews will bow before Gentile (Christians) rather than vice versa. As in the imagery of 2:26–27, Christian readers do not really expect or want Jews to grovel someday before them. Again the imagery reflects Christians sharing in the ultimate reign of Christ, who has redefined the meaning of "reigning" (see 2:26).

3:10 I will keep you from the hour of trial: This does not mean that Christians will be spared the future troubles that are **coming on the whole world**. Revelation does not picture a "rapture" in which Christians will be taken out of the world's final troubles, but that they will be strengthened to endure them, even to death (see on 6:9–11; 7:14; 1 Thess. 4:13–5:11). John sees the harassment and sporadic persecution of his own time as the leading edge of a worldwide persecution, which was not yet present but which he believed was soon to come.

3:10–11 can be seen as a thumbnail sketch of the major themes of the whole book: (1) the coming persecution, "the hour of trial coming on the whole world," which is the prelude to (2) the return of Christ as the final coming of God's kingdom (**I am coming soon**), and (3) the Christian responsibility to remain firm, to bear witness to the faith, to keep **my word of patient endurance**. Revelation is about history, eschatology, and Christian responsibility.

3:12 I will make you a pillar in the temple of my God: The promise of eschatological reward is to be included in God's eschatological temple, not as a visitor, but as a *part* of it. Christian leaders had been called "pillars" (Gal. 2:9), but in the final temple all faithful Christians will share this role. But there will be no temple in the new Jerusalem (21:22; see there)! Such conflicting imagery may point to the use of different sources or traditions by the author, but this is somewhat beside the point. The author could have revised his sources to present one consistent picture, but he did not. The point illustrated here, in fact, is twofold: (1) all such language of ultimate things is metaphorical, so that one should not ask whether the new Jerusalem "really" has pillars or not, and (2) all talk of ultimate things requires more than one picture, whether or not they can be harmonized. Both Rev. 3:12 (temple) and Rev. 21:22 (no temple) have their own valid theological point to make and should not be superficially "harmonized," as though their truth depended on their being objectifying language (see on Matt. 2:16; Acts 1:9; Rev. 6:15, excursus 3.b).

3:14–22
The Message to the Church in Laodicea

3:14 Laodicea: A large and wealthy city in the Lycus valley on the major road forty miles southeast of Philadelphia and one hundred miles east of Ephesus, only a few miles from Colossae. It was destroyed by an earthquake in 60 CE, but wealthy enough to decline Roman help in rebuilding. The church was founded in Paul's times, though not by Paul himself, and according to Col. 4:16 received a letter from him. **The Amen:** Reflects the Hebrew text of Isa. 65:16, where "the God of faithfulness" is literally "the God of Amen," i.e., "Amen" is understood to be a title of God. See 2 Cor. 1:19–20. The **Origin** (NRSV) or **Ruler** (NIV) of God's creation likewise associates Christ with the Creator (see John 1:1–4; 1 Cor. 8:5–6; Col. 1:15–20; Heb. 1:1–4; all reflecting the role of Wisdom in Prov. 8:22–36).

3:15 Neither cold nor hot: In the ancient world, the metaphor "cold" did not mean "passive" and "hot" did not mean "enthusiastic," but these words were rather used in the sense of "against me" and "for me." The Laodiceans attempted to be neither for nor against. Their problem was not lack of enthusiasm but wavering in the either/or choice. It is not only Revelation that insists there is no middle way. The Jesus of the Gospels likewise defines only two groups, those who are for and those who are against; those who gather with him and those who scatter (see Matt. 12:30).

3:16 Lukewarm: There is some evidence that the water supply of Laodicea, which came through an aqueduct from hot springs several miles away, delivered tepid and barely drinkable water to the city. This is one of several indications that the author knew the circumstances of each city and tailored the message to each church.

3:17 For you say, 'I am rich': Laodicea was literally a wealthy city, but this claim is more likely metaphorical, referring to the charismatic "spiritual experiences" they enjoyed. The reputation of Sardis as a "live" church (3:1) and the Laodiceans' view of themselves as "rich" (3:17) probably refer to the charismatic enthusiasm of their realized eschatology. (See 1 Cor. 1:5 and Paul's ironic comments to the Corinthians, 1 Cor. 4:8; 2 Cor. 4:12.) Like Paul earlier, John acknowledges that his churches were well supplied with charismatic phenomena, but charges them with abandoning the love that had characterized their Christian lives earlier. Other, more spectacular manifestations of what they supposed was the spiritual life had become more important than the commonplace, selfless care for others represented by love in its Christian meaning (see 1 Cor. 13).

3:19 I reprove . . . those whom I love: This concluding word of the risen Christ applies to the whole set of seven messages 2:1–3:22 and

places their somewhat harsh and moralistic tone in different light.

3:20 I stand at the door and knock (NIV): Despite the famous painting *The Light of the World* by Holman Hunt, John does not portray Christ as knocking at the "heart's door" of the individual. Rather, the Christ who walks in the midst of his churches (1:20; 2:1) here finds himself on the outside of one of them, and wants in. The door is to be opened by individuals, and when this happens there is personal communion with Christ, but the picture is in a corporate, churchly context. The invitation is to share in the joy of the final messianic banquet, with overtones of the Eucharist, which already anticipates the final celebration.

3:21 I will give a place with me on my throne: That Christians share in Christ's eschatological rule is a persistent theme in Revelation (1:6; 5:10; 20:4, 6; 22:5; see 2 Tim. 2:12). The image of the throne forms the transition to the next section.

4:1–18:24
GOD JUDGES THE "GREAT CITY"

4:1–5:14
THE HEAVENLY THRONE ROOM

4:1–11
Praise to God the Creator of All

At 4:1 the scene moves from the earthly location on Patmos (1:9), where the initial vision was received, to the heavenly world. Chapters 4 and 5 portray the heavenly throne room and provide the setting for the remainder of the book. John sees God enthroned as the Creator, the Lamb who opens the scroll sealed with seven seals. Since the seventh seal unfolds into the seven trumpets (8:1–2), and the last trumpet leads into the seven bowls (11:15; 15:7; 16:1–21), all the series of sevens that comprise the body of the book are already contained in the initial heavenly scene. This is theologically important, in that the series of terrible hardships and sufferings that the world experiences are not pictured as independent random disasters with which believers must cope, but as in the hand of the Creator and the Lamb from the very beginning.

4:1 In heaven a door stood open: Literally, "opened," i.e., by God. John does not seek a revelation and finally succeed in being enlightened. The initiative is with God. As in 5:13 and 7:1, the cosmology assumed is that of the triple-decker universe with the flat earth situated between heaven above and the underworld below (which also is entered through a door or pit, to which there are keys; see 1:18; 9:2; 20:3). The triple-decker model of the universe is also found elsewhere in the New Testament (e.g., Phil. 2:5–11), but there are other models as well. Gnosticizing Christianity pictured the earth as the lowest level, with cosmic powers located between the earth and heaven (Eph. 2:2; 4:7–10). The more common apocalyptic view that there are seven heavens above the earth is also reflected in the New Testament (2 Cor. 12:2, where paradise is located in the "third heaven"). In the first century this cosmology was giving way to the "new" view that regarded the earth as a sphere surrounded by seven concentric "planetary" spheres (the sun, moon, and five planets), beyond which was the realm of the gods. John reflects one version of the older Jewish and biblical view, but his revelation is not intended to give astronomical or cosmological information. As elsewhere in the Bible, his message is expressed within the worldview he assumes to be real. The modern interpreter must distinguish between the truth of the message itself and the ancient worldview within which it is expressed. The variety of such views contained in the Bible already encourages the reader not to take any of them literally.

Come up here: This is the divine invitation and command to be transported to the heavenly world to receive the revelation. It is typical of apocalyptic literature, refers to John's experience in the first century as he received the revelation, and has nothing to do with modern speculations about a "rapture" of later believers.

What must take place after this: The same phrase as in the 1:1 title of the book, referring to its contents as a whole. Like the reference to the **first voice,** this connects the vision to follow with the initial revelation.

4:2 I was in the Spirit: See on 1:10. **There in heaven stood a throne:** As in the Old Testament, the picture of the heavenly world is modeled on that of an earthly monarch, where the king or queen is surrounded by assistants and courtiers. The monarch delegates authority to subordinate officials, who are responsible to the absolute ruler. This idea was elaborated in nonbiblical apocalyptic (e.g., *1 Enoch*), which explained that some of the subordinate angels exceeded their authority, overdid the punishment that God had decreed

for his people, and they themselves would be punished at the final judgment, an idea reflected in some biblical documents (see Gen. 6:1–4; Deut. 32:8–9; 1 Pet. 3:18–20; 2 Pet. 2:4; Jude 6). The image is theologically helpful, for it affirms that God governs the universe, but is not directly responsible for everything that happens, and will finally settle all cosmic accounts with justice for all concerned. The Old Testament sometimes pictured God's governance of the universe as presiding over a divine council (Pss. 82:1–8; 89:7; Job 1:6; Dan. 7:9–10). To be a true prophet was sometimes portrayed as being caught up into the heavenly world and overhearing the divine decrees made in this heavenly council (1 Kgs. 22:1–28; Jer. 23:18). John's description is thus not merely the objective reporting of a personal experience, but reflects a long stream of biblical tradition.

One seated on the throne: John writes not to satisfy curiosity about "what heaven is like" but in response to the burning question in the churches of his time, "Who is in charge of the world?" To all appearances, the Roman Caesar ruled the world, and through the governmental machinery held the lives of Christians in his hand (see Pliny's *Letter to Trajan* in the introduction to Revelation). John gets a look behind the scenes, and reassures his readers that there is a mission control to the whole universe, and it is not vacant.

4:3 Around the throne is a rainbow: Unlike Ezek. 1 and Dan. 7, from which much of his imagery is drawn, John gives no description of the One on the throne. The reader gets the splendor of precious stones—**jasper and carnelian**—but no mental image to fill in the picture of God. This is finally done with the definitive image of the Lamb. The **rainbow** surrounding the throne is not mere decoration, but the sign of hope. After the destructive flood expressing the judgment of God against human sin, God placed the rainbow in the sky as the sign of God's covenant with all the earth (Gen. 9:13–16). All the terrors that unfold in Revelation are surrounded by this sign of the ultimate faithfulness of God to his creation.

4:4 Twenty-four thrones . . . twenty-four elders: individual elements of the heavenly court should not be "decoded" as though each "represents" one objective reality (see on symbolic language in the introduction to Revelation). Such language functions by evoking associations and meanings. While there were various series of twenty-four in the Old Testament, ancient Judaism, and the Hellenistic world, the only association John himself makes is the twelve tribes of Israel and the twelve apostles (21:12–14), i.e., the whole people of God, Old Testament and New Testament. Without claiming to explain, John's picture suggests that somehow the people of God on earth—Israel and the church—are not just earthly realities, but participate in the transcendent world (see on the "angels of the seven churches," 1:20, and the cosmic woman, 12:1–17). Like the church, these heavenly beings participate in God's rule (see on 1:9; 2:26). They have thrones and crowns, but they bow before the one Ruler of the universe and are "casting down their golden crowns beside the crystal sea" (4:10–11; see the Christian hymn "Holy, Holy, Holy," inspired by this scene). Like the church on earth, their essential role is worship. They present before God the prayers of the church on earth (5:8). Since in the Greek text the verbs are in the past and present until 4:10–11, where they shift to the future, John may be indicating that the heavenly worship of the full complement of the people of God still awaits its consummation.

4:5 Lightning, rumblings, peals of thunder: Often in Revelation, reflecting the manifestation and presence of God as originally on Mount Sinai (see Exod. 19:16–18). **Seven spirits of God:** See on 1:4.

4:6 Sea of glass, like crystal: See 15:2; Ezek. 1:22. Some biblical cosmology pictured a heavenly ocean as the source of rain, caused by opening the "windows of heaven," and an ocean under the earth, the source of rivers and springs (see Gen. 7:11). John has a theological point to make, not merely a cosmological description. The theme of this vision is God the Creator. In the Gen. 1 account of creation, God makes a habitable world by driving the waters back and creating space for human and animal life. This account reflects the ancient Near East mythology in which creation is the overcoming of the chaos monster represented by the sea. In this perspective, uncreation, disorder, always threatens the created order, and human life is always lived on the thin line between chaos and creation, so that sometimes chaos reinvades the created order and devastates it. John pictures the absolute victory and rule of God the Creator, who does not struggle with an implacable sea (monster). In this vision, the sea is no longer the enemy, but a good part of God's creation, as calm and beautiful as crystal (see Ps. 104, esp. vv. 24–26).

4:6–8 Four living creatures: God is the Creator of all life. The heavenly court includes not only representations of humanity, but creatures that combine wild and domestic animals, birds, and humans. Their description is a kaleidoscope of imagery from Ezek. 1 and Isa. 6. **Full of eyes all around and inside** is a reminder that Revelation's imagery cannot be represented graphically, even to the mind, but frustrates all attempts to picture what it is "really" like. This is John's way of saying that finite beings of this world "know in part and prophesy in part" (1 Cor. 13:9), that human language shatters on the effort to express the transcendent. And yet the imagery evokes the awareness of the all-seeing nature of the heavenly world.

Holy, holy, holy: From Isa. 6:3. "Holy" is not essentially a moral designation, but means "apart, different, special, other." When applied to God, it means that God is Other, not a part or aspect of the universe, but its Creator. The only response can be praise and adoration, not explanation. When the term "holy" is applied to human beings (as in 5:8; 8:3), usually translated "saints," it means "set apart for a special purpose." **Lord God the Almighty:** The emperor Domitian was signing his decrees with the title "Lord and God" and requiring that he be addressed as such. John pictures the only One whom Christians can address with these words. That God is praised as the Almighty does not mean that God possesses all the power there is, for other beings, human and demonic, also have power—good, bad, and indifferent. Rather, "Almighty" means that God is the Creator of all, that nothing is independent of God, that God prevails above all powers, that God never comes into a situation where he is finally defeated. As the Creator, God does not confront the world as though it were a given reality to which he must adjust. God the Creator can never be victimized by "nature" or "the way things are," for there are no "things" independent of God, and no things "are" independent of the One who says "I am" (Exod. 3:13–15). This was not apparent to John's beleaguered readers, just as it is not obvious to us. Thus John begins with a vision of God the Creator.

4:11 You are worthy: The word "worship" is derived from "worth-ship," in which the suffix "ship" denotes quality, state, rank (as in "fellowship," "scholarship," "kingship"). To worship God is to acknowledge God's worthiness, to acknowledge God as God and oneself as creature (see Ps. 100:3). Worship thus must be God-centered, directed to God. Authentic worship is not a matter of subjective feelings, or cultivating personal religious excitement, but of turning toward God in praise and thanksgiving. John pictures the church's worship as joining with the heavenly world representing all creation.

Revelation is thus dominated by this grand vision of the one God, the Creator. That *God is one* is the primary creed of Judaism and was adopted without qualification by Christianity (Deut. 6:4; see Mark 12:39, 32; Rom. 3:30; 1 Cor. 8:4). In the face of the radical evil in the world, it is not a casual confession. Some alternatives to monotheism are conceptually easier to affirm:

Evil is unreal. One way of handling the problem of evil is to affirm that there is really no evil, it is all a matter of perspective. There is only one God, this God is good and all powerful. Therefore whatever is, is good, and there can be no actual evil in the world. Revelation rejects this option in all its forms.

Atheism. If there is no God or gods, there is no problem of an almighty and loving God who rules a world in which babies are napalmed. In this view the reality of God cannot be combined with the reality of evil. Revelation rejects the atheistic option in all its forms.

Polytheism. If there are several gods, then ours may be the best and even the most powerful, but need not be charged with the evil in the world. He/she/it is struggling against evil like the rest of us. Though there are few explicit idolaters these days, there are many whose understanding of God is a functional polytheism. God is only one of the contending powers in the universe, "the Force," or some such. Some understandings of Christian theology have made Christ and the Spirit into separate deities, as though Jews and Muslims have only one God, but Christians have two or three, in effect a kind of polytheism. Trinitarian theology is not an expression of this option, but was developed to oppose it. Revelation rejects the polytheistic option in all its forms.

Dualism. This is a subheading of polytheism, but handles the problem by having only two powers that struggle against each other. The evil in the world can be attributed to the other power. Much popular talk of the devil is in this category. Revelation's theology includes an important role for the devil, but not as a separate god. Revelation utilizes the dualistic imagery of traditional apocalypti-

cism, but rejects an ultimate dualism in all its forms. On the language of demons, Satan, and exorcism, see the excursus at Mark 5:1.

Revelation, like the Bible in general, affirms the oneness of God as the Creator who is almighty and loving, without giving a coherent explanation of how this could be true, and lives with the consequences. This faith is oriented toward the ultimate future when God will be seen to be just, loving, and almighty, and is communicated in images rather than propositions, a form of reflection and communication that allows it to hold together conflicting views.

5:1–7
The Christological Redefinition
of Winning

The chapter division here is unfortunate, since chaps. 4 and 5 compose one scene.

5:1 A scroll written on the inside and on the back: The Greek word can refer to a codex (a book with leaves) or a roll. The subsequent imagery indicates a roll sealed in such a manner that when a seal is broken it can be unrolled partway and the contents of that part disclosed, then unsealed and disclosed until the whole scroll has been opened. The model for a scroll written on both sides (suggesting the fullness of its contents) is Ezek. 2:9–10. The scroll has several possible connotations: (1) the scroll of the law, which contains God's will and the judgments against those that violate it, an image corresponding to the elements in this vision that suggest a heavenly counterpart to the synagogue; (2) the book of the prophets, containing God's threats of future judgment and promises of future victory, sometimes portrayed as sealed up for a future day (Isa. 8:16; 29:11; Dan. 12:4); (3) the prophetic scroll given to Ezekiel, written like this one on both sides (Ezek. 2:10); (4) the heavenly tablets of destiny that contain the gods' decisions about the future, a motif of Babylonian religion often adopted in Jewish apocalyptic (e.g., *1 En.* 81:1–3); (5) the book of life, in which the redeemed are inscribed (Pss. 69:28; 139:16; *1 En.* 104:1; Luke 10:20; Phil. 4:3; Heb. 12:23; John makes use of this image in 3:5; 13:8; 17:8; and 21:27); (6) the heavenly books in which the deeds of human beings are recorded for future judgment (Dan. 7:10; 12:1; 2 Esd. 6:20; *1 En.* 47:1, *2 Bar.* 24:1; see Rev. 20:12, 15); (7) a last will and testament, normally sealed with seven seals; this document evoking the image of a will that is to be executed by being opened.

John's imagery is evocative, not code (see see introduction to Revelation). The scroll evokes a variety of images in the reader's imagination, but is not "really" any one of these. What is important is the function of the scroll in the vision, which is clear in the remainder of the book. As the scroll is opened one seal at a time, the final acts of history take place. These events are not arbitrary, but represent the will of God in bringing history to its conclusion as the triumph of God. The execution of this plan is in the hands of God as represented by the Lamb.

5:2 Who is worthy?: As in Isa. 6:8 and 1 Kgs. 22:20, the divine council is convened to seek someone to carry out God's purpose. The question echoes the acclamation of 4:11, in which God the Creator is worthy, though no part of creation is. The one who opens this scroll must somehow be identified with God himself. **To open the scroll:** Not just so that it can be read, but so that its contents, the will of God, can be implemented.

5:4 I began to weep: The imagery reflects Isa. 29:11. If God's will for the future is a sealed book, then all who pray for God's kingdom to come, God's will to be done on earth as it is in heaven, will join John in this weeping (see Ezek. 9; Matt. 5:4; 6:10).

5:5 The Lion of the tribe of Judah: See Gen. 49:9, interpreted as a prediction of the Messiah in first-century Judaism. **The root of David:** The mighty king God would send in the future is pictured as the shoot or branch of the Davidic tree that had been cut down (Isa. 11:1; Jer. 23:5; Rev. 22:16; see the frequent New Testament image of the Messiah as the "Son of David"; see on Luke 1:28–33; 3:23; 20:41–44; Acts 13:22–23). **Has conquered:** The Messiah was expected to establish God's reign of justice by the violent destruction of the unrighteous (see Isa. 11:2–9). It is a hope with which all the oppressed can resonate, for it seems so right.

5:6 I saw . . . a Lamb: The slot to be filled by the violent lionlike Messiah is filled with the Lamb who has been killed. He accomplished God's redemptive purpose not by killing others, but by being killed by them. This is why he is praised as worthy (5:9–10). This is perhaps the most mind-wrenching reversal of imagery in all literature, but it is simply a graphic way of expressing the basic Christian confession: Jesus is the Christ (better: the Christ is Jesus, the crucified and risen man of Nazareth—see on Mark 8:29; Acts 17:3; 18:5, 23).

The image of the lamb was used to interpret the meaning of the Christ event by several New Testament authors (John 1:29, 36; Acts 8:26–35; 1 Cor. 5:7; 1 Pet. 1:19), but more frequently in Revelation than any other New Testament book (twenty-eight references to Christ as the Lamb, plus 13:11 of the beast that imitates Christ). The image is derived from the Old Testament, where lambs are sacrificed as offerings for sin (Lev. 4:1–5:13), as an expression of communion and peace between human beings and between God and humanity (Exod. 29:38–46), as a means of liberation and a memorial of the achieved deliverance (the Passover lamb, Exod. 12:1–31, 43–49). The Suffering Servant of Isa. 53:1–12, through whom God accomplishes salvation, is pictured as a lamb.

The relation of Lion and Lamb has been (mis)handled several ways in Christian history:

"First the Lamb, then the Lion." The church has sometimes come to terms with these two pictures of the Messiah by speaking of Jesus' "first coming" as a lamb and his "second coming" as a lion. Those who do not respond to the love offered by Jesus in his first coming get the apocalyptic violence of the second. This is the polar opposite of the meaning of the text of Revelation, in which the lion image is reinterpreted and replaced by the Lamb. It represents a retrogression from a Christian understanding of the meaning of messiahship to the pre-Christian apocalyptic idea. In Revelation, the Lamb is the "slaughtered" Lamb, slain not only on the cross but on the transcendent altar. In Revelation the participle "slaughtered" is always in the perfect tense, representing the *continuing* effects of a once-for-all past act. Love was not a provisional strategy of the earthly Jesus, to be eventually replaced by transcendent, eschatological violence when "they've had their chance" and love has not "worked."

"Lamb to some, Lion to others." Another way of relating Lion and Lamb is to think of the Christ as having both lion and lamb aspects, for example, showing his lamb side to believers and reserving his lion nature for unbelievers. Again, there is no suggestion in Revelation of this parceling out of the Christ into part lion, part lamb.

"The Lamb is really a Lion." Another effort to come to terms with this imagery is to understand "Lamb" as simply another image for the power and violence of the Lion. Such interpreters could point to the **seven horns** as an indication of the Lamb's power, and to such phrases as "the wrath of the Lamb" (6:16). The

Lamb is indeed powerful, representing in fact the ultimate power of God. But Revelation is true to the New Testament in general in affirming that this power is not violence but love, and that it will finally prevail (= "conquer'").

"The Lion is really the Lamb, representing the ultimate power of God." This is the meaning of John's dramatic rebirth of images. The Lamb is indeed powerful, for as the Messiah he represents God, takes the scroll from his hand, and puts it into effect. Breaking the seals of the scroll does not mean merely making known but making effective. The Lamb has seven horns (fullness of power!) and seven eyes (fullness of insight!) and is thus the fulfillment of the hopes of the scion of David of Isa. 11.

In the center of the throne (NIV): This translation of the peculiar Greek expression (literally "in the midst of the throne") is better than the NRSV's attempt to make the scene more imaginable, "Between the throne and the four living creatures." While the image is strange, it is John's way of saying that the slain Lamb is identified with God, is the functional equivalent of God. This identification is not merely speculative theology, but is important for understanding the claim that "in Christ God was reconciling the world to himself" (2 Cor. 5:19). What God does for humanity through the Lamb is not a three-party transaction (God, Jesus, and humanity), but a two-party transaction: God and humanity. This is John's understanding, and is why his evocative images of God and Christ tend to fade into each other (see 3:21, where Christ shares God's throne, and 14:4; 22:1, 22; 22:3, where "God" and "Lamb" are functionally identified). The seven ascriptions of praise in 5:12 are usually reserved for God, but here addressed to the Lamb. The "seven eyes" of the Lamb (5:6) are the seven spirits *of God*. John wants his hearer-readers to grasp how close the relationship is between Christ, God, and the Spirit, to relate the living Christ to the Spirit who speaks in the churches, and to relate this Spirit to the crucified and exalted Christ. In Revelation, God finally conquers, prevails, "wins," but the meaning of "being a winner" has been radically redefined.

5:8–14
Universal Victory and Universal Praise

5:9 New song: See on 14:3.

5:13 Every creature: The victory is universal. Just as God is the Creator of all, so God is the Redeemer of all. Here is a grand vision of the whole creation joining in praise to God the Creator and God the Redeemer, the one God. It is a mistake to try to locate this chronologically or to try to harmonize it conceptually with other pictures in which God is the judge who finally separates the saved from the damned. The Bible contains both pictures of universal salvation such as this one, and pictures of a final separation, in which not everyone is saved (see excursus at 22:21). Yet as the reader proceeds through the book with its violent imagery of God's judgment, this vision should not be forgotten.

6:1–7:17
THE HEAVENLY WORSHIP:
OPENING THE SEALED SCROLL

When the Lamb opens each of the seals, horrifying events occur on earth. Those who interpret Revelation as predicting the long-range future have attempted to identify these with historical catastrophes, either those already past (various wars, earthquakes, and plagues) or those that are about to happen in the interpreter's own time (see "Four Main Types of Interpretation" in the introduction to Revelation). However, John is not predicting particular events that will occur generations or centuries later, but presenting images of the troubles the world will experience just before the return of Christ, which he sees as coming soon (see on 1:3). He thus places the troubles and persecution already being experienced by the church of his day in a meaningful context within the framework of God's plan for history.

The pattern of **seven seals** is constructed of 4 + 3 (so also the seven trumpets; see 8:2–9:21; 11:15–18). The first unit comprises the vision of the four horsemen, John's reconfiguration of the imagery of Zech. 1:7–11 and 6:1–8.

6:1–8
The First Four Seals:
The Four Horsemen of the Apocalypse

6:1 "Come!": This is an echo of the prayer of the church for the coming of Christ (22:17, 20), the longing for God to end the persecution and establish the final justice of the kingdom of God (see Matt. 5:4, 6; 6:10; 1 Cor. 6:22). The prayer is also represented in heaven, as the divine beings call out, "Come."

6:2 A white horse ... a crown ... conquering and to conquer: At first it appears that Christ appears in response to the church's prayer, for the first horseman resembles the figure of 19:11, who is certainly the returning Christ. Yet as the vision develops, it becomes clear that the rider is not Christ, but like the other horsemen brings only war and devastation to the earth. The story of Jesus is the model: just as the way to resurrection and exaltation was not an alternative to suffering and death, but went by way of the cross, so John's message is that the way to the final triumph of Christ and his disciples leads through the sufferings of the last days.

6:6 A quart of wheat for a day's pay: These are the inflated prices of famine, corresponding to the scarcity of grain in 90–91 CE. While the four horsemen are not predictions of particular events, they do seem to reflect features of the troubles and anxieties of John's own time that his readers would recognize. For example, a horseman on a white horse with a bow is characteristic of the mounted archers of the dreaded Parthians on the eastern edge of the empire, never subdued by the Romans, and feared by the Roman world as barbarians at the edges of civilization (see on 9:13–19).

Do not damage the olive oil and the wine: In 91–92 CE the emperor Domitian decreed that half the vines and olive trees in the empire should be cut down, apparently to encourage the raising of grain crops. This decree, which apparently was never carried out, caused great consternation in Asia Minor, where oil and wine were crucial elements of the economy.

6:7 A pale green horse: The final horseman representing **Death** and **Hades** is the color of sickness and death and sums up the meaning of all four horsemen: **to kill with sword, famine, pestilence** (plague), **and wild animals.**

John intends these pictures to have a threefold significance: (1) they are the prelude to the end, the final troubles the world must endure before the kingdom of God comes; (2) since John's churches are already suffering, their troubles are placed in a meaningful context as part of God's plan; and (3) they are intended to produce repentance among the peoples of the earth, to make clear that they are not in control of their own destinies, and to lead them to turn to God (9:20–21; 16:9)—though this does not happen.

6:9–11
The Fifth Seal: The Cry of the Martyrs

6:9 Under the altar: In biblical imagery the life of the person was thought to reside in the blood (e.g., Gen. 9:4; Lev. 17:11, 14; Jonah 1:14). The blood of sacrificial victims ran down to the base of the altar. Thus the "souls" (= lives, selves) have been sacrificed on the (heavenly)

altar. John's vision puts the death of Christians who have died for the faith in a meaningful context: it is a martyr death, sanctified on the heavenly altar (see on 11:3).

The souls of those who had been slaughtered: The vision is not intended to communicate objective data about "what happens after death." The Christian conviction that death is not the end but that the dead are in the hands of God is expressed in two basic pictures in the New Testament (see on Luke 20:27–40; Matt. 28:1): (1) At death the dead go to the grave, the world of the dead, but at the end of history God will raise them to eternal life. (2) The dead are taken directly and immediately into God's presence. This second picture requires thinking of the person as somehow alive apart from the body. Both pictures are used in Revelation, as by other New Testament writers. Neither picture is to be taken literally, and they are not to be combined or harmonized; each in its own way expresses the Christian hope of the gift of eternal life given by God. The "souls" are not some ghostly "part" of the person, but the persons themselves. While "soul" can sometimes mean the inner life of the person in contrast to the physical body (e.g., Matt. 10:28), in the Bible it often means simply "self," "person," as when we say, "I didn't see a soul" (see, e.g., 14:22; 2 Pet. 2:14; in Ezek. 18:4, 20 the same word is translated "soul" in the NIV but "person" in the NRSV).

6:10 How long?: Except for John's own words, this is the first human word recorded in Revelation. It reflects the language of the Psalms used in worship that call out for God to act, to remedy the injustice in the world (Pss. 6:3–4; 13:1–2; 35:17; 74:9–10; 79:5; 80:4; 89:6). It is not merely a cry for personal vengeance and has parallels in the teaching of Jesus (Luke 18:1–8).

6:11 A little longer: Another indication that Revelation expects the end to come soon (see on 1:3). Such words function not to give chronological information, but to provide encouragement to suffering people. **Until the number would be complete:** Such language portrays a set number of martyrs that must die before the end will come. It is not to be taken literally, but is a way of saying the present sufferings fit into God's plan, that things are not out of control. Even such apocalyptic plans are not unchangeable; it is the personal God who is in control, not a schedule that must be maintained (see Mark 13:20). John's vision does not promise that if Christians know how to pray, the persecution will go away. There will be many more martyrdoms before the end comes. He does not offer a superficial optimism, but the realism of the Christian hope.

6:12–17
The Sixth Seal:
The Cosmos Shakes at God's Approach

The progression moves from the historical catastrophes of war, famine, and plague (the first four seals) through persecution (the fifth seal) to the cosmic disintegration immediately prior to the end. As God prepares for the renewal of the cosmos, the present form of the world disintegrates (21:1; see Isa. 51:6; 65:17; 66:22; 1 Cor. 7:31). The pattern is typical of apocalyptic (see, e.g., Mark 13:3–8 [historical tragedies]; 9–23 [persecution]; 24–27 [cosmic dissolution]).

6:12–14 A great earthquake: John is not predicting earthquakes of the distant future. Asia Minor was prone to earthquakes; twelve cities had been leveled in 17 CE, and there had been many since—see commentary on 3:14. In the biblical world, earthquakes were not thought of as "natural" disasters, but the effect and sign of God's presence: the advent of God causes the earth to shake (see, e.g., Judg. 5:4–5; Ps. 18:6–7; Isa. 6:4). The imagery of darkened **sun**, bloody **moon**, falling **stars** and disappearing **sky** is a fusion of elements drawn from Isa. 13:10; 34:4; 50:3; Ezek. 26:15; 32:7–8; Amos 8:9; and Joel 2:31. Falling stars is not thought of in terms of modern astronomy, but refers to meteorites. The imagery is not peculiar to the Bible, but is typical of apocalyptic. See, e.g., *Testament of Moses* 10:5–6:

> The sun will not give light.
> And in darkness the horns of the moon
>   will flee.
> Yea, they will be broken in pieces.
> It will be turned wholly into blood.
> Yea, even the circles of the stars will be
>   thrown into disarray.

6:15 Everyone: The response to the collapse of the cosmos is fear and consternation, as it is recognized as the approach of God and the final judgment. While Revelation is a document opposing all forms of human oppression in the name of the final justice of God, it is not merely a document advocating the rights of the poor against the rich and the slaves against their masters. Both rich and poor, both slave and free, tremble before God's coming judgment, which is universal.

6:16–17 The one seated on the throne and from the wrath of the Lamb: The two figures repre-

sent the one God (see on 1:8; 4:11). Thus **their wrath** is in some manuscripts **his wrath**, which is more likely original, the figures of God and Christ being collapsed into one. **Who is able to stand?** The implied answer is "no one," but the agonized question sets the stage for the vision of chap. 7, in which the answer is given.

EXCURSUS:
INTERPRETING REVELATION'S
VIOLENT IMAGERY

Not only are mind and imagination overwhelmed by the quantity and unrelenting intensity of the violence that is perpetrated against both humans and the cosmos itself; the theological problem is compounded by the fact that the source of violence is God and the Lamb, sometimes invoked with cries for vengeance. This whole range of imagery has posed a severe problem for interpreting Revelation as a Christian book, particularly when compared with the portrayals of Jesus in the Gospels. The picture of sinners being tormented forever in the presence of the Lamb (14:10) seems to present a different world from the picture of the Jesus who prays for his tormentors and teaches his disciples to do the same (Luke 23:34; Matt. 5:43–44). The following observations, perspectives, and principles may be found helpful in interpreting the violent/ "vindictive" language of Revelation.

1. The Givenness of John's Situation of Suffering

John's thought began not with visions about future suffering, but with the fact of suffering in his own present. Apocalyptic thought gives experienced suffering a meaning by placing it in a cosmic context, functioning as an interpretation of the present, not speculation about the future. As illustrated by Israel's imprecatory psalms (Pss. 35; 55; 69; 109; 137), a community that feels itself pushed to the edge of society and the edges of its own endurance will, in its worship, give vent to the natural feelings of resentment, even revenge, as it anticipates the eschatological turning of the tables. Even then, cries for "revenge" are not personal, but a plea for the justice of God to be manifest publicly.

2. John's Appropriation of Tradition

John did not devise this violent language and imagery himself. In both form and content, most of it was adopted and adapted by him from his Bible and his Jewish and Christian tradition.

  a. *The Ancient Near Eastern Combat Myth.* In the background of much of the religious imagery that pervaded John's world was the mythical story of creation in which the chaos monster (the Sea, Tiamat, Lotan [= Leviathan], etc.) was subdued and held at bay at creation, but was still there at the "edges" of the secure created world, still threatening and disrupting the ordered creation. The evil of the present world is understood as the remnants of uncreation, so that the present world has a built-in tension. There will be a final abolition of the uncreation, and a new creation will emerge. But just before the final victory of the Creator, the forces of chaos will make a final reassertion of their threat, causing great havoc to the creation before chaos is finally destroyed forever. The portrayal of this final victory includes pictures of violence.

b. *The Apocalyptic Scheme of the "Messianic Woes."* Jewish apocalyptic developed a "standard" pattern that interpreted the present troubles of the faithful community as the leading edge of the period of suffering that must come just before the final victory, just as labor pains precede birth. John's theology was worked out within the framework of traditional apocalyptic thought, which included the "messianic woes" as an integral part of the plot. John takes over this language, including its macabre details. For instance, the image of horses wading up to their bridles in blood (Rev. 14:19–20) was not originated by John, but was already a proverbial picture of the woes of the last days (*1 En.* 100:3; see 2 Esd. 15:35–36). The world heaves and groans in labor pains as it brings forth the Messiah and the new age. The terrible period of suffering is not the last word, but the harbinger of good news. It is in this sense that the announcement of the coming violence of God's judgment can be called "good news" in 14:6–7.

c. *The Language of Scripture.* Almost everything in the violent pictures of the seals, trumpets, and bowls of chaps. 6–19 is derived from biblical pictures and is described in biblical language. The language and imagery of the exodus naturally becomes John's means of expression of the eschatological deliverance from the contemporary (Roman) "Pharaoh." By labeling the eschatological disasters "plagues" (15:6), which God will visit on the arrogance of the contemporary "Pharaoh"/"Egypt" before the evil empire will "let my people go," he interprets the present Roman pressures and their anticipated intensification as an extension of the biblical story into his churches' own experience.

The terminology of God's "wrath" (6:16–17; 11:18; 14:10; 16:19; 19:15) is not John's creation, but a dimension of a deep stream of biblical theology (only a sampling, including the great prophets

of Israel, the Gospels, and Paul: Exod. 22:21–24; Deut. 9:7–8; Pss. 2:5; 78:21–22; 90:7–9; Isa. 1:24; 9:19; 13:9, 13; 51:17, 22; Jer. 4:4; 10:10, 25; 25:15; Ezek. 7:8, 12; 13:13; 20:8, 13; Hos. 5:10; 13:11; Mic. 5:15; Matt. 3:7; John 3:36; Rom. 1:18 (!); 2:5; 5:9; 9:22; 12:19; 1 Thess. 1:10; 2:16; 5:9). The stream of biblical theology represented by these texts pictures not a petty deity overcome by emotional outbursts, but the relentless, inexorable punishment of sin by a God of justice.

The biblical prophets' woes against Babylon as the enemy of God's people (e.g., Isa. 13; Jer. 51:1–19) are transmuted into the eschatological woes against the "Babylon" of John's time. The source of John's language is not his bitterness against his oppressors, but his Bible. Again, imagery from the imprecatory psalms is used in portraying God's wrath against the contemporary embodiment of evil (Ps. 69:24/Rev. 16:1).

John also makes extensive use of the theophany language of his Scripture. Some of the imagery, e.g., earthquakes, hail, is intended to communicate not the punishment of humanity, but the awesome glory accompanying the appearance of God. It is not punishment language, but theophany language: the earth reels because it cannot *stand* in the presence of God. (See such scenes as 8:7 and 11:19, and see Exod. 9:23–25; 19:18–19; Judg. 5:4–5; 1 Kgs. 19:11–13; Pss. 18:7–15; 29:3–9; Ezek. 38:22; Joel 3:16.)

The other side of this is to show human dependence; water, sun, etc., are not under human control. As human beings, we live in Somebody Else's world, and this truth is eschatologically demonstrated, i.e., *pictured* for us. In the portrayals of the terrors of earthquake, plague, and other catastrophes that afflict the cosmos just before the final victory, the community confesses its faith that it does not control the universe and its destiny, but acknowledges that that destiny is in the hands of an indescribably awesome power over which we have no control. *This,* and not the fate of those portrayed as suffering the final woes and its justice or injustice, is the "point" of such imagery—as in Exodus and the Psalter!

3. John's Use of Language

a. *Visionary/metaphorical.* None of the violence in the scenes of chaps. 6–16 is literal violence against the real world; it is violence in a visionary scene of the future, expressed in metaphorical language (9:7!). The bloody hail and fire launched from heaven against the earth (8:7) are pictures of something, and something terrible, and though not "just" pictures, they are still pictures. The sword and fire by which the evil of the earth is judged (and even "tormented") are not literal swords and fire, but metaphors for the cutting, searing *word* (1:16; 11:5).

b. *Confessional language*. John's imagery portraying violent judgment upon God's enemies is the insider language of the confessing community that expresses their praise and gratitude for salvation, not objectifying language, (on "objectifying language" see on Matt. 2:16; Acts 1:9). The language of worship and prayer is not objectifying description of the fate of outsiders, but the confession of faith of insiders.

The language of the plague stories of Exodus, one of the quarries from which John hews his own imagery, is confessional language glorifying God's deliverance of Israel. It does not function to make statements about God's lack of care for the Egyptian mothers who mourn the loss of their firstborn sons, and God's care for the children themselves. The story is told from inside the faith of the confessing community and makes its "point" from this one perspective. To misconstrue such language as making objective statements about the fate of the Egyptians, from which inferences about the character of God could be drawn, is to misconstrue the genre of the language.

Psalm 91:1–8 is one of many examples of the Bible's confessional language of the worshiping community:

You who dwell in the shelter of the
   Most High,
who abide in the shadow of the Almighty,
will say to the LORD, "My refuge and
   my fortress;
my God, in whom I trust."
For he will deliver you from the snare of
   the fowler
and from the deadly pestilence;
he will cover you with his pinions,
and under his wings you will find refuge;
his faithfulness is a shield and buckler.
You will not fear the terror of the night,
or the arrow that flies by day,
or the pestilence that stalks in darkness,
or the destruction that wastes at noonday.
*A thousand may fall at your side,
ten thousand at your right hand;
but it will not come near you.*
You will only look with your eyes
and see the punishment of the wicked.

We rightly read such words as expressing a profound faith in God's protection and care, and do not ask about the ten thousand that are incidentally mentioned. Such language is noninferential;

it does not presuppose a logical system within which inferences about the fate of the ten thousand that fall at your right hand can be made. Such language functions to make only one "point"—God's protective care for the confessing worshiper. It must never be forgotten that Revelation was written to be read in a service of prayer and praise of worshiping congregations, and is expressed in language that functions within that context.

That Revelation was intended to be read in worship, all at one sitting, also helps appropriate its violent imagery properly. As when watching a violent movie that "turns out right in the end," the violent scenes are not dwelt on as something significant in themselves. The hearer/viewer is taken in a relatively short time from the vision of the Creator God who holds all things in his hand (chaps. 4–5) through the terrors that precede the end (chaps. 6–18) to the dramatic victory at the coming of God's kingdom (chaps. 19–22).

4. John's Theology and Purpose

a. *Sin, Repentance, Judgment.* The violent imagery repeatedly expresses John's conviction of universal human sinfulness. As in the plagues of the exodus story, events intended by God to call people to repentance (see 11:13) serve only to reveal how hardened are their hearts (9:20). Like Paul's, John's theology, too, assumes that Christians, insiders, are also sinners (1:5). John does not picture innocent or self-righteous Christians suffering at the hands of sinful Romans, but sinful humans reeling under the judgment of the holy God. The catastrophes are not simply terrible, tragic events—they are repeatedly placed in the category of God's judgments: 6:10; 11:18; 14:7; 16:5, 7; 17:1; 18:8, 10, 20; 19:2, 11; 20:12, 13. The eschatological terrors are therefore an expression of John's sense of justice. Considering the situation, this is done in a remarkably nonsmug manner. The us/them mentality, while present, is not absolute: *we* are also judged as sinners; *they* are not excluded from salvation.

b. *Christological Transformation of Traditional Imagery.* The traditional imagery of apocalyptic terror is adopted and used by John, but like everything else in his revelation it is transformed within his christological perspective. The imagery of the lion is still used, but the Messiah is the slain Lamb. In mathematics when one changes the valence of the sign outside the parentheses, the formulae within the parentheses are retained, but all their values are reversed. So in Revelation the same imagery is used, but its valence is changed.

Every event of apocalyptic violence in chaps. 6–19 must be seen as *derived from* the scene of chaps. 4–5. This means that *all* of chaps. 6–19 transpires from the hand of the Lamb. These texts must be read only in relation to the love that sacrifices itself even for those who reject it. The *Lamb* is the controlling image throughout. The Messiah is still clothed in the bloody garments of the eschatological victory (19:13), but the blood is his own (1:5). The scenes are scenes of "wrath," but it is the "wrath of the Lamb" (6:16). Death and Hades still rampage through the final scenes (6:7–8), but the Messiah holds the keys to Death and Hades (1:18) and will finally cast them—and not their victims—into the lake of fire (20:14).

c. *Universal Salvation.* The violent imagery is presented within a Revelation that also has scenes of universal salvation (see on 22:21). The world not only reels under the hammer blows of God's wrath; it is also redeemed and released from the power of Satan (20:1–6). The kings of the earth are not only destroyed and their flesh eaten by vultures (19:17–21); they are also redeemed and make their contribution to the new Jerusalem (21:24–26). Revelation does not advocate a theology of revenge or resentment, but a theology of justice.

The above perspectives may permit the aweful imagery of Revelation's eschatological woes to appear in a new light. This is intended not to "water down" the terror of their imagery, but to allow it to function in its full force.

7:1–17
Interlude: The Church Militant
and Triumphant

One expects the series of eschatological woes to proceed, but before the final seal is opened, the scene shifts to characterize the people of God and to answer the question "Who is able to stand?" (6:17).

7:1–8 *The Church Militant*

7:1 Four angels standing at the four corners of the earth: A good example of John expressing his faith within his own worldview, a flat earth with four corners. No one (except perhaps members of The Flat Earth Society) insists on taking this literally. The modern reader understands that John means "the whole earth" and is untroubled by John's mistaken view of the shape of the earth. The same procedure is to be used in interpreting other aspects of John's worldview (see excursus at 1:3, on interpreting John's view of the "near end").

John sees devastating, worldwide winds threatening the earth, and pauses to character-

ize the people of God who will be able to endure the eschatological terrors. The Christians in the tiny, threatened churches in Asia needed a vision of the kind of community to which they belonged. Instead of giving a "doctrine of the church," John's vision evokes in their imaginations several images that help them understand what it means to say, "I belong to the church."

7:3 The servants of our God: Literally "slaves." They have been ransomed (bought) by the blood of Christ (5:9), and owe their new master obedience. **A seal on their foreheads:** Slaves were sometimes "sealed," i.e., marked with a brand or tattoo to identify them as belonging to their master. The image has other connotations: In Ezek. 9:4, from which John draws it, the seal is given to the faithful remnant of God's people, who lament the evils that are committed within the holy city by those who claim to be God's people. In the Pauline churches of Asia from which John draws some traditions, incorporation into the body of Christ by baptism (1 Cor. 12:13) was sometimes pictured as the seal that stamped the new Christian as belonging to God (2 Cor. 1:22; Eph. 1:13; 4:30). In the midst of the Roman threat, baptism comes to have a new meaning: those who bear the mark of God are kept through (not from!) the coming great ordeal, whatever the beastly powers of evil may be able to do to them (see 9:4). John has woven yet another meaning into the image of the seal. He has not yet specifically mentioned the "beast," one of his primary symbols for the persecuting power of Rome (11:7; 13:1–18; 14:9–11; 17:3–17; 19:19–20; 20:4, 10). This "beast" will also give his followers a special mark on their foreheads (13:16–17; 14:9), but this will only be a pale counterfeit of the mark Christ has already given his followers.

7:4 The number of those who were sealed, one hundred forty-four thousand: It is a large number. The church was a small community in the Mediterranean world (see statistics at 2:9 above). Each "congregation" would have been only a handful of people gathered to worship and to wonder what to do in the face of the Roman harassment. While 144,000 seems like a relatively small number from our perspective, the first impression it would have made on John's hearers is that "we belong to something big." John resists the temptation to think of those who are being obedient by holding fast to their faith as the "faithful few."

The number is not only large, it represents wholeness, completion. The number is not found in the Old Testament or elsewhere in Jewish apocalyptic, but is John's own composition: 12 × 12 × 1000. Like the combination of twelves in 21:12–14, it apparently represents the whole people of God, twelve tribes of Israel and twelve apostles.

"Twelve" is the number of Israel, and connotes the Christian community as the continuation of Israel, the Old Testament people of God (see Acts 15:14–18; Rom. 11:17–24; Gal. 6:16; Phil. 3:3; Jas. 1:1; 1 Pet. 1:1; 2:9). Because of deportation and exile, the twelve tribes no longer existed in John's day (Jer. 16:10–15; 2 Kgs. 17; Ezek. 47:13–48:29), but the Jewish hope was that Israel would be restored to its wholeness in the messianic age. "Thousand" is not merely a statistic but has a military connotation, a division of the army. The phrase "the thousands of Israel" is used of Israel's army and has the same ring to it as "the battalions of Israel" (see Num. 31:14, 48; Deut. 1:15; 1 Sam 8:12; 22:7; 2 Sam. 18:1, 4). John uses much battle imagery, transformed by the paradigmatic symbol of the Lion who has become the Lamb. He here pictures the church in its aspect of earthly struggle, the "church militant," as though drawn up in battle array to face its spiritual enemies (see Eph. 6:10–17).

7:5–8 Judah . . . Benjamin: A variety of lists of the twelve tribes exists in the Old Testament (Gen. 35:22–26; 46:8–27; Exod. 1:2–4; Num. 1:4–15; 13:4–16) and Jewish literature, differing in both contents and order. John's own list corresponds with no known list, omitting the tribe of Dan and including both Joseph and Manasseh, though Manasseh was part of the tribe of Joseph. All this shows that the exact "personnel" of Israel was not important either for the Old Testament or for John, but that twelve symbolized "all Israel" (on the symbolism of the "twelve apostles" and the varying lists, see on Matt. 10:1–5).

7:9–17 The Church Triumphant

7:9 A great multitude that no one could count: This is often seen as a separate vision, as though John had seen two groups, that of vv. 4–8 and that of vv. 9–17, sometimes interpreted as Jewish Christians and Gentile Christians. It is better to see this as the continuing portrayal of the one church of God, characterized in two different ways: the first group is on earth, marked, embattled, limited in numbers and religious/ethnic identification. The second group is in heaven, unmarked, at peace, and unlimited either in size or religious/

ethnic identification. But this group too stands in the tradition of those who by faith are "children of Abraham" (Gal. 3:7, 29), for the two key aspects of the promise to Abraham and Sarah was that their descendants would be innumerable and international (Gen. 12:1–3; 15:5–6; 17:5–8). It is too mechanical and code-like to make one Jewish Christians and the other Gentile Christians, or the one church now and the other the church later. The people of God are to be thought of both ways, though they resist conceptual clarity. To belong to the people of God is to belong to a specific, embattled group, but also to belong to that innumerable host that gathers around the throne of God in gratitude and praise.

It is significant that the first group, the 144,000, is only announced, not actually seen. It represents the more traditional understanding of the people of God as a distinct, sealed, group of a particular number. But just as the messianic Lion is announced, but the messianic Lamb is what appears (5:1–7), so the limited, distinct group of "Israel" is announced, but what appears is the unlimited, uncountable multitude of all nations. Here is a vision of the people of God that makes contact with and affirms its limited, particular nature, but is then transformed into the unlimited universal community of those who celebrate God's grace.

Palm branches in their hands: A sign of victory. Although the church is embattled with a hostile culture, it already celebrates the victory of God (see on 12:10–12). The innumerable host is pictured as martyrs, but this does not mean that nonmartyrs are not there. While John did expect that faithful Christians in his situation would be martyred, the point is that the church as such is a martyr church.

7:10 Salvation belongs to our God: The word translated "salvation" in this context is better translated "victory" (as 12:10; 19:1). "Salvation to our God" is not a descriptive statement, but an acclamation of praise, like "Hail to thee," or "Thine is the kingdom, and the power, and the glory," which concludes the Lord's Prayer (Matt. 6:13 KJV). It is the language of confession and worship, not the language of description.

7:13 Who are these? . . . those who have come out of the great ordeal: They have been preserved through the persecution not by escaping death, but by being victorious over it. As in 6:9–11, those who have "conquered" are dressed in the **white robes** of the victors; as there, martyrdom is seen only from its heavenward side. Again, they have "won" only from the heavenly perspective of the Lamb's redefinition of winning; on earth they have been killed.

7:14–17 Washed their robes and made them white in the blood of the Lamb: The description strains language to the breaking point. John's mind-jarring rebirth of imagery continues in paradoxical juxtapositions and deformation of language. The victorious martyrs celebrate before God's throne not because of their own achievement in shedding their own blood, but because of the blood of the Lamb, i.e., the death of Jesus. The **Lamb** is their **shepherd,** and is at the **center of the throne** (see on 5:6). He occupies the place of God and functions as God, and God-language is used of him. The Lord who is our shepherd (Ps. 23:1) is the one definitively revealed in Jesus Christ. At the heart of the universe, at the center of the throne, is the God revealed in the Lamb.

Day and night within his temple: Like the heavenly beings of 4:8, the victorious martyr church joins in continuous, unceasing worship. The scene portrays the final destiny of God's people, in which **God will wipe away every tear** and there will no longer be **hunger or thirst or** pain (see 21:4). It is pointless to ask whether heaven has day and night (21:24), or whether this scene is prior to the final salvation in which there is no temple (21:21). Each of such "conflicting" pictures has its own message and is not to be systematically "harmonized" with other pictures of eschatological salvation (see on 3:21; 19:11–22:5).

8:1–11:19
THE HEAVENLY WORSHIP:
SOUNDING THE SEVEN TRUMPETS

8:1–5
The Prayers of the Church
in the Heavenly Worship

After the intensifying crescendo of the opening of the first six seals and the sealing of God's people, the reader expects the final end. Instead, as the seventh seal is opened, there is a deafening prolonged silence. In some apocalyptic traditions the cosmos returns to its primeval silence just before the end. In Zeph. 1:7 and Zech. 2:13 silence is the prelude to the divine epiphany. Silence was also a ritual prelude to prayer, both among the Greeks and in the Jerusalem temple, just preceding the incense offering. John may also include the silence here for a literary and dramatic purpose.

Great music has rests as well as trumpets and cymbals, and the hearer/readers need a silent pause before the imagery continues.

Before proceeding with his visions of disaster, John sets the whole in the context of heavenly worship. The "book" of Revelation was composed to be read aloud in a worship service of prayer and praise. The struggling church on earth knows that it prays; during the hard times of persecution it may wonder what happens to its prayers. John's revelation lets the worshiping church see its prayer from the heavenward side. As the incense ascends before the heavenly throne, the distressed Christians on earth recognize their own prayers. This has the effect of revealing the earthly church as participating in the worship of heaven, and creating one continuous community embracing the heavenly temple and the struggling churches of Asia. This is John's apocalyptic pictorial version of the communion of saints. Through its worship and prayer, the church is intimately linked with the real world, the world of God.

The prayers are heard, i.e., they have an effect. The effect is not merely a subjective release in the worshiper, but the prayers of the saints on earth cause things to happen on earth (8:4–5; see 9:13–14). The saints' prayers do not result in a deliverance from historical troubles, but the deliverance of the world and history by the eschatological appearance of God's kingdom. But the immediate result of their prayers is not the glorious coming of the kingdom—though that is the ultimate result—but the precipitation of the series of eschatological woes. The path to the kingdom goes through, not around, the woes of history.

Like the liturgy of the earthly temple, the worship in the heavenly court includes not only the burning of incense but the sounding of trumpets (2 Chr. 5:12–13). A number of other images had become associated with trumpets in Jewish tradition. They represented the call to festive assembly and battle, announced both warning and victory, were instrumental in the holy war in which God alone gave the victory, were sounded on New Year's Day and the accession of a king, and were an element in the sound and fury of the theophany (Exod. 19:16; Num. 10:2–10; Josh. 6:4; Ezek. 33:3; Amos 3:6; Joel 2:1, 15). The prophets thus easily adapted the image of sounding the trumpet for their pictures of the eschatological day of the Lord and the related motifs of assembly, battle, judgment, and the new order, with the result that the last trumpet(s) became a standard feature of the eschatological signs (Isa. 27:13; 1 Thess. 4:16; 1 Cor. 15:52; Matt. 24:31).

John sees the terrors to come as analogous to the plagues with which God struck Egypt in the exodus story, i.e., as the means of God's liberating act. While Exod. 7–12 recounts a series of ten plagues, John seems to reflect the tradition that there were seven plagues, found in Ps. 78:43–51 and Ps. 105:27–36. Points of contact with the Egyptian plagues are seen in the hail and fire of 8:7 (Exod. 9:23–25), the sea becoming blood in 8:8–9 (Exod. 7:20), the darkness of 8:12 (Exod. 10:21), and the locustlike beings of 9:1–12 (Exod. 10:12). Casting the imagery in the mold of the exodus story places it in the framework not only of judgment, but of God's liberating activity. Even the plagues can be seen as good news and endured, because the ultimate exodus is about to occur!

The plague imagery is transposed into a transcendent, mythological key and projected onto a cosmic screen in which not only are the Egyptian oppressors struck down within history, but all oppressive worldly powers are judged as history itself is brought to an end. The world itself has been corrupted by human sin (see Gen. 3:17–18; Isa. 24:4–6; Rom. 8:19–23), so not only human beings suffer in the eschatological plagues. The cosmos itself is struck, as the land (8:7), sea (8:8–9), rivers (8:10–11), and the heavenly bodies (8:12) experience the onslaughts of divine judgment.

8:2 The seven angels who stand before God: By John's time, in Jewish tradition there were seven archangels (see Tob. 12:15), and devout Jews knew their names (Uriel, Raphael, Raguel, Michael, Sariel, Gabriel, Remeiel), two of which are reflected in the Bible: Michael (Dan. 10:13, 21; 12:1; Jude 1:9; Rev. 12:7) and Gabriel (Dan. 8:16; 9:21; Luke 1:19, 26). Though the four living creatures and the twenty-four elders are portrayed as sitting, angels are always pictured as **standing,** the posture of reverence before God. Rabbinic tradition explained that they had no knees, since they always stood, apparently based on the phrase from Ezek. 1:7, "and their legs were straight." John utilizes this world of ideas in order to portray the execution of God's plan in bringing history to a conclusion, but is interested neither in the hierarchical structure of the heavenly court nor the names and physiognomy of angels.

Seven trumpets: The opening of the seventh seal turns out to be not the end, but another series of seven (like the first series, divided in the pattern of 4 + 3 [see on 6:1–17]). So also the seventh trumpet does not bring the absolute end, but opens the way to other series of sevens. This structure shows John's literary

craftsmanship and communications strategy. John has much more to say to the reader, but instead of announcing an unmanageable and forbidding twenty-one or twenty-eight items in advance, he announces the symbolic seven, with the "final" one opening into a new series.

8:3 Prayers of all the saints: On **saints,** see 4:8. On the relation of the church's prayers to God's final judgments, see on 6:9–10. On the relation of prayer and incense, see Ps. 141:2; Luke 1:9–11.

8:6–13
The First Four Trumpets:
The Final Troubles Intensify

8:7 Hail and fire mixed with blood: John reflects not only biblical imagery (Exod. 9:23–25; Ezek. 3:22; Joel 2:30–31), but Greek and Roman traditions also were familiar with the portent of blood raining from heaven. **All green grass was burned up:** See 9:4, where the grass is still there. One should not imagine that it has regrown in the time between chaps. 8 and 9, but that John uses differing pictures without being concerned to harmonize them (see on 3:12; 7:16).

8:8 A great mountain, burning with fire: The imagery may reflect the eruption of Vesuvius on the west coast of Italy on 24 August 79, about sixteen years before John writes. John magnifies the familiar imagery to planetary proportions.

8:11 Wormwood: Literally absinthe, a bitter herb used for medicine and for flavoring drinks. In Jer. 9:15; 23:15 it is a prophetic symbol of judgment.

8:12 A third of the sun was struck . . . the moon . . . the stars: As in the sequence of seals, the destructiveness progresses to cosmic proportions. John is not picturing the diminishing of the intensity of the light of the heavenly luminaries, but seems to imagine the heavenly lights to be like torches that normally burn a certain length of time, which is here reduced by a third, thus making the days and nights one-third shorter.

8:13 Woe, woe, woe: The 4 + 3 pattern (see on 6:1–17) here results in each of the last three trumpets being identified as a "woe" (see 9:12; 11:14). A woe in biblical tradition is a prophetic pronouncement of the coming judgment of God, a form also used by Jesus in the Gospels (see, e.g., Isa. 3:9, 11; Jer. 23:1; Ezek. 24:6, 9; Matt. 11:21; 18:7; 23:13, 15, 16, 23, 25, 27, 29; Luke 6:24–26). The fifth trumpet is the first woe (see 9:12); the sixth trumpet is the second woe (see 11:14); the third woe is not specified, but see 12:12.

9:1–12
The Fifth Trumpet/The First Woe: Swarms of Demon Locusts

This vision does not literally correspond to any event in John's past, present, or future. With a montage of images from mythology and tradition, he bombards the hearer-readers' imaginations with yet another evocative image of eschatological calamity.

9:1 I saw a star that had fallen: The stars were personified as deities in ancient paganism and were sometimes identified with angels in the Old Testament and in Jewish tradition (e.g., Job 38:7; *Testament of Solomon* 8).

9:2 The shaft of the bottomless pit: See 20:1. In both places the cosmos is thought of as having three layers, heaven/earth/under the earth (see on 4:1). The earth is protected as long as the shaft to the abyss is kept shut. Only God has the key. But here God allows the demonic powers to torment the world in the last time before the end.

9:3 From the smoke came locusts: The terror of the locust plague, still known in Africa and the eastern Mediterranean, becomes in John's imagination the this-worldly launching pad for his portrayal of the demonic terror of the eschaton. John reflects the shifting of the imagery of the locust plague from the historical to the transcendent mythological plane that had already occurred in Joel 1–2. This-worldly locusts devour vegetation but do not harm humans. The locusts of John's vision disregard vegetation and attack human beings. This-worldly locusts proverbially have no king (Prov. 30:27). In 9:11, the "angel of the bottomless pit" is called *basileus* ("king"), used also for the Roman emperor (thus the Jerusalem Bible translates "their Emperor, the angel of the abyss"). He is also called "Apollyon," a pun for "Apollo," the divine name the emperor Domitian liked to use for himself. Nero also claimed to have a special connection with Apollo, and Domitian is pictured by John as the return of Nero (see on 13:1–4). Further, the locust was the symbol for the god Apollo. Typical for John, the imagery here is not consistent as in a system of codelike symbols—Rome is both subject to the divine judgment and demonic instrument of the divine judgment. Through (but not from!) it all, those who bear God's mark are preserved (9:4).

9:5 Allowed to torture them . . . but not to kill them: See Job 2:6, where Satan is allowed to torment Job but not to kill him. In both texts God is ultimately, but not directly, responsible for the troubles that test human beings. See on the picture of the divine administration of the universe at 4:2.

9:11 The angel of the bottomless pit: The vision concludes with the declaration that the demon-locusts are led by their "king/emperor," the angel of the abyss. Canaanite mythology knew the story of how one of the gods, Athtar the "Day Star" (Venus), had been proposed to take the place of Baal, but did not succeed and had to come down to earth, where he reigns as "god of it all." In Isa. 14:4–20 this mythical pattern is mockingly applied to the pretensions of the king of Babylon, who is pictured as aspiring to attain the divine throne, but instead was cast down to the pit of Sheol, the abode of the dead. In Isa. 14:12 the Babylonian king is taunted: "How you are fallen from heaven, O Day Star (*Hêlêl*, "Luminous," translated "Lucifer" in the KJV), son of Dawn (*Shahar*, the name of a Canaanite deity)." Although the myth originally and in Isa. 14:12 had nothing to do with the idea of Satan and the origin of evil, this connection was later made in (Jewish and) Christian tradition. In other Jewish adaptations of the myth, a whole order of angels came down from heaven and corrupted earth by teaching humanity various skills (such as writing!), but the good angels defeated them and imprisoned them in the abyss (see Gen. 6:1–4; 1 En. 6–10; 54; 2 Bar. 56). In various versions of the myth, evil angels were not destroyed, but placed in the pit for future judgment (2 Pet. 2:4). An additional apocalyptic motif was that the evil which is now restrained will experience a resurgence just before the end, will explode in one final futile paroxysm before being destroyed forever. John uses this general pattern in his apocalyptic understanding of history as a whole, particularly in his description of the final events in 19:11–20:15. The vision of 9:1–12 represents another example of John's adaptation of this myth. The evil powers now restrained in the abyss will be released just before the end. Before their own final destruction, they serve God's purpose by inflicting the eschatological plagues on the rebellious world. It should be noted, however, that John distinguishes the star/angel who descends from heaven in 9:1 from the angel who ascends from the pit in 9:11. John knows nothing of a myth of the origin of Satan as a fallen angel; "explanations" of this sort are found in extracanonical literature, but not in the Bible.

9:13–21
The Sixth Trumpet/The Second Woe:
Hordes of Demon Cavalry

9:13–21 The sixth trumpet: The second woe is an enormous horde of demon cavalry. As in the first seal (see on 6:2), John uses the almost paranoid Roman fear of the Parthian threat on the eastern boundary of the empire as the raw material for his vision of the final devastation before the end. The **bound** angels at the edge of John's world is another allusion to the mythical pattern of fallen angels discussed above. By picturing the incursion of the unimaginably vast army of demonic cavalry (200 million!) into the world of Western civilization as the result of releasing these angels, John again elevates a historical anxiety to the level of eschatological myth. The bizarre description of the horses is reminiscent of the Parthians, but they belong to the other, demonic world.

"Repentance" is a key word in this terrible scene (9:20–21; for meaning see on Luke 3:7–9). Despite the horrors of the last days, rebellious humanity does not **repent.** In the face of such suffering and the dramatic evidence that they are not in charge of the world, human beings, like the Pharaoh/Egyptians of the exodus story, do not repent but are only further confirmed in their rebellion (see Exod. 7–12, where repeatedly Pharaoh hardens his heart/God hardens Pharaoh's heart). Though attacked by beastly hordes, they continue to worship the demonic cultural images and to live by the ungodly values that result. The word "repent" calls a particular meaning to the mind of John's hearer-readers. If the situation and terminology described in Pliny's *Letter to Trajan* (see the introduction to Revelation) is also representative of John's time, "repent" meant from the Roman side the turning away from commitment to Christ as Lord in order to conform to the imperial cult. Just as faithful Christians refused to "repent" in the Roman sense, the Roman world refuses to repent in the Christian sense by turning away from the false values of their culture to worship the Creator.

The imagery of the trumpets in 8:1–9:21 would not have communicated predictions about future generations to the embattled readers of Asia at the end of the first century. The prophetic word they received would have communicated:

1. *The terror of history.* Though humans are not innocent of the tragedies of history, they are not finally in control. This awareness should lead people to repent, but it does not. Violence, even from God or demonic powers, does not change human hearts or accomplish the divine purpose.

2. *Worship as imperative.* Human beings are not complete and self-contained, but require something outside themselves to fulfill the meaning of their lives. To be human is to worship something or someone. "Worship God" is the one imperative of Revelation (19:10; 22:9). The visions show human resistance to this first commandment (Exod. 20:1–6).

3. *Worship related to ethics.* Those who worship God keep his commandments (9:21; 12:17; 14:12)

10:1–11:14
Interlude: The Church of
Prophets and Martyrs

*10:1–11 The Bittersweet Vocation
of Christian Prophecy*

The six angels have sounded six of the seven trumpets, and the reader anticipates the final trumpet that will signal the coming of the kingdom of God and the fulfillment of God's purpose for the creation (10:7; 11:15; see Matt. 24:31; 1 Cor. 15:22; 1 Thess. 4:16). But as there was a break between the sixth and seventh seals (7:1–17), so again the suspense is maintained—John is given two visions of the prophetic mission of the church before the final end comes.

10:1–3 Another mighty angel: The only previous "mighty angel" is that of 5:1, connected with the sealed book in the hand of God. **Wrapped in a cloud . . . rainbow over his head . . . face . . . like the sun . . . legs like pillars of fire . . . like a lion roaring:** The description combines features used elsewhere of God, Christ, and the revelatory angel (see 1:16; 4:3; Exod. 13:21; Job 37; Ps. 18:7–15; Dan. 12:7; Amos 3:8; Zech. 10:1). As in 1:1–2 and throughout Revelation, the images of God, Christ, and Spirit/angel collapse into each other. The ultimate Revealer is God, who defines and represents himself in Christ and communicates with the prophet by means of the angel. Although the figures are kept somewhat distinct, the imagery overlaps in such a way that God/Christ/angel are all presented to the mind's eye by the one picture. The **rainbow** is a reminder that though the revelation of God's truth will be bitter (10:10), it all stands under the sign of hope (see 4:3; Gen. 9:1–17).

A little scroll open in his hand: The contrast is not between "large" and "small," but between "sealed" and "open." The sealed scroll of God's purpose for the end time (Dan. 12:4, 9; Rev. 5:1) is no longer sealed. The Lamb has won the right to open it, and has done so (5:1–10; 6:1–8:1).

10:4 Seal up what the seven thunders have said: John prepares to write the visions of the seven thunders, just as he had written the visions of the seven seals and the seven trumpets, but he is forbidden to do so. Two complementary interpretations seem to be suggested by the context and John's theology:

1. As was the case with Paul, the claim to have some divinely inspired insights into God's purposes does not mean that the Christian prophet claims to know everything (14:3; 1 Cor. 13:12; see 2 Cor. 12:4; see Job 26:14). John acknowledges that his revelation is only fragmentary. His God is the God of Israel, who reveals what his people need to know in order to live faithfully before him, but does not deal in speculative revelations, so that he preserves the divine mystery (Deut. 29:29). In scene after scene John has testified that the sealed book of heavenly mystery (5:1) is now opened, but in this scene he hears a command to seal up divine truth with a seal that is *never* broken. John's claim to provide a revelation of Jesus Christ (1:1) does not include the claim to know everything, does not remove the distinction between divine knowledge and human ignorance and fallibility, even for a prophet who has toured heaven.

2. God interrupts the apocalyptic system of sevens and decides that there will be "no more delay" before the end, even though the traditional apocalyptic scheme of sevens might call for further disasters. This is like other New Testament apocalyptic (Mark 13:20) and in contrast to extrabiblical apocalyptic writings in which the apocalyptic system is more absolute than God, who has no choice but to follow it himself (2 Esdras). John does not present us with an enslavingly consistent logic or inexorable, impersonal fate, but a God who is free to revise the system en route. This is the God of the Hebrew Scriptures, who responds to his creation and even repents (Jer. 9:5; 18:8; Jonah 3:9). A person, not a cosmic computer, is seated on the throne of the universe.

10:6 No more delay: The connection of this scene with Dan. 12:1–10 is extremely important, for it is the key source for John's reformulation of Old Testament imagery. There a mighty angel speaks of a great tribulation to come, followed by resurrection and judgment, and commands that the revelation be sealed until the time of the end. Then two other angels appear, one on each bank of the stream (John's fluid imagery has one figure of cosmic proportions with one foot on the continent and one on the ocean). In the Old Testament scene, Daniel asks the poignant question of suffering apocalyptic communities, "How long?" The angelic figure raises both hands to heaven and swears by the eternal God that the end time period would be three and one-half years ("time, two times, and half a time," Dan. 12:7; see 7:25; 8:14, and the later recalculations in 12:11–12). This is the Danielic picture John receives from his Bible: mighty angels standing on water and dry land, arms uplifted, swearing by God, a long delay, a sealed book to be opened at the end time period of three and one-half years.

In the light of John's conviction that he lives in the eschatological time begun by the advent of the Christ, his inspired prophetic imagination reconfigures these elements into one dramatic picture of an angel with an *un*sealed book in one hand, and the other hand lifted up to heaven and swearing by the Creator that there will be no more delay. The time of waiting and hoping is over; the time of fulfillment already dawns. But before it arrives, there is the predawn darkness of the final tribulation, the "time of trouble such as never has been" of Dan. 12:1, that must be negotiated. John believes he and his churches are already entering into this final terrible period. The 1260 days that he derives from Scripture does not function for him as speculative prediction, but as encouragement: hold firm to your faith, because the tribulation will not last long!

10:7 The mystery of God: God's plan for history, not obvious to human understanding, requiring a revelation. **As he announced to his servants the prophets:** John believes the announcements of God's plan and purpose made by the Old Testament prophets are now being fulfilled. This view was especially prominent in the tradition of the Pauline churches John has inherited (see Rom. 16:25–26; Col. 1:26–27; Eph. 3:5, 9–10; see 2 Tim. 1:9–10; Titus 1:2–3; 1 Pet. 1:20).

10:10 Sweet as honey . . . my stomach was made bitter: John is not merely the spectator and reporter of this scene; he becomes a main character, for the opened book in the hand of the mighty angel is meant for him. He is commanded to take it and—not read, but—*eat* it! Again, what seems a bizarre incident is seen on closer reflection to be John's reimaging of biblical pictures. As a part of his call to be a prophet, Ezekiel was given a book of "lamentation, mourning, and woe" and told to "fill his stomach" with it (Ezek. 2:8–3:3). Ezekiel ate the book, which as word of the Lord was sweet as honey in his mouth (Ezek. 3:3; see Pss. 19:10; 119:103; Jer. 15:16). John sees himself as a prophet in this tradition. He is called to "devour" the book that contains the plan of God for his creation, the bittersweet message of judgment and salvation. Every person who struggles to preach and teach the word of God knows this taste, this satisfaction and this sickness in the stomach.

10:11 Prophesy again: John's prophetic call is renewed. **About many peoples:** The phrase is better translated **against many peoples.** See Ezek. 4:7; 6:12; Jer. 25:30, where the same Greek phrase is translated "prophesy against." John is not called to prophesy **about** future nations, but to speak **against** the idolatry of his own time and call his contemporaries to repentance.

11:1–14 The Prophethood of All Believers
In this vision the temple is measured, part of it is assigned to the nations who will trample on it, and God's two prophets are persecuted, killed, and vindicated. This section is dense with allusions from the Old Testament and earlier apocalyptic traditions. It is not to be "decoded," but does imaginatively place the experience of the church of John's day in the context of extravagant biblical imagery.

11:1–2 A measuring rod like a staff: The image is drawn from Ezek. 40:3, which introduces an elaborate section in which the dimensions of the renewed eschatological temple are given. **Measure the temple . . . and (count [NIV]) those who worship there:** As in Ezekiel, measuring here means marking for eschatological protection. Those outside will be subject to **the nations,** which in John's time meant to yield to the Roman authorities. Those inside are like the 144,000 sealed of 7:1–8, who are protected by God from the eschatological enemy. Yet here as there, it is necessary immediately to point out that being "sealed" or "measured" for God's protection does not mean that Christians will be shielded from suffering and death, but that they are stamped with the sign of God's security even if they have to die.

Since the temple had in fact been totally destroyed by the Romans in 70 CE, it did not exist in John's day. John here probably preserves a fragment of earlier prophecy delivered after the Romans had taken Jerusalem but before the temple was destroyed. We know from the Jewish historian Josephus that Jewish Zealot prophets encouraged the people by proclaiming that though the city and outer courts of the temple had been given over by God to the enemy, the inner court and those within it would be spared. This, of course, turned out to be mistaken, but John takes up this older prophecy and reinterprets it in his own sense, i.e., he uses it to communicate his own prophetic message.

11:3 My two witnesses authority to prophesy: The **two witnesses** are not particular individuals, but symbolize the prophetic ministry of the church during the time of threat and persecution. As a prophet, John belonged to a special group within the church (see the introduction to Revelation). Yet John is concerned to communicate that the prophetic ministry is not confined to persons like himself who receive dramatic revelations. While in the Old Testament only particular persons had the gift of prophecy, it already expressed the hope that the prophetic gift would be democratized, that the people of God as such would receive the prophetic gift (Num. 11:24–29; Joel 2:28–29). The early church believed that they were living in the time of the fulfillment of those hopes and promises, which they expressed in different ways: all members of the Christian community participate in the body of Christ and thus in the breath/Spirit that animates the body, and thus receive the gifts of the Spirit, including prophecy (1 Cor. 2:12–14; 12:4–13; 14:1–5; see Rom. 8:9–11; 12:6–8). All Christians receive the Spirit at baptism (Acts 2:38) and thus inherit the promise that the gift of prophecy will be distributed to the whole believing community (Acts 2:17–18, quoting Joel 2:28–29). After Jesus' departure the Paraclete/Spirit will continue to speak new truths in the name of Christ (John 14–16). John too believes that the Spirit that inspires prophecy functions within the whole Christian community, not individualistically in special persons such as himself. He can thus apply prophetic descriptions such as "servants" to Christians as such (see 1:1a, 1:1b; 2:20; 7:3; 10:7; 11:18; 15:3; 19:5; 22:6). In the vision of 11:1–13, John pictures the whole church in their role as the eschatological prophetic people of God; he affirms the "prophethood of all believers."

One thousand two hundred and sixty days: Although the symbolic connotations of this evocative picture are subtle and complex, the general picture is quite clear: pagans trod down the holy city for 1260 days, but the temple and those worshiping in it are spared. During this same 1260 days of the end time tribulation, the two witnesses, representing the church, exercise their prophetic ministry. They are killed by the powers of evil, but vindicated by God, who raises them and calls them into the courts of the heavenly temple.

The number, derived from Dan. 7:25; 12:7, can be expressed as three and a half years, forty-two months, or "a time, times, and half a time" (= a year, two years, and half a year). Under the influence of Daniel, it became the traditional standard period of eschatological threat, the short time just before the end in which evil is intensified before its final destruction by God (see on Luke 4:25; James 5:17). It is found elsewhere in Revelation at 12:6, 14; 13:5, and is reflected in the three and one-half days of 11:9, 11.

The two figures are "prophets" (11:10) whose ministry is "to prophesy" (11:3). This does not mean that they spent three and a half years making predictions; "prophesy" means "speak and act for God" (see the introduction to Revelation).

Witnesses: As prophets, their ministry is martyrdom. In John's context, martyrdom is not something additional to being a prophet, but is inherent in the prophetic role itself. By the first century, Jewish tradition had developed the idea that true prophets are those who suffer for their faith (Matt. 23:29–35; Acts 7:52; Heb. 11:32–38 reflect this development). It is important to understand these words in their biblical senses when interpreting Revelation. "Martyr" in our time is used in the vocabulary of international terrorism for suicidal fanatical devotees of political causes, and in popular psychology for persons of low self-esteem who invite or imagine persecution. "Witness" and "testimony" has in the jargon of pietistic Christians become synonymous with "relate my own personal religious experiences, telling 'what the Lord has done for me.'" Revelation's meaning is quite different. John makes extensive use of the martyr/witness word group, which derived from the courtroom. "Witness," "martyr," and "testimony" preserve their legal connotations and already have the overtones of holding fast to one's Christian convictions when tried before the pagan courts, even to the point of death, thereby giving testimony to the truth of the

Christian message. It means being willing to be killed by others as a witness to the truth of God, not killing oneself and others. In this sense Jesus was the prototypical martyr (1:5; 3:14; 22:20). Language about Jesus (and his martyrdom) is used interchangeably with language about Christians (and their martyrdom): 2:17/19:12; 2:17/3:12; 2:26–28; 3:21; 12:13/12:17.

The doctrine of God the Almighty affirmed throughout Revelation is also implicit in John's theology of martyrdom (1:8; 4:8; 11:17; 15:3; 16:7, 14; 19:6, 15; 21:22). A god who is only relatively stronger and better than we are, a god who is part of the world process and is himself subject to it, cannot ask for absolute commitment, nor can we give it. To give absolute loyalty to, i.e., to be willing to die for, that which is only relative is to make an idol of it, even if this idol be called "God." God's almightiness was not an item of doctrine for John, but the basis for his call to a commitment that might mean sacrificing life itself.

11:4 Two olive trees and two lampstands: These are examples of John's "prophetic" interpretation of the Old Testament (see v. 8). Joshua the priest and Zerubbabel the king of Zech. 4:1–14 are John's major source for the imagery in this vision. They represent the channels through which God's power becomes effective, and are thus appropriate symbols for the church. That the church is a community of "priests" and "kings," assuming the priestly-royal role of Israel (Exod. 19:6), is one of Revelation's themes throughout (1:6; 5:10; see 20:6). The witnesses are called "lampstands" (11:4), explained as "churches" in 1:20. From Isaiah (42:6; 49:6; 51:4) through the teaching of Jesus (Matt. 5:14) and Paul (1 Thess. 5:5; Phil. 2:15), the people of God are pictured as the bearers of God's light to the nations. When they are killed, people in every city gaze on the dead bodies of the witnesses (11:9)—this is a picture of the church scattered throughout the empire.

11:6 Authority to shut the sky . . . to strike the earth with every kind of plague: The two witnesses are pictured as the eschatological prophets Moses and Elijah. Some streams of Jewish tradition understood that before the Messiah and the end he brings could come, one or both of the two biblical prophetic figures who had not died but had been taken bodily to heaven must return to prepare the way for the coming of God or the Messiah at the end (Mal. 4:5–6; 2 Esd. 6:28). Though Moses' death is reported in Deut. 34:5, the indication in the next verse that God buried him secretly gave rise to the tradition common in the first century that he had not died but, like Elijah, had been taken directly to heaven. Early Christianity had to come to terms with the Jewish view that the eschatological times could not dawn until Moses and/or Elijah had returned, and did so in a variety of ways (Mark 9:2–13; Luke 1:15–17; 4:25–26; 7:11–17). *John meets this condition by casting the faithful church in the role of Elijah and Moses.* Like both Moses (in Jewish tradition) and Elijah (2 Kgs. 2:11), they are vindicated by God by being taken up to heaven. Like Moses (who was considered the prophet par excellence by first-century Judaism; see Deut. 18:15–18; 34:10–11; Hos. 12:13), the two martyr-prophets turn water to blood and strike the earth with every plague (11:6; see Exod. 7:17–19). Here once again the persecution and troubles of the end time are interpreted as God's latter-day "plagues" against the rebellious "Egyptians" (see v. 8—the persecution of Christians takes place in "Egypt"). Like Elijah they have power to shut the sky and stop the rain (1 Kgs. 17:1, see Jas. 5:17), and like Elijah send forth "fire" to destroy their enemies (2 Kgs. 1:10–12). Jesus' disciples had once mistakenly wanted to do the same to the Samaritans who rejected them (Luke 9:51–56), but were rebuked by Jesus, who simply absorbed and accepted their rejection. Likewise in Revelation, the "false prophet" who gets people to worship the beast mimics Elijah by making fire come down from heaven (13:13). In contrast, the two prophet-martyrs of 11:1–13, while they are cast in the role of Elijah and operate with the prophetic power of God, do not, Elijah-like, bring down fire from heaven. **Fire pours from their mouth** (v. 5), i.e., it is their powerful word of witness, a fulfillment of the promise to Jeremiah: "Behold, I am making my words in your mouth a fire, and this people wood, and the fire shall devour them" (5:14; this tradition was already applied to Elijah in Sir. 48:1). Just as their Lord's "terrible swift sword" of justice is the sword that proceeds from his mouth, his judging and purifying word (1:16; 2:12; 19:15), so the "fire" with which his servants "torment" (11:10) their oppressors is their unbearable word. Our society sometimes pretends not to believe in the power of words, but in our better moments we know that words can wound and kill, and that words can bind up wounds and restore life.

11:7 The beast that comes up from the bottomless pit: Mentioned here for the first time, receives a full treatment in chaps. 12–13. The beast opposes the witnesses, "conquers," them, i.e., kills them. To all ordinary observation, the "witnesses" have no power at all. What John has been describing is perceivable only to the eyes of faith. The faithful Christian martyrs/ witnesses are easily dispatched by the pagan courts. Yet they do not die without completing their testimony; their death is not a meaningless tragedy (see 12:11). John holds up an utterly realistic picture before the churches, who must decide how to respond to the Roman pressures: God will not intervene to deliver them; faithfulness does not deliver them from death, but causes it.

11:8 Prophetically called Sodom and Egypt: Sodom was proverbial as the evil city destroyed by God (Gen. 18–19; Isa. 3:9; Jer. 23:14; Amos 4:11; Matt. 11:23). Egypt was the oppressive power that had enslaved Israel (Exod. 1–12). Just as the two prophets are a symbol of the whole believing church, the holy city Jerusalem, killer of the prophets (Matt. 23:37) has become a symbol for the whole unbelieving world. The city is both judged and redeemed. God does not give up on even the worst unbelievers and abandon Jerusalem, but renews it (21:1–22:7).

11:11 The breath of life from God entered them: The Beast does not have the last word. At the end of the brief period of persecution, the same event happens as in Ezek. 37's picture of God's restoring his vanquished people, pictured as a "valley of dry bones" (John using Ezekiel again!): "the breath/spirit of life from God entered them, and they stood on their feet" (11:11; see Ezek. 37:5, 10). They hear exactly the same words addressed to John in 4:1, "Come up here," and ascend to heaven in the sight of all their enemies. The destiny of the prophets corresponds to that of Jesus; he suffered the Roman cross, but was vindicated by God. Here the "after three days" of Jesus' resurrection has been made analogous to the three and a half years of the final persecution. For the church, the experience of being called into God's heavenly world is no escapist "rapture"; in John's revelation Christians go to the presence of God through tribulation and martyrdom, not instead of it. In the present, the kingdom of God is hidden and ambiguous, but the eschatological day comes when it will be public and clear. John is already making the transition to his next scene, the last trumpet and coming of the kingdom.

11:13 The rest were terrified and gave glory to the God of heaven: The phrase means they repented, were converted (see 16:9). Usually in Revelation the eschatological terrors do not cause repentance, but only hardens the hearts of those who endure them (see 9:20). Here, most of the unbelieving world is converted to worship God, like the persecuting King Nebuchadnezzar of Dan. 4:34. John has both pictures, which he does not harmonize: eschatological judgment and eschatological salvation (see excursus at 22:21).

11:14 The second woe has passed: See on 8:13.

11:15–19
The Seventh Trumpet: The Kingdom Comes as Salvation and Woe

The last trumpet sounds, and the glad announcement is proclaimed in heaven that God, the rightful sovereign of the universe, has taken his power and begun to reign. On "kingdom of God," see on Luke 4:43–44. The word usually translated "kingdom" is an active noun, designating an action, not an object or territory: "kinging," "acting as king," "ruling," "rulership." The prayer "thy kingdom come" is the prayer for God, who is the sovereign of the universe, to exercise his power, put down the rebellious claimants to sovereignty over the world, vanquish all that opposes his will, and establish his gracious reign of justice over all his creation. It is a magnificent image, and John dares to announce that it will be fulfilled in reality. In John's vision of the future, his churches are allowed to hear the thanksgivings and praises that already echo through the heavenly world, and in their own worship can themselves already join in the celebration, even as they continue to pray, "Thy kingdom come."

11:15 Our Lord and his Messiah: Already in the Old Testament, God's rule is portrayed in this "double" manner (1 Sam. 12:3; Ps. 2:2). On Messiah/Christ, see on Mark 8:29. **He will reign:** The subject and verb are singular, though the rulership belongs to God and Christ. To ask whether the "he" refers to God or Christ is a false question (as in the "him" of John 3:16). As elsewhere in Revelation, the throne is shared by God and Christ (3:17; 12:5; 22:1, 3; see 5:13). This does not mean there are two eternal kings, but that the one God is represented by Christ, the two figures merge into the one God. The later Trinitarian theology attempted to set forth the pictorial language of the New Testament in more coherent propositional language (see on 1:4, 18; 4:11)

11:16 Twenty-four elders: See on 4:4, 10.

11:17 We give you thanks: Thanksgiving to the gods is rare in pagan religion, but is the basic

Christian posture, the essence of Christian worship, represented already in the heavenly world. Final salvation is celebrated not as an achievement by the believers, but in thanksgiving for God's act. **You ... who are and who were:** In this proleptic vision, God is praised as "the one who is" and "the one who was," but the customary third member of the formula, "the one who is to come" (1:4, 8; 4:8), is missing, because in the "now" of the vision, he *has* come.

11:18 Your wrath has come: There is also a dark side to the announcement. The coming of the final kingdom is also the coming of the last "woe" (see 8:13; 9:12; 11:14). The final picture of this series portrays not only the good news of the arrival of God's kingdom, it also announces wrath, the rage of nations, and the destruction of those who destroy the earth. John is not yet ready to give the full details of the final picture which he is withholding for the detailed visions of 19:1–22:5.

11:19 The ark of the covenant: Only one tantalizing glimpse, a detail to provoke the imagination, comes into focus in his vision: in the heavenly temple John makes out the contours of the ark! This symbol of God's covenant and presence with Israel (Exod. 25:10–22; 1 Sam 4–5; 2 Sam. 6; 1 Kgs. 8) had disappeared at the time of the destruction of the first temple by Babylon. The second temple, standing in Jesus' day but not in John's, had been destroyed by the latter-day "Babylon" (= Rome, 17:5, 18). The second temple had contained a Holy of Holies as the designated place for the ark, but it was empty. Various legends had grown up about the destiny of the original ark, which was supposed to reappear in the eschatological restoration of the temple. When John sees the ark of the covenant in the heavenly temple in this scene of the final coming of the kingdom, not only is it the ultimate sign that the prayer "thy kingdom come" has been finally answered, but also all the Wailing Wall prayers of all the ages also finally find their fulfillment.

12:1–14:20
EXPOSÉ OF THE POWERS OF EVIL
(See excursus, "Satan, the Devil, and Demons in Biblical Theology," at Mark 5:1)

12:1–13:18
Behind the Scenes at the Drama

Structurally, this new vision seems to be part of the seventh trumpet (11:15), the third woe (8:13; see 12:12). The final series of seven does not begin until 15:1. Chapters 12–14 are a series of visions that take a more comprehensive view of the eschatological times in which the church lives, from the birth of Jesus to the end. The troubles experienced by the churches to whom John writes represent something deeper than appears on the surface. It is not merely a matter of a religious and cultural conflict in a Roman province. John lets the reader see behind the scenes of the cosmic drama in which his readers are involved.

The *plot and action* of the drama are clear: a cosmic woman in labor is threatened by a cosmic dragon, but her son is not destroyed by the dragon but taken to heaven. War then breaks out in the heavenly world, and the dragon is defeated and thrown down to earth, where he tries to destroy the woman, but she is protected, so he wars against her other children. (Such a summary, of course, is no substitute for the solemn reading aloud in worship of the biblical narrative itself.)

Some of the *characters* of the drama are clearly identified: the *dragon* is explicitly designated as Satan in all the traditional language (12:9). The *child* is implicitly identified as the Messiah, the one who will rule all nations (12:5; see Ps. 2:9; see on 2:26; 19:15) and who has been taken up to God's throne (see 3:21).

12:1–17 The Woman, the Child, and the Dragon

12:1 A woman clothed with the sun: The identity of the woman is more fluid and allusive, again warning against interpreting Revelation as "code" language (see the introduction to Revelation). Since she is the mother of the Messiah, and since her newborn son is threatened with death, as Jesus was threatened by Herod in Matt. 2:1–18, some interpreters have identified the woman as Mary. The Roman Catholic Church reads this passage on August 15, the Feast of the Assumption of the Blessed Virgin Mary. The birth of the son pictured here is not merely a mythical event, but clearly refers to the actual birth of the historical Jesus. The woman, however, is portrayed as more than a particular historical figure. The Messiah comes not only from Mary but from Israel the people of God, and Israel is sometimes portrayed as a woman suffering labor pains (Isa. 21:3; 26:17–18; 37:3; Jer. 4:31; 6:24; 13:21; 22:23; 30:6; Mic. 4:9; see also Mark 13:8). In the old myth that underlies this imagery, the **crown of twelve stars** was an astrological motif, but for John "twelve" is the mark of the people of God (see on 7:1–8; 21:12–14). The

woman has other children who are persecuted by the dragon (12:17). The scene in which the dragon tries to destroy the child thus represents not Herod in the birth story, but Rome's attempt to destroy Jesus in the passion story. The woman is the Old Testament people of God, who brings forth the Messiah, the Lion of Judah and the Root of David (see on 5:5; see Matt. 1:2–17; Rom. 1:3).

12:3 A great red dragon: The mythical folklore of many peoples contains a story with the same basic plot: a cosmic monster tries to destroy a newborn king, is foiled, and the king returns in triumph. It is a variation of the story of how the forces of darkness, disorder, and sterility/death rebelled against the divine king of light, order, and fertility/life, attempting to overthrow the divine order, kill the newborn king and/or seize the kingship and establish the rule of darkness. In one version of the story the divine Apollo had been born on the island of Delos, not far from Patmos, where John is exiled (1:9). Apollo's mother Leto had fled to Delos to escape the dragon Python, who wanted to kill the newborn son of Zeus. Instead of being killed, Apollo returns to Delphi and kills the dragon. Prior to John's time, Jewish tradition had adapted the story by making the chaos monster Satan and identifying the child as the Messiah. John stands in this tradition, but has Christianized the Jewish imagery in the light of the Christ event. **Seven heads and ten horns:** See on 17:3, 9–14; see Isa. 14:29; 27:1; Dan. 7:7.

12:5 Her child was . . . taken to God and his throne: John's imagery reflects the older version of the myth in which the child is protected from harm and taken to heaven, but John and his readers know that though the "dragon" did not destroy Jesus, his exaltation to heaven was via the cross.

12:6 The woman fled into the wilderness: The people of God continue to exist despite the dragon/devil's attacks (Matt. 16:18); like the Old Testament Israel, the continuing people of God finds the wilderness to be a place of refuge and protection. **One thousand two hundred sixty days:** See on 11:2–3.

12:7 War broke out in heaven: Two motifs are interwoven. (1) The dragon and his angels are defeated by **Michael** (see on 8:2) and thrown out of the heavenly world. "Heaven" here refers to the sky, the realm of demonic powers between heaven and earth inhabited (in some ancient views of the world) by demonic powers (see Rom. 8:38–39; Eph. 2:2; 6:12). The ejection of the Accuser from heaven is not (as in Milton's *Paradise Lost*) the story of the origin of Satan as an angel who rebelled against God in primeval times. Neither here nor elsewhere do biblical authors give speculative "explanations" about the origin of Satan or evil. Such a myth had developed in pre-Christian Judaism (*1–2 En.*), and there are fragmentary echoes of it in the New Testament (Jude 6; 2 Pet. 2:4). That is not the picture in this story, which does not take place in primeval times but at the eschatological time of the establishment of God's kingdom by the life, death, and exaltation of Jesus (see Luke 10:18; John 12:31). (2) Satan is pictured as the heavenly prosecuting attorney who accused God's people on earth in the heavenly court (see 12:10; Job 1:9–11). The point is that though Christians are accused and sometimes condemned in earthly Roman courts (see Pliny's *Letter to Trajan* in the introduction to Revelation), in the heavenly world the Accuser has already lost his case and been ejected from the heavenly court.

12:10 Now the . . . kingdom of our God: Though Revelation emphasizes the "not yet" of God's kingdom, it also knows the "already." While John lives in the time of persecution and looks forward to the time of the final triumph of God's kingdom (see on Luke 4:43–44), he hears the heavenly voice already announcing the victory. The church that prays, "Thy kingdom come," can also already join in this celebration. This anticipatory celebration of God's rule is at the heart of the Christian eucharistic celebration; Revelation was written for reading in such a worship service. When it is read aloud in worship, the prayers and praises of the earthly church join these heavenly voices in celebrating God's universal saving act.

12:11 They have conquered him: The heavenly voice anticipates the triumph of those who conquer, the disciples of Jesus (see on 2:1–3:21; 5:5–6; 7:13; 11:7).

12:12 With great wrath, because he knows that his time is short: The dragon/devil is pictured as a wounded animal who knows it is beaten, and therefore does all the damage it can in its dying gasps. The very fury of the persecution in the times in which John's readers live is itself a sign of the defeat of Satan. On the language of demons, Satan, and exorcism, see the excursus at Mark 5:1.

12:13 He pursued the woman: Having failed in his attempt to destroy the messianic ruler, and having been cast out of heaven, the dragon now attempts to destroy the woman, who represents the continuing people of God—no longer only Israel, but Christians, those who **hold the testimony of Jesus** (12:17).

12:14 Given the two wings of the great eagle: See Exod. 19:4; Deut. 32:11–12; Ps. 74:12–15; Isa. 40:31. Language expressing God's care for Israel is here applied to the church as the continuing people of God.

12:16 The earth came to the help of the woman: As the devil tries to destroy the church, the earth, God's creation, is not neutral, but is on the side of the woman. As in the Old Testament the earth swallows the enemies of God (Exod. 15:12; Num. 16:32–34), so here the earth swallows the flood so that the woman is not overwhelmed and endures through the **time, times, and half a time** (v. 14), the brief period of persecution before the end (see on 11:3–4).

12:17 Make war on the rest of her children: The woman representing the people of God as a whole is protected and will not be destroyed (Matt. 16:18), but the devil still persecutes individual Christians. This scene brings the drama to the point where John's reader-hearers could recognize their own situation. The harassment and persecution they are called on to endure is to be seen in the context of this grand drama.

12:18–13:18 The Two Beasts

In this vision a beast comes from the sea and receives power and authority from the dragon. A second beast from the land compels people to worship the first beast, and marks his followers with a mysterious number. Those who do not worship the beast and have his mark are killed. *This imagery was transparent to John's first readers,* who were living through the history it symbolized. Their question was not *who* the persecuting power was, but *what* it was. This is what is communicated in John's revelatory letter to them. Unlike the first readers, the modern reader needs explanations in order to grasp the meaning of the symbolic language.

12:18 The dragon stood on the shore (NIV): Some manuscripts read "I" (John) rather than "he" (the dragon). Both NRSV and NIV correctly translate "the dragon" as the subject. Frustrated by his failure to destroy the woman (12:13–17), the dragon awaits the arrival of his representative who will continue his war against the church.

13:1 A beast rising out of the sea: In the background is the myth of the sea monster, Leviathan in Old Testament and Jewish tradition (see Job 3:8; 41:1; Ps. 74:14; Isa. 27:1), who often played a role in Jewish apocalyptic documents. It is clear from 13:7 and 17:3, 9–10, 18 that the beast represents the Roman Empire. The governors of Asia, appointed for a one-year term, arrived annually at Ephesus, where they literally came from the sea. **Seven heads:** Explained as emperors in 17:9. See the English phrase "head of state" for a ruler. **Ten horns:** Minor kings who have not yet received power, 17:12. The imagery associates the beast both with the dragon of chap. 12 and with the fourth beast of Dan. 7:7–8, 19–25. **Blasphemous names:** Names that belong only to God. The Roman emperor referred to himself as "son of God," "Lord," "Savior," "King of kings and Lord of lords." Especially Domitian, emperor during John's time, insisted on being addressed as "Lord and God."

13:2 Leopard . . . bear . . . lion: See Dan. 7:1–8, 15–20, where the beasts represent four successive world empires. The beast of John's vision combines and sums up all four. Since one of Daniel's beasts had four heads, the seven heads of John's beast are the sum of the heads of all four of Daniel's beasts. In John's view the Roman Empire inherits and brings to a head the evil of all previous empires. **The dragon gave it his power and his throne:** In a parody of Christ receiving power from God and sharing his throne (3:21; 5:5–12; 12:5; see Matt. 28:18), Satan confers power and authority on Rome. As a parody of the revelatory chain of 1:1–2, the demonic "chain of command" is dragon → beast from the sea → beast from the land.

13:3 One of its heads: One of the emperors, 17:9. **Seemed to have received a death-blow:** After being deposed by the Roman senate in 68 CE, Nero, the first emperor to persecute Christians, had committed suicide by stabbing himself in the throat. Sacrificial lambs were killed by cutting their throats. This is a parody of Jesus the Lamb. Since few had witnessed Nero's death and burial, it was widely believed that he had not really died, but had joined the dreaded Parthians on the eastern border of the empire, from which he would return at the head of an enormous army. By John's time an alternate myth had developed: Nero had indeed died, but would return from the underworld to wreak vengeance on his enemies. This myth of Nero *redivivus* ("Nero back from the dead") was widespread in John's time. Since Domitian was behaving like Nero—claiming divine honors and persecuting those who resisted his claim—he could be

pictured as a second Nero, or Nero returned. Just as a modern racist dictator might be described as "Hitler," so the image of Nero is applied to Domitian. John's first readers did not need such an explanation—the imagery was powerfully clear to them.

13:4 They worshiped the dragon: What was not clear to all the members of John's churches was that participation in the emperor cult was really worship of Satan. Some within the church argued that since Christians know there is only one God, there is no harm in participating in the pagan ceremonies (see 1 Cor. 8:1–13; 10:14–33). This was apparently the view of "Jezebel" (see on 2:6, 20). The modern reader might reflect on John's view that "Satan worship" is not only participation in strange cults and obscene practices, but the adoration of the cultural god. Few readers of this text today are tempted to join a Satanist cult, but John wants to disclose what is really going on in the adoration of the cultural gods, which for us might be consumerism, nationalism, and race.

13:5 Was given: This phrase in the passive voice is used repeatedly as an indirect reference to God. Although the dragon and his agents suppose they are free and independent agents, John's revelation is that ultimately all things rest in one hand. He uses dualistic imagery, but is no dualist (see on 1:18; 4:11). **Forty-two months:** See on 11:3. The Roman harassment and persecution will last only a short time; it was literally true that Rome's days were numbered.

13:7 The saints: See on 4:8. **Make war . . . conquer:** See 12:17. The empire's conquest of God's people will not be final, but John offers no encouragement to his readers that if they are faithful God will deliver them from the Roman persecution (see on 2:10; Dan. 3:18). Faithfulness to God is not motivated by the promise that those who are faithful will be spared; he is utterly realistic on this point—with a realism that affirms even beyond death God is faithful and able to deliver, as he was with Jesus.

13:8 Book of life: See on 3:5. **From the foundation of the world:** The Greek grammar is ambiguous, so that the phrase may belong with "written" (as in the NRSV) or with "slain" (as in the NIV; see NRSV note). In the former case, the meaning is that Christians who choose to be faithful are those whom God has already chosen, a paradoxical affirmation of human responsibility and divine sovereignty, of human decision and the grace of

God (see at Rom. 8:28–30). In the latter case, the meaning is that Christ's death was not a contingent accident of history, but was a part of the divine plan from the beginning. Both understandings are true to John's theology, but the NRSV is probably correct here, as suggested by vv. 9–10.

13:9–10 Into captivity you go: John's reformulation of Jer. 15:2 and 43:11, again affirming that what seem to be human decisions are included within the sovereignty of God. **A call for endurance and faith:** John does not understand predestination in a way that cuts the nerve of human action, but braces believers to act courageously (see excursus at Rom. 8:28–30).

13:11 Another beast . . . out of the earth: Ancient Mediterranean mythology knew not only of Leviathan the sea monster, but of Behemoth the land monster, also reflected in the Old Testament and Apocrypha (Job 40:15; 2 Esd. 6:49, 51). It too is a parody of the **lamb,** but it speaks **like a dragon,** i.e., it resembles Christ, but when it speaks it becomes clear that it represents the devil.

13:12–14 It makes the earth and its inhabitants worship the first beast: Its function is to promote, even to require, participation in the worship of Rome (see the introduction to Revelation, Pliny's *Letter to Trajan*). This beast is often understood to represent the priesthood of the emperor cult in Asia. Since it is later called the "false prophet" (16:13; 19:10; 20:10), it may also represent those Christian prophets who encouraged participation in the Roman cult and culture on the basis that it was "harmless." Since it makes **fire come down from heaven,** it resembles the prophet Elijah (1 Kgs. 18:20–39) and **performs great signs,** it is like the false Christian prophets against which the church was warned (Mark 13:21–23; 2 Thess. 2:9–10). On distinguishing true from false prophets, see the excursus at 2:20.

13:15 To cause those who would not worship the image of the beast to be killed: This had already happened to a limited extent in John's own time (2:13; 6:9–11). He expected the persecution to intensify to universal proportions. He was historically wrong in his expectation, but this does not affect the validity of his call to commitment (see the reinterpretation of Mark 8:34 in Luke 9:23).

13:16 All, small and great, rich and poor, both free and slave: John is not the champion of the poor against the rich or the slave against the free. His theology does not represent a religious version of the class struggle, Marxism with God thrown in. All are challenged as to whether or not they worship the one God.

13:16 Marked on the right hand or the forehead: The symbolism is not literal, but may point to something concrete, such as the use of Roman money (with its pagan symbols) or membership in trade unions and guilds that made employment and business possible. Such organizations always had a religious dimension, so that participation in them meant involvement in Roman sacrifice and worship. For most people, this was only a matter of conventional patriotism, like saluting or pledging allegiance to the flag, but John sees a deeper issue involved. He expects that only those who participate in the Roman worship will be able to participate in the economic life.

13:17 The number of its name: In contrast to modern English, all the languages used in John's time and place represented numbers by letters of the alphabet (e.g., Roman numerals). In Greek, Hebrew, and Latin, every letter was thus also a number. This means that every word is also a numerical sum obtained by totaling all its letters. It is thus easy to go from a word to its number; there is only one possibility, which anyone who can spell and add can readily compute. The opposite process, however, is not easy at all. Given a number, there are many possible words whose letters might add up to that number. This means that the procedure functions only for those who know in advance the word it designates. The number does not serve to identify the name, *but to say something about its significance.* When Revelation was read aloud in the worship of the Asian churches, the call for wisdom to calculate the number of the beast (13:18) was not a challenge to identify *who* the beast, the persecuting authority, was—they knew that well enough already—but to recognize *what* it was, that it was in fact the beast empowered by Satan, not the cultural savior it claimed to be.

The passage is thus important, and its misuse by calendarizers and religious hobbyists who regard 666 as something of a religious crossword puzzle should not deter more serious interpreters from seeking its authentic meaning. A perusal of all John's references to the mark of the beast (13:16–18; 14:9–11; 16:2; 19:20; 20:4) indicates that it is one expression of his "dualism of decision." As a sign of ownership and security, the Lamb marks his followers on the forehead with the seal of the living God, his name and the name of his Father (7:1–8; 14:1–5). The beast imitates the

Lamb, marking his followers on the forehead or the right hand. For John, there are only these two groups, these two choices—everyone bears one mark or the other, and conspicuously! There are no anonymous Christians, no middle-of-the-road, no nonaligned.

The "mark of the beast" occurs as part of a visionary drama. It is to be taken seriously but not literally. Just as John does not want his hearer-readers literally to suppose that their spiritual enemy and threat is a monster with seven heads, so he does not want them literally to expect any time, then or later, when it would be impossible for Christians to buy or sell unless they had a certain mark on their hand or forehead. Yet the picture is to be taken seriously, for it represented something all too real to the members of John's churches, who felt the economic pressure inherent in Christian commitment.

The number 666 has a generic significance that made it particularly appropriate for John's purpose. John shares the broad apocalyptic tradition in which *seven* is the complete number, and has used it as such throughout. The seventh seal, trumpet, and bowl are always the last, that represents the coming of God and his kingdom. But six is often the penultimate number, the number of lack and incompleteness. It is also the number of judgment. As the kingdom of God comes in the seventh and last of each series, the judgment of God comes in the sixth seal, trumpet, and bowl (6:12–17; 9:13–21; 16:12–16)—and John himself and his parishioners live in the time of the sixth emperor, the time of idolatry and eschatological plagues (17:10). Thus 666 is the intensive symbolic expression of incompleteness, idolatry, judgment, nonfulfillment, evil itself raised to the third power. The number communicated as symbol, not by code or analysis.

There is an element of evocative mystery in the symbol that functions whether or not a particular referent is also in mind. Thus the symbol of the beast and his mysterious number can continue to have evocative power in situations where the original reference has long since been forgotten. The symbolic meaning of John's imagery is clear whether or not we can identify the particular meaning evoked in the imaginations of John's audience. The exhortation of v. 18 can well be translated, "It is the moment to have discernment," and challenges the modern interpreter not to historical decoding, but to discern where in our own time propaganda is used to deify political power. The whole passage calls responsible interpreters of the Bible not to "decoding" a "puzzle," but to alertness in discerning the nature and consequences of one's commitments.

Yet it is likely that John intended his readers to think of a particular individual, one already known to them, by this number, which is designated as "a man's name" (13:18 NEB, TEV). Nero is by far the most likely candidate, supported by the majority of contemporary scholars, since the letters "Neron Caesar" in the Hebrew spelling add up to precisely 666: nun (50) + resh (200) + waw (6) and nun (50) + qof (100) + samech (60) + resh (200) = 666. That John expected his hearer-readers to think of Nero is supported by the fact that he uses the myth of the returning Nero elsewhere in Revelation (13:3; 17:9–11), and by the ancient interpretation as Nero, documented in the reading 616 in some manuscripts (Nero spelled in the normal Greek manner without the extra "nun" [50] results in 616).

14:1–20
The Truth about Salvation and Judgment

Before the final series of plagues is described as the pouring out of the seven bowls (15:1–16:21), the reader is given anticipatory visions of the ultimate victory of God. In 12:1–13:18, John has unmasked the powers that lurk behind and in the historical threats to his churches. "Salvation" seemed to call for worshiping the beast. "Judgment" seemed to be what was meted out in the Roman courts for those who refused to acknowledge the cultural values as supreme. In the preceding section, John has let us see how things presently *are*. In 14:1–20 he turns to the other side of the coin of this disclosure/exposé—he will let us see how things *finally* are. First there is a picture of the salvation of those sealed with the mark of the Lamb (14:1–6), then a picture of the judgment of those who bear the mark of the beast (14:7–20).

14:1–5 Real Salvation: The Lamb, His Mark, His Followers

14:1 The Lamb: See on 5:6. **Mount Zion:** The holy mountain in Jerusalem on which the temple was built. **One hundred forty-four thousand:** See on 7:1–8. **Name . . . on their foreheads:** In contrast to those who bear the mark of the beast (13:16).

14:3 New song: As in 5:9, not only a new composition to celebrate a special occasion (see Pss. 33:3; 40:3; 96:1; Isa. 42:10), but connoting eschatological renewal, like "new covenant," "new Jerusalem," and "new creation" (see on Luke 5:36–38; 22:20). Like these, "new song" is an absolute term, not a relative one—the "new song" will not be replaced by a "newer song." The redeemed community is a worshiping, celebrating community that learns the new song of the new age.

14:4 Have not defiled themselves with women: We should not take offense at the word "defile"; in John's usage, it does not suggest that women or sex are "dirty." John here speaks of ritual defilement, of ceremonial impurity. The word is used as we in the nuclear age speak of objects that have been exposed to powerful radiation as "contaminated." John stands in the Hebrew tradition that regarded sex, fertility, and all associated with them as the good gifts of God potent with the mysterious power of life (see the regulations for the ritual containment of the power of menstrual blood that "defiles" [Lev. 15:19–31]). Because these forces are so powerful, they must be ritually insulated from normal life. The same was true of the Scriptures, which were said to "defile the hands." This meant that persons engaged in special occupations or missions such as the priesthood or God's army were, during the time of their service, expected to refrain from sex, not for moralistic reasons, but to insulate the sacred service from other powers (Deut. 20:1–9; 23:9–10; 1 Sam. 21:5). Since John pictures the church as the army of God—the very word "thousands" here conjures up military units (see on 7:1–8)—and as priests (1:6; 5:10), it is therefore pictured as a community of chaste **virgins.** Another of John's images for the church is that of the ideal prophetic community (see on 11:1–13). Since in early Christianity prophets lived a somewhat ascetic lifestyle, leaving home and family and traveling wherever needed in the service of Christ, here the whole church is presented as virgins that **follow the Lamb wherever he goes.** "Virgin" also connotes the pure bride of Christ, in contrast to the harlotry with which idolatry was equated (21:2 vs. 17:1). All these converging and overlapping symbols that characterize the nature of the church are suggested by John's evocative language.

First fruits: Like Christ in his resurrection (1 Cor. 15:20–23), the first sheaf of grain harvested from the fields and presented to God in gratitude for the pledge of the full harvest to come (see Exod. 34:22; Lev. 23:15–22; Num. 28:26; Deut. 16:9–12).

14:5 No lie: Unlike the false prophet, no lie is found in their mouths, and they are **blameless.** Neither of these statements is a moralistic description of the church's piety; their refusal to lie means their resistance to the idolatrous propaganda of the false prophet, the master of the lie; "blameless" is the character of a sacrifice, as their martyrs' deaths were understood to be (see 6:9–11).

14:6–20 Real Judgment:
God the Creator and Judge

In this section the reality of God's judgment appears in contrast to the sham judgment delivered when Christians were condemned in the Roman courts. As 14:1–5 anticipates the eschatological salvation of the new Jerusalem, 14:6–20 anticipates the coming fall of Babylon and God's judgment on those who bear the mark of the beast.

The section is structured as another series of seven (though unnumbered): a series of three angels, then a vision of one like the Son of Man, then the messages of three other angels.

14:6 Another angel . . . with an eternal gospel: The judgment of God is called *euaggelion* ("gospel," "good news"), a word used in the emperor cult of the words and deeds of Caesar. The good news is that God is the Creator of all (see on 4:1–11) and is the judge who will finally establish justice (see on 6:10; 11:18; 19:2, 11; 20:12–13). True judgment will be held by the one God, the Creator—in contrast to the forces of chaos that seem to hold judgment in 13:1–18.

14:8 Fallen is Babylon: On Rome as Babylon, see the introduction to Revelation, and comments on 1 Pet. 5:13. While Babylon/Rome seems to prevail on earth, John lets his hearer-readers hear a second angel announce that Babylon is already fallen (17:1–18:24). It was unthinkable that Rome, "the eternal city," would ever fall, just as it was unthinkable that the Christian message would turn out to be the **eternal gospel.** John's revelation lets the reader see the reality of things.

14:10 Tormented with fire and sulphur . . . in the presence of the Lamb: Anyone who tries to imagine this infinitely-worse-than-Auschwitz picture as somehow objectively real must ask whether God or John does not here overdo it. Such a picture calls into question both the justice and the character of God. (For general principles in interpreting the violent and vindictive language of Revelation, see excursus, "Interpreting Revelation's Violent Imagery," at 6:15 and the excursus, "Universal Salvation and Paradoxical Language," at 22:21.) Here, we only point out that such language does not function to give an objective picture of what shall in fact happen to God's enemies, the outsiders. Even to ask whether Revelation "teaches" eternal torment for the damned is to misconstrue the book as a source of doctrines, to mistake its pictures for propositions. John's language does not deliver a doctrine about the fate of outsiders, but functions to warn insiders, who ponder the question "Is it really so bad to participate in the Roman worship?" John regards this worship as making a this-worldly substitute for the one Creator and Lord, and answers, "More terrible than you can imagine!" Christians who refused such participation were risking death, and must ask, "Is there anything worse than death?" John's answer: "The judgment of God that lies beyond death, the second death, the lake of fire" (20:14). As objectifying language about what shall happen to our enemies, it is cruel beyond imagination; as confessional language, intended not to describe the fate of outsiders but to encourage insiders to remain faithful, it functions precisely like the language of Jesus in the Gospels (Matt. 10:28; 25:30, 46). On confessional language, see at Matt. 2:16.

14:11 Forever and ever: Since the same language is used for the smoke of destroyed "Babylon" (= Rome) in 19:3, this language cannot be understood in a mechanical chronological way. It does not answer the question "How long will they burn?" but "How terrible is it to reject God?" **14:12 The faith of Jesus:** Literally, the "Jesus-faith," which can mean either faith in Jesus, or the kind of faithfulness to death Jesus himself had.

14:13 Blessed are the dead: One of seven beatitudes in Revelation (see on 1:3; 16:15; 19:9; 20:6; 22:7, 14). **In the Lord:** Reflects the Pauline understanding of Christians as being "in Christ" (see on 2 Cor. 5:17). While John affirms the gift of eternal life for all God's people, he here has in mind the Christian martyrs of his own time (6:9–11; 7:13–14). **Their deeds:** Though salvation is by God's grace manifested in the death of Christ (1:4–6; 14:3; 22:1), this does not diminish the importance of human responsibility and "works" (2:2 and in each of the seven messages in chaps. 2–3; 19:8; 20:12).

14:14 One like the Son of Man: See 1:13–16; on the Son of Man imagery, see on Mark 2:10. The figure may be understood either as the exalted

Christ or as an angel; these images flow into each other, and both represent God (see on 1:1–2).

14:16–20 The earth was reaped . . . the great wine press of the wrath of God: The grain harvest of the one "like the Son of Man" is followed by the grape harvest executed by (other) angels. The clusters are thrown into the winepress of God's wrath, and blood flows in unimaginable depth and extent. The main issue in interpreting these images is whether these visions express unqualified judgment in a negative sense, or whether they also somehow represent God's redemptive work, not only through the blood of Christ but through the blood of the martyrs. The whole series can be interpreted as unrelieved judgment, so that both the grain harvest and the winepress are images for the destiny of the wicked, as in John's prototype Joel 3:13. Another view sees some images of salvation mixed with images of judgment, so that the grain harvest is the ingathering of the saved, as in the parables of Jesus, while the winepress is a picture of God's wrath upon the condemned. A third view sees the whole drama in terms of ultimate salvation, a rebirth of images that transforms traditional pictures of judgment into pictures of salvation. The reader should resist the temptation to "decode" these evocative pictures into one consistent "meaning" that can be stated as a clear doctrine. The pictures of blood, torment, divine wrath, and judgment all exceed what the imagination can comprehend, but the reader should also remember that the unthinkable has already happened in the transformation of the lion of God's wrath into the Lamb (5:5–14), and that the wrath is the wrath of the Lamb (6:16). The great quantities of blood that flow in Revelation are the blood of God's enemies, the blood of the martyrs, and the redeeming blood of the Son of God, and these do not flow in separate channels (see on 19:13).

15:1–16:21
THE SEVEN LAST PLAGUES

Chapters 15 and 16 are one unit; The seven last plagues are announced in 15:1, and the last plague is referred to in 16:21. By now the reader might anticipate that the seventh plague will not really be the last, but that the seventh bowl will become another numbered series of seven, but this time there is no "cancelled conclusion," and the vision proceeds to the end without interruption.

15:1–8
The Victory Celebration in
the Heavenly Worship

15:2 What appeared to be a sea: As Israel once stood on the banks of the Red Sea and celebrated God's liberating act of the exodus, the church will stand on the shore of the heavenly sea and sing the song of Moses and the Lamb. This section 15:1–16:21 represents John's most thorough use of the exodus motif in Revelation. "Egypt" is Rome; "Pharaoh" is Caesar; the "plagues" are eschatological woes (16:2 sores/Exod. 9:10–11; 16:3–4 sea and rivers become blood/Exod. 7:17–21; 16:10 darkness/Exod. 10:22; 16:12 drying up the waters/ Exod. 14:21–22; 16:13 frogs/Exod. 8:3; 16:18, 21 thunder, fire, hail/Exod. 9:24); the passover lamb is the exalted Christ, the Lamb who has accomplished eschatological deliverance; the flood of troubles through which the church must pass is the Red Sea; the triumph song is the Song of Moses (and the Lamb). Even the smoke of Sinai (15:8) and the tabernacle containing the law of God's justice appears (15:5; throughout this scene the heavenly sanctuary is pictured as the tabernacle accompanying Israel in the wilderness, see Exod. 40:34–38). As the Red Sea (Exod. 14:21) and the Jordan (Josh. 4:23) were "dried up" as part of God's liberating activity of the exodus, here the Euphrates is dried up to facilitate the final events (16:12).

A Worship Scene: Christian Worship Transfigured. At the Red Sea, God's people celebrated after the fact; in Revelation, the final victory is not yet realized (on earth) but is already accomplished and celebrated in heaven, the ultimately real world, and can thus already be celebrated in this world, where the worship of the earthly church participates in the worship of the heavenly sanctuary (see on 4:1–11). Christian worship anticipates the eschatological victory and celebrates it in the present. Christian worship, especially its eucharistic dimension, points "backward" to the past and understands the present in its light (the "new exodus"), points "forward" to the future victory and celebrates its reality in the present, and points "upward" to the transcendent reality of God's world, participating in the worship of the heavenly sanctuary that unites past, future, and present (see on Luke 22:14–20; 1 Cor. 11:23–32).

15:4 All nations will come and worship: Biblical and apocalyptic tradition pictured the final triumph of God's kingdom in two contrasting ways. In one picture, the pagan nations are defeated and destroyed in a climactic last battle (Ezek. 38–39; Joel 3:2; Zech. 14:2; Ps. 2:1–2; and several noncanonical apocalyptic texts such as the War Scroll, one of the Dead Sea Scrolls). In the other picture, the pagan nations are converted and become worshipers of the one God (Isa. 2:1–4; Isa. 19:24–25; Ezek. 16:52–63; Mic. 4:1–4; Ps. 86:9–10; and several noncanonical apocalyptic documents). John juxtaposes these pictures without harmonizing them, including both in this one scene (see 16:12–16; and 19:11–21/21:24–26).

15:5–7 The temple of the tent of witness in heaven: The imagery of the Old Testament temple in Jerusalem and tabernacle of the exodus wanderings is combined. The language throughout this vision is the language of worship and praise: **harps** (15:2) and songs of praise (15:3–4), in the heavenly temple (15:5), from which come angels dressed in the liturgical attire of **bright linen** and **golden sashes** (15:6). The **seven golden bowls** are of the type used in worship for pouring out libation offerings.

16:1–21
The Seven Bowls of the Wrath of God

The final series of eschatological woes is not a chronological continuation of the preceding ones. It refers to the same period but presents it from a different perspective. It is a vision of cosmic catastrophe in which the preceding visions are paralleled but intensified. Not merely a fourth or third of the world, as in the first two septets, but *all* the world is struck by the blow against the sun and by the darkness, and everything in the sea dies. Not just the earth, but the cosmos itself (heavens, sun, dry land, sea, rivers) is struck (16:1–8). Human rebellion against God has infected the creation itself (see Gen. 3:17; Isa. 24:5–6). As the created world is not finally to be destroyed but to be renewed and redeemed (21:1–22:6; see Rom. 8:18–23), so it passes through the judgment.

The terror of the eschatological plagues is pictured by John as a manifestation of the righteous judgment of God. The establishment of God's reign as the goal of history is a matter not of vengeance but of justice. The present world is not just, but no injustice happens at the eschaton. John inserts into the vivid images of terror interpretive heavenly voices that speak of God's justice (16:5, 7). When the plagues are called expressions of the "wrath of God" (introduced for the first time in 14:10, 19, and then repeatedly in this section: 15:1, 7; 16:1, 19; see 19:15), the expression is to be understood forensically, not emotionally.

16:1–11 The seven bowls of the wrath of God: For parallels to the exodus plagues, see above at 15:2.

16:12 The great river Euphrates ... was dried up: The Euphrates was the largest river in southwest Asia and formed the natural eastern boundary of the Roman Empire. Just as God dried up the Jordan to allow his people to attack the idolatrous Canaanites (Josh. 3:1–4:18), so God will dry up the Euphrates to allow the dreaded **kings from the east** to destroy the arrogant Roman civilization. We are presented with another mind-wrenching rebirth of imagery, in which not only the "Parthians," but the demonic powers behind them—**dragon, beast,** and **false prophet**—are used by God to facilitate eschatological judgment. The call goes forth to assemble **for battle on the great day** of the Lord.

16:15 See, I am coming like a thief: In the midst of these graphic scenes of the eschatological future already breaking in, a voice is heard, the direct voice of Christ speaking through his prophet. While disruptive to the individual reader of the written text, it is appropriate in the oral reading of the book during worship. This is not a misplaced verse more at home among the messages of 2:1–3:21 (see 3:3). It is John's way of reminding his hearer-readers that the visions are to provide not speculative information about the future, but a challenge from the living Christ to orient their lives in the present toward the coming eschatological reality.

16:16 Harmagedon (NRSV)/**Armageddon** (NIV): The different spellings in English translations reflect the variety of names given the location in the ancient Greek manuscripts of Revelation. Popular, uncritical interpretations of this text have often supposed that it predicts some great battle at Megiddo in northern Israel, as part of the final events of history. Both of these assumptions are wrong. That John is writing "prophecy" does not mean that he is predicting historical events of the long-range future, but that he is presenting an inspired interpretation of contemporary events for the Christians of his own time (see the introduction to Revelation). John does not predict any historical event beyond his own generation. Nor is there any "battle" described. John uses the traditional military imagery to portray the final victory of God, but in his own theology the decisive victory was already won at the cross and resurrection of Jesus (see above on 5:1–14;

12:7–12). Revelation thus contains no descriptions of eschatological battles (see 19:11–21; 20:7–10).

The popular identification of Armageddon with Megiddo in Israel is likewise questionable. John specifies that he is giving the name in Hebrew, which must therefore be significant. Since the first part of the word ("har") corresponds to the word for "mountain" in Hebrew, the name would mean "Mountain of Mageddon." There is no such place in the Bible or Palestinian geography, but by a slight adjustment in spelling, the name can be seen as referring to biblical Megiddo, a fortress city in northern Israel where some battles important for biblical history were fought (Judg. 4:4–5:31; see 5:19; 2 Kgs. 23:28–29). There is, however, as modern visitors to Megiddo are surprised to learn, no mountain at Megiddo! Like many ancient cities, the town itself is built in the plain atop a small artificial tell. The Bible speaks of the "waters" and "plain" of Megiddo (Judg. 5:19; 2 Chr. 35:22), but never of a "mountain of Megiddo." There may be a connection to the nearest mountain, Mount Carmel, where Elijah defeated the idolatrous prophets of Baal (1 Kgs. 18:20–46). This would indeed fit John's view that the prophetic Christian community stands in the tradition of Elijah in resisting Roman idolatry (see on 11:4–13). Another possibility argued by some scholars also calls for slightly adjusting the spelling of the mysterious "Mageddon" so that in Hebrew it would read "Assembly." "Armageddon" would then mean "Mount of Assembly." This not only fits the context ("assemble," 16:14), but associates this text with the passage about the "mountain of assembly" in Isa. 14:12–15, a text that portrays the "king of Babylon" in mythological terms.

16:17–21 It is done: The **great city** (Rome) splits **into three parts** (as by a great earthquake), and the **cities of the nations** fall amidst the terror of the appearance of God, who has not forgotten the injustice of the arrogant human city, **great Babylon,** and now appears as her judge. John saves the details for 20:1–22:6.

17:1–18:24
THE FALL OF BABYLON AND THE LAMENT

17:1–18
Rome Is Babylon

The seventh bowl as the climax of God's judgment announced the fall of "Babylon" (Rome); this is now elaborated.

17:1 Come I will show you: In 21:9 the same angel uses exactly the same formula for the bride, the wife of the Lamb, who also represents a city. As two women are contrasted (whore/bride), so two cities are contrasted (Babylon/new Jerusalem). A city is pictured as a woman often in the Old Testament (e.g., Lam. 2:13; Isa. 1:21; 23:16–17; 37:22; 66:7–14; Nah. 3:4). It is clear that the **great whore** is Rome (17:18). **Seated on many waters:** The imagery is taken from Jer. 51:13 and was literally true of Babylon, surrounded by a moat, the Euphrates running through the city, crisscrossed by many irrigation canals. Rome was on the Tiber, but the image applies to the empire as a whole, which sat astride the Mediterranean and the major rivers of the world.

17:2 Fornication: Idolatry (see on 2:14; 14:4). Isaiah 23:17 is the source of John's imagery. **The inhabitants of the earth have become drunk:** They are responsible for their own sins, but also have been victimized, intoxicated by the grandeur and achievements of Rome. See Jer. 51:7, where Babylon was a golden cup in God's hand making all the earth drunk. John's recombination of biblical imagery pictures human responsibility, the victimization of humans by being entrapped in the systemic evil of a powerful culture, and all things ultimately in God's hand (see 17:17).

17:3 In the Spirit: See on 1:10. **Seven heads and ten horns:** The Roman emperors and their subordinate kingdoms. See 13:1; 17:9–14.

17:4 Gold, jewels, pearls: Like the new Jerusalem, the whore is adorned with gold, jewels, and pearls (v. 4; see 21:18–21).

17:6 Drunk with the blood of the saints: Some Christians had already been martyred by Rome; John expects many more (see 2:13; 6:9–11).

17:8 The beast is embodied in the emperors and in each of them. **Was . . . is not . . . is to come:** Another parody of the true God (1:4, 8; 4:8; 11:17; 16:5). On the "evil trinity" of dragon/beast/false prophet as a parody of the true God, see 13:2, 3, 11. The life history of the beast is represented by one of the heads, which once was alive, which was killed and presently does not exist, which shall soon reappear, but whose fate is already sealed because it will **go to destruction.** This reflects one form of the Nero *redivivus* myth (see on 13:3). The beast will require people to worship the power he represents. John sees all succumbing to this pressure except those **written in the book of**

life from the foundation of the world (see on 3:5).

17:9 This calls for a mind that has wisdom: See 13:18. This section is more like typical Jewish apocalyptic in that there is a detailed interpretation of the vision given by an interpreting angel. This is the only section of Revelation of which this is true, and may be an indication that John is here reinterpreting older materials. **Seven heads are seven hills** (NIV): Here the NIV "hills" is a better translation than NRSV "mountains." The Greek word can be correctly translated either way, but in English, Rome is traditionally identified as the "city on seven hills," and John wants to make it clear that the woman represents Rome. **Also, they are seven kings:** John's imagery is fluid and evocative, not mechanical and codelike, but has more than one level of meaning. "Seven kings" is not literal, but refers to the total number of Roman emperors. The emperors and the dates of their reigns are as follows:

Julius Caesar	d. 44 BCE
Augustus (Octavian)	31 BCE–14 CE
Tiberius	14–37
Gaius (Caligula)	37–41
Claudius	41–54
Nero	54–68
Galba	68–69
Otho	69
Vitellius	69
Vespasian	69–79
Titus	79–81
Domitian	81–96
Nerva	96–98
Trajan	98–117
Hadrian	117–138

17:10 Five have fallen: Attempts to calculate from this listing which emperor is reigning as John writes have not been successful, for several reasons: (1) It is not clear with which emperor John begins. Some ancient historians considered Julius Caesar, and others Augustus, to be the first emperor. Some interpreters begin with Caligula, the first emperor after Jesus' death and resurrection, and the first to publicly consider himself to be divine. (2) It is not clear which emperors are to be counted among the "seven." All of them? Only those who had "fallen" in the sense of suffering violent deaths? Only those that had been declared divine by the Senate? Are Galba, Otho, and Vitellius, who held power only briefly in the confusion after Nero's death, to be counted? By juggling different combinations of these possibilities, various scholars have identified every emperor from Nero to Trajan as the emperor under whom John is writing (though the great majority locate the time of writing in Domitian's reign—see the introduction to Revelation).

However, it is likely that John does not understand the number seven literally. Based on his practice elsewhere, it seems more likely that it is a symbolic number standing for the whole line of Roman emperors, whatever their actual number (just as the "seven" churches of chaps. 2–3 represent the churches of Asia—and the world). John wants the imagery to convey to his readers that the series of Roman emperors, though it appears to be "eternal," is coming to an end, that "Nero" shall appear as the leader of a final great persecution, but the kingdom of God will replace the Roman power. The present distress under Domitian was only the leading edge of the great persecution to follow immediately, for when the beast appeared again, though appearing to be powerful, it would last only a little while, since it was already destined to go to perdition. All this John wanted to disclose in his evocative revelation of how things ultimately are, to Christians who had to decide how to evaluate the rival claims to ultimate allegiance made by the god represented in Rome and the God represented in Jesus Christ.

17:14 The Lamb will conquer them: That John is not interested in portraying a strict chronology is clear in that here the Lamb destroys the ten kings and their armies before they are portrayed as uniting to destroy Rome (17:16). The image is fluid, intended to assure the reader of the ultimate victory of the Lamb, not to predict particular historical events.

17:17 God has put it into their hearts: The ten kings are subject to the satanic power, yet they serve God's ultimate purpose—as did Assyria and Babylon in the Old Testament (see, e.g., Isa. 7:17; Jer. 20:4). **Words of God . . . fulfilled:** The rise and fall of empires and the final destruction of evil are embraced in God's plan as the Lord of history, as disclosed to his prophets (see 10:7).

18:1–24
The Fall of Babylon
Celebrated/Lamented

This lamentation borrows much of the language and imagery of Old Testament lamentations that both protest and lament the sins of Israel and Jerusalem, protest and lament their destruction, combined with prophetic judgments that celebrate the fall of Assyria and Babylon (see Ps. 137:8; Isa. 13:21–22; 21:9; 23:8, 17; 34:11, 14; 40:2; 47:8–9; 48:20; Jer. 7:34; 9:10; 16:9; 25:10, 15; 50:8, 15, 29, 31; 51:6, 7, 9, 45; Ezek. 26:16–17; 27:12–22, 30–34, 36; Nah. 3:4). John's lamentation is thus double-pronged. On the one hand, he celebrates the final demise of the oppressive world power that had lived in luxury at the expense of the suffering of others. On the other hand, he mourns the passing away of the great city that had facilitated vitality and the joy of life. John's application of biblical language used against Israel and Jerusalem to Babylon/Rome shows that he is not against civilization itself, but its perversion. His final scenes will picture not the destruction of city life, but its redemption, including the "kings of the earth" (see on 21:1–2, 24–25). None of this should mitigate the readers' hearing John's unqualified condemnation of the oppression and luxury of the great city, and his celebration that it will soon pass away.

18:1 Fallen is Babylon: See on 14:8. Like other prophets, John announces what is *sure* to happen as *already* having happened.

18:4 Come out of her, my people: See Isa. 48:20–22; Jer. 50:8–10; 51:6–10. This is not a literal call for Christians in Rome to leave the city, for it is the Roman power as such, the whole empire centered in Rome, that John opposes. Christians cannot literally leave the empire, but they can disengage from the Roman culture and orient their lives to the present and coming kingdom of God.

18:11 The merchants of the earth weep: Rome was the center of a comprehensive economic system, importing wares from all over the known world. The collapse of Rome means the collapse of world economy.

18:13 Slaves—and human lives: Better translated **slaves—that is, human beings.** Roman commercial success was built upon the backs of slave labor, which it considered a commodity to be traded.

18:20 God has given judgment for you against her: See the prayer of the martyrs (6:10), which is here answered. The whole scene is pictured not as vengeance—John refuses to dance on the grave of his oppressors—but as the righteous judgment of God.

18:24 And of all who have been slaughtered on earth: Here the picture of historical Rome fades into that of universal oppressive empire. It is not only the Christian martyrs that are here lamented and finally vindicated, but all the innocent victims of all the oppressive empires of history.

19:1–22:21
GOD REDEEMS THE "HOLY CITY"

19:1–10
HALLELUJAH CHORUSES
PRAISE GOD'S VICTORY

Each of the three major divisions of Revelation begins with a transcendent scene of the glory of God and/or Christ, from which proceeds a sevenfold vision (see "Outline" in the introduction to Revelation). Revelation comes to its climactic conclusion with seven scenes of the final victory of God, preceded by the setting in heavenly worship:

19:1–10	Heavenly Worship
19:11–16	Picture One: The Return of Christ
19:17–21	Picture Two: The Last Battle
20:1–3	Picture Three: The Binding of Satan
20:4–6	Picture Four: The Millennium
20:7–10	Picture Five: The Defeat of Gog and Magog
20:11–15	Picture Six: The Last Judgment
21:1–22:5	Picture Seven: The New Jerusalem

Though the literary presentation requires that they be presented one after the other, they are not a strict chronology, but seven different pictures of the meaning of the triumph of God at the end of history. Each picture is intended to say something about the character of the end as such, not merely describe one part of the final drama. Here is no chronological calendar of the events of the end time, but a tour through an eschatological art gallery in which the theme of God's victory at the end of history is treated in seven different pictures, each complete in itself.

19:1 Hallelujah: A Hebrew word taken from the biblical and liturgical tradition of Israel that means "Praise the LORD." **Salvation:** Here better translated "victory," an acclamation as in 7:10; 12:10.

19:2: Great whore: See chaps. 17–18.

19:3 Forever and ever: See on 14:10. Rome does not literally burn forever, but along with the rest of this world passes away, is transformed and renewed in the final scene of the historical drama (21:1).

19:4 Twenty-four elders and the four living creatures: See on 4:4, 6–8.

19:6 The Lord our God the Almighty reigns: Better translated "has begun to reign," i.e., has made his eternal kingdom concrete reality. See on 11:15–17 and the discussion of "kingdom

of God" at Luke 4:43–44. One could see this declaration as the key statement of the whole document. The issue in John's situation was "who reigns?" i.e., "who's in charge?" To all appearances the secular culture as embodied in Rome was the reigning power, with which all had to come to terms. The good news of Revelation is that God reigns.

19:7 The marriage of the Lamb: On "Lamb" as a title of Christ, see on 5:6. As a way of expressing the meaning of God's covenant with Israel, the people of God were often pictured as the bride or wife of God in the Old Testament (Isa. 49:18; 50:1; 54:1–6; 62:5; Jer. 3:20; Ezek. 16:8–14; esp. Hos. 1–3). This image was adopted by early Christianity to portray the church as the continuing people of God (Matt. 9:15; 25:1–13; Mark 2:20; Luke 5:35; John 3:29; 2 Cor. 11:2; Eph. 5:25–32). In Revelation, the bride as God's faithful people is contrasted with the great whore, who represents unfaithfulness and idolatry (chaps. 17–18).

19:9 Blessed: The fourth of seven beatitudes in Revelation (see on 1:3). **Those . . . invited to the marriage supper:** These, too, are faithful Christians, who will participate in the messianic banquet, of which the Eucharist is already a foretaste (see excursus, "The Lord's Supper in the New Testament," at 1 Cor. 11:24). They are not a separate group from the "bride," who also represents the faithful church. Here as elsewhere, John's imagery is fluid and is not to be mechanically allegorized or decoded. The marriage supper takes up the Jewish image of the messianic banquet, which sometimes pictured the final inclusion of the Gentiles, as in *3 En.* 48:10: "The kingdom of Israel, gathered from the four corners of the world, shall dine with the Messiah, and the Gentiles shall eat with them." **These are the true words of God:** The reader should not ask which words, as though one could go through Revelation and separate out God's words from the words of Christ, the angel, John himself, and the numerous other voices that are heard in Revelation. The document as a whole is the word of God in the sense that it mediates God's message to the hearers. The words of John, the angel, Christ, and God collapse into each other (see on 1:1–2).

19:10 You must not do that!: The churches of Asia Minor were sometimes fascinated with angels and tended to confuse them with God and to honor them too highly, i.e., to "worship" them (see on Col. 2:18; Heb. 1:4–14). John twice presents a scene in which his mistaken efforts to honor the angel are redirected toward the one God. **I am a fellow servant:** Angels are colleagues of the Christian prophets in delivering the word of God. **The testimony of Jesus:** This can mean the testimony that the risen Jesus himself bears as he speaks through his prophetic messengers, or the testimony about Jesus borne by the prophets, or both. Both are true: the risen Christ speaks in Revelation, and Revelation is a message about Christ.

Now follow the seven pictures of the goal of history and the final coming of God's kingdom.

19:11–22:5
SEVEN VISIONS OF THE END

19:11–16
Picture One: The Return of Christ

The idea of a "second coming" of Christ is one aspect of a set of tensive symbolic pictures that are not to be rationalized or harmonized. John is in accord with New Testament theology in general in holding together several pictures of the advent of Christ without forcing them into a false conceptual consistency.

1. *Christ came* as the revelation of God *and never left*. Christ remains in the world and is present not only to and with his church, but in the lives of those who do not recognize him (Matt. 1:23; 18:20; 25:31–46; 28:20). All the indications of the Holy Spirit's presence in the church and the world, identified as the continuing presence of Christ, belong to this way of thinking (Mark 13:11; John 14:15–17, 25–26; 15:26; 16:7–15; Rom. 8:9–10). John affirms this view in Revelation (1:13, 20; 2:1).

2. Alongside this view, often in the same author and document, is the view that *Christ has* in fact *departed, but* that *from time to time he makes himself present*, he "comes" again in judgment and grace, within the events of history and the experience of the church and individuals (John 14:1–3). This view is conditional: Christ comes in judgment if the church or individual does not repent; Christ comes in grace to make himself known in the church's worship (Luke 24:35). John affirms this view in Revelation (2:5, 16; 3:3, 20).

3. Not as an alternative to the first two views, but also not reducible to them, is the view that *the ascended, heavenly Christ is absent from the earth, but will return at the end of history* to bring this age to fulfillment and establish God's new order. John affirms this view in the text before us.

From heaven comes a **rider on a white horse. He makes war in righteousness** (v. 11; see Isa.

11:4, understood of the Messiah in early Christianity and still read at Advent). He will **rule the nations with a rod of iron** (v. 15), an image from Ps. 2:9 applied to the Messiah in both early Judaism and early Christianity. He has **eyes like a flame of fire** (v. 12; see 1:14). **From his mouth comes a sharp sword** (v. 15; see 1:16; 2:12). Though neither "Jesus" nor "Christ" is used, the other messianic names make it clear the rider is the returning Christ: he is called **Faithful and True** (v. 11; see 1:5; 3:14), the **Word of God** (v. 13; see John 1:1, 14; 1 John 1:1), **King of kings and Lord of lords** (v. 16; see 17:14). Yet these exalted names do not do him justice; his transcendent authority cannot be expressed in any name human ears can hear, so he has **a name inscribed that no one knows but himself** (v. 12; see on 10:4 and 2 Cor. 12:4).

The figure is the returning Jesus, but he appears to be very different from the Jesus of the Gospels, who rides humbly on a donkey rather than a warhorse (Matt. 21:1–9) and who dies for others rather than killing them (Matt. 26:51–56). Thus some have interpreted the "first coming" of Jesus as his advent in love, but the "second coming" as his advent in violent power. This is a fundamental mistake (see on 5:6). The good news of the Christian faith is that at our own death or the end of history we do not meet someone different from the One we have already met in Jesus of Nazareth. Here as elsewhere, John adopts the traditional imagery of the conquering Messiah, but reverses its valences in the light of Jesus the crucified one.

19:13 He is clothed in a robe dipped in blood: The image is from Isa. 63:1–3, where God is pictured as the divine warrior red with the blood of his enemies, the Edomites. In first-century Judaism, this passage had already been understood as applying to the Messiah, with "Edom" understood as a code word for Rome. John takes over this image and reinterprets it in terms of Jesus who dies for others, whose own blood is the price of their salvation (1:5; 5:9; 7:14), and whose only **sword** is the judging and redeeming word that comes **from his mouth** (v. 15; 1:16; 2:16; 19:21). This is the one we meet at the end of history—not an abyss of nothingness, but a person, the same person we have already met in Jesus of Nazareth.

19:17–21
Picture Two: The Last Battle

The second image of the goal of history is that of the last battle, in which God once and for all defeats the enemies of life and the created world.

Not eternal struggle, but final victory is the destiny of the world. In apocalyptic literature, God's salvation of Israel from historical enemies, the wartime longing for the return to the good life, and the joyous celebration of victory when the conflict is finally over are all projected onto a cosmic, eschatological screen, where God defeats the ultimate enemy in a final battle (Ezek. 38–39; 2 Esd. 12). John's Christianized version of this apocalyptic picture is presented in 19:17–21.

19:17 The great supper of God: See Isa. 25:6–7. In some versions of the grand victory banquet, the chaos monsters Leviathan and Behemoth that personify the powers of chaos and evil are served up as the menu. In John's vision the motif of the invitation to the messianic banquet, the wedding feast of the Lamb (19:9), is here taken up again, this time in a grisly ironic tone. John offers his hearer-readers an invitation to an eschatological meal, and lets us choose whether it is to be the wedding celebration of the Lamb or the slaughter meal of the vanquished. As in the eschatological reversal of Zeph. 1:7–9 and with the language and imagery of Ezek. 39:4, 17–20, those who supposed they were to be guests turn out to be the menu (19:21). It is a fearfully revolting picture. Yet this is not the only, or final, picture that we see of them. In 20:9 the evil kings and their armies are destroyed (again!), while in 21:24 they are welcomed into the New Jerusalem, and in 22:2 the nations are healed, rather than destroyed and consumed. All this shows that though John's gruesome pictures are to be taken with utmost seriousness, they cannot be taken literally or fitted into a chronology.

19:18 Free and slave, small and great: See 13:16.

19:20 The beast: The Roman Empire; see on 13:1; 16:12–17. **The false prophet:** See on 13:13; 20:10. **Thrown alive into the lake of fire:** On the model of what happened to the enemies of God in the Old Testament (Num. 16:33); though "lake of fire" is a late picture of divine punishment not found in the Old Testament, fiery rivers are frequent in later Jewish apocalyptic literature. The lake of fire is the place where God's transcendent enemies are destroyed, but in Revelation no human beings are pictured as actually thrown there.

19:21 The rest were killed by the sword: No battle is described, nor could there be in John's theology. The decisive battle had already been won long ago, at the Christ event in which Jesus "conquered" (see on 5:6–14). The end only makes that victory effective and mani-

fest. Without a struggle, in a manner reminiscent of the messianic king of Isa. 11:1–5, the transcendent powers of evil are taken and cast into the transcendent place of destruction, the lake of fire (19:20). The historically rebellious human community, the "kings of the earth" and the "peoples" that follow them, "great and small," are **killed** with the **sword** and receive the awful judgment reserved for those who have rebelled against God. John's imagery gives us compelling pictures that communicate both the terror of rejecting the Creator and the celebration that follows from receiving his grace. But the impossibility of fitting them into one conceptual picture makes clear that both God's judgment and God's grace are more than we can imagine.

20:1–3
Picture Three: The Binding of Satan

In a way that does not reduce personal human responsibility, Satan has been pictured throughout Revelation as the transcendent cause of human evil and misery. As the story comes to a close, two pictures are given of Satan's end: he is thrown into the abyss (20:1–3) and into the lake of fire (20:10). In order to utilize both of these traditional pictures, John "must" allow Satan to be released (20:3). Each picture is complete in itself, however, and each in its own way promises the reader that the reign of evil is not permanent, for God will bring it to an end with the final coming of the kingdom of God. On the language of demons, Satan, and exorcism, see the excursus at Mark 5:1.

20:2 Bound him: The binding of the powers of evil was a traditional apocalyptic motif, already reflected in the Old Testament (Isa. 24:21–22), elaborated in apocalyptic writings such as *1 En.*, and reflected elsewhere in the New Testament (Matt. 12:25–29; Mark 3:27; Jude 6).

20:3 Deceive the nations no more: Satan is pictured as the cause of systemic evil, not only of personal peccadilloes. "Satan" as a symbolic way of thinking of the super-personal power of evil is a valuable dimension of biblical theology. (On the language of demons, Satan, and exorcism, see excursus at Mark 5:1.) The power of evil is bigger than individual sins. John consistently speaks in political and national terms when he talks of the power of Satan (13:7; 18:3, 23; 20:3, 8). Satan is not merely the individualistic tempter to petty sins; he is the deceiver of the nations (20:7–8). We might now label this as "systemic evil," or picture it more in accord with our own times as a vast impersonal computer-like network of evil in which our lives are enmeshed and which influence us quite apart from our wills. A valuable dimension of this imagery is that it pictures the vastness of the reservoir of evil by which we are threatened and from which we cannot deliver ourselves. "Cosmic" is not too big a word; "dragon" is not too bizarre an image. One of the major functions of the prophetic revelation of the power of Satan behind the scenes was to disclose to the Asian Christians that their real enemy was not the Jews and Romans harassing and even imprisoning and killing them, but the power of evil of which they, too, were the victims.

20:4–6
Picture Four: The Millennium

The prophets and seers of the Old Testament had developed basically two different pictures to express the triumph of God at the end of history, which may be called the "prophetic" and the "apocalyptic." In the "prophetic" view, the world's evil would be overcome and life would come into its own as it was intended to be in God's good creation (Isa. 65:17–25; Ezek. 34:25–31). Prophetic eschatology understood salvation in continuity with this world and its history; this world would be the setting for eschatological bliss. In contrast, apocalyptic eschatology saw this world as already too overwhelmed with evil for redemption to occur from within it. The present world must pass away to make way for eschatological fulfillment in the setting of new heavens and a new earth (Isa. 65:17; 66:22; 1 En. 91:15–16; 2 Pet. 3:12–13). In this frame of reference, the Messiah was not thought of as a this-worldly royal figure empowered by God, but as a transcendent figure who brings salvation from the other world. In apocalyptic eschatology, the final kingdom of God does not grow out of this world, but breaks into it from the beyond.

By John's time, these two views had already been combined into a scheme in which a this-worldly messiah brought this-worldly salvation during a transitional kingdom, which was then superseded by eternal apocalyptic salvation in the new world. The "two ages" were bridged by an intermediate period resulting in the scheme "this age" / "the days of the Messiah" / "the age to come." The intermediate period of the Messiah's rule was ascribed various lengths: 40 years (*Apocalypse of Elijah*), 400 years (2 Esd. 7:28), 1000 years (2 En. 32–33), with various rabbis inter-

preting selected texts to yield periods of 365, 365,000, and 7,000 years for the "millennium." In addition, John inherits from his Jewish background both the tradition that only the righteous are raised (Isa. 26:19; *Ps. Sol.* 3:13–14; 1 En. 83–90) and the tradition that all the dead, good and bad alike, are raised (Ezek. 37; Dan. 12:2–3; 2 Esd. 7:37; 2 Bar. 50–51; 1 En. 46:6; 58:3–5). By adopting the scheme of an intermediate eschatological period, he is given a conceptual means of affirming both traditions. It was not only the Jewish tradition that provided the elements for John's picture. The Christian tradition in which he stood, particularly the Pauline stream, could speak of Christians reigning and judging as part of the eschatological scenario (1 Cor. 4:8; 6:2–3).

As one of his pictures of the triumph of God, John portrays Christ reigning with his people on earth for a thousand years. This earth, not some otherworldly place, finally gets to enjoy the good existence for which it was created (Gen. 1) and for which it sighs (Rom. 8:19–24). Later interpreters, who misunderstood John's pictorial language as objectifying, propositional, and chronological, developed the terms "premillennial" (Christ returns to earth before the millennium), "postmillennial" (the Parousia occurs only after the triumph of the kingdom of God on earth for a millennial period), and "amillennial" (there will be no literal millennium, either before or after Christ's return). If John himself is forced into this scheme, he should be labeled premillennial," since the Parousia occurs in 19:11–16, and the millennium not until 20:4–6. If forced into this scheme, the interpretation offered in this commentary is amillennial. Yet both labels would indicate a major misunderstanding of the nature of John's eschatological language. To understand the millennium only as a segment in a chronological series of events that may be plotted on a calendar or chart is to miss the theological message communicated by its own pictorial medium. It is better to remember that no one picture of the end can do justice to the eschatological message John proclaims, so that the message of *each* picture will be allowed to impress itself on the imagination of the interpreter.

20:4 Thrones, and those seated on them were given authority to judge: To participate in God's kingdom means to share God's reign (1:6; 3:21; 5:10). This can also be pictured as sharing the role of final judge (Matt. 19:28; 1 Cor. 6:2). **The souls of those who had been beheaded for their testimony to Jesus:** See 6:9–11; 13:11–15. John sees only the Christian martyrs as participating in the millennial reign. This can be understood as a "special prize" for the martyrs, with other Christians resurrected only later (20:5). It is better, however, not to understand the imagery so mechanically and chronologically, but to see the picture as representing the whole church, characterized as a martyr church. Just as 11:1–13 pictures the church in its prophetic dimension (though not every individual was a prophet), so here the church is portrayed as the martyr church, without claiming that every individual is a martyr. The imagery communicates that it is the nature of the church to bear witness to Christ, to suffer for this testimony, but finally to share Christ's messianic reign.

20:5 This is the first resurrection: By announcing that this resurrection, which happens in the eschatological future, is the first, John probably does not have a subsequent "second" resurrection in mind (which is never mentioned). He is better understood as addressing the claims made by prophet-theologians of the Johannine and Pauline traditions in his own churches that the resurrection has already happened (see John 11:1–44, esp. vv. 25–26; Col. 2:12; 3:1; Eph. 2:1–7; contrast 2 Tim. 2:18). Like his predecessor Paul, John opposes this spiritualizing of the Christian hope of resurrection, emphasizing that there is no resurrection presently experienced—the *first* resurrection will occur at the eschaton (see Phil. 3:7–16).

20:6 Blessed: The fifth of seven beatitudes (see on 1:3).

20:7–10
Picture Five: The Defeat of Gog and Magog

In 19:19–20 the "ordinary" nations of the earth had already been defeated and destroyed at the return of Christ. Now 20:7–10 describes the enemies of God, who are defeated in the last battle in a more mythological manner. They are from "the four corners of the earth" (v. 8), which may mean they represent the earth in its totality, or that they are not human armies at all, but quasi-mythological hordes from the edges of the universe.

20:7 The nations at the four corners of the earth, Gog and Magog: In Ezek. 38–39 Gog was the prince and Magog was the land, but by John's day Jewish tradition had reinterpreted these mysterious names in a variety of ways. John sees both Gog and Magog as personal beings who are deceived by Satan to lead the ultimate enemies of God's people to destruction in the eschatological battle. For John, evil as embod-

ied in historical individuals and nations is not the ultimate enemy. We should not think of Gog and Magog as historical nations that have had a continuing existence during the preceding scene of John's drama, having lived out the millennium in some parenthetical existence, nor of nations of our own time "predicted" by biblical prophecy. John presents before our imaginations a picture of the ultimate destruction of evil, and he needs for this scene antagonists to God who are larger than life. Evil must be magnified to its fullest before being destroyed forever. In order to participate in this mythical scene, the devil "must" be released to engage in his characteristic activity of "deceiving the nations."

20:9 Surrounded the camp of the saints: The saints are the people of God (see on 4:8). "Camp" is interchangeable with "city" in this text as an indication of the pilgrim existence of God's people in this world. "Here we have no lasting city" (Heb. 13:14). **The beloved city:** Jerusalem, which has also been described as "Sodom" and "Egypt" (11:8). Rebellion and rejection of God is not necessarily ultimate; judgment by God does not exclude redemption. **Fire came down from heaven:** As in 11:17–19 and 19:17–21, the "last battle" is no battle at all. There is no other victory than that long since won by God the victor in the cross of Christ. We have only the paradigmatic scene in which all the forces of evil, with Satan at their head, surround the embattled "camp" of the people of God. It is not an objectifying prediction of something that will literally occur in some particular geographical spot, but a picture of the essential nature of the embattled church. Without a struggle, **fire** comes **from heaven** and destroys the enemies of God's people, and the devil disappears **into the lake of fire** forever. This is another affirmation of the apocalyptist's view that, while we must responsibly resist evil, "deliver us from evil" is a prayer that finally must be answered from God's side.

20:11–15
Picture Six: The Last Judgment

Even at its best, the present world is a fusion of good and evil; at its worst, it is an unbearable and lethal mixture. Human judges at best can never achieve final justice, for they are involved in the mixture themselves. What is needed is someone good enough, wise enough, and powerful enough to sort it out, to redeem the good and destroy the evil. Thus one way the coming of

God's kingdom was portrayed was an ultimate courtroom scene. In some scenes God is the judge (Dan. 7), in some scenes God's representative (Isa. 11). The final judgment scene is one of John's pictures of the meaning of the end of history.

20:11 A great white throne and the one who sat on it: Not named, but throughout the phrase has referred to God (e.g., 4:1, 3, 9; 5:1). Elsewhere God's throne is sometimes pictured as shared by Christ and Christians (3:21; see 20:4–6). The various pictures are not to be combined, but each is to be seen as having its own message. **The earth and the heaven:** The whole created universe, Gen. 1:1. **Fled from his presence:** The unbearable holiness of God cannot be endured by the sinful creation (see Isa. 6:5; Luke 5:8; 1 Tim. 6:16). **No place was found for them:** Were it not so deadly serious, one could see a touch of humor here (If you're the universe and want to flee, where can you go?).

20:12 Great and small: See on 13:16. The judgment is universal, of all humans who have lived (20:13). **Books were opened:** See Dan. 7:10. The records of the good and bad deeds of those who are being judged. In this set of books, judgment and salvation are according to works (see 2:23; 18:6). **Another book . . . the book of life:** See on 3:5; 13:8; 17:8; 21:17. This is the book of grace, in which names were enrolled from the foundation of the world. Throughout, John (like the New Testament in general) has affirmed the absolute responsibility of human beings, in tandem with the absolute sovereignty and grace of God. That which is paradoxical, frustrating all logic, is here communicated pictorially: human beings are absolutely (not partially!) responsible, and are judged by their works; God is absolutely sovereign and gracious (not partially!), and saves by grace. Those who insist on a logically clear picture of God and how God works will have a small God and will have reduced salvation to manageable proportions.

20:14 Death and Hades: See 1:18; 6:8. The transcendent power of death is the enemy of life that not only cuts its cord at the end, but distorts it throughout. This last enemy shall finally be destroyed (see 1 Cor. 15:26, 54–55). **The lake of fire . . . is the second death:** The ultimate destruction, beyond physical death. John has not depicted human beings as cast into the lake of fire, but only their transcendent enemies, the Beast and the false prophet (19:20), the dragon Satan (20:10), Death and Hades (20:14). For humans, the possibility of this final rejection remains in the realm of pos-

sibility and threat: **If anyone's name was not found** (NIV): The NRSV has removed the Greek conditional construction and made it into a statement in order to preserve gender-inclusive language—to which the theological point is here sacrificed. In John's theology, the book of life, the book of God's grace, stands between humans and the lake of fire.

21:1–22:7
Picture Seven: The New Jerusalem

21:1 New heaven and a new earth: The phrase does not mean that God wipes out the previous creation and starts all over again, but refers to the eschatological renewal and fulfillment of creation (see Isa. 65:17; 66:22; Matt. 5:18; 19:28; 2 Pet. 3:13). **The sea was no more:** The sea had always symbolized the anticreation forces of chaos. In 4:6 it is part of the heavenly worship scene, tamed and part of God's good creation. Here it disappears entirely. There may be a personal note as well: the sea separated John from his churches, but in the final picture there is no more separation.

21:2 The holy city, the new Jerusalem: John's final and climactic picture of the goal to which God is guiding history is a city. One might have supposed that he would have portrayed the end of the world as a return to Eden, a going back to the garden before the evils of history—concentrated in its cities—had begun. Instead of picturing the abolition of history, he pictures its redemption. A city represents human community, life together. Eschatological existence is not individualistic, but communal. The church, the community of faith, the people of God, is the anticipation of this. **"New"** means "eschatologically renewed," "ultimately and finally transformed"—not merely a new and improved version of the old that might also later be improved (see on 14:3). **Coming down out of heaven:** See v. 10. Human effort does not finally bring the goal of history; it is finally the gift of God rather than the achievement of human beings.

The idea of a heavenly Jerusalem that will become the ultimate home of the people of God is not original with John. Like other Christian authors before and beside him (Phil. 3:20; Gal. 4:24–31; Heb. 11:10; 12:22; 13:14), John found this idea already present in the apocalyptic tradition that came to him. This tradition included even such details as the "descent" of the holy city to earth on the last day (i.e., its establishment by God rather than human effort, see Pss. 46; 48; Isa. 2:1–4; 65:17–25; *Sib.*

Or. 5:420–25; *1 En.* 90:29), the imagery of God's throne (Ps. 47:7; *1 En.* 24:4–5); seeing the face of God (2 Esd. 7:98); the tree of life (*Test. Levi* 18:11; *1 En.* 25:5); jeweled construction (Exod. 25:5–14, 17–29; 39:8–22; Isa. 54:11–14; Ezek. 28:11–17; Tob. 13:16–18); golden streets and gates of pearl (Tob. 13:16–18; Isa. 60:11–14). The many fragments of the Dead Sea Scrolls that have parallels to the new Jerusalem show that John is utilizing a tradition widespread in Judaism.

21:3 They will be his peoples: Although some manuscripts read the singular, the plural is original. John has reinterpreted Ezek. 37:27 in an ultimately inclusive sense (see 22:2).

21:4 Death will be no more: One mode of representing the future world is the *via negativa*. While the future transcendent world can hardly be represented in this-worldly terms (see on 10:4) by saying what it *is*, it can be portrayed by saying what will *not* be there: the **sea** (20:1); **tears, death, mourning, crying, pain** (21:4); the **cowardly, faithless, polluted, murderers, fornicators, sorcerers, idolaters, liars** (21:8; 22:15); the **temple** (21:22); **sun, moon** (21:23); **night** (22:5) and **shut gates** (21:25); ritually **unclean** things (21:27); **anyone who practices abomination or falsehood** (21:27); anything **accursed** (22:3). The evils of historical existence will have been eliminated and transformed.

21:5 "I am making all things new": This is different from "I am making all new things." The present world is God's creation and will receive the transformation for which it longs (see Rom. 8:18–25).

21:8 Their place will be in the lake that burns with fire: See on 20:10 and the excursus at 22:21.

21:9 The bride, the wife of the Lamb: The community of the redeemed is pictured as both woman and city (see on 17:1).

21:11 The glory of God and a radiance like a very rare jewel: The streets of gold, gates of pearl, and walls of jewels portray the beauty of the city. The point is not that we'll all be rich, but that the goal of history is indescribably beautiful.

21:12–14 Twelve tribes . . . twelve apostles: New Jerusalem includes the history of Israel and the church, the one people of God of the Old and New Testaments.

21:16 Foursquare . . . fifteen hundred miles: Like the Most Holy Place, the inner sanctum of the tabernacle and the temple where God himself was present (Exod. 21–35; 8:1–13), the new Jerusalem is a cube—a spacious cube in which

there is room for all. John resists the temptation to depict a small town where the "faithful few" are finally saved; his final vision portrays an indescribably large city in which all God's people can dwell together.

21:22 No temple: The different picture of 3:12 should not be "harmonized" with this, for each has its distinctive message. Here the point is that the whole city will be a temple, the place where God is present with all his people.

21:24 The nations . . . the kings of the earth: These have been presented as hostile to God throughout Revelation and have been "destroyed" more than once. Here, they are part of the new creation, living in God's light and honoring God. Again, each picture has its own message, and each warns against taking the other with exclusive literalism.

21:26 The glory and honor of the nations: At one level, this represents the old picture of the pagan nations finally acknowledging the role of Israel and bringing their gifts to show their subjection to the Israelite monarchy. John has transformed this traditional image so that the nations now participate in God's final salvation. This picture represents not the abolition but the redemption of civilization, of all human efforts to have a decent city and worthwhile culture. Not only religious works, but all the efforts of all human history to construct a good society are here taken into the eternal city. Nothing good is lost.

22:2 The tree of life: Like that of the river, this image is from the garden of Eden (Gen. 2:9–10). John does not have history return to its idyllic prehistoric beginnings before cities were founded, but brings the beginnings into the final city. **The leaves of the tree are for the healing of the nations:** In the original imagery of Ezek. 47:12, the leaves were for healing, i.e., there will be no sickness in the restored Jerusalem, for God has made provision for miraculous medicine. By adding **of the nations,** he transforms this into a social, geopolitical image: in the new Jerusalem all the clashes of warring tribes and nations are resolved and healed (see Isa. 2:2–4; 11:6–9; 65:17–25).

22:3 His servants will worship him: Revelation has been a worship book throughout. Here the goal of creation is not eternal passivity or self-indulgence, but that all things join in worship of God their Creator (see 5:13–14).

John lets his picture speak for itself. His language throughout this vision is indicative:

"This is how it will be." And yet as always the indicatives of biblical theology contain an implicit imperative, the gift becomes an assignment. If this is where the world, under the sovereign grace of God, is finally going, then every thought, move, deed in some other direction is out of step with reality and is finally wasted. The picture is offered not to answer speculative questions about the future, but as an orientation for life in the present.

22:6–7 What must soon take place . . . I am coming soon: See on 1:3. **Blessed:** The sixth of Revelation's seven beatitudes (see on 1:3).

22:8–21
LETTER CONCLUSION

22:8 I, John: The document returns to its letter form (see 1:4–5, 9). Here too the "I, John" modulates into the "I, Jesus" of 22:16.

22:9 Worship God: The repetition of this scene (see on 19:9–10) does not mean that John has forgotten, but that he wants to emphasize the major message of the book and the First Commandment (Exod. 20:1–6; see Deut. 6:4–6).

22:10 Do not seal: In contrast to the typical apocalypse, as represented by Dan. 12:4, 9.

22:14 Blessed: The seventh of Revelation's seven beatitudes (see on 1:3).

22:16 It is I, Jesus, who sent my angel to you: The voices of John, the angel, and Jesus modulate into the voice of God. See on 1:1–2; 19:19.

22:17 The Spirit and the bride: The Spirit speaks through the Christian prophets. The bride is the church (see on 17:1). **Come:** The prayer is both for the final coming of Jesus at the eschaton and for the presence of Christ at the Eucharist (see on 1 Cor. 16:22). The letter was read during the worship service and was probably followed by the Eucharist.

22:18–19 I warn everyone: In the time before printed books, it was easy to modify circulated manuscripts by adding, subtracting, or modifying their contents to suit one's taste. Thus many ancient documents contained curses against those who tampered with their contents and did not transmit them faithfully, something like the ancient equivalent of a copyright notice. This practice was sometimes adopted in the transmission of Israel's sacred texts (Deut. 4:2; 12:32; Ezra 6:11) and is reflected here. It has nothing to with the formulation of the wording of translations, and here applies to the text of Revelation rather than "the Bible," which did not exist in John's day. Nonetheless, it shows that John considered his letter a message from God to the churches, and that it should be handled with the same reverence the church expresses when dealing with its Scriptures.

22:21 Grace . . . be with all (the saints) (NRSV)/ **(God's people)** (NIV): This was simply John's benediction at the close of a Christian letter, but the variety of manuscript readings is symbolic of John's paradoxical affirmation throughout. This concluding word, which became the last word of the Bible, is a word of the grace of God to "all." This is the reading of the best Greek texts; some manuscripts added "the saints," finding the word of universal grace too much to bear and limiting the pronouncement of God's grace to the church. Whatever may have been John's original ending, the ambiguity of this final word is symbolic of the provocative tension of the revelation as a whole, guarding us from both the despair of limited hope and the complacency of cheap grace.

EXCURSUS:
UNIVERSAL SALVATION
AND PARADOXICAL LANGUAGE

Revelation contains two sets of texts picturing the final destiny of human beings (on the language of salvation, see on Acts 16:31). Some texts in Revelation portray or imply limited salvation, i.e., that only faithful believers will finally be saved: 14:9–10; 20:11–15; 21:7–8. Other texts in Revelation portray or imply universal salvation, i.e., that the final victory of God means salvation for the whole creation: 1:7; 4:3; 5:13; 14:14; 15:4; 21:5; 21:22–22:3. Each group of texts belongs to a significant stream of biblical theology. One stream maintains that ultimate salvation is limited; some passages that indicate this are Isa. 26:20–21; 27:12–13; 51:22–23; 66:15–16, 24; Matt. 25:31–46; John 3:16, 36; 2 Thess. 1:6–10. Another stream tends toward or explicitly affirms inclusive, universal salvation; some passages that belong to this stream are Gen. 12:1–3; Ps. 86:9; Isa. 2:2–4; 19:24–25; 25:6–10a; 40:5; 43:25; 44:2–5; 45:22–23; 48:9–11; 49:6; 51:4–6; 52:7–10; 66:18–23; Ezek. 16:49–63; Matt. 20:1–16; John 3:17; 12:32; Rom. 5:15–21; 11:32–36; 1 Cor. 15:20–28; Phil. 2:6–11; Col. 1:15–20; 2:15; Eph. 1:3–22; 3:20; 1 Tim. 2:3–4; 4:10; Titus 2:11.

Three Options in Understanding
This Dual Set of Data

1. The first option is that John's "real" view is limited salvation. Texts that seem to imply universal salvation are actually to be understood in the light of the limited texts.

2. The second option is that John's "real" view is universal salvation. Texts that seem to imply limited, conditional salvation are actually to be understood in the light of the universalistic texts.

3. The third option is that John has no one consistent view. Neither group of texts can be subordinated to the other. This is the view affirmed in the preceding comments. John was a profound thinker, a dialectical theologian who intends to present both sets of pictures, and does so using paradoxical language. Revelation intends to present pictures in which the one sovereign and gracious God is finally victorious and restores all his creation to its intended blessedness, redeeming all his creatures (pictures in which all are saved unconditionally because of God's decision to accept them). John also intends to present pictures which portray human beings as responsible for their decisions, pictures of how inexpressibly terrible it is to reject one's Creator and live one's life in allegiance to false gods (pictures in which the faithful are saved and unbelievers are damned because they did not decide to accept God). By offering pictures of both unconditional/universal and conditional/limited salvation and thus affirming both poles of the dialectic, John, in accord with biblical theology in general, guards against the dangers inherent in a superficial "consistency" obtained by affirming only one side of the issue. The interpreter's task is not to seek ways to reconcile the tension in the text, but to find the thrust of Revelation's message precisely in this tension.

With Regard to the Doctrine of Conditional, Limited Salvation

1. Limited-salvation pictures of judgment and damnation should not be affirmed in such a way that God is pictured as vindictive or frustrated. The logic of some nondialectical affirmations of God's judgment and final damnation of sinners leads to the inescapable picture of a deity who punishes beyond measure (eternally for finite sins), a vindictive god whose lust for revenge is never satisfied as the smoke from the torture of his enemies ascends for all eternity (Rev. 14:9–10). This is not the God revealed in Jesus Christ portrayed in Revelation. Likewise, John's method of dialectical pictures avoids the picture of a frustrated God who wanted to save his whole creation but was able to salvage only a small fraction of it. Revelation delivers us from a picture of a deity who wants to save but must finally throw up his cosmic hands to most of a rebellious creation and say, "All right! Have it your way." This too is unworthy of the Lord God Almighty praised in Revelation (19:6).

2. Limited-salvation pictures of judgment and damnation should not be affirmed in such a way that a doctrine of conditional salvation is *necessary*. The urgency and necessity of evangelism and the believer's response in faith can wrongly be made into an axiom to which all other Christian truth must be subject. A doctrine of limited salvation may be affirmed because it is necessary in order to maintain the coherence of one's theological system or the meaning of one's own salvation: "If all are going to be saved anyway, what is the use of evangelism and faith?" John does not do this. Only an impoverished understanding of evangelism and faith makes these human acts as important as the act of God in Christ. This can lead to a heretical (synergistic) understanding of salvation in which it does not matter that God has sent Christ for the world's salvation unless the Christian evangelist and believer also do their "parts," thus placing the acts of Christian preaching and belief on the same plane as God's act in Christ. John's dialectical affirmation of both sets of pictures avoids this arrogance. Likewise, it is a petty, insecure understanding of salvation that derives its meaning and value from the reassurance that most will be damned.

With Regard to the Doctrine of Universal Salvation

1. The doctrine of universal salvation should not be held in an undialectical way that relativizes the ultimate revelation-salvation event of Jesus Christ. Universal salvation can be affirmed in a way that makes Jesus Christ only one of many paths to God. John does not do this. There are not many gods, but one God, and this God is the God definitively revealed in Jesus for all peoples, whether or not they know and acknowledge it. For John, creation is not saved by being converted to the Christian religion. God saves humanity. But for John, the God who saves humanity is the God who has definitively acted to reveal himself as the savior of all in the eschatological event of Jesus Christ.

2. The doctrine of universal salvation should not be held in such a way that it permits the relaxation of human responsibility. Universal salvation can be affirmed in such a way that salvation becomes a fate rather than a gift, robbing human beings of their ability and responsibility to decide and the church of its evangelistic mission. John's dialectic avoids this. He also has pictures in which we are responsible for our own destiny.

3. The doctrine of universal salvation should not be held in such a way that it minimizes God's judgment on human sin. An undialectical affirmation of universal salvation has difficulty doing justice to the stern side of God's justice and portraying the

awfulness of rebellion against God. Alongside pictures of universal salvation, John offers pictures of the terror of God's judgment.

4. The doctrine of universal salvation should not be held in such a way that it minimizes the importance of faith and the urgency of evangelism. As affirmed by John and the New Testament generally, the implication of the doctrine of universal salvation is not that there is nothing for the church to do, since the whole creation will be saved anyway. Rather, the good news of the one God who brings final salvation to all demands to be lived out and shared in the present, and the pictures of God's judgment against unbelievers and the necessity of human decision for God prevent the universalistic pictures from cutting the nerve of action and mission.

For Further Reading

General and Reference Books on the Whole Bible

Achtemeier, Paul J., ed. *HarperCollins Bible Dictionary*. San Francisco: Harper & Row, 1996.
Dunn, James D. G. and John W. Rogerson, eds. *Eerdmans Commentary on the Bible*. Grand Rapids: Eerdmans, 2003.
Metzger, Bruce G. *The Bible in Translation: Ancient and English Versions*. Grand Rapids: Baker, 2001.
Newsom, Carol A., and Sharon Ringe. *The Women's Bible Commentary*. Louisville, KY: Westminster/ John Knox, 1992.

Extracanonical Texts

Charlesworth, James H., ed. *The Old Testament Pseudepigrapha*. 2 vols. Garden City, NY: Doubleday, 1983, 1985.
Hennecke, Edgar, and Wilhelm Schneemelcher, eds. *New Testament Apocrypha*, 2 vols. Philadelphia: Westminster Press, 1964, and Louisville, KY: Westminster/John Knox Press, 1991.

General Reference Books on the New Testament

Brown, Raymond E. *An Introduction to the New Testament*. New York: Doubleday, 1997.
Harris, Stephen L. *The New Testament: A Student's Introduction*. 4th edition. Boston: McGraw Hill, 2002.

Jesus and the Four Gospels

Boring, M. Eugene. *Truly Human/ Truly Divine: Christological Language and the Gospel Form*. St. Louis: Christian Board of Publication, 1984.
Craddock, Fred B. *The Gospels*. Interpreting Biblical Texts. Nashville: Abingdon, 1981.
Keck, Leander E. *Who Is Jesus? History in the Perfect Tense*. Columbia: University of South Carolina Press, 2000.
Tatum, W. Barnes. *In Quest of Jesus*. Revised and enlarged edition. Nashville, Abingdon, 1999.

Matthew

Boring, M. Eugene. "The Gospel of Matthew." In *The New Interpreter's Bible*, vol. 8. Nashville: Abingdon, 1995.
Meier, John P. *Matthew*. New Testament Message 3. Collegeville, MN: Liturgical Press, 1980.
Pregeant, Russell. *Matthew*. Chalice Commentaries for Today. St. Louis: Chalice Press, 2004.

Mark

Marcus, Joel. *Mark 1–8: A New Translation with Introduction and Commentary*. Anchor Bible 27. New York: Doubleday, 2000.
Hooker, Morna D. *The Gospel according to Saint Mark*. Black's New Testament Commentary. Peabody, MA: Hendrickson, 1991.

Luke

Craddock, Fred B. *Luke*. Interpretation: A Bible Commentary for Teaching and Preaching. Louisville, KY: John Knox Press, 1990.
Culpepper, R. Alan. "The Gospel of Luke." In *The New Interpreter's Bible*, vol. 9. Nashville: Abingdon, 1995.

John

Smith, D. Moody. *John*. Abingdon New Testament Commentaries. Nashville: Abingdon, 1999.
O'Day, Gail R. "The Gospel of John." In *The New Interpreter's Bible*, vol. 9. Nashville: Abingdon, 1995.

Acts

Dunn, J. D. G. *The Acts of the Apostles.* Valley Forge, PA: Trinity, 1996.

Gaventa, Beverly Roberts. *Acts.* Abingdon New Testament Commentary. Nashville: Abingdon, 2003.

Paul and the Epistles

Barrett, C. K. *Paul: An Introduction to His Thought.* Louisville, KY: Westminster John Knox, 1994.

Cousar, Charles B. *The Letters of Paul.* Interpreting Biblical Texts. Nashville: Abingdon, 1996.

Keck, Leander, and Victor Paul Furnish. *The Pauline Letters.* Interpreting Biblical Texts. Nashville: Abingdon, 1984.

Romans

Achtemeier, Paul J. *Romans.* Interpretation: A Bible Commentary for Teaching and Preaching. Atlanta: John Knox Press, 1985.

Barrett, C. K. *The Epistle to the Romans.* Black's New Testament Commentaries. London: Adam & Charles Black, 1957.

1 Corinthians

Fee, Gordon D. *The First Epistle to the Corinthians.* The New International Commentary on the New Testament. Grand Rapids: Eerdmans, 1987.

Hays, Richard B. *First Corinthians.* Interpretation: A Bible Commentary for Teaching and Preaching. Louisville, KY: John Knox Press, 1997.

2 Corinthians

Best, Ernest. *Second Corinthians.* Interpretation: A Bible Commentary for Teaching and Preaching. Louisville, KY: John Knox Press, 1987.

Furnish, Victor Paul. *II Corinthians.* Anchor Bible. Garden City, NY: Doubleday, 1984.

Galatians

Cousar, Charles B. *Galatians.* Interpretation: A Bible Commentary for Teaching and Preaching. Louisville, KY: John Knox Press, 1982.

Martyn, J. Louis. *Galatians.* Anchor Bible. New York: Doubleday, 1997.

Ephesians

Perkins, Pheme. "The Letter to the Ephesians." In *The New Interpreter's Bible,* vol. 11. Nashville: Abingdon, 2000.

Martin, Ralph P. *Ephesians, Colossians, and Philemon.* Interpretation: A Bible Commentary for Teaching and Preaching. Atlanta: John Knox Press, 1991.

Philippians

Craddock, Fred B. *Philippians.* Interpretation: A Bible Commentary for Teaching and Preaching. Atlanta: John Knox Press, 1985.

Osiek, Carolyn. *Philippians, Philemon.* Abingdon New Testament Commentaries. Nashville: Abingdon, 2000.

Colossians

Lincoln, Andrew T. "The Letter to the Colossians." In *The New Interpreter's Bible,* vol. 11. Nashville: Abingdon, 2000.

Lohse, Eduard. *Colossians and Philemon. A Commentary on the Epistles to the Colossians and to Philemon.* Hermeneia. Philadelphia: Fortress, 1971.

1 Thessalonians and 2 Thessalonians

Gaventa, Beverly Roberts. *First and Second Thessalonians.* Interpretation: A Bible Commentary for Teaching and Preaching. Louisville, KY: John Knox Press, 1998.

Smith, Abraham. "The First Letter to the Thessalonians." In *The New Interpreter's Bible,* vol. 11. Nashville: Abingdon, 2000.

1 Timothy, 2 Timothy, Titus

Bassler, Jouette. *1 Timothy, 2 Timothy, Titus.* Nashville: Abingdon, 1996.

Collins, Raymond F. *I and II Timothy and Titus: A Commentary.* New Testament Library. Louisville, KY: Westminster John Knox, 2002.

Philemon

Fitzmyer, Joseph A. *The Letter to Philemon: A New Translation with Introduction and Commentary.* Anchor Bible 32C. New York: Doubleday, 2000.

See also Osiek on *Philippians* and Lohse on *Colossians* above.

Hebrews

Craddock, Fred B. "Hebrews." In *The New Interpreter's Bible,* vol. 12. Nashville: Abingdon, 1998.

Williams, R. M. *Hebrews.* New Century Biblical Commentary. Grand Rapids: Eerdmans, 1987.

James

Johnson, Luke T. "The Letter of James." In *The New Interpreter's Bible,* vol. 12. Nashville: Abingdon, 1998.

Sleeper, C. Freeman. *James.* Abingdon New Testament Commentary. Nashville: Abingdon, 1998.

1 Peter, 2 Peter, Jude

Craddock, Fred B. *First and Second Peter and Jude.* Westminster Bible Commentary. Louisville, KY: Westminster John Knox, 1995.

Boring, M. Eugene. *1 Peter.* Abingdon New Testament Commentary. Nashville: Abingdon, 1999.

Watson, Duane F. "The Second Letter of Peter," "The Letter of Jude." In *The New Interpreter's Bible,* vol. 12. Nashville: Abingdon, 1998.

1–3 John

Rensberger, David. *1 John, 2 John, 3 John.* Abingdon New Testament Commentary. Nashville: Abingdon, 1997.

Smith, D. Moody. *First, Second, and Third John*: Interpretation: A Bible Commentary for Teaching and Preaching. Louisville, KY: John Knox Press, 1991.

Revelation

Boring, M. Eugene. *Revelation.* Interpretation: A Bible Commentary for Teaching and Preaching. Louisville, KY: John Knox Press, 1989.

González, Catherine Gunsalus, and Justo L. González. *Revelation.* Westminster Bible Companion. Louisville, KY: Westminster John Knox, 1997.

Hill, Craig C. *In God's Time: The Bible and the Future.* Grand Rapids: Eerdmans, 2002.

Index of Excursuses

List of Figures